THE NORTON
INTRODUCTION TO
LITERATURE

Fourth Edition

W · W · NORTON & COMPANY · NEW YORK · LONDON

Carl E. Bain
Jerome Beaty
J. Paul Hunter

THE NORTON
INTRODUCTION TO
LITERATURE

Fourth Edition

Published simultaneously in Canada by Penguin Books Canada Ltd,
2801 John Street, Markham, Ontario L3R 1B4

Printed in the United States of America.

Library of Congress Cataloging in Publication Data
Main entry under title:

The Norton introduction to literature.

Includes indexes.
1. Literature—Collections. I. Bain, Carl E.
II. Beaty, Jerome, 1924—   . III. Hunter,
J. Paul, 1934—   .
PN6014.N67   1986   808.8   85–13870
ISBN 0-393-95441-2

W.W. Norton & Company, Inc., 500 Fifth Avenue,
New York, N.Y. 10110
W.W. Norton & Company Ltd., 37 Great Russell Street,
London WC1B 3NU

1 2 3 4 5 6 7 8 9 0

Contents

v

CONTEXT

POETRY

TEXT

Contents

8 SOUND AND SIGHT   667

The Sounds of Poetry   667

The Way a Poem Looks   684

9 STANZAS AND VERSE FORMS   690

POEMS FOR FURTHER READING 799

DRAMA

PLAYS FOR FURTHER READING

WRITING ABOUT LITERATURE

xviii   *Contents*

FOREWORD TO THE FOURTH EDITION

The Norton Introduction to Literature offers in a single volume a complete course in reading and writing about literature. It is both an anthology and a textbook—a "teaching anthology"—for the indispensable course in which college student and college teacher begin to read literature seriously together.

New to this edition is a section on "Writing about Literature." In it we deal both with the writing process as applied to literary works—choosing a topic, gathering evidence, developing an argument, and so forth—and with the varieties of a reader's written responses—from copying and paraphrase to analysis and interpretation: we explore not merely the *hows*, but the *whats* and *whys* as well.

The Fourth Edition includes 47 stories and brief narratives, 16 of which are new; 322 poems, 65 of which are new; and 13 plays, 7 of which are new.

The drama section, especially, has been reinvigorated. New selections include Harold Pinter's sketch *The Black and White* and Anton Chekhov's one-act play *The Brute*; Samuel Beckett's *Krapp's Last Tape*; Charles Fuller's *A Soldier's Play*; Moliere's *The Misanthrope*; and Marsha Norman's *The Laundromat*. *A Streetcar Named Desire* replaces *The Glass Menagerie* (the long last scene of which, however, is still included, along with a crucial scene from *Cat on a Hot Tin Roof* and selections from Tennessee Williams's Essays and *Memoirs*).

In fiction, we now offer four stories by William Faulkner (including the often taught classics *A Rose for Emily* and *Barn Burning*). We have also added stories by Henry James, Ursula K. Le Guin, Bobbie Ann Mason, Guy de Maupassant, Katherine Anne Porter, Leo Tolstoy, William Trevor, and Alice Walker, as well as narratives from native American, African, Chinese, and Persian traditions.

The poetry section has been similarly infused with selections familiar and fresh, with newly included works by Diane Ackerman, James Agee, Margaret Atwood, Carol Jane Bangs, Wendell Berry, Anne Bradstreet, Sterling A. Brown, Amy Clampitt, Lucille Clifton, Hart Crane, Robert Creeley, Waring Cuney, Emily Dickinson, David Donnell, Alan Dugan, Richard Eberhart, James A. Emanuel, Robert Frost, Sandra Gilbert, Thomas Hardy, James Harrison, Robert Hayden, Seamus Heaney, A. D. Hope, Gerard Manley Hopkins, Langston Hughes, Richard Hugo, Paulette Jiles, X. J. Kennedy, Galway Kinnell, Denise Levertov, James Merrill, Edna St. Vincent Millay, Ogden Nash, Sharon Olds, Wilfred Owen, Dorothy Parker, Marge Piercy, Sylvia Plath, Jarold Ramsey, Adrienne Rich, Louis Simpson, Kay Smith, Francis Sparshot, William Stafford, Alfred, Lord Tennyson, Edward Thomas, Ellen Bryant Voigt, Miriam Waddington, Walt Whitman, Richard Wilbur, and John Witte.

But *The Norton Introduction to Literature* remains more than a grab-bag of good things to read. The works are not only selected but arranged in order to introduce a reader to the serious study of literature. Each genre—fiction, poetry, drama—is approached in three logical steps. Fiction, for example, is introduced by "Experiencing Fiction," which treats the purpose and nature of fiction and the reading experience generally. This is followed by the five-chapter section called "Text," in which stories are analyzed by questions of craft, the so-called elements of fiction. The second section, "Context," suggests some ways of seeing a work of literature within its temporal and cultural contexts, the last of the chapters in the section offering a sample of narratives other than "the short story," the form with which we in the Western tradition are most familiar. There follows a group of "Stories for Further Reading," a reservoir of additional examples, for independent study or a different approach. The book's arrangement seeks to facilitate the reader's movement from narrower to broader questions, mirroring the way people read—wanting to learn more as they experience more.

Certain editorial procedures that proved their usefulness in earlier editions have been retained. First of all, the works are annotated, as is customary in Norton anthologies; the notes are informational and not interpretative, for the aim is to help readers understand and appreciate the work, not to dictate a meaning or a response. To offer the texts in the form most immediately available to their particular audience, we have normalized spelling according to modern American usage. In order to avoid giving the impression that all literature was written at the same time, we have noted for each selection the date of first book publication (or, when preceded by a *p*, first periodical publication).

In all our work on this edition we have been guided by teachers in other English departments and in our own, and by students who wrote us as the authors of the textbook they were using and by those who were able to approach us after class as their teachers. We hope that with such help we have been able to offer you a solid and stimulating introduction to the experience of literature.

J.B., J.P.H.

ACKNOWLEDGMENTS

We would like to thank our teachers, for their example in the love of literature and in the art of sharing that love; our students, for their patience as we are learning from them to be better teachers of literature; our wives and children, for their understanding when the work of preparing this text made us seem less than perfectly loving husbands and fathers.

We would also like to thank our colleagues, many of whom have taught our book and evaluated our efforts, for their constant encouragement and enlightenment. Of our colleagues at Emory University, we would like especially to thank Michaelyn Burnette, Lore Metzger, Lee Pederson, Harry Rusche, Ronald Schuchard, Kristina Straub, Floyd C. Watkins, and Sally Wolff. And we thank also Paula R. Backscheider (University of Rochester); T. E. Blom (University of British Columbia); Patricia Brocker; Thomas R. Carper (University of Maine); Frank W. Childrey (Northwest Mississippi Junior College); Randy R. Conine (El Centro College); Michael P. Dean (University of Mississippi); Stephen F. Evans (University of Kansas); Norman Feltes (York University); Lila F. Fink (Pepperdine University); Frederick Goldberg (Clayton Junior College); Larry Gray (Southeastern Louisiana University); Alan Grob (Rice University); Christopher Hudgins (University of Nevada); Kristin Hunter (University of Pennsylvania); Lisa Hunter; Elizabeth Lunz; William Morgan (Illinois State University); Nils Peterson (San Jose State University); Ellanor Pruitt (Oxford College); Richard Quaintance (Douglass College); Joseph N. Riddell (University of California at Los Angeles); Ronald Schleifer (University of Oklahoma); John Shaw (Florida State University); John R. Shriver (Wayne State University); Irwin Simpkins (DeKalb College); Frederick Stocking (Williams College); Rae Thompson (University of Guelph); Dennis Todd (Wayne State University); Richard Turner (Indiana University-Purdue University at Indianapolis); Patricia Vicari (Scarborough College of the University of Toronto); Melissa Walker (Mercer University); Arthur Williams (Oxford College); Dorothy A. Winsor (Wayne State University); and Curt R. Zimansky (University of Colorado).

On several occasions during the preparation of this work a retreat from everyday was needed. The Ossabaw Island Project provided it, and we wish to thank the Ossabaw Island Foundation and particularly Eleanor West for the provision and for the grace with which it was offered.

We would also like to thank our friends at W. W. Norton & Company, especially John Benedict, Fred McFarland, Diane O'Connor, Roy Tedoff, Victoria Thys, and Barry Wade.

J.B., J.P.H.

THE NORTON
INTRODUCTION TO
LITERATURE

Fourth Edition

1 EXPERIENCING FICTION

SPENCER HOLST

The Zebra Storyteller

Once upon a time there was a Siamese cat who pretended to be a lion and spoke inappropriate Zebraic.

That language is whinnied by the race of striped horses in Africa.

Here now: An innocent zebra is walking in a jungle and approaching from another direction is the little cat; they meet.

"Hello there!" says the Siamese cat in perfectly pronounced Zebraic. "It certainly is a pleasant day, isn't it? The sun is shining, the birds are singing, isn't the world a lovely place to live today!"

The zebra is so astonished at hearing a Siamese cat speaking like a zebra, why—he's just fit to be tied.

So the little cat quickly ties him up, kills him, and drags the better parts of the carcass back to his den.

The cat successfully hunted zebras many months in this manner, dining on filet mignon of zebra every night, and from the better hides he made bow neckties and wide belts after the fashion of the decadent princes of the Old Siamese court.

He began boasting to his friends he was a lion, and he gave them as proof the fact that he hunted zebras.

The delicate noses of the zebras told them there was really no lion in the neighborhood. The zebra deaths caused many to avoid the region. Superstitious, they decided the woods were haunted by the ghost of a lion.

One day the storyteller of the zebras was ambling, and through his mind ran plots for stories to amuse the other zebras, when suddenly his eyes brightened, and he said, "That's it! I'll tell a story about a Siamese cat who learns to speak our language! What an idea! That'll make 'em laugh!"

Just then the Siamese cat appeared before him, and said, "Hello there! Pleasant day today, isn't it!"

The zebra storyteller wasn't fit to be tied at hearing a cat speaking his language, because he'd been thinking about that very thing.

He took a good look at the cat, and he didn't know why, but there was something about his looks he didn't like, so he kicked him with a hoof and killed him.

That is the function of the storyteller.

1971

The Zebra Storyteller suggests that the purpose of stories is to prepare us for the unexpected. Though the storyteller thinks he is just spinning stories out of his own imagination, in order to amuse, his stories prove to be practical. When the extraordinary, the unheard-of occurs—like a Siamese cat speaking Zebraic—he is prepared because he has already imagined it, and he alone is able to protect his tribe against the unusual.

Other storytellers make the function of fiction less extraordinary. According to them, fiction enables readers to avoid projecting false hopes and fears (such as the zebras' superstitious belief that they are being preyed on by the ghost of a lion) and shows them what they can actually expect in their everyday lives, so that they can prepare themselves. In George Eliot's novel *Adam Bede*, Hetty Sorrel is being paid admiring attention by the young squire, and she dreams of elopement, marriage, all sorts of vague pleasures. She does not dream that she will be seduced, made pregnant, abandoned. Her imagination has not been trained to project any "narrative" other than her dreams: "Hetty had never read a novel," George Eliot tells us, "[so] how could she find a shape for her expectations?"

We are all storytellers, then, of one stripe or another. Whenever we plan the future or ponder a decision, we are telling stories—projecting expectations through narrative. Whenever we tell stories or read them, we are educating our imaginations, either extending our mental experience in the actual, as Hetty might have done by reading novels, or preparing ourselves for the extraordinary and unexpected, like the zebra storyteller.

The actual and the extraordinary suggest two different uses readers make of fiction. Sometimes we want to read about people like ourselves, or about places, things, experiences, and ideas that are familiar and agreeable. Most of us initially prefer American literature and twentieth-century literature to literature remote in time or place. Indeed, stories must somehow be related to our own lives before we can find them intellectually or emotionally meaningful. No matter what our literary experience and taste, most of us relate in a special way to stories about people like us, experiences like our own, and especially to a story that mentions our hometown or neighborhood or the name of the street that we used to walk along on our way to school. Whether we call this reading for identification or for relevance, no one would deny that one of the many things that fiction may be "for" is learning about ourselves and the world around us.

But at other times the last thing we want is a story about people like ourselves, experiences like those of our everyday lives, and places and times like here and now. At such times we want (or are accused of wanting) to escape. If fiction must be relevant enough to relate meaningfully to us, it must also be "irrelevant," different, other, strange—as strange, perhaps, as a Siamese cat speaking Zebraic. It must take us out of ourselves, out of the confining vision of our own eyes, conditioned by our own background and experience, and show us that there are ways of looking at the world other than our own. So, in addition to many stories about approximately our own time and place, this collection includes a sprinkling of stories written in the last century, a few written in vastly different cultures, and a fair number written about worlds that have not existed or do not (yet) exist.

What a story shows us or teaches us we may call its **message**—an
objective, universal truth that we were unaware of before reading the
story. We gradually learn, however, that stories tell us not so much
what life means as what it's like. Rather than abstract or "objective"
truths, stories deal with perceptions. These perceptions may be translated into messages, but we soon discover that the messages boil down
to things like "There's good and bad in everybody," "Hurting people is
wrong," and "Everything is not what it seems"—messages that Western Union, much less Western literature, might not find too urgent or
startlingly illuminating. Indeed, we do not have to agree with what a
story says or shows so long as we are convinced that if we had *those*
eyes and were *there*, this is what we might see.

Whenever we can say yes, we are convinced, then we have been
able to go beyond the limitations of our own vision, our own past
and conditions, and we are able to see a new world, or the same old
world in a new way. And by recognizing that we can see things
differently, we realize that things we used to think were fixed, objective
entities "out there" were fixed only in our perceptions. Or, as is too
often the case, we realize that we have been accepting things at face
value; we have been perceiving what habit and convention have told
us is "really there." This, then, may awaken us to look at things for
ourselves rather than accept them at conventional face value. For
example, we "know" a table top is square, but in a story we are told
it is diamond-shaped. We understand that if we were to look at the
table top from a certain angle it would look diamond-shaped. But
doesn't that imply that the table top is square only when we look from
a certain angle? And are we looking at it from that angle? We look
again, and we recognize that though we've always *known* it's a square,
we've never really *seen* it as one. The story has not only allowed us to
see reality from another angle, but it has helped us to sharpen our own
vision, our own experience.

Reading fiction may ultimately contribute significantly to the way
we understand and experience our own lives, but what kind of an
experience is reading fiction itself? What is going on inside us while we
are reading? What are we thinking? What are we feeling?

One way to find out is by an act of mental contortion: try looking
over your own shoulder while you read. Try it with this next story,
Guy de Maupassant's *The Jewelry*, paying more attention than you
usually do not just to the story but to your own thoughts and responses while you are reading it. You may want to pause a few extra
heartbeats after each sentence, fifteen to thirty extra seconds after
each paragraph, and two or three minutes after you finish reading the
whole thing.

Consider the title first. *The Jewelry*—Will it be lost? Will it be
stolen? Inherited? Something else? What will happen? What kind of
story will it be? Read the one-sentence first paragraph: nothing about
jewelry! But we have a young man and a young woman and love. M.
Lantin is "enveloped in love as in a net." This does not sound very
promising, does it? What are these people like? What is their situation?
As you read along how do your expectations change? How does your

view of the characters deepen? change? As you get into the story
notice what you remember of the early portions and any details in mid-
story that remind you of earlier ones. There are other questions, but
perhaps some of them can wait until after you have watched yourself
read the story.

GUY DE MAUPASSANT

The Jewelry °

Having met the girl one evening, at the house of the office-superinten-
dent, M. Lantin became enveloped in love as in a net.

She was the daughter of a country-tutor, who had been dead for
several years. Afterward she had come to Paris with her mother, who
made regular visits to several bourgeois families of the neighborhood,
in hopes of being able to get her daughter married. They were poor
and respectable, quiet and gentle. The young girl seemed to be the
very ideal of that pure good woman to whom every young man dreams
of entrusting his future. Her modest beauty had a charm of angelic
shyness; and the slight smile that always dwelt about her lips seemed a
reflection of her heart.

Everybody sang her praises; all who knew her kept saying: "The
man who gets her will be lucky. No one could find a nicer girl than
that."

M. Lantin, who was then chief clerk in the office of the Minister of
the Interior, with a salary of 3,500 francs[1] a year, demanded her
hand, and married her.

He was unutterably happy with her. She ruled his home with an
economy so adroit that they really seemed to live in luxury. It would
be impossible to conceive of any attentions, tendernesses, playful
caresses which she did not lavish upon her husband; and such was the
charm of her person that, six years after he married her, he loved her
even more than he did the first day.

There were only two points upon which he ever found fault with
her—her love of the theater, and her passion for false jewelry.

Her lady-friends (she was acquainted with the wives of several
small office holders) were always bringing her tickets for the theaters;
whenever there was a performance that made a sensation, she always
had her *loge* secured, even for first performances; and she would drag
her husband with her to all these entertainments, which used to tire
him horribly after his day's work. So at last he begged her to go to the
theater with some lady-acquaintances who would consent to see her

---

° Translated by Lafcadio Hearn.
1. The rate of exchange was five francs
to the dollar, but in purchasing power
those francs would now be worth about
five dollars or more.

home afterward. She refused for quite a while—thinking it would not look very well to go out thus unaccompanied by her husband. But finally she yielded, just to please him; and he felt infinitely grateful to her therefor.

Now this passion for the theater at last evoked in her the desire of dress. It was true that her toilette remained simple, always in good taste, but modest; and her sweet grace, her irresistible grace, ever smiling and shy, seemed to take fresh charm from the simplicity of her robes. But she got into the habit of suspending in her pretty ears two big cut pebbles, fashioned in imitation of diamonds; and she wore necklaces of false pearls, bracelets of false gold, and haircombs studded with paste-imitations of precious stones.

Her husband who felt shocked by this love of tinsel and show, would often say—"My dear, when one has not the means to afford real jewelry, one should appear adorned with one's natural beauty and grace only—and these gifts are the rarest of jewels."

But she would smile sweetly and answer: "What does it matter? I like those things—that is my little whim. I know you are right; but one can't make oneself over again. I've always loved jewelry so much!"

And then she would roll the pearls of the necklaces between her fingers, and make the facets of the cut crystals flash in the light, repeating: "Now look at them—see how well the work is done. You would swear it was real jewelry."

He would then smile in his turn, and declare to her: "You have the tastes of a regular Gypsy."

Sometimes, in the evening, when they were having a chat by the fire, she would rise and fetch the morocco box in which she kept her "stock" (as M. Lantin called it)—would put it on the tea-table, and begin to examine the false jewelry with passionate delight, as if she experienced some secret and mysterious sensations of pleasure in their contemplation; and she would insist on putting one of the necklaces round her husband's neck, and laugh till she couldn't laugh any more, crying out: "Oh! how funny you look!" Then she would rush into his arms, and kiss him furiously.

One winter's night, after she had been to the Opera, she came home chilled through, and trembling. Next day she had a bad cough. Eight days after that, she died of pneumonia.

Lantin was very nearly following her into the tomb. His despair was so frightful that in one single month his hair turned white. He wept from morning till night, feeling his heart torn by inexpressible suffering—ever haunted by the memory of her, by the smile, by the voice, by all the charm of the dead woman.

Time did not assuage his grief. Often during office hours his fellow-clerks went off to a corner to chat about this or that topic of the day—his cheeks might have been seen to swell up all of a sudden, his nose wrinkle, his eyes fill with water—he would pull a frightful face, and begin to sob.

He had kept his dead companion's room just in the order she had left it, and he used to lock himself up in it every evening to think about her—all the furniture, and even all her dresses, remained in the same place they had been on the last day of her life.

But life became hard for him. His salary, which, in his wife's hands, had amply sufficed for all household needs, now proved scarcely sufficient to supply his own few wants. And he asked himself in astonishment how she had managed always to furnish him with excellent wines and with delicate eating which he could not now afford at all with his scanty means.

He got a little into debt, like men obliged to live by their wits. At last one morning that he happened to find himself without a cent in his pocket, and a whole week to wait before he could draw his monthly salary, he thought of selling something; and almost immediately it occurred to him to sell his wife's "stock"—for he had always borne a secret grudge against the flash-jewelry that used to annoy him so much in former days. The mere sight of it, day after day, somewhat spoiled the sad pleasure of thinking of his darling.

He tried a long time to make a choice among the heap of trinkets she had left behind her—for up to the very last day of her life she had kept obstinately buying them, bringing home some new thing almost every night—and finally he resolved to take the big pearl necklace which she used to like the best of all, and which he thought ought certainly to be worth six or eight francs, as it was really very nicely mounted for an imitation necklace.

He put it in his pocket, and walked toward the office, following the boulevards, and looking for some jewelry-store on the way, where he could enter with confidence.

Finally he saw a place and went in; feeling a little ashamed of thus exposing his misery, and of trying to sell such a trifling object.

"Sir," he said to the jeweler, "please tell me what this is worth."

The jeweler took the necklace, examined it, weighed it, took up a magnifying glass, called his clerk, talked to him in whispers, put down the necklace on the counter, and drew back a little bit to judge of its effect at a distance.

M. Lantin, feeling very much embarrassed by all these ceremonies, opened his mouth and began to declare—"Oh! I know it can't be worth much" . . . when the jeweler interrupted him saying:

"Well, sir, that is worth between twelve and fifteen thousand francs; but I cannot buy it unless you can let me know exactly how you came by it."

The widower's eyes opened enormously, and he stood gaping—unable to understand. Then after a while he stammered out: "You said? . . . Are you sure?" The jeweler, misconstruing the cause of this astonishment, replied in a dry tone—"Go elsewhere if you like, and see if you can get any more for it. The very most I would give for it is fifteen thousand. Come back and see me again, if you can't do better."

M. Lantin, feeling perfectly idiotic, took his necklace and departed; obeying a confused desire to find himself alone and to get a chance to think.

But the moment he found himself in the street again, he began to laugh, and he muttered to himself: "The fool!—oh! what a fool; If I had only taken him at his word. Well, well!—a jeweler who can't tell paste from real jewelry!"

And he entered another jewelry-store, at the corner of the Rue de la Paix. The moment the jeweler set eyes on the necklace, he exclaimed —"Hello! I know that necklace well—it was sold here!"

M. Lantin, very nervous, asked:

"What's it worth?"

"Sir, I sold it for twenty-five thousand francs. I am willing to buy it back again for eighteen thousand—if you can prove to me satis-factorily, according to legal prescriptions, how you came into posses-sion of it"—This time, M. Lantin was simply paralyzed with astonishment. He said: "Well . . . but please look at it again, sir. I always thought until now that it was . . . was false."

The jeweler said:

"Will you give me your name, sir?"

"Certainly. My name is Lantin; I am employed at the office of the Minister of the Interior. I live at No. 16, Rue des Martyrs."

The merchant opened the register, looked, and said: "Yes; this necklace was sent to the address of Madame Lantin, 16 Rue des Martyrs, on July 20th, 1876."

And the two men looked into each other's eyes—the clerk wild with surprise; the jeweler suspecting he had a thief before him.

The jeweler resumed:

"Will you be kind enough to leave this article here for twenty-four hours only—I'll give you a receipt."

M. Lantin stuttered: "Yes—ah! certainly." And he went out, fold-ing up the receipt, which he put in his pocket.

Then he crossed the street, went the wrong way, found out his mistake, returned by way of the Tuileries, crossed the Seine, found out he had taken the wrong road again, and went back to the Champs-Elysées without being able to get one clear idea into his head. He tried to reason, to understand. His wife could never have bought so valu-able an object as that. Certainly not. But then, it must have been a present! . . . A present from whom? What for?

He stopped and stood stock-still in the middle of the avenue.

A horrible suspicion swept across his mind. . . . She? . . . But then all those other pieces of jewelry must have been presents also! . . . Then it seemed to him that the ground was heaving under his feet; that a tree, right in front of him, was falling toward him; he thrust out his arms instinctively, and fell senseless.

He recovered his consciousness again in a drug-store to which some bystanders had carried him. He had them lead him home, and he locked himself into his room.

Until nightfall he cried without stopping, biting his handkerchief to keep himself from screaming out. Then, completely worn out with grief and fatigue, he went to bed, and slept a leaden sleep.

A ray of sunshine awakened him, and he rose and dressed himself slowly to go to the office. It was hard to have to work after such a shock. Then he reflected that he might be able to excuse himself to the superintendent, and he wrote to him. Then he remembered he would have to go back to the jeweler's; and shame made his face purple. He remained thinking a long time. Still he could not leave the necklace there; he put on his coat and went out.

It was a fine day; the sky extended all blue over the city, and seemed to make it smile. Strollers were walking aimlessly about, with their hands in their pockets.

Lantin thought as he watched them passing: "How lucky the men are who have fortunes! With money a man can even shake off grief— you can go where you please—travel—amuse yourself! Oh! if I were only rich!"

He suddenly discovered he was hungry—not having eaten anything since the evening before. But his pockets were empty; and he remembered the necklace. Eighteen thousand francs! Eighteen thousand francs!—that was a sum—that was!

He made his way to the Rue de la Paix and began to walk backward and forward on the sidewalk in front of the store. Eighteen thousand francs! Twenty times he started to go in; but shame always kept him back.

Still he was hungry—very hungry—and had not a cent. He made one brusque resolve, and crossed the street almost at a run, so as not to let himself have time to think over the matter; and he rushed into the jeweler's.

As soon as he saw him, the merchant hurried forward, and offered him a chair with smiling politeness. Even the clerks came forward to stare at Lantin, with gaiety in their eyes and smiles about their lips.

The jeweler said: "Sir, I made inquiries; and if you are still so disposed, I am ready to pay you down the price I offered you."

The clerk stammered: "Why, yes—sir, certainly."

The jeweler took from a drawer eighteen big bills,[2] counted them, and held them out to Lantin, who signed a little receipt, and thrust the money feverishly into his pocket.

Then, as he was on the point of leaving, he turned to the ever-smiling merchant, and said, lowering his eyes: "I have some—I have some other jewelry, which came to me in the same—from the same inheritance. Would you purchase them also from me?"

The merchant bowed, and answered: "Why, certainly, sir— certainly. . . ." One of the clerks rushed out to laugh at his ease; another kept blowing his nose as hard as he could.

Lantin, impassive, flushed and serious, said: "I will bring them to you."

And he hired a cab to get the jewelry.

When he returned to the store, an hour later, he had not yet breakfasted. They examined the jewelry—piece by piece—putting a value on each. Nearly all had been purchased from that very house.

Lantin, now, disputed estimates made, got angry, insisted on seeing the books, and talked louder and louder the higher the estimates grew.

The big diamond earrings were worth 20,000 francs; the bracelets, 35,000; the brooches, rings, and medallions, 16,000; a set of emeralds and sapphires, 14,000; solitaire, suspended to a gold neckchain, 40,000; the total value being estimated at 196,000 francs.

2. French paper money varies in size, the larger the bill the larger the denomination.

The merchant observed with mischievous good nature: "The person who owned these must have put all her savings into jewelry."

Lantin answered with gravity: "Perhaps that is as good a way of saving money as any other." And he went off, after having agreed with the merchant that an expert should make a counter-estimate for him the next day.

When he found himself in the street again, he looked at the Column Vendôme[3] with the desire to climb it, as if it were a May pole. He felt jolly enough to play leapfrog over the Emperor's head—up there in the blue sky.

He breakfasted at Voisin's[4] restaurant, and ordered wine at 20 francs a bottle.

Then he hired a cab and drove out to the Bois.[5] He looked at the carriages passing with a sort of contempt, and a wild desire to yell out to the passers-by: "I am rich, too—I am! I have 200,000 francs!"

The recollection of the office suddenly came back to him. He drove there, walked right into the superintendent's private room, and said: "Sir, I come to give you my resignation. I have just come into a fortune of *three* hundred thousand francs." Then he shook hands all round with his fellow-clerks; and told them all about his plans for a new career. Then he went to dinner at the Café Anglais.

Finding himself seated at the same table with a man who seemed to him quite genteel, he could not resist the itching desire to tell him, with a certain air of coquetry, that he had just inherited a fortune of *four* hundred thousand francs.

For the first time in his life he went to the theater without feeling bored by the performance; and he passed the night in revelry and debauch.

Six months after he married again. His second wife was the most upright of spouses, but had a terrible temper. She made his life very miserable.

1883

Did you notice the "seemed" in the second paragraph? If you did, it probably alerted you to the fact that the girl may not have been what she appeared to be. Were you surprised by the "boy-gets-girl" phase ending so abruptly with the one-sentence fourth paragraph? Surely most readers have some expectations of a typical, drawn-out love story, full of difficulties. In the fifth paragraph—a little longer, three sentences, one of them longish—six years pass and all is going well. You've probably read enough stories to know that this cannot go on; something has to interrupt their perfect happiness. So you are prepared for the turn in the next paragraph—she has faults. But such

3. Famous column with statue of Napoleon at the top.

4. Like the Café Anglais below, a well-known and high-priced restaurant. When, at Christmas 1870, Paris was under siege and thousands were starving, Voisin's served elephant soup, stuffed head of donkey, jugged kangaroo, roast camel, and cat dressed with rats—some, but obviously not all, the delicacies from the zoo.

5. Large Parisian park where the rich took their outings.

little faults. Why are such little faults dwelt on for a page when it took less space than that for M. Lantin to fall in love, marry, and have six years of bliss? Then, all of a sudden—we're scarcely a third of the way into the story—she dies, as abruptly and with as little fuss as she was married. Where do we go from here?

Did you notice that the wife's first name is never mentioned? What do we know about her? How do we learn it? What kind of a person is she? How do our early opinions or suppositions fare as we read the story to the end?

What we know of her is limited by the fact that we see and know of her only what M. Lantin knows and sees, and we learn what we learn only as he learns it. We do not know much more about him, however, for though we follow him and his experiences through the story we rarely get into his mind and never get in very deeply. Of course if we knew all there was to know, what Lantin did not know, there would not be much of a story.

How much of a story is there, in fact? What does it amount to? Well, it is about a woman who is not exactly what she seems to be, and it is called *The Jewelry*, and the jewelry is not exactly what it seems to be either. That's how we learn that she was not what she seemed to be, so the title and the jewelry itself offer an insight into what the story is all about.

If someone told you about a story in which jewels were not what they seemed, you would more than likely expect the story to be about fake jewelry that was supposed to be real (and indeed de Maupassant did write another story in which that is the case). The idea would still be the same—things are not always what they seem to be. We would be readier for that kind of switch, however: that people are greedy and some will try to substitute worthless things for those of real value may be disappointing but not surprising. But vice versa? Who ever substitutes real money for counterfeit or tries to pass off an original composition as a plagiarism?

Is the twist just a gimmick? It certainly is a flouting of expectations. So is tossing off the marriage and the death of M. Lantin's wife in a sentence or two, without a dramatized scene. And how about the ending? Though upset at his discovery and ashamed at first, it takes Lantin less than a day to recognize how rich he is and what such riches mean. Not many of us, I should think, expected him to shrug off his shame so quickly and debauch so rapidly and deeply. Was his earlier morality destroyed when he recognized his wife's deception, or was it too superficial, "fake," based upon his own modest means and lack of opportunity? So the flouting of narrative convention, the twists on the expected, are echoed in the story's flouting of moral conventions, its cynicism: things are not what they seem, and those "things" include human values, moral precepts, as well as jewels—and wives.

The final twist, the almost gratuitous last short paragraph would seem to confirm this cynicism: Lantin's upright wife made his life miserable. Or does it? We are so used to twisting by now we might find de Maupassant doing it again: although the story seems to suggest the ironical view that Lantin was better off with his "fake jewel" of a first wife than with his truly upright second wife, in terms of Lantin's conduct he got what he deserved in very conventional terms. *He* married his first wife for love; *he* led a decent life; *he* was happy. Then *he* grew cynical and debauched; and now *he* is miserable.

We have read of Lantin's love and of his grief, of his shock and shame, his exhilaration, revelry, and misery. We have imagined what such experiences were like and, to a degree, shared them with him, but we have also had other responses as well—surprise; a different kind of shock; disgust perhaps, perhaps a wrenching feeling of the cruelty, injustice, meaninglessness of life as seen from a certain cynical angle. Each of the elements of the story has contributed to our intellectual and emotional experience of it. We will now look more closely at each of these elements of fiction in turn, and see how they work in other stories. And we will then broaden our perspectives, looking at stories in biographical, cultural, and literary contexts. Our aim will be to learn to read in a more informed, sensitive, receptive, and perceptive way, getting more enjoyment and insight out of each story.

Text

2 PLOT

In *The Zebra Storyteller* you can see the skeleton of the typical short story **plot** or **plot structure**. Plot simply means the arrangement of the **action,** an imagined event or a series of such events.

Action usually involves **conflict,** a struggle between opposing forces, and it often falls into something like the same five parts that we find in a play: exposition, rising action, turning point (or climax), falling action, conclusion (or catastrophe). The conflict in this little tale is between the Siamese cat and the zebras, especially the zebra story-teller. The first part of the action, called the **exposition,** introduces characters, situation, and, usually, time and place. The exposition here is achieved in three sentences: the time is "once upon a," the place Africa, the characters a Siamese cat who speaks Zebraic and an innocent zebra, and the situation their meeting. We then enter the second part of the plot, the **rising action:** events that complicate the situation and intensify or complicate the conflict or introduce new ones. The first event here is the meeting between an innocent zebra and the Zebraic-speaking cat. That initial conflict of zebra and cat is over in a hurry—the zebra who is "fit to be tied" is tied up and eaten. Complications build with the cat's continuing success in killing zebras, and the zebras' growing fears and consequent superstitious belief that the ghost of a lion haunts the region preying on zebras. The **turning point** or **climax** of the action is the third part of the story, the appearance of the zebra storyteller: until now the cat has had it all going his way, but his luck is about to change. From this point on the complications that grew in the first part of the story are untangled—the zebra story-teller, for example, is not surprised when he meets a Siamese cat speaking Zebraic, "because he'd been thinking about that very thing" —this is the fourth part of the story, the reverse movement or **falling action.** The story ends at the fifth part, the **conclusion** or **catastrophe:** the point at which the situation that was destabilized at the beginning of the story (when the Zebraic-speaking cat appears) becomes stable once more: Africa is once again free of cats speaking the language of zebras.

Before the parts of the action can be arranged, of course, they must be selected. The opening passages of the first two stories in this chapter may show some of the issues involved in **selection.**

"The thousand injuries of Fortunato I had borne as I best could, but when he ventured upon insult I vowed revenge." So begins Edgar Allan Poe's *The Cask of Amontillado.* What kinds of injuries? Were there actually that many? Were they real injuries or imaginary? What was the insult? Why was the insult worse than all the injuries? Poe could have invented answers for these questions, but he chose not to.

The first scene of Richard Connell's *The Most Dangerous Game* provides some information—the general location of the yacht, the superstition about the island, the fact that Rainsford is an expert hunter—but it is a rather full scene for one that, on first reading at least, seems to have no essential connection with the exciting events that follow. And Whitney, who appears to be a major character here, we see no more. Why does Connell include this scene and this character?

Authors leave out some things that seem at first to be important to the story and include some things that do not seem very important. **Selection** of events is a significant element of storytelling.

But what do we mean when we say an author selects events? Selects from where? It's not as if these events exist somewhere, as historical events do. Like scientists with their hypotheses and philosophers with their premises, many of us who talk or write about fiction begin with a fiction: we speak as if the people and places exist and the events of a story take place in a world of the author's imagination, a world from which he or she chooses the story elements, a world we can understand and almost re-create in terms of our own. We call this world the **history** behind the story.

Once events have been selected, they must be connected. In the history, events take place in simple chronological sequence: "The king died and then the queen died," to use one critic's example. This sequential narrative of events, the critic says, is not a plot. But if we connect the events, if we structure the history—"The king died and then the queen died of grief"—we have a plot.

Many of us are used to thinking of cause and effect as a natural part of an event, as somehow *in* the event, rather than as an interpretation of a relationship between two events. Often authors, bent on getting us to accept the fiction as a kind of truth, try to hide their structuring of that history from us. Montresor's scheme of revenge against Fortunato in *The Cask of Amontillado* is not the author's plot, Poe leads us to believe, but Montresor's; and, while reading, we probably accept that it is Montresor who, interpreting Fortunato's insult as cause for revenge, generates the events that follow. Only later, putting the story down, do we bother to think that it was Poe who invented and arranged the events, created the plot.

Sometimes, when the characters do not make the connections that turn history to plot, the author makes the reader do it. Hemingway, for example, is very reluctant to structure his stories by connecting events or other details. He just puts down one after another, as if they came into the story that way directly from the history. He uses few connectives, and most of these are neutral, noninterpretive *ands*. In the eleventh paragraph of *The Short Happy Life of Francis Macomber*, for example, an *and* appears where many of us would expect (and perhaps silently insert) a *so*: Macomber is waiting for his wife to enter their tent: "She did not speak to him when she came in *and* he left the tent at once. . . ." Poe's characters make the connections; Heming-way's reader must make them.

In the history, events exist in chronological sequence, and they can be reported that way in the story: "The king died and then the queen died." But the story can be ordered differently: "The queen died after the king died" recounts the same history, but the sequence of events has been changed. The history has been structured. The reader of the first sentence focuses on the king first, the reader of the second sentence on the queen. The difference in emphasis can be significant.

In some stories, such as *The Most Dangerous Game,* the events seem to come unstructured from the history: Rainsford speaks with Whitney aboard the yacht; Whitney goes below; Rainsford falls over-board. . . . The events are presented one after another in the same sequence as in the history. The reader reads along finding out what happens next. In a detective story, on the other hand, the major action (the crime) has taken place before the story begins, and the forward action of the story is the detective's attempt to re-create the past and figure out what happened. The reader does not ask *What will happen?* but *What has happened?* In some other stories, like Faulkner's *A Rose for Emily* in the next chapter, readers may not feel compelled to ask themselves *What happened?* until the end of the story, when a sudden revelation from the fictional past forces them to reconsider all that has gone before. In such stories it is obvious that the author is creating a plot, ordering the events in the story in a sequence different from that in which they occurred, but just as Poe disguised his plot as his narrator's, so Faulkner disguises his reordering of events as the order of the recollections of his narrator followed by that narrator's learning a new fact about the past at the end of the story.

Though the sequence of events in the detective story is reordered in terms of the reader's knowledge of the events—we learn who done it in the past only long after the story beings—the past is not usually replayed. We do not see the crime reenacted before us (although the detective may describe the crime when he gives his solution). The story simply begins in the middle of the history—after the crime—and moves forward as the detective figures out what happened. In *The Short Happy Life of Francis Macomber,* however, there is a replay or flashback. As in a detective story, *Macomber* begins in the middle of the history, which is made up essentially of two hunting episodes. The story begins not with the first but between the two. The first sentence of the story ends, "pretending that nothing had happened," clearly suggesting that, as in a detective story, something significant *had* happened. The reader asks what it was, with curiosity and interest aroused. There are some clues in the first few pages, but neither a detective nor the reader has to reconstruct the past episode from clues. That episode is brought forward into the fictional present and re-presented. About six pages into the story we are told, "It had started the night before," and the following paragraph begins a scene that took place earlier.

One reason for structuring the history into plot is to engage the reader's attention, to make the reader read on. The story of a crime can be written chronologically, so that we know who done it from the beginning and are just reading on to discover if or when or how the criminal is caught; Dostoevsky tells the story of *Crime and Punishment* this way. Such stories are not, strictly speaking, detective stories: they do not play so much on **curiosity**—the desire to know what is happening or has happened. It is the sheer power of curiosity that keeps us reading intensely when we know as little as Watson or Sherlock Holmes himself at the beginning. Nor is it only the detective story that plays upon our curiosity. We have already seen how the phrase "pretending that nothing had happened" at the end of the first sentence of *Macomber* sets us to wondering just what had happened; by the time we find out, six pages later, we are already deep into the characters and situation—we're hooked. Even titles, such as *A Very Old Man with Enormous Wings* or *The Rocking-Horse Winner*, can make us pick up a story; after that, it's up to the story to keep us engaged.

Perhaps stronger than curiosity, or interest in what *is* happening, is **suspense**, the expectation of and doubt about what is *going* to happen next, as in the lion hunt in *Macomber*. The very title of *The Most Dangerous Game* arouses suspense. What *is* the most dangerous game? Russian roulette, perhaps? Within the first fifty words we run across such terms as *mystery, suggestive, curious dread, superstition*, and we may begin to think of the supernatural (but what kind of "game" does that suggest?). In the same passage is *Ship-Trap Island*, and another possible meaning for game, another direction for our anticipation, opens up: hunting and trapping game. This is reinforced in the next twenty-five lines by the talk of hunting. The game must be some exceedingly fierce animal. All sorts of expectations build: supernatural animals, monsters, prehistoric animals, cannibals, Satan himself—worse! By the time Whitney says good night and we come to the first break in the story, our expectations are at a pretty high pitch. There's a good deal of suspense, and our minds are actively scanning four, five, maybe six possibilities of what kinds of things might happen next.

Try reading another couple of pages—say, down to Rainsford's introducing himself ("I'm Sanger Rainsford of New York")—watching yourself anticipate and put together details or clues. What kind of reinforcement do those early references to mystery and superstition get from the unexpected, mirage-like appearance of a palatial chateau, a tall spiked iron gate, a gargoyle on the door knocker, and a gigantic man opening the door? Don't you find yourself trying to fit these things into a pattern? Sooner or later some possibilities are eliminated and one pattern dominates; the story may at some point simply tell you what possibility will be pursued. It is not too long before you learn for sure what the game is. But by that time there are new reasons for suspense—how will it come out? You get to another layer of suspense following Rainsford through a **serial ordeal**, a series of dangerous episodes.

Stories are not all fun and games, no matter how dangerous. Many of them seek to give you new insights into human perception, experience, meaning. They strive to tell truths—new, subjective truths, but truths—even though they "lie" about the actuality of the people and events represented. But first they have to get your attention, and one way is by arousing your curiosity and exciting your anticipation; that's what plot is primarily for. In order to keep you engaged and alert, a story must make you ask questions about what will happen or what will be revealed next. To respond fully to a story you must be alert to the signals and guess along with the author. At least in one aspect, fiction is a guessing game.

Like all guessing games, from quiz shows to philosophy, the plot game in fiction has certain guidelines. A well-structured plot will play fair with you, offering at appropriate points all the necessary indicators or clues to what will happen next, not just springing new and essential information on you at the last minute ("Meanwhile, unknown to our hero, the Marines were just on the other side of the hill . . ."). It is this playing fair that makes the ending of a well-structured story satisfying or, when you look back on it, inevitable. Most stories also offer a number of reasonable but false signals (red herrings) to get you off the scent, so that in a well-structured story the ending, though inevitable, is also surprising. And though there is usually an overarching action from beginning to end, in many stories there are layers of expectation or suspense, so that as soon as one question is answered another comes forth to replace it, keeping you in doubt and suspense as to the final outcome.

Unlike most guessing games, however, the reward is not for the right guess—anticipating the outcome before the final paragraph—but for the number of guesses, right *and* wrong, that you make, the number of signals you respond to. If you are misled by none of the false signals in the early pages of *The Most Dangerous Game*, you may be closer to being "right," but you may have missed many of the implications of the story. But, more important, you have missed the pleasure of learning the "truth" offered by the story for yourself, and you know how much less meaningful it is to be told something than it is to learn it for yourself, through your own experience. Fiction is a way of transmitting not just perception but experience.

How do you react, in *The Cask of Amontillado*, to Montresor's concern for Fortunato's coughing? What do you anticipate? What is it that you later discover? Alertness to signals, anticipating what is to come next, and remembering what has been said and signaled earlier are essential to fully appreciating and understanding stories. By the time you finish the Connell story, you should be able to figure out why he structured it so, why the first scene was there. You might have some idea—though not necessarily a firm and simple answer—as to why, in addition to arousing suspense, Hemingway wanted *The Short Happy Life of Francis Macomber* to begin in the middle of the history and later flash back to the beginning. You may know why insult is more important to Montresor than injury; you may even be able to suggest why Poe did not recount the thousand injuries or the fatal insult.

EDGAR ALLAN POE

The Cask of Amontillado

The thousand injuries of Fortunato I had borne as I best could, but when he ventured upon insult I vowed revenge. You, who so well know the nature of my soul, will not suppose, however, that I gave utterance to a threat. *At length* I would be avenged; this was a point definitely settled—but the very definitiveness with which it was resolved precluded the idea of risk. I must not only punish but punish with impunity. A wrong is unredressed when retribution overtakes its redresser. It is equally unredressed when the avenger fails to make himself felt as such to him who has done the wrong.

It must be understood that neither by word nor deed had I given Fortunato cause to doubt my good will. I continued, as was my wont, to smile in his face, and he did not perceive that my smile *now* was at the thought of his immolation.

He had a weak point—this Fortunato—although in other regards he was a man to be respected and even feared. He prided himself on his connoisseurship in wine. Few Italians have the true virtuoso spirit. For the most part their enthusiasm is adopted to suit the time and opportunity, to practice imposture upon the British and Austrian millionaires. In painting and gemmary, Fortunato, like his countrymen, was a quack, but in the matter of old wines he was sincere. In this respect I did not differ from him materially;—I was skilful in the Italian vintages myself, and bought largely whenever I could.

It was about dusk, one evening during the supreme madness of the carnival season, that I encountered my friend. He accosted me with excessive warmth, for he had been drinking much. The man wore motley. He had on a tight-fitting parti-striped dress, and his head was surmounted by the conical cap and bells. I was so pleased to see him that I thought I should never have done wringing his hand.

I said to him—"My dear Fortunato, you are luckily met. How remarkably well you are looking to-day. But I have received a pipe[1] of what passes for Amontillado, and I have my doubts."

"How?" said he. "Amontillado? A pipe? Impossible! And in the middle of the carnival!"

"I have my doubts," I replied; "and I was silly enough to pay the full Amontillado price without consulting you in the matter. You were not to be found, and I was fearful of losing a bargain."

"Amontillado!"

"I have my doubts."

"Amontillado!"

"And I must satisfy them."

"Amontillado!"

"As you are engaged, I am on my way to Luchresi. If any one has a critical turn, it is he. He will tell me——"

1. A cask holding 126 gallons.

"Luchresi cannot tell Amontillado from Sherry."

"And yet some fools will have it that his taste is a match for your own."

"Come, let us go."

"Whither?"

"To your vaults."

"My friend, no; I will not impose upon your good nature. I perceive you have an engagement. Luchresi——"

"I have no engagement;—come."

"My friend, no. It is not the engagement, but the severe cold with which I perceive you are afflicted. The vaults are insufferably damp. They are encrusted with niter."

"Let us go, nevertheless. The cold is merely nothing. Amontillado! You have been imposed upon. And as for Luchresi, he cannot distinguish Sherry from Amontillado."

Thus speaking, Fortunato possessed himself of my arm; and putting on a mask of black silk and drawing a *roquelaire*[2] closely about my person, I suffered him to hurry me to my palazzo.

There were no attendants at home; they had absconded to make merry in honor of the time. I had told them that I should not return until the morning, and had given them explicit orders not to stir from the house. These orders were sufficient, I well knew, to insure their immediate disappearance, one and all, as soon as my back was turned.

I took from their sconces two flambeaux, and giving one to Fortunato, bowed him through several suites of rooms to the archway that led into the vaults. I passed down a long and winding staircase, requesting him to be cautious as he followed. We came at length to the foot of the descent, and stood together on the damp ground of the catacombs of the Montresors.

The gait of my friend was unsteady, and the bells upon his cap jingled as he strode.

"The pipe?" said he.

"It is farther on," said I; "but observe the white web-work which gleams from these cavern walls."

He turned towards me, and looked into my eyes with two filmy orbs that distilled the rheum of intoxication.

"Niter?" he asked, at length.

"Niter," I replied. "How long have you had that cough?"

"Ugh! ugh! ugh!—ugh! ugh! ugh!—ugh! ugh! ugh! ugh! ugh! ugh!—ugh! ugh! ugh!"

My poor friend found it impossible to reply for many minutes.

"It is nothing," he said, at last.

"Come," I said, with decision, "we will go back; your health is precious. You are rich, respected, admired, beloved; you are happy, as once I was. You are a man to be missed. For me it is no matter. We will go back; you will be ill, and I cannot be responsible. Besides, there is Luchresi——"

2. Roquelaure, man's heavy, knee-length cloak, usually trimmed in fur and silklined, 18th century.

"Enough," he said; "the cough is a mere nothing; it will not kill me. I shall not die of a cough."

"True—true," I replied; "and, indeed, I had no intention of alarming you unnecessarily—but you should use all proper caution. A draft of this Medoc will defend us from the damps."

Here I knocked off the neck of a bottle which I drew from a long row of its fellows that lay upon the mold.

"Drink," I said, presenting him the wine.

He raised it to his lips with a leer. He paused and nodded to me familiarly, while his bells jingled.

"I drink," he said, "to the buried that repose around us."

"And I to your long life."

He again took my arm, and we proceeded.

"These vaults," he said, "are extensive."

"The Montresors," I replied, "were a great and numerous family."

"I forget your arms."

"A huge human foot d'or,[3] in a field azure; the foot crushes a serpent rampant whose fangs are imbedded in the heel."

"And the motto?"

"Nemo me impune lacessit."[4]

"Good!" he said.

The wine sparkled in his eyes and the bells jingled. My own fancy grew warm with the Medoc. We had passed through long walls of piled skeletons, with casks and puncheons intermingling, into the inmost recesses of the catacombs. I paused again, and this time I made bold to seize Fortunato by an arm above the elbow.

"The niter!" I said; "see, it increases. It hangs like moss upon the vaults. We are below the river's bed. The drops of moisture trickle among the bones. Come, we will go back ere it is too late. Your cough——"

"It is nothing," he said; "let us go on. But first, another draft of the Medoc."

I broke and reached him a flagon of De Grâve.[5] He emptied it at a breath. His eyes flashed with a fierce light. He laughed and threw the bottle upward with a gesticulation I did not understand.

I looked at him in surprise. He repeated the movement—a grotesque one.

"You do not comprehend?" he said.

"Not I," I replied.

"Then you are not of the brotherhood."

"How?"

"You are not of the masons."[6]

"Yes, yes," I said; "yes, yes."

"You? Impossible! A mason?"

"A mason," I replied.

---

3. Of gold.
4. No one provokes me with impunity.
5. Like Médoc, a French wine.
6. Masons or Freemasons, an international secret society condemned by the Catholic church. Montresor means by mason one who builds with stone, brick, etc.

"A sign," he said, "a sign."

"It is this," I answered, producing from beneath the folds of my *roquelaire* a trowel.

"You jest," he exclaimed, recoiling a few paces. "But let us proceed to the Amontillado."

"Be it so," I said, replacing the tool beneath the cloak and again offering him my arm. He leaned upon it heavily. We continued our route in search of the Amontillado. We passed through a range of low arches, descended, passed on, and descending again, arrived at a deep crypt, in which the foulness of the air caused our flambeaux rather to glow than flame.

At the most remote end of the crypt there appeared another less spacious. Its walls had been lined with human remains, piled to the vault overhead, in the fashion of the great catacombs of Paris. Three sides of this interior crypt were still ornamented in this manner. From the fourth the bones had been thrown down, and lay promiscuously upon the earth, forming at one point a mound of some size. Within the wall thus exposed by the displacing of the bones, we perceived a still interior crypt or recess, in depth about four feet, in width three, in height six or seven. It seemed to have been constructed for no especial use within itself, but formed merely the interval between two of the colossal supports of the roof of the catacombs, and was backed by one of their circumscribing walls of solid granite.

It was in vain that Fortunato, uplifting his dull torch, endeavored to pry into the depth of the recess. Its termination the feeble light did not enable us to see.

"Proceed," I said; "herein is the Amontillado. As for Luchresi——"

"He is an ignoramus," interrupted my friend, as he stepped unsteadily forward, while I followed immediately at his heels. In an instant he had reached the extremity of the niche, and finding his progress arrested by the rock, stood stupidly bewildered. A moment more and I had fettered him to the granite. In its surface were two iron staples, distant from each other about two feet, horizontally. From one of these depended a short chain, from the other a padlock. Throwing the links about his waist, it was but the work of a few seconds to secure it. He was too much astounded to resist. Withdrawing the key I stepped back from the recess.

"Pass your hand," I said, "over the wall; you cannot help feeling the niter. Indeed it is *very* damp. Once more let me *implore* you to return. No? Then I must positively leave you. But I must first render you all the little attentions in my power."

"The Amontillado!" ejaculated my friend, not yet recovered from his astonishment.

"True," I replied; "the Amontillado."

As I said these words I busied myself among the pile of bones of which I have before spoken. Throwing them aside, I soon uncovered a quantity of building stone and mortar. With these materials and with the aid of my trowel, I began vigorously to wall up the entrance of the niche.

I had scarcely laid the first tier of the masonry when I discovered that the intoxication of Fortunato had in a great measure worn off. The earliest indication I had of this was a low moaning cry from the depth of the recess. It was *not* the cry of a drunken man. There was then a long and obstinate silence. I laid the second tier, and the third, and the fourth; and then I heard the furious vibrations of the chain. The noise lasted for several minutes, during which, that I might hearken to it with the more satisfaction, I ceased my labors and sat down upon the bones. When at last the clanking subsided, I resumed the trowel, and finished without interruption the fifth, the sixth, and the seventh tier. The wall was now nearly upon a level with my breast. I again paused, and holding the flambeaux over the mason-work, threw a few feeble rays upon the figure within.

A succession of loud and shrill screams, bursting suddenly from the throat of the chained form, seemed to thrust me violently back. For a brief moment I hesitated, I trembled. Unsheathing my rapier, I began to grope with it about the recess; but the thought of an instant reassured me. I placed my hand upon the solid fabric of the catacombs, and felt satisfied. I reapproached the wall. I replied to the yells of him who clamored. I reechoed, I aided, I surpassed them in volume and in strength. I did this, and the clamorer grew still.

It was now midnight, and my task was drawing to a close. I had completed the eighth, the ninth and the tenth tier. I had finished a portion of the last and the eleventh; there remained but a single stone to be fitted and plastered in. I struggled with its weight; I placed it partially in its destined position. But now there came from out the niche a low laugh that erected the hairs upon my head. It was succeeded by a sad voice, which I had difficulty in recognizing as that of the noble Fortunato. The voice said—

"Ha! ha! ha!—he! he! he!—a very good joke, indeed—an excellent jest. We will have many a rich laugh about it at the palazzo[7]—he! he! he!—over our wine—he! he! he!"

"The Amontillado!" I said.

"He! he! he!—he! he! he!—yes, the Amontillado. But is it not getting late? Will not they be awaiting us at the palazzo, the Lady Fortunato and the rest? Let us be gone."

"Yes," I said, "let us be gone."

"For the love of God, Montresor!"

"Yes," I said, "for the love of God!"

But to these words I hearkened in vain for a reply. I grew impatient. I called aloud—

"Fortunato!"

No answer. I called again—

"Fortunato!"

No answer still. I thrust a torch through the remaining aperture and let it fall within. There came forth in return only a jingling of the bells. My heart grew sick; it was the dampness of the catacombs

7. Palace.

that made it so. I hastened to make an end of my labor. I forced the last stone into its position; I plastered it up. Against the new masonry I re-erected the old rampart of bones. For the half of a century no mortal has disturbed them. *In pace requiescat!*[8]

p. 1846

RICHARD CONNELL

The Most Dangerous Game

"Off there to the right—somewhere—is a large island," said Whitney. "It's rather a mystery—"

"What island is it?" Rainsford asked.

"The old charts call it 'Ship-Trap Island,'" Whitney replied. "A suggestive name, isn't it? Sailors have a curious dread of the place. I don't know why. Some superstition—"

"Can't see it," remarked Rainsford, trying to peer through the dank tropical night that was palpable as it pressed its thick warm blackness in upon the yacht.

"You've good eyes," said Whitney, with a laugh, "and I've seen you pick off a moose moving in the brown fall bush at four hundred yards, but even you can't see four miles or so through a moonless Caribbean night."

"Nor four yards," admitted Rainsford. "Ugh! It's like moist black velvet."

"It will be light in Rio," promised Whitney. "We should make it in a few days. I hope the jaguar guns have come from Purdey's. We should have some good hunting up the Amazon. Great sport, hunting."

"The best sport in the world," agreed Rainsford.

"For the hunter," amended Whitney. "Not for the jaguar."

"Don't talk rot, Whitney," said Rainsford. "You're a big-game hunter, not a philosopher. Who cares how a jaguar feels?"

"Perhaps the jaguar does," observed Whitney.

"Bah! They've no understanding."

"Even so, I rather think they understand one thing—fear. The fear of pain and the fear of death."

"Nonsense," laughed Rainsford. "This hot weather is making you soft, Whitney. Be a realist. The world is made up of two classes—the hunters and the huntees. Luckily, you and I are hunters. Do you think we've passed that island yet?"

"I can't tell in the dark. I hope so."

"Why?" asked Rainsford.

"The place has a reputation—a bad one."

"Cannibals?" suggested Rainsford.

"Hardly. Even cannibals wouldn't live in such a God-forsaken place.

---

8. May he rest in peace.

But it's gotten into sailor lore, somehow. Didn't you notice that the crew's nerves seemed a bit jumpy today?"

"They were a bit strange, now you mention it. Even Captain Nielsen—"

"Yes, even that tough-minded old Swede, who'd go up to the devil himself and ask him for a light. Those fishy blue eyes held a look I never saw there before. All I could get out of him was: 'This place has an evil name among sea-faring men, sir.' Then he said to me, very gravely: 'Don't you feel anything?'—as if the air about us was actually poisonous. Now, you mustn't laugh when I tell you this—I did feel something like a sudden chill.

"There was no breeze. The sea was as flat as a plate-glass window. We were drawing near the island then. What I felt was a—a mental chill; a sort of sudden dread."

"Pure imagination," said Rainsford. "One superstitious sailor can taint the whole ship's company with his fear."

"Maybe. But sometimes I think sailors have an extra sense that tells them when they are in danger. Sometimes I think evil is a tangible thing—with wave lengths, just as sound and light have. An evil place can, so to speak, broadcast vibrations of evil. Anyhow, I'm glad we're getting out of this zone. Well, I think I'll turn in now, Rainsford."

"I'm not sleepy," said Rainsford. "I'm going to smoke another pipe up on the after deck."

"Good night, then, Rainsford. See you at breakfast."

"Right. Good night, Whitney."

There was no sound in the night as Rainsford sat there, but the muffled throb of the engine that drove the yacht swiftly through the darkness, and the swish and ripple of the wash of the propeller.

Rainsford, reclining in a steamer chair, indolently puffed on his favorite brier. The sensuous drowsiness of the night was on him. "It's so dark," he thought, "that I could sleep without closing my eyes; the night would be my eyelids—"

An abrupt sound startled him. Off to the right he heard it, and his ears, expert in such matters, could not be mistaken. Again he heard the sound, and again. Somewhere, off in the blackness, some one had fired a gun three times.

Rainsford sprang up and moved quickly to the rail, mystified. He strained his eyes in the direction from which the reports had come, but it was like trying to see through a blanket. He leaped upon the rail and balanced himself there, to get greater elevation; his pipe, striking a rope, was knocked from his mouth. He lunged for it; a short, hoarse cry came from his lips as he realized he had reached too far and had lost his balance. The cry was pinched off short as the blood-warm waters of the Caribbean Sea closed over his head.

He struggled up to the surface and tried to cry out, but the wash from the speeding yacht slapped him in the face and the salt water in his open mouth made him gag and strangle. Desperately he struck out with strong strokes after the receding lights of the yacht, but he stopped before he had swum fifty feet. A certain cool-headedness had come to him; it was not the first time he had been in a tight place. There was a chance that his cries could be heard by some one aboard the yacht, but that chance was slender, and grew more slender as the yacht raced on. He wrestled himself out of his clothes, and shouted with all his power. The lights of the yacht became faint and ever-vanishing fireflies; then they were blotted out entirely by the night.

Rainsford remembered the shots. They had come from the right, and doggedly he swam in that direction, swimming with slow, deliberate strokes, conserving his strength. For a seemingly endless time he fought the sea. He began to count his strokes; he could do possibly a hundred more and then—

Rainsford heard a sound. It came out of the darkness, a high scream-ing sound, the sound of an animal in an extremity of anguish and terror.

He did not recognize the animal that made the sound; he did not try to; with fresh vitality he swam toward the sound. He heard it again; then it was cut short by another noise, crisp, staccato.

"Pistol shot," muttered Rainsford, swimming on.

Ten minutes of determined effort brought another sound to his ears —the most welcome he had ever heard—the muttering and growling of the sea breaking on a rocky shore. He was almost on the rocks before he saw them; on a night less calm he would have been shattered against them. With his remaining strength he dragged himself from the swirling waters. Jagged crags appeared to jut into the opaqueness; he forced himself upward, hand over hand. Gasping, his hands raw, he reached a flat place at the top. Dense jungle came down to the very edge of the cliffs. What perils that tangle of trees and under-brush might hold for him did not concern Rainsford just then. All he knew was that he was safe from his enemy, the sea, and that utter weariness was on him. He flung himself down at the jungle edge and tumbled headlong into the deepest sleep of his life.

When he opened his eyes he knew from the position of the sun that it was late in the afternoon. Sleep had given him new vigor; a sharp hunger was picking at him. He looked about him, almost cheerfully.

"Where there are pistol shots, there are men. Where there are men, there is food," he thought. But what kind of men, he wondered, in so forbidding a place? An unbroken front of snarled and ragged jungle fringed the shore.

He saw no sign of a trail through the closely knit web of weeds and trees; it was easier to go along the shore, and Rainsford floundered along by the water. Not far from where he had landed, he stopped.

Some wounded thing, by the evidence a large animal, had thrashed about in the underbrush; the jungle weeds were crushed down and the moss was lacerated; one patch of weeds was stained crimson. A small, glittering object not far away caught Rainsford's eye and he picked it up. It was an empty cartridge.

"A twenty-two," he remarked. "That's odd. It must have been a fairly large animal too. The hunter had his nerve with him to tackle it with a light gun. It's clear that the brute put up a fight. I suppose the first three shots I heard was when the hunter flushed his quarry and wounded it. The last shot was when he trailed it here and finished it."

He examined the ground closely and found what he had hoped to find—the print of hunting boots. They pointed along the cliff in the direction he had been going. Eagerly he hurried along, now slipping on a rotten log or a loose stone, but making headway; night was beginning to settle down on the island.

Bleak darkness was blacking out the sea and jungle when Rainsford sighted the lights. He came upon them as he turned a crook in the coast line, and his first thought was that he had come upon a village, for there were many lights. But as he forged along he saw to his great astonishment that all the lights were in one enormous building—a lofty structure with pointed towers plunging upward into the gloom. His eyes made out the shadowy outlines of a palatial château; it was set on a high bluff, and on three sides of it cliffs dived down to where the sea licked greedy lips in the shadows.

"Mirage," thought Rainsford. But it was no mirage, he found, when he opened the tall spiked iron gate. The stone steps were real enough; the massive door with a leering gargoyle for a knocker was real enough; yet about it all hung an air of unreality.

He lifted the knocker, and it creaked up stiffly, as if it had never before been used. He let it fall, and it startled him with its booming loudness. He thought he heard steps within; the door remained closed. Again Rainsford lifted the heavy knocker, and let it fall. The door opened then, opened as suddenly as if it were on a spring, and Rainsford stood blinking in the river of glaring gold light that poured out. The first thing Rainsford's eyes discerned was the largest man Rainsford had ever seen—a gigantic creature, solidly made and black-bearded to the waist. In his hand the man held a long-barreled revolver, and he was pointing it straight at Rainsford's heart.

Out of the snarl of beard two small eyes regarded Rainsford.

"Don't be alarmed," said Rainsford, with a smile which he hoped was disarming. "I'm no robber. I fell off a yacht. My name is Sanger Rainsford of New York City."

The menacing look in the eyes did not change. The revolver pointed as rigidly as if the giant were a statue. He gave no sign that he understood Rainsford's words, or that he had even heard them. He was dressed in uniform, a black uniform trimmed with gray astrakhan.

"I'm Sanger Rainsford of New York," Rainsford began again. "I fell off a yacht. I am hungry."

The man's only answer was to raise with his thumb the hammer of his revolver. Then Rainsford saw the man's free hand go to his forehead in a military salute, and he saw him click his heels together and stand at attention. Another man was coming down the broad marble steps, an erect, slender man in evening clothes. He advanced to Rainsford and held out his hand.

In a cultivated voice marked by a slight accent that gave it added precision and deliberateness, he said: "It is a very great pleasure and honor to welcome Mr. Sanger Rainsford, the celebrated hunter, to my home."

Automatically Rainsford shook the man's hand.

"I've read your book about hunting snow leopards[1] in Tibet, you see," explained the man. "I am General Zaroff."

Rainsford's first impression was that the man was singularly handsome; his second was that there was an original, almost bizarre quality about the general's face. He was a tall man past middle age, for his hair was a vivid white; but his thick eyebrows and pointed military mustache were as black as the night from which Rainsford had come. His eyes, too, were black and very bright. He had high cheek bones, a sharp-cut nose, a spare, dark face, the face of a man used to giving orders, the face of an aristocrat. Turning to the giant in uniform, the general made a sign. The giant put away his pistol, saluted, withdrew.

"Ivan is an incredibly strong fellow," remarked the general, "but he has the misfortune to be deaf and dumb. A simple fellow, but, I'm afraid, like all his race, a bit of a savage."

"Is he Russian?"

"He is a Cossack,"[2] said the general, and his smile showed red lips and pointed teeth. "So am I."

"Come," he said, "we shouldn't be chatting here. We can talk later. Now you want clothes, food, rest. You shall have them. This is a most restful spot."

Ivan had reappeared, and the general spoke to him with lips that moved but gave forth no sound.

"Follow Ivan, if you please, Mr. Rainsford," said the general. "I was about to have my dinner when you came. I'll wait for you. You'll find that my clothes will fit you, I think."

It was to a huge, beam-ceilinged bedroom with a canopied bed big enough for six men that Rainsford followed the silent giant. Ivan laid out an evening suit, and Rainsford, as he put it on, noticed that it came from a London tailor who ordinarily cut and sewed for none below the rank of duke.

The dining room to which Ivan conducted him was in many ways remarkable. There was a medieval magnificence about it; it suggested a baronial hall of feudal times with its oaken panels, its high ceiling, its vast refectory table where twoscore men could sit down to eat. About the hall were the mounted heads of many animals—lions, tigers, elephants, moose, bears; larger or more perfect specimens Rainsford had never seen. At the great table the general was sitting, alone.

"You'll have a cocktail, Mr. Rainsford," he suggested. The cocktail was surpassingly good; and, Rainsford noted, the table appointments were of the finest—the linen, the crystal, the silver, the china.

They were eating *borsch*, the rich, red soup with whipped cream so dear to Russian palates. Half apologetically General Zaroff said: "We do our best to preserve the amenities of civilization here. Please forgive any lapses. We are well off the beaten track, you know. Do you think the champagne has suffered from its long ocean trip?"

---

1. The ounce, native to the Himalayas, and quite rare.
2. From the southern part of European Russia, the Cossacks were known as exceptionally fine horsemen and light cavalrymen and, under the Czars, were feared for their ruthless raids.

"Not in the least," declared Rainsford. He was finding the general a most thoughtful and affable host, a true cosmopolite. But there was one small trait of the general's that made Rainsford uncomfortable. Whenever he looked up from his plate he found the general studying him, appraising him narrowly.

"Perhaps," said General Zaroff, "you were surprised that I recognized your name. You see, I read all books on hunting published in English, French, and Russian. I have but one passion in my life, Mr. Rainsford, and it is the hunt."

"You have some wonderful heads here," said Rainsford as he ate a particularly well cooked filet mignon. "That Cape buffalo[3] is the largest I ever saw."

"Oh, that fellow. Yes, he was a monster."

"Did he charge you?"

"Hurled me against a tree," said the general. "Fractured my skull. But I got the brute."

"I've always thought," said Rainsford, "that the Cape buffalo is the most dangerous of all big game."

For a moment the general did not reply; he was smiling his curious red-lipped smile. Then he said slowly: "No. You are wrong, sir. The Cape buffalo is not the most dangerous big game." He sipped his wine. "Here in my preserve on this island," he said in the same slow tone, "I hunt more dangerous game."

Rainsford expressed his surprise. "Is there big game on this island?"

The general nodded. "The biggest.".

"Really?"

"Oh, it isn't here naturally, of course. I have to stock the island."

"What have you imported, general?" Rainsford asked. "Tigers?"

The general smiled. "No," he said. "Hunting tigers ceased to interest me some years ago. I exhausted their possibilities, you see. No thrill left in tigers, no real danger. I live for danger, Mr. Rainsford."

The general took from his pocket a gold cigarette case and offered his guest a long black cigarette with a silver tip; it was perfumed and gave off a smell like incense.

"We will have some capital hunting, you and I," said the general. "I shall be most glad to have your society."

"But what game—" began Rainsford.

"I'll tell you," said the general. "You will be amused, I know. I think I may say, in all modesty, that I have done a rare thing. I have invented a new sensation. May I pour you another glass of port, Mr. Rainsford?"

"Thank you, general."

The general filled both glasses, and said: "God makes some men poets. Some He makes kings, some beggars. Me He made a hunter. My hand was made for the trigger, my father said. He was a very rich man with a quarter of a million acres in the Crimea, and he was an ardent sportsman. When I was only five years old he gave me a little gun, specially made in Moscow for me, to shoot sparrows with. When I shot some of his prize turkeys with it, he did not punish me; he

3. Big, quick, intelligent, when separated from the herd ("rogue"), one of the most dangerous of African game animals.

complimented me on my marksmanship. I killed my first bear in the Caucasus when I was ten. My whole life has been one prolonged hunt. I went into the army—it was expected of noblemen's sons—and for a time commanded a division of Cossack cavalry, but my real interest was always the hunt. I have hunted every kind of game in every land. It would be impossible for me to tell you how many animals I have killed."

The general puffed at his cigarette.

"After the debacle in Russia[4] I left the country, for it was imprudent for an officer of the Czar to stay there. Many noble Russians lost everything. I, luckily, had invested heavily in American securities, so I shall never have to open a tea room in Monte Carlo or drive a taxi in Paris. Naturally, I continued to hunt—grizzlies in your Rockies, crocodiles in the Ganges, rhinoceroses in East Africa. It was in Africa that the Cape buffalo hit me and laid me up for six months. As soon as I recovered I started for the Amazon to hunt jaguars, for I had heard they were unusually cunning. They weren't." The Cossack sighed. "They were no match at all for a hunter with his wits about him, and a high-powered rifle. I was bitterly disappointed. I was lying in my tent with a splitting headache one night when a terrible thought pushed its way into my mind. Hunting was beginning to bore me! And hunting, remember, had been my life. I have heard that in America business men often go to pieces when they give up the business that has been their life."

"Yes, that's so," said Rainsford.

The general smiled. "I had no wish to go to pieces," he said. "I must do something. Now, mine is an analytical mind, Mr. Rainsford. Doubtless that is why I enjoy the problems of the chase."

"No doubt, General Zaroff."

"So," continued the general, "I asked myself why the hunt no longer fascinated me. You are much younger than I am, Mr. Rainsford, and have not hunted as much, but you perhaps can guess the answer."

"What was it?"

"Simply this: hunting had ceased to be what you call 'a sporting proposition.' It had become too easy. I always got my quarry. Always. There is no greater bore than perfection."

The general lit a fresh cigarette.

"No animal had a chance with me any more. That is no boast; it is a mathematical certainty. The animal had nothing but his legs and his instinct. Instinct is no match for reason. When I thought of this it was a tragic moment for me, I can tell you."

Rainsford leaned across the table, absorbed in what his host was saying.

"It came to me as an inspiration what I must do," the general went on.

"And that was?"

The general smiled the quiet smile of one who had faced an obstacle and surmounted it with success. "I had to invent a new animal to hunt," he said.

"A new animal? You're joking."

4. **The Revolution of 1917 which overthrew the Czar and prepared the way for Communist rule.**

"Not at all," said the general. "I never joke about hunting. I needed a new animal. I found one. So I bought this island, built this house, and here I do my hunting. The island is perfect for my purposes—there are jungles with a maze of trails in them, hills, swamps—"

"But the animal, General Zaroff?"

"Oh," said the general, "it supplies me with the most exciting hunting in the world. No other hunting compares with it for an instant. Every day I hunt, and I never grow bored now, for I have a quarry with which I can match my wits."

Rainsford's bewilderment showed in his face.

"I wanted the ideal animal to hunt," explained the general. "So I said: 'What are the attributes of an ideal quarry?' And the answer was, of course: 'It must have courage, cunning, and, above all, it must be able to reason.'"

"But no animal can reason," objected Rainsford.

"My dear fellow," said the general, "there is one that can."

"But you can't mean—" gasped Rainsford.

"And why not?"

"I can't believe you are serious, General Zaroff. This is a grisly joke."

"Why should I not be serious? I am speaking of hunting."

"Hunting? Good God, General Zaroff, what you speak of is murder."

The general laughed with entire good nature. He regarded Rainsford quizzically. "I refuse to believe that so modern and civilized a young man as you seem to be harbors romantic ideas about the value of human life. Surely your experiences in the war—"

"Did not make me condone cold-blooded murder," finished Rainsford stiffly.

Laughter shook the general. "How extraordinarily droll you are!" he said. "One does not expect nowadays to find a young man of the educated class, even in America, with such a naïve, and, if I may say so, mid-Victorian point of view. It's like finding a snuff-box in a limousine. Ah, well, doubtless you had Puritan ancestors. So many Americans appear to have had. I'll wager you'll forget your notions when you go hunting with me. You've a genuine new thrill in store for you, Mr. Rainsford."

"Thank you, I'm a hunter, not a murderer."

"Dear me," said the general, quite unruffled, "again that unpleasant word. But I think I can show you that your scruples are quite ill founded."

"Yes?"

"Life is for the strong, to be lived by the strong, and, if need be, taken by the strong. The weak of the world were put here to give the strong pleasure. I am strong. Why should I not use my gift? If I wish to hunt, why should I not? I hunt the scum of the earth—sailors from tramp ships—lascars, blacks, Chinese, whites, mongrels—a thoroughbred horse or hound is worth more than a score of them."

"But they are men," said Rainsford hotly.

"Precisely," said the general. "That is why I use them. It gives me pleasure. They can reason, after a fashion. So they are dangerous."

"But where do you get them?"

The general's left eyelid fluttered down in a wink. "This island is

called Ship-Trap," he answered. "Sometimes an angry god of the high
seas sends them to me. Sometimes, when Providence is not so kind, I
help Providence a bit. Come to the window with me."

Rainsford went to the window and looked out toward the sea.

"Watch! Out there!" exclaimed the general, pointing into the night.
Rainsford's eyes saw only blackness, and then, as the general pressed
a button, far out to sea Rainsford saw the flash of lights.

The general chuckled. "They indicate a channel," he said, "where
there's none: giant rocks with razor edges crouch like a sea monster
with wide-open jaws. They can crush a ship as easily as I crush this
nut." He dropped a walnut on the hardwood floor and brought his heel
grinding down on it. "Oh, yes," he said, casually, as if in answer to a
question, "I have electricity. We try to be civilized here."

"Civilized? And you shoot down men?"

A trace of anger was in the general's black eyes, but it was there for
but a second, and he said, in his most pleasant manner: "Dear me,
what a righteous young man you are! I assure you I do not do the thing
you suggest. That would be barbarous. I treat these visitors with every
consideration. They get plenty of good food and exercise. They get into
splendid physical condition. You shall see for yourself tomorrow."

"What do you mean?"

"We'll visit my training school," smiled the general. "It's in the cellar.
I have about a dozen pupils down there now. They're from the Spanish
bark San Lucar that had the bad luck to go on the rocks out there. A
very inferior lot, I regret to say. Poor specimens and more accustomed
to the deck than to the jungle."

He raised his hand, and Ivan, who served as waiter, brought thick
Turkish coffee. Rainsford, with an effort, held his tongue in check.

"It's a game, you see, pursued the general blandly. "I suggest to one
of them that we go hunting. I give him a supply of food and an excellent hunting knife. I give him three hours' start. I am to follow, armed
only with a pistol of the smallest caliber and range. If my quarry eludes
me for three whole days, he wins the game. If I find him"—the general
smiled—"he loses."

"Suppose he refuses to be hunted?"

"Oh," said the general, "I give him his option, of course. He need
not play that game if he doesn't wish to. If he does not wish to hunt,
I turn him over to Ivan. Ivan once had the honor of serving as official
knouter[5] to the Great White Czar,[6] and he has his own ideas of sport.
Invariably, Mr. Rainsford, invariably they choose the hunt."

"And if they win?"

The smile on the general's face widened. "To date I have not lost,"
he said.

Then he added, hastily: "I don't wish you to think me a braggart,
Mr. Rainsford. Many of them afford only the most elementary sort of
problem. Occasionally I strike a tartar. One almost did win. I eventually had to use the dogs."

"The dogs?"

5. In Czarist Russia the official flogger
of criminals.
6. Probably Nicholas II (1868–1918)
who was overthrown by the Revolution and
executed; "White" designates those opposed to the Communists, or "Reds."

"This way, please. I'll show you."

The general steered Rainsford to a window. The lights from the windows sent a flickering illumination that made grotesque patterns on the courtyard below, and Rainsford could see moving about there a dozen or so huge black shapes; as they turned toward him, their eyes glittered greenly.

"A rather good lot, I think," observed the general. "They are let out at seven every night. If anyone should try to get into my house—or out of it—something extremely regrettable would occur to him." He hummed a snatch of song from the Folies Bergère.[7]

"And now," said the general, "I want to show you my new collection of heads. Will you come with me to the library?"

"I hope," said Rainsford, "that you will excuse me tonight, General Zaroff. I'm really not feeling at all well."

"Ah, indeed?" the general inquired solicitously. "Well, I suppose that's only natural, after your long swim. You need a good, restful night's sleep. Tomorrow you'll feel like a new man, I'll wager. Then we'll hunt, eh? I've one rather promising prospect—"

Rainsford was hurrying from the room.

"Sorry you can't go with me tonight," called the general. "I expect rather fair sport—a big, strong black. He looks resourceful—Well, good night, Mr. Rainsford; I hope you have a good night's rest."

The bed was good, and the pajamas of the softest silk, and he was tired in every fiber of his being, but nevertheless Rainsford could not quiet his brain with the opiate of sleep. He lay, eyes wide open. Once he thought he heard stealthy steps in the corridor outside his room. He sought to throw open the door; it would not open. He went to the window and looked out. His room was high up in one of the towers. The lights of the château were out now; and it was dark and silent, but there was a fragment of sallow moon, and by its wan light he could see, dimly, the courtyard; there, weaving in and out in the pattern of shadow, were black, noiseless forms; the hounds heard him at the window and looked up, expectantly, with their green eyes. Rainsford went back to bed and lay down. By many methods he tried to put himself to sleep. He had achieved a doze when, just as morning began to come, he heard, far off in the jungle, the faint report of a pistol.

General Zaroff did not appear until luncheon. He was dressed faultlessly in the tweeds of a country squire. He was solicitous about the state of Rainsford's health.

"As for me," sighed the general, "I do not feel so well. I am worried, Mr. Rainsford. Last night I detected traces of my old complaint."

To Rainsford's questioning glance the general said: "Ennui. Boredom."

Then, taking a second helping of *crêpes suzette*, the general explained: "The hunting was not good last night. The fellow lost his head. He made a straight trail that offered no problems at all. That's the trouble with these sailors; they have dull brains to begin with, and they do not know how to get about in the woods. They do excessively stupid and obvious things. It's most annoying. Will you have another

---

7. Paris theater and music hall which in 1918 reestablished itself as the scene for revues, spectaculars, etc.

glass of Chablis, Mr. Rainsford?"

"General," said Rainsford firmly, "I wish to leave this island at once."

The general raised his thickets of eyebrows; he seemed hurt. "But, my dear fellow," the general protested, "you've only just come. You've had no hunting—"

"I wish to go today," said Rainsford. He saw the dead black eyes of the general on him, studying him. General Zaroff's face suddenly brightened.

He filled Rainsford's glass with venerable Chablis from a dusty bottle.

"Tonight," said the general, "we will hunt—you and I."

Rainsford shook his head. "No, general," he said, "I will not hunt."

The general shrugged his shoulders and delicately ate a hothouse grape. "As you wish, my friend," he said. "The choice rests entirely with you. But may I not venture to suggest that you will find my idea of sport more diverting than Ivan's?"

He nodded toward the corner to where the giant stood, scowling, his thick arms crossed on his hogshead of a chest.

"You don't mean—" cried Rainsford.

"My dear fellow," said the general, "have I not told you I always mean what I say about hunting? This is really an inspiration. I drink to a foeman worthy of my steel—at last."

The general raised his glass, but Rainsford sat staring at him.

"You'll find this game worth playing," the general said enthusiastically. "Your brain against mine. Your woodcraft against mine. Your strength and stamina against mine. Outdoor chess! And the stake is not without value, eh?"

"And if I win—" began Rainsford huskily.

"I'll cheerfully acknowledge myself defeated if I do not find you by midnight of the third day," said General Zaroff. "My sloop will place you on the mainland near a town."

The general read what Rainsford was thinking.

"Oh, you can trust me," said the Cossack. "I will give you my word as a gentleman and a sportsman. Of course you, in turn, must agree to say nothing of your visit here."

"I'll agree to nothing of the kind," said Rainsford.

"Oh," said the general, "in that case—But why discuss that now? Three days hence we can discuss it over a bottle of Veuve Cliquot,[8] unless—"

The general sipped his wine.

Then a businesslike air animated him. "Ivan," he said to Rainsford, "will supply you with hunting clothes, food, a knife. I suggest you wear moccasins; they leave a poorer trail. I suggest too that you avoid the big swamp in the southeast corner of the island. We call it Death Swamp. There's quicksand there. One foolish fellow tried it. The deplorable part of it was that Lazarus followed him. You can imagine my feelings, Mr. Rainsford. I loved Lazarus; he was the finest hound in my pack. Well, I must beg you to excuse me now. I always take a siesta after lunch. You'll hardly have time for a nap, I fear. You'll want to start, no doubt. I shall not follow till dusk. Hunting at night is so

---

8. A fine champagne; Chablis, above, is a very dry white Burgundy table wine; Chambertin, later, is a highly esteemed red Burgundy wine.

much more exciting than by day, don't you think? Au revoir, Mr. Rainsford, au revoir."

General Zaroff, with a deep, courtly bow, strolled from the room.

From another door came Ivan. Under one arm he carried khaki hunting clothes, a haversack of food, a leather sheath containing a long-
bladed hunting knife; his right hand rested on a cocked revolver thrust
in the crimson sash about his waist. . . .

Rainsford had fought his way through the bush for two hours. "I
must keep my nerve. I must keep my nerve," he said through tight
teeth.

He had not been entirely clear-headed when the château gates
snapped shut behind him. His whole idea at first was to put distance
between himself and General Zaroff, and, to this end, he had plunged
along, spurred on by the sharp rowels of something very like panic.
Now he had got a grip on himself, had stopped, and was taking stock
of himself and the situation.

He saw that straight flight was futile; inevitably it would bring him
face to face with the sea. He was in a picture with a frame of water,
and his operations, clearly, must take place within that frame.

"I'll give him a trail to follow," muttered Rainsford, and he struck
off from the rude paths he had been following into the trackless wilderness. He executed a series of intricate loops; he doubled on his trail
again and again, recalling all the lore of the fox hunt, and all the dodges
of the fox. Night found him leg-weary, with hands and face lashed by
the branches, on a thickly wooded ridge. He knew it would be insane
to blunder on through the dark, even if he had the strength. His need
for rest was imperative and he thought: "I have played the fox, now I
must play the cat of the fable."[9] A big tree with a thick trunk and outspread branches was nearby, and, taking care to leave not the slightest
mark, he climbed up into the crotch, and stretching out on one of the
broad limbs, after a fashion, rested. Rest brought him new confidence
and almost a feeling of security. Even so zealous a hunter as General
Zaroff could not trace him there, he told himself; only the devil himself
could follow that complicated trail through the jungle after dark. But,
perhaps, the general was a devil—

An apprehensive night crawled slowly by like a wounded snake,
and sleep did not visit Rainsford, although the silence of a dead world
was on the jungle. Toward morning when a dingy gray was varnishing
the sky, the cry of some startled bird focused Rainsford's attention in
that direction. Something was coming through the bush, coming
slowly, carefully, coming by the same winding way Rainsford had
come. He flattened himself down on the limb, and through a screen of
leaves almost as thick as tapestry, he watched. The thing that was approaching was a man.

It was General Zaroff. He made his way along with his eyes fixed in
utmost concentration on the ground before him. He paused, almost
beneath the tree, dropped to his knees and studied the ground. Rainsford's impulse was to hurl himself down like a panther, but he saw

---

9. The fox boasts of his many tricks to
elude the hounds; the cat responds he knows
only one—to climb the nearest tree—but that
this is worth more than all the fox's tricks.

that the general's right hand held something metallic—a small automatic pistol.

The hunter shook his head several times, as if he were puzzled. Then he straightened up and took from his case one of his black cigarettes; its pungent incense-like smoke floated up to Rainsford's nostrils.

Rainsford held his breath. The general's eyes had left the ground and were traveling inch by inch up the tree. Rainsford froze there, every muscle tensed for a spring. But the sharp eyes of the hunter stopped before they reached the limb where Rainsford lay; a smile spread over his brown face. Very deliberately he blew a smoke ring into the air; then he turned his back on the tree and walked carelessly away, back along the trail he had come. The swish of the underbrush against his hunting boots grew fainter and fainter.

The pent-up air burst hotly from Rainsford's lungs. His first thought made him feel sick and numb. The general could follow a trail through the woods at night; he could follow an extremely difficult trail; he must have uncanny powers; only by the merest chance had the Cossack failed to see his quarry.

Rainsford's second thought was even more terrible. It sent a shudder of cold horror through his whole being. Why had the general smiled? Why had he turned back?

Rainsford did not want to believe what his reason told him was true, but the truth was as evident as the sun that had by now pushed through the morning mists. The general was playing with him! The general was saving him for another day's sport! The Cossack was the cat; he was the mouse.[1] Then it was that Rainsford knew the full meaning of terror.

"I will not lose my nerve. I will not."

He slid down from the tree, and struck off again into the woods. His face was set and he forced the machinery of his mind to function. Three hundred yards from his hiding place he stopped where a huge dead tree leaned precariously on a smaller, living one. Throwing off his sack of food, Rainsford took his knife from its sheath and began to work with all his energy.

The job was finished at last, and he threw himself down behind a fallen log a hundred feet away. He did not have to wait long. The cat was coming again to play with the mouse.

Following the trail with the sureness of a bloodhound, came General Zaroff. Nothing escaped those searching black eyes, no crushed blade of grass, no bent twig, no mark, no matter how faint, in the moss. So intent was the Cossack on his stalking that he was upon the thing Rainsford had made before he saw it. His foot touched the protruding bough that was the trigger. Even as he touched it, the general sensed his danger and leaped back with the agility of an ape. But he was not quite quick enough; the dead tree, delicately adjusted to rest on the cut living one, crashed down and struck the general a glacing blow on the shoulder as it fell; but for his alertness, he must have been smashed beneath it. He staggered, but he did not fall; nor did he drop his revolver. He stood there, rubbing his injured shoulder, and Rainsford,

---

1. A cat, sure of his prey, plays with a mouse before killing him.

with fear again gripping his heart, heard the general's mocking laugh ring through the jungle.

"Rainsford," called the general, "if you are within sound of my voice, as I suppose you are, let me congratulate you. Not many men know how to make a Malay man-catcher. Luckily, for me, I too have hunted in Malacca. You are proving interesting, Mr. Rainsford. I am going now to have my wound dressed; it's only a slight one. But I shall be back. I shall be back."

When the general, nursing his bruised shoulder, had gone, Rainsford took up his flight again. It was flight now, a desperate, hopeless flight, that carried him on for some hours. Dusk came, then darkness, and still he pressed on. The ground grew softer under his moccasins; the vegetation grew ranker, denser; insects bit him savagely. Then, as he stepped forward, his foot sank into the ooze. He tried to wrench it back, but the muck sucked viciously at his foot as if it were a giant leech. With a violent effort, he tore his foot loose. He knew where he was now. Death Swamp and its quicksand.

His hands were tight closed as if his nerve were something tangible that someone in the darkness was trying to tear from his grip. The softness of the earth had given him an idea. He stepped back from the quicksand a dozen feet or so and, like some huge prehistoric beaver, he began to dig.

Rainsford had dug himself in in France[2] when a second's delay meant death. That had been a placid pastime compared to his digging now. The pit grew deeper; when it was above his shoulders, he climbed out and from some hard saplings cut stakes and sharpened them to a fine point. These stakes he planted in the bottom of the pit with the points sticking up. With flying fingers he wove a rough carpet of weeds and branches and with it he covered the mouth of the pit. Then, wet with sweat and aching with tiredness, he crouched behind the stump of a lightning-charred tree.

He knew his pursuer was coming; he heard the padding sound of feet on the soft earth, and the night breeze brought him the perfume of the general's cigarette. It seemed to Rainsford that the general was coming with unusual swiftness; he was not feeling his way along, foot by foot. Rainsford, crouching there, could not see the general, nor could he see the pit. He lived a year in a minute. Then he felt an impulse to cry aloud with joy, for he heard the sharp crackle of the breaking branches as the cover of the pit gave way; he heard the sharp scream of pain as the pointed stakes found their mark. He leaped up from his place of concealment. Then he cowered back. Three feet from the pit a man was standing, with an electric torch in his hand.

"You've done well, Rainsford," the voice of the general called. "Your Burmese tiger pit has claimed one of my best dogs. Again you score. I think, Mr. Rainsford, I'll see what you can do against my whole pack. I'm going home for a rest now. Thank you for a most amusing evening."

At daybreak Rainsford, lying near the swamp, was awakened by a sound that made him know that he had new things to learn about

2. During World War I he had quickly dug a hole or trench to shelter himself from exploding shells, bullets, etc.

fear. It was a distant sound, faint and wavering, but he knew it. It was the baying of a pack of hounds.

Rainsford knew he could do one of two things. He could stay where he was and wait. That was suicide. He could flee. That was postponing the inevitable. For a moment he stood there, thinking. An idea that held a wild chance came to him, and, tightening his belt, he headed away from the swamp.

The baying of the hounds drew nearer, then still nearer, nearer, ever nearer. On a ridge Rainsford climbed a tree. Down a watercourse, not a quarter of a mile away, he could see the bush moving. Straining his eyes, he saw the lean figure of General Zaroff; just ahead of him Rainsford made out another figure whose wide shoulders surged through the tall jungle weeds; it was the giant Ivan, and he seemed pulled forward by some unseen force; Rainsford knew that Ivan must be holding the pack in leash.

They would be on him any minute now. His mind worked frantically. He thought of a native trick he had learned in Uganda. He slid down the tree. He caught hold of a springy young sapling and to it he fastened his hunting knife, with the blade pointing down the trail; with a bit of wild grapevine he tied back the sapling. Then he ran for his life. The hounds raised their voices as they hit the fresh scent. Rainsford knew now how an animal at bay feels.

He had to stop to get his breath. The baying of the hounds stopped abruptly, and Rainsford's heart stopped too. They must have reached the knife.

He shinned excitedly up a tree and looked back. His pursuers had stopped. But the hope that was in Rainsford's brain when he climbed died, for he saw in the shallow valley that General Zaroff was still on his feet. But Ivan was not. The knife, driven by the recoil of the spring-ing tree, had not wholly failed.

Rainsford had hardly tumbled to the ground when the pack took up the cry again.

"Nerve, nerve, nerve!" he panted, as he dashed along. A blue gap showed between the trees dead ahead. Ever nearer drew the hounds. Rainsford forced himself on toward that gap. He reached it. It was the shore of the sea. Across a cove he could see the gloomy gray stone of the château. Twenty feet below him the sea rumbled and hissed. Rainsford hesitated. He heard the hounds. Then he leaped far out into the sea. . . .

When the general and his pack reached the place by the sea, the Cossack stopped. For some minutes he stood regarding the blue-green expanse of water. He shrugged his shoulders. Then he sat down, took a drink of brandy from a silver flask, lit a perfumed cigarette, and hummed a bit from "Madame Butterfly."

General Zaroff had an exceedingly good dinner in his great paneled dining hall that evening. With it he had a bottle of Pol Roger and half a bottle of Chambertin. Two slight annoyances kept him from perfect enjoyment. One was the thought that it would be difficult to replace Ivan; the other was that his quarry had escaped him; of course the American hadn't played the game—so thought the general as he tasted his after-dinner liqueur. In his library he read, to soothe himself, from the works of Marcus Aurelius.[3] At ten he went up to his bedroom. He was deliciously tired, he said to himself, as he locked himself in. There was a little moonlight, so, before turning on his light, he went to the window and looked down at the courtyard. He could see the great hounds, and he called: "Better luck another time," to them. Then he switched on the light.

A man, who had been hiding in the curtains of the bed, was standing there.

"Rainsford!" screamed the general. "How in God's name did you get here?"

"Swam," said Rainsford. "I found it quicker than walking through the jungle."

The general sucked in his breath and smiled. "I congratulate you," he said. "You have won the game."

Rainsford did not smile. "I am still a beast at bay," he said, in a low, hoarse voice. "Get ready, General Zaroff."

The general made one of his deepest bows. "I see," he said. "Splendid! One of us is to furnish a repast for the hounds. The other will sleep in this very excellent bed. On guard, Rainsford. . . ."

He had never slept in a better bed, Rainsford decided.

1924

ERNEST HEMINGWAY

The Short Happy Life of Francis Macomber

It was now lunch time and they were all sitting under the double green fly of the dining tent pretending that nothing had happened.

"Will you have lime juice or lemon squash?" Macomber asked.

"I'll have a gimlet,"[1] Robert Wilson told him.

"I'll have a gimlet too. I need something," Macomber's wife said.

"I suppose it's the thing to do," Macomber agreed. "Tell him to make three gimlets."

The mess boy had started them already, lifting the bottles out of the canvas cooling bags that sweated wet in the wind that blew through the trees that shaded the tents.

"What had I ought to give them?" Macomber asked.

"A quid[2] would be plenty," Wilson told him. "You don't want to spoil them."

"Will the headman distribute it?"

"Absolutely."

---

3. Roman Emperor (A.D. 161–180), Stoic philosopher, writer, and humanitarian, who, though good to the poor and opposed to the cruelty of gladiatorial shows, persecuted early Christians.

1. Drink of lime juice, gin, and soda or water.

2. Slang for a British pound.

Francis Macomber had, half an hour before, been carried to his tent from the edge of the camp in triumph on the arms and shoulders of the cook, the personal boys, the skinner and the porters. The gun-bearers had taken no part in the demonstration. When the native boys put him down at the door of his tent, he had shaken all their hands, received their congratulations, and then gone into the tent and sat on the bed until his wife came in. She did not speak to him when she came in and he left the tent at once to wash his face and hands in the portable wash basin outside and go over to the dining tent to sit in a comfortable canvas chair in the breeze and the shade.

"You've got your lion," Robert Wilson said to him, "and a damned fine one too."

Mrs. Macomber looked at Wilson quickly. She was an extremely handsome and well-kept woman of the beauty and social position which had, five years before, commanded five thousand dollars as the price of endorsing, with photographs, a beauty product which she had never used. She had been married to Francis Macomber for eleven years.

"He is a good lion, isn't he?" Macomber said. His wife looked at him now. She looked at both these men as though she had never seen them before.

One, Wilson, the white hunter, she knew she had never truly seen before. He was about middle height with sandy hair, a stubby mustache, a very red face and extremely cold blue eyes with faint white wrinkles at the corners that grooved merrily when he smiled. He smiled at her now and she looked away from his face at the way his shoulders sloped in the loose tunic he wore with the four big cartridges held in loops where the left breast pocket should have been, at his big brown hands, his old slacks, his very dirty boots and back to his red face again. She noticed where the baked red of his face stopped in a white line that marked the circle left by his Stetson hat[3] that hung now from one of the pegs of the tent pole.

"Well, here's to the lion," Robert Wilson said. He smiled at her again and, not smiling, she looked curiously at her husband.

Francis Macomber was very tall, very well built if you did not mind that length of bone, dark, his hair cropped like an oarsman, rather thin-lipped, and was considered handsome. He was dressed in the same sort of safari clothes that Wilson wore except that his were new, he was thirty-five years old, kept himself very fit, was good at court games, had a number of big-game fishing records, and had just shown himself, very publicly, to be a coward.

"Here's to the lion," he said. "I can't ever thank you for what you did."

Margaret, his wife, looked away from him and back to Wilson.

"Let's not talk about the lion," she said.

Wilson looked over at her without smiling and now she smiled at him.

"It's been a very strange day," she said. "Hadn't you ought to

---

3. Cowboy-type hat.

put your hat on even under the canvas at noon? You told me that, you know."

"Might put it on," said Wilson.

"You know you have a very red face, Mr. Wilson," she told him and smiled again.

"Drink," said Wilson.

"I don't think so," she said. "Francis drinks a great deal, but his face is never red."

"It's red today," Macomber tried a joke.

"No," said Margaret. "It's mine that's red today. But Mr. Wilson's is always red."

"Must be racial," said Wilson. "I say, you wouldn't like to drop my beauty as a topic, would you?"

"I've just started on it."

"Let's chuck it," said Wilson.

"Conversation is going to be so difficult," Margaret said.

"Don't be silly, Margot," her husband said.

"No difficulty," Wilson said. "Got a damn fine lion."

Margot looked at them both and they both saw that she was going to cry. Wilson had seen it coming for a long time and he dreaded it. Macomber was past dreading it.

"I wish it hadn't happened. Oh, I wish it hadn't happened," she said and started for her tent. She made no noise of crying but they could see that her shoulders were shaking under the rose-colored, sun-proofed shirt she wore.

"Women upset," said Wilson to the tall man. "Amounts to nothing. Strain on the nerves and one thing'n another."

"No," said Macomber. "I suppose that I rate that for the rest of my life now."

"Nonsense. Let's have a spot of the giant killer," said Wilson. "Forget the whole thing. Nothing to it anyway."

"We might try," said Macomber. "I won't forget what you did for me though."

"Nothing," said Wilson. "All nonsense."

So they sat there in the shade where the camp was pitched under some wide-topped acacia trees with a boulder-strewn cliff behind them, and a stretch of grass that ran to the bank of a boulder-filled stream in front with forest beyond it, and drank their just-cool lime drinks and avoided one another's eyes while the boys set the table for lunch. Wilson could tell that the boys all knew about it now and when he saw Macomber's personal boy looking curiously at his master while he was putting dishes on the table he snapped at him in Swahili. The boy turned away with his face blank.

"What were you telling him?" Macomber asked.

"Nothing. Told him to look alive or I'd see he got about fifteen of the best."

"What's that? Lashes?"

"It's quite illegal," Wilson said. "You're supposed to fine them."

"Do you still have them whipped?"

"Oh, yes. They could raise a row if they chose to complain. But they don't. They prefer it to the fines."

"How strange!" said Macomber.

"Not strange, really," Wilson said. "Which would you rather do? Take a good birching or lose your pay?"

Then he felt embarrassed at asking it and before Macomber could answer he went on, "We all take a beating every day, you know, one way or another."

This was no better. "Good God," he thought. "I am a diplomat, aren't I?"

"Yes, we take a beating," said Macomber, still not looking at him. "I'm awfully sorry about that lion business. It doesn't have to go any further, does it? I mean no one will hear about it, will they?"

"You mean will I tell it at the Mathaiga Club?" Wilson looked at him now coldly. He had not expected this. So he's a bloody four-letter man as well as a bloody coward, he thought. I rather liked him too until today. But how is one to know about an American?

"No," said Wilson. "I'm a professional hunter. We never talk about our clients. You can be quite easy on that. It's supposed to be bad form to ask us not to talk though."

He had decided now that to break would be much easier. He would eat, then, by himself and could read a book with his meals. They would eat by themselves. He would see them through the safari on a very formal basis—what was it the French called it? Distinguished consideration[4]—and it would be a damn sight easier than having to go through this emotional trash. He'd insult him and make a good clean break. Then he could read a book with his meals and he'd still be drinking their whisky. That was the phrase for it when a safari went bad. You ran into another white hunter and you asked, "How is everything going?" and he answered, "Oh, I'm still drinking their whisky," and you knew everything had gone to pot.

"I'm sorry," Macomber said and looked at him with his American face that would stay adolescent until it became middle-aged, and Wilson noted his crew-cropped hair, fine eyes only faintly shifty, good nose, thin lips and handsome jaw. "I'm sorry I didn't realize that. There are lots of things I don't know."

So what could he do, Wilson thought. He was all ready to break it off quickly and neatly and here the beggar was apologizing after he had just insulted him. He made one more attempt. "Don't worry about me talking," he said. "I have a living to make. You know in Africa no woman ever misses her lion and no white man ever bolts."

"I bolted like a rabbit," Macomber said.

Now what in hell were you going to do about a man who talked like that, Wilson wondered.

Wilson looked at Macomber with his flat, blue, machine-gunner's eyes and the other smiled back at him. He had a pleasant smile if you did not notice how his eyes showed when he was hurt.

"Maybe I can fix it up on buffalo," he said. "We're after them next, aren't we?"

"In the morning if you like," Wilson told him. Perhaps he had been wrong. This was certainly the way to take it. You most cer-

4. Highest regard.

tainly could not tell a damned thing about an American. He was
all for Macomber again. If you could forget the morning. But, of
course, you couldn't. The morning had been about as bad as they
come.

"Here comes the Memsahib," he said. She was walking over from
her tent looking refreshed and cheerful and quite lovely. She had a
very perfect oval face, so perfect that you expected her to be stupid.
But she wasn't stupid, Wilson thought, no, not stupid.

"How is the beautiful red-faced Mr. Wilson? Are you feeling
better, Francis, my pearl?"

"Oh, much," said Macomber.

"I've dropped the whole thing," she said, sitting down at the table.
"What importance is there to whether Francis is any good at killing
lions? That's not his trade. That's Mr. Wilson's trade. Mr. Wilson is
really very impressive killing anything. You do kill anything, don't
you?"

"Oh, anything," said Wilson. "Simply anything." They are, he
thought, the hardest in the world; the hardest, the cruelest, the most
predatory and the most attractive and their men have softened or
gone to pieces nervously as they have hardened. Or is it that they
pick men they can handle? They can't know that much at the age
they marry, he thought. He was grateful that he had gone through
his education on American women before now because this was a
very attractive one.

"We're going after buff in the morning," he told her.

"I'm coming," she said.

"No, you're not."

"Oh, yes, I am. Mayn't I, Francis?"

"Why not stay in camp?"

"Not for anything," she said. "I wouldn't miss something like today
for anything."

When she left, Wilson was thinking, when she went off to cry,
she seemed a hell of a fine woman. She seemed to understand, to
realize, to be hurt for him and for herself and to know how things
really stood. She is away for twenty minutes and now she is back,
simply enamelled in that American female cruelty. They are the
damnedest women. Really the damnedest.

"We'll put on another show for you tomorrow," Francis Macomber
said.

"You're not coming," Wilson said.

"You're very mistaken," she told him. "And I want *so* to see you
perform again. You were lovely this morning. That is if blowing
things' heads off is lovely."

"Here's the lunch," said Wilson. "You're very merry, aren't you?"

"Why not? I didn't come out here to be dull."

"Well, it hasn't been dull," Wilson said. He could see the boulders
in the river and the high bank beyond with the trees and he remembered the morning.

"Oh, no," she said. "It's been charming. And tomorrow. You don't
know how I look forward to tomorrow."

"That's eland he's offering you," Wilson said.

"They're the big cowy things that jump like hares, aren't they?"

"I suppose that describes them," Wilson said.

"It's very good meat," Macomber said.

"Didn't you shoot it, Francis?" she asked.

"Yes."

"They're not dangerous, are they?"

"Only if they fall on you," Wilson told her.

"I'm so glad."

"Why not let up on the bitchery just a little, Margot," Macomber said, cutting the eland steak and putting some mashed potato, gravy and carrot on the down-turned fork that tined through the piece of meat.

"I suppose I could," she said, "since you put it so prettily."

"Tonight we'll have champagne for the lion," Wilson said. "It's a bit too hot at noon."

"Oh, the lion," Margot said. "I'd forgotten the lion!"

So, Robert Wilson thought to himself, she *is* giving him a ride, isn't she? Or do you suppose that's her idea of putting up a good show? How should a woman act when she discovers her husband is a bloody coward? She's damn cruel but they're all cruel. They govern, of course, and to govern one has to be cruel sometimes. Still, I've seen enough of their damn terrorism.

"Have some more eland," he said to her politely.

That afternoon, late, Wilson and Macomber went out in the motor car with the native driver and the two gun-bearers. Mrs. Macomber stayed in the camp. It was too hot to go out, she said, and she was going with them in the early morning. As they drove off Wilson saw her standing under the big tree, looking pretty rather than beautiful in her faintly rosy khaki, her dark hair drawn back off her forehead and gathered in a knot low on her neck, her face as fresh, he thought, as though she were in England. She waved to them as the car went off through the swale of high grass and curved around through the trees into the small hills of orchard bush.

In the orchard bush they found a herd of impala,[5] and leaving the car they stalked one old ram with long, wide-spread horns and Macomber killed it with a very creditable shot that knocked the buck down at a good two hundred yards and sent the herd off bounding wildly and leaping over one another's backs in long, leg-drawn-up leaps as unbelievable and as floating as those one makes sometimes in dreams.

"That was a good shot," Wilson said. "They're a small target."

"Is it a worthwhile head?" Macomber asked.

"It's excellent," Wilson told him. "You shoot like that and you'll have no trouble."

"Do you think we'll find buffalo tomorrow?"

"There's a good chance of it. They feed out early in the morning and with luck we may catch them in the open."

"I'd like to clear away that lion business," Macomber said. "It's not very pleasant to have your wife see you do something like that."

5. Antelope of bush country of east and south Africa with lyre-shaped horns.

I should think it would be even more unpleasant to do it, Wilson thought, wife or no wife, or to talk about it having done it. But he said, "I wouldn't think about that any more. Anyone could be upset by his first lion. That's all over."

But that night after dinner and a whisky and soda by the fire before going to bed, as Francis Macomber lay on his cot with the mosquito bar over him and listened to the night noises, it was not all over. It was neither all over nor was it beginning. It was there exactly as it happened with some parts of it indelibly emphasized and he was miserably ashamed at it. But more than shame he felt cold, hollow fear in him. The fear was still there like a cold slimy hollow in all the emptiness where once his confidence had been and it made him feel sick. It was still there with him now.

It had started the night before when he had wakened and heard the lion roaring somewhere up along the river. It was a deep sound and at the end there were sort of coughing grunts that made him seem just outside the tent, and when Francis Macomber woke in the night to hear it he was afraid. He could hear his wife breathing quietly, asleep. There was no one to tell he was afraid, nor to be afraid with him, and, lying alone, he did not know the Somali proverb that says a brave man is always frightened three times by a lion; when he first sees his track, when he first hears him roar and when he first confronts him. Then while they were eating breakfast by lantern light out in the dining tent, before the sun was up, the lion roared again and Francis thought he was just at the edge of camp.

"Sounds like an old-timer," Robert Wilson said, looking up from his kippers and coffee. "Listen to him cough."

"Is he very close?"

"A mile or so up the stream."

"Will we see him?"

"We'll have a look."

"Does his roaring carry that far? It sounds as though he were right in camp."

"Carries a hell of a long way," said Robert Wilson. "It's strange the way it carries. Hope he's a shootable cat. The boys said there was a very big one about here."

"If I get a shot, where should I hit him," Macomber asked, "to stop him?"

"In the shoulders," Wilson said. "In the neck if you can make it. Shoot for bone. Break him down."

"I hope I can place it properly," Macomber said.

"You shoot very well," Wilson told him. "Take your time. Make sure of him. The first one in is the one that counts."

"What range will it be?"

"Can't tell. Lion has something to say about that. Won't shoot unless it's close enough so you can make sure."

"At under a hundred yards?" Macomber asked.

Wilson looked at him quickly.

"Hundred's about right. Might have to take him a bit under. Shouldn't chance a shot at much over that. A hundred's a decent range. You can hit him wherever you want at that. Here comes the Memsahib."

"Good morning," she said. "Are we going after that lion?"

"As soon as you deal with your breakfast," Wilson said. "How are you feeling?"

"Marvellous," she said. "I'm very excited."

"I'll just go and see that everything is ready," Wilson went off. As he left the lion roared again.

"Noisy beggar," Wilson said. "We'll put a stop to that."

"What's the matter, Francis?" his wife asked him.

"Nothing," Macomber said.

"Yes, there is," she said. "What are you upset about?"

"Nothing," he said.

"Tell me," she looked at him. "Don't you feel well?"

"It's that damned roaring," he said. "It's been going on all night, you know."

"Why didn't you wake me," she said. "I'd love to have heard it."

"I've got to kill the damned thing," Macomber said, miserably.

"Well, that's what you're out here for, isn't it?"

"Yes. But I'm nervous. Hearing the thing roar gets on my nerves."

"Well then, as Wilson said, kill him and stop his roaring."

"Yes, darling," said Francis Macomber. "It sounds easy, doesn't it?"

"You're not afraid, are you?"

"Of course not. But I'm nervous from hearing him roar all night."

"You'll kill him marvellously," she said. "I know you will. I'm awfully anxious to see it."

"Finish your breakfast and we'll be starting."

"It's not light yet," she said. "This is a ridiculous hour."

Just then the lion roared in a deep-chested moaning, suddenly guttural, ascending vibration that seemed to shake the air and ended in a sigh and a heavy, deep-chested grunt.

"He sounds almost here," Macomber's wife said.

"My God," said Macomber. "I hate that damned noise."

"It's very impressive."

"Impressive. It's frightful."

Robert Wilson came up then carrying his short, ugly, shockingly big-bored .505 Gibbs and grinning.

"Come on," he said. "Your gun-bearer has your Springfield and the big gun. Everything's in the car. Have you solids?"[6]

"Yes."

"I'm ready," Mrs. Macomber said.

"Must make him stop that racket," Wilson said. "You get in front. The Memsahib can sit back here with me."

They climbed into the motor car and, in the gray first daylight, moved off up the river through the trees. Macomber opened the breech of his rifle and saw he had metal-cased bullets, shut the bolt and put the rifle on safety. He saw his hand was trembling. He felt in his pocket for more cartridges and moved his fingers over the cartridges in the loops of his tunic front. He turned back to where

6. They are using jacketed bullets for quick, clean kill; the Springfield is a thirty-caliber rifle as opposed to Wilson's fifty-caliber Gibbs.

Wilson sat in the rear seat of the doorless, box-bodied motor car beside his wife, them both grinning with excitement, and Wilson leaned forward and whispered,

"See the birds dropping. Means the old boy has left his kill."

On the far bank of the stream Macomber could see, above the trees, vultures circling and plummeting down.

"Chances are he'll come to drink along here," Wilson whispered. "Before he goes to lay up. Keep an eye out."

They were driving slowly along the high bank of the stream which here cut deeply to its boulder-filled bed, and they wound in and out through big trees as they drove. Macomber was watching the opposite bank when he felt Wilson take hold of his arm. The car stopped.

"There he is," he heard the whisper. "Ahead and to the right. Get out and take him. He's a marvellous lion."

Macomber saw the lion now. He was standing almost broadside, his great head up and turned toward them. The early morning breeze that blew toward them was just stirring his dark mane, and the lion looked huge, silhouetted on the rise of bank in the gray morning light, his shoulders heavy, his barrel of a body bulking smoothly.

"How far is he?" asked Macomber, raising his rifle.

"About seventy-five. Get out and take him."

"Why not shoot from where I am?"

"You don't shoot them from cars," he heard Wilson saying in his ear. "Get out. He's not going to stay there all day."

Macomber stepped out of the curved opening at the side of the front seat, onto the step and down onto the ground. The lion still stood looking majestically and coolly toward this object that his eyes only showed in silhouette, bulking like some super-rhino. There was no man smell carried toward him and he watched the object, moving his great head a little from side to side. Then watching the object, not afraid, but hesitating before going down the bank to drink with such a thing opposite him, he saw a man figure detach itself from it and he turned his heavy head and swung away toward the cover of the trees as he heard a cracking crash and felt the slam of a .30-06 220-grain solid bullet that bit his flank and ripped in sudden hot scalding nausea through his stomach. He trotted, heavy, big-footed, swinging wounded full-bellied, through the trees toward the tall grass and cover, and the crash came again to go past him ripping the air apart. Then it crashed again and he felt the blow as it hit his lower ribs and ripped on through, blood sudden hot and frothy in his mouth, and he galloped toward the high grass where he could crouch and not be seen and make them bring the crashing thing close enough so he could make a rush and get the man that held it.

Macomber had not thought how the lion felt as he got out of the car. He only knew his hands were shaking and as he walked away from the car it was almost impossible for him to make his legs move. They were stiff in the thighs, but he could feel the muscles fluttering. He raised the rifle, sighted on the junction of the lion's head and shoulders and pulled the trigger. Nothing happened though he pulled until he thought his finger would break. Then he knew he had the safety on and as he lowered the rifle to move the safety over he moved another frozen pace forward, and the lion seeing his silhouette now clear of the silhouette of the car, turned and started off at a trot, and, as Macomber fired, he heard a whunk that meant that the bullet was home; but the lion kept on going. Macomber shot again and everyone saw the bullet throw a spout of dirt beyond the trotting lion. He shot again, remembering to lower his aim, and they all heard the bullet hit, and the lion went into a gallop and was in the tall grass before he had the bolt pushed forward.

Macomber stood there feeling sick at his stomach, his hands that held the Springfield still cocked, shaking, and his wife and Robert Wilson were standing by him. Beside him too were the two gun-bearers chattering in Wakamba.[7]

"I hit him," Macomber said. "I hit him twice."

"You gut-shot him and you hit him somewhere forward," Wilson said without enthusiasm. The gun-bearers looked very grave. They were silent now.

"You may have killed him," Wilson went on. "We'll have to wait a while before we go in to find out."

"What do you mean?"

"Let him get sick before we follow him up."

"Oh," said Macomber.

"He's a hell of a fine lion," Wilson said cheerfully. "He's gotten into a bad place though."

"Why is it bad?"

"Can't see him until you're on him."

"Oh," said Macomber.

"Come on," said Wilson. "The Memsahib can stay here in the car. We'll go to have a look at the blood spoor."

"Stay here, Margot," Macomber said to his wife. His mouth was very dry and it was hard for him to talk.

"Why?" she asked.

"Wilson says to."

"We're going to have a look," Wilson said. "You stay here. You can see even better from here."

"All right."

Wilson spoke in Swahili to the driver. He nodded and said, "Yes, Bwana."

Then they went down the steep bank and across the stream, climbing over and around the boulders and up the other bank, pulling up by some projecting roots, and along it until they found where the lion had been trotting when Macomber first shot. There was dark blood on the short grass that the gun-bearers pointed out with grass stems, and that ran away behind the river bank trees.

"What do we do?" asked Macomber.

"Not much choice," said Wilson. "We can't bring the car over. Bank's too steep. We'll let him stiffen up a bit and then you and

7. A Bantu dialect spoken in Kenya.

I'll go in and have a look for him."

"Can't we set the grass on fire?" Macomber asked.

"Too green."

"Can't we send beaters?"

Wilson looked at him appraisingly. "Of course we can," he said. "But it's just a touch murderous. You see we know the lion's wounded. You can drive an unwounded lion—he'll move on ahead of a noise—but a wounded lion's going to charge. You can't see him until you're right on him. He'll make himself perfectly flat in cover you wouldn't think would hide a hare. You can't very well send boys in there to that sort of a show. Somebody bound to get mauled."

"What about the gun-bearers?"

"Oh, they'll go with us. It's their *shauri*.[8] You see, they signed on for it. They don't look too happy though, do they?"

"I don't want to go in there," said Macomber. It was out before he knew he'd said it.

"Neither do I," said Wilson very cheerily. "Really no choice though." Then, as an afterthought, he glanced at Macomber and saw suddenly how he was trembling and the pitiful look on his face.

"You don't have to go in, of course," he said. "That's what I'm hired for, you know. That's why I'm so expensive."

"You mean you'd go in by yourself? Why not leave him there?"

Robert Wilson, whose entire occupation had been with the lion and the problem he presented, and who had not been thinking about Macomber except to note that he was rather windy, suddenly felt as though he had opened the wrong door in a hotel and seen something shameful.

"What do you mean?"

"Why not just leave him?"

"You mean pretend to ourselves he hasn't been hit?"

"No. Just drop it."

"It isn't done."

"Why not?"

"For one thing, he's certain to be suffering. For another, some one else might run onto him."

"I see."

"But you don't have to have anything to do with it."

"I'd like to," Macomber said. "I'm just scared, you know."

"I'll go ahead when we go in," Wilson said, "with Kongoni tracking. You keep behind me and a little to one side. Chances are we'll hear him growl. If we see him we'll both shoot. Don't worry about anything. I'll keep you backed up. As a matter of fact, you know, perhaps you'd better not go. It might be much better. Why don't you go over and join the Memsahib while I just get it over with?"

"No, I want to go."

"All right," said Wilson. "But don't go in if you don't want to. This is my *shauri* now, you know."

"I want to go," said Macomber.

They sat under a tree and smoked.

8. Problem (a Swahili word).

"Want to go back and speak to the Memsahib while we're waiting?" Wilson asked.

"No."

"I'll just step back and tell her to be patient."

"Good," said Macomber. He sat there, sweating under his arms, his mouth dry, his stomach hollow feeling, wanting to find courage to tell Wilson to go on and finish off the lion without him. He could not know that Wilson was furious because he had not noticed the state he was in earlier and sent him back to his wife. While he sat there Wilson came up. "I have your big gun," he said. "Take it. We've given him time, I think. Come on."

Macomber took the big gun and Wilson said:

"Keep behind me and about five yards to the right and do exactly as I tell you." Then he spoke in Swahili to the two gun-bearers, who looked the picture of gloom.

"Let's go," he said.

"Could I have a drink of water?" Macomber asked. Wilson spoke to the older gun-bearer, who wore a canteen on his belt, and the man unbuckled it, unscrewed the top and handed it to Macomber, who took it noticing how heavy it seemed and how hairy and shoddy the felt covering was in his hand. He raised it to drink and looked ahead at the high grass with the flat-topped trees behind it. A breeze was blowing toward them and the grass rippled gently in the wind. He looked at the gun-bearer and he could see the gun-bearer was suffering too with fear.

Thirty-five yards into the grass the big lion lay flattened out along the ground. His ears were back and his only movement was a slight twitching up and down of his long, black-tufted tail. He had turned at bay as soon as he had reached this cover and he was sick with the wound through his full belly, and weakening with the wound through his lungs that brought a thin foamy red to his mouth each time he breathed. His flanks were wet and hot and flies were on the little openings the solid bullets had made in his tawny hide, and his big yellow eyes, narrowed with hate, looked straight ahead, only blinking when the pain came as he breathed, and his claws dug in the soft baked earth. All of him, pain, sickness, hatred and all of his remaining strength, was tightening into an absolute concentration for a rush. He could hear the men talking and he waited, gathering all of himself into this preparation for a charge as soon as the men would come into the grass. As he heard their voices his tail stiffened to twitch up and down, and, as they came into the edge of the grass, he made a coughing grunt and charged.

Kongoni, the old gun-bearer, in the lead watching the blood spoor, Wilson watching the grass for any movement, his big gun ready, the second gun-bearer looking ahead and listening, Macomber close to Wilson, his rifle cocked, they had just moved into the grass when Macomber heard the blood-choked coughing grunt, and saw the swishing rush in the grass. The next thing he knew he was running; running wildly, in panic in the open, running toward the stream.

He heard the *ca-ra-wong!* of Wilson's big rifle, and again in a second crashing *carawong!* and turning saw the lion, horrible-looking now, with half his head seeming to be gone, crawling toward Wilson in the edge of the tall grass while the red-faced man worked the bolt on the short ugly rifle and aimed carefully as another blasting *carawong!* came from the muzzle, and the crawling, heavy, yellow bulk of the lion stiffened and the huge, mutilated head slid forward and Macomber, standing by himself in the clearing where he had run, holding a loaded rifle, while two black men and a white man looked back at him in contempt, knew the lion was dead. He came toward Wilson, his tallness all seeming a naked reproach, and Wilson looked at him and said:

"Want to take pictures?"

"No," he said.

That was all any one had said until they reached the motor car. Then Wilson had said:

"Hell of a fine lion. Boys will skin him out. We might as well stay here in the shade."

Macomber's wife had not looked at him nor he at her and he had sat by her in the back seat with Wilson sitting in the front seat. Once he had reached over and taken his wife's hand without looking at her and she had removed her hand from his. Looking across the stream to where the gun-bearers were skinning out the lion he could see that she had been able to see the whole thing. While they sat there his wife had reached forward and put her hand on Wilson's shoulder. He turned and she had leaned forward over the low seat and kissed him on the mouth.

"Oh, I say," said Wilson, going redder than his natural baked color.

"Mr. Robert Wilson," she said. "The beautiful red-faced Mr. Robert Wilson."

Then she sat down beside Macomber again and looked away across the stream to where the lion lay, with uplifted, white-muscled, tendon-marked naked forearms, and white bloating belly, as the black men fleshed away the skin. Finally the gun-bearers brought the skin over, wet and heavy, and climbed in behind with it, rolling it up before they got in, and the motor car started. No one had said anything more until they were back in camp.

That was the story of the lion. Macomber did not know how the lion had felt before he started his rush, nor during it when the unbelievable smash of the .505 with a muzzle velocity of two tons had hit him in the mouth, nor what kept him coming after that, when the second ripping crash had smashed his hind quarters and he had come crawling on toward the crashing, blasting thing that had destroyed him. Wilson knew something about it and only expressed it by saying, "Damned fine lion," but Macomber did not know how Wilson felt about things either. He did not know how his wife felt except that she was through with him.

His wife had been through with him before but it never lasted. He was very wealthy, and would be much wealthier, and he knew she would not leave him ever now. That was one of the few things that he really knew. He knew about that, about motorcycles—that was earliest—about motor cars, about duck-shooting, about fishing,

trout, salmon and big-sea, about sex in books, many books, too many
books, about all court games, about dogs, not much about horses,
about hanging on to his money, about most of the other things his
world dealt in, and about his wife not leaving him. His wife had been
a great beauty and she was still a great beauty in Africa, but she was
not a great enough beauty any more at home to be able to leave him
and better herself and she knew it and he knew it. She had missed
the chance to leave him and he knew it. If he had been better with
women she would probably have started to worry about him getting
another new, beautiful wife; but she knew too much about him to
worry about him either. Also, he had always had a great tolerance
which seemed the nicest thing about him if it were not the most
sinister.

All in all they were known as a comparatively happily married
couple, one of those whose disruption is often rumored but never
occurs, and as the society columnist put it, they were adding more
than a spice of *adventure* to their much envied and ever-enduring
Romance by a *Safari* in what was known as *Darkest Africa* until the
Martin Johnsons lighted it on so many silver screens where they were
pursuing *Old Simba* the lion, the buffalo, *Tembo* the elephant and
as well collecting specimens for the Museum of Natural History.[9]
This same columnist had reported them *on the verge* at least three
times in the past and they had been. But they always made it up.
They had a sound basis of union. Margot was too beautiful for
Macomber to divorce her and Macomber had too much money for
Margot ever to leave him.

It was now about three o'clock in the morning and Francis Macomber, who had been asleep a little while after he had stopped
thinking about the lion, wakened and then slept again, woke suddenly, frightened in a dream of the bloody-headed lion standing over
him, and listening while his heart pounded, he realized that his wife
was not in the other cot in the tent. He lay awake with that knowledge for two hours.

At the end of that time his wife came into the tent, lifted her
mosquito bar and crawled cozily into bed.

"Where have you been?" Macomber asked in the darkness.

"Hello," she said. "Are you awake?"

"Where have you been?"

"I just went out to get a breath of air."

"You did, like hell."

"What do you want me to say, darling?"

"Where have you been?"

"Out to get a breath of air."

"That's a new name for it. You *are* a bitch."

"Well, you're a coward."

"All right," he said. "What of it?"

"Nothing as far as I'm concerned. But please let's not talk, darling,
because I'm very sleepy."

"You think that I'll take anything."

9. Martin and Osa Johnson from 1921 to 1936 made nature films in Africa.

"I know you will, sweet."

"Well, I won't."

"Please, darling, let's not talk. I'm so very sleepy."

"There wasn't going to be any of that. You promised there wouldn't be."

"Well, there is now," she said sweetly.

"You said if we made this trip that there would be none of that. You promised."

"Yes, darling. That's the way I meant it to be. But the trip was spoiled yesterday. We don't have to talk about it, do we?"

"You don't wait long when you have an advantage, do you?"

"Please let's not talk. I'm so sleepy, darling."

"I'm going to talk."

"Don't mind me then, because I'm going to sleep." And she did.

At breakfast they were all three at the table before daylight and Francis Macomber found that, of all the many men that he had hated, he hated Robert Wilson the most.

"Sleep well?" Wilson asked in his throaty voice, filling a pipe.

"Did you?"

"Topping," the white hunter told him.

You bastard, thought Macomber, you insolent bastard.

So she woke him when she came in, Wilson thought, looking at them both with his flat, cold eyes. Well, why doesn't he keep his wife where she belongs? What does he think I am, a bloody plaster saint? Let him keep her where she belongs. It's his own fault.

"Do you think we'll find buffalo?" Margot asked, pushing away a dish of apricots.

"Chance of it," Wilson said and smiled at her. "Why don't you stay in camp?"

"Not for anything," she told him.

"Why not order her to stay in camp?" Wilson said to Macomber.

"You order her," said Macomber coldly.

"Let's not have any ordering, nor," turning to Macomber, "any silliness, Francis," Margot said quite pleasantly.

"Are you ready to start?" Macomber asked.

"Any time," Wilson told him. "Do you want the Memsahib to go?"

"Does it make any difference whether I do or not?"

The hell with it, thought Robert Wilson. The utter complete hell with it. So this is what it's going to be like. Well, this is what it's going to be like, then.

"Makes no difference," he said.

"You're sure you wouldn't like to stay in camp with her yourself and let me go out and hunt the buffalo?" Macomber asked.

"Can't do that," said Wilson. "Wouldn't talk rot if I were you."

"I'm not talking rot. I'm disgusted."

"Bad word, disgusted."

"Francis, will you please try to speak sensibly?" his wife said.

"I speak too damned sensibly," Macomber said. "Did you ever eat such filthy food?"

"Something wrong with the food?" asked Wilson quietly.

"No more than with everything else."

"I'd pull yourself together, laddybuck," Wilson said very quietly. "There's a boy waits at table that understands a little English."

"The hell with him."

Wilson stood up and puffing on his pipe strolled away, speaking a few words in Swahili to one of the gun-bearers who was standing waiting for him. Macomber and his wife sat on at the table. He was staring at his coffee cup.

"If you make a scene I'll leave you, darling," Margot said quietly.

"No, you won't."

"You can try it and see."

"You won't leave me."

"No," she said. "I won't leave you and you'll behave yourself."

"Behave myself? That's a way to talk. Behave myself."

"Yes. Behave yourself."

"Why don't *you* try behaving?"

"I've tried it so long. So very long."

"I hate that red-faced swine," Macomber said. "I loathe the sight of him."

"He's really *very* nice."

"Oh, *shut up,*" Macomber almost shouted. Just then the car came up and stopped in front of the dining tent and the driver and the two gun-bearers got out. Wilson walked over and looked at the husband and wife sitting there at the table.

"Going shooting?" he asked.

"Yes," said Macomber, standing up. "Yes."

"Better bring a woolly. It will be cool in the car," Wilson said.

"I'll get my leather jacket," Margot said.

"The boy has it," Wilson told her. He climbed into the front with the driver and Francis Macomber and his wife sat, not speaking, in the back seat.

Hope the silly beggar doesn't take a notion to blow the back of my head off, Wilson thought to himself. Women *are* a nuisance on safari.

The car was grinding down to cross the river at a pebbly ford in the gray daylight and then climbed, angling up the steep bank, where Wilson had ordered a way shovelled out the day before so they could reach the parklike wooded rolling country on the far side.

It was a good morning, Wilson thought. There was a heavy dew and as the wheels went through the grass and low bushes he could smell the odor of the crushed fronds. It was an odor like verbena and he liked this early morning smell of the dew, the crushed bracken and the look of the tree trunks showing black through the early morning mist, as the car made its way through the untracked, parklike country. He had put the two in the back seat out of his mind now and was thinking about buffalo. The buffalo that he was after stayed in the daytime in a thick swamp where it was impossible to get a shot, but in the night they fed out into an open stretch of country and if he could come between them and their swamp with the car, Macomber would have a good chance at them in the open. He did not want to hunt buff with Macomber in thick cover. He did not want to hunt buff or anything else with Macomber at all, but he was a professional hunter and he had hunted with some rare ones in his time. If they got buff today there would only be rhino to come and the poor man would have gone through his dangerous game and things might pick up. He'd have nothing more to do with the woman and Macomber would get over that too. He must have gone through plenty of that before by the look of things. Poor beggar. He must have a way of getting over it. Well, it was the poor sod's[1] own bloody fault.

He, Robert Wilson, carried a double size cot on safari to accommodate any windfalls he might receive. He had hunted for a certain clientele, the international, fast, sporting set, where the women did not feel they were getting their money's worth unless they had shared that cot with the white hunter. He despised them when he was away from them although he liked some of them well enough at the time, but he made his living by them; and their standards were his standards as long as they were hiring him.

They were his standards in all except the shooting. He had his own standards about the killing and they could live up to them or get some one else to hunt them. He knew, too, that they all respected him for this. This Macomber was an odd one though. Damned if he wasn't. Now the wife. Well, the wife. Yes, the wife. Hm, the wife. Well he'd dropped all that. He looked around at them. Macomber sat grim and furious. Margot smiled at him. She looked younger today, more innocent and fresher and not so professionally beautiful. What's in her heart God knows, Wilson thought. She hadn't talked much last night. At that it was a pleasure to see her.

The motor car climbed up a slight rise and went on through the trees and then out into a grassy prairie-like opening and kept in the shelter of the trees along the edge, the driver going slowly and Wilson looking carefully out across the prairie and all along its far side. He stopped the car and studied the opening with his field glasses. Then he motioned to the driver to go on and the car moved slowly along, the driver avoiding wart-hog holes and driving around the mud castles ants had built. Then, looking across the opening, Wilson suddenly turned and said,

"By God, there they are!"

And looking where he pointed, while the car jumped forward and Wilson spoke in rapid Swahili to the driver, Macomber saw three huge, black animals looking almost cylindrical in their long heaviness, like big black tank cars, moving at a gallop across the far edge of the open prairie. They moved at a stiff-necked, stiff bodied gallop and he could see the upswept wide black horns on their heads as they galloped heads out; the heads not moving.

"They're three old bulls," Wilson said. "We'll cut them off before they get to the swamp."

The car was going a wild forty-five miles an hour across the open and as Macomber watched, the buffalo got bigger and bigger until he could see the gray, hairless, scabby look of one huge bull and how his neck was a part of his shoulders and the shiny black of his

---

1. Chap or fellow, now nonpejorative but originally "sodomite" (cp. "bugger").

horns as he galloped a little behind the others that were strung out in that steady plunging gait; and then, the car swaying as though it had just jumped a road, they drew up close and he could see the plunging hugeness of the bull, and the dust in his sparsely haired hide, the side boss of horn and his outstretched, wide-nostrilled muzzle, and he was raising his rifle when Wilson shouted, "Not from the car, you fool!" and he had no fear, only hatred of Wilson, while the brakes clamped on and the car skidded, plowing sideways to an almost stop and Wilson was out on one side and he on the other, stumbling as his feet hit the still speeding-by of the earth, and then he was shooting at the bull as he moved away, hearing the bullets whunk into him, emptying his rifle at him as he moved steadily away, finally remembering to get his shots forward into the shoulder, and as he fumbled to re-load, he saw the bull was down. Down on his knees, his big head tossing, and seeing the other two still galloping he shot at the leader and hit him. He shot again and missed and he heard the *carawonging* roar as Wilson shot and saw the leading bull slide forward onto his nose.

"Get that other," Wilson said. "Now you're shooting!"

But the other bull was moving steadily at the same gallop and he missed, throwing a spout of dirt, and Wilson missed and the dust rose in a cloud and Wilson shouted, "Come on. He's too far!" and grabbed his arm and they were in the car again, Macomber and Wilson hanging on the sides and rocketing swayingly over the un-even ground, drawing up on the steady, plunging, heavy-necked, straight-moving gallop of the bull.

They were behind him and Macomber was filling his rifle, dropping shells onto the ground, jamming it, clearing the jam, then they were almost up with the bull when Wilson yelled "Stop," and the car skidded so that it almost swung over and Macomber fell forward onto his feet, slammed his bolt forward and fired as far forward as he could aim into the galloping, rounded black back, aimed and shot again, then again, then again, and the bullets, all of them hitting, had no effect on the buffalo that he could see. Then Wilson shot, the roar deafening him, and he could see the bull stagger. Macomber shot again, aiming carefully, and down he came, onto his knees.

"All right," Wilson said. "Nice work. That's the three."

Macomber felt a drunken elation.

"How many times did you shoot?" he asked.

"Just three," Wilson said. "You killed the first bull. The biggest one. I helped you finish the other two. Afraid they might have got into cover. You had them killed. I was just mopping up a little. You shot damn well."

"Let's go to the car," said Macomber. "I want a drink."

"Got to finish off that buff first," Wilson told him. The buffalo was on his knees and he jerked his head furiously and bellowed in pig-eyed, roaring rage as they came toward him.

"Watch he doesn't get up," Wilson said. Then, "Get a little broad-side and take him in the neck just behind the ear."

Macomber aimed carefully at the center of the huge, jerking, rage-driven neck and shot. At the shot the head dropped forward.

"That does it," said Wilson. "Got the spine. They're a hell of a looking thing, aren't they?"

"Let's get the drink," said Macomber. In his life he had never felt so good.

In the car Macomber's wife sat very white faced. "You were marvellous, darling," she said to Macomber. "What a ride."

"Was it rough?" Wilson asked.

"It was frightful. I've never been more frightened in my life."

"Let's all have a drink," Macomber said.

"By all means," said Wilson. "Give it to the Memsahib." She drank the neat whisky from the flask and shuddered a little when she swallowed. She handed the flask to Macomber who handed it to Wilson.

"It was frightfully exciting," she said. "It's given me a dreadful headache. I didn't know you were allowed to shoot them from cars though."

"No one shot from cars," said Wilson coldly.

"I mean chase them from cars."

"Wouldn't ordinarily," Wilson said. "Seemed sporting enough to me though while we were doing it. Taking more chance driving that way across the plain full of holes and one thing and another than hunting on foot. Buffalo could have charged us each time we shot if he liked. Gave him every chance. Wouldn't mention it to any one though. It's illegal if that's what you mean."

"It seemed very unfair to me," Margot said, "chasing those big helpless things in a motor car."

"Did it?" said Wilson.

"What would happen if they heard about it in Nairobi?"

"I'd lose my license for one thing. Other unpleasantnesses," Wilson said, taking a drink from the flask. "I'd be out of business."

"Really?"

"Yes, really."

"Well," said Macomber, and he smiled for the first time all day. "Now she has something on you."

"You have such a pretty way of putting things, Francis," Margot Macomber said. Wilson looked at them both. If a four-letter man marries a five-letter woman, he was thinking, what number of letters would their children be? What he said was, "We lost a gun-bearer. Did you notice it?"

"My God, no," Macomber said.

"Here he comes," Wilson said. "He's all right. He must have fallen off when we left the first bull."

Approaching them was the middle-aged gun-bearer, limping along in his knitted cap, khaki tunic, shorts and rubber sandals, gloomy-faced and disgusted looking. As he came up he called out to Wilson in Swahili and they all saw the change in the white hunter's face.

"What does he say?" asked Margot.

"He says the first bull got up and went into the bush," Wilson said with no expression in his voice.

"Oh," said Macomber blankly.

"Then it's going to be just like the lion," said Margot, full of anticipation.

"It's not going to be a damned bit like the lion," Wilson told her.

"Did you want another drink, Macomber?"

"Thanks, yes," Macomber said. He expected the feeling he had had about the lion to come back but it did not. For the first time in his life he really felt wholly without fear. Instead of fear he had a feeling of definite elation.

"We'll go and have a look at the second bull," Wilson said. "I'll tell the driver to put the car in the shade."

"What are you going to do?" asked Margaret Macomber.

"Take a look at the buff," Wilson said.

"I'll come."

"Come along."

The three of them walked over to where the second buffalo bulked blackly in the open, head forward on the grass, the massive horns swung wide.

"He's a very good head," Wilson said. "That's close to a fifty-inch spread."

Macomber was looking at him with delight.

"He's hateful looking," said Margot. "Can't we go into the shade?"

"Of course," Wilson said. "Look," he said to Macomber, and pointed. "See that patch of bush?"

"Yes."

"That's where the first bull went in. The gun-bearer said when he fell off the bull was down. He was watching us helling along and the other two buff galloping. When he looked up there was the bull up and looking at him. Gun-bearer ran like hell and the bull went off slowly into that bush."

"Can we go in after him now?" asked Macomber eagerly.

Wilson looked at him appraisingly. Damned if this isn't a strange one, he thought. Yesterday he's scared sick and today he's a ruddy[2] fire eater.

"No, we'll give him a while."

"Let's please go into the shade," Margot said. Her face was white and she looked ill.

They made their way to the car where it stood under a single, wide-spreading tree and all climbed in.

"Chances are he's dead in there," Wilson remarked. "After a little we'll have a look."

Macomber felt a wild unreasonable happiness that he had never known before.

"By God, that was a chase," he said. "I've never felt any such feeling. Wasn't it marvellous, Margot?"

"I hated it."

"Why?"

"I hated it," she said bitterly. "I loathed it."

"You know I don't think I'd ever be afraid of anything again," Macomber said to Wilson. "Something happened in me after we first saw the buff and started after him. Like a dam bursting. It was pure excitement."

"Cleans out your liver," said Wilson. "Damn funny things happen to people."

2. Euphemism for the stronger "bloody."

Macomber's face was shining. "You know something did happen to me," he said. "I feel absolutely different."

His wife said nothing and eyed him strangely. She was sitting far back in the seat and Macomber was sitting forward talking to Wilson who turned sideways talking over the back of the front seat.

"You know, I'd like to try another lion," Macomber said. "I'm really not afraid of them now. After all, what can they do to you?"

"That's it," said Wilson. "Worst one can do is kill you. How does it go? Shakespeare. Damned good. See if I can remember. Oh, damned good. Used to quote it to myself at one time. Let's see. 'By my troth, I care not; a man can die but once; we owe God a death and let it go which way it will he that dies this year is quit for the next.'[3] Damned fine, eh?"

He was very embarrassed, having brought out this thing he had lived by, but he had seen men come of age before and it always moved him. It was not a matter of their twenty-first birthday.

It had taken a strange chance of hunting, a sudden precipitation into action without opportunity for worrying beforehand, to bring this about with Macomber, but regardless of how it had happened it had most certainly happened. Look at the beggar now, Wilson thought. It's that some of them stay little boys so long, Wilson thought. Sometimes all their lives. Their figures stay boyish when they're fifty. The great American boy-men. Damned strange people. But he liked this Macomber now. Damned strange fellow. Probably meant the end of cuckoldry too. Well, that would be a damned good thing. Damned good thing. Beggar had probably been afraid all his life. Don't know what started it. But over now. Hadn't had time to be afraid with the buff. That and being angry too. Motor car too. Motor cars made it familiar. Be a damn fire eater now. He'd seen it in the war work the same way. More of a change than any loss of virginity. Fear gone like an operation. Something else grew in its place. Main thing a man had. Made him into a man. Women knew it too. No bloody fear.

From the far corner of the seat Margaret Macomber looked at the two of them. There was no change in Wilson. She saw Wilson as she had seen him the day before when she had first realized what his great talent was. But she saw the change in Francis Macomber now.

"Do you have that feeling of happiness about what's going to happen?" Macomber asked, still exploring his new wealth.

"You're not supposed to mention it," Wilson said, looking in the other's face. "Much more fashionable to say you're scared. Mind you, you'll be scared too, plenty of times."

"But you *have* a feeling of happiness about action to come?"

"Yes," said Wilson. "There's that. Doesn't do to talk too much about all this. Talk the whole thing away. No pleasure in anything if you mouth it up too much."

"You're both talking rot," said Margot. "Just because you've chased

3. Shakespeare, *Henry IV Part 2*, III, 2, 250–55. There are some differences in punctuation, and after "owe God a death," the following is omitted: "I'll ne'er bear a base mind. An't be my destiny, so; an't be not, so. No man's too good to serve's prince."

some helpless animals in a motor car you talk like heroes."

"Sorry," said Wilson. "I have been gassing too much." She's worried about it already, he thought.

"If you don't know what we're talking about why not keep out of it?" Macomber asked his wife.

"You've gotten awfully brave, awfully suddenly," his wife said contemptuously, but her contempt was not secure. She was very afraid of something.

Macomber laughed, a very natural hearty laugh. "You know I *have*," he said. "I really have."

"Isn't it sort of late?" Margot said bitterly. Because she had done the best she could for many years back and the way they were together now was no one person's fault.

"Not for me," said Macomber.

Margot said nothing but sat back in the corner of the seat.

"Do you think we've given him time enough?" Macomber asked Wilson cheerfully.

"We might have a look," Wilson said. "Have you any solids left?"

"The gun-bearer has some."

Wilson called in Swahili and the older gun-bearer, who was skinning out one of the heads, straightened up, pulled a box of solids out of his pocket and brought them over to Macomber, who filled his magazine and put the remaining shells in his pocket.

"You might as well shoot the Springfield," Wilson said. "You're used to it. We'll leave the Mannlicher in the car with the Memsahib. Your gun-bearer can carry your heavy gun. I've this damned cannon. Now let me tell you about them." He had saved this until the last because he did not want to worry Macomber. "When a buff comes he comes with his head high and thrust straight out. The boss of the horns covers any sort of a brain shot. The only shot is straight into the nose. The only other shot is into his chest or, if you're to one side, into the neck or the shoulders. After they've been hit once they take a hell of a lot of killing. Don't try anything fancy. Take the easiest shot there is. They've finished skinning out that head now. Should we get started."

He called to the gun-bearers, who came up wiping their hands, and the older one got into the back.

"I'll only take Kongoni," Wilson said. "The other can watch to keep the birds away."

As the car moved slowly across the open space toward the island of brushy trees that ran in a tongue of foliage along a dry water course that cut the open swale, Macomber felt his heart pounding and his mouth was dry again, but it was excitement, not fear.

"Here's where he went in," Wilson said. Then to the gun-bearer in Swahili, "Take the blood spoor."

The car was parallel to the patch of bush. Macomber, Wilson and the gun-bearer got down. Macomber, looking back, saw his wife, with the rifle by her side, looking at him. He waved to her and she did not wave back.

The brush was very thick ahead and the ground was dry. The middle-aged gun-bearer was sweating heavily and Wilson had his hat down over his eyes and his red neck showed just ahead of Macomber. Suddenly the gun-bearer said something in Swahili to Wilson and ran forward.

"He's dead in there," Wilson said. "Good work," and he turned to grip Macomber's hand and as they shook hands, grinning at each other, the gun-bearer shouted wildly and they saw him coming out of the brush sideways, fast as a crab, and the bull coming, nose out, mouth tight closed, blood dripping, massive head straight out, coming in a charge, his little pig eyes bloodshot as he looked at them. Wilson, who was ahead was kneeling shooting, and Macomber, as he fired, unhearing his shot in the roaring of Wilson's gun, saw fragments like slate burst from the huge boss of the horns, and the head jerked, he shot again at the wide nostrils and saw the horns jolt again and fragments fly, and he did not see Wilson now and, aiming carefully, shot again with the buffalo's huge bulk almost on him and his rifle almost level with the on-coming head, nose out, and he could see the little wicked eyes and the head started to lower and he felt a sudden white-hot, blinding flash explode inside his head and that was all he ever felt.

Wilson had ducked to one side to get in a shoulder shot. Macomber had stood solid and shot for the nose, shooting a touch high each time and hitting the heavy horns, splintering and chipping them like hitting a slate roof, and Mrs. Macomber, in the car, had shot at the buffalo with the 6.5 Mannlicher as it seemed about to gore Macomber and had hit her husband about two inches up and a little to one side of the base of his skull.

Francis Macomber lay now, face down, not two yards from where the buffalo lay on his side and his wife knelt over him with Wilson beside her.

"I wouldn't turn him over," Wilson said.

The woman was crying hysterically.

"I'd get back in the car," Wilson said. "Where's the rifle?"

She shook her head, her face contorted. The gun-bearer picked up the rifle.

"Leave it as it is," said Wilson. Then, "Go get Abdulla so that he may witness the manner of the accident."

He knelt down, took a handkerchief from his pocket, and spread it over Francis Macomber's crew-cropped head where it lay. The blood sank into the dry, loose earth.

Wilson stood up and saw the buffalo on his side, his legs out, his thinly-haired belly crawling with ticks. "Hell of a good bull," his brain registered automatically. "A good fifty inches, or better. Better." He called to the driver and told him to spread a blanket over the body and stay by it. Then he walked over to the motor car where the woman sat crying in the corner.

"That was a pretty thing to do," he said in a toneless voice. "He *would* have left you too."

"Stop it," she said.

"Of course it's an accident," he said. "I know that."

"Stop it," she said.

"Don't worry," he said. "There will be a certain amount of unpleasantness but I will have some photographs taken that will be very useful at the inquest. There's the testimony of the gun-bearers and the driver too. You're perfectly all right."

"Stop it," she said.

"There's a hell of a lot to be done," he said. "And I'll have to send a truck off to the lake to wireless for a plane to take the three of us into Nairobi. Why didn't you poison him? That's what they do in England."

"Stop it. Stop it. Stop it," the woman cried.

Wilson looked at her with his flat blue eyes.

"I'm through now," he said. "I was a little angry. I'd begun to like your husband."

"Oh, please stop it," she said. "Please, please stop it."

"That's better," Wilson said. "Please is much better. Now I'll stop."

p. 1936

3   FOCUS AND VOICE

Who is telling us the story—whose words are we reading? Where does this person stand in relation to what is going on in the story? In narrative someone is always between us and the events—a viewer, a speaker, or both; narrative, unlike drama, is always mediated. The way a story is mediated is a key element in fictional structure. This mediation involves both the angle of vision, the point from which the people, events, and other details are viewed, and also the words of the story lying between us and the history. The viewing aspect is called the **focus** or **point of view**, and the verbal aspect the **voice**.

Focus acts much as a movie camera does, choosing what we can look at and the angle at which we can view it, framing, proportioning, emphasizing—even distorting. Plot is a structure that places us in a time relationship to the history; focus places us in a spatial relationship.

We must pay careful attention to the focus at any given point in a story. Is it fixed or mobile? Does it stay at more or less the same angle to, and at the same distance from, the characters and action, or does it move around or in and out? In the first three and a half paragraphs of *An Occurrence at Owl Creek Bridge*, for example, we seem to be seeing through the lens of a camera that can swing left or right, up or down, but that stays pretty much at the same angle and distance from the bridge. By the middle of the fourth paragraph, however, we're inside the mind of the man who's about to be hanged: "The arrangement commended itself to his judgment. . . . He looked a moment. . . . A piece of dancing driftwood caught his attention. . . . How slowly it appeared to move!" From now on we are inside the condemned man's head. The focus is more limited in scope—for almost all the rest of the story we can see and hear only what he sees and hears. But because the focus is internal as well as limited, we can also know what he thinks. This limited, internal focus, used here as well as in *The Most Dangerous Game*, is usually called the **centered** or **central consciousness.**

The centered consciousness has been perhaps the most popular focus in fiction for the past hundred years—through most of the history of the modern short story, in fact—and its tightly controlled range and concentration on a single individual seem particularly suited for the short form. During much of this period, fiction, both long and short, has been in one sense realistic—that is, treating the everyday and the natural. It has become increasingly clear, however, that the apparently real is not necessarily what "is" but what is *perceived* by the senses and mind of the individual. (This is sometimes called **psychological realism.**) The centered consciousness, in which things, people, and events are narrated as if they have been perceived through the filter of an individual character's consciousness, has therefore seemed the more realistic way to tell a story. It is a comfortable focus for readers, too. On the one hand, they can identify with someone whose thoughts and perception they share, even if the character is fallible, like Rainsford in *The Most Dangerous Game*, or reprehensible, like the womanizing Gurov at the beginning of Chekhov's *The Lady with the Dog.* We can identify with the focus in a story told in the first person ("I"), too, but we are too close at times. We cannot escape. The camera cannot pull back as it can in a third-person story.

First-person stories, like *The Summer My Grandmother Was Supposed to Die*, are always limited too, and almost all the time are internal as well (though Montresor, in *The Cask of Amontillado*, hides his plans from us). While they cannot retract spatially from the narrator, they almost always are withdrawn temporally: that is, the "I" telling the story is older than the "I" experiencing the events of the story.

The psychological realism gained by having a limited narrator exacts a price from the reader. If we don't hold the author (or the story) responsible for the absolute truth, validity, accuracy, and opinions of the focal character—if he or she is just telling us what he or she thinks, feels, sees—we must accept the possibility that the narrator's vision may be **unreliable.** At a significant point in *Owl Creek Bridge*, for example, you will find that the camera pulls back from Peyton Farquhar and we are made to recognize to what extent his consciousness is a reliable witness to what has been going on. The history here is only an occurrence; the limited focus structures the mere occurrence into a story.

When the focus is limited, whether to a first-person narrator or to a centered consciousness, it is tied to that individual. When he or she leaves the room, the camera must go too, and if we are to know what happens in the room when the focal character is gone, some means of bringing the information to that character must be devised, such as a

letter or a report by another character. The camera may pull back out
of the character's mind or even, as in *Owl Creek Bridge,* above and
away from the character, but it does not generally jump around. The
somewhat unusual first-person plural focus of *A Rose for Emily* is not
limited to a single individual; anything the town of Jefferson in general
can know of past or present, the narrative can know. But neither is it
an unlimited focus; "we" could not get into Emily's house before she
died and could never get into her mind.

An **unlimited focus** permits such freedom. In *The Short Happy Life
of Francis Macomber* we enter the minds of each of the main characters periodically throughout the story. We get inside Margot Macomber's consciousness on the first page as she looks at Wilson and
knows she hasn't seen him before, and on another page Macomber
and Robert Wilson "both saw that she was going to cry. Wilson had
seen it coming for a long time and he dreaded it. Macomber was
past dreading it." Throughout, the story seems free to dip inside one
consciousness or another, and can move with any of the characters.
This unlimited, internal/external focus is called **omniscient** and the
all-knowing narrator is the **omniscient observer.**

There are no laws governing focus in fiction, but there is a general
feeling that once a focus is chosen that ought to be the law for that
story. Do you feel manipulated when the focus, which has been on
Rainsford for the entire length of *The Most Dangerous Game,* shifts,
very near the end, from him to the general, apparently just to heighten
our suspense? Do you feel betrayed by the fact that we are not allowed
to enter Margot Macomber's mind at one crucial moment, even
though the focus has shifted freely at less crucial times?

Focus and voice often coincide. There is no discrepancy that I can
see (or hear) between the viewing and the telling in *The Cask of
Amontillado,* for example. But in *The Summer My Grandmother Was
Supposed to Die,* the "I" telling the story is older than the "I" experiencing the events of the story. Notice how many phrases there are
like "years later I was shown the telegram" and "In those days . . ."
So, too, the language of the story is clearly not that of a young boy:
"She arrived punctually at noon"; "I've been told that to study Talmud
with him had been a rare pleasure"; "lots of slender volumes of sermons, chassidic tales, and rabbinical commentaries." Such expressions
may deal with incidents and information within the boy's perception,
but the language in which they are expressed is clearly beyond him.

Like the focus, the voice in *Owl Creek Bridge* at the beginning of
the story is not centered in Peyton Farquhar, but even when the focus
narrows on him the voice telling the story is not his; note, for example, "As these thoughts, *which have here to be set down in words,*
were flashed into the doomed man's brain" (emphasis added). The
discrepancy may prepare a careful reader for later developments in the
story.

I have used the common term **narrator** in the usual way—to mean
the person who tells the story. You will have noticed that often the
narrator really is a person in the story, like Muttel, the narrator in *The
Summer My Grandmother Was Supposed to Die.* But how about the

narrator in *Owl Creek Bridge* or in *Macomber?* Who is it who sets down Farquhar's words and can say things like this: "Death is a dignitary who when he comes announced is to be received with formal manifestations of respect, even by those most familiar with him. In the code of military etiquette silence and fixity are forms of deference." Where is he or she standing? What kind of person is this narrator? We might ask the same question of the elusive, unnamed spokesman for the town of Jefferson in *A Rose for Emily.* Close attention to the language and chronology of the story, to the references to race and gender, to the use of "they" and "we" reveals that the narrator is an educated white male who at the time of Emily's death is probably a boy or very young man.

Is he Faulkner? Where the narrator plays some role in the story we are less likely to routinely identify him with the author, though we sometimes thoughtlessly do. Where the narrator is more of a disembodied voice and there is no indication to the contrary we often do tend to identify him or her with the author. We call the narrator of *Owl Creek Bridge* "Bierce," of *Macomber* "Hemingway." This is not necessarily wrong, but it can be misleading. We can dig up a few facts about the author's life and read them into the story, or, worse, read the character or detail of the story into the author's life. It is more prudent, therefore, especially on the basis of a single story, not to speak of the author but of the author's **persona,** the voice or figure of the author who tells and structures the story, who may or may not resemble in nature or values the actual person of the author. Mary Anne Evans wrote novels under the name of George Eliot; her first-person narrator speaks of "himself." That male narrator may be a good example of the persona or representative that most authors construct to "write" their stories.

We say *write* the stories. The narrator of *Owl Creek Bridge* has to "set down in words" what Farquhar is thinking. But, just as poets write of singing their songs (poems), so we often speak of telling a story, and we speak of a narrator, which means a teller. There are stories, usually with first-person narrators, that make much of the convention of oral storytelling: *My Man Bovanne,* for example, or *Spotted Horses.* Often these stories not only have an "oral" taleteller but imply a certain audience. Sometimes, as in *The Celebrated Jumping Frog of Calaveras County,* there is a narrator who tells the story within the story to someone else who retells it or writes it down, and the nature and response of this **auditor** can be a significant part of the meaning and effect of the story.

We are used to thinking of a story in terms of its plot, so that to summarize a story usually means giving a plot summary. But if you shift focus and voice you will often find that though the history has not changed, the story has. You might want to test this out by rewriting *Macomber* with any one character as the focus, or *The Summer My Grandmother Was Supposed to Die* with the focus and perhaps with the voice of Muttel's mother. An element is a basic, irreducible part of something; in fiction, focus and voice are elementary.

AMBROSE BIERCE

An Occurrence at Owl Creek Bridge

I

A man stood upon a railroad bridge in northern Alabama, looking down into the swift water twenty feet below. The man's hands were behind his back, the wrists bound with a cord. A rope closely encircled his neck. It was attached to a stout cross-timber above his head and the slack fell to the level of his knees. Some loose boards laid upon the sleepers[1] supporting the metals of the railway supplied a footing for him and his executioners—two private soldiers of the Federal army, directed by a sergeant who in civil life may have been a deputy sheriff. At a short remove upon the same temporary platform was an officer in the uniform of his rank, armed. He was a captain. A sentinel at each end of the bridge stood with his rifle in the position known as "support," that is to say, vertical in front of the left shoulder, the hammer resting on the forearm thrown straight across the chest—a formal and unnatural position, enforcing an erect carriage of the body. It did not appear to be the duty of these two men to know what was occurring at the center of the bridge; they merely blockaded the two ends of the foot planking that traversed it.

Beyond one of the sentinels nobody was in sight; the railroad ran straight away into a forest for a hundred yards, then, curving, was lost to view. Doubtless there was an outpost farther along. The other bank of the stream was open ground—a gentle acclivity topped with a stockade of vertical tree trunks, loopholed for rifles, with a single embrasure through which protruded the muzzle of a brass cannon commanding the bridge. Midway of the slope between bridge and fort were the spectators—a single company of infantry in line, at "parade rest," the butts of the rifles on the ground, the barrels inclining slightly backward against the right shoulder, the hands crossed upon the stock. A lieutenant stood at the right of the line, the point of his sword upon the ground, his left hand resting upon his right. Excepting the group of four at the center of the bridge, not a man moved. The company faced the bridge, staring stonily, motionless. The sentinels, facing the banks of the stream, might have been statues to adorn the bridge. The captain stood with folded arms, silent, observing the work of his subordinates, but making no sign. Death is a dignitary who when he comes announced is to be received with formal manifestations of respect, even by those most familiar with him. In the code of military etiquette silence and fixity are forms of deference.

The man who was engaged in being hanged was apparently about thirty-five years of age. He was a civilian, if one might judge from his habit, which was that of a planter. His features were good—a straight nose, firm mouth, broad forehead, from which his long, dark hair was combed straight back, falling behind his ears to the collar of his well-

1. Crossties that support railroad track.

fitting frock coat. He wore a mustache and pointed beard, but no whiskers; his eyes were large and dark gray, and had a kindly expression which one would hardly have expected in one whose neck was in the hemp. Evidently this was no vulgar assassin. The liberal military code makes provision for hanging many kinds of persons, and gentlemen are not excluded.

The preparations being complete, the two private soldiers stepped aside and each drew away the plank upon which he had been standing. The sergeant turned to the captain, saluted and placed himself immediately behind that officer, who in turn moved apart one pace. These movements left the condemned man and the sergeant standing on the two ends of the same plank, which spanned three of the crossties of the bridge. The end upon which the civilian stood almost, but not quite, reached a fourth. This plank had been held in place by the weight of the captain; it was now held by that of the sergeant. At a signal from the former the latter would step aside, the plank would tilt and the condemned man go down between two ties. The arrangement commended itself to his judgment as simple and effective. His face had not been covered nor his eyes bandaged. He looked a moment at his "unsteadfast footing," then let his gaze wander to the swirling water of the stream racing madly beneath his feet. A piece of dancing driftwood caught his attention and his eyes followed it down the current. How slowly it appeared to move! What a sluggish stream!

[margin note: inside man's mind]

He closed his eyes in order to fix his last thoughts upon his wife and children. The water, touched to gold by the early sun, the brooding mists under the banks at some distance down the stream, the fort, the soldiers, the piece of drift—all had distracted him. And now he became conscious of a new disturbance. Striking through the thought of his dear ones was a sound which he could neither ignore nor understand, a sharp, distinct, metallic percussion like the stroke of a blacksmith's hammer upon the anvil; it had the same ringing quality. He wondered what it was, and whether immeasurably distant or near by—it seemed both. Its recurrence was regular, but as slow as the tolling of a death knell. He awaited each stroke with impatience and—he knew not why —apprehension. The intervals of silence grew progressively longer; the delays became maddening. With their greater infrequency the sounds increased in strength and sharpness. They hurt his ear like the thrust of a knife; he feared he would shriek. What he heard was the ticking of his watch.

He unclosed his eyes and saw again the water below him. "If I could free my hands," he thought, "I might throw off the noose and spring into the stream. By diving I could evade the bullets and, swimming vigorously, reach the bank, take to the woods and get away home. My home, thank God, is as yet outside their lines; my wife and little ones are still beyond the invader's farthest advance."

As these thoughts, which have here to be set down in words, were flashed into the doomed man's brain rather than evolved from it the captain nodded to the sergeant. The sergeant stepped aside.

II

Peyton Farquhar was a well-to-do planter, of an old and highly respected Alabama family. Being a slave owner and like other slave
owners a politician he was naturally an original secessionist and ardently devoted to the Southern cause. Circumstances of an imperious
nature, which it is unnecessary to relate here, had prevented him from
taking service with the gallant army that had fought the disastrous
campaigns ending with the fall of Corinth,[2] and he chafed under the
inglorious restraint, longing for the release of his energies, the larger
life of the soldier, the opportunity for distinction. That opportunity,
he felt, would come, as it comes to all in war time. Meanwhile he did
what he could. No service was too humble for him to perform in aid
of the South, no adventure too perilous for him to undertake if consistent with the character of a civilian who was at heart a soldier, and
who in good faith and without too much qualification assented to at
least a part of the frankly villainous dictum that all is fair in love and
war.

One evening while Farquhar and his wife were sitting on a rustic
bench near the entrance to his grounds, a gray-clad soldier rode up to
the gate and asked for a drink of water. Mrs. Farquhar was only too
happy to serve him with her own white hands. While she was fetching the water her husband approached the dusty horseman and inquired eagerly for news from the front.

"The Yanks are repairing the railroads," said the man, "and are
getting ready for another advance. They have reached the Owl Creek
bridge, put it in order and built a stockade on the north bank. The
commandant has issued an order, which is posted everywhere, declaring that any civilian caught interfering with the railroad, its
bridges, tunnels or trains will be summarily hanged. I saw the order."

"How far is it to the Owl Creek bridge?" Farquhar asked.

"About thirty miles."

"Is there no force on this side the creek?"

"Only a picket post half a mile out, on the railroad, and a single
sentinel at this end of the bridge."

"Suppose a man—a civilian and student of hanging—should elude the
picket post and perhaps get the better of the sentinel," said Farquhar,
smiling, "what could he accomplish?"

The soldier reflected. "I was there a month ago," he replied. "I observed that the flood of last winter had lodged a great quantity of
driftwood against the wooden pier at this end of the bridge. It is now
dry and would burn like tow."

The lady had now brought the water, which the soldier drank. He
thanked her ceremoniously, bowed to her husband and rode away.
An hour later, after nightfall, he repassed the plantation, going northward in the direction from which he had come. He was a Federal
scout.

---

2. Corinth, Mississippi, captured by General Grant in April 1862.

III

As Peyton Farquhar fell straight downward through the bridge he lost consciousness and was as one already dead. From this state he was awakened—ages later, it seemed to him—by the pain of a sharp pressure upon his throat, followed by a sense of suffocation. Keen, poignant agonies seemed to shoot from his neck downward through every fiber of his body and limbs. These pains appeared to flash along well-defined lines of ramification and to beat with an inconceivably rapid periodicity. They seemed like streams of pulsating fire heating him to an intolerable temperature. As to his head, he was conscious of nothing but a feeling of fulness—of congestion. These sensations were unaccompanied by thought. The intellectual part of his nature was already effaced; he had power only to feel, and feeling was torment. He was conscious of motion. Encompassed in a luminous cloud, of which he was now merely the fiery heart, without material substance, he swung through unthinkable arcs of oscillation, like a vast pendulum. Then all at once, with terrible suddenness, the light about him shot upward with the noise of a loud plash; a frightful roaring was in his ears, and all was cold and dark. The power of thought was restored; he knew that the rope had broken and he had fallen into the stream. There was no additional strangulation; the noose about his neck was already suffocating him and kept the water from his lungs. To die of hanging at the bottom of a river!—the idea seemed to him ludicrous. He opened his eyes in the darkness and saw above him a gleam of light, but how distant, how inaccessible! He was still sinking, for the light became fainter and fainter until it was a mere glimmer. Then it began to grow and brighten, and he knew that he was rising toward the surface—knew it with reluctance, for he was now very comfortable. "To be hanged and drowned," he thought, "that is not so bad; but I do not wish to be shot. No; I will not be shot; that is not fair."

He was not conscious of an effort, but a sharp pain in his wrist appraised him that he was trying to free his hands. He gave the struggle his attention, as an idler might observe the feat of a juggler, without interest in the outcome. What splendid effort!—what magnificent, what superhuman strength! Ah, that was a fine endeavor! Bravo! The cord fell away; his arms parted and floated upward, the hands dimly seen on each side in the growing light. He watched them with a new interest as first one and then the other pounced upon the noose at his neck. They tore it away and thrust it fiercely aside, its undulations resembling those of a water snake. "Put it back, put it back!" He thought he shouted these words to his hands, for the undoing of the noose had been succeeded by the direct pang that he had yet experienced. His neck ached horribly; his brain was on fire; his heart, which had been fluttering faintly, gave a great leap, trying to force itself out at his mouth. His whole body was racked and wrenched with an insupportable anguish! But his disobedient hands gave no heed to the command. They beat the water vigorously with quick, downward strokes, forcing him to the surface. He felt his head emerge; his eyes were blinded by the sunlight; his chest expanded convulsively, and with a supreme and crowning agony his lungs engulfed a great draught of air, which instantly he expelled in a shriek!

He was now in full possession of his physical senses. They were, indeed, preternaturally keen and alert. Something in the awful disturbance of his organic system had so exalted and refined them that they made record of things never before perceived. He felt the ripples upon his face and heard their separate sounds as they struck. He looked at the forest on the bank of the stream, saw the individual trees, the leaves and the veining of each leaf—saw the very insects upon them: the locusts, the brilliant-bodied flies, the gray spiders stretching their webs from twig to twig. He noted the prismatic colors in all the dewdrops upon a million blades of grass. The humming of the gnats that danced above the eddies of the stream, the beating of the dragonflies' wings, the strokes of the waterspiders' legs, like oars which had lifted their boat—all these made audible music. A fish slid along beneath his eyes and he heard the rush of its body parting the water.

He had come to the surface facing down the stream; in a moment the visible world seemed to wheel slowly round, himself the pivotal point, and he saw the bridge, the fort, the soldiers upon the bridge, the captain, the sergeant, the two privates, his executioners. They were in silhouette against the blue sky. They shouted and gesticulated, pointing at him. The captain had drawn his pistol, but did not fire; the others were unarmed. Their movements were grotesque and horrible, their forms gigantic.

Suddenly he heard a sharp report and something struck the water smartly within a few inches of his head, spattering his face with spray. He heard a second report, and saw one of the sentinels with his rifle at his shoulder, a light cloud of blue smoke rising from the muzzle. The man in the water saw the eye of the man on the bridge gazing into his own through the sights of the rifle. He observed that it was a gray eye and remembered having read that gray eyes were keenest, and that all famous marksmen had them. Nevertheless, this one had missed.

A counter-swirl had caught Farquhar and turned him half round; he was again looking into the forest on the bank opposite the fort. The sound of a clear, high voice in a monotonous singsong now rang out behind him and came across the water with a distinctness that pierced and subdued all other sounds, even the beating of the ripples in his ears. Although no soldier, he had frequented camps enough to know the dread significance of that deliberate, drawling, aspirated chant; the lieutenant on shore was taking a part in the morning's work. How coldly and pitilessly—with what an even, calm intonation, presaging, and enforcing tranquility in the men—with what accurately measured intervals fell those cruel words:

"Attention, company! . . . Shoulder arms! . . . Ready! . . . Aim! . . . Fire!"

Farquhar dived—dived as deeply as he could. The water roared in his ears like the voice of Niagara, yet he heard the dulled thunder of the volley and, rising again toward the surface, met shining bits of metal, singularly flattened, oscillating slowly downward. Some of them touched him on the face and hands, then fell away, continuing their descent. One lodged between his collar and neck; it was uncomfortably warm and he snatched it out.

As he rose to the surface, gasping for breath, he saw that he had been a long time under water; he was perceptibly farther downstream —nearer to safety. The soldiers had almost finished reloading; the metal ramrods flashed all at once in the sunshine as they were drawn from the barrels, turned in the air, and thrust into their sockets. The two sentinels fired again, independently and ineffectually.

The hunted man saw all this over his shoulder; he was now swimming vigorously with the current. His brain was as energetic as his arms and legs; he thought with the rapidity of lightning.

"The officer," he reasoned, "will not make that martinet's error a second time. It is as easy to dodge a volley as a single shot. He has probably already given the command to fire at will. God help me, I cannot dodge them all!"

An appalling plash within two yards of him was followed by a loud, rushing sound, diminuendo, which seemed to travel back through the air to the fort and died in an explosion which stirred the very river to its deeps! A rising sheet of water curved over him, fell down upon him, blinded him, strangled him! The cannon had taken a hand in the game. As he shook his head free from the commotion of the smitten water he heard the deflected shot humming through the air ahead, and in an instant it was cracking and smashing the branches in the forest beyond.

"They will not do that again," he thought; "the next time they will use a charge of grape.[3] I must keep my eye upon the gun; the smoke will apprise me—the report arrives too late; it lags behind the missile. That is a good gun."

Suddenly he felt himself whirled round and round—spinning like a top. The water, the banks, the forests, the now distant bridge, fort and men—all were commingled and blurred. Objects were represented by their colors only; circular horizontal streaks of color—that was all he saw. He had been caught in a vortex and was being whirled on with a velocity of advance and gyration that made him giddy and sick. In a few moments he was flung upon the gravel at the foot of the left bank of the stream—the southern bank—and behind a projecting point which concealed him from his enemies. The sudden arrest of his motion, the abrasion of one of his hands on the gravel, restored him, and he wept with delight. He dug his fingers into the sand, threw it over himself in handfuls and audibly blessed it. It looked like diamonds, rubies, emeralds; he could think of nothing beautiful which it did not resemble. The trees upon the bank were giant garden plants; he noted a definite order in their arrangement, inhaled the fragrance of their blooms. A strange, roseate light shone through the spaces among their trunks and the wind made in their branches the music of aeolian harps. He had no wish to perfect his escape—was

3. Grapeshot, a cluster of small iron balls that scatter when fired from cannon.

content to remain in that enchanting spot until retaken.

A whiz and rattle of grapeshot among the branches high above his head roused him from his dream. The baffled cannoneer had fired him a random farewell. He sprang to his feet, rushed up the sloping bank, and plunged into the forest.

All that day he traveled, laying his course by the rounding sun. The forest seemed interminable; nowhere did he discover a break in it, not even a woodman's road. He had not known that he lived in so wild a region. There was something uncanny in the revelation.

By nightfall he was fatigued, footsore, famishing. The thought of his wife and children urged him on. At last he found a road which led him in what he knew to be the right direction. It was as wide and straight as a city street, yet it seemed untraveled. No fields bordered it, no dwelling anywhere. Not so much as the barking of a dog suggested human habitation. The black bodies of the trees formed a straight wall on both sides, terminating on the horizon in a point, like a diagram in a lesson in perspective. Overhead, as he looked up through this rift in the wood, shone great golden stars looking unfamiliar and grouped in strange constellations. He was sure they were arranged in some order which had a secret and malign significance. The wood on either side was full of singular noises, among which—once, twice, and again—he distinctly heard whispers in an unknown tongue.

His neck was in pain and lifting his hand to it he found it horribly swollen. He knew that it had a circle of black where the rope had bruised it. His eyes felt congested; he could no longer close them. His tongue was swollen with thirst; he relieved its fever by thrusting it forward from between his teeth into the cold air. How softly the turf had carpeted the untraveled avenue—he could no longer feel the roadway beneath his feet!

Doubtless, despite his suffering, he had fallen asleep while walking, for now he sees another scene—perhaps he has merely recovered from a delirium. He stands at the gate of his own home. All is as he left it, and all bright and beautiful in the morning sunshine. He must have traveled the entire night. As he pushes upon the gate and passes up the wide white walk, he sees a flutter of female garments; his wife, looking fresh and cool and sweet, steps down from the veranda to meet him. At the bottom of the steps she stands waiting, with a smile of ineffable joy, an attitude of matchless grace and dignity. Ah, how beautiful she is! He springs forward with extended arms. As he is about to clasp her he feels a stunning blow upon the back of the neck; a blinding white light blazes all about him with a sound like the shock of a cannon—then all is darkness and silence!

Peyton Farquhar was dead; his body, with a broken neck, swung gently from side to side beneath the timbers of the Owl Creek bridge.

1891

WILLIAM FAULKNER

A Rose for Emily

I

When Miss Emily Grierson died, our whole town went to her funeral: the men through a sort of respectful affection for a fallen monument, the women mostly out of curiosity to see the inside of her house, which no one save an old manservant—a combined gardener and cook—had seen in at least ten years.

It was a big, squarish frame house that had once been white, decorated with cupolas and spires and scrolled balconies in the heavily lightsome style of the seventies, set on what had once been our most select street. But garages and cotton gins had encroached and obliterated even the august names of that neighborhood; only Miss Emily's house was left, lifting its stubborn and coquettish decay above the cotton wagons and the gasoline pumps—an eyesore among eyesores. And now Miss Emily had gone to join the representatives of those august names where they lay in the cedar-bemused cemetery among the ranked and anonymous graves of Union and Confederate soldiers who fell at the battle of Jefferson.

Alive, Miss Emily had been a tradition, a duty, and a care; a sort of hereditary obligation upon the town, dating from that day in 1894 when Colonel Sartoris, the mayor—he who fathered the edict that no Negro woman should appear on the streets without an apron—remitted her taxes, the dispensation dating from the death of her father on into perpetuity. Not that Miss Emily would have accepted charity. Colonel Sartoris invented an involved tale to the effect that Miss Emily's father had loaned money to the town, which the town, as a matter of business, preferred this way of repaying. Only a man of Colonel Sartoris' generation and thought could have invented it, and only a woman could have believed it.

When the next generation, with its more modern ideas, became mayors and aldermen, this arrangement created some little dissatisfaction. On the first of the year they mailed her a tax notice. February came, and there was no reply. They wrote her a formal letter, asking her to call at the sheriff's office at her convenience. A week later the mayor wrote her himself, offering to call or to send his car for her, and received in reply a note on paper of an archaic shape, in a thin, flowing calligraphy in faded ink, to the effect that she no longer went out at all. The tax notice was also enclosed, without comment.

They called a special meeting of the Board of Aldermen. A deputation waited upon her, knocked at the door through which no visitor had passed since she ceased giving china-painting lessons eight or ten years earlier. They were admitted by the old Negro into a dim hall from which a stairway mounted into still more shadow. It smelled of dust and disuse—a close, dank smell. The Negro led them into the parlor. It was furnished in heavy, leather-covered furniture. When the Negro opened the blinds of one window, they could see that the leather was cracked; and when they sat down, a faint dust rose sluggishly about their thighs, spinning with slow motes in the single sun-ray. On a tarnished gilt easel before the fireplace stood a crayon portrait of Miss Emily's father.

They rose when she entered—a small, fat woman in black, with a thin gold chain descending to her waist and vanishing into her belt, leaning on an ebony cane with a tarnished gold head. Her skeleton was small and spare; perhaps that was why what would have been merely plumpness in another was obesity in her. She looked bloated, like a body long submerged in motionless water, and of that pallid hue. Her eyes, lost in the fatty ridges of her face, looked like two small pieces of coal pressed into a lump of dough as they moved from one face to another while the visitors stated their errand.

She did not ask them to sit. She just stood in the door and listened quietly until the spokesman came to a stumbling halt. Then they could hear the invisible watch ticking at the end of the gold chain.

Her voice was dry and cold. "I have no taxes in Jefferson. Colonel Sartoris explained it to me. Perhaps one of you can gain access to the city records and satisfy yourselves."

"But we have. We are the city authorities, Miss Emily. Didn't you get a notice from the sheriff, signed by him?"

"I received a paper, yes," Miss Emily said. "Perhaps he considers himself the sheriff . . . I have no taxes in Jefferson."

"But there is nothing on the books to show that, you see. We must go by the—"

"See Colonel Sartoris. I have no taxes in Jefferson."

"But, Miss Emily—"

"See Colonel Sartoris." (Colonel Sartoris had been dead almost ten years.) "I have no taxes in Jefferson. Tobe!" The Negro appeared. "Show these gentlemen out."

II

So she vanquished them, horse and foot, just as she had vanquished their fathers thirty years before about the smell. That was two years after her father's death and a short time after her sweetheart—the one we believed would marry her—had deserted her. After her father's death she went out very little; after her sweetheart went away, people hardly saw her at all. A few of the ladies had the temerity to call, but were not received, and the only sign of life about the place was the Negro man—a young man then—going in and out with a market basket.

"Just as if a man—any man—could keep a kitchen properly," the ladies said; so they were not surprised when the smell developed. It was another link between the gross, teeming world and the high and mighty Griersons.

A neighbor, a woman, complained to the mayor, Judge Stevens, eighty years old.

"But what will you have me do about it, madam?" he said.

"Why, send her word to stop it," the woman said. "Isn't there a law?"

"I'm sure that won't be necessary," Judge Stevens said. "It's probably just a snake or a rat that nigger of hers killed in the yard. I'll speak to him about it."

The next day he received two more complaints, one from a man who came in diffident deprecation. "We really must do something about it, Judge. I'd be the last one in the world to bother Miss Emily, but we've got to do something." That night the Board of Aldermen met—three graybeards and one younger man, a member of the rising generation.

"It's simple enough," he said. "Send her word to have her place cleaned up. Give her a certain time to do it in, and if she don't . . ."

"Dammit, sir," Judge Stevens said, "will you accuse a lady to her face of smelling bad?"

So the next night, after midnight, four men crossed Miss Emily's lawn and slunk about the house like burglars, sniffing along the base of the brickwork and at the cellar openings while one of them performed a regular sowing motion with his hand out of a sack slung from his shoulder. They broke open the cellar door and sprinkled lime there, and in all the outbuildings. As they recrossed the lawn, a window that had been dark was lighted and Miss Emily sat in it, the light behind her, and her upright torso motionless as that of an idol. They crept quietly across the lawn and into the shadow of the locusts that lined the street. After a week or two the smell went away.

That was when people had begun to feel really sorry for her. People in our town, remembering how old lady Wyatt, her great-aunt, had gone completely crazy at last, believed that the Griersons held themselves a little too high for what they really were. None of the young men were quite good enough for Miss Emily and such. We had long thought of them as a tableau, Miss Emily a slender figure in white in the background, her father a spraddled silhouette in the foreground, his back to her and clutching a horsewhip, the two of them framed by the back-flung front door. So when she got to be thirty and was still single, we were not pleased exactly, but vindicated; even with insanity in the family she wouldn't have turned down all of her chances if they had really materialized.

When her father died, it got about that the house was all that was left to her; and in a way, people were glad. At last they could pity Miss Emily. Being left alone, and a pauper, she had become humanized. Now she too would know the old thrill and the old despair of a penny more or less.

The day after his death all the ladies prepared to call at the house and offer condolence and aid, as is our custom. Miss Emily met them at the door, dressed as usual and with no trace of grief on her face. She told them that her father was not dead. She did that for three days, with the ministers calling on her, and the doctors, trying to persuade her to let them dispose of the body. Just as they were about to resort to law and force, she broke down, and they buried her father quickly.

We did not say she was crazy then. We believed she had to do that. We remembered all the young men her father had driven away, and we knew that with nothing left, she would have to cling to that which had robbed her, as people will.

III

She was sick for a long time. When we saw her again, her hair was cut short, making her look like a girl, with a vague resemblance to those angels in colored church windows—sort of tragic and serene.

The town had just let the contracts for paving the sidewalks, and in the summer after her father's death they began the work. The construction company came with niggers and mules and machinery, and a foreman named Homer Barron, a Yankee—a big, dark, ready man, with a big voice and eyes lighter than his face. The little boys would follow in groups to hear him cuss the niggers, and the niggers singing in time to the rise and fall of picks. Pretty soon he knew everybody in town. Whenever you heard a lot of laughing anywhere about the square, Homer Barron would be in the center of the group. Presently we began to see him and Miss Emily on Sunday afternoons driving in the yellow-wheeled buggy and the matched team of bays from the livery stable.

At first we were glad that Miss Emily would have an interest, because the ladies all said, "Of course a Grierson would not think seriously of a Northerner, a day laborer." But there were still others, older people, who said that even grief could not cause a real lady to forget *noblesse oblige*—without calling it *noblesse oblige*. They just said, "Poor Emily. Her kinsfolk should come to her." She had some kin in Alabama; but years ago her father had fallen out with them over the estate of old lady Wyatt, the crazy woman, and there was no communication between the two families. They had not even been represented at the funeral.

And as soon as the old people said, "Poor Emily," the whispering began. "Do you suppose it's really so?" they said to one another. "Of course it is. What else could . . ." This behind their hands; rustling of craned silk and satin behind jalousies closed upon the sun of Sunday afternoon as the thin, swift clop-clop-clop of the matched team passed: "Poor Emily."

She carried her head high enough—even when we believed that she was fallen. It was as if she demanded more than ever the recognition of her dignity as the last Grierson; as if it had wanted that touch of earthiness to reaffirm her imperviousness. Like when she bought the rat poison, the arsenic. That was over a year after they had begun to say "Poor Emily," and while the two female cousins were visiting her.

"I want some poison," she said to the druggist. She was over thirty then, still a slight woman, though thinner than usual, with cold, haughty black eyes in a face the flesh of which was strained across the temples and about the eye-sockets as you imagine a lighthouse-keeper's face ought to look. "I want some poison," she said.

"Yes, Miss Emily. What kind? For rats and such? I'd recom—"

"I want the best you have. I don't care what kind."

The druggist named several. "They'll kill anything up to an elephant. But what you want is—"

"Arsenic," Miss Emily said. "Is that a good one?"

"Is . . . arsenic? Yes, ma'am. But what you want—"

"I want arsenic."

The druggist looked down at her. She looked back at him, erect, her face like a strained flag. "Why, of course," the druggist said. "If that's what you want. But the law requires you to tell what you are going to use it for."

Miss Emily just stared at him, her head tilted back in order to look him eye for eye, until he looked away and went and got the arsenic and wrapped it up. The Negro delivery boy brought her the package; the druggist didn't come back. When she opened the package at home there was written on the box, under the skull and bones: "For rats."

IV

So the next day we all said, "She will kill herself"; and we said it would be the best thing. When she had first begun to be seen with Homer Barron, we had said, "She will marry him." Then we said, "She will persuade him yet," because Homer himself had remarked— he liked men, and it was known that he drank with the younger men in the Elks' Club—that he was not a marrying man. Later we said, "Poor Emily" behind the jalousies as they passed on Sunday afternoon in the glittering buggy, Miss Emily with her head high and Homer Barron with his hat cocked and a cigar in his teeth, reins and whip in a yellow glove.

Then some of the ladies began to say that it was a disgrace to the town and a bad example to the young people. The men did not want to interfere, but at last the ladies forced the Baptist minister—Miss Emily's people were Episcopal—to call upon her. He would never divulge what happened during that interview, but he refused to go back again. The next Sunday they again drove about the streets, and the following day the minister's wife wrote to Miss Emily's relations in Alabama.

So she had blood-kin under her roof again and we sat back to watch developments. At first nothing happened. Then we were sure that they were to be married. We learned that Miss Emily had been to the jeweler's and ordered a man's toilet set in silver, with the letters H. B. on each piece. Two days later we learned that she had bought a complete outfit of men's clothing, including a nightshirt, and we said, "They are married." We were really glad. We were glad because the two female cousins were even more Grierson than Miss Emily had ever been.

So we were not surprised when Homer Barron—the streets had been finished some time since—was gone. We were a little disappointed that there was not a public blowing-off, but we believed that he had gone on to prepare for Miss Emily's coming, or to give her a chance to get rid of the cousins. (By that time it was a cabal, and we were all Miss Emily's allies to help circumvent the cousins.) Sure enough, after another week they departed. And, as we had expected all along, within three days Homer Barron was back in town. A neighbor saw the Negro man admit him at the kitchen door at dusk one evening.

And that was the last we saw of Homer Barron. And of Miss Emily for some time. The Negro man went in and out with the market basket, but the front door remained closed. Now and then we would see her at a window for a moment, as the men did that night when they sprinkled the lime, but for almost six months she did not appear on the streets. Then we knew that this was to be expected too; as if that quality of her father which had thwarted her woman's life so many times had been too virulent and too furious to die.

When we next saw Miss Emily, she had grown fat and her hair was turning gray. During the next few years it grew grayer and grayer until it attained an even pepper-and-salt iron-gray, when it ceased turning. Up to the day of her death at seventy-four it was still that vigorous iron-gray, like the hair of an active man.

From that time on her front door remained closed, save for a period of six or seven years, when she was about forty, during which she gave lessons in china-painting. She fitted up a studio in one of the downstairs rooms, where the daughters and granddaughters of Colonel Sartoris' contemporaries were sent to her with the same regularity and in the same spirit that they were sent to church on Sundays with a twenty-five-cent piece for the collection plate. Meanwhile her taxes had been remitted.

Then the newer generation became the backbone and the spirit of the town, and the painting pupils grew up and fell away and did not send their children to her with boxes of color and tedious brushes and pictures cut from the ladies' magazines. The front door closed upon the last one and remained closed for good. When the town got free postal delivery, Miss Emily alone refused to let them fasten the metal numbers above her door and attach a mailbox to it. She would not listen to them.

Daily, monthly, yearly we watched the Negro grow grayer and more stooped, going in and out with the market basket. Each December we sent her a tax notice, which would be returned by the post office a week later, unclaimed. Now and then we would see her in one of the downstairs windows—she had evidently shut up the top floor of the house—like the carven torso of an idol in a niche, looking or not looking at us, we could never tell which. Thus she passed from generation to generation—dear, inescapable, impervious, tranquil, and perverse.

And so she died. Fell ill in the house filled with dust and shadows, with only a doddering Negro man to wait on her. We did not even know she was sick; we had long since given up trying to get any information from the Negro. He talked to no one, probably not even to her, for his voice had grown harsh and rusty, as if from disuse.

She died in one of the downstairs rooms, in a heavy walnut bed with a curtain, her gray head propped on a pillow yellow and moldy with age and lack of sunlight.

V

The Negro met the first of the ladies at the front door and let them in, with their hushed, sibilant voices and their quick, curious glances, and then he disappeared. He walked right through the house and out the back and was not seen again.

The two female cousins came at once. They held the funeral on the second day, with the town coming to look at Miss Emily beneath a mass of bought flowers, with the crayon face of her father musing profoundly above the bier and the ladies sibilant and macabre; and the very old men—some in their brushed Confederate uniforms—on the porch and the lawn, talking of Miss Emily as if she had been a contemporary of theirs, believing that they had danced with her and courted her perhaps, confusing time with its mathematical progression, as the old do, to whom all the past is not a diminishing road but, instead, a huge meadow which no winter ever quite touches, divided from them now by the narrow bottle-neck of the most recent decade of years.

Already we knew that there was one room in that region above stairs which no one had seen in forty years, and which would have to be forced. They waited until Miss Emily was decently in the ground before they opened it.

The violence of breaking down the door seemed to fill this room with pervading dust. A thin, acrid pall as of the tomb seemed to lie everywhere upon this room decked and furnished as for a bridal: upon the valance curtains of faded rose color, upon the rose-shaded lights, upon the dressing table, upon the delicate array of crystal and the man's toilet things backed with tarnished silver, silver so tarnished that the monogram was obscured. Among them lay a collar and tie, as if they had just been removed, which, lifted, left upon the surface a pale crescent in the dust. Upon a chair hung the suit, carefully folded; beneath it the two mute shoes and the discarded socks.

The man himself lay in the bed.

For a long while we just stood there, looking down at the profound and fleshless grin. The body had apparently once lain in the attitude of an embrace, but now the long sleep that outlasts love, that conquers even the grimace of love, had cuckolded him. What was left of him, rotted beneath what was left of the nightshirt, had become inextricable from the bed in which he lay; and upon him and upon the pillow beside him lay that even coating of the patient and biding dust.

Then we noticed that in the second pillow was the indentation of a head. One of us lifted something from it, and leaning forward, that faint and invisible dust dry and acrid in the nostrils, we saw a long strand of iron-gray hair.

1931

MORDECAI RICHLER

The Summer My Grandmother Was Supposed to Die

Dr. Katzman discovered the gangrene on one of his monthly visits. "She won't last a month," he said.

He repeated that the second month, the third, and the fourth, and now she lay dying in the heat of the back bedroom.

"If only she'd die," my mother said. "Oh, God, why doesn't she die? God in heaven, what's she holding on for?"

The summer my grandmother was supposed to die we did not chip in with the Breenbaums to take a cottage in the Laurentians.[1] It wouldn't have been practical. The old lady couldn't be moved, the nurse came daily and the doctor twice a week, and so it seemed best to stay in the city and wait for her to die or, as my mother said, pass away. It was a hot summer, her bedroom was just behind the kitchen, and when we sat down to eat we could smell her. The dressings on my grandmother's left leg had to be changed several times a day and, according to Dr. Katzman, her condition was hopeless. "It's in the hands of the Almighty," he said.

"It won't be long now," my father said, "and she'll be better off, if you know what I mean."

"Please," my mother said.

A nurse came every day from the Royal Victorian Order.[2] She arrived punctually at noon and at five to twelve I'd join the rest of the boys under the outside staircase to look up her dress as she climbed to our second-story flat. Miss Monohan favored lacy pink panties and that was better than waiting under the stairs for Cousin Bessie, for instance. She wore enormous cotton bloomers, rain or shine.

I was sent out to play as often as possible, because my mother felt it was not good for me to see somebody dying. Usually I'd just roam the scorched streets shooting the breeze. There was Arty, Gas sometimes, Hershey, Stan, and me. We talked about everything from A to Z.

"Why is it," Arty wanted to know, "that Tarzan never shits?"

"Dick Tracy too."

"Or Wonder Woman."

"She's a dame."

"So?"

"Jees, wouldn't it be something if Superman crapped in the sky? He could just be flying over Waverly Street when, whamo, Mr. Rabinovitch catches it right in the kisser."

Mr. Rabinovitch was our Hebrew teacher.

"But there's Tarzan," Arty insisted, "in the jungle, week in and week out, and never once does he need to go to the toilet. It's not real, that's all."

Arty told me, "Before your grandma dies she's going to roll her eyes and gurgle. That's what they call the death-rattle."

"Aw, you know everything. Big shot."

"I *read* it, you jerk," Arty said, whacking me one, "in Perry Mason."

Home again I'd find my mother weeping.

"She's dying by inches," she said to my father one stifling night, "and none of them even come to see her. Oh, such children! They should only rot in hell."

---

1. Mountains in eastern Canada between Hudson Bay and the St. Lawrence River.   2. The Victorian Order of Nurses for Canada.

"They're not behaving right. It's certainly not according to Hoyle," my father said.

"When I think of all the money and effort that went into making a rabbi out of Israel—the way Mother doted on him—and for what? Oh, what's the world coming to? God."

"It's not right."

Dr. Kaztman was amazed. "I never believed she'd last this long. Really, it must be will-power alone that keeps her going. And your excellent care."

"I want her to die, Doctor. That's not my mother in the back room. It's an animal. I want her to please please die."

"Hush. You don't mean it. You're tired." And Dr. Katzman gave my father some pills for my mother to take. "A remarkable woman," he said. "A born nurse."

At night in bed my brother Harvey and I used to talk about our grandmother. "After she dies," I said, "her hair will go on growing for another twenty-four hours."

"Sez who?"

"Arty. It's a scientific fact. Do you think Uncle Lou will come from New York for the funeral?"

"Sure."

"Boy, that means another fiver for me. You too."

"You shouldn't say things like that, kiddo, or *her ghost will come back to haunt you.*"

"Well," I said, "I'll be able to go to her funeral, anyway. I'm not too young any more."

I was only six years old when my grandfather died, and I wasn't allowed to go to his funeral.

I have only one memory of my grandfather. Once he called me into his study, set me down on his lap, and made a drawing of a horse for me. On the horse he drew a rider. While I watched and giggled he gave the rider a beard and the round fur-trimmed cap of a rabbi.

My grandfather was a Zaddik,[3] one of the Righteous, and I've been told that to study Talmud with him had been a rare pleasure. I wasn't allowed to go to his funeral, but years after I was shown the telegram of condolence that had come from Eire and Poland and Israel and even Japan. My grandfather had written many books: a translation of the Zohar[4] into modern Hebrew—some twenty years' work—and lots of slender volumes of sermons, chassidic tales, and rabbinical commentaries. His books had been published in Warsaw and later in New York. He had been famous.

"At the funeral," my mother told me, "they had to have six motorcycle policemen to control the crowds. It was such a heat that twelve women fainted—and I'm *not* counting Mrs. Waxman from upstairs. With her, you know, *anything* to fall into a man's arms. Even Pinsky's. And did I tell you that there was even a French-Canadian priest there?"

---

3. "Righteous man" in Hebrew.
4. "The Book of Splendor," the central part of the Kabbalah, the esoteric teach-ings of Judaism and the source of Jewish mysticism.

"No kidding?"

"The priest was a real big *knacker*.[5] A bishop maybe. He used to study with the *zeyda*.[6] The *zeyda* was some personality, you know. Spiritual and wordly-wise at the same time. Such personalities they don't make any more. Today, rabbis and peanuts are the same size."

But, according to my father, the *zeyda* (his father-in-law) hadn't been as famous as all that. "There are things I could say," he told me. "There was another side to him."

My grandfather had come from generations and generations of rabbis, his youngest son was a rabbi, but none of his grandchildren would be one. My brother Harvey was going to be a dentist and at the time, 1937, I was interested in flying and my cousin Jerry was already a communist. I once heard Jerry say, "Our grandpappy wasn't all he was cracked up to be." When the men at the kosher bakeries went out on strike he spoke up against them on the streets where they were picketing and in the *shule*.[7] It was of no consequence to him that they were grossly underpaid. His superstitious followers had to have bread. "Grandpappy," Jerry said, "was a prize reactionary."

A week after my grandfather died my grandmother suffered a stroke. Her right side was completely paralyzed. She couldn't speak. At first, it's true, my grandmother could say a few words and move her right hand enough to write her name in Hebrew. Her name was Malka. But her condition soon began to deteriorate.

My grandmother had six children and seven stepchildren, for my grandfather had been married before. His first wife had died in the old country. Two years later he had married my grandmother, the only daughter of the richest man in the village, and their marriage had been a singularly happy one. My grandmother had been a beautiful girl. She had also been a wise, resourceful, and patient wife. Qualities, I fear, indispensable to life with a Zaddik. For the synagogue had paid my grandfather no stipulated salary and much of the money he had picked up here and there he had habitually distributed among rabbinical students, needy immigrants, and widows. A vice, and such it was to his hard-pressed family, which made him as unreliable a provider as a drunkard. And indeed, to carry the analogy further, my grandmother had had to make many hurried trips to the pawnbroker with her jewelry. Not all of it had been redeemed, either. But her children had been looked after. The youngest, her favorite, was a rabbi in Boston, the eldest was the actor-manager of a Yiddish theater in New York, and another was a lawyer. One daughter lived in Toronto, two in Montreal. My mother was the youngest daughter, and when my grandmother had her stroke there was a family meeting and it was decided that my mother would take care of her. This was my father's fault. All the other husbands spoke up—they protested their wives had too much work, they could never manage it—but my father detested quarrels, and he was silent. So my grandmother came to stay with us.

5. Big shot.   7. Synagogue.
6. Grandfather.

Her bedroom, the back bedroom, had actually been promised to me for my seventh birthday. But all that was forgotten now, and I had to go on sharing a bedroom with my brother Harvey. So naturally I was resentful when each morning before I left for school my mother said, "Go in and kiss the *baba*[8] good-bye."

All the same I'd go into the bedroom and kiss my grandmother hastily. She'd say "Bouyo-bouyo," for that was the only sound she could make. And after school it was, "Go in and tell the *baba* you're home."

"I'm home, *baba.*"

"Bouyo-bouyo."

During those first hopeful months—"Twenty years ago who would have thought there'd be a cure for diabetes?" my father asked; "where there's life there's hope, you know"—she'd smile at me and try to speak, her eyes charged with effort. And even later there were times when she pressed my head urgently to her bosom with her surprisingly strong left arm. But as her illness dragged on and on and she became a condition in the house, something beyond hope or reproach, like the leaky icebox, there was less recognition and more ritual in those kisses. I came to dread her room. A clutter of sticky medicine bottles and the cracked toilet chair beside the bed; glazed but imploring eyes and a feeble smile, the wet slap of her lips against my cheeks. I flinched from her touch. After two years of it I protested to my mother. "Look, what's the use of telling her I'm going or I'm here. She doesn't even recognize me any more."

"Don't be fresh. She's your grandmother."

My uncle who was in the theater in New York sent money regularly to help support my grandmother and, for the first few months, so did the other children. But once the initial and sustaining excitement had passed and it became likely that my grandmother might linger in her invalid condition for two or maybe even three more years, the checks began to drop off, and the children seldom came to our house any more. Anxious weekly visits—"and how is she today, poor lamb?"—quickly dwindled to a dutiful monthly looking in, then a semi-annual visit, and these always on the way to somewhere.

"The way they act," my father said, "you'd think that if they stayed long enough to take off their coats we'd make them take the *baba* home with them."

When the children did come to visit, my mother made it difficult for them.

"It's killing me," she said. "I have to lift her onto that chair three times a day maybe. Have you any idea how heavy she is? And what makes you think I always catch her in time? Sometimes I have to change her bed twice a day. That's a job I'd like to see your wife do," she said to my uncle, the rabbi.

"We could send her to the Old People's Home," the rabbi said.

"Now there's an idea," my father said.

But my mother began to sob. "Not as long as I'm alive," she said. And she gave my father a stony look. "Say something."

8. Grandma.

"It wouldn't be according to Hoyle."

"You want to be able to complain to everybody in town about all the other children," the rabbi said. "You've got a martyr complex."

"Everybody has a point of view, you know. You know what I mean?" my father said. "So what's the use of fighting?"

Meanwhile, Dr. Katzman came once a month to examine my grandmother. "It's remarkable, astonishing," he'd say each time. "She's as strong as a horse."

"Some life for a person," my father said. "She can't speak—she doesn't recognize anybody—what is there for her?"

The doctor was a cultivated man; he spoke often for women's clubs, sometimes on Yiddish literature and other times, his rubicund face hot with impatience, the voice taking on a doomsday tone, on the cancer threat.

"Who are we to judge?" he asked.

Every evening, during the first months of my grandmother's illness, my mother read her a story by Sholem Aleichem.[9] "Tonight she smiled," my mother would say. "She understood. I can tell." And my father, my brother, and I would not comment. Once a week my mother used to give the old lady a manicure. Sunny afternoons she'd lift her into a wheelchair and put her out in the sun. Somebody always had to stay in the house in case my grandmother called. Often, during the night, she would begin to wail unaccountably, and my mother would get up and rock the old lady in her arms for hours. But in the fourth year of my grandmother's illness the strain and fatigue began to tell on my mother. Besides looking after my grandmother—"and believe you me," the doctor assured her with a clap on the back, "it would be a full-time job for a professional nurse"—she had to keep house for a husband and two sons. She began to quarrel with my father and she became sharp with Harvey and me. My father started to spend his evenings playing pinochle at Tansky's Cigar & Soda. Weekends he took Harvey and me to visit his brothers and sisters. And everywhere he went people had little bits of advice for him.

"Sam, you might as well be a bachelor. You're just going to have to put your foot down for once."

"Yeah, in your face maybe."

My cousin Libby, who was at McGill,[1] said, "This could have a very damaging effect on the development of your boys. These are their formative years, Uncle Samuel, and the omnipresence of death in the house . . ."

"What you need," my father said, "is a boy friend. *And how.*"

At Tansky's Cigar & Soda it was, "Come clean, Sam. It's no hardship. If I know you, the old lady's got a big insurance policy and when the time comes . . ."

My mother lost lots of weight. After dinner she'd fall asleep in her chair in the middle of Lux Radio Theater.[2] One minute she'd be sewing a patch on my breeches or be making a list of girls to call

9. "Peace be with you," pen name of Yiddish author and humorist Shalom Rabinovitz (1859–1916).

1. University in Montreal.
2. Radio weekly drama sponsored by Lux soap.

for a bingo party (proceeds for the Talmud Torah),[3] and the next she'd be snoring. Then, one morning, she just couldn't get out of bed, and Dr. Katzman came round a week before his regular visit. "Well, well, this won't do, will it?" He sat in the kitchen with my father and the two men drank apricot brandy out of small glasses.

"Your wife is a remarkable woman," Dr. Katzman said.

"You don't say?"

"She's got a gallstone condition."

My father shrugged. "Have another one for the road," he said.

"Thank you, but I have several more calls to make." Dr. Katzman rose, sighing. "There she lies in that back room, poor old woman," he said, "hanging desperately onto life. There's food for thought there."

My grandmother's children met again, and the five of them sat around my mother's bed embarrassed, irritated, and quick to take insult. All except my uncle who was in the theater. He sucked a cigar and drank whisky. He teased my mother, the rabbi, and my aunts, and if not for him I think they would have been at each other's throats. It was decided, over my mother's protests, to send my grandmother to the Old People's Home on Esplanade Street. An ambulance came to take my grandmother away and Dr. Katzman said, "It's for the best." But my father had been in the back bedroom when the old lady had held on tenaciously to the bedpost, not wanting to be moved by the two men in white—"Easy does it, granny," the younger one had said—and afterwards he could not go in to see my mother. He went out for a walk.

"She looked at me with such a funny expression," he told my brother. "Is it my fault?"

My mother stayed in bed for another two weeks. My father cooked for us and we hired a woman to do the housework. My mother put on weight quickly, her cheeks regained their normal pinkish hue and, for the first time in months, she actually joked with Harvey and me. She became increasingly curious about our schools and whether or not we shined our shoes regularly. She began to cook again, special dishes for my father, and she resumed old friendships with women on the parochial school board. The change reflected on my father. Not only did his temper improve, but he stopped going to Tansky's every other night, and began to come home early from work. Life at home had never been so rich. But my grandmother's name was never mentioned. The back bedroom remained empty and I continued to share a room with Harvey. I couldn't see the point and so one evening I said, "Look, why don't I move into the back bedroom?"

My father glared at me across the table.

"But it's empty like."

My mother left the table. And the next afternoon she put on her best dress and coat and new spring hat.

"Where are you going?" my father asked.

"To see my mother."

"Don't go looking for trouble."

"It's been a month. Maybe they're not treating her right."

3. Orthodox Jewish school for boys.

"They're experts."

"Did you think I was never going to visit her? I'm not inhuman, you know."

"All right, go," he said.

But after she'd gone my father went to the window and said, "Son-of-a-bitch."

Harvey and I sat outside on the steps watching the cars go by. My father sat on the balcony above, cracking peanuts. It was six o'clock, maybe later, when the ambulance turned the corner, slowed down, and parked right in front of the house.

"Son-of-a-bitch," my father said. "I knew it."

My mother got out first, her eyes red and swollen, and hurried upstairs to make my grandmother's bed.

"I'm sorry, Sam, I had to do it."

"You'll get sick again, that's what."

"You think she doesn't recognize people. From the moment she saw me she cried and cried. Oh, it was terrible."

"They're experts there. They know how to handle her better than you do."

"Experts? Expert murderers you mean. She's got bedsores, Sam. Those dirty little Irish nurses they don't change her linen often enough, they hate her. She must have lost twenty pounds there."

"Another month and you'll be flat on your back again."

"Sam, what could I do? Please Sam."

"She'll outlive all of us. Even Muttel.[4] I'm going out for a walk."

She was back and I was to blame.

My father became a regular at Tansky's Cigar & Soda again and every morning I had to go in and kiss my grandmother. She began to look like a man. Little hairs had sprouted on her chin, she had a spiky gray mustache and, of course, she was practically bald. This near-baldness, I guess, sprang from the fact that she had been shaving her head ever since she had married my grandfather the rabbi.[5] My grandmother had four different wigs, but she had not worn one since the first year of her illness. She wore a little pink cap instead. And so, as before, she said, "bouyo-bouyo," to everything.

Once more uncles and aunts sent five-dollar bills, though erratically, to help pay for my grandmother's support. Elderly people, former followers of my grandfather, came to inquire after the old lady's health. They sat in the back bedroom with her for hours, leaning on their canes, talking to themselves, rocking, always rocking to and fro. "The Holy Shakers," my father called them, and Harvey and I avoided them, because they always wanted to pinch our cheeks, give us a dash of snuff and laugh when we sneezed, or offer us a sticky old candy from a little brown bag with innumerable creases in it. When the visit was done the old people would unfailingly sit in the kitchen with my mother for another hour, watching her make lockshen[6] or bake bread. My mother always served them lemon tea and

---

4. The narrator's Yiddish name; could be the equivalent of Mordecai.
5. Married Orthodox Jewish women customarily either shave their heads or cover their hair.
6. Noodles.

they would talk about my grandfather, recalling his books, his sayings, and his charitable deeds.

And so another two years passed, with no significant change in my grandmother's condition. But fatigue, bad temper, and even morbidity enveloped my mother again. She fought with her brothers and sisters and once, when I stepped into the living room, I found her sitting with her head in her hands, and she looked up at me with such anguish that I was frightened.

"What did I do now?" I asked.

"If, God forbid, I had a stroke, would you send me to the Old People's Home?"

"Don't be a joke. Of course not."

"I hope that never in my life do I have to count on my children for anything."

The summer my grandmother was supposed to die, the seventh year of her illness, my brother took a job as a shipper and he kept me awake at night with stories about the factory. "What we do, see, is clear out the middle of a huge pile of lengths of material. That makes for a kind of secret cave. A hideout. Well, then you coax one of the *shiksas*[7] inside and hi-diddle-diddle."

One night Harvey waited until I had fallen asleep and then he wrapped himself in a white sheet, crept up to my bed, and shouted, "Bouyo-bouyo."

I hit him. He shouted.

"Children. Children, please," my mother called. "I must get some rest."

As my grandmother's condition worsened—from day to day we didn't know when she'd die—I was often sent out to eat at my aunt's or at my other grandmother's house. I was hardly ever at home. On Saturday mornings I'd get together with the other guys and we'd walk all the way past the mountain to Eaton's, which was our favorite department store for riding up and down escalators and stealing.

In those days they let boys into the left-field bleachers free during the week and we spent many an afternoon at the ball park. The Montreal Royals, part of the Dodger farm system, was some ball club too. There was Jackie Robinson and Roy Campanella, Honest John Gabbard, Chuck Connors, and Kermit Kitman was our hero. It used to kill us to see that crafty little hebe[8] running around there with all those tall dumb *goyim*.[9] "Hey, Kitman," we'd yell. "Hey, hey, sho-head,[1] if your father knew you played ball on *shabus*—"[2] Kitman, unfortunately, was all field and no hit. He never made the majors. "There goes Kermit Kitman," we'd yell, after he'd gone down swinging again, "the first Jewish strike-out king of the International League." This we usually followed up by bellowing some choice imprecations in Yiddish.

7. Gentile girls.
8. Hebrew, Jew.
9. Gentiles.
1. Possibly *shorn-head* (?), referring to short hair or crew cut of athlete, in contrast to traditional long locks of Orthodox Jews (?).
2. Sabbath.

It was after one of these games, on a Friday afternoon, that I came home to find a small crowd gathered in front of the house.

"That's the grandson."

"Poor kid."

Old people stood silent and expressionless across the street staring at our front door. A taxi pulled up and my aunt hurried out, hiding her face in her hands.

"After so many years," somebody said.

"And probably next year they'll discover a cure. Isn't that *always* the case?"

I took the stairs two at a time. The flat was full. Uncles and aunts from my father's side of the family, odd old people, Dr. Katzman, Harvey, neighbors, were all standing around and talking in hushed voices in the living room. I found my father in the kitchen, getting out the apricot brandy. "Your grandmother's dead," he said.

"She didn't suffer," somebody said. "She passed away in her sleep."

"A merciful death."

"Where's Maw?"

"In the bedroom with . . . you'd better not go in," my father said.

"I want to see her."

My mother's face was long with grief. She wore a black shawl, and glared down at a knot of handkerchief clutched in a fist that had been cracked by washing soda. "Don't come in here," she said.

Several bearded, round-shouldered men in black shiny coats stood round the bed. I couldn't see my grandmother.

"Your grandmother's dead."

"Daddy told me."

"Go and wash your face and comb your hair. You'll have to get your own supper."

"O.K."

"One minute. The *baba* left some jewelry. The ring is for Harvey's wife and the necklace is for yours."

"Who's getting married?"

"Better go and wash your face. And remember behind the ears, Muttel."

Telegrams were sent, long-distance calls were made, and all through the evening relatives and neighbors came and went like swarms of fish when crumbs have been dropped into the water.

"When my father died," my mother said, "they had to have *six* motorcycle policemen to control the crowds. Twelve people fainted, such a heat . . ."

The man from the funeral parlor came.

"There goes the only Jewish businessman in town," my Uncle Harry said, "who wishes all his customers were Germans."

"This is no time for jokes."

"Listen, life goes on."

My cousin Jerry had begun to use a cigarette holder. "Everyone's going to be sickeningly sentimental," he said. "Soon the religious mumbo-jumbo starts. I can hardly wait."

Tomorrow was the Sabbath and so, according to the law, my grandmother couldn't be buried until Sunday. She would have to lie on the floor all night. Two old grizzly women in white came to move and wash the body and a professional mourner arrived to sit up and pray for her.

"I don't trust his face," my mother said. "He'll fall asleep. You watch him, Sam."

"A fat lot of good prayers will do her now."

"Will you just watch him, please."

"I'll watch him, I'll watch him." My father was livid about my Uncle Harry. "The way he's gone after that apricot brandy you'd think that guy never saw a bottle in his life before."

Harvey and I were sent to bed, but we couldn't sleep. My aunt was sobbing over the body in the living room—"That dirty hypocrite," my mother said—there was the old man praying, coughing, and spitting into his handkerchief each time he woke; and hushed voices and whimpering from the kitchen, where my father and mother sat. Harvey was in a good mood, he let me have a few puffs of his cigarette.

"Well, kiddo, this is our last night together. Tomorrow you can take over the back bedroom."

"*Are you crazy?*"

"You always wanted it for yourself."

"She died in there, but. You think I'm going to sleep in there?"

"Good night. Happy dreams, kiddo."

"Hey, let's talk some more."

Harvey told me a ghost story. "Did you know that when they hang a man," he said, "the last thing that happens is that he has an orgasm?"

"A what?"

"Forget it. I forgot you were still in kindergarten."

"I know plenty. Don't worry."

"At the funeral they're going to open her coffin to throw dirt in her face. It's supposed to be earth from Eretz.[3] They open it and you're going to have to look." Harvey stood up on his bed, holding his hands over his head like claws. He made a hideous face. "Bouyo-bouyo. Who's that sleeping in my bed? Woo-woo."

My uncle who was in the theater, the rabbi, and my aunt from Toronto, all came to Montreal for the funeral. Dr. Katzman came too.

"As long as she was alive," my mother said, "he couldn't even send five dollars a month. Some son! What a rabbi! I don't want him in my house, Sam. I can't bear the sight of him."

"You don't mean a word of that and you know it," Dr. Katzman said.

"Maybe you'd better give her a sedative," the rabbi said.

"Sam. Sam, will you say something, please."

My father stepped up to the rabbi, his face flushed. "I'll tell you this straight to your face, Israel," he said. "You've gone down in my estimation."

"Really," the rabbi said, smiling a little.

3. Eretz Yisrael, the Land of Israel.

My father's face burned a deeper red. "Year by year," he said, "your stock has gone down with me."

And my mother began to weep bitterly, helplessly, without control. She was led unwillingly to bed. While my father tried his best to comfort her, as he said consoling things, Dr. Katzman plunged a needle into her arm. "There we are," he said.

I went to sit in the sun on the outside stairs with Arty. "I'm going to the funeral," I said.

"I couldn't go anyway."

Arty was descended from the tribe of high priests and so was not allowed to be in the presence of a dead body. I was descended from the Yisroelis.[4]

"The lowest of the low," Arty said.

"Aw."

My uncle, the rabbi, and Dr. Katzman stepped into the sun to light cigarettes.

"It's remarkable that she held out for so long," Dr. Katzman said.

"Remarkable?" my uncle said. "It's written that if a man has been married twice he will spend as much time with his first wife in heaven as he did on earth. My father, may he rest in peace, was married to his first wife for seven years and my mother, may she rest in peace, has managed to keep alive for seven years. Today in heaven she will be able to join my father, may he rest in peace."

Dr. Katzman shook his head, he pursed his lips. "It's amazing," he said. "The mysteries of the human heart. Astonishing."

My father hurried outside. "Dr. Katzman, please. It's my wife. Maybe the injection wasn't strong enough? She just doesn't stop crying. It's like a tap. Could you come please?"

"Excuse me," Dr. Katzman said to my uncle.

"Of course."

My uncle approached Arty and me.

"Well, boys," he said, "what would you like to be when you grow up?"

1961

4   CHARACTERIZATION

In a good many stories the narrator is a disembodied offstage voice, without an identity or a personal history, without influence on the action, without qualities other than those that a voice and style may suggest. So it is in most of the earlier stories in this volume—*The Most Dangerous Game, Macomber, Owl Creek Bridge.* Poe's narrator, however, not only tells us the story but acts out the action; without him we not only would not know the story, there just would not be any. Richler's narrator looks back into his past; he is there *in* the

---

4. The lowest of the three categories into which the Jewish people are traditionally divided.

story, speaking, listening, reacting. In addition to being the narrator, he is a **character:** someone who acts, appears, or is referred to in a work.

The most common term for the character with the leading male role is **hero,** the "good guy" who opposes the **villain,** or "bad guy." The leading female character is the **heroine.** Heroes are usually larger than life, stronger or better than most human beings, almost godlike (and there's even a brand of heroes nowadays so close to being godlike that they are called superheroes). In most modern fiction, however, the leading character is much more ordinary, more like the rest of us. Such a character is called the **antihero,** not because he opposes the hero but because he is not like a hero in stature or perfection. An older and more neutral term than *hero* for the leading character, a term that does not imply either the presence or absence of outstanding virtue (and with the added advantage of referring equally to male and female), is **protagonist,** whose opponent is the **antagonist.** You might get into long and pointless arguments by calling Montresor or Macomber a hero, but either is his story's protagonist.

The major characters are those we see more of over a longer period of time; we learn more about them, and we think of them as more complex and frequently therefore more "realistic" than the minor characters, the figures who fill out the story. These major characters can grow and change, as Macomber does and as Judith does in Doris Lessing's *Our Friend Judith*; by the end of these stories both protagonists have acted in a way not predictable from what we learned about them and their past actions earlier in the story. Characters who can thus "surprise convincingly," an influential critic says, are **round characters.** Poe's and Connell's characters are not very complex and they do not change in surprising ways; they are therefore called **flat.** But we must be careful not to let terms like *flat* and *round* turn into value judgments. Because flat characters are less complex than round ones it is easy to assume they are artistically inferior; we need only to think of the characters of Charles Dickens, almost all of whom are flat, to realize that this is not always true.

The terms *flat* and *round*, like the terms *hero* and *antihero*, are not absolute or precise. They designate extremes or tendencies, not pigeonholes. Is Poe's Montresor entirely flat? Is Shakespeare's Iago? Falstaff? Charlie Chaplin's Little Tramp? Little Orphan Annie? Archie Bunker? Are all these characters equally flat? We will probably agree that Francis Macomber is a round character, for he is complex and changes before our eyes, but what about the hunter Wilson in the same story? Is he more or less flat than the hunter Rainsford in *The Most Dangerous Game*? Our answers are less important than our looking carefully at these characters to see what we know about each of them, to what degree they can be summed up in a phrase or a sentence; to discover how we learned what we know about them and how our judgment has been controlled by the story; to think about and perhaps judge the assumptions about human motivation, behavior, and nature that underlie the character and his or her characterization. Flat and round are useful as categories but are even more useful as tools of investigation, ways of focusing our attention and sharpening our perception.

Though most of Dickens's flat characters are highly individualized, not to say unique, some, like Fagin, the avaricious Jewish money-lender, are stereotypes: characters based on conscious or unconscious cultural assumptions that sex, age, ethnic or national identification, occupation, marital status, and so on are predictably accompanied by certain character traits, actions, even values.

The stereotype may be very useful in creating a round character, one who can surprise convincingly: Macomber is a spoiled, rich American; Judith, according to a Canadian woman, "one of your typical English spinsters." Both Macomber and Judith, however, act in ways that deny the limitations of the stereotype. A stereotype is, after all, only a quick—and somewhat superficial—form of classification, and classification is a common first step in definitions. One of the chief ways we have of describing or defining is by placing the thing to be defined in a category or class and then distinguishing it from the other members of that class. A good deal of **characterization**—the art, craft, method of presentation, or creation of fictional personages—involves a similar process. Characters are almost inevitably identified by category —by sex, age, nationality, occupation, etc. We soon learn that the narrator of *My Man Bovanne* is a middle-aged urban black woman, that Major Monarch is a middle-aged English gentleman, and, as we have seen, that Judith is an English spinster.

You may have noticed something that may seem odd at first: putting a character in more than one general group does not make that character more generalized or stereotyped, but more individual. The category *middle-aged* includes the narrator of *Bovanne*, Major and Mrs. Monarch, and Judith. That Major Monarch is male separates him from the other three; that the narrator of *Bovanne* is American and black separates her from the others, though she is, like Mrs. Monarch and Judith, a woman. So Hazel is to some degree particularized by being identified as a member of three general categories.

Not all generalizations involve cultural stereotypes, of course. Some may involve generalized character traits that the story or narrator defines for us (and that we must accept unless events in the story prove otherwise). Bovanne is said to be "just a nice old gent from the block," the kind of man whose conversation is "Comfy and cheery." Physical characteristics also serve as categories. Bovanne is blind. Before we are introduced to him, we are told that blind people hum, and that a blind man call Shakey Bee hums. Only then are we told that there is a blind man named Bovanne who also has the habit of humming. As physical characteristics are multiplied, the result is more and more particularizing or individualizing. The detailed physical description of Judith makes it possible to visualize her rather fully, almost to recognize her as an individual:

> Judith is tall, small-breasted, slender. Her light brown hair is parted in the center and cut straight around her neck. A high straight forehead, straight nose, a full grave mouth are setting for her eyes, which are green, large and prominent. Her lids are very white, fringed with gold, and molded close over the eyeball. . . .

There are many other ways in which a character is characterized and individualized besides stereotyping and "de-stereotyping," and besides classifying and particularizing by physical description. In most cases we see what characters do and hear what they say; we sometimes learn what they think, and what other people think or say about them; we often know what kind of clothes they wear, what and how much they own, treasure, or covet; we may be told about their childhood, parents, or some parts of their past. We learn a bit about Hazel, the narrator of *Bovanne*, from her age, sex, and ethnic identification. We learn a great deal more from the way she talks to her children and they to her, from the fact that men call her "long distance and in the middle of the night for a little Mama comfort," the fact that she carried her baby daughter strapped to her chest until the baby was nearly two years old, and from her short, low-cut dress. We even know what she is thinking.

No matter how many methods of characterization are employed, however, at some point the particularization of the individual stops. No matter how individualized the character may be, he or she remains a member of a number of groups, and we make certain assumptions about the character based on our fixed or stereotyped notions of the groups. To destroy a stereotype, a story must introduce a stereotype to destroy. And somehow the de-stereotyped character, no matter how particularized, remains to some degree representative. If Judith turns out to be not as prudish and prissy as the stereotype of the English spinster has led us to believe, we may well conclude that the stereotype is false and Judith is more representative of the real English spinster than the stereotype is. Indeed, this tendency to generalize from the particulars of a story extends beyond cultural groups, sometimes to human character at large: if Francis Macomber can change his ways after years of habitual conduct, then human character, the story might seem to say, is not permanently fixed at birth, in infancy, childhood, ever.

One of the reasons it is so difficult to discuss character is precisely that the principles of definition and evaluation of fictional characters (not of their characterization, the way they are presented) are the same as those we use for real people, an area of violent controversy and confusion. The very term *character* itself, when it refers not to a fictional personage but to a combination of qualities in a human being, is somewhat ambiguous. It usually has moral overtones, often favorable (a man of character); it is sometimes neutral but evaluative (character reference). Judgment about character (not characterization, remember) usually involves moral terms like *good* and *bad* and *strong* and *weak*. *Personality* usually implies that which distinguishes or individualizes a person, and the judgment called for is not so much moral as social—*pleasing* or *displeasing*. An older term, *nature* (it is his nature to be so or do such), usually implies something inherent or inborn, something fixed and thus predictable. The **existential character** implies the opposite; that is, whatever our past, our conditioning, our pattern or previous behavior, we can, by an act of will, change all that right this minute, as Macomber does.

Fictional characters thus frequently seem to be part of the history that lies behind the story or beyond the story as part of our own world, to exist in a reality that is detachable from the words and events of the story in which they appear. We feel we might recognize Tom Jones, Jane Eyre, or Sherlock Holmes on the street, and we might be able to anticipate what they might say or do in *our* world, outside the story. Fictional characters are neither real nor detachable, of course, and they exist only in the words of the works in which they are presented. We must not forget the distinction between the character and the characterization, the method by which he or she is presented; so we must be careful to distinguish the *good character,* meaning someone whom, if real, we would consider virtuous, and the *good characterization,* meaning a fictional person who, no matter what his or her morality or behavior, is well presented.

Henry James's story *The Real Thing* is about the difference between reality and art, character and characterization. Major Monarch is described as a "gentleman, a man of fifty, very high and very straight, with a mustache slightly grizzled and a dark gray walking-coat admirably fitted, . . ." He looks like the stereotype of a celebrity. The painter-narrator of *The Real Thing,* however, immediately recognizes that, because of a "paradoxical law," Major Monarch's appearance means that he is *not* a celebrity: celebrities are not often so "striking." It does not take the narrator long to recognize the Major's real type. Just by the Major's appearance, the painter can "see" the Major's whole gentlemanly life: his hunting, his clothes, his umbrellas, his luggage, his servants, and he can see as well Mrs. Monarch's lady's life, clothes, etc. They are "the real thing," a real gentleman and a real lady. They are therefore useless as models for the artist. Not only are they so much *one* real thing that they can pose only for that type and no other, but even as a lady or gentleman they are so stereotypical they are useful only for illustrations of bad, stereotyped novels. James seems to be distinguishing *character* and *characterization*: the first is "the real thing" which will not do for art or the *representation* of the real; the second, "the alchemy of art," offers not a copy of reality but an *illusion* of reality, an illusion that seems more real in its representation than the real thing would.

Even if we entirely agree with Henry James—and not all readers do—his distinction between reality and its representation does not mean that we cannot learn from one about the other. We must recognize that characters are not finally detachable—that they have roles, functions, limitations, and their very existence in the context of other elements in the story; we must not confuse fictional characters with real people, or character with characterization. This is not to say, however, that we may not learn about real people from characters in fiction or learn to understand fictional characters in part from what we know about real people. For real people too exist in a context of other people and other elements, their history and geography and their "narrator," the one who is representing them—that is, *you*. Indeed, it may be worth paying particular attention to how stories create the images of people and what those images assume about human character pre-

cisely because this process and these assumptions are so similar to the
way we get to know and understand real people. For we are all artists
representing reality to ourselves. If we study the art of characterization
we may become better artists, able to enrich both our reading and our
lives.

TONI CADE BAMBARA

My Man Bovanne

Blind people got a hummin jones[1] if you notice. Which is understandable completely once you been around one and notice what no eyes
will force you into to see people, and you get past the first time,
which seems to come out of nowhere, and it's like you in church
again with fat-chest ladies and old gents gruntin a hum low in the
throat to whatever the preacher be saying. Shakey Bee bottom lip
all swole up with Sweet Peach[2] and me explainin how come the
sweet-potato bread was a dollar-quarter this time stead of dollar regular and he say uh hunh he understand, then he break into this
thizzin kind of hum which is quiet, but fiercesome just the same, if
you ain't ready for it. Which I wasn't. But I got used to it and the
onliest time I had to say somethin bout it was when he was playin
checkers on the stoop one time and he commenst to hummin quite
churchy seem to me. So I says, "Look here Shakey Bee, I can't beat
you and Jesus too." He stop.

  So that's how come I asked My Man Bovanne to dance. He ain't
my man mind you, just a nice ole gent from the block that we all
know cause he fixes things and the kids like him. Or used to fore
Black Power got hold their minds and mess em around till they
can't be civil to ole folks. So we at this benefit for my niece's cousin
who's runnin for somethin with this Black party somethin or other behind her. And I press up close to dance with Bovanne who blind
and I'm hummin and he hummin, chest to chest like talkin. Not jam-
min my breasts into the man. Wasn't bout tits. Was bout vibrations.
And he dug it and asked me what color dress I had on and how my
hair was fixed and how I was doin without a man, not nosy but
nice-like, and who was at this affair and was the canapés dainty-
stingy or healthy enough to get hold of proper. Comfy and cheery
is what I'm tryin to get across. Touch talkin like the heel of the hand
on the tambourine or on a drum.

  But right away Joe Lee come up on us and frown for dancin so
close to the man. My own son who knows what kind of warm I am
about; and don't grown men all call me long distance and in the

1. A compelling need.   2. A brand of dipping snuff.

middle of the night for a little Mama comfort? But he frown. Which ain't right since Bovanne can't see and defend himself. Just a nice old man who fixes toasters and busted irons and bicycles and things and changes the lock on my door when my men friends get messy. Nice man. Which is not why they invited him. Grass roots you see. Me and Sister Taylor and the woman who does heads at Mamies and the man from the barber shop, we all there on account of we grass roots. And I ain't never been souther than Brooklyn Battery and no more country than the window box on my fire escape. And just yesterday my kids tellin me to take them countrified rags off my head and be cool. And now can't get Black enough to suit em. So everybody passin sayin My Man Bovanne. Big deal, keep steppin and don't even stop a minute to get the man a drink or one of them cute sandwiches or tell him what's goin on. And him standin there with a smile ready case someone do speak he want to be ready. So that's how come I pull him on the dance floor and we dance squeezin past the tables and chairs and all them coats and people standin round up in each other face talkin bout this and that but got no use for this blind man who mostly fixed skates and skooters for all these folks when they was just kids. So I'm pressed up close and we touch talkin with the hum. And here come my daughter cuttin her eye[3] at me like she do when she tell me about my "apolitical" self like I got hoof and mouf disease and there ain't no hope at all. And I don't pay her no mind and just look up in Bovanne shadow face and tell him his stomach like a drum and he laugh. Laugh real loud. And here come my youngest, Task, with a tap on my elbow like he the third grade monitor and I'm cuttin up on the line to assembly.

"I was just talkin on the drums," I explained when they hauled me into the kitchen. I figured drums was my best defense. They can get ready for drums what with all this heritage business. And Bovanne stomach just like that drum Task give me when he come back from Africa. You just touch it and it hum thizzz, thizzm. So I stuck to the drum story. "Just drummin that's all."

"Mama, what are you talkin about?"

"She had too much to drink," say Elo to Task cause she don't hardly say nuthin to me direct no more since that ugly argument about my wigs.

"Look here Mama," say Task, the gentle one. "We just tryin to pull your coat. You were makin a spectacle of yourself out there dancing like that."

"Dancin like what?"

Task run a hand over his left ear like his father for the world and his father before that.

"Like a bitch in heat," say Elo.

"Well uhh, I was goin to say like one of them sex-starved ladies gettin on in years and not too discriminating. Know what I mean?"

I don't answer cause I'll cry. Terrible thing when your own children talk to you like that. Pullin me out the party and hustlin me into some

3. Giving a sharp look.

stranger's kitchen in the back of a bar just like the damn police. And ain't like I'm old old. I can still wear me some sleeveless dresses without the meat hangin off my arm. And I keep up with some thangs through my kids. Who ain't kids no more. To hear them tell it. So I don't say nuthin.

"Dancin with that tom," say Elo to Joe Lee, who leanin on the folks' freezer. "His feet can smell a cracker a mile away and go into their shuffle number post haste. And them eyes. He could be a little considerate and put on some shades. Who wants to look into them blown-out fuses that—"

"Is this what they call the generation gap?" I say.

"Generation gap," spits Elo, like I suggested castor oil and fricassee possum in the milk-shakes or somethin. "That's a white concept for a white phenomenon. There's no generation gap among Black people. We are a col—"

"Yeh, well never mind," says Joe Lee. "The point is Mama . . . well, it's pride. You embarrass yourself and us too dancin like that."

"I wasn't shame." Then nobody say nuthin. Them standin there in they pretty clothes with drinks in they hands and gangin up on me, and me in the third-degree chair and nary a olive to my name. Felt just like the police got hold to me.

"First of all," Task say, holdin up his hand and tickin off the offenses, "the dress. Now that dress is too short, Mama, and too low-cut for a woman your age. And Tamu's going to make a speech tonight to kick off the campaign and will be introducin you and expecting you to organize the council of elders—"

"Me? Didn nobody ask me nuthin. You mean Nisi? She change her name?"

"Well, Norton was supposed to tell you about it. Nisi wants to introduce you and then encourage the older folks to form a Council of the Elders to act as an advisory—"

"And you going to be standing there with your boobs out and that wig on your head and that hem up to your ass. And people'll say, 'Ain't that the horny bitch that was grindin with the blind dude?' "

"Elo, be cool a minute," say Task, gettin to the next finger. "And then there's the drinkin. Mama, you know you can't drink cause next thing you know you be laughin loud and carryin on," and he grab another finger for the loudness. "And then there's the dancin. You been tattooed on the man for four records straight and slow draggin even on the fast numbers. How you think that look for a woman your age?"

"What's my age?"

"What?"

"I'm axin you all a simple question. You keep talkin bout what's proper for a woman my age. How old am I anyhow?" And Joe Lee slams his eyes shut and squinches up his face to figure. And Task run a hand over his ear and stare into his glass like the ice cubes goin calculate for him. And Elo just starin at the top of my head like she goin rip the wig off any minute now.

"Is your hair braided up under that thing? If so, why don't you take it off? You always did do a neat cornroll."[4]

"Uh huh," cause I'm thinkin how she couldn't undo her hair fast enough talking bout cornroll so countrified. None of which was the subject. "How old, I say?"

"Sixtee-one or—"

"You a damn lie Joe Lee Peoples."

"And that's another thing," say Task on the fingers.

"You know what you all can kiss," I say, gettin up and brushin the wrinkles out my lap.

"Oh, Mama," Elo say, puttin a hand on my shoulder like she hasn't done since she left home and the hand landin light and not sure it supposed to be there. Which hurt me to my heart. Cause this was the child in our happiness fore Mr. Peoples die. And I carried that child strapped to my chest till she was nearly two. We was close is what I'm tryin to tell you. Cause it was more me in the child than the others. And even after Task it was the girlchild I covered in the night and wept over for no reason at all less it was she was a chub-chub like me and not very pretty, but a warm child. And how did things get to this, that she can't put a sure hand on me and say Mama we love you and care about you and you entitled to enjoy your-self cause you a good woman?

4.   "And then there's Reverend Trent," say Task, glancin from left to right like they hatchin a plot and just now lettin me in on it. "You were suppose to be talking with him tonight, Mama, about giving us his basement for campaign headquarters and—"

"Didn nobody tell me nuthin. If grass roots mean you kept in the dark I can't use it. I really can't. And Reven Trent a fool anyway the way he tore into the widow man up there on Edgecomb cause he wouldn't take in three of them foster children and the woman not even comfy in the ground yet and the man's mind messed up and—"

"Look here," say Task. "What we need is a family conference so we can get all this stuff cleared up and laid out on the table. In the meantime I think we better get back into the other room and tend to business. And in the meantime, Mama, see if you can't get to Reverend Trent and—"

"You want me to belly rub with the Reven, that it?"

"Oh damn," Elo say and go through the swingin door.

"We'll talk about all this at dinner. How's tomorrow night, Joe Lee?" While Joe Lee being self-important I'm wonderin who's doin the cookin and how come no body ax me if I'm free and do I get a corsage and things like that. Then Joe nod that it's O.K. and he go through the swingin door and just a little hubbub come through from the other room. Then Task smile his smile, lookin just like his daddy, and he leave. And it just me in this stranger's kitchen, which was a mess I wouldn't never let my kitchen look like. Poison you just to look at the pots. Then the door swing the other way and it's My Man Bo-vanne standin there sayin Miss Hazel but lookin at the deep fry and

4. Cornrow, a hairstyle in which all the hair is interwoven from the scalp into small braids.

then at the steam table, and most surprised when I come up on him from the other direction and take him on out of there. Pass the folks pushin up towards the stage where Nisi and some other people settin and ready to talk, and folks gettin to the last of the sandwiches and the booze fore they settle down in one spot and listen serious. And I'm thinkin bout tellin Bovanne what a lovely long dress Nisi got on and the earrings and her hair piled up in a cone and the people bout to hear how we all gettin screwed and gotta form our own party and everybody there listenin and lookin. But instead I just haul the man on out of there, and Joe Lee and his wife look at me like I'm terrible, but they ain't said boo to the man yet. Cause he blind and old and don't nobody there need him since they grown up and don't need they skates fixed no more.

"Where we goin, Miss Hazel?" Him knowin all the time.

"First we gonna buy you some dark sunglasses. Then you comin with me to the supermarket so I can pick up tomorrow's dinner, which is goin to be a grand thing proper and you invited. Then we goin to my house."

"That be fine. I surely would like to rest my feet." Bein cute, but you got to let men play out they little show, blind or not. So he chat on bout how tired he is and how he appreciate me takin him in hand this way. And I'm thinkin I'll have him change the lock on my door first thing. Then I'll give the man a nice warm bath with jasmine leaves in the water and a little Epsom salt on the sponge to do his back. And then a good rubdown with rose water and olive oil. Then a cup of lemon tea with a taste in it. And a little talcum, some of that fancy stuff Nisi mother sent over last Christmas. And then a massage, a good face massage round the forehead which is the worryin part. Cause you gots to take care of the older folks. And let them know they still needed to run the mimeo machine and keep the spark plugs clean and fix the mailboxes for folks who might help us get the breakfast program goin, and the school for the little kids and the campaign and all. Cause old folks in the nation. That what Nisi was sayin and I mean to do my part.

"I imagine you are a very pretty woman, Miss Hazel."

"I surely am," I say just like the hussy my daughter always say I was.

1972

HENRY JAMES

The Real Thing

I

When the porter's wife, who used to answer the house-bell, announced "A gentleman and a lady, sir," I had, as I often had in those days—the wish being father to the thought—an immediate vision of sitters. Sitters my visitors in this case proved to be; but not in the sense I should have preferred. There was nothing at first however to indicate that they mightn't have come for a portrait. The gentleman, a man of fifty, very high and very straight, with a mustache slightly grizzled and a dark gray walking-coat admirably fitted, both of which I noted professionally—I don't mean as a barber or yet as a tailor—would have struck me as a celebrity if celebrities often were striking. It was a truth of which I had for some time been conscious that a figure with a good deal of frontage was, as one might say, almost never a public institution. A glance at the lady helped to remind me of this paradoxical law: she also looked too distinguished to be a "personality." Moreover one would scarcely come across two variations together.

Neither of the pair immediately spoke—they only prolonged the preliminary gaze suggesting that each wished to give the other a chance. They were visibly shy; they stood there letting me take them in—which, as I afterwards perceived, was the most practical thing they could have done. In this way their embarrassment served their cause. I had seen people painfully reluctant to mention that they desired anything so gross as to be represented on canvas; but the scruples of my new friends appeared almost insurmountable. Yet the gentleman might have said "I should like a portrait of my wife," and the lady might have said "I should like a portrait of my husband." Perhaps they weren't husband and wife—this naturally would make the matter more delicate. Perhaps they wished to be done together—in which case they ought to have brought a third person to break the news.

"We come from Mr. Rivet," the lady finally said with a dim smile that had the effect of a moist sponge passed over a "sunk" piece of painting, as well as of a vague allusion to vanished beauty. She was as tall and straight, in her degree, as her companion, and with ten years less to carry. She looked as sad as a woman could look whose face was not charged with expression; that is her tinted oval mask showed waste as an exposed surface shows friction. The hand of time had played over her freely, but to an effect of elimination. She was slim and stiff, and so well-dressed, in dark blue cloth, with lappets and pockets and buttons, that it was clear she employed the same tailor as her husband. The couple had an indefinable air of prosperous thrift—they evidently got a good deal of luxury for their money. If I was to be one of their luxuries it would behove me to consider my terms.

"Ah Claude Rivet recommended me?" I echoed; and I added that it was very kind of him, though I could reflect that, as he only painted landscape, this wasn't a sacrifice.

The lady looked very hard at the gentleman, and the gentleman looked round the room. Then staring at the floor a moment and stroking his mustache, he rested his pleasant eyes on me with the remark: "He said you were the right one."

"I try to be, when people want to sit."

"Yes, we should like to," said the lady anxiously.

"Do you mean together?"

My visitors exchanged a glance. "If you could do anything with *me* I suppose it would be double," the gentleman stammered.

"Oh yes, there's naturally a higher charge for two figures than for one."

"We should like to make it pay," the husband confessed.

"That's very good of you," I returned, appreciating so unwonted a sympathy—for I supposed he meant pay the artist.

A sense of strangeness seemed to dawn on the lady. "We mean for the illustrations—Mr. Rivet said you might put one in."

"Put in—an illustration?" I was equally confused.

"Sketch her off, you know" said the gentleman, coloring.

It was only then that I understood the service Claude Rivet had rendered me; he had told them how I worked in black-and-white, for magazines, for storybooks, for sketches of contemporary life, and consequently had copious employment for models. These things were true, but it was not less true—I may confess it now; whether because the aspiration was to lead to everything or to nothing I leave the reader to guess—that I couldn't get the honors, to say nothing of the emoluments, of a great painter of portraits out of my head. My "illustrations" were my pot-boilers; I looked to a different branch of art—far and away the most interesting it had always seemed to me—to perpetuate my fame. There was no shame in looking to it also to make my fortune; but that fortune was by so much further from being made from the moment my visitors wished to be "done" for nothing. I was disappointed; for in the pictorial sense I had immediately *seen* them. I had seized their type—I had already settled what I would do with it. Something that wouldn't absolutely have pleased them, I afterwards reflected.

"Ah you're—you're—a—?" I began as soon as I had mastered my surprise. I couldn't bring out the dingy word "models": it seemed so little to fit the case.

"We haven't had much practice," said the lady.

"We've got to *do* something, and we've thought that an artist in your line might perhaps make something of us," her husband threw off. He further mentioned that they didn't know many artists and that they had gone first, on the off-chance—he painted views of course, but sometimes put in figures; perhaps I remembered—to Mr. Rivet, whom they had met a few years before at a place in Norfolk where he was sketching.

"We used to sketch a little ourselves," the lady hinted.

"It's very awkward, but we absolutely *must* do something," her husband went on.

"Of course we're not so *very* young," she admitted with a wan smile.

With the remark that I might as well know something more about them the husband had handed me a card extracted from a neat new pocket-book—their appurtenances were all of the freshest—and inscribed with the words "Major Monarch." Impressive as these words were they didn't carry my knowledge much further; but my visitor presently added: "I've left the army and we've had the misfortune to lose our money. In fact our means are dreadfully small."

"It's awfully trying—a regular strain," said Mrs. Monarch.

They evidently wished to be discreet—to take care not to swagger because they were gentlefolk. I felt them willing to recognize this as something of a drawback, at the same time that I guessed at an underlying sense—their consolation in adversity—that they *had* their points. They certainly had; but these advantages struck me as preponderantly social; such for instance as would help to make a drawing-room look well. However, a drawing-room was always, or ought to be, a picture.

In consequence of his wife's allusion to their age Major Monarch observed: "Naturally it's more for the figure that we thought of going in. We can still hold ourselves up." On the instant I saw that the figure was indeed their strong point. His "naturally" didn't sound vain, but it lighted up the question. "*She* has the best one," he continued, nodding at his wife with a pleasant after-dinner absence of circumlocution. I could only reply, as if we were in fact sitting over our wine, that this didn't prevent his own from being very good; which led him in turn to make answer: "We thought that if you ever have to do people like us we might be something like it. *She* particularly—for a lady in a book, you know."

I was so amused by them that, to get more of it, I did my best to take their point of view; and though it was an embarrassment to find myself appraising physically, as if they were animals on hire or useful blacks, a pair whom I should have expected to meet only in one of the relations in which criticism is tacit, I looked at Mrs. Monarch judicially enough to be able to exclaim after a moment with conviction: "Oh yes, a lady in a book!" She was singularly like a bad illustration.

"We'll stand up, if you like," said the Major; and he raised himself before me with a really grand air.

I could take his measure at a glance—he was six feet two and a perfect gentleman. It would have paid any club in process of formation and in want of a stamp to engage him at a salary to stand in the principal window. What struck me at once was that in coming to me they had rather missed their vocation; they could surely have been turned to better account for advertising purposes. I couldn't of course see the thing in detail, but I could see them make somebody's fortune —I don't mean their own. There was something in them for a waistcoat-maker, a hotel-keeper or a soap-vendor. I could imagine "We always use it" pinned on their bosoms with the greatest effect; I had a vision of the brilliancy with which they would launch a table d'hôte.

Mrs. Monarch sat still, not from pride but from shyness, and presently her husband said to her: "Get up, my dear, and show how smart you are." She obeyed, but she had no need to get up to show it. She walked to the end of the studio and then came back blushing, her fluttered eyes on the partner of her appeal. I was reminded of an incident I had accidentally had a glimpse of in Paris—being with a friend there, a dramatist about to produce a play, when an actress came to him to ask to be entrusted with a part. She went through her paces before him, walked up and down as Mrs. Monarch was doing. Mrs. Monarch did it quite as well, but I abstained from applauding. It was very odd to see such people apply for such poor pay. She looked as if she had ten thousand a year. Her husband had used the word that described her: she was in the London current jargon essentially and typically "smart." Her figure was, in the same order of ideas, conspicuously and irreproachably "good." For a woman of her age her waist was surprisingly small; her elbow moreover had the orthodox crook. She held her head at the conventional angle, but why did she come to *me?* She ought to have tried on jackets at a big shop. I feared my visitors were not only destitute but "artistic"—which would be a great complication. When she sat down again I thanked her, observing that what a draftsman most valued in his model was the faculty of keeping quiet.

"Oh *she* can keep quiet," said Major Monarch. Then he added jocosely: "I've always kept her quiet."

"I'm not a nasty fidget, am I?" It was going to wring tears from me, I felt, the way she hid her head, ostrich-like, in the other broad bosom.

The owner of this expanse addressed his answer to me. "Perhaps it isn't out of place to mention—because we ought to be quite business-like, oughtn't we?—that when I married her she was known as the Beautiful Statue."

"Oh dear!" said Mrs. Monarch ruefully.

"Of course I should want a certain amount of expression," I rejoined.

"Of *course!*"—and I had never heard such unanimity.

"And then I suppose you know that you'll get awfully tired."

"Oh we *never* get tired!" they eagerly cried.

"Have you had any kind of practice?"

They hesitated—they looked at each other. "We've been photographed—*immensely*," said Mrs. Monarch.

"She means the fellows have asked us themselves," added the Major.

"I see—because you're so good-looking."

"I don't know what they thought, but they were always after us."

"We always got our photographs for nothing," smiled Mrs. Monarch.

"We might have brought some, my dear," her husband remarked.

"I'm not sure we have any left. We've given quantities away," she explained to me.

"With our autographs and that sort of thing," said the Major.

"Are they to be got in the shops?" I enquired as a harmless pleasantry.

"Oh yes, *hers*—they used to be."

"Not now," said Mrs. Monarch with her eyes on the floor.

II

I could fancy the "sort of thing" they put on the presentation copies of their photographs, and I was sure they wrote a beautiful hand. It was odd how quickly I was sure of everything that concerned them. If they were now so poor as to have to earn shillings and pence they could never have had much of a margin. Their good looks had been

their capital, and they had good-humoredly made the most of the
career that this resource marked out for them. It was in their faces,
the blankness, the deep intellectual repose of the twenty years of
country-house visiting that had given them pleasant intonations. I
could see the sunny drawing-rooms, sprinkled with periodicals she
didn't read, in which Mrs. Monarch had continuously sat; I could see
the wet shrubberies in which she had walked, equipped to admiration
for either exercise. I could see the rich covers[1] the Major had helped
to shoot and the wonderful garments in which, late at night, he repaired to the smoking-room to talk about them. I could imagine their
leggings and waterproofs, their knowing tweeds and rugs, their rolls of
sticks and cases of tackle and neat umbrellas; and I could evoke the
exact appearance of their servants and the compact variety of their
luggage on the platforms of country stations.

They gave small tips, but they were liked; they didn't do anything
themselves, but they were welcome. They looked so well everywhere;
they gratified the general relish for stature, complexion and "form."
They knew it without fatuity or vulgarity, and they respected themselves in consequence. They weren't superficial; they were thorough
and kept themselves up—it had been their line. People with such a
taste for activity had to have some line. I could feel how even in a dull
house they could have been counted on for the joy of life. At present
something had happened—it didn't matter what, their little income
had grown less, it had grown least—and they had to do something for
pocket-money. Their friends could like them, I made out, without
liking to support them. There was something about them that represented credit—their clothes, their manners, their type; but if credit is a
large empty pocket in which an occasional chink reverberates, the
chink at least must be audible. What they wanted of me was to help to
make it so. Fortunately they had no children—I soon divined that.
They would also perhaps wish our relations to be kept secret: this was
why it was "for the figure"—the reproduction of the face would betray
them.

I liked them—I felt, quite as their friends must have done—they
were so simple; and I had no objection to them if they would suit. But
somehow with all their perfections I didn't easily believe in them.
After all they were amateurs, and the ruling passion of my life was the
detestation of the amateur. Combined with this was another perversity
—an innate preference for the represented subject over the real one:
the defect of the real one was so apt to be a lack of representation. I
liked things that appeared; then one was sure. Whether they *were* or
not was a subordinate and almost always a profitless question. There
were other considerations, the first of which was that I already had
two or three recruits in use, notably a young person with big feet, in
alpaca, from Kilburn, who for a couple of years had come to me
regularly for my illustrations and with whom I was still—perhaps
ignobly—satisfied. I frankly explained to my visitors how the case
stood, but they had taken more precautions than I supposed. They had
reasoned out their opportunity, for Claude Rivet had told them of the

1. Flocks of game birds.

projected *édition de luxe* of one of the writers of our day—the rarest of the novelists—who, long neglected by the multitudinous vulgar and dearly prized by the attentive (need I mention Philip Vincent?), had had the happy fortune of seeing, late in life, the dawn and then the full light of a higher criticism; an estimate in which on the part of the public there was something really of expiation. The edition preparing, planned by a publisher of taste, was practically an act of high reparation; the wood-cuts with which it was to be enriched were the homage of English art to one of the most independent representatives of English letters. Major and Mrs. Monarch confessed to me they had hoped I might be able to work *them* into my branch of the enterprise. They knew I was to do the first of the books, "Rutland Ramsay," but I had to make clear to them that my participation in the rest of the affair—this first book was to be a test—must depend on the satisfaction I should give. If this should be limited my employers would drop me with scarce common forms. It was therefore a crisis for me, and naturally I was making special preparations, looking about for new people, should they be necessary and securing the best types. I admitted however that I should like to settle down to two or three good models who would do for everything.

"Should we have often to—a—put on special clothes?" Mrs. Monarch timidly demanded.

"Dear yes—that's half the business."

"And should we be expected to supply our own costumes?"

"Oh no; I've got a lot of things. A painter's models put on—or put off—anything he likes."

"And you mean—a—the same?"

"The same?"

Mrs. Monarch looked at her husband again.

"Oh she was just wondering," he explained, "if the costumes are in *general* use." I had to confess that they were, and I mentioned further that some of them—I had a lot of genuine greasy last-century things—had served their time, a hundred years ago, on living world-stained men and women; on figures not perhaps so far removed, in that vanished world, from *their* type, the Monarchs', *quoi!*[2] of a breeched and bewigged age. "We'll put on anything that *fits*," said the Major.

"Oh I arrange that—they fit in the pictures."

"I'm afraid I should do better for the modern books. I'd come as you like," said Mrs. Monarch.

"She has got a lot of clothes at home: they might do for contemporary life," her husband continued.

"Oh I can fancy scenes in which you'd be quite natural." And indeed I could see the slipshod rearrangements of stale properties—the stories I tried to produce pictures for without the exasperation of reading them—whose sandy tracts the good lady might help to people. But I had to return to the fact that for this sort of work—the daily mechanical grind—I was already equipped: the people I was working with were fully adequate.

"We only thought we might be more like *some* characters," said

2. What!

Mrs. Monarch mildly, getting up.

Her husband also rose; he stood looking at me with a dim wistful-
ness that was touching in so fine a man. "Wouldn't it be rather a pull
sometimes to have—a—to have—?" He hung fire; he wanted me to
help him by phrasing what he meant. But I couldn't—I didn't know.
So he brought it out awkwardly: "The *real* thing; a gentleman, you
know, or a lady." I was quite ready to give a general assent—I admitted that there was a great deal in that. This encouraged Major
Monarch to say, following up his appeal with an unacted gulp: "It's
awfully hard—we've tried everything." The gulp was communicative;
it proved too much for his wife. Before I knew it Mrs. Monarch had
dropped again upon a divan and burst into tears. Her husband sat
down beside her, holding one of her hands; whereupon she quickly
dried her eyes with the other, while I felt embarrassed as she looked
up at me. "There isn't a confounded job I haven't applied for—waited
for—prayed for. You can fancy we'd be pretty bad first. Secretary-
ships and that sort of thing? You might as well ask for a peerage. I'd
be *anything*—I'm strong; a messenger or a coalheaver. I'd put on a
gold-laced cap and open carriage-doors in front of the haberdasher's;
I'd hang about a station to carry portmanteaux; I'd be a postman.
But they won't *look* at you; there are thousands as good as yourself
already on the ground. *Gentlemen,* poor beggars, who've drunk their
wine, who've kept their hunters!"

I was as reassuring as I knew how to be, and my visitors were
presently on their feet again while, for the experiment, we agreed on
an hour. We were discussing it when the door opened and Miss
Churm came in with a wet umbrella. Miss Churm had to take the
omnibus to Maida Vale and then walk half a mile. She looked a trifle
blowzy and slightly splashed. I scarcely ever saw her come in without
thinking afresh how odd it was that, being so little in herself, she
should yet be so much in others. She was a meager little Miss Churm,
but was such an ample heroine of romance. She was only a freckled
cockney, but she could represent everything, from a fine lady to a
shepherdess; she had the faculty as she might have had a fine voice or
long hair. She couldn't spell and she loved beer, but she had two or
three "points," and practice, and a knack, and mother-wit, and a
whimsical sensibility, and a love of the theater, and seven sisters, and
not an ounce of respect, especially for the *h*.[3] The first thing my
visitors saw was that her umbrella was wet, and in their spotless
perfection they visibly winced at it. The rain had come on since their
arrival.

"I'm all in a soak; there *was* a mess of people in the 'bus. I wish you
lived near a styion," said Miss Churm. I requested her to get ready as
quickly as possible, and she passed into the room in which she always
changed her dress. But before going out she asked me what she was
to get into this time.

"It's the Russian princess, don't you know?" I answered; "the one
with the 'golden eyes,' in black velvet, for the long thing in the
Cheapside."

3. Working-class Londoners, especially in the East End (cockneys), drop *h*'s
'orribly.

"Golden eyes? I *say!*" cried Miss Churm, while my companions watched her with intensity as she withdrew. She always arranged herself, when she was late, before I could turn round; and I kept my visitors a little on purpose, so that they might get an idea, from seeing her, what would be expected of themselves. I mentioned that she was quite my notion of an excellent model—she was really very clever.

"Do you think she looks like a Russian princess?" Major Monarch asked with lurking alarm.

"When I make her, yes."

"Oh if you have to *make* her—!" he reasoned, not without point.

"That's the most you can ask. There are so many who are not makeable."

"Well now, *here's* a lady"—and with a persuasive smile he passed his arm into his wife's—"who's already made!"

"Oh I'm not a Russian princess," Mrs. Monarch protested a little coldly. I could see she had known some and didn't like them. There at once was a complication of a kind I never had to fear with Miss Churm.

This young lady came back in black velvet—the gown was rather rusty and very low on her lean shoulders—and with a Japanese fan in her red hands. I reminded her that in the scene I was doing she had to look over someone's head. "I forgot whose it is; but it doesn't matter. Just look over a head."

"I'd rather look over a stove," said Miss Churm; and she took her station near the fire. She fell into position, settled herself into a tall attitude, gave a certain backward inclination to her head and a certain forward droop to her fan, and looked, at least to my prejudiced sense, distinguished and charming, foreign and dangerous. We left her looking so while I went downstairs with Major and Mrs. Monarch.

"I believe I could come about as near it as that," said Mrs. Monarch.

"Oh you think she's shabby, but you must allow for the alchemy of art."

However, they went off with an evident increase of comfort founded on their demonstrable advantage in being the real thing. I could fancy them shuddering over Miss Churm. She was very droll about them when I went back, for I told her what they wanted.

"Well, if *she* can sit I'll tyke to bookkeeping," said my model.

"She's very ladylike," I replied as an innocent form of aggravation.

"So much the worse for *you.* That means she can't turn round."

"She'll do for the fashionable novels."

"Oh yes, she'll *do* for them!" my model humorously declared. "Ain't they bad enough without her?" I had often sociably denounced them to Miss Churm.

III

It was for the elucidation of a mystery in one of these works that I first tried Mrs. Monarch. Her husband came with her, to be useful if necessary—it was sufficiently clear that as a general thing he would prefer to come with her. At first I wondered if this were for "propriety's" sake—if he were going to be jealous and meddling. The idea was too tiresome, and if it had been confirmed it would speedily have brought our acquaintance to a close. But I soon saw there was nothing in it and that if he accompanied Mrs. Monarch it was—in addition to the chance of being wanted—simply because he had nothing else to do. When they were separate his occupation was gone and they never *had* been separate. I judged rightly that in their awkward situation their close union was their main comfort and that this union had no weak spot. It was a real marriage, an encouragement to the hesitating, a nut for pessimists to crack. Their address was humble—I remember afterwards thinking it had been the only thing about them that was really professional—and I could fancy the lamentable lodgings in which the Major would have been left alone. He could sit there more or less grimly with his wife—he couldn't sit there anyhow without her.

He had too much tact to try and make himself agreeable when he couldn't be useful; so when I was too absorbed in my work to talk he simply sat and waited. But I liked to hear him talk—it made my work, when not interrupting it, less mechanical, less special. To listen to him was to combine the excitement of going out with the economy of staying at home. There was only one hindrance—that I seemed not to know any of the people this brilliant couple had known. I think he wondered extremely, during the term of our intercourse, whom the deuce I *did* know. He hadn't a stray sixpence[4] of an idea to fumble for, so we didn't spin it very fine; we confined ourselves to questions of leather and even of liquor—saddlers and breeches-makers and how to get excellent claret cheap—and matters like "good trains" and the habits of small game. His lore on these last subjects was astonishing—he managed to interweave the station-master with the ornithologist. When he couldn't talk about greater things he could talk cheerfully about smaller, and since I couldn't accompany him into reminiscences of the fashionable world he could lower the conversation without a visible effort to my level.

So earnest a desire to please was touching in a man who could so easily have knocked one down. He looked after the fire and had an opinion on the draft of the stove without my asking him, and I could see that he thought many of my arrangements not half knowing. I remember telling him that if I were only rich I'd offer him a salary to come and teach me how to live. Sometimes he gave a random sigh of which the essence might have been: "Give me even such a bare old barrack as *this*, and I'd do something with it!" When I wanted to use him he came alone; which was an illustration of the superior courage of women. His wife could bear her solitary second floor, and she was in general more discreet; showing by various small reserves that she was alive to the propriety of keeping our relations markedly professional—not letting them slide into sociability. She wished it to remain clear that she and the Major were employed, not cultivated, and if she approved of me as a superior, who could be kept in his place, she never thought me quite good enough for an equal.

She sat with great intensity, giving the whole of her mind to it, and was capable of remaining for an hour almost as motionless as before a photographer's lens. I could see she had been photographed often, but

4. Roughly, "a dime's worth."

somehow the very habit that made her good for that purpose unfitted her for mine. At first I was extremely pleased with her ladylike air, and it was a satisfaction, on coming to follow her lines, to see how good they were and how far they could lead the pencil. But after a little skirmishing I began to find her too insurmountably stiff; do what I would with it my drawing looked like a photograph or a copy of a photograph. Her figure had no variety of expression—she herself had no sense of variety. You may say that this was my business and was only a question of placing her. Yet I placed her in every conceivable position and she managed to obliterate their differences. She was always a lady certainly, and into the bargain was always the same lady. She was the real thing, but always the same thing. There were moments when I rather writhed under the serenity of her confidence that she *was* the real thing. All her dealings with me and all her husband's were an implication that this was lucky for *me*. Meanwhile I found myself trying to invent types that approached her own, instead of making her own transform itself—in the clever way that was not impossible for instance to poor Miss Churm. Arrange as I would and take the precautions I would, she always came out, in my pictures, too tall—landing me in the dilemma of having represented a fascinating woman as seven feet high, which (out of respect perhaps to my own very much scantier inches) was far from my idea of such a personage.

The case was worse with the Major—nothing I could do would keep *him* down, so that he became useful only for the representation of brawny giants. I adored variety and range, I cherished human accidents, the illustrative note; I wanted to characterize closely, and the thing in the world I most hated was the danger of being ridden by a type. I had quarreled with some of my friends about it; I had parted company with them for maintaining that one *had* to be, and that if the type was beautiful—witness Raphael and Leonardo[5]—the servitude was only a gain. I was neither Leonardo nor Raphael—I might only be a presumptuous young modern searcher; but I held that everything was to be sacrificed sooner than character. When they claimed that the obsessional form could easily *be* character I retorted, perhaps superficially, "Whose?" It couldn't be everybody's—it might end in being nobody's.

After I had drawn Mrs. Monarch a dozen times I felt surer even than before that the value of such a model as Miss Churm resided precisely in the fact that she had no positive stamp, combined of course with the other fact that what she did have was a curious and inexplicable talent for imitation. Her usual appearance was like a curtain which she could draw up at request for a capital performance. This performance was simply suggestive; but it was a word to the wise—it was vivid and pretty. Sometimes even I thought it, though she was plain herself, too insipidly pretty; I made it a reproach to her that the figures drawn from her were monotonously (*bêtement,*[6] as we used to say) graceful. Nothing made her more angry; it was so much

5. Raffaello Sanzio (1483–1520), Leonardo, da Vinci (1452–1519), famous Italian Renaissance painters. Leonardo, of course, was also an inventor, military engineer, architect, sculptor, anatomist, etc.

6. Foolishly.

her pride to feel she could sit for characters that had nothing in common with each other. She would accuse me at such moments of taking away her "reputytion."

It suffered a certain shrinkage, this queer quantity, from the repeated visits of my new friends. Miss Churm was greatly in demand, never in want of employment, so I had no scruple in putting her off occasionally, to try them more at my ease. It was certainly amusing at first to do the real thing—it was amusing to do Major Monarch's trousers. They *were* the real thing, even if he did come out colossal. It was amusing to do his wife's back hair—it was so mathematically neat—and the particular "smart" tension of her tight stays. She lent herself especially to positions in which the face was somewhat averted or blurred; she abounded in ladylike back views and *profils perdus*.[7] When she stood erect she took naturally one of the attitudes in which court-painters represent queens and princesses; so that I found myself wondering whether, to draw out this accomplishment, I couldn't get the editor of the *Cheapside* to publish a really royal romance, "A Tale of Buckingham Palace." Sometimes however the real thing and the make-believe came into contact; by which I mean that Miss Churm, keeping an appointment or coming to make one on days when I had much work in hand, encountered her invidious rivals. The encounter was not on their part, for they noticed her no more than if she had been the housemaid; not from intentional loftiness, but simply because as yet, professionally, they didn't know how to fraternize, as I could imagine they would have liked—or at least that the Major would. They couldn't talk about the omnibus—they always walked; and they didn't know what else to try—she wasn't interested in good trains or cheap claret. Besides, they must have felt—in the air—that she was amused at them, secretly derisive of their ever knowing how. She wasn't a person to conceal the limits of her faith if she had had a chance to show them. On the other hand Mrs. Monarch didn't think her tidy; for why else did she take pains to say to me—it was going out of the way, for Mrs. Monarch—that she didn't like dirty women?

One day when my young lady happened to be present with my other sitters—she even dropped in, when it was convenient, for a chat—I asked her to be so good as to lend a hand in getting tea, a service with which she was familiar and which was one of a class that, living as I did in a small way, with slender domestic resources, I often appealed to my models to render. They liked to lay hands on my property, to break the sitting, and sometimes the china—it made them feel Bohemian. The next time I saw Miss Churm after this incident she surprised me greatly by making a scene about it—she accused me of having wished to humiliate her. She hadn't resented the outrage at the time, but had seemed obliging and amused, enjoying the comedy of asking Mrs. Monarch, who sat vague and silent, whether she would have cream and sugar, and putting an exaggerated simper into the question. She had tried intonations—as if she too wished to pass for the real thing—till I was afraid my other visitors would take offense. Oh they were determined not to do this, and their touching patience

---

7. Incomplete profile, showing more of the back of the head and less of the face.

was the measure of their great need. They would sit by the hour, uncomplaining, till I was ready to use them; they would come back on the chance of being wanted and would walk away cheerfully if it failed. I used to go to the door with them to see in what magnificent order they retreated. I tried to find other employment for them—I introduced them to several artists. But they didn't "take," for reasons I could appreciate, and I became rather anxiously aware that after such disappointments they fell back upon me with a heavier weight. They did me the honor to think me most *their* form. They weren't romantic enough for the painters, and in those days there were few serious workers in black-and-white. Besides, they had an eye to the great job I had mentioned to them—they had secretly set their hearts on supplying the right essence for my pictorial vindication of our fine novelist. They knew that for this undertaking I should want no costume-effects, none of the frippery of past ages—that it was a case in which everything would be contemporary and satirical and presumably genteel. If I could work them into it their future would be assured, for the labor would of course be long and the occupation steady.

One day Mrs. Monarch came without her husband—she explained his absence by his having had to go to the City.[8] While she sat there in her usual relaxed majesty there came at the door a knock which I immediately recognized as the subdued appeal of a model out of work. It was followed by the entrance of a young man whom I at once saw to be a foreigner and who proved in fact an Italian acquainted with no English word but my name, which he uttered in a way that made it seem to include all others. I hadn't then visited his country, nor was I proficient in his tongue; but as he was not so meanly constituted—what Italian is?—as to depend only on that member for expression he conveyed to me, in familiar but graceful mimicry, that he was in search of exactly the employment in which the lady before me was engaged. I was not struck with him at first, and while I continued to draw I dropped few signs of interest or encouragement. He stood his ground however—not importunately, but with a dumb dog-like fidelity in his eyes that amounted to innocent impudence, the manner of a devoted servant—he might have been in the house for years—unjustly suspected. Suddenly it struck me that this very attitude and expression made a picture; whereupon I told him to sit down and wait till I should be free. There was another picture in the way he obeyed me, and I observed as I worked that there were others still in the way he looked wonderingly, with his head thrown back, about the high studio. He might have been crossing himself in Saint Peter's. Before I finished I said to myself "The fellow's a bankrupt orange-monger, but a treasure."

When Mrs. Monarch withdrew he passed across the room like a flash to open the door for her, standing there with the rapt pure gaze of the young Dante spellbound by the young Beatrice.[9] As I never

8. Financial and legal center of London.

9. Dante Alighieri (1265–1321), Italian poet, author of *The Divine Comedy*, was inspired for his whole lifetime poetically and spiritually by Beatrice Fortinari whom he first saw when they were children and saw only infrequently thereafter.

insisted, in such situations, on the blankness of the British domestic, I reflected that he had the making of a servant—and I needed one, but couldn't pay him to be only that—as well as of a model; in short I resolved to adopt my bright adventurer if he would agree to officiate in the double capacity. He jumped at my offer, and in the event my rashness—for I had really known nothing about him—wasn't brought home to me. He proved a sympathetic though a desultory ministrant, and had in a wonderful degree the *sentiment de la pose.*[1] It was uncultivated, instinctive, a part of the happy instinct that had guided him to my door and helped him to spell out my name on the card nailed to it. He had had no other introduction to me than a guess, from the shape of my high north window, seen outside, that my place was a studio and that as a studio it would contain an artist. He had wandered to England in search of fortune, like other itinerants, and had embarked, with a partner and a small green hand-cart, on the sale of penny ices. The ices had melted away and the partner had dissolved in their train. My young man wore tight yellow trousers with reddish stripes and his name was Oronte. He was sallow but fair, and when I put him into some old clothes of my own he looked like an Englishman. He was as good as Miss Churm, who could look, when requested, like an Italian.

IV

I thought Mrs. Monarch's face slightly convulsed when, on her coming back with her husband, she found Oronte installed. It was strange to have to recognize in a scrap of a lazzarone[2] a competitor to her magnificent Major. It was she who scented danger first, for the Major was anecdotically unconscious. But Oronte gave us tea, with a hundred eager confusions—he had never been concerned in so queer a process—and I think she thought better of me for having at last an "establishment." They saw a couple of drawings that I had made of the establishment, and Mrs. Monarch hinted that it never would have struck her he had sat for them. "Now the drawings you make from *us,* they look exactly like us," she reminded me, smiling in triumph; and I recognized that this was indeed just their defect. When I drew the Monarchs I couldn't anyhow get away from them—get into the character I wanted to represent; and I hadn't the least desire my model should be discoverable in my picture. Miss Churm never was, and Mrs. Monarch thought I hid her, very properly, because she was vulgar; whereas if she was lost it was only as the dead who go to heaven are lost—in the gain of an angel the more.

By this time I had got a certain start with "Rutland Ramsay," the first novel in the great projected series; that is I had produced a dozen drawings, several with the help of the Major and his wife, and I had sent them in for approval. My understanding with the publishers, as I have already hinted, had been that I was to be left to do my work, in this particular case, as I liked, with the whole book committed to me; but my connection with the rest of the series was only contingent. There were moments when, frankly, it *was* a comfort to have the real

1. **Instinct for striking poses.**   2. **Street-person.**

thing under one's hand; for there were characters in "Rutland Ramsay" that were very much like it. There were people presumably as erect as the Major and women of as good a fashion as Mrs. Monarch. There was a great deal of country-house life—treated, it is true, in a fine fanciful ironical generalized way—and there was a considerable implication of knickerbockers and kilts.[3] There were certain things I had to settle at the outset; such things for instance as the exact appearance of the hero and the particular bloom and figure of the heroine. The author of course gave me a lead, but there was a margin for interpretation. I took the Monarchs into my confidence, I told them frankly what I was about, I mentioned my embarrassments and alternatives. "Oh take *him!*" Mrs. Monarch murmured sweetly, looking at her husband; and "What could you want better than my wife?" the Major inquired with the comfortable candor that now prevailed between us.

I wasn't obliged to answer these remarks—I was only obliged to place my sitters. I wasn't easy in mind, and I postponed a little timidly perhaps the solving of my question. The book was a large canvas, the other figures were numerous, and I worked off at first some of the episodes in which the hero and the heroine were not concerned. When once I had set *them* up I should have to stick to them—I couldn't make my young man seven feet high in one place and five feet nine in another. I inclined on the whole to the latter measurement, though the Major more than once reminded me that *he* looked about as young as anyone. It was indeed quite possible to arrange him, for the figure, so that it would have been difficult to detect his age. After the spontaneous Oronte had been with me a month, and after I had given him to understand several times over that his native exuberance would presently constitute an insurmountable barrier to our further intercourse, I waked to a sense of his heroic capacity. He was only five feet seven, but the remaining inches were latent. I tried him almost secretly at first, for I was really rather afraid of the judgment my other models would pass on such a choice. If they regarded Miss Churm as little better than a snare what would they think of the representation by a person so little the real thing as an Italian street-vendor of a protagonist formed by a public school?

If I went a little in fear of them it wasn't because they bullied me, because they had got an oppressive foothold, but because in their really pathetic decorum and mysteriously permanent newness they counted on me so intensely. I was therefore very glad when Jack Hawley came home: he was always of such good counsel. He painted badly himself, but there was no one like him for putting his finger on the place. He had been absent from England for a year; he had been somewhere—I don't remember where—to get a fresh eye. I was in a good deal of dread of any such organ, but we were old friends; he had been away for months and a sense of emptiness was creeping into my life. I hadn't dodged a missile for a year.

He came back with a fresh eye, but with the same old black velvet blouse, and the first evening he spent in my studio we smoked ciga-

3. Country-house-type outdoor clothing.

rettes till the small hours. He had done no work himself, he had only got the eye; so the field was clear for the production of my little things. He wanted to see what I had produced for the *Cheapside*, but he was disappointed in the exhibition. That at least seemed the meaning of two or three comprehensive groans which, as he lounged on my big divan, his leg folded under him, looking at my latest drawings, issued from his lips with the smoke of the cigarette.

"What's the matter with you?" I asked.

"What's the matter with *you?*"

"Nothing save that I'm mystified."

"You are indeed. You're quite off the hinge. What's the meaning of this new fad?" And he tossed me, with visible irreverence, a drawing in which I happened to have depicted both my elegant models. I asked if he didn't think it good, and he replied that it struck him as execrable, given the sort of thing I had always represented myself to him as wishing to arrive at; but I let that pass—I was so anxious to see exactly what he meant. The two figures in the picture looked colossal, but I supposed this was *not* what he meant, inasmuch as, for aught he knew to the contrary, I might have been trying for some such effect. I maintained that I was working exactly in the same way as when he last had done me the honor to tell me I might do something some day. "Well, there's a screw loose somewhere," he answered, "wait a bit and I'll discover it." I depended upon him to do so: where else was the fresh eye? But he produced at last nothing more luminous than "I don't know—I don't like your types." This was lame for a critic who had never consented to discuss with me anything but the question of execution, the direction of strokes and the mystery of values.

"In the drawings you've been looking at I think my types are very handsome."

"Oh they won't do!"

"I've been working with new models."

"I see you have. *They* won't do."

"Are you very sure of that?"

"Absolutely—they're stupid."

"You mean *I* am—for I ought to get round that."

"You *can't*—with such people. Who are they?"

I told him, so far as was necessary, and he concluded heartlessly: "Ce sort des gens qu'il faut mettre à la porte."[4]

"You've never seen them; they're awfully good"—I flew to their defense.

"Not seen them? Why all this recent work of yours drops to pieces with them. It's all I want to see of them."

"No one else has said anything against it—the *Cheapside* people are pleased."

"Every one else is an ass, and the *Cheapside* people the biggest asses of all. Come, don't pretend at this time of day to have pretty illusions about the public, especially about publishers and editors. It's not for *such* animals you work—it's for those who know, *coloro che sanno;*[5]

---

4. That kind of person should be shown the door.

5. Dante, *The Divine Comedy,* "The Inferno," 4:131: actually, *color che sanno* —"those who know."

so keep straight for *me* if you can't keep straight for yourself. There was a certain sort of thing you used to try for—and a very good thing it was. But this twaddle isn't *in* it." When I talked with Hawley later about "Rutland Ramsay" and its possible successors he declared that I must get back into my boat again or I should go to the bottom. His voice in short was the voice of warning.

I noted the warning, but I didn't turn my friends out of doors. They bored me a good deal; but the very fact that they bored me admonished me not to sacrifice them—if there was anything to be done with them—simply to irritation. As I look back at this phase they seem to me to have pervaded my life not a little. I have a vision of them as most of the time in my studio, seated against the wall on an old velvet bench to be out of the way, and resembling the while a pair of patient courtiers in a royal ante-chamber. I'm convinced that during the coldest weeks of the winter they held their ground because it saved them fire. Their newness was losing its gloss, and it was impossible not to feel them objects of charity. Whenever Miss Churm arrived they went away, and after I was fairly launched in "Rutland Ramsay" Miss Churm arrived pretty often. They managed to express to me tacitly that they supposed I wanted her for the low life of the book, and I let them suppose it, since they had attempted to study the work—it was lying about the studio—without discovering that it dealt only with the highest circles. They had dipped into the most brilliant of our novelists without deciphering many passages. I still took an hour from them, now and again, in spite of Jack Hawley's warning: it would be time enough to dismiss them, if dismissal should be necessary, when the rigor of the season was over. Hawley had made their acquaintance—he had met them at my fireside—and thought them a ridiculous pair. Learning that he was a painter they tried to approach him, to show him too that they were the real thing; but he looked at them, across the big room, as if they were miles away: they were a compendium of everything he most objected to in the social system of his country. Such people as that, all convention and patent-leather, with ejaculations that stopped conversation, had no business in a studio. A studio was a place to learn to see, and how could you see through a pair of feather-beds?

The main inconvenience I suffered at their hands was that at first I was shy of letting it break upon them that my artful little servant had begun to sit to me for "Rutland Ramsay." They knew I had been odd enough—they were prepared by this time to allow oddity to artists—to pick a foreign vagabond out of the streets when I might have had a person with whiskers and credentials; but it was some time before they learned how high I rated his accomplishments. They found him in an attitude more than once, but they never doubted I was doing him as an organ-grinder. There were several things they never guessed, and one of them was that for a striking scene in the novel, in which a footman briefly figured, it occurred to me to make use of Major Monarch as the menial. I kept putting this off, I didn't like to ask him to don the livery—besides the difficulty of finding a livery to fit him. At last, one day late in the winter, when I was at work on the despised Oronte, who caught one's idea on the wing, and was in the glow of feeling myself go very straight, they came in, the Major and his wife, with their society laugh about nothing(there was less and less to laugh at); came in like country-callers—they always reminded me of that— who have walked across the park after church and are presently persuaded to stay to luncheon. Luncheon was over, but they could stay to tea—I knew they wanted it. The fit was on me, however, and I couldn't let my ardor cool and my work wait, with the fading daylight, while my model prepared it. So I asked Mrs. Monarch if she would mind laying it out—a request which for an instant brought all the blood to her face. Her eyes were on her husband's for a second, and some mute telegraphy passed between them. Their folly was over the next instant; his cheerful shrewdness put an end to it. So far from pitying their wounded pride, I must add, I was moved to give it as complete a lesson as I could. They bustled about together and got out the cups and saucers and made the kettle boil. I know they felt as if they were waiting on my servant, and when the tea was prepared I said: "He'll have a cup, please—he's tired." Mrs. Monarch brought him one where he stood, and he took it from her as if he had been a gentleman at a party squeezing a crush-hat with an elbow.

Then it came over me that she had made a great effort for me— made it with a kind of nobleness—and that I owed her a compensation. Each time I saw her after this I wondered what the compensation could be. I couldn't go on doing the wrong thing to oblige them. Oh it *was* the wrong thing, the stamp of the work for which they sat— Hawley was not the only person to say it now. I sent in a large number of the drawings I had made for "Rutland Ramsay," and I received a warning that was more to the point than Hawley's. The artistic adviser of the house for which I was working was of opinion that many of my illustrations were not what had been looked for. Most of these illustrations were the subjects in which the Monarchs had figured. Without going into the question of what *had* been looked for, I had to face the fact that at this rate I shouldn't get the other books to do. I hurled myself in despair on Miss Churm—I put her through all her paces. I not only adopted Oronte publicly as my hero, but one morning when the Major looked in to see if I didn't require him to finish a *Cheapside* figure for which he had begun to sit the week before, I told him I had changed my mind—I'd do the drawing from my man. At this my visitor turned pale and stood looking at me. "Is *he* your idea of an English gentleman?" he asked.

I was disappointed, I was nervous, I wanted to get on with my work; so I replied with irritation: "Oh my dear Major—I can't be ruined for *you!*"

It was a horrid speech, but he stood another moment—after which, without a word, he quitted the studio. I drew a long breath, for I said to myself that I shouldn't see him again. I hadn't told him definitely that I was in danger of having my work rejected, but I was vexed at his not having felt the catastrophe in the air, read with me the moral of our fruitless collaboration, the lesson that in the deceptive atmosphere of art even the highest respectability may fail of being plastic.

I didn't owe my friends money, but I did see them again. They reappeared together three days later, and, given all the other facts, there was something tragic in that one. It was a clear proof they could find nothing else in life to do. They had threshed the matter out in a dismal conference—they had digested the bad news that they were not in for the series. If they weren't useful to me even for the *Cheapside* their function seemed difficult to determine, and I could only judge at first that they had come, forgivingly, decorously, to take a last leave. This made me rejoice in secret that I had little leisure for a scene; for I had placed both my other models in position together and I was pegging at a drawing from which I hoped to derive glory. It had been suggested by the passage in which Rutland Ramsay, drawing up a chair to Artemisia's piano-stool, says extraordinary things to her while she ostensibly fingers out a difficult piece of music. I had done Miss Churm at the piano before—it was an attitude in which she knew how to take on an absolutely poetic grace. I wished the two figures to "compose" together with intensity, and my little Italian had entered perfectly into my conception. The pair were vividly before me, the piano had been pulled out; it was a charming show of blended youth and murmured love, which I had only to catch and keep. My visitors stood and looked at it, and I was friendly to them over my shoulder.

They made no response, but I was used to silent company and went on with my work, only a little disconcerted—even though exhilarated by the sense that *this* was at least the ideal thing—at not having got rid of them after all. Presently I heard Mrs. Monarch's sweet voice beside or rather above me: "I wish her hair were a little better done." I looked up and she was staring with a strange fixedness at Miss Churm, whose back was turned to her. "Do you mind my just touching it?" she went on—a question which made me spring up for an instant as with the instinctive fear that she might do the young lady a harm. But she quieted me with a glance I shall never forget—I confess I should like to have been able to paint *that*—and went for a moment to my model. She spoke to her softly, laying a hand on her shoulder and bending over her; and as the girl, understanding, gratefully assented, she disposed her rough curls, with a few quick passes, in such a way as to make Miss Churm's head twice as charming. It was one of the most heroic personal services I've ever seen rendered. Then Mrs. Monarch turned away with a low sigh and, looking about her as if for something to do, stooped to the floor with a noble humility and picked up a dirty rag that had dropped out of my paint-box.

The Major meanwhile had also been looking for something to do, and, wandering to the other end of the studio, saw before him my breakfast-things neglected, unremoved. "I say, can't I be useful *here?*" he called out to me with an irrepressible quaver. I assented with a laugh that I fear was awkward, and for the next ten minutes, while I worked, I heard the light clatter of china and the tinkle of spoons and glass. Mrs. Monarch assisted her husband—they washed up my crockery, they put it away. They wandered off into my little scullery, and I afterwards found that they had cleaned my knives and that my slender stock of plate had an unprecedented surface. When it came over me, the latent eloquence of what they were doing, I confess that my drawing was blurred for a moment—the picture swam. They had accepted their failure, but they couldn't accept their fate. They had

heads in bewilderment to the perverse and cruel law in
ich the real thing could be so much less precious than the
hey didn't want to starve. If my servants were my models,
dels might be my servants. They would reverse the parts—
the others would sit for the ladies and gentlemen and *they* would do
the work. They would still be in the studio—it was an intense dumb
appeal to me not to turn them out. "Take us on," they wanted to
say—"we'll do *anything*."

My pencil dropped from my hand; my sitting was spoiled and I got
rid of my sitters, who were also evidently rather mystified and awe-
struck. Then, alone with the Major and his wife I had a most uncomfortable moment. He put their prayer into a single sentence: "I say,
you know—just let *us* do for you, can't you?" I couldn't—it was
dreadful to see them emptying my slops; but I pretended I could, to
oblige them, for about a week. Then I gave them a sum of money to
go away, and I never saw them again. I obtained the remaining books,
but my friend Hawley repeats that Major and Mrs. Monarch did me a
permanent harm, got me into false ways. If it be true I'm content to
have paid the price—for the memory.

1893

DORIS LESSING

Our Friend Judith

I stopped inviting Judith to meet people when a Canadian woman
remarked, with the satisfied fervor of one who has at last pinned a
label on a rare specimen: "She is, of course, one of your typical English
spinsters."

This was a few weeks after an American sociologist, having elicited
from Judith the facts that she was fortyish, unmarried, and living
alone, had inquired of me: "I suppose she has given up?" "Given up
what?" I asked; and the subsequent discussion was unrewarding.

Judith did not easily come to parties. She would come after pressure, not so much—one felt—to do one a favor, but in order to correct
what she believed to be a defect in her character. "I really ought to
enjoy meeting new people more than I do," she said once. We reverted to an earlier pattern of our friendship: odd evenings together,
an occasional visit to the cinema, or she would telephone to say: "I'm
on my way past you to the British Museum. Would you care for a
cup of coffee with me? I have twenty minutes to spare."

It is characteristic of Judith that the word "spinster," used of her,
provoked fascinated speculation about other people. There are my
aunts, for instance: aged seventy-odd, both unmarried, one an ex-
missionary from China, one a retired matron of a famous London hospital. These two old ladies live together under the shadow of the
cathedral in a country town. They devote much time to the Church,

to good causes, to letter writing with friends all over the world, to the grandchildren and the great-grandchildren of relatives. It would be a mistake, however, on entering a house in which nothing has been moved for fifty years, to diagnose a condition of fossilized late-Victorian integrity. They read every book reviewed in the *Observer* or the *Times*,[1] so that I recently got a letter from Aunt Rose inquiring whether I did not think that the author of *On the Road*[2] was not—perhaps?—exaggerating his difficulties. They know a good deal about music, and write letters of encouragement to young composers they feel are being neglected—"You must understand that anything new and original takes time to be understood." Well-informed and critical Tories, they are as likely to dispatch telegrams of protest to the Home Secretary[3] as letters of support. These ladies, my aunts Emily and Rose, are surely what is meant by the phrase "English spinster." And yet, once the connection has been pointed out, there is no doubt that Judith and they are spiritual cousins, if not sisters. Therefore it follows that one's pitying admiration for women who have supported manless and uncomforted lives needs a certain modification?

One will, of course, never know; and I feel now that it is entirely my fault that I shall never know. I had been Judith's friend for upwards of five years before the incident occurred which I involuntarily thought of—stupidly enough—as the first time Judith's mask slipped.

A mutual friend, Betty, had been given a cast-off Dior[4] dress. She was too short for it. Also she said: "It's not a dress for a married woman with three children and a talent for cooking. I don't know why not, but it isn't." Judith was the right build. Therefore one evening the three of us met by appointment in Judith's bedroom, with the dress. Neither Betty nor I was surprised at the renewed discovery that Judith was beautiful. We had both often caught each other, and ourselves, in moments of envy when Judith's calm and severe face, her undemonstratively perfect body, succeeded in making everyone else in a room or a street look cheap.

Judith is tall, small-breasted, slender. Her light brown hair is parted in the center and cut straight around her neck. A high straight forehead, straight nose, a full grave mouth are setting for her eyes, which are green, large and prominent. Her lids are very white, fringed with gold, and molded close over the eyeball, so that in profile she has the look of a staring gilded mask. The dress was of dark green glistening stuff, cut straight, with a sort of loose tunic. It opened simply at the throat. In it Judith could of course evoke nothing but classical images. Diana, perhaps, back from the hunt, in a relaxed moment? A rather intellectual wood nymph who had opted for an afternoon in the British Museum Reading Room? Something like that. Neither Betty nor I said a word, since Judith was examining herself in a long mirror, and must know she looked magnificent.

---

1. Prestigious London newspapers representing roughly the younger more liberal establishment and the Establishment proper.
2. Jack Kerouac (1922–69), leader of the beatniks, 1950s forerunners of the hippies. Kerouac heroes felt themselves completely cut off from and victimized by American society.
3. Head of the British government department responsible for domestic matters.
4. Famous French designer of high fashions.

Slowly she drew off the dress and laid it aside. Slowly she put on the old cord skirt and woolen blouse she had taken off. She must have surprised a resigned glance between us, for she then remarked, with the smallest of mocking smiles: "One surely ought to stay in character, wouldn't you say?" She added, reading the words out of some invisible book, written not by her, since it was a very vulgar book, but perhaps by one of us: "It does everything *for* me, I must admit."

"After seeing you in it," Betty cried out, defying her, "I can't bear for anyone else to have it. I shall simply put it away." Judith shrugged, rather irritated. In the shapeless skirt and blouse, and without makeup, she stood smiling at us, a woman at whom forty-nine out of fifty people would not look twice.

A second revelatory incident occurred soon after. Betty telephoned me to say that Judith had a kitten. Did I know that Judith adored cats? "No, but of course she would," I said.

Betty lived in the same street as Judith and saw more of her than I did. I was kept posted about the growth and habits of the cat and its effect on Judith's life. She remarked for instance that she felt it was good for her to have a tie and some responsibility. But no sooner was the cat out of kittenhood than all the neighbors complained. It was a tomcat, ungelded, and making every night hideous. Finally the landlord said that either the cat or Judith must go, unless she was prepared to have the cat "fixed."[5] Judith wore herself out trying to find some person, anywhere in Britain, who would be prepared to take the cat. This person would, however, have to sign a written statement not to have the cat "fixed." When Judith took the cat to the vet to be killed, Betty told me she cried for twenty-four hours.

"She didn't think of compromising? After all, perhaps the cat might have preferred to live, if given the choice?"

"Is it likely I'd have the nerve to say anything so sloppy to Judith? It's the nature of a male cat to rampage lustfully about, and therefore it would be morally wrong for Judith to have the cat fixed, simply to suit her own convenience."

"She said that?"

"She wouldn't have to *say* it, surely?"

A third incident was when she allowed a visiting young American, living in Paris, the friend of a friend and scarcely known to her, to use her flat while she visited her parents over Christmas. The young man and his friends lived it up for ten days of alcohol and sex and marijuana, and when Judith came back it took a week to get the place clean again and the furniture mended. She telephoned twice to Paris, the first time to say that he was a disgusting young thug and if he knew what was good for him he would keep out of her way in the future; the second time to apologize for losing her temper. "I had a choice either to let someone use my flat, or to leave it empty. But having chosen that you should have it, it was clearly an unwarrantable infringement of your liberty to make any conditions at all.

---

5. Gelded, castrated.

her. He can't possibly understand her. He calls her Judy."

"Good God."

"Yes. But I was wondering. Suppose the other two called her Judy '—little Judy'—imagine it! Isn't it awful? But it does rather throw a light on Judith?"

"It's rather touching."

"I suppose it's touching. But *I* was embarrassed—oh, not because of the situation. Because of how she was, with him. 'Judy, is there another cup of tea in that pot?' And she, rather daughterly and demure, pouring him one."

"Three of the nights he went to her bedroom with her—very casual about it, because she was being. But he was not there in the mornings. So I asked her. You know how it is when you ask her a question. As if you've been having long conversations on that very subject for years and years, and she is merely continuing where you left off last. So when she says something surprising, one feels such a fool to be surprised?"

"Yes. And then?"

"I asked her if she was sorry not to have children. She said yes, but one couldn't have everything."

"One can't have everything, she said?"

"Quite clearly feeling she *has* nearly everything. She said she thought it was a pity, because she would have brought up children very well."

"When you come to think of it, she would, too."

"I asked about marriage, but she said on the whole the role of a mistress suited her better."

"She used the word 'mistress'?"

"You must admit it's the accurate word."

"I suppose so."

"And then she said that while she liked intimacy and sex and everything, she enjoyed waking up in the morning alone and *her own person*."

"Yes, *of course*."

"Of course. but now she's bothered because the professor would like to marry her. Or he feels he ought. At least, he's getting all guilty and obsessive about it. She says she doesn't see the point of divorce, and anyway, surely it would be very hard on his poor old wife after all these years, particularly after bringing up two children so satisfactorily. She talks about his wife as if she's a kind of nice old charwoman, and it wouldn't be *fair* to sack her, you know. Anyway. What with one thing and another. Judith's going off to Italy soon in order *to collect herself*."

"But how's she going to pay for it?"

"Luckily the Third Program's[8] commissioning her to do some arty programs. They offered her a choice of The Cid—El Thid,[9] you know

---

8. British Broadcasting Corporation public radio service (and now also television channel) specializing in classical music, literature and plays, lectures, etc.

9. Castilian, standard Spanish, pronunciation of El Cid, the title of an eleventh-century soldier-hero and hero of many works of literature.

—and the Borgias. Well, the Borghese, then. And Judith settled for the Borgias."

"The Borgias," I said, "*Judith?*"

"Yes, quite. I said that too, in that tone of voice. She saw my point. She says the epic is right up her street, whereas the Renaissance has never been on her wave length. Obviously it couldn't be, all the magnificence and cruelty and *dirt*. But of course chivalry and a high moral code and all those idiotically noble goings-on are right on her wave length."

"Is the money the same?"

"Yes. But is it likely Judith would let money decide? No, she said that one should always choose something new, that isn't up one's street. Well, because it's better for her character, and so on, to get herself unsettled by the Renaissance. She didn't say *that*, of course."

"Of course not."

Judith went to Florence; and for some months postcards informed us tersely of her doings. Then Betty decided she must go by herself for a holiday. She had been appalled by the discovery that if her husband was away for a night she couldn't sleep; and when he went to Australia for three weeks, she stopped living until he came back. She had discussed this with him, and he had agreed that if she really felt the situation to be serious, he would dispatch her by air, to Italy, in order to recover her self-respect. As she put it.

I got this letter from her: "It's no use, I'm coming home. I might have known. Better face it, once you're really married you're not fit for man nor beast. And if you remember what I used to be like! *Well!* I moped around Milan. I sunbathed in Venice, then I thought my tan was surely worth something, so I was on the point of starting an affair with another lonely soul, but I lost heart, and went to Florence to see Judith. She wasn't there. She'd gone to the Italian Riviera. I had nothing better to do, so I followed her. When I saw the place I wanted to laugh, it's so much not Judith, you know, all those palms and umbrellas and gaiety at all costs and ever such an ornamental blue sea. Judith is in an enormous stone room up on the hillside above the sea, with grape vines all over the place. You should see her, she's got beautiful. It seems for the last fifteen years she's been going to Soho[1] every Saturday morning to buy food at an Italian shop. I must have looked surprised, because she explained she liked Soho. I suppose because all that dreary vice and nudes and prostitutes and everything prove how right she is to be as she is? She told the people in the shop she was going to Italy, and the *signora*[2] said, what a coincidence, she was going back to Italy too, and she did hope an old friend like Miss Castlewell would visit her there. Judith said to me: 'I felt lacking, when she used the word friend. Our relations have always been formal. Can you understand it?' she said to me. 'For fifteen years,' I said to her. She said: 'I think I must feel it's a kind of imposition, don't you know, expecting people to feel friendship for

1. A section of London roughly equivalent to Greenwich Village in New York— foreign restaurants and groceries, haunt of writers, painters, etc.—but in recent years increasingly known for prostitutes and pornography.
2. Proprietress.

one.' *Well.* I said: 'You ought to understand it, because you're like that yourself.' 'Am I?' she said. 'Well, think about it,' I said. But I could see she didn't want to think about it. Anyway, she's here, and I've spent a week with her. The widow Maria Rineiri inherited her mother's house, so she came home, from Soho. On the ground floor is a tatty little *rosticceria*[3] patronized by the neighbors. They are all working people. This isn't tourist country, up on the hill. The widow lives above the shop with her little boy, a nasty little brat of about ten. Say what you like, the English are the only people who know how to bring up children, I don't care if that's insular. Judith's room is at the back, with a balcony. Underneath her room is the barber's shop, and the barber is Luigi Rineiri, the widow's younger brother. Yes, I was keeping him until the last. He is about forty, tall dark handsome, a great *bull*, but rather a sweet fatherly bull. He has cut Judith's hair and made it lighter. Now it looks like a sort of gold helmet. Judith is all brown. The widow Rineiri has made her a white dress and a green dress. They fit, for a change. When Judith walks down the street to the lower town, all the Italian males take one look at the golden girl and melt in their own oil like ice cream. Judith takes all this in her stride. She sort of acknowledges the homage. Then she strolls into the sea and vanishes into the foam. She swims five miles every day. *Naturally.* I haven't asked Judith whether she has collected herself, because you can see she hasn't. The widow Rineiri is matchmaking. When I noticed this I wanted to laugh, but luckily I didn't because Judith asked me, really wanting to know: 'Can you see me married to an Italian barber?' (Not being snobbish, but stating the position, so to speak.) 'Well yes,' I said, 'you're the only woman I know who I can see married to an Italian barber.' Because it wouldn't matter who she married, she'd always be her *own person.* 'At any rate, for a time,' I said. At which she said, asperously:[4] 'You can use phrases like for a time in England but not in Italy.' Did you ever see England, at least London, as the home of license, liberty and free love? No, neither did I, but of course she's right. Married to Luigi it would be the family, the neighbors, the church and the *bambini.*[5] All the same she's thinking about it, believe it or not. Here she's quite different, all relaxed and free. She's melting in the attention she gets. The widow mothers her and makes her coffee all the time, and listens to a lot of good advice about how to bring up that nasty brat of hers. Unluckily she doesn't take it. Luigi is crazy for her. At mealtimes she goes to the *trattoria*[6] in the upper square and all the workmen treat her like a goddess. Well, a film star then. I said to her, you're mad to come home. For one thing her rent is ten bob[7] a week, and you eat *pasta* and drink red wine till you bust for about one and sixpence. No, she said, it would be nothing but self-indulgence to stay. Why? I said. She said, she's got nothing to stay for. (Ho ho.) And besides, she's done her research on the Borghese, though so far she can't see her way to an honest presentation of the facts. What made these people

3. Grill.
4. Sharply, harshly.
5. Children.
6. Restaurant.
7. Shillings. There are twenty shillings to the pound; *one and sixpence* below is one and a half shillings. Living in Italy at the time was very inexpensive by British standards.

tick? she wants to know. And so she's only staying because of the cat. I forgot to mention the cat. This is a town of cats. The Italians here love their cats. I wanted to feed a stray cat at the table, but the waiter said no; and after lunch, all the waiters came with trays crammed with leftover food and stray cats came from everywhere to eat. And at dark when the tourists go in to feed and the beach is empty—you know how empty and forlorn a beach is at dusk?—well cats appear from everywhere. The beach seems to move, then you see it's cats. They go stalking along the thin inch of gray water at the edge of the sea, shaking their paws crossly at each step, snatching at the dead little fish, and throwing them with their mouths up onto the dry sand. Then they scamper after them. You've never seen such a snarling and fighting. At dawn when the fishing boats come in to the empty beach, the cats are there in dozens. The fishermen throw them bits of fish. The cats snarl and fight over it. Judith gets up early and goes down to watch. Sometimes Luigi goes too, being tolerant. Because what he really likes is to join the evening promenade with Judith on his arm around and around the square of the upper town. Showing her off. Can you *see* Judith? But she does it. Being tolerant. But she smiles and enjoys the attention she gets, there's no doubt of it.

"She has a cat in her room. It's a kitten really, but it's pregnant. Judith says she can't leave until the kittens are born. The cat is too young to have kittens. Imagine Judith. She sits on her bed in that great stone room, with her bare feet on the stone floor, and watches the cat, and tries to work out why a healthy uninhibited Italian cat always fed on the best from the *rosticceria* should be neurotic. Because it is. When it sees Judith watching it gets nervous and starts licking at the roots of its tail. But Judith goes on watching, and says about Italy that the reason why the English love the Italians is because the Italians make the English feel superior. They have no discipline. And that's a despicable reason for one nation to love another. Then she talks about Luigi and says he has no sense of guilt, but a sense of sin; whereas she has no sense of sin but she has guilt. I haven't asked her if this has been an insuperable barrier, because judging from how she looks, it hasn't. She says she would rather have a sense of sin, because sin can be attoned for, and if she understood sin, perhaps she would be more at home with the Renaissance. Luigi is very healthy, she says, and not neurotic. He is a Catholic of course. He doesn't mind that she's an atheist. His mother has explained to him that the English are all pagans, but good people at heart. I suppose he thinks a few smart sessions with the local priest would set Judith on the right path for good and all. Meanwhile the cat walks nervously around the room, stopping to lick, and when it can't stand Judith watching it another second, it rolls over on the floor, with its paws tucked up, and rolls up its eyes, and Judith scratches its lumpy pregnant stomach and tells it to relax. It makes *me* nervous to see her, it's not like her. I don't know why. Then Luigi shouts up from the barber's shop, then he comes up and stands at the door laughing, and Judith laughs, and the widow says: Children, enjoy yourselves. And off they go, walking down to the town eating ice cream. The cat

"Yes, I know."

"He said she was too young, and she was badly frightened and very hurt. He took the alive kitten to her but she got up and walked away. She didn't want it. Then Luigi told me not to look. But I followed him. He held the kitten by the tail and he banged it against the wall twice. Then he dropped it into the rubbish heap. He moved aside some rubbish with his toe, and put the kitten there and pushed rubbish over it. Then Luigi said the cat should be destroyed. He said she was badly hurt and it would always hurt her to have kittens."

"He hasn't destroyed her. She's still alive. But it looks to me as if he were right."

"Yes, I expect he was."

"What upset you—that he killed the kitten?"

"Oh no, I expect the cat would if he hadn't. But that isn't the point, is it?"

"What is the point?"

"I don't think I really know." She had been speaking breathlessly, and fast. Now she said slowly: "It's not a question of right or wrong, is it? Why should it be? It's a question of what one is. That night Luigi wanted to go promenading with me. For him, that was *that*. Something had to be done, and he'd done it. But I felt ill. He was very nice to me. He's a very good person," she said, defiantly.

"Yes, he looks it."

"That night I couldn't sleep. I was blaming myself. I should never have left the cat to go swimming. Well, and then I decided to leave the next day. And I did. And that's all. The whole thing was a mistake from start to finish."

"Going to Italy at all?"

"Oh, to go for a holiday would have been all right."

"You've done all that work for nothing? You mean you aren't going to make use of all that research?"

"No. It was a mistake."

"Why don't you leave it a few weeks and see how things are then?"

"Why?"

"You might feel differently about it."

"What an extraordinary thing to say. Why should I? Oh, you mean, time passing, healing wounds—that sort of thing? What an extraordinary idea. It's always seemed to me an extraordinary idea. No, right from the beginning I've felt ill at ease with the whole business, not myself at all."

"Rather irrationally, I should have said."

Judith considered this, very seriously. She frowned while she thought it over. Then she said: "But if one cannot rely on what one feels, what can one rely on?"

"On what one thinks, I should have expected you to say."

"Should you? Why? Really, you people are all very strange. I don't understand you." She turned off the electric fire, and her face closed up. She smiled, friendly and distant, and said: "I don't really see any point at all in discussing it."

1963

5   SYMBOLS

One of the chief devices for bridging the gap between the writer's vision and the reader's is the **symbol,** commonly defined as something that stands for something else: a flower, for example, may be seen as a symbol of a particular state. But notice that symbols are generally **figurative;** that is, they compare or put together two *unlike* things. A senator may represent a state, but he represents it *literally*: the state is a governmental unit, and the senator is a member of the government. But the flower has little to do with governing the state, and so represents it only figuratively.

But why speak of anything in terms of something else? Is there no nonarbitrary reason why snakes are commonly symbolic of evil? Sure, some snakes are poisonous, but for some people so are bees, and a lot of snakes are not only harmless but actually helpful ecologically. (In Kipling's *The Jungle Book* the python Ka, while frightening, is on the side of Law and Order.) Through repeated use over the centuries, the snake has become a traditional symbol of Evil—not just danger, sneakiness, repulsiveness, but theological, absolute Evil. Had Macomber been startled by a snake during the lion hunt, we would not necessarily have said, "Aha—snake, symbol of Evil," though that potential meaning might have hovered around the incident and sent us looking backward and forward in the story for supporting evidence that this snake was indeed being used symbolically. However, when we discover that the stranger in *Young Goodman Brown* has a walking stick upon which is carved the image of a snake, we are much more likely to find it such a symbol because of other, related potential symbols or meanings in the context: the term *Goodman* in the title of the story sets up the distinct possibility that Brown (how common a name) stands for more than a "mere" individual young man. Brown's bride is named Faith—a common name among the early Puritans, but, together with Goodman, suggesting symbolic possibilities. Then, just before the stranger with the walking stick appears, Brown says, "What if the devil himself should be at my very elbow!"

A single item, even something as traditionally fraught with meaning as a snake or a rose, becomes a symbol only when its potentially symbolic meaning is confirmed by something else in the story, just as a point needs a second point to define a line. Multiple symbols, potential symbols, direct and indirect hints, such as Brown's mention of the devil: these are among the ways in which details may be identified as symbols (for interpreting symbols is relatively easy once you know what is and what is probably not a symbol).

One form of what may be called an indirect hint is repetition. That an "old maid" like Judith should have a cat seems so ordinary it borders on the trite. But when she chooses to have her male cat put to death rather than neutered, it makes us sit up and take notice, doesn't it? This choice may suggest something about the unconventional in her character, but we probably don't think of the cat in itself representing anything. What happens, though, when there appears another cat, a female this time, whose sex life calls forth strange behavior on

Judith's part? And when the killing of a kitten interrupts Judith's affair with Luigi? It is difficult to say when or if the literal cats shade off into symbols, for they remain so solidly cats in the story. All we can say for sure is that cats become more important in reading and understanding this story than, say, the cask of Amontillado does in the Poe story. The cask remains a thing pure and simple. Repetition, then, calls attention to details and may alert us to potential symbolic overtones, but it does not necessarily turn a thing into a symbol; so long as we get the suggestions of significance, however, agreeing on exactly what—or when—something can be called a symbol is not important.

Direct hints may take the form of explicit statements. (Authors are not so anxious to hide their meanings as some readers are prone to believe.) We also may be alerted to the fact that something is standing for something else when the something does not seem to make literal sense in itself. It does not take us long to realize that *Young Goodman Brown* is not entirely as realistic a story as *Bovanne* or *Macomber*. When things do not seem explicable in terms of everyday reality, we often look beyond them for some meaning, as we do in *The Lottery*. Roses are real enough, but neither Faulkner's narrator nor anyone else in the story gives Emily a real rose. What, then, does the rose in the title *A Rose for Emily* suggest?

We must remember, however, that symbols do not exist solely for the transmission of a meaning we can paraphrase; they do not disappear from the story, our memory, or our response once their "meaning" has been sucked out of them, any more than Francis Macomber ceases to exist as an individual after we recognize his representative or universal nature. Faith's pink ribbons and Judith's cats are objects in their stories, whatever meanings or suggestions of meanings they have given rise to.

As I've often implied and occasionally said, few symbols can be exhausted, translated into an abstract phrase or equivalent: the "something else" that the "something" stands for is ultimately elusive. When you get to the scene in *The Artificial Nigger* in which Nelson and his grandfather are brought back together by their puzzlement over the function of the statue of a little black jockey, a once-common and now unlamentably rare suburban lawn decoration, try to paraphrase exactly what the "artificial nigger" stands for. Or explain with certainty what Faith's pink ribbon symbolizes. It is not that the statue and the ribbon mean nothing but that they mean so many things that no one equivalence will do; even an abstract statement seems to reduce rather than fully explain the significance for the reader. Yes, the "artificial nigger" is a mystery that unites the boy and his grandfather in their ignorance, but is that the whole meaning of the story's description of the statue as "some monument to another's victory that brought them together in their common defeat"? Do any other incidents involving blacks in the story—on the train, on the city streets— relate to the statue? How does "artificial" fit in? And how about the tone? The phrase is offensive and suggests prejudice and ignorance; but the incident and ignorance are a little funny, too, and pathetic. Are this incident and this symbol representative of the tone of the story as a whole? Or disruptive of it? It seems to me the statue appropriately encapsulates the unsettling, frightening, and revealing experiences of grandfather and grandson in the city, but I'm not sure I could say everything I think the "artificial nigger" means or all the feelings it generates.

When a figure is expressed as an explicit comparison, often signaled by *like* or *as*, it is called a **simile**: "eyes as blue as the sky"; "the baby brother I'd never known looked out from the depths of his private life, like an animal waiting to be coaxed into the light" (*Sonny's Blues*). An implicit comparison or identification of one thing with another unlike itself, without a verbal signal but just seeming to say "A *is* B," is called a **metaphor**: "The sea was a sheet of glass"; "the grass was a green carpet"; "there was a boiling wave of dogs about them" (*The Old People*). Sometimes all figures are loosely referred to as metaphors. There is another figure of speech, which seems to border on the one hand on representation and on the other on symbol —the **synechdoche**, a figure in which the part stands for the whole, as when a whole creature of terror is called up by the word "Jaws."

An **allegory** is like a metaphor in that one thing (usually non-rational, abstract, religious) is implicitly spoken of in terms of something that is concrete and usually sensuous (perceptible by the senses), but the comparison in allegory is extended to include a whole work or a large portion of a work. *The Pilgrim's Progress* is probably the most famous prose allegory in English; its central character is named Christian; he was born in the City of Destruction and sets out for the Celestial City, passes through the Slough of Despond and Vanity Fair, meets men named Pliable and Obstinate, and so on.

When an entire story, like *The Lottery*, is symbolic, it is sometimes called a **myth**. *Myth* originally meant a story of communal origin that provided an explanation or religious interpretation of man, nature, the universe, and the relation between them. From the vantage point of another culture or set of beliefs, the word usually implied that the story was false: we speak of classical myths, but Christians do not speak of Christian myth. We also apply the term *myth* now to stories by individuals, sophisticated authors, but often there is still the implication that the mythic story relates to a communal or group experience, whereas a symbolic story may be more personal or private. It is hard to draw the line firmly: *The Lottery* seems to have clearly national, American implications, while *The Rocking-Horse Winner* may be a private Lawrencian symbol or a myth of modern bourgeois society. A plot or character element that recurs in cultural or cross-cultural myths, such as images of the devil, as in *Young Goodman Brown*, is now widely called an **archetype**.

A symbol can be as brief and local as a metaphor or as extended as an allegory, and like an allegory usually speaks in concrete terms of the non- or super-rational, the abstract, that which is not immediately perceived by the senses. Though some allegories can be complex, with many layers or levels of equivalence, and some symbols can be very simple, with paraphrasable equivalences, allegory usually refers to a one-to-one relationhip (as the names from *The Pilgrim's Progress* imply), and literary symbols usually have highly complex or even inexpressible equivalences. *The Lottery* may be considered a symbolic story, but precisely what it "stands for" is extremely difficult to express briefly and satisfactorily—New England Puritanism? Man's cruelty to man? Original Sin? The dulling of human sensibility by ritualistic actions? The use of a scapegoat to suffer for the sins of the community? The operation of chance rather than justice or morality in the universe? It seems to partake of all these meanings but to limit itself to none. It creates a new meaning which seems to stand for a kind of human communal activity for which there is no other satisfactory name. That is what we mean by a symbol—something that cannot be paraphrased, something that has areas of meaning or implication that cannot be wholly rendered in other terms or conveniently separated from the particulars of the work. The unparaphrasable nature of symbolic images or stories is not vagueness but richness, not disorder but complexity.

NATHANIEL HAWTHORNE

Young Goodman Brown

Young Goodman Brown came forth, at sunset, into the street of Salem village,[1] but put his head back, after crossing the threshold, to exchange a parting kiss with his young wife. And Faith, as the wife was aptly named, thrust her own pretty head into the street, letting the wind play with the pink ribbons of her cap, while she called to Goodman Brown.

"Dearest heart," whispered she, softly and rather sadly, when her lips were close to his ear, "pr'y thee, put off your journey until sunrise, and sleep in your own bed tonight. A lone woman is troubled with such dreams and such thoughts, that she's afeard of herself, sometimes. Pray, tarry with me this night, dear husband, of all nights in the year!"

"My love and my Faith," replied young Goodman Brown, "of all nights in the year, this one night must I tarry away from thee. My journey, as thou callest it, forth and back again, must needs be done 'twixt now and sunrise. What, my sweet, pretty wife, dost thou doubt me already, and we but three months married!"

"Then, God bless you!" said Faith, with the pink ribbons, "and may you find all well, when you come back."

"Amen!" cried Goodman Brown. "Say thy prayers, dear Faith, and go to bed at dusk, and no harm will come to thee."

So they parted; and the young man pursued his way, until, being about to turn the corner by the meeting-house, he looked back, and saw the head of Faith still peeping after him, with a melancholy air, in spite of her pink ribbons.

"Poor little Faith!" thought he, for his heart smote him. "What a

1. Salem, Massachusetts, Hawthorne's birthplace (1804) was the scene of the famous witch trials of 1692; *Goodman:* husband, master of household.

wretch am I, to leave her on such an errand! She talks of dreams, too. Methought, as she spoke, there was trouble in her face, as if a dream had warned her what work is to be done tonight. But, no, no! 'twould kill her to think it. Well; she's a blessed angel on earth; and after this one night, I'll cling to her skirts and follow her to Heaven."

With this excellent resolve for the future, Goodman Brown felt himself justfiied in making more haste on his present evil purpose. He had taken a dreary road, darkened by all the gloomiest trees of the forest, which barely stood aside to let the narrow path creep through, and closed immediately behind. It was all as lonely as could be; and there is this peculiarity in such a solitude, that the traveler knows not who may be concealed by the innumerable trunks and the thick boughs overhead; so that, with lonely footsteps, he may yet be passing through an unseen multitude.

"There may be a devilish Indian behind every tree," said Goodman Brown, to himself; and he glanced fearfully behind him, as he added, "What if the devil himself should be at my very elbow!"

His head being turned back, he passed a crook of the road, and looking forward again, beheld the figure of a man, in grave and decent attire, seated at the foot of an old tree. He arose, at Goodman Brown's approach, and walked onward, side by side with him.

"You are late, Goodman Brown," said he. "The clock of the Old South[2] was striking as I came through Boston; and that is full fifteen minutes agone."

"Faith kept me back awhile," replied the young man, with a tremor in his voice, caused by the sudden appearance of his companion, though not wholly unexpected.

It was now deep dusk in the forest, and deepest in that part of it where these two were journeying. As nearly as could be discerned, the second traveler was about fifty years old, apparently in the same rank of life as Goodman Brown, and bearing a considerable resemblance to him, though perhaps more in expression than features. Still, they might have been taken for father and son. And yet, though the elder person was as simply clad as the younger, and as simple in manner too, he had an indescribable air of one who knew the world, and would not have felt abashed at the governor's dinner table, or in King William's[3] court, were it possible that his affairs should call him thither. But the only thing about him, that could be fixed upon as remarkable, was his staff, which bore the likeness of a great black snake, so curiously wrought, that it might almost be seen to twist and wriggle itself, like a living serpent. This, of course, must have been an ocular deception, assisted by the uncertain light.

"Come, Goodman Brown!" cried his fellow-traveler, "this is a dull pace for the beginning of a journey. Take my staff, if you are so soon weary."

"Friend," said the other, exchanging his slow pace for a full stop, "having kept covenant by meeting thee here, it is my purpose now

2. The Third Church of Boston, established in 1669 in opposition to the requirement of church membership for political rights and thus a landmark of religious freedom.

3. William III—William of Orange—1650-1702, ruled England from 1689 to 1702, until 1694 jointly with his wife, Mary II.

to return whence I came. I have scruples, touching the matter thou wot'st of."

"Sayest thou so?" replied he of the serpent, smiling apart. "Let us walk on, nevertheless, reasoning as we go, and if I convince thee not, thou shalt turn back. We are but a little way in the forest, yet."

"Too far, too far!" exclaimed the goodman, unconsciously resuming his walk. "My father never went into the woods on such an errand, nor his father before him. We have been a race of honest men and good Christians, since the days of the martyrs. And shall I be the first of the name of Brown, that ever took this path, and kept—"

"Such company, thou wouldst say," observed the elder person, interpreting his pause. "Well said, Goodman Brown! I have been as well acquainted with your family as with ever a one among the Puritans; and that's no trifle to say. I helped your grandfather, the constable, when he lashed the Quaker woman so smartly through the streets of Salem. And it was I that brought your father a pitch-pine knot, kindled at my own hearth, to set fire to an Indian village, in King Philip's war.[4] They were my good friends, both; and many a pleasant walk have we had along this path, and returned merrily after midnight. I would fain be friends with you, for their sake."

"If it be as thou sayest," replied Goodman Brown, "I marvel they never spoke of these matters. Or, verily, I marvel not, seeing that the least rumor of the sort would have driven them from New England. We are a people of prayer, and good works, to boot, and abide no such wickedness."

"Wickedness or not," said the traveler with the twisted staff, "I have a very general acquaintance here in New England. The deacons of many a church have drunk the communion wine with me; the selectmen, of divers towns, make me their chairman; and a majority of the Great and General Court are firm supporters of my interest. The governor and I, too—but these are state secrets."

"Can this be so!" cried Goodman Brown, with a stare of amazement at his undisturbed companion. "Howbeit, I have nothing to do with the governor and council; they have their own ways, and are no rule for a simple husbandman, like me. But, were I to go on with thee, how should I meet the eye of that good old man, our minister, at Salem village? Oh, his voice would make me tremble, both Sabbath-day and lecture-day!"[5]

Thus far, the elder traveler had listened with due gravity, but now burst into a fit of irrepressible mirth, shaking himself so violently, that his snake-like staff actually seemed to wriggle in sympathy.

"Ha! ha! ha!" shouted he, again and again; then composing himself, "Well, go on, Goodman Brown, go on; but pr'y thee, don't kill me with laughing!"

"Well, then, to end the matter at once," said Goodman Brown, considerably nettled, "there is my wife, Faith. It would break her

4. Metacom or Metacomet, chief of the Wampanoag Indians, known as King Philip, led a war against the New England colonists in 1675–76 which devastated many frontier communities.

5. The day—in the New England colonies usually a Thursday—appointed for a periodical lecture, the lecture being less formal than a sermon or delivered on a different occasion.

dear little heart; and I'd rather break my own!"

"Nay, if that be the case," answered the other, "e'en[6] go thy ways, Goodman Brown. I would not, for twenty old women like the one hobbling before us, that Faith should come to any harm."

As he spoke, he pointed his staff at a female figure on the path, in whom Goodman Brown recognized a very pious and exemplary dame, who had taught him his catechism, in youth, and was still his moral and spiritual adviser, jointly with the minister and Deacon Gookin.

"A marvel, truly, that Goody[7] Cloyse should be so far in the wilderness, at nightfall!" said he. "But, with your leave, friend, I shall take a cut through the woods, until we have left this Christian woman behind. Being a stranger to you, she might ask whom I was consorting with, and whither I was going."

"Be it so," said his fellow-traveler. "Betake you to the woods, and let me keep the path."

Accordingly, the young man turned aside, but took care to watch his companion, who advanced softly along the road, until he had come within a staff's length of the old dame. She, meanwhile, was making the best of her way, with singular speed for so aged a woman, and mumbling some indistinct words, a prayer, doubtless, as she went. The traveler put forth his staff, and touched her withered neck with what seemed the serpent's tail.

"The devil!" screamed the pious old lady.

"Then Goody Cloyse knows her old friend?" observed the traveler, confronting her, and leaning on his writhing stick.

"Ah, forsooth, and is it your worship, indeed?" cried the good dame. "Yea, truly is it, and in the very image of my old gossip, Goodman Brown, the grandfather of the silly fellow that now is. But—would your worship believe it?—my broomstick hath strangely disappeared, stolen, as I suspect, by that unhanged witch, Goody Cory, and that, too, when I was all anointed with the juice of smallage and cinque-foil and wolf's-bane—"

"Mingled with fine wheat and the fat of a new-born babe," said the shape of old Goodman Brown.

"Ah, your worship knows the receipt," cried the old lady, cackling aloud. "So, as I was saying, being all ready for the meeting, and no horse to ride on, I made up my mind to foot it; for they tell me, there is a nice young man to be taken into communion tonight. But now your good worship will lend me your arm, and we shall be there in a twinkling."

"That can hardly be," answered her friend. "I may not spare you my arm, Goody Cloyse, but here is my staff, if you will."

So saying, he threw it down at her feet, where, perhaps, it assumed life, being one of the rods which its owner had formerly lent to the Egyptian Magi.[8] Of this fact, however, Goodman Brown could not

6. Just.

7. Short for "goodwife" or housewife.

8. *Exodus* 7:9-12. The Lord instructs Moses to have his prophet Aaron throw down his rod before the Pharaoh, whereupon it will be turned into a serpent, and by which miracle the Pharaoh will be persuaded to let the Jews go into the wilderness to sacrifice to God. The Pharaoh has his magicians (Magi) do likewise, "but Aaron's rod swallowed up their rods."

take cognizance. He had cast up his eyes in astonishment, and look-ing down again, beheld neither Goody Cloyse nor the serpentine staff, but his fellow-traveler alone, who waited for him as calmly as if nothing had happened.

"That old woman taught me my catechism!" said the young man; and there was a world of meaning in this simple comment.

They continued to walk onward, while the elder traveler exhorted his companion to make good speed and persevere in the path, dis-coursing so aptly, that his arguments seemed rather to spring up in the bosom of his auditor, than to be suggested by himself. As they went, he plucked a branch of maple, to serve for a walking stick, and began to strip it of the twigs and little boughs, which were wet with evening dew. The moment his fingers touched them, they be-came strangely withered and dried up, as with a week's sunshine. Thus the pair proceeded, at a good free pace, until suddenly, in a gloomy hollow of the road, Goodman Brown sat himself down on the stump of a tree, and refused to go any farther.

"Friend," said he, stubbornly, "my mind is made up. Not another step will I budge on this errand. What if a wretched old woman do choose to go to the devil, when I thought she was going to Heaven! Is that any reason why I should quit my dear Faith, and go after her?"

"You will think better of this, by-and-by," said his acquaintance, composedly. "Sit here and rest yourself awhile; and when you feel like moving again, there is my staff to help you along."

Without more words, he threw his companion the maple stick, and was as speedily out of sight, as if he had vanished into the deepen-ing gloom. The young man sat a few moments, by the roadside, applauding himself greatly, and thinking with how clear a conscience he should meet the minister, in his morning walk, nor shrink from the eye of good old Deacon Gookin. And what calm sleep would be his, that very night, which was to have been spent so wickedly, but purely and sweetly now, in the arms of Faith! Amidst these pleasant and praiseworthy meditations, Goodman Brown heard the tramp of horses along the road, and deemed it advisable to conceal himself within the verge of the forest, conscious of the guilty purpose that had brought him thither, though now so happily turned from it.

On came the hoof-tramps and the voices of the riders, two grave old voices, conversing soberly as they drew near. These mingled sounds appeared to pass along the road, within a few yards of the young man's hiding-place; but owing, doubtless, to the depth of the gloom, at that particular spot, neither the travelers nor their steeds were visible. Though their figures brushed the small boughs by the wayside, it could not be seen that they intercepted, even for a moment, the faint gleam from the strip of bright sky, athwart which they must have passed. Goodman Brown alternately crouched and stood on tiptoe, pulling aside the branches, and thrusting forth his head as far as he durst, without discerning so much as a shadow. It vexed him the more, because he could have sworn, were such a thing possible, that he recognized the voices of the minister and Deacon Gookin, jogging along quietly, as they were wont to do, when bound to some ordination or ecclesiastical council. While yet within hearing, one of the riders stopped to pluck a switch.

"Of the two, reverend Sir," said the voice like the deacon's, "I had rather miss an ordination-dinner than tonight's meeting. They tell me that some of our community are to be here from Falmouth[9] and beyond, and others from Connecticut and Rhode Island; besides several of the Indian powows, who, after their fashion, know almost as much deviltry as the best of us. Moreover, there is a goodly young woman to be taken into communion."

"Mighty well, Deacon Gookin!" replied the solemn old tones of the minister. "Spur up, or we shall be late. Nothing can be done, you know, until I get on the ground."

The hoofs clattered again, and the voices, talking so strangely in the empty air, passed on through the forest, where no church had ever been gathered, nor solitary Christian prayed. Whither, then, could these holy men be journeying, so deep into the heathen wilderness? Young Goodman Brown caught hold of a tree, for support, being ready to sink down on the ground, faint and overburdened with the heavy sickness of his heart. He looked up to the sky, doubting whether there really was a Heaven above him. Yet there was the blue arch, and the stars brightening in it.

"With Heaven above, and Faith below, I will yet stand firm against the devil!" cried Goodman Brown.

While he still gazed upward, into the deep arch of the firmament, and had lifted his hands to pray, a cloud, though no wind was stirring, hurried across the zenith, and hid the brightening stars. The blue sky was still visible, except directly overhead, where this black mass of cloud was sweeping swiftly northward. Aloft in the air, as if from the depths of the cloud, came a confused and doubtful sound of voices. Once, the listener fancied that he could distinguish the accents of townspeople of his own, men and women, both pious and ungodly, many of whom he had met at the communion-table, and had seen others rioting at the tavern. The next moment, so indistinct were the sounds, he doubted whether he had heard aught but the murmur of the old forest, whispering without a wind. Then came a stronger swell of those familiar tones, heard daily in the sunshine, at Salem village, but never, until now, from a cloud of night. There was one voice, of a young woman, uttering lamentations, yet with an uncertain sorrow, and entreating for some favor, which, perhaps, it would grieve her to obtain. And all the unseen multitude, both saints and sinners, seemed to encourage her onward.

"Faith!" shouted Goodman Brown, in a voice of agony and desperation; and the echoes of the forest mocked him, crying—"Faith! Faith!" as if bewildered wretches were seeking her, all through the wilderness.

The cry of grief, rage, and terror, was yet piercing the night, when the unhappy husband held his breath for a response. There was a scream, drowned immediately in a louder murmur of voices, fading into far-off laughter, as the dark cloud swept away, leaving

9. A port in extreme southern Massachusetts; Salem is in northern Massachusetts.

the clear and silent sky above Goodman Brown. But something
fluttered lightly down through the air, and caught on the branch
of a tree. The young man seized it, and beheld a pink ribbon.

"My Faith is gone!" cried he, after one stupefied moment. "There
is no good on earth; and sin is but a name. Come, devil! for to thee
is this world given."

And maddened with despair, so that he laughed loud and long,
did Goodman Brown grasp his staff and set forth again, at such a
rate, that he seemed to fly along the forest path, rather than to walk
or run. The road grew wilder and drearier, and more faintly traced,
and vanished at length, leaving him in the heart of the dark wilderness, still rushing onward, with the instinct that guides mortal man
to evil. The whole forest was peopled with frightful sounds; the
creaking of the trees, the howling of wild beasts, and the yell of
Indians; while, sometimes, the wind tolled like a distant church bell,
and sometimes gave a broad roar around the traveler, as if all Nature
were laughing him to scorn. But he was himself the chief horror of
the scene, and shrank not from its other horrors.

"Ha! ha! ha!" roared Goodman Brown, when the wind laughed
at him. "Let us hear which will laugh loudest! Think not to frighten
me with your deviltry! Come witch, come wizard, come Indian
powow, come devil himself! and here comes Goodman Brown. You
may as well fear him as he fear you!"

In truth, all through the haunted forest, there could be nothing
more frightful than the figure of Goodman Brown. On he flew,
among the black pines, brandishing his staff with frenzied gestures,
now giving vent to an inspiration of horrid blasphemy, and now
shouting forth such laughter, as set all the echoes of the forest laughing like demons around him. The fiend in his own shape is less
hideous, than when he rages in the breast of man. Thus sped the
demoniac on his course, until, quivering among the trees, he saw a
red light before him, as when the felled trunks and branches of a
clearing have been set on fire, and throw up their lurid blaze against
the sky, at the hour of midnight. He paused, in a lull of the tempest
that had driven him onward, and heard the swell of what seemed a
hymn, rolling solemnly from a distance, with the weight of many
voices. He knew the tune; it was a familiar one in the choir of the
village meeting-house. The verse died heavily away, and was lengthened by a chorus, not of human voices, but of all the sounds of the
benighted wilderness, pealing in awful harmony together. Goodman
Brown cried out; and his cry was lost to his own ear, by its unison
with the cry of the desert.

In the interval of silence, he stole forward, until the light glared
full upon his eyes. At one extremity of an open space, hemmed in by
the dark wall of the forest, arose a rock, bearing some rude, natural
resemblance either to an altar or a pulpit, and surrounded by four
blazing pines, their tops aflame, their stems untouched, like candles
at an evening meeting. The mass of foliage, that had overgrown the
summit of the rock, was all on fire, blazing high into the night, and
fitfully illuminating the whole field. Each pendent twig and leafy
festoon was in a blaze. As the red light arose and fell, a numerous con-

gregation alternately shone forth, then disappeared in shadow, and again grew, as it were, out of the darkness, peopling the heart of the solitary woods at once.

"A grave and dark-clad company!" quoth Goodman Brown.

In truth, they were such. Among them, quivering to-and-fro, between gloom and splendor, appeared faces that would be seen, next day, at the council-board of the province, and others which, Sabbath after Sabbath, looked devoutly heavenward, and benignantly over the crowded pews, from the holiest pulpits in the land. Some affirm, that the lady of the governor was there. At least, there were high dames well known to her, and wives of honored husbands, and widows, a great multitude, and ancient maidens, all of excellent repute, and fair young girls, who trembled, lest their mothers should espy them. Either the sudden gleams of light, flashing over the obscure field, bedazzled Goodman Brown, or he recognized a score of the church-members of Salem village, famous for their especial sanctity. Good old Deacon Gookin had arrived, and waited at the skirts of that venerable saint, his revered pastor. But, irreverently consorting with these grave, reputable, and pious people, these elders of the church, these chaste dames and dewy virgins, there were men of dissolute lives and women of spotted fame, wretches given over to all mean and filthy vice, and suspected even of horrid crimes. It was strange to see, that the good shrank not from the wicked, nor were the sinners abashed by the saints. Scattered, also, among their pale-faced enemies, were the Indian priests, or powows, who had often scared their native forest with more hideous incantations than any known to English witchcraft.

"But, where is Faith?" thought Goodman Brown; and, as hope came into his heart, he trembled.

Another verse of the hymn arose, a slow and mournful strain, such as the pious love, but joined to words which expressed all that our nature can conceive of sin, and darkly hinted at far more. Unfathomable to mere mortals is the lore of fiends. Verse after verse was sung, and still the chorus of the desert swelled between, like the deepest tone of a mighty organ. And, with the final peal of that dreadful anthem, there came a sound, as if the roaring wind, the rushing streams, the howling beasts, and every other voice of the unconverted wilderness, were mingling and according with the voice of guilty man, in homage to the prince of all. The four blazing pines threw up a loftier flame, and obscurely discovered shapes and visages of horror on the smoke-wreaths, above the impious assembly. At the same moment, the fire on the rock shot redly forth, and formed a glowing arch above its base, where now appeared a figure. With reverence be it spoken, the figure bore no slight similitude, both in garb and manner, to some grave divine of the New England churches.

"Bring forth the converts!" cried a voice, that echoed through the field and rolled into the forest.

At the word, Goodman Brown stepped forth from the shadow of the trees, and approached the congregation, with whom he felt a loathful brotherhood, by the sympathy of all that was wicked in his heart. He could have well nigh sworn, that the shape of his own dead father beckoned him to advance, looking downward from a smoke-wreath, while a woman, with dim features of despair, threw out her hand to warn him back. Was it his mother? But he had no power to retreat one step, nor to resist, even in thought, when the minister and good old Deacon Gookin seized his arms, and led him to the blazing rock. Thither came also the slender form of a veiled female, led between Goody Cloyse, that pious teacher of the catechism, and Martha Carrier, who had received the devil's promise to be queen of hell. A rampant hag was she! And there stood the proselytes, beneath the canopy of fire.

"Welcome, my children," said the dark figure, "to the communion of your race! Ye have found, thus young, your nature and your destiny. My children, look behind you!"

They turned; and flashing forth, as it were, in a sheet of flame, the fiend-worshippers were seen; the smile of welcome gleamed darkly on every visage.

"There," resumed the sable form, "are all whom ye have reverenced from youth. Ye deemed them holier than yourselves, and shrank from your own sin, contrasting it with their lives of righteousness, and prayerful aspirations heavenward. Yet, here are they all, in my worshipping assembly! This night it shall be granted you to know their secret deeds; how hoary-bearded elders of the church have whispered wanton words to the young maids of their households; how many a woman, eager for widow's weeds, has given her husband a drink at bedtime, and let him sleep his last sleep in her bosom; how beardless youths have made haste to inherit their fathers' wealth; and how fair damsels—blush not, sweet ones!—have dug little graves in the garden, and bidden me, the sole guest, to an infant's funeral. By the sympathy of your human hearts for sin, ye shall scent out all the places—whether in church, bedchamber, street, field, or forest—where crime has been committed, and shall exult to behold the whole earth one stain of guilt, one mighty bloodspot. Far more than this! It shall be yours to penetrate, in every bosom, the deep mystery of sin, the fountain of all wicked arts, and which inexhaustibly supplies more evil impulses than human power—than my power, at its utmost!—can make manifest in deeds. And now, my children, look upon each other."

They did so; and, by the blaze of the hell-kindled torches, the wretched man beheld his Faith, and the wife her husband, trembling before that unhallowed altar.

"Lo! there ye stand, my children," said the figure, in a deep and solemn tone, almost sad, with its despairing awfulness, as if his once angelic nature could yet mourn for our miserable race. "Depending upon one another's hearts, ye had still hoped, that virtue were not all a dream. Now are ye undeceived! Evil is the nature of mankind. Evil must be your only happiness. Welcome, again, my children, to the communion of your race!"

"Welcome!" repeated the fiend-worshippers, in one cry of despair and triumph.

And there they stood, the only pair, as it seemed, who were yet hesitating on the verge of wickedness, in this dark world. A basin was hollowed, naturally, in the rock. Did it contain water, reddened by the lurid light? or was it blood? or, perchance, a liquid flame? Herein did the Shape of Evil dip his hand, and prepare to lay the mark of baptism upon their foreheads, that they might be partakers of the mystery of sin, more conscious of the secret guilt of others, both in deed and thought, than they could now be of their own. The husband cast one look at his pale wife, and Faith at him. What polluted wretches would the next glance shew them to each other, shuddering alike at what they disclosed and what they saw!

"Faith! Faith!" cried the husband. "Look up to Heaven, and resist the Wicked One!"

Whether Faith obeyed, he knew not. Hardly had he spoken, when he found himself amid calm night and solitude, listening to a roar of the wind, which died heavily away through the forest. He staggered against the rock and felt it chill and damp, while a hanging twig, that had been on fire, besprinkled his cheek with the coldest dew.

The next morning, young Goodman Brown came slowly into the street of Salem village, staring around him like a bewildered man. The good old minister was taking a walk along the graveyard, to get an appetite for breakfast and meditate his sermon, and bestowed a blessing, as he passed, on Goodman Brown. He shrank from the venerable saint, as if to avoid an anathema. Old Deacon Gookin was at domestic worship, and the holy words of his prayer were heard though the open window. "What God doth the wizard pray to?" quoth Goodman Brown. Goody Cloyse, that excellent old Christian, stood in the early sunshine, at her own lattice, catechizing a little girl, who had brought her a pint of morning's milk. Goodman Brown snatched away the child, as from the grasp of the fiend himself. Turning the corner by the meeting-house, he spied the head of Faith, with the pink ribbons, gazing anxiously forth, and bursting into such joy at sight of him, that she skipped along the street, and almost kissed her husband before the whole village. But, Goodman Brown looked sternly and sadly into her face, and passed on without a greeting.

Had Goodman Brown fallen asleep in the forest, and only dreamed a wild dream of a witch-meeting?

Be it so, if you will. But, alas! it was a dream of evil omen for young Goodman Brown. A stern, a sad, a darkly meditative, a distrustful, if not a desperate man, did he become, from the night of that fearful dream. On the Sabbath day, when the congregation were singing a holy psalm, he could not listen, because an anthem of sin rushed loudly upon his ear, and drowned all the blessed strain. When the minister spoke from the pulpit, with power and fervid eloquence, and, with his hand on the open Bible, of the sacred truths of our religion, and of saint-like lives and triumphant deaths, and of future bliss or misery unutterable, then did Goodman Brown turn pale, dreading, lest the roof should thunder down upon the gray blasphemer and his hearers. Often, awakening suddenly at midnight, he shrank from the bosom of Faith, and at morning or eventide, when the family knelt down at prayer, he scowled, and muttered to himself, and gazed sternly at his wife, and turned away. And when he had lived long, and was borne to his grave, a hoary corpse, followed by Faith, an aged woman, and children and grandchildren, a goodly procession, besides neighbors, not a few, they carved no hopeful verse upon his tombstone; for his dying hour was gloom.

1846

SHIRLEY JACKSON

The Lottery

The morning of June 27th was clear and sunny, with the fresh warmth of a full-summer day; the flowers were blossoming profusely and the grass was richly green. The people of the village began to gather in the square, between the post office and the bank, around ten o'clock; in some towns there were so many people that the lottery took two days and had to be started on June 26th, but in this village, where there were only about three hundred people, the whole lottery took less than two hours, so it could begin at ten o'clock in the morning and still be through in time to allow the villagers to get home for noon dinner.

The children assembled first, of course. School was recently over for the summer, and the feeling of liberty sat uneasily on most of them; they tended to gather together quietly for a while before they broke into boisterous play, and their talk was still of the classroom and the teacher, of books and reprimands. Bobby Martin had already stuffed his pockets full of stones, and the other boys soon followed his example, selecting the smoothest and roundest stones; Bobby and Harry Jones and Dickie Delacroix—the villagers pronounced this name "Dellacroy" —eventually made a great pile of stones in one corner of the square and guarded it against the raids of the other boys. The girls stood aside, talking among themselves, looking over their shoulders at the boys, and the very small children rolled in the dust or clung to the hands of their older brothers or sisters.

Soon the men began to gather, surveying their own children, speaking of planting and rain, tractors and taxes. They stood together, away from the pile of stones in the corner, and their jokes were quiet and they smiled rather than laughed. The women, wearing faded house dresses and sweaters, came shortly after their menfolk. They greeted one another and exchanged bits of gossip as they went to join their husbands. Soon the women, standing by their husbands, began to call to their children, and the chidren came reluctantly, having to be called four or five times. Bobby Martin ducked under his mother's grasping hand and ran, laughing, back to the pile of stones. His father spoke up sharply, and Bobby came quickly and took his place between his father and his oldest brother.

The lottery was conducted—as were the square dances, the teenage club, the Halloween program—by Mr. Summers, who had time and energy to devote to civic activities. He was a round-faced, jovial man and he ran the coal business, and people were sorry for him, because he had no children and his wife was a scold. When he arrived in the square, carrying the black wooden box, there was a murmur of conversation among the villagers, and he waved and called, "Little late today, folks." The postmaster, Mr. Graves, followed him, carrying a three-legged stool, and the stool was put in the center of the square and Mr. Summers set the black box down on it. The villagers kept their distance, leaving a space between themselves and the stool, and when Mr. Summers said, "Some of you fellows want to give me a hand?" there was a hesitation before two men, Mr. Martin and his oldest son, Baxter, came forward to hold the box steady on the stool while Mr. Summers stirred up the papers inside it.

The original paraphernalia for the lottery had been lost long ago, and the black box now resting on the stool had been put into use even before Old Man Warner, the oldest man in town, was born. Mr. Summers spoke frequently to the villagers about making a new box, but no one liked to upset even as much tradition as was represented by the black box. There was a story that the present box had been made with some pieces of the box that had preceded it, the one that had been constructed when the first people settled down to make a village here. Every year, after the lottery, Mr. Summers began talking again about a new box, but every year the subject was allowed to fade off without anything's being done. The black box grew shabbier each year; by now it was no longer completely black but splintered badly along one side to show the original wood color, and in some places faded or stained.

Mr. Martin and his oldest son, Baxter, held the black box securely on the stool until Mr. Summers had stirred the papers thoroughly with his hand. Because so much of the ritual had been forgotten or discarded, Mr. Summers had been successful in having slips of paper substituted for the chips of wood that had been used for generations. Chips of wood, Mr. Summers had argued, had been all very well when the village was tiny, but now that the population was more than three hundred and likely to keep on growing, it was necessary to use something that would fit more easily into the black box. The night before the lottery, Mr. Summers and Mr. Graves made up the slips of paper and put them in the box, and it was then taken to the safe of Mr. Summers' coal company and locked up until Mr. Summers was ready to take it to the square next morning. The rest of the year, the box was put away, sometimes one place, sometimes another; it had spent one year in Mr. Graves's barn and another year underfoot in the post office, and sometimes it was set on a shelf in the Martin grocery and left there.

There was a great deal of fussing to be done before Mr. Summers declared the lottery open. There were the lists to make up—of heads of families, heads of households in each family, members of each household in each family. There was the proper swearing-in of Mr. Summers by the postmaster, as the official of the lottery; at one time, some people remembered, there had been a recital of some sort, performed by the official of the lottery, a perfunctory, tuneless chant that had been rattled off duly each year; some people believed that the official of the lottery used to stand just so when he said or sang it, others believed that he was supposed to walk among the people, but years and years ago this part of the ritual had been allowed to lapse. There had been, also, a ritual salute, which the official of the lottery had had to use in addressing each person who came up to draw from the box, but this also had changed with time, until now it was felt necessary only for the official to speak to each person approaching. Mr. Summers was very good at all this; in his clean white shirt and blue jeans, with one hand resting carelessly on the black box, he seemed very proper and important as he talked interminably to Mr. Graves and the Martins.

Just as Mr. Summers finally left off talking and turned to the assembled villagers, Mrs. Hutchinson came hurriedly along the path to the square, her sweater thrown over her shoulders, and slid into place in the back of the crowd. "Clean forgot what day it was," she said to Mrs. Delacroix, who stood next to her, and they both laughed softly. "Thought my old man was out back stacking wood," Mrs. Hutchinson went on, "and then I looked out the window and the kids was gone, and then I remembered it was the twenty-seventh and came a-running." She dried her hands on her apron, and Mrs. Delacroix said, "You're in time, though. They're still talking away up there."

Mrs. Hutchinson craned her neck to see through the crowd and found her husband and children standing near the front. She tapped Mrs. Delacroix on the arm as a farewell and began to make her way through the crowd. The people separated good-humoredly to let her through; two or three people said, in voices just loud enough to be heard across the crowd, "Here comes your Missus, Hutchinson," and "Bill, she made it after all." Mrs. Hutchinson reached her husband, and Mr. Summers, who had been waiting, said cheerfully, "Thought we were going to have to get on without you, Tessie." Mrs. Hutchinson said, grinning, "Wouldn't have me leave m'dishes in the sink, now, would you, Joe?," and soft laughter ran through the crowd as the people stirred back into position after Mrs. Hutchinson's arrival.

"Well, now," Mr. Summers said soberly, "guess we better get started, get this over with, so's we can go back to work. Anybody ain't here?"

"Dunbar," several people said. "Dunbar, Dunbar."

Mr. Summers consulted his list. "Clyde Dunbar," he said. "That's right. He's broke his leg, hasn't he? Who's drawing for him?"

"Me, I guess," a woman said, and Mr. Summers turned to look at her. "Wife draws for her husband," Mr. Summers said. "Don't you have a grown boy to do it for you, Janey?" Although Mr. Summers and everyone else in the village knew the answer perfectly well, it was the business of the official of the lottery to ask such questions formally. Mr. Summers waited with an expression of polite interest while Mrs. Dunbar answered.

"Horace's not but sixteen yet," Mrs. Dunbar said regretfully. "Guess I gotta fill in for the old man this year."

"Right," Mr. Summers said. He made a note on the list he was holding. Then he asked, "Watson boy drawing this year?"

A tall boy in the crowd raised his hand. "Here," he said. "I'm drawing for m'mother and me." He blinked his eyes nervously and ducked his head as several voices in the crowd said things like "Good fellow, Jack," and "Glad to see your mother's got a man to do it."

"Well," Mr. Summers said, "guess that's everyone. Old Man Warner make it?"

"Here," a voice said, and Mr. Summers nodded.

A sudden hush fell on the crowd as Mr. Summers cleared his throat and looked at the list. "All ready?" he called. "Now, I'll read the names —heads of families first—and the men come up and take a paper out of the box. Keep the paper folded in your hand without looking at it until everyone has had a turn. Everything clear?"

The people had done it so many times that they only half listened to the directions; most of them were quiet, wetting their lips, not looking around. Then Mr. Summers raised one hand high and said, "Adams." A man disengaged himself from the crowd and came forward. "Hi, Steve," Mr. Summers said, and Mr. Adams said, "Hi, Joe." They grinned at one another humorlessly and nervously. Then Mr. Adams reached into the black box and took out a folded paper. He held it firmly by one corner as he turned and went hastily back to his place in the crowd, where he stood a little apart from his family, not looking down at his hand.

"Allen," Mr. Summers said. "Anderson. . . . Bentham."

"Seems like there's no time at all between lotteries any more," Mrs. Delacroix said to Mrs. Graves in the back row. "Seems like we got through with the last one only last week."

"Time sure goes fast," Mrs. Graves said.

"Clark. . . . Delacroix."

"There goes my old man," Mrs. Delacroix said. She held her breath while her husband went forward.

"Dunbar," Mr. Summers said, and Mrs. Dunbar went steadily to the box while one of the women said, "Go on, Janey," and another said, "There she goes."

"We're next," Mrs. Graves said. She watched while Mr. Graves came around from the side of the box, greeted Mr. Summers gravely, and selected a slip of paper from the box. By now, all through the crowd there were men holding the small folded papers in their large hands, turning them over and over nervously. Mrs. Dunbar and her two sons stood together, Mrs. Dunbar holding the slip of paper.

"Harburt. . . . Hutchinson."

"Get up there, Bill," Mrs. Hutchinson said, and the people near her laughed.

"Jones."

"They do say," Mr. Adams said to Old Man Warner, who stood next to him, "that over in the north village they're talking of giving up the lottery."

Old Man Warner snorted. "Pack of crazy fools," he said. "Listening to the young folks, nothing's good enough for *them*. Next thing you know, they'll be wanting to go back to living in caves, nobody work any more, live *that* way for a while. Used to be a saying about 'Lottery in June, corn be heavy soon.' First thing you know, we'd all be eating stewed chickweed and acorns. There's *always* been a lottery," he added petulantly. "Bad enough to see young Joe Summers up there joking with everybody."

"Some places have already quit lotteries," Mrs. Adams said.

"Nothing but trouble in *that*," Old Man Warner said stoutly. "Pack of young fools."

"Martin." And Bobby Martin watched his father go forward. "Over-dyke. . . . Percy."

"I wish they'd hurry," Mrs. Dunbar said to her older son. "I wish they'd hurry."

"They're almost through," her son said.

"You get ready to run tell Dad," Mrs. Dunbar said.

Mr. Summers called his own name and then stepped forward precisely and selected a slip from the box. Then he called, "Warner."

"Seventy-seventh year I been in the lottery," Old Man Warner said as he went through the crowd. "Seventy-seventh time."

"Watson." The tall boy came awkwardly through the crowd. Someone said, "Don't be nervous, Jack," and Mr. Summers said, "Take your time, son."

"Zanini."

After that, there was a long pause, a breathless pause, until Mr. Summers, holding his slip of paper in the air, said, "All right, fellows." For a minute, no one moved, and then all the slips of paper were opened. Suddenly, all the women began to speak at once, saying, "Who is it?," "Who's got it?," "Is it the Dunbars?," "Is it the Watsons?" Then the voices began to say, "It's Hutchinson. It's Bill," "Bill Hutchinson's got it."

"Go tell your father," Mrs. Dunbar said to her older son.

People began to look around to see the Hutchinsons. Bill Hutchinson was standing quiet staring down at the paper in his hand. Suddenly, Tessie Hutchinson shouted to Mr. Summers, "You didn't give him time enough to take any paper he wanted. I saw you. It wasn't fair."

"Be a good sport, Tessie," Mrs. Delacroix called, and Mrs. Graves said, "All of us took the same chance."

"Shut up, Tessie," Bill Hutchinson said.

"Well, everyone," Mr. Summers said, "that was done pretty fast, and now we've got to be hurrying a little more to get done in time." He consulted his next list. "Bill," he said, "you draw for the Hutchinson family. You got any other households in the Hutchinsons?"

"There's Don and Eva," Mrs. Hutchinson yelled. "Make *them* take their chance!"

"Daughters draw with their husbands' families, Tessie," Mr. Summers said gently. "You know that as well as anyone else."

"It wasn't *fair*," Tessie said.

"I guess not, Joe," Bill Hutchinson said regretfully. "My daughter draws with her husband's family, that's only fair. And I've got no other family except the kids."

"Then, as far as drawing for families is concerned, it's you," Mr. Summers said in explanation, "and as far as drawing for households is concerned, that's you, too. Right?"

"Right," Bill Hutchinson said.

"How many kids, Bill?" Mr. Summers asked formally.

"Three," Bill Hutchinson said. "There's Bill, Jr., and Nancy, and little Dave. And Tessie and me."

"All right, then," Mr. Summers said. "Harry, you got their tickets back?"

Mr. Graves nodded and held up the slips of paper. "Put them in the box, then," Mr. Summers directed. "Take Bill's and put it in."

"I think we ought to start over," Mrs. Hutchinson said, as quietly as she could. "I tell you it wasn't *fair*. You didn't give him time enough to choose. *Every*body saw that."

Mr. Graves had selected the five slips and put them in the box, and he dropped all the papers but those onto the ground, where the breeze caught them and lifted them off.

"Listen, everybody," Mrs. Hutchinson was saying to the people around her.

"Ready, Bill?" Mr. Summers asked, and Bill Hutchinson, with one quick glance around at his wife and children, nodded.

"Remember," Mr. Summers said, "take the slips and keep them folded until each person has taken one. Harry, you help little Dave." Mr. Graves took the hand of the little boy, who came willingly with him up to the box. "Take a paper out of the box, Davy," Mr. Summers said. Davy put his hand into the box and laughed. "Take just *one* paper." Mr. Summers said. "Harry, you hold it for him." Mr. Graves took the child's hand and removed the folded paper from the tight fist and held it while little Dave stood next to him and looked up at him wonderingly.

"Nancy next," Mr. Summers said. Nancy was twelve, and her school friends breathed heavily as she went forward, switching her skirt, and took a slip daintily from the box. "Bill, Jr.," Mr. Summers said, and Billy, his face red and his feet over-large, nearly knocked the box over as he got a paper out. "Tessie," Mr. Summers said. She hesitated for a minute, looking around defiantly, and then set her lips and went up to the box. She snatched a paper out and held it behind her.

"Bill," Mr. Summers said, and Bill Hutchinson reached into the box and felt around, bringing his hand out at last with the slip of paper in it.

The crowd was quiet. A girl whispered, "I hope it's not Nancy," and the sound of the whisper reached the edges of the crowd.

"It's not the way it used to be," Old Man Warner said clearly. "People ain't the way they used to be."

"All right," Mr. Summers said. "Open the papers. Harry, you open little Dave's."

Mr. Graves opened the slip of paper and there was a general sigh through the crowd as he held it up and everyone could see that it was blank. Nancy and Bill, Jr., opened theirs at the same time, and both beamed and laughed, turning around to the crowd and holding their slips of paper above their heads.

"Tessie," Mr. Summers said. There was a pause, and then Mr. Summers looked at Bill Hutchinson, and Bill unfolded his paper and showed it. It was blank.

"It's Tessie," Mr. Summers said, and his voice was hushed. "Show us her paper, Bill."

Bill Hutchinson went over to his wife and forced the slip of paper out of her hand. It had a black spot on it, the black spot Mr. Summers had made the night before with the heavy pencil in the coal-company office. Bill Hutchinson held it up, and there was a stir in the crowd.

"All right, folks," Mr. Summers said. "Let's finish quickly."

Although the villagers had forgotten the ritual and lost the original black box, they still remembered to use stones. The pile of stones the boys had made earlier was ready; there were stones on the ground with the blowing scraps of paper that had come out of the box. Mrs. Delacroix selected a stone so large she had to pick it up with both hands and turned to Mrs. Dunbar. "Come on," she said. "Hurry up."

Mrs. Dunbar had small stones in both hands, and she said, gasping for breath, "I can't run at all. You'll have to go ahead and I'll catch up with you."

The children had stones already, and someone gave little Davy Hutchinson a few pebbles.

Tessie Hutchinson was in the center of a cleared space by now, and she held her hands out desperately as the villagers moved in on her. "It isn't fair," she said. A stone hit her on the side of the head.

Old Man Warner was saying, "Come on, come on, everyone." Steve Adams was in the front of the crowd of villagers, with Mrs. Graves beside him.

"It isn't fair, it isn't right," Mrs. Hutchinson screamed, and then they were upon her.

1948

FLANNERY O'CONNOR

The Artificial Nigger

Mr. Head awakened to discover that the room was full of moonlight. He sat up and stared at the floor boards—the color of silver—and then at the ticking on his pillow, which might have been brocade, and after a second, he saw half of the moon five feet away in his shaving mirror, paused as if it were waiting for his permission to enter. It rolled forward and cast a dignifying light on everything. The straight chair against the wall looked stiff and attentive as if it were awaiting an order and Mr. Head's trousers, hanging to the back of it, had an almost noble air, like the garment some great man had just flung to his servant; but the face on the moon was a grave one. It gazed across the room and out the window where it floated over the horse stall and appeared to contemplate itself with the look of a young man who sees his old age before him.

Mr. Head could have said to it that age was a choice blessing and that only with years does a man enter into that calm understanding of life that makes him a suitable guide for the young. This, at least, had been his own experience.

He sat up and grasped the iron posts at the foot of his bed and raised himself until he could see the face on the alarm clock which sat on an overturned bucket beside the chair. The hour was two in the morning. The alarm on the clock did not work but he was not dependent on any mechanical means to awaken him. Sixty years had not dulled his responses; his physical reactions, like his moral ones, were guided by his will and strong character, and these could be seen plainly in his features. He had a long tube-like face with a long rounded open jaw and a long depressed nose. His eyes were alert but quiet, and in the miraculous moonlight they had a look of composure and of ancient wisdom as if they belonged to one of the great guides of men. He might have been Vergil summoned in the middle of the night to go to Dante, or better, Raphael, awakened by a blast of God's light to fly to the side of Tobias.[1] The only dark spot in the room was Nelson's pallet, underneath the shadow of the window.

Nelson was hunched over on his side, his knees under his chin and his heels under his bottom. His new suit and hat were in the boxes that they had been sent in and these were on the floor at the foot of the pallet where he could get his hands on them as soon as he woke up. The slop jar, out of the shadow and made snow-white in the moonlight, appeared to stand guard over him like a small personal angel. Mr. Head lay back down, feeling entirely confident that he could carry out the moral mission of the coming day. He meant to be up before Nelson and to have the breakfast cooking by the time he awakened. The boy was always irked when Mr. Head was the first up. They would have to leave the house at four to get to the railroad junction by five-thirty. The train was to stop for them at five forty-five and they had to be there on time for this train was stopping merely to accommodate them.

This would be the boy's first trip to the city though he claimed it would be his second because he had been born there. Mr. Head had tried to point out to him that when he was born he didn't have the intelligence to determine his whereabouts but this had made no impression on the child at all and he continued to insist that this was to be his second trip. It would be Mr. Head's third trip. Nelson had said, "I will've already been there twict and I ain't but ten."

Mr. Head had contradicted him.

"If you ain't been there in fifteen years, how you know you'll be able to find your way about?" Nelson had asked. "How you know it hasn't changed some?"

"Have you ever," Mr. Head had asked, "seen me lost?"

Nelson certainly had not but he was a child who was never satisfied until he had given an impudent answer and he replied, "It's nowhere around here to get lost at."

"The day is going to come," Mr. Head prophesied, "when you'll find you ain't as smart as you think you are." He had been thinking about this trip for several months but it was for the most part in moral terms that he conceived it. It was to be a lesson that the boy would never forget. He was to find out from it that he had no cause for pride merely because he had been born in a city. He was to find out that the city is not a great place. Mr. Head meant him to see everything there

<hr />

1. Vergil, Publius Vergilius Maro (70–19 B.C.), author of the *Aeneid,* in *The Divine Comedy* of Dante Alighieri (1265–1321), is summoned by Beatrice (*Inferno,* II, 49–70) to assist Dante and serves as his guide through Hell and Purgatory; the angel Raphael in the Book of Tobit in the *Apocrypha* serves as Tobias's instructor and companion in the overcoming of the demon Asmodeus.

is to see in a city so that he would be content to stay at home for the rest of his life. He fell asleep thinking how the boy would at last find out that he was not as smart as he thought he was.

He was awakened at three-thirty by the smell of fatback frying and he leaped off his cot. The pallet was empty and the clothes boxes had been thrown open. He put on his trousers and ran into the other room. The boy had a corn pone on cooking and had fried the meat. He was sitting in the half-dark at the table, drinking cold coffee out of a can. He had on his new suit and his new gray hat pulled low over his eyes. It was too big for him but they had ordered it a size large because they expected his head to grow. He didn't say anything but his entire figure suggested satisfaction at having arisen before Mr. Head.

Mr. Head went to the stove and brought the meat to the table in the skillet. "It's no hurry," he said. "You'll get there soon enough and it's no guarantee you'll like it when you do neither," and he sat down across from the boy whose hat teetered back slowly to reveal a fiercely expressionless face, very much the same shape as the old man's. They were grandfather and grandson but they looked enough alike to be brothers and brothers not too far apart in age, for Mr. Head had a youthful expression by daylight, while the boy's look was ancient, as if he knew everything already and would be pleased to forget it.

Mr. Head had once had a wife and daughter and when the wife died, the daughter ran away and returned after an interval with Nelson. Then one morning, without getting out of bed, she died and left Mr. Head with sole care of the year-old child. He had made the mistake of telling Nelson that he had been born in Atlanta. If he hadn't told him that, Nelson couldn't have insisted that this was going to be his second trip.

"You may not like it a bit," Mr. Head continued. "It'll be full of niggers."

The boy made a face as if he could handle a nigger.

"All right," Mr. Head said. "You ain't ever seen a nigger."

"You wasn't up very early," Nelson said.

"You ain't ever seen a nigger," Mr. Head repeated. "There hasn't been a nigger in this county since we run that one out twelve years ago and that was before you were born." He looked at the boy as if he were daring him to say he had ever seen a Negro.

"How you know I never saw a nigger when I lived there before?" Nelson asked. "I probably saw a lot of niggers."

"If you seen one you didn't know what he was," Mr. Head said, completely exasperated. "A six-month-old child don't know a nigger from anybody else."

"I reckon I'll know a nigger if I see one," the boy said and got up and straightened his slick sharply creased gray hat and went outside to the privy.

They reached the junction some time before the train was due to arrive and stood about two feet from the first set of tracks. Mr. Head carried a paper sack with some biscuits and a can of sardines in it for their lunch. A coarse-looking orange-colored sun coming up behind the east range of mountains was making the sky a dull red behind them, but in front of them it was still gray and they faced a gray transparent

moon, hardly stronger than a thumbprint and completely without light.
A small tin switch box and a black fuel tank were all there was to
mark the place as a junction; the tracks were double and did not converge again until they were hidden behind the bends at either end of
the clearing. Trains passing appeared to emerge from a tunnel of trees
and, hit for a second by the cold sky, vanish terrified into the woods
again. Mr. Head had had to make special arrangements with the ticket
agent to have this train stop and he was secretly afraid it would not, in
which case, he knew Nelson would say, "I never thought no train was
going to stop for you." Under the useless morning moon the tracks
looked white and fragile. Both the old man and the child stared ahead
as if they were awaiting an apparition.

Then suddenly, before Mr. Head could make up his mind to turn
back, there was a deep warning bleat and the train appeared, gliding
very slowly, almost silently around the bend of trees about two hundred yards down the track, with one yellow front light shining. Mr.
Head was still not certain it would stop and he felt it would make an
even bigger idiot of him if it went by slowly. But he and Nelson, however, were prepared to ignore the train if it passed them.

The engine charged by, filling their noses with the smell of hot
metal and then the second coach came to a stop exactly where they
were standing. A conductor with the face of an ancient bloated bulldog
was on the step as if he expected them, though he did not look as if it
mattered one way or the other to him if they got on or not. "To the
right," he said.

Their entry took only a fraction of a second and the train was already speeding on as they entered the quiet car. Most of the travelers
were still sleeping, some with their heads hanging off the chair arms,
some stretched across two seats, and some sprawled out with their
feet in the aisle. Mr. Head saw two unoccupied seats and pushed
Nelson toward them. "Get in there by the winder," he said in his normal
voice which was very loud at this hour of the morning. "Nobody cares
if you set there because it's nobody in it. Sit right there."

"I heard you," the boy muttered. "It's no use in you yelling," and
he sat down and turned his head to the glass. There he saw a pale
ghost-like face scowling at him beneath the brim of a pale ghost-like
hat. His grandfather, looking quickly too, saw a different ghost, pale
but grinning, under a black hat.

Mr. Head sat down and settled himself and took out his ticket and
started reading aloud everything that was printed on it. People began
to stir. Several woke up and stared at him. "Take off your hat," he said
to Nelson and took off his own and put it on his knee. He had a small
amount of white hair that had turned tobacco-colored over the years
and this lay flat across the back of his head. The front of his head was
bald and creased. Nelson took off his hat and put it on his knee and
they waited for the conductor to come ask for their tickets.

The man across the aisle from them was spread out over two seats,
his feet propped on the window and his head jutting into the aisle. He
had on a light blue suit and a yellow shirt unbuttoned at the neck. His
eyes had just opened and Mr. Head was ready to introduce himself
when the conductor came up from behind and growled, "Tickets."

When the conductor had gone, Mr. Head gave Nelson the return half of his ticket and said, "Now put that in your pocket and don't lose it or you'll have to stay in the city."

"Maybe I will," Nelson said as if this were a reasonable suggestion.

Mr. Head ignored him. "First time this boy has ever been on a train," he explained to the man across the aisle, who was sitting up now on the edge of his seat with both feet on the floor.

Nelson jerked his hat on again and turned angrily to the window.

"He's never seen anything before," Mr. Head continued. "Ignorant as the day he was born, but I mean for him to get his fill once and for all."

The boy leaned forward, across his grandfather and toward the stranger. "I was born in the city," he said. "I was born there. This is my second trip." He said it in a high positive voice but the man across the aisle didn't look as if he understood. There were heavy purple circles under his eyes.

Mr. Head reached across the aisle and tapped him on the arm. "The thing to do with a boy," he said sagely, "is to show him all it is to show. Don't hold nothing back."

"Yeah," the man said. He gazed down at his swollen feet and lifted the left one about ten inches from the floor. After a minute he put it down and lifted the other. All through the car people began to get up and move about and yawn and stretch. Separate voices could be heard here and there and then a general hum. Suddenly Mr. Head's serene expression changed. His mouth almost closed and a light, fierce and cautious both, came into his eyes. He was looking down the length of the car. Without turning, he caught Nelson by the arm and pulled him forward. "Look," he said.

A huge coffee-colored man was coming slowly forward. He had on a light suit and a yellow satin tie with a ruby pin in it. One of his hands rested on his stomach which rode majestically under his buttoned coat, and in the other he held the head of a black walking stick that he picked up and set down with a deliberate outward motion each time he took a step. He was proceeding very slowly, his large brown eyes gazing over the heads of the passengers. He had a small white mustache and white crinkly hair. Behind him there were two young women, both coffee-colored, one in a yellow dress and one in a green. Their progress was kept at the rate of his and they chatted in low throaty voices as they followed him.

Mr. Head's grip was tightening insistently on Nelson's arm. As the procession passed them, the light from a sapphire ring on the brown hand that picked up the cane reflected in Mr. Head's eye, but he did not look up nor did the tremendous man look at him. The group proceeded up the rest of the aisle and out of the car. Mr. Head's grip on Nelson's arm loosened. "What was that?" he asked.

"A man," the boy said and gave him an indignant look as if he were tired of having his intelligence insulted.

"What kind of a man?" Mr. Head persisted, his voice expressionless.

"A fat man," Nelson said. He was beginning to feel that he had better be cautious.

"You don't know what kind?" Mr. Head said in a final tone.

"An old man," the boy said and had a sudden foreboding that he was not going to enjoy the day.

"That was a nigger," Mr. Head said and sat back.

Nelson jumped up on the seat and stood looking backward to the end of the car but the Negro had gone.

"I'd of thought you'd know a nigger since you seen so many when you was in the city on your first visit," Mr. Head continued. "That's his first nigger," he said to the man across the aisle.

The boy slid down into the seat. "You said they were black," he said in an angry voice. "You never said they were tan. How do you expect me to know anything when you don't tell me right?"

"You're just ignorant is all," Mr. Head said and he got up and moved over in the vacant seat by the man across the aisle.

Nelson turned backward again and looked where the Negro had disappeared. He felt that the Negro had deliberately walked down the aisle in order to make a fool of him and he hated him with a fierce raw fresh hate; and also, he understood now why his grandfather disliked them. He looked toward the window and the face there seemed to suggest that he might be inadequate to the day's exactions. He wondered if he would even recognize the city when they came to it.

After he had told several stories, Mr. Head realized that the man he was talking to was asleep and he got up and suggested to Nelson that they walk over the train and see the parts of it. He particularly wanted the boy to see the toilet so they went first to the men's room and examined the plumbing. Mr. Head demonstrated the ice-water cooler as if he had invented it and showed Nelson the bowl with the single spigot where the travelers brushed their teeth. They went through several cars and came to the diner.

This was the most elegant car in the train. It was painted a rich egg-yellow and had a wine-colored carpet on the floor. There were wide windows over the tables and great spaces of the rolling view were caught in miniature in the sides of the coffee pots and in the glasses. Three very black Negroes in white suits and aprons were running up and down the aisle, swinging trays and bowing and bending over the travelers eating breakfast. One of them rushed up to Mr. Head and Nelson and said, holding up two fingers, "Space for two!" but Head replied in a loud voice, "We eaten before we left!"

The waiter wore large brown spectacles that increased the size of his eye whites. "Stan' aside then please," he said with an airy wave of the arm as if he were brushing aside flies.

Neither Nelson nor Mr. Head moved a fraction of an inch. "Look," Mr. Head said.

The near corner of the diner, containing two tables, was set off from the rest by a saffron-colored curtain. One table was set but empty but at the other, facing them, his back to the drape, sat the tremendous Negro. He was speaking in a soft voice to the two women while he buttered a muffin. He had a heavy sad face and his neck bulged over his white collar on either side. "They rope them off," Mr. Head explained. Then he said, "Let's go see the kitchen," and they walked the length of the diner but the black waiter was coming fast behind them.

"Passengers are not allowed in the kitchen!" he said in a haughty voice. "Passengers are NOT allowed in the kitchen!"

Mr. Head stopped where he was and turned. "And there's good reason for that," he shouted into the Negro's chest, "because the cockroaches would run the passengers out!"

All the travelers laughed and Mr. Head and Nelson walked out, grinning. Mr. Head was known at home for his quick wit and Nelson felt a sudden keen pride in him. He realized the old man would be his only support in the strange place they were approaching. He would be entirely alone in the world if he were ever lost from his grandfather. A terrible excitement shook him and he wanted to take hold of Mr. Head's coat and hold on like a child.

As they went back to their seats they could see through the passing windows that the countryside was becoming speckled with small houses and shacks and that a highway ran alongside the train. Cars sped by on it, very small and fast. Nelson felt that there was less breath in the air than there had been thirty minutes ago. The man across the aisle had left and there was no one near for Mr. Head to hold a conversation with so he looked out the window, through his own reflection, and read aloud the names of the buildings they were passing. "The Dixie Chemical Corp!" he announced. "Southern Maid Flour! Dixie Doors! Southern Belle Cotton Products! Patty's Peanut Butter! Southern Mammy Cane Syrup!"

"Hush up!" Nelson hissed.

All over the car people were beginning to get up and take their luggage off the overhead racks. Women were putting on their coats and hats. The conductor stuck his head in the car and snarled, "Firstoppppmry,"[2] and Nelson lunged out of his sitting position, trembling. Mr. Head pushed him down by the shoulder.

"Keep your seat," he said in dignified tones. "The first stop is on the edge of town. The second stop is at the main railroad station." He had come by this knowledge on his first trip when he had got off at the first stop and had had to pay a man fifteen cents to take him into the heart of town. Nelson sat back down, very pale. For the first time in his life, he understood that his grandfather was indispensable to him.

The train stopped and let off a few passengers and glided on as if it had never ceased moving. Outside, behind rows of brown rickety houses, a line of blue buildings stood up, and beyond them a pale rosegray sky faded away to nothing. The train moved into the railroad yard. Looking down, Nelson saw lines and lines of silver tracks multiplying and criss-crossing. Then before he could start counting them, the face in the window stared out at him, gray but distinct, and he looked the other way. The train was in the station. Both he and Mr. Head jumped up and ran to the door. Neither noticed that they had left the paper sack with the lunch in it on the seat.

They walked stiffly through the small station and came out of a heavy door into the squall of traffic. Crowds were hurrying to work. Nelson didn't know where to look. Mr. Head leaned against the side

---

2. "First stop, Emory," station in suburban Atlanta.

of the building and glared in front of him.

Finally Nelson said, "Well, how do you see what all it is to see?"

Mr. Head didn't answer. Then as if the sight of people passing had given him the clue, he said, "You walk," and started off down the street. Nelson followed, steadying his hat. So many sights and sounds were flooding in on him that for the first block he hardly knew what he was seeing. At the second corner, Mr. Head turned and looked behind him at the station they had left, a putty-colored terminal with a concrete dome on top. He thought that if he could keep the dome always in sight, he would be able to get back in the afternoon to catch the train again.

As they walked along, Nelson began to distinguish details and take note of the store windows, jammed with every kind of equipment—hardware, drygoods, chicken feed, liquor. They passed one that Mr. Head called his particular attention to where you walked in and sat on a chair with your feet upon two rests and let a Negro polish your shoes. They walked slowly and stopped and stood at the entrances so he could see what went on in each place but they did not go into any of them. Mr. Head was determined not to go into any city store because on his first trip here, he had got lost in a large one and had found his way out only after many people had insulted him.

They came in the middle of the next block to a store that had a weighing machine in front of it and they both in turn stepped up on it and put in a penny and received a ticket. Mr. Head's ticket said, "You weigh 120 pounds. You are upright and brave and all your friends admire you." He put the ticket in his pocket, surprised that the machine should have got his character correct but his weight wrong, for he had weighed on a grain scale not long before and knew he weighed 110. Nelson's ticket said, "You weigh 98 pounds. You have a great destiny ahead of you but beware of dark women." Nelson did not know any women and he weighed only 68 pounds but Mr. Head pointed out that the machine had probably printed the number upsidedown, meaning the 9 for a 6.

They walked on and at the end of five blocks the dome of the terminal sank out of sight and Mr. Head turned to the left. Nelson could have stood in front of every store window for an hour if there had not been another more interesting one next to it. Suddenly he said, "I was born here!" Mr. Head turned and looked at him with horror. There was a sweaty brightness about his face. "This is where I come from!" he said.

Mr. Head was appalled. He saw the moment had come for drastic action. "Lemme show you one thing you ain't seen yet," he said and took him to the corner where there was a sewer entrance. "Squat down," he said, "and stick you head in there," and he held the back of the boy's coat while he got down and put his head in the sewer. He drew it back quickly, hearing a gurgling in the depths under the sidewalk. Then Mr. Head explained the sewer system, how the entire city was underlined with it, how it contained all the drainage and was full of rats and how a man could slide into it and be sucked along down endless pitchblack tunnels. At any minute any man in the city might be sucked into the sewer and never heard from again. He described it so well that Nelson was for some seconds shaken. He connected the sewer passages with the entrance to hell and understood for the first time how the world was put together in its lower parts. He drew away from the curb.

Then he said, "Yes, but you can stay away from the holes," and his face took on that stubborn look that was so exasperating to his grandfather. "This is where I come from!" he said.

Mr. Head was dismayed but he only muttered, "You'll get your fill," and they walked on. At the end of two more blocks he turned to the left, feeling that he was circling the dome, and he was correct for in a half-hour they passed in front of the railroad station again. At first Nelson did not notice that he was seeing the same stores twice but when they passed the one where you put your feet on the rests while the Negro polished your shoes, he perceived that they were walking in a circle.

"We done been here!" he shouted. "I don't believe you know where you're at!"

"The direction just slipped my mind for a minute," Mr. Head said and they turned down a different street. He still did not intend to let the dome get too far away and after two blocks in their new direction, he turned to the left. This street contained two- and three-story wooden dwellings. Anyone passing on the sidewalk could see into the rooms and Mr. Head, glancing through one window, saw a woman lying on an iron bed, looking out, with a sheet pulled over her. Her knowing expression shook him. A fierce-looking boy on a bicycle came driving down out of nowhere and he had to jump to the side to keep from being hit. "It's nothing to them if they knock you down," he said. "You better keep closer to me."

They walked on for some time on streets like this before he remembered to turn again. The houses they were passing now were all unpainted and the wood in them looked rotten; the street between was narrower. Nelson saw a colored man. Then another. Then another. "Niggers live in these houses," he observed.

"Well come on and we'll go somewhere else," Mr. Head said. "We didn't come to look at niggers," and they turned down another street but they continued to see Negroes everywhere. Nelson's skin began to prickle and they stepped along at a faster pace in order to leave the neighborhood as soon as possible. There were colored men in their undershirts standing in the doors and colored women rocking on the sagging porches. Colored children played in the gutters and stopped what they were doing to look at them. Before long they began to pass rows of stores with colored customers in them but they didn't pause at the entrances of these. Black eyes in black faces were watching them from every direction. "Yes," Mr. Head said, "this is where you were born—right here with all these niggers."

Nelson scowled. "I think you done got us lost," he said.

Mr. Head swung around sharply and looked for the dome. It was nowhere in sight. "I ain't got us lost either," he said. "You're just tired of walking."

"I ain't tired, I'm hungry," Nelson said. "Give me a biscuit."

They discovered then that they had lost the lunch.

"You were the one holding the sack," Nelson said. "I would have kepaholt of it."

"If you want to direct this trip, I'll go on by myself and leave you right here," Mr. Head said and was pleased to see the boy turn white. However, he realized they were lost and drifting farther every minute from the station. He was hungry himself and beginning to be thirsty and since they had been in the colored neighborhood, they had both begun to sweat. Nelson had on his shoes and he was unaccustomed to them. The concrete sidewalks were very hard. They both wanted to find a place to sit down but this was impossible and they kept on walking, the boy muttering under his breath, "First you lost the sack and then you lost the way," and Mr. Head growling from time to time, "Anybody wants to be from this nigger heaven can be from it!"

By now the sun was well forward in the sky. The odor of dinners cooking drifted out to them. The Negroes were all at their doors to see them pass. "Whyn't you ast one of these niggers the way?" Nelson said. "You got us lost."

"This is where you were born," Mr. Head said. "You can ast one yourself if you want to."

Nelson was afraid of the colored men and he didn't want to be laughed at by the colored children. Up ahead he saw a large colored woman leaning in a doorway that opened onto the sidewalk. Her hair stood straight out from her head for about four inches all around and she was resting on bare brown feet that turned pink at the sides. She had on a pink dress that showed her exact shape. As they came abreast of her, she lazily lifted one hand to her head and her fingers disappeared into her hair.

Nelson stopped. He felt his breath drawn up by the woman's dark eyes. "How do you get back to town?" he said in a voice that did not sound like his own.

After a minute she said, "You in town now," in a rich low tone that made Nelson feel as if a cool spray had been turned on him.

"How do you get back to the train?" he said in the same reed-like voice.

"You can catch you a car," she said.

He understood she was making fun of him but he was too paralyzed even to scowl. He stood drinking in every detail of her. His eyes traveled up from her great knees to her forehead and then made a triangular path from the glistening sweat on her neck down and across her tremendous bosom and over her bare arm back to where her fingers lay hidden in her hair. He suddenly wanted her to reach down and pick him up and draw him against her and then he wanted to feel her breath on his face. He wanted to look down and down into her eyes while she held him tighter and tighter. He had never had such a feeling before. He felt as if he were reeling down through a pitchblack tunnel.

"You can go a block down yonder and catch you a car take you to the railroad station, Sugarpie," she said.

Nelson would have collapsed at her feet if Mr. Head had not pulled him roughly away. "You act like you don't have any sense!" the old man growled.

They hurried down the street and Nelson did not look back at the woman. He pushed his hat sharply forward over his face which was already burning with shame. The sneering ghost he had seen in the train window and all the foreboding feelings he had on the way returned to him and he remembered that his ticket from the scale had said to beware of dark women and that his grandfather's had said he was upright and brave. He took hold of the old man's hand, a sign of dependence that he seldom showed.

They headed down the street toward the car tracks where a long yellow rattling trolley was coming. Mr. Head had never boarded a streetcar and he let that one pass. Nelson was silent. From time to time his mouth trembled slightly but his grandfather, occupied with his own problems, paid him no attention. They stood on the corner and neither looked at the Negroes who were passing, going about their business just as if they had been white, except that most of them stopped and eyed Mr. Head and Nelson. It occurred to Mr. Head that since the streetcar ran on tracks, they could simply follow the tracks. He gave Nelson a slight push and explained that they would follow the tracks on into the railroad station, walking, and they set off.

Presently to their great relief they began to see white people again and Nelson sat down on the sidewalk against the wall of a building. "I got to rest myself some," he said. "You lost the sack and the direction. You can just wait on me to rest myself."

"There's the tracks in front of us," Mr. Head said. "All we got to do is keep them in sight and you could have remembered the sack as good as me. This is where you were born. This is your old home town. This is your second trip. You ought to know how to do," and he squatted down and continued in this vein but the boy, easing his burning feet out of his shoes, did not answer.

"And standing there grinning like a chim-pan-zee while a nigger woman gives you directions. Great Gawd!" Mr. Head said.

"I never said I was nothing but born here," the boy said in a shaky voice. "I never said I would or wouldn't like it. I never said I wanted to come. I only said I was born here and I never had nothing to do with that. I want to go home. I never wanted to come in the first place. It was all your big idea. How you know you ain't following the tracks in the wrong direction?"

This last had occurred to Mr. Head too. "All these people are white," he said.

"We ain't passed here before," Nelson said. This was a neighborhood of brick buildings that might have been lived in or might not. A few empty automobiles were parked along the curb and there was an occasional passer-by. The heat of the pavement came up through Nelson's thin suit. His eyelids began to droop, and after a few minutes his head tilted forward. His shoulders twitched once or twice and then he fell over on his side and lay sprawled in an exhausted fit of sleep.

Mr. Head watched him silently. He was very tired himself but they could not both sleep at the same time and he could not have slept anyway because he did not know where he was. In a few minutes Nelson would wake up, refreshed by his sleep and very cocky, and would begin complaining that he had lost the sack and the way. You'd have a mighty sorry time if I wasn't here, Mr. Head thought; and then another idea occurred to him. He looked at the sprawled figure for several minutes; presently he stood up. He justified what he was going to do on the grounds that it is sometimes necessary to teach a child a lesson he won't forget, particularly when the child is always reasserting his position with some new impudence. He walked without a sound to the corner about twenty feet away and sat down on a covered garbage can in the alley where he could look out and watch Nelson wake up alone.

The boy was dozing fitfully, half conscious of vague noises and black forms moving up from some dark part of him into the light. His face worked in his sleep and he had pulled his knees up under his chin. The sun shed a dull dry light on the narrow street; everything looked like exactly what it was. After a while Mr. Head, hunched like an old monkey on the garbage can lid, decided that if Nelson didn't wake up soon, he would make a loud noise by bamming his foot against the can. He looked at his watch and discovered that it was two o'clock. Their train left at six and the possibility of missing it was too awful for him to think of. He kicked his foot backwards on the can and a hollow boom reverberated in the alley.

Nelson shot up onto his feet with a shout. He looked where his grandfather should have been and stared. He seemed to whirl several times and then, picking up his feet and throwing his head back, he dashed down the street like a wild maddened pony. Mr. Head jumped off the can and galloped after but the child was almost out of sight. He saw a streak of gray disappearing diagonally a block ahead. He ran as fast as he could, looking both ways down every intersection, but without sight of him again. Then as he passed the third intersection completely winded, he saw about half a block down the street a scene that stopped him altogether. He crouched behind a trash box to watch and get his bearings.

Nelson was sitting with both legs spread out and by his side lay an elderly woman, screaming. Groceries were scattered about the sidewalk. A crowd of women had already gathered to see justice done and Mr. Head distinctly heard the old woman on the pavement shout, "You've broken my ankle and your daddy'll pay for it! Every nickel! Police! Police!" Several of the women were plucking at Nelson's shoulder but the boy seemed too dazed to get up.

Something forced Mr. Head from behind the trash box and forward, but only at a creeping pace. He had never in his life been accosted by a policeman. The women were milling around Nelson as if they might suddenly all dive on him at once and tear him to pieces, and the old woman continued to scream that her ankle was broken and to call for an officer. Mr. Head came on so slowly that he could have been taking a backward step after each forward one, but when he was about ten feet away, Nelson saw him and sprang. The child caught him around the hips and clung panting against him.

The women all turned on Mr. Head. The injured one sat up and shouted, "You sir! You'll pay every penny of my doctor's bill that your boy has caused. He's a juve-nile delinquent! Where is an officer? Somebody take this man's name and address!"

Mr. Head was trying to detach Nelson's fingers from the flesh in the back of his legs. The old man's head had lowered itself into his collar like a turtle; his eyes were glazed with fear and caution.

"Your boy has broken my ankle!" the old woman shouted. "Police!"

Mr. Head sensed the approach of the policeman from behind. He stared straight ahead at the women who were massed in their fury like a solid wall to block his escape. "This is not my boy," he said. "I never seen him before."

He felt Nelson's fingers fall out of his flesh.

Peter's denial

The women dropped back, staring at him with horror, as if they were so repulsed by a man who could deny his own image and likeness that they could not bear to lay hands on him. Mr. Head walked on, through a space they silently cleared, and left Nelson behind. Ahead of him he saw nothing but a hollow tunnel that had once been the street.

The boy remained standing where he was, his neck craned forward and his hands hanging by his sides. His hat was jammed on his head so that there were no longer any creases in it. The injured woman got up and shook her fist at him and the others gave him pitying looks, but he didn't notice any of them. There was no policeman in sight.

In a minute he began to move mechanically, making no effort to catch up with his grandfather but merely following at about twenty paces. They walked on for five blocks in this way. Mr. Head's shoulders were sagging and his neck hung forward at such an angle that it was not visible from behind. He was afraid to turn his head. Finally he cut a short hopeful glance over his shoulder. Twenty feet behind him, he saw two small eyes piercing into his back like pitchfork prongs.

The boy was not of a forgiving nature but this was the first time he had ever had anything to forgive. Mr. Head had never disgraced himself before. After two more blocks, he turned and called over his shoulder in a high desperately gay voice, "Let's us go get a Co' Cola somewheres!"

Nelson, with a dignity he had never shown before, turned and stood with his back to his grandfather.

Mr. Head began to feel the depth of his denial. His face as they walked on became all hollows and bare ridges. He saw nothing they were passing but he perceived that they had lost the car tracks. There was no dome to be seen anywhere and the afternoon was advancing. He knew that if dark overtook them in the city, they would be beaten and robbed. The speed of God's justice was only what he expected for himself, but he could not stand to think that his sins would be visited upon Nelson and that even now, he was leading the boy to his doom.

They continued to walk on block after block through an endless section of small brick houses until Mr. Head almost fell over a water spigot sticking up about six inches off the edge of a grass plot. He had not had a drink of water since early morning but he felt he did not deserve it now. Then he thought that Nelson would be thirsty and they would both drink and be brought together. He squatted down and put his mouth to the nozzle and turned a cold stream of water into his throat. Then he called out in the high desperate voice, "Come on and getcher some water!"

This time the child stared through him for nearly sixty seconds. Mr. Head got up and walked on as if he had drunk poison. Nelson, though he had not had water since some he had drunk out of a paper cup on the train, passed by the spigot, disdaining to drink where his grandfather had. When Mr. Head realized this, he lost all hope. His face in the waning afternoon light looked ravaged and abandoned. He could feel the boy's steady hate, traveling at an even pace behind him and he knew that (if by some miracle they escaped being murdered in the city) it would continue just that way for the rest of his life. He knew that now he was wandering into a black strange place where nothing was like it had even been before, a long old age without respect and an end that would be welcome because it would be the end.

As for Nelson, his mind had frozen around his grandfather's treachery as if he were trying to preserve it intact to present at the final judgment. He walked without looking to one side or the other, but every now and then his mouth would twitch and this was when he felt, from some remote place inside himself, a black mysterious form reach up as if it would melt his frozen vision in one hot grasp.

The sun dropped down behind a row of houses and hardly noticing, they passed into an elegant suburban section where mansions were set back from the road by lawns with birdbaths on them. Here everything was entirely deserted. For blocks they didn't pass even a dog. The big white houses were like partially submerged icebergs in the distance. There were no sidewalks, only drives and these wound around and around in endless ridiculous circles. Nelson made no move to come nearer to Mr. Head. The old man felt that if he saw a sewer entrance he would drop down into it and let himself be carried away; and he could imagine the boy standing by, watching with only a slight interest, while he disappeared.

A loud bark jarred him to attention and he looked up to see a fat man approaching with two bulldogs. He waved both arms like someone shipwrecked on a desert island. "I'm lost!" he called. "I'm lost and can't find my way and me and this boy have got to catch this train and I can't find the station. Oh Gawd I'm lost! Oh hep me Gawd I'm lost!"

The man, who was bald-headed and had on golf knickers, asked him what train he was trying to catch and Mr. Head began to get out his tickets, trembling so violently he could hardly hold them. Nelson had come up to within fifteen feet and stood watching.

"Well," the fat man said, giving him back the tickets, "you won't have time to get back to town to make this but you can catch it at the suburb stop. That's three blocks from here," and he began explaining how to get there.

Mr. Head stared as if he were slowly returning from the dead and when the man had finished and gone off with the dogs jumping at his heels, he turned to Nelson and said breathlessly, "We're going to get home!"

The child was standing about ten feet away, his face bloodless under the gray hat. His eyes were triumphantly cold. There was no light in them, no feeling, no interest. He was merely there, a small figure, waiting. Home was nothing to him.

Mr. Head turned slowly. He felt he knew now what time would be like without seasons and what heat would be like without light and what man would be like without salvation. He didn't care if he never made the train and if it had not been for what suddenly caught his attention, like a cry out of the gathering dusk, he might have forgotten there was a station to go to.

He had not walked five hundred yards down the road when he saw, within reach of him, the plaster figure of a Negro sitting bent over on a low yellow brick fence that curved around a wide lawn. The Negro was about Nelson's size and he was pitched forward at an unsteady angle because the putty that held him to the wall had cracked. One of his eyes was entirely white and he held a piece of brown watermelon.

Mr. Head stood looking at him silently until Nelson stopped at a little distance. Then as the two of them stood there, Mr. Head breathed, "An artificial nigger!"

It was not possible to tell if the artificial Negro were meant to be young or old; he looked too miserable to be either. He was meant to look happy because his mouth was stretched up at the corners but the chipped eye and the angle he was cocked at gave him a wild look of misery instead.

"An artificial nigger!" Nelson repeated in Mr. Head's exact tone. The two of them stood there with their necks forward at almost the same angle and their shoulders curved in almost exactly the same way and their hands trembling identically in their pockets. Mr. Head looked like an ancient child and Nelson like a miniature old man. They stood gazing at the artificial Negro as if they were faced with some great mystery, some monument to another's victory that brought them together in their common defeat. They could both feel it dissolving their differences like an action of mercy. Mr. Head had never known before what mercy felt like because he had been too good to deserve any, but he felt he knew now. He looked at Nelson and understood that he must say something to the child to show that he was still wise and in the look the boy returned he saw a hungry need for that assurance. Nelson's eyes seemed to implore him to explain once and for all the mystery of existence.

Mr. Head opened his lips to make a lofty statement and heard himself say, "They ain't got enough real ones here. They got to have an artificial one."

After a second, the boy nodded with a strange shivering about his mouth, and said, "Let's go home before we get ourselves lost again."

Their train glided into the suburb stop just as they reached the station and they boarded it together, and ten minutes before it was due to arrive at the junction, they went to the door and stood ready to jump off if it did not stop; but it did, just as the moon, restored to its full splendor, sprang from a cloud and flooded the clearing with light. As they stepped off, the sage grass was shivering gently in shades of silver and the clinkers under their feet glittered with a fresh black light. The treetops, fencing the junction like the protecting walls of a garden, were darker than the sky which was hung with gigantic white clouds illuminated like lanterns.

Mr. Head stood very still and felt the action of mercy touch him again but this time he knew that there were no words in the world that could name it. He understood that it grew out of agony, which is not denied to any man and which is given in strange ways to children. He understood it was all a man could carry into death to give his Maker and he suddenly burned with shame that he had so little of it to take with him. He stood appalled, judging himself with the thoroughness of God, while the action of mercy covered his pride like a flame and consumed it. He had never thought himself a great sinner before but he saw now that his true depravity had been hidden from him lest it cause him despair. He realized that he was forgiven for sins from the beginning of time, when he had conceived in his own heart the sin of Adam, until the present, when he had denied poor Nelson. He saw that no sin was too monstrous for him to claim as his own, and since God loved in proportion as He forgave, he felt ready at that instant to enter Paradise.

Nelson, composing his expression under the shadow of his hat brim, watched him with a mixture of fatigue and suspicion, but as the train glided past them and disappeared like a frightened serpent into the woods, even his face lightened and he muttered, "I'm glad I've went once, but I'll never go back again!"

1955

6   THEME

If you ask what a story is "about," an author is likely to answer by telling you the subject. Indeed, many authors tell you the subject in their titles: *An Occurrence at Owl Creek Bridge, The Lottery, Our Friend Judith, Her First Ball.* Though a subject is always concrete, it may be stated at somewhat greater length than the few words of a title: "a man's thoughts as he faces execution for spying during the Civil War" (*Owl Creek Bridge*); "a young girl's excitement at her first grown-up dance and an incident that temporarily depresses her" (*Her First Ball*).

A friend might be more likely to tell you what a story is about by giving you a summary of the action: "This guy shoots a lion but is too chicken to go in and put it out of its misery, so his wife. . . ." (We sometimes call this a **plot summary**, but you will notice that this summary is of the history, of the events in more or less chronological order, while the plot is an arrangement or structuring of that history; in *Macomber*, remember, the lion incident is not told to us first, thought it did happen first.)

Your teacher may well tell you what a story is about by summarizing its **theme.** Some refer to the central idea, the thesis, or even the message of a story, and that is roughly what we mean by theme: a generalization or abstraction from the story.

The subject of *Young Goodman Brown* may be said to be a coven (witches' meeting) or, more fully, "a young colonial New England husband is driven mad by finding everyone he thought good and pure attending a witches' meeting." The theme may be "everyone partakes of evil," or, more succinctly, "the Fall." There are, as you can see, degrees of generalization and abstraction; subject (a young man finds that everyone is evil) shades off into theme, which itself can be more or less general and abstract.

Discussions of literature in or out of class sometimes seem to suggest that stories exist for their themes, that we read only to get the "point" or message. But most themes, you must admit, are somewhat less than earth-shattering. That all men and women are evil may be debatable, but it certainly isn't news. That living beings, human and otherwise, should not be divided into exploiters (hunters) and exploited (hunted)—the apparent theme of *The Most Dangerous Game* —is pretty obvious, something we don't need to read fifteen pages of fiction to find out. No wonder, then, that some of our more skeptical friends contend that stories are only elaborate ways of "saying something simple," that literature is a game in which authors hide their meanings under shells of words.

Of course, reading fifteen pages of a story like *The Most Dangerous Game* can be fun. Could it be that we really read fiction for the fun, and all our talk about themes is just hiding from our Puritan natures the fact that we are goofing off?

I don't believe that articulating the theme of a story is either the purpose of or the excuse for reading fiction, or that authors hide their meanings like Easter eggs. In order to relate his or her unique vision of reality to an absent and unknown reader, a writer must find a way of communicating—some common ground on which to meet the various unique individuals who will read the story. Common experiences, common assumptions, common language, and commonplaces offer such ground. Readers reach out from their own subjective worlds toward that new and different vision of the author with the help of the common elements (the general), and especially through the commonplaces of theme, bringing back the particulars and generalizations of the story to their own reading and living experience. The reader sees a spoiled Easterner on safari in Africa overcome his cowardice in an attempt to put a dangerous animal out of its misery. Generalizing, the reader may conclude that what the story says (its theme) is that life (or happy life) is more than survival, that honor is more important than existence, and that when one's values change one's behavior can be changed. Not planning to go on safari in the very near future, the reader may test out the experience of the story by translating it through its theme to his or her own experience: does this mean that I can change long-standing patterns of behavior that I know are wrong? Do I have any ideals I believe greater than life itself?

We should not confuse these questions with the story, but the significance of any story is modified to some extent by the reader's experience of books and life. This does not imply that you are to reduce every story to the dimensions of what you already know and feel, but rather that you reach out to the story and bring it back to your own experience as an addition and modification. If you're going to make a story yours, and if you are going to make it more than a yarn about a guy who drinks a lot, has an unfaithful wife, and hunts lions and water buffaloes, you will translate it somehow into terms that, while not necessarily psychological or moral precepts, alter or broaden to some degree your own vision of yourself, others, life in general.

When I discussed symbols, I said that, even while a symbol suggests a meaning beyond the particulars of the fiction it remains a detail in the fictional world—the snakelike staff of the stranger in *Young Goodman Brown* remains a staff, Judith's cats remain cats. Some critics would say that this is true also of theme and that theme is related to the story as integrally as symbolic meaning is to detail; that is, rather than *Young Goodman Brown* telling us something we did not know before, its theme and its story modify each other. The theme as I've stated it relates to spiritual evil, the kind of evil suggested by the snake and Satan figures. But this theme is not entirely portable—it cannot be taken out of the story and used as substitute for what the story "means"—nor can it, without qualification, be used to explain all the significant details in the story—the facts that Brown is a newly-wed, that Faith wears pink (coquettish?) ribbons, and that she, whom Brown thought so pure and innocent, shows up at the meeting of witches and sinners suggest a more specific kind of evil than the spiritual or theological evil suggested by the snake and Satan: moral or, even more specifically, sexual evil. This means we must modify our definition of the theme. But how? What does the story imply about the relationship of sex and evil? Is all sex evil? Is original sin sexual? Some details—the snake, the Satanic guide—suggest a theme, other details modify it; still others—Brown's behavior after the night of the witches' meeting—may modify it still further, so that the theme, though an approximate version of it may be abstracted from the story, remains embedded in it, ultimately inseparable from the details of plot, character, setting, and symbol.

A statement that can do justice to all the complexity and all the particulars of the story is not likely to take the simple form of a message. Indeed, it is the complex particularity of literature, its ultimate irreducibility, that makes critics and teachers reject *message* (which suggests a simple packaged statement) as a suitable term even for the paraphrasable thematic content of a story.

Young Goodman Brown is an allegorical story whose details do function as symbols with paraphrasable meanings, yet even its theme refuses to be reduced to a simple statement. *How Much Land Does a Man Need?* is a **parable**, a short fiction that illustrates an explicit moral lesson. That lesson, the theme, is implied in the title. (And here the devil appears not only, at times, in disguise, but also in his proper person.) Even so, Tolstoy's story is not without complexity. How do you account for the first section of the story? Does your paraphrase of the theme accommodate the conversation between the sisters there?

Her First Ball is not allegorical and neither is it parabolic. Though realistic, however, it is a short, rather simple story that seems to have a simple theme overtly enunciated by one of the characters: Leila's elderly partner suggests that her first ball is "only the beginning of her last ball." That youth and life itself are fleeting (scarcely a new truth, but one that we must be reminded of from time to time, no doubt) would seem to be the simple theme of this story. But the scene with the elderly partner is not the end of the story. Leila goes on to dance with a young partner, doesn't recognize her former partner, has fun, and seems to have completely forgotten the man's "message." What is the story "saying"? Is her forgetting "bad"? Or "sad"? Or "good"? Does the theme suggest the thoughtlessness of youth, the incom-municability of experience, trapping us in inescapable patterns, doom-ing us to repeat the experiences of our predecessors? Or is it better for Leila to live while she's young, to make the most of life, rather than dwelling on life's brevity? The specifics of the story modify and enrich all the generalizations we can abstract from it, while these themes and questions, if we recognize them, modify and enrich our reading, our experience of the story.

I realize I have been talking as if a theme or themes spring out at the reader, while to some of you my inference of themes may seem more like pulling rabbits out of hats. *How Much Land Does a Man Need?* does not involve much of a trick: the title asks the question that, once answered, suggests the theme. But there isn't even too much conjuring with *Young Goodman Brown*: I derived the theme of the-ological evil from the symbols (the snake-staff, Satan figure, names) and I tested physical details—like pink ribbons and the narrative situa-tion (the three-month marriage)—which had sexual implications against the theme to see if I would have to modify my paraphrase. In *Her First Ball* a character raises a general issue that is tested by subsequent events in the story and modified by them. In *The Most Dangerous Game* the opening conversation raises thematic issues (the morality of hunting) that are dramatically reinforced by the subse-quent action of the story (Rainsford now the hunted rather than hunter). The title *Beyond the Pale* hints at a theme but too faintly and obliquely to signify until it comes to the surface toward the end of the story. The story itself seems almost to break in half, the first part treating the superficial lives and relationships of four upper-middle-class Britons vacationing in Northern Ireland, the second half threat-ening to become a political tract about the troubled past and present of Ireland. But Cynthia Strafe, one of the four British vacationers, connects their attitudes towards the strife in Ireland and towards their own lives and conduct in a way that profoundly illuminates the title and theme of the story.

There are, of course, other means by which details suggest generali-zations or meaning or by which meaning may be abstracted from detail. You no doubt noticed in *The Most Dangerous Game* the his-torical **allusions**—references outside the story, in this case to history but sometimes to literature, the Bible, and so on. Zaroff is a White Russian general, Ivan a Cossack flogger. The time is not long after the

First World War and the Russian Revolution. The theme of hunter and hunted expands into the historical context as exploiter and exploited and the theme seems to support the weak, the underdog, and predict the overthrow of tyrants like Zaroff or the Czar (-ov or -off is a Russian suffix meaning "son of," so Zaroff implies "son" or product of the Czar). So allusion as well as symbols, plot, focus and voice, and character are elements that contribute to and must be accounted for in paraphrasing a theme. That is why theme is important, and why it comes last in a dicussion of the elements of fiction.

But remember, the theme is an inadequate abstraction from the story; the story and its details do not disappear or lose significance once distilled into theme, nor could you reconstruct a story merely from its paraphrased theme. Indeed, theme and story, history and structure, do not so much interact, are not so much interrelated, as they are fused, inseparable.

Is the connection between the private lives of the vacationing Englishmen in *Beyond the Pale* and the Irish "troubles" part of the plot or part of the theme of that story? Is Pahóm's greed a constituent of character or of theme in *How Much Land Does a Man Need?*

Though they are useful, may be necessary, and seem reasonable or even obvious, constructs, the elements of fiction—plot, focus and voice, character, symbol, and theme—do not, in a sense, really exist. They are convenient ways for us to extricate inextricable threads from the fabric of fiction. As the Old Master Henry James said a hundred years ago:

> A novel is a living thing, all one and continuous, like any other organism, and in proportion as it lives will it be found . . . that in each of its parts there is something of each of the other parts. The critic who over the close texture of a finished work shall pretend to trace a geography of items will mark some frontiers as artificial, I fear, as any that have been known to history. . . . What is character but the determination of incident? What is incident but the illustration of character?

LEO TOLSTOY

How Much Land Does a Man Need?*

I

An elder sister came to visit her younger sister in the country. The elder was married to a tradesman in town, the younger to a peasant in the village. As the sisters sat over their tea talking, the elder began to boast of the advantages of town life: saying how comfortably they lived there, how well they dressed, what fine clothes her children wore, what good things they ate and drank, and how she went to the theater, promenades, and entertainments.

* Translated by Louise and Aylmer Maude.

The younger sister was piqued, and in turn disparaged the life of a tradesman, and stood up for that of a peasant.

"I would not change my way of life for yours," said she. "We may live roughly, but at least we are free from anxiety. You live in better style than we do, but though you often earn more than you need, you are very likely to lose all you have. You know the proverb, 'Loss and gain are brothers twain.' It often happens that people who are wealthy one day are begging their bread the next. Our way is safer. Though a peasant's life is not a fat one, it is a long one. We shall never grow rich, but we shall always have enough to eat."

The elder sister said sneeringly:

"Enough? Yes, if you like to share with the pigs and the calves! What do you know of elegance or manners! However much your goodman may slave, you will die as you are living—on a dung heap— and your children the same."

"Well, what of that?" replied the younger. "Of course our work is rough and coarse. But, on the other hand, it is sure, and we need not bow to anyone. But you, in your towns, are surrounded by temptations; to-day all may be right, but to-morrow the Evil One may tempt your husband with cards, wine, or women, and all will go to ruin. Don't such things happen often enough?"

Pahóm, the master of the house, was lying on the top of the stove and he listened to the women's chatter.

"It is perfectly true," thought he. "Busy as we are from childhood tilling mother earth, we peasants have no time to let any nonsense settle in our heads. Our only trouble is that we haven't land enough. If I had plenty of land, I shouldn't fear the Devil himself!"

The women finished their tea, chatted a while about dress, and then cleared away the tea-things and lay down to sleep.

But the Devil had been sitting behind the stove, and had heard all that was said. He was pleased that the peasant's wife had led her husband into boasting, and that he had said that if he had plenty of land he would not fear the Devil himself.

"All right," thought the Devil. "We will have a tussle. I'll give you land enough; and by means of that land I will get you into my power."

II

Close to the village there lived a lady, a small land-owner who had an estate of about three hundred acres.[1] She had always lived on good terms with the peasants until she engaged as her steward an old soldier, who took to burdening the people with fines. However careful Pahóm tried to be, it happened again and again that now a horse of his got among the lady's oats, now a cow strayed into her garden, now his calves found their way into her meadows—and he always had to pay a fine.

Pahóm paid up, but grumbled, and going home in a temper, was rough with his family. All through that summer, Pahóm had much

1. 120 *desyatíns*. The *desyatína* is properly 2.7 acres but in this story round numbers are used [Maude note].

trouble because of this steward, and he was even glad when winter came and the cattle had to be stabled. Though he grudged the fodder when they could no longer graze on the pasture-land, at least he was free from anxiety about them.

In the winter the news got about that the lady was going to sell her land and that the keeper of the inn on the high road was bargaining for it. When the peasants heard this they were very much alarmed.

"Well," thought they, "if the innkeeper gets the land, he will worry us with fines worse than the lady's steward. We all depend on that estate."

So the peasants went on behalf of their Commune, and asked the lady not to sell the land to the innkeeper, offering her a better price for it themselves. The lady agreed to let them have it. Then the peasants tried to arrange for the Commune to buy the whole estate, so that it might be held by them all in common. They met twice to discuss it, but could not settle the matter; the Evil One sowed discord among them and they could not agree. So they decided to buy the land individually, each according to his means; and the lady agreed to this plan as she had to the other.

Presently Pahóm heard that a neighbor of his was buying fifty acres, and that the lady had consented to accept one half in cash and to wait a year for the other half. Pahóm felt envious.

"Look at that," thought he, "the land is all being sold, and I shall get none of it." So he spoke to his wife.

"Other people are buying," said he, "and we must also buy twenty acres or so. Life is becoming impossible. That steward is simply crushing us with his fines."

So they put their heads together and considered how they could manage to buy it. They had one hundred rúbles[2] laid by. They sold a colt and one half of their bees, hired out one of their sons as a laborer and took his wages in advance; borrowed the rest from a brother-in-law, and so scraped together half the purchase money.

Having done this, Pahóm chose out a farm of forty acres, some of it wooded, and went to the lady to bargain for it. They came to an agreement, and he shook hands with her upon it and paid her a deposit in advance. Then they went to town and signed the deeds; he paying half the price down, and undertaking to pay the remainder within two years.

So now Pahóm had land of his own. He borrowed seed, and sowed it on the land he had bought. The harvest was a good one, and within a year he had managed to pay off his debts both to the lady and to his brother-in-law. So he became a landowner, plowing and sowing his own land, making hay on his own land, cutting his own trees, and feeding his cattle on his own pasture. When he went out to plow his fields, or to look at his growing corn, or at his grass-meadows, his heart would fill with joy. The grass that grew and the flowers that bloomed there seemed to him unlike any that grew elsewhere. Formerly, when he had passed by that land, it had appeared the same as any other land, but now it seemed quite different.

_____

2. That is, about fifty dollars.

III

So Pahóm was well-contented, and everything would have been right if the neighboring peasants would only not have trespassed on his corn-fields and meadows. He appealed to them most civilly, but they still went on: now the Communal herdsmen would let the village cows stray into his meadows, then horses from the night pasture would get among his corn. Pahóm turned them out again and again, and forgave their owners, and for a long time he forbore to prosecute anyone. But at last he lost patience and complained to the District Court. He knew it was the peasants' want of land, and no evil intent on their part, that caused the trouble, but he thought:

"I cannot go on overlooking it or they will destroy all I have. They must be taught a lesson."

So he had them up, gave them one lesson, and then another, and two or three of the peasants were fined. After a time Pahóm's neighbors began to bear him a grudge for this, and would now and then let their cattle on to his land on purpose. One peasant even got into Pahóm's wood at night and cut down five young lime trees for their bark. Pahóm passing through the wood one day noticed something white. He came nearer and saw the stripped trunks lying on the ground, and close by stood the stumps where the trees had been. Pahóm was furious.

"If he had only cut one here and there it would have been bad enough," thought Pahóm, "but the rascal has actually cut down a whole clump. If I could only find out who did this, I would pay him out."

He racked his brains as to who it could be. Finally he decided: "It must be Simon—no one else could have done it." So he went to Simon's homestead to have a look round, but he found nothing, and only had an angry scene. However, he now felt more certain than ever that Simon had done it, and he lodged a complaint. Simon was summoned. The case was tried, and retried, and at the end of it all Simon was acquitted, there being no evidence against him. Pahóm felt still more aggrieved, and let his anger loose upon the Elder and the Judges.

"You let thieves grease your palms," said he. "If you were honest folk yourselves you would not let a thief go free."

So Pahóm quarreled with the Judges and with his neighbors. Threats to burn his building began to be uttered. So though Pahóm had more land, his place in the Commune was much worse than before.

About this time a rumor got about that many people were moving to new parts.

"There's no need for me to leave my land," thought Pahóm. "But some of the others might leave our village and then there would be more room for us. I would take over their land myself and make my estate a bit bigger. I could then live more at ease. As it is, I am still too cramped to be comfortable."

One day Pahóm was sitting at home when a peasant, passing through the village, happened to call in. He was allowed to stay the night, and supper was given him. Pahóm had a talk with this peasant and asked him where he came from. The stranger answered that he

came from beyond the Vólga, where he had been working. One word led
to another, and the man went on to say that many people were settling
in those parts. He told how some people from his village had settled
there. They had joined the Commune, and had had twenty-five acres
per man granted them. The land was so good, he said, that the rye
sown on it grew as high as a horse, and so thick that five cuts of a
sickle made a sheaf. One peasant, he said, had brought nothing with
him but his bare hands, and now he had six horses and two cows of his
own.

Pahóm's heart kindled with desire. He thought:

"Why should I suffer in this narrow hole, if one can live so well
elsewhere? I will sell my land and my homestead here, and with the
money I will start afresh over there and get everything new. In this
crowded place one is always having trouble. But I must first go and
find out all about it myself."

Towards summer he got ready and started. He went down the Vólga
on a steamer to Samára, then walked another three hundred miles on
foot, and at last reached the place. It was just as the stranger had said.
The peasants had plenty of land: every man had twenty-five acres of
Communal land given him for his use, and any one who had money
could buy, besides, at two shillings an acre[3] as much good freehold
land as he wanted.

Having found out all he wished to know, Pahóm returned home as
autumn came on, and began selling off his belongings. He sold his
land at a profit, sold his homestead and all his cattle, and withdrew
from membership of the Commune. He only waited till the spring, and
then started with his family for the new settlement.

IV

As soon as Pahóm and his family reached their new abode, he applied
for admission into the Commune of a large village. He stood treat to
the Elders and obtained the necessary documents. Five shares of
Communal land were given him for his own and his sons' use: that is
to say—125 acres (not all together, but in different fields) besides the
use of the Communal pasture. Pahóm put up the buildings he needed,
and bought cattle. Of the Communal land alone he had three times as
much as at his former home, and the land was good corn-land. He was
ten times better off than he had been. He had plenty of arable land
and pasturage, and could keep as many head of cattle as he liked.

At first, in the bustle of building and settling down, Pahóm was
pleased with it all, but when he got used to it he began to think that
even here he had not enough land. The first year, he sowed wheat on
his share of the Communal land and had a good crop. He wanted to
go on sowing wheat, but had not enough Communal land for the
purpose, and what he had already used was not available; for in those
parts wheat is only sown on virgin soil or on fallow land. It is sown
for one or two years, and then the land lies fallow till it is again
overgrown with prairie grass. There were many who wanted such land
and there was not enough for all; so that people quarreled about it.

3. Three rubles per *desyatína* [Maude note]; that is, about a half-dollar an acre.

Those who were better off wanted it for growing wheat, and those who were poor wanted it to let to dealers, so that they might raise money to pay their taxes. Pahóm wanted to sow more wheat, so he rented land from a dealer for a year. He sowed much wheat and had a fine crop, but the land was too far from the village—the wheat had to be carted more than ten miles. After a time Pahóm noticed that some peasant-dealers were living on separate farms and were growing wealthy; and he thought:

"If I were to buy some freehold land and have a homestead on it, it would be a different thing altogether. Then it would all be nice and compact."

The question of buying freehold land recurred to him again and again.

He went on in the same way for three years, renting land and sowing wheat. The seasons turned out well and the crops were good, so that he began to lay money by. He might have gone on living contentedly, but he grew tired of having to rent other people's land every year, and having to scramble for it. Wherever there was good land to be had, the peasants would rush for it and it was taken up at once, so that unless you were sharp about it you got none. It happened in the third year that he and a dealer together rented a piece of pasture land from some peasants; and they had already plowed it up, when there was some dispute and the peasants went to law about it, and things fell out so that the labor was all lost.

"If it were my own land," thought Pahóm, "I should be independent, and there would not be all this unpleasantness."

So Pahóm began looking out for land which he could buy; and he came across a peasant who had bought thirteen hundred acres, but having got into difficulties was willing to sell again cheap. Pahóm bargained and haggled with him, and at last they settled the price at 1,500 rúbles, part in cash and part to be paid later. They had all but clinched the matter when a passing dealer happened to stop at Pahóm's one day to get a feed for his horses. He drank tea with Pahóm and they had a talk. The dealer said that he was just returning from the land of the Baskírs,[4] far away, where he had bought thirteen thousand acres of land, all for 1,000 rúbles. Pahóm questioned him further, and the tradesman said:

"All one need do is to make friends with the chiefs. I gave away about one hundred rúbles' worth of silk robes and carpets, besides a case of tea, and I gave wine to those who would drink it; and I got the land for less than a penny an acre."[5] And he showed Pahóm the title-deeds, saying:

"The land lies near a river, and the whole prairie is virgin soil."

Pahóm plied him with questions, and the tradesman said:

"There is more land there than you could cover if you walked a year, and it all belongs to the Bashkírs. They are as simple as sheep, and land can be got almost for nothing."

---

4. Extreme eastern European Russia, extending southwest from the Ural mountains; the land is chiefly steppes with fertile meadows in the valleys.

5. Five *kopeks* for a *desyatína* [Maude note]. There are 100 *kopeks* to the *rúble*. The English penny (240 to the pound) was roughly equal to two American cents.

"There now," thought Pahóm, "with my one thousand rúbles, why should I get only thirteen hundred acres, and saddle myself with a debt besides? If I take it out there, I can get more than ten times as much for the money."

V

Pahóm inquired how to get to the place, and as soon as the tradesman had left him, he prepared to go there himself. He left his wife to look after the homestead, and started on his journey taking his man with him. They stopped at a town on their way and bought a case of tea, some wine, and other presents, as the tradesman had advised. On and on they went until they had gone more than three hundred miles, and on the seventh day they came to a place where the Bashkírs had pitched their tents. It was all just as the tradesman had said. The people lived on the steppes, by a river, in felt-covered tents. They neither tilled the ground, nor ate bread. Their cattle and horses grazed in herds on the steppe. The colts were tethered behind the tents, and the mares were driven to them twice a day. The mares were milked, and from the milk kumiss was made. It was the women who prepared kumiss, and they also made cheese. As far as the men were concerned, drinking kumiss and tea, eating mutton, and playing on their pipes was all they cared about. They were all stout and merry, and all the summer long they never thought of doing any work. They were quite ignorant, and knew no Russian, but were good-natured enough.

As soon as they saw Pahóm, they came out of their tents and gathered round their visitor. An interpreter was found, and Pahóm told them he had come about some land. The Bashkírs seemed very glad; they took Pahóm and led him into one of the best tents, where they made him sit on some down cushions placed on a carpet, while they sat round him. They gave him some tea and kumiss, and had a sheep killed, and gave him mutton to eat. Pahóm took presents out of his cart and distributed them among the Bashkírs, and divided the tea amongst them. The Bashkírs were delighted. They talked a great deal among themselves, and then told the interpreter to translate.

"They wish to tell you," said the interpreter, "that they like you, and that it is our custom to do all we can to please a guest and to repay him for his gifts. You have given us presents, now tell us which of the things we possess please you best, that we may present them to you."

"What pleases me best here," answered Pahóm, "is your land. Our land is crowded and the soil is exhausted; but you have plenty of land and it is good land. I never saw the like of it."

The interpreter translated. The Bashkírs talked among themselves for a while. Pahóm could not understand what they were saying, but saw that they were much amused and that they shouted and laughed. Then they were silent and looked at Pahóm while the interpreter said:

"They wish me to tell you that in return for your presents they will gladly give you as much land as you want. You have only to point it out with your hand and it is yours."

The Bashkírs talked again for a while and began to dispute. Pahóm asked what they were disputing about, and the interpreter told him that some of them thought they ought to ask their Chief about the land and not act in his absence, while others thought there was no need to wait for his return.

VI

While the Bashkírs were disputing, a man in a large fox-fur cap appeared on the scene. They all became silent and rose to their feet. The interpreter said, "This is our Chief himself."

Pahóm immediately fetched the best dressing-gown and five pounds of tea, and offered these to the Chief. The Chief accepted them, and seated himself in the place of honor. The Bashkírs at once began telling him something. The Chief listened for a while, then made a sign with his head for them to be silent, and addressing himself to Pahóm, said in Russian:

"Well, let it be so. Choose whatever piece of land you like; we have plenty of it."

"How can I take as much as I like?" thought Pahóm. "I must get a deed to make it secure, or else they may say, 'It is yours,' and afterwards may take it away again."

"Thank you for your kind words," he said aloud. "You have much land, and I only want a little. But I should like to be sure which bit is mine. Could it not be measured and made over to me? Life and death are in God's hands. You good people give it to me, but your children might wish to take it away again."

"You are quite right," said the Chief. "We will make it over to you."

"I heard that a dealer had been here," continued Pahóm, "and that you gave him a little land, too, and signed title-deeds to that effect. I should like to have it done in the same way."

The Chief understood.

"Yes," replied he, "that can be done quite easily. We have a scribe, and we will go to town with you and have the deed properly sealed."

"And what will be the price?" asked Pahóm.

'Our price is always the same: one thousand rúbles a day."

Pahóm did not understand.

"A day? What measure is that? How many acres would that be?"

"We do not know how to reckon it out," said the Chief. "We sell it by the day. As much as you can go round on your feet in a day is yours, and the price is one thousand rúbles a day."

Pahóm was surprised.

"But in a day you can get round a large tract of land," he said.

The Chief laughed.

"It will all be yours!" said he. "But there is one condition: If you don't return on the same day to the spot whence you started, your money is lost."

"But how am I to mark the way that I have gone?"

"Why, we shall go to any spot you like, and stay there. You must start from that spot and make your round, taking a spade with you.

Wherever you think necessary, make a mark. At every turning, dig a hole and pile up the turf; then afterwards we will go round with a plow from hole to hole. You may make as large a circuit as you please, but before the sun sets you must return to the place you started from. All the land you cover will be yours."

Pahóm was delighted. It was decided to start early next morning. They talked a while, and after drinking some more kumiss and eating some more mutton, they had tea again, and then the night came on. They gave Pahóm a feather-bed to sleep on, and the Bashkírs dispersed for the night, promising to assemble the next morning at daybreak and ride out before sunrise to the appointed spot.

VII

Pahóm lay on the feather-bed, but could not sleep. He kept thinking about the land.

"What a large tract I will mark off!" thought he. "I can easily do thirty-five miles in a day. The days are long now, and within a circuit of thirty-five miles what a lot of land there will be! I will sell the poorer land, or let it to peasants, but I'll pick out the best and farm it. I will buy two ox-teams, and hire two more laborers. About a hundred and fifty acres shall be plow-land, and I will pasture cattle on the rest."

Pahóm lay awake all night, and dozed off only just before dawn. Hardly were his eyes closed when he had a dream. He thought he was lying in that same tent and heard somebody chuckling outside. He wondered who it could be, and rose and went out, and he saw the Bashkír Chief sitting in front of the tent holding his sides and rolling about with laughter. Going nearer to the Chief, Pahóm asked: "What are you laughing at?" But he saw that it was no longer the Chief, but the dealer who had recently stopped at his house and had told him about the land. Just as Pahóm was going to ask, "Have you been here long?" he saw that it was not the dealer, but the peasant who had come up from the Vólga, long ago, to Pahóm's old home. Then he saw that it was not the peasant either, but the Devil himself with hoofs and horns, sitting there and chuckling, and before him lay a man barefoot, prostrate on the ground, with only trousers and a shirt on. And Pahóm dreamt that he looked more attentively to see what sort of a man it was that was lying there, and he saw that the man was dead, and that it was himself! He awoke horror-struck.

"What things one does dream," thought he.

Looking round he saw through the open door that the dawn was breaking.

"It's time to wake them up," thought he. "We ought to be starting."

He got up, roused his man (who was sleeping in his cart), bade him harness; and went to call the Bashkírs.

"It's time to go to the steppe to measure the land," he said.

The Bashkírs rose and assembled, and the Chief came too. Then they began drinking kumiss again, and offered Pahóm some tea, but he would not wait.

"If we are to go, let us go. It is high time," said he.

VIII

The Bashkírs got ready and they all started: some mounted on horses, and some in carts. Pahóm drove in his own small cart with his servant and took a spade with him. When they reached the steppe, the morning red was beginning to kindle. They ascended a hillock (called by the Bashkírs a *shikhan*) and dismounting from their carts and their horses, gathered in one spot. The Chief came up to Pahóm and stretching out his arm towards the plain:

"See," said he, "all this, as far as your eye can reach, is ours. You may have any part of it you like."

Pahóm's eyes glistened: it was all virgin soil, as flat as the palm of your hand, as black as the seed of a poppy, and in the hollows different kinds of grasses grew breast high.

The Chief took off his fox-fur cap, placed it on the ground and said:

"This will be the mark. Start from here, and return here again. All the land you go round shall be yours."

Pahóm took out his money and put it on the cap. Then he took off his outer coat, remaining in his sleeveless under-coat. He unfastened his girdle and tied it tight below his stomach, put a little bag of bread into the breast of his coat, and tying a flask of water to his girdle, he drew up the tops of his boots, took the spade from his man, and stood ready to start. He considered for some moments which way he had better go—it was tempting everywhere.

"No matter," he concluded, "I will go towards the rising sun."

He turned his face to the east, stretched himself, and waited for the sun to appear above the rim.

"I must lose no time," he thought, "and it is easier walking while it is still cool."

The sun's rays had hardly flashed above the horizon, before Pahóm, carrying the spade over his shoulder, went down into the steppe.

Pahóm started walking neither slowly nor quickly. After having gone a thousand yards he stopped, dug a hole, and placed pieces of turf one on another to make it more visible. Then he went on; and now that he had walked off his stiffness he quickened his pace. After a while he dug another hole.

Pahóm looked back. The hillock could be distinctly seen in the sunlight, with the people on it, and the glittering tires of the cart-wheels. At a rough guess Pahóm concluded that he had walked three miles. It was growing warmer; he took off his under-coat, flung it across his shoulder, and went on again. It had grown quite warm now; he looked at the sun, it was time to think of breakfast.

"The first shift is done, but there are four in a day, and it is too soon yet to turn. But I will just take off my boots," said he to himself.

He sat down, took off his boots, stuck them into his girdle, and went on. It was easy walking now.

"I will go on for another three miles," thought he, "and then turn to the left. This spot is so fine, that it would be a pity to lose it. The further one goes, the better the land seems."

He went straight on for a while, and when he looked round, the hillock was scarcely visible and the people on it looked like black ants, and he could just see something glistening there in the sun.

"Ah," thought Pahóm, "I have gone far enough in this direction, it is time to turn. Besides I am in a regular sweat, and very thirsty."

He stopped, dug a large hole, and heaped up pieces of turf. Next he untied his flask, had a drink, and then turned sharply to the left. He went on and on; the grass was high, and it was very hot.

Pahóm began to grow tired: he looked at the sun and saw that it was noon.

"Well," he thought, "I must have a rest."

He sat down, and ate some bread and drank some water; but he did not lie down, thinking that if he did he might fall asleep. After sitting a little while, he went on again. At first he walked easily: the food had strengthened him; but it had become terribly hot and he felt sleepy, still he went on, thinking: "An hour to suffer, a life-time to live."

He went a long way in this direction also, and was about to turn to the left again, when he perceived a damp hollow: "It would be a pity to leave that out," he thought. "Flax would do well there." So he went on past the hollow, and dug a hole on the other side of it before he turned the corner. Pahóm looked towards the hillock. The heat made the air hazy: it seemed to be quivering, and through the haze the people on the hillock could scarcely be seen.

"Ah!" thought Pahóm, "I have made the sides too long; I must make this one shorter." And he went along the third side, stepping faster. He looked at the sun: it was nearly half-way to the horizon, and he had not yet done two miles of the third side of the square. He was still ten miles from the goal.

"No," he thought, "though it will make my land lop-sided, I must hurry back in a straight line now. I might go too far, and as it is I have a great deal of land."

So Pahóm hurriedly dug a hole, and turned straight towards the hillock.

IX

Pahóm went straight towards the hillock, but he now walked with difficulty. He was done up with the heat, his bare feet were cut and bruised, and his legs began to fail. He longed to rest, but it was impossible if he meant to get back before sunset. The sun waits for no man, and it was sinking lower and lower.

"Oh dear," he thought, "if only I have not blundered trying for too much! What if I am too late?"

He looked towards the hillock and at the sun. He was still far from his goal, and the sun was already near the rim.

Pahóm walked on and on; it was very hard walking but he went quicker and quicker. He pressed on, but was still far from the place. He began running, threw away his coat, his boots, his flask, and his cap, and kept only the spade which he used as a support.

"What shall I do," he thought again, "I have grasped too much and ruined the whole affair. I can't get there before the sun sets."

And this fear made him still more breathless. Pahóm went on running, his soaking shirt and trousers stuck to him and his mouth was parched. His breast was working like a blacksmith's bellows, his heart was beating like a hammer, and his legs were giving way as if they did not belong to him. Pahóm was seized with terror lest he should die of the strain.

Though afraid of death, he could not stop. "After having run all that way they will call me a fool if I stop now," thought he. And he ran on and on, and drew near and heard the Bashkírs yelling and shouting to him, and their cries inflamed his heart still more. He gathered his last strength and ran on.

The sun was close to the rim, and cloaked in mist looked large, and red as blood. Now, yes now, it was about to set! The sun was quite low, but he was also quite near his aim. Pahóm could already see the people on the hillock waving their arms to hurry up. He could see the fox-fur cap on the ground and the money on it, and the Chief sitting on the ground holding his sides. And Pahóm remembered his dream.

"There is plenty of land," thought he, "but will God let me live on it? I have lost my life, I have lost my life! I shall never reach that spot!"

Pahóm looked at the sun, which had reached the earth: one side of it had already disappeared. With all his remaining strength he rushed on, bending his body forward so that his legs could hardly follow fast enough to keep him from falling. Just as he reached the hillock it suddenly grew dark. He looked up—the sun had already set! He gave a cry: "All my labor has been in vain," thought he, and was about to stop, but he heard the Bashkírs still shouting, and remembered that though to him, from below, the sun seemed to have set, they on the hillock could still see it. He took a long breath and ran up the hillock. It was still light there. He reached the top and saw the cap. Before it sat the Chief laughing and holding his sides. Again Pahóm remembered his dream, and he uttered a cry: his legs gave way beneath him, he fell forward and reached the cap with his hands.

"Ah, that's a fine fellow!" exclaimed the Chief. "He has gained much land!"

Pahóm's servant came running up and tried to raise him, but he saw that blood was flowing from his mouth. Pahóm was dead!

The Bashkírs clicked their tongues to show their pity.

His servant picked up the spade and dug a grave long enough for Pahóm to lie in, and buried him in it. Six feet from his head to his heels was all he needed.

1886

Her First Ball

Exactly when the ball began Leila would have found it hard to say. Perhaps her first real partner was the cab. It did not matter that she shared the cab with the Sheridan girls and their brother. She sat back in her own little corner of it, and the bolster on which her hand rested felt like the sleeve of an unknown young man's dress suit; and away they bowled, past waltzing lampposts and houses and fences and trees.

"Have you really never been to a ball before, Leila? But, my child, how too weird—" cried the Sheridan girls.

"Our nearest neighbor was fifteen miles," said Leila softly, gently opening and shutting her fan.

Oh, dear, how hard it was to be indifferent like the others! She tried not to smile too much; she tried not to care. But every single thing was so new and exciting . . . Meg's tuberoses, Jose's long loop of amber, Laura's little dark head, pushing above her white fur like a flower through snow. She would remember for ever. It even gave her a pang to see her cousin Laurie throw away the wisps of tissue paper he pulled from the fastenings of his new gloves. She would like to have kept those wisps as a keepsake, as a remembrance. Laurie leaned forward and put his hand on Laura's knee.

"Look here, darling," he said. "The third and the ninth as usual. Twig?"

Oh, how marvellous to have a brother! In her excitement Leila felt that if there had been time, if it hadn't been impossible, she couldn't have helped crying because she was an only child, and no brother had ever said "Twig?" to her; no sister would ever say, as Meg said to Jose that moment, "I've never known your hair go up more successfully than it has tonight!"

But, of course, there was no time. They were at the drill hall already; there were cabs in front of them and cabs behind. The road was bright on either side with moving fan-like lights, and on the pavement gay couples seemed to float through the air; little satin shoes chased each other like birds.

"Hold on to me, Leila; you'll get lost," said Laura.

"Come on, girls, let's make a dash for it," said Laurie.

Leila put two fingers on Laura's pink velvet cloak, and they were somehow lifted past the big golden lantern, carried along the passage, and pushed into the little room marked "Ladies." Here the crowd was so great there was hardly space to take off their things; the noise was deafening. Two benches on either side were stacked high with wraps. Two old women in white aprons ran up and down tossing fresh armfuls. And everybody was pressing forward trying to get at the little dressing table and mirror at the far end.

A great quivering jet of gas lighted the ladies' room. It couldn't wait; it was dancing already. When the door opened again and there came a burst of tuning from the drill hall, it leaped almost to the ceiling.

Dark girls, fair girls were patting their hair, tying ribbons again, tucking handkerchiefs down the fronts of their bodices, smoothing marble-white gloves. And because they were all laughing it seemed to Leila that they were all lovely.

"Aren't there any invisible hairpins?" cried a voice. "How most extraordinary! I can't see a single invisible hairpin."

"Powder my back, there's a darling," cried some one else.

"But I must have a needle and cotton. I've torn simply miles and miles of the frill," wailed a third.

Then, "Pass them along, pass them along!" The straw basket of programs was tossed from arm to arm. Darling little pink-and-silver programs, with pink pencils and fluffy tassels. Leila's fingers shook as she took one out of the basket. She wanted to ask someone, "Am I meant to have one too?" but she had just time to read: "Waltz 3. *Two, Two in a Canoe.* Polka 4. *Making the Feathers Fly,*" when Meg cried, "Ready, Leila?" and they pressed their way through the crush in the passage towards the big double doors of the drill hall.

Dancing had not begun yet, but the band had stopped tuning, and the noise was so great it seemed that when it did begin to play it would never be heard. Leila, pressing close to Meg, looking over Meg's shoulder, felt that even the little quivering colored flags strung across the ceiling were talking. She quite forgot to be shy; she forgot how in the middle of dressing she had sat down on the bed with one shoe off and one shoe on and begged her mother to ring up her cousins and say she couldn't go after all. And the rush of longing she had had to be sitting on the veranda of their forsaken upcountry home, listening to the baby owls crying "More pork" in the moonlight, was changed to a rush of joy so sweet that it was hard to bear alone. She clutched her fan, and, gazing at the gleaming, golden floor, the azaleas, the lanterns, the stage at one end with its red carpet and gilt chairs and the band in a corner, she thought breathlessly, "How heavenly; how simply heavenly!"

All the girls stood grouped together at one side of the doors, the men at the other, and the chaperones in dark dresses, smiling rather foolishly, walked with little careful steps over the polished floor towards the stage.

"This is my little country cousin Leila. Be nice to her. Find her partners; she's under my wing," said Meg, going up to one girl after another.

Strange faces smiled at Leila—sweetly, vaguely. Strange voices answered, "Of course, my dear." But Leila felt the girls didn't really see her. They were looking towards the men. Why didn't the men begin? What were they waiting for? There they stood, smoothing their gloves, patting their glossy hair and smiling among themselves. Then, quite suddenly, as if they had only just made up their minds that that was what they had to do, the men came gliding over the parquet. There was a joyful flutter among the girls. A tall, fair man flew up to Meg, seized her program, scribbled something; Meg passed him on to Leila. "May I have the pleasure?" He ducked and smiled. There came a dark man wearing an eyeglass, then cousin Laurie with a friend, and Laura with a little freckled fellow whose tie was crooked. Then quite an old man—fat, with a big bald patch on his head—took her program and murmured, "Let me see, let me see!" And he was a long time comparing his program, which looked black with names, with hers. It seemed to give him so much trouble that Leila was ashamed. "Oh, please don't bother," she said eagerly. But instead of replying the fat man wrote something, glanced at her again. "Do I remember this bright little face?" he said softly. "Is it known to me of yore?" At that moment the band began playing; the fat man disappeared. He was tossed away on a great wave of music that came flying over the gleaming floor, breaking the groups up into couples, scattering them, sending them spinning. . . .

Leila had learned to dance at boarding school. Every Saturday afternoon the boarders were hurried off to a little corrugated iron mission hall where Miss Eccles (of London) held her "select" classes. But the difference between that dusty-smelling hall—with calico texts on the walls, the poor terrified little woman in a brown velvet toque with rabbit's ears thumping the cold piano, Miss Eccles poking the girls' feet with her long white wand—and this was so tremendous that Leila was sure if her partner didn't come and she had to listen to that marvelous music and to watch the others sliding, gliding over the golden floor, she would die at least, or faint, or lift her arms and fly out of one of those dark windows that showed the stars.

"Ours, I think—" Some one bowed, smiled, and offered her his arm; she hadn't to die after all. Some one's hand pressed her waist, and she floated away like a flower that is tossed into a pool.

"Quite a good floor, isn't it?" drawled a faint voice close to her ear.

"I think it's most beautifully slippery," said Leila.

"Pardon!" The faint voice sounded surprised. Leila said it again. And there was a tiny pause before the voice echoed, "Oh, quite!" and she was swung round again.

He steered so beautifully. That was the great difference between dancing with girls and men, Leila decided. Girls banged into each other, and stamped on each other's feet; the girl who was gentleman always clutched you so.

The azaleas were separate flowers no longer; they were pink and white flags streaming by.

"Were you at the Bells' last week." the voice came again. It sounded tired. Leila wondered whether she ought to ask him if he would like to stop.

"No, this is my first dance," said she.

Her partner gave a little gasping laugh. "Oh, I say," he protested.

"Yes, it is really the first dance I've ever been to." Leila was most fervent. It was such a relief to be able to tell somebody. "You see, I've lived in the country all my life up until now. . . ."

At that moment the music stopped, and they went to sit on two chairs against the wall. Leila tucked her pink satin feet under and fanned herself, while she blissfully watched the other couples passing and disappearing through the swing doors.

"Enjoying yourself, Leila?" asked Jose, nodding her golden head.

Laura passed and gave her the faintest little wink; it made Leila wonder for a moment whether she was quite grown up after all. Certainly her partner did not say very much. He coughed, tucked his handkerchief away, pulled down his waistcoat, took a minute thread off his sleeve. But it didn't matter. Almost immediately the band started, and her second partner seemed to spring from the ceiling.

"Floor's not bad," said the new voice. Did one always begin with the floor? And then, "Were you at the Neaves' on Tuesday?" And again Leila explained. Perhaps it was a little strange that her partners were not more interested. For it was thrilling. Her first ball! She was only at the beginning of everything. It seemed to her that she had never known what the night was like before. Up till now it had been dark, silent, beautiful very often—oh, yes—but mournful somehow. Solemn. And now it would never be like that again—it had opened dazzling bright.

"Care for an ice?" said her partner. And they went through the swing doors, down the passage, to the supper room. Her cheeks burned, she was fearfully thirsty. How sweet the ices looked on little glass plates, and how cold the frosted spoon was, iced too! And when they came back to the hall there was the fat man waiting for her by the door. It gave her quite a shock again to see how old he was; he ought to have been on the stage with the fathers and mothers. And when Leila compared him with her other partners he looked shabby. His waistcoat was creased, there was a button off his glove, his coat looked as if it was dusty with French chalk.

'Come along, little lady," said the fat man. He scarcely troubled to clasp her, and they moved away so gently, it was more like walking than dancing. But he said not a word about the floor. "Your first dance, isn't it?" he murmured.

"How *did* you know?"

"Ah," said the fat man, "that's what it is to be old!" He wheezed faintly as he steered her past an awkward couple. "You see, I've been doing this kind of thing for the last thirty years."

"Thirty years?" cried Leila. Twelve years before she was born!

"It hardly bears thinking about, does it?" said the fat man gloomily. Leila looked at his bald head, and she felt quite sorry for him.

"I think it's marvelous to be still going on," she said kindly.

"Kind little lady," said the fat man, and he pressed her a little closer, and hummed a bar of the waltz. "Of course," he said, "you can't hope to last anything like as long as that. No-o," said the fat man, "long before that you'll be sitting up there on the stage, looking on, in your nice black velvet. And these pretty arms will have turned into little short fat ones, and you'll beat time with such a different kind of fan—a black bony one." The fat man seemed to shudder. "And you'll smile away like the poor old dears up there, and point to your daughter, and tell the elderly lady next to you how some dreadful man tried to kiss her at the club ball. And your heart will ache, ache"—the fat man squeezed her closer still, as if he really was sorry for that poor heart—"because no one wants to kiss you now. And you'll say how unpleasant these polished floors are to walk on, how dangerous they are. Eh, Mademoiselle Twinkletoes?" said the fat man softly.

Leila gave a light little laugh, but she did not feel like laughing. Was it—could it all be true? It sounded terribly true. Was this first ball only the beginning of her last ball after all? At that the music seemed to change; it sounded sad, sad it rose upon a great sigh. Oh, how quickly things changed! Why didn't happiness last for ever? For ever wasn't a bit too long.

"I want to stop," she said in a breathless voice. The fat man led her to the door.

"No," she said, "I won't go outside. I won't sit down. I'll just stand here, thank you." She leaned against the wall, tapping with her foot, pulling up her gloves and trying to smile. But deep inside her a little girl threw her pinafore over her head and sobbed. Why had he spoiled it all?

"I say, you know," said the fat man, "you mustn't take me seriously, little lady."

"As if I should!" said Leila, tossing her small dark head and sucking her underlip. . . .

Again the couples paraded. The swing doors opened and shut. Now new music was given out by the bandmaster. But Leila didn't want to dance any more. She wanted to be home, or sitting on the veranda listening to those baby owls. When she looked through the dark windows at the stars, they had long beams like wings. . . .

But presently a soft, melting, ravishing tune began, and a young man with curly hair bowed before her. She would have to dance, out of politeness, until she could find Meg. Very stiffly she walked into the middle; very haughtily she put her hand on his sleeve. But in one minute, in one turn, her feet glided, glided. The lights, the azaleas, the dresses, the pink faces, the velvet chairs, all became one beautiful flying wheel. And when her next partner bumped her into the fat man and he said, "Par*don*," she smiled at him more radiantly than ever. She didn't even recognize him again.

1922

WILLIAM TREVOR

Beyond the Pale

We always went to Ireland in June.

Ever since the four of us began to go on holidays together, in 1965 it must have been, we had spent the first fortnight of the month at Glencorn Lodge in Co. Antrim.[1] Perfection, as Dekko put it once, and none of us disagreed. It's a Georgian house by the sea, not far

---

1. County in Northern Ireland containing the national capital, Belfast.

from the village of Ardbeag. It's quite majestic in its rather elegant way, a garden running to the very edge of a cliff, its long rhododendron drive—or avenue, as they say in Ireland. The English couple who bought the house in the early sixties, the Malseeds, have had to build on quite a bit but it's all been discreetly done, the Georgian style preserved throughout. Figs grow in the sheltered gardens, and apricots, and peaches in the greenhouses which old Mr. Saxton presides over. He's Mrs. Malseed's father actually. They brought him with them from Surrey, and their Dalmatians, Charger and Snooze.

It was Strafe who found Glencorn for us. He'd come across an advertisement in the *Lady* in the days when the Malseeds still felt the need to advertise. "How about this?" he said one evening at the end of the second rubber, and then read out the details. We had gone away together the summer before, to a hotel that had been recommended on the Costa del Sol, but it hadn't been a success because the food was so appalling. "We could try this Irish one," Dekko suggested cautiously, which is what we eventually we did.

The four of us have been playing bridge together for ages, Dekko, Strafe, Cynthia and myself. They call me Milly, though strictly speaking my name is Dorothy Milson. Dekko picked up his nickname at school, Dekko Deakin sounding rather good, I dare say. He and Strafe were in fact at school together, which must be why we all call Strafe by his surname: Major R. B. Strafe he is, the initials standing for Robert Buchanan. We're of an age, the four of us, all in the early fifties: the prime of life, so Dekko insists. We live quite close to Leatherhead, where the Malseeds were before they decided to make the change from Surrey to Co. Antrim. Quite a coincidence, we always think.

"How *very* nice," Mrs. Malseed said, smiling her welcome again this year. Some instinct seems to tell her when guests are about to arrive, for she's rarely not waiting in the large low-ceilinged hall that always smells of flowers. She dresses beautifully, differently every day, and changing of course in the evening. Her blouse on this occasion was scarlet and silver, in stripes, her skirt black. This choice gave her a brisk look, which was fitting because being so busy she often has to be a little on the brisk side. She has smooth gray hair which she once told me she entirely looks after herself, and she almost always wears a black velvet band in it. Her face is well made up, and for one who arranges so many vases of flowers and otherwise has to use her hands she manages to keep them marvelously in condition. Her fingernails are varnished a soft pink, and a small gold bangle always adorns her right wrist, a wedding present from her husband.

"Arthur, take the party's luggage," she commanded the old porter, who doubles as odd-job man. "Rose, Geranium, Hydrangea, Fuchsia." She referred to the titles of the rooms reserved for us: in winter, when no one much comes to Glencorn Lodge, pleasant little details like that are seen to. Mrs. Malseed herself painted the flower-plaques that are attached to the doors of the hotel instead of numbers; her husband sees to redecoration and repairs.

"Well, well, well," Mr. Malseed said now, entering the hall through the door that leads to the kitchen regions. "A hundred thousand welcomes," he greeted us in the Irish manner. He's rather shorter than Mrs. Malseed, who's handsomely tall. He wears Donegal[2] tweed suits and is brown as a berry, including his head, which is bald. His dark brown eyes twinkle at you, making you feel rather more than just another hotel guest. They run the place like a country house, really.

"Good trip?" Mr. Malseed inquired.

"Super," Dekko said. "Not a worry all the way."

"Splendid."

"The wretched boat sailed an hour early one day last week," Mrs. Malseed said. "Quite a little band were left stranded at Stranraer."

Strafe laughed. Typical of that steamship company, he said. "Catching the tide, I dare say?"

"They caught a rocket from me," Mrs. Malseed replied good-humoredly. "A couple of old dears were due with us on Tuesday and had to spend the night in some awful Scottish lodging-house. It nearly finished them."

Everyone laughed, and I could feel the others thinking that our holiday had truly begun. Nothing had changed at Glencorn Lodge, all was well with its Irish world. Kitty from the dining-room came out to greet us, spotless in her uniform. "Ach, you're looking younger," she said, paying the compliment to all four of us, causing everyone in the hall to laugh again. Kitty's a bit of a card.

Arthur led the way to the rooms called Rose, Geranium, Hydrangea and Fuchsia, carrying as much of our luggage as he could manage and returning for the remainder. Arthur has a beaten, fisherman's face and short gray hair. He wears a green baize apron, and a white shirt with an imitation-silk scarf tucked into it at the neck. The scarf, in different swirling greens which blend nicely with the green of his apron, is an idea of Mrs. Malseed's and one appreciates the effort, if not at a uniform, at least at tidiness.

"Thank you very much," I said to Arthur in my room, smiling and finding him a coin.

We played a couple of rubbers after dinner as usual, but not of course going on for as long as we might have because we were still quite tired after the journey. In the lounge there was a French family, two girls and their parents, and a honeymoon couple—or so we had speculated during dinner—and a man on his own. There had been other people at dinner of course, because in June Glencorn Lodge is always full: from where we sat in the window we could see some of them strolling about the lawns, a few taking the cliff path down to the seashore. In the morning we'd do the same: we'd walk along the sands to Ardbeag and have coffee in the hotel there, back in time for lunch. In the afternoon we'd drive somewhere.

I knew all that because over the years this kind of pattern had developed. We had our walks and our drives, tweed to buy in Cushendall, Strafe's and Dekko's fishing day when Cynthia and I just sat on

---

2. County in the northern portion of the Irish Republic.

the beach, our visit to the Giant's Causeway[3] and one to Donegal perhaps, though that meant an early start and taking pot-luck for dinner somewhere. We'd come to adore Co. Antrim, its glens and coastline, Rathlin Island and Tievebulliag. Since first we got to know it, in 1965, we'd all four fallen hopelessly in love with every variation of this remarkable landscape. People in England thought us mad of course: they see so much of the troubles on television that it's natu- rally difficult for them to realize that most places are just as they've always been. Yet coming as we did, taking the road along the coast, dawdling through Ballygally, it was impossible to believe that some- where else the unpleasantness was going on. We'd never seen a thing, nor even heard people talking about incidents that might have taken place. It's true that after a particularly nasty carry-on a few winters ago we did consider finding somewhere else, in Scotland perhaps, or Wales. But as Strafe put it at the time, we felt we owed a certain loyalty to the Malseeds and indeed to everyone we'd come to know round about, people who'd always been glad to welcome us back. It seemed silly to lose our heads, and when we returned the following summer we knew immediately we'd been right. Dekko said that noth- ing could be further away from all the violence than Glencorn Lodge, and though his remark could hardly be taken literally I think we all knew what he meant.

"Cynthia's tired," I said because she'd been stifling yawns. "I think we should call it a day."

"Oh, not at all," Cynthia protested. "No, please."

But Dekko agreed with me that she was tired, and Strafe said he didn't mind stopping now. He suggested a nightcap, as he always does, and as we always do also, Cynthia and I declined. Dekko said he'd like a Cointreau.

The conversation drifted about. Dekko told us an Irish joke about a drunk who couldn't find his way out of a telephone box, and then Strafe remembered an incident at school concerning his and Dekko's housemaster, A. D. Cowley-Stubbs, and the house wag, Thrive Major. A. D. Cowley-Stubbs had been known as Cows and often featured in our after-bridge reminiscing. So did Thrive Major.

"Perhaps I *am* sleepy," Cynthia said. "I don't think I closed my eyes once last night."

She never does on a sea crossing. Personally I'm out like a light the moment my head touches the pillow; I often think it must be the salt in the air because normally I'm an uneasy sleeper at the best of times.

"You run along, old girl," Strafe advised.

"Brekky at nine," Dekko said.

Cynthia said good-night and went, and we didn't remark on her tiredness because as a kind of unwritten rule we never comment on one another. We're four people who play bridge. The companionship it offers, and the holidays we have together, are all part of that. We share everything: the cost of petrol, the cups of coffee or drinks we

3. A formation of basalt cliffs projecting several hundred feet into the sea on the north coast of Antrim.

have; we even each make a contribution towards the use of Strafe's car because it's always his we go on holiday in, a Rover it was on this occasion.

"Funny, being here on your own," Strafe said, glancing across what the Malseeds call the After-Dinner Lounge at the man who didn't have a companion. He was a red-haired man of about thirty, not wearing a tie, his collar open at the neck and folded back over the jacket of his blue serge suit. He was uncouth-looking, though it's a hard thing to say, not at all the kind of person one usually sees at Glencorn Lodge. He sat in the After-Dinner Lounge as he had in the dining-room, lost in some concentration of his own, as if calculating sums in his mind. There had been a folded newspaper on his table in the dining-room. It now reposed tidily on the arm of his chair, still unopened.

"Commercial gent," Dekko said. "Fertilizers."

"Good heavens, never. You wouldn't get a rep in here."

I took no part in the argument. The lone man didn't much interest me, but I felt that Strafe was probably right: if there was anything dubious about the man's credentials he might have found it difficult to secure a room. In the hall of Glencorn Lodge there's a notice which reads: *We prefer not to feature in hotel guides, and we would be grateful to our guests if they did not seek to include Glencorn Lodge in the Good Food Guide, the Good Hotel Guide, the Michelin, Egon Ronay or any others. We have not advertized Glencorn since our early days, and prefer our recommendations to be by word of mouth.*

"Ah, thank you," Strafe said when Kitty brought his whisky and Dekko's Cointreau. "Sure you won't have something?" he said to me, although he knew I never did.

Strafe is on the stout side, I suppose you could say, with a gingery moustache and gingery hair, hardly touched at all by gray. He left the Army years ago, I suppose because of me in a sense, because he didn't want to be posted abroad again. He's in the Ministry of Defense now.

I'm still quite pretty in my way, though nothing like as striking as Mrs. Malseed, for I've never been that kind of woman. I've put on weight, and wouldn't have allowed myself to do so if Strafe hadn't kept saying he can't stand a bag of bones. I'm careful about my hair and, unlike Mrs. Malseed, I have it very regularly seen to because if I don't it gets a salt and pepper look, which I hate. My husband, Ralph, who died of food-poisoning when we were still quite young, used to say I wouldn't lose a single look in middle age, and to some extent that's true. We were still putting off having children when he died, which is why I haven't any. Then I met Strafe, which meant I didn't marry again.

Strafe is married himself, to Cynthia. She's small and ineffectual, I suppose you'd say without being untruthful or unkind. Not that Cynthia and I don't get on or anything like that, in fact we get on extremely well. It's Strafe and Cynthia who don't seem quite to hit it off, and I often think how much happier all round it would have been if Cynthia had married someone completely different, someone like Dekko in a way, except that that mightn't quite have worked out

either. The Strafes have two sons, both very like their father, both of
them in the Army. And the very sad thing is they think nothing of
poor Cynthia.

"Who's that chap?" Dekko asked Mr. Malseed, who'd come over to
wish us good-night.

"Awfully sorry about that, Mr. Deakin. My fault entirely, a booking that came over the phone."

"Good heavens, not at all," Strafe protested, and Dekko looked
horrified in case it should be thought he was objecting to the locals.
"Splendid-looking fellow," he said, overdoing it.

Mr. Malseed murmured that the man had only booked in for a
single night, and I smiled the whole thing away, reassuring him with a
nod. It's one of the pleasantest of the traditions at Glencorn Lodge
that every evening Mr. Malseed makes the rounds of his guests just to
say good-night. It's because of little touches like that that I, too,
wished Dekko hadn't questioned Mr. Malseed about the man because
it's the kind of thing one doesn't do at Glencorn Lodge. But Dekko is
a law unto himself, very tall and gangling, always immaculately suited,
a beaky face beneath mousy hair in which flecks of gray add a certain
distinction. Dekko has money of his own and though he takes out girls
who are half his age he has never managed to get around to marriage.
The uncharitable might say he has a rather gormless laugh; certainly
it's sometimes on the loud side.

We watched while Mr. Malseed bade the lone man good-night. The
man didn't respond, but just sat gazing. It was ill-mannered, but this
lack of courtesy didn't appear to be intentional: the man was clearly
in a mood of some kind, miles away.

"Well, I'll go up," I said. "Good-night, you two."

"Cheery-bye, Milly," Dekko said. "Brekky at nine, remember."

"Good-night, Milly," Strafe said.

The Strafes always occupy different rooms on holidays, and at
home also. This time he was in Geranium and she in Fuchsia. I was in
Rose, and in a little while Strafe would come to see me. He stays
with her out of kindness, because he fears for her on her own. He's a
sentimental, good-hearted man, easily moved to tears: he simply cannot bear the thought of Cynthia with no one to talk to in the evenings,
with no one to make her life around. "And besides," he often says
when he's being jocular, "it would break up our bridge four." Naturally we never discuss her shortcomings or in any way analyze the
marriage. The unwritten rule that exists among the four of us seems to
extend as far as that.

He slipped into my room after he'd had another drink or two, and I
was waiting for him as he likes me to wait, in bed not quite undressed.
He has never said so, but I know that that is something Cynthia would
not understand in him, or ever attempt to comply with. Ralph, of
course, would not have understood either; poor old Ralph would have
been shocked. Actually it's all rather sweet, Strafe and his little ways.

"I love you, dear," I whispered to him in the darkness, but just then
he didn't wish to speak of love and referred instead to my body.

If Cynthia hadn't decided to remain in the hotel the next morning instead of accompanying us on our walk to Ardbeag everything might have been different. As it happened, when she said at breakfast she thought she'd just potter about the garden and sit with her book out of the wind somewhere, I can't say I was displeased. For a moment I hoped Dekko might say he'd stay with her, allowing Strafe and myself to go off on our own, but Dekko—who doesn't go in for saying what you want him to say—didn't. "Poor old sausage,"[4] he said instead, examining Cynthia with a solicitude that suggested she was close to the grave, rather than just a little lowered by the change of life or whatever it was.

"I'll be perfectly all right," Cynthia assured him. "Honestly."

"Cynthia likes to mooch,[5] you know," Strafe pointed out, which of course is only the truth. She reads too much, I always think. You often see her putting down a book with the most melancholy look in her eyes, which can't be good for her. She's an imaginative woman, I suppose you would say, and of course her habit of reading so much is often useful on our holidays: over the years she has read her way through dozen of Irish guide-books. "That's where the garrison pushed the natives over the cliffs," she once remarked on a drive. "Those rocks are known as the Maidens," she remarked on another occasion. She has led us to places of interest which we had no idea existed: Garron Tower on Garron Point, the mausoleum at Bonamargy, the Devil's Backbone.[6] As well as which, Cynthia is extremely knowledgeable about all matters relating to Irish history. Again she has read endlessly: biographies and autobiographies, long accounts of the centuries of battling and politics there've been. There's hardly a town or village we ever pass through that hasn't some significance for Cynthia, although I'm afraid her impressive fund of information doesn't always receive the attention it deserves. Not that Cynthia ever minds; it doesn't seem to worry her when no one listens. My own opinion is that she'd have made a much better job of her relationship with Strafe and her sons if she could have somehow developed a bit more character.

We left her in the garden and proceeded down the cliff path to the shingle beneath. I was wearing slacks and a blouse, with the arms of a cardigan looped round my neck in case it turned chilly: the outfit was new, specially bought for the holiday, in shades of tangerine. Strafe never cares how he dresses and of course she doesn't keep him up to the mark: that morning, as far as I remember, he wore rather shapeless corduroy trousers, the kind men sometimes garden in, and a navy-blue fisherman's jersey. Dekko as usual was a fashion plate: a plane green linen suit with pleated jacket pockets, a maroon shirt open at the neck, revealing a medallion on a fine gold chain. We didn't converse as we crossed the rather difficult shingle, but when we reached the sand Dekko began to talk about some girl or other,

---

4. Soul. (Cockney rhyming slang: "sausage [roll]" = soul.)

5. Wander about.

6. The Tower, now a hotel, was formerly a government center; the mausoleum is in the ruins of a monastery near Ballygalley Castle; the Backbone (Knockalla Mountain) is to the west of Lough Swelly in Donegal.

someone called Juliet who had apparently proposed marriage to him just before we'd left Surrey. He'd told her, so he said, that he'd think about it while on holiday and he wondered now about dispatching a telegram from Ardbeag saying, *Still thinking*. Strafe, who has a simple sense of humor, considered this hugely funny and spent most of the walk persuading Dekko that the telegram must certainly be sent, and other telegrams later on, all with the same message. Dekko kept laughing, throwing his head back in a way that always reminds me of an Australian bird I once saw in a nature film on television. I could see this was going to become one of those jokes that would accompany us all through the holiday, a man's thing really, but of course I didn't mind. The girl called Juliet was nearly thirty years younger than Dekko. I supposed she knew what she was doing.

Since the subject of telegrams had come up, Strafe recalled the occasion when Thrive Major had sent one to A. D. Cowley-Stubbs: *Darling regret three months gone love Rowena*. Carefully timed, it had arrived during one of Cows' Thursday evening coffee sessions. Rowena was a maid, known as the Bicycle, who had been sacked the previous term, and old Cows had something of a reputation as a misogynist. When he read the message he apparently went white and collapsed into an armchair. Warrington P. J. managed to read it too, and after that the fat was in the fire. The consequences went on rather, but I never minded listening when Strafe and Dekko drifted back to their schooldays. I just wish I'd known Strafe then, before either of us had gone and got married.

We had our coffee at Ardbeag, the telegram was sent off, and then Strafe and Dekko wanted to see a man called Henry O'Reilly whom we'd met on previous holidays, who organizes mackerel-fishing trips. I waited on my own, picking out postcards in the village shop that sells almost everything, and then I wandered down towards the shore. I knew that they would be having a drink with the boatman because a year had passed since they'd seen him last. They joined me after about twenty minutes, Dekko apologizing but Strafe not seeming to be aware that I'd had to wait because Strafe is not a man who notices little things. It was almost one o'clock when we reached Glencorn Lodge and were told by Mr. Malseed that Cynthia needed looking after.

The hotel, in fact, was in a turmoil. I have never seen anyone as ashen-faced as Mr. Malseed; his wife, in a forget-me-not[7] dress, was limp. It wasn't explained to us immediately what had happened, because in the middle of telling us that Cynthia needed looking after Mr. Malseed was summoned to the telephone. I could see through the half-open door of their little office a glass of whisky or brandy on the desk and Mrs. Malseed's bangled arm reaching out for it. Not for ages did we realize that it all had to do with the lone man whom we'd speculated about the night before.

"He just wanted to talk to me," Cynthia kept repeating hysterically in the hall. "He sat with me by the magnolias."

I made her lie down. Strafe and I stood on either side of her bed as

7. Blue.

she lay there with her shoes off, her rather unattractively cut plain pink dress crumpled and actually damp from her tears. I wanted to make her take it off and to slip under the bed-clothes in her petticoat but somehow it seemed all wrong, in the circumstances, for Strafe's wife to do anything so intimate in my presence.

"I couldn't stop him," Cynthia said, the rims of her eyes crimson by now, her nose beginning to run again. "From half past ten till well after twelve. He had to talk to someone, he said."

I could sense that Strafe was thinking precisely the same as I was: that the red-haired man had insinuated himself into Cynthia's company by talking about himself and had then put a hand on her knee. Instead of simply standing up and going away Cynthia would have stayed where she was, embarrassed or tongue-tied, at any rate unable to cope. And when the moment came she would have turned hysterical. I could picture her screaming in the garden, running across the lawn to the hotel, and then the pandemonium in the hall. I could sense Strafe picturing that also.

"My God, it's terrible," Cynthia said.

"I think she should sleep," I said quietly to Strafe. "Try to sleep, dear," I said to her, but she shook her head, tossing her jumble of hair about on the pillow.

"Milly's right," Strafe urged. "You'll feel much better after a little rest. We'll bring you a cup of tea later on."

"My God!" she cried again. "My God, how could I sleep?"

I went away to borrow a couple of mild sleeping pills from Dekko, who is never without them, relying on the things too much in my opinion. He was tidying himself in his room, but found the pills immediately. Strangely enough, Dekko's always sound in a crisis.

I gave them to her with water and she took them without asking what they were. She was in a kind of daze, one moment making a fuss and weeping, the next just peering ahead of her, as if frightened. In a way she was like someone who'd just had a bad nightmare and hadn't yet completely returned to reality. I remarked as much to Strafe while we made our way down to lunch, and he said he quite agreed.

"Poor old Cynth!" Dekko said when we'd all ordered lobster bisque and entrecôte[8] béarnaise. "Poor old sausage."

You could see that the little waitress, a new girl this year, was bubbling over with excitement; but Kitty, serving the other half of the dining-room, was grim, which was most unusual. Everyone was talking in hushed tones and when Dekko said, "Poor old Cynth!" a couple of heads were turned in our direction because he can never keep his voice down. The little vases of roses with which Mrs. Malseed must have decorated each table before the fracas had occurred seemed strangely out of place in the atmosphere which had developed.

The waitress had just taken away our soup-plates when Mr. Malseed hurried into the dining-room and came straight to our table. The lobster bisque surprisingly hadn't been quite up to scratch, and in passing I couldn't help wondering if the fuss had caused the kitchen to go to pieces also.

8. Steak cut from between ribs.

"I wonder if I might have a word, Major Strafe," Mr. Malseed said, and Strafe rose at once and accompanied him from the dining-room. A total silence had fallen, everyone in the dining-room pretending to be intent on eating. I had an odd feeling that we had perhaps got it all wrong, that because we'd been out for our walk when it had happened all the other guests knew more of the details than Strafe and Dekko and I did. I began to wonder if poor Cynthia had been raped.

Afterwards Strafe told us what occurred in the Malseeds' office, how Mrs. Malseed had been sitting there, slumped, as he put it, and how two policemen had questioned him. "Look, what on earth's all this about?" he had demanded rather sharply.

"It concerns this incident that's taken place, sir," one of the police-men explained in an unhurried voice. "On account of your wife—"

"My wife's lying down. She must not be questioned or in any way disturbed."

"Ach, we'd never do that, sir."

Strafe does a good Co. Antrim brogue and in relating all this to us he couldn't resist making full use of it. The two policemen were in uniform and their natural slowness of intellect was rendered more noticeable by the lugubrious air the tragedy had inspired in the hotel. For tragedy was what it was; after talking to Cynthia for nearly two hours the lone man had walked down to the rocks and been drowned.

When Strafe finished speaking I placed my knife and fork together on my plate, unable to eat another mouthful. The facts appeared to be that the man, having left Cynthia by the magnolias, had clambered down the cliff to a place no one ever went to, on the other side of the hotel from the sands we had walked along to Ardbeag. No one had seen him except Cynthia, who from the cliff-top had apparently witnessed his battering by the treacherous waves. The tide had been coming in, but by the time old Arthur and Mr. Malseed reached the rocks it had begun to turn, leaving behind it the fully dressed corpse. Mr. Malseed's impression was that the man had lost his footing on the seaweed and accidentally stumbled into the depths, for the rocks were so slip-pery it was difficult to carry the corpse more than a matter of yards. But at least it had been placed out of view, while Mr. Malseed hurried back to the hotel to telephone for assistance. He told Strafe that Cynthia had been most confused, insisting that the man had walked out among the rocks and then into the sea, knowing what he was doing.

Listening to it all, I no longer felt sory for Cynthia. It was typical of her that she should so sillily have involved us in all this. Why on earth had she sat in the garden with a man of that kind instead of standing up and making a fuss the moment he'd begun to paw her? If she'd acted intelligently the whole unfortunate episode could clearly have been avoided. Since it hadn't, there was no point whatsoever in insisting that the man had committed suicide when at that distance no one could possibly be sure.

"It really does astonish me," I said at the lunch table, unable to prevent myself from breaking our unwritten rule. "Whatever came over her?"

"It can't be good for the hotel," Dekko commented, and I was glad to see Strafe giving him a little glance of irritation.

"It's hardly the point," I said coolly.

"What I meant was, hotels occasionally hush things like this up."

"Well, they haven't this time." It seemed an age since I had waited for them in Ardbeag, since we had been so happily laughing over the effect of Dekko's telegram. He'd included his address in it so that the girl could send a message back, and as we'd returned to the hotel along the seashore there's been much speculation between the two men about the form this would take.

"I suppose what Cynthia's thinking," Strafe said, "is that after he'd tried something on with her he became depressed."

"Oh, but he could just as easily have lost his footing. He'd have been on edge anyway, worried in case she reported him."

"Dreadful kind of death," Dekko said. His tone suggested that that was that, that the subject should now be closed, and so it was.

After lunch we went to our rooms, as we always do at Glencorn Lodge, to rest for an hour. I took my slacks and blouse off, hoping that Strafe would knock on my door, but he didn't and of course, that was understandable. Oddly enough I found myself thinking of Dekko, picturing his long form stretched out in the room called Hydrangea, his beaky face in profile on his pillow. The precise nature of Dekko's relationship with these girls he picks up has always privately intrigued me: was it really possible that somewhere in London there was a girl called Juliet who was prepared to marry him for his not inconsiderable money?

I slept and briefly dreamed. Thrive Major and Warrington P. J. were running the post office in Ardbeag, sending telegrams to everyone they could think of, including Dekko's friend Juliet. Cynthia had been found dead beside the magnolias and people were waiting for Hercule Poirot[9] to arrive. "Promise me you didn't do it," I whispered to Strafe, but when Strafe replied it was to say that Cynthia's body reminded him of a bag of old chicken bones.

Strafe and Dekko and I met for tea in the tea-lounge. Strafe had looked in to see if Cynthia had woken, but apparently she hadn't. The police officers had left the hotel, Dekko said, because he'd noticed their car wasn't parked at the front anymore. None of the three of us said, but I think we presumed, that the man's body had been removed from the rocks during the quietness of the afternoon. From where we sat I caught a glimpse of Mrs. Malseed passing quite briskly through the hall, seeming almost herself again. Certainly our holiday would be affected, but it might not be totally ruined. All that remained to hope for was Cynthia's recovery, and then everyone could set about forgetting the unpleasantness. The nicest thing would be if a jolly young couple turned up and occupied the man's room, exorcising the incident, as newcomers would.

The family from France—the two little girls and their parents—were chattering away in the tea-lounge, and an elderly trio who'd

9. Detective in many of Agatha Christie's murder mysteries.

arrived that morning were speaking in American accents. The honeymoon couple appeared, looking rather shy, and began to whisper and giggle in a corner. People who occupied the table next to ours in the dining-room, a Wing-Commander Orfell and his wife, from Guildford,[1] nodded and smiled as they passed. Everyone was making an effort, and I knew it would help matters further if Cynthia felt up to a rubber or two before dinner. That life should continue as normally as possible was essential for Glencorn Lodge, the example already set by Mrs. Malseed.

Because of our interrupted lunch I felt quite hungry, and the Malseeds pride themselves on their teas. The chef, Mr. McBride, whom of course we've met, has the lightest touch I know with sponge cakes and little curranty scones. I was, in fact, buttering a scone when Strafe said:

"Here she is."

And there indeed she was. By the look of her she had simply pushed herself off her bed and come straight down. Her pink dress was even more crumpled than it had been. She hadn't so much as run a comb through her hair, her face was puffy and unpowdered. For a moment I really thought she was walking in her sleep.

Strafe and Dekko stood up. "Feeling better, dear?" Strafe said, but she didn't answer.

"Sit down, Cynth," Dekko urged, pushing back a chair to make room for her.

"He told me a story I can never forget. I've dreamed about it all over again." Cynthia swayed in front of us, not even attempting to sit down. To tell the truth, she sounded inane.

"Story, dear?" Strafe inquired, humoring her.

She said it was the story of two children who had apparently ridden bicycles through the streets of Belfast, out into Co. Antrim. The bicycles were dilapidated, she said; she didn't know if they were stolen or not. She didn't know about the children's home because the man hadn't spoken of them, but she claimed to know instinctively that they had ridden away from poverty and unhappiness. "From the clatter and the quarreling," Cynthia said. "Two children who later fell in love."

"Horrid old dream," Strafe said. "Horrid for you, dear."

She shook her head, and then sat down. I poured another cup of tea. "I had the oddest dream myself," I said. "Thrive Major was running the post office in Ardbeag."

Strafe smiled and Dekko gave his laugh, but Cynthia didn't in any way acknowledge what I'd said.

"A fragile thing the girl was, with depths of mystery in her wide brown eyes. Red-haired of course he was himself, thin as a rake in those days. Glencorn Lodge was derelict then."

"You've had a bit of a shock, old thing," Dekko said.

Strafe agreed, kindly adding, "Look dear, if the chap actually interfered with you—"

"Why on earth should he do that?" Her voice was shrill in the tea-lounge, edged with a note of hysteria. I glanced at Strafe, who was frowning into his tea-cup. Dekko began to say something, but broke off before his meaning emerged. Rather more calmly Cynthia said:

"It was summer when they came here. Honeysuckle he described. And mother of thyme.[2] He didn't know the name of either."

No one attempted any kind of reply, not that it was necessary, for Cynthia just continued.

"At school there were the facts of geography and arithmetic. And the legends of scholars and of heroes, of Queen Maeve and Finn MacCool. There was the coming of St. Patrick[3] to a heathen people. History was full of kings and high-kings, and Silken Thomas and Wolfe Tone, the Flight of the Earls, the Siege of Limerick."[4]

When Cynthia said that, it was impossible not to believe that the unfortunate events of the morning had touched her with some kind of madness. It seemed astonishing that she had walked into the tea-lounge without having combed her hair, and that she'd stood there swaying before sitting down, that out of the blue she had started on about two children. None of it made an iota of sense, and surely she could see that the nasty experience she'd suffered should not be dwelt upon? I offered her the plate of scones, hoping that if she began to eat she would stop talking, but she took no notice of my gesture.

"Look, dear," Strafe said, "there's not one of us who knows what you're talking about."

"I'm talking about a children's story, I'm talking about a girl and a boy who visited this place we visit also. He hadn't been here for years, but he returned last night, making one final effort to understand. And then he walked out into the sea."

She had taken a piece of her dress and was agitatedly crumpling it between the finger and thumb of her left hand. It was dreadful really, having her so grubby-looking. For some odd reason I suddenly thought of her cooking, how she wasn't in the least interested in it or in anything about the house. She certainly hadn't succeeded in making a home for Strafe.

"They rode those worn-out bicycles through a hot afternoon. Can you feel all that? A newly surfaced road, the snap of chippings beneath their tires, the smell of tar? Dust from a passing car, the city they left behind?"

"Cynthia dear," I said, "drink your tea, and why not have a scone?"

"They swam and sunbathed on the beach you walked along today. They went to a spring for water. There were no magnolias then. There was no garden, no neat little cliff paths to the beach. Surely you can

---

2. A low-growing, wide-spreading variety of the aromatic thyme.

3. Maeve, first-century (A.D.) ruler of Connaught who reputedly invaded Ulster and in folk tradition is queen of the fairies; Finn MacCumhaill, third-century chieftain who reputedly possessed gifts of poetry, second sight, and healing; Patrick converted the Irish to Catholicism and reputedly freed Ireland of snakes.

4. Thomas Fitzgerald, tenth Earl of Kildare, rebelled against Henry VIII when he heard his father had been executed and adorned his helmet and those of his supporters with silken fringe; Theobald Wolfe Tone, a founder and leader of the United Irishmen, supported religious toleration, separation from England, and was sentenced to death as a traitor. In 1607 almost a hundred leaders ("Earls") of the North fled rather than serve England and James I, a flight that some believe permanently damaged the Celtic cause; the town of Limerick in southwest Ireland was, in 1791, besieged by troops of King William, and the Irish Army, loyal to the Catholic James II who had been forced off the British throne, was defeated.

see it clearly?"

"No," Strafe said. "No, we really cannot, dear."

"This place that is an idyll for us was an idyll for them too: the trees, the ferns, the wild rose near the water spring, the very sea and sun they shared. There was a cottage lost in the middle of the woods: they sometimes looked for that. They played a game, a kind of hide and seek. People in a white farmhouse gave them milk."

For the second time I offered Cynthia the plate of scones and for the second time she pointedly ignored me. Her cup of tea hadn't been touched. Dekko took a scone and cheerfully said:

"All's well that's over."

But Cynthia appeared to have drifted back into a daze, and I wondered again if it could really be possible that the experience had unhinged her. Unable to help myself, I saw her being led away from the hotel, helped into the back of a blue van, something like an ambulance. She was talking about the children again, how they had planned to marry and keep a sweetshop.

"Take it easy, dear," Strafe said, which I followed up by suggesting for the second time that she should make an effort to drink her tea.

"Has it to do with the streets they came from? Or the history they learnt, he from his Christian Brothers, she from her nuns? History is unfinished in this island; long since it has come to a stop in Surrey."

Dekko said, and I really had to hand it to him:

"Cynth, we have to put it behind us."

It didn't do any good. Cynthia just went rambling on, speaking again of the girl being taught by nuns, and the boy by Christian Brothers. She began to recite the history they might have learnt, the way she sometimes did when we were driving through an area that had historical connections. "Can you imagine," she embarrassingly asked, "our very favorite places bitter with disaffection, with plotting and revenge? Can you imagine the treacherous murder of Shane O'Neill the Proud?"[5]

Dekko made a little sideways gesture of his head, politely marveling. Strafe seemed about to say something, but changed his mind. Confusion ran through Irish history, Cynthia said, like convolvulus in a hedgerow. On May 24th, 1487, a boy of ten called Lambert Simnel, brought to Dublin by a priest from Oxford, was declared Edward VI of all England and Ireland, crowned with a golden circlet taken from a statue of the Virgin Mary. On May 24th, 1798, here in Antrim, Presbyterian farmers fought for a common cause with their Catholic laborers.[6] She paused and looked at Strafe. Chaos and contradiction, she informed him, were hidden everywhere beneath nice-sounding names. "The Battle of the Yellow Ford," she suddenly chanted in a sing-song way that sounded thoroughly peculiar, "the Statues of

5. Sixteenth-century leader who tried to take control of Ulster from England (Elizabeth); when the O'Donnells, egged on by the government, defeated Shane (1567), he fled to Scotland, where, though received peacefully, he was mur- dered.

6. "Edward VI's" rebel forces were defeated by Henry VII and he and the priest were jailed; Antrim was one of the sites of the uprising of the United Irishmen.

Kilkenny. The Battle of Glenmama, the Convention of Drumceat.[7]
The Act of Settlement, the Renunciation Act. The Act of Union, the
Toleration Act.[8] Just so much history it sounds like now, yet people
starved or died while other people watched. A language was lost, a
faith forbidden. Famine followed revolt, plantation followed that. But
it was people who were struck into the soil of other people's land, not
forests of new trees; and it was greed and treachery that spread as a
disease among them all. No wonder unease clings to these shreds of
history and shots ring out in answer to the mockery of drums. No
wonder the air is nervy with suspicion."

There was an extremely awkward silence when she ceased to speak.
Dekko nodded, doing his best to be companionable. Strafe nodded
also. I simply examined the pattern of roses on our tea-time china, not
knowing what else to do. Eventually Dekko said:

"What an awful lot you know, Cynth!"

"Cynthia's always been interested," Strafe said. "Always had a first-
rate memory."

"Those children of the streets are part of the battles and the Acts,"
she went on, seeming quite unaware that her talk was literally almost
crazy. "They're part of the blood that flowed around those nice-sounding names." She paused, and for a moment seemed disinclined to
continue. Then she said:

"The second time they came here the house was being built. There
were concrete-mixers, and lorries drawn up on the grass, noise and
scaffolding everywhere. They watched all through another afternoon
and then they went their different ways: their childhood was over, lost
with their idyll. He became a dockyard clerk. She went to London, to
work in a betting shop."

"My dear," Strafe said very gently, "it's interesting, everything you
say, but it really hardly concerns us."

"No, of course not." Quite emphatically Cynthia shook her head,
appearing wholly to agree. "They were degenerate, awful creatures.
They must have been."

"No one's saying that, my dear."

"Their story should have ended there, he in the docklands of Belfast, she recording bets. Their complicated childhood love should just
have dissipated, as such love often does. But somehow nothing was as
neat as that."

Dekko, in an effort to lighten the conversation, mentioned a boy
called Gollsol who'd been at school with Strafe and himself, who'd

7. At the Battle of Yellow Ford, 1598,
Hugh O'Neill, nephw of Shane, Earl of
Tyrone, in his struggle to prevent anglici-
zation of Ireland, defeated the English.
The statutes, 1366, ordered English (Norman) settlers not to intermarry with Irish,
speak their language, or adopt their customs. At Glenmama, near Dublin, in 999,
the Irish defeated the Danes. Dalriada
was a kingdom, partly in northeastern
Ireland, partly in southwestern Scotland,
and in 590 a convention was called at
Drumceat County, Londonderry, to see if
Scots should give allegiance to the Irish
"high king."
8. Under the Settlement of 1652, those

not friendly to Cromwell's Puritan English
government could forfeit part or all of
their property. In 1783 the English Parliament recognized Irish independence, rights
of Irish courts, and as valid for Ireland
only those laws enacted by English king
and Irish Parliament. Not much later,
1800, the Act of Union united the parliament and kingdoms (thus the United
Kingdom or U.K.). Earlier, 1719, the
Toleration Act, forced on the Irish Parliament, allowed the Irish freedom to
worship and to serve in parish offices if
they would swear civil allegiance and renounce "popish" doctrines.

formed a romantic attachment for the daughter of one of the grounds-
men and had later actually married her. There was a silence for a
moment, then Cynthia, without emotion, said:

"You none of you care. You sit there not caring that two people are
dead."

"Two people, Cynthia?" I said.

"For God's sake, I'm telling you!" she cried. "That girl was murdered in a room in Maida Vale."[9]

Although there is something between Strafe and myself, I do try my
best to be at peace about it. I go to church and take communion, and I
know Strafe occasionally does too, though not as often as perhaps he
might. Cynthia has no interest in that side of life, and it rankled with
me now to hear her blaspheming so casually, and so casually speaking
about death in Maida Vale on top of all this stuff about history and
children. Strafe was shaking his head, clearly believing that Cynthia
didn't know what she was talking about.

"Cynthia dear," I began, "are you sure you're not muddling something up here? You've been upset, you've had a nightmare: don't you
think your imagination, or something you've been reading—"

"Bombs don't go off on their own. Death doesn't just happen to
occur in Derry and Belfast, in London and Amsterdam and Dublin, in
Berlin and Jerusalem. There are people who are murderers: that is
what this children's story is about."

A silence fell, no one knowing what to say. It didn't matter of
course because without any prompting Cynthia continued.

"We drink our gin with Angostura bitters, there's lamb or chicken
Kiev. Old Kitty's kind to us in the dining-room and old Arthur in the
hall. Flowers are everywhere, we have our special table."

"Please let us take you to your room now," Strafe begged, and as he
spoke I reached out a hand in friendship and placed it on her arm.
"Come on, old thing," Dekko said.

"The limbless are left on the streets, blood spatters the car-parks.
Brits Out it says on a rockface, but we know it doesn't mean us."

I spoke quietly then, measuring my words, measuring the pause
between each so that its effect might be registered. I felt the statement
had to be made, whether it was my place to make it or not. I said:

"You are very confused, Cynthia."

The French family left the tea-lounge. The two Dalmatians,
Charger and Snooze, ambled in and sniffed and went away again.
Kitty came to clear the French family's tea things. I could hear her
speaking to the honeymoon couple, saying the weather forecast was
good.

"Cynthia," Strafe said, standing up, "we've been very patient with
you but this is now becoming silly."

I nodded just a little. "I really think," I softly said, but Cynthia
didn't permit me to go on.

"Someone told him about her. Someone mentioned her name, and
he couldn't believe it. She sat alone in Maida Vale, putting together
the mechanisms of her bombs: this girl who had laughed on the

9. Section of London with many foreign transients and rooming houses.

seashore, whom he had loved."

"Cynthia," Strafe began, but he wasn't permitted to continue either. Hopelessly, he just sat down again.

"Whenever he heard of bombs exploding he thought of her, and couldn't understand. He wept when he said that; her violence haunted him, he said. He couldn't work, he couldn't sleep at night. His mind filled up with images of her, their awkward childhood kisses, her fingers working neatly now. He saw her with a carrier-bag, hurrying it through a crowd, leaving it where it could cause most death. In front of the moldering old house that had once been Glencorn Lodge they'd made a fire and cooked their food. They'd lain for ages on the grass. They'd cycled home to their city streets."

It suddenly dawned on me that Cynthia was knitting this whole fantasy out of nothing. It all worked backwards from the moment when she'd had the misfortune to witness the man's death in the sea. A few minutes before he'd been chatting quite normally to her, he'd probably even mentioned a holiday in his childhood and some girl there'd been: all of it would have been natural in the circumstances, possibly even the holiday had taken place at Glencorn. He'd said good-bye and then unfortunately he'd had his accident. As she watched from the cliff edge, something had cracked in poor Cynthia's brain, she having always been a prey to melancholy. I suppose it must be hard having two sons who don't think much of you, and a marriage not offering you a great deal, bridge and holidays probably the best part of it. For some odd reason of her own she'd created her fantasy about a child turning into a terrorist. The violence of the man's death had clearly filled her imagination with Irish violence, so regularly seen on television. If we'd been on holiday in Suffolk I wondered how it would have seemed to the poor creature.

I could feel Strafe and Dekko beginning to put all that together also, beginning to realize that the whole story of the red-haired man and the girl was clearly Cynthia's invention. "Poor creature," I wanted to say, but did not do so.

"For months he searched for her, pushing his way among the people of London, the people who were her victims. When he found her she just looked at him, as if the past hadn't even existed. She didn't smile, as if incapable of smiling. He wanted to take her away, back to where they came from, but she didn't reply when he suggested that. Bitterness was like a disease in her, and when he left her he felt the bitterness in himself."

Again Strafe and Dekko nodded, and I could feel Strafe thinking that there really was no point in protesting further. All we could hope for was that the end of the saga was in sight.

"He remained in London, working on the railways. But in the same way as before he was haunted by the person she'd become, and the haunting was more awful now. He bought a gun from a man he'd been told about and kept it hidden in a shoe-box in his rented room. Now and again he took it out and looked at it, then put it back. He hated the violence that possessed her, yet he was full of it himself: he knew he couldn't betray her with anything but death. Humanity had left both of them when he visited her again in Maida Vale."

To my enormous relief and, I could feel, to Strafe's and Dekko's too, Mr. and Mrs. Malseed appeared beside us. Like his wife, Mr. Malseed had considerably recovered. He spoke in an even voice, clearly wishing to dispose of the matter. It was just the diversion we needed.

"I must apologize, Mr. Strafe," he said. "I cannot say how sorry we are that you were bothered by that man."

"My wife is still a little dicky,"[1] Strafe explained, "but after a decent night's rest I think we can say she'll be as right as rain again."

"I only wish, Mrs. Strafe, you had made contact with my wife, or myself when he first approached you." There was a spark of irritation in Mr. Malseed's eyes, but his voice was still controlled. "I mean, the unpleasantness you suffered might just have been averted."

"Nothing would have been averted, Mr. Malseed, and certainly not the horror we are left with. Can you see her as the girl she became, seated at a chipped white table, her wires and fuses spread around her? What were her thoughts in that room, Mr. Malseed? What happens in the mind of anyone who wishes to destroy? In a back street he bought his gun for too much money. When did it first occur to him to kill her?"

"We really are a bit at sea," Mr. Malseed replied without the slightest hesitation. He humored Cynthia by displaying no surprise, by speaking very quietly.

"All I am saying, Mr. Malseed, is that we should root our heads out of the sand and wonder about two people who are beyond the pale."

"My dear," Strafe said, "Mr. Malseed is a busy man."

Still quietly, still perfectly in control of every intonation, without a single glance around the tea-lounge to ascertain where his guests' attention was, Mr. Malseed said:

"There is unrest here, Mrs. Strafe, but we do our best to live with it."

"All I am saying is that perhaps there can be regret when two children end like this."

Mr. Malseed did not reply. His wife did her best to smile away the awkwardness. Strafe murmured privately to Cynthia, no doubt beseeching her to come to her senses. Again I imagined a blue van drawn up in front of Glencorn Lodge, for it was quite understandable now that an imaginative woman should go mad, affected by the ugliness of death. The garbled speculation about the man and the girl, the jumble in the poor thing's mind—a children's story as she called it—all somehow hung together when you realized they didn't have to make any sense whatsoever.

"Murderers are beyond the pale, Mr. Malseed, and England has always had its pales. The one in Ireland began in 1395."[2]

"Dear," I said, "what has happened has nothing whatsoever to do with calling people murderers and placing them beyond some pale or other. You witnessed a most unpleasant accident, dear, and it's only to

1. Shaky.
2. Richard II visited Ireland 1394–95 to bolster royal authority and (unsuccess- fully) to extend English control over lands.

be expected that you've become just a little lost. The man had a chat with you when you were sitting by the magnolias and then the shock of seeing him slip on the seaweed—"

"He didn't slip on the seaweed," she suddenly screamed. "My God, he didn't slip on the seaweed."

Strafe closed his eyes. The other guests in the tea-lounge had fallen silent ages ago, openly listening. Arthur was standing near the door and was listening also. Kitty was waiting to clear away our tea things, but didn't like to because of what was happening.

"I must request you to take Mrs. Strafe to her room, Major," Mr. Malseed said. "And I must make it clear that we cannot tolerate further upset in Glencorn Lodge."

Strafe reached for her arm, but Cynthia took no notice.

"An Irish joke," she said, and then she stared at Mr. and Mrs. Malseed, her eyes passing over each feature of their faces. She stared at Dekko and Strafe, and last of all at me. She said eventually:

"An Irish joke, an unbecoming tale: of course it can't be true. Ridiculous, that a man returned here. Ridiculous, that he walked again by the seashore and through the woods, hoping to understand where a woman's cruelty had come from."

"This talk is most offensive," Mr. Malseed protested, his calmness slipping just a little. The ashen look that had earlier been in his face returned. I could see he was beside himself with rage. "You are trying to bring something to our doorstep which most certainly does not belong there."

"On your doorstep they talked about a sweetshop: Cadbury's bars and different-flavored creams, nut-milk toffee, Aero and Crunchie."

"For God's sake pull yourself together," I clearly heard Strafe whispering, and Mrs. Malseed attempted to smile. "Come along now, Mrs. Strafe," she said, making a gesture. "Just to please us, dear. Kitty wants to clear away the dishes. Kitty!" she called out, endeavoring to bring matters down to earth.

Kitty crossed the lounge with her tray and gathered up the cups and saucers. The Malseeds, naturally still anxious, hovered. No one was surprised when Cynthia began all over again, by crazily asking Kitty what she thought of us.

"I think, dear," Mrs. Malseed began, "Kitty's quite busy really."

"Stop this at once," Strafe quietly ordered.

"For fourteen years, Kitty, you've served us with food and cleared away the tea-cups we've drunk from. For fourteen years we've played our bridge and walked about the garden. We've gone for drives, we've bought our tweed, we've bathed as those children did."

"Stop it," Strafe said again, a little louder. Bewildered and getting red in the face, Kitty hastily bundled china on to her tray. I made a sign at Strafe because for some reason I felt that the end was really in sight. I wanted him to retain his patience, but what Cynthia said next was almost unbelievable.

"In Surrey we while away the time, we clip our hedges. On a bridge night there's coffee at nine o'clock, with macaroons or *petits fours*. Last thing of all we watch the late-night News, packing away our

cards and scoring-pads, our sharpened pencils. There's been an incident in Armagh, one soldier's had his head shot off, another's run
amok. Our lovely Glens of Antrim, we all four think, our coastal
drives: we hope that nothing disturbs the peace. We think of Mr.
Malseed, still busy in Glencorn Lodge, and Mrs. Malseed finishing her
flower-plaques for the rooms of the completed annex."

"Will you for God's sake shut up?" Strafe suddenly shouted. I could
see him struggling with himself, but it didn't do any good. He called
Cynthia a bloody spectacle, sitting there talking rubbish. I don't believe she even heard him.

"Through honey-tinted glasses we love you and we love your island,
Kitty. We love the lilt of your racy history, we love your earls and
heroes. Yet we made a sensible pale here once, as civilized people
create a garden, pretty as a picture."

Strafe's outburst had been quite noisy and I could sense him being
ashamed of it. He muttered that he was sorry, but Cynthia simply took
advantage of his generosity, continuing about a pale.

"Beyond it lie the bleak untouchables, best kept as dots on the
horizon, too terrible to contemplate. How can we be blamed if we
make neither head nor tail of anything, Kitty, your past and your
present, those battles and Acts of Parliament? We people of Surrey:
how can we know? Yet I stupidly thought, you see, that the tragedy of
two children could at least be understood. He didn't discover where
her cruelty had come from because perhaps you never can: evil breeds
evil in a mysterious way. That's the story the red-haired stranger
passed on to me, the story you huddle away from."

Poor Strafe was pulling at Cynthia, pleading with her, still saying he
was sorry.

"Mrs. Strafe," Mr. Malseed tried to say, but got no further. To my
horror Cynthia abruptly pointed at me.

"That woman," she said, "is my husband's mistress, a fact I am
supposed to be unaware of, Kitty."

"My God!" Strafe said.

"My husband is perverted in his sexual desires. His friend, who
shared his schooldays, has never quite recovered from that time. I
myself am a pathetic creature who has closed her eyes to a husband's
infidelity and his mistress's viciousness. I am dragged into the days of
Thrive Major and A. D. Cowley-Stubbs: mechanically I smile. I
hardly exist, Kitty."

There was a most unpleasant silence, and then Strafe said:

"None of that's true. For God's sake, Cynthia," he suddenly
shouted, "go and rest yourself."

Cynthia shook her head and continued to address the waitress.
She'd had a rest, she told her. "But it didn't do any good, Kitty,
because hell has invaded the paradise of Glencorn, as so often it has
invaded your island. And we, who have so often brought it, pretend it
isn't there. Who cares about children made into murderers?"

Strafe shouted again. "You fleshless ugly bitch!" he cried. "You
bloody old fool!" He was on his feet, trying to get her to hers. The
blood was thumping in his bronzed face, his eyes had a fury in them

I'd never seen before. "Fleshless!" he shouted at her, not caring that so many people were listening. He closed his eyes in misery and in shame again, and I wanted to reach out and take his hand but of course I could not. You could see the Malseeds didn't blame him, you could see them thinking that everything was ruined for us. I wanted to shout at Cynthia too, to batter the silliness out of her, but of course I could not do that. I feel the tears behind my eyes, and I couldn't help noticing that Dekko's hands were shaking. He's quite sensitive behind his joky manner, and had quite obviously taken to heart her statement that he had never recovered from his schooldays. Nor had it been pleasant, hearing myself described as vicious.

"No one cares," Cynthia said in the same unbalanced way, as if she hadn't just been called ugly and a bitch. "No one cares, and on our journey home we shall all four be silent. Yet is the truth about ourselves at least a beginning? Will we wonder in the end about the hell that frightens us?"

Strafe still looked wretched, his face deliberately turned away from us. Mrs. Malseed gave a little sigh and raised the fingers of her left hand to her cheek, as if something tickled it. Her husband breathed heavily. Dekko seemed on the point of tears.

Cynthia stumbled off, leaving a silence behind her. Before it was broken I knew she was right when she said we would just go home, away from this country we had come to love. And I knew as well that neither here nor at home would she be led to a blue van that was not quite an ambulance. Strafe would stay with her because Strafe is made like that, honorable in his own particular way. I felt a pain where perhaps my heart is, and again I wanted to cry. Why couldn't it have been she who had gone down to the rocks and slipped on the seaweed or just walked into the sea, it didn't matter which? Her awful rigmarole hung about us as the last of the tea things were gathered up—the earls who'd fled, the famine and the people planted. The children were there too, grown up into murdering riff-raff.

1981

Context

7   THE AUTHOR'S WORK

Even if it were desirable to read a story as a thing in itself, separate from everything else we had ever read or seen and from everything else the author had written, this is in practice impossible. We can *first* look into Chapman's Homer or Faulkner's fiction only once. After we read a second and then a third story by an author, we recognize the voice and have a sense of familiarity, as we would with a growing acquaintance. Each story is part of the author's entire body of work— the **canon**—which, taken together, forms something like a huge single entity, a vision, a world, a "superwork."

The author's voice and vision soon create in us certain expectations —of action, structure, characterization, world view, language. We come to expect short sentences from Hemingway, long ones from Faulkner, a certain amount of violence from both; we are not surprised if a Hemingway story is set in Michigan or Montmartre or on Mount Kilimanjaro, but we are surprised if a Faulkner story takes place outside Mississippi (his portion of which, we soon learn, he calls Yoknapatawpha). We inevitably bring to our interpretations of Mrs. Macomber's actions what we have learned about Hemingway's view of women from his other writings.

When we find an author's vision attractive or challenging, we naturally want to find out more about it, reading not only the literary works in the canon but the author's nonfictional prose—essays, letters, anything we can find that promises a fuller or clearer view of that unique way of looking at the world. Such knowledge is helpful— within limits. It was D. H. Lawrence, whose stories and statements we are about to read, who warned us to trust the tale and not the teller. A statement of beliefs or of intentions is not necessarily the same as what a given work may show or achieve; and, on the other hand, writers often embody in their art what they cannot articulate, what indeed may not be expressible, in discursive prose.

The three short stories and brief selections from Lawrence's letters and criticism in this chapter are meant to make you feel more at home(and interested) in Lawrence's world and to raise questions about the relationship of the individual work to an author's work as a whole. Of course, short stories and a few pages of nonfiction alone cannot adequately represent the career of a writer who was a novelist, poet, critic, and essayist as well as short story writer, nor can three stories represent the richness and variety of the fifty or more that he published. However, as each story comes from a different decade, they do represent somewhat the continuities and changes within the three decades of his career. Two of the stories, *Odour of Chrysanthemums* and *The Horse Dealer's Daughter*, are characteristically set in the coal-mining region of his native English Midlands, the scene of many of his

novels, including three of the most famous, which also span his career
—*Sons and Lovers* (1913), *The Rainbow* (1915), and *Lady Chatter-
ley's Lover* (1928). The emphasis on the Midlands setting may be
justified in terms of the canon, but can be misleading; there is no way
in' so few selections to represent both the emphasis on the Midlands
and the scope of Lawrence's settings—his stories take place all over
Western Europe, in the Americas, and in Australia. The London setting of *The Rocking-Horse Winner* only faintly indicates Lawrence's
growing cosmopolitanism socially as well as geographically. It also
suggests, though superficially, his developing interest in the superreal
and the mythic—concerns most fully developed in *The Plumed Serpent* (1926) and *The Man Who Died* (1929)—and his movement in
content and style away from nineteenth-century notions of realism.

It may be useful to see the first story here (one of Lawrence's very
first stories) through the eys of its first "professional" reader as he
remembers the experience. Not long before World War I, a young
woman sent to Ford Madox Ford, then editor of *The English Review,*
three poems and a short story written by a schoolmaster friend of
hers, the then unknown D. H. Lawrence. Ford read the story first and,
he recalls, knew immediately that he had a genius on his hands, "a big
one." The very title, *Odour of Chrysanthemums,* Ford noted, "makes
an impact on the mind," indicates that the writer is observant (not
many people realize that chrysanthemums have an odor), and sets the
dark autumnal tone of the story. From the very first sentence, Ford
goes on to say,

> . . . you know that this fellow with the power of observation is going to
> write whatever he writes about from the inside. The "Number 4" shows
> that. He will be the sort of fellow who knows that for the sort of people
> who work about engines, engines have a sort of individuality. He had to
> give the engine the personality of a number. . . . "With seven full
> wagons". . . . The "seven" is good. The ordinary careless writer would
> say "some small wagons." This man knows what he wants. He sees the
> scene of his story exactly. He has an authoritative mind.
>
> "It appeared round the corner with loud threats of speed." . . . Good
> writing; slightly, but not *too* arresting. . . . "But the colt that it startled
> from among the gorse . . . out-distanced it at a canter." Good again.
> This fellow does not "state." He doesn't say: "It was coming slowly," or
> —what would have been a little better—"at seven miles an hour." Be-
> cause even "seven miles an hour" means nothing definite for the untrained
> mind. It might mean something for a trainer or pedestrian racers. The
> imaginative writer writes for all humanity; he does not limit his desired
> readers to specialists. . . . But anyone knows that an engine that makes a
> great deal of noise and yet cannot overtake a colt at a canter must be a
> ludicrously ineffective machine. We know then that this fellow knows his
> job.
>
> "The gorse still flickered indistinctly in the raw afternoon. . . ." Good
> too, distinctly good. This is the just-sufficient observation of Nature that
> gives you, in a single phrase, landscape, time of day, weather, season. It
> is a raw afternoon in autumn in a rather accented countryside. The
> engine would not come round a bend if there were not some obstacle

to a straight course—a watercourse, a chain of hills. Hills, probably, because gorse grows on dry, broken-up waste country. There won't also be
mountains or anything spectacular or the writer would have mentioned
them. It is, then, just "country." . . .

You are, then, . . . to be in one of those untidy, unfinished landscapes
where locomotives wander innocuously amongst women with baskets.
. . . you are going to learn how what we used to call "the other half"—
though we might as well have said other ninety-nine hundredths—lives.
. . . [T]his man knows. He knows how to open a story with a sentence of
the right cadence for holding the attention. He knows how to construct a
paragraph. He knows the life he is writing about in a landscape just
sufficiently constructed with a casual word here and there. You can trust
him for the rest. . . .

—from "Before the Wars," *Selected Memories, The Bodley Head Ford
Madox Ford* (London, 1962), I, 322–323

You will find the same precision of detail, suggesting the author's
"inside view," his mastery of his material, in *The Horse Dealer's
Daughter*—in paragraph six, for example, or the later description of
the cemetery and the pond. You will find it even in that strange and
strangely different story *The Rocking-Horse Winner*, in the first description of Paul's riding the horse, for example; in the description of
the horse's "lowered face" ("Its red mouth was slightly open, its big
eye was wide and glassy-bright") and in the precise accounting of the
races, the odds, the money.

Ford read *Odour of Chrysanthemums* outside the context available
to us. He did not know anything of the author and had read nothing
else by him. Ford was an excellent editor (as well as writer) and to his
credit spotted Lawrence's genius, a genius quite different from his
own. Lawrence's mastery of detail made Ford trust him, but what he
trusted him for seems to have been knowledge of the "other ninety-
nine hundredths" of the population, the working class. An English
writer of genius with knowledge of the working class was no doubt
rare and notable in those pre-war days, and Lawrence's early works
are full of details of the lives of miners and their families. But Lawrence, we now know, considered not class but the man-woman relationship the "great relationship of humanity," all others being subsidiary. Because we know that, know of Lawrence's notoriety for
describing sexual relations, know his later works in which sexual
relations are the major or basic concern—and perhaps because of the
emphasis on sex in our own time—in reading *Odour of Chrysanthemums* we focus our attention not on the working-class mores but
on the strange relationship between the Bateses. We ponder over
Elizabeth's recognition that she not only had never really known her
husband as himself despite their marital intimacy, but that by thinking
of him only as her husband she had denied his individual selfhood and
his otherness. The class element is still in the story, but the context of
Lawrence's other works and utterances highlights this other human
relationship.

What is implied about "real" or "true" love in the criticism of
Elizabeth Bates's possessive love? There is nothing in that story that

would specifically suggest the terrible risk of loving or the inexplicable descent of love on the soul beyond all reason and intent, or love as transfiguration and new birth, the kind of love we see in *The Horse Dealer's Daughter*. We cannot legitimately go back and put that kind of love in the earlier story, and yet, knowing Lawerence's later work, we can see its potential definition lying there, can see in what Elizabeth Bates's love was not the shadowy suggestion of what love must be. At least love defined in *The Horse Dealer's Daughter* is not inconsistent with what real love might be in *Chrysanthemums*. Similarly, the notion of an emotional knowledge deeper than reason, language, and appearance that we see in Fergusson's loving Mabel, the horse dealer's daughter—

> With an inward groan he gave way, and let his heart yield towards her. A sudden gentle smile came on his face. And her eyes, which never left his face, slowly, slowly filled with tears. He watched the strange water rise in her eyes, like some slow fountain coming up. And his heart seemed to burn and melt away in his breast.

—prepares us for the same kind of deep emotional knowledge in the mother of Paul, the rocking-horse rider—

> . . . when her children were present, she always felt the center of her heart go hard. This troubled her, and in her manner she was all the more gentle and anxious for her children, as if she loved them very much. Only she herself knew that at the center of her heart was a hard little place that could not feel love, no, not for anybody. Everybody else said of her: "She is such a good mother. She adores her children." Only she herself, and her children themselves, knew it was not so.

—only in her case the knowledge is of lack of love.

The central, sometimes obsessive concerns and assumptions that permeate an author's work not only relate the individual stories to each other, mutually illuminating and enriching them, but they also serve as the author's trademark. It is not difficult to recognize or even parody a story by Lawrence.

Embodying these larger concerns and underlying such larger structures as plot, focus, and voice are the basic characteristics of the author's language, such as **diction,** the choice and use of words; sentence structure; **rhetorical tropes,** figures of thought and speech; **imagery;** and **rhythm**—in other words, the author's style.

Perhaps because of the uniqueness of style, the vocabulary for discussing stylistic elements is not very precise or accessible. We can broadly characterize diction as **formal** (*The Cask of Amontillado*) or **informal** (most of the stories in this collection), and within the broad term **informal** we can identify a level of language that approximates the speech of ordinary people and call it **colloquial** (*My Man Bovanne*). But to characterize precisely an author's diction so that it adequately describes his or her work and marks it off from the works of contemporaries is a very difficult task indeed. We can note Hemingway's short sentences and Faulkner's long sentences, but it is hard to get much definition in the stylistic fingerprint of an author merely by measuring the lengths of sentences or tabulating connectives (though these qualities no doubt do subliminally contribute to the effect of the works on readers and do help them identify an author's work).

Diction and sentence structure contribute to the tone of a work, or the implied attitude or stance of the author toward the characters and events, an aspect somewhat analogous to tone of voice. When what is being said and the tone are consistent, it is difficult to separate one from the other; when there seems to be a discrepancy, we have some words that are useful to describe the difference. If the language seems exaggerated, we call it **overstatement**. The narrator of *Spotted Horses* is very fond of overstatement: "Flem Snopes had filled that whole country full of spotted horses," he says, and one "flew right over my team, big as a billboard and flying through the air like a hawk." When Wilson, in *Macomber*, admits that if the authorities discovered they had used cars in their hunting he would lose his license and there might be "Other unpleasantness," he is indulging in a bit of obvious **understatement**. When a word or expression carries not only its literal meaning, but for the speaker has a different meaning we have an example of **verbal irony**. When Fortunato says, "I shall not die of a cough," Montresor's "True—true" may seem reassuring but we learn later in the story why it is both accurate and ominous. There are also nonverbal forms of irony, the most common of which is **dramatic irony**, in which a character holds a position or has an expectation that is reversed or fulfilled in an unexpected way. Knowing her husband's habit of drinking himself into unconsciousness, Elizabeth Bates expects him to be brought home like a log. How is her expectation fulfilled? She had also said bitterly, "But he needn't come rolling in here in his pit-dirt, for *I* won't wash him," and yet she does. Why is her determination altered? As you read through, or look back over this story, watch for other reversed or unexpectedly fulfilled expectations.

Another, highly emphasized element of style is **imagery**. In its broadest sense imagery includes any sensory detail or evocation in a work. Note how much more imagery in that sense we find in *The Old People* than in, say, *The Lottery*. Imagery in this broad sense, however, is so prevalent in literature that it would take exhaustive statistics to differentiate styles by counting the number of sensory elements per hundred or thousand words, categorizing the images as primarily visual, tactile, etc. In a more restricted sense imagery refers to figurative language (see Chapter 5 on symbols), particularly that which defines an abstraction or any emotional or psychological state with a sensory comparison. The opening paragraph of *Odour of Chrysanthemums* illustrates the broader definition of imagery, and this passage from later in the same story may represent the figurative sense: "Life with its smoky burning gone from him, had left him apart. . . . In her womb was ice of fear. . . ."

We might say that if an author's vision gives us his or her profile, the style gives us a fingerprint—though the fingerprint is unique and definitive, it is also harder to come by than a glimpse of a profile. Ultimately, however, vision and style are less distinguishable from each other than the profile-fingerprint image suggests. For vision and style, just like history and structure, do more than interact: they are inextricably fused or compounded. Let us look back at the Ford passage. He says this of "the gorse, which still flickered indistinctly in the raw afternoon" (though he misquotes it slightly and rather loosely calls it a phrase):

> . . . Good too, distinctly good. This is the just-sufficient observation of Nature that gives you, in a single phrase, landscape, time of day, weather, season.

Is this vision or style? The observation of Nature is clearly vision, but expressing that vision economically, tautly, is style. The two merge.

Whatever else this passage is, it is vintage, typical Lawrence. Perhaps it would take more than just these ten words, but surely in a paragraph or two we know we're in the fictional world that he perceived and that he embodied in his stories, novels, and poems in a language of his own created out of that language we share.

D. H. LAWRENCE

Odour of Chrysanthemums

1

The small locomotive engine, Number 4, came clanking, stumbling down from Selston with seven full wagons. It appeared round the corner with loud threats of speed, but the colt that it startled from among the gorse, which still flickered indistinctly in the raw afternoon, out-distanced it at a canter. A woman, walking up the railway line to Underwood, drew back into the hedge, held her basket aside, and watched the footplate of the engine advancing. The trucks thumped heavily past, one by one, with slow inevitable movement, as she stood insignificantly trapped between the jolting black wagons and the hedge; then they curved away towards the coppice where the withered oak leaves dropped noiselessly, while the birds, pulling at the scarlet hips beside the track, made off into the dusk that had already crept into the spinney. In the open, the smoke from the engine sank and cleaved to the rough grass. The fields were dreary and forsaken, and in the marshy strip that led to the whimsey, a reedy pit-pond, the fowls had already abandoned their run among the alders, to roost in the tarred fowl-house. The pit-bank loomed up beyond the pond, flames like red sores licking its ashy sides, in the afternoon's stagnant light. Just beyond rose the tapering chimneys and the clumsy black headstocks of Brinsley Colliery. The two wheels were spinning fast up against the sky, and the winding engine rapped out its little spasms. The miners were being turned up.

The engine whistled as it came into the wide bay of railway lines[1] beside the colliery, where rows of trucks stood in harbor.

Miners, single, trailing and in groups, passed like shadows diverging home. At the edge of the ribbed level of sidings squat a low cottage, three steps down from the cinder track. A large bony vine clutched at the house, as if to claw down the tiled roof. Round the bricked yard grew a few wintry primroses. Beyond, the long garden sloped down to a bush-covered brook course. There were some twiggy apple trees, winter-crack trees, and ragged cabbages. Beside the path hung dishevelled pink chrysanthemums, like pink cloths hung on bushes. A woman came stooping out of the felt-covered fowl-house, half-way down the garden. She closed and padlocked the door, then drew herself erect, having brushed some bits from her white apron.

She was a tall woman of imperious mien, handsome, with definite black eyebrows. Her smooth black hair was parted exactly. For a few moments she stood steadily watching the miners as they passed along the railway; then she turned towards the brook course. Her face was calm and set, her mouth was closed with disillusionment. After a moment she called:

"John!" There was no answer. She waited, and then said distinctly: "Where are you?"

"Here!" replied a child's sulky voice from among the bushes. The woman looked piercingly through the dusk.

"Are you at that brook?" she asked sternly.

For answer the child showed himself before the raspberry-canes that rose like whips. He was a small, sturdy boy of five. He stood quite still, defiantly.

"Oh!" said the mother, conciliated. "I thought you were down at that wet brook—and you remember what I told you——"

The boy did not move or answer.

"Come, come on in," she said more gently, "it's getting dark. There's your grandfather's engine coming down the line!"

The lad advanced slowly, with resentful, taciturn movement. He was dressed in trousers and waistcoat of cloth that was too thick and hard for the size of the garments. They were evidently cut down from a man's clothes.

As they went slowly towards the house he tore at the ragged wisps of chrysanthemums and dropped the petals in handfuls along the path.

"Don't do that—it does look nasty," said his mother. He refrained, and she, suddenly pitiful, broke off a twig with three or four wan flowers and held them against her face. When mother and son reached the yard her hand hesitated, and instead of laying the flower aside, she pushed it in her apron-band. The mother and son stood at the foot of the three steps looking across the bay of lines at the passing home of the miners. The trundle of the small train was imminent. Suddenly the engine loomed past the house and came to a stop opposite the gate.

The engine-driver, a short man with round gray beard, leaned out of the cab high above the woman.

1. Flat, level area of railroad tracks, probably bending away.

"Have you got a cup of tea?" he said in a cheery, hearty fashion.

It was her father. She went in, saying she would mash.[2] Directly, she returned.

"I didn't come to see you on Sunday," began the little gray-bearded man.

"I didn't expect you," said his daughter.

The engine-driver winced; then, reassuming his cheery, airy manner, he said:

"Oh, have you heard then? Well, and what do you think——?"

"I think it is soon enough," she replied.

At her brief censure the little man made an impatient gesture, and said coaxingly, yet with dangerous coldness:

"Well, what's a man to do? It's no sort of life for a man of my years, to sit at my own hearth like a stranger. And if I'm going to marry again it may as well be soon as late—what does it matter to anybody?"

The woman did not reply, but turned and went into the house. The man in the engine-cab stood assertive, till she returned with a cup of tea and a piece of bread and butter on a plate. She went up the steps and stood near the footplace of the hissing engine.

"You needn't 'a' brought me bread an' butter," said her father. "But a cup of tea"—he sipped appreciatively—"it's very nice." He sipped for a moment or two, then: "I hear as Walter's got another bout on," he said.

"When hasn't he?" said the woman bitterly.

"I heerd tell of him in the 'Lord Nelson'[3] braggin' as he was going to spend that b—— afore he went: half a sovereign[4] that was."

"When?" asked the woman.

"A' Sat'day night—I know that's true."

"Very likely," she laughed bitterly. "He gives me twenty-three shillings."

"Aye, it's a nice thing, when a man can do nothing with his money but make a beast of himself!" said the gray-whiskered man. The woman turned her head away. Her father swallowed the last of his tea and handed her the cup.

"Aye," he sighed, wiping his mouth. "It's a settler, it is——"

He put his hand on the lever. The little engine strained and groaned, and the train rumbled towards the crossing. The woman again looked across the metals. Darkness was settling over the spaces of the railway and trucks; the miners, in gray somber group, were still passing home. The winding engine pulsed hurriedly, with brief pauses. Elizabeth Bates looked at the dreary flow of men, then she went indoors. Her husband did not come.

The kitchen was small and full of firelight; red coals piled glowing up the chimney mouth. All the life of the room seemed in the white, warm hearth and the steel fender reflecting the red fire. The cloth was laid for tea; cups glinted in the shadows. At the back, where the lowest stairs protruded into the room, the boy sat struggling with a knife and a

2. Prepare (tea).
3. A public house, pub.
4. A sovereign is an English pound, then

worth $4.86+; there are 20 shillings (see below) to the pound.

piece of white wood. He was almost hidden in the shadow. It was half-past four. They had but to await the father's coming to begin tea. As the mother watched her son's sullen little struggle with the wood, she saw herself in his silence and pertinacity; she saw the father in her child's indifference to all but himself. She seemed to be occupied by her husband. He had probably gone past his home, slunk past his own door, to drink before he came in, while his dinner spoiled and wasted in waiting. She glanced at the clock, then took the potatoes to strain them in the yard. The garden and fields beyond the brook were closed in uncertain darkness. When she rose with the saucepan, leaving the drain steaming into the night behind her, she saw the yellow lamps were lit along the high road that went up the hill away beyond the space of the railway lines and the field.

Then again she watched the men trooping home, fewer now and fewer.

Indoors the fire was sinking and the room was dark red. The woman put her saucepan on the hob, and set a batter-pudding near the mouth of the oven. Then she stood unmoving. Directly, gratefully, came quick young steps to the door. Someone hung on the latch a moment, then a little girl entered and began pulling off her outdoor things, dragging a mass of curls, just ripening from gold to brown, over her eyes with her hat.

Her mother chid her for coming late from school, and said she would have to keep her at home the dark winter days.

"Why, mother, it's hardly a bit dark yet. The lamp's not lighted, and my father's not home."

"No, he isn't. But it's a quarter to five! Did you see anything of him?"

The child became serious. She looked at her mother with large wistful blue eyes.

"No, mother, I've never seen him. Why? Has he come up an' gone past, to Old Brinsley? He hasn't, mother, 'cos I never saw him."

"He'd watch that," said the mother bitterly, "he'd take care as you didn't see him. But you may depend upon it, he's seated in the 'Prince o' Wales.' He wouldn't be this late."

The girl looked at her mother piteously.

"Let's have our teas, mother, should we?" said she.

The mother called John to table. She opened the door once more and looked out across the darkness of the lines. All was deserted: she could not hear the winding engines.

"Perhaps," she said to herself, "he's stopped to get some ripping[5] done."

They sat down to tea. John, at the end of the table near the door, was almost lost in the darkness. Their faces were hidden from each other. The girl crouched against the fender slowly moving a thick piece of bread before the fire. The lad, his face a dusky mark on the shadow, sat watching her who was transfigured in the red glow.

"I do think it's beautiful to look in the fire," said the child.

"Do you?" said her mother. "Why?"

---

5. Coal-mining term for taking down the roof of an underground road in order to make it higher.

"It's so red, and full of little caves—and it feels so nice, and you can fair smell it."

"It'll want mending directly," replied her mother, "and then if your father comes he'll carry on and say there never is a fire when a man comes home sweating from the pit. A public house is always warm enough."

There was silence till the boy said complainingly: "Make haste, our Annie."

"Well, I am doing! I can't make the fire do it no faster, can I?"

"She keeps wafflin'[6] it about so's to make 'er slow," grumbled the boy.

"Don't have such an evil imagination, child," replied the mother.

Soon the room was busy in the darkness with the crisp sound of crunching. The mother ate very little. She drank her tea determinedly, and sat thinking. When she rose her anger was evident in the stern unbending of her head. She looked at the pudding in the fender, and broke out:

"It is a scandalous thing as a man can't even come home to his dinner! If it's crozzled[7] up to a cinder I don't see why I should care. Past his very door he goes to get to a public house, and here I sit with his dinner waiting for him——"

She went out. As she dropped piece after piece of coal on the red fire, the shadows fell on the walls, till the room was almost in total darkness.

"I canna see," grumbled the invisible John. In spite of herself, the mother laughed.

"You know the way to your mouth," she said. She set the dustpan outside the door. When she came again like a shadow on the hearth, the lad repeated, complaining sulkily:

"I canna see."

"Good gracious!" cried the mother irritably, "you're as bad as your father if it's a bit dusk!"

Nevertheless, she took a paper spill from a sheaf on the mantelpiece and proceeded to light the lamp that hung from the ceiling in the middle of the room. As she reached up, her figure displayed itself just rounding with maternity.

"Oh, mother——!" exclaimed the girl.

"What?" said the woman, suspended in the act of putting the lamp-glass over the flame. The copper reflector shone handsomely on her, as she stood with uplifted arm, turning to face her daughter.

"You've got a flower in your apron!" said the child, in a little rapture at this unusual event.

"Goodness me!" exclaimed the woman, relieved. "One would think the house was afire." She replaced the glass and waited a moment before turning up the wick. A pale shadow was seen floating vaguely on the floor.

"Let me smell!" said the child, still rapturously, coming forward and putting her face to her mother's waist.

"Go along, silly!" said the mother, turning up the lamp. The light

6. Waving.   7. Shriveled.

revealed their suspense so that the woman felt it almost unbearable. Annie was still bending at her waist. Irritably, the mother took the flowers out from her apron-band.

"Oh, mother—don't take them out!" Annie cried, catching her hand and trying to replace the sprig.

"Such nonsense!" said the mother, turning away. The child put the pale chrysanthemums to her lips, murmuring:

"Don't they smell beautiful!"

Her mother gave a short laugh.

"No," she said, "not to me. It was chrysanthemums when I married him, and chrysanthemums when you were born, and the first time they ever brought him home drunk, he'd got brown chrysanthemums in his buttonhole."

She looked at the children. Their eyes and their parted lips were wondering. The mother sat rocking in silence for some time. Then she looked at the clock.

"Twenty minutes to six!" In a tone of fine bitter carelessness she continued: "Eh, he'll not come now till they bring him. There he'll stick! But he needn't come rolling in here in his pit-dirt, for *I* won't wash him. He can lie on the floor—Eh, what a fool I've been, what a fool! And this is what I came here for, to this dirty hole, rats and all, for him to slink past his very door. Twice last week—he's begun now———"

She silenced herself, and rose to clear the table.

While for an hour or more the children played, subduedly intent, fertile of imagination, united in fear of the mother's wrath, and in dread of their father's homecoming, Mrs. Bates sat in her rocking-chair making a "singlet" of thick cream-colored flannel, which gave a dull wounded sound as she tore off the gray edge. She worked at her sewing with energy, listening to the children, and her anger wearied itself, lay down to rest, opening its eyes from time to time and steadily watching, its ears raised to listen. Sometimes even her anger quailed and shrank, and the mother suspended her sewing, tracing the footsteps that thudded along the sleepers outside; she would lift her head sharply to bid the children "hush," but she recovered herself in time, and the footsteps went past the gate, and the children were not flung out of their play-world.

But at last Annie sighed, and gave in. She glanced at her wagon of slippers, and loathed the game. She turned plaintively to her mother.

"Mother!"—but she was inarticulate.

John crept out like a frog from under the sofa. His mother glanced up.

"Yes," she said, "just look at those shirtsleeves!"

The boy held them out to survey them, saying nothing. Then somebody called in a hoarse voice away down the line, and suspense bristled in the room, till two people had gone by outside, talking.

"It is time for bed," said the mother.

"My father hasn't come," wailed Annie plaintively. But her mother was primed with courage.

"Never mind. They'll bring him when he does come—like a log." She meant there would be no scene. "And he may sleep on the floor till he wakes himself. I know he'll not go to work tomorrow after this!"

The children had their hands and faces wiped with a flannel.[8] They were very quiet. When they had put on their nightdresses, they said their prayers, the boy mumbling. The mother looked down at them, at the brown silken bush of intertwining curls in the nape of the girl's neck, at the little black head of the lad, and her heart burst with anger at their father, who caused all three such distress. The children hid their faces in her skirts for comfort.

When Mrs. Bates came down, the room was strangely empty, with a tension of expectancy. She took up her sewing and stitched for some time without raising her head. Meantime her anger was tinged with fear.

2

The clock struck eight and she rose suddenly, dropping her sewing on her chair. She went to the stair-foot door, opened it, listening. Then she went out, locking the door behind her.

Something scuffled in the yard, and she started, though she knew it was only the rats with which the place was overrun. The night was very dark. In the great bay of railway lines, bulked with trucks, there was no trace of light, only away back she could see a few yellow lamps at the pit-top, and the red smear of the burning pit-bank on the night. She hurried along the edge of the track, then, crossing the converging lines, came to the stile by the white gates, whence she emerged on the road. Then the fear which had led her shrank. People were walking up to New Brinsley; she saw the lights in the houses; twenty yards farther on were the broad windows of the 'Prince of Wales,' very warm and bright, and the loud voices of men could be heard distinctly. What a fool she had been to imagine that anything had happened to him! He was merely drinking over there at the 'Prince of Wales.' She faltered. She had never yet been to fetch him, and she never would go. So she continued her walk toward the long straggling line of houses, standing back on the highway. She entered a passage between the dwellings.

"Mr. Rigley?—Yes! Did you want him? No, he's not in at this minute."

The raw-boned woman leaned forward from her dark scullery and peered at the other, upon whom fell a dim light through the blind of the kitchen window.

"Is it Mrs. Bates?" she asked in a tone tinged with respect.

"Yes. I wondered if your Master was at home. Mine hasn't come yet."

"'Asn't 'e! Oh, Jack's been 'ome an' 'ad 'is dinner an' gone out. 'E's just gone for 'alf an hour afore bed-time. Did you call at the 'Prince of Wales'?"

"No——"

"No, you didn't like——! It's not very nice." The other woman was indulgent. There was an awkward pause. "Jack never said nothink about—about your Master," she said.

"No!—I expect he's stuck in there!"

Elizabeth Bates said this bitterly, and with recklessness. She knew that the woman across the yard was standing at her door listening, but

8. Washrag.

she did not care. As she turned:

"Stop a minute! I'll just go an' ask Jack if 'e knows anythink," said Mrs. Rigley.

"Oh no—I wouldn't like to put——!"

"Yes, I will, if you'll just step inside an' see as th' childer doesn't come downstairs and set theirselves afire."

Elizabeth Bates, murmuring a remonstrance, stepped inside. The other woman apologized for the state of the room.

The kitchen needed apology. There were little frocks and trousers and childish undergarments on the squab[9] and on the floor, and a litter of playthings everywhere. On the black American cloth[1] of the table were pieces of bread and cake, crusts, slops, and a teapot with cold tea.

"Eh, ours is just as bad," said Elizabeth Bates, looking at the woman, not at the house. Mrs. Rigley put a shawl over her head and hurried out, saying:

"I shanna be a minute."

The other sat, noting with faint disapproval the general untidiness of the room. Then she fell to counting the shoes of various sizes scattered over the floor. There were twelve. She sighed and said to herself: "No wonder!"—glancing at the litter. There came the scratching of two pairs of feet on the yard, and the Rigleys entered. Elizabeth Bates rose. Rigley was a big man, with very large bones. His head looked particularly bony. Across his temple was a blue scar, caused by a wound got in the pit, a wound in which the coal-dust remained blue like tattooing.

"'Asna 'e come whoam yit?" asked the man, without any form of greeting, but with deference and sympathy. "I couldna say wheer he is—'e's non ower theer!"—he jerked his head to signify the 'Prince of Wales.'

"'E's 'appen[2] gone up to th' 'Yew,' " said Mrs. Rigley.

There was another pause. Rigley had evidently something to get off his mind:

"Ah left 'im finishin' a stint," he began. "Loose-all[3] 'ad bin gone about ten minutes when we com'n away, an' I shouted: 'Are ter comin', Walt?' an' 'e said: 'Go on, Ah shanna be but a'ef a minnit,' so we com'n ter th' bottom, me an' Bowers, thinkin' as 'e wor just behint, an' 'ud come up i' th' next bantle[4]——"

He stood perplexed, as if answering a charge of deserting his mate. Elizabeth Bates, now again certain of disaster, hastened to reassure him:

"I expect 'e's gone up to th' 'Yew Tree,' as you say. It's not the first time. I've fretted myself into a fever before now. He'll come home when they carry him."

"Ay, isn't it too bad!" deplored the other woman.

"I'll just step up to Dick's an' see if 'e *is* theer," offered the man, afraid of appearing alarmed, afraid of taking liberties.

"Oh, I wouldn't think of bothering you that far," said Elizabeth Bates, with emphasis, but he knew she was glad of his offer.

9. Sofa.
1. Enameled oilcloth.
2. Perhaps.
3. Signal to quit work and come to the surface.
4. An open seat or car of the lift or elevator that takes the miners to the surface.

As they stumbled up the entry, Elizabeth Bates heard Rigley's wife run across the yard and open her neighbor's door. At this, suddenly all the blood in her body seemed to switch away from her heart.

"Mind!"[5] warned Rigley. "Ah've said many a time as Ah'd fill up them ruts in this entry, sumb'dy 'll be breakin' their legs yit."

She recovered herself and walked quickly along with the miner.

"I don't like leaving the children in bed, and nobody in the house," she said.

"No, you dunna!" he replied courteously. They were soon at the gate of the cottage.

"Well, I shanna be many minnits. Dunna you be frettin' now, 'e'll be all right," said the butty.[6]

"Thank you very much, Mr. Rigley," she replied.

"You're welcome!" he stammered, moving away. "I shanna be many minnits."

The house was quiet. Elizabeth Bates took off her hat and shawl, and rolled back the rug. When she had finished, she sat down. It was a few minutes past nine. She was startled by the rapid chuff of the winding engine at the pit, and the sharp whirr of the brakes on the rope as it descended. Again she felt the painful sweep of her blood, and she put her hand to her side, saying aloud: "Good gracious!—it's only the nine o'clock deputy going down," rebuking herself.

She sat still, listening. Half an hour of this, and she was wearied out.

"What am I working myself up like this for?" she said pitiably to herself, "I s'll only be doing myself some damage."

She took out her sewing again.

At a quarter to ten there were footsteps. One person! She watched for the door to open. It was an elderly woman, in a black bonnet and a black woollen shawl—his mother. She was about sixty years old, pale, with blue eyes, and her face all wrinkled and lamentable. She shut the door and turned to her daughter-in-law peevishly.

"Eh, Lizzie, whatever shall we do, whatever shall we do!" she cried.

Elizabeth drew back a little, sharply.

"What is it, mother?" she said.

The elder woman seated herself on the sofa.

"I don't know, child, I can't tell you!"—she shook her head slowly. Elizabeth sat watching her, anxious and vexed.

"I don't know," replied the grandmother, sighing very deeply. "There's no end to my troubles, there isn't. The things I've gone through, I'm sure it's enough——!" She wept without wiping her eyes, the tears running.

"But, mother," interrupted Elizabeth, "what do you mean? What is it?"

The grandmother slowly wiped her eyes. The fountains of her tears were stopped by Elizabeth's directness. She wiped her eyes slowly.

"Poor child! Eh, you poor thing!" she moaned. "I don't know what we're going to do, I don't—and you as you are—it's a thing, it is indeed!"

Elizabeth waited.

"Is he dead?" she asked, and at the words her heart swung violently, though she felt a slight flush of shame at the ultimate extravagance of the question. Her words sufficiently frightened the old lady, almost brought her to herself.

"Don't say so, Elizabeth! We'll hope it's not as bad as that; no, may the Lord spare us that, Elizabeth. Jack Rigley came just as I was sittin' down to a glass afore going to bed, an' 'e said: ' 'Appen you'll go down th' line, Mrs. Bates. Walt's had an accident. 'Appen you'll go an' sit wi' 'er till we can get him home.' I hadn't time to ask him a word afore he was gone. An' I put my bonnet on an' come straight down, Lizzie. I thought to myself: 'Eh, that poor blessed child, if anybody should come an' tell her of a sudden, there's no knowin' what'll 'appen to 'er.' You mustn't let it upset you, Lizzie—or you know what to expect. How long is it, six months—or is it five, Lizzie? Ay!"—the old woman shook her head—"time slips on, it slips on! Ay!"

Elizabeth's thoughts were busy elsewhere. If he was killed—would she be able to manage on the little pension and what she could earn? —she counted up rapidly. If he was hurt—they wouldn't take him to the hospital—how tiresome he would be to nurse!—but perhaps she'd be able to get him away from the drink and his hateful ways. She would—while he was ill. The tears offered to come to her eyes at the picture. But what sentimental luxury was this she was beginning? She turned to consider the children. At any rate she was absolutely necessary for them. They were her business.

"Ay!" repeated the old woman, "it seems but a week or two since he brought me his first wages. Ay—he was a good lad, Elizabeth, he was, in his way. I don't know why he got to be such a trouble, I don't. He was a happy lad at home, only full of spirits. But there's no mistake he's been a handful of trouble, he has! I hope the Lord'll spare him to mend his ways. I hope so, I hope so. You've had a sight o' trouble with him, Elizabeth, you have indeed. But he was a jolly enough lad wi' me, he was, I can assure you. I don't know how it is. . . ."

The old woman continued to muse aloud, a monotonous irritating sound, while Elizabeth thought concentratedly, startled once, when she heard the winding-engine chuff quickly, and the brakes skirr with a shriek. Then she heard the engine more slowly, and the brakes made no sound. The old woman did not notice. Elizabeth waited in suspense. The mother-in-law talked, with lapses into silence.

"But he wasn't your son, Lizzie, an' it makes a difference. Whatever he was, I remember him when he was little, an' I learned to understand him and to make allowances. You've got to make allowances for them——"

It was half-past ten, and the old woman was saying: "But it's trouble from beginning to end; you're never too old for trouble, never too old for that——" when the gate banged back, and there were heavy feet on the steps.

"I'll go, Lizzie, let me go," cried the old woman, rising. But Elizabeth was at the door. It was a man in pit-clothes.

"They're bringin' 'im, Missis," he said. Elizabeth's heart halted a moment. Then it surged on again, almost suffocating her.

"Is he—is it bad?" she asked.

The man turned away, looking at the darkness:

"The doctor says 'e'd been dead hours. 'E saw 'im i' th' lamp-cabin."

The old woman, who stood just behind Elizabeth, dropped into a chair, and folded her hands, crying:·"Oh, my boy, my boy!"

"Hush!" said Elizabeth, with a sharp twitch of a frown. "Be still, mother, don't waken th' children: I wouldn't have them down for anything!"

The old woman moaned softly, rocking herself. The man was drawing away. Elizabeth took a step forward.

"How was it?" she asked.

"Well, I couldn't say for sure," the man replied, very ill at ease. " 'E wor finishin' a stint an' th' butties 'ad gone, an' a lot o' stuff come down atop 'n 'im.'

"And crushed him?" cried the widow, with a shudder.

"No," said the man, "it fell at th' back of 'im. 'E wor under th' face, an' it niver touched 'im. It shut 'im in. It seems 'e wor smothered."

Elizabeth shrank back. She heard the old woman behind her cry: "What?—what did 'e say it was?"

The man replied, more loudly: " 'E wor smothered!"

Then the old woman wailed aloud, and this relieved Elizabeth.

"Oh, mother," she said, putting her hand on the old woman, "don't waken th' children, don't waken th' children."

She wept a little, unknowing, while the old mother rocked herself and moaned. Elizabeth remembered that they were bringing him home, and she must be ready. "They'll lay him in the parlor," she said to herself, standing a moment pale and perplexed.

Then she lighted a candle and went into the tiny room. The air was cold and damp, but she could not make a fire, there was no fireplace. She set down the candle and looked round. The candlelight glittered on the luster-glasses[7] on the two vases that held some of the pink chrysanthemums, and on the dark mahogany. There was a cold, deathly smell of chrysanthemums in the room. Elizabeth stood looking at the flowers. She turned away, and calculated whether there would be room to lay him on the floor, between the couch and the chiffonier. She pushed the chairs aside. There would be room to lay him down and to step round him. Then she fetched the old red tablecloth, and another old cloth, spreading them down to save her bit of carpet. She shivered on leaving the parlor; so, from the dresser drawer she took a clean shirt and put it at the fire to air. All the time her mother-in-law was rocking herself in the chair and moaning.

"You'll have to move from there, mother," said Elizabeth. "They'll be bringing him in. Come in the rocker."

The old mother rose mechanically, and seated herself by the fire, continuing to lament. Elizabeth went into the pantry for another candle, and there, in the little pent-house[8] under the naked tiles, she

---

7. Glass pendants around the edge of an ornamental vase.

8. Structure, usually with a sloping roof, attached to house.

heard them coming. She stood still in the pantry doorway, listening. She heard them pass the end of the house, and come awkwardly down the three steps, a jumble of shuffling footsteps and muttering voices. The old woman was silent. The men were in the yard.

Then Elizabeth heard Matthews, the manager of the pit, say: "You go in first, Jim. Mind!"

The door came open, and the two women saw a collier backing into the room, holding one end of a stretcher, on which they could see the nailed pit-boots of the dead man. The two carriers halted, the man at the head stooping to the lintel of the door.

"Wheer will you have him?" asked the manager, a short, white-bearded man.

Elizabeth roused herself and came from the pantry carrying the unlighted candle.

"In the parlor," she said.

"In there, Jim!" pointed the manager, and the carriers backed round into the tiny room. The coat with which they had covered the body fell off as they awkwardly turned through the two doorways, and the women saw their man, naked to the waist, lying stripped for work. The old woman began to moan in a low voice of horror.

"Lay th' stretcher at th' side," snapped the manager, "an' put 'im on th' cloths. Mind now, mind! Look you now——!"

One of the men had knocked off a vase of chrysanthemums. He stared awkwardly, then they set down the stretcher. Elizabeth did not look at her husband. As soon as she could get in the room, she went and picked up the broken vase and the flowers.

"Wait a minute!" she said.

The three men waited in silence while she mopped up the water with a duster.

"Eh, what a job, what a job, to be sure!" the manager was saying, rubbing his brow with trouble and perplexity. "Never knew such a thing in my life, never! He'd no business to ha' been left. I never knew such a thing in my life! Fell over him clean as a whistle, an' shut him in. Not four foot of space, there wasn't—yet it scarce bruised him."

He looked down at the dead man, lying prone, half naked, all grimed with cold-dust.

" 'Sphyxiated,' the doctor said. It *is* the most terrible job I've ever known. Seems as if it was done o' purpose. Clean over him, an' shut 'im in, like a mouse-trap"—he made a sharp, descending gesture with his hand.

The colliers standing by jerked aside their heads in hopeless comment.

The horror of the thing bristled upon them all.

Then they heard the girl's voice upstairs calling shrilly: "Mother, mother—who is it? Mother, who is it?"

Elizabeth hurried to the foot of the stairs and opened the door:

"Go to sleep!" she commanded sharply. "What are you shouting about? Go to sleep at once—there's nothing——"

Then she began to mount the stairs. They could hear her on the boards, and on the plaster floor of the little bedroom. They could hear her distinctly:

"What's the mater now?—what's the matter with you, silly thing?" —her voice was much agitated, with an unreal gentleness.

"I thought it was some men come," said the plaintive voice of the child. "Has he come?"

"Yes, they've brought him. There's nothing to make a fuss about. Go to sleep now, like a good child."

They could hear her voice in the bedroom, they waited whilst she covered the children under the bedclothes.

"Is he drunk?" asked the girl, timidly, faintly.

"No! No—he's not! He—he's asleep."

"Is he asleep downstairs?"

"Yes—and don't make a noise."

There was silence for a moment, then the men heard the frightened child again:

"What's that noise?"

"It's nothing, I tell you, what are you bothering for?"

The noise was the grandmother moaning. She was oblivious of everything, sitting on her chair rocking and moaning. The manager put his hand on her arm and bade her "Sh—sh!!"

The old woman opened her eyes and looked at him. She was shocked by this interruption, and seemed to wonder.

"What time is it?" the plaintive thin voice of the child, sinking back unhappily into sleep, asked this last question.

"Ten o'clock," answered the mother more softly. Then she must have bent down and kissed the children.

Matthews beckoned to the men to come away. They put on their caps and took up the stretcher. Stepping over the body, they tiptoed out of the house. None of them spoke till they were far from the wakeful children.

When Elizabeth came down she found her mother alone on the parlor floor, leaning over the dead man, the tears dropping on him.

"We must lay him out," the wife said. She put on the kettle, then returning knelt at the feet, and began to unfasten the knotted leather laces. The room was clammy and dim with only one candle, so that she had to bend her face almost to the floor. At last she got off the heavy boots and put them away.

"You must help me now," she whispered to the old woman. Together they stripped the man.

When they arose, saw him lying in the naïve dignity of death, the women stood arrested in fear and respect. For a few moments they remained still, looking down, the old mother whimpering. Elizabeth felt countermanded. She saw him, how utterly inviolable he lay in himself. She had nothing to do with him. She could not accept it. Stooping, she laid her hand on him, in claim. He was still warm, for the mine was hot where he had died. His mother had his face between her hands, and was murmuring incoherently. The old tears fell in succession as drops from wet leaves; the mother was not weeping, merely her tears flowed. Elizabeth embraced the body of her husband, with cheek and lips. She seemed to be listening, inquiring, trying to get some connection. But she could not. She was driven away. He was impregnable.

She rose, went into the kitchen, where she poured warm water into a bowl, brought soap and flannel and a soft towel.

"I must wash him," she said.

Then the old mother rose stiffly, and watched Elizabeth as she carefully washed his face, carefully brushing the big blond moustache from his mouth with the flannel. She was afraid with a bottomless fear, so she ministered to him. The old woman, jealous, said:

"Let me wipe him!"—and she kneeled on the other side drying slowly as Elizabeth washed, her big black bonnet sometimes brushing the dark head of her daughter-in-law. They worked thus in silence for a long time. They never forgot it was death, and the touch of the man's dead body gave them strange emotions, different in each of the women; a great dread possessed them both, the mother felt the lie was given to her womb, she was denied; the wife felt the utter isolation of the human soul, the child within her was a weight apart from her.

At last it was finished. He was a man of handsome body, and his face showed no traces of drink. He was blond, full-fleshed, with fine limbs. But he was dead.

"Bless him," whispered his mother, looking always at his face, and speaking out of sheer terror. "Dear lad—bless him!" She spoke in a faint, sibilant ecstasy of fear and mother love.

Elizabeth sank down again to the floor, and put her face against his neck, and trembled and shuddered. But she had to draw away again. He was dead, and her living flesh had no place against his. A great dread and weariness held her: she was so unavailing. Her life was gone like this.

"White as milk he is, clear as a twelve-month baby, bless him, the darling!" the old mother murmured to herself. "Not a mark on him, clear and clean and white, beautiful as ever a child was made," she murmured with pride. Elizabeth kept her face hidden.

"He went peaceful, Lizzie—peaceful as sleep. Isn't he beautiful, the lamb? Ay—he must ha' made his peace, Lizzie. 'Appen he made it all right, Lizzie, shut in there. He'd have time. He wouldn't look like this if he hadn't made his peace. The lamb, the dear lamb. Eh, but he had a hearty laugh. I loved to hear it. He had the heartiest laugh, Lizzie, as a lad——"

Elizabeth looked up. The man's mouth was fallen back, slightly open under the cover of the moustache. The eyes, half shut, did not show glazed in the obscurity. Life with its smoky burning gone from him, had left him apart and utterly alien to her. And she knew what a stranger he was to her. In her womb was ice of fear, because of this separate stranger with whom she had been living as one flesh. Was this what it all meant—utter, intact separateness, obscured by heat of living? In dread she turned her face away. The fact was too deadly. There had been nothing between them, and yet they had come together, exchanging their nakedness repeatedly. Each time he had taken her, they had been two isolated beings, far apart as now. He was no more responsible than she. The child was like ice in her womb. For as she looked at the dead man, her mind, cold and detached, said clearly: "Who am I? What have I been doing? I have been fighting a husband who did not exist. *He* existed all the time. What wrong have I done? What was that I have been living with? There lies the reality, this man." And her soul died in her for fear: she knew she had never seen him, he had never seen her, they had met in the dark and had fought in the dark, not knowing whom they met nor whom they fought. And now she saw, and turned silent in seeing. For she had been wrong. She had said he was something he was not; she had felt familiar with him. Whereas he was apart all the while, living as she never lived, feeling as she never felt.

In fear and shame she looked at his naked body, that she had known falsely. And he was the father of her children. Her soul was torn from her body and stood apart. She looked at his naked body and was ashamed, as if she had denied it. After all, it was itself. It seemed awful to her. She looked at his face, and she turned her own face to the wall. For his look was other than hers, his way was not her way. She had denied him what he was—she saw it now. She had refused him as himself. And this had been her life, and his life. She was grateful to death, which restored the truth. And she knew she was not dead.

And all the while her heart was bursting with grief and pity for him. What had he suffered? What stretch of horror for this helpless man! She was rigid with agony. She had not been able to help him. He had been cruelly injured, this naked man, this other being, and she could make no reparation. There were the children—but the children belonged to life. This dead man had nothing to do with them. He and she were only channels through which life had flowed to issue in the children. She was a mother—but how awful she knew it now to have been a wife. And he, dead now, how awful he must have felt it to be a husband. She felt that in the next world he would be a stranger to her. If they met there, in the beyond, they would only be ashamed of what had been before. The children had come, for some mysterious reason, out of both of them. But the children did not unite them. Now he was dead, she knew how eternally he was apart from her, how eternally he had nothing more to do with her. She saw this episode of her life closed. They had denied each other in life. Now he had withdrawn. An anguish came over her. It was finished then: it had become hopeless between them long before he died. Yet he had been her husband. But how little!

"Have you got his shirt, 'Lizabeth?"

Elizabeth turned without answering, though she strove to weep and behave as her mother-in-law expected. But she could not, she was silenced. She went into the kitchen and returned with the garment.

"It is aired," she said, grasping the cotton shirt here and there to try. She was almost ashamed to handle him; what right had she or anyone to lay hands on him; but her touch was humble on his body. It was hard work to clothe him. He was so heavy and inert. A terrible dread gripped her all the while: that he could be so heavy and utterly inert, unresponsive, apart. The horror of the distance between them was almost too much for her—it was so infinite a gap she must look across.

At last it was finished. They covered him with a sheet and left him lying, with his face bound. And she fastened the door of the little parlor, lest the children should see what was lying there. Then, with peace sunk heavy on her heart, she went about making tidy the kitchen. She knew she submitted to life, which was her immediate master. But from death, her ultimate master, she winced with fear and shame.

1914

D. H. LAWRENCE

The Horse Dealer's Daughter

"Well, Mabel, and what are you going to do with yourself?" asked Joe, with foolish flippancy. He felt quite safe himself. Without listening for an answer, he turned aside, worked a grain of tobacco to the tip of his tongue, and spat it out. He did not care about anything, since he felt safe himself.

The three brothers and the sister sat round the desolate breakfast table, attempting some sort of desultory consultation. The morning's post had given the final tap to the family fortunes, and all was over. The dreary dining room itself, with its heavy mahogany furniture, looked as if it were waiting to be done away with.

But the consultation amounted to nothing. There was a strange air of ineffectuality about the three men, as they sprawled at table, smoking and reflecting vaguely on their own condition. The girl was alone, a rather short, sullen-looking young woman of twenty-seven. She did not share the same life as her brothers. She would have been good-looking, save for the impassive fixity of her face, "bull dog," as her brothers called it.

There was a confused tramping of horses' feet outside. The three men all sprawled round in their chairs to watch. Beyond the dark holly bushes that separated the strip of lawn from the highroad, they could see a cavalcade of shire horses swinging out of their own yard, being taken for exercise. This was the last time. These were the last horses that would go through their hands. The young men watched with critical, callous look. They were all frightened at the collapse of their lives, and the sense of disaster in which they were involved left them no inner freedom.

Yet they were three fine, well-set fellows enough. Joe, the eldest, was a man of thirty-three, broad and handsome in a hot, flushed way. His face was red, he twisted his black mustache over a thick finger, his eyes were shallow and restless. He had a sensual way of uncovering his teeth when he laughed, and his bearing was stupid. Now he watched the horses with a glazed look of helplessness in his eyes, a certain stupor of downfall.

The great draft-horses swung past. They were tied head to tail, four of them, and they heaved along to where a lane branched off

from the highroad, planting their great hoofs floutingly in the fine
black mud, swinging their great rounded haunches sumptuously,
and trotting a few sudden steps as they were led into the lane, round
the corner. Every movement showed a massive, slumbrous strength,
and a stupidity which held them in subjection. The groom at the
head looked back, jerking the leading rope. And the cavalcade
moved out of sight up the lane, the tail of the last horse, bobbed up
tight and stiff, held out taut from the swinging great haunches as
they rocked behind the hedges in a motion-like sleep.

Joe watched with glazed hopeless eyes. The horses were almost
like his own body to him. He felt he was done for now. Luckily he
was engaged to a woman as old as himself, and therefore her father,
who was steward of a neighboring estate, would provide him with a
job. He would marry and go into harness. His life was over, he
would be a subject animal now.

He turned uneasily aside, the retreating steps of the horses echoing
in his ears. Then, with foolish restlessness, he reached for the scraps
of bacon-rind from the plates, and making a faint whistling sound,
flung them to the terrier that lay against the fender.[1] He watched the
dog swallow them, and waited till the creature looked into his eyes.
Then a faint grin came on his face, and in a high, foolish voice he
said:

"You won't get much more bacon, shall you, you little b——?"

The dog faintly and dismally wagged its tail, then lowered its
haunches, circled round, and lay down again.

There was another helpless silence at the table. Joe sprawled
uneasily in his seat, not willing to go till the family conclave was
dissolved. Fred Henry, the second brother, was erect, clean-limbed,
alert. He had watched the passing of the horses with more sang-froid.
If he was an animal, like Joe, he was an animal which controls,
not one which is controlled. He was master of any horse, and he
carried himself with a well-tempered air of mastery. But he was not
master of the situations of life. He pushed his coarse brown mustache
upwards, off his lip, and glanced irritably at his sister, who sat
impassive and inscrutable.

"You'll go and stop with Lucy for a bit, shan't you?" he asked.
The girl did not answer.

"I don't see what else you can do," persisted Fred Henry.

"Go as a skivvy,"[2] Joe interpolated laconically.

The girl did not move a muscle.

"If I was her, I should go in for training for a nurse," said Malcolm, the youngest of them all. He was the baby of the family, a
young man of twenty-two, with a fresh, jaunty *museau*.[3]

But Mabel did not take any notice of him. They had talked at
her and round her for so many years, that she hardly heard them
at all.

The marble clock on the mantelpiece softly chimed the half-hour,
the dog rose uneasily from the hearthrug and looked at the party

1. Fire-screen or -guard.   3. Face, "mug" (slightly derogatory).
2. Servant.

at the breakfast table. But still they sat on in ineffectual conclave.

"Oh, all right," said Joe suddenly, apropos of nothing. "I'll get a move on."

He pushed back his chair, straddled his knees with a downward jerk, to get them free, in horsey fashion, and went to the fire. Still he did not go out of the room; he was curious to know what the others would do or say. He began to charge his pipe, looking down at the dog and saying, in a high, affected voice:

"Going wi' me? Going wi' me are ter? Tha'rt goin' further than tha counts on just now, dost hear?"

The dog faintly wagged its tail, the man stuck out his jaw and covered his pipe with his hands, and puffed intently, losing himself in the tobacco, looking down all the while at the dog with an absent brown eye. The dog looked up at him in mournful distrust. Joe stood with his knees stuck out, in real horsey fashion.

"Have you had a letter from Lucy?" Fred Henry asked of his sister.

"Last week," came the neutral reply.

"And what does she say?"

There was no answer.

"Does she *ask* you to go and stop there?" persisted Fred Henry.

"She says I can if I like."

"Well, then, you'd better. Tell her you'll come on Monday."

This was received in silence.

"That's what you'll do then, is it?" said Fred Henry, in some exasperation.

But she made no answer. There was a silence of futility and irritation in the room. Malcolm grinned fatuously.

"You'll have to make up your mind between now and next Wednesday," said Joe loudly, "or else find yourself lodgings on the curbstone."

The face of the young woman darkened, but she sat on immutable.

"Here's Jack Fergusson!" exclaimed Malcolm, who was looking aimlessly out of the window.

"Where?" exclaimed Joe, loudly.

"Just gone past."

"Coming in?"

Malcolm craned his neck to see the gate.

"Yes," he said.

There was a silence. Mabel sat on like one condemned, at the head of the table. Then a whistle was heard from the kitchen. The dog got up and barked sharply. Joe opened the door and shouted: "Come on."

After a moment a young man entered. He was muffled up in overcoat and a purple woolen scarf, and his tweed cap, which he did not remove, was pulled down on his head. He was of medium height, his face was rather long and pale, his eyes looked tired.

"Hello, Jack! Well, Jack!" exclaimed Malcolm and Joe. Fred Henry merely said, "Jack."

"What's doing?" asked the newcomer, evidently addressing Fred Henry.

"Same. We've got to be out by Wednesday. Got a cold?"

"I have—got it bad, too."

"Why don't you stop in?"[4]

"*Me* stop in? When I can't stand on my legs, perhaps I shall have a chance." The young man spoke huskily. He had a slight Scotch accent.

"It's a knockout, isn't it," said Joe, boisterously, "if a doctor goes round croaking with a cold. Looks bad for the patients, doesn't it?"

The young doctor looked at him slowly.

"Anything the matter with *you*, then?" he asked sarcastically.

"Not as I know of. Damn your eyes, I hope not. Why?"

"I thought you were very concerned about the patients, wondered if you might be one yourself."

"Damn it, no, I've never been patient to no flaming[5] doctor, and hope I never shall be," returned Joe.

At this point Mabel rose from the table, and they all seemed to become aware of her existence. She began putting the dishes together. The young doctor looked at her, but did not address her. He had not greeted her. She went out of the room with the tray, her face impassive and unchanged.

"When are you off then, all of you?" asked the doctor.

"I'm catching the eleven-forty," replied Malcolm. "Are you goin' down wi' th' trap, Joe?"

"Yes, I've told you I'm going down wi' th' trap, haven't I?"

"We'd better be getting her in then. So long, Jack, if I don't see you before I go," said Malcolm, shaking hands.

He went out, followed by Joe, who seemed to have his tail between his legs.

"Well, this is the devil's own," exclaimed the doctor, when he was left alone with Fred Henry. "Going before Wednesday, are you?"

"That's the orders," replied the other.

"Where, to Northampton?"[6]

"That's it."

"The devil!" exclaimed Fergusson, with quiet chagrin.

And there was silence between the two.

"All settled up, are you?" asked Fergusson.

"About."

There was another pause.

"Well, I shall miss yer, Freddy, boy," said the young doctor.

"And I shall miss thee, Jack," returned the other.

"Miss you like hell," mused the doctor.

Fred Henry turned aside. There was nothing to say. Mabel came in again, to finish clearing the table.

"What are *you* going to do, then, Miss Pervin?" asked Fergusson. "Going to your sister's, are you?"

Mabel looked at him with her steady, dangerous eyes, that always made him uncomfortable, unsettling his superficial ease.

"No," she said.

"Well, what in the name of fortune *are* you going to do? Say

---

4. Stay home.
5. Euphemism for "bloody," roughly equivalent to "darned."

6. Town about 65 miles north and slightly west of London.

what you mean to do," cried Fred Henry, with futile intensity.

But she only averted her head, and continued her work. She folded the white tablecloth, and put on the chenille cloth.

"The sulkiest bitch that ever trod!" muttered her brother.

But she finished her task with perfectly impassive face, the young doctor watching her interestedly all the while. Then she went out.

Fred Henry stared after her, clenching his lips, his blue eyes fixing in sharp antagonism, as he made a grimace of sour exasperation.

"You could bray[7] her into bits, and that's all you'd get out of her," he said, in a small, narrowed tone.

The doctor smiled faintly.

"What's she *going* to do, then?" he asked.

"Strike me if *I* know!" returned the other.

There was a pause. Then the doctor stirred.

"I'll be seeing you tonight, shall I?" he said to his friend.

"Ay—where's it to be? Are we going over to Jessdale?"[8]

"I don't know. I've got such a cold on me. I'll come round to the Moon and Stars, anyway."

"Let Lizzie and May miss their night for once, eh?"

"That's it—if I feel as I do now."

"All's one——"

The two young men went through the passage and down to the back door together. The house was large, but it was servantless now, and desolate. At the back was a small bricked house-yard, and beyond that a big square, graveled fine and red, and having stables on two sides. Sloping, dank, winter-dark fields stretched away on the open sides.

But the stables were empty. Joseph Pervin, the father of the family, had been a man of no education, who had become a fairly large horse dealer. The stables had been full of horses, there was a great turmoil and come-and-go of horses and of dealers and grooms. Then the kitchen was full of servants. But of late things had declined. The old man had married a second time, to retrieve his fortunes. Now he was dead and everything was gone to the dogs, there was nothing but debt and threatening.

For months, Mabel had been servantless in the big house, keeping the home together in penury for her ineffectual brothers. She had kept house for ten years. But previously it was with unstinted means. Then, however brutal and coarse everything was, the sense of money had kept her proud, confident. The men might be foul-mouthed, the women in the kitchen might have bad reputations, her brothers might have illegitimate children. But so long as there was money, the girl felt herself established, and brutally proud, reserved.

No company came to the house, save dealers and coarse men. Mabel had no associates of her own sex, after her sister went away. But she did not mind. She went regularly to church, she attended to her father. And she lived in the memory of her mother, who had died when she was fourteen, and whom she had loved. She had

7. Crush.   8. Apparently a fictional name.

loved her father, too, in a different way, depending upon him, and feeling secure in him, until at the age of fifty-four he married again. And then she had set hard against him. Now he had died and left them all hopelessly in debt.

She had suffered badly during the period of poverty. Nothing, however, could shake the curious sullen, animal pride that dominated each member of the family. Now, for Mabel, the end had come. Still she would not cast about her. She would follow her own way just the same. She would always hold the keys of her own situation. Mindless and persistent, she endured from day to day. Why should she think? Why should she answer anybody? It was enough that this was the end, and there was no way out. She need not pass any more darkly along the main street of the small town, avoiding every eye. She need not demean herself any more, going into the shops and buying the cheapest food. This was at an end. She thought of nobody, not even of herself. Mindless and persistent, she seemed in a sort of ecstasy to be coming nearer to her fulfilment, her own glorification, approaching her dead mother, who was glorified.

In the afternoon she took a little bag, with shears and sponge and a small scrubbing brush, and went out. It was a gray, wintry day, with saddened, dark green fields and an atmosphere blackened by the smoke of foundries not far off. She went quickly, darkly along the causeway, heeding nobody, through the town to the churchyard.

There she always felt secure, as if no one could see her, although as a matter of fact she was exposed to the stare of every one who passed along under the churchyard wall. Nevertheless, once under the shadow of the great looming church, among the graves, she felt immune from the world, reserved within the thick churchyard wall as in another country.

Carefully she clipped the grass from the grave, and arranged the pinky white, small chrysanthemums in the tin cross. When this was done, she took an empty jar from a neighboring grave, brought water, and carefully, most scrupulously sponged the marble headstone and the coping-stone.[9]

It gave her sincere satisfaction to do this. She felt in immediate contact with the world of her mother. She took minute pains, went through the park in a state bordering on pure happiness, as if in performing this task she came into a subtle, intimate connection with her mother. For the life she followed here in the world was far less real than the world of death she inherited from her mother.

The doctor's house was just by the church. Fergusson, being a mere hired assistant, was slave to the countryside. As he hurried now to attend to the outpatients in the surgery, glancing across the graveyard with his quick eye, he saw the girl at her task at the grave. She seemed so intent and remote, it was like looking into another world. Some mystical element was touched in him. He slowed down as he walked, watching her as if spellbound.

She lifted her eyes, feeling him looking. Their eyes met. And each looked again at once, each feeling, in some way, found out by

9. Copestone, stone on top layer.

the other. He lifted his cap and passed on down the road. There remained distinct in his consciousness, like a vision, the memory of her face, lifted from the tombstone in the churchyard, and looking at him with slow, large, portentous eyes. It *was* portentous, her face. It seemed to mesmerize him. There was a heavy power in her eyes which laid hold of his whole being, as if he had drunk some powerful drug. He had been feeling weak and done before. Now the life came back into him, he felt delivered from his own fretted, daily self.

He finished his duties at the surgery as quickly as might be, hastily filling up the bottles of the waiting people with cheap drugs. Then, in perpetual haste, he set off again to visit several cases in another part of his round, before teatime. At all times he preferred to walk if he could, but particularly when he was not well. He fancied the motion restored him.

The afternoon was falling. It was gray, deadened, and wintry, with a slow, moist, heavy coldness sinking in and deadening all the faculties. But why should he think or notice? He hastily climbed the hill and turned across the dark green fields, following the black cinder-track. In the distance, across a shallow dip in the country, the small town was clustered like smouldering ash, a tower, a spire, a heap of low, raw, extinct houses. And on the nearest fringe of the town, sloping into the dip, was Oldmeadow, the Pervins' house. He could see the stables and the outbuildings distinctly, as they lay towards him on the slope. Well, he would not go there many more times! Another resource would be lost to him, another place gone: the only company he cared for in the alien, ugly little town he was losing. Nothing but work, drudgery, constant hastening from dwelling to dwelling among the colliers and the ironworkers. It wore him out, but at the same time he had a craving for it. It was a stimulant to him to be in the homes of the working people, moving as it were through the innermost body of their life. His nerves were excited and gratified. He could come so near, into the very lives of the rough, inarticulate, powerfully emotional men and women. He grumbled, he said he hated the hellish hole. But as a matter of fact it excited him, the contact with the rough, strongly-feeling people was a stimulant applied direct to his nerves.

Below Oldmeadow, in the green, shallow, soddened hollow of fields, lay a square, deep pond. Roving across the landscape, the doctor's quick eye detected a figure in black passing through the gate of the field, down towards the pond. He looked again. It would be Mabel Pervin. His mind suddenly became alive and attentive.

Why was she going down there? He pulled up on the path on the slope above, and stood staring. He could just make sure of the small black figure moving in the hollow of the failing day. He seemed to see her in the midst of such obscurity, that he was like a clairvoyant, seeing rather with the mind's eye than with ordinary sight. Yet he could see her positively enough, whilst he kept his eye attentive. He felt, if he looked away from her, in the thick, ugly, falling dusk, he would lose her altogether.

He followed her minutely as she moved, direct and intent, like something transmitted rather than stirring in voluntary activity,

234 D. H. Lawrence

straight down the field towards the pond. There she stood on the
bank for a moment. She never raised her head. Then she waded
slowly into the water.

He stood motionless as the small black figure walked slowly and
deliberately towards the center of the pond, very slowly, gradually
moving deeper into the motionless water, and still moving forward
as the water got up to her breast. Then he could see her no more
in the dusk of the dead afternoon.

"There!" he exclaimed. "Would you believe it?"

And he hastened straight down, running over the wet, soddened
fields, pushing through the hedges, down into the depression of
callous wintry obscurity. It took him several minutes to come to the
pond. He stood on the bank, breathing heavily. He could see nothing. His eyes seemed to penetrate the dead water. Yes, perhaps that
was the dark shadow of her black clothing beneath the surface of
the water.

He slowly ventured into the pond. The bottom was deep, soft
clay, he sank in, and the water clasped dead cold round his legs.
As he stirred he could smell the cold, rotten clay that fouled up into
the water. It was objectionable in his lungs. Still, repelled and yet
not heeding, he moved deeper into the pond. The cold water rose
over his thighs, over his loins, upon his abdomen. The lower part
of his body was all sunk in the hideous cold element. And the bottom was so deeply soft and uncertain, he was afraid of pitching
with his mouth underneath. He could not swim, and was afraid.

He couched a little, spreading his hands under the water and
moving them round, trying to feel for her. The dead cold pond
swayed upon his chest. He moved again, a little deeper, and again,
with his hands underneath, he felt all around under the water. And
he touched her clothing. But it evaded his fingers. He made a
desperate effort to grasp it.

And so doing he lost his balance and went under, horribly, suffocating in the foul earthy water, struggling madly for a few moments.
At last, after what seemed an eternity, he got his footing, rose again
into the air and looked around. He gasped, and knew he was in
the world. Then he looked at the water. She had risen near him.
He grasped her clothing, and drawing her nearer, turned to take his
way to land again.

He went very slowly, carefully, absorbed in the slow progress. He
rose higher, climbing out of the pond. The water was now only
about his legs; he was thankful, full of relief to be out of the clutches
of the pond. He lifted her and staggered on to the bank, out of the
horror of wet, gray clay.

He laid her down on the bank. She was quite unconscious and
running with water. He made the water come from her mouth, he
worked to restore her. He did not have to work very long before he
could feel the breathing begin again in her; she was breathing
naturally. He worked a little longer. He could feel her live beneath
his hands; she was coming back. He wiped her face, wrapped her
in his overcoat, looked round into the dim, dark gray world, then
lifted her and staggered down the bank and across the fields.

It seemed an unthinkably long way, and his burden so heavy he
felt he would never get to the house. But at last he was in the stable-
yard, and then in the house-yard. He opened the door and went into
the house. In the kitchen he laid her down on the hearthrug, and
called. The house was empty. But the fire was burning in the grate.

Then again he kneeled to attend to her. She was breathing regularly, her eyes were wide open and as if conscious, but there seemed
something missing in her look. She was conscious in herself, but unconscious of her surroundings.

He ran upstairs, took blankets from a bed, and put them before
the fire to warm. Then he removed her saturated, earthy-smelling
clothing, rubbed her dry with a towel, and wrapped her naked in
the blankets. Then he went into the diningroom, to look for spirits.
There was a little whisky. He drank a gulp himself, and put some
into her mouth.

The effect was instantaneous. She looked full into his face, as if
she had been seeing him for some time, and yet had only just
become conscious of him.

"Dr. Fergusson?" she said.

"What?" he answered.

He was divesting himself of his coat, intending to find some dry
clothing upstairs. He could not bear the smell of the dead, clayey
water, and he was mortally afraid for his own health.

"What did I do?" she asked.

"Walked into the pond," he replied. He had begun to shudder
like one sick, and could hardly attend to her. Her eyes remained full
on him, he seemed to be going dark in his mind, looking back at
her helplessly. The shuddering became quieter in him, his life came
back in him, dark and unknowing, but strong again.

"Was I out of my mind?" she asked, while her eyes were fixed
on him all the time.

"Maybe, for the moment," he replied. He felt quiet, because his
strength had come back. The strange fretful strain had left him.

"Am I out of my mind now?" she asked.

"Are you?" he reflected a moment. "No," he answered truthfully,
"I don't see that you are." He turned his face aside. He was afraid
now, because he felt dazed, and felt dimly that her power was
stronger than his, in this issue. And she continued to look at him
fixedly all the time. "Can you tell me where I shall find some dry
things to put on?" he asked.

"Did you dive into the pond for me?" she asked.

"No," he answered. "I walked in. But I went in overhead as well."

There was silence for a moment. He hesitated. He very much
wanted to go upstairs to get into dry clothing. But there was another
desire in him. And she seemed to hold him. His will seemed to
have gone to sleep, and left him, standing there slack before her.
But he felt warm inside himself. He did not shudder at all, though
his clothes were sodden on him.

"Why did you?" she asked.

"Because I didn't want you to do such a foolish thing," he said.

"It wasn't foolish," she said, still gazing at him as she lay on the floor, with a sofa cushion under her head. "It was the right thing to do. *I* knew best, then."

"I'll go and shift [1] these wet things," he said. But still he had not the power to move out of her presence, until she sent him. It was as if she had the life of his body in her hands, and he could not extricate himself. Or perhaps he did not want to.

Suddenly she sat up. Then she became aware of her own immediate condition. She felt the blankets about her, she knew her own limbs. For a moment it seemed as if her reason were going. She looked round, with wild eye, as if seeking something. He stood still with fear. She saw her clothing lying scattered.

"Who undressed me?" she asked, her eyes resting full and inevitable on his face.

"I did," he replied, "to bring you round."

For some moments she sat and gazed at him awfully, her lips parted.

"Do you love me, then?" she asked.

He only stood and stared at her, fascinated. His soul seemed to melt.

She shuffled forward on her knees, and put her arms round him, round his legs, as he stood there, pressing her breasts against his knees and thighs, clutching him with strange, convulsive certainty, pressing his thighs against her, drawing him to her face, her throat, as she looked up at him with flaring, humble eyes of transfiguration, triumphant in first possession.

"You love me," she murmured, in strange transport, yearning and triumphant and confident. "You love me. I know you love me, I know."

And she was passionately kissing his knees, through the wet clothing, passionately and indiscriminately kissing his knees, his legs, as if unaware of everything.

He looked down at the tangled wet hair, the wild, bare, animal shoulders. He was amazed, bewildered, and afraid. He had never thought of loving her. He had never wanted to love her. When he rescued her and restored her, he was a doctor, and she was a patient. He had had no single personal thought of her. Nay, this introduction of the personal element was very distasteful to him, a violation of his professional honor. It was horrible to have her there embracing his knees. It was horrible. He revolted from it, violently. And yet—and yet—he had not the power to break away.

She looked at him again, with the same supplication of powerful love, and that same transcendent, frightening light of triumph. In view of the delicate flame which seemed to come from her face like a light, he was powerless. And yet he had never intended to love her. He had never intended. And something stubborn in him could not give way.

"You love me," she repeated, in a murmur of deep, rhapsodic assurance. "You love me."

Her hands were drawing him, drawing him down to her. He was

1. Change.

afraid, even a little horrified. For he had, really, no intention of loving her. Yet her hands were drawing him towards her. He put out his hand quickly to steady himself, and grasped her bare shoulder. A flame seemed to burn the hand that grasped her soft shoulder. He had no intention of loving her: his whole will was against his yielding. It was horrible. And yet wonderful was the touch of her shoulders, beautiful the shining of her face. Was she perhaps mad? He had a horror of yielding to her. Yet something in him ached also.

He had been staring away at the door, away from her. But his hand remained on her shoulder. She had gone suddenly very still. He looked down at her. Her eyes were now wide with fear, with doubt, the light was dying from her face, a shadow of terrible grayness was returning. He could not bear the touch of her eyes' question upon him, and the look of death behind the question.

With an inward groan he gave way, and let his heart yield towards her. A sudden gentle smile came on his face. And her eyes, which never left his face, slowly, slowly filled with tears. He watched the strange water rise in her eyes, like some slow fountain coming up. And his heart seemed to burn and melt away in his breast.

He could not bear to look at her any more. He dropped on his knees and caught her head with his arms and pressed her face against his throat. She was very still. His heart, which seemed to have broken, was burning with a kind of agony in his breast. And he felt her slow, hot tears wetting his throat. But he could not move.

He felt the hot tears wet his neck and the hollows of his neck, and he remained motionless, suspended through one of man's eternities. Only now it had become indispensable to him to have her face pressed close to him; he could never let her go again. He could never let her head go away from the close clutch of his arm. He wanted to remain like that for ever, with his heart hurting him in a pain that was also life to him. Without knowing, he was looking down on her damp, soft brown hair.

Then, as it were suddenly, he smelt the horrid stagnant smell of that water. And at the same moment she drew away from him and looked at him. Her eyes were wistful and unfathomable. He was afraid of them, and he fell to kissing her, not knowing what he was doing. He wanted her eyes not to have that terrible, wistful, unfathomable look.

When she turned her face to him again, a faint delicate flush was glowing, and there was again dawning that terrible shining of joy in her eyes, which really terrified him, and yet which he now wanted to see, because he feared the look of doubt still more.

"You love me?" she said, rather faltering.

"Yes." The word cost him a painful effort. Not because it wasn't true. But because it was too newly true, the *saying* seemed to tear open again his newly-torn heart. And he hardly wanted it to be true, even now.

She lifted her face to him, and he bent forward and kissed her on the mouth, gently, with the one kiss that is an eternal pledge. And as he kissed her his heart strained again in his breast. He never intended to love her. But now it was over. He had crossed over the gulf to her, and all that he had left behind had shriveled and become void.

After the kiss, her eyes again slowly filled with tears. She sat still, away from him, with her face drooped aside, and her hands folded in her lap. The tears fell very slowly. There was complete silence. He too sat there motionless and silent on the hearthrug. The strange pain of his heart that was broken seemed to consume him. That he should love her? That this was love! That he should be ripped open in this way! Him, a doctor! How they would all jeer if they knew! It was agony to him to think they might know.

In the curious naked pain of the thought he looked again to her. She was sitting there drooped into a muse. He saw a tear fall, and his heart flared hot. He saw for the first time that one of her shoulders was quite uncovered, one arm bare, he could see one of her small breasts; dimly, because it had become almost dark in the room.

"Why are you crying?" he asked, in an altered voice.

She looked up at him, and behind her tears the consciousness of her situation for the first time brought a dark look of shame to her eyes.

"I'm not crying, really," she said, watching him half frightened.

He reached his hand, and softly closed it on her bare arm.

"I love you! I love you!" he said in a soft, low vibrating voice, unlike himself.

She shrank, and dropped her head. The soft, penetrating grip of his hand on her arm distressed her. She looked up at him.

"I want to go," she said. "I want to go and get you some dry things."

"Why?" he said. "I'm all right."

"But I want to go," she said. "And I want you to change your things."

He released her arm, and she wrapped herself in the blanket, looking at him rather frightened. And still she did not rise.

"Kiss me," she said wistfully.

He kissed her, but briefly, half in anger.

Then, after a second, she rose nervously, all mixed up in the blanket. He watched her in her confusion, as she tried to extricate herself and wrap herself up so that she could walk. He watched her relentlessly, as she knew. And as she went, the blanket trailing, and as he saw a glimpse of her feet and her white leg, he tried to remember her as she was when he had wrapped her in the blanket. But then he didn't want to remember, because she had been nothing to him then, and his nature revolted from remembering her as she was when she was nothing to him.

A tumbling, muffled noise from within the dark house startled him. Then he heard her voice—"There are clothes." He rose and went to the foot of the stairs, and gathered up the garments she had thrown down. Then he came back to the fire, to rub himself down and dress. He grinned at his own appearance when he had finished.

The fire was sinking, so he put on coal. The house was now quite dark, save for the light of a street-lamp that shone in faintly from beyond the holly trees. He lit the gas with matches he found on the mantelpiece. Then he emptied the pockets of his own clothes, and threw all his wet things in a heap into the scullery. After which he gathered up her sodden clothes, gently, and put them in a separate heap on the copper-top[2] in the scullery.

It was six o'clock on the clock. His own watch had stopped. He ought to go back to the surgery. He waited, and still she did not come down. So he went to the foot of the stairs and called:

"I shall have to go."

Almost immediately he heard her coming down. She had on her best dress of black voile, and her hair was tidy, but still damp. She looked at him—and in spite of herself, smiled.

"I don't like you in those clothes," she said.

"Do I look a sight?" he answered.

They were shy of one another.

"I'll make you some tea," she said.

"No, I must go."

"Must you?" And she looked at him again with the wide, strained, doubtful eyes. And again, from the pain of his breast, he knew how he loved her. He went and bent to kiss her, gently, passionately, with his heart's painful kiss.

"And my hair smells so horrible," she murmured in distraction. "And I'm so awful, I'm so awful! Oh, no, I'm too awful." And she broke into bitter, heartbroken sobbing. "You can't want to love me, I'm horrible."

"Don't be silly, don't be silly," he said, trying to comfort her, kissing her, holding her in his arms. "I want you, I want to marry you, we're going to be married, quickly, quickly—tomorrow if I can."

But she only sobbed terribly, and cried:

"I feel awful. I feel awful. I feel I'm horrible to you."

"No, I want you, I want you," was all he answered, blindly, with that terrible intonation which frightened her almost more than her horror lest he should *not* want her.

1922

D. H. LAWRENCE

The Rocking-Horse Winner

There was a woman who was beautiful, who started with all the advantages, yet she had no luck. She married for love, and the love turned to dust. She had bonny children, yet she felt they had been thrust upon her, and she could not love them. They looked at her coldly, as if they were finding fault with her. And hurriedly she felt she must cover up some fault in herself. Yet what it was that she must cover up she never knew. Nevertheless, when her children were present, she always felt the center of her heart go hard. This troubled her, and in her manner she was all the more gentle and anxious for her

---

2. Top of a washtub or cooking vessel, now usually made of iron.

children, as if she loved them very much. Only she herself knew that at the center of her heart was a hard little place that could not feel love, no, not for anybody. Everybody else said of her: "She is such a good mother. She adores her children." Only she herself, and her children themselves, knew it was not so. They read it in each other's eyes.

There were a boy and two little girls. They lived in a pleasant house, with a garden, and they had discreet servants, and felt themselves superior to anyone in the neighborhood.

Although they lived in style, they felt always an anxiety in the house. There was never enough money. The mother had a small income, and the father had a small income, but not nearly enough for the social position which they had to keep up. The father went into town to some office. But though he had good prospects, these prospects never materialized. There was always the grinding sense of the shortage of money, though the style was always kept up.

At last the mother said: "I will see if *I* can't make something." But she did not know where to begin. She racked her brains, and tried this thing and the other, but could not find anything successful. The failure made deep lines come into her face. Her children were growing up, they would have to go to school. There must be more money, there must be more money. The father, who was always very handsome and expensive in his tastes, seemed as if he never *would* be able to do anything worth doing. And the mother, who had a great belief in herself, did not succeed any better, and her tastes were just as expensive.

And so the house came to be haunted by the unspoken phrase: *There must be more money! There must be more money!* The children could hear it all the time, though nobody said it aloud. They heard it at Christmas, when the expensive and splendid toys filled the nursery. Behind the shining modern rocking-horse, behind the smart doll's house, a voice would start whispering: "There *must* be more money! There *must* be more money!" And the children would stop playing, to listen for a moment. They would look into each other's eyes, to see if they had all heard. And each one saw in the eyes of the other two that they too had heard. "There *must* be more money! There *must* be more money!"

It came whispering from the springs of the still-swaying rocking-horse, and even the horse, bending his wooden, champing head, heard it. The big doll, sitting so pink and smirking in her new pram,[1] could hear it quite plainly, and seemed to be smirking all the more self-consciously because of it. The foolish puppy, too, that took the place of the teddy bear, he was looking so extraordinarily foolish for no other reason but that he heard the secret whisper all over the house: "There *must* be more money!"

Yet nobody ever said it aloud. The whisper was everywhere, and therefore no one spoke it. Just as no one ever says: "We are breathing!" in spite of the fact that breath is coming and going all the time.

"Mother," said the boy Paul one day, "why don't we keep a car of our own? Why do we always use uncle's, or else a taxi?"

"Because we're the poor members of the family," said the mother.

---

1. Baby carriage.

"But why *are* we, mother?"

"Well—I suppose," she said slowly and bitterly, "it's because your father has no luck."

The boy was silent for some time.

"Is luck money, mother?" he asked, rather timidly.

"No, Paul. Not quite. It's what causes you to have money."

"Oh!" said Paul vaguely. "I thought when Uncle Oscar said *filthy lucker*, it meant money."

"*Filthy lucre* does mean money," said the mother. "But it's lucre, not luck."

"Oh!" said the boy. "Then what *is* luck, mother?"

"It's what causes you to have money. If you're lucky you have money. That's why it's better to be born lucky than rich. If you're rich, you may lose your money. But if you're lucky, you will always get more money."

"Oh! Will you? And is father not lucky?"

"Very unlucky, I should say," she said bitterly.

The boy watched her with unsure eyes.

"Why?" he asked.

"I don't know. Nobody ever knows why one person is lucky and another unlucky."

"Don't they? Nobody at all? Does *nobody* know?"

"Perhaps God. But He never tells."

"He ought to, then. And aren't you lucky either, mother?"

"I can't be, if I married an unlucky husband."

"But by yourself, aren't you?"

"I used to think I was, before I married. Now I think I am very unlucky indeed."

"Why?"

"Well—never mind! Perhaps I'm not really," she said.

The child looked at her to see if she meant it. But he saw, by the lines of her mouth, that she was only trying to hide something from him.

"Well, anyhow," he said stoutly, "I'm a lucky person."

"Why?" said his mother, with a sudden laugh.

He stared at her. He didn't even know why he had said it.

"God told me," he asserted, brazening it out.

"I hope He did, dear!" she said, again with a laugh, but rather bitter.

"He did, mother!"

"Excellent!" said the mother, using one of her husband's exclamations.

The boy saw she did not believe him; or rather, that she paid no attention to his assertion. This angered him somewhat, and made him want to compel her attention.

He went off by himself, vaguely, in a childish way, seeking for the clue to "luck." Absorbed, taking no heed of other people, he went about with a sort of stealth, seeking inwardly for luck. He wanted luck, he wanted it, he wanted it. When the two girls were playing dolls in the nursery, he would sit on his big rocking-horse, charging madly into space, with a frenzy that made the little girls peer at him uneasily.

Wildly the horse careered, the waving dark hair of the boy tossed, his eyes had a strange glare in them. The little girls dared not speak to him.

When he had ridden to the end of his mad little journey, he climbed down and stood in front of his rocking-horse, staring fixedly into its lowered face. Its red mouth was slightly open, its big eye was wide and glassy-bright.

"Now!" he would silently command the snorting steed. "Now, take me to where there is luck! Now take me!"

And he would slash the horse on the neck with the little whip he had asked Uncle Oscar for. He *knew* the horse could take him to where there was luck, if only he forced it. So he would mount again and start on his furious ride, hoping at last to get there. He knew he could get there.

"You'll break your horse, Paul!" said the nurse.

"He's always riding like that! I wish he'd leave off!" said his elder sister Joan.

But he only glared down on them in silence. Nurse gave him up. She could make nothing of him. Anyhow, he was growing beyond her.

One day his mother and his Uncle Oscar came in when he was on one of his furious rides. He did not speak to them.

"Hallo, you young jockey! Riding a winner?" said his uncle.

"Aren't you growing too big for a rocking-horse? You're not a very little boy any longer, you know," said his mother.

But Paul only gave a blue glare from his big, rather close-set eyes. He would speak to nobody when he was in full tilt. His mother watched him with an anxious expression on her face.

At last he suddenly stopped forcing his horse into the mechanical gallop and slid down.

"Well, I got there!" he announced fiercely, his blue eyes still flaring, and his sturdy long legs straddling apart.

"Where did you get to?" asked his mother.

"Where I wanted to go," he flared back at her.

"That's right, son!" said Uncle Oscar. "Don't you stop till you get there. What's the horse's name?"

"He doesn't have a name," said the boy.

"Gets on without all right?" asked the uncle.

"Well, he has different names. He was called Sansovino last week."

"Sansovino, eh? Won the Ascot. How did you know this name?"

"He always talks about horse-races with Bassett," said Joan.

The uncle was delighted to find that his small nephew was posted with all the racing news. Bassett, the young gardener, who had been wounded in the left foot in the war[2] and had got his present job through Oscar Cresswell, whose batman he had been, was a perfect blade[3] of the "turf." He lived in the racing events, and the small boy lived with him.

Oscar Cresswell got it all from Bassett.

"Master Paul comes and asks me, so I can't do more than tell him, sir," said Bassett, his face terribly serious, as if he were speaking of religious matters.

2. World War I, 1914–1918.   3. Dashing young man.

"And does he ever put anything on a horse he fancies?"

"Well—I don't want to give him away—he's a young sport, a fine sport, sir. Would you mind asking him himself? He sort of takes a pleasure in it, and perhaps he'd feel I was giving him away, sir, if you don't mind."

Bassett was serious as a church.

The uncle went back to his nephew and took him off for a ride in the car.

"Say, Paul, old man, do you ever put anything on a horse?" the uncle asked.

The boy watched the handsome man closely.

"Why, do you think I ougntn't to?" he parried.

"Not a bit of it! I thought perhaps you might give me a tip for the Lincoln."[4]

The car sped on into the country, going down to Uncle Oscar's place in Hampshire.

"Honor bright?" said the nephew.

"Honor bright, son!" said the uncle.

"Well, then, Daffodil."

"Daffodil! I doubt it, sonny. What about Mirza?"

"I only know the winner," said the boy. "That's Daffodil."

"Daffodil, eh?"

There was a pause. Daffodil was an obscure horse comparatively.

"Uncle!"

"Yes, son?"

"You won't let it go any further, will you? I promised Bassett."

"Bassett be damned, old man! What's he got to do with it?"

"We're partners. We've been partners from the first. Uncle, he lent me my first five shillings,[5] which I lost. I promised him, honor bright, it was only between me and him; only you gave me that ten-shilling note I started winning with, so I thought you were lucky. You won't let it go any further, will you?"

The boy gazed at his uncle from those big, hot, blue eyes, set rather close together. The uncle stirred and laughed uneasily.

"Right you are, son! I'll keep your tip private. Daffodil, eh? How much are you putting on him?"

"All except twenty pounds," said the boy. "I keep that in reserve."

The uncle thought it a good joke.

"You keep twenty pounds in reserve, do you, you young romancer? What are you betting, then?"

"I'm betting three hundred," said the boy gravely. "But it's between you and me, Uncle Oscar! Honor bright?"

The uncle burst into a roar of laughter.

"It's between you and me all right, you young Nat Gould,"[6] he said, laughing. "But where's your three hundred?"

4. Lincolnshire Handicap race then run at Lincoln Downs. Other races mentioned in the story include the St. Leger Stakes (the Leger) run at Doncaster; the Grand National Steeplechase run at Aintree, the most famous steeplechase in the world; the famous Derby, a mile-and-a-half race for three-year-olds run at Epsom Downs, and the Ascot (above) run at the course of that name in Berkshire.

5. Then just over a dollar. The English pound after World War I fluctuated considerably but was generally less than the $4.86 of the pre-War period and more than $4. There are 20 shillings to the pound.

6. Nathaniel Gould (1857–1919) novelist and journalist whose writings in both genres concerned horse-racing.

"Bassett keeps it for me. We're partners."

"You are, are you! And what is Bassett putting on Daffodil?"

"He won't go quite as high as I do, I expect. Perhaps he'll go a hundred and fifty."

"What, pennies?" laughed the uncle.

"Pounds," said the child, with a surprised look at his uncle. "Bassett keeps a bigger reserve than I do."

Between wonder and amusement Uncle Oscar was silent. He pursued the matter no further, but he determined to take his nephew with him to the Lincoln races.

"Now, son," he said, "I'm putting twenty on Mirza, and I'll put five on for you on any horse you fancy. What's your pick?"

"Daffodil, uncle."

"No, not the fiver on Daffodil!"

"I should if it was my own fiver," said the child.

"Good! Good! Right you are! A fiver for me and a fiver for you on Daffodil."

The child had never been to a race-meeting before, and his eyes were blue fire. He pursed his mouth tight and watched. A Frenchman just in front had put his money on Lancelot. Wild with excitement, he flayed his arms up and down, yelling *Lancelot! Lancelot!* in his French accent.

Daffodil came in first, Lancelot second, Mirza third. The child, flushed and with eyes blazing, was curiously serene. His uncle brought him four five-pound notes, four to one.

"What am I to do with these?" he cried, waving them before the boy's eyes.

"I suppose we'll talk to Bassett," said the boy. "I expect I have fifteen hundred now; and twenty in reserve; and this twenty."

His uncle studied him for some moments.

"Look here, son!" he said. "You're not serious about Bassett and that fifteen hundred, are you?"

"Yes, I am. But it's between you and me, uncle. Honor bright?"

"Honor bright all right, son! But I must talk to Bassett."

"If you'd like to be a partner, uncle, with Bassett and me, we could all be partners. Only, you'd have to promise, honor bright, uncle, not to let it go beyond us three. Bassett and I are lucky, and you must be lucky, because it was your ten shillings I started winning with. . . ."

Uncle Oscar took both Bassett and Paul into Richmond Park for an afternoon, and there they talked.

"It's like this, you see, sir," Bassett said. "Master Paul would get me talking about racing events, spinning yarns, you know, sir. And he was always keen on knowing if I'd made or if I'd lost. It's about a year since, now, that I put five shillings on Blush of Dawn for him: and we lost. Then the luck turned, with that ten shillings, he had from you: that we put on Singhalese. And since that time, it's been pretty steady, all things considering. What do you say, Master Paul?"

"We're all right when we're sure," said Paul. "It's when we're not quite sure that we go down."

"Oh, but we're careful then," said Bassett.

"But when are you *sure?*" smiled Uncle Oscar.

"It's Master Paul, sir," said Bassett in a secret, religious voice. "It's as if he had it from heaven. Like Daffodil, now, for the Lincoln. That was as sure as eggs."

"Did you put anything on Daffodil?" asked Oscar Cresswell.

"Yes, sir. I made my bit."

"And my nephew?"

Bassett was obstinately silent, looking at Paul.

"I made twelve hundred, didn't I, Bassett? I told uncle I was putting three hundred on Daffodil."

"That's right," said Bassett, nodding.

"But where's the money?" asked the uncle.

"I keep it safe locked up, sir. Master Paul he can have it any minute he likes to ask for it."

"What, fifteen hundred pounds?"

"And twenty! And *forty*, that is, with the twenty he made on the course."

"It's amazing!" said the uncle.

"If Master Paul offers you to be partners, sir, I would, if I were you: if you'll excuse me," said Bassett.

Oscar Cresswell thought about it.

"I'll see the money," he said.

They drove home again, and, sure enough, Bassett came round to the garden-house with fifteen hundred pounds in notes. The twenty pounds reserve was left with Joe Glee, in the Turf Commission deposit.

"You see, it's all right, uncle, when I'm *sure!* Then we go strong, for all we're worth. Don't we, Bassett?"

"We do that, Master Paul."

"And when are you sure?" said the uncle, laughing.

"Oh, well, sometimes I'm *absolutely* sure, like about Daffodil," said the boy; "and sometimes I have an idea; and sometimes I haven't even an idea, have I, Bassett? Then we're careful, because we mostly go down."

"You do, do you! And when you're sure, like about Daffodil, what makes you sure, sonny?"

"Oh, well, I don't know," said the boy uneasily. "I'm sure, you know, uncle; that's all."

"It's as if he had it from heaven, sir," Bassett reiterated.

"I should say so!" said the uncle.

But he became a partner. And when the Leger was coming on, Paul was "sure" about Lively Spark, which was a quite inconsiderable horse. The boy insisted on putting a thousand on the horse, Bassett went for five hundred, and Oscar Cresswell two hundred. Lively Spark came in first, and the betting had been ten to one against him. Paul had made ten thousand.

"You see," he said, "I was absolutely sure of him."

Even Oscar Cresswell had cleared two thousand.

"Look here, son," he said, "this sort of thing makes me nervous."

"It needn't, uncle! Perhaps I shan't be sure again for a long time."

"But what are you going to do with your money?" asked the uncle.

"Of course," said the boy, "I started it for mother. She said she had no luck, because father is unlucky, so I thought if *I* was lucky, it might stop whispering."

"What might stop whispering?"

"Our house. I *hate* our house for whispering."

"What does it whisper?"

"Why—why"—the boy fidgeted—"why, I don't know. But it's always short of money, you know, uncle."

"I know it, son, I know it."

"You know people send mother writs, don't you, uncle?"

"I'm afraid I do," said the uncle.

"And then the house whispers, like people laughing at you behind your back.. It's awful, that is! I thought if I was lucky—"

"You might stop it," added the uncle.

The boy watched him with big blue eyes, that had an uncanny cold fire in them, and he said never a word.

"Well, then!" said the uncle. "What are we doing?"

"I shouldn't like mother to know I was lucky," said the boy.

"Why not, son?"

"She'd stop me."

"I don't think she would."

"Oh!"—and the boy writhed in an odd way—"I *don't* want her to know, uncle."

"All right, son! We'll manage it without her knowing."

They managed it very easily. Paul, at the other's suggestion, handed over five thousand pounds to his uncle, who deposited it with the family lawyer, who was then to inform Paul's mother that a relative had put five thousand pounds into his hands, which sum was to be paid out a thousand pounds at a time, on the mother's birthday, for the next five years.

"So she'll have a birthday present of a thousand pounds for five successive years," said Uncle Oscar. "I hope it won't make it all the harder for her later."

Paul's mother had her birthday in November. The house had been "whispering" worse than ever lately, and, even in spite of his luck, Paul could not bear up against it. He was very anxious to see the effect of the birthday letter, telling his mother about the thousand pounds.

When there were no visitors, Paul now took his meals with his parents, as he was beyond the nursery control. His mother went into town nearly every day. She had discovered that she had an odd knack of sketching furs and dress materials, so she worked secretly in the studio of a friend who was the chief "artist" for the leading drapers. She drew the figures of ladies in furs and ladies in silk and sequins for the newspaper advertisements. This young woman artist earned several thousand pounds a year, but Paul's mother only made several hundreds, and she was again dissatisfied. She so wanted to be first in something, and she did not succeed, even in making sketches for drapery advertisements.

She was down to breakfast on the morning of her birthday. Paul watched her face as she read her letters. He knew the lawyer's letter. As his mother read it, her face hardened and became more expressionless. Then a cold, determined look came on her mouth. She hid the letter under the pile of others, and said not a word about it.

"Didn't you have anything nice in the post for your birthday, mother?" said Paul.

"Quite moderately nice," she said, her voice cold and absent.

She went away to town without saying more.

But in the afternoon Uncle Oscar appeared. He said Paul's mother had had a long interview with the lawyer, asking if the whole five thousand could not be advanced at once, as she was in debt.

"What do you think, uncle?" said the boy.

"I leave it to you, son."

"Oh, let her have it, then! We can get some more with the other," said the boy.

"A bird in the hand is worth two in the bush, laddie!" said Uncle Oscar.

"But I'm sure to *know* for the Grand National; or the Lincolnshire; or else the Derby. I'm sure to know for one of them," said Paul.

So Uncle Oscar signed the agreement, and Paul's mother touched the whole five thousand. Then something very curious happened. The voices in the house suddenly went mad, like a chorus of frogs on a spring evening. There were certain new furnishings, and Paul had a tutor. He was *really* going to Eton, his father's school, in the following autumn. There were flowers in the winter, and a blossoming of the luxury Paul's mother had been used to. And yet the voices in the house, behind the sprays of mimosa and almond-blossom, and from under the piles of iridescent cushions, simply trilled and screamed in a sort of ecstasy: "There *must* be more money! Oh-h-h; there *must* be more money. Oh, now, now-w! Now-w-w—there *must* be more money! —more than ever! More than ever!"

It frightened Paul terribly. He studied away at his Latin and Greek with his tutor. But his intense hours were spent with Bassett. The Grand National had gone by: he had not "known," and had lost a hundred pounds. Summer was at hand. He was in agony for the Lincoln. But even for the Lincoln he didn't "know," and he lost fifty pounds. He became wild-eyed and strange, as if something were going to explode in him.

"Let it alone, son! Don't you bother about it!" urged Uncle Oscar. But it was as if the boy couldn't really hear what his uncle was saying.

"I've got to know for the Derby! I've got to know for the Derby!" the child reiterated, his big blue eyes blazing with a sort of madness.

His mother noticed how overwrought he was.

"You'd better go to the seaside. Wouldn't you like to go now to the seaside, instead of waiting? I think you'd better," she said, looking down at him anxiously, her heart curiously heavy because of him.

But the child lifted his uncanny blue eyes.

"I couldn't possibly go before the Derby, mother!" he said. "I couldn't possibly!"

"Why not?" she said, her voice becoming heavy when she was opposed. "Why not? You can still go from the seaside to see the Derby with your Uncle Oscar, if that's what you wish. No need for you to wait here. Besides, I think you care too much about these races. It's a bad sign. My family has been a gambling family, and you won't know till you grow up how much damage it has done. But it has done damage. I shall have to send Bassett away, and ask Uncle Oscar not to talk racing to you, unless you promise to be reasonable about it: go away to the seaside and forget it. You're all nerves!"

"I'll do what you like, mother, so long as you don't send me away till after the Derby," the boy said.

"Send you away from where? Just from this house?"

"Yes," he said, gazing at her.

"Why, you curious child, what makes you care about this house so much, suddenly? I never knew you loved it."

He gazed at her without speaking. He had a secret within a secret, something he had not divulged, even to Bassett or to his Uncle Oscar.

But his mother, after standing undecided and a little bit sullen for some moments, said:

"Very well, then! Don't go to the seaside till after the Derby, if you don't wish it. But promise me you won't let your nerves go to pieces. Promise you won't think so much about horse-racing and *events,* as you call them!"

"Oh, no," said the boy casually. "I won't think much about them, mother. You needn't worry. I wouldn't worry, mother, if I were you."

"If you were me and I were you," said his mother, "I wonder what we *should* do!"

"But you know you needn't worry, mother, don't you?" the boy repeated.

"I should be awfully glad to know it," she said wearily.

"Oh, well, you *can,* you know. I mean, you *ought* to know you needn't worry," he insisted.

"Ought I? Then I'll see about it," she said.

Paul's secret of secrets was his wooden horse, that which had no name. Since he was emancipated from a nurse and a nursery-governess, he had had his rocking-horse removed to his own bedroom at the top of the house.

"Surely you're too big for a rocking-horse!" his mother had remonstrated.

"Well, you see, mother, till I can have a *real* horse, I like to have *some* sort of animal about," had been his quaint answer.

"Do you feel he keeps you company?" she laughed.

"Oh, yes! He's very good, he always keeps me company, when I'm there," said Paul.

So the horse, rather shabby, stood in an arrested prance in the boy's bedroom.

The Derby was drawing near, and the boy grew more and more tense. He hardly heard what was spoken to him, he was very frail, and his eyes were really uncanny. His mother had sudden strange seizures of uneasiness about him. Sometimes, for half an hour, she would feel a sudden anxiety about him that was almost anguish. She wanted to rush to him at once, and know he was safe.

Two nights before the Derby, she was at a big party in town, when one of her rushes of anxiety about her boy, her first-born, gripped her heart till she could hardly speak. She fought with the feeling, might and main, for she believed in common sense. But it was too strong. She had to leave the dance and go downstairs to telephone to the country. The children's nursery-governess was terribly surprised·and startled at being rung up in the night.

"Are the children all right, Miss Wilmot?"

"Oh, yes, they are quite all right."

"Master Paul? Is he all right?"

"He went to bed as right as a trivet. Shall I run up and look at him?"

"No," said Paul's mother reluctantly. "No! Don't trouble. It's all right. Don't sit up. We shall be home fairly soon." She did not want her son's privacy intruded upon.

"Very good," said the governess.

It was about one o'clock when Paul's mother and father drove up to their house. All was still. Paul's mother went to her room and slipped off her white fur cloak. She had told her maid not to wait up for her. She heard her husband downstairs, mixing a whisky and soda.

And then, because of the strange anxiety at her heart, she stole upstairs to her son's room. Noiselessly she went along the upper corridor. Was there a faint noise? What was it?

She stood, with arrested muscles, outside his door, listening. There was a strange, heavy, and yet not loud noise. Her heart stood still. It was a soundless noise, yet rushing and powerful. Something huge, in violent, hushed motion. What was it? What in God's name was it? She ought to know. She felt that she knew the noise. She knew what it was.

Yet she could not place it. She couldn't say what it was. And on and on it went, like a madness.

Softly, frozen with anxiety and fear, she turned the door-handle.

The room was dark. Yet in the space near the window, she heard and saw something plunging to and fro. She gazed in fear and amazement.

Then suddenly she switched on the light, and saw her son, in his green pajamas, madly surging on the rocking-horse. The blaze of light suddenly lit him up, as he urged the wooden horse, and lit her up, as she stood, blonde, in her dress of pale green and crystal, in the doorway.

"Paul!" she cried. "Whatever are you doing?"

"It's Malabar!" he screamed, in a powerful, strange voice. "It's Malabar!"

His eyes blazed at her for one strange and senseless second, as he ceased urging his wooden horse. Then he fell with a crash to the ground, and she, all her tormented motherhood flooding upon her, rushed to gather him up.

But he was unconscious, and unconscious he remained, with some brain-fever. He talked and tossed, and his mother sat stonily by his side.

"Malabar! It's Malabar! Bassett, Bassett, I *know*! It's Malabar!"

So the child cried, trying to get up and urge the rocking-horse that gave him his inspiration.

"What does he mean by Malabar?" asked the heart-frozen mother.

"I don't know," said the father stonily.

"What does he mean by Malabar?" she asked her brother Oscar.

"It's one of the horses running for the Derby," was the answer.

And, in spite of himself, Oscar Cresswell spoke to Bassett, and himself put a thousand on Malabar: at fourteen to one.

The third day of the illness was critical: they were waiting for a change. The boy, with his rather long, curly hair, was tossing ceaselessly on the pillow. He neither slept nor regained consciousness, and his eyes were like blue stones. His mother sat, feeling her heart had gone, turned actually into a stone.

In the evening, Oscar Cresswell did not come, but Bassett sent a message, saying could he come up for one moment, just one moment? Paul's mother was very angry at the intrusion, but on second thought she agreed. The boy was the same. Perhaps Bassett might bring him to consciousness.

The gardener, a shortish fellow with a little brown moustache and sharp little brown eyes, tiptoed into the room, touched his imaginary cap to Paul's mother, and stole to the bedside, staring with glittering, smallish eyes, at the tossing, dying child.

"Master Paul!" he whispered. "Master Paul! Malabar came in first all right, a clean win. I did as you told me. You've made over seventy thousand pounds, you have; you've got over eighty thousand. Malabar came in all right, Master Paul."

"Malabar! Malabar! Did I say Malabar, mother? Did I say Malabar? Do you think I'm lucky, mother? I knew Malabar, didn't I? Over eighty thousand pounds! I call that lucky, don't you, mother? Over eighty thousand pounds! I knew, didn't I know I knew? Malabar came in all right. If I ride my horse till I'm sure, then I tell you, Bassett, you can go as high as you like. Did you go for all you were worth, Bassett?"

"I went a thousand on it, Master Paul."

"I never told you, mother, that if I can ride my horse, and *get there*, then I'm absolutely sure—oh, absolutely! Mother, did I ever tell you? I *am* lucky!"

"No, you never did," said the mother.

But the boy died in the night.

And even as he lay dead, his mother heard her brother's voice saying to her: "My God, Hester, you're eighty-odd thousand to the good, and a poor devil of a son to the bad. But, poor devil, poor devil, he's best gone out of a life where he rides his rocking-horse to find a winner."

1932

D. H. LAWRENCE

Passages from Essays and Letters

from "Nottingham and the Mining Countryside"

I was born . . . in Eastwood, a mining village of some three thousand souls, about eight miles from Nottingham. . . . It is hilly country. . . . To me it seemed, and still seems, an extremely beautiful countryside, just between the red sandstone and the oak-trees of Nottingham, and the cold limestone, the ash-trees, the stone fences of Derbyshire. To me, as a child and a young man, it was still the old England of the forest and agricultural past; there were no motor-cars, the mines were, in a sense, an accident in the landscape, and Robin Hood and his merry men were not very far away.

. . . The people lived almost entirely by instinct, men of my father's age could not really read. And the pit did not mechanize men. . . . My father loved the pit. He was hurt badly, more than once, but he would never stay away. He loved the contact, the intimacy, as men in the war loved the intense male comradeship of the dark days.

Now the colliers had also an instinct for beauty. The colliers' wives had not. The colliers were deeply alive, instinctively. But they had no daytime ambition, and no daytime intellect. They avoided, really, the rational aspect of life. . . . They didn't even care very profoundly about wages. It was the women, naturally, who nagged on this score. . . . The collier went to the pub and drank in order to continue the intimacy with his mates.

. . . Life for him did not consist of facts, but in a flow. Very often he loved his garden. And very often he had a genuine love of the beauty of flowers. . . .

. . . Most women love flowers as possessions, and as trimmings. They can't look at a flower, and wonder a moment, and pass on. If they see a flower that arrests their attention, they must at once pick it, pluck it. Possession! A possession! Something added on to *me!*

from "Love"

. . . the love between a man and a woman . . . is dual. It is the melting into pure communion, and it is the friction of sheer sensuality, both. In pure communion I become whole in love. And in pure, fierce passion of sensuality, I am burned into essentiality. I am driven from the matrix unto sheer separate distinction. I become my single self, inviolable and unique, as the gems were perhaps once driven into themselves out of the confusion of earths. . . .

from "Women Are So Cocksure"

. . . [My mother] was convinced . . . that a man ought not to drink beer. This conviction developed from the fact, naturally, that my father drank beer. He sometimes drank too much. He sometimes boozed away the money necessary for the young family. When my father came in tipsy, she saw scarlet.

from "Art and Morality"

Apples are always apples! says Vox Populi, Vox Dei.[1]

Sometimes they're sin, sometimes they're a knock on the head, sometimes they're a bellyache, sometimes they're part of a pie, sometimes they're sauce for a goose.

1. The voice of the people [is] the voice of God.

What art has got to do, and will go on doing, is to reveal things in their different relationships. That is to say, you've got to see in the apples the bellyache, Sir Isaac's knock on the cranium, the vast, moist wall through which the insect bores to lay her eggs in the middle, and the untasted, unknown quality which Eve saw hanging on a tree.

from "Morality and the Novel"

The business of art is to reveal the relation between man and his circumambient universe, at the living moment. As mankind is always struggling in the toils of old relationships, art is always ahead of the "times," which themselves are always far in the rear of the living moment.

When Van Gogh paints sunflowers, he reveals, or achieves, the vivid relation between himself, as man, and the sunflowers, as sunflower, at that quick moment of time. His painting does not represent the sunflower itself. We shall never know what the sunflower itself is. And the camera will *visualize* the sunflower far more perfectly than van Gogh can.

The vision on the canvas is a third thing, utterly intangible and inexplicable, the offspring of the sunflower itself and van Gogh himself. . . .

. . . The novel is the highest example of subtle interrelatedness that man has discovered. Everything is true in its own time, place, and circumstance, and untrue outside of its own place, time, circumstance. If you try to nail anything down, in the novel, either it kills the novel, or the novel gets up and walks away with the nail.

. . . Love is a great emotion. But if you set out to write a novel, and you yourself are in the throes of the great predilection for love, love as the supreme, the only emotion worth living for, then you will write an immoral novel.

Because *no* emotion is supreme, or exclusively worth living for. *All* emotions go to the achieving of a living relationship between a human being and the other human being or creature or thing he becomes purely related to. All emotions, including love and hate, and rage and tenderness, go to the adjusting of the oscillating, unestablished balance between two people who amount to anything.

A new relation, a new relatedness hurts somewhat in the attaining; and will always hurt. So life will always hurt. . . .

Each time we strive to a new relation, with anyone or anything, it is bound to hurt somewhat. Because it means the struggle with and the displacing of old connections, and this is never pleasant. And, moreover, between living things at least, an adjustment means also a fight, for each party, inevitably, must "seek its own" in the other, and be denied. When, in the two parties, each of them seeks his own, her own, absolutely, then it is a fight to the death. And this is true of the thing called "passion."

The great relationship for humanity will always be the relation between man and woman. The relation between man and man, woman and woman, parent and child, will always be subsidiary.

And the relation between man and woman will change forever, and will forever be the new central clue to human life. It is the *relation itself* which is the quick and the central clue to life, not the man, nor the woman, nor the children that result from the relationship, as a contingency.

from "Why the Novel Matters"

We have curious ideas of ourselves. We think of ourselves as a body with a spirit in it, or a body with a soul in it, or a body with a mind in it. . . .

It is a funny sort of superstition. Why should I look at my hand, as it so cleverly writes these words, and decide that it is a mere nothing compared to the mind that directs it? Why should I imagine that there is a *me* which is more *me* than my hand is? Since my hand is absolutely alive, me alive.

And that's what you learn, when you're a novelist. And that's what you are liable *not* to know, if you're a parson, or a philosopher, or a scientist, or a stupid person.

Now I absolutely flatly deny that I am a soul, or a body, or a mind, or an intelligence, or a brain, or a nervous system, or a bunch of glands, or any of the rest of these bits of me. The whole is greater than the part. And therefore, I, who am man alive, am greater than my soul, or spirit, or body, or mind, or consciousness, or anything else that is merely a part of me. I am man a man, and alive. I am man alive, and as long as I can, I intend to go on being man alive.

For this reason I am a novelist. And being a novelist, I consider myself superior to the saint, the scientist, the philosopher, and the poet, who are all great masters of different bits of man alive, but never get the whole thing.

We should ask for no absolutes, or absolute. . . . There is no absolute good, there is nothing absolutely right. All things flow and change, and even change is not absolute. . . .

. . . If the one I love remains unchanged and unchanging, I shall cease to love her. It is only because she changes and startles me into change and defies my inertia, and is herself staggered in her inertia by my changing, that I can continue to love her. If she stayed put, I might as well love the pepper-pot.

In life, there is right and wrong, good and bad, all the time. But what is right in one case is wrong in another. And in the novel you see one man becoming a corpse, because of his so-called goodness, another going dead because of his so-called wickedness. Right and wrong is an instinct: but an instinct of the whole consciousness in a man, bodily, mental, spiritual at once. And only in the novel are *all* things given full play, or at least, they may be given full play, when we realize that life itself, and not inert safety, is the reason for living. For out of the full play of all things emerges the only thing that is anything, the wholeness of a man, the wholeness of a woman, man alive, and live woman.

from Autobiographical Sketch

They ask me; "Did you find it very hard to get on and to become a success?" And I have to admit that if I can be said to have got on, and if I can be called a success, then I *did not* find it hard.

I never starved in a garret, nor waited in anguish for the post to bring me an answer from editor or publisher, nor did I struggle in sweat and blood to bring forth mighty works, nor did I ever wake up and find myself famous.

. . . My father was a collier, and only a collier, nothing praiseworthy about him. He wasn't even respectable, in so far as he got drunk rather frequently, never went near a chapel, and was usually rather rude to his little immediate bosses at the pit.

My mother was, I suppose, superior. She came from town, and belonged really to the lower bourgeoisie. She spoke King's English, without an accent, and never in her life could even imitate a sentence of the dialect which my father spoke, and which we children spoke out of doors.

I have *wanted* to feel truly friendly with some, at least of my fellow-men. Yet I have never quite succeeded. Whether I got on *in* the world is a question; but I certainly don't get on very well *with* the world. And whether I am a worldly success or not I really don't know. But I feel, somehow, not much of a human success.

By which I mean that I don't feel there is any very cordial of fundamental contact between me and society, or me and other people. There is a breach. And my contact is with something that is nonhuman, nonvocal.

[Why?] The answer, as far as I can see, has something to do with class. Class makes a gulf, across which all the best human flow is lost. It is not exactly the triumph of the middle classes that has made the deadness, but the triumph of the middle-class *thing*.

As a man from the working class, I feel that the middle class cut off some of my vital vibration when I am ·with them. I admit them charming and educated and good people often enough. *But they just stop some part of me from working. . . .*

Then why don't I live with my working people? Because their vibration is limited in another direction. They are narrow, but still fairly deep and passionate, whereas the middle class is broad and shallow and passionless.

I cannot make the transfer from my own class into the middle class. I cannot, not for anything in the world, forfeit my passional consciousness and my old blood-affinity with my fellow-men and the animals and the land, for that other thin, spurious mental conceit which is all that is left of the mental consciousness once it has made itself exclusive.

from the Letters

TO A. W. McLEOD, 26 APRIL 1913

I am so sure that only through a readjustment between men and women, and a making free and healthy of this sex, will she [England] get out of her present atrophy. Oh, Lord, and if I don't "subdue my art to a metaphysic," as somebody very beautifully said of Hardy, I do write because I want folk—English folk—to alter, and have more sense.

TO A. W. McLEOD, 2 JUNE 1914

I think the only re-sourcing of art, revivifying it, is to make it more the joint work of man and woman. I think *the* one thing to do, is for men to have courage to draw nearer to women, expose themselves to them, and be altered by them; and for women to accept and admit men. That is the start—by bringing themselves together, men and women—revealing themselves to each other, gaining great blind knowledge and suffering and joy, which it will take a big further lapse of civilization to exploit and work out. Because the source of all life and knowledge is in man and woman, and the source of all living is in the interchange and the meeting and mingling of these two: man-life and woman-life, man-knowledge and woman-knowledge, man-being and woman-being.

TO J. B. PINKER, 16 DECEMBER 1915

. . . Tell Arnold Bennett [2] that all rules of construction hold good only for novels which are copies of other novels. A book which is not a copy of other books has its own construction and what he calls faults, he being an old imitator, I call characteristics.

TO ROLF GARDINER, 9 AUGUST 1924

What we need is to smash a few big holes in European sub-urbanity, let in a little real fresh air.

TO LADY OTTOLINE MORRELL, 5 FEBRUARY 1929

. . . Don't you think it's nonsense when Murry says that my world is not the ordinary man's world and that I am a sort of animal with a sixth sense. Seems to me more likely he's a sort of animal with only four senses—the real sense of touch missing. They all seem determined to make a freak of me—to save their own short-failings, and make them "normal."

---

2. An early twentieth-century novelist (1867–1931) whose major works—*The Old Wives' Tale* (1908) and *The Clayhanger Trilogy* (1910–15)—treat the middle classes in the pottery country of the English Midlands in a naturalistic manner (usually criticizing the money-grubbing, social-climbing selfishness of the society). In his later years he more or less turned into a hack, though a clever one, and it is to Bennett as a very popular, successful hack that Lawrence is referring.

8   SETTING

All stories, like all individuals, are obviously part of their time, place, and culture, and are conditioned by them. The more we understand of the historical and cultural context, the more we may come to understand about a story (or about a person). The close relationship between historical, geographical, and cultural context—or setting—on the one hand, and people and events on the other, offers the author a means of reinforcing and communicating his or her vision and the reader therefore a means of understanding more fully the details of the story.

Setting is an important aspect of almost all stories. Take *The Cask of Amontillado*, for example. Montresor's character and plot can be called Machiavellian (characterized by subtle or unscrupulous cunning; after the Italian Renaissance politician and writer Niccolo Machiavelli, 1469–1527); no wonder Poe's story is set in Renaissance Italy. The Puritan Goodman Brown lives in the reign of King William (1689–1702) in Salem, Massachusetts, where in 1692 the famous witch trials were held—what better place for a story whose subject is a witches' meeting and whose theme is man's natural depravity? An *English* spinster seems (or seemed) much more prudish and virginal than just any old spinster, Italian lovers seem more sensual than Anglo-Saxon ones, and *Our Friend Judith* takes advantage of that cultural convention. And in Conrad's *Heart of Darkness*, the journey to the interior of the Dark Continent and the journey into the dark interior recesses of the human heart are parallel.

I've mentioned a number of other stories here to emphasize what I hope you long ago understood: almost any story can be put in almost any chapter of this book; almost every aspect of fiction can be seen in almost any story. The stories here illustrate how geographical, historical, and cultural contexts may inform a work, but they are not exclusively local-color, historical, or sociological stories.

Beyond the Bayou, like *Heart of Darkness*, makes parallel, or analogous, psychic areas and geographical ones. La Folle, frightened "out of her senses" during the Civil War, deadens large areas of her emotional life and restricts herself to a narrow corner of her small world. Another trauma opens her to life, and she crosses into the territory "beyond the bayou." Besides this central analogy, the cultural context—the complex racial mix of Louisiana, which made race relations even in the time of slavery and Reconstruction unique, and even the physical nature of the bayou country—subtly modifies and defines the characters and their actions. While we can learn a good deal about that context from the story, we can also learn a good deal about the story from increased awareness of and knowledge of the context.

Charlie, in *Babylon Revisited*, so reflects his historical and cultural context that it is difficult to say whether he is a symbol or a product of his time and nation and social set; is he merely representative, or does the story imply that one's life is virtually determined by and therefore a reflection of its context? During the prosperous, dissolute Roaring

Twenties, Charlie was prosperous and dissolute; an American in Paris, he roared with the loudest. Now, in the depressed thirties, he, like the times, has sobered up.

Many of the geographical and historical details in these two stories need footnotes in order for us more fully to understand the relation between the individuals and their background and even the authors and their assumptions (since the first story was written nearly a hundred years ago and the second almost fifty). Now, however, even white readers may understand more of what it means to be a black living in Harlem in the mid-twentieth century than such readers would have a hundred years ago or will a hundred years from now. There is some question whether a white reader ever can understand a story like *Sonny's Blues* as well as a black reader can, whether it is ever possible to make the imaginative leap across ethnic, cultural, or historical dividing lines with complete success. Surely detailed knowledge and a sympathetic imagination sensitized by literature may at least help us approach such understanding, and understanding other subjective visions of the world is, after all, what literature is all about.

KATE CHOPIN

Beyond the Bayou

The bayou curved like a crescent around the point of land on which La Folle's cabin stood. Between the stream and the hut lay a big abandoned field, where cattle were pastured when the bayou supplied them with water enough. Through the woods that spread back into unknown regions the woman had drawn an imaginary line, and past this circle she never stepped. This was the form of her only mania.

She was now a large, gaunt black woman, past thirty-five. Her real name was Jacqueline, but everyone on the plantation called her La Folle,[1] because in childhood she had been frightened literally "out of her senses," and had never wholly regained them.

It was when there had been skirmishing and sharpshooting all day in the woods. Evening was near when P'tit Maître,[2] black with powder and crimson with blood, had staggered into the cabin of Jacqueline's mother, his pursuers close at his heels. The sight had stunned her childish reason.

She dwelt alone in her solitary cabin, for the rest of the quarters had long since been removed beyond her sight and knowledge. She had more physical strength than most men, and made her patch of cotton and corn and tobacco like the best of them. But of the world

1. The crazy woman.   2. Little Master.

beyond the bayou she had long known nothing, save what her morbid fancy conceived.

People at Bellissime had grown used to her and her way, and they thought nothing of it. Even when "Old Mis' " died, they did not wonder that La Folle had not crossed the bayou, but had stood upon her side of it, wailing and lamenting.

P'tit Maître was now the owner of Bellissime. He was a middle-aged man, with a family of beautiful daughters about him, and a little son whom La Folle loved as if he had been her own. She called him Chéri,[3] and so did every one else because she did.

None of the girls had ever been to her what Chéri was. They had each and all loved to be with her, and to listen to her wondrous stories of things that always happened "yonda, beyon' de bayou."

But none of them had stroked her black hand quite as Chéri did, nor rested their heads against her knee so confidingly, nor fallen asleep in her arms as he used to do. For Chéri hardly did such things now, since he had become the proud possessor of a gun, and had had his black curls cut off.

That summer—the summer Chéri gave La Folle two black curls tied with a knot of red ribbon—the water ran so low in the bayou that even the little children at Bellissime were able to cross it on foot, and the cattle were sent to pasture down by the river. La Folle was sorry whan they were gone, for she loved these dumb companions well, and liked to feel that they were there, and to hear them browsing by night up to her own enclosure.

It was Saturday afternoon, when the fields were deserted. The men had flocked to a neighboring village to do their week's trading, and the women were occupied with household affairs—La Folle as well as the others. It was then she mended and washed her handful of clothes, scoured her house, and did her baking.

In this last employment she never forgot Chéri. Today she had fashioned croquignoles[4] of the most fantastic and alluring shapes for him. So when she saw the boy come trudging across the old field with his gleaming little new rifle on his shoulder, she called out gaily to him, "Chéri! Chéri!"

But Chéri did not need the summons, for he was coming straight to her. His pockets all bulged out with almonds and raisins and an orange that he had secured for her from the very fine dinner which had been given that day up at his father's house.

He was a sunny-faced youngster of ten. When he had emptied his pockets, La Folle patted his round red cheek, wiped his soiled hands on her apron, and smoothed his hair. Then she watched him as, with his cakes in his hand, he crossed her strip of cotton back of the cabin, and disappeared into the wood.

He had boasted of the things he was going to do with his gun out there.

"You think they got plenty deer in the wood, La Folle?" he had inquired, with the calculating air of an experienced hunter.

"*Non, non!*" the woman laughed. "Don't you look fo' no deer, Chéri.

---

3. Darling.   4. Biscuits.

Dat 's too big. But you bring La Folle one good fat squirrel fo' her dinner to-morrow, an' she goin' be satisfi'."

"One squirrel ain't a bit. I'll bring you mo' 'an one, La Folle," he had boasted pompously as he went away.

When the woman, an hour later, heard the report of the boy's rifle close to the wood's edge, she would have thought nothing of it if a sharp cry of distress had not followed the sound.

She withdrew her arms from the tub of suds in which they had been plunged, dried them upon her apron, and as quickly as her trembling limbs would bear her, hurried to the spot whence the ominous report had come.

It was as she feared. There she found Chéri stretched upon the ground, with his rifle beside him. He moaned piteously:

"I'm dead, La Folle! I'm dead! I'm gone!"

"*Non, non!*" she exclaimed resolutely, as she knelt beside him. "Put you' arm 'roun' La Folle's nake, Chéri. Dat's nuttin'; dat goin' be nuttin'." She lifted him in her powerful arms.

Chéri had carried his gun muzzle-downward. He had stumbled, he did not know how. He only knew that he had a ball lodged somewhere in his leg, and he thought that his end was at hand. Now, with his head upon the woman's shoulder, he moaned and wept with pain and fright.

"Oh, La Folle! La Folle! it hurt so bad! I can' stan' it, La Folle!"

"Don't cry, *mon bébé,*[5] *mon bébé, mon Chéri!*" the woman spoke soothingly as she covered the ground with long strides. "La Folle goin' mine you; Doctor Bonfils goin' come make *mon Chéri* well agin."

She had reached the abandoned field. As she crossed it with her precious burden, she looked constantly and restlessly from side to side. A terrible fear was upon her—the fear of the world beyond the bayou, the morbid and insane dread she had been under since childhood.

When she was at the bayou's edge she stood there, and shouted for help as if a life depended upon it:

"Oh, P'tit Maître! P'tit Maître! *Venez donc! Au secours! Au secours!*"[6]

No voice responded. Chéri's hot tears were scalding her neck. She called for each and every one upon the place, and still no answer came.

She shouted, she wailed; but whether her voice remained unheard or unheeded, no reply came to her frenzied cries. And all the while Chéri moaned and wept and entreated to be taken home to his mother.

La Folle gave a last despairing look around her. Extreme terror was upon her. She clasped the child close against her breast, where he could feel her heart beat like a muffled hammer. Then shutting her eyes, she ran suddenly down the shallow bank of the bayou, and never stopped till she had climbed the opposite shore.

She stood there quivering an instant as she opened her eyes. Then she plunged into the footpath through the trees.

She spoke no more to Chéri, but muttered constantly, "*Bon Dieu, ayez pitié La Folle! Bon Dieu, ayez pitié moi!*"[7]

5. My baby.
6. Come here! Help! Help!

7. Good Lord, have pity on La Folle! Good Lord, have pity on me!

Instinct seemed to guide her. When the pathway spread clear and smooth enough before her, she again closed her eyes tightly against the sight of that unknown and terrifying world.

A child, playing in some weeds, caught sight of her as she neared the quarters. The little one uttered a cry of dismay.

"La Folle!" she screamed, in her piercing treble. "La Folle done cross de bayer!"

Quickly the cry passed down the line of cabins.

"Yonda, La Folle done cross de bayou!"

Children, old men, old women, young ones with infants in their arms, flocked to doors and windows to see this awe-inspiring spectacle. Most of them shuddered with superstitious dread of what it might portend. "She totin' Chéri!" some of them shouted.

Some of the more daring gathered about her, and followed at her heels, only to fall back with new terror when she turned her distorted face upon them. Her eyes were bloodshot and the saliva had gathered in a white foam on her black lips.

Some one had run ahead of her to where P'tit Maître sat with his family and guests upon the gallery.

"P'tit Maître! La Folle done cross de bayou! Look her! Look her yonda totin' Chéri!" This startling intimation was the first which they had of the woman's approach.

She was now near at hand. She walked with long strides. Her eyes were fixed desperately before her, and she breathed heavily, as a tired ox.

At the foot of the stairway, which she could not have mounted, she laid the boy in his father's arms. Then the world that had looked red to La Folle suddenly turned black—like that day she had seen powder and blood.

She reeled for an instant. Before a sustaining arm could reach her, she fell heavily to the ground.

When La Folle regained consciousness, she was at home again, in her own cabin and upon her own bed. The moon rays, streaming in through the open door and windows, gave what light was needed to the old black mammy who stood at the table concocting a tisane of fragrant herbs. It was very late.

Others who had come, and found that the stupor clung to her, had gone again. P'tit Maître had been there, and with him Doctor Bonfils, who said that La Folle might die.

But death had passed her by. The voice was very clear and steady with which she spoke to Tante[8] Lizette, brewing her tisane there in a corner.

"Ef you will give me one good drink tisane, Tante Lizette, I b'lieve I'm goin' sleep, me."

And she did sleep; so soundly, so healthfully, that old Lizette without compunction stole softly away to creep back through the moonlit fields to her own cabin in the new quarters.

The first touch of the cool gray morning awoke La Folle. She arose, calmly, as if no tempest had shaken and threatened her exis-

8. Aunt.

tence but yesterday.

She donned her new blue cottonade[9] and white apron, for she remembered that this was Sunday. When she had made for herself a cup of strong black coffee, and drunk it with relish, she quitted the cabin and walked across the old familiar field to the bayou's edge again.

She did not stop there as she had always done before, but crossed with a long, steady stride as if she had done this all her life.

When she had made her way through the brush and scrub cottonwood-trees that lined the opposite bank, she found herself upon the border of a field where the white, bursting cotton, with the dew upon it, gleamed for acres and acres like frosted silver in the early dawn.

La Folle drew a long, deep breath as she gazed across the country. She walked slowly and uncertainly, like one who hardly knows how, looking about her as she went.

The cabins, that yesterday had sent a clamor of voices to pursue her, were quiet now. No one was yet astir at Bellissime. Only the birds that darted here and there from hedges were awake, and singing their matins.

When La Folle came to the broad stretch of velvety lawn that surrounded the house, she moved slowly and with delight over the springy turf, that was delicious beneath her tread.

She stopped to find whence came those perfumes that were assailing her senses with memories from a time far gone.

There they were, stealing up to her from the thousand blue violets that peeped out from green, luxuriant beds. There they were, showering down from the big waxen bells of the magnolias far above her head, and from the jessamine clumps around her.

There were roses, too, without number. To right and left palms spread in broad and graceful curves. It all looked like enchantment beneath the sparkling sheen of dew.

When La Folle had slowly and cautiously mounted the many steps that led up to the veranda, she turned to look back at the perilous ascent she had made. Then she caught sight of the river, bending like a silver bow at the foot of Bellissime. Exultation possessed her soul.

La Folle rapped softly upon a door near at hand. Chéri's mother soon cautiously opened it. Quickly and cleverly she dissembled the astonishment she felt at seeing La Folle.

"Ah, La Folle? Is it you, so early?"

"*Oui,*[1] madame. I come ax how my po' li'le Chéri to, 's mo'nin'."

"He is feeling easier, thank you, La Folle. Dr. Bonfils says it will be nothing serious. He's sleeping now. Will you come back when he awakes?"

"*Non,* madame. I'm goin' wait yair tell Chéri wake up." La Folle seated herself upon the topmost step of the veranda.

A look of wonder and deep content crept into her face as she watched for the first time the sun rise upon the new, the beautiful world beyond the bayou.

1894

---

9. Cotton fabric made to resemble wool. 1. Yes.

F. SCOTT FITZGERALD

Babylon Revisited

"And where's Mr. Campbell?" Charlie asked.

"Gone to Switzerland. Mr. Campbell's a pretty sick man, Mr. Wales."

"I'm sorry to hear that. And George Hardt?" Charlie inquired.

"Back in America, gone to work."

"And where is the Snow Bird?"

"He was in here last week. Anyway, his friend, Mr. Schaeffer, is in Paris."

Two familiar names from the long list of a year and a half ago. Charlie scribbled an address in his notebook and tore out the page.

"If you see Mr. Schaeffer, give him this," he said. "It's my brother-in-law's address. I haven't settled on a hotel yet."

He was not really disappointed to find Paris was so empty. But the stillness in the Ritz bar was strange and portentous. It was not an American bar any more—he felt polite in it, and not as if he owned it. It had gone back into France. He felt the stillness from the moment he got out of the taxi and saw the doorman, usually in a frenzy of activity at this hour, gossiping with a *chasseur*[1] by the servants' entrance.

Passing through the corridor, he heard only a single, bored voice in the once-clamorous women's room. When he turned into the bar he traveled the twenty feet of green carpet with his eyes fixed straight ahead by old habit; and then, with his foot firmly on the rail, he turned and surveyed the room, encountering only a single pair of eyes that fluttered up from a newspaper in the corner. Charlie asked for the head barman, Paul, who in the latter days of the bull market[2] had come to work in his own custom-built car—disembarking, however, with due nicety at the nearest corner. But Paul was at his country house today and Alix giving him information.

"No, no more," Charlie said, "I'm going slow these days."

Alix congratulated him: "You were going pretty strong a couple of years ago."

"I'll stick to it all right," Charlie assured him. "I've stuck to it for over a year and a half now."

"How do you find conditions in America?"

"I haven't been to America for months. I'm in business in Prague, representing a couple of concerns there. They don't know about me down there."

Alix smiled.

"Remember the night of George Hardt's bachelor dinner here?" said Charlie. "By the way, what's become of Claude Fessenden?"

Alix lowered his voice confidentially: "He's in Paris, but he doesn't come here any more. Paul doesn't allow it. He ran up a bill of thirty thousand francs,[3] charging all his drinks and his lunches, and usually

---

1. Hotel errand boy.
2. Rising stock market. The crash came in October 1929, beginning the Depression.

3. About $7,500. Below, 4 Swiss francs equals 18¢.

his dinner, for more than a year. And when Paul finally told him he had to pay, he gave him a bad check."

Alix shook his head sadly.

"I don't understand it, such a dandy fellow. Now he's all bloated up—" He made a plump apple of his hands.

Charlie watched a group of strident queens installing themselves in a corner.

"Nothing affects them," he thought. "Stocks rise and fall, people loaf or work, but they go on forever." The place oppressed him. He called for the dice and shook with Alix for the drink.

"Here for long, Mr. Wales?"

"I'm here for four or five days to see my little girl."

"Oh-h! You have a little girl?"

Outside, the fire-red, gas-blue, ghost-green signs shone smokily through the tranquil rain. It was late afternoon and the streets were in movement; the bistros gleamed. At the corner of the Boulevard des Capucines he took a taxi. The Place de la Concorde moved by in pink majesty; they crossed the logical Seine, and Charlie felt the sudden provincial quality of the Left Bank.[4]

Charlie directed his taxi to the Avenue de l'Opéra, which was out of his way. But he wanted to see the blue hour spread over the magnificent façade, and imagine that the cab horns, playing endlessly the first few bars of *Le Plus que Lent*,[5] were the trumpets of the Second Empire.[6] They were closing the iron grill in front of Brentano's Bookstore, and people were already at dinner behind the trim little bourgeois hedge of Duval's. He had never eaten at a really cheap restaurant in Paris. Five-course dinner, four francs fifty, eighteen cents, wine included. For some odd reason he wished that he had.

As they rolled on to the Left Bank and he felt its sudden provincialism, he thought, "I spoiled this city for myself. I didn't realize it, but the days came along one after another, and then two years were gone, and everything was gone, and I was gone."

He was thirty-five, and good to look at. The Irish mobility of his face was sobered by a deep wrinkle between his eyes. As he rang his brother-in-law's bell in the Rue Palatine, the wrinkle deepened till it pulled down his brows; he felt a cramping sensation in his belly. From behind the maid who opened the door darted a lovely little girl of nine who shrieked "Daddy!" and flew up, struggling like a fish, into his arms. She pulled his head around by one ear and set her cheek against his.

"My old pie," he said.

"Oh, daddy, daddy, daddy, daddy, dads, dads, dads!"

She drew him into the salon, where the family waited, a boy and a girl his daughter's age, his sister-in-law and her husband. He greeted Marion with his voice pitched carefully to avoid either feigned enthusiasm or dislike, but her response was more frankly tepid, though she minimized her expression of unalterable distrust by directing her

---

4. South of the Seine River; site of the student quarter and Bohemian section of Paris.

5. "More than Slow," a Debussy piano piece.

6. Reign of Louis Napoleon, 1852–1870; glamorous "good old days."

regard toward his child. The two men clasped hands in a friendly way and Lincoln Peters rested his for a moment on Charlie's shoulder.

The room was warm and comfortably American. The three children moved intimately about, playing through the yellow oblongs that led to other rooms; the cheer of six o'clock spoke in the eager smacks of the fire and the sounds of French activity in the kitchen. But Charlie did not relax; his heart sat up rigidly in his body and he drew confidence from his daughter, who from time to time came close to him, holding in her arms the doll he had brought.

"Really extremely well," he declared in answer to Lincoln's question. "There's a lot of business there that isn't moving at all, but we're doing even better than ever. In fact, damn well. I'm bringing my sister over from America next month to keep house for me. My income last year was bigger than it was when I had money. You see, the Czechs———"

His boasting was for a specific purpose; but after a moment, seeing a faint restiveness in Lincoln's eye, he changed the subject:

"Those are fine children of yours, well brought up, good manners."

"We think Honoria's a great little girl too."

Marion Peters came back from the kitchen. She was a tall woman with worried eyes, who had once possessed a fresh American loveliness. Charlie had never been sensitive to it and was always surprised when people spoke of how pretty she had been. From the first there had been an instinctive antipathy between them.

"Well, how do you find Honoria?" she asked.

"Wonderful. I was astonished how much she's grown in ten months. All the children are looking well."

"We haven't had a doctor for a year. How do you like being back in Paris?"

"It seems very funny to see so few Americans around."

"I'm delighted," Marion said vehemently. "Now at least you can go into a store without their assuming you're a millionaire. We've suffered like everybody, but on the whole it's a good deal pleasanter."

"But it was nice while it lasted," Charlie said. "We were a sort of royalty, almost infallible, with a sort of magic around us. In the bar this afternoon"—he stumbled, seeing his mistake—"there wasn't a man I knew."

She looked at him keenly. "I should think you'd have had enough of bars."

"I only stayed a minute. I take one drink every afternoon, and no more."

"Don't you want a cocktail before dinner?" Lincoln asked.

"I take only one drink every afternoon, and I've had that."

"I hope you keep to it," said Marion.

Her dislike was evident in the coldness with which she spoke, but Charlie only smiled; he had larger plans. Her very aggressiveness gave him an advantage, and he knew enough to wait. He wanted them to initiate the discussion of what they knew had brought him to Paris.

At dinner he couldn't decide whether Honoria was most like him or her mother. Fortunate if she didn't combine the traits of both that had brought them to disaster. A great wave of protectiveness went over him. He thought he knew what to do for her. He believed in character; he wanted to jump back a whole generation and trust in character again as the eternally valuable element. Everything else wore out.

He left soon after dinner, but not to go home. He was curious to see Paris by night with clearer and more judicious eyes than those of other days. He bought a *strapontin*[7] for the Casino and watched Josephine Baker go through her chocolate arabesques.

After an hour he left and strolled toward Montmartre, up the Rue Pigalle into the Place Blanche. The rain had stopped and there were a few people in evening clothes disembarking from taxis in front of cabarets, and *cocottes*[8] prowling singly or in pairs, and many Negroes. He passed a lighted door from which issued music, and stopped with the sense of familiarity; it was Bricktop's, where he had parted with so many hours and so much money. A few doors farther on he found another ancient rendezvous and incautiously put his head inside. Immediately an eager orchestra burst into sound, a pair of professional dancers leaped to their feet and a maître d'hôtel swooped toward him, crying, "Crowd just arriving, sir!" But he withdrew quickly.

"You have to be damn drunk," he thought.

Zelli's was closed, the bleak and sinister cheap hotels surrounding it were dark; up in the Rue Blanche there was more light and a local, colloquial French crowd. The Poet's Cave had disappeared, but the two great mouths of the Café of Heaven and the Café of Hell still yawned—even devoured, as he watched, the meager contents of a tourist bus—a German, a Japanese, and an American couple who glanced at him with frightened eyes.

So much for the effort and ingenuity of Montmartre. All the catering to vice and waste was on an utterly childish scale, and he suddenly realized the meaning of the word "dissipate"—to dissipate into thin air; to make nothing out of something. In the little hours of the night every move from place to place was an enormous human jump, an increase of paying for the privilege of slower and slower motion.

He remembered thousand-franc notes given to an orchestra for playing a single number, hundred-franc notes tossed to a doorman for calling a cab.

But it hadn't been given for nothing.

It had been given, even the most wildly squandered sum, as an offering to destiny that he might not remember the things most worth remembering, the things that now he would always remember—his child taken from his control, his wife escaped to a grave in Vermont.

In the glare of a *brasserie*[9] a woman spoke to him. He bought her some eggs and coffee, and then, eluding her encouraging stare, gave her a twenty-franc note and took a taxi to his hotel.

II

He woke upon a fine fall day—football weather. The depression of yesterday was gone and he liked the people on the streets. At noon he

---

7. Cheap seat in the aisle. Josephine Baker (1906–1975) was a celebrated black singer of the blues in Paris in the 1920s.
8. Prostitutes.
9. Small restaurant and bar.

sat opposite Honoria at Le Grand Vatel, the only restaurant he could
think of not reminiscent of champagne dinners and long luncheons
that began at two and ended in a blurred and vague twilight.

"Now, how about vegetables? Oughtn't you to have some vegetables?"

"Well, yes."

"Here's *épinards* and *chou-fleur* and carrots and *haricots*."[1]

"I'd like *chou-fleur*."

"Wouldn't you like to have two vegetables?"

"I usually only have one at lunch."

The waiter was pretending to be inordinately fond of children.
"*Qu'elle est mignonne la petite! Elle parle exactement comme une
française.*"[2]

"How about dessert? Shall we wait and see?"

The waiter disappeared. Honoria looked at her father expectantly.

"What are we going to do?"

"First, we're going to that toy store in the Rue Saint-Honoré and
buy you anything you like. And then we're going to the vaudeville
at the Empire."

She hesitated. "I like it about the vaudeville, but not the toy store."

"Why not?"

"Well, you brought me this doll." She had it with her. "And I've got
lots of things. And we're not rich any more, are we?"

"We never were. But today you are to have anything you want."

"All right," she agreed resignedly.

When there had been her mother and a French nurse he had been
inclined to be strict; now he extended himself, reached out for a new
tolerance; he must be both parents to her and not shut any of her out
of communication.

"I want to get to know you," he said gravely. "First let me introduce
myself. My name is Charles J. Wales, of Prague."

"Oh, daddy!" her voice cracked with laughter.

"And who are you, please?" he persisted, and she accepted a role
immediately: "Honoria Wales, Rue Palatine, Paris."

"Married or single?"

"No, not married. Single."

He indicated the doll. "But I see you have a child, madame."

Unwilling to disinherit it, she took it to her heart and thought
quickly: "Yes, I've been married, but I'm not married now. My husband is dead."

He went on quickly, "And the child's name?"

"Simone. That's after my best friend at school."

"I'm very pleased that you're doing so well at school."

"I'm third this month," she boasted. "Elsie"—that was her cousin—
"is only about eighteenth, and Richard is about at the bottom."

"You like Richard and Elsie, don't you?"

"Oh, yes. I like Richard quite well and I like her all right."

Cautiously and casually he asked: "And Aunt Marion and Uncle

1. Spinach, cauliflower, and beans.   just like a French girl."
2. "What a cute little girl! She talks

Lincoln—which do you like best?"

"Oh, Uncle Lincoln, I guess."

He was increasingly aware of her presence. As they came in, a murmur of ". . . adorable" followed them, and now the people at the next table bent all their silences upon her, staring as if she were something no more conscious than a flower.

"Why don't I live with you?" she asked suddenly. "Because mamma's dead?"

"You must stay here and learn more French. It would have been hard for daddy to take care of you so well."

"I don't really need much taking care of any more. I do everything for myself."

Going out of the restaurant, a man and a woman unexpectedly hailed him.

"Well, the old Wales!"

"Hello there, Lorraine. . . . Dunc."

Sudden ghosts out of the past: Duncan Schaeffer, a friend from college. Lorraine Quarrles, a lovely, pale blonde of thirty; one of a crowd who had helped them make months into days in the lavish times of three years ago.

"My husband couldn't come this year," she said, in answer to his question. "We're poor as hell. So he gave me two hundred a month and told me I could do my worst on that. . . . This your little girl?"

"What about coming back and sitting down?" Duncan asked.

"Can't do it." He was glad for an excuse. As always, he felt Lorraine's passionate, provocative attraction, but his own rhythm was different now.

"Well, how about dinner?" she asked.

"I'm not free. Give me your address and let me call you."

"Charlie, I believe you're sober," she said judicially. "I honestly believe he's sober, Dunc. Pinch him and see if he's sober."

Charlie indicated Honoria with his head. They both laughed.

"What's your address?" said Duncan skeptically.

He hesitated, unwilling to give the name of his hotel.

"I'm not settled yet. I'd better call you. We're going to see the vaudeville at the Empire."

"There! That's what I want to do," Lorraine said. "I want to see some clowns and acrobats and jugglers. That's just what we'll do, Dunc."

"We've got to do an errand first," said Charlie. "Perhaps we'll see you there."

"All right, you snob. . . . Good-by, beautiful little girl."

"Good-by."

Honoria bobbed politely.

Somehow, an unwelcome encounter. They liked him because he was functioning, because he was serious; they wanted to see him, because he was stronger than they were now, because they wanted to draw a certain sustenance from his strength.

At the Empire, Honoria proudly refused to sit upon her father's folded coat. She was already an individual with a code of her own, and Charlie was more and more absorbed by the desire of putting a little of himself into her before she crystallized utterly. It was hopeless to try to know her in so short a time.

Between the acts they came upon Duncan and Lorraine in the lobby where the band was playing.

"Have a drink?"

"All right, but not up at the bar. We'll take a table."

"The perfect father."

Listening abstractedly to Lorraine, Charlie watched Honoria's eyes leave their table, and he followed them wistfully about the room, wondering what they saw. He met her glance and she smiled.

"I liked that lemonade," she said.

What had she said? What had he expected? Going home in a taxi afterward, he pulled her over until her head rested against his chest.

"Darling, do you ever think about your mother?"

"Yes, sometimes," she answered vaguely.

"I don't want you to forget her. Have you got a picture of her?"

"Yes, I think so. Anyhow, Aunt Marion has. Why don't you want me to forget her?"

"She loved you very much."

"I loved her too."

They were silent for a moment.

"Daddy, I want to come and live with you," she said suddenly.

His heart leaped; he had wanted it to come like this.

"Aren't you perfectly happy?"

"Yes, but I love you better than anybody. And you love me better than anybody, don't you, now that mummy's dead?"

"Of course I do. But you won't always like me best, honey. You'll grow up and meet somebody your own age and go marry him and forget you ever had a daddy."

"Yes, that's true," she agreed tranquilly.

He didn't go in. He was coming back at nine o'clock and he wanted to keep himself fresh and new for the thing he must say then.

"When you're safe inside, just show yourself in that window."

"All right. Good-by, dads, dads, dads, dads."

He waited in the dark street until she appeared, all warm and glowing, in the window above and kissed her fingers out into the night.

III

They were waiting. Marion sat behind the coffee service in a dignified black dinner dress that just faintly suggested mourning. Lincoln was walking up and down with the animation of one who had already been talking. They were as anxious as he was to get into the question. He opened it almost immediately:

"I suppose you know what I want to see you about—why I really came to Paris."

Marion played with the black stars on her necklace and frowned.

"I'm awfully anxious to have a home," he continued. "And I'm awfully anxious to have Honoria in it. I appreciate your taking in Honoria for her mother's sake, but things have changed now"—he hesitated and then continued more forcibly—"changed radically with me, and I want to ask you to reconsider the matter. It would be silly for me to deny that about three years ago I was acting badly——"

Marion looked up at him with hard eyes.

"—but all that's over. As I told you, I haven't had more than a drink a day for over a year, and I take that drink deliberately, so that the idea of alcohol won't get too big in my imagination. You see the idea?"

"No," said Marion succinctly.

"It's a sort of stunt I set myself. It keeps the matter in proportion."

"I get you," said Lincoln. "You don't want to admit it's got any attraction for you."

"Something like that. Sometimes I forget and don't take it. But I try to take it. Anyhow, I couldn't afford to drink in my position. The people I represent are more than satisfied with what I've done, and I'm bringing my sister over from Burlington to keep house for me, and I want awfully to have Honoria too. You know that even when her mother and I weren't getting along well we never let anything that happened touch Honoria. I know she's fond of me and I know I'm able to take care of her and—well, there you are. How do you feel about it?"

He knew that now he would have to take a beating. It would last an hour or two hours, and it would be difficult, but if he modulated his inevitable resentment to the chastened attitude of the reformed sinner, he might win his point in the end.

Keep your temper, he told himself. You don't want to be justified. You want Honoria.

Lincoln spoke first: "We've been talking it over ever since we got your letter last month. We're happy to have Honoria here. She's a dear little thing, and we're glad to be able to help her, but of course that isn't the question——"

Marion interrupted suddenly. "How long are you going to stay sober, Charlie?" she asked.

"Permanently, I hope."

"How can anybody count on that?"

"You know I never did drink heavily until I gave up business and came over here with nothing to do. Then Helen and I began to run around with——"

"Please leave Helen out of it. I can't bear to hear you talk about her like that."

He stared at her grimly; he had never been certain how fond of each other the sisters were in life.

"My drinking only lasted about a year and a half—from the time we came over until I—collapsed."

"It was time enough."

"It was time enough," he agreed.

"My duty is entirely to Helen," she said. "I try to think what she would have wanted me to do. Frankly, from the night you did that terrible thing you haven't really existed for me. I can't help that. She was my sister."

"Yes."

"When she was dying she asked me to look out for Honoria. If you hadn't been in a sanitarium then, it might have helped matters."

He had no answer.

"I'll never in my life be able to forget the morning when Helen knocked at my door, soaked to the skin and shivering, and said you'd locked her out."

Charlie gripped the sides of the chair. This was more difficult than he expected; he wanted to launch out into a long expostulation and explanation, but he only said: "The night I locked her out—" and she interrupted, "I don't feel up to going over that again."

After a moment's silence Lincoln said: "We're getting off the subject. You want Marion to set aside her legal guardianship and give you Honoria. I think the main point for her is whether she has confidence in you or not."

"I don't blame Marion," Charlie said slowly, "but I think she can have entire confidence in me. I had a good record up to three years ago. Of course, it's within human possibilities I might go wrong any time. But if we wait much longer I'll lose Honoria's childhood and my chance for a home." He shook his head. "I'll simply lose her, don't you see?"

"Yes, I see," said Lincoln.

"Why didn't you think of all this before?" Marion asked.

"I suppose I did, from time to time, but Helen and I were getting along badly. When I consented to the guardianship, I was flat on my back in a sanitarium and the market had cleaned me out. I knew I'd acted badly, and I thought if it would bring any peace to Helen, I'd agree to anything. But now it's different. I'm functioning, I'm behaving damn well, so far as——"

"Please don't swear at me," Marion said.

He looked at her, startled. With each remark the force of her dislike became more and more apparent. She had built up all her fear of life into one wall and faced it toward him. This trivial reproof was possibly the result of some trouble with the cook several hours before. Charlie became increasingly alarmed at leaving Honoria in this atmosphere of hostility against himself; sooner or later it would come out, in a word here, a shake of the head there, and some of that distrust would be irrevocably implanted in Honoria. But he pulled his temper down out of his face and shut it up inside him; he had won a point, for Lincoln realized the absurdity of Marion's remark and asked her lightly since when she had objected to the word "damn."

"Another thing," Charlie said: "I'm able to give her certain advantages now. I'm going to take a French governess to Prague with me. I've got a lease on a new apartment——"

He stopped, realizing that he was blundering. They couldn't be expected to accept with equanimity the fact that his income was again twice as large as their own.

"I suppose you can give her more luxuries than we can," said Marion. "When you were throwing away money we were living along watching every ten francs. . . . I suppose you'll start doing it again."

"Oh, no," he said. "I've learned. I worked hard for ten years, you know—until I got lucky in the market, like so many people. Terribly lucky. It won't happen again."

There was a long silence. All of them felt their nerves straining, and for the first time in a year Charlie wanted a drink. He was sure now that Lincoln Peters wanted him to have his child.

Marion shuddered suddenly; part of her saw that Charlie's feet were planted on the earth now, and her own maternal feeling recognized the naturalness of his desire; but she had lived for a long time with a prejudice—a prejudice founded on a curious disbelief in her sister's happiness, which, in the shock of one terrible night, had turned to hatred for him. It had all happened at a point in her life where the discouragement of ill health and adverse circumstances made it necessary for her to believe in tangible villainy and a tangible villain.

"I can't help what I think!" she cried out suddenly. "How much you were responsible for Helen's death, I don't know. It's something you'll have to square with your own conscience."

An electric current of agony surged through him; for a moment he was almost on his feet, an unuttered sound echoing in his throat. He hung on to himself for a moment, another moment.

"Hold on there," said Lincoln uncomfortably. "I never thought you were responsible for that."

"Helen died of heart trouble," Charlie said dully.

"Yes, heart trouble." Marion spoke as if the phrase had another meaning for her.

Then, in the flatness that followed her outburst, she saw him plainly and she knew he had somehow arrived at control over the situation. Glancing at her husband, she found no help from him, and as abruptly as if it were a matter of no importance, she threw up the sponge.

"Do what you like!" she cried, springing up from her chair. "She's your child. I'm not the person to stand in your way. I think if it were my child I'd rather see her—" She managed to check herself. "You two decide it. I can't stand this. I'm sick. I'm going to bed."

She hurried from the room; after a moment Lincoln said:

"This has been a hard day for her. You know how strongly she feels—" His voice was almost apologetic: "When a woman gets an idea in her head."

"Of course."

"It's going to be all right. I think she sees now that you—can provide for the child, and so we can't very well stand in your way or Honoria's way."

"Thank you, Lincoln."

"I'd better go along and see how she is."

"I'm going."

He was still trembling when he reached the street, but a walk down the Rue Bonaparte to the *quais*[3] set him up, and as he crossed the Seine, fresh and new by the *quai* lamps, he felt exultant. But back in his room he couldn't sleep. The image of Helen haunted him. Helen

3. Paved walks along the Seine River.

whom he had loved so until they had senselessly begun to abuse each other's love, tear it into shreds. On that terrible February night that Marion remembered so vividly, a slow quarrel had gone on for hours. There was a scene at the Florida, and then he attempted to take her home, and then she kissed young Webb at a table; after that there was what she had hysterically said. When he arrived home alone he turned the key in the lock in wild anger. How could he know she would arrive an hour later alone, that there would be a snow storm in which she wandered about in slippers, too confused to find a taxi? Then the aftermath, her escaping pneumonia by a miracle, and all the attendant horror. They were "reconciled," but that was the beginning of the end, and Marion, who had seen with her own eyes and who imagined it to be one of many scenes from her sister's martyrdom, never forgot.

Going over it again brought Helen nearer, and in the white, soft light that steals upon half sleep near morning he found himself talking to her again. She said that he was perfectly right about Honoria and that she wanted Honoria to be with him. She said she was glad he was being good and doing better. She said a lot of other things—very friendly things—but she was in a swing in a white dress, and swinging faster and faster all the time, so that at the end he could not hear clearly all that she said.

IV

He woke up feeling happy. The door of the world was open again. He made plans, vistas, futures for Honoria and himself, but suddenly he grew sad, remembering all the plans he and Helen had made. She had not planned to die. The present was the thing—work to do and someone to love. But not to love too much, for he knew the injury that a father can do to a daughter or a mother to a son by attaching them too closely: afterward, out in the world, the child would seek in the marriage partner the same blind tenderness and, failing probably to find it, turn against love and life.

It was another bright, crisp day. He called Lincoln Peters at the bank where he worked and asked if he could count on taking Honoria when he left for Prague. Lincoln agreed that there was no reason for delay. One thing—the legal guardianship. Marion wanted to retain that a while longer. She was upset by the whole matter, and it would oil things if she felt that the situation was still in her control for another year. Charlie agreed, wanting only the tangible, visible child.

Then the question of a governess. Charles sat in a gloomy agency and talked to a cross Béarnaise and to a buxom Breton peasant,[4] neither of whom he could have endured. There were others whom he would see tomorrow.

He lunched with Lincoln Peters at Griffons, trying to keep down his exultation.

"There's nothing quite like your own child," Lincoln said. "But you understand how Marion feels too."

"She's forgotten how hard I worked for seven years there," Charlie said. "She just remembers one night."

4. Woman from Béarn, a region of southwestern France; peasant from Brittany.

"There's another thing." Lincoln hesitated. "While you and Helen were tearing around Europe throwing money away, we were just getting along. I didn't touch any of the prosperity because I never got ahead enough to carry anything but my insurance. I think Marion felt there was some kind of injustice in it—you not even working toward the end, and getting richer and richer."

"It went just as quick as it came," said Charlie.

"Yes, a lot of it stayed in the hands of *chasseurs* and saxophone players and maitres d'hôtel—well, the big party's over now. I just said that to explain Marion's feeling about those crazy years. If you drop in about six o'clock tonight before Marion's too tired, we'll settle the details on the spot."

Back at his hotel, Charlie found a *pneumatique*[5] that had been redirected from the Ritz bar, where Charlie had left his address for the purpose of finding a certain man.

> DEAR CHARLIE: You were so strange when we saw you the other day that I wondered if I did something to offend you. If so, I'm not conscious of it. In fact, I have thought about you too much for the last year, and it's always been in the back of my mind that I might see you if I came over here. We *did* have such good times that crazy spring, like the night you and I stole the butcher's tricycle, and the time we tried to call on the president and you had the old derby rim and the wire cane. Everybody seems so old lately, but I don't feel old a bit. Couldn't we get together some time today for old time's sake? I've got a vile hangover for the moment, but will be feeling better this afternoon and will look for you about five in the sweatshop at the Ritz.
>
> Always devotedly,
> Lorraine

His first feeling was one of awe that he had actually, in his mature years, stolen a tricycle and pedaled Lorraine all over the Etoile between the small hours and dawn. In retrospect it was a nightmare. Locking out Helen didn't fit in with any other act of his life, but the tricycle incident did—it was one of many. How many weeks or months of dissipation to arrive at that condition of utter irresponsibility?

He tried to picture how Lorraine had appeared to him then—very attractive; Helen was unhappy about it, though she said nothing. Yesterday, in the restaurant, Lorraine had seemed trite, blurred, worn away. He emphatically did not want to see her, and he was glad Alix had not given away his hotel address. It was a relief to think, instead, of Honoria, to think of Sundays spent with her and of saying good morning to her and of knowing she was there in his house at night, drawing her breath in the darkness.

At five he took a taxi and bought presents for all the Peterses—a piquant cloth doll, a box of Roman soldiers, flowers for Marion, big linen handkerchiefs for Lincoln.

He saw, when he arrived in the apartment, that Marion had accepted the inevitable. She greeted him now as though he were a re-

5. Express message sent through Pariswide system of air tubes.

calcitrant member of the family, rather than a menacing outsider. Honoria had been told she was going; Charlie was glad to see that her tact made her conceal her excessive happiness. Only on his lap did she whisper her delight and the question "When?" before she slipped away with the other children.

He and Marion were alone for a minute in the room, and on an impulse he spoke out boldly:

"Family quarrels are bitter things. They don't go according to any rules. They're not like aches or wounds; they're more like splits in the skin that won't heal because there's not enough material. I wish you and I could be on better terms."

"Some things are hard to forget," she answered. "It's a question of confidence." There was no answer to this and presently she asked, "When do you propose to take her?"

"As soon as I can get a governess. I hoped the day after tomorrow."

"That's impossible. I've got to get her things in shape. Not before Saturday."

He yielded. Coming back into the room, Lincoln offered him a drink.

"I'll take my daily whisky," he said.

It was warm here, it was a home, people together by a fire. The children felt very safe and important; the mother and father were serious, watchful. They had things to do for the children more important than his visit here. A spoonful of medicine was, after all, more important than the strained relations between Marion and himself. They were not dull people, but they were very much in the grip of life and circumstances. He wondered if he couldn't do something to get Lincoln out of his rut at the bank.

A long peal at the doorbell; the *bonne à tout faire*[6] passed through and went down the corridor. The door opened upon another long ring, and then voices, and the three in the salon looked up expectantly; Richard moved to bring the corridor within his range of vision, and Marion rose. Then the maid came back along the corridor, closely followed by the voices, which developed under the light into Duncan Schaeffer and Lorraine Quarrles.

They were gay, they were hilarious, they were roaring with laughter. For a moment Charlie was astounded; unable to understand how they ferreted out the Peterses' address.

"Ah-h-h!" Duncan wagged his finger roguishly at Charlie. "Ah-h-h!"

They both slid down another cascade of laughter. Anxious and at a loss, Charlie shook hands with them quickly and presented them to Lincoln and Marion. Marion nodded, scarcely speaking. She had drawn back a step toward the fire; her little girl stood beside her, and Marion put an arm about her shoulder.

With growing annoyance at the intrusion, Charlie waited for them to explain themselves. After some concentration Duncan said:

"We came to invite you out to dinner. Lorraine and I insist that all this shishi,[7] cagy business 'bout your address got to stop."

6. Maid of all work.   7. Chichi, showy.

Charlie came closer to them, as if to force them backward down the corridor.

"Sorry, but I can't. Tell me where you'll be and I'll phone you in half an hour."

This made no impression. Lorraine sat down suddenly on the side of a chair, and focusing her eyes on Richard, cried, "Oh, what a nice little boy! Come here, little boy." Richard glanced at his mother, but did not move. With a perceptible shrug of her shoulders, Lorraine turned back to Charlie:

"Come and dine. Sure your cousins won' mine. See you so sel'om. Or solemn."

"I can't," said Charlie sharply. "You two have dinner and I'll phone you."

Her voice became suddenly unpleasant. "All right, we'll go. But I remember once when you hammered on my door at four A.M. I was enough of a good sport to give you a drink. Come on, Dunc."

Still in slow motion, with blurred, angry faces, with uncertain feet, they retired along the corridor.

"Good night," Charlie said.

"Good night!" responded Lorraine emphatically.

When he went back into the salon Marion had not moved, only now her son was standing in the circle of her other arm. Lincoln was still swinging Honoria back and forth like a pendulum from side to side.

"What an outrage!" Charlie broke out. "What an absolute outrage!"

Neither of them answered. Charlie dropped into an armchair, picked up his drink, set it down again and said:

"People I haven't seen for two years having the colossal nerve——"

He broke off. Marion had made the sound "Oh!" in one swift, furious breath, turned her body from him with a jerk and left the room.

Lincoln set down Honoria carefully.

"You children go in and start your soup," he said, and when they obeyed, he said to Charlie:

"Marion's not well and she can't stand shocks. That kind of people make her really physically sick."

"I didn't tell them to come here. They wormed your name out of somebody. They deliberately——"

"Well, it's too bad. It doesn't help matters. Excuse me a minute."

Left alone, Charlie sat tense in his chair, In the next room he could hear the children eating, talking in monosyllables, already oblivious to the scene between their elders. He heard a murmur of conversation from a farther room and then the ticking bell of a telephone receiver picked up, and in a panic he moved to the other side of the room and out of earshot.

In a minute Lincoln came back. "Look here, Charlie. I think we'd better call off dinner for tonight. Marion's in bad shape."

"Is she angry with me?"

"Sort of," he said, almost roughly. "She's not strong and——"

"You mean she's changed her mind about Honoria?"

"She's pretty bitter right now. I don't know. You phone me at the bank tomorrow."

"I wish you'd explain to her I never dreamed these people would come here. I'm just as sore as you are."

"I couldn't explain anything to her now."

Charlie got up. He took his coat and hat and started down the corridor. Then he opened the door of the dining room and said in a strange voice, "Good night, children."

Honoria rose and ran around the table to hug him.

"Good night, sweetheart," he said vaguely, and then trying to make his voice more tender, trying to conciliate something, "Good night, dear children."

V

Charlie went directly to the Ritz bar with the furious idea of finding Lorraine and Duncan, but they were not there, and he realized that in any case there was nothing he could do. He had not touched his drink at the Peters, and now he ordered a whisky-and-soda. Paul came over to say hello.

"It's a great change," he said sadly. "We do about half the business we did. So many fellows I hear about back in the States lost everything, maybe not in the first crash, but then in the second. Your friend George Hardt lost every cent, I hear. Are you back in the States?"

"No, I'm in business in Prague."

"I heard that you lost a lot in the crash."

"I did," and he added grimly, "but I lost everything I wanted in the boom."

"Selling short."[8]

"Something like that."

Again the memory of those days swept over him like a nightmare —the people they had met traveling; then people who couldn't add a row of figures or speak a coherent sentence. The little man Helen had consented to dance with at the ship's party, who had insulted her ten feet from the table; the women and girls carried screaming with drink or drugs out of public places——

The men who locked their wives out in the snow, because the snow of twenty-nine wasn't real snow. If you didn't want it to be snow, you just paid some money.

He went to the phone and called the Peterses' apartment; Lincoln answered.

"I called up because this thing is on my mind. Has Marion said anything definite?"

"Marion's sick" Lincoln answered shortly. "I know this thing isn't altogether your fault, but I can't have her go to pieces about it. I'm afraid we'll have to let it slide for six months; I can't take the chance of working her up to this state again."

"I see."

"I'm sorry, Charlie."

He went back to his table. His whisky glass was empty, but he

---

8. Selling at too low a price.

shook his head when Alix looked at it questioningly. There wasn't much he could do now except send Honoria some things; he would send her a lot of things tomorrow. He thought rather angrily that this was just money—he had given so many people money. . . .

"No, no more," he said to another waiter. "What do I owe you?"

He would come back some day; they couldn't make him pay forever. But he wanted his child, and nothing was much good now, beside that fact. He wasn't young any more, with a lot of nice thoughts and dreams to have by himself. He was absolutely sure Helen wouldn't have wanted him to be so alone.

1931

JAMES BALDWIN

Sonny's Blues

I read about it in the paper, in the subway, on my way to work. I read it, and I couldn't believe it, and I read it again. Then perhaps I just stared at it, at the newsprint spelling out his name, spelling out the story. I stared at it in the swinging lights of the subway car, and in the faces and bodies of the people, and in my own face, trapped in the darkness which roared outside.

It was not to be believed and I kept telling myself that, as I walked from the subway station to the high school. And at the same time I couldn't doubt it. I was scared, scared for Sonny. He became real to me again. A great block of ice got settled in my belly and kept melting there slowly all day long, while I taught my classes algebra. It was a special kind of ice. It kept melting, sending trickles of ice water all up and down my veins, but it never got less. Sometimes it hardened and seemed to expand until I felt my guts were going to come spilling out or that I was going to choke or scream. This would always be at a moment when I was remembering some specific thing Sonny had once said or done.

When he was about as old as the boys in my classes his face had been bright and open, there was a lot of copper in it; and he'd had wonderfully direct brown eyes, and great gentleness and privacy. I wondered what he looked like now. He had been picked up, the evening before, in a raid on an apartment downtown, for peddling and using heroin.

I couldn't believe it: but what I mean by that is that I couldn't find any room for it anywhere inside me. I had kept it outside me for a long time. I hadn't wanted to know. I had had suspicions, but I didn't name them, I kept putting them away. I told myself that Sonny was wild, but he wasn't crazy. And he'd always been a good boy, he hadn't ever turned hard or evil or disrespectful, the way kids can, so quick, so quick, especially in Harlem. I didn't want to believe that I'd ever see my brother going down, coming to nothing, all that light in his face gone out, in the condition I'd already seen so many others. Yet it had happened and here I was, talking about algebra to a lot of boys who might, every one of them for all I knew, be popping off needles every time they went to the head.[1] Maybe it did more for them than algebra could.

I was sure that the first time Sonny had ever had horse,[2] he couldn't have been much older than these boys were now. These boys, now, were living as we'd been living then, they were growing up with a rush and their heads bumped abruptly against the low ceiling of their actual possibilities. They were filled with rage. All they really knew were two darknesses, the darkness of their lives, which was now closing in on them, and the darkness of the movies, which had blinded them to that other darkness, and in which they now, vindictively, dreamed, at once more together than they were at any other time, and more alone.

When the last bell rang, the last class ended, I let out my breath. It seemed I'd been holding it for all that time. My clothes were wet—I may have looked as though I'd been sitting in a steam bath, all dressed up, all afternoon. I sat alone in the classroom a long time. I listened to the boys outside, downstairs, shouting and cursing and laughing. Their laughter struck me for perhaps the first time. It was not the joyous laughter which—God knows why—one associates with children. It was mocking and insular, its intent was to denigrate. It was disenchanted, and in this, also, lay the authority of their curses. Perhaps I was listening to them because I was thinking about my brother and in them I heard my brother. And myself.

One boy was whistling a tune, at once very complicated and very simple, it seemed to be pouring out of him as though he were a bird, and it sounded very cool and moving through all that harsh, bright air, only just holding its own through all those other sounds.

I stood up and walked over to the window and looked down into the courtyard. It was the beginning of the spring and the sap was rising in the boys. A teacher passed through them every now and again, quickly, as though he or she couldn't wait to get out of that courtyard, to get those boys out of their sight and off their minds. I started collecting my stuff. I thought I'd better get home and talk to Isabel.

The courtyard was almost deserted by the time I got downstairs. I saw this boy standing in the shadow of a doorway, looking just like Sonny. I almost called his name. Then I saw that it wasn't Sonny, but somebody we used to know, a boy from around our block. He'd been Sonny's friend. He'd never been mine, having been too young for me, and, anyway, I'd never liked him. And now, even though he was a grown-up man, he still hung around that block, still spent hours on the street corners, was always high and raggy. I used to run into him from time to time and he'd often work around to asking me for a quarter or fifty cents. He always had some real good excuse, too, and I always gave it to him, I don't know why.

But now, abruptly, I hated him. I couldn't stand the way he looked at me, partly like a dog, partly like a cunning child. I wanted to ask him what the hell he was doing in the school courtyard.

He sort of shuffled over to me, and he said, "I see you got the papers. So you already know about it."

"You mean about Sonny? Yes, I already know about it. How come they didn't get you?"

---

1. Lavatory.   2. Heroin.

He grinned. It made him repulsive and it also brought to mind what he'd looked like as a kid. "I wasn't there. I stay away from them people."

"Good for you." I offered him a cigarette and I watched him through the smoke. "You come all the way down here just to tell me about Sonny?"

"That's right." He was sort of shaking his head and his eyes looked strange, as though they were about to cross. The bright sun deadened his damp dark brown skin and it made his eyes look yellow and showed up the dirt in his kinked hair. He smelled funky.[3] I moved a little away from him and I said, "Well, thanks. But I already know about it and I got to get home."

"I'll walk you a little ways," he said. We started walking. There were a couple of kids still loitering in the courtyard and one of them said goodnight to me and looked strangely at the boy beside me.

"What're you going to do?" he asked me. "I mean, about Sonny?"

"Look. I haven't seen Sonny for over a year, I'm not sure I'm going to do anything. Anyway, what the hell *can* I do?"

"That's right," he said quickly, "ain't nothing you can do. Can't much help old Sonny no more, I guess."

It was what I was thinking and so it seemed to me he had no right to say it.

"I'm surprised at Sonny, though," he went on—he had a funny way of talking, he looked straight ahead as though he were talking to himself—"I thought Sonny was a smart boy, I thought he was too smart to get hung."

"I guess he thought so too," I said sharply, "and that's how he got hung. And how about you? You're pretty goddamn smart, I bet."

Then he looked directly at me, just for a minute. "I ain't smart," he said. "If I was smart, I'd have reached for a pistol a long time ago."

"Look. Don't tell *me* your sad story, if it was up to me, I'd give you one." Then I felt guilty—guilty, probably, for never having supposed that the poor bastard *had* a story of his own, much less a sad one, and I asked, quickly, "What's going to happen to him now?"

He didn't answer this. He was off by himself some place.

"Funny thing," he said, and from his tone we might have been discussing the quickest way to get to Brooklyn, "when I saw the papers this morning, the first thing I asked myself was if I had anything to do with it. I felt sort of responsible."

I began to listen more carefully. The subway station was on the corner, just before us, and I stopped. He stopped, too. We were in front of a bar and he ducked slightly, peering in, but whoever he was looking for didn't seem to be there. The juke box was blasting away with something black and bouncy and I half watched the barmaid as she danced her way from the juke box to her place behind the bar. And I watched her face as she laughingly responded to something someone said to her, still keeping time to the music. When she smiled one saw the little girl, one sensed the doomed, still-struggling woman beneath the battered face of the semi-whore.

"I never *give* Sonny nothing," the boy said finally, "but a long time ago I come to school high and Sonny asked me how it felt." He paused,

3. Obnoxious.

I couldn't bear to watch him, I watched the barmaid, and I listened to the music which seemed to be causing the pavement to shake. "I told him it felt great." The music stopped, the barmaid paused and watched the juke box until the music began again. "It did."

All this was carrying me some place I didn't want to go. I certainly didn't want to know how it felt. It filled everything, the people, the houses, the music, the dark, quicksilver barmaid, with menace; and this menace was their reality.

"What's going to happen to him now?" I asked again.

"They'll send him away some place and they'll try to cure him." He shook his head. "Maybe he'll even think he's kicked the habit. Then they'll let him loose"—he gestured, throwing his cigarette into the gutter. "That's all."

"What do you mean, that's *all?*"

But I knew what he meant.

"I *mean*, that's *all*." He turned his head and looked at me, pulling down the corners of his mouth. "Don't you know what I mean?" he asked, softly.

"How the hell *would* I know what you mean?" I almost whispered it, I don't know why.

"That's right," he said to the air, "how would *he* know what I mean?" He turned toward me again, patient and calm, and yet I somehow felt him shaking, shaking as though he were going to fall apart. I felt that ice in my guts again, the dread I'd felt all afternoon; and again I watched the barmaid, moving about the bar, washing glasses, and singing. "Listen. They'll let him out and then it'll just start all over again. That's what I mean."

"You mean—they'll let him out. And then he'll just start working his way back in again. You mean he'll never kick the habit. Is that what you mean?"

"That's right," he said, cheerfully. "*You* see what I mean."

"Tell me," I said at last, "why does he want to die? He must want to die, he's killing himself, why does he want to die?"

He looked at me in surprise. He licked his lips. "He don't want to die. He wants to live. Don't nobody want to die, ever."

Then I wanted to ask him—too many things. He could not have answered, or if he had, I could not have borne the answers. I started walking. "Well, I guess it's none of my business."

"It's going to be rough on old Sonny," he said. We reached the subway station. "This is your station?" he asked. I nodded. I took one step down. "Damn!" he said, suddenly. I looked up at him. He grinned again. "Damn it if I didn't leave all my money home. You ain't got a dollar on you, have you? Just for a couple of days, is all."

All at once something inside gave and threatened to come pouring out of me. I didn't hate him any more. I felt that in another moment I'd start crying like a child.

"Sure," I said. "Don't sweat." I looked in my wallet and didn't have a dollar, I only had a five. "Here," I said. "That hold you?"

He didn't look at it—he didn't want to look at it. A terrible, closed look came over his face, as though he were keeping the number on the bill a secret from him and me. "Thanks," he said, and now he was

dying to see me go. "Don't worry about Sonny. Maybe I'll write him
or something."

"Sure," I said. "You do that. So long."

"Be seeing you," he said. I went on down the steps.

And I didn't write Sonny or send him anything for a long time.
When I finally did, it was just after my little girl died, he wrote me
back a letter which made me feel like a bastard.

Here's what he said:

Dear brother,

You don't know how much I needed to hear from you. I wanted
to write you many a time but I dug how much I must have hurt
you and so I didn't write. But now I feel like a man who's been
trying to climb up out of some deep, real deep and funky hole and
just saw the sun up there, outside. I got to get outside.

I can't tell you much about how I got here. I mean I don't know
how to tell you. I guess I was afraid of something or I was trying to
escape from something and you know I have never been very strong
in the head (smile). I'm glad Mama and Daddy are dead and can't
see what's happened to their son and I swear if I'd known what I
was doing I would never have hurt you so, you and a lot of other
fine people who were nice to me and who believed in me.

I don't want you to think it had anything to do with me being a
musician. It's more than that. Or maybe less than that. I can't get
anything straight in my head down here and I try not to think about
what's going to happen to me when I get outside again. Sometime
I think I'm going to flip and *never* get outside and sometime I think
I'll come straight back. I tell you one thing, though, I'd rather blow
my brains out than go through this again. But that's what they all
say, so they tell me. If I tell you when I'm coming to New York and
if you could meet me, I sure would appreciate it. Give my love to
Isabel and the kids and I was sure sorry to hear about little Gracie.
I wish I could be like Mama and say the Lord's will be done, but I
don't know it seems to me that trouble is the one thing that never
does get stopped and I don't know what good it does to blame it
on the Lord. But maybe it does some good if you believe it.

Your brother,
Sonny

Then I kept in constant touch with him and I sent him whatever I
could and I went to meet him when he came back to New York. When
I saw him many things I thought I had forgotten came flooding back
to me. This was because I had begun, finally, to wonder about Sonny,
about the life that Sonny lived inside. This life, whatever it was, had
made him older and thinner and it had deepened the distant stillness in
which he had always moved. He looked very unlike my baby brother.
Yet, when he smiled, when we shook hands, the baby brother I'd never
known looked out from the depths of his private life, like an animal
waiting to be coaxed into the light.

"How you been keeping?" he asked me.

"All right. And you?"

"Just fine." He was smiling all over his face. "It's good to see you again."

"It's good to see you."

The seven years' difference in our ages lay between us like a chasm: I wondered if these years would ever operate between us as a bridge. I was remembering, and it made it hard to catch my breath, that I had been there when he was born; and I had heard the first words he had ever spoken. When he started to walk, he walked from our mother straight to me. I caught him just before he fell when he took the first steps he ever took in this world.

"How's Isabel?"

"Just fine. She's dying to see you."

"And the boys?"

"They're fine, too. They're anxious to see their uncle."

"Oh, come on. You know they don't remember me."

"Are you kidding? Of course they remember you."

He grinned again. We got into a taxi. We had a lot to say to each other, far too much to know how to begin.

As the taxi began to move, I asked, "You still want to go to India?"

He laughed. "You still remember that. Hell, no. This place is Indian enough for me."

"It used to belong to them," I said.

And he laughed again. "They damn sure knew what they were doing when they got rid of it."

Years ago, when he was around fourteen, he'd been all hipped on the idea of going to India. He read books about people sitting on rocks, naked, in all kinds of weather, but mostly bad, naturally, and walking barefoot through hot coals and arriving at wisdom. I used to say that it sounded to me as though they were getting away from wisdom as fast as they could. I think he sort of looked down on me for that.

"Do you mind," he asked, "if we have the driver drive alongside the park? On the west side—I haven't seen the city in so long."

"Of course not," I said. I was afraid that I might sound as though I were humoring him, but I hoped he wouldn't take it that way.

So we drove along, between the green of the park and the stony, lifeless elegance of hotels and apartment buildings, toward the vivid, killing streets of our childhood. These streets hadn't changed, though housing projects jutted up out of them now like rocks in the middle of a boiling sea. Most of the houses in which we had grown up had vanished, as had the stores from which we had stolen, the basements in which we had first tried sex, the rooftops from which we had hurled tin cans and bricks. But houses exactly like the houses of our past yet dominated the landscape, boys exactly like the boys we once had been found themselves smothering in these houses, came down into the streets for light and air and found themselves encircled by disaster. Some escaped the trap, most didn't. Those who got out always left something of themselves behind, as some animals amputate a leg and leave it in the trap. It might be said, perhaps, that I had escaped, after all, I was a school teacher; or that Sonny had, he hadn't lived in

Harlem for years. Yet, as the cab moved uptown through streets which seemed, with a rush, to darken with dark people, and as I covertly studied Sonny's face, it came to me that what we both were seeking through our separate cab windows was that part of ourselves which had been left behind. It's always at the hour of trouble and confrontation that the missing member aches.

We hit 110th Street and started rolling up Lenox Avenue. And I'd known this avenue all my life, but it seemed to me again, as it had seemed on the day I'd first heard about Sonny's trouble, filled with a hidden menace which was its very breath of life.

"We almost there," said Sonny.

"Almost." We were both too nervous to say anything more.

We live in a housing project. It hasn't been up long. A few days after it was up it seemed uninhabitably new, now, of course, it's already rundown. It looks like a parody of the good, clean, faceless life—God knows the people who live in it do their best to make it a parody. The beat-looking grass lying around isn't enough to make their lives green, the hedges will never hold out the streets, and they know it. The big windows fool no one, they aren't big enough to make space out of no space. They don't bother with the windows, they watch the TV screen instead. The playground is most popular with the children who don't play at jacks, or skip rope, or roller skate, or swing, and they can be found in it after dark. We moved in partly because it's not too far from where I teach, and partly for the kids; but it's really just like the houses in which Sonny and I grew up. The same things happen, they'll have the same things to remember. The moment Sonny and I started into the house I had the feeling that I was simply bringing him back into the danger he had almost died trying to escape.

Sonny has never been talkative. So I don't know why I was sure he'd be dying to talk to me when supper was over the first night. Everything went fine, the oldest boy remembered him, and the youngest boy liked him, and Sonny had remembered to bring something for each of them; and Isabel, who is really much nicer than I am, more open and giving, had gone to a lot of trouble about dinner and was genuinely glad to see him. And she's always been able to tease Sonny in a way that I haven't. It was nice to see her face so vivid again and to hear her laugh and watch her make Sonny laugh. She wasn't, or, anyway, she didn't seem to be, at all uneasy or embarrassed. She chatted as though there were no subject which had to be avoided and she got Sonny past his first, faint stiffness. And thank God she was there, for I was filled with that icy dread again. Everything I did seemed awkward to me, and everything I said sounded freighted with hidden meaning. I was trying to remember everything I'd heard about dope addiction and I couldn't help watching Sonny for signs. I wasn't doing it out of malice. I was trying to find out something about my brother. I was dying to hear him tell me he was safe.

"Safe!" my father grunted, whenever Mama suggested trying to move to a neighborhood which might be safer for children. "Safe, hell! Ain't no place safe for kids, nor nobody."

He always went on like this, but he wasn't, ever, really as bad as he sounded, not even on weekends, when he got drunk. As a matter of fact, he was always on the lookout for "something a little better," but he died before he found it. He died suddenly, during a drunken weekend in the middle of the war, when Sonny was fifteen. He and Sonny hadn't ever got on too well. And this was partly because Sonny was the apple of his father's eye. It was because he loved Sonny so much and was frightened for him, that he was always fighting with him. It doesn't do any good to fight with Sonny. Sonny just moves back, inside himself, where he can't be reached. But the principal reason that they never hit it off is that they were so much alike. Daddy was big and rough and loud-talking, just the opposite of Sonny, but they both had—that same privacy.

Mama tried to tell me something about this, just after Daddy died. I was home on leave from the army.

This was the last time I ever saw my mother alive. Just the same, this picture gets all mixed up in my mind with pictures I had of her when she was younger. The way I always see her is the way she used to be on a Sunday afternoon, say, when the old folks were talking after the big Sunday dinner. I always see her wearing pale blue. She'd be sitting on the sofa. And my father would be sitting in the easy chair, not far from her. And the living room would be full of church folks and relatives. There they sit, in chairs all around the living room, and the night is creeping up outside, but nobody knows it yet. You can see the darkness growing against the windowpanes and you hear the street noises every now and again, or maybe the jangling beat of a tambourine from one of the churches close by, but it's real quiet in the room. For a moment nobody's talking, but every face looks darkening, like the sky outside. And my mother rocks a little from the waist, and my father's eyes are closed. Everyone is looking at something a child can't see. For a minute they've forgotten the children. Maybe a kid is lying on the rug, half asleep. Maybe somebody's got a kid in his lap and is absent-mindedly stroking the kid's head. Maybe there's a kid, quiet and big-eyed, curled up in a big chair in the corner. The silence, the darkness coming, and the darkness in the faces frighten the child obscurely. He hopes that the hand which strokes his forehead will never stop—will never die. He hopes that there will never come a time when the old folks won't be sitting around the living room, talking about where they've come from, and what they've seen, and what's happened to them and their kinfolk.

But something deep and watchful in the child knows that this is bound to end, is already ending. In a moment someone will get up and turn on the light. Then the old folks will remember the children and they won't talk any more that day. And when light fills the room, the child is filled with darkness. He knows that every time this happens he's moved just a little closer to that darkness outside. The darkness outside is what the old folks have been talking about. It's what they've come from. It's what they endure. The child knows that they won't talk any more because if he knows too much about what's happened to *them,* he'll know too much too soon, about what's going to happen to *him.*

The last time I talked to my mother, I remember I was restless. I wanted to get out and see Isabel. We weren't married then and we had a lot to straighten out between us.

There Mama sat, in black, by the window. She was humming an old church song, *Lord, you brought me from a long ways off*. Sonny was out somewhere. Mama kept watching the streets.

"I don't know," she said, "if I'll ever see you again, after you go off from here. But I hope you'll remember the things I tried to teach you."

"Don't talk like that," I said, and smiled. "You'll be here a long time yet."

She smiled, too, but she said nothing. She was quiet for a long time. And I said, "Mama, don't you worry about nothing. I'll be writing all the time, and you be getting the checks. . . ."

"I want to talk to you about your brother," she said, suddenly. "If anything happens to me he ain't going to have nobody to look out for him."

"Mama," I said, "ain't nothing going to happen to you *or* Sonny. Sonny's all right. He's a good boy and he's got good sense."

"It ain't a question of his being a good boy," Mama said, "nor of his having good sense. It ain't only the bad ones, nor yet the dumb ones that gets sucked under." She stopped, looking at me. "Your Daddy once had a brother," she said, and she smiled in a way that made me feel she was in pain. "You didn't never know that, did you?"

"No," I said, "I never knew that," and I watched her face.

"Oh, yes," she said, "your Daddy had a brother." She looked out of the window again. "I know you never saw your Daddy cry. But I did —many a time, through all these years."

I asked her, "What happened to his brother? How come nobody's ever talked about him?"

This was the first time I ever saw my mother look old.

"His brother got killed," she said, "when he was just a little younger than you are now. I knew him. He was a fine boy. He was maybe a little full of the devil, but he didn't mean nobody no harm."

Then she stopped and the room was silent, exactly as it had sometimes been on those Sunday afternoons. Mama kept looking out into the streets.

"He used to have a job in the mill," she said, "and, like all young folks, he just liked to perform on Saturday nights. Saturday nights, him and your father would drift around to different place, go to dances and things like that, or just sit around with people they knew, and your father's brother would sing, he had a fine voice, and play along with himself on his guitar. Well, this particular Saturday night, him and your father was coming home from some place, and they were both a little drunk and there was a moon that night, it was bright like day. Your father's brother was feeling kind of good, and he was whistling to himself, and he had his guitar slung over his shoulder. They was coming down a hill and beneath them was a road that turned off from the highway. Well, your father's brother, being always kind of frisky, decided to run down this hill, and he did, with that guitar banging and clanging behind him, and he ran across the road, and he was making water behind a tree. And your father was sort of amused at him and he was still coming down the hill, kind of slow. Then he heard a car motor and that same minute his brother stepped from behind the tree, into the road, in the moonlight. And he started to cross the road. And your father started to run down the hill, he says he don't know why. This car was full of white men. They was all drunk, and when they seen your father's brother they let out a great whoop and holler and they aimed the car straight at him. They was having fun, they just wanted to scare him, the way they do sometimes, you know. But they was drunk. And I guess the boy, being drunk, too, and scared, kind of lost his head. By the time he jumped it was too late. Your father says he heard his brother scream when the car rolled over him, and he heard the wood of that guitar when it give, and he heard them strings go flying, and he heard them white men shouting, and the car kept on a-going and it ain't stopped till this day. And, time your father got down the hill, his brother weren't nothing but blood and pulp."

Tears were gleaming on my mother's face. There wasn't anything I could say.

"He never mentioned it," she said, "because I never let him mention it before you children. Your Daddy was like a crazy man that night and for many a night thereafter. He says he never in his life seen anything as dark as that road after the lights of that car had gone away. Weren't nothing, weren't nobody on that road, just your Daddy and his brother and that busted guitar. Oh, yes. Your Daddy never did really get right again. Till the day he died he weren't sure but that every white man he saw was the man that killed his brother."

She stopped and took out her handkerchief and dried her eyes and looked at me.

"I ain't telling you all this," she said, "to make you scared or bitter or to make you hate nobody. I'm telling you this because you got a brother. And the world ain't changed."

I guess I didn't want to believe this. I guess she saw this in my face. She turned away from me, toward the window again, searching those streets.

"But I praise my Redeemer," she said at last, "that He called your Daddy home before me. I ain't saying it to throw no flowers at myself, but, I declare, it keeps me from feeling too cast down to know I helped your father get safely through this world. Your father always acted like he was the roughest, strongest man on earth. And everybody took him to be like that. But if he hadn't had *me* there—to see his tears!"

She was crying again. Still, I couldn't move. I said, "Lord, Lord, Mama, I didn't know it was like that."

"Oh, honey," she said, "there's a lot that you don't know. But you are going to find out." She stood up from the window and came over to me. "You got to hold on to your brother," she said, "and don't let him fall, no matter what it looks like is happening to him and no matter how evil you gets with him. You going to be evil with him many a time. But don't you forget what I told you, you hear?"

"I won't forget," I said. "Don't you worry, I won't forget. I won't let nothing happen to Sonny."

My mother smiled as though she were amused at something she saw in my face. Then, "You may not be able to stop nothing from happening. But you got to let him know you's *there*."

Two days later I was married, and then I was gone. And I had a lot of things on my mind and I pretty well forgot my promise to Mama until I got shipped home on a special furlough for her funeral.

And, after the funeral, with just Sonny and me alone in the empty kitchen, I tried to find out something about him.

"What do you want to do?" I asked him.

"I'm going to be a musician," he said.

For he had graduated, in the time I had been away, from dancing to the juke box to finding out who was playing what, and what they were doing with it, and he had bought himself a set of drums.

"You mean, you want to be a drummer?" I somehow had the feeling that being a drummer might be all right for other people but not for my brother Sonny.

"I don't think," he said, looking at me very gravely, "that I'll ever be a good drummer. But I think I can play a piano."

I frowned. I'd never played the role of the older brother quite so seriously before, had scarcely ever, in fact, *asked* Sonny a damn thing. I sensed myself in the presence of something I didn't really know how to handle, didn't understand. So I made my frown a little deeper as I asked: "What kind of musician do you want to be?"

He grinned. "How many kinds do you think there are?"

"Be *serious*," I said.

He laughed, throwing his head back, and then looked at me. "I *am* serious."

"Well, then, for Christ's sake, stop kidding around and answer a serious question. I mean, do you want to be a concert pianist, you want to play classical music and all that, or—or what?" Long before I finished he was laughing again. "For Christ's *sake*, Sonny!"

He sobered, but with difficulty. "I'm sorry. But you sound so— *scared!*" and he was off again.

"Well, you may think it's funny now, baby, but it's not going to be so funny when you have to make your living at it, let me tell you *that*." I was furious because I knew he was laughing at me and I didn't know why.

"No," he said, very sober now, and afraid, perhaps, that he'd hurt me, "I don't want to be a classical pianist. That isn't what interests me. I mean"—he paused, looking hard at me, as though his eyes would help me to understand, and then gestured helplessly, as though perhaps his hand would help—"I mean, I'll have a lot of studying to do, and I'll have to study *everything*, but, I mean, I want to play *with*—jazz musicians." He stopped. "I want to play jazz," he said.

Well, the word had never before sounded as heavy, as real, as it sounded that afternoon in Sonny's mouth. I just looked at him and I was probably frowning a real frown by this time. I simply couldn't see why on earth he'd want to spend his time hanging around nightclubs, clowning around on bandstands, while people pushed each other

around a dance floor. It seemed—beneath him, somehow. I had never
thought about it before, had never been forced to, but I suppose I
had always put jazz musicians in a class with what Daddy called
"good-time people."

"Are you *serious?*"

"Hell, *yes,* I'm serious."

He looked more helpless than ever, and annoyed, and deeply hurt.

I suggested, helpfully: "You mean—like Louis Armstrong?"

His face closed as though I'd struck him. "No. I'm not talking about
none of that old-time, down home crap."

"Well, look, Sonny, I'm sorry, don't get mad. I just don't altogether
get it, that's all. Name somebody—you know, a jazz musician you admire."

"Bird."

"Who?"

"Bird! Charlie Parker![4] Don't they teach you nothing in the goddamn army?"

I lit a cigarette. I was surprised and then a little amused to discover
that I was trembling. "I've been out of touch," I said. "You'll have to
be patient with me. Now. Who's this Parker character?"

"He's just one of the greatest jazz musicians alive," said Sonny,
sullenly, his hands in his pockets, his back to me. "Maybe *the* greatest,"
he added, bitterly, "that's probably why *you* never heard of him."

"All right," I said, "I'm ignorant. I'm sorry. I'll go out and buy all
the cat's records right away, all right?"

"It don't," said Sonny, with dignity, "make any difference to me. I
don't care what you listen to. Don't do me no favors."

I was beginning to realize that I'd never seen him so upset before.
With another part of my mind I was thinking that this would probably
turn out to be one of those things kids go through and that I shouldn't
make it seem important by pushing it too hard. Still, I didn't think it
would do any harm to ask: "Doesn't all this take a lot of time? Can you
make a living at it?"

He turned back to me and half leaned, half sat, on the kitchen table.
"Everything takes time," he said, "and—well, yes, sure, I can make a
living at it. But what I don't seem to be able to make you understand is
that it's the only thing I want to do."

"Well, Sonny," I said, gently, "you know people can't always do
exactly what they *want* to do—"

"*No,* I don't know that," said Sonny, surprising me. "I think people
ought to do what they want to do, what else are they alive for?"

"You getting to be a big boy," I said desperately, "it's time you
started thinking about your future."

"I'm thinking about my future," said Sonny, grimly. "I think about it
all the time."

I gave up. I decided, if he didn't change his mind, that we could
always talk about it later. "In the meantime," I said, "you got to
finish school." We had already decided that he'd have to move in with

4. Charlie ("Bird") Parker (1920–1955), for whom Birdland in New York was named, perhaps the greatest saxophonist and innovator of jazz; cofounder, with Dizzy Gillespie, of the new jazz, once called "bebop"; narcotics addict.

Isabel and her folks. I knew this wasn't the ideal arrangement because Isabel's folks are inclined to be dicty[5] and they hadn't especially wanted Isabel to marry me. But I didn't know what else to do. "And we have to get you fixed up at Isabel's."

There was a long silence. He moved from the kitchen table to the window. "That's a terrible idea. You know it yourself."

"Do you have a *better* idea?"

He just walked up and down the kitchen for a minute. He was as tall as I was. He had started to shave. I suddenly had the feeling that I didn't know him at all.

He stopped at the kitchen table and picked up my cigarettes. Looking at me with a kind of mocking, amused defiance, he put one between his lips. "You mind?"

"You smoking already?"

He lit the cigarette and nodded, watching me through the smoke. "I just wanted to see if I'd have the courage to smoke in front of you." He grinned and blew a great cloud of smoke to the ceiling. "It was easy." He looked at my face. "Come on, now. I bet you was smoking at my age, tell the truth."

I didn't say anything but the truth was on my face, and he laughed. But now there was something very strained in his laugh. "Sure. And I bet that ain't all you was doing."

He was frightening me a little. "Cut the crap," I said. "We already decided that you was going to go and live at Isabel's. Now what's got into you all of a sudden?"

"*You* decided it," he pointed out. "*I* didn't decide nothing." He stopped in front of me, leaning against the stove, arms loosely folded. "Look, brother. I don't want to stay in Harlem no more, I really don't." He was very earnest. He looked at me, then over toward the kitchen window. There was something in his eyes I'd never seen before, some thoughtfulness, some worry all his own. He rubbed the muscle of one arm. "It's time I was getting out of here."

"Where do you want to *go*, Sonny?"

"I want to join the army. Or the navy, I don't care. If I say I'm old enough, they'll believe me."

Then I got mad. It was because I was so scared. "You must be crazy. You goddamn fool, what the hell do you want to go and join the *army* for?"

"I just told you. To get out of Harlem."

"Sonny, you haven't even finished *school*. And if you really want to be a musician, how do you expect to study if you're in the *army*?"

He looked at me, trapped, and in anguish. "There's ways. I might be able to work out some kind of deal. Anyway, I'll have the G.I. Bill when I come out."

"*If* you come out." We stared at each other. "Sonny, please. Be reasonable. I know the setup is far from perfect. But we got to do the best we can."

"I ain't learning nothing in school," he said. "Even when I go." He turned away from me and opened the window and threw his cigarette

5. Snobbish, bossy.

out into the narrow alley. I watched his back. "At least, I ain't learning nothing you'd want me to learn." He slammed the window so hard I thought the glass would fly out, and turned back to me. "And I'm sick of the stink of these garbage cans!"

"Sonny," I said, "I know how you feel. But if you don't finish school now, you're going to be sorry later that you didn't." I grabbed him by the shoulders. "And you only got another year. It ain't so bad. And I'll come back and I swear I'll help you do *whatever* you want to do. Just try to put up with it till I come back. Will you please do that? For me?"

He didn't answer and he wouldn't look at me.

"Sonny. You hear me?"

He pulled away. "I hear you. But you never hear anything *I* say."

I didn't know what to say to that. He looked out of the window and then back at me. "OK," he said, and sighed. "I'll try."

Then I said, trying to cheer him up a little, "They got a piano at Isabel's. You can practice on it."

And as a matter of fact, it did cheer him up for a minute. "That's right," he said to himself. "I forgot that." His face relaxed a little. But the worry, the thoughtfulness, played on it still, the way shadows play on a face which is staring into the fire.

But I thought I'd never hear the end of that piano. At first, Isabel would write me, saying how nice it was that Sonny was so serious about his music and how, as soon as he came in from school, or wherever he had been when he was supposed to be at school, he went straight to that piano and stayed there until suppertime. And, after supper, he went back to that piano and stayed there until everybody went to bed. He was at the piano all day Saturday and all day Sunday. Then he bought a record player and started playing records. He'd play one record over and over again, all day long sometimes, and he'd improvise along with it on the piano. Or he'd play one section of the record, one chord, one change, one progression, then he'd do it on the piano. Then back to the record. Then back to the piano.

Well, I really don't know how they stood it. Isabel finally confessed that it wasn't like living with a person at all, it was like living with sound. And the sound didn't make any sense to her, didn't make any sense to any of them—naturally. They began, in a way, to be afflicted by this presence that was living in their home. It was as though Sonny were some sort of god, or monster. He moved in an atmosphere which wasn't like theirs at all. They fed him and he ate, he washed himself, he walked in and out of their door; he certainly wasn't nasty or unpleasant or rude, Sonny isn't any of those things; but it was as though he were all wrapped up in some cloud, some fire, some vision all his own; and there wasn't any way to reach him.

At the same time, he wasn't really a man yet, he was still a child, and they had to watch out for him in all kinds of ways. They certainly couldn't throw him out. Neither did they dare to make a great scene about that piano because even they dimly sensed, as I sensed, from so many thousands of miles away, that Sonny was at that piano playing for his life.

But he hadn't been going to school. One day a letter came from the school board and Isabel's mother got it—there had, apparently, been other letters but Sonny had torn them up. This day, when Sonny came in, Isabel's mother showed him the letter and asked where he'd been spending his time. And she finally got it out of him that he'd been down in Greenwich Village, with musicians and other characters, in a white girl's apartment. And this scared her and she started to scream at him and what came up, once she began—though she denies it to this day—was what sacrifices they were making to give Sonny a decent home and how little he appreciated it.

Sonny didn't play the piano that day. By evening, Isabel's mother had calmed down but then there was the old man to deal with, and Isabel herself. Isabel says she did her best to be calm but she broke down and started crying. She says she just watched Sonny's face. She could tell, by watching him, what was happening with him. And what was happening was that they penetrated his cloud, they had reached him. Even if their fingers had been a thousand times more gentle than human fingers ever are, he could hardly help feeling that they had stripped him naked and were spitting on that nakedness. For he also had to see that his presence, that music, which was life or death to him, had been torture for them and that they had endured it, not at all for his sake, but only for mine. And Sonny couldn't take that. He can take it a little better today than he could then but he's still not very good at it and, frankly, I don't know anybody who is.

The silence of the next few days must have been louder than the sound of all the music ever played since time began. One morning, before she went to work, Isabel was in his room for something and she suddenly realized that all of his records were gone. And she knew for certain that he was gone. And he was. He went as far as the navy would carry him. He finally sent me a postcard from some place in Greece and that was the first I knew that Sonny was still alive. I didn't see him any more until we were both back in New York and the war had long been over.

He was a man by then, of course, but I wasn't willing to see it. He came by the house from time to time, but we fought almost every time we met. I didn't like the way he carried himself, loose and dreamlike all the time, and I didn't like his friends, and his music seemed to be merely an excuse for the life he led. It sounded just that weird and disordered.

Then we had a fight, a pretty awful fight, and I didn't see him for months. By and by I looked him up, where he was living, in a furnished room in the Village, and I tried to make it up. But there were lots of other people in the room and Sonny just lay on his bed, and he wouldn't come downstairs with me, and he treated these other people as though they were his family and I weren't. So I got mad and then he got mad, and then I told him that he might just as well be dead as live the way he was living. Then he stood up and he told me not to worry about him any more in life, that he *was* dead as far as I was concerned. Then he pushed me to the door and the other people looked on as though nothing were happening, and he slammed the door behind me. I stood in the hallway, staring at the door. I heard somebody laugh in the room and then the tears came to my eyes. I started down the steps, whistling to keep from crying, I kept whistling to myself, *You going to need me, baby, one of these cold, rainy days.*

I read about Sonny's trouble in the spring. Little Grace died in the fall. She was a beautiful little girl. But she only lived a little over two years. She died of polio and she suffered. She had a slight fever for a couple of days, but it didn't seem like anything and we just kept her in bed. And we would certainly have called the doctor, but the fever dropped, she seemed to be all right. So we thought it had just been a cold. Then, one day, she was up, playing, Isabel was in the kitchen fixing lunch for the two boys when they'd come in from school, and she heard Grace fall down in the living room. When you have a lot of children you don't always start running when one of them falls, unless they start screaming or something. And, this time, Gracie was quiet. Yet, Isabel says that when she heard that *thump* and then that silence, something happened in her to make her afraid. And she ran to the living room and there was little Grace on the floor, all twisted up, and the reason she hadn't screamed was that she couldn't get her breath. And when she did scream, it was the worst sound, Isabel says, that she'd ever heard in all her life, and she still hears it sometimes in her dreams. Isabel will sometimes wake me up with a low, moaning, strangled sound and I have to be quick to awaken her and hold her to me and where Isabel is weeping against me seems a mortal wound.

I think I may have written Sonny the very day that little Grace was buried. I was sitting in the living room in the dark, by myself, and I suddenly thought of Sonny. My trouble made his real.

One Saturday afternoon, when Sonny had been living with us, or anyway, been in our house, for nearly two weeks, I found myself wandering aimlessly about the living room, drinking from a can of beer, and trying to work up courage to search Sonny's room. He was out, he was usually out whenever I was home, and Isabel had taken the children to see their grandparents. Suddenly I was standing still in front of the living room window, watching Seventh Avenue. The idea of searching Sonny's room made me still. I scarcely dared to admit to myself what I'd be searching for. I didn't know what I'd do if I found it. Or if I didn't.

On the sidewalk across from me, near the entrance to a barbecue joint, some people were holding an old-fashioned revival meeting. The barbecue cook, wearing a dirty white apron, his conked[6] hair reddish and metallic in the pale sun, and a cigarette between his lips, stood in the doorway, watching them. Kids and older people paused in their errands and stood there, along with some older men and a couple of very tough-looking women who watched everything that happened on the avenue, as though they owned it, or were maybe owned by it. Well, they were watching this, too. The revival was being carried on by three sisters in black, and a brother. All they had were their voices and their Bibles and a tambourine. The brother was testifying[7] and while he testified two of the sisters stood together, seeming to say, amen, and the third sister walked around with the tambourine outstretched and a

6. Processed: straightened and greased.   7. Publicly professing belief.

couple of people dropped coins into it. Then the brother's testimony ended and the sister who had been taking up the collection dumped the coins into her palm and transferred them to the pocket of her long black robe. Then she raised both hands, striking the tambourine against the air, and then against one hand, and she started to sing. And the two other sisters and the brother joined in.

It was strange, suddenly, to watch, though I had been seeing these meetings all my life. So, of course, had everybody else down there. Yet, they paused and watched and listened and I stood still at the window. *" 'Tis the old ship of Zion,"* they sang, and the sister with the tambourine kept a steady, jangling beat, *"it has rescued many a thousand!"* Not a soul under the sound of their voices was hearing this song for the first time, not one of them had been rescued. Nor had they seen much in the way of rescue work being done around them. Neither did they especially believe in the holiness of the three sisters and the brother, they knew too much about them, knew where they lived, and how. The woman with the tambourine, whose voice dominated the air, whose face was bright with joy, was divided by very little from the woman who stood watching her, a cigarette between her heavy, chapped lips, her hair a cuckoo's nest, her face scarred and swollen from many beatings, and her black eyes glittering like coal. Perhaps they both knew this, which was why, when, as rarely, they addressed each other, they addressed each other as Sister. As the singing filled the air the watching, listening faces underwent a change, the eyes focusing on something within; the music seemed to soothe a poison out of them; and time seemed, nearly, to fall away from the sullen, belligerent, battered faces, as though they were fleeing back to their first condition, while dreaming of their last. The barbecue cook half shook his head and smiled, and dropped his cigarette and disappeared into his joint. A man fumbled in his pockets for change and stood holding it in his hand impatiently, as though he had just remembered a pressing appointment further up the avenue. He looked furious. Then I saw Sonny, standing on the edge of the crowd. He was carrying a wide, flat notebook with a green cover, and it made him look, from where I was standing, almost like a schoolboy. The coppery sun brought out the copper in his skin, he was very faintly smiling, standing very still. Then the singing stopped, the tambourine turned into a collection plate again. The furious man dropped in his coins and vanished, so did a couple of the women, and Sonny dropped some change in the plate, looking directly at the woman with a little smile. He started across the avenue, toward the house. He has a slow, loping walk, something like the way Harlem hipsters walk, only he's imposed on this his own half-beat. I had never really noticed it before.

I stayed at the window, both relieved and apprehensive. As Sonny disappeared from my sight, they began singing again. And they were still singing when his key turned in the lock.

"Hey," he said.

"Hey, yourself. You want some beer?"

"No. Well, maybe." But he came up to the window and stood beside me, looking out. "What a warm voice," he said.

They were singing *If I could only hear my mother pray again!*

"Yes," I said, "and she can sure beat that tambourine."

"But what a terrible song," he said, and laughed. He dropped his notebook on the sofa and disappeared into the kitchen. "Where's Isabel and the kids?"

"I think they went to see their grandparents. You hungry?"

"No." He came back into the living room with his can of beer. "You want to come some place with me tonight?"

I sensed, I don't know how, that I couldn't possibly say no. "Sure. Where?"

He sat down on the sofa and picked up his notebook and started leafing through it. "I'm going to sit in with some fellows in a joint in the Village."

"You mean, you're going to play, tonight?"

"That's right." He took a swallow of his beer and moved back to the window. He gave me a sidelong look. "If you can stand it."

"I'll try," I said.

He smiled to himself and we both watched as the meeting across the way broke up. The three sisters and the brother, heads bowed, were singing *God be with you till we meet again.* The faces around them were very quiet. Then the song ended. The small crowd dispersed. We watched the three women and the lone man walk slowly up the avenue.

"When she was singing before," said Sonny, abruptly, "her voice reminded me for a minute of what heroin feels like sometimes—when it's in your veins. It makes you feel sort of warm and cool at the same time. And distant. And—and sure." He sipped his beer, very deliberately not looking at me. I watched his face. "It makes you feel—in control. Sometimes you've got to have that feeling."

"Do you?" I sat down slowly in the easy chair.

"Sometimes." He went to the sofa and picked up his notebook again. "Some people do."

"In order," I asked, "to play?" And my voice was very ugly, full of contempt and anger.

"Well"—he looked at me with great, troubled eyes, as though, in fact, he hoped his eyes would tell me things he could never otherwise say—"they *think* so. And if they think so—!"

"And what do *you* think?" I asked.

He sat on the sofa and put his can of beer on the floor. "I don't know," he said, and I couldn't be sure if he were answering my question or pursuing his thoughts. His face didn't tell me. "It's not so much to *play*. It's to *stand* it, to be able to make it at all. On any level." He frowned and smiled: "In order to keep from shaking to pieces."

"But these friends of yours," I said, "they seem to shake themselves to pieces pretty goddamn fast."

"Maybe." He played with the notebook. And something told me that I should curb my tongue, that Sonny was doing his best to talk, that I should listen. "But of course you only know the ones that've gone to pieces. Some don't—or at least they haven't *yet* and that's just about all *any* of us can say." He paused. "And then there are some who just live, really, in hell, and they know it and they see what's happening and they go right on. I don't know." He sighed, dropped the notebook, folded his arms. "Some guys, you can tell from the way they play, they on something *all* the time. And you can see that, well, it makes something real for them. But of course," he picked up his beer from the floor and sipped it and put the can down again, "they *want* to, too, you've got to see that. Even some of them that say they don't—*some,* not all."

"And what about you?" I asked—I couldn't help it. "What about you? Do *you* want to?"

He stood up and walked to the window and I remained silent for a long time. Then he sighed. "Me," he said. Then: "While I was downstairs before, on my way here, listening to that woman sing, it struck me all of a sudden how much suffering she must have had to go through—to sing like that. It's *repulsive* to think you have to suffer that much."

I said: "But there's no way not to suffer—is there, Sonny?"

"I believe not," he said and smiled, "but that's never stopped anyone from trying." He looked at me. "Has it?" I realized, with this mocking look, that there stood between us, forever, beyond the power of time or forgiveness, the fact that I had held silence—so long!—when he had needed human speech to help him. He turned back to the window. "No, there's no way not to suffer. But you try all kinds of ways to keep from drowning in it, to keep on top of it, and to make it seem—well, like *you.* Like you did something, all right, and now you're suffering for it. You know?" I said nothing. "Well you know," he said, impatiently, "why *do* people suffer? Maybe it's better to do something to give it a reason, *any* reason."

"But we just agreed," I said, "that there's no way not to suffer. Isn't it better, then, just to—take it?"

"But nobody just takes it," Sonny cried, "that's what I'm telling you! *Everybody* tries not to. You're just hung up on the *way* some people try—it's not *your* way!"

The hair on my face began to itch, my face felt wet. "That's not true," I said, "that's not true. I don't give a damn what other people do, I don't even care how they suffer. I just care how *you* suffer." And he looked at me. "Please believe me," I said, "I don't want to see you— die—trying not to suffer."

"I won't," he said flatly, "die trying not to suffer. At least, not any faster than anybody else."

"But there's no need," I said, trying to laugh, "is there? in killing yourself."

I wanted to say more, but I couldn't. I wanted to talk about will power and how life could be—well, beautiful. I wanted to say that it was all within; but was it? or, rather, wasn't that exactly the trouble? And I wanted to promise that I would never fail him again. But it would all have sounded—empty words and lies.

So I made the promise to myself and prayed that I would keep it.

"It's terrible sometimes, inside," he said, "that's what's the trouble. You walk these streets, black and funky and cold, and there's not really a living ass to talk to, and there's nothing shaking, and there's no way of getting it out—that storm inside. You can't talk it and you can't make love with it, and when you finally try to get with it and play it, you realize *nobody's* listening. So *you've* got to listen. You got to find a way to listen."

And then he walked away from the window and sat on the sofa again, as though all the wind had suddenly been knocked out of him. "Sometimes you'll do *anything* to play, even cut your mother's throat." He laughed and looked at me. "Or your brother's." Then he sobered. "Or your own." Then: "Don't worry. I'm all right now and I think I'll *be* all right. But I can't forget—where I've been. I don't mean just the physical place I've been, I mean where I've *been*. And *what* I've been."

"What have you been, Sonny?" I asked.

He smiled—but sat sideways on the sofa, his elbow resting on the back, his fingers playing with his mouth and chin, not looking at me. "I've been something I didn't recognize, didn't know I could be. Didn't know anybody could be." He stopped, looking inward, looking help-lessly young, looking old. "I'm not talking about it now because I feel *guilty* or anything like that—maybe it would be better if I did, I don't know. Anyway, I can't really talk about it. Not to you, not to anybody," and now he turned and faced me. "Sometimes, you know, and it was ac-tually when I was most *out* of the world, I felt that I was in it, that I was *with* it, really, and I could play or I didn't really have to *play*, it just came out of me, it was there. And I don't know how I played, thinking about it now, but I know I did awful things, those times, sometimes, to people. Or it wasn't that I *did* anything to them—it was that they weren't real." He picked up the beer can; it was empty; he rolled it between his palms: "And other times—well, I needed a fix, I needed to find a place to lean, I needed to clear a space to *listen*—and I couldn't find it, and I—went crazy, I did terrible things to *me*, I was terrible *for* me." He began pressing the beer can between his hands, I watched the metal begin to give. It glittered, as he played with it like a knife, and I was afraid he would cut himself, but I said nothing. "Oh well. I can never tell you. I was all by myself at the bottom of some-thing, stinking and sweating and crying and shaking, and I smelled it, you know? *my* stink, and I thought I'd die if I couldn't get away from it and yet, all the same, I knew that everything I was doing was just locking me in with it. And I didn't know," he paused, still flattening the beer can, "I didn't know, I still *don't* know, something kept telling me that maybe it was good to smell your own stink, but I didn't think that *that* was what I'd been trying to do—and—who can stand it?" and he abruptly dropped the ruined beer can, looking at me with a small, still smile, and then rose, walking to the window as though it were the lodestone rock. I watched his face, he watched the avenue. "I couldn't tell you when Mama died—but the reason I wanted to leave Harlem so bad was to get away from drugs. And then, when I ran away, that's what I was running from—really. When I came back, noth-ing had changed, *I* hadn't changed, I was just—older." And he stopped, drumming with his fingers on the windowpane. The sun had vanished, soon darkness would fall. I watched his face. "It can come again," he said, almost as though speaking to himself. Then he turned to me. "It can come again," he repeated. "I just want you to know that."

"All right," I said, at last. "So it can come again. All right."

He smiled, but the smile was sorrowful. "I had to try to tell you," he said.

"Yes," I said. "I understand that."

"You're my brother," he said, looking straight at me, and not smiling at all.

"Yes," I repeated, "yes. I understand that."

He turned back to the window, looking out. "All that hatred down there," he said, "all that hatred and misery and love. It's a wonder it doesn't blow the avenue apart."

We went to the only nightclub on a short, dark street, downtown. We squeezed through the narrow, chattering, jampacked bar to the entrance of the big room, where the bandstand was. And we stood there for a moment, for the lights were very dim in this room and we couldn't see. Then, "Hello, boy," said a voice and an enormous black man, much older than Sonny or myself, erupted out of all that atmospheric lighting and put an arm around Sonny's shoulder. "I been sitting right here," he said, "waiting for you."

He had a big voice, too, and heads in the darkness turned toward us.

Sonny grinned and pulled a little away, and said, "Creole, this is my brother. I told you about him."

Creole shook my hand. "I'm glad to meet you, son," he said, and it was clear that he was glad to meet me *there,* for Sonny's sake. And he smiled, "You got a real musician in *your* family," and he took his arm from Sonny's shoulder and slapped him, lightly, affectionately, with the back of his hand.

"Well. Now I've heard it all," said a voice behind us. This was another musician, and a friend of Sonny's, a coal-black, cheerful-looking man, built close to the ground. He immediately began confiding to me, at the top of his lungs, the most terrible things about Sonny, his teeth gleaming like a lighthouse and his laugh coming up out of him like the beginning of an earthquake. And it turned out that everyone at the bar knew Sonny, or almost everyone; some were musicians, working there, or nearby, or not working, some were simply hangers-on, and some were there to hear Sonny play. I was introduced to all of them and they were all very polite to me. Yet, it was clear that, for them, I was only Sonny's brother. Here, I was in Sonny's world. Or, rather: his kingdom. Here, it was not even a question that his veins bore royal blood.

They were going to play soon and Creole installed me, by myself, at a table in a dark corner. Then I watched them, Creole, and the little black man, and Sonny, and the others, while they horsed around, standing just below the bandstand. The light from the bandstand spilled just a little short of them and, watching them laughing and gesturing and moving about, I had the feeling that they, nevertheless, were being most careful not to step into that circle of light too suddenly: that if they moved into the light too suddenly, without thinking, they would perish in flame. Then, while I watched, one of them, the small black man, moved into the light and crossed the bandstand and started fooling around with his drums. Then—being funny and being, also, extremely ceremonious—Creole took Sonny by the arm and led him to the piano. A woman's voice called Sonny's name and a few hands started clapping. And Sonny, also being funny and being ceremonious, and so touched, I think, that he could have cried, but neither hiding it nor showing it, riding it like a man, grinned, and put both hands to his heart and bowed from the waist.

Creole then went to the bass fiddle and a lean, very bright-skinned brown man jumped up on the bandstand and picked up his horn. So there they were, and the atmosphere on the bandstand and in the room began to change and tighten. Someone stepped up to the microphone and announced them. Then there were all kinds of murmurs. Some people at the bar shushed others. The waitress ran around, frantically getting in the last orders, guys and chicks got closer to each other, and the lights on the bandstand, on the quartet, turned to a kind of indigo. Then they all looked different there. Creole looked about him for the last time, as though he were making certain that all his chickens were in the coop, and then he—jumped and struck the fiddle. And there they were.

All I know about music is that not many people ever really hear it. And even then, on the rare occasions when something opens within, and the music enters, what we mainly hear, or hear corroborated, are personal, private, vanishing evocations. But the man who creates the music is hearing something else, is dealing with the roar rising from the void and imposing order on it as it hits the air. What is evoked in him, then, is of another order, more terrible because it has no words, and triumphant, too, for that same reason. And his triumph, when he triumphs, is ours. I just watched Sonny's face. His face was troubled, he was working hard, but he wasn't with it. And I had the feeling that, in a way, everyone on the bandstand was waiting for him, both waiting for him and pushing him along. But as I began to watch Creole, I realized that it was Creole who held them all back. He had them on a short rein. Up there, keeping the beat with his whole body, wailing on the fiddle, with his eyes half closed, he was listening to everything, but he was listening to Sonny. He was having a dialogue with Sonny. He wanted Sonny to leave the shoreline and strike out for the deep water. He was Sonny's witness that deep water and drowning were not the same thing—he had been there, and he knew. And he wanted Sonny to know. He was waiting for Sonny to do the things on the keys which would let Creole know that Sonny was in the water.

And, while Creole listened, Sonny moved, deep within, exactly like someone in torment. I had never before thought of how awful the relationship must be between the musician and his instrument. He has to fill it, this instrument, with the breath of life, his own. He has to make it do what he wants it to do. And a piano is just a piano. It's made out of so much wood and wires and little hammers and big ones, and ivory. While there's only so much you can do with it, the only way to find this out is to try; to try and make it do everything.

And Sonny hadn't been near a piano for over a year. And he wasn't on much better terms with his life, not the life that stretched before him now. He and the piano stammered, started one way, got scared, stopped; started another way, panicked, marked time, started again; then seemed to have found a direction, panicked again, got stuck.

And the face I saw on Sonny I'd never seen before. Everything had been burned out of it, and, at the same time, things usually hidden were being burned in, by the fire and fury of the battle which was occurring in him up there.

Yet, watching Creole's face as they neared the end of the first set, I had the feeling that something had happened, something I hadn't heard. Then they finished, there was scattered applause, and then, without an instant's warning, Creole started into something else, it was almost sardonic, it was *Am I Blue*.[8] And, as though he commanded, Sonny began to play. Something began to happen. And Creole let out the reins. The dry, low, black man said something awful on the drums, Creole answered, and the drums talked back. Then the horn insisted, sweet and high, slightly detached perhaps, and Creole listened, commenting now and then, dry, and driving, beautiful and calm and old. Then they all came together again, and Sonny was part of the family again. I could tell this from his face. He seemed to have found, right there beneath his fingers, a damn brand-new piano. It seemed that he couldn't get over it. Then, for a while, just being happy with Sonny, they seemed to be agreeing with him that brand-new pianos certainly were a gas.

Then Creole stepped forward to remind them that what they were playing was the blues. He hit something in all of them, he hit something in me, myself, and the music tightened and deepened, apprehension began to beat the air. Creole began to tell us what the blues were all about. They were not about anything very new. He and his boys up there were keeping it new, at the risk of ruin, destruction, madness, and death, in order to find new ways to make us listen. For, while the tale of how we suffer, and how we are delighted, and how we may triumph is never new, it always must be heard. There isn't any other tale to tell, it's the only light we've got in all this darkness.

And this tale, according to that face, that body, those strong hands on those strings, has another aspect in every country, and a new depth in every generation. Listen, Creole seemed to be saying, listen. Now these are Sonny's blues. He made the little black man on the drums know it, and the bright, brown man on the horn. Creole wasn't trying any longer to get Sonny in the water. He was wishing him Godspeed. Then he stepped back, very slowly, filling the air with the immense suggestion that Sonny speak for himself.

Then they all gathered around Sonny and Sonny played. Every now and again one of them seemed to say, amen. Sonny's fingers filled the air with life, his life. But that life contained so many others. And Sonny went all the way back, he really began with the spare, flat statement of the opening phrase of the song. Then he began to make it his. It was very beautiful because it wasn't hurried and it was no longer a lament. I seemed to hear with what burning he had made it his, with what burning we had yet to make it ours, how we could cease lamenting. Freedom lurked around us and I understood, at last, that he could help us to be free if we would listen, that he would never be free until

8. By Grant Clark and Harry Akst, sung by Ethel Waters in 1929 film, "On with the Show," brilliantly recorded by Billy Holiday, and a favorite blues piece.

we did. Yet, there was no battle in his face now, I heard what he had
gone through, and would continue to go through until he came to rest
in earth. He had made it his: that long line, of which we knew only
Mama and Daddy. And he was giving it back, as everything must be
given back, so that, passing through death, it can live forever. I saw
my mother's face again, and felt, for the first time, how the stones of
the road she had walked on must have bruised her feet. I saw the
moonlit road where my father's brother died. And it brought something else back to me, and carried me past it, I saw my little girl again
and felt Isabel's tears again, and I felt my own tears begin to rise. And
I was yet aware that this was only a moment, that the world waited
outside, as hungry as a tiger, and that trouble stretched above us,
longer than the sky.

Then it was over. Creole and Sonny let out their breath, both soaking wet, and grinning. There was a lot of applause and some of it was
real. In the dark, the girl came by and I asked her to take drinks to
the bandstand. There was a long pause, while they talked up there in
the indigo light and after awhile I saw the girl put a Scotch and milk
on top of the piano for Sonny. He didn't seem to notice it, but just
before they started playing again, he sipped from it and looked
toward me, and nodded. Then he put it back on top of the piano. For
me, then, as they began to play again, it glowed and shook above my
brother's head like the very cup of trembling.[9]

1965

9. See *Isaiah* 51:17, 22–23: "Awake,
awake, stand up, O Jerusalem, which hast
drunk at the hand of the Lord the cup of
his fury; thou hast drunken the dregs of
the cup of trembling, and wrung them
out. . . . Behold, I have taken out of thine
hand the cup of trembling, even the dregs
of the cup of my fury; thou shalt no more
drink it again: But I will put it into the
hands of them that afflict thee; . . . ."

9   A KIND: INITIATION

Themes are useful for grouping stories together for comparison, both to highlight similarities and to reveal differences in history and structure and so to discover the uniqueness of the work. Types of characters—stereotypes—are useful for the same purpose: to show both the common qualities and the unique combination of qualities in a particular character in a story. Though all grouping and classification, used poorly, can blur distinctions and make all members of a group seem the same, when used well they do not blur but bring into focus the individuality of the individual thing or being.

Literary criticism lacks the specific and agreed-on system of classification of biology, so that its terms are not so fixed as *phylum, genus, species,* even in the editors' own usage. In general, we use the term **genre** for the largest commonly agreed-on categories: fiction, poetry, drama, When I'm trying to be consistent, I use the term **subgenre** for the divisions of fiction—novel, novella, short story, etc. A **kind** is a species or subcategory within a subgenre.

There is one kind of short story that is so common that there are those who maintain it is not a kind but is equivalent to the subgenre short story itself. That pervasive kind is the **initiation** story, in which a character—often but not always a child or young person—first learns a significant, even life-determining, truth about the universe, about reality, about society, about people or a person, or about himself or herself. Such a subject tends to dictate the main outlines of the action of the story: it begins with the protagonist in a state of innocence or mistaken belief (exposition); it leads up to the moment of illumination or the discovery of the truth (rising action to climax or turning point), and ends usually with some indication of the result of that discovery (falling action to conclusion). This kind is particularly suitable to a short story because it lends itself to brief treatment: the illumination is more or less sudden—there is no need for lengthy development, for multiple scenes or settings, for much time to pass, for too many complications of action or a large cast of characters— yet it can encapsulate a whole life or important segment of a life and wide-ranging, significant themes.

If you've been reading this anthology from the beginning, you have already run into a number of initiation stories, and you may have some idea of what kinds of truths their protagonists discover. Young Goodman Brown discovers the universality of evil in human beings. Nelson Head (*The Artificial Nigger*) discovers the ubiquity of evil in the world outside his Edenic rural home, while his grandfather—not a young person, but described as having a youthful expression and looking more like Nelson's brother than his grandfather—learns of his own capacity for evil. Leila (*Her First Ball*) comes across the truth that youth is fleeting (you cannot say she really learns it, since by the end of that very short story she has forgotten it). We have also seen that one may retreat from the truth physically or psychologically, as do Brown and Nelson, or remain unchanged or revert to one's former state, as Leila does.

Since to the young all things seem possible—one can be a doctor, novelist, tennis star, saint, and swinger, serially or simultaneously—many of the truths learned in initiation stories have to do with limitation. The girl in *Boys and Girls* learns that she is "only a girl." Fortunately, growing up is not just loss, and there are positive or "happy" initiation stories. The boy in *The Old People* is initiated first into "manhood," and takes his place among "the hunters," and then into a more exclusive, privileged fraternity, that of the owners or, as Faulkner would no doubt prefer it, "custodians" of the land.

Sometimes, the initiation takes place as an unscheduled event, as in *Araby*. At other times there is a scheduled event, a ritual or **rite of passage,** such as a formal entry into society (*Her First Ball*). What do we usually think of as the purpose of a debut? How does the society intend to induct its new member? As you read *Her First Ball*, think about these questions and watch how Leila's debut fulfills its ritual role, how it differs from it, and how it may induct Leila into society more truly than intended. The ritual in *The Old People* is formal, communal, and ceremonial. The formalities of the rite in this story may bring to the surface elements in the pattern that lie beneath the surface in other stories.

By the time you finish this chapter you should have some idea of the variations possible within the initiation story, and as you go on to read such stories as *Flowering Judas* or the short novel *Heart of Darkness* and think back over *The Horse Dealer's Daughter* and *Macomber*, you should have a still better idea of the range of stories in this kind. Adults may be initiated as well as children and adolescents; the truths may be bitter or pleasing, cosmic, social, psychological; the initiates may change forever, retreat, shrug off what they have learned. By seeing all these stories as part of the large group of initiation stories you may the more readily notice the differences in the protagonists, in the learning experience, in the results of the initiation on the protagonists and whether they are permanent or temporary, life-denying or life-enhancing. You may, in other words, have gone a long way toward defining the unique vision of the story, its precise and individual illumination of reality. And that's the function of classification in the first place.

JAMES JOYCE

Araby

North Richmond Street, being blind,[1] was a quiet street except at the hour when the Christian Brothers'[2] School set the boys free. An uninhabited house of two stories stood at the blind end, detached from its neighbors in a square ground. The other houses of the street,

1. Dead-end street. The story takes place in Dublin.　　2. Conservative Irish lay order.

conscious of decent lives within them, gazed at one another with brown imperturbable faces.

The former tenant of our house, a priest, had died in the back drawing room. Air, musty from having been long enclosed, hung in all the rooms, and the waste room behind the kitchen was littered with old useless papers. Among these I found a few paper-covered books, the pages of which were curled and damp: *The Abbot,* by Walter Scott, *The Devout Communicant* and *The Memoirs of Vidocq.*[3] I liked the last best because its leaves were yellow. The wild garden behind the house contained a central apple tree and a few straggling bushes under one of which I found the late tenant's rusty bicycle pump. He had been a very charitable priest; in his will he had left all his money to institutions and the furniture of his house to his sister.

When the short days of winter came dusk fell before we had well eaten our dinners. When we met in the street the houses had grown somber. The space of sky above us was the color of ever-changing violet and towards it the lamps of the street lifted their feeble lanterns. The cold air stung us and we played till our bodies glowed. Our shouts echoed in the silent street. The career of our play brought us through the dark muddy lanes behind the houses where we ran the gantlet of the rough tribes from the cottages, to the back doors of the dark dripping gardens where odors arose from the ashpits,[4] to the dark odorous stables where a coachman smoothed and combed the horse or shook music from the buckled harness. When we returned to the street light from the kitchen windows had filled the areas. If my uncle was seen turning the corner we hid in the shadow until we had seen him safely housed. Or if Mangan's sister came out on the doorstep to call her brother in to his tea we watched her from our shadow peer up and down the street. We waited to see whether she would remain or go in and, if she remained, we left our shadow and walked up to Mangan's steps resignedly. She was waiting for us, her figure defined by the light from the half-opened door. Her brother always teased her before he obeyed and I stood by the railings looking at her. Her dress swung as she moved her body and the soft rope of her hair tossed from side to side.

Every morning I lay on the floor in the front parlor watching her door. The blind was pulled down to within an inch of the sash so that I could not be seen. When she came out on the doorstep my heart leaped. I ran to the hall, seized my books and followed her. I kept her brown figure always in my eye and, when we came near the point at which our ways diverged, I quickened my pace and passed her. This happened morning after morning. I had never spoken to her, except for a few casual words, and yet her name was like a summons to all my foolish blood.

Her image accompanied me even in places the most hostile to romance. On Saturday evenings when my aunt went marketing I had

---

3. The 1820 novel by Sir Walter Scott (1771–1834) is a romance about the Catholic Mary Queen of Scots (1542–87), who was beheaded; a Catholic religious tract: *The Devout Communicant: or Pious Meditations and Aspirations for the Three Days Before and Three Days After Receiv-* ing the Holy Eucharist (1813); François Vidocq (1775–1857), a French criminal who became chief of detectives, who died poor and disgraced for his part in a crime that he solved, and who probably did not write the book called his memoirs.

4. Where fireplace ashes were dumped.

to go to carry some of the parcels. We walked through the flaring
streets, jostled by drunken men and bargaining women, amid the
curses of laborers, the shrill litanies of shop-boys who stood on guard
by the barrels of pigs' cheeks, the nasal chanting of street-singers, who
sang a *come-all-you* about O'Donovan Rossa,[5] or a ballad about the
troubles in our native land. These noises converged in a single sensation of life for me: I imagined that I bore my chalice safely through
a throng of foes. Her name sprang to my lips at moments in strange
prayers and praises which I myself did not understand. My eyes were
often full of tears (I could not tell why) and at times a flood from
my heart seemed to pour itself out into my bosom. I thought little
of the future. I did not know whether I would ever speak to her or
not or, if I spoke to her, how I could tell her of my confused adoration. But my body was like a harp and her words and gestures were
like fingers running upon the wires.

One evening I went into the back drawing room in which the
priest had died. It was a dark rainy evening and there was no sound
in the house. Through one of the broken panes I heard the rain im-
pinge upon the earth, the fine incessant needles of water playing
in the sodden beds. Some distant lamp or lighted window gleamed
below me. I was thankful that I could see so little. All my senses
seemed to desire to veil themselves and, feeling that I was about
to slip from them, I pressed the palms of my hands together until
they trembled, murmuring: *O love! O love!* many times.

At last she spoke to me. When she addressed the first words to me
I was so confused that I did not know what to answer. She asked me
was I going to *Araby*.[6] I forget whether I answered yes or no. It
would be a splendid bazaar, she said; she would love to go.

—And why can't you? I asked.

While she spoke she turned a silver bracelet round and round her
wrist. She could not go, she said, because there would be a retreat
that week in her convent. Her brother and two other boys were
fighting for their caps and I was alone at the railings. She held one
of the spikes, bowing her head towards me. The light from the lamp
opposite our door caught the white curve of her neck, lit up her
hair that rested there and, falling, lit up the hand upon the railing.
It fell over one side of her dress and caught the white border of a
petticoat, just visible as she stood at ease.

—It's well for you, she said.

—If I go, I said, I will bring you something.

What innumerable follies laid waste my waking and sleeping
thoughts after that evening! I wished to annihilate the tedious intervening days. I chafed against the work of school. At night in my bedroom and by day in the classroom her image came between me and
the page I strove to read. The syllables of the word *Araby* were
called to me through the silence in which my soul luxuriated and

5. A song, of which there were many, which began "Come, all you Irishmen." Jeremiah ("Dynamite Rossa") O'Donovan (1831–1915) was a militant Irish nation-alist who fought on despite terms in prison and banishment.
6. A bazaar billed as a "Grand Orien-tal Fête," Dublin, May 1894.

cast an Eastern enchantment over me. I asked for leave to go to the bazaar on Saturday night. My aunt was surprised and hoped it was not some Freemason[7] affair. I answered few questions in class. I watched my master's face pass from amiability to sternness; he hoped I was not beginning to idle. I could not call my wandering thoughts together. I had hardly any patience with the serious work of life which, now that it stood between me and my desire, seemed to me child's play, ugly monotonous child's play.

On Saturday morning I reminded my uncle that I wished to go to the bazaar in the evening. He was fussing at the hallstand, looking for the hat brush, and answered me curtly:

—Yes, boy, I know.

As he was in the hall I could not go into the front parlor and lie at the window. I left the house in bad humor and walked slowly towards the school. The air was pitilessly raw and already my heart misgave me.

When I came home to dinner my uncle had not yet been home. Still it was early. I sat staring at the clock for some time and, when its ticking began to irritate me, I left the room. I mounted the staircase and gained the upper part of the house. The high cold empty gloomy rooms liberated me and I went from room to room singing. From the front window I saw my companions playing below in the street. Their cries reached me weakened and indistinct and, leaning my forehead against the cool glass, I looked over at the dark house where she lived. I may have stood there for an hour, seeing nothing but the brown-clad figure cast by my imagination, touched discreetly by the lamplight at the curved neck, at the hand upon the railings and at the border below the dress.

When I came downstairs again I found Mrs. Mercer sitting at the fire. She was an old garrulous woman, a pawnbroker's widow, who collected used stamps for some pious purpose. I had to endure the gossip of the tea-table. The meal was prolonged beyond an hour and still my uncle did not come. Mrs. Mercer stood up to go: she was sorry she couldn't wait any longer, but it was after eight o'clock and she did not like to be out late, as the night air was bad for her. When she had gone I began to walk up and down the room, clenching my fists. My aunt said:

—I'm afraid you may put off your bazaar for this night of Our Lord.

At nine o'clock I heard my uncle's latchkey in the hall door. I heard him talking to himself and heard the hall stand rocking when it had received the weight of his overcoat. I could interpret these signs. When he was midway through his dinner I asked him to give me the money to go to the bazaar. He had forgotten.

—The people are in bed and after their first sleep now, he said.

I did not smile. My aunt said to him energetically:

—Can't you give him the money and let him go? You've kept him late enough as it is.

My uncle said he was very sorry he had forgotten. He said he

---

7. The Masons, or Freemasons, were considered enemies of the Catholics.

believed in the old saying: *All work and no play makes Jack a dull boy.* He asked me where I was going and, when I had told him a second time he asked me did I know *The Arab's Farewell to His Steed.*[8] When I left the kitchen he was about to recite the opening lines of the piece to my aunt.

I held a florin[9] tightly in my hand as I strode down Buckingham Street towards the station. The sight of the streets thronged with buyers and glaring with gas recalled to me the purpose of my journey. I took my seat in a third-class carriage of a deserted train. After an intolerable delay the train moved out of the station slowly. It crept onward among ruinous houses and over the twinkling river. At Westland Row Station a crowd of people pressed to the carriage doors; but the porters moved them back, saying that it was a special train for the bazaar. I remained alone in the bare carriage. In a few minutes the train drew up beside an improvised wooden platform. I passed out on to the road and saw by the lighted dial of a clock that it was ten minutes to ten. In front of me was a large building which displayed the magical name.

I could not find any sixpenny entrance and, fearing that the bazaar would be closed, I passed in quickly through a turnstile, handing a shilling to a weary-looking man. I found myself in a big hall girdled at half its height by a gallery. Nearly all the stalls were closed and the greater part of the hall was in darkness. I recognized a silence like that which pervades a church after a service. I walked into the center of the bazaar timidly. A few people were gathered about the stalls which were still open. Before a curtain, over which the words *Café Chantant*[1] were written in colored lamps, two men were counting money on a salver. I listened to the fall of the coins.

Remembering with difficulty why I had come, I went over to one of the stalls and examined porcelain vases and flowered tea-sets. At the door of the stall a young lady was talking and laughing with two young gentlemen. I remarked their English accents[2] and listened vaguely to their conversation.

—O, I never said such a thing!

—O, but you did!

—O, but I didn't!

—Didn't she say that?

—Yes. I heard her.

—O, there's a . . . fib!

Observing me the young lady came over and asked me did I wish to buy anything. The tone of her voice was not encouraging; she seemed to have spoken to me out of a sense of duty. I looked humbly at the great jars that stood like eastern guards at either side of the dark entrance to the stall and murmured:

—No, thank you.

The young lady changed the position of one of the vases and went

---

8. Or *The Arab's Farewell to His Horse*, sentimental nineteenth-century poem by Caroline Norton. The speaker has sold the horse.

9. Two-shilling piece; thus four times the "sixpenny entrance" fee.
1. Café with music.
2. Remember, the story is set in Ireland.

back to the two young men. They began to talk of the same subject. Once or twice the young lady glanced at me over her shoulder.

I lingered before her stall, though I knew my stay was useless, to make my interest in her wares seem the more real. Then I turned away slowly and walked down the middle of the bazaar. I allowed the two pennies to fall against the sixpence in my pocket. I heard a voice call from one end of the gallery that the light was out. The upper part of the hall was now completely dark.

Gazing up into the darkness I saw myself as a creature driven and derided by vanity; and my eyes burned with anguish and anger.

1914

ALICE MUNRO

Boys and Girls

My father was a fox farmer. That is, he raised silver foxes, in pens; and in the fall and early winter, when their fur was prime, he killed them and skinned them and sold their pelts to the Hudson's Bay Company or the Montreal Fur Traders. These companies supplied us with heroic calendars to hang, one on each side of the kitchen door. Against a background of cold blue sky and black pine forests and treacherous northern rivers, plumed adventurers planted the flags of England or of France; magnificent savages bent their backs to the portage.

For several weeks before Christmas, my father worked after supper in the cellar of our house. The cellar was whitewashed, and lit by a hundred-watt bulb over the worktable. My brother Laird and I sat on the top step and watched. My father removed the pelt inside-out from the body of the fox, which looked surprisingly small, mean and rat-like, deprived of its arrogant weight of fur. The naked, slippery bodies were collected in a sack and buried at the dump. One time the hired man, Henry Bailey, had taken a swipe at me with this sack, saying, "Christmas present!" My mother thought that was not funny. In fact she disliked the whole pelting operation—that was what the killing, skinning, and preparation of the furs was called—and wished it did not have to take place in the house. There was the smell. After the pelt had been stretched inside-out on a long board my father scraped away delicately, removing the little clotted webs of blood vessels, the bubbles of fat; the smell of blood and animal fat, with the strong primitive odor of the fox itself, penetrated all parts of the house. I found it reassuringly seasonal, like the smell of oranges and pine needles.

Henry Bailey suffered from bronchial troubles. He would cough and cough until his narrow face turned scarlet, and his light blue, derisive eyes filled up with tears; then he took the lid off the stove, and, standing well back, shot out a great clot of phlegm—hsss—straight into the heart of the flames. We admired him for this performance and for his ability to make his stomach growl at will, and for his laughter, which was full of high whistlings and gurglings and involved the whole faulty machinery of his chest. It was sometimes hard to tell what he was laughing at, and always possible that it might be us.

After we had been sent to bed we could still smell fox and still hear Henry's laugh, but these things, reminders of the warm, safe, brightly lit downstairs world, seemed lost and diminished, floating on the stale cold air upstairs. We were afraid at night in the winter. We were not afraid of *outside* though this was the time of year when snowdrifts curled around our house like sleeping whales and the wind harassed us all night, coming up from the buried fields, the frozen swamp, with its old bugbear chorus of threats and misery. We were afraid of *inside,* the room where we slept. At this time the upstairs of our house was not finished. A brick chimney went up one wall. In the middle of the floor was a square hole, with a wooden railing around it; that was where the stairs came up. On the other side of the stairwell were the things that nobody had any use for any more—a soldiery roll of linoleum, standing on end, a wicker baby carriage, a fern basket, china jugs and basins with cracks in them, a picture of the Battle of Balaclava,[1] very sad to look at. I had told Laird, as soon as he was old enough to understand such things, that bats and skeletons lived over there; whenever a man escaped from the county jail, twenty miles away, I imagined that he had some-how let himself in the window and was hiding behind the linoleum. But we had rules to keep us safe. When the light was on, we were safe as long as we did not step off the square of worn carpet which defined our bedroom-space; when the light was off no place was safe but the beds themselves. I had to turn out the light kneeling on the end of my bed, and stretching as far as I could to reach the cord.

In the dark we lay on our beds, our narrow life rafts, and fixed our eyes on the faint light coming up the stairwell, and sang songs. Laird sang "Jingle Bells," which he would sing any time, whether it was Christmas or not, and I sang "Danny Boy." I loved the sound of my own voice, frail and supplicating, rising in the dark. We could make out the tall frosted shapes of the windows now, gloomy and white. When I came to the part, *When I am dead, as dead I well may be*—a fit of shivering caused not by the cold sheets but by pleasurable emotion almost silenced me. *You'll kneel and say, an Ave there above me*—What was an Ave? Every day I forgot to find out.

Laird went straight from singing to sleep. I could hear his long, satisfied, bubbly breaths. Now for the time that remained to me, the most perfectly private and perhaps the best time of the whole day, I arranged myself tightly under the covers and went on with one of the stories I was telling myself from night to night. These stories were about myself, when I had grown a little older; they took place in a world that was recognizably mine, yet one that presented oppor-

---

1. An indecisive Crimean War battle fought on October 25, 1854.

tunities for courage, boldness and self-sacrifice, as mine never did. I rescued people from a bombed building (it discouraged me that the real war had gone on so far away from Jubilee). I shot two rabid wolves who were menacing the schoolyard (the teachers cowered terrified at my back). I rode a fine horse spiritedly down the main street of Jubilee, acknowledging the townspeople's gratitude for some yet-to-be-worked-out piece of heroism (nobody ever rode a horse there, except King Billy in the Orangemen's Day[2] parade). There was always riding and shooting in these stories, though I had only been on a horse twice—bareback because we did not own a saddle— and the second time I had slid right around and dropped under the horse's feet; it had stepped placidly over me. I really was learning to shoot, but I could not hit anything yet, not even tin cans on fence posts.

Alive, the foxes inhabited a world my father made for them. It was surrounded by a high guard fence, like a medieval town, with a gate that was padlocked at night. Along the streets of this town were ranged large, sturdy pens. Each of them had a real door that a man could go through, a wooden ramp along the wire, for the foxes to run up and down on, and a kennel—something like a clothes chest with airholes—where they slept and stayed in winter and had their young. There were feeding and watering dishes attached to the wire in such a way that they could be emptied and cleaned from the outside. The dishes were made of old tin cans, and the ramps and kennels of odds and ends of old lumber. Everything was tidy and ingenious; my father was tirelessly inventive and his favorite book in the world was Robinson Crusoe.[3] He had fitted a tin drum on a wheelbarrow, for bringing water down to the pens. This was my job in summer, when the foxes had to have water twice a day. Between nine and ten o'clock in the morning, and again after supper, I filled the drum at the pump and trundled it down through the barnyard to the pens, where I parked it, and filled my watering can and went along the streets. Laird came too, with his little cream and green gardening can, filled too full and knocking against his legs and slopping water on his canvas shoes. I had the real watering can, my father's, though I could only carry it three-quarters full.

The foxes all had names, which were printed on a tin plate and hung beside their doors. They were not named when they were born, but when they survived the first year's pelting and were added to the breeding stock. Those my father had named were called names like Prince, Bob, Wally and Betty. Those I had named were called Star or Turk, or Maureen or Diana. Laird named one Maud after a hired girl we had when he was little, one Harold after a boy at school, and one Mexico, he did not say why.

Naming them did not make pets out of them, or anything like it.

2. The Orange Society is an Irish Protestant group named after William of Orange, who, as King William III of England, defeated the Catholic James II. The Society sponsors an annual procession on July 12 to commemorate the victory of William III at the Battle of the Boyne.

3. Novel (1719) by Daniel Defoe that is about a man shipwrecked on a desert island and that goes into great detail about his ingenious contraptions.

Nobody but my father ever went into the pens, and he had twice had blood-poisoning from bites. When I was bringing them their water they prowled up and down on the paths they had made inside their pens, barking seldom—they saved that for nighttime, when they might get up a chorus of community frenzy—but always watching me, their eyes burning, clear gold, in their pointed, malevolent faces. They were beautiful for their delicate legs and heavy, aristocratic tails and the bright fur sprinkled on dark down their backs—which gave them their name—but especially for their faces, drawn exquisitely sharp in pure hostility, and their golden eyes.

Besides carrying water I helped my father when he cut the long grass, and the lamb's quarter and flowering money-musk, that grew between the pens. He cut with the scythe and I raked into piles. Then he took a pitchfork and threw fresh-cut grass all over the top of the pens, to keep the foxes cooler and shade their coats, which were browned by two much sun. My father did not talk to me unless it was about the job we were doing. In this he was quite different from my mother, who, if she was feeling cheerful, would tell me all sorts of things—the name of a dog she had had when she was a little girl, the names of boys she had gone out with later on when she was grown up, and what certain dresses of hers had looked like—she could not imagine now what had become of them. Whatever thoughts and stories my father had were private, and I was shy of him and would never ask him questions. Nevertheless I worked willingly under his eyes, and with a feeling of pride. One time a feed salesman came down into the pens to talk to him and my father said, "Like to have you meet my new hired man." I turned away and raked furiously, red in the face with pleasure.

"Could of fooled me," said the salesman. "I thought it was only a girl."

After the grass was cut, it seemed suddenly much later in the year. I walked on stubble in the earlier evening, aware of the reddening skies, the entering silences, of fall. When I wheeled the tank out of the gate and put the padlock on, it was almost dark. One night at this time I saw my mother and father standing talking on the little rise of ground we called the gangway, in front of the barn. My father had just come from the meathouse; he had his stiff bloody apron on, and a pail of cut-up meat in his hand.

It was an odd thing to see my mother down at the barn. She did not often come out of the house unless it was to do something—hang out the wash or dig potatoes in the garden. She looked out of place, with her bare lumpy legs, not touched by the sun, her apron still on and damp across the stomach from the supper dishes. Her hair was tied up in a kerchief, wisps of it falling out. She would tie her hair up like this in the morning, saying she did not have time to do it properly, and it would stay tied up all day. It was true, too; she really did not have time. These days our back porch was piled with baskets of peaches and grapes and pears, bought in town, and onions and tomatoes and cucumbers grown at home, all waiting to be made into jelly and jam and preserves, pickles and chili sauce. In the kitchen there was a fire in the stove all day, jars clinked in boiling water, sometimes a cheesecloth bag was strung on a pole between two chairs straining blue-black grape pulp for jelly. I was given jobs to do and I would sit at the table peeling peaches that had been soaked in the hot water, or cutting up onions, my eyes smarting and streaming. As soon as I was done I ran out of the house, trying to get out of earshot before my mother thought of what she wanted me to do next. I hated the hot dark kitchen in summer, the green blinds and the flypapers, the same old oilcloth table and wavy mirror and bumpy linoleum. My mother was too tired and preoccupied to talk to me, she had no heart to tell about the Normal School Graduation Dance; sweat trickled over her face and she was always counting under her breath, pointing at jars, dumping cups of sugar. It seemed to me that work in the house was endless, dreary and peculiarly depressing; work done out of doors, and in my father's service, was ritualistically important.

I wheeled the tank up to the barn, where it was kept, and I heard my mother saying, "Wait till Laird gets a little bigger, then you'll have a real help."

What my father said I did not hear. I was pleased by the way he stood listening, politely as he would to a salesman or a stranger, but with an air of wanting to get on with his real work. I felt my mother had no business down here and I wanted him to feel the same way. What did she mean about Laird? He was no help to anybody. Where was he now? Swinging himself sick on the swing, going around in circles, or trying to catch caterpillars. He never once stayed with me till I was finished.

"And then I can use her more in the house," I heard my mother say. She had a dead-quiet, regretful way of talking about me that always made me uneasy. "I just get my back turned and she runs off. It's not like I had a girl in the family at all."

I went and sat on a feed bag in the corner of the barn, not wanting to appear when this conversation was going on. My mother, I felt, was not to be trusted. She was kinder than my father and more easily fooled, but you could not depend on her, and the real reasons for the things she said and did were not to be known. She loved me, and she sat up late at night making a dress of the difficult style I wanted, for me to wear when school started, but she was also my enemy. She was always plotting. She was plotting now to get me to stay in the house more, although she knew I hated it (*because* she knew I hated it) and keep me from working for my father. It seemed to me she would do this simply out of perversity, and to try her power. It did not occur to me that she could be lonely, or jealous. No grown-up could be; they were too fortunate. I sat and kicked my heels monotonously against a feed bag, raising dust, and did not come out till she was gone.

At any rate, I did not expect my father to pay any attention to what she said. Who could imagine Laird doing my work—Laird remembering the padlock and cleaning out the watering dishes with a leaf on the end of a stick, or even wheeling the tank without it tumbling over? It showed how little my mother knew about the way things really were.

I have forgotten to say what the foxes were fed. My father's bloody apron reminded me. They were fed horsemeat. At this time most farmers still kept horses, and when a horse got too old to work, or broke a leg or got down and would not get up, as they sometimes did, the owner would call my father, and he and Henry went out to the farm in the truck. Usually they shot and butchered the horse there, paying the farmer from five to twelve dollars. If they had already too much meat on hand, they would bring the horse back alive, and keep it for a few days or weeks in our stable, until the meat was needed. After the war the farmers were buying tractors and gradually getting rid of horses altogether, so it sometimes happened that we got a good healthy horse, that there was just no use for any more. If this happened in the winter we might keep the horse in our stable till spring, for we had plenty of hay and if there was a lot of snow—and the plow did not always get our road cleared—it was convenient to be able to go to town with a horse and cutter.[4]

The winter I was eleven years old we had two horses in the stable. We did not know what names they had had before, so we called them Mack and Flora. Mack was an old black workhorse, sooty and indifferent. Flora was a sorrel mare, a driver. We took them both out in the cutter. Mack was slow and easy to handle. Flora was given to fits of violent alarm, veering at cars and even at other horses, but we loved her speed and high-stepping, her general air of gallantry and abandon. On Saturdays we went down to the stable and as soon as we opened the door on its cosy, animal-smelling darkness Flora threw up her head, rolled her eyes, whinnied despairingly and pulled herself through a crisis of nerves on the spot. It was not safe to go into her stall; she would kick.

This winter also I began to hear a great deal more on the theme my mother had sounded when she had been talking in front of the barn. I no longer felt safe. It seemed that in the minds of the people around me there was a steady undercurrent of thought, not to be deflected, on this one subject. The word *girl* had formerly seemed to me innocent and unburdened, like the word *child*; now it appeared that it was no such thing. A girl was not, as I had supposed, simply what I was; it was what I had to become. It was a definition, always touched with emphasis, with reproach and disappointment. Also it was a joke on me. Once Laird and I were fighting, and for the first time ever I had to use all my strength against him; even so, he caught and pinned my arm for a moment, really hurting me. Henry saw this, and laughed, saying, "Oh, that there Laird's gonna show you, one of these days!" Laird was getting a lot bigger. But I was getting bigger too.

My grandmother came to stay with us for a few weeks and I heard other things. "Girls don't slam doors like that." "Girls keep their knees together when they sit down." And worse still, when I asked some questions, "That's none of girls' business." I continued to slam the doors and sit as awkwardly as possible, thinking that by such measures I kept myself free.

4. A small, light, one-horse sleigh.

When spring came, the horses were let out in the barnyard. Mack stood against the barn wall trying to scratch his neck and haunches, but Flora trotted up and down and reared at the fences, clattering her hooves against the rails. Snow drifts dwindled quickly, revealing the hard gray and brown earth, the familiar rise and fall of the ground, plain and bare after the fantastic landscape of winter. There was a great feeling of opening-out, of release. We just wore rubbers now, over our shoes; our feet felt ridiculously light. One Saturday we went out to the stable and found all the doors open, letting in the unaccustomed sunlight and fresh air. Henry was there, just idling around looking at his collection of calendars which were tacked up behind the stalls in a part of the stable my mother had probably never seen.

"Come to say goodbye to your old friend Mack?" Henry said. "Here, you give him a taste of oats." He poured some oats into Laird's cupped hands and Laird went to feed Mack. Mack's teeth were in bad shape. He ate very slowly, patiently shifting the oats around in his mouth, trying to find a stump of a molar to grind it on. "Poor old Mack," said Henry mournfully. "When a horse's teeth's gone, he's gone. That's about the way."

"Are you going to shoot him today?" I said. Mack and Flora had been in the stable so long I had almost forgotten they were going to be shot.

Henry didn't answer me. Instead he started to sing in a high, trembly, mocking-sorrowful voice, *Oh, there's no more work, for poor Uncle Ned, he's gone where the good darkies go.*[5] Mack's thick, blackish tongue worked diligently at Laird's hand. I went out before the song was ended and sat down on the gangway.

I had never seen them shoot a horse, but I knew where it was done. Last summer Laird and I had come upon a horse's entrails before they were buried. We had thought it was a big black snake, coiled up in the sun. That was around in the field that ran up beside the barn. I thought that if we went inside the barn, and found a wide crack or a knothole to look through, we would be able to see them do it. It was not something I wanted to see; just the same, if a thing really happened, it was better to see it, and know.

My father came down from the house, carrying the gun.

"What are you doing here?" he said.

"Nothing."

"Go on up and play around the house."

He sent Laird out of the stable. I said to Laird, "Do you want to see them shoot Mack?" and without waiting for an answer led him around to the front door of the barn, opened it carefully, and went in. "Be quiet or they'll hear us," I said. We could hear Henry and my father talking in the stable, then the heavy, shuffling steps of Mack being backed out of his stall.

In the loft it was cold and dark. Thin, crisscrossed beams of sunlight fell through the cracks. The hay was low. It was a rolling country, hills and hollows, slipping under our feet. About four feet

5. Lines from the Stephen Foster song "Old Uncle Ned."

up was a beam going around the walls. We piled hay up in one corner and I boosted Laird up and hoisted myself. The beam was not very wide; we crept along it with our hands flat on the barn walls. There were plenty of knotholes, and I found one that gave me the view I wanted—a corner of the barnyard, the gate, part of the field. Laird did not have a knothole and began to complain.

I showed him a widened crack between two boards. "Be quiet and wait. If they hear you you'll get us in trouble."

My father came in sight carrying the gun. Henry was leading Mack by the halter. He dropped it and took out his cigarette papers and tobacco; he rolled cigarettes for my father and himself. While this was going on Mack nosed around in the old, dead grass along the fence. Then my father opened the gate and they took Mack through. Henry led Mack way from the path to a patch of ground and they talked together, not loud enough for us to hear. Mack again began searching for a mouthful of fresh grass, which was not to be found. My father walked away in a straight line, and stopped short at a distance which seemed to suit him. Henry was walking away from Mack too, but sideways, still negligently holding on to the halter. My father raised the gun and Mack looked up as if he had noticed something and my father shot him.

Mack did not collapse at once but swayed, lurched sideways and fell, first on his side; then he rolled over on his back and, amazingly, kicked his legs for a few seconds in the air. At this Henry laughed, as if Mack had done a trick for him. Laird, who had drawn a long, groaning breath of surprise when the shot was fired, said out loud, "He's not dead." And it seemed to me it might be true. But his legs stopped, he rolled on his side again, his muscles quivered and sank. The two men walked over and looked at him in a businesslike way; they bent down and examined his forehead where the bullet had gone in, and now I saw his blood on the brown grass.

"Now they just skin him and cut him up," I said. "Let's go." My legs were a little shaky and I jumped gratefully down into the hay. "Now you've seen how they shoot a horse," I said in a congratulatory way, as if I had seen it many times before. "Let's see if any barn cat's had kittens in the hay." Laird jumped. He seemed young and obedient again. Suddenly I remembered how, when he was little, I had brought him into the barn and told him to climb the ladder to the top beam. That was in the spring, too, when the hay was low. I had done it out of a need for excitement, a desire for something to happen so that I could tell about it. He was wearing a little bulky brown and white checked coat, made down from one of mine. He went all the way up just as I told him, and sat down on the top beam with the hay far below him on one side, and the barn floor and some old machinery on the other. Then I ran screaming to my father, "Laird's up on the top beam!" My father came, my mother came, my father went up the ladder talking very quietly and brought Laird down under his arm, at which my mother leaned against the ladder and began to cry. They said to me, "Why weren't you watching him?" but nobody ever knew the truth. Laird did not know enough to tell. But whenever I saw the brown and white checked coat hanging in the closet, or at the bottom of the rag bag, which was where it ended up, I felt a weight in my stomach, the sadness of unexorcised guilt.

I looked at Laird, who did not even remember this, and I did not like the look on this thin, winter-pale face. His expression was not frightened or upset, but remote, concentrating. "Listen," I said, in an unusually bright and friendly voice, "you aren't going to tell, are you?"

"No," he said absently.

"Promise."

"Promise," he said. I grabbed the hand behind his back to make sure he was not crossing his fingers. Even so, he might have a nightmare; it might come out that way. I decided I had better work hard to get all thoughts of what he had seen out of his mind—which, it seemed to me, could not hold very many things at a time. I got some money I had saved and that afternoon we went into Jubilee and saw a show, with Judy Canova,[6] at which we both laughed a great deal. After that I thought it would be all right.

Two weeks later I knew they were going to shoot Flora. I knew from the night before, when I heard my mother ask if the hay was holding out all right, and my father said, "Well, after tomorrow there'll just be the cow, and we should be able to put her out to grass in another week." So I knew it was Flora's turn in the morning.

This time I didn't think of watching it. That was something to see just one time. I had not thought about it very often since, but sometimes when I was busy, working at school, or standing in front of the mirror combing my hair and wondering if I would be pretty when I grew up, the whole scene would flash into my mind: I would see the easy, practiced way my father raised the gun, and hear Henry laughing when Mack kicked his legs in the air. I did not have any great feeling of horror and opposition, such as a city child might have had; I was too used to seeing the death of animals as a necessity by which we lived. Yet I felt a little ashamed, and there was a new wariness, a sense of holding-off, in my attitude to my father and his work.

It was a fine day, and we were going around the yard picking up tree branches that had been torn off in winter storms. This was something we had been told to do, and also we wanted to use them to make a teepee. We heard Flora whinny, and then my father's voice and Henry's shouting, and we ran down to the barnyard to see what was going on.

The stable door was open. Henry had just brought Flora out, and she had broken away from him. She was running free in the barnyard, from one end to the other. We climbed up on the fence. It was exciting to see her running, whinnying, going up on her hind legs, prancing and threatening like a horse in a Western movie, an unbroken ranch horse, though she was just an old driver, an old sorrel mare. My father and Henry ran after her and tried to grab the dangling

6. American comedian best known for her yodeling in hillbilly movies of the 1940s.

halter. They tried to work her into a corner, and they had almost succeeded when she made a run between them, wild-eyed, and disappeared around the corner of the barn. We heard the rails clatter down as she got over the fence, and Henry yelled, "She's into the field now!"

That meant she was in the long L-shaped field that ran up by the house. If she got around the center, heading towards the lane, the gate was open; the truck had been driven into the field this morning. My father shouted to me, because I was on the other side of the fence, nearest the lane, "Go shut the gate!"

I could run very fast. I ran across the garden, past the tree where our swing was hung, and jumped across a ditch into the lane. There was the open gate. She had not got out, I could not see her up on the road; she must have run to the other end of the field. The gate was heavy. I lifted it out of the gravel and carried it across the roadway. I had it halfway across when she came in sight, galloping straight towards me. There was just time to get the chain on. Laird came scrambling through the ditch to help me.

Instead of shutting the gate, I opened it as wide as I could. I did not make any decision to do this, it was just what I did. Flora never slowed down; she galloped straight past me, and Laird jumped up and down, yelling, "Shut it, shut it!" even after it was too late. My father and Henry appeared in the field a moment too late to see what I had done. They only saw Flora heading for the township road. They would think I had not got there in time.

They did not waste any time asking about it. They went back to the barn and got the gun and the knives they used, and put these in the truck; then they turned the truck around and came bouncing up the field toward us. Laird called to them, "Let me go too, let me go too!" and Henry stopped the truck and they took him in. I shut the gate after they were all gone.

I supposed Laird would tell. I wondered what would happen to me. I had never disobeyed my father before, and I could not understand why I had done it. Flora would not really get away. They would catch up with her in the truck. Or if they did not catch her this morning somebody would see her and telephone us this afternoon or tomorrow. There was no wild country here for her to run to, only farms. What was more, my father had paid for her, we needed the meat to feed the foxes, we needed the foxes to make our living. All I had done was make more work for my father who worked hard enough already. And when my father found out about it he was not going to trust me any more; he would know that I was not entirely on his side. I was on Flora's side, and that made me no use to anybody, not even to her. Just the same, I did not regret it; when she came running at me and I held the gate open, that was the only thing I could do.

I went back to the house, and my mother said, "What's all the commotion?" I told her that Flora had kicked down the fence and got away. "Your poor father," she said, "now he'll have to go chasing over the countryside. Well, there isn't any use planning dinner before one." She put up the ironing board. I wanted to tell her, but thought better of it and went upstairs and sat on my bed.

Lately I had been trying to make my part of the room fancy, spreading the bed with old lace curtains, and fixing myself a dressing table with some leftovers of cretonne for a skirt. I planned to put up some kind of barricade between my bed and Laird's, to keep my section separate from his. In the sunlight, the lace curtains were just dusty rags. We did not sing at night any more. One night when I was singing Laird said, "You sound silly," and I went right on but the next night I did not start. There was not so much need to anyway, we were no longer afraid. We knew it was just old furniture over there, old jumble and confusion. We did not keep to the rules. I still stayed awake after Laird was asleep and told myself stories, but even in these stories something different was happening, mysterious alterations took place. A story might start off in the old way, with a spectacular danger, a fire or wild animals, and for a while I might rescue people; then things would change around, and instead, somebody would be rescuing me. It might be a boy from our class at school, or even Mr. Campbell, our teacher, who tickled girls under the arms. And at this point the story concerned itself at great length with what I looked like—how long my hair was, and what kind of dress I had on; by the time I had these details worked out the real excitement of the story was lost.

It was later than one o'clock when the truck came back. The tarpaulin was over the back, which meant there was meat in it. My mother had to heat dinner up all over again. Henry and my father had changed from their bloody overalls into ordinary working overalls in the barn, and they washed their arms and necks and faces at the sink, and splashed water on their hair and combed it. Laird lifted his arm to show off a streak of blood. "We shot old Flora," he said, "and cut her up in fifty pieces."

"Well I don't want to hear about it," my mother said. "And don't come to my table like that."

My father made him go and wash the blood off.

We sat down and my father said grace and Henry pasted his chewing gum on the end of his fork, the way he always did; when he took it off he would have us admire the pattern. We began to pass the bowls of steaming, overcooked vegetables. Laird looked across the table at me and said proudly, distinctly, "Anyway it was her fault Flora got away."

"What?" my father said.

"She could of shut the gate and she didn't. She just open' it up and Flora run out."

"Is that right?" my father said.

Everybody at the table was looking at me. I nodded, swallowing food with great difficulty. To my shame, tears flooded my eyes.

My father made a curt sound of disgust. "What did you do that for?"

I did not answer. I put down my fork and waited to be sent from the table, still not looking up.

But this did not happen. For some time nobody said anything, then Laird said matter-of-factly, "She's crying."

"Never mind," my father said. He spoke with resignation, even good humor, the words which absolved and dismissed me for good. "She's only a girl," he said.

I didn't protest that, even in my heart. Maybe it was true.

1968

WILLIAM FAULKNER

The Old People

At first there was nothing. There was the faint, cold, steady rain, the gray and constant light of the late November dawn, with the voices of the hounds converging somewhere in it and toward them. Then Sam Fathers, standing just behind the boy as he had been standing when the boy shot his first running rabbit with his first gun and almost with the first load it ever carried, touched his shoulder and he began to shake, not with any cold. Then the buck was there. He did not come into sight; he was just there, looking not like a ghost but as if all of light were condensed in him and he were the source of it, not only moving in it but disseminating it, already running, seen first as you always see the deer, in that split second after he has already seen you, already slanting away in that first soaring bound, the antlers even in that dim light looking like a small rocking-chair balanced on his head.

"Now," Sam Fathers said, "shoot quick, and slow."

The boy did not remember that shot at all. He would live to be eighty, as his father and his father's twin brother and their father in his turn had lived to be, but he would never hear that shot nor remember even the shock of the gun-butt. He didn't even remember what he did with the gun afterward. He was running. Then he was standing over the buck where it lay on the wet earth still in the attitude of speed and not looking at all dead, standing over it shaking and jerking, with Sam Fathers beside him again, extending the knife. "Don't walk up to him in front," Sam said. "If he ain't dead, he will cut you all to pieces with his feet. Walk up to him from behind and take him by the horn first, so you can hold his head down until you can jump away. Then slip your other hand down and hook your fingers in his nostrils."

The boy did that—drew the head back and the throat taut and drew Sam Fathers' knife across the throat and Sam stooped and dipped his hands in the hot smoking blood and wiped them back and forth across the boy's face. Then Sam's horn rang in the wet gray woods and again and again; there was a boiling wave of dogs about them, with Tennie's Jim and Boon Hogganbeck whipping them back after each had had a taste of the blood, then the men, the true hunters—Walter Ewell whose rifle never missed, and Major de Spain and old General Compson and the boy's cousin, McCaslin Edmonds, grandson of his father's sister, sixteen years his senior and, since both he and McCaslin were only children and the boy's father had been nearing seventy when he was born, more his brother than his cousin and more his father than either —sitting their horses and looking down at them: at the old man of seventy who had been a Negro for two generations now but whose face and bearings were still those of the Chickasaw chief who had been his father; and the white boy of twelve with the prints of the bloody hands on his face, who had nothing to do now but stand straight and not let the trembling show.

"Did he do all right, Sam?" his cousin McCaslin said.

"He done all right," Sam Fathers said.

They were the white boy, marked forever, and the old dark man sired on both sides by savage kings, who had marked him, whose bloody hands had merely formally consecrated him to that which, under the man's tutelage, he had already accepted, humbly and joyfully, with abnegation and with pride too; the hands, the touch, the first worthy blood which he had been found at last worthy to draw, joining him and the man forever, so that the man would continue to live past the boy's seventy years and then eighty years, long after the man himself had entered the earth as chiefs and kings entered it;—the child, not yet a man, whose grandfather had lived in the same country and in almost the same manner as the boy himself would grow up to live, leaving his descendants in the land in his turn as his grandfather had done, and the old man past seventy whose grandfathers had owned the land long before the white men ever saw it and who had vanished from it now with all their kind, what of blood they left behind them running now in another race and for a while even in bondage and now drawing toward the end of its alien and irrevocable course, barren, since Sam Fathers had no children.

His father was Ikkemotubbe himself, who had named himself Doom. Sam told the boy about that—how Ikkemotubbe, old Issetibbeha's sister's son, had run away to New Orleans in his youth and returned seven years later with a French companion calling himself the Chevalier Soeur-Blonde de Vitry, who must have been the Ikkemotubbe of his family too and who was already addressing Ikkemotubbe as *Du Homme;*[1]—returned, came home again, with his foreign Aramis[2] and the quadroon slave woman who was to be Sam's mother, and a gold-laced hat and coat and a wicker wine-hamper containing a litter of month-old puppies and a gold snuff-box filled with a white powder resembling fine sugar. And how he was met at the River landing by three or four companions of his bachelor youth, and while the light of a smoking torch gleamed on the glittering braid of the hat and coat Doom squatted in the mud of the land and took one of the puppies from the hamper and put a pinch of the white powder on its tongue and the puppy died before the one who was holding it could cast it away. And how they returned to the Plantation where Issetibbeha,

---

1. Mistaken or provincialized French for "The Man," with overtones of nobility. French nobility usually have, following their title, *de* or *d'* followed by a place name indicating their residence or seat—   e.g., Duc d'Orléans. Even if "The Man," *l'homme*, were preceded by *de*, the proper form would be *de l'homme*.
2. One of Alexandre Dumas' three musketeers.

dead now, had been succeeded by his son, Doom's fat cousin Moketubbe, and the next day Moketubbe's eight-year-old son died suddenly and that afternoon, in the presence of Moketubbe and most of
the others (the People, Sam Fathers called them) Doom produced
another puppy from the wine-hamper and put a pinch of the white
powder on its tongue and Moketubbe abdicated and Doom became
in fact The Man which his French friend already called him. And how
on the day after that, during the ceremony of accession, Doom pronounced a marriage between the pregnant quadroon and one of the
slave men which he had just inherited (that was how Sam Fathers got
his name, which in Chickasaw had been Had-Two-Fathers) and two
years later sold the man and woman and the child who was his own
son to his white neighbor, Carothers McCaslin.

That was seventy years ago. The Sam Fathers whom the boy knew
was already sixty—a man not tall, squat rather, almost sedentary,
flabby-looking though he actually was not, with hair like a horse's mane
which even at seventy showed no trace of white and a face which
showed no age until he smiled, whose only visible trace of Negro blood
was a slight dullness of the hair and the fingernails, and something
else which you did notice about the eyes, which you noticed because
it was not always there, only in repose and not always then—something
not in their shape nor pigment but in their expression, and the boy's
cousin McCaslin told him what that was: not the heritage of Ham, not
the mark of servitude but of bondage; the knowledge that for a while
that part of his blood had been the blood of slaves. "Like an old lion
or a bear in a cage," McCaslin said. "He was born in the cage and has
been in it all his life; he knows nothing else. Then he smells something.
It might be anything, any breeze blowing past anything and then into
his nostrils. But there for a second was the hot sand or the cane-brake
that he never even saw himself, might not even know if he did see it
and probably does know he couldn't hold his own with it if he got
back to it. But that's not what he smells then. It was the cage he
smelled. He hadn't smelled the cage until that minute. Then the hot
sand or the brake blew into his nostrils and blew away, and all he could
smell was the cage. That's what makes his eyes look like that."

"Then let him go!" the boy cried. "Let him go!"

His cousin laughed shortly. Then he stopped laughing, making the
sound that is. It had never been laughing. "His cage ain't McCaslins,"
he said. "He was a wild man. When he was born, all his blood on both
sides, except the little white part, knew things that had been tamed out
of our blood so long ago that we have not only forgotten them, we
have to live together in herds to protect ourselves from our own
sources. He was the direct son not only of a warrior but of a chief.
Then he grew up and began to learn things, and all of a sudden one
day he found out that he had been betrayed, the blood of the warriors
and chiefs had been betrayed. Not by his father," he added quickly.
"He probably never held it against old Doom for selling him and his
mother into slavery, because he probably believed the damage was
already done before then and it was the same warriors' and chiefs'
blood in him and Doom both that was betrayed through the black blood
which his mother gave him. Not betrayed by the black blood and not

wilfully betrayed by his mother, but betrayed by her all the same, who had bequeathed him not only the blood of slaves but even a little of the very blood which had enslaved it; himself his own battleground, the scene of his own vanquishment and the mausoleum of his defeat. His cage aint us," McCaslin said. "Did you ever know anybody yet, even your father and Uncle Buddy, that ever told him to do or not do anything that he ever paid any attention to?"

That was true. The boy first remembered him as sitting in the door of the plantation blacksmith-shop, where he sharpened plow-points and mended tools and even did rough carpenter-work when he was not in the woods. And sometimes, even when the woods had not drawn him, even with the shop cluttered with work which the farm waited on, Sam would sit there, doing nothing at all for half a day or a whole one, and no man, neither the boy's father and twin uncle in their day nor his cousin McCaslin after he became practical though not yet titular master, ever to say to him, "I want this finished by sundown" or "why wasn't this done yesterday?" And once each year, in the late fall, in November, the boy would watch the wagon, the hooped canvas top erected now, being loaded—the food, hams and sausage from the smokehouse, coffee and flour and molasses from the commissary, a whole beef killed just last night for the dogs until there would be meat in camp, the crate containing the dogs themselves, then the bedding, the guns, the horns and lanterns and axes, and his cousin McCaslin and Sam Fathers in their hunting clothes would mount to the seat and with Tennie's Jim sitting on the dog-crate they would drive away to Jefferson, to join Major de Spain and General Compson and Boon Hogganbeck and Walter Ewell and go on into the big bottom of the Tallahatchie where the deer and bear were, to be gone two weeks. But before the wagon was even loaded the boy would find that he could watch no longer. He would go away, running almost, to stand behind the corner where he could not see the wagon and nobody could see him, not crying, holding himself rigid except for trembling, whispering to himself: "Soon now. Soon now. Just three more years" (or two more or one more) "and I will be ten. Then Cass said I can go."

White man's work, when Sam did work. Because he did nothing else: farmed no allotted acres of his own, as the other ex-slaves of old Carothers McCaslin did, performed no field-work for daily wages as the younger and newer Negroes did—and the boy never knew just how that had been settled between Sam and old Carothers, or perhaps with old Carothers' twin sons after him. For, although Sam lived among the Negroes, in a cabin among the other cabins in the quarters, and consorted with Negroes (what of consorting with anyone Sam did after the boy got big enough to walk alone from the house to the blacksmith-shop and then to carry a gun) and dressed like them and talked like them and even went with them to the Negro church now and then, he was still the son of that Chickasaw chief and the Negroes knew it. And, it seemed to the boy, not only Negroes. Boon Hogganbeck's grandmother had been a Chickasaw woman too, and although the blood had run white since and Boon was a white man, it was not chief's blood. To the boy at least, the difference was apparent immediately you saw Boon and Sam together, and even Boon seemed to know it was there—even

Boon, to whom in his tradition it had never occurred that anyone might be better born than himself. A man might be smarter, he admitted that, or richer (luckier, he called it) but not better born. Boon was a mastiff, absolutely faithful, dividing his fidelity equally between Major de Spain and the boy's cousin McCaslin, absolutely dependent for his very bread and dividing that impartially too between Major de Spain and McCaslin, hardy, generous, courageous enough, a slave to all the appetites and almost unratiocinative. In the boy's eyes at least it was Sam Fathers, the Negro, who bore himself not only toward his cousin McCaslin and Major de Spain but toward all white men, with gravity and dignity and without servility or recourse to that impenetrable wall of ready and easy mirth which Negroes sustain between themselves and white men, bearing himself toward his cousin McCaslin not only as one man to another but as an older man to a younger.

He taught the boy the woods, to hunt, when to shoot and when not to shoot, when to kill and when not to kill, and better, what to do with it afterward. Then he would talk to the boy, the two of them sitting beneath the close fierce stars on a summer hilltop while they waited for the hounds to bring the fox back within hearing, or beside a fire in the November or December woods while the dogs worked out a coon's trail along the creek, or fireless in the pitch dark and heavy dew of April mornings while they squatted beneath a turkey-roost. The boy would never question him; Sam did not react to questions. The boy would just wait and then listen and Sam would begin, talking about the old days and the People whom he had not had time ever to know and so could not remember (he did not remember ever having seen his father's face), and in place of whom the other race into which his blood had run supplied him with no substitute.

And as he talked about those old times and those dead and vanished men of another race from either that the boy knew, gradually to the boy those old times would cease to be old times and would become a part of the boy's present, not only as if they had happened yesterday but as if they were still happening, the men who walked through them actually walking in breath and air and casting an actual shadow on the earth they had not quitted. And more: as if some of them had not happened yet but would occur tomorrow, until at last it would seem to the boy that he himself had not come into existence yet, that none of his race nor the other subject race which his people had brought with them into the land had come here yet; that although it had been his grandfather's and then his father's and uncle's and was now his cousin's and someday would be his own land which he and Sam hunted over, their hold upon it actually was as trivial and without reality as the now faded and archaic script in the chancery book[3] in Jefferson which allocated it to them and that it was he, the boy, who was the guest here and Sam Fathers' voice the mouthpiece of the host.

Until three years ago there had been two of them, the other a full-blood Chickasaw, in a sense even more incredibly lost than Sam Fathers. He called himself Jobaker, as if it were one word. Nobody knew his history at all. He was a hermit, living in a foul little shack at

3. Public records or archives.

the forks of the creek five miles from the plantation and about that far from any other habitation. He was a market hunter and fisherman and he consorted with nobody, black or white; no Negro would even cross his path and no man dared approach his hut except Sam. And perhaps once a month the boy would find them in Sam's shop—two old men squatting on their heels on the dirt floor, talking in a mixture of Negroid English and flat hill dialect and now and then a phrase of that old tongue which as time went on and the boy squatted there too listening, he began to learn. Then Jobaker died. That is, nobody had seen him in some time. Then one morning Sam was missing, nobody, not even the boy, knew when nor where, until that night when some Negroes hunting in the creek bottom saw the sudden burst of flame and approached. It was Jobaker's hut, but before they got anywhere near it, someone shot at them from the shadows beyond it. It was Sam who fired, but nobody ever found Jobaker's grave.

The next morning, sitting at breakfast with his cousin, the boy saw Sam pass the dining-room window and he remembered then that never in his life before had he seen Sam nearer the house than the blacksmith-shop. He stopped eating even; he sat there and he and his cousin both heard the voices from beyond the pantry door, then the door opened and Sam entered, carrying his hat in his hand but without knocking as anyone else on the place except a house servant would have done, entered just far enough for the door to close behind him and stood looking at neither of them—the Indian face above the nigger clothes, looking at something over their heads or at something not even in the room.

"I want to go," he said. "I want to go to the Big Bottom to live."

"To live?" the boy's cousin said.

"At Major de Spain's and your camp, where you go to hunt," Sam said. "I could take care of it for your all while you aint there. I will build me a little house in the woods, if you rather I didn't stay in the big one."

"What about Isaac here?" his cousin said. "How will you get away from him? Are you going to take him with you?" But still Sam looked at neither of them, standing just inside the room with that face which showed nothing, which showed that he was an old man only when it smiled.

"I want to go," he said. "Let me go."

"Yes," the cousin said quietly. "Of course. I'll fix it with Major de Spain. You want to go soon?"

"I'm going now," Sam said. He went out. And that was all. The boy was nine then; it seemed perfectly natural that nobody, not even his cousin McCaslin, should argue with Sam. Also, since he was nine now, he could understand that Sam could leave him and their days and nights in the woods together without any wrench. He believed that he and Sam both knew that this was not only temporary but that the exigencies of his maturing, of that for which Sam had been training him all his life some day to dedicate himself, required it. They had settled that one night last summer while they listened to the hounds bringing a fox back up the creek valley; now the boy discerned in that very talk under the high, fierce August stars a presage, a warning, of this moment today. "I done taught you all there is of this settled country," Sam said. "You can hunt it good as I can now. You are ready for the Big Bottom now, for bear and deer. Hunter's meat," he said. "Next year you will be ten. You will write your age in two numbers and you will be ready to become a man. Your pa" (Sam always referred to the boy's cousin as his father, establishing even before the boy's orphanhood did that relation between them not of the ward to his guardian and kinsman and chief and head of his blood, but of the child to the man who sired his flesh and his thinking too.) "promised you can go with us then." So the boy could understand Sam's going. But he couldn't understand why now, in March, six months before the moon for hunting.

"If Jobaker's dead like they say," he said, "and Sam hasn't got anybody but us at all kin to him, why does he want to go to the Big Bottom now, when it will be six months before we get there?"

"Maybe that's what he wants," McCaslin said. "Maybe he wants to get away from you a little while."

But that was all right. McCaslin and other grown people often said things like that and he paid no attention to them, just as he paid no attention to Sam saying he wanted to go to the Big Bottom to live. After all, he would have to live there for six months, because there would be no use in going at all if he was going to turn right around and come back. And, as Sam himself had told him, he already knew all about hunting in this settled country that Sam or anybody else could teach him. So it would be all right. Summer, then the bright days after the first frost, then the cold and himself on the wagon with McCaslin this time and the moment would come and he would draw the blood, the big blood which would make him a man, a hunter, and Sam would come back home with them and he too would have outgrown the child's pursuit of rabbits and 'possums. Then he too would make one before the winter fire, talking of the old hunts and the hunts to come as hunters talked.

So Sam departed. He owned so little that he could carry it. He walked. He would neither let McCaslin send him in the wagon, nor take a mule to ride. No one saw him go even. He was just gone one morning, the cabin which had never had very much in it, vacant and empty, the shop in which there never had been very much done, standing idle. Then November came at last, and now the boy made one—himself and his cousin McCaslin and Tennie's Jim, and Major de Spain and General Compson and Walter Ewell and Boon and old Uncle Ash to do the cooking, waiting for them in Jefferson with the other wagon, and the surrey in which he and McCaslin and General Compson and Major de Spain would ride.

Sam was waiting at the camp to meet them. If he was glad to see them, he did not show it. And if, when they broke camp two weeks later to return home, he was sorry to see them go, he did not show that either. Because he did not come back with them. It was only the boy who returned, returning solitary and alone to the settled familiar land, to follow for eleven months the childish business of rabbits and such while he waited to go back, having brought with him, even from his brief first sojourn, an unforgettable sense of the big woods—not a quality dangerous or particularly inimical, but profound, sentient, gigantic and brooding, amid which he had been permitted to go to and fro at will, unscathed, why he knew not, but dwarfed and, until he had drawn honorably blood worthy of being drawn, alien.

Then November, and they would come back. Each morning Sam would take the boy out to the stand allotted him. It would be one of the poorer stands of course, since he was only ten and eleven and twelve and he had never even seen a deer running yet. But they would stand there, Sam a little behind him and without a gun himself, as he had been standing when the boy shot the running rabbit when he was eight years old. They would stand there in the November dawns, and after a while they would hear the dogs. Sometimes the chase would sweep up and past quite close, belling and invisible; once they heard the two heavy reports of Boon Hogganbeck's old gun with which he had never killed anything larger than a squirrel and that sitting, and twice they heard the flat unreverberant clap of Walter Ewell's rifle, following which you did not even wait to hear his horn.

"I'll never get a shot," the boy said. "I'll never kill one."

"Yes, you will," Sam said. "You wait. You'll be a hunter. You'll be a man."

But Sam wouldn't come out. They would leave him there. He would come as far as the road where the surrey waited, to take the riding horses back, and that was all. The men would ride the horses and Uncle Ash and Tennie's Jim and the boy would follow in the wagon with Sam, with the camp equipment and the trophies, the meat, the heads, the antlers, the good ones, the wagon winding on among the tremendous gums and cypresses and oaks where no axe save that of the hunter had ever sounded between the impenetrable walls of cane and brier—the two changing yet constant walls just beyond which the wilderness whose mark he had brought away forever on his spirit even from that first two weeks seemed to lean, stooping a little, watching them and listening, not quite inimical because they were too small, even those such as Walter and Major de Spain and old General Compson who had killed many deer and bear, their sojourn too brief and too harmless to excite to that, but just brooding, secret, tremendous, almost inattentive.

Then they would emerge, they would be out of it, the line as sharp as the demarcation of a doored wall. Suddenly skeleton cotton- and corn-fields would flow away on either hand, gaunt and motionless beneath the gray rain; there would be a house, barns, fences, where the hand of man had clawed for an instant, holding, the wall of the wilderness behind them now, tremendous and still and seemingly impenetrable in the gray and fading light, the very tiny orifice through which they had emerged apparently swallowed up. The surrey would be waiting, his cousin McCaslin and Major de Spain and General Compson and Walter and Boon dismounted beside it. Then Sam would get down from the wagon and mount one of the horses and, with the others on a rope behind him, he would turn back. The boy would watch him for a while against that tall and secret wall, growing smaller and smaller against it, never looking back. Then he would enter it, returning to what the boy believed, and thought that his cousin McCaslin believed, was his loneliness and solitude.

2   *return to present*

So the instant came. He pulled trigger and Sam Fathers marked his face with the hot blood which he had spilled and he ceased to be a child and became a hunter and a man. It was the last day. They broke camp that afternoon and went out, his cousin and Major de Spain and General Compson and Boon on the horses. Walter Ewell and the Negroes in the wagon with him and Sam and his hide and antlers. There could have been (and were) other trophies in the wagon. But for him they did not exist, just as for all practical purposes he and Sam Fathers were still alone together as they had been that morning. The wagon wound and jolted between the slow and shifting yet constant walls from beyond and above which the wilderness watched them pass, less than inimical now and never to be inimical again since the buck still and forever leaped, the shaking gun-barrels coming constantly and forever steady at last, crashing, and still out of his instant of immortality the buck sprang, forever immortal;—the wagon jolting and bouncing on, the moment of the buck, the shot, Sam Fathers and himself and the blood with which Sam had marked him forever one with the wilderness which had accepted him since Sam said that he had done all right, when suddenly Sam reined back and stopped the wagon and they all heard the unmistakable and unforgettable sound of a deer breaking cover.

Then Boon shouted from beyond the bend of the trail and while they sat motionless in the halted wagon. Walter and the boy already reaching for their guns, Boon came galloping back, flogging his mule with his hat, his face wild and amazed as he shouted down at them. Then the other riders came around the bend, also spurring.

"Get the dogs!" Boon cried. "Get the dogs! If he had a nub on his head, he had fourteen points! Laying right there by the road in that pawpaw[4] thicket! If I'd a knowed he was there, I could have cut his throat with my pocket knife!"

"Maybe that's why he run," Walter said. "He saw you never had your gun." He was already out of the wagon with his rifle. Then the boy was out too with his gun, and the other riders came up and Boon got off his mule somehow and was scrabbling and clawing among the duffel[5] in the wagon, still shouting, "Get the dogs! Get the dogs!" And it seemed to the boy too that it would take them forever to decide what to do—the old men in whom the blood ran cold and slow, in whom during the intervening years between them and himself the blood had become a different and colder substance from that which ran in him and even in Boon and Walter.

"What about it, Sam?" Major de Spain said. "Could the dogs bring him back?"

"We wont need the dogs," Same said. "If he dont hear the dogs behind him, he will circle back in here about sundown to bed."

"All right," Major de Spain said. "You boys take the horses. We'll go on out to the road in the wagon and wait there." He and General Compson and McCaslin got into the wagon and Boon and Walter and Sam and the boy mounted the horses and turned back and out of

4. Papaw, tree of custard apple family.   5. Campers' personal gear.

the trail. Sam led them for an hour through the gray and unmarked afternoon whose light was little different from what it had been at dawn and which would become darkness without any graduation between. Then Sam stopped them.

"This is far enough," he said. "He'll be coming upwind, and he dont want to smell the mules." They tied the mounts in a thicket. Sam led them on foot now, unpathed through the markless afternoon, the boy pressing close behind him, the two others, or so it seemed to the boy, on his heels. But they were not. Twice Sam turned his head slightly and spoke back to him across his shoulder, still walking: "You got time. We'll get there fore he does."

So he tried to go slower. He tried deliberately to decelerate the dizzy rushing of time in which the buck which he had not even seen was moving, which it seemed to him must be carrying the buck farther and farther and more and more irretrievably away from them even though there were no dogs behind him now to make him run, even though, according to Sam, he must have completed his circle now and was heading back toward them. They went on; it could have been another hour or twice that or less than half, the boy could not have said. Then they were on a ridge. He had never been in here before and he could not see that it was a ridge. He just knew that the earth had risen slightly because the underbrush had thinned a little, the ground sloping invisibly away toward a dense wall of cane. Sam stopped. "This is it," he said. He spoke to Walter and Boon: "Follow this ridge and you will come to two crossings. You will see the tracks. If he crosses, it will be at one of these three."

Walter looked about for a moment. "I know it," he said. "I've even seen your deer. I was in here last Monday. He aint nothing but a yearling."

"A yearling?" Boon said. He was panting from the walking. His face still looked a little wild. "If the one I saw was any yearling, I'm still in kindergarden."

"Then I must have seen a rabbit," Walter said. "I always heard you quit school altogether two years before the first grade."

Boon glared at Walter. "If you dont want to shoot him, get out of the way," he said. "Set down somewhere. By God, I—"

"Aint nobody going to shoot him standing here," Sam said quietly.

"Sam's right," Walter said. He moved, slanting the worn, silver-colored barrel of his rifle downward to walk with it again. "A little more moving and a little more quiet too. Five miles is still Hogganbeck range, even if he wasn't downwind." They went on. The boy could still hear Boon talking, though presently that ceased too. Then once more he and Sam stood motionless together against a tremendous pin oak in a little thicket, and again there was nothing. There was only the soaring and somber solitude in the dim light, there was the thin murmur of the faint cold rain which had not ceased all day. Then, as if it had waited for them to find their positions and become still, the wilderness breathed again. It seemed to lean inward above them, above himself and Sam and Walter and Boon in their separate lurking-places, tremendous, attentive, impartial and omniscient, the buck moving in it somewhere, not running yet since he had not been pursued, not

frightened yet and never fearsome but just alert also as they were
alert, perhaps already circling back, perhaps quite near, perhaps conscious also of the eye of the ancient immortal Umpire. Because he was
just twelve then, and that morning something had happened to him: in
less than a second he had ceased forever to be the child he was yesterday. Or perhaps that made no difference, perhaps even a city-bred man,
let alone a child, could not have understood it; perhaps only a country-
bred one could comprehend loving the life he spills. He began to shake
again.

"I'm glad it's started now," he whispered. He did not move to speak;
only his lips shaped the expiring words: "Then it will be gone when I
raise the gun—"

Nor did Sam. "Hush," he said.

"Is he that near?" the boy whispered. "Do you think—"

"Hush," Sam said. So he hushed. But he could not stop the shaking.
He did not try, because he knew it would go away when he needed the
steadiness—had not Sam Fathers already consecrated and absolved
him from weakness and regret too?—not from love and pity for all
which lived and ran and then ceased to live in a second in the very
midst of splendor and speed, but from weakness and regret. So they
stood motionless, breathing deep and quiet and steady. If there had
been any sun, it would be near to setting now; there was a condensing,
a densifying, of what he had thought was the gray and unchanging light
until he realized suddenly that it was his own breathing, his heart, his
blood—something, all things, and that Sam Fathers had marked him
indeed, not as a mere hunter, but with something Sam had had in his
turn of his vanished and forgotten people. He stopped breathing then;
there was only his heart, his blood, and in the following silence the
wilderness ceased to breathe also, leaning, stooping overhead with its
breath held, tremendous and impartial and waiting. Then the shaking
stopped too, as he had known it would, and he drew back the two
heavy hammers of the gun.

Then it had passed. It was over. The solitude did not breathe again
yet; it had merely stopped watching him and was looking somewhere
else, even turning its back on him, looking on away up the ridge at
another point, and the boy knew as well as if he had seen him that the
buck had come to the edge of the cane and had either seen or scented
them and faded back into it. But the solitude did not breathe again. It
should have suspired again then but it did not. It was still facing, watching, what it had been watching and it was not here, not where he and
Sam stood; rigid, not breathing himself, he thought, cried *No! No!*,
knowing already that it was too late, thinking with the old despair of
two and three years ago: *I'll never get a shot.* Then he heard it—the
flat single clap of Walter Ewell's rifle which never missed. Then the
mellow sound of the horn came down the ridge and something went
out of him and he knew then he had never expected to get the shot
at all.

"I reckon that's it," he said. "Walter got him." He had raised the
gun slightly without knowing it. He lowered it again and had lowered
one of the hammers and was already moving out of the thicket when
Sam spoke.

"Wait."

"Wait?" the boy cried. And he would remember that—how he turned upon Sam in the truculence of a boy's grief over the missed opportunity, the missed luck. "What for? Dont you hear that horn?"

And he would remember how Sam was standing. Sam had not moved. He was not tall, squat rather and broad, and the boy had been growing fast for the past year or so and there was not much difference between them in height, yet Sam was looking over the boy's head and up the ridge toward the sound of the horn and the boy knew that Sam did not even see him; that Sam knew he was still there beside him but he did not see the boy. Then the boy saw the buck. It was coming down the ridge, as if it were walking out of the very sound of the horn which related its death. It was not running, it was walking, tremendous, unhurried, slanting and tilting its head to pass the antlers through the undergrowth, and the boy standing with Sam beside him now instead of behind him as Sam always stood, and the gun still partly aimed and one of the hammers still cocked.

Then it saw them. And still it did not begin to run. It just stopped for an instant, taller than any man, looking at them; then its muscles suppled, gathered. It did not even alter its course, not fleeing, not even running, just moving with that winged and effortless ease with which deer move, passing within twenty feet of them, its head high and the eye not proud and not haughty but just full and wild and unafraid, and Sam standing beside the boy now, his right arm raised at full length, palm-outward, speaking in that tongue which the boy had learned from listening to him and Jobaker in the blacksmith shop, while up the ridge Walter Ewell's horn was still blowing them in to a dead buck.

"Oleh, Chief," Sam said. "Grandfather."

When they reached Walter, he was standing with his back toward them, quite still, bemused almost, looking down at his feet. He didn't look up at all.

"Come here, Sam," he said quietly. When they reached him he still did not look up, standing above a little spike buck which had still been a fawn last spring. "He was so little I pretty near let him go," Walter said. "But just look at the track he was making. It's pretty near big as a cow's. If there were any more tracks here beside the ones he is laying in, I would swear there was another buck here that I never even saw."

3

It was dark when they reached the road where the surrey waited. It was turning cold, the rain had stopped, and the sky was beginning to blow clear. His cousin and Major de Spain and General Compson had a fire going. "Did you get him?" Major de Spain said.

"Got a good-sized swamp-rabbit with spike horns," Walter said. He slid the little buck down from his mule. The boy's cousin McCaslin looked at it.

"Nobody saw the big one?" he said.

"I dont even believe Boon saw it," Walter said. "He probably jumped somebody's stray cow in that thicket." Boon started cursing, swearing at Walter and at Sam for not getting the dogs in the first place and at the buck and all.

"Never mind," Major de Spain said. "He'll be here for us next fall. Let's get started home."

It was after midnight when they let Walter out at his gate two miles from Jefferson and later still when they took General Compson to his house and then returned to Major de Spain's, where he and McCaslin would spend the rest of the night, since it was still seventeen miles home. It was cold, the sky was clear now; there would be a heavy frost by sunup and the ground was already frozen beneath the horses' feet and the wheels and beneath their own feet as they crossed Major de Spain's yard and entered the house, the warm dark house, feeling their way up the dark stairs until Major de Spain found a candle and lit it, and into the strange room and the big deep bed, the still cold sheets until they began to warm to their bodies and at last the shaking stopped and suddenly he was telling McCaslin about it while McCaslin listened, quietly until he had finished. "You dont believe it," the boy said. "I know you dont—"

"Why not?" McCaslin said. "Think of all that has happened here, on this earth. All the blood hot and strong for living, pleasuring, that has soaked back into it. For grieving and suffering too, of course, but still getting something out of it for all that, getting a lot out of it, because after all you dont have to continue to bear what you believe is suffering; you can always choose to stop that, put an end to that. And even suffering and grieving is better than nothing; there is only one thing worse than not being alive, and that's shame. But you cant be alive forever, and you always wear out life long before you have exhausted the possibilities of living. And all that must be somewhere; all that could not have been invented and created just to be thrown away. And the earth is shallow; there is not a great deal of it before you come to the rock. And the earth dont want to just keep things, hoard them; it wants to use them again. Look at the seed, the acorns, at what happens even to carrion when you try to bury it: it refuses too, seethes and struggles too until it reaches light and air again, hunting the sun still. And they—" the boy saw his hand in silhouette for a moment against the window beyond which, accustomed to the darkness now, he could see sky where the scoured and icy stars glittered "—they dont want it, need it. Besides, what would it want, itself, knocking around out there, when it never had enough time about the earth as it was, when there is plenty of room about the earth, plenty of places still unchanged from what they were when the blood used and pleasured in them while it was still blood?"

"But we want them," the boy said. "We want them too. There is plenty of room for us and them too."

"That's right," McCaslin said. "Suppose they dont have substance, cant cast a shadow—"

"But I saw it!" the boy cried. "I saw him!"

"Steady," McCaslin said. For an instant his hand touched the boy's flank beneath the covers. "Steady. I know you did. So did I. Sam took me in there once after I killed my first deer."

1942

10 A MODE: FANTASY

There is a looser and wider-ranging system of literary classification than genres and kinds, one that looks at works (or even parts of works) not as organisms but in terms of **modes,** ways of perceiving or presenting experience. If we call the conventional literary genres poetry, drama, fiction, we call the conventional modes the **poetic** (or **lyric**), the **dramatic,** and the **narrative.** A work that is classified in the subgenre short story, within the genre fiction, may have passages in the poetic mode—passages marked by heightened and highly figurative language, intensification of rhythms and emotions, often focusing on the ideal or spiritual. The final paragraphs of *The Artificial Nigger,* Gurov standing by the sea or contemplating the nails in the gray fence around Anna's home in *The Lady with the Dog,* the boy wandering through the Dublin streets full of frustration and shame in *Araby* are examples of poetic passages. Some portion of a story, even a whole story, may be in the dramatic mode, like a play, with unmediated or unnarrated dialogue or action. In *The Most Dangerous Game,* General Zaroff and Rainsford's conversation at their first dinner seems like a scene from a play; it could be transferred to the stage almost without change. *The Lottery,* made up of dialogue and seemingly objective descriptions of action, comes about as close as a short story can to being fully dramatic, short of being reduced to pure dialogue.

Befitting the looseness of the term, modes do not descend in an orderly way through subheadings, as do genres through subgenres and kinds. **Fantasy,** for example, a literary mode involving the consciously unreal—places, societies, or beings that never existed, do not exist, or do not yet exist, or with qualities that are beyond or counter to the ordinary or commonsensical—can be found in fiction, poetry, or drama.

Fantastic fiction sometimes signals its fictionality immediately or very soon: "Once upon a time. . . ." At other times, it goes to some lengths to establish its "reality": many eighteenth-century novels about medieval castles and ghosts (Gothic novels) pretend to be editions of some monk's dusty manuscript, for example. Still other stories, such as *A Very Old Man with Enormous Wings,* simply treat the incredible as perfectly natural, if not perfectly common.

Much fantasy has as its aim to stretch or expand our consciousness, our perception and conception of reality. Some stories seek to open us up to possibilities by disorienting us, alternating or mixing the realistic, the fictional, the fantastic in dizzying patterns. *The Garden of Forking Paths* begins realistically, with documentation and an essay-like manner that makes it seem not like a story at all. Then the confession begins, and we recognize that we are in the midst of a common fictional kind, the spy story or thriller. The shift does not bother us too much—it's like the dusty-manuscript device, and the fictional kind we've entered on is so familiar that we're reasonably comfortable. Suddenly the spy story shifts once again, toward fantasy and, just as we're getting used to fantasy, to mysterious Chinese gardens and riddles. The fantasy is used to question whether it is the fantastic that is incredible, or whether our assumption that time is uniform and absolute is merely arbitrary and too restrictrive—itself a fantasy. Given eternity, we must admit that everything that might possibly happen *will* happen. So when we make a choice, the choice we did not make but might have made will yet be made; its potential must be realized; it must exist somewhere in the vastness of eternity in a world of events parallel to our own. No wonder, then, when we return to the world of the spy story, which, though fictional, operates within the same notions of uniform, absolute time, it seems credible that the writer of the confession is not concerned with whether he lives or dies, realities that are now "unreal, insignificant."

I don't think what I have told you about *Forking Paths* will destroy your interest in the story—indeed, everyone can probably do with a little help in reading this fascinating story for the first time. Its questioning of our assumptions about reality is not too different from what's going on in modern thought. It is precisely because history, psychology, science, philosophy—almost all the intellectual disciplines —have in recent years most urgently called into question our long-standing assumptions about reality that fantasy seems so congenial a mode for us today.

From the middle of the nineteenth century to the middle of ours, the rise of the novel and the rise of realism were assumed to be the same thing, and we looked back on literary history as progress toward the literal, the factual, the ordinary (just as some art historians saw the Renaissance and what followed as demonstrating progress in man's ability to represent things "as they really are"). Long narratives that dwelled on the extraordinary, unusual, bizarre, or supernatural were called **romances**, as opposed to the more realistic **novel**. The early modern short story leaned more heavily toward romance. Poe was perhaps our most widely respected writer, and you can see that *The Cask of Amontillado* is not exactly a story of everyday life. Late in the century, with Maupassant in France (see *The Jewelry*) and Chekhov in Russia (see *The Lady with the Dog*), the realistic short story seemed to have caught up with the novel.

But already in the nineteenth century "common sense" notions of realism were beginning to give way before the discovery of worlds beyond our unaided senses, observable through microscope and telescope. Darwin, with his notion that species themselves were not fixed but moving and changing in time, made the solid earth under our feet a little less solid. With the rise of psychology, which too was meant to capture more realms for consciousness and science, we became more and more aware that there were realities only dreamed of in our philosophies. When physics, the most advanced and scientific of the sciences, began to tell us that all our knowledge is, if not subjective, at least limited to what the human brain and its instruments can perceive, and is altered by our perception, we were not so sure anymore that reality was what existed "out there" or that we were contained between our hat and boots.

Perhaps the unsettling "retrogression" of science toward subjectivity has spurred on our most recent spate of the unreal or superreal; perhaps it was the nightmare of a human reality that could create a barbaric holocaust at Dachau or a scientific one at Hiroshima that made *rationality* and *science* and *realism* less automatically terms of positive value. Even the positive side of scientific achievement—space travel, walking on the moon, television and laser beams—destroyed our sense of a real and stable world and opened up other possibilities.

A generation or two ago, *Rosemary's Baby* or *The Exorcist* could have had only one ending—a rational explanation for the appearance of the supernatural. Few viewers or readers then would take seriously a work that was not embedded in a world of more or less everyday reality. The supernatural or fantastic in such a world had to be explained away as a dream, hallucination, or other psychological aberration, or as a hoax of some sort, set up to take in the foolish or credulous. Similarly, we would have had to explain away stories like *The Lottery* and García Márquez's *Very Old Man* by treating them as allegories. Now we can accept them as symbolic, as experiences that cannot be explained away or reduced to everyday terms, but that exist on their own terms, explaining in fantasy more than we might in our discursive prose, our scientific formulas, graphs, and charts.

The fantasy land of science fiction is usually the future—not so much never-never as never-yet land—which does not necessarily undermine or question conventional reality but projects potential consequences of present knowledge. There are those who maintain that for this very reason it is a mistake to call sci-fi fantasy. Fantasy, they say, involves the incredible or impossible. Science fiction, while it may take place in the future or outside earthly reality, is neither incredible nor impossible but wholly logical, often based on real scientific principles. Others say that's exactly why it's fantasy: historical reality is never predictable, and certainly not by that fantasy called logic.

Science-fiction people are passionate, dedicated, and argumentative, so if it's risky to suggest that science fiction is in the mode of fantasy, it's even riskier to try to define science fiction as a kind, even though everyone will grant that generic definitions are at best only loose approximations. Approximately, **science fiction** is a narrative about events outside the bounds of Earth history in which science or advanced technology is often centrally important. The term **Earth history** allows for both space travel (to imaginary life on real or imaginary planets) in the present and time travel to prehistory. Science and technology in the stories can be merely a plot device or be important as a means of transhistorical travel, or in the operation or perception of that imaginary world, as in *The Eye Altering*. I'm sure this loose baggy monster of a definition leaves something out or includes too much, but at least it separates *The Eye Altering* from the other two fantasy stories here, and from *The Lottery* and *The Rocking-Horse Winner*, and, in "Stories for Further Reading," from *The Kugelmass Episode* and *A Hunger Artist*.

GABRIEL GARCÍA MÁRQUEZ

A Very Old Man with Enormous Wings*

A TALE FOR CHILDREN

On the third day of rain they had killed so many crabs inside the house that Pelayo had to cross his drenched courtyard and throw them into the sea, because the newborn child had a temperature all night and they thought it was due to the stench. The world had been sad since Tuesday. Sea and sky were a single ash-gray thing and the sands of the beach, which on March nights glimmered like powdered light, had become a stew of mud and rotten shellfish. The light was so weak at noon that when Pelayo was coming back to the house after throwing away the crabs, it was hard for him to see what it was that was moving and groaning in the rear of the courtyard. He had to go very close to see that it was an old man, a very old man, lying face down in the mud, who, in spite of his tremendous efforts, couldn't get up, impeded by his enormous wings.

Frightened by that nightmare, Pelayo ran to get Elisenda, his wife, who was putting compresses on the sick child, and he took her to the rear of the courtyard. They both looked at the fallen body with mute stupor. He was dressed like a ragpicker. There were only a few faded hairs left on his bald skull and very few teeth in his mouth, and his pitiful condition of a drenched great-grandfather had taken away any sense of grandeur he might have had. His huge buzzard wings, dirty and half-plucked, were forever entangled in the mud. They looked at him so long and so closely that Pelayo and Elisenda very soon overcame their surprise and in the end found him familiar. Then they dared speak to him, and he answered in an incomprehensible dialect with a strong sailor's voice. That was how they skipped over the inconvenience of the wings and quite intelligently concluded that he was a lonely castaway from some foreign ship wrecked by the storm. And yet, they called in a neighbor woman who knew everything about life and death to see him, and all she needed was one look to show them their mistake.

"He's an angel," she told them. "He must have been coming for the child, but the poor fellow is so old that the rain knocked him down."

On the following day everyone knew that a flesh-and-blood angel was held captive in Pelayo's house. Against the judgment of the wise neighbor woman, for whom angels in those times were the fugitive survivors of a celestial conspiracy, they did not have the heart to club him to death. Pelayo watched over him all afternoon from the kitchen, armed with his bailiff's club, and before going to bed he dragged him out of the mud and locked him up with the hens in the wire chicken coop. In the middle of the night, when the rain stopped, Pelayo and Elisenda were still killing crabs. A short time afterward the child woke up without a fever and with a desire to eat. Then they

* Translated by Gregory Rabassa.

felt magnanimous and decided to put the angel on a raft with fresh water and provisions for three days and leave him to his fate on the high seas. But when they went out into the courtyard with the first light of dawn, they found the whole neighborhood in front of the chicken coop having fun with the angel, without the slightest reverence, tossing him things to eat through the openings in the wire as if he weren't a supernatural creature but a circus animal.

Father Gonzaga arrived before seven o'clock, alarmed at the strange news. By that time onlookers less frivolous than those at dawn had already arrived and they were making all kinds of conjectures concerning the captive's future. The simplest among them thought that he should be named mayor of the world. Others of sterner mind felt that he should be promoted to the rank of five-star general in order to win all wars. Some visionaries hoped that he could be put to stud in order to implant on earth a race of winged wise men who could take charge of the universe. But Father Gonzaga, before becoming a priest, had been a robust woodcutter. Standing by the wire, he reviewed his catechism in an instant and asked them to open the door so that he could take a close look at that pitiful man who looked more like a huge decrepit hen among the fascinated chickens. He was lying in a corner drying his open wings in the sunlight among the fruit peels and breakfast leftovers that the early risers had thrown him. Alien to the impertinences of the world, he only lifted his antiquarian eyes and murmured something in his dialect when Father Gonzaga went into the chicken coop and said good morning to him in Latin. The parish priest had his first suspicion of an imposter when he saw that he did not understand the language of God or know how to greet His ministers. Then he noticed that seen close up he was much too human: he had an unbearable smell of the outdoors, the back side of his wings was strewn with parasites and his main feathers had been mistreated by terrestrial winds, and nothing about him measured up to the proud dignity of angels. Then he came out of the chicken coop and in a brief sermon warned the curious against the risks of being ingenuous. He reminded them that the devil had the bad habit of making use of carnival tricks in order to confuse the unwary. He argued that if wings were not the essential element in determining the difference between a hawk and an airplane, they were even less so in the recognition of angels. Nevertheless, he promised to write a letter to his bishop so that the latter would write to his primate so that the latter would write to the Supreme Pontiff in order to get the final verdict from the highest courts.

His prudence fell on sterile hearts. The news of the captive angel spread with such rapidity that after a few hours the courtyard had the bustle of a marketplace and they had to call in troops with fixed bayonets to disperse the mob that was about to knock the house down. Elisenda, her spine all twisted from sweeping up so much marketplace trash, then got the idea of fencing in the yard and charging five cents admission to see the angel.

The curious came from far away. A traveling carnival arrived with a flying acrobat who buzzed over the crowd several times, but no one paid any attention to him because his wings were not those of an

angel but, rather, those of a sidereal bat. The most unfortunate invalids on earth came in search of health: a poor woman who since
childhood had been counting her heartbeats and had run out of numbers; a Portuguese man who couldn't sleep because the noise of the
stars disturbed him; a sleepwalker who got up at night to undo the
things he had done while awake; and many others with less serious
ailments. In the midst of that shipwreck disorder that made the
earth tremble, Pelayo and Elisenda were happy with fatigue, for in
less than a week they had crammed their rooms with money and the
line of pilgrims waiting their turn to enter still reached beyond the
horizon.

The angel was the only one who took no part in his own act. He
spent his time trying to get comfortable in his borrowed nest, be-
fuddled by the hellish heat of the oil lamps and sacramental candles
that had been placed along the wire. At first they tried to make him
eat some mothballs, which, according to the wisdom of the wise
neighbor woman, were the food prescribed for angels. But he turned
them down, just as he turned down the papal lunches[1] that the peni-
tents brought him, and they never found out whether it was because
he was an angel or because he was an old man that in the end he
ate nothing but eggplant mush. His only supernatural virtue seemed
to be patience. Especially during the first days, when the hens pecked
at him, searching for the stellar parasites that proliferated in his
wings, and the cripples pulled out feathers to touch their defective
parts with, and even the most merciful threw stones at him, trying to
get him to rise so they could see him standing. The only time they
succeeded in arousing him was when they burned his side with an
iron for branding steers, for he had been motionless for so many hours
that they thought he was dead. He awoke with a start, ranting in his
hermetic language and with tears in his eyes, and he flapped his wings
a couple of times, which brought on a whirlwind of chicken dung and
lunar dust and a gale of panic that did not seem to be of this world.
Although many thought that his reaction had been one not of rage
but of pain, from then on they were careful not to annoy him, because
the majority understood that his passivity was not that of a hero
taking his ease but that of a cataclysm in repose.

Father Gonzaga held back the crowd's frivolity with formulas of
maidservant inspiration while awaiting the arrival of a final judgment on the nature of the captive. But the mail from Rome showed no
sense of urgency. They spent their time finding out if the prisoner had
a navel, if his dialect had any connection with Aramaic, how many
times he could fit on the head of a pin, or whether he wasn't just a
Norwegian with wings. Those meager letters might have come and
gone until the end of time if a providential event had not put an end
to the priest's tribulations.

It so happened that during those days, among so many other
carnival attractions, there arrived in town the traveling show of the
woman who had been changed into a spider for having disobeyed
her parents. The admission to see her was not only less than the ad-

---

1. Choice, extremely expensive meals.

mission to see the angel, but people were permitted to ask her all manner of questions about her absurd state and to examine her up and down so that no one would ever doubt the truth of her horror. She was a frightful tarantula the size of a ram and with the head of a sad maiden. What was most heart-rending, however, was not her outlandish shape but the sincere affliction with which she recounted the details of her misfortune. While still practically a child she had sneaked out of her parents' house to go to a dance, and while she was coming back through the woods after having danced all night without permission, a fearful thunderclap rent the sky in two and through the crack came the lightning bolt of brimstone that changed her into a spider. Her only nourishment came from the meatballs that charitable souls chose to toss into her mouth. A spectacle like that, full of so much human truth and with such a fearful lesson, was bound to defeat without even trying that of a haughty angel who scarcely deigned to look at mortals. Besides, the few miracles attributed to the angel showed a certain mental disorder, like the blind man who didn't recover his sight but grew three new teeth, or the paralytic who didn't get to walk but almost won the lottery, and the leper whose sores sprouted sunflowers. Those consolation miracles, which were more like mocking fun, had already ruined the angel's reputation when the woman who had been changed into a spider finally crushed him completely. That was how Father Gonzaga was cured forever of his insomnia and Pelayo's courtyard went back to being as empty as during the time it had rained for three days and crabs walked through the bedrooms.

The owners of the house had no reason to lament. With the money they saved they built a two-story mansion with balconies and gardens and high netting so that crabs wouldn't get in during the winter, and with iron bars on the windows so that angels wouldn't get in. Pelayo also set up a rabbit warren close to town and gave up his job as bailiff for good, and Elisenda bought some satin pumps with high heels and many dresses of iridescent silk, the kind worn on Sunday by the most desirable women in those times. The chicken coop was the only thing that didn't receive any attention. If they washed it down with creolin[2] and burned tears of myrrh inside it every so often, it was not in homage to the angel but to drive away the dungheap stench that still hung everywhere like a ghost and was turning the new house into an old one. At first, when the child learned to walk, they were careful that he not get too close to the chicken coop. But then they began to lose their fears and got used to the smell, and before the child got his second teeth he'd gone inside the chicken coop to play, where the wires were falling apart. The angel was no less standoffish with him than with other mortals, but he tolerated the most ingenious infamies with the patience of a dog who had no illusions. They both came down with chicken pox at the same time. The doctor who took care of the child couldn't resist the temptation to listen to the angel's heart, and he found so much whistling in the heart and so many sounds in his kidneys that it seemed impossible for him to be alive.

2. A disinfectant.

338   *Gabriel García Márquez*

What surprised him most, however, was the logic of his wings. They seemed so natural on that completely human organism that he couldn't understand why other men didn't have them too.

When the child began school it had been some time since the sun and rain had caused the collapse of the chicken coop. The angel went dragging himself about here and there like a stray dying man. They would drive him out of the bedroom with a broom and a moment later find him in the kitchen. He seemed to be in so many places at the same time that they grew to think that he'd been duplicated, that he was reproducing himself all through the house, and the exasperated and unhinged Elisenda shouted that it was awful living in that hell full of angels. He could scarcely eat and his antiquarian eyes had also become so foggy that he went about bumping into posts. All he had left were the bare cannulae of his last feathers. Pelayo threw a blanket over him and extended him the charity of letting him sleep in the shed, and only then did they notice that he had a temperature at night, and was delirious with the tongue twisters of an old Norwegian. That was one of the few times they became alarmed, for they thought he was going to die and not even the wise neighbor woman had been able to tell them what to do with dead angels.

And yet he not only survived his worst winter, but seemed improved with the first sunny days. He remained motionless for several days in the farthest corner of the courtyard, where no one would see him, and at the beginning of December some large, stiff feathers began to grow on his wings, the feathers of a scarecrow, which looked more like another misfortune of decrepitude. But he must have known the reason for those changes, for he was quite careful that no one should notice them, that no one should hear the sea chanteys that he sometimes sang under the stars. One morning Elisenda was cutting some bunches of onions for lunch when a wind that seemed to come from the high seas blew into the kitchen. Then she went to the window and caught the angel in his first attempts at flight. They were so clumsy that his fingernails opened a furrow in the vegetable patch and he was on the point of knocking the shed down with the ungainly flapping that slipped on the light and couldn't get a grip on the air. But he did manage to gain altitude. Elisenda let out a sigh of relief, for herself and for him, when she saw him pass over the last houses, holding himself up in some way with the risky flapping of a senile vulture. She kept watching him even when she was through cutting the onions and she kept on watching until it was no longer possible for her to see him, because then he was no longer an annoyance in her life but an imaginary dot on the horizon of the sea.

1972

URSULA K. LE GUIN

The Eye Altering

Miriam stood at the big window of the infirmary ward and looked out at the view and thought, For twenty-five years I have been standing at this window and looking out at this view. And never once have I seen what I wanted to see.

If I forget thee, O Jerusalem—[1]

The pain was forgotten, yes. The hatred and the fear, forgotten. In exile you don't remember the gray days and the black years. You remember the sunlight, the orchards, the white cities. Even when you try to forget it you remember that Jerusalem was golden.

The sky outside the ward window was dulled with haze. Over the low ridge called Ararat the sun was setting; setting slowly, for New Zion had a slower spin than Old Earth, and a twenty-eight-hour day; settling, rather than setting, dully down onto the dull horizon. There were no clouds to gather the colors of sunset. There were seldom any clouds. When the haze thickened there might be a misty, smothering rain; when the haze was thin, as now, it hung high and vague, formless. It never quite cleared. You never saw the color of the sky. You never saw the stars. And through the haze the sun, no, not the sun, but NSC 641 (Class G)[2] burned swollen and vaporous, warty as an orange—remember oranges? the sweet juice on the tongue? the orchards of Hafia?—NSC 641 stared, like a bleary eye. You could stare back at it. No glory of gold to blind you. Two imbeciles staring at each other.

Shadows stretched across the valley towards the buildings of the Settlement. In shadows the fields and woods were black; in the light they were brown, purplish, and dark red. Dirty colors, the colors you got when you scrubbed your watercolors too much and the teacher came by and said, You'd better use some fresh water, Mimi, it's getting muddy. Because the teacher had been too kind to say to a ten-year-old, That picture's a total loss, Mimi, throw it away and start fresh.

She had thought of that before—she had thought all her thoughts before, standing at this window—but this time it reminded her of Genya, because of the painting, and she turned to see how he was doing. The shock symptoms were almost gone, his face was no longer so pale and his pulse had steadied. While she held his wrist he sighed a bit and opened his eyes. Lovely eyes he had, gray in the thin face. He had never been much but eyes, poor Genya. Her oldest patient. Twenty-four years he had been her patient, right from the moment of his birth, five pounds, purplish-blue like a fetal rat, a month premature and half dead of cyanosis: the fifth child born on New Zion, the first in Ararat Settlement. A native. A feeble and unpromising native. He

---

1. ". . . let my right hand forget her cunning," Psalm 137:5; the psalm begins, "By the rivers of Babylon, there we sat down, yea, we wept, when we remembered Zion," Zion being both another name for Jerusalem and for the congregation of Jews in exile. Below: Ararat, in present-day Turkey, was the mountain where Noah's ark landed after the Flood.

2. I.e., the same kind of star as our sun. *NSC 641*: The catalogue number of a fictional star. *Haifa*: An Israeli port.

hadn't even had the strength, or the sense, to cry at his first breath of this alien air. Sofia's other children had been full-term and healthy, two girls, both married and mothers now, and fat Leon who could hoist a seventy-kilo sack of grain when he was fifteen. Good young colonists, strong stock. But Miriam had always loved Genya, and all the more after her own years of miscarriages and stillbirths, and the last birth, the girl who had lived two hours, whose eyes had been clear gray like Genya's. Babies never have gray eyes, the eyes of the newborn are blue, that was all sentimental rubbish. But how could you ever make sure of what color things were under this damned warty-orange sun? Nothing ever looked right. "So there you are, Gennady Borisovich," she said, "back home, eh?"

It had been their joke when he was a child; he had spent so much time in the infirmary that whenever he came in with one of his fevers or fainting spells or gasping asthma he would say, "Here I am, back home, Auntie Doctor. . . ."

"What happened?" he asked.

"You collapsed. Hoeing down in the South Field. Aaron and Tina brought you up here on the tractor. Touch of sunstroke, maybe? You've been doing all right, haven't you?"

He shrugged and nodded.

"Dizzy? Short of breath?"

"On and off."

"Why didn't you come to the clinic?"

"It's no good, Miriam."

Since he was grown he had called her Miriam. She missed "Auntie Doctor." He had grown away from her, these last few years, withdrawn from her into his painting. He had always sketched and painted, but now, all his free time and whatever energy he had left when his Settlement duties were done, he spent in the loft of the generator building where he'd made a kind of studio, grinding colors from rocks and mixing dyes from native plants, making brushes by begging pigtail ends off little girls, and painting—painting on scraps from the lumber mill, on bits of rag, on precious scraps of paper, on smooth slabs of slate from the quarry on Ararat if nothing better was at hand. Painting portraits, scenes of Settlement life, buildings, machinery, still-lifes, plants, landscapes, inner visions. Painting anything, everything. His portraits had been much in demand—people were always kind to Genya and the other sicklies—but lately he had not done any portraits; he had gone in for queer muddy jumbles of forms and lines all in a dark haze, like worlds half created. Nobody liked those paintings, but nobody ever told Genya he was wasting his time. He was a sickly; he was an artist; O.K. Healthy people had no time to be artists. There was too much work to do. But it was good to have an artist. It was human. It was like Earth. Wasn't it?

They were kind to Toby, too, whose stomach troubles were so bad that at sixteen he weighed eighty-four pounds; kind to little Shura, who was just learning to talk at six, and whose eyes wept and wept all day long, even when she was smiling; kind to all their sicklies, the ones whose bodies could not adjust to this alien world, whose stomachs could not digest the native proteins even with the help of the metabolizing pills which every colonist must take twice a day every day of his life on New Zion. Hard as life was in the Twenty Settlements, much as they needed every hand to work, they were gentle with their useless ones, their afflicted. In affliction the hand of God is visible. They remembered the words civilization, humanity. They remembered Jerusalem.

"Genya, my dear, what do you mean, it's no good?"

His quiet voice had frightened her. "It's no good," he had said, smiling. And the gray eyes not clear but veiled, hazy.

"Medicine," he said, "Pills. Cures."

"Of course you know more about medicine than I do," Miriam said. "You're a much better doctor than I am. Or are you giving up? Is that it, Genya? Giving up?" Anger had come upon her so suddenly, from so deep within, from anxiety so long and deeply hidden, that it shook her body and cracked her voice.

"I'm giving up one thing. The metas."

"Metas? Giving them up? What are you talking about?"

"I haven't taken any for two weeks."

The despairing rage swelled in her. She felt her face go hot, so that it felt twice its normal size. "Two weeks! And so, and so, and so you're here! Where did you think you'd end up, you terrible fool? Lucky you're not dead!"

"I haven't been any worse since I stopped taking them, Miriam. Better, this whole last week. Until today. It can't be that. It must have been heatstroke. I forgot to wear a hat. . . . He too flushed faintly, in the eagerness of his pleading, or with shame. It was stupid to work in the fields bareheaded; for all its dull look NSC 641 could hit the unsheltered human head quite as hard as fiery Sol, and Genya was apologetic for his carelessness. "You see, I was feeling fine this morning, really good, I kept right up with the others hoeing. Then I felt a bit dizzy, but I didn't want to stop, it was so good to be able to work right with the others, I never thought about heatstroke."

Miriam found that there were tears in her eyes, and this made her so ultimately and absolutely angry that she couldn't speak at all. She got up off Genya's bed and strode down the ward between the rows of beds, four on one side, four on the other. She strode back and stood staring out the window at the mud-colored shapeless ugly world.

Genya was saying something—"Miriam, honestly, couldn't it be that the metas are worse for me than the native proteins are?"—but she did not listen; the grief and wrath and fear swelled in her and swelled in her, and broke, and she cried out, "Oh, Genya, Genya, how could you? Not you, to give up now, after fighting so long—I can't bear it! I can't bear it!" But she did not cry it out aloud. Not one word of it. Never. She cried out in her mind, and some tears came out and ran down her cheeks, but her back was turned to the patient. She looked through distorting tears at the flat valley and the dull sun and said to them, silent, "I hate you." Then after a while she could turn around and say aloud, "Lie down,"—for he had sat up, distressed by her long silence—"lie down, be quiet. You'll take two metas before dinner. If you need anything, Geza's in the nurse's station." And she walked out.

As she left the infirmary she saw Tina climbing up the back path from the fields, coming to see how Genya was, no doubt. For all his wheezes and fevers Genya had never wanted for girl friends. Tina, and Shoshanna, and Bella, and Rachel, he could have had his pick. But last year when he and Rachel were living together, they had got contraceptives from the clinic regularly, and then they had separated; they hadn't married, though by his age, twenty-four, Settlement kids were married and parents. He hadn't married Rachel, and Miriam knew why. Moral genetics. Bad genes. Shouldn't pass them on to the next generation. Weed out the sicklies. No procreation for him, and therefore no marriage; he couldn't ask Rachel to live barren for the love of him. What the Settlements needed was children, plenty of healthy young natives who, with the help of the meta pills, could survive on this planet.

Rachel hadn't taken up with anybody else. But she was only eighteen. She'd get over it. Marry a boy from another Settlement, most likely, and move away, away from Genya's big gray eyes. It would be best for her. And for him.

No wonder Genya was suicidal! Miriam thought, and put the thought away from her fiercely, wearily. She was very weary. She had meant to go to her room and wash, change her clothes, change her mood, before dinner; but the room was so lonesome with Leonid away at Salem Settlement and not due back for at least another month, she couldn't stand it. She went straight across the dusty central square of the Settlement to the refectory building, and into the Living Room. To get away, clear away, from the windless haze and the gray sky and the ugly sun.

Nobody was in the Living Room but Commander Marca, fast asleep on one of the padded wooden couches, and Reine, reading. The two oldest members of the Settlement. Commander Marca was in fact the oldest person in the world. He had been forty-four when he piloted the Exile Fleet from Old Earth to New Zion; he was seventy now, and very frail. People didn't wear well here. They aged early, died at fifty, sixty. Reine, the biochemist, was forty-five now but looked twenty years older. It's a damned geriatric club, Miriam thought sourly; and it was true that the young, the Zionborn, seldom used the Living Room. They came there to read, as it held the Settlement's library of books and tapes and microfilm, but not many of them read much, or had much time to read. And maybe the April light and the pictures made them a little uneasy. They were such moral, severe, serious young people; there was no leisure in their lives, no beauty in their world; how could they approve of this luxury their elders needed, this one haven, this one place like home. . . .

The Living Room had no windows. Avram, a wizard with anything electrical, had done the indirect lighting, deliberately reproducing the color and quality of sunlight—not NSC 641 light, but sunlight—so that to enter the Living Room was to enter a room in a house on Earth on a warm sunny day of April or early May, to see all things in that clear, clean, lovely light. Avram and several others had worked on the pictures, enlarging colored photos to a meter or so square: scenes of Earth, photographs and paintings brought by the colonists—

Venice, the Negev, the domes of the Kremlin, a farm in Portugal, the Dead Sea, Hampstead Heath, a beach in Oregon, a meadow in Poland, cities, forests, mountains, Van Gogh's cypresses, Bierstadt's Rocky Mountains, Monet's waterlilies, Leonardo's blue mysterious caves.[3] Every wall of the room was covered with pictures, dozens of pictures, all the beauty of the Earth. So that the Earthborn could see and remember, so that the Zionborn could see and know.

There had been some discussion about the pictures, twenty years ago when Avram had started putting them up: Was it really wise? Should we look back? And so on. But then Commander Marca had come by on a visit, seen the Living Room of Ararat Settlement, and said, "This is where I'll stay." With every Settlement vying to have him, he had chosen Ararat. Because of the pictures of Earth, because of the light of Earth in that room, shining on the green fields, the snowy peaks, the golden forests of autumn, the flight of gulls above the sea, the white and red and rose of waterlilies on blue pools—clear colors, true, pure, the colors of the Earth.

He slept there now, a handsome old man. Outside, in the hard, dull, orange daylight, he would look sick and old, his cheeks veined and muddy. Here you could see what he looked like.

Miriam sat down near him, facing her favorite picture, a quiet landscape by Corot, trees over a silvery stream.[4] She was so tired that for once she was willing to just sit, in a mild stupor. Through the stupor, faintly, idly, words came floating. Couldn't it be . . . honestly, couldn't it be that the metas are worse . . . Miriam, honestly, couldn't it be . . .

"Do you think I never thought of that?" she retorted in silence. "Idiot! Do you think I don't know the metas are hard on your guts? Didn't I try fifty different combinations while you were a kid, trying to get rid of the side effects? But it's not as bad as being allergic to the whole damn planet! You know better than the doctor, do you? Don't give me that. You're trying to—" But she broke off the silent dialogue abruptly. Genya was not trying to kill himself. He was not. He would not. He had courage, that one. And brains.

"All right," she said to the quiet young man in her mind. "All right! If you'll stay in the infirmary, under observation—for two weeks, and do exactly what I say—all right, I'll try it!"

Because, said another, even quieter voice deep in her, it doesn't really matter. Whatever you do or don't do, he will die. This year; next year. Two hours; twenty-four years. The sicklies can't adjust to this world. And neither can we, neither can we. We weren't meant to live here, Genya my dear. We weren't made for this world, nor it for us. We were made of Earth, by Earth, to live on Earth, under the blue sky and the golden sun.

The dinner gong began to ring. Going into the refectory she met little Shura. The child carried a bunch of the repulsive blackish-purple

3. I.e., familiar scenes from their homes on earth, including those in the paintings of the Dutch Vincent Van Gogh (1853–90), the German-born American Albert Bierstadt (1830–1902), the French Claude Monet (1840–1926), and the Italian Leonardo da Vinci (1452–1519).

4. I.e., a typical work by French painter Jean-Baptiste-Camille Corot (1796–1875).

native weeds, as a child at home would carry a bunch of white daisies, red poppies picked in the fields. Shura's eyes were teary as usual, but she smiled up at Auntie Doctor. Her lips looked pallid in the red-orange light of sunset through the windows. Everybody's lips looked pallid. Everybody's face looked tired, set, stoical, after the long day's work, as they went into the Settlement dining hall, all together, the three hundred exiles of Ararat on Zion, the eleventh lost tribe.[5]

He was doing very well. She had to admit it. "You're doing well," she said, and he, with his grin, "I told you so!"

"It could be because you're not doing anything else," she said, "smart ass."

"Not doing anything? I filed health records for Geza all morning, I played games with Rosie and Moishe for two hours, I've been grinding colors all afternoon—say, I need more mineral oil, can I have another liter? It's a much better pigment vehicle than the vegetable oil."

"Sure. But listen. I have something for you better than that. Little Tel Aviv has got their pulp mill going full time. They sent a truck over yesterday with paper—"

"Paper?"

"Half a ton of it! I took two hundred sheets for you. It's in the office." He was off like a shot, and was into the bundle of paper before she even got there. "Oh, God," he said, holding up a sheet, "beautiful, it's beautiful!" And she thought how often she had heard him say that, "beautiful!" of one drab useful thing or another. He didn't know what beauty was; he'd never seen any. The paper was thick, substantial, grayish, in big sheets, intended to be cut small and used sparingly, of course; but let him have it for his painting. There was little enough else she could give him.

"When you let me out of here," Genya said, hugging the unwieldy bundle with both arms, "I'll go over to Tel Aviv and paint their pulp mill, I'll immortalize their pulp mill!"

"You'd better go lie down."

"No, listen, I promised Moishe I'd beat him at chess. What's wrong with him, anyhow?"

"Rashes, edema."

"He's like me?"

Miriam shrugged. "He was fine till this year. Puberty triggered something. Not unusual with allergic symptoms."

"What is allergy, anyhow?"

"Well, call it a failure of adaptation. Back home, people used to feed babies cows' milk, from bottles. Some of the babies could adapt to it, but some got rashes, breathing trouble, colic. The cow's key didn't fit their metabolic lock. Well, New Zion's protein keys don't fit our locks; so we have to change our metabolism with the metas."

"Would Moishe or I have been an allergic on Earth?"

"I don't know. Prematures often are. Irving, he died, oh, twenty years ago, he was allergic to this terrible list of things on Earth, they

---

5. In popular legend, the ten northern Israeli tribes captured by the Assyrians in the eighth century B.C. have reappeared at various times and places.

should never have let him come, poor thing, he spends his life on Earth half suffocated and comes here and starves to death even on a quadruple dose of metas."

"Aha," said Genya, "you shouldn't have given him metas at all. Just Zion mush."

"Zion mush?" Only one of the native grains yielded enough to be worth harvesting, and it produced a gluey meal which could not be baked.

"I ate three bowls of it for lunch."

"He lies around the hospital all day complaining," Miriam said, "and then stuffs his belly with that slop. How can an artistic soul eat something that tastes like jellied bilge?"

"You feed it to your helpless child patients in your own hospital! I just ate the leftovers."

"Oh, get along with you."

"I am. I want to paint while the sun's still up. On a piece of new paper, a whole piece of new paper. . . ."

It had been a long day at the clinic, but there were no inpatients. She had sent Osip home last night in a cast with a good scolding for being so careless as to tip his tractor over, endangering not only his life but the tractor, which was even harder to replace. And young Moishe had gone back to the children's house, though she didn't like the way his rash kept coming back. And Rosie was over her asthma, and the Commander's heart was doing as well as could be expected; so the ward was empty, except for her permanent inmate of the past two weeks, Genya.

He was sprawled out on his bed under the window, so lax and still that she had a moment of alarm; but his color was good, he breathed evenly, he was simply asleep, deeply asleep, the way people slept after a hard day in the fields, exhausted.

He had been painting. He had cleaned up the rags and brushes, he always cleaned up promptly and thoroughly, but the picture stood on his makeshift easel. Usually these days he was secretive about his paintings, hid them, since people had stopped admiring them. The Commander had murmured to her, "What ugly stuff, poor boy!" But she had heard young Moishe, watching Genya paint, say, "How do you do it, Genya, how do you make it so pretty?" and Genya answer, "Beauty's in the eye, Moishe."

Well, that was true, and she went closer to look at the painting in the dull afternoon light. Genya had painted the view out the big window of the ward. Nothing vague and half created this time: realistic, all too realistic. Hideously recognizable. There was the flat ridge of Ararat, the mud-colored trees and fields, the hazy sky, the storage barn and a corner of the school building in the foreground. Her eyes went from the painted scene to the real one. To spend hours, days, painting that! What a waste, what a waste.

It was hard on Genya, it was sad, the way he hid his paintings now, knowing that nobody would want to see them, except maybe a child like Moishe fascinated with the mere skill of the hand, the craftsman's dexterity.

That night as Genya helped her straighten up the injection cabinets

—he was a good deal of help around the infirmary these days—she said, "I like the picture you painted today."

"I finished it today," he corrected her. "Damn thing took all week. I'm just beginning to learn to see."

"Can I put it up in the Living Room?"

He looked at her across a tray of hypodermic needles, his eyes quiet and a little quizzical. "In the Living Room? But that's all pictures of Home."

"It's time maybe we had some pictures of our new home there."

"A moral gesture, eh? Sure. If you like it."

"I like it very much," she lied blandly.

"It isn't bad," he said. "I'll do better, though, when I've learned how to fit myself to the pattern."

"What pattern?"

"Well, you know, you have to look until you *see* the pattern, till it makes sense, and then you have to get that into your hand, too." He made large, vague, shaping gestures with a bottle of absolute alcohol.

"Anybody who asks a painter a question in words deserves what they get, I guess," said Miriam. "Babble, babble. You take the picture over tomorrow and put it up. Artists are so temperamental about where they get their pictures hung, and the lighting. Besides, it's time you were getting out. A little. An hour or two a day. No more."

"Can I eat dinner in the dining hall, then?"

"All right. It'll keep Tina from coming here to keep you from being lonely and eating up all the infirmary rations. That girl eats like a vacuum pump. Listen, if you go out in the middle of the day, will you kindly take the trouble to wear a hat?"

"You think I'm right, then."

"Right?"

"That it was sunstroke."

"That was *my* diagnosis, if you will recall."

"All right: but my addition was that I do better without metas."

"I have no idea. You've got along fine before for weeks, and then poof, down again. Nothing whatever has been proved."

"But a pattern has been established! I've lived a month without metas, and gained six pounds."

"And edema of the head, Mr. Know It All?"

She saw him the next day sitting with Rachel, just before dinner-time, on the slope below the storage barn. Rachel had not come to see him in the infirmary. They sat side by side, very close together, motionless, not talking.

Miriam went on to the Living Room. A half hour there before dinner had become a habit with her lately. It seemed to rest her from the weariness of the day. But the room was less peaceful than usual this evening; the Commander was awake, and talking with Reine and Avram. "Well, where did it come from then?" he was saying in his heavy Italian accent—he had not learned Hebrew till he was forty, in the Transit Camp. "Who put it there?" Then seeing Miriam he greeted her as always with a grand cordiality of voice and gesture. "Ah, Doctor! Please, join us, come, solve our mystery for us. You know each picture in this room as well as I do. Where, do you think, and when did we acquire the new one? You see?"

It's Genya's, Miriam was about to say, when she saw the new picture. It wasn't Genya's. It was a painting, all right, a landscape, but a landscape of the Earth: a wide valley, the fields green and green-gold, orchards coming into flower, the sweeping slope of a mountain in the distance, a tower, perhaps a castle or medieval farm building, in the foreground, and over all the pure, subtle, sunlit sky. It was a complex and happy painting, a celebration of the spring, an act of praise.

"How beautiful," she said, her voice catching. "Didn't you put it up, Avram?"

"Me? I can photograph, I can't paint. Look at it, it's no reproduction. Some kind of tempera or oils, see?"

"Somebody brought it from Home. Had it in their baggage," Reine suggested.

"For twenty-five years?" said the Commander. "Why? And who? We all know what all the others have!"

"No. I think"—Miriam was confused, and stammered—"I think it's something Genya did. I asked him to put up one of his paintings here. Not this one. How did he do this?"

"Copied from a photograph," Avram suggested.

"No no no no, impossible," old Marca said, outraged. "That is a painting, not a copy! That is a work of art, that was seen, seen with the eyes and the heart!"

With the eyes and the heart.

Miriam looked, and she saw. She saw what the light of NSC 641 had hidden from her, what the artificial Earth daylight of the room revealed to her. She saw what Genya saw: the beauty of the world.

"I think it must be in Central France, the Auvergne," Reine was saying wistfully, and the Commander, "Oh no no no, it's near Lake Como, I am certain," and Avram, "Well it looks to me like where I grew up in the Caucasus," when they all turned to look at Miriam. She had made a strange noise, a gasp or laugh or sob. "It's here," she said. "Here. That's Ararat. The mountain. That's the fields, our fields, our trees. That's the corner of the school, that tower. See it? It's here. Zion. It's how Genya sees it. With the eyes and the heart."

"But look, the trees are green, look at the colors, Miriam. It's Earth—"

"Yes! It is Earth. Genya's Earth!"

"But he can't—"

"How do we know? How do we know what a child of Zion sees? We can see the picture in this light that's like Home. Take it outside, into the daylight, and you'll see what we always see, the ugly colors, the ugly planet where we're not at home. But he is at home! He is! It's we," Miriam said, laughing in tears, looking at them all, the anxious, tired, elderly faces, "*we* who lack the key. We with our—with our—" she stumbled and leapt at the idea like a horse at a high wall, "with our meta pills!"

They all stared at her.

"With our meta pills, we can survive here, just barely, right? But don't you see, he *lives* here! We were all perfectly adjusted to Earth, too well, we can't fit anywhere else—he wasn't, wouldn't have been; allergic, a misfit—the pattern a little wrong, see? The pattern. But there are many patterns, infinite patterns, he fits this one a little better than we do—"

Avram and the Commander continued to stare. Reine shot an alarmed glance at the picture, but asked gamely, "You're saying that Genya's allergies—"

"Not just Genya! All the sicklies, maybe! For twenty-five years I've been feeding them metas, and they're allergic to *Earth* proteins, the metas just foul them up, they're a different pattern, oh, idiot! Idiot! Oh, my God, he and Rachel can get married. They've got to marry, he should have kids. What about Rachel taking metas while she's pregnant, the fetus. I can work it out, I can work it out. I must call Leonid. And Moishe, thank God! maybe he's another one! Listen, I must go talk to Genya and Rachel, immediately. Excuse me!" She left, a short, gray woman moving like a lightning bolt.

Marca, Avram, and Reine stood staring after her, at each other, and finally back at Genya's painting.

It hung there before them, serene and joyful, full of light.

"I don't understand," said Avram.

"Patterns," Reine said thoughtfully.

"It is very beautiful," said the old Commander of the Exile Fleet. "Only, it makes me homesick."

1982

JORGE LUIS BORGES

The Garden of Forking Paths[*]

On page 22 of Liddell Hart's *History of World War I* you will read that an attack against the Serre-Montauban[1] line by thirteen British divisions (supported by 1,400 artillery pieces), planned for the 24th of July, 1916, had to be postponed until the morning of the 29th. The torrential rains, Captain Liddell Hart comments, caused this delay, an insignificant one, to be sure.

The following statement, dictated, reread and signed by Dr. Yu Tsun, former professor of English at the *Hochschule* at Tsingtao,[2] throws an unsuspected light over the whole affair. The first two pages of the document are missing.

[*]Translated by Donald A. Yates.

1. Liddell Hart's work is entitled *The Real War, 1914–1918* (1930) and *A History of the World War, 1914–1918* in the enlarged English-language edition (1934). The events of July 1916 do not appear on page 22 in the first and are unlikely to appear so early in any edition. A line between Serre and Montauban forms a defensive position about a hundred miles north-northeast of Paris, north of the Somme River. There is a dizzying mixture of factual references and fiction in this story, the most unlikely often being the factual.

2. The high school in what was the capital of the German colonial enclave until the First World War.

". . . and I hung up the receiver. Immediately afterwards, I recognized the voice that had answered in German. It was that of Captain Richard Madden. Madden's presence in Viktor Runeberg's apartment meant the end of our anxieties and—but this seemed, *or should have seemed*, very secondary to me—also the end of our lives. It meant that Runeberg had been arrested or murdered.[3] Before the sun set on that day, I would encounter the same fate. Madden was implacable. Or rather, he was obliged to be so. An Irishman at the service of England, a man accused of laxity and perhaps of treason, how could he fail to seize and be thankful for such a miraculous opportunity: the discovery, capture, maybe even the death of two agents of the German Reich? I went up to my room; absurdly I locked the door and threw myself on my back on the narrow iron cot. Through the window I saw the familiar roofs and the cloud-shaded six o'clock sun. It seemed incredible to me that that day without premonitions or symbols should be the one of my inexorable death. In spite of my dead father, in spite of having been a child in a symmetrical garden of Hai Feng,[4] was I—now—going to die? Then I reflected that everything happens to a man precisely, precisely *now*. Centuries of centuries and only in the present do things happen; countless men in the air, on the face of the earth and the sea, and all that really is happening is happening to me . . . The almost intolerable recollection of Madden's horselike face banished these wanderings. In the midst of my hatred and terror (it means nothing to me now to speak of terror, now that I have mocked Richard Madden, now that my throat yearns for the noose) it occurred to me that that tumultuous and doubtless happy warrior did not suspect that I possessed the Secret. The name of the exact location of the new British artillery park on the River Ancre.[5] A bird streaked across the gray sky and blindly I translated it into an airplane and that airplane into many (against the French sky) annihilating the artillery station with vertical bombs. If only my mouth, before a bullet shattered it, could cry out that secret name so it could be heard in Germany . . . My human voice was very weak. How might I make it carry to the ear of the Chief? To the ear of that sick and hateful man who knew nothing of Runeberg and me save that we were in Staffordshire[6] and who was waiting in vain for our report in his arid office in Berlin, endlessly examining newspapers . . . I said out loud: *I must flee*. I sat up noiselessly, in a useless perfection of silence, as if Madden were already lying in wait for me. Something—perhaps the mere vain ostentation of proving my resources were nil—made me look through my pockets. I found what I knew I would find. The American watch, the nickel chain and the square coin, the key ring with the incriminating useless keys to Runeberg's apartment, the notebook, a letter which I resolved to

3. An hypothesis both hateful and odd. The Prussian spy Hans Rabener, alias Viktor Runeberg, attacked with drawn automatic the bearer of the warrant for his arrest, Captain Richard Madden. The latter, in self-defense, inflicted the wound which brought about Runeberg's death. (Borges's note.)

4. Chinese gardens usually aim for the appearance of nature, so a symmetrical garden would be unusual. Hai Feng seems fictional, as many names here are, but Hai-fang is Chinese for the Vietnamese city of Haiphong and is near the Yunnan province mentioned later.

5. River in northeastern France.

6. County in English midlands.

destroy immediately (and which I did not destroy), a crown, two
shillings and a few pence,[7] the red-and-blue pencil, the handkerchief,
the revolver with one bullet. Absurdly, I took it in my hand and
weighed it in order to inspire courage within myself. Vaguely I thought
that a pistol report can be heard at a great distance. In ten minutes
my plan was perfected. The telephone book listed the name of the
only person capable of transmitting the message; he lived in a suburb
of Fenton, less than a half hour's train ride away.

I am a cowardly man. I say it now, now that I have carried to its
end a plan whose perilous nature no one can deny. I know its execution was terrible. I didn't do it for Germany, no. I care nothing for
a barbarous country which imposed upon me the abjection of being
a spy. Besides, I know of a man from England—a modest man—who
for me is no less great than Goethe. I talked with him for scarcely an
hour, but during that hour he was Goethe . . . I did it because I
sensed that the Chief somehow feared people of my race—for the innumerable ancestors who merge within me. I wanted to prove to him
that a yellow man could save his armies. Besides, I had to flee from
Captain Madden. His hands and his voice could call at my door at
any moment. I dressed silently, bade farewell to myself in the mirror,
went downstairs, scrutinized the peaceful street and went out. The
station was not far from my home, but I judged it wise to take a cab.
I argued that in this way I ran less risk of being recognized; the fact
is that in the deserted street I felt myself visible and vulnerable,
infinitely so. I remember that I told the cab driver to stop a short
distance before the main entrance. I got out with voluntary, almost
painful slowness; I was going to the village of Ashgrove but I bought
a ticket for a more distant station. The train left within a very few
minutes, at eight-fifty. I hurried; the next one would leave at nine-
thirty. There was hardly a soul on the platform. I went through the
coaches; I remember a few farmers, a woman dressed in mourning,
a young boy who was reading with fervor the *Annals* of Tacitus,[8] a
wounded and happy soldier. The coaches jerked forward at last. A
man whom I recognized ran in vain to the end of the platform. It
was Captain Richard Madden. Shattered, trembling, I shrank into the
far corner of the seat, away from the dreaded window.

From this broken state I passed into an almost abject felicity. I
told myself that the duel had already begun and that I had won the
first encounter by frustrating, even if for forty minutes, even if by a
stroke of fate, the attack of my adversary. I argued that this slightest
of victories foreshadowed a total victory. I argued (no less falla-
ciously) that my cowardly felicity proved that I was a man capable
of carrying out the adventure successfully. From this weakness I took
strength that did not abandon me. I foresee that man will resign himself each day to more atrocious undertakings; soon there will be no
one but warriors and brigands; I give them this counsel: *The author*

---

7. Though the two dollars' worth of
coins would be worth quite a bit more
at present, it still is not much for a middle-class person to be carrying.
8. The Annals of Cornelius Tacitus (55?–

117?) treat the history of Rome from the
death of Augustus in 14 to the end of
Nero's reign in 68, and the military events
of the period.

*of an atrocious undertaking ought to imagine that he has already
accomplished it, ought to impose upon himself a future as irrevocable
as the past.* Thus I proceeded as my eyes of a man already dead
registered the elapsing of that day, which was perhaps the last, and
the diffusion of the night. The train ran gently along, amid ash trees.
It stopped, almost in the middle of the fields. No one announced the
name of the station. "Ashgrove?" I asked a few lads on the platform.
"Ashgrove," they replied. I got off.

A lamp enlightened the platform but the faces of the boys were
in shadow. One questioned me, "Are you going to Dr. Stephen Albert's house?" Without waiting for my answer, another said, "The
house is a long way from here, but you won't get lost if you take
this road to the left and at every crossroads turn again to your left."
I tossed them a coin (my last), descended a few stone steps and
started down the solitary road. It went downhill, slowly. It was of
elemental earth; overhead the branches were tangled; the low, full
moon seemed to accompany me.

For an instant, I thought that Richard Madden in some way had
penetrated my desperate plan. Very quickly, I understood that that
was impossible. The instructions to turn always to the left reminded
me that such was the common procedure for discovering the central
point of certain labyrinths. I have some understanding of labyrinths:
not for nothing am I the great grandson of that Ts'ui Pên who was
governor of Yunnan[9] and who renounced worldly power in order to
write a novel that might be even more populous than the *Hung Lu
Meng*[1] and to construct a labyrinth in which all men would become
lost. Thirteen years he dedicated to these heterogeneous tasks, but
the hand of a stranger murdered him—and his novel was incoherent
and no one found the labyrinth. Beneath English trees I meditated
on that lost maze: I imagined it inviolate and perfect at the secret
crest of a mountain; I imagined it erased by rice fields or beneath the
water; I imagined it infinite, no longer composed of octagonal kiosks
and returning paths, but of rivers and provinces and kingdoms . . . I
thought of a labyrinth of labyrinths, of one sinuous spreading labyrinth that would encompass the past and the future and in some
way involve the stars. Absorbed in these illusory images, I forgot my
destiny of one pursued. I felt myself to be, for an unknown period of
time, an abstract perceiver of the world. The vague, living countryside,
the moon, the remains of the day worked on me, as well as the
slope of the road, which eliminated any possibility of weariness. The
afternoon was intimate, infinite. The road descended and forked among
the now confused meadows. A high-pitched, almost syllabic music
approached and receded in the shifting of the wind, dimmed by leaves
and distance. I thought that a man can be an enemy of other men,
of the moments of other men, but not of a country: not of fireflies,
words, gardens, streams of water, sunsets. Thus I arrived before a

9. Southwesternmost of China's eighteen
traditional provinces; beautiful but sparsely
populated, damp and malarial (the name
means "Cloudy South"); not an ideal
diplomatic assignment.

1. *Dream of the Red Chamber*, long,
semiautobiographical novel by Ts'ao Chan
(1715–1763) about the decay of a wealthy
noble family.

tall, rusty gate. Between the iron bars I made out a poplar grove and a pavilion. I understood suddenly two things, the first trivial, the second almost unbelievable: the music came from the pavilion, and the music was Chinese. For precisely that reason I had openly accepted it without paying it any heed. I do not remember whether there was a bell or whether I knocked with my hand. The sparkling of the music continued.

From the rear of the house within a lantern approached: a lantern that the trees sometimes striped and sometimes eclipsed, a paper lantern that had the form of a drum and the color of the moon. A tall man bore it. I didn't see his face for the light blinded me. He opened the door and said slowly, in my own language: "I see that the pious Hsi P'êng persists in correcting my solitude. You no doubt wish to see the garden?"

I recognized the name of one of our consuls and I replied, disconcerted, "The garden?"

"The garden of forking paths."

Something stirred in my memory and I uttered with incomprehensible certainty, "The garden of my ancestor Ts'ui Pên."

"Your ancestor? Your illustrious ancestor? Come in."

The damp path zigzagged like those of my childhood. We came to a library of Eastern and Western books. I recognized bound in a yellow silk several volumes of the Lost Encyclopedia, edited by the Third Emperor of the Luminous Dynasty[2] but never printed. The record on the phonograph revolved next to a bronze phoenix. I also recall a *famille rose*[3] vase and another, many centuries older, of that shade of blue which our craftsmen copied from the potters of Persia . . .

Stephen Albert observed me with a smile. He was, as I have said, very tall, sharp-featured, with gray eyes and a gray beard. He told me that he had been a missionary in Tientsin "before aspiring to become a Sinologist."

We sat down—I on a long, low divan, he with his back to the window and a tall circular clock. I calculated that my pursuer, Richard Madden, could not arrive for at least an hour. My irrevocable determination could wait.

"An astounding fate, that of Ts'ui Pên," Stephen Albert said. "Governor of his native province, learned in astronomy, in astrology and in the tireless interpretation of the canonical books,[4] chess player, famous poet and calligrapher—he abandoned all this in order to compose a book and a maze. He renounced the pleasures of both tyranny and justice, of his populous couch, of his banquets and even of erudition—all to close himself up for thirteen years in the Pavilion of the Limpid Solitude.[5] When he died, his heirs found nothing save

2. The "Luminous" Dynasty is the Ming; its third emperor, Yung-lo, reigned 1402–1424. He commissioned a compilation of all significant work done on Chinese history, government, philosophy, geography, etc., which, though incomplete, ran to over 11,000 of the small Chinese volumes—too long to be printed.

3. "Rose family" Chinese porcelain, characterized by rose glaze over the decoration.
4. The Confucian classics which officials had to know thoroughly and apply to contemporary social and political issues.
5. The names of both Ts'ui Pên and the Pavilion seem fictitious.

chaotic manuscripts. His family, as you may be aware, wished to condemn them to the fire, but his executor—a Taoist or Buddhist monk—insisted on their publication."

"We descendants of Ts'ui Pên," I replied, "continue to curse that monk. Their publication was senseless. The book is an indeterminate heap of contradictory drafts. I examined it once: in the third chapter the hero dies, in the fourth he is alive. As for the other undertaking of Ts'ui Pên, his labyrinth . . ."

"Here is Ts'ui Pên's labyrinth," he said, indicating a tall lacquered desk.

"An ivory labyrinth!" I exclaimed. "A minimum labyrinth."

"A labyrinth of symbols," he corrected. "An invisible labyrinth of time. To me, a barbarous Englishman, has been entrusted the revelation of this diaphanous mystery. After more than a hundred years, the details are irretrievable; but it is not hard to conjecture what happened. Ts'ui Pên must have said once: *I am withdrawing to write a book*. And another time: *I am withdrawing to construct a labyrinth*. Everyone imagined two works; to no one did it occur that the book and the maze were one and the same thing. The Pavilion of the Limpid Solitude stood in the center of a garden that was perhaps intricate; that circumstance could have suggested to the heirs a physical labyrinth. Ts'ui Pên died; no one in the vast territories that were his came upon the labyrinth; the confusion of the novel suggested to me that *it* was the maze. Two circumstances gave me the correct solution of the problem. One: the curious legend that Ts'ui Pên had planned to create a labyrinth which would be strictly infinite. The other: a fragment of a letter I discovered."

Albert rose. He turned his back on me for a moment; he opened a drawer of the black and gold desk. He faced me and in his hands he held a sheet of paper that had once been crimson, but was now pink and tenuous and cross-sectioned. The fame of Ts'ui Pên as a calligrapher had been justly won. I read, uncomprehendingly and with fervor, these words written with a minute brush by a man of my blood: *I leave to the various futures (not to all) my garden of forking paths*. Wordlessly, I returned the sheet. Albert continued:

"Before unearthing this letter, I had questioned myself about the ways in which a book can be infinite. I could think of nothing other than a cyclic volume, a circular one. A book whose last page was identical with the first, a book which had the possibility of continuing indefinitely. I remembered too that night which is at the middle of the Thousand and One Nights when Scheherazade (through a magical oversight of the copyist) begins to relate word for word the story of the Thousand and One Nights, establishing the risk of coming once again to the night when she must repeat it, and thus on to infinity. I imagined as well a Platonic, hereditary work, transmitted from father to son, in which each new individual adds a chapter or corrects with pious care the pages of his elders. These conjectures diverted me; but none seemed to correspond, not even remotely, to the contradictory chapters of Ts'ui Pên. In the midst of this perplexity, I received from Oxford the manuscript you have examined. I lingered, naturally, on the sentence: *I leave to the various futures (not to all) my garden of forking paths.* Almost instantly, I understood: 'the garden of forking paths' was the chaotic novel; the phrase 'the various futures (not to all)' suggested to me the forking in time, not in space. A broad rereading of the work confirmed the theory. In all fictional works, each time a man is confronted with several alternatives, he chooses one and eliminates the others; in the fiction of Ts'ui Pên, he chooses—simultaneously—all of them. *He creates,* in this way, diverse futures, diverse times which themselves also proliferate and fork. Here, then, is the explanation of the novel's contradictions. Fang, let us say, has a secret; a stranger calls at his door; Fang resolves to kill him. Naturally, there are several possible outcomes: Fang can kill the intruder, the intruder can kill Fang, they both can escape, they both can die, and so forth. In the work of Ts'ui Pên, all possible outcomes occur; each one is the point of departure for other forkings. Sometimes, the paths of this labyrinth converge: for example, you arrive at this house, but in one of the possible pasts you are my enemy, in another, my friend. If you will resign yourself to my incurable pronunciation, we shall read a few pages."

His face, within the vivid circle of the lamplight, was unquestionably that of an old man, but with something unalterable about it, even immortal. He read with slow precision two versions of the same epic chapter. In the first, an army marches to a battle across a lonely mountain; the horror of the rocks and shadows makes the men undervalue their lives and they gain an easy victory. In the second, the same army traverses a palace where a great festival is taking place; the resplendent battle seems to them a continuation of the celebration and they win the victory. I listened with proper veneration to these ancient narratives, perhaps less admirable in themselves than the fact that they had been created by my blood and were being restored to me by a man of a remote empire, in the course of a desperate adventure, on a Western isle. I remember the last words, repeated in each version like a secret commandment: *Thus fought the heroes, tranquil their admirable hearts, violent their swords, resigned to kill and to die.*

From that moment on, I felt about me and within my dark body an invisible, intangible swarming. Not the swarming of the divergent, parallel and finally coalescent armies, but a more inaccessible, more intimate agitation that they in some manner prefigured. Stephen Albert continued:

"I don't believe that your illustrious ancestor played idly with these variations. I don't consider it credible that he would sacrifice thirteen years to the infinite execution of a rhetorical experiment. In your country, the novel is a subsidiary form of literature; in Ts'ui Pên's time it was a despicable form. Ts'ui Pên was a brilliant novelist, but he was also a man of letters who doubtless did not consider himself a mere novelist. The testimony of his contemporaries proclaims—and his life fully confirms—his metaphysical and mystical interests. Philosophic controversy usurps a good part of the novel. I know that of all problems, none disturbed him so greatly nor worked upon him so much as the abysmal problem of time. Now then, the latter is the only problem that does not figure in the pages of the *Garden.* He does not even use the word that signifies *time*. How do you explain this voluntary omission?"

I proposed several solutions—all unsatisfactory. We discussed them. Finally, Stephen Albert said to me:

"In a riddle whose answer is chess, what is the only prohibited word?"

I thought a moment and replied, "The word *chess*."

"Precisely," said Albert. "*The Garden of Forking Paths* is an enormous riddle, or parable, whose theme is time; this recondite cause prohibits its mention. To omit a word always, to resort to inept metaphors and obvious periphrases, is perhaps the most emphatic way of stressing it. That is the tortuous method preferred, in each of the meanderings of his indefatigable novel, by the oblique Ts'ui Pên. I have compared hundreds of manuscripts, I have corrected the errors that the negligence of the copyists has introduced, I have guessed the plan of this chaos, I have re-established—I believe I have re-established—the primordial organization, I have translated the entire work: it is clear to me that not once does he employ the word 'time.' The explanation is obvious: *The Garden of Forking Paths* is an incomplete, but not false, image of the universe as Ts'ui Pên conceived it. In contrast to Newton and Schopenhauer, your ancestor did not believe in a uniform, absolute time. He believed in an infinite series of times, in a growing, dizzying net of divergent, convergent and parallel times. This network of times which approached one another, forked, broke off, or were unaware of one another for centuries, embraces *all* possibilities of time. We do not exist in the majority of these times; in some you exist, and not I; in others I, and not you; in others, both of us. In the present one, which a favorable fate has granted me, you have arrived at my house; in another, while crossing the garden, you found me dead; in still another, I utter these same words, but I am a mistake, a ghost."

"In every one," I pronounced, not without a tremble to my voice, "I am grateful to you and revere you for your re-creation of the garden of Ts'ui Pên."

"Not in all," he murmured with a smile. "Time forks perpetually toward innumerable futures. In one of them I am your enemy."

Once again I felt the swarming sensation of which I have spoken. It seemed to me that the humid garden that surrounded the house was infinitely saturated with invisible persons. Those persons were Albert and I, secret, busy and multiform in other dimensions of time. I raised my eyes and the tenuous nightmare dissolved. In the yellow and black garden there was only one man; but this man was as strong as a statue . . . this man was approaching along the path and he was Captain Richard Madden.

"The future already exists," I replied, "but I am your friend. Could I see the letter again?"

Albert rose. Standing tall, he opened the drawer of the tall desk; for the moment his back was to me. I had readied the revolver. I fired with extreme caution. Albert fell uncomplainingly, immediately. I swear his death was instantaneous—a lightning stroke.

The rest is unreal, insignificant. Madden broke in, arrested me. I have been condemned to the gallows. I have won out abominably; I have communicated to Berlin the secret name of the city they must attack. They bombed it yesterday; I read it in the same papers that offered to England the mystery of the learned Sinologist Stephen Albert, who was murdered by a stranger, one Yu Tsun. The Chief had deciphered this mystery. He knew my problem was to indicate (through the uproar of the war) the city called Albert[6] and that I had found no other means to do so than to kill a man of that name. He does not know (no one can know) my innumerable contrition and weariness.

For Victoria Ocampo   p. 1958

11   THE SHORT STORY AND OTHER NARRATIVES

Elsewhere in this book I have talked about short stories without ever defining the term, assuming that the selections were short stories (and so far they have been), and that they could be discussed as such.

This chapter, however, includes six brief narratives that are short and that tell stories, but that are not really *short stories*. The distinction between the narratives in this chapter and the short stories in the other chapters should lead us toward a definition of the short story as a fictional genre.

Short stories are short. Short stories can be very short indeed, perhaps no longer than a few words, though the median length is about 8,000 words (a dozen or so pages in this book). The longer short stories get, the more they become something else ·

Short stories are written down (the root of the word literature means *letter*). **Narrative,** a mode that includes stories and accounts, real or fictional, usually connecting a series of events, derives from a root word meaning *to tell,* and began indeed as an oral form, long before there were alphabets or writing, no doubt—stories told around a campfire (if there were campfires). Narrative is still an essentially oral form in many cultures and exists as an oral form in all—in our culture as jokes, anecdotes, tall tales, and so forth. All of the stories in this volume are written down—or printed, rather—but some in this chapter were first "told," and were probably passed down by word of mouth from generation to generation. These tales are not necessarily "primitive" in the sense of artless or unsophisticated, for oral narrative has its own qualities and requires its own skills in construction, but

---

6. City on the Paris side (southwest) of the River Ancre.

they do not as a rule follow the same structural patterns of rising and falling action or of causal, logical connection or articulation that we customarily find in short stories.

Short stories are original. An Eskimo, Lamba, or Kiowa narrative is presented as a story that belongs not to the teller but to the culture as a whole; a tale that has existed in one form or another over a long time, perhaps from the dawn of the culture itself. Though some short stories may use traditional patterns—the journey in *The Artificial Nigger*, the scapegoat in *The Lottery*—or traditional material—like the ritual initiation in *The Old People* or the trickster in *Jumping Frog*—the story itself, in its details and in most of its elements, is new or original. Originality implies and sometimes emphasizes the author or creator of the story. The Eskimo, Lamba, or Kiowa narrator is usually effaced, and if he has any identity it is usually either that of an elder whose memory goes back to historical events or to tales he heard as a child or youth from his elders, or that of a performer, newly presenting old tales. Even short stories such as *My Man Bovanne* and *Spotted Horses*, which sound like oral narratives written down, deal with unique, new, or original events and characters, and are "told" by narrators who participate in or observe the "actual" story.

One universal kind of communal oral narrative whose origins lie in the shadowy past is the **myth**, a tale that has to do with matters beyond human memory or knowledge: the gods, the origins of the world, of man, of the tribe, or of various animals and plants. Another common kind is the **legend**, the tale of a human hero, often with divine qualities, and his exploits, often with divine assistance. **Fables**—narratives in prose or verse that point a moral and often use animals as characters—were originally an oral form. They proved so popular that not only were many written down, but more were invented, and the fable has become a literary genre, as we can see in *The Zebra Storyteller*. **Parables** are short narratives that make or illustrate a moral point; they are sometimes short allegories in which each of the details contributes to that moral meaning. They often begin as oral narratives and are later written down as the sayings of great teachers. *The Brigand and the Sage* is such a parable. Most of us are familiar with the parables in the New Testament, such as that of the talents (Matthew 25:14–30) or of the Good Samaritan (Luke 10:30–37).

Short stories are fictional. Though the short story as we are defining it is a subgenre of the genre fiction, even the assertion that a short story is fictional needs qualification. I read the autobiographical portions of N. Scott Momaday's *The Way to Rainy Mountain* as nonfiction. I think Momaday wants me to believe that what he says about himself and his experiences is true and that he believes it to be true. It is not necessary that it *be* true: memory inevitably distorts somewhat, and some details he "remembers" he may have dreamed or heard from older friends or relatives so often that he only thinks he remembers them. On the other hand, I read Mordecai Richler's *The Day My Grandmother Was Supposed to Die* as fiction, as a short story. While it is conceivable that every word of the story is true, that Richler may be reporting an episode from his childhood (the narrator's Yiddish name Muttel can be translated Mordecai), Richler has structured the piece like a short story—with beginning, middle, and end, for example —and we can read it as a story without concern for its actuality. This appearance of arrangement and structuring, of being made, of being *artificial*, in its best sense, is sometimes as important as the relation of a story to actuality in defining its fictionality. (Both *artificial* and *fiction* come from root words having to do with *making* or *molding*.)

Short stories are narratives. This, surely would seem to need no qualification. The middle sections of the Momaday selections, however —especially the passages from the work of an anthropologist—we recognize not as narrative but as **exposition,** a subgenre of nonfictional prose that serves to explain, or as a mixture of exposition and **description.** But all narratives are "impure," having passages of description and exposition in them. What we mean when we say a short story is a narrative is not that every word, sentence, or passage is in some special narrative language that could be identified as such outside the context of the story, but only that the piece as a whole tells a story and that the non-narrative elements contribute to that story.

The short story, then, may be defined as a brief, written, original, fictional narrative in prose.

This chapter makes no attempt to represent all the various kinds of narratives other than the short story, nor does it sample representative narratives that preceded the short story in Western culture. To some extent it represents prose narratives that are most "other": primarily oral narratives; non-Western narratives from American Indian, Eskimo, African, Middle Eastern, and Oriental cultures; and even a bit of nonfictional narrative. It seeks to push toward the outer limits of narrative, to the most strange and different.

The purpose is not only to make us less provincial in thinking about brief narratives, but to open us up to what in fact has been happening in the short story of our own time. A tendency toward the realistic or everyday was long thought to be one of the defining qualities of the modern short story—and a few years ago I might easily have added *realistic* to the list of adjectives in my generic definition. As suggested in the previous chapter, the line from Poe through Maupassant to Chekhov and Joyce was long considered the history of artistic progress —not just in the quality of the individual authors named, which may be valid enough, but in writers' mastery of the art of representing reality. Just as the camera jolted painters in the last hundred years or so to open their eyes to alternative ways of looking at reality and led them to non-Western traditions of representation as one means of broadening human vision, so the writer of narrative, such as Spencer Holst or Gabriel García Márquez, seems to have turned to older oral or other modes. One way of reading *The Way to Rainy Mountain* is to use the nonfiction narrative sections to understand the "reality" behind the Kiowa myths and legends and oral history; another, however, is to recognize that Momaday and the anthropologist he quotes in exposition and autobiography are also only giving fallible human versions of reality, not necessarily more valid (though more acceptable because more familiar) than the Kiowa. Many recent stories, such as Grace Paley's *A Conversation with My Father*, acknowledge within the narrative the artificiality or arbitrariness of narrative itself, the inevitable subjective distortion of reality by an author, the imposition of art upon the actual.

A Note on Dates

Oral narrative is, by its very nature, difficult if not impossible to date accurately. Some of the Kiowa legends that N. Scott Momaday reports in the 1960s probably go back two or three centuries, but they have been passed on to him by his elders. So, too, the Iroquois, Lamba, and Eskimo stories are both old and new. Chuang Tzu lived about the fourth century B.C. but some of the stories and sayings attributed to him have no doubt been added and most have been changed. Sir Richard Burton's translation of *The Thousand Nights and a Night* was published between 1885 and 1888; Western translations date to the early eighteenth century. The actual origin of the tales is obscure, though Harun-al-Rashid, the Persian caliph in the tales, reigned from A.D. 786 to 809. Some of the tales may well have earlier Indian origins.

CORNPLANTER

The Great Mosquito*

An immense bird preyed upon the red men in all parts of the country. Their homes were at no time safe from its ravages. Often it would carry away children playing beside the wigwams, or, like a bolt of lightning, dart from the sky and strike a woman or man bleeding and dying to the earth. Whole fields of corn had been destroyed in a single night by its ravages, and its coming was so swift and terrible that the Indians hardly dared stir from the shelter of their houses. A strong party of Cayugas and Onondagas[1] finally determined upon its death, no matter at what cost to themselves. A young warrior offered himself for the sacrifice. He was provided with a quantity of rawhide thongs, and repaired to one of the open spaces, where it was believed the dreaded monster would discover and descend upon him. The young brave was to bind one of the thongs upon the bird's feet or upon some portion of its body, if possible, before he killed him, and then his companions, rushing from their place of concealment, would try to slay the enemy that had been snared with such difficulty. The preparations were elaborately made, and the young brave went forth on his dangerous mission.

Three days he sat, chanting his death-song and awaiting the coming of his terrible fate. On the morning of the fourth day the sky was suddenly darkened and the watchers saw that the great bird was slowly circling above the heroic young Cayuga. He ceased his

* Translated by William Canfield.
1. Two American Indian nations within the Iroquois Confederacy, which was founded about 1570 in New York state.

chanting, and, standing upright, shouted defiance to the almost certain death that awaited him.

With a scream that turned the hearts of the waiting Indians cold with terror, the bird dropped upon its victim like a panther on his prey. A short and terrible struggle took place and then the concealed warriors rushed forth to finish the work of their brave young companion, who had succeeded in throwing one of the thongs over the great mosquito's neck. They brought willing and ready hands to the battle, and the arrows poured upon the struggling mass like a storm of hail. After a long encounter the bird was killed, and the young Cayuga smiled in triumph as his last glance rested upon the dead body of the monster.

Runners were at once dispatched to the villages to inform the Indians of the victory, and soon vast numbers of them came to look upon their long-dreaded enemy that had been slain at such cost. Its body was larger than that of the largest bear they had ever seen, and the breadth of its outstretched wings was as great as the height of three men. Its talons were as long as arrows, and its monstrous beak was lined with sharp teeth. There was much rejoicing over the great mosquito's death, and for several days feasting and dancing were held in honor of the bravery of those who had rid the country of such a terrible scourge. Soon, however, swarms of the poisonous little flies that have been the pests of all nations since that time, infested the woods, and the Indians discovered that they came from the body of the dead bird. Too late they realized that the body of the great mosquito should have been burned when it was first slain, for fire is ever the destroyer of evil spirits.

OHAYOHOK

A Human Kayak*

This is the story of two brothers who lived in the south part of the village of Keengegan. They had just passed the tests that would permit them to be considered among the regular hunters of the village. After each had brought home a seal and delivered it to the old chief, who would cut it up and pass the meat around to all the homes, they became producers instead of dependents. It was in the spring of the year. The warm south winds had broken up the great ice fields and had brought with them a great abundance of seal to become the prey of *Innuit*[1] hunters. On this particular day the two brothers agreed to go out to the edge of the shore ice and hunt seal. How proud their old father, the Chief, would be to see his two sons dragging their first seal over the ice to the village. Thereafter, they would

---

* Translated by Clark M. Garber.   1. "People," i.e., Eskimo people.

be considered full-fledged hunters and would take their place with the other hunters.

Taking their bows, arrows, spears, *pooksaks*,[2] and other necessary hunting equipment, they traveled almost half of the day before they came to the edge of the shore ice. Around the open patches of water, they hunted until darkness began to overtake them. This brought them to the realization that they had better return to the village regardless of the fact that they had failed to kill a single seal and would be the subjects of many chiding remarks and laughter when they reached the village empty-handed. When they came to a point about halfway on their homeward journey, they discovered that they were on a very large pan of ice which had broken away from the shore and had already left a wide stretch of water between them and the village. The wind and current carried them farther and farther away on their enormous raft of ice. As darkness fell, they could see the land gradually disappearing from sight.

Their plight offered no serious difficulties to the problem of procuring food. They could always rely on their bows and arrows and spears to provide the food they would need. But they realized that unless their ice raft brought them again to land they would finally find themselves in the land of Peeleeuktuk, the land of missing men, from which no man ever returned. Then their relatives and friends would hear of them no more. In their feather parkas and fur pants and *mukluks*[3] they could not freeze, or even suffer from the cold. As long as they could kill seal or other game, they were in no danger of starving.

The boys could hardly wait for daylight to come the next morning so they could set to work building a shelter of snow and ice blocks. In this kind of a shelter, even though it were small, they would be safe from the blizzards which so often raged across the ocean ice. In their little snow hut they lived for many days while their big raft of ice carried them farther and farther from home. Apparently the spirits of the sea were unfavorable to them because they had been so careless as to get caught on the drifting ice. Therefore the seal and other game animals failed to come near them. It was not long until they became very hungry. One day, when the older boy returned from a hunt for food he found his brother had fallen sick in their snow hut. Thereupon a great fear began to creep into their hearts. A longing to return to their father's *innie*[4] possessed them and made them very sad.

On the following day, the younger brother said, "One has conversed with the spirits during the night. They have said that one's body will turn cold in death before two more suns pass."

On the second day thereafter, the younger brother went to their customary lookout on top of a large ice ridge to search with his keen eyes the endless expanse of ice for some sign of land. Toward midday, he sighted a low dark streak of land. Waiting long enough to be

2. Hunter's bag, usually sealskin.
3. Fur or leather boots.
4. Underground house.

sure that they were approaching the shore, he rushed back to the snow hut thinking that such glad tidings would bring rapid recovery to his brother. When he entered the hut, he found his brother dead. Thus his brother's body had turned cold in death just as he had said it would. What could he do now? Land was in sight and the big ice raft on which he was drifting would soon touch the shore. He could not leave his brother's body on the drifting ice. That would offend the spirits of the sea animals beyond repair and would bring famine upon all his people.

There was only one thing to do. Dragging his brother's body by the parka hood, he came as quickly as possible to the edge of the ice nearest to the land. But here he was again thwarted in his purpose. The large ice floe had already touched the shore and was again drifting away from the land. How to get to land across the rapidly widening open water, and at the same time take his brother's body ashore, gave him a problem almost beyond his ability to solve. At length, after many trials and failures, he struck upon the plan of using his brother's body as a means to reach the shore. With his hunting knife he quickly opened the body of his brother and removed the viscera. Then he lashed the shaft of his harpoon to the back of the corpse in order to hold it rigid. He then placed the corpse in the water with the face turned up, and carefully assumed a position within the body cavity, as he would sit in his kayak. In this manner he had converted the body of his brother into a human kayak. After much hard paddling with his bare hands and very slow progress, he finally reached the shore ice safely.

By this time he was becoming very weak from hunger. However, he managed, by great will power and effort, to drag his brother's body to the mountain side and bury it among the rocks. Then he began journeying along the beach in the direction of his home. Day after day he walked alowly along the rock-strewn shore and sandy beach. After many days of slow and difficult traveling with nothing to eat but bits of decaying matter which he picked up along the beach, he came upon a village. When he first caught sight of the village, his strength suddenly left him and he fell prone upon the ground. By sheer will power he forced himself to crawl along on his hands and knees. In this manner he came to the first *innie* of the village. Darkness had fallen, so there were no people about to witness his slow and laborious approach. When he crawled into the entrance of the *innie*, he came upon a mother dog with a litter of pups. There his progress was halted with great commotion.

The *innie* door opened and out through the tunnellike entrance came a beautiful girl to discover the cause of such an unusual disturbance. No sooner did she discover the young man in his weak and starving condition than she sounded an alarm and summoned help from within. Her father came to help her, and soon the young man was lying upon a soft bed of skins noisily devouring a large dish of *okpone*, blood stew. Under the kind treatment of these good people and the excellent food, which the very nice girl prepared for him, his strength soon returned. In a few days, he was ready to add his hunting skill to the problem of keeping food supplied for the family. It was not long until he had become the best hunter in the village. Thereupon he married the lovely girl who had saved him and had nursed him back to health. Thereafter, for a long time, he lived with his wife's people and became the main support of her family.

Until many moons later, life ran along smoothly for the young hunter and his wife. One day his wife came to him and said with much concern, "One's man is a very good hunter. Every time he goes hunting he returns after a short time with a very fine catch. How does one do it?"

"Someday one will tell his woman all about it," replied the young husband.

When another moon had passed, his wife again asked him about his wonderful skill as a hunter. To her query he replied, "First you must get your man some water from the ocean." With her small pail, she hastened to the beach and dipped it full of salty brine. Returning quickly to the *innie*, she placed the pail of water on the floor before her husband. From his parka sleeve her husband drew the skin of a bird. He wet the bird skin in his mouth and then stretched it over his body, thereby transforming himself into a bird. Then he began to fly about inside of the *innie*. After flying about the *innie* for a while, he suddenly dived into the pail of water and came out with a small fish in his beak. Flying as high as possible in the *innie*, he dropped the little fish onto the floor. To the great amazement of his wife, the little fish suddenly turned into a seal. Again the bird man dived into the pail of water and this time brought up a larger fish. This one turned into an *oogrook*[5] when dropped upon the floor. Suddenly the bird man flew through the window of the *innie*. His wife called to him, "Come back my husband. Come back my man. Do not leave your woman in this way."

"This is why one did not wish to tell his lovely wife about his hunting skill. Now one must leave his woman and never return," replied the young birdlike husband, as he flew over the *innie* endeavoring to find his bearings.

In his bird plumage, the young hunter began the journey to his own home. When he arrived in the village of his own people after many days of flying along the coast, his people did not know him from the other birds which flew about the village. Many times, he slept near his mother's *innie* but she did not know that this little bird was one of her long-lost sons. All the time, the little bird stayed near the window of his mother's *eeah*, kitchen, where the smoke from the seal oil lamps and stoves came out. At length the smoke and soot had turned his plumage black so that he looked like a raven.

One day, he fell asleep while perched on the edge of the *eeah* window, and fell into the kitchen. His mother struck him with a wooden spoon with which she was stirring the *okpone,* blood stew. The blow bursted the bird plumage open and out stepped her son. His mother's feelings at finding her long-lost son so unexpectedly

5. Large bearded seal.

brought tears of joy which were mingled with sobs of sorrow when she learned about the death of her other son.

Thereafter, the young man used the bird skin when hunting food for his own people. It brought him great success, and soon he was a very rich man. At length he found himself a wife among his own people. Unfortunately she gave him nothing but girl babies but she was a very devoted wife and kept his *innie* in good order. As his fortune increased his desire for sons became greater. He must have sons to carry on his skill and position among the people. Eventually, he took a second wife who was especially skilled at sewing, tanning and making fur garments. His second wife gave him four sons who, like their father, grew to be famous hunters.

AFRICAN FOLK TALE

What a Little Thing Did*

And one daughter and a son were born. And a man, her cousin, married the girl; and on the morrow he went hunting. His first father-in-law died, and his mother-in-law remained. One day a certain man came and said, "I want to marry your mother-in-law, my son-in-law." And that son-in-law of his said, "Marry, am I to deny my mother-in-law?" And sure enough he came and married his mother-in-law.

One day he said to his son-in-law, "Come, son-in-law, let us go into the bush,[1] that we may eat some honey." Ah, and the son-in-law went with him into the bush. Then as they went along, the father-in-law said, "Son-in-law, here are the bees!" When the son-in-law had gone, he found the bees in a grass-stalk,[2] and the son-in-law thought, "What sort of a father-in-law is this, who calls me to bees in a grass-stalk?" And he cut out the honey from the grass-stalk there. Then his father-in-law said, "Eat the honey that you have cut out." The son-in-law refused, saying, "I have not yet eaten honey from a grass-stalk." And his father-in-law ate alone.

And again they went on. Again he located bees in a tremendously high Wanga[3] tree. Again he called his son-in-law; and when the son-in-law came he said, "Here are bees in the Wanga tree." And he replied, "Am I to climb right high up there?" And his father-in-law said, "Go!" And the son-in-law climbed up above, and the son-in-law cut out the bees, and called saying, "Father-in-law, now I have cut out the honey; give me some bark rope that I may tie up the bark dish." And his father-in-law stripped a bundle of bark rope, and his father-in-law hoisted it up above, and he tied the bark plate. Then he

---

* As told by Clement M. Doke in *Lamba Folk-Lore* (1927). The Awalamba live in what is now Zambia and Zaire in central Africa.
1. Uncleared scrubland.

2. An impossible place in which to find a nest of bees. (Doke's note)
3. A tree of such hard wood that natives seldom attempt to cut out a nest of bees located in it. (Doke's note)

said, "Now father-in-law, take the honey that I have tied." And his father-in-law took the honey, and put it down, and the son-in-law came down from above. And he ordered his son-in-law saying. "Eat up the honey, son-in-law!" And the son-in-law refused even as he had done at the first over the honey from the grass-stalk. Then he carried the honey. And off they went to the village, and slept.

Again when morning dawned, he went early to his son-in-law. And he said, "Son-in-law, let us go today also, and let us cut out some honey." And the son-in-law came out, and off they both went, he and his father-in-law. Again his father-in-law did the same as he had priorly done, and again located it in a grass-stalk; and he called saying, "Father,[4] cut out these bees here." And the son-in-law came, and found them just in the grass-stalk. The son-in-law just stared, saying, "My father-in-law is a worry to me; he is always locating bees in a grass-stalk; he is acting as though he has tricks." Then he said, "Son-in-law, cut out the bees!" Then the son-in-law began to cut them out from the grass-stalk, and took out a barkplate. Then his father-in-law said, "Father, let us eat the honey." And the son-in-law refused, saying, "I don't eat honey from a grass-stalk." Then his father-in-law said, "Carry it, and let us go on walking"; and they departed, and off they went, son-in-law as well. Then as they passed along, he said, "There are some more bees here!" And when the son-in-law went, he found them even in a Wanga tree. And he said, "Climb up, son-in-law!" And the other said, "My father-in-law compels me, he wants his son-in-law to die." And the son-in-law climbed up above to a great height in the Wanga tree; and the son-in-law cut out the honey up there. Then he said, "Now I have cut out the honey, bring the bark rope!" And his father-in-law, who remained below stripped off the bark rope. And he who was above tied up the honey. And he said, "Now take the honey that I have tied up." And then his father-in-law went to the foot of the tree, and held out his hands, that the plate might come into his hands; and the father-in-law received the honey; and placed it on the ground. And the son-in-law descended from above where he was. Then his father-in-law said, "Son-in-law, let us eat the honey." And the son-in-law said, "No, I shall not eat it!" and he refused. Then the other said, "Carry the honey then, and let us go to the village." And they reached the village, and slept.

When it was morning, the father-in-law said, "Come, son-in-law, today also into the bush, and let us cut out some honey." Again he located bees, saying, "Son-in-law, here are some bees in a grass-stalk." The son-in-law came and found the bees even in the grass-stalk, even as he had done before. And the son-in-law said, "Every day you are locating bees right in a grass-stalk, father-in-law; why do you do this?" But his father-in-law said, "Cut out the bees, son-in-law!" And so the son-in-law began to cut out the bees from the grass-stalk, and removed a bark plate, and took the honey. Then his father-in-law said, "Son-in-law, let us eat the honey." His son-in-law refused. Then he said, "Take the honey, and let us go walking on." And the son-in-

4. Form of address.

law took the plate of honey, and carried it. Then off he went with his father-in-law. And then where his father-in-law passed, he located them on the top of a Wanga tree; and then he called his son-in-law saying, "Cut out these bees here." And his son-in-law came; and he stared at them in the Wanga tree, saying, "To what a height my father-in-law sends me to cut out bees!" And the son-in-law climbed up, and cut out the honey.

And he said (to himself), "Today I won't call for a bark plate from below, I will remove a plate from the side of my leg." And he removed a plate from the side of his leg, and it was just there on his leg that he stripped off the string; and he tied the plate with the string that he stripped off from his very leg. Then his father-in-law said, "Lower the honey, son-in-law." And he said, "Hold out your hands, and take the honey." And his father-in-law received the honey. Then his father-in-law said, "What about this string, son-in-law, where did you strip it off?" Then his father-in-law went to the village, saying in his heart, "This son-in-law of mine is a man of tricks." And he reached the village and slept.

When morning came, he went early to his son-in-law. He said, "Today also let us go out walking." Where they went his father-in-law came upon a herd of buffalo. And the son-in-law said, "Wait, father-in-law, let me stalk them." And his father-in-law refused saying, "Stop, let me go, and let me kill them." And he took one arrow, and set it in the bow-string, and shot the arrow, and it went into an animal, and went through this one, and went through that one and it died, and it went through that one and it died, and it went through that one and it died; and the last one also it entered, and he who shot the arrow also entered the animals. Then the son-in-law said, "My father-in-law who killed these animals, where has he gone?" And he went to the first animal, and said, "Father-in-law come out!" He did not come out. And he reached another, and said, "Father-in-law come out!" But his father-in-law did not come out. And to another, but he did not come out. Then it was that he reached the last, and said, "Father-in-law come out, let us go to the village!" Then it was that his father-in-law came out with his bow in his hand. And off they went to the village; and the son-in-law was thinking all the while of his father-in-law's tricks. And the people came to fetch that meat to take it to the village.

Again another day the son-in-law and his father-in-law went into the bush to kill animals. Where they went they came upon many eland. And the father-in-law said, "I am going, let me kill them!" But the son-in-law said, "Let me go today, I know how to kill animals." And the son-in-law took one arrow, and shot it into the herd of eland. It went through this one, and it died; and it went through this one, and it died; and it went through this one, and it died; and when it came to the last one, the arrow went right through, and entered a wild orange. The wild orange fell into the water, and a crocodile swallowed the orange. And in its turn a hippopotamus swallowed the crocodile. The father-in-law went to the animals, and said, "Son-in-law come out!" He did not come out. And he reached another, and said, "Son-in-law come out!" He did not come out. And yet another, but he did not come out. And the last one, but he did not come out. Then he said, "But where has my son-in-law gone? I have finished asking all the animals!" And the father-in-law went off along to the village.

When it was morning, he said, "Where am I to find my son-in-law? Today I am going to dig a pitfall at the side of the river." And he dug the pitfall, and left it covered over, and went away. In the morning when he went early, he found that a hippopotamus had died in it. And he went to the village and said, "Come, mates, let us cut up a hippo, it has died in the pitfall."

And they pierced that hippopotamus, and took out a crocodile from the stomach of the hippopotamus. Then he said, "But where is my son-in-law?" He said, "Now men, pierce this crocodile." And they pierced the crocodile, and took out a wild orange. Then he said, "My son-in-law, come out!" Then it was that he came out of the wild orange with his bow in his hand. His father-in-law sat and marveled, saying, "Son-in-law of mine, why do you do these wonderful things to me, because you have worried me, and have entered many animals?" And he went to the village with his father-in-law, and the people carried that meat.

And he went out early with his son-in-law to cut out honey; and again located bees in a very tall Wanga tree. And he said, "Son-in-law cut out these bees in the Wanga tree." And the son-in-law came, and climbed that Wanga tree, and the son-in-law cut out the honey. And he said, "Father-in-law, take this honey that I have cut out!" Ah, and he received the honey; and then the son-in-law fell hurtling down, and broke and smashed to pieces, and not even a little bit of him was seen; and he entirely crumbled up, and turned into dust. His father-in-law became afraid, and said, "Today my son-in-law is dead, he has broken to pieces." And off he went to the village, and reached the village and said, "My son-in-law is dead, I don't see him."

There where he remained, he revived, and joined himself together piece by piece, and changed into a woman. In the morning his father-in-law came saying, "Just let me go to where my son-in-law died." When he had gone some distance, he met that woman. He said, "Woman, where have you come from?" She said, "I have come from here in this country." Then he said, "I am going to divorce my old wife, and I shall marry this beautiful one that I have seen." All the time it was his son-in-law who had turned into a woman. And she said, "Marry me then." There and then he built a zareba. And night fell. And he lay with that woman. When it was morning, he wanted to return to the village, to fetch something to smoke; and off he went to the village. Where the woman remained, she turned back into the man that she was before. On the father-in-law's return, to his surprise he found the dwelling empty, she had gone out. Then he began calling out, "O my wife, where have you gone?" And she didn't reply; how could she when she had already gone to the village. Then where she went, she turned back into the very son-in-law; and then it was that his father-in-law said, "My son-in-law has bothered me, now

I am going to gather all the people together, that I may tell them how sons-in-law behave." Then it was that he gathered together all his companions. And he said, "Friends do you associate with a son-in-law who is always performing wonderful miracles?" And his companions asked, "What has he done?" He said, "I saw some honey in a Wanga tree; my son-in-law went to cut it out, and he peeled off a bark plate from the side of his leg!" Then all the people said, "Is that what your son-in-law does?" He said, "Yes!" Then all his companions said, "You son-in-law of his, explain what your father-in-law has said." And he said, "It was my father-in-law who began by locating bees in a grass-stalk. Again another day he located bees in a Wanga tree; and I went up above to cut them out. And that was why I started, for why should my father-in-law start his cunning? And so I too one day revealed my cunning, that of peeling a bark plate off my leg." And he added, "And my falling from a tall tree also was in order that my father-in-law might today be met by a devil!"

Then everybody said, "It was you, father-in-law, who began it!" Then the son-in-law said, "That was why I changed into a woman; and you did not know me, you thought I was a woman, and all the time I was your son-in-law." That was how they settled the case.

CHUANG TZU

The Brigand and the Sage*

Confucius was on friendly terms with the sage Liu-hsia Hui. Liu-hsia Hui had a younger brother who was known as the Brigand Chih. This brigand and the nine thousand followers who formed his band swept through the country, pillaging and despoiling every kingdom under Heaven, burrowing their way into houses, wrenching doors, driving off men's cattle and horses, seizing their wives and daughters. In his greed for gain the brigand forgot all ties of kinship, paid no heed to father, mother, or brothers young and old, and made no offerings to his ancestors. Whenever he approached a town, if it was a big place the people manned the city-walls and if it was a small place they ensconced themselves behind their barrows. The whole countryside groaned under the affliction.

Confucius said to Liu-hsia Hui, "A father who is worthy of the name ought to be able to correct his son; an elder brother who is worthy of the name ought to be capable of instructing his younger brother. If it is not the duty of fathers to call their sons to order and of elder brothers to instruct their younger brothers, the whole importance that we attach to those relationships at once disappears. But here are you, admittedly one of the most gifted men of your generation; yet your younger brother is known as 'the Brigand Chih,' has become a curse to the whole land, and you have failed to teach

* Translated by Arthur Waley.

him better ways. Forgive me for saying so, but I blush on your behalf. I hope you will not take it amiss if I go in your stead and have a talk with him." "You say," replied Liu-hsia Hui, "that a father ought to be able to correct his son, that an elder brother ought to be capable of instructing his younger brother. But suppose the son does not listen to his father, suppose the younger brother does not accept the elder brother's advice? In the present case even such eloquence as yours cannot possibly have the slightest effect. My brother Chih is a remarkable man. His passions, once aroused, leap like a fountain; his calculations are swift as a whirlwind. Not only is he strong enough to defy every foe; he is also clever enough to justify every crime. Humor him, and he is friendly; thwart him and he flies into a rage. On such occasions the language he uses is far from flattering; I certainly advise you not to go near him."

Confucius did not listen to this warning, but taking his disciple Yen Hui to drive the carriage and putting Tzu-kung on his right, he set off to visit the Brigand Chih. The brigand and his men happened at the time to be resting on the southern slopes of the T'ai-shan, and were enjoying a supper of minced human liver. Confucius got down from his carriage and went toward the camp. Being confronted by a sentinel he said to him: "Pray inform the General that K'ung Ch'iu[1] of the land of Lu, having heard of his Excellency as a champion of morality, has come to pay his respects." And so saying he prostrated himself twice before the sentinel with solemnity. When the message was brought, the Brigand Chih fell into a mighty rage. His eyes blazed like fiery comets, his hair stood on end so that his hat was lifted off his head. "Why this is that crafty fraud from Lu, K'ung Ch'iu, isn't it? Tell him from me that it is mere talk for the sake of talking—all this random chatter about his heroes king Wên and king Wu. Dresses up in a forked hat that looks as though a tree had taken root on his head, puts the whole flank of a dead ox round his belly and then chatters unceasingly, heaping nonsense upon nonsense; eats what others have grown, wears what others have woven, wags his lips and drums his tongue, deluding all the rulers under heaven with his own private notions of right and wrong and preventing the scholars who come to him from every corner of the land from using the powers that are in them! Pretends to be interested only in filial piety and brotherly obedience, but spends his time currying favor with landed lords, with the rich and great! Tell the fellow that he is a scoundrel for whom no punishment would be too great, and that if he does not clear out of here at once, we shall add his liver to our morning stew."

The message was delivered; but Confucius again asked for an interview. "Being fortunate enough to know your brother Liu-hsia Hui," he said, "I desire to look at your feet beneath the curtain."[2]

The sentinel brought in the message, and this time the brigand Chih said, "Bring him in!" Confucius advanced at a brisk trot,[3] carefully avoided treading upon the brigand's mat, ran backwards a few steps, and prostrated himself twice.

1. I.e., Confucius. (Waley's note)
2. I.e., to be allowed even the most
cursory contact with you. (Waley's note)
3. A sign of respect. (Waley's note)

The brigand was evidently in a great rage. His feet were planted wide apart, he was fingering the blade of his sword, his eyes glared, and finally with a voice like that of a suckling tigress he roared out, "Come here, Ch'iu! And remember, if what you say is acceptable to me, you live; if it is not acceptable, you die!"

"I have heard," said Confucius, "that there are among the men of the world three kinds of personal power (*tê*). To grow to a stature so commanding, to possess beauty and grace so incomparable as to delight the eyes of all men, high or humble, young or old—this is the highest sort of power. To have a knowledge that embraces heaven above and earth below, to have abilities that can cope with every possible situation—this is the second and lower sort of power. To be bold, ruthless, undeterred by any hazard, a gatherer of multitudes and a causer of wars—this is the third and lowest kind of personal power. To possess any one of these three is sufficient to set a man with his face turned to the south and to give him the title of Lonely One.[4] You, my General, possess all three. Your stature is 8 feet 2 inches,[5] your countenance is dazzling, your lips are as though smeared with cinnabar, your teeth are like a row of shells; your voice booms like the tone-note of the scale. And yet for all this, men call you the Brigand Chih! I confess I am ashamed on your behalf and cannot reconcile myself to this. But if you will listen to me, I will go as your ambassador to the courts of Wu and Yüeh in the south, of Ch'i and Lu in the north, of Sung and Wei in the east, of Chin and Ch'u in the west,[6] and arrange that a great walled city shall be built for you, several hundred leagues in circumference, with quarters for many hundred thousand inhabitants. You shall be raised to the dignity of a feudal prince, and under your sway the whole world shall begin anew. You will lay down your arms, disband your followers, gather about you brothers old and young, and see to it that they lack nothing; and make due offering to your ancestors. You will thus be behaving like a Sage and Hero and at the same time giving to the world that for which it ardently longs."

"Listen here," cried the Brigand Chih, in a great rage. "It is only the ignorant low rabble who allow themselves to be beguiled by promises of gain or scolded into altering their ways. My tall stature and my good looks which delight the eyes of all who see me—these are advantages that I inherited from my parents. I am the person most likely to be aware of them and stand in no need of your approbation. Moreover, it is commonly said that those who are prone to praise men to their faces, are quick to speak ill of them behind their backs.

"And now as to your talk of a great city and a multitude of inhabitants—this is merely an attempt to dazzle me by promises of gain, and is treating me as though I were a common, witless peasant. And even if such success were attainable, how long would it be secured? The biggest city cannot be larger than the world. The Emperors Yao

---

4. When the ruler faces his subjects, he alone faces to the south; his subjects face north. He is the Lonely One (Orphan) because his position is unique and perhaps also because the father whom he has suc-

ceeded is necessarily dead. (Waley's note)
  5. About 5 feet 8 inches in our measurement. (Waley's note)
  6. The geography of this promise is somewhat confused. (Waley's note)

and Shun[7] possessed the whole world, yet their sons and grandsons had not so much as a pin-point of land. T'ang of the Yin dynasty, Wu of the Chou dynasty rose to be Sons of Heaven; but their posterity is extinct. Was not this just because what they sought and won was far too large a prize? . . . Neither Yao nor Shun could set a son upon the throne; both made way for subjects. T'ang of Yin banished his sovereign; King Wu of Chou slew Chieh[8] of Yin. And from that day onward the strong have crushed the weak, the many have maltreated the few; nor since the time of T'ang and Wu has there been a single ruler who was not as great a ruffian as they. Yet here come you, earnestly applying yourself to the Way of king Wên and king Wu and using every sophistry under heaven in order to inculcate it upon generations to come. You dress up in a wide cloak and belt of clipped bull's hide, and by your cant and humbug delude the princes of the world into giving you the wealth and honors that are your only real ambition. There can be no greater brigand than you, and instead of talking so much about the Brigand Chih, I wonder people do not call you the Brigand Confucius! . . .

"There is no need for you to say a word more. If you could tell me about the affairs of ghosts or hobgoblins, it would be another matter. About them I admit I know nothing at all. But concerning human affairs nothing you say can possibly carry me any further. I shall have heard it all before. I, on the other hand, intend to tell you something about man and his natural desires. He has an eye that longs for beauty, an ear that longs for music, a mouth that longs for sweet flavors, ambitions and energies that crave fulfillment. Some few may live to eighty years, some fewer to a hundred; but one who lives till sixty has still not died young. And during these sixty years, if we take away the time that is spent in sickness, mourning and trouble, in all this time there will not be more than four or five days in each month when his lips are opened and laughter comes.

"Heaven and earth are illimitable; to man a term is set. Furnished only with the scrap of time that is his span, he is committed to a place amid the illimitables. A flash, and all is over, like a racehorse seen through a crack. He who by the enjoyment of his senses can use this brief moment to the full alone can claim to have found the Way. All that you acclaim, I utterly discard. Be off with you as fast as you can, and never dare prate to me again! This Way of yours is nothing but noise and babble, humbug and empty fraud, such as could never help any man to perfect the unalloyed that is within him; is in fact not worth a moment's discussion."

Confucius prostrated himself twice, and retired at full speed. When he had reached the gate of the camp and regained his carriage, his hands were trembling to such an extent that three times the reins fell out of them, there was a cloud before his eyes and his face was ashen gray. He leant over the fore-rail with sunken head, gasping for breath. At last he reached Lu, and outside the eastern gate happened to meet

7. Legendary "good kings." (Waley's note)   8. Semi-legendary tyrant. (Waley's note)

Liu-hsia Hui. "What has become of you lately?" asked Liu-hsia Hui. "I have not seen you for several days. Judging by the appearance of your horses and carriage, I should think you have been on a journey. Is it possible that, despite my warning, you have been to see my brother Chih?" Confucius gazed upwards at the sky and sighed. "I have indeed," he said. "And Chih," said Liu-hsia Hui, "did not take to your ideas any more kindly than I predicted?" "That is true," said Confucius. "I must confess that, as the saying goes, I poulticed myself with moxa[9] when there was nothing wrong with me. I rushed off to dress a tiger's head and plait its beard. Small wonder if I nearly landed in the tiger's maw!"

N. SCOTT MOMADAY

from The Way to Rainy Mountain

IV

They lived at first in the mountains. They did not yet know of Tai-me,[1] but this is what they knew: There was a man and his wife. They had a beautiful child, a little girl whom they would not allow to go out of their sight. But one day a friend of the family came and asked if she might take the child outside to play. The mother guessed that would be all right, but she told the friend to leave the child in its cradle and to place the cradle in a tree. While the child was in the tree, a redbird came among the branches. It was not like any bird that you have seen; it was very beautiful, and it did not fly away. It kept still upon a limb, close to the child. After a while the child got out of its cradle and began to climb after the redbird. And at the same time the tree began to grow taller, and the child was borne up into the sky. She was then a woman, and she found herself in a strange place. Instead of a redbird, there was a young man standing before her. The man spoke to her and said: "I have been watching you for a long time, and I knew that I would find a way to bring you here. I have brought you here to be my wife." The woman looked all around; she saw that he was the only living man there. She saw that he was the sun.

There the land itself ascends into the sky. These mountains lie at the top of the continent, and they cast a long rain shadow on the sea of grasses to the east. They arise out of the last North American wilder-

---

9. An ointment burned on the skin.

1. Legendary creature with feet of deer and body covered with feathers, protector of the Kiowa Indians. Represented by a two-foot green stone doll shaped like a hu- man with robe of white feathers, feather and ermine-skin headdress, blue beads, and painted with symbols of sun and moon; the effigy is kept hidden except during Sun Dance ceremony.

ness, and they have wilderness names: Wasatch, Bitterroot, Bighorn, Wind River.[2]

I have walked in a mountain meadow bright with Indian paintbrush, lupine, and wild buckwheat, and I have seen high in the branches of a lodgepole pine the male pine grosbeak, round and rose-colored, its dark, striped wings nearly invisible in the soft, mottled light. And the uppermost branches of the tree seemed very slowly to ride across the blue sky.

V

After that the woman grew lonely. She thought about her people, and she wondered how they were getting on. One day she had a quarrel with the sun, and the sun went away. In her anger she dug up the root of a bush which the sun had warned her never to go near. A piece of earth fell from the root, and she could see her people far below. By that time she had given birth; she had a child—a boy by the sun. She made a rope out of sinew and took her child upon her back; she climbed down upon the rope, but when she came to the end, her people were still a long way off, and there she waited with her child on her back. It was evening; the sun came home and found his woman gone. At once he thought of the bush and went to the place where it had grown. There he saw the woman and the child, hanging by the rope halfway down to the earth. He was very angry, and he took up a ring, a gaming wheel, in his hand. He told the ring to follow the rope and strike the woman dead. Then he threw the ring and it did what he told it to do; it struck the woman and killed her, and then the sun's child was all alone.

The plant is said to have been the pomme blanche, *or* pomme de prairie, *of the voyageurs, whose chronicles refer time and again to its use by the Indians. It grows on the high plains and has a farinaceous root that is turniplike in taste and in shape. This root is a healthful food, and attempts have been made to cultivate the plant as a substitute for the potato.*

The anthropologist Mooney wrote in 1896: "Unlike the neighboring Cheyenne and Arapaho, who yet remember that they once lived east of the Missouri and cultivated corn, the Kiowa have no tradition of ever having been an agricultural people or anything but a tribe of hunters."

Even now they are meateaters; I think it is not in them to be farmers. My grandfather, Mammedaty, worked hard to make wheat and cotton grow on his land, but it came to very little in the end. Once when I was a small boy I went across the creek to the house where the old woman Keahdinekeah lived. Some men and boys came in from the pasture, where a calf had just been killed and butchered. One of the boys held the calf's liver—still warm and wet with life—in his hand, eating of it with great relish. I have heard that the old hunters of the Plains prized the raw liver and tongue of the buffalo above all other delicacies.

VI

The sun's child was big enough to walk around on the earth, and he saw a camp nearby. He made his way to it and saw that a great spider—that which is called a grandmother—lived there. The spider spoke to the sun's child, and the child was afraid. The grandmother was full of resentment; she was jealous, you see, for the child had not yet been weaned from its mother's breasts. She wondered whether the child were a boy or a girl, and therefore she made two things, a pretty ball and a bow and arrows. These things she left alone with the child all the next day. When she returned, she saw that the ball was full of arrows, and she knew then that the child was a boy and that he would be hard to raise. Time and again the grandmother tried to capture the boy, but he always ran away. Then one day she made a snare out of rope. The boy was caught up in the snare, and he cried and cried, but the grandmother sang to him and at last he fell asleep.

> Go to sleep and do not cry.
> Your mother is dead, and still you feed
>   upon her breasts.
> Oo-oo-la-la-la-la, oo-oo.

In the autumn of 1874, the Kiowas were driven southward towards the Staked Plains. Columns of troops were converging upon them from all sides, and they were bone-weary and afraid. They camped on Elk Creek, and the next day it began to rain. It rained hard all that day, and the Kiowas waited on horseback for the weather to clear. Then, as evening came on, the earth was suddenly crawling with spiders, great black tarantulas, swarming on the flood.

I know of spiders. There are dirt roads in the Plains. You see them, and you wonder where and how far they go. They seem very old and untraveled, as if they all led away to deserted houses. But creatures cross these roads: dung beetles and grasshoppers, sidewinders and tortoises. Now and then there comes a tarantula, at evening, always larger than you imagine, dull and dark brown, covered with long, dusty hairs. There is something crochety about them; they stop and go and angle away.

VII

The years went by, and the boy still had the ring which killed his mother. The grandmother spider told him never to throw the ring into the sky, but one day he threw it up, and it fell squarely on top of his head and cut him in two. He looked around, and there was another boy, just like himself, his twin. The two of them laughed and laughed, and then they went to the grandmother spider. She nearly cried aloud when she saw them, for it had been hard enough to raise the one. Even so, she cared for them well and made them fine clothes to wear.

Mammedaty owned horses. And he could remember that it was essentially good to own horses, that it was hard to be without horses. There was a day: Mammedaty got down from a horse for the last time. Of all the tribes of the Plains, the Kiowas owned the greatest number of horses per person.

On summer afternoons I went swimming in the Washita River.[3] The current was slow, and the warm, brown water seemed to be standing still. It was a secret place. There in the deep shade, inclosed in the dense, overhanging growth of the banks, my mind fixed on the wings of a dragonfly or the flitting motion of a water strider, the great open land beyond was all but impossible to imagine. But it was there, a stone's throw away. Once, from the limb of a tree, I saw myself in the brown water; then a frog leaped from the bank, breaking the image apart.

XVII

Bad women are thrown away. Once there was a handsome young man. He was wild and reckless, and the chief talked to the wind about him. After that, the man went hunting. A great whirlwind passed by, and he was blind. The Kiowas have no need of a blind man; they left him alone with his wife and child. The winter was coming on and food was scarce. In four days the man's wife grew tired of caring for him. A herd of buffalo came near, and the man knew the sound. He asked his wife to hand him a bow and an arrow. "You must tell me," he said, "when the buffalo are directly in front of me." And in that way he killed a bull, but his wife said that he had missed. He asked for another arrow and killed another bull, but again his wife said that he had missed. Now the man was a hunter, and he knew the sound an arrow makes when it strikes home, but he said nothing. Then his wife helped herself to the meat and ran away with her child. The man was blind; he ate grass and kept himself alive. In seven days a band of Kiowas found him and took him to their camp. There in the firelight a woman was telling a story. She told of how her husband had been killed by enemy warriors. The blind man listened, and he knew her voice. That was a bad woman. At sunrise they threw her away.

In the Kiowa calendars there is graphic proof that the lives of women were hard, whether they were "bad women" or not. Only the captives, who were slaves, held lower status. During the Sun Dance of 1843, a man stabbed his wife in the breast because she accepted Chief Dohasan's invitation to ride with him in the ceremonial procession. And in the winter of 1851–52, Big Bow stole the wife of a man who was away on a raiding expedition. He brought her to his father's camp and made her wait outside in the bitter cold while he went in to collect his things. But his father knew what was going on, and he held Big Bow and would not let him go. The woman was made to wait in the snow until her feet were frozen.

---

3. In Oklahoma.

Mammedaty's grandmother, Kau-au-ointy, was a Mexican captive, taken from her homeland when she was a child of eight or ten years. I never knew her, but I have been to her grave at Rainy Mountain.

KAU-AU-OINTY
BORN 1834
DIED 1929
AT REST

She raised a lot of eyebrows, they say, for she would not play the part of a Kiowa woman. From slavery she rose up to become a figure in the tribe. She owned a great herd of cattle, and she could ride as well as any man. She had blue eyes.

1969

from The Thousand Nights and a Night*

. . . but sleep gave no sign of visiting the Caliph that night and he lay awake pondering the mishaps of the three Kalandar[1]-princes and impatient to know the history of the ladies and the two black bitches. No sooner had morning dawned than he went forth and sat upon the throne of his sovereignty; and, turning to Ja'afar,[2] after all his Grandees and Officers of state were gathered together, he said, "Bring me the three ladies and the two bitches and the three Kalandars." So Ja'afar fared forth and brought them all before him (and the ladies were veiled); then the Minister turned to them and said in the Caliph's name, "We pardon you your maltreatment of us and your want of courtesy, in consideration of the kindness which forewent it, and because you knew us not: now however I would have you to know that you stand in presence of the fifth of the sons of Abbas, Harun al-Rashid, brother of Caliph Músá al-Hádi, son of Al-Mansúr; son of Mohammed the brother of Al-Saffáh bin Mohammed who was first of the royal house. Speak therefore before him the truth and the whole truth!" When the ladies heard Ja'afar's words touching the Commander of the Faithful, the eldest came forward and said, "O Prince of True Believers, my story is one which, were it graven with needlegravers upon the eye-corners were a warning for whoso would be warned[3] and an example for whoso can take profit from example."—And Shahrazad perceived the dawn of day and ceased to say her permitted say.

---

* Translated by Sir Richard Burton.
1. Beggar monks.
2. The Wazir, or chief counselor of Harun al-Rashid the Caliph. Both are historical personages.
3. A common play on the Arabic word *ibrat*, which means both engraving needle and warning or example.

Now when it was the Seventeenth Night,

She said, It has reached me, O auspicious King, that she stood forth before the Commander of the Faithful and began to tell

The Eldest Lady's Tale

Verily a strange tale is mine and it is this:—Those two black bitches are my eldest sisters by one mother and father; and these two others, she who bears upon her the signs of stripes and the third our procuratrix are my sisters by another mother. When my father died, each took her share of the heritage and, after a while my mother also deceased, leaving me and my sisters three thousand dinars; so each daughter received her portion of a thousand dinars and I the same, though the youngest. In due course of time my sisters married with the usual festivities and lived with their husbands, who bought merchandise with their wives' money and set out on their travels together. Thus they threw me off. My brothers-in-law were absent with their wives five years, during which period they spent all the money they had and, becoming bankrupt, deserted my sisters in foreign parts amid stranger folk. After five years my eldest sister returned to me in beggar's gear with her clothes in rags and tatters and a dirty old mantilla;[4] and truly she was in the foulest and sorriest plight. At first sight I did not know my own sister; but presently I recognized her and said, "What state is this?" "O our sister," she replied, "Words cannot undo the done; and the reed of Destiny has run through what Allah decreed." Then I sent her to the bath and dressed her in a suit of my own, and boiled for her a bouillon and brought her some good wine and said to her, "O my sister, you are the eldest, who still stand to us in the place of father and mother; and, as for the inheritance which came to me as to you two, Allah has blessed it and prospered it to me with increase; and my circumstances are easy, for I have made much money by spinning and cleaning silk; and I and you will share my wealth alike." I entreated her with all kindliness and she abode with me a whole year, during which our thoughts and fancies were always full of our other sister. Shortly after she too came home in yet fouler and sorrier plight than that of my eldest sister; and I dealt by her still more honorably than I had done by the first, and each of them had a share of my substance. After a time they said to me, "O our sister, we desire to marry again, for indeed we have not patience to drag on our days without husbands and to lead the lives of widows bewitched"; and I replied, "O eyes of me![5] you have hitherto seen scanty weal in wedlock, for nowadays good men and true are become rarities and curiosities; nor do I deem your projects advisable, as you have already made trial of matrimony and have failed." But they would not accept my advice and married without my consent: nevertheless I gave them outfit and dowries out of my

---

4. Sheet of white calico covering head or hands, worn by poor Egyptian women out of doors.
5. I.e., "My dears." (Burton's note)

money; and they fared forth with their mates. In a mighty little time their husbands played them false and, taking whatever they could lay hands upon, ran off and left them in the lurch. Thereupon they came to me ashamed and in abject case and made their excuses to me, saying, "Pardon our fault and do not be angry with us; for although you are younger in years yet are you older in wit; henceforth we will never make mention of marriage; so take us back as your hand-maidens that we may eat our mouthful." I said, "Welcome to you, O my sisters, there is nothing dearer to me than you." And I took them in and redoubled my kindness to them. We ceased not to live after this loving fashion for a full year, when I resolved to sell my wares abroad and first to fit me a conveyance for Bassorah; so I equipped a large ship, and loaded her with merchandise and valuable goods for traffic, and with provisions and all needful for a voyage, and said to my sisters, "Will you stay at home while I travel, or would you prefer to accompany me on the voyage?" "We will travel with you," they answered, "for we cannot bear to be parted from you." So I divided my money into two parts, one to accompany me and the other to be left in charge of a trusty person, for, as I said to myself, "Perhaps some accident may happen to the ship and yet we remain alive; in which case we shall find on our return what may stand us in good stead. I took my two sisters and we went a-voyaging some days and nights; but the master was careless enough to miss his course, and the ship went astray with us and entered a sea other than the sea we sought. For a time we knew naught of this; and the wind blew fair for us ten days, after which the look-out man went aloft to see about him and cried, "Good news!" Then he came down rejoicing and said, "I have seen what seems to be a city as 'twere a pigeon." We rejoiced and, before an hour of the day had passed, the buildings showed plain in the offing and we asked the Captain, "What is the name of yonder city?" and he answered, "By Allah I know not, for I never saw it before and never sailed these seas in my life: but, since our troubles have ended in safety, it remains for you only to land there with your merchandise and, if you find selling profitable, sell and make your market of what is there; and if not, we will rest here two days and provision ourselves and fare away. So we entered the port and the Captain went up town and was absent awhile, after which he returned to us and said, "Arise; go up into the city and marvel at the works of Allah with His creatures and pray to be preserved from His righteous wrath!" So we landed and going up into the city, saw at the gate men holding staves, but when we drew near them, behold, they had been transformed by the anger of Allah and had become stones. Then we entered the city and found all who lived there turned into black stones: not an inhabited house appeared to the espier, nor was there a blower of fire. We were awe-struck at the sight and threaded the market streets where we found the goods and gold and silver left lying in their places; and we were glad and said, "Doubtless there is some mystery in all this." Then we dispersed about the thoroughfares and each busied himself with collecting the wealth and money and rich stuffs, taking scanty heed of friend or comrade. As for myself I went up to the castle which was strongly fortified; and, entering the King's palace by its gate of red gold, found all the vessel of gold and silver, and the King himself seated in the midst of his Chamberlains and Nabobs and Emirs and Wazirs; all clad in raiment which confounded man's art. I drew nearer and saw him sitting on a throne incrusted and inlaid with pearls and gems; and his robes were of gold-cloth adcrned with jewels of every kind, each one flashing like a star. Around him stood fifty Mamelukes, white slaves, clothed in silks of diverse sorts holding their drawn swords in their hands; but when I drew near to them lo! all were black stones. My understanding was confounded at the sight, but I walked on and entered the great hall of the harem, whose walls I found hung with tapestries of gold-striped silk and spread with silken carpets embroidered with golden flowers. Here I saw the Queen lying at full length arrayed in robes purfled with fresh young[6] pearls; on her head was a diadem set with many sorts of gems each fit for a ring and around her neck hung collars and necklaces. All her raiment and her ornaments were in natural state but she had been turned into a black stone by Allah's wrath. Presently I espied an open door for which I made straight and found leading to it a flight of seven steps. So I walked up and came upon a place pargeted with marble and spread and hung with gold-worked carpets and tapestry, in the middle of which stood a throne of juniper-wood inlaid with pearls and precious stones and set with bosses of emeralds. In the further wall was an alcove whose curtains, bestrung with pearls, were let down and I saw a light issuing therefrom; so I drew near and perceived that the light came from a precious stone as big as an ostrich egg, set at the upper end of the alcove upon a little chryselephantine couch of ivory and gold; and this jewel, blazing like the sun, cast its rays wide and side. The couch also was spread with all manner of silken stuffs amazing the gazer with their richness and beauty. I marveled much at all this, especially when seeing in that place candles ready lighted; and I said in my mind, "Some one must have lighted these candles." Then I went forth and came to the kitchen and thence to the buttery and the King's treasure-chambers; and continued to explore the palace and to pace from place to place; I forgot myself in my awe and marvel at these matters and I was drowned in thought till the night came on. Then I would have gone forth, but not knowing the gate I lost my way, so I returned to the alcove whither the lighted candles directed me and sat down upon the couch; and wrapping myself in a coverlet, after I had repeated somewhat from the Koran, I would have slept but could not, for restlessness possessed me. When night was at its noon I heard a voice chanting the Koran in sweetest accents; but the tone was weak; so I rose, glad to hear the silence broken, and followed the sound until I reached a closet whose door stood ajar. Then, peeping through a chink, I considered the place and lo! it was an oratory wherein was a prayer-niche[7]

6. The pearl is supposed in the East to lose 1 percent per ann. of its splendor and value. (Burton's note)

7. The arch-headed niche in the mosque wall facing Mecca.

with two wax candles burning and lamps hanging from the ceiling. In it too was spread a prayer-carpet whereupon sat a youth fair to see; and before him on its stand[8] was a copy of the Koran, from which he was reading. I marveled to see him alone alive amongst the people of the city and entering saluted him; whereupon he raised his eyes and returned my salam. I said, "Now by the Truth of what you read in Allah's Holy Book, I conjure you to answer my question." He looked at me with a smile and said, "O handmaid of Allah, first tell me the cause of your coming here, and I in turn will tell what has befallen both me and the people of this city, and what was the reason of my escaping their doom." So I told him my story whereat he wondered; and I questioned him of the people of the city, when he replied, "Have patience with me for awhile, O my sister!" and, reverently closing the Holy Book, he laid it up in a satin bag. Then he seated me by his side; and I looked at him and behold, he was as the moon at its full, fair of face and rare of form, soft-sided and slight, of well-proportioned height, and cheek smoothly bright and diffusing light; in brief a sweet, a sugar-stick, even as the poet says of the like of him in these couplets:—

That night th' astrologer a scheme of planets drew, / And lo! a grace-
    ful shape of youth appeared in view:
Saturn had stained his locks with Saturninest jet, / And spots of
    nut-brown musk on rosey side-face blew:[9]
Mars tinctured either cheek with tinct of martial red; / Sagittal
    shots from eyelids Sagittarius threw:
Dowered him Mercury with bright mercurial wit; / Bore off the Bear[1]
    what all man's evil glances grew:
Amazed stood Astrophil[2] to sight the marvel-birth / When louted low
    the Moon at full to buss the Earth.

And of a truth Allah the Most High had robed him in the raiment of perfect grace and had purfled and fringed it with a cheek all beauty and loveliness, even as the poet says of such a one:—

By his eyelids shedding perfume and his fine slim waist I swear, / By
    the shooting of his shafts barbed with sorcery passing rare;
By the softness of his sides, and glances' lingering light; / And brow
    of dazzling day-tide ray and night within his hair;
By his eyebrows which deny to who look upon them rest, / Now
    bidding now forbidding, ever dealing joy and care;
By the rose that decks his cheek, and the myrtle of its moss[3]; / By
    jacinths bedded in his lips and pearl his smile lays bare;
By his graceful bending neck and the curving of his breast; / Whose
    polished surface beareth those granados,[4] lovely pair;

8. A stool of palm-fronds, etc., X-shaped.
9. The Persian poets have a thousand conceits in praise of the "mole." (Burton's note)
1. That is, a bright star in the constellation called The Great Bear drew off the "evil eye" of those who might have envied him his beauty and virtues.
2. The name of the astrologer, from the Greek words for *star* and *lover of knowledge.*
3. Young face hair.
4. Pomegranates (?).

By his heavy hips that quiver as he passeth in his pride; / Or he
resteth with that waist which is slim beyond compare;
By the satin of his skin, by that fine unsullied sprite; / By the beauty
that containeth all things bright and debonair;
By that ever-open hand; by the candor of his tongue; / By noble
blood and high degree whereof he's hope and heir;
Musk from him borrows muskiness she loveth to exhale / And all
the airs of ambergris through him perfume the air;
The sun, methinks, the broad bright sun, before my love would pale/
And sans his splendor would appear a paring of his nail.

I glanced at him with one glance of eyes which caused me a thousand sighs; and my heart was at once taken captive; so I asked him,
"O my lord and my love, tell me what I questioned you about"; and
he answered, "Hearing is obeying! Know, O handmaid of Allah, that
this city was the capital of my father who is the King you saw on
the throne transfigured by Allah's wrath to a black stone, and the
Queen you found in the alcove is my mother. They and all the
people of the city were Magians who adored fire instead of the Omnipotent Lord and swore by flame and heat and shade and light,
and the spheres revolving day and night. My father never had a son
till he was blessed with me near the last of his days; and he reared
me till I grew up and prosperity anticipated me in all things. Now it
so happened there was with us an old woman well stricken in years,
a Moslem who, inwardly believing in Allah and His Apostle, conformed outwardly with the religion of my people; and my father
placed thorough confidence in her for he knew her to be trustworthy
and virtuous; and he treated her with ever-increasing kindness, believing her to be of his own belief. So when I was well-nigh grown up
my father committed me to her charge saying:—Take him and educate
him and teach him the rules of our faith; let him have the best instructions and do not cease your fostering care of him. So she took
me and taught me the tenets of Al-Islam with the divine orders given
in the Koran and the five daily prayers and she made me learn the
Koran by rote, often repeating:—Serve none save Allah Almighty!
When I had mastered this much of knowledge she said to me:—O
my son, keep this matter concealed from your sire and reveal nothing
to him lest he slay you. So I hid it from him and I lived like this
for a term of days when the old woman died, and the people of the
city redoubled in their impiety and arrogance and the error of their
ways. One day, while they were as usual, behold, they heard a loud
and terrible sound and a crier crying out with a voice like roaring
thunder so every ear could hear, far and near:—O folk of this city
leave your fire-worshipping and adore Allah the All-compassionate
King! At this, fear and terror fell upon the citizens and they crowded
to my father (he being King of the city) and asked him:—What
is the awesome voice we have heard, for it has confounded us with
the excess of its terror?; and he answered:—Let not a voice fright
you nor shake your steadfast spirit nor turn you back from the faith
which is right. Their hearts inclined to his words and they continued
to worship the fire and they persisted in rebellion for a full year from

the time they heard the first voice; and on the anniversary came a second cry and a third at the head of the third year, each year once. Still they persisted in their malpractices till one day at break of dawn, judgment and the wrath of Heaven descended upon them with all suddenness, and by the visitation of Allah all were metamorphosed into black stones, they and their beasts and their cattle; and none was saved save myself who at the time was engaged in my devotions. From that day to this I am as you see me, constant in prayer and fasting and reading and reciting the Koran; but I am indeed grown weary by reason of my loneliness, having none to bear me company." Then I said to him (for in very sooth he had won my heart and was the lord of my life and soul), "O youth, will you fare with me to Baghdad city and visit the Olema, men learned in the law and doctors of divinity, and increase your wisdom and understanding and theology? And know that she who stands in your presence will be your handmaid, though she is head of her family and mistress over men and eunuchs and servants and slaves. Indeed my life was no life before it fell in with your youth. I have here a ship laden with merchandise; and in very truth Destiny drove me to this city that I might come to the knowledge of these matters, for it was fated that we should meet." And I continued to persuade him and speak him fair and use every art till he consented."——And Shahrazad perceived the dawn of day and ceased to say her permitted say.

Now when it was the Eighteenth Night,

She continued, It hath reached me, O auspicious King, that the lady ceased not persuading with soft speech the youth to depart with her till he consented and said "Yes." She slept that night lying at his feet and hardly knowing where she was for excess of joy. As soon as the next morning dawned (she pursued, addressing the Caliph), I arose and we entered the treasuries and took whatever was light in weight and great in worth; then we went down side by side from the castle to the city, where we were met by the Captain and my sisters and slaves who had been seeking for me. When they saw me they rejoiced and asked what had kept me, and I told them all I had seen and related to them the story of the young Prince and the transformation with which the citizens had been justly visited. All marveled, but when my two sisters (these two bitches, O Commander of the Faithful!) saw me by the side of my young lover they were jealous of me on his account and were angry and plotted mischief against me. We awaited a fair wind and went on board rejoicing and ready to fly for joy by reason of the goods we had gotten, but my own greatest joyance was in the youth; and we waited awhile till the wind blew fair for us and then we set sail and fared forth. Now as we sat talking, my sisters asked me, "And what will you do with this handsome young man?"; and I answered, "I purpose to make him my husband!" Then I turned to him and said, "O my lord, I have something to propose to you in which you must not cross me; and it is that, when we reach Baghdad, my native city, I offer you my life as your handmaiden in holy matrimony, and you shall be to me baron and I will be femme to thee." He answered, "I hear and

I obey!; you are my lady and my mistress and whatso you do I will
not gainsay." Then I turned to my sisters and said, "This is my gain;
I content me with this youth and those who have gotten any of my
property let them keep it as their gain with my good will." "You say
and do well," answered the two, but they imagined mischief against
me. We ceased not spooning before a fair wind till we had exchanged the sea of peril for the seas of safety and, in a few days,
we made Bassorah-city, whose buildings loomed clear before us as
evening fell. But after we had retired to rest and were sound asleep,
my two sisters arose and took me up, bed and all, and threw me
into the sea: they did the same with the young Prince who, as he
could not swim, sank and was drowned and Allah enrolled him in
the noble army of Martyrs.[5] As for me would Heaven I had been
drowned with him, but Allah deemed that I should be of the saved;
so when I awoke and found myself in the sea and saw the ship making off like a flash of lightning, He threw in my way a piece of timber
which I bestrided, and the waves tossed me to and fro till they cast
me upon an island coast, a high land and an uninhabited one. I
landed and walked about the island the rest of the night and, when
morning dawned, I saw a rough track barely fit for child of Adam
to tread, leading to what proved a shallow ford connecting island
and mainland. As soon as the sun had risen I spread my garments
to dry in its rays; and ate of the fruits of the island and drank of
its waters; then I set out along the foot-track and walked till I
reached the mainland. Now where there remained between me and
the city but a two hours' journey, behold, a great serpent, the bigness of a date-palm, came fleeing towards me in all haste, gliding
along now to the right then to the left till she was close upon me,
while her tongue lolled groundwards a span long and swept the dust
as she went. She was pursued by a Dragon who was not longer
than two lances, and of slender build about the bulk of a spear and,
although her terror lent her speed, and she kept wriggling from side
to side, he overtook her and seized her by the tail, whereat her
tears streamed down and her tongue was thrust out in her agony. I
took pity on her and, picking up a stone and calling upon Allah for
aid, threw it at the Dragon's head with such force that he died then
and there; and the serpent opening a pair of wings flew into the air
and disappeared from before my eyes. I sat down marveling over
that adventure, but I was weary and, drowsiness overcoming me, I
slept where I was for a while. When I awoke I found a jet-black
damsel sitting at my feet shampooing them; and by her side stood
two black bitches (my sisters, O Commander of the Faithful!). I was
ashamed before her[6] and, sitting up, asked her, "O my sister, who
and what?"; and she answered, "How soon you have forgotten me! I

5. The Martyrs-category is extensive, including those killed by falling walls; victims of the plague, pleurisy and pregnancy;
travelers drowned or otherwise lost when
journeying honestly, and chaste lovers who
die of "broken hearts," i.e., impaired di-
gestion. Their souls are at once stowed
away in the crops of green birds where
they remain till Resurrection Day, "eating
of the fruits and drinking of the streams
of Paradise," a place however, whose
topography is wholly uncertain. Thus the
young Prince was rewarded with a manner
of anti-Purgatory, a preparatory heaven.
(Burton's note)
6. She was ashamed to see the lady
doing servile duty by rubbing her feet.
(Burton's note)

am she for whom you did a good deed and sowed the seed of gratitude and slew her foe; for I am the serpent whom by Allah's aid you did just now deliver from the Dragon. I am a Jinniyah and he was a Jinn who hated me, and none saved my life from him but you. As soon as you freed me from him I flew on the wind to the ship whence your sisters threw you, and removed all that was there to your house. Then I ordered my attendant Marids[7] to sink the ship and I transformed your two sisters into these black bitches; for I know all that has passed between them and you; but as for the youth, of a truth he is drowned." So saying she flew up with me and the bitches, and presently set us down on the terrace-roof of my house, where I found already stored the whole of what property was in my ship, nor was any of it missing. "Now (continued the serpent that was), I swear by all engraven on the seal-ring of Solomon[8] (with whom be peace!) unless you deal to each of these bitches three hundred stripes every day I will come and imprison you forever under the earth." I answered, "Hearkening and obedience!"; and away she flew. But before going she again charged me saying, "I again swear by Him who made the two seas[9] flow (and this be my second oath) if you contradict me I will come and transform you like your sisters." Since then I have never failed, O Commander of the Faithful, to beat them with that number of blows till their blood flows with my tears, I pitying them the while, and well they know that their being scourged is no fault of mine and they accept my excuses. And this is my tale and my history! The Caliph marveled at her adventures and then signed to Ja'afar who said to the second lady, the Portress, "And you, how did you come by the welts and wheals upon your body?" So she began the

Tale of the Portress. . . .

---

7. One of the tribes of the Jinn, generally but not always hostile to man. (Burton's note)
8. Alluding to the Most High Name, the hundredth name of God. (Burton's note)
9. I.e., the Mediterranean and the Indian Ocean. (Burton's note)

Stories for Further Reading

JOSEPH CONRAD

The Secret Sharer

1

On my right hand there were lines of fishing-stakes resembling a
mysterious system of half-submerged bamboo fences, incomprehensible in its division of the domain of tropical fishes, and crazy[1] of
aspect as if abandoned for ever by some nomad tribe of fishermen
now gone to the other end of the ocean; for there was no sign of
human habitation as far as the eye could reach. To the left a group
of barren islets, suggesting ruins of stone walls, towers, and block-
houses, had its foundations set in a blue sea that itself looked solid,
so still and stable did it lie below my feet; even the track of light
from the westering sun shone smoothly, without that animated glitter
which tells of an imperceptible ripple. And when I turned my head
to take a parting glance at the tug which had just left us anchored
outside the bar, I saw the straight line of the flat shore joined to
the stable sea, edge to edge, with a perfect and unmarked closeness, in one leveled floor half brown, half blue under the enormous
dome of the sky. Corresponding in their insignificance to the islets
of the sea, two small clumps of trees, one on each side of the only
fault in the impeccable joint, marked the mouth of the river Meinam[2]
we had just left on the first preparatory stage of our homeward
journey; and, far back on the inland level, a larger and loftier mass,
the grove surrounding the great Paknam pagoda, was the only thing
on which the eye could rest from the vain task of exploring the
monotonous sweep of the horizon. Here and there gleams as of a
few scattered pieces of silver marked the windings of the great river;
and on the nearest of them, just within the bar, the tug steaming
right into the land became lost to my sight, hull and funnel and
masts, as though the impassive earth had swallowed her up without
an effort, without a tremor. My eye followed the light cloud of her
smoke, now here, now there, above the plain, according to the

1. Irregular, rickety.
2. The Menan (Chao Phraya) runs
through Bangkok into the Gulf of Siam.
The Paknam Pagoda (Wat Prachadi
Klang-nam) is behind the Fort of Paknam at the mouth of the river. H. Warrington Smyth, in *Five Years in Siam*
(1898), describes Bangkok as "a land
of myths and terror," and says that when
he first crossed the bar of the river his
heart sank at the sight: "All around an
expanse of dirty mud-brown water . . .
stuck here and there with fishing stakes,
which gave to the whole scene a disorderly, ragged sort of look. . . ."

devious curves of the stream, but always fainter and farther away, till I lost it at last behind the mitre-shaped hill of the great pagoda. And then I was left alone with my ship, anchored at the head of the Gulf of Siam.

She floated at the starting-point of a long journey, very still in an immense stillness, the shadows of her spars flung far to the eastward by the setting sun. At that moment I was alone on her decks. There was not a sound in her—and around us nothing moved, nothing lived, not a canoe on the water, not a bird in the air, not a cloud in the sky. In this breathless pause at the threshold of a long passage we seemed to be measuring our fitness for a long and arduous enterprise, the appointed task of both our existences to be carried out, far from all human eyes, with only sky and sea for spectators and for judges.

There must have been some glare in the air to interfere with one's sight, because it was only just before the sun left us that my roaming eyes made out beyond the highest ridge of the principal islet of the group something which did away with the solemnity of perfect solitude. The tide of darkness flowed on swiftly; and with tropical suddenness a swarm of stars came out above the shadowy earth, while I lingered yet, my hand resting lightly on my ship's rail as if on the shoulder of a trusted friend. But, with all that multitude of celestial bodies staring down at one, the comfort of quiet communion with her was gone for good. And there were also disturbing sounds by this time—voices, footsteps forward; the steward flitted along the main deck, a busily ministering spirit; a hand-bell tinkled urgently under the poop deck. . . .

I found my two officers waiting for me near the supper table, in the lighted cuddy. We sat down at once, and as I helped the chief mate, I said:

"Are you aware that there is a ship anchored inside the islands? I saw her mast-heads above the ridge as the sun went down."

He raised sharply his simple face, overcharged by a terrible growth of whisker, and emitted his usual ejaculations, "Bless my soul, sir! You don't say so!"

My second mate was a round-cheeked, silent young man, grave beyond his years, I thought; but as our eyes happened to meet I detected a slight quiver on his lips. I looked down at once. It was not my part to encourage sneering on board my ship. It must be said, too, that I knew very little of my officers. In consequence of certain events of no particular significance, except to myself, I had been appointed to the command only a fortnight before. Neither did I know much of the hands forward. All these people had been together for eighteen months or so, and my position was that of the only stranger on board. I mention this because it has some bearing on what is to follow. But what I felt most was my being a stranger to the ship; and if all the truth must be told, I was somewhat of a stranger to myself. The youngest man on board (barring the second mate), and untried as yet by a position of the fullest responsibility, I was willing to take the adequacy of the others for granted. They had simply to be equal to their tasks; but I wondered how far I should turn out faithful to that ideal conception of one's own personality every man sets up for himself secretly.

Meantime the chief mate, with an almost visible effect of collaboration on the part of his round eyes and frightful whiskers, was trying to evolve a theory of the anchored ship. His dominant trait was to take all things into earnest consideration. He was of a painstaking turn of mind. As he used to say, he "liked to account to himself" for practically everything that came in his way, down to a miserable scorpion he had found in his cabin a week before. The why and the wherefore of that scorpion—how it got on board and came to select his room rather than the pantry (which was a dark place and more what a scorpion would be partial to), and how on earth it managed to drown itself in the inkwell of his writing-desk—had exercised him infinitely. The ship within the islands was much more easily accounted for; and just as we were about to rise from table he made his pronouncement. She was, he doubted not, a ship from home lately arrived. Probably she drew too much water to cross the bar except at the top of spring tides. Therefore she went into that natural harbor to wait for a few days in preference to remaining in an open roadstead.

"That's so," confirmed the second mate suddenly, in his slightly hoarse voice. "She draws over twenty feet. She's the Liverpool ship *Sephora*[3] with a cargo of coal. Hundred and twenty-three days from Cardiff."

We looked at him in surprise.

"The tugboat skipper told me when he come on board for your letters, sir," explained the young man. "He expects to take her up the river the day after tomorrow."

After thus overwhelming us with the extent of his information he slipped out of the cabin. The mate observed regretfully that he "could not account for that young fellow's whims." What prevented him telling us all about it at once, he wanted to know.

I detained him as he was making a move. For the last two days the crew had had plenty of hard work, and the night before they had very little sleep. I felt painfully that I—a stranger—was doing something unusual when I directed him to let all hands turn in without setting an anchor-watch.[4] I proposed to keep on deck myself till one o'clock or thereabouts. I would get the second mate to relieve me at that hour.

"He will turn out the cook and the steward at four," I concluded, "and then give you a call. Of course at the slightest sign of any sort of wind we'll have the hands up and make a start at once."

He concealed his astonishment. "Very well, sir." Outside the cuddy he put his head in the second mate's door to inform him of my unheard-of caprice to take a five hours' anchor-watch on myself. I heard the other raise his voice incredulously—"What? The captain

3. See *Leviticus* 23:15–16, for the system of counting days for offerings; *sephor*, to count, refers to a forty-day period during which no marriages can take place.

4. A detachment of seamen kept on deck while the ship lies at anchor.

himself?" Then a few more murmurs, a door closed, then another. A few moments later I went on deck.

My strangeness, which had made me sleepless, had prompted that unconventional arrangement, as if I had expected in those solitary hours of the night to get on terms with the ship of which I knew nothing, manned by men of whom I knew very little more. Fast alongside a wharf, littered like any ship in port with a tangle of unrelated things, invaded by unrelated shore people, I had hardly seen her yet properly. Now, as she lay cleared for sea, the stretch of her main deck seemed to me very fine under the stars. Very fine, very roomy for her size, and very inviting. I descended the poop and paced the waist, my mind picturing to myself the coming passage through the Malay Archipelago, down the Indian Ocean, and up the Atlantic. All its phases were familiar enough to me, every characteristic, all the alternatives which were likely to face me on the high seas—everything! . . . except the novel responsibility of command. But I took heart from the reasonable thought that the ship was like other ships, the men like other men, and that the sea was not likely to keep any special surprises expressly for my discomfiture.

Arrived at that comforting conclusion, I bethought myself of a cigar and went below to get it. All was still down there. Everybody at the after end of the ship was sleeping profoundly. I came out again on the quarter-deck, agreeably at ease in my sleeping suit on that warm, breathless night, barefooted, a glowing cigar in my teeth, and, going forward, I was met by the profound silence of the fore end of the ship. Only as I passed the door of the forecastle I heard a deep, quiet, trustful sigh of some sleeper inside. And suddenly I rejoiced in the great security of the sea as compared with the unrest of the land, in my choice of that untempted life presenting no disquieting problems, invested with an elementary moral beauty by the absolute straightforwardness of its appeal and by the singleness of its purpose.

The riding-light [5] in the fore-rigging burned with a clear, untroubled, as if symbolic, flame, confident and bright in the mysterious shades of the night. Passing on my way aft along the other side of the ship, I observed that the rope side-ladder, put over, no doubt, for the master of the tug when he came to fetch away our letters, had not been hauled in as it should have been. I became annoyed at this, for exactitude in small matters is the very soul of discipline. Then I reflected that I had myself peremptorily dismissed my officers from duty, and by my own act had prevented the anchor-watch being formally set and things properly attended to. I asked myself whether it was wise ever to interfere with the established routine of duties even from the kindest of motives. My action might have made me appear eccentric. Goodness only knew how that absurdly whiskered mate would "account" for my conduct, and what the whole ship thought of that informality of their new captain. I was vexed with myself.

5. Special light displayed by ship while ("riding") at anchor.

Not from compunction certainly, but, as it were mechanically, I proceeded to get the ladder in myself. Now a side-ladder of that sort is a light affair and comes in easily, yet my vigorous tug, which should have brought it flying on board, merely recoiled upon my body in a totally unexpected jerk. What the devil! . . . I was so astounded by the immovableness of that ladder that I remained stock-still, trying to account for it to myself like that imbecile mate of mine. In the end, of course, I put my head over the rail.

The side of the ship made an opaque belt of shadow on the dark-ling glassy shimmer of the sea. But I saw at once something elongated and pale floating very close to the ladder. Before I could form a guess a faint flash of phosphorescent light, which seemed to issue suddenly from the naked body of a man, flickered in the sleeping water with the elusive, silent play of summer lightning in a night sky. With a gasp I saw revealed to my stare a pair of feet, the long legs, a broad livid back immersed right up to the neck in a greenish cadaverous glow. One hand, awash, clutched the bottom rung of the ladder. He was complete but for the head. A headless corpse! The cigar dropped out of my gaping mouth with a tiny plop and a short hiss quite audible in the absolute stillness of all things under heaven. At that I suppose he raised up his face, a dimly pale oval in the shadow of the ship's side. But even then I could only barely make out down there the shape of his black-haired head. However, it was enough for the horrid, frost-bound sensation which had gripped me about the chest to pass off. The moment of vain exclamations was past too. I only climbed on the spare spar and leaned over the rail as far as I could, to bring my eyes nearer to that mystery floating alongside.

As he hung by the ladder, like a resting swimmer, the sea-lightning played about his limbs at every stir; and he appeared in it ghastly, silvery, fish-like. He remained as mute as a fish, too. He made no motion to get out of the water, either. It was inconceivable that he should not attempt to come on board, and strangely troubling to suspect that perhaps he did not want to. And my first words were prompted by just that troubled incertitude.

"What's the matter?" I asked in my ordinary tone, speaking down to the face upturned exactly under mine.

"Cramp," it answered, no louder. Then slightly anxious, "I say, no need to call any one."

"I was not going to," I said.

"Are you alone on deck?"

"Yes."

I had somehow the impression that he was on the point of letting go the ladder to swim away beyond my ken—mysterious as he came. But, for the moment, this being appearing as if he had risen from the bottom of the sea (it was certainly the nearest land to the ship) wanted only to know the time. I told him. And he, down there, tentatively:

"I suppose your captain's turned in?"

"I am sure he isn't," I said.

He seemed to struggle with himself, for I heard something like the

low, bitter murmur of doubt. "What's the good?" His next words came
out with a hesitating effort.

"Look here, my man. Could you call him out quietly?"

I thought the time had come to declare myself.

"*I* am the captain."

I heard a "By Jove!" whispered at the level of the water. The
phosphorescence flashed in the swirl of the water all about his limbs,
his other hand seized the ladder.

"My name's Leggatt."

The voice was calm and resolute. A good voice. The self-possession
of that man had somehow induced a corresponding state in myself.
It was very quietly that I remarked:

"You must be a good swimmer."

"Yes. I've been in the water practically since nine o'clock. The
question for me now is whether I am to let go this ladder and go
on swimming till I sink from exhaustion or—to come on board here."

I felt this was no mere formula of desperate speech, but a real
alternative in the view of a strong soul. I should have gathered from
this that he was young; indeed, it is only the young who are ever
confronted by such clear issues. But at the time it was pure intuition
on my part. A mysterious communication was established already between us two—in the face of that silent, darkened tropical sea. I was
young, too; young enough to make no comment. The man in the
water began suddenly to climb up the ladder, and I hastened away
from the rail to fetch some clothes.

Before entering the cabin I stood still, listening in the lobby at
the foot of the stairs. A faint snore came through the closed door of
the chief mate's room. The second mate's door was on the hook,
but the darkness in there was absolutely soundless. He, too, was young
and could sleep like a stone. Remained the steward, but he was not
likely to wake up before he was called. I got a sleeping suit out of
my room, and, coming back on deck, saw the naked man from the sea
sitting on the main-hatch, glimmering white in the darkness, his elbows on his knees and his head in his hands. In a moment he had
concealed his damp body in a sleeping suit of the same gray-stripe
pattern as the one I was wearing, and followed me like my double
on the poop. Together we moved right aft, barefooted, silent.

"What is it?" I asked in a deadened voice, taking the lighted
lamp out of the binnacle, and raising it to his face.

"An ugly business."

He had rather regular features; a good mouth; light eyes under
somewhat heavy, dark eyebrows; a smooth, square forehead; no
growth on his cheeks; a small, brown mustache, and a well-shaped,
round chin. His expression was concentrated, meditative, under the
inspecting light of the lamp I held up to his face; such as a man
thinking hard in solitude might wear. My sleeping suit was just right
for his size. A well-knit young fellow of twenty-five at most. He caught
his lower lip with the edge of white, even teeth.

"Yes," I said, replacing the lamp in the binnacle. The warm, heavy
tropical night closed upon his head again.

"There's a ship over there," he murmured.

"Yes, I know. The *Sephora*. Did you know of us?"

"Hadn't the slightest idea. I am the mate of her—" He paused and corrected himself. "I should say I *was*."

"Aha! Something wrong?"

"Yes. Very wrong indeed. I've killed a man."

"What do you mean? Just now?"

"No, on the passage. Weeks ago. Thirty-nine south. When I say a man—"

"Fit of temper," I suggested confidently.

The shadowy, dark head, like mine, seemed to nod imperceptibly above the ghostly gray of my sleeping suit. It was, in the night, as though I had been faced by my own reflection in the depths of a sombre and immense mirror.

"A pretty thing to have to own up to for a Conway boy," [6] murmured my double distinctly.

"You're a Conway boy?"

"I am," he said, as if startled. Then, slowly . . . "Perhaps you too . . ."

It was so; but being a couple of years older I had left before he joined. After a quick interchange of dates a silence fell; and I thought suddenly of my absurd mate with his terrific whiskers and the "Bless my soul—you don't say so" type of intellect. My double gave me an inkling of his thoughts by saying:

"My father's a parson in Norfolk. Do you see me before a judge and jury on that charge? For myself I can't see the necessity. There are fellows that an angel from heaven—And I am not that. He was one of those creatures that are just simmering all the time with a silly sort of wickedness. Miserable devils that have no business to live at all. He wouldn't do his duty and wouldn't let anybody else do theirs. But what's the good of talking! You know well enough the sort of ill-conditioned snarling cur . . ."

He appealed to me as if our experiences had been as identical as our clothes. And I knew well enough the pestiferous danger of such a character where there are no means of legal repression. And I knew well enough also that my double there was no homicidal ruffian. I did not think of asking him for details, and he told me the story roughly in brusque, disconnected sentences. I needed no more. I saw it all going on as though I were myself inside that other sleeping suit.

"It happened while we were setting a reefed foresail, at dusk. Reefed foresail! You understand the sort of weather. The only sail we had left to keep the ship running; so you may guess what it had been like for days. Anxious sort of job, that. He gave me some of his cursed insolence at the sheet.[7] I tell you I was overdone with this terrific weather that seemed to have no end to it. Terrific, I tell you— and a deep ship. I believe the fellow himself was half crazed with

6. The wooden battleship Conway, which was used to train young officers for the Royal Navy and merchant service. She ran aground in the Menai Straits (Wales) in 1953 and burned in 1956.

7. Rope or chain attached to lower corner of sail used for shortening or slackening it.

funk. It was no time for gentlemanly reproof, so I turned round and felled him like an ox. He up and at me. We closed just as an awful sea made for the ship. All hands saw it coming and took to the rigging, but I had him by the throat, and went on shaking him like a rat, the men above us yelling. 'Look out! Look out!' Then a crash as if the sky had fallen on my head. They say that for over ten minutes hardly anything was to be seen of the ship—just the three masts and a bit of the forecastle head and of the poop all awash driving along in a smother of foam. It was a miracle that they found us, jammed together behind the forebits. It's clear that I meant business, because I was holding him by the throat still when they picked us up. He was black in the face. It was too much for them. It seems they rushed us aft together, gripped as we were, screaming 'Murder!' like a lot of lunatics, and broke into the cuddy. And the ship running for her life, touch and go all the time, any minute her last in a sea fit to turn your hair gray only a-looking at it. I understand that the skipper, too, started raving like the rest of them. The man had been deprived of sleep for more than a week, and to have this sprung on him at the height of a furious gale nearly drove him out of his mind. I wonder they didn't fling me overboard after getting the carcass of their precious shipmate out of my fingers. They had rather a job to separate us, I've been told. A sufficiently fierce story to make an old judge and a respectable jury sit up a bit. The first thing I heard when I came to myself was the maddening howling of that endless gale, and on that the voice of the old man. He was hanging on to my bunk, staring into my face out of his sou'wester.

"'Mr. Leggatt, you have killed a man. You can act no longer as chief mate of this ship.'"

His care to subdue his voice made it sound monotonous. He rested a hand on the end of the skylight to steady himself with, and all that time did not stir a limb, so far as I could see. "Nice little tale for a quiet tea party," he concluded in the same tone.

One of my hands, too, rested on the end of the skylight; neither did I stir a limb, so far as I knew. We stood less than a foot from each other. It occurred to me that if old "Bless my soul—you don't say so" were to put his head up the companion and catch sight of us, he would think he was seeing double, or imagine himself come upon a scene of weird witchcraft: the strange captain having a quiet confabulation by the wheel with his own gray ghost. I became very much concerned to prevent anything of the sort. I heard the other's soothing undertone:

"My father's a parson in Norfolk," it said. Evidently he had forgotten he had told me this important fact before. Truly a nice little tale.

"You had better slip down into my stateroom now," I said, moving off stealthily. My double followed my movements; our bare feet made no sound; I let him in, closed the door with care, and, after giving a call to the second mate, returned on deck for my relief.

"Not much sign of any wind yet," I remarked when he approached.

"No, sir. Not much," he assented sleepily in his hoarse voice, with just enough deference, no more, and barely suppressing a yawn.

"Well, that's all you have to look out for. You have got your orders."

"Yes, sir."

I paced a turn or two on the poop and saw him take up his position face forward with his elbow in the ratlines of the mizzen-rigging before I went below. The mate's faint snoring was still going on peacefully. The cuddy lamp was burning over the table on which stood a vase with flowers, a polite attention from the ship's provision merchant —the last flowers we should see for the next three months at the very least. Two bunches of bananas hung from the beam symmetrically, one on each side of the rudder-casing. Everything was as before in the ship—except that two of her captain's sleeping suits were simultaneously in use, one motionless in the cuddy, the other keeping very still in the captain's stateroom.

It must be explained here that my cabin had the form of the capital letter L, the door being within the angle and opening into the short part of the letter. A couch was to the left, the bedplace to the right; my writing-desk and the chronometers' table faced the door. But any one opening it, unless he stepped right inside, had no view of what I call the long (or vertical) part of the letter. It contained some lockers surmounted by a bookcase; and a few clothes, a thick jacket or two, caps, oilskin coat, and such-like, hung on hooks. There was at the bottom of that part a door opening into my bathroom, which could be entered also directly from the saloon. But that way was never used.

The mysterious arrival had discovered the advantage of this particular shape. Entering my room, lighted strongly by a big bulkhead lamp swung on gimbals above my writing-desk, I did not see him anywhere till he stepped out quietly from behind the coats hung in the recessed part.

"I heard somebody moving about, and went in there at once," he whispered.

I, too, spoke under my breath.

"Nobody is likely to come in here without knocking and getting permission."

He nodded. His face was thin and the sunburn faded, as though he had been ill. And no wonder. He had been, I heard presently, kept under arrest in his cabin for nearly nine weeks. But there was nothing sickly in his eyes or in his expression. He was not a bit like me, really; yet, as we stood leaning over my bedplace, whispering side by side, with our dark heads together and our backs to the door, anybody bold enough to open it stealthily would have been treated to the uncanny sight of a double captain busy talking in whispers with his other self.

"But all this doesn't tell me how you came to hang on to our side-ladder," I inquired, in the hardly audible murmurs we used, after he had told me something more of the proceedings on board the *Sephora* once the bad weather was over.

"When we sighted Java Head[8] I had had time to think all those matters out several times over. I had six weeks of doing nothing else, and with only an hour or so every evening for a tramp on the quarterdeck."

He whispered, his arms folded on the side of my bedplace, staring through the open port. And I could imagine perfectly the manner of this thinking out—a stubborn if not a steadfast operation; something of which I should have been perfectly incapable.

"I reckoned it would be dark before we closed with the land," he continued, so low that I had to strain my hearing, near as we were to each other, shoulder touching shoulder almost. "So I asked to speak to the old man. He always seemed very sick when he came to see me—as if he could not look me in the face. You know, that fore-sail saved the ship. She was too deep to have run long under bare poles. And it was I that managed to set it for him. Anyway, he came. When I had him in my cabin—he stood by the door looking at me as if I had the halter round my neck already—I asked him right away to leave my cabin door unlocked at night while the ship was going through Sunda Straits. There would be the Java coast within two or three miles, off Anjer Point. I wanted nothing more. I've had a prize for swimming my second year in the Conway."

"I can believe it," I breathed out.

"God only knows why they locked me in every night. To see some of their faces you'd have thought they were afraid I'd go about at night strangling people. Am I a murdering brute? Do I look it? By Jove! if I had been he wouldn't have trusted himself like that into my room. You'll say I might have chucked him aside and bolted out, there and then—it was dark already. Well, no. And for the same reason I wouldn't think of trying to smash the door. There would have been a rush to stop me at the noise, and I did not mean to get into a confounded scrimmage. Somebody else might have got killed— for I would not have broken out only to get chucked back, and I did not want any more of that work. He refused, looking more sick than ever. He was afraid of the men, and also of that old second mate of his who had been sailing with him for years—a gray-headed old humbug; and his steward, too, had been with him devil knows how long—seventeen years or more—a dogmatic sort of loafer who hated me like poison, just because I was the chief mate. No chief mate ever made more than one voyage in the *Sephora*, you know. Those two old chaps ran the ship. Devil only knows what the skipper wasn't afraid of (all his nerve went to pieces altogether in that hellish spell of bad weather we had)—of what the law would do to him— of his wife, perhaps. Oh yes! she's on board. Though I don't think she would have meddled. She would have been only too glad to have me out of the ship in any way. The 'brand of Cain' business, don't you see? That's all right. I was ready enough to go off wandering on the face of the earth—and that was price enough to pay for an Abel[9] of that sort. Anyhow, he wouldn't listen to me. 'This thing must take its course. I represent the law here.' He was shaking like a leaf. 'So you won't?' 'No!' 'Then I hope you will be able to sleep on that," I said, and turned my back on him. 'I wonder that *you* can,' cries he, and locks the door.

"Well, after that, I couldn't. Not very well. That was three weeks ago. We have had a slow passage through the Java Sea; drifted about Carimata[1] for ten days. When we anchored here they thought, I suppose, it was all right. The nearest land (and that's five miles) is the ship's destination; the consul would soon set about catching me; and there would have been no object in bolting to these islets there. I don't suppose there's a drop of water on them. I don't know how it was, but tonight that steward, after bringing me my supper, went out to let me eat it, and left the door unlocked. And I ate it—all there was, too. After I had finished I strolled out on the quarter-deck. I don't know that I meant to do anything. A breath of fresh air was all I wanted, I believe. Then a sudden temptation came over me. I kicked off my slippers and was in the water before I had made up my mind fairly. Somebody heard the splash and they raised an awful hullabaloo. 'He's gone! Lower the boats! He's committed suicide! No, he's swimming.' Certainly I was swimming. It's not easy for a swimmer like me to commit suicide by drowning. I landed on the nearest islet before the boat left the ship's side. I heard them pulling about in the dark, hailing, and so on, but after a bit they gave up. Everything quieted down and the anchorage became as still as death. I sat down on a stone and began to think. I felt certain they would start searching for me at daylight. There was no place to hide on those stony things—and if there had been, what would have been the good? But now I was clear of that ship, I was not going back. So after a while I took off all my clothes, tied them up in a bundle with a stone inside, and dropped them in the deep water on the outer side of that islet. That was suicide enough for me. Let them think what they liked, but I didn't mean to drown myself. I meant to swim till I sank—but that's not the same thing. I struck out for another of these little islands, and it was from that one that I first saw your riding-light. Something to swim for. I went on easily, and on the way I came upon a flat rock a foot or two above water. In the daytime, I dare say, you might make it out with a glass from your poop. I scrambled up on it and rested myself for a bit. Then I made another start. That last spell must have been over a mile."

His whisper was getting fainter and fainter, and all the time he stared straight out through the porthole, in which there was not even a star to be seen. I had not interrupted him. There was something that made comment impossible, in his narrative, or perhaps in himself; a sort of feeling, a quality, which I can't find a name for. And when

---

9. In *Genesis* (4:14-15) Cain says to the Lord, "Behold, though hast driven me out this day from the face of the earth; and from thy face shall I be hid; and I shall be a fugitive and a vagabond in the earth; and it shall come to pass, that every one that findeth me shall slay me. And the Lord said unto him, Therefore whosoever slayeth Cain, vengeance shall be taken on him sevenfold. And the Lord set a mark upon Cain, lest any finding him should kill him."

1. The Karimata Islands in the straits between Borneo and Sumatra, some three hundred miles northeast of the Sunda Straits.

he ceased, all I found was a futile whisper, "So you swam for our light?"

"Yes—straight for it. It was something to swim for. I couldn't see any stars low down because the coast was in the way, and I couldn't see the land, either. The water was like glass. One might have been swimming in a confounded thousand feet deep cistern with no place for scrambling out anywhere; but what I didn't like was the notion of swimming round and round like a crazed bullock before I gave out; and as I didn't mean to go back . . . No. Do you see me being hauled back, stark naked, off one of these little islands by the scruff of the neck and fighting like a wild beast? Somebody would have got killed for certain, and I did not want any of that. So I went on. Then your ladder—"

"Why didn't you hail the ship?" I asked, a little louder.

He touched my shoulder lightly. Lazy footsteps came right over our heads and stopped. The second mate had crossed from the other side of the poop and might have been hanging over the rail, for all we knew.

"He couldn't hear us talking—could he?" My double breathed into my very ear anxiously.

His anxiety was an answer, a sufficient answer, to the question I had put to him. An answer containing all the difficulty of that situation. I closed the porthole quietly, to make sure. A louder word might have been overheard.

"Who's that?" he whispered then.

"My second mate. But I don't know much more of the fellow than you do."

And I told him a little about myself. I had been appointed to take charge while I least expected anything of the sort, not quite a fortnight ago. I didn't know either the ship or the people. Hadn't had the time in port to look about me or size anybody up. And as to the crew, all they knew was that I was appointed to take the ship home. For the rest, I was almost as much of a stranger on board as himself, I said. And at the moment I felt it most acutely. I felt that it would take very little to make me a suspect person in the eyes of the ship's company.

He had turned about meantime; and we, the two strangers in the ship, faced each other in identical attitudes.

"Your ladder—" he murmured, after a silence. "Who'd have thought of finding a ladder hanging over at night in a ship anchored out here! I felt just then a very unpleasant faintness. After the life I've been leading for nine weeks, anybody would have got out of condition. I wasn't capable of swimming round as far as your rudder-chains. And, lo and behold! there was a ladder to get hold of. After I gripped it I said to myself, 'What's the good?' When I saw a man's head looking over I thought I would swim away presently and leave him shouting—in whatever language it was. I didn't mind being looked at. I—I liked it. And then you speaking to me so quietly—as if you had expected me—made me hold on a little longer. It had been a confounded lonely time—I don't mean while swimming. I was glad to talk a little to somebody that didn't belong to the *Sephora*. As to asking for the captain, that was a mere impulse. It could have been no use, with all the ship knowing about me and the other people pretty certain to be round here in the morning. I don't know—I wanted to be seen, to talk with somebody, before I went on. I don't know what I would have said. . . . 'Fine night, isn't it?' or something of the sort."

"Do you think they will be round here presently?" I asked, with some incredulity.

"Quite likely," he said faintly.

He looked extremely haggard all of a sudden. His head rolled on his shoulders.

"H'm. We shall see then. Meantime get into that bed," I whispered. "Want help? There."

It was a rather high bedplace with a set of drawers underneath. This amazing swimmer really needed the lift I gave him by seizing his leg. He tumbled in, rolled over on his back, and flung one arm across his eyes. And then, with his face nearly hidden, he must have looked exactly as I used to look in that bed. I gazed upon my other self for a while before drawing across carefully the two green serge curtains which ran on a brass rod. I thought for a moment of pinning them together for greater safety, but I sat down on the couch, and once there I felt unwilling to rise and hunt for a pin. I would do it in a moment. I was extremely tired, in a peculiarly intimate way, by the strain of stealthiness, by the effort of whispering, and the general secrecy of this excitement. It was three o'clock by now, and I had been on my feet since nine, but I was not sleepy; I could not have gone to sleep. I sat there, fagged out, looking at the curtains, trying to clear my mind of the confused sensation of being in two places at once, and greatly bothered by an exasperating knocking in my head. It was a relief to discover suddenly that it was not in my head at all, but on the outside of the door. Before I could collect myself, the words "Come in" were out of my mouth, and the steward entered with a tray, bringing in my morning coffee. I had slept, after all, and I was so frightened that I shouted, "This way! I am here, steward," as though he had been miles away. He put down the tray on the table next the couch and only then said, very quietly, "I can see you are here, sir." I felt him give me a keen look, but I dared not meet his eyes just then. He must have wondered why I had drawn the curtains of my bed before going to sleep on the couch. He went out, hooking the door open as usual.

I heard the crew washing decks above me. I knew I would have been told at once if there had been any wind. Calm, I thought, and I was doubly vexed. Indeed, I felt dual more than ever. The steward reappeared suddenly in the doorway. I jumped up from the couch so quickly that he gave a start.

"What do you want here?"

"Close your port, sir—they are washing decks."

"It is closed," I said, reddening.

"Very well, sir." But he did not move from the doorway and returned my stare in an extraordinary, equivocal manner for a time. Then his eyes wavered, all his expression changed, and in a voice unusually gentle, almost coaxingly.

"May I come in to take the empty cup away, sir?"

"Of course!" I turned my back on him while he popped in and out. Then I unhooked and closed the door and even pushed the bolt. This sort of thing could not go on very long. The cabin was as hot as an oven, too. I took a peep at my double, and discovered that he had not moved; his arm was still over his eyes; but his chest heaved, his hair was wet, his chin glistened with perspiration. I reached over him and opened the port.

"I must show myself on deck," I reflected.

Of course, theoretically, I could do what I liked, with no one to say nay to me within the whole circle of the horizon; but to lock my cabin door and take the key away I did not dare. Directly I put my head out of the companion I saw the group of my two officers, the second mate barefooted, the chief mate in long india-rubber boots, near the break of the poop, and the steward half-way down the poop ladder talking to them eagerly. He happened to catch sight of me and dived, the second ran down on the main deck shouting some order or other, and the chief mate came to meet me, touching his cap.

There was a sort of curiosity in his eye that I did not like. I don't know whether the steward had told them that I was "queer" only, or downright drunk, but I know the man meant to have a good look at me. I watched him coming with a smile which, as he got into point-blank range, took effect and froze his very whiskers. I did not give him time to open his lips.

"Square the yards by lifts and braces before the hands go to breakfast."

It was the first particular order I had given on board that ship; and I stayed on deck to see it executed too. I had felt the need of asserting myself without loss of time. That sneering young cub got taken down a peg or two on that occasion, and I also seized the opportunity of having a good look at the face of every foremast man as they filed past me to go to the after braces. At breakfast time, eating nothing myself, I presided with such frigid dignity that the two mates were only too glad to escape from the cabin as soon as decency permitted; and all the time the dual working of my mind distracted me almost to the point of insanity. I was constantly watching myself, my secret self, as dependent on my actions as my own personality, sleeping in that bed, behind that door which faced me as I sat at the head of the table. It was very much like being mad, only it was worse, because one was aware of it.

I had to shake him for a solid minute, but when at last he opened his eyes it was in the full possession of his senses, with an inquiring look.

"All's well so far," I whispered. "Now you must vanish into the bathroom."

He did so, as noiseless as a ghost, and I then rang for the steward, and facing him boldly, directed him to tidy up my stateroom while I was having my bath—"and be quick about it." As my tone admitted of no excuses, he said, "Yes, sir," and ran off to fetch his dustpan and brushes. I took a bath and did most of my dressing, splashing, and whistling softly for the steward's edification, while the secret sharer of my life stood drawn bolt upright in that little space, his face looking very sunken in daylight, his eyelids lowered under the stern, dark line of his eyebrows drawn together by a slight frown.

When I left him there to go back to my room the steward was finishing dusting. I sent for the mate and engaged him in some insignificant conversation. It was, as it were, trifling with the terrific character of his whiskers; but my object was to give him an opportunity for a good look at my cabin. And then I could at last shut, with a clear conscience, the door of my stateroom and get my double back into the recessed part. There was nothing else for it. He had to sit still on a small folding stool, half smothered by the heavy coats hanging there. We listened to the steward going into the bathroom out of the saloon, filling the water-bottles there, scrubbing the bath, setting things to rights, whisk, bang, clatter—out again into the saloon—turn the key—click. Such was my scheme for keeping my second self invisible. Nothing better could be contrived under the circumstances. And there we sat: I at my writing-desk ready to appear busy with some papers, he behind me, out of sight of the door. It would not have been prudent to talk in daytime; and I could not have stood the excitement of that queer sense of whispering to myself. Now and then, glancing over my shoulder, I saw him far back there, sitting rigidly on the low stool, his bare feet close together, his arms folded, his head hanging on his breast—and perfectly still. Anybody would have taken him for me.

I was fascinated by it myself. Every moment I had to glance over my shoulder. I was looking at him when a voice outside the door said:

"Beg pardon, sir."

"Well!" . . . I kept my eyes on him, and so when the voice outside the door announced, "There's a ship's boat coming our way, sir," I saw him give a start—the first movement he had made for hours. But he did not raise his bowed head.

"All right. Get the ladder over."

I hesitated. Should I whisper something to him? But what? His immobility seemed to have been never disturbed. What could I tell him he did not know already? . . . Finally I went on deck.

2

The skipper of the *Sephora* had a thin, red whisker all round his face, and the sort of complexion that goes with hair of that color; also the particular, rather smeary shade of blue in the eyes. He was not exactly a showy figure; his shoulders were high, his stature but middling—one leg slightly more bandy than the other. He shook hands, looking vaguely around. A spiritless tenacity was his main characteristic, I judged. I behaved with a politeness which seemed to disconcert him. Perhaps he was shy. He mumbled to me as if he were ashamed of what he was saying; gave his name (it was some-thing like Archbold—but at this distance of years I hardly am sure), his ship's name, and a few other particulars of that sort, in the manner of a criminal making a reluctant and doleful confession. He had had terrible weather on the passage out—terrible—terrible—wife aboard, too.

By this time we were seated in the cabin and the steward brought in a tray with a bottle and glasses. "Thanks! No." Never took liquor. Would have some water, though. He drank two tumblerfuls. Terrible thirsty work. Ever since daylight had been exploring the islands round his ship.

"What was that for—fun?" I asked with an appearance of polite interest.

"No!" He sighed. "Painful duty."

As he persisted in his mumbling and I wanted my double to hear every word, I hit upon the notion of informing him that I regretted to say I was hard of hearing.

"Such a young man too!" he nodded, keeping his smeary, blue, unintelligent eyes fastened upon me. "What was the cause of it—some disease?" he inquired, without the least sympathy and as if he thought that, if so, I'd got no more than I deserved.

"Yes; disease," I admitted in a cheerful tone which seemed to shock him. But my point was gained, because he had to raise his voice to give me his tale. It is not worth while to record that ver-sion. It was just over two months since all this had happened, and he had thought so much about it that he seemed completely muddled as to its bearings, but still immensely impressed.

"What would you think of such a thing happening on board your own ship? I've had the *Sephora* for these fifteen years. I am a well-known shipmaster."

He was densely distressed—and perhaps I should have sympathized with him if I had been able to detach my mental vision from the unsuspected sharer of my cabin as though he were my second self. There he was on the other side of the bulkhead, four or five feet from us, no more, as we sat in the saloon. I looked politely at Cap-tain Archbold (if that was his name), but it was the other I saw, in a gray sleeping suit, seated on a low stool, his bare feet close to-gether, his arms folded, and every word said between us falling into the ears of his dark head bowed on his chest.

"I have been at sea now, man and boy, for seven and thirty years, and I've never heard of such a thing happening in an Eng-lish ship. And that it should be my ship. Wife on board, too."

I was hardly listening to him.

"Don't you think," I said, "that the heavy sea which, you told me, came aboard just then might have killed the man? I have seen the sheer weight of a sea kill a man very neatly, by simply breaking his neck."

"Good God!" he uttered impressively, fixing his smeary blue eyes on me. "The sea! No man killed by the sea ever looked like that." He seemed positively scandalized at my suggestion. And as I gazed at him, certainly not prepared for anything original on his part, he

advanced his head close to mine and thrust his tongue out at me so
suddenly that I couldn't help starting back.

After scoring over my calmness in this graphic way he nodded
wisely. If I had seen the sight, he assured me, I would never forget
it as long as I lived. The weather was too bad to give the corpse
a proper sea burial. So next day at dawn they took it up on the
poop, covering its face with a bit of bunting; he read a short prayer,
and then, just as it was, in its oilskins and long boots, they launched
it amongst those mountainous seas that seemed ready every moment
to swallow up the ship herself and the terrified lives on board of
her.

"That reefed foresail saved you," I threw in.

"Under God—it did," he exclaimed fervently. "It was by a special
mercy, I firmly believe, that it stood some of those hurricane squalls."

"It was the setting of that sail which—" I began.

"God's own hand in it," he interrupted me. "Nothing less could
have done it. I don't mind telling you that I hardly dared give the
order. It seemed impossible that we could touch anything without
losing it, and then our last hope would have been gone."

The terror of that gale was on him yet. I let him go on for a bit,
then said casually—as if returning to a minor subject:

"You were very anxious to give up your mate to the shore people,
I believe?"

He was. To the law. His obscure tenacity on that point had in it
something incomprehensible and a little awful; something, as it were,
mystical, quite apart from his anxiety that he should not be suspected
of "countenancing any doings of that sort." Seven and thirty virtuous years at sea, of which over twenty of immaculate command,
and the last fifteen in the *Sephora*, seemed to have laid him under
some pitiless obligation.

"And you know," he went on, groping shamefacedly amongst his
feelings, "I did not engage that young fellow. His people had some
interest with my owners. I was in a way forced to take him on. He
looked very smart, very gentlemanly, and all that. But do you know—
I never liked him, somehow. I am a plain man. You see, he wasn't
exactly the sort for the chief mate of a ship like the *Sephora*."

I had become so connected in thoughts and impressions with the
secret sharer of my cabin that I felt as if I, personally, were being
given to understand that I, too, was not the sort that would have
done for the chief mate of a ship like the *Sephora*. I had no doubt
of it in my mind.

"Not at all the style of man. You understand," he insisted superfluously, looking hard at me.

I smiled urbanely. He seemed at a loss for a while.

"I suppose I must report a suicide."

"Beg pardon?"

"Sui-cide! That's what I'll have to write to my owners directly I
get in."

"Unless you manage to recover him before tomorrow," I assented
dispassionately. . . . "I mean, alive."

He mumbled something which I really did not catch, and I turned my ear to him in a puzzled manner. He fairly bawled:

"The land—I say, the mainland is at least seven miles off my anchorage."

"About that."

My lack of excitement, of curiosity, of surprise, of any sort of pronounced interest, began to arouse his distrust. But except for the felicitous pretense of deafness I had not tried to pretend anything. I had felt utterly incapable of playing the part of ignorance properly, and therefore was afraid to try. It is also certain that he had brought some ready-made suspicions with him, and that he viewed my politeness as a strange and unnatural phenomenon. And yet how else could I have received him? Not heartily! That was impossible for psychological reasons, which I need not state here. My only object was to keep off his inquiries. Surlily? Yes, but surliness might have provoked a point-blank question. From its novelty to him and from its nature, punctilious courtesy was the manner best calculated to restrain the man. But there was the danger of his breaking through my defense bluntly. I could not, I think, have met him by a direct lie, also for psychological (not moral) reasons. If he had only known how afraid I was of his putting my feeling of identity with the other to the test! But, strangely enough (I thought of it only afterward), I believe that he was not a little disconcerted by the reverse side of that weird situation, by something in me that reminded him of the man he was seeking—suggested a mysterious similitude to the young fellow he had distrusted and disliked from the first.

However that might have been, the silence was not very prolonged. He took another oblique step.

"I reckon I had no more than a two-mile pull to your ship. Not a bit more."

"And quite enough, too, in this awful heat," I said.

Another pause full of mistrust followed. Necessity, they say, is mother of invention, but fear, too, is not barren of ingenious suggestions. And I was afraid he would ask me point-blank for news of my other self.

"Nice little saloon, isn't it?" I remarked, as if noticing for the first time the way his eyes roamed from one closed door to the other. "And very well fitted out, too. Here, for instance," I continued, reaching over the back of my seat negligently and flinging the door open, "is my bathroom."

He made an eager movement, but hardly gave it a glance. I got up, shut the door of the bathroom, and invited him to have a look round, as if I were very proud of my accommodation. He had to rise and be shown round, but he went through the business without any raptures whatever.

"And now we'll have a look at my stateroom," I declared, in a voice as loud as I dared to make it, crossing the cabin to the starboard side with purposely heavy steps.

He followed me in and gazed around. My intelligent double had vanished. I played my part.

"Very convenient—isn't it?"

"Very nice. Very comf . . ." He didn't finish, and went out brusquely as if to escape from some unrighteous wiles of mine. But it was not to be. I had been too frightened not to feel vengeful; I felt I had him on the run, and I meant to keep him on the run. My polite insistence must have had something menacing in it, because he gave in suddenly. And I did not let him off a single item: mates' rooms, pantry, storerooms, the very sail-locker, which was also under the poop—he had to look into them all. When at last I showed him out on the quarter-deck he drew a long, spiritless sigh, and mumbled dismally that he must really be going back to his ship now. I desired my mate, who had joined us, to see to the captain's boat.

The man of whiskers gave a blast on the whistle which he used to wear hanging round his neck, and yelled, "*Sephora's* away!" My double down there in my cabin must have heard, and certainly could not feel more relieved than I. Four fellows came running out from somewhere forward and went over the side, while my own men, appearing on deck too, lined the rail. I escorted my visitor to the gangway ceremoniously, and nearly overdid it. He was a tenacious beast. On the very ladder he lingered, and in that unique, guiltily conscientious manner of sticking to the point:

"I say . . . you . . . you don't think that—"

I covered his voice loudly.

"Certainly not. . . . I am delighted. Goodbye."

I had an idea of what he meant to say, and just saved myself by the privilege of defective hearing. He was too shaken generally to insist, but my mate, close witness of that parting, looked mystified and his face took on a thoughtful cast. As I did not want to appear as if I wished to avoid all communication with my officers, he had the opportunity to address me.

"Seems a very nice man. His boat's crew told our chaps a very extraordinary story, if what I am told by the steward is true. I suppose you had it from the captain, sir?"

"Yes. I had a story from the captain."

"A very horrible affair—isn't it, sir?"

"It is."

"Beats all these tales we hear about murders in Yankee ships."

"I don't think it beats them. I don't think it resembles them in the least."

"Bless my soul—you don't say so! But of course I've no acquaintance whatever with American ships, not I, so I couldn't go against your knowledge. It's horrible enough for me. . . . But the queerest part is that those fellows seemed to have some idea the man was hidden aboard here. They had really. Did you ever hear of such a thing?"

"Preposterous—isn't it?"

We were walking to and fro athwart the quarter-deck. No one of the crew forward could be seen (the day was Sunday), and the mate pursued:

"There was some little dispute about it. Our chaps took offense. 'As if we would harbor a thing like that,' they said. 'Wouldn't you like to look for him in our coal-hole?' Quite a tiff. But they made it up in the end. I suppose he did drown himself. Don't you, sir?"

"I don't suppose anything."

"You have no doubt in the matter, sir?"

"None whatever."

I left him suddenly. I felt I was producing a bad impression, but with my double down there it was most trying to be on deck. And it was almost as trying to be below. Altogether a nerve-trying situation. But on the whole I felt less torn in two when I was with him. There was no one in the whole ship whom I dared take into my confidence. Since the hands had got to know his story, it would have been impossible to pass him off for any one else, and an accidental discovery was to be dreaded now more than ever. . . .

The steward being engaged in laying the table for dinner, we could talk only with our eyes when I first went down. Later in the afternoon we had a cautious try at whispering. The Sunday quietness of the ship was against us; the stillness of air and water around her was against us; the elements, the men were against us—everything was against us in our secret partnership; time itself—for this could not go on for ever. The very trust in Providence was, I supposed, denied to his guilt. Shall I confess that this thought cast me down very much? And as to the chapter of accidents which counts for so much in the book of success, I could only hope that it was closed. For what favorable accident could be expected?

"Did you hear everything?" were my first words as soon as we took up our position side by side, leaning over my bedplace.

He had. And the proof of it was his earnest whisper, "The man told you he hardly dared to give the order."

I understood the reference to be to that saving foresail.

"Yes. He was afraid of it being lost in the setting."

"I assure you he never gave the order. He may think he did, but he never gave it. He stood there with me on the break of the poop after the maintopsail blew away, and whimpered about our last hope —positively whimpered about it and nothing else—and the night coming on! To hear one's skipper go on like that in such weather was enough to drive any fellow out of his mind. It worked me up into a sort of desperation. I just took it into my own hands and. went away from him, boiling, and—But what's the use telling you? *You* know! . . . Do you think that if I had not been pretty fierce with them I should have got the men to do anything? Not it! The boss'en[2] perhaps? Perhaps! It wasn't a heavy sea—it was a sea gone mad! I suppose the end of the world will be something like that; and a man may have the heart to see it coming once and be done with it—but to have to face it day after day . . . I don't blame anybody. I was precious little better than the rest. Only—I was an officer of that old coal-wagon, anyhow. . . ."

"I quite understand," I conveyed that sincere assurance into his ear. He was out of breath with whispering; I could hear him pant slightly. It was all very simple. The same strung-up force which had given twenty-four men a chance, at least, for their lives had, in a sort of recoil, crushed an unworthy mutinous existence.

2. *Bosun* or *boatswain*, petty officer in charge of deck crew and of rigging.

But I had no leisure to weigh the merits of the matter—footsteps in the saloon, a heavy knock. "There's enough wind to get under way with, sir." Here was the call of a new claim upon my thoughts and even upon my feelings.

"Turn the hands up," I cried through the door. "I'll be on deck directly."

I was going out to make the acquaintance of my ship. Before I left the cabin our eyes met—the eyes of the only two strangers on board. I pointed to the recessed part where the little camp-stool awaited him and laid my finger on my lips. He made a gesture—somewhat vague—a little mysterious, accompanied by a faint smile, as if of regret.

This is not the place to enlarge upon the sensations of a man who feels for the first time a ship move under his feet to his own independent word. In my case they were not unalloyed. I was not wholly alone with my command; for there was that stranger in my cabin. Or, rather, I was not completely and wholly with her. Part of me was absent. That mental feeling of being in two places at once affected me physically as if the mood of secrecy had penetrated my very soul. Before an hour had elapsed since the ship had begun to move, having occasion to ask the mate (he stood by my side) to take a compass bearing of the Pagoda, I caught myself reaching up to his ear in whispers. I say I caught myself, but enough had escaped to startle the man. I can't describe it otherwise than by saying that he shied. A grave, preoccupied manner, as though he were in possession of some perplexing intelligence, did not leave him henceforth. A little later I moved away from the rail to look at the compass with such a stealthy gait that the helmsman noticed it—and I could not help noticing the unusual roundness of his eyes. These are trifling instances, though it's to no commander's advantage to be suspected of ludicrous eccentricities. But I was also more seriously affected. There are to a seaman certain words, gestures, that should in given conditions come as naturally, as instinctively, as the winking of a menaced eye. A certain order should spring on to his lips without thinking; a certain sign should get itself made, so to speak, without reflection. But all unconscious alertness had abandoned me. I had to make an effort of will to recall myself back (from the cabin) to the conditions of the moment. I felt that I was appearing an irresolute commander to those people who were watching me more or less critically.

And, besides, there were the scares. On the second day out, for instance, coming off the deck in the afternoon (I had straw slippers on my bare feet) I stopped at the open pantry door and spoke to the steward. He was doing something there with his back to me. At the sound of my voice he nearly jumped out of his skin, as the saying is, and incidentally broke a cup.

"What on earth's the matter with you?" I asked, astonished.

He was extremely confused. "Beg your pardon, sir. I made sure you were in your cabin."

"You see I wasn't."

"No, sir. I could have sworn I had heard you moving in there not a moment ago. It's most extraordinary . . . very sorry, sir."

I passed on with an inward shudder. I was so identified with my secret double that I did not even mention the fact in those scanty, fearful whispers we exchanged. I suppose he had made some slight noise of some kind or other. It would have been miraculous if he hadn't at one time or another. And yet, haggard as he appeared, he looked always perfectly self-controled, more than calm—almost invulnerable. On my suggestion he remained almost entirely in the bathroom, which, upon the whole, was the safest place. There could be really no shadow of an excuse for any one ever wanting to go in there, once the steward had done with it. It was a very tiny place. Sometimes he reclined on the floor, his legs bent, his head sustained on one elbow. At others I would find him on the camp-stool, sitting in his gray sleeping suit and with his cropped dark hair like a patient, unmoved convict. At night I would smuggle him into my bedplace, and we would whisper together, with the regular footfalls of the officer of the watch passing and repassing over our heads. It was an infinitely miserable time. It was lucky that some tins of fine preserves were stowed in a locker in my stateroom; hard bread I could always get hold of; and so he lived on stewed chicken, pâté de foie gras, asparagus, cooked oysters, sardines—on all sorts of abominable sham-delicacies out of tins. My early morning coffee he always drank; and it was all I dared do for him in that respect.

Every day there was the horrible maneuvering to go through so that my room and then the bathroom should be done in the usual way. I came to hate the sight of the steward, to abhor the voice of that harmless man. I felt that it was he who would bring on the disaster of discovery. It hung like a sword over our heads.

The fourth day out, I think (we were then working down the east side of the Gulf of Siam, tack for tack,[3] in light winds and smooth water)—the fourth day, I say, of this miserable juggling with the unavoidable, as we sat at our evening meal, that man, whose slightest movement I dreaded, after putting down the dishes ran up on deck busily. This could not be dangerous. Presently he came down again; and then it appeared that he had remembered a coat of mine which I had thrown over a rail to dry after having been wetted in a shower which had passed over the ship in the afternoon. Sitting stolidly at the head of the table I became terrified at the sight of the garment on his arm. Of course he made for my door. There was no time to lose.

"Steward!" I thundered. My nerves were so shaken that I could not govern my voice and conceal my agitation. This was the sort of thing that made my terrifically whiskered mate tap his forehead with his forefinger. I had detected him using that gesture while talking on deck with a confidential air to the carpenter. It was too far to hear a word, but I had no doubt that this pantomime could only refer to the strange new captain.

"Yes, sir," the pale-faced steward turned resignedly to me. It was this maddening course of being shouted at, checked without rhyme or reason, arbitrarily chased out of my cabin, suddenly called into it, sent flying out of his pantry on incomprehensible errands, that ac-

3. By a series of shiftings back and forth of sails.

counted for the growing wretchedness of his expression.

"Where are you going with that coat?"

"To your room, sir."

"Is there another shower coming?"

"I'm sure I don't know, sir. Shall I go up again and see, sir?"

"No! never mind."

My object was attained, as of course my other self in there would have heard everything that passed. During this interlude my two officers never raised their eyes off their respective plates; but the lip of that confounded cub, the second mate, quivered visibly.

I expected the steward to hook my coat on and come out at once. He was very slow about it; but I dominated my nervousness sufficiently not to shout after him. Suddenly I became aware (it could be heard plainly enough) that the fellow for some reason or other was opening the door of the bathroom. It was the end. The place was literally not big enough to swing a cat in. My voice died in my throat and I went stony all over. I expected to hear a yell of surprise and terror, and made a movement, but had not the strength to get on my legs. Everything remained still. Had my second self taken the poor wretch by the throat? I don't know what I could have done next moment if I had not seen the steward come out of my room, close the door, and then stand quietly by the sideboard.

"Saved," I thought. "But, no! Lost! Gone! He was gone!"

I laid my knife and fork down and leaned back in my chair. My head swam. After a while, when sufficiently recovered to speak in a steady voice, I instructed my mate to put the ship round at eight o'clock himself.

"I won't come on deck," I went on. "I think I'll turn in, and unless the wind shifts I don't want to be disturbed before midnight. I feel a bit seedy."

"You did look middling bad a little while ago," the chief mate remarked without showing any great concern.

They both went out, and I stared at the steward clearing the table. There was nothing to be read on that wretched man's face. But why did he avoid my eyes? I asked myself. Then I thought I should like to hear the sound of his voice.

"Steward!"

"Sir!" Startled as usual.

"Where did you hang up that coat?"

"In the bathroom, sir." The usual anxious tone. "It's not quite dry yet, sir."

For some time longer I sat in the cuddy. Had my double vanished as he had come? But of his coming there was an explanation, whereas his disappearance would be inexplicable. . . . I went slowly into my dark room, shut the door, lighted the lamp, and for a time dared not turn round. When at last I did I saw him standing bolt upright in the narrow recessed part. It would not be true to say I had a shock, but an irresistible doubt of his bodily existence flitted through my mind. Can it be, I asked myself, that he is not visible to other eyes than mine? It was like being haunted. Motionless, with a grave face, he raised his hands slightly at me in a gesture which meant clearly, "Heavens! what a narrow escape!" Narrow indeed. I think I had come creeping quietly as near insanity as any man who his not actually gone over the border. That gesture restrained me, so to speak.

The mate with the terrific whiskers was now putting the ship on the other tack. In the moment of profound silence which follows upon the hands going to their stations I heard on the poop his raised voice: "Hard alee!"[4] and the distant shout of the order repeated on the main deck. The sails, in that light breeze, made but a faint fluttering noise. It ceased. The ship was coming round slowly; I held my breath in the renewed stillness of expectation; one wouldn't have thought that there was a single living soul on her decks. A sudden brisk shout, "Mainsail haul!" broke the spell, and in the noisy cries and rush over-head of the men running away with the main brace we two, down in my cabin, came together in our usual position by the bedplace.

He did not wait for my question. "I heard him fumbling here and just managed to squat myself down in the bath," he whispered to me. "The fellow only opened the door and put his arm in to hang the coat up. All the same. . . ."

"I never thought of that," I whispered back, even more appalled than before at the closeness of the shave, and marveling at that some-thing unyielding in his character which was carrying him through so finely. There was no agitation in his whisper. Whoever was being driven distracted, it was not he. He was sane. And the proof of his sanity was continued when he took up the whispering again.

"It would never do for me to come to life again."

It was something that a ghost might have said. But what he was alluding to was his old captain's reluctant admission of the theory of suicide. It would obviously serve his turn—if I had understood at all the view which seemed to govern the unalterable purpose of his action.

"You must maroon me as soon as ever you can get amongst these islands off the Cambodje[5] shore," he went on.

"Maroon you! We are not living in a boy's adventure tale," I protested. His scornful whispering took me up.

"We aren't indeed! There's nothing of a boy's tale in this. But there's nothing else for it. I want no more. You don't suppose I am afraid of what can be done to me? Prison or gallows or whatever they may please. But you don't see me coming back to explain such things to an old fellow in a wig and twelve respectable tradesmen, do you? What can they know whether I am guilty or not—or of *what* I am guilty, either? That's my affair. What does the Bible say? 'Driven off the face of the earth.'[6] Very well. I am off the face of the earth now. As I came at night so I shall go."

"Impossible!" I murmured. "You can't."

"Can't? . . . Not naked like a soul on the Day of Judgment. I shall freeze on to this sleeping suit. The Last Day is not yet—and . . . you have understood thoroughly. Didn't you?"

4. Put the helm all the way over to the side away from the wind.
5. Cambodian.
6. See note 9 above.

I felt suddenly ashamed of myself. I may say truly that I understood—and my hesitation in letting that man swim away from my ship's side had been a mere sham sentiment, a sort of cowardice.

"It can't be done now till next night," I breathed out. "The ship is on the offshore tack and the wind may fail us."

"As long as I know that you understand," he whispered. "But of course you do. It's a great satisfaction to have got somebody to understand. You seem to have been there on purpose." And in the same whisper, as if we two whenever we talked had to say things to each other which were not fit for the world to hear, he added, "It's very wonderful."

We remained side by side talking in our secret way—but sometimes silent or just exchanging a whispered word or two at long intervals. And as usual he stared through the port. A breath of wind came now and again into our faces. The ship might have been moored in dock, so gently and on an even keel she slipped through the water, that did not murmur even at our passage, shadowy and silent like a phantom sea.

At midnight I went on deck, and to my mate's great surprise put the ship round on the other tack. His terrible whiskers flitted round me in silent criticism. I certainly should not have done it if it had been only a question of getting out of that sleepy gulf as quickly as possible. I believe he told the second mate, who relieved him, that it was a great want of judgment. The other only yawned. That intolerable cub shuffled about so sleepily and lolled against the rails in such a slack, improper fashion that I came down on him sharply.

"Aren't you properly awake yet?"

"Yes, sir! I am awake."

"Well, then, be good enough to hold yourself as if you were. And keep a look out. If there's any current we'll be closing with some islands long before daylight."

The east side of the gulf is fringed with islands, some solitary, others in groups. On the blue background of the high coast they seem to float on silvery patches of calm water, arid and gray, or dark green and rounded like clumps of evergreen bushes, with the larger ones, a mile or two long, showing the outlines of ridges, ribs of gray rock under the dank mantle of matted leafage. Unknown to trade, to travel, almost to geography, the manner of life they harbor is an unsolved secret. There must be villages—settlements of fishermen at least —on the largest of them, and some communication with the world is probably kept up by native craft. But all that forenoon, as we headed for them, fanned along by the faintest of breezes, I saw no sign of man or canoe in the field of the telescope I kept on pointing at the scattered group.

At noon I gave no orders for a change of course, and the mate's whiskers became much concerned and seemed to be offering themselves unduly to my notice. At last I said:

"I am going to stand right in. Quite in—as far as I can take her."

The stare of extreme surprise imparted an air of ferocity also to his eyes, and he looked truly terrific for a moment.

"We're not doing well in the middle of the gulf," I continued casually. "I am going to look for the land breezes tonight."

"Bless my soul! Do you mean, sir, in the dark amongst the lot of all them islands and reefs and shoals?"

"Well, if there are any regular land breezes at all on this coast one must get close inshore to find them—mustn't one?"

"Bless my soul!" he exclaimed again under his breath. All that afternoon he wore a dreamy, comtemplative appearance which in him was a mark of perplexity. After dinner I went into my state-room as if I meant to take some rest. There we two bent our dark heads over a half-unrolled chart lying on my bed.

"There," I said. "It's got to be Koh-ring.[7] I've been looking at it ever since sunrise. It has got two hills and a low point. It must be inhabited. And on the coast opposite there is what looks like the mouth of a biggish river—with some town, no doubt, not far up. It's the best chance for you that I can see."

"Anything. Koh-ring let it be."

He looked thoughtfully at the chart as if surveying chances and distances from a lofty height—and following with his eyes his own figure wandering on the blank land of Cochin-China, and then passing off that piece of paper clean out of sight into uncharted regions. And it was as if the ship had two captains to plan her course for her. I had been so worried and restless running up and down that I had not had the patience to dress that day. I had remained in my sleeping suit, with straw slippers and a soft floppy hat. The closeness of the heat in the gulf had been most oppressive, and the crew were used to see me wandering in that airy attire.

"She will clear the south point as she heads now," I whispered into his ear. "Goodness only knows when, though—but certainly after dark. I'll edge her in to half a mile, as far as I may be able to judge in the dark . . ."

"Be careful," he murmured warningly—and I realized suddenly that all my future, the only future for which I was fit, would perhaps go irretrievably to pieces in any mishap to my first command.

I could not stop a moment longer in the room. I motioned him to get out of sight and made my way on the poop. That unplayful cub had the watch. I walked up and down for a while thinking things out, then beckoned him over."

"Send a couple of hands to open the two quarter-deck ports," I said mildly.

He actually had the impudence, or else so forgot himself in his wonder at such an incomprehensible order, as to repeat:

"Open the quarter-deck ports! What for, sir?"

"The only reason you need concern yourself about is because I tell you to do so. Have them opened wide and fastened properly."

He reddened and went off, but I believe made some jeering re-mark to the carpenter as to the sensible practice of ventilating a ship's quarter-deck. I know he popped into the mate's cabin to impart the

---

7. *Koh* or *Ko* means *island;* there are a large number of islands with that prefix at the head of the Gulf of Siam, but not, apparently, a Koh-ring.

fact to him, because the whiskers came on deck, as it were by chance, and stole glances at me from below—for signs of lunacy or drunkenness, I suppose.

A little before supper, feeling more restless than ever, I rejoined, for a moment, my second self. And to find him sitting so quietly was surprising, like something against nature, inhuman.

I developed my plan in a hurried whisper.

"I shall stand in as close as I dare and then put her round. I shall presently find means to smuggle you out of here into the sail-locker, which communicates with the lobby. But there is an opening, a sort of square for hauling the sails out, which gives straight on the quarter-deck and which is never closed in fine weather, so as to give air to the sails. When the ship's way is deadened in stays[8] and all the hands are aft at the main braces you shall have a clear road to slip out and get overboard through the open quarter-deck port. I've had them both fastened up. Use a rope's end to lower yourself into the water so as to avoid a splash—you know. It could be heard and cause some beastly complication."

He kept silent for a while, then whispered, "I understand."

"I won't be there to see you go," I began with an effort. "The rest . . . I only hope I have understood too."

"You have. From first to last"—and for the first time there seemed to be a faltering, something strained in his whisper. He caught hold of my arm, but the ringing of the supper bell made me start. He didn't, though; he only released his grip.

After supper I didn't come below again till well past eight o'clock. The faint, steady breeze was loaded with dew; and the wet, darkened sails held all there was of propelling power in it. The night, clear and starry, sparkled darkly, and the opaque, lightless patches shifting slowly amongst the low stars were the drifting islets. On the port bow there was a big one more distant and shadowily imposing by the great space of sky it eclipsed.

On opening the door I had a back view of my very own self looking at a chart. He had come out of the recess and was standing near the table.

"Quite dark enough," I whispered.

He stepped back and leaned against my bed with a level, quiet glance. I sat on the couch. We had nothing to say to each other. Over our heads the officer of the watch moved here and there. Then I heard him move quickly. I knew what that meant. He was making for the companion; and presently his voice was outside my door.

"We are drawing in pretty fast, sir. Land looks rather close."

"Very well," I answered. "I am coming on deck directly."

I waited till he was gone out of the cuddy, then rose. My double moved too. The time had come to exchange our last whispers, for neither of us was ever to hear each other's natural voice.

"Look here!" I opened a drawer and took out three sovereigns. "Take this, anyhow. I've got six and I'd give you the lot, only I

---

8. When the ship's forward motion is slowed or stopped while its head is being turned toward the wind for the purpose of shifting the sail.

must keep a little money to buy some fruit and vegetables for the crew from native boats as we go through Sunda Straits."

He shook his head.

"Take it," I urged him, whispering desperately. "No one can tell what . . ."

He smiled and slapped meaningly the only pocket of the sleeping jacket. It was not safe, certainly. But I produced a large old silk handkerchief of mine, and tying the three pieces of gold in a corner, pressed it on him. He was touched, I suppose, because he took it at last and tied it quickly round his waist under the jacket, on his bare skin.

Our eyes met; several seconds elapsed, till, our glances still mingled, I extended my hand and turned the lamp out. Then I passed through the cuddy, leaving the door of my room wide open. . . . "Steward!"

He was still lingering in the pantry in the greatness of his zeal, giving a rub-up to a plated cruet stand the last thing before going to bed. Being carful not to wake up the mate, whose room was opposite, I spoke in an undertone.

He looked round anxiously. "Sir!"

"Can you get me a little hot water from the galley?"

"I am afraid, sir, the galley fire's been out for some time now."

"Go and see."

He fled up the stairs.

"Now," I whispered loudly into the saloon—too loudly, perhaps, but I was afraid I couldn't make a sound. He was by my side in an instant—the double captain slipped past the stairs—through a tiny dark passage . . . a sliding door. We were in the sail-locker, scrambling on our knees over the sails. A sudden thought struck me. I saw myself wandering barefooted, bareheaded, the sun beating on my dark poll. I snatched off my floppy hat and tried hurriedly in the dark to ram it on my other self. He dodged and fended off silently. I wonder what he thought had come to me before he understood and suddenly desisted. Our hands met gropingly, lingered united in a steady, motionless clasp for a second. . . . No word was breathed by either of us when they separated.

I was standing quietly by the pantry door when the steward returned.

"Sorry, sir. Kettle barely warm. Shall I light the spirit-lamp?"

"Never mind."

I came out on deck slowly. It was now a matter of conscience to shave the land as close as possible—for now he must go overboard whenever the ship was put in stays. Must! There could be no going back for him. After a moment I walked over to leeward and my heart flew into my mouth at the nearness of the land on the bow. Under any other circumstances I would not have held on a minute longer. The second mate had followed me anxiously.

I looked on till I felt I could command my voice.

"She will weather," I said then in a quiet tone.

"Are you going to try that, sir?" he stammered out incredulously.

I took no notice of him and raised my tone just enough to be
heard by the helmsman.

"Keep her good full "[9]

"Good full, sir."

The wind fanned my cheek, the sails slept, the world was silent.
The strain of watching the dark loom of the land grow bigger and
denser was too much for me. I had to shut my eyes—because the
ship must go closer. She must! The stillness was intolerable. Were we
standing still?

When I opened my eyes the second view started my heart with a
thump. The black southern hill of Koh-ring seemed to hang right
over the ship like a towering fragment of the everlasting night. On
that enormous mass of blackness there was not a gleam to be seen,
not a sound to be heard. It was gliding irresistibly towards us and
yet seemed already within reach of the hand. I saw the vague figures
of the watch grouped in the waist, gazing in awed silence.

"Are you going on, sir?" inquired an unsteady voice at my elbow.
I ignored it. I had to go on.

"Keep her full. Don't check her way. That won't do now," I said
warningly.

"I can't see the sails very well," the helmsman answered me, in
strange, quavering tones.

Was she close enough? Already she was, I won't say in the shadow
of the land, but in the very blackness of it, already swallowed up as
it were, gone too close to be recalled, gone from me altogether.

"Give the mate a call," I said to the young man who stood at my
elbow as still as death. "And turn all hands up."

My tone had a borrowed loudness reverberated from the height of
the land. Several voices cried out together, "We are all on deck, sir."

Then stillness again, with the great shadow gliding closer, towering
higher, without a light, without a sound. Such a hush had fallen on
the ship that she might have been a bark of the dead floating in
slowly under the very gate of Erebus.

"My God! Where are we?"

It was the mate moaning at my elbow. He was thunderstruck,
and as it were deprived of the moral support of his whiskers. He
clapped his hands and absolutely cried out, "Lost!"

"Be quiet," I said sternly.

He lowered his tone, but I saw the shadowy gesture of his despair.
"What are we doing here?"

"Looking for the land wind."

He made as if to tear his hair, and addressed me recklessly.

"She will never get out. You have done it, sir. I knew it'd end
in something like this. She will never weather, and you are too close
now to stay. She'll drift ashore before she's round. O my God!"

I caught his arm as he was raising it to batter his poor devoted
head, and shook it violently.

9. Keep the ship's sails filled with wind.

"She's ashore already," he wailed, trying to tear himself away.

"Is she? . . . Keep good full there!"

"Good full, sir," cried the helmsman in a frightened, thin, childlike voice.

I hadn't let go the mate's arm and went on shaking it. "Ready about,[1] do you hear? You go forward"—shake—"and stop there"—shake —"and hold your noise"—shake—"and see these head-sheets properly overhauled"—shake, shake—shake.

And all the time I dared not look towards the land lest my heart should fail me. I released my grip at last and he ran forward as if fleeing for dear life.

I wondered what my double there in the sail-locker thought of this commotion. He was able to hear everything—and perhaps he was able to understand why, on my conscience, it had to be thus close— no less. My first order "Hard alee!" re-echoed ominously under the towering shadow of Koh-ring as if I had shouted in a mountain gorge. And then I watched the land intently. In that smooth water and light wind it was impossible to feel the ship coming-to.[2] No! I could not feel her. And my second self was making now ready to slip out and lower himself overboard. Perhaps he was gone already . . . ?

The great black mass brooding over our very mast-heads began to pivot away from the ship's side silently. And now I forgot the secret stranger ready to depart, and remembered only that I was a total stranger to the ship. I did not know her. Would she do it? How was she to be handled?

I swung the mainyard and waited helplessly. She was perhaps stopped, and her very fate hung in the balance, with the black mass of Koh-ring like the gate of the everlasting night towering over her taffrail. What would she do now? Had she way on her yet? I stepped to the side swiftly, and on the shadowy water I could see nothing except a faint phosphorescent flash revealing the glassy smoothness of the sleeping surface. It was impossible to tell—and I had not learned yet the feel of my ship. Was she moving? What I needed was something easily seen, a piece of paper, which I could throw overboard and watch. I had nothing on me. To run down for it I didn't dare. There was no time. All at once my strained, yearning stare distinguished a white object floating within a yard of the ship's side— white, on the black water. A phosphorescent flash passed under it. What was that thing? . . . I recognized my own floppy hat. It must have fallen off his head . . . and he didn't bother. Now I had what I wanted—the saving mark for my eyes. But I hardly thought of my other self, now gone from the ship, to be hidden for ever from all friendly faces, to be a fugitive and a vagabond on the earth, with no brand of the curse on his sane forehead to stay a slaying hand . . . too proud to explain.

---

1. Be ready to shift the sails (tack). The head-sheets, below, are the lines attached to the sails of the forward mast, and to overhaul is to slacken a rope by pulling it in the opposite direction to that used in hoisting a sail and thus loosening the blocks.

2. Coming to a standstill.

And I watched the hat—the expression of my sudden pity for his mere flesh. It had been meant to save his homeless head from the dangers of the sun. And now—behold—it was saving the ship, by serving me for a mark to help out the ignorance of my strangeness. Ha! It was drifting forward, warning me just in time that the ship had gathered sternway.

"Shift the helm," I said in a low voice to the seaman standing still like a statue.

The man's eyes glistened wildly in the binnacle light as he jumped round to the other side and spun round the wheel.

I walked to the break of the poop. On the overshadowed deck all hands stood by the forebraces waiting for my order. The stars ahead seemed to be gliding from right to left. And all was so still in the world that I heard the quiet remark, "She's round," passed in a tone of intense relief between two seamen.

"Let go and haul."

The foreyards ran round with a great noise, amidst cheery cries. And now the frightful whiskers made themselves heard giving various orders. Already the ship was drawing ahead. And I was alone with her. Nothing! no one in the world should stand now between us, throwing a shadow on the way of silent knowledge and mute affection; the perfect communion of a seaman with his first command.

Walking to the taffrail, I was in time to make out, on the very edge of a darkness thrown by a towering black mass like the very gateway of Erebus—yes, I was in time to catch an evanescent glimpse of my white hat left behind to mark the spot where the secret sharer of my cabin and of my thoughts, as though he were my second self, had lowered himself into the water to take his punishment: a free man, a proud swimmer striking out for a new destiny.

1912

ANTON CHEKHOV

The Lady with the Dog

1

People were telling one another that a newcomer had been seen on the promenade—a lady with a dog. Dmitri Dmitrich Gurov had been a fortnight in Yalta, and was accustomed to its ways, and he, too, had begun to take an interest in fresh arrivals. From his seat in Vernet's outdoor café, he caught sight of a young woman in a toque, passing along the promenade; she was fair and not very tall; after her trotted a white pomeranian.

Later he encountered her in the municipal park, and in the square, several times a day. She was always alone, wearing the same toque, and the pomeranian always trotted at her side. Nobody knew who she was, and people referred to her simply as "the lady with the dog."

"If she's here without her husband, and without any friends," thought Gurov, "it wouldn't be a bad idea to make her acquaintance."

He was not yet forty, but had a twelve-year-old daughter and two schoolboy sons. He had been talked into marrying in his second year at college, and his wife now looked nearly twice as old as he was. She was a tall, black-browed woman, erect, dignified, imposing, and, as she said of herself, a "thinker." She was a great reader, omitted the "hard sign"[1] at the end of words in her letters, and called her husband "Dimitri" instead of Dmitri; and though he secretly considered her shallow, narrow-minded, and dowdy, he stood in awe of her, and disliked being at home. It was long since he had first begun deceiving her and he was now constantly unfaithful to her, and this was no doubt why he spoke slightingly of women, to whom he referred as *the lower race*.

He considered that the ample lessons he had received from bitter experience entitled him to call them whatever he liked, but without this "lower race" he could not have existed a single day. He was bored and ill-at-ease in the company of men, with whom he was always cold and reserved, but felt quite at home among women, and knew exactly what to say to them, and how to behave; he could even be silent in their company without feeling the slightest awkwardness. There was an elusive charm in his appearance and disposition which attracted women and caught their sympathies. He knew this and was himself attracted to them by some invisible force.

Repeated and bitter experience had taught him that every fresh intimacy, while at first introducing such pleasant variety into everyday life, and offering itself as a charming, light adventure, inevitably developed, among decent people (especially in Moscow, where they are so irresolute and slow to move), into a problem of excessive complication leading to an intolerably irksome situation. But every time he encountered an attractive woman he forgot all about this experience, the desire for life surged up in him, and everything suddenly seemed simple and amusing.

One evening, then, while he was dining at the restaurant in the park, the lady in the toque came strolling up and took a seat at a neighboring table. Her expression, gait, dress, coiffure, all told him that she was from the upper classes, that she was married, that she was in Yalta for the first time, alone and bored. . . . The accounts of the laxity of morals among visitors to Yalta are greatly exaggerated, and he paid no heed to them, knowing that for the most part they were invented by people who would gladly have transgressed themselves, had they known how to set about it. But when the lady sat down at a neighboring table a few yards away from him, the stories of easy conquests, of excursions to the mountains, came back to him, and the seductive idea of a brisk transitory liaison, an affair with a woman whose very name he did not know, suddenly took possession of his mind.

1. Conventional sign that was used following consonants; to omit it was then "progressive," and it has in fact been eliminated in the reformed alphabet adopted by the Soviet government.

He snapped his fingers at the pomeranian, and when it trotted up to him, shook his forefinger at it. The pomeranian growled. Gurov shook his finger again.

The lady glanced at him and instantly lowered her eyes.

"He doesn't bite," she said, and blushed.

"May I give him a bone?" he asked, and on her nod of consent added in friendly tones: "Have you been in Yalta long?"

"About five days."

"And I am dragging out my second week here."

Neither spoke for a few minutes.

"The days pass quickly, and yet one is so bored here," she said, not looking at him.

"It's the thing to say it's boring here. People never complain of boredom in God-forsaken holes like Belyev or Zhizdra, but when they get here it's: 'Oh, the dullness! Oh, the dust!' You'd think they'd come from Granada,[2] to say the least."

She laughed. Then they both went on eating in silence, like complete strangers. But after dinner they left the restaurant together, and embarked upon the light, jesting talk of people free and contented, for whom it is all the same where they go, or what they talk about. They strolled along, remarking on the strange light over the sea. The water was a warm, tender purple, the moonlight lay on its surface in a golden strip. They said how close it was, after the hot day. Gurov told her he was from Moscow, that he was really a philologist,[3] but worked in a bank; that he had at one time trained himself to sing in a private opera company, but had given up the idea; that he owned two houses in Moscow. . . . And from her he learned that she had grown up in Petersburg, but had got married in the town of S., where she had been living two years, that she would stay another month in Yalta, and that perhaps her husband, who also needed a rest, would join her. She was quite unable to explain whether her husband was a member of the gubernia[4] council, or on the board of the Zemstvo,[5] and was greatly amused at herself for this. Further, Gurov learned that her name was Anna Sergeyevna.

Back in his own room he thought about her, and felt sure he would meet her the next day. It was inevitable. As he went to bed he reminded himself that only a very short time ago she had been a schoolgirl, like his own daughter, learning her lessons; he remembered how much there was of shyness and constraint in her laughter, in her way of conversing with a stranger—it was probably the first time in her life that she found herself alone, and in a situation in which men could follow her and watch her, and speak to her, all the time with a secret aim she could not fail to divine. He recalled her slender, delicate neck, her fine gray eyes.

"And yet there's something pathetic about her," he thought to himself as he fell asleep.

---

2. City in southern Spain, site of the Alhambra and once capital of the Moorish kingdom.
3. In the older sense, classical scholar.

4. Czarist province.
5. In Czarist Russia an elective provincial council responsible for local government.

2

A week had passed since the beginning of their acquaintance. It was a holiday. Indoors it was stuffy, but the dust rose in clouds out of doors, and people's hats blew off. It was a thirsty day and Gurov kept going to the outdoor café for fruit-drinks and ices to offer Anna Sergeyevna. The heat was overpowering.

In the evening, when the wind had dropped, they walked to the pier to see the steamer come in. There were a great many people strolling about the landing-place; some, bunches of flowers in their hands, were meeting friends. Two peculiarities of the smart Yalta crowd stood out distinctly—the elderly ladies all tried to dress very young, and there seemed to be an inordinate number of generals about.

Owing to the roughness of the sea the steamer arrived late, after the sun had gone down, and it had to maneuver for some time before it could get alongside the pier. Anna Sergeyevna scanned the steamer and passengers through her lorgnette, as if looking for someone she knew, and when she turned to Gurov her eyes were glistening. She talked a great deal, firing off abrupt questions and forgetting immediately what it was she had wanted to know. Then she lost her lorgnette in the crush.

The smart crowd began dispersing, features could no longer be made out, the wind had quite dropped, and Gurov and Anna Sergeyevna stood there as if waiting for someone else to come off the steamer. Anna Sergeyevna had fallen silent, every now and then smelling her flowers, but not looking at Gurov.

"It's turned out a fine evening," he said. "What shall we do? We might go for a drive."

She made no reply.

He looked steadily at her and suddenly took her in his arms and kissed her lips, and the fragrance and dampness of the flowers closed round him, but the next moment he looked behind him in alarm—had anyone seen them?

"Let's go to your room," he murmured.

And they walked off together, very quickly.

Her room was stuffy and smelled of some scent she had bought in the Japanese shop. Gurov looked at her, thinking to himself: "How full of strange encounters life is!" He could remember carefree, good-natured women who were exhilarated by love-making and grateful to him for the happiness he gave them, however short-lived; and there had been others—his wife among them—whose caresses were insincere, affected, hysterical, mixed up with a great deal of quite unnecessary talk, and whose expression seemed to say that all this was not just love-making or passion, but something much more significant; then there had been two or three beautiful, cold women, over whose features flitted a predatory expression, betraying a determination to wring from life more than it could give, women no longer in their first youth, capricious, irrational, despotic, brainless, and when Gurov had cooled to these, their beauty aroused in him nothing but repulsion, and the lace trimming on their underclothes reminded him of fish-scales.

But here the timidity and awkwardness of youth and inexperience were still apparent; and there was a feeling of embarrassment in the atmosphere, as if someone had just knocked at the door. Anna Sergeyevna, "the lady with the dog," seemed to regard the affair as something very special, very serious, as if she had become a fallen woman, an attitude he found odd and disconcerting. Her features lengthened and drooped, and her long hair hung mournfully on either side of her face. She assumed a pose of dismal meditation, like a repentant sinner in some classical painting.

"It isn't right," she said. "You will never respect me anymore."

On the table was a watermelon. Gurov cut himself a slice from it and began slowly eating it. At least half an hour passed in silence.

Anna Sergeyevna was very touching, revealing the purity of a decent, naïve woman who had seen very little of life. The solitary candle burning on the table scarcely lit up her face, but it was obvious that her heart was heavy.

"Why should I stop respecting you?" asked Gurov. "You don't know what you're saying."

"May God forgive me!" she exclaimed, and her eyes filled with tears. "It's terrible."

"No need to seek to justify yourself."

"How can I justify myself? I'm a wicked, fallen woman, I despise myself and have not the least thought of self-justification. It isn't my husband I have deceived, it's myself. And not only now, I have been deceiving myself for ever so long. My husband is no doubt an honest, worthy man, but he's a flunkey. I don't know what it is he does at his office, but I know he's a flunkey. I was only twenty when I married him, and I was devoured by curiosity, I wanted something higher. I told myself that there must be a different kind of life. I wanted to live, to live. . . . I was burning with curiosity . . . you'll never understand that, but I swear to God I could no longer control myself, nothing could hold me back, I told my husband I was ill, and I came here. . . . And I started going about like one possessed, like a madwoman . . . and now I have become an ordinary, worthless woman, and everyone has the right to despise me."

Gurov listened to her, bored to death. The naïve accents, the remorse, all was so unexpected, so out of place. But for the tears in her eyes, she might have been jesting or play-acting.

"I don't understand," he said gently. "What is it you want?"

She hid her face against his breast and pressed closer to him.

"Do believe me, I implore you to believe me," she said. "I love all that is honest and pure in life, vice is revolting to me, I don't know what I'm doing. The common people say they are snared by the devil. And now I can say that I have been snared by the devil, too."

"Come, come," he murmured.

He gazed into her fixed, terrified eyes, kissed her, and soothed her with gentle affectionate words, and gradually she calmed down and regained her cheerfulness. Soon they were laughing together again.

When, a little later, they went out, there was not a soul on the promenade, the town and its cypresses looked dead, but the sea was still roaring as it dashed against the beach. A solitary fishing-boat tossed on the waves, its lamp blinking sleepily.

They found a droshky[6] and drove to Oreanda.

"I discovered your name in the hall, just now," said Gurov, "written up on the board. Von Diederitz. Is your husband a German?"

"No. His grandfather was, I think, but he belongs to the Orthodox church himself."

When they got out of the droshky at Oreanda they sat down on a bench not far from the church, and looked down at the sea, without talking. Yalta could be dimly discerned through the morning mist, and white clouds rested motionless on the summits of the mountains. Not a leaf stirred, the grasshoppers chirruped, and the monotonous hollow roar of the sea came up to them, speaking of peace, of the eternal sleep lying in wait for us all. The sea had roared like this long before there was any Yalta or Oreanda, it was roaring now, and it would go on roaring, just as indifferently and hollowly, when we have passed away. And it may be that in this continuity, this utter indifference to life and death, lies the secret of our ultimate salvation, of the stream of life on our planet, and of its never-ceasing movement toward perfection.

Side by side with a young woman, who looked so exquisite in the early light, soothed and enchanted by the sight of all this magical beauty—sea, mountains, clouds and the vast expanse of the sky—Gurov told himself that, when you came to think of it, everything in the world is beautiful really, everything but our own thoughts and actions, when we lose sight of the higher aims of life, and of our dignity as human beings.

Someone approached them—a watchman, probably—looked at them and went away. And there was something mysterious and beautiful even in this. The steamer from Feodosia could be seen coming toward the pier, lit up by the dawn, its lamps out.

"There's dew on the grass," said Anna Sergeyevna, breaking the silence.

"Yes. Time to go home."

They went back to the town.

After this they met every day at noon on the promenade, lunching and dining together, going for walks, and admiring the sea. She complained of sleeplessness, of palpitations, asked the same questions over and over again, alternately surrendering to jealousy and the fear that he did not really respect her. And often, when there was nobody in sight in the square or the park, he would draw her to him and kiss her passionately. The utter idleness, these kisses in broad daylight, accompanied by furtive glances and the fear of discovery, the heat, the smell of the sea, and the idle, smart, well-fed people continually crossing their field of vision, seemed to have given him a new lease on life. He told Anna Sergeyevna she was beautiful and seductive, made love to her with impetuous passion, and never left her side, while she was always pensive, always trying to force from him the admission that he did not respect her, that he did not love her a bit, and considered her

6. Horse-drawn, four-wheeled open carriage.

just an ordinary woman. Almost every night they drove out of town, to Oreanda, the waterfall, or some other beauty spot. And these excursions were invariably a success, each contributing fresh impressions of majestic beauty.

All this time they kept expecting her husband to arrive. But a letter came in which he told his wife that he was having trouble with his eyes, and implored her to come home as soon as possible. Anna Sergeyevna made hasty preparations for leaving.

"It's a good thing I'm going," she said to Gurov. "It's the intervention of fate."

She left Yalta in a carriage, and he went with her as far as the railway station. The drive took nearly a whole day. When she got into the express train, after the second bell had been rung, she said:

"Let me have one more look at you. . . . One last look. That's right."

She did not weep, but was mournful, and seemed ill, the muscles of her cheeks twitching.

"I shall think of you . . . I shall think of you all the time," she said. "God bless you! Think kindly of me. We are parting for ever, it must be so, because we ought never to have met. Good-bye—God bless you."

The train steamed rapidly out of the station, its lights soon disappearing, and a minute later even the sound it made was silenced, as if everything were conspiring to bring this sweet oblivion, this madness, to an end as quickly as possible. And Gurov, standing alone on the platform and gazing into the dark distance, listened to the shrilling of the grasshoppers and the humming of the telegraph wires, with a feeling that he had only just waked up. And he told himself that this had been just one more of the many adventures in his life, and that it, too, was over, leaving nothing but a memory. . . . He was moved and sad, and felt a slight remorse. After all, this young woman whom he would never again see had not been really happy with him. He had been friendly and affectionate with her, but in his whole behavior, in the tones of his voice, in his very caresses, there had been a shade of irony, the insulting indulgence of the fortunate male, who was, moreover, almost twice her age. She had insisted in calling him good, remarkable, high-minded. Evidently he had appeared to her different from his real self, in a word he had involuntarily deceived her. . . .

There was an autumnal feeling in the air, and the evening was chilly.

"It's time for me to be going north, too," thought Gurov, as he walked away from the platform. "High time!"

3

When he got back to Moscow it was beginning to look like winter, the stoves were heated every day, and it was still dark when the children got up to go to school and drank their tea, so that the nurse had to light the lamp for a short time. Frost had set in. When the first snow falls, and one goes for one's first sleigh-ride, it is pleasant to see the white ground, the white roofs; one breathes freely and lightly, and remembers the days of one's youth. The ancient lime-trees and birches, white with rime, have a good-natured look, they are closer to the heart than cypresses and palms, and beneath their branches one is no longer haunted by the memory of mountains and the sea.

Gurov had always lived in Moscow, and he returned to Moscow on a fine frosty day, and when he put on his fur-lined overcoat and thick gloves, and sauntered down Petrovka Street, and when, on Saturday evening, he heard the church bells ringing, his recent journey and the places he had visited lost their charm for him. He became gradually immersed in Moscow life, reading with avidity three newspapers a day, while declaring he never read Moscow newspapers on principle. Once more he was caught up in a whirl of restaurants, clubs, banquets, and celebrations, once more glowed with the flattering consciousness that well-known lawyers and actors came to his house, that he played cards in the Medical Club opposite a professor.

He had believed that in a month's time Anna Sergeyevna would be nothing but a vague memory, and that hereafter, with her wistful smile, she would only occasionally appear to him in dreams, like others before her. But the month was now well over and winter was in full swing, and all was as clear in his memory as if he had only parted with Anna Sergeyevna the day before. And his recollections grew ever more insistent. When the voices of his children at their lessons reached him in his study through the evening stillness, when he heard a song, or the sounds of a musical-box in a restaurant, when the wind howled in the chimney, it all came back to him: early morning on the pier, the misty mountains, the steamer from Feodosia, the kisses. He would pace up and down his room for a long time, smiling at his memories, and then memory turned into dreaming, and what had happened mingled in his imagination with what was going to happen. Anna Sergeyevna did not come to him in his dreams, she accompanied him everywhere, like his shadow, following him everywhere he went. When he closed his eyes, she seemed to stand before him in the flesh, still lovelier, younger, tenderer than she had really been, and looking back, he saw himself, too, as better than he had been in Yalta. In the evenings she looked out at him from the bookshelves, the fireplace, the corner; he could hear her breathing, the sweet rustle of her skirts. In the streets he followed women with his eyes, to see if there were any like her. . . .

He began to feel an overwhelming desire to share his memories with someone. But he could not speak of his love at home, and outside his home who was there for him to confide in? Not the tenants living in his house, and certainly not his colleagues at the bank. And what was there to tell? Was it love that he had felt? Had there been anything exquisite, poetic, anything instructive or even amusing about his relations with Anna Sergeyevna? He had to content himself with uttering vague generalizations about love and women, and nobody guessed what he meant, though his wife's dark eyebrows twitched as she said:

"The role of a coxcomb doesn't suit you a bit, Dimitri."

One evening, leaving the Medical Club with one of his card-partners, a government official, he could not refrain from remarking:

"If you only knew what a charming woman I met in Yalta!"

The official got into his sleigh, and just before driving off turned and called out:

"Dmítri Dmítrich!"

"Yes?"

"You were quite right, you know—the sturgeon was just a *leetle* off."

These words, in themselves so commonplace, for some reason infuriated Gurov, seemed to him humiliating, gross. What savage manners, what people! What wasted evenings, what tedious, empty days! Frantic card-playing, gluttony, drunkenness, perpetual talk always about the same thing. The greater part of one's time and energy went on business that was no use to anyone, and on discussing the same thing over and over again, and there was nothing to show for it all but a stunted, earth-bound existence and a round of trivialities, and there was nowhere to escape to, you might as well be in a madhouse or a convict settlement.

Gurov lay awake all night, raging, and went about the whole of the next day with a headache. He slept badly on the succeeding nights, too, sitting up in bed, thinking, or pacing the floor of his room. He was sick of his children, sick of the bank, felt not the slightest desire to go anywhere or talk about anything.

When the Christmas holidays came, he packed his things, telling his wife he had to go to Petersburg in the interests of a certain young man, and set off for the town of S. To what end? He hardly knew himself. He only knew that he must see Anna Sergeyevna, must speak to her, arrange a meeting, if possible.

He arrived at S. in the morning and engaged the best room in the hotel, which had a carpet of gray military frieze, and a dusty ink-pot on the table, surmounted by a headless rider, holding his hat in his raised hand. The hall porter told him what he wanted to know: von Diederitz had a house of his own in Staro-Goncharnaya Street. It wasn't far from the hotel, he lived on a grand scale, luxuriously, kept carriage-horses, the whole town knew him. The hall porter pronounced the name "Drideritz."

Gurov strolled over to Staro-Goncharnaya Street and discovered the house. In front of it was a long gray fence with inverted nails hammered into the tops of the palings.

"A fence like that is enough to make anyone want to run away," thought Gurov, looking at the windows of the house and the fence.

He reasoned that since it was a holiday, her husband would probably be at home. In any case it would be tactless to embarrass her by calling at the house. And a note might fall into the hands of the husband, and bring about catastrophe. The best thing would be to wait about on the chance of seeing her. And he walked up and down the street, hovering in the vicinity of the fence, watching for his chance. A beggar entered the gate, only to be attacked by dogs; then, an hour later, the faint, vague sounds of a piano reached his ears. That would be Anna Sergeyevna playing. Suddenly the front door opened and an old woman came out, followed by a familiar white pomeranian. Gurov tried to call to it, but his heart beat violently, and in his agitation he could not remember its name.

He walked on, hating the gray fence more and more, and now ready to tell himself irately that Anna Sergeyevna had forgotten him, had already, perhaps, found distraction in another—what could be more natural in a young woman who had to look at this accursed fence from morning to night? He went back to his hotel and sat on the sofa in his room for some time, not knowing what to do, then he ordered dinner, and after dinner, had a long sleep.

"What a foolish, restless business," he thought, waking up and looking toward the dark windowpanes. It was evening by now. "Well, I've had my sleep out. And what am I to do in the night?"

He sat up in bed, covered by the cheap gray quilt, which reminded him of a hospital blanket, and in his vexation he fell to taunting himself.

"You and your lady with a dog . . . there's adventure for you! See what you get for your pains."

On his arrival at the station that morning he had noticed a poster announcing in enormous letters the first performance at the local theater of *The Geisha*.[7] Remembering this, he got up and made for the theater.

"It's highly probable that she goes to first-nights," he told himself.

The theater was full. It was a typical provincial theater, with a mist collecting over the chandeliers, and the crowd in the gallery fidgeting noisily. In the first row of the stalls[8] the local dandies stood waiting for the curtain to go up, their hands clasped behind them. There, in the front seat of the Governor's box, sat the Governor's daughter, wearing a boa, the Governor himself hiding modestly behind the drapes, so that only his hands were visible. The curtain stirred, the orchestra took a long time tuning up their instruments. Gurov's eyes roamed eagerly over the audience as they filed in and occupied their seats.

Anna Sergeyevna came in, too. She seated herself in the third row of the stalls and when Gurov's glance fell on her, his heart seemed to stop, and he knew in a flash that the whole world contained no one nearer or dearer to him, no one more important to his happiness. This little woman, lost in the provincial crowd, in no way remarkable, holding a silly lorgnette in her hand, now filled his whole life, was his grief, his joy, all that he desired. Lulled by the sounds coming from the wretched orchestra, with its feeble, amateurish violinists, he thought how beautiful she was . . . thought and dreamed. . . .

Anna Sergeyevna was accompanied by a tall, round-shouldered young man with small whiskers, who nodded at every step before taking the seat beside her and seemed to be continually bowing to someone. This must be her husband, whom, in a fit of bitterness, at Yalta, she had called a "flunkey." And there really was something of the lackey's servility in his lanky figure, his side-whiskers, and the little bald spot on the top of his head. And he smiled sweetly, and the badge of some scientific society gleaming in his buttonhole was like the number on a footman's livery.

The husband went out to smoke in the first interval, and she was left alone in her seat. Gurov, who had taken a seat in the stalls, went up to her and said in a trembling voice, with a forced smile: "How d'you do?"

She glanced up at him and turned pale, then looked at him again in alarm, unable to believe her eyes, squeezing her fan and lorgnette in one hand, evidently struggling to overcome a feeling of faintness.

7. Operetta by Sidney Jones (1861–1946) which toured Eastern Europe in 1898–99.

8. Seats at the front of a theater, near the stage and separated from nearby seats by a railing.

Neither of them said a word. She sat there, and he stood beside her, disconcerted by her embarrassment, and not daring to sit down. The violins and flutes sang out as they were tuned, and there was a tense sensation in the atmosphere, as if they were being watched from all the boxes. At last she got up and moved rapidly toward one of the exits. He followed her and they wandered aimlessly along corridors, up and down stairs; figures flashed by in the uniforms of legal officials, high-school teachers, and civil servants, all wearing badges; ladies' coats hanging on pegs, flashed by; there was a sharp draft, bringing with it an odor of cigarette stubs. And Gurov, whose heart was beating violently, thought:

"What on earth are all these people, this orchestra for? . . ."

The next minute he suddenly remembered how, after seeing Anna Sergeyevna off that evening at the station, he had told himself that all was over, and they would never meet again. And how far away the end seemed to be now!

She stopped on a dark narrow staircase over which was a notice bearing the inscription "To the upper circle."

"How you frightened me!" she said, breathing heavily, still pale and half-stunned. "Oh, how you frightened me! I'm almost dead! Why did you come? Oh, why?"

"But, Anna," he said, in low, hasty tones. "But, Anna. . . . Try to understand . . . do try. . . ."

She cast him a glance of fear, entreaty, love, and then gazed at him steadily, as if to fix his features firmly in her memory.

"I've been so unhappy," she continued, taking no notice of his words. "I could think of nothing but you the whole time, I lived on the thoughts of you. I tried to forget—why, oh, why did you come?"

On the landing above them were two schoolboys, smoking and looking down, but Gurov did not care, and, drawing Anna Sergeyevna toward him, began kissing her face, her lips, her hands.

"What are you doing, oh, what are you doing?" she said in horror, drawing back. "We have both gone mad. Go away this very night, this moment. . . . By all that is sacred, I implore you. . . . Somebody is coming."

Someone was ascending the stairs.

"You must go away," went on Anna Sergeyevna in a whisper. "D'you hear me, Dmitri Dmitrich? I'll come to you in Moscow. I have never been happy, I am unhappy now, and I shall never be happy—never! Do not make me suffer still more! I will come to you in Moscow, I swear it! And now we must part! My dear one, my kind one, my darling, we must part."

She pressed his hand and hurried down the stairs, looking back at him continually, and her eyes showed that she was in truth unhappy. Gurov stood where he was for a short time, listening, and when all was quiet went to look for his coat, and left the theater.

4

And Anna Sergeyevna began going to Moscow to see him. Every

two or three months she left the town of S., telling her husband that she was going to consult a specialist on female diseases, and her husband believed her and did not believe her. In Moscow she always stayed at the "Slavyanski Bazaar," sending a man in a red cap to Gurov the moment she arrived. Gurov went to her, and no one in Moscow knew anything about it.

One winter morning he went to see her as usual (the messenger had been to him the evening before, but had not found him at home). His daughter was with him for her school was on the way, and he thought he might as well see her to it.

"It is three degrees above zero,"[9] said Gurov to his daughter, "and yet it is snowing. You see it is only above zero close to the ground, the temperature in the upper layers of the atmosphere is quite different."

"Why doesn't it ever thunder in winter, Papa?"

He explained this, too. As he was speaking, he kept reminding himself that he was going to a rendezvous and that not a living soul knew about it, or, probably, ever would. He led a double life—one in public, in the sight of all whom it concerned, full of conventional truth and conventional deception, exactly like the lives of his friends and acquaintances, and another which flowed in secret. And, owing to some strange, possibly quite accidental chain of circumstances, everything that was important, interesting, essential, everything about which he was sincere and never deceived himself, everything that composed the kernel of his life, went on in secret, while everything that was false in him, everything that composed the husk in which he hid himself and the truth which was in him—his work at the bank, discussions at the club, his "lower race," his attendance at anniversary celebrations with his wife—was on the surface. He began to judge others by himself, no longer believing what he saw, and always assuming that the real, the only interesting life of every individual goes on as under cover of night, secretly. Every individual existence revolves around mystery, and perhaps that is the chief reason that all cultivated individuals insisted so strongly on the respect due to personal secrets.

After leaving his daughter at the door of her school Gurov set off for the "Slavyanski Bazaar." Taking off his overcoat in the lobby, he went upstairs and knocked softly on the door. Anna Sergeyevna, wearing the gray dress he liked most, exhausted by her journey and by suspense, had been expecting him since the evening before. She was pale and looked at him without smiling, but was in his arms almost before he was fairly in the room. Their kiss was lingering, prolonged, as if they had not met for years.

"Well, how are you?" he asked. "Anything new?"

"Wait. I'll tell you in a minute. . . . I can't. . . ."

She could not speak, because she was crying. Turning away, she held her handkerchief to her eyes.

"I'll wait till she's had her cry out," he thought, and sank into a chair.

9. Probably Réaumur thermometer; about 39 degrees Fahrenheit.

He rang for tea, and a little later, while he was drinking it, she was still standing there, her face to the window. She wept from emotion, from her bitter consciousness of the sadness of their life; they could only see one another in secret, hiding from people, as if they were thieves. Was not their life a broken one?

"Don't cry," he said.

It was quite obvious to him that this love of theirs would not soon come to an end, and that no one could say when this end would be. Anna Sergeyevna loved him ever more fondly, worshipped him, and there would have been no point in telling her that one day it must end. Indeed, she would not have believed him.

He moved over and took her by the shoulders, intending to fondle her with light words, but suddenly he caught sight of himself in the looking-glass.

His hair was already beginning to turn gray. It struck him as strange that he should have aged so much in the last few years. The shoulders on which his hands lay were warm and quivering. He felt a pity for this life, still so warm and exquisite, but probably soon to fade and droop like his own. Why did she love him so? Women had always believed him different from what he really was, had loved in him not himself but the man their imagination pictured him, a man they had sought for eagerly all their lives. And afterwards when they discovered their mistake, they went on loving him just the same. And not one of them had ever been happy with him. Time had passed, he had met one woman after another, become intimate with each, parted with each, but had never loved. There had been all sorts of things between them, but never love.

And only now, when he was gray-haired, had he fallen in love properly, thoroughly, for the first time in his life.

He and Anna Sergeyevna loved one another as people who are very close and intimate, as husband and wife, as dear friends love one another. It seemed to them that fate had intended them for one another, and they could not understand why she should have a husband, and he a wife. They were like two migrating birds, the male and the female, who had been caught and put into separate cages. They forgave one another all that they were ashamed of in the past, in their present, and felt that this love of theirs had changed them both.

Formerly, in moments of melancholy, he had consoled himself by the first argument that came into his head, but now arguments were nothing to him, he felt profound pity, desired to be sincere, tender.

"Stop crying, my dearest," he said. "You've had your cry, now stop. . . . Now let us have a talk, let us try and think what we are to do."

Then they discussed their situation for a long time, trying to think how they could get rid of the necessity for hiding, deception, living in different towns, being so long without meeting. How were they to shake off these intolerable fetters?

"How? How?" he repeated, clutching his head. "How?"

And it seemed to them that they were within an inch of arriving at a decision, and that then a new, beautiful life would begin. And they both realized that the end was still far, far away, and that the hardest, the most complicated part was only just beginning.

1899

FRANZ KAFKA

A Hunger Artist *

During these last decades the interest in professional fasting has markedly diminished. It used to pay very well to stage such great performances under one's own management, but today that is quite impossible. We live in a different world now. At one time the whole town took a lively interest in the hunger artist; from day to day of his fast the excitement mounted; everybody wanted to see him at least once a day; there were people who bought season tickets for the last few days and sat from morning till night in front of his small barred cage; even in the nighttime there were visiting hours, when the whole effect was heightened by torch flares; on fine days the cage was set out in the open air, and then it was the children's special treat to see the hunger artist; for their elders he was often just a joke that happened to be in fashion, but the children stood open-mouthed, holding each other's hands for greater security, marveling at him as he sat there pallid in black tights, with his ribs sticking out so prominently, not even on a seat but down among straw on the ground, sometimes giving a courteous nod, answering questions with a constrained smile, or perhaps stretching an arm through the bars so that one might feel how thin it was, and then again withdrawing deep into himself, paying no attention to anyone or anything, not even to the all-important striking of the clock that was the only piece of furniture in his cage, but merely staring into vacancy with half-shut eyes, now and then taking a sip from a tiny glass of water to moisten his lips.

Besides casual onlookers there were also relays of permanent watchers selected by the public, usually butchers, strangely enough, and it was their task to watch the hunger artist day and night, three of them at a time, in case he should have some secret recourse to nourishment. This was nothing but a formality, instituted to reassure the masses, for the initiates knew well enough that during his fast the artist would never in any circumstances, not even under forcible compulsion, swallow the smallest morsel of food; the honor of his profession forbade it. Not every watcher, of course, was capable of understanding this, there were often groups of night watchers who were very lax in carrying out their duties and deliberately huddled together in a retired corner to play cards with great absorption, obviously intending to give the hunger artist the chance of a little refresh-

* Translated by Willa and Edwin Muir.

ment, which they supposed he could draw from some private hoard. Nothing annoyed the artist more than such watchers; they made him miserable; they made his fast seem unendurable; sometimes he mastered his feebleness sufficiently to sing during their watch for as long as he could keep going, to show them how unjust their suspicions were. But that was of little use; they only wondered at his cleverness in being able to fill his mouth even while singing. Much more to his taste were the watchers who sat close up to the bars, who were not content with the dim night lighting of the hall but focused him in the full glare of the electric pocket torch given them by the impresario. The harsh light did not trouble him at all. In any case he could never sleep properly, and he could always drowse a little, whatever the light, at any hour, even when the hall was thronged with noisy onlookers. He was quite happy at the prospect of spending a sleepless night with such watchers; he was ready to exchange jokes with them, to tell them stories out of his nomadic life, anything at all to keep them awake and demonstrate to them again that he had no eatables in his cage and that he was fasting as not one of them could fast. But his happiest moment was when the morning came and an enormous breakfast was brought them, at his expense, on which they flung themselves with the keen appetite of healthy men after a weary night of wakefulness. Of course there were people who argued that this breakfast was an unfair attempt to bribe the watchers, but that was going rather too far, and when they were invited to take on a night's vigil without a breakfast, merely for the sake of the cause, they made themselves scarce, although they stuck stubbornly to their suspicions.

Such suspicions, anyhow, were a necessary accompaniment to the profession of fasting. No one could possibly watch the hunger artist continuously, day and night, and so no one could produce first-hand evidence that the fast had really been rigorous and continuous; only the artist himself could know that; he was therefore bound to be the sole completely satisfied spectator of his own fast. Yet for other reasons he was never satisfied; it was not perhaps mere fasting that had brought him to such skeleton thinness that many people had regretfully to keep away from his exhibitions, because the sight of him was too much for them, perhaps it was dissatisfaction with himself that had worn him down. For he alone knew, what no other initiate knew, how easy it was to fast. It was the easiest thing in the world. He made no secret of this, yet people did not believe him; at the best they set him down as modest; most of them, however, thought he was out for publicity or else was some kind of cheat who found it easy to fast because he had discovered a way of making it easy, and then had the impudence to admit the fact, more or less. He had to put up with all that, and in the course of time had got used to it, but his inner dissatisfaction always rankled, and never yet, after any term of fasting—this must be granted to his credit—had he left the cage of his own free will. The longest period of fasting was fixed by his impresario at forty days, beyond that term he was not allowed to go, not even in great cities, and there was good reason for it, too. Experience had proved that for about forty days the interest of the public could be stimulated by a steadily increasing pressure of advertisement, but after that the town began to lose interest, sympathetic support began notably to fall off; there were of course local variations as between one town and another or one country and another, but as a general rule forty days marked the limit. So on the fortieth day the flower-bedecked cage was opened, enthusiastic spectators filled the hall, a military band played, two doctors entered the cage to measure the results of the fast, which were announced through a megaphone, and finally two young ladies appeared, blissful at having been selected for the honor, to help the hunger artist down the few steps leading to a small table on which was spread a carefully chosen invalid repast. And at this very moment the artist always turned stubborn. True, he would entrust his bony arms to the outstretched helping hands of the ladies bending over him, but stand up he would not. Why stop fasting at this particular moment, after forty days of it? He had held out for a long time, an illimitably long time; why stop now, when he was in his best fasting form, or rather, not yet quite in his best fasting form? Why should he be cheated of the fame he would get for fasting longer, for being not only the record hunger artist of all time, which presumably he was already, but for beating his own record by a performance beyond human imagination, since he felt that there were no limits to his capacity for fasting? His public pretended to admire him so much, why should it have so little patience with him; if he could endure fasting longer, why shouldn't the public endure it? Besides, he was tired, he was comfortable sitting in the straw, and now he was supposed to lift himself to his full height and go down to a meal the very thought of which gave him a nausea that only the presence of the ladies kept him from betraying, and even that with an effort. And he looked up into the eyes of the ladies who were apparently so friendly and in reality so cruel, and shook his head, which felt too heavy on its strengthless neck. But then there happened yet again what always happened. The impresario came forward, without a word—for the band made speech impossible—lifted his arms in the air above the artist, as if inviting Heaven to look down upon its creature here in the straw, this suffering martyr, which indeed he was, although in quite another sense; grasped him round the emaciated waist, with exaggerated caution, so that the frail condition he was in might be appreciated; and committed him to the care of the blenching ladies, not without secretly giving him a shaking so that his legs and body tottered and swayed. The artist now submitted completely; his head lolled on his breast as if it had landed there by chance; his body was hollowed out; his legs in a spasm of self-preservation clung close to each other at the knees, yet scraped on the ground as if it were not really solid ground, as if they were only trying to find solid ground; and the whole weight of his body, a featherweight after all, relapsed onto one of the ladies, who, looking round for help and panting a little —this post of honor was not at all what she had expected it to be— first stretched her neck as far as she could to keep her face at least free from contact with the artist, then finding this impossible, and her more

fortunate companion not coming to her aid but merely holding extended on her own trembling hand the little bunch of knucklebones
that was the artist's, to the great delight of the spectators burst into
tears and had to be replaced by an attendant who had long been stationed in readiness. Then came the food, a little of which the impresario managed to get between the artist's lips, while he sat in a kind
of half-fainting trance, to the accompaniment of cheerful patter designed to distract the public's attention from the artist's condition;
after that, a toast was drunk to the public, supposedly prompted by a
whisper from the artist in the impresario's ear; the band confirmed it
with a mighty flourish, the spectators melted away, and no one
had any cause to be dissatisfied with the proceedings, no one except
the hunger artist himself, he only, as always.

So he lived for many years, with small regular intervals of recupera-
tion, in visible glory, honored by the world, yet in spite of that troubled
in spirit, and all the more troubled because no one would take his
trouble seriously. What comfort could he possibly need? What more
could he possibly wish for? And if some good-natured person, feeling
sorry for him, tried to console him by pointing out that his melancholy was probably caused by fasting, it could happen, especially
when he had been fasting for some time, that he reacted with an outburst of fury and to the general alarm began to shake the bars of his
cage like a wild animal. Yet the impresario had a way of punishing
these outbreaks which he rather enjoyed putting into operation. He
would apologize publicly for the artist's behavior, which was only to
be excused, he admitted, because of the irritability caused by fasting;
a condition hardly to be understood by well-fed people; then by
natural transition he went on to mention the artist's equally incomprehensible boast that he could fast for much longer than he was doing;
he praised the high ambition, the good will, the great self-denial undoubtedly implicit in such a statement; and then quite simply countered it by bringing out photographs, which were also on sale to the
public, showing the artist on the fortieth day of a fast lying in bed
almost dead from exhaustion. This perversion of the truth, familiar to
the artist though it was, always unnerved him afresh and proved too
much for him. What was a consequence of the premature ending of his
fast was here presented as the cause of it! To fight against this lack
of understanding, against a whole world of non-understanding, was
impossible. Time and again in good faith he stood by the bars listening to the impresario, but as soon as the photographs appeared he
always let go and sank with a groan back on to his straw, and the
reassured public could once more come close and gaze at him.

A few years later when the witnesses of such scenes called them to
mind, they often failed to understand themselves at all. For meanwhile
the aforementioned change in public interest had set in; it seemed to
happen almost overnight; there may have been profound causes for it,
but who was going to bother about that; at any rate the pampered
hunger artist suddenly found himself deserted one fine day by the
amusement seekers, who went streaming past him to other more
favored attractions. For the last time the impresario hurried him over
half Europe to discover whether the old interest might still survive

here and there; all in vain; everywhere, as if by secret agreement, a positive revulsion from professional fasting was in evidence. Of course it could not really have sprung up so suddenly as all that, and many premonitory symptoms which had not been sufficiently remarked or suppressed during the rush and glitter of success now came retrospectively to mind, but it was now too late to take any countermeasures. Fasting would surely come into fashion again at some future date, yet that was no comfort for those living in the present. What, then, was the hunger artist to do? He had been applauded by thousands in his time and could hardly come down to showing himself in a street booth at village fairs, and as for adopting another profession, he was not only too old for that but too fanatically devoted to fasting. So he took leave of the impresario, his partner in an unparalleled career, and hired himself to a large circus; in order to spare his own feelings he avoided reading the conditions of his contract.

A large circus with its enormous traffic in replacing and recruiting men, animals and apparatus can always find a use for people at any time, even for a hunger artist, provided of course that he does not ask too much, and in this particular case anyhow it was not only the artist who was taken on but his famous and long-known name as well; indeed considering the peculiar nature of his performance, which was not impared by advancing age, it could not be objected that here was an artist past his prime, no longer at the height of his professional skill, seeking a refuge in some quiet corner of a circus; on the contrary, the hunger artist averred that he could fast as well as ever, which was entirely credible; he even alleged that if he were allowed to fast as he liked, and this was at once promised him without more ado, he could astound the world by establishing a record never yet achieved, a statement which certainly provoked a smile among the other professionals, since it left out of account the change in public opinion, which the hunger artist in his zeal conveniently forgot.

He had not, however, actually lost his sense of the real situation and took it as a matter of course that he and his cage should be stationed, not in the middle of the ring as a main attraction, but outside, near the animal cages, on a site that was after all easily accessible. Large and gaily painted placards made a frame for the cage and announced what was to be seen inside it. When the public came thronging out in the intervals to see the animals, they could hardly avoid passing the hunger artist's cage and stopping there for a moment; perhaps they might even have stayed longer had not those pressing behind them in the narrow gangway, who did not understand why they should be held up on their way towards the excitements of the menagerie, made it impossible for anyone to stand gazing quietly for any length of time. And that was the reason why the hunger artist, who had of course been looking forward to these visiting hours as the main achievement of his life, began instead to shrink from them. At first he could hardly wait for the intervals; it was exhilarating to watch the crowds come streaming his way, until only too soon—not even the most obstinate self-deception, clung to almost consciously, could hold out against the fact —the conviction was borne in upon him that these people, most of them, to judge from their actions, again and again, without exception, were all on their way to the menagerie. And the first sight of them from the distance remained the best. For when they reached his cage he was at once deafened by the storm of shouting and abuse that arose from the two contending factions, which renewed themselves continuously, of those who wanted to stop and stare at him—he soon began to dislike them more than the others—not out of real interest but only out of obstinate self-assertiveness, and those who wanted to go straight on to the animals. When the first great rush was past, the stragglers came along, and these, whom nothing could have prevented from stopping to look at him as long as they had breath, raced past with long strides, hardly even glancing at him, in their haste to get to the menagerie in time. And all too rarely did it happen that he had a stroke of luck, when some father of a family fetched up before him with his children, pointed a finger at the hunger artist and explained at length what the phenomenon meant, telling stories of earlier years when he himself had watched similar but much more thrilling performances, and the children, still rather uncomprehending, since neither inside nor outside school had they been sufficiently prepared for this lesson—what did they care about fasting?—yet showed by the brightness of their intent eyes that new and better times might be coming. Perhaps, said the hunger artist to himself many a time, things would be a little better if his cage were set not quite so near the menagerie. That made it too easy for people to make their choice, to say nothing of what he suffered from the stench of the menagerie, the animals' restlessness by night, the carrying past of raw lumps of flesh for the beasts of prey, the roaring at feeding times, which depressed him continually. But he did not dare to lodge a complaint with the management; after all, he had the animals to thank for the troops of people who passed his cage, among whom there might always be one here and there to take an interest in him, and who could tell where they might seclude him if he called attention to his existence and thereby to the fact that, strictly speaking, he was only an impediment on the way to the menagerie.

A small impediment, to be sure, one that grew steadily less. People grew familiar with the strange idea that they could be expected, in times like these, to take an interest in a hunger artist, and with this familiarity the verdict went out against him He might fast as much as he could, and he did so; but nothing could save him now, people passed him by. Just try to explain to anyone the art of fasting! Anyone who has no feeling for it cannot be made to understand it. The fine placards grew dirty and illegible, they were torn down; the little notice board telling the number of fast days achieved, which at first was changed carefully every day, had long stayed at the same figure, for after the first few weeks even this small task seemed pointless to the staff; and so the artist simply fasted on and on, as he had once dreamed of doing, and it was no trouble to him, just as he had always foretold, but no one counted the days, no one, not even the artist himself, knew what records he was already breaking, and his heart grew heavy. And when once in a time some leisurely passer-by stopped, made merry over the old figure on the board and spoke of swindling, that was in its way the stupidest lie ever invented by indifference and inborn malice, since it was not the hunger artist who was cheating; he was working honestly, but the world was cheating him of his reward.

Many more days went by, however, and that too came to an end. An overseer's eye fell on the cage one day and he asked the attendants why this perfectly good cage should be left standing there unused with dirty straw inside it; nobody knew, until one man, helped out by the notice board, remembered about the hunger artist. They poked into the straw with sticks and found him in it. "Are you still fasting?" asked the overseer. "When on earth do you mean to stop?" "Forgive me, everybody," whispered the hunger artist; only the overseer, who had his ear to the bars, understood him. "Of course," said the overseer, and tapped his forehead with a finger to let the attendants know what state the man was in, "we forgive you." "I always wanted you to admire my fasting," said the hunger artist. "We do admire it," said the overseer, affably. "But you shouldn't admire it," said the hunger artist. "Well, then we don't admire it," said the overseer, "but why shouldn't we admire it?" "Because I have to fast, I can't help it," said the hunger artist. "What a fellow you are," said the overseer, "and why can't you help it?" "Because," said the hunger artist, lifting his head a little and speaking, with his lips pursed, as if for a kiss, right into the overseer's ear, so that no syllable might be lost, "because I couldn't find the food I liked. If I had found it, believe me, I should have made no fuss and stuffed myself like you or anyone else." These were his last words, but in his dimming eyes remained the firm though no longer proud persuasion that he was still continuing to fast.

"Well, clear this out now!" said the overseer, and they buried the hunger artist, straw and all. Into the cage they put a young panther. Even the most insensitive felt it refreshing to see this wild creature leaping around the cage that had so long been dreary. The panther was all right. The food he liked was brought him without hesitation by the attendants; he seemed not even to miss his freedom; his noble body, furnished almost to the bursting point with all that it needed, seemed to carry freedom around with it too; somewhere in his jaws it seemed to lurk; and the joy of life streamed with such ardent passion from his throat that for the onlookers it was not easy to stand the shock of it. But they braced themselves, crowded round the cage, and did not want ever to move away.

1924

KATHERINE ANNE PORTER

Flowering Judas

Braggioni sits heaped upon the edge of a straight-backed chair much too small for him, and sings to Laura in a furry, mournful voice.

Laura has begun to find reasons for avoiding her own house until the latest possible moment, for Braggioni is there almost every night. No matter how late she is, he will be sitting there with a surly, waiting expression, pulling at his kinky yellow hair, thumbing the strings of his guitar, snarling a tune under his breath. Lupe the Indian maid meets Laura at the door, and says with a flicker of a glance towards the upper room, "He waits."

Laura wishes to lie down, she is tired of her hairpins and the feel of her long tight sleeves, but she says to him, "Have you a new song for me this evening?" If he says yes, she asks him to sing it. If he says no, she remembers his favorite one, and asks him to sing it again. Lupe brings her a cup of chocolate and a plate of rice, and Laura eats at the small table under the lamp, first inviting Braggioni, whose answer is always the same: "I have eaten, and besides, chocolate thickens the voice."

Laura says, "Sing, then," and Braggioni heaves himself into song. He scratches the guitar familiarly as though it were a pet animal, and sings passionately off key, taking the high notes in a prolonged painful squeal. Laura, who haunts the markets listening to the ballad singers, and stops every day to hear the blind boy playing his reed-flute in Sixteenth of September Street,[1] listens to Braggioni with pitiless courtesy, because she dares not smile at his miserable performance. Nobody dares to smile at him. Braggioni is cruel to everyone, with a kind of specialized insolence, but he is so vain of his talents, and so sensitive to slights, it would require a cruelty and vanity greater than his own to lay a finger on the vast cureless wound of his self-esteem. It would require courage, too, for it is dangerous to offend him, and nobody has this courage.

Braggioni loves himself with such tenderness and amplitude and eternal charity that his followers—for he is a leader of men, a skilled revolutionist, and his skin has been punctured in honorable warfare—warm themselves in the reflected glow, and say to each other: "He has a real nobility, a love of humanity raised above mere personal affections." The excess of this self-love has flowed out, inconveniently for her, over Laura, who, with so many others, owes her comfortable situation and her salary to him. When he is in a very good humor, he tells her, "I am tempted to forgive you for being a *gringa, gringita!*"[2] and Laura, burning, imagines herself leaning forward suddenly, and with a sound back-handed slap wiping the suety smile from his face. If he notices her eyes at these moments he gives no sign.

She knows what Braggioni would offer her, and she must resist tenaciously without appearing to resist, and if she could avoid it she would not admit even to herself the slow drift of his intention. During these long evenings which have spoiled a long month for her, she sits in her deep chair with an open book on her knees, resting her eyes on the consoling rigidity of the printed page when the sight and sound of Braggioni singing threaten to identify themselves with all her remem-

1. Street in Mexico City, as are all those streets named later.
2. Fair-haired (American) woman—the regular and the diminutive forms of the word. Like most racial terms, not particularly complimentary.

bered afflictions and to add their weight to her uneasy premonitions of the future. The gluttonous bulk of Braggioni has become a symbol of her many disillusions, for a revolutionist should be lean, animated by heroic faith, a vessel of abstract virtues. This is nonsense, she knows it now and is ashamed of it. Revolution must have leaders, and leadership is a career for energetic men. She is, her comrades tell her, full of romantic error, for what she defines as cynicism in them is merely "a developed sense of reality." She is almost too willing to say, "I am wrong, I suppose I don't really understand the principles," and afterward she makes a secret truce with herself, determined not to surrender her will to such expedient logic. But she cannot help feeling that she has been betrayed irreparably by the disunion between her way of living and her feeling of what life should be, and at times she is almost contented to rest in this sense of grievance as a private store of consolation. Sometimes she wishes to run away, but she stays. Now she longs to fly out of this room, down the narrow stairs, and into the street where the houses lean together like conspirators under a single mottled lamp, and leave Braggioni singing to himself.

Instead she looks at Braggioni, frankly and clearly, like a good child who understands the rules of behavior. Her knees cling together under sound blue serge, and her round white collar is not purposely nun-like. She wears the uniform of an idea, and has renounced vanities. She was born Roman Catholic, and in spite of her fear of being seen by someone who might make a scandal of it, she slips now and again into some crumbling little church, kneels on the chilly stone, and says a Hail Mary on the gold rosary she bought in Tehuantepec.[3] It is no good and she ends by examining the altar with its tinsel flowers and ragged brocades, and feels tender about the battered doll-shape of some male saint whose white, lace-trimmed drawers hang limply around his ankles below the hieratic dignity of his velvet robe. She has encased herself in a set of principles derived from her early training, leaving no detail of gesture or of personal taste untouched, and for this reason she will not wear lace made on machines. This is her private heresy, for in her special group the machine is sacred, and will be the salvation of the workers. She loves fine lace, and there is a tiny edge of fluted cobweb on this collar, which is one of twenty precisely alike, folded in blue tissue paper in the upper drawer of her clothes chest.

Braggioni catches her glance solidly as if he had been waiting for it, leans forward, balancing his paunch between his spread knees, and sings with tremendous emphasis, weighing his words. He has, the song relates, no father and no mother, nor even a friend to console him; lonely as a wave of the sea he comes and goes, lonely as a wave. His mouth opens round and yearns sideways, his balloon cheeks grow oily with the labor of song. He bulges marvelously in his expensive garments. Over his lavender collar, crushed upon a purple necktie, held by a diamond hoop: over his ammunition belt of tooled leather worked in silver, buckled cruelly around his gasping middle: over the tops of his glossy yellow shoes Braggioni swells with ominous ripeness,

3. City in southern Mexico.

his mauve silk hose stretched taut, his ankles bound with the stout leather thongs of his shoes.

When he stretches his eyelids at Laura she notes again that his eyes are the true tawny yellow cat's eyes. He is rich, not in money, he tells her, but in power, and this power brings with it the blameless ownership of things, and the right to indulge his love of small luxuries. "I have a taste for the elegant refinements," he said once, flourishing a yellow silk handkerchief before her nose. "Smell that? It is Jockey Club, imported from New York." Nonetheless he is wounded by life. He will say so presently. "It is true everything turns to dust in the hand, to gall on the tongue." He sighs and his leather belt creaks like a saddle girth. "I am disappointed in everything as it comes. Everything." He shakes his head. "You, poor thing, you will be disappointed too. You are born for it. We are more alike than you realize in some things. Wait and see. Some day you will remember what I have told you, you will know that Braggioni was your friend."

Laura feels a slow chill, a purely physical sense of danger, a warning in her blood that violence, mutilation, a shocking death, wait for her with lessening patience. She has translated this fear into something homely, immediate, and sometimes hesitates before crossing the street. "My personal fate is nothing, except as the testimony of a mental attitude," she reminds herself, quoting from some forgotten philosophic primer, and is sensible enough to add, "Anyhow, I shall not be killed by an automobile if I can help it."

"It may be true I am as corrupt, in another way, as Braggioni," she thinks in spite of herself, "as callous, as incomplete," and if this is so, any kind of death seems preferable. Still she sits quietly, she does not run. Where could she go? Uninvited she has promised herself to this place; she can no longer imagine herself as living in another country, and there is no pleasure in remembering her life before she came here.

Precisely what is the nature of this devotion, its true motives, and what are its obligations? Laura cannot say. She spends part of her days in Xochimilco, nearby, teaching Indian children to say in English, "The cat is on the mat." When she appears in the classroom they crowd about her with smiles on their wise, innocent, clay-colored faces; crying, "Good morning, my titcher!" in immaculate voices, and they make of her desk a fresh garden of flowers every day.

During her leisure she goes to union meetings and listens to busy important voices quarreling over tactics, methods, internal politics. She visits the prisoners of her own political faith in their cells, where they entertain themselves with counting cockroaches, repenting of their indiscretions, composing their memoirs, writing out manifestoes and plans for their comrades who are still walking about free, hands in pockets, sniffing fresh air. Laura brings them food and cigarettes and a little money, and she brings messages disguised in equivocal phrases from the men outside who dare not set foot in the prison for fear of disappearing into the cells kept empty for them. If the prisoners confuse night and day, and complain, "Dear little Laura, time doesn't pass in this infernal hole, and I won't know when it is time to sleep unless I have a reminder," she brings them their favorite narcotics, and says in a tone that does not wound them with pity, "Tonight will really be night for you," and though her Spanish amuses them they find her comforting, useful. If they lose patience and all faith, and curse the slowness of their friends in coming to their rescue with money and influence, they trust her not to repeat everything, and if she inquires, "Where do you think we can find money, or influence?" they are certain to answer, "Well, there is Braggioni, why doesn't he do something?"

She smuggles letters from headquarters to men hiding from firing squads in back streets in mildewed houses, where they sit in tumbled beds and talk bitterly as if all Mexico were at their heels, when Laura knows positively they might appear at the band concert in the Alameda[4] on Sunday morning, and no one would notice them. But Braggioni says, "Let them sweat a little. The next time they may be careful. It is very restful to have them out of the way for a while." She is not afraid to knock on any door in any street after midnight, and enter in the darkness, and say to one of these men who is really in danger: "They will be looking for you—seriously—tomorrow morning after six. Here is some money from Vicente. Go to Vera Cruz[5] and wait."

She borrows money from the Roumanian agitator to give to his bitter enemy the Polish agitator. The favor of Braggioni is their disputed territory, and Braggioni holds the balance nicely, for he can use them both. The Polish agitator talks love to her over café tables, hoping to exploit what he believes is her secret sentimental preference for him, and he gives her misinformation which he begs her to repeat as the solemn truth to certain persons. The Roumanian is more adroit. He is generous with his money in all good causes, and lies to her with an air of ingenuous candor, as if he were her good friend and confidant. She never repeats anything they may say. Braggioni never asks questions. He has other ways to discover all that he wishes to know about them.

Nobody touches her, but all praise her gray eyes, and the soft, round under lip which promises gaiety, yet is always grave, nearly always firmly closed: and they cannot understand why she is in Mexico. She walks back and forth on her errands, with puzzled eyebrows, carrying her little folder of drawings and music and school papers. No dancer dances more beautifully than Laura walks, and she inspires some amusing, unexpected ardors, which cause little gossip, because nothing comes of them. A young captain who had been a soldier in Zapata's[6] army attempted, during a horseback ride near Cuernavaca, to express his desire for her with the noble simplicity befitting a rude folk-hero: but gently, because he was gentle. This gentleness was his defeat, for when he alighted, and removed her foot from the stirrup, and essayed to draw her down into his arms, her horse, ordinarily a tame one, shied fiercely, reared and plunged away. The young hero's

4. A public square.
5. Mexican port on the Gulf.
6. Emiliano Zapata (1883–1919), Mexican revolutionary leader who, with Pancho Villa, was able, in 1914, to take Mexico City; but they were forced to withdraw toward Cuernavaca, fifty miles south, in Zapata's native Morelos province. He was known both as an agrarian reformer and as the Attila of the South.

horse careened blindly after his stable-mate, and the hero did not
return to the hotel until rather late that evening. At breakfast he came
to her table in full charro dress, gray buckskin jacket and trousers
with strings of silver buttons down the leg, and he was in a humorous,
careless mood. "May I sit with you?" and "You are a wonderful rider.
I was terrified that you might be thrown and dragged. I should never
have forgiven myself. But I cannot admire you enough for your riding."

"I learned to ride in Arizona," said Laura.

"If you will ride with me again this morning, I promise you a horse
that will not shy with you," he said. But Laura remembered that she
must return to Mexico City at noon.

Next morning the children made a celebration and spent their play-
time writing on the blackboard, "We lov ar titcher," and with tinted
chalks they drew wreaths of flowers around the words. The young
hero wrote her a letter: "I am a very foolish, wasteful, impulsive man.
I should have first said I love you, and then you would not have run
away. But you shall see me again." Laura thought, "I must send him a
box of colored crayons," but she was trying to forgive herself for
having spurred her horse at the wrong moment.

A brown shock-haired youth came and stood in her patio one night
and sang like a lost soul for two hours, but Laura could think of
nothing to do about it. The moonlight spread a wash of gauzy silver
over the clear spaces of the garden, and the shadows were cobalt blue.
The scarlet blossoms of the Judas tree[7] were dull purple, and the
names of the colors repeated themselves automatically in her mind,
while she watched not the boy, but his shadow, fallen like a dark
garment across the fountain rim, trailing in the water. Lupe came
silently and whispered expert counsel in her ear: "If you will throw
him one little flower, he will sing another song or two and go away."
Laura threw the flower, and he sang a last song and went away with the
flower tucked in the band of his hat. Lupe said, "He is one of the
organizers of the Typographers Union, and before that he sold cor-
ridos[8] in the Merced market, and before that, he came from Guanajuato, where I was born. I would not trust any man, but I trust least
those from Guanajuato."

She did not tell Laura that he would be back again the next day,
and the next, nor that he would follow her at a certain fixed distance
around the Merced market, through the Zocolo, up Francesco I.
Madero Avenue, and so along the Paseo de la Reforma to Chapul-
tepec Park, and into the Philosopher's Footpath, still with that flower
withering in his hat, and an indivisible attention in his eyes.

Now Laura is accustomed to him, it means nothing except that he is
nineteen years old and is observing a convention with all propriety, as
though it were founded on a law of nature, which in the end it might
very well prove to be. He is beginning to write poems which he prints
on a wooden press, and he leaves them stuck like handbills in her
door. She is pleasantly disturbed by the abstract, unhurried watch-
fulness of his black eyes which will in time turn easily towards another

7. Judas Iscariot, who betrayed Christ,   tree.
is said to have hanged himself on such a   8. Bullfights tickets.

object. She tells herself that throwing the flower was a mistake, for she is twenty-two years old and knows better; but she refuses to regret it, and persuades herself that her negation of all external events as they occur is a sign that she is gradually perfecting herself in the stoicism she strives to cultivate against that disaster she fears, though she cannot name it.

She is not at home in the world. Every day she teaches children who remain strangers to her, though she loves their tender round hands and their charming opportunistic savagery. She knocks at unfamiliar doors not knowing whether a friend or a stranger shall answer, and even if a known face emerges from the sour gloom of that unknown interior, still it is the face of a stranger. No matter what this stranger says to her, nor what her message to him, the very cells of her flesh reject knowledge and kinship in one monotonous word. No. No. No. She draws her strength from this one holy talismanic word which does not suffer her to be led into evil. Denying everything, she may walk anywhere in safety, she looks at everything without amazement.

No, repeats this firm unchanging voice of her blood; and she looks at Braggioni without amazement. He is a great man, he wishes to impress this simple girl who covers her great round breasts with thick dark cloth, and who hides long, invaluably beautiful legs under a heavy skirt. She is almost thin except for the incomprehensible fullness of her breasts, like a nursing mother's, and Braggioni, who considers himself a judge of women, speculates again on the puzzle of her notorious virginity, and takes the liberty of speech which she permits without a sign of modesty, indeed, without any sort of sign, which is disconcerting.

"You think you are so cold, *gringita*! Wait and see. You will surprise yourself someday! May I be there to advise you!" He stretches his eyelids at her, and his ill-humored cat's eyes waver in a separate glance for the two points of light marking the opposite ends of a smoothly drawn path between the swollen curve of her breasts. He is not put off by that blue serge, nor by her resolutely fixed gaze. There is all the time in the world. His cheeks are bellying with the wind of song. "O girl with the dark eyes," he sings, and reconsiders. "But yours are not dark. I can change all that. O girl with the green eyes, you have stolen my heart away." Then his mind wanders to the song, and Laura feels the weight of his attention being shifted elsewhere. Singing thus, he seems harmless, he is quite harmless, there is nothing to do but sit patiently and say "No," when the moment comes. She draws a full breath, and her mind wanders also, but not far. She dares not wander too far.

Not for nothing has Braggioni taken pains to be a good revolutionist and a professional lover of humanity. He will never die of it. He has the malice, the cleverness, the wickedness, the sharpness of wit, the hardness of heart, stipulated for loving the world profitably. *He will never die of it.* He will live to see himself kicked out from his feeding trough by other hungry world-saviours. Traditionally he must sing in spite of his life which drives him to bloodshed, he tells Laura, for his father was a Tuscany peasant who drifted to Yucatan and married a Maya woman:[9] a woman of race, an aristocrat. They gave him the love and knowledge of music, thus: and under the rip of his thumbnail, the strings of the instrument complain like exposed nerves.

Once he was called Delgadito[1] by all the girls and married women who ran after him; he was so scrawny all his bones showed under his thin cotton clothing, and he could squeeze his emptiness to the very backbone with his two hands. He was a poet and the revolution was only a dream then; too many women loved him and sapped away his youth, and he could never find enough to eat anywhere, anywhere! Now he is a leader of men, crafty men who whisper in his ear, hungry men who wait for hours outside his office for a word with him, emaciated men with wild faces who waylay him at the street gate with a timid, "Comrade, let me tell you . . ." and they blow the foul breath from their empty stomachs in his face.

He is always sympathetic. He gives them handfuls of small coins from his own pockets, he promises them work, there will be demonstrations, they must join the unions and attend the meetings, above all they must be on the watch for spies. They are closer to him than his own brothers, without them he can do nothing—until tomorrow, comrade!

Until tomorrow. "They are stupid, they are lazy, they are treacherous, they would cut my throat for nothing," he says to Laura. He has good food and abundant drink, he hires an automobile and drives in the Paseo on Sunday morning, and enjoys plenty of sleep in a soft bed beside a wife who dares not disturb him; and he sits pampering his bones in easy billows of fat, singing to Laura, who knows and thinks these things about him. When he was fifteen, he tried to drown himself because he loved a girl, his first love, and she laughed at him. "A thousand woman have paid for that," and his tight little mouth turns down at the corners. Now he perfumes his hair with Jockey Club, and confides to Laura: "One woman is really as good as another for me in the dark. I prefer them all."

His wife organizes unions among the girls in the cigarette factories, and walks in picket lines, and even speaks at meetings in the evening. But she cannot be brought to acknowledge the benefits of true liberty. "I tell her I must have my freedom, net.[2] She does not understand my point of view." Laura has heard this many times. Braggioni scratches the guitar and meditates. "She is an instinctively virtuous woman, pure gold, no doubt of that. If she were not, I should lock her up, and she knows it."

His wife, who works so hard for the good of the factory girls, employs part of her leisure lying on the floor weeping because there are so many women in the world, and only one husband for her, and she never knows where nor when to look for him. He told her: "Unless you can learn to cry when I am not here, I must go away for good." That day he went away and took a room at the Hotel Madrid.

9. The Mayan Indians had a highly developed civilization from about A.D. 300 to almost 1000. The surviving Mayans live chiefly in Yucatan, a province at the top of the horn of Mexico that juts northward into the Gulf. Tuscany is an Italian region somewhat north and west of Rome.
1. Little skinny one.
2. Clear and final.

It is this month of separation for the sake of higher principles that has been spoiled not only for Mrs. Braggioni, whose sense of reality is beyond criticism, but for Laura, who feels herself bogged in a nightmare. Tonight Laura envies Mrs. Braggioni, who is alone, and free to weep as much as she pleases about a concrete wrong. Laura has just come from a visit to the prison, and she is waiting for tomorrow with a bitter anxiety as if tomorrow may not come, but time may be caught immovably in this hour, with herself transfixed, Braggioni singing on forever, and Eugenio's body not yet discovered by the guard.

Braggioni says: "Are you going to sleep?" Almost before she can shake her head, he begins telling her about the May-day disturbances coming on in Morelia,[3] for the Catholics hold a festival in honor of the Blessed Virgin, and the Socialists celebrate their martyrs on that day. "There will be two independent processions, starting from either end of town, and they will march until they meet, and the rest depends . . ." He asks her to oil and load his pistols. Standing up, he unbuckles his ammunition belt, and spreads it laden across her knees. Laura sits with the shells slipping through the cleaning cloth dipped in oil, and he says again he cannot understand why she works so hard for the revolutionary idea unless she loves some man who is in it. "Are you not in love with someone?" "No," says Laura. "And no one is in love with you?" "No." "Then it is your own fault. No woman need go begging. Why, what is the matter with you? The legless beggar woman in the Alameda has a perfectly faithful lover. Did you know that?"

Laura peers down the pistol barrel and says nothing, but a long, slow faintness rises and subsides in her; Braggioni curves his swollen finger around the throat of the guitar and softly smothers the music out of it, and when she hears him again he seems to have forgotten her, and is speaking in the hypnotic voice he uses when talking in small rooms to a listening, close-gathered crowd. Some day this world, now seemingly so composed and eternal, to the edges of every sea shall be merely a tangle of gaping trenches, of crashing walls and broken bodies. Everything must be torn from its accustomed place where it has rotted for centuries, hurled skyward and distributed, cast down again clean as rain, without separate identity. Nothing shall survive that the stiffened hands of poverty have created for the rich and no one shall be left alive except the elect spirits destined to procreate a new world cleansed of cruelty and injustice, ruled by benevolent anarchy: "Pistols are good, I love them, cannon are even better, but in the end I pin my faith to good dynamite," he concludes, and strokes the pistol lying in her hands. "Once I dreamed of destroying this city, in case it offered resistance to General Ortiz,[4] but it fell into his hands like an overripe pear."

He is made restless by his own words, rises and stands waiting. Laura holds up the belt to him: "Put that on, and go kill somebody in Morelia, and you will be happier," she says softly. The presence of death in the room makes her bold. "Today, I found Eugenio going into a stupor. He refused to allow me to call the prison doctor. He had

3. City about 125 miles west of Mexico City.
4. Pascual Oritiz Rubio (1877–1963), revolutionary military officer, later diplomat and, in 1930, president of Mexico.

taken all the tablets I brought him yesterday. He said he took them because he was bored."

"He is a fool, and his death is his own business," says Braggioni, fastening his belt carefully.

"I told him if he had waited only a little while longer, you would have got him set free," says Laura. "He said he did not want to wait."

"He is a fool and we are well rid of him," says Braggioni, reaching for his hat.

He goes away. Laura knows his mood has changed, she will not see him anymore for a while. He will send word when he needs her to go on errands into strange streets, to speak to the strange faces that will appear, like clay masks with the power of human speech, to mutter their thanks to Braggioni for his help. Now she is free, and she thinks, I must run while there is time. But she does not go.

Braggoni enters his own house where for a month his wife has spent many hours every night weeping and tangling her hair upon her pillow. She is weeping now, and she weeps more at the sight of him, the cause of all her sorrows. He looks about the room. Nothing is changed, the smells are good and familiar, he is well acquainted with the woman who comes toward him with no reproach except grief on her face. He says to her tenderly: "You are so good, please don't cry anymore, you dear good creature." She says, "Are you tired, my angel? Sit here and I will wash your feet." She brings a bowl of water, and kneeling, unlaces his shoes, and when from her knees she raises her sad eyes under her blackened lids, he is sorry for everything, and bursts into tears. "Ah, yes, I am hungry, I am tired, let us eat something together," he says, between sobs. His wife leans her head on his arm and says, "Forgive me!" and this time he is refreshed by the solemn, endless rain of her tears.

Laura takes off her serge dress and puts on a white linen nightgown and goes to bed. She turns her head a little to one side, and lying still, reminds herself that it is time to sleep. Numbers tick in her brain like little clocks, soundless doors close of themselves around her. If you would sleep, you must not remember anything, the children will say tomorrow, good morning, my teacher, the poor prisoners who come every day bringing flowers to their jailor. 1–2–3–4–5—it is monstrous to confuse love with revolution, night with day, life with death —ah Eugenio!

The tolling of the midnight bell is a signal, but what does it mean? Get up, Laura, and follow me: come out of your sleep, out of your bed, out of this strange house. What are you doing in this house? Without a word, without fear she rose and reached for Eugenio's hand, but he eluded her with a sharp, sly smile and drifted away. This is not all, you shall see—Murderer, he said, follow me, I will show you a new country, but it is far away and we must hurry. No, said Laura, not unless you take my hand, no; and she clung first to the stair rail, and then to the topmost branch of the Judas tree that bent down slowly and set her upon the earth, and then to the rocky ledge of a cliff, and then to the jagged wave of a sea that was not water but a desert of crumbling stone. Where are you taking me? she asked in wonder but without fear. To death, and it is a long way off, and we must hurry, said Eugenio. No, said Laura, not unless you take my hand. Then eat these flowers, poor prisoner, said Eugenio in a voice of pity, take and eat: and from the Judas tree he stripped the warm bleeding flowers, and held them to her lips. She saw that his hand was fleshless, a cluster of small white petrified branches, and his eye sockets were without light, but she ate the flowers greedily for they satisfied both hunger and thirst. Murderer! said Eugenio, and Cannibal! This is my body and my blood.[5] Laura cried No! and at the sound of her own voice, she awoke trembling, and was afraid to sleep again.

1930

WILLIAM FAULKNER

Barn Burning

The store in which the Justice of the Peace's court was sitting smelled of cheese. The boy, crouched on his nail keg at the back of the crowded room, knew he smelled cheese, and more: from where he sat he could see the ranked shelves close-packed with the solid, squat, dynamic shapes of tin cans whose labels his stomach read, not from the lettering which meant nothing to his mind but from the scarlet devils and the silver curve of fish—this, the cheese which he knew he smelled and the hermetic meat which his intestines believed he smelled coming in intermittent gusts momentary and brief between the other constant one, the smell and sense just a little of fear because mostly of despair and grief, the old fierce pull of blood. He could not see the table where the Justic sat and before which his father and his father's enemy (*our enemy* he thought in that despair; *ourn! mine and hisn both! He's my father!*) stood, but he could hear them, the two of them that is, because his father had said no word yet:

"But what proof have you, Mr. Harris?"

"I told you. The hog got into my corn. I caught it up and sent it back to him. He had no fence that would hold it. I told him so, warned him. The next time I put the hog in my pen. When he came to get it. I gave him enough wire to patch up his pen. The next time I put the hog up and kept it. I rode down to his house and saw the wire I gave him still rolled on to the spool in his yard. I told him he could have the hog when he paid me a dollar pound fee. That evening a nigger came with the dollar and got the hog. He was a strange nigger. He said, 'He say to tell you wood and hay kin burn.' I said, 'What?' 'That whut he say to tell you,' the nigger said. 'Wood and

---

5. Christ's words at the Last Supper—"And he took bread, and gave thanks, and brake it, and gave unto them saying, This is my body which is given for you: this do in remembrance of me. Likewise also the cup after supper, saying, This cup is the new testament in my blood, which is shed for you" (Luke 22:19–20).

hay kin burn.' That night my barn burned. I got the stock out but I
lost the barn."

"Where is the nigger? Have you got him?"

"He was a strange nigger, I tell you. I don't know what became of
him."

"But that's not proof. Don't you see that's not proof?"

"Get that boy up here. He knows." For a moment the boy thought
too that the man meant his older brother until Harris said, "Not
him. The little one. The boy," and, crouching, small for his age,
small and wiry like his father, in patched and faded jeans even too
small for him, with straight, uncombed, brown hair and eyes gray
and wild as storm scud, he saw the men between himself and the
table part and become a lane of grim faces, at the end of which he
saw the Justice, a shabby, collarless, graying man in spectacles,
beckoning him. He felt no floor under his bare feet; he seemed to
walk beneath the palpable weight of the grim turning faces. His father,
stiff in his black Sunday coat donned not for the trial but for the
moving, did not even look at him. *He aims for me to lie, he thought,*
again with that frantic grief and despair. *And I will have to do hit.*

"What's your name, boy?" the Justice said.

"Colonel Sartoris Snopes," the boy whispered.

"Hey?" the Justice said. "Talk louder. Colonel Sartoris? I reckon
anybody named for Colonel Sartoris in this country can't help but
tell the truth, can they?" The boy said nothing. *Enemy! Enemy!* he
thought; for a moment he could not even see, could not see that the
Justice's face was kindly nor discern that his voice was troubled when
he spoke to the man named Harris: "Do you want me to question
this boy?" But he could hear, and during those subsequent long seconds while there was absolutely no sound in the crowded little room
save that of quiet and intent breathing it was as if he had swung
outward at the end of a grape vine, over a ravine, and at the top of
the swing had been caught in a prolonged instant of mesmerized
gravity, weightless in time.

"No!" Harris said violently, explosively. "Damnation! Send him
out of here!" Now time, the fluid world, rushed beneath him again,
the voices coming to him again through the smell of cheese and
sealed meat, the fear and despair and the old grief of blood:

"This case is closed. I can't find against you, Snopes, but I can
give you advice. Leave this country and don't come back to it."

His father spoke for the first time, his voice cold and harsh, level,
without emphasis: "I aim to. I don't figure to stay in a country among
people who . . ." he said something unprintable and vile, addressed
to no one.

"That'll do," the Justice said. "Take your wagon and get out of
this country before dark. Case dismissed."

His father turned, and he followed the stiff black coat, the wiry
figure walking a little stiffly from where a Confederate provost's man's[1]
musket ball had taken him in the heel on a stolen horse thirty years
ago, followed the two backs now, since his older brother had appeared

---

1. Military policeman.

from somewhere in the crowd, no taller than the father but thicker, chewing tobacco steadily, between the two lines of grim-faced men and out of the store and across the worn gallery and down the sagging steps and among the dogs and half-grown boys in the mild May dust, where as he passed a voice hissed:

"Barn burner!"

Again he could not see, whirling; there was a face in a red haze, moonlike, bigger than the full moon, the owner of it half again his size, he leaping in the red haze toward the face, feeling no blow, feeling no shock when his head struck the earth, scrabbling up and leaping again, feeling no blow this time either and tasting no blood, scrabbling up to see the other boy in full flight and himself already leaping into pursuit as his father's hand jerked him back, the harsh, cold voice speaking above him: "Go get in the wagon."

It stood in a grove of locusts and mulberries across the road. His two hulking sisters in their Sunday dresses and his mother and her sister in calico and sunbonnets were already in it, sitting on and among the sorry residue of the dozen and more movings which even the boy could remember—the battered stove, the broken beds and chairs, the clock inlaid with mother-of-pearl, which would not run, stopped at some fourteen minutes past two o'clock of a dead and forgotten day and time, which had been his mother's dowry. She was crying, though when she saw him she drew her sleeve across her face and began to descend from the wagon. "Get back," the father said.

"He's hurt. I got to get some water and wash his. . . ."

"Get back in the wagon," his father said. He got in too, over the tail-gate. His father mounted to the seat where the older brother already sat and struck the gaunt mules two savage blows with the peeled willow, but without heat. It was not even sadistic; it was exactly that same quality which in later years would cause his descendants to over-run the engine before putting a motor car into motion, striking and reining back in the same movement. The wagon went on, the store with its quiet crowd of grimly watching men dropped behind; a curve in the road hid it. *Forever* he thought. *Maybe he's done satisfied now, now that he has* . . . stopping himself, not to say it aloud even to himself. His mother's hand touched his shoulder.

"Does hit hurt?" she said.

"Naw," he said. "Hit don't hurt. Lemme be."

"Can't you wipe some of the blood off before hit dries?"

"I'll wash to-night," he said. "Lemme be, I tell you."

The wagon went on. He did not know where they were going. None of them ever did or ever asked, because it was always somewhere, always a house of sorts waiting for them a day or two days or even three days away. Likely his father had already arranged to make a crop on another farm before he . . . Again he had to stop himself. He (the father) always did. There was something about his wolflike independence and even courage when the advantage was at least neutral which impressed strangers, as if they got from his latent ravening ferocity not so much a sense of dependability as a feeling that his ferocious conviction in the rightness of his own actions would be of advantage to all whose interest lay with his.

That night they camped, in a grove of oaks and beeches where a spring ran. The nights were still cool and they had a fire against it, of a rail lifted from a nearby fence and cut into lengths—a small fire, neat, niggard almost, a shrewd fire; such fires were his father's habit and custom always, even in freezing weather. Older, the boy might have remarked this and wondered why not a big one; why should not a man who had not only seen the waste and extravagance of war, but who had in his blood an inherent voracious prodigality with material not his own, have burned everything in sight? Then he might have gone a step farther and thought that that was the reason: the niggard blaze was the living fruit of nights passed during those four years in the woods hiding from all men, blue or gray,[2] with his strings of horses (captured horses, he called them). And older still, he might have divined the true reason: that the element of fire spoke to some deep mainspring of his father's being, as the element of steel or of powder spoke to other men, as the one weapon for the preservation of integrity, else breath were not worth the breathing, and hence to be regarded with respect and used with discretion.

But he did not think this now and he had seen those same niggard blazes all his life. He merely ate his supper beside it and was already half asleep over his iron plate when his father called him, and once more he followed the stiff back, the stiff and ruthless limp, up the slope and on to the starlit road where, turning, he could see his father against the stars but without face or depth—a shape black, flat, and bloodless as though cut from tin in the iron folds of the frockcoat which had not been made for him, the voice harsh like tin and without heat like tin:

"You wre fixing to tell them. You would have told them." He didn't answer. His father struck him with the flat of his hand on the side of the head, hard but without heat, exactly as he had struck the two mules at the store, exactly as he would strike either of them with any stick in order to kill a horse fly, his voice still without heat or anger: "You're getting to be a man. You got to learn. You got to learn to stick to your own blood or you ain't going to have any blood to stick to you. Do you think either of them, any man there this morning, would? Don't you know all they wanted was a chance to get at me because they knew I had them beat? Eh?" Later, twenty years later, he was to tell himself, "If I had said they wanted only truth, justice, he would have hit me again." But now he said nothing. He was not crying. He just stood there. "Answer me," his father said.

"Yes," he whispered. His father turned.

"Get on to bed. We'll be there tomorrow."

To-morrow they were there. In the early afternoon the wagon stopped before a paintless two-room house identical almost with the dozen others it had stopped before even in the boy's ten years, and again, as on the other dozen occasions, his mother and aunt got

2. In the Civil War (1861–1865), Union soldiers wore blue and Confederate soldiers gray uniforms.

down and began to unload the wagon, although his two sisters and his father and brother had not moved.

"Likely hit ain't fitten for hawgs," one of the sisters said.

"Nevertheless, fit it will and you'll hog it and like it," his father said. "Get out of them chairs and help your Ma unload."

The two sisters got down, big, bovine, in a flutter of cheap ribbons; one of them drew from the jumbled wagon bed a battered lantern, the other a worn broom. His father handed the reins to the older son and began to climb stiffly over the wheel. "When they get unloaded, take the team to the barn and feed them." Then he said, and at first the boy thought he was still speaking to his brother: "Come with me."

"Me?" he said.

"Yes," his father said. "You."

"Abner," his mother said. His father paused and looked back— the harsh level stare beneath the shaggy, graying, irascible brows.

"I reckon I'll have a word with the man that aims to begin tomorrow owning me body and soul for the next eight months."

They went back up the road. A week ago—or before last night, that is—he would have asked where they were going, but not now. His father had struck him before last night but never before had he paused afterward to explain why; it was as if the blow and the following calm, outrageous voice still rang, repercussed, divulging nothing to him save the terrible handicap of being young, the light weight of his few years, just heavy enough to prevent his soaring free of the world as it seemed to be ordered but not heavy enough to keep him footed solid in it, to resist it and try to change the course of its events.

Presently he could see the grove of oaks and cedars and the other flowering trees and shrubs where the house would be, though not the house yet. They walked beside a fence massed with honeysuckle and Chrokee roses and came to a gate swinging open between two brick pillars, and now, beyond a sweep of drive, he saw the house for the first time and at that instant he forgot his father and the terror and despair both, and even when he remembered his father again (who had not stopped) the terror and despair did not return. Because, for all the twelve movings, they had sojourned until now in a poor country, a land of small farms and fields and houses, and he had never seen a house like this before. *Hit's big as a courthouse* he thought quietly, with a surge of peace and joy whose reason he could not have thought into words, being too young for that: *They are safe from him. People whose lives are a part of this peace and dignity are beyond his touch, he no more to them than a buzzing wasp: capable of stinging for a little moment but that's all; the spell of this peace and dignity rendering even the barns and stable and cribs which belong to it impervious to the puny flames he might contrive . . .* this, the peace and joy, ebbing for an instant as he looked again at the stiff black back, the stiff and implacable limp of the figure which was not dwarfed by the house, for the reason that it had never looked big anywhere and which now, against the serene columned backdrop, had more than ever that impervious quality of something cut ruthlessly from tin, depthless, as though, sidewise to the sun, it would cast no shadow. Watching him, the boy remarked the absolutely undeviating course which his father held and saw the stiff foot come squarely down in a pile of fresh droppings where a horse had stood in the drive and which his father could have avoided by a simple change of stride. But it ebbed only for a moment, though he could not have thought this into words either, walking on in the spell of the house, which he could even want but without envy, without sorrow, certainly never with that ravening and jealous rage which unknown to him walked in the ironlike black coat before him: *Maybe he will feel it too. Maybe it will even change him now from what maybe he couldn't help but be.*

They crossed the portico. Now he could hear his father's stiff foot as it came down on the boards with clocklike finality, a sound out of all proportion to the displacement of the body it bore and which was not dwarfed either by the white door before it, as though it had attained to a sort of vicious and ravening minimum not to be dwarfed by anything—the flat, wide, black hat, the formal coat of broadcloth which had once been black but which had now that friction-glazed greenish cast of the bodies of old house flies, the lifted sleeve which was too large, the lifted hand like a curled claw. The door opened so promptly that the boy knew the Negro must have been watching them all the time, an old man with neat grizzled hair, in a linen jacket, who stood barring the door with his body, saying, "Wipe you foots, white man, fo you come in here. Major ain't home nohow."

"Get out of my way, nigger," his father said, without heat too, flinging the door back and the Negro also and entering, his hat still on his head. And now the boy saw the prints of the stiff foot on the doorjamb and saw them appear on the pale rug behind the machine-like deliberation of the foot which seemed to bear (or transmit) twice the weight which the body compassed. The Negro was shouting "Miss Lula! Miss Lula!" somewhere behind them, then the boy, deluged as though by a warm wave by a suave turn of carpeted stair and a pendant glitter of chandeliers and a mute gleam of gold frames, heard the swift feet and saw her too, a lady—perhaps he had never seen her like before either—in a gray, smooth gown with lace at the throat and an apron tied at the waist and the sleeves turned back, wiping cake or biscuit dough from her hands with a towel as she came up the hall, looking not at his father at all but at the tracks on the blond rug with an expression of incredulous amazement.

"I tried," the Negro cried. "I tole him to . . ."

"Will you please go away?" she said in a shaking voice. "Major de Spain is not at home. Will you please go away?"

His father had not spoken again. He did not speak again. He did not even look at her. He just stood stiff in the center of the rug, in his hat, the shaggy iron-gray brows twitching slightly above the pebble-colored eyes as he appeared to examine the house with brief deliberation. Then with the same deliberation he turned; the boy watched him pivot on the good leg and saw the stiff foot drag round the arc of the turning, leaving a final long and fading smear. His father never looked at it, he never once looked down at the rug. The Negro held the door. It closed behind them, upon the hysteric and indistinguishable woman-wail. His father stopped at the top of the steps and scraped his boot clean on the edge of it. At the gate he stopped again. He stood for a moment, planted stiffly on the stiff foot, looking back at the house. "Pretty and white, ain't it?" he said. "That's sweat. Nigger sweat. Maybe it ain't white enough yet to suit him. Maybe he wants to mix some white sweat with it."

Two hours later the boy was chopping wood behind the house within which his mother and aunt and the two sisters (the mother and aunt, not the two girls, he knew that; even at this distance and muffled by walls the flat loud voices of the two girls emanated an incorrigible idle inertia) were setting up the stove to prepare a meal, when he heard the hooves and saw the linen-clad man on a fine sorrel mare, whom he recognized even before he saw the rolled rug in front of the Negro youth following on a fat bay carriage horse—a suffused, angry face vanishing, still at full gallop, beyond the corner of the house where his father and brother were sitting in the two tilted chairs; and a moment later, almost before he could have put the axe down, he heard the hooves again and watched the sorrel mare go back out of the yard, already galloping again. Then his father began to shout one of the sisters' names, who presently emerged backward from the kitchen door dragging the rolled rug along the ground by one end while the other sister walked behind it.

"If you ain't going to tote, go on and set up the wash pot," the first said.

"You, Sarty!" the second shouted. "Set up the wash pot!" His father appeared at the door, framed against that shabbiness, as he had been against that other bland perfection, impervious to either, the mother's anxious face at his shoulder.

"Go on," the father said. "Pick it up." The two sisters stooped, broad, lethargic; stooping, they presented an incredible expanse of pale cloth and a flutter of tawdry ribbons.

"If I thought enough of a rug to have to git hit all the way from France I wouldn't keep hit where folks coming in would have to tromp on it," the first said. They raised the rug.

"Abner," the mother said. "Let me do it."

"You go back and git dinner," his father said. "I'll tend to this."

From the woodpile through the rest of the afternoon the boy watched them, the rug spread flat in the dust beside the bubbling wash-pot, the two sisters stooping over it with that profound and lethargic reluctance, while the father stood over them in turn, implacable and grim, driving them though never raising his voice again. He could smell the harsh homemade lye they were using; he saw his mother come to the door once and look toward them with an expression not anxious now but very like despair; his saw his father turn, and he fell to with the axe and saw from the corner of his eye his father raise from the ground a flattish fragment of field stone and examine it and return to the pot, and this time his mother actually spoke: "Abner. Abner. Please don't. Please, Abner."

Then he was done too. It was dusk; the whippoorwills had already begun. He could smell coffee from the room where they would presently eat the cold food remaining from the mid-afternoon meal, though when he entered the house he realized they were having coffee again probably because there was a fire on the hearth, before which the rug now lay spread over the backs of the two chairs. The tracks of his father's foot were gone. Where they had been were now long, water-cloudy scoriations resembling the sporadic course of a liliputian mowing machine.

It still hung there while they ate the cold food and then went to bed, scattered without order or claim up and down the two rooms, his mother in one bed, where his father would later lie, the older brother in the other, himself, the aunt, and the two sisters on pallets on the floor. But his father was not in bed yet. The last thing the boy remembered was the depthless, harsh silhouette of the hat and coat bending over the rug and it seemed to him that he had not even closed his eyes when the silhouette was standing over him, the fire almost dead behind it, the stiff foot prodding him awake. "Catch up the mule," his father said.

When he returned with the mule his father was standing in the black door, the rolled rug over his shoulder. "Ain't you going to ride?" he said.

"No. Give me your foot."

He bent his knee into his father's hand, the wiry, surprising power flowed smoothly, rising, he rising with it, on to the mule's bare back (they had owned a saddle once; the boy could remember it though not when or where) and with the same effortlessness his father swung the rug up in front of him. Now in the starlight they retraced the afternoon's path, up the dusty road rife with honeysuckle, through the gate and up the black tunnel of the drive to the lightless house, where he sat on the mule and felt the rough warp of the rug drag across his thighs and vanish.

"Don't you want me to help?" he whispered. His father did not answer and now he heard again that stiff foot striking the hollow portico with that wooden and clocklike deliberation, that outrageous overstatement of the weight it carried. The rug, hunched, not flung (the boy could tell that even in the darkness) from his father's shoulder struck the angle of wall and floor with a sound unbelievably loud, thunderous, then the foot again, unhurried and enormous; a light came on in the house and the boy sat, tense, breathing steadily and quietly and just a little fast, though the foot itself did not increase its beat at all, descending the steps now, now the boy could see him.

"Don't you want to ride now?" he whispered. "We kin both ride now," the light within the house altering now, flaring up and sinking. *He's coming down the stairs now,* he thought. He had already ridden the mule up beside the horse block; presently his father was up behind him and he doubled the reins over and slashed the mule across the neck, but before the animal could begin to trot the hard, thin arm came round him, the hard, knotted hand jerking the mule back to a walk.

In the first red rays of the sun they were in the lot, putting plow gear on the mules. This time the sorrel mare was in the lot before he heard it at all, the rider collarless and even bareheaded, trembling, speaking in a shaking voice as the woman in the house had done, his father merely looking up once before stooping again to the hame he was buckling, so that the man on the mare spoke to his stooping back:

"You must realize you have ruined that rug. Wasn't there anybody here, any of your women . . ." he ceased, shaking, the boy watching him, the older brother leaning now in the stable door, chewing, blinking slowly and steadily at nothing apparently. "It cost a hundred dollars. But you never had a hundred dollars. You never will. So I'm going to charge you twenty bushels of corn against your crop. I'll add it in your contract and when you come to the commissary you can sign it. That won't keep Mrs. de Spain quiet but maybe it will teach you to wipe your feet off before you enter her house again."

Then he was gone. The boy looked at his father, who still had not spoken or even looked up again, who was now adjusting the loggerhead in the hame.

"Pap," he said. His father looked at him—the inscrutable face, the shaggy brows beneath which the gray eyes glinted coldly. Suddenly the boy went toward him, fast, stopping as suddenly. "You done the best you could!" he cried. "If he wanted hit done different why didn't he wait and tell you how? He won't git no twenty bushels! He won't git none! We'll gether hit and hide hit! I kin watch . . ."

"Did you put the cutter back in that straight stock like I told you?"

"No, sir," he said.

"Then go do it."

That was Wednesday. During the rest of that week he worked steadily, at what was within his scope and some which was beyond it, with an industry that did not need to be driven nor even commanded twice; he had this from his mother, with the difference that some at least of what he did he liked to do, such as splitting wood with the half-size axe which his mother and aunt had earned, or saved money somehow, to present him with at Christmas. In company with the two older women (and on one afternoon, even one of the sisters), he built pens for the shoat and the cow which were a part of his father's contract with the landlord, and one afternoon, his father being absent, gone somewhere on one of the mules, he went to the field.

They were running a middle buster[3] now, his brother holding the plow straight while he handled the reins, and walking beside the straining mule, the rich black soil shearing cool and damp against his bare ankles, he thought *Maybe this is the end of it. Maybe even that twenty bushels that seems hard to have to pay for just a rug will be a cheap price for him to stop forever and always from being what he used to be;* thinking, dreaming now, so that his brother had to speak sharply to him to mind the mule: *Maybe he even won't collect the twenty bushels. Maybe it will all add up and balance and vanish—corn, rug, fire; the terror and grief, the being pulled two ways like between two teams of horses—gone, done with for ever and ever.*

Then it was Saturday; he looked up from beneath the mule he was

---

3. A double moldboard plow that throws a ridge of earth both ways.

harnessing and saw his father in the black coat and hat. "Not that," his father said. "The wagon gear." And then, two hours later, sitting in the wagon bed behind his father and brother on the seat, the wagon accomplished a final curve, and he saw the weathered paint-less store with its tattered tobacco- and patent-medicine posters and the tethered wagons and saddle animals below the gallery. He mounted the gnawed steps behind his father and brother, and there again was the lane of quiet, watching faces for the three of them to walk through. He saw the man in spectacles sitting at the plank table and he did not need to be told this was a Justice of the Peace; he sent one glare of fierce, exultant, partisan defiance at the man in collar and cravat now, whom he had seen but twice before in his life, and that on a galloping horse, who now wore on his face an expression not of rage but of amazed unbelief which the boy could not have known was at the incredible circumstance of being sued by one of his own tenants, and came and stood against his father and cried at the Justice: "He ain't done it! He ain't burnt . . ."

"Go back to the wagon," his father said.

"Burnt?" the Justice said. "Do I understand this rug was burned too?"

"Does anybody here claim it was?" his father said. "Go back to the wagon." But he did not, he merely retreated to the rear of the room, crowded as that other had been, but not to sit down this time, instead, to stand pressing among the motionless bodies, listening to the voices:

"And you claim twenty bushels of corn is too high for the damage you did to the rug?"

"He brought the rug to me and said he wanted the tracks washed out of it. I washed the tracks out and took the rug back to him."

"But you didn't carry the rug back to him in the same condition it was in before you made the tracks on it."

His father did not answer, and now for perhaps half a minute there was no sound at all save that of breathing, the faint, steady suspiration of complete and intent listening.

"You decline to answer that, Mr. Snopes?" Again his father did not answer. "I'm going to find against you, Mr. Snopes. I'm going to find that you were responsible for the injury to Major de Spain's rug and hold you liable for it. But twenty bushels of corn seems a little high for a man in your circumstances to have to pay. Major de Spain claims it cost a hundred dollars. October corn will be worth about fifty cents. I figure that if Major de Spain can stand a ninety-five dollar loss on something he paid cash for, you can stand a five-dollar loss you haven't earned yet. I hold you in damages to Major de Spain to the amount of ten bushels of corn over and above your contract with him, to be paid to him out of your crop at gathering time. Court adjourned."

It had taken no time hardly, the morning was but half begun. He thought they would return home and perhaps back to the field, since they were late, far behind all other farmers. But instead his father passed on behind the wagon, merely indicating with his hand for the older brother to follow with it, and crossed the road toward the blacksmith shop opposite, pressing on after his father, overtaking him, speaking, whispering up at the harsh, calm face beneath the weathered hat: "He won't git no ten bushels neither. He won't git one. We'll . . ." until his father glanced for an instant down at him, the face absolutely calm, the grizzled eyebrows tangled above the cold eyes, the voice almost pleasant, almost gentle:

"You think so? Well, we'll wait till October anyway."

The matter of the wagon—the setting of a spoke or two and the tightening of the tires—did not take long either, the business of the tires accomplished by driving the wagon into the spring branch behind the shop and letting it stand there, the mules nuzzling into the water from time to time, and the boy on the seat with the idle reins, looking up the slope and through the sooty tunnel of the shed where the slow hammer rang and where his father sat on an upended cypress bolt, easily, either talking or listening, still sitting there when the boy brought the dripping wagon up out of the branch and halted it before the door.

"Take them on to the shade and hitch," his father said. He did so and returned. His father and the smith and a third man squatting on his heels inside the door were talking, about crops and animals; the boy, squatting too in the ammoniac dust and hoof-parings and scales of rust, heard his father tell a long and unhurried story out of the time before the birth of the older brother even when he had been a professional horsetrader. And then his father came up beside him where he stood before a tattered last year's circus poster on the other side of the store, gazing rapt and quiet at the scarlet horses, the incredible poisings and convolutions of tulle and tights and the painted leers of comedians, and said, "It's time to eat."

But not at home. Squatting beside his brother against the front wall, he watched his father emerge from the store and produce from a paper sack a segment of cheese and divide it carefully and deliberately into three with his pocket knife and produce crackers from the same sack. They all three squatted on the gallery and ate, slowly, without talking; then in the store again, they drank from a tin dipper tepid water smelling of the cedar bucket and of living beech trees. And still they did not go home. It was a horse lot this time, a tall rail fence upon and along which men stood and sat and out of which one by one horses were led, to be walked and trotted and then cantered back and forth along the road while the slow swapping and buying went on and the sun began to slant westward, they—the three of them—watching and listening, the older brother with his muddy eyes and his steady, inevitable tobacco, the father commenting now and then on certain of the animals, to no one in particular.

It was after sundown when they reached home. They ate supper by lamplight, then, sitting on the doorstep, the boy watched the night fully accomplish, listening to the whippoorwills and the frogs, when he heard his mother's voice: "Abner! No! No! Oh, God. Oh, God. Abner!" and he rose, whirled, and saw the altered light through the door where a candle stub now burned in a bottle neck on the table and his father, still in the hat and coat, at once formal and burlesque as though dressed carefully for some shabby and ceremonial violence, emptying the reservoir of the lamp back into the five-gallon kerosene can from which it had been filled, while the mother tugged at his arm until he shifted the lamp to the other hand and flung her back, not savagely or viciously, just hard, into the wall, her hands flung out against the wall for balance, her mouth open and in her face the same quality of hopeless despair as had been in her voice. Then his father saw him standing in the door.

"Go to the barn and get that can of oil we were oiling the wagon with," he said. The boy did not move. Then he could speak.

"What . . ." he cried. "What are you . . ."

"Go get that oil," his father said. "Go."

Then he was moving, running, outside the house, toward the stable: this the old habit, the old blood which he had not been permitted to choose for himself, which had been bequeathed him willy nilly and which had run for so long (and who knew where, battening on what of outrage and savagery and lust) before it came to him. *I could keep on,* he thought. *I could run on and on and never look back, never need to see his face again. Only I can't. I can't,* the rusted can in his hand now, the liquid sploshing in it as he ran back to the house and into it, into the sound of his mother's weeping in the next room, and handed the can to his father.

"Ain't you going to even send a nigger?" he cried. "At least you sent a nigger before!"

This time his father didn't strike him. The hand came even faster than the blow had, the same hand which had set the can on the table with almost excruciating care flashing from the can toward him too quick for him to follow it, gripping him by the back of his shirt and on to tiptoe before he had seen it quit the can, the face stooping at him in breathless and frozen ferocity, the cold, dead voice speaking over him to the older brother, who leaned against the table, chewing with that steady, curious, sidewise motion of cows:

"Empty the can into the big one and go on. I'll catch up with you."

"Better tie him up to the bedpost," the brother said.

"Do like I told you," the father said. Then the boy was moving, his bunched shirt and the hard, bony hand between his shoulder-blades, his toes just touching the floor, across the room and into the other one, past the sisters sitting with spread heavy thighs in the two chairs over the cold hearth, and to where his mother and aunt sat side by side on the bed, the aunt's arms about his mother's shoulders.

"Hold him," the father said. The aunt made a startled movement. "Not you," the father said. "Lennie. Take hold of him. You'll hold him better than that. If he gets loose don't you know what he is going to do? He will go up yonder." He jerked his head toward the road. "Maybe I'd better tie him."

"I'll hold him," his mother whispered.

"See you do then." Then his father was gone, the stiff foot heavy and measured upon the boards, ceasing at last.

Then he began to struggle. His mother caught him in both arms, he jerking and wrenching at them. He would be stronger in the end, he knew that. But he had no time to wait for it. "Lemme go!" he cried. "I don't want to have to hit you!"

"Let him go!" the aunt said. "If he don't go, before God, I am going up there myself!"

"Don't you see I can't?" his mother cried. "Sarty! Sarty! No! No! Help me, Lizzie!"

Then he was free. His aunt grasped at him but it was too late. He whirled, running, his mother stumbled forward on to her knees behind him, crying to the nearer sister: "Catch him, Net! Catch him!" But that was too late too, the sister (the sisters were twins, born at the same time, yet either of them now gave the impression of being, encompassing as much living meat and volume and weight as any other two of the family) not yet having begun to rise from the chair, her head, face, alone merely turned, presented to him in the flying instant an astonishing expanse of young female features untroubled by any surprise even, wearing only an expression of bovine interest. Then he was out of the room, out of the house, in the mild dust of the starlit road and the heavy rifeness of honeysuckle, the pale ribbon unspooling with terrific slowness under his running feet, reaching the gate at last and turning in, running, his heart and lungs drumming, on up the drive toward the lighted house, the lighted door. He did not knock, he burst in, sobbing for breath, incapable for the moment of speech; he saw the astonished face of the Negro in the linen jacket without knowing when the Negro had appeared.

"De Spain!" he cried, panted. "Where's . . ." then he saw the white man too emerging from a white door down the hall. "Barn!" he cried. "Barn!"

"What?" the white man said. "Barn?"

"Yes!" the boy cried. "Barn!"

"Catch him!" the white man shouted.

But it was too late this time too. The Negro grasped his shirt, but the entire sleeve, rotten with washing, carried away, and he was out that door too and in the drive again, and had actually never ceased to run even while he was screaming into the white man's face.

Behind him the white man was shouting, "My horse! Fetch my horse!" and he thought for an instant of cutting across the park and climbing the fence into the road, but he did not know the park nor how high the vine-massed fence might be and he dared not risk it. So he ran on down the drive, blood and breath roaring; presently he was in the road again though he could not see it. He could not hear either: the galloping mare was almost upon him before he heard her, and even then he held his course, as if the very urgency of his wild grief and need must in a moment more find his wings, waiting until the ultimate instant to hurl himself aside and into the weed-choked roadside ditch as the horse thundered past and on, for an instant in furious silhouette against the stars, the tranquil early summer night sky which, even before the shape of the horse and rider vanished, stained abruptly and violently upward: a long, swirling roar incredible and soundless, blotting the stars, and he springing up and into the road again, running again, knowing it was too late yet still running even after he heard the shot and, an instant later, two shots, pausing now without knowing he had ceased to run, crying "Pap! Pap!", running again before he knew he had begun to run, stumbling, tripping over something and scrabbling up again without ceasing to run, looking backward over his shoulder at the glare as he got up, running on among the invisible trees, panting, sobbing, "Father! Father!"

At midnight he was sitting on the crest of a hill. He did not know it was midnight and he did not know how far he had come. But there was no glare behind him now and he sat now, his back toward what he had called home for four days anyhow, his face toward the dark woods which he would enter when breath was strong again, small, shaking steadily in the chill darkness, hugging himself into the remainder of his thin, rotten shirt, the grief and despair now no longer terror and fear but just grief and despair. *Father. My father,* he thought. "He was brave!" he cried suddenly, aloud but not loud, no more than a whisper: "He was! He was in the war! He was in Colonel Sartoris' cav'ry!" not knowing that his father had gone to that war a private in the fine old European sense, wearing no uniform, admitting the authority of and giving fidelity to no man or army or flag, going to war as Malbrouck[4] himself did: for booty—it meant nothing and less than nothing to him if it were enemy booty or his own.

The slow constellations wheeled on. It would be dawn and then sun-up after a while and he would be hungry. But that would be tomorrow and now he was only cold, and walking would cure that. His breathing was easier now and he decided to get up and go on, and then he found that he had been asleep because he knew it was almost dawn, the night almost over. He could tell that from the whippoorwills. They were everywhere now among the dark trees below him, constant and inflectioned and ceaseless, so that, as the instant for giving over to the day birds drew nearer and nearer, there was no interval at all between them. He got up. He was a little stiff, but walking would cure that too as it would the cold, and soon there would be the sun. He went on down the hill, toward the dark woods within which the liquid silver voices of the birds called unceasing— the rapid and urgent beating of the urgent and quiring heart of the late spring night. He did not look back.

1939

---

4. The Duke of Marlborough (1650–1722), an English general whose name became distorted as Malbrough and Malbrouch in English and French popular songs celebrating his exploits.

WILLIAM FAULKNER

Spotted Horses

Yes, sir. Flem Snopes has filled that whole country full of spotted
horses. You can hear folks running them all day and all night, whooping and hollering, and the horses running back and forth across them
little wooden bridges ever now and then kind of like thunder. Here
I was this morning pretty near halfway to town, with the team ambling along and me setting in the buckboard about half asleep, when
all of a sudden something come swurging[1] up outen the bushes and
jumped the road clean, without touching hoof to it. It flew right over
my team, big as a billboard and flying through the air like a hawk.
It taken me thirty minutes to stop my team and untangle the harness
and the buckboard and hitch them up again.

That Flem Snopes. I be dog if he ain't a case, now. One morning
about ten years ago, the boys was just getting settled down on Varner's porch for a little talk and tobacco, when here come Flem out
from behind the counter, with his coat off and his hair all parted
like he might have been clerking for Varner for ten years already.
Folks all knowed him; it was a big family of them about five miles
down the bottom. That year, at least. Share-cropping. They never
stayed on any place over a year. Then they would move on to
another place, with the chap or maybe the twins of that year's litter.
It was a regular nest of them. But Flem. The rest of them stayed
tenant farmers, moving ever year, but here come Flem one day, walking out from behind Jody Varner's counter like he owned it. And he
wasn't there but a year or two before folks knowed that, if him and
Jody was both still in that store in ten years more, it would be Jody
clerking for Flem Snopes. Why, that fellow could make a nickel where
it wasn't but four cents to begin with. He skun[2] me in two trades,
myself, and the fellow that can do that, I just hope he'll get rich
before I do; that's all.

All right. So here Flem was, clerking at Varner's, making a nickel
here and there and not telling nobody about it. No, sir. Folks never
knowed when Flem got the better of somebody lessen the fellow he
beat told it. He'd just set there in the store-chair, chewing his tobacco
and keeping his own business to hisself, until about a week later we'd
find out it was somebody else's business he was keeping to hisself—
provided the fellow he trimmed was mad enough to tell it. That's
Flem.

We give him ten years to own everything Jody Varner had. But he
never waited no ten years. I reckon you-all know that gal of Uncle
Billy Varner's, the youngest one; Eula. Jody's sister. Ever Sunday
ever yellow-wheeled buggy and curried riding horse in that country
would be hitched to Bill Varner's fence, and the young bucks setting
on the porch, swarming around Eula like bees around a honey pot.
One of these here kind of big, soft-looking gals that could giggle

1. Surging.   2. Skinned, cheated.

richer than plowed newground. Wouldn't none of them leave before
the others, and so they would set there on the porch until time to go
home, with some of them with nine and ten miles to ride and then
get up tomorrow and go back to the field. So they would all leave
together and they would ride in a clump down to the creek ford
and hitch them curried horses and yellow-wheeled buggies and get
out and fight one another. Then they would get in the buggies again
and go on home.

Well, one day about a year ago, one of them yellow-wheeled buggies and one of them curried saddle-horses quit this country. We
heard they was heading for Texas. The next day Uncle Billy and
Eula and Flem come in to town in Uncle Bill's surrey, and when they
come back, Flem and Eula was married. And on the next day we
heard that two more of them yellow-wheeled buggies had left the
country. They mought have gone to Texas, too. It's a big place.

Anyway, about a month after the wedding, Flem and Eula went
to Texas, too. They was gone pretty near a year. Then one day last
month, Eula come back. with a baby. We figgered up, and we decided that it was as well-growed a three-months-old baby as we ever
see. It can already pull up on a chair. I reckon Texas makes big men
quick, being a big place. Anyway, if it keeps on like it started, it'll
be chewing tobacco and voting time it's eight years old.

And so last Friday here come Flem himself. He was on a wagon
with another fellow. The other fellow had one of these two-gallon
hats and a ivory-handled pistol and a box of gingersnaps sticking out
of his hind pocket, and tied to the tailgate of the wagon was about
two dozen of them Texas ponies, hitched to one another with barbed
wire. They was colored like parrots and they was quiet as doves, and
ere a one of them would kill you quick as a rattlenake. Nere a one
of them had two eyes the same color, and nere a one of them had ever
see a bridle, I reckon; and when that Texas man got down offen the
wagon and walked up to them to show how gentle they was, one of
them cut his vest clean offen him, same as with a razor.

Flem had done already disappeared; he had went on to see his
wife, I reckon, and to see if that ere baby had done gone on to the
field to help Uncle Billy plow, maybe. It was the Texas man that taken
the horses on to Mrs. Littlejohn's lot. He had a little trouble at first,
when they come to the gate, because they hadn't never see a fence
before, and when he finally got them in and taken a pair of wire
cutters and unhitched them and got them into the barn and poured
some shell corn into the trough, they durn nigh tore down the barn.
I reckon they thought that shell corn was bugs, maybe. So he left
them in the lot and he announced that the auction would begin at
sunup tomorrow.

That night we was setting on Mrs. Littlejohn's porch. You-all mind
the moon was nigh full that night, and we could watch them spotted
varmints swirling along the fence and back and forth across the lot
same as minnows in a pond. And then now and then they would
all kind of huddle up against the barn and rest themselves by biting
and kicking one another. We would hear a squeal, and then a set of
hoofs would go Bam! against the barn, like a pistol. It sounded

just like a fellow with a pistol, in a nest of cattymounts,[3] taking his time.

II

It wasn't ere[4] a man knowed yet if Flem owned them things or not. They just knowed one thing: that they wasn't never going to know for sho if Flem did or not, or if maybe he didn't just get on that wagon at the edge of town, for the ride or not. Even Eck Snopes didn't know, Flem's own cousin. But wasn't nobody surprised at that. We knowed that Flem would skin Eck quick as he would ere a one of us.

They was there by sunup next morning, some of them come twelve and sixteen miles, with seed-money tied up in tobacco sacks in their overalls, standing along the fence, when the Texas man come out of Mrs. Littlejohn's after breakfast and clumb onto the gate post with that ere white pistol butt sticking outen his hind pocket. He taken a new box of gingersnaps outen his pocket and bit the end offen it like a cigar and spit out the paper, and said the auction was open. And still they was coming up in wagons and a horse-and-mule-back and hitching the teams across the road and coming to the fence. Flem wasn't nowhere in sight.

But he couldn't get them started. He begun to work on Eck, because Eck holp him last night to get them into the barn and feed them that shell corn. Eck got out jist in time. He come outen that barn like a chip of the crest of a busted dam of water, and clumb into the wagon just in time.

He was working on Eck when Henry Armstid come up in his wagon. Eck was saying he was skeered to bid on one of them, because he might get it, and the Texas man says, "Them ponies? Them little horses?" He clumb down offen the gate post and went toward the horses. They broke and run, and him following them, kind of chirping to them, with his hand out like he was fixing to catch a fly, until he got three or four of them cornered. Then he jumped into them, and then we couldn't see nothing for a while because of the dust. It was a big cloud of it, and them blare-eyed, spotted things swoaring outen it twenty foot to a jump, in forty directions without counting up. Then the dust settled and there they was, that Texas man and the horse. He had its head twisted clean around like a owl's head. Its legs was braced and it was trembling like a new bride and groaning like a saw mill, and him holding its head wrung clean around on its neck so it was snuffing sky. "Look it over," he says, with his heels dug too and that white pistol sticking outen his pocket and his neck swole up like a spreading adder's until you could just tell what he was saying, cussing the horse and talking to us all at once: "Look him over, the fiddle-headed son of fourteen fathers. Try him, buy him; you will get the best–" Then it was all dust again, and we couldn't see nothing but spotted hide and mane, and that ere Texas man's boot-heels like a couple of walnuts on two

---

3. Panthers. 4. There was not one.

strings, and after a while that two-gallon hat come sailing out like a fat old hen crossing a fence.

When the dust settled again, he was just getting outen the far fence corner, brushing himself off. He come and got his hat and brushed it off and come and clumb onto the gate post again. He was breathing hard. He taken the gingersnap box outen his pocket and et one, breathing hard. The hammer-head horse was still running round and round the lot like a merry-go-round at a fair. That was when Henry Armstid come shoving up to the gate in them patched overalls and one of them dangle-armed shirts of hisn. Hadn't nobody noticed him until then. We was all watching the Texas man and the horses. Even Mrs. Littlejohn; she had done come out and built a fire under the washpot in her back yard, and she would stand at the fence a while and then go back into the house and come out again with a armful of wash and stand at the fence again. Well, here comes Henry shoving up, and then we see Mrs. Armstid right behind him, in that ere faded wrapper and sunbonnet and them tennis shoes. "Git on back to that wagon," Henry says.

"Henry," she says.

"Here, boys," the Texas man says; "make room for missus to git up and see. Come on, Henry," he says; "here's your chance to buy that saddle-horse missus has been wanting. What about ten dollars, Henry?"

"Henry," Mrs. Armstid says. She put her hand on Henry's arm. Henry knocked her hand down.

"Git on back to that wagon, like I told you," he says.

Mrs. Armstid never moved. She stood behind Henry, with her hands rolled into her dress, not looking at nothing. "He hain't no more despair[5] than to buy one of them things," she says. "And us not five dollars ahead of the porehouse, he hain't no more despair." It was the truth, too. They ain't never made more than a bare living offen that place of theirs, and them with four chaps and the very clothes they wears she earns by weaving by the firelight at night while Henry's asleep.

"Shut your mouth and git on back to that wagon," Henry says. "Do you want I taken a wagon stake to you here in the big road?"

Well, that Texas man taken one look at her. Then he begun on Eck again, like Henry wasn't even there. But Eck was skeered. "I can git me a snapping turtle or a water moccasin for nothing. I ain't going to buy none."

So the Texas man said he would give Eck a horse. "To start the auction, and because you holp me last night. If you'll start the bidding on the next horse," he says, "I'll give you that fiddle-head horse."

I wish you could have seen them, standing there with their seed-money in their pockets, watching that Texas man give Eck Snopes a live horse, all fixed to call him a fool if he taken it or not. Finally Eck says he'll take it. "Only I just starts the bidding," he says. "I don't have to buy the next one lessen I ain't overtopped." The Texas

5. To spare.

man said all right, and Eck bid a dollar on the next one, with Henry Armstid standing there with his mouth already open, watching Eck and the Texas man like a mad dog or something. "A dollar," Eck says.

The Texas man looked at Eck. His mouth was already open too, like he had started to say something and what he was going to say had up and died on him. "A dollar?" he says. "One dollar? You mean, *one* dollar, Eck?"

"Durn it," Eck says; "two dollars, then."

Well, sir, I wish you could a seen that Texas man. He taken out that gingersnap box and held it up and looked into it, careful, like it might have been a diamond ring in it, or a spider. Then he throwed it away and wiped his face with a bandanna. "Well," he says. "Well. Two dollars. Two dollars. Is your pulse all right, Eck?" he says. "Do you have ager-sweats[6] at night, maybe?" he says. "Well," he says, "I got to take it. But are you boys going to stand there and see Eck get two horses at a dollar a head?"

That done it. I be dog if he wasn't nigh as smart as Flem Snopes. He hadn't no more than got the words outen his mouth before here was Henry Armstid, waving his hand. "Three dollars," Henry says. Mrs. Armstid tried to hold him again. He knocked her hand off, shoving up to the gate post.

"Mister," Mrs. Armstid says, "we got chaps in the house and not corn to feed the stock. We got five dollars I earned my chaps a-weaving after dark, and him snoring in the bed. And he hain't no more despair."

"Henry bids three dollars," the Texas man says. "Raise him a dollar, Eck, and the horse is yours."

"Henry," Mrs. Armstid says.

"Raise him, Eck," the Texas man says.

"Four dolars," Eck says.

"Five dollars," Henry says, shaking his fist. He shoved up right under the gate post. Mrs. Armstid was looking at the Texas man too.

"Mister," she says, "if you take that five dollars I earned my chaps a-weaving for one of them things, it'll be a curse onto you and yourn during all the time of man."

But it wasn't no stopping Henry. He had shoved up, waving his fist at the Texas man. He opened it; the money was in nickels and quarters, and one dollar bill that looked like a cow's cud. "Five dollars," he says. "And the man that raises it'll have to beat my head off, or I'll beat hisn."

"All right," the Texas man says. "Five dollars is bid. But don't you shake your hand at me."

III

It taken till nigh sundown before the last one was sold. He got them hotted up once and the bidding got up to seven dollars and a quarter, but most of them went around three or four dollars, him setting on the gate post and picking the horses out one at a time by mouth-

6. Cold sweats, as in malaria.

word, and Mrs. Littlejohn pumping up and down at the tub and
stopping and coming to the fence for a while and going back to the
tub again. She had done got done too, and the wash was hung on
the line in the back yard, and we could smell supper cooking. Finally
they was all sold; he swapped the last two and the wagon for a
buckboard.

We was all kind of tired, but Henry Armstid looked more like a
mad dog than ever. When he bought, Mrs. Armstid had went back to
the wagon, setting in it behind them two rabbit-sized, bone-pore
mules, and the wagon itself looking like it would fall all to pieces soon
as the mules moved. Henry hadn't even waited to pull it outen the
road; it was still in the middle of the road and her setting in it, not
looking at nothing, ever since this morning.

Henry was right up against the gate. He went up to the Texas man.
"I bought a horse and I paid cash," Henry says. "And yet you expect
me to stand around here until they are all sold before I can get my
horse. I'm going to take my horse outen that lot."

The Texas man looked at Henry. He talked like he might have
been asking for a cup of coffee at the table. "Take your horse," he
says.

Then Henry quit looking at the Texas man. He begun to swallow,
holding onto the gate. "Ain't you going to help me?" he says.

"It ain't my horse," the Texas man says.

Henry never looked at the Texas man again, he never looked at
nobody. "Who'll help me catch my horse?" he says. Never nobody said
nothing. "Bring the plowline," Henry says. Mrs. Armstid got outen
the wagon and brought the plowline. The Texas man got down
offen the post. The woman made to pass him, carrying the rope.

"Don't you go in there, missus," the Texas man says.

Henry opened the gate. He didn't look back. "Come on here," he
says.

"Don't you go in here, missus," the Texas man says.

Mrs. Armstid wasn't looking at nobody, neither, with her hands
across her middle, holding the rope. "I reckon I better," she says.
Her and Henry went into the lot. The horses broke and run. Henry
and Mrs. Armstid followed.

"Get him into the corner," Henry says. They got Henry's horse
cornered finally, and Henry taken the rope, but Mrs. Armstid let the
horse get out. They hemmed it up again, but Mrs. Armstid let it get
out again, and Henry turned and hit her with the rope. "Why didn't
you head him back?" Henry says. He hit her again. "Why didn't you?"
It was about that time I looked around and see Flem Snopes standing
there.

It was the Texas man that done something. He moved fast for a
big man. He caught the rope before Henry could hit the third time,
and Henry whirled and made like he would jump at the Texas man.
But he never jumped. The Texas man went and taken Henry's arm and
led him outen the lot. Mrs. Armstid come behind them and the Texas
man taken some money outen his pocket and he give it into Mrs.
Armstid's hand. "Get him into the wagon and take him on home,"

the Texas man says, like he might have been telling them he enjoyed his supper.

Then here come Flem. "What's that for, Buck?" Flem says.

"Thinks he bought one of them ponies," the Texas man says. "Get him on away, missus."

But Henry wouldn't go. "Give him back that money," he says. "I bought that horse and I aim to have him if I have to shoot him."

And there was Flem, standing there with his hands in his pockets, chewing, like he had just happened to be passing.

"You take your money and I take my horse," Henry says. "Give it back to him," he says to Mrs. Armstid.

"You don't own no horse of mine," the Texas man says. "Get him on home, missus."

Then Henry seen Flem. "You got something to do with these horses," he says. "I bought one. Here's the money for it." He taken the bill outen Mrs. Armstid's hand. He offered it to Flem. "I bought one. Ask him. Here. Here's the money," he says, giving the bill to Flem.

When Flem taken the money, the Texas man dropped the rope he had snatched outen Henry's hand. He had done sent Eck Snopes's boy up to the store for another box of gingersnaps, and he taken the box of gingersnaps, and he taken the box outen his pocket and looked into it. It was empty and he dropped it on the ground. "Mr. Snopes will have your money for you tomorrow," he says to Mrs. Amstid. "You can get it from him tomorrow. He don't own no horse. You get him into the wagon and get him on home." Mrs. Armstid went back to the wagon and got in. "Where's that ere buckboard I bought?" the Texas man says. It was after sundown then. And then Mrs. Littlejohn come out on the porch and rung the supper bell.

IV

I come on in and et supper. Mrs. Littlejohn would bring in a pan of bread or something, then she would go out to the porch a minute and come back and tell us. The Texas man had hitched his team to the buckboard he had swapped them last two horses for, and him and Flem had gone, and then she told that the rest of them that never had ropes had went back to the store with I. O. Snopes to get some ropes, and wasn't nobody at the gate but Henry Armstid, and Mrs. Armstid setting in the wagon in the road, and Eck Snopes and that boy of hisn. "I don't care how many of them fool men gets killed by them things," Mrs. Littlejohn says, "but I ain't going to let Eck Snopes take that boy into that lot again." So she went down to the gate, but she come back without the boy or Eck neither.

"It ain't no need to worry about that boy," I says. "He's charmed." He was right behind Eck last night when Eck went to help feed them. The whole drove of them jumped clean over that boy's head and never touched him. It was Eck that touched him. Eck snatched him into the wagon and taken a rope and frailed the tar outen him.

So I had done et and went to my room and was undressing, long as I had a long trip to make next day; I was trying to sell a machine to Mrs. Bundren up past Whiteleaf; when Henry Armstid

opened that gate and went in by hisself. They couldn't make him wait
for the balance of them to get back with their ropes. Eck Snopes said
he tried to make Henry wait, but Henry wouldn't do it. Eck said
Henry walked right up to them and that when they broke, they run
clean over Henry like a hay-mow breaking down. Eck said he snatched
that boy of hisn out of the way just in time and that them things
went through that gate like a creek flood and into the wagons and
teams hitched side the road, busting wagon tongues and snapping
harness like it was fishing line, with Mrs. Armstid still setting in their
wagon in the middle of it like something carved outen wood. Then
they scattered, wild horses and tame mules with pieces of harness and
single trees dangling offen them, both ways up and down the road.

"There goes ourn, paw!" Eck says his boy said. "There it goes, into
Mrs. Littlejohn's house." Eck says it run right up the steps and into
the house like a boarder late for supper. I reckon so. Anyway, I was
in my room, in my underclothes, with one sock on and one sock in my
hand, leaning out the window when the commotion busted out, when
I heard something run into the melodeon in the hall; it sounded like a
railroad engine. Then the door to my room come sailing in like when
you throw a tin bucket top into the wind and I looked over my
shoulder and see something that looked like a fourteen-foot pinwheel
a-blaring its eyes at me. It had to blare them fast, because I was already done jumped out the window.

I reckon it was anxious, too. I reckon it hadn't never seen barbed
wire or shell corn before, but I know it hadn't never seen underclothes before, or maybe it was a sewing-machine agent it hadn't never
seen. Anyway, it swirled and turned to run back up the hall and
outen the house, when it met Eck Snopes and that boy just coming in,
carrying a rope. It swirled again and run down the hall and out the
back door just in time to meet Mrs. Littlejohn. She had just gathered
up the clothes she had washed, and she was coming onto the back
porch with a armful of washing in one hand and a scrubbing board
in the other, when the horse skidded up to her, trying to stop and
swirl again. It never taken Mrs. Littlejohn no time a-tall.

"Git outen here, you son," she says. She hit it across the face with
the scrubbing board; that ere scrubbing board split as neat as ere a
axe could have done it, and when the horse swirled to run back up
the hall, she hit it again with what was left of the scrubbing board,
not on the head this time. "And stay out," she says.

Eck and that boy was halfway down the hall by this time. I reckon
that horse looked like a pinwheel to Eck too. "Git to hell outen here,
Ad!" Eck says. Only there wasn't time. Eck dropped flat on his face,
but the boy never moved. The boy was about a yard tall maybe, in
overhalls just like Eck's; that hoarse swoared over his head without
touching a hair. I saw that, because I was just coming back up the
front steps, still carrying that ere sock and still in my underclothes,
when the horse come onto the porch again. It taken one look at me
and swirled again and run to the end of the porch and jumped the
banisters and the lot fence like a hen-hawk and lit in the lot running
and went out the gate again and jumped eight or ten upside-down
wagons and went on down the road. It was a full moon then. Mrs.

Armstid was still setting in the wagon like she had done been
carved outen wood and left there and forgot.

That horse. It ain't never missed a lick. It was going about forty
miles a hour when it come to the bridge over the creek. It would
have had a clear road, but it so happened that Vernon Tull was already using the bridge when it got there. He was coming back from
town; he hadn't heard about the auction; him and his wife and three
daughters and Mrs. Tull's aunt, all setting in chairs in the wagon bed,
and all asleep, including the mules. They waked up when the horse
hit the bridge one time, but Tull said the first he knew was when the
mules tried to turn the wagon around in the middle of the bridge and
he seen that spotted varmint run right twixt the mules and run up
the wagon tongue like a squirrel. He said he just had time to hit it
across the face with his whip-stock, because about that time the
mules turned the wagon around on that ere one-way bridge and that
horse clumb across one of the mules and jumped down on to the bridge
again and went on, with Vernon standing up in the wagon and
kicking at it.

Tull said the mules turned in the harness and clumb back into the
wagon too, with Tull trying to beat them out again, with the reins
wrapped around his wrist. After that he says all he seen was overturned chairs and womenfolks' legs and white drawers shining in the
moonlight, and his mules and that spotted horse going on up the road
like a ghost.

The mules jerked Tull outen the wagon and drug him a spell on the
bridge before the reins broke. They thought at first that he was dead,
and while they was kneeling around him, picking the bridge splinters
outen him, here come Eck and that boy, still carrying the rope. They
was running and breathing a little hard. "Where'd he go?" Eck says.

V

I went back and got my pants and shirt and shoes on just in time to
go and help get Henry Armstid outen the trash in the lot. I be dog[7]
if he didn't look like he was dead, with his head hanging back and
his teeth showing in the moonlight, and a little rim of white under his
eyelids. We could still hear them horses, here and there; hadn't none
of them got more than four–five miles away yet, not knowing the
country, I reckon. So we could hear them and folks yelling now
and then: "Whooey, Head him!"

We toted Henry into Mrs. Littlejohn's. She was in the hall; she
hadn't put down the armful of clothes. She taken one look at us, and
she laid down the busted scrubbing board and taken up the lamp and
opened a empty door. "Bring him in here," she says.

We toted him in and laid him on the bed. Mrs. Littlejohn set the
lamp on the dresser, still carrying the clothes. "I'll declare, you men,"
she says. Our shadows was way up the wall, tiptoeing too; we could
hear ourselves breathing. "Better get his wife," Mrs. Littlejohn says.
She went out, carrying the clothes.

"I reckon we had," Quick says. "Go get her, somebody."

7. Darned.

"Whyn't you go?" Winterbottom says.

"Let Ernest git her," Durley says. "He lives neighbors with them."

Ernest went to fetch her. I be dog if Henry didn't look like he was dead. Mrs. Littlejohn come back, with a kettle and some towels. She went to work on Henry, and then Mrs. Armstid and Ernest come in. Mrs. Armstid come to the foot of the bed and stood there, with her hands rolled into her apron, watching what Mrs. Littlejohn was doing, I reckon.

"You men get outen the way," Mrs. Littlejohn says. "Git outside," she says. "See if you can't find something else to play with that will kill some more of you."

"Is he dead?" Winterbottom says.

"It ain't your fault if he ain't," Mrs. Littlejohn says. "Go tell Will Varner to come up here. I reckon a man ain't so different from a mule, come long come short. Except maybe a mule's got more sense."

We went to get Uncle Billy. It was a full moon. We could hear them, now and then, four mile away: "Whooey. Head him." The country was full of them, one on ever wooden bridge in the land, running across it like thunder: "Whooey. There he goes. Head him."

We hadn't got far before Henry begun to scream. I reckon Mrs. Littlejohn's water had brung him to; anyway, he wasn't dead. We went on to Uncle Billy's. The house was dark. We called to him, and after a while the window opened and Uncle Billy put his head out, peart as a peckerwood,[8] listening. "Are they still trying to catch them durn rabbits?" he says.

He come down, with his britches on over his nightshirt and his suspenders dangling, carrying his horse-doctoring grip. "Yes, sir," he says, cocking his head like a woodpecker; "they're still a-trying."

We could hear Henry before we reached Mrs. Littlejohn's. He was going Ah-Ah-Ah. We stopped in the yard. Uncle Billy went on in. We could hear Henry. We stood in the yard, hearing them on the bridges, this-a-way and that: "Whooey. Whooey."

"Eck Snopes ought to caught hisn," Ernest says.

"Looks like he ought," Winterbottom said.

Henry was going Ah-Ah-Ah steady in the house; then he begun to scream. "Uncle Billy's started," Quick says. We looked into the hall. We could see the light where the door was. Then Mrs. Littlejohn come out.

"Will needs some help," she says. "You, Ernest. You'll do." Ernest went into the house.

"Hear them?" Quick said. "That one was on Four Mile bridge." We could hear them; it sounded like thunder a long way off; it didn't last long:

"Whooey."

We could hear Henry: "Ah-Ah-Ah-Ah-Ah."

"They are both started now," Winterbottom says. "Ernest too."

That was early in the night. Which was a good thing, because it taken a long night for folks to chase them things right and for Henry to lay there and holler, being as Uncle Billy never had none of this here chloryfoam to set Henry's leg with. So it was considerate in Flem

8. Woodpecker.

to get them started early. And what do you reckon Flem's com-ment was?

That's right. Nothing. Because he wasn't there. Hadn't nobody see him since that Texas man left.

VI

That was Saturday night. I reckon Mrs. Armstid got home about day-light, to see about the chaps. I don't know where they thought her and Henry was. But lucky the oldest one was a gal, about twelve, big enough to take care of the little ones. Which she did for the next two days. Mrs. Armstid would nurse Henry all night and work in the kitchen for hern and Henry's keep, and in the afternoon she would drive home (it was about four miles) to see to the chaps. She would cook up a pot of victuals and leave it on the stove, and the gal would bar the house and keep the little ones quiet. I would hear Mrs. Littlejohn and Mrs. Armstid talking in the kitchen. "How are the chaps making out?" Mrs. Littlejohn says.

"All right," Mrs. Armstid says.

"Don't they git skeered at night?" Mrs. Littlejohn says.

"Ina May bars the door when I leave," Mrs. Armstid says. "She's got the axe in bed with her. I reckon she can make out."

I reckon they did. And I reckon Mrs. Armstid was waiting for Flem to come back to town; hadn't nobody seen him until this morning; to get her money the Texas man said Flem was keeping for her. Sho. I reckon she was.

Anyway, I heard Mrs. Armstid and Mrs. Littlejohn talking in the kitchen this morning while I was eating breakfast. Mrs. Littlejohn had just told Mrs. Armstid that Flem was in town. "You can ask him for that five dollars," Mrs. Littlejohn says.

"You reckon he'll give it to me?" Mrs. Armstid says.

Mrs. Littlejohn was washing dishes, washing them like a man, like they was made out of iron. "No," she says. "But asking him won't do no hurt. It might shame him. I don't reckon it will, but it might."

"If he wouldn't give it back, it ain't no use to ask," Mrs. Armstid says.

"Suit yourself," Mrs. Littlejohn says. "It's your money."

I could hear the dishes.

"Do you reckon he might give it back to me?" Mrs. Armstid says. "That Texas man said he would. He said I could get it from Mr. Snopes later."

"Then go and ask him for it," Mrs. Littlejohn says.

I could hear the dishes.

"He won't give it back to me," Mrs. Armstid says.

"All right," Mrs. Littlejohn says. "Don't ask him for it, then."

I could hear the dishes; Mrs. Armstid was helping. "You don't reckon he would, do you?" she says. Mrs. Littlejohn never said noth-ing. It sounded like she was throwing the dishes at one another. "Maybe I better go and talk to Henry about it," Mrs. Armstid says.

"I would," Mrs. Littlejohn says. I be dog if it didn't sound like she had two plates in her hands, beating them together. "Then Henry can buy another five-dollar horse with it. Maybe he'll buy one next time that will out and out kill him. If I thought that, I'd give you back the money, myself."

"I reckon I better talk to him first," Mrs. Armstid said. Then it sounded like Mrs. Littlejohn taken up all the dishes and throwed them at the cookstove, and I come away.

That was this morning. I had been up to Bundren's and back, and I thought that things would have kind of settled down. So after breakfast, I went up to the store. And there was Flem, setting in the store chair and whittling, like he might not have ever moved since he come to clerk for Jody Varner. I. O. was leaning in the door, in his shirt sleeves and with his hair parted too, same as Flem was before he turned the clerking job over to I. O. It's a funny thing about them Snopes: they all looks alike, yet there ain't ere a two of them that claims brothers. They're always just cousins, like Flem and Eck and Flem and I. O. Eck was there too, squatting against the wall, him and that boy, eating cheese and crackers outen a sack; they told me that Eck hadn't been home a-tall. And that Lon Quick hadn't got back to town, even. He followed his horse clean down to Samson's Bridge, with a wagon and a camp outfit. Eck finally caught one of hisn. It run into a blind lane at Freeman's and Eck and the boy taken and tied their rope across the end of the lane, about three foot high. The horse come to the end of the lane and whirled and run back without ever stopping. Eck says it never seen the rope a-tall. He says it looked just like one of these here Christmas pinwheels. "Didn't it try to run again?" I says.

"No," Eck says, eating a bit of cheese offen his knife blade. "Just kicked some."

"Kicked some?" I says.

"It broke its neck," Eck says.

Well, they was squatting there, about six of them, talking, talking at Flem; never nobody knowed yet if Flem had ere a interest in them horses or not. So finally I come right out and asked him. "Flem's done skun all of us so much," I says, "that we're proud of him. Come on, Flem," I says, "How much did you and that Texas man make offen them horses? You can tell us. Ain't nobody here but Eck that bought one of them; the others ain't got back to town yet, and Eck's your own cousin; he'll be proud to hear, too. How much did you-all make?"

They was all whittling, not looking at Flem, making like they was studying. But you could a heard a pin drop. And I. O. He had been rubbing his back up and down on the door, but he stopped now, watching Flem like a pointing dog. Flem finished cutting the sliver offen his stick. He spit across the porch, into the road. " 'Twarn't none of my horses," he says.

I. O. cackled, like a hen, slapping his legs with both hands. "You boys might just as well quit trying to get ahead of Flem," he said.

Well, about that time I see Mrs. Armstid come outen Mrs. Little-john's gate, coming up the road. I never said nothing. I says, "Well, if a man can't take care of himself in a trade, he can't blame the man that trims him."

Flem never said nothing, trimming at the stick. He hadn't seen

Mrs. Armstid. "Yes, sir," I says. "A fellow like Henry Armstid ain't got nobody but hisself to blame."

"Course he ain't," I. O. says. He ain't seen her, neither. "Henry Armstid's a born fool. Always is been. If Flem hadn't a got his money, somebody else would."

We looked at Flem. He never moved. Mrs. Armstid come on up the road.

"That's right," I says. "But, come to think of it, Henry never bought no horse." We looked at Flem; you could a heard a match drop. "That Texas man told her to get that five dollars back from Flem next day. I reckon Flem's done already taken that money to Mrs. Little-john's and give it to Mrs. Armstid."

We watched Flem. I. O. quit rubbing his back against the door again. After a while Flem raised his head and spit across the porch, into the dust. I. O. cackled, just like a hen. "Ain't he a beating fellow, now?" I. O. says.

Mrs. Armstid was getting closer, so I kept on talking, watching to see if Flem would look up and see her. But he never looked up. I went on talking about Tull, about how he was going to sue Flem, and Flem setting there, whittling his stick, not saying nothing else after he said they wasn't none of his horses.

Then I. O. happened to look around. He seen Mrs. Armstid. "Psssst!" he says. Flem looked up. "Here she comes!" I. O. says. "Go out the back. I'll tell her you done went in to town today."

But Flem never moved. He just set there, whittling, and we watched Mrs. Armstid come up onto the porch, in that ere faded sun-bonnet and wrapper and them tennis shoes that made a kind of hissing noise on the porch. She come onto the porch and stopped, her hands rolled into her dress in front, not looking at nothing.

"He said Saturday," she says, "that he wouldn't sell Henry no horse. He said I could get the money from you."

Flem looked up. The knife never stopped. It went on trimming off a sliver same as if he was watching it. "He taken that money off with him when he left," Flem says.

Mrs. Armstid never looked at nothing. We never looked at her, neither, except the boy of Eck's. He had a half-et cracker in his hand, watching her, chewing.

"He said Henry hadn't bought no horse," Mrs. Armstid says. "He said for me to get the money from you today."

"I reckon he forgot about it," Flem said. "He taken that money off with him Saturday." He whittled again. I. O. kept on rubbing his back, slow. He licked his lips. After a while the woman looked up the road, where it went on up the hill, toward the graveyard. She looked up that way for a while, with that boy of Eck's watching her and I. O. rubbing his back slow against the door. Then she turned back toward the steps.

"I reckon it's time to get dinner started," she says.

"How's Henry this morning, Mrs. Armstid?" Winterbottom says.

She looked at Winterbottom; she almost stopped. "He's resting, I thank you kindly," she says.

Flem got up, outen the chair, putting his knife away. He spit across the porch. "Wait a minute, Mrs. Armstid," he says. She stopped again. She didn't look at him. Flem went on into the store, with I. O. done quit rubbing his back now, with his head craned after Flem, and Mrs. Armstid standing there with her hands rolled into her dress, not looking at nothing. A wagon come up the road and passes; it was Freeman, on the way to town. Then Flem come out again, with I. O. still watching him. Flem had one of these little striped sacks of Jody Varner's candy; I bet he still owes Jody that nickel, too. He put the sack into Mrs. Armstid's hand, like he would have put it into a hollow stump. He spit again across the porch. "A little sweetening for the chaps," he says.

"You're right kind," Mrs. Armstid says. She held the sack of candy in her hand, not looking at nothing. Eck's boy was watching the sack, the half-et cracker in his hand; he wasn't chewing now. He watched Mrs. Armstid roll the sack into her apron. "I reckon I better get on back and help with dinner," she says. She turned and went back across the porch. Flem set down in the chair again and opened his knife. He spit across the porch again, past Mrs. Armstid where she hadn't went down the steps yet. Then she went on, in that ere sunbonnet and wrapper all the same color, back down the road toward Mrs. Littlejohn's. You couldn't see her dress move, like a natural woman walking. She looked like an old snag still standing up and moving along on a high water. We watched her turn in at Mrs. Littlejohn's and go outen sight. Flem was whittling. I. O. begun to rub his back on the door. Then he begun to cackle, just like a durn hen.

"You boys might just as well quit trying," I. O. says. "You can't git ahead of Flem. You can't touch him. Ain't he a sight, now?"

I be dog if he ain't. If I had brung a herd of wild cattymounts into town and sold them to my neighbors and kinfolks, they would have lynched me. Yes, sir.

1931

ISAAC BASHEVIS SINGER

Tanhum

Tanhum Makover buttoned his gaberdine and twisted his earlocks into curls. He wiped his feet on the straw mat before the door, as he had been told to. His prospective father-in-law, Reb Bendit Waldman, often reminded him that one could study the Torah and serve

the Almighty and still not behave like an idle dreamer. Reb Bendit
Waldman offered himself as an example. He was everything at once—
a scholar, a fervent Chassid of the Sadgora rabbi [1] as well as a successful lumber merchant, a chess player, and the proprietor of a
water mill. There was time for everything if one wasn't lazy, Reb
Bendit said—even to teach yourself Russian and Polish and glance
into a newspaper. How his prospective father-in-law managed all this
was beyond Tanhum. Reb Bendit never seemed to hurry. He had a
friendly word for everyone, even an errand boy or servant girl. Women
burdened down by a heavy spirit came to him for advice. Nor did he
neglect to visit the sick or—God forbid—to escort a corpse. Tanhum
often resolved to be like his prospective father-in-law, but he simply
couldn't manage it. He would grow absorbed in some sacred book
and before he knew it half the day had gone by. He tried to maintain a proper appearance, but a button would loosen and dangle by
a thread until it dropped off and got lost. His boots were always
muddied, his shirt collars frayed. As often as he knotted the band
of his breeches it always came untied again. He resolved to commit
two pages of the Gemara [2] to memory each day so that in three and
a half years he might finish with the Talmud, but he couldn't manage
even this. He would become preoccupied with some Talmudic controversy and linger over it for weeks on end. The questions and doubts
wouldn't let him rest. Certainly there was mercy in Heaven, but
why did little children or even dumb animals have to suffer? Why did
man have to end up dying, and a steer under the slaughterer's knife?
Why had the miracles ceased and God's chosen people been forced
to suffer exile for two thousand years? Tanhum probed in the Chassidic lore, the cabala[3] volumes, the ancient philosophy books. The
questions they raised in his mind plagued him like flies. There were
mornings when Tanhum awoke with a weight in his limbs, a pain
in his temples, and no urge at all to study, pray, or even perform
his ablutions. Today was one of those days. He opened the Gemara
and sat there for two hours without turning a page. At prayer, he
couldn't seem to grasp the meaning of the words. While reciting the
eighteen benedictions,[4] he transposed the blessings. And it just so
happened that today he was invited for lunch at his prospective
father-in-law's.

Reb Bendit Waldman's house was constructed in such a way
that one had to pass through the kitchen to get to the dining room.
The kitchen was aswarm with women—Tanhum's prospective mother-
in-law, her daughters-in-law, her daughters, including Tanhum's
bride-to-be, Mira Fridl. Even before entering the house he heard the
racket and commotion inside. The women of the house were all noisy
and inclined to laughter, and often there were neighbors present.

---

1. A member of the Jewish mystic order
that orginated in Poland in the eighteenth
century, stressing the pure heart and devotion but not asceticism and, in Poland,
learning. Sadgora, a small town in Buko-
vina (now U.S.S.R.), whose Jewish residents in the nineteenth century were
mostly Chassidim.
2. The supplementary second part of

the Talmud, commentary on the first part
(Mishnah), together making up the Jewish
civil and religious law.
3. Mystical interpretation of Scriptures.
4. The principal Jewish prayer, which
includes blessings of praise, prayer re-
quests (for understanding, redemption,
etc.), and thanksgiving.

The cooking, baking, knitting, and needlepoint went on with a vengeance, and games of checkers, knucklebones, hide-and-seek, and wolf-and-goat[5] were played. On Chanukkah they rendered chicken fat; after Sukkoth they made coleslaw and pickled cucumbers; in the summers they put up jam. A fire was always kept going in the stove and under a tripod. The kitchen smelled of chicken soup, braised meat, cinnamon, and saffron. Cakes and cookies were baked for the Sabbath and holidays, to go with the roast geese, chickens, and ducks. One day they prepared for a circumcision and another day for the ceremony of redeeming the firstborn son;[6] now one of the family was becoming engaged, and now they all trouped off to a wedding. Tailors fitted coats, cobblers measured feet for shoes. At Reb Bendit Waldman's there was ample occasion to have a drink of cherry or sweet brandy and to nibble at an almond cookie, a babka,[7] or a honey cake. If a guest from another town came to visit, half the town sent over a kugel.[8] Reb Bendit made fun of the women of the house and their exaggerated sense of hospitality, but apparently he, too, enjoyed having his house full of people. Each time he went to Warsaw or Krakow he brought back all kinds of trinkets for the women—embroidered headkerchiefs, rings, shawls, and pins— and for the boys, pocketknives, pens, gold embossed skullcaps, and ornate phylactery bags. Apart from the usual wedding gifts—a set of the Talmud, a gold watch, a wine goblet, a spice box, a prayer shawl with silver brocade—Tanhum had already received all kinds of other presents. It wasn't mere talk when Tanhum's former fellow-students at the Brisk Yeshiva[9] said that he had fallen into a gravy pot. His bride-to-be, Mira Fridl, was considered a beauty, but Tanhum had not yet had a good look at her. How could he? During the signing of the marriage contract the women's parlor was jammed, and in the kitchen Mira Fridl was always surrounded by her sisters and sisters-in-law.

The moment Tanhum crossed the threshhold he lowered his eyes. True, everyone had his destined mate; forty days before he, Tanhum, had been born it had already been decided that Mira Fridl would become his spouse.[1] Still, he fretted that he wasn't a suitable enough son-in-law for Reb Bendit Waldman. All the members of the family were jolly, while he was reticent. He wasn't good at business or quick of tongue, not playful, not good at games, unable to perform stunts or do swimming tricks in the river. At twelve he already had to take free board at the homes of strangers in the towns where he was sent to study at the various yeshivas. His father died when Tanhum was still a child. His mother had remarried. Tanhum's stepfather was a poor peddler and had six children from a previous marriage. From childhood on, Tanhum went around in rags and was

5. Unidentified: there are, however, a Russian children's game and a chess game called wolf-and-sheep.

6. Every firstborn of the womb, man or animal, belongs to the Lord; clean animals must be sacrificed and humans redeemed, usually by the payment of money or its equivalent to the rabbi thirty days after the birth of the firstborn son. See *Exodus* 13:11–16, *Leviticus* 27:26.

7. A cake marblized with soft chocolate.

8. Pudding of noodles or potatoes.

9. The seminary of Brest-Litovsk, Lithuania.

1. Not a contractual arrangement; legend has it that a child's mate is determined in heaven forty days before he or she is born.

neglected. He constantly berated himself for not praying fervently enough or devoting himself sufficiently to Jewishness, and he warred eternally with evil thoughts.

This day, the tumult in the kitchen was louder than ever. Some-one had apparently just told a joke or performed some antic, for the women laughed and clapped their hands. Usually when Tanhum came in, a respectful path was cleared for him, but now he had to push his way through the throng. Who knows, maybe they were making fun of him? The back of his neck felt hot and damp. He must be late, for Reb Bendit was already seated at the table, with his sons and sons-in-law, waiting for him to appear. Reb Bendit, in a flowered robe, his silver-white beard combed into two points and a silk skullcap down over his forehead, lolled grandly in his armchair at the head of the table. The men had apparently had a drink, for a carafe and glasses stood on the table, along with wafers to crunch on. The company was in a joking mood. Reb Bendit's eldest son, Leibush Meir, a big, fleshy fellow with a huge potbelly and a round reddish beard circling his fat face, shook with laughter. Yoshe, a son-in-law—short and round as a barrel and with liquid black eyes and thick lips—giggled into a handkerchief. Another son-in-law, Shlomele, the wag, jokester, and mimic, impudently imitated some-one's gestures.

Reb Bendit asked Tanhum amiably, "You have a gold watch. Why aren't you on time?"

"It stopped running."

"You probably didn't wind it."

"He needs an alarm clock," Schlomele jested.

"Well, go wash your hands," and Reb Bendit pointed to the washstand.

While washing his hands Tanhum wet his sleeves. There was a towel hanging on the rack, but he stood helplessly dripping water on the floor. He often tripped, caught his clothing, and bumped into things, and he constantly had to be told where to go and what to do. There was a mirror in the dining room and Tanhum caught a glimpse of himself—a stooped figure with sunken cheeks, dark eyes below dishevelled brows, a tiny beard on the tip of the chin, a pale nose, and a pointed Adam's apple. It took him a few seconds to realize that he was looking at his reflection. At the table, Reb Bendit praised the dish of groats and asked the woman who had prepared it what ingredients she had used. Leibush Meir demanded a second helping as usual. Shlomele complained that he had found only one mushroom in his portion. After the soup, the conversation turned serious. Reb Bendit had bought a tract of forest in partnership with a Zamosc merchant, Reb Nathan Vengrover. The two partners had fallen out, and Reb Nathan had summoned Reb Bendit to the rabbi's the following Saturday night for a hearing. Reb Bendit complained to the company at lunch that his partner was totally lacking in com-mon sense, a dolt, a ninny, a dunderhead. The sons and sons-in-law agreed that he was a jackass. Tanhum sat in terror. This was evil talk, slander, and who knows what else! According to the Gemara, one lost the world to come for speaking so disrespectfully of another man. Had they forgotten this or did they only pretend to forget? Tanhum

wanted to warn them that they were violating the law: Thou shalt
not go up and down as a talebearer among thy people. According to
the Gemara, he should have stuffed up his ears with the lobes so as
not to hear, but he couldn't embarrass his prospective father-in-law
this way. He sank even lower in his chair. Two women now brought
in the main course—a platter of beef cutlets and a tray of roast
chicken floating in sauce. Tanhum grimaced. How could one eat such
a repast on a weekday? Didn't they remember the destruction of the
Temple?[2]

"Tanhum, are you eating or sleeping?"

It was his intended, Mira Fridl, speaking. Tanhum came to with a
start. He saw her now for the first time—of medium build, fair, with
golden hair and blue eyes, wearing a red dress. She smiled at him
mischievously and even winked.

"Which would you prefer—beef or chicken?"

Tanhum wanted to answer, but the words stuck in his throat. For
some time already, he had felt an aversion to meat. No doubt everything here was strictly kosher, but it seemed to him that the meat
smelled of blood and that he could hear the bellowing of the cow
writhing beneath the slaughterer's knife.

Reb Bendit said, "Give him some of each."

Mira Fridl served a cutlet and then, with her serving spoon poised
over the platter of chicken, asked, "Which would you like—the breast
or a leg?"

Again Tanhum was unable to answer. Instead, Shlomele the wag
said with a leer, "He lusts for both."

As Mira Fridl bent over Tanhum to put a chicken leg on his plate,
her bosom touched his shoulder. She added potatoes and carrots
and Tanhum shrank away from her. He heard Shlomele snicker, and
he was overcome with shame. I don't belong among them, he thought.
They're making a fool of me. . . . He had an urge to stand up and
flee.

"Eat, Tanhum, don't dillydally," Reb Bendit said. "One must have
strength for the Torah."

Tanhum put his fork into the sauce and dug out a sliver of meat,
doused it in horseradish, and sprinkled it with salt to blot out the
taste. He ate a slice of bread. He was intimidated by Mira Fridl.
What would they talk about after the wedding? She was a rich man's
daughter, accustomed to a life of luxury. Her mother had told him
that a goldsmith from Lublin had fashioned jewelry for Mira Fridl.
All kinds of fur coats, jackets, and capes were being sewn for her,
and she would be provided with furniture, rugs, and porcelain. How
could he, Tanhum, exercise control over such a pampered creature?
And why would she want him for a husband? Her father had undoubtedly coerced her into it. He wanted a Talmudist for a son-in-
law. Tanhum envisioned himself standing under the wedding canopy
with Mira Fridl, eating the golden soup,[3] dancing the wedding dance,

2. 2 *Chronicles* 36:19. Because of the
wickedness of Israel and its kings, the
Lord allows the Chaldeans to kill young
men in Solomon's temple, burn it down,
and break down the walls of Jerusalem.

3. The Jewish wedding ceremony takes
place under a canopy (*chuppah*). The
bride and groom fast until after the ceremony, then immediately go into a separate
room to eat, sometimes a more or less
ceremonial food—here, apparently, chicken
soup.

and then being led off to the marriage chamber. He felt a sense of panic. None of this seemed fitting for his oppressed spirit. He began to sway and to beg the Almighty to guard him from temptations, impure thoughts, Satan's net. *Father in Heaven, save me!*

Leibush Meir burst into laughter. "What are you swaying for? It's a chicken leg, not Rashi's commentary."[4]

Reb Nathan was expected to bring his arbitrator, Reb Feivel, to the hearing. Reb Bendit Waldman also had his own arbitrator, Reb Fishel, but nevertheless he invited Tanhum to attend the proceedings too. He said that it would do Tanhum good to learn something about practical matters. If he turned to the rabbinate, he would have to know a little about business. It was entirely feasible that that stubborn villain, Reb Nathan, wouldn't agree to a compromise and would insist on the strict letter of the law, and Reb Bendit asked Tanhum therefore to take down the books and go over the sections that dealt with the codes governing business partnerships. Tanhum agreed reluctantly. The entire Torah was holy, of course, but Tanhum wasn't drawn to those laws dealing with money, manipulation, interests, and swindle. In former years when he studied these subjects in the Gemara, it hadn't occurred to him that there really were Jews who reneged on written agreements, stole, swore falsely, and cheated. The idea of meeting in the flesh a person who would deny a debt, violate a trust, and grow rich from deception was too painful to contemplate. Tanhum wanted to tell Reb Bendit that he had no intention of becoming a rabbi, and that it would be hard for him now to lay aside the treatise in which he was absorbed and turn to matters that were alien to him. But how could he refuse Reb Bendit, who had raised him out of poverty, and given him his daughter for a bride, and provided him with overcoats, underwear, a sheepskin coat, a residence, holy books, a prayer shawl with silver brocade, and a thirteen-pointed fur hat besides? This would have enraged his future mother-in-law and turned Mira Fridl against him. It would have incited a feud and provoked evil gossip. It would have led to who knows what quarrels.

During the next few days, Tanhum didn't have enough time to get deeply into "The Breastplate of Judgment"[5] and its many commentaries. He quickly scanned the text of Rabbi Caro and the annotations of Rabbi Moshe Isserles. He hummed and bit his lips. Obviously even in the old days there had been no lack of frauds and of rascals. Was it any wonder? Even the generation that received the Torah had its Korah, its Dathan, its Abiram.[6] Still, how could theft be reconciled with faith? How could one whose soul had stood on Mount Sinai defile it with crime?

The Din Torah, the hearing, began on Saturday evening, and it

4. Solomon Yitzhaki Rashi (1040–1105), French rabbinical scholar, whose commentary on the whole Talmud helped to establish the text, and whose commentary on the Pentateuch has served as the basis for most later scholarship.

5. The Talmud. Joseph Caro (1488–1575) author of a commentary and its abridgment, *Shulhan Arukh* ("The Pre-pared Table," 1564–65), which, with Moses Isserles' (c.1525–72) critical strictures, *Ha Mappah* ("The Tablecloth") are still considered authoritative by Orthodox Jews.

6. Leaders of the revolt against Moses in the desert who were destroyed by fire and earthquake. *Numbers* 16 and 26:9–11.

looked as though it would last a whole week. The rabbi, Reb Efraim Engel, a patriarch of seventy and author of a book of legal opinions, told his wife to send all those who came seeking advice about other matters to the assistant rabbi. He bolted the door of his study and ordered his beadle to let only the participants enter. On the table stood the candles that had ushered out the Sabbath. The room smelled of wine, wax, and the spice box. From the way the family had decribed Reb Nathan Vengrover as a tough man and a specu- lator, Tanhum expected him to be tall, dark, and with the wild gaze of a gypsy, but in came a thin, stooped little man with a sparse beard the color of pepper, with a milky-white cataract in his left eye, and wearing a faded gaberdine, a sheepskin hat, and coarse boots. Pouches of bluish flesh dangled beneath his eyes and he had warts on his nose. Being the plaintiff, he was the first to speak. He im- mediately began to shout in a hoarse voice, and he kept on shouting and grunting throughout the proceedings.

Reb Bendit smoked an aromatic blend of tobacco in a pipe with an amber cover; Reb Nathan rolled cigarettes of cheap, stinking to- bacco. Reb Bendit spoke deliberately and graced his words with proverbs and quotations from the saints; Reb Nathan slammed the table with his fist, yanked hairs from his beard, and called Reb Bendit a thief. He wouldn't even let his own arbitrator, Reb Feivel—who was the size of a cheder boy,[7] with eyes green as gooseberries and a red beard that fell to his loins—get a word in edgewise. Reb Bendit re- called the details of the agreement from memory, but Reb Nathan consulted whole stackfuls of papers that were filled with row upon row of a clumsy scribble and stained with erasures and blots. He didn't sit in the chair provided for him but paced to and fro, coughed, and spat into a handkerchief. Reb Bendit was sent all kinds of re- freshments and drinks from home, but Reb Nathan didn't even go near the tea that the rabbi's wife brought in. From day to day his face grew more drawn, and was gray as dust and wasted as if from consumption. From nervous tension, he chewed his fingernails and tore his own notes into tiny shreds.

For the first two days, Tanhum was completely bewildered by what went on. The rabbi again and again implored Reb Nathan to speak to the point, not to mix up dates or inject matters that had no bear- ing on the subject. But it all came gushing out of Reb Nathan like water fom a pump. Gradually Tanhum came to understand that his prospective father-in-law was being accused of holding back profits and falsifying accounts. Reb Nathan Vengrover maintained that Reb Bendit had bribed Prince Sapieha's steward to chop down more acres of timber than had been stipulated in the contract. Nor would Reb Bendit allow Reb Nathan and his associate near the Squire, or to get in contact with the merchants who purchased the timber, which was tied in rafts and floated down the Vistula to Danzig. Reb Bendit had allegedly announced one price to Reb Na- than, when he had in fact got a higher one from the merchants. Reb Bendit had claimed to have paid the brokers, loggers, and sawyers

7. Schoolboy.

more than he actually did. He employed every trick and device to oust Reb Nathan from the partnership and to seize all the profits for himself. Reb Nathan pointed out that Reb Bendit had already twice gone bankrupt and subsequently settled for a third of his debts.

Reb Bendit had kept silent most of the time, awaiting his turn to speak, but finally he lost his patience. "Savage!" he shouted. "Hothead! Lunatic!"

"Usurer! Swindler! Robber!" Reb Nathan responded.

On the third day, Reb Bendit calmly began to refute Reb Nathan's charges. He proved that Reb Nathan contradicted himself, exaggerated, and didn't know a pine from an oak. How could he be allowed near the Squire when his Polish was so broken? How could he lay claim to half the income when he, Reb Bendit, had to lay out hush money to the gentry, stave off unfavorable decrees, shower assessors and marshals with gifts out of his own pocket? The more glibly Reb Bendit spoke, the more apparent it became to Tanhum that his prospective father-in-law had broken his agreement and had indeed sought to rob Reb Nathan of the profits and even part of his original investment. But how could this be, Tanhum wondered. How could Reb Bendit, a man in his sixties, a scholar, and a Chassid, commit such iniquities? What was his justification? He knew all the laws. He knew that no repentance could excuse the sin of robbery and theft unless one paid back every penny. The Day of Atonement[8] didn't forgive such transgressions. Could a man who believed in the Creator, in reward and punishment and in immortality of the soul, risk the world to come for the sake of a few thousand gulden?[9] Or was Reb Bendit a secret heretic?

In the closing days, Reb Bendit, his arbitrator, Reb Fishel, and Tanhum didn't go home for dinner—the maid brought them meat and soup. But Tanhum didn't touch the food. There was a gnawing in his stomach. His tongue was dry. He had a bad taste in his mouth, and he felt like vomiting. Although he fasted, his belly was bloated. A lump formed in his throat that he could neither swallow nor disgorge. He didn't weep but his eyes kept tearing over, and he saw everything as if through a mist. Tanhum reminded himself that only that past Sukkoth, when Reb Bendit had gone to the Sadgora rabbi, he had brought the rabbi an ivory ethrog box that was decorated with silver and embossed in gold. Inside, couched in flax, lay an ethrog[10] from Corfu that was pocked and budding. The Chassidim knew that besides contributing generously to the community, of which he was an elder, Reb Bendit also gave the rabbi a tithe. But what was the sense of robbing one person to give to another? Did he do all this to be praised in the Sadgora study houses and be seated at the rabbi's table? Had the greed for money and honors so blinded him that he didn't know the wrongs he committed? Yes, so it seemed, for during evening prayers Reb Bendit piously washed

---

8. Yom Kippur, last of the ten days of Penitence, upon which, by fasting and prayer one may be released from sins or promises made to God, but vows to other men, community, court, or political regime are not annulled.
9. Gold or silver coin of Austria and Germany in wide use through eastern Europe.
10. Citron fruit which, with palm branch (lulab) was used to celebrate—and still symbolizes—the festival of Sukkoth.

his fingers in the basin, girdled his loins with a sash, stationed himself to pray at the eastern wall, swayed, bowed, beat his breast, and sighed. From time to time he stretched his hands up to Heaven. Several times during the arbitration he had invoked God's name.

Thursday night, when it came time to pass judgment, Reb Nathan Vengrover demanded a clear-cut decision: "No compromises! If the law says that what my partner did was right, then I don't demand even a groschen."[1]

"According to law, Reb Bendit has to take an oath," Reb Nathan's arbitrator Reb Feivel, asserted.

"I wouldn't swear even for a sackful of gold," Reb Bendit countered.

"In that case, pay up!"

"Not on your life!"

Both arbitrators, Reb Feivel and Reb Fishel, began to dispute the law. The rabbi drew "The Breastplate of Judgment" down from the bookcase.

Reb Bendit cast a glance at Tanhum. "Tanhum, why don't you speak up?"

Tanhum wanted to say that to appropriate another's possession was as serious an offense as swearing falsely. He also wanted to ask, "Why did you do it?" But he merely mumbled, "Since Father-in-Law signed an agreement, he must honor it."

"So you, too, turn on me, eh?"

"God forbid, but—"

" 'Art thou for us or for our adversaries?' " Reb Bendit quoted from the Book of Joshua,[2] in a dry voice.

"We don't live forever," Tanhum said haltingly.

"You go home!" Reb Bendit ordered.

Tanhum left the rabbi's study and went straight to his room at the inn. He didn't recite the Shema,[3] or undress, but sat on the edge of his cot the whole night. When the light began to break, he packed his Sabbath gaberdine, a few shirts, socks, and books in a straw basket, and walked down Synagogue Street to the bridge that led out of town. Months went by without any news of him. They even dredged the river for his body. Reb Bendit Waldman and Reb Nathan Vengrover reached an agreement. The rabbi and the arbitrators wouldn't permit it to come to oath-taking. Mira Fridl became engaged to a youth from Lublin, the son of a sugar manufacturer. Tanhum had left all his presents behind at the inn, and the bridegroom from Lublin inherited them. One winter day, a shipping agent brought news of Tanhum: he had gone back to the Brisk Yeshiva, from which Reb Bendit originally brought him to his town. Tanhum had become a recluse. He ate no meat, drank no wine, put pebbles inside his shoes, and slept on a bench behind the stove at the study house. When a new match was proposed to him in Brisk, he responded, "My soul yearns for the Torah."

1975

1. I.e., not even a thin dime.
2. *Joshua* 5:13. Before Jericho, Joshua sees a man with drawn sword and asks him this question; the answer: "captain of the host of the Lord."

3. *Shema Yisrael,* "Hear O Israel," the Jewish confession of faith, proclaiming the unity of God, recited morning and evening and on certain special occasions.

JOHN CHEEVER

The Country Husband

To begin at the beginning, the airplane from Minneapolis in which Francis Weed was traveling East ran into heavy weather. The sky had been a hazy blue, with the clouds below the plane lying so close together that nothing could be seen of the earth. Then mist began to form outside the windows, and they flew into a white cloud of such density that it reflected the exhaust fires. The color of the cloud darkened to gray, and the plane began to rock. Francis had been in heavy weather before, but he had never been shaken up so much. The man in the seat beside him pulled a flask out of his pocket and took a drink. Francis smiled at his neighbor, but the man looked away; he wasn't sharing his painkiller with anyone. The plane had begun to drop and flounder wildly. A child was crying. The air in the cabin was overheated and stale, and Francis' left foot went to sleep. He read a little from a paper book that he had bought at the airport, but the violence of the storm divided his attention. It was black outside the ports. The exhaust fires blazed and shed sparks in the dark, and, inside, the shaded lights, the stuffiness, and the window curtains gave the cabin an atmosphere of intense and misplaced domesticity. Then the lights flickered and went out. "You know what I've always wanted to do?" the man beside Francis said suddenly. "I've always wanted to buy a farm in New Hampshire and raise beef cattle." The stewardess announced that they were going to make an emergency landing. All but the child saw in their minds the spreading wings of the Angel of Death. The pilot could be heard singing faintly, "I've got sixpence, jolly, jolly sixpence. I've got sixpence to last me all my life . . ."[1] There was no other sound.

The loud groaning of the hydraulic valves swallowed up the pilot's song, and there was a shrieking high in the air, like automobile brakes, and the plane hit flat on its belly in a cornfield and shook them so violently that an old man up forward howled, "Me kidneys! Me kidneys!" The stewardess flung open the door, and someone opened an emergency door at the back, letting in the sweet noise of their continuing mortality—the idle splash and smell of a heavy rain. Anxious for their lives, they filed out of the doors and scattered over the cornfield in all directions, praying that the thread would hold. It did. Nothing happened. When it was clear that the plane would not burn or explode, the crew and the stewardess gathered the passengers together and led them to the shelter of a barn. They were not far from Philadelphia, and in a little while a string of taxis took them into the city. "It's just like the Marne,"[2] someone said, but there was surprisingly little relaxation of that suspiciousness with which many Americans regard their fellow-travelers.

In Philadelphia, Francis Weed got a train to New York. At the end of that journey, he crossed the city and caught, just as it was about to

1. Song popular with Allied troops in World War II.
2. On September 8, 1914, over 1000 Paris taxicabs were requisitioned to move troops to the Marne River to halt the encircling Germans in what turned out to be the first German defeat of World War I.

pull out, the commuting train that he took five nights a week to his home in Shady Hill.

He sat with Trace Bearden. "You know, I was in that plane that just crashed outside Philadelphia," he said. "We came down in a field . . ." He had traveled faster than the newspapers or the train, and the weather in New York was sunny and mild. It was a day in late September, as fragrant and shapely as an apple. Trace listened to the story, but how could he get excited? Francis had no powers that would let him re-create a brush with death—particularly in the atmosphere of a commuting train, journeying through a sunny countryside where already, in the slum gardens, there were signs of harvest. Trace picked up his newspaper, and Francis was left alone with his thoughts. He said good night to Trace on the platform at Shady Hill and drove in his secondhand Volkswagen up to the Blenhollow neighborhood, where he lived.

The Weeds' Dutch Colonial house was larger than it appeared to be from the driveway. The living room was spacious and divided like Gaul into three parts.[3] Around an ell to the left as one entered from the vestibule was the long table, laid for six, with candles and a bowl of fruit in the center. The sounds and smells that came from the open kitchen door were appetizing, for Julia Weed was a good cook. The largest part of the living room centered around a fireplace. On the right were some bookshelves and a piano. The room was polished and tranquil, and from the windows that opened to the west there was some late-summer sunlight, brilliant and as clear as water. Nothing here was neglected; nothing had not been burnished. It was not the kind of household where, after prying open a stuck cigarette box, you would find an old shirt button and a tarnished nickel. The hearth was swept, the roses on the piano were reflected in the polish of the broad top, and there was an album of Schubert waltzes on the rack. Louisa Weed, a pretty girl of nine, was looking out the western windows. Her younger brother Henry was standing beside her. Her still younger brother, Toby, was studying the figures of some tonsured monks drinking beer on the polished brass of the wood box. Francis, taking off his hat and putting down his paper, was not consciously pleased with the scene; he was not that reflective. It was his element, his creation, and he returned to it with that sense of lightness and strength with which any creature returns to its home. "Hi, everybody," he said. "The plane from Minneapolis . . ."

Nine times out of ten, Francis would be greeted with affection, but tonight the children are absorbed in their own antagonisms. Francis has not finished his sentence about the plane crash before Henry plants a kick in Louisa's behind. Louisa swings around, saying, "*Damn* you!" Francis makes the mistake of scolding Louisa for bad language before he punishes Henry. Now Louisa turns on her father and accuses him of favoritism. Henry is always right; she is persecuted and lonely; her lot is hopeless. Francis turns to his son, but the boy has justification for the kick—she hit him first; she hit him on the ear, which is dangerous. Louisa agrees with this passionately. She hit him on the ear, and she

---

3. Ancient France (Gaul) is so described by Julius Caesar in *The Gallic War*.

meant to hit him on the ear, because he messed up her china collection. Henry says that this is a lie. Little Toby turns away from the wood box to throw in some evidence for Louisa. Henry claps his hand over little Toby's mouth. Francis separates the two boys but accidentally pushes Toby into the wood box. Toby begins to cry. Louisa is already crying. Just then, Julia Weed comes into that part of the room where the table is laid. She is a pretty, intelligent woman, and the white in her hair is premature. She does not seem to notice the fracas. "Hello, darling," she says serenely to Francis. "Wash your hands, everyone. Dinner is ready." She strikes a match and lights the six candles in this vale of tears.[4]

This simple announcement, like the war cries of the Scottish chieftains, only refreshes the ferocity of the combatants. Louisa gives Henry a blow on the shoulder. Henry, although he seldom cries, has pitched nine innings and is tired. He bursts into tears. Little Toby discovers a splinter in his hand and begins to howl. Francis says loudly that he has been in a plane crash and that he is tired. Julia appears again, from the kitchen, and, still ignoring the chaos, asks Francis to go upstairs and tell Helen that everything is ready. Francis is happy to go; it is like getting back to headquarters company.[5] He is planning to tell his oldest daughter about the airplane crash, but Helen is lying on her bed reading a *True Romance* magazine, and the first thing Francis does is to take the magazine from her hand and remind Helen that he has forbidden her to buy it. She did not buy it, Helen replies. It was given to her by her best friend, Bessie Black. Everybody reads *True Romance*. Bessie Black's father reads *True Romance*. There isn't a girl in Helen's class who doesn't read *True Romance*. Francis expresses his detestation of the magazine and then tells her that dinner is ready— although from the sounds downstairs it doesn't seem so. Helen follows him down the stairs. Julia has seated herself in the candlelight and spread a napkin over her lap. Neither Louisa nor Henry has come to the table. Little Toby is still howling, lying face down on the floor. Francis speaks to him gently: "Daddy was in a plane crash this afternoon, Toby. Don't you want to hear about it?" Toby goes on crying. "If you don't come to the table now, Toby," Francis says, "I'll have to send you to bed without any supper." The little boy rises, gives him a cutting look, flies up the stairs to his bedroom, and slams the door. "Oh dear," Julia says, and starts to go after him. Francis says that she will spoil him. Julia says that Toby is ten pounds underweight and has to be encouraged to eat. Winter is coming, and he will spend the cold months in bed unless he has his dinner. Julia goes upstairs. Francis sits down at the table with Helen. Helen is suffering from the dismal feeling of having read too intently on a fine day, and she gives her father and the room a jaded look. She doesn't understand about the plane crash, because there wasn't a drop of rain in Shady Hill.

Julia returns with Toby, and they all sit down and are served. "Do I have to look at that big, fat slob?" Henry says, of Louisa. Everybody but Toby enters into this skirmish, and it rages up and down the table for five minutes. Toward the end, Henry puts his napkin over his

---

4. Common figurative reference to earthly life (vale is valley), though here the tears are literal.

5. That is, like escaping from combat to relative safety behind the lines.

head and, trying to eat that way, spills spinach all over his shirt. Francis asks Julia if the children couldn't have their dinner earlier. Julia's guns are loaded for this. She can't cook two dinners and lay two tables. She paints with lightning strokes that panorama of drudgery in which her youth, her beauty, and her wit have been lost. Francis says that he must be understood; he was nearly killed in an airplane crash, and he doesn't like to come home every night to a battlefield. Now Julia is deeply committed. Her voice trembles. He doesn't come home every night to a battlefield. The accusation is stupid and mean. Everything was tranquil until he arrived. She stops speaking, puts down her knife and fork, and looks into her plate as if it is a gulf. She begins to cry. "Poor Mummy!" Toby says, and when Julia gets up from the table, drying her tears with a napkin, Toby goes to her side. "Poor Mummy," he says. "Poor Mummy!" And they climb the stairs together. The other children drift away from the battlefield, and Francis goes into the back garden for a cigarette and some air.

It was a pleasant garden, with walks and flower beds and places to sit. The sunset had nearly burned out, but there was still plenty of light. Put into a thoughtful mood by the crash and the battle, Francis listened to the evening sounds of Shady Hill. "Varmints! Rascals!" old Mr. Nixon shouted to the squirrels in his bird-feeding station. "Avaunt and quit my sight!" A door slammed. Someone was playing tennis on the Babcocks' court; someone was cutting grass. Then Donald Goslin, who lived at the corner, began to play the "Moonlight Sonata."[6] He did this nearly every night. He threw the tempo out the window and played it *rubato*[7] from beginning to end, like an outpouring of tearful petulance, lonesomeness, and self-pity—of everything it was Beethoven's greatness not to know. The music rang up and down the street beneath the trees like an appeal for love, for tenderness, aimed at some lonely housemaid—some fresh-faced, homesick girl from Galway, looking at old snapshots in her third-floor room. "Here, Jupiter, here, Jupiter," Francis called to the Mercers' retriever. Jupiter crashed through the tomato vines with the remains of a felt hat in his mouth.

Jupiter was an anomaly. His retrieving instincts and his high spirits were out of place in Shady Hill. He was as black as coal, with a long, alert, intelligent, rakehell face. His eyes gleamed with mischief, and he held his head high. It was the fierce, heavily collared dog's head that appears in heraldry, in tapestry, and that used to appear on umbrella handles and walking sticks. Jupiter went where he pleased, ransacking wastebaskets, clotheslines, garbage pails, and shoe bags. He broke up garden parties and tennis matches, and got mixed up in the processional at Christ Church on Sunday, barking at the men in red dresses.[8] He crashed through old Mr. Nixon's rose garden two or three times a day, cutting a wide swath through the Condesa de Sastagos,[9] and as soon as Donald Goslin lighted his barbecue fire on Thursday nights, Jupiter would get the scent. Nothing the Goslins did could drive him

6. Common title of Beethoven's *Sonata Quasi una Fantasia* (1802), one of the most famous, frequently played, and sentimentalized piano compositions.
7. With intentional deviations from strict tempo.
8. Probably the choir.
9. Rather uncommon yellow and red roses difficult to grow.

away. Sticks and stones and rude commands only moved him to the edge of the terrace, where he remained, with his gallant and heraldic muzzle, waiting for Donald Goslin to turn his back and reach for the salt. Then he would spring onto the terrace, lift the steak lightly off the fire, and run away with the Goslins' dinner. Jupiter's days were numbered. The Wrightsons' German gardener or the Farquarsons' cook would soon poison him. Even old Mr. Nixon might put some arsenic in the garbage that Jupiter loved. "Here, Jupiter, Jupiter!" Francis called, but the dog pranced off, shaking the hat in his white teeth. Looking in at the windows of his house, Francis saw that Julia had come down and was blowing out the candles.

Julia and Francis Weed went out a great deal. Julia was well liked and gregarious, and her love of parties sprang from a most natural dread of chaos and loneliness. She went through her morning mail with real anxiety, looking for invitations, and she usually found some, but she was insatiable, and if she had gone out seven nights a week, it would not have cured her of a reflective look—the look of someone who hears distant music—for she would always suppose that there was a more brilliant party somewhere else. Francis limited her to two week-night parties, putting a flexible interpretation on Friday, and rode through the weekend like a dory in a gale. The day after the airplane crash, the Weeds were to have dinner with the Farquarsons.

Francis got home late from town, and Julia got the sitter while he dressed, and then hurried him out of the house. The party was small and pleasant, and Francis settled down to enjoy himself. A new maid passed the drinks. Her hair was dark, and her face was round and pale and seemed familiar to Francis. He had not developed his memory as a sentimental faculty. Wood smoke, lilac, and other such perfumes did not stir him, and his memory was something like his appendix—a vestigial repository. It was not his limitation at all to be unable to escape the past; it was perhaps his limitation that he had escaped it so successfully. He might have seen the maid at other parties, he might have seen her taking a walk on Sunday afternoons, but in either case he would not be searching his memory now. Her face was, in a wonderful way, a moon face—Norman or Irish—but it was not beautiful enough to account for his feeling that he had seen her before, in circumstances that he ought to be able to remember. He asked Nellie Farquarson who she was. Nellie said that the maid had come through an agency, and that her home was Trénon, in Normandy—a small place with a church and a restaurant that Nellie had once visited. While Nellie talked on about her travels abroad, Francis realized where he had seen the woman before. It had been at the end of the war. He had left a replacement depot with some other men and taken a three-day pass in Trénon. On their second day, they had walked out to a crossroads to see the public chastisement of a young woman who had lived with the German commandant during the Occupation.

It was a cool morning in the fall. The sky was overcast, and poured down onto the dirt crossroads a very discouraging light. They were on high land and could see how like one another the shapes of the clouds and the hills were as they stretched off toward the sea. The prisoner arrived sitting on a three-legged stool in a farm cart. She stood by the cart while the mayor read the accusation and the sentence. Her head was bent and her face was set in that empty half smile behind which the whipped soul is suspended. When the mayor was finished, she undid her hair and let it fall across her back. A little man with a gray mustache cut off her hair with shears and dropped it on the ground. Then, with a bowl of soapy water and a straight razor, he shaved her skull clean. A woman approached and began to undo the fastenings of her clothes, but the prisoner pushed her aside and undressed herself. When she pulled her chemise over her head and threw it on the ground, she was naked. The women jeered; the men were still. There was no change in the falseness or the plaintiveness of the prisoner's smile. The cold wind made her white skin rough and hardened the nipples of her breasts. The jeering ended gradually, put down by the recognition of their common humanity. One woman spat on her, but some inviolable grandeur in her nakedness lasted through the ordeal. When the crowd was quiet, she turned—she had begun to cry—and, with nothing on but a pair of worn black shoes and stockings, walked down the dirt road alone away from the village. The round white face had aged a little, but there was no question but that the maid who passed his cocktails and later served Francis his dinner was the woman who had been punished at the crossroads.

The war seemed now so distant and that world where the cost of partisanship had been death or torture so long ago. Francis had lost track of the men who had been with him in Vésey. He could not count on Julia's discretion. He could not tell anyone. And if he had told the story now, at the dinner table, it would have been a social as well as a human error. The people in the Farquarsons' living room seemed united in their tacit claim that there had been no past, no war—that there was no danger or trouble in the world. In the recorded history of human arrangements, this extraordinary meeting would have fallen into place, but the atmosphere of Shady Hill made the memory unseemly and impolite. The prisoner withdrew after passing the coffee, but the encounter left Francis feeling languid; it had opened his memory and his senses, and left them dilated. He and Julia drove home when the party ended, and Julia went into the house. Francis stayed in the car to take the sitter home.

Expecting to see Mrs. Henlein, the old lady who usually stayed with the children, he was surprised when a young girl opened the door and came out onto the lighted stoop. She stayed in the light to count her textbooks. She was frowning and beautiful. Now, the world is full of beautiful young girls, but Francis saw here the difference between beauty and perfection. All those endearing flaws, moles, birthmarks, and healed wounds were missing, and he experienced in his consciousness that moment when music breaks glass, and felt a pang of recognition as strange, deep, and wonderful as anything in his life. It hung from her frown, from an impalpable darkness in her face—a look that impressed him as a direct appeal for love. When she had counted her books, she came down the steps and opened the car door. In the light, he saw that her cheeks were wet. She got in and shut the door.

"You're new," Francis said.

"Yes. Mrs. Henlein is sick. I'm Anne Murchison."

"Did the children give you any trouble?"

"Oh, no, no." She turned and smiled at him unhappily in the dim dashboard light. Her light hair caught on the collar of her jacket, and she shook her head to set it loose.

"You've been crying."

"Yes."

"I hope it was nothing that happened in our house."

"No, no, it was nothing that happened in your house." Her voice was bleak. "It's no secret. Everybody in the village knows. Daddy's an alcoholic, and he just called me from some saloon and gave me a piece of his mind. He thinks I'm immoral. He called just before Mrs. Weed came back."

"I'm sorry."

"Oh, *Lord!*" She gasped and began to cry. She turned toward Francis, and he took her in his arms and let her cry on his shoulder. She shook in his embrace, and this movement accentuated his sense of the fineness of her flesh and bone. The layers of their clothing felt thin, and when her shuddering began to diminish, it was so much like a paroxysm of love that Francis lost his head and pulled her roughly against him. She drew away. "I live on Belleview Avenue," she said. "You go down Lansing Street to the railroad bridge."

"All right." He started the car.

"You turn left at that traffic light. . . . Now you turn right here and go straight on toward the tracks."

The road Francis took brought him out of his own neighborhood, across the tracks, and toward the river, to a street where the near-poor lived, in houses whose peaked gables and trimmings of wooden lace conveyed the purest feelings of pride and romance, although the houses themselves could not have offered much privacy or comfort, they were all so small. The street was dark, and, stirred by the grace and beauty of the troubled girl, he seemed, in turning in to it, to have come into the deepest part of some submerged memory. In the distance, he saw a porch light burning. It was the only one, and she said that the house with the light was where she lived. When he stopped the car, he could see beyond the porch light into a dimly lighted hallway with an old-fashioned clothes tree. "Well, here we are," he said, conscious that a young man would have said something different.

She did not move her hands from the books, where they were folded, and she turned and faced him. There were tears of lust in his eyes. Determinedly—not sadly—he opened the door on his side and walked around to open hers. He took her free hand, letting his fingers in between hers, climbed at her side the two concrete steps, and went up a narrow walk through a front garden where dahlias, marigolds, and roses—things that had withstood the light frosts—still bloomed, and made a bittersweet smell in the night air. At the steps, she freed her hand and then turned and kissed him swiftly. Then she crossed the porch and shut the door. The porch light went out, then the light in the hall. A second later, a light went on upstairs at the side of the house, shining into a tree that was still covered with leaves. It took her only a few minutes to undress and get into bed, and then the house was dark.

Julia was asleep when Francis got home. He opened a second window and got into bed to shut his eyes on that night, but as soon as they were shut—as soon as he had dropped off to sleep—the girl entered his mind, moving with perfect freedom through its shut doors and filling chamber after chamber with her light, her perfume, and the music of her voice. He was crossing the Atlantic with her on the old *Mauretania*[1] and, later, living with her in Paris. When he woke from his dream, he got up and smoked a cigarette at the open window. Getting back into bed, he cast around in his mind for something he desired to do that would injure no one, and he thought of skiing. Up through the dimness in his mind rose the image of a mountain deep in snow. It was late in the day. Wherever his eyes looked, he saw broad and heartening things. Over his shoulder, there was a snow-filled valley, rising into wooded hills where the trees dimmed the whiteness like a sparse coat of hair. The cold deadened all sound but the loud, iron clanking of the lift machinery. The light on the trails was blue, and it was harder than it had been a minute or two earlier to pick the turns, harder to judge—now that the snow was all deep blue—the crust, the ice, the bare spots, and the deep piles of dry powder. Down the mountain he swung, matching his speed against the contours of a slope that had been formed in the first ice age, seeking with ardor some simplicity of feeling and circumstance. Night fell then, and he drank a Martini with some old friend in a dirty country bar.

In the morning, Francis' snow-covered mountain was gone, and he was left with his vivid memories of Paris and the *Mauretania*. He had been bitten gravely. He washed his body, shaved his jaws, drank his coffee, and missed the seven-thirty-one. The train pulled out just as he brought his car to the station, and the longing he felt for the coaches as they drew stubbornly away from him reminded him of the humors of love. He waited for the eight-two, on what was now an empty platform. It was a clear morning; the morning seemed thrown like a gleaming bridge of light over his mixed affairs. His spirits were feverish and high. The image of the girl seemed to put him into a relationship to the world that was mysterious and enthralling. Cars were beginning to fill up the parking lot, and he noticed that those that had driven down from the high land above Shady Hill were white with hoarfrost. This first clear sign of autumn thrilled him. An express train—a night train from Buffalo or Albany—came down the tracks between the platforms, and he saw that the roofs of the foremost cars were covered with a skin of ice. Struck by the miraculous physicalness of everything, he smiled at the passengers in the dining car, who could be seen eating eggs and wiping their mouths with napkins as they traveled. The sleeping-car compartments, with their soiled bed linen, trailed through the fresh morning like a string of rooming-house windows. Then he saw an extraordinary thing; at one of the bedroom windows sat an unclothed woman of exceptional beauty, combining her golden hair. She passed like an apparition through Shady Hill, combing and combing her hair, and Francis followed her with his eyes until she was out of sight. Then old Mrs. Wrightson joined him on the platform and began to talk.

1. The original *Mauretania* (1907–1935), sister ship of the *Lusitania*, which was sunk by the Germans in 1915, was the most famous transatlantic liner of its day and held speed records for more than 20 years.

"Well, I guess you must be surprised to see me here the third morning in a row," she said, "but because of my window curtains I'm becoming a regular commuter. The curtains I bought on Monday I returned on Tuesday, and the curtains I bought Tuesday I'm returning today. On Monday, I got exactly what I wanted—it's a wool tapestry with roses and birds—but when I got them home, I found they were the wrong length. Well, I exchanged them yesterday, and when I got them home, I found they were still the wrong length. Now I'm praying to high Heaven that the decorator will have them in the right length, because you know my house, you *know* my living-room windows, and you can imagine what a problem they present. I don't know what to do with them."

"I know what to do with them," Francis said.

"What?"

"Paint them black on the inside, and shut up."

There was a gasp from Mrs. Wrightson, and Francis looked down at her to be sure that she knew he meant to be rude. She turned and walked away from him, so damaged in spirit that she limped. A wonderful feeling enveloped him, as if light were being shaken about him, and he thought again of Venus combing and combing her hair as she drifted through the Bronx. The realization of how many years had passed since he had enjoyed being deliberately impolite sobered him. Among his friends and neighbors, there were brilliant and gifted people—he saw that—but many of them, also, were bores and fools, and he had made the mistake of listening to them all with equal attention. He had confused a lack of discrimination with Christian love, and the confusion seemed general and destructive. He was grateful to the girl for this bracing sensation of independence. Birds were singing—cardinals and the last of the robins. The sky shone like enamel. Even the smell of ink from his morning paper honed his appetite for life, and the world that was spread out around him was plainly a paradise.

If Francis had believed in some hierarchy of love—in spirits armed with hunting bows, in the capriciousness of Venus and Eros[2]—or even in magical potions, philters, and stews, in scapulae and quarters of the moon,[3] it might have explained his susceptibility and his feverish high spirits. The autumnal loves of middle age are well publicized, and he guessed that he was face to face with one of these, but there was not a trace of autumn in what he felt. He wanted to sport in the green woods, scratch where he itched, and drink from the same cup.

His secretary, Miss Rainey, was late that morning—she went to a psychiatrist three mornings a week—and when she came in, Francis wondered what advice a psychiatrist would have for him. But the girl promised to bring back into his life something like the sound of music. The realization that this music might lead him straight to a trial for statutory rape[4] at the county courthouse collapsed his happiness. The photograph of his four children laughing into the camera on the beach at Gay Head reproached him. On the letterhead of his firm there was

2. The Roman name for the goddess of love (Greek Aphrodite) and the Greek name for her son (Roman Cupid).

3. Love-inducing and predictive magic; *scapulae* are shoulderblades or bones of the back.

4. Criminal charge involving sexual relations with someone below the legal age of consent.

a drawing of the Laocoön[5] and the figure of the priest and his sons in the coils of the snake appeared to him to have the deepest meaning. He had lunch with Pinky Trabert. At a conversational level, the mores of his friends were robust and elastic, but he knew that the moral card house would come down on them all—on Julia and the children as well—if he got caught taking advantage of a babysitter. Looking back over the recent history of Shady Hill for some precedent, he found there was none. There was no turpitude; there had not been a divorce since he lived there; there had not even been a breath of scandal. Things seemed arranged with more propriety even than in the Kingdom of Heaven. After leaving Pinky, Francis went to a jeweler's and bought the girl a bracelet. How happy this clandestine purchase made him, how stuffy and comical the jeweler's clerks seemed, how sweet the women who passed at his back smelled! On Fifth Avenue, passing Atlas with his shoulders bent under the weight of the world,[6] Francis thought of the strenuousness of containing his physicalness within the patterns he had chosen.

He did not know when he would see the girl next. He had the bracelet in his inside pocket when he got home. Opening the door of his house, he found her in the hall. Her back was to him, and she turned when she heard the door close. Her smile was open and loving. Her perfection stunned him like a fine day—a day after a thunderstorm. He seized her and covered her lips with his, and she struggled but she did not have to struggle for long, because just then little Gertrude Flannery appeared from somewhere and said, "Oh, Mr. Weed . . ."

Gertrude was a stray. She had been born with a taste for exploration, and she did not have it in her to center her life with her affectionate parents. People who did not know the Flannerys concluded from Gertrude's behavior that she was the child of a bitterly divided family, where drunken quarrels were the rule. This was not true. The fact that little Gertrude's clothing was ragged and thin was her own triumph over her mother's struggle to dress her warmly and neatly. Garrulous, skinny, and unwashed, she drifted from house to house around the Blenhollow neighborhood, forming and breaking alliances based on an attachment to babies, animals, children her own age, adolescents, and sometimes adults. Opening your front door in the morning, you would find Gertrude sitting on your stoop. Going into the bathroom to shave, you would find Gertrude using the toilet. Looking into your son's crib, you would find it empty, and, looking further, you would find that Gertrude had pushed him in his baby carriage into the next village. She was helpful, pervasive, honest, hungry, and loyal. She never went home of her own choice. When the time to go arrived, she was indifferent to all its signs: "Go home, Gertrude," people could be heard saying in one house or another, night after night. "Go home, Gertrude. It's time for you to go home now, Gertrude." "You had better go home and get your supper, Gertrude." "I told you to go home twenty min-

5. Famous Greek statue, described here, now in the Vatican museum; the "meaning" for Weed seems to reside in the physical struggle, not in the legend (in which the priest and his sons were punished for warning the Trojans about the wooden horse).

6. In Greek legend the Titan Atlas supported the heavens on his shoulders but has come to be depicted as bearing the globe; the statue is at Rockefeller Center.

utes ago, Gertrude." "Your mother will be worrying about you, Gertrude." "Go home, Gertude, go home."

There are times when the lines around the human eye seem like shelves of eroded stone and when the staring eye itself strikes us with such a wilderness of animal feeling that we are at a loss. The look Francis gave the little girl was ugly and queer, and it frightened her. He reached into his pocket—his hands were shaking—and took out a quarter. "Go home, Gertrude, go home, and don't tell anyone, Gertrude. Don't—" He choked and ran into the living room as Julia called down to him from upstairs to hurry and dress.

The thought that he would drive Anne Murchison home later that night ran like a golden thread through the events of the party that Francis and Julia went to, and he laughed uproariously at dull jokes, dried a tear when Mabel Mercer told him about the death of her kitten, and stretched, yawned, sighed, and grunted like any other man with a rendezvous at the back of his mind. The bracelet was in his pocket. As he sat talking, the smell of grass was in his nose, and he was wondering where he would park the car. Nobody lived in the old Parker mansion, and the driveway was used as a lovers' lane. Townsend Street was a dead end, and he could park there, beyond the last house. The old lane that used to connect Elm Street to the riverbanks was overgrown, but he had walked there with his children, and he could drive his car deep enough into the brushwoods to be concealed.

The Weeds were the last to leave the party, and their host and hostess spoke of their own married happiness while they all four stood in the hallway saying good night. "She's my girl," their host said, squeezing his wife. "She's my blue sky. After sixteen years, I still bite her shoulders. She makes me feel like Hannibal crossing the Alps."[7]

The Weeds drove home in silence. Francis brought the car up the driveway and sat still, with the motor running. "You can put the car in the garage," Julia said as she got out. "I told the Murchison girl she could leave at eleven. Someone drove her home." She shut the door, and Francis sat in the dark. He would be spared nothing then, it seemed, that a fool was not spared: ravening lewdness, jealousy, this hurt to his feelings that put tears in his eyes, even scorn—for he could see clearly the image he now presented, his arms spread over the steering wheel and his head buried in them for love.

Francis had been a dedicated Boy Scout when he was young, and, remembering the precepts of his youth, he left his office early the next afternoon and played some round-robin squash, but, with his body toned up by exercise and a shower, he realized that he might better have stayed at his desk. It was a frosty night when he got home. The air smelled sharply of change. When he stepped into the house, he sensed an unusual stir. The children were in their best clothes, and when Julia came down, she was wearing a lavender dress and her diamond sunburst. She explained the stir: Mr. Hubber was coming at seven to take their photograph for the Christmas card. She had put out Francis' blue suit and a tie with some color in it, because the picture was going to be in color this year. Julia was lighthearted at the

7. The Carthaginian general (274–183 B.C.) attacked the Romans from the rear by crossing the Alps, considered impregnable, with the use of elephants.

thought of being photographed for Christmas. It was the kind of ceremony she enjoyed.

Francis went upstairs to change his clothes. He was tired from the day's work and tired with longing, and sitting on the edge of the bed had the effect of deepening his weariness. He thought of Anne Murchison, and the physical need to express himself, instead of being restrained by the pink lamps on Julia's dressing table, engulfed him. He went to Julia's desk, took a piece of writing paper, and began to write on it. "Dear Anne, I love you, I love you, I love you . . ." No one would see the letter, and he used no restraint. He used phrases like "heavenly bliss," and "love nest." He salivated, sighed, and trembled. When Julia called him to come down, the abyss between his fantasy and the practical world opened so wide that he felt it affect the muscles of his heart.

Julia and the children were on the stoop, and the photographer and his assistant had set up a double battery of floodlights to show the family and the architectural beauty of the entrance to their house. People who had come home on a late train slowed their cars to see the Weeds being photographed for their Christmas card. A few waved and called to the family. It took half an hour of smiling and wetting their lips before Mr. Hubber was satisfied. The heat of the lights made an unfresh smell in the frosty air, and when they were turned off, they lingered on the retina of Francis' eyes.

Later that night, while Francis and Julia were drinking their coffee in the living room, the doorbell rang. Julia answered the door and let in Clayton Thomas. He had come to pay her for some theater tickets that she had given his mother some time ago, and that Helen Thomas had scrupulously insisted on paying for, though Julia had asked her not to. Julia invited him in to have a cup of coffee. "I won't have any coffee," Clayton said, "but I will come in for a minute." He followed her into the living room, said good evening to Francis, and sat awkwardly in a chair.

Clayton's father had been killed in the war, and the young man's fatherlessness surrounded him like an element. This may have been conspicuous in Shady Hill because the Thomases were the only family that lacked a piece; all the other marriages were intact and productive. Clayton was in his second or third year of college, and he and his mother lived alone in a large house, which she hoped to sell. Clayton had once made some trouble. Years ago, he had stolen some money and run away; he had got to California before they caught up with him. He was tall and homely, wore horn-rimmed glasses, and spoke in a deep voice.

"When do you go back to college, Clayton?" Francis asked.

"I'm not going back," Clayton said. "Mother doesn't have the money, and there's no sense in all this pretense. I'm going to get a job, and if we sell the house, we'll take an apartment in New York."

"Won't you miss Shady Hill?" Julia asked.

"No," Clayton said. "I don't like it."

"Why not?" Francis asked.

"Well, there's a lot here I don't approve of," Clayton said gravely. "Things like the club dances. Last Saturday night, I looked in toward the end and saw Mr. Granner trying to put Mrs. Minot into the trophy case. They were both drunk. I disapprove of so much drinking."

"It was Saturday night," Francis said.

"And all the dovecotes are phony," Clayton said. "And the way people clutter up their lives. I've thought about it a lot, and what seems to me to be really wrong with Shady Hill is that it doesn't have any future. So much energy is spent in perpetuating the place—in keeping out undesirables, and so forth—that the only idea of the future anyone has is just more and more commuting trains and more parties. I don't think that's healthy. I think people ought to be able to dream big dreams about the future. I think people ought to be able to dream great dreams."

"It's too bad you couldn't continue with college," Julia said.

"I wanted to go to divinity school," Clayton said.

"What's your church?" Francis asked.

"Unitarian, Theosophist, Transcendentalist, Humanist,"[8] Clayton said.

"Wasn't Emerson a transcendentalist?" Julia asked.

"I mean the English transcendentalists," Clayton said. "All the American transcendentalists were goops."

"What kind of a job do you expect to get?" Francis asked.

"Well, I'd like to work for a publisher," Clayton said, "but everyone tells me there's nothing doing. But it's the kind of thing I'm interested in. I'm writing a long verse play about good and evil. Uncle Charlie might get me into a bank, and that would be good for me. I need the discipline. I have a long way to go in forming my character. I have some terrible habits. I talk too much. I think I ought to take vows of silence. I ought to try not to speak for a week, and discipline myself. I've thought of making a retreat at one of the Episcopalian monasteries, but I don't like the Trinitarianism."

"Do you have any girl friends?" Francis asked.

"I'm engaged to be married," Clayton said. "Of course, I'm not old enough or rich enough to have my engagement observed or respected or anything, but I bought a simulated emerald for Anne Murchison with the money I made cutting lawns this summer. We're going to be married as soon as she finishes school."

Francis recoiled at the mention of the girl's name. Then a dingy light seemed to emanate from his spirit, showing everything—Julia, the boy, the chairs—in their true colorlessness. It was like a bitter turn of the weather.

"We're going to have a large family," Clayton said. "Her father's a terrible rummy, and I've had my hard times, and we want to have lots of children. Oh, she's wonderful, Mr. and Mrs. Weed, and we have so much in common. We like all the same things. We sent out the same Christmas card last year without planning it, and we both have an allergy to tomatoes, and our eyebrows grow together in the middle. Well, good night."

Julia went to the door with him. When she returned. Francis said that Clayton was lazy, irresponsible, affected, and smelly. Julia said

8. All are deviations from orthodox Christianity and tend to be more man-than God-oriented, though their differences hardly seem reconcilable; the American Transcendentalists (see below) tended to change the emphasis from the study of thought rather than of sense objects among the English Transcendentalists to belief in "intuition."

that Francis seemed to be getting intolerant; the Thomas boy was young and should be given a chance. Julia had noticed other cases where Francis had been short-tempered. "Mrs. Wrightson has asked everyone in Shady Hill to her anniversary party but us," she said.

"I'm sorry, Julia."

"Do you know why they didn't ask us?"

"Why?"

"Because you insulted Mrs. Wrightson."

"Then you know about it?"

"June Masterson told me. She was standing behind you."

Julia walked in front of the sofa with a small step that expressed, Francis knew, a feeling of anger.

"I did insult Mrs. Wrightson, Julia, and I meant to. I've never liked her parties, and I'm glad she's dropped us."

"What about Helen?"

"How does Helen come into this?"

"Mrs. Wrightson's the one who decides who goes to the assemblies."

"You mean she can keep Helen from going to the dances?"

"Yes."

"I hadn't thought of that."

"Oh, I knew you hadn't thought of it," Julia cried, thrusting hilt-deep into this chink of his armor. "And it makes me furious to see this kind of stupid thoughtlessness wreck everyone's happiness."

"I don't think I've wrecked anyone's happiness."

"Mrs. Wrightson runs Shady Hill and has run it for the last forty years. I don't know what makes you think that in a community like this you can indulge every impulse you have to be insulting, vulgar, and offensive."

"I have very good manners," Francis said, trying to give the evening a turn toward the light.

"Damn you, Francis Weed!" Julia cried, and the spit of her words struck him in the face. "I've worked hard for the social position we enjoy in this place, and I won't stand by and see you wreck it. You must have understood when you settled here that you couldn't expect to live like a bear in a cave."

"I've got to express my likes and dislikes."

"You can conceal your dislikes. You don't have to meet everything head-on, like a child. Unless you're anxious to be a social leper. It's no accident that we get asked out a great deal. It's no accident that Helen has so many friends. How would you like to spend your Saturday nights at the movies? How would you like to spend your Sundays raking up dead leaves? How would you like it if your daughter spent the assembly nights sitting at her window, listening to the music from the club? How would you like it—" He did something then that was, after all, not so unaccountable, since her words seemed to raise up between them a wall so deadening that he gagged: He struck her full in the face. She staggered and then, a moment later, seemed composed. She went up the stairs to their room. She didn't slam the door. When Francis followed, a few minutes later, he found her packing a suitcase.

"Julia, I'm very sorry."

"It doesn't matter," she said. She was crying.

"Where do you think you're going?"

"I don't know. I just looked at a timetable. There's an eleven-sixteen into New York. I'll take that."

"You can't go, Julia."

"I can't stay. I know that."

"I'm sorry about Mrs. Wrightson, Julia, and I'm—"

"It doesn't matter about Mrs. Wrightson. That isn't the trouble."

"What is the trouble?"

"You don't love me."

"I do love you, Julia."

"No, you don't."

"Julia, I do love you, and I would like to be as we were—sweet and bawdy and dark—but now there are so many people."

"You hate me."

"I don't hate you, Julia."

"You have no idea of how much you hate me. I think it's subconscious. You don't realize the cruel things you've done."

"What cruel things, Julia?"

"The cruel acts your subconscious drives you to in order to express your hatred of me."

"What, Julia?"

"I've never complained."

"Tell me."

"You don't know what you're doing."

"Tell me."

"Your clothes."

"What do you mean?"

"I mean the way you leave your dirty clothes around in order to express your subconscious hatred of me."

"I don't understand."

"I mean your dirty socks and your dirty pajamas and your dirty underwear and your dirty shirts!" She rose from kneeling by the suitcase and faced him, her eyes blazing and her voice ringing with emotion. "I'm talking about the fact that you've never learned to hang up anything. You just leave your clothes all over the floor where they drop, in order to humiliate me. You do it on purpose!" She fell on the bed, sobbing.

"Julia, darling!" he said, but when she felt his hand on her shoulder she got up.

"Leave me alone," she said. "I have to go." She brushed past him to the closet and came back with a dress. "I'm not taking any of the things you've given me," she said. "I'm leaving my pearls and the fur jacket."

"Oh, Julia!" Her figure, so helpless in its self-deceptions, bent over the suitcase made him nearly sick with pity. She did not understand how desolate her life would be without him. She didn't understand the hours that working women have to keep. She didn't understand that most of her friendships existed within the framework of their marriage, and that without this she would find herself alone. She didn't understand about travel, about hotels, about money. "Julia, I can't let you go! What you don't understand, Julia, is that you've come to be dependent on me."

She tossed her head back and covered her face with her hands. "Did you say that I was dependent on you?" she asked. "Is that what you said? And who is it that tells you what time to get up in the morning and when to go to bed at night? Who is it that prepares your meals and picks up your dirty clothes and invites your friends to dinner? If it weren't for me, your neckties would be greasy and your clothing would be full of moth holes. You were alone when I met you, Francis Weed, and you'll be alone when I leave. When Mother asked you for a list to send out invitations to our wedding, how many names did you have to give her? Fourteen!"

"Cleveland wasn't my home, Julia."

"And how many of your friends came to the church? Two!"

"Cleveland wasn't my home, Julia."

"Since I'm not taking the fur jacket," she said quietly, "you'd better put it back into storage. There's an insurance policy on the pearls that comes due in January. The name of the laundry and the maid's telephone number—all those things are in my desk. I hope you won't drink too much, Francis. I hope that nothing bad will happen to you. If you do get into serious trouble, you can call me."

"Oh, my darling, I can't let you go!" Francis said. "I can't let you go, Julia!" He took her in his arms.

"I guess I'd better stay and take care of you for a little while longer," she said.

Riding to work in the morning, Francis saw the girl walk down the aisle of the coach. He was surprised; he hadn't realized that the school she went to was in the city, but she was carrying books, she seemed to be going to school. His surprise delayed his reaction, but then he got up clumsily and stepped into the aisle. Several people had come between them, but he could see her ahead of him, waiting for someone to open the car door, and then, as the train swerved, putting out her hand to support herself as she crossed the platform into the next car. He followed her through that car and halfway through another before calling her name—"Anne! Anne!"—but she didn't turn. He followed her into still another car, and she sat down in an aisle seat. Coming up to her, all his feelings warm and bent in her direction, he put his hand on the back of her seat—even this touch warmed him—and, leaning down to speak to her, he saw that it was not Anne. It was an older woman wearing glasses. He went on deliberately into another car, his face red with embarrassment and the much deeper feeling of having his good sense challenged; for if he couldn't tell one person from another, what evidence was there that his life with Julia and the children had as much reality as his dreams of iniquity in Paris or the litter, the grass smell, and the cave-shaped trees in Lovers' Lane.

Late that afternoon, Julia called to remind Francis that they were going out for dinner. A few minutes later, Trace Bearden called. "Look, fellar," Trace said. "I'm calling for Mrs. Thomas. You know? Clayton, that boy of hers, doesn't seem able to get a job, and I wondered if you could help. If you'd call Charlie Bell—I know he's indebted to you—and say a good word for the kid, I think Charlie would—"

"Trace, I hate to say this," Francis said, "but I don't feel that I can do anything for that boy. The kid's worthless. I know it's a harsh thing to say, but it's a fact. Any kindness done for him would backfire in everybody's face. He's just a worthless kid, Trace, and there's nothing

to be done about it. Even if we got him a job, he wouldn't be able to
keep it for a week. I know that to be a fact. It's an awful thing, Trace,
and I know it is, but instead of recommending that kid, I'd feel obliged
to warn people against him—people who knew his father and would
naturally want to step in and do something. I'd feel obliged to warn
them. He's a thief . . ."

The moment this conversation was finished. Miss Rainey came in
and stood by his desk. "I'm not going to be able to work for you any
more, Mr. Weed," she said. "I can stay until the seventeenth if you
need me, but I've been offered a whirlwind of a job, and I'd like to
leave as soon as possible."

She went out, leaving him to face alone the wickedness of what he
had done to the Thomas boy. His children in their photograph laughed
and laughed, glazed with all the bright colors of summer, and he remembered that they had met a bagpiper on the beach that day and
he had paid the piper a dollar to play them a battle song of the Black
Watch.[9] The girl would be at the house when he got home. He would
spend another evening among his kind neighbors, picking and choosing
dead-end streets, cart tracks, and the driveways of abandoned houses.
There was nothing to mitigate his feeling—nothing that laughter or
a game of softball with the children would change—and, thinking
back over the plane crash, the Farquarsons' new maid, and Anne
Murchison's difficulties with her drunken father, he wondered how he
could have avoided arriving at just where he was. He was in trouble.
He had been lost once in his life, coming back from a trout stream in
the north woods, and he had now the same bleak realization that no
amount of cheerfulness or hopefulness or valor or perseverance could
help him find, in the gathering dark, the path that he'd lost. He
smelled the forest. The feeling of bleakness was intolerable, and he
saw clearly that he had reached the point where he would have to
make a choice.

He could go to a psychiatrist, like Miss Rainey; he could go to
church and confess his lusts; he could go to a Danish massage parlor[1]
in the West Seventies that had been recommended by a salesman; he
could rape the girl or trust that he would somehow be prevented from
doing this; or he could get drunk. It was his life, his boat, and, like every
other man, he was made to be the father of thousands, and what harm
could there be in a tryst that would make them both feel more kindly
toward the world? This was the wrong train of thought, and he came
back to the first, the psychiatrist. He had the telephone number of
Miss Rainey's doctor, and he called and asked for an immediate appointment. He was insistent with the doctor's secretary—it was his
manner in business—and when she said that the doctor's schedule was
full for the next few weeks, Francis demanded an appointment that day
and was told to come at five.

The psychiatrist's office was in a building that was used mostly by
doctors and dentists, and the hallways were filled with the candy smell
of mouthwash and memories of pain. Francis' character had been
formed upon a series of private resolves—resolves about cleanliness,

---

9. Originally a British Highland regiment that became a line regiment and distinguished itself in battle, including World
War II battles.
1. Sometimes "fronts" for houses of
prostitution.

about going off the high diving board or repeating any other feat that challenged his courage, about punctuality, honesty, and virtue. To abdicate the perfect loneliness in which he had made his most vital decisions shattered his concept of character and left him now in a condition that felt like shock. He was stupefied. The scene for his *miserere mei Deus*[2] was, like the waiting room of so many doctors' offices, a crude token gesture toward the sweets of domestic bliss: a place arranged with antiques, coffee tables, potted plants, and etchings of snow-covered bridges and geese in flight, although there were no children, no marriage bed, no stove, even, in this travesty of a house, where no one had ever spent the night and where the curtained windows looked straight onto a dark air shaft. Francis gave his name and address to a secretary and then saw, at the side of the room, a policeman moving toward him. "Hold it, hold it," the policeman said. "Don't move. Keep your hands where they are."

"I think it's all right, officer," the secretary began. "I think it will be—"

"Let's make sure," the policeman said, and he began to slap Francis' clothes, looking for what—pistols, knives, an icepick? Finding nothing, he went off, and the secretary began a nervous apology: "When you called on the telephone, Mr. Weed, you seemed very excited, and one of the doctor's patients has been threatening his life, and we have to be careful. If you want to go in now?" Francis pushed open a door connected to an electrical chime, and in the doctor's lair sat down heavily, blew his nose into a handkerchief, searched in his pockets for cigarettes, for matches, for something, and said hoarsely, with tears in his eyes, "I'm in love, Dr. Herzog."

It is a week or ten days later in Shady Hill. The seven-fourteen has come and gone, and here and there dinner is finished and the dishes are in the dish-washing machine. The village hangs, morally and economically, from a thread; but it hangs by its thread in the evening light. Donald Goslin has begun to worry the "Moonlight Sonata" again. *Marcato ma sempre pianissimo!*[3] He seems to be wringing out a wet bath towel, but the housemaid does not heed him. She is writing a letter to Arthur Godfrey.[4] In the cellar of his house, Francis Weed is building a coffee table. Dr. Herzog recommended woodwork as a therapy, and Francis finds some true consolation in the simple arithmetic involved and in the holy smell of new wood. Francis is happy. Upstairs, little Toby is crying, because he is tired. He puts off his cowboy hat, gloves, and fringed jacket, unbuckles the belt studded with gold and rubies, the silver bullets and holsters, slips off his suspenders, his checked shirt, and Levis, and sits on the edge of his bed to pull off his high boots. Leaving this equipment in a heap, he goes to the closet and takes his space suit off a nail. It is a struggle for him to get into the long tights, but he succeeds. He loops the magic cape over his shoulders and, climbing onto the footboard of his bed, he spreads his arms and flies the short distance to the floor, landing with a thump that is audible to everyone in the house but himself.

---

2. "Have mercy upon me, O God"; first words of 51st Psalm.
3. Stressed but still very softly.

4. At the time of the story, host of a daytime radio program especially popular with housewives.

"Go home, Gertrude, go home," Mrs. Masterson says. "I told you to go home an hour ago, Gertrude. It's way past your suppertime, and your mother will be worried. Go home!" A door on the Babcocks' terrace flies open, and out comes Mrs. Babcock without any clothes on, pursued by her naked husband. (Their children are away at boarding school, and their terrace is screened by a hedge.) Over the terrace they go and in at the kitchen door, as passionate and handsome a nymph and satyr[5] as you will find on any wall in Venice. Cutting the last of the roses in her garden, Julia hears old Mr. Nixon shouting at the squirrels in his bird-feeding station. "Rapscallions! Varmints! Avaunt and quit my sight!" A miserable cat wanders into the garden, sunk in spiritual and physical discomfort. Tied to its head is a small straw hat—a doll's hat—and it is securely buttoned into a doll's dress, from the skirts of which protrudes its long, hairy tail. As it walks, it shakes its feet, as if it had fallen into water.

"Here, pussy, pussy, pussy!" Julia calls.

"Here, pussy, here, poor pussy!" But the cat gives her a skeptical look and stumbles away in its skirts. The last to come is Jupiter. He prances through the tomato vines, holding in his generous mouth the remains of an evening slipper. Then it is dark; it is a night where kings in golden suits ride elephants over the mountains.

1958

GRACE PALEY

A Conversation with My Father

My father is eighty-six years old and in bed. His heart, that bloody motor, is equally old and will not do certain jobs any more. It still floods his head with brainy light. But it won't let his legs carry the weight of his body around the house. Despite my metaphors, this muscle failure is not due to his old heart, he says, but to a potassium shortage. Sitting on one pillow, leaning on three, he offers last-minute advice and makes a request.

"I would like you to write a simple story just once more," he says, "the kind de Maupassant wrote, or Chekhov,[1] the kind you used to write. Just recognizable people and then write down what happened to them next."

I say, "Yes, why not? That's possible." I want to please him, though I don't remember writing that way. I *would* like to try to tell such a story, if he means the kind that begins: "There was a woman . . ." followed by plot, the absolute line between two points which I've always despised. Not for literary reasons, but because it takes all hope

5. Minor nature goddesses and mythical woodland gods half man, half goat; the terms are often used to refer to beautiful young girls and to lecherous men.
1. Guy de Maupassant (1850–93) wrote

heavily plotted, ironic stories, Chekhov realistic stories that often had no resolution (see *Lady with the Dog*) and sometimes with little plot.

away. Everyone, real or invented, deserves the open destiny of life.

Finally I thought of a story that had been happening for a couple of years right across the street. I wrote it down, then read it aloud. "Pa," I said, "how about this? Do you mean something like this?"

Once in my time there was a woman and she had a son. They lived nicely, in a small apartment in Manhattan. This boy at about fifteen became a junkie, which is not unusual in our neighborhood. In order to maintain her close friendship with him, she became a junkie too. She said it was part of the youth culture, with which she felt very much at home. After a while, for a number of reasons, the boy gave it all up and left the city and his mother in disgust. Hopeless and alone, she grieved. We all visit her.

"O.K., Pa, that's it," I said, "an unadorned and miserable tale."

"But that's not what I mean," my father said. "You misunderstood me on purpose. You know there's a lot more to it. You know that. You left everything out. Turgenev[2] wouldn't do that. Chekhov wouldn't do that. There are in fact Russian writers you never heard of, you don't have an inkling of, as good as anyone, who can write a plain ordinary story, who would not leave out what you have left out. I object not to facts but to people sitting in trees talking senselessly, voices from who knows where . . ."

"Forget that one, Pa, what have I left out now? In this one?"

"Her looks, for instance."

"Oh. Quite handsome, I think. Yes."

"Her hair?"

"Dark, with heavy braids, as though she were a girl or a foreigner."

"What were her parents like, her stock? That she became such a person. It's interesting, you know."

"From out of town. Professional people. The first to be divorced in their county. How's that? Enough?" I asked.

"With you, it's all a joke," he said. "What about the boy's father? Why didn't you mention him? Who was he? Or was the boy born out of wedlock?"

"Yes," I said. "He was born out of wedlock."

"For Godsakes, doesn't anyone in your stories get married? Doesn't anyone have the time to run down to City Hall before they jump into bed?"

"No," I said. "In real life, yes. But in my stories, no."

"Why do you answer me like that?"

"Oh, Pa, this is a simple story about a smart woman who came to N.Y.C. full of interest love trust excitement very up to date, and about her son, what a hard time she had in this world. Married or not, it's of small consequence."

"It is of great consequence," he said.

"O.K.," I said.

2. Ivan Sergevich Turgenev (1818–1883) wrote stories and novels deeply embedded in the culture of his time; his best-known novel, *Fathers and Sons*, deals with the conflict between generations.

"O.K. O.K. yourself," he said, "but listen. I believe you that she's good-looking, but I don't think she was so smart."

"That's true," I said. "Actually that's the trouble with stories. People start out fantastic. You think they're extraordinary, but it turns out as the work goes along, they're just average with a good education. Sometimes the other way around, the person's a kind of dumb innocent, but he outwits you and you can't even think of an ending good enough."

"What do you do then?" he asked. He had been a doctor for a couple of decades and then an artist for a couple of decades and he's still interested in details, craft, technique.

"Well, you just have to let the story lie around till some agreement can be reached between you and the stubborn hero."

"Aren't you talking silly, now?" he asked. "Start again," he said. "It so happens I'm not going out this evening. Tell the story again. See what you can do this time."

"O.K.," I said. "But it's not a five-minute job." Second attempt:

Once, across the street from us, there was a fine handsome woman, our neighbor. She had a son whom she loved because she'd known him since birth (in helpless chubby infancy, and in the wrestling, hugging ages, seven to ten, as well as earlier and later). This boy, when he fell into the fist of adolescence, became a junkie. He was not a hopeless one. He was in fact hopeful, an ideologue and successful converter. With his busy brilliance, he wrote persuasive articles for his high-school newspaper. Seeking a wider audience, using important connections, he drummed into Lower Manhattan newsstand distribution a periodical called *Oh! Golden Horse!*

In order to keep him from feeling guilty (because guilt is the stony heart of nine tenths of all clinically diagnosed cancers in America today, she said), and because she had always believed in giving bad habits room at home where one could keep an eye on them, she too became a junkie. Her kitchen was famous for a while—a center for intellectual addicts who knew what they were doing. A few felt artistic like Coleridge and others were scientific and revolutionary like Leary.[3] Although she was often high herself, certain good mothering reflexes remained, and she saw to it that there was lots of orange juice around and honey and milk and vitamin pills. However, she never cooked anything but chili, and that no more than once a week. She explained, when we talked to her, seriously, with neighborly concern, that it was her part in the youth culture and she would rather be with the young, it was an honor, than with her own generation.

One week, while nodding through an Antonioni[4] film, this boy was severely jabbed by the elbow of a stern and proselytizing girl, sitting beside him. She offered immediate apricots and nuts for his sugar level, spoke to him sharply, and took him home.

3. Samuel Taylor Coleridge (1772–1834), English Romantic poet, says he wrote his allegedly unfinished poem *Kubla Khan* in an opium dream. Timothy Leary (b. 1920), American psychologist who promoted the use of psychedelic drugs.

4. Michelangelo Antonioni (b. 1912), Italian director (*Blow-Up*, *Zabriskie Point*), whose neo-realist, often slow-moving films investigate society.

She had heard of him and his work and she herself published, edited, and wrote a competitive journal called *Man Does Live By Bread Alone.* In the organic heat of her continuous presence he could not help but become interested once more in his muscles, his arteries, and nerve connections. In fact he began to love them, treasure them, praise them with funny little songs in *Man does Live* . . .

> *the fingers of my flesh transcend*
> *my transcendental soul*
> *the tightness in my shoulders end*
> *my teeth have made me whole*

To the mouth of his head (that glory of will and determination) he brought hard apples, nuts, wheat germ, and soybean oil. He said to his old friends, From now on, I guess I'll keep my wits about me. I'm going on the natch. He said he was about to begin a spiritual deep-breathing journey. How about you too, Mom? he asked kindly.

His conversion was so radiant, splendid, that neighborhood kids his age began to say that he had never been a real addict at all, only a journalist along for the smell of the story. The mother tried several times to give up what had become without her son and his friends a lonely habit. This effort only brought it to supportable levels. The boy and his girl took their electronic mimeograph and moved to the bushy edge of another borough. They were very strict. They said they would not see her again until she had been off drugs for sixty days.

At home alone in the evening, weeping, the mother read and reread the seven issues of *Oh! Golden Horse!* They seemed to her as truthful as ever. We often crossed the street to visit and console. But if we mentioned any of our children who were at college or in the hospital or dropouts at home, she would cry out, My baby! My baby! and burst into terrible, face-scarring, time-consuming tears. The End.

First my father was silent, then he said, "Number One: You have a nice sense of humor. Number Two: I see you can't tell a plain story. So don't waste time." Then he said sadly, "Number Three: I suppose that means she was alone, she was left like that, his mother. Alone. Probably sick?"

I said, "Yes."

"Poor woman. Poor girl, to be born in a time of fools, to live among fools. The end. The end. You were right to put that down. The end."

I didn't want to argue, but I had to say, "Well, it is not necessarily the end, Pa."

"Yes," he said, "what a tragedy. The end of a person."

"No, Pa," I begged him. "It doesn't have to be. She's only about forty. She could be a hundred different things in this world as time goes on. A teacher or a social worker. An ex-junkie! Sometimes it's better than having a master's in education."

"Jokes," he said. "As a writer that's your main trouble. You don't want to recognize it. Tragedy! Plain tragedy! Historical tragedy! No hope. The end."

"Oh, Pa," I said. "She could change."

"In your own life, too, you have to look it in the face." He took a couple of nitroglycerin.[5] "Turn to five," he said, pointing to the dial on the oxygen tank. He inserted the tubes into his nostrils and breathed deep. He closed his eyes and said, "No."

I had promised the family to always let him have the last word when arguing, but in this case I had a different responsibility. That woman lives across the street. She's my knowledge and my invention. I'm sorry for her. I'm not going to leave her there in that house crying. (Actually neither would Life, which unlike me has no pity.)

Therefore: She did change. Of course her son never came home again. But right now, she's the receptionist in a storefront community clinic in the East Village. Most of the customers are young people, some old friends. The head doctor has said to her, "If we only had three people in this clinic with your experiences . . ."

"The doctor said that?" My father took the oxygen tubes out of his nostrils and said, "Jokes. Jokes again."

"No, Pa, it could really happen that way, it's a funny world nowadays."

"No," he said. "Truth first. She will slide back. A person must have character. She does not."

"No, Pa," I said. "That's it. She's got a job. Forget it. She's in that storefront working."

"How long will it be?" he asked. "Tragedy! You too. When will you look it in the face?"

1974

WOODY ALLEN

The Kugelmass Episode

Kugelmass, a professor of humanities at City College, was unhappily married for the second time. Daphne Kugelmass was an oaf. He also had two dull sons by his first wife, Flo, and was up to his neck in alimony and child support.

"Did I know it would turn out so badly?" Kugelmass whined to his analyst one day. "Daphne had promise. Who suspected she'd let herself go and swell up like a beach ball? Plus she had a few bucks, which is not in itself a healthy reason to marry a person, but it doesn't hurt, with the kind of operating nut[1] I have. You see my point?"

Kugelmass was bald and as hairy as a bear, but he had soul.

"I need to meet a new woman," he went on. "I need to have an affair. I may not look the part, but I'm a man who needs romance. I need softness, I need flirtation. I'm not getting younger, so before it's too late I want to make love in Venice, trade quips at '21,'[2] and exchange coy glances over red wine and candlelight. You see what I'm saying?"

5. Medicine for certain heart conditions.   2. Celebrity nightclub and restaurant.
1. Budget, expenses.

Dr. Mandel shifted in his chair and said, "An affair will solve nothing. You're so unrealistic. Your problems run much deeper."

"And also this affair must be discreet," Kugelmass continued. "I can't afford a second divorce. Daphne would really sock it to me."

"Mr. Kugelmass—"

"But it can't be anyone at City College, because Daphne also works there. Not that anyone on the faculty at C.C.N.Y. is any great shakes, but some of those coeds . . ."

"Mr. Kugelmass—"

"Help me. I had a dream last night. I was skipping through a meadow holding a picnic basket and the basket was marked 'Options.' And then I saw there was a hole in the basket."

"Mr. Kugelmass, the worst thing you could do is act out. You must simply express your feelings here, and together we'll analyze them. You have been in treatment long enough to know there is no overnight cure. After all, I'm an analyst, not a magician."

"Then perhaps what I need is a magician," Kugelmass said, rising from his chair. And with that he terminated his therapy.

A couple of weeks later, while Kugelmass and Daphne were moping around in their apartment one night like two pieces of old furniture, the phone rang.

"I'll get it," Kugelmass said. "Hello."

"Kugelmass?" a voice said. "Kugelmass, this is Persky."

"Who?"

"Persky. Or should I say The Great Persky?"

"Pardon me?"

"I hear you're looking all over town for a magician to bring a little exotica into your life? Yes or no?"

"Sh-h-h," Kugelmass whispered. "Don't hang up. Where are you calling from, Persky?"

Early the following afternoon, Kugelmass climbed three flights of stairs in a broken-down apartment house in the Bushwick section of Brooklyn. Peering through the darkness of the hall, he found the door he was looking for and pressed the bell. I'm going to regret this, he thought to himself.

Seconds later, he was greeted by a short, thin, waxy-looking man.

"*You're* Persky the Great?" Kugelmass said.

"The Great Persky. You want a tea?"

"No, I want romance. I want music. I want love and beauty."

"But not tea, eh? Amazing. O.K., sit down."

Persky went to the back room, and Kugelmass heard the sounds of boxes and furniture being moved around. Persky reappeared, pushing before him a large object on squeaky roller-skate wheels. He removed some old silk handkerchiefs that were lying on its top and blew away a bit of dust. It was a cheap-looking Chinese cabinet, badly lacquered.

"Persky," Kugelmass said, "what's your scam?"[3]

"Pay attention," Persky said. "This is some beautiful effect. I developed it for a Knights of Pythias[4] date last year, but the booking fell through. Get into the cabinet."

---

3. Scheme, confidence trick.   4. Secret fraternal society.

"Why, so you can stick it full of swords or something?"

"You see any swords?"

Kugelmass made a face and, grunting, climbed into the cabinet. He couldn't help noticing a couple of ugly rhinestones glued onto the raw plywood just in front of his face. "If this is a joke," he said.

"Some joke. Now, here's the point. If I throw any novel into this cabinet with you, shut the doors, and tap it three times, you will find yourself projected into that book."

Kugelmass made a grimace of disbelief.

"It's the emess,"[5] Persky said. "My hand to God. Not just a novel, either. A short story, a play, a poem. You can meet any of the women created by the world's best writers. Whoever you dreamed of. You could carry on all you like with a real winner. Then when you've had enough you give a yell, and I'll see you're back here in a split second."

"Persky, are you some kind of outpatient?"

"I'm telling you it's on the level," Persky said.

Kugelmass remained skeptical. "What are you telling me—that this cheesy homemade box can take me on a ride like you're describing?"

"For a double sawbuck."[6]

Kugelmass reached for his wallet. "I'll believe this when I see it," he said.

Persky tucked the bills in his pants pocket and turned toward his bookcase. "So who do you want to meet? Sister Carrie? Hester Prynne? Ophelia? Maybe someone by Saul Bellow? Hey, what about Temple Drake?[7] Although for a man your age she'd be a workout."

"French. I want to have an affair with a French lover."

"Nana?"[8]

"I don't want to have to pay for it."

"What about Natasha in 'War and Peace'?"[9]

"I said French. I know! What about Emma Bovary? That sounds to me perfect."

"You got it, Kugelmass. Give me a holler when you've had enough." Persky tossed in a paperback copy of Flaubert's novel.

"You sure this is safe?" Kugelmass asked as Persky began shutting the cabinet doors.

"Safe. Is anything safe in this crazy world?" Persky rapped three times on the cabinet and then flung open the doors.

Kugelmass was gone. At the same moment, he appeared in the bedroom of Charles and Emma Bovary's house at Yonville.[1] Before him was a beautiful woman, standing alone with her back turned to him as she folded some linen. *I can't believe this,* thought Kugelmass, staring at the doctor's ravishing wife. *This is uncanny. I'm here. It's her.*

Emma turned in surprise. "Goodness, you startled me," she said.

---

5. Truth.
6. Twenty dollars.
7. Respectively, the fallen heroine of Theodore Dreiser's *Sister Carrie* (1900); the adulterous heroine of Nathaniel Hawthorne's *The Scarlet Letter* (1850); Hamlet's fiancée, who drowns herself; Bellow's heroines are intensely neurotic, sexual, and vindictive; the victim of a bizarre rape in Faulkner's *Sanctuary* (1931), who is also the heroine of his *Requiem for a Nun* (1950).
8. Prostitute-heroine of Émile Zola's *Nana* (1880).
9. Saucy heroine of the novel (1865–1869) by Tolstoy.
1. Town in Normandy, France, where much of Flaubert's novel *Madame Bovary* (1857) is set.

"Who are you?" She spoke in the same fine English translation as the paperback.

It's simply devastating, he thought. Then, realizing that it was he whom she had addressed, he said, "Excuse me. I'm Sidney Kugelmass. I'm from City College. A professor of humanities. C.C.N.Y.? Uptown. I—oh, boy!"

Emma Bovary smiled flirtatiously and said, "Would you like a drink? A glass of wine, perhaps?"

She is beautiful, Kugelmass thought. What a contrast with the troglodyte who shared his bed! He felt a sudden impulse to take this vision into his arms and tell her she was the kind of woman he had dreamed of all his life.

"Yes, some wine," he said hoarsely. "White. No, red. No, white. Make it white."

"Charles is out for the day," Emma said, her voice full of playful implication.

After the wine, they went for a stroll in the lovely French countryside. "I've always dreamed that some mysterious stranger would appear and rescue me from the monotony of this crass rural existence," Emma said, clasping his hand. They passed a small church. "I love what you have on," she murmured. "I've never seen anything like it around here. It's so . . . so modern."

"It's called a leisure suit," he said romantically. "It was marked down." Suddenly he kissed her. For the next hour they reclined under a tree and whispered together and told each other deeply meaningful things with their eyes. Then Kugelmass sat up. He had just remembered he had to meet Daphne at Bloomingdale's.[2] "I must go," he told her. "But don't worry, I'll be back."

"I hope so," Emma said.

He embraced her passionately, and the two walked back to the house. He held Emma's face cupped in his palms, kissed her again, and yelled, "O.K., Persky! I got to be at Bloomingdale's by three-thirty."

There was an audible pop, and Kugelmass was back in Brooklyn.

"So? Did I lie?" Persky asked triumphantly.

"Look, Persky, I'm right now late to meet the ball and chain at Lexington Avenue, but when can I go again? Tomorrow?"

"My pleasure. Just bring a twenty. And don't mention this to anybody."

"Yeah. I'm going to call Rupert Murdoch."[3]

Kugelmass hailed a cab and sped off to the city. His heart danced on point. I am in love, he thought, I am the possessor of a wonderful secret. What he didn't realize was that at this very moment students in various classrooms across the country were saying to their teachers, "Who is this character on page 100? A bald Jew is kissing Madame Bovary?" A teacher in Sioux Falls, South Dakota, sighed and thought, Jesus, these kids, with their pot and acid. What goes through their minds!

2. Chic New York department store.
3. Australian newspaper baron, who, in addition to several British papers, owns the New York *Post*, the *Village Voice*, and *New York* magazine.

Daphne Kugelmass was in the bathroom-accessories department at Bloomingdale's when Kugelmass arrived breathlessly. "Where've you been?" she snapped. "It's four-thirty."

"I got held up in traffic," Kugelmass said.

Kugelmass visited Persky the next day, and in a few minutes was again passed magically to Yonville. Emma couldn't hide her excitement at seeing him. The two spent hours together, laughing and talking about their different backgrounds. Before Kugelmass left, they made love. "My God, I'm doing it with Madame Bovary!" Kugelmass whispered to himself. "Me, who failed freshman English."

As the months passed, Kugelmass saw Persky many times and developed a close and passionate relationship with Emma Bovary. "Make sure and always get me into the book before page 120," Kugelmass said to the magician one day. "I always have to meet her before she hooks up with this Rodolphe character."[4]

"Why?" Persky asked. "You can't beat his time?"

"Beat his time. He's landed gentry. Those guys have nothing better to do than flirt and ride horses. To me, he's one of those faces you see in the pages of *Women's Wear Daily*. With the Helmut Berger[5] hairdo. But to her he's hot stuff."

"And her husband suspects nothing?"

"He's out of his depth. He's a lackluster little paramedic who's thrown in his lot with a jitterbug. He's ready to go to sleep by ten, and she's putting on her dancing shoes. Oh, well . . . See you later."

And once again Kugelmass entered the cabinet and passed instantly to the Bovary estate at Yonville. "How you doing, cupcake?" he said to Emma.

"Oh, Kugelmass," Emma sighed. "What I have to put up with. Last night at dinner, Mr. Personality dropped off to sleep in the middle of the dessert course. I'm pouring my heart out about Maxim's[6] and the ballet, and out of the blue I hear snoring."

"It's O.K., darling. I'm here now," Kugelmass said, embracing her. I've earned this, he thought, smelling Emma's French perfume and burying his nose in her hair. I've suffered enough. I've paid enough analysts. I've searched till I'm weary. She's young and nubile, and I'm here a few pages after Léon and just before Rodolphe. By showing up during the correct chapters, I've got the situation knocked.

Emma, to be sure, was just as happy as Kugelmass. She had been starved for excitement, and his tales of Broadway night life, of fast cars and Hollywood and TV stars, enthralled the young French beauty.

"Tell me again about O.J. Simpson,"[7] she implored that evening, as she and Kugelmass strolled past Abbé Bournisien's church.

"What can I say? The man is great. He sets all kinds of rushing records. Such moves. They can't touch him."

---

4. The provincial aristocratic womanizer who seduces Emma, after she has a first romantic, idealistic flirtation with the mooning young Léon (who is mentioned below). The Abbé Bournisien and Binet, mentioned later, are minor characters in the novel.

5. Gossipy New York fashion newspaper; handsome German actor (b. 1942) who often plays decadent characters (*The Damned, Portrait of Dorian Gray*).

6. Fashionable Paris restaurant.

7. Famous football running back, recently retired, though he's still seen running through airports in TV commercials.

"And the Academy Awards?" Emma said wistfully. "I'd give anything to win one."

"First you've got to be nominated."

"I know. You explained it. But I'm convinced I can act. Of course, I'd want to take a class or two. With Strasberg[8] maybe. Then, if I had the right agent—"

"We'll see, we'll see. I'll speak to Persky."

That night, safely returned to Persky's flat, Kugelmass brought up the idea of having Emma visit him in the big city.

"Let me think about it," Persky said. "Maybe I could work it. Stranger things have happened." Of course, neither of them could think of one.

"Where the hell do you go all the time?" Daphne Kugelmass barked at her husband as he returned home late that evening. "You got a chippie stashed somewhere?"

"Yeah, sure, I'm just the type," Kugelmass said wearily. "I was with Leonard Popkin. We were discussing Socialist agriculture in Poland. You know Popkin. He's a freak on the subject."

"Well, you've been very odd lately," Daphne said. "Distant. Just don't forget about my father's birthday. On Saturday?"

"Oh, sure, sure," Kugelmass said, heading for the bathroom.

"My whole family will be there. We can see the twins. And Cousin Hamish. You should be more polite to Cousin Hamish—he likes you."

"Right, the twins," Kugelmass said, closing the bathroom door and shutting out the sound of his wife's voice. He leaned against it and took a deep breath. In a few hours, he told himself, he would be back in Yonville again, back with his beloved. And this time, if all went well, he would bring Emma back with him.

At three-fifteen the following afternoon, Persky worked his wizardry again. Kugelmass appeared before Emma, smiling and eager. The two spent a few hours at Yonville with Binet and then remounted the Bovary carriage. Following Persky's instructions, they held each other tightly, closed their eyes, and counted to ten. When they opened them, the carriage was just drawing up at the side door of the Plaza Hotel, where Kugelmass had optimistically reserved a suite earlier in the day.

"I love it! It's everything I dreamed it would be," Emma said as she swirled joyously around the bedroom, surveying the city from their window. "There's F.A.O. Schwarz.[9] And there's Central Park, and the Sherry[1] is which one? Oh, there—I see. It's too divine."

On the bed there were boxes from Halston and Saint Laurent.[2] Emma unwrapped a package and held up a pair of black velvet pants against her perfect body.

"The slacks suit is by Ralph Lauren," Kugelmass said. "You'll look like a million bucks in it. Come on, sugar, give us a kiss."

8. Lee Strasberg's acting school taught the natural acting style known as "The Method" to such stars as Marlon Brando.
9. Well-known toy store.
1. Sherry-Netherland Hotel, also in Central Park area.
2. Famous and expensive fashion designers and couturiers, as is Ralph Lauren, below.

"I've never been so happy!" Emma squealed as she stood before the mirror. "Let's go out on the town. I want to see 'Chorus Line' and the Guggenheim and this Jack Nicholson[3] character you always talk about. Are any of his flicks showing?"

"I cannot get my mind around this," a Stanford professor said. "First a strange character named Kugelmass, and now she's gone from the book. Well, I guess the mark of a classic is that you can reread it a thousand times and always find something new."

The lovers passed a blissful weekend. Kugelmass had told Daphne he would be away at a symposium in Boston and would return Monday. Savoring each moment, he and Emma went to the movies, had dinner in Chinatown, passed two hours at a discothèque, and went to bed with a TV movie. They slept till noon on Sunday, visited SoHo, and ogled celebrities at Elaine's.[4] They had caviar and champagne in their suite on Sunday night and talked until dawn. That morning, in the cab taking them to Persky's apartment, Kugelmass thought, It was hectic, but worth it. I can't bring her here too often, but now and then it will be a charming contrast with Yonville.

At Persky's, Emma climbed into the cabinet, arranged her new boxes of clothes neatly around her, and kissed Kugelmass fondly. "My place next time," she said with a wink. Persky rapped three times on the cabinet. Nothing happened.

"Hmm," Persky said, scratching his head. He rapped again, but still no magic. "Something must be wrong," he mumbled.

"Persky, you're joking!" Kugelmass cried. "How can it not work?"

"Relax, relax. Are you still in the box, Emma?"

"Yes."

Persky rapped again—harder this time.

"I'm still here, Persky."

"I know, darling. Sit tight."

"Persky, we *have* to get her back," Kugelmass whispered. "I'm a married man, and I have a class in three hours. I'm not prepared for anything more than a cautious affair at this point."

"I can't understand it," Persky muttered. "It's such a reliable little trick."

But he could do nothing. "It's going to take a little while," he said to Kugelmass. "I'm going to have to strip it down. I'll call you later."

Kugelmass bundled Emma into a cab and took her back to the Plaza. He barely made it to his class on time. He was on the phone all day, to Persky and to his mistress. The magician told him it might be several days before he got to the bottom of the trouble.

"How was the symposium?" Daphne asked him that night.

"Fine, fine," he said, lighting the filter end of a cigarette.

"What's wrong? You're as tense as a cat."

"Me? Ha, that's a laugh. I'm as calm as a summer night. I'm

---

3. A Broadway musical; the Solomon R. Guggenheim Museum; Nicholson starred in the films *Easy Rider, One Flew Over the Cuckoo's Nest, Five Easy Pieces*.

4. SoHo is the new center of the contemporary art scene south of Greenwich Village. Elaine's restaurant is frequented by publishing and newspaper notables.

just going to take a walk." He eased out the door, hailed a cab, and flew to the Plaza.

"This is no good," Emma said. "Charles will miss me."

"Bear with me, sugar," Kugelmass said. He was pale and sweaty. He kissed her again, raced to the elevators, yelled at Persky over a pay phone in the Plaza lobby, and just made it home before midnight.

"According to Popkin, barley prices in Kraków have not been this stable since 1971," he said to Daphne, and smiled wanly as he climbed into bed.

The whole week went by like that. On Friday night, Kugelmass told Daphne there was another symposium he had to catch, this one in Syracuse. He hurried back to the Plaza, but the second weekend there was nothing like the first. "Get me back into the novel or marry me," Emma told Kugelmass. "Meanwhile, I want to get a job or go to class, because watching TV all day is the pits."

"Fine. We can use the money," Kugelmass said. "You consume twice your weight in room service."

"I met an Off Broadway producer in Central Park yesterday, and he said I might be right for a project he's doing," Emma said.

"Who is this clown?" Kugelmass asked.

"He's not a clown. He's sensitive and kind and cute. His name's Jeff Something-or-Other, and he's up for a Tony."[5]

Later that afternoon, Kugelmass showed up at Persky's drunk.

"Relax," Persky told him. "You'll get a coronary."

"Relax. The man says relax. I've got a fictional character stashed in a hotel room, and I think my wife is having me tailed by a private shamus."[6]

"O.K., O.K. We know there's a problem." Persky crawled under the cabinet and started banging on something with a large wrench.

"I'm like a wild animal," Kugelmass went on. "I'm sneaking around town, and Emma and I have had it up to here with each other. Not to mention a hotel tab that reads like the defense budget."

"So what should I do? This is the world of magic," Persky said. "It's all nuance."

"Nuance, my foot. I'm pouring Dom Pérignon and black eggs[7] into this little mouse, plus her wardrobe, plus she's enrolled at the Neighborhood Playhouse[8] and suddenly needs professional photos. Also, Persky, Professor Fivish Kopkind, who teaches Comp Lit and who has always been jealous of me, has identified me as the sporadically appearing character in the Flaubert book. He's threatened to go to Daphne. I see ruin and alimony jail. For adultery with Madame Bovary, my wife will reduce me to beggary."

"What do you want me to say? I'm working on it night and day. As far as your personal anxiety goes, that I can't help you with. I'm a magician, not an analyst."

5. Broadway Drama Critics' Award comparable to Oscar.
6. Detective.
7. An especially fine champagne and caviar.
8. Founded in 1915 to bring drama to the lower East Side of New York City, its productions tended to have social implications or to be experimental. The theater closed in 1927, but its production company continues to perform.

By Sunday afternoon, Emma had locked herself in the bathroom and refused to respond to Kugelmass's entreaties. Kugelmass stared out the window at the Wollman Rink[9] and contemplated suicide. Too bad this is a low floor, he thought, or I'd do it right now. Maybe if I ran away to Europe and started life over . . . Maybe I could sell the *International Herald Tribune,* like those young girls used to.[1]

The phone rang. Kugelmass lifted it to his ear mechanically.

"Bring her over," Persky said. "I think I got the bugs out of it."

Kugelmass's heart leaped. "You're serious?" he said. "You got it licked?"

"It was something in the transmission. Go figure."

"Persky, you're a genius. We'll be there in a minute. Less than a minute."

Again the lovers hurried to the magician's apartment, and again Emma Bovary climbed into the cabinet with her boxes. This time there was no kiss. Persky shut the doors, took a deep breath, and tapped the box three times. There was the reassuring popping noise, and when Persky peered inside, the box was empty. Madame Bovary was back in her novel. Kugelmass heaved a great sigh of relief and pumped the magician's hand.

"It's over," he said. "I learned my lesson. I'll never cheat again, I swear it." He pumped Persky's hand again and made a mental note to send him a necktie.

Three weeks later, at the end of a beautiful spring afternoon, Persky answered his doorbell. It was Kugelmass, with a sheepish expression on his face.

"O.K., Kugelmass," the magician said. "Where to this time?"

"It's just this once," Kugelmass said. "The weather is so lovely, and I'm not getting any younger. Listen, you've read 'Portnoy's Complaint'? Remember The Monkey?"[2]

"The price is now twenty-five dollars, because the cost of living is up, but I'll start you off with one freebie, due to all the trouble I caused you."

"You're good people," Kugelmass said, combing his few remaining hairs as he climbed into the cabinet again. "This'll work all right?"

"I hope. But I haven't tried it much since all that unpleasantness."

"Sex and romance," Kugelmass said from inside the box. "What we go through for a pretty face."

Persky tossed in a copy of "Portnoy's Complaint" and rapped three times on the box. This time, instead of a popping noise there was a dull explosion, followed by a series of crackling noises and a shower of sparks. Persky leaped back, was seized by a heart attack, and dropped dead. The cabinet burst into flames, and eventually the entire house burned down.

Kugelmass, unaware of this catastrophe, had his own problems. He had not been thrust into "Portnoy's Complaint," or into any other

9. Skating rink in Central Park.
1. This was what some American dropouts of the 1950s did; Jean Seberg portrayed one in the 1959 film *Breathless.*

2. The leading character in Philip Roth's 1969 novel, The Monkey is less romantic than Flaubert's Emma Bovary and sexually carefree and . . . experimental.

novel, for that matter. He had been projected into an old textbook, "Remedial Spanish," and was running for his life over a barren, rocky terrain as the word *"tener"* ("to have")—a large and hairy irregular verb—raced after him on its spindly legs.

p. 1977

BOBBIE ANN MASON

Shiloh

Leroy Moffitt's wife, Norma Jean, is working on her pectorals. She lifts three-pound dumbbells to warm up, then progresses to a twenty-pound barbell. Standing with her legs apart, she reminds Leroy of Wonder Woman.

"I'd give anything if I could just get these muscles to where they're real hard," says Norma Jean. "Feel this arm. It's not as hard as the other one."

"That's 'cause you're right-handed," says Leroy, dodging as she swings the barbell in an arc.

"Do you think so?"

"Sure."

Leroy is a truckdriver. He injured his leg in a highway accident four months ago, and his physical therapy, which involves weights and a pulley, prompted Norma Jean to try building herself up. Now she is attending a body-building class. Leroy has been collecting temporary disability since his tractor-trailer jackknifed in Missouri, badly twisting his left leg in its socket. He has a steel pin in his hip. He will probably not be able to drive his rig again. It sits in the backyard, like a gigantic bird that has flown home to roost. Leroy has been home in Kentucky for three months, and his leg is almost healed but the accident frightened him and he does not want to drive any more long hauls. He is not sure what to do next. In the meantime, he makes things from craft kits. He started by building a miniature log cabin from notched Popsicle sticks. He varnished it and placed it on the TV set, where it remains. It reminds him of a rustic Nativity scene. Then he tried string art (sailing ships on black velvet), a macramé owl kit, a snap-together B-17 Flying Fortress,[1] and a lamp made out of a model truck, with a light fixture screwed in the top of the cab. At first the kits were diversions, something to kill time, but now he is thinking about building a full-scale log house from a kit. It would be considerably cheaper than building a regular house, and besides, Leroy has grown to appreciate how things are put together. He has begun to realize that in all the years he was on the road he never took time to examine anything. He was always flying past scenery.

"They won't let you build a log cabin in any of the new subdivisions," Norma Jean tells him.

"They will if I tell them it's for you," he says, teasing her. Ever since they were married, he has promised Norma Jean he would build her a new home one day. They have always rented, and the house they live in is small and nondescript. It does not even feel like a home, Leroy realizes now.

Norma Jean works at the Rexall drugstore, and she has acquired an amazing amount of information about cosmetics. When she explains to Leroy the three stages of complexion care, involving creams, toners, and moisturizers, he thinks happily of other petroleum products—axle grease, diesel fuel. This is a connection between him and Norma Jean. Since he has been home, he has felt unusually tender about his wife and guilty over his long absences. But he can't tell what she feels about him. Norma Jean has never complained about his traveling; she has never made hurt remarks, like calling his truck a "widow-maker." He is reasonably certain she has been faithful to him, but he wishes she would celebrate his permanent homecoming more happily. Norma Jean is often startled to find Leroy at home, and he thinks she seems a little disappointed about it. Perhaps he reminds her too much of the early days of their marriage, before he went on the road. They had a child who died as an infant, years ago. They never speak about their memories of Randy, which have almost faded, but now that Leroy is home all the time, they sometimes feel awkward around each other, and Leroy wonders if one of them should mention the child. He has the feeling that they are waking up out of a dream together—that they must create a new marriage, start afresh. They are lucky they are still married. Leroy has read that for most people losing a child destroys the marriage—or else he heard this on *Donahue*. He can't always remember where he learns things anymore.

At Christmas, Leroy bought an electric organ for Norma Jean. She used to play the piano when she was in high school. "It don't leave you," she told him once. "It's like riding a bicycle."

The new instrument had so many keys and buttons that she was bewildered by it at first. She touched the keys tentatively, pushed some buttons, then pecked out "Chopsticks." It came out in an amplified fox-trot rhythm, with marimba sounds.

"It's an orchestra!" she cried.

The organ had a pecan-look finish and eighteen preset chords, with optional flute, violin, trumpet, clarinet, and banjo accompaniments. Norma Jean mastered the organ almost immediately. At first she played Christmas songs. Then she bought *The Sixties Songbook* and learned every tune in it, adding variations to each with the rows of brightly colored buttons.

"I didn't like these old songs back then," she said. "But I have this crazy feeling I missed something."

"You didn't miss a thing," said Leroy.

Leroy likes to lie on the couch and smoke a joint and listen to Norma Jean play "Can't Take My Eyes Off You"[2] and "I'll Be Back."

2. A 1967 song by Bob Crewe and Bob Gaudio; best-selling records in 1967 by Frankie Valli, 1968 by The Lettermen, and 1969–70 by Nancy Wilson. *Below:* "I'll Be Back," 1964, by John Lennon and Paul McCartney and recorded by the Beatles.

He is back again. After fifteen years on the road, he is finally settling down with the woman he loves. She is still pretty. Her skin is flawless. Her frosted curls resemble pencil trimmings.

Now that Leroy has come home to stay, he notices how much the town has changed. Subdivisions are spreading across western Kentucky like an oil slick. The sign at the edge of town says "Pop: 11,500"—only seven hundred more than it said twenty years before. Leroy can't figure out who is living in all the new houses. The farmers who used to gather around the courthouse square on Saturday afternoons to play checkers and spit tobacco juice have gone. It has been years since Leroy has thought about the farmers, and they have disappeared without his noticing.

Leroy meets a kid named Stevie Hamilton in the parking lot at the new shopping center. While they pretend to be strangers meeting over a stalled car, Stevie tosses an ounce of marijuana under the front seat of Leroy's car. Stevie is wearing orange jogging shoes and a T-shirt that says CHATTAHOOCHEE SUPER-RAT. His father is a prominent doctor who lives in one of the expensive subdivisions in a new white-columned brick house that looks like a funeral parlor. In the phone book under his name there is a separate number, with the listing "Teenagers."

"Where do you get this stuff?" asks Leroy. "From your pappy?"

"That's for me to know and you to find out," Stevie says. He is slit-eyed and skinny.

"What else you got?"

"What you interested in?"

"Nothing special. Just wondered."

Leroy used to take speed on the road. Now he has to go slowly. He needs to be mellow. He leans back against the car and says, "I'm aiming to build me a log house, soon as I get time. My wife, though, I don't think she likes the idea."

"Well, let me know when you want me again," Stevie says. He has a cigarette in his cupped palm, as though sheltering it from the wind. He takes a long drag, then stomps it on the asphalt and slouches away.

Stevie's father was two years ahead of Leroy in high school. Leroy is thirty-four. He married Norma Jean when they were both eighteen, and their child Randy was born a few months later, but he died at the age of four months and three days. He would be about Stevie's age now. Norma Jean and Leroy were at the drive-in, watching a double feature (*Dr. Strangelove* and *Lover Come Back*),[3] and the baby was sleeping in the back seat. When the first movie ended, the baby was dead. It was the sudden infant death syndrome. Leroy remembers handing Randy to a nurse at the emergency room, as though he were offering her a large doll as a present. A dead baby feels like a sack of flour. "It just happens sometimes," said the doctor, in what Leroy always recalls as a nonchalant tone. Leroy can hardly remember the child anymore, but he still sees vividly a scene from *Dr. Strangelove* in which the President of the United States was talking in a folksy voice

_____

3. A 1963 satire on nuclear war and a   comedy satirizing the advertising business.
1961 Rock Hudson–Doris Day romantic

on the hot line to the Soviet premier about the bomber accidentally headed toward Russia. He was in the War Room, and the world map was lit up. Leroy remembers Norma Jean standing catatonically beside him in the hospital and himself thinking: Who is this strange girl? He had forgotten who she was. Now scientists are saying that crib death is caused by a virus. Nobody knows anything, Leroy thinks. The answers are always changing.

When Leroy gets home from the shopping center, Norma Jean's mother, Mabel Beasley, is there. Until this year, Leroy has not realized how much time she spends with Norma Jean. When she visits, she inspects the closets and then the plants, informing Norma Jean when a plant is droopy or yellow. Mabel calls the plants "flowers," although there are never any blooms. She always notices if Norma Jean's laundry is piling up. Mabel is a short, overweight woman whose tight, brown-dyed curls look more like a wig than the actual wig she sometimes wears. Today she has brought Norma Jean an off-white dust ruffle she made for the bed; Mabel works in a custom-upholstery shop.

"This is the tenth one I made this year," Mabel says. "I got started and couldn't stop."

"It's real pretty," says Norma Jean.

"Now we can hide things under the bed," says Leroy, who gets along with his mother-in-law primarily by joking with her. Mabel has never really forgiven him for disgracing her by getting Norma Jean pregnant. When the baby died, she said that fate was mocking her.

"What's that thing?" Mabel says to Leroy in a loud voice, pointing to a tangle of yarn on a piece of canvas.

Leroy holds it up for Mabel to see. "It's my needlepoint," he explains. "This is a *Star Trek* pillow cover."

"That's what a woman would do," says Mabel. "Great day in the morning!"

"All the big football players on TV do it," he says.

"Why, Leroy, you're always trying to fool me. I don't believe you for one minute. You don't know what to do with yourself—that's the whole trouble. Sewing!"

"I'm aiming to build us a log house," says Leroy. "Soon as my plans come."

"Like *heck* you are," says Norma Jean. She takes Leroy's needlepoint and shoves it into a drawer. "You have to find a job first. Nobody can afford to build now anyway."

Mabel straightens her girdle and says, "I still think before you get tied down y'all ought to take a little run to Shiloh."

"One of these days, Mama," Norma Jean says impatiently.

Mabel is talking about Shiloh, Tennessee. For the past few years, she has been urging Leroy and Norma Jean to visit the Civil War battleground there.[4] Mabel went there on her honeymoon—the only

4. Where, in April 1862, more than 23,000 troops of the North and South, one-quarter of those who fought there, died. This was the first real indication of how bitter and bloody the war was to be. General Ulysses S. Grant, when reinforcements arrived, drove the Confederate forces, which had gained an initial victory by a surprise attack, back to their base in Corinth, Mississippi.

real trip she ever took. Her husband died of a perforated ulcer when Norma Jean was ten, but Mabel, who was accepted into the United Daughters of the Confederacy in 1975, is still preoccupied with going back to Shiloh.

"I've been to kingdom come and back in that truck out yonder," Leroy says to Mabel, "but we never yet set foot in that battleground. Ain't that something? How did I miss it?"

"It's not even that far," Mabel says.

After Mabel leaves, Norma Jean reads to Leroy from a list she has made. "Things you could do," she announces. "You could get a job as a guard at Union Carbide, where they'd let you set on a stool. You could get on at the lumberyard. You could do a little carpenter work, if you want to build so bad. You could—"

"I can't do something where I'd have to stand up all day."

"You ought to try standing up all day behind a cosmetics counter. It's amazing that I have strong feet, coming from two parents that never had strong feet at all." At the moment Norma Jean is holding on to the kitchen counter, raising her knees one at a time as she talks. She is wearing two-pound ankle weights.

"Don't worry," says Leroy. "I'll do something."

"You could truck calves to slaughter for somebody. You wouldn't have to drive any big old truck for that."

"I'm going to build you this house," says Leroy. "I want to make you a real home."

"I don't want to live in any log cabin."

"It's not a cabin. It's a house."

"I don't care. It looks like a cabin."

"You and me together could lift those logs. It's just like lifting weights."

Norma Jean doesn't answer. Under her breath, she is counting. Now she is marching through the kitchen. She is doing goose steps.

Before his accident, when Leroy came home he used to stay in the house with Norma Jean, watching TV in bed and playing cards. She would cook fried chicken, picnic ham, chocolate pie—all his favorites. Now he is home alone much of the time. In the mornings, Norma Jean disappears, leaving a cooling place in the bed. She eats a cereal called Body Buddies, and she leaves the bowl on the table, with the soggy tan balls floating in a milk puddle. He sees things about Norma Jean that he never realized before. When she chops onions, she stares off into a corner, as if she can't bear to look. She puts on her house slippers almost precisely at nine o'clock every evening and nudges her jogging shoes under the couch. She saves bread heels for the birds. Leroy watches the birds at the feeder. He notices the peculiar way goldfinches fly past the window. They close their wings, then fall, then spread their wings to catch and lift themselves. He wonders if they close their eyes when they fall. Norma Jean closes her eyes when they are in bed. She wants the lights turned out. Even then, he is sure she closes her eyes.

He goes for long drives around town. He tends to drive a car rather carelessly. Power steering and an automatic shift make a car feel so small and inconsequential that his body is hardly involved in the driving process. His injured leg stretches out comfortably. Once or twice he has almost hit something, but even the prospect of an accident seems minor in a car. He curses the new subdivisions, feeling like a criminal rehearsing for a robbery. Norma Jean is probably right about a log house being inappropriate here in the new subdivisions. All the houses look grand and complicated. They depress him.

One day when Leroy comes home from a drive he finds Norma Jean in tears. She is in the kitchen making a potato and mushroom-soup casserole, with grated-cheese topping. She is crying because her mother caught her smoking.

"I didn't hear her coming. I was standing here puffing away pretty as you please," Norma Jean says, wiping her eyes.

"I knew it would happen sooner or later," says Leroy, putting his arm around her.

"She don't know the meaning of the word 'knock,' " says Norma Jean. "It's a wonder she hadn't caught me years ago."

"Think of it this way," Leroy says. "What if she caught me with a joint?"

"You better not let her!" Norma Jean shrieks. "I'm warning you, Leroy Moffitt!"

"I'm just kidding. Here, play me a tune. That'll help you relax."

Norma Jean puts the casserole in the oven and sets the timer. Then she plays a ragtime tune, with horns and banjo, as Leroy lights up a joint and lies on the couch, laughing to himself about Mabel's catching him at it. He thinks of Stevie Hamilton—a doctor's son pushing grass. Everything is funny. The whole town seems crazy and small. He is reminded of Virgil Mathis, a boastful policeman Leroy used to shoot pool with. Virgil recently led a drug bust in a back room at a bowling alley, where he seized ten thousand dollars' worth of marijuana. The newspaper had a picture of him holding up the bags of grass and grinning widely. Right now, Leroy can imagine Virgil breaking down the door and arresting him with a lungful of smoke. Virgil would probably have been alerted to the scene because of all the racket Norma Jean is making. Now she sounds like a hard-rock band. Norma Jean is terrific. When she switches to a Latin-rhythm version of "Sunshine Superman,"[5] Leroy hums along. Norma Jean's foot goes up and down, up and down.

"Well, what do you think?" Leroy says, when Norma Jean pauses to search through her music.

"What do I think about what?"

His mind has gone blank. Then he says, "I'll sell my rig and build us a house." That wasn't what he wanted to say. He wanted to know what she thought—what she *really* thought—about them.

"Don't start in on that again," says Norma Jean. She begins playing "Who'll Be the Next in Line?"

---

5. A 1966 song by Donovan Leitch, best-selling record by "Donovan"; *below:* "Who'll Be Next in Line," also British, 1965, by Ray Davies, best-selling record by The Kinks.

Leroy used to tell hitchhikers his whole life story—about his travels, his hometown, the baby. He would end with a question: "Well, what do you think?" It was just a rhetorical question. In time, he had the feeling that he'd been telling the same story over and over to the same hitchhikers. He quit talking to hitchhikers when he realized how his voice sounded—whining and self-pitying, like some teenage-tragedy song. Now Leroy has the sudden impulse to tell Norma Jean about himself, as if he had just met her. They have known each other so long they have forgotten a lot about each other. They could become reacquainted. But when the oven timer goes off and she runs to the kitchen, he forgets why he wants to do this.

The next day, Mabel drops by. It is Saturday and Norma Jean is cleaning. Leroy is studying the plans of his log house, which have finally come in the mail. He has them spread out on the table—big sheets of stiff blue paper, with diagrams and numbers printed in white. While Norma Jean runs the vacuum, Mabel drinks coffee. She sets her coffee cup on a blueprint.

"I'm just waiting for time to pass," she says to Leroy, drumming her fingers on the table.

As soon as Norma Jean switches off the vacuum, Mabel says in a loud voice, "Did you hear about the datsun dog that killed the baby?"

Norma Jean says, "The word is 'dachshund.'"

"They put the dog on trial. It chewed the baby's legs off. The mother was in the next room all the time." She raises her voice. "They thought it was neglect."

Norma Jean is holding her ears. Leroy manages to open the refrigerator and get some Diet Pepsi to offer Mabel. Mabel still has some coffee and she waves away the Pepsi.

"Datsuns are like that," Mabel says. "They're jealous dogs. They'll tear a place to pieces if you don't keep an eye on them."

"You better watch out what you're saying, Mabel," says Leroy.

"Well, facts is facts."

Leroy looks out the window at his rig. It is like a huge piece of furniture gathering dust in the backyard. Pretty soon it will be an antique. He hears the vacuum cleaner. Norma Jean seems to be cleaning the living room rug again.

Later, she says to Leroy, "She just said that about the baby because she caught me smoking. She's trying to pay me back."

"What are you talking about?" Leroy says, nervously shuffling blueprints.

"You know good and well," Norma Jean says. She is sitting in a kitchen chair with her feet up and her arms wrapped around her knees. She looks small and helpless. She says, "The very idea, her bringing up a subject like that! Saying it was neglect."

"She didn't mean that," Leroy says.

"She might not have *thought* she meant it. She always says things like that. You don't know how she goes on."

"But she didn't really mean it. She was just talking."

Leroy opens a king-sized bottle of beer and pours it into two glasses, dividing it carefully. He hands a glass to Norma Jean and she takes it from him mechanically. For a long time, they sit by the kitchen window watching the birds at the feeder.

Something is happening. Norma Jean is going to night school. She has graduated from her six-week body-building course and now she is taking an adult-education course in composition at Paducah Community College. She spends her evenings outlining paragraphs.

"First you have a topic sentence," she explains to Leroy. "Then you divide it up. Your secondary topic has to be connected to your primary topic."

To Leroy, this sounds intimidating. "I never was any good in English," he says.

"It makes a lot of sense."

"What are you doing this for, anyhow?"

She shrugs. "It's something to do." She stands up and lifts her dumbbells a few times.

"Driving a rig, nobody cared about my English."

"I'm not criticizing your English."

Norma Jean used to say, "If I lose ten minutes' sleep, I just drag all day." Now she stays up late, writing compositions. She got a B on her first paper—a how-to theme on soup-based casseroles. Recently Norma Jean has been cooking unusual foods—tacos, lasagna, Bombay chicken. She doesn't play the organ anymore, though her second paper was called "Why Music Is Important to Me." She sits at the kitchen table, concentrating on her outlines, while Leroy plays with his log house plans, practicing with a set of Lincoln Logs. The thought of getting a truckload of notched, numbered logs scares him, and he wants to be prepared. As he and Norma Jean work together at the kitchen table, Leroy has the hopeful thought that they are sharing something, but he knows he is a fool to think this. Norma Jean is miles away. He knows he is going to lose her. Like Mabel, he is just waiting for time to pass.

One day, Mabel is there before Norma Jean gets home from work, and Leroy finds himself confiding in her. Mabel, he realizes, must know Norma Jean better than he does.

"I don't know what's got into that girl," Mabel says. "She used to go to bed with the chickens. Now you say she's up all hours. Plus her a-smoking. I like to died."

"I want to make her this beautiful home," Leroy says, indicating the Lincoln logs. "I don't think she even wants it. Maybe she was happier with me gone."

"She don't know what to make of you, coming home like this."

"Is that it?"

Mabel takes the roof off his Lincoln Log cabin. "You couldn't get *me* in a log cabin," she says. "I was raised in one. It's no picnic, let me tell you."

"They're different now," says Leroy.

"I tell you what," Mabel says, smiling oddly at Leroy.

"What?"

"Take her on down to Shiloh. Y'all need to get out together, stir a little. Her brain's all balled up over them books."

Leroy can see traces of Norma Jean's features in her mother's face. Mabel's worn face has the texture of crinkled cotton, but suddenly she looks pretty. It occurs to Leroy that Mabel has been hinting all along that she wants them to take her with them to Shiloh.

"Let's all go to Shiloh," he says. "You and me and her. Come Sunday."

Mabel throws up her hands in protest. "Oh, no, not me. Young folks want to be by theirselves."

When Norma Jean comes in with groceries, Leroy says excitedly, "Your mama here's been dying to go to Shiloh for thirty-five years. It's about time we went, don't you think?"

"I'm not going to butt in on anybody's second honeymoon," Mabel says.

"Who's going on a honeymoon, for Christ's sake?" Norma Jean says loudly.

"I never raised no daughter of mine to talk that-a-way," Mabel says.

"You ain't seen nothing yet," says Norma Jean. She starts putting away boxes and cans, slamming cabinet doors.

"There's a log cabin at Shiloh," Mabel says. "It was there during the battle. There's bullet holes in it."

"When are you going to *shut up* about Shiloh, Mama?" asks Norma Jean.

"I always thought Shiloh was the prettiest place, so full of history," Mabel goes on. "I just hoped y'all could see it once before I die, so you could tell me about it." Later, she whispers to Leroy, "You do what I said. A little change is what she needs."

"Your name means 'the king,'" Norma Jean says to Leroy that evening. He is trying to get her to go to Shiloh, and she is reading a book about another century.

"Well, I reckon I ought to be right proud."

"I guess so."

"Am I still king around here?"

Norma Jean flexes her biceps and feels them for hardness. "I'm not fooling around with anybody, if that's what you mean," she says.

"Would you tell me if you were?"

"I don't know."

"What does *your* name mean?"

"It was Marilyn Monroe's real name."

"No kidding!"

"Norma comes from the Normans. They were invaders," she says. She closes her book and looks hard at Leroy. "I'll go to Shiloh with you if you'll stop staring at me."

On Sunday, Norma Jean packs a picnic and they go to Shiloh. To Leroy's relief, Mabel says she does not want to come with them. Norma Jean drives, and Leroy, sitting beside her, feels like some boring hitchhiker she has picked up. He tries some conversation, but she answers him in monosyllables. At Shiloh, she drives aimlessly through the park, past bluffs and trails and steep ravines. Shiloh is an immense place, and Leroy cannot see it as a battleground. It is not what he expected. He thought it would look like a golf course. Monuments are everywhere, showing through the thick clusters of trees. Norma Jean passes the log cabin Mabel mentioned. It is surrounded by tourists looking for bullet holes.

"That's not the kind of log house I've got in mind," says Leroy apologetically.

"I know *that*."

"This is a pretty place. Your mama was right."

"It's O.K.," says Norma Jean. "Well, we've seen it. I hope she's satisfied."

They burst out laughing together.

At the park museum, a movie on Shiloh is shown every half hour, but they decide that they don't want to see it. They buy a souvenir Confederate flag for Mabel, and then they find a picnic spot near the cemetery. Norma Jean has brought a picnic cooler, with pimiento sandwiches, soft drinks, and Yodels. Leroy eats a sandwich and then smokes a joint, hiding it behind the picnic cooler. Norma Jean has quit smoking altogether. She is picking cake crumbs from the cellophane wrapper, like a fussy bird.

Leroy says, "So the boys in gray ended up in Corinth. The Union soldiers zapped 'em finally. April 7, 1862."

They both know that he doesn't know any history. He is just talking about some of the historical plaques they have read. He feels awkward, like a boy on a date with an older girl. They are still just making conversation.

"Corinth is where Mama eloped to," says Norma Jean.

They sit in silence and stare at the cemetery for the Union dead and, beyond, at a tall cluster of trees. Campers are parked nearby, bumper to bumper, and small children in bright clothing are cavorting and squealing. Norma Jean wads up the cake wrapper and squeezes it tightly in her hand. Without looking at Leroy, she says, "I want to leave you."

Leroy takes a bottle of Coke out of the cooler and flips off the cap. He holds the bottle poised near his mouth but cannot remember to take a drink. Finally he says, "No, you don't."

"Yes, I do."

"I won't let you."

"You can't stop me."

"Don't do me that way."

Leroy knows Norma Jean will have her own way. "Didn't I promise to be home from now on?" he says.

"In some ways, a woman prefers a man who wanders," says Norma Jean. "That sounds crazy, I know."

"You're not crazy."

Leroy remembers to drink from his Coke. Then he says, "Yes, you *are* crazy. You and me could start all over again. Right back at the beginning."

"We *have* started all over again," says Norma Jean. "And this is how it turned out."

"What did I do wrong?"

"Nothing."

"Is this one of those women's lib things?" Leroy asks.

"Don't be funny."

The cemetery, a green slope dotted with white markers, looks like a subdivision site. Leroy is trying to comprehend that his marriage is breaking up, but for some reason he is wondering about white slabs in a graveyard.

"Everything was fine till Mama caught me smoking," says Norma Jean, standing up. "That set something off."

"What are you talking about?"

"She won't leave me alone—*you* won't leave me alone." Norma Jean seems to be crying, but she is looking away from him. "I feel eighteen again. I can't face that all over again." She starts walking away. "No, it *wasn't* fine. I don't know what I'm saying. Forget it."

Leroy takes a lungful of smoke and closes his eyes as Norma Jean's words sink in. He tries to focus on the fact that thirty-five hundred soldiers died on the grounds around him. He can only think of that war as a board game with plastic soldiers. Leroy almost smiles, as he compares the Confederates' daring attack on the Union camps and Virgil Mathis's raid on the bowling alley. General Grant, drunk and furious, shoved the Southerners back to Corinth, where Mabel and Jet Beasley were married years later, when Mabel was still thin and good-looking. The next day, Mabel and Jet visited the battleground, and then Norma Jean was born, and then she married Leroy and they had a baby, which they lost, and now Leroy and Norma Jean are here at the same battleground. Leroy knows he is leaving out a lot. He is leaving out the insides of history. History was always just names and dates to him. It occurs to him that building a house out of logs is similarly empty—too simple. And the real inner workings of a marriage, like most of history, have escaped him. Now he sees that building a log house is the dumbest idea he could have had. It was clumsy of him to think Norma Jean would want a log house. It was a crazy idea. He'll have to think of something else, quickly. He will wad the blueprints into tight balls and fling them into the lake. Then he'll get moving again. He opens his eyes. Norma Jean has moved away and is walking through the cemetery, following a serpentine brick path.

Leroy gets up to follow his wife, but his good leg is asleep and his bad leg still hurts him. Norma Jean is far away, walking rapidly toward the bluff by the river, and he tries to hobble toward her. Some children run past him, screaming noisily. Norma Jean has reached the bluff, and she is looking out over the Tennessee River. Now she turns toward Leroy and waves her arms. Is she beckoning to him? She seems to be doing an exercise for her chest muscles. The sky is unusually pale—the color of the dust ruffle Mabel made for their bed.

1982

ALICE WALKER

The Revenge of Hannah Kemhuff

In grateful memory of Zora Neale Hurston

1

Two weeks after I became Tante Rosie's apprentice we were visited by a very old woman who was wrapped and contained, almost smothered, in a half-dozen skirts and shawls. Tante Rosie (pronounced Ro'*zee*) told the woman she could see her name, Hannah Kemhuff, written in the air. She told the woman further that she belonged to the Order of the Eastern Star.[1]

The woman was amazed. (And I was, too! Though I learned later that Tante Rosie held extensive files on almost everybody in the county, which she kept in long cardboard boxes under her bed.) Mrs. Kemhuff quickly asked what else Tante Rosie could tell her.

Tante Rosie had a huge tank of water on a table in front of her, like an aquarium for fish, except there was no fish in it. There was nothing but water and I never was able to see anything in it. Tante Rosie, of course, could. While the woman waited Tante Rosie peered deep into the tank of water. Soon she said the water spoke to her and told her that although the woman looked old, she was not. Mrs. Kemhuff said that this was true, and wondered if Tante Rosie knew the reason she looked so old. Tante Rosie said she did not and asked if she would mind telling us about it. (At first Mrs. Kemhuff didn't seem to want me there, but Tante Rosie told her I was trying to learn the rootworking trade[2] and she nodded that she understood and didn't mind. I scrooched down as small as I could at the corner of Tante Rosie's table, smiling at her so she wouldn't feel embarrassed or afraid.)

"It was during the Depression," she began, shifting in her seat and adjusting the shawls. She wore so many her back appeared to be humped!

"Of course," said Tante Rosie, "and you were young and pretty."

"How do you know that?" exclaimed Mrs. Kemhuff. "That is true. I had been married already five years and had four small children and a husband with a wandering eye. But since I married young—"

"Why, you were little more than a child," said Tante Rosie.

"Yes," said Mrs. Kemhuff. "I were not quite twenty years old. And it was hard times everywhere, all over the country and, I suspect, all over the world. Of course, no one had television in those days, so we didn't know. I don't even now know if it was invented. We had a radio before the Depression which my husband won in a poker game, but we sold it somewhere along the line to buy a meal. Anyway, we lived for as long as we could on the money I brought in as a cook in a sawmill. I cooked cabbage and cornpone for twenty men for two

---

1. Service-oriented Masonic order made up of Master Masons, wives, sisters, daughters, etc.

2. The making of charms (often evil-working ones).

dollars a week. But then the mill closed down, and my husband had already been out of work for some time. We were on the point of starvation. We was so hungry, and the children were getting so weak, that after I had crapped off the last leaves from the collard stalks I couldn't wait for new leaves to grow back. I dug up the collards, roots and all. After we ate that there was nothing else.

"As I said, there was no way of knowing whether hard times was existing around the world because we did not then have a television set. And we had sold the radio. However, as it happened, hard times hit everybody we knew in Cherokee County.[3] And for that reason the government sent food stamps which you could get if you could prove you were starving. With a few of them stamps you could go into town to a place they had and get so much and so much fat back, so much and so much of corn meal, and so much and so much of (I think it was) red beans. As I say, we was, by then, desperate. And my husband pervailed on me for us to go. I never wanted to do it, on account of I have always been proud. My father, you know, used to be one of the biggest colored peanut growers in Cherokee County and we never had to ask nobody for nothing.

"Well, what had happened in the meantime was this: My sister, Carrie Mae—"

"A tough girl, if I remember right," said Tante Rosie.

"Yes," said Mrs. Kemhuff, "bright, full of spunk. Well, she were at that time living in the North. In Chicago. And she were working for some good white people that give her they old clothes to send back down here. And I tell you they were good things. And I was glad to get them. So, as it was gitting to be real cold, I dressed myself and my husband and the children up in them clothes. For see, they was made up North to be worn up there where there's snow at and they were warm as toast."

"Wasn't Carrie Mae later killed by a gangster?" asked Tante Rosie.

"Yes, she were," said the woman, anxious to go on with her story. "He were her husband."

"Oh," said Tante Rosie quietly.

"Now, so I dresses us all up in our new finery and with our stomachs growling all together we goes marching off to ask for what the government said was due us as proud as ever we knew how to be. For even my husband, when he had on the right clothes, could show some pride, and me, whenever I remembered how fine my daddy's peanut crops had provided us, why there was nobody with stiffer backbone."

"I see a pale and evil shadow looming ahead of you in this journey," said Tante Rosie, looking into the water as if she'd lost a penny while we weren't looking.

"That shadow was sure pale and evil all right," said Mrs. Kemhuff. "When we got to the place there was a long line, and we saw all of our friends in this line. On one side of the big pile of food was the white line—and some rich peoples was in that line too—and on the other

____

3. Fictional; there are many Cherokee counties, but none in peanut-growing country.

side there was the black line. I later heard, by the by, that the white folks in the white line got bacon and grits, as well as meal, but that is neither here nor there. What happened was this. As soon as our friends saw us all dressed up in our nice warm clothes, though used and castoff they were, they began saying how crazy we was to have worn them. And that's when I began to notice that all the people in the black line had dressed themselves in tatters. Even people what had good things at home, and I knew some of them did. What does this mean? I asked my husband. But he didn't know. He was too busy strutting about to even pay much attention. But I began to be terribly afraid. The baby had begun to cry and the other little ones, knowing I was nervous, commenced to whine and gag. I had a time with them.

"Now, at this time my husband had been looking around at other women and I was scared to death I was going to lose him. He already made fun of me and said I was arrogant and proud. I said that was the way to be and that he should try to be that way. The last thing I wanted to happen was for him to see me embarrassed and made small in front of a lot of people because I knew if that happened he would quit me.

"So I was standing there hoping that the white folks what give out the food wouldn't notice that I was dressed nice and that if they did they would see how hungry the babies was and how pitiful we all was. I could see my husband over talking to the woman he was going with on the sly. She was dressed like a flysweep![4] Not only was she raggedy, she was dirty! Filthy dirty, and with her filthy slip showing. She looked so awful she disgusted me. And yet there was my husband hanging over her while I stood in the line holding on to all four of our children. I guess he knew as well as I did what that woman had in the line of clothes at home. She was always much better dressed than me and much better dressed than many of the white peoples. That was because, they say she was a whore and took money. Seems like people want that and will pay for it even in a depression!"

There was a pause while Mrs. Kemhuff drew a deep breath. Then she continued.

"So soon I was next to get something from the young lady at the counter. All around her I could smell them red beans and my mouth was watering for a taste of fresh-water cornpone. I was proud, but I wasn't fancy. I just wanted something for me and the children. Well, there I was, with the children hanging to my dresstails, and I drew myself up as best I could and made the oldest boy stand up straight, for I had come to ask for what was mine, not to beg. So I wasn't going to be acting like a beggar. Well, I want you to know that that little slip of a woman, all big blue eyes and yellow hair, that little *girl*, took my stamps and then took one long look at me and my children and across at my husband—all of us dressed to kill I guess she thought—and she took my stamps in her hand and looked at them like they was dirty, and then she give them to an old gambler who was next in line behind me! 'You don't need nothing to eat from the way you all dressed up, Hannah Lou,' she said to me. 'But Miss Sadler,' I said, 'my children is

4. Flue-, i.e., chimney-sweep.

hungry.' 'They don't look hungry,' she said to me. 'Move along now, somebody here may really need our help!' The whole line behind me began to laugh and snigger, and that little white moppet sort of grinned behind her hands. She give the old gambler double what he would have got otherwise. And there me and my children about to keel over from want.

"When my husband and his woman saw and heard what happened they commenced to laugh, too, and he reached down and got her stuff, piles and piles of it, it seemed to me then, and helped her put it in somebody's car and they drove off together. And that was about the last I seen of him. Or her."

"Weren't they swept off a bridge together in the flood that wiped out Tunica City?"[5] asked Tante Rosie.

"Yes," said Mrs. Kemhuff. "Somebody like you might have helped me then, too, though looks like I didn't need it."

"So—"

"So after that looks like my spirit just wilted. Me and my children got a ride home with somebody and I tottered around like a drunken woman and put them to bed. They was sweet children and not much trouble, although they was about to go out of their minds with hunger."

Now a deep sadness crept into her face, which until she reached this point had been still and impassive.

"First one then the other of them took sick and died. Though the old gambler came by the house three or four days later and divided what he had left with us. He had been on his way to gambling it all away. The Lord called him to have pity on us and since he knew us and knew my husband had deserted me he said he were right glad to help out. But it was mighty late in the day when he thought about helping out and the children were far gone. Nothing could save them except the Lord and he seemed to have other things on his mind, like the wedding that spring of the mean little moppet."

Mrs. Kemhuff now spoke through clenched teeth.

"My spirit never recovered from that insult, just like my heart never recovered from my husband's desertion, just like my body never recovered from being almost starved to death. I started to wither in that winter and each year found me more hacked and worn down than the year before. Somewhere along them years my pride just up and left altogether and I worked for a time in a whorehouse just to make some money, just like my husband's woman. Then I took to drinking to forget what I was doing, and soon I just broke down and got old all at once, just like you see me now. And I started about five years ago to going to church. I was converted again, 'cause I felt the first time he had done got worn off. But I am not restful. I dream and have nightmares still about the little moppet, and always I feel the moment when my spirit was trampled down within me while they all stood and laughed and she stood there grinning behind her hands."

"Well," said Tante Rosie. "There are ways that the spirit can be

---

5. Tunica, Mississippi, in Tunica County, is about five miles from the Mississippi River.

mended just as there are ways that the spirit can be broken. But one such as I am cannot do both. If I am to take away the burden of shame which is upon you I must in some way inflict it on someone else."

"I do not care to be cured," said Mrs. Kemhuff. "It is enough that I have endured my shame all these years and that my children and my husband were taken from me by one who knew nothing about us. I can survive as long as I need with the bitterness that has laid every day in my soul. But I could die easier if I knew something, after all these years, had been done to the little moppet. God cannot be let to make her happy all these years and me miserable. What kind of justice would that be? It would be monstrous!"

"Don't worry about it, my sister," said Tante Rosie with gentleness. "By the grace of the Man-God I have use of many powers. Powers given me by the Great One Herself. If you can no longer bear the eyes of the enemy that you see in your dreams the Man-God, who speaks to me from the Great Mother of Us All, will see that those eyes are eaten away. If the hands of your enemy have struck you they can be made useless." Tante Rosie held up a small piece of what was once lustrous pewter. Now it was pock-marked and blackened and deteriorating.

"Do you see this metal?" she asked.

"Yes, I see it," said Mrs. Kemhuff with interest. She took it in her hands and rubbed it.

"The part of the moppet you want destroyed will rot away in the same fashion."

Mrs. Kemhuff relinquished the piece of metal to Tante Rosie.

"You are a true sister," she said.

"Is it enough?" Tante Rosie asked.

"I would give anything to stop her grinning behind her hands," said the woman, drawing out a tattered billfold.

"Her hands or the grinning mouth?" asked Tante Rosie.

"The mouth grinned and the hands hid it," said Mrs. Kemhuff.

"Ten dollars for one area, twenty for two," said Tante Rosie.

"Make it the mouth," said Mrs. Kemhuff. "That is what I see most vividly in my dreams." She laid a ten-dollar bill in the lap of Tante Rosie.

"Let me explain what we will do," said Tante Rosie, coming near the woman and speaking softly to her, as a doctor would speak to a patient. "First we will make a potion that has a long history of use in our profession. It is a mixture of hair and nail parings of the person in question, a bit of their water and feces, a piece of their clothing heavy with their own scents, and I think in this case we might as well add a pinch of goober dust; that is, dust from the graveyard. This woman will not outlive you by more than six months."

I had thought the two women had forgotten about me, but now Tante Rosie turned to me and said, "You will have to go out to Mrs. Kemhuff's house. She will have to be instructed in the recitation of the curse-prayer. You will show her how to dress the black candles and how to pay Death for his interception in her behalf."

Then she moved over to the shelf that held her numerous supplies:

oils of Bad and Good Luck Essence, dried herbs, creams, powders, and candles. She took two large black candles and placed them in Mrs. Kemhuff's hands. She also gave her a small bag of powder and told her to burn it on her table (as an altar) while she was praying the curse-prayer. I was to show Mrs. Kemhuff how to "dress" the candles in vinegar so they would be purified for her purpose.

She told Mrs. Kemhuff that each morning and evening for nine days she was to light the candles, burn the powder, recite the curse-prayer from her knees and concentrate all her powers on getting her message through to Death and the Man-God. As far as the Supreme Mother of Us All was concerned, She could only be moved by the pleas of the Man-God. Tante Rosie herself would recite the curse-prayer at the same time that Mrs. Kemhuff did, and together she thought the two prayers, prayed with respect, could not help but move the Man-God, who, in turn, would unchain Death, who would already be eager to come down on the little moppet. But her death would be slow in coming because first the Man-God had to hear all of the prayers.

"We will take those parts of herself that we collect, the feces, water, nail parings, et cetera, and plant them where they will bring for you the best results. Within a year's time the earth will be rid of the woman herself, even as almost immediately you will be rid of her grin. Do you want something else for only two dollars that will make you feel happy even today?" asked Tante Rosie.

But Mrs. Kemhuff shook her head. "I'm carefree enough already, knowing that her end will be before another year. As for happiness, it is something that deserts you once you know it can be bought and sold. I will not live to see the end results of your work, Tante Rosie, but my grave will fit nicer, having someone proud again who has righted a wrong and by so doing lies straight and proud throughout eternity."

And Mrs. Kemhuff turned and left, bearing herself grandly out of the room. It was as if she had regained her youth; her shawls were like a stately toga, her white hair seemed to sparkle.

2

To the Man-God: O great One, I have been sorely tried by my enemies and have been blasphemed and lied against. My good thoughts and my honest actions have been turned to bad actions and dishonest ideas. My home has been disrespected, my children have been cursed and ill-treated. My dear ones have been backbitten and their virtue questioned. O Man-God, I beg that this that I ask for my enemies shall come to pass:

That the South wind shall scorch their bodies and make them wither and shall not be tempered to them. That the North wind shall freeze their blood and numb their muscles and that it shall not be tempered to them. That the West wind shall blow away their life's breath and will not leave their hair grow, and that their fingernails shall fall off and their bones shall crumble. That the East wind shall make their minds grow dark, their sight shall fail and their seed dry up so that they shall not multiply.

I ask that their fathers and mothers from their furtherest generation will not intercede for them before the great throne, and the wombs of their women shall not bear fruit except for strangers, and that they shall become extinct. I pray that the children who may come shall be weak of mind and paralyzed of limb and that they themselves shall curse them in their turn for ever turning the breath of life into their bodies. I pray that disease and death shall be forever with them and that their worldly goods shall not prosper, and that their crops shall not multiply and that their cows, their sheep, and their hogs and all their living beasts shall die of starvation and thirst. I pray that their house shall be unroofed and that the rain, the thunder and lightning shall find the innermost recesses of their home and that the foundation shall crumble and the floods tear it asunder. I pray that the sun shall not shed its rays on them in benevolence, but instead it shall beat down on them and burn them and destroy them. I pray that the moon shall not give them peace, but instead shall deride them and decry them and cause their minds to shrivel. I pray that their friends shall betray them and cause them loss of power, of gold and of silver, and that their enemies shall smite them until they beg for mercy which shall not be given them. I pray that their tongues shall forget how to speak in sweet words, and that it shall be paralyzed and that all about them will be desolation, pestilence and death. O Man-God, I ask you for all these things because they have dragged me in the dust and destroyed my good name; broken my heart and caused me to curse the day that I was born. So be it.

This curse-prayer was regularly used and taught by rootworkers, but since I did not know it by heart, as Tante Rosie did, I recited it straight from Zora Neale Hurston's book, *Mules and Men*,[6] and Mrs. Kemhuff and I learned it on our knees together. We were soon dressing the candles in vinegar, lighting them, kneeling and praying—intoning the words rhythmically—as if we had been doing it this way for years. I was moved by the fervor with which Mrs. Kemhuff prayed. Often she would clench her fists before her closed eyes and bite the insides of her wrists as the women do in Greece.

3

According to courthouse records Sarah Marie Sadler, "the little moppet," was born in 1910. She was in her early twenties during the Depression. In 1932 she married Ben Jonathan Holley, who later inherited a small chain of grocery stores and owned a plantation and an impressive stand of timber. In the spring of 1963, Mrs. Holley was fifty-three years old. She was the mother of three children, a boy and two girls; the boy a floundering clothes salesman, the girls married and oblivious, mothers themselves.

The elder Holleys lived six miles out in the country, their house was large, and Mrs. Holley's hobbies were shopping for antiques, gossiping with colored women, discussing her husband's health and her chil-

6. Volume of folklore published in 1935; Hurston (1901–60), black writer to whose memory this story is dedicated.

dren's babies, and making spoon bread. I was able to glean this much from the drunken ramblings of the Holleys' cook, a malevolent nanny with gout, who had raised, in her prime, at least one tan Holley, a preacher whom the Holleys had sent to Morehouse.[7]

"I bet I could get the nanny to give us all the information and nail parings we could ever use," I said to Tante Rosie. For the grumpy woman drank muscatel like a sow and clearly hated Mrs. Holley. However, it was hard to get her tipsy enough for truly revealing talk and we were quickly running out of funds.

"That's not the way," Tante Rosie said one evening as she sat in her car and watched me lead the nanny out of the dreary but secret-evoking recesses of the Six Forks Bar. We had already spent six dollars on muscatel.

"You can't trust gossips or drunks," said Tante Rosie. "You let the woman we are working on give you everything you need, and from her own lips."

"But that is the craziest thing I have ever heard," I said. "How can I talk to her about putting a fix on her without making her mad, or maybe even scaring her to death?"

Tante Rosie merely grunted.

"Rule number one. OBSERVATION OF SUBJECT. Write that down among your crumpled notes."

"In other words—?"

"Be direct, but not blunt."

On my way to the Holley plantation I came up with the idea of pretending to be searching for a fictitious person. Then I had an even better idea. I parked Tante Rosie's Bonneville at the edge of the spacious yard, which was dotted with mimosas and camellias. Tante Rosie had insisted I wear a brilliant orange robe and as I walked it swished and blew about my legs. Mrs. Holley was on the back patio steps, engaged in conversation with a young and beautiful black girl. They stared in amazement at the length and brilliance of my attire.

"Mrs. Holley, I think it's time for me to go," said the girl.

"Don't be silly," said the matronly Mrs. Holley. "She is probably just a light-skinned African who is on her way somewhere and got lost." She nudged the black girl in the ribs and they both broke into giggles.

"How do you do?" I asked.

"Just fine, how you?" said Mrs. Holley, while the black girl looked on askance. They had been talking with their heads close together and stood up together when I spoke.

"I am looking for a Josiah Henson"—a runaway slave and the original Uncle Tom in Harriet Beecher Stowe's novel, I might have added. "Could you tell me if he lives on your place?"

"That name sounds awful familiar," said the black girl.

"Are you *the* Mrs. Holley?" I asked gratuitously, while Mrs. Holley was distracted. She was sure she had never heard the name.

"Of course," she said, and smiled, pleating the side of her dress. She was a grayish blonde with an ashen untanned face, and her hands

---

7. Predominantly black college, founded 1867, now part of Atlanta University.

were five blunt and pampered fingers each. "And this is my . . . ah . . . my friend, Caroline Williams."

Caroline nodded curtly.

"Somebody told me ole Josiah might be out this way. . . ."

"Well, we hadn't seen him," said Mrs. Holley. "We were just here shelling some peas, enjoying this nice sunshine."

"Are you a light African?" asked Caroline.

"No," I said. "I work with Tante Rosie, the rootworker. I'm learning the profession."

"Whatever *for*?" asked Mrs. Holley. "I would have thought a nice-looking girl like yourself could find a better way to spend her time. I been hearing about Tante Rosie since I was a little bitty child, but everybody always said that rootworking was just a whole lot of n——, I mean colored foolishness. Of course we don't believe in that kind of thing, do we, Caroline?"

"Naw."

The younger woman put a hand on the older woman's arm, possessively, as if to say "You get away from here, bending my white folks' ear with your crazy mess!" From the kitchen window a dark remorseful face worked itself into various messages of "Go away!" It was the drunken nanny.

"I wonder if you would care to prove you do not believe in root-working?"

"Prove?" said the white woman indignantly.

"Prove?" asked the black woman with scorn.

"That is the word," I said.

"Why, not that I'm afraid of any of this nigger magic!" said Mrs. Holley staunchly, placing a reassuring hand on Caroline's shoulder. *I* was the nigger, not she.

"In that case won't you show us how much you don't have fear of it." With the word *us* I placed Caroline in the same nigger category with me. Let her smolder! Now Mrs. Holley stood alone, the great white innovator and scientific scourge, forced to man the Christian fort against heathen nigger paganism.

"Of course, if you like," she said immediately, drawing herself up in the best English manner. Stiff upper lip, what? and all that. She had been grinning throughout. Now she covered her teeth with her scant two lips and her face became flat and resolute. Like so many white women in sections of the country where the race was still "pure" her mouth could have been formed by the minute slash of a thin sword.

"Do you know a Mrs. Hannah Lou Kemhuff?" I asked.

"No I do not."

"She is not white, Mrs. Holley, she is black."

"Hannah Lou, Hannah Lou . . . do we know a Hannah Lou?" she asked, turning to Caroline.

"No, ma'am, we don't!" said Caroline.

"Well, she knows you. Says she met you on the bread lines during the Depression and that because she was dressed up you wouldn't give her any corn meal. Or red beans. Or something like that."

"Bread lines, Depression, dressed up, corn meal . . . ? I don't know what you're talking about!" No shaft of remembrance probed the depth of what she had done to colored people more than twenty years ago.

"It doesn't really matter, since you don't believe . . . but she says you did her wrong, and being a good Christian, she believes all wrongs are eventually righted in the Lord's good time. She came to us for help only when she began to feel the Lord's good time might be too far away. Because we do not deal in the work of unmerited destruction, Tante Rosie and I did not see how we could take the case." I said this humbly, with as much pious intonation as I could muster.

"Well, I'm glad," said Mrs. Holley, who had been running through the back years on her fingers.

"But," I said, "we told her what she could do to bring about restitution of peaceful spirit, which she claimed you robbed her of in a moment during which, as is now evident, you were not concerned. You were getting married the following spring."

"That was '32," said Mrs. Holley. "Hannah *Lou?*"

"The same."

"How black *was* she? Sometimes I can recall colored faces that way."

"That is not relevant," I said, "since you do not believe. . . ."

"Well of *course* I don't believe!" said Mrs. Holley.

"I am nothing in this feud between you," I said. "Neither is Tante Rosie. Neither of us had any idea until after Mrs. Kemhuff left that you were the woman she spoke of. We are familiar with the deep and sincere interest you take in the poor colored children at Christmastime each year. We know you have gone out of your way to hire needy people to work on your farm. We know you have been an example of Christian charity and a beacon force of brotherly love. And right before my eyes I can see it is true you have Negro friends."

"Just what is it you want?" asked Mrs. Holley.

"What *Mrs. Kemhuff* wants are some nail parings, not many, just a few, some hair (that from a comb will do), some water and some feces—and if you don't feel like doing either number one or number two, I will wait—and a bit of clothing, something that you have worn in the last year. Something with some of your odor on it."

"What!" Mrs. Holley screeched.

"They say this combination, with the right prayers, can eat away part of a person just like the disease that ruins so much fine antique pewter."

Mrs. Holley blanched. With a motherly fluttering of hands Caroline helped her into a patio chair.

"Go get my medicine," said Mrs. Holley, and Caroline started from the spot like a gazelle.

"Git away from here! Git away!"

I spun around just in time to save my head from a whack with a gigantic dust mop. It was the drunken nanny, drunk no more, flying to the defense of her mistress.

"She just a tramp and a phony!" she reassured Mrs. Holley, who was caught up in an authentic faint.

4

Not long after I saw Mrs. Holley, Hannah Kemhuff was buried. Tante Rosie and I followed the casket to the cemetery. Tante Rosie most elegant in black. Then we made our way through briers and grass to the highway. Mrs. Kemhuff rested in a tangly grove, off to herself, though reasonably near her husband and babies. Few people came to the funeral, which made the faces of Mrs. Holley's nanny and husband stand out all the more plainly. They had come to verify the fact that this dead person was indeed *the* Hannah Lou Kemhuff whom Mr. Holley had initiated a search for, having the entire county militia at his disposal.

Several months later we read in the paper that Sarah Marie Sadler Holley had also passed away. The paper spoke of her former beauty and vivacity, as a young woman, and of her concern for those less fortunate than herself as a married woman and pillar of the community and her church. It spoke briefly of her harsh and lengthy illness. It said all who knew her were sure her soul would find peace in heaven, just as her shrunken body had endured so much pain and heartache here on earth.

Caroline had kept us up to date on the decline of Mrs. Holley. After my visit, relations between them became strained and Mrs. Holley eventually became too frightened of Caroline's darkness to allow her close to her. A week after I'd talked to them Mrs. Holley began having her meals in her bedroom upstairs. Then she started doing everything else there as well. She collected stray hairs from her head and comb with the greatest attention and consistency, not to say desperation. She ate her fingernails. But the most bizarre of all was her response to Mrs. Kemhuff's petition for a specimen of feces and water. Not trusting any longer the earthen secrecy of the water mains, she no longer flushed. Together with the nanny Mrs. Holley preferred to store those relics of what she ate (which became almost nothing and then nothing, the nanny had told Caroline) and they kept it all in barrels and plastic bags in the upstairs closets. In a few weeks it became impossible for anyone to endure the smell of the house, even Mrs. Holley's husband, who loved her but during the weeks before her death slept in a spare room of the nanny's house.

The mouth that had grinned behind the hands grinned no more. The constant anxiety lest a stray strand of hair be lost and the foul odor of the house soon brought to the hands a constant seeking motion, to the eyes a glazed and vacant stare, and to the mouth a tightly puckered frown, one which only death might smooth.

1973

POETRY

1   EXPERIENCING POETRY

People seldom feel neutral about poetry. Those who love it sometimes give the impression that it is an adequate substitute for food, shelter, and love. It isn't. It won't feed you or do your work for you or help you defeat your enemies, and, however satisfying words can be, they are never an equivalent for life itself and its human experiences. Those who dislike poetry on principle sometimes claim, on the other hand, that poetry is only words and good for nothing. That's not true either. It is easy to become frustrated by words—in poetry or in life—but when words represent, express, and recreate genuine human feelings, as they often do in poetry, they can be crucially important. Poetry is, in fact, more than just words. It is an *experience* of words, and those who know how to read poetry can easily extend their experience of life, their sense of what other people are like, and especially their awareness of personal feelings.

Feelings. One reason why poetry can be so important is that it is so intimately concerned with feelings. Poetry is often full of ideas, too, and sometimes poems can be powerful experiences of the mind, but most poems are primarily about how people feel rather than how people think. Poems provide, in fact, a language for feeling, and one of poetry's most insistent virtues involves its attempt to express the inexpressible. How can anyone, for example, put into words what it means to be in love? or what it feels like to lose to death someone one cares about? Poetry tries, and it often captures exactly the shade of emotion that feels just right to the reader. No one poem can be said to express all the things that love or death feels like, or means, but one of the joys of experiencing poetry occurs when we read a poem and want to say, "Yes, that is just what it is like; I know exactly what that line means but I've never been able to express it so well." Poetry can be the mouthpiece of our feelings even when our minds are speechless with grief or joy.

Here are two poems that talk about the sincerity and depth of love between two people. Each is written as if it were spoken or read by one person to his or her lover, and each is definite and powerful about the intensity and quality of love; but the poems work in quite different ways—the first one asserting the strength and depth of love, the second implying intense feeling by reminiscing about events in the relationship between the two people.

ELIZABETH BARRETT BROWNING

How Do I Love Thee?

How do I love thee? Let me count the ways.
I love thee to the depth and breadth and height
My soul can reach, when feeling out of sight
For the ends of Being and ideal Grace.
I love thee to the level of every day's   5
Most quiet need, by sun and candlelight.
I love thee freely, as men strive for Right;
I love thee purely, as they turn from Praise;
I love thee with the passion put to use
In my old griefs, and with my childhood's faith.   10
I love thee with a love I seemed to lose
With my lost saints—I love thee with the breath,
Smiles, tears of all my life!—and, if God choose,
I shall but love thee better after death.

                                              1850

JAROLD RAMSEY

The Tally Stick

Here from the start, from our first of days, look:
I have carved our lives in secret on this stick
of mountain mahogany the length of your arms
outstretched, the wood clear red, so hard and rare.
It is time to touch and handle what we know we share.   5

Near the butt, this intricate notch where the grains
converge and join: it is our wedding.
I can read it through with a thumb and tell you now
who danced, who made up the songs, who meant us joy.
These little arrowheads along the grain,   10
they are the births of our children. See,
they make a kind of design with these heavy crosses,
the deaths of our parents, the loss of friends.

Over it all as it goes, of course, I
have chiseled Events, History—random   15
hashmarks cut against the swirling grain.
See, here is the Year the World Went Wrong,
we thought, and here the days the Great Men fell.
The lengthening runes of our lives run through it all.

See, our tally stick is whittled nearly end to end;   20
delicate as scrimshaw, it would not bear you up.

Regrets have polished it, hand over hand.
Yet let us take it up, and as our fingers
like children leading on a trail cry back
our unforgotten wonders, sign after sign,   25
we will talk softly as of ordinary matters,
and in one another's blameless eyes go blind.

p. 1977

The first poem is direct, but fairly abstract. It lists several ways in which the poet feels love and connects them to some noble ideas of higher obligations—to justice (line 7), for example, and to spiritual aspiration (lines 2–4). It suggests a wide range of things that love can mean and notices a variety of emotions. It is an ardent statement of feeling and asserts a permanence that will extend even beyond death. It contains admirable thoughts and memorable phrases that many lovers would like to hear said to themselves. What it does not do is say very much about what the relationship between the two lovers is like on an everyday basis, what experiences they have had together, what distinguishes their relationship from that of other devoted or ideal lovers. Its appeal is to our general sense of what love is like and how intense feelings can be; it does not offer everyday details. Love may differ from person to person and even from moment to moment, and so can poems about love.

The Tally Stick is much more concrete. The whole poem concentrates on a single object that, like the poem above, "counts" or "tallies" the ways in which this couple love one another. The stick stands for their love and becomes a kind of physical reminder of it: its natural features—the notches and arrowheads and cross marks (lines 6, 10, and 12) along with the marks carved on it (lines 15–16, 20–21)—indicate events in the story of the relationship. (We could say that the stick *symbolizes* their love; later on, we will look at a number of terms like this that can be used to make it easier to talk about some aspects of poems, but for now it is enough to notice that the stick serves the lovers as a reminder of some specific details of their love.) It is a special kind of reminder to them because its language is "secret" (line 2), something they can share privately (except that we as readers of the poem are sort of looking over their shoulders, not intruding but sharing their secret). The poet interprets the particular features of the stick as standing for particular events—their wedding and the births of their children, for example—and carves marks into it as reminders of other events (lines 15ff.). The stick itself becomes a very personal object, and in the last stanza of the poem it is as if we watch the lovers touching the stick together and reminiscing over it, gradually dissolving into their emotions and each other as they recall the "unforgotten wonders" (line 25) of their lives together.

Both poems are powerful statements of feelings, each in its own way. Some readers will prefer one and some the other. Personal preference does not mean that objective standards for poetry cannot be found (some poems are better than others, and later we will look in detail at features which help us to evaluate poems), but we need have no preconceived standard that all poetry must be one thing or another or work in one particular way. Some good poems are quite abstract, others quite specific. Any poem that helps us to articulate and clarify human feelings and ideas has a legitimate claim on us as readers. We tend to like poems (or people) for what they do, what they are, and what they represent to us.

Both *How Do I Love Thee* and *The Tally Stick* are written as if they were addressed to the partner in the love relationship, and both talk directly about the intensity of the love. The next poem we will look at talks only indirectly about the quality and intensity of love. It is written as if it were a letter from a woman to her husband who has gone on a long journey on business, and it clearly expresses how much she misses him, but indirectly suggests how much she cares about him.

EZRA POUND

The River-Merchant's Wife: A Letter

(*after Rihaku*[1])

While my hair was still cut straight across my forehead
I played about the front gate, pulling flowers.
You came by on bamboo stilts, playing horse,
You walked about my seat, playing with blue plums.
And we went on living in the village of Chokan: 5
Two small people, without dislike or suspicion.

At fourteen I married My Lord you.
I never laughed, being bashful.
Lowering my head, I looked at the wall.
Called to, a thousand times, I never looked back.   10

At fifteen I stopped scowling,
I desired my dust to be mingled with yours
For ever and for ever and for ever.
Why should I climb the look out?

At sixteen you departed,   15
You went into far Ku-to-yen, by the river of swirling eddies,
And you have been gone five months.
The monkeys make sorrowful noise overhead.

You dragged your feet when you went out.
By the gate now, the moss is grown, the different mosses,   20

1. The Japanese name for Li Po, an 8th-century Chinese poet. Pound's poem is a loose paraphrase of Li Po's.

Too deep to clear them away!
The leaves fall early this autumn, in wind.
The paired butterflies are already yellow with August
Over the grass in the West garden;
They hurt me. I grow older.   25
If you are coming down through the narrows of the river Kiang,
Please let me know beforehand,
And I will come out to meet you
        As far as Cho-fu-Sa.

                                                              1915

   The "letter" tells us only a few facts about the nameless merchant's wife: that she is about sixteen and a half years old, that she married at fourteen and fell in love with her husband a year later, that she is now very lonely. And about their relationship we know only that they were childhood playmates in a small Chinese village, that their marriage originally was not a matter of personal choice, and that the husband unwillingly went away on a long journey five months ago. But the words tell us a great deal about how the young wife feels, and the simplicity of her language suggests her sincere and deep longing. The daily noises she hears seem "sorrowful" (line 18), and she worries about the dangers of the far-away place where her husband is, thinking of it in terms of its perilous "river of swirling eddies" (line 16). She thinks of how moss has grown up over the unused gate, and more time seems to her to have passed than actually has (lines 22–25). She remembers nostalgically their innocent childhood, when they played together without deeper love or commitment (lines 1–6), and contrasts that with her later satisfaction in their love (lines 11–14) and with her present anxiety, loneliness, and desire. We do not need to know the details of the geography of the river Kiang or how far Cho-fu-Sa is to sense that her wish to see him is very strong, that her desire is powerful enough to make her venture beyond the ordinary geographical bounds of her existence so that their reunion will come sooner. The closest she comes to a direct statement about her love is her statement that she desired that her dust be mingled with his "For ever and for ever and for ever" (lines 12–13). But her single-minded vision of the world, her perception of even the beauty of nature as only a record of her husband's absence and the passage of time, and her plain, apparently uncalculated language about her rejection of other suitors and her shutting out of the rest of the world all show her to be committed, desirous, nearly desperate for his presence. In a different sense, she has also counted the ways that she loves her man.
   Here is another poem that similarly expresses a woman's intense desire for her lover, but here the expression is much more openly physical and sexual.

DIANE WAKOSKI

Uneasy Rider[2]

Falling in love with a mustache
is like saying
you can fall in love with
the way a man polishes his shoes
      which,   5
      of course,
      is one of the things that turns on
      my tuned-up engine

      those trim buckled boots

      (I feel like an advertisement   10
        for men's fashions
          when I think of your ankles)

Yeats was hung up with a girl's beautiful face[3]

and I find myself

a bad moralist,   15

a failing aesthetician,

a sad poet,

wanting to touch your arms and feel the muscles
that make a man's body have so much substance,
that makes a woman   20
lean and yearn in that direction
that makes her melt/ she is a rainy day
in your presence
the pool of wax under a burning candle
the foam from a waterfall   25

You are more beautiful than any Harley-Davidson
She is the rain,
waits in it for you,
finds blood spotting her legs
from the long ride.   30
                1971

distancing

2. From Wakoski's volume, *The Motorcycle Betrayal Poems. Easy Rider* was one of the most popular motorcycle films of the late 1960s and early '70s.
3. See, for example, Yeats's "Among School Children," p. 793.

Physical details of the man's body and his clothing are plentiful here, and the woman is very direct about their effects—emotional and physical—upon her as she talks about what "turns on" her "tuned-up engine" (lines 7–8), and how his muscles make her "lean and yearn" and her body "melt" (lines 18–22). So vivid and intense are the various pictures of melting ("a rainy day," "a pool of wax," and "foam from a waterfall") that the poem pulls its focus back a bit from the couple near the end and talks of them as "a man" and "a woman": the woman who is speaking the poem adopts the third-person "she" to distance herself (and us) from the fire and energy of passion.

Poems can, of course, be about the meaning of a relationship or about disappointment just as easily as about sex or emotional fulfillment, and poets are often very good at suggesting the contradictions and uncertainties that tend to affect most relationships. Like other people, poets often find love and its complications quaint or downright funny, too, mainly because it involves human beings who, however serious their intentions and concerns, are often inept, uncertain, and self-contradictory—in short, human. Showing us ourselves as others see us is one of the more useful tasks that poems perform, but the poems that result can be just as entertaining and pleasurable as they are educational. Here is a poem which imagines a very strange scene, a kind of fantasy of what happens when we *think* too much about the implications of sex or love, and it is likely to leave us laughing, whether or not we take it seriously as a statement of human anxiety and of the tendency to intellectualize too much.

TOM WAYMAN

Wayman in Love

At last Wayman gets the girl into bed.
He is locked in one of those embraces
so passionate his left arm is asleep
when suddenly he is bumped in the back.
"Excuse me," a voice mutters, thick with German.   5
Wayman and the girl sit up astounded
as a furry gentleman in boots and a frock coat
climbs in under the covers.

"My name is Doktor Marx," the intruder announces
settling his neck comfortably on the pillow.   10
"I'm here to consider for you the cost of a kiss."
He pulls out a notepad. "Let's see now,
we have the price of the mattress, this room must be rented,
your time off work, groceries for two,
medical fees in case of accidents . . ."   15

"Look," Wayman says,
"couldn't we do this later?"
The philosopher sighs, and continues: "You are affected too,
    Miss.
If you are not working, you are going to resent   20
your dependent position. This will influence
I assure you, your most intimate moments . . ."

"Doctor, please," Wayman says. "All we want
is to be left alone."
But another beard, more nattily dressed,   25
is also getting into the bed.
There is a shifting and heaving of bodies
as everyone wriggles out room for themselves.
"I want you to meet a friend from Vienna,"
Marx says. "This is Doktor Freud."   30

The newcomer straightens his glasses,
peers at Wayman and the girl.
"I can see," he begins,
"that you two have problems . . ."

1973

Another traditional subject of poetry is death, and on this subject, too, poets often describe frequent, recurrent human emotions in a variety of ways. In the following poem, a father struggles to understand and control his grief.

BEN JONSON

On My First Son

Farewell, thou child of my right hand,[4] and joy;
My sin was too much hope of thee, loved boy:
Seven years thou'wert lent to me, and I thee pay,
Exacted by thy fate, on the just [5]day.
O could I lose all father now! for why   5
Will man lament the state he should envý,
To have so soon 'scaped world's and flesh's rage,
And, if no other misery, yet age?
Rest in soft peace, and asked, say, "Here doth lie

4. A literal translation of the son's name, Benjamin.
5. Exact; the son died on his seventh birthday, in 1603.

Ben Jonson his[6] best piece of poetry."   10
For whose sake henceforth all his vows be such
As what he loves may never like too much.

                                                                    1616

The poem's attempts to rationalize the death are quite conventional,
and although the father tries to be comforted by pious thoughts,
his feelings keep showing through. The poem's beginning—with its
formal "farewell" and the rather distant-sounding address to the dead
boy ("child of my right hand")—cannot be sustained for long: both
of the first two lines end with bursts of emotion. It is as if the father
is trying to explain the death to himself and to keep his emotions
under control, but cannot quite manage it. Even the punctuation suggests the way his feelings compete with conventional attempts to put
the death into some sort of perspective that will soften the grief, and
the comma near the end of each of the first two lines marks a pause
that cannot quite hold back the overflowing emotion. But finally the
only "idea" that the poem supports is that the father wishes he did not
feel so intensely; in the fifth line he fairly blurts that he wishes he
could lose his fatherly emotions, and in the final lines he resolves
never again to "like" so much that he can be this deeply hurt. Philosophy and religion offer their useful counsels in this poem, but they
prove far less powerful than feeling; and rather than drawing some
kind of moral about what death means, the poem presents the actuality of feeling as inevitable and nearly all-consuming.

The poem that follows similarly tries to suppress the rawness of
feelings about the death of a loved one, but here the survivor is
haunted by memories of his wife when he sees a physical object—a
vacuum cleaner—that was important in her life.

HOWARD NEMEROV

The Vacuum

The house is so quiet now
The vacuum cleaner sulks in the corner closet,
Its bag limp as a stopped lung, its mouth
Grinning into the floor, maybe at my
Slovenly life, my dog-dead youth.   5

I've lived this way long enough,
But when my old woman died her soul
Went into that vacuum cleaner, and I can't bear
To see the bag swell like a belly, eating the dust
And the woolen mice, and begin to howl   10

6. Ben Jonson's (a common Renaissance form of the possessive).

Because there is old filth everywhere
She used to crawl, in the corner and under the stair.
I know now how life is cheap as dirt,
And still the hungry, angry heart
Hangs on and howls, biting at air.   15

1955

The poem is about a vacuum in the husband's life, but the title refers most obviously to the vacuum cleaner that, like the tally stick we
looked at earlier, seems to stand for many of the things that were once
important in their life together. The cleaner is a reminder of the dead
wife ("my old woman," line 7) because of her devotion to cleanliness,
but to the surviving husband buried in the filth of his life it seems as
if the machine has become almost human, a kind of ghost of her: it
"sulks" (line 2), it has lungs and a mouth (line 3), and it seems to
grin, making fun of what has become of him. He "can't bear" (line 8)
to see it in action because it then seems too much alive, too much a
reminder of her life. The poem records his paralysis, his inability to do
more than discover that life is "cheap as dirt" without her ordering
and cleansing presence for him. At the end it is *his* angry heart that
acts like the haunting machine, howling and biting at air as if he has
merged with her spirit and the physical object that memorializes her.
This poem puts a strong emphasis on the stillness of death and the way
it makes things seem to stop; it captures in words the hurt, the anger,
the inability to understand, the vacuum that remains when a loved one
dies and leaves a vacant space. But here we do not see the body or
hear a direct good-bye to the dead person; rather we encounter the
feeling that lingers and won't go away, recalled through memory by
an especially significant object, a mere thing but one that has been
personalized to the point of becoming nearly human in itself. (The
event described here is, by the way, fictional; the poet's wife did not
in fact die. Like a dramatist or writer of fiction, the poet may simply
imagine an event in order to analyze and articulate how such an event
might feel in certain circumstances.)

Sometimes poems are a way of confronting feelings. Sometimes they
explore feelings in detail and try to intellectualize or rationalize them.
At other times, poems generate feelings by recalling an experience
many years in the past. In the following poem, for example, memories
of early childhood—warm, close, secure even during a trip into strange
territory—are vividly recalled much, much later, and the juxtaposition
of adult perspective and childhood discovery give the poem a dramatic
force.

JOHN STONE

Coming Home

About two thousand miles
into my life
the family bounced south
west   east
in an old Oldsmobile.   5

Two brothers tumbled
on the back seat
watching the world blur
upside down right side up
through windows   10
time fogged in
slowly from the corners.

Nights
cars came at us
wall-eyed   15
their lights sliding
over the ceiling
like night fighters

while in the front
they talked parental   low   20
in a drone
we didn't hear .
tossing through Arkansas
toward Mississippi.

When our eyes grew red   25
and blood bulged
in our heads from laughing
we slept
he on the seat
and I bent over   30
the humped transmission

close to the only motor
in the world.

1972

There is much more going on in the poems that we have glanced
at than we have taken time to consider, but even the quickest look at
these poems suggests something of the range of feelings that poems
can offer—the depth of feeling, the clarity, the experience that may be
articulately and precisely shared. Later we will look more carefully at
how these things happen.

THEODORE ROETHKE

I Knew a Woman

I knew a woman, lovely in her bones,
When small birds sighed, she would sigh back at them;
Ah, when she moved, she moved more ways than one:
The shapes a bright container can contain!
Of her choice virtues only gods should speak,   5
Or English poets who grew up on Greek
(I'd have them sing in chorus, cheek to cheek).

How well her wishes went! She stroked my chin,
She taught me Turn, and Counter-turn, and Stand;[1]
She taught me Touch, that undulant white skin;   10
I nibbled meekly from her proffered hand;
She was the sickle; I, poor I, the rake,
Coming behind her for her pretty sake
(But what prodigious mowing we did make).

Love likes a gander, and adores a goose: 15
Her full lips pursed, the errant note to seize;
She played it quick, she played it light and loose;
My eyes, they dazzled at her flowing knees;
Her several parts could keep a pure repose,
Or one hip quiver with a mobile nose   20
(She moved in circles, and those circles moved).

Let seed be grass, and grass turn into hay:
I'm martyr to a motion not my own;
What's freedom for? To know eternity.
I swear she cast a shadow white as stone.   25
But who would count eternity in days?
These old bones live to learn her wanton ways:
(I measure time by how a body sways).

1958

MARGARET ATWOOD

Variation on the Word *Sleep*

I would like to watch you sleeping,
which may not happen.

3. Literary terms for the parts of a Pindaric ode.

I would like to watch you,
sleeping. I would like to sleep
with you, to enter   5
your sleep as its smooth dark wave
slides over my head

and walk with you through that lucent
wavering forest of bluegreen leaves
with its watery sun & three moons   10
towards the cave where you must descend,
towards your worst fear

I would like to give you the silver
branch, the small white flower, the one
word that will protect you   15
from the grief at the center
of your dream, from the grief
at the center. I would like to follow
you up the long stairway
again & become   20
the boat that would row you back
carefully, a flame
in two cupped hands
to where your body lies
beside me, and you enter   25
it as easily as breathing in

I would like to be the air
that inhabits you for a moment
only. I would like to be that unnoticed   30
& that necessary.

1981

AUDRE LORDE

Recreation

Coming together
it is easier to work
after our bodies
meet
paper and pen   5
neither care nor profit
whether we write or not
but as your body moves
under my hands
charged and waiting   10
we cut the leash
you create me against your thighs

hilly with images
moving through our word countries
my body   15
writes into your flesh
the poem
you make of me.

Touching you I catch midnight
as moon fires set in my throat   20
I love you flesh into blossom
I made you
and take you made
into me.

1978

WILLIAM SHAKESPEARE

Let Me Not to the Marriage of True Minds

Let me not to the marriage of true minds
Admit impediments.[2] Love is not love
Which alters when it alteration finds,
Or bends with the remover to remove:
Oh, no! it is an ever-fixéd mark, (béacon)   5
That looks on tempests and is never shaken;
It is the star to every wandering bark,   *North Star*
Whose worth's unknown, although his height be taken.[3]
Love's not Time's fool, though rosy lips and cheeks
Within his bending sickle's compass come;   10
Love alters not with his brief hours and weeks,
But bears it out even to the edge of doom.[4]   *endures*
If this be error and upon me proved,
I never writ, nor no man ever loved.

1609

2. The Marriage Service contained this address to the observers: "If any of you know cause or just impediments why these persons should not be joined together . . .".

3. I.e., measuring the altitude of stars (for purposes of navigation) is not a measurement of value.
4. End of the world.

ANONYMOUS

Western Wind

Western wind, when wilt thou blow,
    The small rain down can rain?
Christ, if my love were in my arms
    And I in my bed again!

ca. 1300   15th century

JOHN DONNE

The Good-Morrow

I wonder, by my troth, what thou and I
    Did, till we loved? were we not weaned till then?
But sucked on country pleasures, childishly?
    Or snorted[5] we in the Seven Sleepers' den?[6]
'Twas so; but[7] this, all pleasures fancies be.   5
If ever any beauty[8] I did see,
Which I desired, and got,[9] 'twas but a dream of thee.

And now good-morrow to our waking souls,
    Which watch not one another out of fear;
For love, all love of other sights controls,   10
    And makes one little room an everywhere.
Let sea-discoverers to new worlds have gone,
Let maps to other,[1] worlds on worlds have shown,
Let us possess one world, each hath one, and is one.

My face in thine eye, thine in mine appears,[2]   15
    And true plain hearts do in the faces rest;
Where can we find two better hemispheres,
    Without sharp north, without declining west?
Whatever dies was not mixed equally,[3]
If our two loves be one, or, thou and I   20
Love so alike that none do slacken, none can die.

1633

5. Snored.
6. According to tradition, seven Christian youths escaped Roman persecution by sleeping in a cave for 187 years.
7. Except for.
8. Beautiful woman.
9. Sexually possessed.

1. Other people.
2. I.e., each is reflected in the other's eyes.
3. Perfectly mixed elements, according to scholastic philosophy, were stable and immortal.

ADRIENNE RICH

Two Songs

1.

Sex, as they harshly call it,
I fell into this morning
at ten o'clock, a drizzling hour
of traffic and wet newspapers.
I thought of him who yesterday   5
clearly didn't
turn me to a hot field
ready for plowing,
and longing for that young man
piercéd me to the roots   10
bathing every vein, etc.[4]
All day he appears to me
touchingly desirable,
a prize one could wreck one's peace for.
I'd call it love if love   15
didn't take so many years
but lust too is a jewel
a sweet flower and what
pure happiness to know
all our high-toned questions   20
breed in a lively animal.

2.

That "old last act"!
And yet sometimes
all seems post coitum triste[5]
and I a mere bystander.   25
Somebody else is going off,
getting shot to the moon.
Or, a moon-race!
my opposite number lands
Split seconds after   30
I make it—
we lie fainting together
at a crater-edge
heavy as mercury in our moonsuits
till he speaks—   35
in a different language
yet one I've picked up
through cultural exchanges . . .
we murmur the first moonwords:
Spasibo. Thanks. O.K.   40

1964

4. See the opening lines of the Prologue to Chaucer's *Canterbury Tales*.
5. Sadness after sexual union.

MARGE PIERCY

To Have Without Holding

Learning to love differently is hard,
love with the hands wide open, love
with the doors banging on their hinges,
the cupboard unlocked, the wind
roaring and whimpering in the rooms   5
rustling the sheets and snapping the blinds
that thwack like rubber bands
in an open palm.

It hurts to love wide open
stretching the muscles that feel   10
as if they are made of wet plaster,
then of blunt knives, then
of sharp knives.

It hurts to thwart the reflexes
of grab, of clutch; to love and let   15
go again and again. It pesters to remember
the lover who is not in the bed,
to hold back what is owed to the work
that gutters like a candle in a cave
without air, to love consciously,   20
conscientiously, concretely, constructively.

I can't do it, you say it's killing
me, but you thrive, you glow
on the street like a neon raspberry,
You float and sail, a helium balloon   25
bright bachelor's button blue and bobbing
on the cold and hot winds of our breath,
as we make and unmake in passionate
diastole and systole the rhythm
of our unbound bonding, to have   30
and not to hold, to love
with minimized malice, hunger
and anger moment by moment balanced.

1980

EDNA ST. VINCENT MILLAY

[I, Being Born a Woman and Distressed]

I, being born a woman and distressed
By all the needs and notions of my kind,

nearness in place or time
Kinship

Am urged by your propinquity to find
Your person fair, and feel a certain zest
To bear your body's weight upon my breast: 5
So subtly is the fume of life designed,   — *gas/smoke/*
To clarify the pulse and cloud the mind,   *something*
And leave me once again undone, possessed.   *that*
Think not for this, however, the poor treason   *impairs*
Of my stout blood against my staggering brain,   *reason*   10
I shall remember you with love, or season
My scorn with pity,—let me make it plain:
I find this frenzy insufficient reason
For conversation when we meet again.

                                              1923

SHARON OLDS

Sex Without Love

How do they do it, the ones who make love
without love? Beautiful as dancers,
gliding over each other like ice-skaters
over the ice, fingers hooked
inside each other's bodies, faces   5
red as steak, wine, wet as the
children at birth whose mothers are going to
give them away. How do they come to the
come to the   come to the   God   come to the
still waters, and not love   10
the one who came there with them, light
rising slowly as steam off their joined
skin? These are the true religious,
the purists, the pros, the ones who will not
accept a false Messiah, love the   15
priest instead of the God. They do not
mistake the lover for their own pleasure,
they are like great runners: they know they are alone
with the road surface, the cold, the wind,
the fit of their shoes, their over-all cardio-   20
vascular health—just factors, like the partner
in the bed, and not the truth, which is the
single body alone in the universe
against its own best time.

                                              1984

ANNE BRADSTREET

To My Dear and Loving Husband

If ever two were one, then surely we.
If ever man were loved by wife, then thee;
If ever wife was happy in a man,
Compare with me ye women if you can.
I prize thy love more than whole mines of gold,   5
Or all the riches that the East doth hold.
My love is such that rivers cannot quench,
Nor ought but love from thee give recompense.
Thy love is such I can no way repay;
The heavens reward thee manifold, I pray.   10
Then while we live, in love let's so persever,
That when we live no more we may live ever.

          1678

SIR THOMAS WYATT

They Flee from Me

They flee from me, that sometime did me seek,
With naked foot stalking in my chamber.
I have seen them, gentle, tame, and meek,
That now are wild, and do not remember
That sometime they put themselves in danger   5
To take bread at my hand; and now they range,
Busily seeking with a continual change.

Thankéd be Fortune it hath been otherwise,
Twenty times better; but once in special,
In thin array, after a pleasant guise,   10
When her loose gown from her shoulders did fall,
And she me caught in her arms long and small.[6]
And therewith all sweetly did me kiss
And softly said, "Dear heart, how like you this?"

It was no dream, I lay broad waking.   15
But all is turned, thorough[7] my gentleness,
Into a strange fashion of forsaking;
And I have leave to go, of her goodness,
And she also to use newfangleness.[8]
But since that I so kindely[9] am servéd,   20
I fain[1] would know what she hath deservéd.

          1557

6. Slender.
7. Through.
8. Fondness for novelty.

9. In a way natural to women.
1. Eagerly.

A Gathering of Poems about Mothers and Fathers

ROBERT CREELEY

Mother's Voice

In these few years
since her death I hear
mother's voice say
under my own, I won't

want any more of that.   5
My cheekbones resonate
with her emphasis. Nothing
of not wanting only

but the distance there from
common fact of others   10
frightens me. I look out
at all this demanding world

and try to put it quietly back,
from me, say, thank you,
I've already had some   15
though I haven't

and would like to
but I've said no, she has,
it's not my own voice anymore.
It's higher as hers was   20

and accommodates too simply
its frustrations when
I at least think I want more
and must have it.

1983

ROBERT HAYDEN

Those Winter Sundays

Sundays too my father got up early
and put his clothes on in the blueblack cold,
then with cracked hands that ached
from labor in the weekday weather made
banked fires blaze. No one ever thanked him.   5

554

I'd wake and hear the cold splintering, breaking.
When the rooms were warm, he'd call,
and slowly I would rise and dress,
fearing the chronic angers of that house,

Speaking indifferently to him,   10
who had driven out the cold
and polished my good shoes as well.
What did I know, what did I know
of love's austere and lonely offices?

                                                          1966

ELLEN BRYANT VOIGT

For My Mother

When does the soul leave the body?
Since early morning you have not moved—
only your head moves, thrown back
with each deliberate breath,
the one sound that matters in the room.   5
My brother is here, my sister,
two of your sisters, ripples
widening from the bed.
The nurses check and measure,
keeping the many records.   10
Are you afraid?
Are you dreaming of what is past, lost,
or is this sleep some other preparation?
My sister has put your rings
on my finger; it seems like your hand   15
stroking the white brow,
unable to release you,
not even after you have asked for death—

And we know nothing about such pain,
except that it has weaned you from us,   20
and from the reedy, rusted
sunflowers outside the window,
drooping over the snow like tongueless bells.

                                                          1983

D. H. LAWRENCE

Piano

Softly, in the dusk, a woman is singing to me;
Taking me back down the vista of years, till I see

A child sitting under the piano, in the boom of the tingling strings
And pressing the small, poised feet of a mother who smiles as she sings.

In spite of myself, the insidious mastery of song   5
Betrays me back, till the heart of me weeps to belong
To the old Sunday evenings at home, with winter outside
And hymns in the cozy parlor, the tinkling piano our guide.

So now it is vain for the singer to burst into clamor
With the great black piano appassionato. The glamour   10
Of childish days is upon me, my manhood is cast
Down in the flood of remembrance, I weep like a child for the past.

                                                        1918

DIANE WAKOSKI

The Photos

My sister in her well-tailored silk blouse hands me
the photo of my father
in naval uniform and white hat.
I say, "Oh, this is the one which Mama used to have on her
    dresser."

My sister controls her face and furtively looks at my mother,   5
a sad rag bag of a woman, lumpy and sagging everywhere,
like a mattress at the Salvation Army, though with no holes or
    tears,
and says, "No."

I look again,
and see that my father is wearing a wedding ring,   10
which he never did
when he lived with my mother. And that there is a legend on it,
"To my dearest wife,
    Love
    Chief"   15
And I realize the photo must have belonged to his second wife,
whom he left our mother to marry.

My mother says, with her face as still as the whole unpopulated
    part of the
state of North Dakota,
"May I see it too?"   20
She looks at it.

I look at my tailored sister
and my own blue-jeaned self. Have we wanted to hurt our
    mother,

sharing these pictures on this, one of the few days I ever visit or
spend with family? For her face is curiously haunted,   25
not now with her usual viperish bitterness,
but with something so deep it could not be spoken.

I turn away and say I must go on, as I have a dinner
    engagement with friends.
But I drive all the way to Pasadena from Whittier,
thinking of my mother's face; how I could never love her;   30
    how my father
could not love her either. Yet knowing I have inherited
the rag-bag body,
stony face with bulldog jaws.

I drive, thinking of that face.
Jeffers' California Medea[1] who inspired me to poetry.   35
I killed my children,
but there as I am changing lanes on the freeway, necessarily
    glancing in the
rearview mirror, I see the face,
not even a ghost, but always with me, like a photo in a   40
    beloved's wallet.

How I hate my destiny.

                                      1978

SHARON OLDS

The Victims

When Mother divorced you, we were glad. She took it and
took it, in silence, all those years and then
kicked you out, suddenly, and her
kids loved it. Then you were fired, and we
grinned inside, the way people grinned when   5
Nixon's helicopter lifted off the South
Lawn for the last time.[2] We were tickled
to think of your office taken away,
your secretaries taken away,
your lunches with three double bourbons,   10
your pencils, your reams of paper. Would they take your
suits back, too, those dark
carcasses hung in your closet, and the black
noses of your shoes with their large pores?
She had taught us to take it, to hate you and take it   15

1. Robinson Jeffers (1887–1962), American poet who migrated to California from the East, retold the Medea story in *Solstice*, 1935. According to Greek legend, Medea was a sorceress who killed her children.
2. When Richard Nixon resigned the U.S. presidency on August 8, 1974, his exit from the White House (by helicopter from the lawn) was televised live.

until we pricked with her for your
annihilation, Father. Now I
pass the bums in doorways, the white
slugs of their bodies gleaming through slits in their
suits of compressed silt, the stained   20
flippers of their hands, the underwater
fire of their eyes, ships gone down with the
lanterns lit, and I wonder who took it and
took it from them in silence until they had
given it all away and had nothing   25
left but this.

1984

SYLVIA PLATH

Daddy

You do not do, you do not do
Any more, black shoe
In which I have lived like a foot
For thirty years, poor and white,
Barely daring to breathe or Achoo.   5

Daddy, I have had to kill you.
You died before I had time——
Marble-heavy, a bag full of God,
Ghastly statue with one gray toe
Big as a Frisco seal   10

And a head in the freakish Atlantic
Where it pours bean green over blue
In the waters off beautiful Nauset.³
I used to pray to recover you.
Ach, du.⁴   15

In the German tongue, in the Polish town
Scraped flat by the roller
Of wars, wars, wars.
But the name of the town is common.
My Polack friend   20

Says there are a dozen or two.
So I never could tell where you
Put your foot, your root,
I never could talk to you.
The tongue stuck in my jaw.   25

3. An inlet on Cape Cod.
4. Literally, "Oh, you" in German.

Plath often portrays herself as Jewish and
her oppressors as German.

It stuck in a barb wire snare.
Ich, ich, ich, ich,
I could hardly speak.
I thought every German was you.
And the language obscene   30

An engine, an engine
Chuffing me off like a Jew.
A Jew to Dachau, Auschwitz, Belsen.[5]
I began to talk like a Jew.
I think I may well be a Jew.   35

The snows of the Tyrol,[6] the clear beer of Vienna
Are not very pure or true.
With my gypsy-ancestress and my weird luck
And my Taroc[7] pack and my Taroc pack
I may be a bit of a Jew.   40

I have always been scared of *you,*
With your Luftwaffe,[8] your gobbledygoo.
And your neat moustache
And your Aryan eye, bright blue.
Panzer-man, panzer-man, O You—   45

Not God but a swastika
So black no sky could squeak through.
Every woman adores a Fascist,
The boot in the face, the brute
Brute heart of a brute like you.   50

You stand at the blackboard, daddy,
In the picture I have of you,
A cleft in your chin instead of your foot
But no less a devil for that, no not
Any less the black man who   55

Bit my pretty red heart in two.
I was ten when they buried you.
At twenty I tried to die
And get back, back, back to you.
I thought even the bones would do   60

But they pulled me out of the sack,
And they stuck me together with glue.
And then I knew what to do.
I made a model of you,
A man in black with a Meinkampf look   65

5. Sites of World War II German death camps.
6. Alpine region in Austria and northern Italy. The snow there is, legendarily, as pure as the beer is clear in Vienna.

7. A variant of Tarot, playing cards used mainly for fortune-telling, said to have been introduced into Europe by gypsies in the 15th century.
8. German air force.

And a love of the rack and the screw.
And I said I do, I do.
So daddy, I'm finally through.
The black telephone's off at the root,
The voices just can't worm through.   70

If I've killed one man, I've killed two——
The vampire who said he was you
And drank my blood for a year,
Seven years, if you want to know.
Daddy, you can lie back now.   75

There's a stake in your fat black heart
And the villagers never like you.
They are dancing and stamping on you.
They always *knew* it was you.
Daddy, daddy, you bastard, I'm through.   80

1966

LUCILLE CLIFTON

Daddy

12/02–5/69

the days have kept on coming,
Daddy or not.   the cracks
in the sidewalk turn green
and the Indian women sell pussywillows
on the corner.   nothing remembers.   5
everything remembers.
in the days where Daddy was
there is a space.

my Daddy died as he lived,
a confident man.   10
"I'll go to Heaven," he said,
"Jesus knows me."
when his leg died, he cut it off.
"It's gone," he said, "it's gone
but I'm still here."   15

what will happen to the days
without you
my baby whispers to me.
the days have kept on coming
and Daddy's gone.   20
He knew.

He must have known and
I comfort my son with the hope
the life in the confident man.

1972

A. M. KLEIN

Heirloom

My father bequeathed me no wide estates;
No keys and ledgers were my heritage;
Only some holy books with *yahrzeit*[9] dates
Writ mournfully upon a blank front page—

Books of the Baal Shem Tov,[1] and of his wonders;   5
Pamphlets upon the devil and his crew;
Prayers against road demons, witches, thunders;
And sundry other tomes for a good Jew.

Beautiful: though no pictures on them, save
The scorpion crawling on a printed track;   10
The Virgin floating on a scriptural wave,
Square letters twinkling in the Zodiac.

The snuff left on this page, now brown and old,
The tallow stains of midnight liturgy—
These are my coat of arms, and these unfold   15
My noble lineage, my proud ancestry!

And my tears, too, have stained this heirloomed ground,
When reading in these treatises some weird
Miracle, I turned a leaf and found
A white hair fallen from my father's beard.   20

1940

GALWAY KINNELL

After Making Love We Hear Footsteps

For I can snore like a bullhorn
or play loud music
or sit up talking with any reasonably sober Irishman
and Fergus will only sink deeper
into his dreamless sleep, which goes by all in one flash,   5
but let there be that heavy breathing
or a stifled come-cry anywhere in the house
and he will wrench himself awake
and make for it on the run—as now, we lie together,
after making love, quiet, touching along the length of our bodies,   10
familiar touch of the long-married,
and he appears—in his baseball pajamas, it happens,
the neck opening so small
he has to screw them on, which one day may make him wonder
about the mental capacity of baseball players—   15
and says, "Are you loving and snuggling? May I join?"
He flops down between us and hugs us and snuggles himself to sleep,
his face gleaming with satisfaction at being this very child.

In the half darkness we look at each other
and smile   20
and touch arms across his little, startlingly muscled body—
this one whom habit of memory propels to the ground of his making,
sleeper only the mortal sounds can sing awake,
this blessing love gives again into our arms.

                                                                    1980

2   EXPECTATION AND SURPRISE

Poetry is full of surprises. Poems express anger or outrage just as effectively as love or sadness, and good poems can be written about going to a rock concert or having lunch or cutting the lawn, as well as about making love or gazing at a cloudless sky or smelling flowers. Even poems on "predictable" subjects can surprise us with unpredicted attitudes, unusual events, or a sudden twist. Knowing that a poem is about some particular subject—love, for example, or death—may give us a general idea of what to expect, but it never tells us altogether what we will find in a particular poem. Experiencing a poem fully means being open to the poem and its surprises, being willing to let the poem guide us to its own attitudes, feelings, and ideas. The following two poems—one about death and one about love—are rather different from those we looked at in Chapter 1.

MARGE PIERCY

Barbie Doll

This girlchild was born as usual
and presented dolls that did pee-pee
and miniature GE stoves and irons
and wee lipsticks the color of cherry candy.
Then in the magic of puberty, a classmate said: 5
You have a great big nose and fat legs.

She was healthy, tested intelligent,
possessed strong arms and back,
abundant sexual drive and manual dexterity.
She went to and fro apologizing.   10
Everyone saw a fat nose on thick legs.

She was advised to play coy,
exhorted to come on hearty,
exercise, diet, smile and wheedle.
Her good nature wore out   15
like a fan belt.
So she cut off her nose and her legs
and offered them up.

In the casket displayed on satin she lay
with the undertaker's cosmetics painted on,   20
a turned-up putty nose,
dressed in a pink and white nightie.
Doesn't she look pretty? everyone said.
Consummation at last.
To every woman a happy ending.   25

1973

564   *Expectation and Surprise*

W. D. SNODGRASS

Leaving the Motel

Outside, the last kids holler
Near the pool: they'll stay the night.
Pick up the towels; fold your collar
Out of sight.

Check: is the second bed   5
Unrumpled, as agreed?
Landlords have to think ahead
In case of need,

Too. Keep things straight: don't take
The matches, the wrong keyrings—   10
We've nowhere we could keep a keepsake—
Ashtrays, combs, things

That sooner or later others
Would accidentally find.
Check: take nothing of one another's   15
And leave behind

Your license number only,
Which they won't care to trace;
We've paid. Still, should such things get lonely,
Leave in their vase   20

An aspirin to preserve
Our lilacs, the wayside flowers
We've gathered and must leave to serve
A few more hours;

That's all. We can't tell when   25
We'll come back, can't press claims;
We would no doubt have other rooms then,
Or other names.

1968

The first poem has the strong note of sadness that characterizes many death poems, but its emphasis is not on the response to the girl's death but on the disappointments in her life. The only "scene" in the poem (lines 19–23) portrays the unnamed girl at rest in her casket, but the still body in the casket contrasts not with vitality but with frustration and anxiety: her life since puberty (lines 5–6) had been full of apologies and attempts to change her physical appearance and emotional makeup. The rest she achieves in death is not, however, a triumph, despite what people say (line 23). Although the poem's last two words are "happy ending" this girl without a name has died in embarrassment and without fulfillment, and the final lines are **ironic**, meaning the opposite of what they say. The cheerful comments at the end lack force and truth because of what we already know; we understand them as ironic because they emphasize how unhappy the girl was and how false her cosmeticized corpse is to the sad truth of her life.

The poem's concern is to suggest the falsity and destructiveness of those standards of beauty which have led to the tragedy of the girl's life. In an important sense, the poem is not really *about* death at all in spite of the fact that the girl's death and her repaired corpse are central to it. As the title suggests, the poem dramatizes how standardized, commercialized notions of femininity and prettiness can be painful and destructive to those whose bodies do not precisely fit the conformist models, and the poem attacks vigorously those conventional standards and the widespread, unthinking acceptance of them.

Leaving the Motel similarly goes in quite a different direction from many poems on the subject of love. Instead of expressing assurance about how love lasts and endures, or about the sincerity and depth of affection, this poem dramatizes a brief sexual encounter. But it does not emphasize sexuality or eroticism in the meeting of the nameless lovers (we see them only as they prepare to leave), nor does it suggest why or how they have found each other, or what either of them is like as a person. Its emphasis is on how careful they must be not to get caught, how exact and calculating they must be in their planning, how finite and limited their encounter must be, how sealed off this encounter is from the rest of their lives. The poem stresses the tiny details the lovers must think of, the agreements they must observe, and the ritual checklist of their duties ("Check . . . Keep things straight . . . Check . . ." lines 5, 9, 15). Affection and sentiment have their small place in the poem (notice the care for the flowers, lines 19–24, and the thought of "pressing claims," line 26), but the emphasis is on temporariness, uncertainty, and limits. The poem is about an illicit, perhaps adulterous sexual encounter, but there is no sex in the poem, only a kind of archeological record of lust.

Labeling a poem as a "love poem" or a "death poem" is primarily a matter of convenience, a grouping based on the **subject matter** in a poem or the event or **topic** it chooses to engage. But as the poems we have been looking at suggest, poems that may be loosely called love poems or death poems may differ widely from one another, express totally different attitudes or ideas, and concentrate on very different aspects of the subject. The main advantages of grouping poems in this way for study is that a reader can become conscious of individual differences: a reading of two poems side by side may suggest how each is distinctive in what it has to say and how it says it.

What a poem has to say is often called its **theme**, the kind of statement it makes about its subject. We could say, for example, that the theme of *Leaving the Motel* is that illicit love is secretive, careful,

transitory, and short on emotion and sentiment, or that secret sexual
encounters tend to be brief, calculated, and characterized by restrained and insecure feelings. The theme of a poem usually may be
expressed in several different ways, and poems often have more than
one theme. *Barbie Doll* suggests that commercialized standards destroy human values; that rigid and idealized notions of normalty cripple people who are different; that false standards of appearance and
behavior can destroy human beings and lead to personal tragedy;
that people are easily and tragically led to accept evaluations thrust
upon them by others; that American consumers tend to be con-
formists, easily influenced in their outlook by advertising and by commercial products; that children who do not conform to middle-class
standards and notions don't have a chance. Each of these statements
could be demonstrated to be said or implied in the poem and rather
central to it. But none of these statements individually nor all of them
together would be an adequate substitute for the poem itself. To state
the theme in such a brief and abstract way—while it may be helpful
in clarifiying what the poem does and does not say—never does justice
to the experience of the poem, the way it works on us as readers.
Poems affect us in all sorts of ways—emotional and psychological as
well as rational—and often a poem's dramatization of a story, an event,
or a moment bypasses our rational responses and affects us far more
deeply than a clear and logical argument would.

Poems, then, may differ widely from one another even when they
share a common subject. And the subjects of poetry also vary widely.
It isn't true that there are certain "poetic" subjects and that there are
others which aren't appropriate to poetry. Any human activity, any
thought or feeling can be the subject of poetry. Poetry often deals with
beauty and the softer, more attractive human emotions, but it can deal
with ugliness and less attractive human conduct as well, for poetry
seeks to mirror human beings and human events, showing us ourselves
not only as we'd like to be but as we are. Good poetry gets written
about all kinds of topics, in all kinds of forms. This poem, for example, celebrates a famous rock concert.

JONI MITCHELL

Woodstock[1]

I came upon a child of God
He was walking along the road
And I asked him, where are you going
And this he told me
I'm going on down to Yasgur's farm   5
I'm going to join in a rock'n'roll band

1. Written after the rock festival there
in 1969, celebrating not only the festival
but what came to be called the "Woodstock Nation."

I'm going to camp out on the land
And try an' get my soul free
  We are stardust
  We are golden   10
  And we've got to get ourselves
  Back to the garden

Then can I walk beside you
I have come here to lose the smog
And I feel to be a cog in something turning   15
Well maybe it is just the time of year
Or maybe it's the time of man
I don't know who I am
But life is for learning
  We are stardust   20
  We are golden
  And we've got to get ourselves
  Back to the garden

By the time we got to Woodstock
We were half a million strong   25
And everywhere there was song and celebration
And I dreamed I saw the bombers
Riding shotgun in the sky
And they were turning into butterflies
Above our nation   30
  We are stardust
  We are golden
  And we've got to get ourselves
  Back to the garden

                  1969

This particular poem is also a song. (The lyrics to some songs "work" as poems; others don't because they aren't sufficiently verbal or because their particular effects depend too much on the music that goes with the words.) The account it gives of Woodstock may now seem rather dated in its optimism about transforming, through love and togetherness, the machines of war (lines 27–30), but its ideals of simplicity and peace are stated powerfully. The recurrent idea of returning somehow to an original ideal of innocence (the Garden of Eden) suggests the high aspirations ("stardust") and urgency ("got to") of the sixties' sense of things gone wrong. The mental pictures portray rural simplicity, freedom, the power of united efforts, and the joys of music as an alternative to urban crowding and pollution (line 14), political conflict (lines 27–28), and confusion over personal identity (lines 18–19). The poem's theme—that human beings can, through

love and working together, recreate a perfect age of innocence and
peace—represents human aspirations at a very high level and does so
persuasively and highmindedly, despite the particular details of time
and place that anchor the poem to a particular moment in history
and a specific experience.

Much less flattering to human nature is this poem about a prison
inmate.

ETHERIDGE KNIGHT

Hard Rock Returns to Prison from the Hospital for the Criminal Insane

Hard Rock was "known not to take no shit
From nobody," and he had the scars to prove it:
Split purple lips, lumped ears, welts above
His yellow eyes, and one long scar that cut
Across his temple and plowed through a thick   5
Canopy of kinky hair.

The WORD was that Hard Rock wasn't a mean nigger
Anymore, that the doctors had bored a hole in his head,
Cut out part of his brain, and shot electricity
Through the rest. When they brought Hard Rock back,   10
Handcuffed and chained, he was turned loose,
Like a freshly gelded stallion, to try his new status.
And we all waited and watched, like indians at a corral,
To see if the WORD was true.

As we waited we wrapped ourselves in the cloak   15
Of his exploits: "Man, the last time, it took eight
Screws[2] to put him in the Hole." "Yeah, remember when he
Smacked the captain with his dinner tray?" "He set
The record for time in the Hole—67 straight days!"
"Ol Hard Rock! man, that's one crazy nigger."   20
And then the jewel of a myth that Hard Rock had once bit
A screw on the thumb and poisoned him with syphilitic spit.

The testing came, to see if Hard Rock was really tame.
A hillbilly called him a black son of a bitch
And didn't lose his teeth, a screw who knew Hard Rock   25
From before shook him down and barked in his face.
And Hard Rock did *nothing*. Just grinned and looked silly,
His eyes empty like knot holes in a fence.

---

2. Guards. "Hole": solitary confinement.

And even after we discovered that it took Hard Rock
Exactly 3 minutes to tell you his first name,   30
We told ourselves that he had just wised up,
Was being cool; but we could not fool ourselves for long,
And we turned away, our eyes on the ground. Crushed.
He had been our Destroyer, the doer of things
We dreamed of doing but could not bring ourselves to do,   35
The fears of years, like a biting whip,
Had cut grooves too deeply across our backs.

                                                              1968

The picture of Hard Rock as a kind of hero to other prison in-
mates is established early in the poem through a retelling of the
legends circulated about him; the straightforward chronology of the
poem sets up the mystery of how he will react after his "treatment"
in the hospital. The poem identifies with those who wait; they are
hopeful that Hard Rock's spirit has not been broken by surgery or shock
treatments, and the lines crawl almost to a stop with disappointment
in stanza four. The "nothing" (line 27) of Hard Rock's response to
teasing and taunting and the emptiness of his eyes ("like knot holes
in a fence," line 28) reduce the heroic hopes and illusions to despair.
The final stanza recounts the observers' attempts to reinterpret, to hang
onto hope that their symbol of heroism could stand up against the
best efforts to tame him, but the spirit has gone out of the hero-
worshipers too, and the poem records them as beaten, conformed,
deprived of their spirit as Hard Rock has been of his. The poem
records the despair of the hopeless and it protests against the exercise
of power that can curb even as rebellious a figure as Hard Rock.

   The following poem is equally full of anger and disappointment,
but it uses a kind of playfulness with words to make the seriousness of
the situation seem all the more relentless.

WILLIAM BLAKE

London

I wander through each chartered street,
Near where the chartered Thames does flow,
And mark in every face I meet
Marks of weakness, marks of woe.

In every cry of every man,   5
In every Infant's cry of fear,
In every voice, in every ban,
The mind-forged manacles I hear.

How the Chimney-sweeper's cry
Every black'ning Church appalls;   10
And the hapless Soldier's sigh
Runs in blood down Palace walls.

But most through midnight streets I hear
How the youthful Harlot's curse
Blasts the new-born Infant's tear,   15
And blights with plagues the Marriage hearse.

1794

The poem gives a strong sense of how London feels to this particular observer; it is cluttered, constricting, oppressive. The wordplay here articulates and connects the strong emotions he associates with London experiences. The repeated words—"every," for example, or "cry"—intensify the sense of total despair in the city and weld connections between things not necessarily related—the cries of street vendors, for example, with the cries for help. The word "chartered" implies strong feelings too, and the word gives a particularly rigid sense of streets. Instead of seeming alive with people or bustling with movement, they are rigidly, coldly determined, controlled, cramped. And the same word is used for the river, as if it too were planned, programed, laid out by an oppressor. In fact, the course of the Thames had been altered (slightly) by the government before Blake's time, but most important is the word's emotional force, the sense it projects of constriction and artificiality: the person speaking experiences London as if human artifice had totally altered nature. According to the poem, people are victimized too, "marked" by their confrontations with urbanness and the power of institutions: the "soldier's sigh" that "runs in blood down Palace walls" vividly suggests, through a metaphor that visually dramatizes the speaker's feelings, both the powerlessness of the individual and the callousness of power. The "description" of the city has clearly become, by now, a subjective, highly emotional, and vivid expression of how the speaker feels about London and what it represents to him.

One more thing about *London:* at first it looks like an account of a personal experience, as if the speaker is describing and interpreting as he goes along: "I wander through each chartered street." But soon it is clear that he is describing many wanderings, putting together impressions from many walks, recreating a generalized or typical walk—which shows him "every" person in the streets, allows him to generalize about the churches being "appalled" (literally, made white) by the cry of the representative Chimney-sweeper, and presents his conclusions about soldiers, prostitutes, and infants. What we are given is not a personal record of an event, but a re-presentation of it, as it seems in the mind in retrospect—not a story, not a narrative or chronological account of events, but a dramatization of self that compresses many experiences into one.

The **tone** of *London* is somber in spite of the poet's playfulness with words. Wordplay may be witty and funny if it calls attention to its own cleverness, but here it involves the discovery of unsuspected (but meaningful) connections between things. The term **tone** is used to describe the attitude the poem takes toward its subject and theme. If the theme of a poem is *what* the poem says, the tone involves *how* one says it. The "how" involves feelings, attitudes that are expressed by how one says the words. The tone of *London* is sad, despairing, and angry; reading *London* aloud, one would try to show in one's voice the strong feelings that the poem expresses, just as one would try to reproduce tenderness and caring in reading aloud *The Tally Stick* or *How Do I Love Thee*.

Subject, theme, and tone. Each of these categories gives us a way to begin considering poems and showing how one poem differs from another. Comparing poems on the same subject, or with a similar theme or tone, can lead to a clearer understanding of each individual poem and can refine our responses to the subtleties of individual differences. The title of a poem (*Leaving the Motel,* for example) or the way the poem first introduces its subject often can give us a sense of what to expect, but we need to be open to surprise too. No two poems are going to be exactly alike in their effect on us; the variety of possible poems multiplies when you think of all the possible themes and tones that can be explored within any single subject. Varieties of feeling often coincide with varieties of thinking, and readers open to the pleasures of the unexpected may find themselves learning, growing, becoming more sensitive to ideas and human issues as well as more articulate about feelings and thoughts they already have.

The following two poems might be said to be about animals, although both of them place their final emphasis on what human beings are like: the animal in each case is only the means to the end of exploring human nature. The poems share a common assumption that animals reflect human habits and conduct and may reveal much about ourselves, and in each case the woman central to the poem is revealed to be surprisingly unlike the way she thinks of herself. But the poems are very different from one another. As you read them, see if you can think of appropriate words to describe the main character and to indicate the right tone of voice to use in reading each poem.

MAXINE KUMIN

Woodchucks

Gassing the woodchucks didn't turn out right.
The knockout bomb from the Feed and Grain Exchange
was featured as merciful, quick at the bone
and the case we had against them was airtight,
both exits shoehorned shut with puddingstone,[3]   5
but they had a sub-sub-basement out of range.

3. A mixture of cement, pebbles, and gravel: a conglomerate.

Next morning they turned up again, no worse
for the cyanide than we for our cigarettes
and state-store Scotch, all of us up to scratch.
They brought down the marigolds as a matter of course   10
and then took over the vegetable patch
nipping the broccoli shoots, beheading the carrots.

The food from our mouths, I said, righteously thrilling
to the feel of the .22, the bullets' neat noses.
I, a lapsed pacifist fallen from grace   15
puffed with Darwinian pieties for killing,
now drew a bead on the littlest woodchuck's face.
He died down in the everbearing roses.

Ten minutes later I dropped the mother. She
flipflopped in the air and fell, her needle teeth   20
still hooked in a leaf of early Swiss chard.
Another baby next. O one-two-three
the murderer inside me rose up hard,
the hawkeye killer came on stage forthwith.

There's one chuck left. Old wily fellow, he keeps   25
me cocked and ready day after day after day.
All night I hunt his humped-up form. I dream
I sight along the barrel in my sleep.
If only they'd all consented to die unseen
gassed underground the quiet Nazi way.   30

1972

ADRIENNE RICH

Aunt Jennifer's Tigers

Aunt Jennifer's tigers prance across a screen,
Bright topaz denizens of a world of green.
They do not fear the men beneath the tree;
They pace in sleek chivalric certainty.

Aunt Jennifer's fingers fluttering through her wool   5
Find even the ivory needle hard to pull.
The massive weight of Uncle's wedding band
Sits heavily upon Aunt Jennifer's hand.

When Aunt is dead, her terrified hands will lie
Still ringed with ordeals she was mastered by.   10
The tigers in the panel that she made
Will go on prancing, proud and unafraid.

1951

How would your tone of voice change if you read *Woodchucks* aloud from beginning to end? What tone would you use to read the ending? How does the hunter feel about her increasing attraction to violence? Why does the poem begin by calling the gassing of the woodchucks "merciful" and end by describing it as "the quiet Nazi way"? What names does the hunter call herself? How does the name-calling affect your feelings about her? Exactly when does the hunter begin to *enjoy* the feel of the gun and the idea of killing? How does the poet make that clear?

Why are tigers a particularly appropriate contrast to the quiet and subdued manner of Aunt Jennifer? What words used to describe the tigers seem particularly significant? In what ways is the tiger an opposite of Aunt Jennifer? In what ways does it externalize her secrets? Why are Aunt Jennifer's hands described as "terrified"? What clues does the poem give about why Aunt Jennifer is so afraid? How does the poem make you feel about Aunt Jennifer? about her tigers? about her life? How would you describe the tone of the poem? How does the poet feel about Aunt Jennifer?

Twenty years after writing *Aunt Jennifer's Tigers*, Adrienne Rich said this about the poem:

> In writing this poem, composed and apparently cool as it is, I thought I was creating a portrait of an imaginary woman. But this woman suffers from the opposition of her imagination, worked out in tapestry, and her life style, "ringed with ordeals she was mastered by." It was important to me that Aunt Jennifer was a person as distinct from myself as possible—distanced by the formalism of the poem, by its objective, observant tone—even by putting the woman in a different generation. In those years formalism was part of the strategy—like asbestos gloves, it allowed me to handle materials I couldn't pick up bare-handed.[4]

Not often do we have such an explicit comment on a poem by its author, and we don't actually have to have it to understand and experience the force of the poem (although such a statement may clarify why the author chose particular modes of presentation and how the poem fits into the author's own patterns of thinking and growing). Most poems contain within them what we need to know in order to tap the human and artistic resources they offer us. Still, it is nice to have comments like this one, and later on (in Chapter 11) we will look at some of the advantages of knowing specific things about an author and other poems that he or she has written. (There, too, you will find a gathering of poems by Adrienne Rich.) In the chapters between now and then we will look at various technical aspects of poetry, considering how poems are put together and what sorts of things we need to know in order to read well, that is, how to experience sensitively and fully other poems you may want to read later. Not all poems are as accessible as those we've looked at so far, and even the

---

4. In *When We Dead Awaken: Writing as Re-Vision*, a talk given in December, 1971, at the Women's Forum of the Modern Language Association.

ones that are accessible usually yield themselves to us more readily and more completely if we approach them systematically by developing specific reading habits and skills—just as someone learning to play tennis systematically learns the rules, the techniques, the things to watch out for that are distinctive to the pleasures and hazards of that skill or craft. It helps if you know what to expect, and the chapters that follow will help you to an understanding of the things that poets can do—and thus to what poems can do for you.

But knowing what to expect isn't everything, and I have one bit of advice to offer every prospective reader of poetry before going any further: Be open. Be open to new experience, be open to new feelings, be open to new ideas. Every poem in the world is a potential new experience, and no matter how sophisticated you become, you can still be surprised (and delighted) by new poems—and by rereading old ones. Good poems bear many, many rereadings, and often one discovers something new with every new reading. Be willing to let poems surprise you when you come to them; let them come on their own terms, let them be themselves. If you are open to poetry, you are open to much that the world can offer you.

No one can give you a method that will offer you total experience of all poems. But because many characteristics of an individual poem are characteristics that one poem shares with other poems, there are guidelines which can prompt you to ask the right questions. The chapters that follow will help you in detail with a variety of problems, but meanwhile here is a checklist of some things to remember:

1. *Identify the poem's situation.* What is said is often conditioned by where it is said and by whom. Identifying the speaker and his or her place in the situation puts what he or she says in perspective.

2. *Read the syntax literally.* What the words say literally in normal sentences is only a starting point, but it is the place to start. Not all poems use normal prose syntax, but most of them do, and you can save yourself embarrassment by paraphrasing accurately (that is, rephrasing what the poem literally says, in plain prose) and not simply free-associating from an isolated word or phrase.

3. *Articulate for yourself what the title, subject, and situation make you expect.* Poets often use false leads and try to surprise you by doing shocking things, but defining expectation lets you be conscious of where you are when you begin.

4. *Be willing to be surprised.* Things often happen in poems that turn them around. A poem may seem to suggest one thing at first, then persuade you to its opposite, or at least to a significant qualification or variation.

5. *Find out what is implied by the traditions behind the poem.* Verse forms, poetic kinds, and metrical patterns all have a frame of reference, traditions of the way they are usually used and for what. For example, the anapest is usually used for comic poems, and if a poet uses it "straight" he is aware of his "departure" and is probably making a point by doing it.

6. *Remember that poems exist in time, and times change.* Not only the meanings of words, but whole ways of looking at the universe and

man's role vary in different ages. Consciousness of time works two ways: your knowledge of history provides a context for reading the poem, and the poem's *use* of a word or idea may modify your notion of a particular age.

7. *Bother the reference librarian.* Look up anything you don't understand: an unfamiliar word (or an ordinary word used in an unfamiliar way), a place, a person, a myth, an idea—anything the poem uses. When you can't find what you need or don't know where to look, ask for help.

8. *Take a poem on its own terms.* Adjust to the poem; don't make the poem adjust to you. Be prepared to hear things you do not want to hear. Not all poems are about your ideas, nor will they always present emotions you want to feel. But be tolerant and listen to the poem's ideas, not only to your desire to revise them for yourself.

9. *Argue.* Discussion usually results in clarification and keeps you from being too dependent on personal biases and preoccupations which sometimes mislead even the best readers. Talking a poem over with someone else (especially someone very different) can expand the limits of a too narrow perspective.

10. *Assume there is a reason for everything.* Poets do make mistakes, but in poems that show some degree of verbal control it is usually safest to assume that the poet chose each word carefully; if the choice seems peculiar to us, it is usually *we* who are missing something. Craftsmanship obliges us to try to account for the specific choices and only settle for conclusions of ineptitude if no hypothetical explanation will make sense.

What *is* poetry? Let your definition be cumulative as you read the poems in this book. No dictionary definition will cover all that you find, and it is better to discover for yourself poetry's many ingredients, its many effects, its many ways of acting. What can it do for you? Wait and see. Begin to add up its effects after you have read carefully —after you have studied and reread—a hundred or so poems; that will be a beginning, and you will be able to add to that total as long as you continue to read new poems or reread old ones.

A Gathering of Poems about Animals

EMILY DICKINSON

A Narrow Fellow in the Grass

A narrow Fellow in the Grass
Occasionally rides—
You may have met Him—did you not
His notice sudden is—

The Grass divides as with a Comb—   5
A spotted shaft is seen—
And then it closes at your feet
And opens further on—

He likes a Boggy Acre
A Floor too cool for Corn—   10
Yet when a Boy, and Barefoot—
I more than once at Noon

Have passed, I thought, a Whip lash
Unbraiding in the Sun
When stooping to secure it   15
It wrinkled, and was gone—

Several of Nature's People
I know, and they know me—
I feel for them a transport
Of cordiality—   20

But never met this Fellow
Attended, or alone
Without a tighter breathing
And Zero at the Bone—

                                                    1866

EDWARD THOMAS

The Owl

Downhill I came, hungry, and yet not starved;
Cold, yet had heat within me that was proof
Against the North wind; tired, yet so that rest
Had seemed the sweetest thing under a roof.

Then at the inn I had food, fire, and rest,   5
Knowing how hungry, cold, and tired was I.
All of the night was quite barred out except
An owl's cry, a most melancholy cry

Shaken out long and clear upon the hill,
No merry note, nor cause of merriment,   10
But one telling me plain what I escaped
And others could not, that night, as in I went.

And salted was my food, and my repose,
Salted and sobered, too, by the bird's voice
Speaking for all who lay under the stars,   15
Soldiers and poor, unable to rejoice.

                                                    1917

OGDEN NASH

The Chipmunk

My friends all know that I am shy,
But the chipmunk is twice as shy as I.
He moves with flickering indecision
Like stripes across the television.
He's like the shadow of a cloud,   5
Or Emily Dickinson read aloud.
Yet his ultimate purpose is obvious, very:
To get back to his chipmonastery.

1953

KARL SHAPIRO

The Fly

O hideous little bat, the size of snot,
With polyhedral eye and shabby clothes,
To populate the stinking cat you walk
The promontory of the dead man's nose,
Climb with the fine leg of a Duncan-Phyfe[1]   5
   The smoking mountains of my food
      And in a comic mood
   In mid-air take to bed a wife.

Riding and riding with your filth of hair
On gluey foot or wing, forever coy,   10
Hot from the compost and green sweet decay,
Sounding your buzzer like an urchin toy—
You dot all whiteness with diminutive stool,
   In the tight belly of the dead
      Burrow with hungry head   15
   And inlay maggots like a jewel.

At your approach the great horse stomps and paws
Bringing the hurricane of his heavy tail;
Shod in disease you dare to kiss my hand
Which sweeps against you like an angry flail;   20
Still you return, return, trusting your wing
   To draw you from the hunter's reach
      That learns to kill to teach
   Disorder to the tinier thing.

1. Furniture of the 19th-century American cabinetmaker Duncan Phyfe sometimes featured delicate, sharply angled legs.

My peace is your disaster. For your death   25
Children like spiders cup their pretty hands
And wives resort to chemistry of war.
In fens of sticky paper and quicksands
You glue yourself to death. Where you are stuck
   You struggle hideously and beg,   30
     You amputate your leg
   Imbedded in the amber muck.

But I, a man, must swat you with my hate,
Slap you across the air and crush your flight,
Must mangle with my shoe and smear your blood,   35
Expose your little guts pasty and white,
Knock your head sidewise like a drunkard's hat,
   Pin your wings under like a crow's,
     Tear off your flimsy clothes
   And beat you as one beats a rat.   40

Then like Gargantua[2] I stride among
The corpses strewn like raisins in the dust,
The broken bodies of the narrow dead
That catch the throat with fingers of disgust.
I sweep. One gyrates like a top and falls   45
   And stunned, stone blind, and deaf
     Buzzes its frightful F
   And dies between three cannibals.

                                        1942

WENDELL BERRY

The Peace of Wild Things

When despair for the world grows in me
and I wake in the night at the least sound
in fear of what my life and my children's lives may be,
I go and lie down where the wood drake
rests in his beauty on the water, and the great heron feeds.   5
I come into the peace of wild things
who do not tax their lives with forethought
of grief. I come into the presence of still water.
And I feel above me the day-blind stars
waiting with their light. For a time   10
I rest in the grace of the world and am free.

                                        1968

---

2. Legendary medieval giant.

WILLIAM STAFFORD

Traveling through the Dark

Traveling through the dark I found a deer
dead on the edge of the Wilson River road.
It is usually best to roll them into the canyon:
that road is narrow; to swerve might make more dead.

By glow of the tail-light I stumbled back of the car   5
and stood by the heap, a doe, a recent killing;
she had stiffened already, almost cold.
I dragged her off; she was large in the belly.

My fingers touching her side brought me the reason—
her side was warm; her fawn lay there waiting,   10
alive, still, never to be born.
Beside that mountain road I hesitated.

The car aimed ahead its lowered parking lights;
under the hood purred the steady engine.
I stood in the glare of the warm exhaust turning red;   15
around our group I could hear the wilderness listen.

I thought hard for us all—my only swerving—,
then pushed her over the edge into the river.

1962

ALAN DUGAN

Funeral Oration for a Mouse

This, Lord, was an anxious brother and
a living diagram of fear: full of health himself,
he brought diseases like a gift
to give his hosts. Masked in a cat's moustache
but sounding like a bird, he was a ghost   5
of lesser noises and a kitchen pest
for whom some ladies stand on chairs. So,
Lord, accept our felt though minor guilt
for an ignoble foe and ancient sin:
the murder of a guest   10
who shared our board: just once he ate
too slowly, dying in our trap
from necessary hunger and a broken back.

Humors of love aside, the mousetrap was our own
opinion of the mouse, but for the mouse   15
it was the tree of knowledge with
its consequential fruit, the true cross
and the gate of hell. Even to approach
it makes him like or better than
its maker: his courage as a spoiler never once   20
impressed us, but to go out cautiously at night,
into the dining room—what bravery, what
hunger! Younger by far, in dying he
was older than us all: his mobile tail and nose
spasmed in the pinch of our annoyance. Why,   25
then, at that snapping sound, did we, victorious,
begin to laugh without delight?

Our stomachs, deep in an analysis
of their own stolen baits
(and asking, "Lord, Host, to whom are we the pests?"),   30
contracted and demanded a retreat
from our machine and its effect of death,
as if the mouse's fingers, skinnier
than hairpins and as breakable as cheese,
could grasp our grasping lives, and in   35
their drowning movement pull us under too,
into the common death beyond the mousetrap.

                                                      1961

MARGE PIERCY

A Story Wet As Tears

Remember the princess who kissed the frog
so he became a prince? At first they danced
all weekend, toasted each other in the morning
with coffee, with champagne at night
and always with kisses. Perhaps it was   5
in bed after the first year had ground
around she noticed he had become cold
with her. She had to sleep
with heating pad and down comforter.
His manner grew increasingly chilly   10
and damp when she entered a room.
He spent his time in water sports,
hydroponics, working on his insect
collection.

Then in the third year   15
when she said to him one day, my dearest,
are you taking your vitamins daily,
you look quite green, he leaped
away from her.
                    Finally on their   20
fifth anniversary she confronted him.
"My precious, don't you love me any
more?" He replied, "Rivet. Rivet."
Though courtship turns frogs into princes,
marriage turns them quietly back.   25

                                                        1983

GALWAY KINNELL

Saint Francis and the Sow

The bud
stands for all things,
even for those things that don't flower,
for everything flowers, from within, of self-blessing;
though sometimes it is necessary   5
to reteach a thing its loveliness,
to put a hand on its brow
of the flower
and retell it in words and in touch
it is lovely   10
until it flowers again from within, of self-blessing;
as Saint Francis[3]
put his hand on the creased forehead
of the sow, and told her in words and in touch
blessings of earth on the sow, and the sow   15
began remembering all down her thick length,
from the earthen snout all the way
through the fodder and slops to the spiritual curl of the tail,
from the hard spininess spiked out from the spine
down through the great broken heart   20
to the blue milken dreaminess spurting and shuddering
from the fourteen teats into the fourteen mouths sucking and blowing
        beneath them:
the long, perfect loveliness of sow.

                                                        1980

3. St. Francis of Assisi, thirteenth-century founder of the Franciscan Order, was famous for his love of all living things, and, according to legend, sometimes preached to "congregations" of animals.

DELMORE SCHWARTZ

The Heavy Bear Who Goes with Me

"the withness of the body" [4]

The heavy bear who goes with me,
A manifold honey to smear his face,
Clumsy and lumbering here and there,
The central ton of every place,
The hungry beating brutish one   5
In love with candy, anger, and sleep,
Crazy factotum, dishevelling all,
Climbs the building, kicks the football,
Boxes his brother in the hate-ridden city.

Breathing at my side, that heavy animal,   10
That heavy bear who sleeps with me,
Howls in his sleep for a world of sugar,
A sweetness intimate as the water's clasp,
Howls in his sleep because the tight-rope
Trembles and shows the darkness beneath.   15
—The strutting show-off is terrified,
Dressed in his dress-suit, bulging his pants,
Trembles to think that his quivering meat
Must finally wince to nothing at all.

That inescapable animal walks with me,   20
Has followed me since the black womb held,
Moves where I move, distorting my gesture,
A caricature, a swollen shadow,
A stupid clown of the spirit's motive,
Perplexes and affronts with his own darkness,   25
The secret life of belly and bone,
Opaque, too near, my private, yet unknown,
Stretches to embrace the very dear
With whom I would walk without him near,
Touches her grossly, although a word   30
Would bare my heart and make me clear,
Stumbles, flounders, and strives to be fed
Dragging me with him in his mouthing care,
Amid the hundred million of his kind,
The scrimmage of appetite everywhere.   35

1938

4. Early editions attributed the epigraph to Alfred North Whitehead, the philosopher.

RICHARD EBERHART

The Groundhog

In June, amid the golden fields,
I saw a groundhog lying dead.
Dead lay he; my senses shook,
And mind outshot our naked frailty.
There lowly in the vigorous summer   5
His form began its senseless change,
And made my senses waver dim
Seeing nature ferocious in him.
Inspecting close his maggots' might
And seething cauldron of his being,   10
Half with loathing, half with a strange love,
I poked him with an angry stick.
The fever rose, became a flame
And Vigour circumscribed the skies,
Immense energy in the sun,   15
And through my frame a sunless trembling.
My stick had done nor good nor harm.
Then stood I silent in the day
Watching the object, as before;
And kept my reverence for knowledge   20
Trying for control, to be still,
To quell the passion of the blood;
Until I had bent down on my knees
Praying for joy in the sight of decay.
And so I left; and I returned   25
In Autumn strict of eye, to see
The sap gone out of the groundhog,
But the bony sodden hulk remained.
But the year had lost its meaning,
And in intellectual chains   30
I lost both love and loathing,
Mured up[1] in the wall of wisdom.
Another summer took the fields again
Massive and burning, full of life,
But when I chanced upon the spot   35
There was only a little hair left,
And bones bleaching in the sunlight
Beautiful as architecture;
I watched them like a geometer,[2]
And cut a walking stick from a birch.   40
It has been three years, now.
There is no sign of the groundhog.

1. Confined.
2. Geometrician, one skilled in measuring properties and arrangement.

I stood there in the whirling summer,
My hand capped a withered heart,
And thought of China and of Greece,   45
Of Alexander in his tent;
Of Montaigne in his tower,
Of Saint Theresa[3] in her wild lament.

1936

RICHARD WILBUR

The Pardon

My dog lay dead five days without a grave
In the thick of summer, hid in a clump of pine
And a jungle of grass and honeysuckle-vine.
I who had loved him while he kept alive

Went only close enough to where he was   5
To sniff the heavy honeysuckle-smell
Twined with another odor heavier still
And hear the flies' intolerable buzz.

Well, I was ten and very much afraid.
In my kind world the dead were out of range   10
And I could not forgive the sad or strange
In beast or man. My father took the spade

And buried him. Last night I saw the grass
Slowly divide (it was the same scene
But now it glowed a fierce and mortal green)   15
And saw the dog emerging. I confess

I felt afraid again, but still he came
In the carnal sun, clothed in a hymn of flies,
And death was breeding in his lively eyes.
I started in to cry and call his name,   20

Asking forgiveness of his tongueless head.
. . . I dreamt the past was never past redeeming:
But whether this was false or honest dreaming
I beg death's pardon now. And mourn the dead.

1950

3. Alexander the Great, ancient king of Macedonia and conqueror of the East; Michel de Montaigne, the Renaissance French essayist who used a tower near his house for a study; and St. Theresa of Spain, famous for intense trances and visions.

Text

3   SPEAKER

Poems are personal. The thoughts and feelings they express belong to a specific person, and however "universal" or general their sentiments seem to be, poems come to us as the expression of a human voice—an individual voice. That voice is often the voice of the poet. But not always. Poets sometimes create a "character" just as writers of fiction or drama do—people who speak for them only indirectly. A character may, in fact, be very different from the poet, just as a character in a play or story is different from the author, and that person, the **speaker** of the poem, may express ideas or feelings very different from the poet's own. In the following poem, *two* individual voices in fact speak, and it is clear that, rather than himself speaking directly to us, the poet has chosen to create two speakers, each of whom has a distinctive voice.

THOMAS HARDY

The Ruined Maid

"O 'Melia,[1] my dear, this does everything crown!
Who could have supposed I should meet you in Town?
And whence such fair garments, such prosperi-ty?"—
"O didn't you know I'd been ruined?" said she.

—"You left us in tatters, without shoes or socks,   5
Tired of digging potatoes, and spudding up docks;[2]
And now you've gay bracelets and bright feathers three!"—
"Yes: that's how we dress when we're ruined," said she.

—"At home in the barton[3] you said 'thee' and 'thou,'
And 'thik oon,' and 'theäs oon,' and 't'other'; but now   10
Your talking quite fits 'ee for high compa-ny!"—
"Some polish is gained with one's ruin," said she.

—"Your hands were like paws then, your face blue and bleak
But now I'm bewitched by your delicate cheek,
And your little gloves fit as on any la-dy!"—   15
"We never do work when we're ruined," said she.

1. Short for Amelia.
2. Spading up weeds.
3. Farmyard.

585

—"You used to call home-life a hag-ridden dream,
And you'd sigh, and you'd sock;[4] but at present you seem
To know not of megrims[5] or melancho-ly!"—
"True. One's pretty lively when ruined," said she.   20

—"I wish I had feathers, a fine sweeping gown,
And a delicate face, and could strut about Town!"—
"My dear—a raw country girl, such as you be,
Cannot quite expect that. You ain't ruined," said she.

1866

The first voice, that of the sister who has stayed home, is designated typographically (that is, by the way the poem is printed):
there are dashes at the beginning and end of each of her speeches.
The second sister regularly gets the last line in each stanza (and in
the last stanza, two lines), so it is easy to tell who is talking at every
point. Also, the two speakers are just as clearly distinguished by what
they say, how they say it, and what sort of person each proves to be.
The nameless stay-at-home shows little knowledge of the world, and
everything surprises her: seeing her sister at all, but especially seeing
her well clothed, cheerful, and polished; and as the poem develops
she shows increasing envy of her more worldly sister. She is the "raw
country girl" (line 23) that her sister says she is, and she still speaks
the country dialect ("fits 'ee," line 11, for example) that she notices
her sister has lost (lines 9–11). The "ruined" sister ('Melia), on the
other hand, says little except to keep repeating the refrain about
having been ruined, but even the slight variations she plays on that
theme suggest her sophistication and amusement at her countrified
sister, although she still uses a rural "ain't" at the end. We are not
told the full story of their lives (was the ruined sister thrown out?
did she run away from home?), but we know enough (that they've
been separated for some time, that the stay-at-home did not know
where her sister had gone) to allow the dialogue to articulate the
contrast between them. The style of speech of each speaker then does
the rest.

It is equally clear that there is a speaker (or, in this case, actually
a singer) in stanzas two through nine of this poem:

X. J. KENNEDY

In a Prominent Bar in Secaucus One Day

*To the tune of "The Old Orange Flute" or
the tune of "Sweet Betsy from Pike!"*

In a prominent bar in Secaucus[6] one day

4. Deliver angry blows.
5. Migraine headaches.
6. A small, smoggy town on the Hackensack River in New Jersey, a few miles
west of Manhattan.

Rose a lady in skunk with a topheavy sway,
Raised a knobby red finger—all turned from their beer—
While with eyes bright as snowcrust she sang high and clear:

"Now who of you'd think from an eyeload of me   5
That I once was a lady as proud as could be?
Oh I'd never sit down by a tumbledown drunk
If it wasn't, my dears, for the high cost of junk.

"All the gents used to swear that the white of my calf
Beat the down of a swan by a length and a half.   10
In the kerchief of linen I caught to my nose
Ah, there never fell snot, but a little gold rose.

"I had seven gold teeth and a toothpick of gold,
My Virginia cheroot was a leaf of it rolled
And I'd light it each time with a thousand in cash—   15
Why the bums used to fight if I flicked them an ash.

"Once the toast of the Biltmore,[7] the belle of the Taft,
I would drink bottle beer at the Drake, never draft,
And dine at the Astor on Salisbury steak
With a clean tablecloth for each bite I did take.   20

"In a car like the Roxy[8] I'd roll to the track,
A steel-guitar trio, a bar in the back,
And the wheels made no noise, they turned over so fast,
Still it took you ten minutes to see me go past.

"When the horses bowed down to me that I might choose,   25
I bet on them all, for I hated to lose.
Now I'm saddled each night for my butter and eggs
And the broken threads race down the backs of my legs.

"Let you hold in mind, girls, that your beauty must pass
Like a lovely white clover that rusts with its grass.   30
Keep your bottoms off barstools and marry you young
Or be left—an old barrel with many a bung.

"For when time takes you out for a spin in his car
You'll be hard-pressed to stop him from going too far
And be left by the roadside, for all your good deeds,   35
Two toadstools for tits and a face full of weeds."

All the house raised a cheer, but the man at the bar
Made a phonecall and up pulled a red patrol car
And she blew us a kiss as they copped her away
From that prominent bar in Secaucus, N.J.   40

                                                          1961

---

7. Like the Taft, Drake, and Astor, a once fashionable New York hotel.
8. A luxurious old New York theater and movie house, the site of many "World Premieres" in the heyday of Hollywood.

588   *Speaker*

Again, we learn about the character primarily through her own words, although we don't have to believe everything she tells us about her past. From her introduction in the first stanza we get some general notion of her appearance and condition, but it is she who tells us that she is a junkie (line 8), a prostitute (line 27), and that her face and figure are pretty well shot (lines 32, 36). That information could make her a sad case, and the poem might lament her state or allow her to lament it, but instead the poem presents her cheerfully. She is anxious to give advice and sound moralistic (line 31, for example), but she's also enormously cheerful about herself, and her spirit repeatedly bursts through her song. Her performance gives her a lot of pleasure as she exaggerates outrageously about her former luxury and prominence, and even her departure in a patrol car she chooses to treat as a grand exit, throwing a kiss to her audience. The comedy is bittersweet, perhaps, but she is allowed to present herself, through her own words and attitudes, as a likable character. The glorious fiction of her life, narrated with energy and polish in the manner of a practiced and accomplished liar, betrays some rather naive notions of good taste and luxurious living (lines 18–26). But this "lady in skunk" has a picturesque and engaging style, a refreshing sense of humor about herself, and (like the cheap fur she wears) her experiences in what she considers high life satisfy her sense of style and drama. The self-portrait accumulates, almost completely through how she talks about herself, and the poet develops our attitude toward her by allowing her to recount her story herself, in her own words—or rather in words chosen for her by the author.

It is, of course, equally possible to create a speaker who makes us dislike himself or herself, also because of what the poet makes him or her say, as the following poem does. Here the speaker, as the title implies, is a monk, but he shows himself to be most unmonklike: mean, self-righteous, and despicable.

ROBERT BROWNING

Soliloquy of the Spanish Cloister[9]

Gr-r-r—there go, my heart's abhorrence!
　　Water your damned flower-pots, do!
If hate killed men, Brother Lawrence,
　　God's blood, would not mine kill you!
What? your myrtle-bush wants trimming?   5
　　Oh, that rose has prior claims—
Needs its leaden vase filled brimming?
　　Hell dry you up with its flames!

9. Monastery.

At the meal we sit together:
   Salve tibi![1] I must hear   10
Wise talk of the kind of weather,
   Sort of season, time of year:
Not a plenteous cork-crop: scarcely
   Dare we hope oak-galls,[2] *I doubt:*
What's the Latin name for "parsley"?   15
   What's the Greek name for Swine's Snout?

Whew! We'll have our platter burnished,
   Laid with care on our own shelf!
With a fire-new spoon we're furnished,
   And a goblet for ourself,   20
Rinsed like something sacrificial
   Ere 'tis fit to touch our chaps[3]—
Marked with L. for our initial!
   (He-he! There his lily snaps!)

Saint, forsooth! While brown Dolores   25
   Squats outside the Convent bank
With Sanchicha, telling stories,
   Steeping tresses in the tank,
Blue-black, lustrous, thick like horsehairs,
   —Can't I see his dead eye glow,   30
Bright as 'twere a Barbary corsair's?[4]
   (That is, if he'd let it show!)

When he finishes refection,[5]
   Knife and fork he never lays
Cross-wise, to my recollection,   35
   As do I, in Jesu's praise.
I the Trinity illustrate,
   Drinking watered orange-pulp—
In three sips the Arian[6] frustrate;
   While he drains his at one gulp.   40

Oh, those melons? If he's able
   We're to have a feast! so nice!
One goes to the Abbot's table,
   All of us get each a slice.
How go on your flowers? None double?   45
   Not one fruit-sort can you spy?
Strange!—And I, too, at such trouble,
   Keep them close-nipped on the sly!

There's a great text in Galatians,[7]

1. Hail to thee. Italics usually indicate the words of Brother Lawrence.
2. Abnormal growth on oak trees, used for tanning.
3. Jaws.
4. African pirate's.
5. A meal.
6. A heretical sect which denied the Trinity.
7. "Cursed is every one that continueth not in all things which are written in the book of law to do them," *Galatians* 3:10. *Galatians* 5:15–23 provides a long list of possible offenses, but they do not add up to 29.

Once you trip on it, entails   50
    Twenty-nine distinct damnations,
  One sure, if another fails:
    If I trip him just a-dying,
  Sure of heaven as sure can be,
Spin him round and send him flying   55
    Off to hell, a Manichee?[8]

Or, my scrofulous French novel
    On gray paper with blunt type!
Simply glance at it, you grovel
    Hand and foot in Belial's gripe:[9]   60
  If I double down its pages
    At the woeful sixteenth print,
When he gathers his greengages,
    Ope a sieve and slip it in't?

Or, there's Satan!—one might venture   65
    Pledge one's soul to him, yet leave
Such a flaw in the indenture
    As he'd miss till, past retrieve,
Blasted lay that rose-acacia
    We're so proud of! *Hy, Zy, Hine* . . .[1]   70
'St, there's Vespers! *Plena gratiâ*
Ave, Virgo.[2] Gr-r-r—you swine!

                                                      1842

Not many poems begin with a growl, and in this one it turns out to be fair warning that we are about to get to know a real beast, even though he is in the clothing of a religious man. In line 1, he has already shown himself to hold a most uncharitable attitude toward his fellow monk, Brother Lawrence, and by line 4 he has uttered two profanities and admitted his intense feelings of hatred and vengefulness. His ranting and roaring is full of exclamation points (four in the first stanza), and he reveals his own personality and character when he imagines curses and unflattering nicknames for Brother Lawrence or plots malicious jokes on him. By the end, we have accumulated no knowledge of Brother Lawrence that makes him seem a fit target for such rage (except that he is pious, dutiful, and pleasant—perhaps enough to make this sort of speaker despise him), but we have discovered the speaker to be lecherous (stanza 4), full of false piety (stanza 5), malicious in trivial matters (stanza 6), ready to use his theological learning to sponsor damnation rather than salvation (stanza 7), a closet reader and viewer of pornography

8. A heretic. According to the Manichean heresy, the world was divided into the forces of good and evil, equally powerful.

9. In the clutches of Satan.

1. Possibly the beginning of an incantation or curse.

2. The opening words of the *Ave Maria*, here reversed: "Full of grace, Hail, Virgin."

within the monastery (stanza 8)—even willing to risk his own soul in order to torment Brother Lawrence (last stanza). The speaker is made to characterize himself; the details accrue and accumulate into a fairly full portrait, and here we do not have even an opening and closing "objective" description (as in *In a Prominent Bar*) or another speaker (as in *The Ruined Maid*) to give us perspective. Except for the moments when the speaker mimics or parodies Brother Lawrence (usually in italic type), we have only the speaker's own words and thoughts. But that is enough; the poet has controlled them so carefully that we clearly know what he thinks of the speaker he has created—that he is a mean-spirited, vengeful hypocrite, a thoroughly disreputable and unlikable character. The whole poem has been about him and his attitudes; the point of the poem has been to characterize the speaker and develop in us a dislike of him and what he stands for—total hypocrisy. In reading a poem like this aloud, we would want our voice to suggest all the unlikable features of a hypocrite. We would also need to suggest, through the tone of voice we used, the author's contemptuous mocking of the rage and hypocrisy, and we would want, like an actor, to create strong disapproval in the hearer. The poem's words (the ones the author has given to the speaker) clearly imply those attitudes, and we would want our voice to express them. Usually there is much more to a poem than the identification and characterization of the speaker, but in many cases it is necessary to identify the speaker and determine his or her character before we can appreciate what else goes on in the poem. And sometimes, as here, in looking for the speaker of the poem, we come near to the center of the poem itself.

The speaker in the following poem is, from the first, clearly much more likable, but we do not get a very full sense of her until the poem is well along. As you read, try to imitate the tone of voice you think this kind of person would use. Exactly when do you begin to feel that you know what she is like?

DOROTHY PARKER

A Certain Lady

Oh, I can smile for you, and tilt my head,
    And drink your rushing words with eager lips,
And paint my mouth for you a fragrant red,
    And trace your brows with tutored finger-tips.
When you rehearse your list of loves to me,   5
    Oh, I can laugh and marvel, rapturous-eyed.
And you laugh back, nor can you ever see
    The thousand little deaths my heart has died.
And you believe, so well I know my part,
    That I am gay as morning, light as snow,   10

And all the straining things within my heart
   You'll never know.

Oh, I can laugh and listen, when we meet,
   And you bring tales of fresh adventurings—
Of ladies delicately indiscreet,   15
   Of lingering hands, and gently whispered things.
And you are pleased with me, and strive anew
   To sing me sagas of your late delights.
Thus do you want me—marveling, gay, and true—
   Nor do you see my staring eyes of nights.   20
And when, in search of novelty, you stray,
   Oh, I can kiss you blithely as you go . . .
And what goes on, my love, while you're away,
   You'll never know.

                                                        1937

To whom does the speaker seem to be talking? What sort of person
is he? How do you feel about him? Which habits and attitudes of
his do you like least? How soon can you tell that the speaker is not
altogether happy about his conversation and conduct? In what tone
of voice would you read the first 22 lines aloud? What attitude
would you try to express toward the person spoken to? What tone
would you use for the last two lines? How would you describe the
speaker's personality? What aspects of her behavior are most crucial
to the poem's effect?

   It is easy to assume that the speaker in a poem is an extension
of the poet. Is the speaker in this poem Dorothy Parker?—Maybe.
A lot of Parker's poems present a similar world-weary posture and a
kind of cynicism about romantic love (look, for example, at *Comment*,
p. 843). But the poem is hardly an example of self-revelation, a
giving away of personal secrets. If it were, it would be silly, not to
say risky, to address her lover in a way that gives damaging facts
about a pose she has been so careful to set up. We may be *tempted*
to think of the speaker as Dorothy Parker, but it is best to resist
the temptation and think of the character as an imagined person.
Besides, the poem is called *A Certain Lady*, as if it were a speaking
portrait of someone. Is the speaker based on any real person at all?
Probably not; we are given no reason to think that the speaker is
anyone in particular or that the poet has done anything but create a
fictional character and situation. In any case, the poem's effect does
not depend on our thinking that the speaker is someone specific and
historical; it depends on our surprise at her honesty and openness in
giving away a secret, something more likely in a fictional speaker than
in real life. In poetry we can be overhearers of a conversation; in real
life such a role could be dangerous to hearer as well as speaker—and
seldom in real life do we get so quick and pointed a characterization
as this poem develops in just a few well-organized and well-calculated
lines.

In poems like *The Ruined Maid, In a Prominent Bar,* and *Soliloquy,* we are in no danger of mistaking the speaker for the poet, once we have recognized that poets may create speakers who participate in specific situations much as in fiction or drama. When there is a pointed discrepancy between the speaker and what we know of the poet—when the speaker is a woman, for example, and the poet is a man—we know we have a created speaker to contend with and that the point (or at least *one* point) in the poem is to observe the characterization carefully. In *A Certain Lady* we may be less sure, and in other poems the discrepancy between speaker and poet may be even more uncertain. What are we to make, for example, of the speaker in *Woodchucks* in the previous chapter (p. 571)? Is that speaker the real Maxine Kumin? At best (without knowing something quite specific about the author) we can only say "maybe" to that question. What we can be sure of is the sort of person the speaker is portrayed to be—someone (man? or woman?) surprised to discover feelings and attitudes that contradict values apparently held confidently. And that is exactly what we need to know for the poem to have its effect.

A similar kind of self-mocking of the speaker is present in the following poem, but here the mockery is put to less revelatory, more comic ends.

A. R. AMMONS

Needs

I want something suited to my special needs
I want chrome hubcaps, pin-on attachments
and year round use year after year
I want a workhorse with smooth uniform cut,
dozer blade and snow blade & deluxe steering   5
wheel
I want something to mow, throw snow, tow
and sow with
I want precision reel blades
I want a console styled dashboard   10
I want an easy spintype recoil starter
I want combination bevel and spur gears, 14
gauge stamped steel housing and
washable foam element air cleaner
I want a pivoting front axle and extrawide   15
turf tires
I want an inch of foam rubber inside a vinyl
covering
and especially if it's not too much, if I
can deserve it, even if I can't pay for it   20
I want to mow while riding.

1970

The poet here may be teasing himself about his desire for comfort and ease—and showing how readily advertisements and catalog descriptions manipulate us. But the speaker doesn't have to be the author for the teasing to work. In fact, the effect is to tease those attitudes no matter who holds them by teasing a speaker who illustrates the attitudes. It doesn't matter to the poem whether the speaker is the poet himself or some totally invented character. If the speaker is a version of the poet himself—perhaps a *side* of his personality that he is exploring—the portrait is still fictional in an important sense. The poem presents not a whole human being (*no* poem could do that) but only a version of him—a mood perhaps, an aspect, an attitude, a part of that person. Here, the poet presents someone with an obsession, in this case a small and not very damaging one, and allows him to spurt phrases as if he were reciting from an ad. Here the "portrait" is made more comic by a clear sense the poem projects that what we have is only a part of the person, an interest grown too intense, gone askew, gotten out of proportion, something that happens to most of us from time to time. The speaker may be a side of the poet, or maybe not. All we know about the speaker is that he has a one-track mind, that he is obsessed by his own luxurious comfort. He may not even be a "he": there is nothing in the poem that makes us certain that the speaker is male. It is customary to think of the speaker in a poem written by a man as "he" and in a poem written by a woman as "she" (as in Maxine Kumin's *Woodchucks*) unless the poem presents contrary evidence, but it is merely a convenience, a habit, nothing more.

Even when poets present themselves as if they were speaking directly to us in their own voices, their poems present only a partial portrait, something considerably less than the full personality of the poet. Even when there is not an obviously created character—someone with distinct characteristics which are different from those of the poet—strategies of characterization are used to present the person speaking in one way and not another. Even in a poem like the following one, it is still a good idea to talk of the speaker instead of the poet, although here it is probable that the poet is writing about a personal, actual experience.

WILLIAM WORDSWORTH

She Dwelt Among the Untrodden Ways

She dwelt among the untrodden ways
    Beside the springs of Dove,[3]
A Maid whom there were none to praise
    And very few to love:

3. A small stream in the Lake District in northern England, near where Wordsworth lived in Dove Cottage at Grasmere.

A violet by a mossy stone   5
   Half hidden from the eye!
—Fair as a star, when only one
   Is shining in the sky.

She lived unknown, and few could know
   When Lucy ceased to be;   10
But she is in her grave, and, oh,
   The difference to me!

                                                          1800

It is hard to say whether this poem is more about Lucy or about how the speaker feels about her death. Her simple life, far removed from fame and known only to a few, is said nevertheless to have been beautiful. We know little else about her beyond her name and where she lived, in a beautiful but then isolated section of northern England. We don't know if she was young or old, only that the speaker thinks of her as "fair" and compares her to a "violet by a mossy stone." What we do know is that the speaker feels her loss deeply, so deeply that he is almost inarticulate with grief, lapsing into simple exclamation ("oh," line 11) and unable to articulate the "difference" that her death makes.

Did Lucy actually live? Was she a friend of the poet? We don't know; the poem doesn't tell us, and even biographers of Wordsworth are unsure. What we do know is that Wordsworth was able to represent grief over the death very powerfully. Whether the speaker is the historical Wordsworth or not, that speaker is a major focus of the poem, and it is his feelings which the poem isolates and expresses. We need to recognize some characteristics of the speaker and be sensitive to his feelings for the poem to work. We may be tempted to identify the speaker with the poet—it seems to be a natural tendency for most readers to make that assumption unless there is overwhelming evidence to the contrary in the poem—but it is still best to think of the voice we hear in the poem as that of the speaker. We don't need to give him a name, but we do need to understand his values as the poem expresses them and to recognize his deep feelings.

The poems we have looked at in this chapter—and the group that follows at the end of the chapter—all suggest the value of beginning the reading of any poem with a simple question: Who is speaking and what do we know about him or her? Putting together the evidence that the poem presents in answer to this question can often take us a long way into the poem. For some poems, this question won't help a great deal because the speaking voice is too indistinct or the character behind the poem too scantily presented, but in many cases asking this question will lead you toward the central experience the poem offers.

HENRY REED

Lessons of the War

Judging Distances

Not only far away, but the way that you say it
Is very important. Perhaps you may never get
The knack of judging a distance, but at least you know
How to report on a landscape: the central sector,
The right of arc and that, which we had last Tuesday,　　　　　5
　　　And at least you know

That maps are of time, not place, so far as the army
Happens to be concerned—the reason being,
Is one which need not delay us. Again, you know
There are three kinds of tree, three only, the fir and the poplar,　　10
And those which have bushy tops to; and lastly
　　　That things only seem to be things.

A barn is not called a barn, to put it more plainly,
Or a field in the distance, where sheep may be safely grazing.
You must never be over-sure. You must say, when reporting:　　15
At five o'clock in the central sector is a dozen
Of what appear to be animals; whatever you do,
　　　Don't call the bleeders *sheep*.

I am sure that's quite clear; and suppose, for the sake of example,
The one at the end, asleep, endeavors to tell us　　　　　20
What he sees over there to the west, and how far away,
After first having come to attention. There to the west,
On the fields of summer the sun and the shadows bestow
　　　Vestments of purple and gold.

The still white dwellings are like a mirage in the heat,　　　　25
And under the swaying elms a man and a woman
Lie gently together. Which is, perhaps, only to say
That there is a row of houses to the left of arc,
And that under some poplars a pair of what appear to be humans
　　　Appear to be loving.　　　　　30

Well that, for an answer, is what we might rightly call
Moderately satisfactory only, the reason being,
Is that two things have been omitted, and those are important.
The human beings, now: in what direction are they,
And how far away, would you say? And do not forget　　　35
　　　There may be dead ground in between.

There may be dead ground in between; and I may not have got
The knack of judging a distance; I will only venture
A guess that perhaps between me and the apparent lovers,
(Who, incidentally, appear by now to have finished,)　　　40

At seven o'clock from the houses, is roughly a distance
　　Of about one year and a half.

1946

AUDRE LORDE

Hanging Fire

I am fourteen
and my skin has betrayed me
the boy I cannot live without
still sucks his thumb
in secret   5
how come my knees are
always so ashy
what if I die
before morning
and momma's in the bedroom   10
with the door closed.

I have to learn how to dance
in time for the next party
my room is too small for me
suppose I die before graduation   15
they will sing sad melodies
but finally
tell the truth about me
There is nothing I want to do
and too much   20
that has to be done
and momma's in the bedroom
with the door closed.

Nobody even stops to think
about my side of it   25
I should have been on Math Team
my marks were better than his
why do I have to be
the one
wearing braces   30
I have nothing to wear tomorrow
will I live long enough
to grow up
and momma's in the bedroom
with the door closed.   35

1978

SEAMUS HEANEY

Mid-Term Break

I sat all morning in the college sick bay
Counting bells knelling classes to a close.
At two o'clock our neighbors drove me home.

In the porch I met my father crying—
He had always taken funerals in his stride—   5
And Big Jim Evans saying it was a hard blow.

The baby cooed and laughed and rocked the pram
When I came in, and I was embarrassed
By old men standing up to shake my hand

And tell me they were "sorry for my trouble,"   10
Whispers informed strangers I was the eldest,
Away at school, as my mother held my hand

In hers and coughed out angry tearless sighs.
At ten o'clock the ambulance arrived
With the corpse, stanched and bandaged by the nurses.   15

Next morning I went up into the room. Snowdrops
And candles soothed the bedside; I saw him
For the first time in six weeks. Paler now,

Wearing a poppy bruise on his left temple,
He lay in the four foot box as in his cot.   20
No gaudy scars, the bumper knocked him clear.

A four foot box, a foot for every year.

1966

JOHN BETJEMAN

In Westminster Abbey[4]

Let me take this other glove off
    As the *vox humana*[5] swells,
And the beauteous fields of Eden
    Bask beneath the Abbey bells.
Here, where England's statesmen lie,   5
    Listen to a lady's cry.

4. The famous Gothic church in London
in which English monarchs are crowned
and famous Englishmen are buried (see
lines 5, 39–40).
5. Organ tones which resemble the human voice.

Gracious Lord, oh bomb the Germans.
  Spare their women for Thy Sake,
And if that is not too easy
  We will pardon Thy Mistake.
But, gracious Lord, whate'er shall be,
Don't let anyone bomb me.

Keep our Empire undismembered
  Guide our Forces by Thy Hand,
Gallant blacks from far Jamaica,
  Honduras and Togoland;
Protect them Lord in all their fights,
And, even more, protect the whites.

Think of what our Nation stands for,
  Books from Boots[6] and country lanes,
Free speech, free passes, class distinction,
  Democracy and proper drains.
Lord, put beneath Thy special care
One-eighty-nine Cadogan Square.[7]

Although dear Lord I am a sinner,
  I have done no major crime;
Now I'll come to Evening Service
  Whensoever I have the time.
So, Lord, reserve for me a crown,
And do not let my shares go down.

I will labor for Thy Kingdom,
  Help our lads to win the war,
Send white feathers to the cowards[8]
  Join the Women's Army Corps,[9]
Then wash the Steps around Thy Throne
In the Eternal Safety Zone.

Now I feel a little better,
  What a treat to hear Thy Word
Where the bones of leading statesmen,
  Have so often been interred.
And now, dear Lord, I cannot wait
Because I have a luncheon date.

1940

6. A chain of London pharmacies.
7. Presumably where the speaker lives, in a fairly fashionable area.
8. White feathers were sometimes given, or sent, to men not in uniform, to suggest that they were cowards and should join the armed forces.
9. The speaker uses the old World War I name (Women's Army Auxiliary Corps) of the Auxiliary Territorial Service, an organization which performed domestic (and some foreign) defense duties.

TOM WAYMAN

Picketing Supermarkets

Because all this food is grown in the store
do not take the leaflet.
Cabbages, broccoli and tomatoes
are raised at night in the aisles.
Milk is brewed in the rear storage areas.   5
Beef produced in vats in the basement.
Do not take the leaflet.
Peanut butter and soft drinks
are made fresh each morning by store employees.
Our oranges and grapes   10
are so fine and round
that when held up to the lights they cast no shadow.
Do not take the leaflet.

And should you take one
do not believe it.   15
This chain of stores has no connection
with anyone growing food someplace else.
How could we have an effect on local farmers?
Do not believe it.

The sound here is Muzak, for your enjoyment.   20
It is not the sound of children crying.
There *is* a lady offering samples
to mark Canada Cheese Month.
There is no dark-skinned man with black hair beside her
wanting to show you the inside of a coffin.   25
You would not have to look if there was.
And there are no Nicaraguan heroes
in any way connected with the bananas.

Pay no attention to these people.
The manager is a citizen.   30
All this food is grown in the store.

                                                          1973

GEORGE HERBERT

The Collar

I struck the board[1] and cried, "No more;
        I will abroad!
What? shall I ever sigh and pine?

1. Table.

My lines[2] and life are free, free as the road,
   Loose as the wind, as large as store.[3] 5
      Shall I be still in suit?[4]
Have I no harvest but a thorn
 To let me blood, and not restore
What I have lost with cordial[5] fruit?
      Sure there was wine 10
Before my sighs did dry it; there was corn
  Before my tears did drown it.
 Is the year only lost to me?
  Have I no bays[6] to crown it,
No flowers, no garlands gay? All blasted? 15
      All wasted?
Not so, my heart; but there is fruit,
    And thou hast hands.
 Recover all thy sigh-blown age
On double pleasures: leave thy cold dispute 20
Of what is fit, and not. Forsake thy cage,
    Thy rope of sands,[7]
Which petty thoughts have made, and made to thee
  Good cable, to enforce and draw,
     And be thy law, 25
While thou didst wink[8] and wouldst not see.
    Away! take heed;
    I will abroad.
Call in thy death's-head[9] there; tie up thy fears.
    He that forbears 30
  To suit and serve his need,
    Deserves his load."
But as I raved and grew more fierce and wild
    At every word,
Methought I heard one calling, *Child!* 35
   And I replied, *My Lord.*

1633

2. Lot.
3. A storehouse; i.e., in abundance.
4. In service to another.
5. Reviving, restorative.
6. Wreaths of triumph.

7. Moral restrictions.
8. I.e., close your eyes to the weaknesses of such restrictions.
9. *Memento mori*, a skull intended to remind men of their mortality.

4   SITUATION AND SETTING

Questions about speaker ("Who?" questions) in a poem almost always lead to questions of "Where?" "When?" and "Why?" Identifying the speaker usually is, in fact, part of a larger process of defining the entire imagined **situation** in a poem: What is happening? Where is it happening? Who is the speaker speaking to? Who else is present? Why is this event occurring? In order to understand the dialogue in *The Ruined Maid,* for example, we need to become aware that the sisters are meeting again after a period of absence and that they are meeting in a town large enough to seem substantially different in setting from the rural area in which they grew up together. And we infer (from the opening lines) that the meeting is accidental, and that no other family members are present for the conversation. The poem's whole "story" depends upon the fact of their situation: after leading separate lives for some time they have some catching up to do. We don't know what specific town is involved, or what year, season, or time of day because those details are not important to the poem's effect. But crucial to the poem are the where and when questions that define the situation and relationship of the two speakers, and the answer to the why question—that the meeting is by chance— is important too. In another poem we looked at in the previous chapter, *A Certain Lady,* the specific moment and place are not important, but we do need to notice that the "lady" is talking to (or having an imaginary conversation with) her man and that they are talking about a relationship of some duration.

Sometimes a *specific* time and place (**setting**) may be important. The "lady in skunk" sings her life story "in a prominent bar in Secaucus, N.J.," a smelly and unfashionable town, but on no particular occasion ("One Day"). In *Soliloquy of the Spanish Cloister,* the setting (a monastery) adds to the irony because of the gross inappropriateness of such sentiments and attitudes in such a supposedly holy place, and the setting of *In Westminster Abbey* similarly helps us to judge the speaker's ideas, attitudes, and self-conception.

The title of the following poem suggests that place may be important, and it is, although you may be surprised to discover exactly what exists at this address and what uses the speaker makes of it.

JAMES DICKEY

Cherrylog Road

Off Highway 106[1]
At Cherrylog Road I entered
The '34 Ford without wheels,

---

1. The poem is set in the mountains of North Georgia.

Smothered in kudzu,[2]
With a seat pulled out to run   5
Corn whiskey down from the hills,

And then from the other side
Crept into an Essex
With a rumble seat of red leather
And then out again, aboard   10
A blue Chevrolet, releasing
The rust from its other color,

Reared up on three building blocks.
None had the same body heat;
I changed with them inward, toward   15
The weedy heart of the junkyard,
For I knew that Doris Holbrook
Would escape from her father at noon

And would come from the farm
To seek parts owned by the sun   20
Among the abandoned chassis,
Sitting in each in turn
As I did, leaning forward
As in a wild stock-car race

In the parking lot of the dead.   25
Time after time, I climbed in
And out the other side, like
An envoy or movie star
Met at the station by crickets.
A radiator cap raised its head,   30

Become a real toad or a kingsnake
As I neared the hub of the yard,
Passing through many states,
Many lives, to reach
Some grandmother's long Pierce-Arrow   35
Sending platters of blindness forth

From its nickel hubcaps
And spilling its tender upholstery
On sleepy roaches,
The glass panel in between   40
Lady and colored driver
Not all the way broken out,

The back-seat phone
Still on its hook.
I got in as though to exclaim,   45

2. A rapidly growing vine, introduced from Japan to combat erosion but now covering whole fields and groves of trees.

"Let us go to the orphan asylum,
John; I have some old toys
For children who say their prayers."

I popped with sweat as I thought
I heard Doris Holbrook scrape   50
Like a mouse in the southern-state sun
That was eating the paint in blisters
From a hundred car tops and hoods.
She was tapping like code,

Loosening the screws,   55
Carrying off headlights,
Sparkplugs, bumpers,
Cracked mirrors and gear-knobs,
Getting ready, already,
To go back with something to show   60

Other than her lips' new trembling
I would hold to me soon, soon,
Where I sat in the ripped back seat
Talking over the interphone,
Praying for Doris Holbrook   65
To come from her father's farm

And to get back there
With no trace of me on her face
To be seen by her red-haired father
Who would change, in the squalling barn,   70
Her back's pale skin with a strop,
Then lay for me

In a bootlegger's roasting car
With a string-triggered 12-gauge shotgun
To blast the breath from the air.   75
Not cut by the jagged windshields,
Through the acres of wrecks she came
With a wrench in her hand,

Through dust where the blacksnake dies
Of boredom, and the beetle knows   80
The compost has no more life.
Someone outside would have seen
The oldest car's door inexplicably
Close from within:

I held her and held her and held her,   85
Convoyed at terrific speed
By the stalled, dreaming traffic around us,
So the blacksnake, stiff
With inaction, curved back
Into life, and hunted the mouse   90

With deadly overexcitement,
The beetles reclaimed their field
As we clung, glued together,
With the hooks of the seat springs
Working through to catch us red-handed   95
Amidst the gray breathless batting

That burst from the seat at our backs.
We left by separate doors
Into the changed, other bodies
Of cars, she down Cherrylog Road   100
And I to my motorcycle
Parked like the soul of the junkyard

Restored, a bicycle fleshed
With power, and tore off
Up Highway 106, continually   105
Drunk on the wind in my mouth,
Wringing the handlebar for speed,
Wild to be wreckage forever.

                                              1964

The *exact* location of the junkyard is not important (there is no Highway 106 near the real Cherrylog Road in North Georgia), but we do need to know that the setting is rural, that the time is summer and that the summer is hot, and that moonshine whiskey is native to the area. Following the story is no problem once we have sorted out these few facts, and we are prepared to meet the cast of characters: Doris Holbrook, her red-haired father, and the speaker. About each we learn just enough to appreciate the sense of vitality, adventure, and power that constitute the major effects of the poem.

The situation of love-making in another setting than the junkyard would not produce the same effects, and the exotic sense of a forbidden meeting in this unlikely place helps to recreate the speaker's sense of the episode. For him, it is memorable (notice all the tiny details he remembers), powerful (notice his reaction when he gets back on his motorcycle), dreamlike (notice the sense of time standing still, especially in lines 85–89), and important (notice how the speaker perceives his environment as changed by their love-making, lines 88–91 and 98–100). The wealth of details about setting also helps us to raise other, related questions. Why does the speaker fantasize about being shot by the father (lines 72–75)? Why, in a poem so full of details, do we find out so little about what Doris Holbrook looks like? What gives us the sense that this incident is a composite of episodes, an event that was repeated many times? What gives us the impression that the events occurred long ago? What makes the speaker feel so powerful at the end? What does he mean when he talks of himself as being "wild to be wreckage forever"? All of the poem's attention to the speaker's reactions, reflections, and memories is intricately tied up with the particulars of setting. Making love in a junkyard is crucial to the speaker's sense of both power and wreckage, and Doris is merely a matter of excitement, adventure, and pretty skin, appreciated because she makes the world seem different and because she is willing to take risks and to suffer for meeting him like this. The more we probe the poem with questions about situation, the more likely we are to catch the poem's full effect.

Cherrylog Road is a fairly easy poem to read, but its effect is more complex than its simple story line suggests. The next poem we will look at is, at first glance, much more difficult to follow. Part of the difficulty is that the poem is from an earlier age, and its language is a little different, and part is because the action in the poem is so closely connected to what is being said. But its opening lines—addressed to someone who is resisting the speaker's suggestions—disclose the situation, and gradually we can figure out the scene: a man is trying to convince a woman that they should make love. When a flea happens by, the speaker uses it for an unlikely example as part of his argument. And once we recognize the situation, we can readily follow (and be amused by) the speaker's witty and intricate argument.

JOHN DONNE

The Flea

Mark but this flea, and mark in this[3]
How little that which thou deny'st me is;
It sucked me first, and now sucks thee,
And in this flea our two bloods mingled be;
Thou know'st that this cannot be said   5
A sin, nor shame, nor loss of maidenhead,
   Yet this enjoys before it woo,
   And pampered[4] swells with one blood made of two,
   And this, alas, is more than we would do.[5]

Oh stay, three lives in one flea spare,   10
Where we almost, yea more than, married are.
This flea is you and I, and this
Our marriage bed, and marriage temple is;
Though parents grudge, and you, we're met
And cloistered in these living walls of jet.   15
   Though use[6] make you apt to kill me,
   Let not to that, self-murder added be,
   And sacrilege, three sins in killing three.

3. Medieval preachers and rhetoricians asked their hearers to "mark" (look at) an object which illustrated a moral or philosophical lesson they wished to emphasize.
4. Fed luxuriously.

5. According to contemporary medical theory, conception involved the literal mingling of the lovers' blood.
6. Habit.

Cruel and sudden, hast thou since
Purpled thy nail in blood of innocence?   20
Wherein could this flea guilty be,
Except in that drop which it sucked from thee?
Yet thou triumph'st, and say'st that thou
Find'st not thyself, nor me, the weaker now;
  'Tis true; then learn how false, fears be;   25
  Just so much honor, when thou yield'st to me,
  Will waste, as this flea's death took life from thee.

1633

The scene in *The Flea* develops almost as in a play. Action even occurs right along with the words. Between stanzas 1 and 2, the woman makes a move to kill the flea (as stanza 2 opens, the speaker is trying to stop her), and between stanzas 2 and 3 the woman has squished the flea with her fingernail. Once we try to make sense of what the speaker says, the action is just as clear from the words as if we had stage directions in the margin. All of the speaker's verbal cleverness and all of his specious arguments follow from the situation, and in this poem (as in *Soliloquy of the Spanish Cloister* or *In Westminster Abbey*) we watch as if we were observing a scene on the stage. The speaker is, in effect, giving a dramatic monologue for our benefit. (You may have noticed that in seduction poems, the seducer usually does all the talking and the seduced seldom gets a chance to speak; for some amusing inversions (reversals) of this pattern, and some witty variations on it, see the group of poems on pp. 769–771).

Neither time nor place is important to *The Flea*, except in the sense that the speaker and his friend have to be assumed to be in the same place and have the leisure for some playfulness. The situation could occur in any place where a man, a woman, and a flea could be together. Indoors, outdoors, morning, evening, city, country, it is all one; the situation could occur in cottage or palace, on a boat or in a bedroom. We do know, from the date of publication of the poem (1633), that the poet was writing about people of more than three centuries ago, but the conduct he describes might equally happen in later ages just as well. Only the habits of language (and perhaps the speaker's religious attitudes) date the poem; the situation could equally be set in any age or place.

Some poems, however, refer to a certain actual place and time. The following poem depends upon historical information (it also assumes that we know the terminology of children's games); if you don't know the history of atomic warfare, you may want to read the footnote before you read the poem.

ROBERT FROST

U. S. 1946 King's X[7]

Having invented a new Holocaust,
And been the first with it to win a war,
How they make haste to cry with fingers crossed,
King's X—no fairs to use it any more!

p. 1946

Our knowledge of the relevant historical facts does not necessarily mean that we will agree with the poet's criticism of U. S. policy at the end of World War II, but we certainly can't understand or appreciate the poem's equation of nuclear policy with a child's fear of consequence unless we do know the facts. Often it is hard to place ourselves fully enough in another time or place to imagine sympathetically what a particular historical moment would have been like, and even the best poetic efforts do not necessarily transport us there. But poets sometimes record a particular moment or event in order to commemorate it or comment upon it. A poem written about a specific occasion is usually called an **occasional poem,** and such a poem is **referential;** that is, it refers to a specific historical moment or event. For such poems we need, at the least, specific historical information—plus a willingness on our part as readers to be transported imaginatively to that particular time, sometimes (as in *U. S. 1946 King's X*) by mentioning explicitly a particular time, sometimes by recreating that moment in a dramatic situation. The poems about World War I on pp. 747–753 suggest something of the range of problems involved in reading consciously historical and referential poetry.

Time or place may, of course, be used much less specifically and still be important to a poem, and the most common uses of setting involve drawing upon common notions of a particular time or place. Setting a poem in a garden, for example, or writing about apples almost inevitably reminds us of the Garden of Eden because it is part of our common heritage of belief or knowledge. Even people who don't read at all or who lack Judaeo-Christian religious commitments are likely to know about Eden, and a poet writing in our culture can count on that. In Joni Mitchell's *Woodstock* (p.566), for example (as we noticed in Chapter 2) the idea of the innocence in Woodstock is drawn into the poem by an allusion to Eden; the final refrain in each stanza of the poem insists that "we've got to get ourselves / Back to the garden." An **allusion** is a reference to something outside the poem that carries a history of meaning and strong emotional associations. For example, gardens may carry suggestions of innocence and order, or temptation and the fall, or both, depending on how the poem handles the allusion. Well-known places from his-

7. Shortly after exploding the two atomic bombs that ended World War II, the United States proposed to share nuclear information with other countries in exchange for an agreement that the information would be used only for peaceful purposes. In children's games, time out is sometimes signaled by crossing fingers and saying "King's X."

tory or myth may be popularly associated with particular ideas or values or ways of life.

The place involved in a poem is its **spatial setting**, and the time is its **temporal setting**. The temporal setting may involve a specific date or an era, a season of the year or a time of day. We tend, for example, to think of spring as a time of discovery and growth, and poems set in spring are likely to draw upon that association; morning usually suggests discovery as well—beginnings, vitality, the world fresh and new—even to those of us who in reality take our waking slow. Temporal or spatial setting are often used to influence our expectation of theme and tone in a specific way, although the poet may then go on to surprise us by making something very different of our expectation. Setting is often an important factor in creating the mood in poems just as in stories, plays, or films. Often the details of setting have a lot to do with the way we ultimately respond to the poem's subject or theme, as in this poem:

SYLVIA PLATH

Point Shirley

From Water-Tower Hill to the brick prison
The shingle booms, bickering under
The sea's collapse.
Snowcakes break and welter. This year
The gritted wave leaps   5
The seawall and drops onto a bier
Of quahog chips,[8]
Leaving a salty mash of ice to whiten

In my grandmother's sand yard. She is dead,
Whose laundry snapped and froze here, who   10
Kept house against
What the sluttish, rutted sea could do.
Squall waves once danced
Ship timbers in through the cellar window;
A thresh-tailed, lanced   15
Shark littered in the geranium bed—

Such collusion of mulish elements
She wore her broom straws to the nub.
Twenty years out
Of her hand; the house still hugs in each drab   20
Stucco socket
The purple egg-stones: from Great Head's knob
To the filled-in Gut
The sea in its cold gizzard ground those rounds.

8. Chips from quahog clam shells, common on the New England coast.

Nobody wintering now behind   25
The planked-up windows where she set
Her wheat loaves
And apple cakes to cool. What is it
Survives, grieves
So, over this battered, obstinate spit   30
Of gravel? The waves'
Spewed relics clicker masses in the wind,

Gray waves the stub-necked eiders ride.
A labor of love, and that labor lost.
Steadily the sea   35
Eats at Point Shirley. She died blessed,
And I come by
Bones, bones only, pawed and tossed,
A dog-faced sea.
The sun sinks under Boston, bloody red.   40

I would get from these dry-papped stones
The milk your love instilled in them.
The black ducks dive.
And though your graciousness might stream,
And I contrive,   45
Grandmother, stones are nothing of home
To that spumiest dove.
Against both bar and tower the black sea runs.

1960

One does not have to know the New England coast by personal
experience to have it vividly recalled by Plath's poem. A reader who
knows that coast or another like it may have an advantage in being
able to respond more quickly to the poem's precision of description,
but the poem does not depend on such knowledge from outside the
poem. The precise location of Point Shirley, near Boston, is not especially important, but visualization of the setting is. Crucial to the poem's
tone and mood is the sense of the sea as aggressor, a force powerful
enough to change the contours of the coast and invade the privacy of
yards and homes. The energy, relentlessness, and impersonality of the
sea met their match, though a temporary one, in the speaker's grandmother who "Kept house against / What the sluttish, rutted sea could
do" (lines 11-12). The grandmother *belonged* in this setting, and it
seemed hers, but twenty years of her absence (since her death) now
begin to show. Still, the marks of her obstinacy and love are there,
although ultimately doomed by the sea's more enduring power.

Details—and how they are amassed—are important here rather than
historic particulars of time and place. The grays and whites and drab
colors of the sea and its leavings provide both a visual sense of the

scene and the mood for the poem. The stubbornness which the
speaker admired in the grandmother comes to seem a part of that
tenacious grayness. Nothing happens rapidly here; things wear down.
Even the "bloody red" (line 40) of the sun's setting—an ominous sign
that adds a vivid fright to the dullness rather than brightening it—
makes promises that seem slow and long-term. The toughness of the
boarded-up house is a monument to the grandmother's loving care
and becomes a way for the speaker to touch her human spirit, but
the poem's final emphasis is on the relentless black sea which continues
to run against the landmarks and fortresses that had been identified
with the setting in the very first line.

Questions about situation and setting begin as simple questions of
identification but often become more complex when we sort out all
the implications. Often it takes only a moment to determine a poem's
situation, but it may take much longer to discover all of the things
that time and place imply, for their meanings may depend upon
visual details, or upon actual historical occurrences, or upon habitual
ways of thinking about certain times and places—or all three at once.
As you read the following poem, notice how the setting—another
shore—prepares us for the speaker's moods and ideas, and then watch
how the movement of his mind is affected by what he sees.

MATTHEW ARNOLD

Dover Beach[9]

The sea is calm tonight.
The tide is full, the moon lies fair
Upon the straits; on the French coast the light
Gleams and is gone; the cliffs of England stand,
Glimmering and vast, out in the tranquil bay. 5
Come to the window, sweet is the night-air!
Only, from the long line of spray
Where the sea meets the moon-blanched land,
Listen! you hear the grating roar
Of pebbles which the waves draw back, and fling, 10
At their return, up the high strand,
Begin, and cease, and then again begin,
With tremulous cadence slow, and bring
The eternal note of sadness in.

Sophocles long ago 15
Heard it on the Aegean, and it brought
Into his mind the turbid ebb and flow

9. At the narrowest point on the English Channel. The lights on the French coast
(lines 3–4) would be about 20 miles away.

Of human misery;[1] we
Find also in the sound a thought,
Hearing it by this distant northern sea.   20

The Sea of Faith
Was once, too, at the full, and round earth's shore
Lay like the folds of a bright girdle furled.
But now I only hear
Its melancholy, long, withdrawing roar,   25
Retreating, to the breath
Of the night-wind, down the vast edges drear
And naked shingles[2] of the world.

Ah, love, let us be true
To one another! for the world, which seems   30
To lie before us like a land of dreams,
So various, so beautiful, so new,

Hath really neither joy, nor love, nor light,
Nor certitude, nor peace, nor help for pain;
And we are here as on a darkling plain   35
Swept with confused alarms of struggle and flight,
Where ignorant armies clash by night.

ca. 1851

Exactly what is the dramatic situation in *Dover Beach?* How soon
are you aware that someone is being spoken to? How much are we
told about the person spoken to? How would you describe the speaker's mood? What does the speaker's mood have to do with time and
place? Do any details of present place and time help to account for
his tendency to talk repeatedly of the past and the future? How
important is it to the poem's total effect that the beach here involves
an international border? What particulars of the Dover Beach seem
especially important to the poem's themes? to its emotional effects?

Not all poems have an identifiable situation or setting, just as not
all poems have a speaker that is distinct from the author. Poems that
simply present a series of thoughts and feelings directly, in a con-
templative, meditative, or reflective way, may not set up any kind of
action, plot, or situation at all, preferring to speak directly without the
intermediary of a dramatic device. But most poems depend crucially
upon a sense of place, a sense of time, and an understanding of human
interaction in scenes that resemble the strategies of drama or film.
And questions about these matters will often lead you to define not
only the "facts" but also the feelings central to a poem's design upon us.

---

1. In *Antigone,* lines 583–91, the chorus   to the waves of the sea.
compares the fate of the house of Oedipus   2. Pebble-strewn beaches.

ROBERT BROWNING

My Last Duchess

Ferrara[3]

That's my last Duchess painted on the wall,
Looking as if she were alive. I call
That piece a wonder, now: Frà Pandolf's hands[4]
Worked busily a day, and there she stands.
Will't please you sit and look at her? I said   5
"Frà Pandolf" by design, for never read
Strangers like you that pictured countenance,
The depth and passion of its earnest glance,
But to myself they turned (since none puts by
The curtain I have drawn for you, but I)   10
And seemed as they would ask me, if they durst,
How such a glance came there; so, not the first
Are you to turn and ask thus. Sir, 'twas not
Her husband's presence only, called that spot
Of joy into the Duchess' cheek: perhaps   15
Frà Pandolf chanced to say "Her mantle laps
Over my lady's wrist too much," or "Paint
Must never hope to reproduce the faint
Half-flush that dies along her throat": such stuff
Was courtesy, she thought, and cause enough   20
For calling up that spot of joy. She had
A heart—how shall I say?—too soon made glad,
Too easily impressed; she liked whate'er
She looked on, and her looks went everywhere.
Sir, 'twas all one! My favor at her breast,   25
The dropping of the daylight in the West,
The bough of cherries some officious fool
Broke in the orchard for her, the white mule
She rode with round the terrace—all and each
Would draw from her alike the approving speech,   30
Or blush, at least. She thanked men,—good! but thanked
Somehow—I know not how—as if she ranked
My gift of a nine-hundred-years-old name
With anybody's gift. Who'd stoop to blame
This sort of trifling? Even had you skill   35
In speech—which I have not—to make your will
Quite clear to such an one, and say, "Just this
Or that in you disgusts me; here you miss,
Or there exceed the mark"—and if she let
Herself be lessoned so, nor plainly set   40

---

3. Alfonso II, Duke of Ferrara in Italy in the mid-16th century, is the presumed speaker of the poem, which is loosely based on historical events. The Duke's first wife —whom he had married when she was 14 —died under suspicious circumstances at 17, and he then negotiated through an agent (to whom the poem is spoken) for the hand of the niece of the Count of Tyrol in Austria.
4. Frà Pandolf is, like Claus (line 56), fictitious.

Her wits to yours, forsooth, and made excuse,
—E'en then would be some stooping; and I choose
Never to stoop. Oh sir, she smiled, no doubt,
Whene'er I passed her; but who passed without
Much the same smile? This grew; I gave commands;   45
Then all smiles stopped together. There she stands
As if alive. Will't please you rise? We'll meet
The company below, then. I repeat,
The Count your master's known munificence
Is ample warrant that no just pretense   50
Of mine for dowry will be disallowed;
Though his fair daughter's self, as I avowed
At starting, is my object. Nay, we'll go
Together down, sir. Notice Neptune, though,
Taming a sea-horse, thought a rarity,   55
Which Claus of Innsbruck cast in bronze for me!

1842

GALWAY KINNELL

To Christ Our Lord

The legs of the elk punctured the snow's crust
And wolves floated lightfooted on the land
Hunting Christmas elk living and frozen;
Inside snow melted in a basin, and a woman basted
A bird spread over coals by its wings and head.   5

Snow had sealed the windows; candles lit
The Christmas meal. The Christmas grace chilled
The cooked bird, being long-winded and the room cold.
During the words a boy thought, it is fitting
To eat this creature killed on the wing?   10

He had killed it himself, climbing out
Alone on snowshoes in the Christmas dawn,
The fallen snow swirling and the snowfall gone,
Heard its throat scream as the rifle shouted,
Watched it drop, and fished from the snow the dead.   15

He had not wanted to shoot. The sound
Of wings beating into the hushed air
Had stirred his love, and his fingers
Froze in his gloves, and he wondered,
Famishing, could he fire? Then he fired.   20

Now the grace praised his wicked act. At its end
The bird on the plate
Stared at his stricken appetite.

There had been nothing to do but surrender,
To kill and to eat; he ate as he had killed, with wonder.   25

At night on snowshoes on the drifting field
He wondered again, for whom had love stirred?
The stars glittered on the snow and nothing answered.
Then the Swan spread her wings, cross of the cold north,
The pattern and mirror of the acts of earth.   30

1960

ANNE SEXTON

The Truth the Dead Know

for my mother, born March 1902, died March 1959
and my father, born February 1900, died June 1959

> Gone, I say and walk from church,
> refusing the stiff procession to the grave,
> letting the dead ride alone in the hearse.
> It is June. I am tired of being brave.

> We drive to the Cape.[5] I cultivate   5
> myself where the sun gutters from the sky,
> where the sea swings in like an iron gate
> and we touch. In another country people die.

> My darling, the wind falls in like stones
> from the whitehearted water and when we touch   10
> we enter touch entirely. No one's alone.
> Men kill for this, or for as much.

> And what of the dead? They lie without shoes
> in their stone boats. They are more like stone
> than the sea would be if it stopped. They refuse   15
> to be blessed, throat, eye and knucklebone.

1962

W. H. AUDEN

Musée des Beaux Arts[6]

About suffering they were never wrong,
The Old Masters: how well they understood

---

5. Cape Cod, in Massachusetts.   6. The Museum of the Fine Arts, in
Brussels.

Its human position; how it takes place
While someone else is eating or opening a window or just walking dully
    along;
How, when the aged are reverently, passionately waiting   5
For the miraculous birth, there always must be
Children who did not specially want it to happen, skating
On a pond at the edge of the wood:
They never forgot
That even the dreadful martyrdom must run its course   10
Anyhow in a corner, some untidy spot
Where the dogs go on with their doggy life and the torturer's horse
Scratches its innocent behind on a tree.

In Brueghel's *Icarus*,[7] for instance: how everything turns away
Quite leisurely from the disaster; the plowman may   15
Have heard the splash, the forsaken cry,
But for him it was not an important failure; the sun shone
As it had to on the white legs disappearing into the green
Water; and the expensive delicate ship that must have seen
Something amazing, a boy falling out of the sky,   20
Had somewhere to get to and sailed calmly on.

                                         1938

JOHN WITTE

Home

    Returning to earth after his life
    of weightlessness, the astronaut cannot
    lift the small bouquet of flowers the child gives him.
    He cannot raise his head off the pillow, pulled down
    by the gravity of a dream.   5

    He remembers nothing, no sound,
    in the absolute zero of deep space,
    the wild pounding of his baffled heart. He lifted
    a building in one hand and a pencil in the other.
    This was what he wanted: the world   10
    like a worn stone cast into the water.
    He wanted to break the promise of the body
    to the earth, to stop the long descent of everyone
    he loved under the ground. He wanted

7. "Landscape with the Fall of Icarus," by Pieter Brueghel the elder, located in the Brussels Museum. According to Greek myth, Daedalus and his son Icarus escaped from imprisonment by using homemade wings of wax; but Icarus flew too near the sun, the wax melted, and he fell into the sea and drowned. In the Brueghel painting the central figure is a peasant plowing, and several other figures are more immediately noticeable than Icarus who, disappearing into the sea, is easy to miss in the lower right-hand corner. Equally ignored by the figures is a dead body in the woods.

to rise, an angel   15
in a paradise of exact data.

He spills his milk on his shirt. The earth
has darkness, and then light. The earth has birds
bickering over the last seeds. His fork slips
clattering on the plate. The road is shining.   20
The magnolia is shameless in the rain.

p. 1984

JOHN DONNE

A Valediction: Forbidding Mourning

As virtuous men pass mildly away,
    And whisper to their souls to go,
Whilst some of their sad friends do say,
    "The breath goes now," and some say, "No,"

So let us melt, and make no noise,   5
    No tear-floods, nor sigh-tempests move;
'Twere profanation of our joys
    To tell the laity our love.

Moving of the earth[8] brings harms and fears,
    Men reckon what it did and meant;   10
But trepidation of the spheres,[9]
    Though greater far, is innocent.

Dull sublunary[1] lovers' love
    (Whose soul is sense) cannot admit
Absence, because it doth remove   15
    Those things which elemented[2] it.

But we, by a love so much refined
    That our selves know not what it is,
Inter-assured of the mind,
    Care less, eyes, lips, and hands to miss.   20

Our two souls therefore, which are one,
    Though I must go, endure not yet
A breach, but an expansion,
    Like gold to airy thinness beat.

8. Earthquakes.
9. The Renaissance hypothesis that the celestial spheres trembled and thus caused unexpected variations in their orbits. Such movements are "innocent" because earthlings do not observe or fret about them.
1. Below the moon; i.e., changeable.

According to the traditional cosmology which Donne invokes here, the moon was considered the dividing line between the immutable celestial world and the earthly mortal one.
2. Comprised.

If they be two, they are two so   25
    As stiff twin compasses are two:
Thy soul, the fixed foot, makes no show
    To move, but doth, if the other do;

And though it in the center sit,
    Yet when the other far doth roam,   30
It leans, and hearkens after it,
    And grows erect, as that comes home.

Such wilt thou be to me, who must,
    Like the other foot, obliquely run;
Thy firmness makes my circle[3] just,   35
    And makes me end where I begun.

                                                            1611(?)

5   WORDS

Fiction and drama depend upon language just as poetry does, but in
a poem almost everything comes down to words. In stories and plays,
we are likely to keep our attention primarily on narrative and plot—
what is happening in front of us or in the action as we imagine it in
our minds—and although words are crucial to how we imagine the
characters and how we respond to what happens to them, we are
less likely to pause over any one word as we may need to in a poem.
Besides, poems often are short and use only a few words, so a lot depends on every single one. Poetry sometimes feels like prose that is
distilled: only the most essential words are there, just barely
enough so that we communicate in the most basic way, using the most
elemental signs of meaning and feeling—and each one chosen for
exactly the right shade of meaning. But elemental does not necessarily
mean simple, and these signs may be very rich in their meanings and
complex in their effects.

Let's look first at two poems, each of which depends heavily upon a
single key word.

RICHARD ARMOUR

Hiding Place

A speaker at a meeting of the New York State Frozen Food Locker Association
declared that the best hiding place in event of an atomic explosion is a frozen-
food locker, where "radiation will not penetrate."[1]   NEWS ITEM.

Move over, ham
And quartered cow,

3. A traditional symbol of perfection.   1. Before home freezers became popular,
                                               many Americans rented lockers in specially
                                               equipped commercial buildings.

My Geiger[2] says
The time is now.

Yes, now I lay me   5
Down to sleep,
And if I die,
At least I'll keep.

1954

YVOR WINTERS

At the San Francisco Airport

To my daughter, 1954

This is the terminal: the light
Gives perfect vision, false and hard;
The metal glitters, deep and bright.
Great planes are waiting in the yard—
They are already in the night.   5

And you are here beside me, small,
Contained and fragile, and intent
On things that I but half recall—
Yet going whither you are bent.
I am the past, and that is all.   10

But you and I in part are one:
The frightened brain, the nervous will,
The knowledge of what must be done,
The passion to acquire the skill
To face that which you dare not shun.   15

The rain of matter upon sense
Destroys me momently. The score:
There comes what will come. The expense
Is what one thought, and something more—
One's being and intelligence.   20

This is the terminal, the break.
Beyond this point, on lines of air,
You take the way that you must take;
And I remain in light and stare—
In light, and nothing else, awake.   25

1954

In *Hiding Place,* almost all the poem's comedy depends on the final
word, "keep." In the child's prayer which the poem echoes, to "pray
the Lord my soul to keep" does not exactly involve cold storage, and

---

2. Geiger counter: used to detect radiation.

so the poem depends upon an outrageous double meaning. The key word is chosen because it can mean more than one thing; in this case, the importance of the word involves its **ambiguity** (an ability to mean more than one thing) rather than its **precision** (exactness).

In the second poem, the several possible meanings of a single word are probed more soberly and thoughtfully. What does it *mean* to be in a place called a "terminal"? the poem asks. As the parting of father and daughter is explored, carefully, the place of parting and the means of transportation begin to take on meanings larger than their simple referential ones. The poem is full of contrasts—young and old, light and dark, past and present, security and adventure—as the parting of generations is pondered. The father ("I am the past," line 10) remains in the light, among known objects and experience familiar to his many years; the daughter is about to depart into the night, the unknown, the uncertain future. But they both share a sense of the necessity of the parting, of the need for the daughter to mature, gain knowledge, acquire experience. Is she going off to school? to college? to her first job? The specifics are not given, but her plane ride clearly means a new departure and a clean break with childhood, dependency, the past.

So much depends upon the meanings of "terminal." It is the airport building, of course, but it also implies a boundary, an extremity, an end, something that is limited, a place where a connection is broken. The clear, crisp meanings of other words are important too. The words "break," "point," "lines," "way," and "remain" all express literally and sharply what the event means. The final stanza of the poem is full of words that state flatly and **denote** exactly, as if the speaker has recovered completely from the momentary confusion of stanza 4, when "being and intelligence" are lost in the emotion of the parting itself. The crisp articulation of the last stanza puts an almost total emphasis on the precise meaning of each word, its **denotation,** what it precisely denotes or refers to. The words "break," "point," "way," and "remain" are almost completely unemotional and colorless; they do not make value judgments or offer personal views, but rather define and describe. It is as if the speaker is trying to disengage himself from the emotion of the situation and just give the facts.

Words, however, are more than hard blocks of meaning on whose sense everyone agrees. They also have a more personal side, and they carry emotional force and shades of suggestion. The words we use indicate not only what we mean but how we feel about it, and we choose words that we hope will carry a persuasive emotional engagement with others, in conversation and daily usage as well as in poems. A person who holds office is, quite literally (and unemotionally), an "officeholder," a word that clearly denotes what he or she does. But if we want to convince someone that an officeholder is wise, trustworthy, and deserving of political support we may call that person a "political leader" or perhaps a "statesman"; whereas if we want to promote distrust or contempt of officeholders we might call them "politicians" or "bureaucrats" or "political hacks." These latter words have clear **connotations**—suggestions of emotional coloration that imply our attitude and invite a similar one on the part of our hearers. What words **connote** can be just as important to a poem as what they denote, although some poems depend primarily on denotation and some more on connotation.

At the San Francisco Airport seems to depend primarily on denotation; the speaker tries to *specify* the meanings and implications of the parting with his daughter, and his tendency to split categories neatly for the two of them at first contributes to the sense of clarity and certainty which the speaker wants to project. He is the past (line 10) and what remains (line 24); he has age and experience, his life is the known quantity, he stands in the light. She, on the other hand, is committed to the adventure of going into the night; she seems small, fragile, and her identity exists in the uncertain future. Yet the connotations of some words carry strong emotional force as well as clear definition: that the daughter seems "small" and "fragile" to the speaker suggests his fear for her, something quite different from her sense of adventure. The neat, clean categories keep breaking down, and the speaker's feelings keep showing through. In stanza 1, the speaker tells us that the light in the terminal gives "perfect vision" but he also notices, indirectly, its artificial quality: it is "false" and "hard," suggesting the limits of the rationalism he tries to maintain. That artificial light shines over most of the poem and honors the speaker's effort, but the whole poem represents his struggle, and in stanza 4 the signals of disturbance are very strong as, despite an insistence on a vocabulary of calculation, his rational facade collapses completely. If we have observed his verbal strategies carefully, we should not be surprised to find him at the end just *staring* in the artificial light, merely awake, although the poem has shown him to be unconsciously awake to much more than he will candidly admit.

At the San Francisco Airport is an unusually intricate and complicated poem, and it offers us, if we are willing to examine very precisely its carefully crafted fabric, an unusually rich insight into how complex a thing it is to be human and have human feelings and foibles when we think we must be rational machines. Connotations often work more simply. The following poem, for example, even though it describes the mixed feelings one person has about another, depends heavily on the common connotations of fairly common words.

WALTER DE LA MARE

Slim Cunning Hands

Slim cunning hands at rest, and cozening eyes—
Under this stone one loved too wildly lies;
How false she was, no granite could declare;
Nor all earth's flowers, how fair.

1950

What the speaker in *Slim Cunning Hands* remembers about the dead woman—her hands, her eyes—tells part of the story; her physical presence was clearly important to him, and the poem's other nouns—

stone, granite, flowers—all remind us of her death and its finality. All
these words denote objects having to do with rituals that memorial-
ize a departed life. Granite and stone connote finality as well, and
flowers connote fragility and suggest the shortness of life (which is
why they have become the symbolic language of funerals). The way
the speaker talks about the woman expresses, in just a few words, how
complexly he feels about his love for her. She was loved, he says,
too "wildly"—by him perhaps, and by others. The excitement she
offered is suggested by the word, and also the lack of control. The
words "cunning" and "cozening" help us interpret both her wildness
and falsity; they suggest her calculation, cleverness, and untrustworthi-
ness as well as her skill, persuasiveness, and ability to place. And the
word "fair," a simple yet very inclusive word, suggests how totally
attractive the speaker finds her: her beauty is just as incapable of
being expressed by flowers as her fickleness is of being expressed in
something as permanent as stone. Simple words here tell us perhaps
all we need to know of a long story.

Words like "fair" and "cozening" are clearly loaded: they have
strong, clear connotations and tell us what to think, what evaluation
to make. The connotations may also suggest or imply the basis for the
evaluation. In the two poems that follow we can readily see why the
specific words are chosen because, although both poems express a
preference for the same sort of feminine appearance, the grounds of
appeal are vastly different.

BEN JONSON

Still to Be Neat[3]

Still[4] to be neat, still to be dressed,
As you were going to a feast;
Still to be powdered, still perfumed;
Lady, it is to be presumed,
Though art's hid causes are not found,   5
All is not sweet, all is not sound.

Give me a look, give me a face
That makes simplicity a grace;
Robes loosely flowing, hair as free;
Such sweet neglect more taketh me   10
Than all th' adulteries of art.
They strike mine eyes, but not my heart.

1609

3. A song from Jonson's play, *The Silent*   4. Continually.
Woman.

ROBERT HERRICK

Delight in Disorder

A sweet disorder in the dress
Kindles in clothes a wantonness.
A lawn[5] about the shoulders thrown
Into a fine distractiön;
An erring lace, which here and there   5
Enthralls the crimson stomacher,[6]
A cuff neglectful, and thereby
Ribbands[7] to flow confusedly;
A winning wave, deserving note,
In the tempestuous petticoat;   10
A careless shoestring, in whose tie
I see a wild civility;
Do more bewitch me than when art
Is too precise[8] in every part.

1648

The poem *Still to Be Neat* begins by describing a woman who looks too neat and orderly; she seems too perfect to be believed, the speaker says, and he has to assume that there is a reason for such overly fastidious grooming, that she is covering up something. He worries that something is wrong underneath—that not all is "sweet" and "sound." "Sweet" could mean several possible things, and its meaning becomes clearer when it is repeated in the next stanza in a more specific context. But "sound" begins to suggest the speaker's moral earnestness: it is a strong word, implying a suspicion that something is deeply wrong.

When "sweet" is repeated in line 10, it has taken on specific attributes from what the speaker has said about things he likes in a less calculated physical appearance. Now it appears to mean easy, attractive, unpremeditated. And when the speaker springs "adulteries" on us in the next line as a description of the woman's cosmeticizing, it is clear what he fears—that the appearance of the too neat, too made-up woman covers serious flaws, things which try to make her appear someone she is not. "Adulteries" suggests the addition of something foreign, something unlike her own nature, and it is a strong, disapproving word. The "soundness" he had worried about involves her integrity; his objection is certainly moral, probably sexual. He wants his women simple and chaste; he wants them to be just what they seem to be.

The speaker in *Delight in Disorder* wants his women easy and sim-

5. Scarf of fine linen.
6. Ornamental covering for the breasts.
7. Ribbons.

8. In the 16th and 17th centuries Puritans were often called Precisians because of their fastidiousness.

ple too, but for different reasons. He finds disorder "sweet" too (line 1), and seems almost to be answering the first speaker, providing a different rationale for artless appearance. His grounds of preference are clear early: his support of "wantonness" (line 2) is close to the opposite in its moral suppositions of the first speaker's disapproval of "adulteries." This speaker wants a careless look because he thinks it's sexy, and many of the words he chooses suggest sensuality and availability: "distraction" (line 4), "erring" (line 5), "tempestuous" (line 10), "wild" (line 12). The speakers in the two poems read informality of dress very differently and have very different expectations of the person who dresses in a particular way. We find out quite a lot about each speaker. Their common subject allows us to see clearly how different they both are, and how what one sees is in the eye of the beholder, how values and assumptions are built into the words one chooses even for description. Jonson has created a speaker who wants an informally clad woman who has a natural grace and ease of manner because she is confident of herself, dependable, and chaste. Herrick has created a speaker who finds informality of dress fetching and sexy and indicative of sensuality and availability.

It would be hard to exaggerate how important words are to poems. Poets who know their craft pick each word with care, so that each word will express exactly what needs to be expressed and suggest every emotional shade that the poem is calculated to evoke in us. Often individual words qualify and amplify one another—suggestions clarify other suggestions, and meanings grow upon meanings— and thus the way the words are put together can be important too. Notice, for example, that in *Slim Cunning Hands* the final emphasis is on how *fair* the speaker's woman was; that is his last word, the thing he can't forget in spite of his distrust of her, and that is where the poem chooses to leave the emphasis, on that one word which, even though it doesn't justify everything else, qualifies all the disappointment and hurt.

That word does not stand all by itself, however, any more than any other word in a poem can be considered all alone. Every word exists within larger units of meaning—sentences, patterns of comparisons and contrasts, the whole poem—and where the word is and how it is used often are very important. The final word or words may be especially emphatic (as in *Slim Cunning Hands*), and words that are repeated take on a special intensity, as "terminal" does in *At the San Francisco Airport* or as "chartered" and "cry" do in *London,* a poem we looked at in Chapter 2. Certain words often stand out, because they are used in an unusual way (like "chartered" in *London* or "adulteries" in *Still To Be Neat*) or because they are given an artificial prominence, through unusual sentence structure, for example, or because the title calls special attention to them. In the following poem, notice how the title calls upon us to wonder, from the beginning, how playful and how patterned the boy's bedtime romp with his father is. As you read it, try to be conscious of the emotional effects created by the choice of words that seem to be key ones. Which words establish the bond between the two males?

THEODORE ROETHKE

My Papa's Waltz

The whiskey on your breath
Could make a small boy dizzy;
But I hung on like death:
Such waltzing was not easy.

We romped until the pans   5
Slid from the kitchen shelf;
My mother's countenance
Could not unfrown itself.

The hand that held my wrist
Was battered on one knuckle;   10
At every step you missed
My right ear scraped a buckle.

You beat time on my head
With a palm caked hard by dirt,
Then waltzed me off to bed   15
Still clinging to your shirt.

                                        1948

Exactly what is the situation in *My Papa's Waltz*? What are the
economic circumstances in the family? How can you tell? What indications are there of the family's social class? of the father's line of work?
How would you characterize the speaker? How does the poem indicate his pleasure in the bedtime ritual? Which words suggest the boy's
excitement? Which suggest his anxiety? How can you tell how the
speaker feels about his father? What clues are there about what the
mother is like? How can you tell that the experience is remembered at
some years' distance? What clues are there in the word choice that
an adult is remembering a childhood experience? In what sense is the
poem a tribute to memories of the father? How would you describe the
poem's tone?

The subtlety and force of word choice is sometimes very much
affected by **word order,** the way the sentences are put together.
Sometimes poems are driven to unusual word order because of the
demands of rhyme and meter, but ordinarily poets use word order
very much as prose writers do, to create a particular emphasis. When
an unusual word order is used, you can be pretty sure that something
worth noticing is going on. Notice, for example, the odd constructions
in the second and third stanzas of *My Papa's Waltz*. In the third
stanza, the way the speaker talks about the abrasion of buckle on ear
is very unusual. He does not say that the buckle scraped his ear, but
rather puts it the other way round—a big difference in the kind of

effect created, for it avoids placing blame and refuses to specify any unpleasant effect. Had he said that the buckle scraped his ear—the normal way of putting it—we would have to worry about the fragile ear. The **syntax** (sentence structure) of the poem channels our feeling and helps to control what we think of the waltz.

The most curious part of the poem is the second stanza, for it is there that the silent mother appears, and the syntax there is peculiar in two places. In lines 5–6, the connection between the romping and the pans falling is stated oddly: "We romped *until* the pans / Slid from the kitchen shelf." The speaker does not say that they knocked down the pans or imply that there was awkwardness, but he does suggest energetic activity and duration. He implies intensity, almost design—as though the romping were not complete until the pans fell. And the sentence about the mother—odd but effective—makes her position clear. She is a silent bystander in this male ritual, and her frown seems molded on her face. It is not as if she is frightened or angry but as if she too is performing a ritual, holding a frown on her face as if it is part of her role in the ritual, as well as perhaps a facet of her stern character. The syntax implies that she *has to* maintain the frown, and the falling of the pans almost seems to be for her benefit. She disapproves, but she is still their audience.

Word order is not always as complicated or crucial as it is in *My Papa's Waltz*, but poets often manipulate the ordinary prose order of a sentence to make a specific point or create a specific emphasis or effect. In the passage below (pp. 629–632) from *Paradise Lost*, for example, notice how the syntax first sets a formal tone for the passage, then calls attention to the complexities of theology which it expresses, and (in lines 44ff.) imitates, by holding back key elements of the grammar, the fall that is being described. The poems that follow suggest some of the ways in which poets use words and word order to create for us the various experiences they want us to have of their words.

GERARD MANLEY HOPKINS

Pied Beauty[9]

Glory be to God for dappled things—
    For skies of couple-color as a brinded[1] cow;
      For rose-moles all in stipple[2] upon trout that swim;
Fresh-firecoal chestnut-falls;[3] finches' wings;
      Landscape plotted and pieced—fold, fallow, and plow;   5
    And all trades, their gear and tackle and trim.

---

9. Particolored beauty: having patches or sections of more than one color.
1. Streaked or spotted.
2. Rose-colored dots or flecks.
3. Fallen chestnuts as red as burning coals.

All things counter, original, spare, strange;
    Whatever is fickle, freckled (who knows how?)
        With swift, slow; sweet, sour; adazzle, dim;
He fathers-forth whose beauty is past change: 10
        Praise him.

1877

EMILY DICKINSON

After Great Pain

After great pain, a formal feeling comes—
The Nerves sit ceremonious, like Tombs—
The stiff Heart questions was it He, that bore,
And Yesterday, or Centuries before?

The Feet, mechanical, go round—   5
Of Ground, or Air, or Ought—
A Wooden way
Regardless grown,
A Quartz contentment, like a stone—

This is the Hour of Lead—   10
Remembered, if outlived,
As Freezing Persons recollect the Snow—
First—Chill—then Stupor—then the letting go—

ca. 1862

WILLIAM CARLOS WILLIAMS

The Red Wheelbarrow

so much depends
upon

a red wheel
barrow

glazed with rain   5
water

beside the white
chickens.

1923

e. e. cummings

anyone lived in a pretty how town

anyone lived in a pretty how town
(with up so floating many bells down)
spring summer autumn winter
he sang his didn't he danced his did.

Women and men (both little and small)   5
cared for anyone not at all
they sowed their isn't they reaped their same
sun moon stars rain

children guessed (but only a few
and down they forgot as up they grew   10
autumn winter spring summer)
that noone loved him more by more

when by now and tree by leaf
she laughed his joy she cried his grief
bird by snow and stir by still   15
anyone's any was all to her

someones married their everyones
laughed their cryings and did their dance
(sleep wake hope and then) they
said their nevers they slept their dream   20

stairs rain sun moon
(and only the snow can begin to explain
how children are apt to forget to remember
with up so floating many bells down)

one day anyone died i guess   25
(and noone stooped to kiss his face)
busy folk buried them side by side
little by little and was by was

all by all and deep by deep
and more by more they dream their sleep   30
noone and anyone earth by april
wish by spirit and if by yes.

Women and men (both dong and ding)
summer autumn winter spring
reaped their sowing and went their came   35
sun moon stars rain

1940

X. J. KENNEDY

Nude Descending a Staircase [4]

Toe upon toe, a snowing flesh,
A gold of lemon, root and rind,
She sifts in sunlight down the stairs
With nothing on. Nor on her mind.

We spy beneath the banister   5
A constant thresh of thigh on thigh—
Her lips imprint the swinging air
That parts to let her parts go by.

One-woman waterfall, she wears
Her slow descent like a long cape   10
And pausing, on the final stair
Collects her motions into shape.

1961

JOHN MILTON

from Paradise Lost [5]

I

Of man's first disobedience, and the fruit [6]
Of that forbidden tree whose mortal taste
Brought death into the world, and all our woe,
With loss of Eden, till one greater Man
Restore us, and regain the blissful seat,   5
Sing, Heav'nly Muse, [7] that, on the secret top
Of Oreb, or Sinai, didst inspire
That shepherd who first taught the chosen seed
In the beginning how the Heav'ns and Earth
Rose out of Chaos: or, if Sion hill   10
Delight thee more, and Siloa's brook that flowed

4. A celebrated cubist-futurist painting by Marcel Duchamp (1913).
5. The opening lines of Books I and II and a short passage from Book III. The first passage states the poem's subject, and the second describes Satan's beginning address to the council of fallen angels meeting to discuss strategy; in the third, God is looking down from Heaven at his new human creation and watching Satan approach the Earth.
6. The apple, but also the consequences.
7. Addressing one of the muses and asking for aid is a convention for the opening lines of an epic; Milton complicates the standard procedure here by describing sources and circumstances of Judeo-Christian revelation rather than specifically invoking one of the nine classical muses. Sinai is the spur of Mount Oreb, where Moses ("That shepherd," line 8, who was traditionally regarded as author of the first five books of the Bible) received the Law; Sion hill and Siloa (lines 10–11), near Jerusalem, correspond to the traditional mountain (Helicon) and springs of classical tradition. Later, in Book VII, Milton calls upon Urania, the muse of astronomy, but he does not mention by name the muse of epic poetry, Calliope.

Fast[8] by the oracle of God, I thence
Invoke thy aid to my adventurous song,
That with no middle flight intends to soar
Above th' Aonian mount,[9] while it pursues   15
Things unattempted yet in prose or rhyme.
And chiefly thou, O Spirit,[1] that dost prefer
Before all temples th' upright heart and pure,
Instruct me, for thou know'st; thou from the first
Wast present, and, with mighty wings outspread,   20
Dovelike sat'st brooding on the vast abyss,
And mad'st it pregnant: what in me is dark
Illumine; what is low, raise and support;
That, to the height of this great argument,[2]
I may assert Eternal Providence,   25
And justify the ways of God to men.
    Say first (for Heav'n hides nothing from thy view,
Nor the deep tract of Hell), say first what cause
Moved our grand parents, in that happy state,
Favored of Heav'n so highly, to fall off   30
From their Creator, and transgress his will
For[3] one restraint, lords of the world besides?
Who first seduced them to that foul revolt?
Th' infernal serpent; he it was, whose guile,
Stirred up with envy and revenge, deceived   35
The mother of mankind, what time[4] his pride
Had cast him out from Heav'n, with all his host
Of rebel angels, by whose aid, aspiring
To set himself in glory above his peers,
He trusted to have equaled the Most High,   40
If he opposed; and with ambitious aim
Against the throne and monarchy of God,
Raised impious war in Heav'n and battle proud,
With vain attempt. Him the Almighty Power
Hurled headlong flaming from th' ethereal sky,   45
With hideous ruin and combustion down
To bottomless perdition, there to dwell
In adamantine chains and penal fire,
Who durst defy th' Omnipotent to arms.[5]

*   *   *

8. Close.
9. Mt. Helicon, home of the classical muses.
1. The divine voice that inspired the Hebrew prophets. *Genesis* 1:2 says that "the Spirit of God moved upon the face of the waters" as part of the process of the original creation; Milton follows tradition in making the inspirational and communicative function of God present in creation itself. The passage echoes and merges many Biblical references to divine creation and revelation.
2. Subject.
3. Because of. "besides": in all other respects.
4. When.
5. After invoking the muse and giving a brief summary of the poem's subject, an epic regularly begins *in medias res* (in the midst of things).

II

High on a throne of royal state, which far
Outshone the wealth of Ormus and of Ind,[6]
Or where the gorgeous East with richest hand
Show'rs on her kings barbaric pearl and gold,
Satan exalted sat, by merit raised   5
To that bad eminence; and, from despair
Thus high uplifted beyond hope, aspires
Beyond thus high, insatiate to pursue
Vain war with Heav'n, and by success[7] untaught,
His proud imaginations thus displayed: 10
    "Powers and Dominions, Deities of Heav'n,
For since no deep within her gulf can hold
Immortal vigor, though oppressed and fall'n,
I give not Heav'n for lost. From this descent
Celestial virtues rising will appear   15
More glorious and more dread than from no fall,
And trust themselves to fear no second fate.
Me though just right and the fixed laws of Heav'n
Did first create your leader, next, free choice,
With what besides, in council or in fight,   20
Hath been achieved of merit, yet this loss,
Thus far at least recovered, hath much more
Established in a safe unenvied throne
Yielded with full consent. The happier state
In Heav'n, which follows dignity, might draw   25
Envy from each inferior; but who here
Will envy whom the highest place exposes
Foremost to stand against the Thunderer's aim
Your bulwark, and condemns to greatest share
Of endless pain? Where there is then no good   30
For which to strive, no strife can grow up there
From faction; for none sure will claim in hell
Precédence, none, whose portion is so small
Of present pain, that with ambitious mind
Will covet more. With this advantage then   35
To union, and firm faith, and firm accord,
More than can be in Heav'n, we now return
To claim our just inheritance of old,
Surer to prosper than prosperity
Could have assured us; and by what best way,   40
Whether of open war or covert guile,
We now debate; who can advise, may speak."

                        *   *   *

III

                        *   *   *

Now had th' Almighty Father from above,   56
From the pure empyrean where he sits

---

6. Hormuz, an island in the Persian
Gulf, famous for pearls, and India.

7. Outcome, either good or bad.

High throned above all height, bent down his eye,
His own works and their works at once to view:
About him all the sanctities of Heav'n [8]   60
Stood thick as stars, and from his sight received
Beatitude past utterance; on his right
The radiant image of his glory sat,
His only Son. On earth he first beheld
Our two first parents, yet the only two   65
Of mankind, in the happy garden placed,
Reaping immortal fruits of joy and love,
Uninterrupted joy, unrivaled love,
In blissful solitude. He then surveyed
Hell and the gulf between, and Satan there   70
Coasting the wall of Heav'n on this side Night
In the dun air sublime,[9] and ready now
To stoop[1] with wearied wings and willing feet
On the bare outside of this world, that seemed
Firm land embosomed without firmament,   75
Uncertain which, in ocean or in air.

                                                            1667

6   FIGURATIVE LANGUAGE

Metaphor and Simile

The language of poetry is almost always picturesque. Rather than
depending primarily on abstract ideas and elaborate reasoning, poems
depend mainly upon the creation of pictures in our minds, helping
us to see things fresh and new, or to feel them suggestively through
our other physical senses, such as hearing or the sense of touch. Poetry
is most often vital in the sense that it helps us form, in our minds,
visual impressions. We "see" a corpse at a funeral, a child chasing
geese in the garden, or two lovers sitting together on the bank of a
stream, so that our response begins from a vivid impression of exactly
what is happening. Some people think that those arts and media
which challenge the imagination of a reader or hearer—radio drama,
for example, or poetry—allow us to respond more fully than arts (such
as film or theater) that actually show things more fully to our physical senses. Certainly they leave more to our imagination, to our
mind's eye.

But being visual does not just mean describing, telling us facts,

8. The hierarchies of angels.   1. Swoop down, like a bird of prey.
9. Aloft in the twilight atmosphere.

indicating shapes, colors, and specific details. Often the vividness of the picture in our minds depends upon comparisons. What we are trying to imagine is pictured in terms of something else familiar to us, and we are asked to think of one thing as if it were something else. Many such comparisons, or **figures of speech,** in which something is pictured or imaged or figured forth in terms of something already familiar to us, are taken for granted in daily life. Things we can't see or which aren't familiar to us are pictured as things we can; for example, God is said to be like a father, Italy is said to be shaped like a boot. Poems use figurative language much of the time. A speaker may tell us that his ladylove is like a red rose, or that the way to imagine how it feels to be spiritually secure is to think of the way a shepherd takes care of his sheep. The pictorialness of our imagination may *clarify* things for us—scenes, states of mind, ideas— but at the same time it stimulates us to think of how those pictures make us *feel*. Pictures, even when they are mental pictures or imagined visions, may be both denotative and connotative, just as individual words are: they may clarify and make precise, and they may channel our feelings. In this chapter, we will look at some of the ways that poets create pictures in our minds—images that help us think clearly about what they are saying and feel clearly the emotions they want us to feel. Most poetry depends, at least in part, on the pictorial quality of words and upon the notion that something becomes clearer when we compare it with something else that is more familiar. In the poem that follows, the poet helps us to visualize the old age and approaching death of the speaker by making comparisons with familiar things—the coming of winter, the approach of sunset, and the dying embers of a fire.

WILLIAM SHAKESPEARE

That Time of Year

That time of year thou mayst in me behold
When yellow leaves, or none, or few, do hang
Upon those boughs which shake against the cold,
Bare ruined choirs, where late the sweet birds sang.
In me thou see'st the twilight of such day   5
As after sunset fadeth in the west;
Which by and by[1] black night doth take away,
Death's second self,[2] that seals up all in rest.
In me thou see'st the glowing of such fire,
That on the ashes of his youth doth lie,   10
As the deathbed whereon it must expire,
Consumed with that which it was nourished by.
This thou perceiv'st, which makes thy love more strong,
To love that well which thou must leave ere long.

1609

1. Shortly.   2. Sleep.

The first four lines of *That Time of Year* make the comparison to seasonal change; but notice that the poet does not have the speaker say directly that his physical condition and age make him resemble autumn. He draws the comparison without stating directly that it is a comparison: you can see, he says, my own state in the coming of winter in late autumn when the leaves are almost all off the trees. The speaker portrays himself *indirectly* by talking about the passing of the year. The poem uses **metaphor**; that is, one thing is pictured *as if* it were something else. *That Time of Year* goes on to another metaphor in lines 5–8 and still another in lines 9–12, and each of the metaphors contributes to our understanding of the speaker's sense of his old age and approaching death. Even more important, however, is the way the metaphors give us feelings, an emotional sense of the speaker's age and of his own attitude toward aging. Through the metaphors we come to understand, appreciate, and to some extent share the increasing sense of anxiety and urgency that the poem expresses. Our emotional sense of the poem is largely influenced by the way each metaphor is developed and by the way each metaphor leads, with its own kind of internal logic, to another.

The images of late autumn in the first four lines all suggest loneliness, loss, and nostalgia for earlier times. As in the rest of the poem, our eyes are imagined to be the main vehicle for noticing the speaker's age and condition; the phrase "thou mayst in me behold" (line 1) introduces what we are asked to see, and in both lines 5 and 9 we are similarly told "In me thou see'st. . . ." The picture of the trees shedding their leaves suggests that autumn is nearly over, and we can imagine trees either with yellow leaves, or without leaves, or with just a trace of foliage remaining—the latter perhaps most feelingly suggesting the bleakness and loneliness that characterize the change of seasons, the ending of the life cycle. But other senses are invoked too. The boughs shaking against the cold represent an appeal to our tactile sense, and the next line appeals to our sense of hearing, although only as a reminder that the birds no longer sing. (Notice how exact the visual representation is of the bare, or nearly bare, limbs, even as the cold and the lack of birds are noted; birds lined up like a choir on risers would have made a striking visual image on the barren limbs one above the other, but now there is only the *reminder* of what used to be. The present is quiet, bleak, trembly, and lonely.)

The next four lines are slightly different in tone, and the color changes. From a black-and-white landscape with a few yellow leaves, we come upon a rich and almost warm reminder of a faded sunset. But a somber note does enter the poem in these lines through another figure of speech, **personification**, which involves treating an abstraction, such as death or justice or beauty, as if it were a person. The poem is talking about the coming of night and of sleep, and Sleep is personified and identified as the "second self" of Death (that is, as a kind of reflection of death). The main emphasis is on how night and sleep close in on our sense of twilight, and only secondarily does a reminder of death enter the poem. But it does enter.

The third metaphor—that of the dying embers of a fire—begins in line 9 and continues to color and warm the bleak cold that the poem began with, but it also sharpens the reminder of death. The three main metaphors in the poem work in a way to make our sense of old age and approaching death more familiar, but also more immediate: moving from barren trees, to fading twilight, to dying embers suggests a sensuous increase of color and warmth, but also an increasing urgency. The first metaphor involves a whole season, or at least a segment of one, a matter of days or possibly weeks; the second involves the passing of a single day, reducing the time scale to a matter of minutes, and the third draws our attention to that split second when a glowing ember fades into a simple ash. The final part of the fire metaphor introduces the most explicit sense of death so far, as the metaphor of embers shifts into a direct reminder of death. Embers which had been a metaphor of the speaker's aging body now themselves become, metaphorically, a deathbed; the vitality that nourishes youth is used up just as a log in a fire is. The urgency of the reminder of coming death has now peaked. It is friendlier but now seems immediate and inevitable, a natural part of the life process, and the final two lines then make an explicit plea to make good and intense use of the remaining moments of human relationship.

That Time of Year represents an unusually intricate use of images to organize a poem and focus its emotional impact. Not all poems are so skillfully made, and not all depend on such a full and varied use of metaphor. But most poems use metaphors for at least part of their effect, and often a poem is based on a single metaphor which is fully developed as the major way of making the poem's statement and impact, as in this poem about the role of a mother and wife.

LINDA PASTAN

Marks

My husband gives me an A
for last night's supper,
an incomplete for my ironing,
a B plus in bed.
My son says I am average,   5
an average mother, but if
I put my mind to it
I could improve.
My daughter believes
in Pass/Fail and tells me   10
I pass. Wait 'til they learn
I'm dropping out.

1978

The speaker in *Marks* is obviously not thrilled with the idea of continually being judged, and the metaphor of marks (or grades) as a way of talking about her performance of roles in the family suggests her irritation. The list of the roles implies the many things expected of her, and the three different systems of marking (letter grades, categories to be checked off on a chart, and pass/fail) detail the difficulties of multiple standards. The poem retains the language of schooldays all the way to the end ("learn," line 11; "dropping out," line 12), and the major effect of the poem depends on the irony of the speaker's agreeing to surrender to the metaphor the family has thrust upon her; if she is to be judged as if she were a student, she retains the right to drop out. Ironically, she joins the system (adopts the metaphor for herself) in order to defeat it.

The difficulty of conveying what some experiences are like and how we feel about them sometimes leads poets to startling comparisons and figures of speech that may at first seem far-fetched but which, in one way or another, do in fact suggest the quality of the experience or the feelings associated with it. Sometimes a series of metaphors is used, as if no one kind of visualization will serve, but several together may suggest the full complexity of the experience or cumulatively define the feeling precisely. Metaphors open up virtually endless possibilities of comparison, giving words a chance to be more than words, offering our mind's eye a challenge to keep up with the fertile and articulate imagination of writers who make it their business to see things that ordinary people miss, noticing the most surprising likenesses.

Sometimes, in poetry as in prose, comparisons are made explicitly, as in the following poem.

ROBERT BURNS

A Red, Red Rose

O, my luve's like a red, red rose
That's newly sprung in June.
O, my luve is like the melodie
That's sweetly played in tune.

As fair art thou, my bonnie lass,   5
So deep in luve am I;
And I will luve thee still, my dear,
Till a' the seas gang³ dry.

Till a' the seas gang dry, my dear,
And the rocks melt wi' the sun;   10
And I will luve thee still, my dear,
While the sands o' life shall run.

And fare thee weel, my only luve,

3. Go.

And fare thee weel a while!
And I will come again, my luve,   15
Though it were ten thousand mile.

                                                                1796

The first four lines make two explicit comparisons: the speaker says that his love is "like a rose" and "like a melodie." Such *explicit* comparison is called a **simile,** and usually (as here) the comparison involves the words "like" or "as." Similes work much as do metaphors, except that they usually are used more passingly, more incidentally; they make a quick comparison and usually do not elaborate, whereas metaphors often extend over a long section of a poem (in which case they are called **extended metaphors**) or even over the whole poem as in Marks (in which case they are called **controlling metaphors**).

The two similes in *A Red, Red Rose* assume that we already have a favorable opinion of roses and of melodies. Here the poet does not develop the comparison or even remind us of attractive details about roses or tunes. He pays the quick compliment and moves on. Similes sometimes develop more elaborate comparisons than this and occasionally even control long sections of a poem (in which case they are called **analogies**), but usually a simile is briefer and relies more fully on something we already know. The speaker in *My Papa's Waltz* says that he hung on "like death"; he doesn't have to explain or elaborate the comparison: we know the anxiety he refers to.

Like metaphors, similes may imply both meaning and feeling; they may both explain something and invoke feelings about it. All figurative language involves an attempt to clarify something *and* to help readers feel a certain way about it. Saying that one's love is like a rose implies a delicate and fragile beauty and invites our senses into play so that we can share sensuously a response to fragrant appeal and soft touch, just as the shivering boughs and dying embers in Shakespeare's poem explain separation and loss at the same time that they allow us to share the cold sense of loneliness and the warmth of old friendship. The poems that follow suggest some other varieties of figures of speech in poems. But you will also find metaphors and similes elsewhere, in fact nearly everywhere. Once you are alerted to look for them you will find figures in poem after poem; they are among the most common devices through which poets share their vision with us.

RANDALL JARRELL

The Death of the Ball Turret Gunner [4]

From my mother's sleep I fell into the State,
And I hunched in its belly till my wet fur froze.
Six miles from earth, loosed from its dream of life,
I woke to black flak and the nightmare fighters.
When I died they washed me out of the turret with a hose.   5

1945

JOHN DONNE

Batter My Heart

Batter my heart, three-personed God; for You
As yet but knock, breathe, shine, and seek to mend;
That I may rise and stand, o'erthrow me, and bend
Your force, to break, blow, burn, and make me new.
I, like an usurped town, to another due,   5
Labor to admit You, but Oh, to no end!
Reason, Your viceroy[5] in me, me should defend,
But is captived, and proves weak or untrue.
Yet dearly I love You, and would be loved fain.[6]
But am betrothed unto Your enemy: 10
Divorce me, untie, or break that knot again,
Take me to You, imprison me, for I,
Except You enthrall me, never shall be free,
Nor ever chaste, except You ravish me.

1633

ANONYMOUS
(Traditionally attributed to King David)

The Twenty-Third Psalm

The Lord is my shepherd; I shall not want.

He maketh me to lie down in green pastures: he leadeth me beside
the still waters.

4. "A ball turret was a plexiglass sphere set into the belly of a B-17 or B-24 and inhabited by two .50 caliber machine-guns and one man, a short, small man. When this gunner tracked with his machine-guns a fighter attacking his bomber from below, he revolved with the turret; hunched upside-down in his little sphere, he looked like the foetus in the womb. The fighters which attacked him were armed with cannon firing explosive shells. The hose was a steam hose." (Jarrell's note)
5. One who rules as the representative of a higher power.
6. Gladly.

He restoreth my soul: he leadeth me in the paths of righteousness
    for his name's sake.
Yea, though I walk through the valley of the shadow of death,
    I will fear no evil: for thou art with me;
    thy rod and thy staff they comfort me.
Thou preparest a table before me in the presence of mine enemies:
    thou anointest my head with oil; my cup runneth over.
Surely goodness and mercy shall follow me all the days of my life:
    and I will dwell in the house of the Lord for ever.

MARGE PIERCY

September Afternoon at Four O'clock

Full in the hand, heavy
with ripeness, perfume spreading
its fan: moments now resemble
sweet russet pears glowing
on the bough, peaches warm   5
from the afternoon sun, amber
and juicy, flesh that can
make you drunk.

There is a turn in things
that makes the heart catch.   10
We are ripening, all the hard
green grasping, the stony will
swelling into sweetness, the acid
and sugar in balance, the sun
stored as energy that is pleasure   15
and pleasure that is energy.

Whatever happens, whatever,
we say, and hold hard and let
go and go on. In the perfect
moment the future coils,   20
a tree inside a pit. Take,
eat, we are each other's
perfection, the wine of our
mouths is sweet and heavy.
Soon enough comes the vinegar.   25
The fruit is ripe for the taking
and we take. There is
no other wisdom.

1980

PHILIP BOOTH

One Man's Wife

Not that he promised not to windowshop,
or refuse free samples; but he gave up
exploring warehouse bargains, and forgot
the trial offers he used to mail away for.

After, that is, she laid on the counter what   5
she'd long kept hidden under the penny-candy,
and demonstrated (one up-country Sunday)
the total inventory of one wife's general store.

1966

Symbol

One can get into a good argument with a literary critic, a philosopher, or just about anybody else simply by mentioning the word symbol. A symbol is many things to many people, and often it means no more than that the person using the term is dealing with something he doesn't know how to describe or think about precisely. The term is difficult to be precise about, but it can be used quite sensibly. A symbol is, put simply, something which stands for something else. The everyday world is full of common examples; a flag, a logo, a trademark, or a skull and crossbones all suggest things beyond themselves, and everyone is likely to understand what their display is meant to signify, whether or not the viewer shares a commitment to what the object represents. In common usage a prison is a symbol of confinement, constriction, and loss of freedom, and in specialized traditional usage a cross may symbolize oppression, cruelty, suffering, death, resurrection, triumph, or the intersection of two separate things, traditions, or ideas (as in crossroads and crosscurrents, for example). The specific symbolic significance is controlled by the context; a reader may often decide by looking at contiguous details in the poem and by examining the poem's attitude toward a particular tradition or body of beliefs. A star means one kind of thing to a Jewish poet and something else to a Christian poet, still something else to a Nazi or to someone whose religion is surfing. In a very literal sense, words themselves are all symbols (they stand for an object, action, or quality, not just for letters or sounds), but symbols in poetry are said to be those words and groups of words which have a range of reference beyond their literal denotation.

Poems sometimes create a symbol out of a thing, action, or event which has no previously agreed upon symbolic significance. In the following poem, for example, a random gesture is given symbolic significance.

SHARON OLDS

Leningrad Cemetery, Winter of 1941[1]

That winter, the dead could not be buried.
The ground was frozen, the gravediggers weak from hunger,
the coffin wood used for fuel. So they were covered with
    something
and taken on a child's sled to the cemetery
in the sub-zero air. They lay on the soil,   5
some of them wrapped in dark cloth
bound with rope like the tree's ball of roots
when it waits to be planted; others wound in sheets,
their pale, gauze, tapered shapes
stiff as cocoons that will split down the center   10
when the new life inside is prepared;
but most lay like corpses, their coverings
coming undone, naked calves
hard as corded wood spilling
from under a cloak, a hand reaching out   15
with no sign of peace, wanting to come back
even to the bread made of glue and sawdust,
even to the icy winter, and the siege.

                                 p. 1979

All of the corpses—frozen, neglected, beginning to be in disarray—vividly stamp upon our minds a sense of the horrors of war, and the detailed picture of the random, uncounted clutter of bodies is likely to stick in our minds long after we have finished reading the poem. Several of the details are striking, and the poem's language heightens our sense of them. The corpses wound in sheets, for example, are described in "their pale, gauze, tapered shapes," and they are compared to cocoons that one day will split and emit new life; and the limbs that dangle loose when the coverings come undone are said to be "hard as corded wood spilling." But clearly the most memorable sight is the hand dangling from one corpse that is coming unwrapped, for the poet invests that hand with special significance, giving its gesture *meaning*. The hand is described as "reaching out . . . wanting to come back": it is as if the dead can still gesture even if they cannot speak, and the gesture seems to signify the desire of the dead to come back at any price. They would be glad to be alive, even under the grim conditions that attend the living in Leningrad during this grim war. Suddenly the grimness which we—living—have been witnessing pales by comparison with what the dead have lost simply by being dead. The hand has been made to **symbolize** the desire of the dead to return, to be alive, to be still among us, anywhere.

1. The 900-day siege of Leningrad during World War II began in September 1941.

The hand reaches out in the poem as a gesture that means; the poet has made it a symbol of desire.

The whole array of dead bodies in the poem might be said to be symbolic as well. As a group, they stand for the human waste that the war has produced, and their dramatic visual presence on the scene provides the poem with a dramatic visualization of how war and its requirements have no time for decency, not even the decency of burial. The bodies are a symbol in the sense that they stand for what the poem as a whole asserts.

This next poem also arises out of a historical moment, but this time the event is a personal one which the poet gives a significance by the interpretation he puts upon it.

JAMES DICKEY

The Leap

The only thing I have of Jane MacNaughton
Is one instant of a dancing-class dance.
She was the fastest runner in the seventh grade,
My scrapbook says, even when boys were beginning
To be as big as the girls,   5
But I do not have her running in my mind,
Though Frances Lane is there, Agnes Fraser,
Fat Betty Lou Black in the boys-against-girls
Relays we ran at recess: she must have run

Like the other girls, with her skirts tucked up   10
So they would be like bloomers,
But I cannot tell; that part of her is gone.
What I do have is when she came,
With the hem of her skirt where it should be
For a young lady, into the annual dance   15
Of the dancing class we all hated, and with a light
Grave leap, jumped up and touched the end
Of one of the paper-ring decorations

To see if she could reach it. She could,
And reached me now as well, hanging in my mind   20
From a brown chain of brittle paper, thin
And muscular, wide-mouthed, eager to prove
Whatever it proves when you leap
In a new dress, a new womanhood, among the boys
Whom you easily left in the dust   25
Of the passionless playground. If I said I saw
In the paper where Jane MacNaughton Hill,

Mother of four, leapt to her death from a window
Of a downtown hotel, and that her body crushed-in
The top of a parked taxi, and that I held   30
Without trembling a picture of her lying cradled
In that papery steel as though lying in the grass,
One shoe idly off, arms folded across her breast,
I would not believe myself. I would say
The convenient thing, that it was a bad dream   35
Of maturity, to see that eternal process

Most obsessively wrong with the world
Come out of her light, earth-spurning feet
Grown heavy; would say that in the dusty heels
Of the playground some boy who did not depend   40
On speed of foot, caught and betrayed her.
Jane, stay where you are in my first mind:
It was odd in that school, at that dance.
I and the other slow-footed yokels sat in corners
Cutting rings out of drawing paper   45

Before you leapt in your new dress
And touched the end of something I began,
Above the couples struggling on the floor,
New men and women clutching at each other
And prancing foolishly as bears: hold on   50
To that ring I made for you, Jane—
My feet are nailed to the ground
By dust I swallowed thirty years ago—
While I examine my hands.

1967

Memory is crucial to *The Leap*. The fact that Jane MacNaughton's
graceful leap in dancing class has stuck in the speaker's mind for
all these years means that this leap was important to him, meant
something to him, stood for something in his mind. For the speaker,
the leap is an "instant" and the "only thing" he has of Jane. Its grace
and ease are what he remembers, and he struggles at several points
to articulate its meaning (lines 15–26, 44–50), but even without articulation or explanation it is there in his head as a visual memory,
a symbol for him of something beyond himself, something he cannot
do, something he wanted to be. What that leap had stood for, or
symbolized, was boldness, confidence, accomplishment, maturity, the
ability to go beyond her fellow students in dancing class—the transcending of childhood by someone beginning to be a woman. Her
feet now seem "earth-spurning" (line 38) in that original leap, and
they separate her from everyone else. Jane MacNaughton was beyond
the speaker's abilities and any attempt he could make to articulate

his hopes, but not beyond his dreams. And even before articulation, she symbolized that dream.

The leap to her death seems cruelly ironic in the context of her earlier leap. In memory she is suspended in air, as if there were no gravity, no coming back to earth, as if life could exist as dream. And so the photograph, recreated in precise detail, is a cruel dashing of the speaker's dream—a detailed record of the ending of a leap, a denial of the suspension in which his memory had held her. His dream is grounded; her mortality is insistent. But what the speaker wants to hang on to (line 42) is still that symbolic moment which, although now confronted in more mature implications, will never be altogether replaced or surrendered.

The leap is ultimately symbolic in the *poem*, too, not just in the speaker's mind. In the poem (and for us as readers) the symbolism of the leap is double: the first leap is aspiration, and the second is frustration of high hopes; the two are complementary, one unable to be imagined without the other. The poem is horrifying in some ways, a dramatic reminder that human beings don't ultimately transcend their mortality, their limits, no matter how heroic or unencumbered by gravity they may seem to an observer. But it is not altogether sad and despairing either, partly because it notices and affirms the validity of the original leap and partly because another symbol is created and elaborated in the poem. That symbol is the paper chain.

The chain connects Jane to the speaker both literally and figuratively. It is, in part, *his* paper chain which she had leaped to touch in dancing class (lines 18–19), and he thinks of her first leap as "touch[ing] the end of something I began" (line 47). He and the other "slow footed," earthbound "yokels" (line 44) were the makers of the chain, and thus they are connected to her original leap, just as a photograph glimpsed in a paper connects the speaker to her second leap. The paper in the chain is "brittle" (line 21), and its creators seem dull artisans compared to the artistic performer that Jane was. They are heavy and left in the dust (lines 25, 52–53), and she is "light" (line 16) and able to transcend them but even in transcendence touching their lives and what they are able to do. And so the paper chain becomes the poem's symbol of linkage, connecting lower accomplishment to higher possibility, the artisan to the artist, material substance to the act of imagination. And the speaker at the end examines the hands that made the chain because those hands certify his connection to her and the imaginative leap she had made for him. The chain thus symbolizes not only the lower capabilities of those who cannot leap like the budding Jane could, but (later) the connection with her leap as both transcendence and mortality. Like the leap itself, the chain has been elevated to special meaning, given symbolic significance, by the poet's treatment of it. A leap and a chain have no necessary significance in themselves to most of us—at least no significance that we have all agreed upon together.

But some objects and acts do have such significance. Over the years some things have acquired an agreed-upon significance, an accepted value in our minds. They already stand for something before the poet cites them; they are **traditional symbols.** Their uses in poetry have to do with the fact that poets can count on a recognition of their traditional suggestions and meanings outside the poem, and the poem does not have to propose or argue a particular symbolic value. Birds, for example, traditionally symbolize flight, freedom from confinement, detachment from earthbound limits, the ability to soar beyond rationality and transcend mortal limits. Traditionally, birds have also been linked with imagination, especially poetic imagination, and poets often identify with them as ideal singers of songs, as in Keats's *Ode to a Nightingale* (p. 710). One of the most traditional symbols is that of the rose. It may be a simple and fairly plentiful flower in its season, but it has been allowed to stand for particular qualities for so long that to name it raises predictable expectations. Its beauty, delicacy, fragility, shortness of life, and depth of color have made it a symbol of the transitoriness of beauty, and countless poets have counted on its accepted symbolism—sometimes to compliment a friend (as Burns does in *A Red, Red Rose*) or sometimes to make a point about the nature of symbolism. The following poem draws on, in a quite traditional way, the traditional meanings.

JOHN CLARE

Love's Emblem

Go, rose, my Chloe's[2] bosom grace:
   How happy should I prove,
Could I supply that envied place
   With never-fading love.

Accept, dear maid, now summer glows,   5
   This pure, unsullied gem,
Love's emblem in a full-blown rose,
   Just broken from the stem.

Accept it as a favorite flower
   For thy soft breast to wear;   10
'Twill blossom there its transient hour,
   A favorite of the fair.

Upon thy cheek its blossom glows,
   As from a mirror clear,
Making thyself a living rose,   15
   In blossom all the year.

It is a sweet and favorite flower
   To grace a maiden's brow,
Emblem of love without its power—
   A sweeter rose art thou.   20

2. A standard "poetic" name for a woman in traditional love poetry.

The rose, like hues of insect wing,
    May perish in an hour;
'Tis but at best a fading thing,
    But thou'rt a living flower.

The roses steeped in morning dews   25
    Would every eye enthrall,
But woman, she alone subdues;
    Her beauty conquers all.

                                                            1873

   The speaker in *Love's Emblem* sends the rose to Chloe to decorate
her bosom (lines 1, 10) and reflect the blush of her cheek and brow
(lines 13, 18), and he goes on to mention some of the standard meanings: the rose is pure (line 6), transitory (line 11), fragrant, beautiful, and always appreciated (line 17). The poet need not elaborate
or argue these things; he can assume the reader's acquiescence. To
say that the rose is an emblem of love is to say that it traditionally
symbolizes love, and the speaker expects Chloe to accept his gift
readily; she will understand it as a compliment, a pledge, and a bond.
She will understand, too, that her admirer is being conventional and
complimentary in going on to call her (and women in general) a
rose (line 20), except that her qualities are said to be more lasting
than those of a momentary flower.
   Several of the poems at the end of this chapter explore the traditional meanings of the rose as symbol, sometimes playing with the
meanings and modifying them, sometimes consciously trying to create
new and untraditional meanings, sometimes calling attention to the
deterioration of nature as well as to the tradition (as in *Southern
Gothic*), or suggesting the primacy of symbol over physical artifact
(*Poem*: "The rose fades").
   Sometimes symbols—traditional or not—become so insistent in the
world of a poem that the larger referential world is left almost totally
behind. In such cases the symbol is everything, and the poem does
not just *use* symbols but becomes a **symbolic poem**.
   Here is an example of such a poem:

WILLIAM BLAKE

The Sick Rose[3]

O rose, thou art sick.
The invisible worm

---

3. In Renaissance emblem books, the
scarab beetle, worm, and rose are closely
associated: The beetle feeds on dung, and
the smell of the rose is fatal to it.

That flies in the night
In the howling storm

Has found out thy bed   5
Of crimson joy,
And his dark secret love
Does thy life destroy.

1794

The poem does not seem to be about a rose, but about what the rose represents—not in this case something altogether understandable through the traditional meanings of rose.

We know that the rose is usually associated with beauty and love, often with sex; and here several key terms have sexual connotations: "bed," "worm," and "crimson joy." The violation of the rose by the worm is the poem's main concern; the violation seems to have involved secrecy, deceit, and "dark" motives, and the result is sickness rather than the joy of love. The poem is sad; it involves a sense of hurt and tragedy, nearly of despair. The poem cries out against the misuse of the rose, against its desecration, implying that instead of a healthy joy in sensuality and sexuality, in this case, there has been destruction and hurt because of misunderstanding and repression and lack of sensitivity.

But to say so much about this poem I have had to extrapolate from other poems by this poet, and have introduced information from outside the poem. Fully symbolic poems often require that, and thus they ask us to go beyond the normal procedures of reading which we have discussed here. As presented in this poem, the rose is not part of the normal world that we ordinarily see, and it is symbolic in a special sense. The poet does not simply take an object from that everyday world and give it special significance, making it a symbol in the same sense that the leap is a symbol, or the corpse's hand. Here the rose seems to belong to its own world, a world made entirely inside the poem. The rose is not referential. The whole poem is symbolic; it is not paraphrasable; it lives in its own world. But what is the rose here a symbol of? In general terms, we can say from what the poem tells us; but we may not be as confident as we can be in the more nearly everyday world of *The Leap* or *Leningrad Cemetery, Winter of 1941*, poems that contain actions we recognize from the world of probabilities in which we live. In *The Sick Rose*, it seems inappropriate to ask the standard questions: What rose? Where? Which worm? What are the particulars here? In the world of this poem worms can fly and may be invisible. We are altogether in a world of meanings.

Negotiation of meanings in symbolic poems can be very difficult indeed. The skill of reading symbolic poems is an advanced skill that depends on special knowledge of authors and of the traditions they work from, and these skills need to be developed carefully and cautiously under the tutelage of a skilled teacher. You will find in this book some examples of symbolic poems (*Sailing to Byzantium*, for example), but the symbols you will usually find in poems are referential, and these meanings are readily discoverable from the careful study of the poems themselves, as in poems like *The Leap* and *Love's Emblem*.

EMILY DICKINSON

Go Not Too Near a House of Rose

Go not too near a House of Rose—
The depredation of a Breeze
Or inundation of a Dew
Alarms its walls away—

Nor try to tie the Butterfly,   5
Nor climb the Bars of Ecstasy,
In insecurity to lie.
Is Joy's insuring quality.

c. 1878

WILLIAM CARLOS WILLIAMS

Poem

The rose fades
and is renewed again
by its seed, naturally
but where

save in the poem   5
shall it go
to suffer no diminution
of its splendor

1962

ROBERT FROST

The Rose Family[4]

The rose is a rose,
And was always a rose.
But the theory now goes
That the apple's a rose,
And the pear is, and so's
The plum, I suppose.
The dear only knows
What will next prove a rose.
You, of course, are a rose—
But were always a rose.

10

1928

DOROTHY PARKER

One Perfect Rose

A single flow'r he sent me, since we met.
  All tenderly his messenger he chose;
Deep-hearted, pure, with scented dew still wet—
  One perfect rose.

I knew the language of the floweret;   5
  "My fragile leaves," it said, "his heart enclose."
Love long has taken for his amulet
  One perfect rose.

Why is it no one ever sent me yet
  One perfect limousine, do you suppose?   10
Ah no, it's always just my luck to get
  One perfect rose.

1937

DONALD JUSTICE

Southern Gothic

(for W.E.B. & P.R.)

Something of how the homing bee at dusk

4. A response to Gertrude Stein's famous line, "A rose is a rose is a rose."

Seems to inquire, perplexed, how there can be
No flowers here, not even withered stalks of flowers,
Conjures a garden where no garden is
And trellises too frail almost to bear   5
The memory of a rose, much less a rose.
Great oaks, more monumentally great oaks now
Than ever when the living rose was new,
Cast shade that is the more completely shade
Upon a house of broken windows merely   10
And empty nests up under broken eaves.
No damask any more prevents the moon,
But it unravels, peeling from a wall,
Red roses within roses within roses.

1960

7   STRUCTURE

"Proper words in proper places": that is the way one great writer of English prose (Jonathan Swift) described good writing. Finding appropriate words is not the easiest of tasks for a poet, and in the last two chapters we have looked at some of the implications for readers of the choices a poet makes. But a poet's decision about where to put those words is also difficult, for individual words, metaphors, and symbols not only exist as part of a phrase or sentence or rhythmic pattern but also as part of the larger whole of the poem itself. How is the whole poem to be organized? What will come first and what last? How is some sort of structure to be created? How are words, sentences, images, ideas, feelings to be put together into something that holds together, seems complete, and will have a certain effect upon us as readers?

Looking at these questions from the point of view of the maker of the poem (What shall I plan? Where shall I begin?) can have the advantage of helping us as readers to notice the effect of structural decisions. In a sense, every single poem is different from every other, and therefore independent, individual decisions must be made about how to organize. But there are also patterns of organization that poems fall into, sometimes because of the subject matter, sometimes because of the effect intended, sometimes for other reasons. Often poets consciously decide on a particular organizational strategy, sometimes they may reach instinctively for one or happen into a structure that suits the needs of the moment, one onto which a creator can hang the words one by one.

When there is a story to be told, the organization of a poem may be fairly simple, as in this popular ballad:

ANONYMOUS

Frankie and Johnny

Frankie and Johnny were lovers,
    Lordy, how they could love,
Swore to be true to each other,
    True as the stars up above,
        He was her man, but he done her wrong.   5

Frankie went down to the corner,
    To buy her a bucket of beer,
Frankie says "Mister Bartender,
    Has my lovin' Johnny been here?
        He is my man, but he's doing me wrong."   10

"I don't want to cause you no trouble
    Don't want to tell you no lie,
I saw your Johnny half-an-hour ago
    Making love to Nelly Bly.
        He is your man, but he's doing you wrong."   15

Frankie went down to the hotel
    Looked over the transom so high,
There she saw her lovin Johnny
    Making love to Nelly Bly.
        He was her man; he was doing her wrong.   20

Frankie threw back her kimono,
    Pulled out her big forty-four;
Rooty-toot-toot: three times she shot
    Right through that hotel door,
        She shot her man, who was doing her wrong.   25

"Roll me over gently,
    Roll me over slow,
Roll me over on my right side,
    'Cause these bullets hurt me so,
        I was your man, but I done you wrong."   30

Bring all your rubber-tired hearses
    Bring all your rubber-tired hacks,
They're carrying poor Johnny to the burying ground
    And they ain't gonna bring him back,
        He was her man, but he done her wrong.   35

Frankie says to the sheriff,
    "What are they going to do?"
The sheriff he said to Frankie,
    "It's the 'lectric chair for you.
        He was your man, and he done you wrong."   40

"Put me in that dungeon,
    Put me in that cell,
Put me where the northeast wind
    Blows from the southeast corner of hell,
        I shot my man, 'cause he done me wrong."   45
                                              (19th century)

When a strict narrative pattern organizes a poem, events follow upon one another in a generally chronological order, but even then a lot of artistic decisions need to be made just as in a short story or novel. Does one begin at the beginning, or begin in the middle at an exciting point, and then circle back and explain earlier events? How much detail should be given? How much description of setting is necessary and where should one stop or slow the narrative to insert it? How much explanation of motives is needed and when should it be provided? Should some details be held back for greater suspense? Should there be subplots or digressions? Is an interpretation or reflection desirable, at the end or at some earlier point?

Even in a poem with as straightforward a **narrative structure** as that of *Frankie and Johnny*, pure chronology is not the only consideration in finding places for the words. The first stanza of the poem provides an overview, some background, and even a hint of the catastrophe ("he done her wrong"). Stanzas 2 and 3 move the story along swiftly, but not by the most economical narrative means possible; instead, the poem adds some color and flavor by including the dialogue between Frankie and the bartender. Except for the repeated refrain (which keeps the whole story continuously in view), the next three stanzas are straightforward, and efficient, up through the shooting and Johnny's confession of infidelity. The final three stanzas also proceed chronologically—through the funeral, the conversation between Frankie and the sheriff, and Frankie's final reflections. The poem does not ever violate chronology, strictly speaking, but one can readily imagine quite a different emphasis from the very same facts told in much the same order. Chronology has guided the construction of the poem, but the final effects depend just as much upon the decision of which details to include, on the decision to include so much dialogue, on the decision to follow Frankie's progress through the events rather than Johnny's, and on the decision to include a summary refrain in each stanza.

Purely narrative poems can often be very long, much longer than can be included in a book like this, and often there are many features that are not, strictly speaking, closely connected to the narrative or linked to a strict chronology. Very often a poem moves on from a narrative of an event to some sort of commentary or reflection upon it, as in *Auto Wreck* (at the end of this chapter) or *When Lilacs Last in the Dooryard Bloomed* (p. 870). Reflection can be included along the way or may be implicit in the way the story is narrated, as in *Woodchucks* (p. 571) where our major attention is more on the narrator and her responses than on the events in the story as such.

Just as they sometimes take on a structure rather like that of a story, poems sometimes borrow the structures of plays. The following poem has a **dramatic structure**; it consists of a series of scenes, each of which is presented vividly and in detail.

HOWARD NEMEROV

The Goose Fish

On the long shore, lit by the moon
To show them properly alone,
Two lovers suddenly embraced
So that their shadows were as one.
The ordinary night was graced   5
For them by the swift tide of blood
That silently they took at flood,
And for a little time they prized
  Themselves emparadised.

Then, as if shaken by stage-fright   10
Beneath the hard moon's bony light,
They stood together on the sand
Embarrassed in each other's sight
But still conspiring hand in hand,
Until they saw, there underfoot,   15
As though the world had found them out,
The goose fish turning up, though dead,
  His hugely grinning head.

There in the china light he lay,
Most ancient and corrupt and gray   20
They hesitated at his smile,
Wondering what it seemed to say
To lovers who a little while
Before had thought to understand,
By violence upon the sand,   25
The only way that could be known
  To make a world their own.

It was a wide and moony grin
Together peaceful and obscene;
They knew not what he would express,   30
So finished a comedian
He might mean failure or success,
But took it for an emblem of
Their sudden, new and guilty love
To be observed by, when they kissed,   35
  That rigid optimist.

So he became their patriarch,
Dreadfully mild in the half-dark.
His throat that the sand seemed to choke,
His picket teeth, these left their mark   40
But never did explain the joke
That so amused him, lying there
While the moon went down to disappear
Along the still and tilted track
    That bears the zodiac.   45

                                                            1955

The first stanza sets the scene—a sandy shore in moonlight—and presents, in fact, the major action of the poem. The rest of the poem
dramatizes the lovers' reactions: their initial embarrassment and feelings of guilt (stanza 2), their attempt to interpret the goose fish's
smile (stanza 3), their decision to make him, whatever his meaning,
the "emblem" of their love (stanza 4), and their acceptance of the
fish's ambiguity and of their own relationship (stanza 5). The five
stanzas do not exactly present five different scenes, but they do
present separate dramatic moments, even if only a few minutes apart.
Almost like a play of five very short acts, the poem traces the drama
of the lovers' discovery of themselves, of their coming to terms with
the meaning of their action. As in many plays, the central event
(their love-making) is not the central focus of the drama, although
the drama is based upon that event and could not take place without it. Here, that event is depicted only briefly but very vividly
through figurative language: "they took at flood" the "swift tide
of blood," and the immediate effect is to make them briefly feel
"emparadised." But the poem concentrates on their later reactions, not
on the act of love itself.

Their sudden discovery of the fish is a rude shock and injects a
grotesque, almost macabre note into the poem. From a vision of
paradise, the poem seems for a moment to turn toward a gothic
horror story when the lovers discover that they have, after all, been
seen—and by such a ghoulish spectator. The last three stanzas gradually recreate the intruder in their minds, as they are forced to admit
that their act of love does not exist in isolation as they had at first
hoped, and they begin to see it as part of a continuum, as part of
their relationship to the larger world, even (at the end) putting it
into the context of the rotating world and its seasons as the moon
disappears into its zodiac. In retrospect, we can see that even at the
moment of passion they were in touch with larger processes controlled
by the presiding mood (the "swift tide of blood"), but neither the
lovers nor we had understood their act as such then, and the poem
is about their gradual recognition.

Stages of feeling and knowing rather than specific visual scenes are
responsible for the poem's progress, and its dramatic structure depends upon internal perceptions and internal states of mind rather

than dialogue and events. Visualization and images help to organize the poem too. Notice in particular how the two most striking visual features of the poem—the fish and the moon—are presented stanza by stanza. In stanza 1, the fish is not yet noticed, and the moon exists plain; it is only mentioned, not described, and its light serves as a stage spotlight to assure not center-stage attention, but rather total privacy: it is a kind of lookout for the lovers. The stage imagery, barely suggested by the light in stanza 1, is articulated in stanza 2, and there the moon is said to be "hard" and its light "bony"; its features have characteristics that seem more appropriate to the fish which has now become visible. In stanza 3, the moon's light has come to seem fragile ("china") as it is said to expose the fish directly; the role of the moon as lookout and protector seems abandoned, or at least endangered. No moon appears in stanza 4, but the fish's grin is described as "wide and moony," almost as if the two onlookers, one earthly and dead, the other heavenly and eternal, had become merged in the poem, as they nearly had been by the imagery in stanza 2. And by stanza 5, the fish has become a friend—by now he is a comedian, optimist, emblem, and a patriarch of their love—and his new position in collaboration with the lovers is presided over by the moon going about its eternal business. The moon has provided the stage light for the poem and the means by which not only the fish but the meaning of the lovers' act has been discovered. The moon has also helped to organize the poem, partly as a dramatic accessory, partly as imagery.

The following poem is also dramatic, but it seems to represent a composite of several similar experiences rather than a single event— a fairly common pattern in dramatic poems.

PHILIP LARKIN

Church Going

Once I am sure there's nothing going on
I step inside, letting the door thud shut.
Another church: matting, seats, and stone,
And little books; sprawlings of flowers, cut
For Sunday, brownish now; some brass and stuff   5
Up at the holy end; the small neat organ;
And a tense, musty, unignorable silence,
Brewed God knows how long. Hatless, I take off
My cycle-clips in awkward reverence,

Move forward, run my hand around the font.[1]   10
From where I stand, the roof looks almost new—
Cleaned, or restored? Someone would know: I don't.
Mounting the lectern, I peruse a few

1. A bowl for baptismal water, mounted on a stone pedestal.

Hectoring[2] large-scale verses, and pronounce
"Here endeth" much more loudly than I'd meant.   15
The echoes snigger briefly. Back at the door
I sign the book, donate an Irish sixpence,
Reflect the place was not worth stopping for.

Yet stop I did: in fact I often do,
And always end much at a loss like this,   20
Wondering what to look for; wondering, too,
When churches fall completely out of use
What we shall turn them into, if we shall keep
A few cathedrals chronically on show,
Their parchment, plate and pyx[3] in locked cases,   25
And let the rest rent-free to rain and sheep.
Shall we avoid them as unlucky places?

Or, after dark, will dubious women come
To make their children touch a particular stone;
Pick simples[4] for a cancer; or on some   30
Advised night see walking a dead one?
Power of some sort or other will go on
In games, in riddles, seemingly at random;
But superstition, like belief, must die,
And what remains when disbelief has gone?   35
Grass, weedy pavement, brambles, buttress, sky,

A shape less recognizable each week,
A purpose more obscure. I wonder who
Will be the last, the very last, to seek
This place for what it was; one of the crew   40
That tap and jot and know what rood-lofts[5] were?
Some ruin-bibber,[6] randy for antique,
Or Christmas-addict, counting on a whiff
Of gown-and-bands and organ-pipes and myrrh?
Or will he be my representative,   45

Bored, uninformed, knowing the ghostly silt
Dispersed, yet tending to this cross of ground
Through suburb scrub because it held unspilt
So long and equally what since is found
Only in separation—marriage, and birth,   50
And death, and thoughts of these—for whom was built
This special shell? For, though I've no idea
What this accoutered frowsty barn is worth,
It pleases me to stand in silence here;

2. Intimidating.
3. A container for the Eucharist.
4. Medicinal herbs.
5. Galleries atop the screens (on which crosses are mounted) which divide the naves or main bodies of churches from the choirs or chancels.
6. Literally, ruin-drinker: someone extremely attracted to antiquarian objects.

A serious house on serious earth it is,   55
In whose blent air all our compulsions meet,
Are recognized, and robed as destinies.
And that much never can be obsolete,
Since someone will forever be surprising
A hunger in himself to be more serious,   60
And gravitating with it to this ground,
Which, he once heard, was proper to grow wise in,
If only that so many dead lie round.

                                                                      1955

Ultimately, the poem's emphasis is upon what it means to visit
churches, what sort of phenomenon church buildings represent, and
what one is to make of the fact that "church going" (in the usual
sense of the word) has declined so much. The poem uses a *different*
sort of church-going (visitation by tourists) to consider larger philosophical questions about the relationship of religion to culture and
history. The poem is, finally, a rather philosophical one about the
directions of English culture, and through an enumeration of religious
objects and rituals it reviews the history of how we got to our
present historical circumstance. It tells a kind of story first, through
one lengthy dramatized scene, in order to comment later on what
the place and the experience may mean, and the larger conclusion
derives from the particulars of what the speaker does and touches.
The action is really over by the end of stanza 2, and that action,
we are told, stands for many such visits to similar churches; after
that, all is reflection and discussion, five stanzas' worth.
    Church Going is a curious, funny poem in many ways. It goes to a
lot of trouble to characterize its speaker, who seems a rather odd
choice as a commentator on the state of religion. His informal attire
(he takes off his cycle-clips at the end of stanza 1) and his not exactly worshipful behavior do not at first make us expect him to be a
serious philosopher about what all this means. He is not disrespectful
or sacrilegious, and before the end of stanza 1 he has tried to describe the "awkward reverence" he feels, but his overly somber imitation of part of the service stamps him as playful and as a tourist here,
not someone who regularly drops in for prayer or meditation in the
usual sense. And yet those early details do give him credentials, in a
way; he clearly knows the names of religious objects and has some of
the history of churches in his grasp. Clearly he does this sort of
church-going often ("Yet stop I did; in fact I often do," line 19) because he wonders seriously what it all means—now—in comparison to
what it meant to religious worshipers in times past. Ultimately, he
takes the church itself seriously and its cultural meaning and function
just as seriously (lines 55ff.), understanding its important place in the
history of his culture. In this poem, the drama is, relatively speaking,
brief, but it gives a context for the more digressive and rambling
free-floating reflections that grow out of the dramatic experience.

Poems often have **discursive structures** too; that is, they are sometimes organized like a treatise, an argument, or an essay. "First,"
they say, "and second . . . and third. . . ." This sort of 1–2–3 structure takes a variety of forms depending on what one is enumerating
or arguing. Here, for example, is a poem that is about three people
who have died. The poem honors all three, but makes clear and sharp
distinctions between them. As you read the poem, try to articulate
just what sort of person each of the three is represented to be.

JAMES WRIGHT

Arrangements with Earth for Three Dead Friends

Sweet earth, he ran and changed his shoes to go
Outside with other children through the fields.
He panted up the hills and swung from trees
Wild as a beast but for the human laughter
That tumbled like a cider down his cheeks.   5
Sweet earth, the summer has been gone for weeks,
And weary fish already sleeping under water
Below the banks where early acorns freeze.
Receive his flesh and keep it cured of colds.
Button his coat and scarf his throat from snow.   10

And now, bright earth, this other is out of place
In what, awake, we speak about as tombs.
He sang in houses when the birds were still
And friends of his were huddled round till dawn
After the many nights to hear him sing.   15
Bright earth, his friends remember how he sang
Voices of night away when wind was one.
Lonely the neighborhood beneath your hill
Where he is waved away through silent rooms.
Listen for music, earth, and human ways.   20

Dark earth, there is another gone away,
But she was not inclined to beg of you
Relief from water falling or the storm.
She was aware of scavengers in holes
Of stone, she knew the loosened stones that fell   25
Indifferently as pebbles plunging down a well
And broke for the sake of nothing human souls.
Earth, hide your face from her where dark is warm.
She does not beg for anything, who knew
The change of tone, the human hope gone gray.   30

1957

Why, in stanza 1, is the earth represented as a parent? What does addressing the earth here as "sweet" seem to mean? How does the address to earth as "bright" fit the dead person described in stanza 2? In what different senses is the person described in stanza 3 "dark"? Why is the earth asked to give attention secretly to this person? Exactly what kind of person was she? How does the poem make you feel about her? Is there any cumulative point in describing three such different people in the same poem? What is accomplished by having the poem's three stanzas addressed to various aspects of earth? Similar discursive structures help to organize poems such as Shelley's *Ode to the West Wind* (p. 664), where the wind is shown driving a leaf in Part I, a cloud in Part II, a wave in Part III, and then, after a summary and statement of the speaker's ambitious hope in Part IV, is asked to make the speaker a lyre in Part V.

Poems may borrow their organizational strategies from many places, imitating chronological, visual, or discursive shapes in reality or in other works of art. Sometimes poems strive to be almost purely descriptive of someone or something (using **descriptive structures**), in which case organizational decisions have to be made much as a painter or photographer would make them, deciding first how the whole scene should look, then putting the parts into proper place for the whole. But there are differences demanded by the poetic medium: a poem has to present the details sequentially, not all at once as an actual picture more or less can, so the poet must decide where the description starts (at the left? center? top?) and what sort of movement to use (linear across the scene? clockwise?). But if having words instead of paint or film has some disadvantages, it also has particular assets: figurative language can be a part of description, or an adjunct to it. A poet can insert a comparison at any point without necessarily disturbing the unity of what he or she describes—as long as the reader's main attention stays riveted on the tenor rather than the vehicle. A poem like Stevens's *Anecdote of the Jar* (p. 860) suggests some other complex things that a descriptive poem can do just *because* it has words to use to offer perspective on an object or scene.

Some poems use **imitative structures**, mirroring as exactly as possible the structure of something that already exists as an object and can be seen (another poem perhaps, as in Koch's *Variations on a Theme by William Carlos Williams*, (p. 771) or a standard visual or vocal format, by asking and answering questions, as Levertov's *What Were They Like* (p. 663) does. Or a poem may use **reflective** (or **meditative**) **structures**, pondering a subject, theme, or event, and letting the mind play with it, skipping (sometimes illogically but still usefully) from one sound to another, or to related thoughts or objects as the mind receives them.

Patterns, forms, structures, models, paradigms—all these terms help to suggest ways that we organize experience every day on the basis of analogy, putting things into an order on the basis of some other order we already know about. And they help with organizing words, with putting together verbal structures into some kind of whole. But the whole process is hardly mechanical. We might try to draw dia-

grams and charts of the organizations of poems, but they wouldn't
be very helpful, not nearly so accurate as a set of plans for a building
or even a sketch of a painting might be. Words reflect and re-
verberate; they are always growing and expanding; they won't stay
put in a single frame. Their shades of meaning, connotations, implications, and their participation in larger syntaxes and pictures mean
that they modify structures even as they fill them out. No one has
ever discovered how to talk precisely about the larger organizations
of words, and yet we need some sense of how attempts are made
to put words into orders that are, to some extent, controlled by larger
principles. And so we use terms such as narrative and imitative
structures as imprecise but suggestive indicators.

The paradigms (or models) for organizing poems are, finally, not
all that different from those of prose. It may be easier to organize
something short rather than something long, but the question of intensity becomes comparatively more important in shorter works. Basically, the problem of how to organize one's material is, for the writer,
first of all a matter of deciding what kind of thing one wants to create,
of having its purposes and effects clearly in mind. That means that
every poem will differ somewhat from every other, but it also means
that patterns of purpose—narrative, dramatic, discursive, descriptive,
imitative, or reflective—may help writers organize and formulate their
ideas. A consciousness of purpose and effect can help the reader see
how a poem proceeds toward its goal. Seeing how a poem is organized is, in turn, often a good way of seeing where it is going and
what its real concerns and purposes may be. Often a poem's organization helps to make clear the particular effects that the poet wishes
to generate. In a good poem, means and end are closely related, and
a reader who is a good observer of one will be able to discover
the other.

ANONYMOUS

Sir Patrick Spens

The king sits in Dumferling toune,[7]
    Drinking the blude-reid[8] wine:
"O whar will I get guid sailor,
    To sail this ship of mine?"

Up and spake an eldern knicht,   5
    Sat at the king's richt knee:
"Sir Patrick Spens is the best sailor
    That sails upon the sea."

7. Town.   8. Blood-red.

The king has written a braid[9] letter
  And signed it wi' his hand,   10
And sent it to Sir Patrick Spens,
  Was walking on the sand.

The first line that Sir Patrick read,
  A loud lauch[1] lauched he;
The next line that Sir Patrick read,   15
  The tear blinded his ee.[2]

"O wha is this has done this deed,
  This il deed done to me,
To send me out this time o' the year,
  To sail upon the sea?   20

"Make haste, make haste, my merry men all,
  Our guid ship sails the morn."
"O say na sae,[3] my master dear,
  For I fear a deadly storm.

"Late, late yestre'en I saw the new moon 25
  Wi' the auld moon in her arm,
And I fear, I fear, my dear mastér,
  That we will come to harm."

O our Scots nobles were richt laith[4]
  To weet their cork-heeled shoon,[5]   30
But lang owre a'[6] the play were played
  Their hats they swam aboon.[7]

O lang, lang, may their ladies sit,
  Wi' their fans into their hand,
Or ere they see Sir Patrick Spens   35
  Come sailing to the land.

O lang, lang, may the ladies stand
  Wi' their gold kems[8] in their hair,
Waiting for their ain[9] dear lords,
  For they'll see them na mair.   40

Half o'er, half o'er to Aberdour
  It's fifty fadom deep,
And there lies guid Sir Patrick Spens
  Wi' the Scots lords at his feet.

(probably 13th century)

9. Broad: explicit.
1. Laugh.
2. Eye.
3. Not so.
4. Right loath: very reluctant.
5. To wet their cork-heeled shoes. Cork was expensive, and therefore such shoes were a mark of wealth and status.
6. Before all.
7. Their hats swam above them.
8. Combs.
9. Own.

KARL SHAPIRO

Auto Wreck

Its quick soft silver bell beating, beating,
And down the dark one ruby flare
Pulsing out red light like an artery,
The ambulance at top speed floating down
Past beacons and illuminated clocks   5
Wings in a heavy curve, dips down,
And brakes speed, entering the crowd.
The doors leap open, emptying light;
Stretchers are laid out, the mangled lifted
And stowed into the little hospital.   10
Then the bell, breaking the hush, tolls once,
And the ambulance with its terrible cargo
Rocking, slightly rocking, moves away,
As the doors, an afterthought, are closed.

We are deranged, walking among the cops   15
Who sweep glass and are large and composed.
One is still making notes under the light.
One with a bucket douches ponds of blood
Into the street and gutter.
One hangs lanterns on the wrecks that cling,   20
Empty husks of locusts, to iron poles.

Our throats were tight as tourniquets,
Our feet were bound with splints, but now,
Like convalescents intimate and gauche,
We speak through sickly smiles and warn   25
With the stubborn saw of common sense,
The grim joke and the banal resolution.
The traffic moves around with care,
But we remain, touching a wound
That opens to our richest horror.   30
Already old, the question Who shall die?
Becomes unspoken Who is innocent?

For death in war is done by hands;
Suicide has cause and stillbirth, logic;
And cancer, simple as a flower, blooms.   35
But this invites the occult mind,
Cancels our physics with a sneer,
And spatters all we knew of denouement
Across the expedient and wicked stones.

1942

LUCILLE CLIFTON

At Last We Killed the Roaches

at last we killed the roaches.
mama and me. she sprayed,
i swept the ceiling and they fell
dying onto our shoulders, in our hair
covering us with red. the tribe was broken,   5
the cooking pots were ours again
and we were glad, such cleanliness was grace
when i was twelve. only for a few nights,
and then not much, my dreams were blood
my hands were blades and it was murder murder   10
all over the place.

                                                      1974

DENISE LEVERTOV

What Were They Like?

1) Did the people of Viet Nam
   use lanterns of stone?
2) Did they hold ceremonies
   to reverence the opening of buds?
3) Were they inclined to rippling laughter?   5
4) Did they use bone and ivory,
   jade and silver, for ornament?
5) Had they an epic poem?
6) Did they distinguish between speech and singing?

1) Sir, their light hearts turned to stone.   10
   It is not remembered whether in gardens
   stone lanterns illumined pleasant ways.
2) Perhaps they gathered once to delight in blossom,
   but after the children were killed
   there were no more buds.   15
3) Sir, laughter is bitter to the burned mouth.
4) A dream ago, perhaps. Ornament is for joy.
   All the bones were charred.
5) It is not remembered. Remember,
   most were peasants; their life   20
   was in rice and bamboo.
   When peaceful clouds were reflected in the paddies
   and the water buffalo stepped surely along terraces,
   maybe fathers told their sons old tales.
   When bombs smashed the mirrors   25
   there was time only to scream.

6) There is an echo yet, it is said,
   of their speech which was like a song.
   It is reported their singing resembled
   the flight of moths in moonlight.   30
   Who can say? It is silent now.

                                                                      1966

PERCY BYSSHE SHELLEY

Ode to the West Wind

I

O wild West Wind, thou breath of Autumn's being,
Thou, from whose unseen presence the leaves dead
Are driven, like ghosts from an enchanter fleeing,

Yellow, and black, and pale, and hectic red,
Pestilence-stricken multitudes: O thou,   5
Who chariotest to their dark wintry bed

The wingéd seeds, where they lie cold and low,
Each like a corpse within its grave, until
Thine azure sister of the Spring shall blow

Her clarion[1] o'er the dreaming earth, and fill   10
(Driving sweet buds like flocks to feed in air)
With living hues and odors plain and hill:

Wild Spirit, which art moving everywhere;
Destroyer and preserver; hear, oh, hear!

II

Thou on whose stream, mid the steep sky's commotion,   15
Loose clouds like earth's decaying leaves are shed,
Shook from the tangled boughs of Heaven and Ocean,

Angels[2] of rain and lightning: there are spread
On the blue surface of thine aëry surge,
Like the bright hair uplifted from the head   20

Of some fierce Maenad,[3] even from the dim verge
Of the horizon to the zenith's height,
The locks of the approaching storm. Thou dirge

Of the dying year, to which this closing night
Will be the dome of a vast sepulcher,   25
Vaulted with all thy congregated might

---

1. Trumpet-call.
2. Messengers.
3. A frenzied female votary of Dionysus, the Greek god of vegetation and fertility who was supposed to die in the fall and rise again each spring.

Of vapors, from whose solid atmosphere
Black rain, and fire, and hail will burst: oh, hear!

III

Thou who didst waken from his summer dreams
The blue Mediterranean, where he lay,   30
Lulled by the coil of his crystálline streams,

Beside a pumice isle in Baiae's bay,[4]
And saw in sleep old palaces and towers
Quivering within the wave's intenser day,

All overgrown with azure moss and flowers   35
So sweet, the sense faints picturing them! Thou
For whose path the Atlantic's level powers

Cleave themselves into chasms, while far below
The sea-blooms and the oozy woods which wear
The sapless foliage of the ocean, know   40

Thy voice, and suddenly grow gray with fear,
And tremble and despoil themselves:[5] oh, hear!

IV

If I were a dead leaf thou mightest bear;
If I were a swift cloud to fly with thee;
A wave to pant beneath thy power, and share   45

The impulse of thy strength, only less free
Than thou, O uncontrollable! If even
I were as in my boyhood, and could be

The comrade by thy wanderings over Heaven,
As then, when to outstrip thy skyey speed   50
Scarce seemed a vision; I would ne'er have striven

As thus with thee in prayer in my sore need.
Oh, lift me as a wave, a leaf, a cloud!
I fall upon the thorns of life! I bleed!

A heavy weight of hours has chained and bowed 55
One too like thee: tameless, and swift, and proud.

V

Make me thy lyre,[6] even as the forest is:
What if my leaves are falling like its own!
The tumult of thy mighty harmonies

Will take from both a deep, autumnal tone,   60
Sweet though in sadness. Be thou, Spirit fierce,

4. Where Roman emperors had erected villas, west of Naples. "pumice": made of porous lava turned to stone.
5. "The vegetation at the bottom of the sea . . . sympathizes with that of the land in the change of seasons." (Shelley's note)
6. Aeolian lyre, a wind harp.

My spirit! Be thou me, impetuous one!

Drive my dead thoughts over the universe
Like withered leaves to quicken a new birth!
And, by the incantation of this verse,   65

Scatter, as from an unextinguished hearth
Ashes and sparks, my words among mankind!
Be through my lips to unawakened earth

The trumpet of a prophecy! O Wind,
If Winter comes, can Spring be far behind?   70

1820

DAVID DONNELL

Potatoes

This poem is about the strength and sadness of potatoes.
Unknown in Portugal or China, England or France,
untasted by the legions of Hannibal or Caesar,
hardy, simple, variable tuber; plain dusty brown,
North Carolina, New Brunswick, Idaho,   5
of the new world, passed over by the Indians
who preferred the bright yellow of corn, its sweetness,
the liquor they made from it, pemmican and wild corn mush.
The potato was seized upon by the more spiritual Puritans
while their companions were enraptured   10
by the beauty of New World tobacco, cotton and squash.

The Puritans recognized something of themselves in the pale
potato. Its simple shape reminded them of the human soul;
the many eyes of the potato amazed them. They split it
in half and saw the indivisibility of man;   15
they looked at the many eyes of the potato
and saw God looking back at them.
Potatoes like many different kinds of soil, resist cold weather,
store well in cool cellars and are more nutritious than beets.
Potato dumplings became the pièce de résistance of eastern Europe.   20
They developed a considerable number of useful proverbs.
For example: "Love is not a potato, do not throw it out the window."
Or the famous Scottish lament—"What good is he to me?
For three days he has not even brought me a potato."

The potato is modest and develops its indivisible bounty   25
under the ground, taking from the ground some of its color
and just enough skin to resist an excess of moisture.
It can be harvested easily by young boys and girls working

in rows with bushel baskets and pausing at lunch
to lift up their skirts and make love under the fences.   30
Truckloads of potatoes can be sent to every part of the world.
The French make frites[7] with them. The Russians make vodka.
The Chinese have white and brown rice but all potatoes are the same.
Potato flour is not as sweet as corn but makes an excellent bread.
In the cellars of poor farmers all over America   35
the potatoes sit quietly on top of each other growing eyes.

                                                                    1980

8   SOUND AND SIGHT

The Sounds of Poetry

A lot of what happens in a poem happens in your mind's eye, but
some of it happens in your voice. Poems are full of sounds and
silences as well as words and sentences that are meaningful. Besides
choosing words for their meanings, poets sometimes choose words
because they involve certain sounds, and use sound effects to create
a mood or establish a tone, just as films do. Sometimes the sounds
of words are crucial to what is happening in the text of the poem.

    The following poem explores the sounds of a particular word, tries
them on, and analyzes them in relation to the word itself.

HELEN CHASIN

The Word *Plum*

The word *plum* is delicious

pout and push, luxury of
self-love, and savoring murmur

full in the mouth and falling
like fruit   5

taut skin
pierced, bitten, provoked into
juice, and tart flesh

7. French fries.

       question
       and reply, lip and tongue   10
       of pleasure.

                                                    1968

The poem savors the sounds of the word as well as the taste and
feel of the fruit itself. It is almost as if the poem is tasting the sounds
and rolling them carefully on the tongue. The second and third lines
even replicate the "p," "l," "uh," and "m" sounds of the word while at
the same time imitating the squishy sounds of eating the fruit. Words
like "delicious" and "luxury" sound juicy, and other words imitate
sounds of satisfaction and pleasure—"murmur," for example. Even the
process of eating is in part recreated aurally. The tight, clipped
sounds of "taut skin / pierced" suggest the sharp breaking of the skin
and solid flesh, and as the tartness is described, the words ("provoked," "question") force the mouth to pucker as it would if it were
savoring a tart fruit. The poet is having fun here recreating the
various sense appeals of a plum, teasing the sounds and meanings out
of available words. The words must mean something appropriate and
describe something accurately first of all, of course, but when they can
also imitate the sounds and feel of the process, they can do double
duty. Not all poems manipulate sound as consciously or as fully as
The Word Plum, but many poems at least contain passages in which
the sounds of life are reproduced by the human voice reading the
poem. To get the full effect of this poem—and of many others—
reading aloud is essential; that way, one can pay attention to the
vocal rhythms and can articulate the sounds as the poem calls for
them to be reproduced by the human voice.
    Almost always a poem's effect will be helped by reading it aloud,
using your voice to pronounce the words so that the poem becomes
a spoken communication. Historically, poetry began as an oral phenomenon, and often poems that seem very difficult when looked at silently
come alive when they are turned into sound. Early bards chanted their
verses, and the music of poetry—its cadences and rhythms—developed
from this kind of performance. Often in primitive poetry (and sometimes in later ages) poetry performances have been accompanied by
some kind of musical instrument. The rhythms of any poem become
clearer when you say or hear them.
    Poetry is, almost always, a vocal art, dependent on the human voice
to become its full self (for some exceptions look at the shaped verse
at the end of this chapter). In a sense, it begins to exist as a real
phenomenon when a reader reads and actualizes it. Poems don't really
achieve their full meaning when they merely exist on a page; a poem
on a page is more a set of stage directions for a poem than a poem
itself. Sometimes, in fact, it is hard to experience the poem at all
unless you hear it. A good poetry reading might easily convince you
of the importance of a good voice sensitive to the poem's requirements,
but you can also persuade yourself by reading poems aloud in the

privacy of your own room. An audience is even better, however, because then there is someone to share the pleasure in the sounds themselves and consider what they imply.

MONA VAN DUYN

What the Motorcycle Said

Br-r-r-am-m-m, rackety-am-m, OM, *Am:*
All—r-r-room, r-r-ram, ala-bas-ter—
Am, the world's my oyster.

I hate plastic, wear it black and slick,
hate hardhats, wear one on my head,   5
that's what the motorcycle said.

Passed phonies in Fords, knocked down billboards, landed
on the other side of The Gap, and Whee,
bypassed history.

When I was born (The Past), baby knew best.   10
They shook when I bawled, took Freud's path,
threw away their wrath.

R-r-rackety-am-m, *Am.* War, rhyme,
soap, meat, marriage, the Phantom Jet
are shit, and like that.   15

Hate pompousness, punishment, patience, am into Love,
hate middle-class moneymakers, live on Dad,
that's what the motorcycle said.

Br-r-r-am-m-m. It's Nowsville, man. Passed Oldies, Uglies,
Straighties, Honkies. I'll never be   20
mean, tired or unsexy.

Passed cigarette suckers, souses, mother-fuckers,
losers, went back to Nature and found
how to get VD, stoned.

Passed a cow, too fast to hear her moo, "*I* rolled   25
our leaves of grass into one ball.
I am the grassy All."

Br-r-r-am-m-m, rackety-am-m, OM, *Am:*
All—gr-r-rin, oooohgah, gl-l-utton—
Am, the world's my smilebutton.   30

1973

Saying this poem as if you were a motorcycle with the power of speech (sort of) is part of the poem's fun, and the rich, loud sounds of a motorcycle revving up concentrate and intensify the effect and enrich the pleasure. It's a shame not to hear a poem like this aloud; a lot of it is missed if you don't try to imitate the sounds or if you don't try to pick up the motor's rhythms in the poem. A performance here is clearly worth it: a human being as motorcycle, motorcycle as human being.

And it's a good poem, too, that does something interesting, important, and maybe a bit subversive. The speaking motorcycle seems to take on the values of some of its riders, the noisy and obtrusive ones that readers are most likely to associate with motorcycles in their minds. The riders made fun of here are themselves sort of mindless and mechanical; they are the sort who have cult feelings about their group, who travel in packs, and who live no life beyond their machines. The speaking motorcycle, like such riders, grooves on power and speed, lives for the moment, and has little respect for people, the past, for institutions, or for anything beyond its own small world. It is self-centered, modish, ignorant, and inarticulate; but proud, mighty proud, and feels important in its own sounds. That's what the motorcycle says.

The following poem uses sound effects efficiently, too.

KENNETH FEARING

Dirge

1-2-3 was the number he played but today the number came 3-2-1;
Bought his Carbide at 30, and it went to 29; had the favorite at Bowie
      but the track was slow—

O executive type, would you like to drive a floating-power, knee-action,
      silk-upholstered six? Wed a Hollywood star? Shoot the course in
      58? Draw to the ace, king, jack?
O fellow with a will who won't take no, watch out for three cigarettes
      on the same, single match; O democratic voter born in August
      under Mars, beware of liquidated rails—

Denouement to denouement, he took a personal pride in the certain,
      certain way he lived his own, private life,   5
But nevertheless, they shut off his gas; nevertheless, the bank foreclosed;
      nevertheless, the landlord called; nevertheless, the radio broke,

And twelve o'clock arrived just once too often,
Just the same he wore one gray tweed suit, bought one straw hat, drank
      one straight Scotch, walked one short step, took one long look,
      drew one deep breath,
Just one too many,

And wow he died as wow he lived,   ¹⁰
Going whop to the office and blooie home to sleep and biff got married
    and bam had children and oof got fired,
Zowie did he live and zowie did he die,

With who the hell are you at the corner of his casket, and where the
    hell're we going on the right-hand silver knob, and who the hell
    cares walking second from the end with an American Beauty
    wreath from why the hell not,

Very much missed by the circulation staff of the New York Evening
Post; deeply, deeply mourned by the B.M.T.[1]
Wham, Mr. Roosevelt; pow, Sears Roebuck; awk, big dipper; bop,
    summer rain;   ¹⁵
Bong, Mr., bong, Mr., bong, Mr., bong.

1935

As the title implies, this poem is a kind of musical lament, in this
case for a certain sort of businessman who took a lot of chances and
saw his investments and life go down the drain in the depression of
the early thirties. Reading this poem aloud is a big help partly because it contains expressive words which echo the action, words like
"oof" and "blooie" (which primarily carry their meaning in their sounds,
for they have no literal or referential meaning). Reading aloud also
helps us notice that the poem employs rhythms much as a song would
and that it frequently shifts its pace and mood. Notice how carefully
the first two lines are balanced, and then how quickly the rhythm
shifts as the "executive type" begins to be addressed directly in line
3. (Line 2 is long and dribbles over in the narrow pages of a book
like this; a lot of the lines here are especially long, and the irregu-
larity of the line lengths is one aspect of the special sound effects
the poem creates.) In the direct address, the poem first picks up a
series of advertising features which it recites in rapid-fire order rather
like the advertising phrases in *Needs* in Chapter 3. In stanza 3 here,
the rhythm shifts again, but the poem gives us helpful clues about
how to read. Line 5 sounds like prose and is long, drawn out, and
rather dull (rather like its subject), but line 6 sets up a regular
(and monotonous) rhythm with its repeated "nevertheless" which
punctuates the rhythm like a drumbeat: "But nevertheless *tuh-tuh-*
tuh-tuh-tuh; nevertheless *tuh-tuh-tuh-tuh*; nevertheless *tuh-tuh-tuh-*
tuh; nevertheless *tuh-tuh-tuh-tuh-tuh.*" In the next stanza, the repetitive phrasing comes again, this time guided by the word "one" in
cooperation with other words of one syllable: "wore *one* gray tweed
suit, bought *one* straw hat, *tuh* one *tuh-tuh*; *tuh* one *tuh-tuh*; *tuh*
one *tuh-tuh*; *tuh* one *tuh-tuh.*" And then a new rhythm and a new
technique in stanza 5 as the language of comic books is imitated

1. A New York subway line.

to describe in violent, exaggerated terms the routine of his life. You have to say words like "whop" and "zowie" aloud and in the rhythm of the whole sentence to get the full effect of how boring his life is, no matter how he tries to jazz it up with exciting words. And so it goes—repeated words, shifting rhythms, emphasis on routine and averageness—until the final bell ("Bong . . . bong . . . bong . . . bong") tolls rhythmically for the dead man in the final clanging line.

Sometimes sounds in poems just provide special effects, rather like a musical score behind a film, setting mood and getting us into an appropriate frame of mind. But often sound and meaning go hand in hand, and the poet finds words that in their sounds echo the action. A word which captures or approximates the sound of what it describes, such as "splash" or "squish" or "murmur" is called an **onomatopoeic** word, and the device itself is called **onomatopoeia**. And similar things can be done poetically with pacing and rhythm, sounds and pauses. The punctuation, the length of vowels, and the combination of consonant sounds help to control the way we read so that we imitate what is being described. The poems at the end of this discussion (pp. 679–684) suggest several ways that such imitations of pace and pause may occur: by echoing the lapping of waves on a shore, for example (*Like as the Waves*), or mimicking the sounds of a train on a variable terrain (*The Express*), or reproducing the rhythms of a musical style (*Dear John, Dear Coltrane*).

Here is a classic passage in which a skillful poet talks about the virtues of making the sound echo the sense—and shows at the same time how to do it:

ALEXANDER POPE

[Sound and Sense][2]

But most by numbers[3] judge a poet's song,   337
And smooth or rough, with them, is right or wrong;
In the bright muse though thousand charms conspire,[4]
Her voice is all these tuneful fools admire,   340
Who haunt Parnassus[5] but to please their ear,
Not mend their minds; as some to church repair,
Not for the doctrine, but the music there.
These, equal syllables[6] alone require,
Though oft the ear the open vowels tire,   345
While expletives[7] their feeble aid do join,
And ten low words oft creep in one dull line,

2. From *An Essay on Criticism*, Pope's poem on the art of poetry and the problems of literary criticism. The passage excerpted here follows a discussion of several common weaknesses of critics: failure to regard an author's intention, for example, or overemphasis on clever metaphors and ornate style.
3. Meter, rhythm, sound.

4. Unite.
5. A mountain in Greece, traditionally associated with the muses and considered the seat of poetry and music.
6. Regular accents.
7. Filler words, such as "do."

While they ring round the same unvaried chimes,
With sure returns of still expected rhymes.
Wheree'er you find "the cooling western breeze,"   350
In the next line, it "whispers through the trees";
If crystal streams "with pleasing murmurs creep,"
The reader's threatened (not in vain) with "sleep."
Then, at the last and only couplet fraught
With some unmeaning thing they call a thought,   355
A needless Alexandrine[8] ends the song,
That, like a wounded snake, drags its slow length along.
Leave such to tune their own dull rhymes, and know
What's roundly smooth, or languishingly slow;
And praise the easy vigor of a line,   360
Where Denham's strength and Waller's[9] sweetness join.
True ease in writing comes from art, not chance,
As those move easiest who have learned to dance.
'Tis not enough no harshness gives offense,
The sound must seem an echo to the sense: 365
Soft is the strain when Zephyr[1] gently blows,
And the smooth stream in smoother numbers flows;
But when loud surges lash the sounding shore,
The hoarse, rough verse should like the torrent roar.
When Ajax[2] strives, some rock's vast weight to throw,   370
The line too labors, and the words move slow;
Not so, when swift Camilla[3] scours the plain,
Flies o'er th' unbending corn, and skims along the main.
Hear how Timotheus'[4] varied lays surprise,
And bid alternate passions fall and rise!   375
While, at each change, the son of Libyan Jove[5]
Now burns with glory, and then melts with love;
Now his fierce eyes with sparkling fury glow,
Now sighs steal out, and tears begin to flow:
Persians and Greeks like turns of nature[6] found,   380
And the world's victor stood subdued by sound!
The pow'r of music all our hearts allow,
And what Timotheus was, is DRYDEN now.

1711

8. A six-foot line, sometimes used in pentameter poems to vary the pace mechanically. Line 357 is an alexandrine.
9. Sir John Denham and Edmund Waller, 17th-century poets credited with perfecting the heroic couplet.
1. The west wind.
2. A Greek hero of the Trojan War, noted for his strength.
3. A woman warrior in *The Aeneid*.
4. The court-musician of Alexander the Great, celebrated in a famous poem by Dryden (see line 383) for the power of his music over Alexander's emotions.
5. In Greek tradition, the chief god of any people was often given the name Zeus (Jove), and the chief god of Libya (the Greek name for all of Africa) was called Zeus Ammon. Alexander visited his oracle and was proclaimed son of the god.
6. Similar alternations of emotion.

A lot of things go on here simultaneously. The poem uses a number of echoic or onomatopoeic words, and pleasant and unpleasant consonant sounds are used in some lines to underline a particular point or add some mood music. When the poet talks about a particular weakness in poetry, he illustrates it at the same time—by using open vowels (line 345), expletives (line 346), monosyllabic words (line 347), predictable rhymes (lines 350–353), or long, slow lines (line 357). And the good qualities of poetry he talks about and illustrates as well (line 360, for example). But the main effects of the passage come from an interaction of several strategies at once. The effects are fairly simple and easy to spot, but their causes involve a lot of poetic ingenuity. In line 340, for example, a careful cacophonous effect is achieved by the repetition of the o͞o vowel sound and the repetition of the L consonant sound together with the interruption (twice) of the rough F sound in the middle; no one wants to be caught admiring that music when the poet gets through with us, but the careful harmony of the preceding sounds has set us up beautifully. And in lines 347, 357, and 359, the pace of the lines is carefully controlled by consonant sounds as well as by the use of long vowels. Line 347 moves incredibly slowly and seems much longer than it is because almost all the one-syllable words end in a consonant which refuses to blend with the beginning of the next word, making the words hard to say without distinct, awkward pauses between them. And in lines 357 and 359, long vowels such as those in "wounded," "snake," "slow," "along," "roundly," and "smooth" help to slow down the pace, and the same trick of juxtaposing awkward, unpronounceable consonants is also employed. The commas also provide nearly a full stop in the midst of each line to slow us down still more. Similarly, the harsh lashing of the shore in lines 368–69 is partly accomplished by onomatopoeia, partly by a shift in the pattern of stress which creates irregular waves in line 368, and partly by the dominance of rough consonants in line 369. (In Pope's time, the English *r* was still trilled gruffly so that it could be made to sound extremely rough and harsh.) Almost every line in this passage could serve as a demonstration of how to make sound echo sense.

As the passage from Pope and the poem *Dirge* suggest, sound is most effectively manipulated in poetry when the rhythm of the voice is carefully controlled so that not only are the proper sounds heard, but they are heard at precisely the right moment. Pace and rhythm are nearly as important to a good poem as they are to a good piece of music. The human voice naturally develops certain rhythms in speech; some syllables and some words receive more stress than others, and a careful poet controls the flow of stresses to that, in many poems, a certain basic rhythm develops almost like a quiet percussion instrument in the background. The most common rhythm in English is the regular alternation of unstressed and stressed syllables, as in the passage from Pope. There, most lines have five sets of unstressed/stressed syllables, although plenty of lines have slight variations so that there is little danger (if you read sensitively) of falling into too expected a rhythm, a dull sing-song. The unstressed/stressed pattern (in that order) is called **iambic** rhythm. Other fairly common rhythms are the **trochaic** (a stressed syllable followed by an unstressed one), the **anapestic** (two unstressed syllables followed by a stressed one), and **dactylic** (a stressed syllable followed by two unstressed ones). Each unit of measurement is called a **foot**. In "A Glossary of Poetic Terms," pp. 882–900, you will find definitions as well for some less frequently used rhythms, a list of terms used to describe lengths of lines, and some directions on how to **scan** (that is, analyze the rhythmic pattern of) metered verse.

Here is a poem which names and illustrates many of the meters. If you read it aloud and chart the unstressed (∪) and stressed (−) syllables you should have a chart similar to that done by the poet himself in the text.

SAMUEL TAYLOR COLERIDGE

Metrical Feet

Lesson for a Boy

Trŏchēe trĭps frŏm lōng tŏ shōrt; [7]
From long to long in solemn sort
Slōw Spōndēe stālks; strōng fōōt! yet ill able
Ēvĕr tŏ cōme ŭp wĭth Dāctȳl trĭsȳllăblĕ.
Īāmbĭcs mārch frŏm shōrt tŏ lōng—   5
Wĭth ă lēap ănd ă bōūnd thĕ swĭft Ānăpĕsts thrōng;
One syllable long, with one short at each side,
Ămphĭbrăchȳs hāstes wĭth ă stātelȳ strīde—
Fīrst ănd lāst bēĭng lōng, mĭddlĕ shōrt, Āmphĭmācer
Strĭkes hĭs thŭndĕrĭng hōofs lĭke ă prōūd hīgh-brĕd Rācer.   10
If Derwent[8] be innocent, steady, and wise,
And delight in the things of earth, water, and skies;
Tender warmth at his heart, with these meters to show it,
With sound sense in his brains, may make Derwent a poet—
May crown him with fame, and must win him the love   15
Of his father on earth and his Father above.
          My dear, dear child!
Could you stand upon Skiddaw,[9] you would not from its whole ridge
See a man who so loves you as your fond s. т. coleridge.
1806

7. The long and short marks over syllables are Coleridge's the kinds of metrical feet named and exemplified here are defined in the glossary, p. 891.
8. Written originally for Coleridge's son Hartley, the poem was later adapted for his younger son, Derwent.
9. A mountain in the lake country of northern England (where Coleridge lived in his early years), near the town of Derwent.

The following poem exemplifies **dactylic** rhythm, and the limericks that follow are written in **anapestic** meter.

ARTHUR W. MONKS

Twilight's Last Gleaming

Higgledy-piggledy
President Jefferson
Gave up the ghost on the
Fourth of July.

So did John Adams, which   5
Shows that such patriots
Propagandistically
Knew how to die.

1967

ANONYMOUS

[A Staid Schizophrenic Named Struther]

A staid schizophrenic named Struther,
When told of the death of his brother,
    Said: "Yes, I am sad;
    It makes me feel bad,
But then, I still have each other."

ANONYMOUS

[There Once Was a Pious Young Priest]

There once was a pious young priest
Who lived almost wholly on yeast.
    He said, "It's so plain
    We must all rise again
That I'd like to get started at least."

ANONYMOUS

[There Once Was a Spinster of Ealing]

There once was a spinster of Ealing,
Endowed with such delicate feeling,

That she thought an armchair
Should not have its legs bare—
So she kept her eyes trained on the ceiling.

This poem is composed in the more common **trochaic** meter.

SIR JOHN SUCKLING

Song

Why so pale and wan, fond Lover?
  Prithee why so pale?
Will, when looking well can't move her,
  Looking ill prevail?
    Prithee why so pale?   5

Why so dull and mute, young Sinner?
  Prithee why so mute?
Will, when speaking well can't win her,
  Saying nothing do 't?
    Prithee why so mute?   10

Quit, quit, for shame, this will not move,
  This cannot take her;
If of her self she will not love,
  Nothing can make her,
    The Devil take her.   15

1646

The basic meter in the following poem is the most common one in English, **iambic**:

JOHN DRYDEN

To the Memory of Mr. Oldham[1]

Farewell, too little, and too lately known,
Whom I began to think and call my own;
For sure our souls were near allied, and thine
Cast in the same poetic mold with mine.
One common note on either lyre did strike,   5
And knaves and fools we both abhorred alike.

---

1. John Oldham (1653–83), who like Dryden (see lines 3–6) wrote satiric poetry.

To the same goal did both our studies drive;
The last set out the soonest did arrive.
Thus Nisus fell upon the slippery place,
While his young friend performed and won the race.[2]   10
O early ripe! to thy abundant store
What could advancing age have added more?
It might (what nature never gives the young)
Have taught the numbers[3] of thy native tongue.
But satire needs not those, and wit will shine   15
Through the harsh cadence of a rugged line.[4]
A noble error, and but seldom made,
When poets are by too much force betrayed.
Thy generous fruits, though gathered ere their prime,
Still showed a quickness; and maturing time   20
But mellows what we write to the dull sweets of rhyme.
Once more, hail and farewell; farewell, thou young,
But ah too short, Marcellus[5] of our tongue;
Thy brows with ivy, and with laurels bound;
But fate and gloomy night encompass thee around.   25

1684

Once you have figured out the basic rhythm of a poem, you can often find some interesting things by looking carefully at the departures from the pattern. Departures from the basic iambic meter of *To the Memory of Mr. Oldham*, for example, suggest some of the imaginative things that poets can do within the apparently very restrictive requirements of traditional meter. Try marking the stressed and unstressed syllables in *To the Memory of Mr. Oldham* and then look carefully at each of the places which vary from the basic iambic pattern. Which of these variations call special attention to a particular sound or action being talked about in the poem? Which ones specifically mimic or echo the sense? Which variations seem to exist primarily for emphasis? Which ones seem primarily intended to mark structural breaks in the poem?

---

2. In Vergil's *Aeneid* (Book V), Nisus (who is leading the race) falls and then trips the second runner so that his friend Euryalus can win.
3. Rhythms.

4. In Dryden's time, R's were pronounced with a harsh, trilling sound.
5. The nephew of the Roman emperor Augustus; he died at 20, and Vergil celebrated him in *The Aeneid*, Book VI.

ALFRED, LORD TENNYSON

Break, Break, Break

Break, break, break,
   On thy cold gray stones, O Sea!
And I would that my tongue could utter
   The thoughts that arise in me.

O well for the fisherman's boy,   5
   That he shouts with his sister at play!
O well for the sailor lad,
   That he sings in his boat on the bay!

And the stately ships go on
   To their haven under the hill;   10
But O for the touch of a vanished hand,
   And the sound of a voice that is still!

Break, break, break,
   At the foot of thy crags, O Sea!
But the tender grace of a day that is dead   15
   Will never come back to me.

ca. 1834

DONALD JUSTICE

Counting the Mad

This one was put in a jacket,
This one was sent home,
This one was given bread and meat
But would eat none,
And this one cried No No No No   5
All day long.

This one looked at the window
As though it were a wall,
This one saw things that were not there,
This one things that were,   10
And this one cried No No No No
All day long.

This one thought himself a bird,
This one a dog,
And this one thought himself a man,   15
An ordinary man,
And cried and cried No No No No
All day long.

1960

JAMES MERRILL

Watching the Dance

1. BALANCHINE'S[6]

Poor savage, doubting that a river flows
But for the myriad eddies made
By unseen powers twirling on their toes,

Here in this darkness it would seem
You had already died, and were afraid.   5
Be still. Observe the powers. Infer the stream.

2. DISCOTHÈQUE.

Having survived entirely your own youth,
Last of your generation, purple gloom
Investing you, sit, Jonah,[7] beyond speech,

And let towards the brute volume VOOM whale mouth   10
VAM pounding viscera VAM VOOM
A teenage plankton luminously twitch.

                                                          1967

GERARD MANLEY HOPKINS

Spring and Fall:

To a Young Child

Márgarét áre you gríeving
Over Goldengrove unleaving?
Leáves, líke the things of man, you
With your fresh thoughts care for, can you?
Áh! ás the heart grows older   5
It will come to such sights colder
By and by, nor spare a sigh
Though worlds of wanwood[8] leafmeal lie;
And yet you wíll weep and know why.
Now no matter, child, the name: 10
Sórrow's spríngs áre the same.
Nor mouth had, no nor mind, expressed
What heart heard of, ghost[9] guessed:
It ís the blight man was born for,
It is Margaret you mourn for.   15

1880

6. George Balanchine, Russian-born (1894) ballet choreographer and teacher.
7. According to *Jonah* 4, Jonah sat in gloom near Nineveh after its residents repented and God decided to spare the city from destruction.
8. Pale, gloomy woods. "leafmeal": broken up, leaf by leaf (analogous to "piecemeal").
9. Soul.

JAMES A. EMANUEL

Wishes, for Alix

Always searching,
may you find;
if you run-down,
may you wind;
every year   5
may you grow
reaping only
what you sow
sowing only in the seed
what will ripen into need   10
what will sweeten to the touch
seeming little, being much.

May your playmates be a song,
may your friends just skip along
laughing you into their game   15
letting you remain the same
in their hearts and on their lips
even when their fingertips
have to let you go your way—
glad they saw Alix today.   20

1985

WILLIAM SHAKESPEARE

Like as the Waves

Like as the waves make towards the pebbled shore,
So do our minutes hasten to their end,
Each changing place with that which goes before,
In sequent[1] toil all forwards do contend.[2]
Nativity,[3] once in the main[4] of light,   5
Crawls to maturity, wherewith being crowned,
Crooked[5] eclipses 'gainst his glory fight,
And Time that gave doth now his gift confound.[6]
Time doth transfix[7] the flourish set on youth
And delves the parallels[8] in beauty's brow,   10
Feeds on the rarities of nature's truth,
And nothing stands but for his scythe to mow.
And yet to times in hope[9] my verse shall stand,
Praising thy worth, despite his cruel hand.

1609

1. Successive.
2. Struggle.
3. New-born life.
4. High seas.
5. Perverse.

6. Bring to nothing.
7. Pierce.
8. Lines, wrinkles.
9. In the future.

STEPHEN SPENDER

The Express

After the first powerful, plain manifesto
The black statement of pistons, without more fuss
But gliding like a queen, she leaves the station.
Without bowing and with restrained unconcern
She passes the houses which humbly crowd outside,   5
The gasworks, and at last the heavy page
Of death, printed by gravestones in the cemetery.
Beyond the town, there lies the open country
Where, gathering speed, she acquires mystery,
The luminous self-possession of ships on ocean.   10
It is now she begins to sing—at first quite low
Then loud, and at last with a jazzy madness—
The song of her whistle screaming at curves,
Of deafening tunnels, brakes, innumerable bolts.
And always light, aerial, underneath,   15
Retreats the elate meter of her wheels.
Steaming through metal landscape on her lines,
She plunges new eras of white happiness,
Where speed throws up strange shapes, broad curves
And parallels clean like trajectories from guns.   20
At last, further than Edinburgh or Rome,
Beyond the crest of the world, she reaches night
Where only a low stream-line brightness
Of phosphorus on the tossing hills is light.
Ah, like a comet through flame, she moves entranced,   25
Wrapt in her music no bird song, no, nor bough
Breaking with honey buds, shall ever equal.

1933

MICHAEL HARPER

Dear John, Dear Coltrane

> *a love supreme, a love supreme*[1]
> *a love supreme, a love supreme*

Sex fingers toes
in the marketplace
near your father's church
in Hamlet, North Carolina—[2]

---

1. Coltrane's record of "A Love Supreme," released in 1965, represents his moment of greatest public acclaim. The record was named Record of the Year and Coltrane was named jazz musician of the year in the *Downbeat* poll.

2. Coltrane's birthplace. His family shared a house with Coltrane's grandfather, who was the minister of St. Stephen's AME Zion Church there.

witness to this love   5
in this calm fallow
of these minds,
there is no substitute for pain:
genitals gone or going,
seed burned out,   10
you tuck the roots in the earth,
turn back, and move
by river through the swamps,
singing: *a love supreme, a love supreme;*
what does it all mean?   15
Loss, so great each black
woman expects your failure
in mute change, the seed gone.
You plod up into the electric city—
your song now crystal and   20
the blues. You pick up the horn
with some will and blow
into the freezing night:
a love supreme, a love supreme—

Dawn comes and you cook   25
up the thick sin 'tween
impotence and death, fuel
the tenor sax cannibal
heart, genitals and sweat
that makes you clean—   30
a love supreme, a love supreme—

Why you so black?
cause I am
why you so funky?
cause I am   35
why you so black?
cause I am
why you so sweet?
cause I am
why you so black?   40
cause I am
a love supreme, a love supreme:

So sick
you couldn't play *Naima*,[3]
so flat we ached   45
for song you'd concealed
with your own blood,
your diseased liver gave
out its purity,
the inflated heart   50

3. Another standard Coltrane song, recorded in 1966 at the Village Vanguard.

pumps out, the tenor kiss,
tenor love:
a love supreme, a love supreme—
a love supreme, a love supreme—

1970

The Way a Poem Looks

The way a poem looks is not nearly so important as the way it sounds—usually. But there are exceptions. A few poems are written to be seen rather than heard or read aloud, and their appearance on the page is crucial to their effect. The poem *l(a,* for example (p. 687), tries to visualize typographically what the poet asks you to see in your mind's eye. Occasionally, too, poems are composed in a specific shape so that the poem looks like a physical object. At the end of this chapter, several poems—some old, some new—illustrate some of the ways in which visual effects may be created. Even though poetry has traditionally been thought of as oral—words to be said, sung, or performed rather than looked at—the idea that poems can also be related to painting and the visual arts is also an old one. Theodoric in ancient Greece is credited with inventing **technopaegnia** —that is, constructing poems with visual appeal. Once, the shaping of words to resemble an object was thought to have mystical power, but more recent attempts at **shaped verse** (the general term that may be applied to any poem that uses visual appeal dramatically) are usually playful exercises (such as Robert Hollander's *You Too? Me Too—Why Not? Soda Pop,* which is shaped like a Coke bottle), attempting to supplement (or replace) verbal meanings with devices from painting and sculpture.

Reading a poem like *Easter Wings* aloud wouldn't make much sense. Our eyes are everything for a poem like that. A more frequent poetic device is to ask us to use our eyes as a guide to sound. The following poem depends upon recognition of some standard typographical symbols and knowledge of their names. We have to say those names to read the poem:

FRANKLIN P. ADAMS

Composed in the Composing Room

At stated .ic times
I love to sit and — off rhymes
Till ,tose at last I fall
Exclaiming "I don't ∧ all."

Though I'm an ° objection
By running this in this here §

5

This 👉 of the Fleeting Hour,
This lofty -ician Tower—

A ¶er's hope dispels   10
All fear of deadly ||.
You think these [] are a pipe?
Well, not on your †eotype.

1914

We create the right term here when we verbalize, putting the visual signs together with the words or letters printed in the poem, for example making the word "periodic" out of ".ic" or "high Phoenician" out of "-ician." This, too, involves an extreme instance and involves a game more than any serious emotional effect. More often poets give us—by the visual placement of sounds—a guide to reading, inviting us to regulate the pace of our reading, notice pauses or silences, pay attention both to the syntax of the poem and to the rhetoric of the voice, thus providing us a set of stage directions for reading.

e. e. cummings

portrait

Buffalo Bill's
defunct
        who used to
        ride a watersmooth-silver
                        stallion   5
and break onetwothreefourfive pigeonsjustlikethat
                        Jesus
he was a handsome man
                        and what i want to know is
how do you like your blueeyed boy   10
Mister Death

1923

The unusual spacing of words here, with some run together and others widely separated, provides a guide to reading, regulating both speed and sense, so that the poem can capture aloud some of the excitement and wonder of a boy's enthusiasm for a theatrical act as spectacular as that of Buffalo Bill. A good reader-aloud, with only this typographical guidance, can capture some of the wide-eyed boy's responses, remembered now in retrospect long after Buffalo Bill's act is out of business and the man himself is dead.

In prose, syntax and punctuation are the main guides to the voice of a reader, providing indicators of emphasis, pace, and speed, and in poetry they are also more conventional and more common guides than extreme forms of unusual typography as in *portrait*. Reading a poem sensitively is in some ways a lot like reading a piece of prose sensitively: one has to pay close attention to the way the sentences are put together and how they are punctuated. A good reader makes use of appropriate pauses as well as thundering emphasis; silence as well as sound is part of any poem, and reading punctuation is as important as knowing how to say the words.

Beyond punctuation, the placement and spacing of lines on the page may be helpful to a reader even when that placement is not as radical as in *portrait*. The fact that poetry looks different from prose is not an accident; decisions to make lines one length instead of another have as much to do with vocal breaks and phrasing as they have to do with functions of syntax or meaning. In a good poem, there are no accidents, not even in the way the poem meets the eye, for as readers our eyes are the most direct route to our voices; they are our scanner and director, our prompter and guide.

GEORGE HERBERT

Easter Wings

Lord, who createdst man in wealth and store,[1]
Though foolishly he lost the same,
Decaying more and more,
Till he became
Most poor:
With thee
O let me rise
As larks,[2] harmoniously,
And sing this day thy victories:
Then shall the fall further the flight in me.

My tender age in sorrow did begin;
And still with sicknesses and shame
Thou didst so punish sin,
That I became
Most thin.
With thee
Let me combine,
And feel this day thy victory;
For, if I imp[3] my wing on thine,
Affliction shall advance the flight in me.

1633

1. In plenty.
2. Which herald the morning.
3. Engraft. In falconry, to engraft feathers in a damaged wing, so as to restore the powers of flight (OED).

ROBERT HERRICK

The Pillar of Fame

Fame's pillar here, at last, we set,
Out-during *Marble, Brass,* or *Jet*,[4]
Charmed and enchanted so,
As to withstand the blow
Of   overthrow:
Nor shall the seas,
Or   OUTRAGES
Of storms o'erbear
What we up-rear,
Tho Kingdoms fall,
This   pillar   never   shall
Decline   or   waste   at   all;
But stand for ever by his own
Firm and well fixed foundation.

1648

e. e. cummings

l(a

l(a

le
af
fa

ll   5

s)
one
l

iness

1958

EDWIN MORGAN

The Computer's First Christmas Card

```
        jollymerry
        hollyberry
        jollyberry
        merryholly
        happyjolly                          5
        jollyjelly
        jellybelly
        bellymerry
        hollyheppy
        jollyMolly                         10
        marryJerry
        merryHarry
        hoppyBarry
        heppyJarry
        boppyheppy                         15
        berryjorry
        jorryjolly
        moppyjelly
        Mollymerry
        Jerryjolly                         20
        bellyboppy
        jorryhoppy
        hollymoppy
        Barrymerry
        Jarryhappy                         25
        happyboppy
        boppyjolly
        jollymerry
        merrymerry
        merrymerry                         30
        merryChris
        ammerryasa
        Chrismerry
        asMERRYCHR
        YSANTHEMUM                         35
```

1968

ROBERT HOLLANDER

You Too? Me Too—Why Not?
Soda Pop

```
        I am
        look
       ing at
       the Co
       caCola
       bottle
      which is
      green wi
      th ridges
      just  like
     c     c     c
      o     o     o
     l     l     l
     u     u     u
      m     m     m
     n     n     n
      s     s     s
    and on itself it says

       COCA-COLA
       reg.u.s.pat.off.
```

exactly like an art pop
statue of that kind of
bottle but not so green
that the juice inside
gives other than the co
lor it has when I pour
it out in a clear glass
glass on this table top
(It's making me thirsty
all this winking and
beading of Hippocrene
please let me pause
drinking the fluid in)
ah! it is enticing how
each color is the same
brown in green bottle
brown in uplifted glass
making each utensil on
the table laid a brown
fork in a brown shade
making me long to watch
them harvesting the crop
which makes the deep-aged
rich brown wine of America
that is to say which makes
soda   pop

p. 1968

Most poems of more than a few lines are divided into **stanzas**, groups of lines divided from other groups by white space on the page. Putting some space between the groupings of lines has the effect of sectioning off the poem, giving its physical appearance a series of divisions that often mark breaks in thought in the poem, or changes of scenery or imagery, or other shifts in the direction of the poem. In *The Flea* (p. 606), for example, the stanza divisions mark distinctive stages in the action; between the first and second stanzas, the speaker stops his companion from killing the flea, and between the second and third stanzas, the companion follows through on her intention and kills the flea. And in *The Goose Fish* (p. 653), the stanzas mark stages in the self-perception of the lovers; each of the stanzas is a more or less distinct scene, and the stanzas unfold almost like a series of slides. Not all stanzas are quite so neatly patterned, but any poem divided into stanzas calls attention on the page to the fact of the divisions and invites some sort of response to what appear to be gaps or silences that may be structural indicators.

Historically, stanzas have most often been organized internally by patterns of rhyme, and thus stanza divisions have been a visual indicator of patterns in sound. In most traditional stanza forms, the pattern of rhyme is repeated in stanza after stanza throughout the poem, and the voice and ear become familiar with the pattern so that, in a sense, we come to depend on it. We can thus "hear" variations, just as we do in music. In a poem of more than a few stanzas, the accumulation of pattern may even mean that our ear comes to expect repetition and finds a kind of comfort in its increasing familiarity. The rhyme thus becomes an organizational device in the poem, and ordinarily the metrical patterns stay constant from stanza to stanza. In Shelley's *Ode to the West Wind,* for example, the first and third lines in each stanza rhyme, and the middle line then rhymes with the first and third lines of the next stanza. (In indicating rhyme, a different letter of the alphabet is conventionally used to represent each sound; in the following example, if we begin with "being" as *a* and "dead" as *b,* then "fleeing" is also *a,* and "red" and "bed" are *b.*)

O wild West Wind, thou breath of Autumn's being,	a
Thou, from whose unseen presence the leaves dead	b
Are driven, like ghosts from an enchanter fleeing,	a
Yellow, and black, and pale, and hectic red,	b
Pestilence-stricken multitudes: O thou,	c
Who chariotest to their dark wintry bed	b
The wingéd seeds, where they lie cold and low,	c
Each like a corpse within its grave, until	d
Thine azure sister of the Spring shall blow	c

In this stanza form, known as **terza rima,** the stanzas are thus linked to each other by a common sound: one rhyme sound from each stanza is picked up in the next stanza, and so on to the end of the group of stanzas. This stanza form is the one used by Dante in *The Divine Comedy;* its use is not all that common in English because it is a rhyme-rich stanza form—that is, it requires many, many rhymes, and English is, relatively speaking, a rhyme-poor language (that is, not so rich in rhyme possibilities as are languages such as Italian or French). One reason for this is that English words derive from so many different language families that we have fewer similar word endings than languages that have remained more "pure," more dependent for vocabulary on roots and patterns in their own language system.

Shortly, we will look at some other stanza forms, but first a brief Defense of Rhyme, or at least an explanation of its uses. Contemporary poets seldom use it, finding it neither necessary nor appealing, but until the last half century or so rhyme was central to most poems. Historically, there are good reasons for rhyme. Why have most recent poets avoided rhyme as vigorously as older poets pursued it? There is no single easy answer, but one can suggest why poetry traditionally found rhyme attractive and notice that some of those needs no longer exist. Because poetry was originally an oral art (and its texts not always written down) various kinds of **memory devices** (sometimes called **mnemonic devices**) were built into poems to help reciters remember them. Rhyme was one such device, and most people still find it easier to memorize poetry that rhymes. The simple pleasure of hearing the repetition of familiar sounds may also help to account for the traditional popularity of rhyme, and perhaps plain habit (for both poets and hearers) had a lot to do with why rhyme flourished for so many centuries as a standard expectation. No doubt, too, rhyme helped to give poetry a special quality that distinguished it from prose, a significant advantage in ages that worried about decorum and propriety and that were anxious to preserve a strong sense of poetic tradition. Some ages have been very concerned that poetry should not in any way be mistaken for prose or made to serve prosaic functions, and the literary critics and theorists in those ages made extraordinary efforts to emphasize the distinctions between poetry, which was thought to be artistically superior, and prose, which was thought to be primarily utilitarian. A pride in elitism and a fear that an expanded reading public could ultimately mean a dilution of the possibilities of traditional art forms have been powerful cultural forces in Western civilization, and if such forces were not themselves responsible for creating rhyme in poetry, they did help to preserve a sense of its necessity.

But there are at least two other reasons for rhyme. One is complex and hard to state justly without long explanations. It involves traditional ideas of the symmetrical relationship of different aspects of the world and ideas about the function of poetry to reflect the universe as human learning understood it. Most poets in earlier centuries assumed that rhyme was proper to verse, perhaps even essential. They would have felt themselves eccentric to compose poems any other way. Some poets did experiment—very successfully—with **blank verse** (that is, verse which did not rhyme but which nevertheless had strict metrical requirements), but the cultural pressure was almost constantly for rhyme. Why? Custom or habit may account for part of the assumption that rhyme was necessary, but probably not all of it. Rather, the poets' sense that poetry was an imitation of larger relationships in the universe made it seem natural to use rhyme to recreate a sense of harmony, correspondence, symmetry, and order. The sounds of poetry were thus faint reminders of the harmonious cosmos, of the music of the spheres that animated the planets, the processes of nature, the interrelationship of all created things and beings. Probably poets never said to themselves, "I shall now tunefully emulate the harmony of God's carefully ordered universe," but the tendency to use rhyme and other repetitions or re-echoings of sound (such as **alliteration** or **assonance**, defined in "A Glossary of Poetic Terms" §8) nevertheless stems ultimately from basic assumptions about how the universe worked. In a modern world increasingly perceived as fragmented, rambling, and unrelated, there is of course a much lessened tendency to testify to a sense of harmony and symmetry. It would be too easy and too mechanical to think that rhyme in a poem specifically means that the poet has a firm sense of cosmic order, and that an unrhymed poem testifies to chaos, but cultural assumptions do affect the expectations of both poets and readers, and cultural tendencies create a kind of pressure upon the individual creator.

One other reason for using rhyme is that it provides a kind of discipline for the poet, a way of harnessing poetic talents and keeping a rein on the imagination, so that the results are ordered, controlled, put into some kind of meaningful and recognizable form. Robert Frost used to be fond of saying that writing poems without rhyme was like playing tennis without a net. Writing good poetry does require a lot of discipline, and Frost speaks for many (perhaps most) traditional poets in suggesting that rhyme can be a major source of that discipline. But it is not the only possible source, and more recent poets have usually felt they would rather play by new rules or invent their own as they go along, and have therefore sought their sources of discipline elsewhere, preferring the more spare tones that unrhymed poetry provides. It is not that contemporary poets cannot think of rhyme words or that they do not care about the sounds of their poetry; rather, recent poets have consciously decided not to work with rhyme and to use instead other aural devices and other strategies for organizing stanzas, just as they have chosen to work with experimental and variable rhythms instead of writing primarily in the traditional English meters. Some few modern poets, though, have protested the abandonment of rhyme and have continued to write rhymed verse successfully in a more or less traditional way.

The amount and density of rhyme varies widely in stanza and verse forms, some requiring elaborate and intricate patterns of rhyme, others more casual or spare sound repetitions. The **Spenserian stanza,** for example, is even more rhyme rich than terza rima, using only three rhyme sounds in nine rhymed lines.

Her falt'ring hand upon the balustrade,   a
Old Angela was feeling for the stair,   b
When Madeline, St. Agnes' charméd maid,   a
Rose, like a missioned spirit, unaware: b
With silver taper's light, and pious care,   b
She turned, and down the agéd gossip led   c
To a safe level matting. Now prepare,   b
Young Porphyro, for gazing on that bed;   c
She comes, she comes again, like ring dove frayed and fled. c

On the other hand, the **ballad stanza** has only one rhyme in four lines; lines 1 and 3 in each stanza do not rhyme at all.

The king sits in Dumferling toune,   a
Drinking the blude-reid wine: b
"O whar will I get guid sailor,   c
To sail this ship of mine?"   b

Most stanzas have a metrical pattern as well as a rhyme scheme. Terza rima, for example, involves five-beat lines (iambic pentameter), and most of the Spenserian stanza (the first 8 lines) is also in iambic pentameter, but the ninth line in each stanza has one extra foot (it is iambic hexameter). The ballad stanza, also iambic as are most English stanza and verse forms, alternates three-beat and four-beat lines; lines 1 and 3 are unrhymed iambic tetrameter, and lines 2 and 4 are rhymed iambic trimeter.

Several stanza forms are exemplified in this book, most of them based on rhyme schemes, but some (such as blank verse or syllabic verse) are based entirely on meter or other measures of sound, or on some more elaborate scheme such as the measured repetition of words, as in the **sestina**, or the repetition of whole lines, as in the **villanelle.** You can probably deduce the principles involved in each of the following stanza or verse forms by looking carefully at a poem which uses it; if you have trouble, look at the definitions in "A Glossary of Poetic Terms," §9.

[Sound and Sense]	heroic couplet	p. 672
To His Coy Mistress	tetrameter couplet	p. 766
There Once Was a Spinster of Ealing	limerick	p. 676
Twilight's Last Gleaming	double dactyl	p. 676
Dirge	free verse	p. 670
from *Paradise Lost*	blank verse	p. 629
Fern Hill	syllabic verse	p. 867
Do Not Go Gentle	villanelle	p. 866

What are stanza forms good for? What use is it to recognize them? Why do poets bother? Matters discussed in this chapter so far have suggested two reasons: 1. Breaks between stanzas provide convenient pauses for reader and writer, something roughly equivalent to paragraphs in prose. The eye thus picks up the places where some kind of pause or break occurs. 2. Poets sometimes use stanza forms, as they do rhyme itself, as a discipline: writing in a certain kind of stanza form imposes a shape on their act of imagination. To suggest some other uses, we will look in more detail at one particular verse form, the **sonnet**. A sonnet has only a single stanza and offers several related possibilities for its rhyme scheme, but it is always fourteen lines long and usually written in iambic pentameter. The sonnet has remained a popular verse form in English for more than four centuries, and even in an age that largely rejects rhyme it continues to attract a variety of poets, including (curiously) radical and even revolutionary poets who find its firm structure very useful. Its uses, although quite varied, can be illustrated fairly precisely.

As a verse form, the sonnet is contained, compact, demanding; whatever it does, it must do concisely and quickly. To be effective, it must take advantage of the possibilities inherent in its shortness and its relative rigidity. It is best suited to intensity of feeling and concentration of expression. Not too surprisingly, one subject it frequently discusses is confinement itself.

WILLIAM WORDSWORTH

Nuns Fret Not

Nuns fret not at their convent's narrow room; a
And hermits are contented with their cells; b
And students with their pensive citadels; b
Maids at the wheel, the weaver at his loom, a
Sit blithe and happy; bees that soar for bloom, a   5
High as the highest Peak of Furness-fells,[1] b
Will murmur by the hour in foxglove bells:[2] b
In truth the prison, unto which we doom a
Ourselves, no prison is: and hence for me, c
In sundry moods, 'twas pastime to be bound d   10
Within the sonnet's scanty plot of ground; d
Pleased if some souls (for such there needs must be) c
Who have felt the weight of too much liberty, c
Should find brief solace there, as I have found. d

1807

1. Mountains in England's Lake District, where Wordsworth lived.

2. Flowers from which digitalis (a heart medicine) began to be made in 1799.

Most sonnets are structured according to one of two principles of division. On one principle, the sonnet divides into three units of four lines each and a final unit of two lines. On the other, the fundamental break is between the first eight lines (called an octave) and the last six (called a sestet). The 4-4-4-2 sonnet is usually called the **English** or **Shakespearean sonnet,** and ordinarily its rhyme scheme reflects the structure: the scheme of *abab cdcd efef gg* is the classic one, but many variations from that pattern still reflect the basic 4-4-4-2 division. The 8-6 sonnet is usually called the **Italian** or **Petrarchan sonnet** (the Italian poet Petrarch was an early master of this structure), and its "typical" rhyme scheme is *abbaabba cdecde,* although it too produces many variations that still reflect the basic division into two parts.

The two kinds of sonnet structures are useful for two different sorts of argument. The 4-4-4-2 structure works very well for constructing a poem that wants to make a three-step argument (with a quick summary at the end), or for setting up brief, cumulative images. *That Time of Year* (p. 633), for example, uses the 4-4-4-2 structure to mark the progressive steps toward death and the parting of friends by using three distinct images, then summarizing. Shakespeare's *Let Me Not to the Marriage of True Minds* (p. 548) works very similarly, following the kind of organization that in Chapter 7 I called the 1-2-3 structure—and doing it compactly and economically.

Here, on the other hand, is a poem which uses the 8-6 pattern:

HENRY CONSTABLE

My Lady's Presence Makes the Roses Red

My lady's presence makes the roses red
Because to see her lips they blush for shame.
The lily's leaves, for envy, pale became,
And her white hands in them this envy bred.
The marigold the leaves abroad doth spread   5
Because the sun's and her power is the same.
The violet of purple color came,
Dyed in the blood she made my heart to shed.
In brief, all flowers from her their virtue take;
From her sweet breath their sweet smells do proceed;   10
The living heat which her eyebeams doth make
Warmeth the ground and quickeneth the seed.
The rain wherewith she watereth the flowers
Falls from mine eyes, which she dissolves in showers.

1594

Here, the first eight lines argue that the lady's presence is responsible for the color of all of nature's flowers, and the final six lines summarize and extend that argument to smells and heat—and finally to the rain that the lady draws from the speaker's eyes. That kind of two-part structure, in which the octave states a proposition or generalization and the sestet provides a particularization or application of it, has a variety of uses. The final lines may, for example, reverse the first eight and achieve a paradox or irony in the poem, or the poem may *nearly* balance two comparable arguments. Basically, the 8-6 structure lends itself to poems with two points to make, or to those which wish to make one fairly brief point and illustrate it.

Sometimes the neat and precise structure I have described is altered—either slightly, as in *Nuns Fret Not* above (where the 8-6 structure is more of an 8½-5½ structure) or more radically as particular needs or effects may demand. And the two basic structures certainly do not define all the structural possibilities within a fourteen-line poem, even if they do suggest the most traditional ways of taking advantage of the sonnet's compact and well-kept container.

The sonnets here by Sidney, Shakespeare, and Constable survive from a golden age of sonnet writing in the late 16th century, an age that set the pattern for expectations of form, subject matter, and tone. The sonnet came to England from Italy via France, and imitations of Petrarch's famous sonnet sequence to Laura became the rage. Thousands upon thousands of sonnets were written in those years, often in sequences of a hundred or more sonnets each; the sequences explored the many moods of love and usually had a light thread of narrative that purported to recount a love affair between the poet and a mistress who was almost always golden-haired, beautiful, disdainful, and inaccessible. Her beauty was described in a series of exaggerated comparisons: her eyes were like the sun (*When Nature Made Her Chief Work, Stella's Eyes*), her teeth like pearls, her cheeks like roses, her skin like ivory, and so on, but the adherence to these conventions was always playful, and it became a game of wit to play variations upon expectations (*My Lady's Presence Makes the Roses Red* and *My Mistress' Eyes Are Nothing Like the Sun*). Almost always teasing and witty, these poems were probably not as true to life as they pretended, but they provided historically an expectation of what sonnets were to be.

Many modern sonnets continue to be about love or private life, and many continue to use a personal, apparently open and sincere tone. But poets often find the sonnet's compact form and rigid demands equally useful for many varieties of subject, theme, and tone. Besides love, sonnets often treat other subjects: politics, philosophy, discovery of a new world. And tones vary widely too, from the anger and remorse of *Th' Expense of Spirit* (p. 856) and righteous outrage of *On the Late Massacre in Piedmont* (p. 699) to the tender awe of *How Do I Love Thee* (p. 536). Many poets seem to take the kind of comfort Wordsworth describes in the careful limits of the form, finding in its two basic variations (the English sonnet such as *My Mistress' Eyes* and the Italian sonnet such as *On First Looking*) a sufficiency of convenient ways to organize their materials into coherent structures.

WILLIAM WORDSWORTH

Scorn Not the Sonnet

Scorn not the Sonnet; Critic, you have frowned,
Mindless of its just honors; with this key
Shakespeare unlocked his heart; the melody
Of this small lute gave ease to Petrarch's[3] wound;
A thousand times this pipe did Tasso sound;   5
With it Camoëns soothed an exile's grief;
The Sonnet glittered a gray myrtle leaf
Amid the cypress with which Dante crowned
His visionary brow: a glow-worm lamp,
It cheered mild Spenser, called from Faeryland   10
To struggle through dark ways; and when a damp
Fell round the path of Milton, in his hand
The Thing became a trumpet; whence he blew
Soul-animating strains—alas, too few!

1827

JOHN KEATS

On the Sonnet   *Variation*

If by dull rhymes our English must be chained,
And like Andromeda,[4] the sonnet sweet
Fettered, in spite of painéd loveliness,
Let us find, if we must be constrained,
Sandals more interwoven and complete   5
To fit the naked foot of Poesy;[5]
Let us inspect the lyre, and weigh the stress
Of every chord,[6] and see what may be gained
By ear industrious, and attention meet;
Misers of sound and syllable, no less   10
Than Midas[7] of his coinage, let us be
Jealous[8] of dead leaves in the bay-wreath crown;[9]
So, if we may not let the Muse be free,
She will be bound with garlands of her own.

1819

3. Petrarch (1304–1374), Italian poet, was the model for English Renaissance sonneteers. The other poets named by Wordsworth—the Italians Tasso and Dante. the Portuguese Camoëns, and the English Shakespeare, Spenser, and Milton—also wrote sonnets extensively.
4. Who, according to Greek myth, was chained to a rock so that she would be devoured by a sea monster. She was rescued by Perseus, who married her. When she died she was placed among the stars.
5. In a letter which contained this sonnet, Keats expressed impatience with the traditional Petrarchan and Shakespearean sonnet forms: "I have been endeavoring to discover a better sonnet stanza than we have."
6. Lyre-string.
7. The legendary king of Phrygia who asked, and got, the power to turn all he touched to gold.
8. Suspiciously watchful.
9. The bay tree was sacred to Apollo, god of poetry, and bay wreaths came to symbolize true poetic achievement. The withering of the bay tree is sometimes considered an omen of death.

PERCY BYSSHE SHELLEY

Ozymandias[1]

I met a traveler from an antique land
Who said: Two vast and trunkless legs of stone
Stand in the desert. . . . Near them, on the sand,
Half sunk, a shattered visage lies, whose frown,
And wrinkled lip, and sneer of cold command,   5
Tell that its sculptor well those passions read
Which yet survive, stamped on these lifeless things,
The hand that mocked them, and the heart that fed:
And on the pedestal these words appear:
"My name is Ozymandias, King of Kings: 10
Look on my works, ye Mighty, and despair!"
Nothing beside remains. Round the decay
Of that colossal wreck, boundless and bare
The lone and level sands stretch far away.

1818

WILLIAM WORDSWORTH

London, 1802

Milton! thou should'st be living at this hour:
England hath need of thee: she is a fen[2]
Of stagnant waters: altar, sword, and pen,
Fireside, the heroic wealth of hall and bower,
Have forfeited their ancient English dower[3]   5
Of inward happiness. We are selfish men;
Oh! raise us up, return to us again;
And give us manners, virtue, freedom, power.
Thy soul was like a star, and dwelt apart:
Thou hadst a voice whose sound was like the sea: 10
Pure as the naked heavens, majestic, free,
So didst thou travel on life's common way,
In cheerful godliness; and yet thy heart
The lowliest duties on herself did lay.

1802

1. The Greek name for Rameses II, 13th-century B.C. pharaoh of Egypt. According to a first century B.C. Greek historian, Diodorus Siculus, the largest statue in Egypt was inscribed: "I am Ozymandias, king of kings; if anyone wishes to know what I am and where I lie, let him surpass me in some of my exploits."
2. Marsh.
3. Inheritance.

JOHN MILTON

On the Late Massacre in Piedmont[4]

Avenge, O Lord, thy slaughtered saints, whose bones
Lie scattered on the Alpine mountains cold;
Ev'n them who kept thy truth so pure of old,
When all our fathers worshiped stocks and stones,
Forget not: in thy book record their groans   5
Who were thy sheep, and in their ancient fold
Slain by the bloody Piedmontese, that rolled
Mother with infant down the rocks. Their moans
The vales redoubled to the hills, and they
To Heav'n. Their martyred blood and ashes sow   10
O'er all th' Italian fields, where still doth sway
The triple Tyrant:[5] that from these may grow
A hundredfold who, having learnt thy way,
Early may fly the Babylonian woe.[6]

1655

JAMES AGEE

We Soldiers of All Nations Who Lie Killed

We soldiers of all nations who lie killed
Ask little: that you never, in our name,
Dare claim we died that men might be fulfilled.
The earth should vomit us, against that shame.

We died; is that enough? Many died well,   5
Of both sides; most of us died senselessly.
Ask soldiers who outlived us; they may tell
How many died to make men slaves, or free.

We died. None knew, few tried to guess, just why.
No one knows now, on either side the grave.   10
If you insist you know, by all means try,
That being your trade, to make the knowledge save.

But never use, not as you honor sorrow,
Our murdered days to garnish your tomorrow.

1945

4. On Easter Sunday, 1655, the Duke of
Savoy's forces massacred 1700 members of
the Waldensian sect in the Piedmont in
northwestern Italy. The sect, founded in
1170, existed at first within the Roman
Catholic Church, but its vigorous con-
demnation of church rites and policies
(especially of the use of icons—see line 4)
led to a total break. Until the year of the
massacre the group had been allowed freedom of worship.
5. The Pope's tiara has three crowns.
6. Protestants in Milton's day associated
Catholicism with Babylonian decadence,
called the church "the whore of Babylon,"
and read the prophecy of *Revelation* 17
and 18 as an allegory of its coming destruction.

GWENDOLYN BROOKS

First Fight. Then Fiddle.

First fight. Then fiddle. Ply the slipping string
With feathery sorcery; muzzle the note
With hurting love; the music that they wrote
Bewitch, bewilder. Qualify to sing
Threadwise. Devise no salt, no hempen thing   5
For the dear instrument to bear. Devote
The bow to silks and honey. Be remote
A while from malice and from murdering.
But first to arms, to armor. Carry hate
In front of you and harmony behind.   10
Be deaf to music and to beauty blind.
Win war. Rise bloody, maybe not too late
For having first to civilize a space
Wherein to play your violin with grace.

1949

SIR PHILIP SIDNEY

When Nature Made Her Chief Work, Stella's Eyes[7]

When Nature made her chief work, Stella's eyes,[8]
In color black[9] why wrapped she beams so bright?
Would she in beamy black, like painter wise,
Frame daintiest luster mixed of shades and light?
Or did she else that sober hue devise,   5
In object best to knit and strength our sight,
Lest if no veil those brave gleams did disguise,
They sunlike should more dazzle than delight?
Or would she her miraculous power show,
That, whereas black seems Beauty's contrary,   10
She even in black doth make all beauties flow?
Both so and thus: she, minding[1] Love should be
Placed ever there, gave him this mourning weed
To honor all their deaths who for her bleed.

1582

---

7. From Sidney's sonnet sequence, *As-trophel and Stella,* usually credited with having started the vogue of sonnet sequences in Elizabethan England.

8. Following Petrarch's lead, Sidney and other English sonneteers developed a series of exaggerated conventions to describe the physical features of the women they cele-brated. The excessive brightness of the eyes—almost always compared favorably with the sun's brightness—was an expected feature.

9. Black was frequently used in the Renaissance to mean absence of light, and ugly or foul (see line 10).

1. Remembering that.

WILLIAM SHAKESPEARE

My Mistress' Eyes Are Nothing like the Sun [2]

My mistress' eyes are nothing like the sun;
Coral is far more red than her lips' red;
If snow be white, why then her breasts are dun; [3]
If hairs be wires, black wires grow on her head. [4]
I have seen roses damasked [5] red and white,   5
But no such roses see I in her cheeks;
And in some perfumes is there more delight
Than in the breath that from my mistress reeks.
I love to hear her speak, yet well I know
That music hath a far more pleasing sound;   10
I grant I never saw a goddess go; [6]
My mistress, when she walks, treads on the ground.
And yet, by heaven, I think my love as rare
As any she belied with false compare.

1609

DIANE ACKERMAN

Sweep Me Through Your Many-Chambered Heart

Sweep me through your many-chambered heart
if you like, or leave me here, flushed
amid the sap-ooze and blossom: one more dish
in the banquet called April, or think me hard-
won all your days full of women. Weeks   5
later, still I felt your arms around
me like a shackle, heard all the sundown
wizardries the fired body speaks.
Tell me why, if it was no more than this,
the unmuddled tumble, the renegade kiss,   10
today, rapt in a still life and unaware,
my paintbrush dropped like an amber hawk;
thinking I'd heard your footfall on the stair,
I listened, heartwise, for the knock.

1978

2. See Sidney's "When Nature Made Her Chief Work, Stella's Eyes," and notes.
3. Mouse-colored.
4. Women in traditional sonnets have hair of gold. Many poets who use the Petrarchan conventions also wrote poems which teased or deflated the conventions.
5. Variegated.
6. Walk.

Context

10 THE AUTHOR'S WORK

Poems are not all written in the same style, as if they were produced by a corporation or put together in a committee. Just as every human individual is unique and has a distinct personality, every poet leaves a distinctive stamp on his or her work. Even though all poets share the same material (language) and usually have some common notions of their craft, they put the unique resources of their individual minds and consciousnesses into what they create. A poet may use the tradition extensively and share the crafts that others have developed without surrendering his or her own individuality, just as the integrity and uniqueness of an individual is not compromised by characteristics the individual may share with others—political affiliations, religious beliefs, tastes in clothes and music. Sometimes the uniqueness is hard to define—what exactly is it that defines the unique personality of an individual?—but it is always there, and the recognition of the distinctive quality is a large part of what we depend upon in our relationship with other people. And so with poets: most poets don't make a conscious effort to put an individual stamp on their work; they don't have to. The stamp is there, just in the way they choose subjects, words, configurations. Every individual's consciousness is unique, and that consciousness uniquely marks what it records, imagines, and decides to print.

Experienced readers can often identify a poem as the distinctive work of an individual poet even though they may never have seen the poem before. That may surprise you, but it is a lot like identifying a particular singer or group after hearing only a few phrases of a new song. Such an ability depends upon experience—a lot of reading of that author, or a lot of listening to music—but any reasonably sensitive reader can learn to do it with great accuracy. Developing such an ability, however, is not really an end in itself; rather, it is a by-product of learning to notice the particular, distinctive qualities in the workmanship of any poet. Once you've read several poems by a particular poet, you will usually begin to notice some features that the poems have in common, and gradually you may come to think of those features as characteristic. The poem that follows was written by Howard Nemerov, whose work you have read in some earlier chapters. Before you read it, you may want to look back at his poems printed earlier in this book and remind yourself of what those poems were like (*The Vacuum*, p. 543 and *The Goose Fish*, p. 653). Three other poems by Nemerov (*Boom!* p. 841; *Epigram: Political Reflexion*, p. 842; and *Life Cycle of the Common Man*, (p. 842) appear in the anthology at the back.

HOWARD NEMEROV

A Way of Life

It's been going on a long time.
For instance, these two guys, not saying much, who slog
Through sun and sand, fleeing the scene of their crime,
Till one turns, without a word, and smacks
His buddy flat with the flat of an axe,   5
Which cuts down on the dialogue
Some, but is viewed rather as normal than sad
By me, as I wait for the next ad.

It seems to me it's been quite a while
Since the last vision of blonde loveliness   10
Vanished, her shampoo and shower and general style
Replaced by this lean young lunk-
head parading along with a gun in his back to confess
How yestereve, being drunk
And in a state of existential despair,   15
He beat up his grandma and pawned her invalid chair.

But here at last is a pale beauty
Smoking a filter beside a mountain stream,
Brief interlude, before the conflict of love and duty
Gets moving again, as sheriff and posse expound,   20
Between jail and saloon, the American Dream
Where Justice, after considerable horsing around,
Turns out to be Mercy; when the villain is knocked off,
A kindly uncle offers syrup for my cough.

And now these clean-cut athletic types   25
In global hats are having a nervous debate
As they stand between their individual rocket ships
Which have landed, appropriately, on some rocks
Somewhere in Space, in an atmosphere of hate
Where one tells the other to pull up his socks   30
And get going, he doesn't say where; they fade,
And an angel food cake flutters in the void.

I used to leave now and again;
No more. A lot of violence in American life
These days, mobsters and cops all over the scene.   35
But there's a lot of love, too, mixed with the strife,
And kitchen-kindness, like a bedtime story
With rich food and a more kissable depilatory.
Still, I keep my weapons handy, sitting here
Smoking and shaving and drinking the dry beer.

1967

What does this poem have in common with Nemerov's other poems? The concern with contemporary life, the tendency to concentrate on modern conveniences and luxuries, and the interest in isolating and defining aspects of the distinctively modern sensibility are all characteristic of Nemerov, and so is the tendency to create a short drama, with a speaker who is not altogether admirable. Several of Nemerov's other poems also share an attitude that seems deeply imbedded in this poem, a kind of anti-romanticism that emerges when someone tries to sound or feel *too* proud or cheerful and is shown, by events in the poem, to be part of a grimmer reality instead. The concentration upon one or more physical objects is also characteristic, and often (as in *The Vacuum*) the main object is a mechanical one that symbolizes modernity and our modern dependency on things rather than our concern with human relationships. Americanness is made emphatic here too, as if the poem were concerned to help us define our culture and its habits and values. The mood of loneliness is also characteristic, and so is the poem's witty conversational style. The verbal wit here, although not as prominent as the puns and double-entendres of *Boom!* and *Life Cycle*, is characteristically informal. Often it seems to derive from the language of commercials and street speech, and the undercutting of this language by the poet—having a paranoid and simple-minded speaker talk about a gangster in "a state of existential despair"—is similar to the strategy of *Boom!* or *The Vacuum*. The regular stanzas, rhymed but not in a traditional or regular way and with a number of near-rhymes, are also typical. Nemerov's thematic interests and ideas, his verbal style, and his cast of mind are all plainly visible in *A Way of Life*.

Noticing common features does not mean that every poem by a particular author will be predictable and contain all these features. Most poets like to experiment with new subjects, tones, forms, and various kinds of poetic strategies and devices. But the way of approach—the distinct stamp imposed by a unique consciousness—is likely to be visible anyway. The work of any writer will have certain *tendencies* that are identifiable, although not every single tendency will show up in any one poem.

Of what practical use is it to notice the distinctive voice and mind of a particular poet? One use (not the most important one for the casual reader, but one that nonetheless gives pleasure) is the pleasant surprise that occurs when you recognize something familiar. Reading a new poem by a poet with whom you are already familiar is a bit like meeting an old friend whose face or conversation reminds you of experiences you have had together. Poetic friendships can be treasures just as personal friendships are, even though they are necessarily more distant and somewhat more abstract. Just as novelty—meeting something or someone altogether new to you—is one kind of pleasure, so revisiting or recalling the familiar is another, its equal and opposite. Just *knowing* and *recognizing* often feel good—in and for themselves.

But there are other reasons, also, to look at the various works of a single writer. Just as you learn from watching other people—seeing how they react and respond to people and events, observing how they cope with their lives—you also learn from watching poets at work, seeing how they learn and develop, how they change their minds about things, how they discover the reach and limits of their minds and talents, how they find their distinctive voices and come to terms with their own identities. Watching someone at work over a period of years (as you can Adrienne Rich in the selection at the end of this chapter) is a little like watching an autobiography unfold, except that the individual poems continue to exist separately and for themselves as well as provide a record of a distinctive but gradually changing and evolving consciousness.

A third reason to study in some detail the work of a single individual is a very practical one: the more you know about the poet, the better a reader you are likely to be of any individual poem by that poet. It is not so much that the external facts of a writer's life find their way into whatever he or she writes—a poem or essay, as well as a letter or an autobiography—but that a reader gets used to habits and manners, of knowing what to expect. Coming to a new poem by a poet you already know is not completely an experience fresh and new. You adjust faster, know better what to look for, have some specific expectations (although they may be unconscious and unarticulated) of what the poem will be like. The more poems you read by any author, the better a reader you are likely to be of any one poem.

Before you read the following poem by John Donne, look at the poems by him that appear elsewhere in this book: *Death Be Not Proud* (p. 813), *Song* (p. 813), *The Flea* (p. 606), *A Valediction: Forbidding Mourning* (p. 617), *Batter My Heart* (p. 638), and *The Canonization* (p. 811). What features in these poems seem most striking and distinctive to you as you review them as a group?

JOHN DONNE

The Sun Rising

Busy old fool, unruly sun,
        Why dost thou thus,
Through windows, and through curtains, call on us?
Must to thy motions lovers' seasons run?
        Saucy pedantic wretch, go chide   5
        Late schoolboys, and sour prentices,[1]
    Go tell court-huntsmen that the king will ride,
    Call country ants[2] to harvest offices;
Love, all alike, no season knows, nor clime,
Nor hours, days, months, which are the rags of time.   10

        Thy beams, so reverend and strong
        Why shouldst thou think?
I could eclipse and cloud them with a wink,
But that I would not lose her sight so long:

1. Apprentices.   2. Farmworkers.

If her eyes have not blinded thine,   15
Look, and tomorrow late, tell me
Whether both the Indias³ of spice and mine
Be where thou left'st them, or lie here with me.
Ask for those kings whom thou saw'st yesterday,
And thou shalt hear, all here in one bed lay.   20

She is all states, and all princes I,
Nothing else is.
Princes do but play us; compared to this,
All honor's mimic,⁴ all wealth alchemy.⁵
Thou, sun, art half as happy as we,   25
In that the world's contracted thus;
Thine age asks⁶ ease, and since thy duties be
To warm the world, that's done in warming us.
Shine here to us, and thou art every where;
This bed thy center⁷ is, these walls thy sphere.   30

1633

Was *The Sun Rising* somewhat easier to read than the first Donne poem you read this term? What kind of expectations did you have of the poem, knowing it was by the same author as other poems you had read? How conscious were you of those expectations? Did those expectations enable you to ask more intelligent questions of the poem as you read it? How conscious were you, as you read, of the subject matter of other Donne poems? of their themes? tone? style? form? sound effects? of other poetic devices? Did you consciously expect a speaker and a dramatic situation? How quickly did you decide what the situation was? How quickly did you identify the setting? Did you find that you had certain expectations of the speaker once you had sensed the poem's subject and situation? In retrospect, how similar to other Donne poems does this one seem? In what specific ways?

The skills involved here are progressive: they don't come all at once like a flash of lightning. Rather, they develop over time, as do most of the more sophisticated reading skills we will be considering in the final chapters of this book, and they develop in conjunction with skills you have already worked on in the previous chapters. Don't worry if you still have difficulty with a new Donne poem. You are in good company: Donne isn't easy. But the more you read, the better you will get. Reading ten or a dozen poems by a single author is better than reading three or four, not only because your generalizations and the expectations they create will be more reliable but also because you will feel increasingly comfortable. Spending some hours in the library reading several new poems by a poet you like and admire can be a very satisfying experience: work with any author long enough, and you will begin to feel positively at home. But even

3. The East and West Indies, commercial sources of spices and gold.
4. Hypocritical.
5. Imposture, like the "scientific" procedures for turning base metals into gold.
6. Requires.
7. Of orbit.

then, a good poet will still surprise you in every new poem, at least to some extent. Being reliable and distinctive is not the same as being totally predictable.

The two groups of poems that follow indicate both the distinctiveness of an individual poet's voice and the variety that often exists within that distinctiveness. The poems by John Keats suggest the pervasive sensuous and sensual quality of his work, his fascination with medieval times and gothic states of mind, his attraction both to nature and to highly ornate artifices, his distinctive patterns of phrasing and use of poetic devices, and the recurrent contrasts in his work between an external world of "objective" reality and internal states of "subjective" consciousness. Prose selections from a preface and from several of Keats's personal letters underscore some of his most persistent poetic and personal concerns. The poems are arranged chronologically, and a chronology of his life suggests the potential relevance of biographical information.

Adrienne Rich's distinctive poetic voice also emerges from the representative selection here, but the corpus of her work also illustrates change and development. Rich herself describes these changes in the prose selections and in notes appended to *Snapshots of a Daughter-in-Law, Orion,* and *Planetarium.* You may also want to look back at what Rich has said about *Aunt Jennifer's Tigers* (p. 572).

JOHN KEATS

On First Looking into Chapman's Homer [8]

Much have I traveled in the realms of gold,
And many goodly states and kingdoms seen;
Round many western islands have I been
Which bards in fealty [9] to Apollo hold.
Oft of one wide expanse had I been told   5
That deep-browed Homer ruled as his demesne; [1]
Yet did I never breathe its pure serene [2]
Till I heard Chapman speak out loud and bold:
Then felt I like some watcher of the skies
When a new planet swims into his ken; [3]   10
Or like stout Cortez [4] when with eagle eyes
He stared at the Pacific—and all his men
Looked at each other with a wild surmise—
Silent, upon a peak in Darien.

1816

8. Chapman's were among the most famous Renaissance translations; his *Iliad* was completed in 1611, *The Odyssey* in 1616. Keats wrote the sonnet after being led to Chapman by his former teacher and reading *The Iliad* all night long.
9. Literally, the loyalty owed by a vas-sal to his feudal lord. Apollo was the Greek and Roman god of poetry and music.
1. Estate, feudal possession.
2. Atmosphere.
3. Range of vision.
4. Actually, Balboa; he first viewed the Pacific from Darien, in Panama.

On the Grasshopper and the Cricket

The poetry of earth is never dead:
When all the birds are faint with the hot sun,
And hide in cooling trees, a voice will run
From hedge to hedge about the new-mown mead;
That is the grasshopper's—he takes the lead   5
In summer luxury—he has never done
With his delights; for when tired out with fun
He rests at ease beneath some pleasant weed.
The poetry of earth is ceasing never:
On a lone winter evening, when the frost   10
Has wrought a silence, from the stove there shrills
The cricket's song, in warmth increasing ever,
And seems to one in drowsiness half lost,
The grasshopper's among some grassy hills.

December 30, 1816

When I Have Fears

When I have fears that I may cease to be
Before my pen has gleaned my teeming brain,
Before high-piléd books, in charact'ry,
Hold like rich garners the full-ripened grain;
When I behold, upon the night's starred face,   5
Huge cloudy symbols of a high romance,
And think that I may never live to trace
Their shadows, with the magic hand of chance;
And when I feel, fair creature of an hour!
That I shall never look upon thee more,   10
Never have relish in the faery power
Of unreflecting love!—then on the shore
Of the wide world I stand alone, and think
Till Love and Fame to nothingness do sink.

1818

Bright Star

Bright star! would I were steadfast as thou art—
    Not in lone splendor hung aloft the night
And watching, with eternal lids apart,
    Like nature's patient, sleepless Eremite,[5]
The moving waters at their priestlike task   5
    Of pure ablution round earth's human shores,
Or gazing on the new soft fallen mask
    Of snow upon the mountains and the moors—
No—yet still steadfast, still unchangeable,

---

5. Religious hermit.

Pillowed upon my fair love's ripening breast,   10
To feel for ever its soft fall and swell,
  Awake for ever in a sweet unrest,
Still, still to hear her tender-taken breath,
And so live ever—or else swoon to death.

1819

La Belle Dame sans Merci[6]

A Ballad
(original version)

O what can ail thee, knight-at-arms,
  Alone and palely loitering?
The sedge has withered from the lake,
  And no birds sing.

O what can ail thee, knight-at-arms,   5
  So haggard and so woe-begone?
The squirrel's granary is full,
  And the harvest's done.

I see a lily on thy brow,
  With anguish moist and fever dew,   10
And on thy cheeks a fading rose
  Fast withereth too.

I met a lady in the meads,[7]
  Full beautiful—a faery's child,
Her hair was long, her foot was light,   15
  And her eyes were wild.

I made a garland for her head,
  And bracelets too, and fragrant zone;[8]
She looked at me as she did love,
  And made sweet moan.   20

I set her on my pacing steed,
  And nothing else saw all day long,
For sidelong would she bend, and sing
  A faery's song.

She found me roots of relish sweet,   25
  And honey wild, and manna dew,
And sure in language strange she said,
  "I love thee true."

6. "The beautiful lady without pity."   Chartier.
The title (but not the subject matter) de-   7. Meadows.
rives from a medieval poem by Alain   8. Girdle.

She took me to her elfin grot,
    And there she wept, and sighed full sore,   30
And there I shut her wild wild eyes
    With kisses four.

And there she lulléd me asleep,
    And there I dreamed—Ah! woe betide!
The latest[9] dream I ever dreamed   35
    On the cold hill side.

I saw pale kings and princes too,
    Pale warriors, death-pale were they all;
They cried—"La Belle Dame sans Merci
    Hath thee in thrall!"   40

I saw their starved lips in the gloam,
    With horrid warning gapéd wide,
And I awoke and found me here,
    On the cold hill's side.

And this is why I sojourn here,   45
    Alone and palely loitering,
Though the sedge has withered from the lake,
    And no birds sing.

April, 1819

Ode to a Nightingale

I

My heart aches, and a drowsy numbness pains
    My sense, as though of hemlock[1] I had drunk,
Or emptied some dull opiate to the drains
    One minute past, and Lethe-wards[2] had sunk:
'Tis not through envy of thy happy lot,   5
    But being too happy in thine happiness,
        That thou, light-wingéd Dryad[3] of the trees,
        In some melodious plot
    Of beechen green, and shadows numberless,
        Singest of summer in full-throated ease.   10

II

O, for a draught of vintage! that hath been
    Cooled a long age in the deep-delvéd earth,
Tasting of Flora[4] and the country green,
    Dance, and Provençal song,[5] and sunburnt mirth!
O for a beaker full of the warm South,   15

9. Last.
1. A poisonous drug.
2. Toward the river of forgetfulness
(Lethe) in Hades.
3. Wood nymph.

4. Roman goddess of flowers.
5. The medieval troubadors of Provence
(in southern France) were famous for their
love songs.

Full of the true, the blushful Hippocrene,[6]
  With beaded bubbles winking at the brim,
    And purple-stainéd mouth;
  That I might drink, and leave the world unseen,
    And with thee fade away into the forest dim: 20

III

Fade far away, dissolve, and quite forget
  What thou among the leaves hast never known,
The weariness, the fever, and the fret
  Here, where men sit and hear each other groan;
Where palsy shakes a few, sad, last gray hairs,   25
  Where youth grows pale, and specter-thin, and dies;
    Where but to think is to be full of sorrow
      And leaden-eyed despairs,
  Where Beauty cannot keep her lustrous eyes,
    Or new Love pine at them beyond tomorrow.   30

IV

Away! away! for I will fly to thee,
  Not charioted by Bacchus and his pards,[7]
But on the viewless wings of Poesy,
  Though the dull brain perplexes and retards:
Already with thee! tender is the night,   35
  And haply the Queen-Moon is on her throne,
    Clustered around by all her starry Fays;[8]
      But here there is no light,
  Save what from heaven is with the breezes blown
    Through verdurous glooms and winding mossy ways.   40

V

I cannot see what flowers are at my feet,
  Nor what soft incense hangs upon the boughs,
But, in embalméd[9] darkness, guess each sweet
  Wherewith the seasonable month endows
The grass, the thicket, and the fruit-tree wild;   45
  White hawthorn, and the pastoral eglantine;[1]
    Fast fading violets covered up in leaves;
      And mid-May's eldest child,
  The coming musk-rose, full of dewy wine,
    The murmurous haunt of flies on summer eves.   50

VI

Darkling[2] I listen; and, for many a time
  I have been half in love with easeful Death,
Called him soft names in many a muséd rhyme,
  To take into the air my quiet breath;

6. The fountain of the Muses on Mt. Helicon, whose waters bring poetic inspiration.
7. The Roman god of wine was sometimes portrayed in a chariot drawn by leopards. "viewless": invisible.
8. Fairies.
9. Fragrant, aromatic.
1. Sweetbriar or honeysuckle.
2. In the dark.

Now more than ever seems it rich to die,   55
   To cease upon the midnight with no pain,
     While thou art pouring forth thy soul abroad
       In such an ecstasy!
   Still wouldst thou sing, and I have ears in vain—
     To thy high requiem become a sod.   60

VII

Thou wast not born for death, immortal Bird!
   No hungry generations tread thee down;
The voice I hear this passing night was heard
   In ancient days by emperor and clown:
Perhaps the selfsame song that found a path   65
   Through the sad heart of Ruth,[3] when, sick for home,
     She stood in tears amid the alien corn;
       The same that ofttimes hath
Charmed magic casements, opening on the foam
   Of perilous seas, in faery lands forlorn.   70

VIII

Forlorn! the very word is like a bell
   To toll me back from thee to my sole self!
Adieu! the fancy cannot cheat so well
   As she is famed to do, deceiving elf.
Adieu! adieu! thy plaintive anthem fades   75
   Past the near meadows, over the still stream,
     Up the hillside; and now 'tis buried deep
       In the next valley-glades:
Was it a vision, or a waking dream?
     Fled is that music:—Do I wake or sleep?   80

May, 1819

Ode on a Grecian Urn

I

Thou still unravished bride of quietness,
   Thou foster-child of silence and slow time,
Sylvan[4] historian, who canst thus express
   A flowery tale more sweetly than our rhyme:
What leaf-fringed legend haunts about thy shape   5
   Of deities or mortals, or of both,
     In Tempe or the dales of Arcady?[5]
What men or gods are these? What maidens loath?
    What mad pursuit? What struggle to escape?
     What pipes and timbrels? What wild ecstasy?   10

---

3. A virtuous Moabite widow who, according to the Old Testament *Book of Ruth*, found a husband while gleaning in the wheat fields of Judah.
4. Rustic. The urn depicts a woodland scene.

5. Arcadia. Tempe is a beautiful valley near Mt. Olympus in Greece, and the valley ("dales") of Arcadia a picturesque section of the Peloponnesus; both came to be associated with the pastoral ideal.

II

Heard melodies are sweet, but those unheard
  Are sweeter; therefore, ye soft pipes, play on;
Not to the sensual[6] ear, but, more endeared,
  Pipe to the spirit ditties of no tone:
Fair youth, beneath the trees, thou canst not leave   15
    Thy song, nor ever can those trees be bare;
      Bold Lover, never, never canst thou kiss,
Though winning near the goal—yet, do not grieve;
    She cannot fade, though thou hast not thy bliss,
      For ever wilt thou love, and she be fair!   20

III

Ah, happy, happy boughs! that cannot shed
  Your leaves, nor ever bid the Spring adieu;
And, happy melodist, unweariéd,
  For ever piping songs for ever new;
More happy love! more happy, happy love!   25
    For ever warm and still to be enjoyed,
      For ever panting, and for ever young;
All breathing human passion far above,
    That leaves a heart high-sorrowful and cloyed,
      A burning forehead, and a parching tongue.   30

IV

Who are these coming to the sacrifice?
  To what green altar, O mysterious priest,
Lead'st thou that heifer lowing at the skies,
  And all her silken flanks with garlands dressed?
What little town by river or sea shore,   35
    Or mountain-built with peaceful citadel,
      Is emptied of this folk, this pious morn?
And, little town, thy streets for evermore
    Will silent be; and not a soul to tell
      Why thou art desolate, can e'er return.   40

V

O Attic[7] shape! Fair attitude! with brede[8]
Of marble men and maidens overwrought,
With forest branches and the trodden weed;
  Thou, silent form, dost tease us out of thought
As doth eternity: Cold Pastoral!   45
    When old age shall this generation waste,
      Thou shalt remain, in midst of other woe
Than ours, a friend to man, to whom thou say'st,
    Beauty is truth, truth beauty[9]—that is all
      Ye know on earth, and all ye need to know.   50

May, 1819

6. Of the senses, as distinguished from the "ear" of the spirit or imagination.
7. Attica was the district of ancient Greece surrounding Athens.
8. Woven pattern. "overwrought": ornamented all over.

9. In some texts of the poem "Beauty is truth, truth beauty" is in quotation marks and in some texts it is not, leading to critical disagreements about whether the last line and a half are also inscribed on the urn or spoken by the poet.

Ode on Melancholy

I

No, no, go not to Lethe,[1] neither twist
  Wolfsbane, tight-rooted, for its poisonous wine;[2]
Nor suffer thy pale forehead to be kissed
  By nightshade, ruby grape of Proserpine;
Make not your rosary of yew-berries,[3]   5
    Nor let the beetle, nor the death-moth be
    Your mournful Psyche,[4] nor the downy owl
A partner in your sorrow's mysteries;
    For shade to shade will come too drowsily,
    And drown the wakeful anguish of the soul.   10

II

But when the melancholy fit shall fall
  Sudden from heaven like a weeping cloud,
That fosters the droop-headed flowers all,
  And hides the green hill in an April shroud;
Then glut thy sorrow on a morning rose,   15
    Or on the rainbow of the salt sand-wave,
    Or on the wealth of globéd peonies;
Or if thy mistress some rich anger shows,
    Emprison her soft hand, and let her rave,
    And feed deep, deep upon her peerless eyes.   20

III

She[5] dwells with Beauty—Beauty that must die;
  And Joy, whose hand is ever at his lips
Bidding adieu; and aching Pleasure nigh,
  Turning to poison while the bee-mouth sips:
Ay, in the very temple of Delight   25
    Veiled Melancholy has her sov'reign shrine,
    Though seen of none save him whose strenuous tongue
Can burst Joy's grape against his palate fine;[6]
    His soul shall taste the sadness of her might,
    And be among her cloudy trophies hung.[7]   30

May, 1819

1. The river of forgetfulness in Hades.
2. Like nightshade (line 4), wolfsbane is a poisonous plant. "Proserpine": Queen of Hades.
3. Which often grow in cemeteries and which are traditionally associated with death.
4. *Psyche* means both "soul" and "breath," and sometimes it was anciently represented by a moth leaving the mouth at death. Owls and beetles were also traditionally associated with darkness and death.
5. The goddess Melancholy, whose chief place of worship ("shrine") is described in lines 25–26.
6. Sensitive, discriminating.
7. The ancient Greeks and Romans hung trophies in their gods' temples.

To Autumn

I

Season of mists and mellow fruitfulness,
  Close bosom-friend of the maturing sun;
Conspiring with him how to load and bless
  With fruit the vines that round the thatch-eves run;
To bend with apples the mossed cottage-trees,   5
  And fill all fruit with ripeness to the core;
    To swell the gourd, and plump the hazel shells
With a sweet kernel; to set budding more,
  And still more, later flowers for the bees,
  Until they think warm days will never cease,   10
    For Summer has o'er-brimmed their clammy cells.

II

Who hath not seen thee oft amid thy store?
  Sometimes whoever seeks abroad may find
Thee sitting careless on a granary floor,
  Thy hair soft-lifted by the winnowing wind;[8]   15
Or on a half-reaped furrow sound asleep,
  Drowsed with the fume of poppies, while thy hook[9]
    Spares the next swath and all its twinéd flowers:
And sometimes like a gleaner thou dost keep
  Steady thy laden head across a brook;   20
  Or by a cider-press, with patient look,
    Thou watchest the last oozings hours by hours.

III

Where are the songs of Spring? Ay, where are they?
  Think not of them, thou hast thy music too—
While barréd clouds bloom the soft-dying day,   25
  And touch the stubble-plains with rosy hue;
Then in a wailful choir the small gnats mourn
  Among the river sallows,[1] borne aloft
    Or sinking as the light wind lives or dies;
And full-grown lambs loud bleat from hilly bourn;[2] 30
  Hedge-crickets sing; and now with treble soft
  The red-breast whistles from a garden-croft;[3]
    And gathering swallows twitter in the skies.
September 19, 1819

from Letter to Benjamin Bailey, November 22, 1817[4]

° ° ° I am certain of nothing but of the holiness of the Heart's affections and the truth of Imagination—What the imagination seizes as
Beauty must be truth—whether it existed before or not—for I have the

8. Which sifts the grain from the chaff.
9. Scythe or sickle.
1. Willows.
2. Domain.

3. An enclosed garden near a house.
4. Keats's private letters, often carelessly
written, are reprinted uncorrected.

same Idea of all our Passions as of Love they are all in their sublime,
creative of essential Beauty ° ° ° The Imagination may be compared to
Adam's dream⁵—he awoke and found it truth. I am the more zealous
in this affair, because I have never yet been able to perceive how any
thing can be known for truth by consequitive reasoning—and yet it
must be—Can it be that even the greatest Philosopher ever ~~when~~ arrived at his goal without putting aside numerous objections—However
it may be, O for a Life of Sensations rather than of Thoughts! It is
"a Vision in the form of Youth" a Shadow of reality to come—and this
consideration has further conv[i]nced me for it has come as auxiliary
to another favorite Speculation of mine, that we shall enjoy ourselves
here after by having what we called happiness on Earth repeated in a
finer tone and so repeated—And yet such a fate can only befall those
who delight in sensation rather than hunger as you do after Truth—
Adam's dream will do here and seems to be a conviction that Imagination and its empyreal reflection is the same as human Life and its
spiritual repetition. But as I was saying—the simple imaginative Mind
may have its rewards in the repeti[ti]on of its own silent Working
coming continually on the spirit with a fine suddenness—to compare
great things with small—have you never by being surprised with an
old Melody—in a delicious place—by a delicious voice, fe[l]t over
again your very speculations and surmises at the time it first operated
on your soul—do you not remember forming to yourself the singer's
face more beautiful that [*for* than] it was possible and yet with the
elevation of the Moment you did not think so—even then you were
mounted on the Wings of Imagination so high—that the Prototype
must be here after—that delicious face you will see—What a time! I
am continually running away from the subject—sure this cannot be
exactly the case with a complex Mind—one that is imaginative and at
the same time careful of its fruits—who would exist partly on sensation
partly on thought—to whom it is necessary that years should bring the
philosophic Mind—such an one I consider your's and therefore it is
necessary to your eternal Happiness that you not only ~~have~~ drink this
old Wine of Heaven which I shall call the redigestion of our most
ethereal Musings on Earth; but also increase in knowledge and know
all things. ° ° °

from Letter to George and Thomas Keats,
December 21, 1817

° ° ° I spent Friday evening with Wells⁶ & went the next morning to
see *Death on the Pale horse.*⁷ It is a wonderful picture, when West's
age is considered; But there is nothing to be intense upon; no women
one feels mad to kiss, no face swelling into reality. the excellence of
every Art is its intensity, capable of making all disagreeables evapo-
rate, from their being in close relationship with Beauty & Truth—

5. In *Paradise Lost.* VIII. 460–90.
6. Charles Wells (1800–1879), an
author.
7. By Benjamin West (1738–1820),

American painter and president of the
Royal Academy; "Christ Rejected" (mentioned below) is also by West.

Examine King Lear & you will find this examplified throughout; but in this picture we have unpleasantness without any momentous depth of speculation excited, in which to bury its repulsiveness—The picture is larger than Christ rejected—I dined with Haydon the sunday after you left, & had a very pleasant day, I dined too (for I have been out too much lately) with Horace Smith & met his two Brothers with Hill & Kingston & one Du Bois,[8] they only served to convince me, how superior humour is to wit in respect to enjoyment—These men say things which make one start, without making one feel, they are all alike; their manners are alike; they all know fashionables; they have a mannerism in their very eating & drinking, in their mere handling a Decanter—They talked of Kean[9] & his low company—Would I were with that company instead of yours said I to myself! I know such like acquaintance will never do for me & yet I am going to Reynolds, on wednesday—Brown & Dilke walked with me & back from the Christmas pantomime. I had not a dispute but a disquisition with Dilke, on various subjects; several things dovetailed in my mind, & at once it struck me, what quality went to form a Man of Achievement especially in Literature & which Shakespeare posessed so enormously—I mean *Negative Capability,* that is when man is capable of being in uncertainties, Mysteries, doubts, without any irritable reaching after fact & reason—Coleridge, for instance, would let go by a fine isolated verisimilitude caught from the Penetralium of mystery, from being incapable of remaining content with half knowledge. This pursued through Volumes would perhaps take us no further than this, that with a great poet the sense of Beauty overcomes every other consideration, or rather obliterates all consideration.

Letter to John Hamilton Reynolds,
February 19, 1818

I have an idea that a Man might pass a very pleasant life in this manner—let him on any certain day read a certain Page of full Poesy or distilled Prose and let him wander with it, and muse upon it, and reflect from it, and bring home to it, and prophesy upon it, and dream upon it—untill it becomes stale—but when will it do so? Never—When Man has arrived at a certain ripeness in intellect any one grand and spiritual passage serves him as a starting post towards all "the two-and-thirty Pallaces"[1] How happy is such a "voyage of conception," what delicious diligent Indolence! A doze upon a Sofa does not hinder it, and a nap upon Clover engenders ethereal finger-pointings—the prattle of a child gives it wings, and the converse of middle age a strength to beat them—a strain of musick conducts to "an odd angle of the Isle",[2] and when the leaves whisper it puts a "girdle round the earth",[3] Nor will this sparing touch of noble Books be any irreverance

---

8. Thomas Hill (1760–1840), a book collector, and Edward duBois (1774–1850), a journalist.
9. Edmund Kean, a famous Shakespearean actor.

1. "Places of delight" in Buddhism.
2. *The Tempest,* Act I, sc. ii, 223.
3. The phrase is from *Midsummer Night's Dream,* Act II, sc. i, 175.

to their Writers—for perhaps the honors paid by Man to Man are trifles in comparison to the Benefit done by great Works to the "Spirit and pulse of good" by their mere passive existence. Memory should not be called knowledge—Many have original minds who do not think it—they are led away by Custom—Now it appears to me that almost any Man may like the Spider spin from his own inwards his own airy Citadel—the points of leaves and twigs on which the Spider begins her work are few and she fills the Air with a beautiful circuiting: man should be content with as few points to tip with the fine Webb of his Soul and weave a tapestry empyrean—full of Symbols for his spiritual eye, of softness for his spiritual touch, of space for his wandering of distinctness for his Luxury—But the Minds of Mortals are so different and bent on such diverse Journeys that it may at first appear impossible for any common taste and fellowship to exist ~~bettween~~ between two or three under these suppositions—It is however quite the contrary—Minds would leave each other in contrary directions, traverse each other in Numberless points, and all [*for* at] last greet each other at the Journeys end—An old Man and a child would talk together and the old Man be led on his Path, and the child left thinking—Man should not dispute or assert but whisper results to his neighbor, and thus by every germ of Spirit sucking the Sap from mould ethereal every human might become great, and Humanity instead of being a wide heath of Furse[4] and Briars with here and there a remote Oak or Pine, would become a grand democracy of Forest Trees. It has been an old Comparison for our urging on—the Bee hive—however it seems to me that we should rather be the flower than the Bee—for it is a false notion that more is gained by receiving than giving—no, the receiver and the giver are equal in their benefits—The f[l]ower I doubt not receives a fair guerdon from the Bee—its leaves blush deeper in the next spring—and who shall say between Man and Woman which is the most delighted? Now it is more noble to sit like Jove that [*for* than] to fly like Mercury—let us not therefore go hurrying about and collecting honey bee like, buzzing here and there impatiently from a knowledge of what is to be arrived at; but let us open our leaves like a flower and be passive and receptive—budding patiently under the eye of Apollo and taking hints from every noble insect that favors us with a visit—sap will be given us for Meat and dew for drink—I was led into these thoughts, my dear Reynolds, by the beauty of the morning operating on a sense of Idleness—I have not read any Books—the Morning said I was right—I had no Idea but of the Morning, and the Thrush said I was right—seeming to say—

> O thou whose face hath felt the Winter's wind,
> Whose eye has seen the snow-clouds hung in mist,
> And the black elm tops 'mong the freezing stars,
> To thee the spring will be a harvest-time.
> O thou, whose only book has been the light
> Of supreme darkness which thou feddest on
> Night after night when Phœbus was away,

4. *The Tempest,* Act I, sc. i, 68–69.

To thee the spring shall be a triple morn.
O fret not after knowledge—I have none,
And yet my song comes native with the warmth.
O fret not after knowledge—I have none,
And yet the Evening listens. He who saddens
At thought of idleness cannot be idle,
And he's awake who thinks himself asleep.

Now I am sensible all this is a mere sophistication, however it may neighbor to any truths, to excuse my own indolence—so I will not deceive myself that Man should be equal with jove—but think himself very well off as a sort of scullion-Mercury, or even a humble Bee—It is not [*for no*] matter whether I am right or wrong either one way or another, if there is sufficient to lift a little time from your Shoulders.

from Letter to John Taylor, February 27, 1818

° ° ° It is a sorry thing for me that any one should have to overcome Prejudices in reading my Verses—that affects me more than any hypercriticism on any particular Passage. In *Endymion* I have most likely but moved into the Go-cart from the leading strings. In Poetry I have a few Axioms, and you will see how far I am from their Centre. 1st I think Poetry should surprise by a fine excess and not by Singularity—it should strike the Reader as a wording of his own highest thoughts, and appear almost a Remembrance—2nd Its touches of Beauty should never be half way therby making the reader breathless instead of content: the rise, the progress, the setting of imagery should like the Sun come natural natural too him—shine over him and set soberly although in magnificence leaving him in the Luxury of twilight—but it is easier to think what Poetry should be than to write it—and this leads me on to another axiom. That if Poetry comes not as naturally as the Leaves to a tree it had better not come at all. However it may be with me I cannot help looking into new countries with "O for a Muse of fire to ascend!"[5]—If Endymion serves me as a Pioneer perhaps I ought to be content. I have great reason to be content, for thank God I can read and perhaps understand Shakspeare to his depths, and I have I am sure many friends, who, if I fail, will attribute any change in my Life and Temper to Humbleness rather than to Pride—to a cowering under the Wings of great Poets rather than to a Bitterness that I am not appreciated. I am anxious to get Endymion printed that I may forget it and proceed. ° ° °

from the Preface to *Endymion,* dated April 10, 1818

The imagination of a boy is healthy, and the mature imagination of a man is healthy; but there is a space of life between, in which the soul is in a ferment, the character undecided, the way of life uncertain, the

5. Shakespeare, *Henry V*, Prologue, 1.

ambition thick-sighted: thence proceeds mawkishness, and all the thousand bitters which those men I speak of must necessarily taste in going over the following pages.

I hope I have not in too late a day touched the beautiful mythology of Greece, and dulled its brightness: for I wish to try once more, before I bid it farewell.

Chronology

1795   John Keats born October 31 at Finsbury, just north of London, the eldest child of Thomas and Frances Jennings Keats. Thomas Keats was head ostler at a livery stable.

1797–1803   Birth of three younger brothers and sisters: George in 1797, Thomas in 1799, Frances Mary (Fanny) in 1803.

1803   With George, begins school in Enfield.

1804   Father killed by a fall from his horse, April 15. On June 27 his mother remarries, and the children go to live with their maternal grandparents at Enfield. The grandfather dies a year later, and the children move with their grandmother to Lower Edmonton.

1809   Begins a literary friendship with Charles Cowden Clarke, the son of the headmaster at the Enfield school, and develops a strong interest in reading.

1810   Mother dies of tuberculosis, after a long illness.

1811   Leaves school to become apprenticed to an apothecary-surgeon in Edmonton; completes a prose translation of the *Aeneid,* begun at school.

1814   Earliest known attempts at writing verse. In December his grandmother dies, and the family home is broken up.

1815   In October moves to next stage of his medical training at Guy's Hospital, south of the Thames in London.

1816   On May 5 his first published poem, *O Solitude,* appears in Leigh Hunt's *Examiner.* In October writes *On First Looking into Chapman's Homer,* published in December. Meets Hunt, Benjamin Haydon, John Hamilton Reynolds, and Shelley. By the spring of 1817, gives up the idea of medical practice.

1817   In March, moves with brothers to Hampstead, sees the Elgin Marbles with Haydon, and publishes his first collection of *Poems.* Composes *Endymion* between April and November. Reads Milton, Shakespeare, Coleridge and rereads Wordsworth during the year.

1818   *Endymion* published in April, unfavorably reviewed in September, defended by Reynolds in October. During the summer goes on walking tour of the lake country and Scotland, but returns to London in mid-August with a sore throat and severe chills. His brother Tom also seriously ill by late summer, dying on December 1. In September, Keats first meets Fanny Brawne (18 years old), with whom he arrives at an "understanding" by Christmas.

1819   Writes *The Eve of St. Agnes* in January, revises it in September. Fanny Brawne and her mother move into the other half of the double house in which Keats lives in April. During April and May writes *La Belle Dame sans Merci* and all the major odes except *To Autumn,*

written in September. Rental arrangements force separation from
Fanny Brawne during the summer (Keats on Isle of Wight from
June to August), and in the fall he tries to break his dependence on
her, but they become engaged by Christmas. Earlier in December
suffers a recurrence of his sore throat.

1820   In February has a severe hemorrhage and in June an attack of
blood-spitting. In July his doctor orders him to Italy for the winter;
he sails in September and finally arrives in Rome on November 15.
In July a volume of poems published, *Lamia, Isabella, The Eve of
St. Agnes and Other Poems.* Fanny Brawne nurses him through the
late summer.

1821   Dies at 11 P.M., February 23. Buried in the English Cemetery at
Rome.

ADRIENNE RICH

At a Bach Concert

Coming by evening through the wintry city
We said that art is out of love with life.
Here we approach a love that is not pity.

This antique discipline, tenderly severe,
Renews belief in love yet masters feeling,   5
Asking of us a grace in what we bear.

Form is the ultimate gift that love can offer—
The vital union of necessity
With all that we desire, all that we suffer.

A too-compassionate art is half an art.   10
Only such proud restraining purity
Restores the else-betrayed, too-human heart.

                                                                 1951

Storm Warnings

The glass has been falling all the afternoon,
And knowing better than the instrument
What winds are walking overhead, what zone
Of gray unrest is moving across the land,
I leave the book upon a pillowed chair   5
And walk from window to closed window, watching
Boughs strain against the sky

And think again, as often when the air
Moves inward toward a silent core of waiting,
How with a single purpose time has traveled   10

By secret currents of the undiscerned
Into this polar realm. Weather abroad
And weather in the heart alike come on
Regardless of prediction.

Between foreseeing and averting change   15
Lies all the mastery of elements
Which clocks and weatherglasses cannot alter.
Time in the hand is not control of time,
Nor shattered fragments of an instrument
A proof against the wind; the wind will rise,   20
We can only close the shutters.

I draw the curtains as the sky goes black
And set a match to candles sheathed in glass
Against the keyhole draught, the insistent whine
Of weather through the unsealed aperture.   25
This is our sole defense against the season;
These are the things that we have learned to do
Who live in troubled regions.

                                                    1951

Snapshots of a Daughter-in-Law

1

You, once a belle in Shreveport,
with henna-colored hair, skin like a peachbud,
still have your dresses copied from that time,
and play a Chopin prelude
called by Cortot: *"Delicious recollections*   5
float like perfume through the memory."

Your mind now, mouldering like wedding-cake,
heavy with useless experience, rich
with suspicion, rumor, fantasy,
crumbling to pieces under the knife-edge   10
of mere fact. In the prime of your life.

Nervy, glowering, your daughter
wipes the teaspoons, grows another way.

2

Banging the coffee-pot into the sink
she hears the angels chiding, and looks out   15
past the raked gardens to the sloppy sky.
Only a week since They said: *Have no patience.*

The next time it was: *Be insatiable.*
Then: *Save yourself; others you cannot save.*[6]

6. According to *Matthew* 27:42, the   the crucified Jesus by saying, "He saved
chief priests, scribes, and elders mocked   others; himself he cannot save."

Sometimes she's let the tapstream scald her arm,   20
a match burn to her thumbnail,

or held her hand above the kettle's snout
right in the woolly steam. They are probably angels,
since nothing hurts her any more, except
each morning's grit blowing into her eyes.   25

3
A thinking woman sleeps with monsters.
The beak that grips her, she becomes. And Nature,
that sprung-lidded, still commodious
steamer-trunk of *tempora* and *mores*[7]
gets stuffed with it all: the mildewed orange-flowers,   30
the female pills, the terrible breasts
of Boadicea[8] beneath flat foxes' heads and orchids.

Two handsome women, gripped in argument,
each proud, acute, subtle, I hear scream
across the cut glass and majolica   35
like Furies[9] cornered from their prey:
The argument *ad feminam*,[1] all the old knives
that have rusted in my back, I drive in yours,
ma semblable, ma soeur![2]

4
Knowing themselves too well in one another: 40
their gifts no pure fruition, but a thorn,
the prick filed sharp against a hint of scorn . . .
Reading while waiting
for the iron to heat,
writing, *My Life had stood—a Loaded Gun—*[3]   45
in that Amherst pantry while the jellies boil and scum,
or, more often,
iron-eyed and beaked and purposed as a bird,
dusting everything on the whatnot every day of life.

5
Dulce ridens, dulce loquens,[4]   50
she shaves her legs until they gleam
like petrified mammoth-tusk.

---

7. Times and customs.
8. Queen of the ancient Britons. When her husband died, the Romans seized the territory he ruled and scourged Boadicea; she then led a heroic but ultimately unsuccessful revolt.
9. In Roman mythology, the three sisters were the avenging spirits of retributive justice.
1. Argument to the woman. The *argumentum ad hominem* (literally, argument to the man) is (in logic) an argument aimed at a person's individual prejudices or special interests.

2. "My mirror-image (or 'double'), my sister." Baudelaire, in the prefatory poem to *Les Fleurs du Mal*, addresses (and attacks) his "hypocrite reader" as "mon semblable, mon frère" (my double, my brother).
3. " 'My Life had stood—a Loaded Gun' [Poem No. 754], Emily Dickinson, *Complete Poems*, ed. T. H. Johnson, 1960, p. 369." (Rich's note)
4. "Sweet (or winsome) laughter, sweet chatter." The phrase (slightly modified here) concludes Horace's *Ode*, 1, 22, describing the appeal of a mistress.

6

When to her lute Corinna sings [5]
neither words nor music are her own;
only the long hair dipping   55
over her check, only the song
of silk against her knees
and these
adjusted in reflections of an eye.

Poised, trembling and unsatisfied, before   60
an unlocked door, that cage of cages,
tell us, you bird, you tragical machine—
is this *fertilisante douleur?*[6] Pinned down
by love, for you the only natural action,
are you edged more keen   65
to prise the secrets of the vault? has Nature shown
her household books to you, daughter-in-law,
that her sons never saw?

7

"To have in this uncertain world some stay
which cannot be undermined, is   70
of the utmost consequence."[7]
                 Thus wrote
a woman, partly brave and partly good,
who fought with what she partly understood.
Few men about her would or could do more,
hence she was labeled harpy, shrew and whore.   75

8

"You all die at fifteen," said Diderot,[8]
and turn part legend, part convention.
Still, eyes inaccurately dream
behind closed windows blankening with steam.
Deliciously, all that we might have been,   80
all that we were—fire, tears,
wit, taste, martyred ambition—
stirs like the memory of refused adultery
the drained and flagging bosom of our middle years.

9

Not that it is done well, but   85
that it is done at all?[9] Yes, think

5. The opening line of a famous Elizabethan lyric (by Thomas Campion) in which Corinna's music is said to control totally the poet's happiness or despair.
6. Enriching pain.
7. "'. . . is of the utmost consequence,' from Mary Wollstonecraft, *Thoughts on the Education of Daughters*, London, 1787." (Rich's note)
8. "'Vous mourez toutes à quinze ans,' from the *Lettres à Sophie Volland*, quoted by Simone de Beauvoir in *Le Deuxième Sexe*, vol. II, pp. 123–4." (Rich's note)

Editor of the *Encyclopédie* (the central document of the French Enlightenment), Diderot became disillusioned with the traditional education of women and undertook an experimental education for his own daughter.
9. Samuel Johnson's comment on women preachers: "Sir, a woman's preaching is like a dog's walking on his hinder legs. It is not done well, but you are surprised to find it done at all." (Boswell's *Life of Johnson*, ed. Birbeck-Hill, I, 463)

of the odds! or shrug them off forever.
This luxury of the precocious child,
Time's precious chronic invalid,—
would we, darlings, resign it if we could?   90
Our blight has been our sinecure:
mere talent was enough for us—
glitter in fragments and rough drafts.

Sigh no more, ladies.
                    Time is male
and in his cups drinks to the fair.   95
Bemused by gallantry, we hear
our mediocrities over-praised,
indolence read as abnegation,
slattern thought styled intuition,
every lapse forgiven, our crime   100
only to cast too bold a shadow
or smash the mould straight off.

For that, solitary confinement,
tear gas, attrition shelling.
Few applicants for that honor.

                    10
                    Well,   105
she's long about her coming, who must be
more merciless to herself than history.[1]
Her mind full to the wind, I see her plunge
breasted and glancing through the currents,
taking the light upon her   110
at least as beautiful as any boy
or helicopter,
                    poised, still coming,
her fine blades making the air wince

but her cargo
no promise then: 115
delivered
palpable
ours.
1958–60

[*In* When We Dead Awaken, *Rich described her consciousness during the time she was writing this poem:* "Over two years I wrote a 10-part poem called 'Snapshots of A Daughter-in-Law,' in a longer, looser mode than I've ever trusted myself with before. It was an extra-

---

1. "Cf. *Le Deuxième Sexe,* vol. II, p. 574: '. . . elle arrive du fond des ages, de Thèbes, de Minos, de Chichen Itza; et elle est aussi le totem planté au coeur de la brousse africaine; c'est un helicoptère et c'est un oiseau; et voilà la plus grande merveille: sous ses cheveux peints le bruissement des feuillages devient une pensée et des paroles s'échappent de ses seins.' " (Rich's note)

ordinary relief to write that poem. It strikes me now as too literary, too
dependent on allusion; I hadn't found the courage yet to do without
authorities, or even to use the pronoun 'I'—the woman in the poem is
always 'she.' One section of it, #2, concerns a woman who thinks she
is going mad; she is haunted by voices telling her to resist and rebel,
voices which she can hear but not obey."]

Orion

Far back when I went zig-zagging
through tamarack pastures
you were my genius, you
my cast-iron Viking, my helmed
lion-heart king in prison.   5
Years later now you're young

my fierce half-brother, staring
down from that simplified west
your breast open, your belt dragged down
by an oldfashioned thing, a sword   10
the last bravado you won't give over
though it weighs you down as you stride

and the stars in it are dim
and maybe have stopped burning.
But you burn, and I know it;   15
as I throw back my head to take you in
an old transfusion happens again:
divine astronomy is nothing to it.

Indoors I bruise and blunder,
break faith, leave ill enough   20
alone, a dead child born in the dark.
Night cracks up over the chimney,
pieces of time, frozen geodes
come showering down in the grate.

A man reaches behind my eyes   25
and finds them empty
a woman's head turns away
from my head in the mirror
children are dying my death
and eating crumbs of my life.   30

Pity is not your forte.
Calmly you ache up there
pinned aloft in your crow's nest,
my speechless pirate!
You take it all for granted   35
and when I look you back

it's with a starlike eye
shooting its cold and egotistical spear
where it can do least damage.
Breathe deep! No hurt, no pardon   40
out here in the cold with you
you with your back to the wall.

1965

[*In* When We Dead Awaken, *Rich described* Orion *as* "a poem of re-construction with a part of myself I had felt I was losing—the active principle, the energetic imagination, the 'half-brother' whom I pro-jected, as I had for many years, into the constellation Orion. It's no ac-cident that the words 'cold and egotistical' appear in this poem, and are applied to myself. The choice still seemed to be between 'love'—womanly, maternal love, altruistic love—a love defined and ruled by the weight of an entire culture—and egotism—a force directed by men into creation, achievement, ambition, often at the expense of others, but justifiably so. For weren't they men, and wasn't that their destiny as womanly love was ours? I know now that the alternatives are false ones—that the word 'love' is itself in need of re-vision."]

Planetarium

*(Thinking of Caroline Herschel, 1750–1848,
astronomer, sister of William; and others)*

A woman in the shape of a monster
a monster in the shape of a woman
the skies are full of them

a woman   "in the snow
among the Clocks and instruments   5
or measuring the ground with poles"

in her 98 years to discover
8 comets

she whom the moon ruled
like us   10
levitating into the night sky
riding the polished lenses

Galaxies of women, there
doing penance for impetuousness
ribs chilled   15
in those spaces   of the mind

An eye,
        "virile, precise and absolutely certain"
    from the mad webs of Uranisborg
                        encountering the NOVA

every impulse of light exploding   20
from the core
as life flies out of us

            Tycho[2] whispering at last
            "Let me not seem to have lived in vain"

What we see, we see   25
and seeing is changing

the light that shrivels a mountain
and leaves a man alive

Heartbeat of the pulsar
heart sweating through my body   30

The radio impulse
pouring in from Taurus
            I am bombarded yet   I stand

I have been standing all my life in the
direct path of a battery of signals   35
the most accurately transmitted most
untranslatable language in the universe
I am a galactic cloud so deep   so invo-
luted that a light wave could take 15
years to travel through me   And has   40
taken   I am an instrument in the shape
of a woman trying to translate pulsations
into images   for the relief of the body
and the reconstruction of the mind.
1968

[*Rich described this poem, in* When We Dead Awaken, *as a* "companion poem to 'Orion,' " *above:* "at last the woman in the poem and
the woman writing the poem become the same person. . . . It was written after a visit to a real planetarium, where I read an account of the
work of Caroline Herschel, the astronomer, who worked with her
brother William, but whose name remained obscure, as his did not."]

---

2. Tycho Brahe (1546–1601), Danish
astronomer whose cosmology tried to fuse
the Ptolemaic and Copernican systems. He
discovered and described (*"De Nova Stella,*
1573) a new star in what had previously
been considered a fixed star-system. Uran-
iborg (line 19) was Tycho's famous and
elaborate palace-laboratory-observatory.

Diving into the Wreck

First having read the book of myths,
and loaded the camera,
and checked the edge of the knife-blade,
I put on
the body-armor of black rubber   5
the absurd flippers
the grave and awkward mask.
I am having to do this
not like Cousteau with his
assiduous team   10
aboard the sun-flooded schooner
but here alone.

There is a ladder.
The ladder is always there
hanging innocently   15
close to the side of the schooner.
We know what it is for,
we who have used it.
Otherwise
it's a piece of maritime floss   20
some sundry equipment.

I go down.
Rung after rung and still
the oxygen immerses me
the blue light   25
the clear atoms
of our human air.
I go down.
My flippers cripple me,
I crawl like an insect down the ladder   30
and there is no one
to tell me when the ocean
will begin.

First the air is blue and then
it is bluer and then green and then   35
black I am blacking out and yet
my mask is powerful
it pumps my blood with power
the sea is another story
the sea is not a question of power   40
I have to learn alone
to turn my body without force
in the deep element.

And now: it is easy to forget
what I came for   45

among so many who have always
lived here
swaying their crenellated fans
between the reefs
and besides   50
you breathe differently down here.

I came to explore the wreck.
The words are purposes.
The words are maps.
I came to see the damage that was done   55
and the treasures that prevail.
I stroke the beam of my lamp
slowly along the flank
of something more permanent
than fish or weed   60

the thing I came for:
the wreck and not the story of the wreck
the thing itself and not the myth
the drowned face always staring
toward the sun   65
the evidence of damage
worn by salt and sway into this threadbare beauty
the ribs of the disaster
curving their assertion
among the tentative haunters.   70

This is the place.
And I am here, the mermaid whose dark hair
streams black, the merman in his armored body
We circle silently
about the wreck   75
we dive into the hold.
I am she: I am he

whose drowned face sleeps with open eyes
whose breasts still bear the stress
whose silver, copper, vermeil cargo lies   80
obscurely inside barrels
half-wedged and left to rot
we are the half-destroyed instruments
that once held to a course
the water-eaten log   85
the fouled compass

We are, I am, you are
by cowardice or courage
the one who find our way
back to this scene   90
carrying a knife, a camera

a book of myths
in which
our names do not appear.

1972

Origins and History of Consciousness

I

Night-life. Letters, journals, bourbon
sloshed in the glass. Poems crucified on the wall,
dissected, their bird-wings severed
like trophies. No one lives in this room
without living through some kind of crisis.   5

No one lives in this room
without confronting the whiteness of the wall
behind the poems, planks of books,
photographs of dead heroines.
Without contemplating last and late   10
the true nature of poetry. The drive
to connect. The dream of a common language.

Thinking of lovers, their blind faith, their
experienced crucifixions,
my envy is not simple. I have dreamed of going to bed   15
as walking into clear water ringed by a snowy wood
white as cold sheets, thinking, *I'll freeze in there.*
My bare feet are numbed already by the snow
but the water
is mild, I sink and float   20
like a warm amphibious animal
that has broken the net, has run
through fields of snow leaving no print;
this water washes off the scent—
You are clear now   25
of the hunter, the trapper
the wardens of the mind—

yet the warm animal dreams on
of another animal
swimming under the snow-flecked surface of the pool,   30
and wakes, and sleeps again.

No one sleeps in this room without
the dream of a common language.

II

It was simple to meet you, simple to take your eyes
into mine, saying: these are eyes I have known   35

from the first. . . . It was simple to touch you
against the hacked background, the grain of what we
had been, the choices, years. . . . It was even simple
to take each other's lives in our hands, as bodies.

What is not simple: to wake from drowning   40
from where the ocean beat inside us like an afterbirth
into this common, acute particularity
these two selves who walked half a lifetime untouching—
to wake to something deceptively simple: a glass
sweated with dew, a ring of the telephone, a scream   45
of someone beaten up far down in the street
causing each of us to listen to her own inward scream

knowing the mind of the mugger and the mugged
as any woman must who stands to survive this city,
this century, this life . . .   50

each of us having loved the flesh in its clenched or loosened
    beauty
better than trees or music (yet loving those too
as if they were flesh—and they are—but the flesh
of beings unfathomed as yet in our roughly literal life).

III

It's simple to wake from sleep with a stranger,   55
dress, go out, drink coffee,
enter a life again. It isn't simple
to wake from sleep into the neighborhood
of one neither strange nor familiar
whom we have chosen to trust. Trusting, untrusting,   60
we lowered ourselves into this, let ourselves
downward hand over hand as on a rope that quivered
over the unsearched. . . . We did this. Conceived
of each other, conceived each other in a darkness
which I remember as drenched in light.   65
                              I want to call this, life.

But I can't call it life until we start to move
beyond this secret circle of fire
where our bodies are giant shadows flung on a wall
where the night becomes our inner darkness, and sleeps   70
like a dumb beast, head on her paws, in the corner.

1972–1974   1978

Coast to Coast

There are days when housework seems the only
outlet   old funnel I've poured caldrons through
old servitude   In grief and fury bending
to the accustomed tasks   the vacuum cleaner plowing
realms of dust   the mirror scoured   gray webs   5
behind framed photographs   brushed away
the gray-seamed sky enormous in the west
snow gathering in corners   of the north

Seeing through the prism
you who gave it me   10
                    You, bearing ceaselessly
yourself, the witness
Rainbow dissolves the Hudson   This chary, stinting
skin of late winter   ice   forming and breaking up

The unprotected seeing it through   15
with their ordinary valor
Rainbow composed of ordinary light
February-flat
gray-white of a cheap enameled pan
breaking into veridian, azure, violet   20
You write: *Three and a half weeks lost from writing. . . .*
I think of the word *protection*
who it is we try to protect   and why

Seeing through the prism   Your face, fog-hollowed   burning
cold of eucalyptus hung with butterflies   25
lavender of rockbloom
O and your anger uttered in silence word and stammer
shattering the fog   lances of sun
piercing the gray Pacific   unanswerable tide
carving itself in clefts and fissures of the rock   30
Beauty of your breasts   your hands
turning a stone a shell a weed a prism   in coastal light
traveler and witness
the passion of the speechless
driving your speech   35
protectless

If you can read and understand this poem
send something back: a burning strand of hair
a still-warm, still-liquid drop of blood
a shell   40
thickened from being battered year on year
send something back.

1979

from Talking with Adrienne Rich[3]

° ° ° I think of myself as using poetry as a chief means of self-exploration—one of several means, of which maybe another would be dreams, really thinking about, paying attention to dreams, but the poem, like the dream, does this through images and it is in the images of my poems that I feel I am finding out more about my own experience, my sense of things. But I don't think of myself as having a position or a self-description which I'm then going to present in the poem.

°   °   °

When I started writing poetry I was tremendously conscious of, and very much in need of, a formal structure that could be obtained from outside, into which I could pour whatever I had, whatever I thought I had to express. But I think that was a part of a whole thing that I see, now as a teacher, very much with young writers, of using language more as a kind of façade than as either self-revelation or as a probe into one's own consciousness. I think I would attribute a lot of the change in my poetry simply to the fact of growing older, undergoing certain kinds of experiences, realizing that formal metrics were not going to suffice me in dealing with those experiences, realizing that experience itself is much more fragmentary, much more sort of battering, much ruder than these structures would allow, and it had to find its own form.

°   °   °

I have a very strong sense about the existence of poetry in daily life and poetry being part of the world as it is, and that the attempt to reduce poetry to what is indited on a page just limits you terribly. . . . The poem is the poetry of things lodged in the innate shape of the experience. My saying "The moment of change is the only poem" is the kind of extreme statement you feel the need to make at certain times if only to force someone to say, "But I always thought a poem is something written on a piece of paper," you know, and to say: "But look, how did those words get on that piece of paper." There had to be a mind; there had to be an experience; the mind had to go through certain shocks, certain stresses, certain strains, and if you're going to carry the poem back to its real beginnings it's that moment of change. I feel that we are always writing.

°   °   °

When I was in my twenties ° ° ° I was going through a very sort of female thing—of trying to distinguish between the ego that is capable of writing poems, and then this other kind of being that you're asked to be if you're a woman, who is, in a sense, denying that ego. I had great feelings of split about that for many years actually, and there are a lot of poems I couldn't write even, because I didn't want to con-

3. A transcript of a conversation recorded March 9, 1971, and printed in *The Ohio Review*, Fall, 1971.

fess to having that much aggression, that much ego, that much sense of myself. I had always thought of my first book as being a book of very well-tooled poems of a sort of very bright student, which I was at that time, but poems in which the unconscious things never got to the surface. But there's a poem in that book about a woman who sews a tapestry and the tapestry has figures of tigers on it. But the woman is represented as being completely—her hand is burdened by the weight of the wedding band, and she's meek, and she's fearful, and the only way in which she can express any other side of her nature is in embroidering these tigers. Well, I thought of that as almost a formal exercise, but when I go back and look at that poem I really think it's saying something about what I was going through. And now that's lessened a great deal for all sorts of reasons—that split.

from An Interview with Adrienne Rich[4]

I would have said ten or fifteen years ago that I would not even want to identify myself as a woman poet. That term *has* been used pejoratively; I just don't think it can be at this point. You know, for a woman the act of creation is prototypically to produce children, while the act of creating with language—I'm not saying that women writers haven't been accepted; certainly, more have been accepted than women lawyers or doctors. Still, a woman writer feels, she is going against the grain—or there has been this sense until very recently (if there isn't still). Okay, it's all right to be a young thing and write verse. But a friend of mine was telling me about meeting a noted poet at a cocktail party. She'd sent him a manuscript for a contest he was judging. She went up to him and asked him about it, and he looked at her and said, "Young girls *are* poems; they shouldn't write them." This attitude toward women poets manifests itself so strongly that you are made to feel you are becoming the thing you are not.

✻   ✻   ✻

If a man is writing, he's gone through all the nonsense and said "Okay, I am a poet and I'm still a man. They don't cancel each other out or, if they do, then I'll opt to be a poet." He's not writing for a hostile sex, a breed of critics who by virtue of their sex are going to look at his language and pass judgment on it. That does happen to a woman. I don't know why the woman poet has been slower than the woman novelist in taking risks though I'm very grateful that this is no longer so. I feel that I dare to think further than I would have dared to think ten years ago—and *that* certainly is going to affect my writing. And I now dare to entertain thoughts and speculations that then would have seemed unthinkable.

✻   ✻   ✻

Many of the male writers whom I very much admire—Galway Kinnell, James Wright, W. S. Merwin—are writing poetry of such great desolation. They come from different backgrounds, write in dif-

4. By David Kalstone, in *The Saturday Review*, April 22, 1972.

ferent ways, and yet all seem to write out of a sense of doom, as if we were fated to carry on these terribly flawed relationships. I think it's expressive of a feeling that "we, the masters, have created a world that's impossible to live in and that probably may not be livable in, in a very literal sense. What we thought, what we'd been given to think is our privilege, our right, and our sexual prerogative has led to this, to our doom." I guess a lot of women—if not a lot of women poets— are feeling that there has to be some other way, that human life is messed-up but that it doesn't have to be *this* desolate.

*   *   *

Today, much poetry by women is charged with anger and uses voices of rage and anger that I don't think were ever used in poetry before. In poets like Sylvia Plath and Diane Wakoski, say, those voices are so convincing that it is impossible to describe them by using those favorite adjectives of phallic criticism—shrill and hysterical. Well, Sylvia Plath is dead. I always maintained from the first time I read her last poems that her suicide was not necessary, that she could have gone on and written poems that would have given us even more insight into the states of anger and willfulness, even of self-destructiveness, that women experience. She didn't need literally to destroy herself in order to reflect and express those things. Diane Wakoski is a young woman. She's changing a lot and will continue to change. What I admire in her, besides her energy and dynamism and quite a beautiful gift for snatching the image that she wants out of the air, is her honesty. No woman has written before about her face and said she hated it, that it had served her ill, that she wished she could throw acid in it. That's very shocking. But I think all women, even the most beautiful women, at times have felt that in a kind of self-hatred. Because the *face* is supposed to be the *woman*.

*   *   *

A lot of poetry is becoming more oral. Certainly, it's true of women and black poets. Reading black poetry on the printed page gives no sense of the poem, if you're going to look at that poetry the way you look at poems by Richard Wilbur. Yet you can hear these poets read and realize it's the oldest kind of poetry.

*   *   *

I think the energy of language comes somewhat from the pressure and need and unbearableness of what's being done to you. It's not the same energy you find in the blues. The blues are a grief language, a lost language, and a cry of pain, usually in a woman's voice, which is interesting. For a long time you sing the blues, and then you begin to say, "I'm tired of singing the blues. I want something else." And that's what you're hearing now. There seems to be a connection between an oppressed condition and having access to certain kinds of energy, vitality, and subjectivity. For women as well as blacks. Though I don't feel there is a necessary cause-and-effect relationship; what seems to happen is that being on top, being in a powerful position leads to a divorce between one's unruly, chaotic, revolutionary sensitivity and one's reason, sense of order and of maintaining a hold. And, therefore, you have at the bottom of the pile, so to speak, a kind of churning energy that gets lost up there among the administrators.

◦   ◦   ◦

I don't know how or whether poetry changes anything. But neither do I know how or whether bombing or even community organizing changes anything when we are pitted against a massive patriarchal system armed with supertechnology. I believe in subjectivity—that a lot of male Left leaders have turned into Omnipotent Administrators, because their "masculinity" forced them to deny their subjectivity. I believe in dreams and visions and "the madness of art." And at moments I can conceive of a women's movement that will show the way to humanizing technology and fusing dreams and skills and visions and reason to begin the healing of the human race. But I don't want women to take over the world and run it the way men have, or to take on—yet again!—the burden of carrying the subjectivity of the race. Women are a vanguard now, and I believe will increasingly become so, because we have—Western women, Third World women, all women— known and felt the pain of the human condition most consistently. But in the end it can't be women alone.

from When We Dead Awaken: Writing as Re-Vision

Most, if not all, human lives are full of fantasy—passive daydreaming which need not be acted on. But to write poetry or fiction, or even to think well, is not to fantasize or to put fantasies on paper. For a poem to coalesce, for a character or an action to take shape, there has to be an imaginative transformation of reality which is in no way passive. And a certain freedom of the mind is needed—freedom to press on, to enter the currents of your thought like a glider pilot, knowing that your motion can be sustained, that the buoyancy of your attention will not be suddenly snatched away. Moreover, if the imagination is to transcend and transform experience it has to question, to challenge, to conceive of alternatives, perhaps to the very life you are living at that moment. You have to be free to play around with the notion that day might be night, love might be hate, nothing can be too sacred for the imagination to turn into its opposite or to call experimentally by another name. For writing is re-naming.

Now, to be maternally with small children all day in the old way, to be with a man in the old way of marriage, requires a holding back, a putting aside of that imaginative activity, and seems to demand instead a kind of conservatism. I want to make it clear that I am *not* saying that in order to write well, or think well, it is necessary to become unavailable to others, or to become a devouring ego. This has been the myth of the masculine artist and thinker; and, I repeat, I do not accept it. But to be a female human being trying to fulfill traditional female functions in a traditional way *is* in direct conflict with the subversive function of the imagination. The word "traditional" is important here. There must be ways, and we will be finding out more and more about them, in which the energy of creation and the energy of relation can be united. But in those earlier years I always felt the conflict as a failure of love in myself. I had thought I was choosing a full life: the life available to most men, in which sexuality, work and parenthood could coexist. But I felt, at 29, guilt toward the people closest to me, and guilty toward my own being.

I wanted, then, more than anything, the one thing of which there was never enough: time to think, time to write. The '50s and early '60s were years of rapid revelations: the sit-ins and marches in the South, the Bay of Pigs, the early antiwar movement, raised large questions—questions for which the masculine world of the academy around me seemed to have expert and fluent answers. But I needed desperately to think for myself—about pacifism and dissent and violence, about poetry and society, and about my own relationship to all these things. For about ten years I was reading in fierce snatches, scribbling in notebooks, writing poetry in fragments; I was looking desperately for clues, because if there were no clues then I thought I might be insane. I wrote in a notebook about this time:

> Paralyzed by the sense that there exists a mesh of relationships
> —e.g. between my anger at the children, my sensual life, pacifism,
> sex (I mean sex in its broadest significance, not merely sexual desire)—an interconnectedness which, if I could see it, make it valid,
> would give me back myself, make it possible to function lucidly
> and passionately. Yet I grope in and out among these dark webs.

I think I began at this point to feel that politics was not something "out there" but something "in here" and of the essence of my condition.

In the late '50s I was able to write, for the first time, directly about experiencing myself as a woman. The poem was jotted in fragments during children's naps, brief hours in a library, or at 3 A.M. after rising with a wakeful child. I despaired of doing any continuous work at this time. Yet I began to feel that my fragments and scraps had a common consciousness and a common theme, one which I would have been very unwilling to put on paper at an earlier time because I had been taught that poetry should be "universal," which meant, of course, nonfemale. Until then I had tried very much *not* to identify myself as a female poet.

Chronology

1929   Born in Baltimore, Maryland, May 16. Began writing poetry as a child under the encouragement and supervision of her father, Dr. Arnold Rich, from whose "very Victorian, pre-Raphaelite" library, Rich later recalled, she read Tennyson, Keats, Arnold, Blake, Rossetti, Swinburne, Carlyle, and Pater.

1951   A.B., Radcliffe College. Phi Beta Kappa. *A Change of World* chosen by W. H. Auden for the Young Poets Award and published.

1952–53   Guggenheim Fellowship; travel in Europe and England. Marriage to Alfred H. Conrad, an economist who taught at Harvard. Residence in Cambridge, Massachusetts, 1953–66.

1955 Birth of David Conrad. Publication of *The Diamond Cutters and Other Poems*, which won the Ridgely Torrence Memorial Award of the Poetry Society of America.

1957 Birth of Paul Conrad.

1959 Birth of Jacob Conrad.

1960 National Institute of Arts and Letters Award for poetry. Phi Beta Kappa poet at William and Mary College.

1961–62 Guggenheim Fellowship; residence with family in the Netherlands.

1962 Bollingen Foundation grant for translation of Dutch poetry.

1962–63 Amy Lowell Travelling Fellowship.

1963 *Snapshots of a Daughter-in-Law* published. Bess Hokin Prize of *Poetry* magazine.

1965 Phi Beta Kappa poet at Swarthmore College.

1966 *Necessities of Life* published, nominated for the National Book Award. Phi Beta Kappa poet at Harvard College. Move to New York City, where Alfred Conrad taught at City College of New York. Residence there from 1966 on. Increasingly active politically in protests against the Indochina war.

1966–68 Lecturer at Swarthmore College.

1967–69 Adjunct Professor of Writing in the Graduate School of the Arts, Columbia University.

1967 *Selected Poems* published in Britain. Litt.D., Wheaton College.

1968 Eunice Tietjens Memorial Prize of *Poetry* magazine. Began teaching in the SEEK and Open Admissions Programs at City College of New York.

1969 *Leaflets* published.

1970 Death of Alfred Conrad.

1971 *The Will to Change* published. Shelley Memorial Award of the Poetry Society of America. Increasingly identifies with the women's movement as a radical feminist.

1972–73 Fanny Hurst Visiting Professor of Creative Literature at Brandeis University.

1973 *Diving into the Wreck* published.

1973–74 Ingram Merrill Foundation research grant; began work on a book on the history and myths of motherhood.

1974 National Book Award for *Diving into the Wreck*. Rich rejected the award as an individual, but accepted it, in a statement written with Audre Lorde and Alice Walker, two other nominees, in the name of all women:

> "We . . . together accept this award in the name of all the women whose voices have gone and still go unheard in a patriarchal world, and in the name of those who, like us, have been tolerated as token women in this culture, often at great cost and in great pain. . . . We symbolically join here in refusing the terms of patriarchal competition and declaring that we will share this prize among us, to be used as best we can for women. . . . We dedicate this occasion to the struggle for self-determination of all women, of every color, identification or derived class . . . the women who will not understand yet; the silent women whose voices have been denied us, the articulate women who have given us strength to do our work."

Professor of English, City College of New York.
1975   *Poems: Selected and New* published.
1976   Professor of English at Douglass College. *Of Woman Born: Motherhood as Experience and Institution* published. *Twenty-one Love Poems* published.
1978   *The Dream of a Common Language: Poems 1974–1977* published.
1979   *On Lies, Secrets, and Silence: Selected Prose 1966–1978* published. Leaves Douglass College and New York City; moves to Montague, Massachusetts; edits, with Michelle Cliff, the lesbian-feminist journal, *Sinister Wisdom*.
1981   *A Wild Patience Has Taken Me This Far: Poems 1978–1981* published.
1984   *The Fact of a Doorframe: Poems Selected and New 1950–1984* published. Moves to Santa Cruz, California.

11   HISTORICAL CONTEXTS

The more you know, the better a reader of poetry you are capable of being. Poems often draw upon a large fund of human knowledge, and sometimes they require a great deal from the reader. The earlier chapters in this book suggest some of the skills one needs to develop in order to cope with the demands they make. In these final chapters we will look at the knowledge poets often expect. Very little that you know will ultimately go to waste in your reading of poetry. The best potential reader of a poem is someone who has already developed reading skills to perfection, read everything, thought deeply about all sorts of things, and who is wise beyond belief—but that is the ideal reader we all strive to be, not the one any of us is, and no poet expects any reader to be all those things. Still, the point is to try. By knowing that these things are important to the reading of poetry, we won't discount too easily what we need, and so we will keep trying to do better, trying to bring more to the poem. The chapters that follow suggest some of the ways that poetry draws specifically upon the traditional fund of human knowledge, how it uses the history of literature, science, philosophy, religion—the "wisdom of the ages" that traditional humanistic education has long relied upon as the cornerstone of its existence. This chapter considers some of the historical particulars, matters that relate specifically to the moment in time when a particular poem was written, for every poem is, in the beginning, a timely act of creation.

Things that happen every day frequently find their way into poetry in an easy and yet often forceful manner. Making love in a junkyard, as in *Cherrylog Road,* is one kind of example; a reader doesn't need to know what particular junkyard was involved—or imaginatively involved—in order to understand the poem, but a reader does need to know what an auto junkyard was like in the middle of the 20th century, with more or less whole car bodies being scattered in various states of disarray over a large plot of ground. But what if, over the next generation or two, another way is developed to dispose of old cars? What if the metal is all melted down, or the junk is orbited into space? If something like that happens, readers then will need a footnote explaining what junkyards were like. The history of junk-yards will not be lost—there will be pictures, films, records, and some-one will write definitive books about the forms and functions of junk-yards, probably even including the fact that lovers occasionally visited them—but the public memory of junkyards will soon disappear. No social customs, no things that are made, no institutions or sites last forever.

Readers may still be able to experience *Cherrylog Road* when that happens, but they will need some help, and they may think its par-ticulars a little quaint, much as we regard literature that involves horses and buggies—or even making love in the back seat of a parked car—as quaint now. Institutions change, habits change, times change, particulars change, even when people's wants, needs, and foibles pretty much go on in the same way. Footnotes never provide a precise or adequate substitute for the ease and pleasure that come from already knowing, but they can help us understand and pave the way for feeling and experience. A kind of imaginative historical sympathy can be simulated and in fact created, for poems from earlier times that refer to specific contemporary details (and that have now become to us, in our own time, *historical* details) often describe human nature and human experiences very much as we still know and experience them. Today's poem may need tomorrow's footnote, but the poem need not be tomorrow's puzzle or only a curiosity or fossil.

The following poem, not many years old, already requires some explanation, not only because the factual details of its occasion may not be known to every reader, but also because the whole spirit of the poem may be difficult to appreciate unless one knows its circumstances.

RAYMOND R. PATTERSON

You Are the Brave

You are the brave who do not break
In the grip of the mob when the blow comes straight
To the shattered bone; when the sockets shriek;
When your arms lie twisted under your back.

Good men holding their courage slack   5
In their frightened pockets see how weak
The work that is done; and feel the weight
Of your blood on the ground for their spirits' sake;

And build their anger, stone on stone;
Each silently, but not alone.   10

1962

I can remember teaching this poem in class during the Viet Nam War and finding that a lot of students were hostile to it because they assumed it to be a poem in praise of patriotism and war. Sometimes the difficulty about factual information is that one doesn't know that one *needs* specific information. In a poem like *You Are the Brave,* it is fairly easy to assume (incorrectly, but understandably) that the conflict involved is a war and that the speaker addresses, and honors, a group of soldiers. Actually, there are clues in the poem that this conflict is, if as bitter as war, one in which mob violence (line 2) and enforced restraint (line 4) are involved. The date of the poem is a clue too—1962, when the American civil rights struggle was at its height. Once that "fact" is noticed, the whole historical context of the poem, if not its *immediate* occasion in terms of one specific civil rights march in one place on one day, becomes clear. In fact, since the poem doesn't mention a particular time and place, we may assume that the poem is not about the particulars of one specific incident, but instead gathers the kind of details that characterized many moments of the early sixties. The poem's details (generalized details about mob resentments and brutalities in a situation of passive resistance), its metaphors in the second and third stanzas, and its dignified tone of praise for "the brave" all make sense readily when the right information is available. The poem does not mention specific time and place because its concern is not confined to one event, but its location in time is important to finding what it refers to. Poems may be referential to one single event or moment, or to some larger situation that may span weeks, months, or even years. The amount of particularity in the poem will tell you.

How do you know what you need to know? The easiest clue is your own puzzlement. When it seems that something is happening in a poem that you don't recognize—and yet the poem makes no apparent effort in itself to clarify it—you have a clue that readers at the time the poem was written must have recognized something that is not now such common knowledge. Once you know you don't know, it's only work to find out: most college libraries contain far more information than you will ever need, and the trick is to learn to search efficiently. Your ability to find the information efficiently will depend upon how well you know the kinds of reference materials available to you. Practice helps. Knowledge accumulates. Most poems printed in textbooks like this one will be annotated for you with minimal facts, but often you may need additional information to interpret the poem's full meaning and resonance. An editor, trying to decide on the needs of a variety of readers, may not always have decided to write the footnote you yourself may need, so there may be digging to be done in the library for any poem you read, certainly for those you may come upon in magazines and books of poetry without footnotes. Few poets like to footnote their own work (they'd rather let you struggle a little to appreciate them), and besides, many things that now need footnotes didn't when they were first written, as in *You Are the Brave.*

To get at appropriate factual and historical information, it is important to learn to ask three kinds of questions. One kind is obvious:

it is the "Do I understand the reference to . . . ?" kind of question. When events, places, or people unfamiliar to you come up, you will need to find out what or who they are. The second kind of question is more difficult: How do you know, in a poem like *You Are the Brave,* that you need to know more? When there are no specific references to look up, no people or events to identify, how do you know that there is a specific context? To get at this sort of question, you have to trust two people: the poet, and yourself. Learning to trust yourself, your own responses, is the more difficult—you can just decide to trust the poet. Usually, good poets know what they are doing. If they do, they will not want to puzzle you more than necessary, so that you can safely assume that something which is not self-explanatory will merit close attention and possibly some digging in the library. (Poets do make mistakes and miscalculations about their readers, but it is safest to assume they know what they are doing and why they are doing it.) When a poem contains things that are not in themselves clear (such as "the grip of the mob" or the "arms . . . twisted under your back" in *You Are the Brave*) those things provide a strong clue that you need more information. And that is why you need to trust yourself: you need to be confident that when something doesn't click, when the information given you does not seem enough, that you trust your puzzlement and try to find the missing facts that will allow the poem to make sense. But how? Often the date of the poem is a help, as in *You Are the Brave*. Sometimes the title gives a clue or a point of departure. Sometimes you can discover, by reading about the author, some of the things he or she was interested in or concerned about. There is no single all-purpose way to discover what to look for, but that kind of research—looking for clues, adding up the evidence—can be interesting in itself and very rewarding when it is successful.

The third question is why? For every factual reference, one needs to ask why. Why does the poem refer to this particular person instead of some other? What function does the reference perform?

Beyond the levels of simply understanding that a particular poem is about a particular event or place or movement is the matter of developing a full sense of historical context, a sense of the larger significance and resonance of the historical occurrence referred to. Often a poem expects you to bring some sense of that significance; equally often it wants to continue your education, telling you more, wanting you to understand and appreciate on a feeling level some further things about this occurrence. A second group of poems at the end of this chapter has as its point of reference World War I. These poems offer a variety of emphases and perspectives, and they isolate quite different facts about the war. What we need to bring to our reading varies from poem to poem. *Dulce et Decorum Est,* for example, needs our knowledge that poison gas was used in the war; the green tint through which the speaker sees the world in lines 13–14, comes from green-lensed glass in the goggles of the gas mask he has just put on. But some broader matters are important as well. Harder to specify but probably even more important is the climate of opinion that surrounded World War I. To idealists, it was "the war to end all wars," and many participants—as well as politicians and propagandists—felt holy about it, regarding the threat of Germany's expansionist policy as the potential destruction of Western civilization.

No doubt you will read the poems more intelligently, and more feelingly, if you know quite a bit about World War I, and the same is true of poems about any historical occurrence or of poems that refer specifically or generally to things that happen or situations that exist in a temporal context. But it is also true that your sense of these events will grow as a result of reading sensitively and thoughtfully the poems themselves. Facts are no substitute for skills. Once you have read individually the poems in this section, try taking a breather, and then at one sitting read them all again. Reading poetry can be a form of gaining knowledge as well as an aesthetic experience. One doesn't go to poetry to seek information as such, but poems often give us more than we came for. The ways to wisdom are paved with facts, and although poetry is not primarily a data-conscious art, it often requires us to be aware, sometimes in detail, of its referents in the real world.

Racial Stress and the Civil Rights Movement

CLAUDE MC KAY

America

Although she feeds me bread of bitterness,
And sinks into my throat her tiger's tooth,
Stealing my breath of life, I will confess
I love this cultured hell that tests my youth!
Her vigor flows like tides into my blood,   5
Giving me strength erect against her hate.
Her bigness sweeps my being like a flood.
Yet as a rebel fronts a king in state,
I stand within her walls with not a shred
Of terror, malice, not a word of jeer.   10
Darkly I gaze into the days ahead,
And see her might and granite wonders there,
Beneath the touch of Time's unerring hand,
Like priceless treasures sinking in the sand.

1922

LANGSTON HUGHES

Harlem (A Dream Deferred)

What happens to a dream deferred?

> Does it dry up
> like a raisin in the sun?
> Or fester like a sore—
> And then run?   5
> Does it stink like rotten meat?
> Or crust and sugar over—
> like a syrupy sweet?
>
> Maybe it just sags
> like a heavy load.   10
>
> *Or does it explode?*

1951

JAMES A. EMANUEL

Emmett Till[1]

> I hear a whistling
> Through the water.
> Little Emmett
> Won't be still.
> He keeps floating   5
> Round the darkness,
> Edging through
> The silent chill.
> Tell me, please,
> That bedtime story   10
> Of the fairy
> River Boy
> Who swims forever,
> Deep in treasures,
> Necklaced in   15
> A coral toy.

1968

1. In 1955, Till, a fourteen-year-old from Chicago, was lynched in Mississippi for allegedly making improper advances toward a white woman.

DUDLEY RANDALL

Ballad of Birmingham

(On the bombing of a church in Birmingham, Alabama, 1963)

"Mother dear, may I go downtown
Instead of out to play,
And march the streets of Birmingham
In a Freedom March today?"

"No, baby, no, you may not go,   5
For the dogs are fierce and wild,
And clubs and hoses, guns and jails
Aren't good for a little child."

"But, mother, I won't be alone.
Other children will go with me,   10
And march the streets of Birmingham
To make our country free."

"No, baby, no, you may not go,
For I fear those guns will fire.
But you may go to church instead   15
And sing in the children's choir."

She has combed and brushed her night-dark hair,
And bathed rose petal sweet,
And drawn white gloves on her small brown hands,
And white shoes on her feet.   20

The mother smiled to know her child
Was in the sacred place,
But that smile was the last smile
To come upon her face.

For when she heard the explosion,   25
Her eyes grew wet and wild.
She raced through the streets of Birmingham
Calling for her child.

She clawed through bits of glass and brick,
Then lifted out a shoe.   30
"Oh, here's the shoe my baby wore,
But, baby, where are you?"

1969

STERLING A. BROWN

Southern Cop[1]

Let us forgive Ty Kendricks.
The place was Darktown. He was young.
His nerves were jittery. The day was hot.
The Negro ran out of the alley.
And so he shot.   5

Let us understand Ty Kendricks.
The Negro must have been dangerous,
Because he ran;
And here was a rookie with a chance
To prove himself a man.   10

Let us condone Ty Kendricks.
When he found what the Negro was running for,
It was too late;
And all we can say for the Negro is
It was unfortunate.   15

Let us pity Ty Kendricks,
He has been through enough,
Standing there, his big gun smoking,
Rabbit-scared, alone,
Having to hear the wenches wail
And the dying Negro to moan.   20

1936

World War I

WILFRED OWEN

Dulce et Decorum Est[1]

Bent double, like old beggars under sacks,
Knock-kneed, coughing like hags, we cursed through sludge,
Till on the haunting flares we turned our backs
And towards our distant rest began to trudge.
Men marched asleep. Many had lost their boots   5
But limped on, blood-shod. All went lame; all blind;
Drunk with fatigue; deaf even to the hoots
Of disappointed shells that dropped behind.

1. Apparently an Atlanta police officer involved in an incident in the 1920s or early 1930s that was widely interpreted by blacks as police brutality.

1. Part of a phrase from Horace, quoted in full in the last lines: "It is sweet and proper to die for one's country."

Gas! Gas! Quick, boys!—An ecstasy of fumbling,
Fitting the clumsy helmets just in time;   10
But someone still was yelling out and stumbling
And floundering like a man in fire or lime.—
Dim, through the misty panes and thick green light
As under a green sea, I saw him drowning.

In all my dreams, before my helpless sight,   15
He plunges at me, guttering, choking, drowning.

If in some smothering dreams you too could pace
Behind the wagon that we flung him in,
And watch the white eyes writhing in his face,
His hanging face, like a devil's sick of sin;   20
If you could hear, at every jolt, the blood
Come gargling from the froth-corrupted lungs,
Obscene as cancer, bitter as the cud
Of vile, incurable sores on innocent tongues,—
My friend, you would not tell with such high zest   25
To children ardent for some desperate glory,
The old Lie: Dulce et decorum est
Pro patria mori.

1917

THOMAS HARDY

Channel Firing[2]

That night your great guns, unawares,
Shook all our coffins as we lay,
And broke the chancel window squares,[3]
We thought it was the Judgment-day[4]

And sat upright. While drearisome   5
Arose the howl of wakened hounds:
The mouse let fall the altar-crumb,[5]
The worms drew back into the mounds,

The glebe cow[6] drooled. Till God called, "No;
It's gunnery practice out at sea   10
Just as before you went below;
The world is as it used to be:

"All nations striving strong to make
Red war yet redder. Mad as hatters

2. Naval practice on the English Channel preceded the outbreak of World War I
in the summer of 1914.
3. The windows near the altar in a
church.

4. When, according to tradition, the
dead will be awakened.
5. Breadcrumbs from the sacrament.
6. Parish cow pastured on the meadow
next to the churchyard.

They do no more for Christés sake   15
Than you who are helpless in such matters.

"That this is not the judgment-hour
For some of them's a blessed thing,
For if it were they'd have to scour
Hell's floor for so much threatening . . .   20

"Ha, ha. It will be warmer when
I blow the trumpet (if indeed
I ever do; for you are men,
And rest eternal sorely need)."

So down we lay again. "I wonder,   25
Will the world ever saner be,"
Said one, "than when He sent us under
In our indifferent century!"

And many a skeleton shook his head.
"Instead of preaching forty year,"   30
My neighbor Parson Thirdly said,
"I wish I had stuck to pipes and beer."

Again the guns disturbed the hour,
Roaring their readiness to avenge.
As far inland as Stourton Tower,   35
And Camelot, and starlit Stonehenge.[7]

April, 1914

ISAAC ROSENBERG

Break of Day in the Trenches

The darkness crumbles away—
It is the same old druid[8] Time as ever.
Only a live thing leaps my hand—
A queer sardonic rat—
As I pull the parapet's poppy[9]   5
To stick behind my ear.
Droll rat, they would shoot you if they knew
Your cosmopolitan sympathies.
Now you have touched this English hand
You will do the same to a German—   10

7. Stourton Tower, built in the 18th century to commemorate King Alfred's ninth-century victory over the Danes, in Stourhead Park, Wiltshire. Camelot is the legendary site of King Arthur's court, said to have been in Cornwall or Somerset. Stonehenge, a circular formation of upright stones dating from about 1800 B.C., is on Salisbury Plain, Wiltshire; it is thought to have been a ceremonial site for political and religious occasions or an early scientific experiment in astronomy.
8. Magician or priest.
9. Flower growing on the earthwork built to shield soldiers from enemy fire. The poppy became a standard symbol for the war dead because a large burial field in Flanders was covered with poppies.

Soon, no doubt, if it be your pleasure
To cross the sleeping green between.
It seems you inwardly grin as you pass
Strong eyes, fine limbs, haughty athletes
Less chanced than you for life,   15
Bonds to the whims of murder,
Sprawled in the bowels of the earth,
The torn fields of France.
What do you see in our eyes
At the shrieking iron and flame   20
Hurled through still heavens?
What quaver—what heart aghast?
Poppies whose roots are in man's veins
Drop, and are ever dropping;
But mine in my ear is safe,   25
Just a little white with the dust.

c. 1917

EZRA POUND

There Died a Myriad[1]

There died a myriad,
And of the best, among them,
For an old bitch gone in the teeth,
For a botched civilization,

Charm, smiling at the good mouth,   5
Quick eyes gone under earth's lid,

For two gross of broken statues,
For a few thousand battered books.

1920

EDGAR A. GUEST

The Things that Make a Soldier Great

The things that make a soldier great and send him out to die,
To face the flaming cannon's mouth, nor ever question why,
Are lilacs by a little porch, the row of tulips red,
The peonies and pansies, too, the old petunia bed,
The grass plot where his children play, the roses on the wall: 5
'Tis these that make a soldier great. He's fighting for them all.

'Tis not the pomp and pride of kings that make a soldier brave;
'Tis not allegiance to the flag that over him may wave;
For soldiers never fight so well on land or on the foam
As when behind the cause they see the little place called home.   10

---

1. Section V of "E. P. Ode pour L'Élection de Son Sépulcre."

Endanger but that humble street whereon his children run—
You make a soldier of the man who never bore a gun.

What is it through the battle smoke the valiant soldier sees?
The little garden far away, the budding apple trees,
The little patch of ground back there, the children at their play,   15
Perhaps a tiny mound behind the simple church of gray.
The golden thread of courage isn't linked to castle dome
But to the spot, where'er it be—the humble spot called home.

And now the lilacs bud again and all is lovely there,
And homesick soldiers far away know spring is in the air;   20
The tulips come to bloom again, the grass once more is green,
And every man can see the spot where all his joys have been.
He sees his children smile at him, he hears the bugle call,
And only death can stop him now—he's fighting for them all.

                                              1918

SIEGFRIED SASSOON

Repression of War Experience

Now light the candles; one; two; there's a moth;
What silly beggars they are to blunder in
And scorch their wings with glory, liquid flame—
No, no, not that,—it's bad to think of war,
When thoughts you've gagged all day come back to scare you;   5
And it's been proved that soldiers don't go mad
Unless they lose control of ugly thoughts
That drive them out to jabber among the trees.

Now light your pipe; look, what a steady hand,
Draw a deep breath; stop thinking; count fifteen,   10
And you're as right as rain. . . .
                            Why won't it rain? . . .
I wish there'd be a thunderstorm to-night,
With bucketsful of water to sluice the dark,
And make the roses hang their dripping heads.   15
Books; what a jolly company they are,
Standing so quiet and patient on their shelves,
Dressed in dim brown, and black, and white, and green,
And every kind of color. Which will you read?
Come on; O *do* read something; they're so wise.   20
I tell you all the wisdom of the world
Is waiting for you on those shelves; and yet
You sit and gnaw your nails, and let your pipe out,
And listen to the silence: on the ceiling
There's one big, dizzy moth that bumps and flutters;   25
And in the breathless air outside the house
The garden waits for something that delays.

There must be crowds of ghosts among the trees,—
Not people killed in battle—they're in France—
But horrible shapes in shrouds—old men who died   30
Slow, natural deaths—old men with ugly souls,
Who wore their bodies out with nasty sins.

You're quiet and peaceful, summering safe at home;
You'd never think there was a bloody war on! . . .
O yes, you would . . . why, you can hear the guns.   35
Hark! Thud, thud, thud—quite soft . . . they never cease—
Those whispering guns—O Christ, I want to go out
And screech at them to stop—I'm going crazy;
I'm going stark, staring mad because of the guns.

                                                      1918

W. B. YEATS

On Being Asked for a War Poem

I think it better that in times like these
A poet's mouth be silent, for in truth
We have no gift to set a statesman right;
He has had enough of meddling who can please
A young girl in the indolence of her youth,   5
Or an old man upon a winter's night.

                                                   p. 1915

WILFRED OWEN

Disabled

He sat in a wheeled chair, waiting for dark,
And shivered in his ghastly suit of grey,
Legless, sewn short at elbow. Through the park
Voices of boys rang saddening like a hymn,
Voices of play and pleasure after day,   5
Till gathering sleep had mothered them from him.

About this time Town used to swing so gay
When glow-lamps budded in the light blue trees,
And girls glanced lovelier as the air grew dim,—
In the old times, before he threw away his knees.   10
Now he will never feel again how slim
Girls' waists are, or how warm their subtle hands;
All of them touch him like some queer disease.

There was an artist silly for his face,
For it was younger than his youth, last year.   15
Now, he is old; his back will never brace;
He's lost his color very far from here,
Poured it down shell-holes till the veins ran dry,

And half his lifetime lapsed in the hot race,
And leap of purple spurted from his thigh.   20

One time he liked a blood-smear down his leg,
After the matches,[2] carried shoulder-high
It was after football, when he'd drunk a peg,[3]
He thought he'd better join.—He wonders why.
Someone had said he'd look a god in kilts,   25
That's why; and may be, too, to please his Meg;
Aye, that was it, to please the giddy jilts
He asked to join. He didn't have to beg;
Smiling they wrote his lie; aged nineteen years.
Germans he scarcely thought of; all their guilt,   30
And Austria's, did not move him. And no fears
Of Fear came yet. He thought of jeweled hilts
For daggers in plaid socks; of smart salutes;
And care of arms; and leave; and pay arrears;
Esprit de corps; and hints for young recruits.   35
And soon, he was drafted out with drums and cheers.

Some cheered him home, but not as crowds cheer Goal.[4]
Only a solemn man who brought him fruits
Thanked him; and then inquired about his soul.
Now, he will spend a few sick years in Institutes,   40
And do what things the rules consider wise,
And take whatever pity they may dole.
Tonight he noticed how the women's eyes
Passed from him to the strong men that were whole.
How cold and late it is! Why don't they come   45
And put him into bed? Why don't they come?

                                                                   1917

Women and Changing Ideas of Self

A. D. HOPE

Advice to Young Ladies

A.U.C. 334:[1] about this date
For a sexual misdemeanor, which she denied,
The vestal virgin[2] Postumia was tried.
Livy records it among affairs of state.

2. Soccer games. See A. E. Housman's *To an Athlete Dying Young*, p. 26.
3. A drink, usually brandy and soda.
4. In soccer.
1. *Ab Urbe Condita*, "from the founding of the city" (Rome), traditionally in 753 B.C. In his *History of Rome from its Foundation*, Livy (59 B.C.–A.D. 17) re-

cords the incident narrated in the first three stanzas.
2. Vestal virgins were the young priest-esses who tended the shrine of Vesta, goddess of the hearth. They were governed by the Pontifex Maximus (line 9), chief priest of the Roman religion.

They let her off: it seems she was perfectly pure;   5
The charge arose because some thought her talk
Too witty for a young girl, her eyes, her walk
Too lively, her clothes too smart to be demure.

The Pontifex Maximus,[3] summing up the case,
Warned her in future to abstain from jokes,   10
To wear less modish and more pious frocks.
She left the court reprieved, but in disgrace.

What then? With her the annalist is less
Concerned than what the men achieved that year:
Plots, quarrels, crimes, with oratory to spare!   15
I see Postumia with her dowdy dress,

Stiff mouth and listless step; I see her strive
To give dull answers. She had to knuckle down.
A vestal virgin who scandalized that town
Had fair trial, then they buried her alive.   20

Alive, bricked up in suffocating dark,
A ration of bread, a pitcher if she was dry,
Preserved the body they did not wish to die
Until her mind was quenched to the last spark.

How many the black maw has swallowed in its time!   25
Spirited girls who would not know their place;
Talented girls who found that the disgrace
Of being a woman made genius a crime;

How many others, who would not kiss the rod[4]
Domestic bullying broke or public shame?   30
Pagan or Christian, it was much the same:
Husbands, St. Paul declared,[5] rank next to God.

Livy and Paul, it may be, never knew
That Rome was doomed; each spoke of her with pride.
Tacitus,[6] writing after both had died,   35
Showed that whole fabric rotten through and through.

Historians spend their lives and lavish ink
Explaining how great commonwealths collapse
From great defects of policy—perhaps
The cause is sometimes simpler than they think.   40

3. Chief priest of the Roman religion who governed the vestal virgins.
4. As the symbol of obedience and chastisement.
5. In Ephesians v.22: "Wives, submit yourselves unto your own husbands, as unto the Lord."
6. Roman historian (c. A.D. 77–117) whose *Histories* of three Roman emperors who ruled and were successively deposed in 68–69 A.D. criticize the degeneracy of the times.

It may not seem so grave an act to break
Postumia's spirit as Galileo's,[7] to gag
Hypatia as crush Socrates, or drag
Joan as Giordano Bruno to the stake.

Can we be sure? Have more states perished, then,   45
For having shackled the inquiring mind,
Than those who, in their folly not less blind,
Trusted the servile womb to breed free men?

1966

RICHARD WILBUR

Playboy

High on his stockroom ladder like a dunce
The stock-boy sits, and studies like a sage
The subject matter of one glossy page,
As lost in curves as Archimedes[8] once.

Sometimes, without a glance, he feeds himself.   5
The left hand, like a mother-bird in flight,
Brings him a sandwich for a sidelong bite,
And then returns it to a dusty shelf.

What so engrosses him? The wild décor
Of this pink-papered alcove into which   10
A naked girl has stumbled, with its rich
Welter of pelts and pillows on the floor,

Amidst which, kneeling in a supple pose,
She lifts a goblet in her farther hand,
As if about to toast a flower-stand   15
Above which hovers an exploding rose

Fired from a long-necked crystal vase that rests
Upon a tasseled and vermilion cloth
One taste of which would shrivel up a moth?
Or is he pondering her perfect breasts?   20

Nothing escapes him of her body's grace
Or of her floodlit skin, so sleek and warm
And yet so strangely like a uniform,
But what now grips his fancy is her face,

7. In 1633 the great Italian astronomer was forced by the Church to condemn his own scientific conclusions and was for a time imprisoned. In 399 B.C. Socrates was sentenced to die by poison on account of his supposedly subversive teachings. Hypatia was a lady of Alexandria, Egypt, noted for her learning and her beauty; she was murdered in 415 A.D., allegedly at the behest of an archbishop. Joan of Arc was burned at the stake in 1431 for heresy and sorcery, Bruno in 1600 for theological and scientific heresies.

8. Greek mathematician and inventor (287?–212 B.C.).

And how the cunning picture holds her still   25
At just that smiling instant when her soul,
Grown sweetly faint, and swept beyond control,
Consents to his inexorable will.

p. 1969

MIRIAM WADDINGTON

Old Women of Toronto

All old women sometimes come to this:
they go to live away, they cross ravines,
mornings they ride the subway, later look below
to read the red of dogwood and the print of snow.
They tread upon the contours of each month   5
with delicate feet that hardly sense its shape,
explore the mouth of March and with a hiss,
they spit at myth and swallow counter-bliss.

Their brows beetle, their plush hats tremble
they specially deplore without preamble   10
the palomino carpets on the lawns
steamy with manure in frosty air;
against all evidence and witnesses they'll swear
they never argued once or schemed to take
the room in front with the old Morris chair,   15
and partial view, at least, of the bright lake.

1972

WARING CUNEY

No Images

She does not know
Her beauty,
She thinks her brown body
Has no glory.

If she could dance   5
Naked,
Under palm trees
And see her image in the river
She would know.

But there are no palm trees   10
On the street,
And dish water gives back no images.

1926

SANDRA GILBERT

Sonnet: The Ladies' Home Journal

The brilliant stills of food, the cozy
glossy, bygone life—mashed potatoes
posing as whipped cream, a neat mom
conjuring shapes from chaos, trimming the flame—
how we ached for all that,   5
that dance of love in the living room,
those paneled walls, that kitchen golden
as the inside of a seed: how we leaned
on those shiny columns of advice,
stroking the *thank yous*, the firm thighs, the wise   10
closets full of soap.
                But even then
we knew it was the lies we loved, the lies
we wore like Dior coats,[9] the clean-cut airtight
lies that laid out our lives in black and white.

                              1984

RICHARD HUGO

To Women

You start it all. You are lovely.
We look at you and we flow.
So a line begins, on the page, on air,
in the all of self. We have misused you,
invested you with primal sin. You bleed   5
for our regret we are not more.
The dragon wins. We come home and sob
and you hold us and say we are brave
and in the future will do better.
So far, so good.   10

Now some of you want out and I don't
blame you, not a tiny bit. You've caught on.
You have the right to veer off flaming
in a new direction, mud flat and diamond mine,
clavicord and dead drum. Whatever.   15
Please know our need remains the same.
It's a new game every time, one on one.

In me today is less rage than ever, less hurt.
When I imagine some good woman young
I no longer imagine her cringing   20
in cornstalks, cruel father four rows away

---

9. Designer coats by Christian Dior.

beating corn leaves aside with a club.
That is release you never expected
from a past you never knew you had.
My horse is not sure he can make it   25
to the next star. You are free.

1980

MARGE PIERCY

What's That Smell in the Kitchen?

All over America women are burning dinners.
It's lambchops in Peoria; it's haddock
in Providence; it's steak in Chicago;
tofu delight in Big Sur; red
rice and beans in Dallas.   5
All over America women are burning
food they're supposed to bring with calico
smile on platters glittering like wax.
Anger sputters in her brainpan, confined
but spewing out missiles of hot fat.   10
Carbonized despair presses like a clinker
from a barbecue against the back of her eyes.
If she wants to grill anything, it's
her husband spitted over a slow fire.
If she wants to serve him anything   15
it's a dead rat with a bomb in its belly
ticking like the heart of an insomniac.
Her life is cooked and digested,
nothing but leftovers in Tupperware.
Look, she says, once I was roast duck   20
on your platter with parsley but now I am Spam.
Burning dinner is not incompetence but war.

1983

KAY SMITH

Annunciation

for Kathy

In all the old paintings
The Virgin is reading—
No one knows what,
When she is disturbed
By an angel with a higher mission,   5
Beyond books.

She looks up reluctantly,
Still marking the place with her finger.
The angel is impressive,
With red shoes and just   10
A hint of wing and shine everywhere.
Listening to the measured message
The Virgin bows her head,
Her eyes aslant
Between the angel and the book.   15

At the Uffizi[1]
We stood
Before a particularly beautiful angel
And a hesitant Sienese Virgin,
We two sometimes women.   20
Believing we could ignore
All messages,
Unobliged to wings or words,
We laughed in the vibrant space
Between the two,   25
Somewhere in the angled focus
Of the Virgin's eye.

Now, in the harder times,
I do not laugh so often;
Still the cheap postcard in my room   30
Glints with the angel's robe.
I look with envy
At the angel and the book,
Wishing I had chosen
One or the other,   35
Anything but the space between.

                                                        1985

PAULETTE   JILES

Paper Matches

My aunts washed dishes while the uncles
squirted each other on the lawn with
   garden hoses. Why are we in here,
I said, and they are out there.
      That's the way it is,   5
      said Aunt Hetty, the shrivelled-up one.

---

1. The richest art gallery in Italy; located in Florence. Its collection includes a painting of the annunciation by the 14th-century Sienese painter Simone Martini.

I have the rages that small animals have,
being small, being animal.
Written on me was a message,
"At Your Service" like a book of   10
paper matches. One by one we were
taken out and struck.
We come bearing supper.
our heads on fire.

1973

CAROL JANE BANGS

Sunday Afternoon

I am sitting in the black chair.
For three hours I have not stirred
more than the smallest shefflera leaf
fixing its aim on the window.

I have been reading the poems   5
of an old, persecuted woman
whose words were ripe Russian pears.
Translation dries them to rich leather,
fragments of skin, tiny seeds.

Whirring machines trouble the air   10
and I believe what a friend once said—
that silence makes life stand still,
or was it darkness, that last authority,
holding our unspoken grief
under his heavy shirt?   15

This morning, walking along the tide,
I couldn't stop humming that song,
the chorus that rises
and falls like breathing.
Even if the world should stop,   20
the checkered circles on the meters
stand still in their glass helmets,
still I would hear her voice,
that sad, unalterable music,
the heavy thumping of this clock   25
winding down in my pocket.

1983

12 LITERARY TRADITION

The more poetry you read, the better a reader of poetry you are likely to be. This is not just because your skills will improve and develop, but also because you will come to know more about the poetic tradition and can thus understand more fully how poets draw upon each other. Poets are conscious of each other, and often they refer to each other's work or use it as a starting point for their own work in ways that may not be immediately obvious to an outsider. Sometimes a quiet (or even noisy) competitiveness is at the bottom of their concern with what other poems have done or can do; at other times, playfulness and a sense of humor about poetic possibilities take over, and the competitiveness dwindles to fun and poetic games. And often they want to tap the rich mine of artistic expression just to share in the bounty of our heritage. In any case, a poet's consciousness of what others have done leads to a sense of tradition that is often hard to articulate but nevertheless is very important to the effects of poetry —and this sense of tradition is something of a problem for a relatively new reader of poetry. How can I possibly read this poem intelligently, sometimes we are likely to ask in exasperation, until I've read all the other poems ever written? It's a real problem. Poets don't actually expect that all of their readers have Ph.D.s in literature, but sometimes it *seems* as if they do. For some poems—T. S. Eliot's *Love Song of J. Alfred Prufrock* (p. 815) is one example—it does help if one has read practically everything imaginable.

Why are poets so dependent on each other? What is the point of their continuous consciousness of what has already been done by others? Why do they repeatedly allude to and echo other poems? Why is a sense of tradition so important to them?

A sense of common task, a kind of communality of purpose, accounts for some traditional poetic practice, and the desire of individual poets to achieve a place in the English and American poetic tradition accounts for some more. Many poets show an anxiety to be counted among those who achieve, through their writing, a place in history, and a way of establishing that place is to define for oneself the relationship between one's own work and that of others whose place is already secure. There is, for many poets, a sense of a serious and abiding cultural tradition which they wish to share and pass on; but also important is a shared sense of playfulness, a kind of poetic gamesmanship. Making words dance on the page or in our heads provides in itself a satisfaction and delight for many writers; pride in craft that is rather like the pride of a painter or potter or tennis player. Often poets set themselves a particular task to see what they can do. One way of doing that is to introduce a standard traditional **motif** (a recurrent device, formula, or situation which deliberately connects a poem with common patterns of existing thought), and then to play variations on it much as a musician might do. Another way is to provide an alternative answer to a question that has repeatedly been asked and answered in a traditional way. Poetic playfulness by no means excludes serious intention—the poems in this chapter often make important statements about their subject, however humorous they may be in their method. Some teasing of the tradition and of other poets is pure fun, a kind of kidding among good friends; some is rather more harsh and represents an attempt to see the world very differently—to define and articulate a very different view.

The English poetic tradition is a rich and varied heritage, and individual poets draw upon it in countless ways. You have probably noticed, in the poems you have read so far, a number of allusions, glances at the tradition or at individual expressions of it, and the more poems you read the better equipped you will be to notice more. The more you read, the more you will yourself become a comfortable member of the audience poets write for. Poets do expect a lot—not always but often enough to make a new reader feel nervous and sometimes inadequate. The other side of that discomfort comes when you begin to notice things that other readers don't.

The three groups of poems in this chapter illustrate some of the ways that the tradition energizes individual poets and suggests some of the things poets like to do with their heritage. The first group consists of poems that share a common subject (love), theme (time is short), and urgency of tone (let's not wait; let's make love now). And most of them seem rather self-conscious—as if each poet is aware of a common tradition and is trying to do something a little bit different. However "sincere" these poems are as seduction poems (many of them do present a convincing sense of love and desire), their sense of play is equally important in its variation upon the standard *carpe diem* (seize the day: live for the moment) motif. The motif is an old one, dating back at least to classical Roman times; several of the poems (*Come, My Celia; Bridal Couch; To the Virgins, to Make Much of Time*) allude specifically to the following lines of a poem by Catullus, which is one of the fountains of the tradition:

> Let us live, my Lesbia, and love
> And not care about the gossip of old men.
> The sun that sets may rise again,
> But when our light has once set
> Our night will be unbroken.

The second group consists of poems that pick on (playfully) Christopher Marlowe's poem *The Passionate Shepherd to His Love*. In effect, all these poems provide "answers" to that poem. It is as if "his love" were telling the shepherd what is the matter with his argument, and the poets are answering Marlowe, too. These poets know full well what Marlowe was doing in the fantasy of his original poem, and they clearly have a lot of fun telling him how people in various circumstances might feel about his fantasy. There is, repeatedly, a lot of joy in their "realistic" deflation of his magic, and not much hostility.

The third group similarly pokes fun at other famous poems, providing another version of what might have happened in each. Koch's *Variations on a Theme by William Carlos Williams* is the only **parody** in the group (that is, it pretends to write in the style of the original poem, but comically exaggerates that style). The other poems use very different styles to alter, totally, the poetic intention of the original. *Ode on a Grecian Urn Summarized* teases Keats as well as the whole notion of poetic summaries; the effects of the summary are not very much like those of the Keats poem. *Leda's Version* offers a different perspective—the woman's—on a famous episode in mythology and thus puts a wholly different interpretation on the event. *The Dover Bitch*, on the other hand, is as its subtitle suggests much more than just a different perspective on the situation portrayed in *Dover Beach*; it uses the tradition to criticize art *and* life.

The Carpe Diem *Motif*

ROBERT HERRICK

To the Virgins, to Make Much of Time

Gather ye rosebuds while ye may,
  Old time is still a-flying;
And this same flower that smiles today
  Tomorow will be dying.

The glorious lamp of heaven, the sun,   5
  The higher he's a-getting,
The sooner will his race be run,
  And nearer he's to setting.

That age is best which is the first,
  When youth and blood are warmer;   10
But being spent, the worse, and worst
  Times still succeed the former.

Then be not coy, but use your time,
  And, while ye may, go marry;
For, having lost but once your prime,   15
  You may forever tarry.

                                        1648

EDMUND WALLER

Song

  Go, lovely rose!
Tell her that wastes her time and me
  That now she knows,
When I resemble¹ her to thee,
How sweet and fair she seems to be.   5

1. Compare.

Tell her that's young,
And shuns to have her graces spied,
That hadst thou sprung
In deserts, where no men abide,
Thou must have uncommended died.   10

Small is the worth
Of beauty from the light retired;
Bid her come forth,
Suffer herself to be desired,
And not blush so to be admired.   15

Then die! that she
The common fate of all things rare
May read in thee;
How small a part of time they share
That are so wondrous sweet and fair!   20

1645

RICHARD LOVELACE

To Amarantha, that She Would Dishevel Her Hair

Amarantha sweet and fair,
Ah, braid no more that shining hair!
As my curious hand or eye
Hovering round thee, let it fly.

Let it fly as unconfined   5
As its calm ravisher, the wind,
Who hath left his darling, th' East,
To wanton o'er that spicy nest.

Every tress must be confessed
But neatly tangled at the best,   10
Like a clue[2] of golden thread,
Most excellently raveléd.

Do not then wind up that light
In ribands, and o'ercloud in night;
Like the sun in's early ray,   15
But shake your head and scatter day.

See, 'tis broke! Within this grove,
The bower and the walks of love,
Weary lie we down and rest
And fan each other's panting breast.   20

Here we'll strip and cool our fire
In cream below, in milk-baths higher;

2. Ball.

And when all wells are drawn dry,
I'll drink a tear out of thine eye.

Which our very joys shall leave,   25
That sorrows thus we can deceive;
Or our very sorrows weep,
That joys so ripe so little keep.

1649

BEN JONSON

Come, My Celia[3]

Come, my Celia, let us prove,[4]
While we can, the sports of love;
Time will not be ours forever:
He at length our good will sever.
Spend not, then, his gifts in vain;   5
Suns that set may rise again,
But if once we lose this light,
'Tis with us perpetual night.
Why should we defer our joys?
Fame and rumor are but toys.   10
Cannot we delude the eyes
Of a few poor household spies?
Or his easier ears beguile,
Thus removéd by our wile?
'Tis no sin love's fruits to steal,   15
But the sweet thefts to reveal;
To be taken, to be seen,
These have crimes accounted been.

1606

ALFRED, LORD TENNYSON

Now Sleeps the Crimson Petal[5]

Now sleeps the crimson petal, now the white;
Nor waves the cypress in the palace walk;
Nor winks the gold fin in the porphyry font;[6]
The firefly wakens; waken thou with me.

Now droops the milk-white peacock like a ghost,   5
And like a ghost she glimmers on to me.

Now lies the Earth all Danaë[7] to the stars,
And all thy heart lies open unto me.

3. A song from *Volpone,* sung by the play's villain and would-be seducer. Part of the poem paraphrases Catullus, V.
4. Try.
5. A song from *The Princess,* in the form of a ghazal.

6. Stone fishbowl. "porphyry": a red stone containing fine white crystals.
7. A princess, confined in a tower, seduced by Zeus after he became a shower of gold in order to gain access to her.

Now slides the silent meteor on, and leaves
A shining furrow, as thy thoughts in me.   10

Now folds the lily all her sweetness up,
And slips into the bosom of the lake;
So fold thyself, my dearest, thou, and slip
Into my bosom and be lost in me.

1847

ANDREW MARVELL

To His Coy Mistress

Had we but world enough, and time,
This coyness,[8] lady, were no crime.
We would sit down, and think which way
To walk, and pass our long love's day.
Thou by the Indian Ganges' side   5
Shouldst rubies[9] find: I by the tide
Of Humber[1] would complain. I would
Love you ten years before the Flood,
And you should if you please refuse
Till the conversion of the Jews.[2]   10
My vegetable love[3] should grow
Vaster than empires, and more slow;
An hundred years should go to praise
Thine eyes, and on thy forehead gaze;
Two hundred to adore each breast,   15
But thirty thousand to the rest.
An age at least to every part,
And the last age should show your heart.
For, lady, you deserve this state;[4]
Nor would I love at lower rate.   20
    But at my back I always hear
Time's wingéd chariot hurrying near;
And yonder all before us lie
Deserts of vast eternity.
Thy beauty shall no more be found,   25
Nor, in thy marble vault, shall sound
My echoing song; then worms shall try
That long preserved virginity,
And your quaint honor turn to dust,
And into ashes all my lust: 30

8. Hesitancy, modesty (not necessarily suggesting calculation).
9. Talismans which are supposed to preserve virginity.
1. A small river which flows through Marvell's home town, Hull. "complain": write love complaints, conventional songs lamenting the cruelty of love.
2. Which, according to popular Christian belief, will occur just before the end of the world.
3. Which is capable only of passive growth, not of consciousness. The "Vegetable Soul" is lower than the other two divisions of the Soul, "Animal" and "Rational."
4. Dignity.

The grave's a fine and private place,
But none, I think, do there embrace.
    Now therefore, while the youthful hue
Sits on thy skin like morning dew,[5]
And while thy willing soul transpires[6]   35
At every pore with instant fires,
Now let us sport us while we may,
And now, like am'rous birds of prey,
Rather at once our time devour
Than languish in his slow-chapped[7] pow'r.   40
Let us roll all our strength and all
Our sweetness up into one ball,
And tear our pleasures with rough strife
Thorough[8] the iron gates of life.
Thus, though we cannot make our sun   45
Stand still,[9] yet we will make him run.[1]

                                                         1681

e. e. cummings

(ponder,darling,these busted statues

(ponder,darling,these busted statues
of yon motheaten forum be aware
notice what hath remained
—the stone cringes
clinging to the stone,how obsolete   5

lips utter their extant smile . . . .
remark

a few deleted of texture
or meaning monuments and dolls

resist Them Greediest Paws of careful   10
time[2] all of which is extremely
unimportant)whereas Life

matters if or

when the your- and my-
idle vertical worthless   15
self unite in a peculiarly
momentary

---

5. The text reads "glew." "Lew" (warmth) has also been suggested as an emendation.
6. Breathes forth.
7. Slow-jawed. Chronos (Time), ruler of the world in early Greek myth, devoured all of his children except Zeus, who was hidden. Later, Zeus seized power (see line 46 and note).
8. Through.
9. To lengthen his night of love with Alcmene, Zeus made the sun stand still.
1. Each sex act was believed to shorten life by one day.
2. See "To His Coy Mistress," above, especially lines 39–40.

partnership (to instigate
constructive
               Horizontal   20
business . . . . even so, let us make haste
—consider well this ruined aqueduct

lady,
which used to lead something into somewhere)

                                                1926

Imitating and Answering

CHRISTOPHER MARLOWE

The Passionate Shepherd to His Love

Come live with me and be my love,
And we will all the pleasures prove[1]
That valleys, groves, hills, and fields,
Woods, or steepy mountain yields.

And we will sit upon the rocks,   5
Seeing the shepherds feed their flocks,
By shallow rivers to whose falls
Melodious birds sing madrigals.

And I will make thee beds of roses
And a thousand fragrant posies,   10
A cap of flowers, and a kirtle[2]
Embroidered all with leaves of myrtle;

A gown made of the finest wool
Which from our pretty lambs we pull;
Fair lined slippers for the cold,   15
With buckles of the purest gold;

A belt of straw and ivy buds,
With coral clasps and amber studs:
And if these pleasures may thee move,
Come live with me, and be my love.   20

The shepherd swains[3] shall dance and sing
For thy delight each May morning:
If these delights thy mind may move,
Then live with me and be my love.

                                              1600

1. Try.
2. Gown.
3. Youths.

SIR WALTER RALEGH

The Nymph's Reply to the Shepherd

If all the world and love were young,
And truth in every shepherd's tongue,
These pretty pleasures might me move
To live with thee and be thy love.

Time drives the flocks from field to fold,   5
When rivers rage, and rocks grow cold,
And Philomel[4] becometh dumb;
The rest complain of cares to come.

The flowers do fade, and wanton fields
To wayward winter reckoning yields: 10
A honey tongue, a heart of gall,
Is fancy's spring, but sorrow's fall.

Thy gowns, thy shoes, they beds of roses,
Thy cap, thy kirtle, and thy posies
Soon break, soon wither, soon forgotten;   15
In folly ripe, in reason rotten.

Thy belt of straw and ivy buds,
Thy coral clasps and amber studs,
All these in me no means can move
To come to thee and be thy love.   20

But could youth last, and love still breed,
Had joys no date,[5] nor age no need,
Then these delights my mind might move
To live with thee and be thy love.

1600

C. DAY LEWIS

Song

Come, live with me and be my love,
And we will all the pleasures prove
Of peace and plenty, bed and board,
That chance employment may afford.

I'll handle dainties on the docks   5
And thou shalt read of summer frocks:
At evening by the sour canals
We'll hope to hear some madrigals.

4. The nightingale.   5. End.

Care on thy maiden brow shall put
A wreath of wrinkles, and thy foot   10
Be shod with pain: not silken dress
But toil shall tire thy loveliness.

Hunger shall make thy modest zone
And cheat fond death of all but bone—
If these delights thy mind may move,   15
Then live with me and be my love.

1935

WILLIAM CARLOS WILLIAMS

Raleigh Was Right

We cannot go to the country
for the country will bring us no peace
What can the small violets tell us
that grow on furry stems in
the long grass among lance shaped leaves?   5

Though you praise us
and call to mind the poets
who sung of our loveliness
it was long ago!
long ago! when country people   10
would plow and sow with
flowering minds and pockets at ease—
if ever this were true.

Not now. Love itself a flower
with roots in a parched ground.   15
Empty pockets make empty heads.
Cure it if you can but
do not believe that we can live
today in the country
for the country will bring us no peace.   20

1941

PETER DE VRIES

Bacchanal[6]

"Come live with me and be my love,"
    He said, in substance. "There's no vine

6. A drunken or riotous celebration.

    We will not pluck the clusters of,
        Or grape we will not turn to wine."

    It's autumn of their second year.   5
        Now he, in seasonal pursuit,
    With rich and modulated cheer,
        Brings home the festive purple fruit;

    And she, by passion once demented
        —That woman out of Botticelli[7]—   10
    She brews and bottles, unfermented,
        The stupid and abiding jelly.

                                                            1959

KENNETH KOCH

Variations on a Theme by William Carlos Williams[8]

1

I chopped down the house that you had been saving to live in next
    summer.
I am sorry, but it was morning, and I had nothing to do
and its wooden beams were so inviting.

2

We laughed at the hollyhocks together
and then I sprayed them with lye.   5
Forgive me. I simply do not know what I am doing.

3

I gave away the money that you had been saving to live on for the
    next ten years.
The man who asked for it was shabby
and the firm March wind on the porch was so juicy and cold.

4

Last evening we went dancing and I broke your leg.   10
Forgive me. I was clumsy, and
I wanted you here in the wards, where I am the doctor!

                                                            1962

---

7. Italian painter (1445–1510) of the Florentine school, famous for his sensuous paintings of Venus and the Virgin Mary.

8. See William Carlos Williams's *This Is Just to Say*, p. 910. Williams was a physician as well as poet (see line 12).

DESMOND SKIRROW

Ode on a Grecian Urn Summarized[9]

Gods chase
Round vase.
What say?
What play?
Don't know.
Nice, though.

p. 1960

JAMES HARRISON

Leda's Version[1]

A furtive blow, more like. There was I
thinking that all he wanted was to take
bread at my hand, not play ducks and drakes
with me and the course of history. Though why
he figured that all that flapping would terrify   5
me I can't imagine. Brute strength's one thing, fake
webbed feet and wet feathers another. It makes
me mad to think about it—lord of the sky
and in just as clumsy a rush as all the rest!
Sad that I could not, at the time, have known   10
how he knew all along the far-flung cost
of his sudden whim. Contempt might then have grown
to pity for so incongruous a lust,
and the whole issue been too much to be borne.

1983

ANTHONY HECHT

The Dover Bitch

A Criticism of Life

for Andrews Wanning

So there stood Matthew Arnold and this girl[2]
With the cliffs of England crumbling away behind them,
And he said to her, "Try to be true to me,
And I'll do the same for you, for things are bad
All over, etc., etc."   5

9. See Keats's *Ode on a Grecian Urn*
(p. 712).
  1. *Leda*—on whom Jupiter dropped in
in the guise of a swan, and who subsequently laid the egg from which were

hatched Helen and the Trojan War.
[Author's note.] See Yeats's *Leda, and the
Swan*, p. 792.
  2. See Arnold's poem *Dover Beach*, p.
611.

Well now, I knew this girl. It's true she had read
Sophocles in a fairly good translation
And caught that bitter allusion to the sea,[3]
But all the time he was talking she had in mind
The notion of what his whiskers would feel like   10
On the back of her neck. She told me later on
That after a while she got to looking out
At the lights across the channel, and really felt sad,
Thinking of all the wine and enormous beds
And blandishments in French and the perfumes.   15
And then she got really angry. To have been brought
All the way down from London, and then be addressed
As a sort of mournful cosmic last resort
Is really tough on a girl, and she was pretty.
Anyway, she watched him pace the room   20
And finger his watch-chain and seem to sweat a bit,
And then she said one or two unprintable things.
But you mustn't judge her by that. What I mean to say is,
She's really all right. I still see her once in a while
And she always treats me right. We have a drink   25
And I give her a good time, and perhaps it's a year
Before I see her again, but there she is,
Running to fat, but dependable as they come.
And sometimes I bring her a bottle of *Nuit d'Amour.*

1968

13   CONTEXTS OF MYTH

Whether or not we are a part of *all* that we have met, we take some
of our identity from the cultures into which we were born and the
traditions that lie behind them. Being so thoroughly culture-bound
doesn't please everybody, and rebels often use a lot of energy kicking
against the values and assumptions built into the people and institutions with whom they have grown up. But even in rebelling, we are
stuck with the terms, values, and assumptions we rebel against. No
matter how "individual" we succeed in being, we are still a part of
something larger, something that has been here longer than we have
and that has managed to clarify and articulate its values over generations and centuries.

Every culture develops stories to explain itself. These stories try to
explain to us who we are and why we are the way we are. Taken
together, they constitute what is often called a **myth.** Calling it a
myth does not mean that it is false. In fact, it means nearly the opposite, for a culture takes its myths seriously as explanations of why
things are the way they are, why the history of the culture has gone
in a particular way. Myth, in the sense in which it is used here, involves the explanations that are more or less universally shared within
a particular culture; it is a frame of reference that people within the

---

3. In *Antigone,* lines 583–91. See *Dover Beach,* lines 9–18.

culture understand and share. A sharing of this frame of reference does not mean that all people within a culture are carbon copies of each other or that popular stereotypes represent reality accurately, nor does it mean that every individual in the culture *knows* the perceived history and can articulate its events, ideas, and values. But it does mean that a shared history and a shared set of symbols lie behind any particular culture and that the culture is to some extent aware of its distinctiveness from other cultures.

A **culture,** in the sense in which it is used here, may be of many sizes and shapes. Often we think of a nation as a culture (and so speak of American culture, American history, the myth of America, the American dream, the American frame of reference), and it is equally useful to make smaller and larger divisions—as long as there is some commonality of history and some cohesiveness of purpose within the group. One can speak of Southern culture, for example, or of urban culture, or of the drug culture, or the rock music culture, or of a culture associated with a particular political belief, economic class, or social group. Most of us belong, willingly or not, to a number of such cultures at one time, and to some extent our identity and destiny are linked with the distinctive features of those cultures and with the ways the culture perceives its identity, values, and history. Some of these cultures we choose to join; some are thrust upon us by birth and circumstances. It is these larger and more persistent kinds of cultures that are illustrated in the frames of reference sampled in this chapter.

Poets, aware of their heritage, often like to probe its history and beliefs and plumb its depths, just as they like to articulate and play variations on the poetic tradition they feel a part of. For poetry written in the English language over the last 400 years or so, both the Judaeo-Christian frame of reference and the classical frame of reference (involving the civilizations of ancient Greece and Rome) have been quite important. Western culture, a broad culture that includes many nations and many sorts of religious and social groups, is largely defined within these two frames of reference—or it has been until quite recently. As religious belief has eroded over the past two or three centuries, and as classical civilization has been less emphasized and less studied, poets have felt increasingly less comfortable in assuming that their audiences share a knowledge of their systems, but they have often continued to use them to isolate and articulate human traits that have cultural continuity and importance. The poems in this chapter exemplify various kinds of attempts to define and investigate cultural contexts and what they continue to mean.

The question of shared values and a common heritage is prominent in all the poems in this chapter. Because communication necessarily involves some kind of common ground, poets in homogeneous cultures have had a relatively easier time of it than poets in very diverse cultures, and modern poets often lament the lack of a received tradition that they can count on. Still, they have to work with what is available, and the poems in the first two subgroups here draw upon two traditional sources of history and myth—the Judaeo-Christian and classical frames of reference. The third subgroup introduces elements from some non-Western frames of reference. The final subgroup represents one modern poet's individual solution to the problem of decaying certitudes in communication; W. B. Yeats's own mythology is highly individual and even eccentric but it amalgamates elements from traditional classical and Judaeo-Christian frames of reference as well as adding novelties of its own.

Judaeo-Christian History and Myth

JOHN MILTON

[Before the Fall][1]

She as a veil down to the slender waist   304
Her unadorned golden tresses wore
Disheveled, but in wanton[2] ringlets waved
As the vine curls her tendrils, which implied
Subjection,[3] but required with gentle sway,
And by her yielded, by him best received,
Yielded with coy[4] submission, modest pride,   310
And sweet reluctant amorous delay.
Nor those mysterious parts were then concealed,
Then was not guilty shame, dishonest shame
Of nature's works, honor dishonorable,
Sin-bred, how have ye troubled all mankind   315
With shows instead, mere shows of seeming pure,
And banished from man's life his happiest life,
Simplicity and spotless innocence.
So passed they naked on, nor shunned the sight
Of God or angel, for they thought no ill.   320
So hand in hand they passed, the loveliest pair
That ever since in love's embraces met,
Adam the goodliest man of men since born
His sons, the fairest of her daughters Eve.
Under a tuft of shade that on a green   325
Stood whispering soft, by a fresh fountain side
They sat them down, and after no more toil
Of their sweet gardening labor than sufficed
To recommend cool zephyr, and made ease
More easy, wholesome thirst and appetite   330
More grateful, to their supper fruits they fell,
Nectarine[5] fruits which the compliant boughs
Yielded them, sidelong as they sat recline
On the soft downy bank damasked[6] with flowers:

1. From *Paradise Lost,* Book IV. For the Biblical description of Eden, see *Genesis* 2:8–25.
2. Luxuriant.
3. The idea derives from *Genesis* 3:16

and *I Corinthians* 11:9–10.
4. Shy.
5. Sweet as nectar, the traditional drink of the gods.
6. Variegated.

The savory pulp they chew, and in the rind   335
Still as they thirsted scoop the brimming stream;
Nor gentle purpose,[7] nor endearing smiles
Wanted,[8] nor youthful dalliance as beseems
Fair couple, linked in happy nuptial league,
Alone as they. About them frisking played   340
All beasts of the earth, since wild, and of all chase[9]
In wood or wilderness, forest or den;
Sporting the lion ramped, and in his paw
Dandled the kid; bears, tigers, ounces,[1] pards,
Gamboled before them, the unwieldy elephant   345
To make them mirth used all his might, and wreathed
His lithe proboscis; close the serpent sly
Insinuating, wove with Gordian[2] twine
His braided train, and of his fatal guile
Gave proof unheeded; others on the grass   350
Couched, and now filled with pasture gazing sat,
Or bedward ruminating: for the sun
Declined was hasting now with prone career
To the Ocean Isles,[3] and in the ascending scale
Of heaven the stars that usher evening rose.   355

1667

A. D. HOPE

Imperial[4] Adam

Imperial Adam, naked in the dew,
Felt his brown flanks and found the rib was gone.
Puzzled he turned and saw where, two and two,
The mighty spoor of Jahweh marked the lawn.

Then he remembered through mysterious sleep   5
The surgeon fingers probing at the bone,
The voice so far away, so rich and deep:
"It is not good for him to live alone."

Turning once more he found Man's counterpart
In tender parody breathing at his side.   10
He knew her at first sight, he knew by heart
Her allegory of sense unsatisfied.

The pawpaw drooped its golden breasts above
Less generous than the honey of her flesh;
The innocent sunlight showed the place of love;   15
The dew on its dark hairs winked crisp and fresh.

---

7. Conversation. "Nor . . . nor": neither
. . . nor (a common 17th-century construction).
8. Were lacking.
9. Tracts of land.
1. Lynxes. "pards": leopards.

2. Like the Gordian knot, a legendary
intricate knot, finally cut by Alexander the
Great.
3. The Azores; i.e., westward.
4. I.e., emperor.

This plump gourd severed from his virile root,
She promised on the turf of Paradise
Delicious pulp of the forbidden fruit;
Sly as the snake she loosed her sinuous thighs,   20

And waking, smiled up at him from the grass;
Her breasts rose softly and he heard her sigh—
From all the beasts whose pleasant task it was
In Eden to increase and multiply

Adam had learned the jolly deed of kind: 25
He took her in his arms and there and then,
Like the clean beasts, embracing from behind,
Began in joy to found the breed of men.

Then from the spurt of seed within her broke
Her terrible and triumphant female cry,   30
Split upward by the sexual lightning stroke.
It was the beasts now who stood watching by:

The gravid [*heavy / pregnant*] elephant, the calving hind,
The breeding bitch, the she-ape big with young
Were the first gentle midwives of mankind;   35
The teeming lioness rasped her with her tongue;

The proud vicuña [*wild remnant, relative of llama and alpaca*] nuzzled her as she slept
Lax on the grass; and Adam watching too
Saw how her dumb breasts at their ripening wept,
The great pod of her belly swelled and grew,   40

And saw its water break, and saw, in fear,
Its quaking muscles in the act of birth,
Between her legs a pigmy face appear,
And the first murderer lay upon the earth.

1955

FRANCIS SPARSHOTT

The Naming of the Beasts

In that lost Caucasian garden
where history began
the nameless beasts paraded
in front of the first man.

Who am I? they asked him   5
and what shall I be
when you have left the garden?
Name me. Name me.

        Poverty cruelty lechery
        rage hate shame   10
        each stalked past the podium
        seeking his name.

        Adam stood to attention
        unable to speak
        his life too short to utter   15
        what was made that week.

        The glum parade stumbles
        from risen to set sun
        past their dumfounded patron.
        But he knows each one   20

        and at last a strange dampness
        salts either cheek.
        That was the language of Eden.
        Not Hebrew, not Greek:

        in grunts, roars, howls   25
        as the first tears fall
        the inarticulate brute
        finds names for them all.

                                           1979

JOHN HOLLANDER

Adam's Task

"And Adam gave names to all cattle, and to the fowl of the air, and to every beast of
the field . . ."—*Gen.* 2:20

    Thou, paw-paw-paw; thou, glurd; thou, spotted
        Glurd; thou, whitestap, lurching through
    The high-grown brush; thou, pliant-footed,
        Implex; thou, awagabu.

    Every burrower, each flier   5
        Came for the name he had to give:
    Gay, first work, ever to be prior,
        Not yet sunk to primitive.

    Thou, verdle; thou, McFleery's pomma;
        Thou; thou; thou—three types of grawl;   10
    Thou, flisket; thou, kabasch; thou, comma-
        Eared mashawk; thou, all; thou, all.

    Were, in a fire of becoming,
        Laboring to be burned away,
    Then work, half-measuring, half-humming,   15
        Would be as serious as play.

Thou, pambler; thou, rivarn; thou, greater
Wherret, and thou, lesser one;
Thou, sproal; thou, zant; thou, lily-eater.
Naming's over. Day is done.   20

                                                      1971

LINDA PASTAN

A Symposium: Apples

> *Eve:* Remember a season
> of apples, the orchard
> full of them, my apron
> full of them. One day
> we wandered from tree   5
> to tree, sharing a basket
> feeling the weight of apples
> increase between us.
> And how your muscles ripened
> with all that lifting.   10
> I felt them round and hard
> under my teeth; white
> and sweet the flesh
> of men and apples.

> *Gabriel:*[5] Nameless in Eden,   15
> the apple itself
> was innocent—an ordinary
> lunchpail fruit.
> Still it reddened
> for the way it was used.   20
> Afterward the apple
> chose for itself
> names untrusting
> on the tongue: stayman,
> gravenstein,   25
> northern spy.

> *The Serpent:* Ordinary, innocent
> yes. But deep
> in each center of whiteness
> one dark star . . .   30

> *Adam:* In the icebox
> an apple
> will keep
> for weeks.
> Then its skin   35
> wrinkles up

5. Traditionally, a messenger of God;   chief of the angelic guards in Paradise.
in *Paradise Lost*, Milton makes Gabriel the

like the skin of the old man
I have become,
from a single
bite.   40

                                                 1975

CHRISTINA ROSSETTI

Eve

"While I sit at the door,
Sick to gaze within,
Mine eye weepeth sore
For sorrow and sin:
As a tree my sin stands   5
To darken all lands;
Death is the fruit it bore.

"How have Eden bowers grown
Without Adam to bend them!
How have Eden flowers blown,   10
Squandering their sweet breath,
Without me to tend them!
The Tree of Life was ours,
Tree twelvefold-fruited,[6]
Most lofty tree that flowers,   15
Most deeply rooted:
I chose the Tree of Death.[7]

"Hadst thou but said me nay,
    Adam, my brother,
I might have pined away—   20
    I, but none other:
God might have let thee stay
Safe in our garden,
By putting me away
Beyond all pardon.   25

"I, Eve, sad mother
Of all who must live,
I, not another,
Plucked bitterest fruit to give
My friend, husband, lover.   30
O wanton eyes run over!
Who but I should grieve?
Cain hath slain his brother:[8]
Of all who must die mother,
Miserable Eve!"   35

6. The tree of life is so described in *Revelation* 22:2, 14, but the account there is of the New Jerusalem, not of Eden.
7. The *Genesis* account distinguishes between the tree of life and the tree of the knowledge of good and evil; the latter is forbidden, and eating of it brings labor, sickness, and death into the world. See *Genesis* 2:9, 3:1–24.
8. Abel (see *Genesis* 4:1–15).

Thus she sat weeping,
Thus Eve our mother,
Where one lay sleeping
Slain by his brother.
Greatest and least   40
Each piteous beast
To hear her voice
Forgot his joys
And set aside his feast.

The mouse paused in his walk   45
And dropped his wheaten stalk:
Grave cattle wagged their heads
In rumination;
The eagle gave a cry
From his cloud station: 50
Larks on thyme beds
Forbore to mount or sing;
Bees drooped upon the wing;
The raven perched on high
Forgot his ration;   55
The conies[9] in their rock,
A feeble nation,
Quaked sympathetical;
The mocking-bird left off to mock;
Huge camels knelt as if   60
In deprecation;
The kind hart's tears were falling;
Chattered the wistful stork;
Dove-voices with a dying fall
Cooed desolation   65
Answering grief by grief.

Only the serpent in the dust,
Wriggling and crawling,
Grinned an evil grin, and thrust
His tongue out with its fork.   70

1865

NANCY SULLIVAN

The Death of the First Man

What was it?
How could they know what it was?
It had never happened before.
No one had ever gone out.
Whatever it was was happening.   5

9. A common term for rabbits, but here probably the small pachyderms mentioned in *Proverbs* 30:26.

Something was over.
Curled in a loose shape
the first dead man
drained out of himself
while the others shifted   10
the dead weight
(because it was dead);
they tried to make him get up.
They kicked and prodded.
Where had he gone?   15
Dead we now call that place
where he stayed in a heap
for maybe a week
until the stink told them
something was wrong.   20
Someone thought to bury him.
How could they know
from the animals that fell to their clubs
that they too could go down?
The first grave   25
mounded up over his weight.

What was it,
this going out?
That was what no one knew
even as it happened.   30
Even as it happens.

                                                              1975

Classical History and Myth

ALFRED, LORD TENNYSON

Ulysses[1]

It little profits that an idle king,
By this still hearth, among these barren crags,
Matched with an agéd wife,[2] I mete and dole
Unequal laws unto a savage race,
That hoard, and sleep, and feed, and know not me.   5
    I cannot rest from travel; I will drink
Life to the lees.[3] All times I have enjoyed
Greatly, have suffered greatly, both with those
That loved me, and alone; on shore, and when

1. After the end of the Trojan War, Ulysses (or Odysseus), King of Ithaca and one of the Greek heroes of the war, returned to his island home (line 34). Homer's account of the situation is in the *Odyssey*, Book XI, but Dante's account of Ulysses in *The Inferno*, XXVI, is the more immediate background of the poem.
2. Penelope.
3. All the way down to the bottom of the cup.

Through scudding drifts the rainy Hyades[4]   10
Vexed the dim sea. I am become a name;
For always roaming with a hungry heart
Much have I seen and known—cities of men
And manners, climates, councils, governments,
Myself not least, but honored of them all—   15
And drunk delight of battle with my peers,
Far on the ringing plains of windy Troy.
I am a part of all that I have met;
Yet all experience is an arch wherethrough
Gleams that untraveled world, whose margin fades   20
For ever and for ever when I move.
How dull it is to pause, to make an end,
To rust unburnished, not to shine in use!
As though to breathe were life. Life piled on life
Were all too little, and of one to me   25
Little remains; but every hour is saved
From that eternal silence, something more,
A bringer of new things; and vile it were
For some three suns to store and hoard myself,
And this gray spirit yearning in desire   30
To follow knowledge like a sinking star,
Beyond the utmost bound of human thought.

    This is my son, mine own Telemachus,
To whom I leave the scepter and the isle—
Well-loved of me, discerning to fulfill   35
This labor by slow prudence to make mild
A rugged people, and through soft degrees
Subdue them to the useful and the good.
Most blameless is he, centered in the sphere
Of common duties, decent not to fail   40
In offices of tenderness, and pay
Meet adoration to my household gods,
When I am gone. He works his work, I mine.

    There lies the port; the vessel puffs her sail:
There gloom the dark, broad seas. My mariners,   45
Souls that have toiled, and wrought, and thought with me—
That ever with a frolic welcome took
The thunder and the sunshine, and opposed
Free hearts, free foreheads—you and I are old;
Old age hath yet his honor and his toil.   50
Death closes all; but something ere the end,
Some work of noble note, may yet be done,
Not unbecoming men that strove with Gods.
The lights begin to twinkle from the rocks;
The long day wanes; the slow moon climbs; the deep   55
Moans round with many voices. Come, my friends.

    4. A group of stars which were supposed to predict rain when they rose at the same time as the sun.

'Tis not too late to seek a newer world.
Push off, and sitting well in order smite
The sounding furrows; for my purpose holds
To sail beyond the sunset, and the baths   60
Of all the western stars, until I die.
It may be that the gulfs will wash us down;[5]
It may be we shall touch the Happy Isles,[6]
And see the great Achilles, whom we knew.
Though much is taken, much abides; and though   65
We are not now that strength which in old days
Moved earth and heaven, that which we are, we are:
One equal temper of heroic hearts,
Made weak by time and fate, but strong in will
To strive, to seek, to find, and not to yield.   70

1833

WALLACE STEVENS

The World as Meditation

J'ai passé trop de temps à travailler mon violon, à voyager. Mais l'exercice essentiel
du compositeur—la méditation—rien ne l'a jamais suspendu en moi . . . Je vis un
rêve permanent, qui ne s'arrête ni nuit ni jour.

                                              GEORGES ENESCO[7]

Is it Ulysses that approaches from the east,[8]
The interminable adventurer? The trees are mended.
That winter is washed away. Someone is moving

On the horizon and lifting himself up above it.
A form of fire approaches the cretonnes of Penelope,   5
Whose mere savage presence awakens the world in which she dwells.

She has composed, so long, a self with which to welcome him,
Companion to his self for her, which she imagined,
Two in a deep-founded sheltering, friend and dear friend.

The trees had been mended, as an essential exercise   10
In an inhuman meditation, larger than her own.
No winds like dogs watched over her at night.

She wanted nothing he could not bring her by coming alone.
She wanted no fetchings. His arms would be her necklace
And her belt, the final fortune of their desire.   15

5. Beyond the Gulf of Gibraltar was
supposed to be a chasm that led to Hades.
6. Elysium, the Islands of the Blessed,
where heroes like Achilles (line 64) abide
after death.
7. Rumanian violinist, conductor, and
composer (1881–1955): "I have spent too
much time working at my violin and traveling. But the essential exercise of the composer—meditation—nothing has ever kept
me from that. I live a permanent dream
which does not stop, night or day."
8. During Ulysses' absence to fight the
Trojan War, Penelope remained at home
for twenty years, besieged by suitors.

But was it Ulysses? Or was it only the warmth of the sun
On her pillow? The thought kept beating in her like her heart.
The two kept beating together. It was only day.

It was Ulysses and it was not. Yet they had met,
Friend and dear friend and a planet's encouragement.   20
The barbarous strength within her would never fail.

She would talk a little to herself as she combed her hair,
Repeating his name with its patient syllables,
Never forgetting him that kept coming constantly so near.

1954

JAMES HARRISON

Penelope[9]

For Ken

Oh, I have no illusions as to what
he's been up to all these years—a sea
nymph here, a minor goddess there, and a free
for all with the odd monster to give the plot
the necessary epic tone. Not   5
that I'm saying he goes out of his way to be
led astray. It happens quite naturally,
I'm sure. But it happens.
                              So, since suitors squat
on my doorstep, why so squeamish? In the first
place because it's the property they're out   10
to get, with me as an afterthought perhaps.
Then they're so callow. But mostly, having nursed
forebearance for twenty years, I'm not about
to have him forgiving me my only lapse.

1983

Non-Western History and Myth

LANGSTON HUGHES

The Negro Speaks of Rivers

I've known rivers:
I've known rivers ancient as the world and older than the flow of human
    blood in human veins.

My soul has grown deep like the rivers.

9. *Penelope*—wife of Ulysses, stuck at
home the ten years he spent fighting Troy,
and the further ten it took him to find his
way back to Ithaca. [Author's note.]

I bathed in the Euphrates when dawns were young.
I built my hut near the Congo and it lulled me to sleep.   5
I looked upon the Nile and raised the pyramids above it.
I heard the singing of the Mississippi when Abe Lincoln went down
    to New Orleans, and I've seen its muddy bosom turn all golden in
    the sunset.

I've known rivers:
Ancient, dusky rivers.

My soul has grown deep like the rivers.   10

                                                    1926

GABRIEL OKARA

Piano and Drums

When at break of day at a riverside
I hear jungle drums telegraphing
the mystic rhythm, urgent, raw
like bleeding flesh, speaking of
primal youth and the beginning,   5
I see the panther ready to pounce,
the leopard snarling about to leap
and the hunters crouch with spears poised;

And my blood ripples, turns torrent,
topples the years and at once I'm   10
in my mother's lap a suckling;
at once I'm walking simple
paths with no innovations,
rugged, fashioned with the naked
warmth of hurrying feet and groping hearts   15
in green leaves and wild flowers pulsing.

Then I hear a wailing piano
solo speaking of complex ways
in tear-furrowed concerto;
of far-away lands   20
and new horizons with
coaxing diminuendo, counterpoint,
crescendo. But lost in the labyrinth
of its complexities, it ends in the middle
of a phrase at a daggerpoint.   25

And I lost in the morning mist
of an age at a riverside keep
wandering in the mystic rhythm
of jungle drums and the concerto.

                                                    1963

MAYA ANGELOU

Africa

Thus she had lain
sugar cane sweet
deserts her hair
golden her feet
mountains her breasts   5
two Niles her tears
Thus she has lain
Black through the years.

Over the white seas
rime white and cold   10
brigands ungentled
icicle bold
took her young daughters
sold her strong sons
churched her with Jesus   15
bled her with guns.
Thus she has lain.

Now she is rising
remember her pain
remember the losses   20
her screams loud and vain
remember her riches
her history slain
now she is striding
although she had lain.   25

1975

BRUCE MCM. WRIGHT

The African Affair

Black is what the prisons are,
The stagnant vortex of the hours
Swept into totality,
Creeping in the perjured heart,
Bitter in the vulgar rhyme,   5
Bitter on the walls;

Black is where the devils dance
With time within
The creviced wall. Time pirouettes
A crippled orbit in a trance,   10

And crawls below, beneath the flesh
Where darkness flows;

Black is where the deserts burn,
The Niger and Sasandra flow,
From where the Middle Passage went   15
Within the Continent of Night
From Cameroons to Carisbrooke
And places conscience cannot go;

Black is where thatched temples burn
Incense to carved ebon-wood;   20
Where traders shaped my father's pain,
His person and his place,
Among dead statues in a frieze,
In the spectrum of his race.

                                                 1963

ISHMAEL REED

Sermonette

a poet was busted by a topless judge
his friends went to morristwn nj & put
black powder on his honah's doorstep
black powder into his honah's car
black powder on his honah's briefs   5
tiny dolls into his honah's mind

by nightfall his honah could a go go no mo
his dog went crazy & ran into a crocodile
his widow fell from a wall &
hanged herself   10
his daughter was run over by a black man
cming home for the wakes the two boys
skidded into mourning
all the next of kin's teeth fell out

gimmie dat ol time   15
                    religion
it's good enough
        for me!

                                                 1972

WILLIAM BUTLER YEATS

Easter 1916[1]

I have met them at close of day
Coming with vivid faces
From counter or desk among gray
Eighteenth-century houses.
I have passed with a nod of the head   5
Or polite meaningless words,
Or have lingered awhile and said
Polite meaningless words,
And thought before I had done
Of a mocking tale or a gibe   10
To please a companion
Around the fire at the club,
Being certain that they and I
But lived where motley[2] is worn:
All changed, changed utterly: 15
A terrible beauty is born.

That woman's[3] days were spent
In ignorant good-will,
Her nights in argument
Until her voice grew shrill.   20
What voice more sweet than hers
When, young and beautiful,
She rode to harriers?[4]
This man[5] had kept a school
And rode our wingéd horse;[6]   25
This other[7] his helper and friend
Was coming into his force;
He might have won fame in the end,
So sensitive his nature seemed,
So daring and sweet his thought.   30

1. The famous Easter uprising began on Easter Monday when an Irish republic was proclaimed by nationalist leaders, but English military forces responded quickly; by April 29, some 300 people were dead and the Nationalists surrendered. Early in May, 15 leaders (including the four mentioned in lines 75–76) were executed, and more than 2,000 were held prisoners.
2. The particolored clothing of a professional fool or jester, at court or in a play.
3. Countess Constance Georgina Markiewicz, a beautiful and well-born young woman from County Sligo who became a vigorous and bitter nationalist. At first condemned to death, she later had her sentence commuted to life imprisonment, and she gained amnesty in 1917.
4. Hounds.
5. Patrick Pearse, who led the assault on the Dublin Post Office from which the proclamation of a republic was issued. A schoolmaster by profession, he had vigorously supported the restoration of the Gaelic language in Ireland and was an active political writer and poet.
6. Pegasus, the traditional symbol of poetic inspiration.
7. Thomas MacDonagh, also a writer and teacher.

This other man[8] I had dreamed
A drunken, vainglorious lout.
He had done most bitter wrong
To some who are near my heart,
Yet I number him in the song;   35
He, too, has resigned his part
In the casual comedy;
He, too, has been changed in his turn,
Transformed utterly:
A terrible beauty is born.   40

Hearts with one purpose alone
Through summer and winter seem
Enchanted to a stone
To trouble the living stream.
The horse that comes from the road,   45
The rider, the birds that range
From cloud to tumbling cloud,
Minute by minute they change;
A shadow of cloud on the stream
Changes minute by minute;   50
A horse-hoof slides on the brim,
And a horse plashes within it;
The long-legged moor-hens dive,
And hens to moor-cocks call;
Minute by minute they live: 55
The stone's in the midst of all.

Too long a sacrifice
Can make a stone of the heart.
O when may it suffice?
That is Heaven's part, our part   60
To murmur name upon name,
As a mother names her child
When sleep at last has come
On limbs that had run wild.
What is it but nightfall?   65
No, no, not night but death;
Was it needless death after all?
For England may keep faith[9]
For all that is done and said.
We know their dream; enough
To know they dreamed and are dead;   70
And what if excess of love
Bewildered them till they died?
I write it out in a verse—
MacDonagh and MacBride   75

8. Major John MacBride, who had married Yeats's beloved Maud Gonne in 1903 but separated from her two years later.

9. Before the uprising the English had promised eventual home rule to Ireland.

And Connolly[1] and Pearse
Now and in time to be,
Wherever green is worn,
Are changed, changed utterly:
A terrible beauty is born.   80

1916

The Second Coming[2]

Turning and turning in the widening gyre[3]
The falcon cannot hear the falconer;
Things fall apart; the center cannot hold;
Mere anarchy is loosed upon the world,
The blood-dimmed tide is loosed, and everywhere   5
The ceremony of innocence is drowned;
The best lack all conviction, while the worst
Are full of passionate intensity.

Surely some revelation is at hand;
Surely the Second Coming is at hand.   10
The Second Coming! Hardly are those words out
When a vast image out of *Spiritus Mundi*[4]
Troubles my sight: somewhere in sands of the desert
A shape with lion body and the head of a man,
A gaze blank and pitiless as the sun,   15
Is moving its slow thighs, while all about it
Reel shadows of the indignant desert birds.[5]
The darkness drops again; but now I know
That twenty centuries of stony sleep
Were vexed to nightmare by a rocking cradle,   20
And what rough beast, its hour come round at last,
Slouches towards Bethlehem to be born?

p. 1920

1. James Connolly, the leader of the Easter uprising.
2. The Second Coming of Christ, according to *Matthew* 24:29–44, will come after a time of "tribulation." Disillusioned by Ireland's continued civil strife, Yeats saw his time as the end of another historical cycle. In *A Vision* (1937) Yeats describes his view of history as dependent on cycles of about 2000 years: the birth of Christ had ended the cycle of Greco-Roman civilization, and now the Christian cycle seemed near an end, to be followed by an antithetical cycle, ominous in its portents.
3. Literally, the widening spiral of a falcon's flight. "Gyre" is Yeats's term for a cycle of history, which he diagramed in terms of a series of interpenetrating cones.
4. Or *Anima Mundi*, the spirit or soul of the world, a consciousness in which the individual participates. Yeats considered this universal consciousness or memory a fund from which poets drew their images and symbols. In *Per Amica Silentia Lunae* he wrote: "Before the mind's eye, whether in sleep or waking, came images that one was to discover presently in some book one had never read, and after looking in vain for explanation . . . , I came to believe in a great memory passing on from generation to generation."
5. Yeats later writes of the "brazen winged beast . . . described in my poem *The Second Coming*" as "associated with laughing, ecstatic destruction." "Our civilization was about to reverse itself, or some new civilization about to be born from all that our age had rejected . . . ; because we had worshipped a single god it would worship many."

Leda and the Swan[6]

A sudden blow: the great wings beating still
Above the staggering girl, her thighs caressed
By the dark webs, her nape caught in his bill,
He holds her helpless breast upon his breast.

How can those terrified vague fingers push   5
The feathered glory from her loosening thighs?
And how can body, laid in that white rush,
But feel the strange heart beating where it lies?

A shudder in the loins engenders there
The broken wall, the burning roof and tower   10
And Agamemnon dead.
                              Being so caught up,
So mastered by the brute blood of the air,
Did she put on his knowledge with his power
Before the indifferent beak could let her drop?

1923

Sailing to Byzantium[7]

I

That[8] is no country for old men. The young
In one another's arms, birds in the trees
—Those dying generations—at their song,
The salmon-falls, the mackerel-crowded seas
Fish, flesh, or fowl, commend all summer long   5
Whatever is begotten, born, and dies.
Caught in that sensual music all neglect
Monuments of unaging intellect.

6. According to Greek myth, Zeus took the form of a swan to seduce Leda, who became the mother of Helen of Troy and also of Clytemnestra, Agamemnon's wife and murderer. Helen's abduction from her husband, Menelaus, brother of Agamemnon, began the Trojan War (line 10). Yeats described the visit of Zeus to Leda as an annunciation like that to Mary (see *Luke* 1:26–38): "I imagine the annunciation that founded Greece as made to Leda. . . ." (*A Vision*).
7. The ancient name of Istanbul, the capital and holy city of Eastern Christendom from the late fourth century until 1453. It was famous for its stylized and formal mosaics, its symbolic, nonnaturalistic art, and its highly developed intellectual life. Yeats repeatedly uses it to symbolize a world of artifice and timelessness, free from the decay and death of the natural and sensual world. In *A Vision*, Yeats wrote: "I think if I could be given a month of Antiquity and leave to spend it where I chose, I would spend it in Byzantium a little before Justinian opened St. Sophia and closed the Academy of Plato [about 535 A.D.]. I think I could find in some little wineshop some philosophical worker in mosaic who could answer all my questions, the supernatural descending nearer to him than to Plotinus even, for the pride of his delicate skill would make what was an instrument of power to princes and clerics, a murderous madness in the mob, show as a lovely flexible presence like that of a perfect human body. I think that in early Byzantium, maybe never before or since in recorded history, religious, aesthetic and practical life were one, that architect and artificers . . . spoke to the multitude and the few alike. The painter, the mosaic worker, the worker in gold and silver, the illuminator of sacred books, were almost impersonal, almost perhaps without the consciousness of individual design, absorbed in their subject-matter and that the vision of the whole people. They could . . . weave all into a vast design, the work of many that seemed the work of one, that made building, picture, metal-work or rail and lamp, seem but a single image. . . ."
8. Ireland, as an instance of the natural, temporal world.

II

An aged man is but a paltry thing,
A tattered coat upon a stick, unless   10
Soul clap its hands and sing, and louder sing
For every tatter in its mortal dress,
Nor is there singing school but studying
Monuments of its own magnificence;
And therefore I have sailed the seas and come   15
To the holy city of Byzantium.

III

O sages standing in God's holy fire
As in the gold mosaic of a wall,
Come from the holy fire, perne in a gyre,[9]
And be the singing-masters of my soul.   20
Consume my heart away; sick with desire
And fastened to a dying animal
It knows not what it is; and gather me
Into the artifice of eternity.

IV

Once out of nature I shall never take   25
My bodily form from any natural thing,
But such a form as Grecian goldsmiths make
Of hammered gold and gold enameling
To keep a drowsy Emperor awake;[1]
Or set upon a golden bough[2] to sing   30
To lords and ladies of Byzantium
Of what is past, or passing, or to come.

1927

Among School Children

I

I walk through the long schoolroom questioning;
A kind old nun in a white hood replies;
The children learn to cipher and to sing,
To study reading-books and history,
To cut and sew, be neat in everything   5
In the best modern way—the children's eyes
In momentary wonder stare upon
A sixty-year-old smiling public man.[3]

9. I.e., whirl in a coiling motion, so that his soul may merge with its motion as the timeless world invades the cycles of history and nature. The gyre in "The Second Coming" moves in the opposite direction, up and out centripetally, so that "things fall apart." "Perne" is Yeats's coinage (from the noun "pirn"): to spin around in the kind of spiral pattern that thread makes as it comes off a bobbin or spool.
1. "I have read somewhere that in the Emperor's palace at Byzantium was a tree made of gold and silver, and artificial birds that sang." (Yeats's note)
2. In Book VI of *The Aeneid*, the sybil tells Aeneas that he must pluck a golden bough from a nearby tree in order to descend to Hades. There is only one such branch there, and when it is plucked an identical one takes its place.
3. At 60 (in 1925) Yeats had been a senator of the Irish Free State.

II

I dream of a Ledaean body,[4] bent
Above a sinking fire, a tale that she   10
Told of a harsh reproof, or trivial event
That changed some childish day to tragedy—
Told, and it seemed that our two natures blent
Into a sphere from youthful sympathy,
Or else, to alter Plato's parable,   15
Into the yolk and white of the one shell.[5]

III

And thinking of that fit of grief or rage
I look upon one child or t'other there
And wonder if she stood so at that age—
For even daughters of the swan can share   20
Something of every paddler's heritage—
And had that color upon cheek or hair,
And thereupon my heart is driven wild:
She stands before me as a living child.

IV

Her present image floats into the mind—   25
Did Quattrocento finger[6] fashion it
Hollow of cheek as though it drank the wind
And took a mess of shadows for its meat?
And I though never of Ledaean kind
Had pretty plumage once—enough of that,   30
Better to smile on all that smile, and show
There is a comfortable kind of old scarecrow.

V

What youthful mother, a shape upon her lap
Honey of generation[7] had betrayed,
And that must sleep, shriek, struggle to escape   35
As recollection or the drug decide,
Would think her son, did she but see that shape

4. Like that of Helen of Troy, daughter of Leda. The memory dream is of Maud Gonne (see also lines 29–30), with whom Yeats had long been hopelessly in love.
5. In Plato's *Symposium*, the origin of human love is explained by parable: Human beings were once spheres, but Zeus was fearful of their power and cut them in half; now each half longs to be reunited with its missing half. Helen and Pollux were hatched from one of two eggs born to Leda after her union with Zeus in the form of a swan; the other contained Castor and Clytemnestra. According to Yeats in *A Vision*, "from one of [Leda's] eggs came Love and from the other War."
6. Fifteenth-century artists, who fall within the 15th Phase of the Christian cycle. Yeats especially admired Botticelli, and in *A Vision* praises his "deliberate strangeness everywhere [which] gives one an emotion of mystery which is new to painting." Botticelli is grouped with those who make "intellect and emotion, *primary* curiosity and the *antithetical* dream . . . for the moment one."
7. "I have taken the 'honey of generation' from Porphyry's essay on 'The Cave of the Nymphs' [*Odyssey*, Book XIII], but find no warrant in Porphyry for considering it the 'drug' that destroys the 'recollection' of prenatal freedom. He blamed a cup of oblivion given in the zodiacal sign of Cancer." (Yeats's note) Porphyry, a third-century Greek scholar and neoplatonic philosopher, says "honey of generation" means the "pleasure arising from copulation" which draws souls "downward" to generation.

With sixty or more winters on its head,
A compensation for the pang of his birth,
Or the uncertainty of his setting forth?   40

VI

Plato thought nature but a spume that plays
Upon a ghostly paradigm of things;[8]
Solider Aristotle played the taws
Upon the bottom of a king of kings;[9]
World-famous golden-thighed Pythagoras[1]   45
Fingered upon a fiddle-stick or strings
What a star sang and careless Muses heard:
Old clothes upon old sticks to scare a bird.

VII

Both nuns and mothers worship images,
But those the candles light are not as those   50
That animate a mother's reveries,
But keep a marble or a bronze repose.
And yet they too break hearts—O Presences
That passion, piety or affection knows,
And that all heavenly glory symbolize—   55
O self-born mockers of man's enterprise;

VIII

Labor is blossoming or dancing where
The body is not bruised to pleasure soul,
Nor beauty born out of its own despair,
Nor blear-eyed wisdom out of midnight oil.   60
O chestnut-tree, great-rooted blossomer,
Are you the leaf, the blossom or the bole?[2]
O body swayed to music, O brightening glance,
How can we know the dancer from the dance?

                                                       1927

Byzantium[3]

The unpurged images of day recede;
The Emperor's drunken soldiery are abed;
Night resonance recedes, night-walkers' song

8. Plato considered the world of nature an imperfect and illusory copy of the ideal world.

9. Aristotle, the teacher of Alexander the Great, disciplined him with a strap ("taw," line 43). His philosophy, insisting on the interdependence of form and matter, took the world of nature far more seriously than did Plato's.

1. Sixth-century B.C. Greek mathematician and philosopher, whose elaborate philosophical system included the doctrine of the harmony of the spheres. He was highly revered, and one legend describes his god-like golden thighs.

2. Trunk.

3. In his diary for April 30, 1930, Yeats sketched the following "Subject for a Poem": "Describe Byzantium as it is in the system towards the end of the first Christian millennium. A walking mummy. Flames at the street corners where the soul is purified, birds of hammered gold singing in the golden trees, in the harbor [dolphins], offering their backs to the wailing dead that they may carry them to paradise."

After great cathedral gong;
A starlit or a moonlit dome[4] disdains   5
All that man is,
All mere complexities,
The fury and the mire of human veins.

Before me floats an image, man or shade,
Shade more than man, more image than a shade;   10
For Hades' bobbin bound in mummy-cloth
May unwind the winding path;[5]
A mouth that has no moisture and no breath
Breathless mouths may summon;
I hail the superhuman;   15
I call it death-in-life and life-in-death.

Miracle, bird or golden handiwork,
More miracle than bird or handiwork,
Planted on the star-lit golden bough,
Can like the cocks of Hades crow,[6]   20
Or, by the moon embittered, scorn aloud
In glory of changeless metal
Common bird or petal
And all complexities of mire or blood.

At midnight on the Emperor's pavement flit   25
Flames that no fagot[7] feeds, nor steel has lit,
Nor storm disturbs, flames begotten of flame,
Where blood-begotten spirits come
And all complexities of fury leave,
Dying into a dance,   30
An agony of trance,
An agony of flame that cannot singe a sleeve.

Astraddle on the dolphin's mire and blood,[8]
Spirit after spirit! The smithies break the flood,
The golden smithies of the Emperor!   35
Marbles of the dancing floor
Break bitter furies of complexity,

4. In *A Vision*, Yeats described the 28 phases of the moon in psychological terms related to his system. In Phase 1, only stars are visible ("starlit") and "body is completely absorbed in its supernatural environment." In its opposite, Phase 15, when the moon is full ("moonlit"), the mind is "completely absorbed in being."

5. A volume in which "Byzantium" appeared, *The Winding Stair and Other Poems*, contains many similar images; of this volume Yeats wrote: "In this book and elsewhere I have used towers, and one tower in particular, as symbols and have compared their winding stairs to the philosophical gyres, but it is hardly necessary to interpret what comes from the main track of thought and expression. Shelley uses towers constantly as symbols, and there are gyres in Swedenborg, and in Thomas Aquinas and certain classical authors."

6. As the bird of dawn, the cock had from antiquity been a symbol of rebirth and resurrection.

7. Bundle of sticks.

8. In ancient art, dolphins symbolize the soul moving from one state to another, and sometimes they provide a vehicle for the dead. Palaemon, for example, in Greek tradition is often mounted on a dolphin.

Those images that yet
Fresh images beget,
That dolphin-torn, that gong-tormented sea.   40

1932

The Circus Animals' Desertion[9]

I

I sought a theme and sought for it in vain,
I sought it daily for six weeks or so.
Maybe at last, being but a broken man,
I must be satisfied with my heart, although
Winter and summer till old age began   5
My circus animals were all on show,
Those stilted boys, that burnished chariot,
Lion and woman and the Lord knows what.

II

What can I but enumerate old themes?
First that sea-rider Oisin[1] led by the nose   10
Through three enchanted islands, allegorical dreams,
Vain gaiety, vain battle, vain repose,
Themes of the embittered heart, or so it seems,
That might adorn old songs or courtly shows;
But what cared I that set him on to ride,   15
I, starved for the bosom of his faery bride?

And then a counter-truth filled out its play,
The Countess Cathleen[2] was the name I gave it;
She, pity-crazed, had given her soul away,
But masterful Heaven had intervened to save it.   20
I thought my dear[3] must her own soul destroy,
So did fanaticism and hate enslave it,
And this brought forth a dream and soon enough
This dream itself had all my thought and love.

And when the Fool and Blind Man stole the bread   25
Cuchulain fought the ungovernable sea;[4]
Heart-mysteries there, and yet when all is said
It was the dream itself enchanted me:
Character isolated by a deed
To engross the present and dominate memory.   30
Players and painted stage took all my love,
And not those things that they were emblems of.

9. The "animals" are early themes and images in Yeats's poetry, and he here reviews some of them.
1. The subject of an 1889 long poem. Oisin was a legendary figure, beguiled to faery land for 150 years, who returned to find his friends dead in his native Ireland.

2. An 1892 play, in which the countess sells her soul to the devil to get food for hungry people but nevertheless gains Heaven.
3. Maud Gonne.
4. In a 1904 play, *On Baile's Strand*.

III

Those masterful images because complete
Grew in pure mind, but out of what began?
A mound of refuse or the sweepings of a street,   35
Old kettles, old bottles, and a broken can,
Old iron, old bones, old rags, that raving slut
Who keeps the till. Now that my ladder's gone,
I must lie down where all the ladders start,
In the foul rag-and-bone shop of the heart.   40

1939

Poems for Further Reading

MARGARET ATWOOD

Death of a Young Son by Drowning

He, who navigated with success
the dangerous river of his own birth
once more set forth

on a voyage of discovery
into the land I floated on   5
but could not touch to claim.

His feet slid on the bank,
the currents took him;
he swirled with ice and trees in the swollen water

and plunged into distant regions,   10
his head a bathysphere;
through his eyes' thin glass bubbles

he looked out, reckless adventurer
on a landscape stranger than Uranus
we have all been to and some remember.   15

There was an accident; the air locked,
he was hung in the river like a heart.
They retrieved the swamped body,

cairn of my plans and future charts,
with poles and hooks   20
from among the nudging logs.

It was spring, the sun kept shining, the new grass
leapt to solidity;
my hands glistened with details.

After the long trip I was tired of waves.   25
My foot hit rock. The dreamed sails
collapsed, ragged.

> I planted him in this country
> like a flag.

1970

W. H. AUDEN

In Memory of W. B. Yeats

(d. January, 1939)

I

He disappeared in the dead of winter:
The brooks were frozen, the airports almost deserted,
And snow disfigured the public statues;
The mercury sank in the mouth of the dying day.
What instruments we have agree   5
The day of his death was a dark cold day.

Far from his illness
The wolves ran on through the evergreen forests,
The peasant river was untempted by the fashionable quays;
By mourning tongues   10
The death of the poet was kept from his poems.

But for him it was his last afternoon as himself,
An afternoon of nurses and rumors;
The provinces of his body revolted,
The squares of his mind were empty,   15
Silence invaded the suburbs,
The current of his feeling failed; he became his admirers.

Now he is scattered among a hundred cities
And wholly given over to unfamiliar affections,
To find his happiness in another kind of wood   20
And be punished under a foreign code of conscience.
The words of a dead man
Are modified in the guts of the living.

But in the importance and noise of tomorrow
When the brokers are roaring like beasts on the floor of the Bourse,[1] 25
And the poor have the sufferings to which they are fairly accustomed,
And each in the cell of himself is almost convinced of his freedom,
A few thousand will think of this day
As one thinks of a day when one did something slightly unusual.
What instruments we have agree   30
The day of his death was a dark cold day.

II

You were silly like us; your gift survived it all:
The parish of rich women, physical decay,
Yourself. Mad Ireland hurt you into poetry.
Now Ireland has her madness and her weather still,   35
For poetry makes nothing happen: it survives
In the valley of its making where executives

---

1. The Paris stock exchange.

Would never want to tamper, flows on south
From ranches of isolation and the busy griefs,
Raw towns that we believe and die in; it survives,   40
A way of happening, a mouth.

III

Earth, receive an honored guest:
William Yeats is laid to rest.
Let the Irish vessel lie
Emptied of its poetry.   45

In the nightmare of the dark
All the dogs of Europe bark,
And the living nations wait,
Each sequestered in its hate;

Intellectual disgrace   50
Stares from every human face,
And the seas of pity lie
Locked and frozen in each eye.

Follow, poet, follow right
To the bottom of the night,   55
With your unconstraining voice
Still persuade us to rejoice;

With the farming of a verse
Make a vineyard of the curse,
Sing of human unsuccess   60
In a rapture of distress;

In the deserts of the heart
Let the healing fountain start,
In the prison of his days
Teach the free man how to praise.   65

1939

WILLIAM BLAKE

Ah Sunflower

Ah Sunflower! weary of time,
Who countest the steps of the Sun,
Seeking after that sweet golden clime
Where the traveler's journey is done,

Where the Youth pined away with desire,   5
And the pale Virgin shrouded in snow,
Arise from their graves and aspire,
Where my Sunflower wishes to go.

1794

WILLIAM BLAKE

The Lamb

Little Lamb, who made thee?
Dost thou know who made thee?
Gave thee life, and bid thee feed
By the stream and o'er the mead;
Gave thee clothing of delight,   5
Softest clothing woolly bright;
Gave thee such a tender voice,
Making all the vales rejoice?
    Little Lamb, who made thee?
    Dost thou know who made thee?   10

Little Lamb, I'll tell thee!
Little Lamb, I'll tell thee:
He is calléd by thy name,
For he calls himself a Lamb,
He is meek and he is mild;   15
He became a little child.
I a child and thou a lamb,
We are calléd by his name.
    Little Lamb, God bless thee!
    Little Lamb, God bless thee!   20

1789

WILLIAM BLAKE

The Tiger

Tiger, Tiger, burning bright
In the forests of the night,
What immortal hand or eye
Could frame thy fearful symmetry?

In what distant deeps or skies   5
Burnt the fire of thine eyes?
On what wings dare he aspire?
What the hand dare seize the fire?

And what shoulder and what art,
Could twist the sinews of thy heart?   10
And when thy heart began to beat,
What dread hand, and what dread feet?

What the hammer? What the chain?
In what furnace was thy brain?
What the anvil? What dread grasp   15
Dare its deadly terrors clasp?

When the stars threw down their spears
And watered heaven with their tears,

Did he smile his work to see?
Did he who made the Lamb make thee?   20

Tiger, Tiger, burning bright
In the forests of the night,
What immortal hand or eye
Dare frame thy fearful symmetry?

1794

AMY CLAMPITT

Time

It may be we are in the last days.
Seven hundred years ago to the week,
on the eleventh of December, the kingdom of Wales went under.
Today, the sixth of the twelfth month of the nineteen-hundred-eighty-
     second year, according to the current reckoning,
there are roses the size of the old English threepenny bit—   5
one fingernail-pink, another minute, extravagant crimson—
flanked by masses of sweet alyssum
and one time-exempt purple pansy
on the site of what was formerly the Women's House of Detention
at the triangular intersection of Tenth Street with Greenwich and Sixth
     Avenues   10
at the back of the old Jefferson Market courthouse,
whose tower clock, revived, goes on keeping time.
And I think again of October violets,
of their hardy refusal to adhere to conventional expectation—
so hardy that I've finally ceased to think of it as startling,   15
this phenomenon which, in fact, I devoted myself in October to looking
     for:
a tame revenant of the blue fire alarm of the original encounter with
     the evidence,
among the dropped leaves and superannuated grass of the season of
     hickory nuts,
that neither time nor place could be counted on to remain self-sufficient,
that you might find yourself slipping back toward the past at any mo-
     ment,   20
or watch it well up in artesian springs of anachronism,
with the prospect of being drowned in that aperture's abrupt blue,
in that twinkling of an eye, at any moment.
It was November, or near then, I found violets massed at the foot of
     the foundations of the castle of Chepstow,
at the edge of Wales—not any longer, as once, covert, fecklessly under-
     mining   25
that sense of fitness, so fragile that at any moment of one's childhood,
whatever sense of continuity has not ebbed or been marked for demo-
     lition,
may break like an eggshell, and be overrun from within by the albumen
     of ruin—

their out-of-season purple not any longer hinting at something, but
    announcing it with a flourish:
the entire gorgeous, intractable realm of the forgotten,   30
the hieratic, the heraldic, the royal, sprung open
at the gouty foot of that anachronism
on the fringes of a kingdom that went under
at or near the downward slope of the thirteenth century. I have seen
the artesian spring of the past foam up at the foot of the castle of
    Chepstow   35
on a day in November, or thereabouts. I have seen a rose the size of a
    perfectly manicured crimson fingernail
alive in a winter that does not arrive, though we plunge again toward
    the solstice.

                      p. 1983

LEONARD COHEN

Suzanne Takes You Down

Suzanne takes you down
to her place near the river,
you can hear the boats go by
you can stay the night beside her.
And you know that she's half crazy   5
but that's why you want to be there
and she feeds you tea and oranges
that come all the way from China.
Just when you mean to tell her
that you have no gifts to give her,   10
she gets you on her wave-length
and she lets the river answer
that you've always been her lover.
    And you want to travel with her,
    you want to travel blind   15
and you know that she can trust you
because you've touched her perfect body
with your mind.

Jesus was a sailor
when he walked upon the water [2]   20
and he spent a long time watching
from a lonely wooden tower
and when he knew for certain
only drowning men could see him
he said All men will be sailors then   25
until the sea shall free them,
but he himself was broken
long before the sky would open,
forsaken, almost human,

2. According to *Matthew* 14:22–26 and *Mark* 6:45–52, Jesus walked upon the water in order to join his disciples in a ship at sea.

he sank beneath your wisdom like a stone.   30
   And you want to travel with him,
   you want to travel blind
   and you think maybe you'll trust him
   because he touched your perfect body
   with his mind.   35

Suzanne takes your hand
and she leads you to the river,
she is wearing rags and feathers
from Salvation Army counters.
The sun pours down like honey   40
on our lady of the harbor
as she shows you where to look
among the garbage and the flowers,
there are heroes in the seaweed
there are children in the morning,   45
they are leaning out for love
they will lean that way forever
while Suzanne she holds the mirror.
   And you want to travel with her
   and you want to travel blind   50
   and you're sure that she can find you
   because she's touched her perfect body
   with her mind.

                               1968

SAMUEL TAYLOR COLERIDGE

Kubla Khan: or, a Vision in a Dream[3]

In Xanadu did Kubla Khan
   A stately pleasure-dome decree:
Where Alph, the sacred river, ran
Through caverns measureless to man
   Down to a sunless sea.   5
So twice five miles of fertile ground
With walls and towers were girdled round:
And here were gardens bright with sinuous rills
Where blossomed many an incense-bearing tree;
And here were forests ancient as the hills,   10
Enfolding sunny spots of greenery.
But oh! that deep romantic chasm which slanted
Down the green hill athwart a cedarn cover![4]
A savage place! as holy and enchanted
As e'er beneath a waning moon was haunted   15
By woman wailing for her demon-lover![5]

3. Coleridge said he wrote this fragment immediately after waking from an opium dream and that after he was interrupted by a caller he was unable to finish the poem.
4. From side to side of a cover of cedar trees.
5. In a famous and often imitated German ballad, the lady Lenore is carried off on horseback by the specter of her lover and married to him at his grave.

And from this chasm, with ceaseless turmoil seething,
As if this earth in fast thick pants were breathing,
A mighty fountain momently was forced,
Amid whose swift half-intermitted burst   20
Huge fragments vaulted like rebounding hail,
Or chaffy grain beneath the thresher's flail:
And 'mid these dancing rocks at once and ever
It flung up momently the sacred river.
Five miles meandering with a mazy motion   25
Through wood and dale the sacred river ran,
Then reached the caverns measureless to man,
And sank in tumult to a lifeless ocean:
And 'mid this tumult Kubla heard from far
Ancestral voices prophesying war!   30

    The shadow of the dome of pleasure
    Floated midway on the waves;
    Where was heard the mingled measure
    From the fountain and the caves.
It was a miracle of rare device,   35
A sunny pleasure-dome with caves of ice!
    A damsel with a dulcimer[6]
    In a vision once I saw:
    It was an Abyssinian maid,
    And on her dulcimer she played,   40
    Singing of Mount Abora.
    Could I revive within me
    Her symphony and song,
    To such a deep delight 'twould win me,
That with music loud and long,   45
I would build that dome in air,
That sunny dome! those caves of ice!
And all who heard should see them there,
And all should cry, Beware! Beware!
His flashing eyes, his floating hair!   50
Weave a circle round him thrice,
And close your eyes with holy dread,
For he on honey-dew hath fed,
And drunk the milk of Paradise.

1798

HART CRANE

To Emily Dickinson

You who desired so much—in vain to ask—
Yet fed your hunger like an endless task,
Dared dignify the labor, bless the quest—
Achieved that stillness ultimately best,

---

6. A stringed instrument, prototype of the piano.

Being, of all, least sought for: Emily, hear!   5
O sweet, dead Silencer, most suddenly clear
When singing that Eternity possessed
And plundered momently in every breast;

—Truly no flower yet withers in your hand,
The harvest you descried and understand   10
Needs more than wit to gather, love to bind.
Some reconcilement of remotest mind—

Leaves Ormus rubyless, and Ophir [7] chill.
Else tears heap all within one clay-cold hill.

                1933

COUNTEE CULLEN

For a Lady I Know

She even thinks that up in heaven
Her class lies late and snores,
While poor black cherubs rise at seven
To do celestial chores.

                1925

e. e. cummings

chanson innocente

in Just-
spring   when the world is mud-
luscious the little
lame balloonman

whistles   far   and wee   5

and eddieandbill come
running from marbles and
piracies and it's
spring

when the world is puddle-wonderful   10

the queer
old balloonman whistles
far   and   wee
and bettyandisbel come dancing

from hop-scotch and jump-rope and   15

7. An ancient country from which Solomon secured gold and precious stones. *Ormus:* Presumably Ormuz, an ancient city on the Persian gulf.

<pre>
it's
spring
and
        the

            goat-footed   20

balloonMan   whistles
far
and
wee[8]
</pre>

                                                                    1923

EMILY DICKINSON

Because I Could Not Stop for Death

Because I could not stop for Death—
He kindly stopped for me—
The Carriage held but just Ourselves—
And Immortality.

We slowly drove—He knew no haste   5
And I had put away
My labor and my leisure too,
For His Civility—

We passed the School, where Children strove
At Recess—in the Ring—   10
We passed the Fields of Gazing Grain—
We passed the Setting Sun—

Or rather—He passed Us—
The Dews drew quivering and chill—
For only Gossamer,[9] my Gown—   15
My Tippet[1]—only Tulle[2]—

We paused before a House that seemed
A Swelling of the Ground—
The Roof was scarcely visible—
The Cornice—in the Ground—   20

Since then—'tis Centuries—and yet
Feels shorter than the Day
I first surmised the Horses' Heads
Were toward Eternity—

ca. 1863

8. Pan, whose Greek name means "everything," is traditionally represented with a syrinx (or the pipes of Pan). The upper half of his body is human, the lower half goat, and as the father of Silenus he is associated with the spring rites of Dionysus.
9. A soft sheer fabric.
1. Scarf.
2. A fine net fabric.

EMILY DICKINSON

The Brain Is Wider than the Sky

The Brain—is wider than the Sky—
For—put them side by side—
The one the other will contain
With ease—and You—beside—

The Brain is deeper than the sea—   5
For—hold them—Blue to Blue—
The one the other will absorb—
As Sponges—Buckets—do—

                                heavier
The Brain is just the weight of God—
For—Heft them—Pound for Pound—   10
And they will differ—if they do—
As Syllable from Sound—

ca. 1862

EMILY DICKINSON

I Dwell in Possibility

I dwell in Possibility—
A fairer House than Prose—
More numerous of Windows—
Superior—for Doors—

Of Chambers as the Cedars—   5
Impregnable of Eye—
And for an Everlasting Roof
The Gambrels[3] of the Sky—

Of Visitors—the fairest—
For Occupation—This—   10
The spreading wide my narrow Hands
To gather Paradise—

ca. 1862

EMILY DICKINSON

I Reckon. When I Count at All

I reckon—when I count at all—
First—Poets—Then the Sun—
Then Summer—Then the Heaven of God—
And then—the List is done—

3. Roofs with double slopes.

But, looking back—the First so seems   5
To Comprehend the Whole—
The Others look a needless Show—
So I write—Poets—All—

Their Summer—lasts a Solid Year—
They can afford a Sun   10
The East—would deem extravagant—
And if the Further Heaven—

Be Beautiful as they prepare
For Those who worship Them—
It is too difficult a Grace—   15
To justify the Dream—

c. 1862

EMILY DICKINSON

My Life Closed Twice

My life closed twice before its close—
It yet remains to see
If Immortality unveil
A third event to me

So huge, so hopeless to conceive   5
As these that twice befell.
Parting is all we know of heaven,
And all we need of hell.

1896

EMILY DICKINSON

My Life Had Stood—A Loaded Gun

My Life had stood—a Loaded Gun—
In Corners—till a Day
The Owner passed—identified—
And carried Me away—

And now We roam in Sovereign Woods—   5
And now We hunt the Doe—
And every time I speak for Him—
The Mountains straight reply—

And do I smile, such cordial light
Upon the Valley glow—   10
It is as a Vesuvian face
Had let its pleasure through—

And when at Night—Our good Day done—
I guard My Master's Head—
'Tis better than the Eider-Duck's   15
Deep Pillow—to have shared—

To foe of His—I'm deadly foe—
None stir the second time—
On whom I lay a Yellow Eye—
Or an emphatic Thumb—   20

Though I than He—may longer live
He longer must—than I—
For I have but the power to kill,
Without—the power to die—

c. 1863

EMILY DICKINSON

Wild Nights! Wild Nights!

Wild Nights—Wild Nights!
Were I with thee
Wild Nights should be
Our luxury!

Futile—the Winds—   5
To a Heart in port—
Done with the Compass—
Done with the Chart!

Rowing in Eden—
Ah, the Sea!   10
Might I but moor—Tonight—
In Thee!

ca. 1861

JOHN DONNE

The Canonization

For God's sake hold your tongue and let me love!
    Or chide my palsy or my gout,
My five gray hairs or ruined fortune flout;
With wealth your state, your mind with arts improve,
    Take you a course, get you a place,   5
    Observe his Honor or his Grace,
Or the king's real or his stampéd face[4]
    Contemplate; what you will, approve,
        So you will let me love.

4. On coins.

Alas, alas, who's injured by my love?   10
    What merchant's ships have my sighs drowned?
Who says my tears have overflowed his ground?
When did my colds a forward spring remove?
    When did the heats which my veins fill
    Add one man to the plaguy bill?[5]   15
Soldiers find wars, and lawyers find out still
    Litigious men which quarrels move,
        Though she and I do love.

Call us what you will, we are made such by love.
    Call her one, me another fly,   20
We're tapers[6] too, and at our own cost die;
And we in us find th' eagle and the dove.[7]
    The phoenix riddle[8] hath more wit[9]
    By us; we two, being one, are it.
So to one neutral thing both sexes fit,   25
    We die and rise the same, and prove
        Mysterious by this love.

We can die by it, if not live by love;
    And if unfit for tombs and hearse
Our legend be, it will be fit for verse;   30
And if no piece of chronicle we prove,[1]
    We'll build in sonnets[2] pretty rooms
    (As well a well-wrought urn becomes[8][3]
The greatest ashes, as half-acre tombs),
    And by these hymns all shall approve   35
        Us canonized for love.

And thus invoke us: "You whom reverent love
    Made one another's hermitage,
You to whom love was peace, that now is rage,
Who did the whole world's soul extract, and drove[4]   40
    Into the glasses of your eyes
    (So made such mirrors and such spies
That they did all to you epitomize)
    Countries, towns, courts; beg from above
        A pattern of your love!"   45
                                                        1633

---

5. List of plague victims.
6. Which consume themselves. To "die" is Renaissance slang for consummating the sexual act, which was popularly believed to shorten life by one day. "fly": a traditional symbol of transitory life.
7. Traditional symbols of strength and purity.
8. According to tradition, only one phoenix existed at a time, dying in a funeral pyre of its own making and being reborn from its own ashes. The bird's existence was thus a riddle akin to a religious mystery (line 27), and a symbol sometimes fused with Christian representations of immortality.
9. Meaning.
1. I.e., if we don't turn out to be an authenticated piece of historical narrative.
2. Love poems. In Italian, *stanza* means rooms.
3. Befits.
4. Compressed.

JOHN DONNE

Death Be Not Proud

Death be not proud, though some have calléd thee
Mighty and dreadful, for thou art not so;
For those whom thou think'st thou dost overthrow
Die not, poor Death, nor yet canst thou kill me.
From rest and sleep, which but thy pictures[5] be,   5
Much pleasure; then from thee much more must flow,
And soonest[6] our best men with thee do go,
Rest of their bones, and soul's delivery.[7]
Thou art slave to Fate, Chance, kings, and desperate men,
And dost with Poison, War, and Sickness dwell;   10
And poppy or charms can make us sleep as well,
And better than thy stroke; why swell'st[8] thou then?
One short sleep past, we wake eternally
And death shall be no more; Death, thou shalt die.

1633

JOHN DONNE

Song

Go, and catch a falling star,
    Get with child a mandrake root,[9]
Tell me, where all past years are,
    Or who cleft the devil's foot,
Teach me to hear mermaids singing   5
Or to keep off envy's stinging,
            And find
            What wind
Serves to advance an honest mind.

If thou beest born to strange sights,[1]   10
    Things invisible to see,
Ride ten thousand days and nights,
    Till age snow white hairs on thee;
Thou, when thou return'st, wilt tell me
All strange wonders that befell thee,   15
            And swear,
            No where
Lives a woman true, and fair.

If thou find'st one, let me know:
    Such a pilgrimage were sweet.   20
Yet do not, I would not go,

5. Likenesses.
6. Most willingly.
7. Deliverance.
8. Puff with pride.

9. The forked mandrake root is said to be shaped like the lower half of a human torso.
1. I.e., if you have supernatural powers.

Though at next door we might meet:
Though she were true when you met her,
And last till you write your letter,
    Yet she   25
    Will be
False, ere I come, to two, or three.

                                                  1633

T. S. ELIOT

Journey of the Magi[2]

"A cold coming we had of it,
Just the worst time of the year
For a journey, and such a long journey:
The ways deep and the weather sharp,
The very dead of winter."[3]   5
And the camels galled, sore-footed, refractory,
Lying down in the melting snow.
There were times we regretted
The summer palaces on slopes, the terraces,
And the silken girls bringing sherbet.   10
Then the camel men cursing and grumbling
And running away, and wanting their liquor and women,
And the night-fires going out, and the lack of shelters,
And the cities hostile and the towns unfriendly
And the villages dirty and charging high prices: 15
A hard time we had of it.
At the end we preferred to travel all night,
Sleeping in snatches,
With the voices singing in our ears, saying
That this was all folly.   20

    Then at dawn we came down to a temperate valley,
Wet, below the snow line, smelling of vegetation;
With a running stream and a water-mill beating the darkness,
And three trees on the low sky,[4]
And an old white horse galloped away in the meadow.   25
Then we came to a tavern with vine-leaves over the lintel,
Six hands at an open door dicing for pieces of silver,
And feet kicking the empty wine-skins.
But there was no information, and so we continued
And arrived at evening, not a moment too soon   30
Finding the place; it was (you may say) satisfactory.

2. The wise men who followed the star of Bethlehem. See *Matthew* 2:1–12.
3. An adaptation of a passage from a 1622 sermon by Lancelot Andrewes.
4. Suggestive of the three crosses of the Crucifixion (*Luke* 23:32–33). The Magi see several objects which suggest later events in Christ's life: pieces of silver (see *Matthew* 26:14–16), the dicing (see *Matthew* 27:35), the white horse (see *Revelation* 6:2 and 19:11–16), and the empty wine-skins (see *Matthew* 9:14–17, possibly relevant also to lines 41–42).

All this was a long time ago, I remember,
And I would do it again, but set down
This set down
This: were we led all that way for   35
Birth or Death? There was a Birth, certainly,
We had evidence and no doubt. I had seen birth and death,
But had thought they were different; this Birth was
Hard and bitter agony for us, like Death, our death.
We returned to our places, these Kingdoms,⁵   40
But no longer at ease here, in the old dispensation,
With an alien people clutching their gods.
I should be glad of another death.

                                                                      1927

T. S. ELIOT

The Love Song of J. Alfred Prufrock

S'io credesse che mia risposta fosse
A persona che mai tornasse al mondo,
Questa fiamma staria senza piu scosse.
Ma perciocche giammai di questo fondo
Non torno vivo alcun, s'i'odo il vero,
*Senza tema d'infamia ti rispondo.*⁶

Let us go then, you and I,
When the evening is spread out against the sky
Like a patient etherized upon a table;
Let us go, through certain half-deserted streets,
The muttering retreats   5
Of restless nights in one-night cheap hotels
And sawdust restaurants with oyster-shells:
Streets that follow like a tedious argument
Of insidious intent
To lead you to an overwhelming question . . .   10
Oh, do not ask, "What is it?"
Let us go and make our visit.

    In the room the women come and go
Talking of Michelangelo.

    The yellow fog that rubs its back upon the window-panes,   15
The yellow smoke that rubs its muzzle on the window-panes,
Licked its tongue into the corners of the evening,

---

5. The Bible only identifies the wise men as "from the East," and subsequent tradition has made them kings. In Persia, Magi were members of an ancient priestly caste.

6. Dante's *Inferno*, XXVII, 61–66. In the Eighth Chasm, Dante and Vergil meet Count Guido de Montefeltrano, one of the False Counselors. The spirits there are in the form of flames, and Guido speaks from the trembling tip of the flame, responding to Dante's request that he tell his life story: "If I thought that my answer were to someone who would ever go back to earth, this flame would be still, without any more movement. But because no one has ever gone back alive from this chasm (if what I hear is true) I answer you without fear of infamy."

Lingered upon the pools that stand in drains,
Let fall upon its back the soot that falls from chimneys,
Slipped by the terrace, made a sudden leap,   20
And seeing that it was a soft October night,
Curled once about the house, and fell asleep.

And indeed there will be time[7]
For the yellow smoke that slides along the street,
Rubbing its back upon the window-panes;   25
There will be time, there will be time
To prepare a face to meet the faces that you meet;
There will be time to murder and create,
And time for all the works and days[8] of hands
That lift and drop a question on your plate;   30
Time for you and time for me,
And time yet for a hundred indecisions,
And for a hundred visions and revisions,
Before the taking of a toast and tea.

In the room the women come and go   35
Talking of Michelangelo.

And indeed there will be time
To wonder, "Do I dare?" and, "Do I dare?"
Time to turn back and descend the stair,
With a bald spot in the middle of my hair—   40
(They will say: "How his hair is growing thin!")
My morning coat, my collar mounting firmly to the chin,
My necktie rich and modest, but asserted by a simple pin—
(They will say: "But how his arms and legs are thin!")
Do I dare   45
Disturb the universe?

In a minute there is time
For decisions and revisions which a minute will reverse.

For I have known them all already, known them all:—
Have known the evenings, mornings, afternoons,   50
I have measured out my life with coffee spoons;
I know the voices dying with a dying fall
Beneath the music from a farther room.
    So how should I presume?

And I have known the eyes already, known them all—   55
The eyes that fix you in a formulated phrase,

7. See *Ecclesiastes* 3:1ff.: "To every-thing there is a season, and a time to every purpose under the heaven: A time to be born, and a time to die; a time to plant, and a time to pluck up that which is planted; A time to kill, and a time to heal. . . ." Also see Marvell's "To His Coy Mistress": "Had we but world enough and time. . . ."
8. Hesiod's ancient Greek didactic poem *Works and Days* prescribed in practical detail how to conduct one's life.

And when I am formulated, sprawling on a pin,
When I am pinned and wriggling on the wall,
Then how should I begin
To spit out all the butt-ends of my days and ways?   60
    And how should I presume?

And I have known the arms already, known them all—
Arms that are braceleted and white and bare
(But in the lamplight, downed with light brown hair!)
Is it perfume from a dress   65
That makes me so digress?
Arms that lie along a table, or wrap about a shawl.
    And should I then presume?
    And how should I begin?
                            . . . .
Shall I say, I have gone at dusk through narrow streets   70
And watched the smoke that rises from the pipes
Of lonely men in shirt-sleeves, leaning out of windows? . . .

    I should have been a pair of ragged claws
    Scuttling across the floors of silent seas.
                            . . . . . .
And the afternoon, the evening, sleeps so peacefully!   75
Smoothed by long fingers,
Asleep . . . tired . . . or it malingers,
Stretched on the floor, here beside you and me.
Should I, after tea and cakes and ices,
Have the strength to force the moment to its crisis?   80
But though I have wept and fasted, wept and prayed,
Though I have seen my head (grown slightly bald) brought in upon
        a platter,⁹
I am no prophet—and here's no great matter;
I have seen the moment of my greatness flicker,
And I have seen the eternal Footman hold my coat, and snicker,   85
And in short, I was afraid.

    And would it have been worth it, after all,
After the cups, the marmalade, the tea,
Among the porcelain, among some talk of you and me,
Would it have been worth while,   90
To have bitten off the matter with a smile,
To have squeezed the universe into a ball¹
To roll it toward some overwhelming question,
To say: "I am Lazarus,² come from the dead,

---

9. See *Matthew* 14:1–12 and *Mark* 6:17–29: John the Baptist was decapitated, upon Salome's request and at Herod's command, and his head delivered on a platter.
  1. See Marvell's "To His Coy Mistress," lines 41–42: "Let us roll all our strength and all / our sweetness up into one ball. . . ."
  2. One Lazarus was raised from the dead by Jesus (see *John* 1:1 to 2:2), and another (in the parable of the rich man Dives) is discussed in terms of returning from the dead to warn the living (*Luke* 16:19–31).

Come back to tell you all, I shall tell you all"—   95
If one, settling a pillow by her head,
   Should say:"That is not what I meant at all.
   That is not it, at all."

   And would it have been worth it, after all,
Would it have been worth while,   100
After the sunsets and the dooryards and the sprinkled streets,
After the novels, after the teacups, after the skirts that trail along the
    floor—
And this, and so much more?—
It is impossible to say just what I mean!
But as if a magic lantern[3] threw the nerves in patterns on a screen: 105
Would it have been worth while
If one, settling a pillow or throwing off a shawl,
And turning toward the window, should say:
   "That is not it at all,
   That is not what I meant, at all."   110
     . . . . . .

No! I am not Prince Hamlet, nor was meant to be;
Am an attendant lord,[4] one that will do
To swell a progress,[5] start a scene or two,
Advise the prince; no doubt, an easy tool,
Deferential, glad to be of use,   115
Politic, cautious, and meticulous;
Full of high sentence, but a bit obtuse;
At times, indeed, almost ridiculous—
Almost, at times, the Fool.

   I grow old . . . I grow old . . .   120
I shall wear the bottoms of my trousers rolled.

   Shall I part my hair behind? Do I dare to eat a peach?
I shall wear white flannel trousers, and walk upon the beach.
I have heard the mermaids singing, each to each.

   I do not think that they will sing to me.   125

   I have seen them riding seaward on the waves
Combing the white hair of the waves blown back
When the wind blows the water white and black.

   We have lingered in the chambers of the sea
By sea-girls wreathed with seaweed red and brown   130
Till human voices wake us, and we drown.

               1917

---

3. **A nonelectric projector used as early**
as the 17th century.
4. Like Polonius in *Hamlet*, who is full
of maxims ("high sentence," line 117).
5. Procession of state.

ROBERT FROST

Fire and Ice

Some say the world will end in fire,
Some say in ice.
From what I've tasted of desire
I hold with those who favor fire.
But if it had to perish twice,   5
I think I know enough of hate
To say that for destruction ice
Is also great
And would suffice.

1923

ROBERT FROST

Range-Finding

The battle rent a cobweb diamond-strung
And cut a flower beside a groundbird's nest
Before it stained a single human breast.
The stricken flower bent double and so hung.
And still the bird revisited her young.   5
A butterfly its fall had dispossessed,
A moment sought in air his flower of rest,
Then lightly stooped to it and fluttering clung.
On the bare upland pasture there had spread
O'ernight 'twixt mullein[6] stalks a wheel of thread   10
And straining cables wet with silver dew.
A sudden passing bullet shook it dry.
The indwelling spider ran to greet the fly,
But finding nothing, sullenly withdrew.

1916

ROBERT FROST

The Road Not Taken

Two roads diverged in a yellow wood,
And sorry I could not travel both
And be one traveler, long I stood
And looked down one as far as I could
To where it bent in the undergrowth;   5

Then took the other, as just as fair,
And having perhaps the better claim,
Because it was grassy and wanted wear;

6. Weed.

Though as for that the passing there
Had worn them really about the same,   10

And both that morning equally lay
In leaves no step had trodden black.
Oh, I kept the first for another day!
Yet knowing how way leads on to 'way,
I doubted if I should ever come back.   15

I shall be telling this with a sigh
Somewhere ages and ages hence:
Two roads diverged in a wood, and I—
I took the one less traveled by,
And that has made all the difference.   20

                                                         1916

ROBERT FROST

Stopping by Woods on a Snowy Evening

Whose woods these are I think I know.
His house is in the village, though;
He will not see me stopping here
To watch his woods fill up with snow.

My little horse must think it queer   5
To stop without a farmhouse near
Between the woods and frozen lake
The darkest evening of the year.

He gives his harness bells a shake
To ask if there is some mistake.   10
The only other sound's the sweep
Of easy wind and downy flake.

The woods are lovely, dark, and deep,
But I have promises to keep,
And miles to go before I sleep,   15
And miles to go before I sleep.

                                                         1923

JOHN GAY

My Own Epitaph

Life is a jest; and all things show it.
I thought so once; but now I know it.

                                                         1720

NIKKI GIOVANNI

Poetry

poetry is motion graceful
as a fawn
gentle as a teardrop
strong like the eye
finding peace in a crowded room   5

we poets tend to think
our words are golden
though emotion speaks too
loudly to be defined
by silence   10

sometimes after midnight or just before
the dawn
we sit typewriter in hand
pulling loneliness around us
forgetting our lovers or children   15
who are sleeping
ignoring the weary wariness
of our own logic
to compose a poem
        no one understands it   20
it never says "love me" for poets are
beyond love
it never says "accept me" for poems seek not
acceptance but controversy
it only says "i am" and therefore   25
i concede that you are too

a poem is pure energy
horizontally contained
between the mind
of the poet and the ear of the reader   30
if it does not sing discard the ear
for poetry is song
if it does not delight discard
the heart for poetry is joy
if it does not inform then close   35
off the brain for it is dead
if it cannot heed the insistent message
that life is precious

which is all we poets
wrapped in our loneliness   40
are trying to say

                                                                       1975

THOMAS HARDY

The Convergence of the Twain

Lines on the loss of the "Titanic"[7]

I

In a solitude of the sea
Deep from human vanity,
And the Pride of Life that planned her, stilly couches she.

II

Steel chambers, late the pyres
Of her salamandrine[8] fires,   5
Cold currents thrid,[9] and turn to rhythmic tidal lyres.

III

Over the mirrors meant
To glass the opulent
The sea-worm crawls—grotesque, slimed, dumb, indifferent.

IV

Jewels in joy designed   10
To ravish the sensuous mind
Lie lightless, all their sparkles bleared and black and blind.

V

Dim moon-eyed fishes near
Gaze at the gilded gear
And query: "What does this vaingloriousness down here?" . . .   15

VI

Well: while was fashioning
This creature of cleaving wing,
The Immanent Will that stirs and urges everything

VII

Prepared a sinister mate
For her—so gaily great—   20
A Shape of Ice, for the time far and dissociate.

VIII

And as the smart ship grew
In stature, grace, and hue,
In shadowy silent distance grew the Iceberg too.

IX

Alien they seemed to be: 25
No mortal eye could see
The intimate welding of their later history,

---

7. On the night of April 14, 1912, the *Titanic*, the largest ship afloat and on her maiden voyage to New York from Southampton, collided with an iceberg in the North Atlantic and sank in less than three hours; 1500 of 2206 passengers were lost.
8. Bright red; the salamander was supposed to be able to live in fire.
9. Thread.

X

Or sign that they were bent
  By paths coincident
On being anon twin halves of one august event,   30

XI

Till the Spinner of the Years
  Said "Now!" And each one hears,
And consummation comes, and jars two hemispheres.

                                                                            1914

THOMAS HARDY

The Darkling Thrush

I leant upon a coppice gate
  When Frost was specter gray,
And Winter's dregs made desolate
  The weakening eye of day.
The tangled bine-stems scored the sky   5
  Like strings of broken lyres,
And all mankind that haunted nigh
  Had sought their household fires.

The land's sharp features seemed to be
  The Century's corpse outleant,   10
His crypt the cloudy canopy,
  The wind his death-lament.
The ancient pulse of germ and birth
  Was shrunken hard and dry,
And every spirit upon earth   15
  Seemed fervorless as I.

At once a voice arose among
  The bleak twigs overhead
In a full-hearted evensong
  Of joy illimited;   20
An aged thrush, frail, gaunt, and small,
  In blast-beruffled plume,
Had chosen thus to fling his soul
  Upon the growing gloom.

So little cause for carolings   25
  Of such ecstatic sound
Was written on terrestrial things
  Afar or nigh around,
That I could think there trembled through
  His happy good-night air   30
Some blessed Hope, whereof he knew
  And I was unaware.

December 31, 1900

THOMAS HARDY

During Wind and Rain

They sing their dearest songs—
He, she, all of them—yea,
Treble and tenor and bass,
    And one to play;
With the candles mooning each face. . . .   5
    Ah, no; the years O!
How the sick leaves reel down in throngs!

They clear the creeping moss—
Elders and juniors—aye,
Making the pathway neat   10
    And the garden gay;
And they build a shady seat. . . .
    Ah, no; the years, the years;
See, the white stormbirds wing across!

They are blithely breakfasting all—   15
Men and maidens—yea,
Under the summer tree,
    With a glimpse of the bay,
While pet fowl come to the knee. . . .
    Ah, no; the years O!   20
And the rotten rose is ripped from the wall.

They change to a high new house,
He, she, all of them—aye,
Clocks and carpets, and chairs
    On the lawn all day,   25
And brightest things that are theirs. . . .
    Ah, no; the years, the years;
Down their carved names the rain drop ploughs.

                              1917

ROBERT HAYDEN

Frederick Douglass[1]

When it is finally ours, this freedom, this liberty, this beautiful
and terrible thing, needful to man as air,
usable as earth; when it belongs at last to all,
when it is truly instinct, brain matter, diastole, systole,
reflex action; when it is finally won; when it is more   5
than the gaudy mumbo jumbo of politicians:
this man, this Douglass, this former slave, this Negro

1. Frederick Douglass (1817–1895), escaped slave. Douglass was involved in the Underground Railroad, and became the publisher of the famous abolitionist newspaper the *North Star*, in Rochester, N.Y.

beaten to his knees, exiled, visioning a world
where none is lonely, none hunted, alien,
this man, superb in love and logic, this man   10
shall be remembered. Oh, not with statues' rhetoric,
not with legends and poems and wreaths of bronze alone,
but with the lives grown out of his life, the lives
fleshing his dream of the beautiful, needful thing.

                                                                      1966

GERARD   MANLEY   HOPKINS

God's Grandeur

The world is charged with the grandeur of God.
    It will flame out, like shining from shook foil;[2]
    It gathers to a greatness, like the ooze of oil
Crushed. Why do men then now not reck his rod?[3]
Generations have trod, have trod, have trod;   5
    And all is seared with trade; bleared, smeared with toil;
    And wears man's smudge and shares man's smell: the soil
Is bare now, nor can foot feel, being shod.

And for all this, nature is never spent;
    There lives the dearest freshness deep down things;   10
And though the last lights off the black West went
    Oh, morning, at the brown brink eastward, springs—
Because the Holy Ghost over the bent
    World broods with warm breast and with ah! bright wings.

                                                                      1918

GERARD   MANLEY   HOPKINS

The Windhover[4]

To Christ Our Lord

I caught this morning morning's minion,[5] king-
        dom of daylight's dauphin,[6] dapple-dawn-drawn Falcon, in his
            riding
    Of the rolling level underneath him steady air, and striding
High there, how he rung upon the rein of a wimpling[7] wing
In his ecstasy! then off, off forth on swing,   5
        As a skate's heel sweeps smooth on a bow-bend: the hurl and
            gliding

---

2. "I mean foil in its sense of leaf or tinsel. . . . Shaken goldfoil gives off broad glares like sheet lightning and also, and this is true of nothing else, owing to its zig-zag dints and creasings and net-work of small many cornered facets, a sort of fork lightning too." *Letters of Gerard Manley Hopkins to Robert Bridges,* ed. C. C. Abbott, 1955, p. 169.
3. Heed his authority.
4. A small hawk, the kestrel, which habitually hovers in the air, headed into the wind.
5. Favorite, beloved.
6. Heir to regal splendor.
7. Rippling.

Rebuffed the big wind. My heart in hiding
Stirred for a bird,—the achieve of, the mastery of the thing!

Brute beauty and valor and act, oh, air, pride, plume, here
    Buckle![8] AND the fire that breaks from thee then, a billion   10
Times told lovelier, more dangerous, O my chevalier![9]

    No wonder of it: sheér plód makes plow down sillion[1]
Shine, and blue-bleak embers, ah my dear,
    Fall, gall themselves, and gash gold-vermilion.
1877

A. E. HOUSMAN

Terence, This Is Stupid Stuff

    "Terence,[2] this is stupid stuff:
You eat your victuals fast enough;
There can't be much amiss, 'tis clear,
To see the rate you drink your beer.
But oh, good Lord, the verse you make,   5
It gives a chap the belly-ache.
The cow, the old cow, she is dead;
It sleeps well, the horned head:
We poor lads, 'tis our turn now
To hear such tunes as killed the cow.   10
Pretty friendship 'tis to rhyme
Your friends to death before their time
Moping melancholy mad:
Come, pipe a tune to dance to, lad."

    Why, if 'tis dancing you would be,   15
There's brisker pipes than poetry.
Say, for what were hop-yards meant,
Or why was Burton built on Trent?[3]
Oh many a peer of England brews
Livelier liquor than the Muse,   20
And malt does more than Milton can
To justify God's ways to man.[4]
Ale, man, ale's the stuff to drink
For fellows whom it hurts to think:
Look into the pewter pot   25
To see the world as the world's not.

8. Several meanings may apply: to join closely, to prepare for battle, to grapple with, to collapse.
9. Horseman, knight.
1. The narrow strip of land between furrows in an open field divided for separate cultivation.
2. Housman originally titled the volume in which this poem appeared "The Poems of Terence Hearsay."
3. Burton was famous for its ales, originally brewed from special springs there.
4. Milton said his purpose in *Paradise Lost* was to "justify the ways of God to men."

And faith, 'tis pleasant till 'tis past:
The mischief is that 'twill not last.
Oh I have been to Ludlow fair[5]
And left my necktie God knows where,   30
And carried half-way home, or near,
Pints and quarts of Ludlow beer:
Then the world seemed none so bad,
And I myself a sterling lad;
And down in lovely muck I've lain,   35
Happy till I woke again.
Then I saw the morning sky:
Heigho, the tale was all a lie;
The world, it was the old world yet,
I was I, my things were wet,   40
And nothing now remained to do
But begin the game anew.

    Therefore, since the world has still
Much good, but much less good than ill,
And while the sun and moon endure   45
Luck's a chance, but trouble's sure,
I'd face it as a wise man would,
And train for ill and not for good.
'Tis true, the stuff I bring for sale
Is not so brisk a brew as ale: 50
Out of a stem that scored the hand
I wrung it in a weary land.
But take it: if the smack is sour,
The better for the embittered hour;
It should do good to heart and head   55
When your soul is in my soul's stead;
And I will friend you, if I may,
In the dark and cloudy day.

    There was a king reigned in the East:
There, when kings will sit to feast,   60
They get their fill before they think
With poisoned meat and poisoned drink.
He gathered all that springs to birth
From the many-venomed earth;
First a little, thence to more,   65
He sampled all her killing store;
And easy, smiling, seasoned sound,
Sate the king when healths went round.
They put arsenic in his meat
And stared aghast to watch him eat;   70
They poured strychnine in his cup
And shook to see him drink it up:

---

5. Ludlow was a market town in Shropshire, and its town fair would be a social high point for a youth growing up in the county.

They shook, they stared as white's their shirt:
Them it was their poison hurt.
—I tell the tale that I heard told.   75
Mithridates,[6] he died old.

                                                              1896

A. E. HOUSMAN

To an Athlete Dying Young

The time you won your town the race
We chaired[7] you through the marketplace;
Man and boy stood cheering by,
And home we brought you shoulder-high.

Today, the road all runners come,   5
Shoulder-high we bring you home,
And set you at your threshold down,
Townsman of a stiller town.

Smart lad, to slip betimes away
From fields where glory does not stay,   10
And early though the laurel[8] grows
It withers quicker than the rose.

Eyes the shady night has shut
Cannot see the record cut,
And silence sounds no worse than cheers   15
After earth has stopped the ears:

Now you will not swell the rout
Of lads that wore their honors out,
Runners whom renown outran
And the name died before the man.   20

So set, before its echoes fade,
The fleet foot on the sill of shade,
And hold to the low lintel[9] up
The still-defended challenge-cup.

And round that early-laureled head   25
Will flock to gaze the strengthless dead,
And find unwithered on its curls
The garland[1] briefer than a girl's.

                                                              1896

---

6. The king of Pontus, he was said to
have developed a tolerance of poison by
taking gradually increasing quantities.
7. Carried aloft in triumph.

8. Wreath of honor.
9. Upper part of a door frame.
1. Wreath of flowers.

LANGSTON HUGHES

Theme for English B

The instructor said,

> *Go home and write*
> *a page tonight.*
> *And let that page come out of you—*
> *Then, it will be true.*   5

I wonder if it's that simple?
I am twenty-two, colored, born in Winston-Salem.
I went to school there, then Durham,[2] then here
to this college[3] on the hill above Harlem.
I am the only colored student in my class.   10
The steps from the hill lead down into Harlem,
through a park, then I cross St. Nicholas,[4]
Eighth Avenue, Seventh, and I come to the Y,
the Harlem Branch Y, where I take the elevator
up to my room, sit down, and write this page: 15

It's not easy to know what is true for you or me
at twenty-two, my age. But I guess I'm what
I feel and see and hear, Harlem, I hear you:
hear you, hear me—we two—you, me, talk on this page.
(I hear New York, too.) Me—who?   20

Well, I like to eat, sleep, drink, and be in love.
I like to work, read, learn, and understand life.
I like a pipe for a Christmas present,
or records—Bessie,[5] bop, or Bach.
I guess being colored doesn't make me *not* like   25
the same things other folks like who are other races.
So will my page be colored that I write?

Being me, it will not be white.
But it will be
a part of you, instructor.   30
You are white—
yet a part of me, as I am a part of you.
That's American.
Sometimes perhaps you don't want to be a part of me.
Nor do I often want to be a part of you.   35
But we are, that's true!
As I learn from you,

2. Cities in North Carolina.
3. Columbia University.
4. An avenue east of Columbia University.
5. Bessie Smith (1898?–1937), famous blues singer.

I guess you learn from me—
although you're older—and white—
and somewhat more free.   40

This is my page for English B.

                                                                1959

RICHARD HUGO

Places and Ways to Live

Note the stump, a peach tree. We had to cut it down.
It banged the window every wind. Our garden
swayed with corn each summer. Our crops were legend
and our kindness. Whatever stranger came, we said,
'Come in.' We ran excited. 'Someone's come to see us.'   5
By night we were exhausted. The dark came early
in that home, came early for the last time soon.

Some nights in motels, I wake bewildered by the room.
Then I remember where I am. I turn the light on
and the girl's still there, smiling from the calendar   10
whatever the year. When I'm traveling, I'm hurt.
I tune in certain radio stations by heart,
the ones that play old tunes like nothing worthwhile's
happened since that funeral in 1949.

When I'm in the house I've bought, I don't dwell on   15
the loss of trees, don't cry when neighbors move away
or dogs get killed by cars. I'm old enough to know
a small girl's tears are fated to return, years from now
in some Berlin hotel, though I seem to sit unfeeling
at the window watching it all like a patron.   20
I'm taking it in, deep where I hope it will bloom.

That is the crude self I've come to. The man who says
suffer, stay poor and I can create. Believe me, friends,
I offer you your homes and wish you well in them.
May kisses rain. May you find warm arms each morning.   25
May your favorite tree be blooming in December.
And may you never be dispossessed, forced to wander
a world the color of salt with no young music in it.

                                                                1975

RICHARD HUGO

What Thou Lovest Well, Remains American

You remember the name was Jensen. She seemed old
always alone inside, face pasted gray to the window,
and mail never came. Two blocks down, the Grubskis
went insane. George played rotten trombone
Easter when they flew the flag. Wild roses   5
remind you the roads were gravel and vacant lots
the rule. Poverty was real, wallet and spirit,
and each day slow as church. You remember threadbare
church groups on the corner, howling their faith
at stars, and the violent Holy Rollers[6]   10
renting the barn for their annual violent sing
and the barn burned down when you came back from war.
Knowing the people you knew then are dead,
you try to believe these roads paved are improved,
the neighbors, moved in while you were away, good-looking,   15
their dogs well fed. You still have need
to remember lots empty and fern.
Lawns well trimmed remind you of the train
your wife took one day forever, some far empty town,
the odd name you never recall. The time: 6:23.   20
The day: October 9. The year remains a blur.
You blame this neighborhood for your failure.
In some vague way, the Grubskis degraded you
beyond repair. And you know you must play again
and again Mrs. Jensen pale at her window, must hear   25
the foul music over the good slide of traffic.
You loved them well and they remain, still with nothing
to do, no money and no will. Loved them, and the gray
that was their disease you carry for extra food
in case you're stranded in some odd empty town   30
and need hungry lovers for friends, and need feel
you are welcome in the secret club they have formed.

                                                                    1975

BEN JONSON

Epitaph on Elizabeth, L. H.

Wouldst thou hear what man can say
In a little? Reader, stay.
Underneath this stone doth lie
As much beauty as could die;
Which in life did harbor give   5
To more virtue than doth live.

6. Slang for emotional evangelical Christians.

If at all she had a fault,
Leave it buried in this vault.
One name was Elizabeth;
Th' other, let it sleep with death: 10
Fitter, where it died, to tell,
Than that it lived at all. Farewell.

1616

ETHERIDGE KNIGHT

The Idea of Ancestry

I

Taped to the wall of my cell[7] are 47 pictures: 47 black
faces: my father, mother, grandmothers (1 dead), grand
fathers (both dead), brothers, sisters, uncles, aunts,
cousins (1st & 2nd), nieces, and nephews. They stare
across the space at my sprawling on my bunk. I know
their dark eyes, they know mine. I know their style,   5
they know mine. I am all of them, they are all of me;
they are farmers, I am a thief, I am me, they are thee.

I have at one time or another been in love with my mother,
1 grandmother, 2 sisters, 2 aunts (1 went to the asylum),   10
and 5 cousins. I am now in love with a 7 yr old niece
(she sends me letters written in large block print, and
her picture is the only one that smiles at me).

I have the same name as 1 grandfather, 3 cousins, 3 nephews,
and 1 uncle. The uncle disappeared when he was 15, just took   15
off and caught a freight (they say). He's discussed each year
when the family has a reunion, he causes uneasiness in
the clan, he is an empty space. My father's mother, who is 93
and who keeps the Family Bible with everybody's birth dates
(and death dates) in it, always mentions him. There is no   20
place in her Bible for "whereabouts unknown."

II

Each Fall the graves of my grandfathers call me, the brown
hills and red gullies of mississippi send out their electric
messages, galvanizing my genes. Last yr/like a salmon quitting
the cold ocean—leaping and bucking up his birthstream/I   25
hitchhiked my way from L.A. with 16 caps[8] in my pocket and a
monkey on my back, and I almost kicked it with the kinfolks.
I walked barefooted in my grandmother's backyard/I smelled
   the old
land and the woods/I sipped cornwhiskey from fruit jars with the
   men/

---

7. This poem is from Knight's volume,   robbery in the Ohio State Penitentiary.
Poems from Prison; Knight began to write   8. Doses of heroin (?); "monkey on
poetry while serving a sentence for armed   my back": drug habit.

I flirted with the women/I had a ball till the caps ran out 30
and my habit came down. That night I looked at my grand-
    mother
and split/my guts were screaming for junk/but I was almost
contented/I had almost caught up with me.
    The next day in Memphis I cracked a croaker's crib[9]/for a fix.

This yr there is a gray stone wall damming my stream, and when 35
the falling leaves stir my genes, I pace my cell or flop on my
    bunk
and stare at 47 black faces across the space. I am all of them,
they are all of me, I am me, they are thee, and I have no sons
to float in the space between.

                                 1968

DENISE LEVERTOV

The Secret

Two girls discover
the secret of life
in a sudden line of
poetry.

I who don't know the 5
secret wrote
the line. They
told me

(through a third person)
they had found it 10
but not what it was
not even

what line it was. No doubt
by now, more than a week
later, they have forgotten 15
the secret,

the line, the name of the poem. I love them
for finding what
I can't find,

and for loving me 20
for the line I wrote,
and for forgetting it
so that

9. Burglarized a doctor's house (or a drugstore).

        a thousand times, till death
        finds them, they may   25
        discover it again, in other
        lines

        in other
        happenings. And for
        wanting to know it,   30
        for

        assuming there is
        such a secret, yes,
        for that
        most of all.   35

                                                            1964

ROBERT LOWELL

Skunk Hour

(For Elizabeth Bishop)

Nautilus Island's hermit
heiress still lives through winter in her Spartan cottage;
her sheep still graze above the sea.
Her son's a bishop. Her farmer
is first selectman[1] in our village,   5
she's in her dotage.

Thirsting for
the hierarchic privacy
of Queen Victoria's century,
she buys up all   10
the eyesores facing her shore,
and lets them fall.

The season's ill—
we've lost our summer millionaire,
who seemed to leap from an L. L. Bean[2]   15
catalogue. His nine-knot yawl
was auctioned off to lobstermen.
A red fox stain covers Blue Hill.

And now our fairy
decorator brightens his shop for fall,   20
his fishnet's filled with orange cork,
orange, his cobbler's bench and awl,
there is no money in his work,
he'd rather marry.

---

1. An elected New England town official.   2. Famous old Maine sporting goods firm.

One dark night,   25
my Tudor Ford climbed the hill's skull,
I watched for love-cars. Lights turned down,
they lay together, hull to hull,
where the graveyard shelves on the town. . . .
My mind's not right.   30

A car radio bleats,
"Love, O careless Love. . . ."³ I hear
my ill-spirit sob in each blood cell,
as if my hand were at its throat. . . .
I myself am hell;   35
nobody's here—

only skunks, that search
in the moonlight for a bite to eat.
They march on their soles up Main Street:
white stripes, moonstruck eyes' red fire   40
under the chalk-dry and spar spire
of the Trinitarian Church.

I stand on top
of our back steps and breathe the rich air—
a mother skunk with her column of kittens swills the garbage pail.   45
She jabs her wedge head in a cup
of sour cream, drops her ostrich tail,
and will not scare.

1959

ARCHIBALD MACLEISH

Ars Poetica⁴

A poem should be palpable and mute
As a globed fruit,

Dumb
As old medallions to the thumb,

Silent as the sleeve-worn stone   5
Of casement ledges where the moss has grown—

A poem should be wordless
As the flight of birds.

A poem should be motionless in time
As the moon climbs,   10

3. A popular song.
4. "The Art of Poetry," title of a poetical   treatise by the Roman poet Horace (65–8
B.C.).

Leaving, as the moon releases
Twig by twig the night-entangled trees,

Leaving, as the moon behind the winter leaves,
Memory by memory the mind—

A poem should be motionless in time   15
As the moon climbs.

A poem should be equal to:
Not true.

For all the history of grief
An empty doorway and a maple leaf.   20

For love
The leaning grasses and two lights above the sea—

A poem should not mean
But be.

                                                    1926

ANDREW MARVELL

The Garden

How vainly men themselves amaze [5]
To win the palm, the oak, or bays,[6]
And their incessant labors see
Crowned from some single herb, or tree,
Whose short and narrow-vergéd[7] shade   5
Does prudently their toils upbraid;
While all flowers and all trees do close[8]
To weave the garlands of repose!

Fair Quiet, have I found thee here,
And Innocence, thy sister dear?   10
Mistaken long, I sought you then
In busy companies of men.
Your sacred plants,[9] if here below,
Only among the plants will grow;
Society is all but rude[1]   15
To[2] this delicious solitude.

No white nor red was ever seen
So am'rous as this lovely green.
Fond lovers, cruel as their flame,

5. Become frenzied.
6. Awards for athletic, civic, and literary
achievements.
7. Narrowly cropped.
8. Unite.
9. Cuttings.
1. Barbarous.
2. Compared to.

Cut in these trees their mistress' name: 20
Little, alas, they know, or heed
How far these beauties hers exceed!
Fair trees, wheresoe'er your barks I wound,
No name shall but your own be found.

When we have run our passion's heat,   25
Love hither makes his best retreat.
The gods, that mortal beauty chase,
Still in a tree did end their race:
Apollo hunted Daphne so,
Only that she might laurel grow;   30
And Pan did after Syrinx speed,
Not as a nymph, but for a reed.[3]

What wondrous life is this I lead!
Ripe apples drop about my head;
The luscious clusters of the vine   35
Upon my mouth do crush their wine;
The nectarine and curious[4] peach
Into my hands themselves do reach;
Stumbling on melons, as I pass,
Insnared with flowers, I fall on grass.   40

Meanwhile the mind, from pleasure less,
Withdraws into its happiness;[5]
The mind, that ocean where each kind
Does straight its own resemblance find;[6]
Yet it creates, transcending these,   45
Far other worlds and other seas,
Annihilating[7] all that's made
To a green thought in a green shade.

Here at the fountain's sliding foot,
Or at some fruit tree's mossy root,   50
Casting the body's vest[8] aside,
My soul into the boughs does glide:
There, like a bird, it sits and sings,
Then whets[9] and combs its silver wings,
And, till prepared for longer flight,   55
Waves in its plumes the various[1] light.

Such was that happy garden-state,
While man there walked without a mate:
After a place so pure, and sweet,

3. In Ovid's *Metamorphoses*, Daphne, pursued by Apollo, is turned into a laurel, and Syrinx, pursued by Pan, into a reed which Pan makes into a flute.
4. Exquisite.
5. I.e., the mind withdraws from lesser sense pleasure into contemplation.
6. All land creatures were supposed to have corresponding sea-creatures.
7. Reducing to nothing by comparison.
8. Vestment, clothing; the flesh is being considered as simply clothing for the soul.
9. Preens.
1. Many-colored.

What other help could yet be meet!²   60
But 'twas beyond a mortal's share
To wander solitary there:
Two paradises 'twere in one
To live in paradise alone.

    How well the skillful gardener drew   65
Of flowers and herbs this dial³ new,
Where, from above, the milder sun
Does through a fragrant zodiac run;
And as it works, th' industrious bee
Computes its time as well as we!   70
How could such sweet and wholesome hours
Be reckoned but with herbs and flowers?

                                                 1681

JAMES MERRILL

Casual Wear

Your average tourist: Fifty. 2.3
Times married. Dressed, this year, in Ferdi Plinthbower
Originals. Odds 1 to 9
Against her strolling past the Embassy

Today at noon. Your average terrorist: 5
Twenty-five. Celibate. No use for trends,
At least in clothing. Mark, though, where it ends.
People have come forth made of colored mist

Unsmiling on one hundred million screens
To tell of his prompt phone call to the station,   10
"Claiming responsibility"—devastation
Signed with a flourish, like the dead wife's jeans.

                                                p. 1984

EDNA ST. VINCENT MILLAY

What Lips My Lips Have Kissed

What lips my lips have kissed, and where, and why,
I have forgotten, and what arms have lain
Under my head till morning; but the rain
Is full of ghosts tonight, that tap and sigh
Upon the glass and listen for reply,   5
And in my heart there stirs a quiet pain
For unremembered lads that not again

---

2. Appropriate.
3. A garden planted in the shape of a sundial, complete with zodiac.

Will turn to me at midnight with a cry.
Nor knows what birds have vanished one by one,   10
Thus in the winter stands the lonely tree,
Yet knows its boughs more silent than before:
I cannot say what loves have come and gone;
I only know that summer sang in me
A little while, that in me sings no more.

                                                                                    1923

CZESLAW MILOSZ

A Poor Christian Looks at the Ghetto[4]

Bees build around red liver,
Ants build around black bone.
It has begun: the tearing, the trampling on silks,
It has begun: the breaking of glass, wood, copper, nickel, silver, foam
Of gypsum, iron sheets, violin strings, trumpets, leaves, balls, crystals.   5
Poof! Phosphorescent fire from yellow walls
Engulfs animal and human hair.

Bees build around the honeycomb of lungs,
Ants build around white bone.
Torn is paper, rubber, linen, leather, flax,   10
Fiber, fabrics, cellulose, snakeskin, wire.
The roof and the wall collapse in flame and heat seizes the foundations.
Now there is only the earth, sandy, trodden down,
With one leafless tree.

Slowly, boring a tunnel, a guardian mole makes his way,   15
With a small red lamp fastened to his forehead.
He touches burned bodies, counts them, pushes on,
He distinguishes human ashes by their luminous vapor,
The ashes of each man by a different part of the spectrum.
Bees build around a red trace.   20
Ants build around the place left by my body.

I am afraid, so afraid of the guardian mole.
He has swollen eyelids, like a Patriarch
Who has sat much in the light of candles
Reading the great book of the species.   25
What will I tell him, I, a Jew of the New Testament,
Waiting two thousand years for the second coming of Jesus?
My broken body will deliver me to his sight
And he will count me among the helpers of death:
The uncircumcised.   30

                                                                                    1943

4. Translated from the Polish by the author.

MARIANNE MOORE

Poetry

I, too, dislike it: there are things that are important beyond all this
            fiddle.
    Reading it, however, with a perfect contempt for it, one discovers in
    it after all, a place for the genuine.
            Hands that can grasp, eyes
            that can dilate, hair that can rise   5
                if it must, these things are important not because a

high-sounding interpretation can be put upon them but because they
            are
    useful. When they become so derivative as to become unintelligible,
    the same thing may be said for all of us, that we
            do not admire what   10
            we cannot understand: the bat
                holding on upside down or in quest of something to

eat, elephants pushing, a wild horse taking a roll, a tireless wolf under
    a tree, the immovable critic twitching his skin like a horse that feels
            a flea, the base-
            ball fan, the statistician—   15
                nor is it valid
                    to discriminate against "business documents and

school-books"[5]; all these phenomena are important. One must make a
            distinction
    however: when dragged into prominence by half poets, the result is
            not poetry.
    nor till the poets among us can be   20
            "literalists of
            the imagination"[6]—above
                insolence and triviality and can present

for inspection, "imaginary gardens with real toads in them," shall we
            have
    it. In the meantime, if you demand on the one hand,   25
    the raw material of poetry in
            all its rawness and
            that which is on the other hand
                genuine, you are interested in poetry.

                                                                        1921

5. *"Diary of Tolstoy,* p. 84: 'Where the
boundary between prose and poetry lies, I
shall never be able to understand. The
question is raised in manuals of style, yet
the answer to it lies beyond me. Poetry is
verse: prose is not verse. Or else poetry is
everything with the exception of business
documents and school books.'" (Moore's
note)
    6. "'Literalists of the imagination.'
Yeats, *Ideas of Good and Evil* (A. H.
Bullen, 1903), p. 182. 'The limitation of
his view was from the too intensity of his
vision; he was a too literal realist of imagination, as others are of nature; and because he believed that the figures seen by
the mind's eye, when exalted by inspiration, were "eternal existences," symbols of
divine essences, he hated every grace of
style that might obscure their linea-
ments.'" (Moore's note)

HOWARD NEMEROV

Boom!

Sees Boom in Religion, Too

Atlantic City, June 23, 1957 (AP).—President Eisenhower's pastor said
tonight that Americans are living in a period of "unprecedented religious
activity" caused partially by paid vacations, the eight-hour day and modern
conveniences.
    "These fruits of material progress," said the Rev. Edward L. R. Elson
of the National Presbyterian Church, Washington, "have provided the
leisure, the energy, and the means for a level of human and spiritual
values never before reached."

Here at the Vespasian-Carlton,[7] it's just one
religious activity after another; the sky
is constantly being crossed by cruciform[8]
airplanes, in which nobody disbelieves
for a second and the tide, the tide   5
of spiritual progress and prosperity
miraculously keeps rising, to a level
never before attained. The churches are full,
the beaches are full, and the filling-stations
are full, God's great ocean is full   10
of paid vacationers praying an eight-hour day
to the human and spiritual values, the fruits,
the leisure, the energy, and the means, Lord,
the means for the level, the unprecedented level,
and the modern conveniences, which also are full.   15
Never before, O Lord, have the prayers and praises
from belfry and phonebooth, from ballpark and barbecue
the sacrifices, so endlessly ascended.

It was not thus when Job in Palestine
sat in the dust and cried, cried bitterly;[9]   20
when Damien kissed the lepers on their wounds
it was not thus;[1] it was not thus
when Francis worked a fourteen-hour day
strictly for the birds;[2] when Dante took
a week's vacation without pay and it rained   25
part of the time,[3] O Lord, it was not thus.

But now the gears mesh and the tires burn
and the ice chatters in the shaker and the priest
in the pulpit and Thy Name, O Lord,

---

7. Vespasian was emperor of Rome 70–
79, shortly after the reign of Nero. In
French, *vespasienne* means public toilet.
    8. Cross-shaped.
    9. According to the *Book of Job*, he
was afflicted with the loss of prosperity,
children, and health as a test of his faith.
His name means, in Hebrew, "he cries";
see especially *Job* 2:7–13.
    1. "Father Damien" (Joseph Damien de
Veuster, 1840–1889), a Roman Catholic
missionary from Belgium, was known for
his work among lepers in Hawaii; he ulti-

mately contracted leprosy himself and died
there.
    2. St. Francis of Assisi, 13th-century
founder of the Franciscan order, was noted
for his love of all living things, and one of
the most famous stories about him tells of
his preaching to the birds. "Strictly for the
birds": a mid-20th-century expression for
worthless or unfashionable activity.
    3. Dante's journey through Hell, Purga-
tory, and Paradise (in *The Divine Comedy*)
takes a week, beginning on Good Friday,
1300. It rains in the third chasm of Hell.

is kept before the public, while the fruits   30
ripen and religion booms and the level rises
and every modern convenience runneth over,
that it may never be with us as it hath been
with Athens and Karnak and Nagasaki,[4]
nor Thy sun for one instant refrain from shining   35
on the rainbow Buick by the breezeway
or the Chris Craft with the uplift life raft;
that we may continue to be the just folks we are,
plain people with ordinary superliners and
disposable diaperliners, people of the stop'n'shop   40
'n'pray as you go, of hotel, motel, boatel,
the humble pilgrims of no deposit no return
and please adjust thy clothing, who will give to Thee,
if Thee will keep us going, our annual
Miss Universe, for Thy Name's Sake, Amen.   45

                                                          1960

HOWARD NEMEROV

Epigram: Political Reflexion

loquitur[5] the sparrow in the zoo.

No bars are set too close, no mesh too fine
To keep me from the eagle and the lion,
Whom keepers feed that I may freely dine.
This goes to show that if you have the wit
To be small, common, cute, and live on shit,   5
Though the cage fret kings, you may make free with it.

                                                          1958

HOWARD NEMEROV

Life Cycle of Common Man

Roughly figured, this man of moderate habits,
This average consumer of the middle class,
Consumed in the course of his average life span
Just under half a million cigarettes,
Four thousand fifths of gin and about   5
A quarter as much vermouth; he drank
Maybe a hundred thousand cups of coffee,
And counting his parents' share it cost
Something like half a million dollars
To put him through life. How many beasts   10

---

4. Athens, the cultural center of ancient civilization; Karnak, a village on the Nile, built on the site of ancient Thebes; Naga- saki, a large Japanese port city, virtually destroyed by a U.S. atomic bomb in 1945.
5. I.e., the sparrow is the speaker.

Died to provide him with meat, belt and shoes
Cannot be certainly said.
                              But anyhow,
It is in this way that a man travels through time,
Leaving behind him a lengthening trail   15
Of empty bottles and bones, of broken shoes,
Frayed collars and worn out or outgrown
Diapers and dinnerjackets, silk ties and slickers.

Given the energy and security thus achieved,
He did . . . ? What? The usual things, of course,   20
The eating, dreaming, drinking and begetting,
And he worked for the money which was to pay
For the eating, et cetera, which were necessary
If he were to go on working for the money, et cetera,
But chiefly he talked. As the bottles and bones   25
Accumulated behind him, the words proceeded
Steadily from the front of his face as he
Advanced into the silence and made it verbal.
Who can tally the tale of his words? A lifetime
Would barely suffice for their repetition;   30
If you merely printed all his commas the result
Would be a very large volume, and the number of times
He said "thank you" or "very little sugar, please,"
Would stagger the imagination. There were also
Witticisms, platitudes, and statements beginning   35
"It seems to me" or "As I always say."

Consider the courage in all that, and behold the man
Walking into deep silence, with the ectoplastic
Cartoon's balloon of speech proceeding
Steadily out of the front of his face, the words   40
Borne along on the breath which is his spirit
Telling the numberless tale of his untold Word[6]
Which makes the world his apple, and forces him to eat.

                                                              1960

DOROTHY PARKER

Comment

Oh, life is a glorious cycle of song,
A medley of extemporanea;
And love is a thing that can never go wrong;
And I am Marie of Rumania.

                                                              1926

6. *Logos*, the principle of creation and order.

DOROTHY PARKER

The Little Old Lady in Lavender Silk

I was seventy-seven, come August,
   I shall shortly be losing my bloom;
I've experienced zephyr and raw gust
   And (symbolical) flood and simoom.

When you come to this time of abatement,   5
   To this passing from Summer to Fall,
It is manners to issue a statement
   As to what you got out of it all.

So I'll say, though reflection unnerves me
   And pronouncements I dodge as I can,   10
That I think (if my memory serves me)
   There was nothing more fun than a man!

In my youth, when the crescent was too wan
   To embarrass with beams from above,
By the aid of some local Don Juan   15
   I fell into the habit of love.

And I learned how to kiss and be merry—an
   Education left better unsung.
My neglect of the waters Pierian[7]
   Was a scandal, when Grandma was young.   20

Though the shabby unbalanced the splendid,
   And the bitter outmeasured the sweet,
I should certainly do as I then did,
   Were I given the chance to repeat.

For contrition is hollow and wraithful,   25
   And regret is no part of my plan,
And I think (if my memory's faithful)
   There was nothing more fun than a man!

                                                    1937

SYLVIA PLATH

Black Rook in Rainy Weather

On the stiff twig up there
Hunches a wet black rook
Arranging and rearranging its feathers in the rain.

7. That is, poetry and learning. In classical mythology, the stream Hippocrene was associated with the Muses (the Pierides) and was sometimes called the Pierian spring.

I do not expect miracle
Or an accident   5

To set the sight on fire
In my eye, nor seek
Any more in the desultory weather some design,
But let spotted leaves fall as they fall,
Without ceremony, or portent   10

Although, I admit, I desire,
Occasionally, some backtalk
From the mute sky, I can't honestly complain:
A certain minor light may still
Leap incandescent   15

Out of kitchen table or chair
As if a celestial burning took
Possession of the most obtuse objects now and then—
Thus hallowing an interval
Otherwise inconsequent   20

By bestowing largesse, honor,
One might say love. At any rate, I now walk
Wary (for it could happen
Even in this dull, ruinous landscape); skeptical,
Yet politic; ignorant   25

Of whatever angel may choose to flare
Suddenly at my elbow. I only know that a rook
Ordering its black feathers can so shine
As to seize my senses, haul
My eyelids up, and grant   30

A brief respite from fear
Of total neutrality. With luck,
Trekking stubborn through this season
Of fatigue, I shall
Patch together a content   35

Of sorts. Miracles occur,
If you care to call those spasmodic
Tricks of radiance miracles. The wait's begun again,
The long wait for the angel,
For that rare, random descent.[8]   40

                                                                 1960

---

8. According to *Acts* 2, the Holy Ghost at Pentecost descended like a dove upon Christ's disciples.

SYLVIA PLATH

Lady Lazarus[9]

I have done it again.
One year in every ten
I manage it——

A sort of walking miracle, my skin
Bright as a Nazi lampshade,   5
My right foot

A paperweight,
My face a featureless, fine
Jew linen.

Peel off the napkin   10
O my enemy.
Do I terrify?——

The nose, the eye pits, the full set of teeth?
The sour breath
Will vanish in a day.   15

Soon, soon the flesh
The grave cave ate will be
At home on me

And I a smiling woman.
I am only thirty.   20
And like the cat I have nine times to die.

This is Number Three.
What a trash
To annihilate each decade.

What a million filaments.   25
The peanut-crunching crowd
Shoves in to see

Them unwrap me hand and foot——
The big strip tease.
Gentlemen, ladies   30

These are my hands
My knees.
I may be skin and bone,

---

9. According to *John* 11, Jesus raised Lazarus, the brother of Mary and Martha, from the dead.

Nevertheless, I am the same, identical woman.
The first time it happened I was ten.   35
It was an accident.

The second time I meant
To last it out and not come back at all.
I rocked shut

As a seashell.   40
They had to call and call
And pick the worms off me like sticky pearls.

Dying
Is an art, like everything else.
I do it exceptionally well.   45

I do it so it feels like hell.
I do it so it feels real.
I guess you could say I've a call.

It's easy enough to do it in a cell.
It's easy enough to do it and stay put.   50
It's the theatrical

Comeback in broad day
To the same place, the same face, the same brute
Amused shout:

"A miracle!"   55
That knocks me out.
There is a charge

For the eyeing of my scars, there is a charge
For the hearing of my heart——
It really goes.   60

And there is a charge, a very large charge
For a word or a touch
Or a bit of blood

Or a piece of my hair or my clothes.
So, so, Herr Doktor.   65
So, Herr Enemy.

I am your opus,
I am your valuable,
The pure gold baby

That melts to a shriek.   70
I turn and burn.
Do not think I underestimate your great concern.

Ash, ash—
You poke and stir.
Flesh, bone, there is nothing there——   75

A cake of soap,
A wedding ring,
A gold filling.

Herr God, Herr Lucifer
Beware   80
Beware.

Out of the ash
I rise with my red hair
And I eat men like air.

1965

MATTHEW PRIOR

A True Maid

No, no; for my virginity,
    When I lose that, says Rose, I'll die:
Behind the elms, last night, cried Dick,
    Rose, were you not extremely sick?

1718

EZRA POUND

In a Station of the Metro[1]

The apparition of these faces in the crowd;
Petals on a wet, black bough.

p. 1913

EZRA POUND

A Virginal

No, no! Go from me. I have left her lately.
I will not spoil my sheath with lesser brightness,
For my surrounding air hath a new lightness;
Slight are her arms, yet they have bound me straitly
And left me cloaked as with a gauze of æther;   5
As with sweet leaves; as with a subtle clearness.
Oh, I have picked up magic in her nearness
To sheathe me half in half the things that sheathe her.
No, no! Go from me, I have still the flavor,
Soft as spring wind that's come from birchen bowers.   10

1. The Paris subway.

Green come the shoots, aye April in the branches,
As winter's wound with her sleight hand she staunches,
Hath of the trees a likeness of the savor:
As white their bark, so white this lady's hours.

1912

JAROLD RAMSEY

Hand-Shadows

(for a daughter, eighteen)

Dear child, first-born, what I could give outright
I've given—now there is only a father's wishing.
What can I hang around your neck for magic,
or smuggle in your pocket? I would draw
you a contour map of the territory ahead   5
but in truth it could only show you *X—you are here.*
The rest would be your Terra Incognita.

Years ago, in the trees beside a mountain lake
after bedtime, your mother and I sat up
together, reading the fire. Each flame, leaping,   10
seemed a stroke of the future, a signal for us
for you asleep in your nest at the rim of firelight
where great jagged shadows danced like knives.
We faced our ignorance until the fire was ash.

Once, in the first transports of adolescence,   15
you wandered over the hills behind the Sky Ranch,
remember? Suddenly beyond your feet
the country plunged away to utter strangeness,
and you were lost. The south wind carried your cries
like birdsong. At last I found you quiet on a stone,   20
your eyes full of the world we do not own.

Now it is all before you—wonderful
beyond a father's bedtime reckoning,
beyond his fears. What is it love must say?
Go forth to the fullness of your being: may   25
a merry kindness look you in the face.
Where home was, may your travels bring
you to a fellowship of open hearts.

So love must change our parts, my child no longer
child. I stand rehearsing at the door,   30
and think how once at bedtime, a dozen years
ago, I taught you how to cross your wrists
in the bright lamp-light, and link your thumbs, *so,*
and there on the wall a great bird arose
and soared on shadow wings, to the wonderment of all.   35

p. 1984

JOHN CROWE RANSOM

Bells for John Whiteside's Daughter

There was such speed in her little body,
And such lightness in her footfall,
It is no wonder her brown study[2]
Astonishes us all.

Her wars were bruited in our high window.   5
We looked among orchard trees and beyond
Where she took arms against her shadow,
Or harried unto the pond

The lazy geese, like a snow cloud
Dripping their snow on the green grass,   10
Tricking and stopping, sleepy and proud,
Who cried in goose, Alas,

For the tireless heart within the little
Lady with rod that made them rise
From their noon apple-dreams and scuttle   15
Goose-fashion under the skies!

But now go the bells, and we are ready,
In one house we are sternly stopped
To say we are vexed at her brown study,
Lying so primly propped.   20

                                                            1924

EDWIN ARLINGTON ROBINSON

Mr. Flood's Party

Old Eben Flood, climbing alone one night
Over the hill between the town below
And the forsaken upland hermitage
That held as much as he should ever know
On earth again of home, paused warily.   5
The road was his and not a native near;
And Eben, having leisure, said aloud,
For no man else in Tilbury Town to hear:

"Well, Mr. Flood, we have the harvest moon
Again, and we may not have many more;   10
The bird is on the wing, the poet says,[3]
And you and I have said it here before.
Drink to the bird." He raised up to the light

2. Stillness, as if in meditation or deep   of Omar Khayyám," so describes the "Bird
thought.   of Time."
3. Edward Fitzgerald, in "The Rubaiyat

The jug that he had gone so far to fill,
And answered huskily: "Well, Mr. Flood,   15
Since you propose it, I believe I will."

Alone, as if enduring to the end
A valiant armor of scarred hopes outworn,
He stood there in the middle of the road
Like Roland's ghost winding a silent horn.⁴   20
Below him, in the town among the trees,
Where friends of other days had honored him,
A phantom salutation of the dead
Rang thinly till old Eben's eyes were dim.

Then, as a mother lays her sleeping child   25
Down tenderly, fearing it may awake,
He set the jug down slowly at his feet
With trembling care, knowing that most things break;
And only when assured that on firm earth
It stood, as the uncertain lives of men   30
Assuredly did not, he paced away,
And with his hand extended paused again:

"Well, Mr. Flood, we have not met like this
In a long time; and many a change has come
To both of us, I fear, since last it was   35
We had a drop together. Welcome home!"
Convivially returning with himself,
Again he raised the jug up to the light;
And with an acquiescent quaver said:
"Well, Mr. Flood, if you insist, I might.   40

"Only a very little, Mr. Flood—
For auld lang syne. No more, sir; that will do."
So, for the time, apparently it did,
And Eben evidently thought so too;
For soon amid the silver loneliness   45
Of night he lifted up his voice and sang,
Secure, with only two moons listening,
Until the whole harmonious landscape rang—

"For auld lang syne." The weary throat gave out,
The last word wavered, and the song was done.   50
He raised again the jug regretfully
And shook his head, and was again alone.
There was not much that was ahead of him,
And there was nothing in the town below—
Where strangers would have shut the many doors   55
That many friends had opened long ago.

1921

4. In French legend Roland's powerful ivory horn was used to warn his allies of impending attack.

EDWIN ARLINGTON ROBINSON

Richard Cory

Whenever Richard Cory went down town,
We people on the pavement looked at him:
He was a gentleman from sole to crown,
Clean favored, and imperially slim.

And he was always quietly arrayed,   5
And he was always human when he talked;
But still he fluttered pulses when he said,
"Good-morning," and he glittered when he walked.

And he was rich—yes, richer than a king—
And admirably schooled in every grace: 10
In fine, we thought that he was everything
To make us wish that we were in his place.

So on we worked, and waited for the light,
And went without the meat, and cursed the bread;
And Richard Cory, one calm summer night,   15
Went home and put a bullet through his head.

1897

ISHMAEL REED

beware : do not read this poem

tonite   ,   thriller was
abt an ol woman   , so vain she
surrounded herself w/
        many mirrors

it got so bad that finally she   5
locked herself indoors & her
whole life became the
        mirrors

one day the villagers broke
into her house   ,   but she was too   10
swift for them .   she disappeared
        into a mirror

each tenant who bought the house
after that   ,   lost a loved one to
        the ol woman in the mirror   :   15
        first a little girl
        then a young woman
        then the young woman/s husband

the hunger of this poem is legendary
it has taken in many victims   20
back off from this poem
it has drawn in yr feet
back off from this poem
it has drawn in yr legs

back off from this poem   25
it is a greedy mirror
you are into this poem   from
    the waist down
nobody can hear you can they   ?
this poem has had you up to here   30
    belch
this poem aint got no manners
you cant call out frm this poem
relax now & go w/ this poem   35
move & roll on to this poem
do not resist this poem
this poem has yr eyes
this poem has his head
this poem has his arms
this poem has his fingers   40
this poem has his fingertips
this poem is the reader & the
reader this poem

statistic   :   the us bureau of missing persons reports
                   that in 1968 over 100,000 people disappeared
                   leaving no solid clues
                          nor trace   only
        a space   in the lives of their friends

                                                                1970

THEODORE ROETHKE

The Dream

1

I met her as a blossom on a stem
Before she ever breathed, and in that dream
The mind remembers from a deeper sleep:
Eye learned from eye, cold lip from sensual lip.
My dream divided on a point of fire;   5
Light hardened on the water where we were;
A bird sang low; the moonlight sifted in;
The water rippled, and she rippled on.

2

She came toward me in the flowing air,
A shape of change, encircled by its fire.   10

I watched her there, between me and the moon;
The bushes and the stones danced on and on;
I touched her shadow when the light delayed;
I turned my face away, and yet she stayed.
A bird sang from the center of a tree;   15
She loved the wind because the wind loved me.

3

Love is not love until love's vulnerable.
She slowed to sigh, in that long interval.
A small bird flew in circles where we stood;
The deer came down, out of the dappled wood.   20
All who remember, doubt. Who calls that strange?
I tossed a stone, and listened to its plunge.
She knew the grammar of least motion, she
Lent me one virtue, and I live thereby.

4

She held her body steady in the wind;   25
Our shadows met, and slowly swung around;
She turned the field into a glittering sea;
I played in flame and water like a boy
And I swayed out beyond the white seafoam;
Like a wet log, I sang within a flame.   30
In that last while, eternity's confine,
I came to love, I came into my own.

1958

THEODORE ROETHKE

Epigram: The Mistake

He left his pants upon a chair:
She was a widow, so she said:
But he was apprehended, bare,
By one who rose up from the dead.

p. 1957

THEODORE ROETHKE

She

I think the dead are tender. Shall we kiss?—
My lady laughs, delighting in what is.
If she but sighs, a bird puts out its tongue.
She makes space lonely with a lovely song.

She lilts a low soft language, and I hear   5
Down long sea-chambers of the inner ear.

We sing together; we sing mouth to mouth.
The garden is a river flowing south.
She cries out loud the soul's own secret joy;
She dances, and the ground bears her away.   10
She knows the speech of light, and makes it plain
A lively thing can come to life again.

I feel her presence in the common day,
In that slow dark that widens every eye.
She moves as water moves, and comes to me,   15
Stayed by what was, and pulled by what would be.

1956

THEODORE ROETHKE

The Waking

I wake to sleep, and take my waking slow.
I feel my fate in what I cannot fear.
I learn by going where I have to go.

We think by feeling. What is there to know?
I hear my being dance from ear to ear.   5
I wake to sleep, and take my waking slow.

Of those so close beside me, which are you?
God bless the Ground! I shall walk softly there,
And learn by going where I have to go.

Light takes the Tree; but who can tell us how?   10
The lowly worm climbs up a winding stair;
I wake to sleep, and take my waking slow.

Great Nature has another thing to do
To you and me; so take the lively air,
And, lovely, learn by going where to go.   15

This shaking keeps me steady. I should know.
What falls away is always. And is near.
I wake to sleep, and take my waking slow.
I learn by going where I have to go.

1953

WILLIAM SHAKESPEARE

Th' Expense of Spirit

Th' expense[5] of spirit in a waste[6] of shame
Is lust in action; and, till action, lust
Is perjured, murderous, bloody, full of blame,
Savage, extreme, rude, cruel, not to trust;
Enjoyed no sooner but despiséd straight: 5
Past reason hunted; and no sooner had,
Past reason hated, as a swallowed bait,
On purpose laid to make the taker mad:
Mad in pursuit, and in possession so;
Had, having, and in quest to have, extreme;   10
A bliss in proof;[7] and proved, a very woe;
Before, a joy proposed; behind, a dream.
All this the world well knows; yet none knows well
To shun the heaven that leads men to this hell.

1609

WILLIAM SHAKESPEARE

Hark, Hark! the Lark[8]

Hark, hark! the lark at heaven's gate sings,
  And Phoebus[9] 'gins arise,
His steeds to water at those springs
  On chaliced[1] flowers that lies;
And winking Mary-buds[2] begin   5
  To ope their golden eyes:
With every thing that pretty is,
  My lady sweet, arise!
  Arise, arise!

ca. 1610

WILLIAM SHAKESPEARE

Not Marble, Nor the Gilded Monuments

Not marble, nor the gilded monuments
Of princes, shall outlive this powerful rhyme;
But you shall shine more bright in these conténts
Than unswept stone, besmeared with sluttish time.
When wasteful war shall statues overturn,   5
And broils root out the work of masonry,
Nor Mars his[3] sword nor war's quick fire shall burn

5. Expending.
6. Using up; also, desert.
7. In the act.
8. From *Cymbeline*, Act II, sc. iii.
9. Apollo, the sun god.

1. Cup-shaped.
2. Buds of marigolds.
3. Mars's (a common Renaissance form of the possessive). "Nor . . . nor": neither . . . nor.

The living record of your memory.
'Gainst death and all-oblivious enmity
Shall you pace forth; your praise shall still find room   10
Even in the eyes of all posterity
That wear this world out to the ending doom.[4]
So, till the judgment that yourself arise,
You live in this, and dwell in lovers' eyes.

                                            1609

WILLIAM SHAKESPEARE

Spring[5]

When daisies pied and violets blue
    And ladysmocks all silver-white
And cuckoobuds of yellow hue
    Do paint the meadows with delight,
The cuckoo then, on every tree,   5
Mocks married men;[6] for thus sings he,
                Cuckoo;
Cuckoo, cuckoo: Oh word of fear,
Unpleasing to a married ear!

When shepherds pipe on oaten straws,   10
    And merry larks are plowmen's clocks,
When turtles tread,[7] and rooks, and daws,
    And maidens bleach their summer smocks,
The cuckoo then, on every tree,
Mocks married men; for thus sings he,   15
                Cuckoo;
Cuckoo, cuckoo: Oh word of fear,
Unpleasing to a married ear!

                                            ca. 1595

WILLIAM SHAKESPEARE

Winter

When icicles hang by the wall
    And Dick the shepherd blows[8] his nail,
And Tom bears logs into the hall,
    And milk comes frozen home in pail.
When blood is nipped and ways be foul,   5
    Then nightly sings the staring owl,
                Tu-who;
Tu-whit, tu-who: a merry note,
While greasy Joan doth keel[9] the pot.

4. Judgment Day.
5. Like "Winter" (below), a song from *Love's Labors Lost*, Act V, sc. ii.
6. By the resemblance of its call to the word "cuckold."

7. Copulate. "turtles": turtledoves.
8. Breathes on for warmth. "nail": fingernail; i.e., hands.
9. Cool: stir to keep it from boiling over.

When all aloud the wind doth blow,   10
  And coughing drowns the parson's saw,[1]
And birds sit brooding in the snow,
  And Marian's nose looks red and raw,
When roasted crabs[2] hiss in the bowl,
Then nightly sings the staring owl,   15
            Tu-who;
Tu-whit, tu-who: a merry note
While greasy Joan doth keel the pot.

                                                              ca. 1595

LOUIS SIMPSON

To the Western World

A siren sang, and Europe turned away
From the high castle and the shepherd's crook.
Three caravels went sailing to Cathay[1]
On the strange ocean, and the captains shook
Their banners out across the Mexique Bay.   5

And in our early days we did the same.
Remembering our fathers in their wreck
We crossed the sea from Palos[2] where they came
And saw, enormous to the little deck,
A shore in silence waiting for a name.   10

The treasures of Cathay were never found.
In this America, this wilderness
Where the axe echoes with a lonely sound,
The generations labor to possess
And grave by grave we civilize the ground.   15

                                                                1959

STEPHEN SPENDER

An Elementary School Classroom in a Slum

Far far from gusty waves these children's faces.
Like rootless weeds, the hair torn round their pallor.
The tall girl with her weighed-down head. The paper-
seeming boy, with rat's eyes. The stunted, unlucky heir
Of twisted bones, reciting a father's gnarled disease,   5
His lesson from his desk. At back of the dim class
One unnoted, sweet and young. His eyes live in a dream
Of squirrel's game, in tree room, other than this.
On sour cream walls, donations. Shakespeare's head,

1. Maxim, proverb.
2. Crabapples.
3. In medieval times, Europeans referred
to northern China as Cathay.
4. The seaport in Spain from which Columbus set sail in 1492.

Cloudless at dawn, civilized dome riding all cities.   10
Belled, flowery, Tyrolese valley.[5] Open-handed map
Awarding the world its world. And yet, for these
Children, these windows, not this world, are world,
Where all their future's painted with a fog,
A narrow street sealed in with a lead sky,   15
Far far from rivers, capes, and stars of words.

Surely, Shakespeare is wicked, the map a bad example
With ships and sun and love tempting them to steal—
For lives that slyly turn in their cramped holes
From fog to endless night? On their slag heap, these children   20
Wear skins peeped through by bones and spectacles of steel
With mended glass, like bottle bits on stones.
All of their time and space are foggy slum.
So blot their maps with slums as big as doom.

Unless, governor, teacher, inspector, visitor,   25
This map becomes their window and these windows
That shut upon their lives like catacombs,
Break O break open till they break the town
And show the children to green fields, and make their world
Run azure on gold sands, and let their tongues   30
Run naked into books, the white and green leaves open
History theirs whose language is the sun.

                                                              1939

STEPHEN SPENDER

Judas Iscariot[6]

The eyes of twenty centuries
Pursue me along corridors to where
I am painted at their ends on many walls.
    Ever-revolving future recognize
This red hair and red beard, where I am seated   5
Within the dark cave of the feast of light.
    Out of my heart-shaped shadow I stretch my hand
Across the white table into the dish
But not to dip the bread. It is as though
The cloth on each side of one dove-bright face   10
Spread dazzling wings on which the apostles ride
Uplifting them into the vision
Where their eyes watch themselves enthroned.
    My russet hand across the dish

Plucks enviously against one feather   15
  —But still the rushing wings spurn me below!

    Saint Sebastian[7] of wickedness
I stand: all eyes legitimate arrows piercing through
The darkness of my wickedness. They recognize
My halo hammered from thirty silver pieces   20
And the hemp rope around my neck
Soft as that Spirit's hanging arms
When on my cheek he answered with the kiss
Which cuts for ever—
                  My strange stigmata,   25
All love and hate, all fire and ice!

    But who betrayed whom? O you,
Whose light gaze forms the azure corridor
Through which those other pouring eyes
Arrow into me—answer! Who   30
Betrayed whom? Who read
In his mind's light from the first day
That the kingdom of heaven on earth must always
Reiterate the garden of Eden,
And each day's revolution be betrayed   35
Within man's heart, each day?
                Who wrapped
The whispering serpent round the tree
And hung between the leaves the glittering purse
And trapped the fangs with God-appointed poison?   40
Who knew
I must betray the truth, and made the lie
Betray its truth in me?

    Those hypocrite eyes which aimed at you
Now aim at me. And yet, beyond their world   45
Each turning on his pole of truth, your pole
Invisible light, and mine
Becoming what man is. We stare
Across two thousand years, and heaven, and hell,
Into each other's gaze.   50

                        1949

WALLACE STEVENS

Anecdote of the Jar

    I placed a jar in Tennessee,
    And round it was, upon a hill.
    It made the slovenly wilderness
    Surround that hill.

7. Early Christian martyr who was a favorite subject of Renaissance painters. According to legend, St. Sebastian was sentenced to be shot with arrows, but his many wounds were miraculously healed.

The wilderness rose up to it,   5
And sprawled around, no longer wild
The jar was round upon the ground
And tall and of a port in air.

It took dominion everywhere.
The jar was gray and bare.   10
It did not give of bird or bush,
Like nothing else in Tennessee.

1923

WALLACE STEVENS

The Idea of Order at Key West

She sang beyond the genius of the sea.
The water never formed to mind or voice,
Like a body wholly body, fluttering
Its empty sleeves; and yet its mimic motion
Made constant cry, caused constantly a cry,   5
That was not ours although we understood,
Inhuman, of the veritable ocean.

The sea was not a mask. No more was she.
The song and water were not medleyed sound
Even if what she sang was what she heard,   10
Since what she sang was uttered word by word.
It may be that in all her phrases stirred
The grinding water and the gasping wind;
But it was she and not the sea we heard.

For she was the maker of the song she sang.   15
The ever-hooded, tragic-gestured sea
Was merely a place by which she walked to sing.
Whose spirit is this? we said, because we knew
It was the spirit that we sought and knew
That we should ask this often as she sang.   20

If it was only the dark voice of the sea
That rose, or even colored by many waves;
If it was only the outer voice of sky
And cloud, of the sunken coral water-walled,
However clear, it would have been deep air,   25
The heaving speech of air, a summer sound
Repeated in a summer without end
And sound alone. But it was more than that,
More even than her voice, and ours, among
The meaningless plungings of water and the wind,   30
Theatrical distances, bronze shadows heaped
On high horizons, mountainous atmospheres
Of sky and sea.

It was her voice that made
The sky acutest at its vanishing.
She measured to the hour its solitude.   35
She was the single artificer of the world
In which she sang. And when she sang, the sea,
Whatever self it had, became the self
That was her song, for she was the maker. Then we,
As we beheld her striding there alone,   40
Knew that there never was a world for her
Except the one she sang and, singing, made.

Ramon Fernandez,[8] tell me, if you know,
Why, when the singing ended and we turned
Toward the town, tell why the glassy lights,   45
The lights in the fishing boats at anchor there,
As the night descended, tilting in the air,
Mastered the night and portioned out the sea,
Fixing emblazoned zones and fiery poles,
Arranging, deepening, enchanting night.   50

Oh! Blessed rage for order, pale Ramon,
The maker's rage to order words of the sea,
Words of the fragrant portals, dimly-starred,
And of ourselves and of our origins,
In ghostlier demarcations, keener sounds.   55

                                                          1935

WALLACE STEVENS

The Emperor of Ice-Cream

Call the roller of big cigars,
The muscular one, and bid him whip
In kitchen cups concupiscent curds.[9]
Let the wenches dawdle in such dress
As they are used to wear, and let the boys   5
Bring flowers in last month's newspapers.
Let be be finale of seem.[1]
The only emperor is the emperor of ice-cream.

8. French classicist and critic, 1894–
1944, who emphasized the ordering role of
a writer's consciousness upon the materials
he used. Stevens denied that he had Fernandez in mind, saying that he combined
a Spanish first name and surname at random: "I knew of Ramon Fernandez, the
critic, and had read some of his criticisms,
but I did not have him in mind." (*Letters*
[New York: Knopf, 1960], p. 798) Later,
Stevens wrote to another correspondent
that he did not have the critic "consciously"
in mind. (*Letters*, p. 823)
9. "The words 'concupiscent curds' have
no genealogy; they are merely expressive:

at least, I hope they are expressive. They
express the concupiscence of life, but, by
contrast with the things in relation in the
poem, they express or accentuate life's des-
titution, and it is this that gives them something more than a cheap lustre" Wallace
Stevens, *Letters* (New York: Knopf, 1960),
p. 500.
1. ". . . the true sense of Let be be the
finale of seem is let being become the conclusion or denouement of appearing to be:
in short, ice cream is an absolute good. The
poem is obviously not about ice cream, but
about being as distinguished from seeming
to be." *Letters*, p. 341.

Take from the dresser of deal,
Lacking the three glass knobs, that sheet   10
On which she embroidered fantails[2] once
And spread it so as to cover her face.
If her horny feet protrude, they come
To show how cold she is, and dumb.
Let the lamp affix its beam.   15
The only emperor is the emperor of ice-cream.

1923

WALLACE STEVENS

Sunday Morning

I

Complacencies of the peignoir, and late
Coffee and oranges in a sunny chair,
And the green freedom of a cockatoo
Upon a rug mingle to dissipate
The holy hush of ancient sacrifice.   5
She dreams a little, and she feels the dark
Encroachment of that old catastrophe,[3]
As a calm darkens among water-lights.
The pungent oranges and bright, green wings
Seem things in some procession of the dead,   10
Winding across wide water, without sound.
The day is like wide water, without sound,
Stilled for the passing of her dreaming feet
Over the seas, to silent Palestine,
Dominion of the blood and sepulchre.   15

II

Why should she give her bounty to the dead?
What is divinity if it can come
Only in silent shadows and in dreams?
Shall she not find in comforts of the sun,
In pungent fruit and bright, green wings, or else   20
In any balm or beauty of the earth,
Things to be cherished like the thought of heaven?
Divinity must live within herself:
Passions of rain, or moods in falling snow;
Grievings in loneliness, or unsubdued   25
Elations when the forest blooms; gusty
Emotions on wet roads on autumn nights;
All pleasures and all pains, remembering
The bough of summer and the winter branch.
These are the measures destined for her soul.   30

2. Fantail pigeons.   3. The Crucifixion.

III

Jove[4] in the clouds had his inhuman birth.
No mother suckled him, no sweet land gave
Large-mannered motions to his mythy mind
He moved among us, as a muttering king,
Magnificent, would move among his hinds,[5]   35
Until our blood, commingling, virginal,
With heaven, brought such requital to desire
The very hinds discerned it, in a star.[6]
Shall our blood fail? Or shall it come to be
The blood of paradise? And shall the earth   40
Seem all of paradise that we shall know?
The sky will be much friendlier then than now,
A part of labor and a part of pain,
And next in glory to enduring love,
Not this dividing and indifferent blue.   45

IV

She says, "I am content when wakened birds,
Before they fly, test the reality
Of misty fields, by their sweet questionings;
But when the birds are gone, and their warm fields
Return no more, where, then, is paradise?"   50
There is not any haunt of prophecy,
Nor any old chimera of the grave,
Neither the golden underground, nor isle
Melodious, where spirits gat[7] them home,
Nor visionary south, nor cloudy palm   55
Remote on heaven's hill, that has endured
As April's green endures, or will endure
Like her remembrance of awakened birds,
Or her desire for June and evening, tipped
By the consummation of the swallow's wings.   60

V

She says, "But in contentment I still feel
The need of some imperishable bliss."
Death is the mother of beauty; hence from her,
Alone, shall come fulfillment to our dreams
And our desires. Although she strews the leaves   65
Of sure obliteration on our paths,
The path sick sorrow took, the many paths
Where triumph rang its brassy phrase, or love
Whispered a little out of tenderness,
She makes the willow shiver in the sun   70
For maidens who were wont to sit and gaze
Upon the grass, relinquished to their feet.
She causes boys to pile new plums and pears

4. Jupiter, the chief Roman god.   6. The star of Bethlehem.
5. Lowliest rural subjects.   7. Got.

On disregarded plate.[8] The maidens taste
And stray impassioned in the littering leaves.   75

VI

Is there no change of death in paradise?
Does ripe fruit never fall? Or do the boughs
Hang always heavy in that perfect sky,
Unchanging, yet so like our perishing earth,
With rivers like our own that seek for seas   80
They never find, the same receding shores
That never touch with inarticulate pang?
Why set the pear upon those river-banks
Or spice the shores with odors of the plum?
Alas, that they should wear our colors there,   85
The silken weavings of our afternoons,
And pick the strings of our insipid lutes!
Death is the mother of beauty, mystical,
Within whose burning bosom we devise
Our earthly mothers waiting, sleeplessly.   90

VII

Supple and turbulent, a ring of men
Shall chant in orgy[9] on a summer morn
Their boisterous devotion to the sun,
Not as a god, but as a god might be,
Naked among them, like a savage source.   95
Their chant shall be a chant of paradise,
Out of their blood, returning to the sky;
And in their chant shall enter, voice by voice,
The windy lake wherein their lord delights,
The trees, like serafin,[1] and echoing hills,   100
That choir among themselves long afterward.
They shall know well the heavenly fellowship
Of men that perish and of summer morn.
And whence they came and whither they shall go
The dew upon their feet shall manifest.   105

VIII

She hears, upon that water without sound,
A voice that cries, "The tomb in Palestine
Is not the porch of spirits lingering.
It is the grave of Jesus, where he lay."
We live in an old chaos of the sun,   110
Or old dependency of day and night,
Or island solitude, unsponsored, free,
Of that wide water, inescapable.

---

8. "Plate is used in the sense ot so-called family plate. Disregarded refers to the disuse into which things fall that have been possessed for a long time. I mean, therefore, that death releases and renews. What the old have come to disregard, the young inherit and make use of" (*Letters of Wallace Stevens* [1966], pp. 183–184).
9. Ceremonial revelry.
1. Seraphim, the highest of the nine orders of angels.

Deer walk upon our mountains, and the quail
Whistle about us their spontaneous cries;   115
Sweet berries ripen in the wilderness;
And, in the isolation of the sky,
At evening, casual flocks of pigeons make
Ambiguous undulations as they sink,
Downward to darkness, on extended wings.   120

1915

JONATHAN SWIFT

On Stella's Birthday, 1719

Stella this day is thirty-four,[2]
(We shan't dispute a year or more)
However Stella, be not troubled,
Although thy size and years are doubled,
Since first I saw thee at sixteen   5
The brightest virgin on the green,
So little is thy form declined
Made up so largely in thy mind.
Oh, would it please the gods to split
Thy beauty, size, and years, and wit,   10
No age could furnish out a pair
Of nymphs so graceful, wise and fair
With half the luster of your eyes,
With half your wit, your years and size:
And then before it grew too late,   15
How should I beg of gentle Fate,
(That either nymph might have her swain,[3])
To split my worship too in twain.

1719

DYLAN THOMAS

Do Not Go Gentle into That Good Night[4]

Do not go gentle into that good night,
Old age should burn and rave at close of day;
Rage, rage against the dying of the light.

Though wise men at their end know dark is right,
Because their words had forked no lightning they
Do not go gentle into that good night.   5

Good men, the last wave by, crying how bright
Their frail deeds might have danced in a green bay,
Rage, rage against the dying of the light.

---

2. Stella is Swift's pet name for Hester
Johnson, a close friend for many years. She
was actually 38.

3. Servant, admirer, lover.
4. Written during the final illness of
the poet's father.

Wild men who caught and sang the sun in flight,   10
And learn, too late, they grieved it on its way,
Do not go gentle into that good night.

Grave men, near death, who see with blinding sight
Blind eyes could blaze like meteors and be gay,
Rage, rage against the dying of the light.   15

And you, my father, there on the sad height,
Curse, bless, me now with your fierce tears, I pray.
Do not go gentle into that good night.
Rage, rage against the dying of the light.

                                                            1952

DYLAN THOMAS

Fern Hill

Now as I was young and easy under the apple boughs
About the lilting house and happy as the grass was green,
      The night above the dingle starry,
            Time let me hail and climb
      Golden in the heydays of his eyes,   5
And honored among wagons I was prince of the apple towns
And once below a time I lordly had the trees and leaves
            Trail with daisies and barley
      Down the rivers of the windfall light.

And as I was green and carefree, famous among the barns   10
About the happy yard and singing as the farm was home,
      In the sun that is young once only,
            Time let me play and be
      Golden in the mercy of his means,
And green and golden I was huntsman and herdsman, the calves   15
Sang to my horn, the foxes on the hills barked clear and cold,
            And the sabbath rang slowly
      In the pebbles of the holy streams.

All the sun long it was running, it was lovely, the hay
Fields high as the house, the tunes from the chimneys, it was air 20
      And playing, lovely and watery
            And fire green as grass.
      And nightly under the simple stars
As I rode to sleep the owls were bearing the farm away,
All the moon long I heard, blessed among stables, the nightjars[5] 25
      Flying with the ricks,[6] and the horses
            Flashing into the dark.

5. Birds.   6. Haystacks.

And then to awake, and the farm, like a wanderer white
With the dew, come back, the cock on his shoulder: it was all
    Shining, it was Adam and maiden,   30
        The sky gathered again
    And the sun grew round that very day.
So it must have been after the birth of the simple light
In the first, spinning place, the spellbound horses walking warm
    Out of the whinnying green stable   35
        On to the fields of praise.

And honored among foxes and pheasants by the gay house
Under the new made clouds and happy as the heart was long,
    In the sun born over and over,
        I ran my heedless ways,   40
    My wishes raced through the house-high hay
And nothing I cared, at my sky-blue trades, that time allows
In all his tuneful turning so few and such morning songs
    Before the children green and golden
        Follow him out of grace,   45

Nothing I cared, in the lamb white days, that time would take me
Up to the swallow-thronged loft by the shadow of my hand,
    In the moon that is always rising,
        Nor that riding to sleep
    I should hear him fly with the high fields   50
And wake to the farm forever fled from the childless land.
Oh as I was young and easy in the mercy of his means,
        Time held me green and dying
    Though I sang in my chains like the sea.

                                       1946

DYLAN THOMAS

The Force that Through the Green Fuse Drives the Flower

The force that through the green fuse drives the flower
Drives my green age; that blasts the roots of trees
Is my destroyer.
And I am dumb to tell the crooked rose
My youth is bent by the same wintry fever.   5

The force that drives the water through the rocks
Drives my red blood; that dries the mouthing streams
Turns mine to wax.
And I am dumb to mouth unto my veins
How at the mountain spring the same mouth sucks.   10

The hand that whirls the water in the pool
Stirs the quicksand; that ropes the blowing wind
Hauls my shroud sail.

And I am dumb to tell the hanging man
How of my clay is made the hangman's lime.   15

The lips of time leech to the fountain head;
Love drips and gathers, but the fallen blood
Shall calm her sores.
And I am dumb to tell a weather's wind
How time has ticked a heaven round the stars.   20

And I am dumb to tell the lover's tomb
How at my sheet goes the same crooked worm.

1934

DYLAN THOMAS

In My Craft or Sullen Art

In my craft or sullen art
Exercised in the still night
When only the moon rages
And the lovers lie abed
With all their griefs in their arms,   5
I labor by singing light
Not for ambition or bread
Or the strut and trade of charms
On the ivory stages
But for the common wages   10
Of their most secret heart.

Not for the proud man apart
From the raging moon I write
On these spindrift[7] pages
Nor for the towering dead   15
With their nightingales and psalms
But for the lovers, their arms
Round the griefs of the ages,
Who pay no praise or wages
Nor heed my craft or art.   20

1946

WALT WHITMAN

I Saw in Louisiana a Live-Oak Growing

I saw in Louisiana a live-oak growing,
All alone stood it and the moss hung down from the branches,
Without any companion it grew there uttering joyous leaves of dark
    green,

· 7. Literally, wind-driven sea spray.

And its look, rude, unbending, lusty, made me think of myself,
But I wonder'd how it could utter joyous leaves standing alone there
    without its friend near, for I knew I could not,   5
And I broke off a twig with a certain number of leaves upon it, and
    twined around it a little moss,
And brought it away, and I have placed it in sight in my room,
It is not needed to remind me as of my own dear friends,
(For I believe lately I think of little else than of them,)
Yet it remains to me a curious token, it makes me think of manly love; 10
For all that, and though the live-oak glistens there in Louisiana solitary
    in a wide flat space,
Uttering joyous leaves all its life without a friend a lover near,
I know very well I could not.

                                                        1860

WALT WHITMAN

When Lilacs Last in the Dooryard Bloomed[8]

1

When lilacs last in the dooryard bloomed,
And the great star early drooped in the western sky in the night,
I mourned, and yet shall mourn with ever-returning spring.

Ever-returning spring, trinity sure to me you bring,
Lilac blooming perennial and drooping star in the west,   5
And thought of him I love.

2

O powerful western fallen star!
O shades of night—O moody, tearful night!
O great star disappeared—O the black murk that hides the star!
O cruel hands that hold me powerless—O helpless soul of me!   10
O harsh surrounding cloud that will not free my soul.

3

In the dooryard fronting an old farm-house near the white-washed
    palings,
Stands the lilac-bush tall-growing with heart-shaped leaves of rich
    green,
With many a pointed blossom rising delicate, with the perfume strong
    I love,
With every leaf a miracle—and from this bush in the dooryard,   15
With delicate-colored blossoms and heart-shaped leaves of rich green,
A sprig with its flower I break.

4

In the swamp in secluded recesses,
A shy and hidden bird is warbling a song.

---

8. The "occasion" of the poem is the assassination of Abraham Lincoln.

Solitary the thrush,   20
The hermit withdrawn to himself, avoiding the settlements,
Sings by himself a song.

Song of the bleeding throat,
Death's outlet song of life (for well dear brother I know,
If thou wast not granted to sing thou would'st surely die).   25

5
Over the breast of the spring, the land, amid cities,
Amid lanes and through old woods, where lately the violets peeped
    from the ground, spotting the gray debris,
Amid the grass in the fields each side of the lanes, passing the endless
    grass,
Passing the yellow-speared wheat, every grain from its shroud in the
    dark-brown fields uprisen,
Passing the apple-tree blows of white and pink in the orchards,   30
Carrying a corpse to where it shall rest in the grave,
Night and day journeys a coffin.

6
Coffin that passes through lanes and streets,[9]
Through day and night with the great cloud darkening the land,
With the pomp of the inlooped flags with the cities draped in black,   35
With the show of the States themselves as of crepe-veiled women
    standing,
With processions long and winding and the flambeaus of the night,
With the countless torches lit, with the silent sea of faces and the un-
    bared heads,
With the waiting depot, the arriving coffin, and the somber faces,
With dirges through the night, with the thousand voices rising strong
    and solemn,
With all the mournful voices of the dirges poured around the coffin,   40
The dim-lit churches and the shuddering organs—where amid these
    you journey,
With the tolling tolling bells' perpetual clang,
Here, coffin that slowly passes,
I give you my sprig of lilac.   45

7
(Nor for you, for one alone,
Blossoms and branches green to coffins all I bring,
For fresh as the morning, thus would I chant a song for you O sane
    and sacred death.

All over bouquets of roses,
O death, I cover you over with roses and early lilies,   50
But mostly and now the lilac that blooms the first,
Copious I break, I break the sprigs from the bushes,
With loaded arms I come, pouring for you,
For you and the coffins all of you O death.)

---

9. The funeral cortege stopped at many towns between Washington and Springfield,
Illinois, where Lincoln was buried.

8

O western orb sailing the heaven,   55
Now I know what you must have meant as a month since I walked,
As I walked in silence the transparent shadowy night,
As I saw you had something to tell as you bent to me night after night,
As you drooped from the sky low down as if to my side (while the
    other stars all looked on),
As we wandered together the solemn night (for something I know
    not what kept me from sleep),   60
As the night advanced, and I saw on the rim of the west how full you
    were of woe,
As I stood on the rising ground in the breeze in the cool transparent
    night,
As I watched where you passed and was lost in the netherward black
    of the night,
As my soul in its trouble dissatisfied sank, as where you sad orb,
Concluded, dropped in the night, and was gone.   65

9

Sing on there in the swamp,
O singer bashful and tender, I hear your notes, I hear your call,
I hear, I come presently, I understand you,
But a moment I linger, for the lustrous star has detained me,
The star my departing comrade holds and detains me.   70

10

O how shall I warble myself for the dead one there I loved?
And how shall I deck my song for the large sweet soul that has gone?
And what shall my perfume be for the grave of him I love?
Sea-winds blown from east and west,
Blown from the Eastern sea and blown from the Western sea, till there
    on the prairies meeting,   75
These and with these and the breath of my chant,
I'll perfume the grave of him I love.

11

O what shall I hang on the chamber walls?
And what shall the pictures be that I hang on the walls,
To adorn the burial-house of him I love?   80

Pictures of growing spring and farms and homes,
With the Fourth-month eve at sundown, and the gray smoke lucid and
    bright,
With floods of the yellow gold of the gorgeous, indolent, sinking sun,
    burning, expanding the air,
With the fresh sweet herbage under foot, and the pale green leaves of
    the trees prolific,
In the distance the flowing glaze, the breast of the river, with a wind-
    dapple here and there,   85
With ranging hills on the banks, with many a line against the sky, and
    shadows,
And the city at hand with dwellings so dense, and stacks of chimneys,

And all the scenes of life and the workshops, and the workmen homeward returning.

12
Lo, body and soul—this land,
My own Manhattan with spires, and the sparkling and hurrying tides,
  and the ships,   90
The varied and ample land, the South and the North in the light,
  Ohio's shores and flashing Missouri,
And ever the far-spreading prairies covered with grass and corn.

Lo, the most excellent sun so calm and haughty,
The violet and purple morn with just-felt breezes,
The gentle soft-born measureless light,   95
The miracle spreading bathing all, the fulfilled noon,
The coming eve delicious, the welcome night and the stars,
Over my cities shining all, enveloping man and land.

13
Sing on, sing on you gray-brown bird,
Sing from the swamps, the recesses, pour your chant from the bushes, 100
Limitless out of the dusk, out of the cedars and pines.

Sing on dearest brother, warble your reedy song,
Loud human song, with voice of uttermost woe.
O liquid and free and tender!
O wild and loose to my soul—O wondrous singer!   105
You only I hear—yet the star holds me (but will soon depart),
Yet the lilac with mastering odor holds me.

14
Now while I sat in the day and looked forth,
In the close of the day with its light and the fields of spring, and the
  farmers preparing their crops,
In the large unconscious scenery of my land with its lakes and forests, 110
In the heavenly aerial beauty (after the perturbed winds and the
  storms),
Under the arching heavens of the afternoon swift passing, and the
  voices of children and women.
The many-moving sea-tides, and I saw the ships how they sailed,
And the summer approaching with richness, and the fields all busy
  with labor,
And the infinite separate houses, how they all went on, each with its
  meals and minutia of daily usages,   115
And the streets how their throbbings throbbed, and the cities pent—lo,
  then and there,
Falling upon them all and among them all, enveloping me with the rest,
Appeared the cloud, appeared the long black trail,
And I knew death, its thought, and the sacred knowledge of death.

Then with the knowledge of death as walking one side of me,   120
And the thought of death close-walking the other side of me,

And I in the middle as with companions, and as holding the hands of
    companions,
I fled forth to the hiding receiving night that talks not,
Down to the shores of the water, the path by the swamp in the dim-
    ness,
To the solemn shadowy cedars and ghostly pines so still.   125

And the singer so shy to the rest received me,
The gray-brown bird I know received us comrades three,
And he sang the carol of death, and a verse for him I love.

From deep secluded recesses,
From the fragrant cedars and the ghostly pines so still,   130
Came the carol of the bird.

And the charm of the carol rapt me,
As I held as if by their hands my comrades in the night,
And the voice of my spirit tallied the song of the bird.

Come lovely and soothing death,   135
Undulate round the world, serenely arriving, arriving,
In the day, in the night, to all, to each,
Sooner or later delicate death.

Praised be the fathomless universe,
For life and joy, and for objects and knowledge curious,   140
And for love, sweet love—but praise! praise! praise!
For the sure-enwinding arms of cool-enfolding death.

Dark mother always gliding near with soft feet,
Have none chanted for thee a chant of fullest welcome?
Then I chant it for thee, I glorify thee above all,   145
I bring thee a song that when thou must indeed come, come unfalter-
    ingly.

Approach strong deliveress,
When it is so, when thou hast taken them I joyously sing the dead,
Lost in the loving floating ocean of thee,
Laved in the flood of thy bliss O death.   150

From me to thee glad serenades,
Dances for thee I propose saluting thee, adornments and feastings for
    thee,
And the sights of the open landscape and the high-spread sky are
    fitting,
And life and the fields, and the huge and thoughtful night.

The night in silence under many a star,   155
The ocean shore and the husky whispering wave whose voice I know,
And the soul turning to thee O vast and well-veiled death,
And the body gratefully nestling close to thee.

Over the tree-tops I float thee a song,
Over the rising and sinking waves, over the myriad fields and the
   prairies wide,   160
Over the dense-packed cities all and the teeming wharves and ways,
I float this carol with joy, with joy to thee O death.

15

To the tally of my soul,
Loud and strong kept up the gray-brown bird,
With pure deliberate notes spreading filling the night.   165

Loud in the pines and cedars dim,
Clear in the freshness moist and the swamp-perfume,
And I with my comrades there in the night.

While my sight that was bound in my eyes unclosed,
As to long panoramas of visions.   170

And I saw askant[1] the armies,
I saw as in noiseless dreams hundreds of battle-flags,
Borne through the smoke of the battles and pierced with missiles I saw
   them,
And carried hither and yon through the smoke, and torn and bloody,
And at last but a few shreds left on the staffs (and all in silence),   175
And the staffs all splintered and broken.

I saw battle-corpses, myriads of them,
And the white skeletons of young men, I saw them,
I saw the debris and debris of all the slain soldiers of the war,
But I saw they were not as was thought,   180
They themselves were fully at rest, they suffered not,
The living remained and suffered, the mother suffered,
And the wife and the child and the musing comrade suffered,
And the armies that remained suffered.

16

Passing the visions, passing the night,   185
Passing, unloosing the hold of my comrades' hands,
Passing the song of the hermit bird and the tallying song of my soul,
Victorious song, death's outlet song, yet varying ever-altering song,
As low and wailing, yet clear the notes, rising and falling, flooding the
   night,
Sadly sinking and fainting, as warning and warning, and yet again
   bursting with joy,   190
Covering the earth and filling the spread of the heaven,
As that powerful psalm in the night I heard from recesses,
Passing, I leave thee lilac with heart-shaped leaves,
I leave thee there in the door-yard, blooming, returning with spring.

---

1. Askance: sideways.

I cease from my song for thee,   195
From my gaze on thee in the west, fronting the west, communing with
    thee,
O comrade lustrous with silver face in the night.

Yet each to keep and all, retrievements out of the night,
The song, the wondrous chant of the gray-brown bird,
And the tallying chant, the echo aroused in my soul,   200
With the lustrous and drooping star with the countenance full of woe,
With the holders holding my hand nearing the call of the bird,
Comrades mine and I in the midst, and their memory ever to keep, for
    the dead I loved so well,
For the sweetest, wisest soul of all my days and lands—and this for his
    dear sake,
Lilac and star and bird twined with the chant of my soul,   205
There in the fragrant pines and the cedars dusk and dim.
1865–66

RICHARD WILBUR

The Beautiful Changes

One wading a Fall meadow finds on all sides
The Queen Anne's Lace[2] lying like lilies
On water; it glides
So from the walker, it turns
Dry grass to a lake, as the slightest shade of you   5
Valleys my mind in fabulous blue Lucernes.[3]

The beautiful changes as a forest is changed
By a chameleon's tuning his skin to it;
As a mantis, arranged
On a green leaf, grows   10
Into it, makes the leaf leafier, and proves
Any greenness is deeper than anyone knows.

Your hands hold roses always in a way that says
They are not only yours; the beautiful changes
In such kind ways,   15
Wishing ever to sunder
Things and things' selves for a second finding, to lose
For a moment all that it touches back to wonder.

1947

2. A delicate-looking plant, with finely divided leaves and flat clusters of small white flowers, sometimes called "wild carrot."
3. Alfalfa, a plant resembling clover, with small purple flowers. Lake Lucerne is famed for deep blue color and its picturesque Swiss setting amid limestone mountains.

RICHARD WILBUR

Love Calls Us to the Things of This World [4]

The eyes open to a cry of pulleys,[5]
And spirited from sleep, the astounded soul
Hangs for a moment bodiless and simple
As false dawn.
            Outside the open window   5
The morning air is all awash with angels.

Some are in bed-sheets, some are in blouses,
Some are in smocks: but truly there they are.
Now they are rising together in calm swells
Of halcyon[6] feeling, filling whatever they wear   10
With the deep joy of their impersonal breathing;
      Now they are flying in place,[7] conveying
The terrible speed of their omnipresence, moving
And staying like white water; and now of a sudden
They swoon down into so rapt a quiet   15
That nobody seems to be there.
                  The soul shrinks

From all that it is about to remember,
From the punctual rape of every blesséd day,
And cries,
        "Oh, let there be nothing on earth but laundry,   20
Nothing but rosy hands in the rising steam
And clear dances done in the sight of heaven."

      Yet, as the sun acknowledges
With a warm look the world's hunks and colors,   25
The soul descends once more in bitter love
To accept the waking body, saying now
In a changed voice as the man yawns and rises,

      "Bring them down from their ruddy gallows;
Let there be clean linen for the backs of thieves;   30
Let lovers go fresh and sweet to be undone,
And the heaviest nuns walk in a pure floating
Of dark habits,
            keeping their difficult balance."

1956

---

4. A phrase from St. Augustine's *Commentary on the Psalms*.
5. Laundry pulleys, designed so that clothes can be hung on the line inside and then sent outdoors to dry.
6. Serene.
7. Like planes in a formation.

WILLIAM CARLOS WILLIAMS

This Is Just to Say

I have eaten
the plums
that were in
the icebox

and which   5
you were probably
saving
for breakfast

Forgive me
they were delicious   10
so sweet
and so cold

1934

WILLIAM WORDSWORTH

Lines Composed a Few Miles above Tintern Abbey on Revisiting the Banks of the Wye During a Tour, July 13, 1798 [8]

Five years have passed; five summers, with the length
Of five long winters! and again I hear
These waters, rolling from their mountain-springs
With a soft inland murmur. Once again
Do I behold these steep and lofty cliffs,   5
That on a wild secluded scene impress
Thoughts of more deep seclusion; and connect
The landscape with the quiet of the sky.
The day is come when I again repose
Here, under this dark sycamore, and view   10
These plots of cottage-ground, these orchard tufts,
Which at this season, with their unripe fruits,
Are clad in one green hue, and lose themselves
'Mid groves and copses.[9] Once again I see
These hedge-rows, hardly hedge-rows, little lines   15
Of sportive wood run wild: these pastoral farms,
Green to the very door; and wreaths of smoke
Sent up, in silence, from among the trees!
With some uncertain notice, as might seem

8. Wordsworth had first visited the Wye valley and the ruins of the medieval abbey there in 1793, while on a solitary walking tour. He was 23 then, 28 when he wrote this poem.
9. Thickets.

Of vagrant dwellers in the houseless woods,   20
Or of some hermit's cave, where by his fire
The hermit sits alone.
                         These beauteous forms,
Through a long absence, have not been to me
As is a landscape to a blind man's eye;
But oft, in lonely rooms, and 'mid the din   25
Of towns and cities, I have owed to them,
In hours of weariness, sensations sweet,
Felt in the blood, and felt along the heart;
And passing even into my purer mind,
With tranquil restoration—feelings too   30
Of unremembered pleasure: such, perhaps,
As have no slight or trivial influence
On that best portion of a good man's life,
His little, nameless, unremembered acts
Of kindness and of love. Nor less, I trust,   35
To them I may have owed another gift,
Of aspect more sublime; that blessèd mood,
In which the burthen[1] of the mystery,
In which the heavy and the weary weight
Of all this unintelligible world,   40
Is lightened—that serene and blessèd mood,
In which the affections gently lead us on—
Until, the breath of this corporeal frame
And even the motion of our human blood
Almost suspended, we are laid asleep   45
In body, and become a living soul;
While with an eye made quiet by the power
Of harmony, and the deep power of joy,
We see into the life of things.
                                  If this
Be but a vain belief, yet, oh! how oft—   50
In darkness and amid the many shapes
Of joyless daylight; when the fretful stir
Unprofitable, and the fever of the world,
Have hung upon the beatings of my heart—
How oft, in spirit, have I turned to thee,   55
O sylvan Wye! thou wanderer through the woods,
How often has my spirit turned to thee!

    And now, with gleams of half-extinguished thought,
With many recognitions dim and faint,
And somewhat of a sad perplexity,   60
The picture of the mind revives again;
While here I stand, not only with the sense
Of present pleasure, but with pleasing thoughts
That in this moment there is life and food
For future years. And so I dare to hope,   65

---

1. Burden.

Though changed, no doubt, from what I was when first
I came among these hills; when like a roe
I bounded o'er the mountains, by the sides
Of the deep rivers, and the lonely streams,
Wherever nature led: more like a man   70
Flying from something that he dreads than one
Who sought the thing he loved. For nature then
(The coarser[2] pleasures of my boyish days,
And their glad animal movements all gone by)
To me was all in all—I cannot paint   75
What then I was. The sounding cataract
Haunted me like a passion; the tall rock,
The mountain, and the deep and gloomy wood,
Their colors and their forms, were then to me
An appetite; a feeling and a love,   80
That had no need of a remoter charm,
By thought supplied, nor any interest
Unborrowed from the eye. That time is past,
And all its aching joys are now no more,
And all its dizzy raptures. Not for this   85
Faint I,[3] nor mourn nor murmur; other gifts
Have followed; for such loss, I would believe,
Abundant recompense. For I have learned
To look on nature, not as in the hour
Of thoughtless youth; but hearing oftentimes   90
The still, sad music of humanity,
Nor harsh nor grating, though of ample power
To chasten and subdue. And I have felt
A presence that disturbs me with the joy
Of elevated thoughts; a sense sublime   95
Of something far more deeply interfused,
Whose dwelling is the light of setting suns,
And the round ocean and the living air,
And the blue sky, and in the mind of man:
A motion and a spirit, that impels   100
All thinking things, all objects of all thought,
And rolls through all things. Therefore am I still
A lover of the meadows and the woods
And mountains; and of all that we behold
From this green earth; of all the mighty world   105
Of eye, and ear—both what they half create,
And what perceive; well pleased to recognize
In nature and the language of the sense
The anchor of my purest thoughts, the nurse,
The guide, the guardian of my heart, and soul   110
Of all my moral being.
                    Nor perchance,
If I were not thus taught, should I the more

2. Physical.   3. Am I discouraged.

Suffer my genial spirits[4] to decay:
For thou art with me here upon the banks
Of this fair river; thou my dearest Friend,[5]   115
My dear, dear Friend; and in thy voice I catch
The language of my former heart, and read
My former pleasures in the shooting lights
Of thy wild eyes. Oh! yet a little while
May I behold in thee what I was once,   120
My dear, dear Sister! and this prayer I make,
Knowing that Nature never did betray
The heart that loved her; 'tis her privilege,
Through all the years of this our life, to lead
From joy to joy: for she can so inform   125
The mind that is within us, so impress
With quietness and beauty, and so feed
With lofty thoughts, that neither evil tongues,
Rash judgments, nor the sneers of selfish men,
Nor greetings where no kindness is, nor all   130
The dreary intercourse of daily life,
Shall e'er prevail against us, or disturb
Our cheerful faith that all which we behold
Is full of blessings. Therefore let the moon
Shine on thee in thy solitary walk;   135
And let the misty mountain-winds be free
To blow against thee: and, in after years,
When these wild ecstasies shall be matured
Into a sober pleasure; when thy mind
Shall be a mansion for all lovely forms,   140
Thy memory be as a dwelling-place
For all sweet sounds and harmonies; oh! then,
If solitude, or fear, or pain, or grief,
Should be thy portion, with what healing thoughts
Of tender joy wilt thou remember me,   145
And these my exhortations! Nor, perchance—
If I should be where I no more can hear
Thy voice, nor catch from thy wild eyes these gleams
Of past existence—wilt thou then forget
That on the banks of this delightful stream   150
We stood together; and that I, so long
A worshiper of Nature, hither came
Unwearied in that service; rather say
With warmer love—oh! with far deeper zeal
Of holier love. Nor wilt thou then forget,   155
That after many wanderings, many years
Of absence, these steep woods and lofty cliffs,
And this green pastoral landscape, were to me
More dear, both for themselves and for thy sake!

                                                                 1798

4. Natural disposition; i.e., the spirits   5. His sister Dorothy.
that are part of his individual genius.

A GLOSSARY OF POETIC TERMS

1. SUBJECT, THEME, AND MEANING

Most readers would agree with Archibald MacLeish that "a poem should not mean but be," but discovering what a poem "is" often involves identifying what it contains. Poets often used to provide an **argument** for their poems, a prose summary of what "happens"; now they seldom provide such a convenience, but to begin interpretation and experience of a poem readers often find it useful to **paraphrase,** put into prose exactly what the poem says, line by line, in words that are different but as nearly equivalent as possible.

The **subject,** or **topic,** of a poem is its general or specific area of concern, usually something categorical such as death (or the death of a particular person), war (or a specific war, or specific battle), love, or the simple life. Most poems make **statements** about a subject and define the degree and kind of their interest in it; a poem about war, for example, may ultimately be more concerned to say something about the nature of man or about honor or about peace than about war itself. Subjects offer a great variety of **themes:** that death is a release from pain, or a gateway to immortality, that war is senseless, or brutal, or a necessary evil, or a heroic quest for justice. A poem's theme is the statement it makes about its subject; summarizing a paraphrase in one or two sentences often yields the theme.

An **explication,** or **exegesis,** explains how all of the elements in an individual poem or passage work; in explication, a critic analyzes the various component parts in order to interpret the poem's statement. Explication takes a step beyond paraphrase in attempting to discover a poem's meaning. The terms **message** and **moral,** once used to summarize the poem's meaning, are now usually considered misleading because they tend to oversimplify and confuse statement with meaning. Similarly objectionable to many is the term **hidden meaning,** which implies that a poem is a puzzle or that the author is deliberately obscuring his or her point. **Meaning** is the poem's combination of themes and statements about a subject or series of subjects *and* the emotions that it artfully evokes toward them by means of poetic devices and strategies. But meaning—however well defined and articulated—is never the precise equivalent of the poem itself.

2. ATTITUDE, TONE, AND AUDIENCE

It is not only what is said that determines a poem's meaning and effect but how it is said and to whom. The term **tone** represents an attempt to be precise about the author's attitude toward what his or her poem literally says. Descriptions of tone try to characterize the way the words of the poem are (or should be) spoken when one sensitively reads the poem aloud. Tone literally tries to describe the vocal sounds which a poem seems to demand, and one may speak of the tone of an individual word or phrase, of a longer passsage, or of a whole poem. Words such as "ironic," "comic," "playful," "sincere," and "straightforward" may sometimes accurately describe tone, as may more particular adjectives such as "angry," "boastful," "taunting," "apologetic," "plaintive," or "bemused."

It is often useful, too, to know about the imagined **audience** of a poem, for much of what poets do involves an attempt to move and influence their hearers. Because poems are meant to be read and experienced by someone besides the poet, they are more than simple records of an event, or idea, or state of mind. Poets fictionalize or imagine circumstances and reflections, and they usually try to communicate by evoking in the reader a particular attitude or emotion.

The means by which poems generate an effect are usually called **poetic** (or **artistic**) **devices** or **strategies.** Almost everything in a poem is in some sense (but not a bad sense) a device: the choice of one word rather than another one, the use of metaphor, of certain sounds and rhythms, of allusions, conventions, forms—all contribute to a total effect. The **rhetoric** of a poem is the sum of the persuasive devices used to affect readers, with or without their consent.

Many of the most important **rhetorical devices** (or **rhetorical figures**) date from classical antiquity, and some of these are so common in ordinary life that we scarcely recognize them as devices, even in a poem. **Comparison** and **contrast** may clarify the identity and properties of a person, place, or thing, but persuasive values may also be built in, depending on what is being compared with what. Acceptance by **association** is as common as guilt by association; naming admired names may lull a reader into easy submission or be part of a complex web of interrelationships in which an author places his or her values among things certain to be admired, or expected to be admired among readers of a certain kind. An **allusion** is a reference to something outside the poem (in history, perhaps, or in another poem) which has built-in emotional associations. **Example** is simply the giving of a specific instance to back up a generalization, and many whole poems are built upon the principle, directly or indirectly.

Several classic figures of speech, though not restricted to poetry, are often found in poems. **Hyperbole** (or extravagant **exaggeration**) may be serious or comic or both at the same time, pushing something so far toward absurdity that its ordinary manifestation may seem normal and acceptable. **Meiosis** (or **understatement**) consciously underrates something or portrays it as lesser than it is usually thought to be; its psychology is to bring the reader instinctively to the defense of the thing being undervalued. It is closely related to **irony** (§3), especially in one of its forms, **litotes,** which affirms something by denying its opposite, as in colloquial expressions such as "He's no Einstein." **Periphrasis** (or **circumlocution**) is deliberate avoidance of the obvious, writing which circles its subject and refuses to take the simplest route toward clear meaning. **Synecdoche** is using a part of something to signify the whole (as in "hired hands" for "workmen"), and **metonymy** is naming something associated with what is being talked about rather than the thing itself, as in the use of "crown" for "king." **Hyperbaton** is the rearrangement of sentence elements for special effects; Milton, in *Paradise Lost,* for example, often uses extreme instances of the figure, as in the sentence beginning in line 44 of Book I (p. 630). **Prolepsis** is the **foreshadowing** of a future event as if it were already influencing the present, as in Eliot's *Journey of the Magi* (p. 814) when the wise men on their way to Bethlehem see objects suggestive of the Crucifixion.

These terms merely describe and categorize standard ways in which words may affect pyschological processes. Many kinds of attempts to persuade—sermons, political speeches, TV commercials, informal conversations—use some version of such devices, although often in more simple and less subtle ways than good poetry. Identifying the devices is only a way of discovering what a poem advocates, how it tries to develop emotional energy, and whether its methods are effective. Being able to identify the devices is useful but only as a means to a more important end.

Poems which openly and directly advocate a particular ideology, argue for a specific cause, or try to teach us something are called **didactic** poems. Critics sometimes distinguish between didactic poems and **mimetic** (or **imaginative**) poems, which are more concerned to present than to persuade. But the distinction is one of degree, for most poems mean at the very least to make their attitudes, their vision, their presentation of reality plausible and attractive. The term **propaganda** is almost always used pejoratively, to suggest that a writer's main aim is to arouse readers toward immediate action in a specific situation; poems so specifically and narrowly directed are usually assumed to be ephemeral, although good "occasional poems" (§11) and "satires" (§10) often transcend their occasions.

3. SPEAKER

It has become traditional to distinguish between the person who wrote the poem and the person who speaks in a poem, for an author often deliberately chooses to speak through a **character** quite different from his or her real self. Poets thus sometimes create a fictional person as a **speaker,** just as playwrights create a character who is then obliged to say things in a way appropriate to the character as created. In many poems the speaker is very like the author, or very like what the author wishes to think he or she is like. Between the speaker who is a fully distinct character and the author speaking honestly and directly are many degrees of detachment.

The term **persona** is often used synonymously with speaker, especially in satire, where the author usually speaks in a voice very like his own except that he often pretends to be more innocent, more earnest, and more pure than he knows himself to be. Such a **pose** (or **posture,** or **mask**) is not really dishonest any more than the creation of a character in a play or story is dishonest; it is part of the author's strategy of making a point effectively and persuasively.

When the author's attitude is different from that of the speaker the poem is said to be ironic, although the term **irony** also means several other things. Irony is not only saying one thing and meaning its opposite; it is also any manner of being oblique rather than straightforward and often involves exaggeration or understatement. A whole poem may be said to be ironic (or to have **structural irony**) when its total effect is to reverse the attitude presented by the speaker, but poems which are not wholly ironic may use ironic words and phrases (**verbal irony**) to generate a more complex statement or attitude. When irony is stark, simple, snide, exactly inverted—that is, when what is said is exactly the opposite of what is meant—it is called **sarcasm**. The term "irony," qualified in various ways, may indicate almost any kind of discrepancy between what is apparent in a literary work and what someone else knows to be so. **Dramatic irony** (which may be used in a poem as well as in a play) occurs when the speaker is unaware of something about himself or his situation but the reader is not.

4. SITUATION AND SETTING

A poem's relationship to time and space is sometimes very simple and sometimes very complicated. Some poems have a **setting** specified as clearly as do stories and plays, and in many cases the effect of a poem may depend heavily upon our recognizing the setting. In *Channel Firing* (p. 748), for example, the setting has to be a graveyard in England just before Britain's entry into World War I for the poem to make any sense. But the poem does not immediately tell us where and when the action is taking place; in *Channel Firing* the facts accumulate: first a dead body awakens and sits up, wondering what the noise is about. A little later we find out that gunnery practice in the English channel is the cause of the commotion, and finally we are given information (about the echoes moving inland) that indicates which side of the channel we are concerned with.

Poems which celebrate a certain occasion (see **occasional poem**, §11) often depend upon a reader's knowledge of the event and its cultural context. Poems about specific events or circumstances may be said to be **referential** in their use of setting, and they generally require us to recognize not only historical facts but the cultural interpretation placed upon the facts at the time. If a poem requires a particular location, there is usually information in the poem that leads to such specificity. When no such information exists in the poem, it is safe to assume that you don't need it to understand the poem's use of setting. Even a general setting may, however, recall other settings in literature, art, history, or myth. Such **allusive settings** (for a definition of **allusion**, see §2) are very common; garden settings, for example, almost inevitably call up memories of the Garden of Eden and its features and events—innocence, perfection, temptation, or the fall. Closely related to allusive settings are **symbolic settings**, which depend upon the psychological association of a particular quality with a particular place.

Temporal settings (that is, settings in time) may be symbolic or allusive or both at the same time. *Sunday Morning* (p. 863) depends upon both the traditional sense of sabbath and the modern custom of using Sunday mornings for luxurious leisure. Temporal settings may also be historically specific, or depend instead upon time of day or season of the year. The temporal setting often helps to set a particular mood in the poem or anchors the poem in a particular psychological reality.

The **situation** may need to be identified even in poems that do not have a specific setting. In *The Flea* (p. 602), for example, a male speaker is delivering a monologue to a woman, but we don't know where or when, the significant thing is that the man is arguing for making love, and the woman is reluctant. In some poems, too, the situation is a remembered one from the distance of later years; such a device is called **retrospection.** *Cherrylog Road* (p. 619), for example, although detailed in its presentation of setting and situation, makes it clear that the speaker is recalling events from many years before.

5.   LANGUAGE AND POETRY

Words are the bricks and mortar of poetry, and whatever design the poet has in mind has to be carried out through the words available in the language. Word choice (**diction**) in poems is usually calculated carefully; often words are chosen because of their **precision** or their **ambiguity,** the multiple possibilities of suggestivity which can complicate reader responses. Where words are placed is important, too; like prose, poetry usually follows the normal **syntax** (word order) of the language in which it is written, but sometimes words are moved around for special effects in sound, emphasis, or meaning.

Most nouns, verbs, adjectives, and adverbs not only **denote** a thing, action, or attribute, but also **connote** feelings and associations suggested by it. A horse is literally a four-legged, whinnying, rideable, workable animal, but the word "horse" connotes to most people strength, vitality, vigor. To be even more emphatic about its vigor and strength and to imply wildness as well, one might call it a steed or stallion. Not all words have clear, universally accepted connotations built into them, and writers often use the more elaborate devices of metaphor and symbolism (§6) to build a specific set of associations and values into the words and combinations of words that they use.

Imagery is used by different critics to mean three related but distinct things: 1. the mental pictures suggested by the verbal descriptions in a poem; 2. the visual descriptions in the poem itself; or 3. the figurative language (including metaphors, similes, and analogies) in the poem. In all three uses, imagery is technically a visual term, though other sense impressions are sometimes included under its large umbrella; imagery which mingles different sense impressions (sound or touch, for exmple, with sight) is said to be **synesthetic imagery.**

The first definition of imagery is the least precise one, for it tries to describe the effect of the poem on the reader; because each reader's response is likely to be a little different from every other reader's, critics usually find it safer and more precise to articulate the poem's efforts to create the effect; the second and third definitions of imagery are attempts to describe these efforts, the *means* of bringing about a certain effect. The third definition is the most common one, and it has the advantage of greater precision in describing different indirect ways that a poem may use to translate words into less abstract sense experience. Critics who use the term "imagery" in this third way may refer to nonfigurative description simply as description and to the presumed effect on the reader of both description and imagery as **visual impressions** or **sense impressions**. Imagery is the collective term for a group of individual **images**. One may speak of an **image cluster** (a group of similar images concentrated in a short passage), of a **controlling image** (when a single image seems to dominate a passage or even a whole poem, making other images subservient to it), or of an **image pattern** (when one or more images recur in a passage or poem). Sometimes it is convenient to speak of **kinds of imagery** ("animal imagery" or "architectural imagery") as well as to define individual images in greater detail. When imagery is defined in the third way, it is **figurative language**, which is defined in §6.

6. FIGURATIVE LANGUAGE

Figurative language (that is, language that uses figures of speech) includes the use of simile, metaphor, analogy, and personification. A **simile** is a direct, explicit comparison of one thing to another and usually uses "like" or "as" in drawing the connection. A simile may **extend** throughout a poem and be elaborated (it is then called an **analogy**) or be used to make a brief comparison in only one specified sense.

A metaphor pretends that one thing is something else, thus making an implicit comparison between the things. Even more than similes, metaphors are often **extended** because, in describing a thing in terms of something else, a metaphor often implies a detailed and complex resemblance between the two, one which may not be obvious at first glance. When a metaphor compares things which seem radically unlike, but which can be developed into a striking parallel, it is called a **conceit**; the "metaphysical poets" of the 17th century specialized in finding surprising likenesses in things usually considered unlike, and their poems often elaborate a single **metaphysical conceit**. The terms **tenor** and **vehicle** are often used to distinguish the primary object of attention from the thing being used to clarify that object. In Shakespeare's *That Time of Year* (p. 633) the primary object of attention (**tenor**) is the aging speaker, and late autumn is the **vehicle** which in the first few lines clarifies his aging. Metaphors are often said to be **extended metaphors** or **controlling metaphors** (in the same sense I have described above for images) when they dominate or organize a passage or poem.

A **mixed metaphor** is one in which terms from one metaphor are incorporated into another one, usually by mistake. A **dead metaphor** is one that has passed into such common usage as to have obscured its origins: we speak of a "leg" of a chair or the "heart" of the problem without remembering that the terms are metaphors implying a comparison to living bodies. When language, metaphorical or not, becomes unnecessarily specialized and self-consciously unavailable to an outsider, it is **jargon**. When such language is used mindlessly, it is called **cant**. When it is slangy and lives the short life of fashion among a select in-group, it is called **argot**. A **cliché** is any expression or idea which, through repeated use, has become commonplace, tiresome, and trite.

Personification (or **prosopopeia**) is the strategy of giving human qualities to abstract concepts or inanimate things: Beauty, Honor, Cruelty, Death, flowers, and various aspects of the natural landscape have been personified in various ages, but the strategy has been largely out of favor except for specialized and comic uses in the 20th century. Closely related is the strategy of ascribing to nature emotions which reflect human happenings (the **pathetic fallacy**), as in *The Darkling Thrush* (p. 823).

A **symbol** is something which stands for something else. In a very literal sense, words themselves are all symbols (they stand for an object, action, or quality, not just for letters or sounds), but symbols in poetry are said to be those words and groups of words which have a range of reference beyond their literal denotation. When a poem pervasively uses symbols as a major strategy and when the poem is more committed to the things which the symbols represent than to everyday reality, it is called a **symbolic poem** and is said to use **symbolism**. Poems, like everyday conversation, may use symbols occasionally and casually without being called symbolic.

In **allegory,** the action of the poem consistently and systematically describes another order of things beyond the obvious one. Spenser's *The Faerie Queene* is allegorical on several levels at the same time; the narrative action makes literal sense as a story, but the characters and actions also stand for political happenings, religious events, and moral values. *The Faerie Queene* is thus said to be a political, religious, and moral allegory.

Poets sometimes develop a highly specialized and personal set of **private symbols**—words, objects, and phrases which take on specific meanings as a result of repeated use by the poet in poem after poem. At the opposite extreme from private symbols are those which are universally shared within a defined culture. The framework of such shared symbols is called a **myth,** and the myth may include characters, events, and recurrent patterns of experience which the culture recognizes as, on some deep level, true. Poets sometimes too use particulars of a myth no longer literally or generally accepted; the wide recognition of standard myths allows writers to employ examples either in or out of their full mythic context. In recent years, critics have been heavily influenced by **myth criticism,** which usually signifies an attempt to discover **archetypes,** patterns of experience and action which are similar in different nations and cultures. In this sense, myth is not restricted to a single system, but rather attempts to transcend the particulars of time and place and locate fundamental recurrent patterns in human nature and human history.

7. FORM AND STRUCTURE

The **form** of a poem has to do with its appearance, just as does the form of a building, and one can describe that form in many different ways, just as a description of the form of a building depends upon the angle of vision (from the ground or from the air), the distance of the viewer, and to what other buildings the building is being compared. The simplest sense of poetic form involves the literal appearance on the page, the poem's shape seen physically, conceived literally. On the page most traditional poems look regular—that is, they are either divided into regular "stanzas" (§9) or they flow continually down the page in lines of more or less equal length. Modern poems tend to be less regular and thus to look more scattered and fragmented on the page, reflecting a general modern attitude that poetic meaning accumulates in a less regular and less programmed way. Occasionally the words are even shaped like a particular object, as in Renaissance **emblem poetry** (or **carmen figuratum** or **shaped verse**) or recent **concrete poetry**.

More enduring, more significant, and more complex senses of form involve less easily seeable ways of classifying external characteristics. Poetry is itself a sort of **formal** classification as distinguished from drama or fiction, and one can also distinguish between kinds of poetry (elegy, for example, or epigram) on the basis of subject matter, tone; conventions, etc. (see §10). Stanza varieties and rhythmic patterns (see §9 and §8) are also formal matters, for each involves external patterns which may be described relative to other poems.

As in a building, **structure** supports form and makes it possible. The order and arrangement of all of a poem's constituent parts—words, images, figures of speech, ideas, everything—involve structure, and the ways of discussing the relationship between parts vary from matters of word arrangement (grammar, syntax) to the development and presentation of ideas. Structure enables the form; the planning and craft of poetry are all, finally, structural matters.

The distinction I have made between form and structure corresponds to distinctions that some critics make between **external** and **internal form** (or external and internal structure). Another frequent distinction is that between **organic** structure or form and **architectonic** structure or form (those who make this distinction do not necessarily use the terms "form" and "structure" as they have been explained above). Things organic are said to take their shape from natural forces, like living organisms, and things architectonic to have shape artificially imposed upon them from without; a strong bias is usually implied toward the former, for the distinction implies the livingness, wholeness, and uniqueness of an individual poem.

Some works are shaped by other works which they **imitate** or **parody**; *The Dover Bitch* (p. 772), for example, is a response to *Dover Beach* (p 611). An **imitation** which makes fun of another work is a **burlesque** or **parody** of it, exaggerating its distinctive features and holding them up to ridicule; it is a parody if its attitude is one of gentle teasing, a burlesque if it is harsh and vicious. Imitation may also be a kind of flattery, honoring the methods, values, and meanings of another work and expropriating them into the new one. Many great poems have their basis in imitation and a good imitation is never a simple copy; it often derives major effects from its similarities to and differences from the original.

Questions of form and structure are related to questions about the integrity and autonomy of individual poems. For many years, critics were reluctant to deal with **parts** of a poem, insisting that as self-existent **wholes** poems deserved to be dealt with **holistically**, as creations having their own laws. More recently, criticism has dealt more directly with parts of poems, admitting that they too have organizational principles and facing squarely the difficulty that knowing whether a poem is whole or not is, even for the author, very nearly a mystical matter. Besides, an individual poem is often part of a larger **sequence** or **cycle**—that is, a group of poems which have significant features in common: they may be about a similar subject, tell a story progressively, or be calculated to produce a particular effect. Almost all poets themselves arrange the poems in their individual volumes, and it is often useful and revealing to read individual poems in the context of these volumes.

8. PROSODY

Prosody is the study of sound and rhythm in poetry. It is not a very exact science, but properly used it can be an aid to reading and *hearing* poems more fully.

The **rhythm** of a passage—in prose or poetry—is the pattern of sound pulsations in the voice as one reads it. Almost all spoken language has some kind of rhythm, however irregular, and simply listening to a human voice reciting, reading, or talking informally reveals recurrent systems of **stress** or **accent**. Stress is a relative matter (and this fact is a major difficulty for prosodic analysis), but in listening to the human voice we can always hear that some words and syllables are **stressed** (**accented**), and that others are, relatively, **unstressed** (**unaccented**). When the stress recurs at quite regular intervals—that is, when the rhythm has a pattern—the result is **meter**. The systematic analysis of patterns of stress, syllable by syllable, sound unit by sound unit, is called **scansion**; a reader who can **scan** a poem will discern the poem's basic rhythmic pattern (meter) and may then notice variations in the pattern or departures from it.

In the sentence,

Throw the ball to me

stresses "naturally" fall on "throw," "ball," and "me," but another context of meaning might considerably alter the stress pattern:

I said, throw the ball to me, not over my head.

Stress here would likely fall on "to," and there might be some other "unusual" stresses, provided by the demands of meaning in particular instances or by particular speakers. When a sentence or phrase appears in a certain rhythmic context (in, for example, a poem written in a certain meter), the sound context also affects it, tending to bend it (or "wrench" it) toward the basic pattern in the surrounding passage. There are, then, three factors which determine stress: (1.) the "natural" stress or stresses of each word; (2.) meaning and emphasis in a sentence or phrase; and (3.) the patterns of stress in the surrounding context.

Meter is measured in feet; a **foot** normally consists of a stressed syllable and one or more unstressed syllables. In the following line, in which stressed syllables have marked "‒" and unstressed syllables "∪," the division into five feet is indicated by a **virgule**, or **slash mark** (/):

$$\text{A lit/tle lear/ning is/a dang/'rous thing}$$

Each of its feet is an *iambic* foot—that is, it has an unstressed syllable followed by a stressed one. Iambic meter is the most common one in English poetry, but three other meters are of some importance:

Trochaic (a stressed syllable followed by an unstressed one):

$$\text{Tell me/ not in/ mourn ful/ num bers}$$

Anapestic (two unstressed syllables followed by a stressed one):

$$\text{'Twas the night/ be fore Christ/ mas and all/ through the house}$$

Dactylic (a stressed syllable followed by two unstressed ones):

$$\text{Hig gle dy/ pig gle dy/ Al fred Lord/ Ten ny son.}$$

Most English poems use one of these meters as their basic meter, but not with absolute regularity. An iambic poem will often contain trochaic feet (for emphasis, perhaps, or just for change), and some variation is almost a requirement if a poem is not to lull the ear into total dull deafness. Besides the standard meters, there are special feet used for variations.

Here is a table of the basic metrical feet and the most frequent variations:

ADJECTIVE FORM OF THE NAME	NOUN FORM	PATTERN
iambic	*iamb* (or *iambus*)	∪ ‒
trochaic	*trochee*	‒ ∪
anapestic	*anapest*	∪ ∪ ‒
dactylic	*dactyl*	‒ ∪ ∪
spondaic	*spondee*	‒ ‒
pyrrhic	*pyrrhic*	∪ ∪
amphibrachic	*amphibrach* (or *amphibrachys* or *rocking foot*)	∪ ‒ ∪
amphimacric	*amphimacer* (or *amphimac* or *cretic*)	‒ ∪ ‒

Coleridge's *Metrical Feet* (p. 675) exemplifies most of them.

The most common line length in English poetry is pentameter, five feet. Here is a table of all the common line lengths:

monometer	one foot
dimeter	two feet
trimeter	three feet
tetrameter	four feet
pentameter	five feet
hexameter	six feet
heptameter	seven feet
octameter	eight feet

Iambic and anapestic meters are sometimes called **rising rhythms** (or **rising meters**) because their basic movement is from unstressed to stressed syllables; and trochaic and dactylic meters are called **falling rhythms** (or **falling meters**). When a foot lacks a syllable it is called **catalectic;** the first foot of anapestic lines is often catalectic, and the final foot of most trochaic lines is catalectic because lines that end with an unstressed syllable are usually thought to "sound funny"; such lines usually occur only in comic poetry. Lines that rhyme by using an unstressed final syllable are said to have **feminine rhyme.** Certain meters are also said to incline toward comic effects; anapestic rhythm tends to produce comic effects, although it can be used to produce more serious tones. Iambic tetrameter also seems more liable than most meters to comic effects, though it also has been used for great varieties of tone. The number and length of pauses in a line affect the speed with which the line is read and, indirectly, the tone in any meter, for a slow-paced line seems less emphatic in its rhythm than a rapid-paced one. Almost all lines contain one or more natural pauses, some very short and some fairly long; any significant pause within a line is called a **caesura,** and in scansion it is indicated by a double virgule (//).

The distinction between stressed and unstressed is not a very precise one, for many degrees of stress are possible, and even an untrained ear can usually hear great variety of stress in the reading of a single line from a single poem. Division into feet is sometimes arbitrary, for there is often more than one way to count the number of feet, even assuming that the stresses are all accurately marked. Students often get bogged down in the technicalities of such matters and lose sight of the point of metrical analysis—which is to *hear* poems more accurately and notice those surprising places when the poem departs from its basic pattern.

Not all English poetry uses meter in the traditional senses I have described. Much modern poetry is in **free verse,** which avoids regularized meter and has no significant recurrent stress rhythms, although it may use other repetitive patterns—of words, phrases, structures—as Whitman often does. (**Free verse** should not be confused with **blank verse,** which is unrhymed but is by definition written in iambic pentameter.) Many modern poems that may appear unpatterned are, however, very tightly controlled metrically; the absence of rhyme does not mean the absence of metrical pattern, and many untradiditional-looking modern poems use traditional meter in traditional ways. Many poems, old as well as new, experiment with meter too, trying odd combinations within the definitions I have given or using different principles altogether. The **sprung rhythm** used by Gerard Manley Hopkins avoids the usual distinctions about kinds of feet and only counts the numbers of stressed syllables; each foot begins with a stressed syllable, but any number of unstressed syllables may follow before the next foot begins, so that traditional scansion would make the pattern seem unpatterned. **Quantitative verse**, imitating the metrical principles used by Latin and Greek poets, has been attempted in almost every age, but seldom with success. Unlike stress meters of any kind, quantitative verse determines pattern by the duration of sounds and sets up various meters in combinations of long and short syllables. Some modern experimenters have fused quantitative and stress patterns, and still others have tried patterns based on the number of sounds (see the discussion of syllabic verse in §9), on the kind of sounds used rather than either duration or stress, or on attempts at precise distinctions in the *amount* of stress in stressed syllables.

Until recently **rhyme** has been nearly as important as meter to most poetry. Rhyme is based on the duplication of the vowel sound and all sounds after the vowel in the relevant words. Most rhyme is **end-rhyme** (that is, the near-duplication of sounds takes place at the ends of the lines), but other patterns are possible. **Internal rhyme** involves rhyming sounds within the same line; in **beginning rhyme**, the first word or syllable rhymes in two or more lines. Not-quite rhyme is often used to vary strict rhyme schemes; the most common form is **slant rhyme** (or **half rhyme**) in which the relevant words have similar but not exactly rhyming sounds because either the vowel or consonant varies slightly (as in backs/box, bent/want, or web/step). **Visual** (or **eye**) **rhyme** uses words with identical endings but different pronunciations (bread/bead), and **rime riche** uses words that sound exactly the same but have different spellings and meanings (knight/night; lead/led; him/hymn). In poetry of earlier ages, one needs to watch, too, for **historical rhyme**—rhyme that was perfect when the poem was written but, because of historical changes in pronunciation, is no longer so; tea/day and join/divine were once good rhymes in the easiest and simplest sense.

Sound effects not involving rhyme continue to be important to poetry, and many of them are (like rhyme and meter) based on the ordering principle of repetition. **Alliteration** is the repetition of sounds in nearby words; usually alliteration involves the initial consonant sounds of words (and sometimes internal consonants in stressed syllables). **Assonance** is a repetition of vowel sounds in a line or series of lines; assonance often affects pace (by unbalancing short and long vowel patterns) and the way words included in the pattern tend to seem underscored. **Consonance** involves a repeated sequence of consonants but with varied vowels (as in stop/step, rope/reap, or hip/hop).

Onomatopoeia is the attempt to imitate or echo sounds being described. Some words are in themselves **onomatopoeic** (buzz, fizz, murmur), and others suggest action or qualities related to their literal meaning (slippery, lull). Passages may use rhythms and vocal sounds for onomatopoeic purposes; the famous "Sound and Sense" passage by Pope (p. 672) exemplifies many of the possibilities of sound to produce imitative, harmonious, or cacophonous effects.

9.   STANZA AND VERSE FORMS

Most poems of more than a few lines are divided into **stanzas,** groups of lines with a specific cogency of their own and usually set off from one another by a space. Traditionally, stanzas are linked by a common **rhyme scheme** (pattern of rhyme words) or by a common pattern of rhythms; modern poems which are divided into stanzas often, however, lack such patterns. Stanza lengths vary considerably, and so do the patterns and complexity of rhyme. Poets often invent distinctive patterns of their own—sometimes for novelty, sometimes to generate a particular effect—but over the years some stanza patterns have proved quite durable.

The **ballad stanza** is one of the oldest; it consists of four lines, the second and fourth of which are iambic trimeter and rhyme with each other. The first and third lines, in iambic tetrameter, do not rhyme. **Terza rima** is the three-line stanza in which Dante wrote *The Divine Comedy;* each iambic pentameter stanza (*aba*) interlocks with the next (*bcb, cdc, ded,* etc.). Among longer stanza forms are **ottava rima,** an Italian form adapted to English as eight lines of iambic pentameter rhyming *abababcc,* and the **Spenserian stanza,** the nine-line form Spenser invented for his *Faerie Queene*—eight lines of iambic pentameter and a ninth line of iambic hexameter, called an **alexandrine,** rhymed *ababbcbcc.* Stanzas with no official names are simply designated by the number of lines; a three-line stanza is called a **tristich, triplet,** or **tercet** (the latter is also a term for part of the sonnet—see the discussion below); a four-line stanza is a **quatrain;** a five-line stanza is a **quintain** or **quintet;** a six-line stanza is a **sextain** or **sixain.**

Many modern poems, rather than using traditional stanzas, are divided spatially according to breaks in syntax, meaning, or tone, and the individual characteristics of a particular poem may dictate such breaks. Some modern experiments have also produced patterns as demanding in their own way as rhyme-based stanzas. **Syllabic verse,** for example, requires that the number of syllables in each line of the first stanza be duplicated in each subsequent stanza; stanzas (and lines within them) may thus be of any length, but the poet commits himself or herself to a pattern in the first stanza and thereafter sticks to it.

The **couplet** is a rather special case among stanza forms. It consists of two lines (of any specifiable length or rhythm) which rhyme with one another, and seldom is one couplet divided by space from another one. Larger divisions within couplet verse are usually indicated (as in blank verse) by indentation, and the units are called **verse paragraphs,** which may or may not be separated by space. The **heroic couplet,** rhyming lines of iambic pentameter, has been the most popular and durable of couplet forms; it dominated English poetry during much of the 17th and 18th centuries and has been used successfully by many earlier and later poets. When the syntax of one couplet carries over into the next couplet, the couplets are said to be **open** or **enjambed; enjambment** is the continuation of syntax beyond the borders of a single couplet. **Closed** (or **end-stopped**) **couplets** are—as far as the technicalities of syntax are concerned—complete in themselves. Couplets written in iambic tetrameter tend to be used for comic effect because of the emphatic regularity of the rhythms and the abrupt underscoring of the rhyme.

Several **fixed poetic forms** (which contain a certain number of stanzas organized in a determined way) have been popular, from time to time, with English poets. Most of them were introduced by French troubadours in Provence, some of them as early as the 12th century. The **villanelle**, for example, contains five three-line stanzas and a final four-line stanza; only two rhyme sounds are permitted in the entire poem, and the first and third lines of the first stanza are repeated, alternately, as the third line of subsequent stanzas until the last. In the last stanza, the repeating lines become the final two lines of the poem. The **sestina** contains six six-line stanzas and a final three-line stanza, all unrhymed; but the final word in each line of the first stanza then becomes the final word in other stanzas (but in a different specified pattern); the final stanza uses these words again in a specified way, one in each half line. Some poets have even written **double** and **triple sestinas,** in which the demands increase geometrically. Repetition (probably originally for mnemonic purposes) is a major feature in fixed poetic forms.

10. GENRES AND KINDS

Here the term **genre** is used to indicate the traditional classroom distinction between fiction, poetry, and drama. Other less inclusive terms may then be used for subdividing genres and for different ways of classifying literary works according to characteristics they have in common.

A **mode** is, literally, a way of doing something; as a literary term it may most usefully be employed to indicate basic literary patterns of organizing experience. The **narrative mode** tells a story and organizes experience along a time continuum. The **dramatic mode** presents a change, usually an abrupt one, and organizes experience emotionally according to the rise and fall of someone's fortunes. The **lyric mode** reflects upon an experience or an idea and organizes experience irrespective of time and space, although it may describe a particular time or specific place. These traditional modes represent basic ways of viewing experience and have been around for a very long time. They obviously influenced the development of genres, which represent a somewhat artificial stiffening or rigidification of the narrative, dramatic, and lyric modes.

One may also think of modes in terms of the conclusions they draw about experience or the dominant emotions they arouse in their presentations of experience. **Tragedy,** or the **tragic mode,** describes someone's downfall, usually in stately language. **Comedy,** or the **comic**

mode, describes in more common language someone's triumph or the successful emergence of some order which encompasses and mutes all disorderly forces. **Romance,** or the **romantic mode,** describes the ideal, or what ought to be, often in terms of nostalgia or fantasy or longing. **Satire,** or the **satiric mode,** attacks the way things are and usually distributes the blame. In *The Anatomy of Criticism,* Northrop Frye argues that these modes correspond to the **myths** of the four seasons (comedy—spring; romance—summer; tragedy—autumn; satire—winter) and thus considers them universal ways of organizing experience.

Poetry considered as a genre may also be subdivided into **kinds** (or **types,** or **subgenres**). The **epic,** or **heroic poetry,** has been traditionally regarded as the highest in a hierarchy of kinds because it describes the great deeds of mighty heroes and heroines, usually in founding a nation or developing a distinctive culture, and uses elevated language and a grand, high style. **Pastoral poetry** describes the simple life of country folk, usually shepherds who live a timeless, painless (and sheepless) life in a world that is full of beauty, music, and love, and that remains forever green. The pastoral poem is also sometimes called an **eclogue,** a **bucolic,** or an **idyll.** The **elegy** was, in classical times, a poem on any subject written in "elegiac" meter, but since the Renaissance the term has usually indicated a formal lament for the death of a particular person; a **dirge,** or **threnody,** is similar but less formal and is supposed to be sung. A dirge or elegy supposed to be sung by one person is called a **monody.** An **epigram** was originally any poem carved in stone (on tombstones, buildings, gates, etc.), but in modern usage it denotes a very short, usually witty verse with a quick turn at the end; it is often, but not always, comic. The **epitaph** is a variety of epigram in which the poem is to be carved on someone's tombstone, but many epitaphs are comic, written about people not yet dead, and of course not really intended for engraving. A **lyric** is a short poem in which a speaker expresses intense personal emotion rather than describing a narrative or dramatic situation; sometimes the term is used even more broadly for *any* short poem. Originally the term "lyric" designated poems meant to be sung to the accompaniment of the lyre, and the names of several other kinds also specify their original connection with music. Many **songs** (whose words are usually called lyrics) are poems which have been set to music. A **ballad** is a narrative poem which is, or originally was, meant to be sung. Characterized by much repetition and often by a repeated **refrain** (recurrent phrase or series of phrases), ballads were originally a folk creation, transmitted orally from person to person and age to age. Once **folk ballads** began to be written down (in the 18th century), **literary ballads** in imitation of folk ballads began to be created by individual authors. A **hymn** is a song of praise, usually in praise of God but sometimes of abstract qualities. A **chanson** (which in French simply means "song") was originally a song written in **couplets** (§9), but the term now describes any simple song. An **aubade** is a morning song in which the coming of dawn is either celebrated or denounced as a nuisance. An **aube** is a more rigidly defined morning poem; the speaker of an aube is the woman in a love triangle, and she expresses regret that dawn is coming so that she and her lover must part. In a **complaint** a lover bemoans his sad condition as a result of neglect by his mistress. In a **palinode**, an author recants his previous attitude toward something, often apologizing for his earlier poetry, which he now claims to have been trivial. The **confessional poem** is a relatively new (or at least only recently defined) kind in which the speaker describes his confused chaotic state, which becomes a metaphor for the state of the world around him. A **meditation** is a contemplation of some physical object as a way of reflecting upon some larger truth, often (but not necessarily) a spiritual one.

Many of the kinds (confessional, complaint, aube, and many others) are traditionally **monologues** (one clearly distinguishable speaker does all the speaking). Monologues are sometimes called **interior monologues** (as in fiction) if the speaker seems to be thinking thoughts rather than speaking to someone. A monologue set in a specific situation and spoken to someone is called **dramatic monologue**; if the character is alone and speaking only to him- or herself, it is called **soliloquy**. **Light verse** encompasses many poems in many kinds; it is not necessarily trivial, but its speaker takes or affects a whimsical, twitting attitude toward his or her subject. Light verse that deals with the manners and mores of polite society is called **vers de société**. And some terms which properly describe a kind also properly describe some other sort of grouping. If **satire**, for example, is in one sense a mode, it is also a kind, for there is **formal verse satire** that attacks a specific vice in the manner of a verse essay. And the term "satire" also describes an attitude toward experience and a tone; as the opposite of **panegyric** (poetry praising something) satire attacks something, usually by analyzing, specifying, and naming names. **Satire** that is mild, civilized, and gentle is called **Horatian satire** (named after the Roman poet Horace); vicious, violent, loud satire is **Juvenalian satire** (named after Juvenal), or **invective**; a satire that attacks a specific person is a **lampoon**.

11. WIDER CONTEXTS

In a sense, every poem creates a world all its own, but every poem also reflects aspects of a larger world from which it derives. Often it is important—and sometimes it is crucial—for a reader to recognize **context**, the circumstances that surrounded the making of the poem. The most obvious and compelling contexts are in poems that refer explicitly to some historical event or situation. A poem written about a specific event or occasion is called an **occasional** poem; the occasion may be a well known public one or a private one. All matters of time and circumstance that might affect either the conception or execution are part of the poem's **historical** or **cultural context**. It is not always easy to determine exactly which factors are relevant to a poem and which are not; deciding just what information is necessary and how to use it once acquired is one of the most delicate tasks in good interpretation.

Literary historians often designate **periods** in which cultural and aesthetic assumptions are more or less shared, speaking, for example, of the Elizabethan period (literally, 1558–1603, the reign of Queen Elizabeth in England) or the Romantic period (approximately 1790–

1830) to describe certain common tendencies in a given historical era. The ideas and assumptions built into poems often reflect trends of thinking in a particular historical period. Poets sometimes consciously evoke their sense of shared ideas by using a **motif** (plural, **motifs** or **motives**): a recurrent device, formula or situation which deliberately connects a poem with common patterns of existing thought. One common motif is that of **carpe diem**. The phrase literally means "seize the day," and *carpe diem* poems invariably remind us of the shortness of life and beauty and the necessity to take advantage of the present. Such recurring situations as temptations in the garden, flights into the country, and journeys into experience are also motifs.

Poets often consciously evoke, too, a particular frame of reference or system of belief as a way of anchoring their own vision in a common pattern of experience that is understandable to an audience. In English poetry, the Judaeo-Christian and classical frames of reference are the most common, and the events and symbols of Biblical and classical history and myth are often prominent. Poets have, however, increasingly worried, especially since the 18th century, about the deterioration of a common heritage that was once based in Judaeo-Christian or classical terms, and the use of other, non-Western myths has become increasingly popular. Some poets have also developed private symbolic systems, sometimes extended into full-blown myths as in the poetry of Yeats. Most authors do not, of course, develop a complex private system of their own, but all authors have individual traits which are a product of their individual consciousness. Reading a group of poems by an author usually clarifies every individual poem, for the reader can develop a sense of the poet's distinctive style, strategies, and ideas. The total work of an author is called a **canon**; one may speak of the Milton canon or the Eliot canon. But even a sampling of a poet's work often leads a reader to expect certain procedures and attitudes, enabling a more exact and intense response. In its broadest sense, the **authorial context** may include biographical detail, psychological analysis, and specific facts about the conditions under which a poem was created, as well as dominant characteristics or tendencies in poems by a certain author.

What kind of contextual knowledge and how much of it a poem requires varies, of course, from poem to poem; many poems are readily accessible without deliberate pursuit of historical, intellectual, or authorial background, but the range and intensity of experience available through a poem is almost always enhanced by more knowledge.

12.   TRADITION AND CONVENTION

In its most inclusive sense, **tradition** is the influence—deliberate or not—of any previous event, technique, or consciousness upon subsequent ways of thought and action. Poetic tradition may involve an influence in ideas, or style, or both. Poets may deliberately seek to follow, refine, or respond to previous thinkers and poets, or they may find themselves conditioned by the past in ways over which they have no control.

Poetry, perhaps more than drama or fiction, is subject to the characteristic habits and limitations of a particular language, and it is common practice to speak of the **English tradition** (or the **English poetic tradition,** or simply the **tradition**) meaning all of the recurrent tendencies over the years, including many which oppose, modify, or contradict other tendencies. The poetry of Pound or cummings, for example, is as surely a part of the tradition as that of Milton or Tennyson, for the tradition is not something which once and for all defines itself but rather consists of continuity marked by continual modification. Participation in the tradition is not always easy to recognize or predict, for some of the English tradition's brightest lights (Shakespeare, Swift, Shelley, and Eliot are examples) at first seemed to their contemporaries most untraditional—in the sense of the tradition then understood. Tradition continually redefines itself to comprehend rebellious sons and daughters born into its line and intent on the old rituals of father-killing and mansion-burning. Sometimes the tradition is defined as if it were already complete, but it is more useful to consider it a living, changing thing which will, by definition, ultimately render any definition incomplete. Much (perhaps most) of what seems new and innovative does not, of course, last long enough in the public memory or evoke a substantial enough response in its audience to become part of the tradition. Contemporary with Shakespeare, for example, were many poets whose innovations did not "catch on" or whose distinctive appeal did not prove to be permanent; it is so in every age, and the process of developing a tradition is a perpetual matter of experimenting and sorting.

Within a language tradition are **national** and **regional traditions** as well; one may speak, for example, of a Canadian tradition, an Irish tradition, or a New England tradition. Such divisions have partly to do with local variations in linguistic usage, but they also relate to ideological concerns, cultural assumptions, and social, political, and economic movements. The same sort of division may be broadened, reaching beyond language barriers to comprehend the **European tradition** or the **Western tradition.** The latter term is often used nearly synonymously with the English tradition; such usage is not entirely precise, but many of the most characteristic features of English poetry do have origins or counterparts in ancient Greece or Rome or in more recent Continental cultures, especially those of France, Italy, and Germany.

Besides definitions based on linguistic, national, and cultural boundaries, there are other, more narrow senses of tradition in common use. Tradition may describe the history and accumulated characteristics of a literary kind or a stanza form (one might speak of the epic tradition, the sonnet tradition, the couplet tradition, or the tradition of free verse, §9 and 10), the recurrent appearances of a motif or theme (the *carpe diem* tradition, §11), the characteristics of a thought or value pattern (the Puritan tradition or the metaphysical tradition), or characteristics associated with a particular time or age (the Elizabethan tradition).

A **convention** is any characteristic which over a period of time has come to be expected in poetry or in a poem of a certain sort. There are conventions of subject matter and conventional ways of using the standard poetic devices, but conventions are especially associated with the older poetic kinds (§10). Following the standard conventions is usually less significant than not following them; when a poem ignores or contradicts a convention, a reader can be pretty sure that the convention is missing or altered for a specific reason. Conventions at their best are shortcuts in communication; they tell a reader what to look for and establish a beginning rapport between poet and reader; what happens as the expectations are satisfied or surprised is then up to the poet. Most conventions originated in the doctrine of **decorum**, which insists on appropriateness in all things: every poetic kind, for example, was assumed to require a certain level of language and persons and incidents of a specific level of dignity. Most conventions begin in necessity, flourish when they are recognizable to a large number of readers, and linger on simply as decoration, a memory of past needs. When specific conventions totally lose their use and force, they become merely ornamental, and sometimes seem amusing or absurd. This is why mechanical repetition of what is expected is often said to be "conventional" (or "merely conventional") in a negative sense. Sensible use of conventions involves taking advantage of the technical solutions and shortcuts they provide, but it involves too the personalized touch of an individual poet. No great poet leaves a convention exactly as he or she found it. In the hands of a shrewd craftsman, tradition and convention may be innovative and exciting; in the hands of a mindless ape of the past, they are nearly always dull and deadly.

DRAMA

1 EXPERIENCING DRAMA

Experiencing a play is very different from experiencing a story or a poem. Plays are written to be performed—by actors, on a stage, for an audience. To see and hear a play—to be a part of an audience responding to it—represents a different kind of experience from the usually solitary act of reading a story or a poem. Watching a performance is, for one thing, much more passive than the act of reading; the play comes to you rather than, as in the act of reading a story, your going to the text. There are, in fact, quite a few differences between performance and reading, and those differences are built into the nature of drama. Plays are written with a public performance in mind. Playwrights create plays in full consciousness of the possibilities that go beyond words and texts and extend to physical actions, stage effects, and other bits of theatricality that can create special effects on an audience.

All good literature tries to engage our imagination actively, inviting us to share feelings or think what it would be like to be a particular person in a particular place, time, or set of circumstances. But plays—when they are acted out on a stage—are more *concrete* than poems or stories: we see actions and hear words spoken through our physical senses; real live human beings stand for imaginary characters and actually say speeches and perform actions that we can hear and watch. Some of the imagination required is provided by the director and by actors who have made choices for us; they are interpreters of the play, and perform for a viewer part of the act of imagination that readers have to perform altogether for themselves. Seeing a play performed does involve an act of imagination, for the audience has to accept the illusion that the stage is actually a hotel room in New York, a meadow in the Midwest, or a court in Denmark, but that act of imagination is quite different from translating words on a page into people and actions.

Because plays are written with the explicit intention that they will be acted out upon a stage, *reading* a play requires an additional act of imagination. Readers of a play need to imagine not just feelings or a flow of action—as in poems and stories—but how the action and characters look in a theater, on a stage, before a live audience. We try to imagine how a character will look and move and talk; in effect, a reader casts a play as he or she reads it, putting actors into roles and making them move and speak in our imaginations. We imagine a whole layer of performance between the words on the page and the way we play out the plot in our minds.

The fact of a stage—physically limited in what it can contain and in what can be done within its confines—conditions the nature of drama, and a student of drama has to confront the particular limitations—and possibilities—that stages and staging are capable of to imagine fully how plays work. Experiencing drama is, thus, both more simple and more complex than experiencing poetry or fiction: more simple because the performance or imagined performance spells out for us far more detail in a far more vivid way than can words on a page, but more complex because as readers we have to construct in our imaginations the precise details our responses will ultimately depend on. In a sense, we become almost collaborators of the playwright as we go along—before we function fully as readers completing the potential of a text.

Drama on a stage often reflects the drama of everyday life, but (like other forms of literature and art) it concentrates life, focuses it, and holds it up to examination. Many scenes in plays could be slices of actual conversations, and sometimes playwrights make a special effort to have their dialogue take on the informality—or even the sloppiness and banality—of ordinary talk. Sometimes, too, the actions portrayed are everyday actions—drinking a cup of coffee, watching a bus go by, working out the subtleties of a relationship with a friend. Not all plays are about grand machinations of state or great loves or noble deeds (although some are), and not all artistic shapings of actuality into drama are formalized into traditional structures (although many are). Plays may be short, have only two or three characters, portray the routine matters of everyday life, and present conflicts that are personal or even trivial as well as great moments of national or cosmic significance. Sometimes it takes greater artistic control to make a very simple scene compelling than it does to portray grander actions that are more laden with deep conflict and greater in import. Here, for example, is a very brief contemporary piece of drama. Its author, Harold Pinter, does not call it a play but only a "sketch," a short piece suitable for staging and containing key elements of dramatic art.

HAROLD PINTER

The Black and White

The First Old Woman is sitting at a milk bar table. Small. A Second Old Woman approaches. Tall. She is carrying two bowls of soup, which are covered by two plates, on each of which is a slice of bread. She puts the bowls down on the table carefully.

SECOND You see that one come up and speak to me at the counter? (*She takes the bread plates off the bowls, takes two spoons from her pocket, and places the bowls, plates and spoons.*)
FIRST You got the bread, then?
SECOND I didn't know how I was going to carry it. In the end I put the plates on top of the soup.

FIRST   I like a bit of bread with my soup. (*They begin the soup. Pause.*)

SECOND   Did you see that one come up and speak to me at the counter?

FIRST   Who?

SECOND   Comes up to me, he says, hullo, he says, what's the time by your clock? Bloody liberty. I was just standing there getting your soup.

FIRST   It's tomato soup.

SECOND   What's the time by your clock? he says.

FIRST   I bet you answered him back.

SECOND   I told him all right. Go on, I said, why don't you get back into your scraghole, I said, clear off out of it before I call a copper. (*Pause.*)

FIRST   I not long got here.

SECOND   Did you get the all-night bus?

FIRST   I got the all-night bus straight here.

SECOND   Where from?

FIRST   Marble Arch.

SECOND   Which one?

FIRST   The two-nine-four, that takes me all the way to Fleet Street.

SECOND   So does the two-nine-one. (*Pause.*) I see you talking to two strangers as I come in. You want to stop talking to strangers, old piece of boot like you, you mind who you talk to.

FIRST   I wasn't talking to any strangers. (*Pause. The First Old Woman follows the progress of a bus through the window.*) That's another all-night bus gone down. (*Pause.*) Going up the other way. Fulham way. (*Pause.*) That was a two-nine-seven. (*Pause.*) I've never been up that way. (*Pause.*) I've been down to Liverpool Street.

SECOND   That's up the other way.

FIRST   I don't fancy going down there, down Fulham way, and all up there.

SECOND   Uh-uh.

FIRST   I've never fancied that direction much. (*Pause.*)

SECOND   How's your bread? (*Pause.*)

FIRST   Eh?

SECOND   Your bread.

FIRST   All right. How's yours? (*Pause.*)

SECOND   They don't charge for the bread if you have soup.

FIRST   They do if you have tea.

SECOND   If you have tea they do. (*Pause.*) You talk to strangers they'll take you in. Mind my word. Coppers'll take you in.

FIRST   I don't talk to strangers.

SECOND   They took me away in the wagon once.

FIRST   They didn't keep you though.

SECOND   They didn't keep me, but that was only because they took a fancy to me. They took a fancy to me when they got me in the wagon.

FIRST   Do you think they'd take a fancy to me?

SECOND   I wouldn't back on it. (*The First Old Woman gazes out of the window.*)

FIRST   You can see what goes on from this top table. (*Pause.*) It's better than going down to that place on the embankment, anyway.

SECOND   Yes, there's not too much noise.

FIRST   There's always a bit of noise.

SECOND   Yes, there's always a bit of life. (*Pause.*)

FIRST   They'll be closing down soon to give it a scrub-round.

SECOND   There's a wind out. (*Pause.*)

FIRST   I wouldn't mind staying.

SECOND   They won't let you.

FIRST   I know. (*Pause.*) Still, they only close hour and half, don't they? (*Pause.*) It's not long. (*Pause.*) You can go along, then come back.

SECOND   I'm going. I'm not coming back.

FIRST   When it's light I come back. Have my tea.

SECOND   I'm going. I'm going up to the Garden.

FIRST   I'm not going down there. (*Pause.*) I'm going up to Waterloo Bridge.

SECOND   You'll just about see the last two-nine-six come up over the river.

FIRST   I'll just catch a look of it. Time I get up there. (*Pause.*) It don't look like an all-night bus in daylight, do it?

1959

All the elements of drama are here in rather elementary form: there is a bit of story, mostly implied, about the lives of the two women; action on a modest scale, with a lot of emphasis on timing and relatively insignificant movements and props in order to emphasize the women's dependence on the everyday; characterization sufficient to give a quite clear idea of what the two women's lives are like; dialogue enough to suggest the characters' thoughts and feelings and to show how their lives intersect. Even a small element of conflict is present, just enough to make the scene interesting and lively and to highlight the quiet desperation of the women's lives.

What is such a sketch about? Why is it interesting? What makes it worth seeing, worth reading, worth studying, worth writing? What makes it "drama"?

It's easy enough to say what it's "about"—the essentially eventless lives of two elderly, lonely women who create a simple kind of sociality between each other and in relation to their rather mechanized, anonymous, modern environment. The order or structure of their lives is built on the predictable schedules of London's night buses and the odd opening and closing hours of an almost-all-night eatery. It reflects human routines in which not much—not even sleep —happens and in which little connection to other people exists. The women therefore create an artificial community with other riders and other patrons who are in fact unknown to them except by rituals, habits, and eccentricities. And with each other they develop some elemental sense of human relationship—a sort of parody of a conventional domestic relationship. One might say (although it sounds almost too pretentious and formal to describe the sketch) that the sketch is about loneliness, ritual, and a quest for meaning. But the point is less to prove or assert something profound or thematic than to present, poignantly, a sense of what life—or a brief slice of life—is like for two isolated people who at this point in their lives feel rather passed by.

The question of what makes the sketch interesting, memorable, and dramatic is more complicated. Once in a while we may witness, in life, a scene or vignette that seems to tell a story or offer a poignant sense of some aspect of human life. When we come upon such a moment, it is sort of art by accident, and in a way that is what Pinter manages to recreate here. We could just walk in on a scene like this, and the sketch goes out of its way to give that impression. The set is simple, the props are few and common, there is nothing especially complicated about the setting or about the way the action is set up. A production of the sketch is not likely to seem much like a production, and one can imagine the actors making it seem as little like a play—as untheatrical—as possible. They probably would not even seem to be actors. This is about as close to a segment of life as one can get, certainly far less portentous than a scene in *Oedipus* or *Hamlet*, far less organized and contrived than a carefully orchestrated confrontation in your favorite soap on television.

Yet the scene is very powerful. The action is efficient, there are no irrelevancies, except in the sense that the whole sketch depends on the conventional perceptions of two lives it presents as marginal. Its two main characters quickly reveal themselves. The setting gives them an opportunity to present, quickly and compactly, their situation and to imply their feelings. The action—almost a non-action—reflects that story of their lives and the theme of the sketch. And the setting and props—in their simplicity and spareness—not only set the stage for the dialogue but also reflect accurately the whole world of the women's lives. All things work together quickly and efficiently to create an impression, a vivid visual sense of the way some people (probably people most members of the audience wouldn't know much about) actually live, and a brief sense both of how those people feel about their lives and how we do.

The play at the end of this chapter—a short one-act play that also isolates quite quickly the lives and feelings of two people—somewhat more fully develops what is possible to do on a stage, in performance, with an audience looking on and responding as a group rather than reading and responding as a series of isolated individuals. In *The Black and White*, the themes of loneliness and isolation are especially touching and sad, in part because we watch the characters from a social perspective of our own, as part of a group that—while made up of individuals who may not know each other—watches together, shares the experience of the sketch, and (in effect) responds communally. If *The Black and White* were written as a story, it would have to use somewhat different strategies to achieve a similar impact. It would, in fact, be an interesting exercise to turn *The Black and White* into a story. How would you, in a narrative about the same two women, gain a similar effect? In *The Brute*, communal response is an equally important part of the play's effect, and in fact would probably be quite a bit more obvious if you were to see a performance of the play because the play is very funny and the audience would be likely to laugh together, creating a more tangible sense of commonality and community response. *The Brute* depends on some standard stereotypes of men and women, and the breaking down of those stereotypes involves some humorous surprises.

Plays are meant to be acted out by real people pretending to be someone else. In poems and stories, only the written text mediates between author and reader, but in plays all of the people involved in a particular production help to interpret the author's text for a specific audience. Not only actors, but directors, producers, even the people who build the sets, place an interpretation on the play, and every production of the play will differ somewhat from all the others. *How* words are spoken, *how* gestures are made, *how* the physical interaction takes place, *how* the set is designed and the place is made visual —all these things affect how an audience will respond to the play itself. Everyone involved in a play's performance is an interpreter— and in a sense a co-author—in a way that has no parallel in poems or stories. Being aware of the features of drama that make it more than a text, more than words on a page, makes the experience of plays take on dimentions that are beyond purely literary effects.

It is no accident that "creative" is one of the highest compliments we pay to performing artists, whether they are musicians, dancers, actors, or stand-up comedians, for no matter who is the author of their play, score, or routine, they bring it to life on the stage, and the original material becomes, in an important sense, theirs. Who gets the major credit for performed art varies considerably (and somewhat irrationally) from art to art. A comedian may sometimes have writers who get no credit at all, while performers of classical music usually take great pains to identify the composers whose music they perform. In drama, the credit is usually distributed fairly evenly between playwrights and leading actors (and sometimes directors). It is common to speak of Olivier's Hamlet (meaning the performance of the title role by Sir Laurence Olivier), of Maggie Smith's or Glenda Jackson's Hedda Gabler, or Zeffirelli's *Romeo and Juliet* (meaning the film interpretation of the play directed by Franco Zeffirelli) because in each case the hand of the actor or director leads to a distinctive interpretation of the play. A particular performance of a given play may well color our interpretation of a play forever after, especially if we see the play before we have read it, for it will influence how we respond to a later performance based on a different interpretation. The power of performance may well be more significant than the interpretive writing of critics which many people consider more abstract. Hamlet may be regarded as indecisive, melancholy, conniving, mad, vindictive, ambitious, or some combination of these things, and individual performances emphasize one attribute or another, always at some expense to other characteristics and interpretations. No play can be all things to an audience in any one performance, although it may be conceived richly enough to support a variety of different performances and different interpretations, so much so that it may appear to be almost a different play in the hands of different directors and actors.

Consciously or not, every director puts an interpretation on every scene by the way he or she stages the action; timing, the choice of actor, physical appearance of people and props, placement on the stage, physical interaction, and the phrasing and tone of every speech affect how the play will play. Every syllable uttered by every actor in some sense affects the outcome; tone of voice and the slightest body gesture are, for an actor, equivalent to the choices of words and sentence rhythm for a writer. Most directors and actors are, in fact, very self-conscious about their art and decide deliberately on a total view of the play. Most playwrights, in turn, leave a certain amount of latitude to performers, opening their plays to some range of interpretations, although they are obviously more pleased by some performances and interpretations than others. Directors and actors could, if they liked (and some historically have done so), undercut and pervert the clear intention of the playwright and meaning of a play, turning tragedy to farce. But most performances involve subtlety of interpretation, and the best of them are in some sense "true" to the written text, or at least to some reasonable interpretation of it. Written texts vary widely in how much direction they give to producers, directors, and actors, sometimes—as in the Pinter sketch—giving full details of what characters are to look like, how the stage is to be set, and how actions and gestures are to be performed.

The fact of a live audience also has an important impact on the way plays are created. The essential feature of an audience at a play involves the fact that they have, at a single instant, a common experience; they have assembled for the explicit purpose of seeing a play. Drama not only plays before a live audience of real people who respond directly and immediately to it (unlike a text that may lie silent and undisturbed in a book for days or even years at a time), but drama is also conceived of by the author in expectation of specific audience response. That is, authors write plays planning for the fact that they will be acted out in front of an audience; they calculate for the effect of a community of watchers rather than for the silent, or at least private, responses of single readers, and they know that the play's actual production may be affected by the way an audience reacts.

Especially in these days of home VCRs, people may watch a film in privacy, but to watch a play by oneself is a highly unusual experience. Drama is meant to be public—a form of collective behavior that persists in many forms in society. We go to football games or rock concerts as our primitive ancestors went to rain dances and fertility rites, to share an experience with others of similar interests or attitudes. When thousands of people gather at a rock concert, they expect something beyond the music. (A purer form of music is usually available more cheaply on records, and they could all be more comfortable and more purely receptive to the music at home.) What they seek is the *experience* of a concert; being there is what is important, and part of that is being there with each other. A live performance can hardly equal one achieved by the sophisticated techniques of the recording studio, but it *is* live and it is shared with thousands of other people. The individual feels the spirit and enthusiasm that makes collective experience meaningful.

Whatever the nature of a public performance, the individuals who make up the audience have made separate but common decisions to attend *Carmen* or *Cats*. They gather at the specified time and place, and in a sense they assume new identities as members of the group, partly expressed in their clothes—people dress one way for a football game and another for the opera—but also in such obvious ways as their new identities as seat numbers (Section 4, Row AA, Seat 103). These group identities strongly influence behavior, as anyone who has laughed at the wrong time in the theater or cheered for the visiting team while sitting among the home fans can testify. The group identity can become so strong that members of the group behave in ways they would not as individuals; cheering loudly, booing, and crying "Encore!" are simple examples. At its worst, the group can become a mob.

Plays are often more topical than poems or stories. They need to engage the audience in a group illusion, and one convenient and popular way to do so is to concentrate on a situation or a theme that broadly concerns the society and time. In recent years, for example, we have seen a number of plays dealing with aging. Arthur Kopit's *Wings* deals with the recovery of a stroke victim, an aging aviatrix. Such plays have more obvious relevance to a society like ours, in which the average age is rising, than to one in which it is falling. A play like *Wings* assumes an audience whose members are interested in a stroke because of either their own situation or that of aging relatives. Plays that aim primarily to entertain may avoid such an issue as aging in favor of examining the prevailing attitudes of the society toward the difference between marrying and living together. What is relevant will vary with the historical situation. Most of Shakespeare's great tragedies, for example, deal with succession to a throne or other positions of power. They were written when Elizabeth I was an aging queen, too old to produce a legitimate heir even if she had chosen to marry. For two centuries England had suffered war and destruction over issues of succession; not surprisingly, Shakespeare's audience was interested in the problems of transfer of power.

The audience also determines what can be seen onstage. In *Oedipus Tyrannus*, for example, Jocasta hangs herself offstage and Oedipus puts out his eyes offstage because the audience did not like to see violence onstage. Shakespeare's audience, on the other hand, seems to have loved onstage violence, if we are to believe the evidence of the last scene of *Hamlet* or the scene in Thomas Kyd's popular *Spanish Tragedy* in which the central character, Hieronimo, bites off his tongue and spits out the piece he has bitten off. In our own day we are witnessing the breakdown of audience taboos against nudity and sexual activity on stage, in films, and on television; audience approval of the mores of a society or a subgroup of that society is crucial for a production to exist.

A play on stage is different from a play on the page, not only because a stage production is transient, but also because every performance is a unique expression of a collaborative effort. Actors must remember hundreds of lines and perform movements on stage at certain times; the stagehands must change sets and install props between scenes; light and sound effects must occur on certain visual and aural cues. In any of these areas a single change or error—a new inflection at the end of a line or a misplaced prop—guarantees that a given performance will be unique. Nor are any two audiences the same, and the character of an audience inevitably affects the performance. A warm, responsive audience will bring out the best in the performers, as any actor will tell you, while a crowd's cold indifference often results in a tepid or stiff production. For these reasons, no staged realization of a play can ever duplicate another.

Not all this potential of dramatic experience is available when you read—rather than see—a play. But, in a way, reading plays draws even more fully on your imagination for as you read you become not only a critic, interpreter, and responder (as in stories and poems), but producer, director, actor, and set designer as well. You have to decide how you would cast the play; do you imagine Cloris Leachman playing the role of Mrs. Popov in *The Brute*? Meryl Streep? Joan Collins? Mia Farrow? How you would stage each scene, how you would coach the actors to walk, gesture, phrase and time their speeches. Those decisions can be difficult, but they are also challenging. And they help to clarify exactly what drama is about, how it differs from other, more purely verbal, forms of art. Ultimately, though, drama belongs in a theater, with actors performing under the supervision of a director in front of an audience. The real experience of drama involves being there.

ANTON CHEKHOV

The Brute[1]

CHARACTERS

MRS. POPOV, *widow and landowner, small, with dimpled cheeks.*
MR. GRIGORY S. SMIRNOV, *gentleman farmer, middle-aged.*
LUKA, *Mrs. Popov's footman, an old man.*
GARDENER, COACHMAN, HIRED MEN.

The drawing room of a country house. MRS. POPOV, *in deep mourning, is staring hard at a photograph.* LUKA *is with her.*

LUKA   It's not right, ma'am, you're killing yourself. The cook has gone off with the maid to pick berries. The cat's having a high old time in the yard catching birds. Every living thing is happy. But you stay moping here in the house like it was a convent, taking no pleasure in nothing. I mean it, ma'am! It must be a full year since you set foot out of doors.

MRS. POPOV   I must never set foot out of doors again, Luka. Never! I have nothing to set foot out of doors *for.* My life is done. *He* is in his grave. I have buried myself alive in this house. We are *both* in our graves.

LUKA   You're off again, ma'am. I just won't listen to you no more. Mr. Popov is dead, but what can we do about that? It's God's doing. God's will be done. You've cried over him, you've done your share of mourning, haven't you? There's a limit to everything. You can't go on weeping and wailing forever. My old lady died, for that matter, and I wept and wailed over her a whole month long. Well, that was it. I couldn't weep and wail all my life, she just wasn't worth it. [*He sighs*] As for the neighbours, you've forgotten all about them, ma'am. You don't visit them and you don't let them visit you. You and I are like a pair of spiders—excuse the expression, ma'am—here we are in this house like a pair of spiders, we never see the light of day. And it isn't like there was no nice people around either. The whole country's swarming with 'em. There's a regiment quartered at Riblov, and the officers are so good-looking! The girls can't take their eyes off them—There's a ball at the camp every Friday—The military band plays most every day of the week —What do you say, ma'am? You're young, you're pretty, you could enjoy yourself! Ten years from now you may want to strut and show your feathers to the officers, and it'll be too late.

MRS. POPOV [*Firmly*]   You must never bring this subject up again, Luka. Since Popov died, life has been an empty dream to me, you know that. *You* may think I am alive. Poor ignorant Luka! You are wrong. I am dead. I'm in my grave. Never more shall I see the

1. Translated by Eric Bentley.

912

light of day, never strip from my body this . . . raiment of death!
Are you listening, Luka? Let this ghost learn how I love him! Yes,
I know, and *you* know, he was often unfair to me, he was cruel to
me, and he was unfaithful to me. What of it? *I* shall be faithful to
him, that's all. I will show him how *I* can love. Hereafter, in a
better world than this, he will welcome me back, the same loyal
girl I always was—

LUKA   Instead of carrying on this way, ma'am, you should go out in
the garden and take a bit of a walk, ma'am. Or why not harness
Toby and take a drive? Call on a couple of the neighbours, ma'am?

MRS. POPOV [*Breaking down*]   Oh, Luka!

LUKA   Yes, ma'am? What have I said, ma'am? Oh dear!

MRS. POPOV   Toby! You said Toby! He adored that horse. When he
drove me out to the Korchagins and the Vlasovs, it was always with
Toby! He was a wonderful driver, do you remember, Luka? So
graceful! So strong! I can see him now, pulling at those reins with
all his might and main! Toby! Luka, tell them to give Toby an
extra portion of oats today.

LUKA   Yes, ma'am.

   [*A BELL rings*]

MRS. POPOV   Who is that? Tell them I'm not at home.

LUKA   Very good, ma'am. [*Exit*]

MRS. POPOV [*Gazing again at the photograph*]   You shall see, my
Popov, how a wife can love and forgive. Till death do us part.
Longer than that. Till death re-unite us forever! [*Suddenly a titter
breaks through her tears*] Aren't you ashamed of yourself, Popov?
Here's your little wife, being good, being faithful, so faithful she's
locked up here waiting for her own funeral, while you—doesn't it
make you ashamed, you naughty boy? You were terrible, you know.
You were unfaithful, and you made those awful scenes about it,
you stormed out and left me alone for weeks—

   [*Enter LUKA*]

LUKA [*Upset*]   There's someone asking for you, ma'am. Says he
must—

MRS. POPOV   I suppose you told him that since my husband's death
I see no one?

LUKA   Yes, ma'am. I did, ma'am. But he wouldn't listen, ma'am. He
says it's urgent.

MRS. POPOV [*Shrilly*]   I see no one!!

LUKA   He won't take no for an answer, ma'am. He just curses and
swears and comes in anyway. He's a perfect monster, ma'am. He's
in the dining room right now.

MRS. POPOV   In the dining room, is he? I'll give him his comeuppance.
Bring him in here this minute.

   [*Exit LUKA*]

[*Suddenly sad again*] Why do they do this to me? Why? Insulting
my grief, intruding on my solitude? [*She sighs*] I'm afraid I'll have
to enter a convent. I will, I *must* enter a convent!

   [*Enter MR. SMIRNOV and LUKA*]

SMIRNOV [*To LUKA*]   Dolt! Idiot! You talk too much! [*Seeing MRS.
POPOV. With dignity*] May I have the honour of introducing myself,

madam? Grigroy S. Smirnov, landowner and lieutenant of artillery, retired. Forgive me, madam, if I disturb your peace and quiet, but my business is both urgent and weighty.

MRS. POPOV [*Declining to offer him her hand*]   What is it you wish, sir?

SMIRNOV   At the time of his death, your late husband—with whom I had the honour to be acquainted, ma'am—was in my debt to the tune of twelve hundred rubles. I have two notes to prove it. Tomorrow, ma'am, I must pay the interest on a bank loan. I have therefore no alternative, ma'am, but to ask you to pay me the money today.

MRS. POPOV   Twelve hundred rubles? But what did my husband owe it to you for?

SMIRNOV   He used to buy his oats from me, madam.

MRS. POPOV [*To* LUKA, *with a sigh*]   Remember what I said. Luka: tell them to give Toby an extra portion of oats today!

[*Exit* LUKA]

My dear Mr.—what was the name again?

SMIRNOV   Smirnov, ma'am.

MRS. POPOV   My dear Mr. Smirnov, if Mr. Popov owed you money, you shall be paid—to the last ruble, to the last kopeck. But today—you must excuse me, Mr.—what was it?

SMIRNOV   Smirnov, ma'am.

MRS. POPOV   Today, Mr. Smirnov, I have no ready cash in the house.
   [SMIRNOV *starts to speak*]
Tomorrow, Mr. Smirnov, no, the day after tomorrow, all will be well. My steward will be back from town. I shall see that he pays what is owing. Today, no. In any case, today is exactly seven months from Mr. Popov's death. On such a day you will understand that I am in no mood to think of money.

SMIRNOV   Madam, if you don't pay up now, you can carry me out feet foremost. They'll seize my estate.

MRS. POPOV   You can have your money.
   [*He starts to thank her*]
Tomorrow.
   [*He again starts to speak*]
That is: the day after tomorrow.

SMIRNOV   I don't need the money the day after tomorrow. I need it today.

MRS. POPOV   I'm sorry, Mr.—

SMIRNOV [*Shouting*]   Smirnov!

MRS. POPOV [*Sweetly*]   Yes, of course. But you can't have it today.

SMIRNOV   But I can't wait for it any longer!

MRS. POPOV   Be sensible, Mr. Smirnov. How can I pay you if I don't have it?

SMIRNOV   You don't have it?

MRS. POPOV   I don't have it.

SMIRNOV   Sure?

MRS. POPOV   Positive.

SMIRNOV   Very well. I'll make a note to that effect. [*Shrugging*] And then they want me to keep cool. I meet the tax commissioner on the street, and he says, 'Why are you always in such a bad humour, Smirnov?' Bad humour! How can I help it, in God's name? I need money, I need it desperately. Take yesterday: I leave home at the crack of dawn, I call on all my debtors. Not a one of them pays up. Footsore and weary, I creep at midnight into some little dive, and try to snatch a few winks of sleep on the floor by the vodka barrel. Then today, I come here, fifty miles from home, saying to myself, 'At last, at last, I can be sure of something,' and you're not in the mood! You give me a mood! Christ, how can I help getting all worked up?

MRS. POPOV I thought I'd made it clear, Mr. Smirnov, that you'll get your money the minute my steward is back from town?

SMIRNOV What the hell do I care about your steward? Pardon the expression, ma'am. But it was you I came to see.

MRS. POPOV What language! What a tone to take to a lady! I refuse to hear another word. [*Quickly, exit*]

SMIRNOV Not in the mood, huh? 'Exactly seven months since Popov's death,' huh? How about me? [*Shouting after her*] Is there this interest to pay, or isn't there? I'm asking you a question: is there this interest to pay, or isn't there? So your husband died, and you're not in the mood, and your steward's gone off some place, and so forth and so on, but what *I* can do about all that, huh? What do you think I should do? Take a running jump and shove my head through the wall? Take off in a balloon? You don't know my *other* debtors. I call on Gruzdeff. Not at home. I look for Yaroshevitch. He's hiding out. I find Kooritsin. He kicks up a row, and I have to throw him through the window. I work my way right down the list. Not a kopeck. Then I come to you, and God damn it to hell, if you'll pardon the expression, you're not in the mood! [*Quietly, as he realizes he's talking to air*] I've spoiled them all, that's what, I've let them play me for a sucker. Well, I'll show them. I'll show this one. I'll stay right her till she pays up. Ugh! [*He shudders with rage*] I'm in a rage! I'm in a positively towering rage! Every nerve in my body is trembling at forty to the dozen! I can't breathe, I feel ill, I think I'm going to faint, hey, you there!

[*Enter* LUKA]

LUKA Yes, sir? Is there anything you wish, sir?

SMIRNOV Water! Water! ! No, make it vodka.

[*Exit* LUKA]

Consider the logic of it. A fellow creature is desperately in need of cash, so desperately in need that he has to seriously contemplate hanging himself, and this woman, this mere chit of a girl, won't pay up, and why not? Because, forsooth, she isn't in the mood! Oh, the logic of women! Come to that, I never have liked them, I could do without the whole sex. Talk to a woman? I'd rather sit on a barrel of dynamite, the very thought gives me gooseflesh. Women! Creatures of poetry and romance! Just to see one in the distance gets me mad. My legs start twitching with rage. I feel like yelling for help.

[*Enter* LUKA, *handing* SMIRNOV *a glass of water*]

LUKA Mrs. Popov is indisposed, sir. She is seeing no one.

SMIRNOV   Get out.

[*Exit* LUKA]

Indisposed, is she? Seeing no one, huh? Well, she can see me or not, but I'll be here, I'll be right here till she pays up. If you're sick for a week, I'll be here for a week. If you're sick for a year, I'll be here for a year. You won't get around *me* with your widow's weeds and your schoolgirl dimples. I know all about dimples. [*Shouting through the window*] Semyon, let the horses out of those shafts, we're not leaving, we're staying, and tell them to give the horses some oats, yes, oats, you fool, what do you think? [*Walking away from the window*] What a mess, what an unholy mess! I didn't sleep last night, the heat is terrific today, not a damn one of 'em has paid up, and here's this—this skirt in mourning that's not in the mood! My head aches, where's that— [*He drinks from the glass*] Water, ugh! You there!

[*Enter* LUKA]

LUKA   Yes, sir. You wish for something, sir?

SMIRNOV   Where's that confounded vodka I asked for?

[*Exit* LUKA]

[SMIRNOV *sits and looks himself over*] Oof! A fine figure of a man *I* am! Unwashed, uncombed, unshaven, straw on my vest, dust all over me. The little woman must've taken me for a highwayman. [*Yawns*] I suppose it wouldn't be considered polite to barge into a drawing room in this state, but who cares? I'm not a visitor, I'm a creditor—most unwelcome of guests, second only to Death.

[*Enter* LUKA]

LUKA   [*Handing him the vodka*] If I may say so, sir, you take too many liberties, sir.

SMIRNOV   What?!

LUKA   Oh, nothing, sir, nothing.

SMIRNOV   Who in hell do you think you're talking to? Shut your mouth!

LUKA   [*Aside*] There's an evil spirit abroad. The Devil must have sent him. Oh! [*Exit* LUKA]

SMIRNOV   What a rage I'm in! I'll grind the whole world to powder. Oh, I feel ill again. You there!

[*Enter* MRS. POPOV]

MRS. POPOV   [*Looking at the floor*] In the solitude of my rural retreat, Mr. Smirnov, I've long since grown unaccustomed to the sound of the human voice. Above all, I cannot bear shouting. I must beg you not to break the silence.

SMIRNOV   Very well. Pay me my money and I'll go.

MRS. POPOV   I told you before, and I tell you again, Mr. Smirnov: I have no cash, you'll have to wait till the day after tomorrow. Can I express myself more plainly?

SMIRNOV   And *I* told *you* before, and *I* tell *you* again, that I need the money today, that the day after tomorrow is too late, and that if you don't, and pay now, I'll have to hang myself in the morning!

MRS. POPOV   But I have no cash. This is quite a puzzle.

SMIRNOV   You won't pay, huh?

MRS. POPOV   I *can't* pay, Mr. Smirnov.

SMIRNOV   In that case, I'm going to sit here and wait. [*Sits down.*] You'll pay up the day after tomorrow? Very good. Till the day after tomorrow, here I sit. [*Pause. He jumps up.*] Now look, do I have to pay that interest tomorrow, or don't I? Or do you think I'm joking?

MRS. POPOV   I must ask you not to raise your voice, Mr. Smirnov. This is not a stable.

SMIRNOV   Who said it was? Do I have to pay the interest tomorrow or not?

MRS. POPOV   Mr. Smirnov, do you know how to behave in the presence of a lady?

SMIRNOV   No, madam, I do not know how to behave in the presence of a lady.

MRS. POPOV   Just what I thought. I look at you, and I say: ugh! I hear you talk, and I say to myself: 'That man doesn't know how to talk to a lady.'

SMIRNOV   You'd like me to come simpering to you in French, I suppose. '*Enchanté, madame! Merci beaucoup* for not paying zee money, *madame! Pardonnez-moi* if I 'ave disturbed you, *madame!* How *charmante*[2] you look in mourning, *madame!*'

MRS. POPOV   Now you're being silly, Mr. Smirnov.

SMIRNOV   [*Mimicking*] 'Now you're being silly, Mr. Smirnov.' 'You don't know how to talk to a lady, Mr. Smirnov.' Look here, Mrs. Popov, I've known more women than you've known pussy cats. I've fought three duels on their account. I've jilted twelve, and been jilted by nine others. Oh, yes, Mrs. Popov, I've played the fool in my time, whispered sweet nothings, bowed and scraped and endeavoured to please. Don't tell me I don't know what it is to love, to pine away with longing, to have the blues, to melt like butter, to be weak as water. I was full of tender emotion. I was carried away with passion. I squandered half my fortune on the sex. I chattered about women's emancipation. But there's an end to everything, dear madam. Burning eyes, dark eyelashes, ripe, red lips, dimpled cheeks, heaving bosoms, soft whisperings, the moon above, the lake below —I don't give a rap for that sort of nonsense any more, Mrs. Popov. I've found out about women. Present company excepted, they're liars. Their behaviour is mere play acting; their conversation is sheer gosip. Yes, dear lady, women, young or old, are false, petty, vain, cruel, malicious unreasonable. As for intelligence, any sparrow could give them points. Appearances, I admit, can be deceptive. In appearance, a woman may be all poetry and romance, goddess and angel, muslin and fluff. To look at her exterior is to be transported to heaven. But I have looked at her interior, Mrs. Popov, and what did I find there—in her very soul? A crocodile. [*He has gripped the back of the chair so firmly that it snaps*] And, what is more revolting, a crocodile with an illusion, a crocodile that imagines tender sentiments are its own special province, a crocodile that

2. Enchanted (to meet you), madame. Thank you very much . . . . Pardon me . . . . How charming . . . .

thinks itself queen of the realm of love! Whereas, in sober fact, dear madam, if a woman can love anything except a lapdog you can hang me by the feet on that nail. For a man, love is suffering, love is sacrifice. A woman just swishes her train around and tightens her grip on your nose. Now, you're a woman, aren't you, Mrs. Popov? You must be an expert on some of this. Tell me, quite frankly, did you ever know a woman to be—faithful, for instance? Or even sincere? Only old hags, huh? Though some women are old hags from birth. But as for the others? You're right: a faithful woman is a freak of nature—like a cat with horns.

MRS. POPOV Who *is* faithful, then? Who *have* you cast for the faithful lover? Not man?

SMIRNOV Right first time, Mrs. Popov: man.

MRS. POPOV [*Going off into a peal of bitter laughter*] Man! Man is faithful! That's a new one! [*Fiercely*] What right do you have to say this, Mr. Smirnov? Men faithful? Let me tell you something. Of all the men I have ever known my late husband Popov was the best. I loved him, and there are women who know how to love, Mr. Smirnov. I gave him my youth, my happiness, my life, my fortune. I worshipped the ground he trod on—and what happened? The best of men was unfaithful to me, Mr. Smirnov. Not once in a while. All the time. After he died, I found his desk drawer full of love letters. While he was alive, he was always going away for the week-end. He squandered my money. He made love to other women before my very eyes. But, in spite of all, Mr. Smirnov, *I* was faithful. Unto death. And beyond. I am *still* faithful, Mr. Smirnov! Buried alive in this house, I shall wear mourning till the day I, too, am called to my eternal rest.

SMIRNOV [*Laughing scornfully*] Expect me to believe that? As if I couldn't see through all this hocus-pocus. Buried alive! Till you're called to your eternal rest! Till when? Till some little poet—or some little subaltern with his first moustache—comes riding by and asks: 'Can that be the house of the mysterious Tamara who for love of her late husband has buried herself alive, vowing to see no man?' Ha!

MRS. POPOV [*Flaring up*] How dare you? How dare you insinuate—?

SMIRNOV You may have buried yourself alive, Mrs. Popov, but you haven't forgotten to powder your nose.

MRS. POPOV [*Incoherent*] How dare you? How—?

SMIRNOV Who's raising his voice now? Just because I call a spade a spade. Because I shoot straight from the shoulder. Well, don't shout at me, I'm not your steward.

MRS. POPOV I'm not shouting, you're shouting! Oh, leave me alone!

SMIRNOV Pay me the money, and I will.

MRS. POPOV You'll get no money out of me!

SMIRNOV Oh, so that's it!

MRS. POPOV Not a ruble, not a kopeck. Get out! Leave me alone!

SMIRNOV Not being your husband, I must ask you not to make scenes with me. [*He sits*] I don't like scenes.

MRS. POPOV [*Choking with rage*] You're sitting down?

SMIRNOV Correct, I'm sitting down.

MRS. POPOV   I asked you to leave!

SMIRNOV   Then give me the money. [*Aside*] Oh, what a rage I'm in, what a rage!

MRS. POPOV   The impudence of the man! I won't talk to you a moment longer. Get out. [*Pause*] Are you going?

SMIRNOV   No.

MRS. POPOV   No?!

SMIRNOV   No.

MRS. POPOV   On your head be it. Luka!

   [*Enter* LUKA]

Show the gentleman out, Luka.

LUKA [*Approaching*]   I'm afraid, sir, I'll have to ask you, um, to leave, sir, now, um—

SMIRNOV [*Jumping up*]   Shut your mouth, you old idiot! Who do you think you're talking to? I'll make mincemeat of you.

LUKA [*Clutching his heart*]   Mercy on us! Holy saints above! [*He falls into an armchair*] I'm taken sick! I can't breathe!!

MRS. POPOV   Then where's Dasha? Dasha! Dasha! Come here at once! [*She rings*]

LUKA   They gone picking berries, ma'am, I'm alone here—Water, water, I'm taken sick!

MRS. POPOV [*To* SMIRNOV]   Get out, you!

SMIRNOV   Can't you even be polite with me, Mrs. Popov?

MRS. POPOV [*Clenching her fists and stamping her feet*]   With you? You're a wild animal, you were never house-broken!

SMIRNOV   What? What did you say?

MRS. POPOV   I said you were a wild animal, you were never house-broken.

SMIRNOV [*Advancing upon her*]   And what right do you have to talk to me like that?

MRS. POPOV   Like what?

SMIRNOV   You have insulted me, madam.

MRS. POPOV   What of it? Do you think I'm scared of you?

SMIRNOV   So you think you can get away with it because you're a woman. A creature of poetry and romance, huh? Well, it doesn't go down with me. I hereby challenge you to a duel.

LUKA   Mercy on us! Holy saints alive! Water!

SMIRNOV   I propose we shoot it out.

MRS. POPOV   Trying to scare me again? Just because you have big fists and a voice like a bull? You're a brute.

SMIRNOV   No one insults Grigory S. Smirnov with impunity! And I don't care if you *are* a female.

MRS. POPOV [*Trying to outshout him*]   Brute, brute, brute!

SMIRNOV   The sexes are equal, are they? Fine: then it's just prejudice to expect men alone to pay for insults. I hereby challenge—

MRS. POPOV [*Screaming*]   All right! You want to shoot it out? All right! Let's shoot it out!

SMIRNOV   And let it be here and now!

MRS. POPOV   Here and now! All right! I'll have Popov's pistols here in one minute! [*Walks away, then turns*] Putting one of Popov's bullets through your silly head will be a pleasure! Au revoir. [*Exit*]

SMIRNOV   I'll bring her down like a duck, a sitting duck. I'm not one of your little poets, I'm no little subaltern with his first moustache. No, sir, there's no weaker sex where I'm concerned!

LUKA   Sir! Master! [*He goes down on his knees*] Take pity on a poor old man, and do me a favour: go away. It was bad enough before, you nearly scared me to death. But a duel—!

SMIRNOV   [*Ignoring him*]   A duel! That's equality of the sexes for you! That's women's emancipation! Just as a matter of principle I'll bring her down like a duck. But what a woman! 'Putting one of Popov's bullets through your silly head . . .' Her cheeks were flushed, her eyes were gleaming! And, by God, she's accepted the challenge! I never knew a woman like this before!

LUKA   Sir! Master! Please go away! I'll always pray for you!

SMIRNOV   [*Again ignoring him*]   What a woman! Phew!! She's no sour puss, *she's* no cry baby. She's fire and brimstone. She's a human cannon ball. What a shame I have to kill her!

LUKA   [*Weeping*]   Please, kind sir, please, go away!

SMIRNOV   [*As before*]   I like her, isn't that funny? With those dimples and all? I like her. I'm even prepared to consider letting her off that debt. And where's my rage? It's gone. I never knew a woman like this before.

[*Enter* MRS. POPOV *with pistols*]

MRS. POPOV   [*Boldly*]   Pistols, Mr. Smirnov! [*Matter of fact*] But before we start, you'd better show me how it's done, I'm not too familiar with these things. In fact I never gave a pistol a second look.

LUKA   Lord, have mercy on us, I must go hunt up the gardener and the coachman. Why has this catastrophe fallen upon us, O Lord? [*Exit*]

SMIRNOV   [*Examining the pistols*]   Well, it's like this. There are several makes: one is the Mortimer, with capsules, especially constructed for duelling. What you have here are Smith and Wesson triple-action revolvers, with extractor, first-rate job, worth ninety rubles at the very least. You hold it this way. [*Aside*] My God, what eyes she has! They're setting me on fire.

MRS. POPOV   This way?

SMIRNOV   Yes, that's right. You cock the trigger, take aim like this, head up, arm out like this. Then you just press with this finger here, and it's all over. The main thing is, keep cool, take slow aim, and don't let your arm jump.

MRS. POPOV   I see. And if it's inconvenient to do the job here, we can go out in the garden.

SMIRNOV   Very good. Of course, I should warn you: I'll be firing in the air.

MRS. POPOV   What? This is the end. Why?

SMIRNOV   Oh, well—because—for private reasons.

MRS. POPOV   Scared, huh? [*She laughs heartily*] Now don't you try to get out of it, Mr. Smirnov. My blood is up. I won't be happy till I've drilled a hole through that skull of yours. Follow me. What's the matter? Scared?

SMIRNOV   That's right. I'm scared.

MRS. POPOV Oh, come on, what's the matter with you?

SMIRNOV Well, um, Mrs. Popov, I, um, I like you.

MRS. POPOV [*Laughing bitterly*] Good God! He likes me, does he?
The gall of the man. [*Showing him the door*] You may leave, Mr.
Smirnov.

SMIRNOV [*Quietly puts the gun down, takes his hat, and walks to the
door. Then he stops and the pair look at each other without a word.
Then, approaching gingerly*] Listen, Mrs. Popov. Are you still mad
at me? I'm in the devil of a temper myself, of course. But then, you
see—what I mean is—it's this way—the fact is—[*Roaring*] Well,
is it my fault, damn it, if I like you. [*Clutches the back of a chair.
It breaks*] Christ, what fragile furniture you have here. I like you.
Know what I mean? I could fall in love with you.

MRS. POPOV I hate you. Get out!

SMIRNOV What a woman! I never saw anything like it. Oh, I'm lost,
I'm done for, I'm a mouse in a trap.

MRS. POPOV Leave this house, or I shoot!

SMIRNOV Shoot away! What bliss to die of a shot that was fired by
that little velvet hand! To die gazing into those enchanting eyes.
I'm out of my mind. I know: you must decide at once. Think for
one second, then decide. Because if I leave now, I'll never be back.
Decide! I'm a pretty decent chap. Landed gentleman, I should say.
Ten thousand a year. Good stable. Throw a kopeck up in the air,
and I'll put a bullet through it. Will you marry me?

MRS. POPOV [*Indignant, brandishing the gun*] We'll shoot it out! Get
going! Take your pistol!

SMIRNOV I'm out of my mind. I don't understand anything any more.
[*Shouting*] You there! That vodka!

MRS. POPOV No excuses! No delays! We'll shoot it out!

SMIRNOV I'm out of my mind. I'm falling in love. I *have* fallen in
love. [*He goes down on his knees*] I love you as I've never loved
before. I jilted twelve, and was jilted by nine others. But I didn't
love a one of them as I love you. I'm full of tender emotion. I'm
melting like butter. I'm weak as water. I'm on my knees like a fool,
and I offer you my hand. It's a shame, it's a disgrace. I haven't
been in love in five years. I took a vow against it. And now, all of
a sudden, to be swept off my feet, it's a scandal. I offer you my
hand, dear lady. Will you or won't you? You won't? Then don't!
[*He rises and walks toward the door*]

MRS. POPOV I didn't say anything.

SMIRNOV [*Stopping*] What?

MRS. POPOV Oh, nothing, you can go. Well, no, just a minute. No,
you can go. Go! I detest you! But, just a moment. Oh, if you knew
how furious I feel! [*Throws the gun on the table*] My fingers have
gone to sleep holding that horrid thing. [*She is tearing her handkerchief to shreds*] And what are you standing around for? Get out
of here!

SMIRNOV Goodbye.

MRS. POPOV Go, go, go! [*Shouting*] Where are you going? Wait a
minute! No, no, it's all right, just go. I'm fighting mad. Don't come
near me, don't come near me!

SMIRNOV [*Who* IS *coming near her*]   I'm pretty disgusted with myself
—falling in love like a kid, going down on my knees like some
moongazing whippersnapper, the very thought gives me gooseflesh.
[*Rudely*] I love you. But it doesn't make sense. Tomorrow, I have
to pay that interest, and we've already started mowing. [*He puts
his arm about her waist*] I shall never forgive myself for this.
MRS. POPOV   Take your hands off me, I hate you! Let's shoot it out!

> [*A long kiss. Enter* LUKA *with an axe, the* GARDENER *with a
> rake, the* COACHMAN *with a pitchwork,* HIRE MEN *with sticks*]

LUKA [*Seeing the kiss*]   Mercy on us! Holy saints above!
MRS. POPOV [*Dropping her eyes*]   Luka, tell them in the stable that
Toby is *not* to have any oats today.

CURTAIN

1888

Text

2 STRUCTURE AND STAGE

An important part of the task of any storyteller, whether the story is to be narrative or dramatic, is the invention, selection, and arrangement of the action: in other words, the creation of the **plot.** Since dramatic plot usually involves **conflict,** dramatic structure centrally concerns the presentation—quite literally the embodiment or fleshing out—of that conflict.

A conflict whose outcome is never in doubt may have other kinds of interest, but it is not truly dramatic, so each of the opposing forces —whether character versus character, character versus society, nature, or whatever—should at some point or other have a chance to triumph. In *Hamlet,* for example, the effectiveness of the struggle between Hamlet and Claudius depends on their being evenly matched. Claudius has possession of the throne and the Queen, but Hamlet has his relation to the late king and his popularity with the people to balance his opponent's strengths. Early in the play Claudius has the upper hand, but he realizes that he has underestimated Hamlet and he overreacts. Until he stops the play-within-the-play, the king seems firmly in command; the odds seem to favor him. The play, however, does not end with Claudius's triumph.

The king's outburst in *Hamlet* is an example of the kind of dramatic event about which the typical structure of a play is built and which is called the **climax.** The typical dramatic structure of a play generally falls into five parts, which may or may not coincide with the division into acts and scenes. The first of these, the **exposition,** presents the situation as it exists at the opening of the play, introducing the characters and defining the relationships among them. In *The Brute* the bulk of the exposition is presented before Luka goes to answer the bell, and the rest of it—the introduction of Smirnov and his information about Popov's debt—is given immediately thereafter. The second part of the dramatic structure of a play, the **rising action,** consists in a series of events that complicate the original situation and create conflicts among the characters. During the rising action, the flow of the action is in a single direction, but at some crucial moment an event occurs that changes the direction of that flow, sometimes just by a sudden revelation: in *The Brute,* for example, the hostile Smirnov suddenly realizes he is falling in love with Mrs. Popov. This is the third part of the play, the **climax,** or **turning point.** The fourth part of a play is the **falling action,** the changes that characterize the unwinding or unknotting of the complication. Generally the falling action requires less time than the rising action. The final part of the play is its **conclusion** or **catastrophe.** The conclusion reestablishes a stable situation to end the drama.

Although this structure does not work the same way in every play, it may be helpful to see in detail how it works in a particular play. In *Hamlet* the exposition sets forth the established situation at the beginning of the play. We need to know about the death of the old king, the accession of Claudius rather than young Hamlet, the marriage of Claudius and Gertrude, Hamlet's return from Wittenberg, and the threat of invasion from Fortinbras. Shakespeare uses two devices to present this information: the recent return of Horatio from Wittenberg (and his need to be brought up to date) and Claudius's speech at the beginning of Act 1, Scene 2. In these and other ways we learn where things stand. At the same time we are witnessing the beginning of the rising action, the introduction of new elements that are to affect the action of the play: the appearance of the ghost, Claudius's refusal to allow Hamlet to return to Wittenberg, Hamlet's growing involvement with Ophelia, the return of Rosencrantz and Guildenstern, and so forth. These and other complications affect the action without changing its basic direction. They also set up events that are to happen later in the play, e.g., Laertes's departure for Paris sets up his return in Act 4. The climax, or turning point, occurs when the King loses control of himself at the play-within-the-play. He loses his advantage over Hamlet, who from then on is more or less in control of the situation. During the falling action the various strands of the plot begin to work themselves out. What happens to Ophelia? What is the result of Rosencrantz and Guildenstern's return? When such questions have been settled, we move to the conclusion of the play, the reestablishment of a new stable situation. In *Hamlet* the conclusion takes place in the final scene, where order is finally restored by the promise of Fortinbras as king.

Even a short play like *The Sacrifice of Isaac* contains all five of the parts: the exposition is presented concisely in Abraham's opening prayer, the action rises from there to the climax—the angel appearing to tell Abraham he need not kill his beloved son—and falls to the conclusion, when Isaac and Abraham head home, a new stability having been restored.

There are other devices by which a play can be made meaningful and effective. One such is called **dramatic irony**, the fulfillment of a plan, action, or expectation in a surprising way, often the opposite of what was intended. *Oedipus Tyrannus* offers a number of parallel instances of such dramatic irony, creating almost unbearable tension and frustration, a sense of powerlessness against the will of the gods. Oedipus opens the action by proclaiming that he will banish the criminal responsible for the plagues upon Thebes, only to discover at play's end that to do so means exiling himself. Oedipus further learns that by fleeing his adoptive parents in Corinth to avoid fulfilling a prophecy, he has in fact murdered his real father and married his mother as foreordained by the gods. And when Oedipus spurns the words of the blind seer Teiresias, Teiresias observes that his own blindness is only physical while Oedipus has eyes but cannot see his own destruction. When Oedipus finally does "see" the truth, he blinds himself. As in the investigation of a detective who discovers that he himself is the criminal he has been looking for, all of Oedipus's words and deeds are ironically reversed as the plot unfolds.

Such paralleled ironies are only one way of achieving thematic resonance through plotting. In *Death of a Salesman*, the unfolding story of Willy's life moves backward and forward through time so that Willy experiences the past as if it were the present, and we hear almost simultaneously conversations between friends inhabiting his grim present and those from an idealized past. These concurrent "plots"—the stories of Willy before and after the Depression—proceed chronologically as revealed to the reader and viewer through Willy's consciousness.

Besides structures like dramatic irony or theme that pull parts of the play together and the five dramatic structural divisions that shape the action, most plays also have formal divisions, such as **acts** and **scenes.** In the Greek theater scenes were separated by choral odes. In many French plays, a new scene begins with any significant entrance or exit. Many "classic" plays have five acts, because the poet Horace suggested that number, but modern plays tend to have two or three acts. Formal divisions are the result of the conventions of the period and the content of the individual play, and may vary from the one-act, one-scene play, such as *The Brute,* to such multi-act plays as O'Neill's *Mourning Becomes Electra.*

Dramatic structures and dramatic irony, even the formal divisions of a play are present to the reader as well as the viewer of the performance of a play, but of course in performance a play takes place on a **stage** or acting area rather than in the reader's mind. The design and significance of the acting area vary in different times and places. In the Greek theater, the audience was seated on a raised semicircle of seats (**amphitheater**) halfway around a circular area (**orchestra**) used primarily for dancing by the chorus. At the back of the orchestra was the **skene** or stage house, which represented the palace or temple before which the action took place. Shakespeare's stage, in contrast, basically involved a rectangular area built inside one end of a generally round enclosure, so that the audience was on three sides of the principal acting area. There were additional acting areas on either side of this stage, as well as a recessed area at the back of the stage, which could represent Gertrude's chamber in *Hamlet,* for example, or the cave in *The Tempest,* and an upper acting area, which could serve as Juliet's balcony, for example.

Modern stages are of three types. The **proscenium** stage evolved during the nineteenth century and is still the most common. For such a stage, the proscenium or proscenium arch is an architectural element that separates the auditorium from the stage and makes the action seem more real because the audience is viewing it through an invisible fourth wall. The proscenium stage lends itself to the use of a curtain, which can be lowered and raised—or closed and parted—between acts or scenes. Sometimes a part of the acting area is on the auditorium side of the proscenium. Such an area is an **apron** or forestage. The second type of modern stage is the **thrust stage,** in which the audience is seated around three-fourths of the major acting area. All of the action may take place on this projecting area, or some may occur in the extended area of the fourth side. In an **arena stage**, the third type, the audience is seated around the acting area. Entrances and exits are made through the auditorium, and restrictions on the sets are required to insure visibility.

At any given time and place the idea of what a stage is like is generally shared by audience and stage personnel, and most authors work with this generally understood notion of the kind of stage involved when they write a play. Of course, authors will sometimes innovate and they, the director, or set designer will work out new ways of using the stage, as in the flashbacks of *Death of a Salesman*. But even then Miller and his associates were working with the general understanding of the nature of one stage. Even greater differences are involved when we examine plays of different periods that have radically different conventions.

One such convention involves the notion of place. The audience knows that the stage is a stage, but they accept it for a public square or a room in a castle or an empty road. In *The Brute* we accept the stage as a drawing room in a Russian country house. There must be at least one door, leading to the entrance of the house, and the rest of the house and a window. There must be at least two (fragile) straight chairs and an armchair. The play is written for a proscenium stage. If the play is to work, the designer must make the audience aware of the objects, doors, windows, chairs, etc., required by the action. By contrast, *The Sacrifice of Isaac* was written to be performed outdoors on a wagon, probably with an elevated area to represent heaven and some indication that one part of the stage represents a field near Abraham's tent and another the place of sacrifice. There are no doors leading to specific places, and only a few objects are required.

The convention of place also involves how place is changed. In *The Sacrifice of Isaac* this was apparently accomplished by moving from one part of the wagon to another. In *The Brute* such a change would involve, if it had been required, lowering a curtain or darkening the stage while the sets and props were changed to produce the new place. In Greek drama, generally there was no change of place and the action was set up to involve only one place. If the presence of Teiresias was required, someone would be sent to bring him.

In *Hamlet* all the conventions are quite different. In Shakespeare's theater the acting area does not represent a specific place, but assumes a temporary identity from the characters who inhabit it, their costumes, and their speeches. At the opening of the play we know we are at a sentry station because a man dressed as a soldier challenges two others. By line 15 we know that we are in Denmark because the actors profess to be "liegemen to the Dane." At the end of the scene the actors leave the stage and in a sense take the sentry station with them. Shortly a group of people dressed in court costumes and a man and a woman wearing crowns appear. The audience knows that the acting area has now become a "chamber of state." As the play progresses, we learn more about the characters and the action, and identification of place become easier. Although the conventions differ, there is always some tacit agreement between playwright and actors on the one hand and the audience on the other about how place is represented as well.

A similar set of conventions governs the treatment of time on stage. Classical theories and practice suggest that in order to insure maximum dramatic impact the action of a play should be restricted to a very short time—sometimes as short as the actual performance (two or three hours), rarely longer than a single day. It is this concentration of time that impels a dramatist to select the moment when a stable situation is on the verge of change and to fill in the necessary prior details by exposition or even by some more elaborate device. In *Death of a Salesman,* you will remember, significant scenes from the past are enacted as dreams or memories on the stage (a device somewhat like the *flashback* in fiction). The action from the beginning to the end of the play thus can be concentrated in a very short period of represented time, rather than spread over fifteen years, moving toward the present crisis scene by scene, act by act. You might look back over the plays you have read so far and note how much time elapses from beginning to end and what devices, if any, preserve the restriction of represented time so as to concentrate the action and thus heighten the impact.

Even within the classical drama with its restricted time-span—or **unity of time**—there are conventions to mark the passing of represented time when it is supposed to pass at a greater rate than that of viewing or reading time. The choral odes in *Oedipus Tyrannus* are an example of one convention for representing the passage of time. The elapsed time between scenes may be that necessary to send for the shepherd from Mount Cithaeron and allow for his return or the much shorter time needed for Oedipus to enter his palace, discover Jocasta's suicide, blind himself, and return. The time covered by the ode is shorter or longer as necessary, without real reference to the length of the ode. In the Elizabethan theater the break between scenes covered whatever time was necessary without a formal device like the choral odes. Sometimes the time was short as the break between Hamlet's departure to see his mother at the end of Act 3, Scene 2, and the opening of the King's prayer at the beginning of the next scene; at other times the elapsed time between might be as long as that between Scenes 4 and 5 of Act 4, in which the news of Polonius's death reached Paris and Laertes returned to Denmark and there rallied his friends. The total elapsed time might be years as in *The Winter's Tale,* where the action begins before Perdita's birth and ends after her marriage. In *Hamlet* we cannot tell exactly what the time span is, but in a time of relatively primitive transportation Laertes goes to Paris, remains there for a time, and returns to Denmark; Fortinbras goes from Norway to Poland, fights a war, and returns to Denmark; and news of the deaths of Rosencrantz and Guildenstern, who left England between Acts 3 and 4, is brought back.

In reading fiction we recognize that what is going on in represented time is often supposed to be taking much longer than it takes us to read the words describing it. The time that is supposed to pass within one sentence can vary greatly from that which passes in another. All this does not bother us. In reading fiction, we are used to making such adjustments. In reading or watching a play, however, we expect the passage of time to be more clearly marked—by stage directions, scene or act endings. Otherwise we assume that the amount of time it takes an actor to walk across the stage or speak a line is exactly the time that has passed within the play while that action or talk has been going on (that is, represented time = reading/viewing time). The duration of a scene for reader or audience is just about the same as the time that is supposed to have passed during that scene.

Not so, necessarily, in Shakespeare. The first scene of *Hamlet,* for example, opens just on the stroke of midnight, yet in less than forty lines—with no obvious warning to the reader that so much time is passing—we learn it is one o'clock. And a hundred lines later the cock crows, and soon Horatio says that it is dawn. If we read this scene as if it were a story, we have no difficulty, perhaps, in adjusting represented time to reading time, but if we enact plays within our imagination while we read them we need to become very aware of this "undramatic handling of time. As a director, even a director of a play on the stage of our own imagination, we need to invent some sort of stage business to suggest the passing of represented time: those watching for the ghost may sit still for what seems to an audience a long time—a couple of minutes—or get up and stretch and walk about the stage, or lie down, toss and turn, perhaps sleep.

Drama is both a literary and performed art, and a play exists separately on page and stage. We must keep this dual nature in mind as we read, and indeed we need to do as much as we can to perform the play in our minds on the stage of our imagination.

ANONYMOUS

The Sacrifice of Isaac *

CHARACTERS

GOD   ISAAC, *his son*
AN ANGEL   A DOCTOR, *a learned man*
ABRAHAM, the patriarch

A field, near ABRAHAM'*s tent.*

ABRAHAM   Father of heaven omnipotent,
       With all my heart to thee I call.
   Thou hast given me both land and rent;
   And my livelihood thou hast me sent.
       I thank thee highly evermore of all.   5

   First of the earth thou madest Adam
       And Eve also to be his wife;
   All others creatures of them two came.
   And now thou hast grant to me, Abraham,
       Here in this land to lead my life.   10

   In my age thou hast granted me this,
       That this young child with me shall wone.[1]
   I love no thing so much, y-wis,[2]
   Except thine own self, dear Father of bliss,
       As Isaac here, my own sweet son.   15

   I have diverse children mo,[3]
       The which I love not half so well;
   This fair child he cheers me so
   In every place where that I go
       That no dis-ease here may I feel.   20

   And therefore, Father of heaven, I thee pray
       For his health and also for his grace.
   Now, Lord, keep him both night and day,
   That never disease nor no fray [4]
       Come to my child in no place.   25

   Now come, Isaac, my own sweet child
       Go we home and take our rest.

ISAAC   Abraham, mine own father so mild,
       To follow you I am full prest,[5]
         Both early and late.   30

---

* Often (and perhaps more accurately) called "The Brome *Sacrifice of Isaac*" (Brome was the name of the 19th-century owner of the manuscript in which the play appears). The events of the play are based on *Genesis* 22.

1. Dwell.
2. Certainly.
3. More.
4. Fright.
5. Ready (Fr. *prêt*).

ABRAHAM   Come on, sweet child. I love thee best
      Of all the children that ever I begat.

    Heaven.

GOD   Mine Angel, fast hie thee thy way
      And unto middle-earth[6] anon thou go;
   Abram's heart now will I assay,   35
      Whether that he be steadfast or no.

Say I commanded him for to take
      Isaac, his young son, that he loves so well,
And with his blood sacrifice he make
      If any of my friendship he will feel.   40

Show him the way unto the hill
      Where that his sacrifice shall be.
I shall assay now his good will,
      Whether he loveth better his child or me.
      All men shall take example by him   45
My commandments how they shall keep.

    The field, near ABRAHAM'S *tent.*

ABRAHAM   Now, Father of heaven, that formed all things,
      My prayers I make to thee again,
For this day my tender offering[7]
      Here must I give to thee certain.   50
Ah! Lord God, almighty king,
      What manner beast will make thee most fain?
If I had thereof very[8] knowing,
      It should be done with all my main[9]
      Full soon anon.   55
To do thy pleasing on an hill,
Verily it is my will,
      Dear Father, God in Trinity.

ANGEL   Abraham! Abraham! will thou rest!
      Our Lord commandeth thee for to take   60
Isaac, thy young son that thou lovest best,
      And with his blood sacrifice that thou make.
Into the Land of Vision[1] thou go,
      And offer thy child unto thy Lord;
I shall thee lead and show also.   65
      Unto God's hest,[2] Abraham, accord.

And follow me upon this green.

---

6. The earth.
7. Periodic sacrifice.
8. True.
9. Strength.
1. A translation of the phrase *in terram visionis* in *Genesis* 22:2 of the Vulgate, the standard Latin Bible of the Middle Ages. Other versions, including the Authorized or King James Version, read "the land of Moriah."
2. Command.

ABRAHAM   Welcome to me be my Lord's sond,[3]
　　　　　And his hest I will not withstand.
　　　　　Yet Isaac, my young son in land,   70
A full dear child to me hath been.

I had liefer,[4] if God had been pleased,
　　　　　For to have forborne all the good that I have
Than Isaac my son should have been dis-eased,
　　　　　So God in heaven my soul might save!   75

I loved never thing so much in earth.
　　　　　And now I must the child go kill.
Ah! Lord God! My conscience is strongly stirred!
And yet, my dear Lord, I am sore a-feared
　　　　　To grudge anything against your will.   80

I love my child as my life;
　　　　　But yet I love my God much more.
For though my heart would make any strife,
Yet will I not spare for child nor wife,
　　　　　But do after my Lord's lore.[5]   85

Though I love my son never so well,
　　　　　Yet smite off his head soon I shall.
Ah! Father of heaven, to thee I kneel;
An hard death my son shall feel
　　　　　For to honor thee, Lord, withall.   90

ANGEL   Abraham! Abraham! This is well said!
　　　　And all these commandments look that thou keep.
But in thy heart be nothing dismayed.
ABRAHAM   Nay, nay, forsooth[6] I hold me well appayed[7]
　　　　　To please my God to the best that I have.   95

For though my heart be heavily set
　　　　　To see the blood of mine own dear son,
Yet for all this I will not let,[8]
But Isaac, my son, I will go fetch,
　　　　　And come as fast as ever we can.   100

　　　　　Another part of the field.

Now, Isaac, my own son dear,
　　　　　Where art thou, child? Speak to me.
ISAAC   My father, sweet father, I am here,
　　　　And make my prayers to the Trinity.

ABRAHAM   Rise up, my child, and fast come hither,   105
　　　　　My gentle bairn[9] that art so wise,

---

3. Messenger.　　　　　　7. Pleased.
4. Rather.　　　　　　　　8. Refrain.
5. Teaching.　　　　　　　9. Child.
6. In truth.

For we two, child, must go together
   And unto my Lord make sacrifice.

ISAAC   I am full ready, my father, lo!
   Even at your hands I stand right here;   110
And whatsoever ye bid me do,
   It shall be done with glad cheer,
      Full well and fine.
ABRAHAM   Ah! Isaac, my own son so dear,
   God's blessing I give thee and mine.   115

Hold this faggot upon thy back,
   And here myself fire shall bring.
ISAAC   Father, all this here will I pack;
   I am full fain to do your bidding.
ABRAHAM [*aside*]   Ah! Lord of heaven my hands I wring,   120
   This child's words all to-wound[1] my heart.

Now, Isaac, son, go we our way
   Unto yon mount, with all our main.[2]
ISAAC   Go we, my dear father, as fast as I may;
   To follow you I am full fain,   125
      Although I be slender.[3]
ABRAHAM [*aside*]   Ah! Lord, my heart breaketh in twain,
   This child's words they be so tender.

      ABRAHAM *and* ISAAC *arrive at the mountain.*

Ah! Isaac, son, anon lay it down;
   No longer upon thy back it hold.   130
For I must make ready bon[4]
   To honor my Lord God as I should.

ISAAC   Lo, my dear father, where it is!
   To cheer you alway I draw me near.
But, father, I marvel sore of this,   135
   Why that ye make this heavy cheer.[5]

And also, father, evermore dread I;
   Where is your quick[6] beast that ye should kill?
Both fire and wood we have ready,
   But quick beast have none on this hill.   140
A quick beast, I wot[7] well, must be dead
   Your sacrifice for to make.
ABRAHAM   Dread thee nought, my child, I thee rede,[8]
Our Lord will send me unto this stead[9]
   Some manner of beast for to take,   145
      Through his sweet sond.[1]

---

1. Wound severely.   6. Live.
2. Strength.   7. Know.
3. Weak.   8. Counsel.
4. Quite ready.   9. Place.
5. Countenance.   1. Messenger.

ISAAC   Yea, father, but my heart beginneth to quake
    To see that sharp sword in your hand.

Why bear ye your sword drawn so?
    Of your countenance I have much wonder.   150
ABRAHAM [*aside*]   Ah! Father of heaven, so I am woe!
    This child here breaketh my heart asunder.

ISAAC   Tell me, dear father, ere that ye cease,
    Bear ye your sword drawn for me?
ABRAHAM   Ah! Isaac, sweet son, peace! peace!   155
    For, y-wis, thou break my heart in three.

ISAAC   Now, truly, somewhat, father, ye think
    That ye mourn thus more and more.
ABRAHAM [*aside*]   Ah! Lord of heaven, thy grace let sink,[2]
    For my heart was never half so sore.   160

ISAAC   I pray you, father, that ye will let me it wit[3]
    Whether shall I have any harm or no.
ABRAHAM   Y-wis, sweet son, I may not tell thee yet;
    My heart is now so full of woe.

ISAAC   Dear father, I pray you, hideth it not from me,   165
    But some of your thought that ye tell me.
ABRAHAM   Ah! Isaac, Isaac I must kill thee!
ISAAC   Kill me, father? Alas, what have I done?

If I have trespassed against you aught,
    With a yard[4] ye may make me full mild;   170
And with your sharp sword kill me nought,
    For, y-wis, father, I am but a child.

ABRAHAM   I am full sorry, son, thy blood for to spill
    But truly, my child, I may not choose.
ISAAC   Now I would to God my mother were here on his hill!   175
    She would kneel for me on both her knees
        To save my life.
And sithen[5] that my mother is not here,
I pray you, father, change your cheer,
        And kill me not with your knife.   180

ABRAHAM   Forsooth, son, but if[6] I thee kill,
    I should grieve God right sore, I dread.
It is his commandment, and also his will,
    That I should do this same deed.

He commanded me, son, for certain,   185
    To make my sacrifice with thy blood.
ISAAC   And is it God's will that I should be slain?
ABRAHAM   Aye, truly, Isaac, my son so good;
    And therefore my hands I wring.

                                           190

2. Descend.
3. Know.
4. Rod.

5. Since.
6. Unless.

ISAAC   Now, father, against my Lord's will
   I will never grudge, loud nor still.[7]
      He might have sent me a better destiny
        If it had have been his pleasure.

ABRAHAM   Forsooth, son, but if I did this deed,
      Grievously displeased our Lord will be.   195
ISAAC   Nay, nay, father, God forbid
      That ever you should grieve him for me.

      Ye have other children, one or two,
        The which ye should love well by kind.[8]
   I pray you, father, make ye no woe;   200
   For be I once dead, and from you go,
      I shall be soon out of your mind.

      Therefore do our Lord's bidding,
        And when I am dead, then pray for me.
   But, good father, tell ye my mother nothing;   205
   Say that I am in another country dwelling.
ABRAHAM   Ah! Isaac, Isaac, blessed might thou be!

      My heart beginneth strongly to rise,
        To see the blood of thy blessed body.
ISAAC   Father, since it may be no other wise.   210
   Let it pass over as well as I.

      But, father, ere I go unto my death,
        I pray you bless me with your hand.
ABRAHAM   Now, Isaac, with all my breath
      My blessing I give thee upon this land,   215
        And God's also thereto, y-wis.
      Isaac, Isaac, son, up thou stand,
        Thy fair sweet mouth that I may kiss.

ISAAC   Now farewell, my own father so fine;
      And greet well my mother in earth.   220
   But I pray you, father, to hide my eyen,[9]
        That I see not the stroke of your sharp sword,
        That my flesh shall defile.
ABRAHAM   Son, thy words make me weep full sore;
   Now, my dear son Isaac, speak no more.   225
ISAAC   Ah! my own dear father, wherefore?
      We shall speak together here but a while.
   And sithen[1] that I must needs be dead,
      Yet, my dear father, to you I pray,
   Smite but few strokes at my head,   230
      And make an end as soon as ye may,
        And tarry not too long.

---

7. In any way.   9. Eyes.
8. Natural affection.   1. Since.

ABRAHAM   Thy meek words, child, make me affray;[2]
            So "Well-a-way!"[3] may be my song,

Except all-only God's will.   235
        Ah! Isaac, my own sweet child,
    Yet kiss me again upon this hill!
        In all this world is none so mild.

ISAAC   Now truly, father, all this tarrying
                It doth my heart but harm;   240
            I pray you, father, make an ending.
ABRAHAM   Come up, sweet son, into my arm.

    I must bind thy hands too,
        Although thou be never so mild.
ISAAC   Ah! mercy, father! Why should ye do so?   245
ABRAHAM   That thou shouldst not let[4] me, my child.

ISAAC   Nay, y-wis, father, I will not let you.
            Do on, for me, your will;
        And on the purpose that ye have set you,
            For God's love keep it forth[5] still.   250

I am full sorry this day to die,
    But yet I keep[6] not my God to grieve.
Do on your list[7] for me hardly;
    My fair sweet father, I give you leave.

But, father, I pray you evermore,   255
    Tell ye my mother no deal;
If she wost[8] it, she would weep full sore,
    For y-wis, father, she loveth me full well.
        God's blessing might she have!

Now farewell, my mother so sweet!   260
We two be like no more to meet,
ABRAHAM   Ah! Isaac, Isaac! son, thou makest me to grate[9]
        And with thy words thou distemperest me.

ISAAC   Y-wis, sweet father, I am sorry to grieve you.
            I cry you mercy of that I have done.   265
        And of all trespass that ever I did move[1] you.
            Now, dear father, forgive me that I have done,
            God of heaven be with me!

ABRAHAM   Ah! dear child, leave off thy moans;
        In all thy life thou grieved me never once.   270
    Now blessed be thou, body and bones,
        That ever thou were bred and born!

---

2. Dread.   7. Pleasure, will.
3. Alas.   8. Knew.
4. Hinder.   9. Gnash my teeth.
5. Pursue it.   1. Perform against.
6. Wish.

Thou hast been to me child full good.
    But, y-wis, child, though I mourn never so fast
    Yet must I needs here at the last   275
In this place shed all thy blood.

Therefore, my dear son, here shall thou lie.
    Unto my work I must me stead.[2]
Y-wis, I had as lief[3] myself to die,
    If God will be pleased with my deed,   280
    And mine own body for to offer
ISAAC Ah! mercy, father. Mourn ye no more!
Your weeping maketh my heart sore,
    As my own death that I shall suffer.

Your kerchief, father, about my eyen[4] ye wind.   285
ABRAHAM So I shall, my sweetest child in earth.
ISAAC Now yet, good father, have this in mind
    And smite me not often with your sharp sword,
    But hastily that it be sped.
ABRAHAM Now farewell, my child, so full of grace.   290
ISAAC Ah! father, father. Turn downward my face,
    For of your sharp sword I am ever a-dread.

ABRAHAM [*aside*] To do this deed I am full sorry,
    But, Lord, thine hest[5] I will not withstand.
ISAAC Ah! Father of heaven, to thee I cry;   295
    Lord, receive me into thy hand.

ABRAHAM [*aside*] Lo! now is the time come, certain,
    That my sword in his neck shall bite.
Ah! Lord, my heart raiseth there-again;[6]
    I may not findeth it in my heart to smite;   300
    My heart will not know thereto.
Yet fain I would work my Lord's will,
But this young innocent lieth so still,
I may not findeth it in my heart him to kill.
    Oh, Father of heaven, what shall I do?   305

ISAAC Ah! mercy, father. Why tarry ye so,
    And let me lay thus long on this heath?
Now I would to God the stroke were do!
Father, I pray you heartily, short me. out of my woe,
    And let me not look thus after my death.   310

ABRAHAM Now, heart, why wouldest not thou break in three?
    Yet shall thou not make me to my God unmild.
I will no longer let[7] for thee,
For that my God a-grieved would be.
    Now hold[8] the stroke, my own dear child.   315

2. Steady myself.
3. Gladly.
4. Eyes.
5. Command.

6. Rises in protest against the act.
7. Refrain.
8. Receive.

ANGEL *appears.*

ANGEL   I am an angel, thou mayest see blithe,[9]
     That from heaven to thee is sent.
Our Lord thank thee an hundred sithe[1]
     For the keeping of his commandment.

He knowest thy will and also thy heart,   320
     That thou dreadest him above all thing;
And some of thy heaviness for to depart[2]
     A fair ram yonder I gan bring;[3]

He standeth tied, lo! among the briars.
     Now, Abraham, amend thy mood,   325
For Isaac, thy young son that here is,
     This day shall not shed his blood.

Go, make thy sacrifice with yon ram.
Now farewell, blessed Abraham,
     For unto Heaven I now go home;   330
     The way is full gain[4] that I must go.
     Take up thy son so free.[5]   *Exit.*

ABRAHAM   Ah! Lord, I thank thee of thy great grace,
Now am I yethed[6] in diverse wise.
Arise up, Isaac, my dear son, arise;   335
     Arise up, sweet child, and come to me.

ISAAC   Ah! mercy, father. Why smite ye nought?
     Ah! smite on, father, once with your knife.
ABRAHAM   Peace, my sweet son, and take no thought,
     For our Lord of heaven hath grant thy life   340
     By his angel now.

That thou shalt not die this day, son, truly.
ISAAC   Ah, father, full glad then were I,
     Y-wis, father, I say, y-wis,
If this tale were true.   345
ABRAHAM   An hundred times, my son fair of hue,
     For joy thy mouth now will I kiss.

ISAAC   Ah! my dear father Abraham,
     Will not God be wroth that we do thus?
ABRAHAM   No, no, hardly, my sweet son,   350
For yon same ram he hath us sent
     Hither down to us.

Yon beast shall die here in thy stead,
     In the worship of our Lord alone.
Go, fetch him hither, my child, indeed.   355

---

9. At once.
1. Times.
2. Remove.
3. Have brought.

4. Straight.
5. Noble.
6. Comforted.

ISAAC   Father, I will go hent[7] him by the head,
        And bring yon beast with me anon.

      Ah! sheep, sheep, blessed might thou be,
        That ever thou were sent down hither!
      Thou shall this day die for me   360
      In the worship of the Holy Trinity.
          Now come fast and go we together
             To my Father of heaven.
      Though thou be never so gentle and good,
      Yet had I liefer[8] thou sheddest thy blood,   365
          Y-wis, sheep, than I.

      Lo! father, I have brought here full smart[9]
         This gentle sheep, and him to you I give.
      But, Lord God, I thank thee with all my heart,
         For I am glad that I shall live,   370
          And kiss once my dear mother.
ABRAHAM   Now be right merry, my sweet child,
      For this quick[1] beast, that is so mild,
         Here I shall present before all other.
ISAAC   And I will fast begin to blow;   375
         This fire shall burn a full good speed.
      But, father, will I stoop down low,
      Ye will not kill me with your sword, I trow?[2]
ABRAHAM   No, hardly, sweet son, have no dread;
         My mourning is past.   380
ISAAC   Aye! but I would that sword were in a gled,[3]
         For, y-wis, father, it makes me full ill aghast.

ABRAHAM   Now, Lord God of heaven in Trinity,
         Almighty God omnipotent,
      My offering I make in worship of thee,   385
         And with this quick beast I thee present.
         Lord, receive thou mine intent,
           As thou art God and ground of our grace.

        GOD *appears above.*

GOD   Abraham, Abraham, well might thou speed,
         And Isaac, thy young son thee by!   390
      Truly, Abraham, for this deed
      I shall multiply your bothers[4] seed
         As thick as stars be in the sky,
           Both more and less;
      And as thick as gravel in the sea,   395
      So thick multiplied your seed shall be.
         This grant I you for your goodness.

7. Seize.
8. Rather.
9. Quickly.
1. Live.

2. Trust.
3. Fire.
4. Both your.

Of you shall come fruit great won,[5]
    And ever be in bliss without end,
For ye dread me as God alone   400
And keep my commandments everyone;
    My blessing I give, wheresoever ye wend.[6]

ABRAHAM   Lo! Isaac, my son, how think ye
    By this work that we have wrought?
Full glad and blithe we may be,   405
    Against the will of God we grudged nought,
        Upon this fair heath.
ISAAC   Ah! father, I thank our Lord every deal,[7]
That my wit served me so well
        For to dread God more than my death.   410

ABRAHAM   Why, dearworthy[8] son, were thou adread?[9]
    Hardly, my child, tell me thy lore.[1]
ISAAC   Aye! by my faith, father, now have I read,
    I was never so afraid before
        As I have been at yon hill.   415
But, by my faith, father, I swear,
I will nevermore come there
        But it be against my will.

ABRAHAM   Aye! come on with me, my own sweet son,
And homeward fast now let us gone.   420
ISAAC   By my faith, father, thereto I grant;
    I had never so good will to go home,
    And to speak with my dear mother.
ABRAHAM   Ah! Lord of heaven, I thank thee,
For now may I lead home with me   425
Isaac, my young son so free,
    The gentlest child above all other.

Now go we forth, my blessed son.
ISAAC   I grant, father, and let us gone;
    For, by my troth, were I at home,   430
    I would never go out under that form;
        This may I well avow.
        I pray God give us grace evermore,
        And all those we be holding to.[2]

DOCTOR *comes forward and addresses the audience.*

DOCTOR   Lo! sovereigns and sires, now have we showed   435
    This solemn story to great and small.
It is good learning to learned and lewd,[3]
    And the wisest of us all,
        Withouten any barring

---

5. In great number.
6. Go.
7. In every way.
8. Beloved.

9. Afraid.
1. Knowledge.
2. To whom we are related.
3. Ignorant.

For this story shows you here   440
How we should keep to our power[4]
    God's commandment without grudging.

Trow ye,[5] sirs, and God sent an angel
   And commanded you your child to slain,
By my troth, is there any of you   445
    That either would grudge or strive thereagainst?

How think ye now, sirs, thereby?
   I trow there be three or four or more,
And these women that weep so sorrowfully
    Then that their children die them from,   450
      As nature will and kind;
It is but folly, I may well avow,
To grudge against God or to grieve you,
For ye shall never see them mischieved,[6] well I know,
    By land nor water, have this in mind.   455
And grudge not against our Lord God
   In wealth or woe, whether[7] that he you send,
Though ye be never so hard bestead;
    For when he will, he may it amend,

His commandments truly if ye keep with good heart,   460
   As this story hath now showed you before,
And faithfully serve him while ye be quart,[8]
    That ye may please God both even and morn.
    Now Jesu, that weareth the crown of thorn,
      Bring us all to heaven's bliss.   465

Finis.[9]

Ms. 1470–1480

---

4. As best we can.
5. Trust.
6. In distress.
7. Whichever.
8. In good health.
9. The end.

WILLIAM SHAKESPEARE

Hamlet

CHARACTERS

CLAUDIUS, *King of Denmark*
HAMLET, *son of the former and nephew to the present King*
POLONIUS, *Lord Chamberlain*
HORATIO, *friend of Hamlet*
LAERTES, *son of Polonius*
VOLTEMAND
CORNELIUS
ROSENCRANTZ
GUILDENSTERN } *courtiers*
OSRIC
A GENTLEMAN
A PRIEST

MARCELLUS
BERNARDO } *officers*
FRANCISCO, *a soldier*
REYNALDO, *servant to Polonius*
PLAYERS
TWO CLOWNS, *gravediggers*
FORTINBRAS, *Prince of Norway*
A NORWEGIAN CAPTAIN
ENGLISH AMBASSADORS
GERTRUDE, *Queen of Denmark, and mother of Hamlet*
OPHELIA, *daughter of Polonius*
GHOST OF HAMLET'S FATHER

LORDS, LADIES, OFFICERS, SOLDIERS, SAILORS, MESSENGERS, *and* ATTENDANTS

SCENE: *The action takes place in or near the royal castle of Denmark at Elsinore.*

Act 1

SCENE 1: *A guard station atop the castle. Enter* BERNARDO *and* FRANCISCO, *two sentinels.*

BERNARDO   Who's there?
FRANCISCO   Nay, answer me. Stand and unfold yourself.
BERNARDO   Long live the king!
FRANCISCO   Bernardo?
BERNARDO   He.   5
FRANCISCO   You come most carefully upon your hour.
BERNARDO   'Tis now struck twelve. Get thee to bed, Francisco.
FRANCISCO   For this relief much thanks. 'Tis bitter cold,
And I am sick at heart.
BERNARDO   Have you had quiet guard?
FRANCISCO   Not a mouse stirring.   10
BERNARDO   Well, good night.
If you do meet Horatio and Marcellus,
The rivals[1] of my watch, bid them make haste.

Enter HORATIO *and* MARCELLUS.

FRANCISCO   I think I hear them. Stand, ho! Who is there?
HORATIO   Friends to this ground.

1. companions

941

| MARCELLUS | And liegemen to the Dane.[2] | 15 |

MARCELLUS   And liegemen to the Dane.[2]   15

FRANCISCO   Give you good night.

MARCELLUS   O, farewell, honest soldier!
Who hath relieved you?

FRANCISCO   Bernardo hath my place.
Give you good night.   *Exit* FRANCISCO.

MARCELLUS   Holla, Bernardo!

BERNARDO   Say—
What, is Horatio there?

HORATIO   A piece of him.

BERNARDO   Welcome, Horatio. Welcome, good Marcellus.   20

HORATIO   What, has this thing appeared again tonight?

BERNARDO   I have seen nothing.

MARCELLUS   Horatio says 'tis but our fantasy,
And will not let belief take hold of him
Touching this dreaded sight twice seen of us.   25
Therefore I have entreated him along
With us to watch the minutes of this night,
That if again this apparition come,
He may approve[3] our eyes and speak to it.

HORATIO   Tush, tush, 'twill not appear.

BERNARDO   Sit down awhile,   30
And let us once again assail your ears,
That are so fortified against our story,
What we have two nights seen.

HORATIO   Well, sit we down,
And let us hear Bernardo speak of this.

BERNARDO   Last night of all,   35
When yond same star that's westward from the pole[4]
Had made his course t' illume that part of heaven
Where now it burns, Marcellus and myself,
The bell then beating one—

Enter GHOST.

MARCELLUS   Peace, break thee off. Look where it comes again.   40

BERNARDO   In the same figure like the king that's dead.

MARCELLUS   Thou art a scholar; speak to it, Horatio.

BERNARDO   Looks 'a[5] not like the king? Mark it, Horatio.

HORATIO   Most like. It harrows me with fear and wonder.

BERNARDO   It would be spoke to.

MARCELLUS   Speak to it, Horatio.   45

HORATIO   What art thou that usurp'st this time of night
Together with that fair and warlike form
In which the majesty of buried Denmark
Did sometimes march? By heaven I charge thee, speak.

MARCELLUS   It is offended.

BERNARDO   See, it stalks away.   50

2. The "Dane" is the King of Denmark, who is also called "Denmark," as in line 48 of this scene. In line 61 the same figure is used for the King of Norway.
3. confirm the testimony of
4. polestar
5. he

HORATIO Stay. Speak, speak. I charge thee, speak. *Exit* GHOST.
MARCELLUS 'Tis gone and will not answer.
BERNARDO How now, Horatio! You tremble and look pale.
Is not this something more than fantasy?
What think you on't?   55
HORATIO Before my God, I might not this believe
Without the sensible[6] and true avouch
Of mine own eyes.
MARCELLUS   Is it not like the king?
HORATIO As thou art to thyself.
Such was the very armor he had on   60
When he the ambitious Norway combated.
So frowned he once when, in an angry parle,[7]
He smote the sledded Polacks on the ice.
'Tis strange.
MARCELLUS Thus twice before, and jump[8] at this dead hour,   65
With martial stalk hath he gone by our watch.
HORATIO In what particular thought to work I know not,
But in the gross and scope of mine opinion,
This bodes some strange eruption to our state.
MARCELLUS Good now, sit down, and tell me he that knows,   70
Why this same strict and most observant watch
So nightly toils the subject[9] of the land,
And why such daily cast of brazen cannon
And foreign mart for implements of war;
Why such impress of shipwrights, whose sore task   75
Does not divide the Sunday from the week.
What might be toward that this sweaty haste
Doth make the night joint-laborer with the day?
Who is't that can inform me?
HORATIO   That can I.
At least, the whisper goes so. Our last king,   80
Whose image even but now appeared to us,
Was as you know by Fortinbras of Norway,
Thereto pricked on by a most emulate pride,
Dared to the combat; in which our valiant Hamlet
(For so this side of our known world esteemed him)   85
Did slay this Fortinbras; who by a sealed compact
Well ratified by law and heraldry,
Did forfeit, with his life, all those his lands
Which he stood seized of,[1] to the conqueror;
Against the which a moiety competent[2]   90
Was gagéd[3] by our king; which had returned
To the inheritance of Fortinbras,
Had he been vanquisher; as, by the same covenant
And carriage of the article designed,
His fell to Hamlet. Now, sir, young Fortinbras,   95

6. of the senses
7. parley
8. precisely
9. people

1. possessed
2. portion of similar value
3. pledged

Of unimprovéd mettle hot and full,
Hath in the skirts of Norway here and there
Sharked up a list of lawless resolutes
For food and diet to some enterprise
That hath a stomach in't; which is no other,   100
As it doth well appear unto our state,
But to recover of us by strong hand
And terms compulsatory, those foresaid lands
So by his father lost; and this, I take it,
Is the main motive of our preparations,   105
The source of this our watch, and the chief head
Of this post-haste and romage[4] in the land.
BERNARDO   I think it be no other but e'en so.
Well may it sort[5] that this portentous figure
Comes arméd through our watch so like the king   110
That was and is the question of these wars.
HORATIO   A mote[6] it is to trouble the mind's eye.
In the most high and palmy state of Rome,
A little ere the mightiest Julius fell,
The graves stood tenantless, and the sheeted dead   115
Did squeak and gibber in the Roman streets;
As stars with trains of fire, and dews of blood,
Disasters in the sun; and the moist star,
Upon whose influence Neptune's empire stands,[7]
Was sick almost to doomsday with eclipse.   120
And even the like precurse[8] of feared events,
As harbingers preceding still the fates
And prologue to the omen coming on,
Have heaven and earth together demonstrated
Unto our climatures[9] and countrymen.   125

    Enter GHOST.

But soft, behold, lo where it comes again!
I'll cross it[1] though it blast me.—Stay, illusion.

                               It spreads [its] arms.

If thou hast any sound or use of voice,
Speak to me.
If there be any good thing to be done,   130
That may to thee do ease, and grace to me,
Speak to me.
If thou art privy to thy country's fate,
Which happily foreknowing may avoid,
O, speak!   135
Or if thou hast uphoarded in thy life

---

4. stir
5. chance
6. speck of dust
7. Neptune was the Roman sea god; the "moist star" is the moon.
8. precursor
9. regions
1. Horatio means either that he will move across the Ghost's path in order to stop him or that he will make the sign of the cross to gain power over him. The stage direction which follows is somewhat ambiguous. "It" seems to refer to the Ghost, but the movement would be appropriate to Horatio.

Extorted treasure in the womb of earth,
For which, they say, you spirits oft walk in death,

The cock crows.

Speak of it. Stay, and speak. Stop it, Marcellus.
MARCELLUS   Shall I strike at it with my partisan[2]?   140
HORATIO   Do, if it will not stand.
BERNARDO   'Tis here.
HORATIO   'Tis here.
MARCELLUS   'Tis gone.   *Exit* GHOST.
We do it wrong, being so majestical,
To offer it the show of violence;
For it is as the air, invulnerable,   145
And our vain blows malicious mockery.
BERNARDO   It was about to speak when the cock crew.
HORATIO   And then it started like a guilty thing
Upon a fearful summons. I have heard
The cock, that is the trumpet to the morn,   150
Doth with his lofty and shrill-sounding throat
Awake the god of day, and at his warning,
Whether in sea or fire, in earth or air,
Th' extravagant and erring[3] spirit hies
To his confine; and of the truth herein   155
This present object made probation.[4]
MARCELLUS   It faded on the crowing of the cock.
Some say that ever 'gainst that season comes
Wherein our Savior's birth is celebrated,
This bird of dawning singeth all night long,   160
And then, they say, no spirit dare stir abroad,
The nights are wholesome, then no planets strike,
No fairy takes,[5] nor witch hath power to charm,
So hallowed and so gracious is that time.
HORATIO   So have I heard and do in part believe it. 165
But look, the morn in russet mantle clad
Walks o'er the dew of yon high eastward hill.
Break we our watch up, and by my advice
Let us impart what we have seen tonight
Unto young Hamlet, for upon my life   170
This spirit, dumb to us, will speak to him.
Do you consent we shall acquaint him with it,
As needful in our loves, fitting our duty?
MARCELLUS   Let's do't, I pray, and I this morning know
Where we shall find him most convenient.   *Exeunt.* 175

SCENE 2. *A chamber of state. Enter* KING CLAUDIUS, QUEEN GER-
TRUDE, HAMLET, POLONIUS, LAERTES, OPHELIA, VOLTEMAND, COR-
NELIUS *and other members of the court.*

---

2. halberd   4. proof
3. wandering out of bounds   5. enchants

KING   Though yet of Hamlet our dear brother's death
    The memory be green, and that it us befitted
    To bear our hearts in grief, and our whole kingdom
    To be contracted in one brow of woe,
    Yet so far hath discretion fought with nature   5
    That we with wisest sorrow think on him,
    Together with remembrance of ourselves.
    Therefore our sometime sister, now our queen,
    Th' imperial jointress[6] to this warlike state,
    Have we, as 'twere with a defeated joy,   10
    With an auspicious and a dropping eye,
    With mirth in funeral, and with dirge in marriage,
    In equal scale weighing delight and dole,
    Taken to wife; nor have we herein barred
    Your better wisdoms, which have freely gone   15
    With this affair along. For all, our thanks.
    Now follows that you know young Fortinbras,
    Holding a weak supposal of our worth,
    Or thinking by our late dear brother's death
    Our state to be disjoint and out of frame,   20
    Colleaguéd with this dream of his advantage,
    He hath not failed to pester us with message
    Importing the surrender of those lands
    Lost by his father, with all bands of law,
    To our most valiant brother. So much for him.   25
    Now for ourself, and for this time of meeting,
    Thus much the business is: we have here writ
    To Norway, uncle of young Fortinbras—
    Who, impotent and bedrid, scarcely hears
    Of this his nephew's purpose—to suppress   30
    His further gait[7] herein, in that the levies,
    The lists, and full proportions are all made
    Out of his subject; and we here dispatch
    You, good Cornelius, and you, Voltemand,
    For bearers of this greeting to old Norway,   35
    Giving to you no further personal power
    To business with the king, more than the scope
    Of these dilated[8] articles allow.
    Farewell, and let your haste commend your duty.

CORNELIUS ⎫
VOLTEMAND ⎬ In that, and all things will we show our duty.   40

KING   We doubt it nothing, heartily farewell.

                Exeunt VOLTEMAND *and* CORNELIUS.

    And now, Laertes, what's the news with you?
    You told us of some suit. What is't, Laertes?
    You cannot speak of reason to the Dane
    And lose your voice. What wouldst thou beg, Laertes,   45

6. A "jointress" is a widow who holds a   7. progress
jointure or life interest in the estate of her   8. fully expressed
deceased husband.

That shall not be my offer, not thy asking?
The head is not more native to the heart,
The hand more instrumental[9] to the mouth,
Than is the throne of Denmark to thy father.
What wouldst thou have, Laertes?

LAERTES   My dread lord,   50
   Your leave and favor to return to France,
   From whence, though willingly, I came to Denmark
   To show my duty in your coronation,
   Yet now I must confess, that duty done,
   My thoughts and wishes bend again toward France,   55
   And bow them to your gracious leave and pardon.

KING   Have you your father's leave? What says Polonius?

POLONIUS   He hath, my lord, wrung from me my slow leave
   By laborsome petition, and at last
   Upon his will I sealed my hard consent.   60
   I do beseech you give him leave to go.

KING   Take thy fair hour, Laertes. Time be thine,
   And thy best graces spend it at thy will.
   But now, my cousin[1] Hamlet, and my son—

HAMLET [*aside*]   A little more than kin, and less than kind.   65

KING   How is it that the clouds still hang on you?

HAMLET   Not so, my lord. I am too much in the sun.

QUEEN   Good Hamlet, cast thy nighted color off,
   And let thine eye look like a friend on Denmark.
   Do not for ever with thy vailéd lids[2]   70
   Seek for thy noble father in the dust.
   Thou know'st 'tis common—all that lives must die,
   Passing through nature to eternity.

HAMLET   Ay, madam, it is common.

QUEEN   If it be,
   Why seems it so particular with thee?   75

HAMLET   Seems, madam? Nay, it is. I know not "seems."
   'Tis not alone my inky cloak, good mother,
   Nor customary suits of solemn black,
   Nor windy suspiration of forced breath,
   No, nor the fruitful river in the eye,   80
   Nor the dejected havior[3] of the visage,
   Together with all forms, moods, shapes of grief,
   That can denote me truly. These indeed seem,
   For they are actions that a man might play,
   But I have that within which passes show—   85
   These but the trappings and the suits of woe.

KING   'Tis sweet and commendable in your nature, Hamlet,
   To give these mourning duties to your father,
   But you must know your father lost a father,
   That father lost, lost his, and the survivor bound   90
   In filial obligation for some term

9. serviceable
1. "Cousin" is used here as a general
term of kinship.

2. lowered eyes
3. appearance

To do obsequious[4] sorrow. But to persever
In obstinate condolement is a course
Of impious stubbornness. 'Tis unmanly grief.
It shows a will most incorrect to[5] heaven,　　　　　　95
A heart unfortified, a mind impatient,
An understanding simple and unschooled.
For what we know must be, and is as common
As any the most vulgar thing to sense,
Why should we in our peevish opposition　　　　　　100
Take it to heart? Fie, 'tis a fault to heaven,
A fault against the dead, a fault to nature,
To reason most absurd, whose common theme
Is death of fathers, and who still hath cried,
From the first corse[6] till he that died today,　　　　　　105
"This must be so." We pray you throw to earth
This unprevailing woe, and think of us
As of a father, for let the world take note
You are the most immediate[7] to our throne,
And with no less nobility of love　　　　　　110
Than that which dearest father bears his son
Do I impart toward you. For your intent
In going back to school in Wittenberg,
It is most retrograde[8] to our desire,
And we beseech you, bend you to remain　　　　　　115
Here in the cheer and comfort of our eye,
Our chiefest courtier, cousin, and our son.
QUEEN　Let not thy mother lose her prayers, Hamlet.
I pray thee stay with us, go not to Wittenberg.
HAMLET　I shall in all my best obey you, madam.　　　　　　120
KING　Why, 'tis a loving and a fair reply.
Be as ourself in Denmark. Madam, come.
This gentle and unforced accord of Hamlet
Sits smiling to my heart, in grace whereof,
No jocund health that Denmark drinks today　　　　　　125
But the great cannon to the clouds shall tell,
And the king's rouse[9] the heaven shall bruit[1] again,
Respeaking earthly thunder. Come away.

Flourish. Exeunt all but HAMLET.

HAMLET　O, that this too too solid flesh would melt,
Thaw, and resolve itself into a dew,　　　　　　130
Or that the Everlasting had not fixed
His canon[2] 'gainst self-slaughter. O God, God,
How weary, stale, flat, and unprofitable
Seem to me all the uses of this world!
Fie on't, ah, fie, 'tis an unweeded garden　　*disorderly kingdom*　135
That grows to seed. Things rank and gross in nature

4. suited for funeral obsequies
5. uncorrected toward
6. corpse
7. next in line
8. contrary
9. carousal
1. echo
2. law

                    entirely
Possess it merely.[3] That it should come to this,
But two months dead, nay, not so much, not two.
So excellent a king, that was to this
Hyperion to a satyr,[4] so loving to my mother,   140
That he might not beteem[5] the winds of heaven
Visit her face too roughly. Heaven and earth,
Must I remember? Why, she would hang on him
As if increase of appetite had grown
By what it fed on, and yet, within a month—   145
Let me not think on't. Frailty, thy name is woman—
A little month, or ere those shoes were old
With which she followed my poor father's body
Like Niobe,[6] all tears, why she, even she—
O God, a beast that wants discourse of reason   150
Would have mourned longer—married with my uncle,
My father's brother, but no more like my father
Than I to Hercules.[7] Within a month,
Ere yet the salt of most unrighteous tears
Had left the flushing in her gallèd eyes,   155
She married. O, most wicked speed, to post
With such dexterity to incestuous sheets!
It is not, nor it cannot come to good.
But break my heart, for I must hold my tongue.

            Enter HORATIO, MARCELLUS, *and* BERNARDO.

HORATIO   Hail to your lordship!
HAMLET   I am glad to see you well.   160
     Horatio—or I do forget myself.
HORATIO   The same, my lord, and your poor servant ever.
HAMLET   Sir, my good friend, I'll change[8] that name with you.
     And what make you from Wittenberg, Horatio?
     Marcellus?   165
MARCELLUS   My good lord!
HAMLET   I am very glad to see you. [*To* BERNARDO.] Good even, sir.—
     But what, in faith, make you from Wittenberg?
HORATIO   A truant disposition, good my lord.
HAMLET   I would not hear your enemy say so,   170
     Nor shall you do my ear that violence
     To make it truster of your own report
     Against yourself. I know you are no truant.
     But what is your affair in Elsinore?
     We'll teach you to drink deep ere you depart.   175
HORATIO   My lord, I came to see your father's funeral.
HAMLET   I prithee do not mock me, fellow-student,
     I think it was to see my mother's wedding.

3. entirely
4. Hyperion, a sun god, stands here for
beauty in contrast to the monstrous satyr,
a lecherous creature, half man and half
goat.
5. permit
6. In Greek mythology Niobe was turned
to stone after a tremendous fit of weeping
over the death of her fourteen children, a
misfortune brought about by her boasting
over her fertility.
7. The demigod Hercules was noted for
his strength and the series of spectacular
labors which it allowed him to accomplish.
8. exchange

HORATIO	Indeed, my lord, it followed hard upon.	
HAMLET	Thrift, thrift, Horatio. The funeral-baked meats	180

Did coldly furnish forth the marriage tables.
Would I had met my dearest[9] foe in heaven
Or ever I had seen that day, Horatio!
My father—methinks I see my father.

HORATIO   Where, my lord?

HAMLET   In my mind's eye, Horatio.   185

HORATIO   I saw him once, 'a was a goodly king.

HAMLET   'A was a man, take him for all in all,
I shall not look upon his like again.

HORATIO   My lord, I think I saw him yesternight.

HAMLET   Saw who?   190

HORATIO   My lord, the king your father.

HAMLET   The king my father?

HORATIO   Season[1] your admiration[2] for a while
With an attent[3] ear till I may deliver[4]
Upon the witness of these gentlemen
This marvel to you.

HAMLET   For God's love, let me hear!   195

HORATIO   Two nights together had these gentlemen,
Marcellus and Bernardo, on their watch
In the dead waste and middle of the night
Been thus encountered. A figure like your father,
Armed at point exactly,[5] cap-a-pe,[6]   200
Appears before them, and with solemn march
Goes slow and stately by them. Thrice he walked
By their oppressed and fear-surprisèd eyes
Within his truncheon's[7] length, whilst they, distilled
Almost to jelly with the act of fear,   205
Stand dumb and speak not to him. This to me
In dreadful secrecy impart they did,
And I with them the third night kept the watch,
Where, as they had delivered, both in time,
Form of the thing, each word made true and good,   210
The apparition comes. I knew your father.
These hands are not more like.

HAMLET   But where was this?

MARCELLUS   My lord, upon the platform where we watch.

HAMLET   Did you not speak to it?

HORATIO   My lord, I did,
But answer made it none. Yet once methought   215
It lifted up it head and did address
Itself to motion, like as it would speak;
But even then the morning cock crew loud,
And at the sound it shrunk in haste away
And vanished from our sight.

---

9. bitterest
1. moderate
2. wonder
3. attentive

4. relate
5. completely
6. from head to toe
7. baton of office

HAMLET	'Tis very strange.	220

HORATIO   As I do live, my honored lord, 'tis true,
   And we did think it writ down in our duty
   To let you know of it.

HAMLET   Indeed, sirs, but
   This troubles me. Hold you the watch tonight?

ALL   We do, my lord.

HAMLET   Armed, say you?

ALL   Armed, my lord.   225

HAMLET   From top to toe?

ALL   My lord, from head to foot.

HAMLET   Then saw you not his face?

HORATIO   O yes, my lord, he wore his beaver[8] up.

HAMLET   What, looked he frowningly?

HORATIO   A countenance more in sorrow than in anger.   230

HAMLET   Pale or red?

HORATIO   Nay, very pale.

HAMLET   And fixed his eyes upon you?

HORATIO   Most constantly.

HAMLET   I would I had been there.

HORATIO   It would have much amazed you.

HAMLET   Very like.
   Stayed it long?   235

HORATIO   While one with moderate haste might tell a hundred.

BOTH   Longer, longer.

HORATIO   Not when I saw't.

HAMLET   His beard was grizzled, no?

HORATIO   It was as I have seen it in his life,
   A sable silvered.

HAMLET   I will watch tonight.   240
   Perchance 'twill walk again.

HORATIO   I warr'nt it will.

HAMLET   If it assume my noble father's person,
   I'll speak to it though hell itself should gape[9]
   And bid me hold my peace. I pray you all,
   If you have hitherto concealed this sight,   245
   Let it be tenable[1] in your silence still,
   And whatsomever else shall hap tonight,
   Give it an understanding but no tongue.
   I will requite your loves. So fare you well.
   Upon the platform 'twixt eleven and twelve   250
   I'll visit you.

ALL   Our duty to your honor.

HAMLET   Your loves, as mine to you. Farewell.

Exeunt all but HAMLET.

My father's spirit in arms? All is not well.
I doubt[2] some foul play. Would the night were come!

---

8. movable face protector
9. open (its mouth) wide

1. held
2. suspect

Till then sit still, my soul. Foul deeds will rise,   255
Though all the earth o'erwhelm them, to men's eyes.   *Exit.*

SCENE 3: *The dwelling of* POLONIUS. *Enter* LAERTES *and* OPHELIA.

LAERTES   My necessaries are embarked. Farewell.
And, sister, as the winds give benefit
And convoy³ is assistant,⁴ do not sleep,
But let me hear from you.
OPHELIA   Do you doubt that?
LAERTES   For Hamlet, and the trifling of his favor,   5
Hold it a fashion and a toy in blood,
A violet in the youth of primy⁵ nature,
Forward, not permanent, sweet, not lasting,
The perfume and suppliance of a minute,
No more.
OPHELIA   No more but so?
LAERTES   Think it no more.   10
For nature crescent⁶ does not grow alone
In thews and bulk, but as this temple⁷ waxes
The inward service of the mind and soul
Grows wide withal. Perhaps he loves you now,
And now no soil nor cautel⁸ doth besmirch   15
The virtue of his will, but you must fear,
His greatness weighed,⁹ his will is not his own,
For he himself is subject to his birth.
He may not, as unvalued persons do,
Carve for himself, for on his choice depends   20
The safety and health of this whole state,
And therefore must his choice be circumscribed
Unto the voice¹ and yielding of that body
Whereof he is the head. Then if he says he loves you,
It fits your wisdom so far to believe it   25
As he in his particular act and place
May give his saying deed, which is no further
Than the main voice of Denmark goes withal.
Then weigh what loss your honor may sustain
If with too credent² ear you list³ his songs,   30
Or lose your heart, or your chaste treasure open
To his unmastered importunity.
Fear it, Ophelia, fear it, my dear sister,
And keep you in the rear of your affection,
Out of the shot and danger of desire.   35
The chariest⁴ maid is prodigal enough
If she unmask her beauty to the moon.
Virtue itself scapes not calumnious strokes.

reveals himself to be cautious & unfeeling

3. means of transport   9. rank considered
4. available   1. assent
5. of the spring   2. credulous
6. growing   3. listen to
7. body   4. most circumspect
8. deceit

The canker[5] galls the infants of the spring   40
Too oft before their buttons[6] be disclosed,
And in the morn and liquid dew of youth
Contagious blastments[7] are most imminent.
Be wary then; best safety lies in fear.
Youth to itself rebels, though none else near.
OPHELIA   I shall the effect of this good lesson keep   45
As watchman to my heart. But, good my brother,
Do not as some ungracious pastors do,
Show me the steep and thorny way to heaven,
Whiles like a puffed and reckless libertine
Himself the primrose path of dalliance treads   50
And recks[8] not his own rede.[9]
LAERTES   O, fear me not.

     Enter POLONIUS.

I stay too long. But here my father comes.
A double blessing is a double grace;
Occasion smiles upon a second leave.
POLONIUS   Yet here, Laertes? Aboard, aboard, for shame!   55
The wind sits in the shoulder of your sail,
And you are stayed for. There—my blessing with thee,
And these few precepts in thy memory
Look thou character.[1] Give thy thoughts no tongue,
Nor any unproportioned thought his act.   60
Be thou familiar, but by no means vulgar.
Those friends thou hast, and their adoption tried,
Grapple them unto thy soul with hoops of steel;
But do not dull[2] thy palm with entertainment
Of each new-hatched, unfledged comrade. Beware   65
Of entrance to a quarrel, but being in,
Bear't[3] that th' opposed[4] may beware of thee.
Give every man thy ear, but few thy voice;[5]
Take each man's censure, but reserve thy judgment.
Costly thy habit as thy purse can buy,   70
But not expressed in fancy; rich not gaudy,
For the apparel oft proclaims the man,
And they in France of the best rank and station
Are of a most select and generous chief[6] in that.
Neither a borrower nor a lender be,   75
For loan oft loses both itself and friend,
And borrowing dulls th' edge of husbandry.
This above all, to thine own self be true,
And it must follow as the night the day
Thou canst not then be false to any man.   80
Farewell. My blessing season this in thee!

[margin annotation: concern with formalities & etiquette]

[margin annotation: ironical]

---

5. rose caterpillar   2. make callous
6. buds   3. conduct it
7. blights   4. opponent
8. heeds   5. approval
9. advice   6. eminence
1. write

LAERTES   Most humbly do I take my leave, my lord.
POLONIUS   The time invites you. Go, your servants tend.[7]
LAERTES   Farewell, Ophelia, and remember well
What I have said to you.
OPHELIA   'Tis in my memory locked,   85
And you yourself shall keep the key of it.
LAERTES   Farewell.   *Exit* LAERTES.
POLONIUS   What is't, Ophelia, he hath said to you?
OPHELIA   So please you, something touching the Lord Hamlet.
POLONIUS   Marry, well bethought.   90
'Tis told me he hath very oft of late
Given private time to you, and you yourself
Have of your audience been most free and bounteous.
If it be so—as so 'tis put on me,
And that in way of caution—I must tell you,   95
You do not understand yourself so clearly
As it behooves my daughter and your honor.
What is between you? Give me up the truth.
OPHELIA   He hath, my lord, of late made many tenders
Of his affection to me.   100
POLONIUS   Affection? Pooh! You speak like a green girl,
Unsifted in such perilous circumstance.
Do you believe his tenders, as you call them?
OPHELIA   I do not know, my lord, what I should think.
POLONIUS   Marry, I will teach you. Think yourself a baby   105
That you have ta'en these tenders for true pay
Which are not sterling. Tender yourself more dearly,
Or (not to crack the wind of the poor phrase,
Running it thus) you'll tender me a fool.
OPHELIA   My lord, he hath importuned me with love   110
In honorable fashion.
POLONIUS   Ay, fashion you may call it. Go to, go to.
OPHELIA   And hath given countenance[8] to his speech, my lord,
With almost all the holy vows of heaven.
POLONIUS   Ay, springes[9] to catch woodcocks. I do know,   115
When the blood burns, how prodigal the soul
Lends the tongue vows. These blazes, daughter,
Giving more light than heat, extinct in both
Even in their promise, as it is a-making,
You must not take for fire. From this time   120
Be something scanter of your maiden presence.
Set your entreatments[1] at a higher rate
Than a command to parle. For Lord Hamlet,
Believe so much in him that he is young,
And with a larger tether may he walk   125
Than may be given you. In few, Ophelia,
Do not believe his vows, for they are brokers,[2]
Not of that dye which their investments[3] show,

---

7. await
8. confirmation
9. snares

1. negotiations before a surrender
2. panders
3. garments

But mere implorators[4] of unholy suits,
Breathing like sanctified and pious bawds,   130
The better to beguile. This is for all:
I would not, in plain terms, from this time forth
Have you so slander any moment leisure
As to give words or talk with the Lord Hamlet.
Look to't, I charge you. Come your ways.   135
OPHELIA   I shall obey, my lord.   *Exeunt.*

SCENE 4: *The guard station. Enter* HAMLET, HORATIO *and*
MARCELLUS.

HAMLET   The air bites shrewdly[5]; it is very cold.
HORATIO   It is a nipping and an eager[6] air.
HAMLET   What hour now?
HORATIO   I think it lacks of twelve.
MARCELLUS   No, it is struck.
HORATIO   Indeed? I heard it not. It then draws near the season   5
Wherein the spirit held his wont to walk.
          A flourish of trumpets, and two pieces go off.
What does this mean, my lord?
HAMLET   The king doth wake tonight and takes his rouse,
Keeps wassail, and the swagg'ring up-spring[7] reels,
And as he drains his draughts of Rhenish down,   10
The kettledrum and trumpet thus bray out
The triumph of his pledge.
HORATIO   Is it a custom?
HAMLET   Ay, marry, is't,
But to my mind, though I am native here
And to the manner born, it is a custom   15
More honored in the breach than the observance.
This heavy-headed revel east and west
Makes us traduced and taxed of other nations.
They clepe[8] us drunkards, and with swinish phrase
Soil our addition,[9] and indeed it takes   20
From our achievements, though performed at height,
The pith and marrow of our attribute.[1]
So oft it chances in particular men,
That for some vicious mole of nature in them,
As in their birth, wherein they are not guilty   25
(Since nature cannot choose his origin),
By the o'ergrowth of some complexion,
Oft breaking down the pales[2] and forts of reason,
Or by some habit that too much o'er-leavens
The form of plausive[3] manners—that these men,   30
Carrying, I say, the stamp of one defect,

[handwritten marginal note: Social consequences of personal incestuous relationship]

4. solicitors   9. reputation
5. sharply   1. honor
6. keen   2. barriers
7. a German dance   3. pleasing
8. call

Being nature's livery or fortune's star,
His virtues else, be they as pure as grace,
As infinite as man may undergo,
Shall in the general censure take corruption   35
From that particular fault. The dram of evil
Doth all the noble substance often doubt[4]
To his own scandal.

        Enter GHOST.

HORATIO   Look, my lord, it comes.
HAMLET   Angels and ministers of grace defend us!
Be thou a spirit of health or goblin damned,   40
Bring with thee airs from heaven or blasts from hell,
Be thy intents wicked or charitable,
Thou com'st in such a questionable[5] shape
That I will speak to thee. I'll call thee Hamlet,
King, father, royal Dane. O, answer me!   45
Let me not burst in ignorance, but tell
Why thy canonized[6] bones, hearséd in death,
Have burst their cerements[7]; why the sepulchre
Wherein we saw thee quietly interred
Hath oped his ponderous and marble jaws   50
To cast thee up again. What may this mean
That thou, dead corse, again in complete steel[8]
Revisits thus the glimpses of the moon,
Making night hideous, and we fools of nature
So horridly to shake our disposition   55
With thoughts beyond the reaches of our souls?
Say, why is this? wherefore? What should we do?

        GHOST *beckons.*

HORATIO   It beckons you to go away it,
As if it some impartment[9] did desire
To you alone.
MARCELLUS   Look with what courteous action   60
It waves[1] you to a more removéd[2] ground.
But do not go with it.
HORATIO   No, by no means.
HAMLET   It will not speak; then I will follow it.
HORATIO   Do not, my lord.
HAMLET   Why, what should be the fear?
I do not set my life at a pin's fee,[3]   65
And for my soul, what can it do to that,
Being a thing immortal as itself?
It waves me forth again. I'll follow it.
HORATIO   What if it tempt you toward the flood, my lord,
Or to the dreadful summit of the cliff   70

4. put out
5. prompting question
6. buried in accordance with church
canons
7. gravecloths

8. armor
9. communication
1. beckons
2. distant
3. price

That beetles[4] o'er his base into the sea,
And there assume some other horrible form,
Which might deprive[5] your sovereignty of reason[6]
And draw you into madness? Think of it.
The very place puts toys of desperation,[7]   75
Without more motive, into every brain
That looks so many fathoms to the sea
And hears it roar beneath.

HAMLET   It waves me still.
Go on. I'll follow thee.
MARCELLUS   You shall not go, my lord.
HAMLET   Hold off your hands.   80
HORATIO   Be ruled. You shall not go.
HAMLET   My fate cries out
And makes each petty artere in this body
As hardy as the Nemean lion's nerve.[8]
Still am I called. Unhand me, gentlemen.
By heaven, I'll make a ghost of him that lets[9] me.   85
I say, away! Go on. I'll follow thee.

Exeunt GHOST *and* HAMLET.

HORATIO   He waxes desperate with imagination.
MARCELLUS   Let's follow. 'Tis not fit thus to obey him.
HORATIO   Have after. To what issue will this come?
MARCELLUS   Something is rotten in the state of Denmark.   90
HORATIO   Heaven will direct it.
MARCELLUS   Nay, let's follow him.   *Exeunt.*

SCENE 5: *Near the guard station. Enter* GHOST *and* HAMLET.

HAMLET   Whither wilt thou lead me? Speak. I'll go no further.
GHOST   Mark me.
HAMLET   I will.
GHOST   My hour is almost come,
When I to sulph'rous and tormenting flames
Must render up myself.
HAMLET   Alas, poor ghost!
GHOST   Pity me not, but lend thy serious hearing   5
To what I shall unfold.
HAMLET   Speak. I am bound to hear.
GHOST   So art thou to revenge, when thou shalt hear.
HAMLET   What?
GHOST   I am thy father's spirit,
Doomed for a certain term to walk the night,   10
And for the day confined to fast in fires,
Till the foul crimes done in my days of nature[1]
Are burnt and purged away. But that I am forbid

4. juts out
5. take away
6. rational power
7. desperate fancies
8. The Nemean lion was a mythological

monster slain by Hercules as one of his
twelve labors.
9. hinders
1. i.e., while I was alive

To tell the secrets of my prison house,
I could a tale unfold whose lightest word   15
Would harrow up thy soul, freeze thy young blood,
Make thy two eyes like stars start from their spheres,
Thy knotted and combinéd[2] locks to part,
And each particular hair to stand an end,
Like quills upon the fretful porpentine.[3]   20
But this eternal blazon[4] must not be
To ears of flesh and blood. List, list, O, list!
If thou didst ever thy dear father love—
HAMLET   O God!
GHOST   Revenge his foul and most unnatural murder.   25
HAMLET   Murder!
GHOST   Murder most foul, as in the best it is,
But this most foul, strange, and unnatural.
HAMLET   Haste me to know't, that I, with wings as swift   *Impulsive*
As meditation or the thoughts of love,   30
May sweep to my revenge.
GHOST   I find thee apt,
And duller shouldst thou be than the fat weed
That rots itself in ease on Lethe[5] wharf,—
Wouldst thou not stir in this. Now, Hamlet, hear.
'Tis given out that, sleeping in my orchard,   35
A serpent stung me. So the whole ear of Denmark
Is by a forgéd process[6] of my death
Rankly abused. But know, thou noble youth,
The serpent that did sting thy father's life
Now wears his crown.
HAMLET   O my prophetic soul!   40
My uncle!
GHOST   Ay, that incestuous, that adulterate beast,
With witchcraft of his wits, with traitorous gifts—
O wicked wit and gifts that have the power
So to seduce!—won to his shameful lust   45
The will of my most seeming virtuous queen.
O Hamlet, what a falling off was there,
From me, whose love was of that dignity
That it went hand in hand even with the vow
I made to her in marriage, and to decline[7]   50
Upon a wretch whose natural gifts were poor
To those of mine!
But virtue, as it never will be moved,
Though lewdness court it in a shape of heaven,
So lust, though to a radiant angel linked,   55
Will sate itself in a celestial bed
And prey on garbage.
But soft, methinks I scent the morning air.

2. tangled
3. porcupine
4. description of eternity
5. The Lethe was one of the rivers of
the classical underworld. Its specific importance was that its waters when drunk
induced forgetfulness. The "fat weed" is
the asphodel which grew there.
6. false report
7. sink

Brief let me be. Sleeping within my orchard,
My custom always of the afternoon, 60
Upon my secure hour thy uncle stole,
With juice of cursed hebona[8] in a vial,
And in the porches of my ears did pour
The leperous distilment, whose effect
Holds such an enmity with blood of man 65
That swift as quicksilver it courses through
The natural gates and alleys of the body,
And with a sudden vigor it doth posset[9]
And curd,[1] like eager[2] droppings into milk,
The thin and wholesome blood. So did it mine, 70
And a most instant tetter[3] barked about[4]
Most lazar-like[5] with vile and loathsome crust
All my smooth body.
Thus was I sleeping by a brother's hand
Of life, of crown, of queen at once dispatched, 75
Cut off even in the blossoms of my sin,
Unhouseled, disappointed, unaneled,[6]
No reck'ning made, but sent to my account
With all my imperfections on my head.
O, horrible! O, horrible! most horrible! 80
If thou hast nature in thee, bear it not.
Let not the royal bed of Denmark be
A couch for luxury[7] and damnéd incest.
But howsomever thou pursues this act,
Taint not thy mind, nor let thy soul contrive 85
Against thy mother aught. Leave her to heaven,
And to those thorns that in her bosom lodge
To prick and sting her. Fare thee well at once.
The glowworm shows the matin[8] to be near,
And gins to pale his uneffectual fire. 90
Adieu, adieu, adieu. Remember me. *Exit.*
HAMLET   O all you host of heaven! O earth! What else?
And shall I couple hell? O, fie! Hold, hold, my heart,
And you, my sinews, grow not instant old,
But bear me stiffly up. Remember thee? 95
Ay, thou poor ghost, whiles memory holds a seat
In this distracted globe.[9] Remember thee?
Yea, from the table[1] of my memory
I'll wipe away all trivial fond[2] records,
All saws of books, all forms, all pressures past 100
That youth and observation copied there,
And thy commandment all alone shall live
Within the book and volume of my brain,

[Margin annotation: King Hamlet's story told under pressure of morning air]

8. a poison
9. coagulate
1. curdle
2. acid
3. a skin disease
4. covered like bark
5. leper-like
6. The Ghost means that he died without the customary rites of the church, that
is, without receiving the sacrament, without
confession, and without extreme unction.
7. lust
8. morning
9. skull
1. writing tablet
2. foolish

Unmixed with baser matter. Yes, by heaven!
O most pernicious woman!   105
O villain, villain, smiling, damnéd villain!
My tables—meet it is I set it down
That one may smile, and smile, and be a villain.
At least I am sure it may be so in Denmark.
So, uncle, there you are. Now to my word[3]:   110
It is "Adieu, adieu. Remember me."
I have sworn't.

     Enter HORATIO *and* MARCELLUS.

HORATIO   My lord, my lord!
MARCELLUS   Lord Hamlet!
HORATIO   Heavens secure him!
HAMLET   So be it!
MARCELLUS   Illo, ho, ho, my lord!   115
HAMLET   Hillo, ho, ho, boy![4] Come, bird, come.
MARCELLUS   How is't, my noble lord?
HORATIO   What news, my lord?
HAMLET   O, wonderful!
HORATIO   Good my lord, tell it.
HAMLET   No, you will reveal it.
HORATIO   Not I, my lord, by heaven.
MARCELLUS   Nor I, my lord.   120
HAMLET   How say you then, would heart of man once think it?
    But you'll be secret?
BOTH   Ay, by heaven, my lord.
HAMLET   There's never a villain dwelling in all Denmark
    But he's an arrant knave.
HORATIO   There needs no ghost, my lord, come from the grave   125
    To tell us this.
HAMLET   Why, right, you are in the right,
    And so without more circumstance at all
    I hold it fit that we shake hands and part,
    You, as your business and desire shall point you,
    For every man hath business and desire   130
    Such as it is, and for my own poor part,
    I will go pray.
HORATIO   These are but wild and whirling words, my lord.
HAMLET   I am sorry they offend you, heartily;
    Yes, faith, heartily.
HORATIO   There's no offence, my lord.   135
HAMLET   Yes, by Saint Patrick, but there is, Horatio,
    And much offence too. Touching this vision here,
    It is an honest ghost, that let me tell you.
    For your desire to know what is between us.
    O'ermaster't as you may. And now, good friends,   140
    As you are friends, scholars, and soldiers,
    Give me one poor request.

HORATIO   What is't, my lord? We will.

HAMLET   Never make known what you have seen tonight.

BOTH   My lord, we will not.

HAMLET   Nay, but swear't.

HORATIO   In faith,   145
My lord, not I.

MARCELLUS   Nor I, my lord, in faith.

HAMLET   Upon my sword.

MARCELLUS   We have sworn, my lord, already.

HAMLET   Indeed, upon my sword, indeed.

GHOST *cries under the stage.*

GHOST   Swear.

HAMLET   Ha, ha, boy, say'st thou so? Art thou there, truepenny[5]?
Come on. You hear this fellow in the cellarage.[6]   150
Consent to swear.

HORATIO   Propose the oath, my lord.

HAMLET   Never to speak of this that you have seen,
Swear by my sword.

GHOST [*beneath*]   Swear.

HAMLET   Hic et ubique?[7] Then we'll shift our ground.   155
Come hither, gentlemen,
And lay your hands again upon my sword.
Swear by my sword
Never to speak of this that you have heard.

GHOST [*beneath*]   Swear by his sword.   160

HAMLET   Well said, old mole! Canst work i' th' earth so fast?
A worthy pioneer![8] Once more remove, good friends.

HORATIO   O day and night, but this is wondrous strange!

HAMLET   And therefore as a stranger give it welcome.
There are more things in heaven and earth, Horatio,   165
Than are dreamt of in your philosophy.
But come.
Here as before, never, so help you mercy,
How strange or odd some'er I bear myself
(As I perchance hereafter shall think meet   170
To put an antic[9] disposition on),
That you, at such times, seeing me, never shall,
With arms encumbered[1] thus, or this head-shake,
Or by pronouncing of some doubtful phrase,
As "Well, well, we know," or "We could, and if we would"   175
Or "If we list to speak," or "There be, and if they might"
Or such ambiguous giving out, to note
That you know aught of me—this do swear,
So grace and mercy at your most need help you.

GHOST [*beneath*]   Swear.   *They swear.* 180

HAMLET   Rest, rest, perturbéd spirit! So, gentlemen,
With all my love I do commend me to you,

5. old fellow   8. soldier who digs trenches
6. below   9. grotesque
7. here and everywhere   1. folded

And what so poor a man as Hamlet is
May do t'express his love and friending[2] to you,
God willing, shall not lack. Let us go in together,   185
And still your fingers on your lips, I pray.
The time is out of joint. O cursèd spite
That ever I was born to set it right!
Nay, come, let's go together.   *Exeunt.*

Act 2

SCENE 1: *The dwelling of* POLONIUS. *Enter* POLONIUS
and REYNALDO.

POLONIUS   Give him this money and these notes, Reynaldo.
REYNALDO   I will, my lord.
POLONIUS   You shall do marvellous wisely, good Reynaldo,
Before you visit him, to make inquire[3]
Of his behavior.   *P. is Suspicious*
REYNALDO   My lord, I did intend it.   5
POLONIUS   Marry, well said, very well said. Look you, sir.
Enquire me first what Danskers[4] are in Paris,
And how, and who, what means, and where they keep,[5]
What company, at what expense; and finding
By this encompassment[6] and drift of question   10
That they do know my son, come you more nearer
Than your particular demands[7] will touch it.
Take you as 'twere some distant knowledge of him,
As thus, "I know his father and his friends,
And in part him." Do you mark this, Reynaldo?   15
REYNALDO   Ay, very well, my lord.
POLONIUS   "And in part him, but," you may say, "not well,
But if't be he I mean, he's very wild,
Addicted so and so." And there put on him
What forgeries[8] you please; marry, none so rank[9]   20
As may dishonor him. Take heed of that.
But, sir, such wanton, wild, and usual slips
As are companions noted and most known
To youth and liberty.
REYNALDO   As gaming, my lord.
POLONIUS   Ay, or drinking, fencing, swearing, quarrelling,   25
Drabbing[1]—you may go so far.
REYNALDO   My lord, that would dishonor him.
POLONIUS   Faith, no, as you may season it in the charge.[2]
You must not put another scandal on him,

2. friendship
3. inquiry
4. Danes
5. live
6. indirect means

7. direct questions
8. lies
9. foul
1. whoring
2. soften the accusation

That he is open to incontinency.[3]   30
That's not my meaning. But breathe his faults so quaintly[4]
That they may seem the taints of liberty,[5]
The flash and outbreak of a fiery mind,
A savageness in unreclaiméd[6] blood,
Of general assault.[7]
REYNALDO   But, my good lord—   35
POLONIUS   Wherefore should you do this?
REYNALDO   Ay, my lord,
I would know that.
POLONIUS   Marry, sir, here's my drift,
And I believe it is a fetch of warrant.[8]
You laying these slight sullies on my son,
As 'twere a thing a little soiled i' th' working,   40
Mark you,
Your party in converse,[9] him you would sound,
Having ever seen in the prenominate[1] crimes
The youth you breathe[2] of guilty, be assured
He closes with you in this consequence,   45
"Good sir," or so, or "friend," or "gentleman,"
According to the phrase or the addition
Of man and country.
REYNALDO   Very good, my lord.
POLONIUS   And then, sir, does 'a this—'a does—What was I about to
    say?   50
By the mass, I was about to say something.
Where did I leave?
REYNALDO   At "closes in the consequence."
POLONIUS   At "closes in the consequence"—ay, marry,
He closes thus: "I know the gentleman.   55
I saw him yesterday, or th' other day,
Or then, or then, with such, or such, and as you say,
There was 'a gaming, there o'ertook in's rouse,
There falling out at tennis," or perchance
"I saw him enter such a house of sale,"   60
Videlicet,[3] a brothel, or so forth.
See you, now—
Your bait of falsehood takes this carp of truth,
And thus do we of wisdom and of reach,[4]
With windlasses and with assays of bias,[5]   65
By indirections find directions out;
So by my former lecture and advice
Shall you my son. You have me, have you not?
REYNALDO   My lord, I have.
POLONIUS   God b'wi' ye; fare ye well.
REYNALDO   Good my lord.   70

3. sexual excess   9. conversation
4. with delicacy   1. already named
5. faults of freedom   2. speak
6. untamed   3. namely
7. touching everyone   4. ability
8. permissible trick   5. indirect tests

POLONIUS   Observe his inclination in yourself.
REYNALDO   I shall, my lord.
POLONIUS   And let him ply[6] his music.
REYNALDO   Well, my lord.
POLONIUS   Farewell.   *Exit* REYNALDO.

    Enter OPHELIA.

               How now, Ophelia, what's the matter?
OPHELIA   O my lord, my lord, I have been so affrighted!   75
POLONIUS   With what, i' th' name of God?
OPHELIA   My lord, as I was sewing in my closet,[7]
    Lord Hamlet with his doublet[8] all unbraced,[9]
    No hat upon his head, his stockings fouled,
    Ungartered and down-gyvéd[1] to his ankle,   80
    Pale as his shirt, his knees knocking each other,
    And with a look so piteous in purport
    As if he had been looséd out of hell
    To speak of horrors—he comes before me.
POLONIUS   Mad for thy love?
OPHELIA   My lord, I do not know,   85
    But truly I do fear it.
POLONIUS   What said he?
OPHELIA   He took me by the wrist, and held me hard,
    Then goes he to the length of all his arm,
    And with his other hand thus o'er his brow,
    He falls to such perusal of my face   90
    As 'a would draw it. Long stayed he so.
    At last, a little shaking of mine arm,
    And thrice his head thus waving up and down,
    He raised a sigh so piteous and profound
    As it did seem to shatter all his bulk,[2]   95
    And end his being. That done, he lets me go,
    And with his head over his shoulder turned
    He seemed to find his way without his eyes,
    For out adoors he went without their helps,
    And to the last bended[3] their light on me.   100
POLONIUS   Come, go with me. I will go seek the king.
    This is the very ecstasy of love,
    Whose violent property[4] fordoes[5] itself,
    And leads the will to desperate undertakings
    As oft as any passion under heaven   105
    That does afflict our natures. I am sorry.
    What, have you given him any hard words of late?
OPHELIA   No, my good lord, but as you did command
    I did repel[6] his letters, and denied
    His access to me.

---

6. practice
7. chamber
8. jacket
9. unlaced
1. fallen down like fetters

2. body
3. directed
4. character
5. destroys
6. refuse

POLONIUS   That hath made him mad.   110
I am sorry that with better heed and judgment
I had not quoted⁷ him. I feared he did but trifle,
And meant to wrack⁸ thee; but beshrew my jealousy.
By heaven, it is as proper to our age
To cast beyond ourselves in our opinions   115
As it is common for the younger sort
To lack discretion. Come, go we to the king.
This must be known, which being kept close, might move
More grief to hide than hate to utter love.
Come.   *Exeunt.* 120

SCENE 2: *A public room. Enter* KING, QUEEN, ROSENCRANTZ
and GUILDENSTERN.

KING   Welcome, dear Rosencrantz and Guildenstern.
Moreover that⁹ we much did long to see you,
The need we have to use you did provoke
Our hasty sending. Something have you heard
Of Hamlet's transformation—so call it,   5
Sith¹ nor th' exterior nor the inward man
Resembles that it was. What it should be,
More than his father's death, that thus hath put him
So much from th' understanding of himself,
I cannot deem of. I entreat you both   10
That, being of so young days² brought up with him,
And sith so neighbored³ to his youth and havior,
That you vouchsafe your rest here in our court
Some little time, so by your companies
To draw him on to pleasures, and to gather   15
So much as from occasion you may glean,
Whether aught to us unknown afflicts him thus,
That opened lies within our remedy.
QUEEN   Good gentlemen, he hath much talked of you,
And sure I am two men there are not living   20
To whom he more adheres. If it will please you
To show us so much gentry⁴ and good will
As to expend your time with us awhile
For the supply and profit of our hope,
Your visitation shall receive such thanks   25
As fits a king's remembrance.
ROSENCRANTZ   Both your majesties
Might, by the sovereign power you have of us,
Put your dread pleasures more into command
Than to entreaty.
GUILDENSTERN   But we both obey,
And here give up ourselves in the full bent⁵   30

7. observed   2. from childhood
8. harm   3. closely allied
9. in addition to the fact that   4. courtesy
1. since   5. completely

To lay our service freely at your feet,
To be commanded.
KING   Thanks, Rosencrantz and gentle Guildenstern.
QUEEN   Thanks, Guildenstern and gentle Rosencrantz.
  And I beseech you instantly to visit   35
  My too much changed son. Go, some of you,
  And bring these gentlemen where Hamlet is.
GUILDENSTERN   Heavens make our presence and our practices
  Pleasant and helpful to him!
QUEEN   Ay, amen!

                                    Exeunt ROSENCRANTZ *and* GUILDENSTERN.

    Enter POLONIUS.

POLONIUS   Th' ambassadors from Norway, my good lord,   40
  Are joyfully returned.
KING   Thou still[6] hast been the father of good news.
POLONIUS   Have I, my lord? I assure you, my good liege,
  I hold my duty as I hold my soul,
  Both to my God and to my gracious king;   45
  And I do think—or else this brain of mine
  Hunts not the trail of policy[7] so sure
  As it hath used to do—that I have found
  The very cause of Hamlet's lunacy.
KING   O, speak of that, that do I long to hear.   50
POLONIUS   Give first admittance to th' ambassadors.
  My news shall be the fruit[8] to that great feast.
KING   Thyself do grace to them, and bring them in.

                                                          Exit POLONIUS.

  He tells me, my dear Gertrude, he hath found
  The head and source of all your son's distemper.   55
QUEEN   I doubt it is no other but the main,
  His father's death and our o'erhasty marriage.
KING   Well, we shall sift[9] him.

    Enter Ambassadors (VOLTEMAND *and* CORNELIUS) *with*
    POLONIUS.
                                    Welcome, my good friends,
  Say, Voltemand, what from our brother Norway?
VOLTEMAND   Most fair return of greetings and desires.   60
  Upon our first,[1] he sent out to suppress
  His nephew's levies, which to him appeared
  To be a preparation 'gainst the Polack,
  But better looked into, he truly found
  It was against your highness, whereat grieved,   65
  That so his sickness, age, and impotence
  Was falsely borne in hand,[2] sends out arrests[3]

---

6. ever
7. statecraft
8. dessert
9. examine

1. i.e., first appearance
2. deceived
3. orders to stop

On Fortinbras, which he in brief obeys,
Receives rebuke from Norway, and in fine,
Makes vow before his uncle never more   70
To give th' assay[4] of arms against your majesty.
Whereon old Norway, overcome with joy,
Gives him threescore thousand crowns in annual fee,
And his commission to employ those soldiers,
So levied as before, against the Polack,   75
With an entreaty, herein further shown,   *Gives* CLAUDIUS *a paper.*
That it might please you to give quiet pass[5]
Through your dominions for this enterprise,
On such regards of safety and allowance
As therein are set down.
KING   It likes[6] us well,   80
And at our more considered time[7] we'll read,
Answer, and think upon this business.
Meantime we thank you for your well-took[8] labor.
Go to your rest; at night we'll feast together.
Most welcome home!   *Exeunt* AMBASSADORS.
POLONIUS   This business is well ended.   85
My liege and madam, to expostulate[9]
What majesty should be, what duty is,
Why day is day, night night, and time is time,
Were nothing but to waste night, day, and time.   *wordiness*
Therefore, since brevity is the soul of wit,   90
And tediousness the limbs and outward flourishes,[1]
I will be brief. Your noble son is mad.
Mad call I it, for to define true madness,
What is't but to be nothing else but mad?
But let that go.
QUEEN   More matter with less art.   95
POLONIUS   Madam, I swear I use no art at all.
That he is mad, 'tis true: 'tis true 'tis pity,
And pity 'tis 'tis true. A foolish figure,
But farewell it, for I will use no art.
Mad let us grant him, then, and now remains   100
That we find out the cause of this effect,
Or rather say the cause of this defect,
For this effect defective comes by cause.
Thus it remains, and the remainder thus.
Perpend.[2]   105
I have a daughter—have while she is mine—
Who in her duty and obedience, mark,
Hath given me this. Now gather, and surmise.
     "To the celestial, and my soul's idol, the most beautified
Ophelia."—That's an ill phrase, a vile phrase, "beautified" is a   110

4. trial   8. successful
5. safe conduct   9. discuss
6. pleases   1. adornments
7. time for more consideration   2. consider

vile phrase. But you shall hear. Thus:
  "In her excellent white bosom, these, etc."
QUEEN   Came this from Hamlet to her?
POLONIUS   Good madam, stay awhile. I will be faithful.

> "Doubt thou the stars are fire,   115
>   Doubt that the sun doth move;
>   Doubt truth to be a liar;
>   But never doubt I love.

O dear Ophelia, I am ill at these numbers.[3]
I have not art to reckon my groans, but that I love thee best, O   120
most best, believe it. Adieu.

> Thine evermore, most dear lady, whilst
>   this machine[4] is to him, HAMLET."

This in obedience hath my daughter shown me,
And more above, hath his solicitings,   125
As they fell out by time, by means, and place,
All given to mine ear.
KING   But how hath she
  Received his love?
POLONIUS   What do you think of me?
KING   As of a man faithful and honorable.
POLONIUS   I would fain prove so. But what might you think,   130
  When I had seen this hot love on the wing,
  (As I perceived it, I must tell you that,
  Before my daughter told me), what might you,
  Or my dear majesty your queen here, think,
  If I had played the desk or table-book,   135
  Or given my heart a winking, mute and dumb,
  Or looked upon this love with idle sight,[5]
  What might you think? No, I went round[6] to work,
  And my young mistress thus I did bespeak:
  "Lord Hamlet is a prince out of thy star.[7]   140
  This must not be." And then I prescripts[8] gave her,
  That she should lock herself from his resort,
  Admit no messengers, receive no tokens.
  Which done, she took[9] the fruits of my advice;
  And he repelled, a short tale to make,   145
  Fell into a sadness, then into a fast,
  Thence to a watch, thence into a weakness,
  Thence to a lightness, and by this declension,
  Into the madness wherein now he raves,
  And all we mourn for.
KING   Do you think 'tis this?   150
QUEEN   It may be, very like.

---

3. verses
4. body
5. Polonius means that he would have been at fault if, having seen Hamlet's attention to Ophelia, he had winked at it or not paid attention, an "idle sight," and if he had remained silent and kept the infor-

mation to himself, as if it were written in a "desk" or "table-book."
6. directly
7. beyond your sphere
8. orders
9. followed

POLONIUS   Hath there been such a time—I would fain know that—
That I have positively said "Tis so,"
When it proved otherwise?
KING   Not that I know.
POLONIUS [*pointing to his head and shoulder*]   Take this from this, if
    this be otherwise.   155
If circumstances lead me, I will find
Where truth is hid, though it were hid indeed
Within the centre.[1]
KING   How may we try it further?
POLONIUS   You know sometimes he walks four hours together
Here in the lobby.
QUEEN   So he does, indeed.   160
POLONIUS   At such a time I'll loose[2] my daughter to him.
Be you and I behind an arras[3] then.
Mark the encounter. If he love her not,
And be not from his reason fall'n thereon,
Let me be no assistant for a state,   165
But keep a farm and carters.
KING   We will try it.

        Enter HAMLET *reading a book.*

QUEEN   But look where sadly the poor wretch comes reading.
POLONIUS   Away, I do beseech you both away,
    I'll board[4] him presently.

                    Exeunt KING *and* QUEEN.

              O, give me leave.
How does my good Lord Hamlet?   170
HAMLET   Well, God-a-mercy.
POLONIUS   Do you know me, my lord?
HAMLET   Excellent well, you are a fishmonger.
POLONIUS   Not I, my lord.
HAMLET   Then I would you were so honest a man.   175
POLONIUS   Honest, my lord?
HAMLET   Ay, sir, to be honest as this world goes, is to be one man
picked out of ten thousand.
POLONIUS   That's very true, my lord.
HAMLET   For if the sun breed maggots in a dead dog, being a god [180]
kissing carrion[5]—Have you a daughter?
POLONIUS   I have, my lord.
HAMLET   Let her not walk i' th' sun. Conception is a blessing, but as
your daughter may conceive—friend, look to 't.
POLONIUS   How say you by that? [*Aside.*] Still harping on my daughter. [185]
Yet he knew me not at first. 'A said I was a fishmonger. 'A is far
gone. And truly in my youth I suffered much extremity for love.
Very near this. I'll speak to him again.—What do you read, my lord?

---

1. of the earth
2. let loose
3. tapestry
4. accost

5. A reference to the belief of the period
that maggots were produced spontaneously
by the action of sunshine on carrion.

HAMLET   Words, words, words.
POLONIUS   What is the matter, my lord?   190
HAMLET   Between who?
POLONIUS   I mean the matter that you read, my lord.
HAMLET   Slanders, sir; for the satirical rogue says here that old men
    have grey beards, that their faces are wrinkled, their eyes purging
    thick amber and plum-tree gum, and that they have a plentiful lack   195
    of wit, together with most weak hams[6]—all which, sir, though I
    most powerfully and potently believe, yet I hold it not honesty to
    have it thus set down, for yourself, sir, shall grow old as I am, if like
    a crab you could go backward.
POLONIUS   [*aside*]   Though this be madness, yet there is method in't.   200
    —Will you walk out of the air, my lord?
HAMLET   Into my grave?
POLONIUS   [*aside*]   Indeed, that's out of the air. How pregnant some-
    time his replies are! a happiness that often madness hits on, which
    reason and sanity could not so prosperously be delivered of. I will   205
    leave him, and suddenly contrive the means of meeting between
    him and my daughter.—My lord. I will take my leave of you.
HAMLET   You cannot take from me anything that I will more willingly
    part withal—except my life, except my life, except my life.

        Enter GUILDENSTERN *and* ROSENCRANTZ.

POLONIUS   Fare you well, my lord.   210
HAMLET   These tedious old fools!
POLONIUS   You go to seek the Lord Hamlet. There he is.
ROSENCRANTZ   [*to* POLONIUS]   God save you, sir!   *Exit* POLONIUS.
GUILDENSTERN   My honored lord!
ROSENCRANTZ   My most dear lord!   215
HAMLET   My excellent good friends! How dost thou, Guildenstern?
    Ah, Rosencrantz! Good lads, how do you both?
ROSENCRANTZ   As the indifferent[7] children of the earth.
GUILDENSTERN   Happy in that we are not over-happy;
    On Fortune's cap we are not the very button.[8]   220
HAMLET   Nor the soles of her shoe?
ROSENCRANTZ   Neither, my lord.
HAMLET   Then you live about her waist, or in the middle of her favors.
GUILDENSTERN   Faith, her privates we.
HAMLET   In the secret parts of Fortune? O, most true, she is a   225
    strumpet.[9] What news?
ROSENCRANTZ   None, my lord, but that the world's grown honest.
HAMLET   Then is doomsday near. But your news is not true. Let me
    question more in particular. What have you, my good friends, de-
    served at the hands of Fortune, that she sends you to prison hither? 230
GUILDENSTERN   Prison, my lord?
HAMLET   Denmark's a prison.

---

6. limbs
7. ordinary
8. i.e., on top
9. Hamlet is indulging in characteristic
ribaldry. Guildenstern means that they are

"privates" = ordinary citizens, but Hamlet
takes him to mean "privates" = sexual organs and "middle of her favors" = waist =
sexual organs.

ROSENCRANTZ   Then is the world one.

HAMLET   A goodly one, in which there are many confines, wards,[1] and
dungeons, Denmark being one o' th' worst.   235

ROSENCRANTZ   We think not so, my lord.

HAMLET   Why then 'tis none to you; for there is nothing either good
or bad, but thinking makes it so. To me it is a prison.

ROSENCRANTZ   Why then your ambition makes it one. 'Tis too narrow
for your mind.   240

HAMLET   O God, I could be bounded in a nutshell and count myself
a king of infinite space, were it not that I have bad dreams.

GUILDENSTERN   Which dreams indeed are ambition; for the very substance of the ambitious is merely the shadow of a dream.

HAMLET   A dream itself is but a shadow.   245

ROSENCRANTZ   Truly, and I hold ambition of so airy and light a quality
that it is but a shadow's shadow.

HAMLET   Then are our beggars bodies, and our monarchs and outstretched heroes the beggars' shadows. Shall we to th' court? for,
by my fay,[2] I cannot reason.   250

BOTH   We'll wait upon you.

HAMLET   No such matter. I will not sort[3] you with the rest of my
servants; for to speak to you like an honest man, I am most dreadfully attended. But in the beaten way of friendship, what make you
at Elsinore?   255

ROSENCRANTZ   To visit you, my lord; no other occasion.

HAMLET   Beggar that I am, I am even poor in thanks, but I thank
you; and sure, dear friends, my thanks are too dear a halfpenny.[4]
Were you not sent for? Is it your own inclining? Is it a free visitation? Come, come, deal justly with me. Come, come, nay speak.   260

GUILDENSTERN   What should we say, my lord?

HAMLET   Why anything but to th' purpose. You were sent for, and
there is a kind of confession in your looks, which your modesties
have not craft enough to color. I know the good king and queen
have sent for you.   265

ROSENCRANTZ   To what end, my lord?

HAMLET   That you must teach me. But let me conjure you by the
rights of our fellowship, by the consonancy of our youth, by the
obligation of our ever-preserved love, and by what more dear a
better proposer can charge you withal, be even and direct[5] with me 270
whether you were sent for or no.

ROSENCRANTZ [*aside to* GUILDENSTERN]   What say you?

HAMLET [*aside*]   Nay, then, I have an eye of you.—If you love me,
hold not off.

GUILDENSTERN   My lord, we were sent for.   275

HAMLET   I will tell you why; so shall my anticipation prevent your
discovery,[6] and your secrecy to the king and queen moult no
feather. I have of late—but wherefore I know not—lost all my
mirth, forgone all custom of exercises; and indeed it goes so heavily
with my disposition, that this goodly frame the earth seems to me   280

1. cells   4. not worth a halfpenny
2. faith   5. straightforward
3. include   6. disclosure

a sterile promontory, this most excellent canopy the air, look you,
this brave o'er-hanging firmament, this majestical roof fretted[7] with
golden fire, why it appeareth nothing to me but a foul and pestilent
congregation of vapors. What a piece of work is a man, how noble in
reason, how infinite in faculties, in form and moving, how express[8] 285
and admirable in action, how like an angel in apprehension, how like
a god: the beauty of the world, the paragon of animals. And yet to
me, what is this quintessence of dust? Man delights not me, nor
woman neither, though by your smiling you seem to say so.

ROSENCRANTZ   My lord, there was no such stuff in my thoughts.   290

HAMLET   Why did ye laugh, then, when I said "Man delights not me"?

ROSENCRANTZ   To think, my lord, if you delight not in man, what
lenten[9] entertainment the players shall receive from you. We coted[1]
them on the way, and hither are they coming to offer you service.

HAMLET   He that plays the king shall be welcome—his majesty shall 295
have tribute on me; the adventurous knight shall use his foil and
target[2]; the lover shall not sigh gratis; the humorous[3] man shall end
his part in peace; the clown shall make those laugh whose lungs are
tickle o' th' sere[4]; and the lady shall say her mind freely, or the
blank verse shall halt for't. What players are they?   300

ROSENCRANTZ   Even those you were wont to take such delight in, the
tragedians of the city.

HAMLET   How chances it they travel? Their residence, both in reputation and profit, was better both ways.

ROSENCRANTZ   I think their inhibition comes by the means of the late 305
innovation.

HAMLET   Do they hold the same estimation they did when I was in
the city? Are they so followed?

ROSENCRANTZ   No, indeed, are they not.

HAMLET   How comes it? Do they grow rusty?   310

ROSENCRANTZ   Nay, their endeavor keeps in the wonted pace; but
there is, sir, an eyrie of children, little eyases,[5] that cry out on the
top of question,[6] and are most tyrannically clapped for't. These are
now the fashion, and so berattle the common stages (so they call
them) that many wearing rapiers are afraid of goose quills[7] and 315
dare scarce come thither.[8]

HAMLET   What, are they children? Who maintains 'em? How are they
escoted[9]? Will they pursue the quality no longer than they can sing?
Will they not say afterwards, if they should grow themselves to
common players (as it is most like, if their means are no better), 320
their writers do them wrong to make them exclaim against their
own succession[1]?

7. ornamented with fretwork
8. well built
9. scanty
1. passed
2. sword and shield
3. eccentric
4. easily set off
5. little hawks
6. with a loud, high delivery
7. pens of satirical writers
8. The passage refers to the emergence

at the time of the play of theatrical companies made up of children from London
choir schools. Their performances became
fashionable and hurt the business of the
established companies. Hamlet says that if
they continue to act, "pursue the quality,"
when they are grown, they will find that
they have been damaging their own future
careers.
9. supported
1. future careers

ROSENCRANTZ   Faith, there has been much to do on both sides; and
the nation holds it no sin to tarre² them to controversy. There was
for a while no money bid for argument,³ unless the poet and the 325
player went to cuffs⁴ in the question.

HAMLET   Is't possible?

GUILDENSTERN   O, there has been much throwing about of brains.

HAMLET   Do the boys carry it away?

ROSENCRANTZ   Ay, that they do, my lord, Hercules and his load too.⁵ 330

HAMLET   It is not very strange, for my uncle is King of Denmark, and
those that would make mouths⁶ at him while my father lived give
twenty, forty, fifty, a hundred ducats apiece for his picture in little.⁷
'Sblood, there is something in this more than natural, if philosophy
could find it out.   *A flourish.* 335

GUILDENSTERN   There are the players.

HAMLET   Gentlemen, you are welcome to Elsinore. Your hands. Come
then, th' appurtenance of welcome is fashion and ceremony. Let me
comply with⁸ you in this garb, lest my extent⁹ to the players, which
I tell you must show fairly outwards, should more appear like enter- 340
tainment¹ than yours. You are welcome. But my uncle-father and
aunt-mother are deceived.

GUILDENSTERN   In what, my dear lord?

HAMLET   I am but mad north-north-west; when the wind is southerly
I know a hawk from a handsaw.²   345

Enter POLONIUS.

POLONIUS   Well be with you, gentlemen.

HAMLET   Hark you, Guildenstern—and you too—at each ear a hearer.
That great baby you see there is not yet out of his swaddling clouts.³

ROSENCRANTZ   Happily he is the second time come to them, for they
say an old man is twice a child.   350

HAMLET   I will prophesy he comes to tell me of the players. Mark it.
—You say right, sir, a Monday morning, 'twas then indeed.

POLONIUS   My lord, I have news to tell you.

HAMLET   My lord, I have news to tell you.
When Roscius was an actor in Rome—⁴   355

POLONIUS   The actors are come hither, my lord.

HAMLET   Buzz, buzz.

POLONIUS   Upon my honor—

HAMLET   Then came each actor on his ass—

POLONIUS   The best actors in the world, either for tragedy, comedy, 360
history, pastoral, pastoral-comical, historical-pastoral, tragical-
historical, tragical-comical-historical-pastoral, scene individable, or

---

2. urge
3. paid for a play plot
4. blows
5. During one of his labors Hercules assumed for a time the burden of the Titan
Atlas, who supported the heavens on his
shoulder. Also a reference to the effect on
business at Shakespeare's theater, the
Globe.
6. sneer

7. miniature
8. welcome
9. fashion
1. cordiality
2. A "hawk" is a plasterer's tool; Hamlet may also be using "handsaw" = hern-
shaw = heron.
3. wrappings for an infant
4. Roscius was the most famous actor of
classical Rome.

poem unlimited. Seneca cannot be too heavy nor Plautus too light.
For the law of writ and the liberty, these are the only men.[5]
HAMLET   O Jephtha, judge of Israel, what a treasure hadst thou![6] 365
POLONIUS   What a treasure had he, my lord?
HAMLET   Why—

> "One fair daughter, and no more,
> The which he loved passing well."

POLONIUS [*aside*]   Still on my daughter.   370
HAMLET   Am I not i' th' right, old Jephtha?
POLONIUS   If you call me Jephtha, my lord, I have a daughter that I
love passing well.
HAMLET   Nay, that follows not.
POLONIUS   What follows then, my lord?   375
HAMLET   Why—

> "As by lot, God wot"

and then, you know,

> "It came to pass, as most like it was."

The first row[7] of the pious chanson[8] will show you more, for look 380
where my abridgement[9] comes.

Enter the PLAYERS.

You are welcome, masters; welcome, all.—I am glad to see thee
well.—Welcome, good friends.—O, old friend! Why thy face is
valanced[1] since I saw thee last. Com'st thou to beard me in Denmark?—What, my young lady and mistress? By'r lady, your ladyship 385
is nearer to heaven than when I saw you last by the altitude of a
chopine.[2] Pray God your voice, like a piece of uncurrent gold, be not
cracked within the ring.—Masters, you are all welcome. We'll e'en
to't like French falconers, fly at anything we see. We'll have a speech
straight. Come give us a taste of your quality,[3] come a passionate 390
speech.
FIRST PLAYER   What speech, my good lord?
HAMLET   I heard thee speak me a speech once, but it was never **acted,**
or if it was, not above once, for the play, I remember, pleased not
the million; 'twas caviary[4] to the general.[5] But it was—as I received 395

5. Seneca and Plautus were Roman writers of tragedy and comedy, respectively. The "law of writ" refers to plays written according to such rules as the three unities; the "liberty" to those written otherwise.
6. To insure victory, Jephtha promised to sacrifice the first creature to meet him on his return. Unfortunately, his only daughter outstripped his dog and was the victim of his vow. The Biblical story is told in *Judges* 11.
7. stanza
8. song
9. that which cuts short by interrupting

1. fringed (with a beard)
2. A reference to the contemporary theatrical practice of using boys to play women's parts. The company's "lady" has grown in height by the size of a woman's thick-soled shoe, "chopine," since Hamlet saw him last. The next sentence refers to the possibility, suggested by his growth, that the young actor's voice may soon begin to change.
3. trade
4. caviar
5. masses

it, and others whose judgments in such matters cried in the top of[6] mine—an excellent play, well digested[7] in the scenes, set down with as much modesty as cunning. I remember one said there were no sallets[8] in the lines to make the matter savory, nor no matter in the phrase that might indict the author of affectation, but called it an 400 honest method, as wholesome as sweet, and by very much more handsome than fine. One speech in't I chiefly loved. 'Twas Æneas' tale to Dido, and thereabout of it especially where he speaks of Priam's slaughter.[9] If it live in your memory, begin at this line—let me see, let me see: 405

"The rugged Pyrrhus, like th' Hyrcanian beast"[1]—

'tis not so; it begins with Pyrrhus—

"The rugged Pyrrhus, he whose sable arms,
Black as his purpose, did the night resemble
When he lay couchéd in th' ominous horse,[2]   410
Hath now this dread and black complexion smeared
With heraldry more dismal; head to foot
Now is he total gules,[3] horridly tricked[4]
With blood of fathers, mothers, daughters, sons,
Baked and impasted[5] with the parching[6] streets,   415
That lend a tyrannous and a damnéd light
To their lord's murder. Roasted in wrath and fire,
And thus o'er-sizéd[7] with coagulate[8] gore,
With eyes like carbuncles, the hellish Pyrrhus
Old grandsire Priam seeks."   420

So proceed you.

POLONIUS   Fore God, my lord, well spoken, with good accent and good discretion.
FIRST PLAYER   "Anon he[9] finds him[1]
Striking too short at Greeks. His antique[2] sword,   425
Rebellious[3] to his arm, lies where it falls,
Repugnant to command. Unequal matched,
Pyrrhus at Priam drives, in rage strikes wide.
But with the whiff and wind of his fell sword
Th' unnervéd father falls. Then senseless[4] Ilium,   430
Seeming to feel this blow, with flaming top
Stoops[5] to his base, and with a hideous crash

6. were weightier than
7. arranged
8. spicy passages
9. Aeneas, fleeing with his band from fallen Troy (Ilium), arrives in Carthage, where he tells Dido, the Queen of Carthage, of the fall of Troy. Here he is describing the death of Priam, the aged king of Troy, at the hands of Pyrrhus, the son of the slain Achilles.
  1. tiger
  2. i.e., the Trojan horse

3. completely red
4. adorned
5. crusted
6. burning
7. glued over
8. clotted
9. Pyrrhus
1. Priam
2. which he used when young
3. refractory
4. without feeling
5. falls

Takes prisoner Pyrrhus' ear. For, lo! his sword,
Which was declining[6] on the milky head
Of reverend Priam, seemed i' th' air to stick.   435
So as a painted tyrant Pyrrhus stood,
And like a neutral to his will and matter,[7]
Did nothing.
But as we often see, against some storm,
A silence in the heavens, the rack[8] stand still,   440
The bold winds speechless, and the orb below
As hush as death, anon the dreadful thunder
Doth rend the region; so, after Pyrrhus' pause,
A rouséd vengeance sets him new awork,[9]
And never did the Cyclops' hammers fall   445
On Mars's armor, forged for proof eterne,[1]
With less remorse than Pyrrhus' bleeding sword
Now falls on Priam.
Out, out, thou strumpet, Fortune! All you gods,
In general synod take away her power,   450
Break all the spokes and fellies[2] from her wheel,
And bowl[3] the round nave[4] down the hill of heaven
As low as to the fiends."
POLONIUS   This is too long.
HAMLET   It shall to the barber's with your beard.—Prithee say on. 455
He's for a jig,[5] or a tale of bawdry, or he sleeps. Say on; come to
Hecuba.[6]
FIRST PLAYER   "But who, ah woe! had seen the mobled[7] queen—"
HAMLET   "The mobled queen"?
POLONIUS   That's good. "Mobled queen" is good.   460
FIRST PLAYER   "Run barefoot up and down, threat'ning the flames
With bisson rheum,[8] a clout[9] upon that head
Where late the diadem stood, and for a robe,
About her lank and all o'er-teeméd loins,
A blanket, in the alarm of fear caught up—   465
Who this had seen, with tongue in venom steeped,
'Gainst Fortune's state[1] would treason have pronounced.
But if the gods themselves did see her then,
When she saw Pyrrhus make malicious sport
In mincing[2] with his sword her husband's limbs,   470
The instant burst of clamor that she made,
Unless things mortal move them not at all,
Would have made milch[3] the burning eyes of heaven,
And passion in the gods."

6. about to fall
7. between his will and the fulfillment of it
8. clouds
9. to work
1. Mars, as befits a Roman war god, had armor made for him by the blacksmith god Vulcan and his assistants, the Cyclops. It was suitably impenetrable, of "proof eterne."
2. parts of the rim
3. roll
4. hub

5. a comic act
6. Hecuba was the wife of Priam and Queen of Troy. Her "loins" are described below as "o'erteemed" because of her unusual fertility. The number of her children varies in different accounts. but twenty is a safe minimum.
7. muffled (in a hood)
8. blinding tears
9. cloth
1. government
2. cutting up
3. tearful (*lit.* milk-giving)

POLONIUS Look whe'r[4] he has not turned his color, and has tears in's 475
eyes. Prithee no more.
HAMLET 'Tis well. I'll have thee speak out the rest of this soon.—
Good my lord, will you see the players well bestowed?[5] Do you
hear, let them be well used, for they are the abstract[6] and brief
chronicles of the time; after your death you were better have a bad 480
epitaph than their ill report while you live.
POLONIUS My lord, I will use them according to their desert.
HAMLET God's bodkin, man, much better. Use every man after his
desert, and who shall 'scape whipping? Use them after your own
honor and dignity. The less they deserve, the more merit is in your 485
bounty. Take them in.
POLONIUS Come, sirs.
HAMLET Follow him, friends. We'll hear a play tomorrow. [*Aside to*
FIRST PLAYER.] Dost thou hear me, old friend, can you play "The
Murder of Gonzago"? 490
FIRST PLAYER Ay, my lord.
HAMLET We'll ha't tomorrow night. You could for a need study a
speech of some dozen or sixteen lines which I would set down and
insert in't, could you not?
FIRST PLAYER Ay, my lord. 495
HAMLET Very well. Follow that lord, and look you mock him not.

Exeunt POLONIUS *and* PLAYERS.

My good friends, I'll leave you till night. You are welcome to
Elsinore.
ROSENCRANTZ Good my lord.

Exeunt ROSENCRANTZ *and* GUILDENSTERN.

HAMLET Ay, so God b'wi'ye. Now I am alone. 500
O, what a rogue and peasant slave am I!
Is it not monstrous that this player here,
But in a fiction, in a dream of passion,
Could force his soul so to his own conceit[7]
That from her working all his visage wanned;[8] 505
Tears in his eyes, distraction in his aspect,[9]
A broken voice, and his whole function suiting
With forms to his conceit? And all for nothing,
For Hecuba!
What's Hecuba to him or he to Hecuba, 510
That he should weep for her? What would he do
Had he the motive and the cue for passion
That I have? He would drown the stage with tears,
And cleave the general ear with horrid speech,
Make mad the guilty, and appal the free, 515
Confound the ignorant, and amaze indeed
The very faculties of eyes and ears.
Yet I,

4. whether
5. provided for
6. summary
7. imagination
8. grew pale
9. face

A dull and muddy-mettled[1] rascal, peak[2]
Like John-a-dreams,[3] unpregnant[4] of my cause,   520
And can say nothing; no, not for a king
Upon whose property and most dear life
A damned defeat was made. Am I a coward?
Who calls me villain, breaks my pate across,
Plucks off my beard and blows it in my face,   525
Tweaks me by the nose, gives me the lie i' th' throat
As deep as to the lungs? Who does me this?
Ha, 'swounds, I should take it; for it cannot be
But I am pigeon-livered and lack gall[5]
To make oppression bitter, or ere this   530
I should 'a fatted all the region kites[6]
With this slave's offal. Bloody, bawdy villain!
Remorseless, treacherous, lecherous, kindless[7] villain!
Why, what an ass am I! This is most brave,
That I, the son of a dear father murdered,   535
Prompted to my revenge by heaven and hell,
Must like a whore unpack[8] my heart with words,
And fall a-cursing like a very drab,
A scullion![9] Fie upon't! foh!
About, my brains. Hum—I have heard   540
That guilty creatures sitting at a play,
Have by the very cunning of the scene
Been struck so to the soul that presently
They have proclaimed[1] their malefactions;
For murder, though it have no tongue, will speak   545
With most miraculous organ. I'll have these players
Play something like the murder of my father
Before mine uncle. I'll observe his looks.
I'll tent[2] him to the quick. If 'a do blench,[3]
I know my course. The spirit that I have seen   550
May be a devil, and the devil hath power
T' assume a pleasing shape, yea, and perhaps
Out of my weakness and my melancholy,
As he is very potent with such spirits,
Abuses me to damn me. I'll have grounds   555
More relative[4] than this. The play's the thing
Wherein I'll catch the conscience of the king.   *Exit.*

1. dull-spirited
2. mope
3. a man dreaming
4. not quickened by
5. bitterness
6. birds of prey of the area
7. unnatural
8. relieve

9. In some versions of the play, the word "stallion," a slang term for a prostitute, appears in place of "scullion."
1. admitted
2. try
3. turn pale
4. conclusive

Act 3

SCENE 1: *A room in the castle. Enter* KING, QUEEN, POLONIUS, OPHELIA, ROSENCRANTZ *and* GUILDENSTERN.

KING   And can you by no drift of conference[5]
Get from him why he puts on this confusion,
Grating so harshly all his days of quiet
With turbulent[6] and dangerous lunacy?
ROSENCRANTZ   He does confess he feels himself distracted,   5
But from what cause 'a will by no means speak.
GUILDENSTERN   Nor do we find him forward[7] to be sounded,[8]
But with a crafty madness keeps aloof
When we would bring him on to some confession
Of his true state.
QUEEN   Did he receive you well?   10
ROSENCRANTZ   Most like a gentleman.
GUILDENSTERN   But with much forcing of his disposition.[9]
ROSENCRANTZ   Niggard of question, but of our demands[1]
Most free in his reply.
QUEEN   Did you assay[2] him
To any pastime?   15
ROSENCRANTZ   Madam, it so fell out that certain players
We o'er-raught[3] on the way. Of these we told him,
And there did seem in him a kind of joy
To hear of it. They are here about the court,
And as I think, they have already order   20
This night to play before him.
POLONIUS   'Tis most true,
And he beseeched me to entreat your majesties
To hear and see the matter.[4]
KING   With all my heart, and it doth much content me
To hear him so inclined.   25
Good gentlemen, give him a further edge,
And drive his purpose[5] into these delights.
ROSENCRANTZ   We shall, my lord.

Exeunt ROSENCRANTZ *and* GUILDENSTERN.

KING   Sweet Gertrude, leave us too,
For we have closely sent for Hamlet hither,
That he, as 'twere by accident, may here   30
Affront[6] Ophelia.
Her father and myself (lawful espials[7])
Will so bestow ourselves that, seeing unseen,
We may of their encounter frankly judge,

5. line of conversation
6. disturbing
7. eager
8. questioned
9. conversation
1. to our questions

2. tempt
3. passed
4. performance
5. sharpen his intention
6. confront
7. justified spies

And gather by him, as he is behaved,   35
If't be th' affliction of his love or no
That thus he suffers for.
QUEEN   I shall obey you.—
    And for your part, Ophelia, I do wish
    That your good beauties be the happy cause
    Of Hamlet's wildness. So shall I hope your virtues   40
    Will bring him to his wonted[8] way again,
    To both your honors.
OPHELIA   Madam, I wish it may.   *Exit* QUEEN.
POLONIUS   Ophelia, walk you here.—Gracious,[9] so please you,
    We will bestow ourselves.—[*To* OPHELIA.] Read on this book,
    That show of such an exercise[1] may color[2]   45
    Your loneliness.—We are oft to blame in this,
    'Tis too much proved, that with devotion's visage
    And pious action we do sugar o'er
    The devil himself.
KING [*aside*]   O, 'tis too true.
    How smart a lash that speech doth give my conscience!   50
    The harlot's cheek, beautied with plast'ring[3] art,
    Is not more ugly to the thing that helps it
    Than is my deed to my most painted word.
    O heavy burden!
POLONIUS   I hear him coming. Let's withdraw, my lord.   55

                              Exeunt KING *and* POLONIUS.

        Enter HAMLET.

HAMLET   To be, or not to be, that is the question:
    Whether 'tis nobler in the mind to suffer
    The slings and arrows of outrageous fortune,
    Or to take arms against a sea of troubles,
    And by opposing end them. To die, to sleep—   60
    No more; and by a sleep to say we end
    The heartache, and the thousand natural shocks
    That flesh is heir to. 'Tis a consummation
    Devoutly to be wished—to die, to sleep—
    To sleep, perchance to dream, ay there's the rub;   65
    For in that sleep of death what dreams may come
    When we have shuffled off this mortal coil[4]
    Must give us pause—there's the respect[5]
    That makes calamity of so long life.
    For who would bear the whips and scorns of time,   70
    Th' oppressor's wrong, the proud man's contumely,[6]
    The pangs of despised love, the law's delay,
    The insolence of office, and the spurns[7]
    That patient merit of th' unworthy takes,

[handwritten marginal note: tone change from end of Act 2]

---

8. usual   3. thickly painted
9. Majesty   4. turmoil
1. act of devotion   5. consideration
2. explain   6. insulting behavior
                                  7. rejections

When he himself might his quietus[8] make   75
With a bare bodkin?[9] Who would fardels[1] bear,
To grunt and sweat under a weary life,
But that the dread of something after death,
The undiscovered country, from whose bourn[2]
No traveller returns, puzzles the will,   80
And makes us rather bear those ills we have
Than fly to others that we know not of?
Thus conscience does make cowards of us all;
And thus the native[3] hue of resolution
Is sicklied o'er with the pale cast of thought,   85
And enterprises of great pitch[4] and moment[5]
With this regard their currents turn awry
And lose the name of action.—Soft you now,
The fair Ophelia.—Nymph, in thy orisons[6]
Be all my sins remembered.

OPHELIA   Good my lord,   90
How does your honor for this many a day?

HAMLET   I humbly thank you, well, well, well.

OPHELIA   My lord, I have remembrances of yours
That I have longed long to re-deliver.
I pray you now receive them.

HAMLET   No, not I,   95
I never gave you aught.

OPHELIA   My honored lord, you know right well you did,
And with them words of so sweet breath composed
As made the things more rich. Their perfume lost,
Take these again, for to the noble mind   100
Rich gifts wax[7] poor when givers prove unkind.
There, my lord.

HAMLET   Ha, ha! are you honest?[8]

OPHELIA   My lord?

HAMLET   Are you fair?   105

OPHELIA   What means your lordship?

HAMLET   That if you be honest and fair, your honesty should admit
no discourse to your beauty.

OPHELIA   Could beauty, my lord, have better commerce[9] than with
honesty?   110

HAMLET   Ay, truly, for the power of beauty will sooner transform
honesty from what it is to a bawd than the force of honesty can
translate beauty into his likeness. This was sometime a paradox, but
now the time gives it proof. I did love you once.

OPHELIA   Indeed, my lord, you made me believe so.   115

HAMLET   You should not have believed me, for virtue cannot so in-
oculate[1] our old stock but we shall relish of it. I loved you not.

OPHELIA   I was the more deceived.

---

8. settlement
9. dagger
1. burdens
2. boundary
3. natural
4. height

5. importance
6. prayers
7. become
8. chaste
9. intercourse
1. change by grafting

HAMLET   Get thee to a nunnery.[2] Why wouldst thou be a breeder of
sinners? I am myself indifferent[3] honest, but yet I could accuse me   120
of such things that it were better my mother had not borne me: I
am very proud, revengeful, ambitious, with more offences at my
beck[4] than I have thoughts to put them in, imagination to give them
shape, or time to act them in. What should such fellows as I do
crawling between earth and heaven? We are arrant[5] knaves all; be-   125
lieve none of us. Go thy ways to a nunnery. Where's your father?
OPHELIA   At home, my lord.
HAMLET   Let the doors be shut upon him, that he may play the fool
nowhere but in's own house. Farewell.
OPHELIA   O, help him, you sweet heavens!   130
HAMLET   If thou dost marry, I'll give thee this plague for thy dowry:
be thou as chaste as ice, as pure as snow, thou shalt not escape
calumny. Get thee to a nunnery, farewell. Or if thou wilt needs
marry, marry a fool, for wise men know well enough what monsters[6]
you make of them. To a nunnery, go, and quickly too. Farewell.   135
OPHELIA   Heavenly powers, restore him!
HAMLET   I have heard of your paintings well enough. God hath given
you one face, and you make yourselves another. You jig, you amble,
and you lisp;[7] you nickname God's creatures, and make your wanton-
ness your ignorance.[8] Go to, I'll no more on't, it hath made me mad.   140
I say we will have no more marriage. Those that are married already,
all but one, shall live. The rest shall keep as they are. To a nunnery,
go.   *Exit.*
OPHELIA   O, what a noble mind is here o'erthrown!
The courtier's, soldier's, scholar's, eye, tongue, sword,   145
Th' expectancy[9] and rose[1] of the fair state,
The glass[2] of fashion and the mould[3] of form,
Th' observed of all observers, quite quite down!
And I of ladies most deject and wretched,
That sucked the honey of his music[4] vows,   150
Now see that noble and most sovereign reason
Like sweet bells jangled, out of time and harsh;
That unmatched form and feature of blown[5] youth
Blasted with ecstasy. O, woe is me
T' have seen what I have seen, see what I see!   155

Enter KING *and* POLONIUS.

KING   Love! His affections do not that way tend,
Nor what he spake, though it lacked form a little,
Was not like madness. There's something in his soul
O'er which his melancholy sits on brood,[6]

And I do doubt[7] the hatch and the disclose[8]   160
Will be some danger; which to prevent,
I have in quick determination
Thus set it down: he shall with speed to England
For the demand of our neglected tribute.
Haply the seas and countries different,   165
With variable objects, shall expel
This something-settled matter in his heart
Whereon his brains still beating puts him thus
From fashion of himself. What think you on't?
POLONIUS   It shall do well. But yet do I believe   170
The origin and commencement of his grief
Sprung from neglected love.—How now, Ophelia?
You need not tell us what Lord Hamlet said,
We heard it all.—My lord, do as you please,
But if you hold it fit, after the play   175
Let his queen-mother all alone entreat him
To show his grief. Let her be round[9] with him,
And I'll be placed, so please you, in the ear[1]
Of all their conference. If she find him not,[2]
To England send him; or confine him where   180
Your wisdom best shall think.
KING   It shall be so.
Madness in great ones must not unwatched go.   *Exeunt.*

SCENE 2: *A public room in the castle. Enter* HAMLET *and three of the* PLAYERS.

HAMLET   Speak the speech, I pray you, as I pronounced it to you, trippingly on the tongue; but if you mouth it as many of our players do, I had as lief the town-crier spoke my lines. Nor do not saw the air too much with your hand thus, but use all gently, for in the very torrent, tempest, and as I may say, whirlwind of your passion, you must   5
acquire and beget a temperance that may give it smoothness. O, it offends me to the soul to hear a robustious[3] periwig-pated[4] fellow tear a passion to tatters, to very rags, to split the ears of the groundlings,[5] who for the most part are capable of[6] nothing but inexplicable dumb shows and noise. I would have such a fellow whipped for   10
o'erdoing Termagant. It out-herods Herod.[7] Pray you avoid it.
FIRST PLAYER   I warrant your honor.
HAMLET   Be not too tame neither, but let your own discretion be your tutor. Suit the action to the word, the word to the action, with this special observance, that you o'erstep not the modesty of nature;   15
for anything so o'erdone is from[8] the purpose of playing, whose end both at the first, and now, was and is, to hold as 'twere the mirror up

7. fear
8. result
9. direct
1. hearing
2. discover his problem
3. noisy
4. bewigged

5. the spectators who paid least
6. i.e., capable of understanding
7. Termagant, a "Saracen" deity, and the Biblical Herod were stock characters in popular drama noted for the excesses of sound and fury used by their interpreters.
8. contrary to

to nature, to show virtue her own feature, scorn her own image, and
the very age and body of the time his form and pressure.[9] Now this
overdone, or come tardy off, though it makes the unskilful[1] laugh,   20
cannot but make the judicious grieve, the censure[2] of the which one
must in your allowance o'erweigh a whole theatre of others. O, there
be players that I have seen play—and heard others praise, and that
highly—not to speak it profanely, that neither having th' accent of
Christians, nor the gait of Christian, pagan, nor man, have so strut-   25
ted and bellowed that I have thought some of nature's journeymen[3]
had made men, and not made them well, they imitated humanity so
abominably.

FIRST PLAYER   I hope we have reformed that indifferently[4] with us.

HAMLET   O, reform it altogether. And let those that play your clowns   30
speak no more than is set down for them, for there be of them that
will themselves laugh, to set on some quantity of barren[5] spectators
to laugh too, though in the meantime some necessary question of the
play be then to be considered. That's villainous, and shows a most
pitiful ambition in the fool that uses it. Go, make you ready.   35

Exeunt PLAYERS.

Enter POLONIUS, GUILDENSTERN, *and* ROSENCRANTZ.

How now, my lord? Will the king hear this piece of work?

POLONIUS   And the queen too, and that presently.

HAMLET   Bid the players make haste.   *Exit* POLONIUS.
Will you two help to hasten them?

ROSENCRANTZ   Ay, my lord.   *Exeunt they two.*   40

HAMLET   What, ho, Horatio!
Enter HORATIO.

HORATIO   Here, sweet lord, at your service.

HAMLET   Horatio, thou art e'en as just a man
As e'er my conversation coped[6] withal.

HORATIO   O my dear lord!

HAMLET   Nay, do not think I flatter,   45
For what advancement may I hope from thee,
That no revenue hast but thy good spirits
To feed and clothe thee? Why should the poor be flattered?
No, let the candied tongue lick absurd pomp,
And crook the pregnant[7] hinges of the knee   50
Where thrift[8] may follow fawning. Dost thou hear?
Since my dear soul was mistress of her choice
And could of men distinguish her election,
S'hath sealed thee for herself, for thou hast been
As one in suff'ring all that suffers nothing,   55
A man that Fortune's buffets and rewards

9. shape
1. ignorant
2. judgment
3. inferior craftsmen
4. somewhat

5. dull-witted
6. encountered
7. quick to bend
8. profit

Hast ta'en with equal thanks; and blest are those
Whose blood and judgment are so well commingled
That they are not a pipe[9] for Fortune's finger
To sound[1] what stop[2] she please. Give me that man   60
That is not passion's slave, and I will wear him
In my heart's core, ay, in my heart of heart,
As I do thee. Something too much of this.
There is a play tonight before the king.
One scene of it comes near the circumstance   65
Which I have told thee of my father's death.
I prithee, when thou seest that act afoot,
Even with the very comment[3] of thy soul
Observe my uncle. If his occulted[4] guilt
Do not itself unkennel[5] in one speech,   70
It is a damnéd ghost that we have seen,
And my imaginations are as foul
As Vulcan's stithy.[6] Give him heedful note,[7]
For I mine eyes will rivet to his face,
And after we will both our judgments join   75
In censure of his seeming.[8]

HORATIO   Well, my lord.
If 'a steal aught the whilst this play is playing,
And 'scape detecting, I will pay[9] the theft.

> *Enter Trumpets and Kettledrums,* KING, QUEEN, POLONIUS,
> OPHELIA, ROSENCRANTZ, GUILDENSTERN, *and other* LORDS *at-*
> *tendant.*

HAMLET   They are coming to the play. I must be idle.
Get you a place.   80
KING   How fares our cousin Hamlet?
HAMLET   Excellent, i' faith, of the chameleon's dish.[1] I eat the air,
promise-crammed. You cannot feed capons so.
KING   I have nothing with this answer, Hamlet. These words are not
mine.   85
HAMLET   No, nor mine now. [*To* POLONIUS.] My lord, you played once
i' th' university, you say?
POLONIUS   That did I, my lord, and was accounted a good actor.
HAMLET   What did you enact?
POLONIUS   I did enact Julius Cæsar. I was killed i' th' Capitol; Brutus   90
killed me.[2]
HAMLET   It was a brute part of him to kill so capital a calf there. Be
the players ready?

9. musical instrument
1. play
2. note
3. keenest observation
4. hidden
5. break loose
6. smithy
7. careful attention
8. manner

9. repay
1. A reference to a popular belief that
the chameleon subsisted on a diet of air.
Hamlet has deliberately misunderstood the
King's question.
2. The assassination of Julius Caesar by
Brutus and others is the subject of another
play by Shakespeare.

ROSENCRANTZ   Ay, my lord, they stay[3] upon your patience.[4]

QUEEN   Come hither, my dear Hamlet, sit by me.   95

HAMLET   No, good mother, here's metal more attractive.

POLONIUS [*to the* KING]   O, ho! do you mark that?

HAMLET   Lady, shall I lie in your lap?

> *Lying down at* OPHELIA's *feet.*

OPHELIA   No, my lord.

HAMLET   I mean, my head upon your lap?   100

OPHELIA   Ay, my lord.

HAMLET   Do you think I meant country matters?[5]

OPHELIA   I think nothing, my lord.

HAMLET   That's a fair thought to lie between maids' legs.

OPHELIA   What is, my lord?   105

HAMLET   Nothing.

OPHELIA   You are merry, my lord.

HAMLET   Who, I?

OPHELIA   Ay, my lord.

HAMLET   O God, your only jig-maker![6] What should a man do but be   110
merry? For look you how cheerfully my mother looks, and my father
died within's two hours.

OPHELIA   Nay, 'tis twice two months, my lord.

HAMLET   So long? Nay then, let the devil wear black, for I'll have a
suit of sables. O heavens! die two months ago, and not forgotten   115
yet? Then there's hope a great man's memory may outlive his life
half a year, but by'r lady 'a must build churches then, or else shall
'a suffer not thinking on, with the hobby-horse, whose epitaph is
"For O, for O, the hobby-horse is forgot!"[7]

tape 3 starts

The trumpets sound. Dumb Show follows. Enter a KING *and a*
QUEEN *very lovingly; the* QUEEN *embracing him and he her.
She kneels, and makes show of protestation unto him. He takes
her up, and declines[8] his head upon her neck. He lies him down
upon a bank of flowers; she, seeing him asleep, leaves him.
Anon come in another man, takes off his crown, kisses it, pours
poison in the sleeper's ears, and leaves him. The* QUEEN *returns,
finds the* KING *dead, makes passionate action. The* POISONER
*with some three or four come in again, seem to condole with
her. The dead body is carried away. The* POISONER *woos the*
QUEEN *with gifts; she seems harsh awhile, but in the end accepts
love.*   *Exeunt.*

OPHELIA   What means this, my lord?   120

HAMLET   Marry, this is miching mallecho;[9] it means mischief.

OPHELIA   Belike this show imports[1] the argument[2] of the play.

---

3. wait
4. leisure
5. Presumably, rustic misbehavior, but here and elsewhere in this exchange Hamlet treats Ophelia to some ribald double meanings.
6. writer of comic scenes
7. In traditional games and dances one of the characters was a man represented as riding a horse. The horse was made of something like cardboard and was worn about the "rider's" waist.
8. lays
9. sneaking crime
1. explains
2. plot

Enter PROLOGUE.

HAMLET   We shall know by this fellow. The players cannot keep counsel; they'll tell all.

OPHELIA   Will 'a tell us what this show meant?   125

HAMLET   Ay, or any show that you will show him. Be not you ashamed to show, he'll not shame to tell you what it means.

OPHELIA   You are naught,[3] you are naught. I'll mark[4] the play.

PROLOGUE   *For us, and for our tragedy,*
            Here stooping to your clemency,   130
            We beg your hearing patiently.   *Exit.*

HAMLET   Is this a prologue, or the posy[5] of a ring?

OPHELIA   'Tis brief, my lord.

HAMLET   As woman's love.

Enter the PLAYER KING *and* QUEEN.

PLAYER KING   *Full thirty times hath Phœbus' cart gone round*   135
    Neptune's salt wash and Tellus' orbéd ground,
    And thirty dozen moons with borrowed sheen[6]
    About the world have times twelve thirties been,
    Since love our hearts and Hymen did our hands
    Unite comutual[7] in most sacred bands.[8]   140

PLAYER QUEEN   *So many journeys may the sun and moon*
    Make us again count o'er ere love be done!
    But woe is me, you are so sick of late,
    So far from cheer and from your former state,
    That I distrust[9] you. Yet though I distrust,   145
    Discomfort you, my lord, it nothing must.
    For women's fear and love hold quantity,[1]
    In neither aught, or in extremity.[2]
    Now what my love is proof hath made you know,
    And as my love is sized,[3] my fear is so.   150
    Where love is great, the littlest doubts are fear;
    Where little fears grow great, great love grows there.

PLAYER KING   *Faith, I must leave thee, love, and shortly too;*
    My operant powers[4] their functions leave[5] to do.
    And thou shalt live in this fair world behind,   155
    Honored, beloved, and haply one as kind
    For husband shalt thou—

PLAYER QUEEN   *O, confound the rest!*
    Such love must needs be treason in my breast.

---

3. obscene
4. attend to
5. motto engraved inside
6. light
7. mutually
8. The speech contains several mythological references. "Phoebus" was a sun god, and his chariot or "cart" the sun. The "salt wash" of Neptune is the ocean; "Tellus" was an earth goddess, and her

"orbed ground" is the earth, or globe. Hymen was the god of marriage.
9. fear for
1. agree in weight
2. The lady means without regard to too much or too little.
3. in size
4. active forces
5. cease

In second husband let me be accurst!
None wed the second but who killed the first.[6]   160
HAMLET   That's wormwood.
PLAYER QUEEN   *The instances*[7] *that second marriage move*
Are base respects[8] *of thrift, but none of love.*
A second time I kill my husband dead,
When second husband kisses me in bed.   165
PLAYER KING   *I do believe you think what now you speak,*
But what we do determine oft we break.
Purpose is but the slave to memory,
Of violent birth, but poor validity;
Which now, like fruit unripe, sticks on the tree,   170
But fall unshaken when they mellow be.
Most necessary 'tis that we forget
To pay ourselves what to ourselves is debt.
What to ourselves in passion we propose,
The passion ending, doth the purpose lose.   175
The violence of either grief or joy
Their own enactures[9] *with themselves destroy.*
Where joy most revels, grief doth most lament;
Grief joys, joy grieves, on slender accident.
This world is not for aye,[1] *nor 'tis not strange*   180
That even our loves should with our fortunes change;
For 'tis a question left us yet to prove,
Whether love lead fortune, or else fortune love.
The great man down, you mark his favorite flies;
The poor advanced makes friends of enemies;   185
And hitherto doth love on fortune tend,
For who not needs shall never lack a friend,
And who in want a hollow[2] *friend doth try,*
Directly seasons him[3] *his enemy.*
But orderly to end where I begun,   190
Our wills and fates do so contrary run
That our devices[4] *still are overthrown;*
Our thoughts are ours, their ends none of our own.
So think thou wilt no second husband wed,
But die thy thoughts when thy first lord is dead.   195
PLAYER QUEEN   *Nor earth to me give food, nor heaven light,*
Sport and repose lock from me day and night,
To desperation turn my trust and hope,
An anchor's cheer[5] *in prison be my scope,*
Each opposite that blanks[6] *the face of joy*   200
Meet what I would have well, and it destroy,
Both here and hence[7] *pursue me lasting strife,*
If once a widow, ever I be wife!

6. Though there is some ambiguity, she seems to mean that the only kind of woman who would remarry is one who has killed or would kill her first husband.
7. causes
8. concerns
9. actions

1. eternal
2. false
3. ripens him into
4. plans
5. anchorite's food
6. blanches
7. in the next world

HAMLET If she should break it now!

PLAYER KING *'Tis deeply sworn. Sweet, leave me here awhile.* 205
My spirits grow dull, and fain I would beguile
The tedious day with sleep. *Sleeps.*

PLAYER QUEEN *Sleep rock thy brain,*
And never come mischance between us twain! *Exit.*

HAMLET Madam, how like you this play?

QUEEN The lady doth protest too much, methinks. 210

HAMLET O, but she'll keep her word.

KING Have you heard the argument? Is there no offence in't?

HAMLET No, no, they do but jest, poison in jest; no offence i' th'
world.

KING What do you call the play? 215

HAMLET "The Mouse-trap." Marry, how? Tropically.[8] This play is the
image of a murder done in Vienna. Gonzago is the duke's name; his
wife, Baptista. You shall see anon. 'Tis a knavish piece of work, but
what of that? Your majesty, and we that have free souls, it touches
us not. Let the galled jade wince, our withers are unwrung.[9] 220

Enter LUCIANUS.

This is one Lucianus, nephew to the king.

OPHELIA You are as good as a chorus, my lord.

HAMLET I could interpret between you and your love, if I could see
the puppets dallying.

OPHELIA You are keen, my lord, you are keen. 225

HAMLET It would cost you a groaning to take off mine edge.

OPHELIA Still better, and worse.

HAMLET So you mis-take your husbands.—Begin, murderer. Leave
thy damnable faces and begin. Come, the croaking raven doth bellow for revenge. 230

LUCIANUS *Thoughts black, hands apt, drugs fit, and time agreeing,*
Confederate season,[1] else no creature seeing,
Thou mixture rank, of midnight weeds collected,
With Hecate's ban thrice blasted, thrice infected,[2]
Thy natural magic[3] and dire property 235
On wholesome life usurps immediately.

Pours the poison in his ears.

HAMLET 'A poisons him i' th' garden for his estate. His name's Gonzago. The story is extant, and written in very choice Italian. You
shall see anon how the murderer gets the love of Gonzago's wife.

OPHELIA The king rises. 240

HAMLET What, frighted with false fire?

QUEEN How fares my lord?

POLONIUS Give o'er the play.

KING Give me some light. Away!

POLONIUS Lights, lights, lights! 245

8. figuratively
9. A "galled jade" is a horse, particularly one of poor quality, with a sore
back. The "withers" are the ridge between
a horse's shoulders; "unwrung withers" are
not chafed by the harness.

1. a helpful time for the crime
2. Hecate was a classical goddess of
witchcraft.
3. native power

Exeunt all but HAMLET *and* HORATIO.

HAMLET   Why, let the strucken deer go weep,
                   The hart ungalléd[4] play.
              For some must watch while some must sleep;
                   Thus runs the world away.
Would not this, sir, and a forest of feathers[5]—if the rest of my for-   250
tunes turn Turk with me—with two Provincial roses on my razed
shoes, get me a fellowship in a cry[6] of players?[7]

HORATIO   Half a share.

HAMLET   A whole one, I.

              For thou dost know, O Damon dear,[8]   255
                 This realm dismantled was
              Of Jove himself, and now reigns here
                 A very, very—peacock.

HORATIO   You might have rhymed.

HAMLET   O good Horatio, I'll take the ghost's word for a thousand   260
pound. Didst perceive?

HORATIO   Very well, my lord.

HAMLET   Upon the talk of the poisoning.

HORATIO   I did very well note[9] him.

HAMLET   Ah, ha! Come, some music. Come, the recorders.[1]   265
For if the king like not the comedy,
Why then, belike he likes it not, perdy.[2]
Come, some music.

Enter ROSENCRANTZ *and* GUILDENSTERN.

GUILDENSTERN   Good my lord, vouchsafe me a word with you.

HAMLET   Sir, a whole history.   270

GUILDENSTERN   The king, sir—

HAMLET   Ay, sir, what of him?

GUILDENSTERN   Is in his retirement[3] marvellous distempered.[4]

HAMLET   With drink, sir?

GUILDENSTERN   No, my lord, with choler.[5]   275

HAMLET   Your wisdom should show itself more richer to signify this
to the doctor, for for me to put him to his purgation[6] would perhaps
plunge him into more choler.

GUILDENSTERN   Good my lord, put your discourse[7] into some frame,[8]
and start not so wildly from my affair.   280

HAMLET   I am tame, sir. Pronounce.

4. uninjured
5. plumes
6. company
7. Hamlet asks Horatio if "this" recitation, accompanied with a player's costume,
including plumes and rosettes on shoes
which have been slashed for decorative effect, might not entitle him to become a
shareholder in a theatrical company in the
event that Fortune goes against him, "turn
Turk."
8. Damon was a common name for a
young man or a shepherd in lyric, espe-

cially pastoral poetry. Jove was the chief
god of the Romans. The Reader may supply for himself the rhyme referred to by
Horatio.
9. observe
1. wooden end-blown flutes
2. *par Dieu* (by God)
3. place to which he has retired
4. vexed
5. bile
6. treatment with a laxative
7. speech
8. order

GUILDENSTERN   The queen your mother, in most great affliction of spirit, hath sent me to you.

HAMLET   You are welcome.

GUILDENSTERN   Nay, good my lord, this courtesy is not of the right 285 breed. If it shall please you to make me a wholesome⁹ answer, I will do your mother's commandment. If not, your pardon and my return¹ shall be the end of my business.

HAMLET   Sir, I cannot.

ROSENCRANTZ   What, my lord? 290

HAMLET   Make you a wholesome answer; my wit's diseased. But, sir, such answer as I can make, you shall command, or rather, as you say, my mother. Therefore no more, but to the matter. My mother, you say—

ROSENCRANTZ   Then thus she says: your behavior hath struck her into 295 amazement and admiration.²

HAMLET   O wonderful son, that can so stonish a mother! But is there no sequel at the heels of this mother's admiration? Impart.³

ROSENCRANTZ   She desires to speak with you in her closet⁴ ere you go to bed. 300

HAMLET   We shall obey, were she ten times our mother. Have you any further trade⁵ with us?

ROSENCRANTZ   My lord, you once did love me.

HAMLET   And do still, by these pickers and stealers.⁶

ROSENCRANTZ   Good my lord, what is your cause of distemper? You 305 do surely bar the door upon your own liberty, if you deny your griefs to your friend.

HAMLET   Sir, I lack advancement.

ROSENCRANTZ   How can that be, when you have the voice of the king himself for your succession in Denmark? 310

HAMLET   Ay, sir, but "while the grass grows"—the proverb⁷ is something musty.

Enter the PLAYERS *with recorders.*

O, the recorders! Let me see one. To withdraw with you⁸—why do you go about to recover the wind of me, as if you would drive me into a toil?⁹ 315

GUILDENSTERN   O my lord, if my duty be too bold, my love is too unmannerly.

HAMLET   I do not well understand that. Will you play upon this pipe?¹

GUILDENSTERN   My lord, I cannot.

HAMLET   I pray you. 320

GUILDENSTERN   Believe me, I cannot.

HAMLET   I do beseech you.

GUILDENSTERN   I know no touch of it,² my lord.

9. reasonable
1. i.e., to the Queen
2. wonder
3. tell me
4. bedroom
5. business
6. hands
7. The proverb ends "the horse starves."

8. let me step aside
9. The figure is from hunting. "You will approach me with the wind blowing from me toward you in order to drive me into the net."
1. recorder
2. have no ability

HAMLET   It is as easy as lying. Govern[3] these ventages[4] with your
fingers and thumb, give it breath with your mouth, and it will 325
discourse most eloquent music. Look you, these are the stops.[5]

GUILDENSTERN   But these cannot I command to any utt'rance of harmony. I have not the skill.

HAMLET   Why, look you now, how unworthy a thing you make of me!
You would play upon me, you would seem to know my stops, you 330
would pluck out the heart of my mystery, you would sound[6] me
from my lowest note to the top of my compass[7]; and there is much
music, excellent voice, in this little organ, yet cannot you make it
speak. 'Sblood, do you think I am easier to be played on than a pipe?
Call me what instrument you will, though you can fret[8] me, you 335
cannot play upon me.

     Enter POLONIUS.

God bless you, sir!

POLONIUS   My lord, the queen would speak with you, and presently.[9]

HAMLET   Do you see yonder cloud that's almost in shape of a camel?

POLONIUS   By th' mass, and 'tis like a camel indeed.   340

HAMLET   Methinks it is like a weasel.

POLONIUS   It is backed like a weasel.

HAMLET   Or like a whale.

POLONIUS   Very like a whale.

HAMLET   Then I will come to my mother by and by. [*Aside.*] They 345
fool me to the top of my bent.[1]—I will come by and by.

POLONIUS   I will say so.   *Exit* POLONIUS.

HAMLET   "By and by" is easily said. Leave me, friends.

     Exeunt all but HAMLET.

'Tis now the very witching time of night,
When churchyards yawn, and hell itself breathes out   350
Contagion to this world. Now could I drink hot blood,
And do such bitter business as the day
Would quake to look on. Soft, now to my mother.
O heart, lose not thy nature; let not ever
The soul of Nero[2] enter this firm bosom.   355
Let me be cruel, not unnatural;
I will speak daggers to her, but use none.
My tongue and soul in this be hypocrites—
How in my words somever she be shent,[3]
To give them seals[4] never, my soul, consent!   *Exit.* 360

SCENE 3: *A room in the castle. Enter* KING, ROSENCRANTZ
and GUILDENSTERN.

---

3. cover and uncover
4. holes
5. wind-holes
6. play
7. range
8. "Fret" is used in a double sense, to annoy and to play a guitar or similar instrument using the "frets" or small bars on the neck.

9. at once
1. treat me as an utter fool
2. The Emperor Nero, known for his excesses, was believed to have been responsible for the death of his mother.
3. shamed
4. fulfillment in action

KING   I like him not,[5] nor stands it safe with us
To let his madness range.[6] Therefore prepare you.
I your commission will forthwith dispatch,
And he to England shall along with you.
The terms of our estate[7] may not endure   5
Hazard so near's as doth hourly grow
Out of his brows.

GUILDENSTERN   We will ourselves provide.[8]
Most holy and religious fear it is
To keep those many many bodies safe
That live and feed upon your majesty.   10

ROSENCRANTZ   The single and peculiar[9] life is bound
With all the strength and armor of the mind
To keep itself from noyance,[1] but much more
That spirit upon whose weal[2] depends and rests
The lives of many. The cess[3] of majesty   15
Dies not alone, but like a gulf[4] doth draw
What's near it with it. It is a massy[5] wheel
Fixed on the summit of the highest mount,
To whose huge spokes ten thousand lesser things
Are mortised and adjoined,[6] which when it falls,   20
Each small annexment, petty consequence,
Attends[7] the boist'rous ruin. Never alone
Did the king sigh, but with a general groan.

KING   Arm you, I pray you, to this speedy voyage,
For we will fetters put about this fear,   25
Which now goes too free-footed.

ROSENCRANTZ   We will haste us.

Exeunt ROSENCRANTZ *and* GUILDENSTERN.

Enter POLONIUS.

POLONIUS   My lord, he's going to his mother's closet.
Behind the arras I'll convey[8] myself
To hear the process.[9] I'll warrant she'll tax him home,[1]
And as you said, and wisely was it said,   30
'Tis meet that some more audience than a mother,
Since nature makes them partial, should o'erhear
The speech, of vantage.[2] Fare you well, my liege.
I'll call upon you ere you go to bed,
And tell you what I know.

KING   Thanks, dear my lord.   35

Exit POLONIUS.

5. distrust him
6. roam freely
7. condition of the state
8. equip (for the journey)
9. individual
1. harm
2. welfare
3. cessation

4. whirlpool
5. massive
6. attached
7. joins in
8. station
9. proceedings
1. sharply
2. from a position of vantage

O, my offence is rank, it smells to heaven;
It hath the primal eldest curse[3] upon't,
A brother's murder. Pray can I not,
Though inclination be as sharp as will.
My stronger guilt defeats my strong intent,   40
And like a man to double business[4] bound,
I stand in pause where I shall first begin,
And both neglect. What if this cursèd hand
Were thicker than itself with brothers' blood,
Is there not rain enough in the sweet heavens   45
To wash it white as snow? Whereto serves mercy
But to confront the visage of offence?
And what's in prayer but this twofold force,
To be forestallèd[5] ere we come to fall,
Or pardoned being down[6]? Then I'll look up.   50
My fault is past. But, O, what form of prayer
Can serve my turn? "Forgive me my foul murder"?
That cannot be, since I am still possessed
Of those effects[7] for which I did the murder—
My crown, mine own ambition, and my queen.   55
May one be pardoned and retain th' offence[8]?
In the corrupted currents of this world
Offence's gilded[9] hand may shove by justice,
And oft 'tis seen the wicked prize itself
Buys out the law. But 'tis not so above.   60
There is no shuffling; there the action[1] lies
In his true nature, and we ourselves compelled,
Even to the teeth and forehead of[2] our faults,
To give in evidence. What then? What rests[3]?
Try what repentance can. What can it not?   65
Yet what can it when one can not repent?
O wretched state! O bosom black as death!
O limèd[4] soul, that struggling to be free
Art more engaged! Help, angels! Make assay.
Bow, stubborn knees, and heart with strings of steel, 70
Be soft as sinews of the new-born babe.
All may be well.   *He kneels.*

    Enter HAMLET.

HAMLET   Now might I do it pat,[5] now 'a is a-praying,
    And now I'll do't—and so 'a goes to heaven,
    And so am I revenged. That would be scanned.[6]   75
    A villain kills my father, and for that,
    I, his sole son, do this same villain send
    To heaven.

3. i.e., of Cain
4. two mutually opposed interests
5. prevented (from sin)
6. having sinned
7. gains
8. i.e., benefits of the offence
9. bearing gold as a bribe

1. case at law
2. face-to-face with
3. remains
4. caught as with bird-lime
5. easily
6. deserves consideration

Why, this is hire and salary, not revenge.
'A took my father grossly, full of bread,[7]   80
With all his crimes broad blown,[8] as flush[9] as May;
And how his audit stands who knows save heaven?
But in our circumstance and course of thought
'Tis heavy with him; and am I then revenged
To take him in the purging of his soul,   85
When he is fit and seasoned[1] for his passage?
No.
Up, sword, and know thou a more horrid hent.[2]
When he is drunk, asleep, or in his rage,
Or in th' incestuous pleasure of his bed,   90
At game a-swearing, or about some act
That has no relish[3] of salvation in't—
Then trip him, that his heels may kick at heaven,
And that his soul may be as damned and black
As hell, whereto it goes. My mother stays.   95
This physic[4] but prolongs thy sickly days.   *Exit.*
KING [*rising*]   My words fly up, my thoughts remain below.
Words without thoughts never to heaven go.   *Exit.*

SCENE 4: *The Queen's chamber. Enter* QUEEN *and* POLONIUS.

POLONIUS   'A will come straight. Look you lay home to[5] him.
Tell him his pranks have been too broad[6] to bear with,
And that your grace hath screen'd[7] and stood between
Much heat and him. I'll silence me even here.
Pray you be round.
QUEEN   I'll warrant you. Fear[8] me not.   5
Withdraw, I hear him coming.

                                POLONIUS *goes behind the arras.*

        Enter HAMLET.

HAMLET   Now, mother, what's the matter?
QUEEN   Hamlet, thou hast thy father much offended.
HAMLET   Mother, you have my father much offended.
QUEEN   Come, come, you answer with an idle tongue.   10
HAMLET   Go, go, you question with a wicked tongue.
QUEEN   Why, how now, Hamlet?
HAMLET   What's the matter now?
QUEEN   Have you forgot me?
HAMLET   No, by the rood,[9] not so.
You are the queen, your husband's brother's wife,
And would it were not so, you are my mother.   15
QUEEN   Nay, then I'll set those to you that can speak.

---

7. in a state of sin and without fasting
8. full-blown
9. vigorous
1. ready
2. opportunity
3. flavor

4. medicine
5. be sharp with
6. outrageous
7. acted as a fire screen
8. doubt
9. cross

HAMLET   Come, come, and sit you down. You shall not budge.
You go not till I set you up a glass[1]
Where you may see the inmost part of you.
QUEEN   What wilt thou do? Thou wilt not murder me?   20
Help, ho!
POLONIUS [*behind*]   What, ho! help!
HAMLET [*draws*]   How now, a rat?
Dead for a ducat, dead!

Kills POLONIUS *with a pass through the arras.*

POLONIUS [*behind*]   O, I am slain!   25
QUEEN   O me, what hast thou done?
HAMLET   Nay, I know not.
Is it the king?
QUEEN   O, what a rash and bloody deed is this!
HAMLET   A bloody deed!—almost as bad, good mother,
As kill a king and marry with his brother.   30
QUEEN   As kill a king?
HAMLET   Ay, lady, it was my word.

Parting the arras.

Thou wretched, rash, intruding fool, farewell!
I took thee for thy better. Take thy fortune.
Thou find'st to be too busy[2] is some danger.—
Leave wringing of your hands. Peace, sit you down   35
And let me wring your heart, for so I shall
If it be made of penetrable stuff,
If damnéd custom have not brazed it[3] so
That it be proof[4] and bulwark against sense.[5]
QUEEN   What have I done that thou dar'st wag thy tongue   40
In noise so rude against me?
HAMLET   Such an act
That blurs the grace and blush of modesty,
Calls virtue hypocrite, takes off the rose
From the fair forehead of an innocent love,
And sets a blister[6] there, makes marriage-vows   45
As false as dicers' oaths. O, such a deed
As from the body of contraction[7] plucks
The very soul, and sweet religion makes
A rhapsody of words. Heaven's face does glow
And this solidity and compound mass[8]   50
With heated visage, as against the doom[9]—
Is thought-sick at the act.
QUEEN   Ay me, what act,
That roars so loud and thunders in the index[1]?
HAMLET   Look here upon this picture[2] and on this,

---

1. mirror
2. officious
3. plated it with brass
4. armor
5. feeling
6. brand

7. the marriage contract
8. meaningless mass (Earth)
9. Judgment Day
1. table of contents
2. portrait

The counterfeit presentment of two brothers.   55
See what a grace was seated on this brow:
Hyperion's curls, the front[3] of Jove himself,
An eye like Mars, to threaten and command,
A station[4] like the herald Mercury[5]
New lighted[6] on a heaven-kissing hill—   60
A combination and a form indeed
Where every god did seem to set his seal,[7]
To give the world assurance of a man.
This was your husband. Look you now what follows.
Here is your husband, like a mildewed ear   65
Blasting his wholesome brother. Have you eyes?
Could you on this fair mountain leave to feed,
And batten[8] on this moor? Ha! have you eyes?
You cannot call it love, for at your age
The heyday in the blood is tame, it's humble,   70
And waits upon the judgment, and what judgment
Would step from this to this? Sense sure you have,
Else could you not have motion, but sure that sense
Is apoplexed[9] for madness would not err,
Nor sense to ecstasy was ne'er so thralled   75
But it reserved some quantity[1] of choice
To serve in such a difference. What devil was't
That thus hath cozened[2] you at hoodman-blind[3]?
Eyes without feeling, feeling without sight,
Ears without hands or eyes, smelling sans[4] all,   80
Or but a sickly part of one true sense
Could not so mope.[5] O shame! where is thy blush?
Rebellious hell,
If thou canst mutine[6] in a matron's bones,
To flaming youth let virtue be as wax   85
And melt in her own fire. Proclaim no shame
When the compulsive ardor gives the charge,[7]
Since frost itself as actively doth burn,
And reason panders[8] will.
QUEEN   O Hamlet, speak no more!
Thou turn'st my eyes into my very soul;   90
And there I see such black and grainéd[9] spots
As will not leave their tinct.[1]
HAMLET   Nay, but to live
In the rank sweat of an enseaméd[2] bed,
Stewed in corruption, honeying and making love
Over the nasty sty—

---

3. forehead
4. bearing
5. Mercury was a Roman god who
served as the messenger of the gods.
6. newly alighted
7. mark of approval
8. feed greedily
9. paralyzed
1. power
2. cheated

3. blindman's buff
4. without
5. be stupid
6. commit mutiny
7. attacks
8. pimps for
9. ingrained
1. lose their color
2. greasy

QUEEN   O, speak to me no more!   95
  These words like daggers enter in my ears;
  No more, sweet Hamlet.
HAMLET   A murderer and a villain,
  A slave that is not twentieth part the tithe[3]
  Of your precedent lord,[4] a vice of kings,[5]
  A cutpurse[6] of the empire and the rule,   100
  That from a shelf the precious diadem stole
  And put it in his pocket—
QUEEN   No more.

          Enter GHOST.

HAMLET   A king of shreds and patches—
  Save me and hover o'er me with your wings,   105
  You heavenly guards! What would your gracious figure?
QUEEN   Alas, he's mad.
HAMLET   Do you not come your tardy[7] son to chide,
  That lapsed in time and passion lets go by
  Th' important acting of your dread command?   110
  O, say!
GHOST   Do not forget. This visitation
  Is but to whet thy almost blunted purpose.
  But look, amazement on thy mother sits.
  O, step between her and her fighting soul!   115
  Conceit[8] in weakest bodies strongest works.
  Speak to her, Hamlet.
HAMLET   How is it with you, lady?
QUEEN   Alas, how is't with you,
  That you do bend[9] your eye on vacancy,
  And with th' incorporal air do hold discourse?   120
  Forth at your eyes your spirits wildly peep,
  And as the sleeping soldiers in th' alarm,
  Your bedded hairs like life in excrements[1]
  Start up and stand an end. O gentle son,
  Upon the heat and flame of thy distemper   125
  Sprinkle cool patience. Whereon do you look?
HAMLET   On him, on him! Look you how pale he glares.
  His form and cause conjoined,[2] preaching to stones,
  Would make them capable.[3]—Do not look upon me,
  Lest with piteous action you convert   130
  My stern effects.[4] Then what I have to do
  Will want true color—tears perchance for blood.
QUEEN   To whom do you speak this?
HAMLET   Do you see nothing there?
QUEEN   Nothing at all, yet all that is I see.   135
HAMLET   Nor did you nothing hear?

3. one-tenth
4. first husband
5. The "Vice," a common figure in the popular drama, was a clown or buffoon.
6. pickpocket
7. slow to act
8. imagination
9. turn
1. nails and hair
2. working together
3. of responding
4. deeds

QUEEN   No, nothing but ourselves.
HAMLET   Why, look you there. Look how it steals away.
My father, in his habit⁵ as he lived!
Look where he goes even now out at the portal.   *Exit* GHOST. ¹⁴⁰
QUEEN   This is the very coinage⁶ of your brain.
This bodiless creation ecstasy⁷
Is very cunning⁸ in.
HAMLET   My pulse as yours doth temperately keep time,
And makes as healthful music. It is not madness   ¹⁴⁵
That I have uttered. Bring me to the test,
And I the matter will re-word, which madness
Would gambol⁹ from. Mother, for love of grace,
Lay not that flattering unction¹ to your soul,
That not your trespass but my madness speaks.   ¹⁵⁰
It will but skin and film the ulcerous place
Whiles rank corruption, mining² all within,
Infects unseen. Confess yourself to heaven,
Repent what's past, avoid what is to come,
And do not spread the compost on the weeds,   ¹⁵⁵
To make them ranker. Forgive me this my virtue,
For in the fatness of these pursy³ times
Virtue itself of vice must pardon beg,
Yea, curb⁴ and woo for leave to do him good.
QUEEN   O Hamlet, thou hast cleft my heart in twain.   ¹⁶⁰
HAMLET   O, throw away the worser part of it,
And live the purer with the other half.
Good night—but go not to my uncle's bed.
Assume a virtue, if you have it not.
That monster custom⁵ who all sense doth eat   ¹⁶⁵
Of habits evil, is angel yet in this,
That to the use of actions fair and good
He likewise gives a frock or livery
That aptly⁶ is put on. Refrain tonight,
And that shall lend a kind of easiness   ¹⁷⁰
To the next abstinence; the next more easy;
For use almost can change the stamp of nature,
And either curb the devil, or throw him out
With wondrous potency. Once more, good night,
And when you are desirous to be blest,   ¹⁷⁵
I'll blessing beg of you. For this same lord
I do repent; but heaven hath pleased it so,
To punish me with this, and this with me,
That I must be their scourge and minister.
I will bestow⁷ him and will answer well   ¹⁸⁰
The death I gave him. So, again, good night.
I must be cruel only to be kind.

5. costume
6. invention
7. madness
8. skilled
9. shy away
1. ointment

2. undermining
3. bloated
4. bow
5. habit
6. easily
7. dispose of

Thus bad begins and worse remains behind.
One word more, good lady.

QUEEN   What shall I do?

HAMLET   Not this, by no means, that I bid you do: 185
Let the bloat[8] king tempt you again to bed,
Pinch wanton[9] on your cheek, call you his mouse,
And let him, for a pair of reechy[1] kisses,
Or paddling in your neck with his damned fingers,
Make you to ravel[2] all this matter out,   190
That I essentially am not in madness,
But mad in craft. 'Twere good you let him know,
For who that's but a queen, fair, sober, wise,
Would from a paddock,[3] from a bat, a gib,[4]
Such dear concernings hide? Who would so do?   195
No, in despite of sense and secrecy,
Unpeg the basket on the house's top,
Let the birds fly, and like the famous ape,
To try conclusions, in the basket creep
And break your own neck down.[5]   200

QUEEN   Be thou assured, if words be made of breath
And breath of life, I have no life to breathe
What thou hast said to me.

HAMLET   I must to England; you know that?

QUEEN   Alack,
I had forgot. 'Tis so concluded on.   205

HAMLET   There's letters sealed, and my two school-fellows,
Whom I will trust as I will adders fanged,
They bear the mandate[6]; they must sweep[7] my way
And marshal me to knavery. Let it work,
For 'tis the sport to have the enginer   210
Hoist with his own petar; and't shall go hard
But I will delve[8] one yard below their mines
And blow them at the moon. O, 'tis most sweet
When in one line two crafts directly meet.[9]
This man shall set me packing.   215
I'll lug the guts into the neighbor room.
Mother, good night. Indeed, this counsellor
Is now most still, most secret, and most grave,
Who was in life a foolish prating knave.
Come sir, to draw toward an end with you.   220
Good night, mother.

Exit the QUEEN. *Then exit* HAMLET *tugging* POLONIUS.

8. bloated
9. lewdly
1. foul
2. reveal
3. toad
4. tomcat
5. Apparently a reference to a now lost fable in which an ape, finding a basket containing a cage of birds on a housetop, opens the cage. The birds fly away. The ape, thinking that if he were in the basket he too could fly, enters, jumps out, and breaks his neck.

6. command
7. prepare
8. dig
9. The "enginer" or engineer is a military man who is here described as being blown up by a bomb of his own construction, "hoist with his own petar." The military figure continues in the succeeding lines where Hamlet describes himself as digging a countermine or tunnel beneath the one Claudius is digging to defeat Hamlet. In line 214 the two tunnels unexpectedly meet.

Act 4

SCENE 1: *A room in tne castle. Enter* KING, QUEEN, ROSENCRANTZ *and* GUILDENSTERN.

KING   There's matter in these sighs, these profound heaves,
You must translate[1]; 'tis fit we understand them.
Where is your son?
QUEEN   Bestow this place on us a little while.

Exeunt ROSENCRANTZ *and* GUILDENSTERN.

Ah, mine own lord, what have I seen tonight!   5
KING   What, Gertrude? How does Hamlet?
QUEEN   Mad as the sea and wind when both contend
Which is the mightier. In his lawless fit,
Behind the arras hearing something stir,
Whips out his rapier, cries "A rat, a rat!"   10
And in this brainish apprehension[2] kills
The unseen good old man.
KING   O heavy deed!
It had been so with us had we been there.
His liberty is full of threats to all—
To you yourself, to us, to every one.   15
Alas, how shall this bloody deed be answered?
It will be laid to us, whose providence[3]
Should have kept short, restrained, and out of haunt,[4]
This mad young man. But so much was our love,
We would not understand what was most fit;   20
But, like the owner of a foul disease,
To keep it from divulging, let it feed
Even on the pith of life. Where is he gone?
QUEEN   To draw apart the body he hath killed,
O'er whom his very madness, like some ore   25
Among a mineral of metals base,
Shows itself pure: 'a weeps for what is done.
KING   O Gertrude, come away!
The sun no sooner shall the mountains touch
But we will ship him hence, and this vile deed   30
We must with all our majesty and skill
Both countenance and excuse. Ho, Guildenstern!

Enter ROSENCRANTZ *and* GUILDENSTERN.

Friends both, go join you with some further aid.
Hamlet in madness hath Polonius slain,
And from his mother's closet hath he dragged him.   35
Go seek him out; speak fair, and bring the body
Into the chapel. I pray you haste in this.

1. explain   3. prudence
2. insane notion   4. away from court

Exeunt ROSENCRANTZ *and* GUILDENSTERN.

Come, Gertrude, we'll call up our wisest friends
And let them know both what we mean to do
And what's untimely done;   40
Whose whisper o'er the world's diameter,
As level[5] as the cannon to his blank,[6]
Transports his poisoned shot—may miss our name,
And hit the woundless air. O, come away!
My soul is full of discord and dismay.   *Exeunt.* 45

SCENE 2: *A passageway. Enter* HAMLET.

HAMLET   Safely stowed.—But soft, what noise? Who calls on Hamlet?
O, here they come.

Enter ROSENCRANTZ, GUILDENSTERN, *and* OTHERS.

ROSENCRANTZ   What have you done, my lord, with the dead body?
HAMLET   Compounded it with dust, whereto 'tis kin.
ROSENCRANTZ   Tell us where 'tis, that we may take it thence   5
And bear it to the chapel.
HAMLET   Do not believe it.
ROSENCRANTZ   Believe what?
HAMLET   That I can keep your counsel and not mine own. Besides, to
be demanded of[7] a sponge—what replication[8] should be made by   10
the son of a king?
ROSENCRANTZ   Take you me for a sponge, my lord?
HAMLET   Ay, sir, that soaks up the king's countenance,[9] his rewards,
his authorities. But such officers do the king best service in the end.
He keeps them like an apple in the corner of his jaw, first mouthed   15
to be last swallowed. When he needs what you have gleaned, it is
but squeezing you and, sponge, you shall be dry again.
ROSENCRANTZ   I understand you not, my lord.
HAMLET   I am glad of it. A knavish speech sleeps in a foolish ear.
ROSENCRANTZ   My lord, you must tell us where the body is, and go   20
with us to the king.
HAMLET   The body is with the king, but the king is not with the body.
The king is a thing—
GUILDENSTERN   A thing, my lord!
HAMLET   Of nothing. Bring me to him. Hide fox, and all after.[1]   25
                                                          Exeunt.

SCENE 3: *A room in the castle. Enter* KING.

KING   I have sent to seek him, and to find the body.
How dangerous is it that this man goes loose!
Yet must not we put the strong law on him.
He's loved of the distracted[2] multitude,

5. direct   9. favor
6. mark   1. Apparently a reference to a children's
7. questioned by   game like hide-and-seek.
8. answer   2. confused

Who like not in their judgment but their eyes,   5
And where 'tis so, th' offender's scourge³ is weighed,
But never the offence. To bear all smooth and even,
This sudden sending him away must seem
Deliberate pause.⁴ Diseases desperate grown
By desperate appliance are relieved,   10
Or not at all.

Enter ROSENCRANTZ, GUILDENSTERN, *and all the rest.*

How now! what hath befall'n?
ROSENCRANTZ   Where the dead body is bestowed, my lord,
We cannot get from him.
KING   But where is he?
ROSENCRANTZ   Without,⁵ my lord; guarded, to know⁶ your pleasure.
KING   Bring him before us.
ROSENCRANTZ   Ho! bring in the lord.   15

They enter with HAMLET.

KING   Now, Hamlet, where's Polonius?
HAMLET   At supper.
KING   At supper? Where?
HAMLET   Not where he eats, but where 'a is eaten. A certain convoca-
tion⁷ of politic⁸ worms are e'en at him. Your worm is your only   20
emperor for diet. We fat all creatures else to fat us, and we fat
ourselves for maggots. Your fat king and your lean beggar is but
variable service—two dishes, but to one table. That's the end.
KING   Alas, alas!
HAMLET   A man may fish with the worm that hath eat of a king, and   25
eat of the fish that hath fed of that worm.
KING   What dost thou mean by this?
HAMLET   Nothing but to show you how a king may go a progress
through the guts of a beggar.
KING   Where is Polonius?   30
HAMLET   In heaven. Send thither to see. If your messenger find him
not there, seek him i' th' other place yourself. But if, indeed, you find
him not within this month, you shall nose⁹ him as you go up the
stairs into the lobby.
KING [*to* ATTENDANTS]   Go seek him there.   35
HAMLET   'A will stay till you come.   *Exeunt* ATTENDANTS.
KING   Hamlet, this deed, for thine especial safety—
Which we do tender,¹ as we dearly² grieve
For that which thou hast done—must send thee hence
With fiery quickness. Therefore prepare thyself.   40
The bark is ready, and the wind at help,
Th' associates tend, and everything is bent
For England.

3. punishment
4. i.e., not an impulse
5. outside
6. await
7. gathering

8. statesmanlike
9. smell
1. consider
2. deeply

HAMLET   For England?
KING   Ay, Hamlet.
HAMLET   Good.
KING   So it is, if thou knew'st our purposes.
HAMLET   I see a cherub that sees them. But come, for England!   45
  Farewell, dear mother.
KING   Thy loving father, Hamlet.
HAMLET   My mother. Father and mother is man and wife, man and
  wife is one flesh. So, my mother. Come, for England.   *Exit.*
KING   Follow him at foot[3]; tempt him with speed aboard.   50
  Delay it not; I'll have him hence tonight.
  Away! for everything is sealed and done
  That else leans on th' affair. Pray you make haste.

                            Exeunt all but the KING.

  And, England, if my love thou hold'st at aught—
  As my great power thereof may give thee sense,[4]   55
  Since yet thy cicatrice[5] looks raw and red
  After the Danish sword, and thy free awe
  Pays homage to us—thou mayst not coldly set[6]
  Our sovereign process,[7] which imports at full
  By letters congruing[8] to that effect   60
  The present death of Hamlet. Do it, England,
  For like the hectic[9] in my blood he rages,
  And thou must cure me. Till I know 'tis done,
  Howe'er my haps, my joys were ne'er begun.   *Exit.*

    SCENE 4: *Near Elsinore. Enter* FORTINBRAS *with his army.*

FORTINBRAS   Go, captain, from me greet the Danish king.
  Tell him that by his license Fortinbras
  Craves the conveyance[1] of a promised march
  Over his kingdom. You know the rendezvous.
  If that his majesty would aught with us,   5
  We shall express our duty in his eye,[2]
  And let him know so.
CAPTAIN   I will do't, my lord.
FORTINBRAS   Go softly on.   *Exeunt all but the* CAPTAIN.

    Enter HAMLET, ROSENCRANTZ, GUILDENSTERN, *and* OTHERS.

HAMLET   Good sir, whose powers are these?
CAPTAIN   They are of Norway, sir.   10
HAMLET   How purposed, sir, I pray you?
CAPTAIN   Against some part of Poland.
HAMLET   Who commands them, sir?
CAPTAIN   The nephew to old Norway, Fortinbras.

---

3. closely   8. agreeing
4. of its value   9. chronic fever
5. wound scar   1. escort
6. set aside   2. presence
7. mandate

HAMLET   Goes it against the main[3] of Poland, sir,   15
Or for some frontier?
CAPTAIN   Truly to speak, and with no addition,[4]
We go to gain a little patch of ground
That hath in it no profit but the name.
To pay five ducats,[5] five, I would not farm it;   20
Nor will it yield to Norway or the Pole
A ranker[6] rate should it be sold in fee.[7]
HAMLET   Why, then the Polack never will defend it.
CAPTAIN   Yes, it is already garrisoned.
HAMLET   Two thousand souls and twenty thousand ducats   25
Will not debate the question of this straw.
This is th' imposthume[8] of much wealth and peace,
That inward breaks, and shows no cause without
Why the man dies. I humbly thank you, sir.
CAPTAIN   God b'wi'ye, sir.   *Exit.*
ROSENCRANTZ   Will't please you go, my lord?   30
HAMLET   I'll be with you straight. Go a little before.

Exeunt all but HAMLET.

How all occasions do inform against me,
And spur my dull revenge! What is a man,
If his chief good and market[9] of his time
Be but to sleep and feed? A beast, no more.   35
Sure he that made us with such large discourse,[1]
Looking before and after, gave us not
That capability and godlike reason
To fust[2] in us unused. Now, whether it be
Bestial oblivion, or some craven scruple   40
Of thinking too precisely on th' event[3]—
A thought which, quartered, hath but one part wisdom
And ever three parts coward—I do not know
Why yet I live to say "This thing's to do,"
Sith[4] I have cause, and will, and strength, and means,   45
To do't. Examples gross as earth exhort me.
Witness this army of such mass and charge,[5]
Led by a delicate and tender prince,
Whose spirit, with divine ambition puffed,
Makes mouths at[6] the invisible event,   50
Exposing what is mortal and unsure
To all that fortune, death, and danger dare,
Even for an eggshell. Rightly to be great
Is not to stir without great argument,
But greatly to find quarrel in a straw   55

3. central part
4. exaggeration
5. i.e., in rent
6. higher
7. outright
8. abscess
9. occupation

1. ample reasoning power
2. grow musty
3. outcome
4. since
5. expense
6. scorns

When honor's at the stake. How stand I then,
That have a father killed, a mother stained,
Excitements of my reason and my blood,
And let all sleep, while to my shame I see
The imminent death of twenty thousand men   60
That for a fantasy and trick of fame
Go to their graves like beds, fight for a plot
Whereon the numbers cannot try the cause,
Which is not tomb enough and continent
To hide the slain?[7] O, from this time forth,   65
My thoughts be bloody, or be nothing worth!   *Exit.*

SCENE 5: *A room in the castle. Enter* QUEEN, HORATIO *and a*
GENTLEMAN.

QUEEN   I will not speak with her.
GENTLEMAN   She is importunate, indeed distract.
　Her mood will needs be pitied.
QUEEN　　　　　　　　　　　　What would she have?
GENTLEMAN   She speaks much of her father, says she hears
　There's tricks i' th' world, and hems, and beats her heart,   5
　Spurns enviously at straws,[8] speaks things in doubt
　That carry but half sense. Her speech is nothing,
　Yet the unshaped use of it doth move
　The hearers to collection[9]; they yawn at it,
　And botch the words up fit to their own thoughts,   10
　Which, as her winks and nods and gestures yield them,
　Indeed would make one think there might be thought,
　Though nothing sure, yet much unhappily.
HORATIO   'Twere good she were spoken with, for she may strew
　Dangerous conjectures in ill-breeding minds.   15
QUEEN   Let her come in.   *Exit* GENTLEMAN.
　[*Aside.*] To my sick soul, as sin's true nature is,
　Each toy[1] seems prologue to some great amiss.[2]
　So full of artless jealousy is guilt,
　It spills itself in fearing to be spilt.   20

　　　　Enter OPHELIA *distracted.*

OPHELIA   Where is the beauteous majesty of Denmark?
QUEEN   How now, Ophelia!
OPHELIA　　　　　　How should I your true love know   *She sings.*
　　　　　　From another one?
　　　　　　By his cockle hat and staff,[3]   25
　　　　　　And his sandal shoon.[4]
QUEEN   Alas, sweet lady, what imports this song?

---

7. The plot of ground involved is so
small that it cannot contain the number of
men involved in fighting nor furnish burial
space for the number of those who will die.
8. takes offense at trifles
9. an attempt to order
1. trifle

2. catastrophe
3. A "cockle hat," one decorated with a
shell, indicated that the wearer had made a
pilgrimage to the shrine of St. James at
Compostela in Spain. The staff also marked
the carrier as a pilgrim.
4. shoes

OPHELIA   Say you? Nay, pray you mark.

> He is dead and gone, lady,
>   He is dead and gone;
> At his head a grass-green turf,
>   At his heels a stone.

O, ho!

QUEEN   Nay, but, Ophelia—

OPHELIA   Pray you mark.
> White his shroud as the mountain snow—

Enter KING.

QUEEN   Alas, look here, my lord.

OPHELIA   Larded all with sweet flowers;
> Which bewept to the grave did not go
>   With true-love showers.

KING   How do you, pretty lady?

OPHELIA   Well, God dild[5] you! They say the owl was a baker's daughter. Lord, we know what we are, but know not what we may be. God be at your table!

KING   Conceit[6] upon her father.

OPHELIA   Pray let's have no words of this, but when they ask you what it means, say you this:

> Tomorrow is Saint Valentine's day,
>   All in the morning betime,
> And I a maid at your window,
>   To be your Valentine.
> Then up he rose, and donn'd his clo'es,
>   And dupped[7] the chamber-door,
> Let in the maid, that out a maid
>   Never departed more.

KING   Pretty Ophelia!

OPHELIA   Indeed, without an oath, I'll make an end on't.

> By Gis[8] and by Saint Charity,
>   Alack, and fie for shame!
> Young men will do't, if they come to't;
>   By Cock,[9] they are to blame.
> Quoth she "Before you tumbled me,
>   You promised me to wed."

He answers:

> "So would I 'a done, by yonder sun,
>   An thou hadst not come to my bed."

KING   How long hath she been thus?

OPHELIA   I hope all will be well. We must be patient, but I cannot choose but weep to think they would lay him i' th' cold ground. My brother shall know of it, and so I thank you for your good counsel.

5. yield
6. thought
7. opened

8. Jesus
9. God

Come, my coach! Good night, ladies, good night. Sweet ladies, good 70
night, good night.   *Exit.*

KING   Follow her close; give her good watch, I pray you.

Exeunt HORATIO *and* GENTLEMAN.

O, this is the poison of deep grief; it springs
All from her father's death, and now behold!
O Gertrude, Gertrude!   75
When sorrows come, they come not single spies,
But in battalions: first, her father slain;
Next, your son gone, and he most violent author
Of his own just remove; the people muddied,[1]
Thick and unwholesome in their thoughts and whispers   80
For good Polonius' death; and we have done but greenly[2]
In hugger-mugger[3] to inter him; poor Ophelia
Divided from herself and her fair judgment,
Without the which we are pictures, or mere beasts;
Last, and as much containing as all these,   85
Her brother is in secret come from France,
Feeds on his wonder, keeps himself in clouds,
And wants not buzzers to infect his ear
With pestilent speeches of his father's death,
Wherein necessity, of matter beggared,[4]   90
Will nothing stick[5] our person to arraign[6]
In ear and ear.[7] O my dear Gertrude, this,
Like to a murd'ring piece,[8] in many places
Gives me superfluous death. Attend,   *A noise within.*

Enter a MESSENGER.

Where are my Switzers[9]? Let them guard the door.   95
What is the matter?
MESSENGER   Save yourself, my lord.
The ocean, overpeering of his list,[1]
Eats not the flats with more impiteous[2] haste
Than young Laertes, in a riotous head,[3]
O'erbears your officers. The rabble call him lord,   100
And as the world were now but to begin,
Antiquity forgot, custom not known,
The ratifiers and props of every word,
They cry "Choose we, Laertes shall be king."
Caps, hands, and tongues, applaud it to the clouds,   105
"Laertes shall be king, Laertes king."
QUEEN   How cheerfully on the false trail they cry[4]!   *A noise within.*
O, this is counter,[5] you false Danish dogs!
KING   The doors are broke.

1. disturbed
2. without judgment
3. haste
4. short on facts
5. hesitate
6. accuse
7. from both sides

8. a weapon designed to scatter its shot
9. Swiss guards
1. towering above its limits
2. pitiless
3. with an armed band
4. as if following the scent
5. backward

Enter LAERTES, *with* OTHERS.

LAERTES   Where is this king?—Sirs, stand you all without.   110
ALL   No, let's come in.
LAERTES   I pray you give me leave.
ALL   We will, we will.   *Exeunt his followers.*
LAERTES   I thank you. Keep[6] the door.—O thou vile king,
    Give me my father!
QUEEN   Calmly, good Laertes.
LAERTES   That drop of blood that's calm proclaims me bastard,   115
    Cries cuckold to my father, brands the harlot
    Even here between the chaste unsmirchéd brow
    Of my true mother.
KING   What is the cause, Laertes,
    That thy rebellion looks so giant-like?
    Let him go, Gertrude. Do not fear[7] our person.   120
    There's such divinity doth hedge a king
    That treason can but peep to[8] what it would,
    Acts little of his will. Tell me, Laertes,
    Why thou art thus incensed. Let him go, Gertrude.
    Speak, man.
LAERTES   Where is my father?
KING   Dead.   125
QUEEN   But not by him.
KING   Let him demand[9] his fill.
LAERTES   How came he dead? I'll not be juggled with.
    To hell allegiance, vows to the blackest devil,
    Conscience and grace to the profoundest pit!
    I dare damnation. To this point I stand,   130
    That both the worlds[1] I give to negligence,[2]
    Let come what comes, only I'll be revenged
    Most throughly for my father.
KING   Who shall stay you?
LAERTES   My will, not all the world's.
    And for my means, I'll husband[3] them so well   135
    They shall go far with little.
KING   Good Laertes,
    If you desire to know the certainty
    Of your dear father, is't writ in your revenge
    That, swoopstake,[4] you will draw both friend and foe,
    Winner and loser?
LAERTES   None but his enemies.   140
KING   Will you know them, then?
LAERTES   To his good friends thus wide I'll ope my arms,
    And like the kind life-rend'ring pelican,[5]
    Repast them with my blood.

---

6. guard
7. fear for
8. look at over or through a barrier
9. question
1. i.e., this and the next

2. disregard
3. manage
4. sweeping the board
5. The pelican was believed to feed her young with her own blood.

1010   *William Shakespeare*

KING   Why, now you speak
Like a good child and a true gentleman.   145
That I am guiltless of your father's death,
And am most sensibly in grief for it,
It shall as level[6] to your judgment 'pear
As day does to your eye.

    A noise within: "Let her come in."

LAERTES   How now? What noise is that?   150

    Enter OPHELIA.

O, heat dry up my brains! tears seven times salt
Burn out the sense[7] and virtue[8] of mine eye!
By heaven, thy madness shall be paid with weight
Till our scale turn the beam. O rose of May,
Dear maid, kind sister, sweet Ophelia!   155
O heavens! is't possible a young maid's wits
Should be as mortal as an old man's life?
Nature is fine[9] in love, and where 'tis fine
It sends some precious instance of itself
After the thing it loves.[1]   160

OPHELIA   They bore him barefac'd on the bier;
        Hey non nonny, nonny, hey nonny;
        And in his grave rain'd many a tear—

Fare you well, my dove!

LAERTES   Hadst thou thy wits, and didst persuade revenge,   165
It could not move thus.

OPHELIA   You must sing "A-down, a-down, and you call him a-down-
a." O, how the wheel becomes it! It is the false steward, that stole his
master's daughter.[2]

LAERTES   This nothing's more than matter.   170

OPHELIA   There's rosemary, that's for remembrance. Pray you, love,
remember. And there is pansies, that's for thoughts.

LAERTES   A document[3] in madness, thoughts and remembrance fitted.

OPHELIA   There's fennel for you, and columbines. There's rue for you,
and here's some for me. We may call it herb of grace a Sundays. O,   175
you must wear your rue with a difference. There's a daisy. I would
give you some violets, but they withered all when my father died.
They say 'a made a good end.

    [*Sings.*]   For bonny sweet Robin is all my joy.

LAERTES   Thought and affliction, passion, hell itself,   180
She turns to favor[4] and to prettiness.

---

6. plain
7. feeling
8. function
9. refined
1. Laertes means that Ophelia, because of her love for her father, gave up her sanity as a token of grief at his death.
2. The "wheel" refers to the *burden* or refrain of a song, in this case "A-down, a-down, and you call him a-down-a." The

ballad to which she refers was about a false steward. Others have suggested that the "wheel" is the Wheel of Fortune, a spinning wheel to whose rhythm such a song might have been sung or a kind of dance movement performed by Ophelia as she sings.
3. lesson
4. beauty

OPHELIA   And will 'a not come again?
            And will 'a not come again?
              No, no, he is dead,
                Go to thy death-bed,   185
              He never will come again.

            His beard was as white as snow,
            All flaxen was his poll⁵;
              He is gone, he is gone,
                And we cast away moan: 190
              God-a-mercy on his soul!

            And of all Christian souls, I pray God. God b'wi'you.   *Exit.*
LAERTES   Do you see this, O God?
KING   Laertes, I must commune with your grief,
            Or you deny me right. Go but apart,   195
            Make choice of whom your wisest friends you will,
            And they shall hear and judge 'twixt you and me.
            If by direct or by collateral⁶ hand
            They find us touched,⁷ we will our kingdom give,
            Our crown, our life, and all that we call ours,   200
            To you in satisfaction; but if not,
            Be you content to lend your patience to us,
            And we shall jointly labor with your soul
            To give it due content.
LAERTES   Let this be so.
            His means of death, his obscure funeral—   205
            No trophy, sword, nor hatchment,⁸ o'er his bones,
            No noble rite nor formal ostentation⁹—
            Cry to be heard, as 'twere from heaven to earth,
            That I must call't in question.
KING   So you shall;
            And where th' offence is, let the great axe fall. 210
            I pray you go with me.   *Exeunt.*

        SCENE 6: *Another room in the castle. Enter* HORATIO *and*
        a GENTLEMAN.

HORATIO   What are they that would speak with me?
GENTLEMAN   Sea-faring men, sir. They say they have letters for you.
HORATIO   Let them come in.   *Exit* GENTLEMAN.
            I do not know from what part of the world
            I should be greeted, if not from Lord Hamlet.   5

        Enter SAILORS.

SAILOR   God bless you, sir.
HORATIO   Let him bless thee too.
SAILOR   'A shall, sir, an't please him. There's a letter for you, sir—it

5. head
6. indirect
7. by guilt

8. coat of arms
9. pomp

came from th' ambassador that was bound for England—if your
name be Horatio, as I am let to know[1] it is.   10

HORATIO [*reads*] "Horatio, when thou shalt have overlooked[2] this,
give these fellows some means[3] to the king. They have letters for
him. Ere we were two days old at sea, a pirate of very warlike appointment[4] gave us chase. Finding ourselves too slow of sail, we put
on a compelled valor, and in the grapple I boarded them. On the in-   15
stant they got clear of our ship, so I alone became their prisoner.
They have dealt with me like thieves of mercy, but they knew what
they did; I am to do a good turn for them. Let the king have the
letters I have sent, and repair thou to me with as much speed as thou
wouldest fly death. I have words to speak in thine ear will make   20
thee dumb; yet are they much too light for the bore of the matter.[5]
These good fellows will bring thee where I am. Rosencrantz and
Guildenstern hold their course for England. Of them I have much to
tell thee. Farewell.
                    He that thou knowest thine, HAMLET."
Come, I will give you way[6] for these your letters,   25
And do't the speedier that you may direct me
To him from whom you brought them.   *Exeunt.*

SCENE 7: *Another room in the castle. Enter* KING *and* LAERTES.

KING Now must your conscience my acquittance seal,[7]
And you must put me in your heart for friend,
Sith you have heard, and with a knowing ear,
That he which hath your noble father slain
Pursued my life.
LAERTES   It well appears. But tell me   5
Why you proceeded not against these feats,
So criminal and so capital in nature,
As by your safety, greatness, wisdom, all things else,
You mainly were stirred up.
KING   O, for two special reasons,
Which may to you, perhaps, seem much unsinewed,[8]   10
But yet to me th' are strong. The queen his mother
Lives almost by his looks, and for myself—
My virtue or my plague, be it either which—
She is so conjunctive[9] to my life and soul
That, as the star moves not but in his sphere,[1]   15
I could not but by her. The other motive,
Why to a public count[2] I might not go,
Is the great love the general gender[3] bear him,
Who, dipping all his faults in their affection,

1. informed
2. read through
3. access
4. equipment
5. A figure from gunnery, referring to shot which is too small for the size of the weapon to be fired.
6. means of delivery
7. grant me innocent

8. weak
9. closely joined
1. A reference to the Ptolemaic cosmology in which planets and stars were believed to revolve about the earth in crystalline spheres concentric with the earth.
2. reckoning
3. common people

Work like the spring that turneth wood to stone,[4] 20
Convert his gyves[5] to graces; so that my arrows,
Too slightly timbered[6] for so loud a wind,
Would have reverted to my bow again,
But not where I have aimed them.

LAERTES   And so have I a noble father lost, 25
A sister driven into desp'rate terms,
Whose worth, if praises may go back again,
Stood challenger on mount of all the age
For her perfections. But my revenge will come.

KING   Break not your sleeps for that. You must not think 30
That we are made of stuff so flat and dull
That we can let our beard be shook with danger,
And think it pastime. You shortly shall hear more.
I loved your father, and we love our self,
And that, I hope, will teach you to imagine— 35

Enter a MESSENGER *with letters.*

MESSENGER   These to your majesty; this to the queen.
KING   From Hamlet! Who brought them?
MESSENGER   Sailors, my lord, they say. I saw them not.
They were given me by Claudio; he received them
Of him that brought them.
KING   Laertes, you shall hear them.— 40
Leave us.   *Exit* MESSENGER.
    [*Reads.*] "High and mighty, you shall know I am set naked on
your kingdom. Tomorrow shall I beg leave to see your kingly eyes;
when I shall, first asking your pardon thereunto, recount the occasion
of my sudden and more strange return. 45
                              HAMLET."
What should this mean? Are all the rest come back?
Or is it some abuse,[7] and no such thing?
LAERTES   Know you the hand?
KING   'Tis Hamlet's character.[8] "Naked"! 50
And in a postscript here, he says "alone."
Can you devise[9] me?
LAERTES   I am lost in it, my lord. But let him come.
It warms the very sickness in my heart
That I shall live and tell him to his teeth 55
"Thus didest thou."
KING   If it be so, Laertes—
As how should it be so, how otherwise?—
Will you be ruled by me?
LAERTES   Ay, my lord,
So you will not o'errule me to a peace.
KING   To thine own peace. If he be now returned, 60

4. Certain English springs contain so
much lime in the water that a lime covering will be deposited on a log placed in
one of them for a length of time.
    5. fetters

6. shafted
7. trick
8. handwriting
9. explain it to

As checking at[1] his voyage, and that he means
No more to undertake it, I will work him
To an exploit now ripe in my device,
Under the which he shall not choose but fall;
And for his death no wind of blame shall breathe   65
But even his mother shall uncharge[2] the practice
And call it accident.

LAERTES   My lord, I will be ruled;
The rather if you could devise it so
That I might be the organ.[3]

KING   It falls right.
You have been talked of since your travel much,   70
And that in Hamlet's hearing, for a quality
Wherein they say you shine. Your sum of parts
Did not together pluck such envy from him
As did that one, and that, in my regard,
Of the unworthiest siege.[4]

LAERTES   What part is that, my lord?   75

KING   A very riband in the cap of youth,
Yet needful too, for youth no less becomes
The light and careless livery that it wears
Than settled age his sables and his weeds,[5]
Importing health and graveness. Two months since   80
Here was a gentleman of Normandy.
I have seen myself, and served against, the French,
And they can[6] well on horseback, but this gallant
Had witchcraft in't. He grew unto his seat,
And to such wondrous doing brought his horse,   85
As had he been incorpsed and demi-natured
With the brave beast. So far he topped my thought
That I, in forgery[7] of shapes and tricks,
Come short of what he did.[8]

LAERTES   A Norman was't?

KING   A Norman.   90

LAERTES   Upon my life, Lamord.

KING   The very same.

LAERTES   I know him well. He is the brooch indeed
And gem of all the nation.

KING   He made confession[9] of you,
And gave you such a masterly report   95
For art and exercise in your defence,[1]
And for your rapier most especial,
That he cried out 'twould be a sight indeed
If one could match you. The scrimers[2] of their nation

1. turning aside from
2. not accuse
3. instrument
4. rank
5. dignified clothing
6. perform
7. imagination
8. The gentleman referred to was so skilled in horsemanship that he seemed to share one body with the horse, "incorpsed." The King further extends the compliment by saying that he appeared like the mythical centaur, a creature who was man from the waist up and horse from the waist down, therefore "demi-natured."
9. gave a report
1. skill in fencing
2. fencers

He swore had neither motion, guard, nor eye,   100
If you opposed them. Sir, this report of his
Did Hamlet so envenom with his envy
That he could nothing do but wish and beg
Your sudden coming o'er, to play with you.
Now out of this—
LAERTES   What out of this, my lord?   105
KING   Laertes, was your father dear to you?
Or are you like the painting of a sorrow,
A face without a heart?
LAERTES   Why ask you this?
KING   Not that I think you did not love your father,
But that I know love is begun by time,   110
And that I see in passages of proof,[3]
Time qualifies the spark and fire of it.
There lives within the very flame of love
A kind of wick or snuff that will abate it,
And nothing is at a like goodness still,   115
For goodness, growing to a plurisy,[4]
Dies in his own too much.[5] That we would do,
We should do when we would; for this "would" changes,
And hath abatements and delays as many
As there are tongues, are hands, are accidents,   120
And then this "should" is like a spendthrift's sigh
That hurts by easing. But to the quick of th' ulcer—
Hamlet comes back; what would you undertake
To show yourself in deed your father's son
More than in words?
LAERTES   To cut his throat i' th' church.   125
KING   No place indeed should murder sanctuarize[6];
Revenge should have no bounds. But, good Laertes,
Will you do this? Keep close within your chamber.
Hamlet returned shall know you are come home.
We'll put on those shall praise your excellence,   130
And set a double varnish[7] on the fame
The Frenchman gave you, bring you in fine[8] together,
And wager on your heads. He, being remiss,[9]
Most generous, and free from all contriving,
Will not peruse[1] the foils, so that with ease,   135
Or with a little shuffling, you may choose
A sword unbated,[2] and in a pass of practice
Requite him for your father.
LAERTES   I will do't,
And for that purpose I'll anoint my sword.
I bought an unction of a mountebank,   140
So mortal that but dip a knife in it,

3. tests of experience   8. in short
4. fullness   9. careless
5. excess   1. examine
6. provide sanctuary for murder 2. not blunted
7. gloss

Where it draws blood no cataplasm[3] so rare,
Collected from all simples[4] that have virtue
Under the moon, can save the thing from death
That is but scratched withal. I'll touch my point   145
With this contagion, that if I gall[5] him slightly,
It may be death.
KING   Let's further think of this,
Weigh what convenience both of time and means
May fit us to our shape. If this should fail,
And that our drift look[6] through our bad performance,   150
'Twere better not assayed. Therefore this project
Should have a back or second that might hold
If this did blast in proof.[7] Soft, let me see.
We'll make a solemn wager on your cunnings—
I ha't.   155
When in your motion you are hot and dry—
As make your bouts more violent to that end—
And that he calls for drink, I'll have preferred him
A chalice for the nonce, whereon but sipping,
If he by chance escape your venomed stuck,[8]   160
Our purpose may hold there.—But stay, what noise?

    Enter QUEEN.

QUEEN   One woe doth tread upon another's heel,
So fast they follow. Your sister's drowned, Laertes.
LAERTES   Drowned? O, where?
QUEEN   There is a willow grows aslant the brook   165
That shows his hoar leaves in the glassy stream.
Therewith fantastic garlands did she make
Of crowflowers, nettles, daisies, and long purples
That liberal[9] shepherds give a grosser[1] name,
But our cold[2] maids do dead men's fingers call them.   170
There on the pendent boughs her coronet weeds
Clamb'ring to hang, an envious[3] sliver broke,
When down her weedy trophies and herself
Fell in the weeping brook. Her clothes spread wide,
And mermaid-like awhile they bore her up,   175
Which time she chanted snatches of old tunes,
As one incapable[4] of her own distress,
Or like a creature native and indued[5]
Unto that element. But long it could not be
Till that her garments, heavy with their drink,   180
Pulled the poor wretch from her melodious lay
To muddy death.
LAERTES   Alas, then she is drowned?
QUEEN   Drowned, drowned.

3. poultice   9. vulgar
4. herbs   1. coarser
5. scratch   2. chaste
6. intent become obvious   3. malicious
7. fail when tried   4. unaware
8. thrust   5. habituated

LAERTES   Too much of water hast thou, poor Ophelia,
And therefore I forbid my tears; but yet   185
It is our trick; nature her custom holds,
Let shame say what it will. When these are gone,
The woman will be out. Adieu, my lord.
I have a speech o' fire that fain would blaze
But that this folly drowns it.   *Exit.*
KING   Let's follow, Gertrude.   190
How much I had to do to calm his rage!
Now fear I this will give it start again;
Therefore let's follow.   *Exeunt.*

Act 5

SCENE 1: *A churchyard. Enter two* CLOWNS.[6]

CLOWN   Is she to be buried in Christian burial when she wilfully
seeks her own salvation?
OTHER   I tell thee she is. Therefore make her grave straight. The
crowner[7] hath sat on her,[8] and finds it Christian burial.
CLOWN   How can that be, unless she drowned herself in her own de- 5
fence?
OTHER   Why, 'tis found so.
CLOWN   It must be "se offendendo";[9] it cannot be else. For here lies
the point: if I drown myself wittingly, it argues an act, and an act
hath three branches—it is to act, to do, to perform; argal,[1] she 10
drowned herself wittingly.
OTHER   Nay, but hear you, Goodman Delver.
CLOWN   Give me leave. Here lies the water; good. Here stands the
man; good. If the man go to this water and drown himself, it is, will
he, nill he, he goes—mark you that. But if the water come to him 15
and drown him, he drowns not himself. Argal, he that is not guilty
of his own death shortens not his own life.
OTHER   But is this law?
CLOWN   Ay, marry, is't; crowner's quest[2] law.
OTHER   Will you ha' the truth on't? If this had not been a gentle- 20
woman, she should have been buried out o' Christian burial.
CLOWN   Why, there thou say'st. And the more pity that great folk
should have count'nance[3] in this world to drown or hang themselves
more than their even-Christen.[4] Come, my spade. There is no ancient
gentlemen but gard'ners, ditchers, and grave-makers. They hold up 25
Adam's profession.
OTHER   Was he a gentleman?
CLOWN   'A was the first that ever bore arms.
OTHER   Why, he had none.
CLOWN   What, art a heathen? How dost thou understand the Scrip- 30

---

6. rustics
7. coroner
8. held an inquest
9. an error for *se defendendo,* in self-
defense

1. therefore
2. inquest
3. approval
4. fellow Christians

ture? The Scripture says Adam digged. Could he dig without arms? I'll put another question to thee. If thou answerest me not to the purpose, confess thyself—

OTHER   Go to.

CLOWN   What is he that builds stronger than either the mason, the 35 shipwright, or the carpenter?

OTHER   The gallows-maker, for that frame outlives a thousand tenants.

CLOWN   I like thy wit well, in good faith. The gallows does well. But how does it well? It does well to those that do ill. Now thou dost ill to say the gallows is built stronger than the church. Argal, the gal- 40 lows may do well to thee. To't again,[5] come.

OTHER   Who builds stronger than a mason, a shipwright, or a carpenter?

CLOWN   Ay tell me that, and unyoke.[6]

OTHER   Marry, now I can tell.   45

CLOWN   To't.

OTHER   Mass, I cannot tell.

CLOWN   Cudgel thy brains no more about it, for your dull ass will not mend his pace with beating. And when you are asked this question next, say "a grave-maker." The houses he makes lasts till doomsday. 50 Go, get thee in, and fetch me a stoup[7] of liquor. *Exit* OTHER CLOWN.

Enter HAMLET *and* HORATIO *as* CLOWN *digs and sings.*

> In youth, when I did love, did love,
>   Methought it was very sweet,
> To contract[8] the time for-a my behove,[9]
>   O, methought there-a was nothing-a meet.[1]   55

HAMLET   Has this fellow no feeling of his business, that 'a sings in grave-making?

HORATIO   Custom hath made it in him a property of easiness.

HAMLET   'Tis e'en so. The hand of little employment hath the daintier sense.   60

CLOWN
> But age, with his stealing steps,
>   Hath clawed me in his clutch,
> And hath shipped me into the land,
>   As if I had never been such.

Throws up a skull.

HAMLET   That skull had a tongue in it, and could sing once. How the 65 knave jowls[2] it to the ground, as if 'twere Cain's jawbone, that did the first murder! This might be the pate of a politician, which this ass now o'erreaches[3]; one that would circumvent God, might it not?

HORATIO   It might, my lord.

HAMLET   Or of a courtier, which could say "Good morrow, sweet lord! 70 How dost thou, sweet lord?" This might be my Lord Such-a-one, that praised my Lord Such-a-one's horse, when 'a meant to beg it, might it not?

5. guess again
6. finish the matter
7. mug
8. shorten
9. advantage
1. The gravedigger's song is a free ver-

sion of "The aged lover renounceth love" by Thomas, Lord Vaux, published in *Tottel's Miscellany*, 1557.
2. hurls
3. gets the better of

HORATIO   Ay, my lord.

HAMLET   Why, e'en so, and now my Lady Worm's, chapless,[4] and   75
knock'd abut the mazzard[5] with a sexton's spade. Here's fine revolution,[6] an we had the trick to see't. Did these bones cost no more the
breeding but to play at loggets with them?[7] Mine ache to think on't.

CLOWN   A pick-axe and a spade, a spade,
                     For and a shrouding sheet: 80
                O, a pit of clay for to be made
                     For such a guest is meet.

Throws up another skull.   trifles, unimportant points

HAMLET   There's another. Why may not that be the skull of a lawyer?
Where be his quiddities now, his quillets, his cases, his tenures, and
his tricks? Why does he suffer this mad knave now to knock him   85
about the sconce[8] with a dirty shovel, and will not tell him of his
action of battery? Hum! This fellow might be in's time a great buyer
of land, with his statutes, his recognizances, his fines, his double
vouchers, his recoveries. Is this the fine[9] of his fines, and the recovery
of his recoveries, to have his fine pate full of fine dirt? Will his vouch-   90
ers vouch him no more of his purchases, and double ones too, than
the length and breadth of a pair of indentures[1]? The very convey-
ances of his lands will scarcely lie in this box, and must th' inheritor
himself have no more, ha?[2]

HORATIO   Not a jot more, my lord.   95

HAMLET   Is not parchment made of sheepskins?

HORATIO   Ay, my lord, and of calves' skins too.

HAMLET   They are sheep and calves which seek out assurance in that.
I will speak to this fellow. Whose grave's this, sirrah?

CLOWN   Mine, sir.   100

            [*Sings.*] O, a pit of clay for to be made—

HAMLET   I think it be thine indeed, for thou liest in't.

CLOWN   You lie out on't, sir, and therefore 'tis not yours. For my part,
I do not lie in't, yet it is mine.

HAMLET   Thou dost lie in't, to be in't and say it is thine. 'Tis for the   105
dead, not for the quick[3]; therefore thou liest.

CLOWN   'Tis a quick lie, sir; 'twill away again from me to you.

HAMLET   What man dost thou dig it for?

CLOWN   For no man, sir.

HAMLET   What woman, then?   110

CLOWN   For none neither.

HAMLET   Who is to be buried in't?

CLOWN   One that was a woman, sir; but, rest her soul, she's dead.

HAMLET   How absolute[4] the knave is! We must speak by the card,[5] or
equivocation will undo us. By the Lord, Horatio, this three years I   115

4. lacking a lower jaw
5. head
6. skill
7. "Loggets" were small pieces of wood
thrown as part of a game.
8. head
9. end

1. contracts
2. In this speech Hamlet reels off a list
of legal terms relating to property trans-
actions.
3. living
4. precise
5. exactly

have took note of it, the age is grown so picked[6] that the toe of the peasant comes so near the heel of the courtier, he galls his kibe.[7] How long hast thou been a grave-maker?

CLOWN   Of all the days i' th' year, I came to't that day that our last King Hamlet overcame Fortinbras.   120

HAMLET   How long is that since?

CLOWN   Cannot you tell that? Every fool can tell that. It was that very day that young Hamlet was born—he that is mad, and sent into England.

HAMLET   Ay, marry, why was he sent into England?   125

CLOWN   Why, because 'a was mad. 'A shall recover his wits there; or, if 'a do not, 'tis no great matter there.

HAMLET   Why?

CLOWN   'Twill not be seen in him there. There the men are as mad as he.   130

HAMLET   How came he mad?

CLOWN   Very strangely, they say.

HAMLET   How strangely?

CLOWN   Faith, e'en with losing his wits.

HAMLET   Upon what ground?   135

CLOWN   Why, here in Denmark. I have been sexton here, man and boy, thirty years.

HAMLET   How long will a man lie i' th' earth ere he rot?

CLOWN   Faith, if 'a be not rotten before 'a die—as we have many pocky[8] corses now-a-days that will scarce hold the laying in—'a will   140 last you some eight year or nine year. A tanner will last you nine year.

HAMLET   Why he more than another?

CLOWN   Why, sir, his hide is so tanned with his trade that 'a will keep out water a great while; and your water is a sore decayer of your   145 whoreson[9] dead body. Here's a skull now hath lien[1] you i' th' earth three and twenty years.

HAMLET   Whose was it?

CLOWN   A whoreson mad fellow's it was. Whose do you think it was?

HAMLET   Nay, I know not.   150

CLOWN   A pestilence on him for a mad rogue! 'A poured a flagon of Rhenish on my head once. This same skull, sir, was, sir, Yorick's skull, the king's jester.

HAMLET   [takes the skull]   This?

CLOWN   E'en that.   155

HAMLET   Alas, poor Yorick! I knew him, Horatio—a fellow of infinite jest, of most excellent fancy. He hath bore me on his back a thousand times, and now how abhorred in my imagination it is! My gorge[2] rises at it. Here hung those lips that I have kissed I know not how oft. Where be your gibes now, your gambols, your songs, your flashes   160 of merriment that were wont to set the table on a roar? Not one now to mock your own grinning? Quite chap-fall'n[3]? Now get you to my

6. refined
7. rubs a blister on his heel
8. corrupted by syphilis
9. bastard (not literally)

1. lain
2. throat
3. lacking a lower jaw

lady's chamber, and tell her, let her paint an inch thick, to this favor[4]
she must come. Make her laugh at that. Prithee, Horatio, tell me one
thing.   165

HORATIO   What's that, my lord?

HAMLET   Dost thou think Alexander looked o' this fashion i' th' earth?

HORATIO   E'en so.

HAMLET   And smelt so? Pah!   *Throws down the skull.*

HORATIO   E'en so, my lord.   170

HAMLET   To what base uses we may return, Horatio! Why may not
imagination trace the noble dust of Alexander till 'a find it stopping
a bung-hole?

HORATIO   'Twere to consider too curiously[5] to consider so.

HAMLET   No, faith, not a jot, but to follow him thither with modesty[6] 175
enough, and likelihood to lead it. Alexander died, Alexander was
buried, Alexander returneth to dust; the dust is earth; of earth we
make loam; and why of that loam whereto he was converted might
they not stop a beer-barrel?

Imperious Cæsar, dead and turned to clay,   180
Might stop a hole to keep the wind away.
O, that that earth which kept the world in awe
Should patch a wall t'expel the winter's flaw![7]

But soft, but soft awhile! Here comes the king,
The queen, the courtiers.

Enter KING, QUEEN, LAERTES, *and the Corse with a* PRIEST *and*
LORDS *attendant.*

                            Who is this they follow?   185
And with such maiméd[8] rites? This doth betoken
The corse they follow did with desperate hand
Fordo[9] it own life. 'Twas of some estate.[1]
Couch[2] we awhile and mark.   *Retires with* HORATIO.

LAERTES   What ceremony else[3]?   190

HAMLET   That is Laertes, a very noble youth. Mark.

LAERTES   What ceremony else?

PRIEST   Her obsequies have been as far enlarged[4]
As we have warranty. Her death was doubtful,
And but that great command o'ersways the order,[5]   195
She should in ground unsanctified been lodged
Till the last trumpet. For charitable prayers,
Shards, flints, and pebbles, should be thrown on her.
Yet here she is allowed her virgin crants,[6]
Her maiden strewments,[7] and the bringing home   200
Of bell and burial.

LAERTES   Must there no more be done?

4. appearance
5. precisely
6. moderation
7. gusty wind
8. cut short
9. destroy. *It*: its.
1. rank

2. conceal ourselves
3. more
4. extended
5. usual rules
6. wreaths
7. flowers strewn on the grave

PRIEST   No more be done.
We should profane the service of the dead
To sing a requiem and such rest to her
As to peace-parted souls.
LAERTES   Lay her i' th' earth,   205
And from her fair and unpolluted flesh
May violets spring! I tell thee, churlish priest,
A minist'ring angel shall my sister be
When thou liest howling.[8]
HAMLET   What, the fair Ophelia!
QUEEN   Sweets to the sweet. Farewell!   *Scatters flowers.*   210
I hoped thou shouldst have been my Hamlet's wife.
I thought thy bride-bed to have decked, sweet maid,
And not have strewed thy grave.
LAERTES   O, treble woe
Fall ten times treble on that cursèd head
Whose wicked deed thy most ingenious sense[9]   215
Deprived thee of! Hold off the earth awhile,
Till I have caught her once more in mine arms.

                                            Leaps into the grave.

Now pile your dust upon the quick and dead,
Till of this flat a mountain you have made
T' o'er-top old Pelion or the skyish head   220
Of blue Olympus.[1]
HAMLET [*coming forward*]   What is he whose grief
Bears such an emphasis, whose phrase of sorrow
Conjures[2] the wand'ring stars, and makes them stand
Like wonder-wounded hearers? This is I,
Hamlet the Dane.   225

      HAMLET *leaps into the grave and they grapple.*

LAERTES   The devil take thy soul!
HAMLET   Thou pray'st not well.
I prithee take thy fingers from my throat,
For though I am not splenitive[3] and rash,
Yet have I in me something dangerous,
Which let thy wisdom fear. Hold off thy hand.   230
KING   Pluck them asunder.
QUEEN   Hamlet! Hamlet!
ALL   Gentlemen!
HORATIO   Good my lord, be quiet.

      The ATTENDANTS *part them, and they come out of the grave.*

HAMLET   Why, I will fight with him upon this theme   235
Until my eyelids will no longer wag.[4]

8. in Hell
9. lively mind
1. The rivalry between Laertes and
Hamlet in this scene extends even to their
rhetoric. Pelion and Olympus, mentioned
here by Laertes, and Ossa, mentioned below by Hamlet, were Greek mountains
noted in mythology for their height. Olym-

pus was the reputed home of the gods, and
the other two were piled one on top of the
other by the Giants in an attempt to reach
the top of Olympus and overthrow the gods.
2. casts a spell on
3. hot-tempered
4. move

QUEEN   O my son, what theme?

HAMLET   I loved Ophelia. Forty thousand brothers
Could not with all their quantity of love
Make up my sum. What wilt thou do for her?   240

KING   O, he is mad, Laertes.

QUEEN   For love of God, forbear[5] him.

HAMLET   'Swounds, show me what th'owt do.
Woo't[6] weep, woo't fight, woo't fast, woo't tear thyself,
Woo't drink up eisel,[7] eat a crocodile?   245
I'll do't. Dost come here to whine?
To outface[8] me with leaping in her grave?
Be buried quick with her, and so will I.
And if thou prate of mountains, let them throw
Millions of acres on us, till our ground,   250
Singeing his pate against the burning zone,[9]
Make Ossa like a wart! Nay, an thou'lt mouth,
I'll rant as well as thou.

QUEEN   This is mere madness;
And thus awhile the fit will work on him.
Anon, as patient as the female dove   255
When that her golden couplets[1] are disclosed,
His silence will sit drooping.

HAMLET   Hear you, sir.
What is the reason that you use me thus?
I loved you ever. But it is no matter.
Let Hercules himself do what he may,   260
The cat will mew, and dog will have his day.

KING   I pray thee, good Horatio, wait upon[2] him.
                         Exeunt HAMLET *and* HORATIO.
[*To* LAERTES.] Strengthen your patience in our last night's speech.
We'll put the matter to the present push.[3]—
Good Gertrude, set some watch over your son.—   265
This grave shall have a living monument.
An hour of quiet shortly shall we see;
Till then in patience our proceeding be.   *Exeunt.*

SCENE 2: *A hall or public room. Enter* HAMLET *and* HORATIO.

HAMLET   So much for this, sir; now shall you see the other.
You do remember all the circumstance?

HORATIO   Remember it, my lord!

HAMLET   Sir, in my heart there was a kind of fighting
That would not let me sleep. Methought I lay   5
Worse than the mutines[4] in the bilboes.[5] Rashly,
And praised be rashness for it—let us know,
Our indiscretion sometime serves us well,

5. bear with
6. will you
7. vinegar
8. get the best of
9. sky in the torrid zone

1. pair of eggs
2. attend
3. immediate trial
4. mutineers
5. stocks

When our deep plots do pall; and that should learn[6] us
There's a divinity that shapes our ends,   10
Rough-hew them how we will—

HORATIO   That is most certain.

HAMLET   Up from my cabin,
My sea-gown scarfed[7] about me, in the dark
Groped I to find out them, had my desire,
Fingered[8] their packet, and in fine[9] withdrew   15
To mine own room again, making so bold,
My fears forgetting manners, to unseal
Their grand commission; where I found, Horatio—
Ah, royal knavery!—an exact[1] command,
Larded[2] with many several sorts of reasons,   20
Importing Denmark's health, and England's too,
With, ho! such bugs and goblins in my life,[3]
That on the supervise,[4] no leisure bated,
No, not to stay the grinding of the axe,
My head should be struck off.

HORATIO   Is't possible?   25

HAMLET   Here's the commission; read it at more leisure.
But wilt thou hear now how I did proceed?

HORATIO   I beseech you.

HAMLET   Being thus benetted[5] round with villainies,
Or I could make a prologue to my brains,   30
They had begun the play. I sat me down,
Devised[6] a new commission, wrote it fair.[7]
I once did hold it, as our statists[8] do,
A baseness to write fair, and labored much
How to forget that learning; but sir, now   35
It did me yeoman's service. Wilt thou know
Th' effect[9] of what I wrote?

HORATIO   Ay, good my lord.

HAMLET   An earnest conjuration from the king,
As England was his faithful tributary,[1]
As love between them like the palm might flourish,   40
As peace should still her wheaten garland wear
And stand a comma 'tween their amities,[2]
And many such like as's of great charge,[3]
That on the view and knowing of these contents,
Without debatement[4] further more or less,   45
He should those bearers put to sudden death,
Not shriving-time allowed.[5]

HORATIO   How was this sealed?

6. teach
7. wrapped
8. stole
9. quickly
1. precisely stated
2. garnished
3. such dangers if I remained alive
4. as soon as the commission was read
5. caught in a net

6. made
7. legibly
8. politicians
9. contents
1. vassal
2. link friendships
3. import
4. consideration
5. without time for confession

HAMLET   Why, even in that was heaven ordinant,[6]
I had my father's signet in my purse,
Which was the model of that Danish seal,   50
Folded the writ up in the form of th' other,
Subscribed it, gave't th' impression,[7] placed it safely,
The changeling[8] never known. Now, the next day
Was our sea-fight, and what to this was sequent[9]
Thou knowest already.   55
HORATIO   So Guildenstern and Rosencrantz go to't.
HAMLET   Why, man, they did make love to this employment.
They are not near[1] my conscience; their defeat[2]
Does by their own insinuation grow.
'Tis dangerous when the baser nature comes   60
Between the pass[3] and fell[4] incenséd points
Of mighty opposites.
HORATIO   Why, what a king is this!
HAMLET   Does it not, think thee, stand me now upon—
He that hath killed my king and whored my mother,
Popped in between th' election and my hopes,   65
Thrown out his angle[5] for my proper life,
And with such coz'nage[6]—is't not perfect conscience
To quit[7] him with this arm? And is't not to be damned
To let this canker of our nature come
In further evil?   70
HORATIO   It must be shortly known to him from England
What is the issue[8] of the business there.
HAMLET   It will be short[9]; the interim is mine.
And a man's life's no more than to say "one."
But I am very sorry, good Horatio,   75
That to Laertes I forgot myself;
For by the image of my cause I see
The portraiture of his. I'll court his favors.
But sure the bravery[1] of his grief did put me
Into a tow'ring passion.
HORATIO   Peace; who comes here?   80

Enter OSRIC.

OSRIC   Your lordship is right welcome back to Denmark.
HAMLET   I humbly thank you, sir. [*Aside to* HORATIO.] Dost know
this water-fly?
HORATIO [*aside to* HAMLET]   No, my good lord.
HAMLET [*aside to* HORATIO]   Thy state is the more gracious, for 'tis a   85
vice to know him. He hath much land, and fertile. Let a beast be
lord of beasts, and his crib shall stand at the king's mess. 'Tis a
chough,[2] but as I say, spacious in the possession of dirt.

6. operative
7. of the seal
8. alteration
9. followed
1. do not touch
2. death
3. thrust
4. cruel

5. fishhook
6. trickery
7. repay
8. outcome
9. soon
1. exaggerated display
2. jackdaw

OSRIC   Sweet lord, if your lordship were at leisure, I should impart a
thing to you from his majesty.   90

HAMLET   I will receive it, sir, with all diligence of spirit. Put your
bonnet to his right use. 'Tis for the head.

OSRIC   I thank your lordship, it is very hot.

HAMLET   No, believe me, 'tis very cold; the wind is northerly.

OSRIC   It is indifferent[3] cold, my lord, indeed.   95

HAMLET   But yet methinks it is very sultry and hot for my complexion.[4]

OSRIC   Exceedingly, my lord; it is very sultry, as 'twere—I cannot tell
how. My lord, his majesty bade me signify to you that 'a has laid
a great wager on your head. Sir, this is the matter—   100

HAMLET   I beseech you, remember.

   HAMLET *moves him to put on his hat.*

OSRIC   Nay, good my lord; for my ease, in good faith. Sir, here is
newly come to court Laertes; believe me, an absolute[5] gentleman,
full of most excellent differences,[6] of very soft society and great
showing.[7] Indeed, to speak feelingly of him, he is the card or cal- 105
endar[8] of gentry, for you shall find in him the continent[9] of what
part a gentleman would see.

HAMLET   Sir, his definement[1] suffers no perdition in you, though I
know to divide him inventorially[2] would dozy[3] th' arithmetic of
memory, and yet but yaw[4] neither in respect of his quick sail. But 110
in the verity of extolment, I take him to be a soul of great article,[5]
and his infusion[6] of such dearth and rareness as, to make true
diction[7] of him, his semblage[8] is his mirror, and who else would
trace[9] him, his umbrage,[1] nothing more.

OSRIC   Your lordship speaks most infallibly of him.   115

HAMLET   The concernancy,[2] sir? Why do we wrap the gentleman in
our more rawer breath?[3]

OSRIC   Sir?

HORATIO   Is't not possible to understand in another tongue? You will
to't, sir, really.   120

HAMLET   What imports the nomination[4] of this gentleman?

OSRIC   Of Laertes?

HORATIO   [*aside*]   His purse is empty already. All's golden words are
spent.

HAMLET   Of him, sir.   125

OSRIC   I know you are not ignorant—

HAMLET   I would you did, sir; yet, in faith, if you did, it would not
much approve me. Well, sir.

OSRIC   You are not ignorant of what excellence Laertes is—

3. moderately
4. temperament
5. perfect
6. qualities
7. good manners
8. measure
9. sum total
1. description
2. examine bit by bit
3. daze

4. steer wildly
5. scope
6. nature
7. telling
8. rival
9. keep pace with
1. shadow
2. meaning
3. cruder words
4. naming

HAMLET I dare not confess that, lest I should compare[5] with him in 130
excellence; but to know a man well were to know himself.

OSRIC I mean, sir, for his weapon; but in the imputation[6] laid on him
by them, in his meed he's unfellowed.[7]

HAMLET What's his weapon?

OSRIC Rapier and dagger. 135

HAMLET That's two of his weapons—but well.

OSRIC The king, sir, hath wagered with him six Barbary horses,
against the which he has impawned,[8] as I take it, six French rapiers
and poniards, with their assigns,[9] as girdle, hangers, and so. Three
of the carriages, in faith, are very dear to fancy,[1] very responsive to 140
the hilts, most delicate[2] carriages, and of very liberal conceit.[3]

HAMLET What call you the carriages?

HORATIO [*aside to* HAMLET] I knew you must be edified by the
margent[4] ere you had done.

OSRIC The carriages, sir, are the hangers. 145

HAMLET The phrase would be more germane to the matter if we
could carry a cannon by our sides. I would it might be hangers till
then. But on! Six Barbary horses against six French swords, their
assigns, and three liberal conceited carriages; that's the French bet
against the Danish. Why is this all impawned, as you call it? 150

OSRIC The king, sir, hath laid, sir, that in a dozen passes between
yourself and him he shall not exceed you three hits; he hath laid on
twelve for nine, and it would come to immediate trial if your lordship would vouchsafe the answer.

HAMLET How if I answer no? 155

OSRIC I mean, my lord, the opposition of your person in trial.

HAMLET Sir, I will walk here in the hall. If it please his majesty, it is
the breathing time[5] of day with me. Let the foils be brought, the
gentleman willing, and the king hold his purpose; I will win for
him an I can. If not, I will gain nothing but my shame and the 160
odd hits.

OSRIC Shall I deliver you so?

HAMLET To this effect, sir, after what flourish your nature will.

OSRIC I commend my duty to your lordship.

HAMLET Yours, yours. [*Exit* OSRIC.] He does well to commend it 165
himself; there are no tongues else for's turn.

HORATIO This lapwing runs away with the shell on his head.[6]

HAMLET 'A did comply,[7] sir, with his dug[8] before 'a sucked it. Thus
has he, and many more of the same bevy that I know the drossy age
dotes on, only got the tune of the time; and out of an habit of en- 170
counter, a kind of yesty[9] collection which carries them through and
through the most fanned and winnowed opinions; and do but blow
them to their trial, the bubbles are out.

---

5. i.e., compare myself
6. reputation
7. unequaled in his excellence
8. staked
9. appurtenances
1. finely designed
2. well adjusted
3. elegant design
4. marginal gloss

5. time for exercise
6. The lapwing was thought to be so
precocious that it could run immediately
after being hatched, even as here with bits
of the shell still on its head.
7. deal formally
8. mother's breast
9. yeasty

Enter a LORD.

LORD   My lord, his majesty commended him to you by young Osric,
who brings back to him that you attend[1] him in the hall. He sends 175
to know if your pleasure hold to play with Laertes, or that you will
take longer time.

HAMLET   I am constant to my purposes; they follow the king's pleasure. If his fitness speaks, mine is ready; now or whensoever, provided
I be so able as now.   180

LORD   The king and queen and all are coming down.

HAMLET   In happy time.

LORD   The queen desires you to use some gentle entertainment[2] to
Laertes before you fall to play.

HAMLET   She well instructs me.   *Exit* LORD. 185

HORATIO   You will lose this wager, my lord.

HAMLET   I do not think so. Since he went into France I have been
in continual practice. I shall win at the odds. But thou wouldst not
think how ill[3] all's here about my heart. But it is no matter.

HORATIO   Nay, good my lord—   190

HAMLET   It is but foolery, but it is such a kind of gaingiving[4] as would
perhaps trouble a woman.

HORATIO   If your mind dislike anything, obey it. I will forestall their
repair[5] hither, and say you are not fit.

HAMLET   Not a whit, we defy augury. There is special providence in 195
the fall of a sparrow. If it be now, 'tis not to come; if it be not to
come, it will be now; if it be not now, yet it will come. The readiness
is all. Since no man of aught he leaves knows, what is't to leave
betimes? Let be.

> *A table prepared. Enter* TRUMPETS, DRUMS, *and* OFFICERS *with
> cushions;* KING, QUEEN, OSRIC *and* ATTENDANTS *with foils,
> daggers, and* LAERTES.

KING   Come, Hamlet, come and take this hand from me.   200

> *The* KING *puts* LAERTES' *hand into* HAMLET'S.

HAMLET   Give me your pardon, sir. I have done you wrong,
But pardon 't as you are a gentleman.
This presence[6] knows, and you must needs have heard,
How I am punished with a sore distraction.
What I have done   205
That might your nature, honor, and exception,[7]
Roughly awake, I here proclaim was madness.
Was 't Hamlet wronged Laertes? Never Hamlet.
If Hamlet from himself be ta'en away,
And when he's not himself does wrong Laertes,   210
Then Hamlet does it not, Hamlet denies it.
Who does it then? His madness. If't be so,

---

1. await
2. cordiality
3. uneasy
4. misgiving

5. coming
6. company
7. resentment

Hamlet is of the faction that is wronged;
His madness is poor Hamlet's enemy.   215
Sir, in this audience,
Let my disclaiming from[8] a purposed evil
Free[9] me so far in your most generous thoughts
That I have shot my arrow o'er the house
And hurt my brother.

LAERTES   I am satisfied in nature,   220
Whose motive in this case should stir me most
To my revenge. But in my terms of honor
I stand aloof, and will no reconcilement
Till by some elder masters of known honor
I have a voice[1] and precedent of peace   225
To keep my name ungored.[2] But till that time
I do receive your offered love like love,
And will not wrong it.

HAMLET   I embrace it freely,
And will this brother's wager frankly[3] play.
Give us the foils.

LAERTES   Come, one for me.

HAMLET   I'll be your foil, Laertes. In mine ignorance   230
Your skill shall, like a star i' th' darkest night,
Stick fiery off[4] indeed.

LAERTES   You mock me, sir.

HAMLET   No, by this hand.

KING   Give them the foils, young Osric. Cousin Hamlet,
You know the wager?

HAMLET   Very well, my lord;   235
Your Grace has laid the odds o' th' weaker side.

KING   I do not fear it, I have seen you both;
But since he is bettered,[5] we have therefore odds.

LAERTES   This is too heavy; let me see another.

HAMLET   This likes[6] me well. These foils have all a[7] length?   240

They prepare to play.

OSRIC   Ay, my good lord.

KING   Set me the stoups of wine upon that table.
If Hamlet give the first or second hit,
Or quit in answer of[8] the third exchange,
Let all the battlements their ordnance fire.   245
The king shall drink to Hamlet's better breath,
And in the cup an union[9] shall he throw,
Richer than that which four successive kings
In Denmark's crown have worn. Give me the cups,
And let the kettle[1] to the trumpet speak,   250
The trumpet to the cannoneer without,

8. denying of
9. absolve
1. authority
2. unshamed
3. without rancor
4. shine brightly

5. reported better
6. suits
7. the same
8. repay
9. pearl
1. kettledrum

The cannons to the heavens, the heaven to earth,
"Now the king drinks to Hamlet." Come, begin—

   Trumpets the while.

And you, the judges, bear a wary eye.
HAMLET   Come on, sir.
LAERTES   Come, my lord.   *They play.*
HAMLET   One.
LAERTES   No.
HAMLET   Judgment?   255
OSRIC   A hit, a very palpable hit.

   Drums, trumpets, and shot. Flourish; a piece goes off.

LAERTES   Well, again.
KING   Stay, give me drink. Hamlet, this pearl is thine.
   Here's to thy health. Give him the cup.
HAMLET   I'll play this bout first; set it by awhile.   260
   Come.   *They play.*
   Another hit; what say you?
LAERTES   I do confess't.
KING   Our son shall win.
QUEEN   He's fat,[2] and scant of breath.
   Here, Hamlet, take my napkin, rub thy brows.   265
   The queen carouses to thy fortune, Hamlet.
HAMLET   Good madam!
KING   Gertrude, do not drink.
QUEEN   I will, my lord; I pray you pardon me.
KING [*aside*]   It is the poisoned cup; it is too late.   270
HAMLET   I dare not drink yet, madam; by and by.
QUEEN   Come, let me wipe thy face.
LAERTES   My lord, I'll hit him now.
KING   I do not think't.
LAERTES [*aside*]   And yet it is almost against my conscience.
HAMLET   Come, for the third, Laertes. You do but dally.   275
   I pray you pass[3] with your best violence;
   I am afeard you make a wanton of me.[4]
LAERTES   Say you so? Come on.   *They play.*
OSRIC   Nothing, neither way.
LAERTES   Have at you now!   280

      LAERTES *wounds* HAMLET: *then, in scuffling, they change*
   rapiers, and HAMLET *wounds* LAERTES.

KING   Part them. They are incensed.
HAMLET   Nay, come again.   *The* QUEEN *falls.*
OSRIC   Look to the queen there, ho!
HORATIO   They bleed on both sides. How is it, my lord?

2. out of shape
3. attack   4. trifle with me

OSRIC   How is't, Laertes?   285

LAERTES   Why, as a woodcock to mine own springe,[5] Osric.
I am justly killed with mine own treachery.

HAMLET   How does the queen?

KING   She swoons to see them bleed.

QUEEN   No, no, the drink, the drink! O my dear Hamlet!
The drink, the drink! I am poisoned.   *Dies.* 290

HAMLET   O, villainy! Ho! let the door be locked.
Treachery! seek it out.

LAERTES   It is here, Hamlet. Hamlet, thou art slain;
No med'cine in the world can do thee good.
In thee there is not half an hour's life.   295
The treacherous instrument is in thy hand,
Unbated[6] and envenomed. The foul practice
Hath turned itself on me. Lo, here I lie,
Never to rise again. Thy mother's poisoned.
I can no more. The king, the king's to blame.   300

HAMLET   The point envenomed too?
Then, venom, to thy work.   *Hurts the* KING.

ALL   Treason! treason!

KING   O, yet defend me, friends. I am but hurt.[7]

HAMLET   Here, thou incestuous, murd'rous, damnéd Dane,   305
Drink off this potion. Is thy union here?
Follow my mother.   *The* KING *dies.*

LAERTES   He is justly served.
It is a poison tempered[8] by himself.
Exchange forgiveness with me, noble Hamlet.
Mine and my father's death come not upon thee,   310
Nor thine on me!   *Dies.*

HAMLET   Heaven make thee free of[9] it! I follow thee.
I am dead, Horatio. Wretched queen, adieu!
You that look pale and tremble at this chance,[1]
That are but mutes or audience to this act,   315
Had I but time, as this fell sergeant Death
Is strict in his arrest,[2] O, I could tell you—
But let it be. Horatio, I am dead:
Thou livest; report me and my cause aright
To the unsatisfied.[3]

HORATIO   Never believe it.   320
I am more an antique Roman than a Dane.
Here's yet some liquor left.

HAMLET   As th'art a man,
Give me the cup. Let go. By heaven, I'll ha't.
O God, Horatio, what a wounded name,
Things standing thus unknown, shall live behind me!   325
If thou didst ever hold me in thy heart,
Absent thee from felicity awhile,

5. snare   9. forgive
6. unblunted   1. circumstance
7. wounded   2. summons to court
8. mixed   3. uninformed

And in this harsh world draw thy breath in pain,
To tell my story.   *A march afar off.*
         What warlike noise is this?
OSRIC   Young Fortinbras, with conquest come from Poland,   330
   To th' ambassadors of England gives
   This warlike volley.[4]
HAMLET   O, I die, Horatio!
   The potent poison quite o'er-crows[5] my spirit.
   I cannot live to hear the news from England,
   But I do prophesy th' election lights   335
   On Fortinbras. He has my dying voice.[6]
   So tell him, with th' occurrents,[7] more and less,
   Which have solicited[8]—the rest is silence.   *Dies.*
HORATIO   Now cracks a noble heart. Good night, sweet prince,
   And flights of angels sing thee to thy rest!   *March within.* 340
   Why does the drum come hither?

         Enter FORTINBRAS, *with the* AMBASSADORS *and with drum,*
         colors, and ATTENDANTS.

FORTINBRAS   Where is this sight?
HORATIO   What is it you would see?
   If aught of woe or wonder, cease your search.
FORTINBRAS   This quarry cries on havoc.[9] O proud death,
   What feast is toward[1] in thine eternal cell   345
   That thou so many princes at a shot
   So bloodily hast struck?
AMBASSADORS   The sight is dismal;
   And our affairs from England come too late.
   The ears are senseless[2] that should give us hearing
   To tell him his commandment is fulfilled,   350
   That Rosencrantz and Guildenstern are dead.
   Where should we have our thanks?
HORATIO   Not from his mouth,
   Had it th' ability of life to thank you.
   He never gave commandment for their death.
   But since, so jump[3] upon this bloody question,   355
   You from the Polack wars, and you from England,
   Are here arrived, give orders that these bodies
   High on a stage be placéd to the view,
   And let me speak to th' yet unknowing world
   How these things came about. So shall you hear   360
   Of carnal, bloody, and unnatural acts;

---

4. The staging presents some difficulties
here. If Osric is not clairvoyant, he must
have left the stage at some point and returned. One possibility is that he might
have left to carry out Hamlet's order to
lock the door (line 291) and returned
when the sound of the distant march is
heard.
5. overcomes

6. support
7. circumstances
8. brought about this scene
9. The game killed in the hunt proclaims a slaughter.
1. in preparation
2. without sense of hearing
3. exactly

Of accidental judgments, casual[4] slaughters;
Of deaths put on by cunning and forced cause;
And, in this upshot,[5] purposes mistook
Fall'n on th' inventors' heads. All this can I   365
Truly deliver.

FORTINBRAS   Let us haste to hear it,
And call the noblest to the audience.[6]
For me, with sorrow I embrace my fortune.
I have some rights of memory[7] in this kingdom,
Which now to claim my vantage[8] doth invite me.   370

HORATIO   Of that I shall have also cause to speak,
And from his mouth whose voice will draw on more.
But let this same be presently performed,
Even while men's minds are wild, lest more mischance
On plots and errors happen.

FORTINBRAS   Let four captains   375
Bear Hamlet like a soldier to the stage,
For he was likely, had he been put on,[9]
To have proved most royal; and for his passage
The soldier's music and the rite of war
Speak loudly for him.   380
Take up the bodies. Such a sight as this
Becomes the field, but here shows much amiss.
Go, bid the soldiers shoot.

> *Exeunt marching. A peal of ordnance shot off.*

> *ca.* 1600

---

4. brought about by apparent accident   7. succession
5. result   8. position
6. hearing   9. elected king

3 CHARACTER AND ACTOR

Human beings are ultimately the subject of almost all literature, and individual works of art—especially narrative works such as novels and short stories, but sometimes poems as well—often explore the lives of individuals in some detail. Most literature tends to be rather analytical about human nature, often suggesting both the great complexity of individual people and the great variety of kinds of people who live in the world that literature reflects. People—their activities, habits, eccentricities, and personalities—are ultimately the center of almost all the stories that literature tells. Just as literature is written for human eyes—and has no meaningful existence as text unless people read it and respond—literature always has people at the center of attention within the text. It is the human fascination with **character**—that is, those qualities of mind, spirit, and behavior that make one individual different from every other—that is the basis for literature and the human interest in it, for literature analyzes, describes, portrays, helps us to understand just what it is about ourselves and others that makes us interesting, or sometimes infuriating, to observe and deal with.

Almost all literature depends for its central interest on the portrayal of character; in fact, we regularly call the people presented in literature "characters," signifying that they are imaginary creatures structured according to some carefully defined idea of individual distinctiveness. The primary act of imagination for writers, prior to verbal and aesthetic considerations, prior even to questions of organization and structure, involves the invention of character. That starting point is basic to any literature that tells a story: novels, short stories, films, narrative or dramatic poems, sometimes even lyric poems that explore an integrated set of feelings. But plays have a special engagement with character because of the visual and concrete manner in which they portray people on the stage. The very process of acting calls extraordinary attention to character—for actors, audience, and even playwrights—simply because actors have to take on, quite specifically, characteristics that are not their own and that therefore have to be defined, studied, and specifically imitated. They have to achieve a specific identity; they try "to get *in* character." Actors quite literally try, for a short while, to *be* someone else, and in that process have to define exactly what about the person (or character) they are playing is distinctive, individual, *character*istic.

Some say that there are Dramas of Plot and Dramas of Character, and it is true that some plays emphasize external action while others place more emphasis on what happens in characters' minds and perceptions. But the difference is really one of degree: all plays tell some sort of story and feature actions that are interesting or significant in themselves. And all depend heavily on the portrayal of people and an understanding of how their individual differences contribute to the action, conflict, and resolution of the plot. Often, an important part of a play's effect depends upon our understanding of the inner life of one or more characters. Always, the first task of a play is to introduce the people with whose lives we are to be concerned and establish the central facts of their characters.

The first page of text of most plays contains a complete list of the *dramatis personae*, that is, the persons whose lives are to be presented dramatically. Often the printed program for a particular performance also contains the list (together with the names of the actors playing each part), sometimes with a brief description of each character and an indication of the relationships among characters. Still, whatever textual aids may be provided for curious readers, the play has to *present* characters on the stage as if from scratch, as if the audience has no notion, until instructed, of what to expect. Stories or poems may comment on a character or editorialize rather directly, but plays have to *reveal* character—that is, let the character dramatize the kind of person he or she is by his or her own words and actions. Other characters may, of course, express opinions about a particular character, and our feelings as members of the audience may be influenced by rumor and innuendo. But all characters who appear on the stage ultimately have to be credible in their own terms, and what they appear to be, through their own appearance, actions, and words, is what they are likely to *be* in the minds of an audience.

Establishing character is one of the first tasks of any play, and the opening minutes of exposition contain an explanation to the audience of who the main characters are as well as what the situation is. One way to handle exposition is to have someone appear before the audience and recite a *prologue* which explains directly what the audience needs to know about plot and character. Most modern plays, however, present the exposition more indirectly. In *The Brute*, for example, the opening conversation between Mrs. Popov and her servant Luka tells us essentially what we need to know about her as well as her situation —not only that her husband has recently died but that she has decided that she will pine away in "grief" at his passing, that her grief is more anger at her dead husband than anything else, and that her notion of her behavior is based on some abstract romantic principle of what is honorable, proper, and likely to gain her the reputation of being a noble, self-sacrificing, and unappreciated widow rather than on personal feelings and desires. The attempts by Luka to talk her out of her silly resolution are primarily a pretense to get the play off the ground; within the first two or three minutes the play is fully set up, and we know what we need to know about Mrs. Popov's character.

The other major character, Smirnov, has not yet been heard of, but the main action of the play has been prepared for because the character of Mrs. Popov—romantic, unfulfilled, long-suffering, unhappy, self-deluded, lonely, adamant but needing to be talked out of her hopelessness—has been sufficiently established to make the subsequent events believable. Then Smirnov reveals himself, without any preparation or exposition, by the way he speaks, rants, and storms about the stage in his desperation and rage. The characters "fit": the resolution, although cleverly arranged and carefully drawn out to maximize the effect, makes sense.

Similarly, in *Hamlet* the opening scenes tell us the situation and set an expectation of the major characters. The hero or heroine of a play seldom appears on stage until he or she has been "prepared for," and some specific expectation has been built up in the audience. As in *Hamlet*, it is often minor (or even inconsequential) characters who provide the initial information, sometimes hardly appearing again after performing their expository function. In *Hamlet*, the exposition is handled with extreme subtlety, and (besides crucial information) an appropriate atmosphere for the play is provided at once: things are misty, dark, mysterious, and the talk of uncertain beings (forces that go beyond individual will or possibly even human power) plunge us at once into a complex world where it is difficult to sort truth from fantasy or fear. The character of Hamlet, like everything else in the play, is terribly complicated, and new wrinkles and revelations are continually occurring. The early exposition of Hamlet's character—through Claudius's patronizing address to him, through his mother's loving but specious concern, and through his own language: the bold expressions of anger, doubt, and self-loathing in his soliloquy and his frank and friendly bantering with Horatio—by no means tells us all we need to know, as might happen in a shorter or simpler play, but it sets us on the right track of expectation.

Titles sometimes give away at once that a play is going to focus on a single individual. *Hamlet, King Lear, Auntie Mame, Evita, Hedda Gabler, Death of a Salesman, The Country Wife, The Brute*—such titles imply that a single character gets the primary stage attention, and in most cases the expectations of titles are fulfilled in the play itself, and the main character (or **protagonist**) is not only at the center of the action but also is the primary object of the playwright's (and the audience's) concern. Defining the character of that protagonist (sometimes by comparison and contrast with a competitor, or **antagonist**) often becomes the consuming interest of the play, and the action seems designed to illustrate, or clarify, or develop that character. Occasionally, of course, a title may be a mere convenience (in which case it means nothing about the play's focus) or it may set up misleading expectations so that our attention can be diverted and responses manipulated. (Does the title of *The Brute* refer to Smirnov or to the absent Popov? Is either the real center of attention?) But in plays that genuinely do follow, relentlessly, the inner life as well as the fortunes of one main character, the revelation of that person's attributes, eccentricities, and effects upon other people continues to occupy center stage throughout the play. In such plays, characters are not just introduced so that their characteristics can play themselves out in the plot; characterization continues throughout the play and new complications and subtleties in the character are revealed in the last act as well as the first.

In *Hedda Gabler*, for example, the protagonist's self-centeredness and cruelty are not fully clear until the play is well along. Our first, indirect impressions of Hedda are rather positive. We hear about what a beauty she is, how sought-after she was and how prominent her family. She has just returned from her honeymoon, and it is from her new husband and his Aunt Juju that we hear about Hedda and learn how lucky they feel that she has—rather inexplicably—chosen to marry the unprepossessing Tesman.

There are cautionary hints that Hedda is less than perfect, however. Tesman says she insisted on having all her baggage with her on the journey. Aunt Juliana is a bit shocked by Hedda's having removed the chintz covers from the furniture and the pretension of using the drawing-room as parlor. When Hedda enters she is a bit snappy with both her husband and his aunt. It is quite possible, however, that the audience shares Hedda's low opinion of her new groom and his family, that we are on her side and are trying to figure out how she was trapped into marrying a rather unattractive, thick-skulled, bloodless oaf like Tesman. (Whether this is a fair estimate of his character remains to be seen.)

We may interpret on the page and an actress portray on the stage the pathetic entrapment of a beautiful but vulnerable aristocrat by a crass, if well-meaning, social-climbing member of the bourgeoisie. Read or acted this way the episode in which Hedda mistakes Aunt Juliana's new hat for an old one that must belong to the maid may well tickle our snobbish sense of ourselves and our superiority to the Tesmans. Later in the play, when Hedda's spoiled, unstable, cruel character has been more and more clearly revealed, we learn that this "mistake" was deliberate, that Hedda was trying to put down Tesman's flighty, doting aunt. First impressions are difficult to overcome, and it may take us much of the play to erase our initial admiration of and pity for Hedda. Indeed, we may never erase it, and the tug of the trapped aristocratic beauty and that of the spoiled bitch may alternate or blend. It is this complexity that makes Hedda such a challenging role for an actress and one that all actresses seem to want to try.

Plays contain all kinds of characters, and the characters may be categorized in a variety of ways. They may be labeled by their importance to the plot: protagonist and antagonist, for example, or hero and heroine; they may be called supporting characters, minor characters, or enclitic characters (that is, who are not important in themselves but merely perform a structural function). They may be categorized by the talents they require in actors—there are demanding and challenging roles, juicy parts and dull or routine ones, roles for stars, character-actors, comedians, straight men, and novices—or by their ethnic, religious, or social identities (Jewish mothers, Roumanian ravenhaired beauties, pious frauds, social climbers), by their body types, personality roles or clichéd behaviors (stringbeans, klutzes, dumb blondes, jocks), etc. However individualized characters ultimately turn out to be, they usually begin as some identifiable "type" of person that the audience will recognize and have certain expectations about. Gangsters, flirts, lawyers, Irishmen, pennypinchers, know-it-alls, and drunks are all common examples (from drama and from life) of character-types who have predictable habits and who evoke stock responses.

The range of characters portrayed in any single play may be limited by the kind of play it is or by particular thematic, ideological, and artistic intentions of the playwright. Most good plays do not set out specifically to include a variety of types, but playwrights often find it convenient to use some stereotypes—stereotypes of a nation, an occupation, or body- or personality-type—for special effects, even in serious plays where the emphasis on complexities of character may be significant elsewhere in the play. Rosencrantz and Guildenstern in *Hamlet,* for example, are stereotypical courtiers of Shakespeare's time: they flatter, dissemble, smile, and double cross. Similarly, Polonius is a foolish old man, given to providing advice that no one wants; he is pompous and ultimately silly, and can readily be played as a comic subtype even though he performs a fairly significant role in the play. Secondary characters in even the best plays are often recognizable "types." And even major characters are sometimes portrayed at first as types—before they are complicated, differentiated, and individualized as the play develops and shows them more fully. Hedda Gabler, for example, at first is a Great Beauty who is beginning to age and panic; she is also rich, spoiled, ambitious, used to having her own way. Less and less attractive as she reveals herself more and more, yet more and more helpless in a trap only in part of her own making, Hedda becomes more and more complex, but she begins as a quite predictable (and at first rather harmless-seeming) stereotype.

Ibsen makes no apparent attempt to determine why Hedda has become the way she is. Plausible contexts exist in her social background and family upbringing, but Ibsen does not seem to explore them. His portrait is starkly realistic, purely dramatic in that no narrator or mediator or interpreter stands between us and Hedda, so we are on our own in attempting to understand her fully. To what degree is Hedda more sinned against than sinning? Should she be played for sympathy, a beautiful, fine lady trapped in an ugly bourgeois world and reduced by frustration and abhorrence to deliberate, almost vicious cruelty? Or should she be played as the thoroughly spoiled brat, used to primacy and getting her own way, who lashes out at the weak and innocent, and uses everyone to satisfy her need and greed? Probably neither, but some subtle mix of the two. No wonder actresses clamor for the part.

Tesman similarly begins almost as a comic type—the otherworldly and somewhat absent-minded professor who doesn't really understand veiled allusions to pregnancy, who has little sense of money, who is affectionate without suspicion, who is generally unsophisticated about the ways of the world and very trusting of human nature. He, too, becomes complicated as the play develops (although he is always more simple and straightforward than Hedda), but his annoying mannerisms (his habit of ending most of his sentences with "what," for example) continue to categorize him.

Most plays offer a related pattern of rising complication in character portrayal, and almost all start out from recognizable "types": types are something to build expectations on, and playwrights use the device as a quick introduction to the audience. Good plays almost never—except in melodrama or farce—settle ultimately for character types in the main roles, but the departure from type is almost always a matter of time and degree. Ultimately a character like Hamlet

cannot be meaningfully pigeonholed as any of the types he is associated with—he is not simply a revenger, or a hesitator, or a son in
love with his mother—but he has elements of several recognizable
types in his personality, and it is part of Shakespeare's skill to build
a full human being so carefully from audience expectations ready at
hand.

Characterization in plays involves four separate processes. The first
involves the **conception** of the character in the playwright's mind, at
the moment when the play begins to be an idea, when the playwright
first begins to construct—or even dream about—a plot, structure, or
theme that will ultimately become drama. Characters may develop
or change radically in this process of conception, and nothing in this
process is really complete or final until the other three processes are
also complete. The second process involves **presentation** of the character by the playwright through the words and actions specified in
the text. The artistic decision about how much to present and when
to present it (structural decisions, really) can have an important effect
on how the audience responds to a character and what sort of character ultimately is realized in the play. But the full effect of characterization in a play ultimately comes only when the play is fleshed
out on the stage with a live actor playing the part and adding the
final personal touches to the character with body gestures, facial expressions and tones of voice. In **casting** a play—that is, in deciding
what actors are to play the parts—a director takes a major step in
determining how a character will seem to the audience, for the choice
of actor determines not only the physical appearance, quality of voice,
and degree of presence that a character will present on stage, but
also more subtle details of presentation. The acting talents of each
individual actor—the ranges of emotion that he or she can project,
the subtleties of facial expression and body language, the quality of
intelligence and understanding of the role that the actor is capable
of—determine how a character will ultimately *seem* to an audience.
The final process, that of **acting** itself, is the last logical step in characterization, for in the actual production the actor makes something
distinctive of her or his talents in relation to the author's original
conception. The embodying of a character onstage in a fully realized
production is the ultimate fulfillment of an art that goes beyond words
and stage directions and is ultimately an exercise in impersonation—
when one person steps out of him- or herself and becomes for a brief
while someone different, someone with different character, someone
who is a character, wholly created in the imagination of playwright,
director, and actor as collaborators.

HENRIK IBSEN

Hedda Gabler*

CHARACTERS

GEORGE TESMAN, *research gradu-*
    ate in cultural history
HEDDA, *his wife*
MISS JULIANA TESMAN, *his aunt*

MRS. ELVSTED
JUDGE BRACK
EILERT LOEVBORG
BERTHA, *a maid*

The action takes place in Tesman's villa, in the fashionable quarter of town.

Act 1

A large drawing room, handsomely and tastefully furnished; decorated in dark colors. In the rear wall is a broad open doorway, with curtains drawn back to either side. It leads to a smaller room, decorated in the same style as the drawing room. In the right-hand wall of the drawing room, a folding door leads out to the hall. The opposite wall, on the left, contains french windows, also with curtains drawn back on either side. Through the glass we can see part of a verandah, and trees in autumn colors. Downstage stands an oval table, covered by a cloth and surrounded by chairs. Downstage right, against the wall, is a broad stove tiled with dark porcelain; in front of it stand a high-backed armchair, a cushioned footrest, and two footstools. Upstage right, in an alcove, is a corner sofa, with a small, round table. Downstage left, a little away from the wall, is another sofa. Upstage of the french windows, a piano. On either side of the open doorway in the rear wall stand what-nots holding ornaments of terra cotta and majolica. Against the rear wall of the smaller room can be seen a sofa, a table, and a couple of chairs. Above this sofa hangs the portrait of a handsome old man in general's uniform. Above the table a lamp hangs from the ceiling, with a shade of opalescent, milky glass. All round the drawing room bunches of flowers stand in vases and glasses. More bunches lie on the tables. The floors of both rooms are covered with thick carpets. Morning light. The sun shines in through the french windows.
    MISS JULIANA TESMAN, *wearing a hat and carrying a parasol, enters from the hall, followed by* BERTHA, *who is carrying a bunch of flowers wrapped in paper.* MISS TESMAN *is about sixty-five, of pleasant and kindly appearance. She is neatly but simply dressed in gray outdoor clothes.* BERTHA, *the maid, is rather simple and rustic-looking. She is getting on in years.*

MISS TESMAN [*stops just inside the door, listens, and says in a hushed voice*] No, bless my soul! They're not up yet.
BERTHA [*also in hushed tones*] What did I tell you, miss? The boat

* Translated by Michael Meyer.

didn't get in till midnight. And when they did turn up—Jesus, miss, you should have seen all the things Madam made me unpack before she'd go to bed!

MISS TESMAN Ah, well. Let them have a good lie in. But let's have some nice fresh air waiting for them when they do come down.

Goes to the french windows and throws them wide open.

BERTHA [*bewildered at the table, the bunch of flowers in her hand*] I'm blessed if there's a square inch left to put anything. I'll have to let it lie here, miss.

Puts it on the piano.

MISS TESMAN Well, Bertha dear, so now you have a new mistress. Heaven knows it nearly broke my heart to have to part with you.

BERTHA [*snivels*] What about me, Miss Juju? How do you suppose I felt? After all the happy years I've spent with you and Miss Rena?

MISS TESMAN We must accept it bravely, Bertha. It was the only way. George needs you to take care of him. He could never manage without you. You've looked after him ever since he was a tiny boy.

BERTHA Oh, but, Miss Juju, I can't help thinking about Miss Rena, lying there all helpless, poor dear. And that new girl! She'll never learn the proper way to handle an invalid.

MISS TESMAN Oh, I'll manage to train her. I'll do most of the work myself, you know. You needn't worry about my poor sister, Bertha dear.

BERTHA But Miss Juju, there's another thing. I'm frightened Madam may not find me suitable.

MISS TESMAN Oh, nonsense, Bertha. There may be one or two little things to begin with—

BERTHA She's a real lady. Wants everything just so.

MISS TESMAN But of course she does! General Gabler's daughter! Think of what she was accustomed to when the General was alive. You remember how we used to see her out riding with her father? In that long black skirt? With the feather in her hat?

BERTHA Oh, yes, miss. As if I could forget! But, Lord! I never dreamed I'd live to see a match between her and Master Georgie.

MISS TESMAN Neither did I. By the way, Bertha, from now on you must stop calling him Master Georgie. You must say: Dr. Tesman.

BERTHA Yes, Madam said something about that too. Last night—the moment they'd set foot inside the door. Is it true, then, miss?

MISS TESMAN Indeed it is. Just imagine, Bertha, some foreigners have made him a doctor.[1] It happened while they were away. I had no idea till he told me when they got off the boat.

BERTHA Well, I suppose there's no limit to what he won't become. He's that clever. I never thought he'd go in for hospital work, though.

MISS TESMAN No, he's not that kind of doctor.

---

1. Awarded him a doctoral degree.

Nods impressively.

In any case, you may soon have to address him by an even grander
title.

BERTHA   You don't say! What might that be, miss?

MISS TESMAN [*smiles*]   Ah! If you only knew!

Moved.

Dear God, if only poor dear Joachim could rise out of his grave
and see what his little son has grown into!

Looks round.

But, Bertha, why have you done this? Taken the chintz covers
off all the furniture!

BERTHA   Madam said I was to. Can't stand chintz covers on chairs,
she said.

MISS TESMAN   But surely they're not going to use this room as a
parlor?

BERTHA   So I gathered, miss. From what Madam said. He didn't say
anything. The Doctor.

> GEORGE TESMAN *comes into the rear room, from the right, hum-*
> *ming, with an open, empty traveling bag in his hand. He is*
> *about thirty-three, of medium height and youthful appearance,*
> *rather plump, with an open, round, contented face, and fair*
> *hair and beard. He wears spectacles, and is dressed in com-*
> *fortable, indoor clothes.*

MISS TESMAN   Good morning! Good morning, George!

TESMAN [*in open doorway*]   Auntie Juju! Dear Auntie Juju!

Comes forward and shakes her hand.

You've come all the way out here! And so early! What?

MISS TESMAN   Well, I had to make sure you'd settled in comfortably.

TESMAN   But you can't have had a proper night's sleep.

MISS TESMAN   Oh, never mind that.

TESMAN   We were so sorry we couldn't give you a lift. But you saw
how it was—Hedda had so much luggage—and she insisted on having it all with her.

MISS TESMAN   Yes, I've never seen so much luggage.

BERTHA [*to* TESMAN]   Shall I go and ask Madam if there's anything
I can lend her a hand with?

TESMAN   Er—thank you, Bertha; no, you needn't bother. She says if
she wants you for anything she'll ring.

BERTHA [*over to right*]   Oh. Very good.

TESMAN   Oh, Bertha—take this bag, will you?

BERTHA [*takes it*]   I'll put it in the attic.

Goes out into the hall.

TESMAN   Just fancy, Auntie Juju, I filled that whole bag with notes for my book. You know, it's really incredible what I've managed to find rooting through those archives. By Jove! Wonderful old things no one even knew existed—

MISS TESMAN   I'm sure you didn't waste a single moment of your honeymoon, George dear.

TESMAN   No, I think I can truthfully claim that. But, Auntie Juju, do take your hat off. Here. Let me untie it for you.

MISS TESMAN [*as he does so*]   Oh dear, oh dear! It's just as if you were still living at home with us.

TESMAN [*turns the hat in his hand and looks at it*]   I say! What a splendid new hat!

MISS TESMAN   I bought it for Hedda's sake.

TESMAN   For Hedda's sake? What?

MISS TESMAN   So that Hedda needn't be ashamed of me, in case we ever go for a walk together.

TESMAN [*pats her cheek*]   You still think of everything, don't you, Auntie Juju?

Puts the hat down on a chair by the table.

Come on, let's sit down here on the sofa. And have a little chat while we wait for Hedda.

They sit. She puts her parasol in the corner of the sofa.

MISS TESMAN [*clasps both his hands and looks at him*]   Oh, George, it's so wonderful to have you back, and be able to see you with my own eyes again! Poor dear Joachim's own son!

TESMAN   What about me! It's wonderful for me to see you again, Auntie Juju. You've been a mother to me. And a father, too.

MISS TESMAN   You'll always keep a soft spot in your heart for your old aunties, won't you, George dear?

TESMAN   I suppose Auntie Rena's no better? What?

MISS TESMAN   Alas, no. I'm afraid she'll never get better, poor dear. She's lying there just as she has all these years. Please God I may be allowed to keep her for a little longer. If I lose her I don't know what I'd do. Especially now I haven't you to look after.

TESMAN [*pats her on the back*]   There, there, there!

MISS TESMAN [*with a sudden change of mood*]   Oh but George, fancy you being a married man! And to think it's you who've won Hedda Gabler! The beautiful Hedda Gabler! Fancy! She was always so surrounded by admirers.

TESMAN [*hums a little and smiles contentedly*]   Yes, I suppose there are quite a few people in this town who wouldn't mind being in my shoes. What?

MISS TESMAN   And what a honeymoon! Five months! Nearly six.

TESMAN   Well, I've done a lot of work, you know. All those archives to go through. And I've had to read lots of books.

MISS TESMAN   Yes, dear, of course.

Lowers her voice confidentially.

But tell me, George—haven't you any—any extra little piece of news to give me?

TESMAN   You mean, arising out of the honeymoon?

MISS TESMAN   Yes.

TESMAN   No, I don't think there's anything I didn't tell you in my letters. My doctorate, of course—but I told you about that last night, didn't I?

MISS TESMAN   Yes, yes, I didn't mean that kind of thing. I was just wondering—are you—are you expecting—?

TESMAN   Expecting what?

MISS TESMAN   Oh, come on George, I'm your old aunt!

TESMAN   Well actually—yes, I am expecting something.

MISS TESMAN   I knew it!

TESMAN   You'll be happy to hear that before very long I expect to become a professor.

MISS TESMAN   Professor?

TESMAN   I think I may say that the matter has been decided. But, Auntie Juju, you know about this.

MISS TESMAN   [*gives a little laugh*]   Yes, of course. I'd forgotten.

Changes her tone.

But we were talking about your honeymoon. It must have cost a dreadful amount of money, George?

TESMAN   Oh well, you know, that big research grant I got helped a good deal.

MISS TESMAN   But how on earth did you manage to make it do for two?

TESMAN   Well, to tell the truth it was a bit tricky. What?

MISS TESMAN   Especially when one's traveling with a lady. A little bird tells me that makes things very much more expensive.

TESMAN   Well, yes, of course it does make things a little more expensive. But Hedda has to do things in style, Auntie Juju. I mean, she has to. Anything less grand wouldn't have suited her.

MISS TESMAN   No, no, I suppose not. A honeymoon abroad seems to be the vogue nowadays. But tell me, have you had time to look round the house?

TESMAN   You bet. I've been up since the crack of dawn.

MISS TESMAN   Well, what do you think of it?

TESMAN   Splendid. Absolutely splendid. I'm only wondering what we're going to do with those two empty rooms between that little one and Hedda's bedroom.

MISS TESMAN   [*laughs slyly*]   Ah, George dear, I'm sure you'll manage to find some use for them—in time.

TESMAN   Yes, of course, Auntie Juju, how stupid of me. You're thinking of my books. What?

MISS TESMAN   Yes, yes, dear boy. I was thinking of your books.

TESMAN   You know, I'm so happy for Hedda's sake that we've managed to get this house. Before we became engaged she often used to say this was the only house in town she felt she could really bear to live in. It used to belong to Mrs. Falk—you know, the Prime Minister's widow.

MISS TESMAN   Fancy that! And what a stroke of luck it happened to come into the market. Just as you'd left on your honeymoon.

TESMAN   Yes, Auntie Juju, we've certainly had all the luck with us. What?

MISS TESMAN   But, George dear, the expense! It's going to make a dreadful hole in your pocket, all this.

TESMAN [*a little downcast*]   Yes, I—I suppose it will, won't it?

MISS TESMAN   Oh, George, really!

TESMAN   How much do you think it'll cost? Roughly, I mean? What?

MISS TESMAN   I can't possibly say till I see the bills.

TESMAN   Well, luckily Judge Brack's managed to get it on very favorable terms. He wrote and told Hedda so.

MISS TESMAN   Don't you worry, George dear. Anyway I've stood security for all the furniture and carpets.

TESMAN   Security? But dear, sweet Auntie Juju, how could you possibly stand security?

MISS TESMAN   I've arranged a mortgage on our annuity.

TESMAN [*jumps up*]   What? On your annuity? And—Auntie Rena's?

MISS TESMAN   Yes. Well, I couldn't think of any other way.

TESMAN [*stands in front of her*]   Auntie Juju, have you gone completely out of your mind? That annuity's all you and Auntie Rena have.

MISS TESMAN   All right, there's no need to get so excited about it. It's a pure formality, you know. Judge Brack told me so. He was so kind as to arrange it all for me. A pure formality; those were his very words.

TESMAN   I dare say. All the same—

MISS TESMAN   Anyway, you'll have a salary of your own now. And, good heavens, even if we did have to fork out a little—tighten our belts for a week or two—why, we'd be happy to do so for your sake.

TESMAN   Oh, Auntie Juju! Will you never stop sacrificing yourself for me?

MISS TESMAN [*gets up and puts her hands on his shoulders*]   What else have I to live for but to smooth your road a little, my dear boy? You've never had any mother or father to turn to. And now at last we've achieved our goal. I won't deny we've had our little difficulties now and then. But now, thank the good Lord, George dear, all your worries are past.

TESMAN   Yes, it's wonderful really how everything's gone just right for me.

MISS TESMAN   Yes! And the enemies who tried to bar your way have been struck down. They have been made to bite the dust. The man who was your most dangerous rival has had the mightiest fall. And now he's lying there in the pit he dug for himself, poor misguided creature.

TESMAN   Have you heard any news of Eilert? Since I went away?

MISS TESMAN   Only that he's said to have published a new book.

TESMAN   What! Eilert Loevborg? You mean—just recently? What?

MISS TESMAN   So they say. I don't imagine it can be of any value, do you? When your new book comes out, that'll be another story. What's it going to be about?

TESMAN   The domestic industries of Brabant[2] in the Middle Ages.

MISS TESMAN   Oh, George! The things you know about!

TESMAN   Mind you, it may be some time before I actually get down to writing it. I've made these very extensive notes, and I've got to file and index them first.

MISS TESMAN   Ah, yes! Making notes; filing and indexing; you've always been wonderful at that. Poor dear Joachim was just the same.

TESMAN   I'm looking forward so much to getting down to that. Especially now I've a home of my own to work in.

MISS TESMAN   And above all, now that you have the girl you set your heart on, George dear.

TESMAN [*embraces her*]   Oh, yes, Auntie Juju, yes! Hedda's the loveliest thing of all!

Looks towards the doorway.

I think I hear her coming. What?

HEDDA *enters the rear room from the left, and comes into the drawing room. She is a woman of twenty-nine. Distinguished, aristocratic face and figure. Her complexion is pale and opalescent. Her eyes are steel-gray, with an expression of cold, calm serenity. Her hair is of a handsome auburn color, but is not especially abundant. She is dressed in an elegant, somewhat loose-fitting morning gown.*

MISS TESMAN [*goes to greet her*]   Good morning, Hedda dear! Good morning!

HEDDA [*holds out her hand*]   Good morning, dear Miss Tesman. What an early hour to call. So kind of you.

MISS TESMAN [*seems somewhat embarrassed*]   And has the young bride slept well in her new home?

HEDDA   Oh—thank you, yes. Passably well.

TESMAN [*laughs*]   Passably. I say, Hedda, that's good! When I jumped out of bed, you were sleeping like a top.

HEDDA   Yes. Fortunately. One has to accustom oneself to anything new, Miss Tesman. It takes time.

Looks left.

Oh, that maid's left the french windows open. This room's flooded with sun.

MISS TESMAN [*goes towards the windows*]   Oh—let me close them.

2. Prosperous duchy (1190–1477), now divided between Belgium and the Netherlands.

HEDDA   No, no, don't do that. Tesman dear, draw the curtains. This light's blinding me.

TESMAN [*at the windows*]   Yes, yes, dear. There, Hedda, now you've got shade and fresh air.

HEDDA   This room needs fresh air. All these flowers— But my dear Miss Tesman, won't you take a seat?

MISS TESMAN   No, really not, thank you. I just wanted to make sure you have everything you need. I must see about getting back home. My poor dear sister will be waiting for me.

TESMAN   Be sure to give her my love, won't you? Tell her I'll run over and see her later today.

MISS TESMAN   Oh yes, I'll tell her that. Oh, George—

Fumbles in the pocket of her skirt.

I almost forgot. I've brought something for you.

TESMAN   What's that, Auntie Juju? What?

MISS TESMAN [*pulls out a flat package wrapped in newspaper and gives it to him*]   Open and see, dear boy.

TESMAN [*opens the package*]   Good heavens! Auntie Juju, you've kept them! Hedda, this is really very touching. What?

HEDDA [*by the what-nots, on the right*]   What is it, Tesman?

TESMAN   My old shoes! My slippers, Hedda!

HEDDA   Oh, them. I remember you kept talking about them on our honeymoon.

TESMAN   Yes, I missed them dreadfully.

Goes over to her.

Here, Hedda, take a look.

HEDDA [*goes away towards the stove*]   Thanks, I won't bother.

TESMAN [*follows her*]   Fancy, Hedda, Auntie Rena's embroidered them for me. Despite her being so ill. Oh, you can't imagine what memories they have for me.

HEDDA [*by the table*]   Not for me.

MISS TESMAN   No, Hedda's right there, George.

TESMAN   Yes, but I thought since she's one of the family now—

HEDDA [*interrupts*]   Tesman, we really can't go on keeping this maid.

MISS TESMAN   Not keep Bertha?

TESMAN   What makes you say that, dear? What?

HEDDA [*points*]   Look at that! She's left her old hat lying on the chair.

TESMAN [*appalled, drops his slippers on the floor*]   But, Hedda—!

HEDDA   Suppose someone came in and saw it?

TESMAN   But, Hedda—that's Auntie Juju's hat.

HEDDA   Oh?

MISS TESMAN [*picks up the hat*]   Indeed it's mine. And it doesn't happen to be old, Hedda dear.

HEDDA   I didn't look at it very closely, Miss Tesman.

MISS TESMAN [*tying on the hat*]   As a matter of fact, it's the first time I've worn it. As the good Lord is my witness.

TESMAN   It's very pretty, too. Really smart.

MISS TESMAN   Oh, I'm afraid it's nothing much really.

> *Looks round.*

My parasol? Ah, here it is.

> *Takes it.*

This is mine, too.

> *Murmurs.*

Not Bertha's.

TESMAN   A new hat and a new parasol! I say, Hedda, fancy that!

HEDDA   Very pretty and charming

TESMAN   Yes, isn't it? What? But Auntie Juju, take a good look at Hedda before you go. Isn't she pretty and charming?

MISS TESMAN   Dear boy, there's nothing new in that. Hedda's been a beauty ever since the day she was born.

> *Nods and goes right.*

TESMAN [*follows her*]   Yes, but have you noticed how strong and healthy she's looking? And how she's filled out since we went away?

MISS TESMAN [*stops and turns*]   Filled out?

HEDDA [*walks across the room*]   Oh, can't we forget it?

TESMAN   Yes, Auntie Juju—you can't see it so clearly with that dress on. But I've good reason to know—

HEDDA [*by the french windows, impatiently*]   You haven't good reason to know anything.

TESMAN   It must have been the mountain air up there in the Tyrol—

HEDDA [*curtly, interrupts him*]   I'm exactly the same as when I went away.

TESMAN   You keep on saying so. But you're not. I'm right, aren't I, Auntie Juju?

MISS TESMAN [*has folded her hands and is gazing at her*]   She's beautiful—beautiful. Hedda is beautiful.

> *Goes over to* HEDDA, *takes her head between her hands, draws it down and kisses her hair.*

God bless and keep you, Hedda Tesman. For George's sake.

HEDDA [*frees herself politely*]   Oh—let me go, please.

MISS TEMAN [*quietly, emotionally*]   I shall come and see you both every day.

TESMAN   Yes, Auntie Juju, please do. What?

MISS TESMAN   Good-bye! Good-bye!

> *She goes out into the hall.* TESMAN *follows her. The door remains open.* TESMAN *is heard sending his love to Aunt Rena and thanking* MISS TESMAN *for his slippers. Meanwhile* HEDDA

walks up and down the room raising her arms and clenching her fists as though in desperation. Then she throws aside the curtains from the french windows and stands there, looking out. A few moments later, TESMAN *returns and closes the door behind him.*

TESMAN [*picks up his slippers from the floor*] What are you looking at, Hedda?

HEDDA [*calm and controlled again*] Only the leaves. They're so golden. And withered.

TESMAN [*wraps up the slippers and lays them on the table*] Well, we're into September now.

HEDDA [*restless again*] Yes. We're already into September.

TESMAN Auntie Juju was behaving rather oddly, I thought, didn't you? Almost as though she was in church or something. I wonder what came over her. Any idea?

HEDDA I hardly know her. Does she often act like that?

TESMAN Not to the extent she did today.

HEDDA [*goes away from the french windows*] Do you think she was hurt by what I said about the hat?

TESMAN Oh, I don't think so. A little at first, perhaps—

HEDDA But what a thing to do, throw her hat down in someone's drawing room. People don't do such things.

TESMAN I'm sure Auntie Juju doesn't do it very often.

HEDDA Oh well, I'll make it up with her.

TESMAN Oh Hedda, would you?

HEDDA When you see them this afternoon invite her to come out here this evening.

TESMAN You bet I will! I say, there's another thing which would please her enormously.

HEDDA Oh?

TESMAN If you could bring yourself to call her Auntie Juju. For my sake, Hedda? What?

HEDDA Oh no, really, Tesman, you mustn't ask me to do that. I've told you so once before. I'll try to call her Aunt Juliana. That's as far as I'll go.

TESMAN [*after a moment*] I say, Hedda, is anything wrong? What?

HEDDA I'm just looking at my old piano. It doesn't really go with all this.

TESMAN As soon as I start getting my salary we'll see about changing it.

HEDDA No, no, don't let's change it. I don't want to part with it. We can move it into that little room and get another one to put in here.

TESMAN [*a little downcast*] Yes, we—might do that.

HEDDA [*picks up the bunch of flowers from the piano*] These flowers weren't here when we arrived last night.

TESMAN I expect Auntie Juju brought them.

HEDDA Here's a card.

Takes it out and reads.

"Will come back later today." Guess who it's from?

TESMAN   No idea. Who? What?

HEDDA   It says: "Mrs. Elvsted."

TESMAN   No, really? Mrs. Elvsted! She used to be Miss Rysing, didn't she?

HEDDA   Yes. She was the one with that irritating hair she was always showing off. I hear she used to be an old flame of yours.

TESMAN   [*laughs*]   That didn't last long. Anyway, that was before I got to know you, Hedda. By Jove, fancy her being in town!

HEDDA   Strange she should call. I only knew her at school.

TESMAN   Yes, I haven't seen her for—oh, heaven knows how long. I don't know how she manages to stick it out up there in the north. What?

HEDDA   [*thinks for a moment, then says suddenly*]   Tell me, Tesman, doesn't he live somewhere up in those parts? You know—Eilert Loevborg?

TESMAN   Yes, that's right. So he does.

BERTHA *enters from the hall.*

BERTHA   She's here again, madam. The lady who came and left the flowers.

Points.

The ones you're holding.

HEDDA   Oh, is she? Well, show her in.

BERTHA *opens the door for* MRS. ELVSTED *and goes out.* MRS. ELVSTED *is a delicately built woman with gentle, attractive features. Her eyes are light blue, large, and somewhat prominent, with a frightened, questioning expression. Her hair is extremely fair, almost flaxen, and is exceptionally wavy and abundant. She is two or three years younger than* HEDDA. *She is wearing a dark visiting dress, in good taste but not quite in the latest fashion.*

HEDDA   [*goes cordially to greet her*]   Dear Mrs. Elvsted, good morning. How delightful to see you again after all this time.

MRS. ELVSTED   [*nervously, trying to control herself*]   Yes, it's many years since we met.

TESMAN   And since *we* met. What?

HEDDA   Thank you for your lovely flowers.

MRS. ELVSTED   Oh, please—I wanted to come yesterday afternoon. But they told me you were away—

TESMAN   You've only just arrived in town, then? What?

MRS. ELVSTED   I got here yesterday, around midday. Oh, I became almost desperate when I heard you weren't here.

HEDDA   Desperate? Why?

TESMAN   My dear Mrs. Rysing—Elvsted—

HEDDA   There's nothing wrong, I hope?

MRS. ELVSTED   Yes, there is. And I don't know anyone else here whom I can turn to.

HEDDA   [*puts the flowers down on the table*]   Come and sit with me on the sofa—

MRS. ELVSTED   Oh, I feel too restless to sit down.

HEDDA   You must. Come along, now.

She pulls MRS. ELVSTED *down on to the sofa and sits beside her.*

TESMAN   Well? Tell us, Mrs.—er—

HEDDA   Has something happened at home?

MRS. ELVSTED   Yes—that is, yes and no. Oh, I do hope you won't misunderstand me—

HEDDA   Then you'd better tell us the whole story, Mrs. Elvsted.

TESMAN   That's why you've come. What?

MRS. ELVSTED   Yes—yes, it is. Well, then—in case you don't already know—Eilert Loevborg is in town.

HEDDA   Loevborg here?

TESMAN   Eilert back in town? By Jove, Hedda, did you hear that?

HEDDA   Yes, of course I heard.

MRS. ELVSTED   He's been here a week. A whole week! In this city. Alone. With all those dreadful people—

HEDDA   But my dear Mrs. Elvsted, what concern is he of yours?

MRS. ELVSTED   [*gives her a frightened look and says quickly*]   He's been tutoring the children.

HEDDA   Your children?

MRS. ELVSTED   My husband's. I have none.

HEDDA   Oh, you mean your stepchildren.

MRS. ELVSTED   Yes.

TESMAN   [*gropingly*]   But was he sufficiently—I don't know how to put it—sufficiently regular in his habits to be suited to such a post? What?

MRS. ELVSTED   For the past two to three years he has been living irreproachably.

TESMAN   You don't say! By Jove, Hedda, hear that?

HEDDA   I hear.

MRS. ELVSTED   Quite irreproachably, I assure you. In every respect. All the same—in this big city—with money in his pockets—I'm so dreadfully frightened something may happen to him.

TESMAN   But why didn't he stay up there with you and your husband?

MRS. ELVSTED   Once his book had come out, he became restless.

TESMAN   Oh, yes—Auntie Juju said he'd brought out a new book.

MRS. ELVSTED   Yes, a big new book about the history of civilization. A kind of general survey. It came out a fortnight ago. Everyone's been buying it and reading it—it's created a tremendous stir—

TESMAN   Has it really? It must be something he's dug up, then.

MRS. ELVSTED   You mean from the old days?

TESMAN   Yes.

MRS. ELVSTED   No, he's written it all since he came to live with us.

TESMAN   Well, that's splendid news, Hedda. Fancy that!

MRS. ELVSTED   Oh, yes! If only he can go on like this!

HEDDA   Have you met him since you came here?

MRS. ELVSTED   No, not yet. I had such dreadful difficulty finding his address. But this morning I managed to track him down at last.

HEDDA [*looks searchingly at her*]   I must say I find it a little strange that your husband—hm—

MRS. ELVSTED [*starts nervously*]   My husband! What do you mean?

HEDDA   That he should send you all the way here on an errand of this kind. I'm surprised he didn't come himself to keep an eye on his friend.

MRS. ELVSTED   Oh, no, no—my husband hasn't the time. Besides. I—er—wanted to do some shopping here.

HEDDA [*with a slight smile*]   Ah. Well, that's different.

MRS. ELVSTED [*gets up quickly, restlessly*]   Please, Mr. Tesman, I beg you—be kind to Eilert Loevborg if he comes here. I'm sure he will. I mean, you used to be such good friends in the old days. And you're both studying the same subject, as far as I can understand. You're in the same field, aren't you?

TESMAN   Well, we used to be, anyway.

MRS. ELVSTED   Yes—so I beg you earnestly, do please, please, keep an eye on him. Oh, Mr. Tesman, do promise me you will.

TESMAN   I shall be only too happy to do so, Mrs. Rysing.

HEDDA   Elvsted.

TESMAN   I'll do everything for Eilert that lies in my power. You can rely on that.

MRS. ELVSTED   Oh, how good and kind you are!

Presses his hands.

Thank you, thank you, thank you.

Frightened.

My husband's so fond of him, you see.

HEDDA [*gets up*]   You'd better send him a note, Tesman. He may not come to you of his own accord.

TESMAN   Yes, that'd probably be the best plan, Hedda. What?

HEDDA   The sooner the better. Why not do it now?

MRS. ELVSTED [*pleadingly*]   Oh yes, if only you would!

TESMAN   I'll do it this very moment. Do you have his address, Mrs.—er—Elvsted?

MRS. ELVSTED   Yes.

Takes a small piece of paper from her pocket and gives it to him.

TESMAN   Good, good. Right, well I'll go inside and—

Looks round.

Where are my slippers? Oh yes, here.

Picks up the package and is about to go.

HEDDA Try to sound friendly. Make it a nice long letter.
TESMAN Right, I will.
MRS. ELVSTED Please don't say anything about my having seen you.
TESMAN Good heavens no, of course not. What?

Goes out through the rear room to the right.

HEDDA [*goes over to* MRS. ELVSTED, *smiles, and says softly*] Well!
Now we've killed two birds with one stone.
MRS. ELVSTED What do you mean?
HEDDA Didn't you realize I wanted to get him out of the room?
MRS. ELVSTED So that he could write the letter?
HEDDA And so that I could talk to you alone.
MRS. ELVSTED [*confused*] About this?
HEDDA Yes, about this.
MRS. ELVSTED [*in alarm*] But there's nothing more to tell, Mrs. Tes-
man. Really there isn't.
HEDDA Oh, yes there is. There's a lot more. I can see that. Come
along, let's sit down and have a little chat.

She pushes MRS. ELVSTED *down into the armchair by the stove
and seats herself on one of the footstools.*

MRS. ELVSTED [*looks anxiously at her watch*] Really, Mrs. Tesman,
I think I ought to be going now.
HEDDA There's no hurry. Well? How are things at home?
MRS. ELVSTED I'd rather not speak about that.
HEDDA But my dear, you can tell me. Good heavens, we were at
school together.
MRS. ELVSTED Yes, but you were a year senior to me. Oh, I used to
be terribly frightened of you in those days.
HEDDA Frightened of me?
MRS. ELVSTED Yes, terribly frightened. Whenever you met me on the
staircase you used to pull my hair.
HEDDA No, did I?
MRS. ELVSTED Yes. And once you said you'd burn it all off.
HEDDA Oh, that was only in fun.
MRS. ELVSTED Yes, but I was so silly in those days. And then after-
wards—I mean, we've drifted so far apart. Our backgrounds were so
different.
HEDDA Well, now we must try to drift together again. Now listen.
When we were at school we used to call each other by our Christian
names—
MRS. ELVSTED No, I'm sure you're mistaken.
HEDDA I'm sure I'm not. I remember it quite clearly. Let's tell each
other our secrets, as we used to in the old days.

Moves closer on her footstool.

There, now.

Kisses her on the cheek.

You must call me Hedda.

MRS. ELVSTED [*squeezes her hands and pats them*] Oh you're so kind. I'm not used to people being so nice to me.

HEDDA Now, now, now. And I shall call you Tora, the way I used to.

MRS. ELVSTED My name is Thea.

HEDDA Yes, of course. Of course. I meant Thea.

Looks at her sympathetically.

So you're not used to kindness, Thea? In your own home?

MRS. ELVSTED Oh, if only I had a home! But I haven't. I've never had one.

HEDDA [*looks at her for a moment*] I thought that was it.

MRS. ELVSTED [*stares blankly and helplessly*] Yes—yes—yes.

HEDDA I can't remember exactly now, but didn't you first go to Mr. Elvsted as a housekeeper?

MRS. ELVSTED Governess, actually. But his wife—at the time, I mean —she was an invalid, and had to spend most of her time in bed. So I had to look after the house too.

HEDDA But in the end, you became mistress of the house.

MRS. ELVSTED [*sadly*] Yes, I did.

HEDDA Let me see. Roughly how long ago was that?

MRS. ELVSTED When I got married, you mean?

HEDDA Yes.

MRS. ELVSTED About five years.

HEDDA Yes; it must be about that.

MRS. ELVSTED Oh, those five years! Especially the last two or three, Oh, Mrs. Tesman, if you only knew—!

HEDDA [*slaps her hand gently*] Mrs. Tesman? Oh, Thea!

MRS. ELVSTED I'm sorry, I'll try to remember. Yes—if you had any idea—

HEDDA [*casually*] Eilert Loevborg's been up there too, for about three years, hasn't he?

MRS. ELVSTED [*looks at her uncertainly*] Eilert Loevborg? Yes, he has.

HEDDA Did you know him before? When you were here?

MRS. ELVSTED No, not really. That is—I knew him by name, of course.

HEDDA But up there, he used to visit you?

MRS. ELVSTED Yes, he used to come and see us every day. To give the children lessons. I found I couldn't do that as well as manage the house.

HEDDA I'm sure you couldn't. And your husband—? I suppose being a magistrate he has to be away from home a good deal?

MRS. ELVSTED Yes. You see, Mrs.—you see, Hedda, he has to cover the whole district.

HEDDA [*leans against the arm of* MRS. ELVSTED'S *chair*]   Poor, pretty little Thea! Now you must tell me the whole story. From beginning to end.

MRS. ELVSTED   Well—what do you want to know?

HEDDA   What kind of a man is your husband, Thea? I mean, as a person. Is he kind to you?

MRS. ELVSTED [*evasively*]   I'm sure he does his best to be.

HEDDA   I only wonder if he isn't too old for you. There's more than twenty years between you, isn't there?

MRS. ELVSTED [*irritably*]   Yes, there's that too. Oh, there are so many things. We're different in every way. We've nothing in common. Nothing whatever.

HEDDA   But he loves you, surely? In his own way?

MRS. ELVSTED   Oh, I don't know. I think he just finds me useful. And then I don't cost much to keep. I'm cheap.

HEDDA   Now you're being stupid.

MRS. ELVSTED [*shakes her head*]   It can't be any different. With him. He doesn't love anyone except himself. And perhaps the children— a little.

HEDDA   He must be fond of Eilert Loevborg, Thea.

MRS. ELVSTED [*looks at her*]   Eilert Loevborg? What makes you think that?

HEDDA   Well, if he sends you all the way down here to look for him—

Smiles almost imperceptibly.

Besides, you said so yourself to Tesman.

MRS. ELVSTED [*with a nervous twitch*]   Did I? Oh yes, I suppose I did.

Impulsively, but keeping her voice low.

Well, I might as well tell you the whole story. It's bound to come out sooner or later.

HEDDA   But my dear Thea—?

MRS. ELVSTED   My husband had no idea I was coming here.

HEDDA   What? Your husband didn't know?

MRS. ELVSTED   No, of course not. As a matter of fact, he wasn't even there. He was away at the assizes. Oh, I couldn't stand it any longer, Hedda! I just couldn't. I'd be so dreadfully lonely up there now.

HEDDA   Go on.

MRS. ELVSTED   So I packed a few things. Secretly. And went.

HEDDA   Without telling anyone?

MRS. ELVSTED   Yes. I caught the train and came straight here.

HEDDA   But my dear Thea! How brave of you!

MRS. ELVSTED [*gets up and walks across the room*]   Well, what else could I do?

HEDDA   But what do you suppose your husband will say when you get back?

MRS. ELVSTED [*by the table, looks at her*]   Back there? To him?

HEDDA   Yes. Surely—?

MRS. ELVSTED   I shall never go back to him.

HEDDA [*gets up and goes closer*]   You mean you've left your home for good?

MRS. ELVSTED   Yes. I didn't see what else I could do.

HEDDA   But to do it so openly!

MRS. ELVSTED   Oh, it's no use trying to keep a thing like that secret.

HEDDA   But what do you suppose people will say?

MRS. ELVSTED   They can say what they like.

Sits sadly, wearily on the sofa.

I had to do it.

HEDDA [*after a short silence*]   What do you intend to do now? How are you going to live?

MRS. ELVSTED   I don't know. I only know that I must live wherever Eilert Loevborg is. If I am to go on living.

HEDDA [*moves a chair from the table, sits on it near* MRS. ELVSTED *and strokes her hands*]   Tell me, Thea, how did this—friendship between you and Eilert Loevborg begin?

MRS. ELVSTED   Oh, it came about gradually. I developed a kind of—power over him.

HEDDA   Oh?

MRS. ELVSTED   He gave up his old habits. Not because I asked him to. I'd never have dared to do that. I suppose he just noticed I didn't like that kind of thing. So he gave it up.

HEDDA [*hides a smile*]   So you've made a new man of him. Clever little Thea!

MRS. ELVSTED   Yes—anyway, he says I have. And he's made a—sort of—real person of me. Taught me to think—and to understand all kinds of things.

HEDDA   Did he give you lessons too?

MRS. ELVSTED   Not exactly lessons. But he talked to me. About—oh, you've no idea—so many things! And then he let me work with him. Oh, it was wonderful. I was so happy to be allowed to help him.

HEDDA   Did he allow you to help him!

MRS. ELVSTED   Yes. Whenever he wrote anything we always—did it together.

HEDDA   Like good pals?

MRS. ELVSTED [*eagerly*]   Pals! Yes—why, Hedda, that's exactly the word he used! Oh, I ought to feel so happy. But I can't. I don't know if it will last.

HEDDA   You don't seem very sure of him.

MRS. ELVSTED [*sadly*]   Something stands between Eilert Loevborg and me. The shadow of another woman.

HEDDA   Who can that be?

MRS. ELVSTED   I don't know. Someone he used to be friendly with in—in the old days. Someone he's never been able to forget.

HEDDA   What has he told you about her?

MRS. ELVSTED   Oh, he only mentioned her once, casually.

HEDDA   Well! What did he say?

MRS. ELVSTED   He said when he left her she tried to shoot him with a pistol.

HEDDA [*cold, controlled*]   What nonsense. People don't do such things. The kind of people we know.

MRS. ELVSTED   No. I think it must have been that red-haired singer he used to—

HEDDA   Ah yes, very probably.

MRS. ELVSTED   I remember they used to say she always carried a loaded pistol.

HEDDA   Well then, it must be her.

MRS. ELVSTED   But, Hedda, I hear she's come back, and is living here. Oh, I'm so desperate—!

HEDDA [*glances towards the rear room*]   Ssh! Tesman's coming.

> *Gets up and whispers.*

Thea, we mustn't breathe a word about this to anyone.

MRS. ELVSTED [*jumps up*]   Oh, no, no! Please don't!

> GEORGE TESMAN *appears from the right in the rear room with a letter in his hand, and comes into the drawing room.*

TESMAN   Well, here's my little epistle all signed and sealed.

HEDDA   Good. I think Mrs. Elvsted wants to go now. Wait a moment —I'll see you as far as the garden gate.

TESMAN   Er—Hedda, do you think Bertha could deal with this?

HEDDA [*takes the letter*]   I'll give her instructions.

> BERTHA *enters from the hall.*

BERTHA   Judge Brack is here and asks if he may pay his respects to Madam and the Doctor.

HEDDA   Yes, ask him to be so good as to come in. And—wait a moment —drop this letter in the post box.

BERTHA [*takes the letter*] Very good, madam.

> *She opens the door for* JUDGE BRACK, *and goes out.* JUDGE BRACK *is forty-five; rather short, but well-built, and elastic in his movements. He has a roundish face with an aristocratic profile. His hair, cut short, is still almost black, and is carefully barbered. Eyes lively and humorous. Thick eyebrows. His moustache is also thick, and is trimmed square at the ends. He is wearing outdoor clothes which are elegant but a little too youthful for him. He has a monocle in one eye; now and then he lets it drop.*

BRACK [*hat in hand, bows*]   May one presume to call so early?

HEDDA   One may presume.

TESMAN [*shakes his hand*]   You're welcome here any time. Judge Brack—Mrs. Rysing.

HEDDA *sighs.*

BRACK [*bows*] Ah—charmed—
HEDDA [*looks at him and laughs*] What fun to be able to see you by daylight for once, Judge.
BRACK Do I look—different?
HEDDA Yes. A little younger, I think.
BRACK Obliged.
TESMAN Well, what do you think of Hedda? What? Doesn't she look well? Hasn't she filled out—?
HEDDA Oh, do stop it. You ought to be thanking Judge Brack for all the inconvenience he's put himself to—
BRACK Nonsense, it was a pleasure—
HEDDA You're a loyal friend. But my other friend is pining to get away. Au revoir, Judge. I won't be a minute.

> *Mutual salutations.* MRS. ELVSTED *and* HEDDA *go out through the hall.*

BRACK Well, is your wife satisfied with everything?
TESMAN Yes, we can't thank you enough. That is—we may have to shift one or two things around, she tells me. And we're short of one or two little items we'll have to purchase.
BRACK Oh? Really?
TESMAN But you mustn't worry your head about that. Hedda says she'll get what's needed. I say, why don't we sit down? What?
BRACK Thanks, just for a moment.

> *Sits at the table.*

There's something I'd like to talk to you about, my dear Tesman.
TESMAN Oh? Ah yes, of course.

> *Sits.*

After the feast comes the reckoning. What?
BRACK Oh, never mind about the financial side—there's no hurry about that. Though I could wish we'd arranged things a little less palatially.
TESMAN Good heavens, that'd never have done. Think of Hedda, my dear chap. You know her. I couldn't possibly ask her to live like a suburban housewife.
BRACK No, no—that's just the problem.
TESMAN Anyway, it can't be long now before my nomination[3] comes through.
BRACK Well, you know, these things often take time.
TESMAN Have you heard any more news? What?
BRACK Nothing definite.

> *Changing the subject.*

3. To a professorship at the university.

Oh, by the way, I have one piece of news for you.

TESMAN   What?

BRACK   Your old friend Eilert Loevborg is back in town.

TESMAN   I know that already.

BRACK   Oh? How did you hear that?

TESMAN   She told me. That lady who went out with Hedda.

BRACK   I see. What was her name? I didn't catch it.

TESMAN   Mrs. Elvsted.

BRACK   Oh, the magistrate's wife. Yes, Loevborg's been living up near them, hasn't he?

TESMAN   I'm delighted to hear he's become a decent human being again.

BRACK   Yes, so they say.

TESMAN   I gather he's published a new book, too. What?

BRACK   Indeed he has.

TESMAN   I hear it's created rather a stir.

BRACK   Quite an unusual stir.

TESMAN   I say, isn't that splendid news! He's such a gifted chap— and I was afraid he'd gone to the dogs for good.

BRACK   Most people thought he had.

TESMAN   But I can't think what he'll do now. How on earth will he manage to make ends meet? What?

> As he speaks his last words, HEDDA *enters from the hall.*

HEDDA   [*to* BRACK, *laughs slightly scornfully*]   Tesman is always worrying about making ends meet.

TESMAN   We were talking about poor Eilert Loevborg, Hedda dear.

HEDDA   [*gives him a quick look*]   Oh, were you?

> *Sits in the armchair by the stove and asks casually.*

Is he in trouble?

TESMAN   Well, he must have run through his inheritance long ago by now. And he can't write a new book every year. What? So I'm wondering what's going to become of him.

BRACK   I may be able to enlighten you there.

TESMAN   Oh?

BRACK   You mustn't forget he has relatives who wield a good deal of influence.

TESMAN   Relatives? Oh, they've quite washed their hands of him, I'm afraid.

BRACK   They used to regard him as the hope of the family.

TESMAN   Used to, yes. But he's put an end to that.

HEDDA   Who knows?

> *With a little smile.*

I hear the Elvsteds have made a new man of him.

BRACK   And then this book he's just published—

TESMAN   Well, let's hope they find something for him. I've just written him a note. Oh, by the way, Hedda, I asked him to come over and see us this evening.

BRACK But my dear chap, you're coming to me this evening. My bachelor party. You promised me last night when I met you at the boat.

HEDDA Had you forgotten, Tesman?

TESMAN Good heavens, yes, I'd quite forgotten.

BRACK Anyway, you can be quite sure he won't turn up here.

TESMAN Why do you think that? What?

BRACK [*a little unwillingly, gets up and rests his hands on the back of his chair*] My dear Tesman—and you, too, Mrs. Tesman—there's something I feel you ought to know.

TESMAN Concerning Eilert?

BRACK Concerning him and you.

TESMAN Well, my dear Judge, tell us, please!

BRACK You must be prepared for your nomination not to come through quite as quickly as you hope and expect.

TESMAN [*jumps up uneasily*] Is anything wrong? What?

BRACK There's a possibility that the appointment may be decided by competition—

TESMAN Competition! By Jove, Hedda, fancy that!

HEDDA [*leans further back in her chair*] Ah! How interesting!

TESMAN But who else—? I say, you don't mean—?

BRACK Exactly. By competition with Eilert Loevborg.

TESMAN [*clasps his hands in alarm*] No, no, but this is inconceivable! It's absolutely impossible! What?

BRACK Hm. We may find it'll happen, all the same.

TESMAN No, but—Judge Brack, they couldn't be so inconsiderate towards me!

Waves his arms.

I mean, by Jove, I—I'm a married man! It was on the strength of this that Hedda and I *got* married! We ran up some pretty hefty debts. And borrowed money from Auntie Juju! I mean, good heavens, they practically promised me the appointment. What?

BRACK Well, well, I'm sure you'll get it. But you'll have to go through a competition.

HEDDA [*motionless in her armchair*] How exciting, Tesman. It'll be a kind of duel, by Jove.

TESMAN My dear Hedda, how can you take it so lightly?

HEDDA [*as before*] I'm not. I can't wait to see who's going to win.

BRACK In any case, Mrs. Tesman, it's best you should know how things stand. I mean before you commit yourself to these little items I hear you're threatening to purchase.

HEDDA I can't allow this to alter my plans.

BRACK Indeed? Well, that's your business. Good-bye.

To TESMAN.

I'll come and collect you on the way home from my afternoon walk.

TESMAN   Oh, yes, yes. I'm sorry, I'm all upside down just now.

HEDDA [*lying in her chair, holds out her hand*]   Good-bye, Judge. See you this afternoon.

BRACK   Thank you. Good-bye, good-bye.

TESMAN [*sees him to the door*]   Good-bye, my dear Judge. You will excuse me, won't you?

JUDGE BRACK *goes out through the hall.*

TESMAN [*pacing up and down*]   Oh, Hedda! One oughtn't to go plunging off on wild adventures. What?

HEDDA [*looks at him and smiles*]   Like you're doing?

TESMAN   Yes. I mean, there's no denying it, it was a pretty big adventure to go off and get married and set up house merely on expectation.

HEDDA   Perhaps you're right.

TESMAN   Well, anyway, we have our home, Hedda. By Jove, yes. The home we dreamed of. And set our hearts on. What?

HEDDA [*gets up slowly, wearily*]   You agreed that we should enter society. And keep open house. That was the bargain.

TESMAN   Yes. Good heavens, I was looking forward to it all so much. To seeing you play hostess to a select circle. By Jove! What? Ah, well, for the time being we shall have to make do with each other's company, Hedda. Perhaps have Auntie Juju in now and then. Oh dear, this wasn't at all what you had in mind—

HEDDA   I won't be able to have a liveried footman. For a start.

TESMAN   Oh no, we couldn't possibly afford a footman.

HEDDA   And that thoroughbred horse you promised me—

TESMAN [*fearfully*]   Thoroughbred horse!

HEDDA   I mustn't even think of that now.

TESMAN   Heaven forbid!

HEDDA [*walks across the room*]   Ah, well. I still have one thing left to amuse myself with.

TESMAN [*joyfully*]   Thank goodness for that. What's that, Hedda? What?

HEDDA [*in the open doorway, looks at him with concealed scorn*]   My pistols, George darling.

TESMAN [*alarmed*]   Pistols!

HEDDA [*her eyes cold*]   General Gabler's pistols.

She goes into the rear room and disappears.

TESMAN [*runs to the doorway and calls after her*]   For heaven's sake, Hedda dear, don't touch those things. They're dangerous. Hedda—please—for my sake! What?

Act 2

The same as in Act One, except that the piano has been removed and an elegant little writing table, with a bookcase, stands in its place. By the sofa on the left a smaller table has been placed. Most of the flowers have been removed. MRS. ELVSTED'S *bouquet stands on the larger table, downstage. It is afternoon.*

HEDDA, *dressed to receive callers, is alone in the room. She is standing by the open french windows, loading a revolver. The pair to it is lying in an open pistol case on the writing table.*

HEDDA [*looks down into the garden and calls*] Good afternoon, Judge.
BRACK [*in the distance, below*] Afternoon, Mrs. Tesman.
HEDDA [*raises the pistol and takes aim*] I'm going to shoot you, Judge Brack.
BRACK [*shouts from below*] No, no, no! Don't aim that thing at me!
HEDDA This'll teach you to enter houses by the back door.

> *Fires.*

BRACK [*below*] Have you gone completely out of your mind?
HEDDA Oh dear! Did I hit you?
BRACK [*still outside*] Stop playing these silly tricks.
HEDDA All right, Judge. Come along in.

> JUDGE BRACK, *dressed for a bachelor party, enters through the french windows. He has a light overcoat on his arm.*

BRACK For God's sake! Haven't you stopped fooling around with those things yet? What are you trying to hit?
HEDDA Oh, I was just shooting at the sky.
BRACK [*takes the pistol gently from her hand*] By your leave, ma'am.

> *Looks at it.*

Ah, yes—I know this old friend well.

> *Looks around.*

Where's the case? Oh, yes.

> *Puts the pistol in the case and closes it.*

That's enough of that little game for today.
HEDDA Well, what on earth *am* I to do?
BRACK You haven't had any visitors?
HEDDA [*closes the french windows*] Not one. I suppose the best people are all still in the country.
BRACK Your husband isn't home yet?
HEDDA [*locks the pistol away in a drawer of the writing table*] No. The moment he'd finished eating he ran off to his aunties. He wasn't expecting you so early.
BRACK Ah, why didn't I think of that? How stupid of me.
HEDDA [*turns her head and looks at him*] Why stupid?
BRACK I'd have come a little sooner.

HEDDA [*walks across the room*] There'd have been no one to receive you. I've been in my room since lunch, dressing.

BRACK You haven't a tiny crack in the door through which we might have negotiated?

HEDDA You forgot to arrange one.

BRACK Another stupidity.

HEDDA Well, we'll have to sit down here. And wait. Tesman won't be back for some time.

BRACK Sad. Well, I'll be patient.

> HEDDA *sits on the corner of the sofa.* BRACK *puts his coat over the back of the nearest chair and seats himself, keeping his hat in his hand. Short pause. They look at each other.*

HEDDA Well?

BRACK [*in the same tone of voice*] Well?

HEDDA I asked first.

BRACK [*leans forward slightly*] Yes, well, now we can enjoy a nice, cozy little chat—Mrs. Hedda.

HEDDA [*leans further back in her chair*] It seems such ages since we had a talk. I don't count last night or this morning.

BRACK You mean: *à deux?*

HEDDA Mm—yes. That's roughly what I meant.

BRACK I've been longing so much for you to come home.

HEDDA So have I.

BRACK You? Really, Mrs. Hedda? And I thought you were having such a wonderful honeymoon.

HEDDA Oh, yes. Wonderful!

BRACK But your husband wrote such ecstatic letters.

HEDDA He! Oh, yes! He thinks life has nothing better to offer than rooting around in libraries and copying old pieces of parchment, or whatever it is he does.

BRACK [*a little maliciously*] Well, that *is* his life. Most of it, anyway.

HEDDA Yes, I know. Well, it's all right for him. But for me! Oh no, my dear Judge. I've been bored to death.

BRACK [*sympathetically*] Do you mean that? Seriously?

HEDDA Yes. Can you imagine? Six whole months without ever meeting a single person who was one of us, and to whom I could talk about the kind of things we talk about.

BRACK Yes, I can understand. I'd miss that, too.

HEDDA That wasn't the worst, though.

BRACK What was?

HEDDA Having to spend every minute of one's life with—with the same person.

BRACK [*nods*] Yes. What a thought! Morning; noon; and—

HEDDA [*coldly*] As I said: every minute of one's life.

BRACK I stand corrected. But dear Tesman is such a clever fellow, I should have thought one ought to be able—

HEDDA Tesman is only interested in one thing, my dear Judge. His special subject.

BRACK True.

HEDDA   And people who are only interested in one thing don't make
the most amusing company. Not for long, anyway.

BRACK   Not even when they happen to be the person one loves?

HEDDA   Oh, don't use that sickly, stupid word.

BRACK [*starts*]   But, Mrs. Hedda—!

HEDDA [*half laughing, half annoyed*]   You just try it, Judge. Listening to the history of civilization morning, noon and—

BRACK [*corrects her*]   Every minute of one's life.

HEDDA   All right. Oh, and those domestic industries of Brabant in the
Middle Ages! That really is beyond the limit.

BRACK [*looks at her searchingly*]   But, tell me—if you feel like this
why on earth did you—? Ha—

HEDDA   Why on earth did I marry George Tesman?

BRACK   If you like to put it that way.

HEDDA   Do you think it so very strange?

BRACK   Yes—and no, Mrs. Hedda.

HEDDA   I'd danced myself tired, Judge. I felt my time was up—

Gives a slight shudder.

No, I mustn't say that. Or even think it.

BRACK   You've no rational cause to think it.

HEDDA   Oh—cause, cause—

Looks searchingly at him.

After all, George Tesman—well, I mean, he's a very respectable
man.

BRACK   Very respectable, sound as a rock. No denying that.

HEDDA   And there's nothing exactly ridiculous about him. Is there?

BRACK   Ridiculous? N-no, I wouldn't say that.

HEDDA   Mm. He's very clever at collecting material and all that, isn't
he? I mean, he may go quite far in time.

BRACK [*looks at her a little uncertainly*]   I thought you believed, like
everyone else, that he would become a very prominent man.

HEDDA [*looks tired*]   Yes, I did. And when he came and begged me
on his bended knees to be allowed to love and to cherish me, I
didn't see why I shouldn't let him.

BRACK   No, well—if one looks at it like that—

HEDDA   It was more than my other admirers were prepared to do,
Judge dear.

BRACK [*laughs*]   Well, I can't answer for the others. As far as I
myself am concerned, you know I've always had a considerable
respect for the institution of marriage. As an institution.

HEDDA [*lightly*]   Oh, I've never entertained any hopes of you.

BRACK   All I want is to have a circle of friends whom I can trust,
whom I can help with advice or—or by any other means, and
into whose houses I may come and go as a—trusted friend.

HEDDA   Of the husband?

BRACK [*bows*]   Preferably, to be frank, of the wife. And of the husband too, of course. Yes, you know, this kind of—triangle is a delightful arrangement for all parties concerned.

HEDDA   Yes, I often longed for a third person while I was away. Oh, those hours we spent alone in railway compartments—

BRACK   Fortunately your honeymoon is now over.

HEDDA [*shakes her head*]   There's a long, long way still to go. I've only reached a stop on the line.

BRACK   Why not jump out and stretch your legs a little, Mrs. Hedda?

HEDDA   I'm not the jumping sort.

BRACK   Aren't you?

HEDDA   No. There's always someone around who—

BRACK [*laughs*]   Who looks at one's legs?

HEDDA   Yes. Exactly.

BRACK   Well, but surely—

HEDDA [*with a gesture of rejection*]   I don't like it. I'd rather stay where I am. Sitting in the compartment. *À deux.*

BRACK   But suppose a third person were to step into the compartment?

HEDDA   That would be different.

BRACK   A trusted friend—someone who understood—

HEDDA   And was lively and amusing—

BRACK   And interested in—more subjects than one—

HEDDA [*sighs audibly*]   Yes, that'd be a relief.

BRACK [*hears the front door open and shut*]   The triangle is completed.

HEDDA [*half under breath*]   And the train goes on.

GEORGE TESMAN, *in gray walking dress with a soft felt hat, enters from the hall. He has a number of paper-covered books under his arm and in his pockets.*

TESMAN [*goes over to the table by the corner sofa*]   Phew! It's too hot to be lugging all this around.

Puts the books down.

I'm positively sweating, Hedda. Why, hullo, hullo! You here already, Judge? What? Bertha didn't tell me.

BRACK [*gets up*]   I came in through the garden.

HEDDA   What are all those books you've got there?

TESMAN [*stands glancing through them*]   Oh, some new publications dealing with my special subject. I had to buy them.

HEDDA   Your special subject?

BRACK   His special subject, Mrs. Tesman.

BRACK *and* HEDDA *exchange a smile.*

HEDDA   Haven't you collected enough material on your special subject?

TESMAN   My dear Hedda, one can never have too much. One must keep abreast of what other people are writing.

HEDDA   Yes. Of course.

TESMAN   [*rooting among the books*]   Look—I bought a copy of Eilert Loevborg's new book, too.

> *Holds it out to her.*

Perhaps you'd like to have a look at it, Hedda? What?

HEDDA   No, thank you. Er—yes, perhaps I will, later.

TESMAN   I glanced through it on my way home.

BRACK   What's your opinion—as a specialist on the subject?

TESMAN   I'm amazed how sound and balanced it is. He never used to write like that.

> *Gathers his books together.*

Well, I must get down to these at once. I can hardly wait to cut the pages. Oh, I've got to change, too.

> *To* BRACK.

We don't have to be off just yet, do we? What?

BRACK   Heavens, no. We've plenty of time yet.

TESMAN   Good, I needn't hurry, then.

> *Goes with his books, but stops and turns in the doorway.*

Oh, by the way, Hedda, Auntie Juju won't be coming to see you this evening.

HEDDA   Won't she? Oh—the hat, I suppose.

TESMAN   Good heavens, no. How could you think such a thing of Auntie Juju? Fancy—! No, Auntie Rena's very ill.

HEDDA   She always is.

TESMAN   Yes, but today she's been taken really bad.

HEDDA   Oh, then it's quite understandable that the other one should want to stay with her. Well, I shall have to swallow my disappointment.

TESMAN   You can't imagine how happy Auntie Juju was in spite of everything. At your looking so well after the honeymoon!

HEDDA   [*half beneath her breath, as she rises*]   Oh, these everlasting aunts!

TESMAN   What?

HEDDA   [*goes over to the french windows*]   Nothing.

TESMAN   Oh. All right.

> *Goes into the rear room and out of sight.*

BRACK   What was that about the hat?

HEDDA   Oh, something that happened with Miss Tesman this morning. She'd put her hat down on a chair.

Looks at him and smiles.

And I pretended to think it was the servant's.

BRACK [*shakes his head*]   But my dear Mrs. Hedda, how could you do such a thing? To that poor old lady?

HEDDA [*nervously, walking across the room*]   Sometimes a mood like that hits me. And I can't stop myself.

Throws herself down in the armchair by the stove.

Oh, I don't know how to explain it.

BRACK [*behind her chair*]   You're not really happy. That's the answer.

HEDDA [*stares ahead of her*]   Why on earth should I be happy? Can you give me a reason?

BRACK   Yes. For one thing you've got the home you always wanted.

HEDDA [*looks at him*]   You really believe that story?

BRACK   You mean it isn't true?

HEDDA   Oh, yes, it's partly true.

BRACK   Well?

HEDDA   It's true I got Tesman to see me home from parties last summer—

BRACK   It was a pity my home lay in another direction.

HEDDA   Yes. Your interests lay in another direction, too.

BRACK [*laughs*]   That's naughty of you, Mrs. Hedda. But to return to you and Tesman—

HEDDA   Well, we walked past this house one evening. And poor Tesman was fidgeting in his boots trying to find something to talk about. I felt sorry for the great scholar—

BRACK [*smiles incredulously*]   Did you? Hm.

HEDDA   Yes, honestly I did. Well, to help him out of his misery, I happened to say quite frivolously how much I'd love to live in this house.

BRACK   Was that all?

HEDDA   That evening, yes.

BRACK   But—afterwards?

HEDDA   Yes. My little frivolity had its consequences, my dear Judge.

BRACK   Our little frivolities do. Much too often, unfortunately.

HEDDA   Thank you. Well, it was our mutual admiration for the late Prime Minister's house that brought George Tesman and me together on common ground. So we got engaged, and we got married, and we went on our honeymoon, and— Ah well, Judge, I've —made my bed and I must lie in it, I was about to say.

BRACK   How utterly fantastic! And you didn't really care in the least about the house?

HEDDA   God knows I didn't.

BRACK   Yes, but now that we've furnished it so beautifully for you?

HEDDA   Ugh—all the rooms smell of lavender and dried roses. But perhaps Auntie Juju brought that in.

BRACK [*laughs*]   More likely the Prime Minister's widow, rest her soul.

HEDDA   Yes, it's got the odor of death about it. It reminds me of the flowers one has worn at a ball—the morning after.

Clasps her hands behind her neck, leans back in the chair and looks up at him.

Oh, my dear Judge, you've no idea how hideously bored I'm going to be out here.

BRACK   Couldn't you find some kind of occupation, Mrs. Hedda? Like your husband?

HEDDA   Occupation? That'd interest me?

BRACK   Well—preferably.

HEDDA   God knows what. I've often thought—

Breaks off.

No, that wouldn't work either.

BRACK   Who knows? Tell me about it.

HEDDA   I was thinking—if I could persuade Tesman to go into politics, for example.

BRACK   [*laughs*]   Tesman! No, honestly, I don't think he's quite cut out to be a politician.

HEDDA   Perhaps not. But if I could persuade him to have a go at it?

BRACK   What satisfaction would that give you? If he turned out to be no good? Why do you want to make him do that?

HEDDA   Because I'm bored.

After a moment.

You feel there's absolutely no possibility of Tesman becoming Prime Minister, then?

BRACK   Well, you know, Mrs. Hedda, for one thing he'd have to be pretty well off before he could become that.

HEDDA   [*gets up impatiently*]   There you are!

Walks across the room.

It's this wretched poverty that makes life so hateful. And ludicrous. Well, it is!

BRACK   I don't think that's the real cause.

HEDDA   What is, then?

BRACK   Nothing really exciting has ever happened to you.

HEDDA   Nothing serious, you mean?

BRACK   Call it that if you like. But now perhaps it may.

HEDDA   [*tosses her head*]   Oh, you're thinking of this competition for that wretched professorship? That's Tesman's affair. I'm not going to waste my time worrying about that.

BRACK   Very well, let's forget about that then. But suppose you were to find yourself faced with what people call—to use the conventional phrase—the most solemn of human responsibilities?

Smiles.   children

A new responsibility, little Mrs. Hedda.

HEDDA [*angrily*] Be quiet! Nothing like that's going to happen.

BRACK [*warily*] We'll talk about it again in a year's time. If not earlier.

HEDDA [*curtly*] I've no leanings in that direction, Judge. I don't want any—responsibilities.

BRACK But surely you must feel some inclination to make use of that —natural talent which every woman—

HEDDA [*over by the french windows*] Oh, be quiet, I say! I often think there's only one thing for which I have any natural talent.

BRACK [*goes closer*] And what is that, if I may be so bold as to ask?

HEDDA [*stands looking out*] For boring myself to death. Now you know.

Turns, looks toward the rear room and laughs.

Talking of boring, here comes the Professor.

BRACK [*quietly, warningly*] Now, now, now, Mrs. Hedda!

GEORGE TESMAN, *in evening dress, with gloves and hat in his hand, enters through the rear room from the right.*

TESMAN Hedda, hasn't any message come from Eilert? What?

HEDDA No.

TESMAN Ah, then we'll have him here presently. You wait and see.

BRACK You really think he'll come?

TESMAN Yes, I'm almost sure he will. What you were saying about him this morning is just gossip.

BRACK Oh?

TESMAN Yes. Auntie Juju said she didn't believe he'd ever dare to stand in my way again. Fancy that!

BRACK Then everything in the garden's lovely.

TESMAN [*puts his hat, with his gloves in it, on a chair, right*] Yes, but you really must let me wait for him as long as possible.

BRACK We've plenty of time. No one'll be turning up at my place before seven or half past.

TESMAN Ah, then we can keep Hedda company a little longer. And see if he turns up. What?

HEDDA [*picks up* BRACK's *coat and hat and carries them over to the corner sofa*] And if the worst comes to the worst, Mr. Loevborg can sit here and talk to me.

BRACK [*offering to take his things from her*] No, please. What do you mean by "if worst comes to worst"?

HEDDA If he doesn't want to go with you and Tesman.

TESMAN [*looks doubtfully at her*] I say, Hedda, do you think it'll be all right for him to stay here with you? What? Remember Auntie Juju isn't coming.

HEDDA Yes, but Mrs. Elvsted is. The three of us can have a cup of tea together.

TESMAN Ah, that'll be all right then.

BRACK [*smiles*] It's probably the safest solution as far as he's concerned.

HEDDA   Why?

BRACK   My dear Mrs. Tesman, you always say of my little bachelor parties that they should be attended only by men of the strongest principles.

HEDDA   But Mr. Loevborg is a man of principle now. You know what they say about a reformed sinner—

BERTHA *enters from the hall.*

BERTHA   Madam, there's a gentleman here who wants to see you—

HEDDA   Ask him to come in.

TESMAN [*quietly*]   I'm sure it's him. By Jove. Fancy that!

EILERT LOEVBORG *enters from the hall. He is slim and lean, of the same age as* TESMAN, *but looks older and somewhat haggard. His hair and beard are of a blackish-brown; his face is long and pale, but with a couple of reddish patches on his cheekbones. He is dressed in an elegant and fairly new black suit, and carries black gloves and a top hat in his hand. He stops just inside the door and bows abruptly. He seems somewhat embarrassed.*

TESMAN [*goes over and shakes his hand*]   My dear Eilert! How grand to see you again after all these years!

EILERT LOEVBORG [*speaks softly*]   It was good of you to write, George.

Goes nearer to HEDDA.

May I shake hands with you, too, Mrs. Tesman?

HEDDA [*accepts his hand*]   Delighted to see you, Mr. Loevborg.

With a gesture.

I don't know if you two gentlemen—

LOEVBORG [*bows slightly*]   Judge Brack, I believe.

BRACK [*also with a slight bow*]   Correct. We—met some years ago—

TESMAN [*puts his hands on* LOEVBORG'S *shoulders*]   Now you're to treat this house just as though it were your own home, Eilert. Isn't that right, Hedda? I hear you've decided to settle here again? What?

LOEVBORG   Yes, I have.

TESMAN   Quite understandable. Oh, by the bye—I've just bought your new book. Though to tell the truth I haven't found time to read it yet.

LOEVBORG   You needn't bother.

TESMAN   Oh? Why?

LOEVBORG   There's nothing much in it.

TESMAN   By Jove, fancy hearing that from you!

BRACK   But everyone's praising it.

LOEVBORG   That was exactly what I wanted to happen. So I only wrote what I knew everyone would agree with.

BRACK   Very sensible.

TESMAN   Yes, but my dear Eilert—

LOEVBORG   I want to try to re-establish myself. To begin again—from the beginning.

TESMAN   [*a little embarrassed*]   Yes, I—er—suppose you do. What?

LOEVBORG   [*smiles, puts down his hat and takes a package wrapped in paper from his coat pocket*]   But when this gets published—George Tesman—read it. This is my real book. The one in which I have spoken with my own voice.

TESMAN   Oh, really? What's it about?

LOEVBORG   It's the sequel.

TESMAN   Sequel? To what?

LOEVBORG   To the other book.

TESMAN   The one that's just come out?

LOEVBORG   Yes.

TESMAN   But my dear Eilert, that covers the subject right up to the present day.

LOEVBORG   It does. But this is about the future.

TESMAN   The future! But, I say, we don't know anything about that.

LOEVBORG   No. But there are one or two things that need to be said about it.

> *Opens the package.*

Here, have a look.

TESMAN   Surely that's not your handwriting?

LOEVBORG   I dictated it.

> *Turns the pages.*

It's in two parts. The first deals with the forces that will shape our civilization.

> *Turns further on towards the end.*

And the second indicates the direction in which that civilization may develop.

TESMAN   Amazing! I'd never think of writing about anything like that.

HEDDA   [*by the french windows, drumming on the pane*]   No. You wouldn't.

LOEVBORG   [*puts the pages back into their cover and lays the package on the table*]   I brought it because I thought I might possibly read you a few pages this evening.

TESMAN   I say, what a kind idea! Oh, but this evening—?

> *Glances at* BRACK.

I'm not quite sure whether—

LOEVBORG   Well, some other time, then. There's no hurry.

BRACK   The truth is, Mr. Loevborg, I'm giving a little dinner this evening. In Tesman's honor, you know.

LOEVBORG [*looks round for his hat*] Oh—then I mustn't—

BRACK   No, wait a minute. Won't you do me the honor of joining us?

LOEVBORG [*curtly, with decision*] No I can't. Thank you so much.

BRACK   Oh, nonsense. Do—please. There'll only be a few of us. And I can promise you we shall have some good sport, as Mrs. Hed—as Mrs. Tesman puts it.

LOEVBORG   I've no doubt. Nevertheless—

BRACK   You could bring your manuscript along and read it to Tesman at my place. I could lend you a room.

TESMAN   By Jove, Eilert, that's an idea. What?

HEDDA [*interposes*] But, Tesman, Mr. Loevborg doesn't want to go. I'm sure Mr. Loevborg would much rather sit here and have supper with me.

LOEVBORG [*looks at her*] With you, Mrs. Tesman?

HEDDA   And Mrs. Elvsted.

LOEVBORG   Oh.

> *Casually.*

I ran into her this afternoon.

HEDDA   Did you? Well, she's coming here this evening. So you really must stay, Mr. Loevborg. Otherwise she'll have no one to see her home.

LOEVBORG   That's true. Well—thank you, Mrs. Tesman, I'll stay then.

HEDDA   I'll just tell the servant.

> *She goes to the door which leads into the hall, and rings.* BERTHA *enters.* HEDDA *talks softly to her and points towards the rear room.* BERTHA *nods and goes out.*

TESMAN [*to* LOEVBORG, *as* HEDDA *does this*] I say, Eilert. This new subject of yours—the—er—future—is that the one you're going to lecture about?

LOEVBORG   Yes.

TESMAN   They told me down at the bookshop that you're going to hold a series of lectures here during the autumn.

LOEVBORG   Yes, I am. I—hope you don't mind, Tesman.

TESMAN   Good heavens, no! But—?

LOEVBORG   I can quite understand it might queer your pitch a little.

TESMAN [*dejectedly*] Oh well, I can't expect you to put them off for my sake.

LOEVBORG   I'll wait till your appointment's been announced.

TESMAN   You'll wait! But—but—aren't you going to compete with me for the post? What?

LOEVBORG   No. I only want to defeat you in the eyes of the world.

TESMAN   Good heavens! Then Auntie Juju was right after all! Oh, I knew it, I knew it! Hear that, Hedda? Fancy! Eilert *doesn't* want to stand in our way.

HEDDA [*curtly*] Our? Leave me out of it, please.

She goes towards the rear room, where BERTHA *is setting a tray with decanters and glasses on the table.* HEDDA *nods approval, and comes back into the drawing room.* BERTHA *goes out.*

TESMAN [*while this is happening*]　Judge Brack, what do you think about all this? What?

BRACK　Oh, I think honor and victory can be very splendid things—

TESMAN　Of course they can. Still—

HEDDA [*looks at* TESMAN *with a cold smile*]　You look as if you'd been hit by a thunderbolt.

TESMAN　Yes, I feel rather like it.

BRACK　There was a black cloud looming up, Mrs. Tesman. But it seems to have passed over.

HEDDA [*points towards the rear room*]　Well, gentlemen, won't you go in and take a glass of cold punch?

BRACK [*glances at his watch*]　A stirrup cup? Yes, why not?

TESMAN　An admirable suggestion, Hedda. Admirable! Oh, I feel so relieved!

HEDDA　Won't you have one, too, Mr. Loevborg?

LOEVBORG　No, thank you. I'd rather not.

BRACK　Great heavens, man, cold punch isn't poison. Take my word for it.

LOEVBORG　Not for everyone, perhaps.

HEDDA　I'll keep Mr. Loevborg company while you drink.

TESMAN　Yes, Hedda dear, would you?

He and BRACK *go into the rear room, sit down, drink punch, smoke cigarettes and talk cheerfully during the following scene.* EILERT LOEVBORG *remains standing by the stove.* HEDDA *goes to the writing table.*

HEDDA [*raising her voice slightly*]　I've some photographs I'd like to show you, if you'd care to see them. Tesman and I visited the Tyrol[4] on our way home.

She comes back with an album, places it on the table by the sofa and sits in the upstage corner of the sofa. EILERT LOEVBORG *comes towards her, stops and looks at her. Then he takes a chair and sits down on her left, with his back towards the rear room.*

HEDDA [*opens the album*]　You see these mountains, Mr. Loevborg? That's the Ortler group. Tesman has written the name underneath. You see: "The Ortler Group near Meran."

LOEVBORG [*has not taken his eyes from her; says softly, slowly*]　Hedda—Gabler!

HEDDA [*gives him a quick glance*]　Ssh!

LOEVBORG [*repeats softly*]　Hedda Gabler!

---

4. Region in the Alps, now primarily in Austria.

HEDDA [*looks at the album*] Yes, that used to be my name. When we first knew each other.

LOEVBORG   And from now on—for the rest of my life—I must teach myself never to say: Hedda Gabler.

HEDDA [*still turning the pages*] Yes, you must. You'd better start getting into practice. The sooner the better.

LOEVBORG [*bitterly*] Hedda Gabler married? And to George Tesman?

HEDDA   Yes. Well—that's life.

LOEVBORG   Oh, Hedda, Hedda! How could you throw yourself away like that?

HEDDA [*looks sharply at him*] Stop it.

LOEVBORG   What do you mean?

TESMAN *comes in and goes towards the sofa.*

HEDDA [*hears him coming and says casually*] And this, Mr. Loevborg, is the view from the Ampezzo valley. Look at those mountains.

Glances affectionately up at TESMAN.

What did you say those curious mountains were called, dear?

TESMAN   Let me have a look. Oh, those are the Dolomites.

HEDDA   Of course. Those are the Dolomites, Mr. Loevborg.

TESMAN   Hedda, I just wanted to ask you, can't we bring some punch in here? A glass for you, anyway. What?

HEDDA   Thank you, yes. And a biscuit or two, perhaps.

TESMAN   You wouldn't like a cigarette?

HEDDA   No.

TESMAN   Right.

He goes into the rear room and over to the right. BRACK *is sitting there, glancing occasionally at* HEDDA *and* LOEVBORG.

LOEVBORG [*softly, as before*] Answer me, Hedda. How could you do it?

HEDDA [*apparently absorbed in the album*] If you go on calling me Hedda I won't talk to you any more.

LOEVBORG   Mayn't I even when we're alone?

HEDDA   No. You can think it. But you mustn't say it.

LOEVBORG   Oh, I see. Because you love George Tesman.

HEDDA [*glances at him and smiles*] Love? Don't be funny.

LOEVBORG   You don't love him?

HEDDA   I don't intend to be unfaithful to him. That's not what I want.

LOEVBORG   Hedda—just tell me one thing—

HEDDA   Ssh!

TESMAN *enters from the rear room, carrying a tray.*

TESMAN   Here we are! Here come the goodies!

Puts the tray down on the table.

HEDDA   Why didn't you ask the servant to bring it in?

TESMAN [*fills the glasses*] I like waiting on you, Hedda.

HEDDA   But you've filled both glasses. Mr. Loevborg doesn't want to drink.

TESMAN Yes, but Mrs. Elvsted'll be here soon.

HEDDA   Oh, yes, that's true. Mrs. Elvsted—

TESMAN Had you forgotten her? What?

HEDDA   We're so absorbed with these photographs.

> *Shows him one.*

You remember this little village?

TESMAN Oh, that one down by the Brenner Pass. We spent a night there—

HEDDA   Yes, and met all those amusing people.

TESMAN Oh yes, it was there, wasn't it? By Jove, if only we could have had you with us, Eilert! Ah, well.

> *Goes back into the other room and sits down with* BRACK.

LOEVBORG Tell me one thing, Hedda.

HEDDA   Yes?

LOEVBORG Didn't you love me either? Not—just a little?

HEDDA   Well now, I wonder? No, I think we were just good pals— Really good pals who could tell each other anything.

> *Smiles.*

You certainly poured your heart out to me.

LOEVBORG You begged me to.

HEDDA   Looking back on it, there was something beautiful and fascinating—and brave—about the way we told each other everything. That secret friendship no one else knew about.

LOEVBORG Yes, Hedda, yes! Do you remember? How I used to come up to your father's house in the afternoon—and the General sat by the window and read his newspaper—with his back towards us—

HEDDA   And we sat on the sofa in the corner—

LOEVBORG Always reading the same illustrated magazine—

HEDDA   We hadn't any photograph album.

LOEVBORG Yes, Hedda. I regarded you as a kind of confessor. Told you things about myself which no one else knew about—then. Those days and nights of drinking and— Oh, Hedda, what power did you have to make me confess such things?

HEDDA   Power? You think I had some power over you?

LOEVBORG Yes—I don't know how else to explain it. And all those— oblique questions you asked me—

HEDDA   You knew what they meant.

LOEVBORG But that you could sit there and ask me such questions! So unashamedly—

HEDDA   I thought you said they were oblique.

LOEVBORG Yes, but you asked them so unashamedly. That you could question me about—about that kind of thing!

HEDDA You answered willingly enough.

LOEVBORG Yes—that's what I can't understand—looking back on it. But tell me, Hedda—what you felt for me—wasn't that—love? When you asked me those questions and made me confess my sins to you, wasn't it because you wanted to wash me clean?

HEDDA No, not exactly.

LOEVBORG Why did you do it, then?

HEDDA Do you find it so incredible that a young girl, given the chance to do so without anyone knowing, should want to be allowed a glimpse into a forbidden world of whose existence she is supposed to be ignorant?

LOEVBORG So that was it?

HEDDA One reason. One reason—I think.

LOEVBORG You didn't love me, then. You just wanted—knowledge. But if that was so, why did you break it off?

HEDDA That was your fault.

LOEVBORG It was you who put an end to it.

HEDDA Yes, when I realized that our friendship was threatening to develop into something—something else. Shame on you, Eilert Loevborg! How could you abuse the trust of your dearest friend?

LOEVBORG [*clenches his fists*] Oh, why didn't you do it? Why didn't you shoot me dead? As you threatened to?

HEDDA I was afraid. Of the scandal.

LOEVBORG Yes, Hedda. You're a coward at heart.

HEDDA A dreadful coward.

> *Changes her tone.*

Luckily for you. Well, now you've found consolation with the Elvsteds.

LOEVBORG I know what Thea's been telling you.

HEDDA I dare say you told her about us.

LOEVBORG Not a word. She's too silly to understand that kind of thing.

HEDDA Silly?

LOEVBORG She's silly about that kind of thing.

HEDDA And I am a coward.

> *Leans closer to him, without looking him in the eyes, and says quietly.*

But let me tell you something. Something you don't know.

LOEVBORG [*tensely*] Yes?

HEDDA My failure to shoot you wasn't my worst act of cowardice that evening.

LOEVBORG [*looks at her for a moment, realizes her meaning and whispers passionately*] Oh, Hedda! Hedda Gabler! Now I see what was behind those questions. Yes! It wasn't knowledge you wanted! It was life!

HEDDA [*flashes a look at him and says quietly*]   Take care! Don't you delude yourself!

> It has begun to grow dark. BERTHA, *from outside, opens the door leading into the hall.*

HEDDA [*closes the album with a snap and cries, smiling*]   Ah, at last! Come in, Thea dear!

> MRS. ELVSTED *enters from the hall, in evening dress. The door is closed behind her.*

HEDDA [*on the sofa, stretches out her arms towards her*]   Thea darling, I thought you were never coming!

> MRS. ELVSTED *makes a slight bow to the gentlemen in the rear room as she passes the open doorway, and they to her. Then she goes to the table and holds out her hand to* HEDDA. EILERT LOEVBORG *has risen from his chair. He and* MRS. ELVSTED *nod silently to each other.*

MRS. ELVSTED   Perhaps I ought to go in and say a few words to your husband?

HEDDA   Oh, there's no need. They're happy by themselves. They'll be going soon.

MRS. ELVSTED   Going?

HEDDA   Yes, they're off on a spree this evening.

MRS. ELVSTED [*quickly, to* LOEVBORG]   You're not going with them?

LOEVBORG   No.

HEDDA   Mr. Loevborg is staying here with us.

MRS. ELVSTED [*takes a chair and is about to sit down beside him*]   Oh, how nice it is to be here!

HEDDA   No, Thea darling, not there. Come over here and sit beside me. I want to be in the middle.

MRS. ELVSTED   Yes, just as you wish.

> She goes round the table and sits on the sofa, on HEDDA'S *right*. LOEVBORG *sits down again in his chair.*

LOEVBORG [*after a short pause, to* HEDDA]   Isn't she lovely to look at?

HEDDA [*strokes her hair gently*]   Only to look at?

LOEVBORG   Yes. We're just good pals. We trust each other implicitly. We can talk to each other quite unashamedly.

HEDDA   No need to be oblique?

MRS. ELVSTED [*nestles close to* HEDDA *and says quietly*]   Oh, Hedda, I'm so happy. Imagine—he says I've inspired him!

HEDDA [*looks at her with a smile*]   Dear Thea! Does he really?

LOEVBORG   She has the courage of her convictions, Mrs. Tesman.

MRS. ELVSTED   I? Courage?

LOEVBORG   Absolute courage. Where friendship is concerned.

HEDDA   Yes. Courage. Yes. If only one had that—

LOEVBORG   Yes?

HEDDA   One might be able to live. In spite of everything.

Changes her tone suddenly.

Well, Thea darling, now you're going to drink a nice glass of cold punch.

MRS. ELVSTED   No, thank you. I never drink anything like that.

HEDDA   Oh. You, Mr. Loevborg?

LOEVBORG   Thank you, I don't either.

MRS. ELVSTED   No, he doesn't either.

HEDDA [*looks into his eyes*]   But if I want you to?

LOEVBORG   That doesn't make any difference.

HEDDA [*laughs*]   Have I no power over you at all? Poor me!

LOEVBORG   Not where this is concerned.

HEDDA   Seriously, I think you should. For your own sake.

MRS. ELVSTED   Hedda!

LOEVBORG   Why?

HEDDA   Or perhaps I should say for other people's sake.

LOEVBORG   What do you mean?

HEDDA   People might think you didn't feel absolutely and unashamedly sure of yourself. In your heart of hearts.

MRS. ELVSTED [*quietly*]   Oh, Hedda, no!

LOEVBORG   People can think what they like. For the present.

MRS. ELVSTED [*happily*]   Yes, that's true.

HEDDA   I saw it so clearly in Judge Brack a few minutes ago.

LOEVBORG   Oh. What did you see?

HEDDA   He smiled so scornfully when he saw you were afraid to go in there and drink with them.

LOEVBORG   Afraid! I wanted to stay here and talk to you.

MRS. ELVSTED   That was only natural, Hedda.

HEDDA   But the Judge wasn't to know that. I saw him wink at Tesman when you showed you didn't dare to join their wretched little party.

LOEVBORG   Didn't dare! Are you saying I didn't dare?

HEDDA   I'm not saying so. But that was what Judge Brack thought.

LOEVBORG   Well, let him.

HEDDA   You're not going, then?

LOEVBORG   I'm staying here with you and Thea.

MRS. ELVSTED   Yes, Hedda, of course he is.

HEDDA [*smiles, and nods approvingly to* LOEVBORG]   Firm as a rock! A man of principle! That's how a man should be!

Turns to MRS. ELVSTED *and strokes her cheek.*

Didn't I tell you so this morning when you came here in such a panic—

LOEVBORG [*starts*]   Panic?

MRS. ELVSTED [*frightened*]   Hedda! But—Hedda!

HEDDA   Well, now you can see for yourself. There's no earthly need for you to get scared to death just because—

Stops.

Well! Let's all three cheer up and enjoy ourselves.

LOEVBORG   Mrs. Tesman, would you mind explaining to me what this is all about?

MRS. ELVSTED   Oh, my God, my God, Hedda, what are you saying? What are you doing?

HEDDA   Keep calm. That horrid Judge has his eye on you.

LOEVBORG   Scared to death, were you? For my sake?

MRS. ELVSTED   [*quietly, trembling*]   Oh, Hedda! You've made me so unhappy!

LOEVBORG   [*looks coldly at her for a moment. His face is distorted*] So that was how much you trusted me.

MRS. ELVSTED   Eilert dear, please listen to me—

LOEVBORG   [*takes one of the glasses of punch, raises it and says quietly, hoarsely*]   Skoal, Thea!

Empties the glass, puts it down and picks up one of the others.

MRS. ELVSTED   [*quietly*]   Hedda, Hedda! Why did you want this to happen?

HEDDA   I—want it? Are you mad?

LOEVBORG   Skoal to you too, Mrs. Tesman. Thanks for telling me the truth. Here's to the truth!

Empties his glass and refills it.

HEDDA   [*puts her hand on his arm*]   Steady. That's enough for now. Don't forget the party.

MRS. ELVSTED   No, no, no!

HEDDA   Ssh! They're looking at you.

LOEVBORG   [*puts down his glass*]   Thea, tell me the truth—

MRS. ELVSTED   Yes!

LOEVBORG   Did your husband know you were following me?

MRS. ELVSTED   Oh, Hedda!

LOEVBORG   Did you and he have an agreement that you should come here and keep an eye on me? Perhaps he gave you the idea? After all, he's a magistrate. I suppose he needed me back in his office. Or did he miss my companionship at the card table?

MRS. ELVSTED   [*quietly, sobbing*]   Eilert, Eilert!

LOEVBORG   [*seizes a glass and is about to fill it*]   Let's drink to him, too.

HEDDA   No more now. Remember you're going to read your book to Tesman.

LOEVBORG   [*calm again, puts down his glass*]   That was silly of me, Thea. To take it like that, I mean. Don't be angry with me, my dear. You'll see—yes, and they'll see, too—that though I fell, I— I have raised myself up again. With your help, Thea.

MRS. ELVSTED   [*happily*]   Oh, thank God!

BRACK *has meanwhile glanced at his watch. He and* TESMAN *get up and come into the drawing room.*

BRACK [*takes his hat and overcoat*]   Well, Mrs. Tesman, it's time for us to go.

HEDDA   Yes, I suppose it must be.

LOEVBORG [*gets up*]   Time for me too, Judge.

MRS. ELVSTED [*quietly, pleadingly*]   Eilert, please don't!

HEDDA [*pinches her arm*]   They can hear you.

MRS. ELVSTED [*gives a little cry*]   Oh!

LOEVBORG [*to* BRACK]   You were kind enough to ask me to join you.

BRACK   Are you coming?

LOEVBORG   If I may.

BRACK   Delighted.

LOEVBORG [*puts the paper package in his pocket and says to* TESMAN]   I'd like to show you one or two things before I send it off to the printer.

TESMAN   I say, that'll be fun. Fancy—! Oh, but, Hedda, how'll Mrs. Elvsted get home? What?

HEDDA   Oh, we'll manage somehow.

LOEVBORG [*glances over towards the ladies*]   Mrs. Elvsted? I shall come back and collect her, naturally.

Goes closer.

About ten o'clock, Mrs. Tesman? Will that suit you?

HEDDA   Yes. That'll suit me admirably.

TESMAN   Good, that's settled. But you mustn't expect me back so early, Hedda.

HEDDA   Stay as long as you c— as long as you like, dear.

MRS. ELVSTED [*trying to hide her anxiety*]   Well then, Mr. Loevborg, I'll wait here till you come.

LOEVBORG [*his hat in his hand*]   Pray do, Mrs. Elvsted.

BRACK   Well, gentlemen, now the party begins. I trust that, in the words of a certain fair lady, we shall enjoy good sport.

HEDDA   What a pity the fair lady can't be there, invisible.

BRACK   Why invisible?

HEDDA   So as to be able to hear some of your uncensored witticisms, your honor.

BRACK [*laughs*]   Oh, I shouldn't advise the fair lady to do that.

TESMAN [*laughs too*]   I say, Hedda, that's good. By Jove! Fancy that!

BRACK   Well, good night, ladies, good night!

LOEVBORG [*bows farewell*]   About ten o'clock, then.

BRACK, LOEVBORG *and* TESMAN *go out through the hall. As they do so,* BERTHA *enters from the rear room with a lighted lamp. She puts it on the drawing-room table, then goes out the way she came.*

MRS. ELVSTED [*has got up and is walking uneasily to and fro*]   Oh, Hedda, Hedda! How is all this going to end?

5. Worshippers of Dionysus, Greek god of vegetation and wine, wore garlands of vine leaves as a sign of divine intoxication.

HEDDA   At ten o'clock, then. He'll be here. I can see him. With a crown of vine-leaves⁵ in his hair. Burning and unashamed!

MRS. ELVSTED   Oh, I do hope so!

HEDDA   Can't you see? Then he'll be himself again! He'll be a free man for the rest of his days!

MRS. ELVSTED   Please God you're right.

HEDDA   That's how he'll come!

Gets up and goes closer.

You can doubt him as much as you like. I believe in him! Now we'll see which of us—

MRS. ELVSTED   You're after something, Hedda.

HEDDA   Yes, I am. For once in my life I want to have the power to shape a man's destiny.

MRS. ELVSTED   Haven't you that power already?

HEDDA   No, I haven't. I've never had it.

MRS. ELVSTED   What about your husband?

HEDDA   Him! Oh, if you could only understand how poor I am. And you're allowed to be so rich, so rich!

Clasps her passionately.

I think I'll burn your hair off after all!

MRS. ELVSTED   Let me go! Let me go! You frighten me, Hedda!

BERTHA   [*in the open doorway*]   I've laid tea in the dining room, madam.

HEDDA   Good, we're coming.

MRS. ELVSTED   No, no, no! I'd rather go home alone! Now—at once!

HEDDA   Rubbish! First you're going to have some tea, you little idiot. And then—at ten o'clock—Eilert Loevborg will come. With a crown of vine-leaves in his hair!

She drags MRS. ELVSTED *almost forcibly towards the open doorway.*

Act 3

The same. The curtains are drawn across the open doorway, and also across the french windows. The lamp, half turned down, with a shade over it, is burning on the table. In the stove, the door of which is open, a fire has been burning, but it is now almost out.

   MRS. ELVSTED, *wrapped in a large shawl and with her feet resting on a footstool, is sitting near the stove, huddled in the armchair.* HEDDA *is lying asleep on the sofa, fully dressed, with a blanket over her.*

MRS. ELVSTED   [*after a pause, suddenly sits up in her chair and listens tensely. Then she sinks wearily back again and sighs*]   Not back yet! Oh, God! Oh, God! Not back yet!

BERTHA *tiptoes cautiously in from the hall. She has a letter in her hand.*

MRS. ELVSTED [*turns and whispers*] What is it? Has someone come?
BERTHA [*quietly*] Yes, a servant's just called with this letter.
MRS. ELVSTED [*quickly, holding out her hand*] A letter! Give it to me!
BERTHA But it's for the Doctor, madam.
MRS. ELVSTED Oh. I see.
BERTHA Miss Tesman's maid brought it. I'll leave it here on the table.
MRS. ELVSTED Yes, do.
BERTHA [*puts down the letter*] I'd better put the lamp out. It's starting to smoke.
MRS. ELVSTED Yes, put it out. It'll soon be daylight.
BERTHA [*puts out the lamp*] It's daylight already, madam.
MRS. ELVSTED Yes. Broad day. And not home yet.
BERTHA Oh dear, I was afraid this would happen.
MRS. ELVSTED Were you?
BERTHA Yes. When I heard that a certain gentleman had returned to town, and saw him go off with them. I've heard all about him.
MRS. ELVSTED Don't talk so loud. You'll wake your mistress.
BERTHA [*looks at the sofa and sighs*] Yes. Let her go on sleeping, poor dear. Shall I put some more wood on the fire?
MRS. ELVSTED Thank you, don't bother on my account.
BERTHA Very good.

Goes quietly out through the hall.

HEDDA [*wakes as the door closes and looks up*] What's that?
MRS. ELVSTED It was only the maid.
HEDDA [*looks round*] What am I doing here? Oh, now I remember.

Sits up on the sofa, stretches herself and rubs her eyes.

What time is it, Thea?
MRS. ELVSTED It's gone seven.
HEDDA When did Tesman get back?
ELVSTED He's not back yet.
HEDDA Not home yet?
MRS. ELVSTED [*gets up*] No one's come.
HEDDA And we sat up waiting for them till four o'clock.
MRS. ELVSTED God! How I waited for him!
HEDDA [*yawns and says with her hand in front of her mouth*] Oh, dear. We might have saved ourselves the trouble.
MRS. ELVSTED Did you manage to sleep?
HEDDA Oh, yes. Quite well, I think. Didn't you get any?
MRS. ELVSTED Not a wink. I couldn't, Hedda. I just couldn't.
HEDDA [*gets up and comes over to her*] Now, now, now. There's nothing to worry about. I know what's happened.
MRS. ELVSTED What? Please tell me.

HEDDA   Well, obviously the party went on very late—
MRS. ELVSTED   Oh dear, I suppose it must have. But—
HEDDA   And Tesman didn't want to come home and wake us all up in the middle of the night.

Laughs.

Probably wasn't too keen to show his face either, after a spree like that.
MRS. ELVSTED   But where could he have gone?
HEDDA   I should think he's probably slept at his aunts'. They keep his old room for him.
MRS. ELVSTED   No, he can't be with them. A letter came for him just now from Miss Tesman. It's over there.
HEDDA   Oh?

Looks at the envelope.

Yes, it's Auntie Juju's handwriting. Well, he must still be at Judge Brack's, then. And Eilert Loevborg is sitting there, reading to him. With a crown of vine-leaves in his hair.
MRS. ELVSTED   Hedda, you're only saying that. You don't believe it.
HEDDA   Thea, you really are a little fool.
MRS. ELVSTED   Perhaps I am.
HEDDA   You look tired to death.
MRS. ELVSTED   Yes. I am tired to death.
HEDDA   Go to my room and lie down for a little. Do as I say, now; don't argue.
MRS. ELVSTED   No, no. I couldn't possibly sleep.
HEDDA   Of course you can.
MRS. ELVSTED   But your husband'll be home soon. And I must know at once—
HEDDA   I'll tell you when he comes.
MRS. ELVSTED   Promise me, Hedda?
HEDDA   Yes, don't worry. Go and get some sleep.
MRS. ELVSTED   Thank you. All right, I'll try.

She goes out through the rear room. HEDDA *goes to the french windows and draws the curtains. Broad daylight floods into the room. She goes to the writing table, takes a small hand mirror from it and arranges her hair. Then she goes to the door leading into the hall and presses the bell. After a few moments,* BERTHA *enters.*

BERTHA   Did you want anything, madam?
HEDDA   Yes, put some more wood on the fire. I'm freezing.
BERTHA   Bless you, I'll soon have this room warmed up.

She rakes the embers together and puts a fresh piece of wood on them. Suddenly she stops and listens.

There's someone at the front door, madam.

HEDDA   Well, go and open it. I'll see to the fire.

BERTHA   It'll burn up in a moment.

> *She goes out through the hall.* HEDDA *kneels on the footstool and puts more wood in the stove. After a few seconds,* GEORGE TESMAN *enters from the hall. He looks tired, and rather worried. He tiptoes towards the open doorway and is about to slip through the curtains.*

HEDDA [*at the stove, without looking up*]   Good morning.

TESMAN [*turns*]   Hedda!

> *Comes nearer.*

Good heavens, are you up already? What?

HEDDA   Yes, I got up very early this morning.

TESMAN   I was sure you'd still be sleeping. Fancy that!

HEDDA   Don't talk so loud. Mrs. Elvsted's asleep in my room.

TESMAN   Mrs. Elvsted? Has she stayed the night here?

HEDDA   Yes. No one came to escort her home.

TESMAN   Oh. No, I suppose not.

HEDDA [*closes the door of the stove and gets up*]   Well. Was it fun?

TESMAN   Have you been anxious about me? What?

HEDDA   Not in the least. I asked if you'd had fun.

TESMAN   Oh yes, rather! Well, I thought, for once in a while— The first part was the best; when Eilert read his book to me. We arrived over an hour too early—what about that, eh? By Jove! Brack had a lot of things to see to, so Eilert read to me.

HEDDA [*sits at the right-hand side of the table*]   Well? Tell me about it.

TESMAN [*sits on a footstool by the stove*]   Honestly, Hedda, you've no idea what a book that's going to be. It's really one of the most remarkable things that's ever been written. By Jove!

HEDDA   Oh, never mind about the book—

TESMAN   I'm going to make a confession to you, Hedda. When he'd finished reading a sort of beastly feeling came over me.

HEDDA   Beastly feeling?

TESMAN   I found myself envying Eilert for being able to write like that. Imagine that, Hedda!

HEDDA   Yes. I can imagine.

TESMAN   What a tragedy that with all those gifts he should be so incorrigible.

HEDDA   You mean he's less afraid of life than most men?

TESMAN   Good heavens, no. He just doesn't know the meaning of the word moderation.

HEDDA   What happened afterwards?

TESMAN   Well, looking back on it I suppose you might almost call it an orgy, Hedda.

HEDDA   Had he vine-leaves in his hair?

TESMAN   Vine-leaves? No, I didn't see any of them. He made a long, rambling oration in honor of the woman who'd inspired him to write this book. Yes, those were the words he used.

HEDDA   Did he name her?

TESMAN   No. But I suppose it must be Mrs. Elvsted. You wait and see!

HEDDA   Where did you leave him?

TESMAN   On the way home. We left in a bunch—the last of us, that is—and Brack came with us to get a little fresh air. Well, then, you see, we agreed we ought to see Eilert home. He'd had a drop too much.

HEDDA   You don't say?

TESMAN   But now comes the funny part, Hedda. Or I should really say the tragic part. Oh, I'm almost ashamed to tell you. For Eilert's sake, I mean—

HEDDA   Why, what happened?

TESMAN   Well, you see, as we were walking towards town I happened to drop behind for a minute. Only for a minute—er—you understand—

HEDDA   Yes, yes—?

TESMAN   Well then, when I ran on to catch them up, what do you think I found by the roadside. What?

HEDDA   How on earth should I know?

TESMAN   You mustn't tell anyone, Hedda. What? Promise me that—for Eilert's sake.

Takes a package wrapped in paper from his coat pocket.

Just fancy! I found this.

HEDDA   Isn't this the one he brought here yesterday?

TESMAN   Yes! The whole of that precious, irreplaceable manuscript! And he went and lost it! Didn't even notice! What about that? By Jove! Tragic.

HEDDA   But why didn't you give it back to him?

TESMAN   I didn't dare to, in the state he was in.

HEDDA   Didn't you tell any of the others?

TESMAN   Good heavens, no. I didn't want to do that. For Eilert's sake, you understand.

HEDDA   Then no one else knows you have his manuscript?

TESMAN   No. And no one must be allowed to know.

HEDDA   Didn't it come up in the conversation later?

TESMAN   I didn't get a chance to talk to him any more. As soon as we got into the outskirts of town, he and one or two of the others gave us the slip. Disappeared, by Jove!

HEDDA   Oh? I suppose they took him home.

TESMAN   Yes, I imagine that was the idea. Brack left us, too.

HEDDA   And what have you been up to since then?

TESMAN   Well, I and one or two of the others—awfully jolly chaps, they were—went back to where one of them lived, and had a cup of morning coffee. Morning-after coffee—what? Ah, well. I'll just lie down for a bit and give Eilert time to sleep it off, poor chap, then I'll run over and give this back to him.

HEDDA [*holds out her hand for the package*]   No, don't do that. Not just yet. Let me read it first.

TESMAN   Oh no, really, Hedda dear, honestly, I daren't do that.

HEDDA   Daren't?

TESMAN   No—imagine how desperate he'll be when he wakes up and finds his manuscript's missing. He hasn't any copy, you see. He told me so himself.

HEDDA   Can't a thing like that be rewritten?

TESMAN   Oh no, not possibly, I shouldn't think. I mean, the inspiration, you know—

HEDDA   Oh, yes. I'd forgotten that.

> *Casually.*

By the way, there's a letter for you.

TESMAN   Is there? Fancy that!

HEDDA [*holds it out to him*]   It came early this morning.

TESMAN   I say, it's from Auntie Juju! What on earth can it be?

> *Puts the package on the other footstool, opens the letter, reads it and jumps up.*

Oh, Hedda! She says poor Auntie Rena's dying.

HEDDA   Well, we've been expecting that.

TESMAN   She says if I want to see her I must go quickly. I'll run over at once.

HEDDA [*hides a smile*]   Run?

TESMAN   Hedda dear, I suppose you wouldn't like to come with me? What about that, eh?

HEDDA [*gets up and says wearily and with repulsion*]   No, no, don't ask me to do anything like that. I can't bear illness or death. I loathe anything ugly.

TESMAN   Yes, yes. Of course.

> *In a dither.*

My hat? My overcoat? Oh yes, in the hall. I do hope I won't get there too late, Hedda? What?

> BERTHA *enters from the hall.*

HEDDA   You'll be all right if you run.

BERTHA   Judge Brack's outside and wants to know if he can come in.

TESMAN   At this hour? No, I can't possibly receive him now.

HEDDA   I can.

> *To* BERTHA.

Ask his honor to come in.

> BERTHA *goes.*

HEDDA [*whispers quickly*]   The manuscript, Tesman.

She snatches it from the footstool.

TESMAN   Yes, give it to me.
HEDDA   No, I'll look after it for now.

She goes over to the writing table and puts it in the bookcase.
TESMAN *stands dithering, unable to get his gloves on.* JUDGE
BRACK *enters from the hall.*

HEDDA [*nods to him*]   Well, you're an early bird.
BRACK   Yes, aren't I?

To TESMAN.

Are you up and about, too?
TESMAN   Yes, I've got to go and see my aunts. Poor Auntie Rena's
dying.
BRACK   Oh dear, is she? Then you mustn't let me detain you. At so
tragic a—
TESMAN   Yes, I really must run. Good-bye! Good-bye!

Runs out through the hall.

HEDDA [*goes nearer*]   You seem to have had excellent sport last night
—Judge.
BRACK   Indeed yes, Mrs. Hedda. I haven't even had time to take my
clothes off.
HEDDA   *You* haven't either?
BRACK   As you see. What's Tesman told you about last night's
escapades?
HEDDA   Oh, only some boring story about having gone and drunk
coffee somewhere.
BRACK   Yes, I've heard about that coffee party. Eilert Loevborg wasn't
with them, I gather?
HEDDA   No, they took him home first.
BRACK   Did Tesman go with him?
HEDDA   No, one or two of the others, he said.
BRACK [*smiles*]   George Tesman is a credulous man, Mrs. Hedda.
HEDDA   God knows. But—has something happened?
BRACK   Well, yes, I'm afraid it has.
HEDDA   I see. Sit down and tell me.

She sits on the left of the table, BRACK *at the long side of it,
near her.*

HEDDA   Well?
BRACK   I had a special reason for keeping track of my guests last
night. Or perhaps I should say some of my guests.
HEDDA   Including Eilert Loevborg?

BRACK   I must confess—yes.

HEDDA   You're beginning to make me curious.

BRACK   Do you know where he and some of my other guests spent the latter half of last night, Mrs. Hedda?

HEDDA   Tell me. If it won't shock me.

BRACK   Oh, I don't think it'll shock you. They found themselves participating in an exceedingly animated *soirée*.

HEDDA   Of a sporting character?

BRACK   Of a highly sporting character.

HEDDA   Tell me more.

BRACK   Loevborg had received an invitation in advance—as had the others. I knew all about that. But he had refused. As you know, he's become a new man.

HEDDA   Up at the Elvsteds', yes. But he went?

BRACK   Well, you see, Mrs. Hedda, last night at my house, unhappily, the spirit moved him.

HEDDA   Yes, I hear he became inspired.

BRACK   Somewhat violently inspired. And as a result, I suppose, his thoughts strayed. We men, alas, don't always stick to our principles as firmly as we should.

HEDDA   I'm sure you're an exception, Judge Brack. But go on about Loevborg.

BRACK   Well, to cut a long story short, he ended up in the establishment of a certain Mademoiselle Danielle.

HEDDA   Mademoiselle Danielle?

BRACK   She was holding the *soirée*. For a selected circle of friends and admirers.

HEDDA   Has she got red hair?

BRACK   She has.

HEDDA   A singer of some kind?

BRACK   Yes—among other accomplishments. She's also a celebrated huntress—of men, Mrs. Hedda. I'm sure you've heard about her. Eilert Loevborg used to be one of her most ardent patrons. In his salad days.

HEDDA   And how did all this end?

BRACK   Not entirely amicably, from all accounts. Mademoiselle Danielle began by receiving him with the utmost tenderness and ended by resorting to her fists.

HEDDA   Against Loevborg?

BRACK   Yes. He accused her, or her friends, of having robbed him. He claimed his pocketbook had been stolen. Among other things. In short, he seems to have made a bloodthirsty scene.

HEDDA   And what did this lead to?

BRACK   It led to a general free-for-all, in which both sexes participated. Fortunately, in the end the police arrived.

HEDDA   The police too?

BRACK   Yes. I'm afraid it may turn out to be rather an expensive joke for Master Eilert. Crazy fool!

HEDDA   Oh?

BRACK   Apparently he put up a very violent resistance. Hit one of the constables on the ear and tore his uniform. He had to accompany them to the police station.

HEDDA   Where did you learn all this?

BRACK   From the police.

HEDDA   [*to herself*]   So that's what happened. He didn't have a crown of vine-leaves in his hair.

BRACK   Vine-leaves, Mrs. Hedda?

HEDDA   [*in her normal voice again*]   But, tell me, Judge, why do you take such a close interest in Eilert Loevborg?

BRACK   For one thing it'll hardly be a matter of complete indifference to me if it's revealed in court that he came there straight from my house.

HEDDA   Will it come to court?

BRACK   Of course. Well, I don't regard that as particularly serious. Still, I thought it my duty, as a friend of the family, to give you and your husband a full account of his nocturnal adventures.

HEDDA   Why?

BRACK   Because I've a shrewd suspicion that he's hoping to use you as a kind of screen.

HEDDA   What makes you think that?

BRACK   Oh, for heaven's sake, Mrs. Hedda, we're not blind. You wait and see. This Mrs. Elvsted won't be going back to her husband just yet.

HEDDA   Well, if there were anything between those two there are plenty of other places where they could meet.

BRACK   Not in anyone's home. From now on every respectable house will once again be closed to Eilert Loevborg.

HEDDA   And mine should be too, you mean?

BRACK   Yes. I confess I should find it more than irksome if this gentleman were to be granted unrestricted access to this house. If he were superfluously to intrude into—

HEDDA   The triangle?

BRACK   Precisely. For me it would be like losing a home.

HEDDA   [*looks at him and smiles*]   I see. You want to be the cock of the walk.

BRACK   [*nods slowly and lowers his voice*]   Yes, that is my aim. And I shall fight for it with—every weapon at my disposal.

HEDDA   [*as her smile fades*]   You're a dangerous man, aren't you? When you really want something.

BRACK   You think so?

HEDDA   Yes, I'm beginning to think so. I'm deeply thankful you haven't any kind of hold over me.

BRACK   [*laughs equivocally*]   Well, well, Mrs. Hedda—perhaps you're right. If I had, who knows what I might not think up?

HEDDA   Come, Judge Brack. That sounds almost like a threat.

BRACK   [*gets up*]   Heaven forbid! In the creation of a triangle—and its continuance—the question of compulsion should never arise.

HEDDA   Exactly what I was thinking.

BRACK   Well, I've said what I came to say. I must be getting back. Good-bye, Mrs. Hedda.

Goes towards the french windows.

HEDDA [*gets up*]   Are you going out through the garden?
BRACK   Yes, it's shorter.
HEDDA   Yes. And it's the back door, isn't it?
BRACK   I've nothing against back doors. They can be quite intriguing —sometimes.
HEDDA   When people fire pistols out of them, for example?
BRACK [*in the doorway, laughs*]   Oh, people don't shoot tame cocks.
HEDDA [*laughs too*]   I suppose not. When they've only got one.

> *They nod good-bye, laughing. He goes. She closes the french windows behind him, and stands for a moment, looking out pensively. Then she walks across the room and glances through the curtains in the open doorway. Goes to the writing table, takes* LOEVBORG's *package from the bookcase and is about to leaf through the pages when* BERTHA *is heard remonstrating loudly in the hall.* HEDDA *turns and listens. She hastily puts the package back in the drawer, locks it and puts the key on the inkstand.* EILERT LOEVBORG, *with his overcoat on and his hat in his hand, throws the door open. He looks somewhat confused and excited.*

LOEVBORG [*shouts as he enters*]   I must come in, I tell you! Let me pass!

> *He closes the door, turns, sees* HEDDA, *controls himself immediately and bows.*

HEDDA [*at the writing table*]   Well, Mr. Loevborg, this is rather a late hour to be collecting Thea.
LOEVBORG   And an early hour to call on you. Please forgive me.
HEDDA   How do you know she's still here?
LOEVBORG   They told me at her lodgings that she has been out all night.
HEDDA [*goes to the table*]   Did you notice anything about their behavior when they told you?
LOEVBORG [*looks at her, puzzled*]   Notice anything?
HEDDA   Did they sound as if they thought it—strange?
LOEVBORG [*suddenly understands*]   Oh, I see what you mean. I'm dragging her down with me. No, as a matter of fact I didn't notice anything. I suppose Tesman isn't up yet?
HEDDA   No, I don't think so.
LOEVBORG   When did he get home?
HEDDA   Very late.
LOEVBORG   Did he tell you anything?
HEDDA   Yes. I gather you had a merry party at Judge Brack's last night.
LOEVBORG   He didn't tell you anything else?
HEDDA   I don't think so. I was so terribly sleepy—

MRS. ELVSTED *comes through the curtains in the open doorway.*

MRS. ELVSTED [*runs towards him*] Oh, Eilert! At last!

LOEVBORG Yes—at last. And too late.

MRS. ELVSTED What is too late?

LOEVBORG Everything—now. I'm finished, Thea.

MRS. ELVSTED Oh, no, no! Don't say that!

LOEVBORG You'll say it yourself, when you've heard what I—

MRS. ELVSTED I don't want to hear anything!

HEDDA Perhaps you'd rather speak to her alone? I'd better go.

LOEVBORG No, stay.

MRS. ELVSTED But I don't want to hear anything, I tell you!

LOEVBORG It's not about last night.

MRS. ELVSTED Then what—?

LOEVBORG I want to tell you that from now on we must stop seeing each other.

MRS. ELVSTED Stop seeing each other!

HEDDA [*involuntarily*] I knew it!

LOEVBORG I have no further use for you, Thea.

MRS. ELVSTED You can stand there and say that! No further use for me! Surely I can go on helping you? We'll go on working together, won't we?

LOEVBORG I don't intend to do any more work from now on.

MRS. ELVSTED [*desperately*] Then what use have I for my life?

LOEVBORG You must try to live as if you had never known me.

MRS. ELVSTED But I can't!

LOEVBORG Try to, Thea. Go back home—

MRS. ELVSTED Never! I want to be wherever you are! I won't let myself be driven away like this! I want to stay here—and be with you when the book comes out.

HEDDA [*whispers*] Ah, yes! The book!

LOEVBORG [*looks at her*] Our book; Thea's and mine. It belongs to both of us.

MRS. ELVSTED Oh, yes! I feel that, too! And I've a right to be with you when it comes into the world. I want to see people respect and honor you again. And the joy! The joy! I want to share it with you!

LOEVBORG Thea—our book will never come into the world.

HEDDA Ah!

MRS. ELVSTED Not—?

LOEVBORG It cannot. Ever.

MRS. ELVSTED Eilert—what have you done with the manuscript? Where is it?

LOEVBORG Oh Thea, please don't ask me that!

MRS. ELVSTED Yes, yes—I must know. I've a right to know. Now!

LOEVBORG The manuscript. I've torn it up.

MRS. ELVSTED [*screams*] No, no!

HEDDA [*involuntarily*] But that's not—!

LOEVBORG [*looks at her*] Not true, you think?

HEDDA [*controls herself*] Why—yes, of course it is, if you say so. It just sounded so incredible—

LOEVBORG   It's true, nevertheless.

MRS. ELVSTED   Oh, my God, my God, Hedda—he's destroyed his own book!

LOEVBORG   I have destroyed my life. Why not my life's work, too?

MRS. ELVSTED   And you—did this last night?

LOEVBORG   Yes, Thea. I tore it into a thousand pieces. And scattered them out across the fjord. It's good, clean, salt water. Let it carry them away; let them drift in the current and the wind. And in a little while, they will sink. Deeper and deeper. As I shall, Thea.

MRS. ELVSTED   Do you know, Eilert—this book—all my life I shall feel as though you'd killed a little child?

LOEVBORG   You're right. It is like killing a child.

MRS. ELVSTED   But how could you? It was my child, too!

HEDDA   [*almost inaudibly*]   Oh—the child—!

MRS. ELVSTED   [*breathes heavily*]   It's all over, then. Well—I'll go now, Hedda.

HEDDA   You're not leaving town?

MRS. ELVSTED   I don't know what I'm going to do. I can't see anything except—darkness.

> *She goes out through the hall.*

HEDDA   [*waits a moment*]   Aren't you going to escort her home, Mr. Loevborg?

LOEVBORG   I? Through the streets? Do you want me to let people see her with me?

HEDDA   Of course I don't know what else may have happened last night. But is it so utterly beyond redress?

LOEVBORG   It isn't just last night. It'll go on happening. I know it. But the curse of it is, I don't want to live that kind of life. I don't want to start all that again. She's broken my courage. I can't spit in the eyes of the world any longer.

HEDDA   [*as though to herself*]   That pretty little fool's been trying to shape a man's destiny.

> *Looks at him.*

But how could you be so heartless towards her?

LOEVBORG   Don't call me heartless!

HEDDA   To go and destroy the one thing that's made her life worth living? You don't call that heartless?

LOEVBORG   Do you want to know the truth, Hedda?

HEDDA   The truth?

LOEVBORG   Promise me first—give me your word—that you'll never let Thea know about this.

HEDDA   I give you my word.

LOEVBORG   Good. Well; what I told her just now was a lie.

HEDDA   About the manuscript?

LOEVBORG   Yes. I didn't tear it up. Or throw it in the fjord.

HEDDA   You didn't? But where is it, then?

LOEVBORG   I destroyed it, all the same. I destroyed it, Hedda!

HEDDA   I don't understand.

LOEVBORG   Thea said that what I had done was like killing a child.

HEDDA   Yes. That's what she said.

LOEVBORG   But to kill a child isn't the worst thing a father can do to it.

HEDDA   What could be worse than that?

LOEVBORG   Hedda—suppose a man came home one morning, after a night of debauchery, and said to the mother of his child: "Look here. I've been wandering round all night. I've been to—such-and-such a place and such-and-such a place. And I had our child with me. I took him to—these places. And I've lost him. Just—lost him. God knows where he is or whose hands he's fallen into."

HEDDA   I see. But when all's said and done, this was only a book—

LOEVBORG   Thea's heart and soul were in that book. It was her whole life.

HEDDA   Yes. I understand.

LOEVBORG   Well, then you must also understand that she and I cannot possibly ever see each other again.

HEDDA   Where will you go?

LOEVBORG   Nowhere. I just want to put an end to it all. As soon as possible.

HEDDA [*takes a step towards him*]   Eilert Loevborg, listen to me. Do it—beautifully!

LOEVBORG   Beautifully?

> *Smiles.*

With a crown of vine-leaves in my hair? The way you used to dream of me—in the old days?

HEDDA   No. I don't believe in that crown any longer. But—do it beautifully, all the same. Just this once. Good-bye. You must go now. And don't come back.

LOEVBORG   Adieu, madam. Give my love to George Tesman.

> *Turns to go.*

HEDDA   Wait. I want to give you a souvenir to take with you.

> *She goes over to the writing table, opens the drawer and the pistol-case, and comes back to* LOEVBORG *with one of the pistols.*

LOEVBORG [*looks at her*]   This? Is this the souvenir?

HEDDA [*nods slowly*]   You recognize it? You looked down its barrel once.

LOEVBORG   You should have used it then.

HEDDA   Here! Use it now!

LOEVBORG [*puts the pistol in his breast pocket*]   Thank you.

HEDDA   Do it beautifully, Eilert Loevborg. Only promise me that!

LOEVBORG   Good-bye, Hedda Gabler.

He goes out through the hall. HEDDA *stands by the door for a
moment, listening. Then she goes over to the writing table,
takes out the package containing the manuscript, glances inside
it, pulls some of the pages half out and looks at them. Then
she takes it to the armchair by the stove and sits down with
the package in her lap. After a moment, she opens the door of
the stove; then she opens the packet.*

HEDDA [*throws one of the pages into the stove and whispers to herself*] I'm burning your child, Thea! You with your beautiful wavy
hair!

She throws a few more pages into the stove.

The child Eilert Loevborg gave you.

Throws the rest of the manuscript in.

I'm burning it! I'm burning your child!

Act 4

*The same. It is evening. The drawing room is in darkness. The small
room is illuminated by the hanging lamp over the table. The curtains
are drawn across the french windows.* HEDDA, *dressed in black, is
walking up and down in the darkened room. Then she goes into the
small room and crosses to the left. A few chords are heard from
the piano. She comes back into the drawing room.*
    BERTHA *comes through the small room from the right with a
lighted lamp, which she places on the table in front of the corner
sofa in the drawing room. Her eyes are red with crying, and she has
black ribbons on her cap. She goes quietly out, right.* HEDDA *goes
over to the french windows, draws the curtains slightly to one side
and looks out into the darkness.*
    A few moments later, MISS TESMAN *enters from the hall. She is
dressed in mourning, with a black hat and veil.* HEDDA *goes to meet
her and holds out her hand.*

MISS TESMAN Well, Hedda, here I am in the weeds of sorrow. My
poor sister has ended her struggles at last.
HEDDA I've already heard. Tesman sent me a card.
MISS TESMAN Yes, he promised me he would. But I thought, no, I
must go and break the news of death to Hedda myself—here, in
the house of life.
HEDDA It's very kind of you.
MISS TESMAN Ah, Rena shouldn't have chosen a time like this to
pass away. This is no moment for Hedda's house to be a place of
mourning.
HEDDA [*changing the subject*] She died peacefully, Miss Tesman?
MISS TESMAN Oh, it was quite beautiful! The end came so calmly.

And she was so happy at being able to see George once again. And say good-bye to him. Hasn't he come home yet?

HEDDA   No. He wrote that I mustn't expect him too soon. But please sit down.

MISS TESMAN   No, thank you, Hedda dear—bless you. I'd like to. But I've so little time. I must dress her and lay her out as well as I can. She shall go to her grave looking really beautiful.

HEDDA   Can't I help with anything?

MISS TESMAN   Why, you mustn't think of such a thing! Hedda Tesman mustn't let her hands be soiled by contact with death. Or her thoughts. Not at this time.

HEDDA   One can't always control one's thoughts.

MISS TESMAN [*continues*]   Ah, well, that's life. Now we must start to sew poor Rena's shroud. There'll be sewing to be done in this house too before long, I shouldn't wonder. But not for a shroud, praise God.

GEORGE TESMAN *enters from the hall.*

HEDDA   You've come at last! Thank heavens!

TESMAN   Are you here, Auntie Juju? With Hedda? Fancy that!

MISS TESMAN   I was just on the point of leaving, dear boy. Well, have you done everything you promised me?

TESMAN   No, I'm afraid I forgot half of it. I'll have to run over again tomorrow. My head's in a complete whirl today. I can't collect my thoughts.

MISS TESMAN   But George dear, you mustn't take it like this.

TESMAN   Oh? Well—er—how should I?

MISS TESMAN   You must be happy in your grief. Happy for what's happened. As I am.

TESMAN   Oh, yes, yes. You're thinking of Aunt Rena.

HEDDA   It'll be lonely for you now, Miss Tesman.

MISS TESMAN   For the first few days, yes. But it won't last long, I hope. Poor dear Rena's little room isn't going to stay empty.

TESMAN   Oh? Whom are you going to move in there? What?

MISS TESMAN   Oh, there's always some poor invalid who needs care and attention.

HEDDA   Do you really want another cross like that to bear?

MISS TESMAN   Cross! God forgive you, child. It's been no cross for me.

HEDDA   But now—if a complete stranger comes to live with you—?

MISS TESMAN   Oh, one soon makes friends with invalids. And I need so much to have someone to live for. Like you, my dear. Well, I expect there'll soon be work in this house too for an old aunt, praise God!

HEDDA   Oh—please!

TESMAN   By Jove, yes! What a splendid time the three of us could have together if—

HEDDA   If?

TESMAN [*uneasily*]   Oh, never mind. It'll all work out. Let's hope so—what?

MISS TESMAN   Yes, yes. Well, I'm sure you two would like to be alone.

Smiles.

Perhaps Hedda may have something to tell you, George. Good-bye. I must go home to Rena.

Turns to the door.

Dear God, how strange! Now Rena is with me and with poor dear Joachim.

TESMAN   Fancy that. Yes, Auntie Juju! What?

MISS TESMAN *goes out through the hall.*

HEDDA [*follows* TESMAN *coldly and searchingly with her eyes*]   I really believe this death distresses you more than it does her.
TESMAN   Oh, it isn't just Auntie Rena. It's Eilert I'm so worried about.
HEDDA [*quickly*]   Is there any news of him?
TESMAN   I ran over to see him this afternoon. I wanted to tell him his manuscript was in safe hands.
HEDDA   Oh? You didn't find him?
TESMAN   No. He wasn't at home. But later I met Mrs. Elvsted and she told me he'd been here early this morning.
HEDDA   Yes, just after you'd left.
TESMAN   It seems he said he'd torn the manuscript up. What?
HEDDA   Yes, he claimed to have done so.
TESMAN   You told him we had it, of course?
HEDDA   No.

Quickly.

Did you tell Mrs. Elvsted?
TESMAN   No, I didn't like to. But you ought to have told him. Think if he should go home and do something desperate! Give me the manuscript, Hedda. I'll run over to him with it right away. Where did you put it?
HEDDA [*cold and motionless, leaning against the armchair*]   I haven't got it any longer.
TESMAN   Haven't got it? What on earth do you mean?
HEDDA   I've burned it.
TESMAN [*starts, terrified*]   Burned it! Burned Eilert's manuscript!
HEDDA   Don't shout. The servant will hear you.
TESMAN   Burned it! But in heaven's name—! Oh, no, no, no! This is impossible!
HEDDA   Well, it's true.
TESMAN   But, Hedda, do you realize what you've done? That's appropriating lost property! It's against the law! By Jove! You ask Judge Brack and see if I'm not right.
HEDDA   You'd be well advised not to talk about it to Judge Brack or anyone else.
TESMAN   But how could you go and do such a dreadful thing? What

on earth put the idea into your head? What came over you? Answer me! What?

HEDDA [*represses an almost imperceptible smile*]   I did it for your sake, George.

TESMAN   For my sake?

HEDDA   When you came home this morning and described how he'd read his book to you—

TESMAN   Yes, yes?

HEDDA   You admitted you were jealous of him.

TESMAN   But, good heavens, I didn't mean it literally!

HEDDA   No matter. I couldn't bear the thought that anyone else should push you into the background.

TESMAN [*torn between doubt and joy*]   Hedda—is this true? But—but—but I never realized you loved me like that! Fancy—   *love?*

HEDDA   Well, I suppose you'd better know. I'm going to have—

> *Breaks off and says violently.*

No, no—you'd better ask your Auntie Juju. She'll tell you.

TESMAN   Hedda! I think I understand what you mean.

> *Clasps his hands.*

Good heavens, can it really be true! What?

HEDDA   Don't shout. The servant will hear you.

TESMAN [*laughing with joy*]   The servant! I say, that's good! The servant! Why, that's Bertha! I'll run out and tell her at once!

HEDDA [*clenches her hands in despair*]   Oh, it's destroying me, all this —it's destroying me!

TESMAN   I say, Hedda, what's up? What?

HEDDA [*cold, controlled*]   Oh, it's all so—absurd—George.

TESMAN   Absurd? That I'm so happy? But surely—? Ah, well—perhaps I won't say anything to Bertha.

HEDDA   No, do. She might as well know too.

TESMAN   No, no, I won't tell her yet. But Auntie Juju—I must let her know! And you—you called me George! For the first time! Fancy that! Oh, it'll make Auntie Juju so happy, all this! So very happy!

HEDDA   Will she be happy when she hears I've burned Eilert Loevborg's manuscript—for your sake?

TESMAN   No, I'd forgotten about that. Of course no one must be allowed to know about the manuscript. But that you're burning with love for me, Hedda, I must certainly let Auntie Juju know that. I say, I wonder if young wives often feel like that towards their husbands? What?

HEDDA   You might ask Auntie Juju about that too.

TESMAN   I will, as soon as I get the chance.

> *Looks uneasy and thoughtful again.*

But I say, you know, that manuscript. Dreadful business. Poor Eilert!

MRS. ELVSTED, *dressed as on her first visit, with hat and over-coat, enters from the hall.*

MRS. ELVSTED [*greets them hastily and tremulously*] Oh, Hedda dear, do please forgive me for coming here again.

HEDDA Why, Thea, what's happened?

TESMAN Is it anything to do with Eilert Loevborg? What?

MRS. ELVSTED Yes—I'm so dreadfully afraid he may have met with an accident.

HEDDA [*grips her arm*] You think so?

TESMAN But, good heavens, Mrs. Elvsted, what makes you think that?

MRS. ELVSTED I heard them talking about him at the boarding-house, as I went in. Oh, there are the most terrible rumors being spread about him in town today.

TESMAN Fancy. Yes, I heard about them too. But I can testify that he went straight home to bed. Fancy that!

HEDDA Well—what did they say in the boarding-house?

MRS. ELVSTED Oh, I couldn't find out anything. Either they didn't know, or else— They stopped talking when they saw me. And I didn't dare to ask.

TESMAN [*fidgets uneasily*] We must hope—we must hope you misheard them, Mrs. Elvsted.

MRS. ELVSTED No, no, I'm sure it was he they were talking about. I heard them say something about a hospital—

TESMAN Hospital!

HEDDA Oh no, surely that's impossible!

MRS. ELVSTED Oh, I became so afraid. So I went up to his rooms and asked to see him.

HEDDA Do you think that was wise, Thea?

MRS. ELVSTED Well, what else could I do? I couldn't bear the uncertainty any longer.

TESMAN But *you* didn't manage to find him either? What?

MRS. ELVSTED No. And they had no idea where he was. They said he hadn't been home since yesterday afternoon.

TESMAN Since yesterday? Fancy that!

MRS. ELVSTED I'm sure he must have met with an accident.

TESMAN Hedda, I wonder if I ought to go into town and make one or two inquiries?

HEDDA No, no, don't you get mixed up in this.

JUDGE BRACK *enters from the hall, hat in hand.* BERTHA, *who has opened the door for him, closes it. He looks serious and greets them silently.*

TESMAN Hullo, my dear Judge. Fancy seeing you!

BRACK I had to come and talk to you.

TESMAN I can see Auntie Juju's told you the news.

BRACK Yes, I've heard about that too.

TESMAN Tragic, isn't it?

BRACK Well, my dear chap, that depends how you look at it.

TESMAN [*looks uncertainly at him*]   Has something else happened?

BRACK   Yes.

HEDDA   Another tragedy?

BRACK   That also depends on how you look at it, Mrs. Tesman.

MRS. ELVSTED   Oh, it's something to do with Eilert Loevborg!

BRACK [*looks at her for a moment*]   How did you guess? Perhaps you've heard already—?

MRS. ELVSTED [*confused*]   No, no, not at all—I—

TESMAN   For heaven's sake, tell us!

BRACK [*shrugs his shoulders*]   Well, I'm afraid they've taken him to the hospital. He's dying.

MRS. ELVSTED [*screams*]   Oh God, God!

TESMAN   The hospital! Dying!

HEDDA [*involuntarily*]   So quickly!

MRS. ELVSTED [*weeping*]   Oh, Hedda! And we parted enemies!

HEDDA [*whispers*]   Thea—Thea!

MRS. ELVSTED [*ignoring her*]   I must see him! I must see him before he dies!

BRACK   It's no use, Mrs. Elvsted. No one's allowed to see him now.

MRS. ELVSTED   But what's happened to him? You must tell me!

TESMAN   He hasn't tried to do anything to himself? What?

HEDDA   Yes, he has. I'm sure of it.

TESMAN   Hedda, how can you—?

BRACK [*who has not taken his eyes from her*]   I'm afraid you've guessed correctly, Mrs. Tesman.

MRS. ELVSTED   How dreadful!

TESMAN   Attempted suicide! Fancy that!

HEDDA   Shot himself!

BRACK   Right again, Mrs. Tesman.

MRS. ELVSTED [*tries to compose herself*]   When did this happen, Judge Brack?

BRACK   This afternoon. Between three and four.

TESMAN   But, good heavens—where? What?

BRACK [*a little hesitantly*]   Where? Why, my dear chap, in his rooms of course.

MRS. ELVSTED   No, that's impossible. I was there soon after six.

BRACK   Well, it must have been somewhere else, then. I don't know exactly. I only know that they found him. He'd shot himself—through the breast.

MRS. ELVSTED   Oh, how horrible! That he should end like that!

HEDDA [*to* BRACK]   Through the breast, you said?

BRACK   That is what I said.

HEDDA   Not through the head?

BRACK   Through the breast, Mrs. Tesman.

HEDDA   The breast. Yes; yes. That's good, too.

BRACK   Why, Mrs. Tesman?

HEDDA   Oh—no, I didn't mean anything.

TESMAN   And the wound's dangerous, you say? What?

BRACK   Mortal. He's probably already dead.

MRS. ELVSTED   Yes, yes—I feel it! It's all over. All over. Oh Hedda—!

TESMAN   But, tell me, how did you manage to learn all this?

BRACK [*curtly*]   From the police. I spoke to one of them.

HEDDA [*loudly, clearly*]   At last! Oh, thank God!

TESMAN [*appalled*]   For God's sake, Hedda, what are you saying?

HEDDA   I am saying there's beauty in what he has done.

BRACK   Hm—Mrs. Tesman—

TESMAN   Beauty! Oh, but I say!

MRS. ELVSTED   Hedda, how can you talk of beauty in connection with a thing like this?

HEDDA   Eilert Loevborg has settled his account with life. He's had the courage to do what—what he had to do.

MRS. ELVSTED   No, that's not why it happened. He did it because he was mad.

TESMAN   He did it because he was desperate.

HEDDA   You're wrong! I know!

MRS. ELVSTED   He must have been mad. The same as when he tore up the manuscript.

BRACK [*starts*]   Manuscript? Did he tear it up?

MRS. ELVSTED   Yes. Last night.

TESMAN [*whispers*]   Oh, Hedda, we shall never be able to escape from this.

BRACK   Hm. Strange.

TESMAN [*wanders round the room*]   To think of Eilert dying like that. And not leaving behind him the thing that would have made his name endure.

MRS. ELVSTED   If only it could be pieced together again!

TESMAN   Yes, fancy! If only it could! I'd give anything—

MRS. ELVSTED   Perhaps it can, Mr. Tesman.

TESMAN   What do you mean?

MRS. ELVSTED [*searches in the pocket of her dress*]   Look! I kept the notes he dictated it from.

HEDDA [*takes a step nearer*]   Ah!

TESMAN   You kept them, Mrs. Elvsted! What?

MRS. ELVSTED   Yes, here they are. I brought them with me when I left home. They've been in my pocket ever since.

TESMAN   Let me have a look.

MRS. ELVSTED [*hands him a wad of small sheets of paper*]   They're in a terrible muddle. All mixed up.

TESMAN   I say, just fancy if we can sort them out! Perhaps if we work on them together—?

MRS. ELVSTED   Oh, yes! Let's try, anyway!

TESMAN   We'll manage it. We must! I shall dedicate my life to this.

HEDDA   *You*, George? Your life?

TESMAN   Yes—well, all the time I can spare. My book'll have to wait. Hedda, you do understand? What? I owe it to Eilert's memory.

HEDDA   Perhaps.

TESMAN   Well, my dear Mrs. Elvsted, you and I'll have to pool our brains. No use crying over spilt milk, what? We must try to approach this matter calmly.

MRS. ELVSTED   Yes, yes, Mr. Tesman. I'll do my best.

TESMAN   Well, come over here and let's start looking at these notes right away. Where shall we sit? Here? No, the other room. You'll excuse us, won't you, Judge? Come along with me Mrs. Elvsted.

MRS. ELVSTED   Oh, God! If only we can manage to do it!

> TESMAN *and* MRS. ELVSTED *go into the rear room. He takes off his hat and overcoat. They sit at the table beneath the hanging lamp and absorb themselves in the notes.* HEDDA *walks across to the stove and sits in the armchair. After a moment,* BRACK *goes over to her.*

HEDDA [*half aloud*]   Oh, Judge! This act of Eilert Loevborg's—doesn't it give one a sense of release!

BRACK   Release, Mrs. Hedda? Well, it's a release for him, of course—

HEDDA   Oh, I don't mean him—I mean me! The release of knowing that someone can do something really brave! Something beautiful!

BRACK [*smiles*]   Hm—my dear Mrs. Hedda—

HEDDA   Oh, I know what you're going to say. You're a bourgeois at heart too, just like—ah, well!

BRACK [*looks at her*]   Eilert Loevborg has meant more to you than you're willing to admit to yourself. Or am I wrong?

HEDDA   I'm not answering questions like that from you. I only know that Eilert Loevborg has had the courage to live according to his own principles. And now, at last, he's done something big! Something beautiful! To have the courage and the will to rise from the feast of life so early!

BRACK   It distresses me deeply, Mrs. Hedda, but I'm afraid I must rob you of that charming illusion.

HEDDA   Illusion?

BRACK   You wouldn't have been allowed to keep it for long, anyway.

HEDDA   What do you mean?

BRACK   He didn't shoot himself on purpose.

HEDDA   Not on purpose?

BRACK   No. It didn't happen quite the way I told you.

HEDDA   Have you been hiding something? What is it?

BRACK   In order to spare poor Mrs. Elvsted's feelings, I permitted myself one or two small—equivocations.

HEDDA   What?

BRACK   To begin with, he is already dead.

HEDDA   He died at the hospital?

BRACK   Yes. Without regaining consciousness.

HEDDA   What else haven't you told us?

BRACK   The incident didn't take place at his lodgings.

HEDDA   Well, that's utterly unimportant.

BRACK   Not utterly. The fact is, you see, that Eilbert Loevborg was found shot in Mademoiselle Danielle's boudoir.

HEDDA [*almost jumps up, but instead sinks back in her chair*]   That's impossible. He can't have been there today.

BRACK   He was there this afternoon. He went to ask for something he claimed they'd taken from him. Talked some crazy nonsense about a child which had got lost—

HEDDA   Oh! So that was the reason!

BRACK   I thought at first he might have been referring to his manuscript. But I hear he destroyed that himself. So he must have meant his pocketbook—I suppose.

HEDDA   Yes, I suppose so. So they found him there?

BRACK   Yes; there. With a discharged pistol in his breast pocket. The shot had wounded him mortally.

HEDDA   Yes. In the breast.

BRACK   No. In the—hm—stomach. The—lower part—

HEDDA   [*looks at him with an expression of repulsion*]   That too! Oh, why does everything I touch become mean and ludicrous? It's like a curse!

BRACK   There's something else, Mrs. Hedda. It's rather disagreeable, too.

HEDDA   What?

BRACK   The pistol he had on him—

HEDDA   Yes? What about it?

BRACK   He must have stolen it.

HEDDA   [*jumps up*]   Stolen it! That isn't true! He didn't.

BRACK   It's the only explanation. He must have stolen it. Ssh!

TESMAN *and* MRS. ELVSTED *have got up from the table in the rear room and come into the drawing room.*

TESMAN   [*his hands full of papers*]   Hedda, I can't see properly under that lamp. Think!

HEDDA   I am thinking.

TESMAN   Do you think we could possibly use your writing table for a little? What?

HEDDA   Yes, of course.

Quickly.

No, wait! Let me tidy it up first.

TESMAN   Oh, don't you trouble about that. There's plenty of room.

HEDDA   No, no, let me tidy it up first, I say. I'll take this in and put them on the piano. Here.

She pulls an object, covered with sheets of music, out from under the bookcase, puts some more sheets on top and carries it all into the rear room and away to the left. TESMAN *puts his papers on the writing table and moves the lamp over from the corner table. He and* MRS. ELVSTED *sit down and begin working again.* HEDDA *comes back.*

HEDDA   [*behind* MRS. ELVSTED'S *chair, ruffles her hair gently*]   Well, my pretty Thea! And how is work progressing on Eilert Loevborg's memorial?

MRS. ELVSTED   [*looks up at her, dejectedly*]   Oh, it's going to be terribly difficult to get these into any order.

TESMAN We've got to do it. We must! After all, putting other people's papers into order is rather my specialty, what?

> HEDDA *goes over to the stove and sits on one of the footstools.*
> BRACK *stands over her, leaning against the armchair.*

HEDDA [*whispers*] What was that you were saying about the pistol?
BRACK [*softly*] I said he must have stolen it.
HEDDA Why do you think that?
BRACK Because any other explanation is unthinkable, Mrs. Hedda,
or ought to be.
HEDDA I see.
BRACK [*looks at her for a moment*] Eilert Loevborg was here this
morning. Wasn't he?
HEDDA Yes.
BRACK Were you alone with him?
HEDDA For a few moments.
BRACK You didn't leave the room while he was here?
HEDDA No.
BRACK Think again. Are you sure you didn't go out for a moment?
HEDDA Oh—yes, I might have gone into the hall. Just for a few
seconds.
BRACK And where was your pistol-case during this time?
HEDDA I'd locked it in that—
BRACK Er—Mrs. Hedda?
HEDDA It was lying over there on my writing table.
BRACK Have you looked to see if both the pistols are still there?
HEDDA No.
BRACK You needn't bother. I saw the pistol Loevborg had when they
found him. I recognized it at once. From yesterday. And other
occasions.
HEDDA Have you got it?
BRACK No. The police have it.
HEDDA What will the police do with this pistol?
BRACK Try to trace the owner.
HEDDA Do you think they'll succeed?
BRACK [*leans down and whispers*] No, Hedda Gabler. Not as long
as I hold my tongue.
HEDDA [*looks nervously at him*] And if you don't?
BRACK [*shrugs his shoulders*] You could always say he'd stolen it.
HEDDA I'd rather die!
BRACK [*smiles*] People say that. They never do it.
HEDDA [*not replying*] And suppose the pistol wasn't stolen? And
they trace the owner? What then?
BRACK There'll be a scandal, Hedda.
HEDDA A scandal!
BRACK Yes, a scandal. The thing you're so frightened of. You'll have
to appear in court. Together with Mademoiselle Danielle. She'll
have to explain how it all happened. Was it an accident, or was it—
homicide? Was he about to take the pistol from his pocket to

threaten her? And did it go off? Or did she snatch the pistol from his hand, shoot him and then put it back in his pocket? She might quite easily have done it. She's a resourceful lady, is Mademoiselle Danielle.

HEDDA   But I had nothing to do with this repulsive business.

BRACK   No. But you'll have to answer one question. Why did you give Eilert Loevborg this pistol? And what conclusions will people draw when it is proved you did give it to him?

HEDDA [*bows her head*]   That's true. I hadn't thought of that.

BRACK   Well, luckily there's no danger as long as I hold my tongue.

HEDDA [*looks up at him*]   In other words, I'm in your power, Judge. From now on, you've got your hold over me.

BRACK [*whispers, more slowly*]   Hedda, my dearest—believe me—I will not abuse my position.

HEDDA   Nevertheless, I'm in your power. Dependent on your will, and your demands. Not free. Still not free!

Rises passionately.

No. I couldn't bear that. No.

BRACK [*looks half-derisively at her*]   Most people resign themselves to the inevitable, sooner or later.

HEDDA [*returns his gaze*]   Possibly they do.

She goes across to the writing table.

HEDDA [*represses an involuntary smile and says in* TESMAN'*s voice*] Well, George. Think you'll be able to manage? What?

TESMAN   Heaven knows, dear. This is going to take months and months.

HEDDA [*in the same tone as before*]   Fancy that, by Jove!

Runs her hands gently through MRS. ELVSTED'*s hair.*

Doesn't it feel strange, Thea? Here you are working away with Tesman just the way you used to work with Eilert Loevborg.

MRS. ELVSTED   Oh—if only I can inspire your husband too!

HEDDA   Oh, it'll come. In time.

TESMAN   Yes—do you know, Hedda, I really think I'm beginning to feel a bit—well—that way. But you go back and talk to Judge Brack.

HEDDA   Can't I be of use to you two in any way?

TESMAN   No, none at all.

Turns his head.

You'll have to keep Hedda company from now on, Judge, and see she doesn't get bored. If you don't mind.

BRACK [*glances at* HEDDA]   It'll be a pleasure.

HEDDA   Thank you. But I'm tired this evening. I think I'll lie down on the sofa in there for a little while.

TESMAN   Yes, dear—do. What?

HEDDA *goes into the rear room and draws the curtains behind her. Short pause. Suddenly she begins to play a frenzied dance melody on the piano.*

MRS. ELVSTED [*starts up from her chair*] Oh, what's that?

TESMAN [*runs to the doorway*] Hedda dear, please! Don't play dance music tonight! Think of Auntie Rena. And Eilert.

HEDDA [*puts her head out through the curtains*] And Auntie Juju. And all the rest of them. From now on I'll be quiet.

Closes the curtains behind her.

TESMAN [*at the writing table*] It distresses her to watch us doing this. I say, Mrs. Elvsted, I've an idea. Why don't you move in with Auntie Juju? I'll run over each evening, and we can sit and work there. What?

MRS. ELVSTED Yes, that might be the best plan.

HEDDA [*from the rear room*] I can hear what you're saying, Tesman. But how shall I spend the evenings out here?

TESMAN [*looking through his papers*] Oh, I'm sure Judge Brack'll be kind enough to come over and keep you company. You won't mind my not being here, Judge?

BRACK [*in the armchair, calls gaily*] I'll be delighted, Mrs. Tesman. I'll be here every evening. We'll have great fun together, you and I.

HEDDA [*loud and clear*] Yes, that'll suit you, won't it, Judge? The only cock on the dunghill—!

A shot is heard from the rear room. TESMAN, MRS. ELVSTED *and* JUDGE BRACK *start from their chairs.*

TESMAN Oh, she's playing with those pistols again.

He pulls the curtains aside and runs in. MRS. ELVSTED *follows him.* HEDDA *is lying dead on the sofa. Confusion and shouting.* BERTHA *enters in alarm from the right.*

TESMAN [*screams to* BRACK] She's shot herself! Shot herself in the head! By Jove! Fancy that!

BRACK [*half paralyzed in the armchair*] But, good God! People don't do such things!

1890

4   LANGUAGE AND PERFORMANCE

The audience at a play sees the stage, the sets, the props, the costumes, the actors, their movements and gestures, their facial expressions. An audience hears sounds and sound effects, voices, spoken
words. The reader of a play has only printed words. Even with stage
directions for assembling a set on the stage of the imagination, for
visualizing the characters and their actions, but it is all in printed
words. For a reader of plays, language is everything, but even for the
audience, despite all the visual effects, the medium of the play is
language.

Sometimes that language is distinctly different from ordinary speech.
Not many of us would say, "Look, the sun's coming up," this way:

> But look, the morn in russet mantle clad
> Walks o'er the dew of yon high eastward hill.

It is no doubt fitting that the high art of traditional tragedy—plays
whose characters are kings and queens, princes and princesses, nobles
and courtiers—should be embodied in elevated language, even, like
Hamlet, in highly figurative and metrical language:

> Mother, for love of grace,
> Lay not that flattering unction to your soul,
> That not your trespass but my madness speaks.
> It will but skin and film the ulcerous place
> Whiles rank corruption, mining all within,
> Infects unseen. Confess yourself to heaven,
> Repent what's past, avoid what is to come,
> And do not spread the compost on the weeds,
> To make them ranker.

Much of the play is in verse like this, with five "beats," or emphasized
syllables, to the line (and typically five less accented syllables). This
rhythm sets up expectations, and one of the pleasures of poetic drama
as in traditional poetry is the delight in fulfilled expectations of sound
and pleasure in modified, modulated, or syncopated, rhythms. To
some extent the meter dictates how an actor reads the lines and, perhaps, how we sound them on our inner ear as we read. An actor,
however, must make a choice whether to emphasize the poetic or the
prose aspect of each line: how much stress or emphasis do you give
the "to" in the second line above or the "on" in the eighth? The text
for a performer is like the score for a musical performer: all the notes
are there but each performance differs. If you can, listen to recordings of John Barrymore and of Maurice Evans, or Richard Burton and
Sir Laurence Olivier, reading this passage and you will hear how
differently the same words can be read. How do you yourself read
the lines? Do you actually sound them out in your mind, choosing
one possibility or the other? Are you, or can you become, aware of
the tug of the meter and meaning simultaneously? Marking the end

of Hamlet's **soliloquy** (speech to oneself) is a beautifully balanced line in which *break* and *heart* in the first half line balance *hold* and *tongue* in the second half, pivoting around the *I*—"But break my heart, for I must hold my tongue." It is doubtful whether this line would have quite the finality and effect were it not for expectations of rhythm built up by the earlier verse.

But isn't poetic drama very artificial, somewhat like opera in which people are singing in each others' faces things like, "Who's at the door?" and "My name is Mimi"? While "artificial" means "unnatural" or "unrealistic," it also means "made by art," and it is possible both to be deeply moved by the human passion and truth of a play like *Hamlet* and thrilled by the skill in structure and language. Indeed, it is possible that our response is fullest and greatest when we are moved by both, conscious of both, even though the two—significance and structure, or meaning and language—are inseparable. Is it the spitting out of the sibilant sounds or the "idea" of his mother's racing into bed with his uncle that makes Hamlet's "O most wicked speed, to post / With such dexterity to incestuous sheets!" so clearly and dramatically reveal his disgust at his mother's marrying Claudius so soon after her husband's death?

The rhythms and sounds, the unseen images called up by the words —russet mantle, flattering unction—are available to reader and audience, as are the statements and implications of the dialogue creating the effects, themes, and significance of the play. The language creates all these things while remaining language, and reader and audience are conscious of the beauty or appropriateness of the sounds and of the precise words, the verbal artistry, even while enthralled by the characters and actions, drawn into the world of the play, and stirred by the resonances of the play's image of man in the world.

The actor's physical presence, the gestures, the intonation and emphasis in the delivery of the lines (as well as sets, costumes, and so on), while they evoke specific emotions and clarify *a* meaning of the play, restrict the audience to the interpretation of the play by director and actor in a way that the words do not. There is no question, for example, that Hamlet is, to put it mildly, upset at his mother's precipitously marrying Claudius, his father's brother, as his language makes clear in the "incestuous sheets" passage and in many others (for example, "to live / In the rank sweat of an enseaméd bed, / Stewed in corruption, honeying, and making love / Over the nasty sty—" 3:4:93–95). But is this the central motivation and meaning of the play? At times an actor and director will play it as if it is, as Sir Laurence Olivier virtually does in his film version. The political and other themes are muted if not cut entirely from the play. The reader, however, though lacking the neatness and clarity of an interpretation, has all the words and so all the themes and possibilities present in the text. In reading, you can perform it one way, unperform it, and reperform it in another, even perform it two ways at once, perhaps, in your imagination as you read. Charles Lamb was so upset by how much the performed play limited his imagination, he vowed not ever again to see Shakespeare on the stage.

Even plays in very prosaic prose frequently call attention to their language, both its use and its limits. At times the characters in Harold Pinter's *The Black and White* converse, that is, they respond to each other:

> FIRST   I not long got here.
> SECOND   Did you get the all-night bus?
> FIRST   I got the all-night bus straight here.
> SECOND   Where from?
> FIRST   Marble Arch.
> SECOND   Which one?
> FIRST   The two-nine-four, that takes me all the way to Fleet Street.
> SECOND   So does the two-nine-one.

The impression is that the conversation is entirely banal, and, while Pinter may be telling us something about the banality of the characters, and the kind of conversation that one hears in an all-night milk bar in central London, there is something uncomfortably familiar about it. So the language calls attention to the way language is used and perhaps to the way we ourselves converse. (The way everyone converses? Is Pinter's dialogue natural or artificial? Is it what two vagrant old dears from London's East End might say, or is it an exaggeration, a stylization? Or is it both? And in either case doesn't its repetition show us something about the nature of our conversation, something very different from the usual representation of speech? And don't its non sequiturs show us that dialogue is often not communication but independent monologues occasionally intersecting?

Notice how each of Pinter's two characters carries on her own half of the conversation without immediately paying much attention to what the other is saying. The sketch opens just that way:

> SECOND   You see that one come up and speak to me at the counter?
> FIRST   You got the bread, then?

A few lines later:

> SECOND   Comes up to me, he says, hullo, he says, what's the time by your clock? Bloody liberty. I was just standing there getting your soup.
> FIRST   It's tomato soup.
> SECOND   What's the time by your clock? he says.

The first woman finally responds. One of the reasons for so much repetition is that people—only such people? all people?—do not listen very carefully, are too wrapped up in their own thoughts and feelings, so that it takes repetition to get their attention.

Pinter's language may seem as stylized and artificial as Shakespeare's blank verse. It certainly is not the language of "realist" drama like that of Ibsen or Miller. There, as in real life, language is a practical tool. We are probably not—and not meant to be—so conscious of the language as language. Tesman's repeated "By Jove" and "what?" (in the translation) do not call attention to themselves as language, even as banal language, but as indication of the kind of conventional character Tesman is: the words are more important for what they point to than they are in themselves as words.

The language in *Death of a Salesman* is frequently of that order. Happy says, "you're the tops," and Willy warns about "counting your chickens," and the waiter Stanley calls it a "dog's life." The clichés in the mouths of the characters are not evidence of poor writing on Miller's part but characterize the ordinariness of the characters (which ordinariness contributes to the pathos of the play: here is no Hamlet, no great matter in the history of the human race, but still a human in moral agony). When they strive to express their emotions, reach for poetry, the very poverty of their language generates a moving pathos, as when Willy is remembering Biff's triumphant day on the football field:

> Like a young god. Hercules—something like that. And the sun, the sun all around him. Remember how he waved to me? Right up from the field, with the representatives of three colleges standing by? And the buyers I brought, and the cheers when he came out—Loman, Loman, Loman! God Almighty, he'll be great yet. A star like that, magnificent, can never really fade away!

Sometimes language, even the very ordinary language that *that* person would use at *that* time in *that* situation, calls attention to itself by its very appropriateness. There are expressions, some sentimental— "he's only a little boat looking for a harbor"—and some more harsh —"spewing out the vomit from his mind"—that reach above the banality of the rest, though they perhaps do not call too much attention to themselves as noticeably expressive language despite their figurativeness. Linda, who can be banal as any in expressing her love for Willy—"He's the dearest man in the world to me"—can also have moments in which the rhythm of her language and the repetitions of words and structure achieve a certain impressive eloquence:

> I don't say he is a great man. Willy Loman never made a lot of money. His name was never in the paper. He's not the finest character that ever lived. But he's a human being, and a terrible thing is happening to him. So attention must be paid. He's not to be allowed to fall into his grave like an old dog. Attention, attention must be finally paid to such a person.

Here the language rises above the merely useful.

There is one scene, in act two, when Willy goes to see Howard Wagner, the son of his late friend and boss, to ask for a non-traveling job with the company, that is a little reminiscent of the Pinter: Willy is down and desperate, Howard is excited with his new toy, a wire-recorder (i.e., early tape recorder). The two men are so entangled in their own affairs they cannot listen to the other (though our sympathies are with Willy, who tries to respond and whose need for dialogue is great). There is also an ironic and wrenching contrast between the emotions of Willy and the mechanically reproduced sounds: the whistling of a popular bar-room song, "Roll Out the Barrel" and the rote repetition by Wagner's five-year-old of the capitals of the states in alphabetical order. When Howard leaves the room there is a macabre incident. The distraught Willy addresses Howard's dead father but accidentally activates the recorder:

> HOWARD'S SON . . . of New York is Albany. The capital of Ohio is Cincinnati, the capital of Rhode Island is . . . *The recitation continues.*

The little boy's voice is no more unresponsive to Willy's plight than Howard was: language is emptied of meaning and feeling.

So even a realistic play can raise our awareness of its language. *Death of a Salesman* is in the flat and empty, inexpressive "real" language of the artificial world of business and the ambition to be wealthy and "number one." The very inexpressiveness of its language helps to define the emptiness of that world, and it is, ironically, through that language that the powerful poignancy of emotions that cannot be articulated is expressed.

Language, then, even in realistic drama is not "merely" realistic: it is crafted to give the illusion of reality, and in its own way embodies and interprets a view of the world seen from a particular vantage point, even as does the language of poetic drama. Consciousness of the language, what it says and what it suggests, how it relates to "real" language and how it differs, how it embodies its world, is essential to understanding and intensifying the experience of reading drama.

ARTHUR MILLER

Death of a Salesman

CHARACTERS

WILLY LOMAN

LINDA

BIFF

HAPPY

BERNARD

THE WOMAN

CHARLEY

UNCLE BEN

HOWARD WAGNER

JENNY

STANLEY

MISS FORSYTHE (GIRL)

LETTA

Act 1

A melody is heard, played upon a flute. It is small and fine, telling of grass and trees and the horizon. The curtain rises.

Before us is the Salesman's house. We are aware of towering, angular shapes behind it, surrounding it on all sides. Only the blue light of the sky falls upon the house and forestage; the surrounding area shows an angry glow of orange. As more light appears, we see a solid vault of apartment houses around the small, fragile-seeming home. An air of the dream clings to the place, a dream rising out of reality. The kitchen at center seems actual enough, for there is a kitchen table with three chairs, and a refrigerator. But no other fixtures are seen. At the back of the kitchen there is a draped entrance, which leads to the living room. To the right of the kitchen, on a level raised two feet, is a bedroom furnished only with a brass bedstead and a straight chair. On a shelf over the bed a silver athletic trophy stands. A window opens onto the apartment house at the side.

Behind the kitchen, on a level raised six and a half feet, is the boys' bedroom, at present barely visible. Two beds are dimly seen, and at the back of the room a dormer window. (This bedroom is above the unseen living room.) At the left a stairway curves up to it from the kitchen.

The entire setting is wholly or, in some places, partially transparent. The roof-line of the house is one-dimensional; under and over it we see the apartment buildings. Before the house lies an apron, curving beyond the forestage into the orchestra. This forward area serves as the back yard as well as the locale of all WILLY'S *imaginings and of his city scenes. Whenever the action is in the present the actors observe the imaginary wall-lines, entering the house only through its door at the left. But in the scenes of the past these boundaries are broken, and characters enter or leave a room by stepping "through" a wall onto the forestage.*

From the right, WILLY LOMAN, *the Salesman, enters, carrying two large sample cases. The flute plays on. He hears but is not aware of it. He is past sixty years of age, dressed quietly. Even as he crosses the stage to the doorway of the house, his exhaustion is apparent. He unlocks the door, comes into the kitchen, and thankfully lets his burden down, feeling the soreness of his palms. A word-sigh escapes his lips—it might be "Oh, boy, oh, boy." He closes the door, then carries his cases out into the living-room, through the draped kitchen doorway.*

LINDA, *his wife, has stirred in her bed at the right. She gets out and puts on a robe, listening. Most often jovial, she has developed an iron repression of her exceptions to* WILLY's *behavior—she more than loves him, she admires him, as though his mercurial nature, his temper, his massive dreams and little cruelties, served her only as sharp reminders of the turbulent longings within him, longings which she shares but lacks the temperament to utter and follow to their end.*

LINDA [*hearing* WILLY *outside the bedroom, calls with some trepidation*]   Willy!

WILLY   It's all right. I came back.

LINDA   Why? What happened? [*Slight pause*]. Did something happen, Willy?

WILLY   No, nothing happened.

LINDA   You didn't smash the car, did you?

WILLY [*with casual irritation*]   I said nothing happened. Didn't you hear me?

LINDA   Don't you feel well?

WILLY   I'm tired to the death. [*The flute has faded away. He sits on the bed beside her, a little numb.*] I couldn't make it. I just couldn't make it, Linda.

LINDA [*very carefully, delicately*]   Where were you all day? You look terrible.

WILLY   I got as far as a little above Yonkers. I stopped for a cup of coffee. Maybe it was the coffee.

LINDA   What?

WILLY [*after a pause*]   I suddenly couldn't drive any more. The car kept going off onto the shoulder, y'know?

LINDA [*helpfully*]   Oh. Maybe it was the steering again. I don't think Angelo knows the Studebaker.

WILLY   No, it's me, it's me. Suddenly I realize I'm goin' sixty miles an hour and I don't remember the last five minutes. I'm—I can't seem to—keep my mind to it.

LINDA   Maybe it's your glasses. You never went for your new glasses.

WILLY   No, I see everything. I came back ten miles an hour. It took me nearly four hours from Yonkers.

LINDA [*resigned*]   Well, you'll just have to take a rest, Willy, you can't continue this way.

WILLY   I just got back from Florida.

LINDA   But you didn't rest your mind. Your mind is overactive, and the mind is what counts, dear.

WILLY I'll start out in the morning. Maybe I'll feel better in the morning. [*She is taking off his shoes.*] These goddam arch supports are killing me.

LINDA Take an aspirin. Should I get you an aspirin? It'll soothe you.

WILLY [*with wonder*] I was driving along, you understand? And I was fine. I was even observing the scenery. You can imagine, me looking at scenery, on the road every week of my life. But it's so beautiful up there, Linda, the trees are so thick, and the sun is warm. I opened the windshield and just let the warm air bathe over me. And then all of a sudden I'm goin' off the road! I'm tellin' ya, I absolutely forgot I was driving. If I'd've gone the other way over the white line I might've killed somebody. So I went on again—and five minutes later I'm dreamin' again, and I nearly—[*He presses two fingers against his eyes.*] I have such thoughts, I have such strange thoughts.

LINDA Willy, dear. Talk to them again. There's no reason why you can't work in New York.

WILLY They don't need me in New York. I'm the New England man. I'm vital in New England.

LINDA But you're sixty years old. They can't expect you to keep traveling every week.

WILLY I'll have to send a wire to Portland. I'm supposed to see Brown and Morrison tomorrow morning at ten o'clock to show the line. Goddammit, I could sell them! [*He starts putting on his jacket.*]

LINDA [*taking the jacket from him*] Why don't you go down to the place tomorrow and tell Howard you've simply got to work in New York? You're too accommodating, dear.

WILLY If old man Wagner was alive I'd a been in charge of New York now! That man was a prince, he was a masterful man. But that boy of his, that Howard, he don't appreciate. When I went north the first time, the Wagner Company didn't know where New England was!

LINDA Why don't you tell those things to Howard, dear?

WILLY [*encouraged*] I will, I definitely will. Is there any cheese?

LINDA I'll make you a sandwich.

WILLY No, go to sleep. I'll take some milk. I'll be up right away. The boys in?

LINDA They're sleeping. Happy took Biff on a date tonight.

WILLY [*interested*] That so?

LINDA It was so nice to see them shaving together, one behind the other, in the bathroom. And going out together. You notice? The whole house smells of shaving lotion.

WILLY Figure it out. Work a lifetime to pay off a house. You finally own it, and there's nobody to live in it.

LINDA Well, dear, life is a casting off. It's always that way.

WILLY No, no, some people—some people accomplish something. Did Biff say anything after I went this morning?

LINDA You shouldn't have criticized him, Willy, especially after he just got off the train. You mustn't lose your temper with him.

WILLY When the hell did I lose my temper? I simply asked him if he was making any money. Is that a criticism?

LINDA   But, dear, how could he make any money?

WILLY [*worried and angered*]   There's such an undercurrent in him. He became a moody man. Did he apologize when I left this morning?

LINDA   He was crestfallen, Willy. You know how he admires you. I think if he finds himself, then you'll both be happier and not fight any more.

WILLY   How can he find himself on a farm? Is that a life? A farm-hand? In the beginning, when he was young, I thought, well, a young man, it's good for him to tramp around, take a lot of different jobs. But it's more than ten years now and he has yet to make thirty-five dollars a week!

LINDA   He's finding himself, Willy.

WILLY   Not finding yourself at the age of thirty-four is a disgrace!

LINDA   Shh!

WILLY   The trouble is he's lazy, goddammit!

LINDA   Willy, please!

WILLY   Biff is a lazy bum!

LINDA   They're sleeping. Get something to eat. Go on down.

WILLY   Why did he come home? I would like to know what brought him home.

LINDA   I don't know. I think he's still lost, Willy. I think he's very lost.

WILLY   Biff Loman is lost. In the greatest country in the world a young man with such—personal attractiveness, gets lost. And such a hard worker. There's one thing about Biff—he's not lazy.

LINDA   Never.

WILLY [*with pity and resolve*]   I'll see him in the morning; I'll have a nice talk with him. I'll get him a job selling. He could be big in no time. My God! Remember how they used to follow him around in high school? When he smiled at one of them their faces lit up. When he walked down the street . . . [*He loses himself in reminiscences.*]

LINDA [*trying to bring him out of it*]   Willy, dear, I got a new kind of American-type cheese today. It's whipped.

WILLY   Why do you get American when I like Swiss?

LINDA   I just thought you'd like a change—

WILLY   I don't want a change! I want Swiss cheese. Why am I always being contradicted?

LINDA [*with a covering laugh*]   I thought it would be a surprise.

WILLY   Why don't you open a window in here, for God's sake?

LINDA [*with infinite patience*]   They're all open, dear.

WILLY   The way they boxed us in here. Bricks and windows, windows and bricks.

LINDA   We should've bought the land next door.

WILLY   The street is lined with cars. There's not a breath of fresh air in the neighborhood. The grass don't grow any more, you can't raise a carrot in the back yard. They should've had a law against apartment houses. Remember those two beautiful elm trees out there? When I and Biff hung the swing between them?

LINDA   Yeah, like being a million miles from the city.

WILLY   They should've arrested the builder for cutting those down.

They massacred the neighborhood. [*Lost*] More and more I think of those days, Linda. This time of year it was lilac and wisteria. And then the peonies would come out, and the daffodils. What fragrance in this room!

LINDA Well, after all, people had to move somewhere.

WILLY No, there's more people now.

LINDA I don't think there's more people. I think—

WILLY There's more people! That's what's ruining this country! Population is getting out of control. The competition is maddening! Smell the stink from that apartment house! And another one on the other side . . . How can they whip cheese?

On WILLY's *last line*, BIFF *and* HAPPY *raise themselves up in their beds, listening.*

LINDA Go down, try it. And be quiet.

WILLY [*turning to Linda, guilty*] You're not worried about me, are you, sweetheart?

BIFF What's the matter?

HAPPY Listen!

LINDA You've got too much on the ball to worry about.

WILLY You're my foundation and my support, Linda.

LINDA Just try to relax, dear. You make mountains out of molehills.

WILLY I won't fight with him any more. If he wants to go back to Texas, let him go.

LINDA He'll find his way.

WILLY Sure. Certain men just don't get started till later in life. Like Thomas Edison, I think. Or B. F. Goodrich. One of them was deaf. [*He starts for the bedroom doorway.*] I'll put my money on Biff.

LINDA And Willy—if it's warm Sunday we'll drive in the country. And we'll open the windshield, and take lunch.

WILLY No, the windshields don't open on the new cars.

LINDA But you opened it today.

WILLY Me? I didn't. [*He stops.*] Now isn't that peculiar! Isn't that a remarkable—[*He breaks off in amazement and fright as the flute is heard distantly.*]

LINDA What, darling?

WILLY That is the most remarkable thing.

LINDA What, dear?

WILLY I was thinking of the Chevvy. [*Slight pause.*] Nineteen twenty-eight . . . when I had that red Chevvy— [*Breaks off.*] That funny? I coulda sworn I was driving that Chevvy today.

LINDA Well, that's nothing. Something must've reminded you.

WILLY Remarkable. Ts. Remember those days? The way Biff used to simonize that car? The dealer refused to believe there was eighty thousand miles on it. [*He shakes his head.*] Heh! [*To Linda*] Close your eyes, I'll be right up. [*He walks out of the bedroom.*]

HAPPY [*to Biff*] Jesus, maybe he smashed up the car again!

LINDA [*calling after Willy*] Be careful on the stairs, dear! The cheese is on the middle shelf! [*She turns, goes over to the bed, takes his jacket, and goes out of the bedroom.*]

Light has risen on the boys' room. Unseen, WILLY *is heard talking to himself, "Eighty thousand miles," and a little laugh.* BIFF *gets out of bed, comes downstage a bit, and stands attentively.* BIFF *is two years older than his brother* HAPPY, *well built, but in these days bears a worn air and seems less self-assured. He has succeeded less, and his dreams are stronger and less acceptable than* HAPPY's. HAPPY *is tall, powerfully made. Sexuality is like a visible color on him, or a scent that many women have discovered. He, like his brother, is lost, but in a different way, for he has never allowed himself to turn his face toward defeat and is thus more confused and hard-skinned, although seemingly more content.*

HAPPY [*getting out of bed*]   He's going to get his license taken away if he keeps that up. I'm getting nervous about him, y'know, Biff?

BIFF   His eyes are going.

HAPPY   No, I've driven with him. He sees all right. He just doesn't keep his mind on it. I drove into the city with him last week. He stops at a green light and then it turns red and he goes. [*He laughs.*]

BIFF   Maybe he's color-blind.

HAPPY   Pop? Why he's got the finest eye for color in the business. You know that.

BIFF [*sitting down on his bed*]   I'm going to sleep.

HAPPY   You're not still sour on Dad, are you, Biff?

BIFF   He's all right, I guess.

WILLY [*underneath them, in the living room*]   Yes, sir, eighty thousand miles—eighty-two thousand!

BIFF   You smoking?

HAPPY [*holding out a pack of cigarettes*]   Want one?

BIFF [*taking a cigarette*]   I can never sleep when I smell it.

WILLY   What a simonizing job, heh!

HAPPY [*with deep sentiment*]   Funny, Biff, y'know? Us sleeping in here again? The old beds. [*He pats his bed affectionately.*] All the talk that went across those two beds, huh? Our whole lives.

BIFF   Yeah. Lotta dreams and plans.

HAPPY [*with a deep and masculine laugh*]   About five hundred women would like to know what was said in this room.

They share a soft laugh.

BIFF   Remember that big Betsy something—what the hell was her name—over on Bushwick Avenue?

HAPPY [*combing his hair*]   With the collie dog!

BIFF   That's the one. I got you in there, remember?

HAPPY   Yeah, that was my first time—I think. Boy, there was a pig! [*They laugh, almost crudely.*] You taught me everything I know about women. Don't forget that.

BIFF   I bet you forgot how bashful you used to be. Especially with girls.

HAPPY   Oh, I still am, Biff.

BIFF   Oh, go on.

HAPPY   I just control it, that's all. I think I got less bashful and you got more so. What happened, Biff? Where's the old humor, the old confidence? [*He shakes* BIFF's *knee.* BIFF *gets up and moves restlessly about the room.*] What's the matter?

BIFF   Why does Dad mock me all the time?

HAPPY   He's not mocking you, he—

BIFF   Everything I say there's a twist of mockery on his face. I can't get near him.

HAPPY   He just wants you to make good, that's all. I wanted to talk to you about Dad for a long time, Biff. Something's—happening to him. He—talks to himself.

BIFF   I noticed that this morning. But he always mumbled.

HAPPY   But not so noticeable. It got so embarrassing I sent him to Florida. And you know something? Most of the time he's talking to you.

BIFF   What's he say about me?

HAPPY   I can't make it out.

BIFF   What's he say about me?

HAPPY   I think the fact that you're not settled, that you're still kind of up in the air . . .

BIFF   There's one or two other things depressing him, Happy.

HAPPY   What do you mean?

BIFF   Never mind. Just don't lay it all to me.

HAPPY   But I think if you just got started—I mean—is there any future for you out there?

BIFF   I tell ya, Hap, I don't know what the future is. I don't know—what I'm supposed to want.

HAPPY   What do you mean?

BIFF   Well, I spent six or seven years after high school trying to work myself up. Shipping clerk, salesman, business of one kind or another. And it's a measly manner of existence. To get on that subway on the hot mornings in summer. To devote your whole life to keeping stock, or making phone calls, or selling or buying. To suffer fifty weeks of the year for the sake of a two-week vacation, when all you really desire is to be outdoors, with your shirt off. And always to have to get ahead of the next fella. And still—that's how you build a future.

HAPPY   Well, you really enjoy it on a farm? Are you content out there?

BIFF   [*with rising agitation*]   Hap, I've had twenty or thirty different kinds of jobs since I left home before the war, and it always turns out the same. I just realized it lately. In Nebraska when I herded cattle, and the Dakotas, and Arizona, and now in Texas. It's why I came home now, I guess, because I realized it. This farm I work on, it's spring there now, see? And they've got about fifteen new colts. There's nothing more inspiring or—beautiful than the sight of a mare and a new colt. And it's cool there now, see? Texas is cool now, and it's spring. And whenever spring comes to where I am, I suddenly get the feeling, my God, I'm not gettin' anywhere! What the hell am I doing, playing around with horses, twenty-eight dollars a week! I'm thirty-four years old, I oughta be makin' my future. That's when I come running home. And now, I get here, and I don't know what to do with myself. [*After a pause*] I've always made a point of not wasting my life, and every time I come back here I know that all I've done is to waste my life.

HAPPY   You're a poet, you know that, Biff? You're a—you're an idealist!

BIFF   No, I'm mixed up very bad. Maybe I oughta get married. Maybe I oughta get stuck into something. Maybe that's my trouble. I'm like a boy. I'm not married, I'm not in business, I just—I'm like a boy. Are you content, Hap? You're a success, aren't you? Are you content?

HAPPY   Hell, no!

BIFF   Why? You're making money, aren't you?

HAPPY   [*moving about with energy, expressiveness*]   All I can do now is wait for the merchandise manager to die. And suppose I get to be merchandise manager? He's a good friend of mine, and he just built a terrific estate on Long Island. And he lived there about two months and sold it, and now he's building another one. He can't enjoy it once it's finished. And I know that's just what I would do. I don't know what the hell I'm workin' for. Sometimes I sit in my apartment—all alone. And I think of the rent I'm paying. And it's crazy. But then, it's what I always wanted. My own apartment, a car, and plenty of women. And still, goddammit, I'm lonely.

BIFF   [*with enthusiasm*]   Listen, why don't you come out West with me?

HAPPY   You and I, heh?

BIFF   Sure, maybe we could buy a ranch. Raise cattle, use our muscles. Men built like we are should be working out in the open.

HAPPY   [*avidly*]   The Loman Brothers, heh?

BIFF   [*with vast affection*]   Sure, we'd be known all over the counties!

HAPPY   [*enthralled*]   That's what I dream about, Biff. Sometimes I want to just rip my clothes off in the middle of the store and outbox that goddam merchandise manager. I mean I can outbox, outrun, and outlift anybody in that store, and I have to take orders from those common, petty sons-of-bitches till I can't stand it any more.

BIFF   I'm tellin' you, kid, if you were with me I'd be happy out there.

HAPPY   [*enthused*]   See, Biff, everybody around me is so false that I'm constantly lowering my ideals . . .

BIFF   Baby, together we'd stand up for one another, we'd have someone to trust.

HAPPY   If I were around you—

BIFF   Hap, the trouble is we weren't brought up to grub for money. I don't know how to do it.

HAPPY   Neither can I!

BIFF   Then let's go!

HAPPY   The only thing is—what can you make out there?

BIFF   But look at your friend. Builds an estate and then hasn't the peace of mind to live in it.

HAPPY   Yeah, but when he walks into the store the waves part in front of him. That's fifty-two thousand dollars a year coming through the revolving door, and I got more in my pinky finger than he's got in his head.

BIFF   Yeah, but you just said—

HAPPY   I gotta show some of those pompous, self-important executives over there that Hap Loman can make the grade. I want to walk into the store the way he walks in. Then I'll go with you, Biff. We'll be together yet, I swear. But take those two we had tonight. Now weren't they gorgeous creatures?

BIFF   Yeah, yeah, most gorgeous I've had in years.

HAPPY   I get that any time I want, Biff. Whenever I feel disgusted. The only trouble is, it gets like bowling or something. I just keep knockin' them over and it doesn't mean anything. You still run around a lot?

BIFF   Naa. I'd like to find a girl—steady, somebody with substance.

HAPPY   That's what I long for.

BIFF   Go on! You'd never come home.

HAPPY   I would! Somebody with character, with resistance! Like Mom, y'know? You're gonna call me a bastard when I tell you this. That girl Charlotte I was with tonight is engaged to be married in five weeks. [*He tries on his new hat.*]

BIFF   No kiddin'!

HAPPY   Sure, the guy's in line for the vice-presidency of the store. I don't know what gets into me, maybe I just have an overdeveloped sense of competition or something, but I went and ruined her, and furthermore I can't get rid of her. And he's the third executive I've done that to. Isn't that a crummy characteristic? And to top it all, I go to their weddings! [*Indignantly, but laughing*] Like I'm not supposed to take bribes. Manufacturers offer me a hundred-dollar bill now and then to throw an order their way. You know how honest I am, but it's like this girl, see. I hate myself for it. Because I don't want the girl, and, still, I take it and—I love it!

BIFF   Let's go to sleep.

HAPPY   I guess we didn't settle anything, heh?

BIFF   I just got one idea that I think I'm going to try.

HAPPY   What's that?

BIFF   Remember Bill Oliver?

HAPPY   Sure, Oliver is very big now. You want to work for him again?

BIFF   No, but when I quit he said something to me. He put his arm on my shoulder, and he said, "Biff, if you ever need anything, come to me."

HAPPY   I remember that. That sounds good.

BIFF   I think I'll go to see him. If I could get ten thousand or even seven or eight thousand dollars I could buy a beautiful ranch.

HAPPY   I bet he'd back you. 'Cause he thought highly of you, Biff. I mean, they all do. You're well liked, Biff. That's why I say to come back here, and we both have the apartment. And I'm tellin' you, Biff, any babe you want . . .

BIFF   No, with a ranch I could do the work I like and still be some-

thing. I just wonder though. I wonder if Oliver still thinks I stole
that carton of basketballs.

HAPPY   Oh, he probably forgot that long ago. It's almost ten years.
You're too sensitive. Anyway, he didn't really fire you.

BIFF   Well, I think he was going to. I think that's why I quit. I was
never sure whether he knew or not. I know he thought the world
of me, though. I was the only one he'd let lock up the place.

WILLY [*below*]   You gonna wash the engine, Biff?

HAPPY   Shh!

> BIFF *looks at* HAPPY, *who is gazing down, listening.* WILLY *is
> mumbling in the parlor.*

HAPPY   You hear that?

> *They listen.* WILLY *laughs warmly.*

BIFF [*growing angry*]   Doesn't he know Mom can hear that?

WILLY   Don't get your sweater dirty, Biff!

> *A look of pain crosses* BIFF's *face.*

HAPPY   Isn't that terrible? Don't leave again, will you? You'll find a
job here. You gotta stick around. I don't know what to do about
him, it's getting embarrassing.

WILLY   What a simonizing job!

BIFF   Mom's hearing that!

WILLY   No kiddin', Biff, you got a date? Wonderful!

HAPPY   Go on to sleep. But talk to him in the morning, will you?

BIFF [*reluctantly getting into bed*]   With her in the house. Brother!

HAPPY [*getting into bed*]   I wish you'd have a good talk with him.

> *The light on their room begins to fade.*

BIFF [*to himself in bed*]   That selfish, stupid . . .

HAPPY   Sh . . . Sleep, Biff.

> *Their light is out. Well before they have finished speaking,*
> WILLY's *form is dimly seen below in the darkened kitchen. He
> opens the refrigerator, searches in there, and takes out a bottle
> of milk. The apartment houses are fading out, and the entire
> house and surroundings become covered with leaves. Music
> insinuates itself as the leaves appear.*

WILLY   Just wanna be careful with those girls, Biff, that's all. Don't
make any promises. No promises of any kind. Because a girl,
y'know, they always believe what you tell 'em, and you're very
young, Biff, you're too young to be talking seriously to girls.

> *Light rises on the kitchen.* WILLY, *talking, shuts the refrigerator*

door and comes downstage to the kitchen table. He pours milk into a glass. He is totally immersed in himself, smiling faintly.

WILLY Too young entirely, Biff. You want to watch your schooling first. Then when you're all set, there'll be plenty of girls for a boy like you. [*He smiles broadly at a kitchen chair.*] That so? The girls pay for you? [*He laughs.*] Boy, you must really be makin' a hit.

WILLY *is gradually addressing—physically—a point offstage, speaking through the wall of the kitchen, and his voice has been rising in volume to that of a normal conversation.*

WILLY I been wondering why you polish the car so careful. Ha! Don't leave the hubcaps, boys. Get the chamois to the hubcaps. Happy, use newspaper on the windows, it's the easiest thing. Show him how to do it, Biff! You see, Happy? Pad it up, use it like a pad. That's it, that's it, good work. You're doin' all right, Hap. [*He pauses, then nods in approbation for a few seconds, then looks upward.*] Biff, first thing we gotta do when we get time is clip that big branch over the house. Afraid it's gonna fall in a storm and hit the roof. Tell you what. We get a rope and sling her around, and then we climb up there with a couple of saws and take her down. Soon as you finish the car, boys, I wanna see ya. I got a surprise for you, boys.

BIFF [*offstage*] Whatta ya got, Dad?

WILLY No, you finish first. Never leave a job till you're finished—remember that. [*Looking toward the "big trees"*] Biff, up in Albany I saw a beautiful hammock. I think I'll buy it next trip, and we'll hang it right between those two elms. Wouldn't that be something? Just swingin' there under those branches. Boy, that would be . . .

YOUNG BIFF *and* YOUNG HAPPY *appear from the direction* WILLY *was addressing.* HAPPY *carries rags and a pail of water.* BIFF, *wearing a sweater with a block "S," carries a football.*

BIFF [*pointing in the direction of the car offstage*] How's that, Pop, professional?

WILLY Terrific. Terrific job, boys. Good work, Biff.

HAPPY Where's the surprise, Pop?

WILLY In the back seat of the car.

HAPPY Boy! [*He runs off.*]

BIFF What is it, Dad? Tell me, what'd you buy?

WILLY [*laughing, cuffs him*] Never mind, something I want you to have.

BIFF [*turns and starts off*] What is it, Hap?

HAPPY [*offstage*] It's a punching bag!

BIFF Oh, Pop!

WILLY It's got Gene Tunney's[1] signature on it!

---

1. Tunney (b. 1897) was world heavy-weight boxing champion from 1926 to 1928.

HAPPY *runs onstage with a punching bag.*

BIFF   Gee, how'd you know we wanted a punching bag?

WILLY   Well, it's the finest thing for the timing.

HAPPY [*lies down on his back and pedals with his feet*]   I'm losing weight, you notice, Pop?

WILLY [*to Happy*]   Jumping rope is good too.

BIFF   Did you see the new football I got?

WILLY [*examining the ball*]   Where'd you get a new ball?

BIFF   The coach told me to practice my passing.

WILLY   That so? And he gave you the ball, heh?

BIFF   Well, I borrowed it from the locker room. [*He laughs confidentially.*]

WILLY [*laughing with him at the theft*]   I want you to return that.

HAPPY   I told you he wouldn't like it!

BIFF [*angrily*]   Well, I'm bringing it back!

WILLY [*stopping the incipient argument, to* HAPPY]   Sure, he's gotta practice with a regulation ball, doesn't he? [*To* BIFF] Coach'll probably congratulate you on your initiative!

BIFF   Oh, he keeps congratulating my initiative all the time, Pop.

WILLY   That's because he likes you. If somebody else took that ball there'd be an uproar. So what's the report, boys, what's the report?

BIFF   Where'd you go this time, Dad? Gee we were lonesome for you.

WILLY [*pleased, puts an arm around each boy and they come down to the apron*]   Lonesome, heh?

BIFF   Missed you every minute.

WILLY   Don't say? Tell you a secret, boys. Don't breathe it to a soul. Someday I'll have my own business, and I'll never have to leave home any more.

HAPPY   Like Uncle Charley, heh?

WILLY   Bigger than Uncle Charley! Because Charley is not—liked. He's liked, but he's not—well liked.

BIFF   Where'd you go this time, Dad?

WILLY   Well, I got on the road, and I went north to Providence. Met the Mayor.

BIFF   The Mayor of Providence!

WILLY   He was sitting in the hotel lobby.

BIFF   What'd he say?

WILLY   He said, "Morning!" And I said, "You got a fine city here, Mayor." And then he had coffee with me. And then I went to Waterbury. Waterbury is a fine city. Big clock city, the famous Waterbury clock. Sold a nice bill there. And then Boston—Boston is the cradle of the Revolution. A fine city. And a couple of other towns in Mass., and on to Portland and Bangor and straight home!

BIFF   Gee, I'd love to go with you sometime, Dad.

WILLY   Soon as summer comes.

HAPPY   Promise?

WILLY   You and Hap and I, and I'll show you all the towns. America is full of beautiful towns and fine, upstanding people. And they know me, boys, they know me up and down New England. The finest people. And when I bring you fellas up, there'll be open sesame for all of us, 'cause one thing, boys: I have friends. I can park my car in any street in New England, and the cops protect it like their own. This summer, heh?

BIFF and HAPPY [*together*]   Yeah! You bet!

WILLY   We'll take our bathing suits.

HAPPY   We'll carry your bags, Pop!

WILLY   Oh, won't that be something! Me comin' into the Boston stores with you boys carryin' my bags. What a sensation!

> BIFF *is prancing around, practicing passing the ball.*

WILLY   You nervous, Biff, about the game?

BIFF   Not if you're gonna be there.

WILLY   What do they say about you in school, now that they made you captain?

HAPPY   There's a crowd of girls behind him everytime the classes change.

BIFF [*taking* WILLY's *hand*]   This Saturday, Pop, this Saturday—just for you, I'm going to break through for a touchdown.

HAPPY   You're supposed to pass.

BIFF   I'm takin' one play for Pop. You watch me, Pop, and when I take off my helmet, that means I'm breakin' out. Then you watch me crash through that line!

WILLY [*kisses* BIFF]   Oh, wait'll I tell this in Boston!

> BERNARD *enters in knickers. He is younger than* BIFF, *earnest and loyal, a worried boy.*

BERNARD   Biff, where are you? You're supposed to study with me today.

WILLY   Hey, looka Bernard. What're you lookin' so anemic about, Bernard?

BERNARD   He's gotta study, Uncle Willy. He's got Regents² next week.

HAPPY [*tauntingly, spinning* BERNARD *around*]   Let's box, Bernard!

BERNARD   Biff! [*He gets away from* HAPPY.] Listen, Biff, I heard Mr. Birnbaum say that if you don't start studyin' math he's gonna flunk you, and you won't graduate. I heard him!

WILLY   You better study with him, Biff. Go ahead now.

BERNARD   I heard him!

BIFF   Oh, Pop, you didn't see my sneakers! [*He holds up a foot for* WILLY *to look at.*]

WILLY   Hey, that's a beautiful job of printing!

BERNARD [*wiping his glasses*]   Just because he printed University of Virginia on his sneakers doesn't mean they've got to graduate him, Uncle Willy!

WILLY [*angrily*]   What're you talking about? With scholarships to three universities they're gonna flunk him?

---

2. A statewide examination administered to New York high school students.

BERNARD But I heard Mr. Birnbaum say—
WILLY Don't be a pest, Bernard! [*To his boys*] What an anemic!
BERNARD Okay, I'm waiting for you in my house, Biff.

BERNARD *goes off. The Lomans laugh.*

WILLY Bernard is not well liked, is he?
BIFF He's liked, but he's not well liked.
HAPPY That's right, Pop.
WILLY That's just what I mean. Bernard can get the best marks in school, y'understand, but when he gets out in the business world, y'understand, you are going to be five times ahead of him. That's why I thank Almighty God you're both built like Adonises.[3] Because the man who makes an appearance in the business world, the man who creates personal interest, is the man who gets ahead. Be liked and you will never want. You take me, for instance. I never have to wait in line to see a buyer. "Willy Loman is here!" That's all they have to know, and I go right through.
BIFF Did you knock them dead, Pop?
WILLY Knocked 'em cold in Providence, slaughtered 'em in Boston.
HAPPY [*on his back, pedaling again*] I'm losing weight, you notice, Pop?

LINDA *enters, as of old, a ribbon in her hair, carrying a basket of washing.*

LINDA [*with youthful energy*] Hello, dear!
WILLY Sweetheart!
LINDA How'd the Chevvy run?
WILLY Chevrolet, Linda, is the greatest car ever built. [*To the boys*] Since when do you let your mother carry wash up the stairs?
BIFF Grab hold there, boy!
HAPPY Where to, Mom?
LINDA Hang them up on the line. And you better go down to your friends, Biff. The cellar is full of boys. They don't know what to do with themselves.
BIFF Ah, when Pop comes home they can wait!
WILLY [*laughs appreciatively*] You better go down and tell them what to do, Biff.
BIFF I think I'll have them sweep out the furnace room.
WILLY Good work, Biff.
BIFF [*goes through wall-line of kitchen to doorway at back and calls down*] Fellas! Everybody sweep out the furnace room! I'll be right down!
VOICES All right! Okay, Biff.
BIFF George and Sam and Frank, come out back! We're hangin' up the wash! Come on, Hap, on the double! [*He and* HAPPY *carry out the basket.*]

3. In Greek mythology Adonis was a beautiful youth, the favorite of Aphrodite, Goddess of Love.

LINDA The way they obey him!

WILLY Well, that's training, the training. I'm tellin' you, I was sellin' thousands and thousands, but I had to come home.

LINDA Oh, the whole block'll be at that game. Did you sell anything?

WILLY I did five hundred gross in Providence and seven hundred gross in Boston.

LINDA No! Wait a minute, I've got a pencil. [*She pulls pencil and paper out of her apron pocket.*] That makes your commission . . . Two hundred—my God! Two hundred and twelve dollars!

WILLY Well, I didn't figure it yet, but . . .

LINDA How much did you do?

WILLY Well, I—I did—about a hundred and eighty gross in Providence. Well, no—it came to—roughly two hundred gross on the whole trip.

LINDA [*without hesitation*] Two hundred gross. That's . . . [*She figures.*]

WILLY The trouble was that three of the stores were half closed for inventory in Boston. Otherwise I woulda broke records.

LINDA Well, it makes seventy dollars and some pennies. That's very good.

WILLY What do we owe?

LINDA Well, on the first there's sixteen dollars on the refrigerator—

WILLY Why sixteen?

LINDA Well, the fan belt broke, so it was a dollar eighty.

WILLY But it's brand new.

LINDA Well, the man said that's the way it is. Till they work themselves in, y'know.

They move through the wall-line into the kitchen.

WILLY I hope we didn't get stuck on that machine.

LINDA They got the biggest ads of any of them!

WILLY I know, it's a fine machine. What else?

LINDA Well, there's nine-sixty for the washing machine. And for the vacuum cleaner there's three and a half due on the fifteenth. Then the roof, you got twenty-one dollars remaining.

WILLY It don't leak, does it?

LINDA No, they did a wonderful job. Then you owe Frank for the carburetor.

WILLY I'm not going to pay that man! That goddam Chevrolet, they ought to prohibit the manufacture of that car!

LINDA Well, you owe him three and a half. And odds and ends, comes to around a hundred and twenty dollars by the fifteenth.

WILLY A hundred and twenty dollars! My God, if business don't pick up I don't know what I'm gonna do!

LINDA Well, next week you'll do better.

WILLY Oh, I'll knock 'em dead next week. I'll go to Hartford. I'm very well liked in Hartford. You know, the trouble is, Linda, people don't seem to take to me.

They move onto the forestage.

LINDA   Oh, don't be foolish.

WILLY   I know it when I walk in. They seem to laugh at me.

LINDA   Why? Why would they laugh at you? Don't talk that way, Willy.

WILLY *moves to the edge of the stage.* LINDA *goes into the kitchen and starts to darn stockings.*

WILLY   I don't know the reason for it, but they just pass me by. I'm not noticed.

LINDA   But you're doing wonderful, dear. You're making seventy to a hundred dollars a week.

WILLY   But I gotta be at it ten, twelve hours a day. Other men—I don't know—they do it easier. I don't know why—I can't stop myself—I talk too much. A man oughta come in with a few words. One thing about Charley. He's a man of few words, and they respect him.

LINDA   You don't talk too much, you're just lively.

WILLY [*smiling*]   Well, I figure, what the hell, life is short, a couple of jokes. [*To himself*] I joke too much! [*The smile goes.*]

LINDA   Why? You're—

WILLY   I'm fat. I'm very—foolish to look at, Linda. I didn't tell you, but Christmas time I happened to be calling on F. H. Stewarts, and a salesman I know, as I was going in to see the buyer I heard him say something about—walrus. And I—I cracked him right across the face. I won't take that. I simply will not take that. But they do laugh at me. I know that.

LINDA   Darling . . .

WILLY   I gotta overcome it. I know I gotta overcome it. I'm not dressing to advantage, maybe.

LINDA   Willy, darling, you're the handsomest man in the world—

WILLY   Oh, no, Linda.

LINDA   To me you are. [*Slight pause.*] The handsomest.

From the darkness is heard the laughter of a woman. WILLY *doesn't turn to it, but it continues through* LINDA's *lines.*

LINDA   And the boys, Willy. Few men are idolized by their children the way you are.

Music is heard as behind a scrim, to the left of the house, THE WOMAN, *dimly seen, is dressing.*

WILLY [*with great feeling*]   You're the best there is, Linda, you're a pal, you know that? On the road—on the road I want to grab you sometimes and just kiss the life outa you.

The laughter is loud now, and he moves into a brightening area at the left, where THE WOMAN *has come from behind the scrim and is standing, putting on her hat, looking into a "mirror" and laughing.*

WILLY 'Cause I get so lonely—especially when business is bad and there's nobody to talk to. I get the feeling that I'll never sell anything again, that I won't make a living for you, or a business, a business for the boys. [*He talks through* THE WOMAN's *subsiding laughter;* THE WOMAN *primps at the "mirror."*] There's so much I want to make for—

THE WOMAN Me? You didn't make me, Willy. I picked you.

WILLY [*pleased*] You picked me?

THE WOMAN [*who is quite proper-looking,* WILLY's *age*] I did. I've been sitting at that desk watching all the salesmen go by, day in, day out. But you've got such a sense of humor, and we do have a good time together, don't we?

WILLY Sure, sure. [*He takes her in his arms.*] Why do you have to go now?

THE WOMAN It's two o'clock . . .

WILLY No, come on in! [*He pulls her.*]

THE WOMAN . . . my sisters'll be scandalized. When'll you be back?

WILLY Oh, two weeks about. Will you come up again?

THE WOMAN Sure thing. You do make me laugh. It's good for me. [*She squeezes his arm, kisses him.*] And I think you're a wonderful man.

WILLY You picked me, heh?

THE WOMAN Sure. Because you're so sweet. And such a kidder.

WILLY Well, I'll see you next time I'm in Boston.

THE WOMAN I'll put you right through to the buyers.

WILLY [*slapping her bottom*] Right. Well, bottoms up!

THE WOMAN [*slaps him gently and laughs*] You just kill me, Willy. [*He suddenly grabs her and kisses her roughly.*] You kill me. And thanks for the stockings. I love a lot of stockings. Well, good night.

WILLY Good night. And keep your pores open!

THE WOMAN Oh, Willy!

> THE WOMAN *bursts out laughing, and* LINDA's *laughter blends in.* THE WOMAN *disappears into the dark. Now the area at the kitchen table brightens.* LINDA *is sitting where she was at the kitchen table, but now is mending a pair of her silk stockings.*

LINDA You are, Willy. The handsomest man. You've got no reason to feel that—

WILLY [*coming out of* THE WOMAN's *dimming area and going over to* LINDA] I'll make it all up to you, Linda, I'll—

LINDA There's nothing to make up, dear. You're doing fine, better than—

WILLY [*noticing her mending*] What's that?

LINDA Just mending my stockings. They're so expensive—

WILLY [*angrily, taking them from her*] I won't have you mending stockings in this house! Now throw them out!

> LINDA *puts the stockings in her pocket.*

BERNARD [*entering on the run*] Where is he? If he doesn't study!

WILLY [*moving to the forestage, with great agitation*] You'll give him the answers!

BERNARD   I do, but I can't on a Regents! That's a state exam! They're liable to arrest me!

WILLY   Where is he? I'll whip him, I'll whip him!

LINDA   And he'd better give back that football, Willy, it's not nice.

WILLY   Biff! Where is he? Why is he taking everything?

LINDA   He's too rough with the girls, Willy. All the mothers are afraid of him!

WILLY   I'll whip him!

BERNARD   He's driving the car without a license!

THE WOMAN's *laugh is heard.*

WILLY   Shut up!

LINDA   All the mothers—

WILLY   Shut up!

BERNARD [*backing quietly away and out*] Mr. Birnbaum says he's stuck up.

WILLY   Get outa here!

BERNARD   If he doesn't buckle down he'll flunk math! [*He goes off.*]

LINDA   He's right, Willy, you've gotta—

WILLY [*exploding at her*] There's nothing the matter with him! You want him to be a worm like Bernard? He's got spirit, personality . . .

As he speaks, LINDA, *almost in tears, exits into the living room.* WILLY *is alone in the kitchen, wilting and staring. The leaves are gone. It is night again, and the apartment houses look down from behind.*

WILLY   Loaded with it. Loaded! What is he stealing? He's giving it back, isn't he? Why is he stealing? What did I tell him? I never in my life told him anything but decent things.

HAPPY *in pajamas has come down the stairs;* WILLY *suddenly becomes aware of* HAPPY's *presence.*

HAPPY   Let's go now, come on.

WILLY [*sitting down at the kitchen table*] Huh! Why did she have to wax the floors herself? Every time she waxes the floors she keels over. She knows that!

HAPPY   Shh! Take it easy. What brought you back tonight?

WILLY   I got an awful scare. Nearly hit a kid in Yonkers. God! Why didn't I go to Alaska with my brother Ben that time! Ben! That man was a genius, that man was success incarnate! What a mistake! He begged me to go.

HAPPY   Well, there's no use in—

WILLY   You guys! There was a man started with the clothes on his back and ended up with diamond mines!

HAPPY   Boy, someday I'd like to know how he did it.

WILLY   What's the mystery? The man knew what he wanted and went out and got it! Walked into a jungle, and comes out, the age of twenty-one, and he's rich! The world is an oyster, but you don't crack it open on a mattress!

HAPPY   Pop, I told you I'm gonna retire you for life.

WILLY   You'll retire me for life on seventy goddam dollars a week? And your women and your car and your apartment, and you'll retire me for life! Christ's sake, I couldn't get past Yonkers today! Where are you guys, where are you? The woods are burning! I can't drive a car!

> CHARLEY *has appeared in the doorway. He is a large man, slow of speech, laconic, immovable. In all he says, despite what he says, there is pity, and, now, trepidation. He has a robe over pajamas, slippers on his feet. He enters the kitchen.*

CHARLEY   Everything all right?

HAPPY   Yeah, Charley, everything's . . .

WILLY   What's the matter?

CHARLEY   I heard some noise. I thought something happened. Can't we do something about the walls? You sneeze in here, and in my house hats blow off.

HAPPY   Let's go to bed, Dad. Come on.

> CHARLEY *signals to* HAPPY *to go.*

WILLY   You go ahead, I'm not tired at the moment.

HAPPY [*to* WILLY]   Take it easy, huh? [*He exits.*]

WILLY   What're you doin' up?

CHARLEY [*sitting down at the kitchen table opposite Willy*]   Couldn't sleep good. I had a heartburn.

WILLY   Well, you don't know how to eat.

CHARLEY   I eat with my mouth.

WILLY   No, you're ignorant. You gotta know about vitamins and things like that.

CHARLEY   Come on, let's shoot. Tire you out a little.

WILLY [*hesitantly*]   All right. You got cards?

CHARLEY [*taking a deck from his pocket*]   Yeah, I got them. Someplace. What is it with those vitamins?

WILLY [*dealing*]   They build up your bones. Chemistry.

CHARLEY   Yeah, but there's no bones in a heartburn.

WILLY   What are you talkin' about? Do you know the first thing about it?

CHARLEY   Don't get insulted.

WILLY   Don't talk about something you don't know anything about.

> *They are playing. Pause.*

CHARLEY   What're you doin' home?

WILLY   A little trouble with the car.

CHARLEY   Oh. [*Pause.*] I'd like to take a trip to California.

WILLY   Don't say.

CHARLEY   You want a job?

WILLY   I got a job, I told you that. [*After a slight pause*] What the hell are you offering me a job for?

CHARLEY   Don't get insulted.

WILLY   Don't insult me.

CHARLEY   I don't see no sense in it. You don't have to go on this way.

WILLY   I got a good job. [*Slight pause.*] What do you keep comin' in here for?

CHARLEY   You want me to go?

WILLY   [*after a pause, withering*]   I can't understand it. He's going back to Texas again. What the hell is that?

CHARLEY   Let him go.

WILLY   I got nothin' to give him, Charley, I'm clean, I'm clean.

CHARLEY   He won't starve. None a them starve. Forget about him.

WILLY   Then what have I got to remember?

CHARLEY   You take it too hard. To hell with it. When a deposit bottle is broken you don't get your nickel back.

WILLY   That's easy enough for you to say.

CHARLEY   That ain't easy for me to say.

WILLY   Did you see the ceiling I put up in the living room?

CHARLEY   Yeah, that's a piece of work. To put up a ceiling is a mystery to me. How do you do it?

WILLY   What's the difference?

CHARLEY   Well, talk about it.

WILLY   You gonna put up a ceiling?

CHARLEY   How could I put up a ceiling?

WILLY   Then what the hell are you bothering me for?

CHARLEY   You're insulted again.

WILLY   A man who can't handle tools is not a man. You're disgusting.

CHARLEY   Don't call me disgusting, Willy.

> UNCLE BEN, *carrying a valise and an umbrella, enters the forestage from around the right corner of the house. He is a stolid man, in his sixties, with a mustache and an authoritative air. He is utterly certain of his destiny, and there is an aura of far places about him. He enters exactly as* WILLY *speaks.*

WILLY   I'm getting awfully tired, Ben.

> BEN'*s music is heard.* BEN *looks around at everything.*

CHARLEY   Good, keep playing; you'll sleep better. Did you call me Ben?

> BEN *looks at his watch.*

WILLY   That's funny. For a second there you reminded me of my brother Ben.

BEN   I only have a few minutes. [*He strolls, inspecting the place.*

WILLY *and* CHARLEY *continue playing.*]

CHARLEY   You never heard from him again, heh? Since that time?

WILLY   Didn't Linda tell you? Couple of weeks ago we got a letter from his wife in Africa. He died.

CHARLEY   That so.

BEN [*chuckling*]   So this is Brooklyn, eh?

CHARLEY   Maybe you're in for some of his money.

WILLY   Naa, he had seven sons. There's just one opportunity I had with that man . . .

BEN   I must make a train, William. There are several properties I'm looking at in Alaska.

WILLY   Sure, sure! If I'd gone with him to Alaska that time, everything would've been totally different.

CHARLEY   Go on, you'd froze to death up there.

WILLY   What're you talking about?

BEN   Opportunity is tremendous in Alaska, William. Surprised you're not up there.

WILLY   Sure, tremendous.

CHARLEY   Heh?

WILLY   There was the only man I ever met who knew the answers.

CHARLEY   Who?

BEN   How are you all?

WILLY [*taking a pot, smiling*]   Fine, fine.

CHARLEY   Pretty sharp tonight.

BEN   Is Mother living with you?

WILLY   No, she died a long time ago.

CHARLEY   Who?

BEN   That's too bad. Fine specimen of a lady, Mother.

WILLY [*to* CHARLEY]   Heh?

BEN   I'd hoped to see the old girl.

CHARLEY   Who died?

BEN   Heard anything from Father, have you?

WILLY [*unnerved*]   What do you mean, who died?

CHARLEY [*taking a pot*]   What're you talkin' about?

BEN [*looking at his watch*]   William, it's half-past eight!

WILLY [*as though to dispel his confusion he angrily stops* CHARLEY'S *hand*]   That's my build!

CHARLEY   I put the ace—

WILLY   If you don't know how to play the game I'm not gonna throw my money away on you!

CHARLEY [*rising*]   It was my ace, for God's sake!

WILLY   I'm through, I'm through!

BEN   When did Mother die?

WILLY   Long ago. Since the beginning you never knew how to play cards.

CHARLEY [*picks up the cards and goes to the door*]   All right! Next time I'll bring a deck with five aces.

WILLY   I don't play that kind of game!

CHARLEY [*turning to him*]   You ought to be ashamed of yourself!

WILLY   Yeah?

CHARLEY   Yeah! [*He goes out.*]

WILLY [*slamming the door after him*]   Ignoramus!

BEN [*as* WILLY *comes toward him through the wall-line of the kitchen*]
So you're William.

WILLY [*shaking* BEN's *hand*]   Ben! I've been waiting for you so long!
What's the answer? How did you do it?

BEN   Oh, there's a story in that.

LINDA *enters the forestage, as of old, carrying the wash basket.*

LINDA   Is this Ben?

BEN [*gallantly*]   How do you do, my dear.

LINDA   Where've you been all these years. Willy's always wondered
why you—

WILLY [*pulling* BEN *away from her impatiently*]   Where is Dad?
Didn't you follow him? How did you get started?

BEN   Well, I don't know how much you remember.

WILLY   Well, I was just a baby, of course, only three or four years
old—

BEN   Three years and eleven months.

WILLY   What a memory, Ben!

BEN   I have many enterprises, William, and I have never kept books.

WILLY   I remember I was sitting under the wagon in—was it
Nebraska?

BEN   It was South Dakota, and I gave you a bunch of wild flowers.

WILLY   I remember you walking away down some open road.

BEN [*laughing*]   I was going to find Father in Alaska.

WILLY   Where is he?

BEN   At that age I had a very faulty view of geography, William. I
discovered after a few days that I was heading due south, so instead of Alaska, I ended up in Africa.

LINDA   Africa!

WILLY   The Gold Coast!

BEN   Principally diamond mines.

LINDA   Diamond mines!

BEN   Yes, my dear. But I've only a few minutes—

WILLY   No! Boys! Boys! [YOUNG BIFF *and* HAPPY *appear.*] Listen to
this. This is your Uncle Ben, a great man! Tell my boys, Ben!

BEN   Why, boys, when I was seventeen I walked into the jungle,
and when I was twenty-one I walked out. [*He laughs.*] And by
God I was rich.

WILLY [*to the boys*]   You see what I been talking about? The greatest
things can happen!

BEN [*glancing at his watch*]   I have an appointment in Ketchikan
Tuesday week.

WILLY   No, Ben! Please tell about Dad. I want my boys to hear. I
want them to know the kind of stock they spring from. All I remember is a man with a big beard, and I was in Mamma's lap,
sitting around a fire, and some kind of high music.

BEN   His flute. He played the flute.

WILLY   Sure, the flute, that's right!

New music is heard, a high, rollicking tune.

BEN   Father was a very great and a very wild-hearted man. We would start in Boston, and he'd toss the whole family into the wagon, and then he'd drive the team right across the country; through Ohio, and Indiana, Michigan, Illinois, and all the Western states. And we'd stop in the towns and sell the flutes that he'd made on the way. Great inventor, Father. With one gadget he made more in a week than a man like you could make in a lifetime.

WILLY   That's just the way I'm bringing them up, Ben—rugged, well liked, all-around.

BEN   Yeah? [*To* BIFF] Hit that, boy—hard as you can. [*He pounds his stomach.*]

BIFF   Oh, no, sir!

BEN   [*taking boxing stance*]   Come on, get to me! [*He laughs.*]

WILLY   Go to it, Biff! Go ahead, show him!

BIFF   Okay! [*He cocks his fists and starts in.*]

LINDA   [*to* WILLY]   Why must he fight, dear?

BEN   [*sparring with* BIFF]   Good boy! Good boy!

WILLY   How's that, Ben, heh?

HAPPY   Give him a left, Biff!

LINDA   Why are you fighting?

BEN   Good boy! [*Suddenly comes in, trips* BIFF, *and stands over him, the point of his umbrella poised over* BIFF's *eye.*]

LINDA   Look out, Biff!

BIFF   Gee!

BEN   [*patting* BIFF's *knee*]   Never fight fair with a stranger, boy. You'll never get out of the jungle that way. [*Taking* LINDA's *hand and bowing*] It was an honor and a pleasure to meet you, Linda.

LINDA   [*withdrawing her hand coldly, frightened*]   Have a nice—trip.

BEN   [*to* WILLY]   And good luck with your—what do you do?

WILLY   Selling.

BEN   Yes. Well . . . [*He raises his hand in farewell to all.*]

WILLY   No, Ben, I don't want you to think . . . [*He takes* BEN's *arm to show him.*] It's Brooklyn, I know, but we hunt too.

BEN   Really, now.

WILLY   Oh, sure, there's snakes and rabbits and—that's why I moved out here. Why, Biff can fell any one of these trees in no time! Boys! Go right over to where they're building the apartment house and get some sand. We're gonna rebuild the entire front stoop right now! Watch this, Ben!

BIFF   Yes, sir! On the double, Hap!

HAPPY   [*as he and* BIFF *run off*]   I lost weight, Pop, you notice?

CHARLEY *enters in knickers, even before the boys are gone.*

CHARLEY   Listen, if they steal any more from that building the watchman'll put the cops on them!

LINDA   [*to* WILLY]   Don't let Biff . . .

BEN *laughs lustily.*

WILLY   You shoulda seen the lumber they brought home last week. At least a dozen six-by-tens worth all kinds of money.

CHARLEY   Listen, if that watchman—

WILLY   I gave them hell, understand. But I got a couple of fearless characters there.

CHARLEY   Willy, the jails are full of fearless characters.

BEN [*clapping* WILLY *on the back, with a laugh at* CHARLEY]   And the stock exchange, friend!

WILLY [*joining in* BEN's *laughter*]   Where are the rest of your pants?

CHARLEY   My wife bought them.

WILLY   Now all you need is a golf club and you can go upstairs and go to sleep. [*To* BEN] Great athlete! Between him and his son Bernard they can't hammer a nail!

BERNARD [*rushing in*]   The watchman's chasing Biff!

WILLY [*angrily*]   Shut up! He's not stealing anything!

LINDA [*alarmed, hurrying off left*]   Where is he? Biff, dear! [*She exits.*]

WILLY [*moving toward the left, away from* BEN]   There's nothing wrong. What's the matter with you?

BEN   Nervy boy. Good!

WILLY [*laughing*]   Oh, nerves of iron, that Biff!

CHARLEY   Don't know what it is. My New England man comes back and he's bleedin', they murdered him up there.

WILLY   It's contacts, Charley, I got important contacts!

CHARLEY [*sarcastically*]   Glad to hear it, Willy. Come in later, we'll shoot a little casino. I'll take some of your Portland money. [*He laughs at* WILLY *and exits.*]

WILLY [*turning to* BEN]   Business is bad, it's murderous. But not for me, of course.

BEN   I'll stop by on my way back to Africa.

WILLY [*longingly*]   Can't you stay a few days? You're just what I need, Ben, because I—I have a fine position here, but I—well, Dad left when I was such a baby and I never had a chance to talk to him and I still feel—kind of temporary about myself.

BEN   I'll be late for my train.

They are at opposite ends of the stage.

WILLY   Ben, my boys—can't we talk? They'd go into the jaws of hell for me, see, but I—

BEN   William, you're being first-rate with your boys. Outstanding, manly chaps!

WILLY [*hanging on to his words*]   Oh, Ben, that's good to hear! Because sometimes I'm afraid that I'm not teaching them the right kind of—Ben, how should I teach them?

BEN [*giving great weight to each word, and with a certain vicious audacity*]   William, when I walked into the jungle, I was seventeen. When I walked out I was twenty-one. And, by God, I was rich! [*He goes off into darkness around the right corner of the house.*]

WILLY   . . . was rich! That's just the spirit I want to imbue them with! To walk into a jungle! I was right! I was right! I was right!

> BEN *is gone, but* WILLY *is still speaking to him as* LINDA, *in nightgown and robe, enters the kitchen, glances around for* WILLY, *then goes to the door of the house, looks out and sees him. Comes down to his left. He looks at her.*

LINDA   Willy, dear? Willy?

WILLY   I was right!

LINDA   Did you have some cheese? [*He can't answer.*] It's very late, darling. Come to bed, heh?

WILLY [*looking straight up*]   Gotta break your neck to see a star in this yard.

LINDA   You coming in?

WILLY   Whatever happened to that diamond watch fob? Remember? When Ben came from Africa that time? Didn't he give me a watch fob with a diamond in it?

LINDA   You pawned it, dear. Twelve, thirteen years ago. For Biff's radio correspondence course.

WILLY   Gee, that was a beautiful thing. I'll take a walk.

LINDA   But you're in your slippers.

WILLY [*starting to go around the house at the left*]   I was right! I was! [*Half to* LINDA, *as he goes, shaking his head*] What a man! There was a man worth talking to. I was right!

LINDA [*calling after* WILLY]   But in your slippers, Willy!

> WILLY *is almost gone when* BIFF, *in his pajamas, comes down the stairs and enters the kitchen.*

BIFF   What is he doing out there?

LINDA   Sh!

BIFF   God Almighty, Mom, how long has he been doing this?

LINDA   Don't, he'll hear you.

BIFF   What the hell is the matter with him?

LINDA   It'll pass by morning.

BIFF   Shouldn't we do anything?

LINDA   Oh, my dear, you should do a lot of things, but there's nothing to do, so go to sleep.

> HAPPY *comes down the stair and sits on the steps.*

HAPPY   I never heard him so loud, Mom.

LINDA   Well, come around more often; you'll hear him. [*She sits down at the table and mends the lining of* WILLY's *jacket.*]

BIFF   Why didn't you ever write me about this, Mom?

LINDA   How would I write to you? For over three months you had no address.

BIFF   I was on the move. But you know I thought of you all the time. You know that, don't you, pal?

LINDA   I know, dear, I know. But he likes to have a letter. Just to know that there's still a possibility for better things.
BIFF   He's not like this all the time, is he?
LINDA   It's when you come home he's always the worst.
BIFF   When I come home?
LINDA   When you write you're coming, he's all smiles, and talks about the future, and—he's just wonderful. And then the closer you seem to come, the more shaky he gets, and then, by the time you get here, he's arguing, and he seems angry at you. I think it's just that maybe he can't bring himself to—to open up to you. Why are you so hateful to each other? Why is that?
BIFF [*evasively*]   I'm not hateful, Mom.
LINDA   But you no sooner come in the door than you're fighting!
BIFF   I don't know why. I mean to change. I'm tryin', Mom, you understand?
LINDA   Are you home to stay now?
BIFF   I don't know. I want to look around, see what's doin'.
LINDA   Biff, you can't look around all your life, can you?
BIFF   I just can't take hold, Mom. I can't take hold of some kind of a life.
LINDA   Biff, a man is not a bird, to come and go with the springtime.
BIFF   Your hair . . . [*He touches her hair*]. Your hair got so gray.
LINDA   Oh, it's been gray since you were in high school. I just stopped dyeing it, that's all.
BIFF   Dye it again, will ya? I don't want my pal looking old. [*He smiles.*]
LINDA   You're such a boy! You think you can go away for a year and . . . You've got to get it into your head now that one day you'll knock on this door and there'll be strange people here—
BIFF   What are you talking about? You're not even sixty, Mom.
LINDA   But what about your father?
BIFF [*lamely*]   Well, I meant him too.
HAPPY   He admires Pop.
LINDA   Biff, dear, if you don't have any feeling for him, then you can't have any feeling for me.
BIFF   Sure I can, Mom.
LINDA   No. You can't just come to see me, because I love him. [*With a threat, but only a threat, of tears*] He's the dearest man in the world to me, and I won't have anyone making him feel unwanted and low and blue. You've got to make up your mind now, darling, there's no leeway any more. Either he's your father and you pay him that respect, or else you're not to come here. I know he's not easy to get along with—nobody knows that better than me—but . . .
WILLY [*from the left, with a laugh*]   Hey, hey, Biffo!
BIFF [*starting to go out after* WILLY]   What the hell is the matter with him? [HAPPY *stops him.*]
LINDA   Don't—don't go near him!
BIFF   Stop making excuses for him! He always, always wiped the floor with you. Never had an ounce of respect for you.
HAPPY   He's always had respect for—
BIFF   What the hell do you know about it?

HAPPY [*surlily*]   Just don't call him crazy!

BIFF   He's got no character— Charley wouldn't do this. Not in his own house—spewing out that vomit from his mind.

HAPPY   Charley never had to cope with what he's got to.

BIFF   People are worse off than Willy Loman. Believe me, I've seen them!

LINDA   Then make Charley your father, Biff. You can't do that, can you? I don't say he's a great man. Willy Loman never made a lot of money. His name was never in the paper. He's not the finest character that ever lived. But he's a human being, and a terrible thing is happening to him. So attention must be paid. He's not to be allowed to fall into his grave like an old dog. Attention, attention must be finally paid to such a person. You called him crazy—

BIFF   I didn't mean—

LINDA   No, a lot of people think he's lost his—balance. But you don't have to be very smart to know what his trouble is. The man is exhausted.

HAPPY   Sure!

LINDA   A small man can be just as exhausted as a great man. He works for a company thirty-six years this March, opens up un-heard-of territories to their trademark, and now in his old age they take his salary away.

HAPPY [*indignantly*]   I didn't know that, Mom.

LINDA   You never asked, my dear! Now that you get your spending money someplace else you don't trouble your mind with him.

HAPPY   But I gave you money last—

LINDA   Christmas time, fifty dollars! To fix the hot water it cost ninety-seven fifty! For five weeks he's been on straight commission, like a beginner, an unknown!

BIFF   Those ungrateful bastards!

LINDA   Are they any worse than his sons? When he brought them business, when he was young, they were glad to see him. But now his old friends, the old buyers that loved him so and always found some order to hand him in a pinch—they're all dead, retired. He used to be able to make six, seven calls a day in Boston. Now he takes his valises out of the car and puts them back and takes them out again and he's exhausted. Instead of walking he talks now. He drives seven hundred miles, and when he gets there no one knows him any more, no one welcomes him. And what goes through a man's mind, driving seven hundred miles home without having earned a cent? Why shouldn't he talk to himself? Why? When he has to go to Charley and borrow fifty dollars a week and pretend to me that it's his pay? How long can that go on? How long? You see what I'm sitting here and waiting for? And you tell me he has no character? The man who never worked a day but for your benefit? When does he get the medal for that? Is this his reward— to turn around at the age of sixty-three and find his sons, who he loved better than his life, one a philandering bum—

HAPPY   Mom!

LINDA   That's what you are, my baby! [*To* BIFF] And you! What happened to the love you had for him? You were such pals! How you used to talk to him on the phone every night! How lonely he was till he could come home to you!

BIFF   All right, Mom. I'll live here in my room, and I'll get a job. I'll keep away from him, that's all.

LINDA   No, Biff. You can't stay here and fight all the time.

BIFF   He threw me out of this house, remember that.

LINDA   Why did he do that? I never knew why.

BIFF   Because I know he's a fake and he doesn't like anybody around who knows!

LINDA   Why a fake? In what way? What do you mean?

BIFF   Just don't lay it all at my feet. It's between me and him—that's all I have to say. I'll chip in from now on. He'll settle for half my pay check. He'll be all right. I'm going to bed. [*He starts for the stairs.*]

LINDA   He won't be all right.

BIFF   [*turning on the stairs, furiously*]   I hate this city and I'll stay here. Now what do you want?

LINDA   He's dying, Biff.

HAPPY *turns quickly to her, shocked.*

BIFF   [*after a pause*]   Why is he dying?

LINDA   He's been trying to kill himself.

BIFF   [*with great horror*]   How?

LINDA   I live from day to day.

BIFF   What're you talking about?

LINDA   Remember I wrote you that he smashed up the car again? In February?

BIFF   Well?

LINDA   The insurance inspector came. He said that they have evidence. That all these accidents in the last year—weren't—weren't—accidents.

HAPPY   How can they tell that? That's a lie.

LINDA   It seems there's a woman . . . [*She takes a breath as*

(BIFF, *sharply but contained*]   What woman?

(LINDA, *simultaneously*] . . . and this woman . . .

LINDA   What?

BIFF   Nothing. Go ahead.

LINDA   What did you say?

BIFF   Nothing. I just said what woman?

HAPPY   What about her?

LINDA   Well, it seems she was walking down the road and saw his car. She says that he wasn't driving fast at all, and that he didn't skid. She says he came to that little bridge, and then deliberately smashed into the railing, and it was only the shallowness of the water that saved him.

BIFF   Oh, no, he probably just fell asleep again.

LINDA   I don't think he fell asleep.

BIFF   Why not?

LINDA   Last month . . . [*With great difficulty*] Oh, boys, it's so hard to say a thing like this! He's just a big stupid man to you, but I tell you there's more good in him than in many other people. [*She chokes, wipes her eyes.*] I was looking for a fuse. The lights blew out, and I went down the cellar. And behind the fuse box—it happened to fall out—was a length of rubber pipe—just short.

HAPPY No kidding?

LINDA There's a little attachment on the end of it. I knew right away. And sure enough, on the bottom of the water heater there's a new little nipple on the gas pipe.

HAPPY [*angrily*] That—jerk.

BIFF Did you have it taken off?

LINDA I'm—I'm ashamed to. How can I mention it to him? Every day I go down and take away that little rubber pipe. But, when he comes home, I put it back where it was. How can I insult him that way? I don't know what to do. I live from day to day, boys. I tell you, I know every thought in his mind. It sounds so old-fashioned and silly, but I tell you he put his whole life into you and you've turned your backs on him. [*She is bent over in the chair, weeping, her face in her hands.*] Biff, I swear to God! Biff, his life is in your hands!

HAPPY [*to* BIFF] How do you like that damned fool!

BIFF [*kissing her*] All right, pal, all right. It's all settled now. I've been remiss. I know that, Mom. But now I'll stay, and I swear to you, I'll apply myself. [*Kneeling in front of her, in a fever of self-reproach.*] It's just—you see, Mom, I don't fit in business. Not that I won't try. I'll try, and I'll make good.

HAPPY Sure you will. The trouble with you in business was you never tried to please people.

BIFF I know, I—

HAPPY Like when you worked for Harrison's. Bob Harrison said you were tops, and then you go and do some damn fool thing like whistling whole songs in the elevator like a comedian.

BIFF [*against* HAPPY] So what? I like to whistle sometimes.

HAPPY You don't raise a guy to a responsible job who whistles in the elevator!

LINDA Well, don't argue about it now.

HAPPY Like when you'd go off and swim in the middle of the day instead of taking the line around.

BIFF [*his resentment rising*] Well, don't you run off? You take off sometimes, don't you? On a nice summer day?

HAPPY Yeah, but I cover myself!

LINDA Boys!

HAPPY If I'm going to take a fade the boss can call any number where I'm supposed to be and they'll swear to him that I just left. I'll tell you something that I hate to say, Biff, but in the business world some of them think you're crazy.

BIFF [*angered*] Screw the business world!

HAPPY All right, screw it! Great, but cover yourself!

LINDA Hap, Hap!

BIFF I don't care what they think! They've laughed at Dad for years, and you know why? Because we don't belong in this nut-house of a city! We should be mixing cement on some open plain, or—or carpenters. A carpenter is allowed to whistle!

WILLY *walks in from the entrance of the house, at left.*

WILLY   Even your grandfather was better than a carpenter. [*Pause. They watch him.*] You never grew up. Bernard does not whistle in the elevator, I assure you.

BIFF [*as though to laugh* WILLY *out of it*]   Yeah, but you do, Pop.

WILLY   I never in my life whistled in an elevator! And who in the business world thinks I'm crazy?

BIFF   I didn't mean it like that, Pop. Now don't make a whole thing out of it, will ya?

WILLY   Go back to the West! Be a carpenter, a cowboy, enjoy yourself!

LINDA   Willy, he was just saying—

WILLY   I heard what he said!

HAPPY [*trying to quiet* WILLY]   Hey, Pop, come on now . . .

WILLY [*continuing over* HAPPY's *line*]   They laugh at me, heh? Go to Filene's, go to the Hub, go to Slattery's, Boston. Call out the name Willy Loman and see what happens! Big shot!

BIFF   All right, Pop.

WILLY   Big!

BIFF   All right!

WILLY   Why do you always insult me?

BIFF   I didn't say a word. [*To* LINDA]   Did I say a word?

LINDA   He didn't say anything, Willy.

WILLY [*going to the doorway of the living room*]   All right, good night, good night.

LINDA   Willy, dear, he just decided . . .

WILLY [*to* BIFF]   If you get tired hanging around tomorrow, paint the ceiling I put up in the living room.

BIFF   I'm leaving early tomorrow.

HAPPY   He's going to see Bill Oliver, Pop.

WILLY [*interestedly*]   Oliver? For what?

BIFF [*with reserve, but trying, trying*]   He always said he'd stake me. I'd like to go into business, so maybe I can take him up on it.

LINDA   Isn't that wonderful?

WILLY   Don't interrupt. What's wonderful about it? There's fifty men in the City of New York who'd stake him. [*To* BIFF] Sporting goods?

BIFF   I guess so. I know something about it and—

WILLY   He knows something about it! You know sporting goods better than Spalding, for God's sake! How much is he giving you?

BIFF   I don't know, I didn't even see him yet, but—

WILLY   Then what're you talkin' about?

BIFF [*getting angry*]   Well, all I said was I'm gonna see him, that's all!

WILLY [*turning away*]   Ah, you're counting your chickens again.

BIFF [*starting left for the stairs*]   Oh, Jesus, I'm going to sleep!

WILLY [*calling after him*]   Don't curse in this house!

BIFF [*turning*] Since when did you get so clean?

HAPPY [*trying to stop them*] Wait a . . .

WILLY Don't use that language to me! I won't have it!

HAPPY [*grabbing* BIFF, *shouts*] Wait a minute! I got an idea. I got a feasible idea. Come here, Biff, let's talk this over now, let's talk some sense here. When I was down in Florida last time, I thought of a great idea to sell sporting goods. It just came back to me. You and I, Biff—we have a line, the Loman Line. We train a couple of weeks, and put on a couple of exhibitions, see?

WILLY That's an idea!

HAPPY Wait! We form two basketball teams, see? Two water polo teams. We play each other. It's a million dollars' worth of publicity. Two brothers, see? The Loman Brothers. Displays in the Royal Palms—all the hotels. And banners over the ring and the basketball court: "Loman Brothers." Baby, we could sell sporting goods!

WILLY That is a one-million-dollar idea!

LINDA Marvelous!

BIFF I'm in great shape as far as that's concerned.

HAPPY And the beauty of it is, Biff, it wouldn't be like a business. We'd be out playin' ball again . . .

BIFF [*enthused*] Yeah, that's . . .

WILLY Million-dollar . . .

HAPPY And you wouldn't get fed up with it, Biff. It'd be the family again. There'd be the old honor, and comradeship, and if you wanted to go off for a swim or somethin'—well, you'd do it! Without some smart cooky gettin' up ahead of you!

WILLY Lick the world! You guys together could absolutely lick the civilized world.

BIFF I'll see Oliver tomorrow. Hap, if we could work that out . . .

LINDA Maybe things are beginning to—

WILLY [*wildly enthused, to* LINDA] Stop interrupting! [*To* BIFF] But don't wear sport jacket and slacks when you see Oliver.

BIFF No, I'll—

WILLY A business suit, and talk as little as possible, and don't crack any jokes.

BIFF He did like me. Always liked me.

LINDA He loved you!

WILLY [*to* LINDA] Will you stop! [*To* BIFF] Walk in very serious. You are not applying for a boy's job. Money is to pass. Be quiet, fine, and serious. Everybody likes a kidder, but nobody lends him money.

HAPPY I'll try to get some myself, Biff. I'm sure I can.

WILLY I see great things for you kids, I think your troubles are over. But remember, start big and you'll end big. Ask for fifteen. How much you gonna ask for?

BIFF Gee, I don't know—

WILLY And don't say "Gee." "Gee" is a boy's word. A man walking in for fifteen thousand dollars does not say "Gee!"

BIFF Ten, I think, would be top though.

WILLY Don't be so modest. You always started too low. Walk in with a big laugh. Don't look worried. Start off with a couple of your good stories to lighten things up. It's not what you say, it's how you say it—because personality always wins the day.

LINDA   Oliver always thought the highest of him—

WILLY   Will you let me talk?

BIFF   Don't yell at her, Pop, will ya?

WILLY [*angrily*]   I was talking, wasn't I?

BIFF   I don't like you yelling at her all the time, and I'm tellin' you, that's all.

WILLY   What're you, takin' over this house?

LINDA   Willy—

WILLY [*turning on her*]   Don't take his side all the time, goddammit!

BIFF [*furiously*]   Stop yelling at her!

WILLY [*suddenly pulling on his cheek, beaten down, guilt ridden*] Give my best to Bill Oliver—he may remember me. [*He exits through the living room doorway.*]

LINDA [*her voice subdued*]   What'd you have to start that for? [BIFF *turns away.*] You see how sweet he was as soon as you talked hopefully? [*She goes over to* BIFF.] Come up and say good night to him. Don't let him go to bed that way.

HAPPY   Come on, Biff, let's buck him up.

LINDA   Please, dear. Just say good night. It takes so little to make him happy. Come. [*She goes through the living room doorway, calling upstairs from within the living room*] Your pajamas are hanging in the bathroom, Willy!

HAPPY [*looking toward where* LINDA *went out*]   What a woman! They broke the mold when they made her. You know that, Biff?

BIFF   He's off salary. My God, working on commission!

HAPPY   Well, let's face it: he's no hot-shot selling man. Except that sometimes, you have to admit, he's a sweet personality.

BIFF [*deciding*]   Lend me ten bucks, will ya? I want to buy some new ties.

HAPPY   I'll take you to a place I know. Beautiful stuff. Wear one of my striped shirts tomorrow.

BIFF   She got gray. Mom got awful old. Gee, I'm gonna go in to Oliver tomorrow and knock him for a—

HAPPY   Come on up. Tell that to Dad. Let's give him a whirl. Come on.

BIFF [*steamed up*]   You know, with ten thousand bucks, boy!

HAPPY [*as they go into the living room*]   That's the talk, Biff, that's the first time I've heard the old confidence out of you! [*From within the living room, fading off*] You're gonna live with me, kid, and any babe you want just say the word . . . [*The last lines are hardly heard. They are mounting the stairs to their parents' bedroom.*]

LINDA [*entering her bedroom and addressing* WILLY, *who is in the bathroom. She is straightening the bed for him*]   Can you do anything about the shower? It drips.

WILLY [*from the bathroom*]   All of a sudden everything falls to pieces! Goddam plumbing, oughta be sued, those people. I hardly finished putting it in and the thing . . . [*His words rumble off.*]

LINDA   I'm just wondering if Oliver will remember him. You think he might?

WILLY [*coming out of the bathroom in his pajamas*]   Remember him? What's the matter with you, you crazy? If he'd've stayed with Oliver he'd be on top by now! Wait'll Oliver gets a look at him. You don't know the average caliber any more. The average young man today—[*he is getting into bed*]—is got a caliber of zero. Greatest thing in the world for him was to bum around.

BIFF *and* HAPPY *enter the bedroom. Slight pause.*

WILLY [*stops short, looking at* BIFF]   Glad to hear it, boy.

HAPPY   He wanted to say good night to you, sport.

WILLY [*to* BIFF]   Yeah. Knock him dead, boy. What'd you want to tell me?

BIFF   Just take it easy, Pop. Good night. [*He turns to go.*]

WILLY [*unable to resist*]   And if anything falls off the desk while you're talking to him—like a package or something—don't you pick it up. They have office boys for that.

LINDA   I'll make a big breakfast—

WILLY   Will you let me finish? [*To* BIFF]   Tell him you were in the business in the West. Not farm work.

BIFF   All right, Dad.

LINDA   I think everything—

WILLY [*going right through her speech*]   And don't undersell yourself. No less than fifteen thousand dollars.

BIFF [*unable to bear him*]   Okay. Good night, Mom. [*He starts moving.*]

WILLY   Because you got a greatness in you, Biff, remember that. You got all kinds a greatness . . . [*He lies back, exhausted.* BIFF *walks out.*]

LINDA [*calling after* BIFF]   Sleep well, darling!

HAPPY   I'm gonna get married, Mom. I wanted to tell you.

LINDA   Go to sleep, dear.

HAPPY [*going*]   I just wanted to tell you.

WILLY   Keep up the good work. [HAPPY *exits.*] God . . . remember that Ebbets Field[4] game? The championship of the city?

LINDA   Just rest. Should I sing to you?

WILLY   Yeah. Sing to me. [LINDA *hums a soft lullaby.*] When that team came out—he was the tallest, remember?

LINDA   Oh, yes. And in gold.

BIFF *enters the darkened kitchen, takes a cigarette, and leaves the house. He comes downstage into a golden pool of light. He smokes, staring at the night.*

WILLY   Like a young god. Hercules—something like that. And the sun all around him. Remember how he waved to me? Right up from the field, with the representatives of three colleges standing by? And the buyers I brought, and the cheers when he came out— Loman, Loman, Loman! God Almighty, he'll be great yet. A star like that, magnificent, can never really fade away!

4. A Brooklyn sports stadium named after Charles H. Ebbets (1859–1925) and torn down in 1960.

The light on WILLY *is fading. The gas heater begins to glow through the kitchen wall, near the stairs, a blue flame beneath red coils.*

LINDA [*timidly*]   Willy dear, what has he got against you?
WILLY   I'm so tired. Don't talk any more.

BIFF *slowly returns to the kitchen. He stops, stares toward the heater.*

LINDA   Will you ask Howard to let you work in New York?
WILLY   First thing in the morning. Everything'll be all right.

BIFF *reaches behind the heater and draws out a length of rubber tubing. He is horrified and turns his head toward* WILLY's *room, still dimly lit, from which the strains of* LINDA's *desperate but monotonous humming rise.*

WILLY [*staring through the window into the moonlight*]   Gee, look at the moon moving between the buildings!

BIFF *wraps the tubing around his hand and quickly goes up the stairs.*

CURTAIN

Act 2

Music is heard, gay and bright. The curtain rises as the music fades away. WILLY, *in shirt sleeves, is sitting at the kitchen table, sipping coffee, his hat in his lap.* LINDA *is filling his cup when she can.*

WILLY   Wonderful coffee. Meal in itself.
LINDA   Can I make you some eggs?
WILLY   No. Take a breath.
LINDA   You look so rested, dear.
WILLY   I slept like a dead one. First time in months. Imagine, sleeping till ten on a Tuesday morning. Boys left nice and early, heh?
LINDA   They were out of here by eight o'clock.
WILLY   Good work!
LINDA   It was so thrilling to see them leaving together. I can't get over the shaving lotion in this house!
WILLY [*smiling*]   Mmm—
LINDA   Biff was very changed this morning. His whole attitude seemed to be hopeful. He couldn't wait to get downtown to see Oliver.
WILLY   He's heading for a change. There's no question, there simply are certain men that take longer to get—solidified. How did he dress?

LINDA His blue suit. He's so handsome in that suit. He could be a—anything in that suit!

WILLY *gets up from the table.* LINDA *holds his jacket for him.*

WILLY There's no question, no question at all. Gee, on the way home tonight I'd like to buy some seeds.

LINDA [*laughing*] That'd be wonderful. But not enough sun gets back there. Nothing'll grow any more.

WILLY You wait, kid, before it's all over we're gonna get a little place out in the country, and I'll raise some vegetables, a couple of chickens . . .

LINDA You'll do it yet, dear.

WILLY *walks out of his jacket.* LINDA *follows him.*

WILLY And they'll get married, and come for a weekend. I'd build a little guest house. 'Cause I got so many fine tools, all I'd need would be a little lumber and some peace of mind.

LINDA [*joyfully*] I sewed the lining . . .

WILLY I could build two guest houses, so they'd both come. Did he decide how much he's going to ask Oliver for?

LINDA [*getting him into the jacket*] He didn't mention it, but I imagine ten or fifteen thousand. You going to talk to Howard today?

WILLY Yeah. I'll put it to him straight and simple. He'll just have to take me off the road.

LINDA And Willy, don't forget to ask for a little advance, because we've got the insurance premium. It's the grace period now.

WILLY That's a hundred . . . ?

LINDA A hundred and eight, sixty-eight. Because we're a little short again.

WILLY Why are we short?

LINDA Well, you had the motor job on the car . . .

WILLY That goddam Studebaker!

LINDA And you got one more payment on the refrigerator . . .

WILLY But it just broke again!

LINDA Well, it's old, dear.

WILLY I told you we should've bought a well-advertised machine. Charley bought a General Electric and it's twenty years old and it's still good, that son-of-a-bitch.

LINDA But, Willy—

WILLY Whoever heard of a Hastings refrigerator? Once in my life I would like to own something outright before it's broken! I'm always in a race with the junkyard! I just finished paying for the car and it's on its last legs. The refrigerator consumes belts like a goddam maniac. They time those things. They time them so when you finally paid for them, they're used up.

LINDA [*buttoning up his jacket as he unbuttons it*] All told, about two hundred dollars would carry us, dear. But that includes the last payment on the mortgage. After this payment, Willy, the house belongs to us.

WILLY   It's twenty-five years!

LINDA   Biff was nine years old when we bought it.

WILLY   Well, that's a great thing. To weather a twenty-five-year mortgage is—

LINDA   It's an accomplishment.

WILLY   All the cement, the lumber, the reconstruction I put in this house! There ain't a crack to be found in it any more.

LINDA   Well, it served its purpose.

WILLY   What purpose? Some stranger'll come along, move in, and that's that. If only Biff would take this house, and raise a family . . . [*He starts to go.*] Good-by, I'm late.

LINDA   [*suddenly remembering*] Oh, I forgot! You're supposed to meet them for dinner.

WILLY   Me?

LINDA   At Frank's Chop House on Forty-eighth near Sixth Avenue.

WILLY   Is that so! How about you?

LINDA   No, just the three of you. They're gonna blow you to a big meal!

WILLY   Don't say! Who thought of that?

LINDA   Biff came to me this morning, Willy, and he said, "Tell Dad, we want to blow him to a big meal." Be there six o'clock. You and your two boys are going to have dinner.

WILLY   Gee whiz! That's really somethin'. I'm gonna knock Howard for a loop, kid. I'll get an advance, and I'll come home with a New York job. Goddammit, now I'm gonna do it!

LINDA   Oh, that's the spirit, Willy!

WILLY   I will never get behind a wheel the rest of my life!

LINDA   It's changing, Willy, I can feel it changing!

WILLY   Beyond a question. G'by, I'm late. [*He starts to go again.*]

LINDA   [*calling after him as she runs to the kitchen table for a hand-kerchief*] You got your glasses?

WILLY   [*feels for them, then comes back in*] Yeah, yeah, got my glasses.

LINDA   [*giving him the handkerchief*] And a handkerchief.

WILLY   Yeah, handkerchief.

LINDA   And your saccharin?

WILLY   Yeah, my saccharin.

LINDA   Be careful on the subway stairs.

> *She kisses him, and a silk stocking is seen hanging from her hand.* WILLY *notices it.*

WILLY   Will you stop mending stockings? At least while I'm in the house. It gets me nervous. I can't tell you. Please.

> LINDA *hides the stocking in her hand as she follows* WILLY *across the forestage in front of the house.*

LINDA   Remember, Frank's Chop House.

WILLY   [*passing the apron*] Maybe beets would grow out there.

LINDA   [*laughing*] But you tried so many times.

WILLY   Yeah. Well, don't work hard today. [*He disappears around the right corner of the house.*]
LINDA   Be careful!

As WILLY *vanishes,* LINDA *waves to him. Suddenly the phone rings. She runs across the stage and into the kitchen and lifts it.*

LINDA   Hello? Oh, Biff! I'm so glad you called, I just . . . Yes, sure, I just told him. Yes, he'll be there for dinner at six o'clock, I didn't forget. Listen, I was just dying to tell you. You know that little rubber pipe I told you about? That he connected to the gas heater? I finally decided to go down the cellar this morning and take it away and destroy it. But it's gone! Imagine? He took it away himself, it isn't there! [*She listens.*] When? Oh, then you took it. Oh—nothing, it's just that I'd hoped he'd taken it away himself. Oh, I'm not worried, darling, because this morning he left in such high spirits, it was like the old days! I'm not afraid any more. Did Mr. Oliver see you? . . . Well, you wait there then. And make a nice impression on him, darling. Just don't perspire too much before you see him. And have a nice time with Dad. He may have big news too! . . . That's right, a New York job. And be sweet to him tonight, dear. Be loving to him. Because he's only a little boat looking for a harbor. [*She is trembling with sorrow and joy.*] Oh, that's wonderful, Biff, you'll save his life. Thanks, darling. Just put your arm around him when he comes into the restaurant. Give him a smile. That's the boy . . . Good-by, dear. . . . You got your comb? . . . That's fine. Good-by, Biff dear.

In the middle of her speech, HOWARD WAGNER, *thirty-six, wheels on a small typewriter table on which is a wire-recording machine and proceeds to plug it in. This is on the left forestage. Light slowly fades on* LINDA *as it rises on* HOWARD. HOWARD *is intent on threading the machine and only glances over his shoulder as* WILLY *appears.*

WILLY   Pst! Pst!
HOWARD   Hello, Willy, come in.
WILLY   Like to have a little talk with you, Howard.
HOWARD   Sorry to keep you waiting. I'll be with you in a minute.
WILLY   What's that, Howard?
HOWARD   Didn't you ever see one of these? Wire recorder.
WILLY   Oh. Can we talk a minute?
HOWARD   Records things. Just got delivery yesterday. Been driving me crazy, the most terrific machine I ever saw in my life. I was up all night with it.
WILLY   What do you do with it?
HOWARD   I bought it for dictation, but you can do anything with it. Listen to this. I had it home last night. Listen to what I picked up. The first one is my daughter. Get this. [*He flicks the switch and "Roll out the Barrel" is heard being whistled.*] Listen to that kid whistle.

WILLY   That is lifelike, isn't it?

HOWARD   Seven years old. Get that tone.

WILLY   Ts, ts. Like to ask a little favor if you . . .

The whistling breaks off, and the voice of HOWARD's *daughter is heard.*

HIS DAUGHTER   "Now you, Daddy."

HOWARD   She's crazy for me! [*Again the same song is whistled.*] That's me! Ha! [*He winks.*]

WILLY   You're very good!

The whistling breaks off again. The machine runs silent for a moment.

HOWARD   Sh! Get this now, this is my son.

HIS SON   "The capital of Alabama is Montgomery; the capital of Arizona is Phoenix; the capital of Arkansas is Little Rock; the capital of California is Sacramento . . ." [*and on, and on.*]

HOWARD [*holding up five fingers*]   Five years old. Willy!

WILLY   He'll make an announcer some day!

HIS SON [*continuing*]   "The capital . . ."

HOWARD   Get that—alphabetical order! [*The machine breaks off suddenly.*] Wait a minute. The maid kicked the plug out.

WILLY   It certainly is a—

HOWARD   Sh, for God's sake!

HIS SON   "It's nine o'clock, Bulova watch time. So I have to go to sleep."

WILLY   That really is—

HOWARD   Wait a minute! The next is my wife.

They wait.

HOWARD'S VOICE   "Go on, say something." [*Pause.*] "Well, you gonna talk?"

HIS WIFE   "I can't think of anything."

HOWARD'S VOICE   "Well, talk—it's turning."

HIS WIFE [*shyly, beaten*]   "Hello." [*Silence.*] "Oh, Howard, I can't talk into this . . ."

HOWARD [*snapping the machine off*]   That was my wife.

WILLY   That is a wonderful machine. Can we—

HOWARD   I tell you, Willy, I'm gonna take my camera, and my band-saw, and all my hobbies, and out they go. This is the most fascinating relaxation I ever found.

WILLY   I think I'll get one myself.

HOWARD   Sure, they're only a hundred and a half. You can't do without it. Supposing you wanna hear Jack Benny,[5] see? But you can't be at home at that hour. So you tell the maid to turn the radio on

5. Jack Benny (1894–1974), a vaude-   star, hosted America's most popular radio
ville, radio, television, and motion picture   show from 1932 to 1955.

when Jack Benny comes on, and this automatically goes on with the radio . . .

WILLY   And when you come home you . . .

HOWARD   You can come home twelve o'clock, one o'clock, any time you like, and you get yourself a Coke and sit yourself down, throw the switch, and there's Jack Benny's program in the middle of the night!

WILLY   I'm definitely going to get one. Because lots of time I'm on the road, and I think to myself, what I must be missing on the radio!

HOWARD   Don't you have a radio in the car?

WILLY   Well, yeah, but who ever thinks of turning it on?

HOWARD   Say, aren't you supposed to be in Boston?

WILLY   That's what I want to talk to you about, Howard. You got a minute? [*He draws a chair in from the wing.*]

HOWARD   What happened? What're you doing here?

WILLY   Well . . .

HOWARD   You didn't crack up again, did you?

WILLY   Oh, no. No . . .

HOWARD   Geez, you had me worried there for a minute. What's the trouble?

WILLY   Well, tell you the truth, Howard. I've come to the decision that I'd rather not travel any more.

HOWARD   Not travel! Well, what'll you do?

WILLY   Remember, Christmas time, when you had the party here? You said you'd try to think of some spot for me here in town.

HOWARD   With us?

WILLY   Well, sure.

HOWARD   Oh, yeah, yeah. I remember. Well, I couldn't think of anything for you, Willy.

WILLY   I tell ya, Howard. The kids are all grown up, y'know. I don't need much any more. If I could take home—well, sixty-five dollars a week, I could swing it.

HOWARD   Yeah, but Willy, see I—

WILLY   I tell ya why, Howard. Speaking frankly and between the two of us, y'know—I'm just a little tired.

HOWARD   Oh, I could understand that, Willy. But you're a road man, Willy, and we do a road business. We've only got a half-dozen salesmen on the floor here.

WILLY   God knows, Howard, I never asked a favor of any man. But I was with the firm when your father used to carry you in here in his arms.

HOWARD   I know that, Willy, but—

WILLY   Your father came to me the day you were born and asked me what I thought of the name of Howard, may he rest in peace.

HOWARD   I appreciate that, Willy, but there just is no spot here for you. If I had a spot I'd slam you right in, but I just don't have a single solitary spot.

He looks for his lighter. WILLY *has picked it up and gives it to him. Pause.*

WILLY [*with increasing anger*] Howard, all I need to set my table is fifty dollars a week.

HOWARD But where am I going to put you, kid?

WILLY Look, it isn't a question of whether I can sell merchandise, is it?

HOWARD No, but it's a business, kid, and everybody's gotta pull his own weight.

WILLY [*desperately*] Just let me tell you a story, Howard—

HOWARD 'Cause you gotta admit, business is business.

WILLY [*angrily*] Business is definitely business, but just listen for a minute. You don't understand this. When I was a boy—eighteen, nineteen—I was already on the road. And there was a question in my mind as to whether selling had a future for me. Because in those days I had a yearning to go to Alaska. See, there were three gold strikes in one month in Alaska, and I felt like going out. Just for the ride, you might say.

HOWARD [*barely interested*] Don't say.

WILLY Oh, yeah, my father lived many years in Alaska. He was an adventurous man. We've got quite a little streak of self-reliance in our family. I thought I'd go out with my older brother and try to locate him, and maybe settle in the North with the old man. And I was almost decided to go when I met a salesman in the Parker House. His name was Dave Singleman. And he was eighty-four years old, and he'd drummed merchandise in thirty-one states. And old Dave, he'd go up to his room, y'understand, put on his green velvet slippers—I'll never forget—and pick up his phone and call the buyers, and without ever leaving his room, at the age of eighty-four, he made his living. And when I saw that, I realized that selling was the greatest career a man could want. 'Cause what could be more satisfying than to be able to go, at the age of eighty-four, into twenty or thirty different cities, and pick up a phone, and be remembered and loved and helped by so many different people? Do you know? when he died—and by the way he died the death of a salesman, in his green velvet slippers in the smoker of the New York, New Haven and Hartford, going into Boston—when he died, hundreds of salesmen and buyers were at his funeral. Things were sad on a lotta trains for months after that. [*He stands up.* HOWARD *has not looked at him.*] In those days there was personality in it, Howard. There was respect, and comradeship, and gratitude in it. Today, it's all cut and dried, and there's no chance for bringing friendship to bear—or personality. You see what I mean? They don't know me any more.

HOWARD [*moving away, to the right*] That's just the thing, Willy.

WILLY If I had forty dollars a week—that's all I'd need. Forty dollars, Howard.

HOWARD Kid, I can't take blood from a stone, I—

WILLY [*desperation is on him now*] Howard, the year Al Smith[6] was nominated, your father came to me and—

HOWARD [*starting to go off*] I've got to see some people, kid.

---

6. Alfred E. Smith (1873–1944) was the Democratic presidential nominee who lost to Herbert Hoover in 1928.

WILLY [*stopping him*] I'm talking about your father! There were promises made across this desk! You mustn't tell me you've got people to see—I put thirty-four years into this firm, Howard, and now I can't pay my insurance! You can't eat the orange and throw the peel away—a man is not a piece of fruit! [*After a pause*] Now pay attention. Your father—in 1928 I had a big year. I averaged a hundred and seventy dollars a week in commissions.

HOWARD [*impatiently*] Now, Willy, you never averaged—

WILLY [*banging his hand on the desk*] I averaged a hundred and seventy dollars a week in the year of 1928! And your father came to me—or rather, I was in the office here—it was right over this desk—and he put his hand on my shoulder—

HOWARD [*getting up*] You'll have to excuse me, Willy, I gotta see some people. Pull yourself together. [*Going out*] I'll be back in a little while.

> On HOWARD's *exit, the light on his chair grows very bright and strange.*

WILLY Pull myself together! What the hell did I say to him? My God, I was yelling at him! How could I! [WILLY *breaks off, staring at the light, which occupies the chair, animating it. He approaches this chair, standing across the desk from it.*] Frank, Frank, don't you remember what you told me that time? How you put your hand on my shoulder, and Frank . . . [*He leans on the desk and as he speaks the dead man's name he accidentally switches on the recorder, and instantly:*]

HOWARD's SON "... of New York is Albany. The capital of Ohio is Cincinnati, the capital of Rhode Island is . . ." [*The recitation continues.*]

WILLY [*leaping away with fright, shouting*] Ha! Howard! Howard! Howard!

HOWARD [*rushing in*] What happened?

WILLY [*pointing at the machine, which continues nasally, childishly, with the capital cities*] Shut it off! Shut it off!

HOWARD [*pulling the plug out*] Look, Willy . . .

WILLY [*pressing his hands to his eyes*] I gotta get myself some coffee. I'll get some coffee . . .

> WILLY *starts to walk out.* HOWARD *stops him.*

HOWARD [*rolling up the cord*] Willy, look . . .

WILLY I'll go to Boston.

HOWARD Willy, you can't go to Boston for us.

WILLY Why can't I go?

HOWARD I don't want you to represent us. I've been meaning to tell you for a long time now.

WILLY Howard, are you firing me?

HOWARD I think you need a good long rest, Willy.

WILLY Howard—

HOWARD And when you feel better, come back, and we'll see if we can work something out.

WILLY   But I gotta earn money, Howard. I'm in no position to—

HOWARD   Where are your sons? Why don't your sons give you a hand?

WILLY   They're working on a very big deal.

HOWARD   This is no time for false pride, Willy. You go to your sons and you tell them that you're tired. You've got two great boys, haven't you?

WILLY   Oh, no question, no question, but in the meantime . . .

HOWARD   Then that's that, heh?

WILLY   All right, I'll go to Boston tomorrow.

HOWARD   No, no.

WILLY   I can't throw myself on my sons. I'm not a cripple!

HOWARD   Look, kid, I'm busy this morning.

WILLY   [*grasping* HOWARD's *arm*]   Howard, you've got to let me go to Boston!

HOWARD   [*hard, keeping himself under control*]   I've got a line of people to see this morning. Sit down, take five minutes, and pull yourself together, and then go home, will ya? I need the office, Willy. [*He starts to go; turns, remembering the recorder, starts to push off the table holding the recorder.*] Oh, yeah. Whenever you can this week, stop by and drop off the samples. You'll feel better, Willy, and then come back and we'll talk. Pull yourself together, kid, there's people outside.

> HOWARD *exits, pushing the table off left.* WILLY *stares into space, exhausted. Now the music is heard—*BEN's *music—first distantly, then closer, closer. As* WILLY *speaks,* BEN *enters from the right. He carries valise and umbrella.*

WILLY   Oh, Ben, how did you do it? What is the answer? Did you wind up the Alaska deal already?

BEN   Doesn't take much time if you know what you're doing. Just a short business trip. Boarding ship in an hour. Wanted to say good-by.

WILLY   Ben, I've got to talk to you.

BEN   [*glancing at his watch*]   Haven't the time, William.

WILLY   [*crossing the apron to* BEN]   Ben, nothing's working out. I don't know what to do.

BEN   Now, look here, William. I've bought timberland in Alaska and I need a man to look after things for me.

WILLY   God, timberland! Me and my boys in those grand outdoors!

BEN   You've a new continent at your doorstep, William. Get out of these cities, they're full of talk and time payments and courts of law. Screw on your fists and you can fight for a fortune up there.

WILLY   Yes, yes! Linda, Linda!

> LINDA *enters as of old, with the wash.*

LINDA   Oh, you're back?

BEN   I haven't much time.

WILLY   No, wait! Linda, he's got a proposition for me in Alaska.

LINDA   But you've got— [*To* BEN]He's got a beautiful job here.

WILLY   But in Alaska, kid, I could—

LINDA   You're doing well enough, Willy!

BEN [*to* LINDA]   Enough for what, my dear?

LINDA [*frightened of* BEN *and angry at him*]   Don't say those things to him! Enough to be happy right here, right now. [*To* WILLY, *while* BEN *laughs*] Why must everybody conquer the world? You're well liked, and the boys love you, and someday—[*to* BEN]—why, old man Wagner told him just the other day that if he keeps it up he'll be a member of the firm, didn't he, Willy?

WILLY   Sure, sure. I am building something with this firm, Ben, and if a man is building something he must be on the right track, mustn't he?

BEN   What are you building? Lay your hand on it. Where is it?

WILLY [*hesitantly*]   That's true, Linda, there's nothing.

LINDA   Why? [*To* BEN] There's a man eighty-four years old—

WILLY   That's right, Ben, that's right. When I look at that man I say, what is there to worry about?

BEN   Bah!

WILLY   It's true, Ben. All he has to do is go into any city, pick up the phone, and he's making his living and you know why?

BEN [*picking up his valise*]   I've got to go.

WILLY [*holding* BEN *back*]   Look at this boy!

> *Biff, in his high school sweater, enters carrying suitcase.* HAPPY *carries* BIFF's *shoulder guards, gold helmet, and football pants.*

WILLY   Without a penny to his name, three great universities are begging for him, and from there the sky's the limit, because it's not what you do, Ben. It's who you know and the smile on your face! It's contacts, Ben, contacts! The whole wealth of Alaska passes over the lunch table at the Commodore Hotel, and that's the wonder, the wonder of this country, that a man can end with diamonds here on the basis of being liked! [*He turns to* BIFF.] And that's why when you get out on that field today it's important. Because thousands of people will be rooting for you and loving you. [*To* BEN, *who has again begun to leave*] And Ben! when he walks into a business office his name will sound out like a bell and all the doors will open to him! I've seen it, Ben, I've seen it a thousand times! You can't feel it with your hand like timber, but it's there!

BEN   Good-by, William.

WILLY   Ben, am I right? Don't you think I'm right? I value your advice.

BEN   There's a new continent at your doorstep, William. You could walk out rich. Rich! [*He is gone.*]

WILLY   We'll do it here, Ben! You hear me? We're gonna do it here!

> YOUNG BERNARD *rushes in. The gay music of the Boys is heard.*

BERNARD   Oh, gee, I was afraid you left already!

WILLY   Why? What time is it?

BERNARD   It's half-past one!

WILLY   Well, come on, everybody! Ebbets Field next stop! Where's the pennants? [*He rushes through the wall-line of the kitchen and out into the living room.*]

LINDA   [*to* BIFF]   Did you pack fresh underwear?

BIFF   [*who has been limbering up*]   I want to go!

BERNARD   Biff, I'm carrying your helmet, ain't I?

HAPPY   No, I'm carrying the helmet.

BERNARD   Oh, Biff, you promised me.

HAPPY   I'm carrying the helmet.

BERNARD   How am I going to get in the locker room?

LINDA   Let him carry the shoulder guards. [*She puts her coat and hat on in the kitchen.*]

BERNARD   Can I, Biff? 'Cause I told everybody I'm going to be in the locker room.

HAPPY   In Ebbets Field it's the clubhouse.

BERNARD   I meant the clubhouse. Biff!

HAPPY   Biff!

BIFF   [*grandly, after a slight pause*]   Let him carry the shoulder guards.

HAPPY   [*as he gives* BERNARD *the shoulder guards*]   Stay close to us now.

WILLY *rushes in with the pennants.*

WILLY   [*handing them out*]   Everybody wave when Biff comes out on the field. [HAPPY *and* BERNARD *run off.*] You set now, boy?

The music has died away.

BIFF   Ready to go, Pop. Every muscle is ready.

WILLY   [*at the edge of the apron*]   You realize what this means?

BIFF   That's right, Pop.

WILLY   [*feeling* BIFF's *muscles*]   You're comin' home this afternoon captain of the All-Scholastic Championship Team of the City of New York.

BIFF   I got it, Pop. And remember, pal, when I take off my helmet, that touchdown is for you.

WILLY   Let's go! [*He is starting out, with his arm around* BIFF, *when* CHARLEY *enters, as of old, in knickers*] I got no room for you, Charley.

CHARLEY   Room? For what?

WILLY   In the car.

CHARLEY   You goin' for a ride? I wanted to shoot some casino.

WILLY   [*furiously*]   Casino! [*Incredulously*]   Don't you realize what today is?

LINDA   Oh, he knows, Willy. He's just kidding you.

WILLY   That's nothing to kid about!

CHARLEY   No, Linda, what's goin' on?

LINDA   He's playing in Ebbets Field.

CHARLEY   Baseball in this weather?

WILLY Don't talk to him. Come on, come on! [*He is pushing them out.*]

CHARLEY Wait a minute, didn't you hear the news?

WILLY What?

CHARLEY Don't you listen to the radio? Ebbets Field just blew up.

WILLY You go to hell! [CHARLEY *laughs. Pushing them out*] Come on, come on! We're late.

CHARLEY [*as they go*] Knock a homer, Biff, knock a homer!

WILLY [*the last to leave, turning to* CHARLEY] I don't think that was funny, Charley. This is the greatest day of his life.

CHARLEY Willy, when are you going to grow up?

WILLY Yeah, heh? When this game is over, Charley, you'll be laughing out the other side of your face. They'll be calling him another Red Grange.[7] Twenty-five thousand a year.

CHARLEY [*kidding*] Is that so?

WILLY Yeah, that's so.

CHARLEY Well, then, I'm sorry, Willy. But tell me something.

WILLY What?

CHARLEY Who is Red Grange?

WILLY Put up your hands. Goddam you, put up your hands!

> CHARLEY, *chuckling, shakes his head and walks away, around the left corner of the stage.* WILLY *follows him. The music rises to a mocking frenzy.*

WILLY Who the hell do you think you are, better than everybody else? You don't know everything, you big, ignorant, stupid . . . Put up your hands!

> *Light rises, on the right side of the forestage, on a small table in the reception room of* CHARLEY'S *office. Traffic sounds are heard.* BERNARD, *now mature, sits whistling to himself. A pair of tennis rackets and an overnight bag are on the floor beside him.*

WILLY [*offstage*] What are you walking away for? Don't walk away! If you're going to say something say it to my face! I know you laugh at me behind my back. You'll laugh out of the other side of your goddam face after this game. Touchdown! Touchdown! Eighty thousand people! Touchdown! Right between the goal posts.

> BERNARD *is a quiet, but self-assured young man.* WILLY'S *voice is coming from right upstage now.* BERNARD *lowers his feet off the table and listens.* JENNY, *his father's secretary, enters.*

JENNY [*distressed*] Say, Bernard, will you go out in the hall?

BERNARD What is that noise? Who is it?

JENNY Mr. Loman. He just got off the elevator.

BERNARD [*getting up*] Who's he arguing with?

---

7. Harold Edward Grange, All-American halfback at the University of Illinois (1923–1925) who played professionally with the Chicago Bears.

JENNY   Nobody. There's nobody with him. I can't deal with him any more, and your father gets all upset everytime he comes. I've got a lot of typing to do, and your father's waiting to sign it. Will you see him?

WILLY [*entering*] Touchdown! Touch— [*He sees* JENNY.] Jenny, Jenny, good to see you. How're ya? Workin'? Or still honest?

JENNY   Fine. How've you been feeling?

WILLY   Not much any more, Jenny. Ha, ha! [*He is surprised to see the rackets.*]

BERNARD   Hello, Uncle Willy.

WILLY [*almost shocked*] Bernard! Well, look who's here! [*He comes quickly, guiltily, to* BERNARD *and warmly shakes his hand.*]

BERNARD   How are you? Good to see you.

WILLY   What are you doing here?

BERNARD   Oh, just stopped by to see Pop. Get off my feet till my train leaves. I'm going to Washington in a few minutes.

WILLY   Is he in?

BERNARD   Yes, he's in his office with the accountant. Sit down.

WILLY [*sitting down*] What're you going to do in Washington?

BERNARD   Oh, just a case I've got there, Willy.

WILLY   That so? [*Indicating the rackets*] You going to play tennis there?

BERNARD   I'm staying with a friend who's got a court.

WILLY   Don't say. His own tennis court. Must be fine people, I bet.

BERNARD   They are, very nice. Dad tells me Biff's in town.

WILLY [*with a big smile*] Yeah, Biff's in. Working on a very big deal, Bernard.

BERNARD   What's Biff doing?

WILLY   Well, he's been doing very big things in the West. But he decided to establish himself here. Very big. We're having dinner. Did I hear your wife had a boy?

BERNARD   That's right. Our second.

WILLY   Two boys! What do you know!

BERNARD   What kind of a deal has Biff got?

WILLY   Well, Bill Oliver—very big sporting-goods man—he wants Biff very badly. Called him from the West. Long distance, carte blanche, special deliveries. Your friends have their own private tennis court?

BERNARD   You still with the old firm, Willy?

WILLY [*after a pause*] I'm—I'm overjoyed to see how you made the grade, Bernard, overjoyed. It's an encouraging thing to see a young man really—really— Looks very good for Biff—very— [*He breaks off, then*] Bernard— [*He is so full of emotion, he breaks off again.*]

BERNARD   What is it, Willy?

WILLY [*small and alone*] What—what's the secret?

BERNARD   What secret?

WILLY   How—how did you? Why didn't he ever catch on?

BERNARD   I wouldn't know that, Willy.

WILLY [*confidentially, desperately*] You were his friend, his boyhood friend. There's something I don't understand about it. His life ended after that Ebbets Field game. From the age of seventeen nothing good ever happened to him.

BERNARD   He never trained himself for anything.

WILLY   But he did, he did. After high school he took so many correspondence courses. Radio mechanics; television; God knows what, and never made the slightest mark.

BERNARD [*taking off his glasses*]   Willy, do you want to talk candidly?

WILLY [*rising, faces* BERNARD]   I regard you as a very brilliant man, Bernard. I value your advice.

BERNARD   Oh, the hell with the advice, Willy. I couldn't advise you. There's just one thing I've always wanted to ask you. When he was supposed to graduate, and the math teacher flunked him—

WILLY   Oh, that son-of-a-bitch ruined his life.

BERNARD   Yeah, but, Willy, all he had to do was go to summer school and make up that subject.

WILLY   That's right, that's right.

BERNARD   Did you tell him not to go to summer school?

WILLY   Me? I begged him to go. I ordered him to go!

BERNARD   Then why wouldn't he go?

WILLY   Why? Why! Bernard, that question has been trailing me like a ghost for the last fifteen years. He flunked the subject, and laid down and died like a hammer hit him!

BERNARD   Take it easy, kid.

WILLY   Let me talk to you—I got nobody to talk to. Bernard, Bernard, was it my fault? Y'see? It keeps going around in my mind, maybe I did something to him. I got nothing to give him.

BERNARD   Don't take it so hard.

WILLY   Why did he lay down? What is the story there? You were his friend!

BERNARD   Willy, I remember, it was June, and our grades came out. And he's flunked math.

WILLY   That son-of-a-bitch!

BERNARD   No, it wasn't right then. Biff just got very angry, I remember, and he was ready to enroll in summer school.

WILLY [*surprised*]   He was?

BERNARD   He wasn't beaten by it·at all. But then, Willy, he disappeared from the block for almost a month. And I got the idea that he'd gone up to New England to see you. Did he have a talk with you then?

WILLY *stares in silence.*

BERNARD   Willy?

WILLY [*with a strong edge of resentment in his voice*]   Yeah, he came to Boston. What about it?

BERNARD   Well, just that when he came back—I'll never forget this, it always mystifies me. Because I'd thought so well of Biff, even though he'd always taken advantage of me. I loved him, Willy, y'know? And he came back after that month and took his sneakers— remember those sneakers with "University of Virginia" printed on them? He was so proud of those, wore them every day. And he took them down in the cellar, and burned them up in the furnace. We had a fist fight. It lasted at least half an hour. Just the two of us, punching each other down the cellar, and crying right through it. I've often thought how strange it was that I knew he'd given up his life. What happened in Boston, Willy?

WILLY *looks at him as at an intruder.*

BERNARD   I just bring it up because you asked me.
WILLY [*angrily*] Nothing. What do you mean, "What happened?" What's that got to do with anything?
BERNARD   Well, don't get sore.
WILLY   What are you trying to do, blame it on me? If a boy lays down is that my fault?
BERNARD   Now, Willy, don't get—
WILLY   Well, don't—don't talk to me that way! What does that mean, "What happened?"

CHARLEY *enters. He is in his vest, and he carries a bottle of bourbon.*

CHARLEY   Hey, you're going to miss that train. [*He waves the bottle.*]
BERNARD   Yeah, I'm going. [*He takes the bottle.*] Thanks, Pop. [*He picks up his rackets and bag.*] Good-by, Willy, and don't worry about it. You know, "If at first you don't succeed . . ."
WILLY   Yes, I believe in that.
BERNARD   But sometimes, Willy, it's better for a man just to walk away.
WILLY   Walk away?
BERNARD   That's right.
WILLY   But if you can't walk away?
BERNARD [*after a slight pause*] I guess that's when it's tough. [*Extending his hand*] Good-by, Willy.
WILLY [*shaking* BERNARD's *hand*] Good-by, boy.
CHARLEY [*an arm on* BERNARD's *shoulder*] How do you like this kid? Gonna argue a case in front of the Supreme Court.
BERNARD [*protesting*] Pop!
WILLY [*genuinely shocked, pained, and happy*] No! The Supreme Court!
BERNARD   I gotta run. 'By, Dad!
CHARLEY   Knock 'em dead, Bernard!

BERNARD *goes off.*

WILLY [*as* CHARLEY *takes out his wallet*] The Supreme Court! And he didn't even mention it!
CHARLEY [*counting out money on the desk*] He don't have to—he's gonna do it.
WILLY   And you never told him what to do, did you? You never took any interest in him.

CHARLEY   My salvation is that I never took any interest in anything. There's some money—fifty dollars. I got an accountant inside.
WILLY   Charley, look . . . [*With difficulty*] I got my insurance to pay. If you can manage it—I need a hundred and ten dollars.

CHARLEY *doesn't reply for a moment; merely stops moving.*

WILLY   I'd draw it from my bank but Linda would know, and I . . .
CHARLEY   Sit down, Willy.
WILLY [*moving toward the chair*]   I'm keeping an account of everything, remember. I'll pay every penny back. [*He sits.*]
CHARLEY   Now listen to me, Willy.
WILLY   I want you to know I appreciate . . .
CHARLEY [*sitting down on the table*]   Willy, what're you doin? What the hell is goin' on in your head?
WILLY   Why? I'm simply . . .
CHARLEY   I offered you a job. You can make fifty dollars a week. And I won't send you on the road.
WILLY   I've got a job.
CHARLEY   Without pay? What kind of a job is a job without pay? [*He rises.*] Now, look, kid, enough is enough. I'm no genius but I know when I'm being insulted.
WILLY   Insulted!
CHARLEY   Why don't you want to work for me?
WILLY   What's the matter with you? I've got a job.
CHARLEY   Then what're you walkin' in here every week for?
WILLY [*getting up*]   Well, if you don't want me to walk in here—
CHARLEY   I am offering you a job.
WILLY   I don't want your goddam job!
CHARLEY   When the hell are you going to grow up?
WILLY [*furiously*]   You big ignoramus, if you say that to me again I'll rap you one! I don't care how big you are! [*He's ready to fight.*]

Pause.

CHARLEY [*kindly, going to him*]   How much do you need, Willy?
WILLY   Charley, I'm strapped. I'm strapped. I don't know what to do. I was just fired.
CHARLEY   Howard fired you?
WILLY   That snotnose. Imagine that? I named him. I named him Howard.
CHARLEY   Willy, when're you gonna realize that them things don't mean anything? You named him Howard, but you can't sell that. The only thing you got in this world is what you can sell. And the funny thing is that you're a salesman, and you don't know that.
WILLY   I've always tried to think otherwise, I guess. I always felt that if a man was impressive, and well liked, that nothing—
CHARLEY   Why must everybody like you? Who liked J. P. Morgan?[8] Was he impressive? In a Turkish bath he'd look like a butcher.

8. John Pierpont Morgan (1887–1943), famous New York banker and financier.

But with his pockets on he was very well liked. Now listen, Willy, I know you don't like me, and nobody can say I'm in love with you, but I'll give you a job because—just for the hell of it, put it that way. Now what do you say?

WILLY   I—I just can't work for you, Charley.

CHARLEY   What're you, jealous of me?

WILLY   I can't work for you, that's all, don't ask me why.

CHARLEY [*angered, takes out more bills*]   You been jealous of me all your life, you damned fool! Here, pay your insurance. [*He puts the money in* WILLY'*s hand.*]

WILLY   I'm keeping strict accounts.

CHARLEY   I've got some work to do. Take care of yourself. And pay your insurance.

WILLY [*moving to the right*]   Funny, y'know? After all the highways, and the trains, and the appointments, and the years, you end up worth more dead than alive.

CHARLEY   Willy, nobody's worth nothin' dead. [*After a slight pause*] Did you hear what I said?

> WILLY *stands still, dreaming.*

CHARLEY   Willy!

WILLY   Apologize to Bernard for me when you see him. I didn't mean to argue with him. He's a fine boy. They're all fine boys, and they'll end up big—all of them. Someday they'll all play tennis together. Wish me luck, Charley. He saw Bill Oliver today.

CHARLEY   Good luck.

WILLY [*on the verge of tears*]   Charley, you're the only friend I got. Isn't that a remarkable thing? [*He goes out.*]

CHARLEY   Jesus!

> CHARLEY *stares after him a moment and follows. All light blacks out. Suddenly raucous music is heard, and a red glow rises behind the screen at right.* STANLEY, *a young waiter, appears, carrying a table, followed by* HAPPY, *who is carrying two chairs.*

STANLEY [*putting the table down*]   That's all right, Mr. Loman, I can handle it myself. [*He turns and takes the chairs from* HAPPY *and places them at the table.*]

HAPPY [*glancing around*]   Oh, this is better.

STANLEY   Sure, in the front there you're in the middle of all kinds a noise. Whenever you got a party, Mr. Loman, you just tell me and I'll put you back here. Y'know, there's a lotta people they don't like it private, because when they go out they like to see a lotta action around them because they're sick and tired to stay in the house by theirself. But I know you, you ain't from Hackensack. You know what I mean?

HAPPY [*sitting down*]   So how's it coming, Stanley?

STANLEY   Ah, it's a dog's life. I only wish during the war they'd a took me in the Army. I coulda been dead by now.

HAPPY   My brother's back, Stanley.
STANLEY   Oh, he come back, heh? From the Far West.
HAPPY   Yeah, big cattle man, my brother, so treat him right. And my father's coming too.
STANLEY   Oh, your father too!
HAPPY   You got a couple of nice lobsters?
STANLEY   Hundred per cent, big.
HAPPY   I want them with the claws.
STANLEY   Don't worry, I don't give you no mice. [HAPPY *laughs.*] How about some wine? It'll put a head on the meal.
HAPPY   No. You remember, Stanley, that recipe I brought you from overseas? With the champagne in it?
STANLEY   Oh, yeah, sure. I still got it tacked up yet in the kitchen. But that'll have to cost a buck apiece anyways.
HAPPY   That's all right.
STANLEY   What'd you, hit a number or somethin'?
HAPPY   No, it's a little celebration. My brother is—I think he pulled off a big deal today. I think we're going into business together.
STANLEY   Great! That's the best for you. Because a family business, you know what I mean?—that's the best.
HAPPY   That's what I think.
STANLEY   'Cause what's the difference? Somebody steals? It's in the family. Know what I mean? [*Sotto voce*] Like this bartender here. The boss is goin' crazy what kinda leak he's got in the cash register. You put it in but it don't come out.
HAPPY [*raising his head*]   Sh!
STANLEY   What?
HAPPY   You notice I wasn't lookin' right or left, was I?
STANLEY   No.
HAPPY   And my eyes are closed.
STANLEY   So what's the—?
HAPPY   Strudel's comin'.
STANLEY [*catching on, looks around*]   Ah, no, there's no—

He breaks off as a furred, lavishly dressed GIRL *enters and sits at the next table. Both follow her with their eyes.*

STANLEY   Geez, how'd ya know?
HAPPY   I got radar or something. [*Staring directly at her profile*] Oooooooo . . . Stanley.
STANLEY   I think that's for you, Mr. Loman.
HAPPY   Look at that mouth. Oh, God. And the binoculars.
STANLEY   Geez, you got a life, Mr. Loman.
HAPPY   Wait on her.
STANLEY [*going to the* GIRL's *table*]   Would you like a menu, ma'am?
GIRL   I'm expecting someone, but I'd like a—
HAPPY   Why don't you bring her—excuse me, miss, do you mind? I sell champagne, and I'd like you to try my brand. Bring her a champagne, Stanley.
GIRL   That's awfully nice of you.
HAPPY   Don't mention it. It's all company money. [*He laughs.*]

GIRL   That's a charming product to be selling, isn't it?

HAPPY   Oh, gets to be like everything else. Selling is selling, y'know.

GIRL   I suppose.

HAPPY   You don't happen to sell, do you?

GIRL   No, I don't sell.

HAPPY   Would you object to a compliment from a stranger? You ought to be on a magazine cover.

GIRL   [*looking at him a little archly*]   I have been.

STANLEY *comes in with a glass of champagne.*

HAPPY   What'd I say before, Stanley? You see? She's a cover girl.

STANLEY   Oh, I could see, I could see.

HAPPY   [*to the* GIRL]   What magazine?

GIRL   Oh, a lot of them. [*She takes the drink.*] Thank you.

HAPPY   You know what they say in France, don't you? "Champagne is the drink of the complexion"—Hya, Biff!

BIFF *has entered and sits with* HAPPY.

BIFF   Hello, kid. Sorry I'm late.

HAPPY   I just got here. Uh, Miss—?

GIRL   Forsythe.

HAPPY   Miss Forsythe, this is my brother.

BIFF   Is Dad here?

HAPPY   His name is Biff. You might've heard of him. Great football player.

GIRL   Really? What team?

HAPPY   Are you familiar with football?

GIRL   No, I'm afraid I'm not.

HAPPY   Biff is quarterback with the New York Giants.

GIRL   Well, that is nice, isn't it? [*She drinks.*]

HAPPY   Good health.

GIRL   I'm happy to meet you.

HAPPY   That's my name. Hap. It's really Harold, but at West Point they called me Happy.

GIRL   [*now really impressed*]   Oh, I see. How do you do? [*She turns her profile.*]

BIFF   Isn't Dad coming?

HAPPY   You want her?

BIFF   Oh, I could never make that.

HAPPY   I remember the time that idea would never come into your head. Where's the old confidence, Biff?

BIFF   I just saw Oliver—

HAPPY   Wait a minute. I've got to see that old confidence again. Do you want her? She's on call.

BIFF   Oh, no. [*He turns to look at the* GIRL.]

HAPPY   I'm telling you. Watch this. [*Turning to the* GIRL] Honey? [*She turns to him.*] Are you busy?

GIRL   Well, I am . . . but I could make a phone call.

HAPPY   Do that, will you, honey? And see if you can get a friend.

We'll be here for a while. Biff is one of the greatest football players in the country.

GIRL [*standing up*]   Well, I'm certainly happy to meet you.

HAPPY   Come back soon.

GIRL   I'll try.

HAPPY   Don't try, honey, try hard.

The GIRL *exits.* STANLEY *follows, shaking his head in bewildered admiration.*

HAPPY   Isn't that a shame now? A beautiful girl like that? That's why I can't get married. There's not a good woman in a thousand. New York is loaded with them, kid!

BIFF   Hap, look—

HAPPY   I told you she was on call!

BIFF [*strangely unnerved*]   Cut it out, will ya? I want to say something to you.

HAPPY   Did you see Oliver?

BIFF   I saw him all right. Now look, I want to tell Dad a couple of things and I want you to help me.

HAPPY   What? Is he going to back you?

BIFF   Are you crazy? You're out of your goddam head, you know that?

HAPPY   Why? What happened?

BIFF [*breathlessly*]   I did a terrible thing today, Hap. It's been the strangest day I ever went through. I'm all numb, I swear.

HAPPY   You mean he wouldn't see you?

BIFF   Well, I waited six hours for him, see? All day. Kept sending my name in. Even tried to date his secretary so she'd get me to him, but no soap.

HAPPY   Because you're not showin' the old confidence, Biff. He remembered you, didn't he?

BIFF [*stopping* HAPPY *with a gesture*]   Finally, about five o'clock, he comes out. Didn't remember who I was or anything. I felt like such an idiot, Hap.

HAPPY   Did you tell him my Florida idea?

BIFF   He walked away. I saw him for one minute. I got so mad I could've torn the walls down! How the hell did I ever get the idea I was a salesman there? I even believed myself that I'd been a salesman for him! And then he gave me one look and—I realized what a ridiculous lie my whole life has been! We've been talking in a dream for fifteen years. I was a shipping clerk.

HAPPY   What'd you do?

BIFF [*with great tension and wonder*]   Well, he left, see. And the secretary went out. I was all alone in the waiting room. I don't know what came over me, Hap. The next thing I know I'm in his office—paneled walls, everything. I can't explain it. I—Hap, I took his fountain pen.

HAPPY   Geez, did he catch you?

BIFF   I ran out. I ran down all eleven flights. I ran and ran and ran.

HAPPY   That was an awful dumb—what'd you do that for?

BIFF [*agonized*]   I don't know, I just—wanted to take something, I don't know. You gotta help me, Hap, I'm gonna tell Pop.

HAPPY   You crazy? What for?

BIFF   Hap, he's got to understand that I'm not the man somebody lends that kind of money to. He thinks I've been spiting him all these years and it's eating him up.

HAPPY   That's just it. You tell him something nice.

BIFF   I can't.

HAPPY   Say you got a lunch date with Oliver tomorrow.

BIFF   So what do I do tomorrow?

HAPPY   You leave the house tomorrow and come back at night and say Oliver is thinking it over. And he thinks it over for a couple of weeks, and gradually it fades away and nobody's the worse.

BIFF   But it'll go on forever!

HAPPY   Dad is never so happy as when he's looking forward to something!

WILLY *enters.*

HAPPY   Hello, scout!

WILLY   Gee, I haven't been here in years!

STANLEY *has followed* WILLY *in and sets a chair for him.* STANLEY *starts off but* HAPPY *stops him.*

HAPPY   Stanley!

STANLEY *stands by, waiting for an order.*

BIFF [*going to* WILLY *with guilt, as to an invalid*]   Sit down, Pop. You want a drink?

WILLY   Sure, I don't mind.

BIFF   Let's get a load on.

WILLY   You look worried.

BIFF   N-no. [*To* STANLEY] Scotch all around. Make it doubles.

STANLEY   Doubles, right. [*He goes.*]

WILLY   You had a couple already, didn't you?

BIFF   Just a couple, yeah.

WILLY   Well, what happened, boy? [*Nodding affirmatively, with a smile*] Everything go all right?

BIFF [*takes a breath, then reaches out and grasps* WILLY'*s hand*] Pal . . . [*He is smiling bravely, and* WILLY *is smiling too.*] I had an experience today.

HAPPY   Terrific, Pop.

WILLY   That so? What happened?

BIFF [*high, slightly alcoholic, above the earth*]   I'm going to tell you everything from first to last. It's been a strange day. [*Silence. He looks around, composes himself as best he can, but his breath keeps breaking the rhythm of his voice.*] I had to wait quite a while for him, and—

WILLY   Oliver?

BIFF   Yeah, Oliver. All day, as a matter of cold fact. And a lot of—instances—facts, Pop, facts about my life came back to me. Who was it, Pop? Who ever said I was a salesman with Oliver?

WILLY   Well, you were.

BIFF   No, Dad, I was a shipping clerk.

WILLY   But you were practically—

BIFF   [*with determination*]   Dad, I don't know who said it first, but I was never a salesman for Bill Oliver.

WILLY   What're you talking about?

BIFF   Let's hold on to the facts tonight, Pop. We're not going to get anywhere bullin' around. I was a shipping clerk.

WILLY   [*angrily*]   All right, now listen to me—

BIFF   Why don't you let me finish?

WILLY   I'm not interested in stories about the past or any crap of that kind because the woods are burning, boys, you understand? There's a big blaze going on all around. I was fired today.

BIFF   [*shocked*]   How could you be?

WILLY   I was fired, and I'm looking for a little good news to tell your mother, because the woman has waited and the woman has suffered. The gist of it is that I haven't got a story left in my head, Biff. So don't give me a lecture about facts and aspects. I am not interested. Now what've you got to say to me?

STANLEY *enters with three drinks. They wait until he leaves.*

WILLY   Did you see Oliver?

BIFF   Jesus, Dad!

WILLY   You mean you didn't go up there?

HAPPY   Sure he went up there.

BIFF   I did. I—saw him. How could they fire you?

WILLY   [*on the edge of his chair*]   What kind of a welcome did he give you?

BIFF   He won't even let you work on commission?

WILLY   I'm out! [*Driving*] So tell me, he gave you a warm welcome?

HAPPY   Sure, Pop, sure!

BIFF   [*driven*]   Well, it was kind of—

WILLY   I was wondering if he'd remember you. [*To* HAPPY] Imagine, man doesn't see him for ten, twelve years and gives him that kind of a welcome!

HAPPY   Damn right!

BIFF   [*trying to return to the offensive*]   Pop, look—

WILLY   You know why he remembered you, don't you? Because you impressed him in those days.

BIFF   Let's talk quietly and get this down to the facts, huh?

WILLY   [*as though* BIFF *had been interrupting*]   Well, what happened? It's great news, Biff. Did he take you into his office or'd you talk in the waiting room?

BIFF   Well, he came in, see, and—

WILLY   [*with a big smile*]   What'd he say? Betcha he threw his arm around you.

BIFF   Well, he kinda—

Arthur Miller

WILLY He's a fine man. [*To* HAPPY] Very hard man to see, y'know.
HAPPY [*agreeing*] Oh, I know.
WILLY [*to* BIFF] Is that where you had the drinks?
BIFF Yeah, he gave me a couple of—no, no!
HAPPY [*cutting in*] He told him my Florida idea.
WILLY Don't interrupt. [*To* BIFF] How'd he react to the Florida idea?
BIFF Dad, will you give me a minute to explain?
WILLY I've been waiting for you to explain since I sat down here!
  What happened? He took you into his office and what?
BIFF Well—I talked. And—and he listened, see.
WILLY Famous for the way he listens, y'know. What was his answer?
BIFF His answer was— [*He breaks off, suddenly angry.*] Dad, you're
  not letting me tell you what I want to tell you!
WILLY [*accusing, angered*] You didn't see him, did you?
BIFF I did see him!
WILLY What'd you insult him or something? You insulted him,
  didn't you?
BIFF Listen, will you let me out of it, will you just let me out of it!
HAPPY What the hell!
WILLY Tell me what happened!
BIFF [*to* HAPPY] I can't talk to him!

> *A single trumpet note jars the ear. The light of green leaves
> stains the house, which holds the air of night and a dream.*
> YOUNG BERNARD *enters and knocks on the door of the house.*

YOUNG BERNARD [*frantically*] Mrs. Loman, Mrs. Loman!
HAPPY Tell him what happened!
BIFF [*to* HAPPY] Shut up and leave me alone!
WILLY No, no! You had to go and flunk math!
BIFF What math? What're you talking about?
YOUNG BERNARD Mrs. Loman, Mrs. Loman!

> LINDA *appears in the house, as of old.*

WILLY [*wildly*] Math, math, math!
BIFF Take it easy, Pop!
YOUNG BERNARD Mrs. Loman!
WILLY [*furiously*] If you hadn't flunked you'd've been set by now!
BIFF Now, look, I'm gonna tell you what happened, and you're going
  to listen to me.
YOUNG BERNARD Mrs. Loman!
BIFF I waited six hours—
HAPPY What the hell are you saying?
BIFF I kept sending in my name but he wouldn't see me. So finally
  he . . . [*He continues unheard as light fades low on the restaurant.*]
YOUNG BERNARD Biff flunked math!
LINDA No!
YOUNG BERNARD Birnbaum flunked him! They won't graduate him!
LINDA But they have to. He's gotta go to the university. Where is he?
  Biff! Biff!

YOUNG BERNARD   No, he left. He went to Grand Central.

LINDA   Grand— You mean he went to Boston!

YOUNG BERNARD   Is Uncle Willy in Boston?

LINDA   Oh, maybe Willy can talk to the teacher. Oh, the poor, poor boy!

Light on house area snaps out.

BIFF [*at the table, now audible, holding up a gold fountain pen*] . . . so I'm washed up with Oliver, you understand? Are you listening to me?

WILLY [*at a loss*]   Yeah, sure. If you hadn't flunked—

BIFF   Flunked what? What're you talking about?

WILLY   Don't blame everything on me! I didn't flunk math—you did! What pen?

HAPPY   That was awful dumb, Biff, a pen like that is worth—

WILLY [*seeing the pen for the first time*]   You took Oliver's pen?

BIFF [*weakening*]   Dad, I just explained it to you.

WILLY   You stole Bill Oliver's fountain pen!

BIFF   I didn't exactly steal it! That's just what I've been explaining to you!

HAPPY   He had it in his hand and just then Oliver walked in, so he got nervous and stuck it in his pocket!

WILLY   My God, Biff!

BIFF   I never intended to do it, Dad!

OPERATOR'S VOICE   Standish Arms, good evening!

WILLY [*shouting*]   I'm not in my room!

BIFF [*frightened*]   Dad, what's the matter? [*He and* HAPPY *stand up.*]

OPERATOR   Ringing Mr. Loman for you!

WILLY   I'm not there, stop it!

BIFF [*horrified, gets down on one knee before* WILLY]   Dad, I'll make good, I'll make good. [WILLY *tries to get to his feet.* BIFF *holds him down.*] Sit down now.

WILLY   No, you're no good, you're no good for anything.

BIFF   I am, Dad, I'll find something else, you understand? Now don't worry about anything. [*He holds up* WILLY'S *face*] Talk to me, Dad.

OPERATOR   Mr. Loman does not answer. Shall I page him?

WILLY [*attempting to stand, as though to rush and silence the Operator*]   No, no, no!

HAPPY   He'll strike something, Pop.

WILLY   No, no . . .

BIFF [*desperately, standing over* WILLY]   Pop listen! Listen to me! I'm telling you something good. Oliver talked to his partner about the Florida idea. You listening? He—he talked to his partner, and he came to me . . . I'm going to be all right, you hear? Dad, listen to me, he said it was just a question of the amount!

WILLY   Then you . . . got it?

HAPPY   He's gonna be terrific, Pop!

WILLY [*trying to stand*]   Then you got it, haven't you? You got it! You got it!

BIFF [*agonized, holds* WILLY *down*]   No, no. Look, Pop. I'm supposed to have lunch with them tomorrow. I'm just telling you this so you'll know that I can still make an impression, Pop. And I'll make good somewhere, but I can't go tomorrow, see?

WILLY   Why not? You simply—

BIFF   But the pen, Pop!

WILLY   You give it to him and tell him it was an oversight!

HAPPY   Sure, have lunch tomorrow!

BIFF   I can't say that—

WILLY   You were doing a crossword puzzle and accidentally used his pen!

BIFF   Listen, kid, I took those balls years ago, now I walk in with his fountain pen? That clinches it, don't you see? I can't face him like that! I'll try elsewhere.

PAGE'S VOICE   Paging Mr. Loman!

WILLY   Don't you want to be anything?

BIFF   Pop, how can I go back?

WILLY   You don't want to be anything, is that what's behind it?

BIFF   [*now angry at* WILLY *for not crediting his sympathy*]   Don't take it that way! You think it was easy walking into that office after what I'd done to him? A team of horses couldn't have dragged me back to Bill Oliver!

WILLY   Then why'd you go?

BIFF   Why did I go? Why did I go! Look at you! Look at what's become of you!

Off left, THE WOMAN *laughs.*

WILLY   Biff, you're going to go to that lunch tomorrow, or—

BIFF   I can't go. I've got no appointment!

HAPPY   Biff, for . . . !

WILLY   Are you spiting me?

BIFF   Don't take it that way! Goddammit!

WILLY   [*strikes* BIFF *and falters away from the table*]   You rotten little louse! Are you spiting me?

THE WOMAN   Someone's at the door, Willy!

BIFF   I'm no good, can't you see what I am?

HAPPY   [*separating them*]   Hey, you're in a restaurant! Now cut it out, both of you! [*The girls enter.*] Hello, girls, sit down.

THE WOMAN *laughs, off left.*

MISS FORSYTHE   I guess we might as well. This is Letta.

THE WOMAN   Willy, are you going to wake up?

BIFF   [*ignoring* WILLY]   How're ya, miss, sit down. What do you drink?

MISS FORSYTHE   Letta might not be able to stay long.

LETTA   I gotta get up very early tomorrow. I got jury duty. I'm so excited! Were you fellows ever on a jury?

BIFF   No, but I been in front of them! [*The girls laugh.*] This is my father.

LETTA Isn't he cute? Sit down with us, Pop.

HAPPY Sit him down, Biff!

BIFF [*going to him*] Come on, slugger, drink us under the table. To hell with it! Come on, sit down, pal.

> On BIFF's *last insistence,* WILLY *is about to sit.*

THE WOMAN [*now urgently*] Willy, are you going to answer the door!

> THE WOMAN's *call pulls* WILLY *back. He starts right, befuddled.*

BIFF Hey, where are you going?

WILLY Open the door.

BIFF The door?

WILLY The washroom . . . the door . . . where's the door?

BIFF [*leading* WILLY *to the left*] Just go straight down.

> WILLY *moves left.*

THE WOMAN Willy, Willy, are you going to get up, get up, get up, get up?

> WILLY *exits left.*

LETTA I think it's sweet you bring your daddy along.

MISS FORSYTHE Oh, he isn't really your father!

BIFF [*at left, turning to her resentfully*] Miss Forsythe, you've just seen a prince walk by. A fine, troubled prince. A hard-working, unappreciated prince. A pal, you understand? A good companion. Always for his boys.

LETTA That's so sweet.

HAPPY Well, girls, what's the program? We're wasting time. Come on, Biff. Gather round. Where would you like to go?

BIFF Why don't you do something for him?

HAPPY Me!

BIFF Don't you give a damn for him, Hap?

HAPPY What're you talking about? I'm the one who—

BIFF I sense it, you don't give a good goddam about him. [*He takes the rolled-up hose from his pocket and puts it on the table in front of* HAPPY.] Look what I found in the cellar, for Christ's sake. How can you bear to let it go on?

HAPPY Me? Who goes away? Who runs off and—

BIFF Yeah, but he doesn't mean anything to you. You could help him—I can't! Don't you understand what I'm talking about? He's going to kill himself, don't you know that?

HAPPY Don't I know it! Me!

BIFF Hap, help him! Jesus . . . help him . . . Help me, help me, I can't bear to look at his face! [*Ready to weep, he hurries out, up right.*]

HAPPY [*starting after him*] Where are you going?

MISS FORSYTHE   What's he so mad about?

HAPPY   Come on, girls, we'll catch up with him.

MISS FORSYTHE [*as* HAPPY *pushes her out*]   Say, I don't like that temper of his!

HAPPY   He's just a little overstrung, he'll be all right!

WILLY [*off left, as* THE WOMAN *laughs*]   Don't answer! Don't answer!

LETTA   Don't you want to tell your father—

HAPPY   No, that's not my father. He's just a guy. Come on, we'll catch Biff, and, honey, we're going to paint this town! Stanley, where's the check! Hey, Stanley!

They exit. STANLEY *looks toward left.*

STANLEY [*calling to* HAPPY *indignantly*]   Mr. Loman! Mr. Loman!

STANLEY *picks up a chair and follows them off. Knocking is heard off left.* THE WOMAN *enters, laughing.* WILLY *follows her. She is in a black slip; he is buttoning his shirt. Raw, sensuous music accompanies their speech.*

WILLY   Will you stop laughing? Will you stop?

THE WOMAN   Aren't you going to answer the door? He'll wake the whole hotel.

WILLY   I'm not expecting anybody.

THE WOMAN   Whyn't you have another drink, honey, and stop being so damn self-centered?

WILLY   I'm so lonely.

THE WOMAN   You know you ruined me, Willy? From now on, whenever you come to the office, I'll see that you go right through to the buyers. No waiting at my desk any more, Willy. You ruined me.

WILLY   That's nice of you to say that.

THE WOMAN   Gee, you are self-centered! Why so sad? You are the saddest, self-centeredest soul I ever did see-saw. [*She laughs. He kisses her.*] Come on inside, drummer boy. It's silly to be dressing in the middle of the night. [*As knocking is heard*] Aren't you going to answer the door?

WILLY   They're knocking on the wrong door.

THE WOMAN   But I felt the knocking. And he heard us talking in here. Maybe the hotel's on fire!

WILLY [*his terror rising*]   It's a mistake.

THE WOMAN   Then tell him to go away!

WILLY   There's nobody there.

THE WOMAN   It's getting on my nerves, Willy. There's somebody standing out there and it's getting on my nerves!

WILLY [*pushing her away from him*]   All right, stay in the bathroom here, and don't come out. I think there's a law in Massachusetts about it, so don't come out. It may be that new room clerk. He looked very mean. So don't come out. It's a mistake, there's no fire.

The knocking is heard again. He takes a few steps away from her, and she vanishes into the wing. The light follows him, and now he is facing YOUNG BIFF, *who carries a suitcase.* BIFF *steps toward him. The music is gone.*

BIFF   Why didn't you answer?

WILLY   Biff! What are you doing in Boston?

BIFF   Why didn't you answer? I've been knocking for five minutes, I called you on the phone—

WILLY   I just heard you. I was in the bathroom and had the door shut. Did anything happen home?

BIFF   Dad—I let you down.

WILLY   What do you mean?

BIFF   Dad . . .

WILLY   Biffo, what's this about? [*Putting his arm around* BIFF] Come on, let's go downstairs and get you a malted.

BIFF   Dad, I flunked math.

WILLY   Not for the term?

BIFF   The term. I haven't got enough credits to graduate.

WILLY   You mean to say Bernard wouldn't give you the answers?

BIFF   He did, he tried, but I only got a sixty-one.

WILLY   And they wouldn't give you four points?

BIFF   Birnbaum refused absolutely. I begged him, Pop, but he won't give me those points. You gotta talk to him before they close the school. Because if he saw the kind of man you are, and you just talked to him in your way, I'm sure he'd come through for me. The class came right before practice, see, and I didn't go enough. Would you talk to him? He'd like you, Pop. You know the way you could talk.

WILLY   You're on. We'll drive right back.

BIFF   Oh, Dad, good work! I'm sure he'll change it for you!

WILLY   Go downstairs and tell the clerk I'm checkin' out. Go right down.

BIFF   Yes, sir! See, the reason he hates me, Pop—one day he was late for class so I got up at the blackboard and imitated him. I crossed my eyes and talked with a lithp.

WILLY [*laughing*]   You did? The kids like it?

BIFF   They nearly died laughing!

WILLY   Yeah? What'd you do?

BIFF   The thquare root of thixthy twee is . . . [WILLY *bursts out laughing;* BIFF *joins him.*] And in the middle of it he walked in!

WILLY *laughs and* THE WOMAN *joins in offstage.*

WILLY [*without hesitation*]   Hurry downstairs and—

BIFF   Somebody in there?

WILLY   No, that was next door.

THE WOMAN *laughs offstage.*

BIFF   Somebody got in your bathroom!

WILLY   No, it's the next room, there's a party—

THE WOMAN [*enters, laughing. She lisps this*]   Can I come in? There's something in the bathtub, Willy, and it's moving!

WILLY *looks at* BIFF, *who is staring open-mouthed and horrified at* THE WOMAN.

WILLY   Ah—you better go back to your room. They must be finished painting by now. They're painting her room so I let her take a shower here. Go back, go back . . . [*He pushes her.*]
THE WOMAN [*resisting*]   But I've got to get dressed, Willy, I can't—
WILLY   Get out of here! Go back, go back . . . [*Suddenly striving for the ordinary*] This is Miss Francis, Biff, she's a buyer. They're painting her room. Go back, Miss Francis, go back . . .
THE WOMAN   But my clothes, I can't go out naked in the hall!
WILLY [*pushing her offstage*]   Get outa here! Go back, go back!

BIFF *slowly sits down on his suitcase as the argument continues offstage.*

THE WOMAN   Where's my stockings? You promised me stockings, Willy!
WILLY   I have no stockings here!
THE WOMAN   You had two boxes of size nine sheers for me, and I want them!
WILLY   Here, for God's sake, will you get outa here!
THE WOMAN [*enters holding a box of stockings*]   I just hope there's nobody in the hall. That's all I hope. [*To* BIFF] Are you football or baseball?
BIFF   Football.
THE WOMAN [*angry, humiliated*]   That's me too. G'night. [*She snatches her clothes from* WILLY, *and walks out.*]
WILLY [*after a pause*]   Well, better get going. I want to get to the school first thing in the morning. Get my suits out of the closet. I'll get my valise. [BIFF *doesn't move.*] What's the matter? [BIFF *remains motionless, tears falling.*] She's a buyer. Buys for J. H. Simmons. She lives down the hall—they're painting. You don't imagine— [*He breaks off. After a pause*] Now listen, pal, she's just a buyer. She sees merchandise in her room and they have to keep it looking just so . . . [*Pause. Assuming command*] All right, get my suits. [BIFF *doesn't move.*] Now stop crying and do as I say. I gave you an order. Biff, I gave you an order! Is that what you do when I give you an order? How dare you cry! [*Putting his arm around* BIFF] Now look, Biff, when you grow up you'll understand about these things. You mustn't—you mustn't overemphasize a thing like this. I'll see Birnbaum first thing in the morning.
BIFF   Never mind.
WILLY [*getting down beside* BIFF]   Never mind! He's going to give you those points. I'll see to it.
BIFF   He wouldn't listen to you.
WILLY   He certainly will listen to me. You need those points for the U. of Virginia.
BIFF   I'm not going there.

WILLY   Heh? If I can't get him to change that mark you'll make it up in summer school. You've got all summer to—

BIFF [*his weeping breaking from him*]   Dad . . .

WILLY [*infected by it*]   Oh, my boy . . .

BIFF   Dad . . .

WILLY   She's nothing to me, Biff. I was lonely, I was terribly lonely.

BIFF   You—you gave her Mama's stockings! [*His tears break through and he rises to go.*]

WILLY [*grabbing for* BIFF]   I gave you an order!

BIFF   Don't touch me, you—liar!

WILLY   Apologize for that!

BIFF   You fake! You phony little fake! You fake! [*overcome, he turns quickly and weeping fully goes out with his suitcase,* WILLY *is left on the floor on his knees.*]

WILLY   I gave you an order! Biff, come back here or I'll beat you! Come back here! I'll whip you!

> STANLEY *comes quickly in from the right and stands in front of* WILLY.

WILLY [*shouts at* STANLEY]   I gave you an order . . .

STANLEY   Hey, let's pick it up, pick it up, Mr. Loman. [*He helps* WILLY *to his feet.*] Your boys left with the chippies. They said they'll see you home.

> *A second waiter watches some distance away.*

WILLY   But we were supposed to have dinner together.

> *Music is heard,* WILLY's *theme.*

STANLEY   Can you make it?

WILLY   I'll—sure, I can make it. [*Suddenly concerned about his clothes*] Do I—I look all right?

STANLEY   Sure, you look all right. [*He flicks a speck off* WILLY's *lapel.*]

WILLY   Here—here's a dollar.

STANLEY   Oh, your son paid me. It's all right.

WILLY [*putting it in* STANLEY's *hand*]   No, take it. You're a good boy.

STANLEY   Oh, no, you don't have to . . .

WILLY   Here—here's some more, I don't need it any more. [*After a slight pause*] Tell me—is there a seed store in the neighborhood?

STANLEY   Seeds? You mean like to plant?

> *As* WILLY *turns,* STANLEY *slips the money back into his jacket pocket.*

WILLY   Yes. Carrots, peas . . .

STANLEY   Well, there's hardware stores on Sixth Avenue, but it may be too late now.

WILLY [*anxiously*]   Oh, I'd better hurry. I've got to get some seeds.

[*He starts off to the right.*] I've got to get some seeds, right away. Nothing's planted. I don't have a thing in the ground.

> WILLY *hurries out as the light goes down.* STANLEY *moves over to the right after him, watches him off. The other waiter has been staring at* WILLY.

STANLEY [*to the waiter*]   Well, whatta you looking at?

> *The waiter picks up the chairs and moves off right.* STANLEY *takes the table and follows him. The light fades on this area. There is a long pause, the sound of the flute coming over. The light gradually rises on the kitchen, which is empty.* HAPPY *appears at the door of the house, followed by* BIFF. HAPPY *is carrying a large bunch of long-stemmed roses. He enters the kitchen, looks around for* LINDA. *Not seeing her, he turns to* BIFF, *who is just outside the house door, and makes a gesture with his hands, indicating "Not here, I guess." He looks into the living room and freezes. Inside,* LINDA, *unseen, is seated,* WILLY'S *coat on her lap. She rises ominously and quietly and moves toward* HAPPY, *who backs up into the kitchen, afraid.*

HAPPY   Hey, what're you doing up? [LINDA *says nothing but moves toward him implacably.*] Where's Pop? [*He keeps backing to the right, and now* LINDA *is in full view in the doorway to the living room.*] Is he sleeping?
LINDA   Where were you?
HAPPY [*trying to laugh it off*]   We met two girls, Mom, very fine types. Here, we brought you some flowers. [*Offering them to her*] Put them in your room, Ma.

> *She knocks them to the floor at* BIFF'S *feet. He has now come inside and closed the door behind him. She stares at* BIFF, *silent.*

HAPPY   Now what'd you do that for? Mom, I want you to have some flowers—
LINDA [*cutting* HAPPY *off, violently to* BIFF]   Don't you care whether he lives or dies?
HAPPY [*going to the stairs*]   Come upstairs, Biff.
BIFF [*with a flare of disgust, to* HAPPY]   Go away from me! [*To* LINDA] What do you mean, lives or dies? Nobody's dying around here, pal.
LINDA   Get out of my sight! Get out of here!
BIFF   I wanna see the boss.
LINDA   You're not going near him!
BIFF   Where is he? [*He moves to the living room and* LINDA *follows.*]
LINDA [*shouting at* BIFF]   You invite him for dinner. He looks forward to it all day—[BIFF *appears in his parents' bedroom, looks around, and exits*]—and then you desert him there. There's no stranger you'd do that to!

HAPPY   Why? He had a swell time with us. Listen, when I—[LINDA *comes back into the kitchen*]—desert him I hope I don't outlive the day!

LINDA   Get out of here!

HAPPY   Now look, Mom . . .

LINDA   Did you have to go to women tonight? You and your lousy rotten whores!

BIFF *re-enters the kitchen.*

HAPPY   Mom, all we did was follow Biff around trying to cheer him up! [*To* BIFF] Boy, what a night you gave me!

LINDA   Get out of here, both of you, and don't come back! I don't want you tormenting him any more. Go on now, get your things together! [*To* BIFF] You can sleep in his apartment. [*She starts to pick up the flowers and stops herself.*] Pick up this stuff, I'm not your maid any more. Pick it up, you bum, you!

HAPPY *turns his back on her in refusal.* BIFF *slowly moves over and gets down on his knees, picking up the flowers.*

LINDA   You're a pair of animals! Not one, not another living soul would have had the cruelty to walk out on that man in a restaurant!

BIFF [*not looking at her*]   Is that what he said?

LINDA   He didn't have to say anything. He was so humiliated he nearly limped when he came in.

HAPPY   But, Mom, he had a great time with us—

BIFF [*cutting him off violently*]   Shut up!

Without another word, HAPPY *goes upstairs.*

LINDA   You! You didn't even go in to see if he was all right!

BIFF [*still on the floor in front of* LINDA, *the flowers in his hand; with self-loathing*]   No. Didn't. Didn't do a damned thing. How do you like that, heh? Left him babbling in a toilet.

LINDA   You louse. You . . .

BIFF   Now you hit it on the nose! [*He gets up, throws the flowers in the wastebasket.*] The scum of the earth, and you're looking at him!

LINDA   Get out of here!

BIFF   I gotta talk to the boss, Mom. Where is he?

LINDA   You're not going near him. Get out of this house!

BIFF [*with absolute assurance, determination*]   No. We're gonna have an abrupt conversation, him and me.

LINDA   You're not talking to him!

Hammering is heard from outside the house, off right. BIFF *turns toward the noise.*

LINDA [*suddenly pleading*]   Will you please leave him alone?

BIFF   What's he doing out there?

LINDA   He's planting the garden!

BIFF [*quietly*]   Now? Oh, my God!

> BIFF *moves outside,* LINDA *following. The light dies down on*
> *them and comes up on the center of the apron as* WILLY *walks*
> *into it. He is carrying a flashlight, a hoe, and a handful of*
> *seed packets. He raps the top of the hoe sharply to fix it*
> *firmly, and then moves to the left, measuring off the distance*
> *with his foot. He holds the flashlight to look at the seed pack-*
> *ets, reading off the instructions. He is in the blue of night.*

WILLY   Carrots . . . quarter-inch apart. Rows . . . one-foot rows. [*He*
measures it off.] One foot. [*He puts down a package and measures*
off.] Beets [*He puts down another package and measures again.*]
Lettuce. [*He reads the package, puts it down.*] One foot— [*He*
breaks off as BEN *appears at the right and moves slowly down to*
him.] What a proposition, ts, ts. Terrific, terrific. 'Cause she's suffered, Ben, the woman has suffered. You understand me? A man
can't go out the way he came in, Ben, a man has got to add up to
something. You can't, you can't— [BEN *moves toward him as though*
to interrupt.] You gotta consider, now. Don't answer so quick. Remember, it's a guaranteed twenty-thousand-dollar proposition. Now
look, Ben, I want you to go through the ins and outs of this thing
with me. I've got nobody to talk to, Ben, and the woman has
suffered, you hear me?

BEN [*standing still, considering*]   What's the proposition?

WILLY   It's twenty thousand dollars on the barrelhead. Guaranteed,
gilt-edged, you understand?

BEN   You don't want to make a fool of yourself. They might not
honor the policy.

WILLY   How can they dare refuse? Didn't I work like a coolie to
meet every premium on the nose? And now they don't pay off?
Impossible!

BEN   It's called a cowardly thing, William.

WILLY   Why? Does it take more guts to stand here the rest of my
life ringing up a zero?

BEN [*yielding*]   That's a point, William. [*He moves, thinking, turns.*]
And twenty thousand—that *is* something one can feel with the hand,
it is there.

WILLY [*now assured, with rising power*]   Oh, Ben, that's the whole
beauty of it! I see it like a diamond, shining in the dark, hard and
rough, that I can pick up and touch in my hand. Not like—like an
appointment! This would not be another damn-fool appointment,
Ben, and it changes all the aspects. Because he thinks I'm nothing,
see, and so he spites me. But the funeral— [*Straightening up*] Ben,
that funeral will be massive! They'll come from Maine, Massachusetts, Vermont, New Hampshire! All the old-timers with the
strange license plates—that boy will be thunder-struck, Ben, because he never realized—I am known! Rhode Island, New York,
New Jersey—I am known, Ben, and he'll see it with his eyes once
and for all. He'll see what I am, Ben! He's in for a shock, that boy!

Death of a Salesman. Act 2 1177
BEN [*coming down to the edge of the garden*] He'll call you a
coward.

WILLY [*suddenly fearful*] No, that would be terrible.

BEN Yes. And a damned fool.

WILLY No, no, he mustn't, I won't have that! [*He is broken and desperate.*]

BEN He'll hate you, William.

The gay music of the Boys is heard.

WILLY Oh, Ben, how do we get back to all the great times? Used to be so full of light, and comradeship, the sleigh-riding in winter, and the ruddiness on his cheeks. And always some kind of good news coming up, always something nice coming up ahead. And never even let me carry the valises in the house, and simonizing, simonizing that little red car! Why, why can't I give him something and not have him hate me?

BEN Let me think about it. [*He glances at his watch.*] I still have a little time. Remarkable proposition, but you've got to be sure you're not making a fool of yourself.

BEN *drifts off upstage and goes out of sight.* BIFF *comes down from the left.*

WILLY [*suddenly conscious of* BIFF, *turns and looks up at him, then begins picking up the packages of seeds in confusion*] Where the hell is that seed? [*Indignantly*] You can't see nothing out here! They boxed in the whole goddam neighborhood!

BIFF There are people all around here. Don't you realize that?

WILLY I'm busy. Don't bother me.

BIFF [*taking the hoe from* WILLY] I'm saying good-by to you, Pop. [WILLY *looks at him, silent, unable to move.*] I'm not coming back any more.

WILLY You're not going to see Oliver tomorrow?

BIFF I've got no appointment, Dad.

WILLY He put his arm around you, and you've got no appointment?

BIFF Pop, get this now, will you? Every time I've left it's been a fight that sent me out of here. Today I realized something about myself and I tried to explain it to you and I—I think I'm just not smart enough to make any sense out of it for you. To hell with whose fault it is or anything like that. [*He takes* WILLY'S *arm.*] Let's just wrap it up, heh? Come on in, we'll tell Mom. [*He gently tries to pull* WILLY *to left.*]

WILLY [*frozen, immobile, with guilt in his voice*] No, I don't want to see her.

BIFF Come on! [*He pulls again, and* WILLY *tries to pull away.*]

WILLY [*highly nervous*] No, no, I don't want to see her.

BIFF [*tries to look into* WILLY'S *face, as if to find the answer there*] Why don't you want to see her?

WILLY [*more harshly now*] Don't bother me, will you?

BIFF   What do you mean, you don't want to see her? You don't want them calling you yellow, do you? This isn't your fault; it's me, I'm a bum. Now come inside! [WILLY *strains to get away.*] Did you hear what I said to you?

> WILLY *pulls away and quickly goes by himself into the house.* BIFF *follows.*

LINDA [*to* WILLY]   Did you plant, dear?

BIFF [*at the door, to* LINDA]   All right, we had it out. I'm going and I'm not writing any more.

LINDA [*going to* WILLY *in the kitchen*]   I think that's the best way, dear. 'Cause there's no use drawing it out, you'll just never get along.

> WILLY *doesn't respond.*

BIFF   People ask where I am and what I'm doing, you don't know, and you don't care. That way it'll be off your mind and you can start brightening up again. All right? That clears it, doesn't it? [WILLY *is silent, and* BIFF *goes to him.*] You gonna wish me luck, scout? [*He extends his hand.*] What do you say?

LINDA   Shake his hand, Willy.

WILLY [*turning to her, seething with hurt*]   There's no necessity to mention the pen at all, y'know.

BIFF [*gently*]   I've got no appointment, Dad.

WILLY [*erupting fiercely*]   He put his arm around . . . ?

BIFF   Dad, you're never going to see what I am, so what's the use of arguing? If I strike oil I'll send you a check. Meantime forget I'm alive.

WILLY [*to* LINDA]   Spite, see?

BIFF   Shake hands, Dad.

WILLY   Not my hand.

BIFF   I was hoping not to go this way.

WILLY   Well, this is the way you're going. Good-by.

> BIFF *looks at him a moment, then turns sharply and goes to the stairs.*

WILLY [*stops him with*]   May you rot in hell if you leave this house!

BIFF [*turning*]   Exactly what is it that you want from me?

WILLY   I want you to know, on the train, in the mountains, in the valleys, wherever you go, that you cut down your life for spite!

BIFF   No, no.

WILLY   Spite, spite, is the word of your undoing! And when you're down and out, remember what did it. When you're rotting some-where beside the railroad tracks, remember, and don't you dare blame it on me!

BIFF   I'm not blaming it on you!

WILLY   I won't take the rap for this, you hear?

HAPPY *comes down the stairs and stands on the bottom step, watching.*

BIFF   That's just what I'm telling you!

WILLY [*sinking into a chair at the table with full accusation*]   You're trying to put a knife in me—don't think I don't know what you're doing!

BIFF   All right, phony! Then let's lay it on the line. [*He whips the rubber tube out of his pocket and puts it on the table.*]

HAPPY   You crazy—

LINDA   Biff! [*She moves to grab the hose, but* BIFF *holds it down with his hand.*]

BIFF   Leave it there! Don't move it!

WILLY [*not looking at it*]   What is that?

BIFF   You know goddam well what that is.

WILLY [*caged, wanting to escape*]   I never saw that.

BIFF   You saw it. The mice didn't bring it into the cellar! What is this supposed to do, make a hero out of you? This supposed to make me sorry for you?

WILLY   Never heard of it.

BIFF   There'll be no pity for you, you hear it? No pity!

WILLY [*to* LINDA]   You hear the spite!

BIFF   No, you're going to hear the truth—what you are and what I am!

LINDA   Stop it!

WILLY   Spite!

HAPPY [*coming down toward* BIFF]   You cut it now!

BIFF [*to* HAPPY]   The man don't know who we are! The man is gonna know! [*To* WILLY] We never told the truth for ten minutes in this house!

HAPPY   We always told the truth!

BIFF [*turning on him*]   You big blow, are you the assistant buyer? You're one of the two assistants to the assistant, aren't you?

HAPPY   Well, I'm practically—

BIFF   You're practically full of it! We all are! And I'm through with it. [*To* WILLY] Now hear this, Willy, this is me.

WILLY   I know you!

BIFF   You know why I had no address for three months? I stole a suit in Kansas City and I was in jail. [*To* LINDA, *who is sobbing*] Stop crying. I'm through with it.

LINDA *turns away from them, her hands covering her face.*

WILLY   I suppose that's my fault!

BIFF   I stole myself out of every good job since high school!

WILLY   And whose fault is that?

BIFF   And I never got anywhere because you blew me so full of hot air I could never stand taking orders from anybody! That's whose fault it is!

WILLY   I hear that!

LINDA   Don't, Biff!

BIFF   It's goddam time you heard that! I had to be boss big shot in two weeks, and I'm through with it!

WILLY   Then hang yourself! For spite, hang yourself!

BIFF   No! Nobody's hanging himself, Willy! I ran down eleven flights with a pen in my hand today. And suddenly I stopped, you hear me? And in the middle of that office building, do you hear this? I stopped in the middle of that building and I saw—the sky. I saw the things that I love in this world. The work and the food and time to sit and smoke. And I looked at the pen and said to myself, what the hell am I grabbing this for? Why am I trying to become what I don't want to be? What am I doing in an office, making a contemptuous, begging fool of myself, when all I want is out there, waiting for me the minute I say I know who I am! Why can't I say that, Willy? [*He tries to make* WILLY *face him, but* WILLY *pulls away and moves to the left.*]

WILLY   [*with hatred, threateningly*]   The door to your life is wide open!

BIFF   Pop! I'm a dime a dozen, and so are you!

WILLY   [*turning on him now in an uncontrolled outburst*]   I am not a dime a dozen! I am Willy Loman, and you are Biff Loman!

> BIFF *starts for* WILLY, *but is blocked by* HAPPY. *In his fury,* BIFF *seems on the verge of attacking his father.*

BIFF   I am not a leader of men, Willy, and neither are you. You were never anything but a hard-working drummer who landed in the ash can like all the rest of them! I'm one dollar an hour, Willy! I tried seven states and couldn't raise it. A buck an hour! Do you gather my meaning? I'm not bringing home any prizes any more, and you're going to stop waiting for me to bring them home!

WILLY   [*directly to* BIFF]   You vengeful, spiteful mut!

> BIFF *breaks from* HAPPY. WILLY, *in fright, starts up the stairs.* BIFF *grabs him.*

BIFF   [*at the peak of his fury*]   Pop, I'm nothing! I'm nothing, Pop. Can't you understand that? There's no spite in it any more. I'm just what I am, that's all.

> BIFF's *fury has spent itself, and he breaks down, sobbing, holding on to* WILLY, *who dumbly fumbles for* BIFF's *face.*

WILLY   [*astonished.*]   What're you doing? What're you doing? [*To* LINDA] Why is he crying?

BIFF   [*crying, broken*]   Will you let me go, for Christ's sake? Will you take that phony dream and burn it before something happens? [*Struggling to contain himself, he pulls away and moves to the stairs.*] I'll go in the morning. Put him—put him to bed. [*Exhausted,* BIFF *moves up the stairs to his room.*]

WILLY [*after a long pause, astonished, elevated*] Isn't that—isn't that remarkable? Biff—he likes me!

LINDA He loves you, Willy!

HAPPY [*deeply moved*] Always did, Pop.

WILLY Oh, Biff! [*Staring wildly*] He cried! Cried to me. [*He is choking with his love, and now cries out his promise*] That boy— that boy is going to be magnificent!

BEN *appears in the light just outside the kitchen.*

BEN Yes, outstanding, with twenty thousand behind him.

LINDA [*sensing the racing of his mind, fearfully, carefully*] Now come to bed, Willy. It's all settled now.

WILLY [*finding it difficult not to rush out of the house*] Yes, we'll sleep. Come on. Go to sleep, Hap.

BEN And it does take a great kind of a man to crack the jungle.

In accents of dread, BEN's *idyllic music starts up.*

HAPPY [*his arm around* LINDA] I'm getting married, Pop, don't for- get it. I'm changing everything. I'm gonna run that department before the year is up. You'll see, Mom. [*He kisses her.*]

BEN The jungle is dark but full of diamonds, Willy.

WILLY *turns, moves, listening to* BEN.

LINDA Be good. You're both good boys, just act that way, that's all.

HAPPY 'Night, Pop. [*He goes upstairs.*]

LINDA [*to* WILLY] Come, dear.

BEN [*with greater force*] One must go in to fetch a diamond out.

WILLY [*to* LINDA, *as he moves slowly along the edge of the kitchen, toward the door*] I just want to get settled down, Linda. Let me sit alone for a little.

LINDA [*almost uttering her fear*] I want you upstairs.

WILLY [*taking her in his arms*] In a few minutes, Linda. I couldn't sleep right now. Go on, you look awful tired. [*He kisses her.*]

BEN Not like an appointment at all. A diamond is rough and hard to the touch.

WILLY Go on now. I'll be right up.

LINDA I think this is the only way, Willy.

WILLY Sure, it's the best thing.

BEN Best thing!

WILLY The only way. Everything is gonna be—go on, kid, get to bed. You look so tired.

LINDA Come right up.

WILLY Two minutes.

LINDA *goes into the living room, then reappears in her bed- room.* WILLY *moves just outside the kitchen door.*

WILLY Loves me. [*Wonderingly*] Always loved me. Isn't that a remarkable thing? Ben, he'll worship me for it!

BEN [*with promise*] It's dark there, but full of diamonds.

WILLY Can you imagine that magnificence with twenty thousand dollars in his pocket?

LINDA [*calling from her room*] Willy! Come up!

WILLY [*calling into the kitchen*] Yes! Coming! It's very smart, you realize that, don't you, sweetheart? Even Ben sees it. I gotta go, baby. 'By! 'By! [*Going over to* BEN, *almost dancing*] Imagine? When the mail comes he'll be ahead of Bernard again!

BEN A perfect proposition all around.

WILLY Did you see how he cried to me? Oh, if I could kiss him, Ben!

BEN Time, William, time!

WILLY Oh, Ben, I always knew one way or another we were gonna make it, Biff and I!

BEN [*looking at his watch*] The boat. We'll be late [*He moves slowly off into the darkness.*]

WILLY [*elegiacally, turning to the house*] Now when you kick off, boy, I want a seventy-yard boot, and get right down the field under the ball, and when you hit, hit low and hit hard, because it's important, boy. [*He swings around and faces the audience.*] There's all kinds of important people in the stands, and the first thing you know . . . [*Suddenly realizing he is alone*] Ben! Ben, where do I . . . [*He makes a sudden movement of search.*] Ben, how do I . . . ?

LINDA [*calling*] Willy, you coming up?

WILLY [*uttering a gasp of fear, whirling about as if to quiet her*] Sh! [*He turns around as if to find his way; sounds, faces, voices, seem to be swarming in upon him and he flicks at them, crying*] Sh! Sh! [*Suddenly music, faint and high, stops him. It rises in intensity, almost to an unbearable scream. He goes up and down on his toes, and rushes off around the house.*] Shhh!

LINDA Willy?

There is no answer. Linda waits. BIFF *gets up off his bed. He is still in his clothes.* HAPPY *sits up.* BIFF *stands listening.*

LINDA [*with real fear*] Willy, answer me! Willy!

There is the sound of a car starting and moving away at full speed.

LINDA No!

BIFF [*rushing down the stairs*] Pop!

As the car speeds off, the music crashes down in a frenzy of sound, which becomes the soft pulsation of a single cello string. BIFF *slowly returns to his bedroom. He and* HAPPY *gravely don their jackets.* LINDA *slowly walks out of her room. The music has developed into a dead march. The leaves of day are appearing over everything.* CHARLEY *and* BERNARD, *somberly dressed, appear and knock on the kitchen door.* BIFF *and* HAPPY *slowly descend the stairs to the kitchen as* CHARLEY *and* BER-NARD *enter. All stop a moment when* LINDA, *in clothes of mourning, bearing a little bunch of roses, comes through the draped doorway into the kitchen. She goes to* CHARLEY *and takes his arm. Now all move toward the audience, through the wall-line of the kitchen. At the limit of the apron,* LINDA *lays down the flowers, kneels, and sits back on her heels. All stare down at the grave.*

Requiem

CHARLEY   It's getting dark, Linda.

LINDA *doesn't react. She stares at the grave.*

BIFF   How about it, Mom? Better get some rest, heh? They'll be closing the gate soon.

LINDA *makes no move. Pause.*

HAPPY [*deeply angered*]   He had no right to do that. There was no necessity for it. We would've helped him.

CHARLEY [*grunting*]   Hmmm.

BIFF   Come along, Mom.

LINDA   Why didn't anybody come?

CHARLEY   It was a very nice funeral.

LINDA   But where are all the people he knew? Maybe they blame him.

CHARLEY   Naa. It's a rough world, Linda. They wouldn't blame him.

LINDA   I can't understand it. At this time especially. First time in thirty-five years we were just about free and clear. He only needed a little salary. He was even finished with the dentist.

CHARLEY   No man only needs a little salary.

LINDA   I can't understand it.

BIFF   There were a lot of nice days. When he'd come home from a trip; or on Sundays, making the stoop; finishing the cellar; putting on the new porch; when he built the extra bathroom; and put up the garage. You know something, Charley, there's more of him in that front stoop than in all the sales he ever made.

CHARLEY   Yeah. He was a happy man with a batch of cement.

LINDA   He was so wonderful with his hands.

BIFF   He had the wrong dreams. All, all, wrong.

HAPPY [*almost ready to fight* BIFF]   Don't say that!

BIFF   He never knew who he was.

CHARLEY [*stopping* HAPPY's *movement and reply. To* BIFF]   Nobody dast blame this man. You don't understand: Willy was a salesman. And for a salesman, there is no rock bottom to the life. He don't put a bolt to a nut, he don't tell you the law or give you medicine. He's a man way out there in the blue, riding on a smile and a shoeshine. And when they start not smiling back—that's an earth-quake. And then you get yourself a couple of spots on your hat, and you're finished. Nobody dast blame this man. A salesman is got to dream, boy. It comes with the territory.

BIFF   Charley, the man didn't know who he was.

HAPPY [*infuriated*]   Don't say that!

BIFF   Why don't you come with me, Happy?

HAPPY   I'm not licked that easily. I'm staying right in this city, and I'm gonna beat this racket! [*He looks at* BIFF, *his chin set.*] The Loman Brothers!

BIFF   I know who I am, kid.

HAPPY   All right, boy. I'm gonna show you and everybody else that Willy Loman did not die in vain. He had a good dream. It's the only dream you can have—to come out number-one man. He fought it out here, and this is where I'm gonna win it for him.

BIFF [*with a hopeless glance at* HAPPY, *bends toward his mother*] Let's go, Mom.

LINDA   I'll be with you in a minute. Go on, Charley. [*He hesitates.*] I want to, just for a minute. I never had a chance to say good-by.

> CHARLEY *moves away, followed by* HAPPY. BIFF *remains a slight distance up and left of* LINDA. *She sits there, summoning herself. The flute begins, not far away, playing behind her speech.*

LINDA   Forgive me, dear. I can't cry. I don't know what it is, but I can't cry. I don't understand it. Why did you ever do that? Help me, Willy, I can't cry. It seems to me that you're just on another trip. I keep expecting you. Willy, dear, I can't cry. Why did you do it? I search and search and search, and I can't understand it, Willy. I made the last payment on the house today. Today, dear. And there'll be nobody home. [*A sob rises in her throat.*] We're free and clear. [*Sobbing more fully, released*] We're free. [BIFF *comes slowly toward her.*] We're free . . . We're free . . .

> BIFF *lifts her to her feet and moves out up right with her in his arms.* LINDA *sobs quietly.* BERNARD *and* CHARLEY *come together and follow them, followed by* HAPPY. *Only the music of the flute is left on the darkening stage as over the house the hard towers of the apartment buildings rise into sharp focus, and*

THE CURTAIN FALLS

1949

Context

5 THE AUTHOR'S WORK

Sometimes playwrights are luckier than writers in other genres: while the act of reading is easily interrupted by the connections we continually make between what is on the page and what is in our minds, it is possible for a play in performance to so hold us that it can shut out other impressions. Once the play is over and we cease to become members of a common audience, however, we turn back into individuals who make comparisons—between this play and bits of our own experience, between this play and other plays of the season, between this play and others by the same dramatist. You have yourself no doubt already been making such comparisons as you've been reading the plays in this book.

Making comparisons is an inevitable activity of the mind, and we can use that activity to enlarge our understanding of a work. Take *Hamlet* as an example: if you have read other tragedies or histories by Shakespeare, you may already be aware how important the question of royal succession was to Shakespeare and his audience, and thus understand the emphasis laid upon it in this play. Moreover, whatever Shakespeare plays you have read or will go on to read, comparisons will show you how Shakespeare continually made his verse line more fluid and dramatic. Thus every new Shakespeare play you encounter will increase your knowledge of Shakespeare's "world." In the present section we provide some materials for the entry into another major playwright's world—that of Tennessee Williams.

Our basic text is *A Streetcar Named Desire* (1947), Williams's second major success and considered by many his finest play. But in order to amplify Williams's world for you beyond that play, we also include crucial scenes from two other masterworks—*The Glass Menagerie* (1945) and *Cat on a Hot Tin Roof* (1955). The scene from *Menagerie* is its conclusion, the final memory of this "memory play." The scene from *Cat* begins at a significant moment in the confrontation between Brick and Big Daddy that closes Act II, a scene that Williams later thought of as one in which "I reached beyond myself" (see our selections from the *Memoirs*). Since Williams wrote and rewrote over twenty full-length plays, as well as works in other genres, our offering can only hint at his vast output, but it may interest you enough to go out and read more.

Before we compare plays, however, we might take a brief look at Williams's life: if he called *The Glass Menagerie* "a memory play," to what extent does it mirror the playwright's own memories? And does his biography infuse the characters or moods of later plays?

Williams's mother, "Miss Edwina," the daughter of an Episcopalian minister, was repressed and genteel, very much the Southern belle in her youth. His father, Cornelius, was a traveling salesman, often away from his family and often violent and drunken when at home. The young Williams was a sickly child, overly protected by his mother; he was closely attached to his sister Rose, repelled by the roughhouse world of boys, and alienated from his father. The family's move from Mississippi to St. Louis, where Cornelius became a sales manager of the shoe company he had traveled for, was a shock to both Mrs. Williams and her young children, used to living in small Southern towns where a minister's daughter was an important person. Yet Mrs. Williams was a woman who could take care of herself, a "survivor." The young Williams went to the University of Missouri, but left after two years; his father then found him a job in the shoe-factory warehouse. He worked there for ten months, writing feverishly at night. His closest friend during the time was a burly co-worker, easy-going and attractive to women, named Stanley Kowalski. Williams found the life so difficult, however, that he succumbed to a nervous breakdown. After recovering at the home of his beloved grandparents, he went on to further studies, finally graduating at twenty-seven. Meanwhile Rose had been suffering increasing mental imbalance; the final trauma was, apparently, brought on by one of Cornelius's alcoholic rages, in which he beat Edwina and, trying to calm Rose, made a gesture that she took to be a sexual one. Shortly thereafter, Edwina signed the papers allowing Rose to be "tragically becalmed" by a prefrontal lobotomy. The next year, Williams left home for New Orleans, determined to become a writer.

"These are the cards life dealt Williams," the novelist Gore Vidal has cynically remarked, "and he played them for the rest of his life." But in comparing his life with the plays, we can see how art can transmute and universalize autobiography. In *Menagerie*, for example, the father has deserted the family years before; while Cornelius never deserted completely, his frequent absences must have made him shadowy indeed, and his presence must have been even harder to bear. Similarly, Edwina's ability to survive, her underlying strength of character, appears in the figure of Amanda in the play. Yet, as our first passage from the *Memoirs* shows, Amanda is not Williams's mother: the character has been transformed into somebody unique and different. Finally, Laura both is and is not Rose. Laura's physical handicap is a transmutation of Rose's emotional one, and the sexuality implicit in Laura's relationship to the glass unicorn with his single phallic horn is based on Williams's intuition of Rose's sexual emotional plight—a plight that possessed him throughout his life, as is evinced by the appearance of a Rose-like character or rose imagery in many later plays.

And even though Elia Kazan, who directed *Streetcar*, said that he "saw Blanche as Williams, an ambivalent figure who is attracted to the harshness and vulgarity around him at the same time that he fears it, because it threatens his life," in this play again art is the transmuting force. There are no incidents in Williams's early life remotely like those that take place in *Streetcar*, despite some similarities between Williams's warehouse friend Kowalski, a lover of Williams's named Pablo, and the Stanley of the play. Williams's biographer tells us that the first image of the earliest drafts of *Streetcar* was "simply that of a woman, sitting with folded hands near a window, while moonlight streamed in and she awaited in vain the arrival of her boy friend"; she was intended first as a younger Amanda. As the drafts began to develop—under the working title *The Poker Night*—Williams invited members of the *Menagerie* stage crew to teach him poker, so that he could consciously use the game in the play.

If we now compare *Streetcar* with our other scenes, we may find that some other aspects of the Williams world open up for us. One of these is what we might call a "Williams language." Amanda and Blanche, especially, speak a heightened, rhythmic, Southern language that may remind us of Flannery O'Connor—a language which differentiates them from the other characters they confront, and which Blanche tries to use to distance herself from her confusion and her doom. It is worth comparing, as well, Stanley's and Big Daddy's speech rhythms as their attacks mount, and the breathlessness of their cornered victims.

Although our excerpts do not include the full opening stage directions for *Menagerie* and *Cat*, you may also notice that Williams had an almost painterly vision of his settings: he asks for a lighting like that of El Greco in *Menagerie*, and he wants Scene 3 of *Streetcar* to look like a Van Gogh painting; he also suggested that the bedroom in *Cat* look like an old photograph of Robert Louis Stevenson's home in the South Seas. More importantly, we see throughout *Streetcar* and in the last scene of *Menagerie* that the action does not remain enclosed within the walls of the Kowalskis' apartment or the Wingfields'; in both plays, it moves freely from the interior to the exterior, with other buildings looming over the protagonists' dwellings. In realizing this movement on the stage—a theatrical innovation at the time—Williams was happily served by his scenic designer Jo Mielziner, who also designed the settings for *Cat* and for *Death of a Salesman*. Mielziner was developing special translucent scenery that, with the proper lighting, could be either opaque or transparent, but he gave some credit to Williams, saying later that "even as an inexperienced young writer, Tennessee Williams revealed a strong instinct for the visual qualities of the theatre. If he had written plays before the technical development of translucent and transparent scenery, I believe he would have invented it.'"

Mielziner went on to say of *Streetcar* that "throughout the play the brooding atmosphere is like an impressionistic X-ray. We are always conscious of the skeleton of this house of terror, even though we have peripheral impressions, like the chant of the Mexican woman which forms a background to a solo scene of Stella in her bedroom downstage." This is enhanced by full orchestration of other theatrical effects: special lighting within the settings, such as Blanche's paper lantern or Laura's candles—lights perhaps symbolic of the characters themselves; music, such as the "Blue Piano" and the "Varsouviana," each of which introduces a mood within the play; and sounds, as in the outside noises and voices that punctuate Brick's and Big Daddy's confrontation. All these, with language and setting, constitute what Williams liked to call "poetic realism" and which is uniquely his.

In reading the selections together, we may also begin to see some characteristic themes that preoccupied Williams's writing throughout his life. One of these is a deep concern, an obsession, with sexuality. For Williams, as for D. H. Lawrence—in whose writings he was, especially in his early career, passionately interested—sexuality was a powerful and intense force: for Wililams, however, the physical aspects of sex are a more dangerous, if not malevolent, force. We may speculate over the extent to which the Gentleman Caller's physicality has made it difficult for Laura to retreat again into her glass menagerie, but there is no doubt that the ever-increasing intensity of Blanche's and Stanley's effect on each other, with its consummation in Scene 10, is what drives her into madness. And in our scene from *Cat on a Hot Tin Roof*, the argument between Brick and his father is about the maiming of more than one life because of unadmitted sexual powers.

In his drinking, Brick seeks always to take himself outside of the ordinary world—if "ordinary" is the way to describe the heated passions of this play. The theme of the outsider is also central for Williams; he once said that he "existed outside of conventional society, while contriving somewhat precariously to remain in contact with it. For me this was not only precarious but a matter of dark unconscious disturbances." If Kazan's remark that Williams *was* Blanche has any meaning, it may be in this sense of what it means to be an outsider. As a close friend said of him, "He was devoted to Rose, but in a way she was an extension of himself. *He* could have had the lobotomy. *He* felt the outsider, marred in some way." Tom in *Menagerie* is only beginning to become an outsider. Blanche is much more so. She has been forced outside the old life of Belle Reve, exiled from Laurel, and is now an outsider, as well, at the Kowalskis—and in turn increasingly disturbs the life the Kowalskis have found. For to be an outsider can be, as well, to disrupt the "conventions" of the society one enters into, as the Gentleman Caller disrupts life in the Wingfield family.

In his *Memoirs* (1975), Williams wrote that "there is more sensibility—which is equivalent to more talent—among the 'gays' of both sexes than among the 'norms' . . . (Why? They must compensate for so much.)" In so saying, he equates the life of the outsider with the idea that art may arise out of suffering and deprivation—a compensation for pain or loss. In *Menagerie*, the unhappiness and the sense of lost or unexperienced adventure make Tom into a poet. Blanche's tattered remnants of culture—her references to Poe or to "Mrs. Browning's" sonnets—do not make her into a poet, any more than her tattered finery makes her into a great lady, but in her destruction we may feel that a light has gone out. In celebrating her, as well as Laura and Brick, Williams makes them speak for his tormented dramatic vision.

TENNESSEE WILLIAMS

A Streetcar Named Desire

And so it was I entered the broken world
To trace the visionary company of love, its voice
An instant in the wind (I know not whither hurled)
But not for long to hold each desperate choice.
"*The Broken Tower*" *by* HART CRANE[1]

THE CHARACTERS

BLANCHE	PABLO
STELLA	A NEGRO WOMAN
STANLEY	A DOCTOR
MITCH	A NURSE
EUNICE	A YOUNG COLLECTOR
STEVE	A MEXICAN WOMAN

Scene One

The exterior of a two-story corner building on a street in New Orleans which is named Elysian Fields and runs between the L & N tracks and the river.[2] The section is poor but, unlike corresponding sections in other American cities, it has a raffish charm. The houses are mostly white frame, weathered grey, with rickety outside stairs and galleries and quaintly ornamented gables. This building contains two flats, upstairs and down. Faded white stairs ascend to the entrances of both.

It is first dark of an evening early in May. The sky that shows around the dim white building is a peculiarly tender blue, almost a turquoise, which invests the scene with a kind of lyricism and gracefully attenuates the atmosphere of decay. You can almost feel the warm breath of the brown river beyond the river warehouses with their faint redolences of bananas and coffee. A corresponding air is evoked by the music of Negro entertainers at a barroom around the corner. In this part of New Orleans you are practically always just around the corner, or a few doors down the street, from a tinny piano being played with the infatuated fluency of brown fingers. This "Blue Piano" expresses the spirit of the life which goes on here.

Two women, one white and one colored, are taking the air on the steps of the building. The white woman is EUNICE, *who occupies the upstairs flat; the colored woman a neighbor, for New Orleans is a cosmopolitan city where there is a relatively warm and easy intermingling of races in the old part of town.*

Above the music of the "Blue Piano" the voices of people on the street can be heard overlapping.

---

1. American poet (1899–1932).
2. Elysian Fields is in fact a New Orleans street at the northern tip of the French Quarter, between the Louisville & Nashville railroad tracks and the Mississippi River. In Greek mythology, the Elysian Fields are the abode of the blessed in the afterlife.

[*Two men come around the corner,* STANLEY KOWALSKI *and*
MITCH. *They are about twenty-eight or thirty years old, roughly
dressed in blue denim work clothes.* STANLEY *carries his bowling jacket and a red-stained package from a butcher's. They
stop at the foot of the steps.*]

STANLEY [*bellowing*]   Hey, there! Stella, baby!

[STELLA *comes out on the first floor landing, a gentle young
woman, about twenty-five, and of a background obviously quite
different from her husband's.*]

STELLA [*mildly*]   Don't holler at me like that. Hi, Mitch.

STANLEY   Catch!

STELLA   What?

STANLEY   Meat!

[*He heaves the package at her. She cries out in protest but
manages to catch it: then she laughs breathlessly. Her husband
and his companion have already started back around the
corner.*]

STELLA [*calling after him*]   Stanley! Where are you going?

STANLEY   Bowling!

STELLA   Can I come watch?

STANLEY   Come on. [*He goes out.*]

STELLA   Be over soon. [*to the white woman*] Hello, Eunice. How are
you?

EUNICE   I'm all right. Tell Steve to get him a poor boy's sandwich[3]
'cause nothing's left here.

[*They all laugh; the colored woman does not stop.* STELLA *goes
out.*]

COLORED WOMAN   What was that package he th'ew at 'er? [*She rises
from steps, laughing louder.*]

EUNICE   You hush, now!

NEGRO WOMAN   Catch *what*!

[*She continues to laugh.* BLANCHE *comes around the corner,
carrying a valise. She looks at a slip of paper, then at the building, then again at the slip and again at the building. Her expression is one of shocked disbelief. Her appearance is incongruous
to this setting. She is daintily dressed in a white suit with a
fluffy bodice, necklace and earrings of pearl, white gloves and
hat, looking as if she were arriving at a summer tea or cocktail
party in the garden district. She is about five years older than*
STELLA. *Her delicate beauty must avoid a strong light. There
is something about her uncertain manner, as well as her white
clothes, that suggests a moth.*]

EUNICE [*finally*]   What's the matter, honey? Are you lost?

BLANCHE [*with faintly hysterical humor*]   They told me to take a
street-car named Desire, and then transfer to one called Cemeteries[4]
and ride six blocks and get off at—Elysian Fields!

EUNICE   That's where you are now.

BLANCHE   At Elysian Fields?

---

3. Usually called just "poor boy" or "po'
boy." Similar to a hero or submarine sandwich.

4. Desire is a street in New Orleans, Cemeteries the end of a streetcar line that
stopped at a cemetery.

EUNICE   This here is Elysian Fields.

BLANCHE   They   mustn't   have—understood—what   number   I   wanted . . .

EUNICE   What number you lookin' for?

[BLANCHE *wearily refers to the slip of paper.*]

BLANCHE   Six thirty-two.

EUNICE   You don't have to look no further.

BLANCHE   [*uncomprehendingly*]   I'm looking for my sister, Stella DuBois. I mean—Mrs. Stanley Kowalski.

EUNICE   That's the party.—You just did miss her, though.

BLANCHE   This—can this be—her home?

EUNICE   She's got the downstairs here and I got the up.

BLANCHE   Oh. She's—out?

EUNICE   You noticed that bowling alley around the corner?

BLANCHE   I'm—not sure I did.

EUNICE   Well, that's where she's at, watchin' her husband bowl. [*There is a pause.*] You want to leave your suitcase here an' go find her?

BLANCHE   No.

NEGRO WOMAN   I'll go tell her you come.

BLANCHE   Thanks.

NEGRO WOMAN   You welcome. [*She goes out.*]

EUNICE   She wasn't expecting you?

BLANCHE   No. No, not tonight.

EUNICE   Well, why don't you just go in and make yourself at home till they get back.

BLANCHE   How could I—do that?

EUNICE   We own this place so I can let you in.

[*She gets up and opens the downstairs door. A light goes on behind the blind, turning it light blue.* BLANCHE *slowly follows her into the downstairs flat. The surrounding areas dim out as the interior is lighted. Two rooms can be seen, not too clearly defined. The one first entered is primarily a kitchen but contains a folding bed to be used by* BLANCHE. *The room beyond this is a bedroom. Off this room is a narrow door to a bathroom.*]

EUNICE   [*defensively, noticing* BLANCHE's *look*]   It's sort of messed up right now but when it's clean it's real sweet.

BLANCHE   Is it?

EUNICE   Uh-huh, I think so. So you're Stella's sister?

BLANCHE   Yes. [*wanting to get rid of her*] Thanks for letting me in.

EUNICE   *Por nada*, as the Mexicans say, *por nada!*[5] Stella spoke of you.

BLANCHE   Yes?

EUNICE   I think she said you taught school.

BLANCHE   Yes.

EUNICE   And you're from Mississippi, huh?

BLANCHE   Yes.

EUNICE   She showed me a picture of your home-place, the plantation.

---

5. "It's nothing."

BLANCHE   Belle Reve?[6]
EUNICE   A great big place with white columns.
BLANCHE   Yes . . .
EUNICE   A place like that must be awful hard to keep up.
BLANCHE   If you will excuse me, I'm just about to drop.
EUNICE   Sure, honey. Why don't you set down?
BLANCHE   What I meant was I'd like to be left alone.
EUNICE [*offended*]   Aw. I'll make myself scarce, in that case.
BLANCHE   I didn't mean to be rude, but—
EUNICE   I'll drop by the bowling alley an' hustle her up. [*She goes out the door.*]

[BLANCHE *sits in a chair very stiffly with her shoulders slightly hunched and her legs pressed close together and her hands tightly clutching her purse as if she were quite cold. After a while the blind look goes out of her eyes and she begins to look slowly around. A cat screeches. She catches her breath with a startled gesture. Suddenly she notices something in a half open closet. She springs up and crosses to it, and removes a whiskey bottle. She pours a half tumbler of whiskey and tosses it down. She carefully replaces the bottle and washes out the tumbler at the sink. Then she resumes her seat in front of the table.*]

BLANCHE [*faintly to herself*]   I've got to keep hold of myself!

[STELLA *comes quickly around the corner of the building and runs to the door of the downstairs flat.*]

STELLA [*calling out joyfully*]   Blanche!

[*For a moment they stare at each other. Then* BLANCHE *springs up and runs to her with a wild cry.*]

BLANCHE   Stella, oh, Stella, Stella! Stella for Star!

[*She begins to speak with feverish vivacity as if she feared for either of them to stop and think. They catch each other in a spasmodic embrace.*]

BLANCHE   Now, then, let me look at you. But don't you look at me, Stella, no, no, no, not till later, not till I've bathed and rested! And turn that over-light off! Turn that off! I won't be looked at in this merciless glare! [STELLA *laughs and complies.*] Come back here now! Oh, my baby! Stella! Stella for Star! [*She embraces her again.*] I thought you would never come back to this horrible place! What am I saying? I didn't mean to say that. I meant to be nice about it and say—Oh, what a convenient location and such—Ha-a-ha! Precious lamb! You haven't said a *word* to me.
STELLA   You haven't given me a chance to, honey! [*She laughs, but her glance at* BLANCHE *is a little anxious.*]
BLANCHE   Well, now you talk. Open your pretty mouth and talk while I look around for some liquor! I know you must have some liquor on the place! Where could it be, I wonder? Oh, I spy, I spy!

[*She rushes to the closet and removes the bottle; she is shaking all over and panting for breath as she tries to laugh. The bottle nearly slips from her grasp.*]

6. "Beautiful Dream."

STELLA [*noticing*]   Blanche, you sit down and let me pour the drinks.
I don't know what we've got to mix with. Maybe a coke in the
icebox. Look'n see, while I'm—

BLANCHE   No coke, honey, not with my nerves tonight! Where—
where—where is—?

STELLA   Stanley? Bowling! He loves it. They're having a—found some
soda!—tournament . . .

BLANCHE   Just water, baby, to chase it! Now don't get worried, your
sister hasn't turned into a drunkard, she's just all shaken up and
hot and tired and dirty! You sit down, now, and explain this place
to me! What are you doing in a place like this?

STELLA   Now, Blanche—

BLANCHE   Oh, I'm not going to be hypocritical, I'm going to be
honestly critical about it! Never, never, never in my worst dreams
could I picture— Only Poe! Only Mr. Edgar Allan Poe!—could
do it justice! Out there I suppose is the ghoul-haunted woodland
of Weir![7] [*She laughs.*]

STELLA   No, honey, those are the L & N tracks.

BLANCHE   No, now seriously, putting joking aside. Why didn't you tell
me, why didn't you write me, honey, why didn't you let me know?

STELLA [*carefully, pouring herself a drink*]   Tell you what, Blanche?

BLANCHE   Why, that you had to live in these conditions!

STELLA   Aren't you being a little intense about it? It's not that bad
at all! New Orleans isn't like other cities.

BLANCHE   This has got nothing to do with New Orleans. You might
as well say—forgive me, blessed baby! [*She suddenly stops short.*]
The subject is closed!

STELLA [*a little drily*]   Thanks.

[*During the pause,* BLANCHE *stares at her. She smiles at*
BLANCHE.]

BLANCHE [*looking down at her glass, which shakes in her hand*]
You're all I've got in the world, and you're not glad to see me!

STELLA [*sincerely*]   Why, Blanche, you know that's not true.

BLANCHE   No?—I'd forgotten how quiet you were.

STELLA   You never did give me a chance to say much, Blanche. So
I just got in the habit of being quiet around you.

BLANCHE [*vaguely*]   A good habit to get into . . . [*then, abruptly*]
You haven't asked me how I happened to get away from the
school before the spring term ended.

STELLA   Well, I thought you'd volunteer that information—if you
wanted to tell me.

BLANCHE   You thought I'd been fired?

STELLA   No, I—thought you might have—resigned . . .

BLANCHE   I was so exhausted by all I'd been through my—nerves
broke. [*nervously tamping cigarette*] I was on the verge of—lunacy,
almost! So Mr. Graves—Mr. Graves is the high school superintendent—he suggested I take a leave of absence. I couldn't put
all of those details into the wire . . . [*She drinks quickly.*] Oh, this
buzzes right through me and feels so *good!*

STELLA   Won't you have another?

---

7. From the refrain of Poe's gothic ballad *Ulalume* (1847).

BLANCHE   No, one's my limit.

STELLA   Sure?

BLANCHE   You haven't said a word about my appearance.

STELLA   You look just fine.

BLANCHE   God love you for a liar! Daylight never exposed so total a ruin! But you—you've put on some weight, yes, you're just as plump as a little partridge! And it's so becoming to you!

STELLA   Now, Blanche—

BLANCHE   Yes, it is, it is or I wouldn't say it! You just have to watch around the hips a little. Stand up.

STELLA   Not now.

BLANCHE   You hear me? I said stand up! [STELLA *complies reluctantly.*] You messy child, you, you've spilt something on that pretty white lace collar! About your hair—you ought to have it cut in a feather bob with your dainty features. Stella, you have a maid, don't you?

STELLA   No. With only two rooms it's—

BLANCHE   What? Two rooms, did you say?

STELLA   This one and—[*She is embarrassed.*]

BLANCHE   The other one? [*She laughs sharply. There is an embarrassed silence.*]

BLANCHE   I am going to take just one little tiny nip more, sort of to put the stopper on, so to speak. . . . Then put the bottle away so I won't be tempted. [*She rises.*] I want you to look at *my* figure! [*She turns around.*] You know I haven't put on one ounce in ten years, Stella? I weigh what I weighed the summer you left Belle Reve. The summer Dad died and you left us . . .

STELLA [*a little wearily*]   It's just incredible, Blanche, how well you're looking.

BLANCHE [*They both laugh uncomfortably.*]   But, Stella, there's only two rooms, I don't see where you're going to put me!

STELLA   We're going to put you in here.

BLANCHE   What kind of bed's this—one of those collapsible things? [*She sits on it.*]

STELLA   Does it feel all right?

BLANCHE [*dubiously*]   Wonderful, honey. I don't like a bed that gives much. But there's no door between the two rooms, and Stanley —will it be decent?

STELLA   Stanley is Polish, you know.

BLANCHE   Oh, yes. They're something like Irish, aren't they?

STELLA   Well—

BLANCHE   Only not so—highbrow? [*They both laugh again in the same way.*] I brought some nice clothes to meet all your lovely friends in.

STELLA   I'm afraid you won't think they are lovely.

BLANCHE   What are they like?

STELLA   They're Stanley's friends.

BLANCHE   Polacks?

STELLA   They're a mixed lot, Blanche.

BLANCHE   Heterogeneous—types?

STELLA   Oh, yes. Yes, types is right!

BLANCHE   Well—anyhow—I brought nice clothes and I'll wear them.
I guess you're hoping I'll say I'll put up at a hotel, but I'm not
going to put up at a hotel. I want to be *near* you, got to be *with*
somebody, I *can't* be alone! Because—as you must have noticed—
I'm—*not* very well . . . [*Her voice drops and her look is frightened.*]

STELLA   You seem a little bit nervous or overwrought or something.

BLANCHE   Will Stanley like me, or will I be just a visiting in-law,
Stella? I couldn't stand that.

STELLA   You'll get along fine together, if you'll just try not to—well
—compare him with men that we went out with at home.

BLANCHE   Is he so—different?

STELLA   Yes. A different species.

BLANCHE   In what way; what's he like?

STELLA   Oh, you can't describe someone you're in love with! Here's
a picture of him! [*She hands a photograph to* BLANCHE.]

BLANCHE   An officer?

STELLA   A Master Sergeant in the Engineers' Corps. Those are
decorations!

BLANCHE   He had those on when you met him?

STELLA   I assure you I wasn't blinded by all the brass.

BLANCHE   That's not what I—

STELLA   But of course there were things to adjust myself to later on.

BLANCHE   Such as his civilian background! [STELLA *laughs uncertainly.*] How did he take it when you said I was coming?

STELLA   Oh, Stanley doesn't know yet.

BLANCHE   [*frightened*]   You—haven't told him?

STELLA   He's on the road a good deal.

BLANCHE   Oh. Travels?

STELLA   Yes.

BLANCHE   Good. I mean—isn't it?

STELLA   [*half to herself*]   I can hardly stand it when he is away for a
night . . .

BLANCHE   Why, Stella!

STELLA   When he's away for a week I nearly go wild!

BLANCHE   Gracious!

STELLA   And when he comes back I cry on his lap like a baby . . .
[*She smiles to herself.*]

BLANCHE   I guess that is what is meant by being in love . . . [STELLA
looks up with a radiant smile.] Stella—

STELLA   What?

BLANCHE   [*in an uneasy rush*]   I haven't asked you the things you
probably thought I was going to ask. And so I'll expect you to be
understanding about what *I* have to tell *you.*

STELLA   What, Blanche? [*Her face turns anxious.*]

BLANCHE   Well, Stella—you're going to reproach me, I know that
you're bound to reproach me—but before you do—take into consideration—you left! I stayed and struggled! You came to New
Orleans and looked out for yourself! *I* stayed at *Belle Reve* and
tried to hold it together! I'm not meaning this in any reproach-
ful way, but *all* the burden descended on *my* shoulders.

STELLA   The best I could do was make my own living, Blanche.

[BLANCHE *begins to shake again with intensity.*]

BLANCHE   I know, I know. But you are the one that abandoned Belle Reve, not I! I stayed and fought for it, bled for it, almost died for it!

STELLA   Stop this hysterical outburst and tell me what's happened? What do you mean fought and bled? What kind of—

BLANCHE   I knew you would, Stella. I knew you would take this attitude about it!

STELLA   About—what?—please!

BLANCHE [*slowly*]   The loss—the loss . . .

STELLA   Belle Reve? Lost, is it? No!

BLANCHE   Yes, Stella.

[*They stare at each other across the yellow-checked linoleum of the table.* BLANCHE *slowly nods her head and* STELLA *looks slowly down at her hands folded on the table. The music of the "Blue Piano" grows louder.* BLANCHE *touches her handkerchief to her forehead.*]

STELLA   But how did it go? What happened?

BLANCHE [*springing up*]   You're a fine one to ask me how it went!

STELLA   Blanche!

BLANCHE   You're a fine one to sit there *accusing me* of it!

STELLA   *Blanche!*

BLANCHE   I, I, *I* took the blows in my face and my body! All of those deaths! The long parade to the graveyard! Father, mother! Margaret, that dreadful way! So big with it, it couldn't be put in a coffin! But had to be burned like rubbish! You just came home in time for the funerals, Stella. And funerals are pretty compared to deaths. Funerals are quiet, but deaths—not always. Sometimes their breathing is hoarse, and sometimes it rattles, and sometimes they even cry out to you, "Don't let me go!" Even the old, sometimes, say, "Don't let me go." As if you were able to stop them! But funerals are quiet, with pretty flowers. And, oh, what gorgeous boxes they pack them away in! Unless you were there at the bed when they cried out, "Hold me!" you'd never suspect there was the struggle for breath and bleeding. You didn't dream, but I saw! *Saw! Saw!* And now you sit there telling me with your eyes that I let the place go! How in hell do you think all that sickness and dying was paid for? Death is expensive, Miss Stella! And old Cousin Jessie's right after Margaret's, hers! Why, the Grim Reaper had put up his tent on our doorstep! . . . Stella. Belle Reve was his headquarters! Honey—that's how it slipped through my fingers! Which of them left us a fortune? Which of them left a cent of insurance even? Only poor Jessie—one hundred to pay for her coffin. That was all, Stella! And I with my pitiful salary at the school. Yes, accuse me! Sit there and stare at me, thinking I let the place go! *I* let the place go? Where were *you!* In bed with your—Polack!

STELLA [*springing*]   Blanche! You be still! That's enough! [*She starts out.*]

BLANCHE   Where are you going?

STELLA   I'm going into the bathroom to wash my face.

BLANCHE   Oh, Stella, Stella, you're crying!

STELLA   Does that surprise you?

BLANCHE   Forgive me—I didn't mean to—

> [*The sound of men's voices is heard.* STELLA *goes into the bathroom, closing the door behind her. When the men appear, and* BLANCHE *realizes it must be* STANLEY *returning, she moves uncertainly from the bathroom door to the dressing table, looking apprehensively toward the front door.* STANLEY *enters, followed by* STEVE *and* MITCH. STANLEY *pauses near his door,* STEVE *by the foot of the spiral stair, and* MITCH *is slightly above and to the right of them, about to go out. As the men enter, we hear some of the following dialogue.*]

STANLEY   Is that how he got it?

STEVE   Sure that's how he got it. He hit the old weather-bird for 300 bucks on a six-number-ticket.

MITCH   Don't tell him those things; he'll believe it.

> [MITCH *starts out.*]

STANLEY   [*restraining* MITCH]   Hey, Mitch—come back here.

> [BLANCHE, *at the sound of voices, retires in the bedroom. She picks up* STANLEY's *photo from dressing table, looks at it, puts it down. When* STANLEY *enters the apartment, she darts and hides behind the screen at the head of bed.*]

STEVE   [*to* STANLEY *and* MITCH]   Hey, are we playin' poker tomorrow?

STANLEY   Sure—at Mitch's.

MITCH   [*hearing this, returns quickly to the stair rail*]   No—not at my place. My mother's still sick!

STANLEY   Okay, at my place . . . [MITCH *starts out again.*]   But you bring the beer!

> [MITCH *pretends not to hear—calls out "Good night, all," and goes out, singing.* EUNICE's *voice is heard, above.*]

Break it up down there! I made the spaghetti dish and ate it myself.

STEVE   [*going upstairs*]   I told you and phoned you we was playing. [*to the men*]   Jax[8] beer!

EUNICE   You never phoned me once.

STEVE   I told you at breakfast—and phoned you at lunch . . .

EUNICE   Well, never mind about that. You just get yourself home here once in a while.

STEVE   You want it in the papers?

> [*More laughter and shouts of parting come from the men.* STANLEY *throws the screen door of the kitchen open and comes in. He is of medium height, about five feet eight or nine, and strongly, compactly built. Animal joy in his being is implicit in all his movements and attitudes. Since earliest manhood the center of his life has been pleasure with women, the giving and taking of it, not with weak indulgence, dependently, but with the power and pride of a richly, feathered male bird among hens. Branching out from this complete and satisfying center are all the auxiliary channels of his life, such as his heartiness with men, his appreciation of rough humor, his love of good drink and food and games, his car, his radio, everything that*

---

8. A local brand of beer.

1198   *Tennessee Williams*

is his, that bears his emblem of the gaudy seed-bearer. He sizes
women up at a glance, with sexual classifications, crude images
flashing into his mind and determining the way he smiles at
them.]

BLANCHE [*drawing involuntarily back from his stare*] You must be
  Stanley. I'm Blanche.
STANLEY Stella's sister?
BLANCHE Yes.
STANLEY H'lo. Where's the little woman?
BLANCHE In the bathroom.
STANLEY Oh. Didn't know you were coming in town.
BLANCHE I—uh—
STANLEY Where you from, Blanche?
BLANCHE Why, I—live in Laurel.
  [*He has crossed to the closet and removed the whiskey bottle.*]
STANLEY In Laurel, huh? Oh, yeah. Yeah, in Laurel, that's right. Not
  in my territory. Liquor goes fast in hot weather. [*He holds the
  bottle to the light to observe its depletion.*] Have a shot?
BLANCHE No, I—rarely touch it.
STANLEY Some people rarely touch it, but it touches them often.
BLANCHE [*faintly*] Ha-ha.
STANLEY My clothes're stickin' to me. Do you mind if I make myself
  comfortable? [*He starts to remove his shirt.*]
BLANCHE Please, please do.
STANLEY Be comfortable is my motto.
BLANCHE It's mine, too. It's hard to stay looking fresh. I haven't
  washed or even powdered my face and—here you are!
STANLEY You know you can catch cold sitting around in damp
  things, especially when you been exercising hard like bowling is.
  You're a teacher, aren't you?
BLANCHE Yes.
STANLEY What do you teach, Blanche?
BLANCHE English.
STANLEY I never was a very good English student. How long you
  here for, Blanche?
BLANCHE I—don't know yet.
STANLEY You going to shack up here?
BLANCHE I thought I would if it's not inconvenient for you all.
STANLEY Good.
BLANCHE Traveling wears me out.
STANLEY Well, take it easy.
  [*A cat screeches near the window.* BLANCHE *springs up.*]
BLANCHE What's that?
STANLEY Cats . . . Hey, Stella!
STELLA [*faintly, from the bathroom*] Yes, Stanley.
STANLEY Haven't fallen in, have you? [*He grins at* BLANCHE. *She
  tries unsuccessfully to smile back. There is a silence.*] I'm afraid
  I'll strike you as being the unrefined type. Stella's spoke of you a
  good deal. You were married once, weren't you?
  [*The music of the polka rises up, faint in the distance.*]
BLANCHE Yes. When I was quite young.

STANLEY   What happened?

BLANCHE   The boy—the boy died. [*She sinks back down.*] I'm afraid I'm—going to be sick! [*Her head falls on her arms.*]

Scene Two

It is six o'clock the following evening. BLANCHE *is bathing.* STELLA *is completing her toilette.* BLANCHE's *dress, a flowered print, is laid out on* STELLA's *bed.*

STANLEY *enters the kitchen from outside, leaving the door open on the perpetual "Blue Piano" around the corner.*

STANLEY   What's all this monkey doings?

STELLA   Oh, Stan! [*She jumps up and kisses him, which he accepts with lordly composure.*] I'm taking Blanche to Galatoire's[9] for supper and then to a show, because it's your poker night.

STANLEY   How about my supper, huh? I'm not going to no Galatoire's for supper!

STELLA   I put you a cold plate on ice.

STANLEY   Well, isn't that just dandy!

STELLA   I'm going to try to keep Blanche out till the party breaks up because I don't know how she would take it. So we'll go to one of the little places in the Quarter afterward and you'd better give me some money.

STANLEY   Where is she?

STELLA   She's soaking in a hot tub to quiet her nerves. She's terribly upset.

STANLEY   Over what?

STELLA   She's been through such an ordeal.

STANLEY   Yeah?

STELLA   Stan, we've—lost Belle Reve!

STANLEY   The place in the country?

STELLA   Yes.

STANLEY   How?

STELLA [*vaguely*]   Oh, it had to be—sacrificed or something. [*There is a pause while* STANLEY *considers.* STELLA *is changing into her dress.*] When she comes in be sure to say something nice about her appearance. And, oh! Don't mention the baby. I haven't said anything yet, I'm waiting until she gets in a quieter condition.

STANLEY [*ominously*]   So?

STELLA   And try to understand her and be nice to her, Stan.

BLANCHE [*singing in the bathroom*]   "From the land of the sky blue water, They brought a captive maid!"

STELLA   She wasn't expecting to find us in such a small place. You see I'd tried to gloss things over a little in my letters.

STANLEY   So?

STELLA   And admire her dress and tell her she's looking wonderful. That's important with Blanche. Her little weakness!

STANLEY   Yeah. I get the idea. Now let's skip back a little to where you said the country place was disposed of.

STELLA   Oh!—yes . . .

9. A famous old restaurant on Bourbon Street in the French Quarter.

STANLEY   How about that? Let's have a few more details on that subjeck.

STELLA   It's best not to talk much about it until she's calmed down.

STANLEY   So that's the deal, huh? Sister Blanche cannot be annoyed with business details right now!

STELLA   You saw how she was last night.

STANLEY   Uh-hum, I saw how she was. Now let's have a gander at the bill of sale.

STELLA   I haven't seen any.

STANLEY   She didn't show you no papers, no deed of sale or nothing like that, huh?

STELLA   It seems like it wasn't sold.

STANLEY   Well, what in hell was it then, give away? To charity?

STELLA   Shhh! She'll hear you.

STANLEY   I don't care if she hears me. Let's see the papers!

STELLA   There weren't any papers, she didn't show any papers, I don't care about papers.

STANLEY   Have you ever heard of the Napoleonic code?[1]

STELLA   No, Stanley, I haven't heard of the Napoleonic code and if I have, I don't see what it—

STANLEY   Let me enlighten you on a point or two, baby.

STELLA   Yes?

STANLEY   In the state of Louisiana we have the Napoleonic code according to which what belongs to the wife belongs to the husband and vice versa. For instance if I had a piece of property, or you had a piece of property—

STELLA   My head is swimming!

STANLEY   All right. I'll wait till she gets through soaking in a hot tub and then I'll inquire if *she* is acquainted with the Napoleonic code. It looks to me like you have been swindled, baby, and when you're swindled under the Napoleonic code I'm swindled too. And I don't like to be *swindled.*

STELLA   There's plenty of time to ask her questions later but if you do now she'll go to pieces again. I don't understand what happened to Belle Reve but you don't know how ridiculous you are being when you suggest that my sister or I or anyone of our family could have perpetrated a swindle on anyone else.

STANLEY   Then where's the money if the place was sold?

STELLA   Not sold—*lost, lost!*

[*He stalks into bedroom, and she follows him.*]

Stanley!

[*He pulls open the wardrobe trunk standing in middle of room and jerks out an armful of dresses.*]

STANLEY   Open your eyes to this stuff! You think she got them out of a teacher's pay?

STELLA   Hush!

STANLEY   Look at these feathers and furs that she come here to preen herself in! What's this here? A solid-gold dress, I believe!

1. This codification of French law (1802), made by Napoleon as emperor, is the basis for Louisiana's civil law.

And this one! What is these here? Fox-pieces! [*He blows on them.*]
Genuine fox fur-pieces, a half a mile long! Where are your fox-
pieces, Stella? Bushy snowwhite ones, no less! Where are your white
fox-pieces?

STELLA   Those are inexpensive summer furs that Blanche has had a
long time.

STANLEY   I got an acquaintance who deals in this sort of merchandise.
I'll have him in here to appraise it. I'm willing to bet you there's
thousands of dollars invested in this stuff here!

STELLA   Don't be such an idiot, Stanley!

     [*He hurls the furs to the day bed. Then he jerks open small
     drawer in the trunk and pulls up a fistful of costume jewelry.*]

STANLEY   And what have we here? The treasure chest of a pirate!

STELLA   Oh, Stanley!

STANLEY   Pearls! Ropes of them! What is this sister of yours, a deep-
sea diver? Bracelets of solid gold, too! Where are your pearls and
gold bracelets?

STELLA   Shhh! Be still, Stanley!

STANLEY   And diamonds! A crown for an empress!

STELLA   A rhinestone tiara she wore to a costume ball.

STANLEY   What's rhinestone?

STELLA   Next door to glass.

STANLEY   Are you kidding? I have an acquaintance that works in a
jewelry store. I'll have him in here to make an appraisal of this.
Here's your plantation, or what was left of it, here!

STELLA   You have no idea how stupid and horrid you're being! Now
close that trunk before she comes out of the bathroom!

     [*He kicks the trunk partly closed and sits on the kitchen table.*]

STANLEY   The Kowalskis and the DuBoises have different notions.

STELLA [*angrily*]   Indeed they have, thank heavens!—*I'm* going outside. [*She snatches up her white hat and gloves and crosses to the
outside door.*] You come out with me while Blanche is getting
dressed.

STANLEY   Since when do you give me orders?

STELLA   Are you going to stay here and insult her?

STANLEY   You're damn tootin' I'm going to stay here.

     [STELLA *goes out to the porch.* BLANCHE *comes out of the
     bathroom in a red satin robe.*]

BLANCHE [*airily*]   Hello, Stanley! Here I am, all freshly bathed and
scented, and feeling like a brand new human being!

     [*He lights a cigarette.*]

STANLEY   That's good.

BLANCHE [*drawing the curtains at the windows*]   Excuse me while I
slip on my pretty new dress!

STANLEY   Go right ahead, Blanche.

     [*She closes the drapes between the rooms.*]

BLANCHE   I understand there's to be a little card party to which we
ladies are cordially *not* invited!

STANLEY [*ominously*]   Yeah?

     [BLANCHE *throws off her robe and slips into a flowered print
     dress.*]

BLANCHE   Where's Stella?

STANLEY   Out on the porch.

BLANCHE   I'm going to ask a favor of you in a moment.

STANLEY   What could that be, I wonder?

BLANCHE   Some buttons in back! You may enter!

[*He crosses through drapes with a smoldering look.*]
How do I look?

STANLEY   You look all right.

BLANCHE   Many thanks! Now the buttons!

STANLEY   I can't do nothing with them.

BLANCHE   You men with your big clumsy fingers. May I have a drag on your cig?

STANLEY   Have one for yourself.

BLANCHE   Why, thanks! . . . It looks like my trunk has exploded.

STANLEY   Me an' Stella were helping you unpack.

BLANCHE   Well, you certainly did a fast and thorough job of it!

STANLEY   It looks like you raided some stylish shops in Paris.

BLANCHE   Ha-ha! Yes—clothes are my passion!

STANLEY   What does it cost for a string of fur-pieces like that?

BLANCHE   Why, those were a tribute from an admirer of mine!

STANLEY   He must have had a lot of—admiration!

BLANCHE   Oh, in my youth I excited some admiration. But look at me now! [*She smiles at him radiantly.*] Would you think it possible that I was once considered to be—attractive?

STANLEY   Your looks are okay.

BLANCHE   I was fishing for a compliment, Stanley.

STANLEY   I don't go in for that stuff.

BLANCHE   What—stuff?

STANLEY   Compliments to women about their looks. I never met a woman that didn't know if she was good-looking or not without being told, and some of them give themselves credit for more than they've got. I once went out with a doll who said to me, "I am the glamorous type, I am the glamorous type!" I said, "So what?"

BLANCHE   And what did she say then?

STANLEY   She didn't say nothing. That shut her up like a clam.

BLANCHE   Did it end the romance?

STANLEY   It ended the conversation—that was all. Some men are took in by this Hollywood glamor stuff and some men are not.

BLANCHE   I'm sure you belong in the second category.

STANLEY   That's right.

BLANCHE   I cannot imagine any witch of a woman casting a spell over you.

STANLEY   That's—right.

BLANCHE   You're simple, straightforward and honest, a little bit on the primitive side I should think. To interest you a woman would have to—[*She pauses with an indefinite gesture.*]

STANLEY [*slowly*]   Lay . . . her cards on the table.

BLANCHE [*smiling*]   Well, I never cared for wishy-washy people. That was why, when you walked in here last night, I said to myself—"My sister has married a man!"—Of course that was all that I could tell about you.

STANLEY [*booming*]   Now let's cut the re-bop![2]

BLANCHE [*pressing hands to her ears*]   Ouuuuu!

STELLA [*calling from the steps*]   Stanley! You come out here and let Blanche finish dressing!

BLANCHE   I'm through dressing, honey.

STELLA   Well, you come out, then.

STANLEY   Your sister and I are having a little talk.

BLANCHE [*lightly*]   Honey, do me a favor. Run to the drugstore and get me a lemon Coke with plenty of chipped ice in it!—Will you do that for me, sweetie?

STELLA [*uncertainly*]   Yes. [*She goes around the corner of the building.*]

BLANCHE   The poor little thing was out there listening to us, and I have an idea she doesn't understand you as well as I do. . . . All right; now, Mr. Kowalski, let us proceed without any more double-talk. I'm ready to answer all questions. I've nothing to hide. What is it?

STANLEY   There is such a thing in this state of Louisiana as the Napoleonic code, according to which whatever belongs to my wife is also mine—and vice versa.

BLANCHE   My, but you have an impressive judicial air!

[*She sprays herself with her atomizer; then playfully sprays him with it. He seizes the atomizer and slams it down on the dresser. She throws back her head and laughs.*]

STANLEY   If I didn't know that you was my wife's sister I'd get ideas about you!

BLANCHE   Such as what!

STANLEY   Don't play so dumb. You know what!

BLANCHE [*she puts the atomizer on the table*]   All right. Cards on the table. That suits me. [*She turns to* STANLEY.] I know I fib a good deal. After all, a woman's charm is fifty per cent illusion, but when a thing is important I tell the truth, and this is the truth: I haven't cheated my sister or you or anyone else as long as I have lived.

STANLEY   Where's the papers? In the trunk?

BLANCHE   Everything that I own is in that trunk.

[STANLEY *crosses to the trunk, shoves it roughly open and begins to open compartments.*]

BLANCHE   What in the name of heaven are you thinking of! What's in the back of that little boy's mind of yours? That I am absconding with something, attempting some kind of treachery on my sister?— Let me do that! It will be faster and simpler . . . [*She crosses to the trunk and takes out a box.*] I keep my papers mostly in this tin box. [*She opens it.*]

STANLEY   What's them underneath? [*He indicates another sheaf of paper.*]

BLANCHE   These are love-letters, yellowing with antiquity, all from one boy. [*He snatches them up. She speaks fiercely.*] Give those back to me!

2. Nonsense syllables (from "bop," a form of jazz).

STANLEY   I'll have a look at them first!

BLANCHE   The touch of your hands insults them!

STANLEY   Don't pull that stuff!

[*He rips off the ribbon and starts to examine them.* BLANCHE *snatches them from him, and they cascade to the floor.*]

BLANCHE   Now that you've touched them I'll burn them!

STANLEY [*staring, baffled*]   What in hell are they?

BLANCHE [*on the floor gathering them up*]   Poems a dead boy wrote. I hurt him the way that you would like to hurt me, but you can't! I'm not young and vulnerable any more. But my young husband was and I—never mind about that! Just give them back to me!

STANLEY   What do you mean by saying you'll have to burn them?

BLANCHE   I'm sorry, I must have lost my head for a moment. Everyone has something he won't let others touch because of their—intimate nature . . . .

[*She now seems faint with exhaustion and she sits down with the strong box and puts on a pair of glasses and goes methodically through a large stack of papers.*]

Ambler & Ambler. Hmmmmm. . . . Crabtree. . . . More Ambler & Ambler.

STANLEY   What is Ambler & Ambler?

BLANCHE   A firm that made loans on the place.

STANLEY   Then it *was* lost on a mortgage?

BLANCHE [*touching her forehead*]   That must've been what happened.

STANLEY   I don't want no ifs, ands or buts! What's all the rest of them papers?

[*She hands him the entire box. He carries it to the table and starts to examine the papers.*]

BLANCHE [*picking up a large envelope containing more papers*] There are thousands of papers, stretching back over hundreds of years, affecting Belle Reve as, piece by piece, our improvident grandfathers and fathers and uncles and brothers exchanged the land for their epic fornications—to put it plainly! [*She removes her glasses with an exhausted laugh.*] The four-letter word deprived us of our plantation, till finally all that was left—and Stella can verify that!—was the house itself and about twenty acres of ground, including a graveyard, to which now all but Stella and I have retreated. [*She pours the contents of the envelope on the table.*] Here all of them are, all papers! I hereby endow you with them! Take them, peruse them—commit them to memory, even! I think it's wonderfully fitting that Belle Reve should finally be this bunch of old papers in your big, capable hands! . . . I wonder if Stella's come back with my lemon Coke . . . [*She leans back and closes her eyes.*]

STANLEY   I have a lawyer acquaintance who will study these out.

BLANCHE   Present them to him with a box of aspirin tablets.

STANLEY [*becoming somewhat sheepish*]   You see, under the Napoleonic code—a man has to take an interest in his wife's affairs—especially now that she's going to have a baby.

[BLANCHE *opens her eyes. The "Blue Piano" sounds louder.*]

BLANCHE   Stella? Stella going to have a baby? [*dreamily*] I didn't
know she was going to have a baby!
> [*She gets up and crosses to the outside door.* STELLA *appears
> around the corner with a carton from the drugstore.* STANLEY
> *goes into the bedroom with the envelope and the box. The
> inner rooms fade to darkness and the outside wall of the house
> is visible.* BLANCHE *meets* STELLA *at the foot of the steps to
> the sidewalk.*]

BLANCHE   Stella, Stella for star! How lovely to have a baby! It's all
right. Everything's all right.

STELLA   I'm sorry he did that to you.

BLANCHE   Oh, I guess he's just not the type that goes for jasmine
perfume, but maybe he's what we need to mix with our blood
now that we've lost Belle Reve. We thrashed it out. I feel a bit
shaky, but I think I handled it nicely, I laughed and treated it all
as a joke. [STEVE *and* PABLO *appear, carrying a case of beer.*] I
called him a little boy and laughed and flirted. Yes, I was flirting
with your husband! [*as the men approach*] The guests are gathering for the poker party. [*The two men pass between them, and
enter the house.*] Which way do we go now, Stella—this way?

STELLA   No, this way. [*She leads* BLANCHE *away.*]

BLANCHE   [*laughing*]   The blind are leading the blind!
> [*A tamale Vendor is heard calling.*]

VENDOR'S VOICE   Red-hot!

Scene Three

THE POKER NIGHT

There is a picture of Van Gogh's of a billiard-parlor at night.[3] *The
kitchen now suggests that sort of lurid nocturnal brilliance, the raw
colors of childhood's spectrum. Over the yellow linoleum of the kitchen
table hangs an electric bulb with a vivid green glass shade. The poker
players—*STANLEY, STEVE, MITCH *and* PABLO—*wear colored shirts, solid
blues, a purple, a red-and-white check, a light green, and they are
men at the peak of their physical manhood, as coarse and direct and
powerful as the primary colors. There are vivid slices of watermelon
on the table, whiskey bottles and glasses. The bedroom is relatively
dim with only the light that spills between the portieres and through
the wide window on the street.*

> *For a moment, there is absorbed silence as a hand is dealt.*

STEVE   Anything wild this deal?

PABLO   One-eyed jacks are wild.

STEVE   Give me two cards.

PABLO   You, Mitch?

MITCH   I'm out.

PABLO   One.

MITCH   Anyone want a shot?

---

3. *The Night Café*, by Vincent Van Gogh, Dutch post-impressionist painter (1853–
90). *The Poker Night* was Williams's first title for *A Streetcar Named Desire*.

STANLEY   Yeah. Me.

PABLO   Why don't somebody go to the Chinaman's and bring back a load of chop suey?

STANLEY   When I'm losing you want to eat! Ante up! Openers? Openers! Get y'r ass off the table, Mitch. Nothing belongs on a poker table but cards, chips and whiskey.

[*He lurches up and tosses some watermelon rinds to the floor.*]

MITCH   Kind of on your high horse, ain't you?

STANLEY   How many?

STEVE   Give me three.

STANLEY   One.

MITCH   I'm out again. I oughta go home pretty soon.

STANLEY   Shut up.

MITCH   I gotta sick mother. She don't go to sleep until I come in at night.

STANLEY   Then why don't you stay home with her?

MITCH   She says to go out, so I go, but I don't enjoy it. All the while I keep wondering how she is.

STANLEY   Aw, for the sake of Jesus, go home, then!

PABLO   What've you got?

STEVE   Spade flush.

MITCH   You all are married. But I'll be alone when she goes.—I'm going to the bathroom.

STANLEY   Hurry back and we'll fix you a sugar-tit.

MITCH   Aw, go rut. [*He crosses through the bedroom into the bathroom.*]

STEVE   [*dealing a hand*]   Seven card stud. [*telling his joke as he deals*] This ole farmer is out in back of his house sittin' down th'owing corn to the chickens when all at once he hears a loud cackle and this young hen comes lickety split around the side of the house with the rooster right behind her and gaining on her fast.

STANLEY   [*impatient with the story*]   Deal!

STEVE   But when the rooster catches sight of the farmer th'owing the corn he puts on the brakes and lets the hen get away and starts pecking corn. And the old farmer says, "Lord God, I hopes I never gits *that* hongry!"

[STEVE *and* PABLO *laugh. The sisters appear around the corner of the building.*]

STELLA   The game is still going on.

BLANCHE   How do I look?

STELLA   Lovely, Blanche.

BLANCHE   I feel so hot and frazzled. Wait till I powder before you open the door. Do I look done in?

STELLA   Why no. You are as fresh as a daisy.

BLANCHE   One that's been picked a few days.

[STELLA *opens the door and they enter.*]

STELLA   Well, well, well. I see you boys are still at it?

STANLEY   Where you been?

STELLA   Blanche and I took in a show. Blanche, this is Mr. Gonzales and Mr. Hubbell.

BLANCHE   Please don't get up.

STANLEY   Nobody's going to get up, so don't be worried.

STELLA   How much longer is this game going to continue?

STANLEY   Till we get ready to quit.

BLANCHE   Poker is so fascinating. Could I kibitz?

STANLEY   You could not. Why don't you women go up and sit with Eunice?

STELLA   Because it is nearly two-thirty. [*Blanche crosses into the bedroom and partially closes the portieres.*] Couldn't you call it quits after one more hand?

>   [*A chair scrapes.* STANLEY *gives a loud whack of his hand on her thigh.*]

STELLA   [*sharply*]   That's not fun, Stanley.

>   [*The men laugh.* STELLA *goes into the bedroom.*]

STELLA   It makes me so mad when he does that in front of people.

BLANCHE   I think I will bathe.

STELLA   Again?

BLANCHE   My nerves are in knots. Is the bathroom occupied?

>   [BLANCHE *knocks.* MITCH *opens the door and comes out, still wiping his hands on a towel.*]

BLANCHE   Oh!—good evening.

MITCH   Hello. [*He stares at her.*]

STELLA   Blanche, this is Harold Mitchell. My sister, Blanche DuBois.

MITCH   [*with awkward courtesy*]   How do you do, Miss DuBois.

STELLA   How is your mother now, Mitch?

MITCH   About the same, thanks. She appreciated your sending over that custard.—Excuse me, please.

>   [*He crosses slowly back into the kitchen, glancing back at* BLANCHE *and coughing a little shyly. He realizes he still has the towel in his hands and with an embarrassed laugh hands it to* STELLA. BLANCHE *looks after him with a certain interest.*]

BLANCHE   That one seems—superior to the others.

STELLA   Yes, he is.

BLANCHE   I thought he had a sort of sensitive look.

STELLA   His mother is sick.

BLANCHE   Is he married?

STELLA   No.

BLANCHE   Is he a wolf?

STELLA   Why, Blanche! [BLANCHE *laughs.*] I don't think he would be.

BLANCHE   What does—what does he do? [*She is unbuttoning her blouse.*]

STELLA   He's on the precision bench in the spare parts department. At the plant Stanley travels for.

BLANCHE   Is that something much?

STELLA   No. Stanley's the only one of his crowd that's likely to get anywhere.

BLANCHE   What makes you think Stanley will?

STELLA   Look at him.

BLANCHE   I've looked at him.

STELLA   Then you should know.

BLANCHE   I'm sorry, but I haven't noticed the stamp of genius even on Stanley's forehead.
[*She takes off the blouse and stands in her pink brassiere and white skirt in the light through the portieres. The game has continued in undertones.*]
STELLA   It isn't on his forehead and it isn't genius.
BLANCHE   Oh. Well, what is it, and where? I would like to know.
STELLA   It's a drive that he has. You're standing in the light, Blanche!
BLANCHE   Oh, am I!
[*She moves out of the yellow streak of light.* STELLA *has removed her dress and put on a light blue satin kimona.*]
STELLA   [*with girlish laughter*]   You ought to see their wives.
BLANCHE   [*laughingly*]   I can imagine. Big, beefy things, I suppose.
STELLA   You know that one upstairs? [*more laughter*] One time [*laughing*] the plaster—[*laughing*] cracked—
STANLEY   You hens cut out that conversation in there!
STELLA   You can't hear us.
STANLEY   Well, you can hear me and I said to hush up!
STELLA   This is my house and I'll talk as much as I want to!
BLANCHE   Stella, don't start a row.
STELLA   He's half drunk!—I'll be out in a minute.
[*She goes into the bathroom.* BLANCHE *rises and crosses leisurely to a small white radio and turns it on.*]
STANLEY   Awright, Mitch, you in?
MITCH   What? Oh!—No, I'm out!
[BLANCHE *moves back into the streak of light. She raises her arms and stretches, as she moves indolently back to the chair. Rhumba music comes over the radio.* MITCH *rises at the table.*]
STANLEY   Who turned that on in there?
BLANCHE   I did. Do you mind?
STANLEY   Turn it off!
STEVE   Aw, let the girls have their music.
PABLO   Sure, that's good, leave it on!
STEVE   Sounds like Xavier Cugat![4]
[STANLEY *jumps up and, crossing to the radio, turns it off. He stops short at the sight of* BLANCHE *in the chair. She returns his look without flinching. Then he sits again at the poker table. Two of the men have started arguing hotly.*]
STEVE   I didn't hear you name it.
PABLO   Didn't I name it, Mitch?
MITCH   I wasn't listenin'.
PABLO   What were you doing, then?
STANLEY   He was looking through them drapes. [*He jumps up and jerks roughly at curtains to close them.*] Now deal the hand over again and let's play cards or quit. Some people get ants when they win.
[MITCH *rises as* STANLEY *returns to his seat.*]
STANLEY   [*yelling*]   Sit down!
MITCH   I'm going to the "head." Deal me out.

4. Cuban band leader, well known for composing and playing rhumbas.

PABLO Sure he's got ants now. Seven five-dollar bills in his pants pocket folded up tight as spitballs.

STEVE Tomorrow you'll see him at the cashier's window getting them changed into quarters.

STANLEY And when he goes home he'll deposit them one by one in a piggy bank his mother give him for Christmas. [*dealing*] This game is Spit in the Ocean.

[MITCH *laughs uncomfortably and continues through the portieres. He stops just inside.*]

BLANCHE [*softly*] Hello! The Little Boys' Room is busy right now.

MITCH We've—been drinking beer.

BLANCHE I hate beer.

MITCH It's—a hot weather drink.

BLANCHE Oh, I don't think so; it always makes me warmer. Have you got any cigs? [*She has slipped on the dark red satin wrapper.*]

MITCH Sure.

BLANCHE What kind are they?

MITCH Luckies.

BLANCHE Oh, good. What a pretty case. Silver?

MITCH Yes. Yes; read the inscription.

BLANCHE Oh, is there an inscription? I can't make it out. [*He strikes a match and moves closer.*] Oh! [*reading with feigned difficulty*] "And if God choose,/I shall but love thee better—after—death!" Why, that's from my favorite sonnet by Mrs. Browning![5]

MITCH You know it?

BLANCHE Certainly I do!

MITCH There's a story connected with that inscription.

BLANCHE It sounds like a romance.

MITCH A pretty sad one.

BLANCHE Oh?

MITCH The girl's dead now.

BLANCHE [*in a tone of deep sympathy*] Oh!

MITCH She knew she was dying when she give me this. A very strange girl, very sweet—very!

BLANCHE She must have been fond of you. Sick people have such deep, sincere attachments.

MITCH That's right, they certainly do.

BLANCHE Sorrow makes for sincerity, I think.

MITCH It sure brings it out in people.

BLANCHE The little there is belongs to people who have experienced some sorrow.

MITCH I believe you are right about that.

BLANCHE I'm positive that I am. Show me a person who hasn't known any sorrow and I'll show you a shuperficial—Listen to me! My tongue is a little—thick! You boys are responsible for it. The show let out at eleven and we couldn't come home on account of the poker game so we had to go somewhere and drink. I'm not accustomed to having more than one drink. Two is the limit—and *three*! [*She laughs.*] Tonight I had three.

---

5. Elizabeth Barrett Browning, 19th-century British poet, was most famous for her sequence of love poems, *Sonnets from the Portuguese.*

STANLEY   Mitch!

MITCH   Deal me out. I'm talking to Miss—

BLANCHE   DuBois.

MITCH   Miss DuBois?

BLANCHE   It's a French name. It means woods and Blanche means white, so the two together mean white woods. Like an orchard in spring! You can remember it by that.

MITCH   You're French?

BLANCHE   We are French by extraction. Our first American ancestors were French Huguenots.

MITCH   You are Stella's sister, are you not?

BLANCHE   Yes, Stella is my precious little sister. I call her little in spite of the fact she's somewhat older than I. Just slightly. Less than a year. Will you do something for me?

MITCH   Sure. What?

BLANCHE   I bought this adorable little colored paper lantern at a Chinese shop on Bourbon. Put it over the light bulb! Will you, please?

MITCH   Be glad to.

BLANCHE   I can't stand a naked light bulb, any more than I can a rude remark or a vulgar action.

MITCH [*adjusting the lantern*]   I guess we strike you as being a pretty rough bunch.

BLANCHE   I'm very adaptable—to circumstances.

MITCH   Well, that's a good thing to be. You are visiting Stanley and Stella?

BLANCHE   Stella hasn't been so well lately, and I came down to help her for a while. She's very run down.

MITCH   You're not—?

BLANCHE   Married? No, no. I'm an old maid schoolteacher!

MITCH   You may teach school but you're certainly not an old maid.

BLANCHE   Thank you, sir! I appreciate your gallantry!

MITCH   So you are in the teaching profession?

BLANCHE   Yes. Ah, yes . . .

MITCH   Grade school or high school or—

STANLEY [*bellowing*]   *Mitch!*

MITCH   Coming!

BLANCHE   Gracious, what lung-power! . . . I teach high school. In Laurel.

MITCH   What do you teach? What subject?

BLANCHE   Guess!

MITCH   I bet you teach art or music? [BLANCHE *laughs delicately.*] Of course I could be wrong. You might teach arithmetic.

BLANCHE   Never arithmetic, sir; never arithmetic! [*with a laugh*] I don't even know my multiplication tables! No, I have the misfortune of being an English instructor. I attempt to instill a bunch of bobby-soxers and drugstore Romeos with reverence for Hawthorne and Whitman and Poe!

MITCH   I guess that some of them are more interested in other things.

BLANCHE   How very right you are! Their literary heritage is not what most of them treasure above all else! But they're sweet things! And in the spring, it's touching to notice them making their first discovery of love! As if nobody had ever known it before!

[*The bathroom door opens and* STELLA *comes out.* BLANCHE *continues talking to* MITCH.]

Oh! Have you finished? Wait—I'll turn on the radio.

[*She turns the knobs on the radio and it begans to play "Wien, Wien, nur du allein."*[6] BLANCHE *waltzes to the music with romantic gestures.* MITCH *is delighted and moves in awkward imitation like a dancing bear.* STANLEY *stalks fiercely through the portieres into the bedroom. He crosses to the small white radio and snatches it off the table. With a shouted oath, he tosses the instrument out the window.*]

STELLA   Drunk—drunk—animal thing, you! [*She rushes through to the poker table.*] All of you—please go home! If any of you have one spark of decency in you—

BLANCHE [*wildly*]   Stella, watch out, he's—

[STANLEY *charges after* STELLA.]

MEN [*feebly*]   Take it easy, Stanley. Easy, fellow.—Let's all—

STELLA   You lay your hands on me and I'll—

[*She backs out of sight. He advances and disappears. There is the sound of a blow.* STELLA *cries out.* BLANCHE *screams and runs into the kitchen. The men rush forward and there is grappling and cursing. Something is overturned with a crash.*]

BLANCHE [*shrilly*]   My sister is going to have a baby!

MITCH   This is terrible.

BLANCHE   Lunacy, absolute lunacy!

MITCH   Get him in here, men.

[STANLEY *is forced, pinioned by the two men, into the bedroom. He nearly throws them off. Then all at once he subsides and is limp in their grasp. They speak quietly and lovingly to him and he leans his face on one of their shoulders.*]

STELLA [*in a high, unnatural voice, out of sight*]   I want to go away, I want to go away!

MITCH   Poker shouldn't be played in a house with women.

[BLANCHE *rushes into the bedroom.*]

BLANCHE   I want my sister's clothes! We'll go to that woman's upstairs!

MITCH   Where is the clothes?

BLANCHE [*opening the closet*]   I've got them! [*She rushes through to* STELLA.] Stella, Stella, precious! Dear, dear little sister, don't be afraid!

[*With her arm around* STELLA, BLANCHE *guides her to the outside door and upstairs.*]

STANLEY [*dully*]   What's the matter; what's happened?

MITCH   You just blew your top, Stan.

PABLO   He's okay, now.

STEVE   Sure, my boy's okay!

MITCH   Put him on the bed and get a wet towel.

PABLO   I think coffee would do him a world of good, now.

STANLEY [*thickly*]   I want water.

6. "Vienna, Vienna, you are my only," a waltz from an operetta by Franz Lehar.

MITCH   Put him under the shower!

[*The men talk quietly as they lead him to the bathroom.*]

STANLEY   Let the rut go of me, you sons of bitches!

[*Sounds of blows are heard. The water goes on full tilt.*]

STEVE   Let's get quick out of here!

[*They rush to the poker table and sweep up their winnings on their way out.*]

MITCH [*sadly but firmly*]   Poker should not be played in a house with women.

[*The door closes on them and the place is still. The Negro entertainers in the bar around the corner play "Paper Doll"[7] slow and blue. After a moment* STANLEY *comes out of the bathroom dripping water and still in his clinging wet polka dot drawers.*]

STANLEY   Stella! [*There is a pause.*] My baby doll's left me!

[*He breaks into sobs. Then he goes to the phone and dials, still shuddering with sobs.*]

Eunice? I want my baby! [*He waits a moment; then he hangs up and dials again.*] Eunice! I'll keep on ringin' until I talk with my baby!

[*An indistinguishable shrill voice is heard. He hurls phone to floor. Dissonant brass and piano sounds as the rooms dim out to darkness and the outer walls appear in the night light. The "Blue Piano" plays for a brief interval. Finally,* STANLEY *stumbles half-dressed out to the porch and down the wooden steps to the pavement before the building. There he throws back his head like a baying hound and bellows his wife's name:* "STELLA! STELLA, *sweetheart!* STELLA!"]

STANLEY   Stell-*lahhhhh!*

EUNICE [*calling down from the door of her upper apartment*]   Quit that howling out there an' go back to bed!

STANLEY   I want my baby down here. Stella, Stella!

EUNICE   She ain't comin' down so you quit! Or you'll git th' law on you!

STANLEY   Stella!

EUNICE   You can't beat on a woman an' then call 'er back! She won't come! And her goin' t' have a baby! . . . You stinker! You whelp of a Polack, you! I hope they do haul you in and turn the fire hose on you, same as the last time!

STANLEY [*humbly*]   Eunice, I want my girl to come down with me!

EUNICE   Hah! [*She slams her door.*]

STANLEY [*with heaven-splitting violence*]   *STELL-LAHHHHH!*

[*The low-tone clarinet moans. The door upstairs opens again.* STELLA *slips down the rickety stairs in her robe. Her eyes are glistening with tears and her hair loose about her throat and shoulders. They stare at each other. Then they come together with low, animal moans. He falls to his knees on the steps and presses his face to her belly, curving a little with maternity. Her eyes go bland with tenderness as she catches his head and*

7. Popular song of the early 1940s.

raises him level with her. He snatches the screen door open and lifts her off her feet and bears her into the dark flat. BLANCHE *comes out the upper landing in her robe and slips fearfully down the steps.*]

BLANCHE   Where is my little sister? Stella? Stella?
[*She stops before the dark entrance of her sister's flat. Then catches her breath as if struck. She rushes down to the walk before the house. She looks right and left as if for a sanctuary. The music fades away.* MITCH *appears from around the corner.*]

MITCH   Miss DuBois?

BLANCHE   Oh!

MITCH   All quiet on the Potomac now?

BLANCHE   She ran downstairs and went back in there with him.

MITCH   Sure she did.

BLANCHE   I'm terrified.

MITCH   Ho-ho! There's nothing to be scared of. They're crazy about each other.

BLANCHE   I'm not used to such—

MITCH   Naw, it's a shame this had to happen when you just got here. But don't take it serious.

BLANCHE   Violence! Is so—

MITCH   Set down on the steps and have a cigarette with me.

BLANCHE   I'm not properly dressed.

MITCH   That don't make no difference in the Quarter.

BLANCHE   Such a pretty silver case.

MITCH   I showed you the inscription, didn't I?

BLANCHE   Yes. [*During the pause, she looks up at the sky.*] There's so much—so much confusion in the world . . . [*He coughs diffidently.*] Thank you for being so kind! I need kindness now.

Scene Four

It is early the following morning. There is a confusion of street cries like a choral chant.

STELLA *is lying down in the bedroom. Her face is serene in the early morning sunlight. One hand rests on her belly, rounding slightly with new maternity. From the other dangles a book of colored comics. Her eyes and lips have that almost narcotized tranquility that is in the faces of Eastern idols.*

The table is sloppy with remains of breakfast and the debris of the preceding night, and STANLEY'S *gaudy pyjamas lie across the threshold of the bathroom. The outside door is slightly ajar on a sky of summer brilliance.*

BLANCHE *appears at this door. She has spent a sleepless night and her appearance entirely contrasts with* STELLA'S. *She presses her knuckles nervously to her lips as she looks through the door, before entering.*

BLANCHE   Stella?

STELLA   [*stirring lazily*]   Hmmh?

[BLANCHE *utters a moaning cry and runs into the bedroom, throwing herself down beside* STELLA *in a rush of hysterical tenderness.*]

BLANCHE   Baby, my baby sister!

STELLA   [*drawing away from her*]   Blanche, what is the matter with you?

[BLANCHE *straightens up slowly and stands beside the bed looking down at her sister with knuckles pressed to her lips.*]

BLANCHE   He's left?

STELLA   Stan? Yes.

BLANCHE   Will he be back?

STELLA   He's gone to get the car greased. Why?

BLANCHE   Why! I've been half crazy, Stella! When I found out you'd been insane enough to come back in here after what happened—I started to rush in after you!

STELLA   I'm glad you didn't.

BLANCHE   What were you thinking of? [STELLA *makes an indefinite gesture.*] Answer me! What? What?

STELLA   Please, Blanche! Sit down and stop yelling.

BLANCHE   All right, Stella. I will repeat the question quietly now. How could you come back in this place last night? Why, you must have slept with him!

[STELLA *gets up in a calm and leisurely way.*]

STELLA   Blanche, I'd forgotten how excitable you are. You're making much too much fuss about this.

BLANCHE   Am I?

STELLA   Yes, you are, Blanche. I know how it must have seemed to you and I'm awful sorry it had to happen, but it wasn't anything as serious as you seem to take it. In the first place, when men are drinking and playing poker anything can happen. It's always a powder-keg. He didn't know what he was doing. . . . He was as good as a lamb when I came back and he's really very, very ashamed of himself.

BLANCHE   And that—that makes it all right?

STELLA   No, it isn't all right for anybody to make such a terrible row, but—people do sometimes. Stanley's always smashed things. Why, on our wedding night—soon as we came in here—he snatched off one of my slippers and rushed about the place smashing light bulbs with it.

BLANCHE   He did—*what?*

STELLA   He smashed all the lightbulbs with the heel of my slipper! [*She laughs.*]

BLANCHE   And you—you *let* him? Didn't *run*, didn't *scream?*

STELLA   I was—sort of—thrilled by it. [*She waits for a moment.*] Eunice and you had breakfast?

BLANCHE   Do you suppose I wanted any breakfast?

STELLA   There's some coffee on the stove.

BLANCHE   You're so—matter of fact about it, Stella.

STELLA   What other can I be? He's taken the radio to get it fixed. It didn't land on the pavement so only one tube was smashed.

BLANCHE   And you are standing there smiling!

STELLA   What do you want me to do?

BLANCHE   Pull yourself together and face the facts.

STELLA   What are they, in your opinion?

BLANCHE   In my opinion? You're married to a madman!

STELLA   No!

BLANCHE   Yes, you are, your fix is worse than mine is! Only you're not being sensible about it. I'm going to *do* something. Get hold of myself and make myself a new life!

STELLA   Yes?

BLANCHE   But you've given in. And that isn't right, you're not old! You can get out.

STELLA [*slowly and emphatically*]   I'm not in anything I want to get out of.

BLANCHE [*incredulously*]   What—Stella?

STELLA   I said I am not in anything that I have a desire to get out of. Look at the mess in this room! And those empty bottles! They went through two cases last night! He promised this morning that he was going to quit having these poker parties, but you know how long such a promise is going to keep. Oh, well, it's his pleasure, like mine is movies and bridge. People have got to tolerate each other's habits, I guess.

BLANCHE   I don't understand you. [*Stella turns toward her.*] I don't understand your indifference. Is this a Chinese philosophy you've —cultivated?

STELLA   Is what—what?

BLANCHE   This—shuffling about and mumbling—'One tube smashed —beer bottles—mess in the kitchen!'—as if nothing out of the ordinary has happened! [STELLA *laughs uncertainly and picking up the broom, twirls it in her hands.*]

BLANCHE   Are you deliberately shaking that thing in my face?

STELLA   No.

BLANCHE   Stop it. Let go of that broom. I won't have you cleaning up for him!

STELLA   Then who's going to do it? Are you?

BLANCHE   I? I!

STELLA   No, I didn't think so.

BLANCHE   Oh, let me think, if only my mind would function! We've got to get hold of some money, that's the way out!

STELLA   I guess that money is always nice to get hold of.

BLANCHE   Listen to me. I have an idea of some kind. [*Shakily she twists a cigarette into her holder.*] Do you remember Shep Huntleigh? [STELLA *shakes her head.*] Of course you remember Shep Huntleigh. I went out with him at college and wore his pin for a while. Well—

STELLA   Well?

BLANCHE   I ran into him last winter. You know I went to Miami during the Christmas holidays?

STELLA   No.

BLANCHE   Well, I did. I took the trip as an investment, thinking I'd meet someone with a million dollars.

STELLA   Did you?

BLANCHE   Yes. I ran into Shep Huntleigh—I ran into him on Biscayne
Boulevard, on Christmas Eve, about dusk . . . getting into his car—
Cadillac convertible; must have been a block long!

STELLA   I should think it would have been—inconvenient in traffic!

BLANCHE   You've heard of oil wells?

STELLA   Yes—remotely.

BLANCHE   He has them, all over Texas. Texas is literally spouting gold
in his pockets.

STELLA   My, my.

BLANCHE   Y'know how indifferent I am to money. I think of money
in terms of what it does for you. But he could do it, he could
certainly do it!

STELLA   Do what, Blanche?

BLANCHE   Why—set us up in a—shop!

STELLA   What kind of shop?

BLANCHE   Oh, a—shop of some kind! He could do it with half what
his wife throws away at the races.

STELLA   He's married?

BLANCHE   Honey, would I be here if the man weren't married?
[STELLA *laughs a little.* BLANCHE *suddenly springs up and crosses
to phone. She speaks shrilly.*] How do I get Western Union?—
Operator! Western Union!

STELLA   That's a dial phone, honey.

BLANCHE   I can't dial, I'm too—

STELLA   Just dial O.

BLANCHE   O?

STELLA   Yes, "O" for Operator! [BLANCHE *considers a moment; then
she puts the phone down.*]

BLANCHE   Give me a pencil. Where is a slip of paper? I've got to
write it down first—the message, I mean . . . [*She goes to the
dressing table, and grabs up a sheet of Kleenex and an eyebrow
pencil for writing equipment.*] Let me see now . . . [*She bites the
pencil.*] 'Darling Shep. Sister and I in desperate situation.'

STELLA   I beg your pardon!

BLANCHE   'Sister and I in desperate situation. Will explain details
later. Would you be interested in—?' [*She bites the pencil again.*]
'Would you be—interested—in . . .' [*She smashes the pencil on the
table and springs up.*] You never get anywhere with direct appeals!

STELLA [*with a laugh*]   Don't be so ridiculous, darling!

BLANCHE   But I'll think of something, I've *got* to think of—*some*-
thing! Don't laugh at me, Stella! Please, please don't—I—I want
you to look at the contents of my purse! Here's what's in it! [*She
snatches her purse open.*] Sixty-five measly cents in coin of the
realm!

STELLA [*crossing to bureau*]   Stanley doesn't give me a regular allowance, he likes to pay bills himself, but—this morning he gave me ten
dollars to smooth things over. You take five of it, Blanche, and I'll
keep the rest.

BLANCHE   Oh, no. No, Stella.

STELLA [*insisting*]   I know how it helps your morale just having a
little pocket-money on you.

BLANCHE   No, thank you—I'll take to the streets!

STELLA   Talk sense! How did you hapen to get so low on funds?

BLANCHE   Money just goes—it goes places. [*She rubs her forehead.*] Sometime today I've got to get hold of a Bromo![8]

STELLA   I'll fix you one now.

BLANCHE   Not yet—I've got to keep thinking!

STELLA   I wish you'd just let things go, at least for a while.

BLANCHE   Stella, I can't live with him! You can, he's your husband. But how could I stay here with him, after last night, with just those curtains between us?

STELLA   Blanche, you saw him at his worst last night.

BLANCHE   On the contrary, I saw him at his best! What such a man has to offer is animal force and he gave a wonderful exhibition of that! But the only way to live with such a man is to—go to bed with him! And that's your job—not mine!

STELLA   After you've rested a little, you'll see it's going to work out. You don't have to worry about anything while you're here. I mean —expenses . . .

BLANCHE   I have to plan for us both, to get us both—out!

STELLA   You take it for granted that I am in something that I want to get out of.

BLANCHE   I take it for granted that you still have sufficient memory of Belle Reve to find this place and these poker players impossible to live with.

STELLA   Well, you're taking entirely too much for granted.

BLANCHE   I can't believe you're in earnest.

STELLA   No?

BLANCHE   I understand how it happened—a little. You saw him in uniform, an officer, not here but—

STELLA   I'm not sure it would have made any difference where I saw him.

BLANCHE   Now don't say it was one of those mysterious electric things between people! If you do I'll laugh in your face.

STELLA   I am not going to say anything more at all about it!

BLANCHE   All right, then, don't!

STELLA   But there are things that happen between a man and a woman in the dark—that sort of make everything else seem— unimportant. [*pause*]

BLANCHE   What you are talking about is brutal desire—just— Desire!—the name of that rattle-trap streetcar that bangs through the Quarter, up one old narrow street and down another . . .

STELLA   Haven't you ever ridden on that streetcar?

BLANCHE   It brought me here.—Where I'm not wanted and where I'm ashamed to be . . .

STELLA   Then don't you think your superior attitude is a bit out of place?

BLANCHE   I am not being or feeling at all superior, Stella. Believe me I'm not! It's just this. This is how I look at it. A man like that is someone to go out with—once—twice—three times when the devil is in you. But live with? Have a child by?

8. Short for "Bromo-seltzer," a headache remedy.

STELLA   I have told you I love him.

BLANCHE   Then I *tremble* for you! I just—*tremble* for you. . . .

STELLA   I can't help your trembling if you insist on trembling!
[*There is a pause.*]

BLANCHE   May I—speak—*plainly?*

STELLA   Yes, do. Go ahead. As plainly as you want to.

> [*Outside, a train approaches. They are silent till the noise sub-
> sides. They are both in the bedroom. Under cover of the
> train's noise* STANLEY *enters from outside. He stands unseen
> by the women, holding some packages in his arms, and over-
> hears their following conversation. He wears an undershirt
> and grease-stained seersucker pants.*]

BLANCHE   Well—if you'll forgive me—he's *common!*

STELLA   Why, yes, I suppose he is.

BLANCHE   Suppose! You can't have forgotten that much of our bringing up, Stella, that you just *suppose* that any part of a gentleman's
in his nature! *Not one particle, no!* Oh, if he was just—*ordinary!*
Just *plain*—but good and wholesome, but—*no*. There's something
downright—*bestial*—about him! You're hating me saying this,
aren't you?

STELLA [*coldly*]   Go on and say it all, Blanche.

BLANCHE   He acts like an animal, has an animal's habits! Eats like
one, moves like one, talks like one! There's even something—sub-
human—something not quite to the stage of humanity yet! Yes,
something—ape-like about him, like one of those pictures I've
seen in—anthropological studies! Thousands and thousands of years
have passed him right by, and there he is—Stanley Kowalski—
survivor of the Stone Age! Bearing the raw meat home from the kill
in the jungle! And you—*you* here—*waiting* for him! Maybe he'll
strike you or maybe grunt and kiss you! That is, if kisses have been
discovered yet! Night falls and the other apes gather! There in the
front of the cave, all grunting like him, and swilling and gnawing
and hulking! His poker night! you call it—this party of apes! Somebody growls—some creature snatches at something—the fight is on!
God! Maybe we are a long way from being made in God's image,
but Stella—my sister—there has been *some* progress since then!
Such things as art—as poetry and music—such kinds of new light
have come into the world since then! In some kinds of people some
tenderer feelings have had some little beginning! That we have
got to make *grow!* And *cling* to, and hold as our flag! In this dark
march toward whatever it is we're approaching. . . . *Don't—don't
hang back with the brutes!*

> [*Another train passes outside.* STANLEY *hesitates, licking his
> lips. Then suddenly he turns stealthily about and withdraws
> through the front door. The women are still unaware of his
> presence. When the train has passed he calls through the
> closed front door.*]

STANLEY   Hey! Hey, Stella!

STELLA [*who has listened gravely to* BLANCHE]   Stanley!

BLANCHE   Stell, I—

[*But* STELLA *has gone to the front door.* STANLEY *enters casually with his packages.*]

STANLEY   Hiyuh, Stella. Blanche back?

STELLA   Yes, she's back.

STANLEY   Hiyuh, Blanche. [*He grins at her.*]

STELLA   You must've got under the car.

STANLEY   Them darn mechanics at Fritz's don't know their ass fr'm —Hey!

[STELLA *has embraced him with both arms, fiercely, and full in the view of* BLANCHE. *He laughs and clasps her head to him. Over her head he grins through the curtains at* BLANCHE. *As the lights fade away, with a lingering brightness on their embrace, the music of the "Blue Piano" and trumpet and drums is heard.*]

Scene Five

BLANCHE *is seated in the bedroom fanning herself with a palm leaf as she reads over a just-completed letter. Suddenly she bursts into a peal of laughter.* STELLA *is dressing in the bedroom.*

STELLA   What are you laughing at, honey?

BLANCHE   Myself, myself, for being such a liar! I'm writing a letter to Shep. [*She picks up the letter.*] "Darling Shep. I am spending the summer on the wing, making flying visits here and there. And who knows, perhaps I shall take a sudden notion to *swoop* down on *Dallas!* How would you feel about that? Ha-ha! [*She laughs nervously and brightly, touching her throat as if actually talking to* SHEP.] Forewarned is forearmed, as they say!"—How does that sound?

STELLA   Uh-huh . . .

BLANCHE [*going on nervously*]   "Most of my sister's friends go north in the summer but some have homes on the Gulf and there has been a continued round of entertainments, teas, cocktails, and luncheons—"

[*A disturbance is heard upstairs at the Hubbell's apartment.*]

STELLA   Eunice seems to be having some trouble with Steve. [EUNICE's *voice shouts in terrible wrath.*]

EUNICE   I heard about you and that blonde!

STEVE   That's a damn lie!

EUNICE   You ain't pulling the wool over my eyes! I wouldn't mind if you'd stay down at the Four Deuces, but you always going up.

STEVE   Who ever seen me up?

EUNICE   I seen you chasing her 'round the balcony—I'm gonna call the vice squad!

STEVE   Don't you throw that at me!

EUNICE [*shrieking*]   You hit me! I'm gonna call the police!

[*A clatter of aluminum striking a wall is heard, followed by a man's angry roar, shouts and overturned furniture. There is a crash; then a relative hush.*]

BLANCHE [*brightly*]   Did he *kill* her?

[EUNICE *appears on the steps in daemonic disorder.*]

STELLA   No! She's coming downstairs.

EUNICE   Call the police, I'm going to call the police! [*She rushes around the corner.*]

[*They laugh lightly.* STANLEY *comes around the corner in his green and scarlet silk bowling shirt. He trots up the steps and bangs into the kitchen.* BLANCHE *registers his entrance with nervous gestures.*]

STANLEY   What's a matter with Eun-uss?

STELLA   She and Steve had a row. Has she got the police?

STANLEY   Naw. She's gettin' a drink.

STELLA   That's much more practical!

[STEVE *comes down nursing a bruise on his forehead and looks in the door.*]

STEVE   She here?

STANLEY   Naw, naw. At the Four Deuces.

STEVE   That rutting hunk! [*He looks around the corner a bit timidly, then turns with affected boldness and runs after her.*]

BLANCHE   I must jot that down in my notebook. Ha-ha! I'm compiling a notebook of quaint little words and phrases I've picked up here.

STANLEY   You won't pick up nothing here you ain't heard before.

BLANCHE   Can I count on that?

STANLEY   You can count on it up to five hundred.

BLANCHE   That's a mighty high number. [*He jerks open the bureau drawer, slams it shut and throws shoes in a corner. At each noise* BLANCHE *winces slightly. Finally she speaks.*] What sign were you born under?

STANLEY [*while he is dressing*]   Sign?

BLANCHE   Astrological sign. I bet you were born under Aries. Aries people are forceful and dynamic. They dote on noise! They love to bang things around! You must have had lots of banging around in the army and now that you're out, you make up for it by treating inanimate objects with such a fury!

[STELLA *has been going in and out of closet during this scene. Now she pops her head out of the closet.*]

STELLA   Stanley was born just five minutes after Christmas.

BLANCHE   Capricorn—the Goat!

STANLEY   What sign were *you* born under?

BLANCHE   Oh, my birthday's next month, the fifteenth of September; that's under Virgo.

STANLEY   What's Virgo?

BLANCHE   Virgo is the Virgin.

STANLEY [*contemptuously*]   Hah! [*He advances a little as he knots his tie.*] Say, do you happen to know somebody named Shaw?

[*Her face expresses a faint shock. She reaches for the cologne bottle and dampens her handkerchief as she answers carefully.*]

BLANCHE   Why, everybody knows somebody named Shaw!

STANLEY   Well, this somebody named Shaw is under the impression he met you in Laurel, but I figure he must have got you mixed up with some other party because this other party is someone he met at a hotel called the Flamingo.

[BLANCHE *laughs breathlessly as she touches the cologne-dampened handkerchief to her temples.*]

BLANCHE   I'm afraid he does have me mixed up with this "other party." The Hotel Flamingo is not the sort of establishment I would dare to be seen in!

STANLEY   You know of it?

BLANCHE   Yes, I've seen it and smelled it.

STANLEY   You must've got pretty close if you could smell it.

BLANCHE   The odor of cheap perfume is penetrating.

STANLEY   That stuff you use is expensive?

BLANCHE   Twenty-five dollars an ounce! I'm nearly out. That's just a hint if you want to remember my birthday! [*She speaks lightly but her voice has a note of fear.*]

STANLEY   Shaw must've got you mixed up. He goes in and out of Laurel all the time so he can check on it and clear up any mistake. [*He turns away and crosses to the portieres.* BLANCHE *closes her eyes as if faint. Her hand trembles as she lifts the handkerchief again to her forehead.* STEVE *and* EUNICE *come around corner.* STEVE's *arm is around* EUNICE's *shoulder and she is sobbing luxuriously and he is cooing love-words. There is a murmur of thunder as they go slowly upstairs in a tight embrace.*]

STANLEY [*to* STELLA]   I'll wait for you at the Four Deuces!

STELLA   Hey! Don't I rate one kiss?

STANLEY   Not in front of your sister. [*He goes out.* BLANCHE *rises from her chair. She seems faint; looks about her with an expression of almost panic.*]

BLANCHE   Stella! What have you heard about me?

STELLA   Huh?

BLANCHE   What have people been telling you about me?

STELLA   Telling?

BLANCHE   You haven't heard any—unkind—gossip about me?

STELLA   Why, no, Blanche, of course not!

BLANCHE   Honey, there was—a good deal of talk in Laurel.

STELLA   About *you,* Blanche?

BLANCHE   I wasn't so good the last two years or so, after Belle Reve had started to slip through my fingers.

STELLA   All of us do things we—

BLANCHE   I never was hard or self-sufficient enough. When people are soft—soft people have got to shimmer and glow—they've got to put on soft colors, the colors of butterfly wings, and put a—paper lantern over the light. . . . It isn't enough to be soft *and attractive.* And I—I'm fading now! I don't know how much longer I can turn the trick. [*The afternoon has faded to dusk.* STELLA *goes into the bedroom and turns on the light under the paper lantern. She holds a bottled soft drink in her hand.*]

BLANCHE   Have you been listening to me?

STELLA   I don't listen to you when you are being morbid! [*She advances with the bottled Coke.*]

BLANCHE [*with abrupt change to gaiety*]   Is that Coke for me?

STELLA   Not for anyone else!

BLANCHE   Why, you precious thing, you! Is it just Coke?

STELLA [*turning*]   You mean you want a shot in it!

BLANCHE   Well, honey, a shot never does a Coke any harm! Let me! You mustn't wait on me!

STELLA   I like to wait on you, Blanche. It makes it seem more like home. [*She goes into the kitchen, finds a glass and pours a shot of whiskey into it.*]

BLANCHE   I have to admit I love to be waited on . . .

[*She rushes into the bedroom.* STELLA *goes to her with the glass.* BLANCHE *suddenly clutches* STELLA's *free hand with a moaning sound and presses the hand to her lips.* STELLA *is embarrassed by her show of emotion.* BLANCHE *speaks in a choked voice.*]

You're—you're so *good* to me! And I—

STELLA   Blanche.

BLANCHE   I know, I won't! You hate me to talk sentimental! But honey, *believe* I feel things more than I *tell* you! I *won't* stay long! I won't, I *promise* I—

STELLA   Blanche!

BLANCHE [*hysterically*]   I won't, I promise, *I'll* go! Go *soon!* I will *really!* I *won't* hang around until he—throws me out . . . .

STELLA   Now will you stop talking foolish?

BLANCHE   Yes, honey. Watch how you pour—that fizzy stuff foams over!

[BLANCHE *laughs shrilly and grabs the glass, but her hand shakes so it almost slips from her grasp.* STELLA *pours the Coke into the glass. It foams over and spills.* BLANCHE *gives a piercing cry.*]

STELLA [*shocked by the cry*]   Heavens!

BLANCHE   Right on my pretty white skirt!

STELLA   Oh . . . Use my hanky. Blot gently.

BLANCHE [*slowly recovering*]   I know—gently—gently . . .

STELLA   Did it stain?

BLANCHE   Not a bit. Ha-ha! Isn't that lucky? [*She sits down shakily, taking a grateful drink. She holds the glass in both hands and continues to laugh a little.*]

STELLA   Why did you scream like that?

BLANCHE   I don't know why I screamed! [*continuing nervously*] Mitch—Mitch is coming at seven. I guess I am just feeling nervous about our relations. [*She begins to talk rapidly and breathlessly.*] He hasn't gotten a thing but a good-night kiss, that's all I have given him, Stella. I want his respect. And men don't want anything they get too easy. But on the other hand men lose interest quickly. Especially when the girl is over—thirty. They think a girl over thirty ought to—the vulgar term is—"put out." . . . And I—I'm not "putting out." Of course he—he doesn't know—I mean I haven't informed him—of my real age!

STELLA   Why are you sensitive about your age?

BLANCHE   Because of hard knocks my vanity's been given. What I mean is—he thinks I'm sort of—prim and proper, you know! [*She laughs out sharply.*] I want to *deceive* him enough to make him—want me . . .

STELLA   Blanche, do you want *him?*

BLANCHE   I want to *rest!* I want to breathe quietly again! Yes—I *want* Mitch . . . *very badly!* Just think! If it happens! I can leave here and not be anyone's problem . . . .

[STANLEY *comes around the corner with a drink under his belt.*]

STANLEY [*bawling*]   Hey, Steve! Hey, Eunice! Hey, Stella!

[*There are joyous calls from above. Trumpet and drums are heard from around the corner.*]

STELLA [*kissing* BLANCHE *impulsively*]   It *will* happen!

BLANCHE [*doubtfully*]   It will?

STELLA   It *will!* [*She goes across the kitchen, looking back at* BLANCHE.] It will, honey, *it will.* . . . But don't take another drink! [*Her voice catches as she goes out the door to meet her husband.*] [BLANCHE *sinks faintly back in her chair with her drink.* EUNICE *shrieks with laughter and runs down the steps.* STEVE *bounds after her with goat-like screeches and chases her around corner.* STANLEY *and* STELLA *twine arms as they follow, laughing. Dusk settles deeper. The music from the Four Deuces is slow and blue.*]

BLANCHE   Ah, me, ah, me, ah, me . . .

[*Her eyes fall shut and the palm leaf fan drops from her fingers. She slaps her hand on the chair arm a couple of times. There is a little glimmer of lightning about the building. A* YOUNG MAN *comes along the street and rings the bell.*]

BLANCHE   Come in.

[*The* YOUNG MAN *appears through the portieres. She regards him with interest.*]

BLANCHE   Well, well! What can I do for *you?*

YOUNG MAN   I'm collecting for *The Evening Star.*

BLANCHE   I didn't know that stars took up collections.

YOUNG MAN   It's the paper.

BLANCHE   I know, I was joking—feebly! Will you—have a drink?

YOUNG MAN   No, ma'am. No, thank you. I can't drink on the job.

BLANCHE   Oh, well, now, let's see. . . . No, I don't have a dime! I'm not the lady of the house. I'm her sister from Mississippi. I'm one of those poor relations you've heard about.

YOUNG MAN   That's all right. I'll drop by later. [*He starts to go out. She approaches a little.*]

BLANCHE   Hey! [*He turns back shyly. She puts a cigarette in a long holder.*] Could you give me a light? [*She crosses toward him. They meet at the door between the two rooms.*]

YOUNG MAN   Sure. [*He takes out a lighter.*] This doesn't always work.

BLANCHE   Its temperamental? [*It flares.*] Ah!—thank you. [*He starts away again*] Hey! [*He turns again, still more uncertainty. She goes close to him.*] Uh—what time is it?

YOUNG MAN   Fifteen of seven, ma'am.

BLANCHE   So late? Don't you just love these long rainy afternoons
in New Orleans when an hour isn't just an hour—but a little piece
of eternity dropped into your hands—and who knows what to do
with it? [*She touches his shoulders.*] You—uh—didn't get wet in
the rain?

YOUNG MAN   No, ma'am. I stepped inside.

BLANCHE   In a drugstore? And had a soda?

YOUNG MAN   Uh-huh.

BLANCHE   Chocolate?

YOUNG MAN   No, ma'am. Cherry.

BLANCHE [*laughing*]   Cherry!

YOUNG MAN   A cherry soda.

BLANCHE   You make my mouth water. [*She touches his cheek lightly,
and smiles. Then she goes to the trunk.*]

YOUNG MAN   Well, I'd better be going—

BLANCHE [*stopping him*]   Young man!

> [*He turns. She takes a large, gossamer scarf from the trunk
> and drapes it about her shoulders. In the ensuing pause, the
> "Blue Piano" is heard. It continues through the rest of this
> scene and the opening of the next. The young man clears his
> throat and looks yearningly at the door.*]

Young man! Young, young, young man! Has anyone ever told you
that you look like a young Prince out of the Arabian Nights?

> [*The* YOUNG MAN *laughs uncomfortably and stands like a
> bashful kid.* BLANCHE *speaks softly to him.*]

Well, you do, honey lamb! Come here. I want to kiss you, just
once, softly and sweetly on your mouth!

> [*Without waiting for him to accept, she crosses quickly to him
> and presses her lips to his.*]

Now run along, now, quickly! It would be nice to keep you, but
I've got to be good—and keep my hands off children.

> [*He stares at her a moment. She opens the door for him and
> blows a kiss at him as he goes down the steps with a dazed
> look. She stands there a little dreamily after he has disappeared.
> Then* MITCH *appears around the corner with a bunch of roses.*]

BLANCHE [*gaily*]   Look who's coming! My Rosenkavalier![9] Bow to me
first . . . now present them! *Ahhhh—Merciiii!*

> [*She looks at him over them, coquettishly pressing them to her
> lips. He beams at her self-consciously.*]

Scene Six

*It is about two A.M. on the same evening. The outer wall of the
building is visible.* BLANCHE *and* MITCH *come in. The utter exhaustion which only a neurasthenic personality can know is evident in*
BLANCHE'*s voice and manner.* MITCH *is stolid but depressed. They
have probably been out to the amusement park on Lake Pontchar-
train, for* MITCH *is bearing, upside down, a plaster statuette of Mae*

---

9. *Knight of the Rose*, title of a romantic opera (1911) by Richard Strauss. "*Merci*":
thank you.

West, the sort of prize won at shooting galleries and carnival games of chance.

BLANCHE [*stopping lifelessly at the steps*] Well—[MITCH *laughs uneasily.*] Well . . .

MITCH I guess it must be pretty late—and you're tired.

BLANCHE Even the hot tamale man has deserted the street, and he hangs on till the end. [MITCH *laughs uneasily again.*] How will you get home?

MITCH I'll walk over to Bourbon and catch an owl-car.

BLANCHE [*laughing grimly*] Is that streetcar named Desire still grinding along the tracks at this hour?

MITCH [*heavily*] I'm afraid you haven't gotten much fun out of this evening, Blanche.

BLANCHE I spoiled it for *you.*

MITCH No, you didn't, but I felt all the time that I wasn't giving you much—entertainment.

BLANCHE I simply couldn't rise to the occasion. That was all. I don't think I've ever tried so hard to be gay and made such a dismal mess of it. I get ten points for trying!—I *did* try.

MITCH Why did you try if you didn't feel like it, Blanche?

BLANCHE I was just obeying the law of nature.

MITCH Which law is that?

BLANCHE The one that says the lady must entertain the gentleman —or no dice! See if you can locate my door key in this purse. When I'm so tired my fingers are all thumbs!

MITCH [*rooting in her purse*] This it?

BLANCHE No, honey, that's the key to my trunk which I must soon be packing.

MITCH You mean you are leaving here soon?

BLANCHE I've outstayed my welcome.

MITCH This it?

[*The music fades away.*]

BLANCHE Eureka! Honey, you open the door while I take a last look at the sky. [*She leans on the porch rail. He opens the door and stands awkwardly behind her.*] I'm looking for the Pleiades,[1] the Seven Sisters, but these girls are not out tonight. Oh, yes they are, there they are! God bless them! All in a bunch going home from their little bridge party. . . . Y' get the door open? Good boy! I guess you—want to go now . . .

[*He shuffles and coughs a little.*]

MITCH Can I—uh—kiss you—good night?

BLANCHE Why do you always ask me if you may?

MITCH I don't know whether you want me to or not.

BLANCHE Why should you be so doubtful?

MITCH That night when we parked by the lake and I kissed you, you—

BLANCHE Honey, it wasn't the kiss I objected to. I liked the kiss very much. It was the other little—familiarity—that I—felt obliged to —discourage. . . . I didn't resent it! Not a bit in the world! In fact,

---

1. The seven daughters of Atlas who were metamorphosed into stars.

I was somewhat flattered that you—desired me! But, honey, you know as well as I do that a single girl, a girl alone in the world, has got to keep a firm hold on her emotions or she'll be lost!

MITCH [*solemnly*]   Lost?

BLANCHE   I guess you are used to girls that like to be lost. The kind that get lost immediately, on the first date!

MITCH   I like you to be exactly the way that you are, because in all my—experience—I have never known anyone like you.

[BLANCHE *looks at him gravely; then she bursts into laughter and then claps a hand to her mouth.*]

MITCH   Are you laughing at me?

BLANCHE   No, honey. The lord and lady of the house have not yet returned, so come in. We'll have a nightcap. Let's leave the lights off. Shall we?

MITCH   You just—do what you want to.

[BLANCHE *precedes him into the kitchen. The outer wall of the building disappears and the interiors of the two rooms can be dimly seen.*]

BLANCHE [*remaining in the first room*]   The other room's more comfortable—go on in. This crashing around in the dark is my search for some liquor.

MITCH   You want a drink?

BLANCHE   I want *you* to have a drink! You have been so anxious and solemn all evening, and so have I; we have both been anxious and solemn and now for these few last remaining moments of our lives together—I want to create—*joie de vivre!* I'm lighting a candle.

MITCH   That's good.

BLANCHE   We are going to be very Bohemian. We are going to pretend that we are sitting in a little artists' cafe on the Left Bank in Paris! [*She lights a candle stub and puts it in a bottle.*] *Je suis la Dame aux Camellias! Vous êtes—Armand!*[2] Understand French?

MITCH [*heavily*]   Naw. Naw, I—

BLANCHE   *Voulez-vous couchez avec moi ce soir? Vous ne comprenez pas? Ah, quelle dommage!*[3]—I mean it's a damned good thing. . . . I've found some liquor! Just enough for two shots without any dividends, honey . . .

MITCH [*heavily*]   That's good.

[*She enters the bedroom with the drinks and the candle.*]

BLANCHE   Sit down! Why don't you take off your coat and loosen your collar?

MITCH   I better leave it on.

BLANCHE   No. I want you to be comfortable.

MITCH   I am ashamed of the way I perspire. My shirt is sticking to me.

BLANCHE   Perspiration is healthy. If people didn't perspire they would die in five mintues. [*She takes his coat from him.*] This is a nice coat. What kind of material is it?

2. "I am the Lady of the Camellias! You are—Armand!" Both are characters in the popular romantic play *La Dame aux Camélias* (1852) by the French author Alexandre Dumas (*fils*); she is a courtesan who gives up her true love, Armand.

3. "Would you like to sleep with me this evening? You don't understand? Ah, what a pity!"

MITCH   They call that stuff alpaca.
BLANCHE   Oh. Alpaca.
MITCH   It's very light-weight alpaca.
BLANCHE   Oh. Light-weight alpaca.
MITCH   I don't like to wear a wash-coat even in summer because I sweat through it.
BLANCHE   Oh.
MITCH   And it don't look neat on me. A man with a heavy build has got to be careful of what he puts on him so he don't look too clumsy.
BLANCHE   You are not too heavy.
MITCH   You don't think I am?
BLANCHE   You are not the delicate type. You have a massive bone-structure and a very imposing physique.
MITCH   Thank you. Last Christmas I was given a membership to the New Orleans Athletic Club.
BLANCHE   Oh, good.
MITCH   It was the finest present I ever was given. I work out there with the weights and I swim and I keep myself fit. When I started there, I was getting soft in the belly but now my belly is hard. It is so hard now that a man can punch me in the belly and it don't hurt me. Punch me! Go on! See? [*She pokes lightly at him.*]
BLANCHE   Gracious. [*Her hand touches her chest.*]
MITCH   Guess how much I weigh, Blanche?
BLANCHE   Oh, I'd say in the vicinity of—one hundred and eighty?
MITCH   Guess again.
BLANCHE   Not that much?
MITCH   No. More.
BLANCHE   Well, you're a tall man and you can carry a good deal of weight without looking awkward.
MITCH   I weigh two hundred and seven pounds and I'm six feet one and one half inches tall in my bare feet—without shoes on. And that is what I weigh stripped.
BLANCHE   Oh, my goodness, me! It's awe-inspiring.
MITCH [*embarrassed*]   My weight is not a very interesting subject to talk about. [*He hesitates for a moment.*] What's yours?
BLANCHE   My weight?
MITCH   Yes.
BLANCHE   Guess!
MITCH   Let me lift you.
BLANCE   Samson![4] Go on, lift me. [*He comes behind her and puts his hands on her waist and raises her lightly off the ground.*] Well?
MITCH   You are light as a feather.
BLANCHE   Ha-ha! [*He lowers her but keeps his hands on her waist. BLANCHE speaks with an affectation of demureness.*] You may release me now.
MITCH   Huh?
BLANCHE [*gaily*]   I said unhand me, sir. [*He fumblingly embraces her. Her voice sounds gently reproving.*] Now, Mitch. Just because Stanley and Stella aren't at home is no reason why you shouldn't behave like a gentleman.

4. Legendary strong man, in the Old Testament.

MITCH   Just give me a slap whenever I step out of bounds.

BLANCHE   That won't be necessary. You're a natural gentleman, one of the very few that are left in the world. I don't want you to think that I am severe and old maid school-teacherish or anything like that. It's just—well—

MITCH   Huh?

BLANCHE   I guess it is just that I have—old-fashioned ideals! [*She rolls her eyes, knowing he cannot see her face.* MITCH *goes to the front door. There is a considerable silence between them.* BLANCHE *sighs and* MITCH *coughs self-consciously.*]

MITCH [*finally*]   Where's Stanley and Stella tonight?

BLANCHE   They have gone out. With Mr. and Mrs. Hubbell upstairs.

MITCH   Where did they go?

BLANCHE   I think they were planning to go to a midnight prevue at Loew's State.

MITCH   We should all go out together some night.

BLANCHE   No. That wouldn't be a good plan.

MITCH   Why not?

BLANCHE   You are an old friend of Stanley's?

MITCH   We was together in the Two-forty-first.[5]

BLANCHE   I guess he talks to you frankly?

MITCH   Sure.

BLANCHE   Has he talked to you about me?

MITCH   Oh—not very much.

BLANCHE   The way you say that, I suspect that he has.

MITCH   No, he hasn't said much.

BLANCHE   But what he *has* said. What would you say his attitude toward me was?

MITCH   Why do you want to ask that?

BLANCHE   Well—

MITCH   Don't you get along with him?

BLANCHE   What do you think?

MITCH   I don't think he understand you.

BLANCHE   That's putting it mildly. If it weren't for Stella about to have a baby, I wouldn't be able to endure things here.

MITCH   He isn't—nice to you?

BLANCHE   He is insufferably rude. Goes out of his way to offend me.

MITCH   In what way, Blanche?

BLANCHE   Why, in every conceivable way.

MITCH   I'm surprised to hear that.

BLANCHE   Are you?

MITCH   Well, I—don't see how anybody could be rude to you.

BLANCHE   It's really a pretty frightful situation. You see, there's no privacy here. There's just these portieres between the two rooms at night. He stalks through the rooms in his underwear at night. And I have to ask him to close the bathroom door. That sort of commonness isn't necessary. You probably wonder why I don't move out. Well, I'll tell you frankly. A teacher's salary is barely sufficient for her living expenses. I didn't save a penny last year

5. Battalion of Engineers, in World War II.

and so I had to come here for the summer. That's why I have to put up with my sister's husband. And he has to put up with me, apparently so much against his wishes. . . . Surely he must have told you how much he hates me!

MITCH   I don't think he hates you.

BLANCHE   He hates me. Or why would he insult me? The first time I laid eyes on him I thought to myself, that man is my executioner! That man will destroy me, unless—

MITCH   Blanche—

BLANCHE   Yes, honey?

MITCH   Can I ask you a question?

BLANCHE   Yes. What?

MITCH   How old are you?
[*She makes a nervous gesture.*]

BLANCHE   Why do you want to know?

MITCH   I talked to my mother about you and she said, "How old is Blanche?" And I wasn't able to tell her. [*There is another pause.*]

BLANCHE   You talked to your mother about me?

MITCH   Yes.

BLANCHE   Why?

MITCH   I told my mother how nice you were, and I liked you.

BLANCHE   Were you sincere about that?

MITCH   You know I was.

BLANCHE   Why did your mother want to know my age?

MITCH   Mother is sick.

BLANCHE   I'm sorry to hear it. Badly?

MITCH   She won't live long. Maybe just a few months.

BLANCHE   Oh.

MITCH   She worries because I'm not settled.

BLANCHE   Oh.

MITCH   She wants me to be settled down before she—[*His voice is hoarse and he clears his throat twice, shuffling nervously around with his hands in and out of his pockets.*]

BLANCHE   You love her very much, don't you?

MITCH   Yes.

BLANCHE   I think you have a great capacity for devotion. You will be lonely when she passes on, won't you? [MITCH *clears his throat and nods.*] I understand what that is.

MITCH   To be lonely?

BLANCHE   I loved someone, too, and the person I loved I lost.

MITCH   Dead? [*She crosses to the window and sits on the sill, looking out. She pours herself another drink.*] A man?

BLANCHE   He was a boy, just a boy, when I was a very young girl. When I was sixteen, I made the discovery—love. All at once and much much too completely. It was like you suddenly turned a blinding light on something that had always been half in shadow, that's how it struck the world for me. But I was unlucky. Deluded. There was something different about the boy, a nervousness, a softness and tenderness which wasn't like a man's, although he wasn't the least bit effeminate looking—still—that thing was there. . . . He came to me for help. I didn't know that. I didn't find out anything till after our marriage when we'd run away and come back and all I knew was I'd failed him in some mysterious way and wasn't able to give the help he needed but couldn't speak of! He was in the quicksands and clutching at me—but I wasn't holding him out, I was slipping in with him! I didn't know that. I didn't know anything except I loved him unendurably but without being able to help him or help myself. Then I found out. In the worst of all possible ways. By coming suddenly into a room that I thought was empty—which wasn't empty, but had two people in it . . . the boy I had married and an older man who had been his friend for years . . . .

[*A locomotive is heard approaching outside. She claps her hands to her ears and crouches over. The headlight of the locomotive glares into the room as it thunders past. As the noise recedes she straightens slowly and continues speaking.*]

Afterward we pretended that nothing had been discovered. Yes, the three of us drove out to Moon Lake Casino, very drunk and laughing all the way.

[*Polka music sounds, in a minor key faint with distance.*]

We danced the Varsouviana![6] Suddenly in the middle of the dance the boy I had married broke away from me and ran out of the casino. A few moments later—a shot!

[*The polka stops abruptly.* BLANCHE *rises stiffly. Then, the polka resumes in a major key.*]

I ran out—all did!—all ran and gathered about the terrible thing at the edge of the lake! I couldn't get near for the crowding. Then somebody caught my arm. "Don't go any closer! Come back! You don't want to see!" See? See what! Then I heard voices say—Allan! Allan! The Grey boy! He'd stuck the revolver into his mouth, and fired—so that the back of his head had been—blown away!

[*She sways and covers her face.*]

It was because—on the dance floor—unable to stop myself—I'd suddenly said—"I saw! I know! You disgust me . . . ." And then the searchlight which had been turned on the world was turned off again and never for one moment since has there been any light that's stronger than this—kitchen—candle . . . .

[MITCH *gets up awkwardly and moves toward her a little. The polka music increases.* MITCH *stands beside her.*]

MITCH [*drawing her slowly into his arms*]   You need somebody. And I need somebody, too. Could it be—you and me, Blanche?

[*She stares at him vacantly for a moment. Then with a soft cry huddles in his embrace. She makes a sobbing effort to speak but the words won't come. He kisses her forehead and her eyes and finally her lips. The Polka tune fades out. Her breath is drawn and released in long, grateful sobs.*]

BLANCHE   Sometimes—there's God—so quickly!

6. Fast Polish dance, similar to the polka.

Scene Seven

It is late afternoon in mid-September.

The portieres are open and a table is set for a birthday supper, with cake and flowers.

STELLA *is completing the decorations as* STANLEY *comes in.*

STANLEY   What's all this stuff for?

STELLA   Honey, it's Blanche's birthday.

STANLEY   She here?

STELLA   In the bathroom.

STANLEY [*mimicking*]   "Washing out some things"?

STELLA   I reckon so.

STANLEY   How long she been in there?

STELLA   All afternoon.

STANLEY [*mimicking*]   "Soaking in a hot tub"?

STELLA   Yes.

STANLEY   Temperature 100 on the nose, and she soaks herself in a hot tub.

STELLA   She says it cools her off for the evening.

STANLEY   And you run out an' get her cokes, I suppose? And serve 'em to Her Majesty in the tub? [STELLA *shrugs*] Set down here a minute.

STELLA   Stanley, I've got things to do.

STANLEY   Set down! I've got th' dope on your big sister, Stella.

STELLA   Stanley, stop picking on Blanche.

STANLEY   That girl calls *me* common!

STELLA   Lately you been doing all you can think of to rub her the wrong way, Stanley, and Blanche is sensitive and you've got to realize that Blanche and I grew up under very different circumstances than you did.

STANLEY   So I been told. And told and told and told! You know she's been feeding us a pack of lies here?

STELLA   No, I don't and—

STANLEY   Well, she has, however. But now the cat's out of the bag! I found out some things!

STELLA   What—things?

STANLEY   Things I already suspected. But now I got proof from the most reliable sources—which I have checked on!

[BLANCHE *is singing in the bathroom a saccharine popular ballad which is used contrapuntally with* STANLEY's *speech.*]

STELLA [*to* STANLEY]   Lower your voice!

STANLEY   Some canary bird, huh!

STELLA   Now please tell me quietly what you think you've found out about by sister.

STANLEY   Lie Number One: All this squeamishness she puts on! You should just know the line she's been feeding to Mitch. He thought she had never been more than kissed by a fellow! But Sister Blanche is no lily! Ha-ha! Some lily she is!

STELLA   What have you heard and who from?

STANLEY   Our supply-man down at the plant has been going through

Laurel for years and he knows all about her and everybody else in the town of Laurel knows all about her. She is as famous in Laurel as if she was the President of the United States, only she is not respected by any party! This supply-man stops at a hotel called the Flamingo.

BLANCHE [*singing blithely*]   "Say, it's only a paper moon. Sailing over a cardboard sea—But it wouldn't be make-believe If you believed in me!"[7]

STELLA   What about the—Flamingo?

STANLEY   She stayed there, too.

STELLA   My sister lived at Belle Reve.

STANLEY   This is after the home-place had slipped through her lily-white fingers! She moved to the Flamingo! A second-class hotel which has the advantage of not interfering in the private social life of the personalities there! The Flamingo is used to all kinds of goings-on. But even the management of the Flamingo was impressed by Dame Blanche! In fact they was so impressed by Dame Blanche that they requested her to turn in her room key—for permanently! This happened a couple of weeks before she showed here.

BLANCHE [*singing*]   "It's a Barnum and Bailey world, Just as phony as it can be—But it wouldn't be make-believe If you believed in me!"

STELLA   What—contemptible lies!

STANLEY   Sure, I can see how you would be supset by this. She pulled the wool over your eyes as much as Mitch's!

STELLA   It's pure invention! There's not a word of truth in it and if I were a man and this creature had dared to invent such things in my presence—

BLANCHE [*singing*]   "Without your love, it's a honky-tonky parade! Without your love, It's a melody played In a penny arcade . . . ."

STANLEY   Honey, I told you I thoroughly checked on these stories! Now wait till I finished. The trouble with Dame Blanche was that she couldn't put on her act any more in Laurel! They got wised up after two or three dates with her and then they quit, and she goes on to another, the same old line, same old act, same old hooey! But the town was too small for this to go on forever! And as time went by she became a town character. Regarded as not just different but downright loco—nuts. [STELLA *draws back.*] That's why she's here this summer, visiting royalty, putting on all this act—because she's practically told by the mayor to get out of town! Yes, did you know there was an army camp near Laurel and your sister's was one of the places called "Out-of-Bounds"?

BLANCHE   "It's only a paper moon, Just as phony as it can be—But it wouldn't be make-believe If you believed in me!"

STANLEY   Well, so much for her being such a refined and particular type of girl. Which brings us to Lie Number Two.

STELLA   I don't want to hear any more!

STANLEY   She's not going back to teach school! In fact I am willing

7. From "It's Only a Paper Moon" (1933), a popular song by Harold Arlen.

to bet you that she never had no idea of returning to Laurel! She didn't resign temporarily from the high school because of her nerves! No, siree, Bob! She didn't. They kicked her out of that high school before the spring term ended—and I hate to tell you the reason that step was taken! A seventeen-year-old boy—she'd gotten mixed up with!

BLANCHE   "It's a Barnum and Bailey world, Just as phony as it can be—"

[*In the bathroom the water goes on loud; little breathless cries and peals of laughter are heard as if a child were frolicking in the tub.*]

STELLA   This is making me—sick!

STANLEY   The boy's dad learned about it and got in touch with the high school superintendent. Boy, oh, boy, I'd like to have been in that office when Dame Blanche was called on the carpet! I'd like to have seen her trying to squirm out of that one! But they had her on the hook good and proper that time and she knew that the jig was all up! They told her she better move on to some fresh territory. Yep, it was prackickly a town ordinance passed against her!

[*The bathroom door is opened and* BLANCHE *thrusts her head out, holding a towel about her hair.*]

BLANCHE   Stella!

STELLA [*faintly*]   Yes, Blanche?

BLANCHE   Give me another bath-towel to dry my hair with. I've just washed it.

STELLA   Yes, Blanche. [*She crosses in a dazed way from the kitchen to the bathroom door with a towel.*]

BLANCHE   What's the matter, honey?

STELLA   Matter? Why?

BLANCHE   You have such a strange expression on your face!

STELLA   Oh—[*She tries to laugh*] I guess I'm a little tired!

BLANCHE   Why don't you bathe, too, soon as I get out?

STANLEY [*calling from the kitchen*]   How soon is that going to be?

BLANCHE   Not so terribly long! Possess your soul in patience!

STANLEY   It's not my soul, it's my kidneys I'm worried about!

[BLANCHE *slams the door.* STANLEY *laughs harshly.* STELLA *comes slowly back into the kitchen.*]

STANLEY   Well, what do you think of it?

STELLA   I don't believe all of those stories and I think your supply-man was mean and rotten to tell them. It's possible that some of the things he said are partly true. There are things about my sister I don't approve of—things that caused sorrow at home. She was always—flighty!

STANLEY   Flighty!

STELLA   But when she was young, very young, she married a boy who wrote poetry. . . . He was extremely good-looking. I think Blanche didn't just love him but worshipped the ground he walked on! Adored him and thought him almost too fine to be human! But then she found out—

STANLEY   What?

STELLA   This beautiful and talented young man was a degenerate.

Didn't your supply-man give you that information?

STANLEY   All we discussed was recent history. That must have been a pretty long time ago.

STELLA   Yes, it was—a pretty long time ago . . .

> [STANLEY *comes up and takes her by the shoulders rather gently. She gently withdraws from him. Automatically she starts sticking little pink candles in the birthday cake.*]

STANLEY   How many candles you putting in that cake?

STELLA   I'll stop at twenty-five.

STANLEY   Is company expected?

STELLA   We asked Mitch to come over for cake and ice-cream.

> [STANLEY *looks a little uncomfortable. He lights a cigarette from the one he has just finished.*]

STANLEY   I wouldn't be expecting Mitch over tonight.

> [STELLA *pauses in her occupation with candles and looks slowly around at* STANLEY.]

STELLA   Why?

STANLEY   Mitch is a buddy of mine. We were in the same outfit to-gether—Two-forty-first Engineers. We work in the same plant and now on the same bowling team. You think I could face him if—

STELLA   Stanley Kowalski, did you—did you repeat what that—?

STANLEY   You're goddam right I told him! I'd have that on my con-science the rest of my life if I knew all that stuff and let my best friend get caught!

STELLA   Is Mitch through with her?

STANLEY   Wouldn't you be if—?

STELLA   I said, *Is Mitch through with her?*

> [BLANCHE'*s voice is lifted again, serenely as a bell. She sings* "But it wouldn't be make-believe If you believed in me."]

STANLEY   No, I don't think he's necessarily through with her—just wised up!

STELLA   Stanley, she thought Mitch was—going to—going to marry her. I was hoping so, too.

STANLEY   Well, he's not going to marry her. Maybe he *was,* but he's not going to jump in a tank with a school of sharks—now! [*He rises.*] Blanche! Oh, Blanche! Can I please get in my bathroom? [*There is a pause.*]

BLANCHE   Yes, indeed, sir! Can you wait one second while I dry?

STANLEY   Having waited one hour I guess one second ought to pass in a hurry.

STELLA   And she hasn't got her job? Well, what will she do!

STANLEY   She's not stayin' here after Tuesday. You know that, don't you? Just to make sure I bought her ticket myself. A bus ticket.

STELLA   In the first place, Blanche wouldn't go on a bus.

STANLEY   She'll go on a bus and like it.

STELLA   No, she won't, no, she won't, Stanley!

STANLEY   *She'll go!* Period. P.S. She'll go *Tuesday!*

STELLA [*slowly*]   What'll—she—do? What on earth will she—*do!*

STANLEY   Her future is mapped out for her.

STELLA   What do you mean?

> [BLANCHE *sings.*]

STANLEY   Hey, canary bird! Toots! Get *OUT* of the *BATHROOM!*
    [*The bathroom door flies open and* BLANCHE *emerges with a
    gay peal of laughter, but as* STANLEY *crosses past her, a fright-
    ened look appears in her face, almost a look of panic. He
    doesn't look at her but slams the bathroom door shut as he
    goes in.*]
BLANCHE   [*snatching up a hair-brush*]   Oh, I feel so good after my
    long, hot bath, I feel so good and cool and—rested!
STELLA   [*sadly and doubtfully from the kitchen*]   Do you, Blanche?
BLANCHE   [*snatching up a hairbrush*]   Yes, I do, so refreshed! [*She
    tinkles her highball glass.*] A hot bath and a long, cold drink always
    give me a brand new outlook on life! [*She looks through the
    portieres at* STELLA, *standing between them, and slowly stops brush-
    ing.*] Something has happened!—What is it?
STELLA   [*turning away quickly*]   Why, nothing has happened, Blanche.
BLANCHE   You're lying! Something has!
        [*She stares fearfully at* STELLA, *who pretends to be busy at
        the table. The distant piano goes into a hectic breakdown.*]

Scene Eight

Three quarters of an hour later.
    *The view through the big windows is fading gradually into a still-
golden dusk. A torch of sunlight blazes on the side of a big water-tank
or oil-drum across the empty lot toward the business district which is
now pierced by pinpoints of lighted windows or windows reflecting
the sunset.*
    The three people are completing a dismal birthday supper. STANLEY
looks sullen. STELLA *is embarrassed and sad.*
    BLANCHE *has a tight, artificial smile on her drawn face. There is a
fourth place at the table which is left vacant.*

BLANCHE   [*suddenly*]   Stanley, tell us a joke, tell us a funny story to
    make us all laugh. I don't know what's the matter, we're all so
    solemn. Is it because I've been stood up by my beau?
        [STELLA *laughs feebly.*]
    It's the first time in my entire experience with men, and I've had
    a good deal of all sorts, that I've actually been stood up by anybody!
    Ha-ha! I don't know how to take it. . . . Tell us a funny little story,
    Stanley! Something to help us out.
STANLEY   I didn't think you liked my stories, Blanche.
BLANCHE   I like them when they're amusing but not indecent.
STANLEY   I don't know any refined enough for your taste.
BLANCHE   Then let me tell one.
STELLA   Yes, you tell one, Blanche. You used to know lots of good
    stories.
        [*The music fades.*]
BLANCHE   Let me see, now. . . . I must run through my repertoire!
    Oh, yes—I love parrot stories! Do you all like parrot stories? Well,
    this one's about the old maid and the parrot. This old maid, she

had a parrot that cursed a blue streak and knew more vulgar expressions than Mr. Kowalski!

STANLEY   Huh.

BLANCHE   And the only way to hush the parrot up was to put the cover back on its cage so it would think it was night and go back to sleep. Well, one morning the old maid had just uncovered the parrot for the day—when who should she see coming up the front walk but the preacher! Well, she rushed back to the parrot and slipped the cover back on the cage and then she let in the preacher. And the parrot was perfectly still, just as quiet as a mouse, but just as she was asking the preacher how much sugar he wanted in his coffee—the parrot broke the silence with a loud—[*She whistles.*]—and said—"God *damn,* but that was a short day!"

   [*She throws back her head and laughs.* STELLA *also makes an ineffectual effort to seem amused.* STANLEY *pays no attention to the story but reaches way over the table to spear his fork into the remaining chop which he eats with his fingers.*]

BLANCHE   Apparently Mr. Kowalski was not amused.

STELLA   Mr. Kowalski is too busy making a pig of himself to think of anything else!

STANLEY   That's right, baby.

STELLA   Your face and your fingers are disgustingly greasy. Go and wash up and then help me clear the table.

   [*He hurls a plate to the floor.*]

STANLEY   That's how I'll clear the table! [*He seizes her arm.*] Don't ever talk that way to me! "Pig—Polack—disgusting—vulgar—greasy!"—them kind of words have been on your tongue and your sister's too much around here! What do you two think you are? A pair of queens? Remember what Huey Long[8] said—"Every Man is a King!" And I am king around here, so don't forget it! [*He hurls a cup and saucer on the floor.*] My place is cleared! You want me to clear your places?

   [STELLA *begins to cry weakly.* STANLEY *stalks out on the porch and lights a cigarette. The Negro entertainers around the corner are heard.*]

BLANCHE   What happened while I was bathing? What did he tell you, Stella?

STELLA   Nothing, nothing, nothing!

BLANCHE   I think he told you something about Mitch and me! You know why Mitch didn't come but you won't tell me! [STELLA *shakes her head helplessly.*] I'm going to call him!

STELLA   I wouldn't call him, Blanche.

BLANCHE   I am, I'm going to call him on the phone.

STELLA [*miserably*]   I wish you wouldn't.

BLANCHE   I intend to be given some explanation from someone!

   [*She rushes to the phone in the bedroom.* STELLA *goes out on the porch and stares reproachfully at her husband. He grunts and turns away from her.*]

STELLA   I hope you're pleased with your doings. I never had so much trouble swallowing food in my life, looking at that girl's face and the empty chair! [*She cries quietly.*]

BLANCHE [*at the phone*]   Hello. Mr. Mitchell, please. . . . Oh. . . . I would like to leave a number if I may. Magnolia 9047. And say it's important to call. . . . Yes, very important. . . . Thank you.

> [*She remains by the phone with a lost, frightened look.*]
> [STANLEY *turns slowly back toward his wife and takes her clumsily in his arms.*]

STANLEY   Stell, it's gonna be all right after she goes and after you've had the baby. It's gonna be all right again between you and me the way that it was. You remember the way that it was? Them nights we had together? God, honey, it's gonna be sweet when we can make noise in the night the way that we used to and get the colored lights going with nobody's sister behind the curtains to hear us!

> [*Their upstairs neighbors are heard in bellowing laughter at something.* STANLEY *chuckles.*] Steve an' Eunice . . .

STELLA   Come on back in. [*She returns to the kitchen and starts lighting the candles on the white cake.*] Blanche?

BLANCHE   Yes. [*She returns from the bedroom to the table in the kitchen.*] Oh, those pretty, pretty little candles! Oh, don't burn them, Stella.

STELLA   I certainly will.

> [STANLEY *comes back in.*]

BLANCHE   You ought to save them for baby's birthdays. Oh, I hope candles are going to glow in his life and I hope that his eyes are going to be like candles, like two blue candles lighted in a white cake!

STANLEY [*sitting down*]   What poetry!

BLANCHE [*she pauses reflectively for a moment*]   I shouldn't have called him.

STELLA   There's lots of things could have happened.

BLANCHE   There's no excuse for it, Stella. I don't have to put up with insults. I won't be taken for granted.

STANLEY   Goddamn, it's hot in here with the steam from the bathroom.

BLANCHE   I've said I was sorry three times. [*The piano fades out.*] I take hot baths for my nerves. Hydrotherapy, they call it. You healthy Polack, without a nerve in your body, of course you don't know what anxiety feels like!

STANLEY   I am not a Polack. People from Poland are Poles, not Polacks. But what I am is one-hundred-per-cent American, born and raised in the greatest country on earth and proud as hell of it, so don't ever call me a Polack.

> [*The phone rings.* BLANCHE *rises expectantly.*]

BLANCHE   Oh, that's for me, I'm sure.

STANLEY   *I'm* not sure. Keep your seat. [*He crosses leisurely to phone.*] H'lo. Aw, yeh, hello, Mac.

> [*He leans against wall, staring insultingly at* BLANCHE. *She sinks back in her chair with a frightened look.* STELLA *leans over and touches her shoulder.*]

BLANCHE   Oh, keep your hands off me, Stella. What is the matter
with you? Why do you look at me with that pitying look?

STANLEY [*bawling*]   QUIET IN THERE!—We've got a noisy woman
on the place.—Go on, Mac. At Riley's? No, I don't wanta bowl at
Riley's. I had a little trouble with Riley last week. I'm the team
captain, ain't I? All right, then, we're not gonna bowl at Riley's,
we're gonna bowl at the West Side or the Gala! All right, Mac.
See you!

> [*He hangs up and returns to the table.* BLANCHE *fiercely con-
> trols herself, drinking quickly from her tumbler of water. He
> doesn't look at her but reaches in a pocket. Then he speaks
> slowly and with false amiability.*]

Sister Blanche, I've got a little birthday remembrance for you.

BLANCHE   Oh, have you, Stanley? I wasn't expecting any, I—I don't
know why Stella wants to observe my birthday! I'd much rather
forget it—when you—reach twenty-seven! Well—age is a subject
that you'd prefer to—ignore!

STANLEY   Twenty-seven?

BLANCHE [*quickly*]   What is it? Is it for *me*?

> [*He is holding a little envelope toward her.*]

STANLEY   Yes, I hope you like it!

BLANCHE   Why, why—Why, it's a—

STANLEY   Ticket! Back to Laurel! On the Greyhound! Tuesday!

> [*The Varsouviana music steals in softly and continues playing.*
> STELLA *rises abruptly and turns her back.* BLANCHE *tries to
> smile. Then she tries to laugh. Then she gives both up and
> springs from the table and runs into the next room. She clutches
> her throat and then runs into the bathroom. Coughing, gagging
> sounds are heard.*]

Well!

STELLA   You didn't need to do that.

STANLEY   Don't forget all that I took off her.

STELLA   You needn't have been so cruel to someone alone as she is.

STANLEY   Delicate piece she is.

STELLA   She is. She was. You didn't know Blanche as a girl. Nobody,
nobody, as tender and trusting as she was. But people like you
abused her, and forced her to change.

> [*He crosses into the bedroom, ripping off his shirt, and changes
> into a brilliant bowling shirt. She follows him.*]

Do you think you're going bowling now?

STANLEY   Sure.

STELLA   You're not going bowling. [*She catches hold of his shirt.*]
Why did you do this to her?

STANLEY   I done nothing to no one. Let go of my shirt. You've torn it.

STELLA   I want to know why. Tell me why.

STANLEY   When we first met, me and you, you thought I was common.
How right you was, baby. I was common as dirt. You showed me
the snapshot of the place with the columns. I pulled you down off
them columns and how you loved it, having them colored lights
going! And wasn't we happy together, wasn't it all okay till she
showed here?

[STELLA *makes a slight movement. Her look goes suddenly inward as if some interior voice had called her name. She begins a slow, shuffling progress from the bedroom to the kitchen, leaning and resting on the back of the chair and then on the edge of a table with a blind look and listening expression.* STANLEY *finishing with his shirt, is unaware of her reaction.*]

And wasn't we happy together? Wasn't it all okay? Till she showed here. Hoity-toity, describing me as an ape. [*He suddenly noices the change in* STELLA.] Hey, what is it, Stel? [*He crosses to her.*]

STELLA [*quietly*]   Take me to the hospital.

[*He is with her now, supporting her with his arm, murmuring indistinguishably as they go outside.*]

Scene Nine

A while later that evening. BLANCHE *is seated in a tense hunched position in a bedroom chair that she has recovered with diagonal green and white stripes. She has on her scarlet satin robe. On the table beside chair is a bottle of liquor and a glass. The rapid, feverish polka tune, the "Varsouviana," is heard. The music is in her mind; she is drinking to escape it and the sense of disaster closing in on her, and she seems to whisper the words of the song. An electric fan is turning back and forth across her.*

MITCH *comes around the corner in work clothes: blue denim shirt and pants. He is unshaven. He climbs the steps to the door and rings.* BLANCHE *is startled.*

BLANCHE   Who is it, please?

MITCH [*hoarsely*]   Me. Mitch.

[*The polka tune stops.*]

BLANCHE   Mitch!—Just a minute.

[*She rushes about farntically, hiding the bottle in a closet, crouching at the mirror and dabbing her face with cologne and powder. She is so excited that her breath is audible as she dashes about. At last she rushes to the door in the kitchen and lets him in.*]

Mitch!—Y'know, I really shouldn't let you in after the treatment I have received from you this evening! So utterly uncavalier! But hello, beautiful!

[*She offers him her lips. He ignores it and pushes past her into the flat. She looks fearfully after him as he stalks into the bedroom.*]

My, my, what a cold shoulder! And such uncouth apparel! Why, you haven't even shaved! The unforgivable insult to a lady! But I forgive you. I forgive you because it's such a relief to see you. You've stopped that polka tune that I had caught in my head. Have you ever had anything caught in your head? No, of course you haven't, you dumb angel-puss, you'd never get anything awful caught in your head!

[*He stares at her while she follows him while she talks. It is obvious that he has had a few drinks on the way over.*]

MITCH   Do we have to have that fan on?

BLANCHE   No!

MITCH   I don't like fans.

BLANCHE   Then let's turn it off, honey. I'm not partial to them!

[*She presses the switch and the fan nods slowly off. She clears her throat uneasily as* MITCH *plumps himself down on the bed in the bedroom and lights a cigarette.*]

I don't know what there is to drink. I—haven't investigated.

MITCH   I don't want Stan's liquor.

BLANCHE   It isn't Stan's. Everything here isn't Stan's. Some things on the premises are actually mine! How is your mother? Isn't your mother well?

MITCH   Why?

BLANCHE   Something's the matter tonight, but never mind. I won't cross-examine the witness. I'll just—[*She touches her forehead vaguely. The polka tune starts up again.*]—pretend I don't notice anything different about you! That—music again . . .

MITCH   What music?

BLANCHE   The "Varsouviana"! The polka tune they were playing when Allan— Wait!

[*A distant revolver shot is heard.* BLANCHE *seems relieved.*]

There now, the shot! It always stops after that.

[*The polka music dies out again.*]

Yes, now it's stopped.

MITCH   Are you boxed out of your mind?

BLANCHE   I'll go and see what I can find in the way of— [*She crosses into the closet, pretending to search for the bottle.*] Oh, by the way, excuse me for not being dressed. But I'd practically given you up! Had you forgotten your invitation to supper?

MITCH   I wasn't going to see you any more.

BLANCHE   Wait a minute. I can't hear what you're saying and you talk so little that when you do say something, I don't want to miss a single syllable of it. . . . What am I looking around here for? Oh, yes—liquor! We've had so much excitement around here this evening that I *am* boxed out of my mind! [*She pretends suddenly to find the bottle. He draws his foot up on the bed and stares at her contemptuously.*] Here's something. Southern Comfort! What is that, I wonder?

MITCH   If you don't know, it must belong to Stan.

BLANCHE   Take your foot off the bed. It has a light cover on it. Of course you boys don't notice things like that. I've done so much with this place since I've been here.

MITCH   I bet you have.

BLANCHE   You saw it before I came. Well, look at it now! This room is almost—dainty! I want to keep it that way. I wonder if this stuff ought to be mixed with something? Ummm, it's sweet! It's terribly, terribly sweet! Why, it's a *liqueur*, I believe! Yes, that's what it *is*, a liqueur! [*Mitch grunts.*] I'm afraid you won't like it, but try it, and maybe you will.

MITCH   I told you already I don't want none of his liquor and I mean it. You ought to lay off his liquor. He says you been lapping it up all summer like a wild cat!

BLANCHE   What a fantastic statement! Fantastic of him to say it, fantastic of you to repeat it! I won't descend to the level of such cheap accusations to answer them, even!

MITCH   Huh.

BLANCHE   What's in your mind? I see something in your eyes!

MITCH [*getting up*]   It's dark in here.

BLANCHE   I like it dark. The dark is comforting to me.

MITCH   I don't think I ever seen you in the light. [BLANCHE *laughs breathlessly.*] That's a fact!

BLANCHE   Is it?

MITCH   I've never seen you in the afternoon.

BLANCHE   Whose fault is that?

MITCH   You never want to go out in the afternoon.

BLANCHE   Why, Mitch, you're at the plant in the afternoon.

MITCH   Not Sunday afternoon. I've asked you to go out with me sometimes on Sundays but you always make an excuse. You never want to go out till after six and then it's always some place that's not lighted much.

BLANCHE   There is some obscure meaning in this but I fail to catch it.

MITCH   What it means is I've never had a real good look at you, Blanche. Let's turn the light on here.

BLANCHE [*fearfully*]   Light? Which light? What for?

MITCH   This one with the paper thing on it. [*He tears the paper lantern off the light bulb. She utters a frightened gasp.*]

BLANCHE   What did you do that for?

MITCH   So I can take a look at you good and plain!

BLANCHE   Of course you don't really mean to be insulting!

MITCH   No, just realistic.

BLANCHE   I don't want realism. I want magic! [MITCH *laughs.*] Yes, yes, magic! I try to give that to people. I misrepresent things to them. I don't tell truth, I tell what *ought* to be truth. And if that is sinful, then let me be damned for it!—*Don't turn the light on!*

    [MITCH *crosses to the switch. He turns the light on and stares at her. She cries out and covers her face. He turns the lights off again.*]

MITCH [*slowly and bitterly*]   I don't mind you being older than what I thought. But all the rest of it—Christ! That pitch about your ideals being so old-fashioned and all the malarkey that you've dished out all summer. Oh, I knew you weren't sixteen any more. But I was a fool enough to believe you was straight.

BLANCHE   Who told you I wasn't—"straight"? My loving brother-in-law. And you believed him.

MITCH   I called him a liar at first. And then I checked on the story. First I asked our supply-man who travels through Laurel. And then I talked directly over long-distance to this merchant.

BLANCHE   Who is this merchant?

MITCH   Kiefaber.

BLANCHE   The merchant Kiefaber of Laurel! I know the man. He

whistled at me. I put him in his place. So now for revenge he makes
up stories about me.

MITCH   Three people, Kiefaber, Stanley and Shaw, swore to them!

BLANCHE   Rub-a-dub-dub, three men in a tub! And such a filthy tub!

MITCH   Didn't you stay at a hotel called The Flamingo?

BLANCHE   Flamingo? No! Tarantula was the name of it! I stayed at a
hotel called The Tarantula Arms!

MITCH [*stupidly*]   Tarantula?

BLANCHE   Yes, a big spider! That's where I brought my victims. [*She
pours herself another drink.*] Yes, I had intimacies with strangers.
After the death of Allan—intimacies with strangers was all I seemed
able to fill my empty heart with. . . . I think it was panic, just panic,
that drove me from one to another, hunting for some protection—
here and there, in the most—unlikely places—even, at last, in a
seventeen-year-old boy but—somebody wrote the superintendent
about it—"This woman is morally unfit for her position!"

[*She throws back her head with convulsive, sobbing laughter.
Then she repeats the statement, gasps, and drinks.*]

True? Yes, I suppose—unfit somehow—anyway. . . . So I came here.
There was nowhere else I could go. I was played out. You know
what played out is? My youth was suddenly gone up the water-
spout, and—I met you. You said you needed somebody. Well, I
needed somebody, too. I thanked God for you, because you seemed
to be gentle—a cleft in the rock of the world that I could hide in!
But I guess I was asking, hoping—too much! Kiefaber, Stanley and
Shaw have tied an old tin can to the tail of the kite.

[*There is a pause.* MITCH *stares at her dumbly.*]

MITCH   You lied to me, Blanche.

BLANCHE   Don't say I lied to you.

MITCH   Lies, lies, inside and out, all lies.

BLANCHE   Never inside, I didn't lie in my heart . . . .

[*A Vendor comes around the corner. She is a blind Mexican
woman in a dark shawl, carrying bunches of those gaudy tin
flowers that lower-class Mexicans display at funerals and other
festive occasions. She is calling barely audibly. Her figure is
only faintly visible outside the building.*]

MEXICAN WOMAN   Flores. Flores. Flores para los muertos.⁹ Flores.
Flores.

BLANCHE   What? Oh! Somebody outside . . . . [*She goes to the door,
opens it and stares at the* MEXICAN WOMAN.]

MEXICAN WOMAN [*she is at the door and offers* BLANCHE *some of her
flowers*]   Flores? Flores para los muertos?

BLANCHE [*frightened*]   No, no! Not now! Not now!

[*She darts back into the apartment, slamming the door.*]

MEXICAN WOMAN [*she turns away and starts to move down the street*]
Flores para los muertos.

[*The polka tune fades in.*]

BLANCHE [*as if to herself*]   Crumble and fade and—regrets—recrim-
inations . . . "If you'd done this, it wouldn't've cost me that!"

9. "Flowers for the dead."

MEXICAN WOMAN   Corones[1] para los muertos. Corones . . . .

BLANCHE   Legacies! Huh. . . . And other things such as bloodstained pillow-slips—"Her linen needs changing"—"Yes, Mother. But couldn't we get a colored girl to do it?" No, we couldn't of course. Everything gone but the—

MEXICAN WOMAN   Flores.

BLANCHE   Death—I used to sit here and she used to sit over there and death was as close as you are. . . . We didn't dare even admit we had ever heard of it!

MEXICAN WOMAN   Flores para los muertos, flores—flores . . .

BLANCHE   The opposite is desire. So do you wonder? How could you possibly wonder! Not far from Belle Reve, before we had lost Belle Reve, was a camp where they trained young soldiers. On Sunday nights they would go in town to get drunk—

MEXICAN WOMAN [*softly*]   Corones . . . .

BLANCHE   —and on the way back they would stagger onto my lawn and call—"Blanche! Blanche!"—the deaf old lady remaining suspected nothing. But sometimes I slipped outside to answer their calls. . . . Later the paddy-wagon would gather them up like daisies . . . the long way home . . . .

> [*The* MEXICAN WOMAN *turns slowly and drifts back off with her soft mournful cries.* BLANCHE *goes to the dresser and leans forward on it. After a moment,* MITCH *rises and follows her purposefully. The polka music fades away. He places his hands on her waist and tries to turn her about.*]

BLANCHE   What do you want?

MITCH [*fumbling to embrace her*]   What I been missing all summer.

BLANCHE   Then marry me, Mitch!

MITCH   I don't think I want to marry you any more.

BLANCHE   No?

MITCH [*dropping his hands from her waist*]   You're not clean enough to bring in the house with my mother.

BLANCHE   Go away, then. [*He stares at her.*] Get out of here quick before I start screaming fire! [*Her throat is tightening with hysteria.*] Get out of here quick before I start screaming fire.

> [*He still remains staring. She suddenly rushes to the big window with its pale blue square of the soft summer light and cries wildly.*]

Fire! Fire! Fire!

> [*With a startled gasp,* MITCH *turns and goes out the outer door, clatters awkwardly down the steps and around the corner of the building.* BLANCHE *staggers back from the window and falls to her knees. The distant piano is slow and blue.*]

Scene Ten

It is a few hours later that night.

BLANCHE *has been drinking fairly steadily since* MITCH *left. She has dragged her wardrobe trunk into the center of the bedroom. It*

1. "Wreaths."

hangs open with flowery dresses thrown across it. As the drinking and packing went on, a mood of hysterical exhilaration came into her and she has decked herself out in a somewhat soiled and crumpled white satin evening gown and a pair of scuffed silver slippers with brilliants set in their heels.

Now she is placing the rhinestone tiara on her head before the mirror of the dressing-table and murmuring excitedly as if to a group of spectral admirers.

BLANCHE   How about taking a swim, a moonlight swim at the old rock-quarry? If anyone's sober enough to drive a car! Ha-ha! Best way in the world to stop your head buzzing! Only you've got to be careful to dive where the deep pool is—if you hit a rock you don't come up till tomorrow . . . .

[*Tremblingly she lifts the hand mirror for a closer inspection. She catches her breath and slams the mirror face down with such violence that the glass cracks. She moans a little and attempts to rise.* STANLEY *appears around the corner of the building. He still has on the vivid green silk bowling shirt. As he rounds the corner the honky-tonk music is heard. It continues softly throughout the scene. He enters the kitchen, slamming the door. As he peers in at* BLANCHE, *he gives a low whistle. He has had a few drinks on the way and has brought some quart beer bottles home with him.*]

BLANCHE   How is my sister?
STANLEY   She is doing okay.
BLANCHE   And how is the baby?
STANLEY   [*grinning amiably*]   The baby won't come before morning so they told me to go home and get a little shut-eye.
BLANCHE   Does that mean we are to be alone in here?
STANLEY   Yep. Just me and you, Blanche. Unless you got somebody hid under the bed. What've you got on those fine feathers for?
BLANCHE   Oh, that's right. You left before my wire came.
STANLEY   You got a wire?
BLANCHE   I received a telegram from an old admirer of mine.
STANLEY   Anything good?
BLANCHE   I think so. An invitation.
STANLEY   What to? A fireman's ball?
BLANCHE   [*throwing back her head*]   A cruise of the Caribbean on a yacht!
STANLEY   Well, well. What do you know?
BLANCHE   I have never been so surprised in my life.
STANLEY   I guess not.
BLANCHE   It came like a bolt from the blue!
STANLEY   Who did you say it was from?
BLANCHE   An old beau of mine.
STANLEY   The one that give you the white fox-pieces?
BLANCHE   Mr. Shep Huntleigh. I wore his ATO pin my last year at college. I hadn't seen him again until last Christmas. I ran in to him on Biscayne Boulevard. Then—just now—this wire—inviting

me on a cruise of the Caribbean! The problem is clothes. I tore into
my trunk to see what I have that's suitable for the tropics!

STANLEY   And come up with that—gorgeous—diamond—tiara?

BLANCHE   This old relic? Ha-ha! It's only rhinestones.

STANLEY   Gosh. I thought it was Tiffany diamonds. [*He unbuttons
his shirt.*]

BLANCHE   Well, anyhow, I shall be entertained in style.

STANLEY   Uh-huh. It goes to show, you never know what is coming.

BLANCHE   Just when I thought my luck had begun to fail me—

STANLEY   Into the picture pops this Miami millionaire.

BLANCHE   This man is not from Miami. This man is from Dallas.

STANLEY   This man is from Dallas?

BLANCHE   Yes, this man is from Dallas where gold spouts out of the
ground!

STANLEY   Well, just so he's from somewhere! [*He starts removing his
shirt.*]

BLANCHE   Close the curtain before you undress any further.

STANLEY   [*amiably*]   This is all I'm going to undress right now. [*He
rips the sack off a quart beer bottle.*] Seen a bottle-opener?

> [*She moves slowly toward the dresser, where she stands with
> her hands knotted together.*]

I used to have a cousin who could open a beer bottle with his
teeth. [*pounding the bottle cap on the corner of table*] That was
his only accomplishment, all he could do—he was just a human
bottle-opener. And then one time, at a wedding party, he broke
his front teeth off! After that he was so ashamed of himself he
used t' sneak out of the house when company came.

> [*The bottle cap pops off and a geyser of foam shoots up.
> Stanley laughs happily, holding up the bottle over his head.*]

Ha-ha! Rain from heaven! [*He extends the bottle toward her*]
Shall we bury the hatchet and make it a loving-cup? Huh?

BLANCHE   No, thank you.

STANLEY   Well, it's a red-letter night for us both. You having an oil
millionaire and me having a baby.

> [*He goes to the bureau in the bedroom and crouches to remove
> something from the bottom drawer.*]

BLANCHE   [*drawing back*]   What are you doing in here?

STANLEY   Here's something I always break out on special occasions
like this. The silk pyjamas I wore on my wedding night!

BLANCHE   Oh.

STANLEY   When the telephone rings and they say, "You've got a
son!" I'll tear this off and wave it like a flag! [*He shakes out a
brilliant pyjama coat.*] I guess we are both entitled to put on the
dog. [*He goes back to the kitchen with the coat over his arm.*]

BLANCHE   When I think of how divine it is going to be to have such
a thing as privacy once more—I could weep with joy!

STANLEY   This millionaire from Dallas is not going to interfere with
your privacy any?

BLANCHE   It won't be the sort of thing you have in mind. This man
is a gentleman and he respects me. [*improvising feverishly*] What

he wants is my companionhip. Having great wealth sometimes makes people lonely! A cultivated woman, a woman of intelligence and breeding, can enrich a man's life—immeasurably! I have those things to offer, and this doesn't take them away. Physical beauty is passing. A transitory possession. But beauty of the mind and richness of the spirit and tenderness of the heart—and I have all of those things—aren't taken away, but grow! Increase with the years! How strange that I should be called a destitute woman! When I have all of these treasures locked in my heart. [*A choked sob comes from her*] I think of myself as a very, very rich woman! But I have been foolish—casting my pearls before swine!

STANLEY   Swine, huh?

BLANCHE   Yes, swine! Swine! And I'm thinking not only of you but of your friend, Mr. Mitchell. He came to see me tonight. He dared to come here in his work clothes! And to repeat slander to me, vicious stories that he had gotten from you! I gave him his walking papers . . . .

STANLEY   You did, huh?

BLANCHE   But then he came back. He returned with a box of roses to beg my forgiveness! He implored my forgiveness. But some things are not forgivable. Deliberate cruelty is not forgivable. It is the one unforgivable thing in my opinion and it is the one thing of which I have never, ever been guilty. And so I told him, I said to him. "Thank you," but it was foolish of me to think that we could ever adapt ourselves to each other. Our ways of life are too different. Our attitudes and our backgrounds are incompatible. We have to be realistic about such things. So farewell, my friend! And let there be no hard feelings . . . .

STANLEY   Was this before or after the telegram came from the Texas oil millionaire?

BLANCHE   What telegram? No! No, after! As a matter of fact, the wire came just as—

STANLEY   As a matter of fact there wasn't no wire at all!

BLANCHE   Oh, oh!

STANLEY   There isn't no millionaire! And Mitch didn't come back with roses 'cause I know where he is—

BLANCHE   Oh!

STANLEY   There isn't a goddam thing but imagination!

BLANCHE   Oh!

STANLEY   And lies and conceit and tricks!

BLANCHE   Oh!

STANLEY   And look at yourself! Take a look at yourself in that worn-out Mardi Gras outfit, rented for fifty cents from some rag-picker! And with the crazy crown on! What queen do you think you are?

BLANCHE   Oh—God . . . .

STANLEY   I've been on to you from the start! Not once did you pull any wool over this boy's eyes! You come in here and sprinkle the place with powder and spray perfume and cover the light-bulb with a paper lantern, and lo and behold the place has turned into Egypt and you are the Queen of the Nile! Sitting on your throne and swilling down my liquor! I say—*Ha!*—*Ha!* Do you hear me? *Ha*—*ha*—*ha!* [*He walks into the bedroom.*]

BLANCHE Don't come in here!

[*Lurid reflections appear on the walls around* BLANCHE. *The shadows are of a grotesque and menacing form. She catches her breath, crosses to the phone and jiggles the hook.* STANLEY *goes into the bathroom and closes the door.*]

Operator, operator! Give me long-distance, please. . . . I want to get in touch with Mr. Shep Huntleigh of Dallas. He's so well known he doesn't require any address. Just ask anybody who—Wait!!— No, I couldn't find it right now. . . . Please understand, I—No! No, wait! . . . One moment! Someone is—Nothing! Hold on, please!

[*She sets the phone down and crosses warily into the kitchen. The night is filled with inhuman voices like cries in a jungle. The shadows and lurid reflections move sinuously as flames along the wall spaces. Through the back wall of the rooms, which have become transparent, can be seen the sidewalk. A prostitute has rolled a drunkard. He pursues her along the walk, overtakes her and there is a struggle. A policeman's whistle breaks it up. The figures disappear. Some moments later the Negro Woman appears around the corner with a sequined bag which the prostitute had dropped on the walk. She is rooting excitedly through it.* BLANCHE *presses her knuckles to her lips and returns slowly to the phone. She speaks in a hoarse whisper.*]

BLANCHE Operator! Operator! Never mind long-distance. Get Western Union. There isn't time to be—Western—Western Union!

[*She waits anxiously.*]

Western Union? Yes! I—want to—Take down this message! "In desperate, desperate circumstances! Help me! Caught in a trap. Caught in—" *Oh!*

[*The bathroom door is thrown open and* STANLEY *comes out in the brilliant silk pyjamas. He grins at her as he knots the tasseled sash about his waist. She gasps and backs away from the phone. He stares at her for a count of ten. Then a clicking becomes audible from the telephone, steady and rasping.*]

STANLEY You left th' phone off th' hook.

[*He crosses to it deliberately and sets it back on the hook. After he has replaced it, he stares at her again, his mouth slowly curving into a grin as he weaves between* BLANCHE *and the outer door. The barely audible "Blue Piano" begins to drum up louder. The sound of it turns into the roar of an approaching locomotive.* BLANCHE *crouches, pressing her fists to her ears until it has gone by.*]

BLANCHE [*finally straightening*] Let me—let me get by you!

STANLEY Get by me? Sure. Go ahead. [*He moves back a pace in the doorway.*]

BLANCHE You—you stand over there! [*She indicates a further position.*]

STANLEY You got plenty of room to walk by me now.

BLANCHE   Not with you there! But I've got to get out somehow!

STANLEY   You think I'll interfere with you? Ha-ha!

[*The "Blue Piano" goes softly. She turns confusedly and makes a faint gesture. The inhuman jungle voices rise up. He takes a step toward her, biting his tongue which protrudes between his lips.*]

STANLEY [*softly*]   Come to think of it—maybe you wouldn't be bad to—interfere with . . . .

[BLANCHE *moves backward through the door into the bedroom.*]

BLANCHE   Stay back! Don't you come toward me another step or I'll—

STANLEY   What?

BLANCHE   Some awful thing will happen! It will!

STANLEY   What are you putting on now?

[*They are now both inside the bedroom.*]

BLANCHE   I warn you, don't, I'm in danger!

[*He takes another step. She smashes a bottle on the table and faces him, clutching the broken top.*]

STANLEY   What did you do that for?

BLANCHE   So I could twist the broken end in your face!

STANLEY   I bet you would do that!

BLANCHE   I would! I will if you—

STANLEY   Oh! So you want some roughhouse! All right, let's have some roughhouse!

[*He springs toward her, overturning the table. She cries out and strikes at him with the bottle top but he catches her wrist.*]

Tiger—tiger—Drop the bottle-top! Drop it! We've had this date with each other from the beginning!

[*She moans. The bottle-top falls. She sinks to her knees. He picks up her inert figure and carries her to the bed. The hot trumpet and drums from the Four Deuces sound loudly.*]

Scene Eleven

It is some weeks later. STELLA *is packing* BLANCHE's *things. Sounds of water can be heard running in the bathroom.*

*The portieres are partly open on the poker players—*STANLEY, STEVE, MITCH *and* PABLO—*who sit around the table in the kitchen. The atmosphere of the kitchen is now the same raw, lurid one of the disastrous poker night.*

The building is framed by the sky of turquoise. STELLA *has been crying as she arranges the flowery dresses in the open trunk.*

EUNICE *comes down the steps from her flat above and enters the kitchen. There is an outburst from the poker table.*

STANLEY   Drew to an inside straight and made it, by God.

PABLO   *Maldita sea tu suerto!*

STANLEY   Put it in English, greaseball.

PABLO   I am cursing your rutting luck.

STANLEY [*prodigiously elated*]   You know what luck is? Luck is believing you're lucky. Take at Salerno.[2] I believed I was lucky. I
figured that 4 out of 5 would not come through but I would . . .
and I did. I put that down as a rule. To hold front position in this
rat-race you've got to believe you are lucky.

MITCH   You . . . you . . . you. . . . Brag . . . brag . . . bull . . . bull.
   [STELLA *goes into the bedroom and starts folding a dress.*]

STANLEY   What's the matter with him?

EUNICE [*walking past the table*]   I always did say that men are callous
things with no feelings but this does beat anything. Making pigs of
yourselves. [*She comes through the portieres into the bedroom.*]

STANLEY   What's the matter with her?

STELLA   How is my baby?

EUNICE   Sleeping like a little angel. Brought you some grapes. [*She
puts them on a stool and lowers her voice.*] Blanche?

STELLA   Bathing.

EUNICE   How is she?

STELLA   She wouldn't eat anything but asked for a drink.

EUNICE   What did you tell her?

STELLA   I—just told her that—we'd made arrangements for her to
rest in the country. She's got it mixed in her mind with Shep
Huntleigh.
   [BLANCHE *opens the bathroom door slightly.*]

BLANCHE   Stella.

STELLA   Yes, Blanche?

BLANCHE   If anyone calls while I'm bathing take the number and
tell them I'll call right back.

STELLA   Yes.

BLANCHE   That cool yellow silk—the bouclé. See if it's crushed. If
it's not too crushed I'll wear it and on the lapel that silver and
turquoise pin in the shape of a seahorse. You will find them in
the heart-shaped box I keep my accessories in. And Stella . . . Try
and locate a bunch of artificial violets in that box, too, to pin with
the seahorse on the lapel of the jacket.
   [*She closes the door.* STELLA *turns to* EUNICE.]

STELLA   I don't know if I did the right thing.

EUNICE   What else could you do?

STELLA   I couldn't believe her story and go on living with Stanley.

EUNICE   Don't ever believe it. Life has got to go on. No matter what
happens, you've got to keep on going.
   [*The bathroom door opens a little.*]

BLANCHE [*looking out*]   Is the coast clear?

STELLA   Yes, Blanche. [*to* EUNICE] Tell her how well she's looking.

BLANCHE   Please close the curtains before I come out.

STELLA   They're closed.

STANLEY   —How many for you?

PABLO   —Two.

STEVE   Three.
   [BLANCHE *appears in the amber light of the door. She has a*

2. Important beachhead in the Allied invasion of Italy in World War II.

tragic radiance in her red satin robe following the sculptural lines of her body. The "Varsouviana" rises audibly as BLANCHE *enters the bedroom.*]

BLANCHE [*with faintly hysterical vivacity*]   I have just washed my hair.

STELLA   Did you?

BLANCHE   I'm not sure I got the soap out.

EUNICE   Such fine hair!

BLANCHE [*accepting the compliment*]   It's a problem. Didn't I get a call?

STELLA   Who from, Blanche?

BLANCHE   Shep Huntleigh . . .

STELLA   Why, not yet, honey!

BLANCHE   How strange! I—

[*At the sound of* BLANCHE's *voice* MITCH's *arm supporting his cards has sagged and his gaze is dissolved into space.* STANLEY *slaps him on the shoulder.*]

STANLEY   Hey, Mitch, come to!

[*The sound of this new voice shocks* BLANCHE. *She makes a shocked gesture, forming his name with her lips.* STELLA *nods and looks quickly away.* BLANCHE *stands quite still for some moments—the silver-backed mirror in her hand and a look of sorrowful perplexity as though all human experience shows on her face.* BLANCHE *finally speaks but with sudden hysteria.*]

BLANCHE   What's going on here?

[*She turns from* STELLA *to* EUNICE *and back to* STELLA. *Her rising voice penetrates the concentration of the game.* MITCH *ducks his head lower but* STANLEY *shoves back his chair as if about to rise.* STEVE *places a restraining hand on his arm.*]

BLANCHE [*continuing*]   What's happened here? I want an explanation of what's happened here.

STELLA [*agonizingly*]   Hush! Hush!

EUNICE   Hush! Hush! Honey.

STELLA   Please, Blanche.

BLANCHE   Why are you looking at me like that? Is something wrong with me?

EUNICE   You look wonderful, Blanche. Don't she look wonderful?

STELLA   Yes.

EUNICE   I understand you are going on a trip.

STELLA   Yes, Blanche *is*. She's going on a vacation.

EUNICE   I'm green with envy.

BLANCHE   Help me, help me get dressed!

STELLA [*handing her dress*]   Is this what you—

BLANCHE   Yes, it will do! I'm anxious to get out of here—this place is a trap!

EUNICE   What a pretty blue jacket.

STELLA   It's lilac colored.

BLANCHE   You're both mistaken. It's Della Robbia blue.[3] The blue of

3. A shade of light blue seen in terra cottas made by the Della Robbia family in the Italian Renaissance.

the robe in the old Madonna pictures. Are these grapes washed?

[*She fingers the bunch of grapes which* EUNICE *had brought in.*]

EUNICE   Huh?

BLANCHE   Washed, I said. Are they washed?

EUNICE   They're from the French Market.

BLANCHE   That doesn't mean they've been washed. [*The cathedral bells chime.*] Those cathedral bells—they're the only clean thing in the Quarter. Well, I'm going now. I'm ready to go.

EUNICE [*whispering*]   She's going to walk out before they get here.

STELLA   Wait, Blanche.

BLANCHE   I don't want to pass in front of those men.

EUNICE   Then wait'll the game breaks up.

STELLA   Sit down and . . . .

[BLANCHE *turns weakly, hesitantly about. She lets them push her into a chair.*]

BLANCHE   I can smell the sea air. The rest of my time I'm going to spend on the sea. And when I die, I'm going to die on the sea. You know what I shall die of? [*She plucks a grape.*] I shall die of eating an unwashed grape one day out on the ocean. I will die—with my hand in the hand of some nice-looking ship's doctor, a very young one with a small blond mustache and a big silver watch. "Poor lady," they'll say, "the quinine did her no good. That unwashed grape has transported her soul to heaven." [*The cathedral chimes are heard.*] And I'll be buried at sea sewn up in a clean white sack and dropped overboard—at noon—in the blaze of summer—and into an ocean as blue as [*chimes again*] my first lover's eyes.

[*A Doctor and a Matron have appeared around the corner of the building and climbed the steps to the porch. The gravity of their profession is exaggerated—the unmistakable aura of the state institution with its cynical detachment. The Doctor rings the doorbell. The murmur of the game is interrupted.*]

EUNICE [*whispering to* STELLA]   That must be them.

[STELLA *presses her fists to her lips.*]

BLANCHE [*rising slowly*]   What is it?

EUNICE [*affectedly casual*]   Excuse me while I see who's at the door.

STELLA   Yes.

[EUNICE *goes into the kitchen.*]

BLANCHE [*tensely*]   I wonder if it's for me.

[*A whispered colloquy takes place at the door.*]

EUNICE [*returning, brightly*]   Someone is calling for Blanche.

BLANCHE   It *is* for me, then! [*She looks fearfully from one to the other and then to the portieres. The "Varsouviana" faintly plays.*] Is it the gentleman I was expecting from Dallas?

EUNICE   I think it is, Blanche.

BLANCHE   I'm not quite ready.

STELLA   Ask him to wait outside.

BLANCHE   I . . .

[EUNICE *goes back to the portieres. Drums sound very softly.*]

STELLA   Everything packed?

BLANCHE   My silver toilet articles are still out.

STELLA   Ah!

EUNICE [*returning*]   They're waiting in front of the house.

BLANCHE   They! Who's "they"?

EUNICE   There's a lady with him.

BLANCHE   I cannot imagine who this "lady" could be! How is she dressed?

EUNICE   Just—just a sort of a—plain-tailored outfit.

BLANCHE   Possibly she's—[*Her voice dies out nervously.*]

STELLA   Shall we go, Blanche?

BLANCHE   Must we go through that room?

STELLA   I will go with you.

BLANCHE   How do I look?

STELLA   Lovely.

EUNICE [*echoing*]   Lovely.

> [BLANCHE *moves fearfully to the portieres.* EUNICE *draws them open for her.* BLANCHE *goes into the kitchen.*]

BLANCHE [*to the men*]   Please don't get up. I'm only passing through.
> [*She crosses quickly to outside door.* STELLA *and* EUNICE *follow. The poker players stand awkwardly at the table—all except* MITCH, *who remains seated, looking down at the table.* BLANCHE *steps out on a small porch at the side of the door. She stops short and catches her breath.*]

DOCTOR   How do you do?

BLANCHE   You are not the gentleman I was expecting. [*She suddenly gasps and starts back up the steps. She stops by* STELLA, *who stands just outside the door, and speaks in a frightening whisper.*] That man isn't Shep Huntleigh.
> [*The "Varsouviana" is playing distantly.* STELLA *stares back at* BLANCHE. EUNICE *is holding* STELLA's *arm. There is a moment of silence—no sound but that of* STANLEY *steadily shuffling the cards.* BLANCHE *catches her breath again and slips back into the flat. She enters the flat with a peculiar smile, her eyes wide and brilliant. As soon as her sister goes past her,* STELLA *closes her eyes and clenches her hands.* EUNICE *throws her arms comfortingly about her. Then she starts up to her flat.* BLANCHE *stops just inside the door.* MITCH *keeps staring down at his hands on the table, but the other men look at her curiously. At last she starts around the table toward the bedroom. As she does,* STANLEY *suddenly pushes back his chair and rises as if to block her way. The* MATRON *follows her into the flat.*]

STANLEY   Did you forget something?

BLANCHE [*shrilly*]   Yes! Yes, I forgot something!
> [*She rushes past him into the bedroom. Lurid reflections appear on the walls in odd, sinuous shapes. The "Varsouviana" is filtered into a weird distortion, accompanied by the cries and noises of the jungle.* BLANCHE *seizes the back of a chair as if to defend herself.*]

STANLEY [*sotto voce*]   Doc, you better go in.

DOCTOR [*sotto voce, motioning to the Matron*]   Nurse, bring her out.
[*The* MATRON *advances on one side,* STANLEY *on the other. Divested of all the softer properties of womanhood, the* MATRON *is a peculiarly sinister figure in her severe dress. Her voice is bold and toneless as a firebell.*]

MATRON   Hello, Blanche.
[*The greeting is echoed and re-echoed by other mysterious voices behind the walls, as if reverberated through a canyon of rock.*]

STANLEY   She says that she forgot something.
[*The echo sounds in threatening whispers.*]

MATRON   That's all right.

STANLEY   What did you forget, Blanche?

BLANCHE   I—I—

MATRON   It don't matter. We can pick it up later.

STANLEY   Sure. We can send it along with the trunk.

BLANCHE [*retreating in panic*]   I don't know you—I don't know you. I want to be—left alone—please!

MATRON   Now, Blanche!

ECHOES [*rising and falling*]   Now, Blanche—now, Blanche—now, Blanche!

STANLEY   You left nothing here but spilt talcum and old empty perfume bottles—unless it's the paper lantern you want to take with you. You want the lantern?
[*He crosses to dressing table and seizes the paper lantern, tearing it off the light bulb, and extends it toward her. She cries out as if the lantern was herself. The* MATRON *steps boldly toward her. She screams and tries to break past the* MATRON. *All the men spring to their feet.* STELLA *runs out to the porch, with* EUNICE *following to comfort her, simultaneously with the confused voices of the men in the kitchen.* STELLA *rushes into* EUNICE's *embrace on the porch.*]

STELLA   Oh, my God, Eunice help me! Don't let them do that to her, don't let them hurt her! Oh, God, oh, please God, don't hurt her! What are they doing to her? What are they doing?
[*She tries to break from* EUNICE's *arms.*]

EUNICE   No. honey, no, no, honey. Stay here. Don't go back in there. Stay with me and don't look.

STELLA   What have I done to my sister? Oh, God, what have I done to my sister?

EUNICE   You done the right thing, the only thing you could do. She couldn't stay here; there wasn't no other place for her to go.
[*While* STELLA *and* EUNICE *are speaking on the porch the voices of the men in the kitchen overlap them.* MITCH *has started toward the bedroom.* STANLEY *crosses to block him.* STANLEY *pushes him aside.* MITCH *lunges and strikes at* STANLEY. STANLEY *pushes* MITCH *back.* MITCH *collapses at the table, sobbing. During the preceding scenes, the* MATRON *catches hold of* BLANCHE's *arm and prevents her flight.* BLANCHE *turns wildly and scratches at the* MATRON. *The heavy woman*]

pinions her arms. BLANCHE *cries out hoarsely and slips to her knees.*]

MATRON   These fingernails have to be trimmed. [*The* DOCTOR *comes into the room and she looks at him.*] Jacket, Doctor?

DOCTOR   Not unless necessary.

[*He takes off his hat and now he becomes personalized. The unhuman quality goes. His voice is gentle and reassuring as he crosses to* BLANCHE *and crouches in front of her. As he speaks her name, her terror subsides a little. The lurid reflections fade from the walls, the inhuman cries and noises die out and her own hoarse crying is calmed.*]

DOCTOR   Miss DuBois.

[*She turns her face to him and stares at him with desperate pleading. He smiles; then he speaks to the* MATRON.]

It won't be necessary.

BLANCHE [*faintly*]   Ask her to let go of me.

DOCTOR [*the the* MATRON]   Let go.

[*The* MATRON *releases her.* BLANCHE *extends her hands toward the* DOCTOR. *He draws her up gently and supports her with his arm and leads her through the portieres.*]

BLANCHE [*holding tight to his arm*]   Whoever you are—I have always depended on the kindness of strangers.

[*The poker players stand back as* BLANCHE *and the* DOCTOR *cross the kitchen to the front door. She allows him to lead her as if she were blind. As they go out on the porch,* STELLA *cries out her sister's name from where she is crouched a few steps up on the stairs.*]

STELLA   Blanche! Blanche! Blanche!

[BLANCHE *walks on without turning, followed by the* DOCTOR *and the* MATRON. *They go around the corner of the building.* EUNICE *descends to* STELLA *and places the child in her arms. It is wrapped in a pale blue blanket.* STELLA *accepts the child, sobbingly.* EUNICE *continues downstairs and enters the kitchen where the men, except for* STANLEY, *are returning silently to their places about the table.* STANLEY *has gone out on the porch and stands at the foot of the steps looking at* STELLA.]

STANLEY [*a bit uncertainly*]   Stella?

[*She sobs with inhuman abandon. There is something luxurious in her complete surrender to crying now that her sister is gone.*]

STANLEY [*voluptuously, soothingly*]   Now, honey. Now, love. Now, now, love. [*He kneels beside her and his fingers find the opening of her blouse.*] Now, now, love, Now, love. . . .

[*The luxurious sobbing, the sensual murmur fade away under the swelling music of the "Blue Piano" and the muted trumpet.*]

STEVE   This game is seven-card stud.

CURTAIN

1947

From The Glass Menagerie

Scene 7. [Conclusion]¹

It is half an hour later. Dinner is just being finished in the dining room, LAURA *is still huddled upon the sofa, her feet drawn under her, her head resting on a pale blue pillow, her eyes wide and mysteriously watchful. The new floor lamp with its shade of rose-colored silk gives a soft, becoming light to her face, bringing out the fragile, unearthly prettiness which usually escapes attention. From outside there is a steady murmur of rain, but it is slackening and soon stops; the air outside becomes pale and luminous as the moon breaks through the clouds. A moment after the curtain rises, the lights in both rooms flicker and go out.*

JIM   Hey, there, Mr. Light Bulb!

AMANDA *laughs nervously.*

*Legend on screen: "Suspension of a public service."*²

AMANDA   Where was Moses when the lights went out? Ha-ha. Do you know the answer to that one, Mr. O'Connor?
JIM   No, Ma'am, what's the answer?
AMANDA   In the dark!

JIM *laughs appreciatively.*

Everybody sit still. I'll light the candles. Isn't it lucky we have them on the table? Where's a match? Which of you gentlemen can provide a match?
JIM   Here.
AMANDA   Thank you, Sir.
JIM   Not at all, Ma'am!
AMANDA [*as she lights the candles*]   I guess the fuse has burnt out. Mr. O'Connor, can you tell a burnt-out fuse? I know I can't and Tom is a total loss when it comes to mechanics. [*They rise from the table and go into the kitchenette, from where their voices are heard.*] Oh, be careful you don't bump into something. We don't

1. At the outset of the play we were informed by Tom, the narrator, that "the play is memory." He lives with his mother Amanda and his sister Laura in a rundown St. Louis apartment. Amanda is fussy, manipulative, doting, and she keeps reminding her children of her youth as a Southern belle, with scores of gentleman callers. Laura, shy and with a slight limp, takes refuge in old phonograph records and her collection of little glass animals. The husband and father has disappeared years before: he was a "telephone man in love with long distances." Tom is forced to help support his family by working in a shoe factory, but he hopes to break the ties and become a footloose poet. Before he does so, however, Amanda prevails on him to bring a co-worker from the factory home for dinner—a desperate attempt to recreate her own past and to provide a "gentleman caller" for Laura.

2. In the published version of the play Williams retained a theatrical device omitted from the acting version: a screen on which are projected appropriate legends and images.

want our gentleman caller to break his neck. Now wouldn't that be a fine howdy-do?

JIM Ha-ha! Where is the fuse-box?

AMANDA Right here next to the stove. Can you see anything?

JIM Just a minute.

AMANDA Isn't electricity a mysterious thing? Wasn't it Benjamin Franklin who tied a key to a kite? We live in such a mysterious universe, don't we? Some people say that science clears up all the mysteries for us. In my opinion it only creates more! Have you found it yet?

JIM No, Ma'am. All these fuses look okay to me.

AMANDA Tom!

TOM Yes, Mother?

AMANDA That light bill I gave you several days ago. The one I told you we got the notices about?

Legend on screen: "Ha!"

TOM Oh—yeah.

AMANDA You didn't neglect to pay it by any chance?

TOM Why, I—

AMANDA Didn't! I might have known it!

JIM Shakespeare probably wrote a poem on that light bill, Mrs. Wingfield.

AMANDA I might have known better than to trust him with it! There's such a high price for negligence in this world!

JIM Maybe the poem will win a ten-dollar prize.

AMANDA We'll just have to spend the remainder of the evening in the nineteenth century, before Mr. Edison made the Mazda lamp!

JIM Candlelight is my favorite kind of light.

AMANDA That shows you're romantic! But that's no excuse for Tom. Well, we got through dinner. Very considerate of them to let us get through dinner before they plunged us into everlasting darkness, wasn't it, Mr. O'Connor?

JIM Ha-ha!

AMANDA Tom, as a penalty for your carelessness you can help me with the dishes.

JIM Let me give you a hand.

AMANDA Indeed you will not!

JIM I ought to be good for something.

AMANDA Good for something? [*Her tone is rhapsodic.*] You? Why, Mr. O'Connor, nobody, *nobody's* given me this much entertainment in years—as you have!

JIM Aw, now, Mrs. Wingfield!

AMANDA I'm not exaggerating, not one bit! But Sister[3] is all by her lonesome. You go keep her company in the parlor! I'll give you this lovely old candelabrum that used to be on the altar at the Church of the Heavenly Rest. It was melted a little out of shape when the church burnt down. Lightning struck it one spring.

3. In many Southern families of Amanda's time, the oldest daughter was called "Sister" by parents and siblings.

Gypsy Jones[4] was holding a revival at the time and he intimated that the church was destroyed because the Episcopalians gave card parties.

JIM   Ha-ha.

AMANDA   And how about you coaxing Sister to drink a little wine? I think it would be good for her! Can you carry both at once?

JIM   Sure. I'm Superman!

AMANDA   Now, Thomas, get into this apron!

> JIM *comes into the dining room, carrying the candelabrum, its candles lighted, in one hand and a glass of wine in the other. The door of the kitchenette swings closed on* AMANDA's *gay laughter; the flickering light approaches the portieres.* LAURA *sits up nervously as* JIM *enters. She can hardly speak from the almost intolerable strain of being alone with a stranger.*
>
> Screen legend: "I don't suppose you remember me at all!"
>
> *At first, before* JIM's *warmth overcomes her paralyzing shyness,* LAURA's *voice is thin and breathless, as though she had just run up a steep flight of stairs.* JIM's *attitude is gently humorous. While the incident is apparently unimportant, it is to* LAURA *the climax of her secret life.*

JIM   Hello there, Laura.

LAURA [*faintly*]   Hello.

> *She clears her throat.*

JIM   How are you feeling now? Better?

LAURA   Yes. Yes, thank you.

JIM   This is for you. A little dandelion wine. [*He extends the glass toward her with extravagant gallantry.*]

LAURA   Thank you.

JIM   Drink it—but don't get drunk!

> *He laughs heartily.* LAURA *takes the glass uncertainly; she laughs shyly.*

Where shall I set the candles?

LAURA   Oh—oh, anywhere . . .

JIM   How about here on the floor? Any objections?

LAURA   No.

JIM   I'll spread a newspaper under to catch the drippings. I like to sit on the floor. Mind if I do?

LAURA   Oh, no.

JIM   Give me a pillow?

LAURA   What?

JIM   A pillow!

---

4. The name was probably suggested by the English evangelist Rodney "Gipsy" Smith (1860–1947), who toured the United States a number of times.

LAURA   Oh . . . [*She hands him one quickly.*]

JIM   How about you? Don't you like to sit on the floor?

LAURA   Oh—yes.

JIM   Why don't you, then?

LAURA   I—will.

JIM   Take a pillow!

[LAURA *does. She sits on the floor on the other side of the candelabrum.* JIM *crosses his legs and smiles engagingly at her.*] I can't hardly see you sitting way over there.

LAURA   I can—see you.

JIM   I know, but that's not fair, I'm in the limelight.

LAURA *moves her pillow closer.*

Good! Now I can see you! Comfortable?

LAURA   Yes.

JIM   So am I. Comfortable as a cow! Will you have some gum?

LAURA   No, thank you.

JIM   I think that I will indulge, with your permission. [*He musingly unwraps a stick of gum and holds it up.*] Think of the fortune made by the guy that invented the first piece of chewing gum. Amazing, huh? The Wrigley Building[5] is one of the sights of Chicago—I saw it when I went up to the Century of Progress. Did you take in the Century of Progress?[6]

LAURA   No, I didn't.

JIM   Well, it was quite a wonderful exposition. What impressed me most was the Hall of Science. Gives you an idea of what the future will be in America, even more wonderful than the present time is! [*There is a pause.* JIM *smiles at her.*] Your brother tells me you're shy. Is that right, Laura?

LAURA   I—don't know.

JIM   I judge you to be an old-fashioned type of girl. Well, I think that's a pretty good type to be. Hope you don't think I'm being too personal—do you?

LAURA [*hastily, out of embarrassment*]   I believe I *will* take a piece of gum, if you—don't mind. [*Clearing her throat.*] Mr. O'Connor, have you—kept up with your singing?

JIM   Singing? Me?

LAURA   Yes. I remember what a beautiful voice you had.

JIM   When did you hear me sing?

LAURA *does not answer, and in the long pause which follows a man's voice is heard singing offstage.*

VOICE:

O blow, ye winds, heigh-ho,
A-roving I will go!
I'm off to my love

5. One of the earliest skyscrapers (1921–24) in the United States.
6. A world's fair held in 1933–34 to celebrate the centennial of the founding of Chicago.

With a boxing glove—
Ten thousand miles away!

JIM   You say you've heard me sing?

LAURA   Oh, yes! Yes, very often . . . I—don't suppose—you remember me—at all?

JIM   [*smiling doubtfully*] You know I have an idea I've seen you before. I had that idea soon as you opened the door. It seemed almost like I was about to remember your name. But the name that I started to call you—wasn't a name! And so I stopped myself before I said it.

LAURA   Wasn't it—Blue Roses?

JIM   [*springing up, grinning*] Blue Roses! My gosh, yes—Blue Roses! That's what I had on my tongue when you opened the door! Isn't it funny what tricks your memory plays? I didn't connect you with high school somehow or other. But that's where it was; it was high school. I didn't even know you were Shakespeare's sister! Gosh, I'm sorry.

LAURA   I didn't expect you to. You—barely knew me!

JIM   But we did have a speaking acquaintance, huh?

LAURA   Yes, we—spoke to each other.

JIM   When did you recognize me?

LAURA   Oh, right away!

JIM   Soon as I came in the door?

LAURA   When I heard your name I thought it was probably you. I knew that Tom used to know you a little in high school. So when you came in the door—well, then I was—sure.

JIM   Why didn't you *say* something, then?

LAURA   [*breathlessly*] I didn't know what to say, I was—too surprised!

JIM   For goodness' sakes! You know, this sure is funny!

LAURA   Yes! Yes, isn't it, though . . .

JIM   Didn't we have a class in something together?

LAURA   Yes, we did.

JIM   What class was that?

LAURA   It was—singing—chorus!

JIM   Aw!

LAURA   I sat across the aisle from you in the Aud.

JIM   Aw.

LAURA   Mondays, Wednesdays, and Fridays.

JIM   Now I remember—you always came in late.

LAURA   Yes, it was so hard for me, getting upstairs. I had that brace on my leg—it clumped so loud!

JIM   I never heard any clumping.

LAURA   [*wincing at the recollection*] To me it sounded like—thunder!

JIM   Well, well, well, I never even noticed.

LAURA   And everybody was seated before I came in. I had to walk in front of all those people. My seat was in the back row. I had to go clumping all the way up the aisle with everyone watching!

JIM   You shouldn't have been self-conscious.

LAURA   I know, but I was. It was always such a relief when the singing started.

JIM   Aw, Yes, I've placed you now! I used to call you Blue Roses. How was it that I got started calling you that?

LAURA   I was out of school a little while with pleurosis. When I came back you asked me what was the matter. I said I had pleurosis—you thought I said *Blue Roses*. That's what you always called me after that!

JIM   I hope you didn't mind.

LAURA   Oh, no—I liked it. You see, I wasn't acquainted with many—people. . . .

JIM   As I remember you sort of stuck by yourself.

LAURA   I—I—never have had much luck at—making friends.

JIM   I don't see why you wouldn't.

LAURA   Well, I—started out badly.

JIM   You mean being—

LAURA   Yes, it sort of—stood between me—

JIM   You shouldn't have let it!

LAURA   I know, but it did, and—

JIM   You were shy with people!

LAURA   I tried not to be but never could—

JIM   Overcome it?

LAURA   No, I—I never could!

JIM   I guess being shy is something you have to work out of kind of gradually.

LAURA [*sorrowfully*]   Yes—I guess it—

JIM   Takes time!

LAURA   Yes—

JIM   People are not so dreadful when you know them. That's what you have to remember! And everybody has problems, not just you, but practically everybody has got some problems. You think of yourself as having the only problems, as being the only one who is disappointed. But just look around you and you will see lots of people as disappointed as you are. For instance, I hoped when I was going to high school that I would be further along at this time, six years later, than I am now. You remember that wonderful write-up I had in *The Torch?*

LAURA   Yes! [*She rises and crosses to the table.*]

JIM   It said I was bound to succeed in anything I went into!

LAURA *returns with the high school yearbook.*

Holy Jeez! *The Torch!*

He accepts it reverently. They smile across the book with mutual wonder. LAURA *crouches beside him and they begin to turn the pages.* LAURA'*s shyness is dissolving in his warmth.*

LAURA   Here you are in *The Pirates of Penzance!*

JIM [*wistfully*]   I sang the baritone lead in that operetta.

LAURA [*raptly*]   So—*beautifully!*

JIM [*protesting*]   Aw—

LAURA   Yes, yes—beautifully—beautifully!

JIM   You heard me?

LAURA   All three times!
JIM   No!
LAURA   Yes!
JIM   All three performances?
LAURA [*looking down*]   Yes.
JIM   Why?
LAURA   I—wanted to ask you to—autograph my program. [*She takes the program from the back of the yearbook and shows it to him.*]
JIM   Why didn't you ask me to?
LAURA   You were always surrounded by your own friends so much that I never had a chance to.
JIM   You should have just—
LAURA   Well, I—thought you might think I was—
JIM   Thought I might think you was—what?
LAURA   Oh—
JIM [*with reflective relish*]   I was beleaguered by females in those days.
LAURA   You were terribly popular!
JIM   Yeah—
LAURA   You had such a—friendly way—
JIM   I was spoiled in high school.
LAURA   Everybody—liked you!
JIM   Including you?
LAURA   I—yes, I—did, too— [*She gently closes the book in her lap.*]
JIM   Well, well, well! Give me that program, Laura.

She hands it to him. He signs it with a flourish.

There you are—better late than never!
LAURA   Oh, I—what a—surprise!
JIM   My signature isn't worth very much right now. But some day—maybe—it will increase in value! Being disappointed is one thing and being discouraged is something else. I am disappointed but I am not discouraged. I'm twenty-three years old. How old are you?
LAURA   I'll be twenty-four in June.
JIM   That's not old age!
LAURA   No, but—
JIM   You finished high school?
LAURA [*with difficulty*]   I didn't go back.
JIM   You mean you dropped out?
LAURA   I made bad grades in my final examinations. [*She rises and replaces the book and the program on the table. Her voice is strained.*] How is—Emily Meisenbach getting along?
JIM   Oh, that kraut-head!
LAURA   Why do you call her that?
JIM   That's what she was.
LAURA   You're not still—going with her?
JIM   I never see her.
LAURA   It said in the "Personal" section that you were—engaged!
JIM   I know, but I wasn't impressed by that—propaganda!
LAURA   It wasn't—the truth?

JIM   Only in Emily's optimistic opinion!
LAURA   Oh—

> *Legend: "What have you done since high school?"*

> JIM *lights a cigarette and leans indolently back on his elbows smiling at* LAURA *with a warmth and charm which lights her inwardly with altar candles. She remains by the table, picks up a piece from the glass menagerie collection, and turns it in her hands to cover her tumult.*

JIM [*after several reflective puffs on his cigarette*]   What have you done since high school?

> *She seems not to hear him.*

Huh?

> LAURA *looks up.*

I said what have you done since high school, Laura?
LAURA   Nothing much.
JIM   You must have been doing something these six long years.
LAURA   Yes.
JIM   Well, then, such as what?
LAURA   I took a business course at business college—
JIM   How did that work out?
LAURA   Well, not very—well—I had to drop out, it gave me—indigestion—

> JIM *laughs gently.*

JIM   What are you doing now?
LAURA   I don't do anything—much. Oh, please don't think I sit around doing nothing! My glass collection takes up a good deal of time. Glass is something you have to take good care of.
JIM   What did you say—about glass?
LAURA   Collection I said—I have one— [*She clears her throat and turns away again, acutely shy.*]
JIM [*abruptly*]   You know what I judge to be the trouble with you? Inferiority complex! Know what that is? That's what they call it when someone low-rates himself! I understand it because I had it too. Although my case was not so aggravated as yours seems to be. I had it until I took up public speaking, developed my voice, and learned that I had an aptitude for science. Before that time I never thought of myself as being outstanding in any way whatsoever! Now I've never made a regular study of it, but I have a friend who says I can analyze people better than doctors that make a profession of it. I don't claim that to be necessarily true, but I can sure guess a person's psychology, Laura! [*He takes out his gum.*] Excuse me, Laura. I always take it out when the flavor is gone. I'll use this

scrap of paper to wrap it in. I know how it is to get it stuck on a shoe. [*He wraps the gum in paper and puts it in his pocket.*] Yep—that's what I judge to be your principal trouble. A lack of confidence in yourself as a person. You don't have the proper amount of faith in yourself. I'm basing that fact on a number of your remarks and also on certain observations I've made. For instance that clumping you thought was so awful in high school. You say that you even dreaded to walk into class. You see what you did? You dropped out of school, you gave up an education because of a clump, which as far as I know was practically nonexistent! A little physical defect is what you have. Hardly noticeable even! Magnified thousands of times by imagination! You know what my strong advice to you is? Think of yourself as *superior* in some way!

LAURA   In what way would I think?

JIM   Why, man alive, Laura! Just look about you a little. What do you see? A world full of common people! All of 'em born and all of 'em going to die! Which of them has one-tenth of your good points! Or mine! Or anyone else's, as far as that goes—gosh! Everybody excels in some one thing. Some in many! [*He unconsciously glances at himself in the mirror.*] All you've got to do is discover in *what!* Take me, for instance. [*He adjusts his tie at the mirror.*] My interest happens to lie in electro-dynamics. I'm taking a course in radio engineering at night school, Laura, on top of a fairly responsible job at the warehouse. I'm taking that course and studying public speaking.

LAURA   Ohhhh.

JIM   Because I believe in the future of television! [*Turning his back to her*] I wish to be ready to go up right along with it. Therefore I'm planning to get in on the ground floor. In fact I've already made the right connections and all that remains is for the industry itself to get under way! Full steam—[*His eyes are starry.*] *Knowledge*—Zzzzzp! *Money*—Zzzzzp!—Power! That's the cycle democracy is built on!

His attitude is convincingly dynamic. LAURA *stares at him, even her shyness eclipsed in her absolute wonder. He suddenly grins.*

I guess you think I think a lot of myself!

LAURA   No—o-o-o, I—

JIM   Now how about you? Isn't there something you take more interest in than anything else?

LAURA   Well, I do—as I said—have my—glass collection—

A peal of girlish laughter rings from the kitchenette.

JIM   I'm not right sure I know what you're talking about. What kind of glass is it?

LAURA   Little articles of it, they're ornaments mostly! Most of them are little animals made out of glass, the tiniest little animals in the world. Mother calls them a glass menagerie! Here's an example of one, if you'd like to see it! This one is one of the oldest. It's nearly thirteen.

Music: "The Glass Menagerie."

He stretches out his hand.

Oh, be careful—if you breathe, it breaks!

JIM   I'd better not take it. I'm pretty clumsy with things.

LAURA   Go, on, I trust you with him! [*She places the piece in his palm.*] There now—you're holding him gently! Hold him over the light, he loves the light! You see how the light shines through him?

JIM   It sure does shine!

LAURA   I shouldn't be partial, but he is my favorite one.

JIM   What kind of a thing is this one supposed to be?

LAURA   Haven't you noticed the single horn on his forehead?

JIM   A unicorn, huh?

LAURA   Mmmm-hmmm!

JIM   Unicorns—aren't they extinct in the modern world?

LAURA   I know!

JIM   Poor little fellow, he must feel sort of lonesome.

LAURA [*smiling*]   Well, if he does, he doesn't complain about it. He stays on a shelf with some horses that don't have horns and all of them seem to get along nicely together.

JIM   How do you know?

LAURA [*lightly*]   I haven't heard any arguments among them!

JIM [*grinning*]   No arguments, huh? Well, that's a pretty good sign! Where shall I set him?

LAURA   Put him on the table. They all like a change of scenery once in a while!

JIM   Well, well, well, well—[*He places the glass piece on the table, then raises his arms and stretches.*] Look how big my shadow is when I stretch!

LAURA   Oh, oh, yes—it stretches across the ceiling!

JIM [*crossing to the door*]   I think it's stopped raining. [*He opens the fire-escape door and the background music changes to a dance tune.*] Where does the music come from?

LAURA   From the Paradise Dance Hall across the alley.

JIM   How about cutting the rug a little, Miss Wingfield?

LAURA   Oh, I—

JIM   Or is your program filled up? Let me have a look at it. [*He grasps an imaginary card.*] Why, every dance is taken! I'll just have to scratch some out.

Waltz music: "La Golondrina."[7]

Ahh, a waltz! [*He executes some sweeping turns by himself, then holds his arms toward* LAURA.]

7. A Mexican song, first printed in 1883, by Narciso Seradell (1843–1910).

LAURA [*breathlessly*]   I—can't dance!

JIM   There you go, that inferiority stuff!

LAURA   I've never danced in my life!

JIM   Come on, try!

LAURA   Oh, but I'd step on you!

JIM   I'm not made out of glass.

LAURA   How—how—how do we start?

JIM   Just leave it to me. You hold your arms out a little.

LAURA   Like this?

JIM [*taking her in his arms*]   A little bit higher. Right. Now don't tighten up, that's the main thing about it— relax.

LAURA [*laughing breathlessly*]   It's hard not to.

JIM   Okay.

LAURA   I'm afraid you can't budge me.

JIM   What do you bet I can't? [*He swings her into motion.*]

LAURA   Goodness, yes, you can!

JIM   Let yourself go, now, Laura, just let yourself go.

LAURA   I'm—

JIM   Come on!

LAURA   —trying!

JIM   Not so stiff—easy does it!

LAURA   I know but I'm—

JIM   Loosen th' backbone! There now, that's a lot better.

LAURA   Am I?

JIM   Lots, better! [*He moves her about the room in a clumsy waltz.*]

LAURA   Oh, my!

JIM   Ha-ha!

LAURA   Oh, my goodness!

JIM   Ha-ha-ha!

> *They suddenly bump into the table, and the glass piece on it falls to the floor.* JIM *stops the dance.*

What did we hit on?

LAURA   Table.

JIM   Did something fall off it? I think—

LAURA   Yes.

JIM   I hope that it wasn't the little glass horse with the horn!

LAURA   Yes. [*She stoops to pick it up.*]

JIM   Aw, aw, aw. Is it broken?

LAURA   Now it is just like all the other horses.

JIM   It's lost its—

LAURA   Horn! It doesn't matter. Maybe it's a blessing in disguise.

JIM   You'll never forgive me. I bet that that was your favorite piece of glass.

LAURA   I don't have favorites much. It's no tragedy, Freckles.[8] Glass breaks so easily. No matter how careful you are. The traffic jars

---

8. In Williams's "Portrait of a Girl in Glass," the story upon which *Menagerie* was based, "Freckles"—a one-armed orphan—was the hero of the one book that Laura constantly read and reread.

the shelves and things fall off them.

JIM   Still I'm awfully sorry that I was the cause.

LAURA [*smiling*]   I'll just imagine he had an operation. The horn was removed to make him feel less—freakish!

They both laugh.

Now he will feel more at home with the other horses, the ones that don't have horns. . . .

JIM   Ha-ha, that's very funny! [*Suddenly he is serious.*] I'm glad to see that you have a sense of humor. You know—you're—well—very different! Surprisingly different from anyone else I know! [*His voice becomes soft and hesitant with a genuine feeling.*] Do you mind me telling you that?

LAURA *is abashed beyond speech.*

I mean it in a nice way—

LAURA *nods shyly, looking away.*

You make me feel sort of—I don't know how to put it! I'm usually pretty good at expressing things, but—this is something that I don't know how to say!

LAURA *touches her throat and clears it—turns the broken unicorn in her hands. His voice becomes softer.*

Has anyone ever told you that you were pretty?

There is a pause, and the music rises slightly. LAURA *looks up slowly, with wonder, and shakes her head.*

Well, you are! In a very different way from anyone else. And all the nicer because of the difference, too.

His voice becomes low and husky. LAURA *turns away, nearly faint with the novelty of her emotions.*

I wish that you were my sister. I'd teach you to have some confidence in yourself. The different people are not like other people, but being different is nothing to be ashamed of. Because other people are not such wonderful people. They're one hundred times one thousand. You're one times one! They walk all over the earth. You just stay here. They're common as—weeds, but—you—well, you're—*Blue Roses!*

Image on screen: Blue Roses.

The music changes.

LAURA   But blue is wrong for—roses. . . .

JIM   It's right for you! You're—pretty!
LAURA   In what respect am I pretty?
JIM   In all respects—believe me! Your eyes—your hair—are pretty!
Your hands are pretty! [*He catches hold of her hand.*] You think I'm
making this up because I'm invited to dinner and have to be nice.
Oh, I could do that! I could put on an act for you, Laura, and say
lots of things without being very sincere. But this time I am. I'm
talking to you sincerely. I happened to notice you had this inferiority
complex that keeps you from feeling comfortable with people. Somebody needs to build your confidence up and make you proud
instead of shy and turning away and—blushing. Somebody—ought
to—*kiss* you, Laura!

> *His hand slips slowly up her arm to her shoulder as the music
> swells tumultuously. He suddenly turns her about and kisses
> her on the lips. When he releases her,* LAURA *sinks on the
> sofa with a bright, dazed look.* JIM *backs away and fishes in
> his pocket for a cigarette.*

> *Legend on screen: "A souvenir."*

Stumblejohn!

> *He lights the cigarette, avoiding her look. There is a peal of
> girlish laughter from* AMANDA *in the kitchenette.* LAURA *slowly
> raises and opens her hand. It still contains the little broken glass
> animal. She looks at it with a tender, bewildered expression.*

Stumblejohn! I shouldn't have done that—that was way off the
beam. You don't smoke, do you?

> *She looks up, smiling, not hearing the question. He sits beside
> her rather gingerly. She looks at him speechlessly—waiting. He
> coughs decorously and moves a little further aside as he con-
> siders the situation and senses her feelings, dimly, with per-
> turbation. He speaks gently.*

Would you—care for a mint?

> *She doesn't seem to hear him but her look grows brighter
> even.*

Peppermint? Life Saver? My pocket's a regular drugstore—
wherever I go. . . . [*He pops a mint in his mouth. Then he
gulps and decides to make a clean breast of it. He speaks slowly and
gingerly.*] Laura, you know, if I had a sister like you, I'd do the same
thing as Tom. I'd bring out fellows and—introduce her to them. The
right type of boys—of a type to—appreciate her. Only—well—he
made a mistake about me. Maybe I've got no call to be saying
this. That may not have been the idea in having me over. But what
if it was? There's nothing wrong about that. The only trouble is
that in my case—I'm not in a situation to—do the right thing. I can't

take down your number and say I'll phone. I can't call up next
week and—ask for a date. I thought I had better explain the situation in case you—misunderstood it and—I hurt your feelings. . . .

> *There is a pause. Slowly, very slowly,* LAURA's *look changes, her
> eyes returning slowly from his to the glass figure in her palm.*
> AMANDA *utters another gay laugh in the kitchenette.*

LAURA [*faintly*] You—won't—call again?
JIM   No, Laura, I can't. [*He rises from the sofa.*] As I was just explaining, I've—got strings on me. Laura, I've—been going steady! I
go out all the time with a girl named Betty. She's a home-girl like
you, and Catholic, and Irish, and in a great many ways we—get
along fine. I met her last summer on a moonlight boat trip up the
river to Alton,[9] on the *Majestic*. Well—right away from the start it
was—love!

> *Legend: Love!*

> LAURA *sways slightly forward and grips the arm of the sofa.
> He fails to notice, now enrapt in his own comfortable being.*

Being in love has made a new man of me!

> *Leaning stiffly forward, clutching the arm of the sofa,* LAURA
> *struggles visibly with her storm. But* JIM *is oblivious; she is a
> long way off.*

The power of love is really pretty tremendous! Love is something
that—changes the whole world, Laura!

> *The storm abates a little and* LAURA *leans back. He notices
> her again.*

It happened that Betty's aunt took sick, she got a wire and had
to go to Centralia.[1] So Tom—when he asked me to dinner—I naturally just accepted the invitation, not knowing that you—that he—that
I —[*He stops awkwardly.*] Huh—I'm a stumblejohn!

> *He flops back on the sofa. The holy candles on the altar of*
> LAURA's *face have been snuffed out. There is a look of almost
> infinite desolation.* JIM *glances at her uneasily.*

I wish that you would—say something.

> *She bites her lip which was trembling and then bravely smiles.
> She opens her hand again on the broken glass figure. Then
> she gently takes his hand and raises it level with her own. She*

9. A city in Illinois about 20 miles   1. A city in Illinois about 60 miles east
north of St. Louis.   of St. Louis.

*carefully places the unicorn in the palm of his hand, then
pushes his fingers closed upon it.*

What are you—doing that for? You want me to have him?
Laura?

She nods.

What for?
LAURA   A—souvenir. . . .

*She rises unsteadily and crouches beside the Victrola to wind
it up.*

*Legend on screen: "Things have a way of turning out so badly!"
Or image: "Gentleman caller waving goodbye—gaily."*

At this moment , AMANDA *rushes brightly back into the living
room. She bears a pitcher of fruit punch in an old-fashioned
cut-glass pitcher, and a plate of macaroons. The plate has a
gold border and poppies painted on it.*

AMANDA   Well, well, well! Isn't the air delightful after the shower?
I've made you children a little liquid refreshment. [*She turns gaily
to* JIM.] Jim, do you know that song about lemonade?
        "Lemonade, lemonade
        Made in the shade and stirred with a spade—
        Good enough for any old maid!"
JIM [*uneasily*]   Ha-ha! No—I never heard it.
AMANDA   Why, Laura! You look so serious!
JIM   We were having a serious conversation.
AMANDA   Good! Now you're better acquainted!
JIM [*uncertainly*]   Ha-ha! Yes.
AMANDA   You modern young people are much more serious-minded
    that my generation. I was so gay as a girl!
JIM   You haven't changed, Mrs. Wingfield.
AMANDA   Tonight I'm rejuvenated! The gaiety of the occasion, Mr.
    O'Connor! [*She tosses her head with a peal of laughter, spilling some
    lemonade.*] Oooo! I'm baptizing myself!
JIM   Here—let me—
AMANDA [*setting the pitcher down*]   There now. I discovered we had
    some maraschino cherries. I dumped them in, juice and all!
JIM   You shouldn't have gone to that trouble, Mrs. Wingfield.
AMANDA   Trouble, trouble? Why, it was loads of fun! Didn't you
    hear me cutting up in the kitchen? I bet your ears were burning! I
    told Tom how outdone with him I was for keeping you to himself
    so long a time! He should have brought you over much, much
    sooner! Well, now that you've found your way, I want you to be a
    very frequent caller! Not just occasional but all the time. Oh, we're
    going to have a lot of gay times together! I see them coming! Mmm,
    just breathe that air! So fresh, and the moon's so pretty! I'll skip

back out—I know where my place is when young folks are having a
—serious conversation!

JIM   Oh, don't go out, Mrs. Wingfield. The fact of the matter is I've
got to be going.

AMANDA   Going, now? You're joking! Why, it's only the shank of the
evening,[2] Mr. O'Connor!

JIM   Well, you know how it is.

AMANDA   You mean you're a young workingman and have to keep
workingmen's hours. We'll let you off early tonight. But only on the
condition that next time you stay later. What's the best night for
you? Isn't Saturday night the best night for you workingmen?

JIM   I have a couple of time-clocks to punch, Mrs. Wingfield. One at
morning, another one at night!

AMANDA   My, but you *are* ambitious! You work at night, too?

JIM   No, Ma'am, not work but—Betty!

*He crosses deliberately to pick up his hat. The band at the
Paradise Dance Hall goes into a tender waltz.*

AMANDA   Betty? Betty? Who's—Betty!

There is an ominous cracking sound in the sky.

JIM   Oh, just a girl. The girl I go steady with!

He smiles charmingly. The sky falls.

Legend: "The Sky Falls."

AMANDA [*a long-drawn exhalation*]   Ohhhh . . . Is it a serious romance,
Mr. O'Connor?

JIM   We're going to be married the second Sunday in June.

AMANDA   Ohhh—how nice! Tom didn't mention that you were engaged to be married.

JIM   The cat's not out of the bag at the warehouse yet. You know
how they are. They call you Romeo and stuff like that. [*He stops
at the oval mirror to put on his hat. He carefully shapes the brim
and the crown to give a discreetly dashing effect.*] It's been a wonderful evening, Mrs. Wingfield. I guess this is what they mean by
Southern hospitality.

AMANDA   It really wasn't anything at all.

JIM   I hope it don't seem like I'm rushing off. But I promised Betty
I'd pick her up at the Wabash depot, an' by the time I get my
jalopy down there her train'll be in. Some women are pretty upset if
you keep 'em waiting.

AMANDA   Yes, I know—the tyranny of women! [*She extends her
hand.*] Goodbye, Mr. O'Connor. I wish you luck—and happiness—and
success! All three of them, and so does Laura! Don't you, Laura?

LAURA   Yes!

2. The best part of the evening.

JIM [*taking* LAURA's *hand*] Goodbye, Laura. I'm certainly going to treasure that souvenir. And don't you forget the good advice I gave you. [*He raises his voice to a cheery shout.*] So long, Shakespeare! Thanks again, ladies. Good night!

> *He grins and ducks jauntily out. Still bravely grimacing,* AMANDA *closes the door on the gentleman caller. Then she turns back to the room with a puzzled expression. She and* LAURA *don't dare to face each other.* LAURA *crouches beside the Victrola to wind it.*

AMANDA [*faintly*] Things have a way of turning out so badly. I don't believe that I would play the Victrola. Well, well—well! Our gentleman caller was engaged to be married! [*She raises her voice.*] Tom!

TOM [*from the kitchenette*] Yes, Mother?

AMANDA Come in here a minute. I want to tell you something awfully funny.

TOM [*entering with a macaroon and a glass of the lemonade*] Has the gentleman caller gotten away already?

AMANDA The gentleman caller has made an early departure. What a wonderful joke you played on us!

TOM How do you mean?

AMANDA You didn't mention that he was engaged to be married.

TOM Jim? Engaged?

AMANDA That's what he just informed us.

TOM I'll be jiggered! I didn't know about that.

AMANDA That seems very peculiar.

TOM What's peculiar about it?

AMANDA Didn't you call your best friend down at the warehouse?

TOM He is, but how did I know?

AMANDA It seems extremely peculiar that you wouldn't know your best friend was going to be married!

TOM The warehouse is where I work, not where I know things about people!

AMANDA You don't know things anywhere! You live in a dream; you manufacture illusions!

> *He crosses to the door.*

Where are you going?

TOM I'm going to the movies.

AMANDA That's right, now that you've had us make such fools of ourselves. The effort, the preparations, all the expense! The new floor lamp, the rug, the clothes for Laura! All for what? To entertain some other girl's fiancé! Go to the movies, go! Don't think about us, a mother deserted, an unmarried sister who's crippled and has no job! Don't let anything interfere with your selfish pleasure! Just go, go, go—to the movies!

TOM All right, I will! The more you shout about my selfishness to me the quicker I'll go, and I won't go to the movies!

AMANDA Go, then! Go to the moon—you selfish dreamer!

TOM *smashes his glass on the floor. He plunges out on the fire escape, slamming the door.* LAURA *screams in fright. The dance-hall music becomes louder.* TOM *stands on the fire escape, gripping the rail. The moon breaks through the storm clouds, illuminating his face.*

Legend on screen: "And so goodbye . . ."

TOM*'s closing speech is timed with what is happening inside the house. We see, as though through soundproof glass, that* AMANDA *appears to be making a comforting speech to* LAURA, *who is huddled upon the sofa. Now that we cannot hear the mother's speech, her silliness is gone and she has dignity and tragic beauty.* LAURA*'s hair hides her face until, at the end of the speech, she lifts her head to smile at her mother.* AMANDA*'s gestures are slow and. graceful, almost dancelike, as she comforts her daughter. At the end of her speech she glances a moment at the father's picture—then withdraws through the portieres. At the close of* TOM*'s speech,* LAURA *blows out the candles, ending the play.*

TOM   I didn't go to the moon, I went much further—for time is the longest distance between two places. Not long after that I was fired for writing a poem on the lid of a shoe-box. I left Saint Louis. I descended the steps of this fire escape for a last time and followed, from then on, in my father's footsteps, attempting to find in motion what was lost in space. I traveled around a great deal. The cities swept about me like dead leaves, leaves that were brightly colored but torn away from the branches. I would have stopped, but I was pursued by something. It always came upon me unwares, taking me altogether by surprise. Perhaps it was a familiar bit of music. Perhaps it was only a piece of transparent glass. Perhaps I am walking along a street at night, in some strange city, before I have found companions. I pass the lighted window of a shop where perfume is sold. The window is filled with pieces of colored glass, tiny transparent bottles in delicate colors, like bits of a shattered rainbow. Then all at once my sister touches my shoulder. I turn around and look into her eyes. Oh, Laura, Laura, I tried to leave you behind me, but I am more faithful than I intended to be! I reach for a cigarette, I cross the street, I run into the movies or a bar, I buy a drink, I speak to the nearest stranger—anything that can blow your candles out!

LAURA *bends over the candles.*

For nowadays the world is lit by lightning! Blow out your candles, Laura—and so goodbye. . . .

She blows the candles out.

1945

From Cat on a Hot Tin Roof

From *Act II. [Brick and Big Daddy]*[1]

BRICK   Big Daddy! Give me my crutch.

[BIG DADDY *throws the crutch out of reach.*]

Give me that crutch, Big Daddy.

BIG DADDY   Why do you drink?

BRICK   Don't know, give me my crutch!

BIG DADDY   You better think why you drink or give up drinking!

BRICK   Will you please give me my crutch so I can get up off this floor?

BIG DADDY   First you answer my question. Why do you drink? Why are you throwing your life away, boy, like somethin' disgusting you picked up on the street?

BRICK [*getting onto his knees*]   Big Daddy, I'm in pain, I stepped on that foot.

BIG DADDY   Good! I'm glad you're not too numb with the liquor in you to feel some pain!

BRICK   You—spilled my—drink. . . .

BIG DADDY   I'll make a bargain with you. You tell me why you drink and I'll hand you one. I'll pour you the liquor myself and hand it to you.

BRICK   Why do I drink?

BIG DADDY   Yea! Why?

BRICK   Give me a drink and I'll tell you.

BIG DADDY   Tell me first!

BRICK   I'll tell you in one word.

BIG DADDY   What word?

BRICK   DISGUST!

[*The clock chimes softly, sweetly.* BIG DADDY *gives it a short, outraged glance.*]

Now how about that drink?

BIG DADDY   What are you disgusted with? You got to tell me that, first. Otherwise being disgusted don't make no sense!

BRICK   Give me my crutch.

BIG DADDY   You heard me, you got to tell me what I asked you first.

BRICK   I told you, I said to kill my disgust!

BIG DADDY   DISGUST WITH WHAT!

BRICK   You strike a hard bargain.

BIG DADDY   What are you disgusted with?—an' I'll pass you the liquor.

BRICK   I can hop on one foot, and if I fall, I can crawl.

BIG DADDY   You want liquor that bad?

---

1. The play is summarized by Donald Spoto: it "is structured as a series of confrontations between members of the Pollitt family: Brick, a former athletic star and current alcoholic; his wife, Maggie, the 'cat,' who is sexually frustrated because of Brick's mysterious distance from her following the suicide of his friend Skipper; Big Daddy, Brick's father, whose imminent death means the transfer of a vast estate; his confused, loyal, long-suffering wife, Big Mama; and Brick's venal brother and sister-in-law, Gooper and Mae." The entire action takes place on the night of Big Daddy's sixty-fifth birthday, in Maggie and Brick's bedroom, which had been occupied long ago by the two men who owned the plantation before Big Daddy took over. It has been established that Brick broke his ankle during a drunken fall on the high school playing fields the night before, and that only Maggie and Brick know the true results of Big Daddy's recent medical examination: he is in fact dying of cancer.

BRICK [*dragging himself up, clinging to bedstead*]   Yeah, I want it that bad.

BIG DADDY   If I give you a drink, will you tell me what it is you're disgusted with, Brick?

BRICK   Yes, sir, I will try to.

[*The old man pours him a drink and solemnly passes it to him.*
[*There is silence as* BRICK *drinks.*]

Have you ever heard the word "mendacity"?

BIG DADDY   Sure. Mendacity is one of them five dollar words that cheap politicians throw back and forth at each other.

BRICK   You know what it means?

BIG DADDY   Don't it mean lying and liars?

BRICK   Yes, sir, lying and liars.

BIG DADDY   Has someone been lying to you?

CHILDREN [*chanting in chorus offstage*]:
We want Big Dad-dee!
We want Big Dad-dee!

[GOOPER *appears in the gallery door.*]

GOOPER   Big Daddy, the kiddies are shouting for you out there.

BIG DADDY [*fiercely*]   Keep out, Gooper!

GOOPER   'Scuse *me!*

[BIG DADDY *slams the doors after* GOOPER.]

BIG DADDY   Who's been lying to you, has Margaret been lying to you, has your wife been lying to you about something, Brick?

BRICK   Not her. That wouldn't matter.

BIG DADDY   Then who's been lying to you, and what about?

BRICK   No one single person and no one lie. . . .

BIG DADDY   Then what, what then, for Christ's sake?

BRICK   —The whole, the whole—thing. . . .

BIG DADDY   Why are you rubbing your head? You got a headache?

BRICK   No, I'm tryin' to—

BIG DADDY   —Concentrate, but you can't because your brain's all soaked with liquor, is that the trouble? Wet brain!

[*He snatches the glass from* BRICK's *hand.*]

What do you know about this mendacity thing? Hell! I could write a book on it! Don't you know that? I could write a book on it and still not cover the subject? Well, I could, I could write a goddam book on it and still not cover the subject anywhere near enough! !— Think of all the lies I got to put up with!—Pretenses! Ain't that mendacity? Having to pretend stuff you don't think or feel or have any idea of? Having for instance to act like I care for Big Mama!— I haven't been able to stand the sight, sound, or smell of that woman for forty years now!—even when I *laid* her!—regular as a piston. . . .

Pretend to love that son of a bitch of a Gooper and his wife Mae and those five same screechers out there like parrots in a jungle? Jesus! Can't stand to look at 'em!

Church!—it bores the bejesus out of me but I go!—I go an' sit there and listen to the fool preacher!

Clubs!—Elks! Masons! Rotary!—*crap!*

[*A spasm of pain makes him clutch his belly. He sinks into a chair and his voice is softer and hoarser.*]

You I *do* like for some reason, did always have some kind of real feeling for—affection—respect—yes, always. . . .

You and being a success as a planter is all I ever had any devotion to in my whole life!—and that's the truth. . . .

I don't know why, but it is!

I've lived with mendacity!—Why can't *you* live with it? Hell, you *got* to live with it, there's nothing *else* to *live* with except mendacity, is there?

BRICK   Yes, sir. Yes, sir there is something else that you can live with!

BIG DADDY   What?

BRICK [*lifting his glass*]   This!—Liquor. . . .

BIG DADDY   That's not living, that's dodging away from life.

BRICK   I want to dodge away from it.

BIG DADDY   Then why don't you kill yourself, man?

BRICK   I like to drink. . . .

BIG DADDY   Oh, God, I can't talk to you. . . .

BRICK   I'm sorry, Big Daddy.

BIG DADDY   Not as sorry as I am. I'll tell you something. A little while back when I thought my number was up—

[*This speech should have torrential pace and fury.*]

—before I found out it was just this—spastic—colon. I thought about you. Should I or should I not, if the jig was up, give you this place when I go—since I hate Gooper an' Mae an' know that they hate me, and since all five same monkeys are little Maes an' Goopers.—And I thought, No!—Then I thought, Yes!—I couldn't make up my mind. I hate Gooper and his five same monkeys and that bitch Mae! Why should I turn over twenty-eight thousand acres of the richest land this side of the valley Nile to not my kind?—But why in hell, on the other hand, Brick—should I subsidize a goddam fool on the bottle?—Liked or not liked, well, maybe even—*loved!*—Why should I do that?—Subsidize worthless behavior? Rot? Corruption?

BRICK [*smiling*]   I understand.

BIG DADDY   Well, if you do, you're smarter than I am, God damn it, because I don't understand. And this I will tell you frankly. I didn't make up my mind at all on that question and still to this day I ain't made out no will!—Well, now I don't *have* to. The pressure is gone. I can just wait and see if you pull yourself together or if you don't.

BRICK   That's right, Big Daddy.

BIG DADDY   You sound like you thought I was kidding.

BRICK [*rising*]   No, sir, I know you're not kidding.

BIG DADDY   But you don't care—?

BRICK [*hobbling toward the gallery door*]   No, sir, I don't care. . . .

Now how about taking a look at your birthday fireworks and getting some of that cool breeze off the river?

[*He stands in the gallery doorway as the night sky turns pink and green and gold with successive flashes of light.*]

BIG DADDY   *WAIT!*—Brick. . . .

[*His voice drops. Suddenly there is something shy, almost tender, in his restraining gesture.*]

Don't let's—leave it like this, like them other talks we've had, we've always—talked around things, we've—just talked around things for some rutten reason, I don't know what, it's always like something was left not spoken, something avoided because neither of us was honest enough with the—other. . . .

BRICK   I never lied to you, Big Daddy.

BIG DADDY   Did I ever to *you?*

BRICK   No, sir. . . .

BIG DADDY   Then there is at least two people that never lied to each other.

BRICK   But we've never *talked* to each other.

BIG DADDY   We can *now.*

BRICK   Big Daddy, there don't seem to be anything much to say.

BIG DADDY   You say that you drink to kill your disgust with lying.

BRICK   You said to give you a reason.

BIG DADDY   Is liquor the only thing that'll kill this disgust?

BRICK   Now. Yes.

BIG DADDY   But not once, huh?

BRICK   Not when I was still young an' believing. A drinking man's someone who wants to forget he isn't still young an' believing.

BIG DADDY   Believing what?

BRICK   Believing. . . .

BIG DADDY   Believing *what?*

BRICK [*stubbornly evasive*]   Believing. . . .

BIG DADDY   I don't know what the hell you mean by believing and I don't think you know what you mean by believing, but if you still got sports in your blood, go back to sports announcing and—

BRICK   Sit in a glass box watching games I can't play? Describing what I can't do while players do it? Sweating out their disgust and confusion in contests I'm not fit for? Drinkin' a coke, half bourbon, so I can stand it? That's no goddam good any more, no help—time just outran me, Big Daddy—got there first. . . .

BIG DADDY   I think you're passing the buck.

BRICK   You know many drinkin' men?

BIG DADDY [*with a slight, charming smile*]   I have known a fair number of that species.

BRICK   Could any of them tell you why he drank?

BIG DADDY   Yep, you're passin' the buck to things like time and disgust with "mendacity" and—crap!—if you got to use that kind of language about a thing, it's ninety-proof bull, and I'm not buying any.

BRICK   I had to give you a reason to get a drink!

BIG DADDY   You started drinkin' when your friend Skipper died.

[*Silence for five beats. The* BRICK *makes a startled movement, reaching for his crutch.*]

BRICK   What are you suggesting?

BIG DADDY   I'm suggesting nothing.

[*The shuffle and clop of* BRICK's *rapid hobble away from his father's steady, grave attention.*]

—But Gooper an' Mae suggested that there was something not right exactly in your—

BRICK [*stopping short downstage as if backed to a wall*]   "Not right"?

BIG DADDY   Not, well, exactly *normal* in your friendship with—

BRICK   They suggested that, too? I thought that was Maggie's suggestion.

[BRICK's *detachment is at last broken through. His heart is accelerated; his forehead sweat-beaded; his breath becomes more rapid and his voice hoarse. The thing they're discussing, timidly and painfully on the side of* BIG DADDY, *fiercely, violently on* BRICK's *side, is the inadmissible thing that Skipper died to disavow between them. The fact that if it existed it had to be disavowed to "keep face" in the world they lived in, may be at the heart of the "mendacity" that* BRICK *drinks to kill his disgust with. It may be the root of his collapse. Or maybe it is only a single manifestation of it, not even the most important. The bird that I hope to catch in the net of this play is not the solution of one man's psychological problem. I'm trying to catch the true quality of experience in a group of people, that cloudy, flickering, evanescent—fiercely charged! —interplay of live human beings in the thundercloud of a common crisis. Some mystery should be left in the revelation of character in a play, just as a great deal of mystery is always left in the revelation of character in life, even in one's own character to himself. This does not absolve the playwright of his duty to observe and probe as clearly and deeply as he legitimately can; but it should steer him away from "pat" conclusions, facile definitions which make a play just a play, not a snare for the truth of human experience.*

[*The following scene should be played with great concentration, with most of the power leashed but palpable in what is left unspoken.*]

Who else's suggestion is it, is it *yours?* How many others thought that Skipper and I were—

BIG DADDY [*gently*]   Now, hold on, hold on a minute, son.—I knocked around in my time.

BRICK   What's that got to do with—

BIG DADDY   I said "Hold on!"—I bummed, I bummed this country till I was—

BRICK   Whose suggestion, who else's suggestion is it?

BIG DADDY   Slept in hobo jungles and railroad Y's and flophouses in all cities before I—

BRICK   Oh, *you* think so, too, you call me your son and a queer. Oh! Maybe that's why you put Maggie and me in this room that was Jack Straw's and Peter Ochello's, in which that pair of old sisters slept in a double bed where both of 'em died!

BIG DADDY   *Now just don't go throwing rocks at—*

[*Suddenly* REVEREND TOOKER *appears in the gallery doors, his head slightly, playfully, fatuously cocked, with a practised clergyman's smile, sincere as a bird call blown on a hunter's whistle, the living embodiment of the pious, conventional lie.*

[BIG DADDY *gasps a little at this perfectly timed, but incongruous, apparition.*]

—What're you lookin' for, Preacher?

REVEREND TOOKER   The gentleman's lavatory, ha ha!—heh, heh . . .

BIG DADDY [*with strained courtesy*]   —Go back out and walk down to the other end of the gallery, Reverend Tooker, and use the bathroom connected with my bedroom, and if you can't find it, ask them where it is!

REVEREND TOOKER   Ah, thanks.

[*He goes out with a deprecatory chuckle.*]

BIG DADDY   It's hard to talk in this place . . .

BRICK   Son of a—!

BIG DADDY [*leaving a lot unspoken*]   —I seen all things and understood a lot of them, till 1910. Christ, the year that—I had worn my shoes through, hocked my—I hopped off a yellow dog freight car half a mile down the road, slept in a wagon of cotton outside the gin—Jack Straw an' Peter Ochello took me in. Hired me to manage this place which grew into this one.—When Jack Straw died—why, old Peter Ochello quit eatin' like a dog does when its master's dead, and died, too!

BRICK   Christ!

BIG DADDY   I'm just saying I understand such—

BRICK [*violently*]   Skipper is dead. I have not quit eating!

BIG DADDY   No, but you started drinking.

[BRICK *wheels on his crutch and hurls his glass across the room shouting.*]

BRICK   YOU THINK SO, TOO?

BIG DADDY   Shhh!

[*Footsteps run on the gallery. There are women's calls.*

[BIG DADDY *goes toward the door.*]

Go way!—Just broke a glass. . . .

[BRICK *is transformed, as if a quiet mountain blew suddenly up in volcanic flame.*]

BRICK   You think so, too? You think so, too? You think me an' Skipper did, did, did!—*sodomy!*—together?

BIG DADDY   Hold—!

BRICK   That what you—

BIG DADDY   —*ON*—a minute!

BRICK   You think we did dirty things between us, Skipper an'—

BIG DADDY   Why are you shouting like that? Why are you—

BRICK   —Me, is that what you think of Skipper, is that—

BIG DADDY   —so excited? I don't think nothing. I don't know nothing. I'm simply telling you what—

BRICK   You think that Skipper and me were a pair of dirty old men?

BIG DADDY   Now that's—

BRICK   Straw? Ochello? A couple of—

BIG DADDY   Now just—

BRICK   —ducking sissies? Queers? Is that what you—

BIG DADDY   Shhh.

BRICK   —think?

[*He loses his balance and pitches to his knees without noticing the pain. He grabs the bed and drags himself up.*]

BIG DADDY   Jesus!—Whew. . . . Grab my hand!

BRICK   Naw, I don't want your hand. . . .

BIG DADDY   Well, I want yours. Git up!

> [*He draws him up, keeps an arm about him with concern and affection.*]

You broken out in a sweat! You're panting like you'd run a race with—

BRICK [*freeing himself from his father's hold*]   Big Daddy, you shock me, Big Daddy, you, you—*shock* me! Talkin' so—

> [*He turns away from his father.*]

—casually!—about a—thing like that . . .

—Don't you know how people *feel* about things like that? How, how *disgusted* they are by things like that? Why, at Ole Miss when it was discovered a pledge to our fraternity, Skipper's and mine, did a, *attempted* to do a, unnatural thing with—

We not only dropped him like a hot rock!—We told him to git off the campus, and he did, he got!—All the way to—

> [*He halts, breathless.*]

BIG DADDY   —Where?

BRICK   —North Africa, last I heard!

BIG DADDY   Well, I have come back from further away than that, I have just now returned from the other side of the moon, death's country, son, and I'm not easy to shock by anything here.

> [*He comes downstage and faces out.*]

Always, anyhow, lived with too much space around me to be infected by ideas of other people. One thing you can grow on a big place more important than cotton!—is *tolerance!*—I grown it.

> [*He returns toward* BRICK.]

BRICK   Why can't exceptional friendship, *real, real, deep, deep friendship!* between two men be respected as something clean and decent without being thought of as—

BIG DADDY   It can, it is, for God's sake.

BRICK—Fairies. . . .

> [*In his utterance of this word, we gauge the wide and profound reach of the conventional mores he got from the world that crowned him with early laurel.*]

BIG DADDY   I told Mae an' Gooper—

BRICK   Frig Mae and Gooper, frig all dirty lies and liars!—Skipper and me had a clean, true thing between us!—had a clean friendship, practically all our lives, till Maggie got the idea you're talking about. Normal? No!—It was too rare to be normal, any true thing between two people is too rare to be normal. Oh, once in a while he put his hand on my shoulder or I'd put mine on his, oh, maybe even, when we were touring the country in pro-football an' shared hotel-rooms we'd reach across the space between the two beds and shake hands to say goodnight, yeah, one or two times we—

BIG DADDY   Brick, nobody thinks that that's not normal!

BRICK   Well, they're mistaken, it was! It was a pure an' true thing an' that's not normal.

> [*They both stare straight at each other for a long moment. The tension breaks and both turn away as if tired.*]

BIG DADDY   Yeah, it's—hard t'—talk. . . .

BRICK   All right, then, let's—let it go. . . .

BIG DADDY   Why did Skipper crack up? Why have you?

[BRICK *looks back at his father again. He has already decided, without knowing that he has made this decision, that he is going to tell his father that he is dying of cancer. Only this could even the score between them: one inadmissible thing in return for another.*]

BRICK [*ominously*]   All right. You're asking for it, Big Daddy. We're finally going to have that real true talk you wanted. It's too late to stop it, now, we got to carry it through and cover every subject.
[*He hobbles back to the liquor cabinet.*]
Uh-huh.
[*He opens the ice bucket and picks up the silver tongs with slow admiration of their frosty brightness.*]
Maggie declares that Skipper and I went into pro-football after we left "Ole Miss" because we were scared to grow up. . . .
[*He moves downstage with the shuffle and clop of a cripple on a crutch. As Margaret did when her speech became "recitative," he looks out into the house,[2] commanding its attention by his direct, concentrated gaze—a broken, "tragically elegant" figure telling simply as much as he knows of "the Truth."*]
—Wanted to—keep on tossing—those long, long!—high high!—passes that—couldn't be intercepted except by time, the aerial attack that made us famous! And so we did, we did, we kept it up for one season, that aerial attack, we held it high!—Yeah, but—
    —that summer, Maggie, she laid the law down to me, said, Now or never, and so I married Maggie. . . .

BIG DADDY   How was Maggie in bed?

BRICK [*wryly*]   Great! the greatest!
[BIG DADDY *nods as if he thought so.*]
She went on the road that fall with the Dixie Stars. Oh, she made a great show of being the world's best sport. She wore a—wore a—tall bearskin cap! A shako, they call it, a dyed moleskin coat, a moleskin coat dyed red!—Cut up crazy! Rented hotel ballrooms for victory celebrations, wouldn't cancel them when it—turned out—defeat. . . .
    MAGGIE THE CAT! Ha ha!
[BIG DADDY *nods.*]
—But Skipper, he had some fever which came back on him which doctors couldn't explain and I got that injury—turned out to be just a shadow on the X-ray plate—and a touch of bursitis. . . .
    I lay in a hospital bed, watched our games on TV, saw Maggie on the bench next to Skipper when he was hauled out of a game for stumbles, fumbles!—Burned me up the way she hung on his arm!—Y'know, I think that Maggie had always felt sort of left out because she and me never got any closer together than two people just get in bed, which is not much closer than two cats on a—fence humping. . . .
    So! She took this time to work on poor dumb Skipper. He was a

2. I.e., out over the audience.

less than average student at Ole Miss, you know that, don't you?!—
Poured in his mind the dirty, false idea that what we were, him
and me, was a frustrated case of that ole pair of sisters that lived
in this room, Jack Straw and Peter Ochello!—He, poor Skipper,
went to bed with Maggie to prove it wasn't true, and when it
didn't work out, he thought it *was* true!—Skipper broke in two like
a rotten stick—nobody ever turned so fast to a lush—or died of it
so quick. . . .

    —Now are you satisfied?

    [BIG DADDY *has listened to this story, dividing the grain from
the chaff. Now he looks at his son.*]

BIG DADDY   Are *you* satisfied?

BRICK   With what?

BIG DADDY   That half-ass story!

BRICK   What's half-ass about it?

BIG DADDY   Something's left out of that story. What did you leave out?

    [*The phone has started ringing in the hall. As if it reminded
him of something,* BRICK *glances suddenly toward the sound
and says:*]

BRICK   Yes!—I left out a long-distance call which I had from Skipper,
in which he made a drunken confession to me and on which I hung
up!—last time we spoke to each other in our lives. . . .

    [*Muted ring stops as someone answers phone in a soft, indis-
tinct voice in hall.*]

BIG DADDY   You hung up?

BRICK   Hung up. Jesus! Well—

BIG DADDY   Anyhow now!—we have tracked down the lie with which
you're disgusted and which you are drinking to kill your disgust
with, Brick. You been passing the buck. This disgust with mendacity
is disgust with yourself.

    You!—dug the grave of your friend and kicked him in it!—before
you'd face truth with him!

BRICK   *His* truth, not *mine!*

BIG DADDY   His truth, okay! But you wouldn't face it with him!

BRICK   Who *can* face truth? Can *you?*

BIG DADDY   Now don't start passin' the rotten buck again, boy!

BRICK   How about these birthday congratulations, these many, many
happy returns of the day, when ev'rybody but you knows there
won't be any!

    [*Whoever has answered the hall phone lets out a high, shrill
laugh; the voice becomes audible saying:* "No, no, you got it
all wrong! Upside down! Are you crazy?"

    [BRICK *suddenly catches his breath as he realized that he has
made a shocking disclosure. He hobbles a few paces, then
freezes, and without looking at his father's shocked face, says:*]

    Let's, let's—go out, now, and—

    [BIG DADDY *moves suddenly forward and grabs hold of the
boy's crutch like it was a weapon for which they were fighting
for possession.*]

BIG DADDY   Oh, no, no! No one's going out! What did you start to say?

BRICK   I don't remember.

BIG DADDY   "Many happy returns when they know there won't be any"?

BRICK   Aw, hell, Big Daddy, forget it. Come on out on the gallery and look at the fireworks they're shooting off for your birthday. . . .

BIG DADDY   First you finish that remark you were makin' before you cut off. "Many happy returns when they know there won't be any"? —Ain't that what you just said?

BRICK   Look, now. I can get around without that crutch if I have to but it would be a lot easier on the furniture an' glassware if I didn' have to go swinging along like Tarzan of th'—

BIG DADDY   FINISH! WHAT YOU WAS SAYIN'!

[*An eerie green glow shows in sky behind him.*]

BRICK [*sucking the ice in his glass, speech becoming thick*]   Leave th' place to Gooper and Mae an' their five little same little monkeys. All I want is—

BIG DADDY   "LEAVE TH' PLACE," did you say?

BRICK [*vaguely*]   All twenty-eight thousand acres of the richest land this side of the valley Nile.

BIG DADDY   Who said I was "leaving the place" to Gooper or anybody? This is my sixty-fifth birthday! I got fifteen years or twenty years left in me! I'll outlive *you!* I'll bury you an' have to pay for your coffin!

BRICK   Sure. Many happy returns. Now let's go watch the fireworks, come on, let's—

BIG DADDY   Lying, have they been lying? About the report from th'— clinic? Did they, did they—find something?—*Cancer.* Maybe?

BRICK   Mendacity is a system that we live in. Liquor is one way out an' death's the other. . . .

[*He takes the crutch from* BIG DADDY's *loose grip and swings out on the gallery leaving the doors open.*

[*A song, "Pick a Bale of Cotton," is heard.*]

MAE [*appearing in door*]   Oh, Big Daddy, the field hands are singin' fo' you!

BIG DADDY [*shouting hoarsely*]   BRICK! BRICK!

MAE   He's outside drinkin', Big Daddy.

BIG DADDY   *BRICK!*

[MAE *retreats, awed by the passion of his voice. Children call* BRICK *in tones mocking* BIG DADDY. *His face crumbles like broken yellow plaster about to fall into dust.*

[*There is a glow in the sky.* BRICK *swings back through the doors, slowly, gravely, quite soberly.*]

BRICK   I'm sorry, Big Daddy. My head don't work any more and it's hard for me to understand how anybody could care if he lived or died or was dying or cared about anything but whether or not there was liquor left in the bottle and so I said what I said without thinking. In some ways I'm no better than the others, in some ways worse because I'm less alive. Maybe it's being alive that makes them lie, and being almost *not* alive makes me sort of accidentally truthful—I don't know but—anyway—we've been friends . . .

—And being friends is telling each other the truth. . . .

[*There is a pause.*]

You told *me!* I told *you!*

[A CHILD *rushes into the room and grabs a fistful of firecrackers and runs out again.*]

CHILD [*screaming*]   Bang, bang, bang, bang, bang, bang, bang, bang, bang!

BIG DADDY [*slowly and passionately*]   CHRIST—DAMN—ALL— LYING SONS OF—LYING BITCHES!

[*He straightens at last and crosses to the inside door. At the door he turns and looks back as if he had some desperate question he couldn't put into words. Then he nods reflectively and says in a hoarse voice:*]

Yes, all liars, all liars, all lying dying liars!

[*This said slowly, slowly, with a fierce revulsion. He goes on out.*]

—Lying! Dying! Liars!

[*His voice dies out. There is the sound of a child being slapped. It rushes, hideously bawling, through room and out the hall door.*

[BRICK *remains motionless as the lights dim out and the curtain falls.*]

CURTAIN

1955

PASSAGES FROM ESSAYS AND *MEMOIRS*

From On a Streetcar Named Success[1]

[*An Artist's Work*]

It is only in his work that an artist can find reality and satisfaction, for the actual world is less intense than the world of his invention, and consequently his life, without recourse to violent disorder, does not seem very substantial. The right condition for him is that in which his work is not only convenient but unavoidable.

From The Timeless World of a Play[2]

Carson McCullers[3] concludes one of her lyric poems with the line: "Time, the endless idiot, runs screaming 'round the world." It is this continual rush of time, so violent that it appears to be screaming, that deprives our actual lives of so much dignity and meaning, and it is, perhaps more than anything else, the *arrest of time* which has taken place in a completed work of art that gives to certain plays their feeling of depth and significance. In the London notices of *Death of a Salesman* a certain notoriously skeptical critic made the remark that

1. First published in the *New York Times* (Nov. 30, 1947), a few days before the opening of *Streetcar*; later collected in *Where I Live* (1978).

2. First published in the *New York Times* (Jan. 14, 1951), and later collected in *Where I Live* (1978).

3. American writer (1917–1967), a close friend of Williams's for a time.

Willy Loman was the sort of man that almost any member of the audience would have kicked out of an office had he applied for a job or detained one for conversation about his troubles. The remark itself possibly holds some truth. But the implication that Willy Loman is consequently a character with whom we have no reason to concern ourselves in drama, reveals a strikingly false conception of what plays are. Contemplation is something that exists outside of time, and so is the tragic sense. Even in the actual world of commerce, there exists in some persons a sensibility to the unfortunate situations of others, a capacity for concern and compassion, surviving from a more tender period of life outside the present whirling wire-cage of business activity. Facing Willy Loman across an office desk, meeting his nervous glance and hearing his querulous voice, we would be very likely to glance at our wrist watch and our schedule of other appointments. We would not kick him out of the office, no, but we would certainly *ease* him out with more expedition than Willy had feebly hoped for. But suppose there had been no wrist watch or office clock and suppose there had *not* been the schedule of pressing appointments, and suppose that we were not actually facing Willy across a desk—and facing a person is *not* the best way to *see* him!—suppose, in other words, that the meeting with Willy Loman had somehow occurred in a world *outside* of time. Then I think we would receive him with concern and kindness and even with respect. If the world of a play did not offer us this occasion to view its characters under that special condition of a *world without time*, then, indeed, the characters and occurrences of drama would become equally pointless, equally trivial, as corresponding meetings and happenings in life.

The classic tragedies of Greece had tremendous nobility. The actors wore great masks, movements were formal, dance-like, and the speeches had an epic quality which doubtless was as removed from the normal conversation of their contemporary society as they seem today. Yet they did not seem false to the Greek audiences: the magnitude of the events and the passions aroused by them did not seem ridiculously out of proportion to common experience. And I wonder if this was not because the Greek audiences knew, instinctively or by training, that the created world of a play is removed from that element which makes people *little* and their emotions fairly inconsequential.

Great sculpture often follows the lines of the human body: yet the repose of great sculpture suddenly transmutes those human lines to something that has an absoluteness, a purity, a beauty, which would not be possible in a living mobile form.

A play may be violent, full of motion: yet it has that special kind of repose which allows contemplation and produces the climate in which tragic importance is a possible thing, provided that certain modern conditions are met.

In actual existence the moments of love are succeeded by the moments of satiety and sleep. The sincere remark is followed by a cynical distrust. Truth is fragmentary, at best: we love and betray each other in not quite the same breath but in two breaths that occur in fairly close sequence. But the fact that passion occurred in *passing,* that it then declined into a more familiar sense of indifference, should not be regarded as proof of its inconsequence. And this is the very truth that drama wished to bring us. . . .

Whether or not we admit it to ourselves, we are all haunted by a truly awful sense of impermanence. . . .

About their lives, people ought to remember that when they are finished, everything in them will be contained in a marvelous state of repose which is the same as that which they unconsciously admired in drama. The rush is temporary. The great and only possible dignity of man lies in his power deliberately to choose certain moral values by which to live as steadfastly as if he, too, like a character in a play, were immured against the corrupting rush of time. Snatching the eternal out of the desperately fleeting is the great magic trick of human existence. . . .

From Person—to—Person[4]

Of course it is a pity that so much of all creative work is so closely related to the personality of the one who does it.

It is sad and embarrassing and unattractive that those emotions that stir him deeply enough to demand expression, and to charge their expression with some measure of light and power, are nearly all rooted, however changed in their surface, in the particular and sometimes peculiar concerns of the artist himself, that special world, the passions and images of it that each of us weaves about him from birth to death, a web of monstrous complexity, spun forth at a speed that is incalculable to a length beyond measure, from the spider mouth of his own singular perceptions.

It is a lonely idea, a lonely condition, so terrifying to think of that we usually don't. And so we talk to each other, write and wire each other, call each other, call each other short and long distance across land and sea, clasp hands with each other at meeting and at parting, fight each other and even destroy each other because of this always somewhat thwarted effort to break through walls to each other. As a character in a play once said, "We're all of us sentenced to solitary confinement inside our own skins."

Personal lyricism is the outcry of prisoner to prisoner from the cell in solitary where each is confined for the duration of his life.

I once saw a group of little girls on a Mississippi sidewalk, all dolled up in their mothers' and sisters' cast-off finery, old raggedy ball gowns and plumed hats and high-heeled slippers, enacting a meeting of ladies in a parlor with a perfect mimicry of polite Southern gush and simper. But one child was not satisfied with the attention paid her enraptured performance by the others, they were too involved in their own performances to suit her, so she stretched out her skinny arms and threw back her skinny neck and shrieked to the deaf heavens and her equally oblivious playmates, "Look at me, look at me, look at me!"

4. First published in the *New York Times* Sunday drama section in 1955; later published as the introduction to *Cat on a Hot Tin Roof* (1955) and collected in *Where I Live* (1978).

And then her mother's high-heeled slippers threw her off balance and she fell to the sidewalk in a great howling tangle of soiled white satin and torn pink net, and still nobody looked at her.

I wonder if she is not, now, a Southern writer.

Of course it is not only Southern writers, of lyrical bent, who engage in such histrionics and shout, "Look at me!" Perhaps it is a parable of all artists. And not always do we topple over and land in a tangle of trappings that don't fit us. However, it is well to be aware of that peril, and not to content yourself with a demand for attention, to know that out of your personal lyricism, your sidewalk histrionics, something has to be created that will not only attract observers but participants in the performance.

I try very hard to do that.

The fact that I want you to observe what I do for your possible pleasure and to give you knowledge of things that I feel I may know better than you, because my world is different from yours, as different as every man's world is from the world of others, is not enough excuse for a personal lyricism that has not yet mastered its necessary trick of rising above the singular to the plural concern, from personal to general import. But for years and years now, which may have passed like a dream because of this obsession, I have been trying to learn how to perform this trick and make it truthful, and sometimes I feel that I am able to do it. Sometimes, when the enraptured street-corner performer in me cries out "Look at me!" I feel that my hazardous footwear and fantastic regalia may not quite throw me off balance. Then, suddenly, you fellow performers in the sidewalk show may turn to give me your attention and allow me to hold it, at least for the interval between 8:40 and 11 something P.M.

From Memoirs[1]

[The Glass Menagerie, *His Mother, and Laurette Taylor*]

On the Broadway opening night of *Menagerie*, the performers took bow after bow, and finally they tried to get me up on the stage. I was sitting in the fourth row, and somebody extended a hand to me and I went up on the stage. And I felt embarrassed; I don't think I felt any great sense of triumph. I think writing is continually a pursuit of a very evasive quarry, and you never quite catch it.

In the essay that accompanies one of the printed editions of *Cat on a Hot Tin Roof*, I talk very honestly about my goal in writing, what I want to do.[2] That goal is just somehow to capture the constantly evanescent quality of existence. When I do that, then I have accomplished something, but I have done it, I think, relatively few times compared to the times I have attempted it. I don't have any sense of being a fulfilled artist. And when I was writing *Menagerie*, I did not know that I was capturing it, and I agree with Brooks Atkinson[3] that

1. Williams published *Memoirs* in 1975, when both his critical reputation and his self-esteem were at a low ebb. As strict autobiography it is not reliable, but it contains extraordinary insights into his life and work.

2. See "Person–to–Person," above.

3. Then drama critic for the *New York Times*.

the narrations are not up to the play. I didn't feel they were at the time, either. Thank God, in the 1973 television version of it, they cut the narrations down. There was too much of them. And the play itself holds without much narration.

Maybe I am a machine, a typist. A compulsive typist and a compulsive writer. But that's my life, and what is in these memoirs is mostly the barest periphery of that which is my intense life, for my intense life is my work.

Mother came up to Chicago for the opening there of *Menagerie* in the late December of 1944. I don't recall her precise reaction to the play but it was probably favorable, for Mother was very concerned with my long-delayed success. I do recall her coming backstage after the performance which she attended and paying her respects to Laurette.[4]

"Well, Mrs. Williams," said Laurette, briefly scrutinizing Edwina Williams in her dressing-room mirror, "how did you like yourself?"

"Myself?" said Mother innocently.

Laurette was as kind a person as I have known in a theatre mostly inhabited by jungle beasts, but even she, being Irish, was not one to pass by an opportunity to be mischievous.

"You notice these bangs I wear? I have to wear them playing this part because it's the part of a fool and I have a high, intellectual forehead."

Miss Edwina did not pick up on this either. She let it go by her without a sign of offense. She was probably bedazzled by Laurette's somewhat supernatural quality on a stage.

[*Craft and* Cat on a Hot Tin Roof]

Well, now, about plays, what about them? Plays are written and then, if they are lucky, they are performed, and if their luck still holds, which is not too frequently the case, their performance is so successful that both audience and critics at the first night are aware that they are being offered a dramatic work which is both honest and entertaining and also somehow capable of engaging their aesthetic appreciation.

I have never liked to talk about the professional side of my life. Am I afraid that it is a bird that will be startled away by discussion, as by a hawk's shadow? Something like that, I suppose.

People are always asking me, at those symposia to which I've been subjected in recent years, which is my favorite among the plays I have written, the number of which eludes my recollection, and I either say to them, "Always the latest" or I succumb to my instinct for the truth and say, "I suppose it must be the published version of *Cat on a Hot Tin Roof*."[5]

That play comes closest to being both a work of art and a work of craft. It is really very well put together, in my opinion, and all its

4. The role of Amanda was created by Laurette Taylor (1884–1946). Her first great success had been in 1912 (*Peg o'My Heart*), and she had been in virtual retirement for a number of years until her performance in this play.

5. The published version includes Williams's original version of Act III, which he preferred to the Broadway version.

characters are amusing and credible and touching. Also it adheres to the valuable edict of Aristotle that a tragedy must have unity of time and place and magnitude of theme.

The set in *Cat* never changes and its running time is exactly the time of its action, meaning that one act, timewise, follows directly upon the other, and I know of no other modern American play in which this is accomplished.

However my reasons for liking *Cat* best are deeper than that. I believe that in *Cat* I reached beyond myself, in the second act, to a kind of crude eloquence of expression in Big Daddy that I have managed to give no other character of my creation.

[*Dramatic Form and "Little People"*]

I realize how very old-fashioned I am as a dramatist to be so concerned with classic form but this does not embarrass me, since I feel that the absence of form is nearly always, if not always, as dissatisfying to an audience as it is to me. I persist in considering *Cat* my best work of the long plays because of its classic unities of time and place and the kingly magnitude of Big Daddy. Yet I seem to contradict myself. I write so often of people with no magnitude, at least on the surface. I write of "little people." But are there "little people"? I sometimes think there are only little conceptions of people. Whatever is living and feeling with intensity is not little and, examined in depth, it would seem to me that most "little people" are living with that intensity that I can use as a writer.

Was Blanche a "little person"? Certainly not. She was a demonic creature, the size of her feeling was too great for her to contain without the escape of madness. . . .

["*Sensations of Being*"]

The work of a fine painter, committed only to vision, abstract and allusive as he pleases, is better able to create for you his moments of intensely perceptive being. Jackson Pollock could paint ecstasy as it could not be written. Van Gogh could capture for you moments of beauty, indescribable as descent into madness.[6]

And those who painted and sculpted the sensuous and the sensual of naked life in its moments of glory made them palpable to you as we can never feel with our fingertips and the erogenous parts of our flesh.

A poet such as the young Rimbaud[7] is the only writer of whom I can think, at this moment, who could escape from words into the sensations of being, through his youth, turbulent with revolution, permitted articulation by nights of absinthe. And of course there is Hart Crane.[8] Both of these poets touched fire that burned them alive. And perhaps it is only through self-immolation of such a nature that we living beings can offer to you the entire truth of ourselves within the reasonable boundaries of a book.

6. Jackson Pollock (1912–1956) American abstract expressionist painter; Vincent Van Gogh (1853–90), Dutch post-impressionist painter.
7. Arthur Rimbaud (1854–91), French poet who deeply influenced the Symbolists.
8. American poet (1899–1932), much admired by Williams. All four of the artists Williams cites combined tempestuous lives with their art.

6   TRAGEDY, COMEDY, AND THE MODERN DRAMA

Genre is the notion that groups of literary works have resemblances that make comparison between them meaningful. We know what a novel is because of the novels we have read. Our earliest surviving notion of tragedy comes from Aristotle's *Poetics*, but even there Aristotle was not defining what tragedy should be but what the tragedies he knew were like. Departures from genre standards may be as important as adherences to them in understanding a particular work. We do not solve the problems of *Hamlet* by saying that it is a tragedy, but saying that it has certain resemblances to *Oedipus Tyrannus* or Racine's *Phèdre* helps us to understand certain aspects better. The play itself is unique, however, and ultimately must be understood on its own terms.

With these points in mind, we will examine three features of several dramatic genres: the order of values implicit in the play, the nature of character in the play, and the nature of the conclusion. The three genres we will examine are **tragedy, comedy,** and the serious modern play, a form for which no really satisfactory critical term has yet been found.

In a tragedy like *Oedipus Turannus*, values are universal and beyond the control of mankind. Right and wrong are determined not by any agreement between men, but by the will of the gods, or some other preterhuman force. When the oracle tells Oedipus that his fate is to kill has father and marry his mother, he is revolted by the prospect. In human terms such a fate is unthinkable, and Oedipus refuses to accept the will of gods. In human terms, Oedipus is certainly right in trying to avoid such a fate—but in terms of the value system that rules the play, his attempt to circumvent the will of the gods is what destroys him.

On the other hand, in a comedy like *The Importance of Being Earnest*, values are social and determined by the general opinion of society. In moral terms there is no reason why Jack and Gwendolen should not marry and get about the business of establishing a family. They are healthy unmarried people of opposite sexes; the only problems about their intention to marry are social ones. Gwendolen's children cannot achieve their "proper" place in society unless her husband is a suitable choice, a man of good family, some social position, and suitable means to provide an appropriate education for them. Implicit in this consideration is the fact that comedy tends to endorse the values of the society. Lady Bracknell may be amusing, but she is also right, because she understands how her society works, what is acceptable and what is not.

Between the two sets of values found in tragedy and comedy are those found in *Krapp's Last Tape*, *Death of a Salesman*, or *A Streetcar Named Desire*. Characters in such plays often feel rootless, aimless, restless, uncertain of their own values or of any accepted standard. Universals often seem missing or inapplicable, and it is often uncertain or unclear whether society holds a clear set of standards that provide guidance for the individual. Often the individual feels lost, with no clear goals or program of conduct. *Krapp's Last Tape* is, for example, a lengthy record of stasis and frustration. In its movement across years and even decades (through the replaying of old tapes) we hear the record of struggle with the same issues and problems— drinking, bowel movement, eating bananas, unsatisfactory human relationships, unsuccessful communication through abortive talk or unsold books—and we see physical evidence only of age and lessened powers, not a clarified set of values, or sharpened determination, or even self-knowledge. Krapp, like many another "hero" in modern plays, bears the full responsibility for his life, such as it is. He seems to have made the choices that have brought him to this place in his life; neither the gods nor society are in control of his life, and Krapp lives primarily with himself, his passion, his guilt, and his memories.

A second characteristic feature of a dramatic genre is its treatment of character. Tragedy, for example, centers around a single individual, a person of high rank who confronts the universe and his fate as an individual, a hero. He is ultimately doomed to defeat because, although a good and noble person, the tragic figure has a flaw of character, a mark of humanity, that offsets all his goodness. Oedipus wishes to know and to control his own destiny, but he learns too much and is destroyed. Had Oedipus been the son of a shepherd rather than of a king, perhaps the gods would not have taken such an unfortunate interest in his fate.

Comic figures are quite different. Since the plays are concerned with society and social roles, comic characters are often defined in those terms. In *The Importance of Being Earnest* both Jack and Algernon are, for plot purposes, unmarried young men who are not eminently eligible husbands-to-be, Jack because of his uncertain parentage and Algernon because of his lack of money. They have individual traits— Algernon eats too much and enjoys pretense, Jack is more straightforward, or wishes to be—but their individuality is not so important as their definition by the common social standard. Many comic characters go even further and become **stereotypes**, characters with little or no individuality, representatives of social types. Lady Bracknell, for example, is a middle-aged meddling matron, ideally placed by age and position to exert tremendous social influence. However ridiculous Lady Bracknell appears, she understands her society and its rules thoroughly. Other stereotypes in the same play are Miss Prism, the desperate spinster, and Dr. Chasuble, the slightly dim clergyman.

Between the poles of character in comedy and tragedy lies the style of characterization in a serious modern play like *Krapp's Last Tape*. About Krapp we actually know little, in spite of the play's exclusive attention to one character and in spite of Krapp's own preoccupation with himself. He is not a "hero" in the traditional sense, and he faces no grand task or dilemma on which the destiny of humanity or a nation depends. He is eccentric, self-absorbed, comic, intelligent, articulate, often bemused, sometimes pathetic. His life is a strange combination of disorder—as indicated by his clothes and miscellaneous bananas—and rigid order, as suggested by the journal and carefully labeled spools. He has measured out his life in reels of tape and has remained, over the years, astonishingly predictable and repetitious. Although neither purely good nor purely evil, Krapp is not a villain and not heroic. He is a complicated human being in a complex, even though solitary, situation. In many ways, he is a "typical" modern man—feeling lonely, even though living in a highly populous world, and unfulfilled in spite of relentless attempts to study and analyze himself. Like Willy Loman in *Death of a Salesman*, Krapp is ordinary in the sense that his unworldly position is neither impressive nor influential; the interest is not in what he does or who he is in some abstract sense, but in how he handles his average life, a mixture of pleasure and sadness, action and passivity, good and evil.

A third feature of the dramatic genres can be found in their endings. In most tragedies, the hero is enlightened; he comes to understand what he has done and to accept his punishment. At the end of *Oedipus Tyrannus* the blind hero sees and understands. He accepts his ostracism and leaves Thebes, a chastened but wiser man. Many tragic heroes die, as Hamlet does, but it is not death that ends the tragedy, it is understanding. Hamlet understands what has happened and in his last moments tries to restore order to the kingdom, asking for himself only that people may know the truth about what he has done. In comedy, on the other hand, the resolution occurs when one or more characters take a proper social role. This is most frequently defined in terms of the marriage of an eligible young woman and an equally eligible young man. The society of *Earnest* believes that young men like Jack and Algernon and young women like Gwendolen and Cecily should marry and get about the business of having children and raising them to provide for the continuation of the society. Even the marriage of Miss Prism and Dr. Chasuble serves social purposes. The society of the play prefers married clergymen to celibates and has no really useful function for a middle-aged spinster. In a serious modern play like *Krapp's Last Tape* the ending is less simple. Despite Krapp's relentless pursuit of pattern and meaning through his journals and tapes, he does not achieve serenity or enlightenment. The protagonists of serious modern plays may mate or marry, suffer or die, but they seldom perform great deeds, accomplish grand tasks, or achieve understanding of their world or themselves. Like Krapp or Willy Loman, they may come to the logical ending of their lives but there is no triumph, no transcendance, no real peace.

SOPHOCLES

Oedipus Tyrannus*

CHARACTERS

OEDIPUS, *Ruler of Thebes*[1]
JOCASTA, *Wife of* OEDIPUS
CREON, *Brother of* JOCASTA
TEIRESIAS, *A Blind Prophet*
A PRIEST
MESSENGER 1
MESSENGER 2

A SHEPHERD
AN ATTENDANT
ANTIGONE } *Daughters of* OEDIPUS *and* JOCASTA
ISMENE
CHORUS OF THEBAN ELDERS

OEDIPUS   What is it, children, sons of the ancient house of Cadmus? Why do you sit as suppliants crowned with laurel branches? What is the meaning of the incense which fills the city? The pleas to end pain? The cries of sorrow? I chose not to hear it from my messengers, but came myself—I came, Oedipus, Oedipus, whose name is known to all. You, old one—age gives you the right to speak for all of them —you tell me why they sit before my altar. Has something frightened you? What brings you here? Some need? Some want? I'll help you all I can. I would be cruel did I not greet you with compassion when you are gathered here before me.

PRIEST   My Lord and King, we represent the young and old; some are priests and some the best of Theban youth. And I—I am a priest of Zeus. There are many more who carry laurel boughs like these— in the market-places, at the twin altars of Pallas, by the sacred ashes of Ismenus' oracle.[2] You see yourself how torn our city is, how she craves relief from the waves of death which now crash over her. Death is everywhere—in the harvests of the land, in the flocks that roam the pastures, in the unborn children of our mothers' wombs. A fiery plague is ravaging the city, festering, spreading its pestilence, wasting the house of Cadmus, filling the house of Hades with screams of pain and of fear. This is the reason why we come to you, these children and I. No, we do not think you a god. But we deem you a mortal set apart to face life's common issues and the trials which the gods dispense to men. It was you who once before came to Thebes and freed us from the spell that hypnotized our lives. You did this, and yet you knew no more than we—less even. You had no help from us. God aided you. Yes, you restored our life. And now a second time, great Oedipus, we turn to you for help. Find some relief for us, whether with god or man to guide your way. You helped us then. Yes. And we believe that you will help us now. O Lord, revive our city; restore her life. Think of your fame, your own repute. The

* Translated by Luci Berkowitz and Theodore F. Brunner.
1. See the note on Thebes and the House of Cadmus, p. 1320.
2. Zeus was the king of the Greek gods. His daughter Pallas, or Athena, was spe-

cifically a goddess of wisdom, but she had played an important part in the founding of Thebes. Apollo (or Phoebus), the sun god, had a shrine near Thebes, close to the river Ismenus.

people know you saved us from our past despair. Let no one say you raised us up to let us fall. Save us and keep us safe. You found good omens once to aid you and brought us fortune then. Find them again. If you will rule this land as king and lord, rule over men and not a wall encircling emptiness. No city wall, no ship can justify its claim to strength if it is stripped of men who give it life.

OEDIPUS   O my children, I know well the pain you suffer and understand what brings you here. You suffer—and yet not one among you suffers more than I. Each of you grieves for himself alone, while my heart must bear the strain of sorrow for all—myself and you and all our city's people. No, I am not blind to it. I have wept and in my weeping set my thoughts on countless paths, searching for an answer. I have sent my own wife's brother Creon, son of Menoeceus, to Apollo's Pythian shrine[3] to learn what I might say or do to ease our city's suffering. I am concerned that he is not yet here—he left many days ago. But this I promise: whenever he returns, whatever news he brings, whatever course the god reveals—*that* is the course that I shall take.

PRIEST   Well spoken. Look! They are giving signs that Creon is returning.

OEDIPUS   O God! If only he brings news as welcome as his smiling face.

PRIEST   I think he does. His head is crowned with laurel leaves.

OEDIPUS   We shall know soon enough. There. My Lord Creon, what word do you bring from the god?

Enter CREON.

CREON   Good news. I tell you this: if all goes well, our troubles will be past.

OEDIPUS   But what was the oracle? Right now I'm swaying between hope and fear.

CREON   If you want to hear it in the presence of these people, I shall tell you. If not, let's go inside.

OEDIPUS   Say it before all of us. I sorrow more for them than for myself.

CREON   Then I shall tell you exactly what the god Apollo answered. These are his words: Pollution. A hidden sore is festering in our land. We are to stop its growth before it is too late.

OEDIPUS   Pollution? How are we to save ourselves?

CREON   Blood for blood. To save ourselves we are to banish a man or pay for blood with blood. It is a murder which has led to this despair.

OEDIPUS   Murder? Whose? Did the god say whose . . . ?

CREON   My Lord, before you came to rule our city, we had a king. His name was Laius . . .

OEDIPUS   I know, although I never saw him.

CREON   He was murdered. And the god's command is clear: we must find the assassin and destroy him.

OEDIPUS   But where? Where is he to be found? How can we find the traces of a crime committed long ago?

---

3. The oracle at Delphi was the principal shrine of Apollo and was called "Pythian" because it celebrated his victory over the monster Python.

CREON   He lives among us. If we seek, we will find; what we do not seek cannot be found.

OEDIPUS   Where was it that Laius met his death? At home? The country? In some foreign land?

CREON   One day he left and told us he would go to Delphi. That was the last we saw of him.

OEDIPUS   And there was no one who could tell what happened? No one who traveled with him? Did no one see? Is there no evidence?

CREON   All perished. All—except one who ran in panic from the scene and could not tell us anything for certain, except . . .

OEDIPUS   Except? What? What was it? One clue might lead to many. We have to grasp the smallest shred of hope.

CREON   He said that robbers—many of them—fell upon Laius and his men and murdered them.

OEDIPUS   Robbers? Who committed *murder*? Why? Unless they were paid assassins?

CREON   We considered that. But the king was dead and we were plagued with trouble. No one came forth as an avenger.

OEDIPUS   Trouble? What could have kept you from investigating the death of your king?

CREON   The Sphinx.[4] The Sphinx was confounding us with her riddles, forcing us to abandon our search for the unknown and to tend to what was then before us.

OEDIPUS   Then I—I shall begin again. I shall not cease until I bring the truth to light. Apollo has shown, and you have shown, the duty which we owe the dead. You have my gratitude. You will find me a firm ally, and together we shall exact vengeance for our land and for the god. I shall not rest till I dispel this defilement—not just for another man's sake, but for my own as well. For whoever the assassin—he might turn his hand against me too. Yes, I shall be serving Laius and myself. Now go, my children. Leave the steps of my altar. Go. Take away your laurel branches. Go to the people of Cadmus. Summon them. Tell them that I, their king, will leave nothing untried. And with the help of God, we shall find success—or ruin.

Exit OEDIPUS.

PRIEST   Come, children. We have learned what we came to learn. Come, Apollo, come yourself, who sent these oracles! Come as our savior! Come! Deliver us from this plague!

CHORUS

O prophecy of Zeus, sweet is the sound of your words
as they come to our glorious city of Thebes
from Apollo's glittering shrine.
Yet I quake and I dread and I tremble at those words.
Io, Delian Lord![5]

4. The Sphinx was a winged monster with the head of a woman and the body of a lion who had terrorized Thebes, demanding the answer to her riddle, "What walks on four feet in the morning, two at noon, and three in the evening?" When the young Oedipus appeared at Thebes, he saved the city by answering her riddle, "Man," thus bringing about her death.

5. "Io" was a cry of generalized meaning used by worshippers in praise or supplication. Apollo was called "Delian Lord" because he had been born on the island of Delos.

What will you bring to pass? Disaster unknown,
or familiar to us, as the ever recurring seasons?
Tell me, O oracle,
heavenly daughter of blessèd hope.

Foremost I call on you, daughter of Zeus,
Athena, goddess supreme;
and on Artemis[6] shielding the world,
shielding this land from her circular shrine
graced with renown.
And on you I call, Phoebus, Lord of the unerring bow.

Come to my aid, you averters of doom!
Come to my aid if ever you came!
Come to my aid as once you did, when you quenched
the fires of doom that fell on our soil!
Hear me, and come to my aid!

Boundless the pain, boundless the grief I bear;
sickness pervades this land,
affliction without reprieve.
Barren the soil, barren of fruit;
children are born no longer to light;
all of us flutter in agony
winging our way into darkness and death.

Countless the number of dead in the land;
corpses of children cover the plain,
children dying before they have lived,
no one to pity them,
reeking, and spreading diseases and death.

Moaning and wailing our wives,
moaning and wailing our mothers
stream to the altars this way and that,
scream to the air with helpless cries.
Hear us, golden daughter of Zeus,
hear us! Send us release!

Ares[7] now rages in our midst
brandishing in his hands
the firebrands of disease,
raving, consuming, rousing the screams of death.
Hear us, O goddess!
Help us, and still his rage!
Turn back his assault!
Help us! Banish him from our land!

6. Artemis (called Diana by the Romans) was the twin sister of Apollo. She was primarily a moon goddess.
7. Ares (Roman Mars) was the war god.

Drive him into the angry sea,
to the wave-swept border of Thrace![8]

We who escape him tonight
will be struck down at dawn.
Help us, O father Zeus,
Lord of the thunderbolt,
crush him! Destroy him!
Burn him with fires of lightning!

Help us, Apollo, Lycean Lord!
Stand at our side with your golden bow!
Artemis, help us!
Come from the Lycian[9] hills!
Come with your torches aflame!
Dionysus,[1] protector, come to our aid,
come with your revelers' band!
Burn with your torch the god
hated among the gods!

    Enter OEDIPUS.   Scene 1

OEDIPUS I have heard your prayers and answer with relief and help, if you will heed my words and tend the sickness with the cure it cries for. My words are uttered as a stranger to the act, a stranger to its tale. I cannot trace its path alone, without a sign. As a citizen newer to Thebes than you, I make this proclamation: If one among you knows who murdered Laius, the son of Labdacus, let him tell us now. If he fears for his life, let him confess and know a milder penalty. He will be banished from this land. Nothing more. Or if you know the assassin to be an alien, do not protect him with your silence. You will be rewarded. But if in fear you protect yourself or any other man and keep your silence, then hear what I say now: Whoever he is, this assassin must be denied entrance to your homes. Any man where I rule is forbidden to receive him or speak to him or share with him his prayers and sacrifice or offer him the holy rites of purification. I command you to drive this hideous curse out of your homes; I command you to obey the will of Pythian Apollo. I will serve the god and the dead. On the assassin or assassins, I call down the most vile damnation—for this vicious act, may the brand of shame be theirs to wear forever. And if I knowingly harbor their guilt within my own walls, I shall not exempt myself from the curse that I have called upon them. It is for me, for God, and for this city that staggers toward ruin that you must fulfill these injunctions. Even if Heaven gave you no sign, you had the sacred duty to insure that this act did not go unexamined, unavenged! It was the assassination of a noble man—your king! Now that I hold the powers that he once held, his bed, his wife—had fate been unopposed, his children would have bound us closer yet—and now on him has this disaster fallen. I will avenge him as I would avenge my own father. I will leave nothing untried to expose the murderer of Laius, the son of Labdacus, heir to the house of Cadmus and Agenor. On those who deny me obedience, I utter this curse: May the gods visit them with barrenness in their harvests, barrenness in their women, barrenness in their fate. Worse still—may they be haunted and tormented and never know the peace that comes with death. But for you, my people, in sympathy with me—I pray that Justice and all the gods attend you forever.

CHORUS   You have made me swear an oath, my Lord, and under oath I speak. I did not kill the king and cannot name the man who did. The question was Apollo's. He could name the man you seek.

OEDIPUS   I know. And yet no mortal can compel a god to speak.

CHORUS   The next-best thing, it seems to me . . .

OEDIPUS   Tell me. Tell me all your thoughts. We must consider everything.

CHORUS   There is one man, second only to Apollo, who can see the truth, who can clearly help us in our search—Teiresias.

OEDIPUS   I thought of this. On Creon's advice, I sent for him. Twice. He should be here.

CHORUS   There were some rumors once, but no one hears them now.

OEDIPUS   What rumors? I want to look at every tale that is told.

CHORUS   They said that travelers murdered Laius.

OEDIPUS   I have heard that too. And yet there's no one to be found who saw the murderer in the act.

CHORUS   He will come forth himself, once he has heard your curse, if he knows what it means to be afraid.

OEDIPUS   Why? Why should a man now fear words if then he did not fear to kill?

CHORUS   But there is one man who can point him out—the man in whom the truth resides, the god-inspired prophet. And there—they are bringing him now.

Enter TEIRESIAS, *guided by a servant.*

OEDIPUS   Teiresias, all things are known to you—the secrets of heaven and earth, the sacred and profane. Though you are blind, you surely see the plague that rakes our city. My Lord Teiresias, we turn to you as our only hope. My messengers may have told you—we have sent to Apollo and he has answered us. We must find Laius' murderers and deal with them. Or drive them out. Then—only then will we find release from our suffering. I ask you not to spare your gifts of prophecy. Look to the voices of prophetic birds or the answers written in the flames. Spare nothing. Save all of us—yourself, your city, your king, and all that is touched by this deathly pollution. We turn to you. My Lord, it is man's most noble role to help his fellow man the best his talents will allow.

TEIRESIAS   O God! How horrible wisdom is! How horrible when it does not help the wise! How could I have forgotten? I should not have come.

OEDIPUS   Why? What's wrong?

TEIRESIAS   Let me go. It will be better if you bear your own distress and I bear mine. It will be better this way.

OEDIPUS   This city gave you life and yet you refuse her an answer! You speak as if you were her enemy.

TEIRESIAS   No! No! It is because I see the danger in your words. And mine would add still more.

OEDIPUS   For God's sake, if you know, don't turn away from us! We are pleading. We are begging you.

TEIRESIAS   Because you are blind! No! I shall not reveal my secrets. I shall not reveal yours.

OEDIPUS   What? You know, and yet you refuse to speak? Would you betray us and watch our city fall helplessly to her death?

TEIRESIAS   I will not cause you further grief. I will not grieve myself. Stop asking me to tell; I will tell you nothing.

OEDIPUS   You will not tell? You monster! You could stir the stones of earth to a burning rage! You will never tell? What will it take?

TEIRESIAS   Know yourself, Oedipus. You denounce me, but you do not yet know yourself.

OEDIPUS   Yes! You disgrace your city. And then you expect us to control our rage!

TEIRESIAS   It does not matter if I speak; the future has already been determined.

OEDIPUS   And if it has, then it is for you to tell me, *prophet!*

TEIRESIAS   I shall say no more. Rage, if you wish.

OEDIPUS   I *am* enraged. And now I will tell you what *I* think. I think this was *your* doing. *You* plotted the crime, *you* saw it carried out. It was *your* doing. All but the actual killing. And had you not been blind, you would have done *that*, too!

TEIRESIAS   Do you believe what you have said? Then accept your own decree! From this day on, deny yourself the right to speak to anyone. You, Oedipus, are the desecrator, the polluter of this land!

OEDIPUS   You traitor! Do you think that you can get away with this?

TEIRESIAS   The truth is my protection.

OEDIPUS   Who taught you this? It did not come from prophecy!

TEIRESIAS   *You* taught me. *You* drove me, *you* forced me to say it against my will.

OEDIPUS   Say it again. I want to make sure that I understand you.

TEIRESIAS   Understand me? Or are you trying to provoke me?

OEDIPUS   No, I want to be sure, I want to know. Say it again.

TEIRESIAS   I say that you, Oedipus Tyrannus, are the murderer you seek.

OEDIPUS   So! A second time! Now twice you will regret what you have said!

TEIRESIAS   Shall I tell you more? Shall I fan your flames of anger?

OEDIPUS   Yes. Tell me more. Tell me more—whatever suits you. It will be in vain.

TEIRESIAS   I say you live in shame with the woman you love, blind to your own calamity.

OEDIPUS   Do you think you can speak like this forever?

TEIRESIAS   I do, if there is any strength in truth.

OEDIPUS   There is—for everyone but you. You—you cripple! Your ears are deaf, your eyes are blind, your mind—your *mind* is crippled!

TEIRESIAS   You fool! You slander me when one day you will hear the same . . .

OEDIPUS   You live in night, Teiresias, in night that never turns to day. And so, you cannot hurt me—or any man who sees the light.

TEIRESIAS   No—it is not I who will cause your fall. That is Apollo's office—and he will discharge it.

OEDIPUS   Was this *your* trick—or Creon's?

TEIRESIAS   No, not Creon's. No, Oedipus. You are destroying yourself!

OEDIPUS   Ah, wealth and sovereignty and skill surpassing skill in life's contentions, why must envy always attend them? This city *gave* me power; I did not ask for it. And Creon, my friend, my trusted friend, would plot to overthrow me—with this charlatan, this impostor, who auctions off his magic wares! His eyes see profit clearly, but they are blind in prophecy. Tell me, Teiresias, what makes you a prophet? Where were you when the monster was here weaving her spells and taunts? What words of relief did Thebes hear from you? Her riddle would stagger the simple mind; it demanded the mind of a seer. Yet, put to the test, all your birds and god-craft proved useless; you had no answer. Then *I* came—ignorant Oedipus—*I* came and smothered her, using only my wit. There were no birds to tell me what to do. I am the man you would overthrow so you can stand near Creon's throne. You will regret—you and your conspirator—you will regret your attempt to purify this land. If you were not an old man, I would make you suffer the pain which you deserve for your audacity.

CHORUS   Both of you, my Lord, have spoken in bitter rage. No more —not when we must direct our every thought to obey the god's command.

TEIRESIAS   Though you are king, the right to speak does not belong to you alone. It is *my* right as well and I shall claim it. I am not your servant and Creon is not my patron. I serve only Loxian Apollo.[2] And I tell you this, since you mock my blindness. You have eyes, Oedipus, and do not see your own destruction. You have eyes and do not see what lives with you. Do you know whose son you are? I say that you have sinned and do not know it; you have sinned against your own—the living and the dead. A double scourge, your mother's and your father's curse, will drive you from this land. Then darkness will shroud those eyes that now can see the light. Cithaeron—the whole earth will resound with your mournful cries when you discover the meaning of the wedding-song that brought you to this place you falsely thought a haven. More sorrow still awaits you—more than you can know—to show you what you are and what our children are. Damn Creon, if you will; damn the words I say. No man on earth will ever know the doom that waits for you.

OEDIPUS   How much of this am I to bear? Leave! Now! Leave my house!

---

2. Apollo was called "Loxian" because the answer given by his oracles at Delphi and elsewhere were frequently ambiguous.

TEIRESIAS   I would not be here had you not sent for me.

OEDIPUS   I never would have sent for you had I known the madness I would hear.

TEIRESIAS   To you, I am mad; but not to your parents . . .

OEDIPUS   Wait! My parents? Who are my parents?

TEIRESIAS   This day shall bring you birth *and* death.

OEDIPUS   Why must you persist with riddles?

TEIRESIAS   Are you not the best of men when it comes to riddles?

OEDIPUS   You mock the very skill that proves me great.

TEIRESIAS   A great misfortune—which will destroy you.

OEDIPUS   I don't care. If I have saved this land, I do not care.

TEIRESIAS   Then I shall go. [*To his servant.*] Come, take me home.

OEDIPUS   Yes, go home. You won't be missed.

TEIRESIAS   I will go when I've said all that I came to say. I am not afraid of you. You cannot hurt me. And I tell you this: The man you seek—the man whose death or banishment you ordered, the man who murdered Laius—that man is here, passing as an alien, living in our midst. Soon it will be known to all of you—he is a native Theban. And he will find no joy in that discovery. His eyes now see, but soon they will be blind: rich now, but soon a beggar. Holding a scepter now, but soon a cane, he will grope for the earth beneath him—in a foreign land. Both brother and father to the children that he loves. Both son and husband to the woman who bore him. Both heir and spoiler of his father's bed and the one who took his life. Go, think on this. And if you find the words I speak are lies, *then* say that I am blind.

Exeunt OEDIPUS, TEIRESIAS.

CHORUS   Ode 1

Who is he? Who is the man?
Who is the man whom the voice of the Delphian shrine
denounced as the killer, the murderer,
the man who committed the terrible crime?
Where is he? Where is he now?
Let him run, let him flee!
Let him rush with the speed of the wind on his flight!
For with fire and lightning the god will attack,
and relentlessy fate will pursue him and haunt him
and drive him to doom.

Do you hear? Do you hear the command of the god?
From Parnassus[3] he orders the hunt.
In vain will the murderer hide,
in vain will he run,
in vain will he lurk in the forests and caves
like an animal roaming the desolate hills.
Let him flee to the edge of the world:
On his heels he will find
the command of the god!

3. Parnassus was a mountain near Delphi, sacred to Apollo and the Muses, minor goddesses associated with the arts.

Confusion and fear
have been spread by the prophet's words.
For I cannot affirm, yet I cannot refute
what he spoke. And I'm lost, I am lost—
What am I to believe?
Now foreboding is gripping my heart.
Was there ever a strife between Laius and Polybus' house?[4]
Can I test? Can I prove?
Can I ever believe that the name of my king
has been soiled by a murder unknown?

It is Zeus and Apollo who know,
who can see the affairs of men.
But the seer and I,
we are mortal, and blind.
Who is right? Who can judge?
We are mortal, our wisdom assigned in degrees.
Does the seer know? Do I?
No, I will not believe in the prophet's charge
till the charge has been proved to my mind.
For I saw how the king
in the test with the Sphinx
proved his wisdom and worth
when he saved this city from doom.
No! I can *never* condemn the king!

    Enter CREON.   Scene 2

CREON My fellow citizens, anger has impelled me to come because
I have heard the accusation which Oedipus has brought against me
—and I will not tolerate it. If he thinks that I—in the midst of this
torment—*I* have thought to harm him in any way, I will not spend
the rest of my life branded by his charge. Doesn't he see the implications of such slander? To you, to my friends, to my city—I would be
a traitor!

CHORUS He spoke in anger—without thinking.

CREON Yes—and who was it who said that the prophet lied on my
advice?

CHORUS It was said, but I don't know how it was meant.

CREON And was this a charge leveled by one whose eyes were clear?
Whose head was clear?

CHORUS I don't know. I do not judge my master's actions. But here he
comes.

    Enter OEDIPUS.   another projection

OEDIPUS Why have you come, Creon? Do you have the audacity to
show your face in my presence? Assassin! And now you would steal
my throne! What drove you to this plot? Did you see cowardice in
me? Stupidity? Did you imagine that I would not see your treachery? Did you expect that I wouldn't act to stop you? You fool! Your

---

4. Polybus, the King of Corinth, and his wife Merope were the reputed parents of
Oedipus.

plot was mad! You go after a throne without money, without friends! How do you think thrones are won?

CREON   You listen to me! And when you have heard me out, when you have heard the truth, *then* judge for yourself.

OEDIPUS   Ah yes, your oratory! I can learn nothing from that. This is what I have learned—you are my enemy!

CREON   Just let me say . . .

OEDIPUS   Say one thing—say that you are not a traitor.

CREON   If you think that senseless stubbornness is a precious gift, you are a fool.

OEDIPUS   If you think that you can threaten the house of Cadmus— your own house—and not pay for it, you are mad.

CREON   I grant you that. But tell me: just what is this terrible thing you say I have done to you?

OEDIPUS   Did you or did you not tell me to send for that—that— prophet?

CREON   I did. And I would again.

OEDIPUS   Then, how long since Laius . . . ?

CREON   What? I do not follow . . .

OEDIPUS   . . . Disappeared?

CREON   A long time ago.

OEDIPUS   Your Teiresias—was he—was he a prophet then?

CREON   Yes—and just as honored and just as wise.

OEDIPUS   Did he ever mention me—then?

CREON   Not in my presence.

OEDIPUS   But didn't you investigate the murder?

CREON   Of course we did—

OEDIPUS   And why didn't the prophet say anything *then*?

CREON   I do not know. It's not for me to try to understand.

OEDIPUS   You know this much which you will try to tell me . . .

CREON   What is it? I will tell you if I can.

OEDIPUS   Just this: Had he not acted under your instructions, he would not have named *me* killer of Laius.

CREON   If this is what he said, you ought to know. You heard him. But now I claim the right to question you, as you have me.

OEDIPUS   Ask what you wish. I am not the murderer.

CREON   Then answer me. Did you marry my sister?

OEDIPUS   Of course I did.

CREON   And do you rule on equal terms with her?

OEDIPUS   She has all that she wants from me.

CREON   And am I not the third and equal partner?

OEDIPUS   You are—and that is where you have proved yourself a traitor.

CREON   Not true. Consider rationally, as I have done. First ask your-self—would any man prefer a life of fear to one in which the self-same rank, the self-same rights are guaranteed untroubled peace? I have no wish to be a king when I can act as one without a throne. And any man would feel the same, if he were wise. I share with you a king's prerogatives, yet you alone must face the danger lurking around the throne. If *I* were king, I would have to act in many ways against my pleasure. What added benefit could kingship hold when

I have rank and rule without the threat of pain? I am not deluded
—no, I would not look for honors beyond the ones which profit me.
I have the favor of every man; each greets me first when he would
hope to have *your* favor. Why should I exchange this for a throne?
Only a fool would. No, I am not a traitor nor would I aid an act of
treason. You want proof? Go to Delphi; ask if I have brought you
the truth. Then, if you find me guilty of conspiracy with the prophet,
command my death. I will face that. But do not condemn me without
proof. You are wrong to judge the guilty innocent, the innocent guilty
—without proof. Casting off a true friend is like casting off your
greatest prize—your life. You will know in time that this is true.
Time alone reveals the just; a single day condemns the guilty.

CHORUS   He is right, my Lord. Respect his words. A man who plans in
haste will gamble the result.

OEDIPUS   This is a plot conceived in rashness. It must be met with
quick response. I cannot sit and wait until the plot succeeds.

CREON   What will you do then? Do you intend to banish me?

OEDIPUS   No. No, not banish you. I want to see you *dead*—to make
you an example for all aspiring to my throne.

CREON   Then you won't do as I suggest? You won't believe me?

OEDIPUS   You have not shown that you deserve belief.

CREON   No, because I see that you are mad.

OEDIPUS   In my own eyes, I am sane.

CREON   You should be sane in mine as well.

OEDIPUS   No. You are a traitor!

CREON   And what if you are wrong?

OEDIPUS   Still—*I* will rule.

CREON   Not when you rule treacherously.

OEDIPUS   Ò Thebes! My city! Listen to him!

CREON   *My* city too!

CHORUS   My Lords, no more. Here comes Jocasta. Perhaps the queen
can end this bitter clash.

Enter JOCASTA.

JOCASTA   Why do you behave like senseless fools and quarrel without
reason? Are you not ashamed to add trouble of your own when your
city is sick and dying? Go, Creon. Go and leave us alone. Forget
those petty grievances which you exaggerate. How important can
they be?

CREON   This important, sister: Oedipus, your husband, in his insanity,
has threatened me with banishment or death.

OEDIPUS   Yes, for I have realized his plot—a plot against my person.

CREON   May the gods haunt me forever, if that is true—if I am guilty
of that charge.

JOCASTA   In the name of God, believe him, Oedipus! Believe him for
the sake of his oath, for my own sake, and for theirs!

CHORUS   Listen to her, my Lord. I beg you to consider and comply.

OEDIPUS   What would you have me do?

CHORUS   Respect the oath that Creon gave you. Respect his past integrity.

OEDIPUS   Do you know what you are asking?

CHORUS   Yes, I know.

OEDIPUS   Then, tell me what you mean.

CHORUS   I mean that you are wrong to charge a friend who has invoked a curse upon his head. You are wrong to slander without proof and be the cause for his dishonor.

OEDIPUS   Then you must know that when you ask for this, you ask for banishment or doom—for *me*.

CHORUS

O God, no!
O Helios,[5] no!
May Heaven and Earth exact my doom
if that is what I thought!
When our city is torn by sickness
and my heart is torn with pain—
do not compound the troubles
that beset us!

OEDIPUS   Then, let him go, although it surely means my death—or banishment with dishonor. *Your* words—not his—have touched my heart. But Creon—wherever he may be—I will hate him.

CREON   You are hard when you should yield, cruel when you should pity. Such natures deserve the pain they bear.

OEDIPUS   Just go—and leave me in peace.

CREON   I will go—my guilt pronounced by you alone. Behold my judge and jury—Oedipus Tyrannus!

Exit CREON.

CHORUS   My queen, persuade your husband to rest awhile.

JOCASTA   I will—when I have learned the truth.

CHORUS   Blind suspicion has consumed the king. And Creon's passions flared beneath the sting of unjust accusations.

JOCASTA   Are *both* at fault?

CHORUS   Yes, both of them.

JOCASTA   But what is the reason for their rage?

CHORUS   Don't ask again. Our city is weary enough from suffering. Enough. Let the matter rest where it now stands.

OEDIPUS   Do you see what you have done? Do you see where you have come—with your good intentions, your noble efforts to dull the sharpness of my anger?

CHORUS

My Lord, I have said before
and now I say again:
I would be mad,
a reckless fool
to turn away my king,
who saved us from a sea of troubles
and set us on a fairer course,
and who will lead us once again
to peace, a haven from our pain.

5. Helios was the name of a sun god, hence Apollo.

JOCASTA   In the name of Heaven, my Lord, tell me the reason for your bitterness.

OEDIPUS   I will—because you mean more to me than anyone. The reason is Creon and his plot against my throne.

JOCASTA   But can you *prove* a plot?

OEDIPUS   He says that I—Oedipus—bear the guilt of Laius' death.

JOCASTA   How does he justify this charge?

OEDIPUS   He does not stain his own lips by saying it. No. He uses that false prophet to speak for him.

JOCASTA   Then, you can exonerate yourself because no mortal has the power of divination. And I can prove it. An oracle came to Laius once from the Pythian priests—I'll not say from Apollo himself— that he would die at the hands of his own child, his child and mine. Yet the story, which *we* heard was that robbers murdered Laius in a place where three roads meet. As for the child—when he was three days old, Laius drove pins into his ankles and handed him to someone to cast upon a deserted mountain path—to die. And so, Apollo's prophecy was unfulfilled—the child did not kill his father. And Laius' fears were unfulfilled—he did not die by the hand of his child. Yet, these had been the prophecies. You need not give them any credence. For the god will reveal what he wants.

OEDIPUS   Jocasta—my heart is troubled at your words. Suddenly, my thoughts are wandering, disturbed . . .

JOCASTA   What is it? What makes you so frightened?

OEDIPUS   Your statement—that Laius was murdered in a place where three roads meet. Isn't that what you said?

JOCASTA   Yes. That was the story then; that is the story now.

OEDIPUS   Where is this place where three roads meet?

JOCASTA   In the land called Phocis where the roads from Delphi and from Daulia converge.[6]

OEDIPUS   How long a time has passed since then?

JOCASTA   We heard it shortly before you came.

OEDIPUS   O God, what have you planned for me?

JOCASTA   What is it, Oedipus? What frightens you?

OEDIPUS   Do not ask me. Do not ask. Just tell me—what was Laius like? How old was he?

JOCASTA   He was tall and his hair was lightly cast with silver tones, the contour of his body much like yours.

OEDIPUS   O God! Am I cursed and cannot see it?

JOCASTA   What is it, Oedipus? You frighten me.

OEDIPUS   It cannot be—that the prophet sees! Tell me one more thing.

JOCASTA   You frighten me, my Lord, but I will try to tell you what I know.

OEDIPUS   Who traveled with the king? Was he alone? Was there a guide? An escort? A few? Many?

JOCASTA   There were five—one of them a herald—and a carriage in which Laius rode.

OEDIPUS   O God! O God! I see it all now! Jocasta, who told you this?

JOCASTA   A servant—the only one who returned alive.

---

6. The Oracle at Delphi was located in the region of central Greece called Phocis. Daulia was a city to the east of Delphi.

OEDIPUS   Is he here now? In our house?

JOCASTA   No. When he came back and saw you ruling where once his master was, he pleaded with me—begged me—to send him to the fields to tend the flocks, far from the city. And so I did. He was a good servant and I would have granted him more than that, if he had asked.

OEDIPUS   Could we arrange to have him here—now?

JOCASTA   Yes, but what do you want with him?

OEDIPUS   I am afraid, Jocasta. I have said too much and now I have to see him.

JOCASTA   Then he shall be brought. But I, too, must know the cause of your distress. I have the right to know.

OEDIPUS   Yes, you have that right. And I must tell you—now. You, more than anyone, will have to know what I am going through. My father was Polybus of Corinth, my mother a Dorian—Merope. I was held in high regard in Corinth until—until something strange occurred—something uncanny and strange, although I might have given it too much concern. There was a man dining with us one day who had had far too much wine and shouted at me—half-drunk and shouting that I was not rightly called my father's son. I could barely endure the rest of that day and on the next I went to my parents and questioned them. They were enraged at the remark. I felt relieved at their response. But still, this—this thing—kept gnawing at my heart. And it was spread about in vulgar whispers. And then, without my parents' knowledge, I went to Delphi, but Apollo did not say what I had gone to hear. Instead, he answered questions I had not asked and told of horror and misery beyond belief—how I would know my mother's bed and bring to the world a race of children too terrible for men to see and cause the death of my own father. I trembled at those words and fled from Corinth—as far as I could—to where no star could ever guide me back, where I could never see that infamous prophecy fulfilled. And as I traveled, I came to that place where you say the king was murdered. This is the truth, Jocasta—I was in that place where the three roads meet. There was a herald leading a carriage drawn by horses and a man riding in the carriage—just as you described. The man in front, and the old one, ordered me out of the path. I refused. The driver pushed. In anger, I struck him. The old man saw it, reached for his lash and waited till I had passed. Then he struck me on the head. But he paid—oh yes, he paid. He lost his balance and fell from the carriage and as he lay there helpless—on his back—I killed him. I killed them all. But if this stranger had any tie with Laius—O God —who could be more hated in the eyes of Heaven and Earth? *I* am the one whom strangers and citizens are forbidden to receive! *I* am the one to whom all are forbidden to speak! *I* am the one who must be driven out! *I* am the one for whom my curse was meant! I have touched his bed with the very hands that killed him! O God! The sin! The horror! *I* am to be banished, never to see my people, never to walk in my fatherland. Or else I must take my mother for a bride and kill my father Polybus, who gave me life and cared for me. What cruel god has sent this torture? Hear me, you gods, you holy gods—I will never see that day! I will die before I ever see the stain of this abominable act!

CHORUS   Your words frighten us, my Lord. But you must have hope until you hear the story from the man who saw.

OEDIPUS   Yes—hope. My only hope is waiting for this shepherd.

JOCASTA   Why? What do you hope to find with him?

OEDIPUS   This—if his story agrees with what you say, then I am safe.

JOCASTA   What did I say that makes you sure of this?

OEDIPUS   You said he told of *robbers*—that *robbers* killed the king If he still says *robbers*, then I am not the guilty one—because no man can talk of many when he means a single one. But if he names a *single* traveler, there will be no doubt—the guilt is mine.

JOCASTA   You can be sure that this was what he said—and he cannot deny it. The whole city heard him—not I alone. But even if he alters what he said before, he cannot prove that Laius met his death as it was prophesied. For Apollo said that he would die at the hand of a child—of mine. And as it happens, the child is dead. So prophecy is worthless. I wouldn't dignify it with a moment's thought.

OEDIPUS   You are right. But still—send someone for the shepherd. Now.

JOCASTA   I shall—immediately. I shall do what you ask. But now— let us go inside.

ode 2   *Exeunt* OEDIPUS, JOCASTA.

CHORUS

I pray, may destiny permit
that honestly I live my life
in word and deed.
That I obey the laws
the heavens have begotten
and prescribed.
Those laws created by Olympus,[7]
laws pure, immortal,
forever lasting, essence of the god
who lives in them.
On arrogance and pride
a tyrant feeds.
The goad of insolence,
of senseless overbearing, blind conceit,
of seeking things unseasonable,
unreasonable,
will prick a man to climb to heights
where he must lose his footing
and tumble to his doom.
Ambition must be used
to benefit the state;
else it is wrong, and God
must strike it from this earth.
Forever, God, I pray,
may you stand at my side!

7. The highest mountain of the Greek peninsula and the reputed home of the gods.

A man who goes through life
with insolence in word and deed,
who lacks respect for law and right,
and scorns the shrines and temples of the gods,
may he find evil fate and doom
as his reward for wantonness,
for seeking ill-begotten gains
and reaching after sacred things
with sacrilegious hands.
No! Surely no such man
escapes the wrath, the vengeance of the god!
For if he did, if he could find reward
in actions which are wrong,
why should I trouble to acclaim,
to honor you, God, in my song?

No longer shall my feet
take me to Delphi's sacred shrine;
no longer shall they Abae or Olympia's altars[8] seek
unless the oracles are shown to tell the truth
to mortals without fail!
Where are you, Zeus, all-powerful, all-ruling?
You must be told,
you must know in your all-pervading power:
Apollo's oracles now fall into dishonor,
and what the god has spoken about Laius
finds disregard.
Could God be dead?

Enter JOCASTA. Scene 3

JOCASTA   My Lords, I want to lay these laurel wreaths and incense
offerings at the shrines of Thebes—for Oedipus is torturing himself,
tearing his heart with grief. His vision to weigh the present against
the past is blurred by fear and terror. He devours every word of
dread, drinks in every thought of pain, destruction, death. And I
no longer have the power to ease his suffering. Now I turn to you,
Apollo, since you are nearest, with prayer and suppliant offerings.
Find some way to free us, end our agony! O God of Light, release
us! You see the fear that grips us—like sailors who watch their captain paralyzed by some unknown terror on the seas.

Enter MESSENGER 1.

MESSENGER 1   Strangers, would you direct me to the house of Oedipus?
Or if you know where I might find the king himself, please tell me.
CHORUS   This is his house, stranger. He is inside. But this is the queen
—his wife, and mother of his children.
MESSENGER 1   Then, blessings on the house of Oedipus—his house,
his children, and his wife.
JOCASTA   Blessings on you as well, stranger. Your words are kind. But
why have you come? What is it?

8. Important oracles were located at Abae and Olympia in ancient times.

MESSENGER 1   Good news, my lady—for your husband and your house.
JOCASTA   What news? Where do you come from?
MESSENGER 1   From Corinth, my lady. My news will surely bring you joy—but sorrow, too.
JOCASTA   What? How can that be?
MESSENGER 1   Your husband now is ruler of the Isthmus!
JOCASTA   Do you mean that Polybus of Corinth has been deposed?
MESSENGER 1   Deposed by death, my lady. He has passed away.
JOCASTA   What! Polybus dead?
MESSENGER 1   I swear on my life that this is true.
JOCASTA   [*to a servant*]   Go! Quickly! Tell your master. [*To the heavens.*] You prophecies—you divinely-uttered prophecies! Where do you stand now? The man that Oedipus feared, the man he dared not face lest he should be his killer—that man is dead! Time claimed his life—not Oedipus!

   Enter OEDIPUS.

OEDIPUS   Why, Jocasta? Why have you sent for me again?
JOCASTA   I want you to listen to this man. Listen to him and judge for yourself the worth of those holy prophecies.
OEDIPUS   Who is he? What news could he have for me?
JOCASTA   He comes from Corinth with the news that—that Polybus—is dead.
OEDIPUS   What! Tell me.
MESSENGER 1   If you must know this first, then I shall tell you—plainly. Polybus has died.
OEDIPUS   How? An act of treason? Sickness? How?
MESSENGER 1   My Lord, only a slight shift in the scales is required to bring the agèd to their rest.
OEDIPUS   Then it was sickness. Poor old man.
MESSENGER 1   Sickness—yes. And the weight of years.
OEDIPUS   Oh, Jocasta! Why? Why should we even look to oracles, the prophetic words delivered at their shrines or the birds that scream above us? They led me to believe that I would kill my father. But he is dead and in his grave, while I stand here—never having touched a weapon. Unless he died of longing for his son. If that is so, then I *was* the instrument of his death. And those oracles! Where are they now? Polybus has taken them to his grave. What worth have they now?
JOCASTA   Have I not been saying this all along?
OEDIPUS   Yes, you have. But I was misled by fear.
JOCASTA   Now you will no longer have to think of it.
OEDIPUS   But—my mother's bed. I still have *that* to fear.
JOCASTA   No. No, mortals have no need to fear when chance reigns supreme. The knowledge of the future is denied to us. It is better to live as you will, live as you can. You need not fear a union with your mother. Men often, in their dreams, approach their mothers' beds, lie with them, possess them. But the man who sees that this is meaningless can live without the threat of fear.
OEDIPUS   You would be right, Jocasta, if my mother were not alive. But she *is* alive. And no matter what you say, I have reason to fear.

JOCASTA   At least your father's death has brought some comfort.

OEDIPUS   Yes—some comfort. But my fear is of *her* as long as she lives.

MESSENGER 1   Who is *she?* The woman you fear?

OEDIPUS   Queen Merope, old man, the wife of Polybus.

MESSENGER 1   But why does *she* instill fear in you?

OEDIPUS   There was an oracle—a dreadful oracle sent by the gods.

MESSENGER 1   Can you tell me—a stranger—what it is?

OEDIPUS   Yes, it is all right to tell. Once Loxian Apollo said that I would take my mother for my bride and murder my father with my own hands. This is the reason that I left Corinth long ago. Fortunately. And yet, I have often longed to see my parents.

MESSENGER 1   Is this the fear that drove you away from Corinth?

OEDIPUS   Yes. I did not want to kill my father.

MESSENGER 1   But I can free you from this fear, my Lord. My purpose for coming was a good one.

OEDIPUS   And I shall see that you receive a fitting reward.

MESSENGER 1   Yes—that's why I came. To fare well myself by your returning home.

OEDIPUS   Home? To Corinth? To my parents? Never.

MESSENGER 1   My son, you do not realize what you are doing.

OEDIPUS   What do you mean, old man? For God's sake, tell me what you mean.

MESSENGER 1   I mean—the reasons why you dread returning home.

OEDIPUS   I dread Apollo's prophecy—and its fulfillment.

MESSENGER 1   You mean the curse—the stain they say lies with your parents?

OEDIPUS   Yes, old man. That is the fear that lives with me.

MESSENGER 1   Then you must realize that this fear is groundless.

OEDIPUS   How can that be—if I am their son?

MESSENGER 1   Because Polybus was no relative of yours.

OEDIPUS   What are you saying! Polybus was *not* my father?

MESSENGER 1   No more than I.

OEDIPUS   No more than you? But you are nothing to me.

MESSENGER 1   He was not your father any more than I.

OEDIPUS   Then why did he call me his son?

MESSENGER 1   You were a gift to him—from me.

OEDIPUS   A gift? From you? And yet he loved me as his son?

MESSENGER 1   Yes, my Lord. He had been childless.

OEDIPUS   And when you gave me to him—had you bought me? Or found me?

MESSENGER 1   I found you—in the hills of Cithaeron.

OEDIPUS   What were you doing there?

MESSENGER 1   Tending sheep along the mountain side.

OEDIPUS   Then you were a—hired shepherd?

MESSENGER 1   Yes, my son—a hired shepherd who saved you at that time.

OEDIPUS   Saved me? Was I in pain when you found me? Was I in trouble?

MESSENGER 1   Yes, your ankles are the proof of that.

OEDIPUS   Ah, you mean this old trouble. What has that to do with it?

MESSENGER 1 When I found you, your ankles were pierced with rivets. And I freed you.

OEDIPUS Yes, I have had this horrible stigma since infancy.

MESSENGER 1 And so it was the swelling in your ankles that caused your name: Oedipus—"Clubfoot."

OEDIPUS Oh! Who did this to me? My father? Or my mother?

MESSENGER 1 I don't know. You will have to ask the man who handed you to me.

OEDIPUS You mean—you did not find me? It was someone else?

MESSENGER 1 Another shepherd.

OEDIPUS Who? Do you remember who he was?

MESSENGER 1 I think—he was of the house of Laius.

OEDIPUS The king who ruled this city?

MESSENGER 1 Yes. He was a shepherd in the service of the king.

OEDIPUS Is he still alive? Can I see him?

MESSENGER 1 [*addressing the* CHORUS] You—you people here—could answer that.

OEDIPUS Do any of you know this shepherd? Have you seen him in the fields? Here in Thebes? Tell me now! Now is the time to unravel this mystery—once and for all.

CHORUS I think it is the shepherd you asked to see before. But the queen will know.

OEDIPUS Jocasta, is that the man he means? Is it the shepherd we have sent for? Is *he* the one?

JOCASTA Why? What difference does it make? Don't think about it. Pay no attention to what he said. It makes no difference.

OEDIPUS No difference? When I must have every clue to untangle the line of mystery surrounding my birth?

JOCASTA In the name of God, if you care at all for your own life, you must not go on with this. I cannot bear it any longer.

OEDIPUS Do not worry, Jocasta. Even if I am a slave—a third-generation slave, it is no stain on your nobility.

JOCASTA Oedipus! I beg you—don't do this!

OEDIPUS I can't grant you that. I cannot leave the truth unknown.

JOCASTA It is for *your* sake that I beg you to stop. For your own good.

OEDIPUS My own good has brought me pain too long.

JOCASTA God help you! May you never know what you are!

OEDIPUS Go, someone, and bring the shepherd to me. Leave the queen to exult in her noble birth.

JOCASTA God help you! This is all that I can say to you—now or ever.

Exit JOCASTA.

CHORUS Why has the queen left like this—grief-stricken and tortured with pain? My Lord, I fear—I fear that from her silence some horror will burst forth.

OEDIPUS Let it explode! I will still want to uncover the secret of my birth—no matter how horrible. She—she is a woman with a woman's pride—and she feels shame for my humble birth. But I am the child of Fortune—beneficent Fortune—and I shall not be shamed! She is my mother. My sisters are the months and they have seen me rise

and fall. This is my family. I will never deny my birth—and I will
learn its secret!

Exit OEDIPUS.

Ode 3

CHORUS
Ah Cithaeron,
if in my judgment I am right,
if I interpret what I hear correctly,
then—by Olympus' boundless majesty!—
tomorrow's full moon will not pass
before, Cithaeron, you will find
that Oedipus will honor you
as mother and as nurse!
That we will praise you in our song,
benevolent and friendly to our king.
Apollo, our Lord, may you find joy in this!

Who bore you, Oedipus? A nymph?
Did Pan beget you in the hills?
Were you begotten by Apollo?
Perhaps so, for he likes the mountain glens.
Could Hermes be your father?[9]
Or Dionysus? Could it be
that he received you as a gift
high in the mountains from a nymph
with whom he lay?

Enter OEDIPUS.

Scene 4

OEDIPUS   My Lords, I have never met him, but could that be the
shepherd we have been waiting for? He seems to be of the same
age as the stranger from Corinth. And I can see now—those are
my servants who are bringing him here. But, perhaps you know—
if you have seen him before. Is he the shepherd?

Enter SHEPHERD.

CHORUS   Yes. I recognize him. He was a shepherd in the service of
Laius—as loyal as any man could be.
OEDIPUS   Corinthian, I ask you—is this the man you mean?
MESSENGER 1   Yes, my Lord. This is the man.
OEDIPUS   And you, old man, look at me and answer what I ask. Were
you in the service of Laius?
SHEPHERD   I was. But not bought. I was reared in his house.
OEDIPUS   What occupation? What way of life?
SHEPHERD   Tending flocks—for most of my life.
OEDIPUS   And where did you tend those flocks?
SHEPHERD   Sometimes Cithaeron, sometimes the neighboring places.
OEDIPUS   Have you ever seen this man before?
SHEPHERD   What man do you mean? Doing what?

9. Pan was a woodland god and a protector of herds. Hermes (Roman Mercury) was
the messenger of the gods.

OEDIPUS   This man. Have you ever met him before?

SHEPHERD   Not that I recall, my Lord.

MESSENGER 1   No wonder, my Lord. But I shall help him to recall. I am sure that he'll remember the time we spent on Cithaeron— he with his two flocks and I with one. Six months—spring to autumn —every year—for three years. In the winter I would drive my flocks to my fold in Corinth, and he to the fold of Laius. Isn't that right, sir?

SHEPHERD   That is what happened. But it was a long time ago.

MESSENGER 1   Then tell me this. Do you remember a child you gave me to bring up as my own?

SHEPHERD   What are you saying? Why are you asking me this?

MESSENGER 1   This, my friend, this—is that child.

SHEPHERD   Damn you! Will you keep your mouth shut!

OEDIPUS   Save your reproaches, old man. It is you who deserve them— your words deserve them.

SHEPHERD   But master—how have I offended?

OEDIPUS   By refusing to answer his question about the child.

SHEPHERD   He doesn't know what he's saying. He's crazy.

OEDIPUS   If you don't answer of your own accord, we'll make you talk.

SHEPHERD   No! My Lord, please! Don't hurt an old man.

OEDIPUS [*to the* CHORUS]   One of you—twist his hands behind his back!

SHEPHERD   Why? Why? What do you want to know?

OEDIPUS   Did you or did you not give him that child?

SHEPHERD   I did. I gave it to him—and I wish that I had died that day.

OEDIPUS   You tell the truth, or you'll have your wish now.

SHEPHERD   If I tell, it will be worse.

OEDIPUS   Still he puts it off!

SHEPHERD   I said that I gave him the child!

OEDIPUS   Where did you get it? Your house? Someone else's? Where?

SHEPHERD   Not mine. Someone else's.

OEDIPUS   Whose? One of the citizens'? Whose house?

SHEPHERD   O God, master! Don't ask me any more.

OEDIPUS   This is the last time that I ask you.

SHEPHERD   It was a child—of the house of Laius.

OEDIPUS   A slave? Or of his own line?

SHEPHERD   Ah master, do I *have* to speak?

OEDIPUS   You have to. And I *have* to hear.

SHEPHERD   They said—it was his child. But the queen could tell you best.

OEDIPUS   Why? Did *she* give you the child?

SHEPHERD   Yes, my Lord.

OEDIPUS   Why?

SHEPHERD   To—kill!

OEDIPUS   Her own child!

SHEPHERD   Yes. Because she was terrified of some dreadful prophecy.

OEDIPUS   What prophecy?

SHEPHERD   The child would kill his father.

OEDIPUS   Then why did you give him to this man?

SHEPHERD   I felt sorry for him, master. And I thought that he would take him to his own home. But he saved him from his suffering—

for worse suffering yet. My Lord, if you are the man he says you are
—O God—you were born to suffering!

OEDIPUS   O God! O no! I see it all now! All clear! O Light! I will never
look on you again! Sin! Sin in my birth! Sin in my marriage! Sin in
blood!

Ode 4

Exit OEDIPUS.

CHORUS
O generations of men, you are nothing!
You are nothing!
And I count you as not having lived at all!
Was there ever a man,
was there ever a man on this earth
who could say he was happy,
who knew happiness, true happiness,
not an image, a dream,
an illusion, a vision, which would disappear?
Your example, Oedipus,
your example, your fate, your disaster,
show that none of us mortals
ever knew, ever felt what happiness truly is.

Here is Oedipus,
fortune and fame and bliss
leading him by the hand,
prodding him on to heights
mortals had never attained.
Zeus, it was he who removed
the scourge of the riddling maid,
of the sharp-clawed, murderous Sphinx!
He restored me to life from the brink
of disaster, of doom and of death.
It was he who was honored and hailed,
who was crowned and acclaimed as our king.

Here is Oedipus:
Who on this earth has been
struck by a harder blow
or stung by a fate more perverse?
Wretched Oedipus!
Father and son alike,
pleasures you took from where
once you were given life.
Furrows your father ploughed
bore you in silence. How, how, oh how could it be?

Time found you out,
all-seeing, irrepressible time.
Time sits in judgment on
the union that never could be;
judges you, father and son,

begot and begetter alike.
Would that I never had
laid eyes on Laius' child!
Now I wail and I weep,
and my lips are drenched in lament.
It was you, who offered me life;
it is you, who now bring me death.

Enter MESSENGER 2.   *Exodos*

MESSENGER 2   O you most honored citizens of Thebes, you will mourn for the things you will hear, you will mourn for the things you will see, and you will ache from the burden of sorrow—if you are true sons of the house of Labdacus, if you care, if you feel. The waters of Ister and Phasis[1] can never cleanse this house of the horrors hidden within it and soon to be revealed—horrors willfully done! Worst of the sorrows we know are those that are willfully done!

CHORUS   We have mourned enough for sorrows we have known. What more is there that you can add?

MESSENGER 2   One more and only one—Jocasta, the queen, is dead.

CHORUS   O God—no! How!

MESSENGER 2   By her own hand. But the most dreadful pain you have not seen. You have not seen the worst. I have seen it and I shall tell you what I can of her terrible suffering. She ran in frenzied despair through the palace halls and rushed straight to her bridal bed—her fingers clutching and tearing at her hair. Then, inside the bedroom, she flung the doors closed and cried out to Laius, long since dead. She cried out to him, remembering the son that she had borne long ago, the son who killed his father, the son who left her to bear a dread curse—the children of her own son! She wept pitifully for that bridal bed which she had twice defiled—husband born of husband, child born of child. I didn't see what happened then. I didn't see her die. At that moment the king rushed in and shrieked in horror. All eyes turned to him as he paced in frantic passion and confusion. He sprang at each of us and begged to have a sword. He begged to know where he could find the wife that was no wife to him, the woman who had been mother to him and to his children. Some power beyond the scope of man held him in its sway and guided him to her. It was none of us. Then—as if somebody had beckoned to him and bade him follow—he screamed in terror and threw himself against the doors that she had locked. His body's weight and force shattered the bolts and thrust them from their sockets and he rushed into the room. There we saw the queen hanging from a noose of twisted cords. And when the king saw her, he cried out and moaned in deep, sorrowful misery. Then he untied the rope that hung about her neck and laid her body on the ground. But what happened then was even worse. Her gold brooches, her pins—he tore them from her gown and plunged them into his eyes again and again and again and screamed, "No longer shall you see the suffering

---

1. The Ister was a name for the lower Danube. The Phasis flowed from the Caucasus to the Black Sea. They are invoked here together as examples of large rivers.

you have known and caused! You saw what was forbidden to be seen, yet failed to recognize those whom you longed to see! Now you shall see only darkness!" And as he cried out in such desperate misery, he struck his eyes over and over—until a shower of blood and tears splattered down his beard, like a torrent of crimson rain and hail. And now suffering is mingled with pain for man and wife for the sins that both have done. Not one alone. Once—long ago—this house was happy—and rightly so. But now—today—sorrow, destruction, death, shame—all torments that have a name—all, all are theirs to endure.

CHORUS   But the king—does he have any relief from his suffering now?

MESSENGER 2   He calls for someone to unlock the gates and reveal to Thebes his father's killer, his mother's—I can't say it. I cannot say this unholy word. He cries out that he will banish himself from the land to free this house of the curse that he has uttered. But he is weak, drained. There is no one to guide his way. The pain is more than he can bear. You will see for yourselves. The palace gates are opening. You will see a sight so hideous that even his most bitter enemy would pity him.

Enter OEDIPUS.

CHORUS
Ah!
Dread horror for men to see!
Most dreadful of all that I have seen!
Ah!
Wretched one,
what madness has possessed you?
What demon has descended upon you
and bound you to this dire fate?
Ah!
Wretched one,
I cannot bear to look at you.
I want to ask you more
and learn still more
and understand—
but I shudder at the sight of you!

OEDIPUS   Ah! Ah! Where has this misery brought me? Is this my own voice I hear—carried on the wings of the air? O Fate! What have you done to me?

CHORUS   Terrible! Too terrible to hear! Too terrible to see!

OEDIPUS   O cloud of darkness! Cruel! Driven by the winds of fate! Assaulting me! With no defense to hold you back! O God! The pain! The pain! My flesh aches from its wounds! My soul aches from the memory of its horrors!

CHORUS   Body and soul—each suffers and mourns.

OEDIPUS   Ah! You still remain with me—a constant friend. You still remain to care for me—a blind man now. Now there is darkness and I cannot see your face. But I can hear your voice and I know that you are near.

CHORUS   O my Lord, how could you have done this? How could you blind yourself? What demon drove you?

OEDIPUS   Apollo! It was Apollo! *He* brought this pain, this suffering to me. But it was my own hand that struck the blow. Not his. O God! Why should I have sight when all that I would see is ugliness?

CHORUS   It is as you say.

OEDIPUS   What is there for me to see and love? What sight would give me joy? What sound? Take me away! Take me out of this land! I am cursed! Doomed! I am the man most hated by the gods!

CHORUS   You have suffered equally for your fortune and for your disaster. I wish that you had never come to Thebes.

OEDIPUS   Damn the man who set me free! Who loosed the fetters from my feet and let me live! I never will forgive him. If he had let me die, I would never have become the cause—the grief . . .

CHORUS   I wish that it had been this way.

OEDIPUS   If it had been, I would not have come to this—killer of my father, bridegroom of the woman who gave me birth, despised by the gods, child of shame, father and brother to my children. Is there any horror worse than these—any horror that has not fallen upon Oedipus.

CHORUS   My Lord, I cannot condone what you have done. You would have been better dead than alive and blind.

OEDIPUS   I did what I had to. You know I did. No more advice. Could these eyes have looked upon my father in the house of Hades? Could these eyes have faced my mother in her agony? I sinned against them both—a sin no suicide could purge. Could I have joy at the sight of my children—born as they were born? With these eyes? Never! Could I look upon the city of Thebes? The turrets that grace her walls? The sacred statues of her gods? Never! Damned! I—the noblest of the sons of Thebes—I have damned myself. It was I who commanded that Thebes must cast out the one who is guilty, unholy, cursed by the heavenly gods. *I* was the curse of Thebes! Could these eyes look upon the people? Never! And if I could raise a wall to channel the fountain of my hearing, I would spare nothing to build a prison for this defiled body where sight and sound would never penetrate. Then only would I have peace—where grief could not reach my mind. O Cithaeron! Why did you receive me? Why did you not let me die then? Why did you let me live to show the world how I was born? O Polybus! O Corinth! My home that was no home! You raised me, thinking I was fair and never knowing the evil that festered beneath. Now—now see the evil from which I was born, the evil I have become. O God! The three roads! The hidden glen! The thickets! The pathway where three roads meet! The blood you drank from my hands—do you not know—it was the blood of my father! Do you remember? Do you remember what I did then and what I did for Thebes? Wedding-rites! You gave me birth and gave my children birth! Born of the same womb that bore my children! Father! Brother! Child! Incestuous sin! Bride! Wife! Mother! All of one union! All the most heinous sins that man can know! The most horrible shame—I can no longer speak of it. For the love of God, hide me somewhere. Hide me away from this land! Kill me! Cast me into the sea where you will never have to look at me again! I beg you—touch me—in my misery. Touch me. Do not be afraid. My sins are mine alone to bear and touch no other man.

Enter CREON.

CHORUS   My Lord, Creon is here to act or counsel in what you ask. In your stead—he is now our sole protector.

OEDIPUS   What can I say to him? How can I ask for his trust? I have wronged him. I know that now.

CREON   I have not come to mock you, Oedipus, nor to reproach you for the past. But you—if you have no respect for men, at least respect the lord of the sun whose fires give life to men. Hide your naked guilt from his sight. No earth or sacred rain or light can endure its presence. [*To a servant.*] Take him inside. It is impious for any but his own family to see and hear his suffering.

OEDIPUS   I ask you in the name of God to grant me one favor. You have been kinder to me than I deserved. But one favor. I ask it for you—not for myself.

CREON   What do you ask of me?

OEDIPUS   Cast me out of this land. Cast me out to where no man can see me. Cast me out now.

CREON   I would have done so, you can be sure. But I must wait and do the will of the god.

OEDIPUS   He has signified his will—with clarity. Destroy the parricide! Destroy the unholy one! Destroy Oedipus!

CREON   That was the god's command, I know. But now—with what has happened—I think it better to wait and learn what we must do.

OEDIPUS   You mean that you would ask for guidance for a man so sorrowful as I?

CREON   Surely, you are ready to put your trust in the god—now.

OEDIPUS   Yes, I am ready now. But I ask this of you. Inside—she is lying inside—give her whatever funeral rites you wish. You will do the right thing for her. She is your sister. But for me—do not condemn this city—my father's city—to suffer any longer from my presence as long as I live. Let me go and live upon Cithaeron—O Cithaeron, your name is ever linked with mine! Where my parents chose a grave for me. Where they would have had me die. Where I shall die in answer to their wish. And yet, I know, neither sickness nor anything else will ever bring me death. For I would not have been saved from death that once. No—I was saved for a more dreadful fate. Let it be. Creon, do not worry about my sons. They are boys and will have all they need, no matter where they go. But my daughters—poor creatures! They never ate a single meal without their father. We shared everything together. Creon, take care of them. Creon, let me touch them one last time. And let me weep—one last time. Please, my Lord, please, allow it—you're generous, you're kind. If I could only touch them and feel that they are with me—as I used to—when I could see them. [*Enter* ANTIGONE *and* ISMENE.] What is that crying? Is it my daughters? Has Creon taken pity on me? Has he sent my daughters to me? Are they here?

CREON Yes, Oedipus, they are here. I had them brought to you. I know how much you love them, how much you have always loved them.

OEDIPUS Bless you for this, Creon. Heaven bless you and grant you greater kindness than it has granted me. Ah, children, where are you? Come—come, touch my hands, the hands of your father, the hands of your brother, the hands that blinded these eyes which once were bright—these eyes—your father's eyes which neither saw nor knew what he had done when he became your father. I weep for you, my children. I cannot see you now. But when I think of the bitterness that waits for you in life, what you will have to suffer—the festivals, the holidays—the sadness you will know when you should share in gaiety! And when you are old enough to marry—who will there be, who will be the man strong enough to bear the slander that will haunt you—because you are *my* children? What disgrace will you not know? Your father killed his father. And lay with the woman that bore him and his children. These are the taunts that will follow you. And what man will marry you? No man, my children. You will spend your lives unwed—without children of your own—barren and wasted. Ah, Creon, you are the only father left to them. We—their parents—are lost. We gave them life. And we are lost to them. Take care of them. See that they do not wander poor and lonely. Do not let them suffer for what I have done. Pity them. They are so young. So lost. They have no one but you. Take my hand and promise me. And oh, my children, if you were older, I could make you understand. But now, make this your prayer—to find some place where you can live and have a better life than what your father knew.

CREON Enough, my Lord. Go inside now.

OEDIPUS Yes. I do not want to, but I will go.

CREON All things have their time and their place.

OEDIPUS I shall go—on this condition.

CREON What condition? I am listening.

OEDIPUS That you will send me away.

CREON That is the god's decision, not mine.

OEDIPUS The gods will not care where I go.

CREON Then you shall have your wish.

OEDIPUS Then—you consent?

CREON It has nothing to do with my consent.

OEDIPUS Let me go away from here.

CREON Go then—but leave the children.

OEDIPUS No! Do not take them away from me!

CREON Do not presume that you are still in power. Your power has not survived with you.

CHORUS
There goes Oedipus—
he was the man who was able
to answer the riddle proposed by the Sphinx.
Mighty Oedipus—
he was an object of envy
to all for his fortune and fame.

There goes Oedipus—
now he is drowning in waves of dread and despair.
Look at Oedipus—
proof that none of us mortals
can truly be thought of as happy
until he is granted deliverance from life,
until he is dead
and must suffer no more.

ca. 429 B.C.

Thebes and the House of Cadmus

Many of the principal myths of the Greeks centered about royal families who seemed particularly susceptible to sensational crimes and punishments. Few families had more lurid histories than that of Cadmus, the founder of Thebes.

When Cadmus' sister Europa was stolen by Zeus, in the form of a white bull, his father, Agenor of Sidon, sent Cadmus and his brothers forth to search for her. After various adventures, Cadmus, led by Athena, set out to establish a city. Led by a cow chosen by the goddess, he came to a spring where he was to establish the city. When most of his men were killed by a serpent who lived there, Cadmus killed the serpent and, again following the instructions of the goddess, sowed its teeth. From the teeth sprang up armed men who began fighting among themselves until Cadmus stopped them by throwing a stone into their midst. These "Sown Men" and their descendants were the great families of Thebes. Among them were Echion, the father of Pentheus, and an ancestor of Menoeceus, the father of Jocasta and Creon.

The chart below shows the relations of the members of the house of Cadmus who are mentioned in *Oedipus Tyrannus* and *The Bacchae*. A number of their relatives with equally spectacular destinies are omitted to make the chart more useful to readers of these two plays.

Although *Oedipus Tyrannus* and *The Bacchae* occur in different generations, the figure of Teiresias, the blind prophet, occurs in both. The name may have designated an office rather than an individual.

Thebes was the principal city of Boeotia, a district to the northwest of Attica in which Athens was located. This may help to explain its prominence in the Athenian drama. The two plays here considered make frequent reference to some of the features of the city, including its seven gates (where *The Seven Against Thebes* fought), the great mountain Cithaeron, which was nearby, the streams Ismenus, Dirce, and Asopus, and the neighboring villages of Hysiae and Erythrae.

OSCAR WILDE

The Importance of Being Earnest

CHARACTERS

JOHN WORTHING, J.P.

ALGERNON MONCRIEFF

REV. CANON CHASUBLE D. D.

LANE, *Manservant*

MERRIMAN, *Butler*

LADY BRACKNELL

HON. GWENDOLEN FAIRFAX

CECILY CARDEW

MISS PRISM, *Governess*

A FOOTMAN

The first act takes place in ALGERNON's *flat in Half-Moon Street, London. The remaining acts take place at the Manor House, Woolton, Hertfordshire, the second in the garden and the third in the drawing-room.*

Act 1

Morning-room in ALGERNON's *flat in Half-Moon Street.*[1] *The room is luxuriously and artistically furnished. The sound of a piano is heard in the adjoining room.*

LANE *is arranging afternoon tea on the table, and after the music has ceased,* ALGERNON *enters.*

ALGERNON   Did you hear what I was playing, Lane?

LANE   I didn't think it polite to listen, sir.

ALGERNON   I'm sorry for that, for your sake. I don't play accurately —any one can play accurately—but I play with wonderful expression. As far as the piano is concerned, sentiment is my forte. I keep science for Life.

LANE   Yes, sir.

ALGERNON   And, speaking of the science of Life, have you got the cucumber sandwiches cut for Lady Bracknell?

LANE   Yes, sir. [*Hands them on a salver.*]

ALGERNON [*inspects them, takes two, and sits down on the sofa*] Oh! . . . by the way, Lane, I see from your book that on Thursday night, when Lord Shoreman and Mr. Worthing were dining with me, eight bottles of champagne are entered as having been consumed.

LANE   Yes, sir; eight bottles and a pint.

ALGERNON   Why is it that at a bachelor's establishment the servants invariably drink the champagne? I ask merely for information.

LANE   I attribute it to the superior quality of the wine, sir. I have often observed that in married households the champagne is rarely of a first-rate brand.

---

1. Half-Moon Street runs north from Piccadilly near Hyde Park. Like many of the addresses in the play, it is in Mayfair, a very fashionable section of London.

ALGERNON   Good heavens! Is marriage so demoralizing as that?

LANE   I believe it is a very pleasant state, sir. I have had very little experience of it myself up to the present. I have only been married once. That was in consequence of a misunderstanding between myself and a young person.

ALGERNON [*languidly*]   I don't know that I am much interested in your family life, Lane.

LANE   No, sir; it is not a very interesting subject. I never think of it myself.

ALGERNON   Very natural, I am sure. That will do, Lane, thank you.

LANE   Thank you, sir. [*Goes out.*]

ALGERNON   Lane's views on marriage seem somewhat lax. Really, if the lower orders don't set us a good example, what on earth is the use of them? They seem, as a class, to have absolutely no sense of moral responsiblity.

Enter LANE.

LANE   Mr. Ernest Worthing.

Enter JACK. LANE *goes out.*

ALGERNON   How are you, my dear Ernest? What brings you up to town?

JACK   Oh, pleasure, pleasure! What else should bring one anywhere? Eating as usual, I see, Algy!

ALGERNON [*stiffly*]   I believe it is customary in good society to take some slight refreshment at five o'clock. Where have you been since last Thursday?

JACK [*sitting down on the sofa*]   In the country.

ALGERNON   What on earth do you do there?

JACK [*pulling off his gloves*]   When one is in town one amuses oneself. When one is in the country one amuses other people. It is excessively boring.

ALGERNON   And who are the people you amuse?

JACK [*airily*]   Oh, neighbors, neighbors.

ALGERNON   Got nice neighbors in your part of Shropshire?

JACK   Perfectly horrid! Never speak to one of them.

ALGERNON   How immensely you must amuse them! [*Goes over and takes sandwich.*] By the way, Shropshire is your county, is it not?

JACK   Eh? Shropshire? Yes, of course.[2] Hallo! Why all these cups? Why cucumber sandwiches? Why such reckless extravagance in one so young? Who is coming to tea?

ALGERNON   Oh! merely Aunt Augusta and Gwendolen.

JACK   How perfectly delightful!

ALGERNON   Yes, that is all very well; but I am afraid Aunt Augusta won't quite approve of your being here.

JACK   May I ask why?

2. As we learn later, Jack's country place is in Hertfordshire, to the north of London. He is attempting to deceive Algernon by giving a false location to the west, on the Welsh border.

ALGERNON   My dear fellow, the way you flirt with Gwendolen is perfectly disgraceful. It is almost as bad as the way Gwendolen flirts with you.

JACK   I am in love with Gwendolen. I have come up to town expressly to propose to her.

ALGERNON   I thought you had come up for pleasure? . . . I call that business.

JACK   How utterly unromantic you are!

ALGERNON   I really don't see anything romantic in proposing. It is very romantic to be in love. But there is nothing romantic about a definite proposal. Why, one may be accepted. One usually is, I believe. Then the excitement is all over. The very essence of romance is uncertainty. If ever I get married, I'll certainly try to forget the fact.

JACK   I have no doubt about that, dear Algy. The Divorce Court was specially invented for people whose memories are so curiously constituted.

ALGERNON   Oh! there is no use speculating on that subject. Divorces are made in Heaven—

> JACK *puts out his hand to take a sandwich.* ALGERNON *at once interferes.*

Please don't touch the cucumber sandwiches. They are ordered specially for Aunt Augusta. [*Takes one and eats it.*]

JACK   Well, you have been eating them all the time.

ALGERNON   That is quite a different matter. She is my aunt. [*Takes plate from below.*] Have some bread and butter. The bread and butter is for Gwendolen. Gwendolen is devoted to bread and butter.

JACK   [*advancing to table and helping himself*]   And very good bread and butter it is too.

ALGERNON   Well, my dear fellow, you need not eat as if you were going to eat it all. You behave as if you were married to her already. You are not married to her already, and I don't think you ever will be.

JACK   Why on earth do you say that?

ALGERNON   Well, in the first place, girls never marry the men they flirt with. Girls don't think it right.

JACK   Oh, that is nonsense!

ALGERNON   It isn't. It is a great truth. It accounts for the extraordinary number of bachelors that one sees all over the place. In the second place, I don't give my consent.

JACK   Your consent!

ALGERNON   My dear fellow, Gwendolen is my first cousin. And before I allow you to marry her, you will have to clear up the whole question of Cecily. [*Rings bell.*]

JACK   Cecily! What on earth do you mean? What do you mean, Algy, by Cecily? I don't know any one of the name of Cecily.

Enter LANE.

ALGERNON   Bring me that cigarette case Mr. Worthing left in the smoking-room the last time he dined here.

LANE   Yes, sir. [*Goes out.*]

JACK   Do you mean to say you have had my cigarette case all this time? I wish to goodness you had let me know. I have been writing frantic letters to Scotland Yard[3] about it. I was very nearly offering a large reward.

ALGERNON   Well, I wish you would offer one. I happen to be more then usually hard up.

JACK   There is no good offering a large reward now that the thing is found.

> Enter LANE *with the cigarette case on a salver.* ALGERNON *takes it at once.* LANE *goes out.*

ALGERNON   I think that is rather mean of you. Ernest, I must say. [*Opens case and examines it.*] However, it makes no matter, for now that I look at the inscription inside, I find that the thing isn't yours after all.

JACK   Of course it's mine. [*Moving to him.*] You have seen me with it a hundred times, and you have no right whatsoever to read what is written inside. It is a very ungentlemanly thing to read a private cigarette case.

ALGERNON   Oh! it is absurd to have a hard and fast rule about what one should read and what one shouldn't. More than half of modern culture depends on what one shouldn't read.

JACK   I am quite aware of the fact, and I don't propose to discuss modern culture. It isn't the sort of thing one should talk of in private. I simply want my cigarette case back.

ALGERNON   Yes; but this isn't your cigarette case. This cigarette case is a present from someone of the name of Cecily, and you said you didn't know anyone of that name.

JACK   Well, if you want to know, Cecily happens to be my aunt.

ALGERNON   Your aunt!

JACK   Yes. Charming old lady she is, too. Lives at Tunbridge Wells.[4] Just give it back to me, Algy.

ALGERNON   [*retreating to back of sofa*]   But why does she call herself little Cecily if she is your aunt and lives at Tunbridge Wells. [*Reading.*] "From little Cecily with her fondest love."

JACK   [*moving to sofa and kneeling upon it*]   My dear fellow, what on earth is there in that? Some aunts are tall, some aunts are not tall. That is a matter that surely an aunt may be allowed to decide for herself. You seem to think that every aunt should be exactly like your aunt! That is absurd. For Heaven's sake give me back my cigarette case. [*Follows* ALGERNON *round the room.*]

ALGERNON   Yes. But why does your aunt call you her uncle? "From little Cecily, with her fondest love to her dear Uncle Jack." There is no objection. I admit, to an aunt being a small aunt, but why an

3. The headquarters of the London Metropolitan Police are in Scotland Yard, near the Houses of Parliament.   4. Tunbridge Wells is a resort town in Kent, to the southeast of London.

aunt, no matter what her size may be, should call her own nephew her uncle, I can't quite make out. Beside, your name isn't Jack at all; it is Ernest.

JACK   It isn't Ernest; it's Jack.

ALGERNON   You have always told me it was Ernest. I have introduced you to everyone as Ernest. You answer to the name of Ernest. You look as if your name was Ernest. You are the most earnest-looking person I ever saw in my life. It is perfectly absurd your saying that your name isn't Ernest. It's on your cards. Here is one of them. [*Taking it from case.*] "Mr. Ernest Worthing, B.4, The Albany."⁵ I'll keep this as a proof that your name is Ernest if ever you attempt to deny it to me, or to Gwendolen, or to any one else. [*Puts the card in his pocket.*]

JACK   Well, my name is Ernest in town and Jack in the country, and the cigarette case was given to me in the country.

ALGERNON   Yes, but that does not account for the fact that your small Aunt Cecily, who lives at Tunbridge Wells, calls you her dear uncle. Come, old boy, you had much better have the thing out at once.

JACK   My dear Algy, you talk exactly as if you were a dentist. It is very vulgar to talk like a dentist when one isn't a dentist. It produces a false impression.

ALGERNON   Well, that is exactly what dentists always do. Now, go on! Tell me the whole thing. I may mention that I have always suspected you of being a confirmed and secret Bunburyist, and I am quite sure of it now.

JACK   Bunburyist? What on earth do you mean by a Bunburyist?

ALGERNON   I'll reveal to you the meaning of that incomparable expression as soon as you are kind enough to inform me why you are Ernest in town and Jack in the country.

JACK   Well, produce my cigarette case first.

ALGERNON   Here it is. [*Hands cigarette case.*] Now produce your explanation, and pray make it improbable. [*Sits on sofa.*]

JACK   My dear fellow, there is nothing improbable about my explanation at all. In fact it's perfectly ordinary. Old Mr. Thomas Cardew, who adopted me when I was a little boy, made me in his will guardian to his granddaughter, Miss Cecily Cardew. Cecily, who addresses me as her uncle from motives of respect that you could not possibly appreciate, lives at my place in the country under the charge of her admirable governess, Miss Prism.

ALGERNON   Where is that place in the country, by the way?

JACK   That is nothing to you, dear boy. You are not going to be invited. . . . I may tell you candidly that the place is not in Shropshire.

ALGERNON   I suspected that, my dear fellow! I have Bunburyed all over Shropshire on two separate occasions. Now, go on. Why are you Ernest in town and Jack in the country?

JACK   My dear Algy, I don't know whether you will be able to understand my real motives. You are hardly serious enough. When

5. An apartment building for single gentlemen on Piccadilly, to the east of Algernon's flat.

one is placed in the position of guardian, one has to adopt a very high moral tone on all subjects. It's one's duty to do so. And as a high moral tone can hardly be said to conduce very much to either one's health or one's happiness, in order to get up to town I have always pretended to have a younger brother of the name of Ernest, who lives in the Albany, and gets into the most dreadful scrapes. That, my dear Algy, is the whole truth pure and simple.

ALGERNON The truth is rarely pure and never simple. Modern life would be very tedious if it were either, and modern literature a complete impossibility!

JACK That wouldn't be at all a bad thing.

ALGERNON Literary criticism is not your forte, my dear fellow. Don't try it. You should leave that to people who haven't been at a University. They do it so well in the daily papers. What you really are is a Bunburyist. I was quite right in saying you were a Bunburyist. You are one of the most advanced Bunburyists I know.

JACK What on earth do you mean?

ALGERNON You have invented a very useful young brother called Ernest, in order that you may be able to come up to town as often as you like. I have invented an invaluable permanent invalid called Bunbury, in order that I may be able to go down into the country whenever I choose. Bunbury is perfectly invaluable. If it wasn't for Bunbury's extraordinary bad health, for instance, I wouldn't be able to dine with you at Willis's[6] tonight, for I have been really engaged to Aunt Augusta for more than a week.

JACK I haven't asked you to dine with me anywhere tonight.

ALGERNON I know. You are absurdly careless about sending out invitations. It is very foolish of you. Nothing annoys people so much as not receiving invitations.

JACK You had much better dine with your Aunt Augusta.

ALGERNON I haven't the smallest intention of doing anything of the kind. To begin with, I dined there on Monday, and once a week is quite enough to dine with one's relations. In the second place, whenever I do dine there I am always treated as a member of the family, and sent down with either no woman at all, or two. In the third place, I know perfectly well whom she will place me next to, tonight. She will place me next to Mary Farquhar, who always flirts with her own husband across the dinner table. That is not very pleasant. Indeed, it is not even decent . . . and that sort of thing is enormously on the increase. The amount of women in London who flirt with their own husbands is perfectly scandalous. It looks so bad. It is simply washing one's clean linen in public. Besides, now that I know you to be a confirmed Bunburyist I naturally want to talk to you about Bunburying. I want to tell you the rules.

JACK I'm not a Bunburyist at all. If Gwendolen accepts me, I am going to kill my brother, indeed I think I'll kill him in any case. Cecily is a little too much interested in him. It is rather a bore. So I am going to get rid of Ernest. And I strongly advise you to

6. A well-known establishment for dining on King Street, off St. James's Street and quite near Piccadilly.

do the same with Mr. . . . with your invalid friend who has the absurd name.

ALGERNON   Nothing will induce me to part with Bunbury, and if you ever get married, which seems to me extremely problematic, you will be very glad to know Bunbury. A man who marries without knowing Bunbury has a very tedious time of it.

JACK   That is nonsense. If I marry a charming girl like Gwendolen, and she is the only girl I every saw in my life that I would marry, I certainly won't want to know Bunbury.

ALGERNON   Then your wife will. You don't seem to realize, that in married life three is company and two is none.

JACK [*sententiously*]   That, my dear young friend, is the theory that the corrupt French Drama has been propounding for the last fifty years.[7]

ALGERNON   Yes! and that the happy English home has proved in half the time.

JACK   For heaven's sake, don't try to be cynical. It's perfectly easy to be cynical.

ALGERNON   My dear fellow, it isn't easy to be anything nowadays. There's such a lot of beastly competition about.

The sound of an electric bell is heard.

Ah! that must be Aunt Augusta, Only relatives, or creditors, ever ring in that Wagnerian manner.[8] Now, if I get her out of the way for ten minutes, so that you can have an opportunity for proposing to Gwendolen, may I dine with you tonight at Willis's?

JACK   I suppose so, if you want to.

ALGERNON   Yes, but you must be serious about it. I hate people who are not serious about meals. It is so shallow of them.

Enter LANE.

LANE   Lady Bracknell and Miss Fairfax.

ALGERNON *goes forward to meet them. Enter* LADY BRACKNELL *and* GWENDOLEN.

LADY BRACKNELL   Good afternoon, dear Algernon, I hope you are behaving very well.

ALGERNON   I'm feeling very well, Aunt Augusta.

LADY BRACKNELL   That's not quite the same thing. In fact the two things rarely go together. [*Sees* JACK *and bows to him with icy coldness.*]

ALGERNON [*to* GWENDOLEN]   Dear me, you are smart!

7. Beginning in the middle of the 19th century, such diverse forces as the theatrical sensationalism of Eugene Scribe (1791–1861) and Victorien Sardou (1832–1908) and the movement toward realism in Alexandre Dumas *fils* (1824–1895) and Emil Augier (1820–1889) produced plays dealing with subjects such as adultery, prostitution, and illegitimacy. The heavily censored English theater either avoided such subjects or dealt with them more circumspectly.

8. Many earlier hearers of the music of Richard Wagner found it extremely loud and, consequently, peremptory in demanding attention.

GWENDOLEN   I am always smart! Am I not, Mr. Worthing?

JACK   You're quite perfect, Miss Fairfax.

GWENDOLEN   Oh! I hope I am not that. I would leave no room for developments, and I intend to develop in many directions.

GWENDOLEN *and* JACK *sit down together in the corner.*

LADY BRACKNELL   I'm sorry if we are a little late, Algernon, but I was obliged to call on dear Lady Harbury. I hadn't been there since her poor husband's death. I never saw a woman so altered; she looks quite twenty years younger. And now I'll have a cup of tea and one of those nice cucumber sandwiches you promised me.

ALGERNON   Certainly, Aunt Augusta. [*Goes over to tea-table.*]

LADY BRACKNELL   Won't you come and sit here, Gwendolen?

GWENDOLEN   Thanks, mamma, I'm quite comfortable where I am.

ALGERNON [*picking up empty plate in horror*]   Good heavens! Lane! Why are there no cucumber sandwiches? I ordered them specially.

LANE [*gravely*]   There were no cucumbers in the market this morning, sir. I went down twice.

ALGERNON.   No cucumbers!

LANE   No, sir. Not even for ready money.

ALGERNON   That will do, Lane, thank you.

LANE   Thank you, sir. [*Goes out.*]

ALGERNON   I am greatly distressed, Aunt Augusta, about there being no cucumbers, not even for ready money.

LADY BRACKNELL   It really makes no matter, Algernon. I had some crumpets with Lady Harbury, who seems to me to be living entirely for pleasure now.

ALGERNON   I hear her hair has turned quite gold from grief.

LADY BRACKNELL   It certainly has changed its color. From what cause I, of course, cannot say.

ALGERNON *crosses and hands tea.*

Thank you. I've quite a treat for you tonight, Algernon. I am going to send you down with Mary Farquhar. She is such a nice woman, and so attentive to her husband. It's delightful to watch them.

ALGERNON   I am afraid, Aunt Augusta, I shall have to give up the pleasure of dining with you tonight after all.

LADY BRACKNELL [*frowning*]   I hope not, Algernon. It would put my table completely out. Your uncle would have to dine upstairs. Fortunately he is accustomed to that.

ALGERNON   It is a great bore, and, I need hardly say, a terrible disappointment to me, but the fact is I have just had a telegram to say that my poor friend Bunbury is very ill again. [*Exchanges glances with* JACK.] They seem to think I should be with him.

LADY BRACKNELL   It is very strange. This Mr. Bunbury seems to suffer from curiously bad health.

ALGERNON   Yes; poor Bunbury is a dreadful invalid.

LADY BRACKNELL   Well, I must say, Algernon, that I think it is high

time that Mr. Bunbury made up his mind whether he was going to
live or to die. This shilly-shallying with the question is absurd. Nor
do I in any way approve of the modern sympathy with invalids. I
consider it morbid. Illness of any kind is hardly a thing to be
encouraged in others. Health is the primary duty of life. I am
always telling that to your poor uncle, but he never seems to take
much notice . . . as far as any improvement in his ailments goes. I
should be much obliged if you would ask Mr. Bunbury, from me,
to be kind enough not to have a relapse on Saturday, for I rely
on you to arrange my music for me. It is my last reception, and one
wants something that will encourage conversation, particularly at
the end of the season when everyone has practically said whatever
they had to say, which, in most cases, was probably not much.

ALGERNON   I'll speak to Bunbury, Aunt Augusta, if he is still conscious, and I think I can promise you he'll be all right by Saturday.
Of course the music is a great difficulty. You see, if one plays good
music, people don't listen, and if one plays bad music, people don't
talk. But I'll run over the program I've drawn out, if you will
kindly come into the next room for a moment.

LADY BRACKNELL   Thank you, Algernon. It is very thoughtful of you.
[*Rising, and following* ALGERNON.] I'm sure the program will be
delightful, after a few expurgations. French songs I cannot possibly
allow. People always seem to think that they are improper, and
either look shocked, which is vulgar, or laugh, which is worse.
But German sounds a thoroughly respectable language, and, indeed
I believe is so. Gwendolen, you will accompany me.

GWENDOLEN   Certainly, mamma.

LADY BRACKNELL *and* ALGERNON *go into the music-room;*
GWENDOLEN *remains behind.*

JACK   Charming day it has been, Miss Fairfax.

GWENDOLEN   Pray don't talk to me about weather, Mr. Worthing.
Whenever people talk to me about the weather, I always feel quite
certain that they mean something else. And that makes me so
nervous.

JACK   I do mean something else.

GWENDOLEN   I thought so. In fact, I am never wrong.

JACK   And I would like to be allowed to take advantage of Lady
Bracknell's temporary absence . . .

GWENDOLEN   I would certainly advise you to do so. Mamma has a
way of coming back suddenly into a room that I have often had to
speak to her about.

JACK [*nervously*]   Miss Fairfax, ever since I met you I have admired
you more than any girl . . . I have ever met since . . . I met you.

GWENDOLEN   Yes, I am quite aware of the fact. And I often wish
that in public, at any rate, you had been more demonstrative. For
me you have always had an irresistible fascination. Even before I
met you I was far from indifferent to you.

JACK *looks at her in amazement.*

We live, as I hope you know, Mr. Worthing, in an age of ideals. The fact is constantly mentioned in the more expensive monthly magazines, and has reached the provincial pulpits, I am told; and my ideal has always been to love some one of the name of Ernest. There is something in that name that inspires absolute confidence. The moment Algernon first mentioned to me that he had a friend called Ernest, I knew I was destined to love you.

JACK   You really love me, Gwendolen?

GWENDOLEN   Passionately!

JACK   Darling! You don't know how happy you've made me.

GWENDOLEN   My own Ernest!

JACK   But you don't really mean to say that you couldn't love me if my name wasn't Ernest?

GWENDOLEN   But your name is Ernest.

JACK   Yes, I know it is. But supposing it was something else? Do you mean to say you couldn't love me then?

GWENDOLEN   [*glibly*]   Ah! that is clearly a metaphysical speculation, and like most metaphysical speculations has very little reference at all to the actual facts of real life, as we know them.

JACK   Personally, darling, to speak quite candidly, I don't much care about the name of Ernest. . . . I don't think the name suits me at all.

GWENDOLEN   It suits you perfectly. It is a divine name. It has a music of its own. It produces vibrations.

JACK   Well, really, Gwendolen, I must say that I think there are lots of other much nicer names. I think Jack, for instance, a charming name.

GWENDOLEN   Jack? . . . No, there is very little music in the name Jack, if any at all, indeed. It does not thrill. It produces absolutely no vibrations. . . . I have known several Jacks, and they all, without exception, were more than usually plain. Besides, Jack is a notorious domesticity for John! And I pity any woman who is married to a man called John. She would probably never be allowed to know the entrancing pleasure of a single moment's solitude. The only really safe name is Ernest.

JACK   Gwendolen, I must get christened at once—I mean we must get married at once. There is no time to be lost.

GWENDOLEN   Married, Mr. Worthing?

JACK   [*astounded*]   Well . . . surely. You know that I love you, and you led me to believe, Miss Fairfax, that you were not absolutely indifferent to me.

GWENDOLEN   I adore you. But you haven't proposed to me yet. Nothing has been said at all about marriage. The subject has not even been touched on.

JACK   Well . . . may I propose to you now?

GWENDOLEN   I think it would be an admirable opportunity. And to spare you any possible disappointment, Mr. Worthing, I think it only fair to tell you quite frankly beforehand that I am fully determined to accept you.

JACK   Gwendolen!

GWENDOLEN   Yes, Mr. Worthing, what have you got to say to me?

JACK   You know what I have got to say to you.

GWENDOLEN   Yes, but you don't say it.

JACK   Gwendolen, will you marry me? [*Goes on his knees.*]

GWENDOLEN   Of course I will, darling. How long you have been about it! I am afraid you have had very little experience in how to propose.

JACK   My own one, I have never loved any one in the world but you.

GWENDOLEN   Yes, but men often propose for practice. I know my brother Gerald does. All my girl-friends tell me so. What wonderfully blue eyes you have, Ernest! They are quite, quite blue. I hope you will always look at me just like that, especially when there are other people present.

> *Enter* LADY BRACKNELL.

LADY BRACKNELL   Mr. Worthing! Rise, sir, from this semi-recumbent posture. It is most indecorous.

GWENDOLEN   Mamma! [*He tries to rise; she restrains him.*] I must beg you to retire. This is no place for you. Besides, Mr. Worthing has not quite finished yet.

LADY BRACKNELL   Finished what, may I ask?

GWENDOLEN   I am engaged to Mr. Worthing, mamma.

> *They rise together.*

LADY BRACKNELL   Pardon me, you are not engaged to anyone. When you do become engaged to some one, I, or your father, should his health permit him, will inform you of the fact. An engagement should come on a young girl as a surprise, pleasant or unpleasant, as the case may be. It is hardly a matter that she could be allowed to arrange for herself. . . . And now I have a few questions to put to you, Mr. Worthing. While I am making these inquiries, you, Gwendolen, will wait for me below in the carriage.

GWENDOLEN [*reproachfully*]   Mamma!

LADY BRACKNELL   In the carriage, Gwendolen!

> GWENDOLEN *goes to the door. She and* JACK *blow kisses to each other behind* LADY BRACKNELL's *back.* LADY BRACKNELL *looks vaguely about as if she could not understand what the noise was. Finally turns around.*

Gwendolen, the carriage!

GWENDOLEN   Yes, mamma. [*Goes out, looking back at* JACK.]

LADY BRACKNELL [*sitting down*]   You can take a seat, Mr. Worthing. [*Looks in her pocket for notebook and pencil.*]

JACK   Thank you, Lady Bracknell, I prefer standing.

LADY BRACKNELL [*pencil and notebook in hand*]   I feel bound to tell you that you are not down on my list of eligible young men, although I have the same list as the dear Duchess of Bolton has. We work together, in fact. However, I am quite ready to enter

your name, should your answers be what a really affectionate
mother requires. Do you smoke?

JACK   Well, yes, I must admit I smoke.

LADY BRACKNELL   I am glad to hear it. A man should always have an
occupation of some kind. There are far too many idle men in
London as it is. How old are you?

JACK   Twenty-nine.

LADY BRACKNELL   A very good age to be married at. I have always
been of the opinion that a man who desires to get married should
know either everything or nothing. Which do you know?

JACK [*after some hestitation*]   I know nothing, Lady Bracknell.

LADY BRACKNELL   I am pleased to hear it. I do not approve of anything that tampers with natural ignorance. Ignorance is like a
delicate exotic fruit; touch it and the bloom is gone. The whole
theory of modern education is radically unsound. Fortunately in
England, at any rate, education produces no effect whatsoever. If
it did, it would prove a serious danger to the upper classes, and
probably lead to acts of violence in Grosvenor Square.⁹ What is
your income?

JACK   Between seven and eight thousand a year.¹

LADY BRACKNELL [*makes a note in her book*]   In land, or in
investments?

JACK   In investments, chiefly.

LADY BRACKNELL   That is satisfactory. What between the duties expected of one during one's lifetime, and the duties exacted from one
after one's death, land has ceased to be either a profit or a
pleasure. It gives one position, and prevents one from keeping it up.
That's all that can be said about land.

JACK   I have a country house with some land, of course, attached to
it, about fifteen hundred acres, I believe; but I don't depend on that
for my real income. In fact, as far as I can make out, the poachers
are the only people who make anything out of it.

LADY BRACKNELL   A country house! How many bedrooms? Well,
that point can be cleared up afterwards. You have a town house,
I hope? A girl with a simple, unspoiled nature, like Gwendolen,
could hardly be expected to reside in the country.

JACK   Well, I own a house in Belgrave Square,² but it is let by the
year to Lady Bloxham. Of course, I can get it back whenever I like,
at six months' notice.

LADY BRACKNELL   Lady Bloxham? I don't know her.

JACK   Oh, she goes about very little. She is a lady considerably advanced in years.

LADY BRACKNELL   Ah, nowadays that is no guarantee of respectability of character. What number in Belgrave Square?

JACK   149.

9. A fashionable location in Mayfair.
1. At the time of the play, the pound
was worth about $4.87. Jack's income was
thus about thirty thousand dollars a year,
a not inconsiderable figure when the New
York *Times* was three cents daily and five
cents on Sundays, when a can of corn was
on sale at nine cents, and when $45 would
purchase first-class passage from New York
to Amsterdam.
2. Belgrave Square is near the southeast corner of Hyde Park in Belgravia,
another fashionable section of London.

LADY BRACKNELL [*shaking her head*] The unfashionable side. I thought there was something. However, that could easily be altered.

JACK Do you mean the fashion, or the side?

LADY BRACKNELL [*sternly*] Both, if necessary, I presume. What are your politics?

JACK Well, I am afraid I really have none. I am a Liberal Unionist.

LADY BRACKNELL Oh, they count as Tories.[3] They dine with us. Or come in the evening, at any rate. Now to minor matters. Are your parents living?

JACK I have lost both my parents.

LADY BRACKNELL To lose one parent, Mr. Worthing, may be regarded as a misfortune; to lose both looks like carelessness. Who was your father? He was evidently a man of some wealth. Was he born in what the Radical papers call the purple of commerce, or did he rise from the ranks of the aristocracy?

JACK I am afraid I really don't know. That fact is, Lady Bracknell, I said I had lost my parents. It would be nearer the truth to say that my parents seem to have lost me. . . . I don't actually know who I am by birth. I was . . . well, I was found.

LADY BRACKNELL Found!

JACK The late Mr. Thomas Cardew, an old gentleman of a very charitable and kindly disposition, found me, and gave me the name of Worthing, because he happened to have a first-class ticket for Worthing in his pocket at the time. Worthing is a place in Sussex. It is a seaside resort.

LADY BRACKNELL Where did the charitable gentleman who had a first-class ticket for this seaside resort find you?

JACK [*gravely*] In a handbag.

LADY BRACKNELL A handbag?

JACK [*very seriously*] Yes, Lady Bracknell. I was in a handbag—a somewhat large, black leather handbag, with handles to it—an ordinary handbag in fact.

LADY BRACKNELL In what locality did this Mr. James, or Thomas, Cardew come across this ordinary handbag?

JACK In the cloakroom at Victoria Station.[4] It was given to him in mistake for his own.

LADY BRACKNELL The cloakroom at Victoria Station?

JACK Yes. The Brighton line.

LADY BRACKNELL The line is immaterial. Mr. Worthing, I confess I feel somewhat bewildered by what you have just told me. To be born, or at any rate bred, in a handbag, whether it had handles or not, seems to me to display a contempt for the ordinary decencies of family life that reminds one of the worst excesses of the French Revolution. And I presume you know what the unfortunate movement led to? As for the particular locality in which the handbag was found, a cloakroom at a railway station might serve to conceal a

3. Liberal Unionists were a late 19th-century political group which had split from the Liberal Party over home rule for Ireland. "Tories" were members of the Conservative Party—the latter was the more customary designation after the First Reform Bill of 1832.

4. Victoria Station is a major railroad terminus in London, particularly for trains to the south of England, including those going to the popular seaside resort of Brighton.

social indiscretion—has probably, indeed, been used for that purpose before now—but it could hardly be regarded as an assured basis for a recognized position in good society.

JACK   May I ask you then what you would advise me to do? I need hardly say I would do anything in the world to ensure Gwendolen's happiness.

LADY BRACKNELL   I would strongly advise you, Mr. Worthing, to try and acquire some relations as soon as possible, and to make a definite effort to produce at any rate one parent, of either sex, before the season is quite over.

JACK   Well, I don't see how I could possibly manage to do that. I can produce the handbag at any moment. It is in my dressing-room at home. I really think that should satisfy you, Lady Bracknell.

LADY BRACKNELL   Me, sir! What has it to do with me? You can hardly imagine that I and Lord Bracknell would dream of allowing our only daughter—a girl brought up with the utmost care—to marry into a cloakroom, and form an alliance with a parcel. Good morning, Mr. Worthing!

LADY BRACKNELL *sweeps out in majestic indignation.*

JACK   Good morning!

ALGERNON, *from the other room, strikes up the Wedding March.* JACK *looks perfectly furious, and goes to the door.*

For goodness' sake don't play that ghastly tune, Algy! How idiotic you are!

The music stops and ALGERNON *enters cheerily.*

ALGERNON   Didn't it go off all right, old boy? You don't mean to say Gwendolen refused you? I know it is a way she has. She is always refusing people. I think it is most ill-natured of her.

JACK   Oh, Gwendolen is as right as a trivet.[5] As far as she is concerned, we are engaged. Her mother is perfectly unbearable. Never met such a Gorgon.[6] . . . I don't really know what a Gorgon is like, but I am quite sure that Lady Bracknell is one. In any case, she is a monster, without being a myth, which is rather unfair. . . . I beg your pardon, Algy, I suppose I shouldn't talk about your own aunt in that way before you.

ALGERNON   My dear boy, I love hearing my relations abused. It is the only thing that makes me put up with them at all. Relations are simply a tedious pack of people, who haven't got the remotest knowledge of how to live, nor the smallest instinct about when to die.

JACK   Oh, that is nonsense!

5. A proverbial expression, referring to the solidity of a tripod on its three legs.
6. A mythological creature of horrible aspect, particularly because the Gorgon

had snakes in place of hair. According to myth, those who looked on a Gorgon were turned to stone by the experience.

ALGERNON It isn't!

JACK Well, I won't argue about the matter. You always want to argue about things.

ALGERNON That is exactly what things were originally made for.

JACK Upon my word, if I thought that, I'd shoot myself. . . . [*A pause.*] You don't think there is any chance of Gwendolen becoming like her mother in about a hundred and fifty years, do you, Algy?

ALGERNON All women become like their mothers. That is their tragedy. No man does. That's his.

JACK Is that clever?

ALGERNON It is perfectly phrased! and quite as true as any observation in civilized life should be.

JACK I am sick to death of cleverness. Everybody is clever nowadays. You can't go anywhere without meeting clever people. The thing has become an absolute public nuisance. I wish to goodness we had a few fools left.

ALGERNON We have.

JACK I should extremely like to meet them. What do they talk about?

ALGERNON The fools? Oh! about the clever people, of course.

JACK What fools.

ALGERNON By the way, did you tell Gwendolen the truth about your being Ernest in town, and Jack in the country?

JACK [*in a very patronizing manner*] My dear fellow, the truth isn't quite the sort of thing one tells to a nice, sweet, refined girl. What extraordinary ideas you have about the way to behave to a woman!

ALGERNON The only way to behave to a woman is to make love to her, if she is pretty, and to someone else, if she is plain.

JACK Oh, that is nonsense.

ALGERNON What about your brother? What about the profligate Ernest?

JACK Oh, before the end of the week I shall have got rid of him. I'll say he died in Paris of apoplexy. Lots of people die of apoplexy, quite suddenly, don't they?

ALGERNON Yes, but it's hereditary, my dear fellow. It's a sort of thing that runs in families. You had much better say a severe chill.

JACK You are sure a severe chill isn't hereditary, or anything of that kind?

ALGERNON Of course it isn't!

JACK Very well, then. My poor brother Ernest is carried off suddenly, in Paris, by a severe chill. That gets rid of him.

ALGERNON But I thought you said that . . . Miss Cardew was a little too much interested in your poor brother Ernest? Won't she feel his loss a good deal?

JACK Oh, that is all right. Cecily is not a silly romantic girl, I am glad to say. She has got a capital appetite, goes on long walks, and pays no attention at all to her lessons.

ALGERNON I would rather like to see Cecily.

JACK I will take very good care you never do. She is excessively pretty, and she is only just eighteen.

ALGERNON   Have you told Gwendolen yet that you have an excessively pretty ward who is only just eighteen?

JACK   Oh! one doesn't blurt these things out to people. Cecily and
Gwendolen are perfectly certain to be extremely great friends. I'll
bet you anything you like that half an hour after they have met,
they will be calling each other sister.

ALGERNON   Women only do that when they have called each other
a lot of other things first. Now, my dear boy, if we want to get a
good table at Willis's, we really must go and dress. Do you know
it is nearly seven?

JACK [*irritably*]   Oh! it always is nearly seven.

ALGERNON   Well, I'm hungry.

JACK   I never knew you when you weren't. . . .

ALGERNON   What shall we do after dinner? Go to a theatre?

JACK   Oh no! I loathe listening.

ALGERNON   Well, let us go to the Club?

JACK   Oh, no! I hate talking.

ALGERNON   Well, we might trot round to the Empire[7] at ten?

JACK   Oh, no! I can't bear looking at things. It is so silly.

ALGERNON   Well, what shall we do?

JACK   Nothing!

ALGERNON   It is awfully hard work doing nothing. However, I don't
mind hard work where there is no definite object of any kind.

Enter LANE.

LANE   Miss Fairfax.

Enter GWENDOLEN. LANE *goes out.*

ALGERNON   Gwendolen, upon my word!

GWENDOLEN   Algy, kindly turn your back. I have something very
particular to say to Mr. Worthing.

ALGERNON   Really, Gwendolen, I don't think I can allow this at all.

GWENDOLEN   Algy, you always adopt a strictly immoral attitude
towards life. You are not quite old enough to do that.

ALGERNON *retires to the fireplace.*

JACK   My own darling!

GWENDOLEN   Ernest, we may never be married. From the expression
on mamma's face I fear we never shall. Few parents nowadays pay
any regard to what their children say to them. The old-fashioned
respect for the young is fast dying out. Whatever influence I ever
had over mamma, I lost at the age of three. But although she may
prevent us from becoming man and wife, and I may marry someone
else, and marry often, nothing that she can possibly do can alter my
eternal devotion to you.

7. The Empire Theatre of Varieties, a music hall on Leicester Square.

JACK   Dear Gwendolen!

GWENDOLEN   The story of your romantic origin, as related to me by
mamma, with unpleasing comments, has naturally stirred the
deeper fibres of my nature. Your Christian name has an irresistible
fascination. The simplicity of your character makes you exquisitely
incomprehensible to me. Your town ·address at the Albany I have.
What is your address in the country?

JACK   The Manor House, Woolton, Hertfordshire.

> ALGERNON, *who has been carefully listening, smiles to himself,
> and writes the address on his shirt-cuff. Then picks up the
> Railway Guide.*

GWENDOLEN   There is a good postal service, I suppose? It may be
necessary to do something desperate. That of course will require
serious consideration. I will communicate with you daily.

JACK   My own one!

GWENDOLEN   How long do you remain in town?

JACK   Till Monday.

GWENDOLEN   Good! Algy, you may turn round now.

ALGERNON   Thanks, I've turned round already.

GWENDOLEN   You may also ring the bell.

JACK   You will let me see you to your carriage, my own darling?

GWENDOLEN   Certainly.

JACK   [*to* LANE, *who now enters*]   I will see Miss Fairfax out.

LANE   Yes, sir.

> JACK *and* GWENDOLEN *go off.* LANE *presents several letters on a
> salver to* ALGERNON. *It is to be surmised that they are bills, as*
> ALGERNON, *after looking at the envelopes, tears them up.*

ALGERNON   A glass of sherry, Lane.

LANE   Yes, sir.

ALGERNON   Tomorrow, Lane, I'm going Bunburying.

LANE   Yes, sir.

ALGERNON   I shall probably not be back till Monday. You can put up
my dress clothes, my smoking jacket, and all the Bunbury suits . . .

LANE   Yes, sir. [*Handing sherry.*]

ALGERNON   I hope tomorrow will be a fine day, Lane.

LANE   It never is, sir.

ALGERNON   Lane, you're a perfect pessimist.

LANE   I do my best to give satisfaction, sir.

> *Enter* JACK. LANE *goes off.*

JACK   There's a sensible, intellectual girl; the only girl I ever cared
for in my life.

> ALGERNON *is laughing immoderately.*

What on earth are you so amused at?

ALGERNON   Oh, I'm a little anxious about poor Bunbury, that is all.

JACK   If you don't take care, your friend Bunbury will get you into a serious scrape some day.

ALGERNON   I love scrapes. They are the only things that are never serious.

JACK   Oh, that's nonsense, Algy. You never talk anything but nonsense.

ALGERNON   Nobody ever does.

JACK *looks indignantly at him, and leaves the room.* ALGERNON *lights a cigarette, reads his shirt-cuff, and smiles.*

Act 2

Garden at the Manor House. A flight of gray stone steps leads up to the house. The garden, an old-fashioned one, full of roses. Time of year, July. Basket chairs, and a table covered with books, are set under a large yew-tree.

MISS PRISM *discovered seated at the table.* CECILY *is at the back, watering flowers.*

MISS PRISM [*calling*]   Cecily, Cecily! Surely such a utilitarian occupation as the watering of flowers is rather Moulton's duty than yours? Especially at a moment when intellectual pleasures await you. Your German grammar is on the table. Pray open it at page fifteen. We will repeat yesterday's lesson.

CECILY [*coming over very slowly*]   But I don't like German. It isn't at all a becoming language. I know perfectly well that I look quite plain after my German lesson.

MISS PRISM   Child, you know how anxious your guardian is that you should improve yourself in every way. He laid particular stress on your German, as he was leaving for town yesterday. Indeed, he always lays stress on your German when he is leaving for town.

CECILY   Dear Uncle Jack is so very serious! Sometimes he is so serious that I think he cannot be quite well.

MISS PRISM [*drawing herself up*]   Your guardian enjoys the best of health, and his gravity of demeanor is especially to be commended in one so comparatively young as he is. I know no one who has a higher sense of duty and responsibility.

CECILY   I suppose that is why he often looks a little bored when we three are together.

MISS PRISM   Cecily! I am surprised at you. Mr. Worthing has many troubles in his life. Idle merriment and triviality would be out of place in his conversation. You must remember his constant anxiety about that unfortunate young man, his brother.

CECILY   I wish Uncle Jack would allow that unfortunate young man, his brother, to come down here sometimes. We might have a good influence over him, Miss Prism. I am sure you certainly would. You know German, and geology, and things of that kind influence a man very much. [CECILY *begins to write in her diary.*]

MISS PRISM [*shaking her head*]   I do not think that even I could produce any effect on a character that according to his own brother's
admission is irretrievably weak and vacillating. Indeed I am not
sure that I would desire to reclaim him. I am not in favor of
this modern mania for turning bad people into good people at
a moment's notice. As a man sows so let him reap. You must put
away your diary, Cecily. I really don't see why you should keep a
diary at all.

CECILY   I keep a diary in order to enter the wonderful secrets of my
life. If I didn't write them down, I should probably forget all about
them.

MISS PRISM   Memory, my dear Cecily, is the diary that we all carry
about with us.

CECILY   Yes, but it usually chronicles the things that have never happened, and couldn't possibly have happened. I believe that Memory
is responsible for nearly all the three-volume novels that Mudie
sends us.[8]

MISS PRISM   Do not speak slightingly of the three-volume novel,
Cecily. I wrote one myself in earlier days.

CECILY   Did you really, Miss Prism? How wonderfully clever you
are! I hope it did not end happily! I don't like novels that end
happily. They depress me so much.

MISS PRISM   The good ended happily, and the bad unhappily. That
is what Fiction means.

CECILY   I suppose so. But it seems very unfair. And was your novel
ever published?

MISS PRISM   Alas! no. The manuscript unfortunately was abandoned.

CECILY *starts.*

I used the word in the sense of lost or mislaid. To your work,
child, these speculations are profitless.

CECILY [*smiling*]   But I see dear Dr. Chasuble coming up through the
garden.

MISS PRISM [*rising and advancing*]   Dr. Chasuble! This is indeed a
pleasure.

Enter CANON CHASUBLE.

CHASUBLE   And how are we this morning? Miss Prism, you are, I
trust, well?

CECILY   Miss Prism has just been complaining of a slight headache. I
think it would do her so much good to have a short stroll with you
in the Park, Dr. Chasuble.

MISS PRISM   Cecily, I have not mentioned anything about a headache.

CECILY   No, dear Miss Prism, I know that, but I felt instinctively that
you had a headache. Indeed I was thinking about that, and not
about my German lesson, when the Rector came in.

8. From the 1860s to the 1880s most novels were published in three volumes. Because of the resultant price, most readers could not afford to buy copies and ob-tained them by subscription from lending libraries, of which Mudie's in London was by far the largest.

CHASUBLE   I hope, Cecily, you are not inattentive.

CECILY   Oh, I am afraid I am.

CHASUBLE   That is strange. Were I fortunate enough to be Miss Prism's pupil, I would hang upon her lips.

MISS PRISM *glares.*

I spoke metaphorically.—My metaphor was drawn from bees. Ahem! Mr. Worthing, I suppose, has not returned from town yet?

MISS PRISM   We do not expect him till Monday afternoon.

CHASUBLE   Ah yes, he usually likes to spend his Sunday in London. He is not one of those whose sole aim is enjoyment, as, by all accounts, that unfortunate young man his brother seems to be. But I must not disturb Egeria[9] and her pupil any longer.

MISS PRISM   Egeria? My name is Laetitia, Doctor.

CHASUBLE   [*bowing*] A classical allusion merely, drawn from the Pagan authors. I shall see you both no doubt at Evensong?

MISS PRISM   I think, dear, Doctor, I will have a stroll with you. I find I have a headache after all, and a walk might do it good.

CHASUBLE   With pleasure, Miss Prism, with pleasure. We might go as far as the schools and back.

MISS PRISM   That would be delightful. Cecily, you will read your Political Economy in my absence.[1] The chapter on the Fall of the Rupee you may omit. It is somewhat too sensational. Even these metallic problems have their melodramatic side. [*Goes down the garden with* DR. CHASUBLE.]

CECILY   [*picks up books and throws them back on table*] Horrid Political Economy! Horrid Geography! Horrid, horrid German!

Enter MERRIMAN *with a card on a salver.*

MERRIMAN   Mr. Ernest Worthing has just driven over from the station. He has brought his luggage with him.

CECILY   [*takes the card and reads it*] "Mr. Ernest Worthing, B.4, The Albany, W." Uncle Jack's brother! Did you tell him Mr. Worthing was in town?

MERRIMAN   Yes, Miss. He seemed very much disappointed. I mentioned that you and Miss Prism were in the garden. He said he was anxious to speak to you privately for a moment.

CECILY   Ask Mr. Ernest Worthing to come here. I suppose you had better talk to the housekeeper about a room for him.

MERRIMAN   Yes, Miss. [*Goes off.*]

CECILY   I have never met any really wicked person before. I feel rather frightened. I am so afraid he will look just like every one else.

Enter ALGERNON, *very gay and debonair.*

9. A nymph in classical mythology, famous as the wise counselor of Numa Pompilius, the second of the legendary kings of Rome.

1. Political Economy was a branch of social science which dealt with the reve-nues and general financial resources of nations. The term came into use at the beginning of the 17th century. In this century it has developed into the study we call Economics. The rupee is the currency unit of India.

He does!

ALGERNON [*raising his hat*]   You are my little cousin Cecily, I'm sure.

CECILY   You are under some strange mistake. I am not little. In fact, I believe I am more than usually tall for my age.

ALGERNON *is rather taken aback.*

But I am your cousin Cecily. You, I see from your card, are Uncle Jack's brother, my cousin Ernest, my wicked cousin Ernest.

ALGERNON   Oh! I am not really wicked at all, Cousin Cecily. You mustn't think that I am wicked.

CECILY   If you are not, then you have certainly been deceiving us all in a very inexcusable manner. I hope you have not been leading a double life, pretending to be wicked and being really good all the time. That would be hypocrisy.

ALGERNON [*looks at her in amazement*]   Oh! Of course I have been rather reckless.

CECILY   I am glad to hear it.

ALGERNON   In fact, now you mention the subject, I have been very bad in my own small way.

CECILY   I don't think you should be so proud of that, though I am sure it must have been very pleasant.

ALGERNON   It is much pleasanter being here with you.

CECILY   I can't understand how you are here at all. Uncle Jack won't be back till Monday afternoon.

ALGERNON   That is a great disappointment. I am obliged to go up by the first train on Monday morning. I have a business appointment that I am anxious . . . to miss!

CECILY   Couldn't you miss it anywhere but in London?

ALGERNON   No: the appointment is in London.

CECILY   Well, I know, of course, how important it is not to keep a business engagement, if one wants to retain any sense of the beauty of life, but still I think you had better wait till Uncle Jack arrives. I know he wants to speak to you about your emigrating.

ALGERNON   About my what?

CECILY   Your emigrating. He has gone up to buy your outfit.

ALGERNON   I certainly wouldn't let Jack buy my outfit. He has no taste in neckties at all.

CECILY   I don't think you will require neckties. Uncle Jack is sending you to Australia.

ALGERNON   Australia! I'd sooner die.

CECILY   Well, he said at dinner on Wednesday night, that you would have to choose between this world, the next world, and Australia.

ALGERNON   Oh, well! The accounts I have received of Australia and the next world are not particularly encouraging. This world is good enough for me, Cousin Cecily.

CECILY   Yes, but are you good enough for it?

ALGERNON   I'm afraid I'm not that. That is why I want you to reform me. You might make that your mission, if you don't mind, Cousin Cecily.

CECILY   I'm afraid I've no time, this afternoon.

ALGERNON   Well, would you mind my reforming myself this afternoon?

CECILY   It is rather Quixotic of you. But I think you should try.

ALGERNON   I will. I feel better already.

CECILY   You are looking a little worse.

ALGERNON   That is because I am hungry.

CECILY   How thoughtless of me. I should have remembered that when one is going to lead an entirely new life, one requires regular and wholesome meals. Won't you come in?

ALGERNON   Thank you. Might I have a buttonhole first?[2] I never have any appetite unless I have a buttonhole first.

CECILY   A Maréchal Niel? [*Picks up scissors.*]

ALGERNON   No, I'd sooner have a pink rose.

CECILY   Why? [*Cuts a flower.*]

ALGERNON   Because you are like a pink rose, Cousin Cecily.

CECILY   I don't think it can be right for you to talk to me like that. Miss Prism never says such things to me.

ALGERNON   Then Miss Prism is a shortsighted old lady.

CECILY *puts the rose in his buttonhole.*

You are the prettiest girl I ever saw.

CECILY   Miss Prism says that all good looks are a snare.

ALGERNON   They are a snare that every sensible man would like to be caught in.

CECILY   Oh, I don't think I would care to catch a sensible man. I shouldn't know what to talk to him about.

They pass into the house. MISS PRISM *and* DR. CHASUBLE *return.*

MISS PRISM   You are too much alone, dear Dr. Chasuble. You should get married. A misanthrope I can understand—a womanthrope, never!

CHASUBLE [*with a scholar's shudder*]   Believe me, I do not deserve so neologistic a phrase. The precept as well as the practice of the Primitive Church was distinctly against matrimony.

MISS PRISM [*sententiously*]   That is obviously the reason why the Primitive Church has not lasted up to the present day. And you do not seem to realize, dear Doctor, that by persistently remaining single, a man converts himself into a permanent public temptation. Men should be more careful; this very celibacy leads weaker vessels astray.

CHASUBLE   But is a man not equally attractive when married?

MISS PRISM   No married man is ever attractive except to his wife.

CHASUBLE   And often, I've been told, not even to her.

MISS PRISM   That depends on the intellectual sympathies of the woman. Maturity can always be depended on. Ripeness can be trusted. Young women are green.

2. A "buttonhole" is a flower to be worn on the lapel of a man's coat, in this case a popular yellow rose of the period. Hardier varieties are available now, and the Maréchal Niel is seldom grown.

DR. CHASUBLE *starts.*

I spoke horticulturally. My metaphor was drawn from fruits. But where is Cecily?

CHASUBLE   Perhaps she followed us to the schools.

Enter JACK *slowly from the back of the garden. He is dressed in the deepest mourning, with crepe hatband and black gloves.*

MISS PRISM   Mr. Worthing!

CHASUBLE   Mr. Worthing?

MISS PRISM   This is indeed a surprise. We did not look for you till Monday afternoon.

JACK [*shakes* MISS PRISM's *hand in a tragic manner*]   I have returned sooner than I expected. Dr. Chasuble, I hope you are well?

CHASUBLE   Dear Mr. Worthing, I trust this garb of woe does not betoken some terrible calamity?

JACK   My brother.

MISS PRISM   More shameful debts and extravagance?

CHASUBLE   Still leading his life of pleasure?

JACK [*shaking his head*]   Dead!

CHASUBLE   Your brother Ernest dead?

JACK   Quite dead.

MISS PRISM   What a lesson for him! I trust he will profit by it.

CHASUBLE   Mr. Worthing, I offer you my sincere condolence. You have at least the consolation of knowing that you were always the most generous and forgiving of brothers.

JACK   Poor Ernest! He had many faults, but it is a sad, sad blow.

CHASUBLE   Very sad indeed. Were you with him at the end?

JACK   No. He died abroad; in Paris, in fact. I had a telegram last night from the manager of the Grand Hotel.

CHASUBLE   Was the cause of death mentioned?

JACK   A severe chill, it seems.

MISS PRISM   As a man sows, so shall he reap.

CHASUBLE [*raising his hand*]   Charity, dear Miss Prism, charity! None of us is perfect. I myself am peculiarly susceptible to drafts. Will the interment take place here?

JACK   No. He seems to have expressed a desire to be buried in Paris.

CHASUBLE   In Paris! [*Shakes his head.*] I fear that hardly points to any very serious state of mind at the last. You would no doubt wish me to make some slight allusion to this tragic domestic affliction next Sunday.

JACK *presses his hand convulsively.*

My sermon on the meaning of the manna in the wilderness can be adapted to almost any occasion, joyful, or, as in the present case, distressing.

All sigh.

I have preached it at harvest celebrations, christenings, confirmations, on days of humiliation and festal days. The last time I delivered it was in the Cathedral, as a charity sermon on behalf of the Society for the Prevention of Discontent among the Upper Orders. The Bishop, who was present, was much struck by some of the analogies I drew.

JACK Ah! that reminds me, you mentioned christenings, I think, Dr. Chasuble? I suppose you know how to christen all right?

DR. CHASUBLE *looks astounded.*

I mean, of course, you are continually christening, aren't you?

MISS PRISM It is, I regret to say, one of the Rector's most constant duties in this parish. I have often spoken to the poorer classes on the subject. But they don't seem to know what thrift is.

CHASUBLE But is there any particular infant in whom you are interested, Mr. Worthing? Your brother was, I believe, unmarried, was he not?

JACK Oh yes.

MISS PRISM [*bitterly*] People who live entirely for pleasure usually are.

JACK But it is not for any child, dear Doctor. I am very fond of children. No! the fact is, I would like to be christened myself, this afternoon, if you have nothing better to do.

CHASUBLE But surely, Mr. Worthing, you have been christened already?

JACK I don't remember anything about it.

CHASUBLE But have you any grave doubts on the subject?

JACK I certainly intend to have. Of course I don't know if the thing would bother you in any way, or if you think I am a little too old now.

CHASUBLE Not at all. The sprinkling, and, indeed, the immersion of adults is a perfectly canonical practice.

JACK Immersion!

CHASUBLE You need have no apprehensions. Sprinkling is all that is necessary, or indeed I think advisable. Our weather is so changeable. At what hour would you wish the ceremony performed?

JACK Oh, I might trot round about five if that would suit you.

CHASUBLE Perfectly, perfectly! In fact I have two similar ceremonies to perform at that time. A case of twins that occurred recently in one of the outlying cottages on your own estate. Poor Jenkins the carter, a most hard-working man.

JACK Oh! I don't see much fun in being christened along with other babies. It would be childish. Would half-past five do?

CHASUBLE Admirably! Admirably! [*Takes out watch.*] And now, dear Mr. Worthing, I will not intrude any longer into a house of sorrow. I would merely beg you not to be too much bowed down by grief. What seem to us bitter trials are often blessings in disguise.

MISS PRISM This seems to me a blessing of an extremely obvious kind.

Enter CECILY *from the house.*

CECILY   Uncle Jack! Oh, I am pleased to see you back. But what horrid clothes you have got on. Do go and change them.

MISS PRISM   Cecily!

CHASUBLE   My child! My child!

> CECILY *goes towards* JACK; *he kisses her brow in a melancholy manner.*

CECILY   What is the matter, Uncle Jack? Do look happy! You look as if you had toothache, and I have got such a surprise for you. Who do you think is in the dining-room? Your brother!

JACK   Who?

CECILY   Your brother Ernest. He arrived about half an hour ago.

JACK   What nonsense! I haven't got a brother.

CECILY   Oh, don't say that. However badly he may have behaved to you in the past he is still your brother. You couldn't be so heartless as to disown him. I'll tell him to come out. And you will shake hands with him, won't you, Uncle Jack? [*Runs back into the house.*]

CHASUBLE   These are very joyful tidings.

MISS PRISM   After we had all been resigned to his loss, his sudden return seems to me peculiarly distressing.

JACK   My brother is in the dining-room? I don't know what it all means. I think it is perfectly absurd.

> *Enter* ALGERNON *and* CECILY *hand in hand. They come slowly up to* JACK.

JACK   Good heavens! [*Motions* ALGERNON *away.*]

ALGERNON   Brother John, I have come down from town to tell you that I am very sorry for all the trouble I have given you, and that I intend to lead a better life in the future.

> JACK *glares at him and does not take his hand.*

CECILY   Uncle Jack, you are not going to refuse your own brother's hand?

JACK   Nothing will induce me to take his hand. I think his coming down here disgraceful. He knows perfectly well why.

CECILY   Uncle Jack, do be nice. There is some good in everyone. Ernest has just been telling me about his poor invalid friend Mr. Bunbury whom he goes to visit so often. And surely there must be much good in one who is kind to an invalid, and leaves the pleasures of London to sit by a bed of pain.

JACK   Oh! he has been talking about Bunbury, has he?

CECILY   Yes, he has told me all about poor Mr. Bunbury, and his terrible state of health.

JACK   Bunbury! Well, I won't have him to talk to you about Bunbury or about anything else. It is enough to drive one perfectly frantic.

ALGERNON   Of course I admit that the faults were all on my side. But I must say that I think that Brother John's coldness to me is peculiarly painful. I expected a more enthusiastic welcome, especially considering it is the first time I have come here.

CECILY   Uncle Jack, if you don't shake hands with Ernest I will never forgive you.

JACK   Never forgive me?

CECILY   Never, never, never!

JACK   Well, this is the last time I shall ever do it. [*Shakes hands with* ALGERNON *and glares.*]

CHASUBLE   It's pleasant, is it not, to see so perfect a reconciliation? I think we might leave the two brothers together.

MISS PRISM   Cecily, you will come with us.

CECILY   Certainly, Miss Prism. My little task of reconciliation is over.

CHASUBLE   You have done a beautiful action today, dear child.

MISS PRISM   We must not be premature in our judgments.

CECILY   I feel very happy.

They all go off except JACK *and* ALGERNON.

JACK   You young scoundrel, Algy, you must get out of this place as soon as possible. I don't allow any Bunburying here.

Enter MERRIMAN.

MERRIMAN   I have put Mr. Ernest's things in the room next to yours, sir. I suppose that is all right?

JACK   What?

MERRIMAN   Mr. Ernest's luggage, sir. I have unpacked it and put it in the room next to your own.

JACK   His luggage?

MERRIMAN   Yes sir. Three portmanteaus, a dressing-case, two hat-boxes, and a large luncheon-basket.

ALGERNON   I am afraid I can't stay more than a week this time.

JACK   Merriman, order the dogcart[3] at once. Mr. Ernest has been suddenly called back to town.

MERRIMAN   Yes, sir. [*Goes back into the house.*]

ALGERNON   What a fearful liar you are, Jack. I have not been called back to town at all.

JACK   Yes, you have.

ALGERNON   I haven't heard any one call me.

JACK   Your duty as a gentleman calls you back.

ALGERNON   My duty as a gentleman has never interfered with my pleasures in the smallest degree.

JACK   I can quite understand that.

ALGERNON   Well, Cecily is a darling.

JACK   You are not to talk of Miss Cardew like that. I don't like it.

ALGERNON   Well, I don't like your clothes. You look perfectly ridiculous in them. Why on earth don't you go up and change? It is perfectly childish to be in deep mourning for a man who is actually staying for a whole week with you in your house as a guest. I call it grotesque.

3. A light, two-wheeled carriage, usually drawn by one horse; it has two transverse seats positioned back to back.

JACK   You are certainly not staying with me for a whole week as a guest or anything else. You have got to leave . . . by the four-five train.

ALGERNON   I certainly won't leave you so long as you are in mourning. It would be most unfriendly. If I were in mourning you would stay with me, I suppose. I should think it very unkind if you didn't.

JACK   Well, will you go if I change my clothes?

ALGERNON   Yes, if you are not too long. I never saw anybody take so long to dress, and with such little result.

JACK   Well, at any rate, that is better than being always overdressed as you are.

ALGERNON   If I am occasionally a little overdressed, I make up for it by being always immensely overeducated.

JACK   Your vanity is ridiculous, your conduct an outrage, and your presence in my garden utterly absurd. However, you have got to catch the four-five, and I hope you will have a pleasant journey back to town. This Bunburying, as you call it, has not been a great success for you. [*Goes into the house.*]

ALGERNON   I think it has been a great success. I'm in love with Cecily, and that is everything.

> *Enter* CECILY *at the back of the garden. She picks up the can and begins to water the flowers.*

But I must see her before I go, and make arrangements for another Bunbury. Ah, there she is.

CECILY   Oh, I merely came back to water the roses. I thought you were with Uncle Jack.

ALGERNON   He's gone to order the dogcart for me.

CECILY   Oh, is he going to take you for a nice drive?

ALGERNON   He's going to send me away.

CECILY   Then have we got to part?

ALGERNON   I am afraid so. It's a very painful parting.

CECILY   It is always painful to part from people whom one has known for a very brief space of time. The absence of old friends one can endure with equanimity. But even a momentary separation from anyone to whom one has just been introduced is almost unbearable.

ALGERNON   Thank you.

> *Enter* MERRIMAN.

MERRIMAN   The dogcart is at the door, sir.

> ALGERNON *looks appealingly at* CECILY.

CECILY   It can wait, Merriman . . . for . . . five minutes.

MERRIMAN   Yes, miss. [*Exit.*]

ALGERNON   I hope, Cecily, I shall not offend you if I state quite frankly and openly that you seem to me to be in every way the visible personification of absolute perfection.

CECILY I think your frankness does you great credit, Ernest. If you will allow me, I will copy your remarks into my diary. [*Goes over to table and begins writing in diary*.]

ALGERNON Do you really keep a diary? I'd give anything to look at it. May I?

CECILY Oh no. [*Puts her hand over it*.] You see, it is simply a very young girl's record of her own thoughts and impressions, and consequently meant for publication. When it appears in volume form I hope you will order a copy. But pray, Ernest, don't stop. I delight in taking down from dictation. I have reached "absolute perfection." You can go on. I am quite ready for more.

ALGERNON [*somewhat taken aback*] Ahem! Ahem!

CECILY Oh, don't cough, Ernest. When one is dictating one should speak fluently and not cough. Besides, I don't know how to spell a cough. [*Writes as* ALGERNON *speaks*.]

ALGERNON [*speaking very rapidly*] Cecily, ever since I first looked upon your wonderful and incomparable beauty, I have dared to love you wildly, passionately, devotedly, hopelessly.

CECILY I don't think that you should tell me that you love me wildly, passionately, devotedly, hopelessly. Hopelessly doesn't seem to make much sense, does it?

ALGERNON Cecily.

Enter MERRIMAN.

MERRIMAN The dogcart is waiting, sir.

ALGERNON Tell it to come round next week, at the same hour.

MERRIMAN [*looks at* CECILY, *who makes no sign*]. Yes, sir. [MERRIMAN *retires*.]

CECILY Uncle Jack would be very much annoyed if he knew you were staying on till next week, at the same hour.

ALGERNON Oh, I don't care about Jack. I don't care for anybody in the whole world but you. I love you, Cecily. You will marry me, won't you?

CECILY You silly boy! Of course. Why, we have been engaged for the last three months.

ALGERNON For the last three months?

CECILY Yes, it will be exactly three months on Thursday.

ALGERNON But how did we become engaged?

CECILY Well, ever since dear Uncle Jack first confessed to us that he had a younger brother who was very wicked and bad, you of course have formed the chief topic of conversation between myself and Miss Prism. And of course a man who is much talked about is always very attractive. One feels there must be something in him, after all. I daresay it was foolish of me, but I fell in love with you, Ernest.

ALGERNON Darling. And when was the engagement actually settled?

CECILY On the 14th of February last. Worn out by your entire ignorance of my existence, I determined to end the matter one way or the other, and after a long struggle with myself I accepted you under this dear old tree here. The next day I bought this little ring in your name, and this is the little bangle with the true lovers' knot I promised you always to wear.

ALGERNON   Did I give you this? It's very pretty, isn't it?

CECILY   Yes, you've wonderfully good taste, Ernest. It's the excuse I've always given for your leading such a bad life. And this is the box in which I keep all your dear letters. [*Kneels at table, opens box, and produces letters tied up with blue ribbon.*]

ALGERNON   My letters! But, my own sweet Cecily, I have never written you any letters.

CECILY   You need hardly remind me of that, Ernest. I remember only too well that I was forced to write your letters for you. I wrote always three times a week, and sometimes oftener.

ALGERNON   Oh, do let me read them, Cecily?

CECILY   Oh, I couldn't possibly. They would make you far too conceited. [*Replaces box.*] The three you wrote me after I had broken off the engagement are so beautiful, and so badly spelled, that even now I can hardly read them without crying a little.

ALGERNON   But was our engagement ever broken off?

CECILY   Of course it was. On the 22nd of last March. You can see the entry if you like. [*Shows diary.*] "Today I broke off my engagement with Ernest. I feel it is better to do so. The weather still continues charming."

ALGERNON   But why on earth did you break it off? What had I done? I had done nothing at all. Cecily, I am very much hurt indeed to hear you broke it off. Particularly when the weather was so charming.

CECILY   It would hardly have been a really serious engagement if it hadn't been broken off at least once. But I forgave you before the week was out.

ALGERNON [*crossing to her, and kneeling*]   What a perfect angel you are, Cecily.

CECILY   You dear romantic boy. [*He kisses her, she puts her fingers through his hair.*]   I hope your hair curls naturally, does it?

ALGERNON   Yes darling, with a little help from others.

CECILY   I am so glad.

ALGERNON   You'll never break off our engagement again, Cecily?

CECILY   I don't think I could break it off now that I have actually met you. Besides, of course, there is the question of your name.

ALGERNON   Yes, of course. [*Nervously.*]

CECILY   You must not laugh at me, darling, but it had always been a girlish dream of mine to love some one whose name was Ernest.

     ALGERNON *rises,* CECILY *also.*

There is something in that name that seems to inspire absolute confidence. I pity any poor married woman whose husband is not called Ernest.

ALGERNON   But, my dear child, do you mean to say you could not love me if I had some other name?

CECILY   But what name?

ALGERNON Oh, any name you like—Algernon—for instance . . .

CECILY But I don't like the name of Algernon.

ALGERNON Well, my own dear sweet, loving little darling, I really can't see why you should object to the name of Algernon. It is not at all a bad name. In fact, it is rather an aristocratic name. Half of the chaps who get into the Bankruptcy Court are called Algernon. But seriously, Cecily . . . [*Moving to her.*] if my name was Algy, couldn't you love me?

CECILY [*rising*] I might respect you, Ernest, I might admire your character, but I fear that I should not be able to give you my undivided attention.

ALGERNON Ahem! Cecily! [*Picking up hat.*] Your Rector here is, I suppose, thoroughly experienced in the practice of all the rites and ceremonials of the Church?

CECILY Oh, yes. Dr. Chasuble is a most learned man. He has never written a single book, so you can imagine how much he knows.

ALGERNON I must see him at once on a most important christening—I mean on most important business.

CECILY Oh!

ALGERNON I shan't be away more than half an hour.

CECILY Considering that we have been engaged since February the 14th, and that I only met you today for the first time, I think it is rather hard that you should leave me for so long a period as half an hour. Couldn't you make it twenty minutes?

ALGERNON I'll be back in no time. [*Kisses her and rushes down the garden.*]

CECILY What an impetuous boy he is! I like his hair so much. I must enter his proposal in my diary.

Enter MERRIMAN.

MERRIMAN A Miss Fairfax just called to see Mr. Worthing. On very important business, Miss Fairfax states.

CECILY Isn't Mr. Worthing in his library?

MERRIMAN Mr. Worthing went over in the direction of the Rectory some time ago.

CECILY Pray ask the lady to come out here; Mr. Worthing is sure to be back soon. And you can bring tea.

MERRIMAN Yes. Miss. [*Goes out.*]

CECILY Miss Fairfax! I suppose one of the many good elderly women who are associated with Uncle Jack in some of his philanthropic work in London. I don't quite like women who are interested in philanthropic work. I think it is so forward of them.

Enter MERRIMAN.

MERRIMAN Miss Fairfax.

Enter GWENDOLEN. *Exit* MERRIMAN.

CECILY [*advancing to meet her*]   Pray let me introduce myself to you. My name is Cecily Cardew.

GWENDOLEN   Cecily Cardew? [*Moving to her and shaking hands.*] What a very sweet name! Something tells me that we are going to be great friends. I like you already more than I can say. My first impressions of people are never wrong.

CECILY   How nice of you to like me so much after we have known each other such a comparatively short time. Pray sit down.

GWENDOLEN [*still standing up*]   I may call you Cecily, may I not?

CECILY   With pleasure!

GWENDOLEN   And you will always call me Gwendolen, won't you?

CECILY   If you wish.

GWENDOLEN   Then that is all quite settled, is it not?

CECILY   I hope so. [*A pause. They both sit down together.*]

GWENDOLEN   Perhaps this might be a favorable opportunity for my mentioning who I am. My father is Lord Bracknell. You have never heard of papa, I suppose?

CECILY   I don't think so.

GWENDOLEN   Outside the family circle, papa, I am glad to say, is entirely unknown. I think that is quite as it should be. The home seems to me to be the proper sphere for the man. And certainly once a man begins to neglect his domestic duties he becomes painfully effeminate, does he not? And I don't like that. It makes men so very attractive. Cecily, mamma, whose views on education are remarkably strict, has brought me up to be extremely short-sighted; it is part of her system; so do you mind my looking at you through my glasses?

CECILY   Oh! not at all, Gwendolen. I am very fond of being looked at.

GWENDOLEN [*after examining* CECILY *carefully through a lorgnette*] You are here on a short visit, I suppose.

CECILY   Oh no! I live here.

GWENDOLEN [*severely*]   Really? Your mother, no doubt, or some female relative of advanced years, resides here also?

CECILY   Oh no! I have no mother, nor, in fact, any relations.

GWENDOLEN   Indeed?

CECILY   My dear guardian, with the assistance of Miss Prism, has the arduous task of looking after me.

GWENDOLEN   Your guardian?

CECILY   Yes, I am Mr. Worthing's ward.

GWENDOLEN   Oh! It is strange he never mentioned to me that he had a ward. How secretive of him! He grows more interesting hourly. I am not sure, however, that the news inspires me with feelings of unmixed delight. [*Rising and going to her.*] I am very fond of you, Cecily; I have liked you ever since I met you! But I am bound to state that now I know that you are Mr. Worthing's ward, I cannot help expressing a wish you were—well, just a little older than you seem to be—and not quite so very alluring in appearance. In fact, if I may speak candidly—

CECILY   Pray do! I think that whenever one has anything unpleasant to say, one should always be quite candid.

GWENDOLEN   Well, to speak with perfect candor, Cecily, I wish that you were fully forty-two, and more than usually plain for your age. Ernest has a strong upright nature. He is the very soul of truth and honor. Disloyalty would be as impossible to him as deception. But even men of the noblest possible moral character are extremely susceptible to the influence of the physical charms of others. Modern, no less than Ancient History, supplies us with many most painful examples of what I refer to. If it were not so, indeed, History would be quite unreadable.

CECILY   I beg your pardon, Gwendolen, did you say Ernest?

GWENDOLEN   Yes.

CECILY   Oh, but it is not Mr. Ernest Worthing who is my guardian. It is his brother—his elder brother.

GWENDOLEN [*sitting down again*]   Ernest never mentioned to me that he had a brother.

CECILY   I am sorry to say they have not been on good terms for a long time.

GWENDOLEN   Ah! that accounts for it. And now that I think of it I have never heard any man mention his brother. The subject seems distasteful to most men. Cecily, you have lifted a load from my mind. I was growing almost anxious. It would have been terrible if any cloud had come across a friendship like ours, would it not? Of course you are quite, quite sure that it is not Mr. Worthing who is your guardian?

CECILY   Quite sure. [*A pause.*] In fact, I am going to be his.

GWENDOLEN [*inquiringly*]   I beg your pardon?

CECILY [*rather shy and confidingly*]   Dearest Gwendolen, there is no reason why I should make a secret of it to you. Our little country newspaper is sure to chronicle the fact next week. Mr. Ernest Worthing and I are engaged to be married.

GWENDOLEN [*quite politely, rising*]   My darling Cecily, I think there must be some slight error. Mr. Ernest Worthing is engaged to me. The announcement will appear in the *Morning Post* on Saturday at the latest.

CECILY [*very politely, rising*]   I am afraid you must be under some misconception. Ernest proposed to me exactly ten minutes ago. [*Shows diary.*]

GWENDOLEN [*examines diary through her lorgnette carefully*]   It is very curious, for he asked me to be his wife yesterday afternoon at 5:30. If you would care to verify the incident, pray do so. [*Produces diary of her own.*] I never travel without my diary. One should always have something sensational to read in the train. I am so sorry, dear Cecily, if it is any disappointment to you, but I am afraid I have the prior claim.

CECILY   It would distress me more than I can tell you, dear Gwendolen, if it caused you any mental or physical anguish, but I feel bound to point out that since Ernest proposed to you he clearly has changed his mind.

GWENDOLEN [*meditatively*]   If the poor fellow has been entrapped into any foolish promise I shall consider it my duty to rescue him at once, and with a firm hand.

CECILY [*thoughtfully and sadly*] Whatever unfortunate entanglement my dear boy may have got into, I will never reproach him with it after we are married.

GWENDOLEN Do you allude to me, Miss Cardew, as an entanglement? You are presumptuous. On an occasion of this kind it becomes more than a moral duty to speak one's mind. It becomes a pleasure.

CECILY Do you suggest, Miss Fairfax, that I entrapped Ernest into an engagement? How dare you? This is no time for wearing the shallow mask of manners. When I see a spade I call it a spade.

GWENDOLEN [*satirically*] I am glad to say that I have never seen a spade. It is obvious that our social spheres have been widely different.

Enter MERRIMAN, *followed by the* FOOTMAN. *He carries a salver, table cloth, and plate stand.* CECILY *is about to retort. The presence of the servants exercises a restraining influence, under which both girls chafe.*

MERRIMAN Shall I lay tea here as usual, Miss?

CECILY [*sternly, in a calm voice*] Yes, as usual.

MERRIMAN *begins to clear table and lay cloth. A long pause.* CECILY *and* GWENDOLEN *glare at each other.*

GWENDOLEN Are there many interesting walks in the vicinity, Miss Cardew?

CECILY Oh! yes! a great many. From the top of one of the hills quite close one can see five counties.

GWENDOLEN Five counties! I don't think I should like that; I hate crowds.

CECILY [*sweetly*] I suppose that is why you live in town?

GWENDOLEN *bites her lip, and beats her foot nervously with her parasol.*

GWENDOLEN [*looking around*] Quite a well-kept garden this is, Miss Cardew.

CECILY So glad you like it, Miss Fairfax.

GWENDOLEN I had no idea there were any flowers in the country.

CECILY Oh, flowers are as common here, Miss Fairfax, as people are in London.

GWENDOLEN Personally I cannot understand how anybody manages to exist in the country, if anybody who is anybody does. The country always bores me to death.

CECILY Ah! This is what the newspapers call agricultural depression, is it not? I believe the aristocracy are suffering very much from it just at present. It is almost an epidemic amongst them, I have been told. May I offer you some tea, Miss Fairfax?

GWENDOLEN [*with elaborate politeness*] Thank you. [*Aside.*] Detestable girl! But I require tea!

CECILY [*sweetly*] Sugar?

GWENDOLEN [*superciliously*] No, thank you. Sugar is not fashionable any more.

> CECILY *looks angrily at her, takes up the tongs and puts four lumps of sugar into the cup.*

CECILY [*severely*] Cake or bread and butter?

GWENDOLEN [*in a bored manner*] Bread and butter, please. Cake is rarely seen at the best houses nowadays.

CECILY [*cuts a very large slice of cake and puts it on the tray*] Hand that to Miss Fairfax.

> MERRIMAN *does so, and goes out with* FOOTMAN. GWENDOLEN *drinks the tea and makes a grimace. Puts down cup at once, reaches out her hand to the bread and butter, looks at it, and finds it is cake. Rises in indignation.*

GWENDOLEN You have filled my tea with lumps of sugar, and though I asked most distinctly for bread and butter, you have given me cake. I am known for the gentleness of my disposition, and the extraordinary sweetness of my nature, but I warn you, Miss Cardew, you may go too far.

CECILY [*rising*] To save my poor, innocent, trusting boy from the machinations of any other girl there are no lengths to which I would not go.

GWENDOLEN From the moment I saw you I distrusted you. I felt that you were false and deceitful. I am never deceived in such matters. My first impressions of people are invariably right.

CECILY It seems to me, Miss Fairfax, that I am trespassing on your valuable time. No doubt you have many other calls of a similar character to make in the neighbourhood.

> *Enter* JACK.

GWENDOLEN [*catching sight of him*] Ernest! My own Ernest!

JACK Gwendolen! Darling! [*Offers to kiss her.*]

GWENDOLEN [*drawing back*] A moment! May I ask if you are engaged to be married to this young lady? [*Points to* CECILY.]

JACK [*laughing*] To dear little Cecily! Of course not! What could have put such an idea into your pretty little head?

GWENDOLEN Thank you. You may! [*Offers her cheek.*]

CECILY [*very sweetly*] I knew there must be some misunderstanding, Miss Fairfax. The gentleman whose arm is at present round your waist is my dear guardian, Mr. John Worthing.

GWENDOLEN I beg your pardon?

CECILY This is Uncle Jack.

GWENDOLEN [*receding*] Jack! Oh!

> *Enter* ALGERNON.

CECILY Here is Ernest.

ALGERNON [*goes straight over to* CECILY *without noticing anyone else*]   My own love! [*Offers to kiss her.*]

CECILY [*drawing back*]   A moment, Ernest! May I ask you—are you engaged to be married to this young lady?

ALGERNON [*looking around*]   To what young lady? Good heavens! Gwendolen!

CECILY   Yes: to good heavens, Gwendolen, I mean to Gwendolen.

ALGERNON [*laughing*]   Of course not! What could have put such an idea into your pretty little head?

CECILY   Thank you. [*Presenting her cheek to be kissed.*] You may.

> ALGERNON *kisses her.*

GWENDOLEN   I felt there was some slight error, Miss Cardew. The gentleman who is now embracing you is my cousin, Mr. Algernon Moncrieff.

CECILY [*breaking away from* ALGERNON]   Algernon Moncrieff! Oh!

> *The two girls move towards each other and put their arms round each other's waists as if for protection.*

CECILY   Are you called Algernon?

ALGERNON   I cannot deny it.

CECILY   Oh!

GWENDOLEN   Is your name really John?

JACK [*standing rather proudly*]   I could deny it if I liked. I could deny anything if I liked. But my name certainly is John. It has been John for years.

CECILY [*to* GWENDOLEN]   A gross deception has been practiced on both of us.

GWENDOLEN   My poor wounded Cecily!

CECILY   My sweet wronged Gwendolen!

GWENDOLEN [*slowly and seriously*]   You will call me sister, will you not?

> *They embrace.* JACK *and* ALGERNON *groan and walk up and down.*

CECILY [*rather brightly*]   There is just one question I would like to be allowed to ask my guardian.

GWENDOLEN   An admirable idea! Mr. Worthing, there is just one question I would like to be permitted to put to you. Where is your brother Ernest? We are both engaged to be married to your brother Ernest, so it is a matter of some importance to us to know where your brother Ernest is at present.

JACK [*slowly and hesitatingly*]   Gwendolen—Cecily—it is very painful for me to be forced to speak the truth. It is the first time in my life that I have ever been reduced to such a painful position, and I am really quite inexperienced in doing anything of the kind. However, I will tell you quite frankly that I have no brother Ernest. I have no brother at all. I never had a brother in my life, and I certainly have not the smallest intention of ever having one in the future.

CECILY [*surprised*]   No brother at all?

JACK [*cheerily*]   None!

GWENDOLEN [*severely*]   Had you never a brother of any kind?

JACK [*pleasantly*]   Never. Not even of any kind.

GWENDOLEN   I am afraid it is quite clear, Cecily, that neither of us is engaged to be married to anyone.

CECILY….It is not a very pleasant position for a young girl suddenly to find herself in. Is it?

GWENDOLEN   Let us go into the house. They will hardly venture to come after us there.

CECILY   No, men are so cowardly, aren't they?

They retire into the house with scornful looks.

JACK   This ghastly state of things is what you call Bunburying, I suppose?

ALGERNON   Yes, and a perfectly wonderful Bunbury it is. The most wonderful Bunbury I have ever had in my life.

JACK   Well, you've no right whatsoever to Bunbury here.

ALGERNON   That is absurd. One has a right to Bunbury anywhere one chooses. Every serious Bunburyist knows that.

JACK   Serious Bunburyist? Good heavens!

ALGERNON   Well, one must be serious about something, if one wants to have any amusement in life. I happen to be serious about Bunburying. What on earth you are serious about I haven't got the remotest idea. About everything, I should fancy. You have such an absolutely trivial nature.

JACK   Well, the only small satisfaction I have in the whole of this wretched business is that your friend Bunbury is quite exploded. You won't be able to run down to the country quite so often as you used to do, dear Algy. And a very good thing too.

ALGERNON   Your brother is a little off color, isn't he, dear Jack? You won't be able to disappear to London quite so frequently as your wicked custom was. And not a bad thing either.

JACK   As for your conduct towards Miss Cardew, I must say that you taking in a sweet, simple, innocent girl like that is quite inexcusable. To say nothing of the fact that she is my ward.

ALGERNON   I can see no possible defense at all for your deceiving a brilliant, clever, thoroughly experienced young lady like Miss Fairfax. To say nothing of the fact that she is my cousin.

JACK   I wanted to be engaged to Gwendolen, that is all. I love her.

ALGERNON   Well, I simply wanted to be engaged to Cecily. I adore her.

JACK   There is certainly no chance of your marrying Miss Cardew.

ALGERNON   I don't think there is much likelihood, Jack, of you and Miss Fairfax being united.

JACK   Well, that is no business of yours.

ALGERNON   If it was my business, I wouldn't talk about it. [*Begins to eat muffins.*] It is very vulgar to talk about one's business. Only people like stockbrokers do that, and then merely at dinner parties.

JACK How you can sit there, calmly eating muffins, when we are in this horrible trouble, I can't make out. You seem to me to be perfectly heartless.

ALGERNON Well, I can't eat muffins in an agitated manner. The butter would probably get on my cuffs. One should always eat muffins quite calmly. It is the only way to eat them.

JACK I say it's perfectly heartless your eating muffins at all, under the circumstances.

ALGERNON When I am in trouble, eating is the only thing that consoles me. Indeed, when I am in really great trouble, as any one who knows me intimately will tell you, I refuse everything except food and drink. At the present moment I am eating muffins because I am unhappy. Besides, I am particularly fond of muffins. [*Rising.*]

JACK [*rising*]....Well, there is no reason why you should eat them all in that greedy way. [*Takes muffins from* ALGERNON.]

ALGERNON [*offering tea-cake*] I wish you would have tea-cake instead. I don't like tea-cake.

JACK Good heavens! I suppose a man may eat his own muffins in his own garden.

ALGERNON But you have just said it was perfectly heartless to eat muffins.

JACK I said it was perfectly heartless of you, under the circumstances. That is a very different thing.

ALGERNON That may be. But the muffins are the same. [*He seizes the muffin-dish from* JACK.]

JACK Algy, I wish to goodness you would go.

ALGERNON You can't possibly ask me to go without having some dinner. It's absurd. I never go without my dinner. No one ever does, except vegetarians and people like that. Besides I have just made arrangements with Dr. Chasuble to be christened at a quarter to six under the name of Ernest.

JACK My dear fellow, the sooner you give up that nonsense the better. I made arrangements this morning with Dr. Chasuble to be christened myself at 5:30, and I naturally will take the name of Ernest. Gwendolen would wish it. We can't both be christened Ernest. It's absurd. Besides, I have a perfect right to be christened if I like. There is no evidence at all that I have ever been christened by anybody. I should think it extremely probable I never was, and so does Dr. Chasuble. It is entirely different in your case. You have been christened already.

ALGERNON Yes, but I have not been christened for years.

JACK Yes, but you have been christened. That is the important thing.

ALGERNON Quite so. So I know my constitution can stand it. If you are not quite sure about your ever having been christened, I must say I think it rather dangerous your venturing on it now. It might make you very unwell. You can hardly have forgotten that someone very closely connected with you was very nearly carried off this week in Paris by a severe chill.

JACK Yes, but you said yourself that a severe chill was not hereditary.

ALGERNON It usen't to be, I know—but I daresay it is now. Science is always making wonderful improvements in things.

JACK [*picking up the muffin-dish*] Oh, that is nonsense; you are always talking nonsense.

ALGERNON Jack, you are at the muffins again! I wish you wouldn't. There are only two left. [*Takes them.*] I told you I was particularly fond of muffins.

JACK But I hate tea-cake.

ALGERNON Why on earth then do you allow tea-cake to be served up for your guests? What ideas you have of hospitality!

JACK Algernon! I have already told you to go. I don't want you here. Why don't you go?

ALGERNON I haven't quite finished my tea yet! and there is still one muffin left.

JACK *groans, and sinks into a chair.* ALGERNON *still continues eating.*

Act 3

Drawing room at the Manor House. GWENDOLEN *and* CECILY *are at the window, looking out into the garden.*

GWENDOLEN The fact that they did not follow us at once into the house, as any one else would have done, seems to me to show that they have some sense of shame left.

CECILY They have been eating muffins. That looks like repentance.

GWENDOLEN [*after a pause*] They don't seem to notice us at all. Couldn't you cough?

CECILY But I haven't got a cough.

GWENDOLEN They're looking at us. What effrontery!

CECILY They're approaching. That's very forward of them.

GWENDOLEN Let us preserve a dignified silence.

CECILY Certainly. It's the only thing to do now.

Enter JACK *followed by* ALGERNON. *They whistle some dreadful popular air from a British opera.*

GWENDOLEN This dignified silence seems to produce an unpleasant effect.

CECILY A most distasteful one.

GWENDOLEN But we will not be the first to speak.

CECILY Certainly not.

GWENDOLEN Mr. Worthing, I have something very particular to ask you. Much depends on your reply.

CECILY Gwendolen, your common sense is invaluable. Mr. Moncrieff, kindly answer me the following question. Why did you pretend to be my guardian's brother?

ALGERNON In order that I might have an opportunity of meeting you.

CECILY [*to* GWENDOLEN]   That certainly seems a satisfactory explanation, does it not?

GWENDOLEN   Yes, dear, if you can believe him.

CECILY   I don't. But that does not affect the wonderful beauty of his answer.

GWENDOLEN   True. In matters of grave importance, style, not sincerity, is the vital thing. Mr. Worthing, what explanation can you offer to me for pretending to have a brother? Was it in order that you might have an opportunity of coming up to town to see me as often as possible?

JACK   Can you doubt it, Miss Fairfax?

GWENDOLEN   I have the gravest doubts about the subject. But I intend to crush them. This is not the moment for German skepticism.[4] [*Moving to* CECILY.] Their explanations appear to be quite satisfactory, especially Mr. Worthing's. That seems to me to have the stamp of truth upon it.

CECILY   I am more than content with what Mr. Moncrieff said. His voice alone inspires one with absolute credulity.

GWENDOLEN   Then you think we should forgive them?

CECILY   Yes. I mean no.

GWENDOLEN   True! I had forgotten. There are principles at stake that one cannot surrender. Which of us should tell them? The task is not a pleasant one.

CECILY   Could we not both speak at the same time?

GWENDOLEN   An excellent idea! I nearly always speak at the same time as other people. Will you take the time from me?

CECILY   Certainly.

GWENDOLEN *beats time with uplifted finger.*

GWENDOLEN *and* CECILY [*speaking together*]   Your Christian names are still an insuperable barrier. That is all!

JACK *and* ALGERNON [*speaking together*]   Our Christian names! Is that all? But we are going to be christened this afternoon.

GWENDOLEN [*to* JACK]   For my sake you are prepared to do this terrible thing?

JACK   I am.

CECILY [*to* ALGERNON]   To please me you are ready to face this fearful ordeal?

ALGERNON   I am!

GWENDOLEN   How absurd to talk of the equality of the sexes! Where questions of self-sacrifice are concerned, men are infinitely beyond us.

JACK   We are. [*Clasps hands with* ALGERNON.]

CECILY   They have moments of physical courage of which we women know absolutely nothing.

GWENDOLEN [*to* JACK]   Darling!

ALGERNON [*to* CECILY]   Darling!

4. A reference to such philosophical movements as the Materialism of Ludwig Feuerbach (1804–1872) and such theological movements as the "Higher Criticism," a movement which subjected the Bible to the same kind of study as that accorded other books.

They fall into each other's arms. Enter MERRIMAN. *When he enters he coughs loudly, seeing the situation.*

MERRIMAN   Ahem! Ahem! Lady Bracknell.
JACK   Good heavens!

Enter LADY BRACKNELL. *The couples separate in alarm. Exit* MERRIMAN.

LADY BRACKNELL   Gwendolen! What does this mean?
GWENDOLEN   Merely that I am engaged to be married to Mr. Worthing, mamma.
LADY BRACKNELL   Come here. Sit down. Sit down immediately. Hesitation of any kind is a sign of mental decay in the young, of physical weakness in the old. [*Turns to* JACK.] Apprised, sir, of my daughter's sudden flight by her trusty maid, whose confidence I purchased by means of a small coin, I followed her at once by a luggage train. Her unhappy father is, I am glad to say, under the impression that she is attending a more than usually lengthy lecture by the University Extension Scheme on the Influence of a Permanent Income on Thought. I do not propose to undeceive him. Indeed I have never undeceived him on any question. I would consider it wrong. But, of course, you will clearly understand that all communication between yourself and my daughter must cease immediately from this moment. On this point, as indeed on all points, I am firm.
JACK   I am engaged to be married to Gwendolen, Lady Bracknell!
LADY BRACKNELL   You are nothing of the kind, sir. And now as regards Algernon! . . . Algernon!
ALGERNON   Yes, Aunt Augusta.
LADY BRACKNELL   May I ask if it is in this house that your invalid friend Mr. Bunbury resides?
ALGERNON [*stammering*]   Oh! no! Bunbury doesn't live here. Bunbury is somewhere else at present. In fact, Bunbury is dead.
LADY BRACKNELL   Dead! When did Mr. Bunbury die? His death must have been extremely sudden.
ALGERNON [*airily*]   Oh! I killed Bunbury this afternoon. I mean poor Bunbury died this afternoon.
LADY BRACKNELL   What did he die of?
ALGERNON   Bunbury? Oh, he was quite exploded.
LADY BRACKNELL   Exploded! Was he the victim of a revolutionary outrage? I was not aware that Mr. Bunbury was interested in social legislation. If so, he is well punished for his morbidity.
ALGERNON   My dear Aunt Augusta, I mean he was found out! The doctors found out that Bunbury could not live, that is what I mean —so Bunbury died.
LADY BRACKNELL   He seems to have had great confidence in the opinion of his physicians. I am glad, however, that he made up his mind at the last to some definite course of action, and acted under proper medical advice. And now that we have finally got rid of

this Mr. Bunbury, may I ask, Mr. Worthing, who is that young person whose hand my nephew Algernon is now holding in what seems to me a peculiarly unnecessary manner?

JACK   That lady is Miss Cecily Cardew, my ward.

LADY BRACKNELL *bows coldly to* CECILY.

ALGERNON   I am engaged to be married to Cecily, Aunt Augusta.

LADY BRACKNELL   I beg your pardon?

CECILY   Mr. Moncrieff and I are engaged to be married, Lady Bracknell.

LADY BRACKNELL [*with a shiver, crossing to the sofa and sitting down*] I do not know whether there is anything peculiarly exciting in the air of this particular part of Hertfordshire, but the number of engagements that go on seems to me considerably above the proper average that statistics have laid down for our guidance. I think some preliminary inquiry on my part would not be out of place. Mr. Worthing, is Miss Cardew at all connected with any of the larger railway stations in London? I merely desire information. Until yesterday I had no idea that there were any families or persons whose origin was a Terminus.

JACK *looks perfectly furious, but restrains himself.*

JACK [*in a cold, clear voice*]   Miss Cardew is the granddaughter of the late Mr. Thomas Cardew of 149 Belgrave Square, S.W.; Gervase Park, Dorking, Surrey; and the Sporran, Fifeshire, N.B.[5]

LADY BRACKNELL   That sounds not unsatisfactory. Three addresses always inspire confidence, even in tradesmen. But what proof have I of their authenticity?

JACK   I have carefully preserved the Court Guides of the period. They are open to your inspection, Lady Bracknell.

LADY BRACKNELL [*grimly*]   I have known strange errors in that publication.

JACK   Miss Cardew's family solicitors are Messrs. Markby, Markby, and Markby.

LADY BRACKNELL   Markby, Markby, and Markby? A firm of the very highest position in their profession. Indeed I am told that one of the Mr. Markbys is occasionally to be seen at dinner parties. So far I am satisfied.

JACK [*very irritably*]   How extremely kind of you, Lady Bracknell! I have also in my possession, you will be pleased to hear, certificates of Miss Cardew's birth, baptism, whooping cough, registration, vaccination, confirmation, and the measles; both the German and the English variety.

LADY BRACKNELL   Ah! A life crowded with incident, I see; though perhaps somewhat too exciting for a young girl. I am not myself in favor of premature experiences. [*Rises, looks at her watch.*] Gwen-

5. In addition to his London residence in Belgrave Square (already referred to in Act 1), Mr. Cardew maintained establish-ments in the south of England (Dorking, Surrey) and in Scotland (Fifeshire).

dolen! the time approaches for our departure. We have not a moment to lose. As a matter of form, Mr. Worthing, I had better ask you if Miss Cardew has any little fortune?

JACK   Oh! about a hundred and thirty thousand pounds in the Funds.[6] That is all. Good-bye, Lady Bracknell. So pleased to have seen you.

LADY BRACKNELL [*sitting down again*]   A moment, Mr. Worthing. A hundred and thirty thousand pounds! And in the Funds! Miss Cardew seems to me a most attractive young lady, now that I look at her. Few girls of the present day have any really solid qualities, any of the qualities that last, and improve with time. We live, I regret to say, in an age of surfaces. [*To* CECILY.] Come over here, dear.

CECILY *goes across.*

Pretty child! your dress is sadly simple, and your hair seems almost as Nature might have left it. But we can soon alter all that. A thoroughly experienced French maid produces a really marvellous result in a very brief space of time. I remember recommending one to young Lady Lancing, and after three months her own husband did not know her.

JACK   And after six months nobody knew her.

LADY BRACKNELL [*glares at* JACK *for a few moments. Then bends, with a practiced smile, to* CECILY]   Kindly turn round, sweet child.

CECILY *turns completely round.*

No, the side view is what I want.

CECILY *presents her profile.*

Yes, quite as I expected. There are distinct social possibilities in your profile. The two weak points in our age are its want of principle and its want of profile. The chin a little higher, dear. Style largely depends on the way the chin is worn. They are worn very high, just at present. Algernon!

ALGERNON   Yes, Aunt Augusta!

LADY BRACKNELL   There are distinct social possibilities in Miss Cardew's profile.

ALGERNON   Cecily is the sweetest, dearest, prettiest girl in the whole world. And I don't care twopence about social possibilities.

LADY BRACKNELL   Never speak disrespectfully of Society, Algernon. Only people who can't get into it do that. [*To* CECILY.] Dear child, of course you know that Algernon has nothing but his debts to depend upon. But I do not approve of mercenary marriages. When I married Lord Bracknell I had no fortune of any kind. But I never dreamed for a moment of allowing that to stand in my way. Well, I suppose I must give my consent.

6. Stock of the British National Debt.

ALGERNON   Thank you, Aunt Augusta.

LADY BRACKNELL   Cecily, you may kiss me!

CECILY [*kisses her*]   Thank you, Lady Bracknell.

LADY BRACKNELL   You may also address me as Aunt Augusta for the future.

CECILY   Thank you, Aunt Augusta.

LADY BRACKNELL   The marriage, I think, had better take place quite soon.

ALGERNON   Thank you, Aunt Augusta.

CECILY   Thank you, Aunt Augusta.

LADY BRACKNELL   To speak frankly, I am not in favor of long engagements. They give people the opportunity of finding out each other's character before marriage, which I think is never advisable.

JACK   I beg your pardon for interrupting you, Lady Bracknell, but this engagement is out of the question. I am Miss Cardew's guardian, and she cannot marry without my consent until she comes of age. That consent I absolutely decline to give.

LADY BRACKNELL   Upon what grounds, may I ask? Algernon is an extremely, I may almost say an ostentatiously, eligible young man. He has nothing, but he looks everything. What more can one desire?

JACK   It pains me very much to have to speak frankly to you, Lady Bracknell, about your nephew, but the fact is that I do not approve at all of his moral character. I suspect him of being untruthful.

ALGERNON *and* CECILY *look at him in indignant amazement.*

LADY BRACKNELL   Untruthful! My nephew Algernon? Impossible! He is an Oxonian.[7]

JACK   I fear there can be no possible doubt about the matter. This afternoon during my temporary absence in London on an important question of romance, he obtained admission to my house by means of the false pretense of being my brother. Under an assumed name he drank, I've just been informed by my butler, an entire pint bottle of my Perrier-Jouet, Brut, '89;[8] wine I was specially reserving for myself. Continuing his disgraceful deception, he succeeded in the course of the afternoon in alienating the affections of my only ward. He subsequently stayed to tea, and devoured every single muffin. And what makes his conduct all the more heartless is, that he was perfectly well aware from the first that I have no brother, that I never had a brother, and that I don't intend to have a brother, not even of any kind. I distinctly told him so myself yesterday afternoon.

LADY BRACKNELL   Ahem! Mr. Worthing, after careful consideration I have decided entirely to overlook my nephew's conduct to you.

JACK   That is very generous of you, Lady Bracknell. My own decision, however, is unalterable. I decline to give my consent.

LADY BRACKNELL [*to* CECILY]   Come here, sweet child.

CECILY *goes over.*

---

7. A graduate of Oxford University.   8. A very dry champagne.

How old are you, dear?

CECILY   Well, I am really only eighteen, but I always admit to twenty when I go to evening parties.

LADY BRACKNELL   You are perfectly right in making some slight alteration. Indeed, no woman should ever be quite accurate about her age. It looks so calculating. . . . [*In a meditative manner.*] Eighteen, but admitting to twenty at evening parties. Well, it will not be very long before you are of age and free from the restraints of tutelage. So I don't think your guardian's consent is, after all, a matter of any importance.

JACK   Pray excuse me, Lady Bracknell, for interrupting you again, but it is only fair to tell you that according to the terms of her grandfather's will Miss Cardew does not come legally of age till she is thirty-five.

LADY BRACKNELL   That does not seem to me to be a grave objection. Thirty-five is a very attractive age. London society is full of women of the very highest birth who have, of their own free choice, remained thirty-five for years. Lady Dumbleton is an instance in point. To my own knowledge she has been thirty-five ever since she arrived at the age of forty, which was many years ago now. I see no reason why our dear Cecily should not be even still more attractive at the age you mention than she is at present. There will be a large accumulation of property.

CECILY   Algy, could you wait for me till I was thirty-five?

ALGERNON   Of course I could, Cecily. You know I could.

CECILY   Yes, I felt it instinctively, but I couldn't wait all that time. I hate waiting even five minutes for anybody. It always makes me rather cross. I am not punctual myself, I know, but I do like punctuality in others, and waiting, even to be married, is quite out of the question.

ALGERNON   Then what is to be done, Cecily?

CECILY   I don't know, Mr. Moncrieff.

LADY BRACKNELL   My dear Mr. Worthing, as Miss Cardew states positively that she cannot wait till she is thirty-five—a remark which I am bound to say seems to me to show a somewhat impatient nature—I would beg of you to reconsider your decision.

JACK   But my dear Lady Bracknell, the matter is entirely in your own hands. The moment you consent to my marriage with Gwendolen, I will most gladly allow your nephew to form an alliance with my ward.

LADY BRACKNELL   [*rising and drawing herself up*]   You must be quite aware that what you propose is out of the question.

JACK   Then a passionate celibacy is all that any of us can look forward to.

LADY BRACKNELL   That is not the destiny I propose for Gwendolen. Algernon, of course, can choose for himself. [*Pulls out her watch.*] Come, dear [GWENDOLEN *rises.*], we have already missed five, if not six, trains. To miss any more might expose us to comment on the platform.

Enter DR. CHASUBLE.

CHASUBLE   Everything is quite ready for the christenings.

LADY BRACKNELL   The christenings, sir! Is not that somewhat premature?

CHASUBLE [*looking rather puzzled, and pointing to* JACK *and* ALGERNON]   Both these gentlemen have expressed a desire for immediate baptism.

LADY BRACKNELL   At their age? The idea is grotesque and irreligious! Algernon, I forbid you to be baptized. I will not hear of such excesses. Lord Bracknell would be highly displeased if he learned that that was the way in which you wasted your time and money.

CHASUBLE   Am I to understand then that there are to be no christenings at all this afternoon?

JACK   I don't think that, as things are now, it would be of much practical value to either of us, Dr. Chasuble.

CHASUBLE   I am grieved to hear such sentiments from you, Mr. Worthing. They savour of the heretical views of the Anbaptists,[9] views that I have completely refuted in four of my unpublished sermons. However, as your present mood seems to be one peculiarly secular, I will return to the church at once. Indeed, I have just been informed by the pew-opener[1] that for the last hour and a half Miss Prism has been waiting for me in the vestry.

LADY BRACKNELL [*starting*]   Miss Prism! Did I hear you mention a Miss Prism?

CHASUBLE   Yes, Lady Bracknell. I am on my way to join her.

LADY BRACKNELL   Pray allow me to detain you for a moment. This matter may prove to be one of vital importance to Lord Bracknell and myself. Is this Miss Prism a female of repellent aspect, remotely connected with education?

CHASUBLE [*somewhat indignantly*]   She is the most cultivated of ladies, and the very picture of respectability.

LADY BRACKNELL   It is obviously the same person. May I ask what position she holds in your household?

CHASUBLE [*severely*]   I am a celibate, madam.

JACK [*interposing*]   Miss Prism, Lady Bracknell, has been for the last three years Miss Cardew's esteemed governess and valued companion.

LADY BRACKNELL   In spite of what I hear of her, I must see her at once. Let her be sent for.

CHASUBLE [*looking off*]   She approaches; she is nigh.

Enter MISS PRISM *hurriedly.*

MISS PRISM   I was told you expected me in the vestry, dear Canon. I have been waiting for you there for an hour and three-quarters. [*Catches sight of* LADY BRACKNELL, *who has fixed her with a stony*

---

9. A 16th-century religious group, most nearly like contemporary Mennonites. Dr. Chasuble, however, is probably using the term loosely to apply to a group more like contemporary Baptists.

1. An usher. Since most pews were completely enclosed, his duties would have included opening the gate that provided entrance for the worshipers. In addition, since most pews were rented for the use of specific persons, he would have been responsible for seeing that worshipers were seated in the correct pews.

glare. MISS PRISM *grows pale and quails. She looks anxiously round as if desirous to escape.*]

LADY BRACKNELL [*in a severe, judicial voice*]   Prism!

MISS PRISM *bows her head in shame.*

Come here, Prism!

MISS PRISM *approaches in a humble manner.*

Prism! Where is that baby?

General consternation. The CANON *starts back in horror.* ALGERNON *and* JACK *pretend to be anxious to shield* CECILY *and* GWENDOLEN *from hearing the details of terrible public scandal.*

Twenty-eight years ago, Prism, you left Lord Bracknell's house, Number 104, Upper Grosvenor Square, in charge of a perambulator that contained a baby of the male sex. You never returned. A few weeks later, through the elaborate investigations of the Metropolitan police, the perambulator was discovered at midnight standing by itself in a remote corner of Bayswater.[2] It contained the manuscript of a three-volume novel of more than usually revolting sentimentality.

MISS PRISM *starts in involuntary indignation.*

But the baby was not there.

Everyone looks at MISS PRISM.

Prism! Where is that baby?

A pause.

MISS PRISM   Lady Bracknell, I admit with shame that I do not know. I only wish I did. The plain facts of the case are these. On the morning of the day you mention, a day that is for ever branded on my memory, I prepared as usual to take the baby out in its perambulator. I had also with me a somewhat old, but capacious handbag in which I had intended to place the manuscript of a work of fiction that I had written during my few unoccupied hours. In a moment of mental abstraction, for which I can never forgive myself, I deposited the manuscript in the bassinette and placed the baby in the handbag.

JACK [*who has been listening attentively*]   But where did you deposit the handbag?

2. Bayswater is a residential section to the north of Hyde Park and Kensington Gardens.

MISS PRISM   Do not ask me, Mr. Worthing.

JACK   Miss Prism, this is a matter of no small importance to me. I insist on knowing where you deposited the handbag that contained that infant.

MISS PRISM   I left it in the cloakroom of one of the larger railway stations in London.

JACK   What railway station?

MISS PRISM [*quite crushed*]   Victoria. The Brighton line. [*Sinks into a chair.*]

JACK   I must retire to my room for a moment. Gwendolen, wait here for me.

GWENDOLEN   If you are not too long, I will wait here for you all my life.

    Exit JACK *in great excitement.*

CHASUBLE   What do you think this means, Lady Bracknell?

LADY BRACKNELL   I dare not even suspect, Dr. Chasuble. I need hardly tell you that in families of high position strange coincidences are not supposed to occur. They are hardly considered the thing.

    Noises heard overhead as if some one was throwing trunks about. Everyone looks up.

CECILY   Uncle Jack seems strangely agitated.

CHASUBLE   Your guardian has a very emotional nature.

LADY BRACKNELL   This noise is extremely unpleasant. It sounds as if he was having an argument. I dislike arguments of any kind. They are always vulgar, and often convincing.

CHASUBLE [*looking up*]   It has stopped now.

    The noise is redoubled.

LADY BRACKNELL   I wish he would arrive at some conclusion.

GWENDOLEN   This suspense is terrible. I hope it will last.

    Enter JACK *with a handbag of black leather in his hand.*

JACK [*rushing over to* MISS PRISM]   Is this the handbag, Miss Prism? Examine is carefully before you speak. The happiness of more than one life depends on your answer.

MISS PRISM [*calmly*]   It seems to be mine. Yes, here is the injury it received through the upsetting of a Gower Street omnibus in younger and happier days. Here is the stain on the lining caused by the explosion of a temperance beverage, an incident that occurred at Leamington. And here, on the lock, are my initials. I had forgotten that in an extravagant mood I had had them placed there. The bag is undoubtedly mine. I am delighted to have it so unexpectedly restored to me. It has been a great inconvenience being without it all these years.

JACK [*in a pathetic voice*]   Miss Prism, more is restored to you than this handbag. I was the baby you placed in it.

MISS PRISM [*amazed*]   You?

JACK [*embracing her*]   Yes . . . mother!

MISS PRISM [*recoiling in indignant astonishment*]   Mr. Worthing, I am unmarried!

JACK   Unmarried! I do not deny that is a serious blow. But after all, who has the right to cast a stone against one who has suffered? Cannot repentance wipe out an act of folly? Why should there be one law for men, and another for women? Mother. I forgive you. [*Tries to embrace her again.*]

MISS PRISM [*still more indignant*]   Mr. Worthing, there is some error. [*Pointing to* LADY BRACKNELL.] There is the lady who can tell you who you really are.

JACK [*after a pause*]   Lady Bracknell, I hate to seem inquisitive, but would you kindly inform me who I am?

LADY BRACKNELL   I am afraid that the news I have to give you will not altogether please you. You are the son of my poor sister, Mrs. Moncrieff, and consequently Algernon's elder brother.

JACK   Algy's elder brother! Then I have a brother after all. I knew I had a brother! I always said I had a brother! Cecily—how could you have ever doubted that I had a brother? [*Seizes hold of* ALGERNON.] Dr. Chasuble, my unfortunate brother. Miss Prism, my unfortunate brother. Gwendolen, my unfortunate brother. Algy, you young scoundrel, you will have to treat me with more respect in the future. You have never behaved to me like a brother in all your life.

ALGERNON   Well, not till today, old boy, I admit. I did my best, however, though I was out of practice. [*Shakes hands.*]

GWENDOLEN [*to* JACK]   My own! But what own are you? What is your Christian name, now that you have become someone else?

JACK   Good heavens! . . . I had quite forgotten that point. Your decision on the subject of my name is irrevocable, I suppose?

GWENDOLEN   I never change, except in my affections.

CECILY   What a noble nature you have, Gwendolen!

JACK   Then the question had better be cleared up at once. Aunt Augusta, a moment. At the time when Miss Prism left me in the handbag, had I been christened already?

LADY BRACKNELL   Every luxury that money could buy, including christening, had been lavished on you by your fond and doting parents.

JACK   Then I was christened! That is settled. Now, what name was I given? Let me know the worst.

LADY BRACKNELL   Being the eldest son you were naturally christened after your father.

JACK [*irritably*]   Yes, but what was my father's Christian name?

LADY BRACKNELL [*meditatively*]   I cannot at the present moment recall what the General's Christian name was. But I have no doubt he had one. He was eccentric, I admit. But only in later years. And that was the result of the Indian climate, and marriage, and indigestion, and other things of that kind.

JACK   Algy! Can't you recollect what our father's Christian name was?

ALGERNON   My dear boy, we were never even on speaking terms. He died before I was a year old.

JACK   His name would appear in the Army Lists of the period, I suppose, Aunt Augusta?

LADY BRACKNELL   The General was essentially a man of peace, except in his domestic life. But I have no doubt his name would appear in any military directory.

JACK   The Army Lists of the last forty years are here. These delightful records should have been my constant study. [*Rushes to bookcase and tears the books out.*] M. Generals . . . Mallam, Maxbohm, Magley—what ghastly names they have—Markby, Migsby, Mobbs, Moncrieff! Lieutenant 1840, Captain, Lieutenant-Colonel, Colonel, General 1869, Christian names, Ernest John. [*Puts book very quietly down and speaks quite calmly.*] I always told you, Gwendolen, my name was Ernest, didn't I? Well, it is Ernest after all. I mean it naturally is Ernest.

LADY BRACKNELL   Yes, I remember now that the General was called Ernest. I knew I had some particular reason for disliking the name.

GWENDOLEN   Ernest! My own Ernest! I felt from the first that you could have no other name!

JACK   Gwendolen, it is a terrible thing for a man to find out suddenly that all his life he has been speaking nothing but the truth. Can you forgive me?

GWENDOLEN   I can. For I feel that you are sure to change.

JACK   My own one!

CHASUBLE [*to* MISS PRISM]   Laetitia! [*Embraces her.*]

MISS PRISM [*enthusiastically*]   Frederick! At last!

ALGERNON   Cecily! [*Embraces her.*] At last!

JACK   Gwendolen! [*Embraces her.*] At last!

LADY BRACKNELL   My nephew, you seem to be displaying signs of triviality.

JACK   On the contrary, Aunt Augusta, I've now realized for the first time in my life the vital Importance of Being Earnest.

1895

SAMUEL BECKETT

Krapp's Last Tape

A late evening in the future.

KRAPP's *den.*

Front centre a small table, the two drawers of which open towards audience.

Sitting at the table, facing front, i.e., across from the drawers, a wearish old man: KRAPP.

Rusty black narrow trousers too short for him. Rusty black sleeveless waistcoat, four capacious pockets. Heavy silver watch and chain. Grimy white shirt open at neck, no collar. Surprising pair of dirty white boots, size ten at least, very narrow and pointed.

White face. Purple nose. Disordered grey hair. Unshaven.

Very near-sighted (but unspectacled). Hard of hearing.

Cracked voice. Distinctive intonation.

Laborious walk.

On the table a tape-recorder with microphone and a number of cardboard boxes containing reels of recorded tapes.

Table and immediately adjacent area in strong white light. Rest of stage in darkness.

KRAPP *remains a moment motionless, heaves a great sigh, looks at his watch, fumbles in his pockets, takes out an envelope, puts it back, fumbles, takes out a small bunch of keys, raises it to his eyes, chooses a key, gets up and moves to front of table. He stoops, unlocks first drawer, peers into it, feels about inside it, takes out a reel of tape, peers at it, puts it back, locks drawer, unlocks second drawer, peers into it, feels about inside it, takes out a large banana, peers at it, locks drawer, puts keys back in his pocket. He turns, advances to edge of stage, halts, strokes banana, peels it, drops skin at his feet, puts end of banana in his mouth and remains motionless, staring vacuously before him. Finally he bites off the end, turns aside and begins pacing to and fro at edge of stage, in the light, i.e. not more than four or five paces either way, meditatively eating banana. He treads on skin, slips, nearly falls, recovers himself, stoops and peers at skin and finally pushes it, still stooping, with his foot over the edge of stage into pit. He resumes his pacing, finishes banana, returns to table, sits down, remains a moment motionless, heaves a great sigh, takes keys from his pockets, raises them to his eyes, chooses key, gets up and moves to front of table, unlocks second drawer, takes out a second large banana, peers at it, locks drawer, puts back keys in his pocket, turns, advances to edge of stage, halts, strokes banana, peels it, tosses skin into pit, puts end of banana in his mouth and remains motionless, staring vacuously before him. Finally he has an idea, puts banana in his waistcoat pocket, the end emerging, and goes with all the speed he can muster backstage into darkness. Ten seconds. Loud pop of cork. Fifteen seconds. He comes back into light carrying an old ledger and sits down at table. He lays ledger on table, wipes his mouth, wipes his hands on the front of his waistcoat, brings them smartly together and rubs them.*

KRAPP [*briskly*]   Ah! [*He bends over ledger, turns the pages, finds the entry he wants, reads.*] Box . . . thrree . . . spool . . . five. [*He raises his head and stares front. With relish.*] Spool! [*Pause.*] Spool! [*Happy smile. Pause. He bends over table, starts peering and poking at the boxes.*] Box . . . thrree . . . thrree . . . four . . . two . . . [*with surprise*] nine! good God! . . . seven . . . ah! the little rascal! [*He takes up box, peers at it.*] Box thrree. [*He lays it on table, opens it and peers at spools inside.*] Spool . . . [*he peers at ledger*] . . . five . . . [*he peers at spools*] . . . five . . . five . . . ah! the little scoundrel! [*He takes out a spool, peers at it.*] Spool five. [*He lays it on table, closes box three, puts it back with the others, takes up the spool.*] Box thrree, spool five. [*He bends over the machine, looks up. With relish.*] Spooool! [*Happy smile. He bends, loads spool on machine, rubs his hands.*] Ah! [*He peers at ledger, reads entry at foot of page.*] Mother at rest at last . . . Hm . . . The black ball . . . [*He raises his head, stares blankly front. Puzzled.*] Black ball? . . . [*He peers again at ledger, reads.*] The dark nurse . . . [*He raises his head, broods, peers again at ledger, reads.*] Slight improvement in bowel condition . . . Hm . . . Memorable . . . what? [*He peers closer.*] Equinox, memorable equinox. [*He raises his head, stares blankly front. Puzzled.*] Memorable equinox? . . . [*Pause. He shrugs his shoulders, peers again at ledger, reads.*] Farewell to—[*He turns the page*]—love.

He raises his head, broods, bends over machine, switches on and assumes listening posture, i.e. leaning forward, elbows on table, hand cupping ear towards machine, face front.

TAPE [*strong voice, rather pompous, clearly* KRAPP's *at a much earlier time.*]   Thirty-nine today, sound as a—[*Settling himself more comfortably he knocks one of the boxes off thte table, curses, switches off, sweeps boxes and ledger violently to the ground, winds tape back to beginning, switches on, resumes posture.*] Thirty-nine today, sound as a bell, apart from my old weakness, and intellectually I have now every reason to suspect at the . . . [*hesitates*] . . . crest of the wave—or thereabouts. Celebrated the awful occasion, as in recent years, quietly at the Winehouse. Not a soul. Sat before the fire with closed eyes, separating the grain from the husks. Jotted down a few notes, on the back of an envelope. Good to be back in my den, in my old rags. Have just eaten I regret to say three bananas and only with difficulty refrained from a fourth. Fatal things for a man with my condition. [*Vehemently.*] Cut 'em out! [*Pause.*] The new light above my table is a great improvement. With all this darkness round me I feel less alone. [*Pause.*] In a way. [*Pause.*] I love to get up and move about in it, then back here to . . . [*hesitates*] . . . me. [*Pause.*] Krapp.

Pause.

The grain, now what I wonder do I mean by that, I mean . . . [*hesitates*] . . . I suppose I mean those things worth having when all the dust has—when all *my* dust has settled. I close my eyes and try and imagine them.

Pause. KRAPP *closes his eyes briefly.*

Extraordinary silence this evening, I strain my ears and do not hear a sound. Old Miss McGlome always sings at this hour. But not tonight. Songs of her girlhood, she says. Hard to think of her as a girl. Wonderful woman though. Connaught, I fancy. [*Pause.*] Shall I sing when I am her age, if I ever am? No. [*Pause.*] Did I sing as a boy? No. [*Pause.*] Did I ever sing? No.

Pause.

Just been listening to an old year, passages at random. I did not check in the book, but it must be at least ten or twelve years ago. At that time I think I was still living on and off with Bianca in Kedar Street. Well out of that, Jesus yes! Hopeless business. [*Pause.*] Not much about her, apart from a tribute to her eyes. Very warm. I suddenly saw them again. [*Pause.*] Incomparable! [*Pause.*] Ah well . . . [*Pause.*] These old P.M.s are gruesome, but I often find them—[KRAPP *switches off, broods, switches on*]—a help before embarking on a new . . . [*hesitates*] . . . retrospect. Hard to believe I was ever that young whelp. The voice! Jesus! And the aspirations! [*Brief laugh in which Krapp joins.*] And the resolutions! [*Brief laugh in which* KRAPP *joins.*] To drink less, in particular. [*Brief laugh of* KRAPP *alone.*] Statistics. Seventeen hundred hours, out of the preceding eight thousand odd, consumed on licensed premises alone. More than 20%, say 40% of his waking life. [*Pause.*] Plans for a less . . . [*hesitates*] . . . engrossing sexual life. Last illness of his father. Flagging pursuit of happiness. Unattainable laxation. Sneers at what he calls his youth and thanks to God that it's over. [*Pause.*] False ring there. [*Pause.*] Shadows of the opus . . . magnum. Closing with a—[*brief laugh*]—yelp to Providence. [*Prolonged laugh in which* KRAPP *joins.*] What remains of all that misery? A girl in a shabby green coat, on a railway-station platform? No?

Pause.

When I look—

> KRAPP *switches off, broods, looks at his watch, gets up, goes backstage into darkness. Ten seconds. Pop of cork. Ten seconds. Second cork. Ten seconds. Third cork. Ten seconds. Brief burst of quavering song.*

KRAPP [*sings*]   Now the days is over,
Night is drawing nigh-igh,
Shadows—

> *Fit of coughing. He comes back into light, sits down, wipes his mouth, switches on, resumes his listening posture.*

TAPE   —back on the year that is gone, with what I hope is perhaps a glint of the old eye to come, there is of course the house on the canal where mother lay a-dying, in the late autumn, after her long viduity [*Krapp gives a start*], and the—[*Krapp switches off, winds back tape a little, bends his ear closer to machine, switches on*]—a-dying, after her long viduity, and the—

> KRAPP *switches off, raises his head, stares blankly before him. His lips move in the syllables of "viduity." No sound. He gets up, goes backstage into darkness, comes back with an enormous dictionary, lays it on table, sits down and looks up the word.*

KRAPP [*reading from dictionary*]   State—or condition of being—or remaining—a widow—or widower. [*Looks up. Puzzled.*] Being—or remaining? . . . [*Pause. He peers again at dictionary. Reading.*] "Deep weeds of viduity" . . . Also of an animal, especially a bird . . . the vidua or weaver-bird . . . Black plumage of male . . . [*He looks up. With relish.*] The vidua-bird!

> *Pause. He closes dictionary, switches on, resumes listening posture.*

TAPE   —bench by the weir from where I could see her window. There I sat, in the biting wind, wishing she were gone. [*Pause.*] Hardly a soul, just a few regulars, nursemaids, infants, old men, dogs. I got to know them quite well—oh by appearance of course I mean! One dark young beauty I recollect particularly, all white and starch, incomparable bosom, with a big black hooded perambulator, most funereal thing. Whenever I looked in her direction she had her eyes on me. And yet when I was bold enough to speak to her—not having been introduced—she threatened to call a policeman. As if I had designs on her virtue! [*Laugh. Pause.*] The face she had! The eyes! Like . . . [*hesitates*] . . . chrysolite! [*Pause.*] Ah well . . . [*Pause.*] I was there when—[KRAPP *switches off, broods, switches on again*]—the blind went down, one of those dirty brown roller affairs, throwing a ball for a little white dog, as chance would have it. I happened to look up and there it was. All over and done with, at last. I sat on for a few moments with the ball in my hand and the dog yelping and pawing at me. [*Pause.*] Moments. Her moments, my moments. [*Pause.*] The dog's moments. [*Pause.*] In the end I held it out to him and he took it in his mouth, gently, gently. A small, old, black, hard, solid rubber ball. [*Pause.*] I shall feel it, in my hand, until my dying day. [*Pause.*] I might have kept it. [*Pause.*] But I gave it to the dog.

Pause.

Ah well . . .

Pause.

Spiritually a year of profound gloom and indigence until that memorable night in March, at the end of the jetty, in the howling wind, never to be forgotten, when suddenly I saw the whole thing. The vision, at last. This I fancy is what I have chiefly to record this evening, against the day when my work will be done and perhaps no place left in my memory, warm or cold, for the miracle that . . . [*hesitates*] . . . for the fire that set it alight. What I suddenly saw then was this, that the belief I had been going on all my life, namely—[KRAPP *switches off impatiently, winds tape forward, switches on again*]—great granite rocks the foam flying up in the light of the lighthouse and the wind-gauge spinning like a propellor, clear to me at last that the dark I have always struggled to keep under is in reality my most—[KRAPP *curses, switches off, winds tape forward, switches on again*]—unshatterable association until my dissolution of storm and night with the light of the understanding and the fire—[KRAPP *curses louder, switches off, winds tape forward, switches on again*]—my face in her breasts and my hand on her. We lay there without moving. But under us all moved, and moved us, gently, up and down, and from side to side.

Pause.

Past midnight. Never knew such silence. The earth might be uninhabited.

Pause.

Here I end—

KRAPP switches off, winds tape back, switches on again.

—upper lake, with punt, bathed off the bank, then pushed out into the stream and drifted. She lay stretched out on the floorboards with her hands under her head and her eyes closed. Sun blazing down, bit of a breeze, water nice and lively. I noticed a scratch on her thigh and asked her how she came by it. Picking gooseberries, she said. I said again I thought it was hopeless and no good going on, and she agreed, without opening her eyes. [*Pause.*] I asked her to look at me and after a few moments—[*pause*]—*after a few moments she did, but the eyes just slits, because of the glare. I bent over her to get them in the shadow and they opened. [*Pause. Low.*] Let me in. [*Pause.*] We drifted in among the flags and stuck. The way they went down, sighing, before the stem! [*Pause.*] I lay down, sighing, before the stem! [*Pause.*] I lay down across her with my face in her breasts and my hand on her. We lay there without moving. But under us all moved, and moved us, gently, up and down, and from side to side.

Pause.

Past midnight. Never knew—

> KRAPP *switches off, broods. Finally he fumbles in his pockets, encounters the banana, takes it out, peers at it, puts it back, fumbles, brings out the envelope, fumbles, puts back envelope, looks at his watch, gets up and goes backstage into darkness. Ten seconds. Sound of bottle against glass, then brief siphon. Ten seconds. Bottle against glass alone. Ten seconds. He comes back a little unsteadily into light, goes to front of table, takes out keys, raises them to his eyes, chooses key, unlocks first drawer, peers into it, feels about inside, takes out reel, peers at it, locks drawer, puts keys back in his pocket, goes and sits down, takes reel off machine, lays it on dictionary, loads virgin reel on machine, takes envelope from his pocket, consults back of it, lays it on table, switches on, clears his throat and begins to record.*

KRAPP   Just been listening to that stupid bastard I took myself for thirty years ago, hard to believe I was ever as bad as that. Thank God that's all done with anyway. [*Pause.*] The eyes she had! [*Broods, realizes he is recording silence, switches off, broods. Finally.*] Everything there, everything, all the—[*Realizes this is not being recorded, switches on.*] Everything there, everything on this old muckball, all the light and dark and famine and feasting of . . . [*hesitates*] . . . the ages! [*In a shout.*] Yes! [*Pause.*] Let that go! Jesus! Take his mind off his homework! Jesus! [*Pause. Weary.*] Ah well, maybe he was right. [*Pause.*] Maybe he was right. [*Broods. Realizes. Switches off. Consults envelope.*] Pah! [*Crumples it and throws it away. Broods. Switches on.*] Nothing to say, not a squeak. What's a year now? The sour cud and the iron stool. [*Pause.*] Revelled in the word spool. [*With relish.*] Spooool! Happiest moment of the past half million. [*Pause.*] Seventeen copies sold, of which eleven at trade price to free circulating libraries beyond the seas. Getting known. [*Pause.*] One pound six and something, eight I have little doubt. [*Pause.*] Crawled out once or twice, before the summer was cold. Sat shivering in the park, drowned in dreams and burning to be gone. Not a soul. [*Pause.*] Last fancies. [*Vehemently.*] Keep 'em under! [*Pause.*] Scalded the eyes out of me reading *Effie* again, a page a day, with tears again. Effie . . . [*Pause.*] Could have been happy with her, up there on the Baltic, and the pines, and the dunes. [*Pause.*] Could I? [*Pause.*] And she? [*Pause.*] Pah! [*Pause.*] Fanny came in a couple of times. Bony old ghost of a whore. Couldn't do much, but I suppose better than a kick in the crutch. The last time wasn't so bad. How do you manage it, she said, at your age? I told her I'd been saving up for her all my life. [*Pause.*] Went to Vespers once, like when I was in short trousers. [*Pause. Sings.*]

> Now the day is over,
> Night is drawing nigh-igh,
> Shadows—[*coughing, then almost
>   inaudible*]—of the evening
> Steal across the sky.

[*Gasping.*] Went to sleep and fell off the pew. [*Pause.*] Sometimes wondered in the night if a last effort mightn't—[*Pause.*] Ah finish your booze now and get to your bed. Go on with this drivel in the morning. Or leave it at that. [*Pause.*] Leave it at that. [*Pause.*] Lie propped up in the dark—and wander. Be again in the dingle on a Christmas Eve, gathering holly, the red-berried. [*Pause.*] Be again on Croghan[1] on a Sunday morning, in the haze, with the bitch, stop and listen to the bells. [*Pause.*] Be again, be again. [*Pause.*] All that old misery. [*Pause.*] Once wasn't enough for you. [*Pause.*] Lie down across her.

> *Long pause. He suddenly bends over machine, switches off, wrenches off tape, throws it away, puts on the other, winds it forward to the passage he wants, switches on, listens staring front.*

TAPE   —gooseberries, she said. I said again I thought it was hopeless and no good going on, and she agreed, without opening her eyes. [*Pause.*] I asked her to look at me and after a few moments—[*Pause*]—after a few moments she did, but the eyes just slits, because of the glare. I bent over her to get them in the shadow and they opened. [*Pause. Low.*] Let me in. [*Pause.*] We drifted in among the flags and stuck. They way they went down, sighing, before the stem! [*Pause.*] I lay down across her with my face in her breasts and my hand on her. We lay there without moving. But under us all moved, and moved us, gently, up and down, and from side to side.

> *Pause.* KRAPP's *lips moved.* No sound.

---

1. Mountain in southeastern Ireland.

Past midnight. Never knew such silence. The earth might be uninhabited.

Pause.

Here I end this reel. Box—[*pause.*]—three, spool—[*pause*]—five. [*Pause.*] Perhaps my best years are gone. When there was a chance of happiness. But I wouldn't want them back. Not with the fire in me now. No, I wouldn't want them back.

KRAPP *motionless staring before him. The tape runs on in silence.*

CURTAIN

1958

7   HISTORICAL SETTING

One of the factors that make drama seem as if it is *happening* is its use of the present tense (as opposed to the conventional past tense of most fiction, where everything has already happened but is only now being told to us). This "presentness" contributes to the dramatic impact. (Indeed, it may be to preserve this sense of the presentness that represented time is so often restricted to something not too different from reading or viewing time.) Presentness also makes drama appear timeless: what is always present seems outside time. So, when we read or watch a 2500-year-old play it still does not seem to be something that has happened long ago and is over with; it is something going on *now*. Its timelessness also makes drama seem not to be historical: Oedipus was not a contemporary even of those watching the first performance of Sophocles' play, but if he was a figure of the past it was of the mythical not the historical past, and myth is eternal, recurrent, or always present.

Every play is, of course, historical in one sense: it was written and performed at a particular time and in a particular culture and tradition. It is the product of and to some extent the producer of its age—or at least our vision of its age: *Hamlet* is an Elizabethan play and we know what the Elizabethan period was like in part because it was that time in which *Hamlet* was produced. No doubt every play has a special pertinence and relationship to its age. Each is embedded in an historical context and that context is worth studying in depth to get some sense of its special nature and contemporary significance. We can of course never "know" the period as a contemporary did, much less in any truly objective sense. What we understand of history depends on what we know—and we should know as much as we can —but it also depends on where we are standing, where we are ourselves in time. Even a casual glance at the various interpretations of *Hamlet* through the ages will reveal that those readings tell you not only about aspects of the play you may have missed without critical guidance, but also about the period or predisposition of the interpreter. To know as much as possible about the period in which *Hamlet* first appeared is therefore valuable not only to our fuller understanding of the play but also to our understanding of our own time, the historical vantage point from which we are reading *Hamlet*. To see in that play some reflection of bitter awareness not just of the rottenness of the Denmark of what was even then long ago but of the "present-day," Elizabethan England in which Essex fell from favor, rebelled, and was beheaded, may illuminate something in *Hamlet* that a modern North American reader could easily miss. To suppose that that is the central concern of the play, however, may tell us more about the troubled times or political views of the interpreter than about Shakespeare and his contemporaries.

Like *Hamlet*, *A Soldier's Play* is about the historical past, but its past is neither so remote nor so vaguely treated: when everyone wears a wristwatch, we expect a bit more temporal precision from our playwrights than those did who relied on sun or sands. Fuller, in fact, immediately indicates the precise historical time—1944, and within a few pages we know that the murder occurred in mid-April and it is now late May. The stage directions for the first scene specify that a picture of President Franklin Delano Roosevelt, who later in 1944 was elected to his fourth term, and a poster of "Pvt. Joe Louis," the black world heavyweight champion since 1938 who had recently been inducted into the army, are on the walls—the first in the room of the white officers, the second in the barracks of the black enlisted men. The place, Louisiana, is also part of the historical setting, since the South was wholly and distinctly segregated, the North extensively but more subtly so. We thus have not only a "wristwatch" sense of time but an historical sense of the times.

Just as a play typically treats conflict and begins just as its characters' lives are about to change, so an historical drama will be set in an historical moment when opposing historical forces clash and things are about to change. The clash in *A Soldier's Play* is racial and it is epitomized not so much by the murder of a black soldier—presumed to have been committed by Southern whites, perhaps by the Klan—for that's an old story, but by the appearance of Captain Davenport, a black captain who is to conduct the murder investigation: the black enlisted men and white officers have never seen a black in a position of power. The most obvious statement of the play is that white society had better get used to seeing blacks in such positions.

The historical moment is also that of the final year of World War II; the black soldiers are eager to join the battle against the Nazis and racism. It is probably no accident that the black army unit in *A Soldier's Play* is described as having been assembled primarily as a baseball team: just three years after the time of the play a black ex-Army officer named Jackie Robinson would bring down the racial barriers of major league baseball.

There is, however, another harbinger of change: the murdered man, Sergeant Waters. He had served in the segregated army since the days of World War I (which ended in 1918) and though he had not risen to the status of officer and gentleman, he had gained a certain amount of authority within the enlisted ranks as a technical sergeant. He had made his way up by playing the game according to the rules laid down by the dominant white society, and he played it to the hilt. There had been a time when he had expected things to change—during World War I, after he had "seen Paree." There had been no changes, but he knows things will change this time, and he has his own agenda: "the only thing that can move the race is power," he says; his son will not go into the army but to "some big white college . . . [to] learn the white man's language—how he does things." (Davenport, on the other hand, has graduated from Howard, a black university.) In trying to succeed in the white world and achieve white man's power, Waters has become something of an anti-black racist himself, wanting to eradicate "Negro-ness."

Given the major roles of Waters and Davenport and the important minor roles of the down-home C. J. and the militant Peterson, the play seems to explore the choice facing black Americans as the old, wholly segregated society is collapsing. What kind of society is likely to emerge? What kind *should* emerge? How should one act to effect the best possible outcome? Should one's primary loyalty be to principles, moral values such as traditional concepts of justice, or first to racial solidarity both to compensate for centuries of injustice and to make sure that white society will have to share its power? To appreciate the play fully you must exercise the same kind of sympathetic imagination you would in reading any other work of literature, but you must also exercise your historical imagination. You must try to understand what it was like "then," with legally enforced segregation, deprivation of voting rights, and illegal but often unprosecuted acts of racial violence like lynchings.

You must also be aware, however, that *A Soldier's Play* was not written in the 1940s and is not addressed to an audience of that time, white or black. In 1981, when it was first performed, the viewers knew about Jackie Robinson and knew that the Thurgood Marshall mentioned early in the play had, in 1967, become the first black Supreme Court Justice. Between the time of the dramatic action and the time of the reading or viewing much had happened in the arena of civil rights: Martin Luther King, Jr.; Black Power; the end of legal segregation; the painfully slow desegregation of schools and of many professions; voting rights; the election of black mayors of major cities, even including those in the South. If all was not well, much had been accomplished. The play, read or seen in 1981, could well seem positive and hopeful.

But even in 1981, there were disquieting realities in the historical background. Of course integration was far from complete, but even leaving that aside, recent events may have cast a shadow on certain aspects of the play. The setting of the play is in World War II and though that war had long been over, a more recent and rather different one, in Vietnam, had barely ended. In the recent war black Americans certainly had more than ample "opportunity" to fight the enemy than they had had early in World War II. The army in Vietnam was so "integrated" it was rather extensively black. And the enemy was not white and racist but non-white and nationalistic. Does that make any difference in our reading or viewing of *A Soldier's Play*? Do later events in history make us ask why it was the Germans and not the Japanese that the black troops in the play were so eager to fight? If the play had been written and performed during the Vietnam War, say in 1971, with that war, its consequences, its controversy foremost in the minds of the audience, such questions would surely be asked. Are they properly asked in 1981—or later; that is, are they appropriate or inevitable questions to ask of the play or would the asking tell you more about the questioner's age or political orientation than about the play itself?

It is, however, no longer even 1981, much less 1971 or 1944. Though 1981 may seem nearly the historical present, time has not stood still. Many now believe there has been a significant pause in the racial integration of American society in the 1980s, and some even believe they see a movement backward toward resegregation or disintegration. Now *A Soldier's Play* may seem less optimistic and more ironic than meets the eye—Davenport rushing toward his own, unseen Water-shed. So even in miniature—within a decade—the gap between first audience and later ones may be pereceived, the relevance of history to our understanding and appreciation of literature may be made visible in the historical setting of the work and where we ourselves are situated in history may be illuminated.

CHARLES FULLER

A Soldier's Play

TIME: 1944

PLACE: Fort Neal, Louisiana

SCENE: *The inner shell of the stage is black. On the stage, in a horse-shoe-like half circle, are several platforms at varying levels.*

On the left side of this horseshoe is a military office arrangement with a small desk (a nameplate on the desk reads: CAPTAIN CHARLES TAYLOR), *two office-type chairs, one straight-backed, a regimental, and an American flag. A picture of F.D.R.[1] is on the wall.*

On the right side of the horseshoe, and curved toward the rear, is a barracks arrangement, with three bunk beds and footlockers set in typical military fashion. The exit to this barracks is a free-standing doorway on the far right. (This barracks should be changeable—these bunks with little movement can look like a different place.) On the edge of this barracks is a poster, semi-blown up, of Joe Louis[2] in an army uniform, helmet, rifle, and bayonet. It reads: PVT. JOE LOUIS SAYS, "WE'RE GOING TO DO OUR PART—AND WE'LL WIN BECAUSE WE'RE ON GOD'S SIDE."

On the rear of the horseshoe, upstage center, is a bare platform, raised several feet above everything else. It can be anything we want it to be—a limbo if you will.

The entire set should resemble a courtroom. The sets, barracks and office, will both be elevated, so that from anywhere on the horseshoe one may look down onto a space at center stage that is on the stage floor. The levels should have easy access by either stairs or ramps, and the entire set should be raked ever so slightly so that one does not perceive much difference between floor and set, and the bottom edges of the horseshoe. There must also be enough area on both sides of the horseshoe to see exits and entrances.

Lighting will play an integral part in the realization of the play. It should therefore be sharp, so that areas are clearly defined, with as little spill into other areas as possible. Lights must also be capable of suggesting mood, time, and place.

As the play opens, the stage is black. In the background, rising in volume, we hear the song "Don't Sit under the Apple Tree," sung by the Andrews Sisters.[3] Quite suddenly, in a sharp though narrow beam of light, in limbo, TECH/SERGEANT VERNON C. WATERS, *a well-built, light-brown-skinned man in a World War II, winter army*

---

1. Franklin Delano Roosevelt (1882–1945), 32nd President of the United States, was, at the time of the opening of the play (Spring, 1944) serving his third term and would soon be elected to his fourth.

2. Joe Louis (1914–81), "The Brown Bomber," world heavyweight boxing champion since 1937, had (in 1944) recently been inducted into the army as a private. He died in April 1981, just a few months before the first production of *A Soldier's Play* in November.

3. *"Don't Sit Under the Apple Tree"* . . . *Andrews Sisters*—Maxine, LaVerne, and Patti Andrews made up the most popular singing group of the 1940s; they had sung this wartime hit song (released 1942) in the film *Private Buckaroo.*

uniform, is seen down on all fours. He is stinking drunk, trying to stand and mumbling to himself.

WATERS [*repeating*] They'll still hate you! They still hate you . . . They still hate you!

> WATERS *is laughing as suddenly someone steps into the light. [We never see this person.] He is holding a .45 caliber pistol. He lifts it swiftly and ominously toward* WATERS*'s head and fires.* WATERS *is knocked over backward. He is dead. The music has stopped and there is a strong silence onstage.*

VOICE Le's go!

> *The man with the gun takes a step, then stops. He points the gun at* WATERS *again and fires a second time. There is another silence as limbo is plunged into darkness, and the barracks is just as quickly lit.*
>
> *We are in the barracks of Company B, 221st Chemical Smoke Generating Company, at Fort Neal. Five black enlisted men stand at "parade rest" with their hands above their heads and submit to a search. They are:* CORPORAL BERNARD COBB, *a man in his mid to late twenties, dressed in a T-shirt, dog tags, fatigues, and slippers.* PRIVATE JAMES WILKIE, *a man in his early forties, a career soldier, is dressed in fatigues from which the stripes have been removed, with a baseball cap on, and smoking a cigar.* PRIVATE LOUIS HENSON, *thin, in his late twenties or early thirties, is wearing a baseball T-shirt that reads "Fort Neal" on the front and "#4" on the back, with fatigues and boots on.* PFC MELVIN PETERSON, *a man in his late twenties, wearing glasses, looks angelic. His shirt is open but he does not look sloppy; of all the men, his stripe is the most visible, his boots the most highly polished.* PRIVATE TONY SMALLS, *a man in his late thirties, a career man, is as small as his name feels. All five men are being searched by* CORPORAL ELLIS, *a soldier who is simply always "spit and polish."* ELLIS *is also black, and moves from man to man, patting them down in a police-like search.* CAPTAIN CHARLES TAYLOR, *a young white man in his mid to late thirties, looks a bit disturbed. All the men's uniforms are from World War II.*

TAYLOR I'm afraid this kind of thing can't be helped, men—you can put your arms down when Ellis finishes. [*Several men drop their arms.* ELLIS *is searching* PVT. HENSON] We don't want anyone from Fort Neal going into Tynin looking for red-necks.

COBB May I speak sir? [TAYLOR *nods*] Why do this, Captain? They got M.P.'s[4] surrounding us, and hell, the Colonel must know nobody colored killed the man!

TAYLOR This is precaution, Cobb. We can't have revenge killings, so we search for weapons.

PETERSON Where'd they find the Sarge, sir?

TAYLOR In the woods out by the Junction—and so we don't have any rumors. Sergeant Waters was shot twice—we don't know that

---

4. Military police.

he was lynched! [*Pause*] Twice. Once in the chest, and a bullet in the head. [ELLIS *finishes with the last man*] You finished in the footlockers?

ELLIS   Yes, sir! There aren't any weapons.

TAYLOR [*relaxes*]   I didn't think there would be. At ease, men! [*The men relax.*] Tech/Sergeant Waters, in my opinion, served the 221st and this platoon in particular with distinction, and I for one shall miss the man. [*Slight pause*] But no matter what we think of the Sergeant's death, we will not allow this incident to make us forget our responsibility to this uniform. We are soldiers, and our war is with the Nazis and Japs, not the civilians in Tynin. Any enlisted man found with unauthorized weapons will be immediately subject to summary court-martial. [*Softens*] Sergeant Waters's replacement won't be assigned for several weeks. Until that time, you will all report to Sergeant Dorsey of C Company. Corporal Cobb will be barracks N.C.O.—any questions?

PETERSON   Who do you think did it, sir?

TAYLOR   At this time there are no suspects.

HENSON   You know the Klan did it, sir.

TAYLOR   Were you an eyewitness, soldier?

HENSON   Who else goes around killin' Negroes in the South?—They lynched Jefferson the week I got here, sir! And that Signal Corps guy, Daniels, two months later!

TAYLOR   Henson, unless you saw it, keep your opinions to yourself! Is that clear? [HENSON *nods.*] And that's an order! It also applies to everybody else!

ALL [*almost simultaneously*]   Yes, sir!

TAYLOR   You men who have details this afternoon, report to the orderly room for your assignments. The rest of you are assigned to the Colonel's quarters—clean-up detail. Cobb, I want to see you in my office at 1350 hours.[5]

COBB   Yes, sir.

TAYLOR   As of 0600 hours this morning, the town of Tynin was placed off-limits to all military personnel. [*Slight groan from the men*] The Friday night dance has also been canceled—[*All the men moan.* TAYLOR *is sympathetic*] O.K., O.K.! Some of the officers are going to the Colonel—I can't promise anything. Right now, it's canceled.

ELLIS   Tenn-hut!

The men snap to. The CAPTAIN *salutes. Only* COBB *salutes him back. The* CAPTAIN *starts out.*

TAYLOR   As you were!

The CAPTAIN *and* ELLIS *exit the barracks. The men move to their bunks or footlockers.* WILKIE *goes to the rear of the bunks and looks out.*

COBB   They still out there, Wilkie?

WILKIE   Yeah. Got the whole place surrounded.

HENSON   I don't know what the hell they thought we'd go into that town with—mops and dishrags?

5. 1:50 P.M. (the army uses a twenty-four-hour clock).

WILKIE   Y'all recruits know what Colonel's clean-up detail is, don't you? Shovelin' horseshit in his stables—

COBB   Ain't no different from what we been doin'. [*He lies down and begins scratching around his groin area*]

PETERSON [*to* COBB]   Made you the barracks Commander-in-Chief, huh? [COBB *nods*] Don't git like ole Stone-ass— What are you doin'?

COBB   Scratchin'!

HENSON [*overlapping*]   Taylor knows the Klan did it—I hope y'all know that!

SMALLS [*sudden*]   Then why are the M.P.'s outside with rifles? Why hold us prisoner?

PETERSON   They scared we may kill a couple of peckerwoods,[6] Smalls. Calm down, man!

WILKIE [*quickly*]   Smalls, you wanna play some coon-can?[7]

SMALLS *shakes his head no. He is quiet, staring.*

COBB [*examining himself*]   Peterson, you know I think Eva gave me the crabs.

HENSON   Cobb, the kinda women you find, it's a wonda your nuts ain't fell off—crabs? You probably got lice, ticks, bedbugs, fleas—tapeworms—

COBB   Shut up, Henson! Pete—I ain't foolin', man! [*He starts to open his pants.*]

PETERSON   Get some powder from the PX.

WILKIE [*almost simultaneously*]   Which one of y'all feels like playin' me some cards? [*He looks at* HENSON.]

HENSON   Me and Peterson's goin' down the mess hall—you still goin', Pete?

PETERSON [*nods*]   Wilkie? I thought all you could do was play go-fer?

HENSON [*slyly*]   Yeah, Wilkie—whose ass can you kiss, now that your number-one ass is dead?

COBB [*laughing*]   That sounds like something C.J. would sing! [*Looks at himself again.*] Ain't this a bitch? [*Picks at himself.*]

WILKIE [*overlapping, to* HENSON]   You know what you can do for me, Henson—you too, Peterson!

PETERSON   Naughty, naughty!

WILKIE *moves to his bunk, justifying.*

WILKIE   I'm the one lost three stripes—and I'm the only man in here with kids, so when the man said jump, I jumped!

HENSON [*derisively*]   Don't put your wife and kids between you and Waters's ass, man!

WILKIE   I wanted my stripes back!

COBB   I'm goin' to sick call after chow.

WILKIE [*continuing*]   Y'all ain't neva' had nothin', that's why you can't understand a man like me! There was a time I was a sergeant major, you know!

HENSON *waves disdainfully at him, turning his attention to* COBB

HENSON   Ole V-girl[8] slipped Cobb the crabs! How you gonna explain

6. Woodpecker—pejorative term used by blacks to denote poor rural whites.

7. A card game.

8. "Victory-girl," one of the young women who hung around military installations, bus and railroad terminals, etc., to pick up soldiers.

that to the girl back home, Corporal? How will that fine, big-thighed Moma feel, when the only ribbon you bring home from this war is the Purple Heart for crab bites? [HENSON *laughs as* SMALLS *stands suddenly*]

SMALLS   Don't any of you guys give a damn?

PETERSON   What's the matta', Smalls?

SMALLS   The man's dead! We saw him alive last night!

COBB [*quickly*]   I saw him, too. At least I know he died good and drunk!

SMALLS [*loud*]   What's the matter with y'all?

HENSON   The man got hisself lynched! We're in the South, and we can't do a goddamn thing about it—you heard the Captain! But don't start actin' like we guilty of somethin'. [*Softens*] I just hope we get lucky enough to get shipped outta this hell-hole to the war! [*To himself*] Besides, whoever did it, didn't kill much anyway.

SMALLS   He deserved better than that!

COBB   Look, everybody feels rotten, Smalls. But it won't bring the man back, so let's forget about it!

PETERSON *moves to pat* SMALLS *on the back.*

PETERSON   Why don't you walk it off, man?

SMALLS *moves away to his bunk.* PETERSON *shrugs.*

HENSON   Yeah—or go turn on a smoke machine, let the fog make you think you in London!

SMALLS *sits down on his bunk and looks at them for a moment, then lies down, his face in the pillow.*

WILKIE [*overlapping*]   Let Cobb bring his Eva over, she'll take his mind off Waters plus give him a bonus of crabs!

The men laughed, but SMALLS *doesn't move at the lights begin slowly to fade out.*

HENSON [*counting*]   —an' blue-balls. Clap. Syphilis. Pimples! [COBB *throws a pillow at* HENSON] Piles! Fever blisters. Cockeyes. Cooties! *The men are laughing as the lights go out. As they do, a rather wiry black officer wearing glasses,* CAPTAIN RICHARD DAVENPORT, *walks across the stage from the wings, dressed sharply in an M.P. uniform, his hat cocked to the side and strapped down, the way airmen wear theirs. He is carrying a brief case, and we are aware of a man who is very confident and self-assured. He is smiling as he faces the audience, cleaning his glasses as he begins to speak.*

DAVENPORT   Call me Davenport—Captain, United States Army, attached to the 343rd Military Police Corps Unit, Fort Neal, Louisiana. I'm a lawyer the segregated Armed Services couldn't find a place for. My job in this war? Policing colored troops. [*Slight pause*] One morning during mid-April 1944, a colored tech/sergeant, Vernon C. Waters, assigned to the 221st Chemical Smoke Generating Company, stationed here before transfer to Europe, was brutally shot to death in a wooded section off the New Post Road and the junction of Highway 51—just two hundred yards from the colored N.C.O. club—by a person or persons unknown. [*Pauses a little.*] Naturally, the unofficial consensus was the local Ku Klux Klan, and for that reason, I was told at the time, Colonel

Barton Nivens ordered the Military Police to surround the enlisted men's quarters—then instructed his company commanders to initiate a thorough search of all personal property for unauthorized knives, guns—weapons of any kind. [*Slight pause*] You see, ninety percent of the Colonel's command—all of the enlisted men stationed here are Negroes, and the Colonel felt—and I suppose justly— that once word of the Sergeant's death spread among his troops, there might be some retaliation against the white citizens of Tynin. [*Shrugs*] What he did worked—there was no retaliation, and no racial incidents. [*Pause*] The week after the killing took place, several correspondents from the Negro press wrote lead articles about it. But the headlines faded—[*Smiles*] The NAACP got me involved in this. Rumor has it, Thurgood Marshall[9] ordered an immediate investigation of the killing, and the army, pressured by Secretary of War Stimson, rather randomly ordered Colonel Nivens to initiate a preliminary inquiry into the Sergeant's death. Now, the Colonel didn't want to rehash the murder, but he complied with the army's order by instructing the Provost Marshal, my C.O., Major Hines, to conduct a *few* question-and-answer sessions among the men of Sergeant Water's platoon and file a report. The matter was to be given the lowest priority. [*Pause*] The case was mine, five minutes later. It was four to five weeks after his death—the month of May. [*He pauses as the light builds in* CAPTAIN TAYLOR'S *office.* TAYLOR *is facing* DAVENPORT, *expressionless.* DAVENPORT *is a bit puzzled.*] Captain?

TAYLOR Forgive me for occasionally staring, Davenport, you're the first colored officer I've ever met. I'd heard you had arrived a month ago, and you're a bit startling. [*Quickly*] I mean you no offense. [*Starts back to his desk and sits on the edge of it, as* DAVENPORT *starts into the office a bit cautiously*] We'll be getting some of you as replacements, but we don't expect them until next month. Sit down, Davenport. [DAVENPORT *sits*] You came out of Fort Benning[1] in '43?

DAVENPORT Yes.

TAYLOR And they assigned a lawyer to the Military Police? I'm Infantry and I've been with the Engineers, Field Artillery, and Signal Corps—this is some army. Where'd you graduate law school?

DAVENPORT Howard University.[2]

TAYLOR Your daddy a rich minister or something? [DAVENPORT *shakes his head no*] I graduated the Point[3]—[*Pause*] We didn't have any Negroes at the Point. I never saw a Negro until I was twelve or thirteen. [*Pause*] You like the army, I suppose, huh?

DAVENPORT Captain, did you see my orders?

TAYLOR [*bristling slightly*] I saw them right after Colonel Nivens sent them to Major Hines. I sent my orderly to the barracks and told him to have the men waiting for you.

9. Black lawyer (b. 1908) with long and distinguished career with the NAACP who in 1967 would be appointed first black justice of the Supreme Court.
1. Large military post, chiefly infantry, in Georgia.
2. Leading black university; in Washington, D.C.
3. The United States Military Academy at West Point, N.Y.

DAVENPORT   Thank you.

TAYLOR   I didn't know at the time that Major Hines was assigning a Negro, Davenport. [DAVENPORT *stiffens.*] My preparations were made in the belief that you'd be a white man. I think it only fair to tell you that had I known what Hines intended I would have requested the immediate suspension of the investigation— May I speak freely?

DAVENPORT   You haven't stopped yet, Captain.

TAYLOR   Look—how far could you get even if you succeed? These local people aren't going to charge a white man in this parish on the strength of an investigation conducted by a Negro!—and Nivens and Hines know that! The Colonel doesn't give a damn about finding the men responsible for this thing! And they're making a fool of you—can't you see that?—and—take off those sunglasses!

DAVENPORT   I intend to carry out my orders—and I like these glasses —they're like MacArthur's.[4]

TAYLOR   You go near that sheriff's office in Tynin in your uniform— carrying a briefcase, looking and sounding white, and. charging local people—and you'll be found just as dead as Sergeant Waters! People around here don't respect the colored!

DAVENPORT   I know that.

TAYLOR   [*annoyed*]   You know how many times I've asked Nivens to look into this killing? Every day, since it happened, Davenport. Major Hines didn't tell you that!

DAVENPORT   Do you suspect someone, Captain?

TAYLOR   Don't play cat-and-mouse with me, soldier!

DAVENPORT   [*calmly*]   Captain, like it or not, I'm all you've got. I've been ordered to look into Sergeant Waters's death, and I intend to do exactly that.

    There is a long pause.

TAYLOR   Can I tell you a little story? [DAVENPORT *nods*] Before you were assigned here Nivens got us together after dinner one night, and all we did was discuss Negroes in the officer ranks. We all commanded Negro troops, but nobody had ever come face to face with colored officers—there were a lot of questions that night— for example, your quarters—had to be equal to ours, but we had none—no mess hall for you! [*Slight pause*] Anyway, Jed Harris was the only officer who defended it—my own feelings were mixed. The only Negroes I've ever known were subordinates— My father hired the first Negro I ever saw—man named Colfax—to help him fix the shed one summer. Nice man—worked hard—did a good job, too. [*Remembering; smiles thoughtfully.*] But I never met a Negro with any education until I graduated the Point—hardly an officer of equal rank. So I frankly wasn't sure how I'd feel—until right now—and——[*Struggles*] I don't want to offend you, but I just cannot get used to it—the bars, the uniform—being in charge just doesn't look right on Negroes!

DAVENPORT   [*rises*]   Captain, are you through?

4. General Douglas MacArthur (1880– 1964), Commander of Allied Forces in the Southwest Pacific during World War II, was often shown wearing wire-framed aviator sunglasses.

TAYLOR   You could ask Hines for another assignment—this case is not for you! By the time you overcome the obstacles to your race, this case would be dead!

DAVENPORT [*sharply*]   I got it. And I *am* in charge! All your orders instruct you to do is cooperate!

> *There is a moment of silence.*

TAYLOR   I won't be made a fool of, Davenport. [*Straightens*] Ellis! You're right, there's no need to discuss this any further.

> ELLIS *appears on the edge of the office.*

ELLIS   Yes, sir!

TAYLOR   Captain Davenport will need assistance with the men—I can't prevent that, Davenport, but I intend to do all I can to have this so-called investigation stopped.

DAVENPORT   Do what you like. If there's nothing else, you'll excuse me, won't you, Captain?

TAYLOR [*sardonically*]   Glad I met you, Captain.

> DAVENPORT *salutes and* TAYLOR *returns salute. For an instant the two men trade cold stares, then* DAVENPORT *gestures to* ELLIS, *and the two of them start out of the office by way of the stage.* DAVENPORT *follows* ELLIS *out. Behind them,* TAYLOR *stares after them as the lights in his office fade out.* DAVENPORT *removes his glasses.*

ELLIS   We heard it was you, sir—you know how the grapevine is. Sad thing—what happened to the Sarge.

DAVENPORT   What's on the grapevine about the killing?

> *The two men stop as slowly, almost imperceptibly, on the right the barracks area is lit. In it, a small table and two chairs have been set up.* ELLIS *shrugs.*

ELLIS   We figure the Klan. They ain't crazy about us tan yanks in this part of the country.

DAVENPORT   Is there anything on the grapevine about trouble in the town before Sergeant Waters was killed?

ELLIS   None that I know of before—after, there were rumors around the post—couple of our guys from the Tank Corps wanted to drive them Shermans into Tynin—then I guess you heard that somebody said two officers did it—I figure that's why the Colonel surrounded our barracks.

DAVENPORT   Was the rumor confirmed—I didn't hear that! Did anything ever come of it?

ELLIS   Not that I know of, sir.

DAVENPORT   Thanks, Ellis—I'd better start seeing the men. [*They start into the barracks from the stage floor.*] Did you set this up? [ELLIS *nods*] Good— [*He sets his briefcase on the table*] Are they ready?

ELLIS   The Captain instructed everybody in the Sarge's platoon to be here, sir. He told them you'd be starting this morning.

> DAVENPORT *smiles.*

DAVENPORT [*to himself*]   Before he found out, huh?

ELLIS [*puzzled*]   Sir?

DAVENPORT   Nothing. Call the first man in, Corporal—and stay loose, I might need you.

ELLIS   Yes, sir! Sir, may I say something? [DAVENPORT *nods*] It sure
is good to see one of us wearin' them Captain's bars, sir.

DAVENPORT   Thank you.

    ELLIS *salutes, does a sharp about-face, and starts out.*

ELLIS [*loud*]   Private Wilkie.

WILKIE [*offstage*]   Yes, sir! [*Almost immediately,* WILKIE *appears in
the doorway. He is dressed in proper uniform of fatigues, boots,
and cap.*]

ELLIS   Cap'n wants to see you!

WILKIE   Yes indeedy! [*Moves quickly to the table, where he comes
to attention and salutes*] Private James Wilkie reporting as ordered,
sir.

DAVENPORT   At ease, Private. Have a seat. [*To* ELLIS *as* WILKIE *sits*]
That will be all, Corporal.

ELLIS   Yes, sir.

    ELLIS *salutes and exits.* DAVENPORT *waits until he leaves before
speaking.*

DAVENPORT   Private Wilkie, I am Captain Davenport—

WILKIE [*interjecting*]   Everybody knows that, sir. You all we got
down here. [*Smiles broadly*] I was on that first detail got your
quarters togetha', sir.

    DAVENPORT *nods.*

DAVENPORT [*coldly*]   I'm conducting an investigation into the events
surrounding Sergeant Waters's death. Everything you say to me
will go in my report, but that report is confidential.

WILKIE   I understand, sir.

    DAVENPORT *removes pad and pencil from the briefcase.*

DAVENPORT   How long did you know Sergeant Waters?

WILKIE   'Bout a year, sir. I met him last March—March 5th—I
remember the date, I had been a staff sergeant exactly two years
the day he was assigned. This company was basically a baseball
team then, sir. See, most of the boys had played for the Negro
League,[5] so naturally the army put us all together. [*Chuckles at
the memory*] We'd be assigned to different companies—Motor Pool
—Dump Truck all week long—made us do the dirty work on the
post—garbage, clean-up—but on Saturdays we were whippin' the
hell out of 'em on the baseball diamond! I was hittin' .352 myself!
And we had a boy, C. J. Memphis? He coulda hit a ball from Fort
Neal to Berlin, Germany—or Tokyo—if he was battin' right-
handed. [*Pauses, catches* DAVENPORT'S *impatience.*] Well, the army
sent Waters to manage the team. He had been in Field Artillery—
Gunnery Sergeant. Had a croix de guerre from the First War, too.

DAVENPORT   What kind of man was he?

WILKIE   All spit and polish, sir.

    At that moment, in limbo, a spotlight hits SERGEANT WATERS.
    He is dressed in a well-creased uniform, wearing a helmet

---

5. The first professional black baseball
league, the Negro National League, was
formed in 1920 and others followed in
1923 and 1937. Major league baseball
was segregated until 1947, when Jackie
Robinson broke in with the Brooklyn
Dodgers.

*liner and standing at parade-rest, facing the audience. The
light around him, however, is strange—it is blue-gray like the
past. The light around* DAVENPORT *and* WILKIE *abates somewhat. Dialogue is continuous.*

DAVENPORT   Tell me about him.

WILKIE   He took my stripes! [*Smiles*] But I was in the wrong, sir!

WATERS *stands at ease. His voice crisp and sharp, his movements minimal. He is the typical hard-nosed N.C.O.—strict,
soldierly.*

WATERS   Sergeant Wilkie! You are a noncommissioned officer in the
army of a country at war—the penalty for being drunk on duty is
severe in peace time, so don't bring me no po'colored-folks-can't-
do-nothin'-unless-they-drunk shit as an excuse! You are supposed
to be an example to your men—so, I'm gonna send you to jail for
ten days *and* take them goddamn stripes. Teach you a lesson— You
in the army! [*Derisively*] Colored folks always runnin' off at the
mouth 'bout what y'all gonna do if the white man gives you a
chance—and you get it, and what do you do with it? You wind up
drunk on guard duty—I don't blame the white man—why the hell
should he put colored and white together in this war? You can't
even be trusted to guard your own quarters—no wonder they treat
us like dogs— Get outta' my sight, *Private!*

Light fades at once on WATERS.

DAVENPORT   What about the other men?

WILKIE   Sometimes the Southern guys caught a little hell—Sarge
always said he was from up North somewhere. He was a good
soldier, sir. I'm from Detroit myself—born and raised there. Joe
Louis started in Detroit—did you know that, sir?

DAVENPORT   What about the Southerners?

WILKIE   Sarge wasn't exactly crazy 'bout 'em—'cept for C.J. Now
C.J. was from the South, but with him Sarge was different—
probably because C.J. was the best ball player we had. He could
sing too! [*Slight pause*] Sarge never got too close to nobody—
maybe me—but he didn't mess with C.J., you know what I mean?
Not like he did with everybody else.

In limbo the spotlight illuminates C.J. MEMPHIS, *a young,
handsome black man. He is in a soldier's uniform, cap on the
side. He is strumming a guitar.* WATERS *is watching him,
smiling. Their light is the strange light of the past.* C.J. *begins
to sing, his voice deep, melodious, and bluesy.*

C.J.   It's a low/it's a low, low/lowdown dirty shame! Yeah, it's a
low/it's a low, low/lowdown dirty shame!

WILKIE [*before* C.J. *finishes*]   Big Mississippi boy!

WILKIE *and* C.J. *simultaneously sing.*

C.J. AND WILKIE   They say we fightin' Hitler! But they won't let us
in the game!

C.J. *strums and hums as* WATERS *looks on.*

WILKIE   Worked harder and faster than everybody—wasn't a man
on the team didn't like him. Sarge took to him the first time he saw
him. "Wilkie," he says.

WILKIE AND WATERS [*simultaneously*]   What have we got here?

WATERS   A guitar-playin' man! Boy, you eva' heard of Blind Willie Reynolds? Son House? Henry Sims?[6]

      C.J. *nods to everything.*

C.J.   You heard them play, Sarge?

WATERS   Every one of 'em. I was stationed in Mississippi couple years ago—you from down that way, ain't you?

C.J.   Yes, sah!

WATERS   Well, they use ta play over at the Bandana Club outside Camp J. J. Riley.

C.J.   I played there once!

WATERS [*smiles*]   Ain't that somethin'? I'd go over there from time to time—people use ta come from everywhere! [*To* WILKIE] Place was always dark, Wilkie—smoky. Folks would be dancin'—sweatin' —guitar pickers strummin', shoutin'—it would be wild in there sometimes. Reminded me of a place I use ta go in France durin' the First War—the women, the whiskey—place called the Café Napoleon.

C.J.   You really like the blues, huh?

WATERS   No other kind of music—where'd you learn to play so good? I came by here yesterday and heard this pickin'—one of the men tol' me it was you.

C.J.   My daddy taught me, Sarge.

WATERS   You play pretty good, boy. Wilkie, wasn't that good?

WILKIE   Yes indeed, Sarge.

WILKIE [*to Davenport*]   I mostly agreed with the Sarge, sir. He was a good man. Good to his men. Talked about his wife and kids all the time— [WATERS *starts down from the limbo area, as the lights around* C.J. *fade out.* WATERS *pulls a pipe from his pocket, lights it as he moves to the edge of the* CAPTAIN's *office and sits on the edge of the platform supporting it. He puffs a few times.* WILKIE's *talk is continuous*] Use ta write home every day. I don't see why nobody would want to kill the Sarge, sir.

      WATERS *smiles.*

WATERS   Wilkie? [WILKIE *rises and walks into the blue-gray light and the scene with* WATERS. DAVENPORT *will watch.*] You know what I'ma get that boy of mine for his birthday? One of them Schwinn bikes. He'll be twelve—time flies, don't it? Let me show you something?

WILKIE [*to* DAVENPORT]   He was always pullin' out snapshots, sir.

      WATERS *hands him a snapshot.*

WATERS   My wife let a neighbor take this a couple weeks ago— ain't he growin' fast?

WILKIE   He's over your wife's shoulder! [*Hands it back.* WATERS *looks at the photo*]

WATERS   I hope this kid never has to be a soldier.

WILKIE   It was good enough for you.

WATERS   I couldn't do any better—and this army was the closest I

6. Southern black blues singers.

figured the white man would let me get to any kind of authority. No, the army ain't for this boy. When this war's over, things are going to change, Wilkie—and I want him to be ready for it—my daughter, too! I'm sendin' bot' of 'em to some big white college— let 'em rub elbows with the whites, learn the white man's language —how he does things. Otherwise, we'll be left behind—you can see it in the army. White man runnin' rings around us.

WILKIE   A lot of us didn't get the chance or the schoolin' the white folks got.

WATERS   That ain't no excuse, Wilkie. Most niggahs just don't care— tomorrow don't mean nothin' to 'em. My daddy shoveled coal from the back of a wagon all his life. He couldn't read or write, but he saw to it we did! Not havin' ain't no excuse for not gettin'.

WILKIE   Can't get pee from a rock, Sarge.

WATERS *rises abruptly.*

WATERS   You just like the rest of 'em, Wilkie—I thought bustin' you would teach you something—we got to challenge this man in his arena—use his weapons, don't you know that? We need lawyers, doctors—generals—senators! Stop thinkin' like a niggah!

WILKIE   All I said—

WATERS   Is the equipment ready for tomorrow's game?

WILKIE   Yeah.

WATERS   Good. You can go now, Wilkie. [WILKIE *is stunned*] That's an order!

> WILKIE *turns toward* DAVENPORT. *In the background, the humming of* C.J. *rises a bit as the light around* WATERS *fades out.*

WILKIE   He could be two people sometimes, sir. Warm one minute— ice the next.

DAVENPORT   How did you feel about him?

WILKIE   Overall—I guess he was all right. You could always borrow a ten-spot off him if you needed it.

DAVENPORT   Did you see the Sergeant any time immediately preceding his death?

WILKIE   I don't know how much before it was, but a couple of us had been over the N.C.O. club that night and Sarge had been juicin' pretty heavy.

DAVENPORT   Did Waters drink a lot?

WILKIE   No more than most—[*Pause*] Could I ask you a question, sir? [DAVENPORT *nods*] Is it true, when they found Sarge all his stripes and insignia were still on his uniform?

DAVENPORT   I don't recall it being mentioned in my preliminary report. Why?

WILKIE   If that's the way they found him, something's wrong, ain't it, sir? Them Klan boys don't like to see us in these uniforms. They usually take the stripes and stuff off, before they lynch us.

> DAVENPORT *is quiet, thoughtful for a moment.*

DAVENPORT   Thank you, Private—I might want to call you again, but for now you're excused.

> WILKIE *rises.*

WILKIE   Yes, sir! [*Sudden mood swing, hesitant*] Sir?

DAVENPORT   Yes?

WILKIE   Can you do something about allotment checks? My wife didn't get hers last month.

DAVENPORT   There's nothing I can do directly—did you see the finance officer? [WILKIE *nods*] Well—I'll—I'll mention it to Captain Taylor.

WILKIE   Thank you, sir. You want me to send the next man in?

> DAVENPORT *nods.* WILKIE *salutes, does an about-face, and exits.* DAVENPORT *returns the salute, then leans back in his chair thoughtfully. In the background, the humming of* C.J. *rises again as the next man,* PFC MELVIN PETERSON, *enters. Dressed in fatigues, he is the model soldier. He walks quickly to the table, stands at attention, and salutes. The humming fades out as* DAVENPORT *returns the salute.*

PETERSON   Private First Class Melvin Peterson reporting as ordered, sir!

DAVENPORT   Sit down, Private. [PETERSON *sits*] Do you know why I'm here?

PETERSON   Yes, sir.

DAVENPORT   Fine. Now, everything you tell me is confidential, so I want you to speak as freely as possible. [PETERSON *nods*] Where are you from?

PETERSON   Hollywood, California—by way of Alabama, sir. I enlisted in '42—thought we'd get a chance to fight.

DAVENPORT   [*ignores the comment*]   Did you know Sergeant Waters well?

PETERSON   No, sir. He was already with the company when I got assigned here. And us common G.I.'s don't mix well with N.C.O.'s.

DAVENPORT   Were you on the baseball team?

PETERSON   Yes, sir—I played shortstop.

DAVENPORT   Did you like the Sergeant?

PETERSON   No, sir.

> *Before* DAVENPORT *can speak,* ELLIS *enters.*

ELLIS   Beg your pardon, sir. Captain Taylor would like to see you in his office at once.

DAVENPORT   Did he say why?

ELLIS   No, sir—just that you should report to him immediately.

DAVENPORT   [*annoyed*]   Tell the men to stick around. When I finish with the Captain, I'll be back.

ELLIS   Yes, sir!

> ELLIS *exits.*

DAVENPORT   [*to* PETERSON]   Feel like walking, Private? We can continue this on the way. [*Begins to put his things in his briefcase.*] Why didn't you like the Sergeant?

> DAVENPORT *and* PETERSON *start out as the light begins to fade in the barracks. They go through doorway, exit, and reenter the stage in full view.*

PETERSON   It goes back to the team, sir. I got here in—baseball season had started, so it had to be June—June of last year. The team had won maybe nine—ten games in a row, there was a rumor that they would even get chance to play the Yankees in exhibition. So when I got assigned to a team like that, sir—I mean, I felt good. Anyway, ole stone-ass—

DAVENPORT   Stone-ass?

PETERSON   I'm the only one called him that—Sergeant Waters, sir. *As the two of them pass in front of the barracks area, the light begins to rise very slowly, but it is the blue-gray light of the past. The chairs and table are gone, and the room looks different.*

DAVENPORT   Respect his rank, with me, Private.

PETERSON   I didn't mean no offense, sir. [*Slight pause*] Well, the Sergeant and that brown-nosin' Wilkie? They ran the team—and like it was a chain gang, sir. A chain gang!

The two men exit the stage. As they do, C.J. MEMPHIS, HENSON, COBB, *and* SMALLS *enter in their baseball uniforms. T-shirts with "Fort Neal" stamped on the fronts, and numbers on the back, and baseball caps. They are carrying equipment—bats, gloves.* C.J. *is carrying his guitar.* SMALLS *enters tossing a baseball into the air and catching it. They almost all enter at once, with the exuberance of young men. Their talk is locker-room loud, and filled with bursts of laughter.*

HENSON   You see the look on that umpire's face when C.J. hit that home run? I thought he was gonna die on the spot, he turned so pale!

They move to their respective bunks.

SMALLS   Serves the fat bastard right! Some of them pitches he called strikes were well ova' my head!

C.J. *strums his guitar.* COBB *begins to brush off his boots.*

COBB   C.J.? Who was that fine, river-hip thing you was talkin' to, homey?[7]

C.J. *shrugs and smiles.*

HENSON   Speakin' of women, I got to write my Lady a letter. [*He begins to dig for his writing things.*]

COBB   She looked mighty good to me, C.J.

SMALLS [*overlapping*]   Y'all hear Henson? Henson, you ain't had a woman since a woman had you!

HENSON *makes an obscene gesture.*

C.J. [*overlapping* SMALLS]   Now, all she did was ask me for my autograph.

COBB   Look like she was askin' you fo' mor'n that. [*To* SMALLS] You see him, Smalls? Leanin' against the fence, all in the woman's face, breathin' heavy—

HENSON   If Smalls couldn't see enough to catch a ground ball right in his glove, how the hell could he see C.J. ova' by the fence?

SMALLS   That ball got caught in the sun!

HENSON   On the ground?

COBB [*at once*]   We beat 'em nine to one! Y'all be quiet, I'm askin' this man 'bout a woman he was with had tits like two helmets!

7. Fellow-countryman; someone from "home."

C.J.   If I had'a give that gal what she asked fo'—she'da give me somethin' I didn't want! Them V-gals git you a bad case a' clap. 'Sides, she wasn' but sixteen.

SMALLS   You shoulda introduced her to Henson—sixteen's about his speed.

HENSON *makes a farting sound in retaliation.*

C.J.   Aroun' home? There's a fella folks use ta call, Lil' Jimmy One Leg—on account of his thing was so big? Two years ago—ole young pretty thing laid clap on Jimmy so bad, he los' the one good leg he had! Now folks jes' call him Little!

Laughter.

C.J.   That young thing talkin' to me ain't look so clean.

HENSON   Dirty or clean, she had them white boys lookin'.

COBB   Eyes popin' out they sockets, wasn't they? Remind me of that pitcher las' week! The one from 35th Ordnance? The one everybody claimed was so good? Afta' twelve straight hits, he looked the same way!

PETERSON *enters, carrying two baseball bats.*

SMALLS   It might be funny ta y'all, but when me and Pete had duty in the Ordnance mess hall, that same white pitcher was the first one started the name-callin'—

HENSON   Forget them dudes in Ordnance—lissen to this! [HENSON *begins to read from a short letter*] "Dear, Louis"—y'all hear that? The name is Louis—

COBB   Read the damn letter!

HENSON [*makes obscene gesture*]   "Dear, Louis. You and the boys keep up the good work. All of us here at home are praying for you and inspired in this great cause by you. We know the Nazis and the Japs can't be stopped unless we all work together, so tell your buddies to press forward and win this war. All our hopes for the future go with you, Louis. Love Mattie." I think I'm in love with the sepia Winston Churchill—what kinda' letter do you write a nut like this?

COBB   Send her a round of ammunition and a bayonet, *Louis!*

HENSON *waves disdainfully.*

PETERSON   Y'all oughta listen to what Smalls said. Every time we beat them at baseball, they get back at us every way they can.

COBB   It's worth it to me just to wipe those superior smiles off they faces.

PETERSON   I don't know—seems like it makes it that much harder for us.

C.J.   They tell me, coupla them big-time Negroes is on the verge a' gittin' all of us togetha'—colored and white—say they want one army.

PETERSON   Forget that, C.J.! White folks'll neva' integrate no army!

C.J. [*strums*]   If they do—I'ma be ready for 'em! [*Sings*] Well, I got me a bright red zoot suit / And a pair a' patent-leatha' shoes / And my woman she sittin' waitin' / Fo' the day we hea' the news! Lawd, lawd, lawd, lawd, / Lawd, lawd, lawd, lawd!

SERGEANT WATERS, *followed by* WILKIE, *enters, immediately*

> *crossing to the center of the barracks, his strident voice*
> *abruptly cutting off* c.j.*'s singing and playing.*

WATERS Listen up! [*To* c.j.] We don't need that guitar playin'-sittin'-round-the-shack music today. C.J.! [*Smiles*] I want all you men out of those baseball uniforms and into work clothes! You will all report to me at 1300 hours in front of the Officers Club. We've got a work detail. We're painting the lobby of the club.

> *Collective groan.*

SMALLS The officers can't paint their own club?

COBB Hell no, Smalls! Let the great-colored-clean-up company do it! Our motto is: Anything you don't want to do, the colored troops will do for you!

HENSON [*like a cheer*] Anything you don't want to do, the colored troops will do for you! [*He starts to lead the others.*]

OTHERS Anything you don't—

WATERS That's enough!

> *The men are instantly silent.*

HENSON When do we get a rest? We just played nine innings of baseball, Sarge!

SMALLS We can't go in the place, why the hell should we paint it?

COBB Amen, brother!

> *There is a moment of quiet before* WATERS *speaks.*

WATERS Let me tell you fancy-assed ball-playin' Negroes somethin'! The *reasons* for any orders given by a superior officer is none of y'all's business! You obey them! This country is at war, and you niggahs are soldiers—nothin' else! So baseball teams—win or lose—get no special privileges; They need to work some of you niggahs till your legs fall off! [*Intense*] And something else—from now on, when I tell you to do something, I want it done—is that clear? [*The men are quiet.*] Now, Wilkie's gonna' take all them funky shirts you got on over to the laundry. I could smell you suckers before I hit the field!

PETERSON What kinda colored man are you?

WATERS I'm a soldier, Peterson! First, last, and always! I'm the kinda colored man that don't like lazy, shiftless Negroes!

PETERSON You ain't got to come in here and call us names!

WATERS The Nazis call you schvatza![8] You gonna tell them they hurt your little feelings?

C.J. Don't look like to me we could do much to them Nazis wit' paint brushes, Sarge.

> *The men laugh. The moment is gone, and though* WATERS *is angry, his tone becomes overly solicitous, smiling.*

WATERS You tryin' to mock me, C.J.?

C.J. No, sah, Sarge.

WATERS Good, because whatever an ignorant, low-class geechy[9] like you has to say isn't worth paying attention to, is it? [*Pause*] Is it?

---

8. *Schwartze,* black or Negro in German, often used pejoratively.

9. Pejorative term used by blacks about other blacks, those from "the back country."

C.J. I reckon not, Sarge.

PETERSON You' a creep, Waters!

WATERS Boy, you are something—ain't been in the company a month, Wilkie, and already everybody's champion!

C.J. [*interjecting*] Sarge was just jokin', Pete—he don't mean no harm!

PETERSON He does! We take enough from the white boys!

WATERS Yes, you do—and if it wasn' for you Southern niggahs, yessahin', bowin' and scrapin', scratchin' your heads, white folks wouldn' think we were all fools!

PETERSON Where you from, England?
    Men snicker.

HENSON [*at once*] Peterson!

WATERS [*immediately*] You got somethin' to say, Henson?

HENSON Nothin', Sarge.
    HENSON *shakes his head as* WATERS *turns back to* PETERSON.

WATERS Peterson, you got a real comic streak in you. Wilkie, looks like we got us a wise-ass Alabama boy here! [*He moves toward* PETERSON] Yes, sir— [*He snatches* PETERSON *in the collar.*] Don't get smart, niggah!
    PETERSON *yanks away.*

PETERSON Get your fuckin' hands off me!
    WATERS *smiles, leans forward.*

WATERS You wanna hit ole Sergeant Waters, boy? [*Whispers*] Come on! Please! Come on, niggah!
    CAPTAIN TAYLOR *enters the barracks quite suddenly, unaware of what is going on.*

HENSON Tenn-hut!
    All the men snap to.

TAYLOR At ease! [*He moves toward* WATERS, *feeling the tension*] What's going on here, Sergeant?

WATERS Nothin', sir—I was going over the *Manual of Arms*. Is there something in particular you wanted, sir? Something I can do?

TAYLOR [*relaxed somewhat*] Nothing— [*To the men*] Men, I congratulate you on the game you won today. We've only got seven more to play, and if we win them, we'll be the first team in Fort Neal history to play the Yanks in exhibition. Everyone in the regiment is counting on you. In times like these, morale is important —and winning can help a lot of things. [*Pause*] Sergeant, as far as I'm concerned, they've got the rest of the day off.
    The men are pleased.

WATERS Begging your pardon, sir, but these men need all the work they can get. They don't need time off—our fellas aren't getting time off in North Africa[1]—besides, we've got orders to report to the Officers Club for a paint detail at 1300 hours.

TAYLOR Who issued that order?

WATERS Major Harris, sir.

1. North Africa was the scene of the first American ground combat operations against the Nazis, who were expelled from North Africa by British and American troops in May 1943. (Flashbacks involving C.J. take place in 1943.)

TAYLOR   I'll speak to the Major.

WATERS   Sir, I don't think it's such a good idea to get a colored N.C.O. mixed up in the middle of you officers, sir.

TAYLOR   I said, I'd speak to him, Sergeant.

WATERS   Yes, sir!

TAYLOR   I respect the men's duty to service, but they need time off.

WATERS   Yes, sir.

   Pause.

TAYLOR   You men played a great game of baseball out there today— that catch you made in center field, Memphis—how the hell'd you get up so high?

C.J.   [*shrugs, smiles*]   They say I got "Bird" in mah blood, sir.

   TAYLOR *is startled by the statement, his smile is an uncomfortable one.* WATERS *is standing on "eggs."*

TAYLOR   American eagle, I hope. [*laughs a little.*]

C.J.   No, sah, crow—[WATERS *starts to move, but* C.J. *stops him by continuing. Several of the men are beginning to get uncomfortable.*] Man tol' my daddy the day I was born, the shadow of a crow's wings—

TAYLOR   [*cutting him off*]   Fine—men, I'll say it again—you played superbly. [*Turns to* WATERS] Sergeant. [*He starts out abruptly.*]

WATERS   Tenn-hut!

   WATERS *salutes as the men snap to.*

TAYLOR   [*exiting*]   As you were.

   TAYLOR *salutes as he goes. There is an instant of quiet. The men relax a little, but their focus is* C.J.

WATERS   [*laughing*]   Ain't these geechies somethin'? How long a story was you gonna tell the man, C.J.? My God! [*The men join him, but as he turns toward* PETERSON, *he stiffens*] Peterson! Oh, I didn't forget you, boy. [*The room quiets.*] It's time to teach you a lesson!

PETERSON   Why don't you drop dead, Sarge?

WATERS   Nooo! I'ma drop you, boy! Out behind the barracks— Wilkie, you go out and make sure it's all set up.

WILKIE   You want all the N.C.O.'s?

   WATERS *nods.* WILKIE *goes out smiling.*

WATERS   I'm going outside and wait for you, geechy! And when you come out, I'm gonna whip your black Southern ass—let the whole company watch it, too! [*Points*] You need to learn respect, boy— how to talk to your betters. [*Starts toward the door*] Fight hard, hea'? I'ma try to bust your fuckin' head open—the rest of you get those goddamn shirts off like I said!

   He exits. The barracks is quiet for a moment.

COBB   You gonna fight him?

HENSON   [*overlapping*]   I tried to warn you!

PETERSON   You ain't do nothin'!

SMALLS   He'll fight you dirty, Pete—don't do it!

   PETERSON *goes to his bunk and throws his cap off angrily.*

COBB   You don't want to do it?

PETERSON   You wanna fight in my place, Cobb? [*He sits*] Shit!

   Slight pause. HENSON *pulls off his shirt.*

c.j.   I got some Farmers Dust—jes' a pinch'll make you strong as a bull—they say it comes from the city of Zar.[2] [*Removes a pouch from his neck.*] I seen a man use this stuff and pull a mule outta a sinkhole by hisself!

PETERSON   Get the hell outta here with that backwater crap—can't you speak up for yourself—let that bastard treat you like a dog!

c.j.   'Long as his han's ain't on me—he ain't done me no harm, Pete. Callin' names ain't nothin', I know what I is. [*Softens*] Sarge ain't so bad—been good to me.

PETERSON   The man despises you!

c.j.   Sarge? You wrong, Pete—plus I feel kinda sorry for him myself. Any man ain't sure where he belongs must be in a whole lotta pain.

PETERSON   Don't y'all care?

HENSON   Don't nobody like it, Pete—but when you here a little longer—I mean, what can you do? This hea's the army and Sarge got all the stripes.

> PETERSON *rises, disgusted, and starts out.* SMALLS *moves at once.*

SMALLS   Peterson, look, if you want me to, I'll get the Captain. You don't have to go out there and get your head beat in!

PETERSON   Somebody's got to fight him.

> *He exits. There is quiet as* SMALLS *walks back to his bunk.*

c.j.   [*singing*] It's a low / it's a low, low / lowdown dirty shame! It's a low / it's a low, low / lowdown dirty shame! Been playin' in this hea' army / an ain't even learned the game! Lawd, lawd, lawd, lawd—

> c.j. *begins to hum as the lights slowly fade out over the barracks. As they do, the lights come up simultaneously in the* CAPTAIN's *office. It is empty.* PETERSON [*in proper uniform*] *and* DAVENPORT *enter from off-stage. They stop outside the* CAPTAIN's *office.*

PETERSON   He beat me pretty bad that day, sir. The man was crazy!

DAVENPORT   Was the incident ever reported?

PETERSON   I never reported it, sir—I know I should have, but he left me alone after that. [*Shrugs*] I just played ball.

DAVENPORT   Did you see Waters the night he died?

PETERSON   No, sir—me and Smalls had guard duty.

DAVENPORT   Thank you, Private. That'll be all for now. [PETERSON *comes to attention.*] By the way, did the team ever get to play the Yankees?

PETERSON   No, sir. We lost the last game to a Sanitation Company.

> *He salutes.* DAVENPORT *returns salute.* PETERSON *does a crisp about-face and exits. Slowly* DAVENPORT *starts into the* CAPTAIN's *office, surprised that no one is about.*

DAVENPORT   Captain? [*There is no response. For a moment or two,*

DAVENPORT [*looks around. He is somewhat annoyed.*] Captain?

> *He starts out.* TAYLOR *enters. He crosses the room to his desk, where he sits.*

---

2. *Farmer's Dust . . . Zar*—Unidentified.

TAYLOR   I asked you back here because I wanted you to see the request I've sent to Colonel Nivens to have your investigation terminated. [*He picks up several sheets of paper on his desk and hands them to* DAVENPORT, *who ignores them.*]

DAVENPORT   What?

TAYLOR   I wanted you to see that my reasons have nothing to do. with you personally—my request will not hurt your army record in any way! [*Pause*] There are other things to consider in this case!

DAVENPORT   Only the color of my skin, Captain.

TAYLOR   [*sharply*]   I want the people responsible for killing one of my men found and jailed, Davenport!

DAVENPORT   So do I!

TAYLOR   Then give this up! [*Rises*] Whites down here won't see their duty—or justice. They'll see *you!* And once they do, the law—due process—it all goes! And what is the point of continuing an investigation that can't possibly get at the truth?

DAVENPORT   Captain, my orders are very specific, so unless you want charges brought against you for interfering in a criminal investigation, stay the hell out of my way and leave me and my investigation alone!

TAYLOR   [*almost sneering*]   Don't take yourself too seriously, Davenport. You couldn't find an officer within five hundred miles who would convey charges to a court-martial board against me for something like that, and you know it!

DAVENPORT   Maybe not, but I'd—I'd see to it that your name, rank, and duty station got into the Negro press! Yeah, let a few colored newspapers call you a Negro-hater! Make you an embarrassment to the United States Army, Captain—like Major Albright at Fort Jefferson, and you'd never command troops again—or wear more than those captain's bars on that uniform, Mr. West Point!

TAYLOR   I'll never be more than a captain, Davenport, because I won't let them get away with dismissing things like Water's death. I've been the commanding officer of three outfits! I raised hell in all of them, so threatening me won't change my request. Let the Negro press print that I don't like being made a fool of with phony investigations!

DAVENPORT   [*studies* TAYLOR *for a moment*]   There are two white officers involved in this, Captain—aren't there?

TAYLOR   I want them in jail—out of the army! And there is no way *you* can get them charged, or court-martialed, or put away! The white officers on this post won't let you—they won't let me!

DAVENPORT   Why wasn't there any mention of them in your preliminary report? I checked my own summary on the way over here, Captain—nothing! You think I'ma let you get away with this? [*There is a long silence.* TAYLOR *walks back to his desk as* DAVENPORT *watches him.* TAYLOR *sits*]Why?

TAYLOR   I couldn't prove the men in question had anything to do with it.

DAVENPORT   Why didn't you report it?

TAYLOR   I was ordered not to. [*Pause*] Nivens and Hines. The doctors took two .45 caliber bullets out of Waters—army issue.

But remember what it was like that morning? If these men had thought a white officer killed Waters, there would have been a slaughter! [*Pause*] Cobb reported the incident innocently the night before—then suddenly it was all over the Fort.

DAVENPORT   Who were they, Captain? I want their names!

TAYLOR   Byrd and Wilcox. Byrd's in Ordnance—Wilcox's with the 12th Hospital Group. I was Captain of the Guard the night Waters was killed. About 2100 hours, Cobb came into my office and told me he'd just seen Waters and two white officers fighting outside the colored N.C.O. club. I called *your* office, and when I couldn't get two M.P.'s, I started over myself to break it up. When I got there —no Waters, no officers. I checked the officers' billet and found Byrd and Wilcox in bed. Several officers verified they'd come in around 2130. I then told Cobb to go back to the barracks and forget it.

DAVENPORT   What made you do that?

TAYLOR   At the time there was no reason to believe anything was wrong! Waters wasn't found until the following morning. I told the Colonel what had happened the previous night, and about the doctor's report, and I was told, since the situation at the Fort was potentially dangerous, to keep my mouth shut until it blew over. He agreed to let me question Byrd and Wilcox, but I've asked him for a follow-up investigation every day since it happened. [*Slight pause*] When I saw you, I exploded—it was like he was laughing at me.

DAVENPORT   Then you never believed the Klan was involved?

TAYLOR   No. Now, you can see why this thing needs—someone else?

DAVENPORT   What did they tell you, Captain? Byrd and Wilcox?

TAYLOR   They're not going to let you charge those two men!

DAVENPORT [*snaps*]   Tell me what they told you!

> TAYLOR *is quiet for a moment. At this time, on center stage in limbo,* SERGEANT WATERS *is staggering. He is dressed as we first saw him. Behind him a blinking light reads: 221st N.C.O. Club. As he staggers toward the stairs leading to center stage, two white officers,* LIEUTENANT BYRD, *a spit-and-polish soldier in his twenties, and* CAPTAIN WILCOX, *a medical officer, walk on-stage. Both are in full combat gear—rifles, pistol belts, packs —and both are tired.* TAYLOR *looks out as if he can see them.*

TAYLOR   They were coming off bivouac.

> *The two men see* WATERS. *In the background is the faint hum of* C.J.*'s music.*

TAYLOR   They saw him outside the club.

> *He rises, as* WATERS *sees* BYRD *and* WILCOX, *and smiles.*

WATERS   Well, if it ain't the white boys!

> WATERS *straightens and begins to march in a mock circle and then down in their direction. He is mumbling, barely audibly: "One, two, three, four! Hup, hup, three, four! Hup, hup, three, four!"* BYRD'S *speech overlaps* WATERS'S.

BYRD   And it wasn't like we were looking for trouble, Captain— were we, Wilcox?

WILCOX *shakes his head no, but he is astonished by* WATERS's
behavior and stares at him, disbelieving.

WATERS   White boys! All starched and stiff! Wanted everybody to
learn all that symphony shit! That's what you were saying in
France—and you know, I listened to you? Am I all right now?
Am I?

BYRD   Boy, you'd better straighten up and salute when you see an
officer, or you'll find yourself without those stripes! [*To* WILCOX
as WATERS *nears them, smiling the "coon" smile and doing a
juba.*][3] Will you look at this niggah? [*Loud*] Come to attention,
Sergeant! That's an order!

WATERS   No, sah! I ain't straightenin' up for y'all no more! I ain't
doin' nothin' white folks say do, no more! [*Sudden change of mood,
smiles, sings*] No more, no more / no more, no more, noooo! No
more, no more / no more, no more, noooooo!

BYRD *faces* TAYLOR *as* WATERS *continues to sing.*

BYRD [*overlapping*]   Sir, I thought the man was crazy!

TAYLOR   And what did you think, Wilcox?

BYRD *moves toward* WATERS, *and* WATERS, *still singing low,
drunk and staggering, moves back and begins to circle* BYRD,
stalk him, shaking his head no as he sings. WILCOX *watches
apprehensively.*

WILCOX [*at once*]   He did appear to be intoxicated, sir—out of his
mind almost! [*He turns to* BYRD] Byrd, listen—

BYRD *ignores him.*

DAVENPORT [*suddenly*]   Did they see anyone else in the area?

TAYLOR   No. [*To* BYRD] I asked them what they did next.

BYRD   I told that niggah to shut up!

WATERS [*sharply*]   No! [*Change of mood*] Followin' behind y'all?
Look what it's done to me!—I hate myself!

BYRD   Don't blame us, boy! God made you black, not me!

WATERS [*smiles*]   My daddy use ta say—

WILCOX   Sergeant, get hold of yourself!

WATERS [*points*]   Listen!

BYRD *steps toward him and shoves him in the face.*

BYRD   I gave you an order, niggah!

WILCOX *grabs* BYRD, *and stops him from advancing, as* WATERS
begins to cry.

WATERS   My daddy said, "Don't talk like dis'—talk like that!" "Don't
live hea'—live there!" [*To them*] I've killed for you! [*To himself;
incredulous*] And nothin' changed!

BYRD *pulls free of* WILCOX *and charges* WATERS.

BYRD   He needs to be taught a lesson!

He shoves WATERS *onto the ground, where he begins to beat
and kick the man, until he is forcibly restrained by* WILCOX.
WATERS *moans.*

WILCOX   Let him be! You'll kill the man! He's sick—leave him alone!

BYRD *pulls away; he is flush.* WATERS *tries to get up.*

3. Compare song: "Juba, Juba, killed a
yellow gal, Juba, Juba."

WATERS   Nothin' changed—see? And I've tried everything! Everything!

BYRD   I'm gonna bust his black ass to buck private!—I should blow his coward's head off! [*Shouts*] There are good men killing for you, niggah! Gettin' their guts all blown to hell for you!

> WILCOX *pulls him away. He pulls* BYRD *offstage as the light around* WATERS *and that section of the stage begins to fade out. As it does, a trace of* C.J.'s *music is left on the air.* WATERS *is on his knees, groveling, as the lights go out around him.*

DAVENPORT   Did they shove Waters again?

TAYLOR   No. But Byrd's got a history of scrapes with Negroes. They told me they left Waters at 2110—and everyone in the officers' billet verifies they were both in by 2130. And neither man left— Byrd had duty the next morning, and Wilcox was scheduled at the hospital at 0500 hours—both men reported for duty.

DAVENPORT   I don't believe it.

TAYLOR   I couldn't shake their stories—

DAVENPORT   That's nothing more than officers lying to protect two of their own and you know it! I'm going to arrest and charge both of them, Captain—and you may consider yourself confined to your quarters pending my charges against *you!*

TAYLOR   What charges?

DAVENPORT   It was *your* duty to go over Nivens's head if you had to!

TAYLOR   Will you arrest Colonel Nivens too, Davenport? Because he's part of their alibi—he was there when they came in—played poker—from 2100 to 0300 hours the following morning, the Colonel—your Major Hines, "Shack" Callahan—Major Callahan, and Jed Harris—and Jed wouldn't lie for either of them!

DAVENPORT   They're all lying!

TAYLOR   Prove it, hotshot—I told you all I know, now you go out and prove it!

DAVENPORT   I will, Captain! You can bet your sweet ass on that! I will!

> DAVENPORT *starts out as the lights begin to fade, and* TAYLOR *looks after him and shakes his head. In the background, the sound of "Don't Sit under the Apple Tree" comes up again and continues to play as the lights fade to black.*

ACT 2

SCENE: *As before.*

> *Light rises slowly over limbo. We hear a snippet of "Don't Sit under the Apple Tree" as* DAVENPORT, *seated on on the edge of a bunk, finishes dressing. He is putting on a shirt, tie, bars, etc., and addresses the audience as he does so.*

DAVENPORT   During May of '44, the Allies were making final preparations for the invasion of Europe. Invasion! Even the sound of it made Negroes think we'd be in it—be swept into Europe in the waves of men and equipment—I know I felt it. [*Thoughtfully*]

We hadn't seen a lot of action except in North Africa—or Sicily.[4] But the rumor in orderly rooms that spring was, pretty soon most of us would be in combat—somebody said Ike[5] wanted to find out if the colored boys could fight—shit, we'd been fighting all along— right here, in these small Southern towns—[*Intense*] I don't have the authority to arrest a white *private* without a white officer present! [*Slight pause*] Then I get a case like this? There was no way I wouldn't see this through to its end. [*Smiles*] And after my first twenty-four hours, I wasn't doing too badly. I had two prime suspects—a motive, and opportunity! [*Pause*] I went to Colonel Nivens and convinced him that word of Byrd's and Wilcox's involve- ment couldn't be kept secret any longer. However, before anyone in the press could accuse him of complicity—I would silence all suspicions by pursuing the investigation openly—on his orders— [*Mimics himself*] "Yes, sir, Colonel, you can even send along a white officer—not Captain Taylor, though—I think he's a little too close to the case, sir." Colonel Nivens gave me permission to ques- tion Byrd and Wilcox, and having succeeded sooo easily, I decided to spend some time finding out more about Waters and Memphis. Somehow the real drama seemed to be there, and my curiosity wouldn't allow me to ignore it.

> DAVENPORT *is dressed and ready to go as a spotlight in the barracks area opens on* PRIVATE HENSON. *He is seated on a footlocker. He rises as* DAVENPORT *descends to the stage. He will not enter the barracks, but will almost handle this like a courtroom interrogation. He returns* HENSON's *salute.*

DAVENPORT   Sit down, Private. Your name is Louis Henson, is that right?

HENSON   Yes, sir.

> HENSON *sits, as* DAVENPORT *paces.*

DAVENPORT   Tell me what you know about Sergeant Waters and C. J. Memphis. [HENSON *looks at him strangely*] Is there something wrong?

HENSON   No, sir—I was just surprised you knew about it.

DAVENPORT   Why?

HENSON   You're an officer.

DAVENPORT [*quickly*]   And?

HENSON [*hesitantly*]   Well—officers are up here, sir—and us enlisted men—down here. [*Slight pause*] C.J. and Waters—that was just between enlisted men, sir. But I guess ain't nothin' a secret around colored folks—not that is was a secret. [*Shrugs*] There ain't that much to tell—sir. Sarge ain't like C.J. When I got to the company in May of las' year, the first person I saw Sarge chew out was C.J.! [*He is quiet*]

DAVENPORT   Go on.

> HENSON's *expression is pained.*

---

4. Island south of Italian peninsula invaded by Allied forces from North Africa in July 1943.

5. Nickname for Dwight D. Eisen- hower (1890–1969), Supreme Comman-

der of the Allied Forces that invaded Europe in June 1944 (and later, of course, 34th President of the United States, 1953–61).

HENSON   Is that an order, sir?

DAVENPORT   Does it have to be?

HENSON   I don't like tattle-talin', sir—an' I don't mean no offense, but I ain't crazy 'bout talkin' to officers—colored or white.

DAVENPORT   It's an order, Henson!

     HENSON *nods.*

HENSON   C.J. wasn' movin' fast enough for *him*. Said C.J. didn' have enough *fire-under-his-behind* out on the field.

DAVENPORT   You were on the team?

HENSON   Pitcher. [*Pause.* DAVENPORT *urges with a look.*] He jus' *stayed* on C.J. all the time—every little thing, it seemed like to me —then the shootin' went down, and C.J. caught all the hell.

DAVENPORT   What shooting?

HENSON   The shootin' at Williams's Golden Palace, sir—here, las' year!—way before you got here. Toward the end of baseball season. [DAVENPORT *nods his recognition*] The night it happened, a whole lotta gunshots went off near the barracks. I had gotten drunk over at the enlisted men's club, so when I got to the barracks I just sat down in a stupor!

     Suddenly shots are heard in the distance and grow ever closer as the eerie blue-gray light rises in the barracks over the sleeping figures of men in their bunks. HENSON *is seated, staring at the ground. He looks up once as the gunshots go off, and as he does, someone—we cannot be sure who—sneaks into the barracks as the men begin to shift and awaken. This person puts something under* C.J.*'s bed and rushes out.* HENSON *watches—surprised at first, rising, then disbelieving. He shakes his head, then sits back down as several men wake up.* DAVENPORT *recedes to one side of the barracks, watching.*

COBB   What the hell's goin' on? Don't they know a man needs his sleep? [*He is quickly back to sleep*]

SMALLS   [*simultaneously*]   Huh? Who is it? [*Looks around, then falls back to sleep*]

DAVENPORT   Are you sure you saw someone?

HENSON   Well—I saw something, sir.

DAVENPORT   What did you do?

     The shooting suddenly stops and the men settle down.

HENSON   I sat, sir—I was juiced— [*Shrugs*] The gunshots weren't any of my business—plus I wasn't sure what I had seen in the first place, then out of nowhere Sergeant Waters, he came in.

     WATERS *enters the barracks suddenly, followed by* WILKIE, HENSON *stands immediately, staggering a bit.*

WATERS   All right, all right! Everybody up! Wake them, Wilkie!

     WILKIE *moves around the bunks, shaking the men.*

WILKIE   Let's go! Up! Let's go, you guys!

     COBB *shoves* WILKIE*'s hand aside angrily as the others awaken slowly.*

WATERS   Un-ass them bunks! Tenn-hut! [*Most of the men snap to.* SMALLS *is the last one, and* WATERS *moves menacingly toward him*] There's been a shooting! One of ours bucked the line[6] at Williams's

6. Charged into the group (football term).

pay phone and three soldiers are dead! Two colored and one white M.P. [*Pauses*] Now, the man who bucked the line, he killed the M.P., and the white boys started shootin' everybody—that's how our two got shot. And this lowdown niggah we lookin' for got chased down here—and was almost caught, 'til somebody in these barracks started shootin' at the men chasin' him. So, we got us a vicious, murderin' piece of black trash in here somewhere—and a few people who helped him. If any of you are in this, I want you to step forward. [*No one moves*] All you baseball niggahs are innocent, huh? Wilkie, make the search. [PETERSON *turns around as* WILKIE *begins*] Eyes front!

PETERSON   I don't want that creep in my stuff!

WATERS   You don't talk at attention!

> WILKIE *will search three bunks, top and bottom, along with footlockers. Under* C.J.*'s bed he will find what he is looking for.*

WATERS   I almost hope it is some of you geechies—get rid of you Southern niggahs! [*To* WILKIE] Anything yet?

WILKIE   Nawwww!

WATERS   Memphis, are you in this?

C.J.   No, sah, Sarge.

WATERS   How many of you were out tonight?

SMALLS   I was over at Williams's around seven—got me some Lucky Strikes—I didn't try to call home, though.

COBB   I was there, this mornin'!

WATERS   Didn't I say tonight—uncle?

WILKIE   Got somethin'!

> WILKIE *is holding up a .45 caliber automatic pistol, army issue. Everyone's attention focuses on it. The men are surprised, puzzled.*

WATERS   Where'd you find it?

> WILKIE *points to* C.J., *who recoils at the idea.*

C.J.   Naaaawww, man!

WATERS   C.J.? This yours?

C.J.   You know it ain't mine, Sarge!

WATERS   It's still warm—how come it's under your bunk?

C.J.   Anybody coulda' put it thea', Sarge!

WATERS   Who? Or maybe this .45 crawled in through an open window—looked around the whole room—passed Cobb's bunk, and decided to snuggle up under yours? Must be voodoo, right, boy, Or some of that Farmers Dust round that neck of yours, huh?

C.J.   That pistol ain't mine!

WATERS   Liar!

C.J.   No, Sarge—I hate guns! Make me feel bad jes' to see a gun!

WATERS   You're under arrest—Wilkie, escort this man to the stockade!

> PETERSON *steps forward.*

PETERSON   C.J. couldn't hurt a fly, Waters, you know that!

WATERS   I found a gun, soldier—now get out of the way!

PETERSON   Goddammit, Waters, you know it ain't him!

WATERS   How do I know?

HENSON   Right before you came in, I though I saw somebody sneak in.

WATERS   You were drunk when you left the club—I saw you myself!

WILKIE   Besides, how you know it wasn't C.J.?

COBB   I was here all night. C.J. didn't go out.

  WATERS *looks at them, intense.*

WATERS   We got the right man. [*Points at* C.J., *impassioned*] You think he's innocent, don't you? C. J. Memphis, playin' cotton-picker singin' the blues, bowin' and scrapin'—smilin' in everybody's face —this man undermined us! You and me! The description of the man who did the shooting fits C.J.! [*To* HENSON] You saw C.J. sneak in here [*Points*] Don't be fooled—that yassah boss is hidin' something—niggahs ain't like that today! This is 1943—he shot that white boy!

  C.J. *is stunned, then suddenly the enormity of his predicament hits him and he breaks free of* WILKIE *and hits* WATERS *in the chest. The blow knocks* WATERS *down, and* C.J. *is immediately grabbed by the other men in the barracks.* COBB *goes to* WATERS *and helps him up slowly. The blow hurts* WATERS, *but he forces a smile at* C.J., *who has suddenly gone immobile, surprised by what he has done.*

WATERS   What did you go and do now, boy? Hit a noncommissioned officer.

COBB   Sarge, he didn't mean it!

  WILKIE *grabs* C.J. *by the arm and leads him out.* C.J. *goes calmly, almost passively.* WATERS *looks at all the men quietly for a moment, then walks out without saying a word. There is a momentary silence in the barracks.*

SMALLS   Niggah like that can't have a mother.

HENSON   I know I saw something!

PETERSON   C.J. was sleepin' when I came in! It's Waters—can't y'all see that? I've seen him before—we had 'em in Alabama! White man gives them a little ass job as a servant—close to the big house, and when the boss ain't lookin,' old copycat niggahs act like they the new owner! They take to soundin' like the boss—shoutin', orderin' people aroun'—and when it comes to you and me—they sell us to continue favor. They think the high-jailers like that. Arrestin' C.J. —that'll get Waters another stripe! Next it'll be you—or you. He can't look good unless he's standin' on you! Cobb tol' him C.J. was in all evening—Waters didn't even listen! Turning somebody in [*mimics*]: "Look what I done, Captain Boss!" They let him in the army 'cause they know he'll do anything they tell him to—I've seen his kind of fool before. Someone's going to kill him.

SMALLS   I heard they killed a sergeant at Fort Robinson—recruit did it—

COBB   It'll just be our luck, Sarge'll come through the whole war without a scratch.

PETERSON   Maybe—but I'm goin' over to the stockade—tell the M.P.'s what I know—C.J. was here all evening. [*He starts dressing*]

SMALLS   I'll go with you!

COBB   Me too, I guess.

  They all begin to dress as the light fades slowly in the barracks area. HENSON *rises and starts toward* DAVENPORT. *In the back-ground,* C.J.*'s music comes up a bit.*

DAVENPORT Could the person you thought you saw have stayed in the barracks—did you actually see someone go out?

HENSON Yes, sir!

DAVENPORT Was Wilkie the only man out of his bunk that night?

HENSON Guess so—he came in with Sarge.

DAVENPORT And Peterson—he did most of the talking?

HENSON As I recall. It's been a while ago—an' I was juiced!

DAVENPORT *rises.*

DAVENPORT Ellis!

ELLIS *appears at the door.*

ELLIS Sir!

DAVENPORT I want Private Wilkie and Pfc Peterson to report to me at once.

ELLIS They're probably on work detail, sir.

DAVENPORT Find them.

ELLIS Yes, sir!

ELLIS *exits quickly and* DAVENPORT *lapses into a quiet thought-fulness.*

HENSON Is there anything else?—Sir

DAVENPORT [*vexed*] No! That'll be all—send in the next man.

HENSON *comes to attention and salutes.* DAVENPORT *returns salute as* HENSON *exits through the barracks.* C.J.*'s music plays in background. There is a silence.* DAVENPORT *rises, mumbling something to himself.* COBB *appears suddenly at the doorway. He watches* DAVENPORT *for a moment.*

COBB Sir? [DAVENPORT *faces him*] Corporal Cobb reporting as ordered, sir. [*He salutes*]

DAVENPORT Have a seat, Corporal [COBB *crosses the room and sits*] And let's get something straight from the beginning—I don't care whether you like officers or not—is that clear?

COBB *looks at him strangely.*

COBB Sir?

Pause. DAVENPORT *calms down somewhat.*

DAVENPORT I'm sorry— Did you know Sergeant Waters well?

COBB As well as the next man, sir—I was already with the team when he took over. Me and C.J., we made the team the same time.

DAVENPORT Were you close to C.J.?

COBB Me and him were "homeys," sir! Both came from Mississippi. C.J. from Carmella—me, I'm from up 'roun' Jutlerville, what they call snake county. Plus, we both played for the Negro League before the war.

DAVENPORT How did you feel about his arrest?

COBB Terrible—C.J. didn't kill nobody, sir.

DAVENPORT He struck Sergeant Waters—

COBB Waters made him, sir! He called that boy things he had never heard of before—C.J., he was so confused he didn't know what else to do—[*Pause*] An' when they put him in the stockade, he jus' seemed to go to pieces. [*Lowly in the background,* C.J.*'s music comes up*] See, we both lived on farms—and even though C.J.'s daddy played music, C.J., he liked the wide-open spaces. [*Shakes his head*] That cell? It started closin' in on him right away. [*Blue-gray light rises in limbo, where* C.J. *is sitting on the edge of a bunk. A shadow of bars cuts across the space. His guitar is on the bunk beside him.*] I went to see him, the second day he was in there. He looked pale and ashy, sir—like something dead.

C.J. *faces* COBB.

C.J.   It's hard to breathe in these little spaces, Cobb—man wasn' made for this hea'—nothin' was! I don't think I'll eva' see a' animal in a cage agin' and not feel sorry for it [*To himself*] I'd rather be on the chain gang.

COBB *loks up at him.*

COBB   Come on, homey! [*He rises, moves toward* C.J.]

C.J.   I don't think I'm comin' outta here, Cobb—feels like I'm goin' crazy. Can't walk in hea'—can't see the sun! I tried singin', Cobb, but nothin' won't come out. I sure don't wanna die in this jail!

COBB [*moving closer*]   Ain't nobody gonna die, C.J.!

C.J.   Yesterday I broke a guitar string—lost my Dust! I got no protection—nothin' to keep the dog from tearin' at my bones!

COBB   Stop talkin' crazy!

C.J. *is quiet for a moment. He starts forward. Slowly, in center stage,* WATERS *emerges. He faces the audience.*

C.J.   You know, he come up hea' las' night? Sergeant Waters?

WATERS *smiles, pulls out his pipe, lights it.*

WATERS [*calmly*]   You should learn never to hit sergeants, boy—man can get in a lot of trouble doin' that kinda thing durin' wartime—they talkin' 'bout givin' you five years—they call what you did mutiny in the navy. Mutiny, boy.

C.J.   That gun ain't mine!

WATERS   Oh, we know that, C.J.! [C.J. *is surprised.*] That gun belonged to the niggah did the shootin' over at Williams's place—me and Wilkie caught him hidin' in the Motor Pool, and he confessed his head off. You're in here for striking a superior officer, boy. And I got a whole barracks full of your friends to prove it! [*Smiles broadly, as* C.J. *shakes his head.*]

DAVENPORT [*To* COBB, *at once*]   Memphis wasn't charged with the shooting?

COBB   No, sir—

WATERS   Don't feel too bad, boy. It's not your fault entirely—it has to be this way. The First War, it didn't change much for us, boy—but this one—it's gonna change a lot of things. Them Nazis ain't all crazy—a whole lot of people just can't fit into where things seem to be goin'—like you, C.J. The black race can't afford you no more. There used ta be a time when we'd see somebody like you, singin, clownin'—yas-sah-bossin'—and we wouldn't do anything. [*Smiles*] Folks liked that—you were good—homey kinda' niggah—they needed somebody to mistreat—call a name, they paraded you, reminded them of the old days—corn-bread bakin', greens and ham cookin'—Daddy out pickin' cotton, Grandmammy sit on the front porch smokin' a pipe. [*Slight pause*] Not no more. The day of the geechy is gone, boy—the only thing that can move the race is power. It's all the white respects—and people like you just make us seem like fools. And we can't let nobody go on believin' we all like you! You bring us down—make people think the whole race is unfit! [*Quietly pleased*] I waited a long time for you, boy, but I gotcha! And I try to git rid of you wherever I go. I put two geechies in jail at Fort Campbell, Kentucky—three at Fort Huachuca. Now I got you—one less fool for the race to be ashamed of! [*Points*] And I'ma git that ole boy Cobb next! [*Light begins to fade around* WATERS]

DAVENPORT [*at once*]   You?

COBB   Yes, sir. [*Slight pause*]

DAVENPORT   Go on.

C.J.   You imagin' anybody sayin' that? I know I'm not gittin' outta' hea', Cobb! [*Quiet*] You remember I tol' you 'bout a place I use ta go outside Carmella? When I was a little ole tiny thing? Place out behind O'Connell's Farm? Place would be stinkin' of plums, Cobb. Shaded—that ripe smell be weavin' through the cotton fields and clear on in ta town on a warm day. First time I had Evelyn? I had her unda' them plum trees. I wrote a song for her— [*Talks, sings*] My ginger-colored Moma—she had thighs the size of hams! [*Chuckles*] And when you spread them, Momaaaa! / [*Talks*] You let me have my jelly roll and jam! [*Pause, mood swing*] O'Connell, he had a dog—meanes' dog I *eva'* did see! An' the only way you could enjoy them plum trees was to outsmart that dog. Waters is like that ole dog, Cobb—you gotta run circles roun' ole Windy— that was his name. They say he tore a man's arm off once, and got to likin' it. So, you had to cheat that dog outta' bitin' you every time. Every time. [*Slowly the light begins to fade around* C.J.]

COBB   He didn't make sense, sir. I tried talkin' about the team—the war—aint nothin' work—seem like he jes' got worse.

DAVENPORT   What happened to him?

COBB *looks at him incredulously.*

COBB   The next day—afta' the day I saw him? C.J., he hung hisself, sir! Suicide—jes' couldn't stand it. M.P.'s found him hung from the bars.

DAVENPORT *is silent for a moment.*

DAVENPORT   What happened after that?

COBB   We lost our last game—we jes' threw it—we did it for C.J.— Captain, he was mad 'cause we ain't git ta play the Yankees. Peterson was right on that one—somebody needed to protest that man!

DAVENPORT   What did Waters do?

COBB   Well, afta' we lost, the commanding officer, he broke up the team, and we all got reassigned to this Smoke Company. Waters, he started actin' funny, sir—stayed drunk—talked to hisself all the time.

DAVENPORT   Did you think you were next?

COBB   I ain't sure I eva' believed Waters said that, sir—C.J. had to be outta' his head or he wouldna' killed hisself—Sarge, he neva' came near me afta' C.J. died.

DAVENPORT   What time did you get back the night Waters was killed?
COBB   I'd say between 2120 and 9:30.
DAVENPORT   And you didn't go out again?
COBB   No, sir—me and Henson sat and listened to the radio till Abbott and Lou Costello[7] went off, then I played checkers with Wilkie for 'notha' hour, then everybody went to bed. What C.J. said about Waters? It ain't botha' me, sir.
    DAVENPORT *is silent.*
DAVENPORT   Who were the last ones in that night?
COBB   Smalls and Peterson—they had guard duty.
    TAYLOR *enters the barracks area and stops just inside the door when he sees* DAVENPORT *isn't quite finished.*
DAVENPORT   Thank you, Corporal.
    COBB *rises at attention and salutes.* DAVENPORT *returns salute and* COBB *starts out. He nods at* TAYLOR, *who advances toward* DAVENPORT.
TAYLOR [*smiling*]   You surprise me, Davenport—I just left Colonel Nivens. He's given you permission to question Byrd and Wilcox? [DAVENPORT *nods*] How'd you manage that? You threatened him with an article in the Chicago *Defender*,[8] I suppose.
DAVENPORT   I convinced the Colonel it was in his best interests to allow it.
TAYLOR   Really? Did he tell you I would assist you?
DAVENPORT   I told him I especially didn't want you.
TAYLOR   That's precisely why he sent me—he didn't want you to think you could get your way entirely—not with him. Then neither Byrd or Wilcox would submit to it without a white officer present. That's how it is. [*There is a rather long silence*] But there's something else, Davenport. The Colonel began talking about the affidavits he and the others signed—and the discrepancies in their statements that night. [*Mimics*] He wants me with you because he doesn't want Byrd and Wilcox giving you the wrong impression— he never elaborated on what he meant by the wrong impression. I want to be there!
DAVENPORT   So you're not on *that* side anymore—you're on *my* side now, right?
TAYLOR [*bristles*]   I want whoever killed my sergeant, Davenport!
DAVENPORT   Bullshit! Yesterday you were daring me to try! And today we're allies? Besides, you don't give that much of a damn about your men! I've been around you a full day and you haven't uttered a word that would tell me you had any more than a minor acquaintance with Waters! He managed your baseball team—was an N.C.O. in your company, and you haven't offered *any* opinion of the man as a soldier—sergeant—platoon leader! Who the hell was he?
TAYLOR   He was one of my men! On my roster—a man these bars make me responsible for! And no, I don't know a helluva lot about him—or a lot of their names or where they come from, but I'm still

7. Highly successful radio (and then movie) comedy team during the 1940s and '50s.

8. Widely distributed weekly newspaper from the black press.

their commanding officer and in a little while I may have to trust them with my life! And I want them to know they can trust me with theirs—here and now! [*Pause*] I have Byrd and Wilcox in my office. [DAVENPORT *stares at him for a long moment, then rises and starts out toward center stage.*] Why didn't you tell Nivens that you'd placed me under arrest?

DAVENPORT *stops.*

DAVENPORT   I didn't find it necessary.

They stare at one another. TAYLOR *is noticeably strained.*

DAVENPORT [*starts away*]   What do you know about C. J. Memphis?

TAYLOR *follows.*

TAYLOR [*shrugs*]   He was a big man as I recall—more a boy than a man, though. Played the guitar sometimes at the Officers Club— there was something embarrassing about him. Committed suicide in the stockade. Pretty good center fielder—

DAVENPORT *stops.*

DAVENPORT   Did you investigate his arrest—the charges against him?

TAYLOR   He was charged with assaulting a noncommissioned officer —I questioned him—he didn't say much. He admitted he struck Waters—I started questioning several of the men in the platoon and he killed himself before I could finish—open-and-shut case.

DAVENPORT   I think Waters tricked C.J. into assaulting him.

TAYLOR   Waters wasn't that kind of a man! He admitted he might have provoked the boy—he accused him of that Golden Palace shooting—

Behind them, the CAPTAIN's *office is lit. In two chairs facing* TAYLOR's *desk are* LIEUTENANT BYRD *and* CAPTAIN WILCOX, *both in dress uniform.*

TAYLOR   Listen, Waters didn't have a fifth-grade education—he wasn't a schemer! And colored soldiers aren't devious like that.

DAVENPORT   What do you mean we aren't devious?

TAYLOR [*sharply*]   You're not as devious—! [DAVENPORT *stares as* TAYLOR *waves disdainfully and starts into the office.*] Anyway, what has that to do with this? [*He is distracted by* BYRD *and* WILCOX *before* DAVENPORT *can answer.* TAYLOR *speaks as he moves to his desk.*] This is *Captain* Davenport—you've both been briefed by Colonel Nivens to give the Captain your full cooperation.

DAVENPORT *puts on his glasses.* TAYLOR *notices and almost smiles.*

BYRD [*to* DAVENPORT]   They tell me you a lawyer, huh?

DAVENPORT   I am not here to answer your questions, Lieutenant. And I am Captain Davenport, is that clear?

BYRD [*to* TAYLOR]   Captain, is he crazy?

TAYLOR   You got your orders.

BYRD   Sir, I vigorously protest as an officer—

TAYLOR [*cuts him off*]   You answer him the way he wants you to, Byrd, or I'll have your ass in a sling so tight you won't be able to pee, soldier!

BYRD *backs off slightly.*

DAVENPORT   When did you last see Sergeant Waters?

BYRD   The night he was killed, but I didn't kill him—I should have blown his head off, the way he spoke to me and Captain Wilcox here.

DAVENPORT   How did he speak to you, Captain?

WILCOX   Well, he was very drunk—and he said a lot of things he shouldn't have. I told the Lieutenant here not to make the situation worse and he agreed, and we left the Sergeant on his knees, wallowing in self-pity. [*Shrugs*]

DAVENPORT   What exactly did he say?

WILCOX   Some pretty stupid things about us—I mean white people, sir.

BYRD *reacts to the term "sir."*

DAVENPORT   What kind of things?

BYRD   [*annoyed*] He said he wasn't going to obey no white man's orders! And that me and Wilcox here were to blame for him being black, and not able to sleep or keep his food down! And I didn't even know the man! Never even spoke to him before that night!

DAVENPORT   Anything else?

WILCOX   Well—he said he'd killed somebody.

DAVENPORT   Did he call a name—or say who?

WILCOX   Not that I recall, sir.

DAVENPORT *looks at* BYRD.

BYRD   No— [*Sudden and sharp*] Look—the goddamn Negro was disrespectful! He wouldn't salute! Wouldn't come to attention! And where I come from, colored don't talk the way he spoke to us—not to white people they don't!

DAVENPORT   Is that the reason you killed him?

BYRD   I killed nobody! I said "where I come from," didn't I? You'd be dead yourself, where I come from! But I didn't kill the—the *Negro!*

DAVENPORT   But you hit him, didn't you?

BYRD   I knocked him down!

DAVENPORT   [*quickens pace*] And when you went to look at him, he was dead, wasn't he?

BYRD   He was alive when we left!

DAVENPORT   You're a liar! You beat Waters up—you went back and you shot him!

BYRD   No! [*Rises*] But you better get outta my face before I kill you!

DAVENPORT *stands firm.*

DAVENPORT   Like you killed Waters?

BYRD   No! [*He almost raises a hand to* DAVENPORT]

TAYLOR   [*at once*] Soldier!

BYRD   He's trying to put it on me!

TAYLOR   Answer his questions, Lieutenant.

DAVENPORT   You were both coming off bivouac, right?

WILCOX   Yes.

DAVENPORT   So you both had weapons?

BYRD   So what? We didn't fire them!

DAVENPORT   Were the weapons turned in immediately?

WILCOX   Yes, sir—Colonel Nivens took our .45's to Major Hines. It was all kept quiet because the Colonel didn't want the colored boys to know that anyone white from the Fort was involved in any way—ballistics cleared them.

DAVENPORT   We can check.

BYRD   Go ahead.

TAYLOR   I don't believe it—why wasn't I told?

WILCOX   The weapons had cleared—and the Colonel felt if he involved you further, you'd take the matter to Washington and there'd be a scandal about colored and white soldiers—as it turned out, he thinks you went to Washington anyway. [*To* DAVENPORT] I'd like to say, Captain, that neither Lieutenant Byrd or myself had anything whatsoever to do with Sergeant Waters's death—I swear that as an officer and a gentleman. He was on the ground when we left him, but very much alive.

TAYLOR   Consider yourselves under arrest, *gentlemen!*

BYRD   On what charge?

TAYLOR   Murder! You think I believe that crap—

DAVENPORT   Let them go, Captain.

TAYLOR   You've got motive—a witness to their being at the scene—

DAVENPORT   Let them go! This is still my investigation—you two are dismissed.

> BYRD *rises quickly.* WILCOX *follows his lead.*

WILCOX   Are we being charged, sir?

DAVENPORT   Not by me.

WILCOX   Thank you.

> WILCOX *comes to attention, joined by a reluctant* BYRD. *They both salute.* DAVENPORT *returns salute.*

BYRD   I expected more from a white man, Captain.

TAYLOR   Get out of here, before I have you cashiered out of the army, Byrd!

> *Both men exit quietly, and for a moment* TAYLOR *and* DAVENPORT *are quiet.*

TAYLOR   What the hell is the matter with you? You could have charged both of them—Byrd for insubordination—Wilcox, tampering with evidence.

DAVENPORT   Neither charge is murder—you think Wilcox would tell a story like that if he didn't have Hines and Nivens to back it up? [*Slightly tired*] They've got a report.

TAYLOR   So what do you do now?

DAVENPORT   Finish the investigation.

TAYLOR   They're lying, dammit! So is the Colonel! You were ordered to investigate and charge the people responsible—charge them! I'll back you up!

DAVENPORT   I'm not satisfied yet, Captain.

TAYLOR   I am! Dammit!—I wish they'd sent somebody else! I do—you—you're afraid! You thought you'd accuse the Klan, didn't you? —and that would be the end of it, right? Another story of midnight riders for your Negro press! And now it's officers—white men in the army. It's too much for you—what will happen when Captain Davenport comes up for promotion to major if he accuses white officers, right?

DAVENPORT   I'm not afraid of white men, Captain.

TAYLOR   Then why the hell won't you arrest them?

DAVENPORT   Because I do what the facts tell me, Captain—not you!

TAYLOR   You don't know what a fact is, Davenport!

ELLIS *enters suddenly and salutes.*

ELLIS   Begging your pardon, sir.

TAYLOR   What is it, Corporal?

ELLIS   Ah—it's for Captain Davenport— [*To* DAVENPORT] We found Private Wilkie, sir. We haven't located Pfc Peterson yet. Seems him and Private Smalls went out on detail together, and neither one of 'em showed up—but I got a few men from the company lookin' for 'em around the N.C.O. club and in the PX, sir.

DAVENPORT   Where's Wilkie?

ELLIS   He's waiting for you in the barracks, Captain.

DAVENPORT *nods, and* ELLIS *goes out after saluting. The lights come up around* WILKIE, *who is seated in a chair in the barracks reading a Negro newspaper.* DAVENPORT *is thoughtful for a moment.*

TAYLOR   Didn't you question Wilkie and Peterson yesterday? [DAVENPORT *starts out*] Davenport? [DAVENPORT *does not answer*] Don't you ignore me!

DAVENPORT   Get off my back! What I do—how I do it—who I interrogate is my business, Captain! This investigation is mine! [*Holds out the back of his hand, showing* TAYLOR *the color of his skin*] Mine!

TAYLOR   Don't treat me with that kind of contempt—I'm not some red-neck cracker!

DAVENPORT   And I'm not your yessirin' colored boy either!

TAYLOR   I asked you a question!

DAVENPORT   I don't have to answer it!

There is a long silence. The two men glare at one another— TAYLOR *in another time, disturbed.*

TAYLOR   Indeed you don't—*Captain.*

Pause.

DAVENPORT   Now, *Captain*—what if Byrd and Wilcox are telling the truth?

TAYLOR   Neither one of us believes that.

DAVENPORT   What if they are?

TAYLOR   Then who killed the goddamn man?

DAVENPORT   I don't know yet. [*Slight pause*] Is there anything else? TAYLOR *shakes his head no as* DAVENPORT *starts toward center stage, headed toward* WILKIE.

TAYLOR   No, hotshot, nothing.

DAVENPORT *enters the barracks area.* WILKIE *quickly puts his paper aside and snaps to attention and salutes.* DAVENPORT *returns salute but remains silent, going right to the desk and removing his pad and pencil. The light around the office fades out.*

DAVENPORT [*snapping at Wilkie*]   When did you lose your stripes? [*He is standing over* WILKIE.]

WILKIE   Couple months before they broke up the team—right after Sergeant Waters got assigned to us, sir.

DAVENPORT   Nervous, Wilkie?

WILKIE   [*smiles haltingly*] I couldn't figure out why you called me back, sir? [*Laughs nervously*]

DAVENPORT   You lost your stripes for being drunk on duty, is that correct?

WILKIE   Yes, sir.

DAVENPORT   You said Waters busted you, didn't you?

WILKIE   He got me busted—he's the one reported me to the Captain.

DAVENPORT   How did you feel? Must have been awful— [DAVENPORT *paces*] Weren't you and the Sergeant good friends? Didn't you tell me he was all right? A nice guy?

WILKIE   Yes, sir.

DAVENPORT   Would a nice guy have gotten a friend busted?

WILKIE   No, sir.

DAVENPORT   So you lied when you said he was a nice guy, right?

WILKIE   No, sir—I mean—

DAVENPORT   Speak up! Speak up! Was the Sergeant a nice guy or not?

WILKIE   No, sir.

DAVENPORT   Why not? Answer me!

WILKIE   Well, you wouldn't turn somebody in over something like that!

DAVENPORT   Not a good friend, right?

WILKIE   Right, sir—I mean, a friend would give you extra duty—I would have—or even call you a whole buncha' names—you'd expect that, sir—but damn! Three stripes? They took ten years to get in this army, sir! Ten years! I started out with the 24th Infantry—I—

DAVENPORT   Made you mad, didn't it?

WILKIE   Yeah, it made me mad—all the things I did for him!

DAVENPORT   [*quickly*] That's right! You were his assistant, weren't you? Took care of the team— [WILKIE *nods*] Ran all his errands, looked at his family snapshots [WILKIE *nods again*], policed his quarters, put the gun under J.C.'s bed—

WILKIE *looks up suddenly.*

WILKIE   No!

DAVENPORT   [*quickly*] It was you Henson saw, wasn't it, Wilkie?

WILKIE   No, sir!

DAVENPORT   Liar! You lied about Waters, and you're lying now! You were the only person out of the barracks that night, and the only one who knew the layout well enough to go straight to C.J.'s bunk! Not even Waters knew the place that well! Henson didn't see who it was, but he saw what the person did—he was positive about that —only you knew the barracks in the dark!

WILKIE   [*pleadingly*] It was the Sarge, Captain—he ordered me to do it—he said I'd get my stripes back—he wanted to scare that boy C.J.! Let him stew in jail! Then C.J. hit him—and he had the boy right where he wanted him— [*Confused*] But it backfired— C.J. killed hisself—Sarge didn't figure on that.

DAVENPORT   Why did he pick Memphis?

WILKIE   He despised him, Captain—he'd hide it, 'cause everybody in the company liked that boy so much. But underneath—it was a crazy hate, sir—he'd go cold when he talked about C.J. You could feel it.

> *In limbo, the blue-gray light rises on* C.J. *and* WATERS. C.J. *is humming a blues song and* WATERS *is standing smiling, smoking a pipe as he was in Act One.* WATERS *turns away from* C.J. *His speech takes place over* C.J.'s *humming.*

WATERS   He's the kinda boy seems innocent, Wilkie. Got everybody around the post thinking he's a strong, black buck! Hits home runs —white boys envy his strength—his speed, the power in his swing. Then this colored champion lets those same white boys call him Shine—or Sambo at the Officers Club. They laugh at his blues songs, and he just smiles—can't talk, barely read or write his own name—and don't care! He'll tell you they like him—or that colored folks ain't supposed to have but so much sense. [*Intense*] Do you know the damage one ignorant *Negro* can do? [*Remembering*] We were in France during the First War, Wilkie. We had won decorations, but the white boys had told all the French gals we had tails. And they found this ignorant colored soldier. Paid him to tie a tail to his ass and parade around naked making monkey sounds. [*Shakes his head*] They sat him on a big, round table in the Café Napoleon, put a reed in his hand, a crown on his head, a blanket on his shoulders, and made him eat bananas in front of them Frenchies. And ohhh, the white boys danced that night—passed out leaflets with that boy's picture on them—called him Moonshine, King of the Monkeys. And when we slit his throat, you know that fool asked us what he had done wrong? [*Pause*] My daddy told me, we got to turn our backs on his kind, Wilkie. Close our ranks to the chittlin's, the collard greens—the corn-bread style. We are men— soldiers, and I don't intend to have our race cheated out of its place of honor and respect in *this* war because of fools like C.J.! You watch everything he does—*everything!*

> *Light fades slowly around* WATERS *and* C.J., *and as it does,* C.J. *stops humming.*

WILKIE   And I watched him, sir—but Waters—he couldn't wait! He wouldn't talk about nothin' else—it was C.J. this—C.J. all the time!

DAVENPORT   [*troubled*]   Why didn't he pick Peterson—they fought—

WILKIE   They fought all the time, sir—but the Sarge, he likes Peterson. [*Nods*] Peterson fought back, and Waters admired that. He promoted Pete! Imagine that—he thought Peterson would make a fine soldier!

DAVENPORT   What was Peterson's reaction—when C.J. died?

WILKIE   Like everybody else, he was sad—he put together that protest that broke up the team, but afta' that he didn't say much. And he usually runs off at the mouth. Kept to himself—or with Smalls.

> *Slight pause.*

DAVENPORT   The night Waters was killed, what time did you get in?

WILKIE   Around nine forty-five—couple of us came from the club

and listened to radio awhile—I played some checkers, then I went
to bed. Sir? I didn't mean to do what I did—it wasn't my fault—
he promised me my stripes!

> *Suddenly, out of nowhere, in the near distance, is the sound of
> gunfire, a bugle blaring, something like a cannon going off.
> The noise is continuous through scene.* DAVENPORT *rises,
> startled.*

DAVENPORT   I'm placing you under arrest, Private!

> ELLIS *bursts into the room.*

ELLIS   Did you hear, sir? [DAVENPORT, *surprised, shakes his head no*]
Our orders! They came down from Washington, Captain! We're
shippin' out! They finally gonna let us Negroes fight!

> DAVENPORT *is immediately elated, and almost forgets* WILKIE
> *as he shakes* ELLIS's *hand.*

DAVENPORT   Axis ain't got a chance!

ELLIS   Surrrre—we'll win this mother in six months now! Afta' what
Jesse Owens did to them people? Joe Louis?[9]

> HENSON *bursts in.*

HENSON   Did y'all hear it? Forty-eight-hour standby alert? We goin'
into combat [*Loud*] Look out, Hitler, the niggahs is comin' to git
your ass through the fog!

ELLIS   With real rifles—it's really O.K., you know?

HENSON   They tell me them girls in England—woooow!

> DAVENPORT *faces* WILKIE *as* COBB *enters, yelling.*

COBB   They gonna let us git in it! We may lay so much smoke the
Germans may never get to see what a colored soldier looks like
'til the war's over! [*To* HENSON] I wrote my woman jes' the otha'
day that we'd be goin' soon!

ELLIS   Go on!

HENSON [*overlapping*]   Man, you ain't nothin'!

> DAVENPORT *begins to move* WILKIE *toward* ELLIS.

HENSON   If the army said we was all discharged, you'd claim you
wrote that! [*He quiets, watching* DAVENPORT.]

COBB [*quickly*]   You hea' this fool, sir?

HENSON   Shhhhh!

DAVENPORT [*To* ELLIS]   Corporal, escort Private Wilkie to the
stockade.

ELLIS [*surprised*]   Yes, sir!

> ELLIS *starts* WILKIE *out, even though he is bewildered by it.*
> *They exit.*

HENSON   Wilkie's under arrest, sir? [DAVENPORT *nods*] How come? I
apologize, sir—I didn't mean that.

DAVENPORT   Do either of you know where Smalls and Peterson can
be located?

> HENSON *shrugs.*

COBB   Your men got Smalls in the stockade, sir!

DAVENPORT   When?

9. At the 1936 Olympics in Germany,
Owens (1913–80) upset Hitler (and his
theories of Aryan superiority) by winning
four gold medals and in the process breaking two world records and tying another;
Louis (see above, n. 2, p. 000) knocked
out the German heavyweight Max Schmel-
ling who had earlier defeated him.

COBB   I saw two colored M.P.'s takin' him through the main gate. Jes' a while ago—I was on my way ova' hea'!

> DAVENPORT *goes to the desk and picks up his things and starts out.*

COBB   Tenn-hut.

> DAVENPORT *stops and salutes.*

DAVENPORT   As you were. By the way—congratulations!

> DAVENPORT *exits the barracks through the doorway.*

HENSON   Look out, Hitler!

COBB   The niggahs is coming to get yo' ass.

HENSON AND COBB   Through the fog.

> *The lights in the barracks go down at once. Simultaneously, they rise in limbo, where* SMALLS *is pacing back and forth. He is smoking a cigarette. There is a bunk, and the shadow of a screen over his cell. In the background, the sounds of celebration continue.* DAVENPORT *emerges from the right, and begins to speak immediately as the noises of celebration fade.*

DAVENPORT   Why'd you go AWOL, soldier?

> SMALLS *faces him, unable to see* DAVENPORT *at first. When he sees him, he snaps to attention and salutes.*

SMALLS   Private Anthony Smalls, sir!

DAVENPORT   At ease—answer my question!

SMALLS   I didn't go AWOL, sir—I—I got drunk in Tynin and fell asleep in the bus depot—it was the only public place I could find to sleep it off.

DAVENPORT   Where'd you get drunk? Where in Tynin?

SMALLS   Jake's—Jake's and Lilly's Golden Slipper—on Melville Street—

DAVENPORT   Weren't you and Peterson supposed to be on detail? [SMALLS *nods*] Where was Peterson? Speak up!

SMALLS   I don't know, sir!

DAVENPORT   You're lying! You just walked off your detail and Peterson did nothing?

SMALLS   No, sir—he warned me, sir—"Listen, Smalls!" he said—

DAVENPORT   [*cutting him off*] You trying to make a fool of me, Smalls? Huh? [*Loud*] Are you?

SMALLS   No, sir!

DAVENPORT   The two of you went A-W-O-L together, didn't you? [SMALLS *is quiet*] Answer me!

SMALLS   Yes!

DAVENPORT   You left together because Peterson knew I would find out the two of you killed Waters, didn't you? [SMALLS *suddenly bursts into quiet tears, shaking his head*] What? I can't hear you! [SMALLS *is sobbing*] You killed Waters, didn't you? I want an answer.

SMALLS   I can't sleep—I can't sleep!

DAVENPORT   Did you kill Sergeant Waters?

SMALLS   It was Peterson, sir! [*As if he can see it*] I watched! It wasn't me!

> *The blue-gray light builds in center stage. As it does,* SERGEANT

WATERS *staggers forward and falls on his knees. He can't get up, he is so drunk. He has been beaten, and looks the way we saw him in the opening of Act One.*

SMALLS   We were changing the guard.

WATERS   Can't be trusted—no matter what we do, there are no guarantees—and your mind won't let you forget it. [*Shakes his head repeatedly.*] No, no, no!

SMALLS [*overlapping*]   On our way back to the Captain's office— and Sarge, he was on the road. We just walked into him! He was ranting, and acting crazy, sir!

PETERSON *emerges from the right. He is dressed in a long coat, pistol belt and pistol, rifle, helmet, his pants bloused over his boots. He sees* WATERS *and smiles.* WATERS *continues to babble.*

PETERSON   Smalls, look who's drunk on his ass, boy! [*He begins to circle* WATERS]

SMALLS [*to* DAVENPORT]   I told him to forget Waters!

PETERSON   Noooo! I'm gonna' enjoy this, Smalls—big, bad Sergeant Waters down on his knees? No, sah—I'm gonna' love this! [*Leans over* WATERS] Hey, Sarge—need some help? [WATERS *looks up; almost smiles. He reaches for* PETERSON, *who pushes him back down.*] That's the kinda help I'll give yah, boy! Let me help you again—all right? [*Kicks* WATERS.] Like that, Sarge? Huh? Like that, dog?

SMALLS [*shouts*]   Peterson!

PETERSON   No! [*Almost pleading*] Smalls—some people, man— If this was a German, would you kill it? If it was Hitler—or that fuckin' Tojo? Would you kill him? [*Kicks* WATERS *again.*]

WATERS [*mumbling throughout*]   There's a trick to it, Peterson—it's the only way you can win—C.J. could never make it—he was a clown! [*Grabs at* PETERSON] A clown in blackface! A niggah!

PETERSON *steps out of reach. He is suddenly expressionless as he easily removes his pistol from his holster.*

WATERS   You got to be like them! And I was! I was—but the rules are fixed. [*Whispers*] Shhhh! Listen. It's C.J.— [*Laughs*] I made him do it, but it doesn't make any difference! They still hate you! [*Looks at* PETERSON, *who has moved closer to him.*] They still hate you! [WATERS *laughs.*]

PETERSON [*to* SMALLS]   Justice, Smalls. [*He raises the pistol.*]

DAVENPORT [*suddenly, harshly*]   That isn't justice!

SMALLS *almost recoils.*

PETERSON [*simultaneously, continuing*]   For C.J.! Everybody!

PETERSON *fires the gun at* WATER's *chest, and the shot stops everything. The celebration noise stops. Even* DAVENPORT *in his way seems to hear it.* PETERSON *fires again. There is a moment of quiet on stage.* DAVENPORT *is angered and troubled.*

DAVENPORT   You call that justice?

SMALLS   No, sir.

DAVENPORT [*enraged*]   Then why the fuck didn't you do something?

SMALLS   I'm scared of Peterson—just scared of him!

PETERSON *has been looking at* WATER's *body throughout. He*

> *now begins to lift* WATERS *as best he can, and pull him off-stage. It is done with some difficulty.*

SMALLS   I tried to get him to go, sir, but he wanted to drag the Sergeant's body back into the woods—

> *Light fades quickly around* PETERSON, *as* DAVENPORT *paces.*

SMALLS   Said everybody would think white people did it.

DAVENPORT   [*somewhat drained*]   Then what happened?

SMALLS   I got sick, sir—and Peterson, when he got done, he helped me back to the barracks and told me to keep quiet. [*Slight pause*] I'm sorry sir.

> *There is a long pause, during which* DAVENPORT *stares at* SMALLS *with disgust, then abruptly starts out without saluting. He almost flees.* SMALLS *rises quickly.*

SMALLS   Sir?

> DAVENPORT *turns around.* SMALLS *comes to attention and salutes.* DAVENPORT *returns salute and starts out of the cell and down toward center stage. He is thoughtful as the light fades around* SMALLS. DAVENPORT *removes his glasses and begins to clean them as he speaks.*

DAVENPORT   Peterson was apprehended a week later in Alabama. Colonel Nivens called it "just another black mess of cuttin', slashin', and shootin'!" He was delighted there were no white officers mixed up in it, and his report to Washington characterized the events surrounding Waters's murder as "the usual, common violence any commander faces in Negro Military units." It was the kind of "mess" that turns up on page 3 in the colored papers—the Cain and Abel story of the week—the headline we Negroes can't quite read in comfort. [*Shakes head and paces*] For me? Two colored soldiers are dead—two on their way to prison. Four less men to fight with—and none of their reasons—nothing anyone *said,* or *did,* would have been worth a life to men with larger hearts—men less split by the madness of race in America. [*Pause*] The case got little attention. The details were filed in my report and I was quickly and rather unceremoniously ordered back to my M.P. unit. [*Smiles*] A style of guitar pickin' and a dance called the C.J. caught on for a while in Tynin saloons during 1945. [*Slight pause*] In northern New Jersey, through a military foul-up, Sergeant Waters's family was informed that he had been killed in action. The Sergeant was, therefore, thought and unofficially rumored to have been the first colored casualty of the war from that county and under the circumstances was declared a hero. Nothing could be done officially, but his picture was hung on a Wall of Honor in the Dorie Miller VFW Post #978. [*Pause*] The men of the 221st Chemical Smoke Generating Company? The entire outfit—officers and enlisted men—was wiped out in the Ruhr Valley during a German advance. [*He turns toward* TAYLOR, *who enters quietly*] Captain?

TAYLOR   Davenport—I see you got your man.

DAVENPORT   I got him—what is it, Captain?

TAYLOR   Will you accept my saying, you did a splendid job?

DAVENPORT   I'll take the praise—but how did I manage it?

TAYLOR   Dammit, Davenport—I didn't come here to be made fun of— [*Slight pause*] The men—the regiment—we all ship out for Europe tomorrow, and [*hesitates*] I was wrong, Davenport—about the bars—the uniform—about Negroes being in charge. [*Slight pause*] I guess I'll *have* to get used to it.

DAVENPORT   Oh, you'll get used to it—you can bet your ass on that. Captain—you will get used to it.

       Lights begin to fade slowly as the music "Don't Sit under the Apple Tree" rises in the background, and the house goes to black.

1982

Plays for Further Reading

MOLIÈRE

The Misanthrope*

CHARACTERS

ALCESTE, *in love with Célimène*
PHILINTE, *Alceste's friend*
ORONTE, *in love with Célimène*
CÉLIMÈNE, *Alceste's beloved*
ÉLIANTE, *Célimène's cousin*
ARSINOÉ, *a friend of Célimène's*

ACASTE
CLITANDRE } *Marquesses*
BASQUE, *Célimène's servant*
A GUARD *of the Marshalsea*
DUBOIS, *Alceste's valet*

The Scene throughout is in Célimène's house at Paris.

Act 1

SCENE 1. [PHILINTE, ALCESTE]

PHILINTE   Now, what's got into you?
ALCESTE [*seated*]   Kindly leave me alone.
PHILINTE   Come, come, what is it? This lugubrious tone . . .
ALCESTE   Leave me, I said; you spoil my solitude.
PHILINTE   Oh, listen to me, now, and don't be rude.
ALCESTE   I choose to be rude, Sir, and to be hard of hearing.   5
PHILINTE   These ugly moods of yours are not endearing;
  Friends though we are, I really must insist . . .
ALCESTE [*abruptly rising*]   Friends? Friends, you say? Well, cross me
  off your list.
  I've been your friend till now, as you well know;
  But after what I saw a moment ago   10
  I tell you flatly that our ways must part.
  I wish no place in a dishonest heart.
PHILINTE   Why, what have I done, Alceste? Is this quite just?
ALCESTE   My God, you ought to die of self-disgust.
  I call your conduct inexcusable, Sir,   15
  And every man of honor will concur.
  I see you almost hug a man to death,
  Exclaim for joy until you're out of breath,
  And supplement these loving demonstrations
  With endless offers, vows, and protestations;   20
  Then when I ask you "Who was that?" I find
  That you can barely bring his name to mind!
  Once the man's back is turned, you cease to love him,
  And speak with absolute indifference of him!
  By God, I say it's base and scandalous   25

* Translated by Richard Wilbur.

1424

To falsify the heart's affections thus;
    If I caught myself behaving in such a way,
    I'd hang myself for shame, without delay.
PHILINTE   It hardly seems a hanging matter to me;
    I hope that you will take it graciously   30
    If I extend myself a slight reprieve,
    And live a little longer, by your leave.
ALCESTE   How dare you joke about a crime so grave?
PHILINTE   What crime? How else are people to behave?
ALCESTE   I'd have them be sincere, and never part   35
    With any word that isn't from the heart.
PHILINTE   When someone greets us with a show of pleasure,
    It's but polite to give him equal measure,
    Return his love the best that we know how,
    And trade him offer for offer, vow for vow.   40
ALCESTE   No, no, this formula you'd have me follow,
    However fashionable, is false and hollow,
    And I despise the frenzied operations
    Of all these barterers of protestations,
    These lavishers of meaningless embraces,   45
    These utterers of obliging commonplaces,
    Who court and flatter everyone on earth
    And praise the fool no less than the man of worth.
    Should you rejoice that someone fondles you,
    Offers his love and service, swears to be true,   50
    And fills your ears with praises of your name,
    When to the first damned fop he'll say the same?
    No, no: no self-respecting heart would dream
    Of prizing so promiscuous an esteem;
    However high the praise, there's nothing worse   55
    Than sharing honors with the universe.
    Esteem is founded on comparison:
    To honor all men is to honor none.
    Since you embrace this indiscriminate vice,
    Your friendship comes at far too cheap a price;   60
    I spurn the easy tribute of a heart
    Which will not set the worthy man apart:
    I choose, Sir, to be chosen; and in fine,
    The friend of mankind is no friend of mine.
PHILINTE   But in polite society, custom decrees   65
    That we show certain outward courtesies. . . .
ALCESTE   Ah, no! we should condemn with all our force
    Such false and artificial intercourse.
    Let men behave like men; let them display
    Their inmost hearts in everything they say;   70
    Let the heart speak, and let our sentiments
    Not mask themselves in silly compliments.
PHILINTE   In certain cases it would be uncouth
    And most absurd to speak the naked truth;
    With all respect for your exalted notions,   75
    It's often best to veil one's true emotions.
    Wouldn't the social fabric come undone

If we were wholly frank with everyone?
Suppose you met with someone you couldn't bear;
Would you inform him of it then and there?   80

ALCESTE   Yes.

PHILINTE   Then you'd tell old Emilie it's pathetic
The way she daubs her features with cosmetic
And plays the gay coquette at sixty-four?

ALCESTE   I would.

PHILINTE   And you'd call Dorilas a bore,
And tell him every ear at court is lame   85
From hearing him brag about his noble name?

ALCESTE   Precisely.

PHILINTE   Ah, you're joking.

ALCESTE   *Au contraire:*[1]
In this regard there's none I'd choose to spare.
All are corrupt; there's nothing to be seen
In court or town but aggravates my spleen.   90
I fall into deep gloom and melancholy
When I survey the scene of human folly,
Finding on every hand base flattery,
Injustice, fraud, self-interest, treachery. . . .
Ah, it's too much; mankind has grown so base,   95
I mean to break with the whole human race.

PHILINTE   This philosophic rage is a bit extreme;
You've no idea how comical you seem;
Indeed, we're like those brothers in the play
Called *School for Husbands*, one of whom was prey . . .[2]   100

ALCESTE   Enough, now! None of your stupid similes.

PHILINTE   Then let's have no more tirades, if you please.
The world won't change, whatever you say or do;
And since plain speaking means so much to you,
I'll tell you plainly that by being frank   105
You've earned the reputation of a crank,
And that you're thought ridiculous when you rage
And rant against the manners of the age.

ALCESTE   So much the better; just what I wish to hear.
No news could be more grateful to my ear.   110
All men are so detestable in my eyes,
I should be sorry if they thought me wise.

PHILINTE   Your hatred's very sweeping, is it not?

ALCESTE   Quite right: I hate the whole degraded lot.

PHILINTE   Must all poor human creatures be embraced,   115
Without distinction, by your vast distaste?
Even in these bad times, there are surely a few . . .

ALCESTE   No, I include all men in one dim view:
Some men I hate for being rogues: the others
I hate because they treat the rogues like brothers,   120
And, lacking a virtuous scorn for what is vile,
Receive the villain with a complaisant smile.

---

1. To the contrary.
2. Molière's play *The School for Hus-* *bands* (*L'École des Maris*) had been writ-ten in 1661.

Notice how tolerant people choose to be
Toward that bold rascal who's at law with me.
His social polish can't conceal his nature;   125
One sees at once that he's a treacherous creature;
No one could possibly be taken in
By those soft speeches and that sugary grin.
The whole world knows the shady means by which
The low-brow's grown so powerful and rich,   130
And risen to a rank so bright and high
That virtue can but blush, and merit sigh.
Whenever his name comes up in conversation,
None will defend his wretched reputation;
Call him knave, liar, scoundrel, and all the rest,   135
Each head will nod, and no one will protest.
And yet his smirk is seen in every house,
He's greeted everywhere with smiles and bows,
And when there's any honor that can be got
By pulling strings, he'll get it, like as not.   140
My God! It chills my heart to see the ways
Men come to terms with evil nowadays;
Sometimes, I swear, I'm moved to flee and find
Some desert land unfouled by humankind.
PHILINTE   Come, let's forget the follies of the times   145
And pardon mankind for its petty crimes;
Let's have an end of rantings and of railings,
And show some leniency toward human failings.
This world requires a pliant rectitude;
Too stern a virtue makes one stiff and rude;   150
Good sense views all extremes with detestation,
And bids us to be noble in moderation.
The rigid virtues of the ancient days
Are not for us; they jar with all our ways
And ask of us too lofty a perfection.   155
Wise men accept their times without objection,
And there's no greater folly, if you ask me,
Than trying to reform society.
Like you, I see each day a hundred and one
Unhandsome deeds that might be better done,   160
But still, for all the faults that meet my view,
I'm never known to storm and rave like you.
I take men as they are, or let them be,
And teach my soul to bear their frailty;
And whether in court or town, whatever the scene,   165
My phlegm's as philosophic as your spleen.[3]
ALCESTE   This phlegm which you so eloquently commend,
Does nothing ever rile it up, my friend?
Suppose some man you trust should treacherously
Conspire to rob you of your property,   170
And do his best to wreck your reputation?

3. According to the psychology of "humors," character was determined by the relative
proportions of four body fluids. An oversupply of *phlegm* produced the stolid, unimagina-
tive character which we still call "phlegmatic."

Wouldn't you feel a certain indignation?
PHILINTE   Why, no. These faults of which you so complain
Are part of human nature, I maintain,
And it's no more a matter for disgust   175
That men are knavish, selfish and unjust,
Than that the vulture dines upon the dead,
And wolves are furious, and apes ill-bred.
ALCESTE   Shall I see myself betrayed, robbed, torn to bits,
And not . . . Oh, let's be still and rest our wits.   180
Enough of reasoning, now. I've had my fill.
PHILINTE   Indeed, you would do well, Sir, to be still.
Rage less at your opponent, and give some thought
To how you'll win this lawsuit that he's brought.
ALCESTE   I assure you I'll do nothing of the sort.   185
PHILINTE   Then who will plead your case before the court?
ALCESTE   Reason and right and justice will plead for me.
PHILINTE   Oh, Lord. What judges do you plan to see?
ALCESTE   Why, none. The justice of my cause is clear.
PHILINTE   Of course, man; but there's politics to fear. . . .   190
ALCESTE   No, I refuse to lift a hand. That's flat.
I'm either right, or wrong.
PHILINTE   Don't count on that.
ALCESTE   No, I'll do nothing.
PHILINTE   Your enemy's influence
Is great, you know . . .
ALCESTE   That makes no difference.
PHILINTE   It will; you'll see.
ALCESTE   Must honor bow to guile?   195
If so, I shall be proud to lose the trial.
PHILINTE   Oh, really . . .
ALCESTE   I'll discover by this case
Whether or not men are sufficiently base
And impudent and villainous and perverse
To do me wrong before the universe.   200
PHILINTE   What a man!
ALCESTE   Oh, I could wish, whatever the cost,
Just for the beauty of it, that my trial were lost.
PHILINTE   If people heard you talking so, Alceste,
They'd split their sides. Your name would be a jest.
ALCESTE   So much the worse for jesters.
PHILINTE   May I enquire   205
Whether this rectitude you so admire,
And these hard virtues you're enamored of
Are qualities of the lady whom you love?
It much surprises me that you, who seem
To view mankind with furious disesteem,   210
Have yet found something to enchant your eyes
Amidst a species which you so despise.
And what is more amazing, I'm afraid,
Is the most curious choice your heart has made.

The honest Éliante is fond of you,   215
Arsinoé, the prude, admires you too;
And yet your spirit's been perversely led
To choose the flighty Célimène instead,
Whose brittle malice and coquettish ways
So typify the manners of our days.   220
How is it that the traits you most abhor
Are bearable in this lady you adore?
Are you so blind with love that you can't find them?
Or do you contrive, in her case, not to mind them?
ALCESTE My love for that young widow's not the kind   225
    That can't perceive defects; no, I'm not blind.
    I see her faults, despite my ardent love,
    And all I see I fervently reprove.
    And yet I'm weak; for all her falsity,
    That woman knows the art of pleasing me,   230
    And though I never cease complaining of her,
    I swear I cannot manage not to love her.
    Her charm outweighs her faults; I can but aim
    To cleanse her spirit in my love's pure flame.
PHILINTE That's no small task; I wish you all success.   235
    You think then that she loves you?
ALCESTE   Heavens, yes!
    I wouldn't love her did she not love me.
PHILINTE Well, if her taste for you is plain to see,
    Why do these rivals cause you such despair?
ALCESTE True love, Sir, is possessive, and cannot bear   240
    To share with all the world. I'm here today
    To tell her she must send that mob away.
PHILINTE If I were you, and had your choice to make,
    Éliante, her cousin, would be the one I'd take;
    That honest heart, which cares for you alone,   245
    Would harmonize far better with your own.
ALCESTE True, true: each day my reason tells me so;
    But reason doesn't rule in love, you know.
PHILINTE I fear some bitter sorrow is in store;
    This love . . .

SCENE 2. [ORONTE, ALCESTE, PHILINTE]

ORONTE [*to* ALCESTE] The servants told me at the door   250
    That Éliante and Célimène were out,
    But when I heard, dear Sir, that you were about,
    I came to say, without exaggeration,
    That I hold you in the vastest admiration,
    And that it's always been my dearest desire   255
    To be the friend of one I so admire.
    I hope to see my love of merit requited,
    And you and I in friendship's bond united.

I'm sure you won't refuse—if I may be frank—
A friend of my devotedness—and rank.   260

> *During this speech of* ORONTE's, ALCESTE *is abstracted, and
> seems unaware that he is being spoken to. He only breaks off his
> reverie when* ORONTE *says:*

It was for you, if you please, that my words were intended.
ALCESTE   For me, Sir?
ORONTE   Yes, for you. You're not offended?
ALCESTE   By no means. But this much surprises me. . . .
The honor comes most unexpectedly. . . .
ORONTE   My high regard should not astonish you;   265
The whole world feels the same. It is your due.
ALCESTE   Sir . . .
ORONTE   Why, in all the State there isn't one
Can match your merits; they shine, Sir, like the sun.
ALCESTE   Sir . . .
ORONTE   You are higher in my estimation
Than all that's most illustrious in the nation.   270
ALCESTE   Sir . . .
ORONTE   If I lie, may heaven strike me dead!
To show you that I mean what I have said,
Permit me, Sir, to embrace you most sincerely,
And swear that I will prize our friendship dearly.
Give me your hand. And now, Sir, if you choose,   275
We'll make our vows.
ALCESTE   Sir . . .
ORONTE   What! You refuse?
ALCESTE   Sir, it's a very great honor you extend:
But friendship is a sacred thing, my friend;
It would be profanation to bestow
The name of friend on one you hardly know.   280
All parts are better played when well-rehearsed;
Let's put off friendship, and get acquainted first.
We may discover it would be unwise
To try to make our natures harmonize.
ORONTE   By heaven! You're sagacious to the core;   285
This speech has made me admire you even more.
Let time, then, bring us closer day by day;
Meanwhile, I shall be yours in every way.
If, for example, there should be anything
You wish at court, I'll mention it to the King.   290
I have his ear, of course; it's quite well known
That I am much in favor with the throne.
In short, I am your servant. And now, dear friend,
Since you have such fine judgment, I intend
To please you, if I can, with a small sonnet   295
I wrote not long ago. Please comment on it,
And tell me whether I ought to publish it.
ALCESTE   You must excuse me, Sir; I'm hardly fit
To judge such matters.

ORONTE   Why not?

ALCESTE   I am, I fear,
  Inclined to be unfashionably sincere.   300

ORONTE   Just what I ask; I'd take no satisfaction
  In anything but your sincere reaction.
  I beg you not to dream of being kind.

ALCESTE   Since you desire it, Sir, I'll speak my mind.

ORONTE   *Sonnet.* It's a sonnet. . . . *Hope* . . . The poem's addressed   305
  To a lady who wakened hopes within my breast.
  Hope . . . this is not the pompous sort of thing,
  Just modest little verses, with a tender ring.

ALCESTE   Well, we shall see.

ORONTE   *Hope* . . . I'm anxious to hear
  Whether the style seems properly smooth and clear,   310
  And whether the choice of words is good or bad.

ALCESTE   We'll see, we'll see.

ORONTE   Perhaps I ought to add
  That it took me only a quarter-hour to write it.

ALCESTE   The time's irrelevant, Sir: kindly recite it.

ORONTE [*reading*]   *Hope comforts us awhile, 'tis true,*   315
              Lulling our cares with careless laughter,
              And yet such joy is full of rue,
              My Phyllis, if nothing follows after.

PHILINTE   I'm charmed by this already; the style's delightful.

ALCESTE [*sotto voce, to* PHILINTE]   How can you say that? Why, the
  thing is frightful.   320

ORONTE   *Your fair face smiled on me awhile,*
              But was it kindness so to enchant me?
              'Twould have been fairer not to smile,
              If hope was all you meant to grant me.

PHILINTE   What a clever thought! How handsomely you phrase it!   325

ALCESTE [*sotto voce, to* PHILINTE]   You know the thing is trash. How
  dare you praise it?

ORONTE   *If it's to be my passion's fate*
              Thus everlastingly to wait,
              Then death will come to set me free:
              For death is fairer than the fair;   330
              Phyllis, to hope is to despair
              When one must hope eternally.

PHILINTE   The close is exquisite—full of feeling and grace.

ALCESTE [*sotto voce, aside*]   Oh, blast the close; you'd better close
    your face
  Before you send your lying soul to hell.   335

PHILINTE   I can't remember a poem I've liked so well.

ALCESTE [*sotto voce, aside*]   Good Lord!

ORONTE [*to* PHILINTE]   I fear you're flattering me a
  bit.

PHILINTE   Oh, no!

ALCESTE [*sotto voce, aside*]   What else d'you call it, you hypocrite?

ORONTE [*to* ALCESTE]   But you, Sir, keep your promise now: don't
  shrink

From telling me sincerely what you think.   340
ALCESTE   Sir, these are delicate matters; we all desire
To be told that we've the true poetic fire.
But once, to one whose name I shall not mention,
I said, regarding some verse of his invention,
That gentlemen should rigorously control   345
That itch to write which often afflicts the soul;
That one should curb the heady inclination
To publicize one's little avocation;
And that in showing off one's works of art
One often plays a very clownish part.   350
ORONTE   Are you suggesting in a devious way
That I ought not . . .
ALCESTE   Oh, that I do not say.
Further, I told him that no fault is worse
Than that of writing frigid, lifeless verse,
And that the merest whisper of such a shame   355
Suffices to destroy a man's good name.
ORONTE   D'you mean to say my sonnet's dull and trite?
ALCESTE   I don't say that. But I went on to cite
Numerous cases of once-respected men
Who came to grief by taking up the pen.   360
ORONTE   And am I like them? Do I write so poorly?
ALCESTE   I don't say that. But I told this person, "Surely
You're under no necessity to compose;
Why you should wish to publish, heaven knows.
There's no excuse for printing tedious rot   365
Unless one writes for bread, as you do not.
Resist temptation, then, I beg of you;
Conceal your pastimes from the public view;
And don't give up, on any provocation,
Your present high and courtly reputation,   370
To purchase at a greedy printer's shop
The name of silly author and scribbling fop."
These were the points I tried to make him see.
ORONTE   I sense that they are also aimed at me;
But now—about my sonnet—I'd like to be told . . .   375
ALCESTE   Frankly, that sonnet should be pigeonholed.
You've chosen the worst models to imitate.
The style's unnatural. Let me illustrate:
        For example, *Your fair face smiled on me awhile,*
        Followed by, *'Twould have been fairer not to smile!*   380
        Or this: *such joy is full of rue;*
        Or this: *For death is fairer than the fair;*
        Or, *Phyllis, to hope is to despair*
                When one must hope eternally!
This artificial style, that's all the fashion,   385
Has neither taste, nor honesty, nor passion;
It's nothing but a sort of wordy play,
And nature never spoke in such a way.

What, in this shallow age, is not debased?
Our fathers, though less refined, had better taste;   390
I'd barter all that men admire today
For one old love song I shall try to say:[4]

  If the King had given me for my own
  Paris, his citadel,
  And I for that must leave alone   395
  Her whom I love so well,
  I'd say then to the Crown,
  Take back your glittering town;
  My darling is more fair, I swear,
  My darling is more fair.   400

The rhyme's not rich, the style is rough and old,
But don't you see that it's the purest gold
Beside the tinsel nonsense now preferred,
And that there's passion in its every word?

  If the King had given me for my own   405
  Paris, his citadel,
  And I for that must leave alone
  Her whom I love so well,
  I'd say then to the Crown,
  Take back your glittering town;   410
  My darling is more fair, I swear,
  My darling is more fair.

There speaks a loving heart. [*To* PHILINTE.] You're laughing, eh?
Laugh on, my precious wit. Whatever you say,
I hold that song's worth all the bibelots   415
That people hail today with ah's and oh's.

ORONTE And I maintain my sonnet's very good.
ALCESTE It's not at all surprising that you should.
 You have your reasons; permit me to have mine
 For thinking that you cannot write a line.   420
ORONTE Others have praised my sonnet to the skies.
ALCESTE I lack their art of telling pleasant lies.
ORONTE You seem to think you've got no end of wit.
ALCESTE To praise your verse, I'd need still more of it.
ORONTE I'm not in need of your approval, Sir.   425
ALCESTE That's good; you couldn't have it if you were.
ORONTE Come now, I'll lend you the subject of my sonnet;
 I'd like to see you try to improve upon it.
ALCESTE I might, by chance, write something just as shoddy;
 But then I wouldn't show it to everybody.   430
ORONTE You're most opinionated and conceited.
ALCESTE Go find your flatterers, and be better treated.
ORONTE Look here, my little fellow, pray watch your tone.
ALCESTE My great big fellow, you'd better watch your own.
PHILINTE [*stepping between them*] Oh, please, please, gentlemen!
 This will never do.   435

4. No origin is known for Alceste's *chanson*.

ORONTE   The fault is mine, and I leave the field to you.
I am your servant, Sir, in every way.
ALCESTE   And I, Sir, am your most abject valet.

SCENE 3. [PHILINTE, ALCESTE]

PHILINTE   Well, as you see, sincerity in excess
Can get you into a very pretty mess;   440
Oronte was hungry for appreciation. . . .
ALCESTE   Don't speak to me.
PHILINTE   What?
ALCESTE   No more conversation.
PHILINTE   Really, now . . .
ALCESTE   Leave me alone.
PHILINTE   If I . . .
ALCESTE   Out of my sight!
PHILINTE   But what . . .
ALCESTE   I won't listen.
PHILINTE   But . . .
ALCESTE   Silence!
PHILINTE   Now, is it polite . . .
ALCESTE   By heaven, I've had enough. Don't follow me.   445
PHILINTE   Ah, you're just joking. I'll keep you company.

Act 2

SCENE 1. [ALCESTE, CÉLIMÈNE]

ALCESTE   Shall I speak plainly, Madam? I confess
Your conduct gives me infinite distress,
And my resentment's grown too hot to smother.
Soon, I foresee, we'll break with one another.
If I said otherwise, I should deceive you;   5
Sooner or later, I shall be forced to leave you,
And if I swore that we shall never part,
I should misread the omens of my heart.
CÉLIMÈNE.   You kindly saw me home, it would appear,
So as to pour invectives in my ear.   10
ALCESTE   I've no desire to quarrel. But I deplore
Your inability to shut the door
On all these suitors who beset you so.
There's what annoys me, if you care to know.
CÉLIMÈNE   Is it my fault that all these men pursue me?   15
Am I to blame if they're attracted to me?
And when they gently beg an audience,
Ought I to take a stick and drive them hence?
ALCESTE   Madam, there's no necessity for a stick;
A less responsive heart would do the trick.   20
Of your attractiveness I don't complain;
But those your charms attract, you then detain
By a most melting and receptive manner,

And so enlist their hearts beneath your banner.
It's the agreeable hopes which you excite   25
That keep these lovers round you day and night;
Were they less liberally smiled upon,
That sighing troop would very soon be gone.
But tell me, Madam, why it is that lately
This man Clitandre interests you so greatly?   30
Because of what high merits do you deem
Him worthy of the honor of your esteem?
Is it that your admiring glances linger
On the splendidly long nail of his little finger?
Or do you share the general deep respect   35
For the blond wig he chooses to affect?
Are you in love with his embroidered hose?
Do you adore his ribbons and his bows?
Or is it that this paragon bewitches
Your tasteful eye with his vast German breeches?   40
Perhaps his giggle, or his falsetto voice,
Makes him the latest gallant of your choice?

CÉLIMÈNE   You're much mistaken to resent him so.
Why I put up with him you surely know:
My lawsuit's very shortly to be tried,   45
And I must have his influence on my side.

ALCESTE   Then lose your lawsuit, Madam, or let it drop;
Don't torture me by humoring such a fop.

CÉLIMÈNE   You're jealous of the whole world, Sir.

ALCESTE   That's true,
Since the whole world is well-received by you.   50

CÉLIMÈNE   That my good nature is so unconfined
Should serve to pacify your jealous mind;
Were I to smile on one, and scorn the rest,
Then you might have some cause to be distressed.

ALCESTE   Well, if I musn't be jealous, tell me, then,   55
Just how I'm better treated than other men.

CÉLIMÈNE   You know you have my love. Will that not do?

ALCESTE   What proof have I that what you say is true?

CÉLIMÈNE   I would expect, Sir, that my having said it
Might give the statement a sufficient credit.   60

ALCESTE   But how can I be sure that you don't tell
The selfsame thing to other men as well?

CÉLIMÈNE   What a gallant speech! How flattering to me!
What a sweet creature you make me out to be!
Well then, to save you from the pangs of doubt,   65
All that I've said I hereby cancel out;
Now, none but yourself shall make a monkey of you:
Are you content?

ALCESTE   Why, why am I doomed to love you?
I swear that I shall bless the blissful hour
When this poor heart's no longer in your power!   70
I make no secret of it: I've done my best
To exorcise this passion from my breast;

But thus far all in vain; it will not go;
It's for my sins that I must love you so.
CÉLIMÈNE   Your love for me is matchless, Sir; that's clear.   75
ALCESTE   Indeed, in all the world it has no peer;
Words can't describe the nature of my passion,
And no man ever loved in such a fashion.
CÉLIMÈNE   Yes, it's a brand-new fashion, I agree:
You show your love by castigating me,   80
And all your speeches are enraged and rude.
I've never been so furiously wooed.
ALCESTE   Yet you could calm that fury, if you chose.
Come, shall we bring our quarrels to a close?
Let's speak with open hearts, then, and begin . . .   85

SCENE 2. [CÉLIMÈNE, ALCESTE, BASQUE]

CÉLIMÈNE   What is it?
BASQUE   Acaste is here.
CÉLIMÈNE   Well, send him in.

SCENE 3. [CÉLIMÈNE, ALCESTE]

ALCESTE   What! Shall we never be alone at all?
You're always ready to receive a call,
And you can't bear, for ten ticks of the clock,
Not to keep open house for all who knock.   90
CÉLIMÈNE   I couldn't refuse him: he'd be most put out.
ALCESTE   Surely that's not worth worrying about.
CÉLIMÈNE   Acaste would never forgive me if he guessed
That I consider him a dreadful pest.
ALCESTE   If he's a pest, why bother with him then?   95
CÉLIMÈNE   Heavens! One can't antagonize such men;
Why, they're the chartered gossips of the court,
And have a say in things of every sort.
One must receive them, and be full of charm;
They're no great help, but they can do you harm,   100
And though your influence be ever so great,
They're hardly the best people to alienate.
ALCESTE   I see, dear lady, that you could make a case
For putting up with the whole human race;
These friendships that you calculate so nicely . . .   105

SCENE 4. [ALCESTE, CÉLIMÈNE, BASQUE]

BASQUE   Madam, Clitandre is here as well.
ALCESTE   Precisely.
CÉLIMÈNE   Where are you going?
ALCESTE   Elsewhere.
CÉLIMÈNE   Stay.
ALCESTE   No, no.

CÉLIMÈNE   Stay, Sir.
ALCESTE   I can't.
CÉLIMÈNE   I wish it.
ALCESTE   No, I must go.
  I beg you, Madam, not to press the matter;
  You know I have no taste for idle chatter.   110
CÉLIMÈNE   Stay. I command you.
ALCESTE   No, I cannot stay.
CÉLIMÈNE   Very well; you have my leave to go away.

   SCENE 5. [ÉLIANTE, PHILINTE, ACASTE, CLITANDRE,
           ALCESTE, CÉLIMÈNE, BASQUE]

   ÉLIANTE [*to* CÉLIMÈNE]   The Marquesses have kindly come to call.
     Were they announced?
   CÉLIMÈNE   Yes. Basque, bring chairs for all.

        BASQUE *provides the chairs, and exits.*

        [*To* ALCESTE.] You haven't gone?

ALCESTE   No; and I shan't depart   115
  Till you decide who's foremost in your heart.
CÉLIMÈNE   Oh, hush.
ALCESTE   It's time to choose; take them, or me.
CÉLIMÈNE   You're mad.
ALCESTE   I'm not, as you shall shortly see.
CÉLIMÈNE   Oh?
ALCESTE   You'll decide.
CÉLIMÈNE   You're joking now, dear friend.
ALCESTE   No, no; you'll choose; my patience is at an end.   120
CLITANDRE   Madam, I come from court, where poor Cléonte
  Behaved like a perfect fool, as is his wont.
  Has he no friend to counsel him, I wonder,
  And teach him less unerringly to blunder?
CÉLIMÈNE   It's true, the man's a most accomplished dunce;   125
  His gauche behavior charms the eye at once;
  And every time one sees him, on my word,
  His manner's grown a trifle more absurd.
ACASTE   Speaking of dunces, I've just now conversed
  With old Damon, who's one of the very worst;   130
  I stood a lifetime in the broiling sun
  Before his dreary monologue was done.
CÉLIMÈNE   Oh, he's a wondrous talker, and has the power
  To tell you nothing hour after hour:
  If, by mistake, he ever came to the point,   135
  The shock would put his jawbone out of joint.
ÉLIANTE [*to* PHILINTE]   The conversation takes its usual turn,
  And all our dear friends' ears will shortly burn.
CLITANDRE   Timante's a character, Madam.
CÉLIMÈNE   Isn't he, though?

A man of mystery from top to toe,   140
Who moves about in a romantic mist
On secret missions which do not exist.
His talk is full of eyebrows and grimaces;
How tired one gets of his momentous faces;
He's always whispering something confidential   145
Which turns out to be quite inconsequential;
Nothing's too slight for him to mystify;
He even whispers when he says "good-by."

ACASTE   Tell us about Géralde.

CÉLIMÈNE   That tiresome ass.
He mixes only with the titled class,   150
And fawns on dukes and princes, and is bored
With anyone who's not at least a lord.
The man's obsessed with rank, and his discourses
Are all of hounds and carriages and horses;
He uses Christian names with all the great,   155
And the word Milord, with him, is out of date.

CLITANDRE   He's very taken with Bélise, I hear.

CÉLIMÈNE   She is the dreariest company, poor dear.
Whenever she comes to call, I grope about
To find some topic which will draw her out,   160
But, owing to her dry and faint replies,
The conversation wilts, and droops, and dies.
In vain one hopes to animate her face
By mentioning the ultimate commonplace;
But sun or shower, even hail or frost   165
Are matters she can instantly exhaust.
Meanwhile her visit, painful though it is,
Drags on and on through mute eternities,
And though you ask the time, and yawn, and yawn,
She sits there like a stone and won't be gone.   170

ACASTE   Now for Adraste.

CÉLIMÈNE   Oh, that conceited elf
Has a gigantic passion for himself;
He rails against the court, and cannot bear it
That none will recognize his hidden merit;
All honors given to others give offense   175
To his imaginary excellence.

CLITANDRE   What about young Cléon? His house, they say,
Is full of the best society, night and day.

CÉLIMÈNE   His cook has made him popular, not he:
It's Cléon's table that people come to see.   180

ÉLIANTE   He gives a splendid dinner, you must admit.

CÉLIMÈNE   But must he serve himself along with it?
For my taste, he's a most insipid dish
Whose presence sours the wine and spoils the fish.

PHILINTE   Damis, his uncle, is admired no end.   185
What's your opinion, Madam?

CÉLIMÈNE   Why, he's my friend.

PHILINTE   He seems a decent fellow, and rather clever.

CÉLIMÈNE   He works too hard at cleverness, however.
I hate to see him sweat and struggle so
To fill his conversation with *bons mots*.[5]   190
Since he's decided to become a wit
His taste's so pure that nothing pleases it;
He scolds at all the latest books and plays,
Thinking that wit must never stoop to praise,
That finding fault's a sign of intellect,   195
That all appreciation is abject,
And that by damning everything in sight
One shows oneself in a distinguished light.
He's scornful even of our conversations:
Their trivial nature sorely tries his patience;   200
He folds his arms, and stands above the battle,
And listens sadly to our childish prattle.
ACASTE   Wonderful, Madam! You've hit him off precisely.
CLITANDRE   No one can sketch a character so nicely.
ALCESTE   How bravely, Sirs, you cut and thrust at all   205
These absent fools, till one by one they fall:
But let one come in sight, and you'll at once
Embrace the man you lately called a dunce,
Telling him in a tone sincere and fervent
How proud you are to be his humble servant.   210
CLITANDRE   Why pick on us? *Madame's* been speaking, Sir.
And you should quarrel, if you must, with her.
ALCESTE   No, no, by God, the fault is yours, because
You lead her on with laughter and applause,
And make her think that she's the more delightful   215
The more her talk is scandalous and spiteful.
Oh, she would stoop to malice far, far less
If no such claque approved her cleverness.
It's flatterers like you whose foolish praise
Nourishes all the vices of these days.   220
PHILINTE   But why protest when someone ridicules
Those you'd condemn, yourself, as knaves or fools?
CÉLIMÈNE   Why, Sir? Because he loves to make a fuss.
You don't expect him to agree with us,
When there's an opportunity to express   225
His heaven-sent spirit of contrariness?
What other people think, he can't abide;
Whatever they say, he's on the other side;
He lives in deadly terror of agreeing;
'Twould make him seem an ordinary being.   230
Indeed, he's so in love with contradiction,
He'll turn against his most profound conviction
And with a furious eloquence deplore it,
If only someone else is speaking for it.
ALCESTE   Go on, dear lady, mock me as you please;   235
You have your audience in ecstasies.

---

5. Witticisms, literally "good words" or "good sayings."

PHILINTE   But what she says is true: you have a way
     Of bridling at whatever people say;
     Whether they praise or blame, your angry spirit
     Is equally unsatisfied to hear it.   240
ALCESTE   Men, Sir, are always wrong, and that's the reason
     That righteous anger's never out of season;
     All that I hear in all their conversation
     Is flattering praise or reckless condemnation.
CÉLIMÈNE   But . . .
ALCESTE   No, no, Madam, I am forced to state   245
     That you have pleasures which I deprecate,
     And that these others, here, are much to blame
     For nourishing the faults which are your shame.
CLITANDRE   I shan't defend myself, Sir; but I vow
     I'd thought this lady faultless until now.   250
ACASTE   I see her charms and graces, which are many;
     But as for faults, I've never noticed any.
ALCESTE   I see them, Sir; and rather than ignore them,
     I strenuously criticize her for them.
     The more one loves, the more one should object   255
     To every blemish, every least defect.
     Were I this lady, I would soon get rid
     Of lovers who approved of all I did,
     And by their slack indulgence and applause
     Endorsed my follies and excused my flaws.   260
CÉLIMÈNE   If all hearts beat according to your measure,
     The dawn of love would be the end of pleasure;
     And love would find its perfect consummation
     In ecstasies of rage and reprobation.
ÉLIANTE   Love, as a rule, affects men otherwise,   265
     And lovers rarely love to criticize.
     They see their lady as a charming blur,
     And find all things commendable in her.
     If she has any blemish, fault, or shame,
     They will redeem it by a pleasing name.   270
     The pale-faced lady's lily-white, perforce;
     The swarthy one's a sweet brunette, of course;
     The spindly lady has a slender grace;
     The fat one has a most majestic pace;
     The plain one, with her dress in disarray,   275
     They classify as *beauté négligée*;[6]
     The hulking one's a goddess in their eyes,
     The dwarf, a concentrate of Paradise;
     The haughty lady has a noble mind;
     The mean one's witty, and the dull one's kind;   280
     The chatterbox has liveliness and verve,
     The mute one has a virtuous reserve.
     So lovers manage, in their passion's cause,
     To love their ladies even for their flaws.

6. Careless beauty or the beauty of the untended.

ALCESTE   But I still say . . .   285
CÉLIMÈNE   I think it would be nice
   To stroll around the gallery once or twice.
   What! You're not going, Sirs?
CLITANDRE *and* ACASTE   No, Madam, no.
ALCESTE   You seem to be in terror lest they go.
   Do what you will, Sirs; leave, or linger on,
   But I shan't go till after you are gone.   290
ACASTE   I'm free to to linger, unless I should perceive
   Madame is tired, and wishes me to leave.
CLITANDRE   And as for me, I needn't go today
   Until the hour of the King's *coucher*.[7]
CÉLIMÈNE [*to* ALCESTE]   You're joking, surely?
ALCESTE   Not in the least; we'll see   295
   Whether you'd rather part with them, or me.

SCENE 6.   [ALCESTE, CÉLIMÈNE, ÉLIANTE, ACASTE,
          PHILINTE, CLITANDRE, BASQUE]

BASQUE [*to* ALCESTE]   Sir, there's a fellow here who bids me state
   That he must see you, and that it can't wait.
ALCESTE   Tell him that I have no such pressing affairs.
BASQUE   It's a long tailcoat that this fellow wears,   300
   With gold all over.
CÉLIMÈNE [*to* ALCESTE]   You'd best go down and see.
   Or—have him enter.

SCENE 7.   [ALCESTE, CÉLIMÈNE, ÉLIANTE, ACASTE,
          PHILINTE, CLITANDRE, GUARD]

ALCESTE [*confronting the* GUARD]   Well, what do you want with me?
   Come in, Sir.
GUARD   I've a word, Sir, for your ear.
ALCESTE   Speak it aloud, Sir; I shall strive to hear.
GUARD   The Marshals have instructed me to say   305
   You must report to them without delay.[8]
ALCESTE   Who? Me, Sir?
GUARD   Yes, Sir; you.
ALCESTE   But what do they want?
PHILINTE [*to* ALCESTE]   To scotch your silly quarrel with Oronte.
CÉLIMÈNE [*to* PHILINTE]   What quarrel?
PHILINTE   Oronte and he have fallen out
   Over some verse he spoke his mind about;   310
   The Marshals wish to arbitrate the matter.
ALCESTE   Never shall I equivocate or flatter!

---

7. At the French court during the period
of the play there were formal ceremonies
connected with both the king's going to bed,
coucher, and his rising from bed, *lever*.
   8. The "Marshals" were high court officers of the period who formed a court to
arbitrate arguments of honor among the
nobility. By this time they no longer had
any military function. The number of marshals varied, reaching a high of twenty
around 1700.

PHILINTE   You'd best obey their summons; come, let's go.
ALCESTE   How can they mend our quarrel, I'd like to know?
    Am I to make a cowardly retraction,   315
    And praise those jingles to his satisfaction?
    I'll not recant; I've judged that sonnet rightly.
    It's bad.
PHILINTE   But you might say so more politely. . . .
ALCESTE   I'll not back down; his verses make me sick.
PHILINTE   If only you could be more politic!   320
    But come, let's go.
ALCESTE   I'll go, but I won't unsay
    A single word.
PHILINTE   Well, let's be on our way.
ALCESTE   Till I am ordered by my lord the King
    To praise that poem, I shall say the thing
    Is scandalous, by God, and that the poet   325
    Ought to be hanged for having the nerve to show it.

        To CLITANDRE *and* ACASTE, *who are laughing.*

    By heaven, Sirs, I really didn't know
    That I was being humorous.
CÉLIMÈNE   Go, Sir, go;
    Settle your business.
ALCESTE   I shall, and when I'm through,
    I shall return to settle things with you.   330

                        Act 3

        SCENE 1. [CLITANDRE, ACASTE]

CLITANDRE   Dear Marquess, how contented you appear;
    All things delight you, nothing mars your cheer.
    Can you, in perfect honesty, declare
    That you've a right to be so debonair?
ACASTE   By Jove, when I survey myself, I find   5
    No cause whatever for distress of mind.
    I'm young and rich; I can in modesty
    Lay claim to an exalted pedigree;
    And owing to my name and my condition
    I shall not want for honors and position.   10
    Then as to courage, that most precious trait,
    I seem to have it, as was proved of late
    Upon the field of honor, where my bearing,
    They say, was very cool and rather daring.
    I've wit, of course; and taste in such perfection   15
    That I can judge without the least reflection,
    And at the theater, which is my delight,
    Can make or break a play on opening night,
    And lead the crowd in hisses or bravos,
    And generally be known as one who knows.   20

I'm clever, handsome, gracefully polite;
My waist is small, my teeth are strong and white;
As for my dress, the world's astonished eyes
Assure me that I bear away the prize.
I find myself in favor everywhere,   25
Honored by men, and worshiped by the fair;
And since these things are so, it seems to me
I'm justified in my complacency.
CLITANDRE   Well, if so many ladies hold you dear,
Why do you press a hopeless courtship here?   30
ACASTE   Hopeless, you say? I'm not the sort of fool
That likes his ladies difficult and cool.
Men who are awkward, shy, and peasantish
May pine for heartless beauties, if they wish,
Grovel before them, bear their cruelties,   35
Woo them with tears and sighs and bended knees,
And hope by dogged faithfulness to gain
What their poor merits never could obtain.
For men like me, however, it makes no sense
To love on trust, and foot the whole expense.   40
Whatever any lady's merits be,
I think, thank God, that I'm as choice as she;
That if my heart is kind enough to burn
For her, she owes me something in return;
And that in any proper love affair   45
The partners must invest an equal share.
CLITANDRE   You think, then, that our hostess favors you?
ACASTE   I've reason to believe that that is true.
CLITANDRE   How did you come to such a mad conclusion?
You're blind, dear fellow. This is sheer delusion.   50
ACASTE   All right, then: I'm deluded and I'm blind.
CLITANDRE   Whatever put the notion in your mind?
ACASTE   Delusion.
CLITANDRE   What persuades you that you're right?
ACASTE   I'm blind.
CLITANDRE   But have you any proofs to cite?
ACASTE   I tell you I'm deluded.
CLITANDRE   Have you, then,   55
Received some secret pledge from Célimène?
ACASTE   Oh, no: she scorns me.
CLITANDRE   Tell me the truth, I beg.
ACASTE   She just can't bear me.
CLITANDRE   Ah, don't pull my leg.
Tell me what hope she's given you, I pray.
ACASTE   I'm hopeless, and it's you who win the day.   60
She hates me thoroughly, and I'm so vexed
I mean to hang myself on Tuesday next.
CLITANDRE   Dear Marquess, let us have an armistice
And make a treaty. What do you say to this?
If ever one of us can plainly prove   65
That Célimène encourages his love,

The other must abandon hope, and yield,
And leave him in possession of the field.
ACASTE   Now, there's a bargain that appeals to me;
With all my heart, dear Marquess, I agree.   70
But hush.

SCENE 2. [CÉLIMÈNE, ACASTE, CLITANDRE]

CÉLIMÈNE   Still here?
CLITANDRE   'Twas love that stayed our feet.
CÉLIMÈNE   I think I heard a carriage in the street.
Whose is it? D'you know?

SCENE 3. [CÉLIMÈNE, ACASTE, CLITANDRE, BASQUE]

BASQUE   Arsinoé is here,
   Madame.
CÉLIMÈNE   Arsinoé, you say? Oh, dear.
BASQUE   Éliante is entertaining her below.   75
CÉLIMÈNE   What brings the creature here, I'd like to know?
ACASTE   They say she's dreadfully prudish, but in fact
I think her piety . . .
CÉLIMÈNE   It's all an act.
At heart she's worldly, and her poor success
In snaring men explains her prudishness.   80
It breaks her heart to see the beaux and gallants
Engrossed by other women's charms and talents,
And so she's always in a jealous rage
Against the faulty standards of the age.
She lets the world believe that she's a prude   85
To justify her loveless solitude,
And strives to put a brand of moral shame
On all the graces that she cannot claim.
But still she'd love a lover; and Alceste
Appears to be the one she'd love the best.   90
His visits here are poison to her pride;
She seems to think I've lured him from her side;
And everywhere, at court or in the town,
The spiteful, envious woman runs me down.
In short, she's just as stupid as can be,   95
Vicious and arrogant in the last degree,
And . . .

SCENE 4. [ARSINOÉ, CÉLIMÈNE, CLITANDRE, ACASTE]

CÉLIMÈNE   Ah! What happy chance has brought you here?
I've thought about you ever so much, my dear.
ARSINOÉ   I've come to tell you something you should know.
CÉLIMÈNE   How good of you to think of doing so!   100

   CLITANDRE *and* ACASTE *go out, laughing.*

SCENE 5. [ARSINOÉ, CÉLIMÈNE]

ARSINOÉ   It's just as well those gentlemen didn't tarry.
CÉLIMÈNE   Shall we sit down?
ARSINOÉ   That won't be necessary.
  Madam, the flame of friendship ought to burn
  Brightest in matters of the most concern,
  And as there's nothing which concerns us more   105
  Than honor, I have hastened to your door
  To bring you, as your friend, some information
  About the status of your reputation.
  I visited last night, some virtuous folk,
  And, quite by chance, it was of you they spoke;   110
  There was, I fear, no tendency to praise
  Your light behavior and your dashing ways.
  The quantity of gentlemen you see
  And your by now notorious coquetry
  Were both so vehemently criticized   115
  By everyone, that I was much surprised.
  Of course, I needn't tell you where I stood;
  I came to your defense as best I could,
  Assured them you were harmless, and declared
  Your soul was absolutely unimpaired.   120
  But there are some things, you must realize,
  One can't excuse, however hard one tries,
  And I was forced at last into conceding
  That your behavior, Madam, is misleading,
  That makes a bad impression, giving rise   125
  To ugly gossip and obscene surmise,
  And that if you were more *overtly* good,
  You wouldn't be so much misunderstood.
  Not that I think you've been unchaste—no! no!
  The saints preserve me from a thought so low!   130
  But mere good conscience never did suffice:
  One must avoid the outward show of vice.
  Madam, you're too intelligent, I'm sure,
  To think my motives anything but pure
  In offering you this counsel—which I do   135
  Out of a zealous interest in you.
CÉLIMÈNE   Madam, I haven't taken you amiss;
  I'm very much obliged to you for this;
  And I'll at once discharge the obligation
  By telling you about *your* reputation.   140
  You've been so friendly as to let me know
  What certain people say of me, and so
  I mean to follow your benign example
  By offering you a somewhat similar sample.
  The other day, I went to an affair   145
  And found some most distinguished people there
  Discussing piety, both false and true.
  The conversation soon came round to you.

Alas! Your prudery and bustling zeal
Appeared to have a very slight appeal.   150
Your affectation of a grave demeanor,
Your endless talk of virtue and of honor,
The aptitude of your suspicious mind
For finding sin where there is none to find,
Your towering self-esteem, that pitying face   155
With which you contemplate the human race,
Your sermonizings and your sharp aspersions
On people's pure and innocent diversions—
All these were mentioned, Madam, and, in fact,
Were roundly and concertedly attacked.   160
"What good," they said, "a e all these outward shows,
When everything belies her pious pose?
She prays incessantly; but then, they say,
She beats her maids and cheats them of their pay;
She shows her zeal in every holy place,   165
But still she's vain enough to paint her face;
She holds that naked statues are immoral,
But with a naked *man* she'd have no quarrel."
Of course, I said to everybody there
That they were being viciously unfair;   170
But still they were disposed to criticize you,
And all agreed that someone should advise you
To leave the morals of the world alone,
And worry rather more about your own.
They felt that one's self-knowledge should be great   175
Before one thinks of setting others straight;
That one should learn the art of living well
Before one threatens other men with hell,
And that the Church is best equipped, no doubt,
To guide our souls and root our vices out.   180
Madam, you're too intelligent, I'm sure,
To think my motives anything but pure
In offering you this counsel—which I do
Out of a zealous interest in you.
ARSINOÉ   I dared not hope for gratitude, but I   185
Did not expect so acid a reply;
I judge, since you've been so extremely tart,
That my good counsel pierced you to the heart.
CÉLIMÈNE   Far from it, Madam. Indeed, it seems to me
We ought to trade advice more frequently.   190
One's vision of oneself is so defective
That it would be an excellent corrective.
If you are willing, Madam, let's arrange
Shortly to have another frank exchange
In which we'll tell each other, *entre nous*,[9]   195
What you've heard tell of me, and I of you.

9. Between ourselves, or between the two of us.

ARSINOÉ   Oh, people never censure you, my dear;
   It's me they criticize. Or so I hear.
CÉLIMÈNE   Madam, I think we either blame or praise
   According to our taste and length of days.   200
   There is a time of life for coquetry,
   And there's a season, too, for prudery.
   When all one's charms are gone, it is, I'm sure,
   Good strategy to be devout and pure:
   It makes one seem a little less forsaken.   205
   Some day, perhaps, I'll take the road you've taken:
   Time brings all things. But I have time aplenty,
   And see no cause to be a prude at twenty.
ARSINOÉ   You give your age in such a gloating tone
   That one would think I was an ancient crone;   210
   We're not so far apart, in sober truth,
   That you can mock me with a boast of youth!
   Madam, you baffle me. I wish I knew
   What moves you to provoke me as you do.
CÉLIMÈNE   For my part, Madam, I should like to know   215
   Why you abuse me everywhere you go.
   Is it my fault, dear lady, that your hand
   Is not, alas, in very great demand?
   If men admire me, if they pay me court
   And daily make me offers of the sort   220
   You'd dearly love to have them make to you,
   How can I help it? What would you have me do?
   If what you want is lovers, please feel free
   To take as many as you can from me.
ARSINOÉ   Oh, come. D'you think the world is losing sleep   225
   Over that flock of lovers which you keep,
   Or that we find it difficult to guess
   What price you pay for their devotedness?
   Surely you don't expect us to suppose
   Mere merit could attract so many beaux?   230
   It's not your virtue that they're dazzled by;
   Nor is it virtuous love for which they sigh.
   You're fooling no one, Madam; the world's not blind;
   There's many a lady heaven has designed
   To call men's noblest, tenderest feelings out,   235
   Who has no lovers dogging her about;
   From which it's plain that lovers nowadays
   Must be acquired in bold and shameless ways,
   And only pay one court for such reward
   As modesty and virtue can't afford.   240
   Then don't be quite so puffed up, if you please,
   About your tawdry little victories;
   Try, if you can, to be a shade less vain,
   And treat the world with somewhat less disdain.
   If one were envious of your amours,   245
   One soon could have a following like yours;
   Lovers are no great trouble to collect

If one prefers them to one's self-respect.
CÉLIMÈNE   Collect them then, my dear; I'd love to see
    You demonstrate that charming theory;   250
    Who knows, you might . . .
ARSINOÉ   Now, Madam, that will do;
    It's time to end this trying interview.
    My coach is late in coming to your door,
    Or I'd have taken leave of you before.
CÉLIMÈNE   Oh, please don't feel that you must rush away;   255
    I'd be delighted, Madam, if you'd stay.
    However, lest my conversation bore you,
    Let me provide some better company for you;
    This gentleman, who comes most apropos,
    Will please you more than I could do, I know.   260

SCENE 6. [ALCESTE, CÉLIMÈNE, ARSINOÉ]

CÉLIMÈNE   Alceste, I have a little note to write
    Which simply must go out before tonight;
    Please entertain *Madame;* I'm sure that she
    Will overlook my incivility.

SCENE 7. [ALCESTE, ARSINOÉ]

ARSINOÉ   Well, Sir, our hostess graciously contrives   265
    For us to chat until my coach arrives;
    And I shall be forever in her debt
    For granting me this little *tête-à-tête.*[1]
    We women very rightly give our hearts
    To men of noble character and parts,   270
    And your especial merits, dear Alceste,
    Have roused the deepest sympathy in my breast.
    Oh, how I wish they had sufficient sense
    At court, to recognize your excellence!
    They wrong you greatly, Sir. How it must hurt you   275
    Never to be rewarded for your virtue!
ALCESTE   Why, Madam, what cause have I to feel aggrieved?
    What great and brilliant thing have I achieved?
    What service have I rendered to the King
    That I should look to him for anything?   280
ARSINOÉ   Not everyone who's honored by the State
    Has done great services. A man must wait
    Till time and fortune offer him the chance.
    Your merit, Sir, is obvious at a glance,
    And . . .
ALCESTE   Ah, forget my merit; I'm not neglected.   285
    The court, I think, can hardly be expected
    To mine men's souls for merit, and unearth
    Our hidden virtues and our secret worth.

---

1. A "face-to-face" meeting or conversation; literally "head-to-head."

ARSINOÉ   *Some* virtues, though, are far too bright to hide;
      Yours are acknowledged, Sir, on every side.   290
      Indeed, I've heard you warmly praised of late
      By persons of considerable weight.
ALCESTE   This fawning age has praise for everyone,
      And all distinctions, Madam, are undone.
      All things have equal honor nowadays,   295
      And no one should be gratified by praise.
      To be admired, one only need exist,
      And every lackey's on the honors list.
ARSINOÉ   I only wish, Sir, that you had your eye
      On some position at court, however high;   300
      You'd only have to hint at such a notion
      For me to set the proper wheels in motion;
      I've certain friendships I'd be glad to use
      To get you any office you might choose.
ALCESTE   Madam, I fear that any such ambition   305
      Is wholly foreign to my disposition.
      The soul God gave me isn't of the sort
      That prospers in the weather of a court.
      It's all too obvious that I don't possess
      The virtues necessary for success.   310
      My one great talent is for speaking plain;
      I've never learned to flatter or to feign;
      And anyone so stupidly sincere
      Had best not seek a courtier's career.
      Outside the court, I know, one must dispense   315
      With honors, privilege, and influence;
      But still one gains the right, foregoing these,
      Not to be tortured by the wish to please.
      One needn't live in dread of snubs and slights,
      Nor praise the verse that every idiot writes,   320
      Nor humor silly Marquesses, nor bestow
      Politic sighs on Madam So-and-So.
ARSINOÉ   Forget the court, then; let the matter rest.
      But I've another cause to be distressed
      About your present situation, Sir.   325
      It's to your love affair that I refer.
      She whom you love, and who pretends to love you,
      Is, I regret to say, unworthy of you.
ALCESTE   Why, Madam? Can you seriously intend
      To make so grave a charge against your friend?   330
ARSINOÉ   Alas, I must. I've stood aside too long
      And let that lady do you grievous wrong;
      But now my debt to conscience shall be paid:
      I tell you that your love has been betrayed.
ALCESTE   I thank you, Madam; you're extremely kind.   335
      Such words are soothing to a lover's mind.
ARSINOÉ   Yes, though she *is* my friend, I say again
      You're very much too good for Célimène.
      She's wantonly misled you from the start.

ALCESTE   You may be right; who knows another's heart?   340
    But ask yourself if it's the part of charity
    To shake my soul with doubts of her sincerity.
ARSINOÉ   Well, if you'd rather be a dupe than doubt her,
    That's your affair. I'll say no more about her.
ALCESTE   Madam, you know that doubt and vague suspicion   345
    Are painful to a man in my position;
    It's most unkind to worry me this way
    Unless you've some real proof of what you say.
ARSINOÉ   Sir, say no more: all doubts shall be removed,
    And all that I've been saying shall be proved.   350
    You've only to escort me home, and there
    We'll look into the heart of this affair.
    I've ocular evidence which will persuade you
    Beyond a doubt, that Célimène's betrayed you.
    Then, if you're saddened by that revelation,   355
    Perhaps I can provide some consolation.

Act 4

SCENE 1. [ÉLIANTE, PHILINTE]

PHILINTE   Madam, he acted like a stubborn child;
    I thought they never would be reconciled;
    In vain we reasoned, threatened, and appealed;
    He stood his ground and simply would not yield.
    The Marshals, I feel sure, have never heard   5
    An argument so splendidly absurd.
    "No, gentlemen," said he, "I'll not retract.
    His verse is bad: extremely bad, in fact.
    Surely it does the man no harm to know it.
    Does it disgrace him, not to be a poet?   10
    A gentleman may be respected still,
    Whether he writes a sonnet well or ill.
    That I dislike his verse should not offend him;
    In all that touches honor, I commend him;
    He's noble, brave, and virtuous—but I fear   15
    He can't in truth be called a sonneteer.
    I'll gladly praise his wardrobe; I'll endorse
    His dancing, or the way he sits a horse;
    But, gentlemen, I cannot praise his rhyme.
    In fact, it ought to be a capital crime   20
    For anyone so sadly unendowed
    To write a sonnet, and read the thing aloud."
    At length he fell into a gentler mood
    And, striking a concessive attitude,
    He paid Oronte the following courtesies: 25
    "Sir, I regret that I'm so hard to please,
    And I'm profoundly sorry that your lyric
    Failed to provoke me to a panegyric."

After these curious words, the two embraced,
And then the hearing was adjourned—in haste.   30
ÉLIANTE   His conduct has been very singular lately;
Still, I confess that I respect him greatly.
The honesty in which he takes such pride
Has—to my mind—its noble, heroic side.
In this false age, such candor seems outrageous;   35
But I could wish that it were more contagious.
PHILINTE   What most intrigues me in our friend Alceste
Is the grand passion that rages in his breast.
The sullen humors he's compounded of
Should not, I think, dispose his heart to love;   40
But since they do, it puzzles me still more
That he should choose your cousin to adore.
ÉLIANTE   It does, indeed, belie the theory
That love is born of gentle sympathy,
And that the tender passion must be based   45
On sweet accords of temper and of taste.
PHILINTE   Does she return his love, do you suppose?
ÉLIANTE   Ah, that's a difficult question, Sir. Who knows?
How can we judge the truth of her devotion?
Her heart's a stranger to its own emotion.   50
Sometimes it thinks it loves, when no love's there;
At other times it loves quite unaware.
PHILINTE   I rather think Alceste is in for more
Distress and sorrow than he's bargained for;
Were he of my mind, Madam, his affection   55
Would turn in quite a different direction,
And we would see him more responsive to
The kind regard which he receives from you.
ÉLIANTE   Sir, I believe in frankness, and I'm inclined,
In matters of the heart, to speak my mind.   60
I don't oppose his love for her; indeed,
I hope with all my heart that he'll succeed,
And were it in my power, I'd rejoice
In giving him the lady of his choice.
But if, as happens frequently enough   65
In love affairs, he meets with a rebuff—
If Célimène should grant some rival's suit—
I'd gladly play the role of substitute;
Nor would his tender speeches please me less
Because they'd once been made without success.   70
PHILINTE   Well, Madam, as for me, I don't oppose
Your hopes in this affair; and heaven knows
That in my conversations with the man
I plead your cause as often as I can.
But if those two should marry, and so remove   75
All chance that he will offer you his love,
Then I'll declare my own, and hope to see
Your gracious favor pass from him to me.
In short, should you be cheated of Alceste,

I'd be most happy to be second best.   80
ÉLIANTE   Philinte, you're teasing.
PHILINTE   Ah, Madam, never fear;
No words of mine were ever so sincere,
And I shall live in fretful expectation
Till I can make a fuller declaration.

SCENE 2. [ALCESTE, ÉLIANTE, PHILINTE]

ALCESTE   Avenge me, Madam! I must have satisfaction.   85
Or this great wrong will drive me to distraction!
ÉLIANTE   Why, what's the matter? What's upset you so?
ALCESTE   Madam, I've had a mortal, mortal blow.
If Chaos repossessed the universe,
I swear I'd not be shaken any worse.   90
I'm ruined. . . . I can say no more. . . . My soul . . .
ÉLIANTE   Do try, Sir, to regain your self-control.
ALCESTE   Just heaven! Why were so much beauty and grace
Bestowed on one so vicious and so base?
ÉLIANTE   Once more, Sir, tell us. . . .
ALCESTE   My world has gone to wrack;   95
I'm—I'm betrayed; she's stabbed me in the back:
Yes, Célimène (who would have thought it of her?)
Is false to me, and has another lover.
ÉLIANTE   Are you quite certain? Can you prove these things?
PHILINTE   Lovers are prey to wild imaginings   100
And jealous fancies. No doubt there's some mistake. . . .
ALCESTE   Mind your own business, Sir, for heaven's sake.
                To ÉLIANTE.

Madam, I have the proof that you demand
Here in my pocket, penned by her own hand.
Yes, all the shameful evidence one could want   105
Lies in this letter written to Oronte—
Oronte! whom I felt sure she couldn't love,
And hardly bothered to be jealous of.
PHILINTE   Still, in a letter, appearances may deceive;
This may not be so bad as you believe.   110
ALCESTE   Once more I beg you, Sir, to let me be;
Tend to your own affairs; leave mine to me.
ÉLIANTE   Compose yourself; this anguish that you feel . . .
ALCESTE   Is something, Madam, you alone can heal.
My outraged heart, beside itself with grief,   115
Appeals to you for comfort and relief.
Avenge me on your cousin, whose unjust
And faithless nature has deceived my trust;
Avenge a crime your pure soul must detest.
ÉLIANTE   But how, Sir?
ALCESTE   Madam, this heart within my breast   120
Is yours; pray take it; redeem my heart from her,
And so avenge me on my torturer.

Let her be punished by the fond emotion,
The ardent love, the bottomless devotion,
The faithful worship which this heart of mine   125
Will offer up to yours as to a shrine.
ÉLIANTE   You have my sympathy, Sir, in all you suffer;
Nor do I scorn the noble heart you offer;
But I suspect you'll soon be mollified,
And this desire for vengeance will subside.   130
When some belovèd hand has done us wrong
We thirst for retribution—but not for long;
However dark the deed that she's committed,
A lovely culprit's very soon acquitted.
Nothing's so stormy as an injured lover,   135
And yet no storm so quickly passes over.
ALCESTE   No, Madam, no—this is no lovers' spat;
I'll not forgive her; it's gone too far for that;
My mind's made up; I'll kill myself before
I waste my hopes upon her any more.   140
Ah, here she is. My wrath intensifies.
I shall confront her with her tricks and lies,
And crush her utterly, and bring you then
A heart no longer slave to Célimène.

SCENE 3. [CÉLIMÈNE, ALCESTE]

ALCESTE [*aside*]   Sweet heaven, help me to control my passion.   145
CÉLIMÈNE [*aside*]   Oh, Lord.
　　　　　To ALCESTE.
　　　　　　　　　　　　Why stand there staring in that fashion?
And what d'you mean by those dramatic sighs,
And that malignant glitter in your eyes?
ALCESTE   I mean that sins which cause the blood to freeze
Look innocent beside your treacheries;   150
That nothing Hell's or Heaven's wrath could do
Ever produced so bad a thing as you.
CÉLIMÈNE   Your compliments were always sweet and pretty.
ALCESTE   Madam, it's not the moment to be witty.
No, blush and hang your head; you've ample reason,   155
Since I've the fullest evidence of your treason.
Ah, this is what my sad heart prophesied;
Now all my anxious fears are verified;
My dark suspicion and my gloomy doubt
Divined the truth, and now the truth is out.   160
For all your trickery, I was not deceived;
It was my bitter stars that I believed.
But don't imagine that you'll go scot-free;
You shan't misuse me with impunity.
I know that love's irrational and blind;   165
I know the heart's not subject to the mind,
And can't be reasoned into beating faster;

I know each soul is free to choose its master;
Therefore had you but spoken from the heart,
Rejecting my attentions from the start,   170
I'd have no grievance, or at any rate
I could complain of nothing but my fate.
Ah, but so falsely to encourage me—
That was a treason and a treachery
For which you cannot suffer too severely,   175
And you shall pay for that behavior dearly.
Yes, now I have no pity, not a shred;
My temper's out of hand; I've lost my head;
Shocked by the knowledge of your double-dealings,
My reason can't restrain my savage feelings;   180
A righteous wrath deprives me of my senses,
And I won't answer for the consequences.

CÉLIMÈNE   What does this outburst mean? Will you please explain?
Have you, by any chance, gone quite insane?

ALCESTE   Yes, yes, I went insane the day I fell   185
A victim to your black and fatal spell,
Thinking to meet with some sincerity
Among the treacherous charms that beckoned me.

CÉLIMÈNE   Pooh. Of what treachery can you complain?

ALCESTE   How sly you are, how cleverly you feign!   190
But you'll not victimize me any more.
Look: here's a document you've seen before.
This evidence, which I acquired today,
Leaves you, I think, without a thing to say.

CÉLIMÈNE   Is this what sent you into such a fit?   195

ALCESTE   You should be blushing at the sight of it.

CÉLIMÈNE   Ought I to blush? I truly don't see why.

ALCESTE   Ah, now you're being bold as well as sly;
Since there's no signature, perhaps you'll claim . . .

CÉLIMÈNE   I wrote it, whether or not it bears my name.   200

ALCESTE   And you can view with equanimity
This proof of your disloyalty to me!

CÉLIMÈNE   Oh, don't be so outrageous and extreme.

ALCESTE   You take this matter lightly, it would seem.
Was it no wrong to me, no shame to you,   205
That you should send Oronte this billet-doux?

CÉLIMÈNE   Oronte! Who said it was for him?

ALCESTE   Why, those
Who brought me this example of your prose.
But what's the difference? If you wrote the letter
To someone else, it pleases me no better.   210
My grievance and your guilt remain the same.

CÉLIMÈNE   But need you rage, and need I blush for shame;
If this was written to a *woman* friend?

ALCESTE   Ah! Most ingenious. I'm impressed no end;
And after that incredible evasion   215
Your guilt is clear. I need no more persuasion.
How dare you try so clumsy a deception?

D'you think I'm wholly wanting in perception?
Come, come, let's see how brazenly you'll try
To bolster up so palpable a lie: 220
Kindly construe this ardent closing section
As nothing more than sisterly affection!
Here, let me read it. Tell me, if you dare to,
That this is for a woman . . .

CÉLIMÈNE   I don't care to.
  What right have you to badger and berate me,   225
And so highhandedly interrogate me?

ALCESTE   Now, don't be angry; all I ask of you
Is that you justify a phrase or two . . .

CÉLIMÈNE   No, I shall not. I utterly refuse,
  And you may take those phrases as you choose.   230

ALCESTE   Just show me how this letter could be meant
For a woman's eyes, and I shall be content.

CÉLIMÈNE   No, no, it's for Oronte; you're perfectly right.
  I welcome his attentions with delight,
  I prize his character and his intellect,   235
  And everything is just as you suspect.
  Come, do your worst now; give your rage free rein;
  But kindly cease to bicker and complain.

ALCESTE [*aside*]   Good God! Could anything be more inhuman?
  Was ever a heart so mangled by a woman?   240
  When I complain of how she has betrayed me,
  She bridles, and commences to upbraid me!
  She tries my tortured patience to the limit;
  She won't deny her guilt; she glories in it!
  And yet my heart's too faint and cowardly   245
  To break these chains of passion, and be free,
  To scorn her as it should, and rise above
  This unrewarded, mad, and bitter love.

      To CÉLIMÈNE.

Ah, traitress, in how confident a fashion
You take advantage of my helpless passion,   250
And use my weakness for your faithless charms
To make me once again throw down my arms!
But do at least deny this black transgression;
Take back that mocking and perverse confession;
Defend this letter and your innocence,   255
  And I, poor fool, will aid in your defense.
Pretend, pretend, that you are just and true,
  And I shall make myself believe in you.

CÉLIMÈNE   Oh, stop it. Don't be such a jealous dunce,
  Or I shall leave off loving you at once.   260
  Just why should I *pretend*? What could impel me
To stoop so low as that? And kindly tell me
Why, if I loved another, I shouldn't merely
Inform you of it, simply and sincerely!
I've told you where you stand, and that admission   265

Should altogether clear me of suspicion;
After so generous a guarantee,
What right have you to harbor doubts of me?
Since women are (from natural reticence)
Reluctant to declare their sentiments,   270
And since the honor of our sex requires
That we conceal our amorous desires,
Ought any man for whom such laws are broken
To question what the oracle has spoken?
Should he not rather feel an obligation   275
To trust that most obliging declaration?
Enough, now. Your suspicions quite disgust me;
Why should I love a man who doesn't trust me?
I cannot understand why I continue,
Fool that I am, to take an interest in you.   280
I ought to choose a man less prone to doubt,
And give you something to be vexed about.
ALCESTE   Ah, what a poor enchanted fool I am;
These gentle words, no doubt, were all a sham,
But destiny requires me to entrust   285
My happiness to you, and so I must.
I'll love you to the bitter end, and see
How false and treacherous you dare to be.
CÉLIMÈNE   No, you don't really love me as you ought.
ALCESTE   I love you more than can be said or thought;   290
Indeed, I wish you were in such distress
That I might show my deep devotedness.
Yes, I could wish that you were wretchedly poor,
Unloved, uncherished, utterly obscure;
That fate had set you down upon the earth   295
Without possessions, rank, or gentle birth;
Then, by the offer of my heart, I might
Repair the great injustice of your plight;
I'd raise you from the dust, and proudly prove
The purity and vastness of my love.   300
CÉLIMÈNE   This is a strange benevolence indeed!
God grant that I may never be in need. . . .
Ah, here's Monsieur Dubois, in quaint disguise.

SCENE 4. [CÉLIMÈNE, ALCESTE, DUBOIS]

ALCESTE   Well, why this costume? Why those frightened eyes?
What ails you?
DUBOIS   Well, Sir, things are most mysterious.   305
ALCESTE   What do you mean?
DUBOIS   I fear they're very serious.
ALCESTE   What?
DUBOIS   Shall I speak more loudly?
ALCESTE   Yes; speak out.
DUBOIS   Isn't there someone here, Sir?
ALCESTE   Speak, you lout!
Stop wasting time.

DUBOIS	Sir, we must slip away.	
ALCESTE	How's that?	
DUBOIS	We must decamp without delay.	310
ALCESTE	Explain yourself.	
DUBOIS	I tell you we must fly.	
ALCESTE	What for?	
DUBOIS	We mustn't pause to say good-by.	
ALCESTE	Now what d'you mean by all of this, you clown?	
DUBOIS	I mean, Sir, that we've got to leave this town.	
ALCESTE	I'll tear you limb from limb and joint from joint	315

ALCESTE   I'll tear you limb from limb and joint from joint
  If you don't come more quickly to the point.
DUBOIS   Well, Sir, today a man in a black suit,
  Who wore a black and ugly scowl to boot,
  Left us a document scrawled in such a hand
  As even Satan couldn't understand.   320
  It bears upon your lawsuit, I don't doubt;
  But all hell's devils couldn't make it out.
ALCESTE   Well, well, go on. What then? I fail to see
  How this event obliges us to flee.
DUBOIS   Well, Sir, an hour later, hardly more,   325
  A gentleman who's often called before
  Came looking for you in an anxious way.
  Not finding you, he asked me to convey
  (Knowing I could be trusted with the same)
  The following message.... Now, what *was* his name?   330
ALCESTE   Forget his name, you idiot. What did he say?
DUBOIS   Well, it was one of your friends, Sir, anyway.
  He warned you to begone, and he suggested
  That if you stay, you may well be arrested.
ALCESTE   What? Nothing more specific? Think, man, think!   335
DUBOIS   No, Sir. He had me bring him pen and ink,
  And dashed you off a letter which, I'm sure,
  Will render things distinctly less obscure.
ALCESTE   Well—let me have it!
CÉLIMÈNE   What *is* this all about?
ALCESTE   God knows; but I have hopes of finding out.   340
  How long am I to wait, you blitherer?
DUBOIS [*after a protracted search for the letter*]   I must have left it on
  your table, Sir.
ALCESTE   I ought to ...
CÉLIMÈNE   No, no, keep your self-control;
  Go find out what's behind his rigmarole.
ALCESTE   It seems to me that fate, no matter what I do,   345
  Has sworn that I may not converse with you;
  But, Madam, pray permit your faithful lover
  To try once more before the day is over.

Act 5

SCENE 1. [ALCESTE, PHILINTE]

ALCESTE   No, it's too much. My mind's made up, I tell you.

PHILINTE   Why should this blow, however hard, compel you . . .
ALCESTE   No, no, don't waste your breath in argument;

Nothing you say will alter my intent;
This age is vile, and I've made up my mind   5
To have no further commerce with mankind.
Did not truth, honor, decency, and the laws
Oppose my enemy and approve my cause?
My claims were justified in all men's sight;
I put my trust in equity and right;   10
Yet, to my horror and the world's disgrace,
Justice is mocked, and I have lost my case!
A scoundrel whose dishonesty is notorious
Emerges from another lie victorious!
Honor and right condone his brazen fraud,   15
While rectitude and decency applaud!
Before his smirking face, the truth stands charmed,
And virtue conquered, and the law disarmed!
His crime is sanctioned by a court decree!
And not content with what he's done to me,   20
The dog now seeks to ruin me by stating
That I composed a book now circulating,
A book so wholly criminal and vicious
That even to speak its title is seditious!
Meanwhile Oronte, my rival, lends his credit   25
To the same libelous tale, and helps to spread it!
Oronte! a man of honor and of rank,
With whom I've been entirely fair and frank,
Who sought me out and forced me, willy-nilly,
To judge some verse I found extremely silly;   30
And who, because I properly refused
To flatter him, or see the truth abused,
Abets my enemy in a rotten slander!
There's the reward of honesty and candor!
The man will hate me to the end of time   35
For failing to commend his wretched rhyme!
And not this man alone, but all humanity
Do what they do from interest and vanity;
They prate of honor, truth, and righteousness,
But lie, betray, and swindle nonetheless.   40
Come then: man's villainy is too much to bear;
Let's leave this jungle and this jackal's lair.
Yes! treacherous and savage race of men,
You shall not look upon my face again.

PHILINTE   Oh, don't rush into exile prematurely;   45
Things aren't as dreadful as you make them, surely.
It's rather obvious, since you're still at large,
That people don't believe your enemy's charge.
Indeed, his tale's so patently untrue
That it may do more harm to him than you.   50

ALCESTE   Nothing could do that scoundrel any harm:
His frank corruption is his greatest charm,

And, far from hurting him, a further shame
Would only serve to magnify his name.

PHILINTE   In any case, his bald prevarication   55
Has done no injury to your reputation,
And you may feel secure in that regard.
As for your lawsuit, it should not be hard
To have the case reopened, and contest
This judgment . . .

ALCESTE   No, no, let the verdict rest.   60
Whatever cruel penalty it may bring,
I wouldn't have it changed for anything.
It shows the times' injustice with such clarity
That I shall pass it down to our posterity
As a great proof and signal demonstration   65
Of the black wickedness of this generation.
It may cost twenty thousand francs; but I
Shall pay their twenty thousand, and gain thereby
The right to storm and rage at human evil,
And send the race of mankind to the devil.[2]   70

PHILINTE   Listen to me . . .

ALCESTE   Why? What can you possibly say?
Don't argue, Sir; your labor's thrown away.
Do you propose to offer lame excuses
For men's behavior and the times' abuses?

PHILINTE   No, all you say I'll readily concede: 75
This is a low, conniving age indeed;
Nothing but trickery prospers nowadays,
And people ought to mend their shabby ways.
Yes, man's a beastly creature; but must we then
Abandon the society of men?   80
Here in the world, each human frailty
Provides occasion for philosophy,
And that is virtue's noblest exercise;
If honesty shone forth from all men's eyes,
If every heart were frank and kind and just,   85
What could our virtues do but gather dust
(Since their employment is to help us bear
The villainies of men without despair)?
A heart well-armed with virtue can endure. . . .
I'm all for those who frankly speak their mind.

ORONTE   Madam, you'll search in vain for a defender.

ALCESTE   You're beaten, Madam, and may as well surrender.

ORONTE   Speak, speak, you must; and end this awful strain.   185

ALCESTE   Or don't, and your position will be plain.

ORONTE   A single word will close this painful scene.

ALCESTE   But if you're silent, I'll know what you mean.

---

2. Since the loss of twenty thousand francs does not apparently threaten Alceste with financial ruin, we may assume that he is rich. Mm. Édouard Lop and André Sauvage, in their edition of the play (*Les Classiques du Peuple*, Paris, Éditions Sociales, 1963) say that in the seventeenth century such a sum would have purchased a small farm near Paris or provided a sufficient dowry for a young woman of the bourgeois to make a marriage which would move her up the social ladder, In Molière's *The Would-Be Gentleman*, the rich and extravagant M. Jourdain, in preparation for the dinner to impress Dorimene, lends Dorante eighteen thousand francs in addition to purchasing a diamond and many other extravagances of his own.

If your heart shares the sweet desires of mine,
Show me as much by some convincing sign;
And here's the sign I urgently suggest:
That you no longer tolerate Alceste,
But sacrifice him to my love, and sever   115
All your relations with the man forever.

CÉLIMÈNE   Why do you suddenly dislike him so?
You praised him to the skies not long ago.

ORONTE   Madam, that's not the point. I'm here to find
Which way your tender feelings are inclined.   120
Choose, if you please, between Alceste and me,
And I shall stay or go accordingly.

ALCESTE [*emerging from the corner*]   Yes, Madam, choose; this gentle-
   man's demand
Is wholly just, and I support his stand.
I too am true and ardent; I too am here   125
To ask you that you make your feelings clear.
No more delays, now; no equivocation;
The time has come to make your declaration.

ORONTE   Sir, I've no wish in any way to be
An obstacle to your felicity.   130

ALCESTE   Sir, I've no wish to share her heart with you;
That may sound jealous, but at least it's true.

ORONTE   If, weighing us, she leans in your direction . . .

ALCESTE   If she regards you with the least affection . . .

ORONTE   I swear I'll yield her to you there and then.   135

ALCESTE   Sir, you're a matchless reasoner, to be sure;   90
Your words are fine and full of cogency;
But don't waste time and eloquence on me.
My reason bids me go, for my own good.
My tongue won't lie and flatter as it should;
God knows what frankness it might next commit,   95
And what I'd suffer on account of it.
Pray let me wait for Célimène's return
In peace and quiet. I shall shortly learn,
By her response to what I have in view,
Whether her love for me is feigned or true.   100

PHILINTE   Till then, let's visit Éliante upstairs.

ALCESTE   No, I am too weighed down with somber cares.
Go to her, do; and leave me with my gloom
Here in the darkened corner of this room.

ALCESTE   I swear I'll never see her face again.

ORONTE   Now, Madam, tell us what we've come to hear.

ALCESTE   Madam, speak openly and have no fear.

ORONTE   Just say which one is to remain your lover.

ALCESTE   Just name one name, and it will all be over.   140

ORONTE   What! Is it possible that you're undecided?

ALCESTE   What! Can your feelings possibly be divided?

CÉLIMÈNE   Enough: this inquisition's gone too far:
How utterly unreasonable you are!
Not that I couldn't make the choice with ease;   145
My heart has no conflicting sympathies;

I know full well which one of you I favor,
And you'd not see me hesitate or waver.
But how can you expect me to reveal
So cruelly and bluntly what I feel?   150
I think it altogther too unpleasant
To choose between two men when both are present;
One's heart has means more subtle and more kind
Of letting its affections be divined,
Nor need one be uncharitably plain   155
To let a lover know he loves in vain.

ORONTE   No, no, speak plainly; I for one can stand it.
I beg you to be frank.

ALCESTE   And I demand it.
The simple truth is what I wish to know,
And there's no need for softening the blow.   160
You've made an art of pleasing everyone,
But now your days of coquetry are done:
You have no choice now, Madam, but to choose,
For I'll know what to think if you refuse;
I'll take your silence for a clear admission   165
That I'm entitled to my worst suspicion.

ORONTE   I thank you for this ultimatum, Sir,
And I may say I heartily concur.

CÉLIMÈNE   Really, this foolishness is very wearing:
Must you be so unjust and overbearing?   170
Haven't I told you why I must demur?
Ah, here's Éliante; I'll put the case to her.

SCENE 3. [ÉLIANTE, PHILINTE, CÉLIMÈNE, ORONTE, ALCESTE]

CÉLIMÈNE   Cousin, I'm being persecuted here
By these two persons, who, it would appear,
Will not be satisfied till I confess   175
Which one I love the more, and which the less,
And tell the latter to his face that he
Is henceforth banished from my company.
Tell me, has ever such a thing been done?

ÉLIANTE   You'd best not turn to me; I'm not the one   180
To back you in a matter of this kind:
To keep my counsel, after what I've heard.
I'm shocked and staggered by your want of morals.
It's not my way to mix in others' quarrels;
But really, when this fine and noble spirit,   270
This man of honor and surpassing merit,
Laid down the offering of his heart before you,
How *could* you . . .

ALCESTE   Madam, permit me, I implore you,
To represent myself in this debate.
Don't bother, please, to be my advocate.   275
My heart, in any case, could not afford
To give your services their due reward;
And if I chose, for consolation's sake,

SCENE 4. [ARSINOÉ, CÉLIMÈNE, ÉLIANTE, ALCESTE,
    PHILINTE, ACASTE, CLITANDRE, ORONTE]

ACASTE [*to* CÉLIMÈNE]   Madam, with all due deference, we two
    Have come back to pick a little bone with you.   190
CLITANDRE [*to* ORONTE *and* ALCESTE]   I'm glad you're present, Sirs,
    as you'll soon learn,
    Our business here is also your concern.
ARSINOÉ [*to* CÉLIMÈNE]   Madam, I visit you so soon again
    Only because of these two gentlemen,
    Who came to me indignant and aggrieved   195
    About a crime too base to be believed.
    Knowing your virtue, having such confidence in it,
    I couldn't think you guilty for a minute,
    In spite of all their telling evidence;
    And, rising above our little difference,   200
    I've hastened here in friendship's name to see
    You clear yourself of this great calumny.
ACASTE   Yes, Madam, let us see with what composure
    You'll manage to respond to this disclosure.
    You lately sent Clitandre this tender note.   205
CLITANDRE   And this one, for Acaste, you also wrote.
ACASTE [*to* ORONTE *and* ALCESTE]   You'll recognize this writing, Sirs, I
    think;
    The lady is so free with pen and ink
    That you must know it all too well, I fear.
    But listen: this is something you should hear.   210
    "How absurd you are to condemn my lightheartedness in society,
    and to accuse me of being happiest in the company of others.
    Nothing could be more unjust; and if you do not come to me in-
    stantly and beg pardon for saying such a thing, I shall never forgive
    you as long as I live. Our big bumbling friend the Viscount . . ."   215
    What a shame that he's not here.
    "Our big bumbling friend the Viscount, whose name stands first
    in your complaint, is hardly a man to my taste; and ever since the
    day I watched him spend three-quarters of an hour spitting into a
    well, so as to make circles in the water, I have been unable to think   220
    highly of him. As for the little Marquess . . ."
    In all modesty, gentlemen, that is I.
    "As for the little Marquess, who sat squeezing my hand for such
    a long while yesterday, I find him in all respects the most trifling
    creature alive; and the only things of value about him are his cape   225
    and his sword. As for the man with the green ribbons . . ."
    [*To* ALCESTE.]   It's your turn now, Sir.
    "As for the man with the green ribbons, he amuses me now and
    then with his bluntness and his bearish ill-humor; but there are
    many times indeed when I think him the greatest bore in the world.   230
    And as for the sonneteer . . ."
    [*To* ORONTE.]   Here's your helping.
    "And as for the sonneteer, who has taken it into his head to be
    witty, and insists on being an author in the teeth of opinion, I

simply cannot be bothered to listen to him, and his prose wearies ²³⁵
me quite as much as his poetry. Be assured that I am not always so
well entertained as you suppose; that I long for your company, more
than I dare to say, at all these entertainments to which people drag
me; and that the presence of those one loves is the true and perfect
seasoning to all one's pleasures."   ²⁴⁰

CLITANDRE   And now for me.

"Clitandre, whom you mention, and who so pesters me with his
saccharine speeches, is the last man on earth for whom I could feel
any affection. He is quite mad to suppose that I love him, and so are
you, to doubt that you are loved. Do come to your senses; exchange ²⁴⁵
your suppositions for his; and visit me as often as possible, to help
me bear the annoyance of his unwelcome attentions."
It's a sweet character that these letters show,
And what to call it, Madam, you well know.
Enough. We're off to make the world acquainted   ²⁵⁰
With this sublime self-portrait that you've painted.

ACASTE   Madam, I'll make you no farewell oration;
No, you're not worthy of my indignation.
Far choicer hearts than yours, as you'll discover,
Would like this little Marquess for a lover.   ²⁵⁵

SCENE 5. [CÉLIMÈNE, ÉLIANTE, ARSINOÉ, ALCESTE,
      ORONTE, PHILINTE]

ORONTE   So! After all those loving letters you wrote,
You turn on me like this, and cut my throat!
And your dissembling, faithless heart, I find,
Has pledged itself by turns to all mankind!
How blind I've been! But now I clearly see;   ²⁶⁰
I thank you, Madam, for enlightening me.
My heart is mine once more, and I'm content;
The loss of it shall be your punishment.

      To ALCESTE.

Sir, she is yours; I'll seek no more to stand
Between your wishes and this lady's hand.   ²⁶⁵

SCENE 6. [CÉLIMÈNE, ÉLIANTE, ARSINOÉ, ALCESTE,
      PHILINTE]

ARSINOÉ [*to* CÉLIMÈNE] Madam, I'm forced to speak. I'm far too
      stirred
PHILINTE   Why, that's no sort of company, my friend;   ¹⁰⁵
I'll see if Éliante will not descend.

SCENE 2. [CÉLIMÈNE, ORONTE, ALCESTE]

ORONTE   Yes, Madam, if you wish me to remain
Your true and ardent lover, you must deign
To give me some more positive assurance.
All this suspense is quite beyond endurance.   ¹¹⁰

Some other lady, 'twould not be you I'd take.

ARSINOÉ   What makes you think you could, Sir? And how dare you   280
Imply that I've been trying to ensnare you?
If you can for a moment entertain
Such flattering fancies, you're extremely vain.
I'm not so interested as you suppose
In Célimène's discarded gigolos.   285
Get rid of that absurd illusion, do.
Women like me are not for such as you.
Stay with this creature, to whom you're so attached;
I've never seen two people better matched.

SCENE 7. [CÉLIMÈNE, ÉLIANTE, ALCESTE, PHILINTE]

ALCESTE [*to* CÉLIMÈNE]   Well, I've been still throughout this exposé,   290
Till everyone but me has said his say.
Come, have I shown sufficient self-restraint?
And may I now . . .
CÉLIMÈNE   Yes, make your just complaint.
Reproach me freely, call me what you will;
You've every right to say I've used you ill.   295
I've wronged you, I confess it; and in my shame
I'll make no effort to escape the blame.
The anger of those others I could despise;
My guilt toward you I sadly recognize.
Your wrath is wholly justified, I fear;   300
I know how culpable I must appear,
I know all things bespeak my treachery,
And that, in short, you've grounds for hating me.
Do so; I give you leave.
ALCESTE   Ah, traitress—how,
How should I cease to love you, even now?   305
Though mind and will were passionately bent
On hating you, my heart would not consent.

        To ÉLIANTE *and* PHILINTE.

Be witness to my madness, both of you;
See what infatuation drives one to;
But wait; my folly's only just begun,   310
And I shall prove to you before I'm done
How strange the human heart is, and how far
From rational we sorry creatures are.

        To CÉLIMÈNE.

Woman, I'm willing to forget your shame,
And clothe your treacheries in a sweeter name;   315
I'll call them youthful errors, instead of crimes,
And lay the blame on these corrupting times.
My one condition is that you agree
To share my chosen fate, and fly with me
To that wild, trackless, solitary place   320
In which I shall forget the human race.

Only by such a course can you atone
For those atrocious letters; by that alone
Can you remove my present horror of you,
And make it possible for me to love you.   325
CÉLIMÈNE   What! I renounce the world at my young age,
And die of boredom in some hermitage?
ALCESTE   Ah, if you really loved me as you ought,
You wouldn't give the world a moment's thought;
Must you have me, and all the world beside?   330
CÉLIMÈNE   Alas, at twenty one is terrified
Of solitude. I fear I lack the force
And depth of soul to take so stern a course.
But if my hand in marriage will content you,
Why, there's a plan which I might well consent to,   335
And . . .
ALCESTE   No, I detest you now. I could excuse
Everything else, but since you thus refuse
To love me wholly, as a wife should do,
And see the world in me, as I in you,
Go! I reject your hand, and disenthrall   340
My heart from your enchantments, once for all.

SCENE 8. [ÉLIANTE, ALCESTE, PHILINTE]

ALCESTE [*to* ÉLIANTE]   Madam, your virtuous beauty has no peer;
Of all this world you only are sincere;
I've long esteemed you highly, as you know;
Permit me ever to esteem you so,   345
And if I do not now request your hand,
Forgive me, Madam, and try to understand.
I feel unworthy of it; I sense that fate
Does not intend me for the married state,
That I should do you wrong by offering you   350
My shattered heart's unhappy residue,
And that in short . . .
ÉLIANTE   Your argument's well taken:
Nor need you fear that I shall feel forsaken.
Were I to offer him this hand of mine,
Your friend Philinte, I think, would not decline.   355
PHILINTE   Ah, Madam, that's my heart's most cherished goal,
For which I'd gladly give my life and soul.
ALCESTE [*to* ÉLIANTE *and* PHILINTE]   May you be true to all you now
     profess,
And so deserve unending happiness.
Meanwhile, betrayed and wronged in everything,   360
I'll flee this bitter world where vice is king,
And seek some spot unpeopled and apart
Where I'll be free to have an honest heart.
PHILINTE   Come, Madam, let's do everything we can
To change the mind of this unhappy man.   365

MARSHA NORMAN

Third and Oak: The Laundromat[1]

CHARACTERS

ALBERTA—a woman who values her education, who cares what she looks like, even at three o'clock in the morning. Alberta listens quietly, and is quite opinionated, but generally expresses her opinions so as to protect the feelings of the other person. She is in her mid to late forties and has spent her life as a teacher. Alberta believes that there is a right way to do things, and that is how she does them. Alberta is a careful woman, verging on being picky, but she is harder on herself than on others in this regard.

DEEDEE—a nineteen year old, chatty and constantly in motion. She eats too much sugar and watches too much TV. She once had a job in an all-night grocery, but she was fired for talking too much. She is attractive, but no matter how long she spends getting dressed, she always looks thrown together.

SHOOTER—a handsome black disc jockey, whose late night radio show has been first in the local ratings for years. He is as smooth as they come.

SET: The play takes place in a standard, dreary laundromat. There are tile floors, washers, dryers, coin-op vending machines for soaps, soft drinks and candy bars. There is a bulletin board on which various notices are posted. There is a table for folding clothes as well as a low table and ugly chair littered with magazines. There is a coffee can ash tray on the table. A clock on the wall reads 3:00 o'clock and should continue to run during the show. One side of The Laundromat will be used as a window looking out into the street.

> As the lights come up, the song "Stand By Your Man" is playing on the radio. The door to the Attendant's room is slightly ajar.

SHOOTER'S VOICE [*over the final chords of the song*] And that's all for tonight, night owls. This is your A-Number-One Night Owl saying it's 3 o'clock, all right, and time to rock your daddy to dreams of delight. And Mama, I'm comin' home. And the rest of you night owls gonna have to make it through the rest of this night by yourself, or with the help of your friends, if you know what I mean. And you know what I mean.

> The radio station goes dead, music replaced by an irritating static.

ALBERTA *opens the door tentatively, looks around and walks in. She has dressed carefully and her laundry basket exhibits the same care. She checks the top of a washer for dust or water before putting down her purse and basket. She walks back to the open Attendant door and is startled briefly when she looks in.*

---

1. As originally performed, *The Laundromat* is the first act of *Third and Oak. The Laundromat* is published separately by Dramatists Play Service, and does not include the Shooter character. This version is the original first act, which includes the Shooter character. [Author's note.]

ALBERTA Hello! [*steps back, seeing that he is asleep*] Sleep? Is that how you do your job? Sleep?

> *She leans in and turns off the radio. We hear the click and the static stops. She walks back toward the basket talking to herself.*

ALBERTA Now just be quiet, Alberta. I mean, you don't want him out here talking to you, do you? [*turning back quickly*] Maybe you should take his cigar out of his . . . [*changing her mind*] It wasn't burning, was it. It's not your cigar, is it? Mind your own business. Do your wash. [*procrastinating*] No, first. . . .

> ALBERTA *takes an index card out of her purse, on which is printed a message. She tacks it up on the bulletin board. We must see that it is very important to her.*
>
> ALBERTA *opens a washer lid and runs her fingers around the soap tray. She takes out the lint and deposits it in one of the coffee cans. As she does this, she accidentally knocks over her purse.*

ALBERTA [*trying to calm down*] It's all right. Everything is all right.

> *She bends down and begins to put the things back in her purse. She cannot see as* DEEDEE *backs in the door of The Laundromat.* DEEDEE *is a wreck. She carries her clothes tied up in a man's shirt. She trips over a wastebasket on the floor and falls on her laundry as it spills out of the shirt.*

DEEDEE Well, poo-rats!

ALBERTA [*stands up, startled, then walks over to* DEEDEE] Are you all right?

DEEDEE [*grudgingly*] Cute, huh?

ALBERTA [*moves the wastebasket out of the way*] Probably a wet spot on the floor. [*goes back to her laundry*]

DEEDEE I already picked these clothes off the floor once tonight. [*no response from* ALBERTA] We been in our apartment two years and Joe still ain't found the closets. He thinks hangers are for when you lock your keys in your car. [*still no response*] I mean, he's got this coat made outta sheep's fur or something and my Mom came over one day and asked where did we git that fuzzy little rug. [*no response from* ALBERTA] He works at the Ford plant. [*getting up and gathering her clothes*] I asked him why they call it that. I said, "How often do you have to water a Ford plant?" [DEEDEE *is very nervous*] It was just a little joke, but he didn't think it was very funny.

ALBERTA They probably do have a sprinkler system.

DEEDEE Huh?

ALBERTA Nothing.

DEEDEE [*doesn't understand, but keeps talking*] Shoulda saved my breath and just tripped over the coffee table. He'd a' laughed at that. [*no response from* ALBERTA] Well, I guess it's just you and me.

ALBERTA Yes.

DEEDEE Guess not too many people suds their duds in the middle of the night.

ALBERTA Suds their duds?

DEEDEE I do mine at Mom's. [DEEDEE *begins to put her clothes in two washers, imitating* ALBERTA] I mean, I take our stuff over to Mom's. She's got matching Maytags. She buys giant size Cheer and we sit around and watch the soaps 'til the clothes come out. Suds the duds, that's what she says. Well, more than that. She wrote it on a little card and sent it in to Cheer so they could use it on their TV ads.

ALBERTA   Gives you a chance to talk, I guess. Visit.

DEEDEE   She says "Just leave em, I'll do em," but that wouldn't be right, so I stay. Course she don't ever say how she likes seein' me, but she holds back, you know. I mean, there's stuff you don't have to say when it's family.

ALBERTA   So, she's not home tonight?

DEEDEE   No, probably just asleep. [ALBERTA *nods.* DEEDEE *reads the washer instructions*] Five Cycle Turbomatic Deluxe. [*punches the buttons on the machine*] Hot wash—warm rinse, warm wash—warm rinse, warm wash—cold rinse, cold wash—cold rinse, cold wash—delicate cycle. Is that like on TV?

ALBERTA   Is what like on TV?

DEEDEE   That hot-cold-warm, thing. Wait, I remember. Whites in hot water, perma press in cold, colors and special fabrics in warm.

ALBERTA   It's the other way around. Perma press in warm, colors and special fabrics in cold.

DEEDEE   What's this? "Add Laundry Aids."

ALBERTA   Your mother does your laundry.

DEEDEE   You don't have a washer either, huh?

ALBERTA   It's broken.

DEEDEE   Get your husband to fix it. [*now looks at* ALBERTA'*s wash*] Got a heap o' shirts, don't he?

ALBERTA   It can't be fixed.

DEEDEE   Where are *your* clothes?

ALBERTA   Mine are mostly hand wash.

DEEDEE   We just dump all our stuff in together.

ALBERTA   That's nice.

DEEDEE   Joe can fix just about anything. He's real good with his hands. [*laughs*] I been sayin' that since high school. [*no response from* ALBERTA] He makes trucks. God, I'd hate to see the truck I'd put together. [*nervous laugh*] Had to work the double shift tonight. [*going on quickly.*] They do all kinds out there. Pick-ups, dump trucks . . . they got this joke, him and his buddies, about what rhymes with pickle truck, but I don't know the end of it, you know, the punch line. Goes like . . . "I'll come to get you baby in a pickle truck. I'll tell you what I'm wanting is a . . . [*stops*] See, that's the part I don't know. The end. [*shrugs her shoulders*]

ALBERTA   Does he do this often? Have to work late?

DEEDEE   A whole lot, here lately. He says people are buyin' more trucks cause farmers have to raise more cows cause we got a population explosion goin' on. Really crummy, you know, people I don't even know having babies means Joe can't come home at the right time. Don't seem fair.

ALBERTA   Or true.

DEEDEE   Huh?

ALBERTA   The population explosion is over. The birthrate is declining now.

DEEDEE   Oh.

ALBERTA   You don't like to be in the house by yourself?

DEEDEE   See, we live over there, on top of the Mexican restaurant. [*goes over to the window*] That window with the blue light in it, that's ours. It's a bunch of blueberries on a stalk, only it's a light. Joe gave it to me. He thinks blue is my favorite color.

ALBERTA   And the restaurant noise was bothering you.

DEEDEE   I guess. They got this bar stays open til 4. That's how Joe picked the apartment. He hates to run out for beer late. Runnin' *down* ain't so bad. [*brightly*] Ole Mexico Taco Tavern. Except Joe says it's sposed to be Olé Mexico, like what they say in bullfights.

ALBERTA   Bullfights are disgusting.

DEEDEE   You've seen a real bullfight?

ALBERTA   We used to travel quite a bit.

DEEDEE   Well, tell me about it!

ALBERTA   There's not much to tell. The bull comes out and they kill it.

DEEDEE   I bet a man thought that up.

ALBERTA   [*a little laugh*]   I'll bet you're right.

DEEDEE   Your husband works nights, too?

ALBERTA   Herb is out of town. [*now seeing what* DEEDEE *is doing*] Did you mean to put that in there?

DEEDEE   [*peering into her washer*]   Huh?

ALBERTA   Your whites will come out green.

DEEDEE   [*retrieving the shirt*]   Joe wouldn't like that. No sir. Be like when Mom's washer chewed this hole in his bowling shirt. Whoo-ee! Was he hot. Kicked the chest of drawers, broke his toe. [*a pause*] Broke the chest of drawers too. [*a pause*] Is Herb picky like that?

ALBERTA   [*reaching for her soap*]   Herb likes to look nice.

DEEDEE   Hey! You forgot one. [*picking the remaining shirt out of* ALBERTA's *basket*] See? [*opens it out, showing an awful stain*] Yuck. Looks like vomit.

ALBERTA   [*reluctantly*]   It's my cabbage soup.

DEEDEE   Well . . . [*helpfully*] in it goes! [*opening one of* ALBERTA's *washers*]

ALBERTA   [*suddenly*]   No!

DEEDEE   [*reaching for the other washer*]   The other one?

ALBERTA   [*taking it away from her*]   I don't want to . . . it's too . . . that stain will never . . . [*enforcing a calm now*] It needs to presoak. I forgot the Woolite.

DEEDEE   Sorry.

ALBERTA   [*putting the shirt back in the basket*]   That's quite all right.

DEEDEE   One of those machines give soap? [ALBERTA *points to one,* DEEDEE *walks to it*] It takes nickels. I only got quarters.

ALBERTA   [*putting her quarters in the washer*]   The attendant will give you change.

DEEDEE   [*looking in his doorway*]   He's asleep. [ALBERTA *nods*] Be terrible to wake him up just for some ol' nickels. Do you have any change?

ALBERTA   No.

DEEDEE   Looks like he's got a pocket full of money. Think it would wake him up if I stuck my hand in there?

ALBERTA   [*feeling bad about not wanting to help*]   Twenty years ago, maybe. [DEEDEE *laughs*] Here, I found some. [DEEDEE *walks back, gives* ALBERTA *the quarters,* ALBERT *counts out the nickels.*] That's ten, twenty, thirty, forty, fifty.

DEEDEE   [*putting the nickles in the soap machine*]   He shouldn't be sleeping like that. Somebody could come in and rob him. You don't thing he's dead, do you? I mean, I probably wouldn't know it if I saw somebody dead.

ALBERTA   [*starting her washer*]   You'd know.

DEEDEE   [*pushing in the coin tray, starting the washers*]   O.K. Cheer up! [*laughs*] That's what Mom always says, "Cheer up!" [*looks over at* ALBERTA *now*] Hey, my name is Deedee. Deedee Johnson.

ALBERTA   [*picking up a magazine*]   Nice to meet you.

DEEDEE   What's yours?

ALBERTA   Alberta.

DEEDEE   Alberta what?

ALBERTA   [*reluctantly*]   Alberta Johnson.

DEEDEE   Hey! We might be related. I mean, Herb and Joe could be cousins or something.

ALBERTA   I don't think so.

DEEDEE   Yeah. Guess there's lots of Johnsons.

ALBERTA   Yes.

DEEDEE   I'm botherin' you, aren't I? [ALBERTA *smiles*] I'd talk to somebody else, but there ain't anybody else. 'Cept Sleepy back there.

ALBERTA   Would you like a magazine?

DEEDEE   No thanks. I brought a Dr. Pepper. You can have it if you want.

ALBERTA   No thank you.

DEEDEE   Sleepy was one of the seven dwarfs. I can still name them all. I couldn't tell you seven presidents of the United States, but I can say the dwarfs. Sleepy, Grumpy, Sneezy, Dopey, Doc and Bashful. [*very proud, doesn't notice she's only named six*]

ALBERTA   You could name seven presidents.

DEEDEE   Oh no.

ALBERTA   Try it.

DEEDEE   O.K. [*takes a big breath*] There's Carter, Nixon, Kennedy, Lincoln, Ben Franklin, George Washington . . . uh . . .

ALBERTA   Think of Mount Rushmore.

DEEDEE   Who?

ALBERTA   How about Eleanor Roosevelt's husband.

DEEDEE   Mr. Roosevelt?

ALBERTA   Mr. Roosevelt. That's seven. Except Benjamin Franklin was never president.

DEEDEE   You're a teacher or something, aren't you.

ALBERTA   I was. Say Mr. Roosevelt again.

DEEDEE   Mr. Roosevelt.

ALBERTA   There. Teddy makes seven.

DEEDEE   Around here? Or in the county schools?

ALBERTA   Ohio. Columbus.

DEEDEE   Great!

ALBERTA   Do you know Columbus?

DEEDEE   Not personally.

ALBERTA   Ah.

DEEDEE   I better be careful, huh? No ain'ts or nuthin.

ALBERTA   You can't say anything I haven't heard before.

DEEDEE   Want me to try?

ALBERTA   No.

DEEDEE   What does Herb do?

ALBERTA   Is Deedee short for something? Deidre, Deborah?

DEEDEE   No, just Deedee. The guys in high school always kidded me about my name. [*affecting a boy's voice*] Hey, Deedee. Is Deedee your name or your bra size?

ALBERTA   That wasn't very nice of them.

DEEDEE   That ain't even the worst. Wanna hear the worst? [ALBERTA *doesn't respond*] Ricky Baker, Icky Ricky Baker and David Duvall said this one. They'd come up to the locker bank, David's locker was right next to mine and Ricky'd say "Hey, you have a good time last night?" and David would say, "Yes, in Deedee." Then they'd slap each other and laugh like idiots.

ALBERTA   You could have had your locker moved.

DEEDEE   I guess. But, see, the basketball players always came down that hall at the end of school. Going to practice, you know.

ALBERTA   One of the basketball players I taught . . . [*begins to chuckle*]

DEEDEE   Yeah?

ALBERTA   . . . thought Herbert Hoover invented the vacuum cleaner. [ALBERTA *laughs at her joke.* DEEDEE *doesn't get it.* ALBERTA *steps back a little.* DEEDEE *tries to laugh*]

DEEDEE   Why did you quit . . . teaching.

ALBERTA   Age.

DEEDEE   You don't look old enough to retire.

ALBERTA   No, not my age. Theirs.

DEEDEE   Mine.

ALBERTA   Actually, mother was very sick then.

DEEDEE   Is she still alive?

ALBERTA   No.

DEEDEE   I'm sorry.

ALBERTA   There was quite a lot of pain at the end. It was a blessing, really.

DEEDEE   For her maybe, but what about you?

ALBERT   She was the one with the pain.

DEEDEE   Sounds like she was lucky to have you there, nursing her and all.

ALBERTA   I read her *Wuthering Heights* five times that year. I kept checking different ones out of the library, you know, *Little Women*, *Jane Eyre*, but each time she'd say, "No, I think I'd like to hear *Wuthering Heights*" like she hadn't heard it in 50 years. But each time, I'd read the last page and look up, and she'd say the same thing.

DEEDEE   What thing?

ALBERTA   She'd say, "I still don't understand it. They didn't have to
have all that trouble. All they had to do was find him someplace to
go every day. All Heathcliff needed was a job. [*pause*] But maybe
I missed something. Read it again."

DEEDEE   My mother thinks Joe's a bum. [*somehow* DEEDEE *thinks this
is an appropriate response, and* ALBERTA *is jolted back to the present*]
No really, she kept paying this guy that worked at Walgreens to
come over and strip our wallpaper. She said, "Deedee, he's gonna
be manager of that drugstore someday." Hell, the only reason he
worked there was getting a discount on his pimple cream. She
thought that would get me off Joe. No way. We've been married
two years last month. Mom says this is the itch year.

ALBERTA   The itch year?

DEEDEE   When guys get the itch, you know, to fool around with other
women. Stayin' out late, comin' in with stories about goin' drinkin'
with the boys or workin' overtime or . . . somethin'. Is that clock
right?

ALBERTA   I think so.

DEEDEE   Bet Herb never did that, huh?

ALBERTA   Be unfaithful, you mean? [DEEDEE *nods*]   No.

DEEDEE   How can you be so sure like that? You keep him in the
refrigerator?

ALBERTA   Well, I suppose he could have . . . [*doesn't believe this for a
minute*]

DEEDEE   Like right now, while he's up in wherever he is . . .

ALBERTA   Akron.

DEEDEE   Akron, he could be sittin' at the bar in some all-night bowling
alley polishin' some big blonde's ball.

ALBERTA   No.

DEEDEE   That's real nice to trust him like that.

ALBERTA   Aren't you afraid Joe will call you on his break and be
worried about where you are?

DEEDEE   You got any kids?

ALBERTA   No.

DEEDEE   Didn't you want some?

ALBERTA   Oh yes.

DEEDEE   Me too. Lots of 'em. But Joe says he's not ready. Wants to
be earning lots of money before we start our family.

ALBERTA   That's why he works this double-shift.

DEEDEE   Yeah. Only now he's fixin' up this '64 Chevy he bought to
drag race. Then when the race money starts comin' in, we can
have them kids. He's really lookin' forward to that—winnin' a big
race and havin' me and the kids run out on the track and him
smilin' and grabbin' up the baby and pourin' beer all over us while
the crowd is yellin' and screamin' . . .

ALBERTA   So all his money goes into this car.

DEEDEE   Hey. I love it too. Sundays we go to the garage and work
on it. [*gets a picture out of her wallet*] That devil painted there on
the door, that cost 200 dollars!

ALBERTA   You help him?

DEEDEE   He says it's a real big help just havin' me there watchin'.

ALBERTA   I never understood that, men wanting you to watch them do whatever it . . . I mean . . . Well . . . [*deciding to tell this story*] Every year at Thanksgiving, Herb would watch over me washing the turkey, making the stuffing, stuffing the turkey. Made me nervous.

DEEDEE   You coulda told him to get lost.

ALBERTA   Actually, the last ten years or so, I sent him out for sage. For the dressing. He'd come in and sit down saying, "Mmmm boy, was this ever going to be the best turkey yet," and rubbing his hands together and I'd push jars around in the cabinet and look all worried and say, "Herb, I don't think I have enough sage." And he'd say, "Well, Bertie, my girl, I'll just run out for some."

DEEDEE   Bet you got a lot of that sage by now.

ALBERTA   I could open a store.

DEEDEE   I saw white pepper at the store last week. How do they do that?

ALBERTA   I don't know.

DEEDEE   Is Dr. Pepper made out of pepper?

ALBERTA   I don't know.

DEEDEE   What did Herb do, that you have to watch, I mean.

ALBERTA   He gardened. I didn't have to watch him plant the seeds or weed the plants or spray for pests or pick okra. But when the day came to turn over the soil, that was the day. Herb would rent a roto-tiller and bring out a lawn chair from the garage. He'd wipe it off and call in the kitchen window, "Alberta, it's so pleasant out here in the sunshine."

DEEDEE   And you watched.

ALBERTA   When he finished he'd bring out this little wooden sign and drive it into the ground.

DEEDEE   What'd it say?

ALBERTA   Herb Garden. [*pauses*] He thought that was funny.

DEEDEE   Did you laugh?

ALBERTA   Every year.

DEEDEE   [*walking to the window*]   He's not doing one this year?

ALBERTA   No.

DEEDEE   [*still staring out the window*]   Why not?

ALBERTA   What's out there?

DEEDEE   Oh nothing.

ALBERTA   You looked like . . .

DEEDEE   Joe should be home soon. I turned all the lights out except the blueberries so I could tell if he comes in, you know, when he turns the lights on.

ALBERTA   When is the shift over?

DEEDEE   Oh . . . [*with enforced cheer*] not for a long time yet. I just thought . . . He might get through early, he said. And we could go have a beer. Course, he might stop off and bowl a few games first.
   [ALBERTA *gets up to check on her wash.* DEEDEE *walks to the bulletin board on the wall.*]

DEEDEE [*reading*] "Typing done. Hourly or by the page. Cheer." What on earth?

ALBERTA Must be "cheap." Better be cheap.

DEEDEE Most of this stuff is over already. [*taking some notices down*] Hey! Here's one for Herb. "Gardening Tools, never used. Rake, hoe, spade and towel."

ALBERTA Trowel.

DEEDEE [*irritated by the correction*] You got great eyes, Alberta. [*continues to read*] 459-4734. A. Johnson. You think this A. Johnson is related to us? [*laughs*] No, that's right, you said Herb wasn't doing a garden any more. No, I got it! This A. Johnson is you. And the reason Herb ain't doin' a garden is you're selling his rakes. But this says "never used." Alberta, you shouldn't try to fool people like that. Washin' up Herb's hoe and selling it like it was new. Bad girl.

ALBERTA Actually, that is me. I bought Herb some new tools for his birthday and then he . . . gave it up . . . gardening.

DEEDEE Before his birthday?

ALBERTA What?

DEEDEE Did you have time to go buy him another present?

ALBERTA Yes . . . well, no. I mean, he told me before his birthday, but I didn't get a chance to get him anything else.

DEEDEE He's probably got everything anyhow.

ALBERTA Just about.

DEEDEE Didn't he get his feelings hurt?

ALBERTA No.

DEEDEE Joe never likes the stuff I give him.

ALBERTA Oh, I'm sure he does. He just doesn't know how to tell you.

DEEDEE No. He doesn't. For our anniversary, I planned real far ahead for this one, I'm tellin' you. I sent off my picture, not a whole body picture, just my face real close up, to this place in Massachusetts, and they painted, well I don't know if they really painted, but somehow or other, they *put* my face on this doll. It was unbelievable how it really looked like me. 'Bout this tall . . . [*indicates about two feet*] with overalls and a checked shirt. I thought it was real cute, and I wrote this card sayin' "From one livin' doll to another. Let's keep playin' house till the day we die."

ALBERTA Wasn't he surprised?

DEEDEE He laughed so hard he fell over backward out of the chair and cracked his head open on the radiator. We had to take him to the emergency room.

ALBERTA Was he hurt very badly?

DEEDEE We were sittin' there waitin' for him to get sewed up and this little kid comes in real sick and I brought the doll along, see, I don't know why, anyway, Joe says to me, [*getting a candy bar out of her purse*] "Deedee, that little girl is so much sicker than me. Let's give her this doll to make her feel better." And they were takin' her right on in to the doctors 'cause she looked pretty bad, and Joe rushes up and puts this doll in her arms.

ALBERTA They let her keep it?

DEEDEE   Her mother said, "Thanks a lot." Real sweet like they didn't have much money to buy the kid dolls or something. It made Joe feel real good.

ALBERTA   But it was your present to him. It was your face on the doll.

DEEDEE   Yeah. [*pause*] But I figure it was his present as soon as I gave it to him, so if he wanted to give it away, that's his business. But . . . [*and she stops*] . . . he didn't like it. I could tell. [*walks to the window again*] They need to wash the window here.

ALBERTA   I gave Herb a fishing pole one year.

DEEDEE [*not interested*]   He fishes?

ALBERTA   No, but I thought he wanted to. He'd cut out a picture of this husky man standing in water practically up to his waist, fishing. I thought he left it out so I'd get the hint.

DEEDEE   But he didn't.

ALBERTA   Oh, it was a hint all right. He wanted the hat.

DEEDEE [*not listening*]   Right.

ALBERTA [*seeing that* DEEDEE *is increasingly upset*]   Do you like the things Joe gives you?

DEEDEE   I'd like it if he came home, that's what I'd like.

ALBERTA   He'll be back soon. You'll probably see those lights go on as soon as your clothes are dry.

DEEDEE   Sure.

ALBERTA   People can't always be where we want them to be, when we want them to be there.

DEEDEE   Well, I don't like it.

ALBERTA   You don't have to like it. You just have to know it.

DEEDEE [*defensive*]   Wouldn't you like for Herb to be home right now?

ALBERTA [*a small forced laugh*]   I made a lemon meringue pie tonight. But I forgot, he's the one who likes lemon meringue.

DEEDEE   'Cause if they were both home where they should be, we wouldn't have to be here in this crappy laundromat washin' fuckin' shirts in the middle of the night. [*kicks a dryer*] I'm sorry. You probably don't use language like that, well, neither do I very often, but I'm . . . [*now doing it on purpose*] pissed as hell at that sunuvabitch.

> ALBERTA *picks up a magazine, trying to withdraw completely. She is offended, but wants to try not to appear self-righteous. The door has opened sometime during* DEEDEE's *fury. Now,* SHOOTER *pushes open the door.* DEEDEE *turns sharply and sees him. She storms back and sits down beside* ALBERTA. *Both women are somewhat alarmed at a black man entering this preserve so late at night.*

> SHOOTER *is poised and handsome. He is dressed neatly, but casually. He is carrying an army duffel bag full of clothes and a sack of tacos. He has a can of beer in one pocket. He moves toward a washer, sets down the duffel bag, pops the cap on the beer. He is aware that he has frightened them. This amuses*

him, but he understands it. Besides, he is so goddamned charming.

SHOOTER [*holding the taco sack so they can see it*]   Would either of you two ladies care to join me in a taco?

ALBERTA [*finally*]   No thank you.

SHOOTER [*as though in an ad*]   Freshly chopped lettuce, firm vine-ripened New Jersey beefsteak tomatoes, a-ged, shred-ded, ched-dar cheese, sweet slivers of Bermunda onion and Ole Mexico's very own, very hot taco sauce.

DEEDEE   That's just what they say on the radio.

SHOOTER   That's because I'm the "they" who says it on the radio.

DEEDEE   You are?

SHOOTER [*walking over*]   Shooter Stevens. [*shakes her hand*]

ALBERTA [*as he shakes her hand*]   Nice to meet you.

DEEDEE   You're the Number One Nightowl?

SHOOTER [*as he said it at the beginning of the act*]   . . . sayin' it's three o'clock, all right, and time to rock your daddy to dreams of de-light.

DEEDEE   You are! You really are! That's fantastic! I always listen to you!

SHOOTER [*walking back to his laundry*]   Yeah?

DEEDEE   Always. Except when . . . I mean, when I get to pick, I pick you. I mean, your station. You're on late.

SHOOTER   You got it.

DEEDEE [*to* ALBERTA]   Terrific. [*disgusted with herself*] I'm telling him he's on late. He knows he's on late. He's the one who's on late. Big news, huh?

SHOOTER   You a reporter?

DEEDEE [*pleased with the question*]   Oh no. [*stands up, stretches*] Gotten so stiff sitting there. [*walks over*] Don't you know what they put in those things?

SHOOTER   The tacos?

DEEDEE   Dog food.

SHOOTER [*laughing*]   Have to eat 'em anyway. Good business. I keep stopping in over there, they keep running the ad. Gonna kill me.

DEEDEE   No kidding. We take our . . . [*quickly*] My garbage cans are right next to theirs and whatta theirs got in em all the time? Dog food cans.

SHOOTER [*he smiles*]   Maybe they have a dog.

ALBERTA   It could be someone else in the building.

SHOOTER   See?

DEEDEE   She didn't mean they have a dog. She meant some old person in the building's eatin' dog food. It happens. A lot around here.

SHOOTER [*to* ALBERTA]   You her Mom?

ALBERTA   No.

DEEDEE   We just met in here. She's Alberta Johnson. I'm Deedee Johnson.

ALBERTA   Shooter is an unusual name.

SHOOTER [*nodding toward the pool hall next door*]   I play some pool.

DEEDEE [*pointing to the cue case*]   What's that?

SHOOTER   My cue.

DEEDEE   You any good?

SHOOTER   At what?

DEEDEE   At pool, dummy.

SHOOTER [*putting his clothes in the washer*]   I do O.K.

DEEDEE   You must do better than O.K. or else why would you have your own cue?

SHOOTER   Willie says, Willie's the guy who owns the place, Willie says pool cues are like women. You gotta have your own and you gotta treat her right.

DEEDEE [*seeing a piece of clothing he's dropped in*]   Did you mean to put that in here?

SHOOTER [*pulling it back out*]   This?

DEEDEE   Your whites will come out green.

SHOOTER [*dropping it back in the washer*]   Uh-uh. It's nylon.

ALBERTA   Your work sounds very interesting.

SHOOTER   Yes, it does.

DEEDEE   What's your real name?

SHOOTER   G.W.

DEEDEE   That's not a real name.

SHOOTER   I don't like my real name.

DEEDEE   Come on . . .

SHOOTER [*disgusted*]   It's Gary Wayne. Now do I look like Gary Wayne to you?

DEEDEE [*laughs*]   No.

SHOOTER   Mom's from Indiana.

ALBERTA   From Gary or Fort Wayne?

DEEDEE   Alberta used to be a teacher.

SHOOTER   It coulda been worse. She coulda named me Clarksville. [DEEDEE *laughs.*]

SHOOTER   Hey! Now why don't the two of you come over and join us for a beer.

ALBERTA   No thank you.

SHOOTER [*pouring in the soap*]   It's just Willie and me this time of night.

ALBERTA   No.

DEEDEE [*with a knowing look at* ALBERTA]   And watch you play pool?

SHOOTER   Actually, what we were planning to do tonight was whip us up a big devil's food cake and pour it in one of the pool tables to bake. Turn up the heat real high . . . watch it rise and then pour on the creamy fudge icing with lots of nuts.

DEEDEE   *You're* nuts.

SHOOTER   Get real sick if we have to eat it all ourselves.

DEEDEE   I've never seen anybody play pool.

SHOOTER   The key to pool's a . . . [*directly seductive now*] real smooth stroke . . . the feel of that stick in your hand . . .

DEEDEE   Feels good?

SHOOTER   You come on over, I'll show you just how it's done.

DEEDEE   Pool.

SHOOTER   Sure. [*smiles, then turns sharply and walks back to* ALBERTA, *depositing an empty soap box in the trash can*]   Willie always keeps hot water. You could have a nice cup of tea.

ALBERTA [*a pointed look at* DEEDEE]   No.

DEEDEE   Our wash is almost done. We have to . . .

SHOOTER   We'll be there quite a while. Gets lonesome this late, you know.

DEEDEE   We know. [*and suddenly, everybody feels quite uncomfortable*]

SHOOTER [*to* ALBERTA]   It was nice meeting you. Hope I didn't interrupt your reading or anything.

DEEDEE   She used to be a teacher.

SHOOTER   That's what you said. [*walking toward the door*] Right next door, now. Can't miss it. [*to* DEEDEE] Give you a piece of that fudge cake.

DEEDEE   Yeah, I'll bet you would.

SHOOTER   Big piece. [*closing the door*]

ALBERTA *watches* DEEDEE *watch to see which direction* SHOOTER *takes*

DEEDEE [*after a moment*]   I thought we'd had it there for a minute, didn't you? [*visibly cheered*] Coulda been a murderer, or a robber or a rapist, just as easy! [*increasingly excited*] We coulda been hostages by now!

ALBERTA   To have hostages you have to commit a hijacking. You do not hijack a laundromat.

DEEDEE   Depends how bad you need clean clothes.

ALBERTA   I didn't like the things he said to you.

DEEDEE   He was just playin'.

ALBERTA   He was not playing.

DEEDEE   Well, what does it hurt? Just words.

ALBERTA   Not those words.

DEEDEE   You don't miss a thing, do you?

ALBERTA   I'm not deaf.

DEEDEE   Just prejudiced.

ALBERTA   That's not true.

DEEDEE   If that was a white DJ comin' in here, you'd still be talkin' to him, I bet. Seein' if he knows your "old" favorites.

ALBERTA   If you don't want to know what I think, you can stop talking to me.

DEEDEE   What you think is what's wrong with the world. People don't trust each other just because they're some other color from them.

ALBERTA   And who was it that said he could be a murderer? That was you, Deedee. Would you have said that if he'd been white?

DEEDEE   It just makes you sick, doesn't it. The thought of me and Shooter over there after you go home.

ALBERTA   It's not my business.

DEEDEE   That's for sure.

ALBERTA *goes back to reading her magazine.* DEEDEE *wanders around.*

DEEDEE You don't listen to him on the radio, but I do. And you know what he says after "rock your daddy to dreams of de-light?" He says, "And Mama, I'm comin' home." Now, if he has a "Mama" to go home to, what's he doing washing his own clothes? So he don't have a "Mama," and that means lonely. And he's loaded, too. So if he's got a wife, she's got a washer, so don't say maybe they don't have a washer. Lonely.

ALBERTA All right. He's a nice young man who washes his own clothes and is "friendly" without regard to race, creed or national origin.

DEEDEE I mean, we're both in here in the middle of the night and it don't mean we're on the make, does it?

ALBERTA It's perfectly respectable.

DEEDEE You always do this when Herb is out of town?

ALBERTA No.

DEEDEE You don't live in this neighborhood, do you?

ALBERTA No.

DEEDEE Know how I knew that? That garden. There ain't a garden for miles around here.

ALBERTA You've been reading Sherlock Holmes.

DEEDEE [*knows she's just been insulted*] So why did you come here?

ALBERTA [*knows she's made a mistake*] I came for the same reason you did. To do my wash.

DEEDEE In the middle of the night! Hah! It's a big mystery, isn't it, and you don't want to tell me. Is some man meetin' you here? Yeah, and you can't have your meetin' out where you live cause your friends might see you and give the word to ol' Herb when he gets back.

ALBERTA No. [*pauses*] I'm sorry I said what I did. Go on over to the pool hall. I'll put your clothes in the dryer. They're almost finished.

DEEDEE [*easily thrown off the track*] And let him think I'm all hot for him? No sir. Besides, Joe might come home.

ALBERTA That's right.

DEEDEE Might just serve him right, though. Come in and see me drinkin' beer and eatin' fudge cake with Willie and Shooter. Joe hates black people. He says even when they're dancin' or playin' ball, they're thinking about killin'. Yeah, that would teach him to run out on me. A little dose of his own medicine. Watch him gag on it.

ALBERTA He's run out on you?

DEEDEE I told you he was working the double shift.

ALBERTA I know you did.

DEEDEE And you don't believe me. You think he just didn't come home, is that it? You think I was over there waitin' and waitin' in in my new nightgown and when the late show went off I turned on the radio and ate a whole pint of chocolate ice cream, and when the radio went off I couldn't stand it any more so I grabbed up all these clothes, dirty or not, and got outta there so he wouldn't come in and find me crying . . . Well . . . [*firmly*] I wasn't cryin'.

ALBERTA [*after a considerable pause*] I haven't cried in forty years.

DEEDEE   Just happy I guess.

ALBERTA   I had an aunt, Dora, who had a rabbit, Puffer, who died. I cried then. I cried for weeks.

DEEDEE   And it wasn't even your rabbit.

ALBERTA   I loved Aunt Dora. And she loved that rabbit. She had a high chair for it—at the table. I'd go visit and she'd tell me stories—what Puffer'd been up to that day—looking through seed catalogues, fingerpainting, telling her stories—Goldilocks and the Three Hares, Sleeping Bunny, The Rabbit Who Ate New York. Then we'd go outside and drink lemonade while Puffer ate lettuce and she'd say, "Now, what has my Bertie been up to today." She grew lettuce just for him. A whole back yard of it.

DEEDEE   [*glad to be on some other subject*]   You're kidding.

ALBERTA   I helped her bury him. Tears were streaming down my face. "Bertie," she said, "tears will not bring Puffer back to us. He didn't mean to go and leave us all alone and he'd feel bad if he knew he made us so miserable." But in the next few weeks, Aunt Dora got quieter and quieter till finally she wasn't talking at all and Mother put her in a nursing home.

DEEDEE   Where she died.

ALBERTA   Yes.

DEEDEE   Little cracked, huh?

ALBERTA   I suppose so, yes.

DEEDEE   Well, you better start cryin', Alberta, or you'll go just like she did. [*a bit too casual*] Hey! Our wash is done. [ALBERTA *doesn't seem to hear her.*] Look, I'll do it. You go sit.

ALBERTA   [*worried*]   No, I . . .

DEEDEE   Let me, really. I know this part. Mom says you can't blow this part, so I do it. She still checks, though, finds some reason to go downstairs and checks the heat I set. I don't mind, really. Can't be too careful.

> DEEDEE *begins to unload the washers and carry the clothes to the dryers.* ALBERTA *walks over to the bulletin board, takes down her notice, reads it, then decides to put it back up again.*

DEEDEE   [*setting the heat*]   Regular for you guys, warm for permos and undies. Now, Herb's shirts and shorts get hot. Pants and socks get . . .

ALBERTA   [*goes to the window*]   Warm.

DEEDEE   What's Herb got left to wear anyhow?

ALBERTA   His gray suit.

DEEDEE   [*laughs at how positive* ALBERTA *is about this*]   What color tie?

ALBERTA   Red with a silver stripe through it.

DEEDEE   [*still merry*]   Shirt?

ALBERTA   White.

DEEDEE   Shoes?

ALBERTA   [*quiet astonishment*]   I don't know.

DEEDEE   Whew! I thought for a minute you were seein' him out the window, telling me all that stuff he had on. Alberta . . .

ALBERTA [*worried, turns to face her*] Yes?

DEEDEE You got any dimes?

ALBERTA [*relieved*] Sure. [*Walks to her purse, starts to check the dryer settings as she goes by them, then changes her mind and doesn't look.* DEEDEE *notices.*] How many do we need?

DEEDEE Two each, I guess. 4 dryers makes 8. [*as* ALBERTA *is getting them out of her wallet*] I don't know what I'd have done if you hadn't been here.

ALBERTA You'd have done fine. Don't forget Sleepy back there.

DEEDEE Men need so much sleep, don't they? Dad was always asleep. Joe can fall asleep right in the middle of what I'm saying. I know he's gotta have his rest, but it makes me feel like I'm the TV and he just changed channels.

ALBERTA He could try to stay awake.

DEEDEE Sometimes he does, try, you know. And sometimes I just go on talking. I mean, if he's already asleep, there's no reason not to.

ALBERTA Sure. People put tape recorders under their pillows to learn foreign languages.

DEEDEE [*doesn't understand*] They do?

ALBERTA They do. So he hears you anyway.

DEEDEE And he doesn't interrupt me or want something to eat.

ALBERTA Exactly.

DEEDEE I wish Mom were more like you.

ALBERTA Stuck up?

DEEDEE Smart. Nice to talk to.

ALBERTA Thank you, but . . .

DEEDEE No, really. You've been to Mexico and you've got a good man.

ALBERTA I'm not much fun though.

DEEDEE Mom's just got me and giant size Cheer. And she don't say two words while I'm there. Ever. I don't blame her, I guess.

ALBERTA Well . . . [*feels a response is called for, but can't figure one out*]

DEEDEE Yeah.

ALBERTA But you're young and pretty. You have a wonderful sense of humor.

DEEDEE Uh-huh.

ALBERTA And you'll have those children some day.

DEEDEE Yeah, I know. [*gloomily*] I have my whole life in front of me.

ALBERTA You could get a job.

DEEDEE Oh, I got one. This company in New Jersey, they send me envelopes and letters and lists of names and I write on the names and addresses and Dear Mr. Wilson or whatever at the top of the letter. I do have nice handwriting. I had to send them a sample first.

ALBERTA I see.

DEEDEE I get so bored doing it. Sometimes I want to take a fat orange crayon and scribble [*making letters in the air*] EAT BEANS, FATSO, and then draw funny faces all over the letter.

ALBERTA I'm sure the extra money comes in handy.

DEEDEE Well, Joe don't know I do it. I hide all the stuff before he comes home. And I keep the money at Mom's. She borrows from it sometimes. She says that makes us even for the water for the washing machine. See, I can't spend it or Joe will know I got it.

ALBERTA   He doesn't want you to work?

DEEDEE [*imitating Joe's voice*]   I'm the head of his house.

ALBERTA   He expects you to sit around all day?

DEEDEE   I guess. [*with good-humored rage*] Oh, I can wash the floor if I want.

ALBERTA   You should tell him how you feel.

DEEDEE   He'd leave me.

ALBERTA   Maybe.

DEEDEE [*getting what she thinks is* ALBERTA's *message*]   So what? Right?

ALBERTA   I just meant, if you give him the chance to understand . . .

DEEDEE   But what would I say?

ALBERTA   You'd figure something out, I'm sure.

DEEDEE   But I can't ever talk to him and just say one thing, you know? Like I keep, well, all this other stuff comes out. See, I'll start out saying we're having tuna casserole for dinner and end up telling him about this girl at the grocery that told me how to cook minute steaks. But by then, he's walked into the bathroom and shut the door, all because I got off the track only I don't know how it happened.

ALBERTA   Then you'll just have to . . .

DEEDEE   Then I'll just have to say, "Joe, I want to get a real job cause I can't just sit around here all day cause I gotta have something to think about besides when are you coming home and how long's it gonna be before you don't come home at all because you're lying to me all the time and I know it. Even tonight, you're not out bowling or working that double shift and I know it and I'm sick of pretending that I don't know it because I do know it!

ALBERTA [*cautioning her against suspicion*]   Now . . .

DEEDEE   No, really. I called the bowling alley and asked for him and the bartender said, "This Patsy? He's on his way, honey!" I hope he falls in the sewer.

ALBERTA   Deedee . . .

DEEDEE   I hope he gets his shirt caught in his zipper. I hope he wore socks with holes in 'em. I hope his baseball cap falls in the toilet. I hope she kills him. [*knocking over one of the carts*]

ALBERTA   Deedee!

DEEDEE   I do. Last night, I thought I'd surprise him and maybe we'd bowl a few . . . well, I was gettin' my shoes and I saw them down at lane 12, laughin' an all. He had one of his hands rubbin' her hair and the other one rubbin' his bowling ball. Boy did I get outta there quick. I've seen her there before. She teaches at the Weight Control upstairs, so she's probably not very strong but maybe she could poison him or something. She wears those pink leotards and I hate him.

ALBERTA   I'm sure you don't really . . .

DEEDEE   I do. He's mean and stupid. I thought he'd get over it, but he didn't. Mean and stupid. And I'm not all that smart, so if I know he's dumb, he must really be dumb. I used to think he just acted mean and stupid. Now I know he really *is* . . .

ALBERTA [*finishing her sentence for her*] . . . mean and stupid.

DEEDEE Why am I tellin' you this? You don't know nuthin about bein' dumped.

ALBERTA At least you have some money saved.

DEEDEE For what?

ALBERTA And your mother would let you stay with her till you got your own place.

DEEDEE She's the *last* person I'm tellin'.

ALBERTA I'll bet you'd like being a telephone operator.

DEEDEE But how's he gonna eat? The only time he ever even fried an egg, he flipped it over and it landed in the sink. It was the last egg, so he grabbed it up and ate it in one bite. [*indicating, however strangely, her perception of his need for her*]

ALBERTA One bite?

DEEDEE [*ready to cry*] Where is he?

ALBERTA He stuffed a whole egg in his mouth?

DEEDEE You're worse than Mom. [*angrily*] He's gonna be a famous race car driver someday and I want to be there.

ALBERTA To have him pour beer all over you.

DEEDEE [*hostile*] Yes. To have him pour beer all over me.

ALBERTA *knows she has said too much. She checks the clothes in one of her dryers.*

ALBERTA He could've come in without turning on the lights. If you want to go check, I'll watch your things here.

DEEDEE You want to get rid of me, don't you? You want to be here all by yourself. Cause you want to take out all those shirts and shorts and fold them up real nice and take them home and put them away cause Herb, good ol' Herb, old herb-garden Herb, he ain't up in Akron at all. Herb is dead. Isn't he? You want me to run off and leave my husband so I'll be all alone too. Like you. And Mom after Dad left. And like your crazy old aunt after her stupid rabbit died. That's what you want, A. Johnson. And you didn't want nobody botherin' you, did you? So you came down to a crummy part of town in the middle of the night so none of your friends would find out Herb didn't even leave you enough money to get your washer fixed. Ain't that right.

ALBERTA [*calmly*] What do I have to do to get you to leave me alone.

DEEDEE [*proud*] I was right.

ALBERTA You were right.

DEEDEE [*feels bad now*] I'm so stupid.

ALBERTA You . . .

DEEDEE What? Tell me. Say something horrible.

ALBERTA [*slowly but now mean*] You just don't know when to shut up.

DEEDEE Worse than that. I don't know how.

ALBERTA But you are not dumb, child. And don't let anybody tell you you are, O.K.? [*takes off her glasses and rubs her eyes*]

DEEDEE   I'm sorry, Mrs. Johnson. I really am sorry. You've probably been plannin' this night for a long time. Washin' his things up. And I barged in and spoiled it all.

ALBERTA   I've been avoiding it for a long time.

DEEDEE *feels terrible. She wants to ask questions, but is trying very hard, for once, to control herself.*

ALBERTA   Herb died last winter, the day before his birthday.

DEEDEE   When you got him the rakes. [*pointing to the bulletin board*]

ALBERTA   He was being nosy, like I told you before, in the kitchen. I was making his cake. So I asked him to take out the garbage.

DEEDEE   How . . .

ALBERTA   I didn't miss him til I put the cake in the oven. Guess I thought he was checking his seed beds in the garage. [*pause*] I yelled out, "Herb, do you want butter cream or chocolate?" and then I saw him. Lying in the alley, covered in my cabbage soup. Paper towels everywhere. I ran out. A cat was watching.

DEEDEE   Did you . . .

ALBERTA   First, I threw a coffee can at that cat. Then I picked up his head in my hand and held it while I cleaned up as much of the stuff as I could. A tuna can, coffee grounds, egg shells, a bologna package . . .

DEEDEE [*carefully*]   You knew he was dead, not just knocked out?

ALBERTA   Yes.

DEEDEE   And you didn't cry?

ALBERTA   No.

DEEDEE   I'm sorry.

ALBERTA   I don't want you to be alone, that's not what I meant before.

DEEDEE   Looks like I'm alone anyway.

ALBERTA   That's what I meant.

DEEDEE   Sometimes I bring in a little stand-up mirror to the coffee table while I'm watchin TV. It's my face over there when I look, but it's a face just the same.

ALBERTA   Being alone isn't so awful. I mean, it's awful, but it's not that awful. There are hard things. [*the dryers stop*]

DEEDEE [*watches* ALBERTA *take a load of clothes from the dryer, holding them up to smell them*]   I'd probably eat pork and beans for weeks.

ALBERTA [*her back to* DEEDEE]   I found our beachball when I cleaned out the basement. I can't let the air out of it. [*turning around to face her now*] It's . . . his breath in there.

ALBERTA *sees that* DEEDEE *is upset. She takes the rest of her clothes out of the dryer.*

ALBERTA   Get your clothes out. They'll wrinkle. [*starting to fold the clothes*] That's amazing about the shoes.

DEEDEE   The shoes?

ALBERTA   Remember before, I was telling you what Herb was wearing?

DEEDEE   Gray suit, red tie . . . [*slowing down, understanding*] with a silver stripe . . .

ALBERTA   I hang onto this shirt he died in, and I don't even know if he's got shoes on in his coffin.

DEEDEE   [*trying to help*] If he's flying around Heaven, he don't need 'em.

ALBERTA   I hope they speak English in Heaven. Herb never was much good at languages.

DEEDEE   You bought him all black socks.

ALBERTA   It was his idea. He thought it would be easier to match them up if they were all the same color.

DEEDEE   Is it?

ALBERTA   No. Now I have to match by length. Just because they're all black doesn't mean they all shrink the same. I guess I don't really have to match them now, though, do I? [*but she continues to pair the socks*]

DEEDEE   I'd like to lose all Joe's white ones.

> *She holds them up over the trash can, but then decides it's not such a good idea.*

ALBERTA   [*going back for a sock that must still be in the dryer*] Your lights are on. [*looking toward the window*]

DEEDEE   You sure?

ALBERTA   Come see. [DEEDEE *walks over to the window*]

DEEDEE   You're right.

ALBERTA   Yes.

DEEDEE   So what do I do now?

ALBERTA   I don't know.

> *They look at each other quietly, then* DEEDEE *breaks the gaze to see that* SHOOTER's *washer has stopped.*

DEEDEE   [*walking over to the washer*] Shooter's clothes are done.

ALBERTA   It won't hurt them to rest a while in there.

DEEDEE   [*picking up the dimes*] Well, look at this. He left dimes on the washer.

ALBERTA   Very clever.

DEEDEE   Look. What will it hurt to dry his clothes for him?

ALBERTA   [*doesn't want to get into this again*] Not a thing.

DEEDEE   You're going to tell me I'm making a big mistake taking his clothes back to him.

ALBERTA   You seem to know it already.

DEEDEE   So, should I rush right home? Ask Joe did he have a good time bowling a few games after his double shift? Listen to him brag about his score? His score he didn't make in the games he didn't bowl after the double shift he didn't work?

ALBERTA   It will be hard, but it's not more trouble. I think if you go see Shooter, you'll just be getting even with Joe for hurting you.

DEEDEE   And what's wrong with that?

ALBERTA   What's wrong with that is you'll forget how mad you are. You don't have to put up with what he's doing. You can if you want to, if you think you can't make it without him, but you don't have to.

DEEDEE   But what should I say? Joe, if you don't stop going out on me, I'm never speaking to you again? That's exactly what he wants.

ALBERTA   I don't know what you should say. But there is something you must remember.

DEEDEE   What is it?

ALBERTA   Your own face in a mirror is better company than a man who would eat a whole fried egg in one bite. [DEEDEE *laughs*] But it won't be easy.

DEEDEE [*cautiously*]   Are you going to wash that other shirt ever?

ALBERTA   The cabbage soup shirt? No, I don't think so.

DEEDEE   Yeah.

ALBERTA   Maybe, in a few months or next year sometime, I'll be able to give these away. They're nice things.

DEEDEE   People do need them. Hey! [*leaving her laundry and going to the bulletin board.* ALBERTA *is loading up her basket.*] I told you there ain't a garden for miles around here. [*takes* ALBERTA'S *notice down and walks back to the folding table*] You better hang onto these hoes. You might get some carrots spring up all by themselves.

ALBERTA   I might at that. [*puts the note in her purse and is ready to go*] Green beans growing out of sheer habit.

DEEDEE   Yeah.

ALBERTA [*looking around the room*]   Well, that's everything. I'll just get my soap and . . .

DEEDEE [*hesitantly*]   Mrs. Johnson?

ALBERTA   Alberta.

DEEDEE   Alberta?

ALBERTA   Yes.

DEEDEE   I'm really lonely.

ALBERTA   I know.

DEEDEE   How can you stand it?

ALBERTA   I can't. [*pause*] But I have to, just the same.

DEEDEE   How do I . . . [*quickly*] How do you do that?

ALBERTA   I don't know. You call me if you think of something.

ALBERTA *gives her a small kiss on the forehead.*

DEEDEE [*asking for it*]   I don't have your number.

ALBERTA [*backing away to get her laundry*]   I really wanted to be alone tonight.

DEEDEE   I know.

ALBERTA   I'm glad you talked me out of it.

DEEDEE   Boy, you can count on me for that. Hey! Don't go yet! I owe you some money.

ALBERTA [*fondly*]   No, everybody deserves a free load now and then.

DEEDEE   Thank you.

ALBERTA   Now, I suggest you go wake up Sleepy back there and see if there's something he needs to talk about. [*opening the door*]

DEEDEE   Tell you the truth, I'm ready for a little peace and quiet.

ALBERTA   Good night. [*leaves*]

DEEDEE   [*going back to her clothes*]   Peace and quiet. [*picking up her Dr. Pepper*] Too bad it don't come in cans.

And DEEDEE *continues to fold her laundry as the lights go down and we have*

THE END

1978

WRITING
ABOUT LITERATURE

INTRODUCTION

Writing about literature ought to be easier than writing about anything else. When you write about painting, for example, you have to translate shapes and colors and textures into words. When you write about music, you have to translate various aspects and combinations of sounds into words. When you write about that complex, mysterious, fleeting thing called "reality" or "life," you have an even more difficult task. Worst of all, perhaps, is trying to put into words all that is going on at any given moment inside your particular and unique self. So you ought to be relieved to know that you are going to write—that is, use words—about literature—again, words. How much easier it is going to be than writing about how you spent your summer vacation or what you think and feel about Van Gogh's sunflowers, capital punishment, or your parents. Or it should be.

But writing about literature will not be easy if you haven't learned to *read* literature, for in order to write about anything you have to know that something rather well. Helping you to learn to read literature is what the rest of this book is about; this chapter is about the writing. (But, as you will see, you cannot fully separate the writing from the reading.)

Another thing keeps writing about literature from being easy: writing itself is not easy. Writing well requires a variety of language skills —a good working vocabulary, for example—and a sense of ordering your ideas, of how to link one idea or statement to another, of what to put in and what to leave out. Worse, writing is not a finite or definite skill or art; you never really "know how to write," you just learn how to write a little better about a little more. It's like maturity: you're always getting there but never quite make it. You no doubt write better than you did in the first grade or in the fifth grade, and perhaps even better than you did last year. If you work at it in this course, you will be able to write a lot better next year. But even then, you will still be able to improve your writing; and even then it may not come easily. These very words you are reading have been written and revised several times, even though your editors have had a good many years in which to practice.

REPRESENTING THE LITERARY TEXT

Copying

If writing about literature is using words about words, what words should you use? Since most writers work very hard to get each word exactly right and in exactly the right order, there are no better words to use in discussing what the literature is about than those of the literary work itself. Faced with writing about a poem, then, you could just write the poem over again, word for word:

> Once upon a midnight dreary, while I pondered weak and weary,
> Over many a quaint and curious volume of forgotten lore. . . .

and so on until the end. Copying texts was useful in medieval monasteries, but nowadays, what with printing and Xerox, it would not seem to be very useful. Besides, if you try to copy a text, you will probably find that spelling or punctuation errors, reversed word order, missing or added or just different words seem mysteriously to appear. Still, it's a good exercise for teaching yourself accuracy and attention to detail, and you will probably discover things about the text you are copying that you would be unlikely to notice otherwise. Early in a literature course, particularly, copying can serve as a useful step in the direction of learning how to read and write about literature; later, being able to copy a passage accurately will help when you want to quote a passage to illustrate or prove a point you are making. But copying is not, in itself, writing *about* literature.

Reading aloud, a variation of copying, may be a more original and interpretive exercise than copying itself, since by tone, emphasis, and pace you are clarifying the text or indicating the way you understand the text. But it, too, is not *writing* about literature, and you will not long be satisfied with merely repeating someone else's words. You will have perceptions, responses, and ideas that you will want to express for yourself about what you are reading. And having something to say, and wanting to say or write it, is the first and most significant step in learning to write about literature.

Paraphrase

If you look away from the text for a while and then write the same material but in your own words, you are writing a **paraphrase**.

For example, let's try to paraphrase the first sentence of Jane Austen's *Pride and Prejudice*: "It is a truth universally acknowledged that a single man in possession of a good fortune, must be in want of a wife." We can start by making "It is a truth" a little less formal: *It's true that*, perhaps. Now "universally acknowledged": *everybody acknowledges*, or, a little more loosely, *everybody agrees*. Now we may choose to drop the whole first clause and begin, *Everybody agrees that* "a single man"—*a bachelor*—" in possession of a good fortune"—*rich* —"must be in want of a wife"—*wants a wife*. Or is it *needs a wife*? Okay, *Everybody agrees that a rich bachelor needs* (or *wants*) *a wife*. You can see that the process of paraphrase is something like that of translation. We are translating Austen's nineteenth-century formal English prose into twentieth-century informal American prose.

But what good is that? First of all, it enables us to test whether we really understand what we are reading. Second, certain elements of the text become clearer: we may see now that Austen's sentence is meant to be ironic or humorous, and we now understand the two possible meanings of "in want of." Third, we can check our paraphrase with those of others, our classmates' versions, for example, to compare our understanding of the passage with theirs. Finally, we have learned how dependent literature is upon words. A paraphrase, no matter how precise, can render only an approximate equivalent of the meaning of a text—how *good* Austen's sentence is, how *flat* our paraphrase.

Paraphrasing, like copying, is not in itself an entirely satisfactory way of writing about literature, but, like copying, it can be a useful tool when you write about literature in other ways. In trying to explain or clarify a literary text for someone, to illustrate a point you are making about that text, or to remind your readers of or to acquaint them with a text or passage you will at times want to paraphrase. Unlike an exact copy, a paraphrase, being in your own words, adds something of yours to the text or passage—your emphasis, your perspective, your understanding.

Summary

Paraphrase follows faithfully the outlines of the text. But if you stand back far enough from the text so as not to see its specific words or smaller details and put down briefly in your own words what you believe the work is about, you will have a **summary**. How briefly? Well, you could summarize the 108 lines of Poe's *The Raven* in about 180 words or so, like this, for example:

> The speaker of Poe's *The Raven* is sitting in his room late at night reading in order to forget the death of his beloved Lenore. There's a tap at the door; after some hesitation he opens it and calls Lenore's name, but there is only an echo. When he goes back into his room he hears the rapping again, this time at his window, and when he opens it a raven enters. He asks the raven its name, and it answers very clearly, "Nevermore." When the speaker says that the bird, like his friends, will leave, the raven again says, "Nevermore." As the speaker's thoughts run back to Lenore, he realizes the aptness of the raven's word: she shall sit there nevermore. But, he says, sooner or later he will forget her and the grief will lessen. "Nevermore," the raven says again, too aptly. Now the speaker wants the bird to leave, but "Nevermore," the raven says once again. At the end, the speaker knows he'll never escape the raven or his dark message.

You could be very brief, summarizing *Hamlet*, for example, in a single sentence: "A young man, seeking to avenge the murder of his father by his uncle, kills his uncle, but he himself and others die in the process." Has *too* much been left out? What do you feel it essential to add? Let's try again: "In Denmark, many centuries ago, a young prince avenged the murder of his father, the king, by his uncle, who had usurped the throne, but the prince himself was killed as were others, and a well-led foreign army had no trouble successfully invading the decayed and troubled state." A classmate may have written this summary: "From the ghost of his murdered father a young prince learns that his uncle, who has married the prince's mother, much to the young man's shame and disgust, is the father's murderer, and he plots revenge, feigning madness, acting erratically—even to insulting the woman he loves—and, though gaining his revenge, causes the suicide of his beloved and the deaths of others and, finally, of himself."

The last two, though accurate enough, sound like two different plays, don't they? To summarize means to select and emphasize and so to interpret: that is, not to replicate the text in miniature, as a reduced photograph might replicate the original, but while reducing it to change the angle of vision and even the filter, to represent the essentials as the reader or summarizer sees them. When you write a summary you should try to be as objective as possible; nevertheless, your summary will reflect not only the literary text but also your own understanding and attitudes. There's nothing wrong with your fingerprints or "mindprints" appearing on the summary, so long as you recognize that in summarizing you are doing more than copying, paraphrasing, or merely reflecting the literary text. You might learn something about both literature and yourself by comparing your summaries of, say, three or four poems, a couple of short stories, or a play with summaries of the same works by several of your classmates. Try to measure the refraction of the text as it passes through the lens of each student's mind. You might then write a composite summary that would include all that any one reader felt important. You might try the same exercise again on different texts. Has the practice made you more careful? More inclusive? Is there a greater degree of uniformity in your summaries?

A good summary can be a form of literary criticism, and learning—largely by practice—how to summarize is an essential part of writing about literature; though you will seldom be called upon merely to summarize a work, a good deal of writing about literature requires that at some point or other you do summarize—a whole work, a particular incident or aspect, a stanza, chapter, or scene. But beware: a summary is not a do-it-yourself critical-essay-kit. A mere summary, no matter how accurate, will seldom satisfy the demand for a critical essay. Furthermore, summary is not, in itself, the answer to any question you may be asked about a text nor the evidence and conclusion for any topic you may be asked to write about.

REPLYING TO THE TEXT

Imitation and Parody

While paraphrase is something like translation—a faithful following of the original text but in different words—and summary is the faithful reduction of the matter, there is another kind of writing about literature that faithfully follows the manner or matter or both of a literary text, but that does so for different ends. It's called **imitation.**

Art students learn to paint by copying the Old Masters, and imitation, especially the variety of imitation that used to be called "writing from models," was for many generations the way students were taught to write. Many poets, novelists, and playwrights have learned to write by imitating literary works. Indeed, many serious works are, in one way or another, imitations: *The Aeneid,* for example, may be said to be an imitation of *The Odyssey,* and, in a very different way, so might James Joyce's *Ulysses.* You too may be able to learn a good deal about writing—and reading—by trying your hand at an imitation.

Some imitations, such as *The Aeneid,* may be the sincerest form of flattery, but not all are entirely flattering. Alexander Pope no doubt meant to pay tribute to John Donne's *Satires* by writing his imitation of them. What he says he is doing, however, is "versifying" them; since Donne's satires are already in verse, this has the effect of saying you are going to write a comic version of *Gilligan's Island.* Pope was not poking fun, good-natured or not, at Donne or his poetry; he was merely "regularizing" Donne's meter and syntax, converting or "translating" the works into the kind of verse admired in Pope's own day.

Sometimes you can poke fun at a work by imitating it—but at the same time exaggerating its style or prominent characteristics, or placing it in an inappropriate context; that kind of imitation, a kind that is still popular, is called a **parody.** T. S. Eliot's *The Love Song of J. Alfred Prufrock* begins,

> Let us go then, you and I,
> When the evening is spread out against the sky
> Like a patient etherized upon a table; . . .

John Abbott Clark's parody of *Prufrock* keeps the same form and some of the same words; it begins,

> Let us go then, you and I,
> When Dartmouth is spread out against the sky
> Like a student cracked-up on a ski run . . .

Eliot's unheroic protagonist, hesitating to ask an "overwhelming question," says,

> I should have been a pair of ragged claws
> Scuttling across the floors of silent seas. . . .

In Clark's parody the passage appears as

> I should have been a pair of shoulder pads
> Scatting across the gridiron, beating Yale. . . .

The title of the parody indicates that the target of the parody is not only T. S. Eliot's poem but also a famous novelist's infamous nostalgia for youth, especially his college days; Clark's poem is called *The Love Song of F. Scott Fitzgerald.*

But how would *you* go about writing an imitation? You first analyze the original—that is, break it down into its characteristics or qualities —and decide just what you want to preserve in your version. The list of qualities and the model might be much the same for a serious imitation and for a parody, only in a parody you can exaggerate a little—or a lot—just as a cartoonist selects Nixon's nose or Carter's teeth as identifying qualities and exaggerates them. To parody Poe's *The Raven*, we may decide to stick closely to Poe's rhythms, his use of repetitive mood words or of several words that mean almost the same thing, and his frequent use of alliteration (words that begin with the same sound). We might want to exaggerate the characteristic stylistic devices as C. L. Edson does in his parody; it begins,

> Once upon a midnight dreary, eerie, scary,
> I was wary, I was weary, full of worry, thinking of my lost Lenore,
> Of my cheery, airy, faerie, fierie Dearie—(Nothing more).

We may choose another kind of parody, keeping the form as close as possible to the original but applying it to a ludicrously unsuitable subject, as Pope does in his mock epic *The Rape of the Lock*, where he uses all the grand epic machinery in a poem about cutting off a lock of a lady's hair. In writing such a parody of *The Raven*, we will keep the rhythm closer to Poe's and the subject matter less close. How about this?

> Once upon a midday murky, crunching on a Christmas turkey,
> And guzzling giant Jereboams of gin . . .

And maybe we could use the "Nevermore" refrain as if it were an antacid commercial.

You will have noticed that in order to write a good imitation or parody you must read and re-read the original very carefully, examine it, and identify just those elements and qualities that go to make it up and be itself. Since you admire works you wish to imitate, such close study should be a pleasure. You may or may not greatly admire a work you wish to parody, but parody itself is fun to do and fun to read. In either case, you are having fun while gaining a deeper, more intimate knowledge of the nature and details of a work of literature. Moreover, such close attention to how a professional piece of writing is put together and how its parts function together to do what it does along with your effort to reproduce the effects in your own imitation or parody are sure to help you understand the process of writing and so help you improve your own ability to write about literature knowledgeably.

Re-creation and Reply

Sometimes a poem, story, or play will seem so partial, biased, or unrealistic that it will stimulate a response that is neither an imitation nor a parody but a retort. While Christopher Marlowe's "shepherd" in *The Passionate Shepherd to His Love* paints an idyllic scene of love in the country for his beloved and pleads, "Come live with me and be my love," Sir Walter Ralegh apparently feels obliged to reply in the name of the beloved "nymph": it won't always be spring, she says in *The Nymph's Reply to the Shepherd*; we won't always be young, and, besides, I can scarcely trust myself to someone who offers me such a phony view of reality.

Ralegh's nymph confronts the invitation and the words of Marlowe's shepherd directly and almost detail for detail. In fiction the reply is less likely to be so directly verbal a retort and is more likely to involve a shift in perspective. It may tell the same story as the original but from a different angle, may not only give a different view of the same events and people but also add details that the original focus ignored or could not perceive. In *Jane Eyre*, for example, Bertha Mason Rochester is the hero's bestial, mad wife, whom he has locked away upstairs and whose existence, when it comes to light, prevents our heroine, our Jane, from marrying her heart's desire; Bertha is, in effect, the villainess. In *The Wide Sargasso Sea*, Jean Rhys not only gives Bertha's side of Charlotte Brontë's story but tells us more details about Bertha's earlier life: poor Bertha was more sinned against than sinning, it turns out. How do you think Margaret Macomber would describe the macho world of the safari, and how did she get involved with Francis and that world in the first place?

We may respond to a work whose view seems partial or distorted by shifting the perspective in time as well as in space. Are Francis Weed's marital and other problems solved by his recognition, at the end of *The Country Husband*, that life in the suburbs can be, in its own way, as adventurous as more romantic kinds of existence? What will happen to him next spring? On his fortieth birthday? As he lies dying? What will the speaker of *My Papa's Waltz* be thinking about as he plays or dances with *his* son or daughter?

You may have noticed that while retorts can often be witty, they are also serious. Usually they say not merely, "That's not how the story went," but "That's not what life is really like," and the latter statement is what a great deal of literature seems to testify to—"It has been written that life is like this, but I say unto you. . . ." Though we must always read literature initially with the aim of understanding it and taking it at its highest value (rather than reducing it and quibbling), and though we must try to "hear" what it is saying and not impose our own notions of reality prematurely upon a work but if possible learn from it and broaden our own views, we must finally read it critically as well, asking, "Is this the way things *really* are?" or, more generously, "If I were standing over there, where the story, poem, play (author, character) is, would things really look that way?"

Works responding to other works need not be negative. Tom Stoppard's *Rosencrantz and Guildenstern Are Dead* views *Hamlet* through two of the play's minor characters (even incorporating pieces of the original play from time to time), not so as to diminish Shakespeare's great tragedy, but to add a humble dimension. And, by writing his play in a manner closer to that of Samuel Beckett's *Waiting for Godot* than Shakespeare's *Hamlet*, Stoppard reveals how universal, how adaptable to other worlds and times *Hamlet* is.

Perhaps the most familiar kind of literary re-creation or reply is the **adaptation,** especially that of fiction into film. (Among the stories in this anthology that have been made into feature-length films are *The Most Dangerous Game, The Short Happy Life of Francis Macomber, An Occurrence at Owl Creek Bridge, The Lady with the Dog,* and *The Rocking-Horse Winner.*) In adaptation, the rather contradictory demands of faithfulness to the original and appropriateness to the new medium can teach us a great deal both about the content and the medium of the original. It is unlikely you will have the opportunity to make a film based on a poem, play, or story in this course, but you can still try your hand at adapting a work or piece of a work to a new medium. You might want to turn *The Cask of Amontillado* into verse (probably as a dramatic monologue) or write a short story called *The Dumb Waiter* or a one-act play called *Young Goodman Brown.* It is quite likely that you will learn not only about the nature of the original work but also something of the nature of the medium in which you are trying to work.

EXPLAINING THE TEXT

Description

To give an account of the form of a work or passage rather than merely a brief version of its content or plot (and a plot summary, even of a poem, is usually what we mean by "summary") you may wish to write a **description.** We have given a summary of Poe's *The Raven* earlier, concentrating there, as summaries tend to do, on subject and plot. A description, on the other hand, may concentrate on the form of the stanzas, the lines, the rhyme scheme, perhaps like this:

> Poe's *The Raven* is a poem of 108 lines divided into eighteen 6-line stanzas. If in describing the rhyme scheme you were to look just at the ends of the lines, you would notice only one or two unusual features: not only is there only one rhyme sound per stanza, lines 2, 4, 5, and 6 rhyming, but that one rhyme sound is the same in all eighteen stanzas, so that there are 72 lines ending with the sound "ore"; in addition, the fourth and fifth lines of each stanza end with the identical word, and in six of the stanzas that word is "door" and in four others "Lenore." There is even more repetition: the last line of six of the first seven stanzas ends with the words "nothing more," and the last eleven

stanzas end with the word "Nevermore." The rhyming lines—other than the last, which is very short—in each stanza are fifteen syllables long, the unrhymed lines sixteen. The longer lines give the effect of shorter ones, however, and add still further to the frequency of repeated sounds, for the first half of each opening line rhymes with the second half of the line, and so do the halves of line three. There is still more: the first half of line 4 rhymes with the halves of line 3 (in the first stanza the rhymes are "dreary"/"weary" and "napping"/"tapping"/"rapping"). So at least nine words in each eight-line stanza are involved in the regular rhyme scheme, and in many stanzas there are added instances of rhyme or repetition. As if this were not enough, all the half-line rhymes are rich feminine rhymes, where both the accented and the following unaccented syllables rhyme—"drēarў"/"wēarў."

This is a detailed and complicated description of a complex and unusual pattern of rhymes. Though there are many other elements of the poem we could describe—images and symbols, for example—the unusual and dominant element in this poem is clearly the intricate and insistent pattern of rhyme and repetition. Moreover, this paragraph shows how you can describe at length, in depth, and with considerable complexity, certain aspects of a work without mentioning the content at all. You can describe a play in comparable terms—acts, scenes, settings, time lapses perhaps—and you might describe a novel in terms of chapters, books, summary narration, dramatized scenes. Frequently, however, descriptions of elements involve content, as in this description of the structure of a short story:

> *The Short Happy Life of Francis Macomber* is made up of two major hunting scenes and a scene at the camp. The story opens with the camp scene though the first hunting episode has actually occurred earlier and is told in the form of a "flashback," through the memory of Macomber. We are not always in Macomber's mind, however: the story moves freely in and out of the minds of the other two main characters—Mrs. Macomber and the hunting guide. And there are bits of exposition: who Macomber is, where he lives when he's not on safari, and so forth—told by an omniscient narrator.

In addition to describing the structure of a short story, you might also describe the diction (word-choice), the sentence structure, the amount of description of the characters or landscape, and so on.

Analysis

Like copying, paraphrase, and summary, a description of a work or passage rarely stands alone as a piece of writing about literature. It is, instead, a tool, a means of supporting a point or opinion. Even the descriptions we have given above border on **analysis**. To analyze is to break something down into its parts to discover what they are and, usually, how they function in or relate to the whole. The description of the rhyme scheme of *The Raven* tells you what that scheme or pattern is but says nothing about how it functions in the poem. If you were to add such an account to the description, then, you would have analyzed one aspect of the poem. In order to do so, however, you would first have to decide what, in a general way, the poem is about: what its *theme* is. If you defined the theme of *The Raven* as "inconsolable grief," you could then write an analytical paper suggesting how the rhyme scheme reinforces that theme. You might begin something like this:

Obsessive Rhyme in The Raven

We all know that gloomy poem with that gloomy bird, Edgar Allan Poe's *The Raven*. The time is midnight, the room is dark, the bird is black, and the poem is full of words like "dreary," "sad," "mystery," and "ghastly." We all know too it has a rather sing-song rhythm and repeated rhymes, but we do not often stop to think how the rhymes contribute to the mood or meaning. Before we do so here, perhaps it would be a good idea to describe in detail just what that rhyme scheme is.

—Then follow with the description of the rhyme scheme, and go on like this:

Of course the most obvious way in which the rhyme scheme reinforces the theme of inconsolable loss is through the emphatic repetition of "Nevermore." Since this refrain comes at the very end of each of the last stanzas it is even more powerful in its effect.

What is not so obvious as the effect of repeating "Nevermore" is the purpose of the over-all abundance and richness of rhyme. Some might say it is not abundant and rich but excessive and cloying. These harsh critics cynically add that in a way the rhymes and repetitions are appropriate to this poem because the whole poem is excessive and cloying: grief over loss, even intense grief, does, human experience tells us, pass away. This criticism is just, however, only if we have accurately defined the theme of the poem as "inconsolable sorrow." The very insistence of the rhyme and repetition, however, suggests we may need to adjust slightly our definition of that theme. Perhaps the poem is not about "inconsolable sorrow" in so neutral a way; maybe it would be better to say it is about obsessive grief. Then the insistent, pounding rhyme and repetition make sense (just as the closed-in dark chamber does). Obsessive repetition of words and sounds thus helps to create the meaning of the poem almost as much as the words themselves do.

Interpretation

Principles and Procedures

If you have been reading carefully, you may have noticed what looks like a catch: to turn description into analysis, you must relate what you are describing to the theme, the over-all effect and meaning of the work of literature. But how do you know what the theme is? If analysis relates the part to the whole, how can you know the "whole" before you have analyzed each part? But then, how can you analyze each part—relating it to the whole—if you don't know what that whole is?

Perhaps if you have been reading *very* carefully, you may have spotted a clue here and there, especially in the last paragraph of the short paper on *The Raven*. There the reader's initial sense of the theme of the poem was "inconsolable sorrow," an assumption good enough to permit an analysis of the rhyme scheme, showing how that element functioned in the poem and supported the theme or meaning of the whole. But that analysis, itself, modified the reader's initial perception of the theme, so that "obsessive grief" now seemed a better rendering. Further analysis—of rhyme scheme or other aspects of the poem—may generate further modifications or "fine tuning" of your understanding of the work.

From this example, several principles and procedures may emerge. **Interpretation,** or the expression of your conception of a literary work and its meaning, involves an initial general impression that is then supported and, often, modified by analysis of the particulars. It involves looking at the whole, the part, the whole, the part, the whole, the part in a series of approximations and adjustments. (Note, too, how you must keep your mind open for modifications or changes rather than forcing your analysis to confirm your first impressions.)

This procedure should in turn suggest something of the nature and even the form of the critical essay, or essay of interpretation. The essay should present the over-all theme and support that generalization with close analyses of the major elements of the text (or, in some essays, an analysis of one significant element)—showing how one or more of such elements as rhyme or speaker, plot or setting reinforce, define, or modify the theme of the poem, story, or play. Often the conclusion of such an essay will be a fuller, refined statement of the theme. If we were to continue the essay on *The Raven* beyond its last sentence—"Obsessive repetition of words and sounds thus helps to create the meaning of the poem almost as much as the words themselves do"—and were to discuss how the kinds of words used, the images, and perhaps other elements reinforce or modify the theme, we would be writing a full-fledged interpretation.

You will have noticed that both the definition of and the procedures for interpreting a work suggest that a literary text is unified, probably around a theme, a meaning and effect. In interpreting, you therefore keep asking of each element or detail, "How does it fit? How does it contribute to *the* theme or whole?" In most instances, especially when you are writing on shorter works, if you dig hard and deep enough, you will find a satisfactory interpretation or central theme. Even after you have done your best, however, you must hold your "reading" or interpretation as a hypothesis rather than a final truth. Your experience of reading criticism has probably already shown you that more than one reading of a literary work is possible and that no reading exhausts the meaning and totality of a work. Essays on *Hamlet*, for example, may offer several convincing but different interpretations of the work, all of which are satisfactory and all of which are incapable of fully "explaining" the play. You may, then, want to settle for description, describing the play in terms of several possible meanings, or you may want to use the fact that a work like *Hamlet* does offer these different meanings or perspectives to make some other point about literature and human experience and understanding. Nonetheless, you must begin reading a literary text, including, no doubt, *Hamlet*, as if it were going to make a central statement and create a single effect, no matter how complex. You must try as conscientiously as you can to "make sense" of the work, to analyze it, show how its elements work together. In analyzing elements, you kept your initial sense of the whole as hypothesis and did not try to force evidence to fit your first impression. So, too, you must hold your interpretation as a hypothesis even in its final stages, even at the end. It is, you must be sure, the fullest and best "reading" of the text you are capable of at this time, with the evidence and knowledge you have at this moment; but only that. In other words, an interpretation is "only an opinion." But just as your political and other opinions are not lightly held but are what you really feel and believe based on all you know and have experienced and all you have thought and felt, so your opinion or interpretation of a literary work should be as responsible as you can make it. Your opinions are a measure of your knowledge, intelligence, and sensibility. They should not be lightly changed but neither should they be obstinately and inflexibly held.

Reading and Theme Making

Because you need a sense of the whole text before you can analyze it—you don't, after all, know or believe that *The Raven* is about "inconsolable loss" until you've read some or all of the poem—analysis and interpretation would seem to be possible only after repeated readings. Though obvious, logical, and partially true, this may not be *entirely* true. In reading, we actually anticipate theme or meaning much as we anticipate what will happen next. Often this anticipation or expectation of theme or effect begins with our first opening a book—or even before, in reading the title. If you were to read *Hamlet* in an edition that gives its full title—*The Tragedy of Hamlet, Prince of Denmark*—even if, as unlikely as it may seem, you had never heard of the play or its author before—you would have some idea or hypothesis about who the protagonist is, where the action will more than likely be set, how the play will end, and even some of the feelings it will arouse.

Such anticipation of theme and effect, projecting and modifying understanding and response, continues as you read. When you read the first four words of *The Zebra Storyteller*—"Once upon a time . . ." —the strange title is to some extent explained and the kind of story you are about to read and its relation to everyday reality has been established. We have already seen in the chapter on plot in fiction (pp. 14–62) how the title and the first short section of *The Most Dangerous Game* arouse expectations of the supernatural, the frightening, the adventurous, creating suspense: "What will happen next?" we ask as we read the first few paragraphs. The brief conversation about hunting, toward the end of that section, not only educates our expectations but also generates a moral and thematic question: "Are there really two animal classes—the hunters and the hunted—and does being lucky enough to be among the hunters justify insensitivity toward the feelings of the hunted?" While the question may recede from the foreground of our attention for a while, it has nonetheless been raised. It is, in addition, reinforced by the break on the page, which forces us to pause and, even if but momentarily, reflect. It comes forward again when General Zaroff introduces the subject of hunting. At these two points, at least, a thematic hypothesis based on hunters and hunted begins forming, however faintly, in our minds. That is enough to give us grounds—even as we read the story for the first time—for an analysis of elements and their relationship to our very tentatively formulated theme, and perhaps for beginning to modify or modulate our articulation of that theme. Many details in the story indicate that there is a political coloring to the theme: Zaroff is a Cossack—a people noted for fierceness—and is, or was, a czarist general; he keeps a giant Cossack servant who was an official flogger under the czar; he refers to the Revolution of 1917 in Russia as a "debacle"; he is clearly a racist. We may want to alter "hunter" and "hunted" in our first version of the anticipated theme to something broader—"strong" and "weak," perhaps, or "privileged" and "underprivileged," or we may need fuller definitions of the implications of the terms "hunter" and "hunted."

Just as we have more than one expectation of what may happen next as we read a poem, play, or story, so we may have more than one expectation of what it is going to be "about" in the more general sense: as we read along we have expectations or hypotheses of meaning, and so we consciously or unconsciously try to fit together the pieces or elements of what we are reading into a pattern of significance. By the end of our first reading we should have a fairly well-defined sense of what the story, poem, or play is "about," what it means, even how some of the elements have worked together to produce that meaning and effect. Indeed, isn't this the way we read when we are not reading for a class or performance? Don't most people read most stories, poems, plays only once? And don't we usually think we have understood what we have read? Shouldn't we be able to read a sonnet or a very short story in class just once and immediately write an interpretive paper based on that first reading?

This is not to say that we cannot understand more about a work by repeated re-readings, or that there is some virtue or purity of response in the naïve first reading that is lost in closer study. Our first "reading" —"reading" both in the sense of "casting our eye over" and "interpretation"—is almost certain to be modified or refined by re-reading: if nothing else, we know from the beginning of our second reading why it is important to be Earnest, know what Keats's urn has to say, what the most dangerous game is, why Macomber's life is short and perhaps why it is happy. This time, then, we can concentrate on such aspects or details as how Lady Bracknell's attitudes toward Algernon function in defining the theme; how the images on the urn relate to what it "says," and so on. The theme or meaning is likely to be modulated by later readings, the way the elements function in defining or embodying meaning is likely to be clearer; the effect of the second reading is certain to be different from that of the first. It may be instructive to re-read several times the short work we interpreted in class after a single reading, write a new interpretive essay, and see how our understanding has been changed and enriched by subsequent readings.

Opinions, Right and Wrong

Just as each of our own separate readings is different, so naturally one reader's fullest and "final" reading, interpretation, or opinion will differ somewhat from another's. Seldom will readers agree entirely with any full statement of the theme of a literary text. Nor is one of these interpretations entirely "right" and all the others necessarily "wrong." For no thematic summary, no analysis or interpretation, no matter how full, can exhaust the affective or intellectual significance of a major literary text. There are various approximate readings of varying degrees of acceptability, various competent or "good" readings, not just one single "right" reading. Anyone who has heard two accomplished musicians faithfully perform the same work, playing all the "same" notes, or anyone who has seen two performances of *Hamlet*, will recognize how "interpretations" can be both correct and different. You might try to get hold of several recordings of one or more of Hamlet's soliloquies—by John Barrymore, Sir John Gielgud, Richard Burton, Sir Lawrence Olivier, for example—and notice how each of these actors lends to identical passages his own emphasis, pacing, tone, color, his own effect, and so, ultimately, his own meaning. These actors reading the identical words are, in effect, "copying," not paraphrasing or putting Shakespeare's Elizabethan poetry into modern American prose, not "interpreting," or putting his play into their own words. If merely performing or reading the words aloud generates significant differences in interpretation, it is no wonder that when you write an interpretive essay about literature, when you give your conception of the meaning and effect of the literary text in your own words, your interpretation will differ from other interpretations, even when each of the different interpretations is competent and "correct."

That quite different interpretations may be "correct" is not to say, with Alice's Humpty-Dumpty, that a word or a work "means just what I choose it to mean." Though there may not be one "right" reading, some readings are more appropriate and convincing than others and some readings are demonstrably wrong. In grammar, "It is I," "It's me," and "It be me" may all be used by native speakers of the English language in certain groups and circumstances. We are used to calling the last two "wrong," but they are not "wrong," merely ineffective or inappropriate when used outside the community in which they are the "standard" and "accepted." (Just as the "correct" form may be inappropriate in some circumstances or for certain purposes.) It is unlikely, however, that any native speaker of the English language would say in any group or under any circumstances, "It are me." That, then, is clearly wrong—anywhere, any time.

What would you say about this reading of *Hamlet*?

> The play is about the hero's sexual love for his mother. He sees his father's "ghost" because he feels guilty, somehow responsible for his father's death, more than likely because he had often wished his father dead. To free himself from this feeling of guilt, he imagines that he sees his father's ghost and that the ghost tells him that his uncle murdered his father. He focuses upon his uncle because he is fiercely jealous that it is his uncle not himself who has replaced his father in his mother's bed. He so resents his mother's choice of so unworthy a mate, he attributes it not to love but to mere lust, clearly a projection of his own lust for his mother, which he calls love. His mother's lust so disgusts him that he hates all women now, even Ophelia. When his father was alive he could be fond of Ophelia, for his sexual feeling for his mother was deflected by his father-the-king's powerful presence. Now, however, he must alienate Ophelia not only because of his new hatred of women but because he has a chance of winning his mother, especially if he can get rid of Claudius, his uncle.

Such a reading explains more or less convincingly certain details in the play, but it wrenches some out of context and it leaves a good deal out and a good deal unexplained: why, for example, do others see the ghost of Hamlet's father if it is just a figment of his imagination? What are Horatio and Fortinbras and the political elements doing in the play? *If* you accept certain Freudian premises about human psychology and see life in Freudian terms; if you see literary texts as the *author's* psychic fantasy stimulating your own psychic fantasies and believe that interpretation of *Hamlet* is not merely a reading of the play itself but an analysis of Shakespeare's psyche, you will find this reading convincing. You will perhaps explain away some of the details of the play that do not seem to fit your Freudian reading as a cover-up, an attempt by Shakespeare to disguise the true but hidden meaning of his dramatic fantasy from others—and from himself. Such a reading is probably neither right nor wrong but only a way of interpreting *Hamlet* based on certain assumptions about psychology and about the way literature *means*. In Scots law there is a legal verdict other than "guilty" or "innocent"—"not proved." Perhaps that is what we should say of such competent but not wholly or universally acceptable interpretations.

Suppose one of your ingenious classmates were to argue that the

real subject of *Hamlet* is that the hero has tuberculosis. This would
explain, your classmate would say, the hero's moodiness, his pretended
madness that sometimes seems real, his rejection of Ophelia (he
wouldn't want their children to suffer from the disease), his father's
ghost (he, too, died of consumption), his anger at his uncle (who
carries the disease, of course) for marrying Hamlet's mother, and so
on. Your classmate might even argue that the text of the play is
flawed, that it was just copied down during a performance by someone
in the audience or was printed from an actor's imperfect copy. Therefore, "O that this too too *solid flesh*" should read "*sullied flesh*," as
many scholars have argued (and might not "sullied flesh" suggest
tuberculosis?). And, therefore, isn't it quite possible that the most
famous soliloquy in the play really began or was meant to begin, "TB
or not TB"? "No way!" we'd say. We would be reasonably sure that
this is not just "not proved" but just plain *wrong*. It might be interesting and illuminating to rebut that reading in a paper of your own and
to notice what kinds of evidence you bring to bear on an interpretive
argument.

But if a piece of literature does not *say* something specific, does not
mean something specific, then what good is it anyway? Why should we
bother to read it at all? Isn't the author trying to say something? And
if he or she cannot say it, say it so we or our professors or anybody
can understand it, then what good is it?

Reader and Text

If it is difficult sometimes to say exactly what a piece of literature *says*,
it is usually not because it is vague or meaningless but because it is too
specific and meaning*ful* to paraphrase satisfactorily in any language
other than its own. Since no two human beings are identical and no
two people can inhabit the same space at the same time, no two people
can see exactly the same reality from the same angle and vantage
point. Most of us get around this awkward truth by saying that we
see—or by only actually seeing—what we are "supposed" to see, a
generalized, common-sense approximation of reality. We "know" a
table is rectangular and so we think we see it that way, whereas if we
really looked we might see it as a diamond or a trapezoid or some
other quadrilateral figure. We are all, in effect, like Polonius in the
third act of *Hamlet*, who sees in a cloud a camel, a weasel, a whale—
whatever Hamlet tells him he sees.

Some individuals resist the communal pressure to accept the generalized version and struggle to see things as fully and clearly as
possible from their own unique vantage point in space and time. Those
who try to communicate to others their particular—even peculiar—
vision in our common language are or seek to be writers of literature.

There is for these authors a constant tug-of-war between the
uniqueness and therefore ultimate inexpressibility of their individual

visions and the generalizing and therefore reductive or distorting nature of language. The battle does not always result in sheer loss, however. Often, in the very struggle to get their own perceptions into language writers sharpen those perceptions or discover in the process what they themselves did not know they knew when they began to write. You have probably made similar discoveries some time or other in the process of writing an assigned paper, or perhaps in writing a letter. Very often too, however, perhaps always, writers find that what they have written does not perfectly embody what they meant it to, just as you perhaps have found that your finished papers have been not quite so brilliant as your original idea.

The first task of the reader, therefore, is to get not to the author's intention, but to the general statement that the work itself makes—that is, its theme or thesis. After a few readings we can usually make a stab at articulating the theme of most works. We have already seen, in the case of *The Raven*, that further reading and analysis can sharpen or modify our rendering of the theme. What a work says in the way of a general theme, however, is not necessarily its full or ultimate meaning; otherwise we would read theme summaries and not stories, poems, or plays. The theme is the meaning accessible to all through close reading of the text and common to all, but a literary text is not all statement. There are often cloudy areas in the text where we cannot be sure what is *implication*, the suggestion of the text, and what is our *inference*, or interpretation, of the text. What is the speaker of *The Raven* doing, for example, in the opening lines of that poem? He is reading, or, rather, pondering over "many a quaint and curious volume of forgotten lore." Now why should a man so stricken by the death of a loved one be reading? The poem does not say, but we might infer from our own experience that he is trying to forget, to distract his attention from his loss, and indeed the final "message" of the raven is that he shall nevermore be able to escape his grief. But why is he reading quaint old educational or instructional books instead of entertaining ones, if he is merely seeking to distract himself? No wonder he's weary. Words like "quaint," "curious," "forgotten," and "lore" in the context of his obsessive grief may suggest to you, especially if other macabre works of Poe's are part of your past reading experience, that he has been studying black magic, some way of raising or communicating with the dead Lenore. The black carrion-eating bird enters then to tell him there is no way, not even by magic; he will see Lenore nevermore. Poe's poem does not *say* what the volumes are about. Many readers, however, will find this inference convincing. If accepted, this changes the theme of the poem to some degree. Still, it need not be accepted; the poem does not, will never say what those volumes contain. The meaning of the poem for the reader who is convinced will differ from the meaning for the reader who is not convinced.

The full meaning of a work for you the reader is not only in its stated theme, one that everyone can agree on, but in the meaning you derive by bringing together that generalized theme, the precise language of the text, and your own applicable experiences—including reading experience—and imagination. That "meaning" is not the total meaning of the work, not what the author originally perceived and "meant to say"; it is the vision of the author as embodied in the work and re-viewed from your own angle of vision.

Your role in producing a meaning from the text does not free you, please note, from paying very close attention to the precise language of the text, the words and their meanings, their order, the syntax of the sentences, and even such mundane details as punctuation. You cannot impose a meaning on the text, no matter how sincerely and intensely you feel it, in defiance of the rules of grammar and the nature of the language.

Or, you should not. Yet we feel this may have happened to one of our favorite poems, William Butler Yeats's *The Second Coming* (p. 791). The poem ends, as you see, with a question mark where the structure of the final sentence leads us to expect a period. Readers have generally (we could say *always*) read the sentence as a question, as the final punctuation gives them the right to do, but they have rarely if ever acknowledged the possibility of reading it as a simple declarative statement, which the sentence structure would seem to dictate. We can choose to read the ending as a query, but we must recognize that such a reading is an interpretation that goes beyond the facts of the text. The reader's license to produce a meaning from the author's text does not give the reader the right to ignore the details of the text that the author has created.

Still, the reader must be an artist too, trying to experience the reality of the work as the author experienced reality, and with the same reverence and sense of responsibility for the original. To write about literature you must try to embody your reading experience—or interpretation—of the work in language. Alas, writing about literature, using words about words, is not as easy as it sounded at first. But it is more exciting, giving you a chance to see with another's eyes, to explore another's perceptions or experiences, and to explore and more fully understand your own in the process, thus expanding the horizon of your experience, perception, consciousness.

When some rich works, like *Hamlet*, then, seem to have more than one meaning or no entirely satisfactory meaning or universally agreed upon single theme, it is not that they are not saying something, and saying something very specific, but that what they are saying is too specific, and complex, and profound, and true, perhaps, to be generalized or paraphrased in a few dozen words. The literary work is meaning*ful*—that is, full of meaning or meanings; but it is the reader who produces each particular meaning from the work, using the work itself, the language of the community and of the work, and his or her own experience and imagination.

As readers trying to understand the unique perception of the author, we must translate the text as best we can into terms we can understand for ourselves. We try not to reduce the text to our own earlier, limited understanding but to stretch our minds and feelings toward its vision.

An interpretation, then, is not a clarification of what the writer "was trying to say"; it is a process that itself says, in effect, "The way I am trying to understand *Hamlet* is. . . ."

WRITING ABOUT STORIES, POEMS, PLAYS

So far we have been discussing writing about literature in general, rather than writing about a story, a poem, or a play in particular, though we have used specific works as examples. There are topics, such as a study of imagery, symbol, or theme, that are equally applicable to all three genres: you can write a paper on the images or symbols in or the theme of a story, a poem, or a play. Indeed, you can write an essay comparing imagery, say, in a story, poem, and play—comparing the water imagery in James Baldwin's story *Sonny's Blues*, for example, with the air or wind imagery in Shelley's *Ode to the West Wind*, and the fire or burning imagery in Ibsen's *Hedda Gabler*. Fiction and drama also have action and character in common, so that you can not only choose to write on the plot of a story or play or on characters or characterization in a particular story or play, but you can compare, for example, a character in a story with a character in a play—Hemingway's Margaret Macomber with Ibsen's Hedda Gabler perhaps.

Narrative

A story has not only elements common to all three genres, such as plot and character, however; it also has something special—a narrator, someone who tells the story. Everything in fiction—action, character, theme, structure, even the language—is mediated: everything comes to us through an intervening mind or voice; we often see the story from a particular vantage point or several vantage points (*focus*) and always are told the story by someone, whether that someone is identified or is merely a disembodied *voice*. We must be aware of the narration, the means by which the story comes to us. We must be aware that the action, characters, all the elements in a story, are always mediated (there is someone between us and the story), and that the mediation contributes greatly to the meaning, structure, and effect of the story. Who is telling us the story of *The Lottery*? What is the physical and emotional relationship of the narrator of that story to its characters? How would you describe the language or voice of the narration? These are essential questions to ask about Shirley Jackson's superb story, and in answering them you may want to write a paper called *The Narrator in "The Lottery"* (or, if you want to be more dramatic, *The Ghostly Reporter of "The Lottery"*). A story is told *to* someone as well as by someone, and you might want to ask yourself what the relationship is supposed to be between us—the audience—, the narrator, and the characters. Would Mr. Head and his grandson, the chief characters of Flannery O'Connor's *The Artificial Nigger*, understand the language and the literary and religious allusions in that story? What kind of reader is the narrator speaking to? How do the answers to these two questions define where we are in relation to the characters, the attitude we are supposed to take toward them, and the effect of the story? Such questions might lead to an analysis of the tone of that story—and a paper we might jazzily call *The Artificial Reader of "The Artificial Nigger."* These are the kinds of questions raised by the simple but central fact that stories do not come to us directly but are narrated; these are therefore the kinds of questions of special importance to readers of fiction and the kinds of questions writing about fiction frequently centers upon.

Even the conventional past tense in fiction that we take for granted implies a narrator. Since the story is not happening "now," in the present, is not being enacted before us but is over with, having already happened in the past, it is being recalled, and someone must be recalling it, someone who knows what happened and how it all came out. That someone is the narrator. Knowing the end, the narrator has been able to select and shape the events and details. For that reason everything in a well-constructed story is relevant and significant.

Even narrative time is purposefully structured. Stories, unlike actual time as we know it, have beginnings and endings, but they do not have to begin at the beginning and proceed in a uniform direction at a uniform pace toward the end. They can be told from end to beginning, or even from middle to beginning to end, as in *Macomber*. In a story an hour, day, or decade can be skipped or condensed into a narrative moment (a phrase or sentence), or a moment can be expanded to fill pages. Since this manipulation of time affects the meaning and effect of the story, we must pay close attention to it and question its significance. For example, the beginning of the third chapter of *An Occurrence at Owl Creek Bridge* follows immediately from the end of the first chapter, so why is the second chapter there at all? Why does the first chapter cover only a few minutes of action but the third chapter, only a little longer, cover what seems to be a whole day? Can you explain why—in terms of meaning and effect—each of the lengthy scenes in *The Lady with the Dog* is dwelled upon? Why other, longer periods are briefly summarized or skipped? Why do some stories, such as *Her First Ball*, cover only a very short period of time, while others, such as *A Rose for Emily*, cover years and years? Why are stories such as *Her First Ball* presented largely through dialogue, while others, such as *A Rose for Emily*, are "told" rather than presented, with few dramatized scenes and little dialogue?

Dramatization

Scenes presented more or less immediately (that is, without mediation) through dialogue and action, taking place over a short period of time, are said to be *dramatized*. Though there may be gaps of time *between* the scenes or acts of a play, once the action begins it takes exactly as much time on the stage as it would in actuality: the actors speak and move in "real" time. Though there is, of course, a play-wright who knew how it would all come out and has shaped the play accordingly, the language of the play that we respond to is in the present tense, the dialogue and action are happening in the present, right before our eyes. And though the playwright has written all the lines, his or her voice is not directly heard: only the characters speak. Neither the playwright nor a surrogate in the form of a narrator stands at your elbow to tell you who are the good guys and who the bad, what each character is like or whether what is being said is true, distorted, false. Only very rarely—as in the Shakespearean soliloquy or aside—do we know what a character is thinking. In plays such as *The Sacrifice of Isaac*, *Oedipus Tyrannus*, and even *Hamlet*, there are only very brief indications of setting, costume, movement of charac-ters, tone of voice, if they are present at all. Such stage directions— which may be as elaborate as the detailed description of setting and costumes and the instructions for action and tone in *Hedda Gabler*— are not, in a sense, purely dramatic. Watching a play being performed on a stage, we do not see or hear these words at all. On the page, they are usually distinguished from the text of the play by italics or some other typographical device, so as we read we register—or are supposed to register—them as separate from "the play itself." They seem to belong to some other dimension and clearly belong to a voice other than that of any character.

When we read a play we tend to imagine it—in the literal sense of putting it into images—in our minds as if it were being performed on a stage. We act, as it were, as our own directors; if we were to put into words all that would be necessary to stage the play as we see it in our minds, we would be writing the stage directions, or narrative, of the play. The relative absence of such narrative in drama makes our part in the imagining or staging of a play as we read more crucial than it is in reading fiction. How you would stage a play or a scene in order to bring out its full meaning and effect as you imagined it can serve as a significant topic for writing about drama. You might ask yourself such questions as, What instructions would I give the actors for speaking the apparently banal lines of *The Black and White* and what effect would I strive for? What scene or passage would I use as the best ex-ample of how the play should be read? How would I costume Oedipus in the first and last scenes in order to bring out the main movement and theme of the play? How can I, in the early scenes, subtly reveal that Oedipus has an injured ankle without detracting from the power and majesty of his presence at that time? . . . In the middle of his stage directions describing the set for *Hedda Gabler*, Isben specifies that on the rear wall of the smaller room there "hangs the portrait of a handsome old man in general's uniform." What, precisely, should this portrait look like? What expression should be on the general's face? How prominent should the picture be in the set as a whole?

Though you may wish to write on the theme, characters, action, imagery, or language of a play from time to time, one central element you will certainly want to write about sooner or later is the staging, or dramatization—the set, costumes, acting, moving of characters about on the stage, even lighting—and how this can enhance the effect and meaning of the play on the page.

Words

Some plays, like *Hamlet*, are written partly or entirely in verse. Though we may be able to make a distinction between poetry and verse, it is reasonable to say that as the term is generally used, poetry itself is not so much a literary genre as it is a medium. It might be more logical to break literature down into "prose" and "poetry" rather than into "fiction," "drama," and "poetry." For besides poetic dramas like *Hamlet*, there are also dramatic poems, such as Browning's *My Last Duchess* and John Donne's *The Flea*, poems in which a distinguishable character speaks in a definable, almost "stageable" situation. There are also narrative poems, those that tell a story through a narrator, such as *Sir Patrick Spens* or *Paradise Lost*. What these and other poems, lyrics, for example, have in common is rhythmical language (and, some people would add, highly figurative language).

All literature is embodied in words, of course, but poetry uses words most intensely, most fully. It uses not only the statements words make, what they signify or *denote*, using them with great precision; not only what words suggest or *connote*, usually with wide-ranging sensitivity and inclusiveness; but the very sounds of the words themselves. Not all poems have highly patterned or very regular meter, but almost all poetry is more highly patterned than almost any prose. Not all poems rhyme, but it seems safe to say that all extensively rhymed works are poems. So much writing about poetry concentrates on the words themselves: some treats the patterns of sounds, the rhythms or rhymes, some the precision or suggestiveness of the language, and some the relation of sounds to shades of meaning. This is not to say that excellent papers may not be written on the themes, characters, settings of poems. There are many excellent topics as well for comparative papers; the themes of a poem and a story may be compared—*Dover Beach* and *The Lady with the Dog*, for example—or of a poem and a play—*The Love Song of J. Alfred Prufrock* and *Hamlet*, perhaps. But in writing about poetry, even when discussing theme or other elements, at some point one usually comes to concentrate on the medium itself, the sound, precision, suggestiveness of the language. The sample paper on Dryden's *To the Memory of Mr. Oldham* (p. 1635) are examples of how one writes about this central element of poetry, words.

Sample Topics and Titles

We have been stressing, on the one hand, writing about the most characteristic elements of stories, plays, and poems—narration, dramatization, and words—and on the other hand, writing about the elements common to all three genres, like theme or symbols. For further hints about likely topics you might look at the chapter headings in the table of contents of this volume and read the introductory material to the chapter, or chapters, that looks most interesting or most promising for your immediate purpose. You might look, too, at the list of sample topics that follows, not so much for the topic that you will actually come to write on but as a trigger for your own imagination and ideas.

Fiction

1. A Plotless Story about Plot: Grace Paley's *A Conversation with My Father?*
2. The Selection and Ordering of the Scenes in *The Country Husband*
3. What does the voice in *Spotted Horses* contribute to the story's structure, tone, and effect?
4. Who Am I? The Nature of the Narrator in *Our Friend Judith*
5. The Self-Characterization of Montresor in *The Cask of Amontillado*
6. Sonny's Brother's Character
7. Beyond the Literal: Symbolism in *Beyond the Pale*
8. The Image and Import of the Sea in *The Lady with the Dog*
9. "Only a Girl": The Theme of *Boys and Girls*
10 What is the theme of *The Rocking-Horse Winner,* and how does it relate to the title of the story?

Poetry

1. Attitudes toward Authority in *Sir Patrick Spens*
2. Scene, Sequence, and Time in *Sir Patrick Spens*
3. Sir Patrick Spens as a Tragic Hero
4. Why "Facts" Are Missing in *Western Wind*
5. Birth and Death Imagery in *The Death of the Ball Turret Gunner*
6. Varieties of Violence in Frost's *Range-Finding*
7. The Characterization of God in *Channel Firing*
8. The Idea of Flight in *Ode to a Nightingale*
9. Attitudes toward the Past in *Mr. Flood's Party* and *They Flee from Me*
10. Satire of Distinctive American Traits in *The Unknown Citizen, Dirge,* and *What the Motorcycle Said*

Drama

1. What is the conflict and what is the reversal (peripety) in *The Brute*?
2. What is the effect on the reader or audience of having so much of the major actions of *Hedda Gabler* (or *Oedipus*) happen offstage?
3. Rosencrantz and Guildenstern as Half-Men in *Hamlet*
4. The Past Recaptured: What We Know (or can Infer) about Blanche's Life in *A Streetcar Named Desire*
5. Varieties of Verbal Wit as a Device of Characterization in *The Importance of Being Earnest*
6. Realistic Drama versus Comedy: Love and Marriage in *Hedda Gabler* and *The Importance of Being Earnest*
7. Write stage directions—including stage sets, costumes, instructions to actors for delivery of lines and gestures—for *The Sacrific of Isaac*.
8. Staging Polonius: Language and Cliché as Guides to Gestures, Facial Expression, and Character in *Hamlet*
9. How important is the visual impression that Hedda makes in *Hedda Gabler*? How would you stage her appearance? How would you clothe her? What gestures would you give her? How would you instruct the actress playing her to speak? What textual clues lead you to your decisions?

Intergeneric Topics

1. Motivation in *Hedda Gabler* and *Richard Cory*
2. The Functions of Spare Language in *The Short Happy Life of Francis Macomber* and *On My First Son*
3. The Uses of Fantasy in *Araby* and *Wild Nights! Wild Nights!*
4. The Disillusioned Lovers in Joyce's *Araby* and Wyatt's *They Flee from Me*
5. The Loyalty of the Survivor: de Maupassant's *The Jewelry* and Chekhov's *The Brute*
6. Hedda Gabler and Margaret Macomber: A Comparison
7. The Murderer Confesses: Browning's Duke of Ferrara and Poe's Montresor
8. Remembering Grandma: Dorothy Livesay's *Green Rain* and Mordecai Richler's *The Summer My Grandmother Was Supposed to Die*

Creative Topics

1. The speaker in *My Last Duchess* has been charged with the murder of his last duchess. On the basis on his words in the poem, prepare a case for the prosecution.

2. Write a "reply" to the speaker of *To His Coy Mistress*, declining his invitation and picking out the flaws in his argument.

3. Write a soliloquy for Gertrude (*Hamlet*) in which she defends herself against the most serious charges made against her motives and conduct.

4. Reconstruct the events and sentiments in *Dover Beach* as a short mood play by writing dialogue and stage directions for a scene between the speaker and the woman.

5. Retell (in poetry or prose) the story in *Cherrylog Road* from the point of view of the woman who is looking back on the experience twenty years later.

6. Using *Fern Hill* as a model, write the kind of imaginary reverie Hedda Gabler might have written about her childhood.

7. What would happen in your neighborhood (town) if one morning there appeared a very old man with enormous wings?

8. Elo's (Joe Lee's) Version of the Dance in *My Man Bovanne*

9. Select three scenes for a one-act play called *The Rocking-Horse Winner*.

10. Choose one of the *Stories for Further Reading* that you have not read before (perhaps *The Secret Sharer*?), read to a crucial point or a pause marked by the author, and describe your expectations of how the story will develop and conclude.

DECIDING WHAT TO WRITE ABOUT

Having Something to Say

Deciding what to write about—what approach to use, which questions to ask—seems like the first step in the process of writing a paper about a work of literature. It isn't. Before that, you have to have confidence that you have something to say. If you are a beginner at this kind of writing, you are likely to have deep doubts about that. Developing confidence is not, at the beginning, easy. Confidence comes with experience and success, and you may feel that you do not yet know what you are doing. That feeling is common. You may feel as if you can *never* begin and want to put off the paper forever. Or you may want to plunge in fast and get it over with. Either of these approaches, though common and tempting, is a mistake. Blustering ahead won't give you confidence, and delay will make you less confident. The best way is to begin preparing for the paper as soon as possible—the moment you know you have one to write—but not to hurry into the writing itself.

The first step in building your confidence is to get close enough to the work to feel comfortable with it. Before you can tell anyone else about what you have read—and writing about literature is just another form of talking about literature, although a more formal and organized one—you need to "know" the work, to have a sure sense of what the work itself is like, how its parts function, what ideas it expresses, how it creates particular effects, how it makes you feel. And the only way you will get to know the work is to spend time with it, reading it carefully and thoughtfully and turning it over in your mind. "Read, read, read, read, my unlearned Reader" is the advice that the author of *Tristram Shandy* gives to those who want to know what his book is about. There is no substitute for reading, several times and with care, the work you are going to write about *before* you pick up a pen and prepare to write. Read carefully, read thoughtfully, read intensely, read in as many different paces and moods as you can. Read sympathetically, taking the work on its own terms; read critically, judging it in terms of your own thought, values, and experience. And then read it again. And let your reading be the *work itself*, not something *about* that work, at least at first. Later, your instructor may steer you to background materials or to critical readings about the work. But at first you should encounter the work alone and become aware, as fully as possible, of your own private responses to the work before you take the next step. Your writing about literature must, after all, come from your experience of reading. You have to trust yourself so that you will have the confidence to begin.

Begin, then, by reading, several times, the work you are going to write about. The first time, read it straight through at one sitting: read slowly, pausing at its natural divisions—between paragraphs, or stanzas, or at the ends of scenes—to consider how you are responding to the work. Trust your instincts, even if they may not always be right. Later, when your knowledge of the work is more nearly complete and when you have the "feel" of the whole, you can compare your early responses with your more considered thoughts about the work, in effect "correcting" your first impressions in whatever way seems necessary on the basis of new and better knowledge. But if you are noncommittal at first, refusing to notice what you think and feel, you will have nothing to correct, and you may cut yourself off from the most direct routes of response. Feelings are not always reliable—about literature any more than about people—but they are always the first point of contact with a literary work: You feel before you think. Try to start with your mind open, as if it were a blank sheet of paper ready to receive an impression from what you read.

When you have finished a first reading, think about your first impressions. If the assignment is a story, think about how it began, how it gained your interest, how its conflicts and issues were resolved, how it ended, how it made you feel from beginning to end. Write down any phrases or events that you remember especially vividly, anything you are afraid you might forget. Look back at any parts that puzzled you at first. Write down in one sentence what you think the story is about.

Then read the story again, this time much more slowly, making notes as you go on any passages that seem especially significant and pausing over any features or passages that puzzle you. Then write a longer statement—three or four sentences—summarizing the story and suggesting more fully what it seems to be about. Try to write the kind of summary described above on pages 1493–1494.

Stop. Do something else for a while, something as different as possible—see a movie, do math problems, ride a bicycle, listen to music, have a meal, take a nap, mow the lawn, build a loft. Do NOT do some other reading you have been meaning to do. When you go back to the story and finish reading it for the third time—rapidly and straight through—write down in a sentence the most important thing you would want to tell someone else who was about to read the story for the first time: not just whether you liked it or not, but what exactly you liked, how the whole story seems to have worked. If your reading is a poem or a play, follow the same basic procedure: read the work, consider what it made you think and how it made you feel; read it again, make notes, and write a summary; then read it once more and make a single significant statement about it, articulating what seems to you most interesting or important about the way it "works."

Now you are ready to choose a topic.

Choosing a Topic

Once you are ready to choose a topic, the chances are that you have already—quietly and unconsciously—chosen one. The clue is in the last statement you wrote. The desire to tell someone about a work of literature is a wonderful place to begin. Good papers almost always grow out of a desire to communicate. Desire is not enough, of course; the substance (and most of the work, sentence by sentence) is still ahead of you. But desire will get you started. Chances are that what you wrote down as the one thing you most wanted to say is close to the heart of the central issue in the work you are going to write about. Your statement will become, perhaps, in somewhat revised form, your *thesis.*

The next step is to convert your personal feelings and desire to communicate into something communicable—into an "objective" statement about the work, a statement that will mean something to someone else. Again, you may already be further along than you realize. Look at the "summary" you wrote after your second reading. The summary will probably sound factual, objective, and general about the work; the personal statement you wrote after the third reading will be more emotional, subjective, and particular about some aspect of the work. In combining the two successfully lies the key to a good paper: what you need to do is to write persuasively an elaboration and explanation of the last statement so that your reader comes to share the "objective" view of the whole work that your summary expresses. The summary you have written will, in short, be implicit in the whole essay; your total essay will suggest to your reader the wholeness of the work you are writing about, but it will do so by focusing its attention on some particular aspect of the work—on a part that leads to, or suggests, or represents the whole. What you want to do is build an essay on the basis of your first statement, taking a firm hold on the handle you have found. The summary is your limit and guide: it reminds you of where you will come out, the bottom line. Any good topic ultimately leads back to the crucial perceptions involved in a summary. Ultimately, any good writing about literature leads to a full and resonant sense of the central thrust of the work, but the most effective way to find that center is by discovering a pathway that particularly interests you. The best writing about literature presents a clear—and well-argued—thesis about a work or works of literature and presents it from the perspective of personal, individual perception. But the thesis should clarify the central thrust of the work, helping the literary work to open itself up to readers more completely and more satisfyingly.

Topics often suggest themselves after a second or third reading, simply because one feature or problem stands out so prominently that it almost demands to be talked about. In *Western Wind*, for example, you almost have to account for what is not said, for the lack of narrative information, and in *My Papa's Waltz* you need to suggest how the boy's strong affections for his father and his pleasure in the "waltz" are expressed. Sometimes you may be lucky: your instructor may *assign* a topic instead of asking you to choose your own. At first glance, that may not seem like a good break: it often feels confining to follow specific directions or to have to operate within limits and rules prescribed by someone else. The advantage is that it may save a lot of time and prevent floundering around. If your instructor assigns a topic, it is almost certain to be one that will work, one that has a payoff if you approach it creatively and without too much resentment at being directed so closely and precisely. It is time consuming, even when you have tentatively picked a topic, to think through its implications and be sure it works. And an instructor's directions, especially if they are detailed and call attention to particular questions or passages, may aid greatly in helping you focus on particular issues or in leading you to evidence crucial to the topic.

If your instructor does *not* give you a topic and if no topic suggests itself to you after you have read a particular work three or four times, you may sometimes have to settle for the kind of topic that will—more or less—be safe for any literary work. Some topics are almost all-purpose. You can always analyze devices of characterization in a story, showing how descriptive detail, dialogue, and the reactions of other people in the story combine to present a particular character and evoke the reader's response to him or her; with a poem you can almost always write an adequate paper analyzing rhythm, or verse form, or imagery, or the connotations of key words. Such "fall-back" topics are, however, best used only as last resorts, when your instincts have

Writing About Literature **1519**

failed you in a particular instance. When choice is free, a more lively and committed paper is likely to begin from a particular insight or question, something that grabs you and makes you want to say something, or solve a problem, or formulate a thesis. The best papers are usually very personal in origin; even when a topic is set by the assignment, the best papers come from a sense of having personally found an answer to a significant question. To turn a promising idea into a good paper, however, personal responses usually need to be supported by a considerable mass of evidence; the process often resembles the testing of "evidence" in a laboratory or the formulation of hypotheses and arguments in a law case—and they will usually need to go through repeated written revisions that will sharpen and refine them.

Considering Your Audience

Thinking of your paper as an argument or an explanation will also help with one of the most sensitive issues in writing about literature. The issue is: Who are you writing for? Who is your audience? The obvious answer is, your instructor, but in an important sense, that is the wrong answer. It is wrong because, although it could literally be true that your instructor will be the only person (besides you) who will ever read your paper, your object in writing about literature is to learn to write for an audience of peers, people a lot like yourself who are sensible, pretty well educated, and need to have something (in this case a literary work) explained to them so that they will be able to understand it more fully. Picture your ideal reader as someone about your own age and with about the same educational background. Assume that that person is intelligent and has some idea of what literature is like and how it works, but that he or she has just read this particular literary work for the first time and has not yet had a chance to think about it carefully. Don't be insulting and explain the obvious, but don't assume either that your reader has noticed and correctly interpreted every detail. The object is to inform and convince your reader, not try to impress.

Should you, then, altogether ignore the obvious fact that it is an instructor—probably with a master's degree or Ph.D. in literature—who is your actual reader? Not altogether: you don't want to get so carried away with speaking to people of your own age and interests that you slip into slang, or feel the need to explain what a stanza is, or leave an allusion to a rock star unexplained, and you do want to learn from the kind of advice your instructor has given in class or from comments he or she may have made on other papers you have written. But don't become preoccupied with the idea that you are writing for someone in "authority" or someone you need to please. Most of all, don't think of yourself as writing for a captive audience, for a reader who *has* to read what you write. It is not always easy to know exactly who your audience is or how interested your readers may be, so you have to pull out all the stops, do the best you can, make the most of every single word. Your roommate or your best friend or your instructor may feel obliged to listen and fake an interest in what you have read—or may even *be* interested—and thus put up with poor sentences and inexact details, with thoughts not fully formulated, or a monologue full of vocal pauses, and "you know's" and "I don't know how to express it." But a stranger—and the person at the other end of what you write is a stranger even if you can pretty well figure out what he or she will want to know—may not be charitable, patient, or interested. It is your job to get his or her attention. And you will have to do it subtly, making conscious assumptions about what your reader already knows and what he or she can readily understand. You cannot, as in a conversation, watch the facial expressions, the eyes, the gestures of your audience and improvise. Writing commits you to assumptions about your audience. Writing is more formal than speech, and a paper about a poem or a play or a story should be "respectable" enough that your grandmother could read it if she ever felt inclined: its tone should be serious and straightforward and its attitude respectful toward the reader, as well as toward the literary work. But its approach and vocabulary, while formal enough for academic writing, should be readily understandable by someone with your own background and reading experience. And it should be lively enough to interest someone like you. Try to imagine, as your ideal reader, the person in your class whom you most respect. Write to get, and hold, that person's serious attention. Try to communicate, try to teach.

FROM TOPIC TO ROUGH DRAFT

Writing about literature is very much like talking about literature. But there is one important difference. When we talk, we organize as we go—trying to get a handle, experimenting, working toward an understanding. And the early stages of preparing a paper—the notetaking, the outlining, the rough drafts—are much like that. A "finished" paper, however, has the uncertainties and tentativeness worked out and presents a smooth argument that moves carefully toward a conclusion. How does one get from here to there?

Once you have decided on a topic, the process of planning is fairly straightforward, but it can be time consuming and (often) frustrating. There are three basic steps in the planning process: first you gather the evidence, then you sort it into order, and (finally) you develop it into a convincing argument. The easiest way is to take these steps one by one.

Gathering Evidence

The first step involves accumulating evidence to support the statement you have decided to make about your topic (that is, your thesis), and (yet once more) it takes you back to the text. But before you read the text again, look over the notes you have already made, in the margin of that text or on separate pieces of paper. Which ones of them have something to do with the topic you have now defined? Which of them will be useful to you in making your main point? Which ones can you now set aside as irrelevant to the topic you have decided on?

Reading over the notes you have already made is a good preparation for re-reading the work again, for this time as you read it (at least the fourth time you will have read it) you will be looking at it in a new and quite specific way, looking for all the things in it that relate to the topic you have decided on. This time you will, in effect, be flagging everything—words, phrases, structural devices, changes of tone, any-thing—that bears upon your topic. As you read—very slowly and single-mindedly, with your topic always in mind—keep your pen con-stantly poised to mark useful points. Be ready to say something about the points as you come upon them; it's a good idea to write down, immediately, any sentences that occur to you as you re-read this time. Some of these sentences will turn out to be useful when you actually begin to write your paper. Some will be incorporated in your paper. But some will not; you will find that a lot of the notes you take, like a lot of the footage shot in making a film, will end up on the cutting room floor. Writing, properly done, is not an efficient process and a lot of the thoughts that will occur to you as you get ready to write will not end up being central to your argument. Don't get retentive about your notes.

No one can tell you exactly how to take notes. Good notetaking is a highly individualized skill; precisely what notes you will need to take and how will depend on the particulars of the paper you are about to write. Ultimately, you will develop a style that is right for you, but some general guidelines may be useful. Here are five hints toward successful notetaking:

1. Keep your topic and your thesis about your topic constantly in mind as you re-read and take notes. Mark all passages in the work that bear on your topic, and for each one write on a note card a single sentence that describes how the passage relates to your topic and thesis. Indicate, for each passage, the specific location in the text—by line number if you are writing about a poem; by page number (and location on the page) if you are working on a story; by act, scene, and line number if you are writing about a play.
2. Keep re-reading and taking notes until one of five things happens:
   (a) You get too tired and lose your concentration. (If that hap-pens, stop and then start again when you are rested, prefer-ably the next day.)
   (b) You stop finding relevant passages or perceive a noticeable

drying up of your ideas. (Again, time to pause; give the work at least one more reading later when your mind is fresh and see whether the juices start anew. If they don't, you may be ready to outline and write.)

(c) You begin to find yourself annotating every single sentence or line, and the evidence all begins to run together into a single blob. (Stop and sort out your thesis again, simplifying and narrowing it so that you don't try to include everything. Then go back to your notetaking and discriminate more carefully between what actually is important to your thesis and what only relates at some distance.)

(d) You become impatient with your notetaking and can't wait to get started writing. (Start writing. Use scrap paper, and be prepared to go back to systematic notetaking if your ideas or your energy fade. The chances are that the prose passages you write this way will find a place in your paper, but they may not belong exactly where you think they do when you first write them down.)

(e) You find that there is insufficient evidence for your thesis, that the evidence points in another direction, or that the evidence contradicts your thesis. (Revise your topic to reflect the evidence, and begin re-reading once more.)

3. When you think you have finished your notetaking, read all your note cards over slowly, one by one, and jot down any further ideas as they occur to you, each one on a separate note card. (Sometimes it will seem as if note cards beget note cards. Too much is better than too little at the notetaking stage: you can always discard them before the final draft. Don't worry if you seem to have too many notes and too much material. But later, when you boil down to essentials, you will have to be ruthless with yourself and omit some of your favorite ideas.)

4. Transfer all of your notes to pieces of paper—or note cards— that are all the same size, one note on each. It is easier to sort them this way when you get ready to organize and outline. If you like to write notes in the margin of your text (or on the backs of envelopes, or on dinner napkins, or shirtsleeves), systematically transfer every note to uniform sheets of paper or cards before you begin to outline. Having everything easily recorded on sortable cards that can be moved from one pile to another makes organizing easier later, especially when you change your mind (as you will) and decide to move a point from one part of your paper to another. Index cards—either 3×5, if you write small and make economical notes, or 4×6, if you need more space— are ideal for notetaking and sorting (perhaps why they are called note cards, or index cards.)

5. When you think you are done taking notes (because you are out of ideas, or out of time, or getting beyond a manageable number of pieces of evidence), read through the whole pile one more time, again letting any new ideas—or ideas that take on a fresh look because you combine them in a new way—spawn new sentences for new note cards.

How many times should you read a story or play before you stop taking notes? There is no right answer. If you have read the work three times before settling on a topic, two more readings may do. But it could take several more. Common sense, endurance, and deadlines will all have an effect on how many re-readings you do. Almost certainly you will read a 20-line poem many more times than you will a 30-page story, not just because it takes less time per reading, but because in short compact works you will find the evidence more tightly interwoven and more in need of a careful unraveling. Let your conscience, your judgment, and your clock be your guide.

Organizing Your Notes

The notes you have taken will become, in the next few hours, almost the whole content of your paper. The task remaining is to give that content the form and shape that will make it appealing and persuasive. But it is not an easy task: the best content in the world isn't worth much if it isn't effectively presented. The key to the task is getting all your ideas into the right order, that is, into a sequence that will allow them to argue your thesis most persuasively. It is worth the trouble: the difference between ideas and evidence scattered randomly and a carefully ordered presentation is the same as the difference between winning and losing an argument or battle when the best resources are clearly on your side—or between failing a paper and writing a respectable one. As in most things, you may have to put a lot of effort into making your prose seem easy and effortless.

In order to put your notes into a proper order, you will need (ironically) to get a little distance from your notes. (The key to good planning and writing—and to many other pursuits—is in knowing when to back away and get some perspective.) Set your notes aside, but not too far away. On a fresh sheet of paper, write down all the major points you want to be sure to make. Write them down randomly, as they occur to you. Now read quickly through your pack of note cards and add to your list any important points you have left out. Then decide which ideas should go first, which should go second, and so on.

Putting your points in order is something of a guess at this point. You may well want to re-order them before you begin to write—or later when you are writing a first (or even later) draft. But make your best guess. The easiest way to try out an order is to take your random list and put a 1 in front of the point you will probably begin with, a 2 before the probable second point, and so on. Then copy the list, in numerical order, onto a clean sheet of paper, revising (if you need to) as you go. Do not be surprised if later you have to revise your list further. Your next task is to match up your note cards (and the examples they contain) with the points on your outline.

Putting things in a particular order is a spatial problem, and by having your notes on cards or pieces of paper of a uniform size you can do much of your organizing physically. Do your sorting on a large table or sit in the middle of the floor. Prepare a title card for each point in your outline, writing on it the point and its probable place in your paper. Then line them up in order, like this:

Point 1	Point 2	Point 3	Point 4
___	___	___	___
	___		
Point 5	Point 6	Point 7	Point 8
___	___	___	___
___		___	
___		___	
Point 9	Point 10	Point 11	Point 12
___	___	___	___
		___	

Etcetera. You may have only three or four points, not twelve, but the principle is the same for a short or a long paper. Now go through your whole pack of cards; the object is to line up each note with its appropriate point by putting all your cards in the appropriate pile. If you have too few piles, you may need to subdivide the piles into subpoints before you begin writing.

Two-thirds of this exercise is quite easy: most examples and ideas you have written down will match quite easily with a particular point. But some cards will resist classification. Some cards will seem to belong in two or more places; others will not seem to belong at all. If a card seems to belong to more than one point, put it in the pile with the lowest number (but write on it the number or numbers of other possible locations). If, for example, a card may belong in point 2, but could also belong in point 6 or 9, put it in the pile of 2s and write "maybe 6 or 9" on the card; if you don't use it in writing about point 2, move it to pile 6; if you don't then use it in 6, move it to 9. Remember that you will work your way through the piles in numerical order, so that you have a safety system for notes that don't seem to belong where you first thought but that still belong somewhere in your paper. Move them to a possible later point, or put them in a special pile (marked "?" or "use in revised draft") and, once you have completed a first draft on your paper, go through this pile, carefully looking for places in your paper where these ideas may belong. Almost never will everything fit neatly into your first draft. If everything does seem to fit exactly as you had originally planned, you have either done an incredible job of planning and guessing about the organization of your paper, or you are forcing things into inappropriate places.

Don't be surprised if you have a large number of left-over note cards, that is, cards whose ideas you haven't yet used, after you have written your first draft. You will probably find places for many of these ideas later, but some just won't fit or won't be needed for the paper you ultimately write, no matter how good the ideas are. No paper will do everything it could do. Writing a paper is a *human* project; it has limits.

Before you actually start writing, you may want to develop a more elaborate outline, incorporating your examples and including topic sentences for each paragraph, or you may wish to work from your sketchy outline and the accompanying packs of cards. Do the more detailed outline if it seems right to you, but don't delay the writing too long. You are probably ready right now, and any exercises you invent to delay writing are probably just excuses.

Developing an Argument

Once you have decided on your major points and assembled your evidence, you have to decide how you are going to present your argument and how you are going to present *yourself*. What you say is, of course, more important than how you say it, but your manner of presentation can make a world of difference. Putting your evidence together effectively—in a coherent and logical order so that your readers' curiosities and questions are answered systematically and fully —is half the task in developing a persuasive argument. The other half involves your choice of a voice and tone that will make your readers want to read on—and make them favorably disposed toward what you say.

Your tone in your paper is just as important in its way as is the tone of the work of literature you are writing about. It is the basis of your relationship with your reader. If you have not done a lot of formal writing, you may feel that you have no *choice* of tone or of how you are going to present yourself. "I will just be *me*," you may say, "and write naturally." But writing is not a "natural" act, any more than swinging a tennis racket, carrying a football, or dancing a pirouette. The "me" you choose to present is only one of several possible me's; you will project a certain mood, a certain attitude toward your subject, a certain confidence. Will you choose to be cocky and arrogant? Tentative and uncertain? Rigid, difficult, and dogmatic? Insecure, bewildered, and hesitant? The question is, how do you want your readers to feel about you and your argument? Being too positive can make your readers feel stupid and inadequate and can turn them into defensive, resistant readers who will rebel at your every point. Friendship with your reader is better than an adversary relationship. Sounding like a nice person who is talking reasonably and sensibly is not enough if in fact you don't make sense or have nothing to say, but the purpose of the tone you choose is to make your reader receptive to your content, not hostile. The rest of the job depends on the argument itself.

It has been said that all good papers should be organized in the same way:

1. Tell 'em what you're going to tell 'em.
2. Tell 'em.
3. Tell 'em what you told 'em.

That description fits—in pretty general terms—the most common kind of organization, which includes an introduction, a body of argument, and a conclusion, but if it is followed too simplistically it can lead to a paper that sounds kind of simple minded. You don't want to say "Dear Reader, what I am going to do is . . ." or "Dear Reader, what I have done is. . . ." The beginning does need to introduce the subject, sort out the essential issues, and suggest what your perspective will be, and the conclusion does need to sum up what you have said in the main part of your paper, but the first paragraph shouldn't give *everything* away, nor should the final one simply repeat what is already clear. Lead into your subject clearly but with a little subtlety and finesse; arrange your main points in the most effective manner you can think of, building a logical argument and supporting your general points with clear textual evidence, concisely phrased and presented, and at the end show *how* your argument has added up—don't just *say* that it did.

There are, of course, other ways to organize than the basic Tell[3] method. Some writers, for example, can develop an argument on the analogy of a mystery story—building suspense in a dramatic way and pulling all the parts of the argument together only at the end. But it is awfully easy to sound precious and cute that way, and such sophisticated devices of organizing are usually best left to more experienced writers.

Experiment with such methods later when you feel more confident, when you have succeeded repeatedly with a more simple structure. The imagination and originality that can be exercised in a straightforward Tell[3] paper are practically unlimited. The challenge is to hold to the basic plan and subtly work enough variation on it that your readers are constantly surprised without ever feeling that they have been tricked or made fools of.

Writing the First Draft

It is now time to set pen to paper. No one can help you much now for a while: you are on your own. The main thing is to get started right with a clear first sentence that expresses your sense of direction and arrests the attention of your readers. (If you can't think of a good first sentence, don't pause over it too long. Write down a paraphrase of what you want it to say—something like the statement you wrote down after your third reading—and go on to start writing about your main points. Your "first" sentence may sometimes be the last one you will write.) And then you inch along, word by word and sentence by sentence, as you follow your outline from one paragraph to another. Keep at it. Struggle. Stare into space. Bite your pen when you feel like it. Get up and stride about the room. Scratch your head. Sharpen a pencil. Run your fingers through your hair. Groan. Snap your fingers. Pray. But keep writing.

It is often frustrating as you search for the right word or struggle to decide how the next sentence begins, but it is satisfying when you get it right. Stay with it until you complete a draft you think you can live with. Write "The End" at the bottom and set it aside. Put your favorite book on it so it won't leap up and fly away from its own excitement. Breathe a sigh of relief and try not to think about the revisions you will do tomorrow.

Welcome to the fellowship of writers.

FROM ROUGH DRAFT TO COMPLETED PAPER

Revising

This final stage of the process is the most important of all, and it is the easiest one to mismanage. The effort that raises a *C* paper to an *A* paper most often takes place here; there is a world of difference between a bunch of ideas that present a decent interpretation of a work of literature and a cogent, coherent, persuasive essay that will stir your readers to a nod of agreement and shared pleasure in a moment of insight—or that will prompt your instructor toward praise and generosity. If you haven't done good literary analysis and sorted out your insights earlier, nothing you do at this stage will help much, but if what you have done so far is satisfactory, this is the stage that can turn your paper into something special.

The important thing is not to allow yourself to be too easily satisfied. If you have struggled with earlier stages (and students who are honest with themselves will all admit that the early stages of writing a paper *are* a struggle), it may be tempting to think you are Finished when you have put a period to the last sentence in your first draft. It will often feel as if you are done: you may feel drained, tired of the subject, anxious to get on to other things, such as sleep or food or friends or another project. And it *is* a good idea to take a break once you've finished a draft and let what you have done settle for a few hours, preferably over night. (The Roman poet and critic Horace suggested putting a draft aside for nine years, but most instructors won't wait that long to grade an assignment.) Re-reading it "cold" may be discouraging, though: all those sentences that felt so good when you wrote them often seem flat and stale, or even worthless, when a little time has elapsed. The biggest battle, in moving from a first draft to a second one, is to keep from throwing what you have written into a wastebasket—or to keep from throwing up on top of it. Resist. It will get better, but not without your help.

It may take *several* more drafts to produce your best work. Often it is tempting to cut corners—to smooth out a troublesome paragraph by obscuring the issue or by omitting the difficult point altogether instead of confronting it, or to ask a roommate or friend for help in figuring out what is wrong with a particular passage. But you will learn more in the long run—and probably do better in the short run as well—if you make yourself struggle a bit. When a particular word or phrase you have used turns out to be imprecise, or misleading, or ambiguous, search until you find the *right* word or phrase. (At the least put a big X in the margin so that you will come back and fix it later; thoughtful revision does not all come at once, and you may sometimes profit from pondering one problem while you go on to something else.) If a paragraph is incomplete or poorly organized, fill it out or reorganize it. If a transition from one point to another does not work, look again at your outline and see if another way of ordering your points would help. *Never* decide that the problem can best be solved by hoping that your reader will not notice. The satisfaction of finally solving the problem will give you confidence, and if you get in the habit of overlooking or covering up little problems, you will build yourself a big long-range problem.

Reviewing Your Work and Revising Again

Precisely how you move from one draft to another is up to you and will properly depend on the ways you work best; the key is to find all the things that bother you (and that *should* bother you) and then gradually correct them, moving toward a better paper with each succeeding draft. Here are some things to watch for.

Thesis and central thrust: It is clear what your main point is? Do you state it clearly, effectively, and early? Do you make clear what the work is about? Are you fair to the spirit and the emphasis of the work? Do you make clear the relationship between your thesis and the central thrust of the work? Do you explain *how* the work creates its effect rather than just asserting it?

Organization: Does your paper move logically from beginning to end? Does your first paragraph set up the main issue you are going to discuss and suggest the direction of your discussion? Do your paragraphs follow each other in a coherent and logical order? Does the first sentence of each paragraph accurately suggest what that paragraph will contain? Does your final paragraph draw a conclusion that follows from the body of your paper? Do you resolve the issues you say you resolve?

Use of evidence: Do you use enough examples? Too many? Does each example prove what you say it does? Do you explain each example fully enough? Are the examples sufficiently varied? Are any of them labored, or over explained, or made to bear more weight than they can stand? Have you left out any examples useful to your thesis? Do you include any gratuitous ones just because you like them? Have you achieved a good balance between examples and generalizations?

Tone: How does your voice sound in the paper? Confident? Arrogant? Boastful? Does it show off too much? Is it too timid or self-effacing? Do you ever sound smug? Scared? Too tentative? Too dogmatic? Would a neutral reader be persuaded by the way you explain? Would such a reader be put off by any of your assertions? By your way of arguing? By your choice of examples? By the language you use?

Sentences: Does each sentence read clearly and crisply? Have you rethought and rewritten any sentences you can't explain? Is the first sentence of your paper a strong, clear one likely to gain the interest of a neutral reader? Is the first sentence of each paragraph an especially vigorous one? Are your sentences varied enough? Do you avoid the passive voice and "there is/there are" sentences?

Word choice: Have you used any words whose meaning you are not sure of? In any cases in which you were not sure of what word to use, did you stay with the problem until you found the exact word? Do your metaphors and figures of speech make literal sense? Are all the idioms used correctly? Is your terminology correct? Are your key words always used to mean *exactly* the same thing? Have you avoided sounding repetitive by varying your sentences rather than using several different terms to mean precisely the same thing?

Conciseness: Have you eliminated all the padding you put in when you didn't think your paper would be long enough? Have you gone through your paper, sentence by sentence, to eliminate all the unnecessary words and phrases? Have you looked for sentences (or even paragraphs) that essentially repeat what you have already said—and eliminated all repetition? Have you checked for multiple examples and pared down to the best and most vivid ones? Have you gotten rid of all inflated phrasing calculated to impress readers? Have you eliminated all roundabout phrases and rewritten long, complicated, or confusing sentences into shorter, clearer ones? Are you convinced that you have trimmed every possible bit of excess and that you cannot say what you have to say any more economically?

Mechanics: Have you checked the syntax in each *separate* sentence? Have you checked the spelling of any words that you are not sure of or that look funny? Have you examined each sentence separately for punctuation? Have you checked every quotation word by word against the original? Have you given proper credit for all material—written or oral—that you have borrowed from others? Have you followed the directions your instructor gave you for citations, footnotes, and form?

The most effective way to revise in the final stages is to read through your paper looking for one problem at a time, that is, to go through it once looking at paragraphing, another time looking at individual sentences, still another for word choice or problems of grammar. It is almost impossible to check too many things too often—although you can get so absorbed with little things that you overlook larger matters. With practice, you will learn to watch carefully for the kinds of mistakes you are most prone to. Everyone has individual weaknesses and flaws. Here are some of the most common temptations that beginning writers fall for:

1. Haste. (Don't start too late, or finish too soon after you begin.)
2. Pretentiousness. (Don't use words you don't understand, tackle problems that are too big for you, or write sentences you can't ex-

plain: it is more important to make sense than to make a big, empty impression.)

3. Boredom. (The quickest way to bore others is to be bored yourself. If you think your paper will be a drag, you are probably right. It is hard to fake interest in something you can't get excited about; keep at it until you find a spark.)

4. Randomness. (Don't try to string together half a dozen unrelated ideas or insights and con yourself into thinking that you have written a paper.)

5. Imprecision. (Don't settle for approximation, either in words or ideas; something that is 50 percent right is also 50 percent wrong.)

6. Universalism. (Don't try to be a philosopher and make grand statements about life; stick to what is in the story, poem, or play you are writing about.)

7. Vagueness. (Don't settle for a general "sense" of the work you are talking about; get it detailed, get it right.)

8. Wandering. (Don't lose track of your subject or the work that you are talking about.)

9. Sloppiness. (Don't sabotage all your hard work on analysis and writing by failing to notice misspelled words, grammatical mistakes, misquotations, incorrect citations or references, or typographical errors. Little oversights make readers suspicious.)

10. Impatience. (Don't be too anxious to get done. Enjoy the experience; savor the process. Have fun watching yourself learn.)

Being flexible—being willing to rethink your ideas and reorder your argument as you go—is crucial to success in writing, especially in writing about literature. You will find different (and better) ways to express your ideas and feelings as you struggle with revisions, and you will also find that—in the course of analyzing the work, preparing to write, writing, and rewriting—your response to the work itself will have grown and shifted somewhat. Part of the reason is that you will have gotten more knowledgeable—maybe even smarter—as a result of the time and effort you have spent, and you will have, by the time you finish, a more subtle understanding of the work. But part of the reason will also be that the work itself will not be exactly the same. Just as a work is a little different for every reader, it is also a little different with every successive reading by the *same* reader, and what you will be capturing in your words is some of the subtlety of the work in its capability of producing effects that are alive and therefore always changing just slightly. You need not, therefore, feel that you must say the final word about the work you are writing about—but you do want to say whatever word you have to say in the best possible way.

You can turn all this into a full-time job, of course, but you needn't. It is hard work, and at first the learning seems slow and the payoff questionable. A basketball novice watching the magic of a Julius Erving may find it hard to see the point of practicing layups, but even creative geniuses have to go through those awful moments of sitting down and putting pen to paper (and then crossing out and rewriting again and again). But that's the way you learn to make it seem easy. Art is mostly craft, and craft means methodical work. As one of our most accomplished poets once put it:

> True ease in writing comes from art, not chance,
> As those move easiest who have learned to dance.

It *will* come more easily with practice. But you needn't aspire to professional writing to take pleasure in what you accomplish. Learning to write well about literature will help you with all sorts of tasks, some of them having little to do with writing. Writing, like most other meaningful exercises in the educational process, trains the mind, creates habits, teaches you procedures that will have all kinds of long-range payoffs that you may not immediately recognize or be able to predict. And ultimately it is very satisfying, even if it is not easy, to be able to stand back and say, "That is mine. Those are my words. I did it. I have gotten it right. I know what I'm talking about. I understand, and I can make someone else understand." Communication through words is one of the activities that make us distinctively human.

One final bit of advice: do not follow, too rigidly or too closely, anyone's advice, including ours. We have suggested some general strategies and listed some common pitfalls. But writing is a very personal experience, and you will have talents (and faults) that are a little different from anyone else's. Learn to play to your own strengths and avoid the weaknesses that you are especially prone to. Pay attention to your instructor's comments; learn from your own mistakes.

A SUMMARY OF THE PROCESS

Here, briefly, is a summary, step by step, of the stages we have suggested you move through in preparing a paper about literature.

Stage One: Deciding what to write about.
- Read the work straight through, thoughtfully. Make notes at the end on any points that caught your special attention.
- Read the work again more slowly, pausing to think through all the parts you don't understand. When you finish, write a three- or four-sentence summary.
- Read the work again, carefully but quite quickly. Decide what you feel most strongly about in the work, and write down the one thing you would most want to explain to a friend about how the story (or poem or play) works, or (if the work still puzzles you) the one question you would most like to be able to answer.
- Decide how the statement you made at the end of your third reading relates to the summary you wrote down after the second reading.
- Write a one-paragraph "promise" of what your paper is going to argue.

Stage Two: Planning your paper
- Read the work at least twice more and make notes on anything that relates to your thesis.

- Read through all your notes so far, and for each write a sentence articulating how it relates to your thesis.
- Transfer all your notes to note cards of uniform size.
- Read through all your notes again and record any new observations or ideas on additional note cards.
- Set aside your note cards for the moment, and make a brief outline of the major points you intend to make.
- Sort the note cards into piles corresponding to the major points in your outline. Sort the cards in each separate pile into the most likely order of their use in the paper.
- Make a more detailed outline (including the most significant examples) from your pile of note cards on each point.
- Reconsider your order of presentation and make any necessary adjustments.
- Begin writing.

Stage Three: Rewriting.
- Go over your writing, word by word, sentence by sentence, and paragraph by paragraph, in draft after draft until your writing is worthy of the ideas you want to express.

SOME FINAL THOUGHTS

Why write about literature? There are two kinds of answers to this question in a literature course. One is that your instructor will probably insist on it. In fact, your college probably insists on it, one way or another, as a requirement for graduation. But there's a larger reason that lies behind your instructor's (and your college's) insistence. That is because writing is a way of knowing, or of coming to know. In a very real sense, you do not actually know whether you know a particular thing until you can explain it to someone else. Are you ever tempted to say: "I know what that poem means but I just can't explain it"? That's a clear sign that you need to read it again, maybe several more times, and try to figure out how to talk about the meaning, or the effect, or the total intellectual and emotional experience of the poem. No interpretation will *be* the poem, of course, or the perfect equivalent of the poem, but as you learn to interpret more precisely and more readily, you will discover that your experience itself is richer. You will get not just vague sensations of pleasure or pain, but more clearly defined responses that will let you know that you know. The old adage that the way to learn something thoroughly and permanently is to teach it to someone else is especially applicable to attempts to interpret literature by writing about it. Years from now you will remember very well the stories, poems, and plays that you write about, while others will have slipped away from you. But even more important, you will have exercised and refined your skills of knowing by applying them in a concentrated way; doing a good paper on one poem or one story or one play will make you a better reader of the next work of literature you read, of whatever kind.

Reading literature, even for students who begin with indifference, usually turns out to be a pleasure; writing about literature sometimes does not. We will not try to kid you: writing about literature is not easy, even though it does use words to describe other words. And even for people who get very good at it, it is hard work. But it can also be very satisfying work if you take the time and trouble to do it well and endure the frustration of confronting your weaknesses and mistakes. You can learn to do it, but it may take a lot of effort and some unsuccessful attempts along the way. You will soon develop your own habits and learn to play to your own strengths and capabilities. Meanwhile, here is a checklist of some things to keep in mind.

1. Begin early. Last minute means last resort.

2. Complete your analysis before you begin to write. It is easier to write when you know what you think.

3. Plan. Don't wait for divine inspiration or trust to luck.

4. Outline. Be sure you know where all your thoughts go and how they fit together.

5. Limit your subject. A paper that is about everything is about nothing.

6. Think clearly all the way to the end. Do not let your sentences or paragraphs trail off into uncertainty, vague attempts to sound impressive, or a hope for supernatural intervention.

7. Argue. A discussion with a friend or roommate will normally clarify what you think. Strong feelings are not enough to make a paper work, but vigor reinforces clarity.

8. Prove. Assertions are for headlines; an essay has to give evidence and convince its audience.

9. Be clear. Fog enlarges objects but does not enhance prose. "Partly cloudy" is not a favorable forecast for your paper.

10. Be varied. Do not write the same paper every week of the term. Once you know what you *can* do well, experiment with other possibilities. You will learn more by taking risks, even if sometimes you do not succeed, than you will by repeated success in the same rut. And most teachers will respect your attempt to improve yourself rather than basking in repeated reflection of past glories.

11. Be hard on yourself. Never settle for a sentence that almost makes sense or a word that is almost right.

12. Rewrite. Getting something right in words takes time and patience. Most papers take several drafts before they begin to seem smooth. It takes a lot of work to sound effortless. Let your prose "cool" between drafts whenever possible; you will find trouble spots more easily when you are a bit removed from the thoughts behind the writing. Sleeping on a paper is not always a good thing (it depends on what you do when you wake up), but it can help provide the distance that can lead to good critical judgment. It is better to find your own problems and correct them than to read about them in your instructor's comments.

13. Type. The chances are that your instructor does not have a

degree in hieroglyphics and did not work as a decoder in World War II.

14. Proofread. Who wants to read a paper you did not care enough about to read yourself?

15. Proofread again. Find your mistakes before someone else does. It is less expensive.

16. Read it one more time.

SAMPLE PAPER

The essay that follows was written by a student in her freshman year at Emory University. We are grateful to Christine Woodside for her kind permission to reprint her paper here.

Metrical Variation and Meaning

in "To the Memory of Mr. Oldham"

Christine Woodside

In his poem "To the Memory of Mr. Oldham," John Dryden rationalizes the death of a fellow satirist by comparing himself to the dead man. He begins by saying they were "cast in the same poetic mold," then considers the fact that Oldham's youth did not prevent him from reaching the "same goal" before the older speaker. Dryden also notes that while age—and thus experience—would have given Oldham a smoother command of the English language, satire and wit do not need such polishing and will "shine"

through a less-experienced poet's "rugged line."

He points out the possible stagnant quality

that experience can nurture and seems to imply

both that experience is unnecessary to produce

good satire and that Oldham's death was timely,

since he had already succeeded. Still, the poem

ends in a tired, labored farewell, suggesting

that Oldham's death was <u>not</u> timely, and that

"fate and gloomy night" surround him. Since this

poem is a single stanza, the shifts in thought

and tone are subtle. The occasional exceptions

to the iambic pentameter emphasize the different

themes Dryden addresses. Although the variations

in meter do not drastically alter the poem's

significance, they do clarify some of the main

<u>ideas</u> in the poem.

The first notable idea is the alliance

Dryden feels with Oldham, which is emphasized

by four separate metrical variations. The word

"allied" in the third line is accented on the

first syllable, which disturbs the metrical

flow that requires a stress on the second. In the next line, "cast in the same" throws off the iambic rhythm with an unexpected stress on the word "cast." (This also highlights the word "same," since two small words are unaccented between the two.) A third metrical surprise is in the fifth line, where the first three words, "One common note," receive accents. These accents not only emphasize the words, but actually slow down the reader. Another emphasis on unity is in the seventh line, where the first two words yield to stresses on the third and fourth in "To the same goal." All of these unsettling accent changes illustrate Dryden's conviction that both he and Oldham had the same goals in their poetry.

There are two variances in meter that emphasize youth. The first of these occurs when Dryden mentions that Oldham has surpassed his older and more experienced ally in a short amount of time: "While his young friend performed and won the race." Here the word "young"

receives the unexpected accent. Not surprisingly, Dryden goes on to discuss Oldham's youth
and youth's lack of control over the language.
The second metrical variation deals with this
inexperience with language, saying that a young
poet's work must show "Through the harsh
cadence of a rugged line." By position, neither
"harsh" nor "cadence" would normally receive
the accent, but both stand out noticeably.
Interestingly, Dryden chooses to emphasize,
metrically, youthful inexperience while at the
same time saying that satire does <u>not</u> need an
experienced control of the language. By doing
this, he is contending that youth is <u>not</u> a
handicap, at least not in satire. Still, he does
choose to emphasize the "harsh cadence" (the
consonants are hard to pronounce) of inexperienced work.

The next three metrical variations shift
the attention to experience, which, he says,
only "mellows what we write to the dull sweets
of rhyme." The word "dull" receives an unex-

pected accent and, together with "sweets," gives
the line a tired, heavy quality. This mirrors
Dryden's thought that "maturing time" will only
make his work "dull." (Also, as he mentions that
rhyme can become stagnant, he has just completed three consecutive rhyming lines; the
pattern calls for two.) The second "dull"
metrical difference appears in line 22. "Once
more, hail" is also slow and heavy because all
three words need an accent. Finally, the last
line contains six iambic feet instead of five,
and the last word is redundant: "But fate and
gloomy night encompass thee around." To say
"encompass thee" would imply the word "around";
the last word does not change or clarify anything. It merely shows that Dryden allows the
"dull sweets of rhyme" to control his choice of
words! In the three metrical variations above,
Dryden generates the very dullness he criticizes
as characteristic of an older, experienced poet
such as himself.

 This poem discusses the "one common note"

Dryden shares with Oldham; it then considers Oldham's youth; then deals with Dryden's age and experience in relation to the dead man's youth. All three of these ideas are reflected in the variations of the iambic pentameter, and the variations strengthen their impact.

ACKNOWLEDGMENTS

Woody Allen: "The Kugelmass Episode" copyright © 1977 by Woody Allen. Reprinted from *Side Effects* by Woody Allen, by permission of Random House, Inc.

James Baldwin: "Sonny's Blues" from *Going to Meet the Man* by James Baldwin. Copyright © 1948, 1951, 1957, 1958, 1960, 1965 by James Baldwin. Reprinted by permission of Doubleday & Company, Inc.

Toni Cade Bambara: "My Man Bovanne" copyright © by Toni Cade Bambara. Reprinted from *Gorilla, My Love*, by Toni Cade Bambara, by permission of Random House, Inc.

Jorge Luis Borges: "Garden of Forking Paths" from *Labyrinths*, translated by Donald A. Yates. Copyright © 1962 by New Directions Publishing Corporation. Reprinted by permission of New Directions.

John Cheever: "The Country Husband" copyright 1954 by John Cheever. Reprinted from *The Stories of John Cheever* by permission of Alfred A. Knopf, Inc.

Richard Connell: "The Most Dangerous Game" by Richard Connell copyright © 1924 by Richard Connell. Copyright renewed 1952 by Louise Connell. Reprinted by permission of Brandt & Brandt Literary Agents, Inc.

William Faulkner: "A Rose for Emily" copyright 1930 and renewed 1958 by William Faulkner. "Barn Burning" copyright 1939 and renewed 1967 by Estelle Faulkner and Jill Faulkner Summers. Reprinted from *Collected Stories of William Faulkner* by permission of Random House, Inc. "The Old People" from *Go Down Moses*. Copyright 1940, 1942; renewed 1968, 1970 by Estelle Faulkner and Jill Summers. Reprinted by permission of Random House, Inc. "Spotted Horses" copyright 1931 and renewed 1959 by William Faulkner. Reprinted from Scribner's Magazine by permission of Random House, Inc. An expanded version of this story appears as part of *The Hamlet* by William Faulkner.

F. Scott Fitzgerald: "Babylon Revisited" from *Taps at Reville* is used with the permission of Charles Scribner's Sons. Copyright 1931 The Curtis Publishing Company; renewal copyright © 1959 Frances S. F. Lanahan.

Gabriel Garcia Marquez: "A Very Old Man with Enormous Wings" from *Leaf Storm and Other Stories* by Gabriel Garcia Marquez. Reprinted by permission of Harper & Row, Publishers, Inc.

Ernest Hemingway: "The Short Happy Life of Francis Macomber" (copyright 1936 Ernest Hemingway) is reprinted by permission of Charles Scribner's Sons from *The Short Stories of Ernest Hemingway*.

Spencer Holst: "The Zebra Storyteller" reprinted by permission of E. P. Dutton from *The Language of Cats and Other Stories* by Spencer Holst. Copyright © 1971 by Spencer Holst. A Saturday Review Press edition.

Shirley Jackson: "The Lottery" from *The Lottery*, copyright 1948, 1949 by Shirley Jackson. Copyright renewed © 1976 by Laurence Hyman, Barry Hyman, Mrs. Sarah Webster, and Mrs. Joanne Schnurer. First published in *The New Yorker*. Reprinted by permission of Farrar, Straus & Giroux, Inc.

James Joyce: "Araby" from *Dubliners* by James Joyce. Copyright © 1967 by the Estate of James Joyce. Reprinted by permission of Viking Penguin, Inc.

Franz Kafka: "A Hunger Artist" reprinted by permission of Schocken Books Inc. from *The Penal Colony* by Franz Kafka, trans. by Willa and Edwin Muir. Copyright © 1948, 1976 by Schocken Books Inc.

D. H. Lawrence: "The Rocking Horse Winner" from *The Complete Short Stories, Vol. I*, copyright © 1962 by Angelo Ravagli and C. M. Weekley, Executors of the Estate of Frieda Lawrence Ravagli. "Odour of Chrysanthemums," copyright © 1962 by Angelo Ravagli and C. M. Weekley, Executors of the Estate of Frieda Lawrence Ravagli, and "Horse Dealer's Daughter," copyright 1922 by Thomas Seltzer, Inc., renewed 1950 by Frieda Lawrence, from *The Complete Short Stories, Vol. II*. Reprinted by permission of Viking Penguin, Inc. Excerpts from *Selected Literary Criticism*, edited by Anthony Beal, Copyright © 1956 by Frieda Lawrence. Selections from *Phoenix I*, edited by Edward O. McDonald, copyright © 1936 by Frieda Lawrence, © renewed 1964 by the Estate of the late Frieda Lawrence Ravagli. Reprinted by permission of Viking Penguin, Inc.

Ursula K. LeGuin: "The Eye-Altering" from *The Compass Rose* by Ursula K. LeGuin. Copyright © 1982 by Ursula K. LeGuin. Reprinted by permission of Harper & Row, Publisher, Inc.

Doris Lessing: "Our Friend Judith" from *A Man and Two Women* by Doris Lessing. Copyright © 1958, 1962, 1963 by Doris Lessing. Reprinted by permission of Simon & Schuster, Inc. and Jonathan Clowes Ltd., London, on behalf of Doris Lessing.

Katherine Mansfield: "Her First Ball," copyright 1922 by Alfred A. Knopf, Inc., and renewed 1950 by John Middleton Murry. Reprinted from *The Short Stories of Katherine Mansfield* by permission of Alfred A. Knopf, Inc.

Bobbie Ann Mason: "Shiloh" from *Shiloh and Other Stories* by Bobbie Ann Mason. Originally appeared in *The New Yorker*. Copyright © 1982 by Bobbie Ann Mason. Reprinted by permission of Harper & Row, Publishers, Inc.

N. Scott Momaday: from *The Way to Rainy Mountain*, © 1969, The University of New Mexico Press. Reprinted by permission.

Alice Munro: "Boys and Girls" from *The Dance of the Happy Shades* by Alice Munro. Copyright © Alice Munro, 1968. Reprinted by permission of McGraw-Hill Ryerson Limited, Toronto.

Flannery O'Connor: "The Artificial Nigger" copyright © 1955 by Flannery O'Connor. Reprinted from her volume *A Good Man is Hard to Find* by permission of Harcourt Brace Jovanovich, Inc.

Grace Paley: "A Conversation With My Father" from *Enormous Changes at the Last Minute* by Grace Paley. Copyright © 1972, 1974 by Grace Paley. Reprinted with the permission of Farrar, Straus & Giroux, Inc.

Katherine Anne Porter: "Flowering Judas" from *Flowering Judas and Other Stories*, copyright 1930, 1958 by Katherine Anne Porter. Reprinted by permission of Harcourt Brace Jovanovich, Inc.

Mordecai Richler: "The Summer My Grandmother Was Supposed to Die" from *The Street* by Mordecai Richler. Copyright © 1975 by Mordecai Richler. Reprinted by permission of

mings, is reprinted by permission of Harcourt Brace Jovanovich.

Walter de la Mare: "Slim Cunning Hands" from *The Complete Poems of Walter de la Mare* is reprinted by permission of the Literary Executors of Walter de la Mare and The Society of Authors as their representative.

Peter deVries: "Bacchanal" from *The Tents of Wickedness* by Peter deVries. Copyright © 1960 by Peter deVries. First appeared in *The New Yorker*.

James Dickey: "Cherrylog Road" and "The Leap" from *Poems 1957–1967*, by James Dickey. Copyright © 1963, 1964 by James Dickey. Reprinted by permission of Wesleyan University Press. "Cherrylog Road" first appeared in *The New Yorker*.

Emily Dickinson: #'s 341, 569, 632, 657, 712, 754, and 986 are reprinted by permission of the Publisher and the Trustees of Amherst College from *The Poems of Emily Dickinson edited* by Thomas H. Johnson, Cambridge, Mass.: The Belknap Press of Harvard University, Copyright 1951, © 1955, 1979, 1983 by The President and Fellows of Harvard College. #'s 341, 569, 657, and 754 are also reprinted by permission of Little, Brown and Company from *The Complete Poems of Emily Dickinson* edited by Thomas H. Johnson copyright 1929 by Martha Dickinson Bianchi; copyright © renewed 1957 by Mary L. Hampson.

David Donnell: "Potatoes" from *Settlements: New and Selected Poems* by David Donnell, published by McClelland & Stewart, Toronto, Canada. Reprinted by permission of the author.

Alan Dugan: "Funeral Oration for a Mouse" copyright © 1961 by Alan Dugan. From *New and Collected Poems, 1961–1983* by Alan Dugan, published by The Ecco Press in 1983. Reprinted by permission.

Richard Eberhart: "The Groundhog" from *Collected Poems 1930–1976* by Richard Eberhart. Copyright © 1976 by Richard Eberhart. Reprinted by permission of Oxford University Press, Inc.

T. S. Eliot: "The Journey of the Magi" and "The Love Song of J. Alfred Prufrock" from *Collected Poems 1909–1962* by T. S. Eliot, copyright 1936 by Harcourt Brace Jovanovich, Inc.; copyright © 1963, 1964 by T. S. Eliot. Reprinted by permission of Harcourt Brace Jovanovich, Inc. and Faber and Faber Ltd.

James A. Emanuel: "Emmett Till" from *The Treehouse and other Poems* © 1968 by James A. Emanuel. Reprinted by permission of Broadside/Crummel Press, Detroit, Michigan. "Wishes, for Alix" from *Black Man Abroad: The Toulouse Poems,* published by Lotus Press, is reprinted by permission of the author.

Kenneth Fearing: "Dirge" from *New and Selected Poems* by Kenneth Fearing. Reprinted by permission of the publisher, Indiana University Press.

Robert Frost: "Fire and Ice," "Range-Finding," "The Road Not Taken," "The Rose Family," "Stopping by Woods on a Snowy Evening," and "U. S. 1946 King's X" from *The Poetry of Robert Frost* edited by Edward Connery Lathem. Copyright 1916, 1923, 1928, 1947, © 1969 by Holt, Rinehart and Winston. Copyright 1944, 1951, © 1956 by Robert Frost. Copyright © 1975 by Leslie Frost Ballentine. Reprinted by permission of Holt, Rinehart and Winston, Publishers.

Sandra Gilbert: "Sonnet: The Ladies' Home Journal" reprinted from *Emily's Bread, Poems* by Sandra M. Gilbert, by permission of W. W. Norton & Company, Inc. Copyright © 1984 by Sandra M. Gilbert.

Nikki Giovanni: "Poetry" from *The Woman and the Men* by Nikki Giovanni. Copyright © 1975 by Nikki Giovanni. By permission of William Morrow & Company.

Edgar A. Guest: "The Things That Make a Soldier Great" reprinted from *The Collected Verse of Edgar A. Guest* by Edgar A. Guest, © 1934, used with permission of Contemporary Books, Inc., Chicago.

Michael Harper: "Dear John, Dear Coltrane" from *Dear John, Dear Coltrane* published by the University of Pittsburgh Press. First published in the *Carolina Quarterly*, 1970. Reprinted by permission.

James Harrison: "Penelope" and "Leda's Version" by James Harrison from *Flying Dutchmen* (1983) reprinted with the permission of Sono Nis Press.

Robert Hayden: "Those Winter Sundays" reprinted from *Angle of Ascent: New and Selected Poems* by Robert Hayden, by permission of Liveright Publishing Corporation. Copyright © 1975, 1972, 1970, 1966 by Robert Hayden.

Seamus Heaney: "Mid-Term Break" from *Poems 1965–1975* by Seamus Heaney. Copyright © 1966, 1969, 1972, 1975, 1980 by Seamus Heaney. Reprinted by permission of Farrar, Straus & Giroux, Inc. Reprinted by permission of Faber and Faber Ltd. from *Death of a Naturalist* by Seamus Heaney.

Anthony Hecht: "The Dover Bitch" used by permission of Atheneum Publishers from *The Hard Hours* by Anthony Hecht. Copyright © 1960, 1967 by Anthony Hecht.

John Hollander: "Adam's Task" from *The Night Mirror*, copyright © 1970, 1971 by John Hollander. Reprinted by permission of Atheneum Publishers.

Robert Hollander: "You Too? Me Too—Why Not? Soda Pop" is reprinted from *The Massachusetts Review* © 1968 by The Massachusetts Review, Inc. by permission of the publisher.

A. D. Hope: "Advice to Young Ladies" and "Imperial Adam" by A. D. Hope from *Collected Poems 1930–1970* are reprinted with the permission of Angus & Robertson (UK) Ltd.

A. E. Housman: "Terence, This is Stupid Stuff" and "To an Athlete Dying Young" from "A Shropshire Lad"—authorized edition—from *The Collected Poems of A. E. Housman.* Copyright 1939, 1940, © 1965 by Holt, Rinehart and Winston. Copyright © 1967, 1968 Copyright 1939, 1940, © 1965 by Holt, Rinehart and Winston. Copyright © 1967, 1968 by Robert E. Symons. Reprinted by permission of Holt, Rinehart and Winston Publishers, The Society of Authors as the literary representative of the Estate of A. E. Housman, and Jonathan Cape Ltd.

Langston Hughes: "The Negro Speaks of Rivers" copyright 1926 by Alfred A. Knopf, Inc. and renewed 1954 by Langston Hughes. Reprinted from *Selected Poems of Langston Hughes,* by permission of Alfred A. Knopf, Inc. "Harlem (A Dream Deferred)" copyright 1959 by Langston Hughes. Reprinted from *The Panther and the Lash,* by Langston Hughes, by permission of Alfred A. Knopf, Inc. "Theme for English B" from

INDEX OF AUTHORS

INDEX OF TITLES AND FIRST LINES

1555